TIMELINE

ARTS, LITERATURE, RELIGION, AND PHILOSOPHY

1805
ARTS
Turner paints "The Shipwreck"
LITERATURE
Chateaubriand's *René*

1810
ARTS
Goya engraves *Los desastres de la guerra*
LITERATURE
Crabbe's *The Borough*

1815
LITERATURE
Beowulf manuscript discovered and published
Schlegel's *Lectures on Dramatic Arts and Literature* translated

1820
ARTS
Sculpture of the Venus de Milo discovered
LITERATURE
Walter Scott's *Ivanhoe*

1825
ARTS
Nash remodels Buckingham Palace
LITERATURE
Hazlitt's *The Spirit of the Age*
PHILOSOPHY
James Mill's *Analysis of the Phenomena of the Human Mind*

1830
ARTS
Delacroix paints "Liberty Leading the People"
LITERATURE
Tennyson's *Poems, Chiefly Lyrical*
PHILOSOPHY
Comte begins publishing *Cours de philosophie positive*

1805 1810 1815 1820 1825 1830

1805
WAR
Nelson defeats Franco-Spanish fleet at Trafalgar
Napoleon defeats Austrians and Russians at Austerlitz
SCIENCE
Mungo Park drowns exploring Niger River
Sartuner isolates morphine

1810
WAR
Wellington defeats French at Salamanca
POLITICS
Reform debated in Parliament
De Maistre's *Essay on the Generation of Political Constitutions*
SCIENCE
Koenig invents power-driven printing press
Appert develops food-canning techniques

1815
WAR
Napoleon is defeated at Waterloo
POLITICS
France bans the slave trade
SCIENCE
Steam warship USS *Fulton* sails
Apothecaries Act establishes standards for medical practice
ECONOMICS
Ricardo's *The Influence of a Low Price of Corn on the Profits of Stock*

1820
POLITICS
Prince Regent becomes George IV
4,000 British settle in South Africa
SCIENCE
Plutonium is discovered in Russian Urals
Scoresby's *Account of the Arctic Regions*
ECONOMICS
Malthus's *Principles of Political Economy*

1825
WAR
Missolonghi falls to the Turks
POLITICS
Adams elected as sixth U.S. president
SCIENCE
Laing becomes first explorer to reach Timbuktu
Stockton-Darlington railway system begins service in England

1830
POLITICS
George IV dies
Louis Phillipe begins reign in France
SCIENCE
Lyle's *Principles of Geology*
Liverpool-Manchester rail line begins service

WAR, POLITICS, SCIENCE, AND ECONOMICS

A comprehensive chronology appears as an appendix.

BRITISH LITERATURE

1780–1830

BRITISH LITERATURE

1780–1830

ANNE K. MELLOR
University of California at Los Angeles

RICHARD E. MATLAK
College of the Holy Cross

Harcourt Brace College Publishers
Fort Worth Philadelphia San Diego New York Orlando Austin San Antonio
Toronto Montreal London Sydney Tokyo

PUBLISHER Ted Buchholz
EXECUTIVE EDITOR Michael Rosenberg
ACQUISITIONS EDITORS Stephen T. Jordan/John Meyers
DEVELOPMENTAL EDITOR Tia Black
PROJECT EDITORS Sarah Sims/Deanna Johnson
PRODUCTION MANAGERS Tad Gaither/Jane Tyndall Ponceti
ART DIRECTOR Pat Bracken

ISBN: 0-15-500260-0

Library of Congress Catalog Card Number: 95-81832

Address for Editorial Correspondence: Harcourt Brace College Publishers, 301 Commerce Street, Suite 3700, Fort Worth, TX 76102.

Address for Orders: Harcourt Brace & Company, 6277 Sea Harbor Drive, Orlando, FL 32887-6777. 1-800-782-4479, or 1-800-433-0001 (in Florida).

(Copyright Acknowledgments begin on page 1441, which constitutes a continuation of this copyright page.)

Printed in the United States of America

7 8 9 0 1 2 3 4 5 039 10 9 8 7 6 5 4

Dedicated with gratitude to the members of my National Endowment for the Humanities Summer Seminars for College Teachers (1982, 1989, 1994), who taught me how to teach.

BY ANNE K. MELLOR

Dedicated to the memory of Richard H. Rodino

BY RICHARD E. MATLAK

PREFACE

In recent years, our understanding of the "Romantic Period" in English literature has changed dramatically. The rediscovery of forgotten women writers and of neglected working-class and regional writers, together with a clearer recognition of the many ways in which all the literary works written in England between 1780 and 1830 responded to the political and social movements of the time, has led many scholars to question the sufficiency of traditional aesthetic definitions of "Romanticism." This is the first anthology of the "Romantic" period to take into account the major role that women played in the production of literature at this time, as well as the wide range of social and political debates to which both canonical and noncanonical writers responded in their writings. By including as many women writers as men, by devoting half of this volume to women and hitherto neglected male writers, and by prefacing all their works with historical documents that help to locate and define the major intellectual and political debates of this period, we hope to make it possible for both teachers and students to pursue these interrogations of English literary Romanticism in the classroom.

Our General Introduction indicates the working principles that guided the selection of specific authors and works for this volume. We have included a wide range of literary genres—poetry, prose, fiction, drama, letters, journals—both because we believe that each genre has its own literary merits and because we believe that such generic variety more accurately reflects the literary culture of this period. By doing so, we also draw attention to the ways in which women excelled in those forms—drama, prose, fiction, letters, and journals—not usually included in anthologies of "Romantic poetry."

Since we believe that authors are influenced by their generational allegiances, we have arranged authors according to birth date. Under each author, works are given in order of publication, rather than composition, because we wish to highlight the ways in which literary works functioned within a *public* literary sphere. The dates of publication and composition (when known) of individual works of literature included in this volume are given both in the Table of Contents and at the beginning of each work. A Comprehensive Chronology appears as an appendix and includes important historical dates that will help to locate specific literary works in relation to major political, intellectual, and social events occurring at the same times. We have provided extensive annotations for each work (many of these works have not previously been edited or annotated for classroom use), as well as introductory headnotes for each author that give essential biographical and literary information. At the back of the volume we have included a selective bibliography, listing a few of the major critical works on each writer so that students who wish to pursue further investigation of an individual writer or literary movement may do so.

Acknowledgments

As coeditors, we collaborated closely on the conceptualization and structure of this anthology, and are jointly responsible for the General Introduction and the working principles of selection and presentation. We divided the actual labor of compiling this anthology roughly in half. Richard Matlak takes responsibility for selecting, annotating, and writing the Headnotes for the Historical Context sections on The French Revolution and Rights of Man, on Science and Nature, and on Society and Political Economy; for Dorothy Wordsworth and all the male writers except William Blake and Olaudah Equiano, and for the Comprehensive Chronology. Anne Mellor takes responsibility for selecting, annotating, and writing the Headnotes for the Historical Context sections on the Rights of Woman, on Slavery, the Slave-Trade, and Abolition in Britain, and on Aesthetic Theory and Literary Criticism; for all the women writers except Dorothy Wordsworth; and for William Blake and Olaudah Equiano. Richard Matlak thanks Zaneta Gaul for clerical and administrative assistance and his colleague, Josh Gidding, for assistance with annotations. For invaluable help with the annotating of previously unedited texts, Anne Mellor thanks Hilary Weeks, Chris Hamilton, and especially Hal Gladfelder.

We particularly wish to thank the editorial staff at Harcourt Brace for their unfailing support of this project: Stephen T. Jordan, former Acquisitions Editor in English, who had the foresight to commission this anthology at a time when few editors would have done so; Michael Rosenberg, Executive Editor in English; and John Meyers, Acquisitions Editor in English, who at the last moment generously allotted us the additional pages we needed to include all the material we considered essential; and above all, Tia Black, our Developmental Editor, whose unfailing courtesy, good humor, efficiency, determination, and belief in the value of this project kept us on track during several trying years.

We also thank the fine production team at Harcourt Brace: Tad Gaither and Jane Ponceti, Production Managers; Sarah Sims and Deanna Johnson, Project Editors; Pat Bracken, Art Director; and Cheri Throop, Permissions.

In addition, we are both extremely grateful to all those who generously gave of their time and advice to help us with this project: reviewers, Stephen Behrendt, University of Nebraska; Catherine Burroughs, Cornell College; Stuart Curran, University of Pennsylvania; Anthony Harding, University of Saskatchewan; Nicholas Jones, Oberlin College; Theresa Kelley, University of Texas at Austin; Peter Manning, University of Southern California; Jerome McGann, University of Virginia; Judith Pascoe, University of Iowa; Alan Richardson, Boston College; and Susan Wolfson, Princeton University; and colleagues and friends, John Anderson, Frederick L. Burwick, Marilyn Butler, Julie Carlson, Morris Eaves, Roxanne Eberle, Robert Essick, Paula Feldman, Kathleen Fowler, James T. Flynn, Kevin Gilmartin, Sonia Hofkosh, Sheila Minn Hwang, Kenneth R. Johnston, Laura Mandell, James McKusick, Mitzi Myers, Frank Petrella, Eric Robinson, Marlon Ross, Philip C. Rule, Esther Schor, Paul Sheats, and Nanora Sweet.

CONTENTS

6. AESTHETIC THEORY AND LITERARY CRITICISM

AUTHOR SELECTIONS

ANNA LETITIA AIKIN BARBAULD (1743–1825)

OLAUDAH EQUIANO (C. 1745–1797)

Hannah More (1745–1833)

Charlotte Turner Smith (1749–1806)

Ann Cromarty Yearsley (1752–1806)

William Blake (1757–1827)

MARY DARBY ROBINSON (1758–1800)

ROBERT BURNS (1759–1796)

Mary Wollstonecraft (1759–1797)

Joanna Baillie (1762–1851)

Helen Maria Williams (1762–1827)

Dorothy Wordsworth (1771–1855)

Walter Scott (1771–1832)

PERCY BYSSHE SHELLEY (1792–1822)

Felicia Dorothea Browne Hemans (1793–1835)

John Clare (1793–1864)

John Keats (1795–1821)

MARY WOLLSTONECRAFT GODWIN SHELLEY (1797–1851)

LETITIA ELIZABETH LANDON (KNOWN AS L. E. L.) (1802–1838)

COMPREHENSIVE CHRONOLOGY AND BIBLIOGRAPHIES

BRITISH LITERATURE

1780–1830

General Introduction

NEW WAYS OF thinking about and teaching literary texts require new pedagogical anthologies. Recent debates over the periodization of literary history, the politics of canon formation, the adequate representation of women and minority writers in the academic curriculum, and the nature of cultural literacy have significantly changed the way many scholars, critics, teachers, and students approach the literature of the past. It is time to offer to teachers of that literary period traditionally called "English Romanticism" a new, comprehensive, and revisionist anthology of writing composed and/or published in Britain between 1780 and 1830. A single text can most conveniently and efficiently satisfy the pedagogical needs of those who wish to utilize recent historical, feminist, textual, and cultural methods and scholarship in the classroom as well as to enhance the intellectual and cultural development of students.

While the principal motivation and goals for this anthology are straightforward, achieving them has been a more complex undertaking. We have attempted to provide a single teaching text suitable for undergraduate and graduate students that includes 1) a generous selection from British men and women writers of the period 1780–1830; 2) adequate representation of the major historical conditions and social and cultural movements to which these writers responded; 3) a selection of the works of a given author that reveals the development of both the public and the private voice; and 4) texts that reflect the most recent authoritative editorial work and critical scholarship. Since not one of these objectives is easily attained in an obvious or efficient way, it may be necessary to explain in more detail the rationale that underlay the execution of this project.

I. SELECTION OF WRITERS

There will always be writers "missing" from any anthology. Many late-nineteenth century anthologies of British writing contain literary works published between 1780 and 1830 that do not appear here or in any other twentieth-century anthology, but which were then read for imperative cultural reasons. What Emerson said of books is equally true of anthologies: every age must write, or create, its own. The canon of literary works that we find essential to know changes over time as the practical outcome of the choices that publishers make as to what works should be printed and kept in print and that teachers make as to what works deserve a place on their syllabi.

The selection of writers for this anthology was motivated by a desire to give a comprehensive sense of the range of writing produced in England between 1780 and 1830, including works by women as well as men, by lower-class as well as middle-class and aristocratic writers, by men and women of differing races and ethnicities, and spanning in genre productions in poetry, drama, fiction, nonfictional prose essays, journals, and letters. Previous anthologists of this time period have selected writers to represent a specific aesthetic or literary movement called "Romanticism." Whether their anthologies included as many as fifty-four writers, as did Russell Noyes' *English Romantic Poetry and Prose* (1956), or as few as six, as did William Heath's *Major British Poets of the Romantic Period* (1973), or some number in between, as the thirty writers represented in David Perkins' original *English Romantic Writers* (1973), the endeavor of all these anthologies was the same. They all were based upon and confirmed the prevailing academic concept of English literary Romanticism as a movement anticipated by Blake, established by Wordsworth and Coleridge, and complicated or refined by three second-generation poets: Shelley, Keats, and Byron. Such anthologies were acceptable in their day because they reflected the dominant interests of academic literary scholarship, the attempt to map in detail the increasingly refined differences between the forms of literary Romanticism, a kind of writing identified with the passionate and rebellious outpourings of young men. So specific and exclusionary had this concept of "Romanticism" become that even the later writings of Wordsworth and Coleridge were ignored or condemned for failing to sustain the radical concerns of their youth.

Recently Jerome McGann in his *The New Oxford Book of Romantic Period Verse* (1993), David Perkins in his revised *English Romantic Writers* (1994) and Duncan Wu in his *Romanticism—An Anthology* (1994) have all claimed to broaden the canon of British Romantic writing by including selections from women writers and less well-known male writers. But all these texts maintain the academic bias described above. They all limit the selections of writings by women to less than ten percent of the volume, they devote at least two-thirds of their anthologies to the six canonical poets, and they represent William Wordsworth in large part by his youthful writings (Wu, for instance, includes the entire *Prelude* of 1805 but only one short poem written by Wordsworth after 1807, while McGann includes only a brief excerpt from "The Excursion" of 1814). None of these anthologies indicate the full range of writing in all the genres published in England between 1780 and 1830.

We have deliberately avoided using the terms "Romantic" or "Romanticism" to describe the historical period represented in this anthology. These terms are themselves the product of a specific historical and critical process that did not begin until the end of the nineteenth century. As the name of a literary movement or a kind of art, "Romantic" or "Romanticism" came into widespread use only in the early twentieth century. Between 1780 and 1830, "romantic" referred to the Greek romances, to the poetic romances of the Middle Ages and the Renaissance, and to seventeenth- and eighteenth-century prose romances (most notably by the Scuderys), and thus to literary works in both poetry and prose that were fanciful, idealistic, focused on courtly or erotic love, and containing elements of the supernatural or the wonderful. The poets now called "Romantic" were at the time called the "Lake Poets" or the "Cockney School" or even the "Satanic School," all labels coined by neoclassical, politically conservative critics such as Francis Jeffrey, John Gibson Lockhart, and John Wilson Croker.

These poets were first named "The Romantic School" by Hippolyte Taine in his *History of English Literature* in 1863. Taine derived his notion of literary Romanticism from French and

German writers, and defined it as a concern with historical relativism and German idealist philosophy. Most British Victorian critics who applied the term "romantic" to literary works intended a specifically *political* connotation, identifying "romantic" poetry with a particular set of responses to the French Revolution, ones that were liberal, radical, even revolutionary. This conception of the romantic movement as a political "spirit of the age" received its fullest exposition in 1910 in William John Courthope's *The Romantic Movement in English Poetry: The Effects of the French Revolution*.

During the late nineteenth century, however, the Pre-Raphaelite writers, and especially Dante Gabriel and William Michael Rossetti, offered an alternative construction of the careers of Keats and Shelley as poets of beauty who valued art for art's sake. This conception of Romanticism as primarily an *aesthetic* term received a fuller exposition in A. O. Lovejoy's famous 1924 essay "On the Discrimination of Romanticisms" and by the mid-twentieth century had come to dominate academic discussions of "the Romantic Movement in England." This aesthetic or literary definition of Romanticism has since been critically expanded by a generous reliance upon the self-descriptions of their literary project provided by Wordsworth, Coleridge, Shelley, Keats, and others. (For a fuller discussion of the content of this "Romantic" poetics, see the following Context Section on AESTHETIC THEORY AND LITERARY CRITICISM.)

Recognizing that the term "Romanticism" has become the subject of interrogation by recent new historical, cultural, and feminist critics, we have set it aside as a principle of selection. Instead, we have used a time line defined by historical developments. The focal point remains the French Revolution and the fierce debates it both consummated and spawned concerning the rights of the individual and the nature of good government. More broadly considered, the period of the French Revolution initiated a period of complex struggle with the lasting problems of liberalism and modernity—the extension of human and political rights, especially suffrage and the abolition of slavery; the dislocation and stress associated with industrialization and urbanization; the economic uncertainties of capitalist economies and empires; and the establishment of constitutional governments. This historical time line—from the rise of liberalism leading to the American and French Revolutions, through the abolition of the slave trade and the extension of suffrage in the early 1830s—does not deny the importance of Romanticism as an aesthetic category. But it does permit us to include other modes of literary reaction to this revolutionary constellation of historical, social, and intellectual events: the dawning of European democracy with the fall of the Bastille in 1789; the rise and vicissitudes of the early feminist movement; the attempts to abolish the slave trade and then slavery itself; the gradual transformation of natural philosophy into modern science; the shifting structure of the class system and new economic theories produced by the Industrial Revolution and colonial expansion; the rise and fall of Napoleon and the restoration of the French monarchy; and the domestic social and political movements that culminated in the Reform Bill of 1832.

Even with this broadened historical perspective, we have not been able to include every writer or work of interest that we wished. Most notably missing from this anthology, simply because of their bulk, are *novels*, already by this historical period the dominant literary genre and one in which women writers excelled (of the dozen most popular and highly respected novelists between 1780 and 1830, ten were women). This anthology is therefore *designed to be used in conjunction with at least two novels:* Mary Shelley's *Frankenstein* (1818) and a novel by Jane Austen. Among Austen's novels, the narrative of *Mansfield Park* (1814), whose title alludes to Lord Mansfield's anti-slavery judgment, perhaps speaks most directly to the issues of the slave trade and women's rights, which we have addressed in our Historical Contexts sections.

II. HISTORICAL CONTEXTS

The historicizing intentions of this anthology are notably represented in the opening Context sections on THE FRENCH REVOLUTION AND THE RIGHTS OF MAN; the RIGHTS OF WOMAN; SLAVERY, THE SLAVE TRADE, AND ABOLITION; SOCIETY AND POLITICAL ECONOMY; SCIENCE AND NATURE; and AESTHETIC THEORY AND LITERARY CRITICISM. We have tried to provide documentary material from a wide range of writing—philosophical, political, scientific, economic, aesthetic, and literary—to represent the major social, cultural, and political debates occurring in England between 1780 and 1830. The specific literary works that follow will gain added significance, we believe, when they are viewed as participating in wider cultural discourses, or as taking positions on divisive contemporary political, social, and moral issues that still trouble us.

We have therefore selected texts that represent opposing arguments on various historical events. Deeply felt public and private conflicts inspired a range of rhetorical disputation that can now help us to better understand "the spirit of the age," in William Hazlitt's phrase. The literature of these fifty years was created out of deep tensions and uncertainties over immense political, economic, social, and scientific changes. We can easily recognize the debate between radical and conservative responses to the doctrine of the rights of man that inspired the revolutions in America and France. More deep-seated anxieties were aroused, however, by the liberal-democratic movement towards the great risks of modernity: universal suffrage, constitutional government, capitalist enterprise, imperialist expansion, industrialization, and technological development. On these issues, even those who shared the same aesthetic concerns—even Coleridge, Wordsworth, and Southey—responsibly differed all their lives. This anthology greatly extends the range of important and well-written literary reactions to this time of social upheaval, dislocation, and fear.

Intellectual debate and emotional conflict is a feature not just of this historical zeitgeist but also of many of its most thoughtful individual literary works, such as Joanna Baillie's *Count Basil,* William Wordsworth's "Elegiac Stanzas," Felicia Hemans' *The Siege of Valencia* and John Keats' Odes. Authors might avoid taking sides by representing all sides, as did Byron in *Don Juan,* in that literary mode we now call "Romantic Irony." Or they might develop the classical rhetorical forms for debate, as did those who worked in the new genre of the meditative-descriptive poem, a genre that includes Coleridge's "The Eolian Harp" and Barbauld's "The First Fire." Some writers actively inserted contradictory texts into their own previously published work, as did Coleridge when he added the prose glosses to his "Rime of the Ancyent Marinere." Other writers represented irresolvable contraries in the juxtaposition of their own works, as William Blake did in his *Songs of Innocence* and *Songs of Experience* or Felicia Hemans in "The Homes of England" and "The Graves of a Household." Many writers entered into calculated dialogues or debates with other literary works, as the dialogue between Wordsworth's "Ode: [There Was a Time]" and Coleridge's "Dejection: An Ode"; between Mary Shelley's

Frankenstein and Byron's *Manfred*; between Wollstonecraft's *Vindication of the Rights of Woman* and Anna Barbauld's "To a Lady, with Some Painted Flowers" and "The Rights of Woman"; between Keats' "La Belle Dame Sans Merci" and Letitia Landon's "The Proud Lady." Our decision to represent the historical contexts as debates both responds to the historical provocations that caused them—Paine and Wollstonecraft did write in response to Burke; Malthus and Opie in response to Godwin—and more importantly, it draws attention to the dynamics of polarity that structure many of these literary works.

III. ORGANIZATION OF WORKS

Our Table of Contents will immediately reveal at least two significant organizational differences from almost all other teaching anthologies and single-author editions of this literary period. First, we have organized texts chronologically according to *date of book publication* rather than date of composition. We hope to encourage a pedagogical attempt to understand this literary period as it developed in the public eye, rather than to reinforce a traditional emphasis upon the biographical development of individual writers. Second, we have applied this principle of chronological organization, with qualifications to be discussed below, without regard to genre; in other words, we have not separated texts generically—letters and journals are intermingled with poetry, fiction, and drama. Finally, we have listed authors themselves chronologically, according to birthdate, since we believe that generational allegiances influenced these writers.

Our rationale for this chronological organization is twofold. We hope to encourage a pedagogical representation of this literature as both participating in and constructing the public sphere. Writers entered into dialogues with the published work of other writers; hence it is critical to know exactly when a given text was widely available to other readers. Moreover, the context of a given poem within a specific published volume is itself an index to its meaning. For instance, knowing that Coleridge's readers first encountered "Frost at Midnight" in a volume entitled *Fears in Solitude* (1798) that included both "France: An Ode" and "Fears in Solitude" enables students and teachers to consider the significance of the volume's implicit political drama. They may reflect on the poem's exclusion from *Lyrical Ballads* (1798). Or they may ignore both to focus on exclusively formal matters, such as the poem's culmination of a line of Coleridgean meditative-descriptive lyrics beginning with "Effusion 35," later entitled "The Eolian Harp." Both teacher and student will have a greater range of pedagogical and scholarly possibilities open to them, however, if they know when and in what volume a given text first appeared.

It is also useful to identify clearly the works that could not have made a direct impact on their age because they remained unpublished. To do this, we have placed POSTHUMOUS PUBLICATIONS at the end of each authorial section. To take the most obvious example, except for the select few of his intimate audience, whatever readers thought of William Wordsworth did not derive from a reading of *The Prelude*, in any of its myriad forms. Nor could her readers know that Mary Shelley in 1819 had penned the first literary analysis of a father-daughter incestuous relationship written by a woman, because William Godwin both refused to send *Mathilda* to a publisher and to return the manuscript to his daughter; the novella was first published in 1959. We have included such works because they add to a fuller understanding of the author and his or her published works and because these texts figure prominently in contemporary scholarship.

We do not wish to erase the pedagogical possibility of thinking about the individual development of a given writer. To preserve this biographical history, we have noted in all cases where the information is available, the year of composition, as well as the date of its publication. We have also included as generous a selection as possible of letters and journal entries, as these often provide an understanding of unique psychological conflicts. In order to enable students to grasp the ways in which specific poems change over time, as poems-in-process, we have also in a few of the most striking instances provided both the poem as originally composed and the poem as published; for instance, we have printed major portions of all forms of William Wordsworth's *The Prelude* (1799, 1805, 1850). Where changes between published versions potentially alter the entire meaning of a poem, as in the case of Coleridge's "The Rime of the Ancyent Marinere," and "The Eolian Harp," we have included both the first and a later version.

HISTORICAL AND CULTURAL CONTEXT SECTIONS

The French Revolution and Rights of Man

Just as the British Industrial Revolution had been inexorably reshaping economic and social institutions since the mid-eighteenth century, the French Revolution of 1789 and its aftermath proved a comparable catalyst for the development of nineteenth-century liberalism and nationalism. Ironically, the French Revolution was more effective in advancing the Rights of Man in England than in France. By 1804, the French had a new despot in the person of Napoleon Bonaparte; in 1815, French monarchy was restored; and by 1830, France required a second revolution to establish a constitutional monarchy. To avoid the peril of comparable upheavals, the British parliament debated and passed by 1832 the first in a series of Reform Bills to extend the franchise to the rising middle class.

In *The Old Regime and the Revolution* (1856), the French sociologist and historian, Alexis de Tocqueville (1805–1859), said that "Never was any such event, stemming from factors so far back in the past, so inevitable yet so completely unforeseen." The Revolution was unforeseen because eighteenth-century France was the admiration of Europe and England for its refined culture, successful economy, and significant intellectual life. The French language was the *lingua communis* of trade and diplomacy. Things French were then (as now) widely imitated. Inspired by the rational religious and social critiques of their major *philosophes*—Diderot, Montesquieu, Rousseau, Voltaire—the revolutionaries of France destroyed the medieval institutions and alliances of Church, State, and Nobility.

At the outset, liberals in England approved. Coming soon after the centenary of Britain's "Glorious Revolution" of 1688, which resulted in the subordination of the monarchy to Parliament, the French Revolution seemed a belated emulation of England's political lead. Whigs, youthful intelligentsia, and activists of the British working class—all of whom were beginning to agitate for parliamentary reform—applauded the storming of France's political prison, the Bastille, on 14 July 1789. Reporting the event, the London *Times* said that "the right hand . . . of tyranny is cut off." Charles James Fox, leader of the Whig party, effused: "How much the greatest event it is that ever happened in the world! and how much the best!" Though only seven inmates were being housed in the dreaded Bastille, the symbolic value of its capitulation to a mob of radicals was stunning. The newly created National Assembly of France passed its "Declaration of the Rights of Man and the Citizen" shortly thereafter (26 August 1789), and English sympathizers began to reflect eloquently on the political and religious significance of events twenty-four miles across the Channel.

Joseph Priestley (1733–1804), the discoverer of oxygen, a Unitarian minister, and a major figure in the development of modern Unitarianism, believed the Revolution to be the fulfillment of biblical prophecy foretelling the peace and brotherhood that would precede the millennium and the world's end. Dissenting divine and founder of actuarial statistics, Richard Price (1723–1791), said in a sermon delivered to the London Revolution Society:

> I have lived to see a diffusion of knowledge, which has undermined superstition and error. I have lived to see the rights of men better understood than ever; and nations panting for liberty which seemed to have lost the idea of it. I have lived to see THIRTY MILLIONS of people, indignant and resolute, spurning at slavery, and demanding liberty with an irresistible voice.

Later that evening, the celebrants composed a congratulatory address to the French Assembly on "the Revolution in that country and on the prospect it gives to the two first Kingdoms in the World of a common participation in the blessings of Civil and Religious Liberty": to wit, that civil and political authority derives from the people; that governmental abuse of power justifies resistance; and that certain liberties and rights, such as liberty of conscience, trial by jury, freedom of the press, and freedom of election, were inviolable. Though the French *Declaration* identified seventeen Rights of Man, Price and the Revolutionists found that even their short list was sufficiently controversial to begin a debate that continued through the 1790s.

In response to unwary British liberals, the great Whig statesman and orator, Edmund Burke,* sounded the clarion of alarm on behalf of British political and domestic values. In *Reflections on the Revolution in France* (1790), Burke specified the grave risks in disposing of monarchy, primogeniture, chivalry, landed interests, and the orderly transition of political power that these assured. He particularly warned his countrymen against the intrusion of the *spirit* of revolution, the birth of which he dated not from the attack on the Bastille, but rather from the storming of the royal palace and arrest of Louis XVI and his queen, Marie Antoinette, on 5–6 October 1789.

Because Burke had an admirable record of support for controversial liberal causes, his vitriolic attack on France astonished his liberal allies. He had once applauded the "fierce spirit of liberty" displayed by English colonists in America during the American Revolution, while reflecting disappointedly that though England "still . . . respects" her freedom, she "formerly adored" it. He argued now that Price's three Rights of Man threatened the fabric of British society.

Burke's defense of traditional values and institutions inspired a great and popular debate by providing liberals with a coherent ideological position to attack. Published on 1 November 1790, *Reflections* sold almost 20,000 copies and went through eleven editions by September 1791. Within four years, *Reflections* spawned over seventy printed responses, including Mary Wollstonecraft's* *A Vindication of the Rights of Men* (1790), which appeared anonymously within a month of its publication, and Thomas Paine's* *Rights of Man* (1791), which sold hundreds of thousands of copies in innumerable cheap editions and became the political bible of working-class radicals for the next half century.

As long as liberals and idealists interpreted the Revolution as a millennial event, Paine, Wollstonecraft, and other radical voices were applauded. "Bliss was it in that dawn to be alive, / But to be young was very heaven!" William Wordsworth* recalls in his autobiographical epic, *The Prelude* (1850), for, "Not favored spots alone, but the whole earth, / The beauty wore of promise." Dire events in France, however, made Burke's *Reflections* a prophecy.

During the September Massacres of 1792, 1,200 to 1,400 priests, aristocrats, and common criminals were taken out of Paris prisons and publicly executed after mob trials. The decapitation of Louis XVI and Marie Antoinette in 1793 then inaugurated an internal Reign of Terror that led thousands from all classes and walks of life to local guillotines. In addition to the execution of its clergy, the Catholic Church also suffered the confiscation and redistribution of its property and lands by the revolutionaries.

Francophobia spread rapidly in England as the 1790s progressed. With a French invasion of England imminent in 1798–1799, political and civil rights were suppressed: *habeas corpus* was suspended, local officials permitted the harassment of French sympathizers, publishers were penalized for inflammatory publications, and government spies infiltrated societies dedicated to constitutional reform.

The rise and fall of the London Corresponding Society (1792–1799) is emblematic of reformist activity during the 1790s. Founded by a shoemaker, Thomas Hardy, the primary goal of the Corresponding Society was "Universal Suffrage and Annual Parliaments," which meant the annual election of parliamentary representatives by all men over the age of twenty-one. Its general mission was to arouse the growing mass of working-class artisans, shopkeepers, and mechanics into political consciousness and class activism through meetings, debates, and pamphleteering. At the time of its greatest influence, the Corresponding Society probably had about 2,000 paying members, with many more in attendance at its outdoor gatherings, where eloquent agitators such as John Thelwall* shaped the opinion of thousands toward radical ends. In 1794, Thelwall and Hardy were both tried for sedition for allegedly attempting to establish a society that would replace Parliament, take over the government by armed force, and execute the prime minister and royal family, in other words, for plotting a homegrown French revolution. They were acquitted, but the government's anti-reformist campaign was successful, as fear of imprisonment, trial, and possible execution silenced radical voices. Police actions against public gatherings, such as the Riot Act, which threatened death to those who refused to disperse within an hour of its reading, caused the zeal for reform to subside. In 1799, Parliament finally squelched the Corresponding Society by passing an act against its existence.

Political intrigue and rebellion made the revolutionary climate of Ireland hotter than England's. Disgruntled Irish Catholic nationalists and some protestants conspired with the French to overthrow the minority protestant government. Although government spies ruined a massive uprising planned by the Society of United Irishmen by having its Dublin leaders arrested, revolutionists in the countryside roused the peasants according to plan. The devastating result was that a quarter of the 100,000 peasants who revolted in the Irish Rebellion of May 1798 were killed within four months. Villages and towns were destroyed and the Irish Parliament was abolished. To add to the complexity of the aftermath, the Catholic bishops supported the Act of Union that closed the Irish Parliament and sent its members to join the British parliament in Westminster, England.

In general, English radicals suffered disenchantment at the Revolution's turn toward wanton internal violence and imperialist designs upon the British Isles. Radicals rationalized that France's continental aggression was justified by England's declaration of war against the infant republic in 1793 and by its collusion with continental despots. However, the rise of Napoleon Bonaparte as the first secular dictator since Alexander the Great was impossible to excuse. The centralized control of Napoleon's Consulate (1799–1804) and his campaign for world conquest during his reign as Emperor (1804–1814) made mockery of the Rights of Man.

Nevertheless, Napoleon's meteoric rise and fall captured the imagination of many in England and Europe and went far to establish the phenomenon of hero worship in the nineteenth century. In the decade between his coronation as emperor in 1804 and his final defeat at Waterloo in 1815, Napoleon astonished the world with a series of swift military victories throughout the Continent. His undoing was the overextension of his ambitions against Russia on land and England at sea. Even so, his demise was spectacular. After suffering defeats in 1814 against the alliance of England, Russia, Prussia, and Austria, Napoleon was exiled, only to flare up again for 100 days when he brazenly returned to Paris to take command of his faithful army against the surprised and embarrassed allies. Napoleon's defeat at Waterloo in 1815 at the hands of Arthur Wellesley, the Duke of Wellington, finally put an end to his feared reign and to the Napoleonic era. Napoleon was exiled to the remote South Atlantic island of St. Helena. The Congress of Vienna (1814–1815) restored the Bourbons to the French throne and reduced France to her borders of 1792.

Louis XVIII, the first monarch of the French restoration, attempted to conduct a reasonable constitutional monarchy to avoid alienating or provoking his subjects. Vengeful aristocrats, however, had no intention of being reasonable. By 1816 ultraroyalists had taken over the lower house, or Chamber of Deputies, and within five years liberals were out of power. After Louis's death in 1824, his brother Charles X acceded to the throne with a royalist agenda to reestablish the *ancien régime*. He required that the Chamber of Deputies raise funds to compensate aristocratic families that had lost their lands; he restored primogeniture; and he provided the Catholic Church governmental support. In July 1830, the middle classes revolted successfully to preserve their power and influence.

Despite England's disappointment with the political vagaries of France, the moral imperative to advance human and political rights lasted, albeit under a cloud of disenchantment and skepticism. There was simultaneously impatience with compromise and distrust of extremism. William Blake asserted that "Opposition is true friendship." The rhetoric of argument and debate permeated the literary imagination. As noted in the General Introduction, almost all major literary works of the period reflect tensions between doubt and affirmation. The following selections from Burke, Wollstonecraft, Paine, and Thomas Babington Macaulay provide textual milestones of England's Rights of Man debate from its opening salvos in the 1790s to its momentous and nervous conclusion in the Houses of Parliament in the early 1830s.

EDMUND BURKE

(1729–1797)

The biographical facts of Burke's life seem to have uniquely prepared him for the contentiousness of his times. As an Irish member of the British Parliament, raised by a Roman Catholic mother and protestant father, he embodied the political and religious schisms of Great Britain. He attempted to appropriate the traditions and culture of England, living in a gentleman's estate at Beaconsfield, yet political opponents demeaned his Irish heritage by remarking that his rhetoric smelled of whiskey and potatoes. Nonetheless, the astute literary critic and steadfast political radical, William Hazlitt,* believed that Burke's prose was incomparable. Thomas Babington Macaulay* claimed that Burke was "the greatest man since Milton" for the profundity of his political thought and for his sustained eloquence.

Edmund Burke was born in Dublin, 12 January 1729, the second son of attorney Richard Burke. The religious tolerance he felt throughout his life is probably due to being raised in a family of mixed religion and then being educated by Quakers. Burke attended Trinity College, Dublin, 1743–1748, and moved to London in 1750 to study law. Literary work seems to have held more appeal for him, however. Burke was never called to the bar, which angered his father into cancelling financial support. Forced to earn a living, Burke published a variety of aesthetic and political works, the most distinguished of which was *The Philosophical Inquiry into the Origin of Our Ideas on the Sublime and the Beautiful* (1757). In 1766, Burke received a seat in Parliament through the influence of a family friend. Despite his Irish accent and harsh tone, his rhetorical powers and innate political sagacity soon "filled the town [London] with wonder." Burke was denied cabinet level responsibilities despite his abilities, however, because Whig oligarchs were jealous of the "Irish adventurer." Burke remained the moral leader of his party until splitting with liberal allies over his denunciation of the French Revolution in *Reflections on the Revolution in France.* George III said that *Reflections* was "a good book, a very good book; every gentleman ought to read it," and tens of thousands of men, and women, did. Burke lost favor with his party, however, and became isolated and embittered until his parliamentary career ended in 1794. He died a "dishonoured prophet" in 1797.

from Reflections on the Revolution in France,

and on the proceedings in certain societies in London relative to that event: in a letter intended to have been sent to a gentleman in Paris

(1790)

Solicitous chiefly for the peace of my own country, but by no means unconcerned for your's, I wish to communicate more largely, what was at first intended only for your private satisfaction. I shall still keep your affairs in my eye, and continue to address myself to you. Indulging myself in the freedom of epistolary intercourse, I beg leave to throw out my thoughts, and express my feelings, just as they arise in my mind, with very little attention to formal method. . . . It looks to me as if I were in a great crisis, not of the affairs of France alone, but of all Europe, perhaps of more than Europe. All circumstances taken together, the French revolution is the most astonishing that has hitherto happened in the world. The most wonderful things are brought about in many instances by means the most absurd and ridiculous; in the most ridiculous modes; and apparently, by the most contemptible instruments. Every thing seems out of nature in this strange chaos of levity and ferocity, and of all sorts of crimes jumbled together with all sorts of follies. In viewing this monstrous tragi-comic scene, the most opposite passions necessarily succeed, and sometimes mix with each other in the mind; alternate contempt and indignation; alternate laughter and tears; alternate scorn and horror. . . .

You will observe, that from Magna Charta to the Declaration of Right,[1] it has been the uniform policy of our constitution to claim and assert our liberties, as an *entailed inheritance* derived to us from our forefathers, and to be transmitted to our posterity; as an estate specially belonging to the people of this kingdom without any reference whatever to any other more general or prior right. By this means our constitution preserves an unity in so great a diversity of its parts. We have an inheritable crown; an inheritable peerage; and an house of commons and a people inheriting privileges, franchises, and liberties, from a long line of ancestors.

This policy appears to me to be the result of profound reflection; or rather the happy effect of following nature, which is wisdom without reflection, and above it. A spirit of innovation is generally the result of a selfish temper and confined views. People will not look forward to posterity, who never look backward to their ancestors. Besides, the people of England well know, that the idea of inheritance furnishes a sure principle of conservation, and a sure principle of transmission; without at all excluding a principle of improvement. It leaves acquisition free; but it secures what it acquires. Whatever advantages are obtained by a state proceeding on these maxims, are locked fast as in a sort of family settlement; grasped as in a kind of mortmain for ever.[2] By a constitutional policy, working after the pattern of nature, we receive, we hold, we transmit our government and our privileges, in the same manner in which we enjoy and transmit our property and our lives. The institutions of policy, the goods of fortune, the gifts of Providence, are handed down, to us and from us, in the same course and order. Our political system is placed in a just correspondence and symmetry with the order of the world, and with the mode of existence decreed to a permanent body composed of transitory parts; wherein, by the disposition of a stupendous wisdom, moulding together the great mysterious incorporation of the human race, the whole, at one time, is never old, or middle-aged, or young, but in a condition of unchangeable constancy, moves on through the varied tenour of perpetual decay, fall, renovation, and progression. Thus, by preserving the method of nature in the conduct of the state, in what we improve we are never wholly new; in what we retain we are never wholly obsolete. By adhering in this manner and on those principles to our forefathers, we are guided not by the superstition of antiquarians, but by the spirit of philosophic analogy. In this choice of inheritance we have given to our frame of polity the image of a relation in blood; binding up the constitution of our country with our dearest domestic ties; adopting our fundamental laws into the bosom of our family affections; keeping inseparable, and cherishing with the warmth of all their combined and mutually reflected charities, our state, our hearths, our sepulchres, and our altars. . . .

Far am I from denying in theory; full as far is my heart from withholding in practice (if I were of power to give or to withhold) the *real* rights of men.[3] In denying their false claims of right, I do not mean to injure those which are real, and are such as their pretended rights would totally destroy. If civil society be made for the advantage of man, all the advantages for which it is made become his right. It is an institution of beneficence; and law itself is only beneficence acting by a rule. Men have a right to live by that rule; they have a right to justice; as between their fellows, whether their fellows are in politic function or in ordinary occupation. They have a right to the fruits of their industry; and to the means of making their industry fruitful. They have a right to the acquisitions of their parents;

[1] The Magna Carta was the result of an agreement in 1215 between King John and various constituencies—lords, high churchmen, and London merchants—that the king would confirm and guarantee historic liberties. The Declaration of Right came out of the "Glorious Revolution" of 1688, which established a limited monarchy. The civil liberties of the privileged classes were guaranteed, the monarch ruled at the consent of Parliament, and monarchs were subject to law.

[2] **mortmain**: In law, "the condition of lands or tenements held inalienably by an ecclesiastical or other corporation" (*Oxford English Dictionary*). Literally *dead hand*, suggesting the posthumous control of such land.

[3] Burke sets out to refute the rights inferred by Price in his sermon, *A Discourse on the Love of Our Country* (November 1789), and comparable rights adopted by the National Assembly of Revolutionary France in its *Rights of Man and the Citizen* (1789). Neither list is incompatible with the rights claimed in the American *Declaration of Independence* (1776).

to the nourishment and improvement of their offspring; to instruction in life, and to consolation in death. Whatever each man can separately do, without trespassing upon others, he has a right to do for himself; and he has a right to a fair portion of all which society, with all its combinations of skill and force, can do in his favour. In this partnership all men have equal rights; but not to equal things. He that has but five shillings in the partnership, has as good a right to it, as he that has five hundred pound has to his larger proportion. But he has not a right to an equal dividend in the product of the joint stock; and as to the share of power, authority, and direction which each individual ought to have in the management of the state, that I must deny to be amongst the direct original rights of man in civil society; for I have in my contemplation the civil social man, and no other. It is a thing to be settled by convention. . . .

. . . History will record, that on the morning of the 6th of October 1789, the king and queen of France, after a day of confusion, alarm, dismay, and slaughter, lay down, under the pledged security of public faith, to indulge nature in a few hours of respite, and troubled melancholy repose. From this sleep the queen was first startled by the voice of the centinel at her door, who cried out to her, to save herself by flight—that this was the last proof of fidelity he could give—that they were upon him, and he was dead. Instantly he was cut down. A band of cruel ruffians and assassins, reeking with his blood, rushed into the chamber of the queen, and pierced with an hundred strokes of bayonets and poniards the bed, from whence this persecuted woman had but just time to fly almost naked, and through ways unknown to the murderers had escaped to seek refuge at the feet of a king and husband, not secure of his own life for a moment.

This king, to say no more of him, and this queen, and their infant children (who once would have been the pride and hope of a great and generous people) were then forced to abandon the sanctuary of the most splendid palace in the world, which they left swimming in blood, polluted by massacre, and strewed with scattered limbs and mutilated carcases. Thence they were conducted into the capital of their kingdom. Two had been selected from the unprovoked, unresisted, promiscuous slaughter, which was made of the gentlemen of birth and family who composed the king's body guard. These two gentlemen, with all the parade of an execution of justice, were cruelly and publickly dragged to the block, and beheaded in the great court of the palace. Their heads were stuck upon spears, and led the procession; whilst the royal captives who followed in the train were slowly moved along, amidst the horrid yells, and shrilling screams, and frantic dances, and infamous contumelies,[4] and all the unutterable abominations of the furies of hell, in the abused shape of the vilest of women. After they had been made to taste, drop by drop, more than the bitterness of death, in the slow torture of a journey of twelve miles, protracted to six hours, they were, under a guard, composed of those very soldiers who had thus conducted them through this famous triumph, lodged in one of the old palaces of Paris,[5] now converted into a Bastile [*sic*] for kings. . . .

I hear that the august person,[6] . . . though he supported himself, felt much on that shameful occasion. As a man, it became him to feel for his wife and his children, and the faithful guards of his person, that were massacred in cold blood about him; as a prince, it became him to feel for the strange and frightful transformation of his civilized subjects, and to be more grieved for them, than solicitous for himself. It derogates little from his fortitude, while it adds infinitely to the honour of his humanity. I am very sorry to say it, very sorry indeed, that such personages are in a situation in which it is not unbecoming in us to praise the virtues of the great.

I hear, and I rejoice to hear, that the great lady,[7] the other object of the triumph, has borne that day (one is interested that beings made for suffering should suffer well) and that she bears all the succeeding days, that she bears the imprisonment of her husband, and her own captivity, and the exile of her friends, and the insulting adulation of addresses, and the whole weight of her accumulated wrongs, with a serene patience, in a manner suited to her rank and race, and becoming the offspring of a sovereign distinguished for her piety and her courage; that like her she has lofty sentiments; that she feels with the dignity of a Roman matron; that in the last extremity she will save herself from the last disgrace, and that if she must fall, she will fall by no ignoble hand.

It is now sixteen or seventeen years since I saw the queen of France, then the dauphiness, at Versailles; and surely never lighted on this orb, which she hardly seemed to touch, a more delightful vision. I saw her just above the

---

[4] **contumelies:** Insolent and rude remarks and acts.

[5] The Tuileries.

[6] Louis XVI.

[7] The queen, Marie Antoinette, daughter of the Austrian Archduchess Maria Theresa and the Holy Roman Emperor Francis I.

horizon, decorating and cheering the elevated sphere she just began to move in,—glittering like the morning-star, full of life, and splendor, and joy. Oh! what a revolution! and what an heart must I have, to contemplate without emotion that elevation and that fall! Little did I dream when she added titles of veneration to those of enthusiastic, distant, respectful love, that she should ever be obliged to carry the sharp antidote against disgrace concealed in that bosom; little did I dream that I should have lived to see such disasters fallen upon her in a nation of gallant men, in a nation of men of honour and of cavaliers. I thought ten thousand swords must have leaped from their scabbards to avenge even a look that threatened her with insult.—But the age of chivalry is gone.—That of sophisters, oeconomists, and calculators,[8] has succeeded; and the glory of Europe is extinguished for ever. Never, never more, shall we behold that generous loyalty to rank and sex, that proud submission, that dignified obedience, that subordination of the heart, which kept alive, even in servitude itself, the spirit of an exalted freedom. The unbought grace of life, the cheap defence of nations, the nurse of manly sentiment and heroic enterprize is gone! It is gone, that sensibility of principle, that chastity of honour, which felt a stain like a wound, which inspired courage whilst it mitigated ferocity, which ennobled whatever it touched, and under which vice itself lost half its evil, by losing all its grossness.

This mixed system of opinion and sentiment had its origin in the antient chivalry; and the principle, though varied in its appearance by the varying state of human affairs, subsisted and influenced through a long succession of generations, even to the time we live in. If it should ever be totally extinguished, the loss I fear will be great. It is this which has given its character to modern Europe. It is this which has distinguished it under all its forms of government, and distinguished it to its advantage, from the states of Asia, and possibly from those states which flourished in the most brilliant periods of the antique world. It was this, which, without confounding ranks, had produced a noble equality, and handed it down through all the gradations of social life. It was this opinion which mitigated kings into companions, and raised private men to be fellows with kings. Without force, or opposition, it subdued the fierceness of pride and power; it obliged sovereigns to submit to the soft collar of social esteem, compelled stern authority to submit to elegance, and gave a domination vanquisher of laws, to be subdued by manners.

But now all is to be changed. All the pleasing illusions, which made power gentle, and obedience liberal, which harmonized the different shades of life, and which, by a bland assimilation, incorporated into politics the sentiments which beautify and soften private society, are to be dissolved by this new conquering empire of light and reason. All the decent drapery of life is to be rudely torn off. All the superadded ideas, furnished from the wardrobe of a moral imagination, which the heart owns, and the understanding ratifies, as necessary to cover the defects of our naked shivering nature, and to raise it to dignity in our own estimation, are to be exploded as ridiculous, absurd, and antiquated fashion.

On this scheme of things, a king is but a man; a queen is but a woman; a woman is but an animal; and an animal not of the highest order. All homage paid to the sex in general as such, and without distinct views, is to be regarded as romance and folly. Regicide, and parricide, and sacrilege, are but fictions of superstition, corrupting jurisprudence by destroying its simplicity. The murder of a king, or a queen, or a bishop, or a father, are only common homicide; and if the people are by any chance, or in any way gainers by it, a sort of homicide much the most pardonable, and into which we ought not to make too severe a scrutiny.

On the scheme of this barbarous philosophy, which is the offspring of cold hearts and muddy understandings, and which is as void of solid wisdom, as it is destitute of all taste and elegance, laws are to be supported only by their own terrors, and by the concern, which each individual may find in them, from his own private speculations, or can spare to them from his own private interests. In the groves of *their* academy, at the end of every visto, you see nothing but the gallows. Nothing is left which engages the affections on the part of the commonwealth. On the principles of this mechanic philosophy, our institutions can never be embodied, if I may use the expression, in persons; so as to create in us love, veneration, admiration, or attachment. But that sort of reason which banishes the affections is incapable of filling their place. These public affections, combined with manners, are required sometimes as supplements, sometimes as correctives, always as aids to law. The precept given by a wise man, as well as a great critic, for the construction of poems, is equally true as to states. *Non satis est pulchra esse*

[8] Burke probably refers to British *philosophes,* such as social reformer Jeremy Bentham (1748–1832), founder of utilitarianism; and economist Adam Smith (1723–1790), advocate of *laissez-faire* economics.

poemata, dulcia sunto.[9] There ought to be a system of manners in every nation which a well-formed mind would be disposed to relish. To make us love our country, our country ought to be lovely.

But power, of some kind or other, will survive the shock in which manners and opinions perish; and it will find other and worse means for its support. The usurpation which, in order to subvert antient institutions, has destroyed antient principles, will hold power by arts similar to those by which it has acquired it. When the old feudal and chivalrous spirit of *Fealty*, which, by freeing kings from fear, freed both kings and subjects from the precautions of tyranny, shall be extinct in the minds of men, plots and assassinations will be anticipated by preventive murder and preventive confiscation, and that long roll of grim and bloody maxims, which form the political code of all power, not standing on its own honour, and the honour of those who are to obey it. Kings will be tyrants from policy when subjects are rebels from principle.

When antient opinions and rules of life are taken away, the loss cannot possibly be estimated. From that moment we have no compass to govern us; nor can we know distinctly to what port we steer. Europe undoubtedly, taken in a mass, was in a flourishing condition the day on which your Revolution was compleated. How much of that prosperous state was owing to the spirit of our old manners and opinions is not easy to say; but as such causes cannot be indifferent in their operation, we must presume, that, on the whole, their operation was beneficial.

We are but too apt to consider things in the state in which we find them, without sufficiently adverting to the causes by which they have been produced, and possibly may be upheld. Nothing is more certain, than that our manners, our civilization, and all the good things which are connected with manners, and with civilization, have, in this European world of ours, depended for ages upon two principles; and were indeed the result of both combined; I mean the spirit of a gentleman, and the spirit of religion. The nobility and the clergy, the one by profession, the other by patronage, kept learning in existence, even in the midst of arms and confusions, and whilst governments were rather in their causes than formed. Learning paid back what it received to nobility and to priesthood; and paid it with usury, by enlarging their ideas and by furnishing their minds. Happy if they had all continued to know their indissoluble union, and their proper place! Happy if learning, not debauched by ambition, had been satisfied to continue the instructor, and not aspired to be the master! Along with its natural protectors and guardians, learning will be cast into the mire, and trodden down under the hoofs of a swinish multitude.

If, as I suspect, modern letters owe more than they are always willing to own to antient manners, so do other interests which we value full as much as they are worth. Even commerce, and trade, and manufacture, the gods of our oeconomical politicians, are themselves perhaps but creatures; are themselves but effects, which, as first causes, we choose to worship. They certainly grew under the same shade in which learning flourished. They too may decay with their natural protecting principles. With you, for the present at least, they all threaten to disappear together. Where trade and manufactures are wanting to a people, and the spirit of nobility and religion remains, sentiment supplies, and not always ill supplies their place; but if commerce and the arts should be lost in an experiment to try how well a state may stand without these old fundamental principles, what sort of a thing must be a nation of gross, stupid, ferocious, and at the same time, poor and sordid barbarians, destitute of religion, honour, or manly pride, possessing nothing at present, and hoping for nothing hereafter?

I wish you may not be going fast, and by the shortest cut, to that horrible and disgustful situation. Already there appears a poverty of conception, a coarseness and vulgarity in all the proceedings of the assembly and of all their instructors. Their liberty is not liberal. Their science is presumptuous ignorance. Their humanity is savage and brutal.

It is not clear, whether in England we learned those grand and decorous principles, and manners, of which considerable traces yet remain, from you, or whether you took them from us. But to you, I think we trace them best. You seem to me to be—*gentis incunabula nostrae.*[10] France has always more or less influenced manners in England; and when your fountain is choaked up and polluted, the stream will not run long, or not run clear with us, or perhaps with any nation. This gives all Europe, in my opinion, but too close and connected a concern in what is done in France. Excuse me, therefore, if I have dwelt too long on the atrocious spectacle of the sixth of October 1789, or have given too much scope to the reflections which have arisen in my mind on occasion of the most

[9] From Horace's *Ars Poetica*, 99–100: "It is not enough that poems be beautiful; let them be tender and affecting."

[10] From Vergil's *Aenead*, III.105: "The cradle of our race."

important of all revolutions, which may be dated from that day, I mean a revolution in sentiments, manners, and moral opinions. As things now stand, with every thing respectable destroyed without us, and an attempt to destroy within us every principle of respect, one is almost forced to apologize for harbouring the common feelings of men.

Why do I feel so differently from the Reverend Dr. Price, and those of his lay flock, who will choose to adopt the sentiments of his discourse?—For this plain reason—because it is *natural* I should; because we are so made as to be affected at such spectacles with melancholy sentiments upon the unstable condition of mortal prosperity, and the tremendous uncertainty of human greatness; because in those natural feelings we learn great lessons; because in events like these our passions instruct our reason; because when kings are hurl'd from their thrones by the Supreme Director of this great drama, and become the objects of insult to the base, and of pity to the good, we behold such disasters in the moral, as we should behold a miracle in the physical order of things. We are alarmed into reflexion; our minds (as it has long since been observed) are purified by terror and pity;[11] our weak unthinking pride is humbled, under the dispensations of a mysterious wisdom.—Some tears might be drawn from me, if such a spectacle were exhibited on the stage. I should be truly ashamed of finding in myself that superficial, theatric sense of painted distress, whilst I could exult over it in real life. With such a perverted mind, I could never venture to shew my face at a tragedy. People would think the tears that Garrick formerly, or that Siddons[12] not long since, have extorted from me, were the tears of hypocrisy; I should know them to be the tears of folly.

. . . I have often been astonished, considering that we are divided from you but by a slender dyke of about twenty-four miles, and that the mutual intercourse between the two countries has lately been very great, to find how little you seem to know of us. I suspect that this is owing to your forming a judgment of this nation from certain publications, which do, very erroneously, if they do at all, represent the opinions and dispositions generally prevalent in England. The vanity, restlessness, petulance, and spirit of intrigue of several petty cabals, who attempt to hide their total want of consequence in bustle and noise, and puffing, and mutual quotation of each other, makes you imagine that our contemptuous neglect of their abilities is a mark of general acquiescence in their opinions. No such thing, I assure you. Because half a dozen grasshoppers under a fern make the field ring with their importunate chink, whilst thousands of great cattle, reposed beneath the shadow of the British oak, chew the cud and are silent, pray do not imagine, that those who make the noise are the only inhabitants of the field; that of course, they are many in number; or that, after all, they are other than the little shrivelled, meagre, hopping, though loud and troublesome insects of the hour.

I almost venture to affirm, that not one in a hundred amongst us participates in the "triumph" of the Revolution Society.[13] If the king and queen of France, and their children, were to fall into our hands by the chance of war, in the most acrimonious of all hostilities (I deprecate such an event, I deprecate such hostility) they would be treated with another sort of triumphal entry into London. We formerly have had a king of France[14] in that situation; you have read how he was treated by the victor in the field; and in what manner he was afterwards received in England. Four hundred years have gone over us; but I believe we are not materially changed since that period. Thanks to our sullen resistance to innovation, thanks to the cold sluggishness of our national character, we still bear the stamp of our forefathers. We have not (as I conceive) lost the generosity and dignity of thinking of the fourteenth century; nor as yet have we subtilized ourselves into savages. We are not the converts of Rousseau; we are not the disciples of Voltaire; Helvetius has made no progress amongst us.[15] Atheists are not our preachers; madmen are not our lawgivers. We know that *we* have made no discoveries; and we think that no discoveries are to be made, in morality; nor many in the great principles of government, nor in the ideas of liberty, which were understood long before we were born, altogether as well as they will be after the grave has heaped its mould upon our presumption, and the silent tomb shall have imposed its law on our pert loquacity. In England we have not yet been completely embowelled of

[11] Burke alludes to Aristotle's claim that *katharsis*, or the proper purgation of "pity and fear," is the chief end of tragedy (*Poetics, VI*).

[12] David Garrick (1717–1779) and Sarah Siddons (1755–1831) were two of the greatest actors of Burke's time.

[13] The London Revolution Society was formed in 1788 to celebrate the centenary of the Glorious Revolution.

[14] During the Hundred Years War, the French king, John II the Good (1319–1364), was brought captive to England after the English victory at Poitiers (1356).

[15] **Voltaire, Rousseau, and Helvetius:** French *philosophes*.

our natural entrails; we still feel within us, and we cherish and cultivate, those inbred sentiments which are the faithful guardians, the active monitors of our duty, the true supporters of all liberal and manly morals. We have not been drawn and trussed, in order that we may be filled, like stuffed birds in a museum, with chaff and rags, and paltry, blurred shreds of paper about the rights of man. We preserve the whole of our feelings still native and entire, unsophisticated by pedantry and infidelity. We have real hearts of flesh and blood beating in our bosoms. We fear God; we look up with awe to kings; with affection to parliaments; with duty to magistrates; with reverence to priests; and with respect to nobility. Why? Because when such ideas are brought before our minds, it is *natural* to be so affected; because all other feelings are false and spurious, and tend to corrupt our minds, to vitiate our primary morals, to render us unfit for rational liberty; and by teaching us a servile, licentious, and abandoned insolence, to be our low sport for a few holidays, to make us perfectly fit for, and justly deserving of slavery, through the whole course of our lives.

You see, Sir, that in this enlightened age I am bold enough to confess, that we are generally men of untaught feelings; that instead of casting away all our old prejudices, we cherish them to a very considerable degree, and, to take more shame to ourselves, we cherish them because they are prejudices; and the longer they have lasted, and the more generally they have prevailed, the more we cherish them. We are afraid to put men to live and trade each on his own private stock of reason; because we suspect that this stock in each man is small, and that the individuals would be better to avail themselves of the general bank and capital of nations, and of ages. Many of our men of speculation, instead of exploding general prejudices, employ their sagacity to discover the latent wisdom which prevails in them. If they find what they seek, and they seldom fail, they think it more wise to continue the prejudice, with the reason involved, than to cast away the coat of prejudice, and to leave nothing but the naked reason; because prejudice, with its reason, has a motive to give action to that reason, and an affection which will give it permanence. Prejudice is of ready application in the emergency; it previously engages the mind in a steady course of wisdom and virtue, and does not leave the man hesitating in the moment of decision, sceptical, puzzled, and unresolved. Prejudice renders a man's virtue his habit; and not a series of unconnected acts. Through just prejudice, his duty becomes a part of his nature.

Your literary men, and your politicians, and so do the whole clan of the enlightened among us, essentially differ in these points. They have no respect for the wisdom of others; but they pay it off by a very full measure of confidence in their own. With them it is a sufficient motive to destroy an old scheme of things, because it is an old one. As to the new, they are in no sort of fear with regard to the duration of a building run up in haste; because duration is no object to those who think little or nothing has been done before their time, and who place all their hopes in discovery. They conceive, very systematically, that all things which give perpetuity are mischievous, and therefore they are at inexpiable war with all establishments. They think that government may vary like modes of dress, and with as little ill effect. . . .

MARY WOLLSTONECRAFT

(1759–1797)

A Vindication of the Rights of Men, in a Letter to the Right Honourable Edmund Burke (1790) was the first of the liberal responses to Burke's *Reflections on the Revolution in France* (1790). It was published by friend and radical publisher, Joseph Johnson, for whom Wollstonecraft worked as reader, translator, reviewer, and editorial assistant for the *Analytical Review*. (See Headnote to WOLLSTONECRAFT.)

from A Vindication of the Rights of Men,

in a Letter to the Right Honourable Edmund Burke[1]
Occasioned by His Reflections on the Revolution in France
(1790)

SIR,

It is not necessary, with courtly insincerity, to apologise to you for thus intruding on your precious time, nor to profess that I think it an honour to discuss an important subject with a man whose literary abilities have raised him to notice in the state. I have not yet learned to twist my periods, nor, in the equivocal idiom of politeness, to disguise my sentiments, and imply what I should be afraid to utter: if, therefore, in the course of this epistle, I chance to express contempt, and even indignation, with some emphasis, I beseech you to believe that it is not a flight of fancy; for truth, in morals, has ever appeared to me the essence of the sublime; and, in taste, simplicity the only criterion of the beautiful. But I war not with an individual when I contend for the *rights of men* and the liberty of reason. You see I do not condescend to cull my words to avoid the invidious phrase, nor shall I be prevented from giving a manly definition of it, by the flimsy ridicule which a lively fancy has interwoven with the present acceptation of the term. Reverencing the rights of humanity, I shall dare to assert them; not intimidated by the horse laugh that you have raised, or waiting till time has wiped away the compassionate tears which you have elaborately laboured to excite.

From the many just sentiments interspersed through the letter before me, and from the whole tendency of it, I should believe you to be a good, though a vain man, if some circumstances in your conduct did not render the inflexibility of your integrity doubtful; and for this vanity a knowledge of human nature enables me to discover such extenuating circumstances, in the very texture of your mind, that I am ready to call it amiable, and separate the public from the private character. . . .

Quitting now the flowers of rhetoric, let us, Sir, reason together; and, believe me, I should not have meddled with these troubled waters, in order to point out your inconsistencies, if your wit had not burnished up some rusty, baneful opinions, and swelled the shallow current of ridicule till it resembled the flow of reason, and presumed to be the test of truth.

I shall not attempt to follow you through 'horse-way and foot-path';[2] but, attacking the foundation of your opinions, I shall leave the superstructure to find a centre of gravity on which it may lean till some strong blast puffs it into the air; or your teeming fancy, which the ripening judgment of sixty years has not tamed, produces another

[1] Edmund Burke (1729–1797), eminent Anglo-Irish orator and politician, was famous as an aesthetician (see AESTHETICS), as a defender of the American colonists and of Irish emancipation, and as an advocate for the establishment of political parties independent of the Crown (in his *Thoughts on the Cause of the Present Discontents*, 1770). However, in his *Reflections on the Revolution in France* (1790), he defended the established monarchies of Europe.

[2] Shakespeare, *King Lear*, IV.i.55.

Chinese erection,[3] to stare, at every turn, the plain country people in the face, who bluntly call such an airy edifice—a folly.

The birthright of man, to give you, Sir, a short definition of this disputed right, is such a degree of liberty, civil and religious, as is compatible with the liberty of every other individual with whom he is united in a social compact, and the continued existence of that compact.[4]

Liberty, in this simple, unsophisticated sense, I acknowledge, is a fair idea that has never yet received a form in the various governments that have been established on our beauteous globe; the demon of property has ever been at hand to encroach on the sacred rights of men, and to fence round with awful pomp laws that war with justice. But that it results from the eternal foundation of right—from immutable truth—who will presume to deny, that pretends to rationality—if reason has led them to build their morality[5] and religion on an everlasting foundation—the attributes of God?

I glow with indignation when I attempt, methodically, to unravel your slavish paradoxes, in which I can find no fixed first principle to refute; I shall not, therefore, condescend to shew where you affirm in one page what you deny in another; and how frequently you draw conclusions without any previous premises:—it would be something like cowardice to fight with a man who had never exercised the weapons with which his opponent chose to combat, and irksome to refute sentence after sentence in which the latent spirit of tyranny appeared.

I perceive, from the whole tenor of your Reflections, that you have a mortal antipathy to reason; but, if there is any thing like argument, or first principles, in your wild declamation, behold the result:—that we are to reverence the rust of antiquity, and term the unnatural customs, which ignorance and mistaken self-interest have consolidated, the sage fruit of experience: nay, that, if we do discover some errors, our *feelings* should lead us to excuse, with blind love, or unprincipled filial affection, the venerable vestiges of ancient days. These are gothic notions of beauty—the ivy is beautiful, but, when it insidiously destroys the trunk from which it receives support, who would not grub it up?

Further, that we ought cautiously to remain for ever in frozen inactivity, because a thaw, whilst it nourishes the soil, spreads a temporary inundation; and the fear of risking any personal present convenience should prevent a struggle for the most estimable advantages. This is sound reasoning, I grant, in the mouth of the rich and short-sighted.

Yes, Sir, the strong gained riches, the few have sacrificed the many to their vices; and, to be able to pamper their appetites, and supinely exist without exercising mind or body, they have ceased to be men.—Lost to the relish of true pleasure, such beings would, indeed, deserve compassion, if injustice was not softened by the tyrant's plea—necessity; if prescription was not raised as an immortal boundary against innovation. Their minds, in fact, instead of being cultivated, have been so warped by education, that it may require some ages to bring them back to nature, and enable them to see their true interest, with that degree of conviction which is necessary to influence their conduct.

The civilization which has taken place in Europe has been very partial, and, like every custom that an arbitrary point of honour has established, refines the manners at the expence of morals, by making sentiments and opinions current in conversation that have no root in the heart, or weight in the cooler resolves of the mind.—And what has stopped its progress?—hereditary property—hereditary honours. The man has been changed into an artificial monster by the station in which he was born, and the consequent homage that benumbed his faculties like the torpedo's[6] touch;—or a being, with a capacity of reasoning, would not have failed to discover, as his faculties unfolded, that true happiness arose from the friendship and intimacy which can only be enjoyed by equals; and that charity is not a condescending distribution of alms, but an intercourse of good offices and mutual benefits, founded on respect for justice and humanity. . . .

---

[3] Chinese pagodas were fashionable garden structures in England in the late eighteenth century.

[4] Cf. John Locke, *Two Treatises of Government* (1690), II, 97: ". . . every Man, by consenting with others to make one Body Politick under one Government, puts himself under an obligation to every one of that Society, to submit to the determination of the *majority*, and to be concluded by it; or else this *original Compact*, whereby he with others incorporates into *one Society*, would signify nothing, and be no Compact."

[5] As religion is included in my idea of morality, I should not have mentioned the term without specifying all the simple ideas which that comprehensive word generalizes; but as the charge of atheism has been very freely banded about in the letter I am considering, I wish to guard against misrepresentation [M. W.].

[6] **torpedo**: flat fish that emits electrical discharges, also called "numb-fish."

It is necessary emphatically to repeat, that there are rights which men inherit at their birth, as rational creatures, who were raised above the brute creation by their improvable faculties; and that, in receiving these, not from their forefathers, but from God, prescription can never undermine natural rights.

A father may dissipate his property without his child having any right to complain;—but should he attempt to sell him for a slave, or fetter him with laws contrary to reason; nature, in enabling him to discern good from evil, teaches him to break the ignoble chain, and not to believe that bread becomes flesh, and wine blood, because his parents swallowed the Eucharist[7] with this blind persuasion.

There is no end to this implicit submission to authority—somewhere it must stop, or we return to barbarism; and the capacity of improvement, which gives us a natural sceptre on earth, is a cheat, an ignis-fatuus,[8] that leads us from inviting meadows into bogs and dung-hills. And if it be allowed that many of the precautions, with which any alteration was made, in our government, were prudent, it rather proves its weakness than substantiates an opinion of the soundness of the stamina, or the excellence of the constitution.

But on what principle Mr Burke could defend American independence, I cannot conceive,[9] for the whole tenor of his plausible arguments settles slavery on an everlasting foundation. Allowing his servile reverence for antiquity, and prudent attention to self-interest, to have the force which he insists on, the slave trade ought never to be abolished; and, because our ignorant forefathers, not understanding the native dignity of man, sanctioned a traffic that outrages every suggestion of reason and religion, we are to submit to the inhuman custom, and term an atrocious insult to humanity the love of our country, and a proper submission to the laws by which our property is secured.—Security of property! Behold, in a few words, the sacrificed.—The Briton takes place of the man, and the image of God is lost in the citizen! But it is not that enthusiastic flame which in Greece and Rome consumed every sordid passion: no, self is the focus; and the disparting rays rise not above our foggy atmosphere. But softly—it is only the property of the rich that is secure; the man who lives by the sweat of his brow has no asylum from oppression; the strong man may enter—when was the castle of the poor sacred?—and the base informer steal him from the family that depend on his industry for subsistence. . . .[10]

A government that acts in this manner cannot be called a good parent, nor inspire natural (habitual is the proper word) affection, in the breasts of children who are thus disregarded.

The game laws are almost as oppressive to the peasantry as press-warrants to the mechanic.[11] In this land of liberty what is to secure the property of the poor farmer when his noble landlord chooses to plant a decoy field[12] near his little property? Game devour the fruit of his labour; but fines and imprisonment await him if he dare to kill any—or lift up his hand to interrupt the pleasure of his lord. How many families have been plunged, in the *sporting* countries, into misery and vice for some paltry transgression of these coercive laws, by the natural consequence of that anger which a man feels when he sees the reward of his industry laid waste by unfeeling luxury?—when his children's bread is given to dogs!

You have shewn, Sir, by your silence on these subjects, that your respect for rank has swallowed up the common feelings of humanity; you seem to consider the poor as only the live stock of an estate, the feather of hereditary nobility.

The only security of property that nature authorizes and reason sanctions is, the right a man has to enjoy the acquisitions which his talents and industry have acquired;

---

[7] **Eucharist**: Christian sacrament that reenacts the last supper of Jesus with his disciples, in which he gave them bread saying, "This is my body" and wine saying, "This is my blood" (Matthew 26, Mark 14, Luke 22).

[8] **ignis-fatuus**: Latin, foolish or false fire; phosphorescent light over marshy ground supposedly caused by the spontaneous combustion of decaying organic matter (also called "will-o'-the-wisp"); hence any delusive guiding principle or hope.

[9] Cf. Burke, *On Conciliation with America* (22 March 1775), in which he argues that the American Revolution is an affirmation of traditional English liberties.

[10] By law, the English King could conscript (or "impress") able-bodied but unwilling men into the army or navy; wealthy conscripts could either purchase their release or pay another man to take their place. Wollstonecraft also refers to the fact that thefts of as little as 5 shillings (about 5 dollars in 1995 US currency) could be punished with death (until 1813).

[11] **game laws**: British law restricting the right to kill game to substantial landowners or long-lease holders (1389–1831); **press-warrants**: "impress" or military draft notices.

[12] **decoy field**: field of unguarded crops designed to lure game.

and to bequeath them to whom he chooses. Happy would it be for the world if there were no other road to wealth or honour; if pride, in the shape of parental affection, did not absorb the man, and prevent friendship from having the same weight as relationship. Luxury and effeminacy would not then introduce so much idiotism into the noble families which form one of the pillars of our state: the ground would not lie fallow, nor would undirected activity of mind spread the contagion of restless idleness, and its concomitant, vice, through the whole mass of society.

Instead of gaming they might nourish a virtuous ambition, and love might take place of the gallantry which you, with knightly fealty, venerate. Women would probably then act like mothers, and the fine lady, become a rational woman, might think it necessary to superintend her family and suckle her children, in order to fulfil her part of the social compact. But vain is the hope, whilst great masses of property are hedged round by hereditary honours; for numberless vices, forced in the hot-bed of wealth, assume a sightly form to dazzle the senses and cloud the understanding. The respect paid to rank and fortune damps every generous purpose of the soul, and stifles the natural affections on which human contentment ought to be built. . . .

I reverence the rights of men.—Sacred rights! for which I acquire a more profound respect, the more I look into my own mind; and, professing these heterodox opinions, I still preserve my bowels; my heart is human, beats quick with human sympathies—and I FEAR God!

I bend with awful reverence when I enquire on what my fear is built.—I fear that sublime power, whose motive for creating me must have been wise and good; and I submit to the moral laws which my reason deduces from this view of my dependence on him.—It is not his power that I fear—it is not to an arbitrary will, but to unerring *reason* I submit.—Submit—yes; I disregard the charge of arrogance, to the law that regulates his just resolves; and the happiness I pant after must be the same in kind, and produced by the same exertions as his—though unfeigned humility overwhelms every idea that would presume to compare the goodness which the most exalted created being could acquire, with the grand source of life and bliss.

This fear of God makes me reverence myself.—Yes, Sir, the regard I have for honest fame, and the friendship of the virtuous, falls far short of the respect which I have for myself. And this enlightened self-love, if an epithet the meaning of which has been grossly perverted will convey my idea, forces me to see; and, if I may venture to borrow a prostituted term, to *feel*, that happiness is reflected, and that, in communicating good, my soul receives its noble aliment.—I do not trouble myself, therefore, to enquire whether this is the fear the *people* of England feel:—and, if it be *natural* to include all the modifications which you have annexed—it is not. . . .[13]

But, among all your plausible arguments, and witty illustrations, your contempt for the poor always appears conspicuous, and rouses my indignation. The following paragraph in particular struck me, as breathing the most tyrannic spirit, and displaying the most factitious feelings. 'Good order is the foundation of all good things. To be enabled to acquire, the people, without being servile, must be tractable and obedient. The magistrate must have his reverence, the laws their authority. The body of the people must not find the principles of natural subordination by art rooted out of their minds. They *must* respect that property of which they *cannot* partake. *They must labour to obtain what by labour can be obtained; and when they find, as they commonly do, the success disproportioned to the endeavour, they must be taught their consolation in the final proportions of eternal justice.* Of this consolation, whoever deprives them, deadens their industry, and strikes at the root of all acquisition as of all conservation. He that does this, is the cruel oppressor, the merciless enemy, of the poor and wretched; at the same time that, by his wicked speculations, he exposes the fruits of successful industry, and the accumulations of fortune, (ah! there's the rub)[14] to the plunder of the negligent, the disappointed, and the unprosperous.'[15]

This is contemptible hard-hearted sophistry, in the specious form of humility, and submission to the will of Heaven.—It is, Sir, *possible* to render the poor happier in this world, without depriving them of the consolation which you gratuitously grant them in the next. They have a right to more comfort than they at present enjoy; and more comfort might be afforded them, without encroaching on the pleasures of the rich: not now waiting to enquire whether the rich have any right to exclusive pleasures. What do I say?—encroaching! No; if an intercourse were established between them, it would impart

[13] See [Burke's] *Reflections*, p. 128: "We fear God; we look up with *awe* to kings; with *affection* to parliaments; with *duty* to magistrates; with *reverence* to priests; and with *respect* to nobility" [M. W.]. The emphases are Wollstonecraft's. Page 19 this text.

[14] **"there's the rub"**: Shakespeare, *Hamlet*, III.i.65.

[15] [Burke, *Reflections*], Page 351 [M. W.]. The emphases are Wollstonecraft's.

the only true pleasure that can be snatched in this land of shadows, this hard school of moral discipline.

I know, indeed, that there is often something disgusting in the distresses of poverty, at which the imagination revolts, and starts back to exercise itself in the more attractive Arcadia[16] of fiction. The rich man builds a house, art and taste give it the highest finish. His gardens are planted, and the trees grow to recreate the fancy of the planter, though the temperature of the climate may rather force him to avoid the dangerous damps they exhale, than seek the umbrageous retreat. Every thing on the estate is cherished but man;—yet, to contribute to the happiness of man, is the most sublime of all enjoyments. But if, instead of sweeping pleasure-grounds, obelisks, temples, and elegant cottages, as *objects* for the eye, the heart was allowed to beat true to nature, decent farms would be scattered over the estate, and plenty smile around. Instead of the poor being subject to the griping hand of an avaricious steward, they would be watched over with fatherly solicitude, by the man whose duty and pleasure it was to guard their happiness, and shield from rapacity the beings who, by the sweat of their brow, exalted him above his fellows.

I could almost imagine I see a man thus gathering blessings as he mounted the hill of life; or consolation, in those days when the spirits lag, and the tired heart finds no pleasure in them. It is not by squandering alms that the poor can be relieved, or improved—it is the fostering sun of kindness, the wisdom that finds them employments calculated to give them habits of virtue, that ameliorates their condition. Love is only the fruit of love; condescension and authority may produce the obedience you applaud; but he has lost his heart of flesh who can see a fellow-creature humbled before him, and trembling at the crown of a being, whose heart is supplied by the same vital current, and whose pride ought to be checked by a consciousness of having the same infirmities.

What salutary dews might not be shed to refresh this thirsty land, if men were more *enlightened!* Smiles and premiums might encourage cleanliness, industry, and emulation.—A garden more inviting than Eden would then meet the eye, and springs of joy murmur on every side. The clergyman would superintend his own flock, the shepherd would then love the sheep he daily tended: the school might rear its decent head, and the buzzing tribe, let loose to play, impart a portion of their vivacious spirits to the heart that longed to open their minds, and lead them to taste the pleasures of men. Domestic comfort, the civilizing relations of husband, brother, and father, would soften labour, and render life contented.

[16] **Arcadia:** Greek land seen as the ideal region of rural happiness and pastoral simplicity.

THOMAS PAINE

(1737–1809)

Thomas Paine was born 29 January 1737 in Thetford, England, to Frances (Cocke) and Joseph Paine, a small farmer, staymaker, and member of the local Society of Friends. He received his earliest and only schooling at a Quaker grammar school. At the age of thirteen, Paine entered his father's business of making corsets. He received an appointment in the excise in 1761, from which he was dismissed for neglect of duty. He received a second chance at collecting taxes, but found more delight in agitating for causes, such as improving the salaries of excisemen. At the age of thirty-seven, Paine moved to America with a letter in hand from Benjamin Franklin recommending him as an "ingenious, worthy young man." Paine proudly displayed his radical colors in writing for the *Pennsylvania Magazine* on behalf of women's rights and for the abolition of slavery. When the British and the colonists exchanged gunfire at Lexington and Concord, the time was ripe for Revolution. Paine's pamphlet, *Common Sense* (1776), rallied near-universal sympathy for the formation of an independent state out of the colonies, and his *Crises* pamphlets, the first of which begins with the famous sentence, "These are the times that try men's souls," became mandatory reading in George Washington's army. After the Revolution, Paine returned to England with a scheme for iron bridges, but revolutionary events again captured his imagination. Paine was in Paris visiting the Marquis de Lafayette when Burke's *Reflections on the Revolution in France* (1790) was published. Paine immediately struck off the first part of *The Rights of Man* (1791) in response to Burke. *The Rights of Man* was a popular success and the inspiration for widespread radical agitation in England. In 1792 Paine was indicted for treason. He fled to France, where he had already been elected to the Convention. He was later imprisoned in France for speaking against the execution of Louis XVI. Legend has it that he avoided execution only because the jailer overlooked the chalk mark above his cell indicating he was to die. Through the influence of James Monroe, the American ambassador to France, Paine was released from prison and returned to America. His virulent attack against Christianity in *The Age of Reason* (1792–1795), however, turned the common man against him. He died ostracized, disgruntled, and financially ruined in 1809. A decade later, sympathetic radical William Cobbett* exhumed his remains for transport back to England, where they eventually passed from the Cobbett family and disappeared.

from The Rights of Man

(1791)

— PART FIRST —

Among the incivilities by which nations or individuals provoke and irritate each other, Mr. Burke's pamphlet on the French Revolution is an extraordinary instance. Neither the people of France, nor the National Assembly, were troubling themselves about the affairs of England, or the English Parliament; and that Mr. Burke should commence an unprovoked attack upon them, both in Parliament and in public, is a conduct that cannot be pardoned on the score of manners, nor justified on that of policy. There is scarcely an epithet of abuse to be found in the English language, with which Mr. Burke has not loaded the French nation and the National Assembly. Every thing which rancor, prejudice, ignorance, or knowledge could suggest are poured forth in the copious fury of near four hundred pages. In the strain and on the plan Mr. Burke was writing, he might have written on to as many thousands. When the tongue or the pen is let loose in a frenzy of passion, it is the man and not the subject that becomes exhausted.

Hitherto Mr. Burke has been mistaken and disappointed in the opinions he had formed of the affairs of France; but such is the ingenuity of his hope, or the malignancy of his despair, that it furnishes him with new pretenses to go on. There was a time when it was impossible to make Mr. Burke believe there would be any revolution in France. His opinion then was, that the French had neither spirit to undertake it, nor fortitude to support it; and now that there is one, he seeks an escape by condemning it. . . .

There never did, there never will, and there never can exist a parliament, or any description of men, or any generation of men, in any country, possessed of the right or the power of binding and controlling posterity to the *"end of time,"* or of commanding forever how the world shall be governed, or who shall govern it; and therefore, all such clauses, acts or declarations, by which the makers of them attempt to do what they have neither the right nor the power to do, nor the power to execute, are in themselves null and void.

Every age and generation must be as free to act for itself, *in all cases,* as the ages and generation which preceded it. The vanity and presumption of governing beyond the grave, is the most ridiculous and insolent of all tyrannies.

Man has no property in man; neither has any generation a property in the generations which are to follow. The Parliament or the people of 1688, or of any other period, had no more right to dispose of the people of the present day, or to bind or to control them *in any shape whatever,* than the Parliament or the people of the present day have to dispose of, bind, or control those who are to live a hundred or a thousand years hence.

Every generation is, and must be, competent to all the purposes which its occasions require. It is the living, and not the dead, that are to be accommodated. When man ceases to be, his power and his wants cease with him; and having no longer any participation in the concerns of this world, he has no longer any authority in directing who shall be its governors, or how its government shall be organized, or how administered.

I am not contending for nor against any form of government, nor for nor against any party here or elsewhere. That which a whole nation chooses to do, it has a right to do. Mr. Burke says, No. Where then *does* the right exist? I am contending for the rights of the *living,* and against their being willed away, and controlled, and contracted for, by the manuscript assumed authority of the dead; and Mr. Burke is contending for the authority of the dead over the rights and freedom of the living.

"We have seen," says Mr. Burke, "the French rebel against a mild and lawful monarch, with more fury, outrage, and insult, than any people has been known to rise against the most illegal usurper, or the most sanguinary tyrant." This is one among a thousand other instances, in which Mr. Burke shows that he is ignorant of the springs and principles of the French Revolution.

It was not against Louis XVI, but against the despotic principles of the government, that the nation revolted. These principles had not their origin in him, but in the original establishment, many centuries back; and they were become too deeply rooted to be removed, and the Augean stable[1] of parasites and plunderers too abominably filthy to be cleansed, by anything short of a complete and universal revolution.

When it becomes necessary to do a thing, the whole heart and soul should go into the measure, or not attempt it. That crisis was then arrived, and there remained no choice but to act with determined vigor, or not to act at all. The King was known to be the friend of the nation, and this circumstance was favorable to the enterprise. Perhaps no man bred up in the style of an absolute king, ever possessed a heart so little disposed to the exercise of that species of power as the present King of France.

But the principles of the government itself still remained the same. The monarch and the monarchy were distinct and separate things; and it was against the established despotism of the latter, and not against the person or principles of the former, that the revolt commenced, and the Revolution has been carried.

Mr. Burke does not attend to the distinction between *men* and *principle;* and therefore, he does not see that a revolt may take place against the despotism of the latter, while there lies no charge of despotism against the former.

The natural moderation of Louis XVI contributed nothing to alter the hereditary despotism of the monarchy. All the tyrannies of the former reigns, acted under that hereditary despotism, were still liable to be revived in the hands of a successor. It was not the respite of a

[1] **Augean:** Exceedingly filthy from years of neglect. After Augeas, King of Elis, who left his stables uncleaned for thirty years.

reign that would satisfy France, enlightened as she was then become.

A casual discontinuance of the *practise* of despotism, is not a discontinuance of its *principles*; the former depends on the virtue of the individual who is in immediate possession of power; the latter, on the virtue and fortitude of the nation. In the case of Charles I and James II of England,[2] the revolt was against the personal despotism of the men; whereas in France, it was against the hereditary despotism of the established government. But men who can consign over the rights of posterity for ever, on the authority of a moldy parchment, like Mr. Burke, are not qualified to judge of this Revolution. It takes in a field too vast for their views to explore, and proceeds with a mightiness of reason they cannot keep pace with.

But there are many points of view in which this Revolution may be considered. When despotism has established itself for ages in a country, as in France, it is not in the person of the king only that it resides. It has the appearance of being so in show, and in nominal authority; but it is not so in practise, and in fact. It has its standard everywhere.

Every office and department has its despotism, founded upon custom and usage. Every place has its Bastille,[3] and every Bastille its despot. The original hereditary despotism, resident in the person of the king, divides and subdivides itself into a thousand shapes and forms, till at last the whole of it is acted by deputation.

This was the case in France; and against this species of despotism, proceeding on through an endless labyrinth of office till the source of it is scarcely perceptible, there is no mode of redress. It strengthens itself by assuming the appearance of duty, and tyrannizes under the pretense of obeying.

When a man reflects on the condition which France was in from the nature of her government, he will see other causes for revolt than those which immediately connect themselves with the person or character of Louis XVI. There were, if I may so express it, a thousand despotisms to be reformed in France, which had grown up under the hereditary despotism of the monarchy, and became so rooted as to be in a great measure independent of it. Between the monarchy, the parliament, and the church, there was a *rivalship* of despotism; besides the feudal despotism operating locally, and the ministerial despotism operating everywhere.

But Mr. Burke, by considering the King as the only possible object of a revolt, speaks as if France was a village, in which every thing that passed must be known to its commanding officer, and no oppression could be acted but what he could conveniently control. Mr. Burke might have been in the Bastille his whole life, as well under Louis XVI and neither the one nor the other have known that such a man as Mr. Burke existed. The despotic principles of the government were the same in both reigns, though the dispositions of the men were as remote as tyranny and benevolence.

What Mr. Burke considers as a reproach to the French Revolution (that of bringing it forward under a reign more mild than the preceding ones), is one of its highest honors. The revolutions that have taken place in other European countries, have been excited by personal hatred. The rage was against the man, and he became the victim. But, in the instance of France, we see a revolution generated in the rational contemplation of the rights of man, and distinguishing from the beginning between persons and principles.

But Mr. Burke appears to have no idea of principles, when he is contemplating governments. "Ten years ago," says he, "I could have felicitated France on her having a government, without inquiring what the nature of that government was, or how it was administered."

Is this the language of a rational man? Is it the language of a heart feeling as it ought to feel for the rights and happiness of the human race? On this ground, Mr. Burke must compliment every government in the world, while the victims who suffer under them, whether sold into slavery, or tortured out of existence, are wholly forgotten. . . .

As to the tragic paintings by which Mr. Burke has outraged his own imagination, and seeks to work upon

---

[2] Charles I of England, son of James I (of England), was beheaded in 1649 for "high treason and other high crimes," which put an end to monarchical rule in England until the restoration of the Stuart monarchy in 1660. James II, son of Charles I and successor to the throne from 1685–1688, sought to establish an absolutist rule and threatened to pass on his throne to a Catholic son. Parliament invited William III of Orange to invade England to preserve "traditional liberties" and to share monarchical power with James's protestant daughter Mary. James fled to France and the protection of Louis XIV. Parliament proclaimed William and Mary monarchs in 1689 to conclude the "Glorious Revolution."

[3] The Bastille was France's notorious political prison and a symbol of abusive royal power. *Lettre de cachet,* or an order under the King's private seal, was sufficient for the incarceration of any subject without charge or trial. The French Revolution of 1789 began with a successful attack on the Bastille.

that of his readers, they are very well calculated for theatrical representation, where facts are manufactured for the sake of show, and accommodated to produce, through the weakness of sympathy, a weeping effect. But Mr. Burke should recollect that he is writing history, and not *plays*; and that his readers will expect truth, and not the spouting rant of high-toned declamation.

When we see a man dramatically lamenting in a publication intended to be believed, that, "*The age of chivalry is gone!* that *The glory of Europe is extinguished forever!* that *The unbought grace of life* (if any one knows what it is), *the cheap defense of nations, the nurse of manly sentiment and heroic enterprise, is gone!*" and all this because the Quixotic age of chivalric nonsense is gone, what opinion can we form of his judgment, or what regard can we pay to his facts?

In the rhapsody of his imagination, he has discovered a world of wind-mills, and his sorrows are, that there are no Quixotes to attack them. But if the age of aristocracy, like that of chivalry, should fall, and they had originally some connection, Mr. Burke, the trumpeter of the order, may continue his parody to the end, and finish with exclaiming, "*Othello's occupation's gone!*"[4]

Notwithstanding Mr. Burke's horrid paintings, when the French Revolution is compared with that of other countries, the astonishment will be, that it is marked with so few sacrifices; but this astonishment will cease when we reflect that *principles* and not *persons*, were the meditated objects of destruction. The mind of the nation was acted upon by a higher stimulus than what the consideration of persons could inspire, and sought a higher conquest than could be produced by the downfall of an enemy.

Among the few who fell, there do not appear to be any that were intentionally singled out. They all of them had their fate in the circumstances of the moment, and were not pursued with that long, cold-blooded, unabated revenge which pursued the unfortunate Scotch, in the affair of 1745.[5]

Through the whole of Mr. Burke's book I do not observe that the Bastille is mentioned more than once, and that with a kind of implication as if he were sorry it was pulled down, and wished it were built up again. "We have rebuilt Newgate," says he, "and tenanted the mansion; and we have prisons almost as strong as the Bastille for those who dare to libel the Queens of France."

As to what a madman, like the person called Lord George Gordon,[6] might say, and to whom Newgate is rather a bedlam than a prison, it is unworthy a rational consideration.

It was a madman that libelled,—and that is sufficient apology; and it afforded an opportunity for confining him, which was the thing which was wished for; but certain it is that Mr. Burke, who does not call himself a madman, whatever other people may do, has libelled, in the most unprovoked manner, and in the grossest style of the most vulgar abuse, the whole representative authority of France; and yet Mr. Burke takes his seat in the British House of Commons!

From his violence and his grief, his silence on some points, and his excess on others, it is difficult not to believe that Mr. Burke is sorry, extremely sorry, that arbitrary power, the power of the Pope, and the Bastille, are pulled down.

Not one glance of compassion, not one commiserating reflection, that I can find throughout his book, has he bestowed on those who lingered out the most wretched of lives, a life without hope, in the most miserable of prisons.

It is painful to behold a man employing his talents to corrupt himself. Nature has been kinder to Mr. Burke than he is to her. He is not affected by the reality of distress touching his heart, but by the showy resemblage of it striking his imagination. He pities the plumage, but forgets the dying bird.

Accustomed to kiss the aristocratical hand that hath purloined him from himself, he degenerates into a composition of art, and the genuine soul of nature forsakes him. His hero or his heroine must be a tragedy-victim expiring in show, and not the real prisoner of mystery, sinking into death in the silence of a dungeon. . . .

---

[4] From Shakespeare's *Othello*, III.iii.348.

[5] **the affair of 1745**: Second Jacobite Rebellion (1745–1746) led by Charles Edward, the Young Pretender, who proclaimed his father as James VIII of Scotland and James III of England. The army of the Jacobites (supporters of the Stuarts after the Glorious Revolution of 1688) was finally defeated, ending Stuart hopes for recovering the throne.

[6] Lord George Gordon, a rabid anti-Catholic, was imprisoned in 1780 for instigating riots over the government's discontinuing of the requirement that military recruits take anti-Catholic oaths.

THOMAS BABINGTON MACAULAY

(1800–1859)

Thomas Babington Macaulay was born on 25 October 1800, the eldest son of Selina Mills and Zachary Macaulay, abolitionist, editor of the *Christian Observor,* and chief of the Evangelical Clapham Sect. He began reading voraciously at the age of three; at age four, Hannah More* took an interest in his moral and intellectual development, often caring for him and presenting him with books for his own library. It seems that his father Zachary's antislavery agitation aroused his interest in politics. In 1818 Macaulay entered Trinity College, Cambridge University, where he became a confirmed Whig. After graduating, he became a lawyer but found haunting the House of Commons and writing on literary and political topics to be more congenial than practicing law. An essay on Milton for the *Edinburgh Review* brought him immediate literary acclaim. In admiration of his articles on James Mill attacking both left- and right-wing radicals, Lord Lansdowne offered him a seat in Parliament for the "pocket borough" of Calne. Macaulay soon received the approval of the entire Parliament, including Sir Robert Peel, leader of the Tories, for his speech on the Great Reform Bill (excerpt follows). Ironically, Macaulay was deprived of his seat when the borough was eliminated by the Reform Bill. He next applied himself to Indian affairs, serving on the Supreme Council of India, from 1834 to 1837. He returned to Parliament as Liberal member for Edinburgh in 1839 and retired from public life after losing his seat in 1847. Macaulay was offered but declined the Regius Chair of History at his alma mater. He spent his remaining years as a man of letters, publishing the immensely popular and influential four-volume *History of England* (1848–1855). He died on 28 December 1859 and was buried in Westminster Abbey.

from A Speech Delivered in the House of Commons on the 2nd of March, 1831.[1]

. . . Sir, every argument which would induce me to oppose Universal Suffrage,[2] induces me to support the plan which is now before us. I am opposed to Universal Suffrage, because I think that it would produce a destructive revolution. I support this plan, because I am sure that it is our best security against a revolution. I, Sir, do entertain great apprehension for the fate of my country. I do in my conscience believe that, unless the plan proposed, or some similar plan, be speedily adopted, great and terrible calamities will befall us. Entertaining this opinion, I think myself bound to state it, not as a threat, but as a reason. I support this bill because it will improve our institutions; but I support it also because it tends to preserve them. That we may exclude those whom it is necessary to exclude, we must admit those whom it may be safe to admit. At present we oppose the schemes of revolutionists with only one half, with only one quarter of our proper force. We say, and we say justly, that it is not by mere numbers, but by property and intelligence, that the nation ought to be governed. Yet, saying this, we exclude from all share in the government great masses of property and intelligence, great numbers of those who are most interested in preserving tranquillity, and who know best how to preserve it. We do more. We drive over to the side

[1] Macaulay's speech was made in support of a motion made by Lord John Russell that the House of Commons consider a bill to extend the franchise. The motion carried after a debate of seven days and nights. The House of Lords then rejected it.

[2] Universal Suffrage did not include women.

of revolution those whom we shut out from power. Is this a time when the cause of law and order can spare one of its natural allies? . . .

If, Sir, I wished to make such a foreigner clearly understand what I consider as the great defects of our system, I would conduct him through that immense city which lies to the north of Great Russell Street and Oxford Street, a city superior in size and in population to the capitals of many mighty kingdoms; and probably superior in opulence, intelligence, and general respectability, to any city in the world. I would conduct him through that interminable succession of streets and squares, all consisting of well built and well furnished houses. I would make him observe the brilliancy of the shops, and the crowd of well appointed equipages. I would show him that magnificent circle of palaces which surrounds the Regent's Park. I would tell him, that the rental of this district was far greater than that of the whole kingdom of Scotland, at the time of the Union. And then I would tell him, that this was an unrepresented district. It is needless to give any more instances. It is needless to speak of Manchester, Birmingham, Leeds, Sheffield, with no representation, or of Edinburgh and Glasgow with a mock representation. . . .

To say that such a system is ancient is no defence. My honourable friend, the Member for the University of Oxford, challenges us to show, that the Constitution was ever better than it is. Sir, we are legislators, not antiquaries. Turn where we may, within, around, the voice of great events is proclaiming to us, Reform, that you may preserve. Now, therefore, while every thing at home and abroad forebodes ruin to those who persist in a hopeless struggle against the spirit of the age, now, while the crash of the proudest throne of the continent is still resounding in our ears, now, while the roof of a British palace affords an ignominious shelter to the exiled heir of forty kings, now, while we see on every side ancient institutions subverted, and great societies dissolved, now, while the heart of England is still sound, now, while old feelings and old associations retain a power and a charm which may too soon pass away, now, in this your accepted time, now, in this your day of salvation, take counsel, not of prejudice, not of party spirit, not of the ignominious pride of a fatal consistency, but of history, of reason, of the ages which are past, of the signs of this most portentous time. Pronounce in a manner worthy of the expectation with which this great debate has been anticipated, and of the long remembrance which it will leave behind. Renew the youth of the State. Save property, divided against itself. Save the multitude, endangered by its own ungovernable passions. Save the aristocracy, endangered by its own unpopular power. Save the greatest, and fairest, and most highly civilised community that ever existed, from calamities which may in a few days sweep away all the rich heritage of so many ages of wisdom and glory. The danger is terrible. The time is short. If this bill should be rejected, I pray to God that none of those who concur in rejecting it may ever remember their votes with unavailing remorse, amidst the wreck of laws, the confusion of ranks, the spoliation of property, and the dissolution of social order.[3]

[3] The Great Reform Bill was passed into law in 1832. The Bill abolished boroughs which had small numbers of voters and replaced them with representatives from areas, especially manufacturing districts and cities, that had undergone significant population increases in the eighteenth century. The number of voters in England and Wales increased by over 200,000.

Rights of Woman

THE "RIGHTS OF WOMAN" question was fiercely debated throughout this historical period (1780–1830). The prevailing belief, based on tradition and upheld by the Church of England and the laws of the nation, assumed that women were innately inferior to men in both rational capacity and ethical development although they possessed souls and could be trained to be virtuous. Therefore they could be held responsible for their sins and any legal crimes they might commit. Increasingly, during this time, medical and scientific treatises insisted on the innate sexual difference between males and females. As females, women were claimed to be more emotional (they possessed greater "sensibility"), more highly sexed (they were frequently referred to as "the sex"), physically frailer, and more beautiful than males. The ultimate social responsibility of women was to bear and nurture young infants and to manage the domestic household under their husband's or father's supervision. Legally, women existed in the condition known as "coverture": their bodies and their possessions, inherited or earned, as well as their children, belonged by law to their fathers or husbands. This dominant domestic ideology or doctrine of the separate spheres was fiercely upheld by the male political and social leaders of this period, receiving one of its more vituperative defenses in the Rev. Richard Polwhele's satiric poem "The Unsex'd Females" (1798).

Feminist thinkers, led by Catherine Macaulay, Mary Hays, and most notably Mary Wollstonecraft in her *Vindication of the Rights of Woman* (1792),* argued that women were the equals of men in all rational and moral capacities; man's only superiority lay in his greater upper-body strength. They insisted that women should be educated in the same way as men, should perform the same economic and social roles as men, and should enjoy the same civil rights, including the vote. More conservative thinkers such as Anna Barbauld in her "The Rights of Woman" (1792),* Hannah More in her "Sensibility" (1782)* and *Strictures on the Modern System of Female Education* (1799),* and Elizabeth Hamilton in her *Letters on Education* (1801–1802) argued that women should be better educated in the methods of rational thought and religious doctrine only in order to become better wives and mothers. Both More and Barbauld argued that women should acknowledge the superiority of men, but that they had an important role to play in both the private and the social sphere, educating the young, caring for the poor and the sick, and providing moral guidance for all.

Between these two poles, women writers of the day staked out other progressive positions. In *Thoughts on the Condition of Women, and on the Injustice of Mental Subordination* (1799), Mary Robinson* attacked the sexual double standard, arguing that male hypocrisy was primarily responsible for female prostitution. At the same time she celebrated the historical accomplishments, both political and cultural, of women. Priscilla Wakefield believed that women should submit to their husbands' superior judgment but insisted that women should be educated to *support themselves,* since the accidents of fortune often left women of all classes without male economic support. Mary Anne Radcliffe, writing from her personal experiences as a landed Scottish heiress whose ne'er-do-well husband had lost all their money, leaving her destitute and in ill health, bitterly attacked the lack of suitable employment available to respectable women in *The Female Advocate* (1799). And Mary Lamb, in her essay "On Needle-Work,"* drew attention to the class differences between female workers. As did both Mary Lamb and Hannah More, Maria Edgeworth* assumed that women would remain within the domestic sphere, but she insisted that they should be the rational and moral partners of their husbands and should take on the primary responsibility for the education of their children and the management of the family household.

All these female defenders of the rights of women were commonly referred to as "blue-stockings." The term was derived from the blue worsted (as opposed to silk) stockings worn by the only man, Benjamin Stillingfleet, who regularly attended the literary salons hosted by Elizabeth Robinson Montagu in the 1760s. Originally applied to male intellectuals, by the 1770s the name had come to refer to the women who gathered for literary and intellectual conversations at the home of Montagu, the "Queen of the Blues," a group that numbered among its members Elizabeth Vesey, Frances Boscawen, Elizabeth Carter, Hester Chapone, Hester Thrale (later Piozzi) and the much younger Frances Burney* and Hannah More* (More celebrated this coterie of women in her poem "Bas Bleu, or Conversation" in 1786). During this historical period, every woman writer or intellectual, including all those in this volume, was popularly dubbed a "female philosopher" or a "blue-stocking." Some women accepted this appellation; others (such as Maria Edgeworth, Jane Austen,* Susan Ferrier, Elizabeth Hamilton, and Jane West) resisted it, writing parodies of those female intellectuals who ostentatiously displayed what little knowledge they had acquired or who demanded "rights," rather than responsibilities, for women. The "Blues" were the subject of several male-authored works, some harshly satirical (e.g., Byron's "The Blues" and Thomas Moore's *M. P. or The Blue-Stocking, A Comic Opera*), some extremely respectful (e.g., Leigh Hunt's "Blue-Stocking Revels, or The Feast of the Violets" and William Scargill's *Blue-Stocking Hall*).

The growth of the social movement for women's rights received a damaging blow from the publication of William Godwin's *Memoirs of the Author of a Vindication of the Rights of Woman* in 1798. Godwin intended to pay an act of public homage to his recently deceased wife, Mary Wollstonecraft, by publishing her unfinished manuscripts and letters together with an account of her life and early death. But his decision to include Wollstonecraft's love letters to Gilbert Imlay and to himself (as well as an account of her love affairs with Fuseli and Imlay, her illegitimate child, her two suicide attempts, and her sexual liaison with Godwin before their marriage) appalled even his friends. The poet Robert Southey* accused Godwin of "a want of all feeling in stripping his dead wife naked." The *Monthly Review,* a journal that had hitherto endorsed Wollstonecraft's demands for the rights of woman, editorialized in May 1798, that "blushes would suffuse the cheeks of most husbands if they were *forced* to relate those anecdotes of their wives which Mr. Godwin voluntarily proclaims to the world. The extreme eccentricity of Mr. Godwin's sentiments will account for this conduct. Virtue and vice are weighed by him in a balance of his own. He neither looks to marriage with respect, nor to suicide with horror." Godwin's *Memoirs* gave his and Wollstonecraft's enemies, led by the passionately conservative journal, the *Anti-Jacobin,* just the ammunition they needed to define Wollstonecraft (and by implication all her followers) as a whore and an atheist, thus discrediting the campaign for the rights of woman.

The outcry against Wollstonecraft forced even her female followers to distance themselves from her. Mary Hays condemned Godwin's *Memoirs* in the *Analytical Review* for his failure to explain the reasons for Wollstonecraft's feminist positions, and then, five years later, omitted Wollstonecraft entirely from her five-volume *Dictionary of Female Biography* (1803), even though she provided lengthy entries for Mary Astell, Catherine Macaulay, and Madame Roland. Amelia Opie* examined the social and psychological havoc that too close an adherence to Godwin's and Wollstonecraft's principles could wreak on an innocent girl in her novel *Adeline Mowbray* (1805). And Maria Edgeworth caricatured the militant feminist in her portrait of Harriet Freke in *Belinda* (1801).* The damage done to the emerging women's rights movement by Godwin's well-intentioned but injudicious publication was overwhelming; even fifty years later, Harriet Martineau (1802–1876), an outspoken Victorian social reformer, insisted that Wollstonecraft was neither "a safe example, nor a successful champion of Woman and her Rights" and further, that "women of the Wollstonecraft order . . . do infinite mischief, and for my part, I do not wish to have any thing to do with them."

In the years that followed, the anti-feminist backlash unleashed by Godwin's four volumes forced respectable women who sympathized with Wollstonecraft's views to express their support for the rights of women through subtle literary ironies masked beneath an overt claim to Christian piety, as did Jane Austen* in *Emma,* Maria Edgeworth in *Belinda,** and Lucy Aikin in her *Epistles on Women.**

CATHERINE SAWBRIDGE MACAULAY

(1731–1791)

A wealthy heiress, the daughter of well-connected Whig merchant and banker families, Catherine Sawbridge was educated at home where she had access to her father's well-stocked library at the Sawbridge country estate in Kent. In 1760 she married the distinguished Scottish obstetrician, George Macaulay, 15 years her senior, who supported her intellectual and literary interests. Three years after the marriage, she published the first of her eight-volume *The History of England, from the Accession of James I to that of the Brunswick Line* (1763–1783), an eloquent defense of Cromwell and the subsequent Whig struggle against the tyrannies of monarchy. In 1766, after she had borne one daughter, her husband died, and Macaulay moved to Bath for her health, where she continued a prolific writing career as a radical Whig historian, political and legal commentator, and authority on medicine. Her critique of Burke in 1770 led him to call her "our republican Virago." A book on natural religion was incorporated into her *Letters on Education* (1790), which Wollstonecraft* enthusiastically reviewed and which directly influenced Wollstonecraft's *Vindication of the Rights of Woman.* A thoughtful, original work, Macaulay's *Letters on Education* argue for the civil rights of women and the need for improved education for both sexes. Macaulay was the first woman admitted to the Reading Room of the British Library, and was widely admired in both England and America for her judicious, progressive views. Her marriage in 1778 to the 21-year-old surgeon's mate William Graham, together with her radical opinions, gave rise to several scurrilous attacks and subjected her, she said, to "long and malevolent prosecution." Wollstonecraft admiringly described Macaulay as "the woman of the greatest abilities, undoubtedly, that this country has ever produced."

from Letters on Education

with Observations on Religious and Metaphysical Subjects
(1801–1802)

— *from* LETTER XXI —

Morals must be taught on immutable Principles.

. . . As you have had patience to go through my whole plan of education, from infancy to manhood, it is but fair that I should attend to your objections, and examine whether my plan is founded on error, or on the principles of reason and truth. Know then, good Hortensia, that I have given similar rules for male and female enducation [sic], on the following grounds of reasoning.

First, That there is but one rule of right for the conduct of all rational beings; consequently that true virtue in one sex must be equally so in the other, whenever a proper opportunity calls for its exertion; and, vice versa, what is vice in one sex, cannot have a different property when found in the other.

Secondly, That true wisdom, which is never found at variance with rectitude, is as useful to women as to men; because it is necessary to the highest degree of happiness, which can never exist with ignorance.

Lastly, That as on our first entrance into another world, our state of happiness may possibly depend on the degree of perfection we have attained in this, we cannot justly lessen, in one sex or the other, the means by which perfection, that is another word for wisdom, is acquired.

It would be paying you a bad compliment, Hortensia, were I to answer all the frivolous objections which prejudice has framed against the giving a learned education to women; for I know of no learning, worth having, that does not tend to free the mind from error, and enlarge our stock of useful knowledge. Thus much it may be proper to observe, that those hours which are spent in studious retirement by learned women, will not in all probability intrude so much on the time for useful avocation, as the wild and spreading dissipations of the present day; that levity and ignorance will always be found in opposition to what is useful and graceful in life; and that the contrary may be expected from a truly enlightened understanding. . . .

MARY HAYS

(1760–1843)

The daughter of middle-class Rational Dissenters living in Southwark, London, Mary Hays educated herself through an extended literary correspondence from 1779 to 1780 with another young Dissenter, John Eccles, with whom she fell passionately in love (their love letters were published in 1925). Eccles died suddenly in 1780, just as they were about to marry. Guided by the Baptist preacher and leading radical Robert Robinson, Mary Hays continued her self-education through the 1780s, reading English and Continental fiction, philosophical tracts, poetry, and religious treatises. Through Robinson, Hays met some of the most influential Dissenters of her day: Dr. Joseph Priestley, Theophilus Lindsay, and John Disney. Her first publication, under the pseudonym "Eusebia," was a spirited defense of Lindsay's Unitarian Church, *Cursory Remarks on an Enquiry into the Expediency and Propriety of Public or Social Worship* (1791).

The success of this pamphlet brought Hays into close contact with the more radical religious dissenters: the poet George Dyer, the Cambridge mathematician William Frend, the radical publisher Joseph Johnson, and his circle: Thomas Paine, Thomas Holcroft, Anna Barbauld, and most important, Mary Wollstonecraft and William Godwin, both of whom became close friends of Hays. Her *Letters and Essays, Moral and Miscellaneous,* published in 1793, eloquently defended Wollstonecraft's feminist opinions (while attacking the social "degrading" of "the female character"), supported Jacobin notions of the rights of man, and upheld Godwin's doctrines of necessity and perfectibility through the agency of reason. She based her first novel *Memoirs of Emma Courtney* (1796) on Godwin's doctrines, as well as on her unrequited love affair, at 35, with William Frend.

Hays' second novel, *The Victim of Prejudice* (1799), explores the unjust treatment given to women who must pay for a moment of sexual pleasure with a lifetime of ruin. Abandoned by her lover, the heroine's mother rapidly sinks into prostitution, is separated from her daughter, and is finally executed as a murderer's accomplice. As she writes to her lover, "I perceived myself the victim of the injustice, of the prejudice, of society, which, by opposing to my return to virtue almost insuperable barriers, had plunged me into irremediable ruin. I grew sullen, desperate, hardened." The virtuous heroine Mary is raped but refuses to marry her traducer; unable to get honest work, she is arrested for debt, sent to prison, where her health is destroyed, and finally dies, still refusing to marry her (supposedly reformed) rapist and thus preserving her independence and integrity.

Hays wrote numerous literary and political reviews for the *Analytical Review,* the *Monthly Magazine,* and other journals. Her feminist tract, *Appeal to the Men of Great Britain in Behalf of Women* (1798), published anonymously in an increasingly conservative political climate, assumes the natural equality of the sexes and passionately challenges both scriptural authority and custom for their unjustified elevation of the male sex. To support her claim for the rational and moral equality of women, Hays then wrote the first history of women, *Female Biography; or, Memoirs of Illustrious and Celebrated Women, of all Ages and Countries,* published in six volumes in 1803. She supported herself through a long life by her writing, producing numerous religious tracts, pedagogical novels for children, and political journalism. Her final attempt to compile images of "female excellence and worth" in order to further "the moral rights and intellectual advancement of *woman,*" *Memoirs of Queens Illustrious and Celebrated,* appeared in 1821. As Hays summarized a lifetime of committed advocacy for the rights of woman in her preface to *Memoirs of Queens*:

> I maintain . . . that there is, there can be, but *one moral standard of excellence for mankind,* whether male or female, and that the licentious distinctions [between the sexes] made by the domineering party, in the spirit of tyranny, selfishness, and sexuality, are at the foundation of the heaviest evils that have afflicted, degraded, and corrupted society: and I found my arguments upon nature, equity, philosophy, and the Christian religion.
>
> The powers and capacity of woman for rational and moral advancement are, at this day, no longer a question: still, her general training — though superior minds, aided by the diffusion of literature, struggle and assert themselves, — is for adornment rather than for use; for exhibition rather than for moral and mental improvement; for the delight of the harem, rather than to render her the friend, the companion, the assistant, the counsellor of man, the former of his infant habits, the instructor of his early years, the source from which his character takes its bias, his principles their rise. (pp. vi–vii)

from Letters and Essays, Moral, and Miscellaneous

(1793)

— No. III

Of all bondage, mental bondage is surely the most fatal; the absurd despotism which has hitherto, with more than gothic barbarity, enslaved the female mind, the enervating and degrading system of manners by which the understandings of women have been chained down to frivolity and trifles, have increased the general tide of effeminacy and corruption. To conform to the perpetual fluctuation of fashion (and few have the courage to dare the "slow and moving finger of scorn,"[1] which is pointed at every external singularity) requires almost their whole time and attention, and leaves little leisure for intellectual improvement.

"Say dreamers of gay dreams!
"How will you weather an eternal night,
"Where such expedients fail?"[2]

It has been alleged, that this constant variation of mode is serviceable to commerce, and promotes a brisk circulation of money; or with more propriety it might be said a quick succession of bankruptcies: but however this may be, it is I conceive making too expensive an offering at the golden shrine of Plutus[3] to sacrifice all the dignified and rational pursuits of life. A few distinguished individuals, feeling the powers of their own minds (for what can curb the celestial energy of genius?) are endeavouring to dispel the magical illusions of custom, and restore degraded woman to the glory of rationality, and to fitness for immortality. The rights of woman, and the name of Woollstonecraft, will go down to posterity with reverence, when the pointless sarcasms of witlings are forgotten. I am aware that some men of real good sense and candor, have supposed that the idea of there being no sexual character, is carried

[1] **"slow and moving finger of scorn"**: Shakespeare, *Othello,* IV.ii.54–56: "but, alas, to make me / A fixed figure for the time of scorn / To point his slow unmoving finger at!" (printed as "His slow and moving finger" in the Knight and Staunton editions of Shakespeare's plays).

[2] **"Say dreamers . . . fail?"**: unidentified.

[3] **Plutus**: Pluto, Classical Greek god of the dead (Gk. *ploutos* means "riches").

in this most admirable work a little too far. Let them reflect for a moment on the extremes which the opposite opinion has produced; and say from whence arises the most formidable danger? Is there any cause to apprehend that we may subject our feelings too much to the guidance of reason? Or that we shall conduct the business of our families with too much order and equity: to the wise and good only, I now appeal! would you not dare to give up any of the allurements of the mistress (if indeed any need be given up worth the preserving) to the refined pleasure of living with a rational and equal companion? In such an intercourse, when enlivened by love, if happiness resides on earth, surely it is to be found! where the advantages are reciprocal, for each reflects back with interest, the light they receive. Similarity of mind and principle is the only true basis of harmony. Great superiority of either side causes a narrow jealousy, or a painful constraint; there is nothing so irksome as to converse with people who cannot understand you.

Others (I mean the vulgar of every rank) terrified at the very idea of our feeling and asserting our rights to rationality, raise innumerable cavils and objections, all originating from the same source, a pertinacious and jealous adherence to a narrow and mistaken self-interest, and the petty word AUTHORITY. It is this which makes the priest on certain occasions raise an alarm about the safety of the church, the sovereign with paternal solicitude endeavour to guard his people from light and knowledge, by royal proclamations and prohibitions, and the Ephesians to exclaim that their "craft" is "in danger."[4] Must I inform these profound politicians, that every infringement of right weakens duty, every stretch of prerogative gives a mortal wound to monarchy, and every weak fence of proscription prepares the way for their utter demolition, and for laying Hierarchy waste? The love of arbitrary power, with morbid influence, corrupts the human mind; and after the factitious strength of the delirium, exhausted by the unnatural exertion, sinks it into helpless effeminacy and cowardly despondence, the usurper must sooner or later be the victim of his usurpation. . . .

[4] **Ephesians:** The Biblical *Epistle to the Ephesians* (attributed to St. Paul), which deals primarily with the moral duties of married persons, parents, and children, and strongly urges its readers to submit to the church's authority.

from Appeal to the Men of Great Britain in Behalf of Women

(1798)

Let it be remembered, that the efficacy of ignorance has been long tried, and has not produced the consequences expected. Let knowledge therefore take its turn, and let the patrons of privation stand a while aside, and admit the operation of positive principles.

JOHNSON[1]

— INTRODUCTION —

It may at first sight appear absurd to address the following pages in behalf of women, to the men of Great Britain; whose apparent interest it perhaps is, in common with that of all other men, that things should remain on the footing they are. But as the men of Great Britain, to whom in particular I chuse to appeal, have to their everlasting honor, always been remarkable for an ardent love of liberty, and high in their pretensions to justice with regard to themselves; it is not to be believed, if the subject of the present work were taken into their serious consideration, but that the same sentiments would be freely and generously extended to that class of beings, in whose cause I though unworthy appear. A class, upon whom the Almighty has stamped so sublime, so unequivocal marks of dignity and importance, that it is difficult to conceive why men should wish to counteract the benevolent designs of Providence in their favour; by leading in chains, too often galling to their sensible and tender natures, those, whom heaven having in its wisdom formed their equals, could never surely, save in its wrath, doom to be the slaves of man. . . .

— ARGUMENTS ADDUCED FROM REASON AGAINST THE SUBJECTION OF WOMEN —

. . . It is necessary to make some attempt at arrangement and method in pursuing my subject; and I shall therefore divide this part of it under the following heads, viz.

[1] **Johnson:** Dr. Samuel Johnson (1709–1784), famous writer and lexicographer.

The erroneous ideas which men have formed, of the characters and abilities of women. — What men would have women to be. — What women are. — And, what women ought to be. — All of which, as they at present stand, I take to be essentially and necessarily different from each other.

— OF THE ERRONEOUS IDEAS WHICH MEN HAVE FORMED, OF THE CHARACTERS AND ABILITIES OF WOMEN —

That 'most women have no character at all,' it is feared men in general endeavour to make themselves believe; and that too perhaps, not from the most upright motives. For confirming and disseminating this pleasant idea, the women of Great Britain are much indebted to the very silly line of Pope's[2] which I have just quoted; — and who by the way, with all his wit, had a great many silly ones on that subject. Upon this principle however, such as it is, men have formed a standard, to which they would willingly reduce the whole sex. Like the barbarous tyrant, who is reported to have stretched or amputated the limbs of his subjects, or strangers, to suit his miserable caprice; so men, not contented with women as they come from the hands of the all-wise Creator, with that endless variety of character, that variety which is the soul of beauty, the most potent charm in society; men will not allow their companions to be, what Heaven has made them, and intended them to remain; but must model them anew after their own fashion; to suit their passions and prejudices; and so as to give the least check possible to that unbounded freedom to which they have always aspired, and the least chance possible for women to emancipate themselves. . . .

Appealing therefore, on the one hand, to men of reading and information, who are able to decide the question upon the evidence of well-known and established facts, which must readily occur to their memory; and appealing on the other to the mass of mankind, who are fully competent to judge, upon the principles of common sense, and from daily observation; I ask those of both classes, who have sufficient strength of mind to cast prejudice aside, whether, taking into account the very few women, who have received a suitable education; the numbers who have shone, as sovereigns, as legislators, in politicks, in literature, and in common life; are not out of all proportion great? . . .

If then it can hardly be disputed that women — the ancients as far as we can learn from the extraordinary panegyricks of historians — the moderns from actual and undoubted proofs — have ruled with as much glory to themselves, as much benefit to their subjects, and as great marks of sound judgment, and knowledge in the arts of government, as the greatest princes their contemporaries; I hope it will not appear presumption to say, that did women receive equal advantages of education, there is every reason to suppose, they would equal men in the sublime science of politicks; which as it includes the whole art of governing the multitude well in the most liberal sense of the word, requires not only such talents, as the one sex is allowed to possess in common with the other; but includes likewise those, which men are fond of arrogating exclusively to themselves. Such as strength of mind — extensive foresight, — genius to plan schemes of importance, — and resolution, and stability to put them in execution; — with a thousand et caeteras which will very readily occur to men, accustomed to string up their own superiorities; and extremely willing to take for granted, without much examination, opinions so creditable and convenient for themselves. . . .

"Implicit faith, all hail! Imperial Man
"Exacts submission."——

YEARSLEY[3]

— WHAT MEN WOULD HAVE WOMEN TO BE —

Of all the systems, — if indeed a bundle of contradictions and absurdities may be called a system, — which human nature in its moments of intoxication has produced; that which men have contrived with a view to forming the minds, and regulating the conduct of women, is perhaps the most completely absurd. And, though the consequences are often very serious to both sexes, yet if one could for a moment forget these, and consider it only as a system, it would rather be found a subject of mirth and ridicule than serious anger.

[2] **the very silly line of Pope's:** "Most women have no characters at all," from Alexander Pope's "Epistle ii.—To a Lady: Of the Characters of Women," 2:46.

[3] **Yearsley:** See ANN CROMARTIE YEARSLEY.*

What a chaos!—What a mixture of strength and weakness,—of greatness and littleness,—of sense and folly,—of exquisite feeling and total insensibility,—have they jumbled together in their imaginations,—and then given to their pretty darling the name of woman!

> —Reason we resign;
> Against our senses we adopt the plan
> Which reverence, fear, and folly think divine.
>
> YEARSLEY[4]

....

— WHAT WOMEN ARE —

To say what women *really* are, would be a very difficult task indeed; we must therefore endeavour, to describe them by negatives. As, perhaps, the only thing that can be advanced with certainty on the subject, is,—what they are *not*. For it is very clear, that they are not what they ought to be, that they are not what men would have them to be, and to finish the portrait, that they are not what they appear to be. Indeed, indeed, they cannot say with honest Hamlet, that they 'know not what seem is.'[5] I hope however that these observations will not be considered as a libel upon the sex; for as this inconsistency and uncertainty of character is a matter of necessity and not of choice, they are rather objects of pity than of blame. And as their defects are generally speaking, I presume, those of education, rather than of nature, the men have more subject for remorse than triumph. . . .

In the first place then, I hold it as an infallible truth, and a truth that few will attempt to deny; that any race of people, or I should rather say any class of rational beings,—though by no means inferior originally in intellectual endowments,—may be held in a state of subjection and dependence from generation to generation, by another party, who, by a variety of circumstances, none of them depending on actual, original superiority of mind, may have established an authority over them. And it must be acknowledged a truth equally infallible, that any class so held in a state of subjection and dependence, will degenerate both in body and mind. . . .

But it must be confessed, that even those who consider the human species, in a more liberal and extensive point of view,—who do not see sufficient grounds for those claims so haughtily advanced on the part of the men,—yet suppose the necessity of subordination on one side unavoidable. They therefore fear, that women, were their eyes opened to their natural equality and consequence, would not so tamely submit to the cruel injustice with which they are treated, in many of the leading points in life. And they know that nothing would tend so much to this *eclaircissement*,[6] as an education, which by exercising their reason, and unfolding their talents, should point out to themselves, how they might exert them to the utmost. Such a development of mind would undoubtedly enable them to see and reason upon what principles, all the other regulations of society were formed,—which however they may deviate in execution, are evidently founded on justice and humanity,—and would consequently enable them to bring home and apply those principles to the situation of their sex in general. Thus awakened to a sense of their injuries, they would behold with astonishment and indignation, the arts which had been employed, to keep them in a state of PERPETUAL BABYISM. . . .

And this is precisely a case in point. For, in the first place it cannot be proved, that men are fitter to govern women, than women are to govern themselves, in the unlimited sense that men aspire to; except comparative experiment had been fairly and repeatedly made. Or, except superiority of mind had from the beginning, been so completely, so distinctly, and so uniformly marked; that it could bear no more dispute, that men should take the whole command into their own hands, than that mature age, should care for helpless infancy.

Men however, having taken for granted, and endeavoured to establish without proof, that they have some degree of intellectual superiority over women; have the consequences of their government, been equal to their declarations of superior wisdom, or answerable to their wishes, or to their ideas, of the possible perfection of the female sex, even in that secondary view in which they chuse to consider them? I apprehend they will not say so. Or if they do, the sex will by no means join them. For chained and blindfolded as they most certainly are, with respect to their own rights;—they know,—they feel conscious—of capability of greater degrees of perfection, than they are permitted to arrive at. Yes they see—there is not an individual among them, who does not at times see,—and feel too with keenest anguish,—that mind, as has been finely said, is of no sex. . . .

---

[4] **Yearsley:** See ANN CROMARTIE YEARSLEY.*

[5] **Hamlet:** Hays paraphrases Shakespeare's *Hamlet* I.ii.76: "Seems, madam! Nay, it is; I know not 'seems.'"

[6] **eclaircissement:** (French) revelation, clarification.

— WHAT WOMEN OUGHT TO BE —

Women then, I must take it upon me to say, ought to be considered as the companions and equals, not as the inferiors,—much less as they virtually are,—as the slaves of men. In every station they are entitled to esteem, as well as love, when deserving, and virtuous, in the different connections of life,—They were originally intended, to be the helpmates of the other sex, as the Scripture most emphatically and explicitly calls them;[7] and not their drudges in the common ranks, and the tools of their passions and prejudices in the higher. . . .

Having said as much on the two first charges, as the limited nature of this sketch will admit; I shall now consider the last—That knowledge renders women masculine, and consequently disgusting in their manners.—In doing this I think my argument will prove a two-edged sword. I think it must prove, that neither has learning a direct, and inevitable tendency to render women masculine; nor if it did so, would it render them consequently, and infallibly disagreeable to the men. . . .

If therefore we are to understand by a masculine woman, one who emulates those virtues and accomplishments, which as common to human nature, are common to both sexes; the attempt is natural, amiable, and highly honorable to that woman, under whatever name her conduct may be disguised or censured.

[7] **Scripture:** Genesis 2:18.

But if on the other hand we mean by a masculine woman, one who apes the exercises, the attributes, the unrestrained passions, and the numberless improprieties, which men fondly *chuse* to think suitable enough for their own sex—and which excesses to say the truth after all, chiefly distinguish their moral characters from those of women—I must say that knowledge has no tendency whatever to produce such aukward imitations; and I must confess, that such are masculine in the worst sense of the word, and as we should imagine consequently disagreeable. This however as we hinted before would be a hasty and ill-grounded conclusion, though apparently founded in reason, for the fact is otherwise; and the present age furnishes examples enough, that women may be truly masculine in their conduct and demeanor, without wounding the delicacy of the men.

I will own, however, that even if the pretensions of the sexes were finally adjusted, and that equilibrium established, which I have endeavoured to point out as necessary to the peace and satisfaction of both; that perfection, or compleat happiness, is not to be expected. Of this however we are certain, that, if universal justice were to prevail among mankind,—in which of course we include womankind,—that we should then be on the high road to happiness; of which we might reasonably hope to taste a competent share in this world, and might safely trust to a good providence for the perfection of it in another. . . .

RICHARD POLWHELE

(1760–1838)

An Anglican clergyman who claimed descent from Drogo de Polwhele, chamberlain of the Empress Matilda, Richard Polwhele was a staunch upholder of the status quo and a frequent contributor to the *Anti-Jacobin Review*, the *Gentleman's Magazine*, and the *Orthodox Churchman's Magazine*. Educated at Christ Church, Oxford, in 1782 he became the curate of Kenton, near Powderham Castle, Devonshire, the seat of the Courtenays, where he joined a nearby literary society at Exeter. The society published *Poems Chiefly by Gentlemen of Devonshire and Cornwall* in 1792, edited by Polwhele, and in 1796 *Essays by a Society of Gentlemen at Exeter*. He wrote incomplete histories of Devon and of his native Cornwall (published between 1793 and 1808). In addition, he wrote many topographical and didactic poems (most notably *Poems* in 1791), and translated the *Idylls, Epigrams,* and *Fragments* of Theocritus, Bion, and Moschus, along with the *Elegies* of Tyrtaeus (1786); this last was his most successful work and was widely reprinted. He addressed his attack on the rights of woman to another conservative critic, T. J. Mathias (1754–1835), from whose poem, "The Pursuits of Literature" (1794–1797), Polwhele borrowed his title. Mathias, in a note, had referred to "our unsex'd female writers" who "now instruct, or confuse, us and themselves, in the labyrinth of politics, or turn us wild with Gallic frenzy." The chief objects of Polwhele's attack are Mary Wollstonecraft,* Anna Barbauld,* Mary Robinson,* Charlotte Smith,* Helen Maria Williams,* Ann Yearsley,* Mary Hays,* Emma Crewe, and the painter Angelica Kauffmann.

from The Unsex'd Females

(1798)

Thou, who with all the poet's genuine rage,
Thy "fine eye rolling" o'er "this aweful age,"
Where polish'd life unfolds its various views,
Hast mark'd the magic influence of the muse;
Sever'd, with nice precision, from her beam
Of genial power, her false or feeble gleam;
Expos'd the Sciolist's[1] vain-glorious claim,
And boldly thwarted Innovation's aim,
Where witlings wildly think or madly dare,
With Honor, Virtue, Truth, announcing war;
Survey with me, what ne'er our fathers saw,
A female band despising NATURE's law,
As "proud defiance" flashes from their arms,[2]
And vengeance smothers all their softer charms.
I shudder at the new unpictur'd scene,
Where unsex'd woman vaunts the imperious mien;
Where girls, affecting to dismiss the heart,
Invoke the Proteus[3] of petrific art;
With equal ease, in body or in mind,
To Gallic freaks or Gallic faith resign'd,
The crane-like neck, as Fashion bids, lay bare,
Or frizzle, bold in front, their borrow'd hair;
Scarce by a gossamery film carest,
Sport, in full view, the meretricious breast;[4]

[1] **Sciolist:** a person of shallow or superficial learning.

[2] "A troop came next, who crowns and armour wore, / And proud defiance in their looks they bore." [Alexander] Pope. The Amazonian band—the female Quixotes of the new philosophy, are, here, too justly characterised [R. P.].

[3] **Proteus:** mythical deity of creation and change.

[4] To "sport a face," is a cant phrase in one of our Universities, by which is meant an impudent obtrusion of a man's person in company. It is not inapplicable, perhaps, to the open bosom—a fashion which we have never invited or sanctioned. The fashions of France, which have been always imitated by the English, were, heretofore, unexceptionable in a moral point of view;

Loose the chaste cincture, where the graces shone,
And languish'd all the Loves, the ambrosial zone;
As lordly domes inspire dramatic rage,
Court prurient Fancy to the private stage;
With bliss botanic as their bosoms heave,[5]
Still pluck forbidden fruit, with mother Eve,
For puberty in sighing florets pant,
Or point the prostitution of a plant;
Dissect its organ of unhallow'd lust,
And fondly gaze the titillating dust;
With liberty's sublimer views expand,
And o'er the wreck of kingdoms sternly stand;[6]
And, frantic, midst the democratic storm,
Pursue, Philosophy! thy phantom-form.
  Far other is the female shape and mind,
By modest luxury heighten'd and refin'd;
Those limbs, that figure, tho' by Fashion grac'd,
By Beauty polish'd, and adorn'd by Taste;
That soul, whose harmony perennial flows,
In Music trembles, and in Color glows;
Which bids sweet Poesy reclaim the praise
With faery light to gild fastidious days,
From sullen clouds relieve domestic care,
And melt in smiles the withering frown of war.
Ah! once the female Muse, to NATURE true,
The unvalued store from FANCY, FEELING drew;
Won, from the grasp of woe, the roseate hours,
Cheer'd life's dim vale, and strew'd the grave with
    flowers.
  But lo! where, pale amidst the wild, she draws
Each precept cold from sceptic Reason's vase;
Pours with rash arm the turbid stream along,
And in the foaming torrent whelms the throng.
  Alas! her pride sophistic flings a gloom,
To chase, sweet Innocence! thy vernal bloom,
Of each light joy to damp the genial glow,
And with new terrors clothe the groupe of woe,
Quench the pure daystar in oblivion deep,
And, Death! restore thy "long, unbroken sleep."[7]
  See Wollstonecraft, whom no decorum checks,
Arise, the intrepid champion of her sex;
O'er humbled man assert the sovereign claim,
And slight the timid blush of virgin fame.
  "Go, go (she cries) ye tribes of melting maids,
"Go, screen your softness in sequester'd shades;
"With plaintive whispers woo the unconscious grove,
"And feebly perish, as depis'd ye love.
"What tho' the fine Romances of Rousseau[8]
"Bid the frame flutter, and the bosom glow;
"Tho' the rapt Bard, your empire fond to own,
"Fall prostrate and adore your living throne,
"The living throne his hands presum'd to rear,
"Its seat a simper, and its base a tear;
"Soon shall the sex disdain the illusive sway,
"And wield the sceptre in yon blaze of day;
"Ere long, each little artifice discard,
"No more by weakness winning fond regard;
"Nor eyes, that sparkle from their blushes, roll,
"Nor catch the languors of the sick'ning soul,
"Nor the quick flutter, nor the coy reserve,
"But nobly boast the firm gymnastic nerve;[9]
"Nor more affect with Delicacy's fan
"To hide the emotion from congenial man;
"To the bold heights where glory beams, aspire,
"Blend mental energy with Passion's fire,
"Surpass their rivals in the powers of mind
"And vindicate *the Rights of womankind.*"
  She spoke: and veteran BARBAULD[10] caught the strain,
And deem'd her songs of Love, her Lyrics vain;
And ROBINSON to Gaul her Fancy gave,
And trac'd the picture of a Deist's grave!
And charming SMITH resign'd her power to please,

since, however ridiculous or absurd, they were innocent. But they have now their source among prostitutes—among women of the most abandoned character [R. P.].

[5] Polwhele here refers to Erasmus Darwin's "The Loves of the Plants" in his *Botanic Garden* (1789, 1803). (See SCIENCE AND NATURE.)

[6] The female advocates of Democracy in this country, though they have had no opportunity of imitating the French ladies, in their atrocious acts of cruelty; have yet assumed a stern serenity in the contemplation of those savage excesses [R. P.].

[7] From the Greek elegiac poet Moschus (2nd century BC).

[8] **Rousseau:** Jean-Jacques Rosseau (1712–1778), French political philosopher, educationalist, and novelist. His "Romances" include *La nouvelle Héloïse* (1760) and *Emile* (1762).

[9] Miss Wollstonecraft seriously laments the neglect of all muscular exercises, at our female Boarding-schools [R. P.].

[10] **Barbauld:** Anna Letitia Barbauld* (1743–1825), poet, critic, essayist, and friend of Joanna Baillie.*

Poetic feeling and poetic ease;[11]
And HELEN, fir'd by Freedom, bade adieu
To all the broken visions of Peru;
And YEARSELEY, who had warbled, Nature's child,
Midst twilight dews, her minstrel ditties wild,
(Tho' soon a wanderer from her meads and milk,
She long'd to rustle, like her sex, in silk)
Now stole the modish grin, the sapient sneer,[12]
And flippant HAYS assum'd a cynic leer;
While classic KAUFFMAN her Priapus drew,
And linger'd a sweet blush with EMMA CREWE. . . .[13]

[11] **Robinson**: Mary Robinson* (1758–1800), actress, playwright, poet, novelist, and radical thinker. Her best known novel, *Walsingham* (1797), expresses Deistic and Godwinian political views. **Smith**: Charlotte Smith* (1749–1806), poet and novelist, author of the extremely successful Gothic novel *The Old Manor House* (1793).

[12] **Helen**: Helen Maria Williams* (1762–1827), poet, novelist, and political commentator. Best known for her *Letters from France* (1790–1798), a pro-Jacobin commentary on the French Revolution. Polwhele here refers to her long poem *Peru*.* **Yearseley**: Mrs. Ann Cromartie Yearsley* (1756–1806), poet and milkwoman. Hannah More* recognized her poetic gifts and revised and published her first volume of poems in 1784.

[13] **Hays**: Mary Hays* (1760–1843), novelist and radical essayist, best known for her novel *Memoirs of Emma Courtney* (1796). **Kauffman**: Angelica Kauffmann (1741–1807), Swiss painter who emigrated to England, where she enjoyed royal patronage and became one of the two female founding members of the Royal Academy of Art. **Priapus**: Greek god of fertility, represented as a grotesque little man with an enormous phallus. The artist obsessed with illustrating the ancient worship of Priapus at this time was Sir Richard Payne Knight. **Crewe**: Emma Crewe, English painter and etcher, active ca. 1783.

PRISCILLA BELL WAKEFIELD

(1751–1832)

The granddaughter and daughter of devout Quakers, Priscilla Bell married Edward Wakefield, a successful London merchant, in 1771 and had three children. She was well-known for her philanthropic works (she founded a lying-in hospital for poor women in 1791 and promoted savings or "frugality" banks for the working classes) and for her especially detailed children's books on botany, entymology, zoology, and the geography of the British Empire, North America, Africa, and London. Her *Reflections on the Present Condition of the Female Sex; with Suggestions for Its Improvement* advocating greater employment opportunities for women, was published in 1798.

from Reflections on the Present Condition of the Female Sex; with Suggestions for Its Improvement

(1798)

— *from* CHAPTER I —

. . . In civilized nations it has ever been the misfortune of the [female] sex to be too highly elevated, or too deeply depressed; now raised above the condition of mortals, upon the score of their personal attractions; and now debased below that of reasonable creatures, with respect to their intellectual endowments. The result of this improper treatment has been a neglect of the mental powers, which women really possess, but know not how to exercise; and they have been contented to barter the dignity of reason, for the imaginary privilege of an empire, of the existence of which they can entertain no reasonable hope beyond the duration of youth and beauty.

Of the few who have raised themselves to preeminence by daring to stray beyond the accustomed path, the envy of their own sex, and the jealousy or contempt of the other, have too often been the attendants; a fate which doubtless has deterred others from attempting to follow them, or emulate, even in an inferior degree, the distinction they have attained.

But notwithstanding these disadvantages, and others of less perceptible influence, the diffusion of christianity, and the progress of civilization, have raised the importance of the female character; and it has become a branch of philosophy, not a little interesting, to ascertain the offices which the different ranks of women are required to fulfil. Their rights and their duties have lately occupied the pens of writers of eminence; the employments which may properly exercise their faculties, and fill up their time in a useful manner, without encroaching upon those professions, which are appropriate to men, remain to be defined. There are many branches of science, as well as useful occupations, in which women may employ their time and their talents, beneficially to themselves and to the community, without destroying the peculiar characteristic of their sex, or exceeding the most exact limits of modesty and decorum. Whatever obliges them to mix in the public haunts of men, or places the young in too familiar a situation with the other sex; whatever is obnoxious to the delicacy and reserve of the female character, or destructive, in the smallest degree, to the strictest moral purity, is inadmissible. The sphere of feminine action is contracted by numberless difficulties, that are no impediments to masculine exertions. Domestic privacy is the only sure asylum for the juvenile part of the sex; nor can the grave matron step far beyond that boundary with propriety. Unfitted, by their relative situation in society, for many honourable and lucrative employments, those only are suitable for them, which can be pursued without endangering their virtue, or corrupting their manners.

But, under these restrictions, there may be found a multitude of objects adapted to the useful exertions of female talents, which it will be the principal design of these Reflections to point out, after making some remarks upon the present state of female education, and suggesting some improvements towards its reformation.

— *from* CHAPTER IV —

. . . The difficulty of meeting with persons properly qualified to be the preceptors and guides of the uncorrupted minds of youth, is allowed to be great, and suggests the advantages which might arise, from the establishment of institutions for the express purpose of educating young women, of small expectations, for the office. These institutions should be sufficiently endowed, to provide masters in every useful science, and to furnish a well-chosen library, consisting of the most approved authors, with globes, and other suitable apparatus for instruction, and after a certain number of years, women only should be nominated to the charge of instruction. The effect of such seminaries would be a constant succession of female teachers properly prepared for their destination, not only by a regular course of study, but also by a thorough initiation into the philosophical principles of education, founded upon the opinions of the most eminent writers upon the subject. Another beneficial consequence would be, the affording a respectable subsistence to great numbers of young women, who are reduced to misery through want of employment, by enabling them to teach those sciences, which are exclusively taught by masters, an evil that calls loudly for redress. Surely it can never be denied, that the instruction of girls in every department of knowledge or art, is a fair field for the exertion of female talents. Is it compatible with propriety or decency, that the persons of girls advancing towards maturity, should be exposed to the wanton eye of a dancing-master? Are not the fascinating tones of music as dangerous as the graces of dancing, in exciting the tender emotions? Women only, therefore, should be permitted to instruct the sex in these seductive arts. It ought to be their privilege to do so in every other. Nature has imposed no invincible barrier to their acquisition and communication of languages, arithmetic, writing, drawing, geography, or any science which is proper for girls to learn. . . .

The necessity of directing the attention of females to some certain occupation is not so apparent, because custom has rendered them dependant upon their fathers and husbands for support; but as some of every class experience the loss of those relations, without inheriting an adequate resource, there would be great propriety in preparing each of them, by an education of energy and useful attainments, to meet such disasters, and to be able, under such circumstances, to procure an independence for themselves. There is scarcely a more helpless object in the wide circle of misery which the vicissitudes of civilized society display, than a woman genteelly educated, whether single or married, who is deprived, by any unfortunate accident, of the protection and support of male relations; unaccustomed to struggle with difficulty, unacquainted with any resource to supply an independent maintenance, she is reduced to the depths of wretchedness, and not unfrequently, if she be young and handsome, is driven by despair to those paths which lead to infamy. Is it not time to find a remedy for such evils, when the contention of nations has produced the most affecting transitions in private life, and transferred the affluent and the noble to the humiliating extremes of want and obscurity? When our streets teem with multitudes of unhappy women, many of whom might have been rescued from their present degradation, or who would perhaps never have fallen into it, had they been instructed in the exercise of some art or profession, which would have enabled them to procure for themselves a respectable support by their own industry.

This reasonable precaution against the accidents of life is resisted by prejudice, which rises like an insurmountable barrier against a woman, of any degree above the vulgar, employing her time and her abilities, towards the maintenance of herself and her family: degradation of rank immediately follows the virtuous attempt, as it did formerly, among the younger branches of the noble families in France. But the nature of truth is immutable, however it may be obscured by error: that which is a moral excellence in one rational being, deserves the same estimation in another; therefore, if it be really honourable in a man, to exert the utmost of his abilities, whether mental or corporal, in the acquisition of a competent support for himself, and for those who have a natural claim upon his protection; it must be equally so in a woman, nay, perhaps still more incumbent, as in many cases, there is nothing so inimical to the preservation of her virtue as a state of poverty, which leaves her dependent upon the generosity of others, to supply those accommodations, which use has rendered necessary to her comfort.

There appears then no moral impediment to prevent women from the application of their talents to purposes of utility; on the contrary, an improvement in public manners must infallibly result from it; as their influence over the other sex is universally acknowledged, it may be boldly asserted, that a conversion of their time from trifling and unproductive employments, to those that are both useful and profitable, would operate as a check upon luxury, dissipation, and prodigality, and retard the progress of that general dissoluteness, the offspring of idleness, which is deprecated by all political writers, as the sure forerunner of national decay. . . .

— *from* CHAPTER X —

. . . Another heavy discouragement to the industry of women, is the inequality of the reward of their labour, compared with that of men, an injustice which pervades every species of employment performed by both sexes.[1]

In employments which depend upon bodily strength the distinction is just; for it cannot be pretended that the generality of women can earn as much as men, where the produce of their labour is the result of corporeal exertion; but it is a subject of great regret, that this inequality should prevail, even where an equal share of skill and application are exerted. Male stay-makers, mantua-makers, and hair-dressers are better paid than female artists of the same professions; but surely it will never be urged as an apology for this disproportion, that women are not as capable of making stays, gowns, dressing hair, and similar arts, as men; if they are not superior to them, it can only be accounted for upon this principle, that the prices they receive for their labour are not sufficient to repay them for the expence of qualifying themselves for their business, and that they sink under the mortification of being regarded as artizans of inferior estimation, whilst the men, who supplant them, receive all the encouragement of large profits and full employment, which is ensured to them by the folly of fashion. The occasion for this remark is a disgrace upon those who patronize such a brood of effeminate beings in the garb of men; when sympathy with their humbler sisters should direct them to act in a manner exactly opposite, by holding out every incitement to the industry of their own sex. This evil indeed calls loudly upon women of rank and fortune for redress: they should determine to employ women only, wherever they can be employed; they should procure female instructors for their children; they should frequent no shops that are not served by women; they should wear no clothes that are not made by them; they should reward them as liberally as they do the men who have hitherto supplanted them. . . .

The serving of retail shops, which deal in articles of female consumption, should be exclusively appropriated to women. For were the multitudes of men, who are constantly employed in measuring linen, gauze, ribbons, and lace; selling perfumes and cosmetics; setting a value on feathers and trinkets; and displaying their talents in praising the elegance of bonnets and caps, to withdraw, they might benefit the community, by exchanging such frivolous avocations for something more worthy of the masculine character, and by this measure afford an opportunity of gaining a creditable livelihood to many destitute women, whom a dreadful necessity drives to the business of prostitution.—The attendance of women in shops, need not be entirely confined to haberdashers, perfumers, and milliners; there are other trades in which they may be employed behind the counter: the familiar offices of trying on gloves and shoes, are more suitably performed by persons of the same sex.

It is wonderful, that amongst the number of modern refinements, an alteration has not been adopted likewise, with respect to an article of clothing, which custom has long placed in the hands of men, at least in the vicinity of London, the measuring and making of which, decency would assign to women. The covering alluded to, by this remark, is the last which is required. Every undertaker should employ women, for the express purpose of supplying the female dead, with those things which are requisite. How shocking is the idea of our persons being exposed, even after death, to the observation of a parcel of undertaker's men. . . .

It is surely unnecessary to insist farther upon the benefits of encouraging the useful industry of women, they are too obvious to need a repetition.—Beside those employments which are commonly performed by women, and those already shewn to be suitable for such persons as are above the condition of hard labour, there are some professions and trades customarily in the hands of men, which might be conveniently exercised by either sex.—Many parts of the business of a stationer, particularly ruling account books or making pens. The compounding of medicines in an apothecary's shop, requires no other talents than care and exactness; and if opening a vein occasionally be an indispensible requisite, a woman may acquire the capacity of doing it for those of her own sex at least, without any reasonable objection.—Cupping is an art, which wants neither strength in the performance, nor medical judgment in the application, as that depends upon the direction of the physician, and might, under the restriction just mentioned with regard to bleeding, be exercised by women.—Pastry and confectionary appear particularly consonant to the habits of women, though generally performed by men: perhaps the heat of the ovens, and the strength requisite to fill and empty them, may render male assistants necessary; but certainly women are most eligible to mix up the ingredients, and

[1] This abuse is in no instance more conspicuous than in the wages of domestic servants. A footman, especially of the higher kind, whose most laborious task is to wait at table, gains, including clothes, vails [tips], and other perquisites, at least £50 [fifty pounds] per annum, whilst a cook-maid, who is mistress of her profession does not obtain £20 [twenty pounds], though her office is laborious, unwholesome, and requires a much greater degree of skill than that of a valet. A similar disproportion is observable among the inferior servants of the establishment [P. B. W.].

prepare the various kinds of cakes for baking.—Light turnery and toy-making, depend more upon dexterity and invention than force, and are therefore suitable work for women and children.

There must be public houses for the reception of travellers, and labourers who are single, and have no homes: it were happy indeed for the community, that they were confined to such purposes, instead of being converted into receptacles for intemperance; but since they are necessary, even in their present corrupt state, some persons must submit to the inconveniences of this disagreeable profession. Without recommending it as an eligible employment for women, reasons may be urged for the widows of publicans, or even other women of a certain age, engaging in it; as houses of this description, which are under female management, are generally the most orderly, and the most successful.

Farming, as far as respects the theory, is commensurate with the powers of the female mind; nor is the practice of inspecting agricultural processes, incompatible with the delicacy of their frames, if their constitution be good. Several instances of successful female farmers have occurred, and Sir Frederic Morton Eden's[2] opinion confirms the propriety of the practice. . . .

[2] Sir Frederick Morton Eden (1766–1809), economic and political writer, author of *The State of the Poor* (1797), an investigation of poverty among the English labouring classes.

MARY LAMB

(1764–1847)

The daughter of upper-domestic servants, her parents, John Lamb, a valet, and Elizabeth Field Lamb, a housekeeper, were both employed by Samuel Salt, a Whig barrister and Member of Parliament. Mary Lamb was educated to a life of obedient service and self-restraint. Largely ignored by her parents, who devoted themselves to the needs of this kindly master, Mary Lamb lavished her affection on her brother Charles, ten years her junior, for whom she was the primary caregiver. Their sibling bond was so close that Charles later described it as "a sort of double singleness." After attending William Bird's 'dames-school' for the impoverished daughters of the working classes for four years, she educated herself by reading the books in Samuel Salt's library and taught herself Latin and Italian. Apprenticed to a mantua-maker, Mary Lamb supported herself and, after Samuel Salt's death in 1792, her parents as well. She worked as a seamstress, sewing at home the short cloaks fashionable among nineteenth-century women. Needle-work by the piece, in Mary Lamb's day, was so badly paid and so difficult to obtain that for many respectable but impoverished working women, it was only one slippery step above prostitution.

Suffering from a genetic predisposition to madness, a severe manic-depressive psychosis shared by her brother Charles, Mary Lamb was frequently institutionalized for short periods in various London mental asylums, condemned to the brutal care available to poor-house lunatics. In a psychotic attack, perhaps triggered by the exhaustion both of sewing and of caring for her totally disabled mother and her senile father, she stabbed her mother to death on 22 September 1796. Her devoted brother Charles, who could not imagine a life apart from her, became her legal guardian and committed himself to caring for her at home, although she returned to mental institutions for short periods throughout her life. Mary Lamb's matricide may also have been motivated by her repressed anger at her mother's life-long coldness toward her despite Mary's devoted nursing of both her aged parents. After her mother's death, Mary Lamb frequently insisted that her mother was in heaven and had forgiven her. When not suffering from a psychotic incident, Mary Lamb was widely acknowledged to be a woman of exceptional mildness and gentleness, one who sought to mediate and resolve any conflict among her friends.

Mary Lamb eagerly assisted her brother in several writing projects, mostly intended for juvenile audiences: the extremely successful and much reprinted *Tales from Shakespeare* (1807), for which she wrote all but the tragedies; *Mrs. Leicester's School* (1808), in which several of the tales, including "Margaret Green, The Young Mahometan," are in part autobiographical; and *Poetry for Children* (1809). Her essay "On Needle-Work," a muted protest against the working conditions of seamstresses which nonetheless endorses an ideology of female service and obedient marriage, appeared in *British Ladies' Magazine* in 1815.

from BRITISH LADIES' MAGAZINE

On Needle-Work
(1815)

Mr. Editor, In early life I passed eleven years in the exercise of my needle for a livelihood. Will you allow me to address your readers, among whom might perhaps be found some of the kind patronesses of my former humble labours, on a subject widely connected with female life—the state of needle-work in this country.

To lighten the heavy burthen which many ladies impose upon themselves is one object which I have in view; but, I confess, my strongest motive is to excite attention towards the industrious sisterhood to which I once belonged.

From books I have been informed of the fact upon which *The British Lady's Magazine* chiefly founds its pretensions; namely, that women have, of late, been rapidly advancing in intellectual improvement. Much may have been gained in this way, indirectly, for that class of females for whom I wish to plead. Needle-work[1] and intellectual improvement are naturally in a state of warfare. But I am afraid the root of the evil has not, as yet, been struck at. Work-women of every description were never in so much distress for want of employment.

Among the present circle of my acquaintance I am proud to rank many that may truly be called respectable; nor do the female part of them in their mental attainments at all disprove the prevailing opinion of that intellectual progression which you have taken as the basis of your work; yet I affirm that I know not a single family where there is not some essential draw-back to its comfort which may be traced to needle-work *done at home,* as the phrase is for all needle-work performed in a family by some of its own members, and for which no remuneration in money is received or expected.

In money alone, did I say? I would appeal to all the fair votaries of voluntary housewifery whether, in the matter of conscience, any one of them ever thought she had done as much needle-work as she ought to have done. Even fancy-work, the fairest of the tribe! How delightful the arrangement of her materials! The fixing upon her happiest pattern, how pleasing an anxiety! How cheerful the commencement of the labour she enjoys! But that lady must be a true lover of the art, and so industrious a pursuer of a predetermined purpose, that it were pity her energy should not have been directed to some wiser end, who can affirm she neither feels weariness during the execution of a fancy piece, nor takes more time than she had calculated for the performance.

Is it too bold an attempt to persuade your readers that it would prove an incalculable addition to general happiness and the domestic comfort of both sexes, if needle-work were never practised but for a remuneration in money? As nearly, however, as this desirable thing can be effected, so much more nearly will women be upon an equality with men as far as respects the mere enjoyment of life. As far as that goes, I believe it is every woman's opinion that the condition of men is far superior to her own.

"They can do as they like," we say. Do not these words generally mean they have time to seek out whatever amusements suit their tastes? We dare not tell them we have not time to do this; for if they should ask in what manner we dispose of our time we should blush to enter upon a detail of the minutiae which compose the sum of a woman's daily employment. Nay, many a lady who allows not herself one quarter of an hour's positive leisure during her waking hours, considers her own husband as the most industrious of men if he steadily pursue his occupation till the hour of dinner,[2] and will be perpetually lamenting her own idleness.

Real business and *real leisure* make up the portions of men's time;—two sources of happiness which we certainly partake of in a very inferior degree. To the execution of employments in which the faculties of the body or mind are called into busy action there must be a consoling importance attached, which feminine duties (that generic name for all our business) cannot aspire to.

In the most meritorious discharge of those duties the highest praise we can aim at is to be accounted the helpmates of *man;* who, in return for all he does for us, expects, and justly expects, us to do all in our power to soften and sweeten life.

In how many ways is a good woman employed in thought or action through the day that her *good man* may be enabled to feel his leisure hours a *real, substantial holiday* and perfect respite from the cares of business? Not the

[1] **Needle-work:** embroidery or fine sewing.

[2] **hour of dinner:** usually at 3 or 4 in the afternoon, since "dinner" was the first meal following breakfast in Mary Lamb's day.

least part to be done to accomplish this end is to fit herself to become a conversational companion; that is to say, she has to study and understand the subjects on which he loves to talk. This part of our duty, if strictly performed, will be found by far our hardest part. The disadvantages we labour under from an education differing from a manly one make the hours in which we *sit and do nothing* in men's company too often anything but a relaxation; although as to pleasure and instruction time so passed may be esteemed more or less delightful.

To make a man's home so desirable a place as to preclude his having a wish to pass his leisure hours at any fireside in preference to his own, I should humbly take to be the sum and substance of woman's domestic ambition. I would appeal to our British ladies, who are generally allowed to be the most jealous and successful of all women in the pursuit of this object, I would appeal to them who have been most successful in the performance of this laudable service, in behalf of father, son, husband or brother, whether an anxious desire to perform this duty well is not attended with enough of *mental* exertion, at least, to incline them to the opinion that women may be more properly ranked among the contributors to, rather than the partakers of, the undisturbed relaxation of men.

If a family be so well ordered that the master is never called in to its direction, and yet he perceives comfort and economy well attended to, the mistress of that family (especially if children form a part of it), has, I apprehend, as large a share of womanly employment as ought to satisfy her own sense of duty; even though the needle-book and threadcase were quite laid aside, and she cheerfully contributed her part to the slender gains of the corset-maker, the milliner, the dressmaker, the plain worker,[3] the embroidress, and all the numerous classifications of females supporting themselves by *needle-work,* that great staple commodity which is alone appropriated to the self-supporting part of our sex.

Much has been said and written on the subject of men engrossing to themselves every occupation and calling. After many years of observation and reflection I am obliged to acquiesce in the notion that it cannot well be ordered otherwise.

If, at the birth of girls, it were possible to foresee in what cases it would be their fortune to pass a single life, we should soon find trades wrested from their present occupiers and transferred to the exclusive possession of our sex. The whole mechanical business of copying writings in the law department, for instance, might very soon be transferred with advantage to the poorer sort of women, who, with very little teaching, would soon beat their rivals of the other sex in facility and neatness. The parents of female children who were known from their birth to be destined to maintain themselves through the whole course of their lives with like certainty as their sons are, would feel it a duty incumbent on themselves to strengthen the minds, and even the bodily constitutions, of their girls so circumstanced, by an education which, without affronting the preconceived habits of society, might enable them to follow some occupation now considered above the capacity, or too robust for the constitutions of our sex. Plenty of resources would then lie open for single women to obtain an independent livelihood, when every parent would be upon the alert to encroach upon some employment, now engrossed by men, for such of their daughters as would then be exactly in the same predicament as their sons now are. Who, for instance, would lay by money to set up his sons in trade, give premiums and in part maintain them through a long apprenticeship; or, which men of moderate incomes frequently do, strain every nerve in order to bring them up to a learned profession; if it were in a very high degree probable that, by the time they were twenty years of age, they would be taken from this trade or profession, and maintained during the remainder of their lives by the *person whom they should marry.* Yet this is precisely the situation in which every parent whose income does not very much exceed the moderate, is placed with respect to his daughters.

Even where boys have gone through a laborious education, superinducing habits of steady attention accompanied with the entire conviction that the business which they learn is to be the source of their future distinction, may it not be affirmed that the persevering industry required to accomplish this desirable end causes many a hard struggle in the minds of young men, even of the most hopeful disposition? What, then, must be the disadvantages under which a very young woman is placed who is required to learn a trade, from which she can never expect to reap any profit, but at the expense of losing that place in society to the possession of which she may reasonably look forward, inasmuch as it is by far the most *common lot,* namely, the condition of a *happy* English wife?

As I desire to offer nothing to the consideration of your readers but what, at least as far as my own observation goes, I consider as truths confirmed by experience, I will only say that, were I to follow the bent of my own

[3] **milliner:** hatmaker. **plain worker:** one who does "plain sewing," i.e., hems sheets, tablecloths, napkins, etc.

speculative opinion, I should be inclined to persuade every female over whom I hope to have any influence to contribute all the assistance in her power to those of her own sex who may need it, in the employments they at present occupy, rather than to force them into situations now filled wholly by men. With the mere exception of the profits which they have a right to derive by their needle, I would take nothing from the industry of man which he already possesses.

"A penny saved is a penny earned," is a maxim not true unless the penny be saved in the same time in which it might have been earned. I, who have known what it is to work for *money earned*, have since had much experience in working for *money saved*; and I consider, from the closest calculation I can make, that a *penny saved* in that way bears about a true proportion to a *farthing*[4] *earned*. I am no advocate for women who do not depend on themselves for subsistence, proposing to themselves to *earn money*. My reasons for thinking it not advisable are too numerous to state—reasons deduced from authentic facts and strict observations on domestic life in its various shades of comfort. But if the females of a family *nominally* supported by the other sex find it necessary to add something to the common stock, why not endeavour to do something by which they may produce money *in its true shape?*

It would be an excellent plan, attended with very little trouble, to calculate every evening how much money has been saved by needle-work *done in the family*, and compare the result with the daily portion of the yearly income. Nor would it be amiss to make a memorandum of the time passed in this way, adding also a guess as to what share it has taken up in the thoughts and conversation. This would be an easy mode of forming a true notion and getting at the exact worth of this species of *home* industry, and perhaps might place it in a different light from any in which it has hitherto been the fashion to consider it.

Needle-work taken up as an amusement may not be altogether unamusing. We are all pretty good judges of what entertains ourselves, but it is not so easy to pronounce upon what may contribute to the entertainment of others. At all events, let us not confuse the motives of economy with those of simple pastime. If *saving* be no object, and long habit have rendered needle-work so delightful an avocation that we cannot think of relinquishing it, there are the good old contrivances in which our grand-dames were wont to beguile and lose their time—knitting, knotting, netting, carpet-work, and the like ingenious pursuits—those so often praised but tedious works which are so long in the operation that purchasing the labour has seldom been thought good economy. Yet, by a certain fascination, they have been found to chain down the great to a self-imposed slavery, from which they considerately or haughtily excused the needy. These may be esteemed lawful and lady-like amusements. But, if those works more usually denominated useful yield greater satisfaction, it might be laudable scruple of conscience, and no bad test to herself of her own motive, if a lady who had no absolute need were to give the money so saved to poor needle-women belonging to those branches of employment from which she has borrowed these shares of pleasurable labour.—*Sempronia*.

[4] **farthing**: a quarter-penny.

3

Slavery, the Slave Trade, and Abolition in Britain

THE ATTEMPT TO end the British involvement in the slave trade and to emancipate the slaves in the British crown colonies in the West Indies was perhaps second only to the French Revolution in its impact on the social consciousness of writers, especially women, in England between 1780 and 1830. On May 14, 1772, William Murray, Lord Mansfield, presiding on the King's Bench, had ruled in the case of James Somerset, a black slave who had been brought to England, versus his master, Mr. Stewart of Virginia, that slavery was not lawful in England, maintaining that England was "a soil whose air is deemed too pure for slaves to breathe in." Somerset thereby gained his freedom, making England a Mecca for slaves in the British West Indies. Significantly, in that case, Mr. Dunning, the lawyer defending Stewart, argued that slavery, *like marriage,* was a "municipal" rather than a "natural" relationship, and thus constructed by legal custom, similar to feudal villenage, rather than subject to "natural" law. The implied parallel between wives and slaves in this argument—and Lord Mansfield's refusal to rule against the "municipal" servitude of wives—did not escape the attention of the women writers of the period.

The legal abolition of slavery in England itself ended neither the slave trade nor the institution of slavery in the colonies. By 1775 the triangular slave trade had reached its peak: typically, British merchants sent "trappers" and ships to the Gold Coast of Africa where they kidnapped or bought 38,000 to 42,000 Africans annually, at a maximum of £15 per head. These Africans were then shipped under appalling conditions on "the Middle Passage" (during which 13 percent typically died; another 33 percent died later during the "seasoning" or breaking-in period at the other end) to the West Indies to work in the tobacco and sugarcane fields, where they were sold at an average of £35 each. The profits from this sale were then used to buy sugar and tobacco that was sold again, at great profit, in England and Europe; total profits ranged from £600,000 to over £1,000,000 annually. Bristol and Liverpool were the center of the British slave trade; their merchants argued persuasively in the Houses of Parliament that the British economy, and the ability to gratify the national addiction to refined sugar and its products, depended on the continuance of the slave trade. In addition, the lobby of the extremely wealthy West Indian planters, the British owners of the slave plantations who lived either in England (as does Sir Thomas

Bertram in Jane Austen's *Mansfield Park*) or abroad, on their plantations (as does Mr. Vincent in Maria Edgeworth's *Belinda*), exerted an enormous influence on British politics.

Between 1778, when the Prime Minister William Pitt introduced the first bill attempting to regulate the slave trade, and 1807, when the practice was legally abolished, debate raged in England concerning its continuance. The powerful Standing Committee of Planters and Merchants argued that both the practice and the institution of slavery in the West Indian colonies were necessary to Britain's economic survival (especially since France and Holland had recently begun to make serious inroads into the slave market). Moreover, both were morally justified on the grounds that the Africans had been slaves in their own countries and, further, were savages or heathen incapable of rational thought or moral feeling and hence unfit for freedom. African slaves should be regarded as "children" who required a "benevolent" master to teach them the civilizing benefits of Christian doctrine and the Protestant work ethic. Maria Edgeworth's novella "The Grateful Negro"* makes this pro-planter argument in a particularly compelling form, even as she acknowledges that slave masters who abuse their slaves do not deserve their loyalty.

On the other hand, the abolitionists who wished to end not only the slave trade but the very institution of slavery in the colonies argued that the institution of slavery was immoral and violated both the rights of man and Christian doctrine. Moreover, they contended that the actual conditions imposed on Africans both during the Middle Passage and on the slave plantations were far more barbaric and uncivilized than anything they had experienced in Africa, and called into question the morality of England as a Christian nation. The infamous legal case of the *Zong*—a slave ship whose captain, Luke Collingwood, in 1781 threw 132 plague-infected Africans to the sharks in order to collect insurance on this jettisoned "cargo"—raised widespread horror at the cruelty of the slave trade. This event was so shocking and memorable to the British public that 50 years later it inspired both J. M. W. Turner's brilliant painting, "The Slave Ship," and John Ruskin's passionate moral denunciation of British imperialism in his essay "Of Water, as painted by Turner."

The leading voices to end the slave trade were Granville Sharp, who brought the Somerset case to trial, and Thomas Clarkson, whose indefatigable research into the living conditions on the slave ships embarking from Liverpool alerted the public to the atrocities of the Middle Passage denied by the West Indian planters. Clarkson's authoritative *History of the Rise, Progress and Accomplishment of the Abolition of the African Slave Trade, by the British Parliament* was published in 1808. He was joined by William Wilberforce, the Member of Parliament from Hull who headed the efforts to introduce bills abolishing the slave trade and slavery in Parliament between 1788 and 1807. The largest outcry against both the slave trade and the institution of slavery was organized by the Quakers, who established Anti-Slavery Societies throughout England and founded the influential *Anti-Slavery Monthly Reporter* in 1823.

Women were major participants in these societies and were leading figures in the social protests against the slave trade; many boycotted sugar (using honey instead), while others wrote poetry, novels, and tracts condemning the slave trade (e.g., Anna Barbauld's "Epistle to William Wilberforce,"* Hannah More's "Slavery, a Poem,"* Helen Maria Williams' "Farewell, for Two Years, to England,"* and Ann Yearsley's "Poem on the Inhumanity of the Slave Trade"*). Gender played a significant role in the arguments for the abolition of slavery. Those writers who subscribed to the ideology of masculine Romanticism tended to attack slavery as a violation of the innate "rights of man" (see William Cowper's "The Negro's Complaint" [1788]* and "Pity for Poor Africans" [1788],* as well as William Blake's "Little Black Boy,"* William Wordsworth's "To Toussaint L'Ouverture,"* Samuel Taylor Coleridge's "On the Slave Trade,"* Robert Southey's "Poems concerning the Slave Trade,"* and Percy Shelley's "Declaration of Rights"*). Those writers who subscribed to the ideology of feminine Romanticism (on masculine and feminine Romanticism, see Mellor, *Romanticism and Gender,* 1993) tended to condemn slavery because it violated the domestic affections, separating mothers from their children, husbands from their wives, and subjecting black women to sexual abuse from their white masters (see the poems by women listed above, as well as Thomas Day's famous "The Dying Negro" [1773], William Wilberforce's *Letter on the Abolition of the Slave Trade,** and Amelia Opie's "The Black Man's Lament, or How to make Sugar" [1826]*). Actual slave narratives, most notably those included here by Ottobah Cugoano,* Olaudah Equiano,* and Mary Prince,* provided searing witness to the atrocities of slavery. Nonetheless, all these abolitionist writers participated in a colonial discourse of Christian "Anglo-Africanism," grounded in the assumption, in Winthrop Jordan's summary, that "to be Christian was to be civilized rather than barbarous, English rather than African, white rather than black."

Between these two poles, many writers argued that the slave *trade* should be abolished, since Christian merchants should not deal in the buying and selling of human flesh, but that the *institution* of slavery in the West Indies should be allowed to continue since it provided "better" living conditions and greater access to Christian teaching than the Africans could receive in their own countries. Abolishing the trade, they argued, would force planters to treat their slaves more humanely since they could no longer be easily replaced. On the other hand, if the slaves were freed, the planters in fairness would have to be financially "compensated" by the king, an enormous expense which no chancellor of the exchequer in this period wished to pay. It was this view that prevailed in the British Parliament, where the slave trade was formally abolished in 1807 (although it continued illegally for several more years). Slavery in the British West Indian colonies remained a legal institution until numerous events brought about its demise. Beginning in 1760, slave revolts arose, occurring most notably in Saint-Domingue (Haiti) in 1791, led by Vincent Oge and Toussaint L'Ouverture, and in Jamaica in 1831. Secondly, the weakening economic contribution of the West Indies to the British commercial empire meant a diminishing of the slave trade's relative importance to the economy of Britain. And, finally, an ever more vigorous campaign by the abolitionists (the Ladies Anti-Slavery Society in 1832 submitted a petition with 187,000 names demanding immediate emancipation of all slaves) made possible the passage of the Abolition Act of 1833. Even after this period, however, the emancipation of slaves required compensation—by the slave or by the government—of the owner, and proceeded only gradually.

from The Mansfield Judgment
(1772)

From *The English Reports* 98 (King's Bench Division 27), Easter Term, 12 Geo. 3, 1772, K. B.: SOMERSET *against* STEWART, May 14, 1772.

On return to an habeas corpus, requiring Captain Knowles to shew cause for the seizure and detainure of the complainant Somerset, a negro—the case appeared to be this—

That the negro had been a slave to Mr. Stewart, in Virginia, had been purchased from the African coast, in the course of the slave trade, as tolerated in the plantations; that he had been brought to England by his master, who intending his return, by force sent him on board of Captain Knowles's vessel, lying in the river; and was there, by the order of his master, in the custody of Captain Knowles, detained against his consent; until returned in obedience to the writ. . . .

Mr. Hargrave [arguing on behalf of Somerset].—The importance of the question will I hope justify to your Lordships the solicitude with which I rise to defend it; and however unequal I feel myself, will command attention. . . . I shall endeavour to state the grounds from which Mr. Stewart's supposed right arises; and then offer, as appears to me, sufficient confutation to his claim over the negro, as property, after having him brought over to England. . . . The question on that is not whether slavery is lawful in the colonies (where a concurrence of unhappy circumstances has caused it to be established as necessary) but whether in England? Not whether it ever has existed in England; but whether it be not now abolished? Various definitions have been given of slavery; one of the most considerable is the following: a service for life, for bare necessaries. Harsh and terrible to human nature as even such a condition is, slavery is very insufficiently defined by these circumstances—it includes not the power of the master over the slave's person, property, and limbs, life only excepted; it includes not the right over all acquirements of the slave's labour; nor includes the alienation of the unhappy object from his original master, to whatever absolute lord, interest, caprice or malice, may chuse to transfer him; it includes not the descendible property from father to son, and in like manner continually of the slave and all his descendants. Let us reflect on the consequences of servitude in a light still more important. The corruption of manners in the master, from the entire subjection of the slaves he possesses to his sole will; from whence spring forth luxury, pride, cruelty, with the infinite enormities appertaining to their train; the danger to the master, from the revenge of his much injured and unredressed dependant; debasement of the mind of the slave, for want of means and motives of improvement; and peril to the constitution under which the slave cannot but suffer, and which he will naturally endeavour to subvert, as the only means of retrieving comfort and security to himself.—The humanity of modern times has much mitigated this extreme rigour of slavery; shall an attempt to introduce perpetual servitude here to this island hope for countenance? Will not all the other mischiefs of mere utter servitude revive, if once the idea of absolute property, under the immediate sanction of the laws of this country extend itself to those who have been brought over to a soil whose air is deemed too pure for slaves to breathe in it; but the laws, the genius and spirit of the constitution, forbid the approach of slavery, will not suffer it's existence here. . . .

Mr. Alleyne [arguing on behalf of Somerset].—. . . But slavery is not a natural, 'tis a municipal relation; an institution therefore confined to certain places, and necessarily dropt by passage into a country where such municipal regulations do not exist.

Mr. Dunning [arguing on behalf of Stewart].—. . . Freedom has been asserted as a natural right, and therefore unalienable and unrestrainable; there is perhaps no branch of this right, but in some places at all times, and in all places at different times, has been restrained: nor could society otherwise be conceived to exist. For the great benefit of the public and individuals, natural liberty, which consists in doing what one likes, is altered to the doing what one ought. . . . A distinction was endeavoured to be established between natural and municipal relations; but the natural relations are not those only which attend the person of the man, political do so too; with which the municipal are most closely connected: municipal laws, strictly, are those confined to a particular place; political, are those in which the municipal laws of many States may and do concur. The relation of husband and wife, I think myself warranted in questioning, as a natural relation: does it subsist for life; or to answer the natural purposes which may reasonably be supposed often to terminate sooner? Yet this is one of these relations which follow a man every where. If only natural relations had that property, the effect would be very limited indeed. In fact the municipal laws are principally employed in determining the manner by which relations are created; and which manner varies in various countries, and in the same country at different periods; the political relation itself continuing usually unchanged by the change of place. There is but one form at present with us, by which the relation of husband and wife can be constituted; there was a time when otherwise. . . . Let me take notice, neither the air of England is too pure for a slave to breathe in, nor the laws of England have rejected servitude. Villenage in this country is said to be worn out; the propriety of the expression strikes me a little. Are the laws not existing by which it was created? . . .

Sergeant Davy [on behalf of Somerset].— . . . Mr. Dunning availed himself of a wrong interpretation of the word natural; 'twas used as moral, which no laws can supercede. All contracts, I do not venture to assert are of a moral nature; but I know not any law to confirm an immoral contract, and execute it. The contract of marriage is a moral contract, established for moral purposes, enforcing moral obligations; the right of taking property by descent, the legitimacy of children; . . . these, and many other consequences, flow from the marriage properly solemnised; are governed by the municipal laws of that particular State, under whose institutions the contracting and disposing parties live as subjects . . . it has been asserted, and is now repeated by me, this air is too pure for a slave to breathe in; I trust, I shall not quit this Court without certain conviction of the truth of that assertion.

Lord Mansfield [presiding judge].— . . . The now question is, whether any dominion, authority or coercion can be exercised in this country, on a slave according to the American laws? . . .

— TRINITY TERM, JUNE 22, 1772 —

Lord Mansfield.— On the part of Somerset, the case which we gave notice should be decided this day, the Court now proceeds to give its opinion. . . . The state of slavery is of such a nature, that it is incapable of being introduced on any reasons, moral or political; but only positive law, which preserves its force long after the reasons, occasion, and time itself from whence it was created, is erased from memory: it's so odious, that nothing can be suffered to support it, but positive law. Whatever inconveniences, therefore, may follow from a decision, I cannot say this case is allowed or approved by the law of England; and therefore the black must be discharged.

OTTOBAH CUGOANO

(1757–?)

Born in the Fanti country of the Gold Coast (near the modern town of Ajumako, Ghana), Ottobah Cugoano was kidnapped and enslaved while still a child and taken to the West Indies. How he achieved his freedom is not known, but by the 1780s he was in London, actively working with Granville Sharpe, Olaudah Equiano,* and others for the abolition of slavery. His book *Thoughts and Sentiments on the Evil and Wicked Traffic of Slavery* (1787) provides both an eloquent account of his own experiences as a West Indian slave and a convincing theoretical attack on the institution of slavery on theological, humanitarian, and economic grounds. Cugoano argues that slavery violates the Christian injunction to love thy neighbor as thyself and is moreover uneconomical, citing Adam Smith's compelling evidence that free labor is cheaper than slave labor. Cugoano's *Thoughts and Sentiments* went into a second edition in 1787 and was translated into French in 1788. Little is known of his life after 1787, save that in 1791 he proposed opening a school for freed African slaves and all those "desirous of being acquainted with the Knowledge of the Christian Religion and the Laws of Civilization."

from Thoughts and Sentiments on the Evil and Wicked Traffic of the Slavery and Commerce of the Human Species

(1787)

As several learned gentlemen of distinguished abilities, as well as eminent for their great humanity, liberality and candour, have written various essays against that infamous traffic of the African Slave Trade, carried on with the West-India planters and merchants, to the great shame and disgrace of all Christian nations wherever it is admitted in any of their territories, or in any place or situation amongst them; it cannot be amiss that I should thankfully acknowledge these truly worthy and humane gentlemen with the warmest sense of gratitude, for their beneficent and laudable endeavours towards a total suppression of that infamous and iniquitous traffic of stealing, kidnapping, buying, selling, and cruelly enslaving men!

Those who have endeavoured to restore to their fellow-creatures the common rights of nature, of which especially the poor unfortunate Black People have been so unjustly deprived, cannot fail in meeting with the applause of all good men, and the approbation of that which will for ever redound to their honor; they have the warrant of that which is divine: *Open thy mouth, judge righteously, plead the cause of the poor and needy; for the liberal deviseth liberal things, and by liberal things shall stand.* And they can say with the pious Job, *Did not I weep for him that was in trouble; was not my soul grieved for the poor?* . . .[1]

It is therefore manifest, that something else ought yet to be done; and what is required, is evidently the incumbent duty of all men of enlightened understanding, and of every man that has any claim or affinity to the name of Christian, that the base treatment which the African Slaves undergo ought to be abolished; and it is moreover evident, that the whole, or any part of that iniquitous traffic of slavery, can nowhere, or in any degree, be admitted, but among those who must eventually resign their own claim to any degree of sensibility and humanity, for that of barbarians and ruffians.

But it would be needless to arrange an history of all the base treatment which the African Slaves are subjected to, in order to shew the exceeding wickedness and evil of that insidious traffic, as the whole may easily appear in every part, and at every view, to be wholly and totally inimical to every idea of justice, equity, reason and humanity. What I intend to advance against that

[1] **Open thy mouth . . . poor and needy:** Proverbs 31:9. **the liberal . . . stand:** Isaiah 32:8. **Did not I . . . poor:** Job 31:25.

evil, criminal and wicked traffic of enslaving men, are only some Thoughts and Sentiments which occur to me, as being obvious from the Scriptures of Divine Truth, or such arguments as are chiefly deduced from thence, with other such observations as I have been able to collect. Some of these observations may lead into a larger field of consideration, than that of the African Slave Trade alone; but those causes from wherever they originate, and become the production of slavery, the evil effects produced by it, must shew that its origin and source is of a wicked and criminal nature.

No necessity, or any situation of men, however poor, pitiful and wretched they may be, can warrant them to rob others, or oblige them to become thieves, because they are poor, miserable and wretched: But the robbers of men, the kid-nappers, ensnarers and slave-holders, who take away the common rights and privileges of others to support and enrich themselves, are universally those pitiful and detestable wretches; for the ensnarings of others, and taking away their liberty by slavery and oppression, is the worst kind of robbery, as most opposite to every precept and injunction of the Divine Law, and contrary to that command which enjoins that *all men should love their neighbours as themselves*, and *that they should do unto others, as they would that men should do to them.*[2] As to any other laws that slave-holders may make among themselves, as respecting slaves, they can be of no better kind, nor give them any better character, than what is implied in the common report—that there may be some honesty among thieves. This may seem a harsh comparison, but the parallel is so coincident that, I must say, I can find no other way of expressing my Thoughts and Sentiments, without making use of some harsh words and comparisons against the carriers on of such abandoned wickedness. But, in this little undertaking, I must humbly hope the impartial reader will excuse such defects as may arise from want of better education; and as to the resentment of those who can lay their cruel lash upon the backs of thousands, for a thousand times less crimes than writing against their enormous wickedness and brutal avarice, is what I may be sure to meet with.

However, it cannot but be very discouraging to a man of my complexion in such an attempt as this, to meet with the evil aspersions of some men, who say "That an African is not entitled to any competent degree of knowledge, or capable of imbibing any sentiments of probity; and that nature designed him for some inferior link in the chain, fitted only to be a slave." But when I meet with those who make no scruple to deal with the human species, as with the beasts of the earth, I must think them not only brutish, but wicked and base; and that their aspersions are insidious and false: And if such men can boast of greater degrees of knowledge, than any African is entitled to, I shall let them enjoy all the advantages of it unenvied, as I fear it consists only in a greater share of infidelity, and that of a blacker kind than only skin deep. And if their complexion be not what I may suppose, it is at least the nearest in resemblance to an infernal hue. A good man will neither speak nor do as a bad man will; but if a man is bad, it makes no difference whether he be a black or a white devil. . . .

But again let me observe, that whatever civilization the inhabitants of Great-Britain may enjoy among themselves, they have seldom maintained their own innocence in that great duty as a Christian nation towards others; and I may say, with respect to their African neighbours, or to any other wheresoever they may go by the way of commerce, they have not regarded them at all. And when they saw others robbing the Africans, and carrying them into captivity and slavery, they have neither helped them, nor opposed their oppressors in the least. But instead thereof they have joined in combination against them with the rest of other profligate nations and people, to buy, enslave and make merchandize of them, because they found them helpless and fit to suit their own purpose, and are become the head carriers on of that iniquitous traffic. But the greater that any reformation and civilization is obtained by any nation, if they do not maintain righteousness, but carry on any course of wickedness and oppression, it makes them appear only the more inconsistent, and their tyranny and oppression the more conspicuous. Wherefore because of the great wickedness, cruelty and injustice done to the Africans, those who are greatest in the transgression give an evident and undubious warrant to all other nations beholding their tyranny and injustice to others, if those nations have any regard to their own innocence and virtue, and wish to maintain righteousness, and to remain clear of the oppression and blood of all men; it is their duty to chastize and suppress such unjust and tyrannical oppressors and enslavers of men. And should none of these be found among the enlightened and civilized nations, who maintain their own innocence and righteousness, with regard to their duty unto all men; and that there may be none to chastize the tyrannical

[2] **all men . . . themselves:** Leviticus 20:18. **they should do . . . do to them:** Tobias 4:15, Matthew 7:12, Luke 6:31.

oppressors of others; then it may be feared, as it has often been, that fierce nations of various insects, and other annoyances, may be sent as a judgment to punish the wicked nations of men. For by some way or other every criminal nation, and all their confederates, who sin and rebel against God, and against his laws of nature and nations, will each meet with some awful retribution at last, unless they repent of their iniquity. And the greater advantages of light, learning, knowledge and civilization that any people enjoy, if they do not maintain righteousness, but do wickedly, they will meet with the more severe rebuke when the visitations of God's judgment cometh upon them. And the prophecy which was given to Moses, is still as much in force against the enlightened nations now for their wickedness, in going after the abominations of heathens and barbarians, for none else would attempt to enslave and make merchandize of men, as it was when denounced against the Israelitish nation of old, when they departed, or should depart, from the laws and statutes of the Most High. *The Lord shall bring a nation against thee, from far, from the ends of the earth, as swift as the eagle flieth, a nation whose tongue thou shalt not understand,* &c. See Deut. xxviii. . . .[3]

But why should total abolition, and an universal emancipation of slaves, and the enfranchisement of all the Black People employed in the culture of the Colonies, taking place as it ought to do, and without any hesitation, or delay for a moment, even though it might have some seeming appearance of loss either to government or to individuals, be feared at all? Their labour, as freemen, would be as useful in the sugar colonies as any other class of men that could be found; and should it even take place in such a manner that some individuals, at first, would suffer loss as a just reward for their wickedness in slave-dealing, what is that to the happiness and good of doing justice to others; and, I must say, to the great danger, otherwise, that must eventually hang over the whole community? It is certain, that the produce of the labour of slaves, together with all the advantages of the West-India traffic, bring in an immense revenue to government; but let that amount be what it will, there might be as much or more expected from the labour of an equal increase of free people, and without the implication of any guilt attending it, and which, otherwise, must be a greater burden to bear, and more ruinous consequences to be feared from it, than if the whole national debt was to sink at once, and to rest upon the heads of all that might suffer by it. Whereas, if a generous encouragement were to be given to a free people, peaceable among themselves, intelligent and industrious, who by art and labour would improve the most barren situations, and make the most of that which is fruitful; the free and voluntary labour of many, would soon yield to any government, many greater advantages than any thing that slavery can produce. And this should be expected, wherever a Christian government is extended, and the true religion is embraced, that the blessings of liberty should be extended likewise, and that it should diffuse its influences first to fertilize the mind, and then the effects of its benignity would extend, and arise with exuberant blessings and advantages from all its operations. Was this to be the case, every thing would increase and prosper at home and abroad, and ten thousand times greater and greater advantages would arise to the state, and more permanent and solid benefit to individuals from the service of freemen, than ever they can reap, or in any possible way enjoy, by the labour of slaves. . . .

And now that blessings may come instead of a curse, and that many beneficent purposes of good might speedily arise and flow from it, and be more readily promoted; I would hereby presume to offer the following considerations, as some outlines of a general reformation which ought to be established and carried on. And first, I would propose, that there ought to be days of mourning and fasting appointed, to make enquiry into that great and preeminent evil for many years past carried on against the Heathen nations, and the horrible iniquity of making merchandize of us, and cruelly enslaving the poor Africans; and that you might seek grace and repentance, and find mercy and forgiveness before God Omnipotent; and that he may give you wisdom and understanding to devise what ought to be done.

Secondly, I would propose that a total abolition of slavery should be made and proclaimed; and that an universal emancipation of slaves should begin from the date thereof, and be carried on in the following manner: That a proclamation should be caused to be made, setting forth the anti-Christian unlawfulness of the slavery and commerce of the human species; and that it should be sent to all the courts and nations in Europe, to require their advice and assistance, and as they may find it unlawful to carry it on, let them whosoever will join to prohibit it. . . .

And, thirdly, I would propose, that a fleet of some ships of war should be immediately sent to the coast of Africa, and particularly where the slave trade is carried on, with faithful men to direct that none should be brought from the coast of Africa without their own

[3] **Deut. xxviii:** Deuteronomy 28:49.

consent and the approbation of their friends, and to intercept all merchant ships that were bringing them away, until such a scrutiny was made, whatever nation they belonged to. . . .

To put an end to the nakedness of slavery and merchandizing of men, and to prevent murder, extirpation and dissolution, is what every righteous nation ought to seek after; and to endeavour to diffuse knowledge and instruction to all the heathen nations wherever they can, is the grand duty of all Christian men. But while the horrible traffic of slavery is admitted and practiced, there can be but little hope of any good proposals meeting with success anywhere; for the abandoned carriers on of it have spread the poison of their iniquity wherever they come, at home and abroad. Were the iniquitous laws in support of it, and the whole of that oppression and injustice abolished, and the righteous laws of Christianity, equity, justice and humanity established in the room thereof, multitudes of nations would flock to the standard of truth, and instead of revolting away, they would count it their greatest happiness to be under the protection and jurisdiction of a righteous government. And in that respect, *in the multitude of the people is the King's honour; but in the want of people, is the destruction of the Prince.*[4]

We would wish to have the grandeur and fame of the British empire to extend far and wide; and the glory and honor of God to be promoted by it, and the interest of Christianity set forth among all the nations wherever its influence and power can extend; but not to be supported by the insidious pirates, depredators,[5] murderers and slave-holders. And as it might diffuse knowledge and instruction to others, that it might receive a tribute of reward from all its territories, forts and garrisons, without being oppressive to any. But contrary to this the wickedness of many of the White People who keep slaves, and contrary to all the laws and duties of Christianity which the Scriptures teach, they have in general endeavoured to keep the Black People in total ignorance as much as they can, which must be a great dishonor to any Christian government, and injurious to the safety and happiness of rulers. . . .

And let me now hope that you will pardon me in all that I have been thus telling you, O ye inhabitants of Great-Britain! to whom I owe the greatest respect; to your king! to yourselves! and to your government! And tho' many things which I have written may seem harsh, it cannot be otherwise evaded when such horrible iniquity is transacted: and tho' to some what I have said may appear as the rattling leaves of autumn, that may soon be blown away and whirled in a vortex where few can hear and know: I must yet say, although it is not for me to determine the manner, that the voice of our complaint implies a vengeance, because of the great iniquity that you have done, and because of the cruel injustice done unto us Africans; and it ought to sound in your ears as the rolling waves around your circumambient shores; and if it is not hearkened unto, it may yet arise with a louder voice, as the rolling thunder, and it may encrease in the force of its volubility, not only to shake the leaves of the most stout in heart, but to rend the mountains before them, and to cleave in pieces the rocks under them, and to go on with fury to smite the stoutest oaks in the forest; and even to make that which is strong, and wherein you think that your strength lieth, to become as stubble, and as the fibres of rotten wood, that will do you no good, and your trust in it will become a snare of infatuation to you!

---

[4] **in the multitude . . . of the Prince:** Proverbs 14:28.

[5] **depredator:** a ravager, plunderer.

WILLIAM COWPER

(1731–1800)

Famous as the author of *The Task* (1785), a long poem that heavily influenced both Wordsworth and Coleridge, William Cowper suffered all his life from severe depression; he twice attempted suicide. His acute melancholia took a religious cast: "conviction of sin and expectation of instant judgment never left me," he wrote in his autobiographical *Memoir* (c. 1767). Turning to evangelical Christianity for salvation, Cowper came under the influence of the Evangelical minister and former slave trader John Newton whose *Authentic Narrative* (1764) had graphically detailed both his voyages and his growing doubts about his profession. Together, Newton and Cowper wrote the much-praised *Olney Hymns* (1779), to which Cowper contributed "God moves in a mysterious way" and "Oh, for a closer walk with God." At Wilberforce's request, he wrote his two poems against the slave trade in 1788; they were widely reprinted in illustrated editions and played a powerful role in rousing British antipathy to the slave trade.

The Negro's Complaint

(1778)

Forc'd from home and all its pleasures,
  Afric's coast I left forlorn;
To increase a stranger's treasures,
  O'er the raging billows borne.

Men from Europe bought and sold me,
  Paid my price in paltry gold;
But, though slave they have enroll'd me,
  Minds are never to be sold.

Still in thought as free as ever,
  What are England's rights, I ask,
Me from my delights to sever,
  Me to torture, me to task?

Fleecy locks and black complexion
  Cannot forfeit Nature's claim;
Skins may differ, but affection
  Dwells in white and black the same.

Why did all-creating Nature
  Make the plant, for which we toil?
Sighs must fan it, tears must water,
  Sweat of ours must dress the soil.

Think, ye masters iron-hearted,
  Lolling at your jovial boards;
Think how many backs have smarted
  For the sweets your cane[1] affords.

Is there, as you sometimes tell us,
  Is there one, who reigns on high?
Has he bid you buy and sell us,
  Speaking from his throne the sky?

Ask him, if your knotted scourges,
  Matches, blood-extorting screws,
Are the means that duty urges
  Agents of his will to use?

Hark! he answers — wild tornadoes,
  Strewing yonder sea with wrecks;
Wasting towns, plantations, meadows,
  Are the voice, with which he speaks.

He, foreseeing what vexations
  Afric's sons should undergo,
Fix'd their tyrant's habitations
  Where his whirlwinds answer — no.

[1] **cane:** sugarcane.

By our blood in Afric wasted,
Ere our necks receiv'd the chain;
By the mis'ries that we tasted,
Crossing in your barks the main;

By our suff'rings, since ye brought us
To the man-degrading mart;
All, sustain'd by patience, taught us
Only by a broken heart:

Deem our nation brutes no longer,
Till some reason ye shall find
Worthier of regard, and stronger
Than the colour of our kind.

Slaves of gold, whose sordid dealings
Tarnish all your boasted pow'rs,
Prove that you have human feelings,
Ere you proudly question ours!

Pity for Poor Africans

(1788)

I own I am shock'd at the purchase of slaves,
And fear those who buy them and sell them are knaves;
What I hear of their hardships, their tortures, and groans,
Is almost enough to draw pity from stones.

I pity them greatly, but I must be mum,
For how could we do without sugar and rum?
Especially sugar, so needful we see?
What, give up our desserts, our coffee, and tea!

Besides, if we do, the French, Dutch, and Danes,
Will heartily thank us, no doubt, for our pains;
If we do not buy the poor creatures, they will,
And tortures and groans will be multiplied still.

If foreigners likewise would give up the trade,
Much more in behalf of your wish might be said;
But, while they get riches by purchasing blacks,
Pray tell me why we may not also go snacks?[2]

Your scruples and arguments bring to my mind
A story so pat, you may think it is coin'd,
On purpose to answer you, out of my mint;
But I can assure you I saw it in print.

A youngster at school, more sedate than the rest,
Had once his integrity put to the test;
His comrades had plotted an orchard to rob,
And ask'd him to go and assist in the job.

He was shock'd, sir, like you, and answer'd—'Oh no!
What! rob our good neighbour! I pray you don't go;
Besides, the man's poor, his orchard's his bread,
Then think of his children, for they must be fed.'

'You speak very fine, and you look very grave,
But apples we want, and apples we'll have;
If you will go with us, you shall have a share,
If not, you shall have neither apple nor pear.'

They spoke, and Tom ponder'd—'I see they will go;
Poor man! what a pity to injure him so!
Poor man! I would save him his fruit if I could,
But staying behind will do him no good.

'If the matter depended alone upon me,
His apples might hang, till they dropp'd from the tree;
But, since they will take them, I think I'll go too,
He will lose none by me, though I get a few.'

[2] **go snacks:** have a share (in something); divide profits.

THOMAS BELLAMY

(1745–1800)

Born at Kingston-on-Thames in 1745, Thomas Bellamy first served as an apprentice to a hosier in Newgate Street. He then opened his own successful hosiery business, which he ran for 20 years. He started writing verse at an early age, an avocation he pursued until he could afford to give up the hosiery business to become a clerk in a bookseller's shop in Paternoster Row. After a quarrel with his employer, in 1787 he started publishing the *General Magazine and Impartial Review.* His *Bellamy's Picturesque Magazine and Literary Museum* and *Monthly Magazine* (a journal devoted to the stage) came after; but none of these journals succeeded with the public. Through his contact with the songwriter Charles Dibdin, Bellamy gained an entree to the London theatre; in 1789 his short play supporting the West Indian lobby, *The Benevolent Planters,* was performed at the Theatre Royal, Haymarket. In 1794, Bellamy collected his verses, the moral tales he had written for his magazines, and his biography of the comedian Parsons and published them in two volumes under the title *Miscellanies in Prose and Verse.* He then established a moderately successful circulating library. When he inherited some property from his mother, he retired to devote himself to writing but he died soon afterwards, on 29 August 1800. His three-volume novel, *The Beggar Boy,* was published posthumously in 1801.

The Benevolent Planters

A Dramatic Piece as performed at the Theatre Royal, Haymarket
(1789)

— SCENE: Jamaica —

CHARACTERS

Planters	Slaves
GOODWIN	ORAN
STEADY	SELIMA
HEARTFREE	ARCHERS, ETC. ETC.

— SCENE 1 —

A Room in GOODWIN*'s House*

Enter GOODWIN, *meeting* STEADY *and* HEARTFREE

GOODWIN: Good morrow, neighbours, friend Steady, is your jetty tribe ready for the diversions?

STEADY: My tribe is prepared and ready to meet thine, and my heart exults on beholding so many happy countenances. But an added joy is come home to my bosom. This English friend, who, some time since, came to settle among us, in order that he might exhibit to his brother Planters, the happy effects of humanity, in the treatment of those who, in the course of human chance, are destined to the bonds of slavery, has honoured my dwelling with his presence, and gladdened my heart with his friendship.

HEARTFREE: A cause like the present, makes brothers of us all, and may heaven increase the brothers of humanity. Friend Steady informs me, that we are to preside as directors of the different diversions.

GOODWIN: It is our wish to prevent a repetition of disorders, that last year disturbed the general happiness. They were occasioned by the admission of one of those games, which, but too often, begin in sport, and end in passion. The offenders, however, were soon made sensible of the folly of attacking each other without provocation, and with no other view than to shew their superior skill, in an art, which white men have introduced among them.[1]

HEARTFREE: If that art was only made use of as a defence against the attacks of an unprincipled and

[1] **art . . . among them:** probably duelling, with either swords or guns.

vulgar violence, no man could with propriety form a wish of checking its progress. But while it opens another field where the gambler fills his pocket at the expence of the credulous and unsuspecting, whose families too often mourn in poverty and distress the effects of their folly; every member of society will hold up his hand against it, if his heart feels as it ought. I am sorry likewise to add, that too many recent instances of its fatal effects among my own countrymen, have convinced me of the guilt and folly of venturing *a life* to display a *skill*.

GOODWIN: We are happy to find our union strengthened by corresponding sentiments.

HEARTFREE: The sports, I find, are to continue six days; repeat your design, respecting the successful archers.

STEADY: The archers, friend, to the number of twelve, consist of selected slaves, whose honest industry and attachment have rendered them deserving of reward. They are to advance in pairs, and the youth who speeds the arrow surest, is to be proclaimed victor.

HEARTFREE: And what is his reward?

STEADY: A portion of land for himself, and his posterity—freedom for his life, and the maiden of his heart.

HEARTFREE: Generous men! humanity confers dignity upon authority. The grateful Africans have hearts as large as ours, and shame on the degrading lash, when it can be spared. Reasonable obedience is what we expect, and let those who look for more, feel and severely feel the sting of disappointment.

STEADY: Will your poor fellow attend the festival?

HEARTFREE: He will. I respect your feelings for the sorrows of the worthy Oran.

GOODWIN: Oran, did you say? What know you of him; pardon my abruptness, but relate his story, it may prove a task of pleasure.

HEARTFREE: By the fate of war, Oran had been torn from his beloved Selima. The conquerors were on the point of setting fire to the consuming pile to which he was bound, while the partner of his heart, who was devoted to the arms of the chief of the adverse party, was rending the air with her cries; at this instant a troop of Europeans broke in upon them, and bore away a considerable party to their ships; among the rest was the rescued Oran, who was happily brought to our mart, where I had the good fortune to become his master—he has since served me well and affectionately. But sorrow for his Selima is so deeply rooted in his feeling bosom, that I fear I shall soon lose an excellent domestic and as valuable a friend, whose only consolation springs from a sense of dying in the possession of Christian principles, from whence he acknowledges to have drawn comforts inexpressible.

GOODWIN: And comfort he shall still draw from a worldly as well as a heavenly source. For know, I can produce the Selima he mourns. She has told me her story, which is indeed a tale of woe. Inward grief has preyed upon her mind, and like her faithful Oran, she is bending to her grave. But happiness, love, and liberty shall again restore them.

HEARTFREE: When the mind has made itself up to misery, discoveries admitting of more than hope, ought ever to be made with caution. But you have a heart to feel for the distress of another, and conduct to guide you in giving relief to sorrow; leave me to my poor fellow, and do you prepare his disconsolate partner.

GOODWIN: I'll see her immediately, and when we take our seats on the plain of sports, we will communicate to each other the result of our considerations.

STEADY: Till then, my worthy associates, farewell.

(Exeunt.)

— SCENE II —

Another Apartment in GOODWIN'*s House.*
(Enter GOODWIN *and* SELIMA.*)*

GOODWIN: Come, my poor disconsolate, be composed, and prepare to meet your friends on those plains, where you never shall experience sorrow; but on the contrary, enjoy every happiness within the power of thy grateful master to bestow; you once told me, Selima, that my participation of your griefs abated their force; will you then indulge me with that pleasing tho' mournful Song you have made, on the loss of him, who, perhaps, may one day be restored?

SELIMA: Good and generous Master! ever consoling me with hope, can I deny you who have given me mind, taught me your language, comforted me with the knowledge of books, and made me every thing I am? Prepared too, my soul for joys, which you say are to succeed the patient bearing of human misery. Oh, Sir, with what inward satisfaction do I answer a request in every way so grateful to my feelings!

— SONG —

SET TO MUSIC BY MR. REEVE[2]

How vain to me the hours of ease,
  When every daily toil is o'er;
In my sad heart no hope I find,
  For Oran is, alas! no more.

Not sunny Africa could please,
  Nor friends upon my native shore,
To me the dreary world's a cave,
  For Oran is, alas! no more.

In bowers of bliss beyond the moon,
  The white man says, his sorrow's o'er,
And comforts me with soothing hope,
  Tho' Oran is, alas! no more.

O come then, messenger of death,
  Convey me to yon starry shore,
Where I may meet with my true love,
  And never part with Oran more.

GOODWIN: There's my kind Selima! and now attend to a discovery, on which depends your future happiness; not only liberty, but love awaits you.

SELIMA: The first I want not — the last can never be! for where shall I find another Oran?

GOODWIN: O my good girl, your song of sorrow shall be changed into that of gladness. For know — the hours of anguish are gone by, — your Oran lives, and lives but to bless his faithful Selima.

SELIMA: *(after a pause)* To that invisible Being who has sustained my suffering heart, I kneel, overwhelmed with an awful sense of his protecting power. But how?

GOODWIN: As we walk on, I will explain every thing. You soon will embrace your faithful Oran, and his beloved Selima shall mourn no more.

(Exeunt.)

— SCENE III —

An open Plain

(On one side a range of men-slaves; on the other a range of women-slaves — at some distance, seated on decorated chairs, HEARTFREE, GOODWIN, *and* STEADY *— twelve archers close the line on the men-side, meeting the audience with* ORAN *at their head, distinguished from the rest by a rich dress —* ORAN *advancing to the front of the stage, stands in a dejected posture.)*

HEARTFREE: Now let the air echo to the sound of the enlivening instruments, and beat the ground to their tuneful melody; while myself and my two worthy friends, who since our last festival have reaped the benefit of your honest labours, in full goblets drink to your happiness.

(Flourish of music, and a dance.)

HEARTFREE: Now let the archers advance in pairs, and again, in replenished cups, health and domestic peace to those who surest speed the arrow.

(Flourish.)

(Here the archers advance in pairs to the middle of the Stage, and discharge their arrows through the side wings — the victor is saluted by two female slaves, who present to him the maiden of his choice — then a flourish of music, and the parties fall back to the side. After the ceremony has been repeated five times to as many pair of archers, and ORAN *and* ALMABOE *only remain to advance as the sixth pair,* ORAN *appears absorbed in grief, which is observed with evident concern by* HEARTFREE.*)*

HEARTFREE: Why Oran, with looks divided between earth and heaven, dost thou appear an alien among those who are encompassed with joy and gladness? Though your beloved Selima is torn from your widowed arms, yet it is a duty you owe yourself, as a man, an obligation due to me, as your friend, to take to your bosom one whom I have provided for you. A contest with Almaboe is needless; he has fixed on his partner, to whom, according to your request, he is now presented.

(A flourish of music — two female slaves advance with a third, who is presented to ALMABOE *— the parties embrace.)*

It remains, therefore, for you to comply with the wishes of those who honour your virtues, and have respected your sorrows.

ORAN: Kind and benevolent masters; I indeed came hither unwillingly, to draw the bow, with a heart already pierced with the arrow of hopeless anguish. You have done generously by my friend, to whom I meant to have relinquished the victor's right, had the chance been mine. For alas, Sirs! Selima was my first and only love; and when I lost her, joy fled from a bosom it will never again revisit. The short date of my existence is therefore devoted alone to that Power whom you have taught me to revere. Sacred

[2] **Mr. Reeve:** William Reeve (1757–1815), actor and musical composer.

to gratitude, and sacred to her whose beckoning spirit seems at this moment to call on me from yonder sky.

GOODWIN: What say you, Oran, if I should produce a maiden whose virtues will bring you comfort, and whose affection you will find as strong as hers, whose loss you so feelingly deplore?

ORAN: O Sirs! had you but known my Selima, you would not attempt to produce her equal! Poor lost excellence! Yes, thy spirit, released from all its sufferings, is now looking down upon its Oran! But let not imagination too far transport me: perhaps she yet lives, a prey to brutal lust. *(Turns to* ALMABOE*)* Brother of my choice, and friend of my adverse hour, long may your Coanzi be happy in the endearments of her faithful Almaboe. And O my friend! when thy poor Oran is no more, if chance that Selima yet lives, if blessed Providence *should* lead her to these happy shores, if she should escape the cruel enemy, and be brought hither with honour unsullied; tell her how much she owes to these generous men; comfort her afflicted spirit, and teach her to adore the God of truth and mercy.

ALMABOE: Oran must himself endeavour to live for that day, and not by encouraging despair, sink self-devoted to the grave. The same Providence, my friend, which has turned the terrors of slavery into willing bondage, may yet restore thy Selima.

ORAN: The words of Almaboe come charged with the force of truth, and erring Oran bends to offended Heaven! Yet erring Oran must still feel his loss, and erring Oran must for ever lament it.

GOODWIN: It is true, Oran, our arguments to urge thee to be happy, have hitherto proved fruitless. But know, thou man of sorrow, we are possessed of the means which will restore thee to thyself and to thy friends. Hear, then, the important secret, and know, that thy Selima yet lives!

ORAN: *(after a pause)* Yet lives! Selima yet lives! what my Selima! my own dear angel! O speak again, your words have visited my heart, and it is lost in rapture.

HEARTFREE: Nay, Oran, but be calm.

ORAN: I am calm. Heaven will permit me to support my joy, but do you relieve me from suspence.

GOODWIN: Let the instruments breathe forth the most pleasing strains. Advance, my happy virgins, with your charge, and restore to Oran his long-lost Selima. You receive her pure as when you parted, with a mind released from the errors of darkness, and refined by its afflictions.

(Soft music. SELIMA *comes down the stage, attended by six virgins in fancied dresses, who present her to* ORAN*. The lovers embrace. Flourish of music, and a shout.)*

ORAN: Lost in admiration, gratitude, and love, Oran has no words, but can only in silence own the hand of Heaven; while to his beating heart he clasps its restored treasure. And O my masters! for such, though free, suffer me still to call you; let my restored partner and myself bend to such exalted worth; while for ourselves, and for our surrounding brethren, we declare, that you have proved yourselves *The Benevolent Planters,* and that under subjection like yours,

SLAVERY IS BUT A NAME

— SONG —

TO THE TUNE OF "RULE BRITANNIA"

In honour of this happy day,
  Let Afric's sable sons rejoice;
To mercy we devote the lay,
  To heaven-born mercy raise the voice.
Long may she reign, and call each heart her own,
And nations guard her sacred throne.
Fair child of heaven, our rites approve,
  With smiles attend the votive song,
Inspire with universal love,
  For joy and peace to thee belong.
Long may'st thou reign, and call each heart thy own,
While nations guard thy sacred throne.

FINIS

ROBERT SOUTHEY
(1774–1843)

Robert Southey met S. T. Coleridge at Oxford in 1792 and they became close friends and political allies. Together they planned to emigrate to America to found a utopian community on "the banks of the Susquehanna" in Pennsylvania, based on Pantisocratic principles. At Oxford, Southey was known for his radical political opinions, expressed most forcefully in his play *Wat Tyler* (1794). Although the emigration scheme fell through, and Southey instead became a lawyer, he continued to write a prodigious amount of politically liberal poetry and drama through the next decade: *Joan of Arc* (1796), *Thalaba* (1801), *Madoc* (1805), and *The Curse of Kehama* (1810). In 1813 he became Poet Laureate of England, which led Byron and Hazlitt to attack him bitterly as a political renegade and turncoat.

Southey wrote "The Sailor, who had served in the Slave Trade" (1798) after he had read Coleridge's "Rime of the Ancyent Mariner," also published in 1798 in the first volume of *Lyrical Ballads*. Echoing Coleridge's ballad-stanza and specific diction, it registers a powerful critique of Coleridge's poetic vision.

from POEMS CONCERNING THE SLAVE TRADE

The Sailor, Who Had Served in the Slave Trade
(1798)

In September, 1798, a Dissenting Minister of Bristol discovered a sailor in the neighbourhood of that City, groaning and praying in a cow-house. The circumstance which occasioned his agony of mind is detailed in the annexed ballad, without the slightest addition or alteration. By presenting it as a Poem the story is made more public, and such stories ought to be made as public as possible.

It was a Christian minister,
Who, in the month of flowers,
Walk'd forth at eve amid the fields
Near Bristol's ancient towers;

When from a lonely out-house breathed,
He heard a voice of woe,
And groans which less might seem from pain,
Than wretchedness to flow;

Heart-rending groans they were, with words
Of bitterest despair,
Yet with the holy name of Christ
Pronounced in broken prayer.

The Christian minister went in,
A Sailor there he sees,
Whose hands were lifted up to Heaven,
And he was on his knees.

Nor did the Sailor so intent
His entering footsteps heed,
But now "Our Father" said, and now
His half-forgotten creed;

And often on our Saviour call'd
With many a bitter groan,
But in such anguish as may spring
From deepest guilt alone.

The miserable man was ask'd
Why he was kneeling there,
And what had been the crime that caused
The anguish of his prayer?

"I have done a cursed thing!" he cried,
"It haunts me night and day,
And I have sought this lonely place
Here undisturb'd to pray.

Aboard I have no place for prayer,
So I came here alone,
That I might freely kneel and pray,
And call on Christ, and groan.

If to the main-mast head I go,
The Wicked One is there;
From place to place, from rope to rope,
He follows every where.

I shut my eyes . . it matters not . .
Still, still the same I see, . .
And when I lie me down at night,
'Tis always day with me!

He follows, follows every where,
And every place is Hell!
O God . . and I must go with Him
In endless fire to dwell!

He follows, follows every where,
He's still above . . below!
Oh, tell me where to fly from him!
Oh, tell me where to go!"

"But tell thou," quoth the stranger then,
"What this thy crime hath been,
So haply I may comfort give
To one who grieves for sin."

"O cursed, cursed is the deed!"
The wretched man replies,
"And night and day and every where
'Tis still before my eyes.

I sail'd on board a Guinea-man,[1]
And to the slave-coast went; . . .
Would that the sea had swallow'd me
When I was innocent!

And we took in our cargo there,
Three hundred negro slaves,
And we sail'd homeward merrily
Over the ocean-waves.

But some were sulky of the slaves,
And would not touch their meat,
So therefore we were forced by threats
And blows to make them eat.

One woman, sulkier than the rest,
Would still refuse her food, . . .
O Jesus God! I hear her cries!
I see her in her blood!

The captain made me tie her up,
And flog while he stood by,
And then he cursed me if I staid
My hand to hear her cry.

She shriek'd, she groan'd, . . I could not spare,
For the Captain he stood by; . . .
Dear God! that I might rest one night
From that poor creature's cry!

What woman's child a sight like that
Could bear to look upon!
And still the Captain would not spare . . .
But made me still flog on.

She could not be more glad than I
When she was taken down:
A blessed minute! . . 't was the last
That I have ever known!

I did not close my eyes all night,
Thinking what I had done;
I heard her groans, and they grew faint
Towards the rising sun.

She groan'd and moan'd, but her voice grew
Fainter at morning tide;
Fainter and fainter still it came
Until at noon she died.

They flung her overboard; . . poor wretch
She rested from her pain, . .
But when . . O Christ! O blessed God!
Shall I have rest again!

I saw the sea close over her
Yet she is still in sight;
I see her twisting every where;
I hear her day and night.

Go where I will, do what I can,
The Wicked One I see:
Dear Christ, have mercy on my soul!
O God, deliver me!

O give me comfort, if you can!
Oh tell me where to fly!
Oh tell me if there can be hope
For one so lost as I!"

---

[1] **Guinea-man**: armed naval ship used for slave trade. Guinea is on the Equatorial coast of Africa.

What said the Minister of Christ?
He bade him trust in Heaven,
And call on Him for whose dear sake
All sins shall be forgiven.

He told him of that precious blood
Which should his guilt efface,
Told him that none are lost, but they
Who turn from proffer'd grace.

He bade him pray, and knelt with him,
And join'd him in his prayers: . . .
And some who read the dreadful tale
Perhaps will aid with theirs.

WILLIAM WILBERFORCE

(1759–1833)

The leading parliamentary advocate for the abolition of the slave trade, the wealthy William Wilberforce was elected as the Member from Hull in 1780. In 1785, under the tutelage of Isaac Milner and John Newton (a former slave trader who had repented of his earlier cruelties), Wilberforce experienced a "conversion" from his earlier dissolute ways to a strictly religious life. When Thomas Clarkson appealed to him in 1787, Wilberforce joined the Quaker Clapham Sect and, with the encouragement of his party leader William Pitt, agreed to raise the question of reforming the slave trade before the House in 1787. Ill health delayed him, but in 1789 Wilberforce moved 12 resolutions condemning the slave trade, based on the researches of Thomas Clarkson. In 1791, his first bill to abolish the slave trade was defeated (largely because of the public alarm at the slave rebellion in Santo Domingo in 1791), but Wilberforce and Pitt persevered and in 1792 a bill was narrowly passed for the *gradual* abolition of the slave trade, to be completed by 1 January 1796. The planters cleverly resisted implementation of this bill, however, and the French Revolution distracted Pitt's government. It was not until 1807, after numerous parliamentary defeats (in 1798, 1799, and 1804), that Wilberforce was able, with the support of Fox and Grenville, finally to gain the approval of both the House of Commons and the House of Lords to declare the slave trade illegal. Wilberforce then became the conscience of the nation, everywhere hailed for his acts of charity and humanity. He supported the attempt to register slaves, believing that this would lead to eventual emancipation, urged the amelioration of the conditions of slavery, and in March 1823 issued an "Appeal" that led to the formation of the first Anti-Slavery Society. Ill health forced him to resign his seat in 1824, although he continued to lecture publicly against slavery until 1830.

from A Letter on the Abolition of the Slave Trade

Addressed to the Freeholders and Other Inhabitants of Yorkshire

(1807)

There is neither Greek nor Jew, circumcision nor uncircumcision, Barbarian, Scythian, bond nor free: but CHRIST is all, and in all. Put on therefore bowels of mercies, kindness, &c. — COL. iii. 11–12.

GOD hath made of one blood all nations of men, for to dwell on all the face of the earth. — ACTS xvii. 26.

— INTRODUCTION —

For many years I have ardently wished that it had been possible for me to plead, in your presence, the great cause of the Abolition of the Slave Trade. Conscious that I was accountable to you for the discharge of the important trust which your kindness had committed to me, I have longed for such an opportunity of convincing you, that it was not without reason that this question had occupied so large a share of my parliamentary life. I wished you to know, that the cause of my complaint was no minute grievance, which, from my eyes having been continually fixed on it, had swelled by degrees into a false shew of magnitude; no ordinary question, on which my mind, warming in the pursuit of its object, and animated by repeated contentions, had at length felt emotions altogether disproportionate to their subject. Had I however erred, unintentionally, I have too long experienced your candour not to have hoped for your ready forgiveness. On the contrary, if the Slave Trade be indeed the foulest blot that ever stained our National character, you will not deem your Representative to have been unworthily employed, in having been among the foremost in wiping it away. . . .

That the Almighty Creator of the universe governs the world which he has made; that the sufferings of nations are to be regarded as the punishment of national crimes; and their decline and fall, as the execution of His sentence; are truths which I trust are still generally believed among us. Indeed to deny them, would be directly to contradict the express and repeated declarations of the Holy Scriptures. If these truths be admitted, and if it be also true, that fraud, oppression, and cruelty, are crimes of the blackest dye, and that guilt is aggravated in proportion as the criminal acts in defiance of clearer light, and of stronger motives to virtue (and these are positions to which we cannot refuse our assent, without rejecting the authority not only of revealed, but even of natural religion); have we not abundant cause for serious apprehension? The course of public events has, for many years, been such as human wisdom and human force have in vain endeavoured to controul or resist. The counsels of the wise have been infatuated;[1] the valour of the brave has been turned to cowardice. Though the storm has been raging for many years, yet, instead of having ceased, it appears to be now increasing in fury; the clouds which have long been gathering around us, have at length almost overspread the whole face of the heavens with blackness. In this very moment of unexampled difficulty and danger, those great political Characters,[2] to the counsels of the one or the other of whom the nation has been used to look in all public exigencies, have both been taken from us. If such be our condition; and if the Slave Trade be a national crime, declared by every wise and respectable man of all parties, without exception, to be a compound of the grossest wickedness and cruelty, a crime to which we cling in defiance of the clearest light, not only in opposition to our own acknowledgments of its guilt, but even of our own declared resolutions to abandon it; is not this then a time in which all who are not perfectly sure that the Providence of God is but a fable, should be strenuous in their endeavours to lighten the vessel of the state, of such a load of guilt and infamy? . . .

And now surely you must be prepared to admit without hesitation, and in its full extent, the declaration made by Mr. Pitt, in the House of Commons, that the Slave Trade was the greatest practical evil that ever had afflicted the human race. Such indeed it would be found, had we but leisure to take the real weight of all the various evils which it includes; and surely it might well become us to enter into this examination. But it would almost exceed the powers of calculation, after having traced the Slave Trade into all its various forms of suffering, to estimate the amount of them all. . . .

. . . The enormous dimensions of this mass of misery are such, that our organs are not fitted for the contemplation of it; our affections are not suited to deal with it; we are lost in the immensity of the prospect; we are distracted by it's variety. We may see highly probable reasons why our allwise Creator has so constituted us, that we are more deeply affected by one single tale of misery, with all the details of which we are acquainted, than by the greatest accumulation of sufferings of which the particulars have not fallen under our notice. Could I but separate this immense aggregate into all its component parts, and present them one by one to your view, in all their particularity of wretchedness, you would then have a more just impression of the immensity of the misery which we wish to terminate. This cannot now be done; but let us, in concluding our melancholy course, employ a few moments in taking some family, or some individual Negro, and following him through all his successive stages of suffering, from his first becoming the victim of some nightly attack on his dwelling, or from his being sentenced to slavery for the benefit of those who condemned him, to the final close of his wretched life. I will not attempt to describe his sufferings; estimate from your own feelings what must be his, in all the various situations through which he passes.

Conceive, if you can, the agony with which, as he is hurried away by his unfeeling captors, he looks back upon the native village which contains his wife and children who are left behind; or, supposing them to have been carried off also, with which he sees their sufferings, and looks forward to the dreadful future; while his own anguish is augmented by witnessing theirs. Accompany him through his long and painful march to the coast; behold him, when the powers of nature are almost exhausted by

[1] **infatuated:** turned into folly, confounded.

[2] **great political Characters:** William Pitt (1759–1806), Prime Minister of England (1783–1806), and Charles James Fox (1749–1806), leader of the Whig opposition who opposed the slave trade and supported the abolition of slavery (in 1806).

fatigue and affliction, urged forward like a brute by the lash, or, with still more bitterness of suffering, seeing the fainting powers of his wretched wife or daughter roused into fresh exertions by the same savage discipline.[3] Behold him next brought on shipboard and delivered over to men, whose colour, appearance, language, are all strange to him, while every object around must excite terror. If his wretched family have not been brought away with him, he is tormented by the consciousness that they are left destitute and unprotected, and that his eyes will see them no more. If his wife and daughter have been carried off with him, he sees them dragged away to another part of the ship, while he is debarred from their society, and often even from the sight of them; what must be his anguish, from being conscious not only that they are suffering many of the same evils as himself, but still more, from knowing that they are exposed to all those brutalities, the idea of which must be most cutting to a husband or a father; while his misery becomes more intense, from the consciousness that they are close to him, though he cannot alleviate their misery, or protect their weakness.

See our wretched family or individual arriving at the destined port, and then call to mind the abominations of the sale of a negro cargo. See the wretched individual or family exposed naked like brutes, and the same methods taken as with their fellow brutes, to ascertain whether or not their limbs and members are perfect. See them forced to jump or dance, to prove their agility; or, still more affecting, see them afraid, each lest the other only should be bought by some particular purchaser, and therefore displaying their agility, while their hearts are wrung with anguish, in order to induce the buyer to take them both. Perhaps the different branches of the family may be bought by different owners; they may probably be taken to different islands, and the poor hope of wearing away together the wretched remainder of their lives is disappointed; or, if they are purchased together, see them taken home to the estate, and entering upon their course of laborious and bitter degradation; while, looking forward to the future, not a single ray of hope breaks in to cheer the prospect, no hope of any alleviation of drudgery or degradation for them or for their children, for ever! Suppose our wretched Slave at length reduced to the level of his condition, and, either with his own family or with a new one, suppose him to have his hard lot in some little measure mitigated by a very slight taste of domestic and social comforts. It might well be thought, that, except for the hardships and sufferings inseparable from such a state of slavery, where even the necessaries of life must depend on an owner's affluence, in a country where we know that an immense majority are extremely embarrassed in their affairs—the bitterness of death would be now past; but a negro Slave does not die so easily; again probably, possibly again and again, he is to be subjected to the brutalities of a sale, and to the pains of separation from all that are most dear to him.[4] He is taken perhaps to form a new settlement, and forced to the severe labour of clearing land, in a pestilential soil and climate, without any of those little accommodations which ingenious and industrious poverty might in a course of years have collected around him, in his old habitation. This, however, if a severe is still a short suffering, from which death soon releases him, and is far preferable to the sad fate of those, who linger out the tedious remainder of life, separated from all who have known them in their better days, and without any of those kindly props to lean upon, which the merciful ordainer of all things has provided, for sustaining the weakness, and mitigating the sorrows of age. To look around, and to see not a single face of friendship or relationship, no eye to cheer, no staff to lean upon; surely the comfortless close of such a Negro's comfortless life, though not of equal intensity of suffering with many of the evils of the former scenes through which he has passed, is yet, from the deep tinge and uniform melancholy of its colouring, as affecting a state, to the humane mind, as any whatever in a life abounding in all the varieties of human wretchedness.

Such from first to last is the condition of human existence, to which that abhorred traffic the Slave Trade annually consigns many thousands of our unoffending fellow creatures. This is a most astonishing phenomenon, when we consider the general character of the people of this country; when we call to mind the unparalleled benevolence and liberality which are found among us; when we take into account, that not a new species of distress can be pointed out, but that almost immediately some meeting takes place, some society is formed, for preventing it. Is it not utterly astonishing, that Great Britain should have been the prime agents in carrying on this trade of blood? Posterity will scarcely believe it. We, the happiest, render the Africans the most miserable of mankind!

---

[3] See Mr. Parke's account of his journey to the coast from the interior [W. W.]. **Parke:** Mungo Park (1771–1806), Scottish explorer, the first European to penetrate the heart of West Africa, recorded in his *Travels in the Interior of Africa* (1799).

[4] Let it be considered what immense numbers of Negroes have of late years been removed from our older islands to Trinidad, or to Guiana [W. W.].

THOMAS CLARKSON

(1760–1846)

The son of an Anglican headmaster and an outstanding student at Cambridge University, Thomas Clarkson found his life's work when in 1785 he wrote a prize Latin essay on the assigned topic *"anne liceat invitos in servitutem dare?"* ("is it right to make men slaves against their wills?"). Arguing in abstract terms against the immorality of slavery and drawing his examples from the Quaker Anthony Benezet's powerful descriptions of the inhumane conditions of slavery in the West Indies, Clarkson became obsessed with the evil he had discovered. On his return from collecting his prize in London, he recalls, ". . . all my pleasure was damped by the facts which were now continually before me. In the daytime, I was uneasy. In the night I had little rest. I sometimes never closed my eyes for grief. . . . I frequently tried to persuade myself that the contents of my essay could not be true . . . coming in sight of Wades Mill in Hertfordshire, I sat down disconsolate on the turf . . . here a thought came into my mind, that if the contents were true, it was time some person should see these calamities to their end."

Pedantic, thorough, and absolutely convinced of the rectitude of his cause, Clarkson never wavered in his commitment to end slavery. In 1786 he published his prize essay *On the Slavery and Commerce of the Human Species, particularly the African* and in 1787 joined the Quaker committee founded by Granville Sharp to abolish the slave trade. He was sent to Bristol and Liverpool by the Committee to determine the actual conditions aboard the slave ships; his indefatigable research, based on numerous interviews with captains, sailors, ships' surgeons, and escaped slaves, formed the backbone of the abolitionists' attacks for years to come. Armed only with pencil and paper, Clarkson crawled through the holds of ships, haunted the waterfront pubs where drunken, rowdy sailors talked most freely, and risked his life to gain access to crew men forbidden to speak with him. He uncovered not only the appalling treatment of the Africans aboard the slave ships and the difference between "loose" and "tight" packing (allowing chained men and women room to turn over or not), but also the brutal floggings, starvings, and even murder of the sailors unlucky enough to sign up for these voyages.

After he presented this documentary evidence to Wilberforce's Privy Council Committee assigned to investigate the slave trade in 1789, Clarkson spent six months in France in an unsuccessful effort to persuade the leaders of the French Revolution to abolish their slave trade and slavery in the French colonies. For the next five years, Clarkson rode thousands of miles, scouring the ports and seagoing vessels of England for witnesses willing to testify to Parliament about the actual practices in the slave trade (so vehemently denied by the ship owners and planters); in 1794, his health completely gave way and he was forced to retire from this work. He continued to write against the slave trade, publishing *An Essay on the Impolicy of the Slave-Trade* in 1788 and in 1808 his most famous work, his unsurpassed *The History of the Rise, Progress and Accomplishment of the Abolition of the African Slave-Trade by the British Parliament.* He joined with Wilberforce in founding the Anti-Slavery Society in 1823, and lived to see the passage of the Emancipation Bill in 1833, which freed 800,000 slaves and compensated their owners over £20,000,000. His last public appearance, recorded in a painting by Benjamin Haydon, was at the Anti-Slavery Convention in London in June,

1840. An indefatigable spokesman for the cause of abolition, Clarkson over his lifetime changed the British public perception of slavery and the slave trade from that of a necessary if unfortunate dimension of the British economy to that of a crime against humanity. Wordsworth, in his sonnet to Thomas Clarkson in 1807, applauded Clarkson's tireless battle for abolition, saying it was "an obstinate hill to climb . . . ," ". . . an enterprise sublime."

from The History of the Rise, Progress and Accomplishment of the Abolition of the African Slave-Trade by the British Parliament

(1808)

— VOLUME I —

from CHAPTER 1

Among the evils, corrected or subdued, either by the general influence of Christianity on the minds of men, or by particular associations of Christians, the African Slave-trade[1] appears to me to have occupied the foremost place. The abolition of it, therefore, of which it has devolved upon me to write the history, should be accounted as one of the greatest blessings, and, as such, should be one of the most copious sources of our joy. Indeed I know of no evil, the removal of which should excite in us a higher degree of pleasure. For in considerations of this kind, are we not usually influenced by circumstances? Are not our feelings usually affected according to the situation, or the magnitude, or the importance of these? Are they not more or less elevated as the evil under our contemplation has been more or less productive of misery, or more or less productive of guilt? Are they not more or less elevated, again, as we have found it more or less considerable in extent? Our sensations will undoubtedly be in proportion to such circumstances, or our joy to the appreciation or mensuration[2] of the evil which has been removed.

To value the blessing of the abolition as we ought, or to appreciate the joy and gratitude which we ought to feel concerning it, we must enter a little into the circumstances of the trade. Our statement, however, of these needs not be long. A few pages will do all that is necessary! A glance only into such a subject as this will be sufficient to affect the heart; to arouse our indignation and our pity; and to teach us the importance of the victory obtained.

The first subject for consideration, towards enabling us to make the estimate in question, will be that of the nature of the evil belonging to the Slave-trade. This may be seen by examining it in three points of view: First, As it has been proved to arise on the continent of Africa in the course of reducing the inhabitants of it to slavery; Secondly, In the course of conveying them from thence to the lands or colonies of other nations; And, Thirdly, In continuing them there as slaves.

To see it as it has been shown to arise in the first case, let us suppose ourselves on the Continent just mentioned. Well then: We are landed; we are already upon our travels; we have just passed through one forest; we are now come to a more open place, which indicates an approach to habitations. And what object is that, which first obtrudes itself upon our sight? Who is that wretched woman, whom we discover under that noble tree, wringing her hands, and beating her breast, as if in the agonies of despair? Three days has she been there at intervals to look and to watch, and this is the fourth morning, and no tidings of her children yet. Beneath its spreading boughs they were accustomed to play: But alas! the savage man-stealer interrupted their playful mirth, and has taken them for ever from her sight.

But let us leave the cries of this unfortunate woman, and hasten into another district: And what do we first see here? Who is he that just now started across the narrow pathway, as if afraid of a human face? What is that sudden rustling among the leaves? Why are those persons flying from our approach, and hiding themselves in yon darkest thicket? Behold, as we get into the plain, a deserted village! The rice-field has been just trodden down around it. An aged man, venerable by his silver beard, lies wounded

[1] Slavery had been before annihilated by Christianity, I mean in the West of Europe, at the close of the twelfth century [T. C.].

[2] **mensuration:** size as measured.

and dying near the threshold of his hut. War, suddenly instigated by avarice, has just visited the dwellings which we see. The old have been butchered, because unfit for slavery, and the young have been carried off, except such as have fallen in the conflict, or have escaped among the woods behind us. . . .

. . . Let us now estimate it as it has been proved to exist in the second; or let us examine the state of the unhappy Africans, reduced to slavery in this manner, while on board the vessels, which are to convey them across the ocean to other lands. And here I must observe at once, that, as far as this part of the evil is concerned, I am at a loss to describe it. Where shall I find words to express properly their sorrow, as arising from the reflection of being parted for ever from their friends, their relatives, and their country? Where shall I find language to paint in appropriate colours the horror of mind brought on by thoughts of their future unknown destination, of which they can augur nothing but misery from all that they have yet seen? How shall I make known their situation, while labouring under painful disease, or while struggling in the suffocating holds of their prisons, like animals inclosed in an exhausted receiver?[3] How shall I describe their feelings as exposed to all the personal indignities, which lawless appetite or brutal passion may suggest? How shall I exhibit their sufferings as determining to refuse sustenance and die, or as resolving to break their chains, and, disdaining to live as slaves, to punish their oppressors? How shall I give an idea of their agony, when under various punishments and tortures for their reputed crimes? Indeed every part of this subject defies my powers, and I must therefore satisfy myself and the reader with a general representation, or in the words of a celebrated member of Parliament, that "Never was so much human suffering condensed in so small a space."[4]

I come now to the evil, as it has been proved to arise in the third case; or to consider the situation of the unhappy victims of the trade, when their painful voyages are over, or after they have been landed upon their destined shores. And here we are to view them first under the degrading light of cattle. We are to see them examined, handled, selected, separated, and sold. Alas, relatives are separated from relatives, as if, like cattle, they had no rational intellect, no power of feeling the nearness of relationship, nor sense of the duties belonging to the ties of life! We are next to see them labouring, and this for the benefit of those, to whom they are under no obligation, by any law either natural or divine, to obey. We are to see them, if refusing the commands of their purchasers, however weary, or feeble, or indisposed, subject to corporal punishments, and, if forcibly resisting them, to death. We are to see them in a state of general degradation and misery. The knowledge, which their oppressors have of their own crime in having violated the rights of nature, and of the disposition of the injured to seek all opportunities of revenge, produces a fear which dictates to them the necessity of a system of treatment by which they shall keep up a wide distinction between the two, and by which the noble feelings of the latter shall be kept down, and their spirits broken. We are to see them again subject to individual persecution, as anger, or malice, or any bad passion may suggest. Hence the whip; the chain; the iron-collar. Hence the various modes of private torture, of which so many accounts have been truly given. Nor can such horrible cruelties be discovered so as to be made punishable, while the testimony of any number of the oppressed is invalid against the oppressors, however they may be offences against the laws. And, lastly, we are to see their innocent offspring, against whose personal liberty the shadow of an argument cannot be advanced, inheriting all the miseries of their parents' lot.

The evil then, as far as it has been hitherto viewed, presents to us in its three several departments a measure of human suffering not to be equalled; not to be calculated; not to be described. But would that we could consider this part of the subject as dismissed! Would that in each of the departments now examined there was no counterpart left us to contemplate! but this cannot be. For if there be persons, who suffer unjustly, there must be others, who oppress. And if there be those who oppress, there must be to the suffering, which has been occasioned, a corresponding portion of immorality or guilt.

We are obliged then to view the counterpart of the evil in question, before we can make a proper estimate of the nature of it. And, in examining this part of it, we shall find that we have a no less frightful picture to behold than in the former cases; or that, while the miseries endured by the unfortunate Africans excite our pity on the one hand, the vices, which are connected with them, provoke our indignation and abhorrence on the other. The Slave-trade, in this point of view, must strike us as an immense mass of evil on account of the criminality attached to it, as displayed in the various branches of it, which have already been examined. For, to take the counterpart of the

[3] **exhausted receiver**: emptied out receptacle or tank.

[4] **"celebrated . . . space"**: William Wilberforce.*

evil in the first of these, can we say, that no moral turpitude is to be placed to the account of those, who living on the continent of Africa give birth to the enormities, which take place in consequence of the prosecution of this trade? Is not that man made morally worse, who is induced to become a tyger to his species, or who, instigated by avarice, lies in wait in the thicket to get possession of his fellow-man? Is no injustice manifest in the land, where the prince, unfaithful to his duty, seizes his innocent subjects, and sells them for slaves? Are no moral evils produced among those communities, which make war upon other communities for the sake of plunder, and without any previous provocation or offence? Does no crime attach to those, who accuse others falsely, or who multiply and divide crimes for the sake of the profit of the punishment, and who for the same reason continue the use of barbarous and absurd ordeals as a test of innocence or guilt?

In the second of these branches the counterpart of the evil is to be seen in the conduct of those, who purchase the miserable natives in their own country, and convey them to distant lands. And here questions, similar to the former, may be asked. Do they experience no corruption of their nature, or become chargeable with no violation of right, who, when they go with their ships to this continent, know the enormities which their visits there will occasion, who buy their fellow-creature man, and this, knowing the way in which he comes into their hands, and who chain, and imprison, and scourge him? Do the moral feelings of those persons escape without injury, whose hearts are hardened? And can the hearts of those be otherwise than hardened, who are familiar with the tears and groans of innocent strangers forcibly torn away from every thing that is dear to them in life, who are accustomed to see them on board their vessels in a state of suffocation and in the agonies of despair, and who are themselves in the habits of the cruel use of arbitrary power?

The counterpart of the evil in its third branch is to be seen in the conduct of those, who, when these miserable people have been landed, purchase and carry them to their respective homes. And let us see whether a mass of wickedness is not generated also in the present case. Can those have nothing to answer for, who separate the faithful ties which nature and religion have created? Can their feelings be otherwise than corrupted, who consider their fellow-creatures as brutes, or treat those as cattle, who may become the temples of the Holy Spirit, and in whom the Divinity disdains not himself to dwell? Is there no injustice in forcing men to labour without wages? Is there no breach of duty, when we are commanded to clothe the naked, and feed the hungry, and visit the sick and in prison, in exposing them to want, in torturing them by cruel punishment, and in grinding them down by hard labour, so as to shorten their days? Is there no crime in adopting a system, which keeps down all the noble faculties of their souls, and which positively debases and corrupts their nature? Is there no crime in perpetuating these evils among their innocent offspring? And finally, besides all these crimes, is there not naturally in the familiar sight of the exercise, but more especially in the exercise itself, of uncontroulled power, that which vitiates the internal man? In seeing misery stalk daily over the land, do not all become insensibly hardened? By giving birth to that misery themselves, do they not become abandoned? In what state of society are the corrupt appetites so easily, so quickly, and so frequently indulged, and where else, by means of frequent indulgence, do these experience such a monstrous growth? Where else is the temper subject to such frequent irritation, or passion to such little controul? Yes; if the unhappy slave is in an unfortunate situation, so is the tyrant who holds him. Action and reaction are equal to each other, as well in the moral as in the natural world. You cannot exercise an improper dominion over a fellow-creature, but by a wise ordering of Providence you must necessarily injure yourself. . . .

from CHAPTER 15

. . In pursuing another object, which was that of going on board the slave-ships, and learning their construction and dimensions, I was greatly struck, and indeed affected, by the appearance of two little sloops, which were fitting out for Africa, the one of only twenty-five tons, which was said to be destined to carry seventy; and the other of only eleven, which was said to be destined to carry thirty slaves. I was told also that which was more affecting, namely, that these were not to act as tenders on the coast, by going up and down the rivers, and receiving three or four slaves at a time, and then carrying them to a large ship, which was to take them to the West Indies, but that it was actually intended, that they should transport their own slaves themselves; that one if not both of them were, on their arrival in the West Indies, to be sold as pleasure-vessels, and that the seamen belonging to them were to be permitted to come home by what is usually called the run.

This account of the destination of these little vessels, though it was distressing at first, appeared to me afterwards, on cool reasoning, to be incredible. I thought that my informants wished to impose upon me, in order that I might make statements which would carry their own refutation with them, and that thus I might injure the great cause which I had undertaken. And I was much inclined to be of this opinion, when I looked again at the least of the two: for any person, who was tall, standing upon dry ground by the side of her, might have overlooked every thing upon her deck. I knew also that she had been built as a pleasure boat for the accommodation of only six persons upon the Severn.[5] I determined, therefore, to suspend my belief till I could take the admeasurement of each vessel. This I did; but lest, in the agitation of my mind on this occasion, I should have made any mistake, I desired my friend George Fisher to apply to the builder for his admeasurement also. With this he kindly complied. When he obtained it he brought it to me. This account, which nearly corresponds with my own, was as follows. . . . In the vessel of twenty-five tons, the length of the upper part of the hold, or roof, of the room, where the seventy slaves were to be stowed, was but little better than ten yards, or thirty-one feet. The greatest breadth of the bottom, or floor, was ten feet four inches, and the least five. Hence, a grown person must sit down all the voyage, and contract his limbs within the narrow limits of three square feet. In the vessel of eleven tons, the length of the room for the thirty slaves was twenty-two feet. The greatest breadth of the floor was eight, and the least four. The whole height from the keel to the beam was but five feet eight inches, three feet of which were occupied by ballast, cargo, and provisions, so that two feet eight inches remained only as the height between the decks. Hence, each slave would have only four square feet to sit in, and, when in this posture, his head, if he were a full-grown person, would touch the ceiling, or upper deck.

Having now received this admeasurement from the builder, which was rather more favourable than my own, I looked upon the destination of these little vessels as yet more incredible than before. Still the different persons, whom I occasionally saw on board them, persisted in it that they were going to Africa for slaves, and also for the numbers mentioned, which they were afterwards to carry to the West Indies themselves. I desired, however, my friends, George Fisher, Truman Harford, Harry Gandy, Walter Chandler, and others, each to make a separate inquiry for me on this subject; and they all agreed that, improbable as the account both of their destination, and of the number they were to take, might appear, they had found it to be too true. I had soon afterwards the sorrow to learn from official documents from the Customhouse, that these little vessels actually cleared out for Africa, and that now nothing could be related so barbarous of this traffic, which might not instantly be believed. . . .

— VOLUME II —

from CHAPTER 10

. . . But though the bill had now passed both houses, there was an awful fear throughout the kingdom, lest it should not receive the royal assent before the ministry was dissolved. This event took place the next day; for on Wednesday the twenty-fifth, at half past eleven in the morning, his majesty's message was delivered to the different members of it, that they were then to wait upon him to deliver up the seals of their offices. It then appeared that a commission for the royal assent to this bill among others had been obtained. This commission was instantly opened by the lord chancellor (Erskine) who was accompanied by the lords Holland and Auckland; and as the clock struck twelve, just when the sun was in its meridian splendour to witness this august act, this establishment of a Magna Charta[6] for Africa in Britain, and to sanction it by its most vivid and glorious beams, it was completed. The ceremony being over, the seals of the respective offices were delivered up; so that the execution of this commission was the last act of the administration of lord Grenville; an administration, which, on account of its virtuous exertions in behalf of the oppressed African race, will pass to posterity, living through successive generations, in the love and gratitude of the most virtuous of mankind.

Thus ended one of the most glorious contests, after a continuance for twenty years, of any ever carried on in any age or country. A contest, not of brutal violence, but of reason. A contest between those, who felt deeply for the happiness and the honour of their fellow-creatures, and those, who, through vicious custom and the impulse of avarice, had trampled under-foot the sacred rights of their nature, and had even attempted to efface all title to the divine image from their minds.

---

[5] **Severn:** river in the west of England.

[6] **Lords Erskine, Holland, Auckland, Grenville:** the leading members of the Whig party in 1807. **Magna Charta:** Magna Carta, the bill of rights signed by King John on 15 June 1215, guaranteeing fundamental rights to his subjects and establishing the principles of a just government.

Of the immense advantages of this contest I know not how to speak. Indeed, the very agitation of the question, which it involved, has been highly important. Never was the heart of man so expanded. Never were its generous sympathies so generally and so perseveringly excited. These sympathies, thus called into existence, have been useful in the preservation of a national virtue. For any thing we know, they may have contributed greatly to form a counteracting balance against the malignant spirit, generated by our almost incessant wars during this period, so as to have preserved us from barbarism.

It has been useful also in the discrimination of moral character. In private life it has enabled us to distinguish the virtuous from the more vicious part of the community.[7] It has shown the general philanthropist. It has unmasked the vicious in spite of his pretension to virtue. It has afforded us the same knowledge in public life. It has separated the moral statesman from the wicked politician. It has shown us who, in the legislative and executive offices of our country are fit to save, and who to destroy, a nation.

It has furnished us also with important lessons. It has proved what a creature man is! how devoted he is to his own interest! to what a length of atrocity he can go, unless fortified by religious principle! But as if this part of the prospect would be too afflicting, it has proved to us, on the other hand, what a glorious instrument he may become in the hands of his Maker; and that a little virtue, when properly leavened, is made capable of counteracting the effects of a mass of vice!

With respect to the end obtained by this contest, or the great measure of the abolition of the Slave-trade as it has now passed, I know not how to appreciate its importance. To our own country, indeed, it is invaluable. We have lived, in consequence of it, to see the day, when it has been recorded as a principle in our legislation, that commerce itself shall have its moral boundaries. We have lived to see the day, when we are likely to be delivered from the contagion of the most barbarous opinions. They, who supported this wicked traffic, virtually denied, that man was a moral being. They substituted the law of force for the law of reason. But the great Act now under our consideration, has banished the impious doctrine, and restored the rational creature to his moral rights. Nor is it a matter of less pleasing consideration, that, at this awful crisis, when the constitutions of kingdoms are on the point of dissolution, the stain of the blood of Africa is no longer upon us, or that we have been freed (alas, if it be not too late!) from a load of guilt, which has long hung like a mill-stone about our necks ready to sink us to perdition.

In tracing the measure still further, or as it will affect other lands, we become only the more sensible of its importance: for can we pass over to Africa; can we pass over to the numerous islands, the receptacles of miserable beings from thence; and can we call to mind the scenes of misery, which have been passing in each of these regions of the earth, without acknowledging, that one of the greatest sources of suffering to the human race has, as far as our own power extends, been done away? Can we pass over to these regions again, and contemplate the multitude of crimes, which the agency necessary for keeping up the barbarous system produced, without acknowledging, that a source of the most monstrous and extensive wickedness has been removed also? But here, indeed, it becomes us peculiarly to rejoice; for though nature shrinks from pain, and compassion is engendered in us when we see it become the portion of others, yet what is physical suffering compared with moral guilt? The misery of the oppressed is, in the first place, not contagious like the crime of the oppressor. Nor is the mischief, which it generates, either so frightful or so pernicious. The body, though under affliction, may retain its shape; and, if it even perish, what is the loss of it but of worthless dust? But when the moral springs of the mind are poisoned, we lose the most excellent part of the constitution of our nature, and the divine image is no longer perceptible in us. Nor are the two evils of similar duration. By a decree of Providence, for which we cannot be too thankful, we are made mortal. Hence the torments of the oppressor are but temporary; whereas the immortal part of us, when once corrupted, may carry its pollutions with it into another world.

[7] I have had occasion to know many thousand persons in the course of my travels on this subject; and I can truly say, that the part which these took on this great question, was always a true criterion of their moral character. Some indeed opposed the abolition who seemed to be so respectable, that it was difficult to account for their conduct; but it invariably turned out in a course of time, either that they had been influenced by interested motives, or that they were not men of steady moral principle. In the year 1792, when the national enthusiasm was so great, the good were as distinguishable from the bad, according to their disposition to this great cause, as if the Divine Being had marked them; or as a friend of mine the other day observed, as we may suppose the sheep to be from the goats on the day of judgment [T. C.].

But independently of the quantity of physical suffering and the innumerable avenues to vice in more than a quarter of the globe, which this great measure will cut off, there are yet blessings, which we have reason to consider as likely to flow from it. Among these we cannot overlook the great probability, that Africa, now freed from the vicious and barbarous effects of this traffic, may be in a better state to comprehend and receive the sublime truths of the Christian religion. Nor can we overlook the probability, that, a new system of treatment necessarily springing up in our islands, the same bright sun of consolation may visit her children there. But here a new hope rises to our view. Who knows but that emancipation, like a beautiful plant, may, in its due season, rise out of the ashes of the abolition of the Slave-trade, and that, when its own intrinsic value shall be known, the seed of it may be planted in other lands? And looking at the subject in this point of view, we cannot but be struck with the wonderful concurrence of events as previously necessary for this purpose, namely, that two nations, England and America, the mother and child, should, in the same month of the same year, have abolished this impious traffic; nations, which at this moment have more than a million of subjects within their jurisdiction to partake of the blessing; and one of which, on account of her local situation and increasing power, is likely in time to give, if not law, at least a tone to the manners and customs of the great continent, on which she is situated.

Reader! Thou art now acquainted with the history of this contest! Rejoice in the manner of its termination! And, if thou feelest grateful for the event, retire within thy closet, and pour out thy thanksgivings to the Almighty for this his unspeakable act of mercy to thy oppressed fellow-creatures.

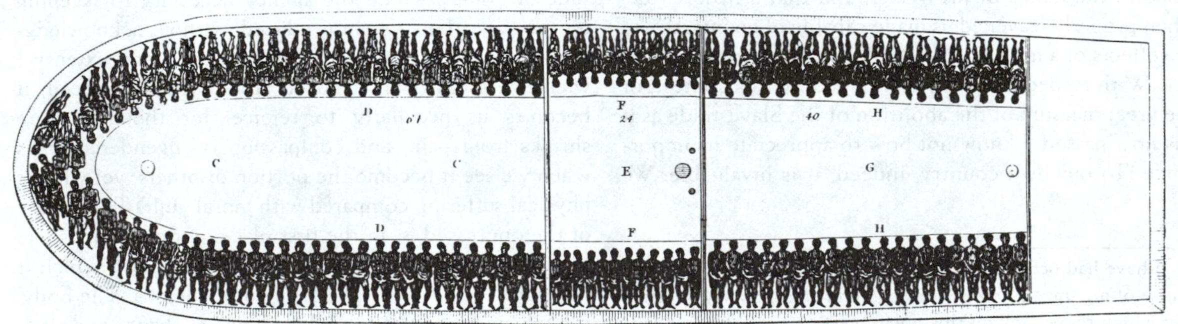

"Slave ship," from Thomas Clarkson, *The History of the Rise, Progress, and Accomplishment of the Abolition of the African Slave-Trade by the British Parliament* (1808), Vol. I, facing p. 110. "Loose packing."

AMELIA ALDERSON OPIE

(1769–1853)

A close friend of Mary Wollstonecraft, William Godwin (who without success proposed to her), Elizabeth Inchbald, and Thomas Holcroft, Amelia Alderson imbibed her republican, pro-Jacobin principles from her father, the dissenting Unitarian minister James Alderson, M.D. In May 1798 she married the ambitious, successful portrait painter John Opie and moved to London, where she began writing novellas, or tales, which explored the difficulties of contemporary women's lives from a distinctively feminist viewpoint. After her husband's death in 1807, she joined the Society of Friends, gave up writing fiction, and devoted the remainder of her life to charitable activities, working to reform the management of workhouses, prisons, and hospitals and ministering to the poor. She ardently opposed the slave trade, joining the Anti-Slavery Society in Norwich, campaigning vigorously for abolition, and attending the anti-slavery convention in London in 1840 as the delegate from Norwich (she appears in Benjamin Haydon's painting of the delegates, now in the National Portrait Gallery in London). Her first widely reprinted and influential abolitionist poem, "The Negro Boy's Tale," appeared in 1802; her second, "The Black Man's Lament, or How to Make Sugar" in 1826.

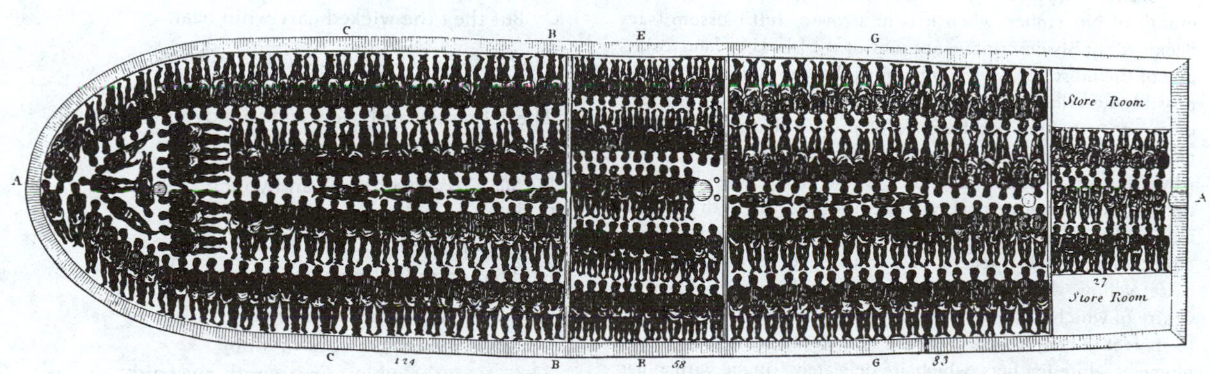

"Slave ship," from Thomas Clarkson, *The History of the Rise, Progress, and Accomplishment of the Abolition of the African Slave-Trade by the British Parliament* (1808), Vol. I, facing p. 110. "Tight packing."

The Black Man's Lament,

or, How to Make Sugar
(1826)

Come, listen to my plaintive ditty,
Ye tender hearts, and children dear!
And, should it move your souls to pity,
Oh! try to *end* the griefs you hear.

There is a beauteous plant,[1] that grows
In western India's[2] sultry clime,
Which makes, alas! the Black man's woes,
And also makes the White man's crime.

For know, its tall gold stems contain
A sweet rich juice, which White men prize;
And that they may this *sugar* gain,
The Negro toils, and bleeds, and *dies*.

But, Negro slave! *thyself* shall tell,
Of past and present wrongs the story;
And would all British hearts could feel,
To *end* those wrongs were *Britain's glory*.

— NEGRO SPEAKS —

First to our own dear Negro land,
His ships the cruel White man sends;
And there contrives, by armed band,
To tear us from our homes and friends;

From parents, brethren's fond embrace;
From tender wife, and child to tear;
Then in a darksome ship to place,
Pack'd close, like bales of cotton there.

Oh! happy those, who, in that hour,
Die from their prison's putrid breath!
Since they escape from White man's pow'r,
From toils and stripes, and lingering death!

For what awaited us on shore,
Soon as the ship had reach'd the strand,
Unloading its degraded store
Of freemen, forc'd from Negro land?

See! eager White men come around,
To choose and claim us for their slaves;
And make us envy those who found
In the dark ship their early graves.

They bid black men and women stand
In lines, the drivers in the rear:
Poor Negroes hold a *hoe* in hand,
But they the wicked cart-whip bear.

Then we, in gangs, like beasts in droves,
Swift to the cane-fields driven are;
There first our toil the weeds removes,
And next we holes for plants prepare.

But woe to all, both old and young,
Women and men, or strong or weak,
Worn out or fresh, those gangs among,
That dare the toilsome line to break!

As holes must all *at once* be made,
Together we must work or stop;
Therefore, the whip our strength must aid,
And lash us when we pause or drop!

When we have dug sufficient space,
The bright-eye top[3] of many a cane,
Lengthways, we in the trenches place,
And *then* we trenches dig again.

[1] **beauteous plant**: "A field of canes, when standing in the month of November, when it is in arrow or full blossom (says Beckford, in his descriptive account of the Island of Jamaica), is one of the most beautiful productions that the pen or pencil can possibly describe. It, in common, rises from three to eight feet, or more, in height; a difference of growth that very strongly marks the difference of soil, or the varieties of culture. It is, when ripe, of a bright and golden yellow; and, where obvious to the sun, is in many parts very beautifully streaked with red. The top is of a darkish green; but the more dry it becomes (from either an excess of ripeness, or a continuance of drought), of a russet yellow, with long and narrow leaves depending; from the centre of which, shoots up an arrow, like a silver wand, from two to six feet in height; and, from the summit of which, grows out a plume of white feathers, which are delicately fringed with a lilac dye, and indeed is, in its appearance, not much unlike the tuft that adorns this particular and elegant tree." [Opie's note, quoting from *A Descriptive Account of the Island of Jamaica, with Remarks upon the Cultivation of the Sugar Cane* (1798), by the historian William Beckford (d.1799).]

[2] **western India**: refers not to the Asian subcontinent but to the West Indies, the islands located between the southeastern United States and the northern coast of South America, separating the Caribbean from the Atlantic Ocean; the group includes Cuba, Puerto Rico, Jamaica, Hispaniola (Haiti and the Dominican Republic), the Bahamas, and the Virgin Islands.

[3] **bright-eye top**: "The top shoots are *full of eyes*, or *gems*, as they are called." [Opie's note: *eye* and *gem* are other names for the buds of plants.]

We cover next the plants with mould;
And e'en, ere fifteen days come round,
We can the slender sprouts behold,
Just shooting greenly from the ground.

The weeds about them clear'd away,
Then mould again by hand we throw;
And, at no very distant day,
Here Negroes plough, and there they hoe.

But when the crops are ripen'd quite,
'Tis then begin our saddest pains;
For then we toil both day and night,
Though fever burns within our veins.

When 18 months complete their growth,
Then the tall canes rich juices fill;
And we, to bring their liquor forth,
Convey them to the bruising-mill.

That mill, our labour, every hour,
Must with fresh loads of canes supply;
And if we faint, the cart-whip's power,
Gives force which *nature's* powers *deny.*

Our task is next to catch the juice
In leaden bed, soon as it flows;
And instant, lest it spoil for use,
It into boiling vessels goes.

Nor one alone: four vessels more
Receive and clear the sugar-tide.
Six coolers next receive the store;
Long vessels, shallow, wooden, *wide.*

While cooling, it begins to grain,
Or form in crystals white and clear;
Then we remove the whole again,
And to the *curing-house* we bear.

Molasses there is drain'd away;
The liquor is through hogsheads pour'd;
The scum falls through, the crystals stay;
The casks are clos'd, and soon on board.

The ships to English country go,
And bear the hardly-gotten treasure.
Oh! that good Englishmen could know
How Negroes suffer for their pleasure!

Five months, we, every week, alas!
Save when we eat, to work are driven:
Six days, three nights; then, to each class,
Just twenty hours of rest are given.

But when the Sabbath-eve comes round,
That eve which White men sacred keep
Again we at our toil are found,
And six days more we work and weep.

"But, Negro slave, some men must toil.
The English peasant works all day;
Turns up, and sows, and ploughs the soil.
Thou wouldst not, sure, have Negroes play?"

"Ah! no. But Englishmen can work
Whene'er they like, and stop for breath;
No driver dares, like any Turk,
Flog peasants on almost to death.

"Who dares an English peasant flog,
Or buy, or sell, or steal away?
Who sheds his blood? treats him like dog,
Or fetters him like beasts of prey?

"He has a cottage, he a wife;
If child he has, that child is free.
I am depriv'd of married life,
And my poor child were *slave* like *me.*

"Unlike his home, ours is a shed
Of pine-tree trunks, unsquar'd, ill-clos'd:
Blanket we have, but not a bed,
Whene'er to short, chill sleep dispos'd.

"Our clothing's ragged. All our food
Is rice, dried fish, and Indian meal.[4]
Hard, scanty fare! Oh, would I could
Make White men Negroes' miseries feel!"

"But could you not, your huts around,
Raise plants for food, and poultry rear?
You might, if willing, till your ground,
And then some wants would disappear."

"Work for ourselves and others too?
When all our master's work is o'er,
How could we bear our own to do?
Poor, weary slaves, hot, scourg'd, and sore!

"Sometimes, 'tis true, when Sabbath-bell
Calls White man to the house of pray'r,
And makes poor blacks more sadly feel
'Tis thought *slaves* have no *business* there:

[4] **Indian meal:** cornmeal.

"Then Negroes try the earth to till,
And raise their food on Sabbath-day;
But Envy's pangs poor Negroes fill,
That we must *work* while others *pray*.

"Then, where have we *one* legal right?
White men may bind, whip, torture slave.
But oh! if we but strike one White,
Who can poor Negro help or save?

"There are, I'm told, upon some isles,
Masters who gentle deign to be;
And there, perhaps, the Negro *smiles*,
But *smiling* Negroes *few* can see.

"Well, I must learn to bear my pain;
And, lately, I am grown more calm;
For Christian men come o'er the main,
To pour in Negro souls a balm.

"They tell us there is one above
Who died to save both bond and free;
And who, with eyes of equal love,
Beholds White man, and *humble me*.

"They tell me if, with patient heart,
I bear my wrongs from day to day,
I shall, at death, to realms depart,
Where God wipes every tear away!

"Yet still, at times, with fear I shrink;
For, when with sense of injury prest,
I burn with rage! and *then* I think
I ne'er can *gain* that place of rest."

He ceas'd; for here his tears would flow,
And ne'er resum'd his tale of *ruth*.[5]
Alas! it rends my heart to know
He only told a *tale of truth*.

---

[5] **ruth:** sorrow or misery; lamentation.

SOCIETY AND POLITICAL ECONOMY

NUMBERS HELD SWAY in nineteenth-century liberal thought. Whether computing votes in an increasingly democratic political system, profits in capitalist business ventures, or data in scientific experimentation, the truth was approached through numbers and statistics. Empiricism provided a rational—as opposed to a traditional or customary—approach to social development. Jeremy Bentham's (1748–1832) nugget of ethical utility from *Introduction to Principles of Morals and Legislation* (1789)—"It is the greatest happiness of the greatest number that is the measure of right and wrong"—in effect made *number* a metonymy for the citizen of the modern state.

The societal revolution of the Industrial Age can also be described fairly adequately with numbers. The total population for England and Wales during this period was about 5.5 million and annual income ranged from £10 to £3,000. At the apex of this range was the oligarchy of Old England (1714–1760), which consisted of about 200 aristocrats—dukes, marquesses, earls, viscounts, and barons—who sat in the House of Lords, and enjoyed an average income of £2,800. On the next level of the pyramid stood 16,000 gentlemen, knights, and baronets, with an income of between £280 and £1,000. Totalling about 2.3 million were merchants, professional men, farmers, shopkeepers, and tradesmen, with incomes from £400 down to £44 per year. The bottom of the pyramid was the "laboring poor"—over 3 million artisans, laborers, cottagers, soldiers, seamen, and paupers, with incomes from £6 to £15 pounds per year.

The stability of this traditional society was founded upon family property inherited in accordance with laws of primogeniture. One's relationship with land was also believed to be the source of domestic and patriotic virtue. A peer might own 10,000 acres, with a grand residence, or "seat," in the country and a townhouse in London. A small proprietor in the North of England might have only a slant hillside for grazing sheep. A village peasant might have little more than a garden plot on the village waste, which he might feel proprietary towards as a squatter. In *The Case of the Labourers in Husbandry* (1795), the Reverend David Davies (17??–1819) extols the importance of land at a time when revolutionary storms abroad made patriotism an urgent concern: "It is plainly agreeable to sound policy, that as many individuals as possible should possess an interest in the soil; because this attaches them strongly to the country and its constitution, and makes them zealous and resolute in defending them." Edmund Burke* argued, "the first link in the series by which we proceed towards a love to our country and to mankind" derives from the "little platoon we belong to in society."

Between 1760 and 1830, England underwent an Industrial Revolution, one of the most powerful catalysts to social change since the technological advances in agriculture which had made permanent settlement possible. Historians have suggested that England was uniquely prepared for an industrial revolution just as France was for a political revolution, because the aristocracy perceived their self-interest as lying in economic development; because the British government was inclined to stay out of business except to fight wars on behalf of economic expansion; and because the values preached by the dissenting churches were conducive to capitalist trade and industry. Population growth, increasing wealth, and social mobility changed at once the physical, cultural, and political landscapes of Great Britain. Investors financed the infrastructure required to transport raw materials to mills and products to market. By the opening of the nineteenth century, canals, locks, bridges, improved waterways, and roads spanned the countryside. The symbol of modernity became the railroad. Construction on the line between Liverpool and Manchester began in 1826.

THE GROWTH AND MOVEMENT OF POPULATION

The population figures of the first census taken in England, Scotland, and Wales indicate that there were 10.6 million inhabitants in 1801. Ireland had another 5.2 million. The census figures of 1811 indicate that for the first time in the history of an advanced nation, more members of society were employed outside of agriculture. While 895,998 families were associated with agrarian employment, 1,129,049 families were employed in trade and manufacturing. By 1831, the population of Great Britain had risen to 14 million.

These statistics indicate that population centers were *perceptibly* growing from 1780 to 1830. A population drift from villages to cities resulted from rural pauperization due to enclosure, lower earnings caused by cheaper products from urban manufacturing centers, and the lure of higher wages. Manchester became the magnet of population drift in the midlands and the best example of industrial development for the kingdom. In 1773, Manchester had a population of 27,000, without a single spinning mill; by 1802, the population had risen to 95,000, with 52 cotton mills.

A fraction of Manchester's population lived in luxury on the breezy hills overlooking the textile empire, but the working class lived in crowded and putrid slums on the banks of the polluted Irk. It was impossible to supplement a population growth of 350 percent in three decades with a tripling of adequate housing and sanitation in an age without plumbing. Food and clothing were intermittently scarce and poor in quality in working-class districts. William Cobbett* in his *Poor Man's Friend* (1826) wrote that in the North, newspapers reported in 1826 that the poor "eat horse-flesh, grains, and have been detected in eating out of pig-troughs," while in the midlands, *"tens of thousands were upon the point of starvation."* In *The State of the Poor* (1797), Sir. F. M. Eden observed that workers in the South of England "are habituated to the unvarying meal of dry bread and cheese from week's end to week's end."

Because capitalism required workers to react predictably to increased and decreased wages, workers had to abandon their traditional country values with their village lives. Protestantism, especially Calvinism, aided in the inculcation of new work values with emphasis upon frugality, industry, devotion to a calling, and sobriety. The ideal worker would become acquisitive rather than satisfied with little, or even enough. The socialist philanthropist Robert Owen (1771–1858) described the deleterious effect of early capitalism on relationships and politics. In "Observations on the Effect of the Manufacturing System" (1815), Owen argued that the principle of buying cheap and selling dear is "destructive of that open, honest sincerity, without which man cannot make others happy, nor enjoy happiness himself." As relations between workers and employers became increasingly strained and hostile, Owen perceived a national risk: "The employer regards the employed as mere instruments of gain, while these acquire a gross ferocity of character, which, . . . will sooner or later plunge the country into a formidable and perhaps inextricable state of danger."

Indeed, the bad harvests and near-famine conditions of the mid-1790s made for a volatile political climate. The cost of wheat almost doubled (from 50 to 92 shillings per imperial quarter), leading to bread riots in Coventry, Nottingham, and Sussex. In a context of continental revolution, hunger was perceived as a possible catalyst for radical political change. Thomas Malthus* argued in his *Essay on the Principle of Population* (1798) that unchecked population growth would inevitably lead to human disaster. He proposed "two postulata" based upon the "fixed laws of our nature": "First, food is necessary to the existence of man. Secondly, that the passion between the sexes is necessary, and will remain nearly in its present state." The resulting inference supported the recent view of Economics as the "dismal science": "Population, when unchecked, increases in a geometrical ratio. Subsistence increases only in an arithmetical ratio." Sexual restraint being no more likely than living on air, simple mathematical calculation brought Malthus to the conclusion that if war, disease, natural disaster, or another species of misery did not "check" the growth of the human race, starvation would inevitably ensue. It was the fallen Adam's curse translated into contemporary history: "O voice once heard / Delightfully, 'Increase and multiply,' / Now death to hear!" (*Paradise Lost*, X.729–31).

One of the first consequences of the movement of populations to cities was thus the need for more efficient farming to feed the urban workforce. This produced the political solution of enclosure, or the combining of village commons, small farms, and wastes into larger, more efficient food-producing enterprises. Between 1781 and 1801, about 2,000 enclosure acts were passed, and another 2,000 between 1802 and 1844. As. J. L. and Barbara Hammond commented in *The Village Labourer* (1912), "every patch of arable land was a gold mine." Because enclosure commissions recognized legal title rather than custom and tenancy, landlords and large farmers tended to fare best, the small farmer and the poor the worst. Many impoverished agrarians enlisted in the military. Over 640,000 men served in the army and navy during the French Wars and Britain's expansion into India and China.

EASTERN IMPERIALISM

Foreign trade with India and China countered the soulful dreariness of domestic industrialism and its plodding material success with the romance of orientalism and the seduction of lucrative imperialism. The heart of British mercantilism abroad was the East India Company, headquartered principally in London and Calcutta. Although its original function had been commerce, by 1800 the India Company was formally committed to a program of administration, expansion, and war. It also collected taxes from the Indians to protect the subcontinent from French invasion, and thereby to protect British investment.

The influence of the East India Company on British society was incalculable. At the highest levels, its money exerted enormous political and personal influence. The company itself made little profit, but employment in its Indian operations placed one in a position of lucrative private opportunities. More generally, daily life at home was affected by its imports, most universally, tea, but also opium from the Bengal region, the location of "the most prosperous and highly organized opium industry in the world." Between 1801 and 1810, Britain imported 24 million pounds of tea a year through the company. However, the greatest revenues were derived from the British monopolies on saltpeter, which is used in gunpowder, and the outlawed opium trade with China.

In 1795, Samuel Taylor Coleridge* harangued against the selfishness of the new Commercial Man, embodied most vividly by the successive governor-generals of the East India Company, Robert Clive and Warren Hastings, who acquired fortunes of £234,000 and £400,000 respectively in India even as the company itself lost money. However, when Coleridge challenged his countrymen to give up the "pestilent Luxuries" that made slavery and enslavement profitable and argued that "Family connections, and the necessity of a maintenance are no excuses!", he indicted his own family and friends in the moral turpitude. Charles Lamb,* his earliest friend, was employed by the home office of the East India Company. William and Dorothy Wordsworth invested heavily in their mariner brother's ill-fated get-rich-quick Indian schemes in 1802 and 1805. Coleridge's brother Francis served militarily for the company, eventually committing suicide after a battle in Seringapatam. Coleridge, along with Thomas De Quincey,* Clive, William Wilberforce,* and countless others, were addicted to the by-products of opium. De Quincey described the "abyss of divine enjoyment" he experienced in his *Confessions of an English Opium-Eater* (1822).* Clive died of an overdose at the age of forty-nine. Mary Shelley's* half-sister Fanny Imlay committed suicide with it.

Almost everyone benefited from the medicinal form of opium, the liquid laudanum, because it was prescribed for everything from syphilis to obstinate constipation. Children received opium in the form of such patent medicines as Godfrey's Cordial, Dalbey's Carminative, McMunn's Elixir, Batley's Sedative Solution, Mother Bailey's Quieting Syrup, etc. Working-class mothers used these sedatives to keep their young children quiet at home while they labored in the factories. Some 1,600 laboring families in one Lancashire town are said to have used Godfrey's Cordial for their children.

Cheaper than beer or gin, laudanum was also the preferred recreation of a Saturday night for the millworkers of the industrial towns of Sheffield, Birmingham, Nottingham, and the counties of Yorkshire, Cambridgeshire, and Lincolnshire. In 1822, Britain imported 22,000 pounds of opium; by 1860, the amount had risen to more than 90,000. Opium dens became the most popular establishments of London underground life.

The following selections speak to the salient controversies of the times regarding economics and social improvement. Godwin's *Enquiry Concerning Political Justice* (1793; 1796; 1798) provided his age with an enlightened critique of social institutions. In this work, he argues that human perfectability can be realized in a world guided by reasoned deliberation rather than tradition and violence. Malthus responds to this philosophical optimism with mathematical calculations to prove that, even if Godwin's dream of free love and communal property were fulfilled, it would be shortlived when competition for survival intensified as a result of unchecked population growth. Jane Marcet represents Adam Smith's argument that liberty advances more assuredly in a capitalism marketplace because the labor of the working poor becomes a valued commodity to exchange for wages. William Cobbett takes the alleged morality of modern economics to task for employing impersonal "laws" that dehumanize the poor and argues for reviving the old laws that require parishes to provide for their needy inhabitants. The reader may turn to *Confessions of an English Opium-Eater* by De Quincey for an extended selection on the contemporary use of the drug and to Samuel Taylor Coleridge's *Preface to "Kubla Khan"* (1816) for an even more famous statement of its effects on the poetic imagination.

WILLIAM GODWIN

(1756–1836)

William Hazlitt* said of Godwin's influence during the 1790s that "wherever liberty, truth, and justice was the theme, his name was not far off . . ." The optimism of Godwin's philosophical treatise, *An Enquiry Concerning Political Justice* (1793), became increasingly important as disenchantment with the French Revolution set in. Godwin philosophized that laws of determinism or necessity applied to humans as physical beings. Humankind is perfectible, however, if reason is permitted to function freely in the light of particular circumstances, rather than in conformity with norms or conventions. The inevitable outcome of reasoned discussion and behavior would be utopia: no wars, jails, social classes, privately owned property, marriage, or government. Democracy is temporarily acceptable, but the ultimate end is anarchy.

William Godwin was the seventh of thirteen children born to a Dissenting minister. He was educated for the ministry and served several parishes until French philosophy undermined his Christian faith. He left the ministry in 1783 to write and soon became a member of London's radical circle. Despite his opposition to marriage, he wed Mary Wollstonecraft* in 1797, who died shortly afterward in childbirth with their daughter, the future Mary Wollstonecraft Godwin Shelley.* In 1801, Godwin married again, and suffered a lifetime of marital discord. With the exception of a few proselytes, his reputation faded as times grew conservative. He published novels, biographies, histories, and political tracts, but none had the popular and financial success of *Political Justice*.

from Enquiry Concerning Political Justice and Its Influence on Morals and Happiness[1]

(1798)

. . . The only things which can be said to compose the nature or constitution of man are our external structure, which itself is capable of being modified with indefinite variety; the appetites and impressions growing out of that structure; and the capacity of combining ideas and inferring conclusions. The appetites common to the species we cannot wholly destroy: the faculty of reason it would be absurd systematically to counteract, since it is only by some sort of reasoning, bad or good, that we can so much as adopt any system. In this sense therefore no doubt we ought to follow nature, that is, to employ our understandings and increase our discernment. But, by conforming ourselves to the principles of our constitution in this respect, we most effectually exclude all following, or implicit assent. If we would fully comport ourselves in a manner correspondent to our properties and powers, we must bring everything to the standard of reason. Nothing must be admitted either as principle or precept that will not support this trial. Nothing must be sustained because it is ancient, because we have been accustomed to regard it as sacred, or because it has been unusual to bring its validity into question. Finally, if by following nature be understood that we must fix our preference upon things that will conduce to human happiness, in this there is some truth. But the truth it contains is extremely darkened by the phraseology in which it is couched. We must consider our external structure so far as relates to the mere question of our preservation. As

[1] Appeared in three editions (1793, 1796, 1798). Selection herein is from the third rather than first edition because improvements in rhetoric and argument make the last edition more useful for anthologizing. The subtitle of the editions also changed from *An Enquiry . . . and Its Influence on General Virtue and Happiness* (1793) to *Enquiry . . . and Its Influence on Modern Morals and Happiness* (1798).

to the rest, whatever will make a reasonable nature happy will make us happy; and our preference ought to be bestowed upon that species of pleasure which has most independence and most animation.

The corollaries respecting political truth, deducible from the simple proposition, which seems clearly established by the reasonings of the present chapter, that the voluntary actions of men are in all instances conformable to the deductions of their understanding, are of the highest importance. Hence we may infer what are the hopes and prospects of human improvement. The doctrine which may be founded upon these principles may perhaps best be expressed in the five following propositions: Sound reasoning and truth, when adequately communicated, must always be victorious over error; Sound reasoning and truth are capable of being so communicated; Truth is omnipotent; The vices and moral weakness of man are not invincible; Man is perfectible, or in other words susceptible of perpetual improvement.

—*from* CHAPTER III—

Benefits Attendant on a System of Equality

Having seen the justice of an equal distribution of the good things of life, let us next proceed to consider, in detail, the benefits with which it would be attended. And here with grief it must be confessed that, however great and extensive are the evils that are produced by monarchies and courts, by the imposture of priests and the iniquity of criminal laws, all these are imbecile and impotent compared with the evils that arise out of the established administration of property.

Its first effect is that we have already mentioned, a sense of dependence. It is true that courts are mean-spirited, intriguing and servile, and that this disposition is transferred by contagion from them to all ranks of society. But accumulation brings home a servile and truckling spirit, by no circuitous method, to every house in the nation. Observe the pauper fawning with abject vileness upon his rich benefactor, speechless with sensations of gratitude, for having received that which he ought to have claimed, not indeed with arrogance, or a dictatorial and overbearing temper, but with the spirit of a man discussing with a man, and resting his cause only on the justice of his claim. Observe the servants that follow in a rich man's train, watchful of his looks, anticipating his commands, not daring to reply to his insolence, all their time and their efforts under the direction of his caprice. Observe the tradesman, how he studies the passions of his customers, not to correct, but to pamper them, the vileness of his flattery and the systematical constancy with which he exaggerates the merit of his commodities. Observe the practices of a popular election, where the great mass are purchased by obsequiousness, by intemperance and bribery, or driven by unmanly threats of poverty and persecution. Indeed, 'the age of chivalry is not gone'.[2] The feudal spirit still survives that reduced the great mass of mankind to the rank of slaves and cattle for the service of a few.

We have heard much of visionary and theoretical improvements. It would indeed be visionary to expect integrity from mankind while they are thus subjected to hourly corruption; and bred, from father to son, to sell their independence and their conscience for the vile rewards that oppression has to bestow. No man can be either useful to others, or happy in himself, who is a stranger to the grace of firmness, or who is not habituated to prefer the dictates of his own understanding to the tyranny of command and the allurements of temptation. Here again, . . . religion comes in to illustrate our thesis. Religion was the generous ebullition of men who let their imagination loose on the grandest subjects, and wandered without restraint in the unbounded field of enquiry. It is not to be wondered at therefore if they brought home imperfect ideas of the sublimest views that intellect can furnish. In this instance, religion teaches that the pure perfection of man is to arm himself against the power of sublunary enticements and sublunary terrors; that he must suffer no artificial wants, sensuality, or fear, to come in competition with the dictates of rectitude and reflection. But to expect a constancy of this sort from the human species, under the present system, is an extravagant speculation. The enquirer after truth, and the benefactor of mankind, will be desirous of removing from them those external impressions by which their evil propensities are cherished. The true object that should be kept in view is to extirpate all ideas of condescension and superiority, to oblige every man to feel that the kindness he exerts is what he is bound to perform, and to examine whether the assistance he asks be what he has a right to claim.

A second evil that arises out of the established administration of property is the continual spectacle of injustice it exhibits. The effect of this consists partly in

---

[2] Allusion to the controversial phrase from Edmund Burke's* *Reflections on the Revolution in France* (1790): "the age of chivalry is gone."

the creation of wrong propensities, and partly in a hostility to right ones. There is nothing more pernicious to the human mind than the love of opulence. Essentially active when the original cravings of appetite have been satisfied, we necessarily fix on some object of pursuit, benevolent or personal, and, in the latter case, on the attainment of some excellence, or something which shall command the esteem and deference of others. Few propensities, absolutely considered, can be more valuable than this. But the established administration of property directs it into the channel of the acquisition of wealth. The ostentation of the rich perpetually goads the spectator to the desire of opulence. Wealth, by the sentiments of servility and dependence it produces, makes the rich man stand forward as the principal object of general esteem and deference. In vain are sobriety, integrity and industry, in vain the sublimest powers of mind, and the most ardent benevolence, if their possessor be narrow in his circumstances. To acquire wealth and to display it is therefore the universal passion. The whole structure of human society is made a system of the narrowest selfishness. If the state of society were such that self-love and benevolence were apparently reconciled as to their object, a man might then set out with the desire of eminence, and yet become every day more generous and philanthropical in his views. But the passion we are here describing is accustomed to be gratified at every step by inhumanly trampling upon the interest of others. Wealth is acquired by overreaching our neighbour, and is spent in insulting him.

The spectacle of injustice which the established administration of property exhibits operates also in the way of hostility to right propensities. If you would cherish in any man the love of rectitude, you must see that its principles be impressed on him, not only by words, but actions. It happens perhaps, during the period of education, that maxims of integrity and consistency are repeatedly enforced, and the preceptor gives no quarter to the base suggestions of selfishness and cunning. But how is the lesson that has been read to the pupil confounded and reversed when he enters upon the scene of the world? If he ask, 'Why is this man honoured?' the ready answer is, 'Because he is rich.' If he enquire further, 'Why is he rich?' the answer, in most cases, is, 'From the accident of birth, or from a minute and sordid attention to the cares of gain.' Humanity weeps over the distresses of the peasantry in all civilized nations; and, when she turns from this spectacle, to behold the luxury of their lords, gross, imperious and prodigal, her sensations certainly are not less acute. This spectacle is the school in which mankind have been educated. They have been accustomed to the sight of injustice, oppression and iniquity, till their feelings are made callous, and their understandings incapable of apprehending the principles of virtue. . . .

How rapid would be the advances of intellect if all men were admitted into the field of knowledge? At present ninety-nine persons in a hundred are no more excited to any regular exertions of general and curious thought than the brutes themselves. What would be the state of public mind in a nation where all were wise, all had laid aside the shackles of prejudice and implicit faith, all adopted, with fearless confidence, the suggestions of reason, and the lethargy of the soul was dismissed for ever? It is to be presumed that the inequality of mind would, in a certain degree, be permanent; but it is reasonable to believe that the geniuses of such an age would greatly surpass the utmost exertions of intellect hitherto known. Genius would not be depressed with false wants and niggardly patronage. It would not exert itself with a sense of neglect and oppression rankling in its bosom. It would be delivered from those apprehensions that perpetually recall us to the thought of personal emolument; and, of consequence, would expatiate freely among sentiments of generosity and public good.

From ideas of intellectual, let us turn to moral, improvement. And here it is obvious that the great occasions of crime would be cut off for ever.

The fruitful source of crimes consists in this circumstance, one man's possessing in abundance that of which another man is destitute. We must change the nature of mind before we can prevent it from being powerfully influenced by this circumstance, when brought strongly home to its perceptions by the nature of its situation. Man must cease to have senses, the pleasures of appetite and vanity must cease to gratify, before he can look on tamely at the monopoly of these pleasures. He must cease to have a sense of justice, before he can clearly and fully approve this mixed scene of superfluity and want. It is true that the proper method of curing this inequality is by reason and not by violence. But the immediate tendency of the established administration is to persuade men that reason is impotent. The injustice of which they complain is upheld by force; and they are too easily induced by force to attempt its correction. All they endeavour is the partial correction of an injustice which education tells them is necessary, but more powerful reason affirms to be tyrannical. . . .

The spirit of oppression, the spirit of servility, and the spirit of fraud, these are the immediate growth of the established administration of property. They are alike hostile to intellectual and moral improvement. The other vices of envy, malice and revenge are their inseparable companions. In a state of society where men lived in the midst of plenty, and where all shared alike the bounties of nature, these sentiments would inevitably expire. The narrow principle of selfishness would vanish. No man being obliged to guard his little store, or provide, with anxiety and pain, for his restless wants, each would lose his individual existence, in the thought of the general good. No man would be an enemy to his neighbour, for they would have no subject of contention; and of consequence, philanthropy would resume the empire which reason assigns her. Mind would be delivered from her perpetual anxiety about corporal support, and free to expatiate in the field of thought which is congenial to her. Each would assist the enquiries of all. . . .

There is one other circumstance which, though inferior to those above enumerated, deserves to be mentioned. This is population. It has been calculated that the average cultivation of Europe might be so improved as to maintain five times her present number of inhabitants. There is a principle in human society by which population is perpetually kept down to the level of the means of subsistence. Thus, among the wandering tribes of America and Asia, we never find, through the lapse of ages, that population has so increased as to render necessary the cultivation of the earth. Thus, among the civilized nations of Europe, by means of territorial monopoly, the sources of subsistence are kept within a certain limit, and, if the population became overstocked, the lower ranks of the inhabitants would be still more incapable of procuring for themselves the necessaries of life. There are, no doubt, extraordinary concurrences of circumstances by means of which changes are occasionally introduced in this respect; but, in ordinary cases, the standard of population is held, in a manner, stationary for centuries. Thus the established administration of property may be considered as strangling a considerable portion of our children in their cradle. Whatever may be the value of the life of man, or rather whatever would be his capability of happiness in a free and equal state of society, the system we are here opposing may be considered as arresting, upon the threshold of existence, four fifths of that value and that happiness.

—*from* APPENDIX—

Co-operation, Cohabitation and Marriage

. . . It would be absurd to say that we are not capable of truth, of evidence and agreement. In these respects, so far as mind is in a state of progressive improvement, we are perpetually coming nearer to each other. But there are subjects about which we shall continually differ, and ought to differ. The ideas, associations and circumstances of each man are properly his own; and it is a pernicious system that would lead us to require all men, however different their circumstances, to act by a precise general rule. Add to this that, by the doctrine of progressive improvement, we shall always be erroneous, though we shall every day become less erroneous. The proper method for hastening the decline of error, and producing uniformity of judgement, is not by brute force, by laws, or by imitation; but, on the contrary, by exciting every man to think for himself.

From these principles it appears that everything that is usually understood by the term co-operation is, in some degree, an evil. A man in solitude is obliged to sacrifice or postpone the execution of his best thoughts, in compliance with his necessities, or his frailties. How many admirable designs have perished in the conception, by means of this circumstance? It is still worse when a man is also obliged to consult the convenience of others. If I be expected to eat or to work in conjunction with my neighbour, it must either be at a time most convenient to me, or to him, or to neither of us. We cannot be reduced to a clockwork uniformity. . . .

Having ventured to state these hints and conjectures, let us endeavour to mark the limits of individuality. Every man that receives an impression from any external object has the current of his own thoughts modified by force; and yet, without external impressions, we should be nothing. Every man that reads the composition of another suffers the succession of his ideas to be, in a considerable degree, under the direction of his author. But it does not seem as if this would ever form a sufficient objection against reading. One man will always have stored up reflections and facts that another wants; and mature and digested discourse will perhaps always, in equal circumstances, be superior to that which is extempore. Conversation is a species of co-operation, one or the other party always yielding to have his ideas guided by the other; yet conversation, and the intercourse of mind with mind, seem to be the most fertile sources of improvement. It is here as it is with punishment. He that in the gentlest manner, undertakes to reason another out of his vices will probably occasion pain; but this species of punishment ought, upon no account, to be superseded.

Let not these views of the future individuality of man be misapprehended, or overstrained. We ought to be able to do without one another. He is the most perfect man to whom society is not a necessary of life, but a luxury, innocent and enviable, in which he joyfully indulges. Such a man will not fly to society, as to something requisite for the consuming of his time, or the refuge of his weakness. In society he will find pleasure; the temper of his mind will prepare him for friendship and for love. But he will resort with a scarcely inferior eagerness to solitude; and will find in it the highest complacence and the purest delight.

Another article which belongs to the subject of co-operation is cohabitation. The evils attendant on this practice are obvious. In order to the human understanding's being successfully cultivated, it is necessary that the intellectual operations of men should be independent of each other. We should avoid such practices as are calculated to melt our opinions into a common mould. Cohabitation is also hostile to that fortitude which should accustom a man, in his actions, as well as in his opinions, to judge for himself, and feel competent to the discharge of his own duties. Add to this, that it is absurd to expect the inclinations and wishes of two human beings to coincide, through any long period of time. To oblige them to act and to live together is to subject them to some inevitable portion of thwarting, bickering and unhappiness. This cannot be otherwise, so long as men shall continue to vary in their habits, their preferences and their views. No man is always cheerful and kind; and it is better that his fits of irritation should subside of themselves, since the mischief in that case is more limited, and since the jarring of opposite tempers, and the suggestions of a wounded pride, tend inexpressibly to increase the irritation. When I seek to correct the defects of a stranger, it is with urbanity and good humour. I have no idea of convincing him through the medium of surliness and invective. But something of this kind inevitably obtains where the intercourse is too unremitted.

The subject of cohabitation is particularly interesting as it includes in it the subject of marriage. It will therefore be proper to pursue the enquiry in greater detail. The evil of marriage, as it is practised in European countries, extends further than we have yet described. The method is for a thoughtless and romantic youth of each sex to come together, to see each other, for a few times and under circumstances full of delusion, and then to vow eternal attachment. What is the consequence of this? In almost every instance they find themselves deceived. They are reduced to make the best of an irretrievable mistake. They are led to conceive it their wisest policy to shut their eyes upon realities, happy, if, by any perversion of intellect, they can persuade themselves that they were right in their first crude opinion of each other. Thus the institution of marriage is made a system of fraud; and men who carefully mislead their judgements in the daily affair of their life must be expected to have a crippled judgement in every other concern.

Add to this that marriage, as now understood, is a monopoly, and the worst of monopolies. So long as two human beings are forbidden, by positive institution, to follow the dictates of their own mind, prejudice will be alive and vigorous. So long as I seek, by despotic and artificial means, to maintain my possession of a woman, I am guilty of the most odious selfishness. Over this imaginary prize, men watch with perpetual jealousy; and one man finds his desire, and his capacity to circumvent, as much excited as the other is excited to traverse his projects, and frustrate his hopes. As long as this state of society continues, philanthropy will be crossed and checked in a thousand ways, and the still augmenting stream of abuse will continue to flow.

The abolition of the present system of marriage appears to involve no evils. We are apt to represent that abolition to ourselves as the harbinger of brutal lust and depravity. But it really happens, in this, as in other cases, that the positive laws which are made to restrain our vices irritate and multiply them. Not to say that the same sentiments of justice and happiness which, in a state of equality, would destroy our relish for expensive gratifications might be expected to decrease our inordinate appetites of every kind, and to lead us universally to prefer the pleasures of intellect to the pleasures of sense.

It is a question of some moment whether the intercourse of the sexes, in a reasonable state of society, would be promiscuous, or whether each man would select for himself a partner to whom he will adhere as long as that adherence shall continue to be the choice of both parties. Probability seems to be greatly in favour of the latter. Perhaps this side of the alternative is most favourable to population. Perhaps it would suggest itself in preference to the man who would wish to maintain the several propensities of his frame, in the order due to their relative importance, and to prevent a merely sensual appetite from engrossing excessive attention. It is scarcely to be imagined that this commerce, in any state of society, will be stripped of its adjuncts, and that men will as willingly hold it with a woman whose personal and mental qualities they disapprove as with one of a different description. But it is the nature of the human mind to persist, for a certain length of time, in its opinion or choice. The parties therefore, having acted upon selection, are not likely to forget this selection when the interview is over. Friendship, if by friendship we understand that affection for an individual which is measured singly by what we know of his worth, is one of the most exquisite gratifications, perhaps one of the most improving exercises, of a rational mind. Friendship therefore may be expected to come in aid of the sexual intercourse, to refine its grossness, and increase its delight. All these arguments are calculated to determine our judgement in favour of marriage as a salutary and respectable institution, but not of that species of marriage in which there is no room for repentance and to which liberty and hope are equally strangers.

Admitting these principles therefore as the basis of the sexual commerce, what opinion ought we to form respecting infidelity to this attachment? Certainly no ties ought to be imposed upon either party, preventing them from quitting the attachment, whenever their judgement directs them to quit it. With respect to such infidelities as are compatible with an intention to adhere to it, the point of principal importance is a determination to have recourse to no species of disguise. In ordinary cases, and where the periods of absence are of no long duration, it would seem that any inconstancy would reflect some portion of discredit on the person that practised it. It would argue that the person's propensities were not under that kind of subordination which virtue and self-government appear to prescribe. But inconstancy, like any other temporary dereliction, would not be found incompatible with a character of uncommon excellence. What, at present, renders it, in many instances, peculiarly loathsome is its being practised in a clandestine manner. It leads to a train of falsehood and a concerted hypocrisy, than which there is scarcely anything that more eminently depraves and degrades the human mind.

The mutual kindness of persons of an opposite sex will, in such a state, fall under the same system as any other species of friendship. Exclusively of groundless and obstinate attachments, it will be impossible for me to live in the world without finding in one man a worth superior to that of another. To this man I shall feel kindness in exact proportion to my apprehension of his worth. The case will be the same with respect to the other sex. I shall assiduously cultivate the intercourse of that woman whose moral and intellectual accomplishments strike me in the most powerful manner. But it may happen that other men will feel for her the same preference that I do. This will create no difficulty. We may all enjoy her conversation; and, her choice being declared, we shall all be wise enough to consider the sexual commerce as unessential to our regard. It is a mark of the extreme depravity of our present habits that we are inclined to suppose the sexual commerce necessary to the advantages arising from the purest friendship. It is by no means indispensable that the female to whom each man attaches himself in that matter should appear to each the most deserving and excellent of her sex. . . .

THOMAS ROBERT MALTHUS

(1766–1834)

On the Principle of Population As It Affects the Future Improvement of Society (1798) was inspired by an argument Malthus had with his father over the feasibility of William Godwin's arguments for utopia in *Enquiry Concerning Political Justice.** Godwin's disregard of the empirical relationship between population growth and food supply made his perfect society a dangerous model for planning social change. After perhaps a few generations of utopian experience, the elimination of restraints on sexual desire and self-preservation would lead to overwhelming population growth and then a fierce struggle for survival. Present social institutions, Malthus argues, are required to control the behavior of beings ruled by self-love rather than benevolence.

Malthus's *Principle of Population* received a hostile reception from an audience that sought optimism in theories of nature and human nature to offset the gloom of contemporary political events, but his later influence on Charles Darwin's *On the Origin of Species* (1859) vindicated his insights on competition and survival. After a contemplative, scholarly life, Malthus died of heart disease on 23 December 1834.

from An Essay on the Principle of Population

(1798)

— *from* CHAPTER I —

The great and unlooked-for discoveries that have taken place of late years in natural philosophy; the increasing diffusion of general knowledge from the extension of the art of printing; the ardent and unshackled spirit of inquiry that prevails throughout the lettered, and even unlettered world; the new and extraordinary lights that have been thrown on political subjects, which dazzle, and astonish the understanding; and particularly that tremendous phenomenon in the political horizon the French Revolution, which, like a blazing comet, seems destined either to inspire with fresh life and vigour, or to scorch up and destroy the shrinking inhabitants of the earth, have all concurred to lead many able men into the opinion, that we were touching on a period big with the most important changes, changes that would in some measure be decisive of the future fate of mankind.

It has been said, that the great question is now at issue, whether man shall henceforth start forwards with accelerated velocity towards illimitable, and hitherto unconceived improvement; or be condemned to a perpetual oscillation between happiness and misery, and after every effort remain still at an immeasurable distance from the wished-for goal. . . .

I have read some of the speculations on the perfectibility of man and of society, with great pleasure.[1] I have been warmed and delighted with the enchanting picture which they hold forth. I ardently wish for such happy improvements. But I see great, and, to my understanding, unconquerable difficulties in the way to them. These difficulties it is my present purpose to state; declaring, at the same time, that so far from exulting in them, as a cause of triumph over the friends of innovation, nothing would give me greater pleasure than to see them completely removed. . . .

I think I may fairly make two postulata.

First, that food is necessary to the existence of man.

Secondly, that the passion between the sexes is necessary, and will remain nearly in its present state.

These two laws ever since we have had any knowledge of mankind, appear to have been fixed laws of our nature; and, as we have not hitherto seen any alteration in them, we have no right to conclude that they will ever cease to be

[1] In English the works of William Godwin, Adam Smith, and Jeremy Bentham, but also the works of French *philosophes*.

what they now are, without an immediate act of power in that Being who first arranged the system of the universe; and for the advantage of his creatures, still executes, according to fixed laws, all its various operations. . . .

Assuming then, my postulata as granted, I say, that the power of population is indefinitely greater than the power in the earth to produce subsistence for man.

Population, when unchecked, increases in a geometrical ratio. Subsistence increases only in an arithmetical ratio. A slight acquaintance with numbers will show the immensity of the first power in comparison of the second.

By that law of our nature which makes food necessary to the life of man, the effects of these two unequal powers must be kept equal.

This implies a strong and constantly operating check on population from the difficulty of subsistence. This difficulty must fall somewhere; and must necessarily be severely felt by a large portion of mankind.

Through the animal and vegetable kingdoms, nature has scattered the seeds of life abroad with the most profuse and liberal hand. She has been comparatively sparing in the room, and the nourishment necessary to rear them. The germs of existence contained in this spot of earth, with ample food, and ample room to expand in, would fill millions of worlds in the course of a few thousand years. Necessity, that imperious all-pervading law of nature, restrains them within the prescribed bounds. The race of plants, and the race of animals shrink under this great restrictive law. And the race of man cannot, by any efforts of reason, escape from it. Among plants and animals its effects are waste of seed, sickness, and premature death. Among mankind, misery and vice. The former, misery, is an absolutely necessary consequence of it. Vice is a highly probable consequence, and we therefore see it abundantly prevail; but it ought not, perhaps, to be called an absolutely necessary consequence. The ordeal of virtue is to resist all temptation to evil.

—*from* CHAPTER X—

The great error under which Mr Godwin labours throughout his whole work, is, the attributing almost all the vices and misery that are seen in civil society to human institutions. Political regulations, and the established administration of property, are with him the fruitful sources of all evil, the hotbeds of all the crimes that degrade mankind. Were this really a true state of the case, it would not seem a hopeless task to remove evil completely from the world; and reason seems to be the proper and adequate instrument for effecting so great a purpose. But the truth is, that though human institutions appear to be the obvious and obtrusive causes of much mischief to mankind; yet, in reality, they are light and superficial, they are mere feathers that float on the surface, in comparison with those deeper-seated causes of impurity that corrupt the springs, and render turbid the whole stream of human life. . . .

I have already pointed out the error of supposing that no distress and difficulty would arise from an overcharged population before the earth absolutely refused to produce any more. But let us imagine for a moment Mr Godwin's beautiful system of equality realized in its utmost purity, and see how soon this difficulty might be expected to press under so perfect a form of society. A theory that will not admit of application cannot possibly be just.

Let us suppose all the causes of misery and vice in this island removed. War and contention cease. Unwholesome trades and manufactories do not exist. Crowds no longer collect together in great and pestilent cities for purposes of court intrigue, of commerce, and vicious gratifications. Simple, healthy, and rational amusements take place of drinking, gaming and debauchery. There are no towns sufficiently large to have any prejudicial effects on the human constitution. The greater part of the happy inhabitants of this terrestrial paradise live in hamlets and farmhouses scattered over the face of the country. Every house is clean, airy, sufficiently roomy, and in a healthy situation. All men are equal. The labours of luxury are at end. And the necessary labours of agriculture are shared amicably among all. The number of persons, and the produce of the island, we suppose to be the same as at present. The spirit of benevolence, guided by impartial justice, will divide this produce among all the members of the society according to their wants. Though it would be impossible that they should all have animal food every day, yet vegetable food, with meat occasionally, would satisfy the desires of a frugal people, and would be sufficient to preserve them in health, strength, and spirits.

Mr Godwin considers marriage as a fraud and a monopoly. Let us suppose the commerce of the sexes established upon principles of the most perfect freedom. Mr Godwin does not think himself that this freedom would lead to a promiscuous intercourse; and in this I perfectly agree with him. The love of variety is a vicious, corrupt, and unnatural taste, and could not prevail in any great degree in a simple and virtuous state of society. Each man would probably select himself a partner, to whom he would adhere as long as that adherence continued to be the choice of both parties. It would be of little consequence, according to Mr Godwin, how many children a woman had, or to whom they belonged. Provisions and assistance would spontaneously flow from the quarter in which they abounded, to the quarter that was deficient. And every man would be ready to furnish instruction to the rising generation according to his capacity.

I cannot conceive a form of society so favourable upon the whole to population. The irremediableness of marriage, as it is at present constituted, undoubtedly deters many from entering into that state. An unshackled intercourse on the contrary, would be a most powerful incitement to early attachments: and as we are supposing no anxiety about the future support of children to exist, I do not conceive that there would be one woman in a hundred, of twenty three, without a family.

With these extraordinary encouragements to population, and every cause of depopulation, as we have supposed, removed, the numbers would necessarily increase faster than in any society that has ever yet been known. . . .

Difficult, however, as it might be, to double the average produce of the island in twenty-five years, let us suppose it effected. At the expiration of the first period therefore, the food, though almost entirely vegetable, would be sufficient to support in health, the doubled population of 14 millions.

During the next period of doubling, where will the food be found to satisfy the importunate demands of the increasing numbers? Where is the fresh land to turn up? Where is the dressing necessary to improve that which is already in cultivation? There is no person with the smallest knowledge of land, but would say, that it was impossible that the average produce of the country could be increased during the second twenty five years by a quantity equal to what it at present yields. Yet we will suppose this increase, however improbable, to take place. The exuberant strength of the argument allows of almost any concession. Even with this concession, however, there would be 7 millions at the expiration of the second term, unprovided for. A quantity of food equal to the frugal support of 21 millions, would be to be divided among 28 millions.

Alas! what becomes of the picture where men lived in the midst of plenty; where no man was obliged to provide with anxiety and pain for his restless wants; where the narrow principle of selfishness did not exist; where mind was delivered from her perpetual anxiety about corporal support, and free to expatiate in the field of thought which is congenial to her. This beautiful fabric of imagination vanishes at the severe touch of truth. The spirit of benevolence, cherished and invigorated by plenty, is repressed by the chilling breath of want. The hateful passions that had vanished, reappear. The mighty law of self-preservation, expels all the softer and more exalted emotions of the soul. The temptations to evil are too strong for human nature to resist. The corn is plucked before it is ripe, or secreted in unfair proportions; and the whole black train of vices that belong to falsehood are immediately generated. Provisions no longer flow in for the support of the mother with a large family. The children are sickly from insufficient food. The rosy flush of health gives place to the pallid cheek and hollow eye of misery. Benevolence yet lingering in a few bosoms, makes some faint expiring struggles, till at length self-love resumes his wonted empire, and lords it triumphant over the world.

No human institutions here existed, to the perverseness of which Mr Godwin ascribes the original sin of the worst men. No opposition had been produced by them between public and private good. No monopoly had been created of those advantages which reason directs to be left in common. No man had been goaded to the breach of order by unjust laws. Benevolence had established her reign in all hearts: and yet in so short a period as within fifty years, violence, oppression, falsehood, misery, every hateful vice, and every form of distress, which degrade and sadden the present state of society, seem to have been generated by the most imperious circumstances, by laws inherent in the nature of man, and absolutely independent of all human regulations. . . .

JANE MARCET

(1769–1858)

Jane Haldimand Marcet was the daughter of a wealthy Swiss merchant based in London. She married Dr. Alexander Marcet in 1799 and began writing on scientific topics to educate a curious lay audience. She became widely known for three textbooks at a time when textbooks in the sciences were unheard of: *Conversations on Chemistry, intended more especially for the Female Sex* (1806), which went into 16 editions and sold over 160,000 copies in the United States alone; *Conversations on Natural Philosophy* (1819), which was directed at young children; and her classic, *Conversations on Political Economy* (1816), which was often reprinted and re-edited (1817, 1821, 1824). The famous utilitarian economist David McCulloch stated in 1845 that *Conversations on Political Economy* was the "best introduction to the science that has yet appeared." It remains a lucid, if elementary, exposition of Adam Smith's economic theory, while also revealing the social perspective and values of a rising middle class.

from Conversations on Political Economy

(1816)

—*from* INTRODUCTION—

CAROLINE: Well, after all, Mrs. B., ignorance of political economy is a very excusable deficiency in women. It is the business of Government to reform the prejudices and errors which prevail respecting it; and, as we are never likely to become legislators, is it not just as well that we should remain in happy ignorance of evils which we have no power to remedy?

MRS. B.: When you plead in favour of ignorance, there is a strong presumption that you are in the wrong. If a more general knowledge of political economy prevented women from propagating errors respecting it, in the education of their children, no trifling good would ensue. Childhood is spent in acquiring ideas, adolescence in discriminating and rejecting those which are false: how greatly we should facilitate this labour by diminishing the number of errors imbibed in early youth, and by inculcating such ideas only as are founded in truth.

—*from* CONVERSATION X—

ON THE CONDITION OF THE POOR

CAROLINE: I have been reflecting ever since our last interview, Mrs. B., whether there were no means of averting or at least alleviating the misery resulting from an excess of population; and it appears to me, that though we have not the same resource in land as America, yet we have large tracts of waste land, which, by being brought into cultivation, would produce an additional stock of subsistence.

MRS. B.: You must remember that industry is limited by the extent of capital, and that no more labourers can be employed than we have the means of maintaining; they work for their daily bread, and without obtaining it, they neither could nor would work. All the labourers which the capital of the country can maintain being disposed of, the only question is, whether it be better to employ them on land already in a state of cultivation, or in breaking up and bringing into culture new lands; and this point may safely be trusted to the decision of the landed proprietors, as it is no less their interest than that of the labouring classes that the greatest possible quantity of produce should be raised. To a certain extent it has been found more advantageous to lay out capital in improving the culture of old land, rather than to employ it in bringing new land into tillage; because the soil of the waste land is extremely poor and ungrateful, and requires a great deal to be laid out on it before it brings in a return. But there is often capital sufficient for both these purposes, and of late years we have seen not only prodigious improvements in the processes of agriculture throughout the country, but a great number of commons inclosed and cultivated.

CAROLINE: I fear you will think me inconsistent, but I cannot help regretting the inclosure of commons; they are the only resource of the cottagers for the maintenance of a few lean cattle. Let me once more quote my favourite Goldsmith:[1]

> Where then, ah! where shall poverty reside,
> To 'scape the pressure of contiguous pride?
> If to some common's fenceless limits stray'd,
> He drives his flock to pick the scanty blade,
> Those fenceless fields the sons of wealth deride,
> And e'en the bare-worn common is deny'd.

MRS. B.: You should recollect that we do not admit poets to be very good authority in political economy. If, instead of feeding a few lean cattle, a common, by being inclosed, will fatten a much greater number of fine cattle, you must allow that the quantity of subsistence will be increased, and the poor, though in a less direct manner, will fare the better for it. Labourers are required to inclose and cultivate those commons, the neighbouring cottagers are employed for that purpose, and this additional demand for labour turns to their immediate advantage. They not only receive an indemnity for their loss of right of common, but they find purchasers for the cattle they can no longer maintain, in the proprietors of the new inclosures.

When Finchley Common was inclosed, it was divided amongst the inhabitants of that parish; and the cottagers and little shopkeepers sold the small slips of land which fell to their share, to men of greater property, who thus became possessed of a sufficient quantity to make it answer to them to inclose and cultivate it; and the poorer classes were amply remunerated for their loss of commonage by the sale of their respective lots. . . .

But, to return to the population of England; the more we find ourselves unable to provide for an overgrown population, the more desirous we should be to avail ourselves of those means which tend to prevent the evil;—such, for instance, as a general diffusion of knowledge, which would excite greater attention in the lower classes to their future interests.

CAROLINE: Surely you would not teach political economy to the labouring classes, Mrs. B.?

MRS. B.: No; but I would endeavour to give the rising generation such an education as would render them not only moral and religious, but industrious, frugal, and provident. In proportion as the mind is informed, we are able to calculate the consequences of our actions: it is the infant and the savage who live only for the present moment; those whom instruction has taught to think, reflect upon the past and look forward to the future. Education gives rise to prudence, not only by enlarging our understandings, but by softening our feelings, by humanising the heart, and promoting amiable affections. The rude and inconsiderate peasant marries without either foreseeing or caring for the miseries he may entail on his wife and children; but he who has been taught to value the comforts and decencies of life, will not heedlessly involve himself and all that is dear to him in poverty, and its long train of miseries.

CAROLINE: I am very happy to hear that you think instruction may produce this desirable end, since the zeal for the education of the poor that has been displayed of late years gives every prospect of success; and in a few years more, it may perhaps be impossible to meet with a child who cannot read and write.

MRS. B.: The highest advantages, both religious, moral, and political, may be expected to result from this general ardour for the instruction of the poor. No great or decided improvement can be effected in the manners of the people but by the education of the rising generation. It is difficult, if not impossible, to change the habits of men whose characters are formed and settled; the prejudices of ignorance that have grown up with us, will not yield to new impressions; whilst youth and innocence may be moulded into any form you choose to give them. . . .

But independently of schools, and the various institutions for the education of youth, there is an establishment among the lower classes which is peculiarly calculated to inculcate lessons of prudence and economy. I mean the Benefit Clubs, or Friendly Societies; the members of which, by contributing a small stipend monthly, accumulate a fund which furnishes them relief and aid in times of sickness or distress. These associations have spread throughout the country, and their good effects are rendered evident by comparing the condition of such of the labouring classes as belong to them, with those of the same district who have no resource in times of distress, but parochial relief or private charity. The

[1] See also John Clare's "The Moors."*

former are comparatively cleanly, industrious, sober, frugal, respecting themselves, and respected by others; depending in times of casual sickness or accident on funds created by their own industry, they maintain an honourable pride and independence of character; whilst the latter, in a season of distress, become a prey to dirt and wretchedness; and being dissatisfied with the scantiness of parish relief, they are often driven to the commission of crimes. . . .

An institution has within a very few years been established in Scotland, and is, I am happy to say, now rapidly spreading in England, which is likely to prove still more advantageous to the lower classes than the benefit clubs. "The object of this institution," says the Edinburgh Review, No. 49., "is to open to the lower orders a place of deposit for their small savings, with the allowance of a reasonable monthly interest, and with full liberty of withdrawing their money, at any time, either in whole or in part,—an accommodation which it is impracticable for the ordinary banks to furnish. Such an establishment has been called *a Saving Bank*."

These institutions afford the greatest encouragement to industry, by securing the property of the labouring poor. How frequently it happens that an industrious man, after having toiled to accumulate a small sum, is tempted to lay it out in a lottery ticket, is inveigled by sharpers to a gambling table, or induced by adventurers to engage in some ill-judged and hazardous speculation; to lend it to a distressed or a treacherous friend,—not to mention the risk of its being lost or stolen. If we succeed in establishing banks in different districts in England, where the poor may without difficulty or trouble deposit the trifle they can spare from their earnings, and where, as an additional inducement, some interest is allowed them for their money, all this mischief will be avoided, and we may hope that the influence of prudential habits will help to raise the poor above the degrading resource of parochial assistance, and prepare the way for the abolition of the poor-rate—a tax which falls so heavily on the middling classes of people, and which is said to give rise to still more poverty than it relieves.

CAROLINE: I cannot understand that.

MRS. B.: The certainty that the parish is bound to succour their wants, renders the poor less apprehensive of indigence than if they were convinced that they must suffer all the wretchedness it entails. When a young man marries, without having the means of supporting his family by his labour, and without having made some little provision against accidents or sickness, he depends upon the parish as a never-failing resource. A profligate man knows that if he spend his wages at the public-house instead of providing for his family, his wife and children can at worst but go to the poor-house. Parish-relief thus becomes the very cause of the mischief which it professes to remedy. . . .

CAROLINE: But what is to be done; the poor cannot be allowed to starve, even when idle and vicious?

MRS. B.: Certainly not; and besides, the wife and children of a profligate man are often the innocent victims of his misconduct. Then there are frequently cases of casual distress, which no prudence could foresee nor guard against; under these circumstances the poor-rate could not be abolished without occasioning the most cruel distress. I know, therefore, of no other remedy to this evil than the slow and gradual effect of education. By enlightening the minds of the lower classes, their moral habits are improved, and they rise above that state of degradation in which all feelings of dignity and independence are extinguished.

CAROLINE: But, alas! how many years will elapse before these happy results can take place. I am impatient that benefits should be immediately and universally diffused; their progress is in general so slow and partial, that there is but a small chance of our living to see their effects.

MRS. B.: There is some gratification in looking forward to an improved state of society, even if we should not live to witness it.

CAROLINE: Since it is so little in our power to accelerate its progress, we must endeavour to be contented with the prospect of improvement: but I confess that I cannot help regretting the want of sovereign power to forward measures so conducive to the happiness of mankind.

. . .

WILLIAM COBBETT

(1763–1835)

William Cobbett published over 20,000,000 words in a lifetime of political journalism in England and America. Although his political sympathies changed from conservative to radical over the course of his career, he always campaigned fiercely against personal abuses of power, regardless of who was in power. Consequently, he was often charged with libel. A conviction in England cost him a large fine and two years in Newgate Prison. Cobbett adopted the pseudonym of Peter Porcupine in America, where he published the popular but pro-British *Porcupine's Gazette* (1797–1799). After libel action was brought against him in Philadelphia, Cobbett returned to England to publish his immensely popular *Political Register* from 1802 on. The son of a farmer, Cobbett was a self-educated man, devoted to educating the poor and voicing their grievances in witty and sometimes scurrilous arguments presented in "plain, broad, downright English" (Hazlitt*). Cobbett was elected a Member of Parliament from Oldham in 1832.

Cobbett's Poor Man's Friend

or Useful Information and Advice for the Working Classes in a Series of Letters, addressed to the Working Classes of Preston.

(1826)

Burghelerz, Hampshire, 22nd August, 1826.

My Excellent Friends,

37. Amongst all the new, the strange, the unnatural, the monstrous things that mark the present times, or, rather, that have grown out of the present system of governing this country, there is, in my opinion, hardly any thing more monstrous, or even so monstrous, as the language that is now become fashionable, relative to the condition and the treatment of that part of the community, which are usually denominated the POOR; by which word I mean to designate the persons who, from age, infirmity, helplessness, or from want of the means of gaining any thing by labour, become destitute of a sufficiency of food, or of raiment, and are in danger of perishing if they be not relieved. Such are the persons that we mean, when we talk of THE POOR; and, I repeat, that, amongst all the monstrous things of these monstrous days, nothing is, in my opinion, so monstrous, as the language which we now constantly hear, relative to the condition and treatment of this part of the community.

38. Nothing can be more common than to read, in the newspapers, descriptions the most horrible of the sufferings of *the Poor,* in various parts of England, but particularly in the North. It is related of them, that they eat horse-flesh, grains, and have been detected in eating out of pig-troughs. In short, they are represented as being far worse fed and worse lodged, than the greater part of the pigs. These statements of the *newspapers* may be false, or, at least, only partially true; but, at a public meeting of rate-payers, at Manchester, on the 17th of August, Mr. Baxter, the Chairman, said, that some of the POOR had been *starved to death,* and that *tens of thousands were upon the point of starving;* and, at the same meeting, Mr. Potter gave a detail, which showed, that Mr. Baxter's general description was true. Other accounts, very nearly official, and, at any rate, being of unquestionable authenticity, concur so fully with the statements made at the Manchester Meeting, that it is impossible not to believe, that a great number of thousands of persons are now on the point of perishing for want of food, and *that many have actually perished from that cause;* and that this has taken place, and is taking place, IN ENGLAND.

39. There is, then, no doubt of the existence of the disgraceful and horrid facts; but, that which is as horrid as are the facts themselves, and even more horrid than those facts, is the cool and *unresentful* language and manner, in which the facts are usually spoken of. Those who write about the misery and starvation, in Lancashire and Yorkshire, never appear to think *that any body is to blame,* even when the poor die with hunger. The Ministers ascribe the

calamity to *"over-trading"*; the cotton and cloth and other master-manufacturers ascribe it to *"a want of paper-money,"* or, to the *Corn-Bill*; others ascribe the calamity to the *taxes.* These last are right; but, what have these things to do with the treatment of the poor? What have these things to do with the horrid facts relative to the condition and starvation of English people? It is very true, that the enormous taxes which we pay on account of loans made to carry on the late unjust wars, on account of a great standing army in time of peace, on account of pensions, sinecures and grants, and on account of *a Church,* which, besides, swallows up so large a part of the produce of the land and the labour; it is very true, that these enormous taxes, co-operating with the paper-money and its innumerable monopolies; it is very true, that *these enormous taxes,* thus associated, have produced the ruin in trade, manufactures and commerce, and have, of course, produced the *low wages* and the *want of employment:* this is very true; but, it is not less true, that, be wages or employment as they may, the poor are not to perish with hunger, or with cold, while the rest of the community have food and raiment more than the latter want for their own sustenance. The LAW OF ENGLAND says, that there shall be no person to suffer from want of food and raiment. It has placed *officers* in every parish to see that no person suffer from this sort of want; and, lest these officers should not do their duty, *it commands all the magistrates* to hear the complaints of the poor, and to compel the officers to do their duty. The LAW OF ENGLAND has provided ample means of relief for the poor; for, it has authorized the officers, or overseers, to get from the rich inhabitants of the parish as much money as *is wanted* for the purpose, without any limit as to amount; and, in order, that the overseers may have no excuse of inability to make people pay, the law has armed them with powers of a nature the most efficacious and the most efficient and most prompt in their operation. In short, the language of the LAW, to the overseer, is this: "Take care that no person suffer from hunger, or from cold; and, that you may be sure not to fail of the means of obeying this my command, I give you, as far as shall be necessary for this purpose, full power over all the lands, all the houses, all the goods, and all the cattle, in your parish." To the justices of the Peace the LAW says: "Lest the overseer should neglect his duty; lest, in spite of my command to him, any one should suffer from hunger or cold, I command you to be ready to hear the complaint of every sufferer from such neglect; I command you to summon the offending overseer, and to compel him to do his duty."

40. Such being the language of the LAW, is it not a monstrous state of things, when we hear it commonly and coolly stated, that many thousands of persons, in England, are *upon the point of starvation*; that *thousands will die of hunger and cold next winter*; that many have *already died of hunger*; and, when we hear all this, unaccompanied with one word of *complaint against any overseer,* or any *justice of the peace!* Is not this state of things perfectly monstrous? A state of things, in which it appears to be taken for granted, that the LAW is nothing, when it is intended to operate as a protection to the poor! Law is always law: if one part of the law may be, with impunity, set at defiance, why not another and every other part of the law? If the law, which provides for the succour of the poor, for the preservation of their lives, may be, with impunity, set at defiance, why should there not be impunity for setting at defiance the law, which provides for the security of the property and the lives of the rich? If you, in Lancashire, were to read, in an account of a meeting in Hampshire, that, here, the farmers and gentlemen were constantly and openly robbed; that the poor were daily breaking into their houses, and knocking their brains out; and that it was expected, that great part of them would be killed very soon: if you, in Lancashire, were to hear this said of the state of Hampshire, what would you say? Say! Why, you would say, to be sure, "Where is the LAW; where are the constables, the justices, the juries, the judges, the sheriffs and the hangmen? Where can that *Hampshire* be? It, surely, never can be in Old England! It must be some savage country, where such enormities can be committed, and where even those, who talk of and who *lament* the evils, never utter one word in the way of *blame* of the perpetrators." And, if you were called upon to pay taxes, or to make subscriptions in money, to furnish the means of protection to the unfortunate rich people in Hampshire, would you not say, and with good reason, "No: what should we do this for? The people of Hampshire have the SAME LAW that we have; they are under the same Government; *let them duly enforce that law*; and, then, they will stand in no need of money from us to provide for their protection."

41. This is what common sense says would be *your* language in such a case; and, does not common sense say, that the people of Hampshire, and of every other part of England, will thus think, when they are told of the sufferings, and the starvation, in Lancashire and Yorkshire? The report of the Manchester ley-payers, which took place on the 17th of August, reached me in a friend's house, in this little village; and, when another friend, who was present, read, in the speeches of Mr. BAXTER and

MR. POTTER, that tens of thousands of Lancashire people were *on the point of starvation,* and that many had already *actually died from starvation*; and when he perceived, that even those gentlemen uttered not a word of *complaint* against either overseer or justices of the peace, he exclaimed: "What! are there *no poor-laws* in Lancashire! Where, amidst all this starvation, is the overseer? Where is the justice of the peace? Surely that Lancashire can never be *in England!*"

42. The observations of this gentleman are those which occur to every man of sense; when he hears the horrid accounts of the sufferings in the manufacturing districts; for, though we are all well aware, that the burden of the poor-rates presses, at this time, with peculiar weight on the landowners and occupiers, and on owners and occupiers of other real property, in those districts, we are equally well aware, that those owners and occupiers *have derived great benefits* from that vast population that now presses upon them. There is *land,* in the parish in which I am now writing, and belonging to the farm in the house of which I am, which land would not let for 20*s.* a statute acre; while land, not so good, would let, in any part of Lancashire, near to the manufactories, at 60*s.* or 80*s.* a statute acre. The same may be said with regard to *houses.* And, pray, are the owners and occupiers, who have gained so largely by the manufacturing works being near their lands and houses; are they, *now,* to complain, if the vicinage of these same works causes a charge of rates *there,* heavier than exists *here?* Are the owners and occupiers of Lancashire to enjoy *an age of advantages* from the labours of the spinners and the weavers; and are they, when a reverse comes, *to bear none of the disadvantages?* Are they to make no sacrifices, in order to save from perishing those industrious and ever-toiling creatures, by the labours of whom their land and houses have been augmented in value, three, five, or perhaps, tenfold? None but the most unjust of mankind can answer these questions in the affirmative.

43. But, as *greediness* is never at a loss for excuses for the hard-heartedness that it is always ready to practise, it is said, that *the whole of the rents* of the land and the houses would not suffice for the purpose; that is to say, that if the poor-rates were to be made so high as to leave the tenant no means of paying rent, even then, some of the poor must go without a sufficiency of food. I have no doubt that, in particular instances, this would be the case. But for cases like this the LAW has amply provided; for, in every case of this sort, *adjoining parishes* may be made to *assist* the hard-pressed parish; and if the pressure become severe on these adjoining parishes, those *next adjoining them* may be made to assist: and thus the call upon adjoining parishes may be extended till it reach *all over the county.* So good, so benignant, so wise, so foreseeing, and so effectual, is this, the very best of all our good old laws! This law, or rather code of laws, distinguishes England from all the other countries in the world, *except the United States of America,* where, while hundreds of other English statutes have been abolished, this law has always remained in full force, this great law of mercy and humanity, which says, that *no human being that treads English ground shall perish for want of food and raiment.* For such poor persons as are *unable to work* the law provides food and clothing; and it commands that *work* shall be provided for such as are able to work; and *cannot otherwise get employment.* This law was passed more than *two hundred years* ago. Many attempts have been made to *chip it away,* and some have been made to destroy it altogether; but it still exists, and every man who does not wish to see general desolation take place, will do his best to cause it to be duly and conscientiously executed.

44. Having now, my friends of Preston, stated what the law is, and also the reasons for its honest enforcement in the particular case immediately before us, I will next endeavour to show you that it is founded in the law of nature, and that, were it not for the provisions of this law, people would, according to the opinions of the greatest lawyers, have *a right* to *take* food and raiment sufficient to preserve them from perishing; and that *such taking* would be neither *felony* nor *larceny.* This is a matter of the greatest importance; it is a most momentous question; for if it be settled in the affirmative—if it be settled that it is *not felony, nor larceny,* to take other men's goods without their assent, and even against their will, when such taking is absolutely necessary to the preservation of life, how great, how imperative, is the duty of affording, if possible, *that relief which will prevent such necessity!* In other words, how imperative it is on all overseers and justices to obey the law with alacrity; and how weak are those persons who look to *"grants"* and *"subscriptions,"* to supply the place of the execution of this, the most important of all the laws that constitute the basis of English society! And if this question be settled in the affirmative; if we find the most learned of lawyers and most wise of men, maintaining the affirmative of this proposition; if we find them maintaining, that it is neither *felony* nor *larceny* to take food, in case of *extreme necessity,* though without the assent, and even against the will of the owner, what are we to think of those, (and they are not few in number, nor weak in power), who, animated with the savage soul of the Scotch *feelosophers,* would wholly abolish the poor-laws, or, at least, render them of little effect, and thereby constantly keep thousands exposed to this dire necessity!

SCIENCE AND NATURE

THE SCIENTIFIC STUDY of nature and the human body during the period of 1780 to 1830 was as revolutionary, as international, and often as contentious as the politics. In England, Joseph Priestley spoke of "few, if any, revolutions in science so great, so sudden, and so general, as . . . *the new system of chemistry.*" The American Samuel Miller attributed scientific advance to "the swarms of inquirers and experimenters every where" flourishing in an age of "free inquiry."

Students of science were sensitive to the ideological and political implications of experimental results, theory, and the life of scientists. Benjamin Franklin became a Promethean hero to the scientists of the Birmingham Lunar Society—Priestley, James Watt, Erasmus Darwin,* Matthew Boulton—for gathering electricity from the heavens and establishing democracy on earth. Darwin hailed the political significance of Lavoisier's *Elements of Chemistry* (published in 1789, the year of the fall of the Bastille) in a letter to Watt, discoverer of the steam engine: "Do you not congratulate your grandchildren on the dawn of universal liberty? I feel myself becoming all french both in chemistry and politics." Priestley wrote in his *Letters to the Philosophers and Politicians of France, on the Subject of Religion* (1793), that "with respect to philosophy, and especially chemistry . . . the age of mystery and deception . . . is now over, and rational and useful science has taken the place of solemn pretensions, absurd systems, and idle tricks."

The historical development of geology offers an especially compelling example of the spirit of the times influencing scientific paradigms. Researchers in geology could neither experimentally control nor reproduce the forces and phenomena they sought to explain. Geology was thus open to the prevailing *zeitgeist* for suggesting conceptual models to account for evidence of vast changes in the earth's surface. The French theory of "catastrophism" argued that the primeval earth had experienced violent and singular upheavals caused by volcanoes, floods, earthquakes, droughts, and storms. The geologist Deluc said that sublime terrestrial features, such as mountains and caverns, were "monuments" of the earth's revolutions. The Old Testament's Seven Days of Creation became in Buffon's *Epochs of Nature* (1778) the seven epochs of geological revolution, culminating in the appearance of early man on the steppes of Asia. Leading British geologist, Charles Lyell,* developed the countertheory of "uniformitarianism," which held that forces of geological change were permanent, rather than terminal, though they might proceed unnoticed because inexorable and gradual, rather than cataclysmal. Lyell's influential *Principles of Geology* (1830–1833) describes the earth as "a theatre of reiterated change, and . . . still the subject of slow, but never-ending fluctuations." Just as catastrophism accorded with French politics, so Lyell's theory suited the penchant of British politics for evolutionary progress towards the fulfillment of constitutional democracy.

In the entirely new field of electricity, there was an air of avid experimentalism, with fascinating speculation on the medical value of results for determining the difference between life and death.[1] Pioneered by Franklin in 1752 with his famous kite-and-key experiment, the study of electricity was encouraged by Priestley, who described it as "a field . . . but just opened, and requir[ing] no great stock of particular preparatory knowledge."

After the Italian Count Alessandro Volta (1745–1827) discovered that electricity could be generated mechanically, it became possible to test its applications in various settings. In 1791, an Italian physiologist, Luigi Galvani (1737–1798), theorized that the life force of the body was an electrical fluid produced in the brain. This theory stimulated experiments in "galvanism" on both dead and living bodies. Giovanni Aldini performed some of the most famous of these in England: in 1802, he wired and applied voltaic shocks to the head of a recently killed ox, which produced a series of reactions that made it appear revived; in 1803, Professor Aldini applied his electro-medical technology to a human corpse, which also displayed muscular and sensory convulsions that appeared weird, but sufficiently life-like to support the speculation that electricity was the principle of life.

Psychology, however, probably had the most pervasive impact on literary works and theory, because of its threat to mind, free will, and soul. As we may infer from our descriptions of chemistry, electricity, and geology, a fundamental assumption of science is that the phenomena of the physical world are causally determined in conformity with natural laws. Eighteenth-century metaphors for Nature emphasized its mechanical qualities. It was a clock that had been created and set in motion by an omnipotent, omniscient, and rational God, who now watched its operation from a distance. The purpose of the scientist was to apply human reason to uncover the inexorable laws of a rational Creator's grand design. But when John Locke (1632–1704) argued that the mind is governed by psychological laws comparable to physical laws, the danger to human freedom became manifest. Locke posited the mind as a blank slate, a *tabula rasa,* void of *a priori* knowledge, that operates by combining sense data according to laws of association. However, associationism inevitably implied predictability and the potential for psychological control. Misguided educationists theorized that behavior and thought might be predetermined by manipulating sense data.

In response to the metaphysical crisis begat by modern science, the German philosopher Friedrich von Schlegel (1772–1829) posited an organic, evolving world. It is difficult to appreciate the great impact of *organicism* on nineteenth-century thought without understanding that the Enlightenment had assumed a constant, perfect, and timeless physical universe, the laws of which obtain eternally. In his *System der Naturphilosophie* (1798–1799), Schlegel argued instead that change is inevitable, that nature is in a constant state of becoming, and that both good and evil are temporary conditions in an evolving universe.

[1] It is useful to know that most scientists of this time were trained in general university courses, especially in medicine, or prepared through apprenticeship. Medicine included anatomy, natural philosophy (physics and chemistry), *materia medica,* therapeutics, including medical botany, and physiology. There were few institutions for establishing norms and not many distinctions were made between "fields," or even between science and the humanities.

Even animate nature is in a process of moving from unconsciousness to consciousness and back again. History is therefore essential because "the explanation of an *organic* product, of an *organic* being, must be *historical,* not mechanical." The power of mind needed to understand a world running organically and unconsciously in an endless process of growth and decay is not reason, but imagination, which can grasp truths holistically, and intuitively, rather than trying to derive them from preconceived axioms and methods of reason and science.

The human imagination thus became the mental power that might overcome the threat of associationism. British poets and essayists of the early nineteenth century made enthusiastic and varied claims for the imagination having sacred powers. For Wordsworth, imagination is "but another name for absolute power / And clearest insight, amplitude of mind, / And Reason in her most exalted mood" (*Prelude,* XIV). Percy Bysshe Shelley finds the empathetic power of imagination to be "the greatest instrument of moral good," and poetry the medium that "administers to the effect [the good] by acting upon the cause [the morally refined imagination]" (*Defence of Poetry*). Coleridge, influenced deeply by Schlegel's organicism, emerged as the most influential literary theorist of the creative imagination.

In his essays on Shakespeare and in fragmentary comments on the nature of imagination in his literary biography, Coleridge claims that the human imagination and its creative acts are analogues to the creative power and acts of divinity. He theorizes that a "Primary Imagination" is the inherently creative faculty that unconsciously organizes and shapes sense-data into meaningful patterns. The primary imagination produces both the interior and the exterior worlds we consciously experience, what Immanuel Kant called the realm of *phenomenon.* A "Secondary Imagination" becomes the "echo of the [primary imagination]" as a willed, and therefore *conscious,* act of shaping or creation that first breaks up the patterns produced by the primary imagination or perception in order to create new patterns, new ideas, new images, which are most clearly articulated as new works of art. Like the "Infinite I AM," each human mind creates both its consciousness of itself *as a self* and the world in which it exists. The Creative Imagination, rather than Reason, or even Soul, becomes the spark of human divinity.

Nevertheless, David Hartley* (1705–1757) and Erasmus Darwin* (1731–1802) were attractive to writers of this period because, as medical scientists, they represented nature and mind in a way that promised reconciliation between matter and spirit. Hartley lived outside the time frame of this anthology, 1780–1830, but his *Observations on Man, His Frame, His Duty, and His Expectations* (1749) was given currency and renewed significance in an edition of 1791, edited (and embellished) by Priestley, who as chemist, political radical, and Unitarian minister, had concerns similar to the poets.

Darwin's merit to romantic writers was his rendering of the thesis of nature's sexual and emotional life in botanical poetry supported by annotations of vast medical and scientific learning. Darwin also developed a theory of evolution that anticipated the later work of his more famous grandson, Charles Darwin, whose *On the Origin of Species by Means of Natural Selection* appeared in 1859. Darwin was bold in arguing for evolution against two tenets of contemporary biology. The first of these was preformationist embryology, which held that either the sperm or the unfertilized embryo was a minute homunculus, "perfectly formed and complete," needing only to unfold and grow. The second, the stability of species, analogous to the Enlightenment's view of nature, held that life-forms are immutable, or constant, since the time of their creation. In his medical-scientific tome *Zoonomia: or the Laws of Organic Life* (1794–1796), Darwin said: "it would appear, that all nature exists in a state of perpetual improvement by laws impressed on the atoms of matter by the great CAUSE OF CAUSES; and that the world may still be in its infancy, and continue to improve FOR EVER AND EVER." In answer to the query, Why must evolution improve rather than abolish a species?, Darwin's answer is that a species develops in relation to its wants and desires because the Cause of Causes wills it so.

The writers included in this section—David Hartley, Erasmus Darwin, Frances Burney, Mary Shelley, and Charles Lyell—provide a multifaceted perspective on science from 1780 to 1830. Hartley, Darwin, and Lyell speak as scientists for the importance and promise of psychology, biology, and geology, respectively. Shelley and Burney speak for the lay point of view on the continuing dangers and shortcomings of modern science.

ERASMUS DARWIN

(1731–1802)

Erasmus Darwin's reputation in general medicine reached George III, who wanted him as court physician, but Darwin refused to move from Lichfield to London. Darwin's medical tome *Zoonomia* (1794–1796) provided both a theory of generation and evolution in its first volume and a compendium of mental and physical pathologies with advice on treatment in its second. In his theory of evolution, Darwin anticipated the French naturalist Lamarck (1744–1829), rather than his more famous grandson, Charles Darwin (1809–1882), in asserting that the "wants" that life-forms experience in adapting to their environment cause physical changes that are passed on through heredity. Regarding human generation, Darwin believed that such wants or intentions are controlled in the imagination of the male during sexual intercourse. Darwin popularized his romantic biology in poems heavily annotated with botanical information. His most popular poetic production, *The Botanic Garden,* was inspired by Anna Seward's verses on his garden at Lichfield. The first part, *The Economy of Vegetation* (1792), deals with the physiology of plants; the second part, the *Loves of the Plants* (1789), allegorizes the sexual systems of plants in heroic couplets inspired by the "Botanic Muse." Contemporary scholarship continues to reveal the pervasive influence of Darwin's thought on many writers of the early nineteenth century.

from THE BOTANIC GARDEN, PART II

The Loves of the Plants

(1789)

— *from* CANTO I[1] —

(lines 1–56, 77–84, 131–142, 247–262, and 413–430)

Descend, ye hovering Sylphs! aerial Quires,
And sweep with little hands your silver lyres;
With fairy foot-steps print your grassy rings,
Ye Gnomes! accordant to the tinkling strings;
While in soft notes I tune to oaten reed
Gay hopes, and amorous sorrows of the mead.—
From giant Oaks, that wave their branches dark,
To the dwarf Moss, that clings upon their bark,
What Beaux and Beauties croud the gaudy groves,
And woo and win their vegetable Loves.[2]
How Snow-drops cold, and blue-eyed Harebels blend
Their tender tears, as o'er the stream they bend;
The love-sick Violet, and the Primrose pale
Bow their sweet heads, and whisper to the gale;
With secret sighs the Virgin Lily droops,
And jealous Cowslips hang their tawny cups.
How the young Rose in beauty's damask pride
Drinks the warm blushes of his bashful bride;
With honey'd lips enamour'd Woodbines meet,
Clasp with fond arms, and mix their kisses sweet.—

Stay thy soft-murmuring waters, gentle Rill;
Hush, whispering Winds, ye rustling Leaves, be still;
Rest, silver Butterflies, your quivering wings;

[1] The poem is organized according to the Linnean classification of 24 classes of plants, with all of their sexual permutations. The opening lines were composed by Anna Seward and appropriated without acknowledgement in Darwin's first anonymous edition of 1789.

[2] **vegetable Loves**: Linneus, the celebrated Swedish naturalist, has demonstrated, that all flowers contain families of male or females, or both; and on their marriages has constructed his invaluable system of Botany [E.D.].

Alight, ye Beetles, from your airy rings;
Ye painted Moths, your gold-eyed plumage furl,
Bow your wide horns, your spiral trunks uncurl;
Glitter, ye Glow-worms, on your mossy beds;
Descend, ye Spiders, on your lengthen'd threads;
Slide here, ye horned Snails, with varnish'd shells;
Ye Bee-nymphs, listen in your waxen cells! —

BOTANIC MUSE! who in this latter age
Led by your airy hand the Swedish sage,
Bad his keen eye your secret haunts explore
On dewy dell, high wood, and winding shore;
Say on each leaf how tiny Graces dwell;
How laugh the Pleasures in a blossom's bell;
How insect-Loves arise on cob-web wings,
Aim their light shafts, and point their little stings.

— [TENDER HUSBAND][3]

"First the tall CANNA[4] lifts his curled brow
Erect to heaven, and plights his nuptial vow;
The virtuous pair, in milder regions born,
Dread the rude blast of Autumn's icy morn;
Round the chill fair he folds his crimson vest,
And clasps the timorous beauty to his breast.

— [SELF-ADMIRER] —

Thy love, CALLITRICHE,[5] *two* Virgins share,
Smit with thy starry eye and radiant hair; —
On the green margin sits the youth, and laves
His floating train of tresses in the waves;
Sees his fair features paint the streams that pass,
And bends for ever o'er the watery glass.

[3] The bracketed subject titles for each section are given by Darwin in "Catalogue of the Poetic Exhibition" at the conclusion of the volume.

[4] **canna**: cane, or Indian reed. One male and one female inhabit each flower. [Throughout, pistils are female; stamens / anthers are male. *Canna* or cane is one of the very few dyads of the garden.] It is brought from between the tropics to our hothouses, and bears a beautiful crimson flower; the seeds are used as shot by the Indians, and are strung for prayer-beads in some catholic countries [E.D.].

[5] **callitriche**: fine-hair, stargrass. One male and two females inhabit each flower. The upper leaves grow in form of a star, whence it is called Stellaria Aquatica by Ray and others; its stems and leaves float far on the water, and are often so matted together, as to bear a person walking on them. The male sometimes lives in a separate flower [E.D.].

— [RIVAL LOVERS] —

Two brother swains of COLLIN'S[6] gentle name,
The same their features, and their forms the same,
With rival love for fair COLLINIA sigh,
Knit the dark brow, and roll the unsteady eye.
With sweet concern the pitying beauty mourns,
And sooths with smiles the jealous pair by turns.

— [MONSTER HUSBAND] —

With strange deformity PLANTAGO[7] treads,
A Monster-birth! and lifts his hundred heads;
Yet with soft love a gentle belle he charms,
And clasps the beauty in his hundred arms.
So hapless DESDEMONA, fair and young,
Won by OTHELLO's captivating tongue,
Sigh'd o'er each strange and pitious tale, distress'd,
And sunk enamour'd on his sooty breast.

— [HARLOTS] —

The fell SILENE[8] and her sisters fair,
Skill'd in destruction, spread the viscous snare.

[6] **collinsonia**: two males, one female. I have lately observed a very singular circumstance in this flower; the two males stand widely diverging from each other, and the female bends herself into contact first with one of them, and after some time leaves this, and applies herself to the other. It is probable one of the anthers may be mature before the other? See note on Gloriosa, and Genista. The females in Nigella, devil in the bush, are very tall compared to the males; and bending over in a circle to them, give the flower some resemblance to a regal crown. The female of the epilobium angustifolium, rose bay willow herb, bends down amongst the males for several days, and becomes upright again, when impregnated [E.D.].

[7] **plantago**: rosea. rose-plantain. In this vegetable monster the bractes, or divisions of the spike, become wonderfully enlarged; and are converted into leaves. The chaffy scales of the calyx in Xeranthemum, and in a species of Dianthus, and the glume in some alpine grasses, and the scales of the ament in the salix rosea, rose-willow, grow into leaves; and produce other kinds of monsters. The double flowers become monsters by the multiplication of their petals or nectaries. See note on Alcea [E.D.].

[8] **silene**: catchfly. Three females and ten males inhabit each flower; the viscous material, which surrounds the stalks under the flowers of this plant, and of the Cucubulus Otites, is a curious contrivance to prevent various insects from plundering the honey, or devouring the seed. In the Dionaea Muscipula there is a still more wonderful contrivance to prevent the

The harlot-band *ten* lofty bravoes screen,
And frowning guard the magic nets, unseen.—
Haste, glittering nations, tenants of the air,
Oh, steer from hence your viewless course afar!
If with soft words, sweet blushes, nods, and smiles,
The *three* dread Sirens lure you to their toils,
Limed with their art in vain you point your stings,
In vain the efforts of your whirring wings!—
Go, seek your gilded mates and infant hives,
Nor taste the honey purchas'd with your lives!

— [SENSIBILITY] —

Weak with nice sense, the chaste MIMOSA[9] stands,
From each rude touch withdraws her timid hands;
Oft as light clouds o'erpass the Summer-glade,
Alarm'd she trembles at the moving shade;
And feels, alive through all her tender form,
The whisper'd murmurs of the gathering storm;
Shuts her sweet eye-lids to approaching night;
And hails with freshen'd charms the rising light.
Veil'd, with gay decency and modest pride,
Slow to the mosque she moves, an eastern bride;
There her soft vows unceasing love record,
Queen of the bright seraglio of her Lord.—
So sinks or rises with the changeful hour
The liquid silver in its glassy tower.
So turns the needle to the pole it loves,
With fine vibrations quivering, as it moves.

. . . .

Here paused the Muse,—across the darken'd pole
Sail the dim clouds, the echoing thunders roll;
The trembling Wood-nymphs, as the tempest lowers,
Lead the gay Goddess to their inmost bowers;
Hang the mute lyre the laurel shade beneath,
And round her temples bind the myrtle wreath.
—Now the light swallow with her airy brood
Skims the green meadow, and the dimpled flood;
Loud shrieks the lone thrush from his leafless thorn,
Th' alarmed beetle sounds his bugle horn;
Each pendant spider winds with fingers fine
His ravel'd clue, and climbs along the line;
Gay Gnomes in glittering circles stand aloof
Beneath a spreading mushroom's fretted roof;
Swift bees returning seek their waxen cells,
And Sylphs cling quivering in the lily's bells.
Through the still air descend the genial showers,
And pearly rain-drops deck the laughing flowers.

---

depredations of insects: The leaves are armed with long teeth, like the antennae of insects, and lie spread upon the ground round the stem; and are so irritable, that when an insect creeps upon them, they fold up, and crush or pierce it to death. The late professor Linneus in his supplementum plantarum, gives the following account of the Arum Muscivorum. The flower has the smell of carrion; by which the flies are invited to lay their eggs in the chamber of the flower, but in vain endeavour to escape, being prevented by the hairs pointing inwards; and thus perish in the flower, whence its name of fly-eater. P. 411, in the Dypsacus is another contrivance for this purpose, a bason of water is placed round each joint of the stem. In the Drosera is another kind of fly trap. See Dypsacus and Drosera; the flowers of Silene and Cucubalus are closed all day, but are open and give an agreeable odour in the night. See Cerea [E.D.].

[9] **mimosa:** the sensitive plant. Of the class Polygamy, one house. Naturalists have not explained the immediate cause of the collapsing of the sensitive plant; the leaves meet and close in the night during the sleep of the plant, or when exposed to much cold in the day time, in the same manner as when they are affected by external violence, folding their upper surfaces together, and in part over each other like scales or tiles; so as to expose as little of the upper surface as may be to the air; but do not indeed collapse quite so far, since I have found, when touched in the night during their sleep, they fall still further; especially when touched on the foot-stalks between the stems and the leaflets, which seems to be their most sensitive or irritable part. Now as their situation after being exposed to external violence resembles their sleep, but with a greater degree of collapse, may it not be owing to a numbness or paralysis consequent to too violent irritation, like the faintings of animals from pain or fatigue? I kept a sensitive plant in a dark room till some hours after day break, its leaves and leaf-stalks were collapsed as in its most profound sleep, and on exposing it to the light, above twenty minutes passed before the plant was thoroughly awake and had quite expanded itself. During the night the upper or smoother surfaces of the leaves are appressed together, this would seem to shew that the office of this surface of the leaf was to expose the fluids of the plant to the light as well as to the air. See note on Helianthus. Many flowers close up their petals during the night. See note on vegetable respiration in part 1st [E.D.].

DAVID HARTLEY

(1705–1757)

David Hartley was educated for the ministry at Jesus College, Cambridge, but turned to medicine over scruples with the Anglican Church. He devoted his leisure to philosophy. Hartley's scientific, philosophical, and religious inclinations are given blended expression in his psychological treatise, *Observations on Man, His Frame, His Duty, and His Expectations* (1749), which applies the law of association to human mental development from a neurophysiological perspective. Psychological development begins from a material base of sensory experience causing "vibrations" or "vibratiuncles" that make impressions in the "medullary substance" of the brain. Simple "ideas" and feelings associated with sensation are stored in the memory. Complex ideas are a coalescence of contiguous simple ideas and feelings. Intellectual and moral pleasure and an understanding of God represent the highest achievement of the meditative mind. In the 1790s, Joseph Priestley's edition of Hartley's *Observations* gave hope to those who sought a way of reconciling Necessity (physical determinism) with Christianity. Hartley's scientism was also attractive for its explanatory power of psychological development. When the reductivism of association in accounting for artistic creation became apparent, Hartley's theory of mind stimulated opposing theories of the romantic imagination. (See AESTHETICS AND LITERARY CRITICISM.)

from Observations on Man, His Frame, His Duty, and His Expectations

(1749; 1791)

—*from* CHAPTER III, SECTION 4— OF MEMORY

Prop. XC: To examine how far the Phaenomena of Memory are agreeable to the foregoing theory.

. . . .

Memory was defined in the introduction to be the faculty by which traces of sensations and ideas recur, or are recalled, in the same order and proportion, accurately or nearly, as they were once presented. . . .[1]

. . . Suppose now a person so far advanced in life, as that he has learnt all these rudiments, i.e., that he has ideas of the common appearances and occurrences of life, under a considerable variety of subordinate circumstances, which recur to his imagination from the slightest causes, and with the most perfect facility; and let us ask, how he can be able to remember or recollect a past fact, consisting of one thousand single particulars, or of one hundred such clusters as are called the rudiments of memory; ten single particulars being supposed to constitute a rudiment? First, then, We may observe, that there are only one hundred links wanting in the chain; for he has already learnt considerable exactness in the subordinate circumstances of the one hundred clusters; and perfect exactness is not to be supposed or required.—Secondly, The one hundred clusters recur again and again to the imagination for some time after the fact, in a quick and transient manner, as those who attend sufficiently to what passes in their own minds may perceive: and this both makes the impression a little deeper, and also serves to preserve the order. If the person attempts to recollect soon after the impression, the effect remaining in the brain is sufficient to enable him to do this with the accuracy required and experienced; if a longer time intervene, before he attempts to recollect, still the number of involuntary recurrences makes up in some measure for the

[1] The following explanation of memory influenced William Wordsworth's discussion of poetic meditation. (See Preface to *Lyrical Ballads*.)

want of this voluntary recollection. However, the power of recollection declines in general, and is entirely lost by degrees. It confirms this reasoning, that a new set of strong impressions destroys this power of recollection. For this must both obliterate the effects of the foregoing impressions, and prevent the recurrency of the ideas.—Thirdly, As the single impressions, which make the small clusters, are not combined together at hazard, but according to a general tenor in nature, so the clusters which make facts succeed each other according to some general tenor likewise. Now this both lessens the number of varieties, and shews that the association between many of the clusters, or rudiments, or one hundred links supposed to be wanting, is cemented already. This may be both illustrated and exemplified by the observation, that it is difficult to remember even well-known words that have no connexion with each other, and more so to remember collections of barbarous terms; whereas adepts in any science remember the things of that science with a surprising exactness and facility.—Fourthly, Some clusters are excluded from succeeding others, by ideas of inconsistency, impossibility, and by the methods of reasoning, of which we become masters as we advance in life.—Fifthly, The visible impressions which concur in the past fact, by being vivid, and preserving the order of place, often contribute greatly to preserve the order of time, and to suggest the clusters which may be wanting.—Sixthly, It is to be observed, that as we think in words, both the impressions and the recurrences of ideas will be attended with words; and these words, from the great use and familiarity of language, will fix themselves strongly in the fancy, and by so doing bring up the associated trains of ideas in the proper order, accurately or nearly. And thus, when a person relates a past fact, the ideas do in some cases suggest the words, whilst in others the words suggest the ideas. Hence illiterate persons do not remember nearly so well as others, *caeteris paribus* [other things being equal]. And I suppose the same is true of deaf persons in a still greater degree. But it arises hence also, that many mistakes in the subordinate circumstances are committed in the relations of past facts, if the relater descend to minute particulars. For the same reasons these mistakes will be so associated with the true facts after a few relations, that the relater himself shall believe that he remembers them distinctly.—Seventhly, The mistakes which are committed both on the foregoing account and others, make considerable abatements in the difficulty here to be solved. . . .

—*from* SECTION 5—
OF IMAGINATION, REVERIES, AND DREAMS

Prop. XCI: To examine how far the Phaenomena of Imagination, Reveries, and Dreams, are agreeable to the foregoing Theory.

....

The recurrence of ideas, especially visible and audible ones, in a vivid manner, but without any regard to the order observed in past facts, is ascribed to the power of imagination or fancy.[2] Now here we may observe, that every succeeding thought is the result either of some new impression, or of an association with the preceding. And this is the common opinion. It is impossible indeed to attend so minutely to the succession of our ideas, as to distinguish and remember for a sufficient time the very impression or association which gave birth to each thought; but we can do this as far as it can be expected to be done, and in so great a variety of instances, that our argument for the prevalence of the foregoing principle of association in all instances, except those of new impressions, may be esteemed a complete induction.

A reverie differs from imagination only in that the person being more attentive to his own thoughts, and less disturbed by foreign objects, more of his ideas are deducible from association, and fewer from new impressions. It is to be observed, however, that in all the cases of imagination and reverie, the thoughts depend, in part, upon the then state of body or mind. A pleasurable or painful state of the stomach or brain, joy or grief, will make all the thoughts warp their own way, little or much. But this exception is as agreeable to the foregoing theory, as the general prevalence of association just laid down.

We come next to dreams. I say then, that dreams are nothing but the imaginations, fancies, or reveries of a sleeping man; and that they are deducible from the three following causes; *viz.* First, The impressions and ideas lately received, and particularly those of the preceding day. Secondly, The state of the body, particularly of the stomach and brain. And, thirdly, Association. . . .

---

[2] Samuel Taylor Coleridge argued against the synonomic equivalence of Fancy and Imagination in *Biographia Literaria*, Chapter 13.

FRANCES BURNEY, later D'ARBLAY

(1752–1840)

One of the two or three leading female novelists in England between 1780 and 1830, Frances (known as Fanny) Burney was the daughter of the eminent musicologist Charles Burney, to whom she was devoted and whose *Memoirs* she published in 1832. A prolific letter-writer and diarist, she published her first novel, *Evelina,* in 1778 to immediate acclaim. Her second novel, *Cecilia* (1782), focuses on a young heiress who marries the man she loves despite his family's opposition and the fact that she must sacrifice her fortune to do so. In 1786, as a result of the king's fondness for *Cecilia,* she was appointed second Keeper of the Robes to Queen Charlotte, and spent five excruciating years at court, which she painfully yet wittily described in her letters. At the age of 41, she married the charming and devoted but penniless French emigre, Alexandre d'Arblay, and gave birth to her only child, a son, in 1794. The d'Arblay family lived on the income from Burney's third novel, *Camilla,* which received an astounding £2,000 from a public subscription before publication. Seeking to reclaim her husband's properties lost during the French Revolution, the d'Arblay family was trapped in France in 1802 and spent the next ten years there, during which Burney suffered and recorded in excruciating detail her mastectomy for breast cancer. In 1814, she published her last and finest novel, *The Wanderer,* a powerful description of the difficulties faced by a well-bred, accomplished young woman who, fleeing the brutalities of the French Revolution and arriving in England nameless, homeless, and destitute, a female Robinson Crusoe, must earn her own living while preserving her respectability. This novel, through the secondary character of Elinor Joddrel, defines Burney's ambivalent attitudes toward the 'rights of woman' issue raised by Mary Wollstonecraft, May Hays, and others.

A Mastectomy

Letter from Frances Burney to Esther Burney
(September 30, 1811)

. . .

About August, in the year 1810, I began to be annoyed by a small pain in my breast, which went on augmenting from week to week, yet, being rather heavy than acute, without causing me any uneasiness with respect to consequences: Alas, *'what was the ignorance?'* The most sympathising of Partners, however, was more disturbed: not a start, not a wry face, not a movement that indicated pain was unobserved, & he early conceived apprehensions to which I was a stranger. He pressed me to see some Surgeon; I revolted from the idea, & hoped, by care & warmth, to make all succour unnecessary. Thus passed some months, during which Madame de Maisonneuve, my particularly intimate friend, joined with M. d'Arblay to press me to consent to an examination. I thought their fears groundless, and could not make so great a conquest over my repugnance. I relate this false confidence, now, as a warning to my dear Esther—my Sisters & Nieces, should any similar sensations excite similar alarm. M. d'A. now revealed his uneasiness to another of our kind friends, Mad^e^ de Tracy, who wrote to me a long & eloquent Letter upon the subject, that began to awaken very unpleasant surmizes; & a conference with her ensued, in which her urgency & representations, aided by her long experience of disease, & most miserable existence by art, subdued me, and, most painfully & reluctantly, I ceased to object, & M. d'A: summoned a physician—M. Bourdois?[1] Maria will cry;—No, my dear Maria, I would not give

[1] **M. Bourdois:** Edme-Joachim Bourdois de la Motte, an eminent physician of the period. He was the brother of Antoine Bourdois, the husband of Burney's niece Hannah Maria—and thus Maria's *beau frere* (brother-in-law).

your *beau frere* that trouble; not him, but Dr. Jouart, the physician of Miss Potts. Thinking but slightly of my statement, he gave me some directions that produced no fruit—on the contrary, I grew worse, & M. d'A. now would take no denial to my consulting M. Dubois,[2] who had already attended & cured me in an abscess of which Maria, my dearest Esther, can give you the history. M. Dubois, the most celebrated surgeon of France, was then appointed *accoucheur* to the Empress, & already lodged in the Tuilleries, & in constant attendance: but nothing could slacken the ardour of M. d'A. to obtain the first advice. Fortunately for his kind wishes, M. Dubois had retained a partial regard for me from the time of his former attendance, &, when applied to through a third person, he took the first moment of liberty, granted by a *promenade* taken by the Empress, to come to me. It was now I began to perceive my real danger, M. Dubois gave me a prescription to be pursued for a month, during which time he could not undertake to see me again, & pronounced nothing—but uttered so many charges to me to be tranquil, & to suffer no uneasiness, that I could not but suspect there was room for terrible inquietude. My alarm was encreased by the non-appearance of M. d'A. after his departure. They had remained together some time in the Book room, & M. d'A. did not return—till, unable to bear the suspence, I begged him to come back. He, also, sought then to tranquilize me—but in words only; his looks were shocking! his features, his whole face displayed the bitterest woe. I had not, therefore, much difficulty in telling myself what he endeavoured not to tell me—that a small operation would be necessary to avert evil consequences! . . .

All hope of escaping this evil being now at an end, I could only console or employ my Mind in considering how to render it less dreadful to M. d'A. M. Dubois had pronounced *'il faut s'attendre à souffrir, Je ne veux pas vous trompez—Vous Souffrirez—vous souffrirez* beaucoup!—,[3] M. Ribe had *charged* me to cry! to withhold or restrain myself might have seriously bad consequences, he said. M. Moreau, in ecchoing this injunction, enquired whether I had cried or screamed at the birth of Alexander—Alas, I told him, it had not been possible to do otherwise; Oh then, he answered, there is no fear!—What terrible inferences were here to be drawn! I desired, therefore, that M. d'A. might be kept in ignorance of the day till the operation should be over. To this they agreed, except M. Larrey, with high approbation: M. Larrey looked dissentient, but was silent. M. Dubois protested he would not undertake to act, after what he had seen of the agitated spirits of M. d'A. if he were present: nor would he suffer me to know the time myself over night; I obtained with difficulty a promise of 4 hours warning, which were essential to me for sundry regulations. . .

After sentence thus passed, I was in hourly expectation of a summons to execution; judge, then, my surprise to be suffered to go on full 3 Weeks in the same state! M. Larrey from time to time visited me, but pronounced nothing, & was always melancholy. At length, M. d'A. was told that he waited himself for a Summons! & that, a formal one, & in writing! *I* could not give one. A *consent* was my utmost effort. But poor M. d'A. wrote a desire that the operation, if necessary, might take place without further delay. In my own mind, I had all this time been persuaded there were hopes of a cure: why else, I thought, let me know my doom thus long? But here I must account for this apparently useless, & therefore cruel measure, though I only learnt it myself 2 months afterwards. M. Dubois had given his opinion that the evil was too far advanced for any remedy; that the cancer was already internally declared; that I was inevitably destined to that most frightful of deaths, & that an operation would but accellerate my dissolution. Poor M. Larrey was so deeply affected by this sentence, that—as he has lately told me,—he regretted to his Soul ever having known me, & was upon the point of demanding a commission to the furthest end of France in order to force me into other hands. I had said, however, he remembered, once, that I would far rather suffer a quick end without, than a lingering life with this dreadfullest of maladies: he finally, therefore, considered it might be possible to save me by the trial, but that without it my case was desperate, & resolved to make the attempt. Nevertheless, the responsibility was too great to rest upon his own head entirely; & therefore he waited the formal summons.—In fine, One morning—the last of September, 1811, while I was still in Bed, & M. d'A. was arranging some papers for his office, I received a Letter written by M. de Lally to a Journalist, in vindication of the honoured memory of his Father against the assertions

[2] **M. Dubois:** Antoine Dubois (1756–1837), the leading obstetrician of the time, as indicated by his position of **accoucheur** (a male midwife or, here, obstetrician) to the Empress Marie Louise.

[3] **. . . vous souffrirez beaucoup!:** "You must be ready to suffer, I don't wish to deceive you—You will suffer—you will suffer *a lot!*"

of Mad^e du Deffand. I read it aloud to My Alexanders,[4] with tears of admiration & sympathy, & then sent it by Alex: to its excellent Author, as I had promised the preceding evening. I then dressed, aided, as usual for many months, by my maid, my right arm being condemned to total inaction; but not yet was the grand business over, when another Letter was delivered to me—another, indeed!—'twas from M. Larrey, to acquaint me that at 10 o'clock he should be with me, properly accompanied, & to exhort me to rely as much upon his sensibility & his prudence, as upon his dexterity & his experience; he charged to secure the absence of M. d'A.: & told me that the young Physician who would deliver me this *announce,* would prepare for the operation, in which he must lend his aid: & also that it had been the decision of the consultation to allow me but two hours notice.—Judge, my Esther, if I read this unmoved! . . .—I walked backwards & forwards till I quieted all emotion, & became, by degrees, nearly stupid—torpid, without sentiment or consciousness;—& thus I remained till the Clock struck three. A sudden spirit of exertion then returned,—I defied my poor arm, no longer worth sparing, & took my long banished pen to write a few words to M. d'A.—& a few more for Alex, in case of a fatal result. These short billets I could only deposit safely, when the Cabriolets—one—two—three—four—succeeded rapidly to each other in stopping at the door. Dr. Moreau instantly entered my room, to see if I were alive. He gave me a wine cordial, & went to the Sallon. I rang for my Maid & Nurses,—but before I could speak to them, my room, without previous message, was entered by 7 Men in black, Dr. Larrey, M. Dubois, Dr. Moreau, Dr. Aumont, Dr. Ribe, & a pupil of Dr. Larrey, & another of M. Dubois. I was now awakened from my stupor—& by a sort of indignation—Why so many? & without leave?—But I could not utter a syllable. M. Dubois acted as Commander in Chief. Dr. Larrey kept out of sight; M. Dubois ordered a Bed stead into the middle of the room. Astonished, I turned to Dr. Larrey, who had promised that an Arm Chair would suffice; but he hung his head, & would not look at me. Two *old mattrasses* M. Dubois then demanded, & an old Sheet. I now began to tremble violently, more with distaste & horrour of the preparations even than of the pain. These arranged to his liking, he desired me to mount the Bed stead. I stood suspended, for a moment, whether I should not abruptly escape—I looked at the door, the windows—I felt desperate—but it was only for a moment, my reason then took the command, & my fears & feelings struggled vainly against it. I called to my maid—she was crying, & the two Nurses stood, transfixed, at the door. Let those women all go! cried M. Dubois. This order recovered me my Voice—No, I cried, let them stay! *qu'elles restent!* This occasioned a little dispute, that re-animated me—The Maid, however, & one of the nurses ran off—I charged the other to approach, & she obeyed. Mr. Dubois now tried to issue his commands *en militaire,* but I resisted all that were resistable—I was compelled, however, to submit to taking off my long robe de Chambre, which I had meant to retain—Ah, then, how did I think of My Sisters!—not one, at so dreadful an instant, at hand, to protect—adjust—guard me—I regretted that I had refused Me de Maisonneuve—Me Chastel—no one upon whom I could rely—my departed Angel![5]—how did I think of her!—how did I long—long for my Esther—my Charlotte!—My distress was, I suppose, apparent, though not my Wishes, for M. Dubois himself now softened, & spoke soothingly. Can *You,* I cried, feel for an operation that, to *You,* must seem so trivial?—Trivial? he repeated—taking up a bit of paper, which he tore, unconsciously, into a million of pieces, *oui—c'est peu de chose—mais—*[6] he stammered, & could not go on. No one else attempted to speak, but I was softened myself, when I saw even M. Dubois grow agitated, while Dr. Larrey kept always aloof, yet a glance shewed me he was pale as ashes. I knew not, positively, then, the immediate danger, but every thing convinced me danger was hovering about me, & that this experiment could alone save me from its jaws. I mounted, therefore, unbidden, the Bed stead—& M. Dubois placed me upon the Mattress, & spread a cambric handkerchief upon my face. It was transparent, however, & I saw, through it, that the Bed stead was instantly surrounded by the 7 men & my nurse. I refused to be held; but when, Bright through the cambric, I saw the glitter of polished Steel—I closed my Eyes. I would not trust to convulsive fear the sight of the terrible incision. A silence the most profound ensued, which lasted for some minutes, during which, I imagine, they took their orders by signs, & made their examination—Oh what a horrible suspension!—I did not breathe—& M. Dubois tried vainly to find any pulse.

[4] **My Alexanders:** Burney's husband and son.

[5] Susanna, Burney's favorite sister, who had died on 6 January 1800.

[6] **oui-c'est peu de chose—mais:** "Yes, it's a small thing, but . . ."

This pause, at length, was broken by Dr. Larrey, who, in a voice of solemn melancholy, said *'Qui me tiendra ce sein?*—'[7]

No one answered; at least not verbally; but this aroused me from my passively submissive state, for I feared they imagined the whole breast infected—feared it too justly,—for, again through the Cambric, I saw the hand of M. Dubois held up, while his forefinger first described a straight line from top to bottom of the breast, secondly a Cross, & thirdly a circle; intimating that the WHOLE was to be taken off. Excited by this idea, I started up, threw off my veil, &, in answer to the demand 'Qui me tiendra ce sein,? cried *'C'est moi, Monsieur!'*[8] & I held My hand under it, & explained the nature of my sufferings, which all sprang from one point, though they darted into every part. I was heard attentively, but in utter silence, & M. Dubois then re-placed me as before, &, as before, spread my veil over my face. How vain, alas, my representation! immediately again I saw the fatal finger describe the Cross—& the circle—Hopeless, then, desperate, & self-given up, I closed once more my Eyes, relinquishing all watching, all resistance, all interference, & sadly resolute to be wholly resigned.

My dearest Esther,—& all my dears to whom she communicates this doleful ditty, will rejoice to hear that this resolution once taken, was firmly adhered to, in defiance of a terror that surpasses all description, & the most torturing pain. Yet—when the dreadful steel was plunged into the breast—cutting through veins—arteries—flesh—nerves—I needed no injunctions not to restrain my cries. I began a scream that lasted unintermittingly during the whole time of the incision—& I almost marvel that it rings not in my Ears still! so excruciating was the agony. When the wound was made, & the instrument was withdrawn, the pain seemed undiminished, for the air that suddenly rushed into those delicate parts felt like a mass of minute but sharp & forked poniards, that were tearing the edges of the wound—but when again I felt the instrument—describing a curve—cutting against the grain, if I may so say, while the flesh resisted in a manner so forcible as to oppose & tire the hand of the operator, who was forced to change from the right to the left—then, indeed, I thought I must have expired. I attempted no more to open my Eyes,—they felt as if hermettically shut, & so firmly closed, that the Eyelids seemed indented into the Cheeks.

[7] **Qui me tiendra ce sein?**: "Who will hold this breast for me?"

[8] **C'est moi, Monsieur!**: "I will, Monsieur."

The instrument this second time withdrawn, I concluded the operation over—Oh no! presently the terrible cutting was renewed—& worse than ever, to separate the bottom, the foundation of this dreadful gland from the parts to which it adhered—Again all description would be baffled—yet again all was not over,—Dr Larrey rested but his own hand, &—Oh Heaven!—I then felt the Knife <rack>ling against the breast bone—scraping it!—This performed, while I yet remained in utterly speechless torture, I heard the Voice of Mr. Larrey,—(all others guarded a dead silence) in a tone nearly tragic, desire every one present to pronounce if any thing more remained to be done; The general voice was Yes,—but the finger of Mr. Dubois—which I literally *felt* elevated over the wound, though I saw nothing, & though he touched nothing, so indescribably sensitive was the spot—pointed to some further requisition—& again began the scraping!—and, after this, Dr. Moreau thought he discerned a peccant attom[9]—and still, & still, M. Dubois demanded attom after attom—My dearest Esther, not for days, not for Weeks, but for Months I could not speak of this terrible business without nearly again going through it! I could not *think* of it with impunity! I was sick, I was disordered by a single question—even now, 9 months after it is over, I have a head ache from going on with the account! & this miserable account, which I began 3 Months ago, at least, I dare not revise, nor read, the recollection is still so painful.

To conclude, the evil was so profound, the case so delicate, & the precautions necessary for preventing a return so numerous, that the operation, including the

[9] **peccant attom**: cancerous tissue. [Cf. Robert Liston (1794–1847), a prominent English surgeon, *Practical Surgery* (1837), pp. 284–7: 'This is a disease in which no half measures will answer; and if a patient has made up her mind, after a severe struggle, to submit to the pain and risk of a very dreadful operation, in the expectation and with the view of saving herself from after-suffering, and enjoying an immunity from a terrible disease, it is not fair, from any slovenliness or carelessness to throw away a chance, or in any way endanger a recurrence of the mischief. The operation is one which must be gone about deliberately and conscientiously, as ought to be the case in undertaking operations of any kind, in any situation. The duration of the proceeding must not be considered. Many operations can be done well, and quickly too, and fully as well when quickly done. This is not one of these; the extirpation should be set about with a thorough determination to free the patient of the whole diseased structure.']

treatment & the dressing, lasted 20 minutes! a time, for sufferings so acute, that was hardly supportable—However, I bore it with all the courage I could exert, & never moved, nor stopt them, nor resisted, nor remonstrated, nor spoke—except once or twice, during the dressings, to say *'Ah Messieurs! que je vous plains!—'*[10] for indeed I was sensible to the feeling concern with which they all saw what I endured, though my speech was principally—*very* principally meant for Dr. Larrey. Except this, I uttered not a syllable, save, when so often they re-commenced, calling out *'Avertissez moi, Messieurs! avertissez moi!—'*[11] Twice, I believe, I fainted; at least, I have two total chasms in my memory of this transaction, that impede my tying together what passed. When all was done, & they lifted me up that I might be put to bed, my strength was so totally annihilated, that I was obliged to be carried, & could not even sustain my hands & arms, which hung as if I had been lifeless; while my face, as the Nurse has told me, was utterly colourless. This removal made me open my Eyes—& I then saw my good Dr. Larrey, pale nearly as myself, his face streaked with blood, & its expression depicting grief, apprehension, & almost horrour.

---

[10] **Ah Messieurs! que je vous plains!:** "Ah, gentlemen, how I feel for you!"

[11] **Avertissez . . . moi:** "Warn me, gentlemen, warn me!"

MARY WOLLSTONECRAFT GODWIN SHELLEY

(1797–1851)

Mary Shelley's *Frankenstein* derives from a ghost-writing contest suggested by Lord Byron in June 1816 while the Shelleys were guests at his residence in Geneva, Switzerland. Byron and Percy Shelley produced nothing consequential. "The illustrious poets . . . annoyed by the platitudes of prose, speedily relinquished their uncongenial task," Mary explains earlier in the Introduction. However, she and Byron's physician and travelling companion, John William Polidori, produced two of the most lasting myths of the nineteenth century. Though a primitive narrative, Polidori's *The Vampyre, a Tale* (1820) became a theatrical hit in dramatized form. Mary Shelley's *Frankenstein* was published in March 1818, to even greater acclaim. (See the headnote to Mary Wollstonecraft Godwin Shelley for further information on the life and work of Mary Shelley.)

from the Introduction *to the third edition of* Frankenstein

or The Modern Prometheus

(1831)

. . . I busied myself *to think of a story,*—a story to rival those which had excited us to this task.[1] One which would speak to the mysterious fears of our nature, and awaken thrilling horror—one to make the reader dread to look round, to curdle the blood, and quicken the beatings of the heart. If I did not accomplish these things, my ghost story would be unworthy of its name. I thought and pondered—vainly. I felt that blank incapability of invention which is the greatest misery of authorship, when dull Nothing replies to our anxious invocations. *Have you thought of a story?* I was asked each morning, and each morning I was forced to reply with a mortifying negative.

Every thing must have a beginning, to speak in Sanchean phrase;[2] and that beginning must be linked to something that went before. The Hindoos give the world an elephant to support it, but they make the elephant stand upon a tortoise. Invention, it must be humbly admitted, does not consist in creating out of void, but out of chaos;[3] the materials must, in the first place, be afforded: it can give form to dark, shapeless substances, but cannot bring into being the substance itself. In all matters of discovery and invention, even of those that appertain to the imagination, we are continually reminded of the story of Columbus and his egg. Invention consists in the capacity of seizing on the capabilities of a subject, and in the power of moulding and fashioning ideas suggested to it.

Many and long were the conversations between Lord Byron and Shelley, to which I was a devout but nearly silent listener. During one of these, various philosophical doctrines were discussed, and among others the nature of the principle of life, and whether there was any probability of its ever being discovered and communicated. They talked of the experiments of Dr. Darwin[4] (I speak not of what the Doctor really did, or said that he did, but, as more to my purpose, of what was then spoken of as having been done by him), who preserved a piece of vermicelli in

[1] The party had been reading German ghost stories.

[2] **Sanchean phrase:** The kind of truism that would be attributable to Sancho Panza, the squire of Don Quixote.

[3] Because *Frankenstein* is permeated by *Paradise Lost* (1667), it is useful to recall that Milton's God creates the universe by ensphering a portion of Chaos with a pair of golden compasses. Shelley might also have in mind recent theories of catastrophic geology, which describe the evolution of the earth in terms of apocalyptic natural occurrences: floods, volcanoes, earthquakes.

[4] Erasmus Darwin.*

a glass case, till by some extraordinary means it began to move with voluntary motion. Not thus, after all, would life be given. Perhaps a corpse would be re-animated; galvanism had given token of such things: perhaps the component parts of a creature might be manufactured, brought together, and endued with vital warmth.[5]

Night waned upon this talk, and even the witching hour had gone by, before we retired to rest. When I placed my head on my pillow, I did not sleep, nor could I be said to think. My imagination, unbidden, possessed and guided me, gifting the successive images that arose in my mind with a vividness far beyond the usual bounds of reverie. I saw—with shut eyes, but acute mental vision—I saw the pale student of unhallowed arts kneeling beside the thing he had put together. I saw the hideous phantasm of a man stretched out, and then, on the working of some powerful engine, show signs of life, and stir with an uneasy, half vital motion. Frightful must it be; for supremely frightful would be the effect of any human endeavour to mock the stupendous mechanism of the Creator of the world. His success would terrify the artist; he would rush away from his odious handywork, horror-stricken. He would hope that, left to itself, the slight spark of life which he had communicated would fade; that this thing, which had received such imperfect animation, would subside into dead matter; and he might sleep in the belief that the silence of the grave would quench for ever the transient existence of the hideous corpse which he had looked upon as the cradle of life. He sleeps; but he is awakened; he opens his eyes; behold the horrid thing stands at his bedside, opening his curtains, and looking on him with yellow, watery, but speculative eyes.

I opened mine in terror. The idea so possessed my mind, that a thrill of fear ran through me, and I wished to exchange the ghastly image of my fancy for the realities around. I see them still; the very room, the dark *parquet*, the closed shutters, with the moonlight struggling through, and the sense I had that the glassy lake and white high Alps were beyond. I could not so easily get rid of my hideous phantom; still it haunted me. I must try to think of something else. I recurred to my ghost story,—my tiresome unlucky ghost story! O! if I could only contrive one which would frighten my reader as I myself had been frightened that night!

Swift as light and as cheering was the idea that broke in upon me. "I have found it! What terrified me will terrify others; and I need only describe the spectre which had haunted my midnight pillow." On the morrow I announced that I had *thought of a story*. I began that day with the words, *It was on a dreary night of November*, making only a transcript of the grim terrors of my waking dream.

At first I thought but of a few pages—of a short tale; but Shelley urged me to develope the idea at greater length. I certainly did not owe the suggestion of one incident, nor scarcely of one train of feeling, to my husband, and yet but for his incitement, it would never have taken the form in which it was presented to the world. From this declaration I must except the preface. As far as I can recollect, it was entirely written by him.

And now, once again, I bid my hideous progeny go forth and prosper. I have an affection for it, for it was the offspring of happy days, when death and grief were but words, which found no true echo in my heart. Its several pages speak of many a walk, many a drive, and many a conversation, when I was not alone; and my companion was one who, in this world, I shall never see more. But this is for myself; my readers have nothing to do with these associations. . . .

---

[5] **Galvanism:** See Introduction to SCIENCE AND NATURE.

CHARLES LYELL

(1797–1875)

Lyell began his life as a scientist by collecting insects as a boy. During his undergraduate years at Oxford (1816–1819), his interest in geology was aroused by the recent publication of William Smith's *Strata Identified by Organized Fossils,* which introduced questions of origin and extinction in its description of differences in fauna. Following graduation, Lyell joined the Geological and the Linnean Societies of London to keep abreast of the sciences he loved. He published the first volume of *Principles of Geology* in 1830 and completed the three-volume project by 1833. Though *Principles* went through 11 editions during his lifetime to form a virtual record of geology's early development as a science, Lyell held fast to the theory of "uniformitarianism," as opposed to "catastrophism": that geologic change was the result of inexorable forces still at work, rather than the result of periodic apocalyptic events—floods, earthquakes, volcanoes—that extinguished species. Originally controversial, uniformitarianism finally prevailed. Lyell was buried in the nave of Westminster Abbey following his death in 1875.

from Principles of Geology

(1830–1833)

Modern Progress of Geology

No period could have been more fortunate for the discovery, in the immediate neighbourhood of Paris, of a rich store of well-preserved fossils, than the commencement of the present century; for at no former era had Natural History been cultivated with such enthusiasm in the French metropolis. The labours of Cuvier[1] in comparative osteology, and of Lamarck[2] in recent and fossil shells, had raised these departments of study to a rank of which they had never previously been deemed susceptible. Their investigations had eventually a powerful effect in dispelling the illusion which had long prevailed concerning the absence of analogy between the ancient and modern state of our planet. A close comparison of the recent and fossil species, and the inferences drawn in regard to their habits, accustomed the geologist to contemplate the earth as having been at successive periods the dwellingplace of animals and plants of different races, some terrestrial, and others aquatic—some fitted to live in seas, others in the waters of lakes and rivers. By the consideration of these topics, the mind was slowly and insensibly withdrawn from imaginary pictures of catastrophes and chaotic confusion, such as haunted the imagination of the early cosmogonists. Numerous proofs were discovered of the tranquil deposition of sedimentary matter, and the slow development of organic life. If many writers, and Cuvier himself in the number, still continued to maintain, that 'the thread of induction was broken,' yet, in reasoning by the strict rules of induction from recent to fossil species, they in a great measure disclaimed the dogma which in theory they professed. The adoption of the same generic, and, in some cases, even of the same specific, names for the exuviae of fossil animals and their living analogues, was an important step towards familiarising the mind with the idea of the identity and unity of the system in distant eras. It was an acknowledgement, as it were, that part at least of the ancient memorials of nature were written in a living language. The growing importance, then, of the natural history of organic remains may be pointed out as the characteristic feature of the progress of the science during the present century. This branch of knowledge has already become an instrument of great utility in geological

[1] **Baron Georges Leopold Cuvier (1769–1832):** French paleontologist and founder of comparative anatomy. In this context, catastrophic theorist.

[2] **Chevalier de Lamarck [Jean Baptiste Pierre Antoine de Monet] (1744–1829):** French naturalist who theorized that a living being could willfully adapt to changes in its environment and pass those changes on through heredity.

classification, and is continuing daily to unfold new data for grand and enlarged views respecting the former changes of the earth.

When we compare the result of observations in the last thirty years with those of the three preceding centuries, we cannot but look forward with the most sanguine expectations to the degree of excellence to which geology may be carried, even by the labours of the present generation. Never, perhaps, did any science, with the exception of astronomy, unfold, in an equally brief period, so many novel and unexpected truths, and overturn so many preconceived opinions. The senses had for ages declared the earth to be at rest, until the astronomer taught that it was carried through space with inconceivable rapidity. In like manner was the surface of this planet regarded as having remained unaltered since its creation, until the geologist proved that it had been the theatre of reiterated change, and was still the subject of slow but never-ending fluctuations. The discovery of other systems in the boundless regions of space was the triumph of astronomy: to trace the same system through various transformations—to behold it at successive eras adorned with different hills and valleys, lakes and seas, and peopled with new inhabitants, was the delightful meed of geological research. By the geometer were measured the regions of space, and the relative distances of the heavenly bodies;—by the geologist myriads of ages were reckoned, not by arithmetical computation, but by a train of physical events—a succession of phenomena in the animate and inanimate worlds—signs which convey to our minds more definite ideas than figures can do of the immensity of time. . . .

Introduction of man, to what extent a change in the system.—But setting aside the question of progressive development, another and a far more difficult one may arise out of the admission that man is comparatively of modern origin.[3] Is not the interference of the human species, it may be asked, such a deviation from the antecedent course of physical events, that the knowledge of such a fact tends to destroy all our confidence in the uniformity of the order of nature, both in regard to time past and future? If such an innovation could take place after the earth had been exclusively inhabited for thousands of ages by inferior animals, why should not other changes as extraordinary and unprecedented happen from time to time? If one new cause was permitted to supervene, differing in kind and energy from any before in operation, why may not others have come into action at different epochs? Or what security have we that they may not arise hereafter? And if such be the case, how can the experience of one period, even though we are acquainted with all the possible effects of the then existing causes, be a standard to which we can refer all natural phenomena of other periods? . . .

. . . We have no reason to suppose, that when man first became master of a small part of the globe, a greater change took place in its physical condition than is now experienced when districts, never before inhabited, became successively occupied by new settlers. When a powerful European colony lands on the shores of Australia, and introduces at once those arts which it has required many centuries to mature; when it imports a multitude of plants and large animals from the opposite extremity of the earth, and begins rapidly to extirpate many of the indigenous species, a mightier revolution is effected in a brief period than the first entrance of a savage horde, or their continued occupation of the country for many centuries, can possibly be imagined to have produced. If there be no impropriety in assuming that the system is uniform when disturbances so unprecedented occur in certain localities, we can with much greater confidence apply the same language to those primeval ages when the aggregate number and power of the human race, or the rate of their advancement in civilisation, must be supposed to have been far inferior. In reasoning on the state of the globe immediately before our species was called into existence, we must be guided by the same rules of induction as when we speculate on the state of America in the interval that elapsed between the introduction of man into Asia, the supposed cradle of our race, and the arrival of the first adventurers on the shores of the New World. In that interval, we imagine the state of things to have gone on according to the order now observed in regions unoccupied by man. Even now, the waters of lakes, seas, and the great ocean, which teem with life, may be said to have no immediate relation to the human race—to be portions of the terrestrial system of which man has never taken, nor ever can take, possession; so that the greater part of the inhabited surface of the planet may remain still as insensible to our presence as before any isle or continent was appointed to be our residence. . . .

Concluding Remarks

In the history of the progress of geology, it has been stated that the opinion originally promulgated by

[3] Catastrophists believed that man was a recent creation between catastrophies.

Hutton,[4] 'that the strata called *primitive* were mere altered sedimentary rocks,' was vehemently opposed for a time, on the ground of its supposed tendency to promote a belief in the past eternity of our planet. Before that period the absence of animal and vegetable remains in the so-called primitive strata had been appealed to, as proving that there had been an era when the planet was uninhabited by living beings, and when, as was also inferred, it was uninhabitable, and, therefore, probably in a nascent state.

The opposite doctrine, that the oldest visible strata might be the monuments of an antecedent period, when the animate world was already in existence, was declared to be equivalent to the assumption that there never was a beginning to the present order of things. The unfairness of this charge was clearly pointed out by Playfair, who observed, 'that it was one thing to declare that we had not yet discovered the traces of a beginning, and another to deny that the earth ever had a beginning.'

I regret, however, to find that the bearing of my arguments in the first book has been misunderstood in a similar manner; for I have been charged with endeavouring to establish the proposition, that 'the existing causes of change have operated with absolute uniformity from all eternity'. . . . [5]

. . . With equal justice might an astronomer be accused of asserting that the works of creation extended throughout *infinite* space, because he refuses to take for granted that the remotest stars now seen in the heavens are on the utmost verge of the material universe. Every improvement of the telescope has brought thousands of new worlds into view; and it would, therefore, be rash and unphilosophical to imagine that we already survey the whole extent of the vast scheme, or that it will ever be brought within the sphere of human observation.

But no argument can be drawn from such premises in favour of the infinity of the space that has been filled with worlds; and if the material universe has any limits, it then follows that it must occupy a minute and infinitesimal point in infinite space.

So if, in tracing back the earth's history, we arrive at the monuments of events which may have happened millions of ages before our times, and if we still find no decided evidence of a commencement, yet the arguments from analogy in support of the probability of a beginning remain unshaken; and if the past duration of the earth be finite, then the aggregate of geological epochs, however numerous, must constitute a mere moment of the past, a mere infinitesimal portion of eternity.

It has been argued, that, as the different states of the earth's surface, and the different species by which it has been inhabited, have all had their origin, and many of them their termination, so the entire series may have commenced at a certain period. It has also been urged, that, as we admit the creation of man to have occurred at a comparatively modern epoch—as we concede the astonishing fact of the first introduction of a moral and intellectual being—so also we may conceive the first creation of the planet itself.

I am far from denying the weight of this reasoning from analogy; but, although it may strengthen our conviction, that the present system of change has not gone on from eternity, it cannot warrant us in presuming that we shall be permitted to behold the signs of the earth's origin, or the evidences of the first introduction into it of organic beings. We aspire in vain to assign limits to the works of creation in *space*, whether we examine the starry heavens, or that world of minute animalcules which is revealed to us by the microscope. We are prepared, therefore, to find that in *time* also the confines of the universe lie beyond the reach of mortal ken. But in whatever direction we pursue our researches, whether in time or space, we discover everywhere the clear proofs of a Creative Intelligence, and of His foresight, wisdom, and power.

As geologists, we learn that it is not only the present condition of the globe which has been suited to the accommodation of myriads of living creatures, but that many former states also have been adapted to the organisation and habits of prior races of beings. The disposition of the seas, continents, and islands, and the climates, have varied; the species likewise have been changed; and yet they have all been so modelled, on types analogous to those of existing plants and animals, as to indicate throughout a perfect harmony of design and unity of purpose. To assume that the evidence of the beginning or end of so vast a scheme lies within the reach of our philosophical inquiries, or even of our speculations, appears to be inconsistent with a just estimate of the relations which subsist between the finite powers of man and the attributes of an Infinite and Eternal Being.

---

[4] **James Hutton (1726–1797):** His *Theory of the Earth with Proofs and Illustrations* (1795) anticipated Lyell's views on geologic change.

[5] A comment from an article in the *Quarterly Review,* 86 (Oct. 1830): 464.

Aesthetic Theory and Literary Criticism

THE WRITERS AND artists of late-eighteenth-century England inherited from the aesthetic theorists of classical antiquity and the English Renaissance the belief that the purpose of art was to imitate nature—in the words of Shakespeare's Hamlet, "to hold, as t'were, the mirror up to nature." As Walter Jackson Bate cogently summarized this aesthetic theory in his *From Classic to Romantic* (1946), the nature to be thus imitated or copied was not primarily the nature one actually sees unfolding around one in all her variety and mutability. Rather, the artist was urged to reveal the eternal, unchanging forms of nature, those rational, objective laws and principles of a harmoniously ordered universe identified by Plato as the ideal forms of which passing appearances are but a dim shadow. For the artist, these ideal forms—or what Sir Joshua Reynolds called the "central forms"—are the essence of beauty. They are also, as Samuel Johnson insisted, the essence of morality, for as he asserted, "He who thinks reasonably must think morally."

The artist should carefully select from the physical universe and actual human beings only those characteristics which possess such universal and enduring beauty and moral virtue. It is a synthesized or generic type that constitutes the form of beauty. Neoclassical aestheticians such as Thomas Rymer, Johann Winckelmann, and René Rapin argued that such forms of beauty were most clearly revealed in the art and writing of the Hellenistic Greeks and their Roman imitators, in the sculptures of Phidias, in the Apollo Belvidere and the Laocoon, in the architecture of the Parthenon, in the epics of Homer and Virgil, in the dramas of Aeschylus, Sophocles, and Euripedes. By copying such classical artistic and literary models, later artists could most closely approximate ideal beauty.

The social purpose of art was therefore both to delight and instruct, as Horace had said. Art provided examples of heroic behavior and moral virtue in such a vivid and pleasing way that the members of its audiences were inspired to imitate such examples in their own lives. To achieve this didactic function, the artist, it was thought, must obey specific rules inherited from antiquity. Art must conform to established generic and aesthetic conventions: for instance, the traditional stanzaic patterns and narrative structures of the poetic epic, the ode, the elegy, and the sonnet; the unities of time, space, and causation of the classical drama; the composition and figural attitudes of the history painting, the portrait, the still life. At all times, the work of art must observe decorum, suiting its language and style to the action displayed.

In the late eighteenth century, this neoclassical, mimetic aesthetic theory was strongly contested. Focussing on the subjective or psychological origins of the experience of aesthetic pleasure rather than on the objective forms of beauty, Edmund Burke powerfully argued for two very different kinds of aesthetic experience, the sublime and the beautiful. The sublime experience occurred when one's instinct for self-preservation was aroused by an image that seemed to threaten one's life, by scenes of the infinite power of God or nature in which the frailty and mortality of human beings are strikingly portrayed. In contrast, the experience of the beautiful was produced when one's instinct for procreation was aroused, by scenes which aroused (masculine) sexual desire. To Burke's categories, William Gilpin added a third, the category of the picturesque. Gilpin argued that beauty in nature consisted of scenes which would form a pleasing pictorial composition. Combining elements from the paintings of the acknowledged master of the sublime in landscape, Salvator Rosa, and the leading painter of the beautiful in landscape, Claude Lorraine, Gilpin argued that the most aesthetically satisfying image was irregular, rough, and varied. Inspired by Gilpin, hundreds of British tourists and hikers set out to find the picturesque in the English landscape. They carried with them their "Claude glasses," a rectangular mirror on a handle, whose glass was tinted either blue (for early morning scenes) or golden-brown (for afternoon scenes). They would stand with their backs to nature, moving the mirror until it framed a scene that contained the elements Gilpin had defined as picturesque.

Burke's emphasis on the psychological origin of aesthetic beauty encouraged a belief that feelings rather than rational objectivity lead to the deepest experience of beauty. Drawing on the earlier work of Lord Shaftesbury (1671–1713) and David Hume (1711–1776), the Scottish moral philosopher and economist Adam Smith argued that sympathy or the capacity to enter into the feelings of those around one was the basis both of morality and of aesthetic beauty. The best works of art aroused pity and compassion for the sufferings of others, a sympathy that brought the reader or viewer to tears and inspired benevolent acts of charity. A cult of sensibility grew up in response to Smith's arguments, championed most famously by the Scottish novelist Henry Mackenzie's *The New Man of Feeling* (1771). The female sex was considered particularly capable of sensibility, since females were thought to possess more refined and sensitive emotions. Several women poets lauded the female capacity for sensibility: see, for examples, Hannah More's "Sensibility,"* Anna Barbauld's "To a Lady, with Some Painted Flowers,"* and Helen Maria Williams' "To Sensibility."* During this historical period, numerous accomplished young ladies demonstrated their delicacy or sensibility by publicly weeping over the sentimental scenes of novels or plays. During her career Mary Wollstonecraft first embraced and then offered a powerful critique of the concept of female sensibility (see below and her *Vindication of the Rights of Woman**).

Responding to all these influences, William Blake in his letters and poetry,* William Wordsworth in his Preface to *Lyrical Ballads,** Samuel Taylor Coleridge in his *Biographia Literaria** and *Lectures on Shakespeare,** William Hazlitt in his essays,* John Keats in his letters,* Percy Shelley in his *Defence of Poetry,** among several others included in this volume, developed alternative aesthetic theories which in the early twentieth century were grouped together under the name "Romanticism." These writers tended to see the work of art not so much as an objective synthesis of universal wisdom and beauty, "what oft was thought but ne'er so well expressed," as Alexander Pope had put it, but rather as a unique and original creation of the subjective imagination that expressed the artist's individual emotional and intellectual response to a particular human or natural event.

Coleridge, deriving his argument from the epistemological theories of Immanuel Kant, asserted that the structure and language of the poem develops organically from and thus gives outward form to the particular subjective or phenomenological movement of the poet's mind and feelings. In creating the work of art, Coleridge further claimed in *Biographia Literaria** that the human imagination participates in the same divine power that created and sustains the universe. The poem is therefore a heterocosm or world in itself: a world that reconciles the multeity of experience into a harmonious unity or whole. The linguistic representation of this fusion of the half-perceiving, half-creating mind with external nature, according to Coleridge, is the symbol, an image that reveals the presence of the infinite within the finite. Since the artist replicates the activity of the divine Creator and constructs the stories or myths which human beings use to make sense of their lives, several of these poets claimed for themselves the social role of the educator, priest, and savior of mankind, the "unacknowledged legislator of the world," as Percy Shelley put it.

Less optimistic supporters of this romantic aesthetic, such as John Keats and Lord Byron, offered as an alternative to the Wordsworthian "egotistical sublime" a more skeptical and questioning version of Romanticism. It is now known, in terms derived from its first theoretician Friedrich Schlegel, as Romantic Irony (for further discussion of this concept, see Anne K. Mellor, *English Romantic Irony,* 1980). Rather than envisioning the universe in Judeo-Christian terms as necessarily and progressively moving toward apocalyptic perfection, they viewed the universe as an unknowable chaos that is constantly creating and decreating life-forms. The artist who seeks to represent this chaos in his art must similarly create and de-create both his narrative fictions and his own selfhood. The work of art, then, like nature itself, is in constant process and can never be more than a fragment, a partial and incomplete representation of an always becoming, never fully comprehensible universe.

The terms "Romantic" or "Romanticism" as the name of a literary movement or a kind of art did not come into widespread use until the early twentieth century. Between 1780 and 1830, "romantic" referred to the romances of the Middle Ages and the Renaissance, to literary works that were fanciful, focussed on courtly love, idealistic, and containing elements of the supernatural or the wonderful. The poets we now call "Romantic" were at the time called the "Lake Poets" or the "Cockney School" or even the "Satanic School," all labels coined by neoclassical, politically conservative, or moderate critics such as Francis Jeffrey, John Gibson Lockhart, and John Wilson Croker. These poets were first named "The Romantic School" by Hippolyte Taine in his *History of English Literature* in 1863. Taine derived his notion of literary Romanticism from French and German writers, and defined it as a concern with historical relativism and Kantian philosophy. On the other hand, most British Victorian critics who applied the term "romantic" to literary works intended a specifically *political* connotation, identifying "romantic" poetry with a particular set of responses to the French Revolution, ones that were liberal, radical, even revolutionary. This conception of the romantic movement as a political "spirit of the age" received its fullest exposition in 1910 in William John Courthope's *The Romantic Movement in English Poetry: The Effects of the French Revolution.* During the late nineteenth century, however, Pre-Raphaelite writers, especially Dante Gabriel Rossetti and William Michael Rossetti, tried to reclaim

Keats and Shelley as poets of beauty who valued art for art's sake. This conception of Romanticism as primarily an *aesthetic* term received a fuller exposition in A. O. Lovejoy's famous 1924 essay "On the Discrimination of Romanticisms." By the mid-twentieth century, this aesthetic definition of Romanticism had come to dominate academic discussions of "the Romantic Movement in England" and has in the last 50 years been generously expanded and refined on the basis of the self-descriptions of their literary project provided by Wordsworth, Coleridge, Shelley, Keats, and many other male writers included in this anthology. This construction of Romanticism was recently identified by Jerome McGann in his *Romantic Ideology* (1983) as an ideological poetics of whose self-interest or class bias we should be aware.

The women writers of this period responded to the dialogue between a mimetic / objective (Neoclassical) and an expressive / subjective (Romantic) aesthetics by staking out a middle ground. Such female literary critics and writers as Clara Reeve in her *Progress of Romance,* Mary Wollstonecraft in her book reviews and essays for *Analytical Review,* Elizabeth Inchbald in her *Remarks for the British Theatre* (1809), Joanna Baillie in her *Introductory Discourse to Plays on the Passions,** and most notably Anna Barbauld in her magisterial essay "On the Origin and Progress of Novel-Writing"* argued that the function of art is to teach morality or right feeling by arousing readers' sympathies through the representation of *probable* or believable examples of virtuous and evil human behavior in contemporary situations. In opposition to a neoclassical hierarchy of the genres which gave priority to epic poetry and tragic drama, they argued that the most realistic and hence the most moral genre was the novel, an eighteenth-century outgrowth of Greek and medieval romances. Not only was the novel capable of depicting a social world that was both more credible and more psychologically complex than that found in epic poetry, tragic drama, or the earlier romance, Barbauld argued, it was also more democratic, because it was a genre that could be read and understood by any literate person and did not require a prior education in the Greek and Latin classics.

Practicing critics relied on these differing aesthetic positions as the basis for their judgments of individual works. The same literary work could arouse violently different reactions from a Neoclassicist, a Romantic, a Probabilist. Critics' responses were further shaped by the political positions supported by the journals for which they wrote. The print culture of this period was extremely, often virulently, partisan. *Blackwood's, The Quarterly,* and *The Anti-Jacobin* were ardent supporters of the king and the Tory faction, while Richard Carlile's *Republican,* Joseph Johnson's *Analytical Review,* Leigh Hunt's *The Examiner,* and *The Edinburgh Review* advocated positions ranging from the radical and liberal to the more moderate reforms endorsed by the Whig faction. John Gibson Lockhart argued from the politically conservative tenets of neoclassical decorum; William Hazlitt,* a liberal, endorsed the ideas of the Romantic aesthetic; while Francis Jeffrey, Clara Reeve, and Anna Barbauld* assumed the reformist or Whig position that the best art combines morality with probability.

JOHANN JOACHIM WINCKELMANN

(1717–1768)

A German classical archeologist and art critic, Winckelmann did more than any other writer in the eighteenth century to establish classical Greek (as opposed to Roman) art and literature as the highest aesthetic achievement of western civilization. After his conversion to Roman Catholicism in 1754, he paid numerous visits to Rome, Florence, Pompeii, and Naples, where he exhaustively studied and compared Greek and Roman antiquities. He was put in charge of the classical antiquities in the Vatican Palace in Rome in 1763, and from this position of authority constantly insisted on the supreme beauty of Hellenistic sculpture and architecture. His writings, which included *Reflections on the Painting and Sculpture of the Greeks* (1755), *The History of Ancient Art* (1764), *Uncatalogued Monuments of Antiquity* (1767), and others, were widely translated and became the bibles of Neoclassical art theory in the eighteenth century. Winckelmann, a practicing homosexual, was murdered in Naples in 1768 by a male prostitute.

from The History of Ancient Art

(1764)

(trans., G. Henry Lodge, 1880)

— UNITY —

The highest beauty is in God; and our idea of human beauty advances towards perfection in proportion as it can be imagined in conformity and harmony with that highest Existence which, in our conception of unity and indivisibility, we distinguish from matter. This idea of beauty is like an essence extracted from matter by fire; it seeks to beget unto itself a creature formed after the likeness of the first rational being designed in the mind of the Divinity. The forms of such a figure are simple and flowing, and various in their unity; and for this reason they are harmonious, just as a sweet and pleasing tone can be extracted from bodies the parts of which are uniform. All beauty is heightened by unity and simplicity, as is everything which we do and say; for whatever is great in itself is elevated, when executed and uttered with simplicity. . . .

— GENERALITY —

From unity proceeds another attribute of lofty beauty, the absence of individuality; that is, the forms of it are described neither by points nor lines other than those which shape beauty merely, and consequently produce a figure which is neither peculiar to any particular individual, nor yet expresses any one state of the mind or affection of the passions, because these blend with it strange lines, and mar the unity. According to this idea, beauty should be like the best kind of water, drawn from the spring itself; the less taste it has, the more healthful it is considered, because free from all foreign admixture. . . .

— THE SHAPE OF BEAUTY —

The shape of beauty is either *individual*—that is, confined to an imitation of one individual—or it is a selection of beautiful parts from many individuals, and their union into one, which we call *ideal*. . . .

But nature and the structure of the most beautiful bodies are rarely without fault. They have forms which can either be found more perfect in other bodies, or which may be imagined more perfect. In conformity to this teaching of experience, those wise artists, the ancients, acted as a skillful gardener does, who ingrafts different shoots of excellent sorts upon the same stock; and, as a bee gathers from many flowers, so were their ideas of beauty not limited to the beautiful in a single individual, but they sought to unite the beautiful parts of many beautiful bodies. They purified their images from all personal feelings, by which the mind is diverted from the truly beautiful.

— THE APOLLO OF BELVEDERE —

Among all the works of antiquity which have escaped destruction the statue of Apollo is the highest ideal of art. The artist has constructed this work entirely on the ideal, and has employed in its structure just so much only of the material as was necessary to carry out his design and render it visible. This Apollo exceeds all other figures of him as much as the Apollo of Homer excels him whom later poets paint. His stature is loftier than that of man, and his attitude speaks of the greatness with which he is filled. An eternal spring, as in the happy fields of Elysium, clothes with the charms of youth the graceful manliness of ripened years, and plays with softness and tenderness about the proud shape of his limbs. Let thy spirit penetrate into the kingdom of incorporeal beauties, and strive to become a creator of a heavenly nature, in order that thy mind may be filled with beauties that are elevated above nature; for there is nothing mortal here, nothing which human necessities require. Neither blood-vessels nor sinews heat and stir this body, but a heavenly essence, diffusing itself like a gentle stream, seems to fill the whole contour of the figure. He has pursued the Python, against which he uses his bow for the first time; with vigorous step he has overtaken the monster and slain it.[1] His lofty look, filled with a consciousness of power, seems to rise far above his victory, and to gaze into infinity. Scorn sits upon his lips, and his nostrils are swelling with suppressed anger, which mounts even to the proud forehead; but the peace which floats upon it in blissful calm remains undisturbed, and his eye is full of sweetness as when the Muses gathered around him seeking to embrace him. The Father of the gods in all the images of him which we have remaining, and which art venerates, does not approach so nearly the grandeur in which he manifested himself to the understanding of the divine poet, as he does here in the countenance of his son, and the individual beauties of the other deities are here as in the person of Pandora assembled together, a forehead of Jupiter, pregnant with the Goddess of Wisdom, and eyebrows the contractions of which express their will, the grandly arched eyes of the queen of the gods, and a mouth shaped like that whose touch stirred with delight the loved Branchus.[2] The soft hair plays about the divine head as if agitated by a gentle breeze, like the slender waving tendrils of the noble vine; it seems to be anointed with the oil of the gods, and tied by the Graces with pleasing display on the crown of his head. In the presence of this miracle of art I forget all else, and I myself take a lofty position for the purpose of looking upon it in a worthy manner. My breast seems to enlarge and swell with reverence, like the breasts of those who were filled with the spirit of prophecy, and I feel myself transported to Delos and into the Lycæan groves—places which Apollo honored by his presence—for my image seems to receive life and motion, like the beautiful creation of Pygmalion.[3] How is it possible to paint and describe it! Art itself must counsel me, and guide my hand in filling up hereafter the first outlines which I here have sketched. As they who were unable to reach the heads of the divinities which they wished to crown deposited the garlands at the feet of them, so I place at the feet of this image the conception which I have presented of it. . . .

---

[1] **Apollo Belvedere**: Roman copy in marble of famous Greek bronze statue, now lost, of Apollo, the Greek god of poetry, music, prophecy, and medicine, now in the Belvedere of the Vatican Museum, Rome. **Python**: in Greek myth, huge serpent slain by the youthful Apollo.

[2] **Father of the Gods**: Jupiter. **Pandora**: In Greek myth, first woman on earth. **Goddess of Wisdom**: Athena. **Queen of the gods**: Juno. **Branchus**: "a youth of Miletus, son of Smicrus, beloved by Apollo, who gave him the gift of prophecy" (Lempriere).

[3] **Pygmalion**: in Greek myth, a sculptor who created the image of a woman so beautiful he fell in love with her; Aphrodite, the goddess of love, intervened and brought the statue, named Galatea, to life.

SIR JOSHUA REYNOLDS

(1723–1792)

The most fashionable portrait-painter in England in the eighteenth century, Joshua Reynolds succeeded in raising the art of portraiture to that of the highest artistic genre, history painting, by presenting his sitters in the guise of classical deities and heroes. Among his most famous idealizing or "classical" portraits are those of the actress Sarah Siddons as "The Tragic Muse" and of the three Montgomery sisters decorating a bust of Hymen as "The Three Irish Graces." He was knighted for his services to the Crown as painter to the king in 1768. When the Royal Academy of Art was founded in 1768, he became its first president, and gave an annual presidential address or discourse on the purposes and value of painting. As president, Reynolds was anxious to gain the same national status for the visual arts as had been achieved by literature; he therefore insisted that his students imitate classical art and obey the rules established by those painters he defined as the "masters" of painting: Raphael, Titian, Rembrandt, and above all, Michelangelo.

from Discourses on Art

—*from* DISCOURSE III: THE GREAT LEADING PRINCIPLES OF THE GRAND STYLE—
(1770)

. . . The principle now laid down, that the perfection of this art does not consist in mere imitation, is far from being new or singular. It is, indeed, supported by the general opinion of the enlightened part of mankind. The poets, orators, and rhetoricians of antiquity, are continually enforcing this position; that all the arts receive their perfection from an ideal beauty, superior to what is to be found in individual nature. They are ever referring to the practice of the painters and sculptors of their times, particularly Phidias (the favourite artist of antiquity) to illustrate their assertions. As if they could not sufficiently express their admiration of this genius by what they knew, they have recourse to poetical enthusiasm. They call it inspiration; a gift from heaven. The artist is supposed to have ascended the celestial regions, to furnish his mind with this perfect idea of beauty. "He," says Proclus, "who takes for his model such forms as nature produces, and confines himself to an exact imitation of them, will never attain to what is perfectly beautiful. For the works of nature are full of disproportion, and fall very short of the true standard of beauty. So that Phidias, when he formed his Jupiter, did not copy any object ever presented to his sight; but contemplated only that image which he had conceived in his mind from Homer's description." And thus Cicero, speaking of the same Phidias: "Neither did this artist," says he, "when he carved the image of Jupiter or Minerva, set before him any one human figure, as a pattern, which he was to copy; but having a more perfect idea of beauty fixed in his mind, this he steadily contemplated, and to the imitation of this all his skill and labour were directed."[1]

The Moderns are not less convinced than the Ancients of this superior power existing in the art; nor less sensible of its effects. Every language has adopted terms expressive of this excellence. The *gusto grande* of the Italians, the *beau ideal* of the French, and the *great style, genius*, and *taste* among the English, are but different appellations of the same thing. It is this intellectual dignity, they say, that ennobles the painter's art; that lays the line between him and the mere mechanick; and produces those great

[1] **Phidias:** Greek sculptor of fifth-century BC Athens; regarded as greatest of ancient Greek sculptors; among his most notable works were the sculptures of the Parthenon and the Propylaeus on the Acropolis at Athens, the statue of Olympian Zeus at Elis, and the statue of an Amazon at Ephesus. **Proclus:** Greek Neoplatonic philosopher (410?–485). **Cicero:** Marcus Tullius Cicero (106–43 BC), Roman orator, statesman, and philosopher.

effects in an instant, which eloquence and poetry, by slow and repeated efforts, are scarcely able to attain. . . .

It is not easy to define in what this great style consists; nor to describe, by words, the proper means of acquiring it, if the mind of the student should be at all capable of such an acquisition. Could we teach taste or genius by rules, they would be no longer taste and genius. But though there neither are, nor can be, any precise invariable rules for the exercise, or the acquisition, of these great qualities, yet we may truly say that they always operate in proportion to our attention in observing the works of nature, to our skill in selecting, and to our care in digesting, methodizing, and comparing our observations. There are many beauties in our art, that seem, at first, to lie without the reach of precept, and yet may easily be reduced to practical principles. Experience is all in all; but it is not every one who profits by experience; and most people err, not so much from want of capacity to find their object, as from not knowing what object to pursue. This great ideal perfection and beauty are not to be sought in the heavens, but upon the earth. They are about us, and upon every side of us. But the power of discovering what is deformed in nature, or in other words, what is particular and uncommon, can be acquired only by experience; and the whole beauty and grandeur of the art consists, in my opinion, in being able to get above all singular forms, local customs, particularities, and details of every kind.

All the objects which are exhibited to our view by nature, upon close examination will be found to have their blemishes and defects. The most beautiful forms have something about them like weakness, minuteness, or imperfection. But it is not every eye that perceives these blemishes. It must be an eye long used to the contemplation and comparison of these forms; and which, by a long habit of observing what any set of objects of the same kind have in common, has acquired the power of discerning what each wants in particular. This long laborious comparison should be the first study of the painter, who aims at the greatest style. By this means, he acquires a just idea of beautiful forms; he corrects nature by herself, her imperfect state by her more perfect. His eye being enabled to distinguish the accidental deficiencies, excrescences, and deformities of things, from their general figures, he makes out an abstract idea of their forms more perfect than any one original; and what may seem a paradox, he learns to design naturally by drawing his figures unlike to any one object. This idea of the perfect state of nature, which the Artist calls the Ideal Beauty, is the great leading principle, by which works of genius are conducted. By this Phidias acquired his fame. He wrought upon a sober principle, what has so much excited the enthusiasm of the world; and by this method you, who have courage to tread the same path, may acquire equal reputation.

This is the idea which has acquired, and which seems to have a right to the epithet of *divine*; as it may be said to preside, like a supreme judge, over all the productions of nature; appearing to be possessed of the will and intention of the Creator, as far as they regard the external form of living beings. When a man once possesses this idea in its perfection, there is no danger, but that he will be sufficiently warmed by it himself, and be able to warm and ravish every one else.

Thus it is from a reiterated experience, and a close comparison of the objects in nature, that an artist becomes possessed of the idea of that central form, if I may so express it, from which every deviation is deformity. But the investigation of this form, I grant, is painful, and I know but of one method of shortening the road; this is, by a careful study of the works of the ancient sculptors; who, being indefatigable in the school of nature, have left models of that perfect form behind them, which an artist would prefer as supremely beautiful, who had spent his whole life in that single contemplation. But if industry carried them thus far, may not you also hope for the same reward from the same labour? We have the same school opened to us, that was opened to them; for nature denies her instructions to none, who desire to become her pupils.

This laborious investigation, I am aware, must appear superfluous to those who think every thing is to be done by felicity, and the powers of native genius. . . .

— *from* DISCOURSE V: RAPHAEL AND MICHELANGELO COMPARED — (1772)

. . . If we put these great artists in a light of comparison with each other, Raphael had more Taste and Fancy, Michael Angelo more Genius and Imagination.[2] The one excelled in beauty, the other in energy. Michael Angelo

[2] **Michael Angelo:** Michelangelo Buonarroti (1475–1564), greatest Italian painter, sculptor, and architect; painted frescoes on ceiling of the Sistine Chapel (Capella Sistina) of the Vatican. **Raphael:** Raffaello Sanzio (1483–1520), Italian painter famed for his Madonnas. **Longinus:** Dionysius Cassius Longinus, first-century AD Greek Platonic philosopher and rhetorician, best known for his treatise *On the Sublime*.

has more of the Poetical Inspiration; his ideas are vast and sublime; his people are a superior order of beings; there is nothing about them, nothing in the air of their actions or their attitudes, or the style and cast of their limbs or features, that reminds us of their belonging to our own species. Raphael's imagination is not so elevated; his figures are not so much disjoined from our own diminutive race of beings, though his ideas are chaste, noble, and of great conformity to their subjects. Michael Angelo's works have a strong, peculiar, and marked character: they seem to proceed from his own mind entirely, and that mind so rich and abundant, that he never needed, or seemed to disdain, to look abroad for foreign help. Raphael's materials are generally borrowed, though the noble structure is his own. The excellency of this extraordinary man lay in the propriety, beauty, and majesty of his characters, the judicious contrivance of his Composition, his correctness of Drawing, purity of Taste, and skilful accommodation of other men's conceptions to his own purpose. Nobody excelled him in that judgement, with which he united to his own observations on Nature, the Energy of Michael Angelo, and the Beauty and Simplicity of the Antique. To the question therefore, which ought to hold the first rank, Raphael or Michael Angelo, it must be answered, that if it is to be given to him who possessed a greater combination of the higher qualities of the art than any other man, there is no doubt but Raphael is the first. But if, as Longinus thinks, the sublime, being the highest excellence that human composition can attain to, abundantly compensates the absence of every other beauty, and atones for all other deficiencies, then Michael Angelo demands the preference.

THE SUBLIME, THE BEAUTIFUL, AND THE PICTURESQUE

EDMUND BURKE

(1729–1797)

Born in Dublin of an Irish Catholic mother and an Anglo-Irish Protestant father, Burke was raised as a Protestant and entered the Middle Temple in London as a lawyer in 1750. He soon gave up his legal studies to pursue a career as a writer, and made his reputation as an aesthetician and literary critic with the publication of his essay *On the Sublime and Beautiful* in 1757. The essay, as Isaac Kramnick has shown in his fine study of Burke, *The Rage of Edmund Burke* (1977), implicitly identifies the sublime with Burke's overbearing father and the beautiful with his submissive, affectionate mother. For Burke's subsequent career as one of the leading conservative ministers of the Tory government and most powerful opponents of Jacobin thought in England, see THE FRENCH REVOLUTION AND RIGHTS OF MAN.

from A Philosophical Enquiry into the Origin of Our Ideas of the Sublime and Beautiful

(1757; 5th edition, 1767)

— PART I, SECT. VI: OF THE PASSIONS WHICH BELONG TO SELF-PRESERVATION —

Most of the ideas which are capable of making a powerful impression on the mind, whether simply of Pain or Pleasure, or of the modifications of those, may be reduced very nearly to these two heads, *self-preservation* and *society*; to the ends of one or the other of which all our passions are calculated to answer. The passions which concern self-preservation, turn mostly on *pain* or *danger*. The ideas of *pain, sickness,* and *death,* fill the mind with strong emotions of horror; but *life* and *health*, though they put us in a capacity of being affected with pleasure, they make no such impression by the simple enjoyment. The passions therefore which are conversant about the preservation of the individual, turn chiefly on *pain* and *danger,* and they are the most powerful of all the passions.

— PART I, SECT. VII: OF THE SUBLIME —

Whatever is fitted in any sort to excite the ideas of pain, and danger, that is to say, whatever is in any sort terrible, or is conversant about terrible objects, or operates in a manner analogous to terror, is a source of the *sublime*; that is, it is productive of the strongest emotion which the mind is capable of feeling. I say the strongest emotion, because I am satisfied the ideas of pain are much more powerful than those which enter on the part of pleasure. Without all doubt, the torments which we may be made to suffer, are much greater in their effect on the body and mind, than any pleasures which the most learned voluptuary could suggest, or than the liveliest imagination, and the most sound and exquisitely sensible body could enjoy. Nay I am in great doubt whether any man could be found who would earn a life of the most perfect satisfaction, at the price of ending it in the torments, which justice inflicted in a few hours on the late unfortunate regicide[1] in France. But as pain is stronger in its operation than pleasure, so death is in general a much more affect-

[1] **late . . . regicide:** Robert François Damiens (1715–1757), fanatic who attempted to assassinate King Louis XV at Versailles (5 January 1757); tortured and executed.

ing idea than pain; because there are very few pains, however exquisite, which are not preferred to death; nay, what generally makes pain itself, if I may say so, more painful, is, that it is considered as an emissary of this king of terrors. When danger or pain press too nearly, they are incapable of giving any delight, and are simply terrible; but at certain distances, and with certain modifications, they may be, and they are delightful, as we every day experience. The cause of this I shall endeavour to investigate hereafter.

— PART I, SECT. VIII: OF THE PASSIONS WHICH BELONG TO SOCIETY —

The other head under which I class our passions, is that of *society,* which may be divided into two sorts. I. The society of the *sexes,* which answers the purposes of propagation; and next, that more *general society,* which we have with men and with other animals, and which we may in some sort be said to have even with the inanimate world. The passions belonging to the preservation of the individual, turn wholly on pain and danger; those which belong to *generation,* have their origin in gratifications and *pleasures;* the pleasure most directly belonging to this purpose is of a lively character, rapturous and violent, and confessedly the highest pleasure of sense; yet the absence of this so great an enjoyment, scarce amounts to an uneasiness; and except at particular times, I do not think it affects at all. When men describe in what manner they are affected by pain and danger; they do not dwell on the pleasure of health and the comfort of security, and then lament the *loss* of these satisfactions; the whole turns upon the actual pains and horrors which they endure. But if you listen to the complaints of a forsaken lover, you observe, that he insists largely on the pleasures which he enjoyed, or hoped to enjoy, and on the perfection of the object of his desires; it is the *loss* which is always uppermost in his mind. . . .

— PART II, SECT. I: OF THE PASSION CAUSED BY THE SUBLIME —

The passion caused by the great and sublime in *nature,* when those causes operate most powerfully, is astonishment; and astonishment is that state of the soul, in which all its motions are suspended, with some degree of horror. In this case the mind is so entirely filled with its object, that it cannot entertain any other, nor by consequence reason on that object which employs it. Hence arises the great power of the sublime, that far from being produced by them, it anticipates our reasonings, and hurries us on by an irresistible force. Astonishment, as I have said, is the effect of the sublime in its highest degree; the inferior effects are admiration, reverence, and respect.

— PART II, SECT. II: TERROR —

No passion so effectually robs the mind of all its powers of acting and reasoning as fear. For fear being an apprehension of pain or death, it operates in a manner that resembles actual pain. Whatever therefore is terrible, with regard to sight, is sublime too, whether this cause of terror, be endued with greatness of dimensions or not . . .

— PART II, SECT. III: OBSCURITY —

To make any thing very terrible, obscurity seems in general to be necessary. . . . No person seems better to have understood the secret of heightening, or of setting terrible things, if I may use the expression, in their strongest light, by the force of a judicious obscurity, than Milton. His description of Death in the second book is admirably studied; it is astonishing with what a gloomy pomp, with what a significant and expressive uncertainty of strokes and colouring he has finished the portrait of the king of terrors.

> The other shape,
> If shape it might be call'd that shape had none
> Distinguishable, in member, joint, or limb;
> Or substance might be call'd that shadow seem'd,
> For each seem'd either; black he stood as night;
> Fierce as ten furies; terrible as hell;
> And shook a deadly dart. What seem'd his head
> The likeness of a kingly crown had on.[2]

In this description all is dark, uncertain, confused, terrible, and sublime to the last degree.

— PART II, SECT. V: POWER —

Besides these things which *directly* suggest the idea of danger, and those which produce a similar effect from a mechanical cause, I know of nothing sublime which is not some modification of power. . . . [P]ain is always inflicted by a power in some way superior, because we never submit to pain willingly. So that strength, violence, pain, and terror, are ideas that rush in upon the mind together. . . . The power which arises from institution in kings and commanders, has the same connection with terror. Sovereigns are frequently addressed with the title of *dread majesty.* And it

[2] Milton, *Paradise Lost,* II.666–673.

may be observed, that young persons little acquainted with the world, and who have not been used to approach men in power, are commonly struck with an awe which takes away the free use of their faculties. . . . I say then, that whilst we consider the Godhead merely as he is an object of the understanding, which forms a complex idea of power, wisdom, justice, goodness, all stretched to a degree far exceeding the bounds of our comprehension, whilst we consider the divinity in this refined and abstracted light, the imagination and passions are little or nothing affected. But because we are bound, by the condition of our nature, to ascend to these pure and intellectual ideas, through the medium of sensible images, and to judge of these divine qualities by their evident acts and exertions, it becomes extremely hard to disentangle our idea of the cause from the effect by which we are led to know it. Thus when we contemplate the Deity, his attributes and their operation coming united on the mind, form a sort of sensible image, and as such are capable of affecting the imagination. Now, though in a just idea of the Deity, perhaps none of his attributes are predominant, yet to our imagination, his power is by far the most striking. Some reflection, some comparing is necessary to satisfy us of his wisdom, his justice, and his goodness. To be struck with his power, it is only necessary that we should open our eyes. But whilst we contemplate so vast an object, under the arm, as it were, of almighty power, and invested upon every side with omnipresence, we shrink into the minuteness of our own nature, and are, in a manner, annihilated before him. And though a consideration of his other attributes may relieve in some measure our apprehensions; yet no conviction of the justice with which it is exercised, nor the mercy with which it is tempered, can wholly remove the terror that naturally arises from a force which nothing can withstand. If we rejoice, we rejoice with trembling; and even whilst we are receiving benefits, we cannot but shudder at a power which can confer benefits of such mighty importance. . . .

— PART II, SECT. VI: PRIVATION —

All *general* privations are great, because they are all terrible; *Vacuity, Darkness, Solitude,* and *Silence.* . . .

— PART II, SECT. VIII: INFINITY —

Another source of the sublime, is *infinity;* if it does not rather belong to the last. Infinity has a tendency to fill the mind with that sort of delightful horror, which is the most genuine effect, and truest test of the sublime. There are scarce any things which can become the objects of our senses, that are really and in their own nature infinite. But the eye not being able to perceive the bounds of many things, they seem to be infinite, and they produce the same effects as if they were really so. We are deceived in the like manner, if the parts of some large object are so continued to any indefinite number, that the imagination meets no check which may hinder its extending them at pleasure. . . .

— PART III, SECT. I: OF BEAUTY —

It is my design to consider beauty as distinguished from the sublime; and, in the course of the enquiry, to examine how far it is consistent with it. . . . By beauty I mean, that quality, or those qualities in bodies, by which they cause love, or some passion similar to it. . . . I likewise distinguish love, by which I mean that satisfaction which arises to the mind upon contemplating any thing beautiful, of whatsoever nature it may be, from desire or lust; which is an energy of the mind, that hurries us on to the possession of certain objects, that do not affect us as they are beautiful, but by means altogether different. . . .

— PART III, SECT. XIII: BEAUTIFUL OBJECTS SMALL —

. . . The sublime, which is the cause of the former, always dwells on great objects, and terrible; the latter on small ones, and pleasing; we submit to what we admire, but we love what submits to us; in one case we are forced, in the other we are flattered into compliance. In short, the ideas of the sublime and the beautiful stand on foundations so different, that it is hard, I had almost said impossible, to think of reconciling them in the same subject, without considerably lessening the effect of the one or the other upon the passions. So that, attending to their quantity, beautiful objects are comparatively small.

— PART III, SECTS. XIV–XVI: SMOOTHNESS —

The next property constantly observable in such objects is *Smoothness:* A quality so essential to beauty, that I do not now recollect any thing beautiful that is not smooth. . . . For take any beautiful object, and give it a broken and rugged surface, and however well formed it may be in other respects, it pleases no longer. . . .

. . . perfectly beautiful bodies are not composed of angular parts, so their parts never continue long in the same right line. . . . In this description I have before me the idea of a dove; it agrees very well with most of the conditions of beauty. It is smooth and downy; its parts are (to use that expression) melted into one another; you are presented with no sudden protuberance through the whole, and yet the whole is continually changing. Observe that part of a beautiful woman where she is perhaps the most beautiful, about the neck and breasts; the smoothness; the softness; the easy and insensible swell; the variety of the surface, which is never for the smallest space the same; the deceitful maze, through which the unsteady eye slides giddily, without knowing where to fix, or whither it is carried. . . .

An air of robustness and strength is very prejudicial to beauty. An appearance of *delicacy*, and even of fragility, is almost essential to it. . . .

— PART III, SECT. XXVII: THE SUBLIME AND BEAUTIFUL COMPARED —

On closing this general view of beauty, it naturally occurs, that we should compare it with the sublime; and in this comparison there appears a remarkable contrast. For sublime objects are vast in their dimensions, beautiful ones comparatively small; beauty should be smooth and polished; the great, rugged and negligent; beauty should shun the right line, yet deviate from it insensibly; the great in many cases loves the right line, and when it deviates, it often makes a strong deviation; beauty should not be obscure; the great ought to be dark and gloomy; beauty should be light and delicate; the great ought to be solid, and even massive. They are indeed ideas of a very different nature, one being founded on pain, the other on pleasure; and however they may vary afterwards from the direct nature of their causes, yet these causes keep up an eternal distinction between them, a distinction never to be forgotten by any whose business it is to affect the passions. . . .

WILLIAM GILPIN

(1724–1804)

William Gilpin was educated at The Queen's College, Oxford, and subsequently became a schoolmaster and vicar of Boldre. His concept of the picturesque was laid out in numerous writings. He defined the theoretical principles of the picturesque in relation to the beautiful in his *Three Essays: On Picturesque Beauty; On Picturesque Travel; and On Sketching Landscape* (1792). This treatise was preceded and followed by numerous illustrated guidebooks to the picturesque in English landscape, including accounts of his walking tours in Wye and South Wales (1782), the Lake District (1789), and the Scottish Highlands (1800). His work was endorsed by William Payne Knight in his *The Landscape* (1794), by Uvedale Price in his *Essays on the Picturesque* (1794), and by the landscape-gardener Humphrey Repton (1752–1818), who constructed numerous picturesque gardens on English country estates.

Gilpin's work became so famous that it inspired an equally well-known burlesque by William Combe, *The Tour of Dr. Syntax in Search of the Picturesque,* written to accompany Thomas Rowlandson's satiric colored prints and drawings. Dr. Syntax is a grotesque figure of a clergyman and schoolmaster who sets out during the school holidays on his old horse Grizzle to "make a TOUR and write it," and meets with a series of absurd misadventures. Originally published in Rudolph Ackermann's *Poetical Magazine* in 1809, it was reissued as a book in 1812 that went into numerous editions. It was so popular that Combe and Rowlandson followed it with *The Second Tour of Dr. Syntax in Search of Consolation* (after his wife died) in 1820 and *The Third Tour of Dr. Syntax in Search of a Wife* in 1821.

from Three Essays: On Picturesque Beauty; On Picturesque Travel; and On Sketching Landscape

(1792)

—*from* ESSAY I: ON PICTURESQUE BEAUTY—

Disputes about beauty might perhaps be involved in less confusion, if a distinction were established, which certainly exists, between such objects as are *beautiful,* and such as are *picturesque*—between those, which please the eye in their *natural state;* and those, which please from some quality, capable of being *illustrated in painting.* . . .

The question simply is, What is that quality in objects, which particularly marks them as picturesque?

In examining the *real object,* we shall find, one source of beauty arises from that species of elegance, which we call *smoothness* or *neatness;* for the terms are nearly synonymous. The higher the marble is polished, the brighter the silver is rubbed, and the more the mahogony shines, the more each is considered as an object of beauty: as if the eye is delighted in gliding smoothly over a surface. . . . Mr. Burke, enumerating the properties of beauty, considers *smoothness* as one of the most essential.

But in *picturesque representation* it seems somewhat odd, yet we shall perhaps find it equally true, that the reverse of this is the case; and that the ideas of *neat* and *smooth,* instead of being picturesque, in fact disqualify the object, in which they reside, from any pretensions to *picturesque beauty.*—Nay farther, we do not scruple to assert, that *roughness* forms the most essential point of difference between the *beautiful,* and the *picturesque;* as it seems to be that particular quality, which makes objects chiefly pleasing in painting.—I use the general term *roughness;* but properly speaking roughness relates only to the surfaces of bodies: when we speak of their delineation, we use the word *ruggedness.* Both ideas however equally enter into the picturesque; and both are observable in the smaller, as well as in the larger parts of nature—in the outline, and bark of a tree, as in the rude summit, and craggy sides of a mountain.

Let us then examine our theory by an appeal to experience; and try how far these qualities enter into the ideal of *picturesque beauty*; and how far they mark that difference among objects, which is the ground of our own inquiry.

A piece of Palladian architecture[1] may be elegant in the last degree. The proportion of its parts—the propriety of its ornaments—and the symmetry of the whole, may be highly pleasing. But if we introduce it in a picture, it immediately becomes a formal object, and ceases to please. Should we wish to give it picturesque beauty, we must use the mallet, instead of the chissel: we must beat down one half of it, deface the other, and throw the mutilated members around in heaps. In short, from a *smooth* building we must turn it into a *rough* ruin. No painter, who had the choice of the two objects, would hesitate a moment.

Again, why does an elegant piece of garden-ground make no figure on canvas? The shape is pleasing; the combination of the objects, harmonious; and the winding of the walk in the very line of beauty. All this is true; but the *smoothness* of the whole, tho right, and as it should be in nature, offends in picture. Turn the lawn into a piece of broken ground; plant rugged oaks instead of flowering shrubs; break the edges of the walk; give it the rudeness of a road; mark it with wheel-tracks; and scatter around a few stones, and brushwood; in a word, instead of making the whole *smooth*, make it *rough*; and you make it also picturesque. All the other ingredients of beauty it already possessed.

You sit for your picture. The master, at your desire, paints your head combed smooth and powdered from the barber's hand. This may give it a more striking likeness, as it is more the resemblance of the real object. But is it therefore a more pleasing picture? I fear not. Leave Reynolds to himself, and he will make it picturesque: he will throw the hair dishevelled about your shoulders. Virgil would have done the same. . . . would you see the human face in its highest form of *picturesque beauty*, examine that patriarchal head. What is it, which gives that dignity of character; that force of expression; those lines of wisdom, and experience; that energetic meaning, so far beyond the rosy hue, or even the bewitching smile of youth? What is it, but the forehead furrowed with wrinkles? the prominent cheekbone, catching the light? the muscles of the cheek strongly marked, and losing themselves in the shaggy beard? and, above all, the austere brow, projecting over the eye—that feature which particularly struck Homer in his idea of Jupiter, and which he had probably seen finely represented in some statue? in a word, what is it, but the *rough* touches of age?

As an object of the mixed kind, partaking both of the *beautiful*, and the *picturesque*, we admire the human form also . . . ; yet the more its *smooth surface is ruffled*, if I may so speak, the more picturesque it appears. When it is agitated by passion, and its muscles swol'n by strong exertion, the whole frame is shewn to the most advantage.

. . . Picturesque composition consists in uniting in one whole a variety of parts; and these parts can only be obtained from rough objects. . . . From *rough* objects also he [the artist] seeks the *effect of light and shade*, which they are as well disposed to produce, as they are the beauty of the composition. One uniform light, or one uniform shade produces no effect. It is the various surfaces of objects, sometimes turning to the light in one way, and sometimes in another, that gives the painter his choice of opportunity in massing, and graduating both his lights, and shades.—The *richness* also of the light depends on the breaks, and little recesses, which it finds on the surfaces of bodies. What the painter calls *richness* on a surface, is only a variety of little parts; on which the light shining, shews all its small inequalities, and roughnesses; and in the painter's language, *inriches* it. . . .

In *colouring* also, *rough* objects give the painter another advantage. Smooth bodies are commonly as uniform in their colour, as they are in their surface. In glossy objects, the smoothness, the colouring may sometimes vary. In general, however, it is of one uniform colour; while the fractured rock presents its grey surface, adorned with patches of greensward running down its guttered sides; and the broken ground is every where varied with an okery tint, a grey gravel, or a leaden-coloured clay: so that in fact the rich colours of the ground arise generally from its broken surface.

From such reasoning then we infer, that it is not merely for the sake of his *execution*, that the painter prefers *rough* objects to *smooth*. The very essence of his art requires it.

—*from* ESSAY II: ON PICTURESQUE TRAVEL—

. . . In treating of picturesque travel, we may consider first its *object*; and secondly its sources of *amusement*.

Its *object* is beauty of every kind, which either art, or nature can produce: but it is chiefly that species of

[1] **Palladian architecture**: style associated with Andrea Palladio (1508–1580), Venetian architect, notable for geometric regularity, use of rounded arches and classical columns.

picturesque beauty, which we have endeavoured to characterise in the preceding essay. This great object we pursue through the scenery of nature; and examine it by the rules of painting. We seek it among all the ingredients of landscape — trees — rocks — broken grounds — woods — rivers — lakes — plains — vallies — mountains — and distances. These objects *in themselves* produce infinite variety. No two rocks, or trees are exactly the same. They are varied, a second time, by *combination,* and almost as much, a third time, by different *lights, and shades,* and other aereal effects. Sometimes we find among them the exhibition of *a whole;* but oftener we find only beautiful *parts.* . . .

But among all the objects of art, the picturesque eye is perhaps most inquisitive after the elegant relics of ancient architecture; the ruined tower, the gothic arch, the remains of castles, and abbeys. These are the richest legacies of art. They are consecrated by time; and almost deserve the veneration we pay to the works of nature itself.

Thus universal are the objects of picturesque travel. We pursue *beauty* in every shape; through nature, through art; and all its various arrangements in form, and colour; admiring it in the grandest objects, and not rejecting it in the humblest.

From the *objects* of picturesque travel, we consider its *sources of amusement* — or in what way the mind is gratified by these objects.

. . . The first source of amusement to the picturesque traveller, is the *pursuit* of his object — the expectation of new scenes continually opening, and arising to his view. We suppose the country to have been unexplored. Under this circumstance the mind is kept constantly in an agreeable suspense. The love of novelty is the foundation of this pleasure. Every distant horizon promises something new; and with this pleasing expectation we follow nature through all her walks. We pursue her from hill to dale; and hunt after those various beauties, with which she everywhere abounds.

The pleasures of the chase are universal. A hare started before dogs is enough to set a whole country in an uproar. The plough and the spade are deserted. Care is left behind; and every human faculty is dilated with joy.

And shall we suppose it a greater pleasure to the sportsman to pursue a trivial animal, than it is to the man of taste to pursue the beauties of nature? to follow her through all her recesses? to obtain a sudden glance, as she flits past him in some airy shape? to trace her through the mazes of the cover? to wind after her along the vale? or along the reaches of the river?

After the pursuit we are gratified with the *attainment* of the object. Our amusement on this head arises from the employment of the mind in examining the beautiful scenes we have found. Sometimes we examine them under the idea of a *whole:* we admire the composition, the colouring, and the light, in one *comprehensive view.* When we are fortunate enough to fall in with scenes of this kind, we are highly delighted. But as we have less frequent opportunities of being thus gratified, we are more commonly employed in analyzing the *parts of scenes;* which may be exquisitely beautiful, tho unable to produce a whole. We examine what would amend the composition; how little is wanting to reduce it to the rules of our art; what a trifling circumstance sometimes forms the limit between beauty, and deformity. Or we compose the objects before us with other objects of the same kind: — or perhaps we compare them with the imitations of art. From all these operations of the mind results great amusement.

But it is not from this *scientifical* employment, that we derive our chief pleasure. We are most delighted, when some grand scene, tho perhaps of incorrect composition, rising before the eye, strikes us beyond the power of thought — when the *vox faucibus haeret;* and every mental operation is suspended. In this pause of intellect; this *deliquium*[2] of the soul, an enthusiastic sensation of pleasure overspreads it, previous to any examination by the rules of art. The general idea of the scene makes an impression, before any appeal is made to the judgement. We rather *feel,* than *survey* it.

. . . The more refined our taste grows from *the study of nature,* the more insipid are the *works of art.* Few of its efforts please. The idea of the great original is so strong, that the copy must be very pure, if it do not disgust. But the varieties of nature's charts are such, that, study them as we can, new varieties will always arise: and let our taste be ever so refined, her works on which it is formed (at least when we consider them as *objects*), must always go beyond it; and furnish fresh sources both of pleasure and amusement.

---

[2] **vox faucibus haeret:** Latin, "the voice sticks in the throat." **deliquium:** Latin, "eclipse" (as of a heavenly body).

ADAM SMITH

(1723–1790)

Best known as the founder of laissez-faire political economy, the Scottish philosopher Adam Smith began his career as a professor of logic and ethics at the University of Glasgow. He was part of a brilliant intellectual circle known as the "Athens of the North," centered in Edinburgh in the mid-eighteenth century, that included David Hume and Dr. Hugh Blair. Smith won his reputation as a specialist in theology, ethics, and jurisprudence with the publication of his *Theory of Moral Sentiments* in 1759. After travelling in France, where he met Voltaire and other French philosophers, he retired in 1767 to complete his life-work on political economy. His *Inquiry into the Nature and Causes of the Wealth of Nations* (1776) postulated the labor theory of value; argued that in a laissez-faire economy, the impulse of self-interest would bring about the public welfare; and opposed monopolies. His pragmatism together with his commitment to social ethics differentiates him from the more utilitarian, rigorously mathematical calculations of such later economists as David Ricardo.

from The Theory of Moral Sentiments

(1759)

from *Part I: Of the Propriety of Action Consisting of Three Sections*

Section I: Of the Sense of Propriety

— CHAP. I: OF SYMPATHY —

How selfish soever man may be supposed, there are evidently some principles in his nature, which interest him in the fortune of others, and render their happiness necessary to him, though he derives nothing from it, except the pleasure of seeing it. Of this kind is pity or compassion, the emotion which we feel for the misery of others, when we either see it, or are made to conceive it in a very lively manner. That we often derive sorrow from the sorrow of others, is a matter of fact too obvious to require any instances to prove it; for this sentiment, like all the other original passions of human nature, is by no means confined to the virtuous and humane, though they perhaps may feel it with the most exquisite sensibility. The greatest ruffian, the most hardened violator of the laws of society, is not altogether without it.

As we have no immediate experience of what other men feel, we can form no idea of the manner in which they are affected, but by conceiving what we ourselves should feel in the like situation. Though our brother is upon the rack, as long as we ourselves are at our ease, our senses will never inform us of what he suffers. They never did and never can carry us beyond our own person, and it is by the imagination only that we can form any conception of what are his sensations. Neither can that faculty help us to this any other way, than by representing to us what would be our own, if we were in his case. It is the impressions of our own senses only, not those of his, which our imaginations copy. By the imagination we place ourselves in his situation, we conceive ourselves enduring all the same torments, we enter as it were into his body and become in some measure him, and thence form some idea of his sensations and even feel something which, though weaker in degree, is not altogether unlike them. His agonies, when they are thus brought home to ourselves, when we have thus adopted and made them our own, begin at last to affect us, and we then tremble and shudder at the thought of what he feels. For as to be in pain or distress of any kind excites the most excessive sorrow, so to conceive or to imagine that we are in it, excites some degree of the same emotion, in proportion to the vivacity or dulness of the conception.

That this is the source of our fellow-feeling for the misery of others, that it is by changing places in fancy with the sufferer, that we come either to conceive or to be affected by what he feels, may be demonstrated by many obvious observations, if it should not be thought sufficiently evident of itself. When we see a stroke aimed and just ready to fall upon the leg or arm of another person, we naturally shrink and draw back our own leg or our own arm; and when it does fall, we feel it in some measure, and are hurt by it as well as the sufferer. The mob, when they are gazing at a dancer on the slack rope, naturally writhe and twist and balance their own bodies, as they see him do, and as they feel that they themselves must do if in his situation. Persons of delicate fibres and a weak constitution of body, complain that in looking on the sores and ulcers which are exposed by beggars in the streets, they are apt to feel an itching or uneasy sensation in the correspondent part of their own bodies. The horror which they conceive at the misery of those wretches affects that particular part in themselves more than any other; because that horror arises from conceiving what they themselves would suffer, if they really were the wretches whom they are looking upon, and if that particular part in themselves was actually affected in the same miserable manner. The very force of this conception is sufficient, in their feeble frames, to produce that itching or uneasy sensation complained of. Men of the most robust make, observe that in looking upon sore eyes they often feel a very sensible soreness in their own, which proceeds from the same reason; that organ being in the strongest man more delicate than any other part of the body is in the weakest.

Neither is it those circumstances only, which create pain or sorrow, that call forth our fellow-feeling. Whatever is the passion which arises from any object in the person principally concerned, an analogous emotion springs up, at the thought of his situation, in the breast of every attentive spectator. Our joy for the deliverance of those heroes of tragedy or romance who interest us, is as sincere as our grief for their distress, and our fellow-feeling with their misery is not more real than that with their happiness. We enter into their gratitude towards those faithful friends who did not desert them in their difficulties; and we heartily go along with their resentment against those perfidious traitors who injured, abandoned, or deceived them. In every passion of which the mind of man is susceptible, the emotions of the by-stander always correspond to what, by bringing the case home to himself, he imagines, should be the sentiments of the sufferer.

Pity and compassion are words appropriated to signify our fellow-feeling with the sorrow of others. Sympathy, though its meaning was, perhaps, originally the same, may now, however, without much impropriety, be made use of to denote our fellow-feeling with any passion whatever. . . .

— CHAP. V: OF THE AMIABLE AND RESPECTABLE VIRTUES —

Upon these two different efforts, upon that of the spectator to enter into the sentiments of the person principally concerned, and upon that of the person principally concerned, to bring down his emotions to what the spectator can go along with, are founded two different sets of virtues. The soft, the gentle, the amiable virtues, the virtues of candid condescension and indulgent humanity, are founded upon the one: the great, the awful and respectable, the virtues of self-denial, of self-government, of that command of the passions which subjects all the movements of our nature to what our own dignity and honour, and the propriety of our own conduct require, derive their origin from the other.

How amiable does he appear to be, whose sympathetic heart seems to re-echo all the sentiments of those with whom he converses, who grieves for their calamities, who resents their injuries, and rejoices at their good fortune! When we bring home to ourselves the situation of his companions, we enter into their gratitude, and feel what consolation they must derive from the tender sympathy of so affectionate a friend. And for a contrary reason, how disagreeable does he appear to be, whose hard and obdurate heart feels for himself only, but is altogether insensible of the happiness or misery of others! We enter, in this case too, into the pain which his presence must give to every mortal with whom he converses, to those especially with whom we are most apt to sympathize, the unfortunate and the injured. . . .

And hence it is, that to feel much for others and little for ourselves, that to restrain our selfish, and to indulge our benevolent affections, constitutes the perfection of human nature; and can alone produce among mankind that harmony of sentiments and passions in which consist their whole grace and propriety. As to love our neighbour as we love ourselves is the great law of christianity, so it is the great precept of nature to love ourselves only as we love our neighbour, or what comes to the same thing, as our neighbour is capable of loving us.

As taste and good judgment, when they are considered as qualities which deserve praise and admiration, are supposed to imply a delicacy of sentiment and an acuteness of understanding not commonly to be met with; so the virtues of sensibility and self-command are not apprehended to consist in the ordinary, but in the uncommon degrees of those qualities. The amiable virtue of humanity requires, surely, a sensibility, much beyond what is possessed by the rude vulgar of mankind. The great and exalted virtue of magnanimity undoubtedly demands much more than that degree of self-command, which the weakest of mortals are capable of exerting. As in the common degree of the intellectual qualities, there are no abilities; so in the common degree of the moral, there is no virtue. Virtue is excellence, something uncommonly great and beautiful, which rises far above what is vulgar and ordinary. The amiable virtues consist in that degree of sensibility which surprizes by its exquisite and unexpected delicacy and tenderness. The awful and respectable, in that degree of self-command which astonishes by its amazing superiority over the most ungovernable passions of human nature. . . .

It is in the same manner that we judge of the productions of all arts which address themselves to the imagination. When a critic examines the work of any of the great masters for poetry or painting, he may sometimes examine it by an idea of perfection, in his own mind, which neither that nor any other human work will ever come up to; and as long as he compares it with this standard, he can see nothing in it but faults and imperfections. But when he come to consider the rank which it ought to hold among other works of the same kind, he necessarily compares it with a very different standard, the common degree of excellence which is usually attained in this particular art; and when he judges of it by this new measure, it may often appear to deserve the highest applause, upon account of its approaching much nearer to perfection than the greater part of those works which can be brought into competition with it.

MARY WOLLSTONECRAFT

(1759–1797)

Wollstonecraft's attitude toward the cult of sensibility changed significantly during her literary career. In her first novel, *Mary, A Fiction* (1788), the eponymous heroine is an exemplar of the virtues of sensibility, filled with compassion for the sufferings of others. In her *Vindication of the Rights of Woman* (1792),* she denounced the cult of sensibility as encouraging feminine irrationality and emotional self-indulgence. But in her final work, the unfinished novel *Maria, or the Wrongs of Woman* (1798), she attempted to distinguish between positive and negative forms of sensibility. In the passage included here, Maria writes to her lost daughter from the madhouse where her husband, George Venable, has imprisoned her.

from Mary, A Fiction

(1788)

— *from* CHAPTER XXIV —

Mary still continued weak and low, though it was spring, and all nature began to look gay; with more than usual brightness the sun shone, and a little robin which she had cherished during the winter sung one of his best songs. The family were particularly civil this fine morning, and tried to prevail on her to walk out. Any thing like kindness melted her; she consented.

Softer emotions banished her melancholy, and she directed her steps to the habitation she had rendered comfortable.

Emerging out of a dreary chamber, all nature looked cheerful; when she had last walked out, snow covered the ground, and bleak winds pierced her through and through: now the hedges were green, the blossoms adorned the trees, and the birds sung. She reached the dwelling, without being much exhausted; and while she rested there, observed the children sporting on the grass, with improved complexions. The mother with tears thanked her deliverer, and pointed out her comforts. Mary's tears flowed not only from sympathy, but a complication of feelings and recollections; the affections which bound her to her fellow creatures began again to play, and reanimated nature. She observed the change in herself, tried to account for it, and wrote with her pencil a rhapsody on sensibility.

"Sensibility is the most exquisite feeling of which the human soul is susceptible: when it pervades us, we feel happy; and could it last unmixed, we might form some conjecture of the bliss of those paradisiacal days, when the obedient passions were under the dominion of reason, and the impulses of the heart did not need correction.

"It is this quickness, this delicacy of feeling, which enables us to relish the sublime touches of the poet, and the painter; it is this, which expands the soul, gives an enthusiastic greatness, mixed with tenderness, when we view the magnificent objects of nature; or hear of a good action. The same effect we experience in the spring, when we hail the returning sun, and the consequent renovation of nature; when the flowers unfold themselves, and exhale their sweets, and the voice of music is heard in the land. Softened by tenderness; the soul is disposed to be virtuous. Is any sensual gratification to be compared to that of feeling the eyes moistened after having comforted the unfortunate?

"Sensibility is indeed the foundation of all our happiness . . ."

from Maria, or the Wrongs of Woman

(1798)

— *from* CHAPTER XIII —

. . . Your improvement, my dearest girl, being ever present to me while I write, I note these feelings, because women, more accustomed to observe manners than actions, are too much alive to ridicule. So much so, that their boasted sensibility is often stifled by false delicacy. True sensibility, the sensibility which is the auxiliary of virtue, and the soul of genius, is in society so occupied with the feelings of others, as scarcely to regard its own sensations. With what reverence have I looked up at my uncle, the dear parent of my mind! when I have seen the sense of his own sufferings, of mind and body, absorbed in a desire to comfort those, whose misfortunes were comparatively trivial. He would have been ashamed of being as indulgent to himself, as he was to others. "Genuine fortitude," he would assert, "consisted in governing our own emotions, and making allowance for the weaknesses in our friends, that we would not tolerate in ourselves. . . ."

SAMUEL TAYLOR COLERIDGE

(1772–1834)

In his *Lectures on Belles Lettres* (1812–1813), his literary biography *Biographia Literaria* (1817),* *The Statesman's Manual* (1816),* and numerous additional essays and notebook entries, Coleridge developed the aesthetic theory that we now call Romanticism. Deeply influenced by the German idealist philosophies of Kant and Schelling, as well as the literary works of A. W. Schlegel, a leader of the Romantic movement in Germany, he developed the concept of the literary work as a heterocosm that reconciles the fundamental polarities of the universe: the tension between the "free life" and the "confining form."

from Lectures on Belles Lettres

(1812)

— MECHANIC AND ORGANIC FORM —

The Subject of the present Lecture is no less than a Question submitted to your Understandings, emancipated from national Prejudice: Are the Plays of *Shakespear* works of rude uncultivated Genius, in which the splendor of the Parts compensates if ought can compensate, for the barbarous Shapelessness & Irregularity of the Whole — To which not only the French Critics, but even his own English Admirers, say — [yes]. Or is the Form equally admirable with the Matter, the Judgement of the great Poet not less deserving of our wonder than his Genius? — Or to repeat the question in other words — Is Shakespear a great Dramatic Poet on account only of those beauties & excellencies which he possesses in common with the Ancients, but with diminished Claims to our Love & Honor to the full extent of his difference from them? — Or are these very differences additional proofs of poetic Wisdom, at once results & symbols of living Power as contrasted with lifeless mechanism, of free & rival originality as contradistinguished from servile Imitation or, more accurately, a blind copying of Effects instead of a true Imitation of the essential Priniciples? — Imagine not I am about to oppose Genius to Rules — No! — the Comparative value of these Rules is the very cause to be tried. — The Spirit of Poetry like all other living Powers, must of necessity circumscribe itself by Rules, were it only to unite Power with Beauty.

It must embody in order to reveal itself; but a living Body is of necessity an organized one — & what is organization, but the connection of Parts to a whole, so that each Part is at once End & Means! — This is no discovery of Criticism — it is a necessity of the human mind — & all nations have felt & obeyed it, in the invention of metre, & measured Sounds, as the vehicle & Involucrum of Poetry, itself, a fellow-growth from the Same Life, even as the Bark is to the Tree. —

No work of true Genius dare want its appropriate Form — neither indeed is there any danger of this — as it must not, so neither can it, be lawless — for it is even this that constitutes its Genius — the power of acting creatively under laws of its own origination —. How then comes it that not only single Zoili,[1] but whole Nations have combined in unhesitating condemnation of our great Dramatist, as a sort of African Nature, fertile in beautiful Monsters, as a wild Heath where Islands of Fertility look greener from the surrounding Waste, where the loveliest Plants now shine out among unsightly weeds and now are choked by their parasitic growth, so intertwined that we cannot disentangle the weed without snapping the Flower? In this statement I have had no reference to the vulgar abuse of Voltaire[2] — save as far as his charges are

[1] **Zoili:** fourth-century BC Greek critic notorious for his savage criticism of Homer; hence a severe critic.

[2] **Voltaire:** François-Marie Arouet de Voltaire (1694–1778), French philosopher and author, major proponent of Enlightenment doctrines of rationality and scepticism.

coincident with the decisions of his Commentators & (so they tell you) his almost idolatrous admirers—The true ground of the mistake, as has been well remarked by a Continental Critic,[3] lies in the confounding mechanical regularity with organic form—The form is mechanic when on any given material we impress a predetermined form, not necessarily arising out of the properties of the material—as when to a mass of wet clay we give whatever shape we wish it to retain when hardened—The organic form on the other hand is innate, it shapes as it developes itself from within, and the fullness of its developement is one & the same with the perfection of its outward Form. Such is the Life, such the form—Nature, the prime Genial Artist, inexhaustible in diverse powers is equally inexhaustible in forms—each Exterior is the physiognomy of the Being within, its true Image reflected & thrown out from the concave mirror—& even such is the appropriate Excellence of her chosen Poet, of our own Shakespear, himself a Nature humanized, a genial Understanding directing self-consciously a power & an implicit wisdom deeper than Consciousness—

from The Statesman's Manual
(1816)

—ALLEGORY AND SYMBOL—

. . . And in nothing is Scriptural history more strongly contrasted with the histories of highest note[1] in the present age than in its freedom from the hollowness of abstractions. While the latter present a shadow-fight of Things and Quantities, the former gives us the history of Men, and balances the important influence of individual Minds with the previous state of the national morals and manners, in which, as constituting a specific susceptibility, it presents to us the true cause both of the Influence itself, and of the Weal or Woe that were its Consequents. How should it be otherwise? The histories and political economy of the present and preceding century partake in the general contagion of its mechanic philosophy, and are the *product* of an unenlivened generalizing Understanding. In the Scriptures they are the living *educts* of the Imagination; of that reconciling and mediatory power, which incorporating the Reason in Images of the Sense, and organizing (as it were) the flux of the Senses by the permanence and self-circling energies of the Reason, gives birth to a system of symbols, harmonious in themselves, and consubstantial with the truths, of which they are the *conductors*. These are the Wheels which Ezekiel beheld, when the hand of the Lord was upon him, and he saw visions of God as he sate among the captives by the river of Chebar. *Whithersoever the Spirit was to go, the wheels went, and thither was their spirit to go: for the spirit of the living creature was in the wheels also.*[2] The truths and the symbols that represent them move in conjunction and form the living chariot that bears up (for *us*) the throne of the Divine Humanity. Hence, by a derivative, indeed, but not a divided, influence, and though in a secondary yet in more than a metaphorical sense, the Sacred Book is worthily intitled *the* WORD OF GOD. Hence too, its contents present to us the stream of time continuous as Life and a symbol of Eternity, inasmuch as the Past and the Future are virtually contained in the Present. According therefore to our relative position on its banks the Sacred History becomes prophetic, the Sacred Prophecies historical, while the power and substance of both inhere in its Laws, its Promises, and its Comminations.[3] In the Scriptures therefore both Facts and Persons must of necessity have a two-fold significance, a past and a future, a temporary and a perpetual, a particular and a universal application. They must be at once Portraits and Ideals.

Eheu! paupertina philosophia in paupertinam religionem ducit:—A hunger-bitten and idea-less philosophy naturally produces a starveling and comfortless religion. It is among the miseries of the present age that it recognizes no medium between *Literal* and *Metaphorical*. Faith is either to be buried in the dead letter, or its name and honors usurped by a counterfeit product of the mechanical understanding, which in the blindness of self-complacency confounds SYMBOLS with ALLEGORIES. Now an Allegory is but a translation of abstract notions into a picture-language which is itself nothing but an abstraction from objects of the senses; the principal being more worthless

[3] **Continental Critic:** August Wilhelm von Schlegel (1767–1845), German Orientalist and man of letters, translator of Shakespeare's plays, brother of Friedrich Schlegel.

[1] **histories of highest note:** those by David Hume (1711–1776), Scottish philosopher and historian, author of *History of England during Reigns of James I and Charles I* (1754 f.), and by Edward Gibbon (1737–1794), author of *The History of the Decline and Fall of the Roman Empire* (1776–1788).

[2] Ezekiel 1:20.

[3] **commination:** denunciation of sinners.

even than its phantom proxy, both alike unsubstantial, and the former shapeless to boot. On the other hand a Symbol (ὁ ἔστιν ἄει ταυτηγόρικον)[4] is characterized by a translucence of the Special in the Individual or of the General in the Especial or of the Universal in the General. Above all by the translucence of the Eternal through and in the Temporal. It always partakes of the Reality which it renders intelligible; and while it enunciates the whole, abides itself as a living part in that Unity, of which it is the representative. The other are but empty echoes which the fancy arbitrarily associates with apparitions of matter, less beautiful but not less shadowy than the sloping orchard or hillside pasture-field seen in the transparent lake below. Alas! for the flocks that are to be led forth to such pastures! . . .

[4] The Greek means "which is always tautegorical," the last word a coinage by Coleridge which means "expressing the *same* subject but with a difference."

WILLIAM HAZLITT

(1778–1830)

The son of a Unitarian minister whose strong liberal political and theological views he endorsed, William Hazlitt became a close friend of Coleridge* and Charles Lamb* in London in 1800. Their example inspired him to give up the Dissenting ministry for which he had been training and to take up instead a career as a man of letters. A prolific journalist, parliamentary reporter, dramatic and literary critic, essayist, and lecturer, he ardently supported the French Revolution and Napoleon. After 1812, his published writings focussed primarily on literature. In *Characters of Shakespeare's Plays* (1817); *The Round Table,* a collection of essays co-authored with Leigh Hunt (1818); *Lectures on the English Poets* (1818), and *Lectures on the English Comic Writers* (1819), he provided the clearest and most insightful exposition of the Romantic aesthetic and its connection to political radicalism that we have.

In 1820 he met Sarah Walker, his landlady's daughter, with whom he fell so obsessively in love that for the next three years his sanity was seriously in question; his moving account of this passionate love and Sarah Walker's resistance to his campaign of sexual harassment is given in his *Liber Amoris* (1823). Arrested for debt and publicly denounced for the behavior revealed in *Liber Amoris,* Hazlitt gradually repaired his fortunes by writing a calmer reflection on love, *Characteristics,* in 1823, and contributing to a new journal, *The Liberal,* founded by Leigh Hunt and Byron. His best known volume of essays, *The Spirit of the Age,* a collection of studies of famous men from his own age and the previous 50 years, appeared in 1826. He devoted the remainder of his life to what he regarded as his best work, a hagiographic account of the career of Napoleon; the first two volumes of his *Life of Napoleon* appeared in 1828, the last two volumes in 1830.

from Lectures on the English Poets
(1818)

—*from* LECTURE I: ON POETRY IN GENERAL—

. . . Poetry then is an imitation of nature, but the imagination and the passions are a part of man's nature. We shape things according to our wishes and fancies, without poetry; but poetry is the most emphatical language that can be found for those creations of the mind "which ecstasy is very cunning in." Neither a mere description of natural objects, nor a mere delineation of natural feelings, however distinct or forcible, constitutes the ultimate end and aim of poetry, without the heightenings of the imagination. The light of poetry is not only a direct but also a reflected light, that while it shows us the object, throws a sparkling radiance on all around it: the flame of the passions, communicated to the imagination, reveals to us, as with a flash of lightning, the inmost recesses of thought, and penetrates our whole being. Poetry represents forms chiefly as they suggest other forms; feelings, as they suggest forms or other feelings. Poetry puts a spirit of life and motion into the universe. It describes the flowing, not the fixed. It does not define the limits of sense, or analyse the distinctions of the understanding, but signifies the excess of the imagination beyond the actual or ordinary impression of any object or feeling. The poetical impression of any object is that uneasy, exquisite sense of beauty or power that cannot be contained within itself; that is impatient of all limit; that (as flame bends to flame) strives to link itself to some other image of kindred beauty or grandeur; to enshrine itself, as it were, in the highest forms of fancy, and to relieve the aching sense of pleasure by expressing it in the boldest manner, and by the most striking examples of the same quality in other instances. Poetry, according to Lord Bacon, for this reason, "has something divine in it, because it raises the mind and hurries it into sublimity, by conforming the shows of things to the desires of the soul, instead of subjecting the soul to external things, as reason and history do."[1] It is strictly the language of the imagination; and the imagination is that faculty which represents objects, not as they are in themselves, but as they are moulded by other thoughts and feelings, into an infinite variety of shapes and combinations of power. This language is not the less true to nature, because it is false in point of fact; but so much the more true and natural, if it conveys the impression which the object under the influence of passion makes on the mind. Let an object, for instance, be presented to the senses in a state of agitation or fear— and the imagination will distort or magnify the object, and convert it into the likeness of whatever is most proper to encourage the fear. "Our eyes are made the fools" of our other faculties. This is the universal law of the imagination. . . . We compare a man of gigantic stature to a tower: not that he is anything like so large, but because the excess of his size beyond what we are accustomed to expect, or the usual size of things of the same class, produces by contrast a greater feeling of magnitude and ponderous strength than another object of ten times the same dimensions. The intensity of the feeling makes up for the disproportion of the objects. Things are equal to the imagination, which have the power of affecting the mind with an equal degree of terror, admiration, delight, or love. When Lear calls upon the heavens to avenge his cause, "for they are old like him," there is nothing extravagant or impious in this sublime identification of his age with theirs; for there is no other image which could do justice to the agonizing sense of his wrongs and his despair!

Poetry is the high-wrought enthusiasm of fancy and feeling. As in describing natural objects, it impregnates sensible impressions with the forms of fancy, so it describes the feelings of pleasure or pain, by blending them with the strongest movements of passion, and the most striking forms of nature. Tragic poetry, which is the most impassioned species of it, strives to carry on the feeling to the utmost point of sublimity or pathos, by all the force of comparison or contrast; loses the sense of present suffering in the imaginary exaggeration of it; exhausts the terror or pity by an unlimited indulgence of it; grapples with impossibilities in its desperate impatience of restraint; throws us back upon the past, forward into the future; brings every moment of our being or object of nature in startling review before us; and in the rapid whirl of events, lifts us from the depths of woe to the highest contemplations on human life. . . .

[1] Francis Bacon (1561–1626), *Advancement of Learning* (1605), II, ch. 4.

from Table Talk, or Original Essays on Men and Manners

(1821)

— *from* ON GENIUS AND COMMON SENSE: THE SAME SUBJECT CONTINUED —

Genius or originality is, for the most part, *some strong quality in the mind, answering to and bringing out some new and striking quality in nature.*

Imagination is, more properly, the power of carrying on a given feeling into other situations, which must be done best according to the hold which the feeling itself has taken of the mind.[1] In new and unknown combinations, the impression must act by sympathy, and not by rule; but there can be no sympathy, where there is no passion, no original interest. The personal interest may in some cases oppress and circumscribe the imaginative faculty, as in the instance of Rousseau:[2] but in general the strength and consistency of the imagination will be in proportion to the strength and depth of feeling; and it is rarely that a man even of lofty genius will be able to do more than carry on his own feelings and character, or some prominent and ruling passion, into fictitious and uncommon situations. Milton has by allusion embodied a great part of his political and personal history in the chief characters and incidents of Paradise Lost. He has, no doubt, wonderfully adapted and heightened them, but the elements are the same; you trace the bias and opinions of the man in the creations of the poet. Shakespear (almost alone) seems to have been a man of genius, raised above the definition of genius. "Born universal heir to all humanity," he was "as one, in

[1] I do not here speak of the figurative or fanciful exercise of the imagination, which consists in finding out some striking object or image to illustrate another [W. H.].

[2] **Rousseau:** Jean-Jacques Rousseau (1712–1778), French philosopher and author of *The Social Contract* (1762), *Emile* (1762), *Julie, or The New Eloisa* (1761) and *Confessions* (1781).

suffering all who suffered nothing;" with a perfect sympathy with all things, yet alike indifferent to all: who did not tamper with nature or warp her to his own purposes; who "knew all qualities with a learned spirit," instead of judging of them by his own predilections; and was rather "a pipe for the Muse's finger to play what stop she pleased," than anxious to set up any character or pretensions of his own. His genius consisted in the faculty of transforming himself at will into whatever he chose: his originality was the power of seeing every object from the exact point of view in which others would see it. He was the Proteus[3] of human intellect. Genius in ordinary is a more obstinate and less versatile thing. It is sufficiently exclusive and self-willed, quaint and peculiar. It does some one thing by virtue of doing nothing else: it excels in some one pursuit by being blind to all excellence but its own. It is just the reverse of the cameleon; for it does not borrow, but lend its colour to all about it: or like the glow-worm, discloses a little circle of gorgeous light in the twilight of obscurity, in the night of intellect, that surrounds it. So did Rembrandt.[4] If ever there was a man of genius, he was one, in the proper sense of the term. He lived in and revealed to others a world of his own, and might be said to have invented a new view of nature. He did not discover things *out* of nature, in fiction or fairy land, or make a voyage to the moon "to descry new lands, rivers, or mountains in her spotty globe," but saw things *in* nature that every one had missed before him, and gave others eyes to see them with. This is the test and triumph of originality, not to shew us what has never been, and what we may therefore very easily never have dreamt of, but to point out to us what is before our eyes and under our feet, though we have had no suspicion of its existence, for want of sufficient strength of intuition, of determined grasp of mind to seize and retain it. . . .

Originality is the seeing nature differently from others, and yet as it is in itself. It is not singularity or affectation, but the discovery of new and valuable truth. All the world do not see the whole meaning of any object they have been looking at. Habit blinds them to some things: short-sightedness to others. Every mind is not a gauge and measure of truth. Nature has her surface and her dark recesses. She is deep, obscure, and infinite. It is only minds on whom she makes her fullest impressions that can penetrate her shrine or unveil her *Holy of Holies.* It is only those whom she has filled with her spirit that have the boldness or the power to reveal her mysteries to others. But nature has a thousand aspects, and one man can only draw out one of them. Whoever does this, is a man of genius. One displays her force, another her refinement, one her power of harmony, another her suddenness of contrast, one her beauty of form, another her splendour of colour. Each does that for which he is best fitted by his particular genius, that is to say, by some quality of mind in which the quality of the object sinks deepest, where it finds the most cordial welcome, is perceived to its utmost extent, and where again it forces its way out from the fulness with which it has taken possession of the mind of the student. The imagination gives out what it has first absorbed by congeniality of temperament, what it has attracted and moulded into itself by elective affinity, as the loadstone draws and impregnates iron. . . .

[3] **Proteus**: in Greek myth, a sea-god able to assume whatever shape he chose.

[4] **Rembrandt**: Rembrandt van Rijn (1606–1669), leading representative of Dutch school of realistic painting.

CLARA REEVE

(1729–1807)

Educated by her father, the Reverend William Smith, at home in Ipswich, Suffolk, Clara Reeve published her first volume of poems in 1769. After writing a play and an oratorio that were not produced, she turned to the novel, and in 1777 anonymously published *The Champion of Virtue.* Retitled *The Old English Baron* and reissued under her own name the following year, this novel became a great success. Here Reeve attempts to show what she later described in *The Progress of Romance:* the transformation of the conventions of the medieval and Gothic romance into the contemporary didactic novel. To write a successful novel, she asserted in the preface to this work, "there is required a sufficient degree of the marvelous, to excite the attention; enough of the manners of real life, to give an air of probability to the work; and enough of the pathetic, to engage the heart in its behalf." *The Old English Baron* traces the fortunes of the Lovel family, from initial glory through ruin at the hands of a villain, to retribution and the triumph of virtue, amidst ruined castles and ghostly visitations. Her three later novels—*The Two Mentors* (1783), *The Exiles* (1788), and *The School for Widows* (1791)—promoted sensibility, the social virtues, and egalitarian marriages.

from The Progress of Romance,

through Times, Countries, and Manners; with Remarks on the Good and Bad Effects of It, on Them Respectively; in a Course of Evening Conversations
(1785)

—*from* EVENING I—

EUPHRASIA: —No writings are more different than the ancient *Romance* and modern *Novel,* yet they are frequently confounded together, and mistaken for each other. There are likewise great distinctions to be made between the *old Greek* Romances,[1] those of the middle ages, and those of the fifteenth and sixteenth centuries. Books of all these kinds have been enthusiastically read and admired; of late years they have been as absurdly censured and condemned. If read indiscriminately they are at best unprofitable, frequently productive of absurdities in manners and sentiments, sometimes hurtful to good morals; and yet from this Genus there may be selected books that are truly respectable, works of genius, taste, and utility, capable of improving the morals and manners of mankind. . . .

. . . I propose to trace Romance to its Origin, to follow its progress through the different periods to its declension, to shew how the modern Novel sprung up out of its ruins, to examine and compare the merits of both, and to remark upon the effects of them.

—*from* EVENING II—

EUPHRASIA: The Origin of Romance is of much higher date, as I hope to convince you,—but first let us speak of the name.

HORTENSIUS: How then would you define it?

EUPHRASIA: By fixing a clear and certain meaning to it, not as of my own invention or judgment; but borrowing the idea of the Latinists, I would call it simply an *Heroic fable,*—a fabulous Story of such actions as are commonly ascribed to heroes, or men of

[1] **Greek romances:** classical tales of love dating from the first century BC; the major writers in this genre of prose fiction were Achilles Tatius, Chariton, Heliodorus, Longus (author of *Daphnis and Chloe*), and Xenophon of Ephesus.

extraordinary courage and abilities.—Or if you would allow of it, I would say an Epic in prose. . . .

. . . Romances or Heroic fables are of very ancient, and I might say universal Origin. We find traces of them in all times, and in all countries: they have always been the favourite entertainment of the most savage, as well as the most civilized people. In the earliest accounts of all nations, we find they had traditional stories of their most eminent persons, that is of their *Heroes*, to which they listened in raptures, and found themselves excited to perform great actions, by hearing them recited;—they had their war-songs—and they had also their prose narratives. . . .

Homer is universally acknowledged as the Prince of Epic poetry. . . . [W]ith all this eclat that surrounds him, *Homer* was the parent of Romance; where ever his works have been known, they have been imitated by the Poets and Romance writers.—I look upon *Virgil* as the most successful of his Imitators. . . .

—*from* EVENING IV—

EUPHRASIA: I hope by this time *Hortensius* is convinced, that Romances, have been written, both in prose and verse; and further that a Romance, is nothing but an Epic in prose. . . .

. . . In early times, in the dawning of literature, these subjects exercised the pens of the ingenious—they were the favourite studies of the young nobility and gentry of those times, and their manners were, in a great measure formed upon the models of those adventurers, whose exploits they continually heard recited. The effects they produced were indeed of so mixed a nature, that it is difficult to separate the good from the bad. Religion and virtue, were so blended with fanaticism and absurdity, that the lustre of the former principles, concealed the blemishes of the latter.—At this distance of time we need not be afraid to give our judgment of them, neither ought we to be ashamed to do justice to works of Genius, by whatever name they are called.

HORTENSIUS: Certainly.—I shall pay them due respect for your sake.

EUPHRASIA: Not so, *Hortensius*, I will not accept such respect for them.—You shall pay it for the sake of those illustrious men, who imbibed their enthusiasm, and carried it into practice.

These were the books that caused such a spirit of Chivalry in the youth of much later times, particularly in Spain; such as raised up a *Cervantes* to attack them; and you will find a curious list of them, in the sixth chapter of the first book of *Don Quixote*, in the conversation between the Priest and the Barber; in which the Author condemns most of them to the flames.

HORTENSIUS: Is it possible to respect that incomparable work, and yet respect the books it condemns and ridicules?

EUPHRASIA: Yes it is; though it may seem at first view a paradox.—This infatuation was so general, that the brightest geniuses, and the wisest men were not exempt from it.—Our Poetry owes more to it, than you imagine; it was calculated to elevate and warm a poetic imagination, of this I shall bring proofs. *Chaucer*, and all our old writers, abound with it,—*Spencer* owes perhaps his immortality to it, it is the Gothic imagery, that gives the principal graces to his work, and without them we should soon grow tired of his Allegories,—but we have a yet stronger instance in our divine *Milton*, whose mind was so deeply impressed by them, and his imagination so warmed, that he frequently recurs to them, of which I shall only give you a few specimens.—

Fairer than feigned of old, or fabled since
Of Fairy damsels met in forest wide
By knights of Logres, or of Lyones,
Lancelot, or *Pelleas*, or *Pellenore*. PAR. REG. b. 2.

And again in the following book.—

When *Agrican* with all his northern powers
Besieged *Albracca*, as *Romances* tell,
The city of Galliphrone;—from thence to win
The fairest of her sex *Angelica*
His daughter; fought by many prowest knights,
Both *Paynim*, and the peers of *Charlemagne*.

There are continual allusions of this kind, sprinkled through all his works; but these may serve as proofs of what I have advanced. . . .

—*from* EVENING V—

EUPHRASIA: We are now to proceed to the modern Romances, which have been so often mistaken for the old ones.—after these had been exploded in a great measure, the taste for them was revived in France, by *Calprenède,*—*D'Urfé,*—the *Scudéry's,*[2] and many others; who wrote new Romances upon a different plan: which in some kinds of refinement were superior to the old ones, but in the greater merits fell very short of them. They were written with more regularity, and brought nearer to probability; but on the other hand by taking for their foundation some obscure parts of true history, and building fictitious stories upon them, truth and fiction were so blended together, that a common reader could not distinguish them, young people especially imbibed such absurd ideas of historical facts and persons, as were very difficult to be rectified. . . .—

The ancient and modern Romance, had each their peculiar *ton,* their *affectation,* their *absurdities:*—at the same time it must be confessed by those who despise them, that the enthusiasm they inspired was that of virtue and honour.

SOPHRONIA: That is indisputable.—I have read many of these you are now speaking of, and I can bear my testimony that they inculcated no principles contrary to any of the moral or social virtues.

EUPHRASIA: You say true.—If it taught young women to deport themselves too much like Queens and Princesses, it taught them at the same time that virtue only could give lustre to every rank and degree.—It taught the young men to look upon themselves as the champions and protectors of the weaker sex;—to treat the object of their passion with the utmost respect;—to avoid all improper familiarities, and, in short, to expect from her the reward of their virtues.

—*from* EVENING VII—

HORTENSIUS: We have now, I presume, done with the Romances, and are expecting your investigation of Novels. . . .

EUPHRASIA: The Romance is an heroic fable, which treats of fabulous persons and things.—The Novel is a picture of real life and manners, and of the times in which it is written. The Romance in lofty and elevated language, describes what never happened nor is likely to happen.—The Novel gives a familiar relation of such things, as pass every day before our eyes, such as may happen to our friend, or to ourselves; and the perfection of it, is to represent every scene, in so easy and natural a manner, and to make them appear so probable, as to deceive us into a persuasion (at least while we are reading) that all is real, until we are affected by the joys or distresses, of the persons in the story, as if they were our own. . . .

—*from* EVENING XI—

EUPHRASIA: Let us then take a brief survey of *Eastern Tales,* a class of no small extent. I have spoken largely of the *Arabian Nights Entertainment* as a work of Originality and Authenticity, and let me add of amusement. The great demand for this book, raised a swarm of imitations, most of which are of the French manufactory, as the *Persian Tales*—*Turkish Tales*—*Tartarian Tales*—*Chinese Tales*—*Peruvian Tales*—*Mogul Tales*—etc.

The stories of this kind are all wild and extravagant to the highest degree; they are indeed so far out of the bounds of Nature and probability, that it is difficult to judge of them by rules drawn from these sources.—It cannot be denied that some of them are amusing, and catch hold of the readers attention.

SOPHRONIA: They do more than catch the attention, for they retain it.—There is a kind of fascination in them,—when once we begin a volume, we cannot lay it aside, but drive through to the end of it, and yet upon reflexion we despise and reject them.

HORTENSIUS: They are certainly dangerous books for youth,—they create and encourage the wildest excursions of imagination, which it is, or ought to be, the care of parents and preceptors to restrain, and to give them a just and true representation of human nature, and of the duties and practice of common life.

EUPHRASIA: You speak as if it was the general study of parents and teachers in our days to educate our youth to wisdom and virtue.—Is it not their ambition to make them knowing rather than wise, and fashionable rather than virtuous?—thus they are hackney'd in the ways of the world, and though ignorant of every thing that is really good and estimable, they are *old* before their days are half spent.

[2] **Gautier de Costes de La Calprenède (1609?–1663):** French novelist and playwright, author of *Cassandre* (1642–1660), *Cleopatre* (1647–1658), etc. **Honore d'Urfé (1568–1625):** French author of chivalric pastoral romance *Astrée.* **Madeleine de Scudéry (1607–1701):** Prolific French novelist, author of *Artamene ou le Grand Cyrus* (10 vols., 1649–1653), and *Clélie* (1656). **Georges de Scudéry (1601–1667):** Author of *L'Amour Tyrannique* (1638), brother of Madeleine de Scudéry.

SOPHRONIA: The books that are put into the hands of youth, do in a great measure direct their pursuits and determine their characters; it is therefore of the first consequence that they should be well chosen. . . .

— *from* EVENING XII —

EUPHRASIA: A Circulating Library[3] is indeed a great evil,—young people are allowed to subscribe to them, and to read indiscriminately all they contain; and thus both food and poison are conveyed to the young mind together.

HORTENSIUS: I should suppose that if books of the worst kind were excluded; still there would be enough to lay a foundation of idleness and folly—A person used to this kind of reading will be disgusted with every thing serious or solid, as a weakened and depraved stomach rejects plain and wholsome food.

SOPHRONIA: There is truth and justice in your observation,—but how to prevent it?

HORTENSIUS: There are yet more and greater evils behind.—The seeds of vice and folly are sown in the heart,—the passions are awakened,—false expectations are raised.—A young woman is taught to expect adventures and intrigues,—she expects to be addressed in the style of these books, with the language of flattery and adulation.—If a plain man addresses her in rational terms and pays her the greatest of compliments,—that of desiring to spend his life with her,—that is not sufficient, her vanity is disappointed, she expects to meet a Hero in Romance.

EUPHRASIA: No *Hortensius,*—not a Hero in Romance, but a fine Gentleman in a Novel:—you will not make the distinction.

HORTENSIUS: I ask your pardon, I agreed to the distinction and therefore ought to observe it. . . .

From this kind of reading, young people fancy themselves capable of judging of men and manners, and that they are knowing, while involved in the profoundest ignorance. They believe themselves wiser than their parents and guardians, whom they treat with contempt and ridicule:—Thus armed with ignorance, conceit, and folly, they plunge into the world and its dissipations, and who can wonder if they become its victims?—For such as the foundation is, such will be the superstructure.

EUPHRASIA: All this is undoubtedly true, but at the same time would you exclude all works of fiction from the young reader?—In this case you would deprive him of the pleasure and improvement he might receive from works of genius, taste and morality.

HORTENSIUS: Yes, I would serve them as the Priest did *Don Quixote*'s library, burn the good ones for being found in bad company. . . .

EUPHRASIA: Pray *Hortensius,* is all this severity in behalf of our sex or your own?

HORTENSIUS: Of both.—Yet yours are most concerned in my remonstrance for they read more of these books than ours, and consequently are most hurt by them.

EUPHRASIA: You will then become a Knight errant, to combat with the windmills, which your imagination represents as Giants; while in the mean time you leave a side unguarded.

HORTENSIUS: And you have found it out.—Pray tell me without metaphors, your meaning in plain English?

EUPHRASIA: It seems to me that you are unreasonably severe upon these books, which you suppose to be appropriated to our sex, (which however is not the case):—not considering how many books of worse tendency, are put into the hands of the youth of your own, without scruple.

HORTENSIUS: Indeed!—how will you bring proofs of that assertion?

EUPHRASIA: I will not go far for them. I will fetch them from the School books, that generally make a part of the education of young men.—They are taught the History—the Mythology—the morals—of the great Ancients, whom you and all learned men revere.—But with these, they learn also—their Idolatry—their follies—their vices—and every thing that is shocking to virtuous manners.—*Lucretius* teaches them that *fear* first made Gods—that men grew out of the earth like trees, and that the indulgence of the passions and appetites, is the truest wisdom.—*Juvenal* and *Persius* describe such scenes, as I may venture to affirm that Romance and Novel-writers of any credit would blush at:—and *Virgil*—the modest and delicate *Virgil,* informs them of many things, they had better be ignorant of.—As a

[3] The first Circulating, or lending, Libraries were created by British booksellers in the 1780s; about three-quarters of their subscribers were female. For the first time, middle-class women had access to a wide range of books (the annual subscription fee was about one pound); this produced both an increased literacy rate and a new audience for literary culture in England.

woman I cannot give this argument its full weight. —But a hint is sufficient, —and I presume you will not deny the truth of my assertion.

HORTENSIUS: I am astonished—admonished—and convinced!—I cannot deny the truth of what you have advanced, I confess that a reformation is indeed wanting in the mode of Education of the youth of our sex.

SOPHRONIA: Of both sexes you may say . . .

. . . It is now that I may enter upon my office of Moderator. —*Hortensius* would prohibit the reading all Novels in order to exclude the bad ones. —*Euphrasia* would make a separation in favour of works of Genius, taste, and morality; she would recommend such methods of preventing the mischiefs arising from novel reading, as are moderate, prudent, and above all *practicable.*—

The objections to bad books of this species, are equally applicable to all other kinds of writing,—indecent novels, indecent plays, essays, memoirs, dialogues are equally to be exploded: but it does not follow that all these kinds of writing are to be extirpated, because some are bad. —By the same kind of reasoning we might plead for the prohibition of all kinds of writing; for excellent and unexceptionable works of every species, may be contrasted with vicious and immoral ones. All these objections amount to no more than that bad books are bad things;—but shall we therefore prohibit reading?

HORTENSIUS: You have spoken to some purpose.—I know that mine is an *Utopian* scheme; and I acknowledge that *Euphrasia*'s is practicable, if parents and guardians would give due attention to it.

EUPHRASIA: Then we are agreed at last,—Selection is to be strongly recommended, and good books to be carefully chosen by all that are concerned in the education of youth. . .

FRANCIS JEFFREY

(1773–1850)

Educated at Edinburgh and Glasgow Universities, Francis Jeffrey became a judge and a Member of Parliament in the Whig party. He founded, with Sydney Smith, the *Edinburgh Review* in 1802 and served as its editor until 1829. He was regarded as a severe but discriminating literary critic. He wrote appreciatively of George Crabbe,* Sir Walter Scott,* Byron,* and Keats,* but followed his review of Wordsworth's *Excursion* with a series of attacks on "a *sect* of poets" he called the Lake Poets (Wordsworth, Coleridge, Southey, and sometimes Thomas De Quincy).

from a review of The Excursion, by William Wordsworth

(November 1814)

This will never do. It bears no doubt the stamp of the author's heart and fancy; but unfortunately not half so visibly as that of his peculiar system. His former poems were intended to recommend that system, and to bespeak favour for it by their individual merit;—but this, we suspect, must be recommended by the system—and can only expect to succeed where it has been previously established. It is longer, weaker, and tamer, than any of Mr. Wordsworth's other productions; with less boldness and originality, and less even of that extreme simplicity and lowliness of tone which wavered so prettily, in the Lyrical Ballads, between silliness and pathos. We have imitations of Cowper, and even of Milton here, engrafted on the natural drawl of the Lakers—and all diluted into harmony by that profuse and irrepressible wordiness which deluges all the blank verse of this school of poetry, and lubricates and weakens the whole structure of their style. . . .

The case of Mr. Wordsworth, we perceive, is now manifestly hopeless; and we give him up as altogether incurable, and beyond the power of criticism. We cannot indeed altogether omit taking precautions now and then against the spreading of the malady;—but for himself, though we shall watch the progress of his symptoms as a matter of professional curiosity and instruction, we really think it right not to harass him any longer with nauseous remedies,—but rather to throw in cordials and lenitives, and wait in patience for the natural termination of the disorder. In order to justify this desertion of our patient, however, it is proper to state why we despair of the success of a more active practice. . . .

. . . We now see clearly, however, how the case stands;—and, making up our minds, though with the most sincere pain and reluctance, to consider him as finally lost to the good cause of poetry, shall endeavour to be thankful for the occasional gleams of tenderness and beauty which the natural force of his imagination and affections must still shed over all his productions,—and to which we shall ever turn with delight, in spite of the affectation and mysticism and prolixity, with which they are so abundantly contrasted.

Long habits of seclusion, and an excessive ambition of originality, can alone account for the disproportion which seems to exist between this author's taste and his genius; or for the devotion with which he has sacrificed so many precious gifts at the shrine of those paltry idols which he has set up for himself among his lakes and his mountains. Solitary musings, amidst such scenes, might no doubt be expected to nurse up the mind to the majesty of poetical conception,—(though it is remarkable, that all the greater poets lived, or had lived, in the full current of society;)—But the collision of equal minds,—the admonition of prevailing impressions—seems necessary to reduce its redundancies, and repress that tendency to extravagance or puerility, into which the self-indulgence and self-admiration of genius is so apt to be betrayed, when it is allowed to wanton, without awe or restraint, in the triumph and delight of its own intoxication. That its flights should be graceful and glorious in the eyes of men, it seems almost to be necessary that they should be made in the consciousness that men's eyes are to behold them,

—and that the inward transport and vigour by which they are inspired, should be tempered by an occasional reference to what will be thought of them by those ultimate dispensers of glory. An habitual and general knowledge of the few settled and permanent maxims, which form the canon of general taste in all large and polished societies—a certain tact, which informs us at once that many things, which we still love and are moved by in secret, must necessarily be despised as childish or derided as absurd, in all such societies—though it will not stand in the place of genius, seems necessary to the success of its exertions; and though it will never enable any one to produce the higher beauties of art, can alone secure the talent which does produce them, from errors that must render it useless. Those who have most of the talent, however, commonly acquire this knowledge with the greatest facility;—and if Mr. Wordsworth, instead of confining himself almost entirely to the society of the dalesmen and cottagers, and little children, who form the subjects of his book, had condescended to mingle a little more with the people that were to read and judge of it, we cannot help thinking, that its texture would have been considerably improved. At least it appears to us to be absolutely impossible, that any one who had lived or mixed familiarly with men of literature and ordinary judgment in poetry, (of course we exclude the coadjutors and disciples of his own school,) could ever have fallen into such gross faults, or so long mistaken them for beauties. His first essays[1] we looked upon in a good degree as poetical paradoxes,—maintained experimentally, in order to display talent, and court notoriety;—and so maintained, with no more serious belief in their truth, than is usually generated by an ingenious and animated defence of other paradoxes. But when we find, that he has been for twenty years exclusively employed upon articles of this very fabric, and that he has still enough of raw material on hand to keep him so employed for twenty years to come, we cannot refuse him the justice of believing that he is a sincere convert to his own system, and must ascribe the peculiarities of his composition, not to any transient affectation, or accidental caprice of imagination, but to a settled perversity of taste or understanding, which has been fostered, if not altogether created, by the circumstances to which we have already alluded.

The volume before us, if we were to describe it very shortly, we should characterize as a tissue of moral and devotional ravings, in which innumerable changes are rung upon a few very simple and familiar ideas:—but with such an accompaniment of long words, long sentences, and unwieldly phrases—and such a hubbub of strained raptures and fantastical sublimities, that it is often extremely difficult for the most skilful and attentive student to obtain a glimpse of the author's meaning—and altogether impossible for an ordinary reader to conjecture what he is about. . . .

The character of the work is decidedly didactic; and more than nine tenths of it are occupied with a species of dialogue, or rather a series of long sermons or harangues which pass between the pedlar, the author, the old chaplain, and a worthy vicar, who entertains the whole party at dinner on the last day of their excursion. The incidents which occur in the course of it are as few and trifling as can be imagined;—and those which the different speakers narrate in the course of their discourses, are introduced rather to illustrate their arguments or opinions, than for any interest they are supposed to possess of their own.—The doctrine which the work is intended to enforce, we are by no means certain that we have discovered. In so far as we can collect, however, it seems to be neither more nor less than the old familiar one, that a firm belief in the providence of a wise and beneficent Being must be our great stay and support under all afflictions and perplexities upon earth—and that there are indications of his power and goodness in all the aspects of the visible universe, whether living or inanimate—every part of which should therefore be regarded with love and reverence, as exponents of those great attributes. We can testify, at least, that these salutary and important truths are inculcated at far greater length, and with more repetitions, than in any ten volumes of sermons that we ever perused. It is also maintained, with equal conciseness and originality, that there is frequently much good sense, as well as much enjoyment, in the humbler conditions of life; and that in spite of great vices and abuses, there is a reasonable allowance both of happiness and goodness in society at large. If there be any deeper or more recondite doctrines in Mr. Wordsworth's book, we must confess that they have escaped us;—and, convinced as we are of the truth and soundness of those to which we have alluded, we cannot help thinking that they might have been better enforced with less parade and prolixity. His effusions on what may be called the physiognomy of external nature, or its moral and theological expression, are eminently fantastic, obscure, and affected. . . .

[1] essays: poems in *Lyrical Ballads,* 1798 [F. J.].

JOHN GIBSON LOCKHART

(1794–1854)

Educated at Glasgow University and Balliol College, Oxford, John Gibson Lockhart was called to the Scottish bar and became one of the principal contributors to *Blackwood's Magazine,* a conservative or Tory rival to the more liberal *Edinburgh Review. Blackwood's* was renowned for its partisan politics and satiric attacks on leading cultural figures. In 1817 John Gibson Lockhart began a long series of attacks on what he dubbed the "Cockney School of Poetry," insisting on the low-born vulgarity of the poetry and criticism of Leigh Hunt, John Keats, and William Hazlitt. From 1825 to 1853 he served as the editor of the Tory journal *The Quarterly Review,* founded by the publisher John Murray to defend established society, Church, and Crown. His critical ferocity was aptly designated by his nom de plume, "The Scorpion."

Cockney School of Poetry, *in* Blackwood's Edinburgh Magazine

(August 1818)

— NO. IV —

________________ OF KEATS,
THE MUSES' SON OF PROMISE, AND WHAT FEATS
HE YET MAY DO, &C.

CORNELIUS WEBB.[1]

Of all the manias of this mad age, the most incurable, as well as the most common, seems to be no other than the Metromanie.[2] The just celebrity of Robert Burns and Miss Baillie has had the melancholy effect of turning the heads of we know not how many farm-servants and unmarried ladies; our very footmen compose tragedies, and there is scarcely a superannuated governess in the island that does not leave a roll of lyrics behind her in her band-box. To witness the disease of any human understanding, however feeble, is distressing; but the spectacle of an able mind reduced to a state of insanity is of course ten times more afflicting. It is with such sorrow as this that we have contemplated the case of Mr John Keats. This young man appears to have received from nature talents of an excellent, perhaps even of a superior order — talents which, devoted to the purposes of any useful profession, must have rendered him a respectable, if not an eminent citizen. His friends, we understand, destined him to the career of medicine, and he was bound apprentice some years ago to a worthy apothecary in town. But all has been undone by a sudden attack of the malady to which we have alluded. Whether Mr John had been sent home with a diuretic or composing draught[3] to some patient far gone in the poetical mania, we have not heard. This much is certain, that he has caught the infection, and that thoroughly. For some time we were in hopes, that he might get off with a violent fit or two; but of late the symptoms are terrible. The phrenzy of the "Poems" was bad enough in its way; but it did not alarm us half so seriously as the calm, settled, imperturbable drivelling idiocy of "Endymion." We hope, however, that in so young a person, and with a constitution originally so good, even now the disease is not utterly incurable. Time, firm treatment, and rational restraint, do much for many apparently hopeless invalids; and if Mr Keats should happen, at some interval of reason, to cast his eye upon our pages, he may perhaps be convinced of the existence of his malady, which, in such cases, is often all that is necessary to put the patient in a fair way of being cured.

The readers of the Examiner newspaper were informed, some time ago, by a solemn paragraph, in Mr

[1] **Cornelius Webb (c. 1790–c. 1848):** an acquaintance of Keats.

[2] **Metromanie:** Lockhart's coinage, "meter-mania" or passion for versifying.

[3] **composing draught:** sleeping potion.

Hunt's best style, of the appearance of two new stars of glorious magnitude and splendour in the poetical horizon of the land of Cockaigne.[4] One of these turned out, by and by, to be no other than Mr John Keats. This precocious adulation confirmed the wavering apprentice in his desire to quit the gallipots,[5] and at the same time excited in his too susceptible mind a fatal admiration for the character and talents of the most worthless and affected of all the versifiers of our time. One of his first productions was the following sonnet, *"written on the day when Mr Leigh Hunt left prison."* It will be recollected, that the cause of Hunt's confinement was a series of libels against his sovereign, and that its fruit was the odious and incestuous "Story of Rimini."

"What though, for shewing truth to flattered state,
Kind Hunt was shut in prison, yet has he,
In his immortal spirit been as free
As the sky-searching lark, and as elate.
Minion of grandeur! think you he did wait?
Think you he nought but prison walls did see,
Till, so unwilling, thou unturn'dst the key?
Ah, no! far happier, nobler was his fate!
In Spenser's halls! he strayed, and bowers fair,
Culling enchanted flowers; and he flew
With daring Milton! through the fields of air;
To regions of his own his genius true
Took happy flights. Who shall his fame impair
When thou art dead, and all thy wretched crew?

The absurdity of the thought in this sonnet is, however, if possible, surpassed in another, *"addressed to Haydon"* the painter, that clever, but most affected artist, who as little resembles Raphael in genius as he does in person, notwithstanding the foppery of having his hair curled over his shoulders in the old Italian fashion. In this exquisite piece it will be observed, that Mr Keats classes together WORDSWORTH, HUNT, and HAYDON, as the three greatest spirits of the age, and that he alludes to himself, and some others of the rising brood of Cockneys, as likely to attain hereafter an equally honourable elevation. Wordsworth and Hunt! what a juxta-position! The purest, the loftiest, and we do not fear to say it, the most classical of living English poets, joined together in the same compliment with the meanest, the filthiest, and the most vulgar of Cockney poetasters. . . .

From his prototype Hunt, John Keats has acquired a sort of vague idea, that the Greeks were a most tasteful people, and that no mythology can be so finely adapted for the purposes of poetry as theirs. It is amusing to see what a hand the two Cockneys make of this mythology; the one confesses that he never read the Greek Tragedians, and the other knows Homer only from Chapman; and both of them write about Apollo, Pan, Nymphs, Muses, and Mysteries, as might be expected from persons of their education. We shall not, however, enlarge at present upon this subject, as we mean to dedicate an entire paper to the classical attainments and attempts of the Cockney poets. As for Mr Keats' "Endymion," it has just as much to do with Greece as it has with "old Tartary the fierce;" no man, whose mind has ever been imbued with the smallest knowledge or feeling of classical poetry or classical history, could have stooped to profane and vulgarise every association in the manner which has been adopted by this "son of promise." Before giving any extracts, we must inform our readers, that this romance is meant to be written in English heroic rhyme. To those who have read any of Hunt's poems, this hint might indeed be needless. Mr Keats has adopted the loose, nerveless versification, and Cockney rhymes of the poet of Rimini; but in fairness to that gentleman, we must add, that the defects of the system are tenfold more conspicuous in his disciple's work than in his own. Mr Hunt is a small poet, but he is a clever man. Mr Keats is a still smaller poet, and he is only a boy of pretty abilities, which he has done every thing in his power to spoil. . . .

We had almost forgot to mention, that Keats belongs to the Cockney School of Politics, as well as the Cockney School of Poetry.

It is fit that he who holds Rimini to be the first poem, should believe the Examiner to be the first politician of the day. We admire consistency, even in folly. Hear how their bantling[6] has already learned to lisp sedition.

[Here follows excerpt from Keats' *Endymion* III.1–22, beginning "There are who lord it o'er their fellow-men."]

And now, good-morrow to "the Muses' son of Promise;" as for "the feats he yet may do," as we do not pretend to say, like himself, "Muse of my native land am I

[4] **Cockaigne:** Lockhart's coinage, "land of the Cockneys," i.e., those of the lowest and most vulgar classes; also, from "cock's eggs," misshapen, effeminate men.

[5] **gallipot:** earthen pot used by apothecaries or pharmacists for ointments.

[6] **bantling:** young child, brat; formerly, a bastard.

inspired," we shall adhere to the safe old rule of *pauca verba.*[7] We venture to make one small prophecy, that his bookseller will not a second time venture £50 upon any thing he can write. It is a better and a wiser thing to be a starved apothecary than a starved poet; so back to the shop Mr John, back to "plasters, pills, and ointment boxes," etc. But, for Heaven's sake, young Sangrado, be a little more sparing of extenuatives and soporifics in your practice than you have been in your poetry.

Z.

---

[7] **pauca verba**: Latin, few words; i.e., the less said the better. **"plasters, pills, and ointment boxes"**: From Joanna Baillie,* "The Kitten." **Sangrado**: Medical quack in Alain Rene Le Sage's novel *Gil Blas* (1715–1735). **Z**: "Z" is the usual signature on the critical attacks on Hunt and other Cockney poets in *Blackwood's*.

AUTHOR SELECTIONS

ANNA LETITIA AIKIN BARBAULD

(1743–1825)

Anna Letitia Aikin was the eldest child of Dr. John Aikin, a theologian and tutor at Warrington Academy, a dissenting presbyterian public school. She received a superior education, studying French, Italian, Latin, and Greek, science and mathematics, as well as the libertarian political principles of Britain's leading dissenters, especially those of her father's friend Joseph Priestley. Ever modest and unassuming, she was urged into print by her brother John, publishing *Miscellaneous Pieces in Prose* with him in 1773 and in that same year a first volume of poems, including "Corsica" and "The Mouse's Petition." In 1774 she married the Rev. Rochemont Barbauld, the son of a French presbyterian minister. The marriage, although childless (the Barbaulds finally adopted her brother's middle son, Charles Rochemont Aikin, as their own), was happy until Rochemont succumbed to insanity in his later years. Resisting Lady Mary Wortley Montagu's suggestion that they open a finishing school for girls, the Barbaulds established their own dissenting academy in Palgrove, Suffolk, where Anna took charge of the education of the younger boys. Her *Hymns in Prose for Children* (1781), written for her students, immediately became enormously popular and was translated into several European languages. Following Locke's dictum that the child's mind is a *tabula rasa,* a "white paper" upon which experience writes, she urged the "child of reason" to observe the natural world carefully for the lessons of divine wisdom inscribed within it. As do Blake's *Songs of Innocence,** these Hymns create a utopian world in which God loves and protects every child and every adult.

Although the school was extremely successful both financially and academically, the workload proved excessive for Rochemont's mental health; he experienced his first episode of insanity in 1785. The Barbaulds then moved to Hampstead, in London, where Rochemont officiated at a small presbyterian chapel and Anna devoted herself to literary labors. She rapidly became the leading female literary and social critic of this period, publishing influential essays on Akenside, Collins, and Richardson. She played an important role in the public opposition to the slave trade, proclaiming her support of Wilberforce in a poetic epistle in 1791. Her program for national reform based on the principles of individual and domestic morality, *Sins of Government, Sins of the Nation,* appeared in 1793.

Her husband's deteriorating mental health persuaded them to move to Stoke Newington to be with her brother in 1802; they returned to London in a final desperate attempt to find adequate treatment for the increasingly deranged Rochemont, but after brutally assaulting his wife, he committed suicide in 1808. Anna Barbauld then returned to Stoke Newington and devoted herself full-time to her literary endeavors, editing the first publishing effort to establish the canon of the English novel, a 50-volume series initiated in 1810 by Rivington and Co., entitled *The British Novel,* that opened with her essay "On the Origin and Progress of Novel-Writing." In 1812 she published the most significant of her poems, *Eighteen Hundred and Eleven,* a prophetic denunciation of British imperialism that was widely condemned in the popular press.

Writing numerous critical essays, carrying on a large correspondence, and regularly visiting the leading literary figures of the period, Anna Barbauld became the primary spokeswoman for a specific aesthetic theory, one that stood in stark contrast to the poetic theory propounded by Samuel Taylor Coleridge,* William Wordsworth,* and Percy Shelley.* (See AESTHETIC THEORY AND LITERARY CRITICISM.) Barbauld believed that the primary goal of literature was to educate the young in rational thought and correct moral principles. Endorsing the neoclassical dictum that literature must "delight and instruct," she further insisted that contemporary literature must teach a new concept of gender-equality, in which both women and men would exercise their rational and moral faculties to their greatest capacity.

To attain these goals, literature must above all be *probable,* showing in detail how characters develop over time, gradually learning to recognize and correct their mistakes in perception and behavior. The genre best suited to this didactic purpose, Barbauld firmly believed, was not poetry but the novel, whose realistic representation of everyday life showed more clearly and vividly than could the imaginative or self-reflective poem exactly how well-principled and well-educated people could lead the good life. Moreover, the novel was inherently a more democratic genre, available to anyone who could read, regardless of whether they had learned Latin and Greek. Above all, the novel was the genre that provided for young women the education that they were otherwise socially denied, an education in rational self-control and moral virtue. In Barbauld's view, it is finally the novelist, and the female novelist in particular, who becomes the unacknowledged legislator of the social world.

from POEMS
(1773)

An Inventory of the Furniture in Dr. Priestley's[1] Study

A map of every country known,
With not a foot of land his own.
A list of folks that kicked a dust
On this poor globe, from Ptol. the First;[2]
He hopes, — indeed it is but fair, —
Some day to get a corner there.
A group of all the British kings,
Fair emblem! on a packthread swings.[3]
The Fathers, ranged in goodly row,
A decent, venerable show,
Writ a great while ago, they tell us,
And many an inch o'ertop their fellows.[4]
A Juvenal to hunt for mottos;
And Ovid's tales of nymphs and grottos.[5]
The meek-robed lawyers, all in white;
Pure as the lamb, — at least, to sight.[6]

[1]**Dr. Joseph Priestley (1733–1804):** chemist, lawyer, and clergyman who taught at the dissenting academy at Warrington, where Anna Barbauld's father also taught. Priestley is best known as the discoverer of oxygen (which he called "dephlogisticated air") in 1774, and as an early analyst of electrical discharges (the "Priestley rings"), explained in his *History and Present State of Electricity* (1767). His ardent support for the French Revolution led the townspeople of Birmingham to burn his house in 1791, forcing him to emigrate to Northumberland, Pennsylvania, in 1794.

[2]**list of folks:** reference to Joseph Priestley's *New Chart of History* (1769), which discusses the rise and fall of the great empires of the world. **Ptol. the First:** Ptolemy Soter (367?–283 BC), the first king of Egypt.

[3]**group . . . swings:** a chart of the succession of the kings of England, hanging on the wall; Barbauld here implies that Priestley, a renowned supporter of the American Revolution, is hanging the kings.

[4]**The Fathers . . . fellows:** the writings of the Fathers of the Holy Roman Catholic Church, printed in large folio volumes.

[5]**Juvenal:** Decimus Junius Juvenalis (60?–?140 AD), Roman satirical poet and lawyer. **Ovid:** Publius Ovidius Naso (43BC–AD?17), Roman poet best known for his *Metamorphoses,* a collection of legends recounting the supernatural transformations of gods and humans.

[6]**lawyers . . . sight:** volumes of jurisprudence, bound in white vellum.

A shelf of bottles, jar and phial,
By which the rogues he can defy all,—
All filled with lightning keen and genuine,
And many a little imp he'll pen you in;
Which, like Le Sage's sprite, let out,
Among the neighbours makes a rout;[7]
Brings down the lightning on their houses,
And kills their geese, and frights their spouses.
A rare thermometer, by which
He settles, to the nicest pitch,
The just degrees of heat, to raise
Sermons, or politics, or plays.
Papers and books, a strange mixed olio,[8]
From shilling touch[9] to pompous folio,
Answer, remark, reply, rejoinder,
Fresh from the mint, all stamped and coined here;
Like new-made glass, set by to cool,
Before it bears the workman's tool.
A blotted proof-sheet, wet from Bowling.[10]
—"How can a man his anger hold in?"—
Forgotten rimes, and college themes,
Worm-eaten plans, and embryo schemes;—
A mass of heterogeneous matter,
A chaos dark, nor land nor water;—
New books, like new-born infants, stand,
Waiting the printer's clothing hand;—
Others, a motley ragged brood,
Their limbs unfashioned all, and rude,
Like Cadmus' half-formed men[11] appear;
One rears a helm, one lifts a spear,
And feet were lopped and fingers torn
Before their fellow limbs were born;
A leg began to kick and sprawl
Before the head was seen at all,
Which quiet as a mushroom lay
Till crumbling hillocks gave it way;
And all, like controversial writing,
Were born with teeth, and sprung up fighting.
"But what is this," I hear you cry,
"Which saucily provokes my eye?"—
A thing unknown, without a name,
Born of the air and doomed to flame.[12]

[7] **phial . . . rout**: Barbauld refers to the "Leyden jar" or phial in which electricity was stored; when this condenser or capacitor was discharged, a spark like lightning was produced. In René Le Sage's *Le Diable Boiteux* (1707), a student releases a spirit from a phial who lifts the roofs off the neighbors' houses, thereby revealing their private lives, to their immense consternation.

[8] **olio**: a collection of various writings, a miscellany.

[9] **shilling touch**: hastily written, cheap pamphlet.

[10] **blotted**: smeared with excess ink. **Bowling**: the name of a printer.

[11] **Cadmus' half-formed men**: in Ovid's *Metamorphoses* (3:88–123), Cadmus, the legendary founder of Thebes, killed a sacred dragon. He was then told by Athena to sow the dragon's teeth in the earth; the teeth sprang up as Sparti (sown men) or warriors, feet first, armed and fighting, the ancestors of the noble families of Thebes.

[12] **born . . . flame**: a gas produced by one of Priestley's numerous experiments, perhaps hydrogen (which he called "inflammable air").

On a Lady's Writing

Her even lines her steady temper show;
Neat as her dress, and polish'd as her brow;
Strong as her judgment, easy as her air;
Correct though free, and regular though fair:
And the same graces o'er her pen preside
That form her manners and her footsteps guide.

To a Lady, with Some Painted Flowers[1]

_________________ tibi lilia plenis
Ecce ferunt nymphae calathis.[2]

VIRGIL

Flowers to the fair: To you these flowers I bring,
And strive to greet you with an earlier spring.
Flowers sweet, and gay, and delicate like you;
Emblems of innocence, and beauty too.
With flowers the Graces bind their yellow hair,
And flowery wreaths consenting lovers wear.
Flowers, the sole luxury which nature knew,

[1] Mary Wollstonecraft reprinted the entire text of this poem in *A Vindication of the Rights of Woman* (1792), Chapter 4, note 7, introducing these lines as "ignoble" and concluding, "So the men tell us; but virtue, says reason, must be acquired by *rough* toils, and useful struggles with worldly *cares*."

[2] **Motto**: from Virgil's *Eclogues*, II.45–46: "Behold, the nymphs bring you lilies in overflowing baskets."

In Eden's pure and guiltless garden grew.
To loftier forms are rougher tasks assign'd;
The sheltering oak resists the stormy wind,
The tougher yew repels invading foes,
And the tall pine for future navies grows;
But this soft family, to cares unknown,
Were born for pleasure and delight alone.
Gay without toil, and lovely without art,
They spring to cheer the sense, and glad the heart.
Nor blush, my fair, to own you copy these;
Your best, your sweetest empire is—to please.

A Summer Evening's Meditation
(1773)

One sun by day, by night ten thousand shine.[1]
YOUNG

'Tis past! The sultry tyrant of the south
Has spent his short-liv'd rage; more grateful hours
Move silent on; the skies no more repel
The dazzled sight, but with mild maiden beams
Of temper'd lustre, court the cherish'd eye
To wander o'er their sphere; where hung aloft
DIAN's bright crescent, like a silver bow
New strung in heaven, lifts high its beamy horns
Impatient for the night, and seems to push
Her brother down the sky. Fair VENUS shines
E'en in the eye of day; with sweetest beam
Propitious shines, and shakes a trembling flood
Of soften'd radiance from her dewy locks.
The shadows spread apace; while meeken'd[2] Eve,
Her cheek yet warm with blushes, slow retires
Thro' the Hesperian gardens of the west,
And shuts the gates of day. 'Tis now the hour
When Contemplation, from her sunless haunts,
The cool damp grotto, or the lonely depth
Of unpierc'd woods, where wrapt in solid shade
She mused away the gaudy hours of noon,
And fed on thoughts unripen'd by the sun,
Moves forward; and with radiant finger points
To yon blue concave swell'd by breath divine,
Where, one by one, the living eyes of heaven
Awake, quick kindling o'er the face of ether
One boundless blaze; ten thousand trembling fires,
And dancing lustres, where th' unsteady eye
Restless and dazzled, wanders unconfin'd
O'er all this field of glories: spacious field!
And worthy of the master: he, whose hand
With hieroglyphics elder than the Nile,
Inscrib'd the mystic tablet; hung on high
To public gaze, and said, adore, O man!
The finger of thy GOD. From what pure wells
Of milky light, what soft o'erflowing urn,
Are all these lamps so fill'd? these friendly lamps,
For ever streaming o'er the azure deep
To point our path, and light us to our home.
How soft they slide along their lucid spheres!
And silent as the foot of time, fulfil
Their destin'd courses: Nature's self is hush'd,
And, but a scatter'd leaf, which rustles thro'
The thick-wove foliage, not a sound is heard
To break the midnight air; tho' the rais'd ear,
Intensely listening, drinks in every breath.
How deep the silence, yet how loud the praise!
But are they silent all? or is there not
A tongue in every star that talks with man,
And wooes him to be wise; nor wooes in vain:
This dead of midnight is the noon of thought,
And wisdom mounts her zenith with the stars.
At this still hour the self-collected soul
Turns inward, and beholds a stranger there
Of high descent, and more than mortal rank;
An embryo God; a spark of fire divine,
Which must burn on for ages, when the sun,
(Fair transitory creature of a day!)
Has clos'd his golden eye, and wrapt in shades
Forgets his wonted journey thro' the east.
Ye citadels of light, and seats of GODS!
Perhaps my future home, from whence the soul
Revolving periods past, may oft look back
With recollected tenderness, on all
The various busy scenes she left below,
Its deep laid projects and its strange events,
As on some fond and doating tale that sooth'd
Her infant hours; O be it lawful now
To tread the hallow'd circles of your courts,
And with mute wonder and delighted awe
Approach your burning confines. Seiz'd in thought,
On fancy's wild and roving wing I sail,
From the green borders of the peopled earth,
And the pale moon, her duteous fair attendant;
From solitary Mars; from the vast orb
Of Jupiter, whose huge gigantic bulk

[1] **Motto:** from Edward Young, *Night Thoughts,* 9:748.
[2] **meeken'd:** humbled, softened, made meek.

Dances in ether like the lightest leaf;
To the dim verge, the suburbs of the system,
Where chearless Saturn 'midst his wat'ry moons
Girt with a lucid zone, in gloomy pomp,
Sits like an exil'd monarch: fearless thence
I launch into the trackless deeps of space,
Where, burning round, ten thousand suns appear,
Of elder beam; which ask no leave to shine
Of our terrestrial star, nor borrow light
From the proud regent of our scanty day;
Sons of the morning, first-born of creation,
And only less than him who marks their track,
And guides their fiery wheels. Here must I stop,
Or is there aught beyond? What hand unseen
Impels me onward thro' the glowing orbs
Of habitable nature; far remote,
To the dread confines of eternal night,
To solitudes of vast unpeopled space,
The desarts of creation, wide and wild;
Where embryo systems and unkindled suns
Sleep in the womb of chaos; fancy droops,
And thought astonish'd stops her bold career.
But oh thou mighty mind! whose powerful word
Said, thus let all things be, and thus they were,
Where shall I seek thy presence? how unblam'd
Invoke thy dread perfection?
Have the broad eye-lids of the morn beheld thee?
Or does the beamy shoulder of Orion
Support thy throne? O look with pity down
On erring guilty man; not in thy names
Of terrour clad; not with those thunders arm'd
That conscious Sinai[3] felt, when fear appall'd
The scatter'd tribes; thou hast a gentler voice,
That whispers comfort to the swelling heart,
Abash'd, yet longing to behold her Maker.
  But now my soul unus'd to stretch her powers
In flight so daring, drops her weary wing,
And seeks again the known accustom'd spot,
Drest up with sun, and shade, and lawns, and streams,
A mansion fair and spacious for its guest,
And full replete with wonders. Let me here
Content and grateful, wait th' appointed time
And ripen for the skies: the hour will come
When all these splendours bursting on my sight
Shall stand unveil'd, and to my ravish'd sense
Unlock the glories of the world unknown.

[3] From Exodus 19. Reference to God's descending in thunder and lightning to deliver the Ten Commandments to Moses on Mount Sinai.

Epistle to William Wilberforce, Esq. on the Rejection of the Bill for Abolishing the Slave Trade[1]

(1791)

Cease, Wilberforce, to urge thy generous aim!
Thy Country knows the sin, and stands the shame!
The Preacher, Poet, Senator in vain
Has rattled in her sight the Negro's chain;
With his deep groans assail'd her startled ear,
And rent the veil that hid his constant tear;
Forc'd her averted eyes his stripes to scan,
Beneath the bloody scourge laid bare the man,
Claim'd Pity's tear, urg'd Conscience' strong controul,
And flash'd conviction on her shrinking soul.
The Muse too, soon awak'd, with ready tongue
At Mercy's shrine applausive peans rung;
And Freedom's eager sons, in vain foretold
A new Astrean reign, an age of gold:
She knows and she persists—Still Afric bleeds,
Uncheck'd, the human traffic still proceeds;
She stamps her infamy to future time,
And on her harden'd forehead seals the crime.
  In vain, to thy white standard gathering round,
Wit, Worth, and Parts and Eloquence are found:
In vain, to push to birth thy great design,
Contending chiefs, and hostile virtues join;
All, from conflicting ranks, of power possest
To rouse, to melt, or to inform the breast.
Where seasoned tools of Avarice prevail,
A Nation's eloquence, combined, must fail:
Each flimsy sophistry by turns they try;
The plausive[2] argument, the daring lye,
The artful gloss, that moral sense confounds,
Th' acknowledged thirst of gain that honour wounds:
Bane of ingenuous minds, th' unfeeling sneer,
Which, sudden, turns to stone the falling tear:
They search assiduous, with inverted skill,
For forms of wrong, and precedents of ill;
With impious mockery wrest the sacred page,
And glean up crimes from each remoter age:

[1] On 18 April 1791, William Wilberforce, M.P., moved the first Parliamentary bill to abolish the slave trade; on April 19, the motion was defeated 163 to 88. (See SLAVERY, THE SLAVE TRADE, AND ABOLITION.)

[2] **plausive**: specious.

Wrung Nature's tortures, shuddering, while you tell,
From scoffing fiends bursts forth the laugh of hell;
In Britain's senate, Misery's pangs give birth
To jests unseemly, and to horrid mirth—
Forbear! — thy virtues but provoke our doom,
And swell th' account of vengeance yet to come;
For, not unmark'd in Heaven's impartial plan,
Shall man, proud worm, contemn his fellow-man?
And injur'd Afric, by herself redrest,
Darts her own serpents at her Tyrant's breast.
Each vice, to minds deprav'd by bondage known,
With sure contagion fastens on his own;
In sickly languors melts his nerveless frame,
And blows to rage impetuous Passion's flame:
Fermenting swift, the fiery venom gains
The milky innocence of infant veins;
There swells the stubborn will, damps learning's fire,
The whirlwind wakes of uncontroul'd desire,
Sears the young heart to images of woe,
And blasts the buds of Virtue as they blow.
  Lo! where reclin'd, pale Beauty courts the breeze,
Diffus'd on sofas of voluptuous ease;
With anxious awe, her menial train around,
Catch her faint whispers of half-utter'd sound;
See her, in monstrous fellowship, unite
At once the Scythian, and the Sybarite;[3]
Blending repugnant vices, misally'd,
Which frugal nature purpos'd to divide;
See her, with indolence to fierceness join'd,
Of body delicate, infirm of mind,
With languid tones imperious mandates urge;
With arm recumbent wield the household scourge;
And with unruffled mien, and placid sounds,
Contriving torture, and inflicting wounds.
  Nor, in their palmy walks and spicy groves,
The form benign of rural Pleasure roves;
No milk-maid's song, or hum of village talk,
Sooths the lone Poet in his evening walk:
No willing arm the flail unweary'd plies,
Where the mix'd sounds of cheerful labour rise;
No blooming maids, and frolic swains are seen
To pay gay homage to their harvest queen:
No heart-expanding scenes their eyes must prove
Of thriving industry, and faithful love:
But shrieks and yells disturb the balmy air,
Dumb sullen looks of woe announce despair,
And angry eyes thro' dusky features glare.
Far from the sounding lash the Muses fly,
And sensual riot drowns each finer joy.
  Nor less from the gay East, on essenc'd wings,
Breathing unnam'd perfumes, Contagion springs;
The soft luxurious plague alike pervades
The marble palaces, and rural shades;
Hence, throng'd Augusta[4] builds her rosy bowers,
And decks in summer wreaths her smoky towers;
And hence, in summer bow'rs, Art's costly hand
Pours courtly splendours o'er the dazzled land:
The manners melt—One undistinguish'd blaze
O'erwhelms the sober pomp of elder days;
Corruption follows with gigantic stride,
And scarce vouchsafes his shameless front to hide:
The spreading leprosy taints ev'ry part,
Infects each limb, and sickens at the heart.
Simplicity! most dear of rural maids,
Weeping resigns her violated shades:
Stern Independance from his glebe[5] retires,
And anxious Freedom eyes her drooping fires;
By foreign wealth are British morals chang'd,
And Afric's sons, and India's, smile aveng'd.
  For you, whose temper'd ardour long has borne
Untir'd the labour, and unmov'd the scorn;
In Virtue's fasti[6] be inscrib'd your fame,
And utter'd your's with Howard's[7] honour'd name,
Friends of the friendless — Hail, ye generous band!
Whose efforts yet arrest Heav'n's lifted hand,
Around whose steady brows, in union bright,
The civic wreath, and Christian's palm unite:
Your merit stands, no greater and no less,
Without, or with the varnish of success;
But seek no more to break a Nation's fall,
For ye have sav'd yourselves — and that is all.
Succeeding times your struggles, and their fate,
With mingled shame and triumph shall relate,
While faithful History, in her various page,
Marking the features of this motley age,
To shed a glory, and to fix a stain,
Tells how you strove, and that you strove in vain.

[3] **Scythian . . . Sybarite:** the ancient Scythians were known for their savagery, the Sybarites for their luxury and decadence.

[4] **Augusta:** London.

[5] **glebe:** cultivated land; field.

[6] **fasti:** annals.

[7] **Howard:** John Howard (1726–1790), prison reformer and philanthropist.

from Sins of Government, Sins of the Nation; Or A Discourse for the Fast[1]

(1793)

. . . Amongst our national faults, have we any instances of *cruelty* or *oppression* to repent of? Can we look round from sea to sea, and from east to west, and say, *that our brother hath not aught against us?* If such instances do not exist under our immediate eye, do they exist any where under our influence and jurisdiction? There are some, whose nerves, rather than whose principles, cannot bear cruelty—like other nuisances, they would not chuse it in sight, but they can be well content to know it exists, and that they are indebted for it to the increase of their income, and the luxuries of their table. Are there not some *darker-coloured* children of the same family, over whom we assume a hard and unjust controul? And have not these our brethren *aught against us?* If we *suspect* they have, would it not become us anxiously to enquire into the truth, that we may deliver our souls; but if we know it, and cannot help knowing it, if such enormities have been pressed and forced upon our notice, till they are become flat and stale in the public ear, from fulness and repetition, and satiety of proof; and if they are still sanctioned by our legislature, defended by our princes—deep indeed is the colour of our guilt.—And do we appoint fasts, and make pretences to religion? Do we pretend to be shocked at the principles or the practices of neighbouring nations, and start with affected horror at the name of Atheist? Are our consciences so tender, and our hearts so hard? Is it possible we should meet as a nation, and knowing ourselves to be guilty of these things, have the confidence to implore the blessing of God upon our commerce and our colonies; preface with prayer our legislative meetings, and then deliberate *how long* we shall continue human sacrifices? Rather let us

Never pray more, abandon all remorse.

Let us lay aside the grimace of hypocrisy, stand up for what we are, and boldly profess, like the emperor of old, that every thing is sweet from which money is extracted, and that we know better than to deprive ourselves of a gain for the sake of a fellow-creature. . .

[1] **Fast:** national day of fasting appointed by the Church of England for 19 April 1793, to pray for peace and prosperity in time of war.

from THE BRITISH NOVELISTS

(1810)

from On the Origin and Progress of Novel-Writing

A collection of Novels has a better chance of giving pleasure than of commanding respect. Books of this description are condemned by the grave, and despised by the fastidious; but their leaves are seldom found unopened, and they occupy the parlour and the dressing-room while productions of higher name are often gathering dust upon the shelf. It might not perhaps be difficult to show that this species of composition is entitled to a higher rank than has been generally assigned it. Fictitious adventures, in one form or other, have made a part of the polite literature of every age and nation. These have been grafted upon the actions of their heroes; they have been interwoven with their mythology; they have been moulded upon the manners of the age,—and, in return, have influenced the manners of the succeeding generation by the sentiments they have infused and the sensibilities they have excited.

Adorned with the embellishments of Poetry, they produce the epic; more concentrated in the story, and exchanging narrative for action, they become dramatic. When allied with some great moral end, as in the *Télémaque* of Fénelon, and Marmontel's *Belisaire,*[1] they may be termed didactic. They are often made the vehicles of satire, as in Swift's *Gulliver's Travels,* and the *Candide* and *Babouc* of Voltaire.[2] They take a tincture from the learning

[1] **Fénelon:** François de Salignac de La Mothe Fénelon (1651–1715), French theologian and writer, author of *Télémaque* (1699). **Marmontel:** Jean-François Marmontel (1723–1799), French critic, dramatist, and author of moral fictions, including *Belisaire* (1767).

[2] **Swift:** Jonathan Swift (1667–1745), Anglo-Irish satirist, author of *Gulliver's Travels* (1726). **Voltaire:** François-Marie Arouet de Voltaire (1694–1778), French philosopher, historian, and author of such philosophical tales as *Babouc* and his masterpiece, *Candide* (1759).

and politics of the times, and are made use of successfully to attack or recommend the prevailing systems of the day. When the range of this kind of writing is so extensive, and its effects so great, it seems evident that it ought to hold a respectable place among the productions of genius; nor is it easy to say, why the poet, who deals in one kind of fiction, should have so high a place allotted him in the temple of fame; and the romance-writer so low a one as in the general estimation he is confined to. To measure the dignity of a writer by the pleasure he affords his readers is not perhaps using an accurate criterion; but the invention of a story, the choice of proper incidents, the ordonnance of the plan, occasional beauties of description, and above all, the power exercised over the reader's heart by filling it with the successive emotions of love, pity, joy, anguish, transport, or indignation, together with the grave impressive moral resulting from the whole, imply talents of the highest order, and ought to be appretiated accordingly. A good novel is an epic in prose, with more of character and less (indeed in modern novels nothing) of the supernatural machinery.

If we look for the origin of fictitious tales and adventures, we shall be obliged to go to the earliest accounts of the literature of every age and country. The Eastern nations have always been fond of this species of mental gratification. The East is emphatically the country of invention. The Persians, Arabians, and other nations in that vicinity have been, and still are, in the habit of employing people whose business it is to compose and to relate entertaining stories; and it is surprising how many stories (as Parnell's Hermit for instance)[3] which have passed current in verse and prose through a variety of forms, may be traced up to this source. From Persia the taste passed into the soft and luxurious Ionia. The *Milesian Tales,* written by Aristides of Miletus,[4] at what time is not exactly known, seem to have been a kind of novel. They were translated into Latin during the civil wars of Marius and Sulla.[5] They consisted of loose love stories, but were very popular among the Romans; and the Parthian general who beat Crassus[6] took occasion, from his finding a copy of them amongst the camp equipage, to reproach that nation with effeminacy, in not being able, even in time of danger, to dispense with such an amusement. From Ionia the taste of romances passed over to the Greeks about the time of Alexander the Great.[7] The *Golden Ass* of Lucian, which is exactly in the manner of the Arabian Tales, is one of the few extant.

The first Gothic romances[8] appeared under the venerable guise of history. Arthur and the knights of the round table, Charlemagne and his peers, were their favourite heroes. The extended empire of Charlemagne and his conquests naturally offered themselves as subjects for recital; but it seems extraordinary that Arthur, a British prince, the scene of whose exploits was in Wales, a country little known to the rest of Europe, and who was continually struggling against ill-fortune, should have been so great a favourite upon the continent. Perhaps, however, the comparative obscurity of his situation might favour the genius of the composition, and the intercourse between Wales and Brittany would contribute to diffuse and exaggerate the stories of his exploits. In fact, every song and record relating to this hero was kept with the greatest care in Brittany, and, together with a chronicle deducing Prince Arthur from Priam king of Troy, was brought to England about the year 1100, by Walter Mapes archdeacon of Oxford,[9] when he returned from the continent through that province. This medley of historical songs, traditions, and invention, was put into Latin by Geoffry of Monmouth,[10] with many additions of his own,

[3] **Parnell:** Thomas Parnell (1679–1718), Irish poet.

[4] **Aristides:** Aristides of Miletus (c. 100 BC), author of lost *Milesian Tales,* reputed to be obscene; "Milesiae" became a generic title for erotic tales in classical Rome.

[5] **Marius and Sulla:** Gaius Marius (c.157 BC–86 BC), and Lucius Cornelius Sulla (138 BC–78 BC), Roman generals whose rivalry led to civil war (88 BC).

[6] **Crassus:** Marcus Licinius Crassus (d. 53 BC), Roman politician and consul, murdered after his military defeat by archers from Parthia (an ancient country corresponding to part of modern Iran).

[7] **Alexander the Great (356–323 BC):** king of Macedon and conqueror of much of Asia. **Lucian:** Evidently mistaken for Lucius Apuleius, Latin satirist, author of *The Golden Ass.*

[8] **Gothic romances:** here used to refer to medieval chivalric tales rather than to the genre of sensational fictions popular in the later eighteenth and nineteenth centuries.

[9] **Walter Mapes:** also, Map (c. 1140–c. 1210), English author and archdeacon of Oxford; the attribution of one or more Arthurian romances to him is no longer credited.

[10] **Geoffry of Monmouth (c. 1100–1154):** English author, noted primarily for his *Historia regum Brittaniae* (History of the Kings of Britain, 1135), among the earliest and fullest treatments of the Arthurian legend.

and from Latin translated into French in the year 1115, under the title of *Brut d' Angleterre*. . . .

In the mean time Europe settled into a state of comparative tranquillity: castles and knights and adventures of distressed damsels ceased to be the topics of the day, and romances founded upon them had begun to be insipid when the immortal satire of Cervantes[11] drove them off the field, and they have never since been able to rally their forces. . . .

Though Cervantes had laid to rest the giants and enchanters, a new style of fictitious writing was introduced, not less remote from nature, in the romances *de longue haleine*,[12] which originated in France, and of which Calprenède and Mad. Scudéry were the most distinguished authors. The principle of these was high honour, impregnable chastity, a constancy unshaken by time or accident, and a species of love so exalted and refined, that it bore little resemblance to a natural passion. These, in the construction of the story, came nearer to real life than the former had done. The adventures were marvellous, but not impossible. The heroes and heroines were taken from ancient history, but without any resemblance to the personages whose names they bore. The manners therefore and passions referred to an ideal world, the creation of the writer; but the situations were often striking, and the sentiments always noble. It is a curious circumstance that Rousseau,[13] who tells us that his childhood was conversant in these romances, (a course of reading which no doubt fed and inflamed his fine imagination) has borrowed from them an affecting incident in his *Nouvelle Héloïse. St. Preux*, when his mistress lies ill of the small-pox, glides into the room, approaches the bed in order to imbibe the danger, and retires without speaking. *Julie*, when recovered, is impressed with a confused idea of having seen him, but whether in a dream, a vision, or a reality, she cannot determine. . . .

Rude times are fruitful of striking adventures; polished times must render them pleasing.—The ponderous volumes of the romance writers being laid upon the shelf, a closer imitation of nature began to be called for . . .—The *Zaide* and the *Princesse de Cleves* of Madame de la Fayette[14] are esteemed to be the first which approach the modern novel of the serious kind, the latter especially. Voltaire[15] says of them, that "They were the first novels which gave the manners of cultivated life and natural incidents related with elegance. Before the time of this lady, the style of these productions was affectedly turgid, and the adventures out of nature." . . .

Marivaux[16] excelled in a different style. . . . He lays open the heart, particularly the female heart, in its inmost folds and recesses; its little vanities and affectations as well as its finer feelings. He abounds in wit, but it is of a refined kind, and requires thought in the reader to enter into it. He has also much humour, and describes comic scenes and characters amongst the lower and middle ranks with a great deal of the comic effect, but without the coarseness, of Fielding. . . .

At the head of writers of this class stands the seductive, the passionate Rousseau,—the most eloquent writer in the most eloquent modern language: whether his glowing pencil paints the strong emotions of passion, or the enchanting scenery of nature in his own romantic country, or his peculiar cast of moral sentiment,—a charm is spread over every part of the work, which scarcely leaves the judgement free to condemn what in it is dangerous or reprehensible. His are truly the "thoughts that breathe and words that burn." He has hardly any thing of story; he has but few figures upon his canvass; he wants them not; his characters are drawn more from a creative imagination than from real life, and we wonder that what has so little to do with nature should have so much to do with

[11] **Cervantes**: Miguel de Cervantes Saavedra (1547–1616), Spanish novelist and playwright, author of *Don Quixote* (1605–1615).

[12] **romances de longue haleine**: literally, long-breathed romances, multivolume quasi-historical stories of love, honor, and nobility, such as *Clélie* (1654–1660) by Madeleine de **Scudéry** (1607?–1701), and *Cassandre* (1642) by Gautier de Costes, sieur de La **Calprenède** (1609?–1663).

[13] **Rousseau**: Jean-Jacques Rousseau (1712–1778), French-Swiss moralist, philosopher, and novelist, author of the autobiographical *Confessions* (1770) and the novel *Julie, ou la Nouvelle Héloïse* (1761).

[14] **Madame de la Fayette**: Marie-Madeleine Pioche de La Vergne, comtesse de La Fayette (1634–1692), French novelist, author of *Zaide* (1669) and *La Princesse de Cleves* (1678), historical romances which exhibited a new kind of psychological realism.

[15] **Voltaire**: See note 2. Barbauld quotes from his *Essay on Epic Poetry* (1727).

[16] **Marivaux**: Pierre Carlet de Marivaux (1688–1763), French dramatist and novelist, author of *La Vie de Marianne* (1731–1741) and *Le Paysan Parvenu* (1735–1736), novels of middle-class life.

the heart. Our censure of the tendency of this work will be softened if we reflect that Rousseau's aim, as far as he had a moral aim, seems to have been to give a striking example of fidelity in the *married* state, which, it is well known, is little thought of by the French; though they would judge with the greatest severity the more pardonable failure of an unmarried woman. But Rousseau has not reflected that *Julie* ought to have considered herself as indissolubly united to *St. Preux*; her marriage with another was the infidelity. . . . For the expression of sentiment in all its various shades, for the most delicate tact, and a refinement and polish, the fruit of high cultivation, the French writers are superior to those of every other nation.

There is one species of this composition which may be called the *Didactic Romance,* which they have particularly made use of as a vehicle for moral sentiment, and philosophical or political systems and opinions.—Of this nature is the beautiful fiction of *Télémaque,* if it be not rather an Epic in prose; the high merit of which cannot be sufficiently appretiated, unless the reader bears in mind when and to whom it was written; that it dared to attack the fondness for war and the disposition to ostentatious profusion, under a monarch the most vain and ambitious of his age, and to draw, expressly as a pattern for his successor, the picture of a prince, the reverse of him in almost every thing. . . .

There is one objection to be made to these romances founded on history, which is, that if the personages are not judiciously selected, they are apt to impress false ideas on the mind. . . . *Telemachus* is a character already within the precincts of poetry and fable, and may illustrate without any objection the graceful fictions of Fénelon. Our own Prince *Arthur* offers himself with equal advantage for poetry or romance. Where history says little, fiction may say much: events and men that are dimly seen through the obscurity of remote periods and countries, may be illuminated with these false lights; but where history throws her light steady and strong, no artificial colouring should be permitted. Impressions of historical characters very remote from the truth, often remain on the mind from dramatic compositions. If we examine into our ideas of the Henries and Richards of English history, we shall perhaps find that they are as much drawn from Shakespear as from Hume[17] or Rapin. Some of our English romances are very faulty in this respect. A lady confessed that she could never get over a prejudice against the character of our Elizabeth, arising from her cruelty to two imaginary daughters of Mary Queen of Scots, who never existed but in the pages of a novel. The more art is shown, and much is often shown, in weaving the fictitious circumstances into the texture of the history, the worse is the tendency. . . .

The Germans, formerly remarkable for the laborious heaviness and patient research of their literary labours, have, within this last century, cultivated with great success the field of polite literature. Plays, tales, and novels of all kinds, many of them by their most celebrated authors, were at first received with avidity in this country, and even made the study of their language popular. The tide has turned, and they are now as much depretiated. The *Sorrows of Werter,* by Goethe,[18] was the first of these with which we were familiarized in this country: we received it through the medium of a French translation. It is highly pathetic, but its tendency has been severely, perhaps justly, censured; yet the author might plead that he has given warning of the probable consequences of illicit and uncontrolled passions by the awful catastrophe. It is certain, however, that the impression made is of more importance than the moral deduced; and if Schiller's[19] fine play of *The Robbers* has had, as we are assured was the case, the effect of leading some well-educated young gentlemen to commit depredations on the public, allured by the splendour of the principal character, we may well suppose that Werter's delirium of passion will not be less seducing. . . .

In England, most of the earlier romances, from the days of Chaucer to James the First, were translations from the Spanish or French. One of the most celebrated of our own growth is Sir Philip Sidney's *Arcadia,*[20] dedicated to his sister the Countess of Pembroke. It is a kind of pastoral romance, mingled with adventures of the heroic and

[17] **Hume**: David Hume (1711–1776), Scottish philosopher and historian, author of a standard *History of England* (1754–1762). **Rapin**: Paul Rapin de Thoyras (1661–1725), French historian of England, author of the *Histoire d'Angleterre* (published 1727–1735).

[18] **Goethe**: Johann Wolfgang von Goethe (1749–1832), German poet, dramatist, and novelist, author of the Romantic novel *The Sorrows of Young Werther* (1774), a story of love and suicidal despair, and the dramatic poem *Faust* (1808–1832).

[19] **Schiller**: Friedrich von Schiller (1759–1805), German poet and playwright, author of the Romantic drama *The Robbers* (1781), a study of political tyranny and rebellion.

[20] **Sidney**: Sir Philip Sidney (1554–1586), English poet and critic, author of the pastoral romance *Arcadia* (1590).

chivalrous kind. It has great beauties, particularly in poetic imagery. It is a book which all have heard of, which some few possess, but which nobody reads. The taste of the times seems to have been for ponderous performances. . . . We had pretty early some celebrated political romances. Sir Thomas More's *Utopia*, Barclay's *Argenis*, and Harrington's *Oceana*,[21] are of this Kind: the two former are written in Latin. The *Utopia*, which is meant as a model of a perfect form of civil polity, is chiefly preserved in remembrance at present by having had the same singular fortune with the *Quixote* of Cervantes, of furnishing a new word, which has been adopted into the language as a permanent part of it; for we speak familiarly of an Utopian scheme and a Quixotish expedition. . . . Mrs. Behn's[22] Novels were licentious; they are also fallen; but it ought not to be forgotten that Southerne borrowed from her his affecting story of *Oroonoko*. Mrs. Haywood was a very prolific genius; her earlier novels are in the style of Mrs. Behn's, and Pope has chastised her in his *Dunciad* without mercy or delicacy, but her later works are by no means void of merit. She wrote *The Invisible Spy*, and *Betsy Thoughtless*, and was the author of *The Female Spectator.*

But till the middle of the last century, theatrical productions and poetry made a far greater part of polite reading than novels, which had attained neither to elegance nor discrimination of character. . . . The first author amongst us who distinguished himself by natural painting, was that truly original genius De Foe.[23] His *Robinson Crusoe* is to this day an *unique* in its kind, and he has made it very interesting without applying to the common resource of love. At length, in the reign of George the Second, Richardson, Fielding, and Smollet,[24] appeared in quick succession; and their success raised such a demand for this kind of entertainment, that it has ever since been furnished from the press, rather as a regular and necessary supply, than as an occasional gratification. Novels have indeed been numerous "as leaves in Vallombrosa."[25] The indiscriminate passion for them, and their bad effects on the female mind, became the object of the satire of Garrick,[26] in a sprightly piece entitled *Polly Honeycomb*. . . .

About fifty years ago a very singular work appeared, somewhat in the guise of a novel, which gave a new impulse to writings of this stamp; namely, *The Life and Opinions of Tristram Shandy*, followed by *The Sentimental Journey*, by the Rev. Mr. Sterne,[27] a clergyman of York. They exhibit much originality, wit, and beautiful strokes of pathos, but a total want of plan or adventure, being made up of conversations and detached incidents. It is the peculiar characteristic of this writer, that he affects the heart, not by long drawn tales of distress, but by light electric touches which thrill the nerves of the reader who possesses a correspondent sensibility of frame. His characters, in like manner, are struck out by a few masterly touches. He resembles those painters who can give expression to a figure by two or three strokes of bold outline, leaving the imagination to fill up the sketch. . . . The two *Shandys*, *Trim*, *Dr. Slop*, are all drawn with a masterly hand. It is one of the merits of Sterne that he has awakened the attention of his readers to the wrongs of the poor negroes, and certainly a great spirit of tenderness and humanity breathes throughout the work. It is rather mortifying to reflect how little the power of expressing these feelings is connected with moral worth; for Sterne was a man by no means attentive to the happiness of those

[21] **Harrington's Oceana**: the *Commonwealth of Oceana* (1656), by James Harrington (1611–1677), is a utopian fiction advocating political reform; it influenced the early government of Pennsylvania and the political theorists of the American and French Revolutions. It was one of a number of political essays written in the form of utopian fictions, including *Argenis* by John **Barclay** (1582–1621), the Scottish-French classical scholar and writer; and, most importantly, the *Utopia* (1516) of Sir Thomas **More** (1478–1535), an early classic of English Humanist thought.

[22] **Mrs. Behn**: Aphra Behn (1640–1689), English playwright, novelist, and spy, author of the anti-slavery novel *Oroonoko* (1688), which was the basis for a play of the same name (1696) by Thomas Southerne (1660–1746). **Mrs. Haywood**: Eliza Haywood (1693?–1756), English novelist and editor, author of *The Invisible Spy* (1755) and the didactic psychological novel *The History of Miss Betsy Thoughtless* (1751), and editor of the periodical *The Female Spectator* (1744–1746).

[23] **De Foe**: Daniel Defoe (1660?–1731), English novelist and journalist, author of *Robinson Crusoe* (1719), *Moll Flanders* (1722), and *Roxana* (1724).

[24] **Richardson**: Samuel Richardson (1689–1761), author of *Clarissa* (1748). **Fielding**: Henry Fielding (1707–1754), author of *Tom Jones* (1749). **Smollet**: Tobias George Smollet (1721–1771), author of *Humphrey Clinker* (1770).

[25] **leaves in Vallombrosa**: Milton, *Paradise Lost*, I. 302–303.

[26] **Garrick**: David Garrick (1717–1779), English actor, dramatist, and stage producer, the most celebrated Shakespearean actor of his day and the author of such comic plays as *Polly Honeycomb* (1760; also attributed to George Colman).

[27] **Sterne**: Laurence Sterne (1713–1768), English clergyman and novelist, author of the parodic, psychological-philosophical anti-novel *Tristram Shandy* (1760–1767), and *A Sentimental Journey through France and Italy* (unfinished; 1768).

connected with him: and we are forced to confess that an author may conceive the idea of "brushing away flies without killing them," and yet behave ill in every relation of life. . . .

. . . This work gave rise to the vapid effusions of a crowd of sentimentalists, many of whom thought they had seized the spirit of Sterne, because they could copy him in his breaks and asterisks. The taste spread, and for a while, from the pulpit to the playhouse, the reign of sentiment was established. Among the more respectable imitators of Sterne may be reckoned Mr. Mackenzie[28] in his *Man of Feeling* and his *Julia de Roubigné*, and Mr. Pratt in his *Emma Corbett*. . . .

Many tears have been shed by the young and tender-hearted over *Sidney Biddulph*, the production of Mrs. Sheridan,[29] the wife of Mr. Thomas Sheridan the lecturer, an ingenious and amiable woman: the sentiments of this work are pure and virtuous, but the author seems to have taken pleasure in heaping distress upon virtue and innocence, merely to prove, what no one will deny, that the best dispositions are not always sufficient to ward off the evils of life. Why is it that women when they write are apt to give a melancholy tinge to their compositions? Is it that they suffer more, and have fewer resources against melancholy? Is it that men, mixing at large in society, have a brisker flow of ideas, and, seeing a greater variety of characters, introduce more of the business and pleasures of life into their productions? Is it that humour is a scarcer product of the mind than sentiment, and more congenial to the stronger powers of man? Is it that women nurse those feelings in secrecy and silence, and diversify the expression of them with endless shades of sentiment, which are more transiently felt, and with fewer modifications of delicacy, by the other sex? The remark, if true, has no doubt many exceptions; but the productions of several ladies, both French and English, seem to countenance it. . . .

. . . —But it is time to retire from the enumeration of these works of fancy, or the reader might be as much startled with the number of heroes and heroines called up around him, as Ulysses[30] was with the troops of shades that came flocking about him in the infernal regions.

If the end and object of this species of writing be asked, many no doubt will be ready to tell us that its object is,—to call in fancy to the aid of reason, to deceive the mind into embracing truth under the guise of fiction:

"Cosi a l' egro fanciul porgiamo aspersi
Di soave licor gli orli del vaso,
Succhi amari, ingannato in tanto ei beve,
E da l' inganno suo vita riceve."[31]

with such-like reasons equally grave and dignified. For my own part, I scruple not to confess that, when I take up a novel, my end and object is entertainment; and as I suspect that to be the case with most readers, I hesitate not to say that entertainment is their legitimate end and object. To read the productions of wit and genius is a very high pleasure to all persons of taste, and the avidity with which they are read by all such shows sufficiently that they are calculated to answer this end. Reading is the cheapest of pleasures: it is a domestic pleasure. Dramatic exhibitions give a more poignant delight, but they are seldom enjoyed in perfection, and never without expense and trouble. Poetry requires in the reader a certain elevation of mind and a practised ear. It is seldom relished unless a taste be formed for it pretty early. But the humble novel is always ready to enliven the gloom of solitude, to soothe the languor of debility and disease, to win the attention from pain or vexatious occurrences, to take man from himself, (at many seasons the worst company he can be in,) and, while the moving picture of life passes before him, to make him forget the subject of his own complaints. It is pleasant to the mind to sport in the boundless regions of possibility; to find relief from the sameness of every-day occurrences by expatiating amidst brighter skies and fairer fields; to exhibit love that is always happy, valour that is always successful; to feed the appetite for

[28] **Mackenzie**: Henry Mackenzie (1745–1831), Scottish novelist, author of the sentimental novels *The Man of Feeling* (1771) and *Julia de Roubigné* (1777). **Pratt**: Samuel Jackson Pratt (1749–1814), English writer, author of the novel, *Emma Corbett, or the Miseries of Civil War* (1780).

[29] **Sheridan**: Frances Sheridan (1724–1766), Irish novelist and dramatist, author of the *Memoirs of Miss Sidney Biddulph* (1761).

[30] **Ulysses**: the Latin name for Odysseus, the hero of Homer's *Odyssey*, who in one episode (Book XI) of his long return to Greece after the end of the Trojan war, visits the dead in the underworld of Hades.

[31] **Cosi a l'egro fanciul** . . . : the passage quoted is from Torquato Tasso's *Gerusalemme Liberata* [Jerusalem Delivered] (1575), an epic of the Crusades: "So when the draught we give to the sick child, / The vessel's edge we touch with syrup sweet; / Cheated, he swift drinks down the bitter brew, / And from the cheat receives his life anew" (translated in *Dictionary of Quotations, French and Italian*, by Harbottle and Dalbiac; New York, n.d.).

wonder by a quick succession of marvellous events; and to distribute, like a ruling providence, rewards and punishments which fall just where they ought to fall.

It is sufficient therefore, as an end, that these writings add to the innocent pleasures of life; and if they do no harm, the entertainment they give is a sufficient good. We cut down the tree that bears no fruit, but we ask nothing of a flower beyond its scent and its colour. The unpardonable sin in a novel is dullness: however grave or wise it may be, if its author possesses no powers of amusing, he has no business to write novels; he should employ his pen in some more serious part of literature.

But it is not necessary to rest the credit of these works on amusement alone, since it is certain they have had a very strong effect in infusing principles and moral feelings. It is impossible to deny that the most glowing and impressive sentiments of virtue are to be found in many of these compositions, and have been deeply imbibed by their youthful readers. They awaken a sense of finer feelings than the commerce of ordinary life inspires. Many a young woman has caught from such works as *Clarissa* or *Cecilia*,[32] ideas of delicacy and refinement which were not, perhaps, to be gained in any society she could have access to. Many a maxim of prudence is laid up in the memory from these stores, ready to operate when occasion offers.

The passion of love, the most seductive of all the passions, they certainly paint too high, and represent its influence beyond what it will be found to be in real life; but if they soften the heart they also refine it. They mix with the common passions of our nature all that is tender in virtuous affection; all that is estimable in high principle and unshaken constancy; all that grace, delicacy, and sentiment can bestow of touching and attractive. Benevolence and sensibility to distress are almost always insisted on in modern works of this kind; and perhaps it is not exaggeration to say, that much of the softness of our present manners, much of that tincture of humanity so conspicuous amidst all our vices, is owing to the bias given by our dramatic writings and fictitious stories. A high regard to female honour, generosity, and a spirit of self-sacrifice, are strongly inculcated. It costs nothing, it is true, to an author to make his hero generous, and very often he is extravagantly so; still, sentiments of this kind serve in some measure to counteract the spirit of the world, where selfish considerations have always more than their due weight. In what discourse from the pulpit are religious feelings more strongly raised than in the prison sermon of *The Vicar of Wakefield*,[33] or some parts of *The Fool of Quality*?

But not only those splendid sentiments with which, when properly presented, our feelings readily take part, and kindle as we read; the more severe and homely virtues of prudence and economy have been enforced in the writings of a Burney and an Edgeworth.[34] Writers of their good sense have observed, that while these compositions cherished even a romantic degree of sensibility, the duties that have less brilliancy to recommend them were neglected. Where can be found a more striking lesson against unfeeling dissipation than the story of the *Harrels*? Where have order, neatness, industry, sobriety, been recommended with more strength than in the agreeable tales of Miss Edgeworth? If a parent wishes his child to avoid caprice, irregularities of temper, procrastination, coquetry, affectation,—all those faults and blemishes which undermine family happiness, and destroy the every-day comforts of common life,—whence can he derive more impressive morality than from the same source? When works of fancy are thus made subservient to the improvement of the rising generation, they certainly stand on a higher ground than mere entertainment, and we revere while we admire.

Some knowledge of the world is also gained by these writings, imperfect indeed, but attained with more ease, and attended with less danger, than by mixing in real life. If the stage is a mirror of life, so is the novel, and perhaps a more accurate one, as less is sacrificed to effect and representation. There are many descriptions of characters in the busy world, which a young woman in the retired scenes of life hardly meets with at all, and many whom it is safer to read of than to meet; and to either sex it must be desirable that the first impressions of fraud, selfishness, profligacy and perfidy should be connected, as in good novels they always will be, with infamy and ruin. At any rate, it is safer to meet with a bad character in the pages of a fictitious story, than in the polluted walks of life; but an author solicitous for the morals of his readers

[32] **Cecilia:** title of the second novel (1782) by Frances Burney (1752–1840) which includes the story of the Harrel family.

[33] **The Vicar of Wakefield:** title of the only novel (1766) of Oliver Goldsmith (1730?–1774), Anglo-Irish poet and dramatist.

[34] **Edgeworth:** Maria Edgeworth* (1767–1849), Irish novelist, author of *Castle Rackrent* (1800), and *Moral Tales* for children (1801).

will be sparing in the introduction of such characters.—It is an aphorism of Pope,[35]

> Vice is a monster of such frightful mien
> As to be hated, needs but to be seen.

But he adds,

> But seen too oft, familiar with her face,
> We first endure, then pity, then embrace.

Indeed the former assertion is not true without considerable modifications. If presented in its naked deformity, vice will indeed give disgust; but it may be so surrounded with splendid and engaging qualities, that the disgust is lost in admiration. Besides, though the selfish and mean propensities are radically unlovely, it is not the same with those passions which all have felt, and few are even desirous to resist. To present these to the young mind in the glowing colours of a Rousseau or a Madame de Staël is to awaken and increase sensibilities, which it is the office of wise restraint to calm and to moderate. Humour covers the disgust which the grosser vices would occasion; passion veils the danger of the more seducing ones.

After all, the effect of novel-reading must depend, as in every other kind of reading, on the choice which is made. If the looser compositions of this sort are excluded, and the sentimental ones chiefly perused, perhaps the danger lies more in fixing the standard of virtue and delicacy too high for real use, than in debasing it. Generosity is carried to such excess as would soon dissipate even a princely fortune; a weak compassion often allows vice to escape with impunity; an overstrained delicacy, or regard to a rash vow, is allowed to mar all the prospects of a long life: dangers are despised, and self is annihilated, to a degree that prudence does not warrant, and virtue is far from requiring. The most generous man living, the most affectionate friend, the most dutiful child, would find his character fall far short of the perfections exhibited in a highly-wrought novel.

Love is a passion particularly exaggerated in novels. It forms the chief interest of, by far, the greater part of them. In order to increase this interest, a false idea is given of the importance of the passion. It occupies the serious hours of life; events all hinge upon it; every thing gives way to its influence, and no length of time wears it out. When a young lady, having imbibed these notions, comes into the world, she finds that this formidable passion acts a very subordinate part on the great theatre of the world; that its vivid sensations are mostly limited to a very early period; and that it is by no means, as the poet sings,

> All the colour of remaining life.

She will find but few minds susceptible of its more delicate influences. Where it is really felt, she will see it continually overcome by duty, by prudence, or merely by a regard for the show and splendour of life; and that in fact it has a very small share in the transactions of the busy world, and is often little consulted even in choosing a partner for life. In civilized life both men and women acquire so early a command over their passions, that the strongest of them are taught to give way to circumstances, and a moderate liking will appear apathy itself, to one accustomed to see the passion painted in its most glowing colours. Least of all will a course of novels prepare a young lady for the neglect and tedium of life which she is perhaps doomed to encounter. If the novels she reads are virtuous, she has learned how to arm herself with proper reserve against the ardour of her lover; she has been instructed how to behave with the utmost propriety when run away with, like *Miss Byron*,[36] or locked up by a cruel parent, like *Clarissa*; but she is not prepared for indifference and neglect. Though young and beautiful, she may see her youth and beauty pass away without conquests, and the monotony of her life will be apt to appear more insipid when contrasted with scenes of perpetual courtship and passion.

It may be added with regard to the knowledge of the world, which, it is allowed, these writings are calculated in some degree to give, that, let them be as well written and with as much attention to real life and manners as they can possibly be, they will in some respects give false ideas, from the very nature of fictitious writing. Every such work is a *whole*, in which the fates and fortunes of the personages are brought to a conclusion, agreeably to the author's own preconceived idea. Every incident in a well written composition is introduced for a certain purpose, and made to forward a certain plan. A sagacious reader is never disappointed in his forebodings. If a prominent

[35] **Pope:** Alexander Pope (1688–1744), English poet and satirist; the lines are misquoted from *Essay on Man* (1730–1732), Epistle II, 217–220.

[36] **Miss Byron:** Harriet Byron, a character in *The History of Sir Charles Grandison* (1753–1754), the third novel by Samuel Richardson (see note 24).

circumstance is presented to him, he lays hold on it, and may be very sure it will introduce some striking event; and if a character has strongly engaged his affections, he need not fear being obliged to withdraw them; the personages never turn out differently from what their first appearance gave him a right to expect; they gradually open, indeed; they may surprise, but they never disappoint him. Even from the elegance of a name he may give a guess at the amenity of the character. But real life is a kind of chance-medley, consisting of many unconnected scenes. The great author of the drama of life has not finished his piece; but the author must finish his; and vice must be punished and virtue rewarded in the compass of a few volumes; and it is a fault in *his* composition if every circumstance does not answer the reasonable expectations of the reader. But in real life our reasonable expectations are often disappointed; many incidents occur which are like "passages that lead to nothing,"[37] and characters occasionally turn out quite different from what our fond expectations have led us to expect.

In short, the reader of a novel forms his expectations from what he supposes passes in the mind of the author, and guesses rightly at his intentions, but would often guess wrong if he were considering the real course of nature. It was very probable, at some periods of his history, that *Gil Blas*, if a real character, would come to be hanged; but the practised novel-reader knows well that no such event can await the hero of the tale. Let us suppose a person speculating on the character of *Tom Jones* as the production of an author, whose business it is pleasingly to interest his readers. He has no doubt but that, in spite of his irregularities and distresses, his history will come to an agreeable termination. He has no doubt but that his parents will be discovered in due time; he has no doubt but that his love for *Sophia* will be rewarded sooner or later with her hand; he has no doubt of the constancy of that young lady, or of their entire happiness after marriage. And why does he foresee all this? Not from the real tendencies of things, but from what he has discovered of the author's intentions. But what would have been the probability in real life? Why, that the parents would either never have been found, or have proved to be persons of no consequence—that *Jones* would pass from one vicious indulgence to another, till his natural good disposition was quite smothered under his irregularities—that *Sophia* would either have married her lover clandestinely, and have been poor and unhappy, or she would have conquered her passion and married some country gentleman with whom she would have lived in moderate happiness, according to the usual routine of married life. But the author would have done very ill so to have constructed his story. If *Booth*[38] had been a real character, it is probable his *Amelia* and her family would not only have been brought to poverty, but left in it; but to the reader it is much more probable that by some means or other they will be rescued from it, and left in possession of all the comforts of life. It is *probable* in *Zeluco*[39] that the detestable husband will some way or other be got rid of; but woe to the young lady, who, when married, should be led, by contemplating the possibility of such an event, to cherish a passion which ought to be entirely relinquished!

Though a great deal of trash is every season poured out upon the public from the English presses, yet in general our novels are not vicious; the food has neither flavour nor nourishment, but at least it is not poisoned. Our national taste and habits are still turned towards domestic life and matrimonial happiness, and the chief harm done by a circulating library is occasioned by the frivolity of its furniture, and the loss of time incurred. Now and then a girl perhaps may be led by them to elope with a coxcomb; or, if she is handsome, to expect the homage of a *Sir Harry* or *My lord*, instead of the plain tradesman suitable to her situation in life; but she will not have her mind contaminated with such scenes and ideas as Crébillon, Louvet,[40] and others of that class have published in France.

And indeed, notwithstanding the many paltry books of this kind published in the course of every year, it may safely be affirmed that we have more good writers in this walk living at the present time, than at any period since the days of Richardson and Fielding. A very great proportion of these are ladies: and surely it will not be said that either taste or morals have been losers by their taking the

[37] **"passages that lead to nothing"**: Thomas Gray (1716–1771), "A Long Story."

[38] **Booth**: William Booth, the troubled protagonist of *Amelia* (1751), the last novel by Henry Fielding.

[39] **Zeluco**: the first novel (1786) by John Moore (1729–1802), English physician and author—it offered a sensational representation of villainy, set in Sicily.

[40] **Louvet**: Jean-Baptiste Louvet de Couvray (1760–1797), French novelist, author of *Les Amours du chevalier de Faublas* [The Loves of the Knight of Faublas] (1787–1789), a libertine novel.

pen in hand. The names of D' Arblay,[41] Edgeworth, Inchbald, Radcliffe, and a number more will vindicate this assertion.

No small proportion of modern novels have been devoted to recommend, or to mark with reprobation, those systems of philosophy or politics which have raised so much ferment of late years. Mr. Holcroft's *Anna St. Ives*[42] is of this number: its beauties, and beauties it certainly has, do not make amends for its absurdities. What can be more absurd than to represent a young lady gravely considering, in the disposal of her hand, how she shall promote the greatest possible good of the system? Mr. Holcroft was a man of strong powers, and his novels are by no means without merit, but his satire is often partial, and his representations of life unfair. On the other side may be reckoned *The Modern Philosophers,* and the novels of Mrs. West.[43] In the war of systems these light skirmishing troops have been often employed with great effect; and, so long as they are content with fair, general warfare, without taking aim at individuals, are perfectly allowable. We have lately seen the gravest theological discussions presented to the world under the attractive form of a novel, and with a success which seems to show that the interest, even of the generality of readers, is most strongly excited when some serious end is kept in view.

It is not the intention in these slight remarks to enumerate those of the present day who have successfully entertained the public: otherwise Mr. Cumberland might be mentioned, that veteran in every field of literature; otherwise a tribute ought to be paid to the peculiarly pathetic powers of Mrs. Opie; nor would it be possible to forget the very striking and original novel of *Caleb Williams,*[44] in which the author, without the assistance of any of the common events or feelings on which these stories generally turn, has kept up the curiosity and interest of the reader in the most lively manner; nor his *St. Leon,* the ingenious speculation of a philosophical mind, which is also much out of the common track. It will bear an advantageous comparison with Swift's picture of the *Strulbrugs* in his *Voyage to Laputa,* the tendency of which seems to be to repress the wish of never-ending life in this world: but in fact it does not bear at all upon the question, for no one ever did wish for immortal life without immortal youth to accompany it, the one wish being as easily formed as the other; but *St. Leon* shows, from a variety of striking circumstances, that both together would pall, and that an immortal *human* creature would grow an insulated unhappy being. . . .

Some perhaps may think that too much importance has been already given to a subject so frivolous, but a discriminating taste is no where more called for than with regard to a species of books which every body reads. It was said by Fletcher of Saltoun,[45] "Let me make the ballads of a nation, and I care not who makes the laws." Might it not be said with as much propriety, Let me make the novels of a country, and let who will make the systems?

[41] **D'Arblay:** married name of Frances Burney.* **Inchbald:** Elizabeth Inchbald (1753–1821), English radical novelist, author of *A Simple Story* (1791) and *Nature and Art* (1796). **Radcliffe:** Ann Radcliffe (1764–1823), English Gothic novelist, author of *The Mysteries of Udolpho* (1794) and *The Italian* (1797).

[42] **Anna St. Ives:** title of a novel (1792) by Thomas Holcroft (1745–1809), English radical novelist of the French Revolutionary period.

[43] **The Modern Philosophers:** a reference to *Memoirs of Modern Philosophers* (1800) by Elizabeth Hamilton, a novel that satirizes Godwin's philosophy of perfectibility and free love, here applied to women with disastrous results. **Mrs. West:** Jane West (1758–1852), author of such novels as *The Advantages of Education: or the History of Maria Williams* (1793) and *A Tale of the Times* (1799).

[44] **Cumberland:** probably Richard Cumberland (1732–1811), English dramatist and author of two novels, *Arundel* (1789) and *Henry* (1795). **Opie:** Amelia Opie* (1769–1853), English novelist, author of *Father and Daughter* (1801) and *Amelia Mowbray, or the Mother and Daughter* (1804). **Caleb Williams:** title of the first novel (1794) by the English anarchist philosopher and novelist William Godwin* (1756–1836), husband of Mary Wollstonecraft and father of Mary Shelley; he later wrote the philosophical romance *St. Leon* (1799).

[45] **Fletcher of Saltoun:** Andrew Fletcher (1655–1716), Scottish nationalist politician and author. The words Barbauld quotes are taken, somewhat loosely, from his *Account of a Conversation concerning a Right Regulation of Governments* (1704).

Eighteen Hundred and Eleven[1]

(1812)

Still the loud death drum, thundering from afar,
O'er the vext nations pours the storm of war:
To the stern call still Britain bends her ear,
Feeds the fierce strife, the alternate hope and fear;
Bravely, though vainly, dares to strive with Fate,
And seeks by turns to prop each sinking state.
Colossal Power with overwhelming force
Bears down each fort of Freedom in its course;
Prostrate she lies beneath the Despot's sway,[2]
While the hushed nations curse him—and obey.
Bounteous in vain, with frantic man at strife,
Glad Nature pours the means—the joys of life;
In vain with orange blossoms scents the gale,
The hills with olives clothes, with corn the vale;
Man calls to Famine, nor invokes in vain,
Disease and Rapine follow in her train;
The tramp of marching hosts disturbs the plough,
The sword, not sickle, reaps the harvest now,
And where the Soldier gleans the scant supply,
The helpless Peasant but retires to die;
No laws his hut from licensed outrage shield,
And war's least horror is the ensanguined field.
Fruitful in vain, the matron counts with pride
The blooming youths that grace her honoured side;
No son returns to press her widow'd hand,
Her fallen blossoms strew a foreign strand.
—Fruitful in vain, she boasts her virgin race,
Whom cultured arts adorn and gentlest grace;
Defrauded of its homage, Beauty mourns,
And the rose withers on its virgin thorns.
Frequent, some stream obscure, some uncouth name
By deeds of blood is lifted into fame;
Oft o'er the daily page some soft-one bends
To learn the fate of husband, brothers, friends,
Or the spread map with anxious eye explores,
Its dotted boundaries and penciled shores,
Asks *where* the spot that wrecked her bliss is found,
And learns its name but to detest the sound.
And think'st thou, Britain, still to sit at ease,
An island Queen amidst thy subject seas,
While the vext billows, in their distant roar,
But soothe thy slumbers, and but kiss thy shore?
To sport in wars, while danger keeps aloof,
Thy grassy turf unbruised by hostile hoof?
So sing thy flatterers; but, Britain, know,
Thou who hast shared the guilt must share the woe.
Nor distant is the hour; low murmurs spread,
And whispered fears, creating what they dread;
Ruin, as with an earthquake shock, is here,
There, the heart-witherings of unuttered fear,
And that sad death, whence most affection bleeds,
Which sickness, only of the soul, precedes.
Thy baseless wealth dissolves in air away,
Like mists that melt before the morning ray:
No more on crowded mart or busy street
Friends, meeting friends, with cheerful hurry greet;
Sad, on the ground thy princely merchants bend
Their altered looks, and evil days portend,
And fold their arms, and watch with anxious breast
The tempest blackening in the distant West.[3]
Yes, thou must droop; thy Midas dream is o'er;
The golden tide of Commerce leaves thy shore,
Leaves thee to prove the alternate ills that haunt
Enfeebling Luxury and ghastly Want;
Leaves thee, perhaps, to visit distant lands,
And deal the gifts of Heaven with equal hands.
Yet, O my Country, name beloved, revered,
By every tie that binds the soul endeared,
Whose image to my infant senses came
Mixt with Religion's light and Freedom's holy flame!
If prayers may not avert, if 'tis thy fate

[1] By 1811, Britain had been at war with France for 17 years, causing high economic inflation, food shortages, frequent conscription (or "impressments") of unwilling peasants, and widespread misery in England with no end in sight. The entire continent of Europe was under the control of Napoleon, who had made a separate peace with Russia. George III had suffered his final mental collapse in 1810, a victim of porphyry; yet his government would not negotiate an end to the blockade, which was creating increasingly hostile relations with America. Nonetheless the public response to Barbauld's poem was universal outrage; she was accused by both the Tories and the liberals of undermining national morale.

[2] **Colossal Power . . . Despot's sway:** the reign of Napoleon, to whom Russia (1807), Spain (1808), and Austria (1809) had all surrendered.

[3] **tempest . . . West:** the long-threatened war with America began in June 1812.

To rank amongst the names that once were great,
Not like the dim cold Crescent[4] shalt thou fade,
Thy debt to Science and the Muse unpaid;
Thine are the laws surrounding states revere,
Thine the full harvest of the mental year,
Thine the bright stars in Glory's sky that shine,
And arts that make it life to live are thine.
If westward streams the light that leaves thy shores,
Still from thy lamp the streaming radiance pours.
Wide spreads thy race from Ganges to the pole,[5]
O'er half the western world thy accents roll:
Nations beyond the Apalachian hills
Thy hand has planted and thy spirit fills:
Soon as their gradual progress shall impart
The finer sense of morals and of art,
Thy stores of knowledge the new states shall know,
And think thy thoughts, and with thy fancy glow;
Thy Lockes, thy Paleys[6] shall instruct their youth,
Thy leading star direct their search for truth;
Beneath the spreading Platan's tent-like shade,
Or by Missouri's rushing waters laid,
"Old father Thames"[7] shall be the Poet's theme,
Of Hagley's woods the enamoured virgin dream,
And Milton's tones the raptured ear enthrall,
Mixt with the roar of Niagara's fall;
In Thomson's[8] glass the ingenuous youth shall learn
A fairer face of Nature to discern;
Nor of the Bards that swept the British lyre
Shall fade one laurel, or one note expire.
Then, loved Joanna, to admiring eyes
Thy storied groups in scenic pomp shall rise;
Their high soul'd strains and Shakespear's nobel rage
Shall with alternate passion shake the stage.
Some youthful Basil from thy moral lay
With stricter hand his fond desires shall sway;
Some Ethwald, as the fleeting shadows pass,
Start at his likeness in the mystic glass;
The tragic Muse resume her just controul,
With pity and with terror purge the soul,
While wide o'er transatlantic realms thy name
Shall live in light, and gather *all* its fame.[9]

Where wanders Fancy down the lapse of years
Shedding o'er imaged woes untimely tears?
Fond moody Power! as hopes—as fears prevail,
She longs, or dreads, to lift the awful veil,
On visions of delight now loves to dwell,
Now hears the shriek of woe or Freedom's knell:
Perhaps, she says, long ages past away,
And set in western waves our closing day,
Night, Gothic night, again may shade the plains
Where Power is seated, and where Science reigns;
England, the seat of arts, be only known
By the gray ruin and the mouldering stone;
That Time may tear the garland from her brow,
And Europe sit in dust, as Asia now.

Yet then the ingenuous youth whom Fancy fires
With pictured glories of illustrious sires,
With duteous zeal their pilgrimage shall take
From the Blue Mountains, or Ontario's lake,
With fond adoring steps to press the sod
By statesmen, sages, poets, heroes trod;
On Isis' banks to draw inspiring air,
From Runnymede to send the patriot's prayer;
In pensive thought, where Cam's slow waters wind,
To meet those shades that ruled the realms of mind;[10]
In silent halls to sculptured marbles bow,
And hang fresh wreaths round Newton's awful brow.
Oft shall they seek some peasant's homely shed,
Who toils, unconscious of the mighty dead,
To ask where Avon's winding waters stray,
And thence a knot of wild flowers bear away;

[4] **Crescent:** the Ottoman Empire of the Middle East.

[5] **Ganges . . . pole:** British colonies were well established in India and the northern reaches of Canada.

[6] **Locke:** John Locke (1632–1704), English philosopher, author of *An Essay Concerning Human Understanding* (1690) and *Two Treatises on Civil Government* (1690). **Paley:** William Paley (1743–1805), English theologian, author of the widely read defenses of Christianity, *A View of the Evidences of Christianity* (1794) and *Natural Theology* (1802).

[7] **Platan:** Oriental plane-tree, thriving in Asia. **Thames:** river running through the center of London.

[8] **Hagley's woods:** estate of Lord Lyttleton in Worcestershire, celebrated for its landscape gardens in James Thomson's *Spring* (1728), ll. 901–59. **Thomson's glass:** refers to the most celebrated poem of the Scottish poet James Thomson (1700–1748), *The Seasons* (1730).

[9] **Joanna . . . fame:** Joanna Baillie* (1762–1851), playwright, poet and literary critic, author of the tragedies *Count Basil** (1798) and *Ethwald* (1802).

[10] **the Blue Mountains:** in central Pennsylvania. **Ontario's lake:** Lake Ontario, in Canada. **Isis' banks:** the Isis is a branch of the river Thames flowing through Oxford. **Runnymede:** meadow in Egham, Surrey, on bank of Thames where King John signed the Magna Carta in 1215. **Cam:** river flowing between the colleges of Cambridge University.

Anxious enquire where Clarkson, friend of man,
Or all-accomplished Jones his race began;
If of the modest mansion aught remains
Where Heaven and Nature prompted Cowper's strains;[11]
Where Roscoe, to whose patriot breast belong
The Roman virtue and the Tuscan song,
Led Ceres to the black and barren moor
Where Ceres never gained a wreath before:
With curious search their pilgrim steps shall rove
By many a ruined tower and proud alcove,
Shall listen for those strains that soothed of yore
Thy rock, stern Skiddaw, and thy fall, Lodore;
Feast with Dun Edin's classic brow their sight,
And visit "Melross by the pale moonlight."[12]
But who their mingled feelings shall pursue
When London's faded glories rise to view?
The mighty city, which by every road,
In floods of people poured itself abroad;
Ungirt by walls, irregularly great,
No jealous drawbridge, and no closing gate;
Whose merchants (such the state which commerce brings)
Sent forth their mandates to dependant kings;
Streets, where the turban'd Moslem, bearded Jew,
And woolly Afric, met the brown Hindu;
Where through each vein spontaneous plenty flowed,
Where Wealth enjoyed, and Charity bestowed.
Pensive and thoughtful shall the wanderers greet
Each splendid square, and still, untrodden street;
Or of some crumbling turret, mined by time,
The broken stairs with perilous step shall climb,
Thence stretch their view the wide horizon round,
By scattered hamlets trace its antient bound,
And, choked no more with fleets, fair Thames survey
Through reeds and sedge pursue his idle way.
With throbbing bosoms shall the wanderers tread
The hallowed mansions of the silent dead,
Shall enter the long isle and vaulted dome
Where Genius and where Valour find a home;
Awe-struck, midst chill sepulchral marbles breathe,
Where all above is still, as all beneath;
Bend at each antique shrine, and frequent turn
To clasp with fond delight some sculptured urn,
The ponderous mass of Johnson's form to greet,
Or breathe the prayer at Howard's sainted feet.[13]
Perhaps some Briton, in whose musing mind
Those ages live which Time has cast behind,
To every spot shall lead his wondering guests
On whose known site the beam of glory rests:
Here Chatham's eloquence in thunder broke,
Here Fox persuaded, or here Garrick spoke;[14]
Shall boast how Nelson, fame and death in view,
To wonted victory led his ardent crew,
In England's name enforced, with loftiest tone,
Their duty,—and too well fulfilled his own:[15]
How gallant Moore, as ebbing life dissolved,
But hoped his country had his fame absolved.
Or call up sages whose capacious mind
Left in its course a track of light behind;
Point where mute crowds on Davy's lips reposed,
And Nature's coyest secrets were disclosed;

[11] **Newton**: Isaac Newton (1642–1727), English philosopher, mathematician and physicist, Lucasian Professor of Mathematics at Cambridge University. **Avon**: river flowing through Stratford-on-Avon, birthplace of Shakespeare. **Clarkson**: Thomas Clarkson (1760–1846), leading opponent of the slave trade. (See SLAVERY, THE SLAVE TRADE, AND ABOLITION.) **Jones**: Sir William Jones (1746–1794), English Orientalist and jurist, founded the Bengal Asiatic Society (1784) and published extensively on the Sanskrit language and the customs of India. **Cowper**: William Cowper (1731–1800), poet; see his evangelical *Olney Hymns* (1779) to which Barbauld here alludes.

[12] **Roscoe**: William Roscoe (1753–1831), scholar, poet, and agriculturalist, had shown that Lancashire moorlands could yield high-quality crops. **Ceres**: Roman goddess of grain. **Skiddaw . . . Lodore**: mountain and waterfall in the Lake District, celebrated by William Wordsworth in *The Prelude** and "An Evening Walk."* **Dun Edin**: archaic name for Edinburgh, capital of Scotland. **Melross . . . moonlight**: from Sir Walter Scott, "The Lay of the Last Minstrel"* (1805), II.i.

[13] **Johnson**: Dr. Samuel Johnson (1709–1784), eminent poet, lexicographer, and literary critic. **Howard**: John Howard (1726–1790), leading prison reformer. Reference to statues of these two men, which stand in St. Paul's Cathedral, London.

[14] **Chatham**: William Pitt, first Earl of Chatham (1708–1778), prime minister during the Seven Years' War, famed for his oratory. **Fox**: Charles James Fox (1749–1806), an eloquent defender of the rights of the American colonists, of the French Revolution, and of abolition in successive Whig administrations. **Garrick**: David Garrick (1717–1779), famous Shakespearean actor.

[15] Every reader will recollect the sublime telegraphic dispatch, "England expects every man to do his duty" [A. L. B.]; this was sent by Admiral Horatio **Nelson** (1758–1805), commander of the British fleet, just before he was killed at the Battle of Trafalgar on 21 October 1805.

Join with their Franklin, Priestley's injured name,
Whom, then, each continent shall proudly claim.[16]
Oft shall the strangers turn their eager feet
The rich remains of antient art to greet,
The pictured walls with critic eye explore,
And Reynolds be what Raphael was before.[17]
On spoils from every clime their eyes shall gaze,
Egyptian granites and the Etruscan vase;
And when midst fallen London, they survey
The stone where Alexander's ashes lay,[18]
Shall own with humbled pride the lesson just
By Time's slow finger written in the dust.
There walks a Spirit o'er the peopled earth,
Secret his progress is, unknown his birth;
Moody and viewless as the changing wind,
No force arrests his foot, no chains can bind;
Where'er he turns, the human brute awakes,
And, roused to better life, his sordid hut forsakes:
He thinks, he reasons, glows with purer fires,
Feels finer wants, and burns with new desires:
Obedient Nature follows where he leads;
The steaming marsh is changed to fruitful meads;
The beasts retire from man's asserted reign,
And prove his kingdom was not given in vain.
Then from its bed is drawn the ponderous ore,
Then Commerce pours her gifts on every shore,
Then Babel's towers and terrassed gardens rise,
And pointed obelisks invade the skies;
The prince commands, in Tyrian purple drest,
And Egypt's virgins weave the linen vest.
Then spans the graceful arch the roaring tide,
And stricter bounds the cultured fields divide.
Then kindles Fancy, then expands the heart,
Then blow the flowers of Genius and of Art;
Saints, Heroes, Sages, who the land adorn,
Seem rather to descend than to be born;
Whilst History, midst the rolls consigned to fame,
With pen of adamant inscribes their name.
The Genius now forsakes the favoured shore,
And hates, capricious, what he loved before;
Then empires fall to dust, then arts decay,
And wasted realms enfeebled despots sway;
Even Nature's changed; without his fostering smile
Ophir no gold, no plenty yields the Nile;
The thirsty sand absorbs the useless rill,
And spotted plagues from putrid fens distill.
In desert solitudes then Tadmor sleeps,
Stern Marius then o'er fallen Carthage weeps;[19]
Then with enthusiast love the pilgrim roves
To seek his footsteps in forsaken groves,
Explores the fractured arch, the ruined tower,
Those limbs disjointed of gigantic power;
Still at each step he dreads the adder's sting,
The Arab's javelin, or the tiger's spring;
With doubtful caution treads the echoing ground,
And asks where Troy or Babylon is found.
And now the vagrant Power no more detains
The vale of Tempe, or Ausonian plains;[20]
Northward he throws the animating ray,
O'er Celtic nations bursts the mental day:
And, as some playful child the mirror turns,
Now here now there the moving lustre burns;
Now o'er his changeful fancy more prevail
Batavia's dykes than Arno's purple vale,
And stinted suns, and rivers bound with frost,

[16] "'I hope England will be satisfied,' were the last words of General Moore" [A. L. B.]; General Sir John **Moore** (1761–1809) led the attack on Napoleon's army at Madrid but was killed at the Battle of Corunna (January 1809). **Davy**: Sir Humphrey Davy (1778–1829), English chemist, first President of the Royal Society for Science (1820). **Franklin**: Benjamin Franklin (1706–1790), American scientist, philosopher, and statesman. **Priestley**: Joseph Priestley (1733–1804), see "An Inventory of the Furniture in Dr. Priestley's Study."

[17] **Reynolds**: Sir Joshua Reynolds (1723–1792), artist and first President of the Royal Academy of Art. (See AESTHETIC THEORY AND LITERARY CRITICISM.) **Raphael**: Raffaello Sanzio (1483–1520), renowned Italian Renaissance painter.

[18] **stone . . . ashes**: a granite sarcophagus thought to be the tomb of Alexander the Great was brought from Italy with the Rosetta Stone to London for display in the newly opened British Museum in 1802.

[19] **Ophir**: Old Testament region famed for its gold mines. **Tadmor**: Biblical name for Palmyra, ancient city in central Syria. **Marius**: Gaius Marius (157–86 BC), Roman consul and military leader, ruled with Sulla and Cinna as a triumvirate (104–88), driven by Sulla to Africa in 88 BC where he was denied access; Plutarch records his response to the governor, "Tell him, then, that thou hast seen Marius a fugitive, seated amid the ruins of Carthage" (Plutarch, *Parallel Lives of the Greeks and Romans*, 9:577).

[20] **vale of Tempe**: in Thessaly, in classical Greek literature. **Ausonian plains**: the plains of Italy, in Virgil; hence a reference to classical Roman literature.

Than Enna's plains or Baia's viny coast;
Venice the Adriatic weds in vain,
And Death sits brooding o'er Campania's plain;
O'er Baltic shores and through Hercynian groves,[21]
Stirring the soul, the mighty impulse moves;
Art plies his tools, and Commerce spreads her sail,
And wealth is wafted in each shifting gale.
The sons of Odin tread on Persian looms,
And Odin's daughters breathe distilled perfumes;
Loud minstrel Bards, in Gothic halls, rehearse
The Runic rhyme, and "build the lofty verse:"[22]
The Muse, whose liquid notes were wont to swell
To the soft breathings of th' Aeolian shell,
Submits, reluctant, to the harsher tone,
And scarce believes the altered voice her own.
And now, where Caesar saw with proud disdain
The wattled hut and skin of azure stain,
Corinthian columns rear their graceful forms,
And light varandas brave the wintry storms,
While British tongues the fading fame prolong
Of Tully's eloquence and Maro's song.
Where once Bonduca[23] whirled the scythed car,
And the fierce matrons raised the shriek of war,
Light forms beneath transparent muslins float,
And tutored voices swell the artful note.
Light-leaved acacias and the shady plane
And spreading cedar grace the woodland reign;
While crystal walls the tenderer plants confine,
The fragrant orange and the nectared pine;
The Syrian grape there hangs her rich festoons,
Nor asks for purer air, or brighter noons:
Science and Art urge on the useful toil,
New mould a climate and create the soil,
Subdue the rigour of the northern Bear,
O'er polar climes shed aromatic air,
On yielding Nature urge their new demands,
And ask not gifts but tribute at her hands.
London exults:—on London Art bestows
Her summer ices and her winter rose;
Gems of the East her mural crown adorn,
And Plenty at her feet pours forth her horn;
While even the exiles her just laws disclaim,
People a continent, and build a name:
August she sits, and with extended hands
Holds forth the book of life to distant lands.
But fairest flowers expand but to decay;
The worm is in thy core, thy glories pass away;
Arts, arms and wealth destroy the fruits they bring;
Commerce, like beauty, knows no second spring.
Crime walks thy streets, Fraud earns her unblest bread,
O'er want and woe thy gorgeous robe is spread,
And angel charities in vain oppose:
With grandeur's growth the mass of misery grows.
For see,—to other climes the Genius soars,
He turns from Europe's desolated shores;
And lo, even now, midst mountains wrapt in storm,
On Andes' heights he shrouds his awful form:
On Chimborazo's summits treads sublime,
Measuring in lofty thought the march of Time;
Sudden he calls:—"'Tis now the hour!" he cries,
Spreads his broad hand, and bids the nations rise.
La Plata hears amidst her torrents' roar,
Potosi[24] hears it, as she digs the ore:
Ardent, the Genius fans the noble strife,
And pours through feeble souls a higher life,
Shouts to the mingled tribes from sea to sea,
And swears—Thy world, Columbus, shall be free.[25]

---

[21] The Power of Genius is moving west from Europe. **Celtic nations:** those continuing to speak Celtic languages after the Roman invasion in the fifth century AD, namely the British Isles and French Brittany. **Batavia's dykes:** Holland. **Arno:** river flowing through Florence, Italy. **Enna:** valley in Sicily. **Baia:** Roman resort on the Bay of Naples. **Venice . . . weds:** in an annual ceremony the city of Venice in Italy "weds" the Adriatic sea. **Campania:** region of central Italy. **Hercynian groves:** Black Forest of southern Germany.

[22] **sons of Odin:** Norsemen. **build . . . verse:** see Milton, "Lycidas," l.11 [misquoted].

[23] **Caesar . . . azure stain:** Julius Caesar noted in his *Bellicum Gallicum* that the ancient Scots warriors painted themselves blue. **Tully:** Marcus Tullius Cicero (106–43 BC), Roman orator and statesman. **Maro:** Publius Vergilius Maro, known as Vergil (70–19 BC), Roman poet, author of *The Aenead.* **Bonduca:** Boudicca or Boadicea (d. 62 AD), Queen of the Ancient Britons or Iceni, defeated by Roman governor Suetonius Paulinus.

[24] **Andes' heights:** mountains in Peru. **Chimborazo:** mountain in Ecuador. **La Plata:** city in Argentina. **Potosi:** city in Bolivia famed for its silver mines.

[25] **Thy . . . free:** Venezuela declared its independence from Spain in 1811. **Columbus:** Christopher Columbus (1451–1506), who arrived in the Caribbean Islands in 1492 and claimed the lands of Central and South America for Spain.

A Thought on Death
(November 1822)

When life, as opening buds, is sweet,
And golden hopes the spirit greet,
And youth prepares his joys to meet,
Alas! how hard it is to die!

When scarce is seiz'd some valu'd prize,
And duties press, and tender ties
Forbid the soul from earth to rise,
How awful then it is to die!

When, one by one, those ties are torn,
And friend from friend is snatched forlorn,
And man is left alone to mourn,
Ah! then, how easy 'tis to die!

When faith is strong, and conscience clear,
And words of peace the spirit cheer,
And vision'd glories half appear,
'Tis joy, 'tis triumph, then to die!

When trembling limbs refuse their weight,
And films, slow gathering, dim the sight,
And clouds obscure the mental light,
'Tis nature's precious boon to die!

POSTHUMOUS PUBLICATIONS

from WORKS OF ANNA LETITIA BARBAULD
(1825)

To Mr. Barbauld, with a Map of the Land of Matrimony[1]
(1825; comp. 1774)

The sailor worn by toil and wet with storms,
As in the wished-for port secure he rides,
With transport numbers o'er the dangers past
From threatning quicksands and from adverse tides.

Joyous he tells among his jocund mates
Of loud alarms that chased his broken sleep,
And blesses every kinder star that led
His favoured vessel through the raging deep.

Thus canst thou, Rochemont, view this pictured chart,
And trace thy voyage to the promised shore;
Thus does thy faithful bosom beat with joy,
To think the tempest past, the wanderings o'er?

Canst thou recall the days when jealous Doubt,
When boding Fears thy anxious heart oppresst,
When Hope, our star, shone faintly through the gloom,
And the pale cheek betrayed the tortured breast?

And say;—the land through Fancy's glass descried,
The bright Elysian fields her pencil drew,—
Has time the dear ideas realized?
Or are her optics false, her tints untrue?

O say they are not!—Though life's ceaseless cares,
Life's ceaseless toils demand thy golden hours,
Tell her glad heart whose hand these lines confess,
That Peace resides in Hymen's happy bowers.

But soon the restless seaman longs to change
His bounded view and tempt the deeps again;
Careless he breaks from weeping Susan's arms,
To fight with billows and to plough the main.

So shalt not thou, for no returning prow
E'er cut the ocean which thy bark has past;
Too strong relentless Fate has fixed her bars,
And I my destined captive hold too fast.

[1] This poem was probably composed by Anna Letitia Barbauld for her husband Rochemont Barbauld on her wedding day, 26 May 1774.

The Rights of Woman[1]
(1825; comp. 1793)

Yes, injured Woman! rise, assert thy right!
Woman! too long degraded, scorned, opprest;
O born to rule in partial Law's despite,
Resume thy native empire o'er the breast!

[1] This poem was composed in 1793 in angry response to Mary Wollstonecraft's contemptuous dismissal of Barbauld's "To a Lady, with some painted Flowers" (see above) in *A Vindication of the Rights of Woman* (1792), Ch. 4, note 7. Barbauld did not publish this poem during her lifetime.

Go forth arrayed in panoply divine;
That angel pureness which admits no stain;
Go, bid proud Man his boasted rule resign,[2]
And kiss the golden sceptre of thy reign.

Go, gird thyself with grace; collect thy store
Of bright artillery glancing from afar;
Soft melting tones thy thundering cannon's roar,
Blushes and fears thy magazine of war.

Thy rights are empire: urge no meaner claim,—
Felt, not defined, and if debated, lost;
Like sacred mysteries, which withheld from fame,
Shunning discussion, are revered the most.

Try all that wit and art suggest to bend
Of thy imperial foe the stubborn knee;
Make treacherous Man thy subject, not thy friend;
Thou mayst command, but never canst be free.

Awe the licentious, and restrain the rude;
Soften the sullen, clear the cloudy brow:
Be, more than princes' gifts, thy favours sued;—
She hazards all, who will the least allow.

But hope not, courted idol of mankind,
On this proud eminence secure to stay;
Subduing and subdued, thou soon shalt find
Thy coldness soften, and thy pride give way.

Then, then, abandon each ambitious thought,
Conquest or rule thy heart shall feebly move,
In Nature's school, by her soft maxims taught,
That separate rights are lost in mutual love.

To a Little Invisible Being Who Is Expected Soon to Become Visible

(1825; comp. 1795)

Germ of new life, whose powers expanding slow
For many a moon their full perfection wait,—
Haste, precious pledge of happy love, to go
Auspicious borne through life's mysterious gate.

What powers lie folded in thy curious frame,—
Senses from objects locked, and mind from thought!
How little canst thou guess thy lofty claim
To grasp at all the worlds the Almighty wrought!

And see, the genial season's warmth to share,
Fresh younglings shoot, and opening roses glow!
Swarms of new life exulting fill the air,—
Haste, infant bud of being, haste to blow!

For thee the nurse prepares her lulling songs,
The eager matrons count the lingering day;
But far the most thy anxious parent longs
On thy soft cheek a mother's kiss to lay.

She only asks to lay her burden down,
That her glad arms that burden may resume;
And nature's sharpest pangs her wishes crown,
That free thee living from thy living tomb.

She longs to fold to her maternal breast
Part of herself, yet to herself unknown;
To see and to salute the stranger guest,
Fed with her life through many a tedious moon.

Come, reap thy rich inheritance of love!
Bask in the fondness of a Mother's eye!
Nor wit nor eloquence her heart shall move
Like the first accents of thy feeble cry.

Haste, little captive, burst thy prison doors!
Launch on the living world, and spring to light!
Nature for thee displays her various stores,
Opens her thousand inlets of delight.

If charmed verse or muttered prayers had power,
With favouring spells to speed thee on thy way,
Anxious I'd bid my beads[1] each passing hour,
Till thy wished smile thy mother's pangs o'erpay.

Washing-Day

(1825; comp. 1797)

. . . . and their voice,
Turning again towards childish treble, pipes
And whistles in its sound.—[1]

The Muses are turned gossips; they have lost
The buskin'd[2] step, and clear high-sounding phrase,

[2] **Go, bid:** see Pope, *Essay on Man,* 2:19–30.

[1] **bid my beads:** pray, as with a rosary.

[1] Motto: Shakespeare, *As You Like It,* II.vii.161–163 [misquoted; Barbauld replaces Shakespeare's "big, manly voice" with "their voice"].

[2] **buskin'd:** wearing the high, thick-soled boot worn in Athenian tragedy; hence tragic.

Language of gods. Come, then, domestic Muse,
In slip-shod measure[3] loosely prattling on
Of farm or orchard, pleasant curds and cream,
Or drowning flies, or shoe lost in the mire
By little whimpering boy, with rueful face;
Come, Muse, and sing the dreaded *Washing-Day*.
—Ye who beneath the yoke of wedlock bend,
With bowed soul, full well ye ken the day
Which week, smooth sliding after week, brings on
Too soon; for to that day nor peace belongs
Nor comfort; ere the first grey streak of dawn,
The red-arm'd washers come and chase repose.
Nor pleasant smile, nor quaint device of mirth,
E'er visited that day; the very cat,
From the wet kitchen scared, and reeking hearth,
Visits the parlour, an unwonted guest.
The silent breakfast-meal is soon dispatch'd,
Uninterrupted, save by anxious looks
Cast at the lowering sky, if sky should lower.
From that last evil, oh preserve us, heavens!
For should the skies pour down, adieu to all
Remains of quiet; then expect to hear
Of sad disasters—dirt and gravel stains
Hard to efface, and loaded lines at once
Snapped short—and linen-horse[4] by dog thrown
 down,
And all the petty miseries of life.
Saints have been calm while stretched upon the rack,
And Guatimozin[5] smil'd on burning coals;
But never yet did housewife notable
Greet with a smile a rainy washing-day.
—But grant the welkin[6] fair, require not thou
Who call'st thyself perchance the master there,
Or study swept, or nicely dusted coat,
Or usual 'tendance; ask not, indiscreet,
Thy stockings mended, tho' the yawning rents
Gape wide as Erebus,[7] nor hope to find
Some snug recess impervious; should'st thou try
The 'customed garden walks, thine eye shall rue
The budding fragrance of thy tender shrubs,
Myrtle or rose, all crushed beneath the weight
Of coarse check'd apron, with impatient hand
Twitch'd off when showers impend: or crossing lines
Shall mar thy musings, as the wet cold sheet
Flaps in thy face abrupt. Woe to the friend
Whose evil stars have urged him forth to claim
On such a day the hospitable rites;
Looks, blank at best, and stinted courtesy,
Shall he receive. Vainly he feeds his hopes
With dinner of roast chicken, savoury pie,
Or tart or pudding:—pudding he nor tart
That day shall eat; nor, tho' the husband try,
Mending what can't be help'd, to kindle mirth
From cheer deficient, shall his consort's brow
Clear up propitious; the unlucky guest
In silence dines, and early slinks away.
 I well remember, when a child, the awe
This day struck into me; for then the maids,
I scarce knew why, looked cross, and drove me from
 them;
Nor soft caress could I obtain, nor hope
Usual indulgencies; jelly or creams,
Relique of costly suppers, and set by
For me their petted one; or butter'd toast,
When butter was forbid; or thrilling tale
Of ghost, or witch, or murder—so I went
And shelter'd me beside the parlour fire:
There my dear grandmother, eldest of forms,
Tended the little ones, and watched from harm,
Anxiously fond, tho' oft her spectacles
With elfin cunning hid, and oft the pins
Drawn from her ravell'd stocking, might have sour'd
One less indulgent.—
At intervals my mother's voice was heard,
Urging dispatch; briskly the work went on,
All hands employed to wash, to rinse, to wring,
To fold, and starch, and clap, and iron, and plait.
Then would I sit me down, and ponder much
Why washings were. Sometimes thro' hollow bole
Of pipe amused we blew, and sent aloft
The floating bubbles, little dreaming then
To see, Mongolfier, thy silken ball
Ride buoyant thro' the clouds[8]—so near approach

[3] **slip-shod measure**: See Pope, *Dunciad,* 3:13–16.

[4] **linen-horse**: wooden structure or sawhorse used for drying heavy wet bedclothes.

[5] **Guatimozin**: Cuauhtemoc, last Emperor of Mexico, nephew and son-in-law of Montezuma, tortured and executed by Hernán Cortés in 1525.

[6] **welkin**: the arch of the heavens, sky, firmament.

[7] **Erebus**: in Greek mythology, a place of darkness, midway between heaven and hades.

[8] **Montgolfier . . . clouds**: Joseph-Michel Montgolfier (1740–1810) and Jacques-Étienne Montgolfier (1745–1799) launched the first hot-air balloon in Annonay, France, in 1783.

The sports of children and the toils of men.
Earth, air, and sky, and ocean, hath its bubbles,
And verse is one of them — this most of all.

To Mr. S. T. Coleridge[1]

(1825; comp. 1797)

Midway the hill of Science, after steep
And rugged paths that tire th' unpractised feet
A Grove extends, in tangled mazes wrought,
And fill'd with strange enchantment: — dubious shapes
Flit thro' dim glades, and lure the eager foot
Of youthful ardour to eternal chase.
Dreams hang on every leaf; unearthly forms
Glide thro' the gloom, and mystic visions swim
Before the cheated sense. Athwart the mists,
Far into vacant space, huge shadows stretch
And seem realities; while things of life,
Obvious to sight and touch, all glowing round
Fade to the hue of shadows. *Scruples*[2] here
With filmy net, most like th' autumnal webs
Of floating Gossamer, arrest the foot
Of generous enterprize; and palsy hope
And fair ambition, with the chilling touch
Of sickly hesitation and blank fear.
Nor seldom *Indolence* these lawns among
Fixes her turf-built seat, and wears the garb
Of deep philosophy, and museful sits,
In dreamy twilight of the vacant mind,
Soothed by the whispering shade; for soothing soft
The shades, and vistas lengthening into air,
With moon beam rainbows tinted. Here each mind
Of finer mold, acute and delicate,
In its high progress to eternal truth
Rests for a space, in fairy bowers entranced;
And loves the softened light and tender gloom;
And, pampered with most unsubstantial food,
Looks down indignant on the grosser world,
And matter's cumbrous[3] shapings. Youth belov'd
Of Science — of the Muse belov'd, not here,
Not in the maze of metaphysic lore
Build thou thy place of resting; lightly tread
The dangerous ground, on noble aims intent;
And be this Circe[4] of the studious cell
Enjoyed, but still subservient. Active scenes
Shall soon with healthful spirit brace thy mind,
And fair exertion, for bright fame sustained,
For friends, for country, chase each spleen-fed fog
That blots the wide creation —
Now Heaven conduct thee with a Parent's love!

[1] Barbauld first met Coleridge in August 1797, at the home of a mutual friend, John Prior Estlin, in Bristol. Coleridge commented on Barbauld in a letter to Estlin on 1 March 1800: "The more I see of Mrs. Barbauld, the more I admire her — that wonderful *Propriety* of mind! — She has great *acuteness*, very great — yet how steadily she keeps it within the bounds of practical Reason. This I almost envy as well as admire — My own Subtleties too often lead me into strange (tho' God be praised) transient Out-of-the-waynesses" (*STC Letters* I:578).

[2] **Scruples:** here, intellectual perplexities as well as moral reservations.

[3] **cumbrous:** oppressive, unwieldy, cumbersome.

[4] **Circe:** in Greek myth, an enchantress who dwelt on the island of Aea and transformed all who drank her potions into swine.

The First Fire

(1825; comp. 1 October 1815)

Ha, old acquaintance! many a month has past
Since last I viewed thy ruddy face; and I,
Shame on me! had mean time well nigh forgot
That such a friend existed. Welcome now! —
When summer suns ride high, and tepid airs
Dissolve in pleasing languor; then indeed
We think thee needless, and in wanton pride
Mock at thy grim attire and sooty jaws,
And breath sulphureous, generating spleen, —
As Frenchmen say; Frenchmen, who never knew
The sober comforts of a good coal fire.[1]
— Let me imbibe thy warmth, and spread myself
Before thy shrine adoring: — magnet thou
Of strong attraction, daily gathering in
Friends, brethren, kinsmen, variously dispersed,
All the dear charities of social life,
To thy close circle. Here a man might stand,
And say, This is my world! Who would not bleed
Rather than see thy violated hearth
Prest by a hostile foot? The winds sing shrill;

[1] The French preferred to burn wood in their fires.

Heap on the fuel! Not the costly board,[2]
Nor sparkling glass, nor wit, nor music, cheer
Without thy aid. If thrifty thou dispense
Thy gladdening influence, in the chill saloon
The silent shrug declares the' unpleased guest.
—How grateful to belated traveller
Homeward returning, to behold the blaze
From cottage window, rendering visible
The cheerful scene within! There sits the sire,
Whose wicker chair, in sunniest nook enshrined,
His age's privilege,—a privilege for which
Age gladly yields up all precedence else
In gay and bustling scenes,—supports his limbs.
Cherished by thee, he feels the grateful warmth
Creep through his feeble frame and thaw the ice
Of fourscore years, and thoughts of youth arise.
—Nor less the young ones press within, to see
Thy face delighted, and with husk of nuts,
Or crackling holly, or the gummy pine,
Feed thy immortal hunger: cheaply pleased
They gaze delighted, while the leaping flames
Dart like an adder's tongue upon their prey;
Or touch with lighted reed thy wreaths of smoke;
Or listen, while the matron sage remarks
Thy bright blue scorching flame and aspect clear,
Denoting frosty skies. Thus pass the hours,
While Winter spends without his idle rage.
—Companion of the solitary man,
From gayer scenes withheld! With thee he sits,
Converses, moralizes; musing asks
How many eras of uncounted time
Have rolled away since thy black unctuous food
Was green with vegetative life, and what
This planet then:[3] or marks, in sprightlier mood,
Thy flickering smiles play round the' illumined room,
And fancies gay discourse, life, motion, mirth,
And half forgets he is a lonely creature.
—Nor less the bashful poet loves to sit
Snug, at the midnight hour, with only thee
Of his lone musings conscious. Oft he writes,
And blots, and writes again; and oft, by fits,
Gazes intent with eyes of vacancy
On thy bright face; and still at intervals,
Dreading the critic's scorn, to thee commits,
Sole confidant and safe, his fancies crude.[4]
—O wretched he, with bolts and massy bars
In narrow cell immured, whose green damp walls,
That weep unwholesome dews, have never felt
Thy purifying influence! Sad he sits
Day after day, till in his youthful limbs
Life stagnates, and the hue of hope is fled
From his wan cheek.—And scarce less wretched he—
When wintry winds blow loud and frosts bite keen,—
The dweller of the clay-built tenement,
Poverty-struck, who, heartless, strives to raise
From sullen turf, or stick plucked from the hedge,
The short-lived blaze; while chill around him spreads
The dreary fen, and Ague, sallow-faced,
Stares through the broken pane;—Assist him, ye
On whose warm roofs the sun of plenty shines,
And feel a glow beyond material fire!

[2] **costly board:** lavish meal.

[3] **black unctuous food . . . planet then:** reference to coal as vegetable matter compressed through eons of time.

[4] See William Cowper, *The Task*, Bk. IV, "The Winter's Evening" (lines 270–307) and S. T. Coleridge, "Frost at Midnight" (1798), to which Barbauld here alludes.

On the Death of the Princess Charlotte[1]

(1825; comp. 1817)

Yes Britain mourns, as with electric shock
For youth, for love, for happiness destroyed.
Her universal population wells
In grief spontaneous; and hard hearts are moved,
And rough unpolished natures learn to feel
For those they envied, humbled in the dust
By fate's impartial hand; and pulpits sound
With vanity and woe to earthly goods,
And urge, and dry the tear—Yet one there is[2]
Who midst this general burst of grief remains

[1] Princess Charlotte Augusta (1796–1817), oldest daughter of King George IV and Caroline of Brunswick, married (1816) to Prince Leopold of Saxe-Coburg. She died a few hours after giving birth to a stillborn son, on 6 November 1817. She had been enormously popular with the British public as a model of female virtue and their future Queen.

[2] **one there is:** probably King George III, the Princess's grandfather, who had become permanently insane seven years before, in 1810.

In strange tranquillity; whom not the stir
And long drawn murmurs of the gathering crowd,
That by his very windows trail the pomp
Of hearse, and blazoned arms, and long array
Of sad funereal rites, nor the loud groans
And deep felt anguish of a husband's heart
Can move to mingle with this flood one tear.
In careless apathy — perhaps in mirth
He spends the day; yet is he near in blood,
The very stem on which this blossom grew,
And at his knees she fondled, in the charm
And grace spontaneous, which alone belongs
To untaught infancy; yet — Oh forbear
Nor deem him hard of heart, for, awful, struck
By heaven's severest visitation, sad,
Like a scathed oak amidst the forest trees
Lonely he stands; leaves sprout, and fade, and fall,
And seasons run their round, to him in vain,
He holds no sympathy with living nature,
Or time's incessant change. Then, in this hour,
While pensive thought is busy with the woes
And restless cares of poor humanity,
Oh think of him, and set apart one sigh,
From the full tide of sorrow spare one tear
For him who does not weep.

OLAUDAH EQUIANO

(c. 1745–1797)

Olaudah Equiano was born in 1745, probably in Essaka, the region lying east of the modern Nigerian city of Onitsha; he was a member of the Ibo tribe. He was captured and taken in a British slave ship first to Barbados, and then to Virginia, where he was purchased by Lieutenant Pascal of the British navy, who renamed him Gustavus Vassa. He served in the Seven Years' War with General Wolfe in Canada in 1758 and with Admiral Boscawen in the Mediterranean in 1761. Captain Pascal then resold him into slavery. Equiano worked for several years aboard the trading ships of Robert King, a Quaker merchant of Philadelphia who helped him purchase his freedom. After his emancipation, he travelled to the Arctic with the Phipps expedition of 1772–73, went on a grand tour of the Mediterranean as the personal servant of an English gentleman, and spent six months among the Miskito Indians of Central America. He was appointed Commissary for Stores to the 1787 expedition to resettle freed slaves in Sierra Leone, but quarreled with the Agent, Joseph Irwin, whom he accused of planning to enslave the freed blacks once they reached Africa; his appointment was terminated in March 1787, and he did not accompany this disastrous, fever-ridden, and poorly prepared expedition.

Equiano became an ardent and effective abolitionist, working closely with Granville Sharp and another freed slave, Ottobah Cugoano; he published his *The Interesting Narrative of the Life of Olaudah Equiano, or Gustavus Vassa, the African* in 1789. This book sold over 5,000 copies and was, as Thomas Digges stated in a letter of 1791, "a principal instrument in bringing about the motion for a repeal of the Slave-Act." He spent the final years of his life lecturing against the slave trade throughout England. In 1792, while on this lecture circuit, he married an Englishwoman, Susanna Cullen, at Soham Church, Cambridgeshire; they had two daughters, Ann Maria and Johanna. He died on 30 April 1797.

from The Interesting Narrative of the Life of Olaudah Equiano, or Gustavus Vassa, the African

(1789)

VOLUME ONE

Behold, God is my salvation; I will trust and not be afraid, for the Lord Jehovah is my strength and my song; he also is become my salvation.

And in that day shall ye say, Praise the Lord, call upon his name, declare his doings among the people.

Isaiah xii. 2, 4.

—TO THE LORDS SPIRITUAL AND TEMPORAL, AND THE COMMONS OF THE PARLIAMENT OF GREAT BRITAIN—

My Lords and Gentlemen,

Permit me, with the greatest deference and respect, to lay at your feet the following genuine Narrative; the chief design of which is to excite in your august assemblies a sense of compassion for the miseries which the Slave-Trade has entailed on my unfortunate countrymen. By the horrors of that trade I was first torn away from all the tender connexions that were naturally dear to my heart; but these, through the mysterious ways of Providence, I ought to regard as infinitely more than compensated by the introduction I have thence obtained to the knowledge of the

Christian religion, and of a nation which, by its liberal sentiments, its humanity, the glorious freedom of its government, and its proficiency in arts and sciences, has exalted the dignity of human nature.

I am sensible I ought to entreat your pardon for addressing to you a work so wholly devoid of literary merit; but, as the production of an unlettered African, who is actuated by the hope of becoming an instrument towards the relief of his suffering countrymen, I trust that *such a man*, pleading in *such a cause*, will be acquitted of boldness and presumption.

May the God of heaven inspire your hearts with peculiar benevolence on that important day when the question of Abolition is to be discussed, when thousands, in consequence of your Determination, are to look for Happiness or Misery!

I am,
My Lords and Gentlemen,
Your most obedient,
And devoted humble Servant,
Olaudah Equiano,
or
Gustavus Vassa

Union-Street, Mary-le-bone, March 24, 1789.

— *from* CHAPTER I —

That part of Africa, known by the name of Guinea, to which the trade for slaves is carried on, extends along the coast above 3400 miles, from the Senegal to Angola, and includes a variety of kingdoms. Of these the most considerable is the kingdom of Benen,[1] both as to extent and wealth, the richness and cultivation of the soil, the power of its king, and the number and warlike disposition of the inhabitants. It is situated nearly under the line,[2] and extends along the coast about 170 miles, but runs back into the interior part of Africa to a distance hitherto I believe unexplored by any traveller; and seems only terminated at length by the empire of Abyssinia,[3] near 1500 miles from its beginning. This kingdom is divided into many provinces or districts: in one of the most remote and fertile of which, called Eboe,[4] I was born, in the year 1745, in a charming fruitful vale, named Essaka.[5] The distance of this province from the capital of Benin and the sea coast must be very considerable; for I had never heard of white men or Europeans, nor of the sea. . . . My father was one of those elders or chiefs I have spoken of, and was styled Embrenche;[6] a term, as I remember, importing the highest distinction, and signifying in our language a *mark* of grandeur. . . .

. . . We have . . . markets, at which I have been frequently with my mother. These are sometimes visited by stout mahogany-coloured men from the south west of us: we call them Oye-Eboe,[7] which term signifies red men living at a distance. They generally bring us fire-arms, gunpowder, hats, beads, and dried fish. The last we esteemed a great rarity, as our waters were only brooks and springs. These articles they barter with us for odoriferous woods and earth, and our salt of wood ashes.[8] They always carry slaves through our land; but the strictest account is exacted of their manner of procuring them before they are suffered to pass. Sometimes indeed we sold slaves to them, but they were only prisoners of war, or such among us as had been convicted of kidnapping, or adultery, and some other crimes, which we esteemed heinous. This practice of kidnapping induces me to think, that, notwithstanding all our strictness, their principal business among us was to trepan[9] our people. I remember too they carried great sacks along with them, which not long after I had an opportunity of fatally seeing applied to that infamous purpose. . . .

[1] **Guinea**: term used by Europeans during the colonial period for the west coast of Africa, from the nation of **Senegal** in the north to **Angola** in the south; it included such nations as present-day Liberia, Ghana, and Nigeria. **Benen**: the kingdom of Benin, which exerted political and cultural influence on Onitsha and other towns on the Niger River.

[2] **under the line**: south of the equator.

[3] **Abyssinia**: former name of Ethiopia, in northeastern Africa.

[4] **Eboe**: Ibo or Igbo, a people and language group of present-day eastern Nigeria.

[5] **Essaka**: the precise location is uncertain; it would have lain somewhere to the southeast of Onitsha, east of the Niger River.

[6] **Embrenche**: term referring to men, such as village elders, with ritual scars.

[7] **Oye-Eboe**: could be related to modern "onye Igbo," Ibo man, for the term Igbo used to refer not to one's own but to the neighboring clan; or to "onye Aboh," man from Aboh, on the Niger River below Onitsha.

[8] **salt of wood ashes**: salt was commonly extracted from the ashes of burnt wood or leaves; mangrove and ironwood were frequent sources.

[9] **trepan**: to ensnare, trap.

. . . Those prisoners which were not sold or redeemed we kept as slaves: but how different was their condition from that of the slaves in the West Indies! With us they do no more work than other members of the community, even their masters; their food, clothing and lodging were nearly the same as theirs, (except that they were not permitted to eat with those who were free-born); and there was scarce any other difference between them, than a superior degree of importance which the head of a family possesses in our state, and that authority which, as such, he exercises over every part of his household. Some of these slaves have even slaves under them as their own property, and for their own use.

As to religion, the natives believe that there is one Creator of all things, and that he lives in the sun, and is girted round with a belt that he may never eat or drink; but, according to some, he smokes a pipe, which is our own favourite luxury. They believe he governs events, especially our deaths or captivity; but, as for the doctrine of eternity, I do not remember to have ever heard of it: some however believe in the transmigration of souls in a certain degree. Those spirits, which are not transmigrated, such as our dear friends or relations, they believe always attend them, and guard them from the bad spirits or their foes. For this reason they always before eating, as I have observed, put some small portion of the meat, and pour some of their drink, on the ground for them; and they often make oblations of the blood of beasts or fowls at their graves. . . .

These instances, and a great many more which might be adduced, while they shew how the complexions of the same persons vary in different climates, it is hoped may tend also to remove the prejudice that some conceive against the natives of Africa on account of their colour. Surely the minds of the Spaniards did not change with their complexions! Are there not causes enough to which the apparent inferiority of an African may be ascribed, without limiting the goodness of God, and supposing he forbore to stamp understanding on certainly his own image, because "carved in ebony." Might it not naturally be ascribed to their situation? When they come among Europeans, they are ignorant of their language, religion, manners, and customs. Are any pains taken to teach them these? Are they treated as men? Does not slavery itself depress the mind, and extinguish all its fire and every noble sentiment? But, above all, what advantages do not a refined people possess over those who are rude and uncultivated. Let the polished and haughty European recollect that his ancestors were once, like the Africans, uncivilized, and even barbarous. Did Nature make *them* inferior to their sons? and should *they too* have been made slaves? Every rational mind answers, No. Let such reflections as these melt the pride of their superiority into sympathy for the wants and miseries of their sable brethren, and compel them to acknowledge, that understanding is not confined to feature or colour. If, when they look round the world, they feel exultation, let it be tempered with benevolence to others, and gratitude to God, "who hath made of one blood all nations of men for to dwell on all the face of the earth; and whose wisdom is not our wisdom, neither are our ways his ways."[10]

— *from* CHAPTER II —

. . . I have already acquainted the reader with the time and place of my birth. My father, besides many slaves, had a numerous family, of which seven lived to grow up, including myself and a sister, who was the only daughter. As I was the youngest of the sons, I became, of course, the greatest favourite with my mother, and was always with her; and she used to take particular pains to form my mind. I was trained up from my earliest years in the art of war; my daily exercise was shooting and throwing javelins; and my mother adorned me with emblems, after the manner of our greatest warriors. In this way I grew up till I was turned the age of eleven, when an end was put to my happiness in the following manner . . . : One day, when all our people were gone out to their works as usual, and only I and my dear sister were left to mind the house, two men and a woman got over our walls, and in a moment seized us both, and, without giving us time to cry out, or make resistance, they stopped our mouths, and ran off with us into the nearest wood. Here they tied our hands, and continued to carry us as far as they could, till night came on, when we reached a small house, where the robbers halted for refreshment, and spent the night. . . . The next morning we left the house, and continued travelling all the day. For a long time we had kept the woods, but at last we came into a road which I believed I knew. I had now some hopes of being delivered; for we had advanced but a little way before I discovered some people at a distance, on which I began to cry out for their assistance: but my cries had no other effect than to make them tie me faster and stop my mouth, and then they put me into a large sack. They also stopped my sister's mouth,

---

[10] **"neither are our ways his ways"**: "Acts, chap. xvii, verse 26" [O.E.].

and tied her hands; and in this manner we proceeded till we were out of the sight of these people. When we went to rest the following night they offered us some victuals; but we refused it; and the only comfort we had was in being in one another's arms all that night, and bathing each other with our tears. But alas! we were soon deprived of even the small comfort of weeping together. The next day proved a day of greater sorrow than I had yet experienced; for my sister and I were then separated, while we lay clasped in each other's arms. It was in vain that we besought them not to part us; she was torn from me, and immediately carried away, while I was left in a state of distraction not to be described. I cried and grieved continually; and for several days I did not eat any thing but what they forced into my mouth. At length, after many days travelling, during which I had often changed masters, I got into the hands of a chieftain, in a very pleasant country. This man had two wives and some children, and they all used me extremely well, and did all they could to comfort me; particularly the first wife, who was something like my mother. . . .

Soon after this my master's only daughter, and child by his first wife, sickened and died . . . and I was again sold. . . .

. . . I had been travelling for a considerable time, when one evening, to my great surprise, whom should I see brought to the house where I was but my dear sister! As soon as she saw me she gave a loud shriek, and ran into my arms—I was quite overpowered: neither of us could speak; but, for a considerable time, clung to each other in mutual embraces, unable to do any thing but weep. Our meeting affected all who saw us; and indeed I must acknowledge, in honour of those sable destroyers of human rights, that I never met with any ill treatment, or saw any offered to their slaves, except tying them, when necessary, to keep them from running away. When these people knew we were brother and sister they indulged us together; and the man, to whom I supposed we belonged, lay with us, he in the middle, while she and I held one another by the hands across his breast all night; and thus for a while we forgot our misfortunes in the joy of being together: but even this small comfort was soon to have an end; for scarcely had the fatal morning appeared, when she was again torn from me for ever! I was now more miserable, if possible, than before. . . .

The first object which saluted my eyes when I arrived on the coast was the sea, and a slave ship, which was then riding at anchor, and waiting for its cargo. These filled me with astonishment, which was soon converted into terror when I was carried on board. I was immediately handled and tossed up to see if I were sound by some of the crew; and I was now persuaded that I had gotten into a world of bad spirits, and that they were going to kill me. Their complexions too differing so much from ours, their long hair, and the language they spoke, (which was very different from any I had ever heard) united to confirm me in this belief. . . . When I looked round the ship too and saw a large furnace or copper boiling, and a multitude of black people of every description chained together, every one of their countenances expressing dejection and sorrow, I no longer doubted of my fate. . . . I asked them if we were not to be eaten by those white men with horrible looks, red faces, and loose hair. They told me I was not. . . . I was not long suffered to indulge my grief; I was soon put down under the decks, and there I received such a salutation in my nostrils as I had never experienced in my life: so that, with the loathsomeness of the stench, and crying together, I became so sick and low that I was not able to eat, nor had I the least desire to taste any thing. I now wished for the last friend, death, to relieve me; but soon, to my grief, two of the white men offered me eatables; and, on my refusing to eat, one of them held me fast by the hands, and laid me across I think the windlass, and tied my feet, while the other flogged me severely. I had never experienced any thing of this kind before; and although, not being used to the water, I naturally feared that element the first time I saw it, yet nevertheless, could I have got over the nettings, I would have jumped over the side, but I could not; and, besides, the crew used to watch us very closely who were not chained down to the decks, lest we should leap into the water: and I have seen some of these poor African prisoners most severely cut for attempting to do so, and hourly whipped for not eating. This indeed was often the case with myself. In a little time after, amongst the poor chained men, I found some of my own nation, which in a small degree gave ease to my mind. I inquired of these what was to be done with us; they gave me to understand we were to be carried to these white people's country to work for them. I then was a little revived, and thought, if it were no worse than working, my situation was not so desperate: but still I feared I should be put to death, the white people looked and acted, as I thought, in so savage a manner; for I had never seen among any people such instances of brutal cruelty; and this not only shewn towards us blacks, but also to some of the whites themselves. One white man in particular I saw, when we were permitted to be on deck, flogged so unmercifully with a large rope near the foremast, that he died in consequence of it; and they tossed him over the side as they would have done a brute. . . . .

. . . At last, when the ship we were in had got in all her cargo, they made ready with many fearful noises, and we were all put under deck, so that we could not see how they managed the vessel. But this disappointment was the least of my sorrow. The stench of the hold while we were on the coast was so intolerably loathsome, that it was dangerous to remain there for any time, and some of us had been permitted to stay on the deck for the fresh air; but now that the whole ship's cargo were confined together, it became absolutely pestilential. The closeness of the place, and the heat of the climate, added to the number in the ship, which was so crowded that each had scarcely room to turn himself, almost suffocated us. This produced copious perspirations, so that the air soon became unfit for respiration, from a variety of loathsome smells, and brought on a sickness among the slaves, of which many died, thus falling victims to the improvident avarice, as I may call it, of their purchasers. This wretched situation was again aggravated by the galling of the chains, now become insupportable; and the filth of the necessary tubs, into which the children often fell, and were almost suffocated. The shrieks of the women, and the groans of the dying, rendered the whole a scene of horror almost inconceivable. Happily perhaps for myself I was soon reduced so low here that it was thought necessary to keep me almost always on deck; and from my extreme youth I was not put in fetters. . . . One day, when we had a smooth sea and moderate wind, two of my wearied countrymen who were chained together (I was near them at the time), preferring death to such a life of misery, somehow made through the nettings and jumped into the sea: immediately another quite dejected fellow, who, on account of his illness, was suffered to be out of irons, also followed their example; and I believe many more would very soon have done the same if they had not been prevented by the ship's crew, who were instantly alarmed. . . . At last we came in sight of the island of Barbadoes,[11] at which the whites on board gave a great shout, and made many signs of joy to us. We did not know what to think of this; but as the vessel drew nearer we plainly saw the harbour, and other ships of different kinds and sizes; and we soon anchored amongst them off Bridge Town.[12] Many merchants and planters now came on board, though it was in the evening. They put us in separate parcels, and examined us attentively. They also made us jump, and pointed to the land, signifying we were to go there. We thought by this we should be eaten by these ugly men, as they appeared to us; and, when soon after we were all put down under the deck again, there was much dread and trembling among us, and nothing but bitter cries to be heard all the night from these apprehensions, insomuch that at last the white people got some old slaves from the land to pacify us. They told us we were not to be eaten, but to work, and were soon to go on land, where we should see many of our country people. This report eased us much; and sure enough, soon after we were landed, there came to us Africans of all languages. We were conducted immediately to the merchant's yard, where we were all pent up together like so many sheep in a fold, without regard to sex or age. As every object was new to me every thing I saw filled me with surprise. What struck me first was that the houses were built with stories, and in every other respect different from those in Africa: but I was still more astonished on seeing people on horseback. I did not know what this could mean; and indeed I thought these people were full of nothing but magical arts. . . . We were not many days in the merchant's custody before we were sold after their usual manner, which is this:—On a signal given, (as the beat of a drum) the buyers rush at once into the yard where the slaves are confined, and make choice of that parcel they like best. The noise and clamour with which this is attended, and the eagerness visible in the countenances of the buyers, serve not a little to increase the apprehensions of the terrified Africans, who may well be supposed to consider them as the ministers of that destruction to which they think themselves devoted. In this manner, without scruple, are relations and friends separated, most of them never to see each other again. . . . O, ye nominal Christians! might not an African ask you, learned you this from your God, who says unto you, Do unto all men as you would men should do unto you? Is it not enough that we are torn from our country and friends to toil for your luxury and lust of gain? Must every tender feeling be likewise sacrificed to your avarice? Are the dearest friends and relations, now rendered more dear by their separation from their kindred, still to be parted from

[11] **Barbadoes:** island in the West Indies; a British colony until 1966, now an independent nation.

[12] **Bridge Town:** capital and chief port of Barbados, founded by the British in 1628.

each other, and thus prevented from cheering the gloom of slavery with the small comfort of being together and mingling their sufferings and sorrows? Why are parents to lose their children, brothers their sisters, or husbands their wives? Surely this is a new refinement in cruelty, which, while it has no advantage to atone for it, thus aggravates distress, and adds fresh horrors even to the wretchedness of slavery.

—*from* CHAPTER III—

. . . I had been some time in this miserable, forlorn, and much dejected state, without having any one to talk to, which made my life a burden, when the kind and unknown hand of the Creator (who in very deed leads the blind in a way they know not) now began to appear, to my comfort; for one day the captain of a merchant ship, called the Industrious Bee, came on some business to my master's house. This gentleman, whose name was Michael Henry Pascal, was a lieutenant in the royal navy, but now commanded this trading ship, which was somewhere in the confines of the county many miles off. While he was at my master's house it happened that he saw me, and liked me so well that he made a purchase of me. . . . I was carried on board a fine large ship, loaded with tobacco, &c. and just ready to sail for England. I now thought my condition much mended; I had sails to lie on, and plenty of good victuals to eat; and every body on board used me very kindly, quite contrary to what I had seen of any white people before; I therefore began to think that they were not all of the same disposition. A few days after I was on board we sailed for England. I was still at a loss to conjecture my destiny. By this time, however, I could smatter a little imperfect English; and I wanted to know as well as I could where we were going. Some of the people of the ship used to tell me they were going to carry me back to my own country, and this made me very happy. I was quite rejoiced at the sound of going back; and thought if I should get home what wonders I should have to tell. But I was reserved for another fate, and was soon undeceived when we came within sight of the English coast. While I was on board this ship, my captain and master named me *Gustavus Vasa*. . . .[13] There was on board the ship a young lad who had never been at sea before, about four or five years older than myself: his name was Richard Baker. He was a native of America, had received an excellent education, and was of a most amiable temper. Soon after I went on board he shewed me a great deal of partiality and attention, and in return I grew extremely fond of him. We at length became inseparable; and, for the space of two years, he was of very great use to me, and was my constant companion and instructor. Although this dear youth had many slaves of his own, yet he and I have gone through many sufferings together on shipboard; and we have many nights lain in each other's bosoms when we were in great distress. Thus such a friendship was cemented between us as we cherished till his death, which, to my very great sorrow, happened in the year 1759, when he was up the Archipelago,[14] on board his majesty's ship the Preston: an event which I have never ceased to regret, as I lost at once a kind interpreter, an agreeable companion, and a faithful friend; who, at the age of fifteen, discovered a mind superior to prejudice; and who was not ashamed to notice, to associate with, and to be the friend and instructor of one who was ignorant, a stranger, of a different complexion, and a slave!

. . . I remained here[15] till the summer of the year 1757; when my master, being appointed first lieutenant of his majesty's ship the Roebuck, sent for Dick and me, and his old mate: on this we all left Guernsey. . . .

—*from* CHAPTER IV—

It was now between two and three years since I first came to England, a great part of which I had spent at sea; so that I became inured to that service, and began to consider myself as happily situated; for my master treated me always extremely well; and my attachment and gratitude to him were very great. From the various scenes I had beheld on ship-board, I soon grew a stranger to terror of every kind, and was, in that respect at least, almost an Englishman. . . . I could now speak English tolerably well, and I perfectly understood every thing that was said. I now not only felt myself quite easy with these new countrymen, but relished their society and manners. I no longer looked upon them as spirits, but as men superior to us; and therefore I had the stronger desire to resemble them; to imbibe their spirit, and imitate their manners; I therefore embraced every occasion of improvement; and

[13] **Gustavus Vasa:** the name of two Swedish kings, Gustavus I (1496–1560), who founded the modern Swedish state, and Gustavus II (1594–1632), who played a crucial role in the Thirty Years' War (1618–1648).

[14] **up the Archipelago:** in the Greek islands of the Aegean Sea.

[15] **here:** on the island of Guernsey in the English Channel, where Captain Pascal left Equiano and his friend Dick in care of one of his mates' families.

every new thing that I observed I treasured up in my memory. I had long wished to be able to read and write; and for this purpose I took every opportunity to gain instruction, but had made as yet very little progress. However, when I went to London with my master, I had soon an opportunity of improving myself, which I gladly embraced. Shortly after my arrival, he sent me to wait upon the Miss Guerins,[16] who had treated me with much kindness when I was there before; and they sent me to school.

While I was attending these ladies their servants told me I could not go to Heaven unless I was baptized. This made me very uneasy; for I had now some faint idea of a future state: accordingly I communicated my anxiety to the eldest Miss Guerin, with whom I was become a favourite, and pressed her to have me baptized; when to my great joy she told me I should. . . .

. . . I thought now of nothing but being freed, and working for myself, and thereby getting money to enable me to get a good education; for I always had a great desire to be able at least to read and write; and while I was on ship-board I had endeavoured to improve myself in both. While I was in the Ætna[17] particularly, the captain's clerk taught me to write, and gave me a smattering of arithmetic as far as the rule of three. . . .[18]

. . . Mr. King, my new master, . . . said the reason he had bought me was on account of my good character; and, as he had not the least doubt of my good behaviour, I should be very well off with him. He also told me he did not live in the West Indies, but at Philadelphia, where he was going soon; and, as I understood something of the rules of arithmetic, when we got there he would put me to school, and fit me for a clerk. . . .

I had the good fortune to please my master in every department in which he employed me; and there was scarcely any part of his business, or household affairs, in which I was not occasionally engaged. I often supplied the place of a clerk, in receiving and delivering cargoes to the ships, in tending stores, and delivering goods: and, besides this, I used to shave and dress my master when convenient, and take care of his horse; and when it was necessary, which was very often, I worked likewise on board of different vessels of his. By these means I became very useful to my master; and saved him, as he used to acknowledge, above a hundred pounds a year. . . .

VOLUME TWO

—*from* CHAPTER ONE—

Every day now brought me[19] nearer my freedom, and I was impatient till we proceeded again to sea, that I might have an opportunity of getting a sum large enough to purchase it. I was not long ungratified. . . .

. . . When we had unladen the vessel, and I had sold my venture, finding myself master of about forty-seven pounds, I consulted my true friend, the Captain, how I should proceed in offering my master the money for my freedom. . . . My master then said, he would not be worse than his promise; and, taking the money, told me to go to the Secretary at the Register Office, and get my manumission drawn up. These words of my master were like a voice from heaven to me: in an instant all my trepidation was turned into unutterable bliss; and I most reverently bowed myself with gratitude, unable to express my feelings, but by the overflowing of my eyes, while my true and worthy friend, the Captain, congratulated us both with a peculiar degree of heart-felt pleasure. . . .

—*from* CONCLUSION—

March the 21st, 1788, I had the honour of presenting the Queen[20] with a petition on behalf of my African brethren, which was received most graciously by her Majesty:

[16] **the Miss Guerins:** sisters of a friend of Captain Pascal.

[17] **the Aetna:** the ship on which Equiano served under Pascal in 1762.

[18] **the rule of three:** a kind of mathematical calculation based on ratios.

[19] **Every day now brought me . . . :** the year is 1766; Equiano has served Mr. King on numerous commercial voyages between Philadelphia and the West Indies for some three years, saving money of his own to purchase his freedom from his master (according to the certificate of manumission, Equiano had to pay King not £40 but £70).

[20] **the Queen:** Charlotte Sophia, wife of King George III. Between the conversion scene and this closing passage, Equiano had travelled among the Miskito Indians of Central America and had been involved in the 1787 mission to resettle freed African slaves in Sierra Leone, from which he was dismissed.

To the Queen's most Excellent Majesty

Madam,

Your Majesty's well known benevolence and humanity emboldens me to approach your royal presence, trusting that the obscurity of my situation will not prevent your Majesty from attending to the sufferings for which I plead.

Yet I do not solicit your royal pity for my own distress; my sufferings, although numerous, are in a measure forgotten. I supplicate your Majesty's compassion for millions of my African countrymen, who groan under the lash of tyranny in the West Indies.

The oppression and cruelty exercised to the unhappy negroes there, have at length reached the British legislature,[21] and they are now deliberating on its redress; even several persons of property in slaves in the West Indies, have petitioned parliament against its continuance, sensible that it is as impolitic as it is unjust — and what is inhuman must ever be unwise.

Your Majesty's reign has been hitherto distinguished by private acts of benevolence and bounty; surely the more extended the misery is, the greater claim it has to your Majesty's compassion, and the greater must be your Majesty's pleasure in administering to its relief.

I presume, therefore, gracious Queen, to implore your interposition with your royal consort,[22] in favour of the wretched Africans; that, by your Majesty's benevolent influence, a period may now be put to their misery; and that they may be raised from the condition of brutes, to which they are at present degraded, to the rights and situation of freemen, and admitted to partake of the blessings of your Majesty's happy government; so shall your Majesty enjoy the heart-felt pleasure of procuring happiness to millions, and be rewarded in the grateful prayers of themselves, and of their posterity.

And may the all-bountiful Creator shower on your Majesty, and the Royal Family, every blessing that this world can afford, and every fulness of joy which divine revelation has promised us in the next.

I am your Majesty's most dutiful and
devoted servant to command,
GUSTAVUS VASSA,
The Oppressed Ethiopean.
No. 53, Baldwin's Gardens.

[21] **the British legislature:** Equiano was active in the antislavery movement in Britain throughout the 1780s and 1790s; the British slave trade was finally outlawed in 1807, and in 1833 slavery was abolished throughout the British Empire.

[22] **your royal consort:** George III.

HANNAH MORE

(1745–1833)

Educated with her four sisters at home by her father, Jacob More, a High Anglican schoolmaster in a poorly endowed charity school at Stapleton, near Bristol, Hannah More was regarded as the "genius" of the family, notable for her ability to learn (her father refused to teach her any more mathematics when she outstripped all his male students) and to write. "Born with more desires than guineas," as her witty sister Sally put it, the five More girls succeeded in supporting themselves by opening an extremely successful private venture school for the girls of the commercial and landed gentry classes in Bristol in 1757. Filling a widespread need for better-educated women, the More sisters taught not only the "accomplishments" of a well-bred lady (English, French, Italian, dancing, music, sketching), but also literature, history, mathematics, and that which contributed most to their resounding success, religious and moral instruction. Hannah More began her career as a writer here, providing plays suitable for respectable Christian schoolgirls to produce, *Sacred Dramas for Young Persons* (published 1782) and *The Search after Happiness* (1773), which was immediately reissued in numerous editions.

When her wealthy middle-aged fiancé, William Turner, thrice jilted her at the altar between 1780 and 1781 (a case, as Charlotte Younge put it, of an "elderly man growing shy"), Hannah More broke her engagement and vowed to remain a spinster (although she accepted the generous annuity Turner, in his embarrassment, bestowed upon her). She left her sisters' school (which would flourish until 1790) and moved to London to pursue a career as a playwright, where she became close friends with David Garrick and his wife. Her tragedies—*The Inflexible Captive* (1774) and especially *Percy* (1777)—were enormously popular (their stilted language and melodramatic plots captured the taste of the time), but when Hannah Cowley publicly accused her of stealing the plot of her next play, *The Fatal Falsehood* (1779), from Cowley's unproduced *Albina*, Hannah More gave up playwriting as too "unchristian." She remained in London, admired by the now aging circle of Bluestockings (see RIGHTS OF WOMAN) and literary intellectuals, including Dr. Johnson, Joshua Reynolds, Edmund Burke, and Horace Walpole. Her combination of extravagant adulation and sabbatarian piety appealed strongly to this circle, for whom she wrote her admiring poem "Bas Bleu" in 1786.

On a visit to her sisters in 1784, she was shown the poems of a local milkwoman, Ann Yearsley,* an impoverished mother with five children and an unemployed husband. Perceiving a diamond in the rough, Hannah More took it upon herself to educate Yearsley in poetic composition, correct her manuscripts, and write over 1,000 letters in a campaign to publish Yearsley's poems by subscription. When Yearsley's poems appeared in 1785, however, More put the £360 profit in a trust for Yearsley and her children that paid out 3 percent annually, since she was convinced that Yearsley was not capable of handling such large amounts wisely. Yearsley attacked More publicly, demanding her money and accusing More of embezzling it; the trust was closed, and Yearsley received her money, but the rift between them never healed.

In the late 1780s Hannah More increasingly distanced herself from the gay society life of London to devote herself to Christian charities. Her *Thoughts on the Importance of the*

Manners of the Great in General Society (1788) criticized the moral laxness of the aristocracy, as did *An Estimate of the Religion of the Fashionable World* (1790). Inspired by Captain Charles Middleton, an ardent abolitionist, she became friends with many of the leading members of the anti-slave trade movement, John Newton, William Cowper, and William Wilberforce, and joined the Evangelical Clapham Sect. Leaving London for a quieter life in a cottage at Cowslip Green, near Wrington Vale, Somerset, she began her most enduring life work, the attempt to educate the children of the impoverished rural working classes. Firmly believing in the rectitude of a divinely ordained class system, she felt that the lives of the lowest classes could only be improved by their conversion to Christian morality and practices of thrift, cleanliness, and sobriety. Offended by Thomas Paine's revolutionary *Rights of Man*, she published *Village Politics*—which has been called a "Burke for Beginners"—in 1792, followed by her critique of the atheism of the leaders of the French Revolution, *Remarks on the Speech of M. Dupont, made in the French Convention*, in 1793.

In 1795, she began the project that more than any other would bring her lasting fame. Wishing to reach the illiterate poor of England, she published between 1795 and 1799 a series of over 100 stories, ballads, and songs in the format of the popular broadsides of the day. Her purpose, as she wrote in the advertisement, was "to improve the habits, and raise the principles of the common people . . . not only to counteract vice and profligacy on the one hand, but error, discontent, and false religion on the other." These *Cheap Repository Tracts*, which sold for no more than a halfpenny, were enormously popular. Bought by churchmen and aristocrats for their parishioners and tenants, they reached every corner of England, often being read where books had never been seen before. They were distributed for free in prisons and workhouses and among the armed forces; the Society for the Promotion of Christian Knowledge recommended their use in Sunday schools; and missionaries carried them abroad to Africa and India. By March 1796, over 2 million copies had been sold. Inculcating the virtues of honesty, thrift, sobriety, cleanliness, and hard work, they upheld the status quo but at the same time made available to the lowest classes an opportunity to read and learn. The popularity of these tracts contributed greatly to raising the general literacy of the population. Since the tracts also criticized the irresponsibility and amorality of the rich, they were more progressive in their political propaganda than many at first realized.

During the 1790s Hannah More, with her sister Patty, began the last of her major charitable projects, the establishment of a series of schools for the children of the lowest classes in the Mendip region of Somerset, a ten-mile area stretching along the Bristol Channel from Bristol south to Cheddar and Wedmore. This project was attacked by the curate at Blagdon, who did not wish the poor to be educated at all. (He involved More in what was known as the Blagdon Controversy, from 1800 to 1803, in which an ardent defense was made for the schoolmaster More had hired for her school at Blagdon). The schools—both day schools and Sunday schools—established a precedent for educating the lowest classes in writing, reading, and arithmetic, as well as in Christian doctrine.

After 1799, More devoted herself to writing educational and Evangelical religious tracts. *Strictures on the Modern System of Female Education* appeared in 1799. This influential treatise on the education of women assumed that there was an innate difference between the sexes and the social roles they should perform, but nonetheless endorsed Wollstonecraft's view that women were rational and should be educated to develop their intellectual and moral capacities to the fullest. After moving with all her sisters to a large house at Barley Wood, Wrington, Somerset, in 1801, More applied her educational theories to a specific case, that of the nine-year-old Princess Charlotte Augusta, in *Hints toward forming the Character of a Young Princess* (1805). She then published her only novel, *Coelebs in Search of a Wife* (1808), in order "to shew how religion may be brought to mix with the concerns of ordinary life, without impairing its activity, lessening its cheerfulness, or diminishing its usefulness." Coelebs seeks, and in Lucilla Stanley finds, the perfect wife, one who can be a "companion" rather than a servant, one who has received an education which "inculcates principles, polishes taste, regulates temper, cultivates reason, subdues the passions, directs the feelings, habituates to reflection, trains to self-denial, and, more especially, . . . refers all actions, feelings, sentiments, tastes, and passions, to the love and fear of God."

Her last books focus directly on issues of Evangelical doctrine and practice: *Practical Piety* in 1811; *Christian Morals* in 1812; *The Character and Practical Writings of St. Paul* (1815); *The Spirit of Prayer* (1825). By the time she died at the age of 88, Hannah More had earned over £30,000 from her writing and done more than any other person to increase the literacy of the lowest classes. Although she did not directly challenge the orthodox Christian doctrine of the separate spheres, her career demonstrated that a rational, well-educated woman could break down the division between the public and the private spheres by playing a major role in society, reforming the education and treatment of both women and the working classes. Her writings everywhere advocated what one critic has described as "a woman's brand of bourgeois progressivism—pedagogy, philanthropy, and purification her cures for the old order's social ills."

from Sensibility: A Poetical Epistle to the Hon. Mrs. Boscawen

(1782)

Accept, BOSCAWEN! these unpolish'd lays,
Nor blame too much the verse you cannot praise.
For you far other bards have wak'd the string;
Far other bards for you were wont to sing.
Yet on the gale their parting music steals,
Yet, your charm'd ear the lov'd impression feels.

. . . .

122 Forgive, BOSCAWEN, if my sorrowing heart,
Intent on grief, forget the rules of art;
Forgive, if wounded recollection melt—
You best can pardon who have oft'nest felt.
You, who for many a friend and hero[1] mourn,
Who bend in anguish o'er the frequent urn;
You who have found how much the feeling heart
Shapes its own wound, and points itself the dart;
You, who from tender sad experience feel
The wounds such minds receive can never heal;
That grief a thousand entrances can find,
Where parts superior dignify the mind;
Wou'd you renounce the pangs those feelings give,
Secure in joyless apathy to live?

For tho' in souls, where taste and sense abound,
Pain thro' a thousand avenues can wound;
Yet the same avenues are open still,
To casual blessings as to casual ill.
Nor is the trembling temper more awake

[1] **hero:** Admiral Boscawen [H. M.]. Admiral Edward Boscawen (1711–1761), known as "Old Dreadnaught," defeated the French Navy off Finistere (1747), at Newfoundland (1755), at Cape Breton (1758), and in Lagos Bay (1759). This poem is addressed to his wife, Frances Boscawen (1719–1805), the mother of a daughter named Leveson and a son named Beaufort, the author of a large and lively correspondence, and a notable patron of literature.

To every wound which misery can make,
Than is the finely-fashion'd nerve alive
To every transport pleasure has to give.
For if, when home-felt joys the mind elate,
It mourns in secret for another's fate;
Yet when its own sad griefs invade the breast,
Abroad, in others blessings, see it blest!
Ev'n the soft sorrow of remember'd woe
A not unpleasing sadness may bestow,

Let not the vulgar read this pensive strain,
Their jests the tender anguish wou'd profane:
Yet these some deem the happiest of their kind,
Whose low enjoyments never reach'd the mind;
Who ne'er a pain but for themselves have known,
Nor ever felt a sorrow but their own;
Who call romantic every finer thought,
Conceiv'd by pity, or by friendship wrought.
Ah! wherefore happy? where's the kindred mind?
Where, the large soul that takes in human kind?
Where, the best passions of the mortal breast?
Where, the warm blessing when another's blest?
Where, the soft lenitives of others' pain,
The social sympathy, the sense humane?
The sigh of rapture, and the tear of joy,
Anguish that charms, and transports that destroy?
For tender Sorrow has her pleasures too;
Pleasures, which prosp'rous Dulness never knew.
She never knew, in all her coarser bliss,
The sacred rapture of a pain like this!
Nor think, the cautious only are the just;
Who never was deceiv'd I wou'd not trust.
Then take, ye happy vulgar! take your part
Of sordid joy, which never touch'd the heart.
Benevolence, which seldom stays to chuse,
Lest pausing Prudence teach her to refuse;
Friendship, which once determin'd, never swerves,
Weighs ere it trusts, but weighs not ere it serves;
And soft-ey'd Pity, and Forgiveness bland,
And melting Charity with open hand;
And artless Love, believing and believ'd,
And gen'rous Confidence which ne'er deceiv'd;
And Mercy stretching out, ere Want can speak,
To wipe the tear from pale Affliction's cheek;
These ye have never known!—then take your part
Of sordid joy, which never touch'd the heart.

Ye, who have melted in bright Glory's flame,
Or felt the spirit-stirring breath of fame!
Ye noble few! in whom her promis'd meed
Wakes the great thought, and makes the wish the deed!
Ye, who have tasted the delight to give,
And, God's own agents, bid the wretched live;
Who the chill haunts of Desolation seek,
Raise the sunk heart, and flush the fading cheek!
Ye, who with pensive Petrarch love to mourn,
Or weave fresh chaplets for Tibullus' urn;
Who cherish both in Hammond's plaintive lay,[2]
The Provence myrtle, and the Roman bay!
Ye, who divide the joys, and share the pains
Which merit feels, or Heav'n-born Fancy feigns;
Wou'd you renounce such joys, such pains as these,
For vulgar pleasures, or for selfish ease?
Wou'd you, to 'scape the pain the joy forego;
And miss the transport, to avoid the woe?
Wou'd you the sense of real sorrow lose,
Or cease to wooe the melancholy Muse?
No, Greville![3] no!—Thy song tho' steep'd in tears,
Tho' all thy soul in all thy strain appears;
Yet wou'dst thou all thy well-sung anguish chuse,
And all th' inglorious peace thou begg'st, refuse.

Or you, BOSCAWEN! when you fondly melt,
In raptures none but mothers ever felt;
And view, enamour'd, in your beauteous race,
All LEVESON's sweetness, and all BEAUFORT's grace!
Yet think what dangers each lov'd child may share,
The youth is valiant, and the maid is fair;
That perils multiply as blessings flow,
And constant sorrows on enjoyments grow:
You, who have felt how fugitive is joy,
That while we clasp the phantom we destroy;
That life's bright sun is dimm'd by clouded views,
And who have most to love have most to lose;
Yet from these fair possessions wou'd you part,
To shield from future pain your guarded heart?
Wou'd your fond mind renounce its tender boast,

[2] **Petrarch**: Francesco Petrarca (1304–1374), Italian humanist and poet, most famous for his love sonnets (*Canzoniere*) to Laura, the wife of Count Hughes de Sade, who died in 1348 after bearing eleven children. **Tibullus**: Albius Tibullus (54?–?18 BC), Roman poet famed for his elegies. **Hammond**: James Hammond, author of *Love Elegies* (1732).

[3] **Greville**: see the beautiful "Ode to Indifference" [H. M.]. Frances Greville (1726?–1789), Anglo-Irish poet, author of "Prayer for Indifference," probably written after the death of her son in 1756.

Or wish their op'ning bloom of promise lost?
Yield the dear hopes, which break upon your view,
For all the quiet, Dulness ever knew?
Debase the objects of your tend'rest pray'r,
To save the dangers of a distant care?
Consent, to shun the anxious fears you prove;
They less shou'd merit, or you less shou'd love?

Yet, while I hail the Sympathy Divine,
Which makes, O man! the wants of others thine:
I mourn heroic JUSTICE, scarcely own'd,
And PRINCIPLE for SENTIMENT dethron'd.
While FEELING boasts her ever-tearful eye,
Stern TRUTH, firm FAITH, and manly VIRTUE fly.

Sweet SENSIBILITY! thou soothing pow'r,
Who shedd'st thy blessings on the natal hour,
Like fairy favours! Art can never seize,
Nor Affectation catch thy pow'r to please:
Thy subtile essence still eludes the chains
Of Definition, and defeats her pains.
Sweet Sensibility! thou keen delight!
Thou hasty moral! sudden sense of right!
Thou untaught goodness! Virtue's precious seed!
Thou sweet precursor of the gen'rous deed!
Beauty's quick relish! Reason's radiant morn,
Which dawns soft light before Reflexion's born!
To those who know thee not, no words can paint!
And those who know thee, know all words are faint!
'Tis not to mourn because a sparrow dies;
To rave in artificial extasies:
'Tis not to melt in tender *Otway's* fires;
'Tis not to faint, when injur'd *Shore* expires:
'Tis not because the ready eye o'erflows
At *Clementina's* or *Clarissa's*, woes.

Forgive, O RICHARDSON![4] nor think I mean,
With cold contempt, to blast thy peerless scene:
If some faint love of virtue glow in me,
Pure spirit! I first caught that flame from thee.

While soft Compassion silently relieves,
Loquacious *Feeling* hints how much she gives;
Laments how oft her wounded heart has bled,
And boasts of many a tear she never shed.

As words are but th' external marks, to tell
The fair ideas in the mind that dwell;
And only are of things the outward sign,
And not the things themselves, they but define;
So exclamations, tender tones, fond tears,
And all the graceful drapery Pity wears;
These are not Pity's self, they but express
Her inward sufferings by their pictur'd dress;
And these fair marks, reluctant I relate,
These lovely symbols may be counterfeit.
Celestial Pity! why must I deplore,
Thy sacred image stamp'd on basest ore?
There are, who fill with brilliant plaints the page
If a poor linnet meet the gunner's rage:
There are, who for a dying fawn display
The tend'rest anguish in the sweetest lay;
Who for a wounded animal deplore,
As if friend, parent, country were no more;
Who boast quick rapture trembling in their eye,
If from the spider's snare they save a fly;
Whose well-sung sorrows every breast inflame,
And break all hearts but his from whom they came:
Yet, scorning life's *dull* duties to attend,
Will persecute a wife, or wrong a friend;
Alive to every woe by *fiction* dress'd;
The innocent he wrong'd, the wretch distress'd,
May plead in vain; their suff'rings come not near,
Or he relieves them cheaply, with a tear.
Not so the tender moralist of Tweed;[5]
His *Man of Feeling* is a man indeed.

Oh, bless'd Compassion! Angel Charity!
More dear one genuine deed perform'd for thee,
Than all the periods Feeling e'er can turn,
Than all thy soothing pages, polish'd STERNE![6]

---

[4] **Otway:** Thomas Otway (1652–1685), author of several great tragedies, *Don Carlos* (1676), *The Orphan* (1680), and *Venice Preserv'd* (1682). **Shore:** Jane Shore (d. 1527), mistress of King Edward IV, accused by Richard III of sorcery and forced to do public penance in 1483; died in poverty. Her tribulations were the subject of many eighteenth-century works, most notably Nicholas Rowe's drama *Jane Shore* (1714). **Richardson:** Samuel Richardson (1689–1761), novelist, author of *Clarissa* (1747–1748), the story of a virtuous heroine who, once raped, prefers to die rather than to marry her seducer Lovelace, and of *Sir Charles Grandison* (1753–1754), which includes the tale of the long-suffering Clementina.

[5] **Tweed:** the Scottish novelist and editor Henry Mackenzie (1745–1831), who celebrated masculine sensibility in his *Man of Feeling* (1771).

[6] **Sterne:** novelist Laurence Sterne (1713–1768), author of *Tristram Shandy* (1760–1767) and *Sentimental Journey* (1768).

Not that by deeds alone this love's exprest,
If so, the affluent only were the blest.
One silent wish, one pray'r, one soothing word,
The precious page of Mercy shall record;
One soul-felt sigh by pow'rless Pity giv'n,
Accepted incense! shall ascend to Heav'n.

Since trifles make the sum of human things,
And half our mis'ry from our foibles springs;
Since life's best joys consist in peace and ease,
And few can save or serve, but all may please:
Oh! let th' ungentle spirit learn from hence,
A small unkindness is a great offence.
Large bounties to bestow we wish in vain;
But all may shun the guilt of giving pain.
To bless mankind with tides of flowing wealth;
With pow'r to grace them, or to crown with health,
Our little lot denies; but Heav'n decrees
To all, the gift of minist'ring to ease.
The gentle offices of patient love,
Beyond all flatt'ry, and all price above;
The mild forbearance at another's fault,
The taunting word, suppress'd as soon as thought;
On these Heav'n bade the bliss of life depend,
And crush'd ill-fortune when he made a FRIEND.

A solitary blessing few can find,
Our joys with those we love are intertwin'd;
And he, whose helpful tenderness removes
Th' obstructing thorn which wounds the breast he
loves,
Smooths not another's rugged path alone,
But scatters roses to adorn his own.
The hint malevolent, the look oblique,
The obvious satire, or implied dislike;
The sneer equivocal, the harsh reply,
And all the cruel language of the eye;
The artful injury, whose venom'd dart,
Scarce wounds the hearing while it stabs the heart;
The guarded phrase whose meaning kills, yet told,
The list'ner wonders how you thought it cold;
Small slights, contempt, neglect unmix'd with hate,
Make up in number what they want in weight.
These, and a thousand griefs minute as these,
Corrode our comfort, and destroy our ease.

As this strong feeling tends to good or ill,
It gives fresh pow'r to vice or principle;
'Tis not peculiar to the wise and good;
'Tis passion's flame, the virtue of the blood.
But to divert it to its proper course,
There Wisdom's pow'r appears, there Reason's force;
If, ill-directed, it pursues the wrong,
It adds new strength to what before was strong;
Breaks out in wild irregular desires,
Disorder'd passions, and illicit fires.
But if the virtuous bias rule the soul,
This lovely feeling then adorns the whole;
Sheds its sweet sunshine on the moral part,
Nor wastes on fancy what shou'd warm the heart.
Cold and inert the mental pow'rs wou'd lie,
Without this quick'ning spark of Deity.
To draw the rich materials from the mine,
To bid the mass of intellect refine;
To melt the firm, to animate the cold,
And Heav'n's own impress stamp on nature's gold;
To give immortal MIND its finest tone,
Oh, SENSIBILITY! is all thy own.
This is th' etherial flame which lights and warms,
In song transports us, and in action charms.
'Tis THIS that makes the pensive strains of GRAY[7]
Win to the open heart their easy way.
Makes the touch'd spirit glow with kindred fire,
When sweet SERENA's poet wakes the lyre.
'Tis THIS, tho' Nature's hidden treasures lie,
Bare to the keen inspection of her eye,
Makes PORTLAND's face its brightest rapture wear,
When her large bounty smooths the bed of care.
'Tis THIS that breathes thro' SEVIGNE's[8] sweet page,
That nameless grace which soothes a second age.
'Tis THIS, whose charms the soul resistless seize,
And gives BOSCAWEN half her pow'r to please.

Yet, why those terrors? why that anxious care,
Since your last hope[9] the deathful war will dare?

---

[7] **Gray**: "This is meant of the *Elegy in a Country Churchyard* [1750, by the English poet Thomas Gray (1716–1771)], of which exquisite Poem, *Sensibility* is, perhaps, the characteristic beauty" [H. M.].

[8] **Serena's poet**: William Hayley (1745–1820); Serena appears in his *Triumphs of Temper* (1781). **Portland**: Margaret Cavendish Holles Harley, the Duchess of Portland (1714–1785), notable for her philanthropy and patronage of the arts; her private art collection was known as "the Portland Museum." **Sévigné**: Marie de Rabutin-Chantal, Marquise de Sévigné (1626–1696), famed for her detailed and moving *Lettres de Mme de Sévigné*, written to her daughter the Comtesse de Grignan.

[9] **last hope**: "Viscount Falmouth, Admiral Boscawen's only remaining son, was then in America, and at the battle of Lexington" [H. M.].

Why dread that energy of soul which leads
To dang'rous glory by heroic deeds?
Why tremble lest this ardent soul aspire?—
You fear the son because you knew the sire.
Hereditary valour you deplore,
And dread, yet wish to find one hero more.

Slavery, A Poem
(1788)

O great design!
Ye sons of mercy! O complete your work;
Wrench from Oppression's hand the iron rod,
And bid the cruel feel the pains they give.
THOMSON's "Liberty"[1]

If Heaven has into being deign'd to call
Thy light, O LIBERTY! to shine on all;
Bright intellectual sun! why does thy ray
To earth distribute only partial day?
Since no resisting cause from spirit flows,
Thy penetrating essence to oppose;
No obstacles by Nature's hand impress'd,
Thy subtle and ethereal beams arrest;
Nor motion's laws can speed thy active course,
Nor strong repulsion's powers obstruct thy force;
Since there is no convexity in MIND,
Why are thy genial beams to parts confined?
While the chill North with thy bright ray is blest,
Why should fell darkness half the South invest?
Was it decreed, fair Freedom! at thy birth,
That thou shouldst ne'er irradiate *all* the earth?
While Britain basks in thy full blaze of light,
Why lies sad Afric quench'd in total night?
Thee only, sober Goddess! I attest,
In smiles chastised, and decent graces dress'd,
Not that unlicensed monster of the crowd,[2]
Whose roar terrific bursts in peals so loud,
Deaf'ning the ear of Peace; fierce Faction's tool,
Of rash Sedition born, and mad Misrule;
Whose stubborn mouth, rejecting Reason's rein,
No strength can govern, and no skill restrain;
Whose magic cries the frantic vulgar draw,
To spurn at Order, and to outrage Law;
To tread on grave Authority and Power,
And shake the work of ages in an hour;
Convulsed her voice, and pestilent her breath,
She raves of mercy, while she deals out death:
Each blast is fate; she darts from either hand
Red conflagration o'er th' astonish'd land;
Clamouring for peace, she rends the air with noise,
And to reform a part, the whole destroys.
Oh, plaintive Southerne![3] whose impassion'd strain
So oft has wak'd my languid Muse in vain!
Now, when congenial themes her cares engage,
She burns to emulate thy glowing page;
Her failing efforts mock her fond desires,
She shares thy feelings, not partakes thy fires.
Strange power of song! the strain that warms the heart
Seems the same inspiration to impart;
Touch'd by the kindling energy alone,
We think the flame which melts us is our own;
Deceived, for genius we mistake delight,
Charm'd as we read, we fancy we can write.
Though not to me, sweet bard, thy powers belong,
Fair Truth, a hallow'd guide! inspires my song.
Here Art would weave her gayest flowers in vain,
For Truth the bright invention would disdain.
For no fictitious ills these numbers flow,
But living anguish, and substantial woe;
No individual griefs my bosom melt
For millions feel what Oroonoko felt:
Fired by no single wrongs, the countless host
I mourn, by rapine dragg'd from Afric's coast.
Perish th' illiberal thought which would debase
The native genius of the sable race!
Perish the proud philosophy, which sought
To rob them of the powers of equal thought!
Does then th' immortal principle within
Change with the casual colour of a skin?
Does matter govern spirit? or is mind
Degraded by the form to which 'tis join'd?

[1] **Thomson's "Liberty":** a political poem by the Scottish poet James Thomson (1700–1748), author of *The Seasons* (1726–1744).

[2] **that unlicensed monster of the crowd:** the imagery of the following 24 lines "allud[es] to the riots of London in the year 1780" (More's note)—i.e., the Gordon riots, in which more than 800 people were killed or injured.

[3] **Southerne:** Thomas Southerne (1660–1746), Anglo-Irish playwright, author of the tragedy *Oroonoko* (1696), based on the novel by Aphra Behn, whose hero is an enslaved African prince struggling for freedom.

No; they have heads to think, and hearts to feel,
And souls to act, with firm, tho' erring zeal;
For they have keen affections, kind desires,
Love strong as death, and active patriot fires;
All the rude energy, the fervid flame,
Of high-soul'd passion, and ingenuous shame:
Strong, but luxuriant virtues boldly shoot
From the wild vigour of a savage root.
Nor weak their sense of honour's proud control,
For pride is virtue in a Pagan soul;
A sense of worth, a conscience of desert,
A high, unbroken haughtiness of heart;
That self-same stuff which erst proud empires sway'd,
Of which the conquerors of the world were made.
Capricious fate of man! that very pride
In Afric scourged, in Rome was deified.
No muse, O Quashi![4] shall thy deeds relate,
No statue snatch thee from oblivious fate!
For thou wast born where never gentle muse
On Valour's grave the flowers of Genius strews;
And thou wast born where no recording page
Plucks the fair deed from Time's devouring rage.
Had Fortune placed thee on some happier coast,
Where polish'd souls heroic virtue boast,
To thee, who sought'st a voluntary grave,
Th' uninjured honours of thy name to save,
Whose generous arm thy barb'rous Master spared,
Altars had smoked, and temples had been rear'd.

[4] **Quashi**: It is a point of honour among negroes of a high spirit, to die rather than to suffer their glossy skin to bear the mark of the whip. Quashi had somehow offended his master, a young planter, with whom he had been bred up in the endearing intimacy of a playfellow. His services had been faithful: his attachment affectionate. The master resolved to punish him, and pursued him for that purpose. In trying to escape, Quashi stumbled and fell; the master fell upon him: they wrestled long with doubtful victory: at length Quashi got uppermost, and being firmly seated on his master's breast, he secured his legs with one hand, and with the other drew a sharp knife; then said, "Master, I have been bred up with you from a child; I have loved you as myself;—in return, you have condemned me to a punishment of which I must ever have borne the marks—thus only I can avoid them;" so saying, he drew the knife with all his strength across his own throat, and fell down dead, without a groan, on his master's body. [James] Ramsay, *An Essay on the Treatment [and Conversion] of African Slaves [in the British Sugar Colonies]* (1784) [More's note].

Whene'er to Afric's shores I turn my eyes,
Horrors of deepest, deadliest guilt arise;
I, by more than Fancy's mirror shown,
The burning village, and the blazing town:
See the dire victim torn from social life,
The shrieking babe, the agonizing wife!
She, wretch forlorn! is dragg'd by hostile hands,
To distant tyrants sold, in distant lands!
Transmitted miseries, and successive chains,
The sole sad heritage her child obtains!
E'en this last wretched boon their foes deny,
To weep together, or together die.
By felon hands, by one relentless stroke,
See the fond links of feeling Nature broke!
The fibres twisting round a parent's heart,
Torn from their grasp, and bleeding as they part.
Hold, murderers, hold! nor aggravate distress;
Respect the passions you yourselves possess;
E'en you, of ruffian heart, and ruthless hand,
Love your own offspring, love your native land.
Ah! leave them holy Freedom's cheering smile,
The heav'n-taught fondness for the parent soil;
Revere affections mingled with our frame,
In every nature, every clime the same;
In all, these feelings equal sway maintain;
In all, the love of HOME and FREEDOM reign:
And Tempe's vale,[5] and parch'd Angola's sand,
One equal fondness of their sons command.
Th' unconquer'd Savage laughs at pain and toil,
Basking in Freedom's beams which gild his native soil.
Does thirst of empire, does desire of fame,
(For these are specious crimes,) our rage inflame?
No: sordid lust of gold their fate controls,
The basest appetite of basest souls:
Gold, better gain'd by what their ripening sky,
Their fertile fields, their arts[6] and mines supply.
What wrongs, what injuries, does Oppression plead,
To smooth the horror of th' unnatural deed?
What strange offence, what aggravated sin?

[5] **Tempe's vale**: the Vale of Tempe in central Greece was sacred to Apollo; its beauty is described in Virgil's *Georgics*. **Angola**: located in southwestern Africa; colonized starting in the sixteenth century by Portugal; the base for the Portuguese slave trade to Brazil.

[6] **arts**: "Besides many valuable productions of the soil, cloths and carpets of exquisite manufacture are brought from the coast of Guinea" [H. M.].

They stand convicted—of a darker skin!
Barbarians, hold! th' opprobrious commerce spare,
Respect *His* sacred image which they bear.
Though dark and savage, ignorant and blind,
They claim the common privilege of kind;
Let Malice strip them of each other plea,
They still are men, and men should still be free.
Insulted Reason loathes th' inverted trade—
Dire change! the agent is the purchase made!
Perplex'd, the baffled Muse involves the tale;
Nature confounded, well may language fail!
The outraged Goddess, with abhorrent eyes,
Sees MAN the traffic, SOULS the merchandise!
  Plead not, in reason's palpable abuse,
Their sense of feeling[7] callous and obtuse:
From heads to hearts lies Nature's plain appeal,
Though few can reason, all mankind can feel.
Though wit may boast a livelier dread of shame,
A loftier sense of wrong, refinement claim;
Though polish'd manners may fresh wants invent,
And nice distinctions nicer souls torment;
Though these on finer spirits heavier fall,
Yet natural evils are the same to all.
Tho' wounds there are which reason's force may heal,
There needs no logic sure to make us feel.
The nerve, howe'er untutor'd, can sustain
A sharp, unutterable sense of pain;
As exquisitely fashion'd in a slave,
As where unequal fate a sceptre gave.
Sense is as keen where Congo's waters glide,
As where proud Tiber[8] rolls his classic tide.
Rhetoric or verse may point the feeling line,
They do not whet sensation, but define.
Did ever slave less feel the galling chain,
When Zeno[9] proved there was no ill in pain?
Their miseries philosophic quirks deride,
Slaves groan in pangs disown'd by Stoic pride.
  When the fierce sun darts vertical his beams,
And thirst and hunger mix their wild extremes;
When the sharp iron[10] wounds his inmost soul,
And his strain'd eyes in burning anguish roll;
Will the parch'd negro find, ere he expire,
No pain in hunger, and no heat in fire?
  For him, when fate his tortur'd frame destroys,
What hope of present fame, or future joys?
For *this,* have heroes shorten'd nature's date;
For *that,* have martyrs gladly met their fate;
But him, forlorn, no hero's pride sustains,
No martyr's blissful visions sooth his pains;
Sullen, he mingles with his kindred dust,
For he has learn'd to dread the Christian's trust;
To him what mercy can that Pow'r display,
Whose servants murder, and whose sons betray?
Savage! thy venial errors I deplore,
They are *not* Christians who infest thy shore.
  O thou sad spirit, whose preposterous yoke
The great deliverer Death, at length, has broke!
Released from misery, and escaped from care,
Go, meet that mercy man denied thee here.
In thy dark home, sure refuge of th' oppress'd,
The wicked vex not, and the weary rest.
And, if some notions, vague and undefined,
Of future terrors have assail'd thy mind;
If such thy masters have presumed to teach,
As terrors only they are prone to preach;
(For should they paint eternal Mercy's reign,
Where were th' oppressor's rod, the captive's chain?)
If, then, thy troubled soul has learn'd to dread
The dark unknown thy trembling footsteps tread;
On HIM, who made thee what thou art, depend;
HE, who withholds the means, accepts the end.
Not *thine* the reckoning dire of LIGHT abused,
KNOWLEDGE disgraced, and LIBERTY misused;
On *thee* no awful judge incensed shall sit
For parts perverted, and dishonour'd wit.

[7] **sense of feeling**: "Nothing is more frequent than this cruel and stupid argument, that they do not *feel* the miseries inflicted on them as Europeans would do" [H. M.].

[8] **Congo's waters**: the Congo River flows 2,720 miles through Zaïre to the Atlantic Ocean in equatorial Africa. **Tiber**: River flowing 250 miles through central Italy, and through the middle of Rome.

[9] **Zeno**: Zeno of Citium (c. 334–c. 262 BC), Greek philosopher and founder of **Stoicism**, a complex philosophy sometimes reduced to a belief that pain, like pleasure, should be borne with indifference.

[10] **sharp iron**: "This is not said figuratively. The writer of these lines has seen a complete set of chains, fitted to every separate limb of these unhappy, innocent men; together with instruments for wrenching open the jaws, contrived with such ingenious cruelty as would gratify the tender mercies of an inquisitor" [H. M.].

Where ignorance will be found the surest plea,
How many learn'd and wise shall envy *thee!*
 And thou, WHITE SAVAGE! whether lust of gold,
Or lust of conquest, rule thee uncontroll'd!
Hero or robber! — by whatever name
Thou plead thy impious claim to wealth or fame;
Whether inferior mischiefs be thy boast,
A petty tyrant rifling Gambia's coast;
Or bolder carnage track thy crimson way,
Kings dispossess'd, and provinces thy prey:
Panting to tame wide earth's remotest bound;
All Cortez[11] murder'd, all Columbus found;
O'er plunder'd realms to reign, detested Lord,
Make millions wretched, and thyself abhorr'd: —
In Reason's eye, in Wisdom's fair account,
Your sum of glory boasts a like amount;
The means may differ, but the end's the same;
Conquest is pillage with a nobler name.
Who makes the sum of human blessings less,
Or sinks the stock of general happiness,
No solid fame shall grace, no true renown
His life shall blazon, or his memory crown.
 Had those advent'rous spirits who explore
Through ocean's trackless wastes the far-sought shore:
Whether of wealth insatiate, or of power,
Conquerors who waste, or ruffians who devour:
Had these possess'd, O Cook![12] thy gentle mind,
Thy love of arts, thy love of human kind;
Had these pursued thy mild and liberal plan,
DISCOVERERS had not been a curse to man!
Then, bless'd Philanthropy! thy social hands
Had link'd dissever'd worlds in brothers' bands;
Careless, if colour, or if clime divide,
Then, loved, and loving, man had lived and died.
 The purest wreaths which hang on glory's shrine,
For empires founded, peaceful PENN![13] are thine;
No blood-stain'd laurels crown'd thy virtuous toil,
No slaughter'd natives drench'd thy fair-earn'd soil.
Still thy meek spirit in thy flock survives,
Consistent still, *their* doctrines rule their lives;
Thy followers only have effaced the shame
Inscribed by SLAVERY on the Christian name.
 Shall Britain, where the soul of Freedom reigns,
Forge chains for others she herself disdains?
Forbid it, Heaven! O let the nations know
The liberty she loves she will bestow;
Not to herself the glorious gift confined,
She spreads the blessing wide as humankind;
And, scorning narrow views of time and place,
Bids all be free in earth's extended space.
 What page of human annals can record
A deed so bright as human rights restored?
O may that godlike deed, that shining page,
Redeem OUR fame, and consecrate OUR age!
 And see, the cherub Mercy from above,
Descending softly, quits the sphere of love!
On feeling hearts she sheds celestial dew,
And breathes her spirit o'er th' enlighten'd few,
From soul to soul the spreading influence steals,
Till every breast the soft contagion feels.
She bears, exulting, to the burning shore,
The loveliest office Angel ever bore:
To vindicate the pow'r in Heaven adored,
To still the clank of chains, and sheathe the sword;
To cheer the mourner, and with soothing hands
From bursting hearts unbind th' Oppressor's bands;
To raise the lustre of the Christian name,
And clear the foulest blot that dims its fame.
 As the mild Spirit hovers o'er the coast,
A fresher hue the wither'd landscapes boast;
Her healing smiles the ruin'd scenes repair,
And blasted Nature wears a joyous air.
She spreads her blest commission from above,
Stamp'd with the sacred characters of love,
She tears the banner stain'd with blood and tears,
And, LIBERTY! thy shining standard rears!
As the bright ensign's glory she displays,
See pale OPPRESSION faints beneath the blaze!
The giant dies! no more his frown appals,
The chain, untouch'd, drops off; the fetter falls.
Astonish'd Echo tells the vocal shore,
Oppression's fall'n, and Slavery is no more!
The dusky myriads crowd the sultry plain,
And hail that mercy long invoked in vain,
Victorious power! she bursts their two-fold bands,
And FAITH and FREEDOM spring from Mercy's hands.

[11] **Cortez:** Hernán Cortés (1485–1547), conqueror of Mexico on behalf of Spain.

[12] **Cook:** James Cook (1728–1779), English navigator and explorer of the south Pacific, Hawaii, and the western coast of North America.

[13] **Penn:** William Penn (1644–1718), English Quaker and founder of the colony of Pennsylvania, which was distinguished for its settlers' amicable relations with the Native Americans and for its religious toleration; further, as More notes, "the Quakers have emancipated all their slaves throughout America."

Village Politics

addressed to all the mechanics, journeymen, and labourers, in Great Britain
by Will Chip, a country carpenter
[Written early in the French Revolution]
(1792)

It is a privilege to be prescribed to in things about which our minds would otherwise be tost with various apprehensions. And for pleasure, I shall profess myself so far from doating on that popular idol, Liberty, that I hardly think it possible for any kind of obedience to be more painful than an unrestrained liberty. Were there not true bounds, of magistrates, of laws, of piety, of reason in the heart, every man would have a fool, nay, a mad tyrant to his master, that would multiply him more sorrows than the briars and thorns did to Adam, when he was freed from the bliss at once, and the restraint of Paradise, and became a greater slave in the wilderness than in the enclosure. —Dr. Hammond's Sermon.[1]

— A DIALOGUE —

BETWEEN JACK ANVIL, THE BLACKSMITH, AND TOM HOD, THE MASON

JACK: What's the matter, Tom? Why dost look so dismal!

TOM: Dismal, indeed! Well enough I may.

JACK: What! is the old mare dead? or work scarce?

TOM: No, no, work's plenty enough, if a man had but the heart to go to it.

JACK: What book art reading? Why dost look so like a hang dog?

TOM: *(Looking on his book.)* Cause enough. Why I find here that I'm very unhappy, and very miserable; which I should never have known if I had not had the good luck to meet with this book. Oh 'tis a precious book!

JACK: A good sign though; that you can't find out you're unhappy without looking into a book for it! What is the matter?

TOM: Matter? Why I want liberty.

JACK: Liberty! That's bad indeed! What! has any one fetched a warrant for thee? Come, man, cheer up, I'll be bound for thee. Thou art an honest fellow in the main, though thou dost tipple and prate a little too much at the Rose and Crown.

TOM: No, no, I want a new constitution.

JACK: Indeed! Why I thought thou hadst been a desperate healthy fellow. Send for the doctor directly.

TOM: I'm not sick; I want liberty and equality, and the rights of man.[2]

JACK: O, now I understand thee. What! thou art a leveller and a republican,[3] I warrant!

TOM: I'm a friend to the people. I want a reform.

JACK: Then the shortest way is to mend thy self.

TOM: But I want a *general reform.*

JACK: Then let every one mend one.

TOM: Pooh! I want freedom and happiness, the same as they have got in France.

JACK: What, Tom, we imitate them? We follow the French! Why they only began all this mischief at first in order to be just what *we* are already; and what a blessed land must this be, to be in actual possession of all they ever hoped to gain by all their hurly-burly. Imitate them indeed! —why I'd sooner go to the negroes to get learning, or to the Turks to get religion, than to the French for freedom and happiness.

TOM: What do you mean by that? ar'n't the French free?

JACK: Free, Tom! ay free with a witness. They are all so free that there's nobody safe. They make free to rob whom they will, and kill whom they will. If they don't like a man's looks, they make free to hang him without judge or jury, and the next lamp-post serves for the gallows; so then they call themselves free, because you see they have no law left to condemn them, and no king to take them up and hang them for it.

---

[1] **Dr. Hammond's Sermon:** probably one of the 21 sermons published in 1664 by Henry Hammond (1605–1660), English theologian and clergyman, active on the side of Charles I during the English Revolution.

[2] **rights of man:** allusion to *The Rights of Man** (1791–1792) by the Anglo-American radical author Thomas Paine* (1737–1809), in which he defended the French Revolution on the basis of a theory of natural rights, and for which he was prosecuted for treason.

[3] **Leveller and republican** were common eighteenth-century terms, often used interchangeably, for those who believed in social and political equality; the Levellers were originally a Puritan sect from the time of the English Civil War (1642–1648) who argued for equality and the abolition of class privilege.

TOM: Ah, but Jack, didn't their king formerly hang people for nothing too? and besides, were they not all papists before the revolution?

JACK: Why, true enough, they had but a poor sort of religion; but bad is better than none, Tom. And so was the government bad enough too; for they could clap an innocent man into prison, and keep him there too as long as they would, and never say, with your leave or by your leave, gentlemen of the jury. But what's all that to us?

TOM: To us! Why don't many of our governors put many of our poor folks in prison against their will? What are all the jails for? Down with the jails, I say; all men should be free.

JACK: Harkee, Tom, a few rogues in prison keep the rest in order, and then honest men go about their business in safety, afraid of nobody; that's the way to be free. And let me tell thee, Tom, thou and I are tried by our peers as much as a lord is. Why the *king* can't send me to prison if I do no harm; and if I do, there's reason good why I should go there. I may go to law with Sir John at the great castle yonder; and he no more dares lift his little finger against me than if I were his equal. A lord is hanged for hanging matter, as thou or I should be; and if it will be any comfort to thee, I myself remember a peer of the realm being hanged for killing his man, just the same as the man would have been for killing *him*.[4]

TOM: A lord! Well, that is some comfort to be sure. But have you read the Rights of Man?

JACK: No, not I: I had rather by half read the *Whole Duty of Man*.[5] I have but little time for reading, and such as I should therefore only read a bit of the best.

TOM: Don't tell me of those old-fashioned notions. Why should not we have the same fine things they have got in France? I'm for a *constitution*, and *organization*, and *equalization*, and *fraternization*.[6]

JACK: Do be quiet. Now, Tom, only suppose this nonsensical equality was to take place; why it would not last while one could say Jack Robinson; or suppose it could—suppose in the general division, our new rulers were to give us half an acre of ground a-piece; we could to be sure raise potatoes on it for the use of our families; but as every other man would be equally busy in raising potatoes for *his* family, why then you see if thou wast to break thy spade, I, whose trade it is, should no longer be able to mend it. Neighbour Snip would have no time to make us a suit of clothes, nor the clothier to weave the cloth; for all the world would be gone a digging. And as to boots and shoes, the want of some one to make them for us, would be a still greater grievance than the tax on leather. If we should be sick, there would be no doctor's stuff for us; for doctors would be digging too. And if necessity did not compel, and if inequality subsisted, we could not get a chimney swept, or a load of coal from pit, for love or money.

TOM: But still I should have no one over my head.

JACK: That's a mistake: I'm stronger than thou; and Standish, the exciseman, is a better scholar; so that we should not remain equal a minute. I should out-*fight* thee, and he'd out-*wit* thee. And if such a sturdy fellow as I am, was to come and break down thy hedge for a little firing, or take away the crop from thy ground, I'm not so sure that these new-fangled laws would see thee righted. I tell thee, Tom, we have a fine constitution already, and our forefathers thought so.

TOM: They were a pack of fools, and had never read the Rights of Man.

JACK: I'll tell thee a story. When Sir John married, my lady, who is a little fantastical, and likes to do every thing like the French, begged him to pull down yonder fine old castle, and build it up in her frippery way. No, says Sir John, what shall I pull down this noble building, raised by the wisdom of my brave ancestors; which outstood the civil wars, and only underwent a little needful repair at the revolution; a castle which all my neighbours come to take a pattern by—shall I pull it all down, I say, only because there may be a dark closet, or an awkward passage, or an inconvenient room or two in it? Our ancestors took *time* for what they did. They understood *foundation* work; no running up your little slight lath and plaster buildings, which are up in a day, and down in a night. My lady mumpt and grumbled; but the castle was let stand, and a glorious building it is;

[4] **for killing him**: "Lord Ferrers was hanged in 1760, for killing his steward" [H. M.].

[5] **the Whole Duty of Man**: title of a work by Richard Allestree (1619–1681), English clergyman and provost of Eton College, who fought on the king's side during the English Revolution.

[6] **constitution, and organization, and equalization, and fraternization**: all terms associated with the French Revolution—as in the motto *"Liberté, Egalité, Fraternité"*—and with the reformist strain in British politics, which has worked (unsuccessfully) for a written constitution since the seventeenth century.

though there may be a trifling fault or two, and though a few decays want stopping; so now and then they mend a little thing, and they'll go on mending, I dare say, as they have leisure, to the end of the chapter, if they are let alone. But no pull-me-down works. What is it you are crying out for, Tom?

TOM: Why for a perfect government.

JACK: You might as well cry for the moon. There's nothing perfect in this world, take my word for it: though Sir John says, we come nearer to it than any country in the world ever did.

TOM: I don't see why we are to work like slaves, while others roll about in their coaches, feed on the fat of the land, and do nothing.

JACK: My little maid brought home a storybook from the charity school[7] t'other day, in which was a bit of a fable about the belly and the limbs. The hands said, I won't work any longer to feed this lazy belly, who sits in state like a lord and does nothing. Said the feet I won't walk and tire myself to carry him about; let him shift for himself; so said all the members; just as your levellers and republicans do now. And what was the consequence? Why the belly was pinched to be sure, and grew thin upon it; but the hands and the feet, and the rest of the members, suffered so much for want of their old nourishment, which the belly had been all the time administering, while they accused him of sitting in idle state, that they all fell sick, pined away, and would have died, if they had not come to their senses just in time to save their lives, as I hope all you will do.

TOM: But the times—but the taxes, Jack.

JACK: Things are dear to be sure, but riot and murder is not the way to make them cheap. And taxes are high; but I'm told there's a deal of old scores paying off, and paying off, by them who did not contract the debt neither, Tom. Besides things are mending, I hope; and what little is done is for us poor people; our candles are somewhat cheaper, and I dare say, if the honest gentleman who has the management of things, is not disturbed by you levellers, things will mend every day. But bear one thing in mind: the more we riot, the more we shall have to pay: the more mischief is done, the more will the repairs cost: the more time we waste in meeting to redress public wrongs, the more we shall increase our private wants. And mind too, that 'tis working, and not murmuring, which puts bread in our children's mouths, and a new coat on our backs. Mind another thing too, we have not the same ground of complaint; in France the poor paid all the taxes, as I have heard 'em say, and the quality paid nothing.

TOM: Well, I know what's what, as well as another; and I'm as fit to govern—

JACK: No, Tom, no. You are indeed as good as another man, seeing you have hands to work, and a soul to be saved. But are all men fit for all kind of things? Solomon says 'How can he be wise whose talk is of oxen?'[8] Every one in his way. I am a better judge of a horse-shoe than Sir John; but he has a deal better notion of state affairs than I; and I can no more do without his employ than he can do without my farriery.[9] Besides, few are so poor but they may get a vote for a parliament-man; and so you see the poor have as much share in the government as they well know how to manage.

TOM: But I say all men are equal. Why should one be above another?

JACK: If that's thy talk, Tom, thou dost quarrel with Providence, and not with government. For the woman is below her husband, and the children are below their mother, and the servant is below his master.

TOM: But the subject is not below the king: all kings are 'crown'd ruffians': and all governments are wicked. For my part, I'm resolv'd I'll pay no more taxes to any of them.

JACK: Tom, Tom, if thou didst go oft'ner to church, thou wouldst know where it is said, 'Render unto Cæsar the things that are Cæsar's'; and also, 'Fear God, honour the king.'[10] *Your* book tells you that we need obey no government but that of the people;

[7] **charity school:** a school established by private contributions for the education of the children of the poor; the charity school movement of the eighteenth and earlier nineteenth centuries was later overtaken by the creation of a system of universal free public education.

[8] **Solomon says:** "How can he get wisdom that holdeth the plough, and that glorieth in the goad, that driveth oxen, and is occupied in their labours, and whose talk is of bullocks?" Ecclesiasticus 38:25.

[9] **farriery:** the shoeing and treatment of horses, including veterinary services.

[10] **Render unto Caesar:** Mark 12:1. **Fear God:** 1 Peter 2:17.

and that we may fashion and alter the government according to our whimsies: but *mine* tells me, 'Let every one be subject to the higher powers,[11] for all power is of God, the powers that be are ordained of God; whosoever therefore resisteth the power, resisteth the ordinance of God.' Thou say'st, thou wilt pay no taxes to any of them.—Dost thou know who it was that worked a miracle, that he might have money to pay tribute with, rather than set you and me an example of disobedience to government? an example, let me tell thee, worth an hundred precepts, and of which all the wit of man can never lessen the value. Then there's another thing worth minding, when St. Paul was giving all those directions, in the epistle to the Romans, for obedience and submission; what sort of a king now dost think they had? Dost think 'twas a *saint* which he ordered them to obey?

TOM: Why it was a kind, merciful, charitable king to be sure; one who put nobody to death or to prison.

JACK: You was never more out in your life. Our parson says he was a monster—that he robbed the rich, and murdered the poor—set fire to his own town, as fine a place as London—fiddled to the flames, and then hanged and burnt the Christians, who were all poor, as if they had burnt the town. Yet there's not a word about rising.—Duties are fixed, Tom.—Laws are settled; a Christian can't pick and choose, whether he will obey or let it alone. But *we* have no such trials.—We have a king the very reverse.

TOM: I say we shall never be happy, till we do as the French have done.

JACK: The French and we contending for liberty, Tom, is just as if thou and I were to pretend to run a race; thou to set out from the starting-post when I am in already; thou to have all the ground to travel when I have reached the end. Why we've got it man! we've no race to run! we're there already! Our constitution is no more like what the French one was, than a mug of our Taunton beer is like a platter of their soup-maigre.

TOM: I know we shall be undone, if we don't get a new *constitution*—that's all.

JACK: And I know we shall be undone if we *do*. I don't know much about politics, but I can see by a little, what a great deal means. Now only to show thee the state of public credit, as I think Tim Standish calls it. There's farmer Furrow, a few years ago he had an odd fifty pounds by him; so to keep it out of harm's way, he put it out to use, on government security, I think he calls it; well, t'other day he married one of his daughters, so he thought he'd give her that fifty pounds for a bit of a portion. Tom, as I'm a living man, when he went to take it out, if his fifty pounds was not almost grown to an hundred! and would have been a full hundred, they say, by this time, if the gentlemen had been let alone.

TOM: Well, still as the old saying is—I should like to do as they do in France.

JACK: What, shouldest like to be murdered with as little ceremony as Hackabout, the butcher, knocks down a calf? or shouldest like to get rid of thy wife for every little bit of tiff? And as for liberty of *conscience*, which they brag so much about, why they have driven away their parsons (ay, and murdered many of 'em) because they would not swear as they would have them. And then they talk of liberty of the press; why, Tom, only t'other day they hang'd a man for printing a book against this pretty government of theirs.

TOM: But you said yourself it was sad times in France, before they pull'd down the old government.

JACK: Well, and suppose the French were as much in the right as I know them to be in the wrong; what does that argue for *us*?—Because my neighbour Furrow, t'other day pulled down a crazy old barn, is that a reason why I must set fire to my tight cottage?

TOM: I don't see for all that why one man is to ride in his coach and six, while another mends the highway for him.

JACK: I don't see why the man in the coach is to *drive over* the man on foot, or hurt a hair of his head, any more than you. And as to our great folks, that you levellers have such a spite against, I don't pretend to say they are a bit better than they should be; but that's no affair of mine; let them look to that they'll answer for that in another place. To be sure, I wish they'd set us a better example about going to church, and those things; but still *hoarding's* not the sin of the age; they don't lock up their *money*—away it goes, and every body's the better for it.—They do spend too much, to be sure, in feastings and

[11] **Let every one be subject to the higher powers:** Romans 13:1–2.

fandangoes; and so far from commending them for it, if I was a parson I'd go to work with 'em, but it should be in another kind of way; but as I am only a poor tradesman, why 'tis but bringing more grist to my mill. It all comes among the people. Their very extravagance, for which, as I said before, their parsons should be at them, is a fault by which, as poor men, we are benefitted; so you cry out just in the wrong place. Their coaches and their furniture, and their buildings, and their planting, employ a power of tradesmen and labourers. Now in this village, what should we do without the castle? Though my lady is too rantipolish,[12] and flies about all summer to hot water and cold water, and fresh water and salt water, when she ought to stay at home with Sir John: yet when she does come down, she brings such a deal of gentry that I have more horses than I can shoe, and my wife more linen than she can wash. Then all our grown children are servants in the family, and rare wages they have got. Our little boys get something every day by weeding their gardens, and the girls learn to sew and knit at Sir John's expense, who sends them all to school of a Sunday besides.

TOM: Ay, but there's not Sir Johns in every village.

JACK: The more's the pity. But there's other help. 'Twas but last year you broke your leg, and was nine weeks in the Bristol Infirmary,[13] where you was taken as much care of as a lord, and your family was maintained all the while by the parish. No poor-rates in France, Tom; and here there's a matter of two million and a half paid for the poor every year, if 'twas but a little better managed.

TOM: Two million and a half!

JACK: Ay, indeed, not translated into tenpences, as your French millions are, but twenty good shillings to the pound. But when this levelling comes about, there will be no infirmaries, no hospitals, no charity-schools, no Sunday-schools, where so many hundred thousand poor souls learn to read the word of God for nothing.—For who is to pay for them? *Equality* can't afford it; and those that may be willing won't be able.

TOM: But we shall be one as good as another for all that.

JACK: Ay, and bad will be the best. But we must work as we do now, and with this difference, that no one will be able to pay us. Tom! I have got the use of my limbs, of my liberty, of the laws, and of my Bible. The two first I take to be my natural rights; the two last my civil and religious rights: these, I take it, are the *true Rights of Man*, and all the rest is no thing but nonsense, and madness, and wickedness. My cottage is my castle; I sit down in it at night in peace and thankfulness, and 'no man maketh me afraid.' Instead of indulging discontent, because another is richer than I in this world (for envy is at the bottom of your equality works) I read my Bible, go to church, and look forward to a treasure in Heaven.

TOM: Ay, but the French have got it in *this* world.

JACK: 'Tis all a lie, Tom. Sir John's butler says his master gets letters which *say* 'tis all a lie. 'Tis all murder, and nakedness, and hunger, many of the poor soldiers fight without victuals, and march without clothes. These are your *democrats!* Tom.

TOM: What then, dost think all the men on our side wicked?

JACK: No—not so neither—If some of the leaders are knaves, more of the followers are fools. Sir John, who is wiser than I, says the whole system is the operation of fraud upon folly. They've made fools of most of you, as I believe. I judge no man Tom; I hate no man. Even republicans and levellers, I hope, will always enjoy the protection of our laws; though I hope they will never be our law *makers*. There are many true dissenters, and there are some hollow churchmen; and a good man is a good man, whether his church has got a steeple to it or not.—The new fashion'd way of proving one's religion is to *hate* somebody. Now, though some folk pretend that a man's hating a papist, or a presbyterian, proves him to be a good *churchman*, it don't prove him to be a good *Christian*, Tom. As much as I hate republican works, I'd scorn to *live* in a country where there was not liberty of conscience; and where every man might not worship God in his own way. Now that liberty they had not in France: the Bible was shut up in an unknown and heathenish tongue.[14]—While

---

[12] **rantipolish**: behaving in a romping, rude, or noisy manner.

[13] **Bristol Infirmary**: hospital for the poor; supported by charity. **Poor-rates**: taxes (usually on property owners) for the relief or support of the poor.

[14] **the Bible was shut up in an unknown and heathenish tongue**: in Roman Catholic countries such as France, Bibles were generally, at least through the eighteenth century, published in Latin, which effectively kept them out of the hands of lay people.

here, thou and I can make as free use of ours as a bishop: can no more be sent to prison unjustly than the judge who tries us; and are as much taken care of by the laws as the parliament-man who makes them.—Then, as to your thinking that the new scheme will make you happy, look among your own set and see if any thing can be so dismal and discontented as a leveller.—Look at France. Those poor French fellows used to be the merriest dogs in the world; but since equality came in, I don't believe a Frenchman has ever laughed.

TOM: What then dost thou take French *liberty* to be?

JACK: To murder more men in one night, than ever their poor king did in his whole life.

TOM: And what dost thou take a *democrat* to be?

JACK: One who lives to be governed by a thousand tyrants, and yet can't bear a king.

TOM: What is *equality*?

JACK: For every man to pull down every one that is above him: while, instead of raising those below him, to his own level, he only makes use of them as steps to raise himself to the place of those he has tumbled down.

TOM: What is the *new Rights of Man*?

JACK: Battle, murder, and sudden death.

TOM: What is it to be *an enlightened people*?

JACK: To put out the light of the Gospel, confound right and wrong, and grope about in pitch darkness.

TOM: What is *philosophy*, that Tim Standish talks so much about?

JACK: To believe that there's neither God, nor devil, nor heaven, nor hell: to dig up a wicked old fellow's[15] rotten bones, whose books, Sir John says, have been the ruin of thousands; and to set his figure up in a church and worship him.

TOM: And what is a *patriot* according to the new school?

JACK: A man who loves every other country better than his own, and France best of all.

TOM: And what is *Benevolence*?

JACK: Why, in the new fangled language, it means contempt of religion, aversion to justice, overturning of law, doating on all mankind in general, and hating every body in particular.

TOM: And what mean the other hard words that Tim talks about—*organization* and *function*, and *civism*, and *incivism*, and *equalization*, and *inviolability*, and *imperscriptible*, and *fraternization*?

JACK: Nonsense, gibberish, downright hocus-pocus. I know 'tis not English; Sir John says 'tis not Latin; and his valet de sham[16] says 'tis not French neither.

TOM: And yet Tim says he never shall be happy till all these fine things are brought over to England.

JACK: What! in this christian country, Tom? Why dost know they have no *Sabbath* in France? Their mob parliament meets on a Sunday to do their wicked work, as naturally as we do to go to church. They have renounced God's word and God's day, and they don't even date in the year of our Lord. Why dost turn pale, man? And the rogues are always making such a noise, Tom, in the midst of their parliament-house, that their speaker rings a bell, like our penny-post man, because he can't keep them in order.

TOM: And dost thou believe they are as cruel as some folks pretend?

JACK: I am sure they are, and I think I know the reason. We Christians set a high value on life, because we know that every fellow-creature has an immortal soul: a soul to be saved or lost, Tom—Whoever believes that, is a little cautious how he sends a soul unprepared to his grand account. But he who believes a man is no better than a dog will make no more scruple of killing one than the other.

TOM: And dost thou think our Rights of Man will lead to all this wickedness?

JACK: As sure as eggs are eggs.

TOM: I begin to think we're better off as we are.

JACK: I'm sure on't. This is only a scheme to make us go back in every thing. 'Tis making ourselves poor when we are getting rich, and discontented when we are comfortable.

TOM: I begin to think I'm not so very unhappy as I had got to fancy.

JACK: Tom, I don't care for drink myself, but thou dost, and I'll argue with thee, not in the way of principle, but in thy own way; when there's all equality there will be no *superfluity*; when there's no wages there'll be no drink: and levelling will rob thee of thy ale more than the malt tax does.

[15] **a wicked old fellow:** "Voltaire" [H. M.]. The French philosopher Voltaire (1694–1778) was among the leading figures of the Enlightenment, an intellectual movement associated with a belief in reason, liberal political reform, secularism, tolerance, and freethinking in religion.

[16] **valet de sham:** *"valet de chambre"* or personal servant.

TOM: But Standish says, if we had a good government, there'd be no want of any thing.

JACK: He is like many others, who take the king's money and betray him: let him give up the profits of his place before he kicks at the hand that feeds him.—Though I'm no scholar, I know that a good government is a good thing. But don't go to make me believe that *any* government can make a bad man good, or a discontented man happy.—What art musing upon, man?

TOM: Let me sum up the evidence, as they say at 'sizes'[17]—Hem! To cut every man's throat who does not think as I do, or hang him up at a lamp-post!—Pretend liberty of conscience, and then banish the parsons only for being conscientious!—Cry out liberty of the press, and hang up the first man who writes his mind!—Lose our poor laws!—Lose one's wife perhaps upon every little tiff!—March without clothes, and fight without victuals!—No trade!—No Bible! No Sabbath nor day of rest!—No safety, no comfort, no peace in this world—and no world to come!—Jack, I never knew thee tell a lie in my life.

JACK: Nor would I now, not even against the French.

TOM: And thou art very sure we are not ruined?

JACK: I'll tell thee how we are ruined. We have a king, so loving, that he would not hurt the people if he could: and so kept in, that he could not hurt the people if he would. We have as much liberty as can make us happy, and more trade and riches than allows us to be good. We have the best laws in the world, if they were more strictly enforced; and the best religion in the world if it was but better followed. While old England is safe, I'll glory in her, and pray for her, and when she is in danger, I'll fight for her, and die for her.

TOM: And so will I too, Jack, that's what I will, *(Sings)* 'O the roast beef of old England!'[18]

JACK: Thou art an honest fellow, Tom.

TOM: This is Rose and Crown night, and Tim Standish is now at his mischief; but we'll go and put an end to that fellow's work, or he'll corrupt the whole club.

JACK: Come along.

TOM: No; first I'll stay to burn my book, and then I'll go and make a bonfire and—

JACK: Hold, Tom. There is but one thing worse than a bitter enemy—and that is an imprudent friend. If thou would'st show thy love to thy king and country, let's have no drinking, no riot, no bonfires: put in practice this text, which our parson preach'd on last Sunday, 'Study to be quiet,[19] work with your own hands, and mind your own business.'

TOM: And so I will, Jack—Come on.

[17] **'sizes:** assizes, court sessions held several times yearly in England and Wales for the trial of civil or criminal cases.

[18] **'O the roast beef of old England:** the first line of a popular song in praise of English life and customs.

[19] **Study to be quiet:** 1 Thessalonians 4:11.

from CHEAP REPOSITORY TRACTS
(1795–1798)

Patient Joe; or, The Newcastle Collier
(1795)

Have you heard of a collier of honest renown,
Who dwelt on the borders of Newcastle[1] town?
His name it was Joseph—you better may know
If I tell you he always was call'd Patient Joe.

Whatever betided, he thought it was right,
And Providence still he kept ever in sight;
To those who love God, let things turn as they would,
He was certain that all work'd together for good.

He praised his Creator whatever befell;
How thankful was Joseph when matters went well!
How sincere were his carols of praise for good health,
And how grateful for any increase in his wealth!

In trouble he bow'd him to God's holy will;
How contented was Joseph when matters went ill!
When rich and when poor, he alike understood
That all things together were working for good.

If the land was afflicted with war, he declared
'Twas a needful correction for sins which he shared:
And when merciful Heaven bade slaughter to cease,
How thankful was Joe for the blessing of peace!

[1] **Newcastle:** Newcastle upon Tyne, a coal-mining and shipping center in northeastern England.

When taxes ran high, and provisions were dear,
Still Joseph declared he had nothing to fear;
It was but a trial he well understood,
From Him who made all work together for good.

Though his wife was but sickly, his gettings but small,
Yet a mind so submissive prepared him for all;
He lived on his gains, were they greater or less,
And the Giver he ceased not each moment to bless.

When another child came he received him with joy,
And Providence bless'd, who had sent him the boy!
But when the child died, said poor Joe, I'm content,
For God had a right to recall what he lent.

It was Joseph's ill-fortune to work in a pit
With some who believed that profaneness was wit;
When disasters befell him, much pleasure they show'd,
And laugh'd and said, "Joseph, will this work for good?"

But ever when these would profanely advance
That this happen'd by luck, and that happen'd by
 chance;
Still Joseph insisted no chance could be found,
Not a sparrow by accident falls to the ground.

Among his companions who work'd in the pit,
And made him the butt of their profligate wit,
Was idle Tim Jenkins, who drank and who gamed,
Who mock'd at his Bible, and was not ashamed.

One day at the pit his old comrades he found,
And they chatted, preparing to go under-ground;
Tim Jenkins, as usual, was turning to jest
Joe's notion—that all things which happen'd were
 best.[2]

As Joe on the ground had unthinkingly laid
His provision for dinner, of bacon and bread,
A dog, on the watch, seized the bread and the meat,
And off with his prey ran with footsteps so fleet.

Now to see the delight that Tim Jenkins express'd;
"Is the loss of thy dinner too, Joe, for the best?"
"No doubt on't," said Joe; "but as I must eat,
'Tis my duty to try to recover my meat."

So saying, he followed the dog a long round,
While Tim, laughing and swearing, went down
 under-ground.
Poor Joe soon return'd, though his bacon was lost,
For the dog a good dinner had made at his cost.

When Joseph came back he expected a sneer,
But the face of each collier spoke horror and fear;
"What a narrow escape hast thou had," they all said,
"The pit is fall'n in, and Tim Jenkins is dead!"

How sincere was the gratitude Joseph express'd!
How warm the compassion which glow'd in his
 breast!
Thus events great and small, if aright understood,
Will be found to be working together for good.[3]

"When my meat," Joseph cried, "was just now stol'n
 away,
"And I had no prospect of eating to-day,
"How could it appear to a short-sighted sinner,
"That my life would be saved by the loss of my dinner?"

[2] **all things . . . were best:** reference to philosophical optimism, ridiculed by Voltaire in *Candide, or Optimism* (1759).

[3] **Thus events . . . for good:** see Pope's *Essay on Man*, I.285–294, which concludes: "Whatever is, is right."

The Riot; or Half a Loaf Is Better Than No Bread

in a dialogue between Jack Anvil and Tom Hod
To the Tune of—"A Cobbler there was."
[Written in Ninety-five, a Year of Scarcity and Alarm[1]]
(1795)

TOM

Come, neighbours, no longer be patient and quiet,
Come let us go kick up a bit of a riot;
I'm hungry, my lads, but I've little to eat,
So we'll pull down the mills, and we'll seize all the
 meat:
I'll give you good sport, boys, as ever you saw,
So a fig for the justice, a fig for the law.
 Derry down.

Then his pitchfork Tom seized—Hold a moment,
 says Jack,
I'll show thee thy blunder, brave boy, in a crack,
And if I don't prove we had better be still,

[1] **Ninety-five, a Year of Scarcity and Alarm:** in the wake of the French Revolution (from 1789) and the military buildup that followed, there were periodic fears in Britain during the 1790s of a French invasion, and the costs of war with France caused considerable economic hardship.

I'll assist thee straightway to pull down every mill;
I'll show thee how passion thy reason does cheat,
Or I'll join thee in plunder for bread and for meat.
Derry down.

What a whimsey to think thus our bellies to fill,
For we stop all the grinding by breaking the mill!
What a whimsey to think we shall get more to eat
By abusing the butchers who get us the meat!
What a whimsey to think we shall mend our spare diet
By breeding disturbance, by murder, and riot!
Derry down.

Because I am dry, 'twould be foolish, I think,
To pull out my tap, and to spill all my drink;
Because I am hungry and want to be fed,
That is sure no wise reason for wasting my bread:
And just such wise reasons for mending their diet
Are used by those blockheads who rush into riot.
Derry down.

I would not take comfort from others' distresses,
But still I would mark how God our land blesses;
For though in Old England the times are but sad,
Abroad, I am told, they are ten times as bad;
In the land of the Pope there is scarce any grain,
And 'tis worse still, they say, both in Holland and Spain.
Derry down.

Let us look to the harvest our wants to beguile,
See the lands with rich crops how they everywhere smile!
Meantime to assist us, by each western breeze,
Some corn is brought daily across the salt seas!
Of tea we'll drink little, of gin none at all,
And we'll patiently wait, and the prices will fall.
Derry down.

But if we're not quiet, then let us not wonder
If things grow much worse by our riot and plunder;
And let us remember whenever we meet,
The more ale we drink, boys, the less we shall eat.
On those days spent in riot, no bread you brought home;
Had you spent them in labour, you must have had some.
Derry down.

A dinner of herbs, says the wise man, with quiet,
Is better than beef amid discord and riot.
If the thing could be help'd, I'm a foe to all strife,
And I pray for a peace every night of my life;
But in matters of state not an inch will I budge,
Because I conceive I'm no very good judge.
Derry down.

But though poor, I can work, my brave boy, with the best,
Let the king and the parliament manage the rest;
I lament both the war and the taxes together,
Though I verily think they don't alter the weather.
The king, as I take it, with very good reason,
May prevent a bad law, but can't help a bad season.
Derry down.

The parliament men, although great is their power,
Yet they cannot contrive us a bit of a shower;
And I never yet heard, though our rulers are wise,
That they know very well how to manage the skies;
For the best of them all, as they found to their cost,
Were not able to hinder last winter's hard frost.
Derry down.

Besides, I must share in the wants of the times,
Because I have had my full share in its crimes;
And I'm apt to believe the distress which is sent,
Is to punish and cure us of all discontent.
But harvest is coming — potatoes are come!
Our prospect clears up; ye complainers, be dumb!
Derry down.

And though I've no money, and though I've no lands,
I've head on my shoulders, and a pair of good hands;
So I'll work the whole day, and on Sundays I'll seek
At church how to bear all the wants of the week.
The gentlefolks too will afford us supplies,
They'll subscribe — and they'll give up their puddings and pies.
Derry down.

Then before I'm induced to take part in a riot,
I'll ask this short question — What shall I get by it?
So I'll e'en wait a little, till cheaper the bread,
For a mittimus[2] hangs o'er each rioter's head;
And when of two evils I'm ask'd which is best,
I'd rather be hungry than hang'd, I protest.
Derry down.

Quoth, Tom, thou art right; if I rise, I'm a Turk;
So he threw down his pitchfork, and went to his work.

---

[2] **mittimus:** a legal writ authorizing arrest and detention.

The Gin Shop; or, A Peep into Prison

(1795)

Look through the land from north to south,
And look from east to west,
And see what is to Englishmen
Of life the deadliest pest.

It is not want, though that is bad,
Nor war, though that is worse;
But Britons brave endure, alas!
A self-inflicted curse.

Go where you will, throughout the realm,
You'll find the reigning sin,
In cities, villages, and towns,
—The monster's name is GIN.

The prince of darkness never sent
To man a deadlier foe;
"My name is Legion," it may say,
The source of many a woe.

Nor does the fiend alone deprive
The labourer of his wealth;
That is not all, it murders too
His honest name and health.

We say the times are grievous hard,
And hard they are, 'tis true,
But, drunkards, to your wives and babes
They're harder made by you.

The drunkard's tax is self-imposed,
Like every other sin:
The taxes altogether lay
No weight so great as gin.

The state compels no man to drink,
Compels no man to game;
'Tis gin and gambling sink him down
To rags, and want, and shame.

The kindest husband, changed by gin,
Is for a tyrant known;
The tenderest heart that nature made
Becomes a heart of stone.

In many a house the harmless babes
Are poorly clothed and fed,
Because the craving gin-shop takes
The children's daily bread.

Come, neighbour, take a walk with me,
Through many a London street,
And see the cause of penury
In hundreds we shall meet.

We shall not need to travel far—
Behold that great man's door,
He well discerns yon idle crew
From the deserving poor.

He will relieve with liberal hand
The child of honest thrift;
But where long scores at gin-shops stand,
He will withhold his gift.

Behold that shivering female there,
Who plies her woeful trade!
'Tis ten to one you'll find that gin
That hopeless wretch has made.

Look down those steps, and view below
Yon cellar under-ground,
There every want and every woe,
And every sin is found.

Those little wretches trembling there,
With hunger and with cold,
Were, by their parents' love of gin,
To sin and misery sold.

Blest be those friends to humankind[1]
Who take these wretches up,
Ere they have drunk the bitter dregs
Of their sad parents' cup.

Look through that prison's iron bars,
Look through that dismal grate,
And learn what dire misfortune brought
So terrible a fate.

The debtor and the felon too,
Though differing much in sin,
Too oft you'll find were thither brought
By all-destroying gin.

Yet Heaven forbid I should confound
Calamity with guilt!
Or name the debtor's lesser fault
With blood of brother spilt.

[1] **friends to humankind**: "The Philanthropic Society" [H. M.].

To prison dire misfortune oft
 The guiltless debtor brings;
Yet oftener far it will be found
 From gin the misery springs.

See the pale manufact'rer there,
 How lank and lean he lies
How haggard is his sickly cheek!
 How dim his hollow eyes!

He plied the loom with good success,
 His wages still were high,
Twice what the village labourer gains
 His master did supply.

No book-debts kept him from his cash,
 All paid as soon as due;
His wages on the Saturday
 To fail he never knew.

How amply had his gains sufficed,
 On wife and children spent!
But all must for his pleasures go,
 All to the gin-shop went.

See that apprentice, young in years,
 But hackney'd[2] long in sin,
What made him rob his master's till?
 Alas! 'twas love of gin.

That serving-man—I knew him once,
 So jaunty, spruce, and smart!
Why did he steal, then pawn the plate?
 'Twas gin ensnared his heart.

But hark! what dismal sound was that
 'Tis Saint Sepulchre's bell![3]
It tolls, alas, for human guilt!
 Some malefactor's knell.

O woful sound! Oh! what could cause
 Such punishment and sin?
Hark! hear his words, he owns the cause—
 Bad company and gin.

And when the future lot is fix'd,
 Of darkness, fire, and chains,
How can the drunkard hope to 'scape
 Those everlasting pains?

For if the murderer's doomed to woe,
 As holy-writ declares,
The drunkard with self-murderers
 That dreadful portion shares.

[2] **hackney'd:** habituated by long practice; experienced.

[3] **Saint Sepulchre's bell:** the bell of St. Sepulchre's Church, London, was rung when condemned criminals passed it on their way to the gallows.

from Strictures on the Modern System of Female Education
(1799)

— INTRODUCTION —

It is a singular injustice which is often exercised towards women, first to give them a very defective education, and then to expect from them the most undeviating purity of conduct; to train them in such a manner as shall lay them open to the most dangerous faults, and then to censure them for not proving faultless. Is it not unreasonable and unjust, to express disappointment if our daughters should, in their subsequent lives, turn out precisely that very kind of character for which it would be evident to an unprejudiced by-stander, that the whole scope and tenor of their instruction had been systematically preparing them?

Some reflections on the present erroneous system are here with great deference submitted to public consideration. The author is apprehensive that she shall be accused of betraying the interests of her sex by laying open their defects; but surely, an earnest wish to turn their attention to objects calculated to promote their true dignity, is not the office of an enemy. So to expose the weakness of the land as to suggest the necessity of internal improvement, and to point out the means of effectual defence, is not treachery, but patriotism. . . .

— *from* CHAPTER I —

. . . The general state of civilized society depends more than those are aware who are not accustomed to scrutinize into the springs of human action, on the prevailing sentiments and habits of women, and on the nature and degree of the estimation in which they are held. Even those who admit the power of female elegance on the manners of men, do not always attend to the influence of female principles on their character. In the former case, indeed, women are apt to be sufficiently conscious of their power, and not backward in turning it to account. But there are nobler objects to be effected by the exertion of their powers; and unfortunately, ladies, who are often unreasonably confident where they ought to be diffident, are sometimes capriciously diffident just when they ought to feel where their true importance lies; and, feeling, to exert it. To use their boasted power over mankind to no higher purpose than the gratification of vanity or the indulgence of pleasure, is the degrading triumph of those fair victims to luxury, caprice, and despotism, whom the laws and the religion of the voluptuous prophet of Arabia[1] exclude from light, and liberty, and knowledge: and it is humbling to reflect, that in those countries in which fondness for the mere persons of women is carried to the highest excess, *they are slaves*; and that their moral and intellectual degradation increases in direct proportion to the adoration which is paid to mere external charms.

But I turn to the bright reverse of this mortifying scene; to a country where our sex enjoys the blessings of liberal instruction, of reasonable laws, of a pure religion, and all the endearing pleasures of an equal, social, virtuous, and delightful intercourse: I turn with an earnest hope, that women, thus richly endowed with the bounties of Providence, will not content themselves with polishing, when they are able to reform; with entertaining, when they may awaken; and with captivating for a day, when they may bring into action powers of which the effects may be commensurate with eternity.

In this moment of alarm and peril, I would call on them with a "warning voice," which should stir up every latent principle in their minds, and kindle every slumbering energy in their hearts; I would call on them to come forward, and contribute their full and fair proportion towards the saving of their country. But I would call on them to come forward, without departing from the refinement of their character, without derogating from the dignity of their rank, without blemishing the delicacy of their sex: I would call them to the best and most appropriate exertion of their power, to raise the depressed tone of public morals, and to awaken the drowsy spirit of religious principle. They know too well how arbitrarily they give the law to manners, and with how despotic a sway they fix the standard of fashion. But this is not enough; this is a low mark, a prize not worthy of their high and holy calling. For, on the use which women of the superior class may now be disposed to make of that power delegated to them by the courtesy of custom, by the honest gallantry of the heart, by the imperious control of virtuous affections, by the habits of civilized states, by the usages of polished society; on the use, I say, which they shall hereafter make of this influence, will depend, in no low degree, the well-being of those states, and the virtue and happiness, nay perhaps the very existence, of that society. . . .

But the great object to which *you*, who are or may be mothers, are more especially called, is the education of your children. If we are responsible for the use of influence in the case of those over whom we have no immediate control, in the case of our children we are responsible for the exercise of acknowledged *power*: a power wide in its extent, indefinite in its effects, and inestimable in its importance. On YOU depend in no small degree the principles of the whole rising generation. To your direction the daughters are almost exclusively committed; and until a certain age, to you also is consigned the mighty privilege of forming the hearts and minds of your infant sons. To YOU is made over the awfully important trust of infusing the first principles of piety into the tender minds of those who may one day be called to instruct, not families merely, but districts; to influence, not individuals, but senates. Your private exertions may at this moment be contributing to the future happiness, your domestic neglect, to the future ruin, of your country. And may you never forget, in this your early instruction of your offspring, nor they, in their future application of it, that religion is the only sure ground of morals; that private principle is the only solid basis of public virtue. O, think that they both may be fixed or forfeited for ever, according to the use you are now making of that power which God has delegated to you, and of which he will demand a strict account. By his blessing on your pious labours, may both sons and daughters hereafter "arise and call you blessed." And in the great day of general account, may every Christian mother be enabled through divine grace to say, with humble confidence, to her Maker and Redeemer, "Behold the children whom thou hast given me!" . . .

—*from* CHAPTER IV—

. . . But, though a well-bred young lady may lawfully learn most of the fashionable arts; yet, let me ask,—Does it seem to be the true end of education to make women of fashion dancers, singers, players, painters, actresses, sculptors, gilders, varnishers, engravers, and embroiderers? Most *men* are commonly destined to some profession, and their minds are consequently turned each to its respective object. Would it not be strange if they were called out to exercise their profession, or to set up their trade, with only a little general knowledge of the trades

[1] **the voluptuous prophet of Arabia:** Mohammed. More was drawing on the conventional European idea that women were uniquely limited or oppressed under Islamic law.

and professions of all other men, and without any previous definite application to their own peculiar calling? The profession of ladies, to which the bent of *their* instruction should be turned, is that of daughters, wives, mothers, and mistresses of families. They should be therefore trained with a view of these several conditions, and be furnished with a stock of ideas, and principles, and qualifications, and habits, ready to be applied and appropriated, as occasion may demand, to each of these respective situations. For though the arts which merely embellish life must claim admiration; yet, when a man of sense comes to marry, it is a companion whom he wants, and not an artist. It is not merely a creature who can paint, and play, and sing, and draw, and dress, and dance; it is a being who can comfort and counsel him; one who can reason, and reflect, and feel, and judge, and discourse, and discriminate; one who can assist him in his affairs, lighten his cares, sooth his sorrows, purify his joys, strengthen his principles, and educate his children. . . .

— *from* CHAPTER V —

. . . Young ladies should also be accustomed to set apart a fixed portion of their time, as sacred to the poor,[2] whether in relieving, instructing, or working for them; and the performance of this duty must not be left to the event of contingent circumstances, or the operation of accidental impressions; but it must be established into a principle, and wrought into a habit. A specific portion of the day must be allotted to it, on which no common engagement must be allowed to intrench. Those periods of time, which are not stated, are seldom turned to their proper use; and nothing short of a regular plan (which must, however, be sometimes made to give way to circumstances) insures the conscientious discharge of any duty. This will help to furnish a powerful remedy for that selfishness, whose strongholds (the truth cannot be too often repeated) it is the grand business of Christian education perpetually to attack. If we were but aware how much better it makes ourselves, to wish to see others better, and to assist in making them so, we should find that the good done would be of as much importance by the habit of doing good which it would induce in our own minds, as by its beneficial effects on the objects of our kindness.

— *from* CHAPTER XIV —

The practical use of female knowledge, with a sketch of the female character, and a comparative view of the sexes.

....

The chief end to be proposed in cultivating the understandings of women, is to qualify them for the practical purposes of life. Their knowledge is not often, like the learning of men, to be reproduced in some literary composition, nor ever in any learned profession; but it is to come out in conduct. It is to be exhibited in life and manners. A lady studies, not that she may qualify herself to become an orator or a pleader; not that she may learn to debate, but to act. She is to read the best books, not so much to enable her to talk of them, as to bring the improvement which they furnish, to the rectification of her principles and the formation of her habits. The great uses of study to a woman are to enable her to regulate her own mind, and to be instrumental to the good of others.

To woman, therefore, whatever be her rank, I would recommend a predominance of those more sober studies, which, not having display for their object, may make her wise without vanity, happy without witnesses, and content without panegyrists; the exercise of which will not bring celebrity, but improve usefulness. She should pursue every kind of study which will teach her to elicit truth; which will lead her to be intent upon realities; will give precision to her ideas; will make an exact mind. She should cultivate every study, which, instead of stimulating her sensibility, will chastise it; which will neither create an excessive or a false refinement; which will give her definite notions; will bring the imagination under dominion; will lead her to think, to compare, to combine, to methodize; which will confer such a power of discrimination, that her judgment shall learn to reject what is dazzling, if it be not solid; and to prefer, not what is striking, or bright, or new, but what is just. That kind of knowledge

[2] **sacred to the poor:** "It would be a noble employment, and well becoming the tenderness of their sex, if ladies were to consider the superintendence of the poor as their immediate office. They are peculiarly fitted for it; for from their own habits of life they are more intimately acquainted with domestic wants than the other sex; and in certain instances of sickness and suffering peculiar to themselves, they should be expected to have more sympathy; and they have obviously more leisure. There is a certain religious society, distinguished by simplicity of dress, manners, and language, whose poor are perhaps better taken care of than any other; and one reason may be, that they are immediately under the inspection of the women" [H. M.].

which is rather fitted for home consumption than foreign exportation, is peculiarly adapted to women.[3]

It is because the superficial nature of their education furnishes them with a false and low standard of intellectual excellence, that women have too often become ridiculous by the unfounded pretensions of literary vanity; for it is not the really learned, but the smatterers, who have generally brought their sex into discredit by an absurd affectation which has set them on despising the duties of ordinary life. There have not, indeed, been wanting (but the character is not now common) *precieuses ridicules*,[4] who, assuming a superiority to the sober cares which ought to occupy their sex, have claimed a lofty and supercilious exemption from the dull and plodding drudgeries

Of this dim speck called earth![5]

There have not been wanting ill-judging females, who have affected to establish an unnatural separation between talents and usefulness, instead of bearing in mind that talents are the great appointed instruments of usefulness; who have acted as if knowledge were to confer on woman a kind of fantastic sovereignty, which should exonerate her from the discharge of female duties; whereas it is only meant the more eminently to qualify her for the performance of them. A woman of real sense will never forget, that while the greater part of her proper duties are such as the most moderately gifted may fulfil with credit, (since Providence never makes that to be very difficult, which is generally necessary,) yet that the most highly endowed are equally bound to fulfil them; and let her remember that the humblest of these offices, performed on Christian principles, are wholesome for the minds even of the most enlightened, as they tend to the casting down of those "high imaginations" which women of genius are too much tempted to indulge. . . .

[3] **peculiarly adapted to women**: "May I be allowed to strengthen my own opinion with the authority of Dr. Johnson, that *a woman cannot have too much arithmetic*? It is a solid, practical acquirement, in which there is much use and little display; it is a quiet sober kind of knowledge, which she acquires for herself and her family, and not for the world" [H. M.].

[4] **precieuses ridicules**: ridiculous women; the phrase is from Molière's play *Les Précieuses ridicules* (1659), which satirizes literary women.

[5] **Of this dim speck called earth**: "Above the smoke and stir of this dim spot / Which men call earth": Milton, *Comus*, lines 5–6.

from Letter to John Bowdler
(1799)

My plan for instructing the poor is very limited and strict. They learn of weekdays such coarse works as may fit them for servants. I allow of no writing. My object has not been to teach dogmas and opinions, but to form the lower class to habits of industry and virtue. I know no way of teaching morals but by infusing principles of Christianity, nor of teaching Christianity without a thorough knowledge of Scripture . . . To make good members of society (and this can only be done by making good Christians) has been my aim . . . Principles not opinions are what I labour to give them.

from Letter to William Wilberforce[1]
(1801)

MY DEAR SIR,

I am truly sorry to hear of your detention at Broomfield,[2] (and more especially for the cause) when I was indulging the idea that you were ranging far and wide, in full liberty and relaxation. I shall rejoice to hear Mrs. W. is recovered, and that you are on the wing. As to your request about giving hints for a school, I know nothing so difficult. To shew, however, my disposition to obey your orders, I have inclosed a sheet of hints, which I fear will be of little use. Indeed, it seems just now particularly wrong in me to attempt to teach others, who am myself so disgraced, traduced, and vilified. Oh! may I be supported as seeing Him who is invisible! It is circulated among the worldly and Socinian clergy,[3] that I have been in the constant habit of praying for the success of the French in my schools! How I shall one day admire that infinite wisdom,

[1] **William Wilberforce***: British political figure, leader of the campaign to abolish the slave trade and organizer of the Society for the Suppression of Vice, which grew out of his Evangelical Christian beliefs.

[2] **your detention at Broomfield**: perhaps alluding to the illness or financial difficulties that beset Wilberforce from 1800 to 1801.

[3] **Socinian clergy**: Socinianism was a religious movement beginning in the sixteenth century which attempted to reconcile Christianity with humanism and rationalism; its adherents, who denied the divinity of Jesus and other doctrines, were persecuted

which has thus decreed that I should be wounded just where I am most vulnerable! My gracious Father, I doubt not, saw (though I knew it not) that I was too anxious about human opinion. You have, doubtless, seen the Anti-Jacobin[4] for June. I could give you a fresh instance of the treachery of that editor, and you would see how every thing has concurred to injure me. O for more faith, and more deadness to such a world! If it does but help to purify and fit me for a better, I ought to count it a light affliction. B[lagdon] is playing some fresh trick daily, refuses to resign, and threatens an appeal to the Archbishop, and to prosecute my Diocesan.[5]

Your's ever.
H. MORE

— HINTS —

(ENCLOSED IN THE ABOVE)

In the morning I open school with one of the Sunday School Prayers, from the Cheap Repository Tract. I have a Bible class — Testament class — Psalter[6] class. Those who cannot read at all, are questioned out of the first little question book for the Mendip schools. In instructing the Bible or Testament class, I always begin with the Parables, which we explain to them in the most familiar manner, one at a time, till they understand that one so perfectly, that they are able to give me back the full sense of it.

We begin with the three parables[7] in the fifteenth chapter of St. Luke, first fixing in their minds the literal sense, and then teaching them to make the practical application. When their understandings are a little exercised, we dwell for a long time on the three first chapters of Genesis,[8] endeavouring from these to establish them in the doctrine of the fall of man. We keep them a good while close to the same subject, making them read the same parts so often, that the most important texts shall adhere to their memories; because upon this knowledge only can I ground my general conversation with them so as to be intelligible. I also encourage them by little bribes of a penny a chapter, to get by heart certain fundamental parts of Scripture, for instance, the promises, and prophecies, and confessions of sin — such as the 9th of Isaiah, 53rd of Isaiah, and 51st Psalm — the beatitudes[9] and indeed the whole sermon on the Mount — together with the most striking parts of our Saviour's discourses in the gospel of St. John. It is my grand endeavour to make every thing as entertaining as I can, and to try to engage their affections; to excite in them the love of God; and particularly to awaken their gratitude to their Redeemer.

When they seem to get a little tired, we change the scene; and by standing up, and singing a hymn, their attention is relieved.

I have never tried the system of terror, because I have found that kindness produces a better end by better means.

About five o'clock we dismiss the little ones with a prayer and a hymn. It would be an excellent method (and has been practised with success,) to invite the grown-up children and their parents, to come to the school at six o'clock, and get some kind lady (which answers better than a teacher,) to read a little sermon to them — 'Burder's Village Sermons'[10] are very proper.

Those who attend four Sundays, without intermission, and come in time for morning prayer, receive a penny every fourth Sunday; but if they fail once, the other three Sundays go for nothing, and they must begin again. Once in every six or eight weeks I give a little gingerbread. Once a year I distribute little books according to merit — those who deserve most, get a Bible — second rate merit gets a prayer-book — the rest, Cheap Repository Tracts.

Once a year, also, each scholar receives some one article of dress; the boy, a hat, shirt, or pair of shoes, according to their wants — the big girls, a calico apron and cap — the little ones, a cap, and a tippet of calico.

---

by the Catholic Church, and the movement dissolved by mid-century. More uses the term to disparage liberal clergymen in general.

[4] **the Anti-Jacobin**: the *Anti-Jacobin Review*, a conservative political and satirical journal patterned on the 1797–1798 *Anti-Jacobin* and edited by John Gifford (pseudonym for John Richards Green), which appeared from 1798 to 1821.

[5] **Blagdon . . . my Diocesan**: allusion to the Blagdon Controversy (1800–1803), a virulent pamphlet campaign against Hannah More in which Bere, the curate of the village of Blagdon, accused her of corrupting the children of the rural poor by sending as schoolmaster to her charity Sunday school a young diocesan, Mr. Younge, whom Bere considered to be a heretical Methodist.

[6] **Psalter**: the book of Psalms.

[7] **three parables**: the parables of the lost sheep, the lost coin, and the prodigal son (Luke 15).

[8] **three first chapters of Genesis**: from the creation to the fall of Adam and Eve.

[9] **the beatitudes**: nine statements of blessedness, such as "Blessed are the meek, for they shall inherit the earth," at the beginning of Jesus' Sermon on the Mount (Matthew 5–7).

[10] **Burder's Village Sermons**: *Village Sermons* (1797–1820) by George Burder (1752–1832), congregationalist minister.

CHARLOTTE TURNER SMITH

(1749–1806)

Born to affluent parents and raised as a pampered, accomplished young lady, Charlotte Smith was forced into a disastrous marriage at the age of sixteen that soon rendered her destitute; she turned to writing for publication, first poetry and then fiction, as the necessary and only respectable means to provide for her growing family. In the process, she both articulated a distinct poetic voice, that of a woman acutely suffering from the inequities of patriarchal privilege, and at the same time developed an artistic craft that powerfully shaped (without acknowledgment) the blank verse and sonnets of her male followers, most notably William Wordsworth.*

The oldest daughter of Nicholas Turner of Bignor Park, Sussex, and Anna Towers, Charlotte Turner was born to a life of upper-class fashion on 4 May 1749. Spending her youth between her father's London townhouse near St. James Park and his country estates at Stoke House, Surrey, and Bignor Park, Sussex, Charlotte received the best education available to a female of her time. At girls' schools in Chichester and Kensington, she was instructed in art by the noted landscape painter George Smith, received extensive lessons in dancing and acting (at which she excelled), and read widely in poetry and fiction. Her childhood was idyllic, despite the death of her mother in childbirth when Charlotte was three.

However, when Charlotte was fifteen her father decided to marry a young heiress, Miss Meriton, whose £20,000 dowry could continue to support his lavish lifestyle as a man of fashion. His new bride was jealous of his attractive adolescent daughter. Charlotte's aunt, thinking she was doing her niece a favor, in 1765 arranged what she thought was an advantageous marriage, to the reluctant 21-year-old Benjamin Smith, the pampered heir to a West Indian slave plantation fortune. An irresponsible, bad-tempered, alcoholic spendthrift, Smith shared none of Charlotte's intellectual or cultural interests. Within five years, Charlotte wrote to her sister, Catherine Anne Dorset, "No disadvantage could equal those I sustained: the more my mind expanded, the more I became sensible of personal slavery; the more I improved and cultivated my understanding, the farther I was removed from those with whom I was condemned to pass my life; and the more clearly I saw by these newly-acquired lights the horror of the abyss into which I had unconsciously plunged."

Until 1776, her father-in-law Richard Smith managed to curb his son's financial profligacy and insure a comfortable household for Charlotte and her growing family (she was pregnant almost annually; by 1774, she had given birth to seven children). In his effort to pass on his estate directly to his grandchildren, however, Richard Smith wrote a will without legal advice that, after his death in 1776, was tied up in the Chancery law courts for 37 years, providing the plot for Dickens' *Bleak House.* Benjamin Smith was able to obtain a lucrative government contract through his family connections with the East India Company, but immediately entered into a profligate lifestyle that far exceeded his means. In December 1783, he was imprisoned for debt, and Charlotte, leaving her children with her brother at Bignor Park, loyally entered the King's Bench Prison with her husband. From there she negotiated with his creditors to gain his release, but within a year Benjamin was forced to flee to France to escape his new debts. In October 1784, Charlotte moved her family to

Dieppe; by spring she was able to negotiate their return. However, Benjamin's acquisition of a French mistress led to a final legal separation between the couple. Benjamin returned to France, and Charlotte, pregnant with her twelfth child, was left in England with no legal control over her own financial affairs to support her children on her own.

She turned to the only lucrative and respectable employment open to her, writing for publication. In 1784, she had published her first volume, the immediately successful *Elegiac Sonnets and Other Poems by Charlotte Smith of Bignor Park, Sussex*, whose title simultaneously asserts her social status and her personal misery. Over the next sixteen years, she published eight more, ever-expanding editions of her *Elegiac Sonnets*. Although Smith considered herself a practitioner of what neoclassical aesthetic theory regarded as the "higher" genre of poetry, she was driven by economic necessity to writing in the more profitable genre of prose fiction. Between 1788 and 1798 she published ten novels, many of which examine the gender inequities of both the British and the French political and legal systems. The first, *Emmeline, or the Orphan of the Castle* (1788), was so highly praised by the reviewers that her publisher, Thomas Cadell, supplemented the amount originally paid for the manuscript. Of her next nine novels, *Celestina* (1792), *Desmond* (1792), *The Old Manor House* (1793), and *The Young Philosopher* (1798) were the best received. Despite her failing health and the heart-wrenching death of her favorite daughter, Anna Augusta de Foville, who died giving birth in 1795, she maintained a cheerful temperament and managed to raise her eight surviving children successfully. She even supported another daughter whose husband had abandoned her and her three children.

Charlotte Smith continued to regard her poetry as her best work. Her examination of political tyranny both at home and abroad, *The Emigrants* (1793), has been hailed by Stuart Curran as "the finest piece of extended blank verse in English between Cowper's *The Task* (1785) and Wordsworth's unpublished initial version of *The Prelude* (1799)." Her extended meditation on the relationship of nature to the human mind, *Beachy Head* (1807), can be read as a challenge to the "egotistical sublime" of Wordsworth's *Prelude** in its insistence on the stubborn otherness and minute particularity of the natural world and on the limitations of human subjectivity. "The playful wit and peculiar vein of humour," which her sister claimed in her *Memoir of Charlotte Smith* were typical of Smith's conversation, are engagingly revealed in the series of bird fables derived from Fontaine which Smith wrote in 1806, at a time when she was crippled by the illness that would lead to her death that year. They were published in the last of her naturalist books for children, *The History of Birds* (1807).

from Elegiac Sonnets and Other Poems

(1784–1797)

— I —

The partial[1] Muse has from my earliest hours
Smiled on the rugged path I'm doom'd to tread,
And still with sportive hand has snatch'd wild flowers,
To weave fantastic garlands for my head:
But far, far happier is the lot of those
Who never learn'd her dear delusive art;
Which, while it decks the head with many a rose,
Reserves the thorn to fester in the heart.
For still she bids soft Pity's melting eye
Stream o'er the ills she knows not to remove,
Points every pang, and deepens every sigh
Of mourning Friendship, or unhappy Love.
Ah! then, how dear the Muse's favours cost,
If those paint sorrow best—who feel it most![2]

— XXVII —

Sighing I see yon little troop at play,
By Sorrow yet untouch'd, unhurt by Care;
While free and sportive they enjoy to-day,
"Content and careless of to-morrow's fare!"[3]
O happy age! when Hope's unclouded ray
Lights their green path, and prompts their simple mirth;
Ere yet they feel the thorns that lurking lay
To wound the wretched pilgrims of the earth,
Making them rue the hour that gave them birth,
And threw them on a world so full of pain,
Where prosperous folly treads on patient worth,
And, to deaf Pride, Misfortune pleads in vain!
Ah!—for their future fate how many fears
Oppress my heart—and fill mine eyes with tears!

— XXXV —

To Fortitude

Nymph of the rock! whose dauntless spirit braves
The beating storm, and bitter winds that howl
Round thy cold breast; and hear'st the bursting waves
And the deep thunder with unshaken soul;
Oh come!—and shew how vain the cares that press
On my weak bosom—and how little worth
Is the false fleeting meteor, Happiness,
That still misleads the wanderers of the earth!
Strenghten'd by thee, this heart shall cease to melt
O'er ills that poor Humanity must bear;
Nor friends estranged, or ties dissolved be felt
To leave regret, and fruitless anguish there:
And when at length it heaves its latest sigh,
Thou and mild Hope shall teach me how to die!

— XLIII —

The unhappy exile, whom his fates confine
To the bleak coast of some unfriendly isle,
Cold, barren, desart, where no harvests smile,
But thirst and hunger on the rocks repine;
When, from some promontory's fearful brow,
Sun after sun he hopeless sees decline
In the broad shipless sea—perhaps may know
Such heartless pain, such blank despair as mine:
And, if a flattering cloud appears to show
The fancied semblance of a distant sail,
Then melts away—anew his spirits fail,
While the lost hope but aggravates his woe!
Ah! so for me delusive Fancy toils,
Then, from contrasted truth—my feeble soul recoils.

— XLIV —

Written in the Church-Yard at Middleton in Sussex[4]

Press'd by the Moon, mute arbitress of tides,
While the loud equinox its power combines,
The sea no more its swelling surge confines,
But o'er the shrinking land sublimely rides.
The wild blast, rising from the Western cave,
Drives the huge billows from their heaving bed;

---

[1] **partial**: biased in one's favour, kindly, sympathetic.

[2] **If those paint . . . most!**: "The well-sung woes shall soothe my pensive ghost; / He best can paint them who shall feel them most." Pope's "Eloisa to Abelard," 366th line [C. S.].

[3] **"Content . . . fare!"**: from James Thomson, *The Seasons*, "Autumn," line 191.

[4] Middleton is a village on the margin of the sea, in Sussex, containing only two or three houses. There were formerly several acres of ground between its small church and the sea, which now, by its continual encroachments, approaches within a few feet of this half-ruined and humble edifice. The wall, which once surrounded the church-yard, is entirely swept away, many of the graves broken up, and the remains of bodies interred washed into the sea; whence human bones are found among the sand and shingles on the shore [C. S.].

Tears from their grassy tombs the village dead,
And breaks the silent sabbath of the grave!
With shells and sea-weed mingled, on the shore
Lo! their bones whiten in the frequent wave;
But vain to them the winds and waters rave;
They hear the warring elements no more:
While I am doom'd—by life's long storm opprest,
To gaze with envy on their gloomy rest.

— XLVII —

TO FANCY[5]

Thee, Queen of Shadows!—shall I still invoke,
Still love the scenes thy sportive pencil drew,
When on mine eyes the early radiance broke
Which shew'd the beauteous rather than the true!
Alas! long since those glowing tints are dead,
And now 'tis thine in darkest hues to dress
The spot where pale Experience hangs her head
O'er the sad grave of murder'd Happiness!
Thro' thy false medium, then, no longer view'd,
May fancied pain and fancied pleasure fly,
And I, as from me all thy dreams depart,
Be to my wayward destiny subdued:
Nor seek perfection with a poet's eye,
Nor suffer anguish with a poet's heart!

— LVII —

TO DEPENDENCE

Dependence! heavy, heavy are thy chains,
And happier they who from the dangerous sea,
Or the dark mine, procure with ceaseless pains
An hard-earn'd pittance—than who trust to thee!
More blest the hind, who from his bed of flock[6]
Starts—when the birds of morn their summons give,
And waken'd by the lark—"the shepherd's clock,"[7]
Lives but to labour—labouring but to live.
More noble than the sycophant, whose art
Must heap with taudry flowers thy hated shrine;
I envy not the meed[8] thou canst impart
To crown *his* service—while, tho' Pride combine
With Fraud to crush me[9]—my unfetter'd heart
Still to the Mountain Nymph[10] may offer mine.

— LIX —

WRITTEN SEPTEMBER 1791, DURING A REMARKABLE THUNDER STORM, IN WHICH THE MOON WAS PERFECTLY CLEAR, WHILE THE TEMPEST GATHERED IN VARIOUS DIRECTIONS NEAR THE EARTH

What awful pageants crowd the evening sky!
The low horizon gathering vapours shroud;
Sudden, from many a deep-embattled cloud
Terrific thunders burst, and lightnings fly—
While in serenest azure, beaming high,
Night's regent,[11] of her calm pavilion proud,
Gilds the dark shadows that beneath her lie,
Unvex'd by all their conflicts fierce and loud.
—So, in unsullied dignity elate,
A spirit conscious of superior worth,
In placid elevation firmly great,
Scorns the vain cares that give Contention birth;
And blest with peace above the shocks of Fate,
Smiles at the tumult of the troubled earth.

— LXV —

TO DR. PARRY OF BATH,[12] WITH SOME BOTANIC DRAWINGS WHICH HAD BEEN MADE SOME YEARS

In happier hours, ere yet so keenly blew
Adversity's cold blight, and bitter storms,
Luxuriant Summer's evanescent forms,
And Spring's soft blooms with pencil light I drew:

[5] **fancy**: the imagination.

[6] **the hind**: a married farm servant, for whom a cottage is provided; a rustic. **bed of flock**: Material consisting of the course tufts and refuse of wool or cotton, used for stuffing beds.

[7] **"the shepherd's clock"**: "And merry larks are ploughman's clocks" (Shakespeare, *Love's Labour's Lost*, V.ii.901).

[8] **meed**: recompense, reward.

[9] **crush me**: a general reference to the problem of patronage in which artists must sacrifice their aesthetic integrity to secure economic support, as well as a specific reference to Charlotte Smith's protracted legal suit to claim the estate her father-in-law had intended for her, and to her estranged husband's legal rights to her earnings; in both these legal situations, as a woman under the British law of couverture, she had no legal standing.

[10] **the Mountain Nymph**: the mountain goddess Liberty, from Milton's *Allegro*, line 36.

[11] **Night's regent**: the moon.

[12] **Dr. Parry of Bath**: to the excellent friend and Physician to whom these lines are addressed, I was obliged for the kindest attention, and for the recovery from one dangerous illness of that beloved child whom a few months afterwards his skill

But as the lovely family of flowers
Shrink from the bleakness of the Northern blast,
So fail from present care and sorrow past
The slight botanic pencil's mimic powers —
Nor will kind Fancy even by Memory's aid,
Her visionary garlands now entwine;
Yet while the wreaths of Hope and Pleasure fade,
Still is one flower of deathless blossom mine,
That dares the lapse of Time, and Tempest rude,
The unfading Amaranth[13] of Gratitude.

— LXX —

On being cautioned against walking on an headland overlooking the sea, because it was frequented by a lunatic

Is there a solitary wretch who hies
To the tall cliff, with starting pace or slow,
And, measuring, views with wild and hollow eyes
Its distance from the waves that chide below;
Who, as the sea-born gale with frequent sighs
Chills his cold bed upon the mountain turf,
With hoarse, half-utter'd lamentation, lies
Murmuring responses to the dashing surf?
In moody sadness, on the giddy brink,
I see him more with envy than with fear;
He has no *nice felicities* that shrink[14]
From giant horrors; wildly wandering here,
He seems (uncursed with reason) not to know
The depth or the duration of his woe.

— LXXIV —

The winter night

"Sleep, that knits up the ravell'd sleeve of care,"[15]
Forsakes me, while the chill and sullen blast,
As my sad soul recalls its sorrows past,
Seems like a summons, bidding me prepare
For the last sleep of death[.] — Murmuring I hear
The hollow wind around the ancient towers,[16]
While night and silence reign; and cold and drear
The darkest gloom of Middle Winter lours;
But wherefore fear existence such as mine,
To change for long and undisturb'd repose?
Ah! when this suffering being I resign,
And o'er my miseries the tomb shall close,
By her, whose loss in anguish I deplore,[17]
I shall be laid, and feel that loss no more!

— LXXXIV —

To the Muse

Wilt thou forsake me who in life's bright May
Lent warmer lustre to the radiant morn;
And even o'er Summer scenes by tempests torn,
Shed with illusive light the dewy ray
Of pensive pleasure? — Wilt thou, while the day
Of saddening Autumn closes, as I mourn
In languid, hopeless sorrow, far away
Bend thy soft step, and never more return? —
Crush'd to the earth, by bitterest anguish prest,
From my faint eyes thy graceful form recedes;
Thou canst not heal an heart like mine that bleeds;
But, when in quiet earth that heart shall rest,
Haply may'st thou one sorrowing vigil keep,
Where Pity and Remembrance bend and weep![18]

— XCI —

Reflections on some drawings of plants

I can in groups these mimic flowers compose,
These bells and golden eyes, embathed in dew;
Catch the soft blush that warms the early Rose,
Or the pale Iris cloud with veins of blue;
Copy the scallop'd leaves, and downy stems,
And bid the pencil's varied shades arrest
Spring's humid[19] buds, and Summer's musky gems:
But, save the portrait on my bleeding breast,

---

and most unremitted and disinterested exertions could not save! [C. S.]. Smith refers to the death of her favourite child, Anna Augusta de Foville, who died in childbirth in 1795.

Dr. Caleb Hillier Parry (1755–1822) was the author of an important treatise on angina pectoris or heart disease, published in 1799.

[13] **Amaranth**: the immortal flower of paradise.

[14] **no nice felicities**: "Tis delicate felicity that shrinks / When rocking winds are loud." Walpole [C. S.].

[15] Shakespeare, *Macbeth*, II.ii.37.

[16] **the ancient towers**: these lines were written in a residence among ancient public buildings [C. S.].

[17] **her . . . deplore**: Smith's favourite child, Anna Augusta de Foville, died in 1795.

[18] **Pity . . . weep!**: "Where melancholy friendship bends and weeps." Thomas Gray [C. S.], "Epitaph on Sir William Williams," line 12.

[19] **humid**: slightly wet, as with mist, vapour.

I have no semblance of that form adored,[20]
That form, expressive of a soul divine,
So early blighted; and while life is mine,
With fond regret, and ceaseless grief deplored—
That grief, my angel! with too faithful art
Enshrines thy image in thy Mother's heart.

THIRTY-EIGHT ADDRESSED TO MRS. H– – – –Y[1] (1789)

In early youth's unclouded scene,
The brilliant morning of eighteen,
With health and sprightly joy elate
We gazed on life's enchanting spring,
Nor thought how quickly time would bring
The mournful period——Thirty-eight.

Then the starch[2] maid, or matron sage,
Already of that sober age,
We view'd with mingled scorn and hate;
In whose sharp words, or sharper face,
With thoughtless mirth we loved to trace
The sad effects of——Thirty-eight.

Till saddening, sickening at the view,
We learn'd to dread what Time might do;
And then preferr'd a prayer to Fate
To end our days ere that arrived;
When (power and pleasure long survived)
We met neglect and——Thirty-eight.

But Time, in spite of wishes, flies,
And Fate our simple prayer denies,
And bids us Death's own hour await:
The auburn locks are mix'd with grey,
The transient roses fade away,
But Reason comes at——Thirty-eight.

Her voice the anguish contradicts
That dying vanity inflicts;
Her hand new pleasures can create,
For us she opens to the view
Prospects less bright—but far more true,
And bids us smile at——Thirty-eight.

No more shall *Scandal*'s breath destroy
The social converse[3] we enjoy
With bard or critic tête à tête;—
O'er Youth's bright blooms her blights shall pour,
But spare the improving friendly hour
That Science[4] gives to——Thirty-eight.

Stripp'd of their gaudy hues by Truth,
We view the glitt'ring toys of youth,
And blush to think how poor the bait
For which to public scenes we ran,
And scorn'd of sober Sense the plan,
Which gives content at——Thirty-eight.

Tho' Time's inexorable sway
Has torn the myrtle bands[5] away,
For other wreaths 'tis not too late,
The amaranth's[6] purple glow survives,
And still Minerva's olive[7] lives
On the calm brow of——Thirty-eight.

With eye more steady we engage
To contemplate approaching age,
And life more justly estimate;
With firmer souls, and stronger powers,
With reason, faith, and friendship ours,
We'll not regret the stealing hours
That lead from Thirty——even to Forty-eight.

---

[20] **form adored:** reference to her daughter, Anna Augusta de Foville.

[1] **Mrs. H– – – –Y:** Eliza Hayley, who married the poet William Hayley in 1769 at the age of 19. Shortly after this poem was written, in 1789, she separated permanently from her husband.

[2] **starch:** stiff, unbending, formal.

[3] **social converse:** conversation free from sexual innuendo.

[4] **Science:** learning, knowledge.

[5] **myrtle bands:** evergreen plant, held sacred to Venus and therefore an emblem of love.

[6] **amaranth:** immortal flower of paradise.

[7] **Minerva's olive:** Minerva (Athena) is the classical goddess of wisdom; the olive is a symbol of peace.

The Emigrants[1]

(1793)

To William Cowper, Esq.

DEAR SIR,

There is, I hope, some propriety in my addressing a Composition to you, which would never perhaps have existed, had I not, amid the heavy pressure of many sorrows, derived infinite consolation from your Poetry, and some degree of animation and of confidence from your esteem.

The following performance is far from aspiring to be considered as an imitation of your inimitable Poem, THE TASK;[2] I am perfectly sensible, that it belongs not to a feeble and feminine hand to draw the Bow of Ulysses.[3]

The force, clearness, and sublimity of your admirable Poem; the felicity, almost peculiar to your genius, of giving to the most familiar objects dignity and effect, I could never hope to reach; yet, having read THE TASK almost incessantly from its first publication to the present time, I felt that kind of enchantment described by Milton, when he says,

> The Angel ended, and in Adam's ear
> So charming left his voice, that he awhile
> Thought him still speaking.—
>
> [*Paradise Lost,* VIII. 1–3]

And from the force of this impression, I was gradually led to attempt, in Blank Verse, a delineation of those interesting objects which happened to excite my attention, and which even pressed upon an heart, that has learned, perhaps from its own sufferings, to feel with acute, though unavailing compassion, the calamity of others.

A Dedication usually consists of praises and of apologies; *my* praise can add nothing to the unanimous and loud applause of your country. She regards you with pride, as one of the few, who, at the present period, rescue her from the imputation of having degenerated in Poetical talents; but in the form of Apology, I should have much to say, if I again dared to plead the pressure of evils, aggravated by their long continuance, as an excuse for the defects of this attempt.

Whatever may be the faults of its execution, let me vindicate myself from those, that may be imputed to the design.—In speaking of the Emigrant Clergy,[4] I beg to be understood as feeling the utmost respect for the integrity of their principles; and it is with pleasure I add my suffrage to that of those, who have had a similar opportunity of witnessing the conduct of the Emigrants of all descriptions during their exile in England; which has been such as does honour to *their* nation, and ought to secure to them in ours the esteem of every liberal mind.

Your philanthropy, dear Sir, will induce you, I am persuaded, to join with me in hoping, that this painful exile may finally lead to the extirpation of that reciprocal hatred so unworthy of great and enlightened nations; that it may tend to humanize both countries, by convincing each, that good qualities exist in the other; and at length annihilate the prejudices that have so long existed to the injury of both.[5]

Yet it is unfortunately but too true, that with the body of the English, this national aversion has acquired

---

[1] **The Emigrants:** as the Revolution unfolded in France, a great many who had enjoyed power and privilege under the *ancien regime* sought refuge in England. Their ranks were of such dimensions that from among the men could be assembled a counter-revolutionary army which then invaded France in a disastrous chivalric gesture, suffering wholesale military defeat. Thus, to the numbers of unprotected women who had been sent abroad with their children for safety were added others whose husbands had emigrated with them but then had returned to France to fight and die, leaving unprovided widows to their fate in a strange land. The extent to which the rules made by men at once keep women dependent and leave them with no recourse when left alone links these distressed emigrants and the poet who observes them [C. S.].

[2] **The Task:** long, meditative poem in blank verse published by William Cowper in 1784.

[3] **the Bow of Ulysses:** in Homer's *Odyssey,* the suitors for Odysseus' wife Penelope lack the strength to string and draw his bow; only the returned Odysseus (Ulysses), disguised as a beggar, can draw his bow and kill the suitors.

[4] **Emigrant Clergy:** Catholic priests who fled from persecution when the new French Republic in 1790 abolished the established Catholic church and confiscated all Church holdings.

[5] **prejudices . . . both:** since the sixteenth century when Henry VIII broke with the Roman Catholic Church and established the independent Anglican Church of England, most English people were extremely hostile to Catholicism. English Roman Catholics were forbidden to vote in Smith's day.

new force by the dreadful scenes which have been acted in France during the last summer[6]—even those who are the victims of the Revolution, have not escaped the odium, which the undistinguishing multitude annex to all the natives of a country where such horrors have been acted: nor is this the worst effect those events have had on the minds of the English; by confounding the original cause with the wretched catastrophes that have followed its ill management; the attempts of public virtue, with the outrages that guilt and folly have committed in its disguise, the very name of Liberty has not only lost the charm it used to have in British ears, but many, who have written, or spoken, in its defence, have been stigmatized as promoters of Anarchy, and enemies to the prosperity of their country. Perhaps even the Author of THE TASK, with all his goodness and tenderness of heart, is in the catalogue of those, who are reckoned to have been too warm in a cause, which it was once the glory of Englishmen to avow and defend—The exquisite Poem, indeed, in which you have honoured Liberty, by a tribute highly gratifying to her sincerest friends, was published some years before the demolition of regal despotism in France, which, in the fifth book, it seems to foretell—All the truth and energy of the passage to which I allude, must have been strongly felt, when, in the Parliament of England, the greatest Orator of our time quoted the sublimest of our Poets—when the eloquence of Fox[7] did justice to the genius of Cowper.

I am, dear SIR, with the most perfect esteem, your obliged and obedient servant,

CHARLOTTE SMITH

Brighthelmstone, May 10, 1793

[6] **scenes . . . summer**: in August 1792, the French king and queen, Louis XVI and Marie Antoinette, were deposed and imprisoned; between September 2 and September 4, invading Austro-Prussian armies provoked the slaughter of hundreds of Royalists in Paris in what were known as the September massacres; during this summer, the moderate Girondists were overthrown by Robespierre and the bloodthirsty Montagnards, who initiated the widespread guillotining of aristocrats and clergy known as the Terror.

[7] **Fox**: Charles James Fox, leader of the Whig opposition in the House of Commons from 1783 to 1796, known for his liberal positions and brilliant oratory. Supported the cause of liberty in France, the abolition of slavery and the slave trade, and the voting rights of Catholics and Dissenters. Passionately opposed England's attacks on France (the sedition and treason acts, the military campaign against Napoleon, etc.).

— BOOK I —

SCENE, *on the Cliffs to the Eastward of the Town of Brighthelmstone*[1] *in Sussex*

TIME, *a Morning in November, 1792*[2]

Slow in the Wintry Morn, the struggling light
Throws a faint gleam upon the troubled waves;
Their foaming tops, as they approach the shore
And the broad surf that never ceasing breaks
On the innumerous pebbles, catch the beams
Of the pale Sun, that with reluctance gives
To this cold northern Isle, its shorten'd day.
Alas! how few the morning wakes to joy!
How many murmur at oblivious night
For leaving them so soon; for bearing thus
Their fancied bliss (the only bliss they taste!),
On her black wings away!—Changing the dreams
That sooth'd their sorrows, for calamities
(And every day brings its own sad proportion)
For doubts, diseases, abject dread of Death,
And faithless friends, and fame and fortune lost;
Fancied or real wants; and wounded pride,
That views the day star,[3] but to curse his beams.

Yet He, whose Spirit into being call'd
This wond'rous World of Waters; He who bids
The wild wind lift them till they dash the clouds,
And speaks to them in thunder; or whose breath,
Low murmuring o'er the gently heaving tides,
When the fair Moon, in summer night serene,
Irradiates with long trembling lines of light
Their undulating surface; that great Power,
Who, governing the Planets, also knows
If but a Sea-Mew falls, whose nest is hid
In these incumbent cliffs;[4] He surely means

[1] **Brighthelmstone**: modern Brighton, near the Cliffs of Dover on the coast of Sussex, across the English Channel from France.

[2] **November, 1792**: by November 1792, Robespierre and the Montagnards had declared France a Republic (on 22 September 1792), seized control of the French Convention or governing body, and promised political and even military support for all other revolutionary movements in Europe and England.

[3] **day star**: the sun.

[4] **Sea-Mew**: the common sea gull. **incumbent cliffs**: superincumbent, lying on top of something else, a technical geological term; the chalk (or white) cliffs of Dover rest on strata of

To us, his reasoning Creatures, whom He bids
Acknowledge and revere his awful hand,
Nothing but good: Yet Man, misguided Man,
Mars the fair work that he was bid enjoy,
And makes himself the evil he deplores.
How often, when my weary soul recoils
From proud oppression, and from legal crimes
(For such are in this Land, where the vain boast
Of equal Law is mockery, while the cost
Of seeking for redress is sure to plunge
Th' already injur'd to more certain ruin
And the wretch starves, before his Counsel pleads),[5]
How often do I half abjure Society,
And sigh for some lone Cottage, deep embower'd
In the green woods, that these steep chalky Hills
Guard from the strong South West;[6] where round
their base
The Beach[7] wide flourishes, and the light Ash
With slender leaf half hides the thymy turf!—
There do I wish to hide me; well content
If on the short grass, strewn with fairy flowers,
I might repose thus shelter'd; or when Eve
In Orient crimson[8] lingers in the west,
Gain the high mound, and mark these waves remote
(Lucid tho' distant), blushing with the rays
Of the far-flaming Orb, that sinks beneath them;
For I have thought, that I should then behold
The beauteous works of God, unspoil'd by Man
And less affected then, by human woes
I witness'd not; might better learn to bear
Those that injustice, and duplicity
And faithlessness and folly, fix on me:
For never yet could I derive relief,
When my swol'n heart was bursting with its sorrows,
From the sad thought, that others like myself
Live but to swell affliction's countless tribes!
—Tranquil seclusion I have vainly sought;
Peace, who delights in solitary shade,
No more will spread for me her downy wings,
But, like the fabled Danaïds[9]—or the wretch,[10]
Who ceaseless, up the steep acclivity,
Was doom'd to heave the still rebounding rock,
Onward I labour; as the baffled wave,
Which yon rough beach repulses, that returns
With the next breath of wind, to fail again.—
Ah! Mourner—cease these wailings: cease and learn,
That not the Cot sequester'd, where the briar
And wood-bine wild, embrace the mossy thatch,
(Scarce seen amid the forest gloom obscure!)
Or more substantial farm, well fenced and warm,
Where the full barn, and cattle fodder'd round
Speak rustic plenty; nor the statelier dome
By dark firs shaded, or the aspiring pine,
Close by the village Church (with care conceal'd
By verdant foliage, lest the poor man's grave
Should mar the smiling prospect of his Lord),[11]
Where offices well rang'd,[12] or dove-cote stock'd,
Declare manorial residence; not these
Or any of the buildings, new and trim
With windows circling towards the restless Sea,
Which ranged in rows,[13] now terminate my walk,
Can shut out for an hour the spectre Care,
That from the dawn of reason, follows still
Unhappy Mortals, 'till the friendly grave
(Our sole secure asylum) "ends the chace."[14]

---

granite and coal. Charlotte Smith here displays her considerable scientific learning in the fields of geology, zoology, and botany.

[5] **legal crimes . . . pleads:** a reference to Charlotte Smith's protracted and failed legal suit to gain legal control of the trust established for her children by her father-in-law. See Headnote and *Elegiac Sonnets,* LVII, "To dependence," note 9.

[6] **South West:** winds off the Atlantic Ocean.

[7] **Beach:** probably refers to the beech tree.

[8] **Eve in Orient crimson:** the sunset.

[9] **the fabled Danaïds:** the fifty daughters of Danaus, who were condemned to an eternity of torture in Tartarus for murdering their husbands on their wedding night: they could draw and drink water only from a sieve.

[10] **the wretch:** Sisyphus, punished for his cunning deception of the gods by being condemned eternally to push an enormous boulder up the slope of a steep mountain, only to have it roll down again just before Sisyphus reached the summit.

[11] **smiling prospect of his Lord:** the view from the manor house whose lord does not wish to be reminded of the sufferings of his tenants.

[12] **offices well rang'd:** buildings attached to the manor house (kitchens, dairy, stables, etc.).

[13] **buildings . . . ranged in rows:** new townhouses built by the luxury-loving aristocrats who in the 1780s followed the Prince of Wales to Brighton, where he set up his summer court and built the lavish Royal Pavilion. Significantly, Smith does not mention the Pavilion, the Prince regent's extravagant architectural folly begun in 1785 and completed in 1810.

[14] **"ends the chace":** I have a confused notion, that this expression, with nearly the same application, is to be found in [the poetry of Edward] Young; but I cannot refer to it [C. S.].

Behold, in witness of this mournful truth,
A group approach me, whose dejected looks,
Sad Heralds of distress! proclaim them Men
Banish'd for ever and for conscience sake
From their distracted Country,[15] whence the name
Of Freedom misapplied, and much abus'd
By lawless Anarchy, has driven them far
To wander; with the prejudice they learn'd
From Bigotry (the Tut'ress of the blind),
Thro' the wide World unshelter'd; their sole hope,
That German spoilers,[16] thro' that pleasant land
May carry wide the desolating scourge
Of War and Vengeance; yet unhappy Men,
Whate'er your errors, I lament your fate:
And, as disconsolate and sad ye hang
Upon the barrier of the rock, and seem
To murmur your despondence, waiting long
Some fortunate reverse that never comes,
Methinks in each expressive face, I see
Discriminated[17] anguish; there droops one,
Who in a moping cloister long consum'd
This life inactive, to obtain a better,
And thought that meagre abstinence, to wake
From his hard pallet with the midnight bell,
To live on eleemosynary bread,[18]
And to renounce God's works, would please that God.
And now the poor pale wretch receives, amaz'd,
The pity, strangers give to his distress,
Because these strangers are, by his dark creed,
Condemn'd as Heretics — and with sick heart
Regrets[19] his pious prison, and his beads.[20]
Another, of more haughty port, declines
The aid he needs not; while in mute despair
His high indignant thoughts go back to France,
Dwelling on all he lost — the Gothic dome,
That vied with splendid palaces;[21] the beds
Of silk and down, the silver chalices,
Vestments with gold enwrought for blazing altars;
Where, amid clouds of incense, he held forth
To kneeling crowds the imaginary bones
Of Saints suppos'd, in pearl and gold enchas'd,
And still with more than living Monarchs' pomp
Surrounded; was believ'd by mumbling bigots
To hold the keys of Heaven, and to admit
Whom he thought good to share it — Now alas!
He, to whose daring soul and high ambition
The World seem'd circumscrib'd; who, wont to dream
Of Fleuri, Richelieu, Alberoni,[22] men
Who trod on Empire, and whose politics
Were not beyond the grasp of his vast mind,
Is, in a Land once hostile, still prophan'd
By disbelief, and rites un-orthodox,
The object of compassion[.] — At his side,
Lighter of heart than these, but heavier far
Than he was wont, another victim comes,
An Abbé — who with less contracted brow
Still smiles and flatters, and still talks of Hope;
Which, sanguine as he is, he does not feel,
And so he cheats the sad and weighty pressure
Of evils present; — Still, as Men misled
By early prejudice (so hard to break),
I mourn your sorrows; for I too have known
Involuntary exile; and while yet
England had charms for me, have felt how sad

[15] **Men Banish'd . . Country**: members of the Catholic clergy banished from revolutionary France.

[16] **German spoilers**: the Austro-Prussian army that invaded France in August 1792, which was repelled, but continued to threaten France.

[17] **discriminated**: distinct.

[18] **eleemosynary bread**: alms.

[19] **regrets**: recalls with regret.

[20] Lest the same attempts at misrepresentation should now be made, as have been made on former occasions, it is necessary to repeat, that nothing is farther from my thoughts, than to reflect invidiously on the Emigrant clergy, whose steadiness of principle excites veneration, as much as their sufferings compassion. Adversity has now taught them the charity and humility they perhaps wanted, when they made it a part of their faith, that salvation could be obtained in no other religion than their own [C. S.].

[21] Let it not be considered as an insult to men in fallen fortune, if these luxuries (undoubtedly inconsistent with their profession) be here enumerated — France is not the only country, where the splendour and indulgences of the higher, and the poverty and depression of the inferior Clergy, have alike proved injurious to the cause of Religion [C. S.].

[22] **Fleuri, Richelieu, Alberoni**: three Catholic cardinals who held high political offices. Cardinal Andre Hercule de Fleury (1653–1743), the former tutor of Louis XV, served as de facto prime minister of France from 1726 to 1743. Armand Jean du Plessis, Duc de Richelieu (1585–1643), was Louis XIII's principal minister. Cardinal Guilio Alberoni (1664–1752) served as de facto prime minister of Spain from 1716 to 1719.

It is to look across the dim cold sea,
That melancholy rolls its refluent[23] tides
Between us and the dear regretted land
We call our own—as now ye pensive wait
On this bleak morning, gazing on the waves
That seem to leave your shore; from whence the wind
Is loaded to your ears, with the deep groans
Of martyr'd Saints and suffering Royalty,
While to your eyes the avenging power of Heaven
Appears in aweful anger to prepare
The storm of vengeance, fraught with plagues and
death.
Even he of milder heart, who was indeed
The simple shepherd in a rustic scene,
And, 'mid the vine-clad hills of Languedoc,[24]
Taught to the bare-foot peasant, whose hard hands
Produc'd[25] the nectar he could seldom taste,
Submission to the Lord for whom he toil'd;
He, or his brethren, who to Neustria's sons[26]
Enforc'd religious patience, when, at times,
On their indignant hearts Power's iron hand
Too strongly struck; eliciting some sparks
Of the bold spirit of their native North;
Even these Parochial Priests, these humbled men,
Whose lowly undistinguish'd cottages
Witness'd a life of purest piety,
While the meek tenants were, perhaps, unknown
Each to the haughty Lord of his domain,
Who mark'd them not; the Noble scorning still
The poor and pious Priest, as with slow pace
He glided thro' the dim arch'd avenue
Which to the Castle led; hoping to cheer
The last sad hour of some laborious life
That hasten'd to its close—even such a Man
Becomes an exile; staying not to try
By temperate zeal to check his madd'ning flock,
Who, at the novel sound of Liberty
(Ah! most intoxicating sound to slaves!),
Start into licence[.]—Lo! dejected now,
The wandering Pastor mourns, with bleeding heart,
His erring people, weeps and prays for them,
And trembles for the account that he must give
To Heaven for souls entrusted to his care.—
Where the cliff, hollow'd by the wintry storm,
Affords a seat with matted sea-weed strewn,
A softer form reclines; around her run,
On the rough shingles, or the chalky bourn,[27]
Her gay unconscious children, soon amus'd;
Who pick the fretted stone, or glossy shell,
Or crimson plant marine: or they contrive
The fairy vessel, with its ribband sail
And gilded paper pennant: in the pool,
Left by the salt wave on the yielding sands,
They launch the mimic navy—Happy age!
Unmindful of the miseries of Man!—
Alas! too long a victim to distress,
Their Mother, lost in melancholy thought,
Lull'd for a moment by the murmurs low
Of sullen billows, wearied by the task
Of having here, with swol'n and aching eyes
Fix'd on the grey horizon, since the dawn
Solicitously watch'd the weekly sail
From her dear native land, now yields awhile
To kind forgetfulness, while Fancy brings,
In waking dreams, that native land again!
Versailles[28] appears—its painted galleries,
And rooms of regal splendour; rich with gold,
Where, by long mirrors multiply'd, the crowd
Paid willing homage—and, united there,
Beauty gave charms to empire—Ah! too soon
From the gay visionary pageant rous'd,
See the sad mourner start!—and, drooping, look
With tearful eyes and heaving bosom round
On drear reality—where dark'ning waves,
Urg'd by the rising wind, unheeded foam
Near her cold rugged seat:—To call her thence
A fellow-sufferer comes: dejection deep
Checks, but conceals not quite, the martial air,

[23] **refluent:** flowing back.

[24] **Languedoc:** region in southern France, bordering the Pyrenees.

[25] See the finely descriptive Verses written at Montaubon in France in 1750, by Dr. Joseph Warton. Printed in Dodsley's *Miscellanies,* Vol. IV. page 203 [C. S.].

Warton's poem begins thus: "Tarn, how delightful wind thy willow'd waves, / But ah! they fructify a land of slaves! . . ."

[26] **Neustria's sons:** inhabitants of French region of Normandy.

[27] **rough shingles:** loose, water-worn pebbles found on the seashore. **chalky bourn:** a small stream or brook cutting through the chalk cliffs along the sea.

[28] **Versailles:** the opulent neoclassical palace built in the mid-1600s by Louis XIV, the "Sun King," to symbolically reflect his magnificence.

And that high consciousness of noble blood,
Which he has learn'd from infancy to think
Exalts him o'er the race of common men:
Nurs'd in the velvet lap of luxury,
And fed by adulation—could *he* learn,
That worth alone is true Nobility?
And that *the peasant* who, "amid the sons
Of Reason, Valour, Liberty, and Virtue,
Displays distinguish'd merit, is a Noble
Of Nature's own creation!"[29]—If even here,
If in this land of highly vaunted Freedom,
Even Britons controvert the unwelcome truth,
Can it be relish'd by the sons of France?
Men, who derive their boasted ancestry
From the fierce leaders of religious wars,
The first in Chivalry's emblazon'd page;
Who reckon Gueslin, Bayard, or De Foix,[30]
Among their brave Progenitors? *Their* eyes,
Accustom'd to regard the splendid trophies
Of Heraldry[31] (that with fantastic hand
Mingles, like images in feverish dreams,
"Gorgons and Hydras, and Chimeras dire,"[32]
With painted puns, and visionary shapes;),
See not the simple dignity of Virtue,
But hold all base, whom honours such as these
Exalt not from the crowd[33]—As one, who long
Has dwelt amid the artificial scenes
Of populous City, deems that splendid shows,
The Theatre, and pageant pomp of Courts,
Are only worth regard; forgets all taste
For Nature's genuine beauty; in the lapse
Of gushing waters hears no soothing sound,
Nor listens with delight to sighing winds,
That, on their fragrant pinions, waft the notes
Of birds rejoicing in the tangled copse;
Nor gazes pleas'd on Ocean's silver breast,
While lightly o'er it sails the summer clouds
Reflected in the wave, that, hardly heard,
Flows on the yellow sands: so to *his* mind,
That long has liv'd where Despotism hides
His features harsh, beneath the diadem[34]
Of worldly grandeur, abject Slavery seems,
If by that power impos'd, slavery no more:
For luxury wreathes with silk the iron bonds,
And hides the ugly rivets with her flowers,
Till the degenerate triflers, while they love
The glitter of the chains, forget their weight.
But more the Men, whose ill acquir'd wealth[35]
Was wrung from plunder'd myriads, by the means
Too often legaliz'd by power abus'd,
Feel all the horrors of the fatal change,
When their ephemeral greatness, marr'd at once
(As a vain toy that Fortune's childish hand
Equally joy'd to fashion or to crush),
Leaves them expos'd to universal scorn
For having nothing else; not even the claim
To honour, which respect for Heroes past

[29] These lines are Thomson's [from James Thomson's adaptation of Shakespeare's *Coriolanus*, III.iii, where they are spoken by Posthumous Cominius], and are among those sentiments which are now called (when used by living writers), not common-place declamation, but sentiments of dangerous tendency [C. S.].

[30] **Gueslin, Bayard, or De Foix**: heroic French warriors. Bertrand De Guesclin (1320?–1380), the "Eagle of Brittany," Constable of France, was instrumental in driving the British out of southern and western France (1342–1380). Pierre Terrail de Bayard (c. 1473–1524), the "Chevalier sans peur et sans reproche" [without fear and above reproach], distinguished himself in the Italian campaigns of Charles VIII, Louis XII, and Francis I. He fought beside Gaston de Foix, Duc de Nemours, "the Thunderbolt of Italy," at the Battle of Ravenna (1512).

[31] **Heraldry**: aristocratic family's coat-of-arms.

[32] **"Gorgons . . . dire"**: Milton, *Paradise Lost,* I.628.

[33] It has been said, and with great appearance of truth, that the contempt in which the Nobility of France held the common people, was remembered, and with all that vindictive asperity which long endurance of oppression naturally excites, when, by a wonderful concurrence of circumstances, the people acquired the power of retaliation. Yet let me here add, what seems to be in some degree inconsistent with the former charge, that the French are good masters to their servants, and that in their treatment of their Negro slaves, that are allowed to be more mild and merciful than other Europeans [C. S.].

[34] **diadem**: crown.

[35] The Financiers and Fermiers Generaux [general bankers] are here intended. In the present moment of clamour against all those who have spoken or written in favour of the first Revolution of France, the declaimers seem to have forgotten, that under the reign of a mild and easy tempered Monarch [Louis XVI], in the most voluptuous Court in the world, the abuses by which men of this description were enriched, had arisen to such height, that their prodigality exhausted the immense resources of France: and, unable to supply the exigencies of Government, the Ministry were compelled to call Le Tiers Etat [the third Estate or merchants]; a meeting that gave birth to the Revolution, which has since been so ruinously conducted [C. S.].

Allows to ancient titles; Men, like these,
Sink even beneath the level, whence base arts
Alone had rais'd them;—unlamented sink,
And know that they deserve the woes they feel.
Poor wand'ring wretches! whosoe'er ye are,
That hopeless, houseless, friendless, travel wide
O'er these bleak russet downs;[36] where, dimly seen,
The solitary Shepherd shiv'ring tends
His dun discolour'd flock (Shepherd, unlike
Him, whom in song the Poet's fancy crowns
With garlands, and his crook with vi'lets binds);
Poor vagrant wretches! outcasts of the world!
Whom no abode receives, no parish owns;
Roving, like Nature's commoners, the land
That boasts such general plenty: if the sight
Of wide-extended misery softens yours
Awhile, suspend your murmurs!—here behold
The strange vicissitudes of fate—while thus
The exil'd Nobles, from their country driven,
Whose richest luxuries were their's, must feel
More poignant anguish, than the lowest poor,
Who, born to indigence, have learn'd to brave
Rigid Adversity's depressing breath!—
Ah! rather Fortune's worthless favourites!
Who feed on England's vitals—Pensioners
Of base corruption, who, in quick ascent
To opulence unmerited, become
Giddy with pride, and as ye rise, forgetting
The dust ye lately left, with scorn look down
On those beneath ye (tho' your *equals* once
In fortune, and *in worth superior still,*
They view the eminence, on which ye stand,
With wonder, not with envy; for they know
The means, by which ye reach'd it, have been such
As, in all honest eyes, degrade ye far
Beneath the poor dependent, whose sad heart
Reluctant pleads for what your pride denies);
Ye venal, worthless hirelings of a Court!
Ye pamper'd Parasites! whom Britons pay
For forging fetters for them; rather here
Study a lesson that concerns ye much;
And, trembling, learn, that if oppress'd too long,
The raging multitude, to madness stung,
Will turn on their oppressors; and, no more
By sounding titles and parading forms
Bound like tame victims, will redress themselves!
Then swept away by the resistless torrent,
Not only all your pomp may disappear,
But, in the tempest lost, fair Order sink
Her decent head, and lawless Anarchy
O'erturn celestial Freedom's radiant throne;—
As now in Gallia;[37] where Confusion, born
Of party rage and selfish love of rule,
Sully the noblest cause that ever warm'd
The heart of Patriot Virtue[.][38]—There arise
The infernal passions; Vengeance, seeking blood,
And Avarice; and Envy's harpy[39] fangs
Pollute the immortal shrine of Liberty,
Dismay her votaries, and disgrace her name.
Respect is due to principle; and they,
Who suffer for their conscience, have a claim,
Whate'er that principle may be, to praise.
These ill-starr'd Exiles then, who, bound by ties,
To them the bonds of honour; who resign'd
Their country to preserve them, and now seek
In England an asylum—well deserve
To find that (every prejudice forgot,
Which pride and ignorance teaches), we for them
Feel as our brethren; and that English hearts,
Of just compassion ever own the sway,
As truly as our element, the deep,
Obeys the mild dominion of the Moon[.]—
This they *have* found; and may they find it still!
Thus may'st thou, Britain, triumph!—May thy foes,
By Reason's gen'rous potency subdued,
Learn, that the God thou worshippest, delights
In acts of pure humanity!—May thine
Be still such bloodless laurels! nobler far
Than those acquir'd at Cressy or Poictiers,[40]
Or of more recent growth, those well bestow'd

[36] **Poor wand'ring wretches . . . downs:** Cf. Shakespeare's *King Lear,* III.iv.28–32: "Poor naked wretches, wheresoe'er you are, / That bide the pelting of this pitiless storm, / How shall your houseless heads and unfed sides, / Your loop'd and window'd raggedness, defend you / From seasons such as these?"

[37] **Gallia:** France.

[38] This sentiment will probably *renew* against me the indignation of those, who have an interest in asserting that no such virtue any where exists [C. S.].

[39] **harpy:** in Greek mythology, a rapacious, filthy monster with a woman's head and body and a bird's wings and claws.

[40] **Cressy . . . Poictiers:** two decisive battles fought by Edward III in 1346 and 1356 to establish his claim to the throne of France.

On him who stood on Calpe's blazing height[41]
Amid the thunder of a warring world,
Illustrious rather from the crowds he sav'd
From flood and fire, than from the ranks who fell
Beneath his valour! — Actions such as these,
Like incense rising to the Throne of Heaven,
Far better justify the pride, that swells
In British bosoms, than the deafening roar
Of Victory from a thousand brazen throats,
That tell with what success wide-wasting War
Has by our brave Compatriots thinned the world.

— BOOK II —

Quippe ubi fas versum atque nefas: tot bella per orbem
Tam multæ scelerum facies; non ullus aratro
Dignus honos: squalent abductis arva colonis,
Et curva[e] rigidum falces conflantur in ensem[.]
Hinc movet Euphrates, illinc Germania bellum[;]
Vicinæ ruptis inter se legibus urbes
Arma ferunt: sævit toto Mars impius orbe.

VERGIL, *Georgics*. lib. i.505–11[1]

SCENE, *on an Eminence on one of those Downs, which afford to the South a View of the Sea; to the North, of the Weald of Sussex*

TIME, *an Afternoon in April, 1793*[2]

Long wintry months are past; the Moon that now
Lights her pale crescent even at noon, has made
Four times her revolution; since with step,
Mournful and slow, along the wave-worn cliff,
Pensive I took my solitary way,[3]
Lost in despondence, while contemplating
Not my own wayward destiny alone,
(Hard as it is, and difficult to bear!)
But in beholding the unhappy lot
Of the lorn Exiles; who, amid the storms
Of wild disastrous Anarchy, are thrown,
Like shipwreck'd sufferers, on England's coast,
To see, perhaps, no more their native land,
Where Desolation riots:[4] They, like me,
From fairer hopes and happier prospects driven,
Shrink from the future, and regret the past.[5]
But on this Upland scene, while April comes,
With fragrant airs, to fan my throbbing breast,
Fain would I snatch an interval from Care,
That weighs my wearied spirit down to earth;
Courting, once more, the influence of Hope
(For "Hope" still waits upon the flowery prime)[6]
As here I mark Spring's humid hand unfold
The early leaves that fear capricious winds,
While, even on shelter'd banks, the timid flowers
Give, half reluctantly, their warmer hues
To mingle with the primroses' pale stars.
No shade the leafless copses yet afford,
Nor hide the mossy labours of the Thrush,
That, startled, darts across the narrow path;
But quickly re-assur'd, resumes his task,
Or adds his louder notes to those that rise
From yonder tufted brake;[7] where the white buds
Of the first thorn are mingled with the leaves
Of that which blossoms on the brow of May.

Ah! 'twill not be: — So many years have pass'd,
Since, on my native hills, I learn'd to gaze

[41] **him who stood . . . height**: George Augustus Eliott (1717–1790) successfully resisted the Spanish siege of Gibraltar (whose ancient name is Calpe) from 1779 to 1783, for which he was knighted.

[1] Epigraph: "Here right has become wrong, and wrong right, so much war spread across the world, so many aspects of evil. The plow is no longer honored; fields have been emptied of their tillers; and the curved sickle is beaten into the unbending sword. War erupts on the Euphrates, in Germany: neighboring states break their treaties and bear forth arms. Uncaring Mars savages the whole world" (Virgil, *Georgics*, Bk. i.505-11, trans. Stuart Curran).

[2] **Weald of Sussex:** tract of wooded country lying between North and South Downs in Sussex. **April, 1793:** Louis XVI was guillotined on 21 January 1793; in February, England and France declared war on each other.

[3] "They hand in hand with wand'ring steps and slow, / Through Eden took their solitary way." *Paradise Lost,* XIII. 648–649.

[4] **Desolation riots:** counterrevolutionary attacks on the new French Republic erupted in the Vendée, the western region of France, in March 1793; they were brutally suppressed.

[5] **regret the past:** look back with regret or nostalgia upon the past.

[6] Shakspeare [C. S.]. The line, "Hope waits upon the flowery prime," in fact comes from Edmund Waller's "To my young Lady Lucy Sidney," line 13, first published in his *Poems* (1645), later retitled "To a Very Young Lady."

[7] **brake:** a clump of bushes, a thicket.

On these delightful landscapes; and those years
Have taught me so much sorrow, that my soul
Feels not the joy reviving Nature brings;
But, in dark retrospect, dejected dwells
On human follies, and on human woes.—
What is the promise of the infant year,
The lively verdure, or the bursting blooms,
To those, who shrink from horrors such as War
Spreads o'er the affrighted world? With swimming eye,
Back on the past they throw their mournful looks,
And see the Temple, which they fondly hop'd
Reason would raise to Liberty, destroy'd
By ruffian hands; while, on the ruin'd mass,
Flush'd with hot blood, the Fiend of Discord sits
In savage triumph; mocking every plea
Of policy and justice, as she shews
The headless corse of one, whose only crime
Was being born a Monarch[8]—Mercy turns,
From spectacle so dire, her swol'n eyes;
And Liberty, with calm, unruffled brow
Magnanimous, as conscious of her strength
In Reason's panoply, scorns to distain[9]
Her righteous cause with carnage, and resigns
To Fraud and Anarchy the infuriate crowd.—
What is the promise of the infant year
To those, who (while the poor but peaceful hind[10]
Pens, unmolested, the encreasing flock
Of his rich master in this sea-fenc'd isle)
Survey, in neighbouring countries, scenes that make
The sick heart shudder; and the Man, who thinks,
Blush for his species? *There* the trumpet's voice[11]
Drowns the soft warbling of the woodland choir;
And violets, lurking in their turfy beds
Beneath the flow'ring thorn, are stain'd with blood.
There fall, at once, the spoiler and the spoil'd;
While War, wide-ravaging, annihilates
The hope of cultivation; gives to Fiends,
The meagre, ghastly Fiends of Want and Woe,
The blasted land—There, taunting in the van
Of vengeance-breathing armies, Insult stalks;
And, in the ranks, "Famine, and Sword, and Fire,
Crouch for employment."[12]—Lo! the suffering world,
Torn by the fearful conflict, shrinks, amaz'd,
From Freedom's name, usurp'd and misapplied,
And, cow'ring to the purple Tyrant's rod,[13]
Deems *that* the lesser ill—Deluded Men!
Ere ye prophane her ever-glorious name,
Or catalogue the thousands that have bled
Resisting her; or those, who greatly died
Martyrs to *Liberty*—revert awhile
To the black scroll, that tells of regal crimes
Committed to destroy her; rather count
The hecatombs[14] of victims, who have fallen
Beneath a single despot; or who gave
Their wasted lives for some disputed claim
Between anointed robbers: Monsters both![15]
"Oh! Polish'd perturbation—golden care!"[16]
So strangely coveted by feeble Man
To lift him o'er his fellows;—Toy, for which
Such showers of blood have drench'd th'affrighted
earth—
Unfortunate *his* lot,[17] whose luckless head
Thy jewel'd circlet, lin'd with thorns, has bound;
And who, by custom's laws, obtains from thee
Hereditary right to rule, uncheck'd,
Submissive myriads: for untemper'd power,
Like steel ill form'd, injures the hand
It promis'd to protect—Unhappy France!
If e'er thy lilies,[18] trampled now in dust,
And blood-bespotted, shall again revive
In silver splendour, may the wreath be wov'n
By voluntary hands; and Freemen, such
As England's self might boast, unite to place
The guarded diadem on *his* fair brow,
Where Loyalty may join with Liberty

[8] **headless corse . . . Monarch:** the French king Louis XVI was beheaded on 21 January 1793.

[9] **distain:** discolor, defile, dishonor.

[10] **hind:** tenant farmer or shepherd.

[11] **trumpet's voice:** call to arms.

[12] **"Famine . . . employment":** Shakspeare [C. S.], *Henry V*, Prologue, 7–8.

[13] **purple Tyrant's rod:** absolute monarchy.

[14] **hecatombs:** public sacrifices.

[15] **Monsters both!:** such was the cause of the quarrel between the Houses of York and Lancaster [in England's Wars of the Roses, 1455–1485]; and of too many others, with which the page of History reproaches the reason of man [C. S.].

[16] **"Oh! Polish'd perturbation . . . care!":** Shakspeare [C. S.], *II Henry IV*, IV.v.23.

[17] **his lot:** Louis XVI.

[18] **thy lilies:** the lily is the symbol of the Bourbon dynasty, the hereditary monarchy of France.

To fix it firmly.—In the rugged school
Of stern Adversity so early train'd,
His future life, perchance, may emulate
That of the brave Bernois,[19] so justly call'd
The darling of his people; who rever'd
The Warrior less, than they ador'd the Man!
But ne'er may Party Rage, perverse and blind,
And base Venality, prevail to raise
To public trust, a wretch,[20] whose private vice
Makes even the wildest profligate recoil;
And who, with hireling ruffians leagu'd, has burst
The laws of Nature and Humanity!
Wading, beneath the Patriot's specious mask,
And in Equality's illusive name,
To empire thro' a stream of kindred blood—
Innocent prisoner![21]—most unhappy heir
Of fatal greatness, who art suffering now
For all the crimes and follies of thy race;
Better for thee, if o'er thy baby brow
The regal mischief never had been held:
Then, in an humble sphere, perhaps content,
Thou hadst been free and joyous on the heights
Of Pyrennean mountains, shagg'd with woods
Of chestnut, pine, and oak: as on these hills
Is yonder little thoughtless shepherd lad,
Who, on the slope abrupt of downy turf
Reclin'd in playful indolence, sends off
The chalky ball, quick bounding far below;
While, half forgetful of his simple task,
Hardly his length'ning shadow, or the bells'
Slow tinkling of his flock, that supping tend
To the brown fallows[22] in the vale beneath,
Where nightly it is folded, from his sport
Recall the happy idler.—While I gaze
On his gay vacant countenance, my thoughts
Compare with his obscure, laborious lot,
Thine, most unfortunate, imperial Boy!
Who round thy sullen prison daily hear'st
The savage howl of Murder, as it seeks
Thy unoffending life: while sad within
Thy wretched Mother,[23] petrified with grief,
Views thee with stony eyes, and cannot weep!—
Ah! much I mourn thy sorrows, hapless Queen!
And deem thy expiation made to Heaven
For every fault, to which Prosperity
Betray'd thee, when it plac'd thee on a throne
Where boundless power was thine, and thou wert rais'd
High (as it seem'd) above the envious reach
Of destiny! Whate'er thy errors were,
Be they no more remember'd; tho' the rage
Of Party swell'd them to such crimes, as bade
Compassion stifle every sigh that rose
For thy disastrous lot—More than enough
Thou hast endur'd; and every English heart,
Ev'n those, that highest beat in Freedom's cause,
Disclaim as base, and of that cause unworthy,
The Vengeance, or the Fear, that makes thee still
A miserable prisoner!—Ah! who knows,
From sad experience, more than I, to feel
For thy desponding spirit, as it sinks
Beneath procrastinated fears for those
More dear to thee than life! But eminence
Of misery is thine, as once of joy;
And, as we view the strange vicissitude,
We ask anew, where happiness is found?—
Alas! in rural life, where youthful dreams
See the Arcadia[24] that Romance describes,
Not even Content resides!—In yon low hut
Of clay and thatch, where rises the grey smoke
Of smold'ring turf,[25] cut from the adjoining moor,
The labourer, its inhabitant, who toils
From the first dawn of twilight, till the Sun
Sinks in the rosy waters of the West,
Finds that with poverty it cannot dwell;
For bread, and scanty bread, is all he earns

[19] **the brave Bernois:** Henry IV of France. It may be said of this monarch, that had all the French sovereigns resembled him, despotism would have lost its horrors; yet he had considerable failings, and his greatest virtues may be chiefly imputed to his education in the School of Adversity [C. S.].

Henry IV, who reigned from 1589 to 1610, founded the Bourbon dynasty and struggled unsuccessfully to reconcile the Catholic and Protestant factions in France.

[20] **a wretch:** probably Jean-Paul Marat, who with Robespierre and St. Just, were the most bloodthirsty leaders of the Montagnard faction that initiated the Reign of Terror. Marat had a skin disease that was popularly attributed to a life of sexual promiscuity. He was assassinated in his bath by Charlotte Corday on 13 July 1793.

[21] **Innocent prisoner:** the Dauphin Louis (1786–1795), heir presumptive to the French throne, in 1793 was in prison with his parents.

[22] **brown fallows:** ploughed but uncultivated fields.

[23] **wretched Mother:** Marie Antoinette, queen of France.

[24] **Arcadia:** mythic Greek land of idyllic pastoral simplicity.

[25] **smold'ring turf:** peat, used as fuel.

For him and for his household[.]—Should Disease,
Born of chill wintry rains, arrest his arm,
Then, thro' his patch'd and straw-stuff'd casement, peeps
The squalid figure of extremest Want;
And from the Parish the reluctant dole,[26]
Dealt by th' unfeeling farmer, hardly saves
The ling'ring spark of life from cold extinction:
Then the bright Sun of Spring, that smiling bids
All other animals rejoice, beholds,
Crept from his pallet, the emaciate wretch
Attempt, with feeble effort, to resume
Some heavy task, above his wasted strength,
Turning his wistful looks (how much in vain!)
To the deserted mansion, where no more
The owner (gone to gayer scenes) resides,
Who made even luxury, Virtue; while he gave
The scatter'd crumbs to honest Poverty.—
But, tho' the landscape be too oft deform'd
By figures such as these, yet Peace is here,
And o'er our vallies, cloath'd with springing corn,
No hostile hoof shall trample, nor fierce flames
Wither the wood's young verdure, ere it form
Gradual the laughing May's luxuriant shade;
For, by the rude sea guarded, we are safe,[27]
And feel not evils such as with deep sighs
The Emigrants deplore, as they recall
The Summer past, when Nature seem'd to lose
Her course in wild distemperature, and aid,
With seasons all revers'd, destructive War.
  Shuddering, I view the pictures they have drawn
Of desolated countries, where the ground,
Stripp'd of its unripe produce, was thick strewn
With various Death—the war-horse falling there
By famine, and his rider by the sword.
The moping clouds sail'd heavy charg'd with rain,
And bursting o'er the mountains['] misty brow,
Deluged, as with an inland sea, the vales;[28]
Where, thro' the sullen evening's lurid gloom,
Rising, like columns of volcanic fire,
The flames of burning villages illum'd
The waste of water; and the wind, that howl'd
Along its troubled surface, brought the groans
Of plunder'd peasants, and the frantic shrieks
Of mothers for their children; while the brave,
To pity still alive, listen'd aghast
To these dire echoes, hopeless to prevent
The evils they beheld, or check the rage,
Which ever, as the people of one land
Meet in contention, fires the human heart
With savage thirst of kindred blood, and makes
Man lose his nature; rendering him more fierce
Than the gaunt monsters of the howling waste.
  Oft have I heard the melancholy tale,
Which, all their native gaiety forgot,
These Exiles tell—How Hope impell'd them on,
Reckless of tempest, hunger, or the sword,
Till order'd to retreat, they know not why,
From all their flattering prospects, they became
The prey of dark suspicion and regret:[29]
Then, in despondence, sunk the unnerv'd arm
Of gallant Loyalty[.]—At every turn
Shame and disgrace appear'd, and seem'd to mock
Their scatter'd squadrons; which the warlike youth,
Unable to endure, often implor'd,
As the last act of friendship, from the hand
Of some brave comrade, to receive the blow
That freed the indignant spirit from its pain.
To a wild mountain, whose bare summit hides
Its broken eminence in clouds; whose steeps

[26] **Parish . . . dole:** under the English Poor Laws, each parish was responsible for the care of its destitute inhabitants, who received minimal charitable contributions or alms (the dole).

[27] **rude sea . . . safe:** as an island nation protected by a powerful navy, England was thought to be safe from foreign invasion.

[28] **rain . . . vales:** from the heavy and incessant rains during the last campaign, the [French Emigrant] armies were often compelled to march for many miles through marshes overflowed; suffering the extremities of cold and fatigue. The peasants frequently misled them; and, after having passed these inundations at the hazard of their lives, they were sometimes under the necessity of crossing them a second and a third time; their evening quarters after such a day of exertion were often in a wood without shelter; and their repast, instead of bread, unripe corn, without any other preparation than being mashed into a sort of paste [C. S.].

[29] **Hope . . . regret:** it is remarkable, that notwithstanding the excessive hardships to which the army of the Emigrants was exposed, very few in it suffered from disease till they began to retreat; then it was that despondence consigned to the most miserable death many brave men who deserved a better fate; and then despair impelled some to suicide, while others fell by mutual wounds, unable to survive disappointment and humiliation [C. S.].

Are dark with woods; where the receding rocks
Are worn by torrents of dissolving snow,
A wretched Woman, pale and breathless, flies!
And, gazing round her, listens to the sound
Of hostile footsteps[.]—No! it dies away:
Nor noise remains, but of the cataract,
Or surly breeze of night, that mutters low
Among the thickets, where she trembling seeks
A temporary shelter—clasping close
To her hard-heaving heart her sleeping child,
All she could rescue of the innocent groupe
That yesterday surrounded her[.]—Escap'd
Almost by miracle! Fear, frantic Fear,
Wing'd her weak feet: yet, half repentant now
Her headlong haste, she wishes she had staid
To die with those affrighted Fancy paints
The lawless soldier's victims[.]—Hark! again
The driving tempest bears the cry of Death,
And, with deep sullen thunder, the dread sound
Of cannon vibrates on the tremulous earth;
While, bursting in the air, the murderous bomb
Glares o'er her mansion. Where the splinters fall,
Like scatter'd comets, its destructive path
Is mark'd by wreaths of flame!—Then, overwhelm'd
Beneath accumulated horror, sinks
The desolate mourner; yet, in Death itself,
True to maternal tenderness, she tries
To save the unconscious infant from the storm
In which she perishes; and to protect
This last dear object of her ruin'd hopes
From prowling monsters, that from other hills,
More inaccessible, and wilder wastes,
Lur'd by the scent of slaughter, follow fierce
Contending hosts, and to polluted fields
Add dire increase of horrors[.]—But alas!
The Mother and the Infant perish both!—
 The feudal Chief, whose Gothic battlements
Frown on the plain beneath, returning home
From distant lands, alone and in disguise,
Gains at the fall of night his Castle walls,
But, at the vacant gate, no Porter sits
To wait his Lord's admittance!—In the courts
All is drear silence!—Guessing but too well
The fatal truth, he shudders as he goes
Thro' the mute hall; where, by the blunted light
That the dim moon thro' painted casements lends,
He sees that devastation has been there:
Then, while each hideous image to his mind
Rises terrific, o'er a bleeding corse
Stumbling he falls; another interrupts
His staggering feet—all, all who us'd to rush
With joy to meet him—all his family
Lie murder'd in his way!—And the day dawns
On a wild raving Maniac, whom a fate
So sudden and calamitous has robb'd
Of reason; and who round his vacant walls
Screams unregarded, and reproaches Heaven!—
Such are thy dreadful trophies, savage War!
And evils such as these, or yet more dire,
Which the pain'd mind recoils from, all are thine—
The purple Pestilence, that to the grave
Sends whom the sword has spar'd, is thine; and thine
The Widow's anguish and the Orphan's tears!—
Woes such as these does Man inflict on Man;
And by the closet murderers, whom we style
Wise Politicians, are the schemes prepar'd,
Which, to keep Europe's wavering balance even,[30]
Depopulate her kingdoms, and consign
To tears and anguish half a bleeding world!—
 Oh! could the time return, when thoughts like these
Spoil'd not that gay delight, which vernal Suns,
Illuminating hills, and woods, and fields,
Gave to my infant spirits—Memory come!
And from distracting cares, that now deprive
Such scenes of all their beauty, kindly bear
My fancy to those hours of simple joy,
When, on the banks of Arun, which I see
Make its irriguous course thro' yonder meads,[31]
I play'd; unconscious then of future ill!
There (where, from hollows fring'd with yellow broom,
The birch with silver rind, and fairy leaf,
Aslant the low stream trembles) I have stood,
And meditated how to venture best
Into the shallow current, to procure
The willow herb of glowing purple spikes,
Or flags,[32] whose sword-like leaves conceal'd the tide,
Startling the timid reed-bird from her nest,
As with aquatic flowers I wove the wreath,
Such as, collected by the shepherd girls,
Deck in the villages the turfy shrine,
And mark the arrival of propitious May.—
How little dream'd I then the time would come,
When the bright Sun of that delicious month
Should, from disturb'd and artificial sleep,

[30] **Europe's . . . even:** the balance of political power.

[31] **Arun:** river in West Sussex, England. **irriguous:** irrigating. **meads:** meadows.

[32] **flags:** wild iris.

Awaken me to never-ending toil,
To terror and to tears!—Attempting still,
With feeble hands and cold desponding heart,
To save my children from the o'erwhelming wrongs,
That have for ten long years been heap'd on me!—
The fearful spectres of chicane and fraud
Have, Proteus[33] like, still chang'd their hideous forms
(As the Law lent its plausible disguise),
Pursuing my faint steps; and I have seen
Friendship's sweet bonds (which were so early form'd,
And once I fondly thought of amaranth[34]
Inwove with silver seven times tried) give way,
And fail; as these green fan-like leaves of fern
Will wither at the touch of Autumn's frost.
Yet there *are those,* whose patient pity still
Hears my long murmurs; who, unwearied, try
With lenient hands to bind up every wound
My wearied spirit feels, and bid me go
"Right onward"[35]—a calm votary of the Nymph,
Who, from her adamantine[36] rock, points out
To conscious rectitude the rugged path,
That leads at length to Peace!—Ah! yes, my friends
Peace will at last be mine; for in the Grave
Is Peace—and pass a few short years, perchance
A few short months, and all the various pain
I now endure shall be forgotten there,
And no memorial shall remain of me,
Save in your bosoms; while even *your* regret
Shall lose its poignancy, as ye reflect
What complicated woes that grave conceals!
But, if the little praise, that may await
The Mother's efforts, should provoke the spleen
Of Priest or Levite,[37] and they then arraign
The dust that cannot hear them; be it yours
To vindicate my humble fame; to say,
That, not in selfish sufferings absorb'd,
"I gave to misery all I had, my tears."[38]
And if, where regulated sanctity
Pours her long orisons[39] to Heaven, my voice
Was seldom heard, that yet *my prayer* was made
To him who hears even silence; not in domes
Of human architecture, fill'd with crowds,
But on these hills, where boundless, yet distinct,
Even as a map, beneath are spread the fields
His bounty cloaths; divided here by woods,
And there by commons rude,[40] or winding brooks,
While I might breathe the air perfum'd with flowers,
Or the fresh odours of the mountain turf;
And gaze on clouds above me, as they sail'd
Majestic: or remark the reddening north,
When bickering arrows of electric fire[41]
Flash on the evening sky—I made my prayer
In unison with murmuring waves that now
Swell with dark tempests, now are mild and blue,
As the bright arch above; for all to me
Declare omniscient goodness; nor need I
Declamatory essays to incite
My wonder or my praise, when every leaf
That Spring unfolds, and every simple bud,
More forcibly impresses on my heart
His power and wisdom—Ah! while I adore
That goodness, which design'd to all that lives
Some taste of happiness, my soul is pain'd
By the variety of woes that Man
For Man creates—his blessings often turn'd
To plagues and curses: Saint-like Piety,
Misled by Superstition, has destroy'd
More than Ambition; and the sacred flame
Of Liberty becomes a raging fire,
When Licence and Confusion bid it blaze.
From thy high throne, above yon radiant stars,
O Power Omnipotent! with mercy view
This suffering globe, and cause thy creatures cease,
With savage fangs, to tear her bleeding breast:
Restrain that rage for power, that bids a Man,
Himself a worm, desire unbounded rule
O'er beings like himself: Teach the hard hearts
Of rulers, that the poorest hind, who dies
For their unrighteous quarrels, in thy sight
Is equal to the imperious Lord, that leads

---

[33] **Proteus:** a Greek sea god who was able to change his shape at will.

[34] **amaranth:** immortal flower of paradise.

[35] **"Right onward":** Milton, Sonnet 22d [C. S.], "Cyriac, this three years' day," line 9.

[36] **adamantine:** unbreakable, of impregnable hardness.

[37] **Levite:** one of the tribe of Levi who acted as assistants to the priests in the temple worship; a Jewish rabbi.

[38] Gray [C. S.]: Thomas Gray, "He gave to Mis'ry all he had, a tear," from the poet's own epitaph included in his "Elegy Written in a Country Church-Yard," line 123.

[39] **regulated sanctity:** formal religion. **orisons:** prayers.

[40] **commons rude:** uncultivated common grazing land.

[41] **reddening north . . . fire:** northern lights, or aurora borealis.

His disciplin'd destroyers to the field.—
May lovely Freedom, in her genuine charms,
Aided by stern but equal Justice, drive
From the ensanguin'd earth the hell-born fiends
Of Pride, Oppression, Avarice, and Revenge,
That ruin what thy mercy made so fair!
Then shall these ill-starr'd wanderers, whose sad fate
These desultory lines lament, regain
Their native country; private vengeance then
To public virtue yield; and the fierce feuds,
That long have torn their desolated land,
May (even as storms, that agitate the air,
Drive noxious vapours from the blighted earth)
Serve, all tremendous as they are, to fix
The reign of Reason, Liberty, and Peace!

POSTHUMOUS PUBLICATIONS

from BEACHY HEAD, AND OTHER POEMS
(1807)

Beachy Head
(1807; comp. 1806)

On thy stupendous summit, rock sublime!
That o'er the channel rear'd, half way at sea
The mariner at early morning hails,[1]
I would recline; while Fancy should go forth,
And represent the strange and awful hour
Of vast concussion;[2] when the Omnipotent
Stretch'd forth his arm, and rent the solid hills,
Bidding the impetuous main flood rush between
The rifted shores, and from the continent
Eternally divided this green isle.
Imperial lord of the high southern coast!
From thy projecting head-land I would mark
Far in the east the shades of night disperse,
Melting and thinned, as from the dark blue wave
Emerging, brilliant rays of arrowy light
Dart from the horizon; when the glorious sun
Just lifts above it his resplendent orb.
Advances now, with feathery silver touched,
The rippling tide of flood; glisten the sands,
While, inmates of the chalky clefts that scar
Thy sides precipitous, with shrill harsh cry,
Their white wings glancing in the level beam,
The terns, and gulls, and tarrocks, seek their food,[3]
And thy rough hollows echo to the voice
Of the gray choughs, and ever restless daws,[4]
With clamour, not unlike the chiding hounds,
While the lone shepherd, and his baying dog,
Drive to thy turfy crest his bleating flock.

The high meridian of the day is past,
And Ocean now, reflecting the calm Heaven,
Is of cerulean hue; and murmurs low
The tide of ebb, upon the level sands.
The sloop, her angular canvas shifting still,
Catches the light and variable airs
That but a little crisp the summer sea,
Dimpling its tranquil surface.

Afar off,
And just emerging from the arch immense
Where seem to part the elements, a fleet
Of fishing vessels stretch their lesser sails;[5]
While more remote, and like a dubious spot
Just hanging in the horizon, laden deep,
The ship of commerce richly freighted, makes
Her slower progress, on her distant voyage,

[1] In crossing the [English] Channel from the coast of France, Beachy Head is the first land made [C. S.]. Beachy Head is the southernmost point in Sussex, between Brighton and Eastbourne, directly across the English Channel from Dieppe.

[2] Alluding to an idea that this Island was once joined to the continent of Europe, and torn from it by some convulsion of Nature. I confess I never could trace the resemblance between the two countries. Yet the cliffs about Dieppe, resemble the chalk cliffs on the Southern coast [of England]. But Normandy has no likeness whatever to the part of England opposite it [C. S.].

[3] **terns . . . tarrocks:** terns. *Sterna hirundo,* or Sea-Swallow. Gulls. *Larus canus* [seagull]. tarrocks. *Larus tridactylus* [common guillemot] [C. S.]. Here, as elsewhere in this poem, Charlotte Smith displays her considerable ornithological, zoological, and botanical learning.

[4] **gray choughs:** *Corvus Graculus,* Cornish Choughs, or, as these birds are called by the Sussex people, Saddle-backed Crows, build in great numbers on this coast [C. S.]. **daws:** *corvus monedula,* a jackdaw or crow.

[5] **lesser sails:** the fishing boats, keeping their main sails furled, sail at half-speed, dragging their nets.

Bound to the orient climates,[6] where the sun
Matures the spice within its odorous shell,
And, rivalling the gray worm's filmy toil,[7]
Bursts from its pod the vegetable down;[8]
Which in long turban'd wreaths, from torrid heat
Defends the brows of Asia's countless casts.[9]
There the Earth hides within her glowing breast
The beamy adamant,[10] and the round pearl
Enchased in rugged covering; which the slave,
With perilous and breathless toil, tears off
From the rough sea-rock, deep beneath the waves.
These are the toys of Nature; and her sport
Of little estimate in Reason's eye:
And they who reason, with abhorrence see
Man, for such gaudes and baubles, violate
The sacred freedom of his fellow man—
Erroneous estimate! As Heaven's pure air,
Fresh as it blows on this aërial height,
Or sound of seas upon the stony strand,
Or inland, the gay harmony of birds,
And winds that wander in the leafy woods;
Are to the unadulterate taste more worth
Than the elaborate harmony, brought out
From fretted stop, or modulated airs
Of vocal science.[11]—So the brightest gems,
Glancing resplendent on the regal crown,
Or trembling in the high born beauty's ear,
Are poor and paltry, to the lovely light
Of the fair star,[12] that as the day declines
Attendent on her queen, the crescent moon,
Bathes her bright tresses in the eastern wave.

[6] **dubious spot . . . orient climates:** the poet is looking southwest, toward Portsmouth, the major southern English shipping port, whence commercial ships embarked for India and the Far East.

[7] **gray worm's . . . toil:** the silkworm.

[8] Cotton. *Gossypium herbaceum* [C. S.]: England's major export in the eighteenth century was textiles.

[9] **casts:** India's castes or hereditary classes.

[10] Diamonds, the hardest and most valuable of precious stones. For the extraordinary exertions of the Indians in diving for the pearl oysters, see the account of the Pearl fisheries in [Robert] Percival's *View of Ceylon* [*An Account of the Island of Cyprus*, 1803] [C. S.].

[11] **fretted stop:** finger position on a stringed instrument. **vocal science:** music.

[12] **fair star:** the evening star, Venus.

For now the sun is verging to the sea,
And as he westward sinks, the floating clouds
Suspended, move upon the evening gale,
And gathering round his orb, as if to shade
The insufferable brightness, they resign
Their gauzy whiteness; and more warm'd, assume
All hues of purple. There, transparent gold
Mingles with ruby tints, and sapphire gleams,
And colours, such as Nature through her works
Shews only in the ethereal canopy.
Thither aspiring Fancy fondly soars,
Wandering sublime thro' visionary vales,
Where bright pavilions rise, and trophies, fann'd
By airs celestial; and adorn'd with wreaths
Of flowers that bloom amid elysian bowers.
Now bright, and brighter still the colours glow,
Till half the lustrous orb within the flood
Seems to retire: the flood reflecting still
Its splendor, and in mimic glory drest;
Till the last ray shot upward, fires the clouds
With blazing crimson; then in paler light,
Long lines of tenderer radiance, lingering yield
To partial darkness; and on the opposing side
The early moon distinctly rising, throws
Her pearly brilliance on the trembling tide.

The fishermen, who at set seasons pass
Many a league off at sea their toiling night,
Now hail their comrades, from their daily task
Returning; and make ready for their own,
With the night tide commencing:—The night tide
Bears a dark vessel on, whose hull and sails
Mark her a coaster from the north. Her keel
Now ploughs the sand; and sidelong now she leans,
While with loud clamours her athletic crew
Unload her; and resounds the busy hum
Along the wave-worn rocks. Yet more remote
Where the rough cliff hangs beetling o'er its base,
All breathes repose; the water's rippling sound
Scarce heard; but now and then the sea-snipe's[13] cry
Just tells that something living is abroad;
And sometimes crossing on the moonbright line,

[13] In crossing the channel this bird is heard at night, uttering a short cry, and flitting along near the surface of the waves. The sailors call it the Sea Snipe; but I can find no species of sea bird of which this is the vulgar name. A bird so called inhabits the Lake of Geneva [in Switzerland] [C. S.].

Glimmers the skiff, faintly discern'd awhile,
Then lost in shadow.

Contemplation here,
High on her throne of rock, aloof may sit,
And bid recording Memory unfold
Her scroll voluminous—bid her retrace
The period, when from Neustria's hostile shore[14]
The Norman launch'd his galleys, and the bay
O'er which that mass of ruin[15] frowns even now
In vain and sullen menace, then received
The new invaders; a proud martial race,
Of Scandinavia[16] the undaunted sons,
Whom Dogon, Fier-a-bras, and Humfroi led
To conquest: while Trinacria to their power
Yielded her wheaten garland; and when thou,

[14] **Neustria's hostile shore**: Normandy.

[15] Pevensey Castle [C. S.].

[16] The Scandinavians (modern Norway, Sweden, Denmark, Lapland, &c.) and other inhabitants of the north, began towards the end of the 8th century, to leave their inhospitable climate in search of the produce of more fortunate countries.

The North-men made inroads on the coasts of France; and carrying back immense booty, excited their compatriots to engage in the same piratical voyages: and they were afterwards joined by numbers of necessitous and daring adventurers from the coasts of Provence and Sicily.

In 844, these wandering innovators had a great number of vessels at sea; and again visiting the coasts of France, Spain, and England, the following year they penetrated even to Paris: and the unfortunate Charles the Bald, king of France, purchased at a high price, the retreat of the banditti he had no other means of repelling.

These successful expeditions continued for some time; till Rollo, otherwise Raoul, assembled a number of followers, and after a descent on England, crossed the channel, and made himself master of Rouen, which he fortified. Charles the Simple, unable to contend with Rollo, offered to resign to him some of the northern provinces, and to give him his daughter in marriage. Neustria, since called Normandy, was granted to him, and afterwards Brittany. He added the more solid virtues of the legislator to the fierce valour of the conqueror—converted to Christianity, he established justice, and repressed the excesses of his Danish subjects, till then accustomed to live only by plunder. . . . The Danes and Francs produced a race of men celebrated for their valour; . . . Soon afterwards three brothers of Coutance, the sons of Tancred de Hauteville, Guillaume Fier-a-bras, Drogon, and Humfroi, joining the Normans established at Aversa, became masters of the fertile island of Sicily; and Robert Guiscard joining them, the Normans became sovereigns both of Sicily and Naples (Parthenope). [C. S.].

Parthenope! within thy fertile bay
Receiv'd the victors—

In the mailed ranks
Of Normans landing on the British coast
Rode Taillefer; and with astounding voice
Thunder'd the war song daring Roland sang
First in the fierce contention: vainly brave,
One not inglorious struggle England made—
But failing, saw the Saxon heptarchy[17]
Finish for ever.——Then the holy pile,[18]
Yet seen upon the field of conquest, rose,
Where to appease heaven's wrath for so much blood,
The conqueror bade unceasing prayers ascend,
And requiems for the slayers and the slain.
But let not modern Gallia[19] form from hence
Presumptuous hopes, that ever thou again,
Queen of the isles! shalt crouch to foreign arms.
The enervate sons of Italy may yield;
And the Iberian,[20] all his trophies torn
And wrapp'd in Superstition's monkish weed,
May shelter his abasement, and put on
Degrading fetters. Never, never thou!
Imperial mistress of the obedient sea;
But thou, in thy integrity secure,
Shalt now undaunted meet a world in arms.

England! 'twas where this promontory rears
Its rugged brow above the channel wave,
Parting the hostile nations, that thy fame,
Thy naval fame was tarnish'd, at what time
Thou, leagued with the Batavian, gavest to France[21]

[17] **Saxon heptarchy**: the seven contiguous kingdoms of Saxon England.

[18] Battle Abbey was raised by [William] the Conqueror [in 1066, after the Battle of Hastings], and endowed with an ample revenue, that masses might be said night and day for the souls of whose who perished in battle [C. S.].

[19] **Gallia**: France.

[20] **Italy . . . Iberian**: Napoleon conquered both Italy and Spain (the Iberian peninsula).

[21] In 1690, King William being then in Ireland, Tourville, the French admiral, arrived on the coast of England. His fleet consisted of seventy-eight large ships, and twenty-two fire-ships. Lord Torrington, the English admiral, lay at St. Helens, with only forty English and a few Dutch ships; and conscious of the disadvantage under which he should give battle, he ran up between the enemy's fleet and the coast, to protect it. The queen's council, dictated to by Russel, persuaded her to order Torrington

One day of triumph—triumph the more loud,
Because even then so rare. Oh! well redeem'd,
Since, by a series of illustrious men,
Such as no other country ever rear'd,
To vindicate her cause. It is a list
Which, as Fame echoes it, blanches the cheek
Of bold Ambition, while the despot feels
The extorted sceptre tremble in his grasp.

From even the proudest roll[22] by glory fill'd,
How gladly the reflecting mind returns
To simple scenes of peace and industry,
Where, bosom'd in some valley of the hills
Stands the lone farm; its gate with tawny ricks[23]
Surrounded, and with granaries and sheds,
Roof'd with green mosses, and by elms and ash
Partially shaded; and not far remov'd
The hut of sea-flints built; the humble home
Of one, who sometimes watches on the heights,[24]
When hid in the cold mist of passing clouds,
The flock, with dripping fleeces, are dispers'd
O'er the wide down; then from some ridged point
That overlooks the sea, his eager eye
Watches the bark that for his signal waits
To land its merchandize:—Quitting for this
Clandestine traffic his more honest toil,
The crook[25] abandoning, he braves himself
The heaviest snow-storm of December's night,
When with conflicting winds the ocean raves,
And on the tossing boat, unfearing mounts
To meet the partners of the perilous trade,
And share their hazard. Well it were for him,
If no such commerce of destruction known,
He were content with what the earth affords
To human labour; even where she seems
Reluctant most. More happy is the hind,
Who, with his own hands rears on some black moor,
Or turbary,[26] his independent hut
Cover'd with heather, whence the slow white smoke
Of smouldering peat arises——A few sheep,
His best possession, with his children share
The rugged shed when wintry tempests blow;
But, when with Spring's return the green blades rise
Amid the russet heath, the household live
Joint tenants of the waste[27] throughout the day,
And often, from her nest, among the swamps,
Where the gemm'd sun-dew grows, or fring'd
buck-bean,
They scare the plover,[28] that with plaintive cries
Flutters, as sorely wounded, down the wind.
Rude, and but just remov'd from savage life
Is the rough dweller among scenes like these,
(Scenes all unlike the poet's fabling dreams
Decribing Arcady)—But he is free;
The dread that follows on illegal acts
He never feels; and his industrious mate
Shares in his labour. Where the brook is traced
By crouding osiers, and the black coot[29] hides
Among the plashy reeds, her diving brood,
The matron wades; gathering the long green rush[30]

---

to venture a battle. The orders Torrington appears to have obeyed reluctantly: his fleet now consisted of twenty-two Dutch and thirty-four English ships. Evertson, the Dutch admiral, was eager to obtain glory; Torrington, more cautious, reflected on the importance of the stake. The consequence was, that the Dutch rashly sailing on were surrounded, and Torrington, solicitous to recover this false step, placed himself with difficulty between the Dutch and French,—but three Dutch ships were burnt, two of their admirals killed, and almost all their ships disabled. The English and Dutch declining a second engagement, retired towards the mouth of the Thames. The French, from ignorance of the coast, and misunderstanding among each other, failed to take all the advantage they might have done of this victory [C. S.].

[22] **roll:** historical chronicle or military list of soldiers wounded or killed in battle.

[23] **tawny ricks:** haystacks.

[24] The shepherds and labourers of this tract of country, a hardy and athletic race of men, are almost universally engaged in the countraband trade, carried on for the coarsest and most destructive spirits, with the opposite coast. When no other vessel will venture to sea, these men hazard their lives to elude the watchfulness of the Revenue officers, and to secure their cargoes [C. S.].

[25] **crook:** shepherd's staff with hooked end, for catching the hind legs of sheep.

[26] **turbary:** peat bog.

[27] **waste:** uncultivated lands.

[28] **sun-dew.** *Drosera rotundifolia.* [small herbs growing in bogs whose leaves secrete viscid drops which glitter in the sun like dew]. **buck-bean.** *Menyanthes trifoliatum.* [water-plant common in bogs in England, bears pinkish white flowers]. **plover.** *Tringa vanellus.* [common bird of snipe family] [C. S.].

[29] **osiers:** species of willow much used in basketwork. **coot:** *Fulica aterrima* [C. S.]: web-footed water bird.

[30] **rush:** dried reeds burned for light instead of the more expensive candles.

That well prepar'd hereafter lends its light
To her poor cottage, dark and cheerless else
Thro' the drear hours of Winter. Otherwhile
She leads her infant group where charlock[31] grows
"Unprofitably gay,"[32] or to the fields,
Where congregate the linnet and the finch,
That on the thistles, so profusely spread,
Feast in the desert; the poor family
Early resort, extirpating with care
These, and the gaudier mischief of the ground;
Then flames the high rais'd heap; seen afar off
Like hostile war-fires flashing to the sky.[33]
Another task is theirs: On fields that shew
As angry Heaven had rain'd sterility,
Stony and cold, and hostile to the plough,
Where clamouring loud, the evening curlew[34] runs
And drops her spotted eggs among the flints;
The mother and the children pile the stones
In rugged pyramids; —and all this toil
They patiently encounter; well content
On their flock bed[35] to slumber undisturb'd
Beneath the smoky roof they call their own.
Oh! little knows the sturdy hind, who stands
Gazing, with looks where envy and contempt
Are often strangely mingled, on the car
Where prosperous Fortune sits; what secret care
Or sick satiety is often hid,
Beneath the splendid outside: *He* knows not
How frequently the child of Luxury
Enjoying nothing, flies from place to place
In chase of pleasure that eludes his grasp;
And that content is e'en less found by him,
Than by the labourer, whose pick-axe smooths
The road before his chariot; and who doffs
What *was* an hat; and as the train pass on,
Thinks how one day's expenditure, like this,
Would cheer him for long months, when to his toil
The frozen earth closes her marble breast.
Ah! who *is* happy? Happiness! a word
That like false fire,[36] from marsh effluvia born,
Misleads the wanderer, destin'd to contend
In the world's wilderness, with want or woe—
Yet *they* are happy, who have never ask'd
What good or evil means. The boy
That on the river's margin gaily plays,
Has heard that Death is there[.]—He knows not
    Death,
And therefore fears it not; and venturing in
He gains a bullrush, or a minnow—then,
At certain peril, for a worthless prize,
A crow's, or raven's nest, he climbs the boll[37]
Of some tall pine; and of his prowess proud,
Is for a moment happy. Are *your* cares,
Ye who despise him, never worse applied?
The village girl is happy, who sets forth
To distant fair, gay in her Sunday suit,
With cherry colour'd knots, and flourish'd shawl,
And bonnet newly purchas'd. So is he
Her little brother, who his mimic drum
Beats, till he drowns her rural lovers' oaths
Of constant faith, and still increasing love;
Ah! yet a while, and half those oaths believ'd,
Her happiness is vanish'd; and the boy
While yet a stripling, finds the sound he lov'd
Has led him on, till he has given up
His freedom, and his happiness together.
I once was happy, when while yet a child,
I learn'd to love these upland solitudes,
And, when elastic[38] as the mountain air,
To my light spirit, care was yet unknown
And evil unforseen:—Early it came,
And childhood scarcely passed, I was condemned,
A guiltless exile, silently to sigh,
While Memory, with faithful pencil, drew
The contrast; and regretting, I compar'd
With the polluted smoky atmosphere
And dark and stifling streets, the southern hills
That to the setting Sun, their graceful heads

[31] **charlock:** wild mustard, poisonous to sheep.

[32] "With blossom'd furze, unprofitably gay." Goldsmith [*The Deserted Village*, line 194] [C. S.].

[33] The Beacons formerly lighted up the hills to give notice of the approach of an enemy. These signals would still be used in case of alarm, if the Telegraph [semaphore signals] now substituted could not be distinguished on account of fire or darkness [C. S.].

[34] curlew. *Charadrius oedienemus* [C. S.].

[35] **flock bed:** mattress stuffed with tufts of waste wool or cotton.

[36] **false fire:** ignis fatuus, will-o'-the-wisp.

[37] **boll:** bole, trunk.

[38] **elastic:** buoyant, flexible, resilient.

Rearing, o'erlook the frith, where Vecta[39] breaks
With her white rocks, the strong impetuous tide,
When western winds the vast Atlantic urge
To thunder on the coast[.]—Haunts of my youth!
Scenes of fond day dreams, I behold ye yet!
Where 'twas so pleasant by thy northern slopes
To climb the winding sheep-path, aided oft
By scatter'd thorns: whose spiny branches bore
Small woolly tufts, spoils of the vagrant lamb
There seeking shelter from the noon-day sun;
And pleasant, seated on the short soft turf,
To look beneath upon the hollow way
While heavily upward mov'd the labouring wain,[40]
And stalking slowly by, the sturdy hind
To ease his panting team, stopp'd with a stone
The grating wheel.

Advancing higher still
The prospect widens, and the village church
But little, o'er the lowly roofs around
Rears its gray belfry, and its simple vane;
Those lowly roofs of thatch are half conceal'd
By the rude arms of trees, lovely in spring,[41]
When on each bough, the rosy-tinctur'd bloom
Sits thick, and promises autumnal plenty.
For even those orchards round the Norman Farms,
Which, as their owners mark the promis'd fruit,
Console them for the vineyards of the south,
Surpass not these.

Where woods of ash, and beech,
And partial copses, fringe the green hill foot,
The upland shepherd rears his modest home,
There wanders by, a little nameless stream
That from the hill wells forth, bright now and clear,
Or after rain with chalky mixture gray,
But still refreshing in its shallow course,
The cottage garden; most for use design'd,
Yet not of beauty destitute. The vine
Mantles the little casement; yet the briar
Drops fragrant dew among the July flowers;
And pansies rayed, and freak'd and mottled pinks
Grow among balm, and rosemary and rue;
There honeysuckles flaunt, and roses blow
Almost uncultured: Some with dark green leaves
Contrast their flowers of pure unsullied white;
Others, like velvet robes of regal state
Of richest crimson, while in thorny moss
Enshrined and cradled, the most lovely, wear
The hues of youthful beauty's glowing cheek.—
With fond regret I recollect e'en now
In Spring and Summer, what delight I felt
Among these cottage gardens, and how much
Such artless nosegays, knotted with a rush
By village housewife or her ruddy maid,
Were welcome to me; soon and simply pleas'd.

An early worshipper at Nature's shrine,
I loved her rudest scenes—warrens,[42] and heaths,
And yellow commons, and birch-shaded hollows,
And hedge rows, bordering unfrequented lanes
Bowered with wild roses, and the clasping woodbine
Where purple tassels of the tangling vetch
With bittersweet, and bryony inweave,
And the dew fills the silver bindweed's cups—
I loved to trace the brooks whose humid banks
Nourish the harebell, and the freckled pagil;[43]
And stroll among o'ershadowing woods of beech,
Lending in Summer, from the heats of noon
A whispering shade; while haply there reclines
Some pensive lover of uncultur'd flowers,
Who, from the tumps[44] with bright green mosses clad,
Plucks the wood sorrel,[45] with its light thin leaves,
Heart-shaped, and triply folded; and its root
Creeping like beaded coral; or who there
Gathers, the copse's pride, anémones,[46]

---

[39] **frith:** firth, long narrow inlet from the sea. **Vecta:** the Isle of Wight, which breaks the force of the waves when they are driven by south-west winds against this long and open coast. It is somewhere described as "Vecta shouldering the Western Waves" [C. S.].

[40] **hollow way:** road through a valley. **wain:** cart.

[41] Every cottage in this country has its orchard; and I imagine that not even those of Herefordshire, or Worcestershire, exhibit a more beautiful prospect, when the trees are in bloom, and the "Primavera candida e vermiglia" ["pure and rosy Spring," Petrarch, Sonnet 310, line 4] is every where so enchanting [C. S.].

[42] **warrens:** a piece of uncultivated ground in which rabbits breed wild in burrows.

[43] **vetch.** *Vicia sylvatica.* **bittersweet.** *Solanum dulcamara.* **bryony.** *Bryonia alba.* **bindweed.** *Convolvulus sepium.* **harebell.** *Hyancinthus non scriptus.* **pagil.** *Primula veris* [C. S.].

[44] **uncultur'd flowers:** wildflowers. **tumps:** hillocks, mounds.

[45] **sorrel.** *Oxalis acetosella* [C. S.].

[46] **anémones.** *Anemóne nemorosa.* It appears to be settled on late and excellent authorities, that this word should not be accented

With rays like golden studs on ivory laid
Most delicate: but touch'd with purple clouds,
Fit crown for April's fair but changeful brow.

Ah! hills so early loved! in fancy still
I breathe your pure keen air; and still behold
Those widely spreading views, mocking alike
The Poet and the Painter's utmost art.
And still, observing objects more minute,
Wondering remark the strange and foreign forms
Of sea-shells; with the pale calcareous[47] soil
Mingled, and seeming of resembling substance.[48]
Tho' surely the blue Ocean (from the heights
Where the downs westward trend, but dimly seen)
Here never roll'd its surge. Does Nature then
Mimic, in wanton mood, fantastic shapes
Of bivalves, and inwreathed volutes,[49] that cling
To the dark sea-rock of the wat'ry world?
Or did this range of chalky mountains, once[50]
Form a vast bason, where the Ocean waves
Swell'd fathomless? What time these fossil shells,
Buoy'd on their native element, were thrown
Among the imbedding calx:[51] when the huge hill
Its giant bulk heaved, and in strange ferment
Grew up a guardian barrier, 'twixt the sea
And the green level of the sylvan weald.[52]

Ah! very vain is Science' proudest boast,
And but a little light its flame yet lends
To its most ardent votaries; since from whence
These fossil forms are seen, is but conjecture,
Food for vague theories, or vain dispute,
While to his daily task the peasant goes,
Unheeding such inquiry; with no care
But that the kindly change of sun and shower,
Fit for his toil the earth he cultivates.
As little recks the herdsman of the hill,
Who on some turfy knoll, idly reclined,
Watches his wether[53] flock, that deep beneath
Rest the remains of men, of whom is left[54]
No traces in the records of mankind,
Save what these half obliterated mounds
And half fill'd trenches doubtfully impart
To some lone antiquary; who on times remote,
Since which two thousand years have roll'd away,
Loves to contemplate. He perhaps may trace,
Or fancy he can trace, the oblong square
Where the mail'd legions, under Claudius,[55] rear'd
The rampire, or excavated fossé delved;[56]
What time the huge unwieldy Elephant[57]

on the second syllable, but on the penultima. I have however ventured the more known accentuation, as more generally used, and suiting better the nature of my verse [C. S.].

[47] **calcareous**: chalky.

[48] Among the crumbling chalk I have often found shells, some quite in a fossil state and hardly distinguishable from chalk. Others appeared more recent; cockles, muscles, and periwinkles, I well remember, were among the number; and some whose names I do not know. A great number were like those of small land snails. It is now many years since I made these observations. The appearance of sea-shells so far from the sea excited my surprise, though I then knew nothing of natural history. I have never read any of the late theories of the earth, nor was I ever satisfied with the attempts to explain many of the phenomena which call forth conjecture in those books I happened to have had access to on this subject [C. S.].

[49] **bivalves**: double-shelled mollusks, such as clams and oysters. **volutes**: spiral-shelled mollusks, such as conches and periwinkles.

[50] The theory here slightly hinted at, is taken from an idea started by Mr. White [Gilbert White (1720–1793), in *The History of Seabourne* (1789)] [C. S.].

[51] **calx**: lime.

[52] **sylvan weald**: the Sussex Weald, the wooded valley lying inland from the downs that border the southwestern English coast.

[53] **wether**: male sheep, ram, often a castrated ram.

[54] These Downs are not only marked with traces of encampments, which from their forms are called Roman or Danish; but there are numerous tumuli [burial mounds] among them. Some of which having been opened a few years ago, were supposed by a learned antiquary to contain the remains of the original natives of the country [C. S.].

[55] That the legions of Claudius [10 BC–54 AD] were in this part of Britain appears certain, since this emperor received the submission of Cantii, Atrebates, Irenobates, and Regni, in which latter denomination were included the people of Sussex [C. S.].

[56] **rampire**: rampart, barrier. **fossé**: ditch, trench. **delved**: dug up.

[57] In the year 1740, some workmen digging in the park at Burton in Sussex, discovered, nine feet below the surface, the teeth and bones of an elephant; two of the former were seven feet eight inches in length. There were besides these, tusks, one of which broke in removing it, a grinder not at all decayed, and a part of the jaw-bone, with bones of the knee and thigh, and

Auxiliary reluctant, hither led,
From Afric's forest glooms and tawny sands,
First felt the Northern blast, and his vast frame
Sunk useless; whence in after ages found,
The wondering hinds, on those enormous bones
Gaz'd; and in giants[58] dwelling on the hills
Believed and marvell'd—
Hither, Ambition come!
Come and behold the nothingness of all
For which you carry thro' the oppressed Earth,
War, and its train of horrors—see where tread
The innumerous hoofs of flocks above the works
By which the warrior sought to register
His glory, and immortalize his name[.]—

several others. Some of them remained very lately at Burton House, the seat of John Biddulph, Esq. Others were in possession of the Rev. Dr. Langrish, minister of Petworth at that period, who was present when some of these bones were taken up, and gave it as his opinion, that they had remained there since the universal deluge [that is, from the time of Noah's Ark]. The Romans under the Emperor Claudius probably brought elephants into Britain. Milton, in the Second Book of his History [of Britain], in speaking of the expedition, says that "He [who waiteth ready with a huge preparation, as if not safe anough amidst the flowr of all his Romans,] like a great eastern king, with armed elephants, marched [marches] through Gallia." This is given on the authority of Dion Cassius, in his Life of the Emperor Claudius. It has therefore been conjectured, that the bones found at Burton might have been those of one of these elephants, who perished there soon after its landing; or dying on the high downs, one of which, called Duncton Hill, rises immediately above Burton Park, the bones might have been washed down by the torrents of rain, and buried deep in the soil. They were not found together, but scattered at some distance from each other. The two tusks were twenty feet apart. I had often heard of the elephant's bones at Burton, but never saw them; and I have no books to refer to. I think I saw, in what is now called the National Museum at Paris, the very large bones of an elephant, which were found in North America: though it is certain that this enormous animal is never seen in its natural state, but in the countries under the torrid zone of the old world. I have, since making this note, been told that the bones of the rhinoceros and hippopotamus have been found in America [C. S.].

58 The peasants believe that the large bones sometimes found belonged to giants, who formerly lived on the hills. The devil also has a great deal to do with the remarkable forms of hill and vale: the Devil's Punch Bowl, the Devil's Leaps, and the Devil's Dyke, are names given to deep hollows, or high and abrupt ridges, in this and the neighboring country [C. S.].

The pirate Dane,[59] who from his circular camp
Bore in destructive robbery, fire and sword
Down thro' the vale, sleeps unremember'd here;
And here, beneath the green sward, rests alike
The savage native,[60] who his acorn meal
Shar'd with the herds, that ranged the pathless woods;
And the centurion, who on these wide hills
Encamping, planted the Imperial Eagle.[61]
All, with the lapse of Time, have passed away,
Even as the clouds, with dark and dragon shapes,
Or like vast promontories crown'd with towers,
Cast their broad shadows on the downs: then sail
Far to the northward, and their transient gloom
Is soon forgotten.
But from thoughts like these,
By human crimes suggested, let us turn
To where a more attractive study courts
The wanderer of the hills; while shepherd girls
Will from among the fescue[62] bring him flowers,
Of wonderous mockery; some resembling bees
In velvet vest, intent on their sweet toil,[63]
While others mimic flies,[64] that lightly sport
In the green shade, or float along the pool,
But here seen perch'd upon the slender stalk,
And gathering honey dew. While in the breeze
That wafts the thistle's plumed seed along,

59 The incursions of the Danes were for many ages the scourge of this island [C. S.].

60 The Aborigines of this country lived in woods, unsheltered but by trees and caves; and were probably as truly savage as any of those who are now termed so [C. S.].

61 **Imperial Eagle**: the emblem of the Roman Empire.

62 The grass called Sheep's Fescue *(Festuca ovina)* clothes these Downs with the softest turf [C. S.].

63 *Ophrys apifera.* Bee Ophrys, or Orchis found plentifully on the hills, as well as the next [C. S.].

64 *Ophrys muscifera.* Fly Orchis. Linnaeus, misled by the variations to which some of this tribe are really subject, has perhaps too rashly esteemed all those which resemble insects, as forming only one species, which he terms Ophrys insectifera. See *English Botany* [C. S.]. **Linnaeus**: Carolus Linnaeus (1707–1778), Swedish botanist and father of modern systematic botany. His most famous treatise, *Systema Naturae,* appeared in 1737; he visited England in 1737 and the translation of his observations, *English Botany,* appeared in 1742.

Blue bells wave tremulous. The mountain thyme[65]
Purples the hassock of the heaving mole,
And the short turf is gay with tormentil,[66]
And bird's foot trefoil, and the lesser tribes
Of hawkweed;[67] spangling it with fringed stars.—
Near where a richer tract of cultur'd land
Slopes to the south; and burnished by the sun,
Bend in the gale of August, floods of corn;
The guardian of the flock, with watchful care,[68]
Repels by voice and dog the encroaching sheep—
While his boy visits every wired trap[69]
That scars the turf; and from the pit-falls takes
The timid migrants,[70] who from distant wilds,
Warrens, and stone quarries, are destined thus
To lose their short existence. But unsought
By Luxury yet, the Shepherd still protects
The social bird,[71] who from his native haunts
Of willowy current, or the rushy pool,
Follows the fleecy croud, and flirts and skims,
In fellowship among them.
                                        Where the knoll
More elevated takes the changeful winds,
The windmill rears its vanes; and thitherward
With his white load,[72] the master travelling,
Scares the rooks rising slow on whispering wings,
While o'er his head, before the summer sun
Lights up the blue expanse, heard more than seen,
The lark sings matins; and above the clouds
Floating, embathes his spotted breast in dew.
Beneath the shadow of a gnarled thorn,
Bent by the sea blast[73] from a seat of turf
With fairy nosegays strewn, how wide the view.[74]
Till in the distant north it melts away,
And mingles indiscriminate with clouds:
But if the eye could reach so far, the mart
Of England's capital, its domes and spires
Might be perceived—Yet hence the distant range
Of Kentish hills,[75] appear in purple haze;
And nearer, undulate the wooded heights,
And airy summits,[76] that above the mole[77]

[65] **Blue bells.** *Campanula rotundifolia.* **Mountain thyme.** *Thymus serpyllum.* "It is a common notion, that the flesh of sheep which feed upon aromatic plants, particularly wild thyme, is superior in flavour to other mutton. The truth is, that sheep do not crop these aromatic plants, unless now and then by accident, or when they are first turned on hungry to downs, heaths, or commons; but the soil and situations favourable to aromatic plants, produce a short sweet pasturage, best adapted to feeding sheep, whom nature designed for mountains, and not for turnip grounds and rich meadows. The attachment of bees to this, and other aromatic plants, is well known." Martyn's Miller [Thomas Martyn, *The Gardener's and Botanist's Dictionary . . . by the late Philip Miller . . . To Which Are Now Added a Complete Enumeration and Description of All Plants* (1797–1807)] [C. S.].

[66] **hassock . . . mole:** matted vegetation or grassy mound being forced up by a ridge forming in watery ground. **tormentil.** *Tormentilla reptans* [C. S.].

[67] **bird's foot trefoil.** *Trifolium ornithopoides.* **hawkweed.** *Hieracium,* many sorts [C. S.].

[68] The downs, especially to the south, where they are less abrupt, are in many places under the plough; and the attention of the shepherds is there particularly required to keep the flocks from trespassing [C. S.].

[69] Square holes cut in the turf, into which a wire noose is fixed, to catch Wheatears. Mr. White *[History of Selbourne]* says, that these birds *(Motacilla oenanthe)* are never taken beyond the river Adur, and Beding Hill; but this is certainly a mistake [C. S.].

[70] These birds are extremely fearful, and on the slightest appearance of a cloud, run for shelter to the first rut, or heap of stone, that they see [C. S.].

[71] The Yellow Wagtail. *Motacilla flava.* It frequents the banks of rivulets in winter, making its nest in meadows and corn-fields. But after the breeding season is over, it haunts downs and sheepwalks, and is seen constantly among the flocks, probably for the sake of the insects it picks up. In France the shepherds call it *La Bergeronette,* and say it often gives them, by its cry, notice of approaching danger [C. S.].

[72] **white load:** grain, to be ground into flour.

[73] The strong winds from the south-west occasion almost all the trees, which on these hills are exposed to it, to grow the other way [C. S.].

[74] So extensive are some of the views from these hills, that only the want of power in the human eye to travel so far, prevents London itself being discerned. Description falls so infinitely short of the reality, that only here and there, distinct features can be given [C. S.].

[75] A scar of chalk in a hill beyond Sevenoaks in Kent, is very distinctly seen of a clear day [C. S.].

[76] The hills above Dorking in Surry; over almost the whole extent of which country the prospect extends [C. S.].

[77] **mole:** ridge of cliffs that descend to the sea.

Rise in green beauty; and the beacon'd ridge
Of Black-down[78] shagg'd with heath, and swelling rude
Like a dark island from the vale; its brow
Catching the last rays of the evening sun
That gleam between the nearer park's old oaks,
Then lighten up the river, and make prominent
The portal, and the ruin'd battlements[79]
Of that dismantled fortress; rais'd what time
The Conqueror's successors fiercely fought,
Tearing with civil feuds the desolate land.
But now a tiller of the soil dwells there,
And of the turret's loop'd and rafter'd halls
Has made an humbler homestead—Where he sees,
Instead of armed foemen, herds that graze
Along his yellow meadows; or his flocks
At evening from the upland driv'n to fold—

In such a castellated mansion once
A stranger chose his home; and where hard by
In rude disorder fallen, and hid with brushwood
Lay fragments gray of towers and buttresses,
Among the ruins, often he would muse—
His rustic meal soon ended, he was wont
To wander forth, listening the evening sounds
Of rushing milldam, or the distant team,
Or night-jar, chasing fern-flies:[80] the tir'd hind
Pass'd him at nightfall, wondering he should sit
On the hill top so late: they from the coast
Who sought bye paths with their clandestine load,
Saw with suspicious doubt, the lonely man
Cross on their way: but village maidens thought
His senses injur'd; and with pity say
That he, poor youth! must have been cross'd in
    love—

For often, stretch'd upon the mountain turf
With folded arms, and eyes intently fix'd
Where ancient elms and firs obscured a grange,[81]
Some little space within the vale below,
They heard him, as complaining of his fate,
And to the murmuring wind, of cold neglect
And baffled hope he told.—The peasant girls
These plaintive sounds remember, and even now
Among them may be heard the stranger's songs.

Were I a Shepherd on the hill
    And ever as the mists withdrew
Could see the willows of the rill
Shading the footway to the mill
    Where once I walk'd with you—

And as away Night's shadows sail,
    And sounds of birds and brooks arise,
Believe, that from the woody vale
I hear your voice upon the gale
    In soothing melodies;

And viewing from the Alpine height,
    The prospect dress'd in hues of air,
Could say, while transient colours bright

[78] This is an high ridge, extending between Sussex and Surry. It is covered with heath, and has almost always a dark appearance. On it is a telegraph [C. S.].

[79] In this country there are several of the fortresses or castles built by Stephen of Blois [King of England, 1135–1154], in his contention for the kingdom, with the daughter of Henry I, the empress Matilda. Some of these are now converted into farm houses [C. S.].

[80] Dr. Aikin remarks, I believe, in his essay "On the Application of Natural History to the Purposes of Poetry," how many of our best poets have noticed the same circumstance, the hum of the Dor Beetle *(Scaraboeus stercorarius)* among the sounds heard by the evening wanderer. [In *An Essay on the Application of Natural History to Poetry* (London: J. Johnson, 1777), 7–8, John Aikin, the brother of Anna Barbauld, compares the usage of Shakespeare's *Macbeth*, Milton's "Lycidas," Gray's "Elegy Written in a Country Church-Yard," and Collins' "Ode to Evening."] I remember only one instance in which the more remarkable, though by no means uncommon noise, of the Fern Owl, or Goatsucker, is mentioned. It is called the Night Hawk, the Jar Bird, the Churn Owl, and the Fern Owl, from its feeding on the *Scaraboeus solstitialis*, or Fern Chafer, which it catches while on the wing with its claws, the middle toe of which is long and curiously serrated, on purpose to hold them. It was this bird that was intended to be described in the Forty-second Sonnet [Smith's *Elegiac Sonnets*]. I was mistaken in supposing it as visible in November; it is a migrant, and leaves this country in August. I had often seen and heard it, but I did not then know its name or history. It is called Goatsucker *(Caprimulgus)*, from a strange prejudice taken against it by the Italians, who assert that it sucks their goats; and the peasants of England still believe that a disease in the backs of their cattle, occasioned by a fly, which deposits its egg under the skin, and raises a boil, sometimes fatal to calves, is the work of this bird, which they call a Puckeridge. Nothing can convince them that their beasts are not injured by this bird, which they therefore hold in abhorrence [C. S.].

[81] **grange:** farm.

Touch'd the fair scene with dewy light,
'Tis, that *her* eyes are there!

I think, I could endure my lot
And linger on a few short years,
And then, by all but you forgot,
Sleep, where the turf that clothes the spot
May claim some pitying tears.

For 'tis not easy to forget
One, who thro' life has lov'd you still,
And you, however late, might yet
With sighs to Memory giv'n, regret
The Shepherd of the Hill.

Yet otherwhile it seem'd as if young Hope
Her flattering pencil gave to Fancy's hand,
And in his wanderings, rear'd to sooth his soul
Ideal bowers of pleasure—Then, of Solitude
And of his hermit life, still more enamour'd,
His home was in the forest; and wild fruits
And bread sustain'd him. There in early spring
The Barkmen[82] found him, e'er the sun arose;
There at their daily toil, the Wedgecutters[83]
Beheld him thro' the distant thicket move.
The shaggy dog following the truffle hunter,[84]
Bark'd at the loiterer; and perchance at night
Belated villagers from fair or wake,
While the fresh night-wind let the moonbeams in
Between the swaying boughs, just saw him pass,
And then in silence, gliding like a ghost
He vanish'd! Lost among the deepening gloom.—
But near one ancient tree, whose wreathed roots
Form'd a rude couch, love-songs and scatter'd rhymes,
Unfinish'd sentences, or half erased,
And rhapsodies like this, were sometimes found—

Let us to woodland wilds repair
While yet the glittering night-dews seem
To wait the freshly-breathing air,
Precursive of the morning beam,
That rising with advancing day,
Scatters the silver drops away.

An elm, uprooted by the storm,
The trunk with mosses gray and green,
Shall make for us a rustic form,
Where lighter grows the forest scene;
And far among the bowery shades,
Are ferny lawns and grassy glades.

Retiring May to lovely June
Her latest garland now resigns:
The banks with cuckoo-flowers[85] are strewn,
The woodwalks blue with columbines,[86]
And with its reeds, the wandering stream
Reflects the flag-flower's[87] golden gleam.

There, feathering down the turf to meet,
Their shadowy arms the beeches spread,
While high above our sylvan seat,
Lifts the light ash its airy head;
And later leaved, the oaks between
Extend their boughs of vernal green.

The slender birch its paper rind
Seems offering to divided love,
And shuddering even without a wind
Aspins, their paler foliage move,
As if some spirit of the air
Breath'd a low sigh in passing there.

The Squirrel in his frolic mood,
Will fearless bound among the boughs;
Yaffils[88] laugh loudly thro' the wood,
And murmuring ring-doves tell their vows;
While we, as sweetest woodscents rise,
Listen to woodland melodies.

[82] As soon as the sap begins to rise, the trees intended for felling are cut and barked. At which time the men who are employed in that business pass whole days in the woods [C. S.].

[83] The wedges used in ship-building are made of beech wood, and great numbers are cut every year in the woods near the Downs [C. S.].

[84] Truffles are found under the beech woods, by means of small dogs trained to hunt them by the scent [C. S.].

[85] **cuckoo-flowers.** *Lychnis dioica.* Shakespeare describes the Cuckoo buds as being yellow [in *Love's Labour's Lost*, V.ii.894]. He probably meant the numerous Ranunculi, or March marigolds (*Caltha palustris*) which so gild the meadows in Spring; but poets have never been botanists. The Cuckoo flower is the *Lychnis floscuculi* [C. S.].

[86] **Columbines.** *Aquilegia vulgaris* [C. S.].

[87] **flag-flower.** *iris pseudacorus* [C. S.].

[88] **Yaffils.** Woodpeckers (*Picus*), three or four species in Britain [C. S.].

And I'll contrive a sylvan room
Against the time of summer heat,
Where leaves, inwoven in Nature's loom,
Shall canopy our green retreat;
And gales that "close the eye of day"[89]
Shall linger, e'er they die away.

And when a sear and sallow hue
From early frost the bower receives,
I'll dress the sand rock cave for you,
And strew the floor with heath and leaves,
That you, against the autumnal air
May find securer shelter there.

The Nightingale will then have ceas'd
To sing her moonlight serenade;
But the gay bird with blushing breast,[90]
And Woodlarks[91] still will haunt the shade,
And by the borders of the spring
Reed-wrens[92] will yet be carolling.

The forest hermit's lonely cave
None but such soothing sounds shall reach,
Or hardly heard, the distant wave
Slow breaking on the stony beach;
Or winds, that now sigh soft and low,
Now make wild music as they blow.

And then, before the chilling North
The tawny foliage falling light,
Seems, as it flits along the earth,
The footfall of the busy Sprite,
Who wrapt in pale autumnal gloom,
Calls up the mist-born Mushroom.

Oh! could I hear your soft voice there,
And see you in the forest green
All beauteous as you are, more fair
You'ld look, amid the sylvan scene,
And in a wood-girl's simple guise,
Be still more lovely in mine eyes.

Ye phantoms of unreal delight,
Visions of fond delirium born!
Rise not on my deluded sight,
Then leave me drooping and forlorn
To know, such bliss can never be,
Unless Amanda loved like me.

The visionary, nursing dreams like these,
Is not indeed unhappy. Summer woods
Wave over him, and whisper as they wave,
Some future blessings he may yet enjoy.
And as above him sail the silver clouds,
He follows them in thought to distant climes,
Where, far from the cold policy of this,
Dividing him from her he fondly loves,
He, in some island of the southern sea,[93]
May haply build his cane-constructed bower
Beneath the bread-fruit, or aspiring palm,
With long green foliage rippling in the gale.
Oh! let him cherish his ideal bliss—
For what is life, when Hope has ceas'd to strew
Her fragile flowers along its thorny way?
And sad and gloomy are his days, who lives
Of Hope abandon'd!

Just beneath the rock
Where Beachy overpeers the channel wave,
Within a cavern mined by wintry tides
Dwelt one,[94] who long disgusted with the world

[89] "And [Thy] liquid notes that close the eye of day." Milton [Sonnet 1, "O Nightingale," line 5]. The idea here meant to be conveyed is of the evening wind, so welcome after a hot day of Summer, and which appears to sooth and lull all nature into tranquillity [C. S.].

[90] **The Robin.** *(Motacilla rubecula)* which is always heard after other songsters have ceased to sing [C. S.].

[91] **The Woodlark,** *(Alauda nemerosa)* sings very late [C. S.].

[92] **Reed-wrens,** *(Motacilla arundinacea)* sing all the summer and autumn, and are often heard during the night [C. S.].

[93] An allusion to the visionary delights of the newly discovered islands [Polynesia, particularly Tahiti], where it was at first believed men lived in a state of simplicity and happiness; but where, as later enquiries have ascertained, that exemption from toil, which the fertility of their country gives them, produces the grossest vices; and a degree of corruption that late navigators think will end in the extirpation of the whole people in a few years [C. S.].

[94] In a cavern almost immediately under the cliff called Beachy Head, there lived, as the people of the country believed, a man of the name of Darby, who for many years had no other abode than this cave, and subsisted almost entirely on shell-fish. He had often administered assistance to ship-wrecked mariners; but venturing into the sea on this charitable mission during a violent equinoctial storm, he himself perished. As it is above thirty years since I heard this tradition of Parson Darby (for so I think he was called): it may now perhaps be forgotten [C. S.].

And all its ways, appear'd to suffer life
Rather than live; the soul-reviving gale,
Fanning the bean-field, or the thymy heath,
Had not for many summers breathed on him;
And nothing mark'd to him the season's change,
Save that more gently rose the placid sea,
And that the birds which winter on the coast
Gave place to other migrants; save that the fog,
Hovering no more above the beetling cliffs
Betray'd not then the little careless sheep[95]
On the brink grazing, while their headlong fall
Near the lone Hermit's flint-surrounded home,
Claim'd unavailing pity; for his heart
Was feelingly alive to all that breath'd;
And outraged as he was, in sanguine youth,
By human crimes, he still acutely felt
For human misery.

Wandering on the beach,
He learn'd to augur from the clouds of heaven,
And from the changing colours of the sea,
And sullen murmurs of the hollow cliffs,
Or the dark porpoises,[96] that near the shore
Gambol'd and sported on the level brine
When tempests were approaching: then at night
He listen'd to the wind; and as it drove
The billows with o'erwhelming vehemence
He, starting from his rugged couch, went forth
And hazarding a life, too valueless,
He waded thro' the waves, with plank or pole
Towards where the mariner in conflict dread
Was buffeting for life the roaring surge;
And now just seen, now lost in foaming gulphs,
The dismal gleaming of the clouded moon
Shew'd the dire peril. Often he had snatch'd
From the wild billows, some unhappy man
Who liv'd to bless the hermit of the rocks.
But if his generous cares were all in vain,
And with slow swell the tide of morning bore
Some blue swol'n cor'se to land; the pale recluse
Dug in the chalk a sepulchre — above
Where the dank sea-wrack[97] mark'd the utmost tide,
And with his prayers perform'd the obsequies
For the poor helpless stranger.

One dark night
The equinoctial wind blew south by west,
Fierce on the shore; — the bellowing cliffs were shook
Even to their stony base, and fragments fell
Flashing and thundering on the angry flood.
At day-break, anxious for the lonely man,
His cave the mountain shepherds visited,
Tho' sand and banks of weeds had choak'd their way —
He was not in it; but his drowned cor'se
By the waves wafted, near his former home
Receiv'd the rites of burial. Those who read
Chisel'd within the rock, these mournful lines,
Memorials of his sufferings, did not grieve,
That dying in the cause of charity
His spirit, from its earthy bondage freed,
Had to some better region fled for ever.

[95] Sometimes in thick weather the sheep feeding on the summit of the cliff, miss their footing, and are killed by the fall [C. S.].

[96] **Dark porpoises.** *Delphinus phocoena* [C. S.].

[97] **sea-wrack:** refuse, especially seaweed, left on the beach by the receding tide.

from THE HISTORY OF BIRDS
(1807)

from Fables
(comp. 1806)

— NOTES TO THE FABLES —

These are old stories, which I have endeavoured to tell with such a degree of novelty as natural history can lend them. They have been so often repeated, that probably the original inventors have been long since forgotten. La Fontaine, whose graceful simplicity in such light narrative has been universally allowed, is the most usually referred to.

La Fontaine, in his manner of telling the story of Les deux Pigeons [Book IX, Fable 2], calls them *Friends.* But the proverbial conjugal fidelity of this race of birds, makes it seem more natural to describe them as the pigeon and his mate. If it be objected, that the Truant Dove is represented as repeating the apology of Henry the Fourth of France — "Toujours perdrix, toujours Chapon bouilli ne vaut rien" [If you always have boiled partridge or capon, it is nothing special]; and that his partner talks from Shakespeare; I must take refuge under the authority of Chaucer; or rather his polisher Dryden; who makes his

Dame Partlet quote Galen and Cato, while Chanticleer explains Latin sentences:

> "For in the days of yore the birds of parts,
> Were bred to speak and sing; and learn the liberal arts."
> ["The Cock and the Fox; or, the Tale of the Nun's Priest," lines 91–92]

In fact, if the mind momentarily acquiesces in the absurdity of animals having the passions and the faculties of man, every thing else may be granted. It might be necessary to apologize for inserting these fables; but that which Prior and Cowper, and so many other of the most eminent writers have not disdained, can never need any defence. . . .

The Truant Dove[1] from Pilpay

(comp. 1806)

A mountain stream its channel deep
Beneath a rock's rough base had torn;
The cliff, like a vast castle wall, was steep
By fretting rains in many a crevice worn;
But the fern wav'd there, and the mosses crept,
And o'er the summit, where the wind
Peel'd from their stems the silver rind,
Depending[2] birches wept—
There, tufts of broom a footing used to find,
And heath and straggling grass to grow,
And half-way down from roots enwreathing, broke
The branches of a scathed[3] oak,
And seem to guard the cave below,
Where each revolving year,
Their twins two faithful Doves were wont to rear.
Choice never join'd a fonder pair;
To each their simple home was dear,
No discord ever enter'd there;
But there the soft affections dwell'd,
And three returning springs beheld
Secure within their fortress high
The little happy family.
"Toujours perdrix, messieurs, ne valent rien"[4]—
So did a Gallic monarch once harangue,
And evil was the day whereon our bird
This saying heard
From certain new acquaintance he had found;
Who at their perfect ease,
Amid a field of pease,
Boasted to him, that all the country round,
The wheat, and oats, and barley, rye and tares,
Quite to the neighb'ring sea, were theirs;
And theirs the oak, and beech-woods, far and near,
For their right noble owner was a peer,
And they themselves luxuriantly were stored
In a great dove-cote—to amuse my lord!
"Toujours perdrix ne valent rien." That's strange!
When people once are happy, wherefore change?
So thought our Stock Dove, but communication
With birds in his new friends' exalted station,
Whose means of information,
And knowledge of all sorts, must be so ample;
Who saw great folks, and follow'd their example,
Made on the dweller of the cave, impression;
And soon, whatever was his best possession,
His sanctuary within the rock's deep breast,
His soft-ey'd partner, and her nest,
He thought of with indiff'rence, then with loathing;
So much insipid love was good for nothing.—
But sometimes tenderness return'd; his dame
So long belov'd, so mild, so free from blame,
How should he tell her, he had learn'd to cavil
At happiness itself, and longed to travel?

[1] The varieties of pigeons here named, as Fantail, Carrier, Pouter, Almond Tumbler, and Nun, with many others, are varieties produced by art from the common pigeon. Societies exist in which prizes are given to those who produce birds nearest to the standard of imaginary perfection. A Pouter is a bird of which the crop [craw or throat] is capable of being so much distended with wind, that the animal appears to be without a head. On this enlargement of the crop depends the beauty and the value of the bird. These Fanciers are to Ornithologists, what Flower Fanciers are to Botanists [C. S.].

[2] **depending:** with hanging branches.

[3] **scathed:** injured by lightning, blasted.

[4] **"Toujours. . .rien:"** "If you always have partridge, gentlemen, it is nothing special." The saying attributed to King Henry IV of France, often cited by Charlotte Smith, in its entirety reads "Toujours perdrix, toujours Chapon bouilli ne vaut rien" ["If you always have boiled partridge or capon, it is worth nothing"]. Here the saying suggests that the "right noble owner" of this estate, having gotten bored with eating partridge, might prefer doves instead.

His heart still smote him, so much wrong to do her,
He knew not how to break the matter to her.
But love, though blind himself, makes some discerning;
His frequent absence, and his late returning,
With ruffled plumage, and with alter'd eyes,
His careless short replies,
And to their couplets[5] coldness or neglect
Had made his gentle wife suspect,
All was not right; but she forbore to teaze[6] him,
Which would but give him an excuse to rove:
She therefore tried by every art to please him,
Endur'd his peevish starts with patient love,
And when (like other husbands from a tavern)
Of his new notions full he sought his cavern,
She with dissembled cheerfulness "beguiled
The thing she was,"[7] and gaily coo'd and smiled.
'Tis not in this most motley sphere uncommon,
For man (and so of course more feeble woman)
Most strongly to suspect, what they're pursuing
Will lead them to inevitable ruin,
Yet rush with open eyes to their undoing;
Thus felt the Dove; but in the cant of fashion
He talk'd of fate, and of predestination,[8]
And in a grave oration,
He to his much affrighted mate related,
How he, yet slumb'ring in the egg, was fated,
To gather knowledge, to instruct his kind,
By observation elevate his mind,
And give new impulse to Columbian[9] life;
"If it be so," exclaim'd his hapless wife,
"It is *my* fate, to pass my days in pain,
To mourn your love estrang'd, and mourn in vain;
Here in our once dear hut to wake and weep,
When your unkindness shall have 'murder'd sleep';[10]
And never that dear hut shall I prepare,
And wait with fondness your arrival there,
While, me and mine forgetting, you will go
To some new love." "Why *no*, I tell you *no*,—
What shall I say such foolish fears to cure?
I only mean to make a little tour,
Just—just to see the world around me; then
With new delight, I shall come home again;
Such tours[11] are quite the rage—at my return
I shall have much to tell, and you to learn;
Of fashions—some becoming, some grotesque;
Of change of empires, and ideas novel;
Of buildings, Grecian, Gothic, Arabesque,
And scenery sublime and picturesque;[12]
And all these things with pleasure we'll discuss—"
"Ah, me! and what are all these things to us?"
"So then, you'd have a bird of genius grovel,
And never see beyond a farmer's hovel?
Ev'n the sand-martin, that inferior creature,
Goes once a year abroad."[13] "It is *his* nature,
But yours, how diff'rent once!" and then she sigh'd,
"There *was* a time, Ah! would that I had died,
Ere you so chang'd! when you'd have perish'd, rather
Than this poor breast should heave a single feather
With grief and care; and all this cant of fashion
Would but have rais'd your anger, or compassion.—
O my dear love! You sought not then to range,
But on my changeful neck as fell the light,
You sweetly said, you wish'd no other change
Than that soft neck could show; to berries bright
Of mountain ash you fondly could compare
My scarlet feet and bill; my shape and air,

[5] **couplets**: twin offspring.

[6] **teaze**: vex, interrogate.

[7] **"beguiled . . . was"**: Cf. Desdemona's aside to Iago, "I am not merry; but I do beguile / The thing I am by seeming otherwise," Shakespeare, *Othello*, II.i.123–24.

[8] **fate . . . predestination**: as did Chaunticleer, in Chaucer's *The Parlement of Foules*.

[9] **Columbian**: a pun combining *colombe* (*dove*, in French) with Christopher Columbus, the explorer.

[10] **'murder'd sleep'**: Shakespeare, *Macbeth*, II.ii.42.

[11] **such tours**: the Grand Tour of Europe was considered essential to the formation of an English gentleman in the eighteenth century.

[12] **grotesque**: bizarre, with particular reference to a style of painting or sculpture in which human and animal forms are fantastically interwoven with foliage and flowers (derived from the domestic wall-paintings in Pompeii and the Golden House, or Grotto, of Nero in Rome, which were excavated in the eighteenth century). **Grecian, Gothic, Arabesque**: current styles of architecture based on classical, medieval, and grotesque patterns. Smith may be alluding to the Pavilion at Brighton built by the Prince Regent, which combined neoclassical, medieval, and oriental motifs. **sublime and picturesque**: aesthetic categories defined by Edmund Burke* and William Gilpin*, the sublime is overwhelming, the picturesque ('like a picture') is domestic and pleasingly varied (see AESTHETIC THEORY AND LITERARY CRITICISM).

[13] **once a year abroad**: the sand-martin, or sandpiper, is a migratory bird.

Ah! faithless flatt'rer, did you not declare
The soul of grace and beauty centred there?
My eyes, you said, were opals, brightly pink,
Enchas'd in onyx, and you seem'd to think,
Each charm might then the coldest heart enthrall,
Those charms were mine. Alas! I gave you all—[14]
Your farthest wand'rings then were but to fetch
The pea, the tare, the beechmast, and the vetch,
For my repast, within my rocky bow'r,
With spleenwort shaded, and the blue-bell's flow'r:
For prospects then you never wish'd to roam,
But the best scen'ry was our happy home;
And when, beneath my breast, then fair and young,
Our first dear pair, our earliest nestlings sprung,
And weakly, indistinctly, tried to coo—
Were not those moments picturesque to you?"
"Yes, faith, my dear; and all you say is true."
"Oh! hear me then; if thus we have been blest,
If on these wings it was your joy to rest,
Love must from habit still new strength be gaining—"
"From habit? 'tis of that, child, I'm complaining:
This everlasting fondness will not be
For birds of flesh and blood. We sha'nt agree,
So why dispute? now prithee don't torment me;
I shall not long be gone; let that content ye:
Pshaw! what a fuss! Come, no more sighs and groans,
Keep up your spirits; mind your little ones;
My journey won't be far—my honour's pledg'd—
I shall be back again before they're fledg'd;[15]
Give me a kiss; and now my dear, adieu!"
So light of heart and plumes away he flew;
And, as above the shelt'ring rock he springs,
She listen'd to the echo of his wings;
Those well-known sounds, so soothing heretofore,
Which her heart whisper'd she should hear no more.
Then to her cold and widow'd bed she crept,
Clasp'd her half-orphan'd young, and wept!
Her recreant mate, by other views attracted,
A very different part enacted;
He sought the dove-cote, and was greeted there
With all that's tonish,[16] elegant, and rare
Among the pigeon tribes; and there the rover
Liv'd quite in clover!
His jolly comrades now were blades[17] of spirit;
Their nymphs possess'd most *fascinating* merit;
Nor fail'd our hero of the rock to prove
He thought not of inviolable love
To his poor spouse at home. He bow'd and sigh'd,
Now to a Fantail's, now a Cropper's bride;
Then cow'ring low to a majestic Powter,
Declar'd he should not suffer life without her!
And then with upturn'd eyes, in phrase still humbler,
Implor'd the pity of an Almond Tumbler;
Next, to a beauteous Carrier's feet he'd run,
And liv'd a week the captive of a Nun:
Thus far in measureless content he revels,
And blest the hour when he began his travels.
Yet some things soon occurr'd not quite so pleasant;
He had observ'd, that an unfeeling peasant,
In silence mounting on a ladder high,
Seiz'd certain pigeons just as they could fly,
Who never figur'd more, but in a pie:
That was but awkward; then, his lordship's son
Heard from the groom, that 'twould be famous fun
To try on others his unpractis'd gun;
Their fall, the rattling shot, his nerves perplex'd;
He thought perhaps it might be his turn next.
It has been seen ere now, that much elated,
To be by some great man caress'd and fêted,
A youth of humble birth, and mind industrious,
Foregoes in evil hour his independence;
And, charm'd to wait upon his friend illustrious,
Gives up his time to flatt'ry and attendance.
His patron, smiling at his folly, lets him—
Some newer whim succeeds, and he forgets him.
So far'd our bird; his new friend's vacant stare
Told him he scarce remember'd he was there;
And, when he talk'd of living more securely,
This very dear friend, yawning, answer'd, "Surely!
You are quite right to do what's most expedient,
So, au revoir!—Good bye! Your most obedient."[18]
Allies in prosp'rous fortune thus he prov'd,
And left them, unregretting, unbelov'd;
Yet much his self-love suffer'd by the shock,
And now, his quiet cabin in the rock,
The faithful partner of his ev'ry care,

[14] **I gave you all:** Cf. Shakespeare, *King Lear,* II.iv.253.

[15] **fledg'd:** having grown the feathers necessary for flight, i.e. ready to leave the nest.

[16] **tonish:** fashionable, having "ton" or being "à la mode."

[17] **blade:** a gallant, a free and easy fellow.

[18] **"Your most obedient.":** with "servant," the formulaic closing of an eighteenth-century letter.

And all the blessings he abandon'd there,
Rush'd on his sick'ning heart; he felt it yearn,
But pride and shame prevented his return;
So wand'ring farther—at the close of day
To the high woods he pensive wing'd his way;
But new distress at ev'ry turn he found—
Struck by a hawk, and stunn'd upon the ground,
He once by miracle escap'd; then fled
From a wild cat, and hid his trembling head
Beneath a dock;[19] recov'ring, on the wind
He rose once more, and left his fears behind;
And, as above the clouds he soar'd, the light
Fell on an inland rock; the radiance bright
Show'd him his long deserted place of rest,
And thitherward he flew; his throbbing breast
Dwelt on his mate, so gentle, and so wrong'd,
And on his mem'ry throng'd
The happiness he once at home had known;
Then to forgive him earnest to engage her,
And for his errours eager to atone,
Onward he went; but ah! not yet had flown
Fate's sharpest arrow: to decide a wager,
Two sportsmen shot at our deserter; down
The wind swift wheeling, struggling, still he fell,
Close to the margin of the stream, that flow'd
Beneath the foot of his regretted cell,
And the fresh grass was spotted with his blood;
To his dear home he turn'd his languid[20] view,

[19] **dock:** coarse weed.

[20] **languid:** faint, weak, spiritless.

Deplor'd his folly, while he look'd his last,
And sigh'd a long adieu!
Thither to sip the brook, his nestlings, led
By their still pensive mother, came;
He saw; and murm'ring forth her dear lov'd name,
Implor'd her pity, and with short'ning breath,
Besought her to forgive him ere his death[.]—
And now, how hard in metre to relate
The tears and tender pity of his mate!
Or with what gen'rous zeal his faithful moitie[21]
Taught her now feather'd young, with duteous piety,
To aid her, on their mutual wings to bear,
With storklike care,
Their suff'ring parent to the rock above;
There, by the best physician, Love,
His wounds were heal'd[.]—His wand'rings at an end,
And sober'd quite, the husband, and the friend,
In proof of reformation and contrition,
Gave to his race this prudent admonition;
Advice, which this, our fabling muse, presumes,
May benefit the *biped without plumes:*
"If of domestic peace you are possess'd,
Learn to believe yourself supremely bless'd;
And, gratefully enjoying your condition,
Frisk not about, on whims and fancies strange,
For, ten to one, you for the worse will change;
And 'tis most wise, to check all vain ambition[.]—
By such aspiring pride the angels fell;
So love your wife, and know when you are well."

[21] **moitie:** moiety, other half.

ANN CROMARTY YEARSLEY

(1752–1806)

The daughter of working-class parents in Clifton Hill, near Bristol (her father was a day laborer and her mother a dairywoman who sold milk door-to-door), Ann Cromarty was taught to read and write by her brother William, but received no formal education. She claimed that she had always felt a compulsion to write poetry. Following in her mother's trade, she married the "honest and sober" John Yearsley in 1774, and bore six children in six years, one of whom died. Sinking into destitution, despite all their efforts, during the harsh winter of 1783 to 1784, the family almost starved to death: her mother died, while Ann, pregnant with her sixth child, and her other children were saved from starvation only by the last minute intervention of a Mr. Vaughan. The story of the starving milkwoman poet reached the ears of Hannah More's cook, from whom Yearsley bought the More's household garbage or "dishwashings" for her pig and who then showed Yearsley's poems to her employer. More* was so impressed by Yearsley's poetry that she informed Elizabeth Robinson Montagu that "it has been denied this poor recluse to drink at the pure well-head of pagan poesy; yet, from the true fountain of divine inspiration, her mind has been wonderfully cherished and enriched; nor has the retailing a few fine maxims in virtue cheated her of the most exact probity of heart: industrious in no common degree, pious, unambitious, simple and unaffected in her manners, of which I have received incontestable proofs." Hannah More visited Yearsley in Clifton Hill, helped her revise her poems, and arranged to publish them by subscription. Yearsley's *Poems on Several Occasions* appeared in June 1785, earning her the sobriquet of "Lactilla, the Bristol Milkwoman."

But when More placed the profits (£360) from the sale of Yearsley's poems in a trust fund for the milkwoman's children, to be administered jointly by More and Montagu (having extracted from Yearsley and her husband their reluctant agreement to forego their financial rights in the publication in favor of their children), Yearsley indignantly demanded the right to administer her own money. Yearsley offered to serve as joint trustee of the trust with More and to guarantee that the principal would be used only by her children at their emancipation, but More refused, fearing that the income from the trust would set Yearsley "above her station." Yearsley angrily denounced More's patronizing treatment of her in her Preface of her next volume, *Poems on Various Subjects* (1787).

Despite her quarrel with More, which was never resolved even after the trust was dissolved and Yearsley received her money, Yearsley continued to write for publication. Her powerful condemnation of slavery, "A Poem on the Inhumanity of the Slave-Trade," designed to compete directly with More's on the same subject, appeared in 1788. When the footman of Levi Eames, the mayor of Bristol, savagely horsewhipped the Yearsley children for playing on the mayor's property, and later turned on her, causing her to miscarry, Yearsley publicly attacked the mayor and the corruption of power in her *Stanzas of Woe* (1790). Her play *Earl Goodwin* (published in 1791) defended the rights of the peasants against both Church and State. With the proceeds of her writing, in 1793 she set up a circulating library for the working classes. Her novel, *The Royal Captive*, a Gothic tale of political and sexual oppression, focussing on the seventeenth-century story of the man in the iron mask, appeared in 1795, and her final collection of poems, *The Rural Lyre*, was published in 1796.

Throughout her writing, she drew on her own experiences as a member of the oppressed, impoverished rural working classes to expose the tyrannies of the rich and the powerful even as she foreswore violent resistence in favor of a peaceful mediation of class conflict through mutual understanding and generosity.

from POEMS ON SEVERAL OCCASIONS
(1785)

from "To Mr. R——,
on his Benevolent Scheme for rescuing Poor Children from Vice and Misery, by promoting Sunday Schools"
(1785)

. . . .

And infants, yet unborn, in choral song,
Shall bless the hand which form'd a social father,
A father on whose lip instruction hangs,
Who snatches from the burning flame the brand!

The poor illiterate, chill'd by freezing want,
Within whose walls pale Penury still sits,
With icy hand impressing every meal,
Cannot divide his slender, hard-earn'd mite
Betwixt his bodily and mental wants,
The soul must go—for hunger loudly pleads,
And Nature will be answer'd; thus his race,
Envelop'd, groping, sink in vulgar toils;
To eat and sleep includes the soul's best wish;
And mean deceit, and treacherous, low-phras'd guile,
Fill the vast space for better purpose given.

. . . .

Listless, inactive, waiting but the call
Of great JEHOVAH, listen to his voice,
A voice ne'er heard in vain; hark! hark! it sounds
From Misery's lowest shed; the accent soft,
The humble sigh, the infant's early tear,
The husband's stifled, sympathetic groan,
The mother's feelings, more than ever felt,
Tho' borne in silence and in pensive mood.
These are all shades in which the Godhead's seen;
Well felt those woes where great Religion sits
On the house-top, and sheds her heavenly dews
On the poor group;—be't your's to fix her there.
In dress like this, Omniscience softly tries
Your friendly doors, and thus disguis'd, oft meets
The stern repulse, and virtue-killing frown.

"To the Same [Stella];
on her Accusing the Author of Flattery, and of Ascribing to the Creature that Praise which is due only to the Creator"
(1785)

Excuse me, Stella,[1] sunk in humble state,
With more than needful awe I view the great;
No glossy diction e'er can aid the thought,
First stamp'd in ignorance, with error fraught.
My friends I've praised—they stood in heavenly guise
When first I saw them, and my mental eyes
Shall in that heavenly rapture view them still,
For mine's a stubborn and a savage will;
No customs, manners, or soft arts I boast,
On my rough soul your nicest rules are lost;
Yet shall unpolish'd gratitude be mine,
While STELLA deigns to nurse the spark divine.
A savage pleads—let e'en her errors move,
And your forgiving spirit melt in love.
O, cherish gentle Pity's lambent[2] flame,
From Heaven's own bosom the soft pleader came!
Then deign to bless a soul, who'll ne'er degrade
Your gift, tho' sharpest miseries invade!
You I acknowledge, next to bounteous Heaven,
Like his, your influence chears where'er 'tis given;

[1] Stella is Yearsley's patroness, Hannah More.*
[2] **lambent:** softly radiant.

Blest in dispensing! gentle STELLA, hear
My only, short, but pity-moving prayer,
That thy great soul may spare the rustic Muse,
Whom Science ever scorn'd, and errors still abuse.

A Poem on the Inhumanity of the Slave-Trade
(1788)

Bristol,[1] thine heart hath throbb'd to glory.—Slaves,
E'en Christian slaves, have shook their chains, and gaz'd
With wonder and amazement on thee. Hence
Ye grov'ling souls, who think the term I give,
Of Christian slave, a paradox! to *you*
I do not turn, but leave you to conception
Narrow; with that be blest, nor dare to stretch
Your shackled souls along the course of *Freedom*.

Yet, Bristol, list! nor deem Lactilla's[2] soul
Lessen'd by distance; snatch her rustic thought,
Her crude ideas, from their panting state,
And let them fly in wide expansion; lend
Thine energy, so little understood
By the rude million, and I'll dare the strain
Of Heav'n-born Liberty till Nature moves
Obedient to her voice. Alas! my friend,
Strong rapture dies within the soul, while Pow'r
Drags on his bleeding victims. Custom, Law,
Ye blessings, and ye curses of mankind,
What evils do ye cause? We feel enslav'd,
Yet move in your direction. Custom, thou
Wilt preach up filial piety; thy sons
Will groan, and stare with impudence at Heav'n,
As if they did abjure the act, where Sin
Sits full on Inhumanity; the church
They fill with mouthing, vap'rous sighs and tears,
Which, like the guileful crocodile's, oft fall,
Nor fall, but at the cost of human bliss.

Custom, thou hast undone us! led us far
From God-like probity, from truth, and heaven.

But come, ye souls who feel for human woe,
Tho' drest in savage guise! Approach, thou son,
Whose heart would shudder at a father's chains,
And melt o'er thy lov'd brother as he lies
Gasping in torment undeserv'd. Oh, sight
Horrid and insupportable! far worse
Than an immediate, an heroic death;
Yet to this sight I summon thee. Approach,
Thou slave of avarice, that canst see the maid
Weep o'er her inky sire! Spare me, thou God
Of all-indulgent Mercy, if I scorn
This gloomy wretch, and turn my tearful eye
To more enlighten'd beings. Yes, my tear
Shall hang on the green furze, like pearly dew
Upon the blossom of the morn. My song
Shall teach sad Philomel[3] a louder note,
When Nature swells her woe. O'er suff'ring *man*
My soul with sorrow bends! Then come, ye few
Who feel a more than cold, material essence;
Here ye may vent your sighs, till the bleak North
Find its adherents aided.—Ah, no more!
The dingy youth comes on, sullen in chains;
He smiles on the rough sailor, who aloud
Strikes at the spacious heav'n, the earth, the sea,
In breath too blasphemous; yet not to *him*
Blasphemous, for *he* dreads not either:—lost
In dear internal imag'ry, the soul
Of Indian Luco rises to his eyes.
Silent, not inexpressive: the strong beams
With eager wildness yet drink in the view
Of his too humble home, where he had left
His mourning father, and his Incilanda.

Curse on the toils spread by a Christian hand
To rob the Indian of his freedom! Curse
On him who from a bending parent steals
His dear support of age, his darling child;
Perhaps a son, or a *more tender* daughter,
Who might have clos'd his eyelids, as the spark

[1] Bristol, where Yearsley lived, was one of the two major slave-trading seaports in England; the other was Liverpool (see SLAVERY, THE SLAVE TRADE, AND ABOLITION).

[2] **Lactilla:** Latin, milkmaid; this is Yearsley's poetic pseudonym—she was known as "Lactilla, the Bristol Milkwoman."

[3] **furze:** evergreen shrub with yellow flowers. **Philomel:** mythological, Greek woman raped by her brother-in-law Tereus, who cut out her tongue; she wove the event into a shroud and then conspired with her sister Procne to kill Tereus' son and feed him to his father. The gods intervened and changed Philomel into a nightingale, Procne into a swallow, Tereus into a buzzard, and his son into a goldfinch.

Of life gently retired. Oh, thou poor world!
Thou fleeting good to individuals! see
How much for thee they care, how wide they ope
Their helpless arms to clasp thee; vapour thou!
More swift than passing wind! thou leav'st them nought
Amid th' unreal scene, but a *scant grave.*

I know the crafty merchant will oppose
The plea of nature to my strain, and urge
His toils are for his children: the soft plea
Dissolves my soul—*but when I sell a son,*
Thou God of nature, let it be my own!

Behold that Christian! see what horrid joy
Lights up his moody features, while he grasps
The wish'd-for gold, purchase of human blood!
Away, thou seller of mankind! Bring on
Thy daughter to this market! bring thy wife!
Thine aged mother, though of little worth,
With all thy ruddy boys! Sell them, thou wretch,
And swell the price of Luco! Why that start?
Why gaze as thou wouldst fright me from my challenge
With look of anguish? Is it *Nature* strains
Thine heart-strings at the image? Yes, my charge
Is full against her, and she rends thy soul,
While I but strike upon thy pityless ear,
Fearing her rights are violated.—Speak,
Astound the voice of *Justice!* bid thy tears
Melt the unpitying pow'r, while thus she claims
The pledges of thy love. Oh, throw thine arm
Around thy little ones, and loudly plead
Thou *canst not* sell thy children.—Yet, beware
Lest Luco's groan be heard; should *that* prevail,
Justice will scorn thee in her turn, and hold
Thine *act* against thy *pray'r.* Why clasp, she cries,
That blooming youth? Is it because thou lov'st him?
Why Luco was belov'd: then wilt thou feel,
Thou selfish Christian, for thy private woe,
Yet cause such pangs to him that is a father?
Whence comes thy right to barter for thy fellows?
Where are thy statutes? Whose the iron pen
That gave thee precedent? Give me the seal
Of virtue, or religion, for thy trade,
And I will ne'er upbraid thee; but if force
Superior, hard brutality alone
Become thy boast, hence to some savage haunt,
Nor claim protection from my social laws.

Luco is gone; his little brothers weep,
While his fond mother climbs the hoary rock
Whose point o'er-hangs the main. No Luco there,
No sound, save the hoarse billows. On she roves,
With love, fear, hope, holding alternate rage
In her too anxious bosom. Dreary main!
Thy murmurs now are riot, while she stands
List'ning to ev'ry breeze, waiting the step
Of gentle Luco. Ah, return! return!
Too hapless mother, thy indulgent arms
Shall never clasp thy fetter'd Luco more.
See Incilanda! artless maid, my soul
Keeps pace with thee, and mourns. Now o'er the hill
She creeps, with timid foot, while Sol[4] embrowns
The bosom of the isle, to where she left
Her faithful lover: here the well-known cave,
By Nature form'd amid the rock, endears
The image of her Luco; here his pipe,
Form'd of the polish'd cane, neglected lies,
No more to vibrate; here the useless dart,
The twanging bow, and the fierce panther's skin,
Salute the virgin's eye. But where is Luco?
He comes not down the steep, tho' he had vow'd,
When the sun's beams at noon should sidelong gild
The cave's wide entrance, he would swift descend
To bless his Incilanda. Ten pale moons
Had glided by, since to his generous breast
He clasp'd the tender maid, and whisper'd love.

Oh, mutual sentiment! thou dang'rous bliss!
So exquisite, that Heav'n had been unjust
Had it bestow'd less exquisite of ill;
When thou art held no more, thy pangs are deep,
Thy joys convulsive to the soul; yet all
Are meant to smooth th' uneven road of life.

For Incilanda, Luco rang'd the wild,
Holding her image to his panting heart;
For her he strain'd the bow, for her he stript
The bird of beauteous plumage; happy hour,
When with these guiltless trophies he adorn'd
The brow of her he lov'd. Her gentle breast
With gratitude was fill'd, nor knew she aught
Of language strong enough to paint her soul,
Or ease the great emotion; whilst her eye
Pursued the gen'rous Luco to the field,
And glow'd with rapture at his wish'd return.

---

[4] **main:** the sea. **Sol:** the sun.

Ah, sweet suspense! betwixt the mingled cares
Of friendship, love, and gratitude, so mix'd,
That ev'n the soul may cheat herself.—Down, down,
Intruding Memory! bid thy struggles cease,
At this soft scene of innate war. What sounds
Break on her ear? She, starting, whispers "Luco."
Be still, fond maid; list to the tardy step
Of leaden-footed woe. A father comes,
But not to seek his son, who from the deck
Had breath'd a last adieu: no, he shuts out
The soft, fallacious gleam of hope, and turns
Within upon the mind: horrid and dark
Are his wild, unenlighten'd pow'rs: no ray
Of *forc'd* philosophy to calm his soul,
But all the anarchy of wounded nature.

Now he arraigns his country's gods, who sit,
In his bright fancy, far beyond the hills,
Unriveting the chains of slaves: his heart
Beats quick with stubborn fury, while he doubts
Their justice to his child. Weeping old man,
Hate not a Christian's God, whose record holds
Thine injured Luco's name. Frighted he starts,
Blasphemes the Deity, whose altars rise
Upon the Indian's helpless neck, and sinks,
Despising comfort, till by grief and age
His angry spirit is forced out. Oh, guide,
Ye angel-forms, this joyless shade to worlds
Where the poor *Indian,* with the *sage,* is prov'd
The work of a Creator. Pause not here,
Distracted maid! ah, leave the breathless form,
On whose cold cheek thy tears so swiftly fall,
Too unavailing! On this stone, she cries,
My Luco sat, and to the wand'ring stars
Pointed my eye, while from his gentle tongue
Fell old traditions of his country's woe.
Where now shall Incilanda seek him? Hence,
Defenceless mourner, ere the dreary night
Wrap thee in added horror. Oh, Despair,
How eagerly thou rend'st the heart! She pines
In anguish deep, and sullen: Luco's form
Pursues her, lives in restless thought, and chides
Soft consolation. Banish'd from his arms,
She seeks the cold embrace of death; her soul
Escapes in one sad sigh. Too hapless maid!
Yet happier far than he thou lov'dst; his tear,
His sigh, his groan avail not, for they plead
Most weakly with a Christian. Sink, thou wretch,
Whose act shall on the cheek of Albion's[5] sons
Throw Shame's red blush: thou, who hast frighted far
Those simple wretches from thy God, and taught
Their erring minds to mourn his[6] partial love,
Profusely pour'd on thee, while they are left
Neglected to *thy* mercy. Thus deceiv'd,
How doubly dark must be *their* road to death!

Luco is borne around the neighb'ring isles,
Losing the knowledge of his native shore
Amid the pathless wave; destin'd to plant
The sweet luxuriant cane.[7] He strives to please,
Nor once complains, but greatly smothers grief.
His hands are blister'd, and his feet are worn,
Till ev'ry stroke dealt by his mattock[8] gives
Keen agony to life; while from his breast
The sigh arises, burthen'd with the name
Of Incilanda. Time inures the youth,
His limbs grow nervous, strain'd by willing toil:
And resignation, or a calm despair,
(Most useful either) lulls him to repose.

A Christian renegade, that from his soul
Abjures the tenets of our schools, nor dreads
A future punishment, nor hopes for mercy,
Had fled from England, to avoid those laws
Which must have made his life a retribution
To violated justice, and had gain'd,
By fawning guile, the confidence (ill placed)
Of Luco's master. O'er the slave he stands
With knotted whip, lest fainting nature shun
The task too arduous, while his cruel soul,
Unnat'ral, ever feeds, with gross delight,
Upon his suff'rings. Many slaves there were,
But none who could supress the sigh, and bend,
So quietly as Luco: long he bore
The stripes, that from his manly bosom drew

[5] **Albion:** England.

[6] Indians [i.e., West Indians, African slaves] have been often heard to say, in their complaining moments, "God Almighty no love us well; he be good to buckera [white man]; he bid buckera burn us; he no burn buckera" [A. Y.].

[7] **cane:** sugarcane, the staple crop of the West Indian slave plantations, processed into refined sugar and rum for sale in Europe.

[8] **mattock:** agricultural tool with socketed steel head, having on one side an adze-shaped blade, on the other a pick, used for loosening hard ground.

The sanguine[9] stream (too little priz'd); at length
Hope fled his soul, giving her struggles o'er,
And he resolv'd to die. The sun had reach'd
His zenith—pausing faintly, Luco stood,
Leaning upon his hoe, while mem'ry brought,
In piteous imag'ry, his aged father,
His poor fond mother, and his faithful maid:
The mental group in wildest motion set
Fruitless imagination; fury, grief,
Alternate shame, the sense of insult, all
Conspire to aid the inward storm; yet words
Were no relief, he stood in silent woe.

Gorgon, remorseless Christian, saw the slave
Stand musing, 'mid the ranks, and, stealing soft
Behind the studious Luco, struck his cheek
With a too-heavy whip, that reach'd his eye,
Making it dark for ever. Luco turn'd,
In strongest agony, and with his hoe
Struck the rude Christian on the forehead. Pride,
With hateful malice, seized on Gorgon's soul,
By nature fierce; while Luco sought the beach,
And plung'd beneath the wave; but near him lay
A planter's barge, whose seamen grasp'd his hair;
Dragging to life a wretch who wish'd to die.

Rumour now spreads the tale, while Gorgon's breath
Envenom'd, aids her blast: imputed crimes
Oppose the plea of Luco, till he scorns
Even a just defence, and stands prepared.
The planters, conscious that to fear alone
They owe their cruel pow'r, resolve to blend
New torment with the pangs of death, and hold
Their victims high in dreadful view, to fright
The wretched number left. Luco is chain'd
To a huge tree, his fellow-slaves are ranged
To share the horrid sight; fuel is plac'd
In an increasing train, some paces back,
To kindle slowly, and approach the youth,
With more than native terror. See, it burns!
He gazes on the growing flame, and calls
For "water, water!" The small boon's deny'd.
E'en Christians throng each other, to behold
The different alterations of his face,
As the hot death approaches. (Oh, shame, shame
Upon the followers of Jesus! shame
On him that dares avow a God!) He writhes,
While down his breast glide the unpity'd tears,
And in their sockets strain their scorched balls.
"Burn, burn me quick! I cannot die!" he cries:
"Bring fire more close!" The planters heed him not,
But still prolonging Luco's torture, threat
Their trembling slaves around. His lips are dry,
His senses seem to quiver, e'er they quit
His frame for ever, rallying strong, then driv'n
From the tremendous conflict. Sight no more
Is Luco's, his parch'd tongue is ever mute;
Yet in his soul his Incilanda stays,
Till both escape together. Turn, my muse,
From this sad scene; lead Bristol's milder soul
To where the solitary spirit roves,
Wrapt in the robe of innocence, to shades
Where pity breathing in the gale, dissolves
The mind, when fancy paints such real woe.

Now speak, ye Christians (who for gain enslave
A soul like Luco's, tearing her from joy
In life's short vale; and if there be a hell,
As ye believe, to *that* ye thrust her down,
A blind, involuntary victim), where
Is your true essence of religion? where
Your proofs of righteousness, when ye conceal
The knowledge of the Deity from those
Who would adore him *fervently*? Your God
Ye rob of worshippers, his altars keep
Unhail'd, while driving from the sacred font
The eager slave, lest *he* should hope in *Jesus*.

Is this your piety? Are these your laws,
Whereby the glory of the Godhead spreads
O'er barb'rous climes? Ye hypocrites, disown
The Christian name, nor shame its cause: yet where
Shall souls like yours find welcome? Would the Turk,
Pagan, or wildest Arab, ope their arms
To gain such proselytes? No: he that owns
The name of Mussulman would start, and shun
Your worse than serpent touch; he frees his slave
Who turns to Mahomet. The Spaniard stands
Your brighter contrast; he condemns the youth
For ever to the mine; but ere the wretch
Sinks to the deep domain, the hand of Faith
Bathes his faint temples in the sacred stream,
Bidding his spirit hope.[10] Briton, dost thou

[9] **stripes:** lashes. **sanguine:** bloody.

[10] The Turk gives freedom to his slave on condition that he embraces Mahometanism. The Spaniard, immediately on purchasing an Indian gives him baptism [A. Y.].

Act up to this? If so, bring on thy slaves
To Calv'ry's mount,[11] raise high their kindred souls
To him who died to save them: this alone
Will teach them calmly to obey thy rage,
And deem a life of misery but a day,
To long eternity. Ah, think how soon
Thine head shall on earth's dreary pillow lie,
With thy poor slaves, each silent, and unknown
To his once furious neighbour. Think how swift
The sands of time ebb out, for him and *thee.*
Why groans that Indian youth, in burning chains
Suspended o'er the beach? The lab'ring sun
Strikes from his full meridian on the slave
Whose arms are blister'd by the heated iron,
Which still corroding, seeks the bone. What crime
Merits so dire a death? Another gasps
With strongest agony, while life declines
From recent amputation.[12] Gracious God!
Why thus in mercy let thy whirlwinds sleep
O'er a vile race of Christians, who profane
Thy glorious attributes? Sweep them from earth,
Or check their cruel pow'r: the savage tribes
Are angels when compared to brutes like these.

Advance, ye Christians, and oppose my strain:
Who dares condemn it? Prove from laws divine,
From deep philosophy, or social love,
That ye derive your privilege. I scorn
The cry of Av'rice, or the trade that drains
A fellow-creature's blood: bid Commerce plead
Her publick good, her nation's many wants,
Her sons thrown idly on the beach, forbade
To seize the image of their God and sell it:—
I'll hear her voice, and Virtue's hundred tongues
Shall sound against her. Hath our public good
Fell rapine[13] for its basis? Must our wants
Find their supply in murder? Shall the sons
Of Commerce shiv'ring stand, if not employ'd
Worse than the midnight robber? Curses fall
On the destructive system that shall need
Such base supports! Doth England need them? No;
Her laws, with prudence, hang the meagre thief
That from his neighbour steals a slender sum,
Tho' famine drove him on. O'er him the priest,
Beneath the fatal tree,[14] laments the crime,
Approves the law, and bids him calmly die.
Say, doth this law, that dooms the thief, protect
The wretch who makes another's life his prey,
By hellish force to take it at his will?
Is this an English law, whose guidance fails
When crimes are swell'd to magnitude so vast,
That *Justice* dare not scan them? Or does *Law*
Bid *Justice* an eternal distance keep
From England's great tribunal, when the slave
Calls loud on *Justice only*? Speak, ye few
Who fill Britannia's senate, and are deem'd
The fathers of your country! Boast your laws,
Defend the *honour* of a land so fall'n,
That Fame from ev'ry battlement is flown,
And Heathens start, e'en at a Christian's name.

Hail, social love! true soul of *order,* hail!
Thy softest emanations, pity, grief,
Lively emotion, sudden joy, and pangs,
Too deep for language, are thy own: then rise,
Thou gentle angel! spread thy silken wings
O'er drowsy *man,* breathe in his *soul,* and give
Her God-like pow'rs thy animating force,
To banish Inhumanity. Oh, loose
The fetters of his mind, enlarge his views,
Break down for him the bound of avarice, lift
His feeble faculties beyond a world
To which he soon must prove a stranger! Spread
Before his ravish'd eye the varied tints
Of future glory; bid them live to *Fame,*
Whose banners wave for ever. Thus inspired,
All that is great and good, and sweetly mild,
Shall fill his noble bosom. He shall melt,
Yea, by thy sympathy unseen, shall feel

[11] Mount Calvary, where Jesus Christ was crucified.

[12] A Coromantin slave in Jamaica (who had escaped to the mountains) was, a few years since, doomed to have his leg cut off. A young practitioner from England (after the surgeon of the estate had refused to be an executioner) undertook the operation, but after the removal of the limb, on the slave's exclaiming, You buckera! God Almighty made dat leg; you cut it off! You put it on again? was so shocked, that the other surgeon was obliged to take up the vessels, apply the dressings, &c. The Negro suffered without a groan, called for his pipe, and calmly smoaked, till the absence of the attendant gave him an opportunity of tearing off his bandages, when he bled to death in an instant. Many will call this act of the Negro's stubbornness; under *such* circumstances, I dare give it a more *glorious* epithet, and that is *fortitude* [A. Y.].

[13] **rapine:** violent plunder, robbery.

[14] **fatal tree:** in London, the Tyburn tree or gallows; any tree from which a criminal is hanged.

Another's pang: for the lamenting maid
His heart shall heave a sigh; with the old slave
(Whose head is bent with sorrow) he shall cast
His eye back on the joys of youth, and say,
"Thou *once* couldst feel, as I do, love's pure bliss;
Parental fondness, and the dear returns
Of filial tenderness were thine, till torn
From the dissolving scene."—Oh, social love,
Thou universal good, thou that canst fill
The vacuum of immensity, and live
In endless void! thou that in motion first
Set'st the long lazy atoms, by thy force
Quickly assimilating, and restrain'd
By strong attraction; touch the soul of man;
Subdue him; make a fellow-creature's woe
His own by heart-felt sympathy, whilst wealth
Is made subservient to his soft disease.

And when thou hast to high perfection wrought
This mighty work, say, "such is Bristol's soul."

from THE RURAL LYRE
(1796)

To Mira, On the Care of Her Infant
(1796; comp. 1795)

Whilst war, destruction, crimes that fiends delight,
Burst on the globe, and millions sink in night;
Whilst here a monarch, there a subject dies,
Equally dear to him who rules the skies;
Whilst man to man oppos'd wou'd shake the world,
And see vast systems into chaos hurl'd,
Rather than turn his face from yon dread field,
Or, by forgiving, teach his foe to yield:
Let us, whose sweet employ the Gods admire,
Serenely blest, to softer joys retire!
Spite of those wars, we will mild pleasure know—
Pleasure, that, long as woman lives, shall flow!
We are not made for Mars;[1] we ne'er could bear
His pond'rous helmet and his burning spear;
Nor in fierce combat prostrate lay that form
That breathes affection whilst the heart is warm:—
No: whilst our heroes from their homes retire,
We'll nurse the infant, and lament the sire.
  I am no Amazon; nor would I give
One silver groat[2] by iron laws to live.
Nay, if, like hers, my heart were iron-bound,
My warmth would melt the fetters to the ground.
  Ah, weep not, Mira! In this cradle view
Thy lovely charge—Amyntor's copy true;
Think, by this pledge the absent sire ensures
Thy constant memory, and thy heart secures.
And, whilst we read, reflect, by turns converse,
Comment on wars in prose or mimic verse,
Permit me, pensive friend, who long have known
A mother's duty, pleasing cares to own,
Teach thee to gently nurse thy beauteous boy—
Lest Custom gentle Nature's pow'r destroy:
So young an infant should reposing lie,
Unswath'd[3] and loose, that the fair limbs may ply
To every motion happy Nature tries,
Whilst life seems fluid, and from pressure flies.
Clothe him with easy warmth. Of ills the worst
Are cruel swathes, of infant griefs the first.
Think what the stomach feels when hardly press'd!—
The breath confin'd swells high the snowy chest:
The pulses throb, the heart with flutt'ring beats;
The eyes roll ghastly; wind the nurture meets;
And, ere the new-born appetite hath din'd,
The food's rejected, and the head reclin'd.
  Be tender, Mira!—Downy beds prepare;
To thy own bosom clasp Amyntor's heir!
See not thy babe pining with speechless grief,
His thirsty lip craving thy kind relief:[4]
Relief that Nature bids the infant claim;
Withheld by healthy mothers, to their shame.
  Behold gay Circe in her gig!—Old Night
Hath from one moon receiv'd her valu'd light,
Since Circe's heir was with his grandsire laid;
And all her grief on yon rich tomb display'd.
  Her child was lovely, strong, and promis'd fair;
His looks transporting, his complexion clear;

[1] **Mars:** the Greek and Roman god of war.

[2] **Amazon:** female warrior. **groat:** four pennies.

[3] **unswath'd:** unswaddled, not bound in the swaddling bandages that were wrapped around newborn infants, like a cocoon, to prevent all movement of the limbs.

[4] Yearsley here urges mothers to breastfeed their own children; (see Wollstonecraft, *Vindication of the Rights of Woman**).

Ardent to seek her bosom, and recline
Where dear affection makes the gift divine!
But no:—could Circe dress renounce, the ball—
For a child's humour suffer TASTE to fall?
'Immensely monstrous! singular!' she cried—
A boist'rous nurse her wish'd-for love supplied.
And soon her babe's wan look proclaim'd the cheat:
He loath'd the bosom he was forc'd to meet;
Refus'd in silence, starv'd in robes of lace,
And oft imploring view'd his mother's face.
Too proud to nurse, maternal fevers came—
Her burthen'd bosom caught th' invited flame;
Too late she woo'd her infant to her breast,
He only sigh'd, and sunk to lasting rest.
  Do thou not, Mira, follow Circe's line—
In thee, let soft maternal pleasure shine;
Pleasure that virtuous mothers highly taste,
When gen'rous Hymen makes them more than chaste.
Benign and social, new affections grow;
Their minds enlarg'd, their noblest spirits flow;
Friendship, compassion, sympathy, and love,
Such as the self-corrected mind may prove,
Stamp ev'ry act.—These gen'rous joys are thine—
Wouldst thou exchange them for Golconda's mine?[5]
  I own such is the force of social law,
The unmarried [mother] loves her babe with awe:
Nurs'd far from public view in yon lone wild,
She sometimes strays to tremble o'er her child.
There coarse rusticity, vice, vulgar sound—
All that can sentiment or wisdom wound,
Breaks on the eye and ear—Unhappy fair!
Yet not condemn'd, if thy sweet pledge be dear—
Leave thy fond soul with him, to him return:
O let his FUTURE on thy fancy burn!
Quick bear him thence! Instruct him, point to Fame—
Neglected, he will moan; ay, seal thy shame!
  Mira, as thy dear Edward's senses grow,
Be sure they all will seek this point—TO KNOW:
Woo to enquiry—strictures long avoid,
By force the thirst of weakly sense is cloy'd:
Silent attend the frown, the gaze, the smile,
To grasp far objects the incessant toil;
So play life's springs with energy, and try
The unceasing thirst of knowledge to supply.
  I saw the beauteous Caleb th' other day
Stretch forth his little hand to touch a spray,
Whilst on the grass his drowsy nurse inhal'd
The sweets of Nature as her sweets exhal'd:
But, ere the infant reach'd the playful leaf,
She pull'd him back—His eyes o'erflow'd with grief;
He check'd his tears—Her fiercer passions strove,
She look'd a vulture cow'ring o'er a dove!
'I'll teach you, brat!' The pretty trembler sigh'd—
When, with a cruel shake, she hoarsely cried—
'Your mother spoils you—everything you see
You covet. It shall ne'er be so with me!
Here, eat this cake, sit still, and don't you rise—
Why don't you pluck the sun down from the skies?
I'll spoil your sport—Come, laugh me in the face—
And henceforth learn to keep your proper place.
You rule me in the house!—To hush your noise
I, like a spaniel, must run for toys:
But here, Sir, let the trees alone, nor cry—
Pluck, if you dare—Who's master? you, or I?'
  O brutal force, to check th' enquiring mind,
When it would pleasure in a rose-bud find!
Whose wondrous strength was never yet discern'd,
By millions gone, by all we yet have learn'd.
  True to the senses, systematic man
Conceives himself a mighty, finish'd plan;
To see, to touch, to taste, and smell and hear,
He strives to prove, make full existence here:
These to the brain exquisite forms convey;
On these she works, these keep her life in play.
  And is this all, Mira, we boast below?
Does not the soul spring forward still to KNOW;
Pant for the future as her pow'rs expand,
And pine for more than sense can understand?
Does she not, when the senses weary lie,
Paint brighter visions on some unknown sky;
Again forego her visionary joy,
To guide the senses in their strong employ;
With life's affections share their gentle flow,
But still, unsated, onward rove to KNOW?
In infancy, when all her force is young,
She patient waits behind the useless tongue;
Silent attunes her senses, silent sees
Objects thro' mists, plainer by swift degrees.
SOUND strikes at first on her new-organ'd ear
As if far off; monotonous comes near.
Her taste yet sleeps, no melody she owns,
Nor wakes to joyous, or to thrilling tones:
Dull indiscrimination blinds her views;

[5] **Golconda's mine:** old name of Hyderabad, celebrated for its diamond mines, hence "a mine of wealth."

But still, the sound once caught, the ear pursues;
Till cadence whispers o'er the eager thought,
And human accents strike, with MEANING fraught;
Then gentle breathings in the babe inspire
Joy, pleasure, sympathy, new-born desire.
He feels instinctive happiness, and tries
To grasp her fully as she onward flies.
Hence Mira's soft endearments shall excite
In her dear Edward exquisite delight.
Wouldst thou Amyntor should adore his child;
Nurse him thyself, for thou canst make him mild;
Grant him the toy that suits his young desire,
Nor, when he pensive moans, his temper tire;
Keep froward[6] passions from his tranquil breast—
By irritation, who were ever blest?—
Distorting frowns delirious fear create;
And blows, a sense of injury and hate.
Long—very long, should surly chiding sleep—
Nay, it were best thy babe should never weep.
No cure, no medicine fills the tear—the eye
Whose owner ne'er offended should be dry.
 I grant, when he the distant toy would reach,
Stern self-denial maiden aunts would preach:
But, contrary to this cold maxim tried,
Bestow the gift, Indulgence be thy guide;
Ay, give unask'd; example has its kind,
Pouring its image on the ductile[7] mind.
Hence nobler spirits shall their likeness breed,
And ONE great virtue take the mental lead:
Hence vice and ignorance (What ills are worse?)
Arise contagious in the artful nurse;
For Virtue's self she ne'er could virtue prize,
O'er THOUGHT deform'd she throws the fair
  disguise;
Coarse in idea—furious in her ire,
Her passions grow amid their smother'd fire.
O trust not Edward to so warm a breast,
Lest she infuse the evils you detest.
 Early instruction does the infant need—
On pictured lessons we are prone to feed:
Thro' ev'ry stage, what strikes the eye bestrides
Attention, judgment follows and decides.

[6] **froward:** disposed to go counter to what is demanded or reasonable, refractory.

[7] **ductile:** malleable, flexible, tractable.

With mental vision deck th' instructive show.
Say what we will, we wish ourselves to know;
For this the child of seventy eager tries—
Explores his inward world—exploring dies!
However, early teach him mind to scan:
And when he's weary, tell him, 'SUCH IS MAN.'
 Next, try thy soothing skill—A challenge make—
An apple, orange, or some gew-gaw stake.
Which shall read best the alphabetic line,
Be his the wish'd reward—the sorrow thine.
This rule perhaps is contrary to those
Who on the failing babe some task impose:
Ah, too severe! they chill the struggling mind—
'Tis hard to learn—the tutor should be kind.
When Edward fails, console him—let him see
Thou mourn'st his loss, and he will mourn with
  thee:
Not long he will thy mimic sorrow view:
Thy point once seen, he will that point pursue.
A rival for perfection, generous shame
Will touch the soul's best spark, and blaze it into fame.
 Thus far I've lightly tripp'd the infant stage:
Truths bold and strong await the second age.
To ancient fathers be thy boy consign'd,
But plant thyself true virtue in his mind.
Watch his belief, his doubts, his fruitless fears;
Convince him, The frail babe of seventy years
Will unresisting slumber on the sod,
The sole undoubted property of GOD!

The Indifferent Shepherdess to Colin

(1796; comp. 1796)

Colin, why this mistake?
  Why plead thy foolish love?
My heart shall sooner break
  Than I a minion[1] prove;
Nor care I half a rush,
  No snare I spread for thee:
Go home, my friend, and blush
  For love and liberty.

[1] **minion:** a beloved one, a lover or mistress.

Remembrance is my own—
  Dominion bright and clear,
Truth there was ever known
  To combat ev'ry care:
One image there imprest
  Thro' life shall ever be,
Whilst my innoxious[2] breast
  Owns love of liberty.

I ever taught thee how
  To prize the soul entire,
When on the mountain's brow
  I tun'd my rural lyre:
Thou servile art and vain,
  Thy love unworthy me!
Away! nor hear my strain,
  Of love or liberty.

What arts need I display
  To woo a soul like thine?
Thou ne'er canst know the way
  My mem'ry to confine;
For my eternal plan
  Is to be calm and free.
Estrang'd from tyrant man
  I'll keep my liberty.

Yon woods their foliage wear,
  Be thou away or nigh;
The warblers of the year
  Instruct me not to sigh:
My tears ne'er roll the steep,
  Nor swell the restless sea,
Except for those who sleep
  Bereft of liberty.

Slave to commanding eyes!
  Those eyes thou wouldst commend
My judgment must despise—
  My pity is thy friend:
If eyes alone can move
  A swain so dull as thee,
They mean but to reprove
  Thy loss of liberty.

I stray o'er rocks and fields
  Where native beauties shine:
All fetter'd fancy yields
  Be, Colin, ever thine.
Complain no more! but rove—
  My cheek from crimson free,[3]
Within my native grove
  I'll guard my liberty.

[2] **innoxious:** innocuous, innocent, blameless.

[3] **from crimson free:** free from immodest blushes.

WILLIAM BLAKE

(1757–1827)

William Blake was a poet, a painter, and an engraver by trade; a radical Christian, and a revolutionary. The son of working-class London artisans (his father, James Blake, apprenticed as a glover and then opened a successful glove and haberdashery shop in which Blake and his mother and three siblings all worked), Blake always identified with the working classes as opposed to the gentry and nobility. Self-educated by choice, his only formal schooling was as an artist: at the age of 10, he took drawing lessons at Henry Pars's academy, and at 14 he was apprenticed as a commercial engraver to the old-fashioned line engraver, James Basire. After an unhappy year at the Royal Academy of Art (1779–1780), he began his career as a professional engraver for the magazine and book trade. On 18 August 1782, he married Catherine Sophia Boucher (or Butcher). The daughter of a Battersea market gardener, she had consoled Blake after he had been jilted by his first love, Polly Wood. Catherine was devoted to Blake, stood by him during his professional disappointments and flirtations with other women, and eventually learned to color by hand his illuminated prints and to share his spiritual visions. This childless marriage was regarded by the Blakes and their friends as an extremely successful one, one that enabled Blake to pursue his own visionary projects unimpeded.

Although Blake clearly loved and appreciated his wife's efforts on his behalf, his most powerful emotional bonding was with his brother Robert, ten years his junior. Blake filled the role of both father and professional mentor to Robert, training him as an artist. Blake never fully recovered from his grief at Robert's early death from tuberculosis in 1787, and continued to have spiritual "conversations" with Robert throughout his life. He credited Robert with the technique of "illuminated printing" that he developed in 1788 and with inspiring many of his long poems, especially *Milton* (1804). Powerful images of homosocial bonding recur throughout Blake's poetry and art, probably influenced by Blake's continuing passion for his younger brother.

Blake's "illuminated printing" was an attempt to create a composite art in which text and visual design would exist in a dynamic, contrapuntal, often ironic relationship to each other, each telling its own story; thus Blake's verbal texts cannot be understood independently of his illuminating designs, and vice versa. Beginning with *There is No Natural Religion* in 1788, Blake used the following technique to produce his illuminated books. He wrote in reverse on a copper plate, using an acid-insoluble gum mixture. He then dipped the copper plate in a strong acid bath, allowing the acid to cut deeply into the plate, thus leaving his writing and designs on raised lines. He then inked the plate and printed the design on paper, usually in a sepia-colored ink. Finally, he watercolored the plate, adding background washes, coloring in his printed designs, and sometimes adding new details. Since each plate was individually hand-painted, usually by Blake himself, but sometimes by Catherine, the coloring varied markedly from one set of printings of a given poem to another set. Sometimes they appeared in a fairly crude coloring; sometimes they approximated the highly detailed, rich coloring of such medieval illustrated manuscripts as the "Bedford Hours," which had been Blake's immediate inspiration (he saw them in the Winchester Abbey library between 1771 and 1772). Blake hoped to find a wide audience for his illuminated poems and to make a large profit on them. Their extremely high price, increasingly radical and difficult language, and his own obscurity, however, meant that very few of his illuminated books were actually purchased (we know of only 29 copies of the *Songs of Innocence* still in existence, for instance).

Since Blake insisted on pursuing an increasingly outdated style of commercial line engraving, which emphasized outlines, as opposed to stipple (or dot-and-lozenge) engraving, which emphasized masses and shadows and could more successfully reproduce the subtle tonalities of oil painting, especially the styles of Rembrandt and the Venetians (Titian, Tintoretto, Georgione), his career as an engraver was less and less successful. He spent most of his life on the edge of poverty, dependent on the goodwill of a few friends who found engraving commissions for him (the painters Flaxman and Fuseli and, in his final years, John Linnell, and the writer William Hayley). He relied also on the patronage of one remarkably tolerant client, Thomas Butts (who bought his series of illustrations to the Bible, to *Job*, and to Milton's *Paradise Lost*). Blake deeply resented his financial dependence and frequently quarrelled with those who tried to employ him, especially the bookseller Richard Cromek and William Hayley, despite Hayley's generous assistance when Blake was arrested and tried for sedition against the king in 1803. Blake had denounced the king to a drunken soldier, John Scolfield, who had invaded his garden at Felpham, where he was living in a cottage owned by Hayley. Blake was later acquitted because Scolfield could not produce a reliable witness at the trial.

Although he and his family lived a lonely and increasingly impoverished life, Blake was consoled throughout by his own visions. As he possessed an extremely highly developed eidetic imagination, in which the mental images perceived by the eyes and those created by the mind appear with equal clarity and depth, Blake considered these visions to be as true as what others called "reality." And he was sustained by the appreciation of a few friends and patrons—especially Thomas Butts and the group of young painters known as the Antients (John Linnell, Richard Calvert, George Richmond, Samuel Palmer, and John Varley), who discovered him in 1818 and hailed him as their Interpreter in his final decade. He died on 12 August 1827, singing "Hallelujahs & songs of joy & Triumph."

Throughout his poetry and art, Blake attacked the hegemonic ideology of late eighteenth-century England: the religious doctrines of the Anglican Church, the moral codes of English society, the political institution of monarchy, the Enlightenment glorification of human reason. He consciously tried to liberate all Englishmen from the "mind-forg'd manacles" imposed on them by stale, limited belief systems. He set out to create a new myth or system that would expand the possibilities of human experience by rejecting each and every mental or psychological restriction—political, intellectual, social, emotional—that inhibited or prevented the gratification of man's (as opposed to woman's) desires.

Blake began with a metaphor, a new vision of God and man. Whereas the eighteenth-century Enlightenment Deists had equated God with Reason and considered man to be good only insofar as he acted and thought rationally, Blake believed that God *is* man, not rational man but natural, spontaneous, innocent man. He concluded his second religious tract, *There is No Natural Religion* (1788), with this assertion: "God becomes as we are, that we may be as he is."

The poems that Blake composed, illuminated, and published the following year, in 1789, explored the implications of this metaphor. The *Songs of Innocence* present a religious vision which sees God as human and man as *potentially* divine. To live in Innocence, as Blake represents it, is to know that God resides both within oneself and without; that every living thing is holy; that one's most intuitive, spontaneous thoughts and acts are manifestations of divine truth and will; and that heaven and earth are potentially one. Blake's metaphor is not new, although he probably expressed it in its most extreme form. St. Paul, Joachim of Flora, and many English Evangelical or Dissenting sects had earlier affirmed the doctrine that God resides in man and that man must be true to the "inner light" of his own divine conscience and intuition.

Blake's *Songs of Innocence* depict the age prophesied by Joachim of Flora and Jacob Boehme, an age when God is fully manifest in man, and man's natural, spontaneous acts instinctively create a world of love and spiritual freedom. Here the "evils" of climate, disease, and death are rendered painless by the inner strength of faith. The man of Innocence knows that God cherishes and protects every living thing in life and in death, and that he has achieved divinity. This conviction brings him intellectual and psychological security, spiritual liberty, and enormous pleasure, love, and peace. Blake's radical immanental Christianity, his vision of Innocence, should not be too quickly dismissed as a limited or naive view of the world. These *Songs,* written when Blake was 32, offer what many would argue is the necessary moral basis upon which any radical reconstruction of human society must build. Blake's assumption—that human nature is essentially good rather than evil—was shared by Rousseau and by Marx, and is the ground of most radical utopian thought. Blake clearly intended his *Songs* for adults as well as for children. He portrays a utopian society of love and freedom which is, he believed, within the capacity of natural man to create.

Nonetheless, Blake's *Songs of Innocence* both verbally and visually construct a bounded, self-enclosed world, in the sense that they look toward a *future* realization of an idyllic, self-sufficient, and eternal society in which man's spiritual needs are completely satisfied. This closed, utopian character of Innocence means, of course, that aspects of the "real" world, of eighteenth-century England as Blake knew it, have been excluded. This exclusion does not mean that the *spiritual* message of the *Songs of Innocence* is necessarily untrue or inadequate as religious faith. However, this exclusion does arouse a feeling of tension in the reader: how are we to relate to the closed and self-sustaining vision of Innocence? Should we dismiss these *Songs* as foolish, sentimental, naive? Or should we see them as a possible blueprint for a future utopian society? And if the latter, then perhaps we should feel anger (rather than cynicism) at the discrepancy between the ideal world Blake portrays and the actual world in which he—and we—live, an anger that might be translated into revolutionary political action.

In the *Songs of Innocence* Blake initiated a system of metaphors grounded on gender that became the foundation of all his later poetry and art. In Blake's aesthetic world, the female is identified with nature, the physical body or matter, and the realm of the domestic. Blake's positive females give birth, raise children, and offer sexual delight and supportive compassion to Blake's males. In their negative forms, Blake's females deny sexual pleasure, oppress children, and exercise what Blake comes to call "the Female Will," an aggressive usurpation of power over men. In contrast, masculinity is identified with imagination, with the spiritual or visionary, and with the realm of the mental or linguistic. Positive males function as protective and democratic fathers and political leaders, as rebels against mental and physical tyranny, as potent sexual initiators, and above all as visionary artists and prophets. The realm of the discursive, the authority to speak, is consistently identified with the masculine.

Blake's negative males are those who exercise this authority at the expense of other males: political tyrants, oppressive fathers, proponents of the constricting lines of reason as opposed to the liberating lines of the imagination. Although Blake radically contested the boundaries between almost all of the binary structures he inherited from his culture (he reconceptualized the relationships between good and evil, man and God, reason and imagination, freedom and slavery, etc.), he never contested the fundamental binary of sexual difference: the ideal human form divine is always in Blake's system male; the female is either an "emanation" from the male (and happily subservient to him), or essentially different from and lesser than the male (and therefore wrong in asserting opposition to him).

In the years of the French Revolution that followed the printing of the *Songs of Innocence* in 1789, Blake optimistically believed that a political revolution overthrowing the British monarchy might be possible. *The Book of Thel* (1789, last plate 1791) had suggested how a female child of Innocence might mature into an eager sexual partner and devoted mother, and how she might resist the social and sexual restrictions of Regency England by choosing instead a life of Innocence in the Vales of Har. In *The Marriage of Heaven and Hell* (1793), *Visions of the Daughters of Albion* (1793), *America* (1793), and *Songs of Experience* (1794), Blake more directly attacked the political and sexual oppressions of his England. Blake's spokesman, the Devil or "Just Man" of *The Marriage of Heaven and Hell,* drawing on the imagery of the radical Swedish theologian Emanuel Swedenborg, hails the advent of a new age when creative energy shall harness the bounding lines of reason to its own emancipatory social and political agenda, while Oothoon in *Visions of the Daughters of Albion* denounces the British institutions of the slave trade, slavery, and sexual repression. In *Songs of Experience,* which Blake added to and never published independently from *Songs of Innocence* (although he continued to print *Songs of Innocence* separately as a self-sufficient utopian tract), the vision of Innocence directly confronts the evils of eighteenth-century London, taking on the voice of satire, the tone of righteous indignation and prophetic denunciation assigned both to the Piper and the Bard.

By the end of 1794, however, Blake's failure to succeed as a commercial engraver, artist, print shop owner, and illuminated printer, combined with the increasingly oppressive political climate in England in response to the Terror in France, produced a period of prolonged depression for Blake, a period that lasted for almost a decade. *The Book of Urizen* (1794); the shorter prophecies of 1794 and 1795; the powerful color print series that Blake created for Thomas Butts between 1795 and 1803 (now housed in large part in the Tate Gallery, London); his illustrations for Edward Young's *Night Thoughts* (1795–1797) and for Robert Blair's *The Grave;* and the manuscript of the first of Blake's long prophetic poems, *Vala* (c. 1796–1804; later revised as *The Four Zoas,* c. 1804–1807) all represent the world of eighteenth-century England as entirely "fallen," dominated by the cruel tyranny of Urizen ("your reason") and Vala (female nature or the mortal body). The only salvation Blake here offers is an escape from the physical body, through death, into the spiritual afterlife envisioned by Young and Blair.

In August 1803, returning to London after three extremely troubled years as Hayley's protégé in Felpham, Sussex, Blake experienced an ecstatic conversion, or what he afterward called "an altered state," which we can more precisely define as a return to his earlier belief in the vision of Innocence. Visiting the art collection of Joseph, Count Truchsess, in a newly opened gallery in the New Road, Marylebone, Blake's faith in his own artistic visions was restored by the contemplation of the old masters (Rembrandt, Rubens, and especially Durer) whom he admired and now believed he could equal: "I was again enlightened with the light I enjoyed in my youth, and which has for exactly twenty years been closed from me as by a door and by window-shutters. . . . [E]xcuse my enthusiasm, or rather madness, for I am really drunk with intellectual vision whenever I take a pencil or graver into my hand, even as I used to be in my youth . . . ." (Letter to Hayley, 23 October 1804). From this point on, in his paintings for Butts (scenes from the Bible), in his illustrations to *Job* and Dante and Milton, and above all in his own illuminated poetry (the epic prophecies of *The Four Zoas, Milton,* and *Jerusalem*), Blake confidently asserted the capacity of the human imagination to achieve *on earth,* in the physical body, the realization of the divine.

Jerusalem (1804–1820) tells the epic story of man's fall into limited states of the mind and the body and of his regeneration or return to the Human Form Divine, the total enactment of his innate divinity. The Human Form Divine is now represented first as a mode of being and acting—specifically, an imitation of the life of Christ as Blake defined it, the life of a proud, angry, sensual, loving man who is humble *only* before his own authentic divinity, the life of a poet/rebel who speaks in parables, the life of one who forgives sin, both his own and others'. Secondly, the Human Form Divine is a mode of *vision,* what Blake calls the Divine Analogy, the capacity to see man as God, to see earth as heaven, "to see a world in a grain of sand." The plot of *Jerusalem* represents the fall of each of man's four dimensions or "Zoas"—his imagination (Urthona), his emotions (Luvah), his physical and sexual desires (Tharmas), and his reason (Urizen). As each Zoa falls away from the One Man, he attempts to seize full control over the other Zoas and over the world; each then falls further apart, separating into a diminished male selfhood and a female emanation; and each must then be saved by being reintegrated into the unified body of the One Man, Albion. This regeneration is accomplished through the labours of Los, the mortal imagination, and *his* emanation, Enitharmon, the physical body (of art as well as of the human body). Finally, the longed-for apocalypse occurs, on Plate 94, line 23: "Time was finished!" The Four Zoas now reunite in Albion, Albion reabsorbs his weeping emanation Jerusalem and recognizes his identity with Jesus, and the One Man expands to include all time and space, an eternal realm of Innocence or what Blake now calls Eden, in which an unending process of visionary creation and mutual love takes place.

There Is No Natural Religion

(1788)

—[a]—

The Argument. Man has no notion of moral fitness but from Education. Naturally he is only a natural organ subject to Sense.

I Man cannot naturally Percieve. but through his natural or bodily organs.

II Man by his reasoning power. can only compare & judge of what he has already perciev'd.

III From a perception of only 3 senses or 3 elements none could deduce a fourth or fifth

IV None could have other than natural or organic thoughts if he had none but organic perceptions

V Mans desires are limited by his perceptions. none can desire what he has not perciev'd

VI The desires & perceptions of man untaught by any thing but organs of sense, must be limited to objects of sense.

Conclusion. If it were not for the Poetic or Prophetic character the Philosophic & Experimental would soon be at the ratio[1] of all things, & stand still unable to do other than repeat the same dull round over again

— [b] —

I Mans perceptions are not bounded by organs of perception. he percieves more than sense (tho' ever so acute) can discover.

II Reason or the ratio of all we have already known. is not the same that it shall be when we know more.

[III lacking]

IV The bounded is loathed by its possessor. The same dull round even of a univer[s]e would soon become a mill with complicated wheels

V If the many become the same as the few when possess'd, More! More! is the cry of a mistaken soul, less than All cannot satisfy Man.

VI If any could desire what he is incapable of possessing, despair must be his eternal lot.

VII The desire of Man being Infinite the possession is Infinite & himself Infinite

Application. He who sees the Infinite in all things sees God. He who sees the Ratio only sees himself only.

Therefore God becomes as we are, that we may be as he is

All Religions Are One

(1788)

The Voice of one crying in the Wilderness[1]

The Argument. As the true method of knowledge is experiment the true faculty of knowing must be the faculty which experiences. This faculty I treat of.

PRINCIPLE 1st That the Poetic Genius is the true Man. and that the body or outward form of Man is derived from the Poetic Genius. Likewise that the forms of all things are derived from their Genius. which by the Ancients was call'd an Angel & Spirit & Demon.

PRINCIPLE 2d As all men are alike in outward form, So (and with the same infinite variety) all are alike in the Poetic Genius

[1] **ratio:** from Latin *ratio* (reason), the sum of knowledge derived from sensory perception.

[1] **The Voice . . . Wilderness:** John the Baptist (Isaiah 40:3).

PRINCIPLE 3d No man can think write or speak from his heart, but he must intend truth. Thus all sects of Philosophy are from the Poetic Genius adapted to the weaknesses of every individual

PRINCIPLE 4. As none by travelling over known lands can find out the unknown. So from already acquired knowledge Man could not acquire more. therefore an universal Poetic Genius exists

PRINCIPLE 5. The Religeons of all Nations are derived from each Nation's different reception of the Poetic Genius which is every where call'd the Spirit of Prophecy.

PRINCIPLE 6 The Jewish & Christian Testaments are An original derivation from the Poetic Genius. this is necessary from the confined nature of bodily sensation

PRINCIPLE 7th As all men are alike (tho' infinitely various) So all Religions & as all similars have one source.

The true Man is the source he being the Poetic Genius

from SONGS OF INNOCENCE[1]

(1789)

Introduction

Piping down the valleys wild
Piping songs of pleasant glee
On a cloud I saw a child.
And he laughing said to me.

Pipe a song about a Lamb;
So I piped with merry chear,
Piper pipe that song again—
So I piped, he wept to hear.

Drop thy pipe thy happy pipe
Sing thy songs of happy chear,
So I sung the same again
While he wept with joy to hear

[1] Blake conceived and engraved the *Songs of Innocence* independently from the *Songs of Experience.* The *Songs of Innocence* were composed between 1784 and 1789, and Blake continued to publish them as a separate volume even after the *Songs of Experience* were added to them in 1794.

Piper sit thee down and write
In a book that all may read—
So he vanish'd from my sight.
And I pluck'd a hollow reed.

And I made a rural pen,
And I stain'd the water clear,
And I wrote my happy songs
Every child may joy to hear

The Shepherd
(1789)

How sweet is the Shepherds sweet lot,
From the morn to the evening he strays:
He shall follow his sheep all the day
And his tongue shall be filled with praise.

For he hears the lambs innocent call,
And he hears the ewes tender reply,
He is watchful while they are in peace,
For they know when their Shepherd is nigh.

The Ecchoing Green
(1789)

The Sun does arise,
And make happy the skies.
The merry bells ring
To welcome the Spring.
The sky-lark and thrush,
The birds of the bush,
Sing louder around,
To the bells chearful sound.
While our sports shall be seen
On the Ecchoing Green.

Old John with white hair
Does laugh away care,
Sitting under the oak,
Among the old folk,
They laugh at our play,
And soon they all say.
Such such were the joys.
When we all girls & boys,
In our youth-time were seen,
On the Ecchoing Green.

Till the little ones weary
No more can be merry
The sun does descend,
And our sports have an end:
Round the laps of their mothers,
Many sisters and brothers,
Like birds in their nest,
Are ready for rest;
And sport no more seen,
On the darkening Green.

The Lamb
(1789)

Little Lamb who made thee
Dost thou know who made thee
Gave thee life & bid thee feed.
By the stream & o'er the mead;
Gave thee clothing of delight,
Softest clothing wooly bright;
Gave thee such a tender voice,
Making all the vales rejoice!
Little Lamb who made thee
Dost thou know who made thee

Little Lamb I'll tell thee,
Little Lamb I'll tell thee!
He is called by thy name,
For he calls himself a Lamb:
He is meek & he is mild,
He became a little child:
I a child & thou a lamb,
We are called by his name.
Little Lamb God bless thee.
Little Lamb God bless thee.

The Little Black Boy[1]
(1789)

My mother bore me in the southern wild,
And I am black, but O! my soul is white;

[1] Design for Plate 2: in some colored copies of this design which depicts the black and white boy leaning on the knee of Christ, the black boy has become white.

White as an angel is the English child:
But I am black as if bereav'd of light.

My mother taught me underneath a tree
And sitting down before the heat of day,
She took me on her lap and kissed me,
And pointing to the east began to say.

Look on the rising sun: there God does live
And gives his light, and gives his heat away.
And flowers and trees and beasts and men recieve
Comfort in morning joy in the noon day.

And we are put on earth a little space,
That we may learn to bear the beams of love,
And these black bodies and this sun-burnt face
Is but a cloud, and like a shady grove.

For when our souls have learn'd the heat to bear
The cloud will vanish we shall hear his voice.
Saying: come out from the grove my love & care,
And round my golden tent like lambs rejoice.

Thus did my mother say and kissed me,
And thus I say to little English boy.
When I from black and he from white cloud free,
And round the tent of God like lambs we joy:

Ill shade him from the heat till he can bear,
To lean in joy upon our fathers knee.
And then I'll stand and stroke his silver hair,
And be like him and he will then love me.

The Blossom
(1789)

Merry Merry Sparrow
Under leaves so green
A happy Blossom
Sees you swift as arrow
Seek your cradle narrow
Near my Bosom.

Pretty Pretty Robin
Under leaves so green
A happy Blossom
Hears you sobbing sobbing
Pretty Pretty Robin
Near my Bosom.

The Chimney Sweeper
(1789)

When my mother died I was very young,
And my father sold me while yet my tongue,
Could scarcely cry weep weep weep weep.[1]
So your chimneys I sweep & in soot I sleep.

Theres little Tom Dacre, who cried when his head
That curl'd like a lambs back, was shav'd, so I said.
Hush Tom never mind it, for when your head's bare,
You know that the soot cannot spoil your white hair.

And so he was quiet, & that very night,
As Tom was a sleeping he had such a sight,
That thousands of sweepers Dick, Joe Ned & Jack
Were all of them lock'd up in coffins of black

And by came an Angel who had a bright key,
And he open'd the coffins & set them all free.
Then down a green plain leaping laughing they run
And wash in a river and shine in the Sun.

Then naked & white, all their bags left behind,
They rise upon clouds, and sport in the wind.
And the Angel told Tom if he'd be a good boy,
He'd have God for his father & never want joy.

And so Tom awoke and we rose in the dark
And got with our bags & our brushes to work.
Tho' the morning was cold, Tom was happy & warm,
So if all do their duty, they need not fear harm.

[1] **weep . . . weep:** a reference to the chimney sweeper's lisping cry, "'weep" (i.e., "sweep, sweep"). In 1788, Jonas Hanway reported to Parliament on the condition and abuse of English chimney sweeps. Typically apprenticed (or "sold") by their parents at the age of six or seven, they were brutally used by their masters, receiving little clothing, food, or shelter, and in constant danger of burning or suffocating as they swept out the narrow, filthy chimneys of London. Many contracted skin cancer and pulmonary diseases which killed them before they reached adulthood; their general dirtiness and their reputation for stealing made them social outcasts.

The Little Boy Lost
(1789; comp. 1784)

Father, father, where are you going
O do not walk so fast.
Speak father, speak to your little boy
Or else I shall be lost,

The night was dark no father was there
The child was wet with dew.
The mire was deep, & the child did weep
And away the vapour flew.

The Little Boy Found
(1789)

The little boy lost in the lonely fen,
Led by the wand'ring light,
Began to cry, but God ever nigh,
Appeard like his father in white.
He kissed the child & by the hand led
And to his mother brought,
Who in sorrow pale, thro' the lonely dale
Her little boy weeping sought.

The Divine Image
(1789)

To Mercy Pity Peace and Love,
All pray in their distress:
And to these virtues of delight
Return their thankfulness.

For Mercy Pity Peace and Love,
Is God our father dear:
And Mercy Pity Peace and Love,
Is Man his child and care.

For Mercy has a human heart
Pity, a human face:
And Love, the human form divine,
And Peace, the human dress.

Then every man of every clime,
That prays in his distress,
Prays to the human form divine
Love Mercy Pity Peace.

And all must love the human form,
In heathen, turk or jew.
Where Mercy, Love & Pity dwell
There God is dwelling too.

Holy Thursday
(1789; comp. 1784)

Twas on a Holy Thursday[1] their innocent faces clean
The children walking two & two in red & blue & green[2]
Grey headed beadles[3] walkd before with wands as white as snow
Till into the high dome of Pauls they like Thames waters flow

O what a multitude they seemd these flowers of London town
Seated in companies they sit with radiance all their own
The hum of multitudes was there but multitudes of lambs
Thousands of little boys & girls raising their innocent hands

Now like a mighty wind they raise to heaven the voice of song
Or like harmonious thunderings the seats of heaven among
Beneath them sit the aged men wise guardians of the poor
Then cherish pity, lest you drive an angel from your door

[1] Ascension Day, in which the 6,000 students attending the Charity Schools in London (i.e., the schools for poor and destitute children funded by private donations) gathered for services in St. Paul's Cathedral.

[2] **red . . . green:** each school had its own colored uniform.

[3] **beadles:** school functionaries who served as ushers to keep order during the religious services.

Nurse's Song
(1789; comp. 1784)

When the voices of children are heard on the green
And laughing is heard on the hill,
My heart is at rest within my breast
And every thing else is still

Then come home my children, the sun is gone down
And the dews of night arise
Come come leave off play, and let us away
Till the morning appears in the skies

No no let us play, for it is yet day
And we cannot go to sleep
Besides in the sky, the little birds fly
And the hills are all coverd with sheep

Well well go & play till the light fades away
And then go home to bed
The little ones leaped & shouted & laugh'd
And all the hills ecchoed

Infant Joy
(1789)

I have no name
I am but two days old.—
What shall I call thee?
I happy am
Joy is my name,—
Sweet joy befall thee!

Pretty joy!
Sweet joy but two days old.
Sweet joy I call thee:
Thou dost smile.
I sing the while
Sweet joy befall thee.

A Dream
(1789)

Once a dream did weave a shade,
O'er my Angel-guarded bed,
That an Emmet[1] lost it's way
Where on grass methought I lay.

Troubled wilderd and folorn
Dark benighted travel-worn,
Over many a tangled spray
All heart-broke I heard her say.

O my children! do they cry
Do they hear their father sigh.
Now they look abroad to see,
Now return and weep for me.

Pitying I drop'd a tear:
But I saw a glow-worm near:
Who replied. What wailing wight
Calls the watchman of the night.

I am set to light the ground,
While the beetle goes his round:
Follow now the beetles hum,
Little wanderer hie thee home.

On Anothers Sorrow
(1789)

Can I see anothers woe,
And not be in sorrow too.
Can I see anothers grief,
And not seek for kind relief.

Can I see a falling tear,
And not feel my sorrows share,
Can a father see his child,
Weep, nor be with sorrow fill'd.

Can a mother sit and hear,
An infant groan an infant fear—
No no never can it be.
Never never can it be.

And can he who smiles on all
Hear the wren with sorrows small,
Hear the small birds grief & care
Hear the woes that infants bear—

And not sit beside the nest
Pouring pity in their breast,
And not sit the cradle near
Weeping tear on infants tear.

[1] Emmet: an ant.

And not sit both night & day,
Wiping all our tears away.
O! no never can it be.
Never never can it be.

He doth give his joy to all.
He becomes an infant small.
He becomes a man of woe
He doth feel the sorrow too.

Think not, thou canst sigh a sigh,
And thy maker is not by.
Think not, thou canst weep a tear,
And thy maker is not near.

O! he gives to us his joy,
That our grief he may destroy
Till our grief is fled & gone
He doth sit by us and moan

The Little Girl Lost[1]

(1789)

In futurity
I prophetic see,
That the earth from sleep,
(Grave the sentence deep)

Shall arise and seek
For her maker meek:
And the desart wild
Become a garden mild.

In the southern clime,
Where the summers prime,
Never fades away;
Lovely Lyca lay.

Seven summers old
Lovely Lyca told,
She had wanderd long,
Hearing wild birds song.

Sweet sleep come to me
Underneath this tree;
Do father, mother weep.—
"Where can Lyca sleep".

Lost in desart wild
Is your little child.
How can Lyca sleep,
If her mother weep.

If her heart does ake,
Then let Lyca wake;
If my mother sleep,
Lyca shall not weep.

Frowning frowning night,
O'er this desart bright,
Let thy moon arise,
While I close my eyes.

Sleeping Lyca lay;
While the beasts of prey,
Come from caverns deep,
View'd the maid asleep

The kingly lion stood
And the virgin view'd,
Then he gambold round
O'er the hallowd ground:

Leopards, tygers play,
Round her as she lay;
While the lion old,
Bow'd his mane of gold.

And her bosom lick,
And upon her neck,
From his eyes of flame,
Ruby tears there came;

While the lioness,
Loos'd her slender dress,
And naked they convey'd
To caves the sleeping maid.

The Little Girl Found

(1789)

All the night in woe
Lyca's parents go:
Over vallies deep,
While the desarts weep.

[1] "The Little Girl Lost," "The Little Girl Found," and "The Voice of the Ancient Bard" were first engraved and published in *Songs of Innocence,* which appeared in independent editions. In editions of *Songs of Innocence and of Experience* published after 1794, these poems appear among the *Songs of Experience.*

Tired and woe-begone,
Hoarse with making moan:
Arm in arm seven days,
They trac'd the desart ways.

Seven nights they sleep,
Among shadows deep:
And dream they see their child
Starv'd in desart wild.

Pale thro pathless ways
The fancied image strays,
Famish'd, weeping, weak
With hollow piteous shriek

Rising from unrest,
The trembling woman prest,
With feet of weary woe;
She could no further go.

In his arms he bore,
Her arm'd with sorrow sore;
Till before their way,
A couching lion lay.

Turning back was vain,
Soon his heavy mane,
Bore them to the ground;
Then he stalk'd around,

Smelling to his prey.
But their fears allay,
When he licks their hands;
And silent by them stands.

They look upon his eyes
Fill'd with deep surprise:
And wondering behold,
A spirit arm'd in gold.

On his head a crown
On his shoulders down,
Flow'd his golden hair.
Gone was all their care.

Follow me he said,
Weep not for the maid;
In my palace deep,
Lyca lies asleep.

Then they followed,
Where the vision led:
And saw their sleeping child,
Among tygers wild.

To this day they dwell
In a lonely dell
Nor fear the wolvish howl,
Nor the lions growl.

The School Boy[1]

(1789)

I love to rise in a summer morn,
When the birds sing on every tree;
The distant huntsman winds his horn,
And the sky-lark sings with me.
O! what sweet company.

But to go to school in a summer morn
O! it drives all joy away;
Under a cruel eye outworn,
The little ones spend the day,
In sighing and dismay.

Ah! then at times I drooping sit,
And spend many an anxious hour.
Nor in my book can I take delight,
Nor sit in learnings bower,
Worn thro' with the dreary shower

How can the bird that is born for joy,
Sit in a cage and sing.
How can a child when fears annoy,
But droop his tender wing,
And forget his youthful spring.

O! father & mother, if buds are nip'd,
And blossoms blown away,
And if the tender plants are strip'd
Of their joy in the springing day,
By sorrow and cares dismay,

How shall the summer arise in joy
Or the summer fruits appear
Or how shall we gather what griefs destroy
Or bless the mellowing year,
When the blasts of winter appear.

[1] Later transferred to *Songs of Experience.*

The Voice of the Ancient Bard

(1789)

Youth of delight come hither:
And see the opening morn,
Image of truth new born
Doubt is fled & clouds of reason
Dark disputes & artful teazing.
Folly is an endless maze,
Tangled roots perplex her ways,
How many have fallen there!
They stumble all night over bones of the dead;
And feel they know not what but care;
And wish to lead others when they should be led.

THE BOOK OF THEL[1]

(1789–1791)

PLATE i

Thel's Motto,

Does the Eagle know what is in the pit?
Or wilt thou go ask the Mole:
Can Wisdom be put in a silver rod?
Or Love in a golden bowl?[2]

PLATE 1

Thel

— I —

The daughters of Mne Seraphim[3] led round their sunny flocks,
All but the youngest. she in paleness sought the secret air.
To fade away like morning beauty from her mortal day:
Down by the river of Adona[4] her soft voice is heard:
And thus her gentle lamentation falls like morning dew.

O life of this our spring! why fades the lotus of the water?
Why fade these children of the spring? born but to smile & fall.
Ah! Thel is like a watry bow, and like a parting cloud,
Like a reflection in a glass. like shadows in the water.
Like dreams of infants. like a smile upon an infants face,
Like the doves voice, like transient day, like music in the air;
Ah! gentle may I lay me down, and gentle rest my head.
And gentle sleep the sleep of death. and gentle hear the voice
Of him that walketh in the garden in the evening time.[5]

The Lilly of the valley breathing in the humble grass
Answer'd the lovely maid and said; I am a watry weed,
And I am very small, and love to dwell in lowly vales;
So weak, the gilded butterfly scarce perches on my head
Yet I am visited from heaven and he that smiles on all.
Walks in the valley. and each morn over me spreads his hand
Saying, rejoice thou humble grass, thou new-born lilly flower,
Thou gentle maid of silent valleys. and of modest brooks;
For thou shalt be clothed in light, and fed with morning manna:
Till summers heat melts thee beside the fountains and the springs
To flourish in eternal vales: then why should Thel complain,

PLATE 2

Why should the mistress of the vales of Har,[6] utter a sigh.

---

[1] Thel is derived from Greek *thelo,* will or desire. Plates 1–5 of this work were etched c. 1789; plate 6 and the Motto were etched c. 1791.

[2] **silver rod . . . golden bowl:** Cf. Ecclesiastes 12:6.

[3] **Mne Seraphim:** perhaps a female form of "Bne Seraphim," an alchemical term used by Cornelius Agrippa (1486–1535) to refer to heavenly agents.

[4] **Adona:** derived from the Greek Adonis, a youth beloved by Venus for his beauty. Cf. *Paradise Lost,* I.450.

[5] **him that walketh:** Cf. Genesis 3:8, "And they heard the voice of the Lord God walking in the garden in the cool of the day."

[6] **vales of Har:** the state of Innocence.

She ceased & smild in tears, then sat down in her silver shrine.

Thel answerd. O thou little virgin of the peaceful valley.
Giving to those that cannot crave, the voiceless, the o'ertired.
Thy breath doth nourish the innocent lamb, he smells thy milky garments,
He crops thy flowers. while thou sittest smiling in his face,
Wiping his mild and meekin[7] mouth from all contagious taints.
Thy wine doth purify the golden honey, thy perfume,
Which thou dost scatter on every little blade of grass that springs
Revives the milked cow, & tames the fire-breathing steed.
But Thel is like a faint cloud kindled at the rising sun:
I vanish from my pearly throne, and who shall find my place.

Queen of the vales the Lilly answerd, ask the tender cloud,
And it shall tell thee why it glitters in the morning sky,
And why it scatters its bright beauty thro' the humid air.
Descend O little cloud & hover before the eyes of Thel.

The Cloud descended, and the Lilly bowd her modest head:
And went to mind her numerous charge among the verdant grass.

PLATE 3

— II —

O little Cloud the virgin said, I charge thee tell to me,
Why thou complainest not when in one hour thou fade away:
Then we shall seek thee but not find; ah Thel is like to Thee.
I pass away. yet I complain, and no one hears my voice.
The Cloud then shew'd his golden head & his bright form emerg'd,
Hovering and glittering on the air before the face of Thel.

O virgin know'st thou not. our steeds drink of the golden springs
Where Luvah[8] doth renew his horses: look'st thou on my youth,
And fearest thou because I vanish and am seen no more.
Nothing remains; O maid I tell thee, when I pass away,
It is to tenfold life, to love, to peace, and raptures holy:
Unseen descending. weigh my light wings upon balmy flowers;
And court the fair eyed dew. to take me to her shining tent;
The weeping virgin, trembling kneels before the risen sun,
Till we arise link'd in a golden band, and never part;
But walk united, bearing food to all our tender flowers

Dost thou O little Cloud? I fear that I am not like thee;
For I walk through the vales of Har. and smell the sweetest flowers;
But I feed not the little flowers: I hear the warbling birds,
But I feed not the warbling birds. they fly and seek their food;
But Thel delights in these no more because I fade away,
And all shall say, without a use this shining woman liv'd,
Or did she only live. to be at death the food of worms.

The Cloud reclind upon his airy throne and answer'd thus.

Then if thou art the food of worms. O virgin of the skies,
How great thy use. how great thy blessing; every thing that lives,
Lives not alone, nor for itself: fear not and I will call
The weak worm from its lowly bed, and thou shalt hear its voice.
Come forth worm of the silent valley, to thy pensive queen.

The helpless worm arose, and sat upon the Lillys leaf,
And the bright Cloud saild on, to find his partner in the vale.

[7] **meekin:** meek, gentle, humble.

[8] **Luvah:** name coined by Blake, an Apollo-like figure who drives the chariot of the sun across the sky.

Plate 4

— III —

Then Thel astonish'd view'd the Worm upon its dewy bed.
Art thou a Worm? image of weakness. art thou but a Worm?
I see thee like an infant wrapped in the Lillys leaf:
Ah weep not little voice, thou can'st not speak. but thou can'st weep;
Is this a Worm? I see thee lay helpless & naked: weeping,
And none to answer, none to cherish thee with mothers smiles.
The Clod of Clay heard the Worms voice, & raisd her pitying head;
She bow'd over the weeping infant, and her life exhal'd
In milky fondness, then on Thel she fix'd her humble eyes.
O beauty of the vales of Har. we live not for ourselves,
Thou seest me the meanest thing, and so I am indeed;
My bosom of itself is cold. and of itself is dark,

Plate 5

But he that loves the lowly, pours his oil upon my head.
And kisses me, and binds his nuptial bands around my breast,
And says; Thou mother of my children, I have loved thee.
And I have given thee a crown that none can take away
But how this is sweet maid, I know not, and I cannot know,
I ponder, and I cannot ponder; yet I live and love.
The daughter of beauty wip'd her pitying tears with her white veil,
And said. Alas! I knew not this, and therefore did I weep:
That God would love a Worm I knew, and punish the evil foot
That wilful, bruis'd its helpless form: but that he cherish'd it
With milk and oil. I never knew: and therefore did I weep,
And I complaind in the mild air, because I fade away,
And lay me down in thy cold bed, and leave my shining lot.
Queen of the vales, the matron Clay answerd; I heard thy sighs.
And all thy moans flew o'er my roof. but I have call'd them down:
Wilt thou O Queen enter my house. 'tis given thee to enter,
And to return; fear nothing. enter with thy virgin feet.

Plate 6

— IV —

The eternal gates terrific porter lifted the northern bar:[9]
Thel enter'd in & saw the secrets of the land unknown;
She saw the couches of the dead, & where the fibrous roots
Of every heart on earth infixes deep its restless twists:
A land of sorrows & of tears where never smile was seen.

She wanderd in the land of clouds thro' valleys dark, listning
Dolours & lamentations: waiting oft beside a dewy grave
She stood in silence. listning to the voices of the ground,
Till to her own grave plot she came, & there she sat down.
And heard this voice of sorrow breathed from the hollow pit.

Why cannot the Ear be closed to its own destruction?
Or the glistning Eye to the poison of a smile!
Why are Eyelids stord with arrows ready drawn,
Where a thousand fighting men in ambush lie?
Or an Eye of gifts & graces, show'ring fruits & coined gold!
Why a Tongue impress'd with honey from every wind?
Why an Ear, a whirlpool fierce to draw creations in?
Why a Nostril wide inhaling terror trembling & affright
Why a tender curb upon the youthful burning boy!
Why a little curtain of flesh on the bed of our desire?

The Virgin started from her seat, & with a shriek.
Fled back unhinderd till she came into the vales of Har

---

[9] **the northern bar**: from the *Odyssey* 13:109–12, where the cave of the Naiads has two gates, the northern one for mortals, the southern one for gods.

THE MARRIAGE OF HEAVEN AND HELL[1]

(1793; comp. 1790–1793)

PLATE 2

— THE ARGUMENT —

Rintrah[2] roars & shakes his fires in the burdend air;
Hungry clouds swag[3] on the deep

Once meek, and in a perilous path,
The just man kept his course along
The vale of death.
Roses are planted where thorns grow.
And on the barren heath
Sing the honey bees.

Then the perilous path was planted:
And a river, and a spring
On every cliff and tomb;
And on the bleached bones
Red clay[4] brought forth.

Till the villain left the paths of ease,
To walk in perilous paths, and drive
The just man into barren climes.

Now the sneaking serpent walks
In mild humility.
And the just man rages in the wilds
Where lions roam.

Rintrah roars & shakes his fires in the burdend air;
Hungry clouds swag on the deep.

PLATE 3

As a new heaven is begun, and it is now thirty-three years since its advent;[5] the Eternal Hell revives. And lo! Swedenborg is the Angel sitting at the tomb; his writings are the linen clothes folded up. Now is the dominion of Edom,[6] & the return of Adam into Paradise; see Isaiah XXXIV & XXXV Chap:[7]

---

[1] Allusion to Emanuel Swedenborg's *Heaven and Hell* (1778), in which Swedenborg (1688–1772), a Swedish engineer and mystic, announced the Second Coming of Christ and the inauguration of his New Church ("the New Jerusalem"). In 1757 Swedenborg claimed he had beheld the Last Judgment and that "a new heaven was begun." He further claimed to have regular conversations or "Memorable Relations" with both angels and devils, conversations which he recorded in his numerous books. Blake read and annotated Swedenborg's *Heaven and Hell, Divine Love and Divine Wisdom* (1788), and *Divine Providence* (1790).

Blake admired several aspects of Swedenborg's theology: his conviction that Jesus Christ was a man, that children are angels, and that the "New Jerusalem" is a heaven on earth. But Swedenborg was a predestinarian who divided humanity into the damned and the saved: the damned were dominated by lust and the pleasures of the body, what Swedenborg called "scoratory love," while the saved experienced only a "holy, pure and clean" spiritual love. According to Swedenborg, the new Eden will be achieved through the reconciliation or "marriage" of heaven and hell, when human physical desires are sublimated into spiritual desires, when lust becomes pure "conjugal love."

[2] **Rintrah:** the angry prophet or "just man" described by Isaiah 35.

[3] **swag:** sway, hang unsteadily, sink down.

[4] **red clay:** In Hebrew, "Adam" means "red clay."

[5] **advent:** thirty-three years before Blake composed *The Marriage* in 1790, in 1757, Blake was born and Swedenborg announced his vision of the Last Judgment. Christ rose from the tomb at the age of 33.

[6] **Edom:** the Edomites are the disinherited descendants of Esau, Isaac's firstborn son, who was cheated out of his father's blessing by the trickery of Jacob. Isaac then prophesied that Esau would serve his younger brother until "it shall come to pass when thou shalt have the dominion, that thou shalt shake his yoke from off thy neck" (Genesis 27:40). Cf. Isaiah 63:1–4.

[7] **Isaiah:** In the Book of Isaiah, the prophet Isaiah condemns the fallen, godless people of Judah and Jerusalem as "lying children, children that will not hear the law of the Lord: Which say to the seers, see not; and to the prophets, Prophesy not unto us right things, speak unto us smooth things, prophesy deceits" (30:9–10).

Isaiah then prophesies that God will destroy all but a tenth of these wicked people, that He will send forth a warrior from the tribe of Jesse, a "just man" who will lead an army, "roaring like young lions," against the fallen, destroying them like "lightning" and "the flame of a devouring fire" (5:29, 10:17). This devastation will bring forth a New Jerusalem, Eden will be restored and swords beaten into ploughshares, and "The wolf also shall dwell with the lamb, and the leopard shall lie down with the kid; and the calf and the young lion and the fatling together; and a little child shall lead them" (11:6). Then, Isaiah prophesies, the desert will "rejoice and blossom as the rose, for in the wilderness shall waters break out and streams in the deserts" (35:1, 6). And in the midst of Jerusalem there shall be a "highway, the way of holiness" and "No lion shall be there, nor any ravenous beast shall

Without Contraries is no progression. Attraction and Repulsion, Reason and Energy, Love and Hate, are necessary to Human existence.

From these contraries spring what the religious call Good & Evil. Good is the passive that obeys Reason[.] Evil is the active springing from Energy.

Good is Heaven. Evil is Hell.

PLATE 4

— THE VOICE OF THE DEVIL —

All Bibles or sacred codes. have been the causes of the following Errors.

1. That Man has two real existing principles Viz: a Body & a Soul.

2. That Energy. calld Evil. is alone from the Body. & that Reason. calld Good. is alone from the Soul.

3. That God will torment Man in Eternity for following his Energies. But the following Contraries to these are True

1. Man has no Body distinct from his Soul for that calld Body is a portion of Soul discernd by the five Senses, the chief inlets of Soul in this age

2. Energy is the only life and is from the Body and Reason is the bound or outward circumference of Energy.

3. Energy is Eternal Delight

PLATE 5

Those who restrain desire, do so because theirs is weak enough to be restrained; and the restrainer or reason usurps its place & governs the unwilling.

And being restraind it by degrees becomes passive till it is only the shadow of desire.

The history of this is written in Paradise Lost. & the Governor or Reason is call'd Messiah.

And the original Archangel or possessor of the command of the heavenly host, is calld the Devil or Satan and his children are call'd Sin & Death[8]

But in the Book of Job[9] Miltons Messiah is call'd Satan.

For this history has been adopted by both parties

It indeed appear'd to Reason as if Desire was cast out, but the Devils account is, that the Messi[PL 6]ah fell. & formed a heaven of what he stole from the Abyss

This is shewn in the Gospel,[10] where he prays to the Father to send the comforter or Desire that Reason may have Ideas to build on, the Jehovah of the Bible being no other than he, who dwells in flaming fire. Know that after Christs death, he became Jehovah.

But in Milton; the Father is Destiny, the Son, a Ratio[11] of the five senses. & the Holy-ghost, Vacuum!

Note. The reason Milton wrote in fetters when he wrote of Angels & God, and at liberty when of Devils & Hell, is because he was a true Poet and of the Devils party without knowing it

— A MEMORABLE FANCY —

As I was walking among the fires of hell, delighted with the enjoyments of Genius; which to Angels look like torment and insanity. I collected some of their Proverbs: thinking that as the sayings used in a nation, mark its character, so the Proverbs of Hell, shew the nature of Infernal wisdom better than any description of buildings or garments.

When I came home; on the abyss of the five senses, where a flat sided steep frowns over the present world. I saw a mighty Devil folded in black clouds, hovering on the sides of the rock, with cor[PL 7]roding fires[12] he wrote the following sentence now percieved by the minds of men, & read by them on earth.

How do you know but ev'ry Bird that cuts the airy way,
Is an immense world of delight, clos'd by your senses five?

— PROVERBS OF HELL —

In seed time learn, in harvest teach, in winter enjoy.
Drive your cart and your plow over the bones of the dead.

go up thereon . . . but the redeemed shall walk there. And the ransomed of the Lord shall return, and come to Zion with songs and everlasting joy upon their heads" (35:9, 10).

8 **The history . . . Death**: in Milton's *Paradise Lost,* Satan, who desires to be as powerful as God, is defeated by Christ the Messiah (Book VI); the birth of Sin and Death occurs in Book II.

9 **Book of Job**: in the Book of Job, God permits Satan to torment Job with logical arguments that "prove" his sinfulness.

10 John 16:7.

11 **Ratio**: from Latin *ratio* (reason), the sum of knowledge derived from sensory perception, what John Locke called "experience." Cf. *There is No Natural Religion,* First Series.

12 **corroding fires**: Blake engraved his designs for his poems with corrosive acid.

The road of excess leads to the palace of wisdom.
Prudence is a rich ugly old maid courted by Incapacity.
He who desires but acts not, breeds pestilence.
The cut worm forgives the plow.
Dip him in the river who loves water.
A fool sees not the same tree that a wise man sees.
He whose face gives no light, shall never become a star.
Eternity is in love with the productions of time.
The busy bee has no time for sorrow.
The hours of folly are measur'd by the clock, but of wisdom: no clock can measure.
All wholsom food is caught without a net or a trap.
Bring out number weight & measure in a year of dearth.
No bird soars too high. if he soars with his own wings.
A dead body. revenges not injuries.
The most sublime act is to set another before you.
If the fool would persist in his folly he would become wise
Folly is the cloke of knavery.
Shame is Prides cloke.

Plate 8

Prisons are built with stones of Law, Brothels with bricks of Religion.
The pride of the peacock is the glory of God.
The lust of the goat is the bounty of God.
The wrath of the lion is the wisdom of God.
The nakedness of woman is the work of God.
Excess of sorrow laughs. Excess of joy weeps.
The roaring of lions, the howling of wolves, the raging of the stormy sea, and the destructive sword. are portions of eternity too great for the eye of man.
The fox condemns the trap, not himself.
Joys impregnate. Sorrows bring forth.
Let man wear the fell of the lion. woman the fleece of the sheep.
The bird a nest, the spider a web, man friendship.
The selfish smiling fool. & the sullen frowning fool. shall be both thought wise. that they may be a rod.
What is now proved was once, only imagin'd.
The rat, the mouse, the fox, the rabbet; watch the roots, the lion, the tyger, the horse, the elephant, watch the fruits.
The cistern contains: the fountain overflows
One thought. fills immensity.
Always be ready to speak your mind, and a base man will avoid you.
Every thing possible to be believ'd is an image of truth.
The eagle never lost so much time, as when he submitted to learn of the crow.

Plate 9

The fox provides for himself. but God provides for the lion.
Think in the morning, Act in the noon, Eat in the evening, Sleep in the night.
He who has sufferd you to impose on him knows you.
As the plow follows words, so God rewards prayers.
The tygers of wrath are wiser than the horses of instruction
Expect poison from the standing water.
You never know what is enough unless you know what is more than enough.
Listen to the fools reproach! it is a kingly title!
The eyes of fire, the nostrils of air, the mouth of water, the beard of earth.
The weak in courage is strong in cunning.
The apple tree never asks the beech how he shall grow, nor the lion. the horse, how he shall take his prey.
The thankful reciever bears a plentiful harvest.
If others had not been foolish, we should be so.
The soul of sweet delight, can never be defil'd,
When thou seest an Eagle, thou seest a portion of Genius. lift up thy head!
As the catterpiller chooses the fairest leaves to lay her eggs on, so the priest lays his curse on the fairest joys.
To create a little flower is the labour of ages.
Damn. braces: Bless relaxes.
The best wine is the oldest. the best water the newest.
Prayers plow not! Praises reap not!
Joys laugh not! Sorrows weep not!

Plate 10

The head Sublime, the heart Pathos, the genitals Beauty, the hands & feet Proportion.
As the air to a bird or the sea to a fish, so is contempt to the contemptible.
The crow wish'd every thing was black, the owl, that every thing was white.
Exuberance is Beauty.
If the lion was advise'd by the fox. he would be cunning.
Improve[me]nt makes strait roads, but the crooked roads without Improvement, are roads of Genius.

Sooner murder an infant in its cradle than nurse unacted desires
Where man is not nature is barren.
Truth can never be told so as to be understood, and not be believ'd.

Enough! or Too much

PLATE 11

The ancient Poets animated all sensible objects with Gods or Geniuses, calling them by the names and adorning them with the properties of woods, rivers, mountains, lakes, cities, nations, and whatever their enlarged & numerous senses could percieve.

And particularly they studied the genius of each city & country. placing it under its mental deity.

Till a system was formed, which some took advantage of & enslav'd the vulgar by attempting to realize or abstract the mental deities from their objects; thus began Priesthood.

Choosing forms of worship from poetic tales.

And at length they pronouncd that the Gods had orderd such things.

Thus men forgot that All deities reside in the human breast.

PLATE 12

— A MEMORABLE FANCY —

The Prophets Isaiah and Ezekiel dined with me, and I asked them how they dared so roundly to assert. that God spake to them; and whether they did not think at the time, that they would be misunderstood, & so be the cause of imposition.

Isaiah answer'd. I saw no God, nor heard any, in a finite organical perception: but my senses discover'd the infinite in every thing, and as I was then perswaded, & remain confirm'd; that the voice of honest indignation is the voice of God, I cared not for consequences but wrote.

Then I asked: does a firm perswasion that a thing is so, make it so?

He replied. All poets believe that it does, & in ages of imagination this firm perswasion removed mountains; but many are not capable of a firm perswasion of any thing.

Then Ezekiel said. The philosophy of the east taught the first principles of human perception some nations held one principle for the origin & some another, we of Israel taught that the Poetic Genius (as you now call it) was the first principle and all the others merely derivative, which was the cause of our despising the Priests & Philosophers of other countries, and prophecying that all Gods [PL 13] would at last be proved to originate in ours & to be the tributaries of the Poetic Genius, it was this. that our great poet King David desired so fervently & invokes so patheticly, saying by this he conquers enemies & governs kingdoms; and we so loved our God. that we cursed in his name all the deities of surrounding nations, and asserted that they had rebelled; from these opinions the vulgar came to think that all nations would at last be subject to the jews.

This said he, like all firm perswasions, is come to pass, for all nations believe the jews code and worship the jews god, and what greater subjection can be

I heard this with some wonder, & must confess my own conviction. After dinner I ask'd Isaiah to favour the world with his lost works, he said none of equal value was lost. Ezekiel said the same of his.

I also asked Isaiah what made him go naked and barefoot three years? he answerd, the same that made our friend Diogenes the Grecian.[13]

I then asked Ezekiel.[14] why he eat dung, & lay so long on his right & left side? he answerd. the desire of raising other men into a perception of the infinite this the North American tribes practise. & is he honest who resists his genius or conscience. only for the sake of present ease or gratification?

PLATE 14

The ancient tradition that the world will be consumed in fire at the end of six thousand years is true. as I have heard from Hell.

For the cherub with his flaming sword is hereby commanded to leave his guard at tree of life,[15] and when he does, the whole creation will be consumed, and appear infinite. and holy whereas it now appears finite & corrupt.

This will come to pass by an improvement of sensual enjoyment.

---

[13] **Isaiah . . . Grecian:** Isaiah 20:3; Diogenes (412?–323 BC), Greek philosopher and cynic.

[14] **Ezekiel:** Ezekiel 4:4–6, 12.

[15] **cherub . . . life:** Genesis 3:24.

But first the notion that man has a body distinct from his soul, is to be expunged; this I shall do, by printing in the infernal method, by corrosives, which in Hell are salutary and medicinal, melting apparent surfaces away, and displaying the infinite which was hid.

If the doors of perception were cleansed every thing would appear to man as it is, infinite.

For man has closed himself up, till he sees all things thro' narrow chinks of his cavern.

PLATE 15

— A MEMORABLE FANCY —

I was in a Printing house in Hell & saw the method in which knowledge is transmitted from generation to generation.

In the first chamber was a Dragon-Man, clearing away the rubbish from a caves mouth; within, a number of Dragons were hollowing the cave,

In the second chamber was a Viper folding round the rock & the cave, and others adorning it with gold silver and precious stones.

In the third chamber was an Eagle with wings and feathers of air, he caused the inside of the cave to be infinite, around were numbers of Eagle like men, who built palaces in the immense cliffs.

In the fourth chamber were Lions of flaming fire raging around & melting the metals into living fluids.

In the fifth chamber were Unnam'd forms, which cast the metals into the expanse.

There they were reciev'd by Men who occupied the sixth chamber, and took the forms of books & were arranged in libraries.

PLATE 16

The Giants who formed this world into its sensual existence and now seem to live in it in chains, are in truth. the causes of its life & the sources of all activity, but the chains are, the cunning of weak and tame minds. which have power to resist energy, according to the proverb, the weak in courage is strong in cunning.

Thus one portion of being, is the Prolific. the other, the Devouring: to the devourer it seems as if the producer was in his chains, but it is not so, he only takes portions of existence and fancies that the whole.

But the Prolific would cease to be Prolific unless the Devourer as a sea recieved the excess of his delights.

Some will say, Is not God alone the Prolific? I answer, God only Acts & Is, in existing beings or Men.

These two classes of men are always upon earth, & they should be enemies; whoever tries [PL 17] to reconcile them seeks to destroy existence.

Religion is an endeavour to reconcile the two.

Note. Jesus Christ did not wish to unite but to separate them, as in the Parable of sheep and goats! & he says I came not to send Peace but a Sword.[16]

Messiah or Satan or Tempter was formerly thought to be one of the Antediluvians who are our Energies.

— A MEMORABLE FANCY —

An Angel came to me and said O pitiable foolish young man! O horrible! O dreadful state! consider the hot burning dungeon thou art preparing for thyself to all eternity, to which thou art going in such career.

I said, perhaps you will be willing to shew me my eternal lot & we will contemplate together upon it and see whether your lot or mine is most desirable

So he took me thro' a stable & thro' a church & down into the church vault at the end of which was a mill: thro' the mill we went, and came to a cave. down the winding cavern we groped our tedious way till a void boundless as a nether sky appeard beneath us. & we held by the roots of trees and hung over this immensity, but I said, if you please we will commit ourselves to this void, and see whether providence is here also, if you will not I will? but he answerd, do not presume O young-man but as we here remain behold thy lot which will soon appear when the darkness passes away

So I remaind with him sitting in the twisted [PL 18] root of an oak. he was suspended in a fungus which hung with the head downward into the deep;

By degrees we beheld the infinite Abyss, fiery as the smoke of a burning city: beneath us at an immense distance was the sun, black but shining[:] round it were fiery tracks on which revolv'd vast spiders, crawling after their prey; which flew or rather swum in the infinite deep, in the most terrific shapes of animals sprung from corruption. & the air was full of them, & seemd composed of them; these are Devils. and are called Powers of the air, I now asked my companion which was my eternal lot? he said, between the black & white spiders

But now, from between the black & white spiders a cloud and fire burst and rolled thro the deep blackning all beneath, so that the nether deep grew black as a sea & rolled with a terrible noise: beneath us was nothing now

[16] **Parable . . . Sword:** Matthew 25:32–3, 10:34.

to be seen but a black tempest, till looking east between the clouds & the waves, we saw a cataract of blood mixed with fire and not many stones throw from us appeard and sunk again the scaly fold of a monstrous serpent[.] at last to the east, distant about three degrees appeard a fiery crest above the waves[.] slowly it reared like a ridge of golden rocks till we discoverd two globes of crimson fire, from which the sea fled away in clouds of smoke, and now we saw, it was the head of Leviathan, his forehead was divided into streaks of green & purple like those on a tygers forehead: soon we saw his mouth & red gills hang just above the raging foam tinging the black deep with beams of blood, advancing toward [PL 19] us with all the fury of a spiritual existence.

My friend the Angel climb'd up from his station into the mill; I remain'd alone, & then this appearance was no more, but I found myself sitting on a pleasant bank beside a river by moon light hearing a harper who sung to the harp, & his theme was, The man who never alters his opinion is like standing water, & breeds reptiles of the mind.

But I arose, and sought for the mill, & there I found my Angel, who surprised asked me, how I escaped?

I answerd. All that we saw was owing to your metaphysics: for when you ran away, I found myself on a bank by moonlight hearing a harper, But now we have seen my eternal lot, shall I shew you yours? he laughd at my proposal; but I by force suddenly caught him in my arms, & flew westerly thro' the night, till we were elevated above the earths shadow: then I flung myself with him directly into the body of the sun, here I clothed myself in white, & taking in my hand Swedenborgs volumes sunk from the glorious clime, and passed all the planets till we came to saturn, here I staid to rest & then leap'd into the void, between saturn & the fixed stars.

Here said I! is your lot, in this space, if space it may be calld, Soon we saw the stable and the church, & I took him to the altar and open'd the Bible, and lo! it was a deep pit, into which I descended driving the Angel before me, soon we saw seven houses of brick,[17] one we enterd; in it were a [PL 20] number of monkeys, baboons, & all of that species chaind by the middle, grinning and snatching at one another, but witheld by the shortness of their chains: however I saw that they sometimes grew numerous, and then the weak were caught by the strong and with a grinning aspect, first coupled with & then devourd, by plucking off first one limb and then another till the body was left a helpless trunk. this after grinning & kissing it with seeming fondness they devourd too; and here & there I saw one savourily picking the flesh off of his own tail; as the stench terribly annoyd us both we went into the mill, & I in my hand brought the skeleton of a body, which in the mill was Aristotles Analytics.

So the Angel said: thy phantasy has imposed upon me & thou oughtest to be ashamed.

I answerd: we impose on one another, & it is but lost time to converse with you whose works are only Analytics

Opposition is true Friendship

Plate 21

I have always found that Angels have the vanity to speak of themselves as the only wise; this they do with a confident insolence sprouting from systematic reasoning;

Thus Swedenborg boasts that what he writes is new; tho' it is only the Contents or Index of already publish'd books

A man carried a monkey about for a shew, & because he was a little wiser than the monkey, grew vain, and conciev'd himself as much wiser than seven men. It is so with Swedenborg; he shews the folly of churches & exposes hypocrites, till he imagines that all are religious. & himself the single [PL 22] one on earth that ever broke a net.

Now hear a plain fact: Swedenborg has not written one new truth: Now hear another: he has written all the old falshoods.

And now hear the reason. He conversed with Angels who are all religious, & conversed not with Devils who all hate religion, for he was incapable thro' his conceited notions.

Thus Swedenborgs writings are a recapitulation of all superficial opinions, and an analysis of the more sublime, but no further.

Have now another plain fact: Any man of mechanical talents may from the writings of Paracelsus or Jacob Behmen,[18] produce ten thousand volumes of equal value

[17] **seven houses of brick**: the seven churches in Asia hailed by St. John the Divine (Revelation 1).

[18] **Paracelsus . . . Behmen**: Paracelsus (1493?–1541), German physician, alchemist, and Neoplatonist; Jakob Behmen or Boehme (1575–1624), an itinerant shoemaker and mystic, known as the "Teutonic Philosopher," whose visionary *Way to Christ* (1623) heavily influenced Blake.

with Swedenborg's. and from those of Dante or Shakespear. an infinite number.

But when he has done this, let him not say that he knows better than his master, for he only holds a candle in sunshine.

— A MEMORABLE FANCY —

Once I saw a Devil in a flame of fire. who arose before an Angel that sat on a cloud. and the Devil utterd these words.

The worship of God is. Honouring his gifts in other men each according to his genius. and loving the [PL 23] greatest men best, those who envy or calumniate great men hate God, for there is no other God.

The Angel hearing this became almost blue but mastering himself he grew yellow, & at last white pink & smiling, and then replied,

Thou Idolater, is not God One? & is not he visible in Jesus Christ? and has not Jesus Christ given his sanction to the law of ten commandments and are not all other men fools, sinners, & nothings?

The Devil answer'd; bray a fool in a morter with wheat. yet shall not his folly be beaten out of him: if Jesus Christ is the greatest man, you ought to love him in the greatest degree; now hear how he has given his sanction to the law of ten commandments: did he not mock at the sabbath, and so mock the sabbaths God? murder those who were murderd because of him? turn away the law from the woman taken in adultery? steal the labor of others to support him? bear false witness when he omitted making a defence before Pilate? covet when he pray'd for his disciples, and when he bid them shake off the dust of their feet against such as refused to lodge them? I tell you, no virtue can exist without breaking these ten commandments. . Jesus was all virtue, and acted from im[PL 24]pulse. not from rules.

When he had so spoken: I beheld the Angel who stretched out his arms embracing the flame of fire & he was consumed and arose as Elijah.

Note. This Angel, who is now become a Devil, is my particular friend: we often read the Bible together in its infernal or diabolical sense which the world shall have if they behave well

I have also: The Bible of Hell: which the world shall have whether they will or no.

One Law for the Lion & Ox is Oppression

PLATE 25

— A SONG OF LIBERTY —

1. The Eternal Female groand![19] it was heard over all the Earth:

2. Albions[20] coast is sick silent; the American meadows faint!

3 Shadows of Prophecy shiver along by the lakes and the rivers and mutter across the ocean? France rend down thy dungeon;

4. Golden Spain burst the barriers of old Rome;

5. Cast thy keys O Rome into the deep down falling, even to eternity down falling,

6. And weep

7. In her trembling hands she took the new born terror howling:

8. On those infinite mountains of light now barr'd out by the atlantic sea,[21] the new born fire stood before the starry king!

9. Flag'd with grey brow'd snows and thunderous visages the jealous wings wav'd over the deep.

10. The speary hand burned aloft, unbuckled was the shield, forth went the hand of jealousy among the flaming hair, and [PL 26] hurl'd the new born wonder thro' the starry night.

11. The fire, the fire, is falling!

12. Look up! look up! O citizen of London. enlarge thy countenance; O Jew, leave counting gold! return to thy oil and wine; O African! black African! (go. winged thought widen his forehead.)

13. The fiery limbs, the flaming hair, shot like the sinking sun into the western sea.

14. Wak'd from his eternal sleep, the hoary element roaring fled away:

15. Down rushd beating his wings in vain the jealous king; his grey brow'd councellors, thunderous warriors, curl'd veterans, among helms, and shields, and chariots[,] horses, elephants: banners, castles, slings and rocks,

16. Falling, rushing, ruining! buried in the ruins, on Urthona's dens.

17. All night beneath the ruins, then their sullen flames faded emerge round the gloomy king,

---

[19] **Female groand!:** in childbirth.

[20] **Albion:** England.

[21] **infinite . . . sea:** the now submerged or "lost continent" of Atlantis.

18. With thunder and fire: leading his starry hosts thro' the waste wilderness [PL 27] he promulgates his ten commands, glancing his beamy eyelids over the deep in dark dismay,

19. Where the son of fire in his eastern cloud, while the morning plumes her golden breast,

20. Spurning the clouds written with curses, stamps the stony law to dust, loosing the eternal horses from the dens of night, crying

Empire is no more! and now the lion & wolf shall cease.

CHORUS

Let the Priests of the Raven of dawn, no longer in deadly black. with hoarse note curse the sons of joy. Nor his accepted brethren whom, tyrant. he calls free: lay the bound or build the roof. Nor pale religious letchery call that virginity, that wishes but acts not!

For every thing that lives is Holy.

VISIONS OF THE DAUGHTERS OF ALBION[1]

(1793)

The Eye sees more than the Heart knows.

PLATE iii

The Argument

I loved Theotormon[2]
And I was not ashamed
I trembled in my virgin fears
And I hid in Leutha's[3] vale!

I plucked Leutha's flower,
And I rose up from the vale;
But the terrible thunders tore
My virgin mantel in twain.

---

[1] **Albion:** England.

[2] **Theotormon:** name coined by Blake, alluding to Greek *theo,* god, and Latin *tormentum,* to twist, torment.

[3] **Leutha:** name coined by Blake, signifies female sexual desire.

PLATE 1

Visions

ENSLAV'D, the Daughters of Albion[4] weep: a trembling lamentation
Upon their mountains; in their valleys. sighs toward America.

For the soft soul of America, Oothoon[5] wanderd in woe,
Along the vales of Leutha seeking flowers to comfort her;
And thus she spoke to the bright Marygold[6] of Leutha's vale

Art thou a flower! art thou a nymph! I see thee now a flower;
Now a nymph! I dare not pluck thee from thy dewy bed?

The Golden nymph replied; pluck thou my flower Oothoon the mild
Another flower shall spring, because the soul of sweet delight
Can never pass away. she ceas'd & closd her golden shrine.

Then Oothoon pluck'd the flower saying, I pluck thee from thy bed
Sweet flower. and put thee here to glow between my breasts
And thus I turn my face to where my whole soul seeks.

---

[4] **Enslav'd . . . Albion:** Blake echoes Mary Wollstonecraft's claim in *A Vindication of the Rights of Woman* (1792) that all English women are "slaves . . . in a political and civil sense."

[5] **soft soul . . . Oothoon:** Oothoon's name is derived by Blake from James Macpherson's *Ossian,* where Oithona, "the virgin of the waves" becomes the bride of Gaul; during her husband's absence, she is kidnapped and raped by a rejected suitor, Dunrommath, Lord of Uthal. Here she also represents the enslaved black women in England's Caribbean colonies and in America. Blake had learned of the oppressive conditions of slavery in the Americas in 1792 to 1793 when he read and engraved most of the plates for John G. Stedman's *A Narrative, of a five Years' expedition, against the Revolted Negroes of Surinam, in Guiana, on the Wild Coast of South America; from the year 1772 to 1777* (London, 1796).

[6] **Marygold:** *caltha palustris,* commonly called mayflower, a symbol of fertility in May Day festivals.

Over the waves she went in wing'd exulting swift delight;
And over Theotormons reign, took her impetuous course.

Bromion[7] rent her with his thunders. on his stormy bed
Lay the faint maid, and soon her woes appalld his thunders hoarse

Bromion spoke. behold this harlot here on Bromions bed,
And let the jealous dolphins sport around the lovely maid;
Thy soft American plains are mine, and mine thy north & south:
Stampt with my signet are the swarthy children of the sun:
They are obedient, they resist not, they obey the scourge:
Their daughters worship terrors and obey the violent:

PLATE 2

Now thou maist marry Bromions harlot, and protect the child
Of Bromions rage, that Oothoon shall put forth in nine moons time

Then storms rent Theotormons limbs; he rolld his waves around.
And folded his black jealous waters round the adulterate pair
Bound back to back in Bromions caves terror & meekness dwell

At entrance Theotormon sits wearing the threshold hard
With secret tears; beneath him sound like waves on a desart shore
The voice of slaves beneath the sun, and children bought with money.
That shiver in religious caves beneath the burning fires
Of lust, that belch incessant from the summits of the earth

Oothoon weeps not: she cannot weep! her tears are locked up;
But she can howl incessant writhing her soft snowy limbs.

---

[7] **Bromion:** name coined by Blake, here a slave owner.

And calling Theotormons Eagles to prey upon her flesh.

I call with holy voice! kings of the sounding air,
Rend away this defiled bosom that I may reflect.
The image of Theotormon on my pure transparent breast.

The Eagles at her call descend & rend their bleeding prey;
Theotormon severely smiles. her soul reflects the smile;
As the clear spring mudded with feet of beasts grows pure & smiles.

The Daughters of Albion hear her woes. & eccho back her sighs.

Why does my Theotormon sit weeping upon the threshold;
And Oothoon hovers by his side, perswading him in vain:
I cry arise O Theotormon for the village dog
Barks at the breaking day. the nightingale has done lamenting.
The lark does rustle in the ripe corn, and the Eagle returns
From nightly prey, and lifts his golden beak to the pure east;
Shaking the dust from his immortal pinions to awake
The sun that sleeps too long. Arise my Theotormon I am pure.
Because the night is gone that clos'd me in its deadly black.
They told me that the night & day were all that I could see;
They told me that I had five senses to inclose me up.
And they inclos'd my infinite brain into a narrow circle.
And sunk my heart into the Abyss, a red round globe hot burning
Till all from life I was obliterated and erased.
Instead of morn arises a bright shadow, like an eye
In the eastern cloud: instead of night a sickly charnel house;
That Theotormon hears me not! to him the night and morn
Are both alike: a night of sighs, a morning of fresh tears;

PLATE 3

And none but Bromion can hear my lamentations.

With what sense is it that the chicken shuns the ravenous hawk?
With what sense does the tame pigeon measure out the expanse?
With what sense does the bee form cells? have not the mouse & frog
Eyes and ears and sense of touch? yet are their habitations.
And their pursuits, as different as their forms and as their joys:
Ask the wild ass why he refuses burdens: and the meek camel
Why he loves man: is it because of eye ear mouth or skin
Or breathing nostrils? No, for these the wolf and tyger have.
Ask the blind worm the secrets of the grave, and why her spires
Love to curl round the bones of death; and ask the rav'nous snake
Where she gets poison: & the wing'd eagle why he loves the sun
And then tell me the thoughts of man, that have been hid of old.

Silent I hover all the night, and all day could be silent.
If Theotormon once would turn his loved eyes upon me;
How can I be defild when I reflect thy image pure?
Sweetest the fruit that the worm feeds on. & the soul prey'd on by woe
The new wash'd lamb ting'd with the village smoke & the bright swan
By the red earth of our immortal river: I bathe my wings.
And I am white and pure to hover round Theotormons breast.

Then Theotormon broke his silence. and he answered.

Tell me what is the night or day to one o'erflowd with woe?
Tell me what is a thought? & of what substance is it made?
Tell me what is a joy? & in what gardens do joys grow?
And in what rivers swim the sorrows? and upon what mountains

PLATE 4

Wave shadows of discontent? and in what houses dwell the wretched
Drunken with woe forgotten. and shut up from cold despair.

Tell me where dwell the thoughts forgotten till thou call them forth
Tell me where dwell the joys of old! & where the ancient loves?
And when will they renew again & the night of oblivion past?
That I might traverse times & spaces far remote and bring
Comforts into a present sorrow and a night of pain
Where goest thou O thought? to what remote land is thy flight?
If thou returnest to the present moment of affliction
Wilt thou bring comforts on thy wings. and dews and honey and balm;
Or poison from the desart wilds, from the eyes of the envier.

Then Bromion said: and shook the cavern with his lamentation

Thou knowest that the ancient trees seen by thine eyes have fruit;
But knowest thou that trees and fruits flourish upon the earth
To gratify senses unknown? trees beasts and birds unknown:
Unknown, not unpercievd, spread in the infinite microscope,
In places yet unvisited by the voyager. and in worlds
Over another kind of seas, and in atmospheres unknown:
Ah! are there other wars, beside the wars of sword and fire!
And are there other sorrows, beside the sorrows of poverty!
And are there other joys, beside the joys of riches and ease?
And is there not one law for both the lion and the ox?
And is there not eternal fire, and eternal chains?
To bind the phantoms of existence from eternal life?

Songs of Innocence, Title page, Keynes Copy B, British Museum Print Room, London

The Book of Thel, Title page, Huntington Library, San Marino, California

Songs of Innocence, Frontispiece, Keynes Copy B, British Museum Print Room, London

"The Lamb," from *Songs of Innocence*, Keynes Copy B, British Museum Print Room, London

"The Marriage of Heaven and Hell," Title page, Copy I, Fitzwilliam Museum, Cambridge, England

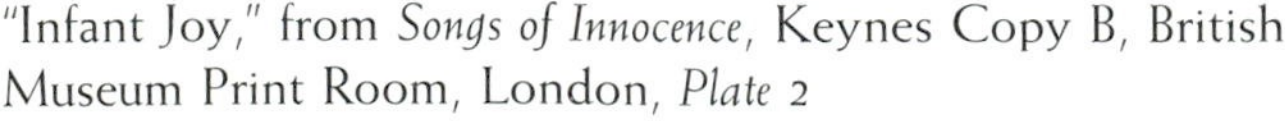

"Infant Joy," from *Songs of Innocence*, Keynes Copy B, British Museum Print Room, London, *Plate* 2

Songs of Innocence and of Experience, Title page, Keynes Copy B, British Museum Print Room, London

Visions of the Daughters of Albion," Tailpiece, Separate Plate, Tate Gallery, London

Songs of Innocence and of Experience, Frontispiece, Keynes Copy B, British Museum Print Room, London

"The Sick Rose," *Songs of Innocence and of Experience*, Keynes Copy B, British Museum Print Room

"The Book of Urizen," Title page, Copy G, Rosenwald Collection, Library of Congress, Washington, DC

"The Tyger," from *Songs of Innocence and of Experience*, Keynes Copy B, British Museum Print Room, London

Then Oothoon waited silent all the day. and all the night,

PLATE 5

But when the morn arose, her lamentation renewd,
The Daughters of Albion hear her woes, & eccho back her sighs.

O Urizen![8] Creator of men! mistaken Demon of heaven:
Thy joys are tears! thy labour vain, to form men to thine image.
How can one joy absorb another? are not different joys
Holy, eternal, infinite! and each joy is a Love.

Does not the great mouth laugh at a gift? & the narrow eyelids mock
At the labour that is above payment, and wilt thou take the ape
For thy councellor? or the dog, for a schoolmaster to thy children?
Does he who contemns poverty, and he who turns with abhorrence
From usury: feel the same passion or are they moved alike?
How can the giver of gifts experience the delights of the merchant?
How the industrious citizen the pains of the husbandman.
How different far the fat fed hireling with hollow drum;
Who buys whole corn fields into wastes, and sings upon the heath:
How different their eye and ear! how different the world to them!
With what sense does the parson claim the labour of the farmer?
What are his nets & gins & traps. & how does he surround him
With cold floods of abstraction, and with forests of solitude,
To build him castles and high spires. where kings & priests may dwell.
Till she who burns with youth. and knows no fixed lot; is bound
In spells of law to one she loaths: and must she drag the chain
Of life, in weary lust! must chilling murderous thoughts. obscure
The clear heaven of her eternal spring? to bear the wintry rage
Of a harsh terror driv'n to madness, bound to hold a rod
Over her shrinking shoulders all the day; & all the night
To turn the wheel of false desire: and longings that wake her womb
To the abhorred birth of cherubs in the human form
That live a pestilence & die a meteor & are no more.
Till the child dwell with one he hates. and do the deed he loaths
And the impure scourge force his seed into its unripe birth
E'er yet his eyelids can behold the arrows of the day.

Does the whale worship at thy footsteps as the hungry dog?
Or does he scent the mountain prey, because his nostrils wide
Draw in the ocean? does his eye discern the flying cloud
As the ravens eye? or does he measure the expanse like the vulture?
Does the still spider view the cliffs where eagles hide their young?
Or does the fly rejoice. because the harvest is brought in?
Does not the eagle scorn the earth & despise the treasures beneath?
But the mole knoweth what is there, & the worm shall tell it thee.
Does not the worm erect a pillar in the mouldering church yard?

PLATE 6

And a palace of eternity in the jaws of the hungry grave
Over his porch these words are written. Take thy bliss O Man!

[8] **Urizen:** name first coined here by Blake, pronounced by Blake with primary stress on the first syllable. If the stress is shifted to the second syllable and the "i" is pronounced as a short "i," the name is a punning allusion to "your reason"; if the "i" is pronounced as long, the name echoes the Greek *ourizein,* the bounding circle (the etymological origin of the English "horizon").

And sweet shall be thy taste & sweet thy infant joys renew!

Infancy, fearless, lustful, happy! nestling for delight
In laps of pleasure; Innocence! honest, open, seeking
The vigorous joys of morning light; open to virgin bliss,
Who taught thee modesty, subtil modesty! child of night & sleep
When thou awakest. wilt thou dissemble all thy secret joys
Or wert thou not, awake when all this mystery was disclos'd!
Then com'st thou forth a modest virgin knowing to dissemble
With nets found under thy night pillow, to catch virgin joy,
And brand it with the name of whore; & sell it in the night,
In silence. ev'n without a whisper, and in seeming sleep:
Religious dreams and holy vespers, light thy smoky fires:
Once were thy fires lighted by the eyes of honest morn
And does my Theotormon seek this hypocrite modesty!
This knowing, artful, secret, fearful, cautious, trembling hypocrite.
Then is Oothoon a whore indeed! and all the virgin joys
Of life are harlots: and Theotormon is a sick mans dream
And Oothoon is the crafty slave of selfish holiness.
But Oothoon is not so, a virgin fill'd with virgin fancies
Open to joy and to delight where ever beauty appears
If in the morning sun I find it: there my eyes are fix'd

PLATE 7

In happy copulation; if in evening mild. wearied with work;
Sit on a bank and draw the pleasures of this free born joy.

The moment of desire! the moment of desire! The virgin
That pines for man; shall awaken her womb to enormous joys
In the secret shadows of her chamber; the youth shut up from
The lustful joy. shall forget to generate. & create an amorous image
In the shadows of his curtains and in the folds of his silent pillow.
Are not these the places of religion? the rewards of continence?
The self enjoyings of self denial? Why dost thou seek religion?
Is it because acts are not lovely, that thou seekest solitude,
Where the horrible darkness is impressed with reflections of desire.

Father of Jealousy.[9] be thou accursed from the earth!
Why hast thou taught my Theotormon this accursed thing?
Till beauty fades from off my shoulders darken'd and cast out,
A solitary shadow wailing on the margin of non-entity.

I cry, Love! Love! Love! happy happy Love! free as the mountain wind!
Can that be Love, that drinks another as a sponge drinks water?
That clouds with jealousy his nights, with weepings all the day:
To spin a web of age around him. grey and hoary! dark!
Till his eyes sicken at the fruit that hangs before his sight.
Such is self-love that envies all! a creeping skeleton
With lamplike eyes watching around the frozen marriage bed.

But silken nets and traps of adamant will Oothoon spread,
And catch for thee girls of mild silver, or of furious gold;
I'll lie beside thee on a bank & view their wanton play
In lovely copulation bliss on bliss with Theotormon:
Red as the rosy morning, lustful as the first born beam,
Oothoon shall view his dear delight, nor e'er with jealous cloud

[9] **Father of Jealousy:** Urizen.

Come in the heaven of generous love; nor selfish blightings bring.

Does the sun walk in glorious raiment. on the secret floor

PLATE 8

Where the cold miser spreads his gold? or does the bright cloud drop
On his stone threshold? does his eye behold the beam that brings
Expansion to the eye of pity? or will he bind himself
Beside the ox to thy hard furrow? does not that mild beam blot
The bat, the owl, the glowing tyger, and the king of night.
The sea fowl takes the wintry blast. for a cov'ring to her limbs:
And the wild snake, the pestilence to adorn him with gems & gold.
And trees. & birds. & beasts. & men. behold their eternal joy.
Arise you little glancing wings, and sing your infant joy!
Arise and drink your bliss, for every thing that lives is holy!
Thus every morning wails Oothoon. but Theotormon sits
Upon the margind ocean conversing with shadows dire.
The Daughters of Albion hear her woes, & eccho back her sighs.

from SONGS OF EXPERIENCE[1]

(1794)

Introduction

Hear the voice of the Bard!
Who Present, Past, & Future sees

[1] The *Songs of Experience* were engraved and first published in 1794 with the *Songs of Innocence* in a volume titled *Songs of Innocence and of Experience—Shewing the Two Contrary States of the Human Soul.* Blake continued to publish the *Songs of Innocence* separately, but never published the *Songs of Experience* independently.

Whose ears have heard,
The Holy Word,
That walk'd among the ancient trees.[1]

Calling the lapsed Soul
And weeping in the evening dew;
That might controll,
The starry pole;
And fallen fallen light renew!

O Earth O Earth return!
Arise from out the dewy grass;
Night is worn,
And the morn
Rises from the slumberous mass.

Turn away no more:
Why wilt thou turn away
The starry floor
The watry shore
Is giv'n thee till the break of day.

[1] walk'd . . . trees: Cf. Genesis 3:8.

Earth's Answer

(1794)

Earth rais'd up her head,
From the darkness dread & drear.
Her light fled:
Stony dread!
And her locks cover'd with grey despair.

Prison'd on watry shore
Starry Jealousy does keep my den
Cold and hoar
Weeping o'er
I hear the Father of the ancient men

Selfish father of men
Cruel jealous selfish fear
Can delight
Chain'd in night
The virgins of youth and morning bear.

Does spring hide its joy
When buds and blossoms grow?
Does the sower?
Sow by night?
Or the plowman in darkness plow?

Break this heavy chain,
That does freeze my bones around
Selfish! vain,
Eternal bane!
That free Love with bondage bound.

The Clod and the Pebble
(1794)

Love seeketh not Itself to please,
Nor for itself hath any care;
But for another gives its ease,
And builds a Heaven in Hells despair.

So sang a little Clod of Clay,
Trodden with the cattles feet:
But a Pebble of the brook,
Warbled out these metres meet.

Love seeketh only Self to please,
To bind another to its delight;
Joys in anothers loss of ease,
And builds a Hell in Heavens despite.

Holy Thursday[1]
(1794)

Is this a holy thing to see,
In a rich and fruitful land,
Babes reducd to misery,
Fed with cold and usurous hand?

Is that trembling cry a song?
Can it be a song of joy?
And so many children poor?
It is a land of poverty!

And their sun does never shine.
And their fields are bleak & bare.
And their ways are fill'd with thorns.
It is eternal winter there.

For where-e'er the sun does shine,
And where-e'er the rain does fall:
Babe can never hunger there,
Nor poverty the mind appall.

[1] On **Holy Thursday,** see note 1 to "Holy Thursday" (poem of same title), in *Songs of Innocence.*

The Chimney Sweeper
(1794; comp. 1790–1792)

A little black thing among the snow:
Crying weep, weep, in notes of woe!
Where are thy father & mother? say?
They are both gone up to the church to pray.

Because I was happy upon the heath,
And smil'd among the winters snow:
They clothed me in the clothes of death,
And taught me to sing the notes of woe,

And because I am happy, & dance & sing,
They think they have done me no injury:
And are gone to praise God & his Priest & King
Who make up a heaven of our misery.

Nurses Song
(1794)

When the voices of children, are heard on the green
And whisprings are in the dale:
The days of my youth rise fresh in my mind,
My face turns green and pale.

Then come home my children, the sun is gone down
And the dews of night arise
Your spring & your day, are wasted in play
And your winter and night in disguise.

The Sick Rose
(1794)

O Rose thou art sick.
The invisible worm,
That flies in the night
In the howling storm:

Has found out thy bed
Of crimson joy:
And his dark secret love
Does thy life destroy.

The Fly

(1794; comp. 1790–1792)

Little Fly
Thy summers play,
My thoughtless hand
Has brush'd away.

Am not I
A fly like thee?
Or art not thou
A man like me?

For I dance
And drink & sing;
Till some blind hand
Shall brush my wing.

If thought is life
And strength & breath;[1]
And the want
Of thought is death;

Then am I
A happy fly,
If I live,
Or if I die.

The Angel

(1794)

I Dreamt a Dream! what can it mean?
And that I was a maiden Queen:
Guarded by an Angel mild;
Witless woe, was ne'er beguil'd!

And I wept both night and day
And he wip'd my tears away
And I wept both day and night
And hid from him my hearts delight

So he took his wings and fled:
Then the morn blush'd rosy red:
I dried my tears & armd my fears,
With ten thousand shields and spears.

Soon my Angel came again:
I was arm'd, he came in vain:
For the time of youth was fled
And grey hairs were on my head.

[1] Cf. Descartes's famous phrase *"cogito, ergo sum,"* "I think, therefore I am."

The Tyger

(1794; comp. 1790–1792)

Tyger Tyger, burning bright,
In the forests of the night;
What immortal hand or eye,
Could frame thy fearful symmetry?

In what distant deeps or skies
Burnt the fire of thine eyes!
On what wings dare he aspire?[1]
What the hand, dare sieze the fire?

And what shoulder, & what art,
Could twist the sinews of thy heart?
And when thy heart began to beat,
What dread hand? & what[2] dread feet?

What the hammer? what the chain,
In what furnace was thy brain?
What the anvil? what dread grasp,
Dare its deadly terrors clasp?

When the stars threw down their spears
And water'd heaven with their tears:
Did he smile his work to see?
Did he who made the Lamb make thee?

Tyger, Tyger burning bright,
In the forests of the night:
What immortal hand or eye,
Dare frame thy fearful symmetry?

[1] **wings . . . aspire:** an allusion to Icarus, who flew too close to the sun with wings constructed by his father, Daedalus, of feathers and wax; the wax melted and Icarus plunged to his death.

[2] **& what:** altered to "formd thy" in ink in a late copy of *Songs of Innocence and of Experience.*

My Pretty Rose Tree
(1794)

A flower was offerd to me;
Such a flower as May never bore.
But I said I've a Pretty Rose-tree,
And I passed the sweet flower o'er.

Then I went to my Pretty Rose-tree;
To tend her by day and by night.
But my Rose turnd away with jealousy:
And her thorns were my only delight.

The Garden of Love
(1794)

I went to the Garden of Love,
And saw what I never had seen:
A Chapel was built in the midst,
Where I used to play on the green.

And the gates of this Chapel were shut,
And Thou shalt not. writ over the door;
So I turn'd to the Garden of Love,
That so many sweet flowers bore,

And I saw it was filled with graves,
And tomb-stones where flowers should be:
And Priests in black gowns, were walking their rounds,
And binding with briars, my joys & desires.

The Little Vagabond
(1794)

Dear Mother, dear Mother, the Church is cold.
But the Ale-house is healthy & pleasant & warm;
Besides I can tell where I am use'd well,
Such usage in heaven will never do well.

But if at the Church they would give us some Ale.
And a pleasant fire, our souls to regale;
We'd sing and we'd pray, all the live-long day;
Nor ever once wish from the Church to stray,
Then the Parson might preach & drink & sing.
And we'd be as happy as birds in the spring:
And modest dame Lurch who is always at
Church,
Wou'ld not have bandy[1] children nor fasting nor
birch.

And God like a father rejoicing to see,
His children as pleasant and happy as he:
Would have no more quarrel with the Devil or
the Barrel
But kiss him & give him both drink and apparel.

London
(1794)

I wander thro' each charter'd street,
Near where the charter'd Thames does flow.
And mark in every face I meet
Marks of weakness, marks of woe.

In every cry of every Man,
In every Infants cry of fear,
In every voice: in every ban,
The mind-forg'd manacles I hear

How the Chimney-sweepers cry
Every blackning Church appalls,
And the hapless Soldiers sigh,
Runs in blood down Palace walls

But most thro' midnight streets I hear
How the youthful Harlots curse
Blasts the new-born Infants tear
And blights with plagues the Marriage hearse

The Human Abstract
(1794; comp 1790–1792)

Pity would be no more,
If we did not make somebody Poor:
And Mercy no more could be,
If all were as happy as we;

[1] **bandy:** legs curved laterally with the concavity inward.

And mutual fear brings peace;
Till the selfish loves increase.
Then Cruelty knits a snare,
And spreads his baits with care.

He sits down with holy fears,
And waters the ground with tears:
Then Humility takes its root
Underneath his foot.

Soon spreads the dismal shade
Of Mystery over his head;
And the Catterpiller and Fly,
Feed on the Mystery.

And it bears the fruit of Deceit,
Ruddy and sweet to eat;
And the Raven his nest has made
In its thickest shade.

The Gods of the earth and sea,
Sought thro' Nature to find this Tree
But their search was all in vain:
There grows one in the Human Brain

Infant Sorrow
(1794)

My mother groand! my father wept.
Into the dangerous world I leapt:
Helpless, naked, piping loud:
Like a fiend hid in a cloud.

Struggling in my fathers hands:
Striving against my swadling bands:[1]
Bound and weary I thought best
To sulk upon my mothers breast.

[1] **swadling bands**: swaddling clothes, i.e., long bandages wrapped around newborn infants to prevent the free movement of their limbs, commonly used in England until the early nineteenth century.

A Poison Tree
(1794)

I was angry with my friend;
I told my wrath, my wrath did end.
I was angry with my foe:
I told it not, my wrath did grow.

And I waterd it in fears,
Night & morning with my tears:
And I sunned it with smiles,
And with soft deceitful wiles.

And it grew both day and night,
Till it bore an apple bright.
And my foe beheld it shine,
And he knew that it was mine.

And into my garden stole,
When the night had veild the pole;
In the morning glad I see;
My foe outstretchd beneath the tree.

A Little Boy Lost
(1794; comp. 1790–1792)

Nought loves another as itself
Nor venerates another so.
Nor is it possible to Thought
A greater than itself to know:

And Father, how can I love you,
Or any of my brothers more?
I love you like the little bird
That picks up crumbs around the door.

The Priest sat by and heard the child.
In trembling zeal he siez'd his hair:
He led him by his little coat:
And all admir'd the Priestly care.

And standing on the altar high,
Lo what a fiend is here! said he:
One who sets reason up for judge
Of our most holy Mystery.

The weeping child could not be heard.
The weeping parents wept in vain:

They strip'd him to his little shirt.
And bound him in an iron chain.

And burn'd him in a holy place,
Where many had been burn'd before:
The weeping parents wept in vain.
Are such things done on Albions shore.

A Little Girl Lost
(1794)

Children of the future age,
Reading this indignant page:
Know that in a former time,
Love! sweet Love! was thought a crime.

In the Age of Gold,
Free from winters cold:
Youth and maiden bright,
To the holy light,
Naked in the sunny beams delight.

Once a youthful pair
Fill'd with softest care:
Met in garden bright,
Where the holy light,
Had just removd the curtains of the night.

There in rising day,
On the grass they play:
Parents were afar:
Strangers came not near:
And the maiden soon forgot her fear.

Tired with kisses sweet
They agree to meet,
When the silent sleep
Waves o'er heavens deep;
And the weary tired wanderers weep.

To her father white
Came the maiden bright:
But his loving look,
Like the holy book,
All her tender limbs with terror shook.

Ona! pale and weak!
To thy father speak:
O the trembling fear!
O the dismal care!
That shakes the blossoms of my hoary hair

To Tirzah[1]
(1803)

Whate'er is Born of Mortal Birth,
Must be consumed with the Earth
To rise from Generation free;
Then what have I to do with thee?

The Sexes sprung from Shame & Pride
Blow'd in the morn: in evening died
But Mercy changd Death into Sleep;
The Sexes rose to work & weep.

Thou Mother of my Mortal part
With cruelty didst mould my Heart,
And with false self-decieving tears,
Didst bind my Nostrils Eyes & Ears.

Didst close my Tongue in senseless clay
And me to Mortal Life betray:
The Death of Jesus set me free,
Then what have I to do with thee?

THE [FIRST] BOOK OF URIZEN[1]
(1794)

PLATE 2

— PRELUDIUM TO THE [FIRST] BOOK OF URIZEN —

Of the primeval Priests[2] assum'd power,
When Eternals spurn'd back his religion;
And gave him a place in the north,
Obscure, shadowy, void, solitary.

Eternals I hear your call gladly,
Dictate swift winged words, & fear not
To unfold your dark visions of torment.

---

[1] This poem was added to the *Songs of Experience* after 1803. **Tirzah:** in the Old Testament, Tirzah was the capital city of the northern fallen kingdom of Israel, as opposed to Jerusalem, the capital of the southern redeemed kingdom of Judah; Cf. Joshua 12:24, 1 Kings 14:17, 15:21, 16.

[1] Originally titled *The First Book of Urizen.* On **Urizen,** see note 8 to *Visions of the Daughters of Albion.*

[2] **the primeval Priest:** Urizen.

PLATE 3

— CHAP. I —

1. Lo, a shadow of horror is risen
In Eternity! Unknown, unprolific!
Self-closd, all-repelling: what Demon
Hath form'd this abominable void
This soul-shudd'ring vacuum?—Some said
"It is Urizen", But unknown, abstracted
Brooding secret, the dark power hid.

2. Times on times he divided, & measur'd
Space by space in his ninefold darkness
Unseen, unknown! changes appeard
In his desolate mountains rifted furious
By the black winds of perturbation

3. For he strove in battles dire
In unseen conflictions with shapes
Bred from his forsaken wilderness,
Of beast, bird, fish, serpent & element
Combustion, blast, vapour and cloud.

4. Dark revolving in silent activity:
Unseen in tormenting passions;
An activity unknown and horrible;
A self-contemplating shadow,
In enormous labours occupied

5. But Eternals beheld his vast forests
Age on ages he lay, clos'd, unknown,
Brooding shut in the deep; all avoid
The petrific abominable chaos

6. His cold horrors silent, dark Urizen
Prepar'd: his ten thousands of thunders
Rang'd in gloom'd array stretch out across
The dread world, & the rolling of wheels
As of swelling seas, sound in his clouds
In his hills of stor'd snows, in his mountains
Of hail & ice; voices of terror,
Are heard, like thunders of autumn,
When the cloud blazes over the harvests

— CHAP. II —

1. Earth was not: nor globes of attraction[3]
The will of the Immortal expanded
Or contracted his all flexible senses.
Death was not, but eternal life sprung

2. The sound of a trumpet[4] the heavens
Awoke & vast clouds of blood roll'd
Round the dim rocks of Urizen, so nam'd
That solitary one in Immensity

3. Shrill the trumpet: & myriads of Eternity,

PLATE 4

Muster around the bleak desarts
Now fill'd with clouds, darkness & waters
That roll'd perplex'd labring & utter'd
Words articulate, bursting in thunders
That roll'd on the tops of his mountains

4. From the depths of dark solitude. From
The eternal abode in my holiness,
Hidden set apart in my stern counsels
Reserv'd for the days of futurity,
I have sought for a joy without pain,
For a solid without fluctuation
Why will you die O Eternals?
Why live in unquenchable burnings?

5. First I fought with the fire; consum'd
Inwards, into a deep world within:
A void immense, wild dark & deep,
Where nothing was; Natures wide womb[.][5]
And self balanc'd stretch'd o'er the void
I alone, even I! the winds merciless
Bound; but condensing, in torrents
They fall & fall; strong I repell'd
The vast waves, & arose on the waters
A wide world of solid obstruction

6. Here alone I in books formd of metals
Have written the secrets of wisdom
The secrets of dark contemplation
By fightings and conflicts dire,
With terrible monsters Sin-bred:
Which the bosoms of all inhabit;
Seven deadly Sins of the soul.

7. Lo! I unfold my darkness: and on
This rock, place with strong hand the Book
Of eternal brass, written in my solitude.

---

[3] **globes of attraction:** a reference to Newtonian physics, which conceived of the universe as ordered by laws of gravity and the forces of magnetic attraction and repulsion.

[4] **sound of a trumpet:** on the day Moses received the stone tablets inscribed with the Ten Commandments, "there were thunders and lightning, and a thick cloud upon the mount [Mount Sinai], and the voice of the trumpet exceeding loud" (Exodus 19:16).

[5] **Natures . . . womb:** chaos, cf. *Paradise Lost*, II.911.

8. Laws of peace, of love, of unity:
Of pity, compassion, forgiveness.
Let each chuse one habitation:
His ancient infinite mansion:
One command, one joy, one desire,
One curse, one weight, one measure
One King, one God, one Law.

— CHAP. III —

1. The voice ended, they saw his pale visage
Emerge from the darkness; his hand
On the rock of eternity unclasping
The Book of brass. Rage siez'd the strong

2. Rage, fury, intense indignation
In cataracts of fire blood & gall
In whirlwinds of sulphurous smoke:
And enormous forms of energy;
All the seven deadly sins of the soul

Plate 5

In living creations appear'd
In the flames of eternal fury.

3. Sund'ring, dark'ning, thund'ring!
Rent away with a terrible crash
Eternity roll'd wide apart
Wide asunder rolling
Mountainous all around
Departing; departing; departing:
Leaving ruinous fragments of life
Hanging frowning cliffs & all between
An ocean of voidness unfathomable.

4. The roaring fires ran o'er the heav'ns
In whirlwinds & cataracts of blood
And o'er the dark desarts of Urizen
Fires pour thro' the void on all sides
On Urizens self-begotten armies.

5. But no light from the fires. all was darkness
In the flames of Eternal fury

6. In fierce anguish & quenchless flames
To the desarts and rocks He ran raging
To hide, but He could not: combining
He dug mountains & hills in vast strength,
He piled them in incessant labour,
In howlings & pangs & fierce madness
Long periods in burning fires labouring
Till hoary, and age-broke, and aged,
In despair and the shadows of death.

7. And a roof, vast petrific around,
On all sides He fram'd: like a womb;
Where thousands of rivers in veins
Of blood pour down the mountains to cool
The eternal fires beating without
From Eternals; & like a black globe
View'd by sons of Eternity, standing
On the shore of the infinite ocean
Like a human heart strugling & beating
The vast world of Urizen appear'd.

8. And Los[6] found the dark globe of Urizen,
Kept watch for Eternals to confine,
The obscure separation alone;
For Eternity stood wide apart,

Plate 6

As the stars are apart from the earth

9. Los wept howling around the dark Demon:
And cursing his lot; for in anguish,
Urizen was rent from his side;
And a fathomless void for his feet;
And intense fires for his dwelling.

10. But Urizen laid in a stony sleep
Unorganiz'd, rent from Eternity

11. The Eternals said: What is this? Death[.]
Urizen is a clod of clay.

Plate 7

12. Los howld in a dismal stupor,
Groaning! gnashing! groaning!
Till the wrenching apart was healed

13. But the wrenching of Urizen heal'd not
Cold, featureless, flesh or clay,
Rifted with direful changes
He lay in a dreamless night

14. Till Los rouz'd his fires, affrighted
At the formless unmeasurable death.

---

[6] Los: name coined by Blake, pronounced to rhyme with "close." An anagram of the Latin *sol*, sun, with an allusion to "loss." Los is one of the all-creating Eternals, here functioning as a guard to prevent the fallen Urizen from returning to Eternity.

PLATE 8

— CHAP. IV[a] —

1. Los smiten with astonishment
Frightend at the hurtling bones

2. And at the surging sulphureous
Perturbed Immortal mad raging

3. In whirlwinds & pitch & nitre
Round the furious limbs of Los

4. And Los formed nets & gins[7]
And threw the nets round about

5. He watch'd in shuddring fear
The dark changes & bound every change
With rivets of iron & brass;

6. And these were the changes of Urizen.

PLATE 10

— CHAP. IV[b] —

1. Ages on ages roll'd over him!
In stony sleep ages roll'd over him!
Like a dark waste stretching chang'able
By earthquakes riv'n. belching sullen fires
On ages roll'd ages in ghastly
Sick torment; around him in whirlwinds
Of darkness the eternal Prophet howl'd
Beating still on his rivets of iron
Pouring sodor[8] of iron; dividing
The horrible night into watches.

2. And Urizen (so his eternal name)
His prolific delight obscurd more & more
In dark secresy hiding in surgeing
Sulphureous fluid his phantasies.
The Eternal Prophet[9] heavd the dark bellows,
And turn'd restless the tongs; and the hammer
Incessant beat; forging chains new & new
Numb'ring with links. hours, days & years

3. The eternal mind bounded began to roll
Eddies of wrath ceaseless round & round,
And the sulphureous foam surgeing thick
Settled, a lake, bright, & shining clear:
White as the snow on the mountains cold.

4. Forgetfulness, dumbness, necessity!
In chains of the mind locked up,
Like fetters of ice shrinking together
Disorganiz'd, rent from Eternity,
Los beat on his fetters of iron;
And heated his furnaces & pour'd
Iron sodor and sodor of brass

5. Restless turnd the immortal inchain'd
Heaving dolorous! anguish'd! unbearable
Till a roof[10] shaggy wild inclos'd
In an orb, his fountain of thought.

6. In a horrible dreamful slumber;
Like the linked infernal chain;
A vast Spine writh'd in torment
Upon the winds; shooting pain'd
Ribs, like a bending cavern
And bones of solidness, froze
Over all his nerves of joy.
And a first Age passed over,
And a state of dismal woe.

PLATE 11

7. From the caverns of his jointed Spine,
Down sunk with fright a red
Round globe hot burning deep
Deep down into the Abyss:
Panting: Conglobing, Trembling
Shooting out ten thousand branches
Around his solid bones.
And a second Age passed over,
And a state of dismal woe.

8. In harrowing fear rolling round;
His nervous brain shot branches
Round the branches of his heart.
On high into two little orbs
And fixed in two little caves
Hiding carefully from the wind,
His Eyes beheld the deep,
And a third Age passed over:
And a state of dismal woe.

9. The pangs of hope began,
In heavy pain striving, struggling.

[7] **gins:** snares, nets, traps.

[8] **sodor:** solder, any fusable metallic alloy used to unite surfaces.

[9] **The Eternal Prophet:** Los, here depicted as a blacksmith, forging chains to bind down Urizen. In general, in Blake's poetry, Los represents the human imagination.

[10] **a roof:** the skull.

Two Ears in close volutions.[11]
From beneath his orbs of vision
Shot spiring out and petrified
As they grew. And a fourth Age passed
And a state of dismal woe.

10. In ghastly torment sick;
Hanging upon the wind;

PLATE 13

Two Nostrils bent down to the deep.
And a fifth Age passed over;
And a state of dismal woe.

11. In ghastly torment sick;
Within his ribs bloated round,
A craving Hungry Cavern;
Thence arose his channeld Throat,
And like a red flame a Tongue.
Of thirst & of hunger appeard.
And a sixth Age passed over:
And a state of dismal woe.

12. Enraged & stifled with torment
He threw his right Arm to the north
His left Arm to the south
Shooting out in anguish deep,
And his Feet stampd the nether Abyss
In trembling & howling & dismay.
And a seventh Age passed over:
And a state of dismal woe.

— CHAP. V —

1. In terrors Los shrunk from his task:
His great hammer fell from his hand:
His fires beheld, and sickening,
Hid their strong limbs in smoke.
For with noises ruinous loud;
With hurtlings & clashings & groans
The Immortal endur'd his chains,
Tho' bound in a deadly sleep.

2. All the myriads of Eternity:
All the wisdom & joy of life:
Roll like a sea around him,
Except what his little orbs
Of sight by degrees unfold.

3. And now his eternal life
Like a dream was obliterated

4. Shudd'ring, the Eternal Prophet smote
With a stroke, from his north to south region
The bellows & hammer are silent now
A nerveless silence, his prophetic voice
Siez'd; a cold solitude & dark void
The Eternal Prophet & Urizen clos'd

5. Ages on ages rolld over them
Cut off from life & light frozen
Into horrible forms of deformity
Los suffer'd his fires to decay
Then he look'd back with anxious desire
But the space undivided by existence
Struck horror into his soul.

6. Los wept obscur'd with mourning:
His bosom earthquak'd with sighs;
He saw Urizen deadly black,
In his chains bound, & Pity began,

7. In anguish dividing & dividing
For pity divides the soul
In pangs eternity on eternity
Life in cataracts pourd down his cliffs
The void shrunk the lymph into Nerves
Wand'ring wide on the bosom of night
And left a round globe of blood
Trembling upon the Void

PLATE 15

Thus the Eternal Prophet was divided
Before the death-image of Urizen
For in changeable clouds and darkness
In a winterly night beneath,
The Abyss of Los stretch'd immense:
And now seen now obscur'd, to the eyes
Of Eternals the visions remote
Of the dark seperation appear'd.
As glasses[12] discover Worlds
In the endless Abyss of space,
So the expanding eyes of Immortals
Beheld the dark visions of Los,
And the globe of life blood trembling.

PLATE 18

8. The globe of life blood trembled
Branching out into roots;
Fibrous, writhing upon the winds;
Fibres of blood, milk and tears;

[11] **close volutions:** the spirals of the inner ear.

[12] **glasses:** telescopes.

In pangs, eternity on eternity.
At length in tears & cries imbodied
A female form trembling and pale
Waves before his deathy face

9. All Eternity shudderd at sight
Of the first female now separate
Pale as a cloud of snow
Waving before the face of Los

10. Wonder, awe, fear, astonishment,
Petrify the eternal myriads;
At the first female form now separate

PLATE 19

They call'd her Pity, and fled

11. "Spread a Tent, with strong curtains around them
"Let cords & stakes bind in the Void
That Eternals may no more behold them"

12. They began to weave curtains of darkness
They erected large pillars round the Void
With golden hooks fastend in the pillars
With infinite labour the Eternals
A woof wove, and called it Science[13]

— CHAP. VI —

1. But Los saw the Female & pitied
He embrac'd her, she wept, she refus'd
In perverse and cruel delight
She fled from his arms, yet he followd

2. Eternity shudder'd when they saw,
Man begetting his likeness,
On his own divided image.

3. A time passed over, the Eternals
Began to erect the tent;
When Enitharmon,[14] sick,
Felt a Worm within her womb.

4. Yet helpless it lay like a Worm
In the trembling womb
To be moulded into existence

5. All day the worm lay on her bosom
All night within her womb
The worm lay till it grew to a serpent
With dolorous hissings & poisons
Round Enitharmons loins folding,

6. Coild within Enitharmons womb
The serpent grew casting its scales,
With sharp pangs the hissings began
To change to a grating cry,
Many sorrows and dismal throes
Many forms of fish, bird & beast,
Brought forth an Infant form
Where was a worm before.

7. The Eternals their tent finished
Alarm'd with these gloomy visions
When Enitharmon groaning
Produc'd a man Child to the light.

8. A shriek ran thro' Eternity:
And a paralytic stroke;
At the birth of the Human shadow.

9. Delving earth in his resistless way;
Howling, the Child with fierce flames
Issu'd from Enitharmon.

10. The Eternals, closed the tent:
They beat down the stakes the cords

PLATE 20

Stretch'd for a work of eternity;
No more Los beheld Eternity.

11. In his hands he siez'd the infant
He bathed him in springs of sorrow
He gave him to Enitharmon.

— CHAP. VII —

1. They named the child Orc,[15] he grew
Fed with milk of Enitharmon

2. Los awoke her; O sorrow & pain!
A tight'ning girdle grew,
Around his bosom. In sobbings
He burst the girdle in twain,
But still another girdle
Oppressd his bosom, In sobbings
Again he burst it. Again
Another girdle succeeds

[13] **Science:** knowledge based on sense perception and rational methods of induction and deduction.

[14] **Enitharmon:** name coined by Blake. Enitharmon is the emanation of Los, the physical embodiment of the created images of the imagination and the body of the female once it has separated itself from the male.

[15] **Orc:** name coined by Blake, derived from Latin *orcus*, hell.

The girdle was form'd by day;
By night was burst in twain.

3. These falling down on the rock
Into an iron Chain
In each other link by link lock'd

4. They took Orc to the top of a mountain.
O how Enitharmon wept!
They chain'd his young limbs to the rock
With the Chain of Jealousy
Beneath Urizens deathful shadow

5. The dead heard the voice of the child
And began to awake from sleep
All things. heard the voice of the child
And began to awake to life.

6. And Urizen craving with hunger
Stung with the odours of Nature
Explor'd his dens around

7. He form'd a line & a plummet
To divide the Abyss beneath.
He form'd a dividing rule:

8. He formed scales to weigh;
He formed massy weights;
He formed a brazen quadrant;
He formed golden compasses[16]
And began to explore the Abyss
And he planted a garden of fruits

9. But Los encircled Enitharmon
With fires of Prophecy
From the sight of Urizen & Orc.

10. And she bore an enormous race

— CHAP. VIII —

1. Urizen explor'd his dens
Mountain, moor, & wilderness,
With a globe of fire lighting his journey
A fearful journey, annoy'd
By cruel enormities: forms

PLATE 23

Of life on his forsaken mountains

2. And his world teemd vast enormities
Frightning; faithless; fawning
Portions of life; similitudes
Of a foot, or a hand, or a head
Or a heart, or an eye, they swam mischevous
Dread terrors! delighting in blood

3. Most Urizen sicken'd to see
His eternal creations appear
Sons & daughters of sorrow on mountains
Weeping! wailing! first Thiriel appear'd
Astonish'd at his own existence
Like a man from a cloud born, & Utha
From the waters emerging, laments!
Grodna rent the deep earth howling
Amaz'd! his heavens immense cracks
Like the ground parch'd with heat; then Fuzon[17]
Flam'd out! first begotten, last born.
All his eternal sons in like manner
His daughters from green herbs & cattle
From monsters, & worms of the pit.

4. He in darkness clos'd, view'd all his race
And his soul sicken'd! he curs'd
Both sons & daughters: for he saw
That no flesh nor spirit could keep
His iron laws one moment.

5. For he saw that life liv'd upon death

PLATE 25

The Ox in the slaughter house moans
The Dog at the wintry door
And he wept, & he called it Pity
And his tears flowed down on the winds

6. Cold he wander'd on high, over their cities
In weeping & pain & woe!
And where-ever he wanderd in sorrows
Upon the aged heavens
A cold shadow follow'd behind him
Like a spiders web, moist, cold, & dim
Drawing out from his sorrowing soul
The dungeon-like heaven dividing
Where ever the footsteps of Urizen
Walk'd over the cities in sorrow.

7. Till a Web dark & cold, throughout all
The tormented element stretch'd
From the sorrows of Urizens soul

---

[16] **compasses:** an allusion to *Paradise Lost,* VII.224–31, where God creates the circumference of the Universe with a pair of golden compasses.

[17] **Thiriel . . . Utha . . . Grodna . . . Fuzon:** names coined by Blake for the four elements: air, water, earth, and fire.

And the Web is a Female in embrio.
None could break the Web, no wings of fire.

8. So twisted the cords, & knotted
The meshes: twisted like to the human brain

9. And all calld it, The Net of Religion.

— CHAP. IX —

1. Then the Inhabitants of those Cities:
Felt their Nerves change into Marrow
And hardening Bones began
In swift diseases and torments,
In throbbings & shootings & grindings
Thro' all the coasts; till weaken'd
The Senses inward rush'd shrinking,
Beneath the dark net of infection.

2. Till the shrunken eyes clouded over
Discernd not the woven hipocrisy
But the streaky slime in their heavens
Brought together by narrowing perceptions
Appeard transparent air; for their eyes
Grew small like the eyes of a man
And in reptile forms shrinking together
Of seven feet stature they remaind

3. Six days they. shrunk up from existence
And on the seventh day they rested
And they bless'd the seventh day, in sick hope:[18]
And forgot their eternal life

4. And their thirty cities divided
In form of a human heart
No more could they rise at will
In the infinite void, but bound down
To earth by their narrowing perceptions

PLATE 28

They lived a period of years
Then left a noisom body
To the jaws of devouring darkness

5. And their children wept, & built
Tombs in the desolate places,
And form'd laws of prudence, and call'd them
The eternal laws of God

6. And the thirty cities remaind
Surrounded by salt floods, now call'd
Africa: its name was then Egypt.

[18] Six days . . . hope: a parody of the six days of expanding creation in Genesis.

7. The remaining sons of Urizen
Beheld their brethren shrink together
Beneath the Net of Urizen;
Perswasion was in vain;
For the ears of the inhabitants
Were wither'd, & deafen'd, & cold.
And their eyes could not discern,
Their brethren of other cities.

8. So Fuzon call'd all together
The remaining children of Urizen:
And they left the pendulous earth
They called it Egypt, & left it.[19]

9. And the salt ocean rolled englob'd

Letter [To] Revd Dr Trusler,[1] Englefield Green, Egham, Surrey

13 Hercules Buildings, Lambeth, August 23, 1799

REVd Sir

I really am sorry that you are falln out with the Spiritual World Especially if I should have to answer for it I feel very sorry that your Ideas & Mine on Moral Painting differ so much as to have made you angry with my method of Study. If I am wrong I am wrong in good company. I had hoped your plan comprehended All Species of this Art & Especially that you would not regret that Species which gives Existence to Every other. namely Visions of Eternity You say that I want somebody to Elucidate my Ideas. But you ought to know that What is Grand is necessarily obscure to Weak men. That which can be made Explicit to the Idiot is not worth my care. The wisest of the Ancients considerd what is not too Explicit as the fittest for Instruction because it rouzes the faculties to act. I name Moses Solomon Esop Homer Plato

[19] left . . . Egypt: an allusion to the Exodus, in which Moses led the Israelites out of Egypt across the Red Sea.

[1] Blake had been introduced to Dr. John Trusler (1735–1820), author of *Hogarth Moralized* and *The Way To Be Rich and Respectable,* as a possible illustrator for his works. The two, however, were incompatible; as Trusler wrote to Blake, "*Your Fancy* seems to be in the other world, or the World of Spirits, which accords not with my Intentions, which, whilst living in This World, Wish to follow *the Nature of it.*" Trusler endorsed the following letter with the comment, "Blake, dim'd with Superstition."

But as you have favord me with your remarks on my Design permit me in return to defend it against a mistaken one, which is. That I have supposed Malevolence without a Cause.[2]—Is not Merit in one a Cause of Envy in another & Serenity & Happiness & Beauty a Cause of Malevolence. But Want of Money & the Distress of A Thief can never be alledged as the Cause of his Thievery. for many honest people endure greater hard ships with Fortitude We must therefore seek the Cause elsewhere than in want of Money for that is the Misers passion, not the Thiefs

I have therefore proved your Reasonings Ill proportiond which you can never prove my figures to be. They are those of Michael Angelo Rafael & the Antique & of the best living Models. I percieve that your Eye[s] is perverted by Caricature Prints, which ought not to abound so much as they do. Fun I love but too much Fun is of all things the most loathsom. Mirth is better than Fun & Happiness is better than Mirth—I feel that a Man may be happy in This World. And I know that This World Is a World of Imagination & Vision I see Every thing I paint In This World, but Every body does not see alike. To the Eyes of a Miser a Guinea is more beautiful than the Sun & a bag worn with the use of Money has more beautiful proportions than a Vine filled with Grapes. The tree which moves some to tears of joy is in the Eyes of others only a Green thing that stands in the way. Some See Nature all Ridicule & Deformity & by these I shall not regulate my proportions, & Some Scarce see Nature at all But to the Eyes of the Man of Imagination Nature is Imagination itself. As a man is So he Sees. As the Eye is formed such are its Powers You certainly Mistake when you say that the Visions of Fancy are not to be found in This World. To Me This World is all One continued Vision of Fancy or Imagination & I feel Flatterd when I am told So. What is it sets Homer Virgil & Milton in so high a rank of Art. Why is the Bible more Entertaining & Instructive than any other book. Is it not because they are addressed to the Imagination which is Spiritual Sensation & but mediately to the Understanding or Reason Such is True Painting and such <was> alone valued by the Greeks & the best modern Artists. Consider what Lord Bacon says "Sense sends over to Imagination before Reason have judged & Reason sends over to Imagination before the Decree can be acted." See Advancem[ent] of Learning Part 2 P 47 of first Edition

But I am happy to find a Great Majority of Fellow Mortals who can Elucidate My Visions & Particularly they have been Elucidated by Children who have taken a greater delight in contemplating my Pictures than I even hoped. Neither Youth nor Childhood is Folly or Incapacity Some Children are Fools & so are some Old Men. But There is a vast Majority on the side of Imagination or Spiritual Sensation

To Engrave after another Painter is infinitely more laborious than to Engrave ones own Inventions. And of the Size you require my price has been Thirty Guineas & I cannot afford to do it for less. I had Twelve for the Head I sent you as a Specimen. but after my own designs I could do at least Six times the quantity of labour in the same time which will account for the difference of price as also that Chalk Engraving is at least six times as laborious as Aqua tinta. I have no objection to Engraving after another Artist. Engraving is the profession I was apprenticed to, & should never have attempted to live by any thing else If orders had not come in for my Designs & Paintings, which I have the pleasure to tell you are Increasing Every Day. Thus If I am a Painter it is not to be attributed to Seeking after. But I am contented whether I live by Painting or Engraving

I am Rev[d] Sir Your very obedient servant

William Blake

Letter [To Thomas Butts, 22 November 1802][1]

Dear Sir

After I had finishd my Letter I found that I had not said half what I intended to say & in particular I wish to ask you what subject you choose to be painted on the remaining Canvas which I brought down with me (for there were

[2] **Malevolence . . . Cause:** Blake here refers to a design that he had shown to Trusler, entitled *Malevolence* and described by Blake as "A Father, taking leave of his Wife & Child, Is watch'd by Two Fiends incarnate, with intention that when his back is turned they will murder the mother & her infant."

[1] Thomas Butts, a wealthy civil servant (he was Chief Clerk in the office of the Commissary General of Musters), real estate developer, and devout Christian, was Blake's chief patron; he commissioned 35 tempera illustrations to the Bible which Blake painted from 1800 to 1803 and 21 watercolor illustrations to The Book of Job which Blake completed from 1805 to 1810.

three) and to tell you that several of the Drawings were in great forwardness you will see by the Inclosed Account that the remaining Number of Drawings which you gave me orders for is Eighteen I will finish these with all possible Expedition if indeed I have not tired you or as it is politely calld Bored you too much already or if you would rather cry out Enough Off Off! tell me in a Letter of forgiveness if you were offended & of accustomd friendship if you were not. But I will bore you more with some Verses which My Wife desires me to Copy out & send you with her kind love & Respect they were Composed <above> a twelve-month ago [*in a*] <while> Walk<ing> from Felpham to Lavant to meet my Sister

With happiness stretchd across the hills
In a cloud that dewy sweetness distills
With a blue sky spread over with wings
And a mild sun that mounts & sings
With trees & fields full of Fairy elves
And little devils who fight for themselves
Remembring the Verses that Hayley sung[2]
When my heart knockd against the root of my tongue
With Angels planted in Hawthorn bowers
And God himself in the passing hours
With Silver Angels across my way
And Golden Demons that none can stay
With my Father hovering upon the wind
And my Brother Robert just behind
And my Brother John the evil one[3]
In a black cloud making his mone
Tho dead they appear upon my path
Notwithstanding my terrible wrath
They beg they intreat they drop their tears
Filld full of hopes filld full of fears
With a thousand Angels upon the Wind
Pouring disconsolate from behind
To drive them off & before my way
A frowning Thistle implores my stay
What to others a trifle appears
Fills me full of smiles or tears
For double the vision my Eyes do see
And a double vision is always with me
With my inward Eye 'tis an old Man grey
With my outward a Thistle across my way
"If thou goest back the thistle said
Thou art to endless woe betrayd
For here does Theotormon lower
And here is Enitharmons bower
And Los the terrible thus hath sworn
Because thou backward dost return
Poverty Envy old age & fear
Shall bring thy Wife upon a bier
And Butts shall give what Fuseli[4] gave
A dark black Rock & a gloomy Cave."
I struck the Thistle with my foot
And broke him up from his delving root
"Must the duties of life each other cross"
"Must every joy be dung & dross"
"Must my dear Butts feel cold neglect"
"Because I give Hayley his due respect"
"Must Flaxman[5] look upon me as wild"
"And all my friends be with doubts beguild"
"Must my Wife live in my Sisters bane"
"Or my sister survive on my Loves pain"
"The curses of Los the terrible shade"
"And his dismal terrors make me afraid"

[2] **Verses that Hayley sung:** probably Hayley's blank verse translation of the first 200 lines of Tasso's *Le Sette Giornale,* titled *Genesis, the Seven Days of the Created World,* which were transcribed by Blake. From 1800 to 1803, Blake, his wife Catherine, and his sister Catherine Elizabeth were the guests of the poet William Hayley at his home in Felpham, between Chichester and Brighton, on the coast of Surrey. Hayley's attempts to guide Blake's work into more conventional channels were deeply resented by Blake, even as Blake acknowledged his gratitude for Hayley's financial support.

[3] **Robert . . . John the evil one:** Robert Blake, the poet's favorite sibling, died of consumption in 1787 at the age of 20; Blake continually invoked him as a source of inspiration. John Blake (b. 1760) failed in several careers, became an alcoholic, and died at an early age.

[4] **Fuseli:** Henri Fuseli (1741–1825), a Swiss painter and revolutionary thinker, who emigrated to England and became a close friend of Blake, by whom his art was much influenced. He frequently employed Blake as an engraver of his paintings. By 1802, however, he had quarrelled with Blake and ceased to employ him.

[5] **Flaxman:** John Flaxman (1755–1826), one of England's leading sculptors. He specialized in the neoclassical style, and in addition to his monumental church and funeral sculptures, illustrated Homer and Virgil in austere outline engravings and provided the bulk of the designs for Wedgwood's pottery. He and his wife Anne had been close friends and patrons of Blake in earlier years, but disapproved of his style of painting and urged him to stick to engraving instead.

So I spoke & struck in my wrath
The old man weltering upon my path
Then Los appeard in all his power
In the Sun he appeard descending before
My face in fierce flames in my double sight
Twas outward a Sun: inward Los in his might

"My hands are labourd day & night"
"And Ease comes never in my sight"
"My Wife has no indulgence given"
"Except what comes to her from heaven"
"We eat little we drink less"
"This Earth breeds not our happiness"
"Another Sun feeds our lifes streams"
"We are not warmed with thy beams"
"Thou measurest not the Time to me"
"Nor yet the Space that I do see"
"My Mind is not with thy light arrayd"
"Thy terrors shall not make me afraid"

When I had my Defiance given
The Sun stood trembling in heaven
The Moon that glowd remote below
Became leprous & white as snow
And every Soul of men on the Earth
Felt affliction & sorrow & sickness & dearth
Los flamd in my path & the Sun was hot
With the bows of my Mind & the Arrows of Thought
My bowstring fierce with Ardour breathes
My arrows glow in their golden sheaves
My brothers & father march before
The heavens drop with human gore

Now I a fourfold vision see
And a fourfold vision is given to me
Tis fourfold in my supreme delight
And three fold in soft Beulahs[6] night
And twofold Always. May God us keep
From Single vision & Newtons sleep[7]

I also inclose you some Ballads by Mr Hayley with prints to them by Your H^ble^. Servt. I should have sent them before now but could not get any thing done for You to please myself for I do assure you that I have truly studied the two little pictures I now send & do not repent of the time I have spent upon them

God bless you
Yours
W B

P.S. I have taken the liberty to trouble you with a letter to my Brother which you will be so kind as to send or give him & oblige yours W B

[6] **Beulah:** Beulah ("married") is the name given to Palestine when it was restored to God's favor (Isaiah 62:4). In John Bunyan's *The Pilgrim's Progress,* the land of Beulah is the Earthly Paradise where pilgrims live until they enter heaven.

[7] **Newtons sleep:** Isaac Newton (1642–1727), who discovered the law of gravity and is the father of contemporary particle physics, was attacked by Blake for reducing the world of the spirit to mere matter.

POSTHUMOUS PUBLICATIONS

from THE PICKERING MANUSCRIPT

(1863)

Auguries of Innocence

(comp. c. 1803)

To see a World in a Grain of Sand
And a Heaven in a Wild Flower
Hold Infinity in the palm of your hand
And Eternity in an hour
A Robin Red breast in a Cage
Puts all Heaven in a Rage
A dove house filld with doves & Pigeons
Shudders Hell thro all its regions
A dog starvd at his Masters Gate
Predicts the ruin of the State
A Horse misusd upon the Road
Calls to Heaven for Human blood
Each outcry of the hunted Hare
A fibre from the Brain does tear
A Skylark wounded in the wing
A Cherubim does cease to sing
The Game Cock clipd & armd for fight
Does the Rising Sun affright
Every Wolfs & Lions howl
Raises from Hell a Human Soul
The wild deer wandring here & there
Keeps the Human Soul from Care
The Lamb misusd breeds Public strife
And yet forgives the Butchers Knife

The Bat that flits at close of Eve
Has left the Brain that wont Believe
The Owl that calls upon the Night
Speaks the Unbelievers fright
He who shall hurt the little Wren
Shall never be belovd by Men
He who the Ox to wrath has movd
Shall never be by Woman lovd
The wanton Boy that kills the Fly
Shall feel the Spiders enmity
He who torments the Chafers sprite[1]
Weaves a Bower in endless Night
The Catterpiller on the Leaf
Repeats to thee thy Mothers grief
Kill not the Moth nor Butterfly
For the Last Judgment draweth nigh
He who shall train the Horse to War
Shall never pass the Polar Bar
The Beggers Dog & Widows Cat
Feed them & thou wilt grow fat
The Gnat that sings his Summers song
Poison gets from Slanders tongue
The poison of the Snake & Newt
Is the sweat of Envys Foot
The Poison of the Honey Bee
Is the Artists Jealousy
The Princes Robes & Beggars Rags
Are Toadstools on the Misers Bags
A truth thats told with bad intent
Beats all the Lies you can invent
It is right it should be so
Man was made for Joy & Woe
And when this we rightly know
Thro the World we safely go
Joy & Woe are woven fine
A Clothing for the Soul divine
Under every grief & pine
Runs a joy with silken twine
The Babe is more than swadling Bands
Throughout all these Human Lands
Tools were made & Born were hands
Every Farmer Understands
Every Tear from Every Eye
Becomes a Babe in Eternity
This is caught by Females bright
And returnd to its own delight

[1] **Chafer:** beetle. **sprite:** sprout or offshoot; spirit or ghost.

The Bleat the Bark Bellow & Roar
Are Waves that Beat on Heavens Shore
The Babe that weeps the Rod beneath
Writes Revenge in realms of death
The Beggars Rags fluttering in Air
Does to Rags the Heavens tear
The Soldier armd with Sword & Gun
Palsied strikes the Summers Sun
The poor Mans Farthing is worth more
Than all the Gold on Africs Shore
One Mite wrung from the Labrers hands
Shall buy & sell the Misers Lands
Or if protected from on high
Does that whole Nation sell & buy
He who mocks the Infants Faith
Shall be mock'd in Age & Death
He who shall teach the Child to Doubt
The rotting Grave shall neer get out
He who respects the Infants faith
Triumphs over Hell & Death
The Childs Toys & the Old Mans Reasons
Are the Fruits of the Two seasons
The Questioner who sits so sly
Shall never know how to Reply
He who replies to words of Doubt
Doth put the Light of Knowledge out
The Strongest Poison ever known
Came from Caesars Laurel Crown
Nought can deform the Human Race
Like to the Armours iron brace
When Gold & Gems adorn the Plow
To peaceful Arts shall Envy Bow
A Riddle or the Crickets Cry
Is to Doubt a fit Reply
The Emmets Inch & Eagles Mile
Make Lame Philosophy to smile
He who Doubts from what he sees
Will neer Believe do what you Please
If the Sun & Moon should doubt
Theyd immediately Go out
To be in a Passion you Good may do
But no Good if a Passion is in you
The Whore & Gambler by the State
Licencd build that Nations Fate
The Harlots cry from Street to Street
Shall weave Old Englands winding Sheet
The Winners Shout the Losers Curse
Dance before dead Englands Hearse
Every Night & every Morn

Some to Misery are Born
Every Morn & every Night
Some are Born to sweet delight
Some are Born to sweet delight
Some are Born to Endless Night
We are led to Believe a Lie
When we see not Thro the Eye
Which was Born in a Night to perish in a Night
When the Soul Slept in Beams of Light
God Appears & God is Light
To those poor Souls who dwell in Night
But does a Human Form Display
To those who Dwell in Realms of day

from ALEXANDER GILCHRIST'S *LIFE OF WILLIAM BLAKE: PICTOR IGNOTUS*

(1863; rev. 1880)

from A VISION OF THE LAST JUDGMENT

(comp. 1810)

For the Year 1810 Additions to Blakes Catalogue of Pictures &c

. . . The Last Judgment is an Overwhelming of Bad Art & Science. Mental Things are alone Real what is Calld Corporeal Nobody Knows of its dwelling Place <it> is in Fallacy & its Existence an Imposture Where is the Existence Out of Mind or Thought Where is it but in the Mind of a Fool. Some People flatter themselves that there will be No Last Judgment & that Bad Art will be adopted & mixed with Good Art That Error or Experiment will make a Part of Truth & they Boast that it is its Foundation these People flatter themselves I will not Flatter them Error is Created Truth is Eternal Error or Creation will be Burned Up & then & not till then Truth or Eternity will appear It is Burnt up the Moment Men cease to behold it I assert for My self that I do not behold the Outward Creation & that to me it is hindrance & not Action it is as the Dirt upon my feet No part of Me. What it will be Questiond When the Sun rises do you not see a round Disk of fire somewhat like a Guinea[1] O no no I see an Innumerable company of the Heavenly host crying Holy Holy Holy is the Lord God Almighty I question not my Corporeal or Vegetative Eye any more than I would Question a Window concerning a Sight I look thro it & not with it.

[1] **guinea:** an English gold coin, first struck in 1663, valued at 21 shillings.

MARY DARBY ROBINSON

(1758–1800)

Mary Darby was born on 27 November 1758, the daughter of Mary Seys and an American whaling captain, John Darby. Mary's father was ruined financially in 1768 in an ill-fated Labrador Eskimo whale-fishery construction scheme and then deserted his family to become a mercenary captain in the Russian navy. He died in Russia in 1786. At the age of 15, the beautiful Mary Darby was pressured by her impoverished mother into marriage to a neighbor, Thomas Robinson, an articled clerk in Lincoln's Fields. He turned out to be a gambler and a libertine who within two years landed his family in debtors' prison. Well-educated (she had attended Hannah More's sisters' school and later been given a "masculine" education by Meribah Lorrington), Mary Robinson began writing to support herself, her husband, and her daughter, Maria Elizabeth (born in 1774). Her first published poem, appropriately titled "Captivity," appeared in her *Poems* in 1775. She soon realized that becoming an actress would earn her a higher income; the following year she made her debut as Juliet at the Drury Lane Theatre to instant acclaim. Having an honorable economic independence, she wrote, "is the one true felicity in this world of humiliations!"

Her successful career on the stage (she played three dozen parts in four seasons, receiving the large sum of £20 for her second portrayal of Juliet in 1778) enabled her to pay her husband's debts, despite his "marked and increasing neglect" (he had taken up with two different mistresses). From 1779 to 1780, she played Perdita in Shakespeare's *The Winter's Tale* so brilliantly that she was ever afterward known as "Perdita" Robinson. Asked to perform the play for the royal family on 3 December 1779, she captivated the seventeen-year-old Prince of Wales who wooed her by letter as "Florizel" and promised her £20,000 if she would become his mistress (she agreed, but the sum was first denied and then reduced to a £500 annuity). Their much publicized affair made her the butt of numerous scurrilous satires, especially after the prince abandoned her the following year, leaving her £7,000 in debt.

Ostracized from society by the resultant scandal, her stage career on hold, Robinson separated from her husband and fled to Paris for six months. She was saved from total financial ruin by the help of Charles James Fox, who negotiated her annuity and persuaded the king to pay her £5,000 in addition for the return of the prince's indiscreet letters and bond. She was accompanied by Col. Banastre Tarleton, a distinguished if ruthless leader of the British troops in the War against the Colonies, to whom she addressed her most passionate poems. Feted in Paris as "la belle Anglaise," she returned to the London stage for the 1782–1783 season, in which she excelled as Rosalind in *As You Like It.* She settled at Windsor with Tarleton, who proved to be an inveterate gambler. In 1783, she was paralyzed from the waist down for six months by a badly handled miscarriage brought on while pursuing Tarleton, who was in debt and fleeing to France. They remained lovers until Tarleton deserted her in 1797. Robinson returned to the stage in Edinburgh for the spring of 1787, playing Lady Macbeth and the title role in *The Irish Widow.*

Increasingly crippled by arthritis and relying on her writing to support herself and her daughter, she began a "poetical correspondence" in 1790 with Robert Merry, who in 1784 had founded the Society della Crusca in Florence. In a widely reprinted series of love poems in 1785, Robert Merry (signing himself Della Crusca) and "Anna Matilda" (the playwright Hannah Cowley) had developed the hallmarks of the Della Cruscan poetic style: a display of poetic language as pure artifice, characterized by a brilliant use of metaphor, imagery and verbal wit, extensive literary allusion, and an affirmation of erotic love as sublime. Robinson worked first in this self-consciously artificial Della Cruscan style (her Della Cruscan name was "Laura Maria") and then turned to more realistic and satiric poetic commentaries on the vices of the aristocracy. Her work was praised both by such upper-class Bluestockings as Georgiana, Duchess of Devonshire, and Lady Mary Wortley Montagu, and by such radical intellectuals and poets as Godwin, Wollstonecraft,* Wordsworth,* and Coleridge* (who called her "an undoubted genius"). She wrote pro-Jacobin essays for *The Morning Post* as "Tabitha Bramble," supported the ideals of the French Revolution (although she condemned the Terror in "The Progress of Liberty" published in 1806), and denounced slavery and the slave trade. Her *Thoughts on the Condition of Women, and on the Injustice of Mental Subordination* (published under the pseudonym Anne Frances Randall in 1799; republished under her own name later that year) attacks male hypocrisy and the sexual double standard, defends the prostitute (whose fall is caused not by her lack of virtue but by economic necessity), and insists upon the equal intelligence and cultural achievements of women.

Her eight novels track the snares laid by vicious aristocrats to entrap virtuous but naive young heroines and heroes. Her poems, which eventually earned her the title of "the English Sappho," relentlessly portray the sufferings of the poor, the disenfranchised, the orphaned or abandoned, the mad, and the female, while vividly cataloguing the unpunished vices of the wealthy and the powerful. Her settings are often Gothic, blurring the boundaries between the rational and the irrational. In Robinson's poetic world, justice does not triumph, merit is not rewarded, love does not endure. Neither religion nor nature comfort the suffering. Her vivid and compelling autobiography, *Memoirs of the Late Mrs. Robinson, written by Herself* (1801) and intended to illustrate "the progressive evils of a too acute sensiblity" in a "world of duplicity and sorrow," was completed by her daughter after her death on 26 December 1800, as an act of filial admiration and duty.

from POEMS
(1791)

Canzonet[1]

SLOW the limpid currents twining,[2]
Brawl along the lonely dell,
'Till in one wild stream combining,
Nought its rapid course can quell;
So at first LOVE's poisons stealing,
Round the heart unheeded play,
While we hope our pangs concealing,
Vainly hope to check his sway.
If amidst the glassy river
Aught impedes its placid course,
Ah! it glides more swift than ever,
While opposing gives it force;
So when HOPE and PASSION blending,
Warm the feeble trembling frame;
REASON sickens by contending,
Fanning only feeds the flame.

[1] A **canzonet** is a short, light song. Robinson probably has in mind a shorter version of the Italian or Provencal *canzone,* or the *Canzoniere* of Petrarch.

[2] **twining:** to wind or twist.

Ode to Beauty
(1791)

Exulting beauty:—phantom of an hour,
Whose magic spells enchain the heart,
Ah! what avails thy fascinating pow'r,
Thy thrilling smile, thy witching art?[1]
Thy lip, where balmy nectar glows;
Thy cheek, where round the damask rose
A thousand nameless Graces move;
Thy mildly speaking azure eyes,
Thy golden hair, where cunning Love
In many a mazy ringlet lies?
Soon as thy radiant form is seen,
Thy native blush, thy timid mien,[2]
Thy hour is past! thy charms are vain!
Ill-Nature haunts thee with her sallow train,
Mean Jealousy deceives thy list'ning ear,
And Slander stains thy cheek with many a bitter tear.

In calm retirement form'd to dwell,
Nature, thy handmaid fair and kind,
For thee a beauteous garland twin'd;
The vale-nurs'd Lily's downcast bell
Thy modest mien display'd,
The snow-drop, April's meekest child,
With myrtle blossoms undefil'd.
Thy mild and spotless mind pourtray'd.
Dear blushing maid, of cottage birth,
'Twas thine, o'er dewy meads to stray,
While sparkling health, and frolic mirth,
Led on thy laughing Day.

Lur'd by the babbling tongue of Fame,
Too soon, insidious Flatt'ry came;
Flush'd Vanity her footsteps led,
To charm thee from thy blest repose,
While Fashion twin'd about thy head
A wreath of wounding woes;
See Dissipation smoothly glide,
Cold Apathy, and puny Pride,
Capricious Fortune, dull, and blind,
O'er splendid Folly throws her veil,
While Envy's meagre tribe assail
Thy gentle form, and spotless mind.

Their spells prevail! no more those eyes
Shoot undulating fires;
On thy wan cheek, the young rose dies,
Thy lip's deep tint expires;
Dark Melancholy chills thy mind;
Thy silent tear reveals thy woe;
Time strews with thorns thy mazy way;
Where'er thy giddy footsteps stray,
Thy thoughtless heart is doom'd to find
An unrelenting foe.

'Tis thus, the infant Forest flow'r,
Bespangled o'er with glitt'ring dew,
At breezy morn's refreshing hour,
Glows with pure tints of varying hue,
Beneath an aged oak's wide spreading shade,
Where no rude winds, or beating storms invade.
Transplanted from its lonely bed,
No more it scatters perfumes round,
No more it rears its gentle head,
Or brightly paints the mossy ground;
For ah! the beauteous bud, too soon,
Scorch'd by the burning eye of day;
Shrinks from the sultry glare of noon,
Droops its enamell'd brow, and blushing, dies away.

[1] **art:** here partakes of the meaning "merely artifice," as well as "a skill that is practiced."

[2] **mien:** aspect or expression of countenance, look, appearance.

from SAPPHO AND PHAON:[1] IN A SERIES OF LEGITIMATE SONNETS
(1796)

Flendus amor meus est; elegeia flebile carmen:
Non facit ad lacrymas barbitos ulla meas.

Ovid

[1] **Sappho and Phaon:** Sappho, an early Greek lyric poet of the sixth century, was most famous for her love poems addressed to other women. According to later legend, probably unfounded, she killed herself for love of a male youth, Phaon, by jumping off mount Leucas into the sea. Robinson's contemporaries drew a parallel between the poet from Lesbos and Robinson by naming her "The English Sappho," and Robinson herself suggests the connection, occasionally signing her poems "Sappho."

Love taught my tears in sadder notes to flow,
And tuned my heart to elegies of wo.
POPE

— SONNET VII —

COME, Reason, come! each nerve rebellious bind,
Lull the fierce tempest of my feverish soul;
Come, with the magic of thy meek control,
And check the wayward wanderings of my mind:
Estranged from thee, no solace can I find;
O'er my [rapt] brain, where pensive visions stole,
Now passion reigns and stormy tumults roll:
So the smooth sea obeys the furious wind!
In vain philosophy unfolds her store,
O'erwhelm'd is every source of pure delight;
Dim is the golden page of wisdom's lore;
All nature fades before my sick'ning sight:
For what bright scene can fancy's eye explore
Midst dreary labyrinths of mental night?

— SONNET XI —
(1796)

O REASON! vaunted sovereign of the mind!
Thou pompous vision with a sounding name!
Canst thou the soul's rebellious passions tame?
Can'st thou in spells the vagrant fancy bind?
Ah, no! capricious as the wavering wind
Are sighs of love that dim thy boasted flame;
While Folly's torch consumes the wreath of fame,
And Pleasure's hands the sheaves of truth unbind
Press'd by the storms of fate, Hope shrinks and dies!
Frenzy darts forth in mightiest ills array'd;
Around thy throne destructive tumults rise,
And hell-fraught jealousies thy rights invade!
Then, what art thou, O idol of the wise?
A visionary theme! — a gorgeous shade![1]

[1] **shade:** shadow. Suggests the Greek conception of the soul as a shade or shadow; an inferior version of one's living self.

from LYRICAL TALES
(1800)

All Alone

AH! wherefore by the Church-yard side,
Poor little lorn[1] one, dost thou stray?
Thy wavy locks but thinly hide
The tears that dim thy blue-eye's ray;
And wherefore dost thou sigh, and moan,
And weep, that thou are left alone?

Thou art not left alone, poor boy,
The Traveller stops to hear thy tale;
No heart, so hard, would thee annoy!
For though thy mother's cheek is pale,
And withers under yon grave stone,
Thou art not, Urchin, left alone.

I know thee well! thy yellow hair
In silky waves I oft have seen;
Thy dimpled face, so fresh and fair,
Thy roguish smile, thy playful mien,
Were all to me, poor Orphan, known,
Ere Fate had left thee — all alone!

Thy russet coat is scant, and torn,
Thy cheek is now grown deathly pale!
Thy eyes are dim, thy looks forlorn,
And bare thy bosom meets the gale;
And oft I hear thee deeply groan,
That thou, poor boy, art left alone.

Thy naked feet are wounded sore
With thorns, that cross thy daily road;
The winter winds around thee roar,
The church-yard is thy bleak abode;
Thy pillow now a cold grave stone —
And there thou lov'st to grieve — alone!

The rain has drench'd thee, all night long;
The nipping frost thy bosom froze;
And still, the yew-tree shades among,
I heard thee sigh thy artless woes;
I heard thee, till the day-star shone
In darkness weep — and weep alone!

[1] **lorn:** lost, abandoned.

Oft have I seen thee, little boy,
Upon thy lovely mother's knee;
For when she lived, thou wert her joy,
Though now a mourner thou must be!
For she lies low, where yon grave stone
Proclaims, that thou art left alone.

Weep, weep no more; on yonder hill
The village bells are ringing, gay;
The merry reed, and brawling rill
Call thee to rustic sports away.
Then wherefore weep, and sigh, and moan,
A truant from the throng—alone?

"I cannot the green hill ascend,
I cannot pace the upland mead;
I cannot in the vale attend
To hear the merry-sounding reed:
For all is still, beneath yon stone,
Where my poor mother's left alone!

"I cannot gather gaudy flowers
To dress the scene of revels loud—
I cannot pass the evening hours
Among the noisy village crowd;
For, all in darkness, and alone
My mother sleeps, beneath yon stone.

"See how the stars begin to gleam,
The sheep-dog barks—'tis time to go;
The night-fly hums, the moonlight beam
Peeps through the yew-trees' shadowy row:
It falls upon the white grave-stone,
Where my dear mother sleeps alone.

"O stay me not, for I must go,
The upland path in haste to tread;
For there the pale primroses grow,
They grow to dress my mother's bed.
They must, ere peep of day, be strown,
Where she lies mould'ring all alone.

"My father o'er the stormy sea
To distant lands was borne away,
And still my mother stay'd with me,
And wept by night and toil'd by day.
And shall I ever quit the stone
Where she is left, to sleep alone.

"My father died, and still I found
My mother fond and kind to me;
I felt her breast with rapture bound
When first I prattled on her knee—
And then she blest my infant tone,
And little thought of yon grave-stone.

"No more her gentle voice I hear,
No more her smile of fondness see;
Then wonder not I shed the tear,
She would have died, to follow me!
And yet she sleeps beneath yon stone
And I still live—to weep alone.

"The playful kid, she loved so well,
From yon high clift was seen to fall;
I heard, afar, his tinkling bell,
Which seem'd in vain for aid to call—
I heard the harmless suff'rer moan,
And grieved that he was left alone.

"Our faithful dog grew mad, and died,
The lightning smote our cottage low—
We had no resting-place beside,
And knew not whither we should go:
For we were poor—and hearts of stone
Will never throb at misery's groan.

"My mother still survived for me,
She led me to the mountain's brow,
She watch'd me, while at yonder tree
I sat, and wove the ozier[2] bough;
And oft she cried, "fear not, mine own!
Thou shalt not, boy, be left alone."

"The blast blew strong, the torrent rose
And bore our shatter'd cot away;
And where the clear brook swiftly flows,
Upon the turf, at dawn of day,
When bright the sun's full lustre shone,
I wander'd, friendless—and alone!"

Thou art not, boy, for I have seen
Thy tiny footsteps print the dew,
And while the morning sky serene
Spread o'er the hill a yellow hue,
I heard thy sad and plaintive moan,
Beside the cold sepulchral stone.

And when the summer noontide hours
With scorching rays the landscape spread,

[2]ozier: a type of willow whose branches are used in basket work.

I mark'd thee, weaving fragrant flowers
To deck thy mother's silent bed!
Nor, at the church-yard's simple stone
Wert thou, poor Urchin, left alone.

I follow'd thee along the dale,
And up the woodland's shad'wy way:
I heard thee tell thy mournful tale
As slowly sunk the star of day:
Nor, when its twinkling light had flown
Wert thou a wand'rer, all alone.

"O! yes, I was! and still shall be
A wand'rer, mourning and forlorn;
For what is all the world to me—
What are the dews and buds of morn?
Since she, who left me sad, alone
In darkness sleeps, beneath yon stone!

"No brother's tear shall fall for me,
For I no brother ever knew;
No friend shall weep my destiny,
For friends are scarce, and tears are few;
None do I see, save on this stone,
Where I will stay, and weep alone.

"My father never will return,
He rests beneath the sea-green wave;
I have no kindred left to mourn
When I am hid in yonder grave:
Not one! to dress with flow'rs the stone!
Then—surely, I AM LEFT ALONE!"

The Poor, Singing Dame
(1800)

BENEATH an old wall, that went round an old castle,
For many a year, with brown ivy o'erspread;
A neat little hovel, its lowly roof raising,
Defied the wild winds that howl'd over its shed:
The turrets, that frown'd on the poor simple dwelling,
Were rock'd to and fro, when the tempest would roar,
And the river, that down the rich valley was swelling,
Flow'd swiftly beside the green step of its door.

The summer sun gilded the rushy-roof slanting,
The bright dews bespangled its ivy-bound hedge,
And above, on the ramparts, the sweet birds were chanting,
And wild buds thick dappled the clear river's edge,
When the castle's rich chambers were haunted, and dreary,
The poor little hovel was still, and secure;
And no robber e'er enter'd, or goblin or fairy,
For the splendours of pride had no charms to allure.

The lord of the castle, a proud surly ruler,
Oft heard the low dwelling with sweet music ring,
For the old dame that lived in the little hut cheerly,
Would sit at her wheel, and would merrily sing:
When with revels the castle's great hall was resounding,
The old dame was sleeping, not dreaming of fear;
And when over the mountains the huntsmen were bounding
She would open her wicket,[1] their clamours to hear.

To the merry-toned horn she would dance on the threshold,
And louder, and louder, repeat her old song:
And when winter its mantle of frost was displaying,
She caroll'd, undaunted, the bare woods among:
She would gather dry fern, ever happy and singing,
With her cake of brown bread, and her jug of brown beer,
And would smile when she heard the great castle-bell ringing,
Inviting the proud to their prodigal cheer.

Thus she lived, ever patient and ever contented
Till envy the lord of the castle possess'd,
For he hated that poverty should be so cheerful,
While care could the fav'rites of fortune molest;
He sent his bold yeomen with threats to prevent her,
And still would she carol her sweet roundelay;[2]
At last, an old steward relentless he sent her—
Who bore her, all trembling, to prison away!

Three weeks did she languish, then died, broken-hearted,
Poor dame! how the death-bell did mournfully sound!

[1] **wicket:** lattice, window shutters.

[2] **roundelay:** a short, simple song with a refrain, as well as a bird's song or carol.

And along the green path six young bachelors bore her,
And laid her, for ever, beneath the cold ground!
And the primroses pale, 'mid the long grass were growing,
The bright dews of twilight bespangled her grave,
And morn heard the breezes of summer soft blowing
To bid the fresh flow'rets in sympathy wave.

The lord of the castle, from that fatal moment
When poor singing Mary was laid in her grave,
Each night was surrounded by screech-owls appalling,
Which o'er the black turrets their pinions would wave!
On the ramparts that frown'd on the river, swift flowing,
They hover'd, still hooting a terrible song,
When his windows would rattle, the winter blast blowing,
They would shriek like a ghost, the dark alleys among!

Wherever he wander'd they followed him crying;
At dawnlight, at eve, still they haunted his way!
When the moon shone across the wide common, they hooted,
Nor quitted his path, till the blazing of day.
His bones began wasting, his flesh was decaying,
And he hung his proud head, and he perish'd with shame;
And the tomb of rich marble, no soft tear displaying,
O'ershadows the grave of the poor singing dame!

The Haunted Beach

(1800)

UPON a lonely desert beach,
Where the white foam was scatter'd,
A little shed uprear'd its head,
Though lofty barks[1] were shatter'd.
The sea-weeds gathering near the door,
A sombre path display'd;
And, all around, the deafening roar
Re-echoed on the chalky shore,
By the green billows made.

Above a jutting cliff was seen
Where sea-birds hover'd, craving;
And all around, the craggs were bound
With weeds—for ever waving.
And here and there, a cavern wide
Its shadowy jaws display'd;
And near the sands, at ebb of tide,
A shiver'd mast was seen to ride
Where the green billows stray'd.

And often, while the moaning wind
Stole o'er the summer ocean,
The moonlight scene was all serene,
The waters scarce in motion;
Then, while the smoothly slanting sand
The tall cliff wrapp'd in shade,
The fisherman beheld a band
Of spectres, gliding hand in hand—
Where the green billows play'd.

And pale their faces were as snow,
And sullenly they wander'd;
And to the skies with hollow eyes
They look'd as though they ponder'd.
And sometimes, from their hammock shroud,
They dismal howlings made,
And while the blast blew strong and loud,
The clear moon mark'd the ghastly crowd,
Where the green billows play'd.

And then above the haunted hut
The curlews[2] screaming hover'd;
And the low door, with furious roar,
The frothy breakers cover'd.
For in the fisherman's lone shed
A murder'd man was laid,
With ten wide gashes in his head,
And deep was made his sandy bed
Where the green billows play'd.

A shipwreck'd mariner was he,
Doom'd from his home to sever
Who swore to be through wind and sea
Firm and undaunted ever!
And when the wave resistless roll'd,
About his arm he made
A packet rich of Spanish gold,
And, like a British sailor bold,
Plung'd where the billows play'd.

[1] **barks:** sailing ships.

[2] **curlews:** long-billed, wading ocean birds.

The spectre band, his messmates brave,
Sunk in the yawning ocean,
While to the mast he lash'd him fast,
And braved the storm's commotion.
The winter moon upon the sand
A silvery carpet made,
And mark'd the sailor reach the land,
And mark'd his murderer wash his hand
Where the green billows play'd.

And since that hour the fisherman
Has toil'd and toil'd in vain;
For all the night the moony light
Gleams on the specter'd main!
And when the skies are veil'd in gloom,
The murderer's liquid way
Bounds o'er the deeply yawning tomb,
And flashing fires the sands illume,
Where the green billows play.

Full thirty years his task has been,
Day after day more weary;
For Heaven design'd his guilty mind
Should dwell on prospects dreary.
Bound by a strong and mystic chain,
He has not power to stray;
But, destined misery to sustain,
He wastes, in solitude and pain,
A loathsome life away.

Deborah's Parrot

A Village Tale
(1800)

'TWAS in a little western town
An ancient maiden dwelt:
Her name was Miss, or Mistress, Brown,
Or Deborah, or Debby: she
Was doom'd a spinster pure to be,
For soft delights her breast ne'er felt:
Yet, she had watchful ears and eyes
For every youthful neighbour,
And never did she cease to labour
A tripping[1] female to surprize.

And why was she so wondrous pure,
So stiff, so solemn — so demure?
Why did she watch with so much care
The roving youth, the wandering fair?
The tatler, Fame, has said that she
A spinster's life had long detested,
But 'twas her quiet destiny
Never to be molested! —
And had Miss Debby's form been graced,
Fame adds, — she had not been so chaste; —
But since for frailty she would roam,
She ne'er was taught — to *look at home.*

Miss Debby was of mien demure,
And blush'd like any maid!
She could not saucy man endure,
Lest she should be betray'd!
She never fail'd at dance or fair
To watch the wily lurcher's snare;
At church she was a model godly!
Though sometimes she had other eyes
Than those uplifted to the skies,
Leering most oddly!
And Scandal, ever busy, thought
She rarely practised — what she taught.

Her dress was always stiff brocade,
With laces broad and dear;
Fine cobwebs! that would thinly shade
Her shrivell'd cheek of sallow hue,
While, like a spider, her keen eye,
Which never shed soft pity's tear,
Small holes in others geer could spy,[2]
And microscopic follies prying view.
And sorely vex'd was every simple thing
That wander'd near her never-tiring sting!

Miss Debby had a parrot, who
If Fame speaks true,
Could prate, and tell what neighbours did,
And yet the saucy rogue was never chid!
Sometimes he talk'd of roving spouses
Who wander'd from their quiet houses:
Sometimes he call'd a spinster pure

[1] **tripping:** stumbling, erring, sinning.

[2] **geer:** one's clothing or equipment, in this case something akin to armor. Robinson puns on the jeering Deborah and her efforts to spot "small holes in others geer," or chinks in one's armor.

By names that virtue can't endure!
And sometimes told an ancient dame
Such tales as made her blush with shame!
Then gabbled how a giddy miss
Would give the boisterous squire a kiss!
But chiefly he was taught to cry,
"Who with the parson toy'd? O fie!"

This little joke Miss Debby taught him,
To vex a young and pretty neighbour;
But by her scandal-zealous labour
To shame she brought him!
For the old parrot, like his teacher,
Was but a false and canting preacher,
And many a gamesome pair had sworn
Such lessons were not to be borne.

At last, Miss Debby sore was flouted,
And by her angry neighbours scouted;
She never knew one hour of rest,—
Of every saucy boor the jest:
The young despised her, and the sage
Look'd back on Time's impartial page:
They knew that youth was given to prove
The season of ecstatic joy,
That none but cynics would destroy
The early buds of love.
They also knew that Debby sigh'd
For charms that envious Time denied;
That she was vex'd with jealous spleen
That Hymen pass'd her by, unseen.

For though the spinster's wealth was known,
Gold will not purchase love—alone.
She and her parrot now were thought
The torments of their little sphere:
He, because mischievously taught,
And she, because a maid austere!—
In short, she deem'd it wise to leave
A place, where none remain'd to grieve.

Soon, to a distant town removed,
Miss Debby's gold a husband brought;
And all she had her parrot taught
(Her parrot now no more beloved)
Was quite forgotten. But, alas!
As Fate would have it come to pass,
Her spouse was given to jealous rage;
For, both in person and in age,
He was the partner of his love,
Ordain'd her second self to prove!

One day, old Jenkins[3] had been out
With merry friends to dine,
And, freely talking, had no doubt
Been also free with wine.
One said, of all the wanton gay
In the whole parish, search it round,
None like the parson could be found,
Where a frail maid was in the way.
Another thought the parson sure
To win the heart of maid or wife;
And would have freely pledged his life
That, young or old, or rich or poor,
None could defy
The magic of his roving eye!

Jenkins went home, but all the night
He dream'd of this strange tale!
Yet bless'd his stars, with proud delight,
His partner was not young, nor frail.
Next morning, at the breakfast table,
The parrot, loud as he was able,
Was heard repeatedly to cry,
"Who with the parson toy'd? O fie!"

Old Jenkins listen'd, and grew pale,
The parrot then more loudly scream'd;
And Mistress Jenkins heard the tale,
And much alarm'd she seem'd!
Trembling, she tried to stop his breath,
Her lips and cheek as pale as death!
The more she trembled, still the more
Old Jenkins view'd her o'er and o'er:
And now her yellow cheek was spread
With blushes of the deepest red.

And now again the parrot's tale
Made his old tutoress doubly pale;
For cowardice and guilt, they say,
Are the twin brothers of the soul:
So Mistress Jenkins her dismay
Could not control!
While the accuser, now grown bold,
Thrice o'er the tale of mischief told.

Now Jenkins from the table rose,
"Who with the parson toy'd?" he cried.

[3]**Jenkins:** this name, and the poem's interest in marital strife, suggest the Wife of Bath's husband Janekin, and the marital strife and wife-beating outlined in her prologue and tale.

"So, Mistress Frailty, you must play
And sport your wanton hours away.
And with your gold, a pretty joke,
You thought to buy a pleasant cloak,
A screen to hide your shame — but know
I will not blind to ruin go. —
I am no modern spouse, d'ye see,
Gold will not gild disgrace, with me!"
Some say he seized his fearful bride,
And came to blows!
Day after day the contest dire
Augmented, with resistless ire!
And many a drubbing Debby bought
For mischief she her parrot taught!

Thus, slander turns against its maker:
And if this little story reaches
A spinster who her parrot teaches,
Let her a better task pursue,
And here the certain vengeance view
Which surely will, in time, o'ertake her.

The Alien Boy
(1800)

'TWAS on a mountain near the western main,
An alien dwelt. A solitary hut
Built on a jutting crag, o'erhung with weeds,
Mark'd the poor exile's home. Full ten long years
The melancholy wretch had lived unseen
By all, save Henry, a loved little son,
The partner of his sorrows. On the day
When persecution, in the sainted guise
Of liberty,[1] spread wide its venom'd power,
The brave Saint Hubert fled his lordly home,
And, with his baby son, the mountain sought,
Resolved to cherish in his bleeding breast
The secret of his birth — Ah! birth too high
For his now humbled state! — from infancy
He taught him labour's task: he bade him cheer
The dreary day of cold adversity
By patience and by toil. The summer morn
Shone on the pillow of his rushy bed;
The noontide, sultry hour, he fearless pass'd
On the shagg'd eminence; while the young kid
Skipp'd, to the cadence of his minstrelsy.

At night young Henry trimm'd the faggot fire,
While oft Saint Hubert wove the ample net
To snare the finny victim. Oft they sang
And talk'd, while sullenly the waves would sound,
Dashing the sandy shore. Saint Hubert's eyes
Would swim in tears of fondness, mix'd with joy,
When he observed the opening harvest rich
Of promised intellect, which Henry's soul,
Whate'er the subject of their talk, display'd.

Oft the bold youth, in question intricate,
Would seek to know the story of his birth;
Oft ask, who bore him: and with curious skill
Enquire, why he, and only one beside,
Peopled the desert mountain? Still his sire
Was slow of answer, and, in words obscure,
Varied the conversation. Still the mind
Of Henry ponder'd; for, in their lone hut,
A daily journal would Saint Hubert make
Of his long banishment: and sometimes speak
Of friends forsaken, kindred massacred;
Proud mansions, rich domains, and joyous scenes
For ever faded, — lost!
One winter time,
'Twas on the eve of Christmas, the shrill blast
Swept o'er the stormy main. The boiling foam
Rose to an altitude so fierce and strong,
That their low hovel totter'd. Oft they stole
To the rock's margin, and with fearful eyes
Mark'd the vex'd deep, as the slow rising moon
Gleam'd on the world of waters. 'Twas a scene
Would make a stoic[2] shudder! For, amid
The wavy mountains, they beheld, alone,
A little boat, now scarcely visible;
And now not seen at all; or, like a buoy,
Bounding, and buffetting, to reach the shore!

Now the full moon in crimson lustre shone
Upon the outstretch'd ocean. The black clouds
Flew swiftly on, the wild blast following,
And, as they flew, dimming the angry main
With shadows horrible! Still the small boat

[1] **persecution, in the sainted guise of liberty:** reference to the Terror of the French Revolution. Although a supporter of the Revolution, Robinson condemned the Terror.

[2] **stoic:** reference to the ancient Greek school of philosophy founded by Zeno and characterized by the repression of emotion and indifference to pleasure or pain.

Struggled amid the waves, a sombre speck
Upon the wide domain of howling death!
Saint Hubert sigh'd! while Henry's speaking eye
Alternately the stormy scene survey'd,
And his low hovel's safety. So pass'd on
The hour of midnight,—and, since first they knew
The solitary scene, no midnight hour
E'er seem'd so long and weary.
While they stood,
Their hands fast link'd together, and their eyes
Fix'd on the troublous ocean, suddenly
The breakers, bounding on the rocky shore,
Left the small wreck; and crawling on the side
Of the rude crag,—a human form was seen!
And now he climb'd the foam-wash'd precipice,
And now the slipp'ry weeds gave way, while he
Descended to the sands. The moon rose high—
The wild blast paused, and the poor shipwreck'd man
Look'd round aghast, when on the frowning steep
He mark'd the lonely exiles. Now he call'd;
But he was feeble, and his voice was lost
Amid the din of mingling sounds that rose
From the wild scene of clamour.
Down the steep
Saint Hubert hurried, boldly venturous,
Catching the slimy weeds, from point to point,
And unappall'd by peril. At the foot
Of the rude rock, the fainting mariner
Seized on his outstretch'd arm, impatient, wild,
With transport exquisite! But ere they heard
The blest exchange of sounds articulate,
A furious billow, rolling on the steep,
Engulph'd them in oblivion!
On the rock
Young Henry stood, with palpitating heart,
And fear-struck, e'en to madness! Now he call'd,
Louder and louder, as the shrill blast blew;
But, 'mid the elemental strife of sounds,
No human voice gave answer! The clear moon
No longer quiver'd on the curling main,
But, mist-encircled, shed a blunted light,
Enough to show all things that moved around,
Dreadful, but indistinctly! The black weeds
Waved, as the night-blast swept them; and along
The rocky shore the breakers, sounding low,
Seem'd like the whispering of a million souls
Beneath the green-deep mourning.
Four long hours
The lorn boy listen'd! four long tedious hours
Pass'd wearily away, when, in the east,
The grey beam coldly glimmer'd. All alone
Young Henry stood aghast, his eye wide fix'd;
While his dark locks, uplifted by the storm,
Uncover'd, met its fury. On his cheek
Despair sat terrible! for, 'mid the woes
Of poverty and toil, he had not known,
Till then, the horror-giving cheerless hour
Of total solitude!
He spoke—he groan'd,
But no responsive voice, no kindred tone,
Broke the dread pause: for now the storm had ceased,
And the bright sun-beams glitter'd on the breast
Of the green placid ocean. To his hut
The lorn boy hasten'd; there the rushy couch,
The pillow still indented, met his gaze,
And fix'd his eye in madness.—From that hour
A maniac wild the alien boy has been;
His garb with sea-weeds fringed, and his wan cheek,
The tablet of his mind, disorder'd, changed,
Fading, and worn with care. And if, by chance,
A sea-beat wanderer from the outstretch'd main
Views the lone exile, and with generous zeal
Hastes to the sandy beach, he suddenly
Darts 'mid the cavern'd cliffs, and leaves pursuit
To track him, where no footsteps but his own
Have e'er been known to venture! Yet he lives
A melancholy proof, that man may bear
All the rude storms of fate, and still suspire[3]
By the wide world forgotten!

POSTHUMOUS PUBLICATIONS

from Memoirs of the Late Mrs. Robinson, Written by Herself

(1801; comp. 1799–1800)

. . . In this venerable mansion [in Bristol] there was one chamber whose dismal and singular constructure left no doubt of its having been a part of the original monastery. It was supported by the mouldering arches of the cloisters; dark, Gothic, and opening on the minster[1] sanctuary,

[3] **suspire:** both meanings of "to breathe" and "to sigh" seem to commingle at this moment.

[1] **minster:** a monastery or Christian religious house.

not only by casement windows that shed a dim mid-day gloom, but by a narrow winding staircase, at the foot of which an iron-spiked door led to the long gloomy path of cloistered solitude. This place remained in the situation in which I describe it in the year 1776, and probably may, in a more ruined state, continue so to this hour.

In this awe-inspiring habitation, which I shall henceforth denominate the Minster-house, during a tempestuous night, on the twenty-seventh of November, 1758, I first opened my eyes to this world of duplicity and sorrow. I have often heard my mother say that a more stormy hour she never remembered. The wind whistled round the dark pinnacles of the minster tower, and the rain beat in torrents against the casements of her chamber. Through life the tempest has followed my footsteps; and I have in vain looked for a short interval of repose from the perseverance of sorrow. . . .

In my early days my father was prosperous, and my mother was the happiest of wives. She adored her children; she devoted her thoughts and divided her affections between them and the tenderest of husbands. Their spirits now, I trust, are in happier regions, blest, and re-united for ever.

If there could be found a fault in the conduct of my mother towards her children, it was that of a too unlimited indulgence, a too tender care, which but little served to arm their breast against the perpetual arrows of mortal vicissitude. My father's commercial concerns were crowned with prosperity. His house was opened by hospitality, and his generosity was only equalled by the liberality of fortune: every day augmented his successes; every hour seemed to increase his domestic felicity, till I attained my ninth year, when a change took place as sudden as it was unfortunate, at a moment when every luxury, every happiness, not only brightened the present, but gave promise of future, felicity: a scheme was suggested to my father, as wild and romantic as it was perilous to hazard, which was no less than that of establishing a whale fishery, on the coast of Labrador; and of civilizing the Esquimaux Indians, in order to employ them in the extensive undertaking. During two years this eccentric plan occupied his thoughts by day, his dreams by night: all the smiles of prosperity could not tranquillize the restless spirit: and, while he anticipated an acquirement of fame, he little considered the perils that would attend his fortune.

My mother (who, content with affluence, and happy in beholding the prosperity of her children, trembled at the fear of endangering either,) in vain endeavoured to dissuade my father from putting his favourite scheme in practice. In the early part of his youth he had been accustomed to a sea life, and, being born an American, his restless spirit was ever busied in plans for the increase of wealth and honour to his native country; whose fame and interest were then united to those of Britain. After many dreams of success and many conflicts betwixt prudence and ambition, he resolved on putting his scheme in practice: the potent witchery possessed his brain, and all the persuasive powers of reason shrunk before its magic.

Full of the important business, my misguided parent repaired to the metropolis;[2] and, on his arrival, laid the plan before the late Earl of Hilsborough, Sir Hugh Palliser, the late Earl of Bristol, Lord Chatham (father to the present William Pitt,[3]) the Chancellor Lord Northington, who was my god-father, and several other equally distinguished personages; who all not only approved the plan but commended the laudable and public spirit which induced my father to suggest it. The prospect appeared full of promise, and the Labrador whale fishery was expected to be equally productive with that of Greenland. My parent's commercial connections were of the highest respectability; while his own name for worth and integrity gave a powerful sanction to the eccentric undertaking.

In order to facilitate this plan, my father deemed it absolutely necessary to reside at least two years in America. My mother, who felt an invincible antipathy to the sea, heard his determination with grief and horror. All the persuasive powers of affection failed to detain him; all the pleadings of reason, prudence, a fond wife, and an infant family, proved ineffectual. My father was determined on departing, and my mother's unconquerable timidity prevented her being the companion of his voyage. From this epocha I date the sorrows of my family. . . .

Many months elapsed, and my mother continued to receive the kindest letters from that husband, whose rash scheme filled her bosom with regret and apprehension. At length the intervals became more frequent and protracted. The professions of regard, no longer flowing from the heart, assumed a laboured style, and seemed rather the

---

[2] **metropolis:** London.

[3] Robinson alludes to her many aristocratic acquaintances throughout her memoirs. **Sir Hugh Palliser** (1723–1796), an admiral, was one of several military figures acquainted with Mary Robinson. A rather malicious man, he unfairly court-martialed a friend and fellow officer. **William Pitt** (1759–1806), as Robinson indicates, was the son of another William Pitt, Lord Chatham (1708–1778). The younger Pitt was a brilliant politician and shrewd leader; he became prime minister at age 24.

efforts of honourable feeling than the involuntary language of confidential affection. My mother felt the change, and her affliction was infinite.

At length a total silence of several months awoke her mind to the sorrows of neglect, the torture of compunction: she now lamented the timidity which had divided her from a husband's bosom, the natural fondness which had bound her to her children;—for, while her heart bled with sorrow and palpitated with apprehension, the dreadful secret was unfolded,—and the cause of my father's silence was discovered to be a new attachment;—a mistress, whose resisting nerves could brave the stormy ocean, and who had consented to remain two years with him in the frozen wilds of America.

This intelligence nearly annihilated my mother, whose mind, though not strongly organized, was tenderly susceptible. She resigned herself to grief. I was then at an age to feel and to participate in her sorrows. I often wept to see her weep: I tried all my little skill to soothe her, but in vain: the first shock was followed by calamities of a different nature. The scheme in which my father had embarked his fortune failed, the Indians rose in a body, burst his settlement, murdered many of his people, and turned the produce of their toil adrift on the wide and merciless ocean. The *noble* patrons of his plan deceived him in their assurances of marine protection, and the island of promise presented a scene of barbarous desolation. This misfortune was rapidly followed by other commercial losses: and to complete the vexations which pressed heavily on my mother, her rash husband gave a bill of sale of his whole property, by the authority of which we were obliged to quit our home, and to endure those accumulated vicissitudes for which there appeared no remedy.

It was at this period of trial that my mother was enabled to prove, by that unerring touchstone adversity, who were her real and disinterested friends.[4] Many with affected commiseration dropped a tear, or rather seemed to drop one, on the disappointments of our family; while others, with a malignant triumph, condemned the expensive style in which my father had reared his children; the studied elegance which had characterized my mother's dress and habitation, and the hospitality which was now marked by the ungrateful epithet of prodigal luxuriance, but which had evinced the open liberality of my father's heart. . . .

This deviation from domestic faith was the only dark shade that marked my father's character. He possessed a soul brave, liberal, enlightened and ingenuous. He felt the impropriety of his conduct. Yet, though his mind was strongly organized, though his understanding was capacious, and his sense of honour delicate even to fastidiousness, he was still the dupe of his passions, the victim of an unfortunate attachment.

Within a few days after our arrival in London we were placed for education in a school at Chelsea. The mistress of this seminary was perhaps one of the most extraordinary women that ever graced, or disgraced, society: her name was Meribah Lorrington. She was the most extensively accomplished female that I ever remember to have met with: her mental powers were no less capable of cultivation than superiorly cultivated. Her father, whose name was Hull, had from her infancy been the master of an academy at Earl's Court, near Fulham; and early after his marriage losing his wife, he resolved on giving this daughter a masculine education. Meribah was early instructed in all the modern accomplishments, as well as in classical knowledge. She was mistress of the Latin, French, and Italian languages; she was said to be a perfect arithmetician and astronomer, and possessed the art of painting on silk to a degree of exquisite perfection. But, alas! with all these advantages she was addicted to one vice, which at times so completely absorbed her faculties, as to deprive her of every power, either mental or corporeal. Thus, daily and hourly, her superior acquirements, her enlightened understanding, yielded to the intemperance of her ruling infatuation, and every power of reflection seemed lost in the unfeminine propensity.

All that I ever learned I acquired from this extraordinary woman. In those hours when her senses were not intoxicated, she would delight in the task of instructing me. She had only five or six pupils, and it was my lot to be her particular favourite. She always, out of school, called me her little friend, and made no scruple of conversing with me, (sometimes half the night, for I slept in her chamber,) on domestic and confidential affairs. I felt for her a very sincere affection, and I listened with peculiar attention to all the lessons she inculcated. Once I recollect her mentioning the particular failing which disgraced so intelligent a being: she pleaded, in excuse of it, the immitigable regret of a widowed heart, and with compunction

---

[4] **disinterested**: not "uninterested," but rather, not concerned merely for personal or selfish interest. Robinson's notion of "real and disinterested" friends may anticipate Hazlitt's notion of the "sympathetic" powers of the imagination, as well as Keat's famous concept of "Negative Capability"; that is, the poet's polymorphic ability to assume the character of anyone or anything (see HAZLITT* and KEATS*).

declared that she flew to intoxication as the only refuge from the pang of prevailing sorrow. . . .

Shortly after my mother had established herself at Chelsea, on a summer's evening, as I was sitting at the window, I heard a deep sigh or rather a groan of anguish, which suddenly attracted my attention. The night was approaching rapidly, and I looked towards the gate before the house, where I observed a woman evidently labouring under excessive affliction; I instantly descended and approached her. She bursting into tears, asked whether I did not know her. Her dress was torn and filthy;—she was almost naked;—and an old bonnet, which nearly hid her face, so completely disfigured her features that I had not the smallest idea of the person who was then almost sinking before me. I gave her a small sum of money, and inquired the cause of her apparent agony: she took my hand and pressed it to her lips.—"Sweet girl," said she, "you are still the angel I ever knew you!"—I was astonished; she raised her bonnet—her fine dark eyes met mine. It was Mrs Lorrington.—I led her into the house; my mother was not at home. I took her to my chamber, and, with the assistance of a lady who was our French teacher, I clothed and comforted her. She refused to say how she came to be in so deplorable a situation; and took her leave. It was in vain that I entreated, that I conjured her to let me know where I might send to her. She refused to give me her address, but promised that in a few days she would call upon me again. It is impossible to describe the wretched appearance of this accomplished woman! The failing to which she had now yielded, as to a monster that would destroy her, was evident even at the moment when she was speaking to me. I saw no more of her: but to my infinite regret I was informed some years after, that she had died, the martyr of a premature decay, brought on by the indulgence of her propensity to intoxication, in the workhouse—of Chelsea! . . .

A few days after, Mr Robinson paid my mother a visit. We had now removed to Villars-street, York-buildings; my mother's fondness for books of a moral and religious character was not lost upon my new lover; and elegantly bound editions of Hervey's Meditations,[5] with some others of a similar description, were presented, as small tokens of admiration and respect. My mother was beguiled by these little interesting attentions, and soon began to feel a strong predilection in favour of Mr Robinson.

Every day some new mark of respect augmented my mother's favourable opinion; till Mr Robinson became so great a favourite, that he seemed to her the most perfect of existing beings. Just at this period my brother George sickened for the small-pox: my mother idolized him; he was dangerously ill:—Mr Robinson was indefatigable in his attentions, and my appearance on the stage was postponed till the period of his perfect recovery. Day and night Mr Robinson devoted himself to the task of consoling my mother, and of attending to her darling boy; hourly, and indeed momentarily, Mr Robinson's praises were reiterated with enthusiasm by my mother. He was "the kindest, the best of mortals!" the least addicted to worldly follies—and the man, of all others, whom she should adore as a *son in law*.

My brother recovered, at the period when I sickened from the infection of his disease. I felt little terror at the approaches of a dangerous and deforming malady; for, I know not why, but personal beauty has never been to me an object of material solicitude. It was now that Mr Robinson exerted all his assiduity to win my affections; it was when a destructive disorder menaced my features, and the few graces that nature had lent them, that he professed a disinterested fondness: every day he attended with the zeal of a brother; and that zeal made an impression of gratitude upon my heart, which was the source of all my succeeding sorrows.

During my illness Mr Robinson so powerfully wrought upon the feelings of my mother, that she prevailed on me to promise, in case I should recover, to give him my hand in marriage. The words of my father were frequently repeated, not without some inuendos that I refused my ready consent to an union with Mr Robinson, from a blind partiality to the libertine Captain *******. Repeatedly urged and hourly reminded of my father's vow, I at last consented; and the bans were published while I was yet lying on a bed of sickness;—I was then only a few months advanced in my sixteenth year.

My mother, whose affection for me was boundless, notwithstanding her hopes of my forming an alliance that would be productive of felicity, still felt the most severe pain at the thought of our approaching separation. She was estranged from a husband's affections: she had treasured up all her fondest hopes in the society of an only daughter: she knew that no earthly pleasure can compensate for the loss of that sweet sympathy which is the bond of union betwixt child and parent. Her regrets were

[5] **Hervey's Meditations**: a collection of devotional writings by James Hervey (1714–1758). Originally published in 1745 as "Meditations and Contemplations," his essays and collections of truisms were quite popular in the eighteenth century. Robinson probably received a later edition of Hervey's works, printed in 1757, simply titled *Meditations*.

infinite as they were evident;—and Mr Robinson, in order to remove any obstacle which this consideration might throw in the way of our marriage, voluntarily proposed that she should reside with us. He represented me as too young and inexperienced to superintend domestic concerns; and while he flattered my mother's *amour propre,*[6] he rather requested her aid as a sacrifice to his interest than as an obligation conferred on her.

The bans were published three successive Sundays at St Martin's church, and the day was fixed for our marriage;—*the twelfth of April.* It was not till all preliminaries were adjusted, that Mr Robinson, with much apparent agitation, suggested the necessity of keeping our union a secret. I was astonished at the proposal: but two reasons were given for his having made it, both of which seemed plausible: the first was, that Mr Robinson had still three months to serve before his articles to Messrs Vernon and Elderton expired; and the second was, the hope which a young lady entertained of forming a matrimonial union with Mr Robinson as soon as that period should arrive. The latter reason alarmed me; but I was most solemnly assured that all the affection was cherished on the lady's part; that Mr Robinson was particularly averse to the idea of such a marriage, and that as soon as he should become of age his independence would place him beyond the control of any person whatsoever.

I now proposed deferring our wedding day till that period. I pleaded that I thought myself too young to encounter the cares and important duties of domestic life: I shrunk from the idea of every thing clandestine, and anticipated a thousand ill consequences that might attend on a concealed marriage. My scruples only seemed to increase Mr Robinson's impatience for that ceremony which should make me his for ever. He represented to my mother the disapprobation which my father would not fail to evince at my adopting a theatrical life, in preference to engaging in an honourable and prosperous connexion. He so powerfully worked upon the credulity of my beloved parent, that she became a decided convert to his opinions. My youth, my person, he represented as the destined snares for my honour, on a public stage, where all the attractions of the mimic scene would combine to render me a fascinating object. He also persuaded her that my health would suffer by the fatigues and exertions of the profession, and that probably I might be induced to marry some man who would not approve of a *mother's* forming a part in our *domestic establishment.*

These circumstances were repeatedly urged in favour of the union. Still I felt an almost instinctive repugnance at the thought of a clandestine marriage. My mother, whose parental fondness was ever watchful for my safety, now imagined that my objections proceeded from a fixed partiality towards the libertine Captain *******, who, though he had not the temerity to present himself before my mother, persisted in writing to me, and in following me whenever I appeared in public. I never spoke to him after the story of his marriage was repeated to my mother; I never corresponded with him; but felt a decided and proud indignation whenever his name was mentioned in my presence.

My appearance on the stage had been put off from time to time, till Mr Garrick became impatient, and desired my mother to allow of his fixing the night of important trial. It was now that Mr Robinson and my mother united in persuading me to relinquish my project; and so perpetually, during three days, was I tormented on the subject,—so ridiculed for having permitted the bans to be published, and afterwards hesitating to fulfil my contract, that I consented—and was married.

As soon as the day of my wedding was fixed, it was deemed necessary that a total revolution should take place in my external appearance. I had till that period worn the habit of a child; and the dress of a woman so suddenly assumed sat rather awkwardly upon me. Still so juvenile was my appearance, that even two years after my union with Mr Robinson I was always accosted with the appellation of *Miss,* whenever I entered a shop, or was in company with strangers. My manners were no less childish than my appearance; only three months before I became a wife, I had dressed a doll; and such was my dislike to the idea of a matrimonial alliance, that the only circumstance which induced me to marry was that of being still permitted to reside with my mother, and to live separated, at least for some time, from my husband.

My heart, even when I knelt at the altar, was as free from any tender impression as it had been at the moment of my birth. I knew not the sensation of any sentiment beyond that of esteem; love was still a stranger to my bosom. I had never, then, seen the being who was destined to inspire a thought which might influence my fancy, or excite an interest in my mind; and I well remember that even while I was pronouncing the marriage vow my fancy involuntarily wandered to that scene where I had hoped to support myself with *éclat*[7] and reputation. . . .

[6] **amour propre:** self-esteem, vanity.

[7] **éclat:** radiance or ostentation; in this case, publicity.

The stated time of concealment elapsed, and still my husband was perpetually at Chambers in Lincoln's Inn. Still he was evidently under the control of his articles, and still desirous that our marriage should be kept a secret. My mother began to feel a considerable degree of inquietude upon the subject; particularly as she was informed that Mr Robinson was not exactly in that state of expectation which he had represented. She found that he was already of age, and that he had still some months to serve of his clerkship. She also heard that he was not the nephew and heir, but the illegitimate son of the man from whom he expected a handsome fortune: though he had an elder brother, now Commodore William Robinson, who was then in India reaping the fruits of industry under the patronage of Lord Clive.

It was now for the first time that my mother repented the influence she had used in promoting our union. She informed Mr Robinson that she apprehended some gross deception on his part, and that she would no longer consent to our marriage being kept a secret. The reputation of a darling child, she alleged, was at stake; and though during a few weeks the world might have been kept in ignorance of my marriage, some circumstances that had transpired now rendered an immediate disclosure absolutely necessary.

Mr Robinson, finding my mother inexorable, resolved on setting out for Wales, in order to avow our marriage and to present me to his *uncle,* for such he still obstinately denominated his father. My mother wished to avail herself of this opportunity to visit her friends at Bristol, and accordingly we set out on the journey; we passed through Oxford; visited the different colleges; proceeded to Blenheim, and made the *tour,* a tour of pleasure; with the hope of soothing my mother's resentment, and exhilarating my spirits, which were now perpetually dejected. I cannot help mentioning that shortly after my marriage I formed an acquaintance with a young lady, whose mind was no less romantic than my own; and while Mr Robinson was occupied at Chambers, we almost daily passed our morning hours in Westminster Abbey. It was to me a soothing and a gratifying scene of meditation.—I have often remained in the gloomy chapels of that sublime fabric,[8] till I became as it were an inhabitant of another world. The dim light of the Gothic windows, the vibration of my footsteps along the lofty aisles, the train of reflections that the scene inspired, were all suited to the temper of my soul: and the melancholy propensities of my earliest infancy seemed to revive with an instinctive energy, which rendered them the leading characteristics of my existence. Indeed the world has mistaken the character of my mind; I have ever been the reverse of volatile and dissipated; I mean not to write my own eulogy; though, with the candid and sensitive mind, I shall I trust succeed in my vindication.

On our arrival at Bristol, Mr Robinson thought it most adviseable to proceed towards Tregunter, the seat of his *uncle,* alone, in order to prepare him for my cordial reception, or to avoid the mortification I should experience, should he refuse to sanction our union. Mr Robinson left me a few guineas, and promised that his absence should be short and his affection increasing.

I had now been married near four months: and, though love was not the basis of my fidelity, honour, and a refined sense of feminine rectitude, attached me to the interest as well as to the person of my husband. I considered chastity as the brightest ornament that could embellish the female mind; and I regulated my conduct to that tenour which has principle more than affection to strengthen its progress. . . .

On the following morning [in London] Lords Northington, Lyttelton, and Colonel Ayscough, made their visits of ceremony. Mr Robinson was not at home, but I received them, though not without some embarrassment. I was yet a child, and wholly unacquainted with the manners of the world. Yet, young as I was, I became the traveller of its mazy and perilous paths;—at an age when girls are generally at school, or indeed scarcely emancipated from the nursery, I was presented in society as a wife,—and very nearly as a mother.

Lord Lyttelton, who was perhaps the most accomplished libertine that any age or country has produced, with considerable artifice inquired after Mr Robinson, professed his earnest desire to cultivate his acquaintance, and, on the following day, sent him a card of invitation. Lyttelton was an adept[9] in the artifices of fashionable intrigue: he

[8] **sublime fabric:** Robinson invokes a Burkean, as opposed to Longinian, sense of the sublime, which involves the simultaneous experiences of beauty and fear in viewing a lofty or grand subject, such as the towering Gothic architecture of Westminster Abbey. The archaic "fabric" for building or edifice reinforces the Gothic mood of this passage.

[9] **adept:** one who is completely skilled in his/her art. **Lord Lyttelton** (1744–1779), commonly called the "wicked Lord Lyttelton," was the opposite of his father, a sober and

plainly perceived that both Mr Robinson and myself were uninitiated in its mysteries: he knew that to undermine a wife's honour, he must become master of the husband's confidence; and Mr Robinson was too much pleased with the society of a man whose wit was only equalled by his profligacy, to shrink from such an association.

Fortunately for me, Lord Lyttelton was uniformly my aversion. His manners were overbearingly insolent, his language licentious, and his person slovenly even to a degree that was disgusting. Mr Robinson was in every respect the very reverse of his companion: he was unassuming, neat, and delicate in his conversation. I had not a wish to descend from the propriety of wedded life; and I abhorred, decidedly abhorred, the acquaintance with Lord Lyttelton.

In the course of a few days his lordship presented me with the works of Miss Aikin, (now Mrs Barbauld).[10] I read them with rapture; I thought them the most beautiful Poems I had ever seen, and considered the woman who could invent such poetry, as the most to be envied of human creatures. Lord Lyttelton had some taste for poetical compositions, and wrote verses with considerable facility.

On the following Monday I again visited the Pantheon. My dress was then white and silver. Again I was followed with attention. Lord Lyttelton was my *caveliere servante*[11] that evening, though, as usual, his chief attention was paid to Mr Robinson. During the concert he presented the Count de Belgioso, the Imperial Ambassador, one of the most accomplished foreigners I ever remember having met with. Lord Valentia was also introduced; but as his Lordship had recently made some éclat by his attentions to the celebrated Mrs Elliot, I rather avoided than wished to cultivate his acquaintance.

Mr Robinson's intercourse with the world was now rapidly augmenting. Every day was productive of some new association. . . .

Of those who frequented our house Lord Lyttelton was most decidedly my abhorrence; I knew that he frequently led my husband from the paths of domestic confidence to the haunts of profligate debasement. Towards me his Lordship affected great indifference; he has even in my presence declared, that no woman under thirty years of age was worth admiring; that even the antiquity of forty was far preferable to the insipidity of sixteen; and he generally concluded his observations by hoping he had not made "the *pretty child* angry."

I soon discovered that his intercourse with Lord Lyttelton produced a very considerable change in Mr Robinson's domestic deportment. They were constantly together, and the neglect which I experienced began to alarm me. I dedicated all my leisure hours to poetry: I wrote verses of all sorts; and Mr Robinson having mentioned that I had purposed appearing on the stage previous to my marriage, in the character of Cordelia, Lord Lyttelton facetiously christened me the Poetess Corry.

It was with extreme regret, and frequently with uncontrolable indignation, that I endured the neglect of my husband and the tauntings of the profligate Lyttelton—"The child," for so he generally called me, was deserted for the society of the most libertine men and the most abandoned women. Mr Robinson became not only careless of his wife, but of his pecuniary finances; while I was kept in total ignorance as to the resources which supported his increasing expenses. . . .

One forenoon Lord Lyttelton called in Hatton-garden, as was almost his daily custom, and, on finding that Mr Robinson was not at home, requested to speak with me on business of importance. I found him seemingly much distressed. He informed me that he had a secret to communicate of considerable moment both to my interest and happiness. I started. "Nothing, I trust in heaven, has befallen my husband!" said I with a voice scarcely articulate. Lord Lyttelton hesitated. "How little does that husband deserve the solicitude of such a wife!" said he; "but," continued his Lordship, "I fear that I have in some degree aided in alienating his conjugal affections. I could not bear to see such youth, such merit, so sacrificed"—"Speak briefly, my Lord," said I.—"Then," replied Lord Lyttelton, "I must inform you, that your husband is the most false and undeserving of that name! He has formed a connection with a woman of abandoned character; he lavishes on her those means of subsistence which you will shortly stand in need of."

---

upright figure in British political life. Eventually, the younger Lyttelton's "loose and prodigal habits occasioned a complete rupture with his family." He died at an early age, under rather unusual circumstances. The cynical Lyttelton made light of a dream in which it was revealed "he had not three days to live," and spread the story of his dream all over London. He died three days later, shortly after retiring to bed, having boasted that he should "bilk the ghost."

[10] **Miss Aikin**: as Robinson notes, "now Mrs. Barbauld." Anna Letitia Barbauld* was an influential poet and critic of the late eighteenth and early nineteenth century.

[11] **caveliere servante**: a lover or suitor.

"I do not believe it," said I, indignantly.—"Then you shall be convinced," answered his Lordship—"but remember, if you betray me, your true and zealous friend, I must fight your husband; for he never will forgive my having discovered his infidelity."

"It cannot be true," said I. "You have been misinformed."

"Then it has been by the woman who usurps your place in the affections of your husband," replied Lord Lyttelton: "from her I received the information: her name is Harriet Wilmot: she resides in Soho: your husband daily visits her."—I thought I should have fainted: but a torrent of tears recalled the ebbing current of my heart, and I grew proud in fortitude, though humbled in self-love.

"Now," said Lord Lyttelton, "if you are a woman of spirit, you will be *revenged!*" I shrunk with horror, and would have quitted the room. "Hear me," said he. "You cannot be a stranger to my motives for thus cultivating the friendship of your husband; my fortune is at your disposal. Robinson is a ruined man; his debts are considerable, and nothing but destruction can await you. Leave him! Command my powers to serve you."

I would hear no more—broke from him, and rushed out of the apartments. My sensations, my sufferings were undescribable.

I immediately took an hackney coach, and proceeded to Prince's-street, Soho;—Lord Lyttleton having given me the address of my rival. Language cannot describe what I suffered till I arrived at the lodgings of Miss Wilmot. The coachman knocked, a dirty servant girl opened the door. Her mistress was not at home, I quitted the coach and ascended to the drawing room: where the servant left me, after informing me that Miss W. would return in a very short time. I was now left alone.

I opened the chamber-door which led from the drawing room: a new white lustring sacque[12] and petticoat lay on the bed. While I was examining the room, a loud knocking at the street door alarmed me. I reentered the front apartment, and waited with a palpitating bosom till the being whose triumph had awakened both my pride and my resentment, appeared before me.

She was a handsome woman, though evidently some years older than myself. She wore a dress of printed Irish muslin, with a black gauze cloak and a chip hat, trimmed with pale lilac ribbons; she was tall, and had a very pleasing countenance: her manner was timid and confused; her lips as pale as ashes. I commiserated her distress, desired her not to be alarmed, and we took our seats, with increased composure.

"I came to inquire whether or not you are acquainted with a Mr Robinson," said I.

"I am," replied Miss Wilmot. "He visits me frequently." She drew off her glove as she spoke, and passing her hand over her eyes, I observed on her finger a ring, which I knew to have been my husband's.

"I have nothing more to say," added I, "but to request that you will favour me with Mr Robinson's address, I have something which I wish to convey to him." She smiled, and cast her eyes over my figure: my dress was a morning *dishabille*[13] of India muslin: with a bonnet of straw: and a white lawn cloak bordered with lace.

"You are Mr Robinson's wife," said she with a trembling voice: "I am sure you are; and probably this ring was yours; pray receive it—"

I declined taking the ring. She continued: "Had I known that Mr Robinson was the husband of such a woman—"

I rose to leave her.—She added: "I never will see him more—unworthy man—I never will again receive him." I could make no reply; but rose and departed. . . .

One day, I particularly remember, Mr Harris had invited a large party to dinner. John and Charles Morgan, Esqrs. members of parliament, with an old clergyman of the name of Jones, and several others were present. I was then within a fortnight of my perilous moment. One of the company expressed his satisfaction that I was come [to Wales] to give Tregunter a little stranger; and turning to Mr Harris, added, "you have just finished your house, in time for a nursery."

"No, no," replied Mr Harris, laughing, "they came here because *prison doors* were open to receive them." I felt my face redden to scarlet: every person present seemed to sympathize in my chagrin, and I was near sinking under the table with confusion. Mr Robinson's indignation was evident; but it was restrained by duty as well as necessity.

The manor-house was not yet finished; and a few days after our arrival Mr Harris informed me that he had

[12] **sacque:** Robinson probably has in mind "a loose gown worn by ladies," although eighteenth-century usage includes "an appendage of silk attached to the shoulders of such a dress, and forming a train."

[13] **dishabille:** literally "undressed," this French word has come to mean a very casual state of dress, such as a robe or nightgown.

no accommodations for my approaching confinement. Where was I to go? was the next question. After many family consultations, it was decided that I should remove to Trevecca-house, about a mile and a half distant, and there give to this miserable world my first born darling.

I removed to Trevecca; it was a spacious mansion at the foot of a stupendous mountain, which, from its form, was called the Sugar-loaf. A part of the building was converted into a flannel manufactory, and the inhabitants were of the Huntingdonian school. Here I enjoyed the sweet repose of solitude: here I wandered about woods entangled by the wild luxuriance of nature, or roved upon the mountain's side, while the blue vapours floated round its summit. O, God of Nature! Sovereign of the universe of wonders! in those interesting moments how fervently did I adore thee!

How often have I sat at my little parlour window and watched the pale moonbeams darting amidst the sombre and venerable yew trees that shed their solemn shade over the little garden. How often have I strolled down the woody paths, spangled with the dew of morning, and shaken off the briery branches that hung about me. How tranquil did I feel, escaped from kindred tyranny, and how little did I regret the busy scenes of fashionable folly. Unquestionably the Creator formed me with a strong propensity to adore the sublime and beautiful of his works! But it has never been my lot to meet with an associating mind, a congenial spirit, who could (as it were abstracted from the world,) find an universe in the sacred intercourse of soul, the sublime union of sensibility.

At Trevecca-house I was tranquil, if not perfectly happy. I there avoided the low taunts of uncultivated natures, the insolent vulgarity of pride, and the overbearing triumphs of a family, *whose loftiest branch* was as inferior to *my stock* as the *small weed* is beneath the *tallest tree* that overshades it. I had formed an union with a family who had neither sentiment nor sensibility: I was doomed to bear the society of ignorance and pride: I was treated as though I had been the most abject of beings, even at a time when my conscious spirit soared as far above their powers to wound it, as the mountain towered over the white battlements of my then solitary habitation.

After my removal to Trevecca I seldom saw Miss Robinson or Mrs Molly; Mr Harris never called on me; though I was not more than a mile and a half from Tregunter. At length the expected, though, to me, most perilous moment arrived, which awoke a new and tender interest in my bosom, which presented to my fondly beating heart my child,—my Maria. I cannot describe the sensations of my soul at the moment when I pressed the little darling to my bosom, my maternal bosom; when I kissed its hands, its cheeks, its forehead, as it nestled closely to my heart, and seemed to claim that affection which has never failed to warm it. She was the most beautiful of infants! I thought myself the happiest of mothers: her first smile appeared like something celestial,—something ordained to irradiate my dark and dreary prospect of existence. . . .

A short time after Mr Robinson was arrested. Now came my hour of trial. He was conveyed to the house of a sheriff's officer, and in a few days, detainers were lodged against him to the amount of twelve hundred pounds, chiefly the arrears of annuities, and other demands from Jew creditors; for I can proudly and with truth declare, that he did not at that time, *or at any period since,* owe fifty pounds for *me,* or to any tradesmen on *my* account whatever.

Mr Robinson knew that it would be useless to ask Mr Harris's assistance: indeed his mind was too much depressed to make an exertion for the arrangement of his affairs. He was, therefore, after waiting three weeks in the custody of a sheriff's officer, (during which time I never left him for a single hour, day or night) obliged to submit to the necessity of becoming a captive.

For myself I cared but little; all my anxiety was for Mr Robinson's repose and the health of my child. The apartment which we obtained was in the upper part of the building, overlooking a racquet-ground. Mr Robinson was expert in all exercises of strength, or activity, and he found that amusement daily which I could not partake of. I had other occupations of a more interesting nature, the care of a beloved and still helpless daughter.

During nine months and three weeks never once did I pass the threshold of our dreary habitation; though every allurement was offered, every effort was made, to draw me from my scene of domestic attachment. Numberless messages and letters from Lords Northington and Lyttelton, from Mr Fitzgerald, and many others, were conveyed to me. But they all, excepting Lord Northington's, were dictated in the language of gallantry, were replete with profusions of *love,* and wishes to release me from my unpleasant and humiliating situation—and were therefore treated with contempt, scorn, and indignation. For God can bear witness that, at that period, my mind had never entertained a thought of violating those vows which I had made to my husband at the altar.

What I suffered during this tedious captivity!—My little volume of Poems sold but indifferently: my health was considerably impaired; and the trifling income which Mr Robinson received from his father was scarcely sufficient to support him. I will not enter into a tedious detail of vulgar sorrows, of vulgar scenes; I seldom quitted my apartment, and never till the evening, when for air and exercise I walked on the racquet-ground with my husband.

It was during one of these night walks that my little daughter first blessed my ears with the articulation of words. The circumstance made a forcible and indelible impression on my mind. It was a clear moonlight evening; the infant was in the arms of her nursery maid; she was dancing her up and down, and I was playing with her; her eyes were fixed upon the moon, to which she pointed with her small forefinger;—on a sudden a cloud passed over it, and the child, with a slow falling of her hand, articulately sighed, *"all gone!"* This had been a customary expression with her maid, whenever the infant wanted any thing which it was deemed prudent to withhold or to hide from her. These little nothings will appear insignificant to the common reader; but to the parent whose heart is ennobled by sensibility, they will become matters of important interest. I can only add, that I walked till near midnight, watching every cloud that passed over the moon, and as often, with a rapturous sensation, hearing my little prattler repeat her observation.

Having much leisure and many melancholy hours, I again turned my thoughts towards the Muses. I chose *Captivity* for the subject of my pen, and soon composed a quarto poem of some length; it was superior to my former productions; but it was full of defects, replete with weak or laboured lines. I never now read my early compositions without a suffusion on my cheek, which marks my humble opinion of them. . . .

Were I to describe one half of what I suffered, during fifteen months captivity, the world would consider it as the invention of a novel. But Mr Robinson knows what I endured, and how patiently, how correctly I suited my mind to the strict propriety of wedded life: he knows, that my duty as a wife was exemplary, my chastity inviolate; he knows that neither poverty nor obscurity, neither the tauntings of the world nor his neglect, could tempt me even to the smallest error: he knows that I bore my afflicting humiliations with a cheerful, uncomplaining spirit; that I toiled honourably for his comfort; and that my attentions were exclusively dedicated to him and to my infant. . . .

Mr Robinson having once more obtained his liberty, how were we to subsist honourably and above reproach? He applied to his father, but every aid was refused; he could not follow his profession, because he had not completed his articles of clerkship. I resolved on turning my thoughts towards literary labour, and projected a variety of works, by which I hoped to obtain at least a decent independence. Alas! how little did I then know either the fatigue or the hazard of mental occupations! How little did I foresee that the day would come, when my health would be impaired, my thoughts perpetually employed, in so destructive a pursuit! At the moment that I write this page I feel in every fibre of my brain the fatal conviction that it is a *destroying labour.*

It was at this moment of anxiety, of hope, of fear, that my thoughts once more were turned to a dramatic life; and, walking with my husband in St James's Park, late in the autumn, we were accosted by Mr Brereton[14] of Drury-lane theatre. I had not seen him during the last two years, and he seemed rejoiced in having met us. At that period we lodged at Lyne's the confectioner in Old Bond-street. Mr Brereton went home and dined with us; and after dinner the conversation turned on my partiality to the stage, which he earnestly recommended as a scene of great promise to what he termed my promising talents. The idea rushed like electricity through my brain: I asked Mr Robinson's opinion, and he now readily consented to my making the trial. He had repeatedly written to his father, requesting even the smallest aid towards our support until he could embark in his profession; but every letter remained unanswered, and we had no hope but in our own mental exertions. . . .

An appointment was made in the Green-room of Drury-lane theatre. Mr Garrick, Mr Sheridan,[15] Mr Brereton, and my husband, were present; I there recited the principal scenes of Juliet, (Mr Brereton repeating those of Romeo,) and Mr Garrick, without hesitation, fixed on that character as the trial of my *début*. . . .

The theatre was crowded with fashionable spectators; the Green-room and Orchestra (where Mr Garrick sat during the night) were thronged with critics. My dress was a pale pink satin, trimmed with crape, richly spangled with silver; my head was ornamented with white

[14] **Brereton**: William Brereton (1751–1787) was an actor at Drury Lane, a prominent London theater, as well as at Covent Garden, a competing theater. He was, by all accounts, rather handsome but lacking in talent.

[15] **David Garrick** (1717–1779) was the most acclaimed actor of the eighteenth century. He was an actor, a manager, a patentee, a playwright, and a poet as well. Garrick was the manager of Drury Lane during Robinson's tenure there. **Richard Sheridan** was an extremely popular dramatist of the eighteenth century, whose masterpieces include *The Rivals* and *School for Scandal.*

feathers, and my monumental suit, for the last scene, was white satin and completely plain; excepting that I wore a veil of the most transparent gauze, which fell quite to my feet from the back of my head, and a string of beads round my waist, to which was suspended a cross appropriately fashioned.

When I approached the side wing my heart throbbed convulsively; I then began to fear that my resolution would fail, and I leaned upon the nurse's arm, almost fainting. Mr Sheridan and several other friends encouraged me to proceed; and at length, with trembling limbs and fearful apprehension, I approached the audience.

The thundering applause that greeted me, nearly over-powered all my faculties. I stood mute and bending with alarm, which did not subside till I had feebly articulated the few sentences of the first short scene, during the whole of which I had never once ventured to look at the audience.

On my return to the Green-room, I was again encouraged, as far as my looks were deemed deserving of approbation; for of my powers nothing yet could be known, my fears having as it were palsied both my voice and action. The second scene being the Masquerade, I had time to collect myself. I never shall forget the sensation which rushed through my bosom when I first looked towards the Pit. I beheld a gradual ascent of heads: all eyes were fixed upon me; and the sensation they conveyed was awfully impressive: but the keen, the penetrating eyes of Mr Garrick, darting their lustre from the centre of the orchestra, were, beyond all others, the objects most conspicuous.

As I acquired courage I found the applause augment; and the night was concluded with peals of clamorous approbation. I was complimented on all sides; but the praise of one object, whom most I wished to please, was flattering even to the extent of human vanity. I then experienced, for the first time in my life, a gratification which language could not utter. I heard one of the most fascinating men and the most distinguished geniuses of the age honour me with partial approbation: a new sensation seemed to awake in my bosom: I felt that emulation which the soul delights to encourage, where the attainment of fame will be pleasing to an esteemed object. I had till that period known no impulse beyond that of friendship; I had been an example of conjugal fidelity; but I had never known the perils to which the feeling heart is subjected in an union of regard wholly uninfluenced by the affections of the soul. . . .

The death of Sophia [her second daughter] so deeply affected my spirits, that I was rendered totally incapable of appearing again that season. I therefore obtained Mr Sheridan's permission to visit Bath for the recovery of my repose. From Bath I went to Bristol—to *Bristol!* Why does my pen seem suddenly arrested while I write the word? I know not why, but an undefinable melancholy always follows the idea of my native birthplace. I instantly beheld the Gothic structure, the lonely cloisters, the lofty aisles, of the antique minster:—for, within a few short paces of its walls, this breast, which has never known *one year of happiness,* first palpitated on inhaling the air of this bad world! Is it within its consecrated precincts that this heart shall shortly moulder? Heaven only knows, and to its will I bow implicitly.

I transcribe this passage on the twenty-ninth of March, 1800. I feel my health decaying, my spirit broken. I look back without regret that so many of my days are numbered; and, were it in my power to choose, I would not wish to measure them again:—but whither am I wandering? I will resume my melancholy story. . . .

It was now that I began to know the perils attendant on a dramatic life. It was at this period that the most alluring temptations were held out to alienate me from the paths of domestic quiet—domestic happiness I cannot say, for it never was my destiny to know it. But I had still the consolation of an unsullied name. I had the highest female patronage, a circle of the most respectable and partial friends. . . .

The flattering and zealous attentions which Mr Sheridan evinced were strikingly contrasting with the marked and increasing neglect of my husband. I now found that he supported two women, in one house, in Maiden-lane, Covent-garden. The one was a figure-dancer at Drury-lane theatre; the other, a woman of professed libertinism. With these he passed all his hours that he could steal from me; and I found that my salary was at times inadequate to the expenses which were incurred by an enlarged circle of new acquaintance, which Mr Robinson had formed since my appearance in the dramatic scene. Added to this, the bond creditors became so clamorous, that the whole of my Benefits were appropriated to their demands; and on the second year after my appearance at Drury-lane theatre, Mr Robinson once more persuaded me to make a visit at Tregunter.

I was now received with more civility, and more warmly welcomed, than I had been on any former arrival. Though the *assumed sanctity* of Miss Robinson's manners condemned a dramatic life, the labour was deemed *profitable,* and the supposed immorality was consequently *tolerated!* However repugnant to my feelings this visit was, still I hoped that it would promote my husband's interest, and confirm his reconciliation to his father; I therefore resolved on undertaking it. I now felt that I could support myself honourably; and the consciousness of independence is the only true felicity in this world of humiliations. . . .

I had then been married more than four years, my daughter Maria Elizabeth nearly three years old. I had been then seen, and known, at all public places from the age of fifteen; yet I knew as little of the world's deceptions, as though I had been educated in the deserts of Siberia. I believed every woman friendly, every man sincere, till I discovered proofs that their characters were deceptive. . . .

The play of The WINTER'S TALE was this season commanded by their Majesties. I never had performed before the royal family; and the first character in which I was destined to appear, was that of PERDITA. I had frequently played the part, both with the Hermione of Mrs Hartley and of Miss Farren:[16] but I felt a strange degree of alarm when I found my name announced to perform it before the royal family.

In the Green-room I was rallied on the occasion; and Mr Smith, whose gentlemanly manners and enlightened conversation rendered him an ornament to the profession, who performed the part of Leontes, laughingly exclaimed, "By Jove, Mrs Robinson, you will make a conquest of the Prince; for to-night you look handsomer than ever." I smiled at the unmerited compliment, and little foresaw the vast variety of events that would arise from that night's exhibition!

As I stood in the wing opposite the Prince's box, waiting to go on the stage, Mr Ford, the manager's son, and now a respectable defender of the laws, presented a friend who accompanied him; this friend was Lord Viscount Malden, now Earl of Essex.

We entered into conversation during a few minutes, the Prince of Wales all the time observing us, and frequently speaking to Colonel (now *General*) Lake, and to the Honourable Mr Legge,[17] brother to Lord Lewisham, who was in waiting on his Royal Highness. I hurried through the first scene, not without much embarrassment, owing to the fixed attention with which the Prince of Wales honoured me. Indeed, some flattering remarks which were made by his Royal Highness met my ear as I stood near his box, and I was overwhelmed with confusion.

The Prince's particular attention was observed by every one, and I was again rallied at the end of the play. On the last curtsy, the royal family condescendingly[18] returned a bow to the performers; but just as the curtain was falling, my eyes met those of the Prince of Wales; and, with a look that I *never shall forget*, he gently inclined his head a second time; I felt the compliment, and blushed my gratitude.

During the entertainment Lord Malden never ceased conversing with me: he was young, pleasing, and perfectly accomplished. He remarked the particular applause which the Prince had bestowed on my performance; said a thousand civil things; and detained me in conversation till the evening's performance was concluded.

I was now going to my chair, which waited, when I met the royal family crossing the stage. I was again honoured with a very marked and low bow from the Prince of Wales.—On my return home, I had a party to supper; and the whole conversation centred in encomiums on the person, graces, and amiable manners, of the illustrious heir apparent.

Within two or three days of this time Lord Malden made me a morning visit: Mr Robinson was not at home, and I received him rather awkwardly. But his Lordship's embarrassment far exceeded mine: he attempted to speak—paused, hesitated, apologized; I knew not why. He hoped I would pardon him; that I would not mention something he had to communicate; that I would consider the peculiar delicacy of his situation, and then act as I thought proper.—I could not comprehend his meaning, and therefore requested that he would be explicit.

---

[16] **Mrs Hartley** (1750?–1824), or Elizabeth Hartley, (maiden name, White), a celebrated actress. The identity of Mr. Hartley remains a secret. If Elizabeth Hartley preferred "Mrs. Hartley" to squelch rumors and discourage suitors, it was to no avail. Her stunning beauty and remarkable talent attracted many of the same figures in Mary Robinson's life, including "the wicked" Lord Lyttelton and Robert Fitzgerald. **Elizabeth Farren** (1762–1829), later Countess of Derby, was a well-beloved actress and singer. She was enormously popular, both for her beauty and her poise, eventually finding herself admitted into the highest stratum of society.

[17] **Colonel Lake** (1744–1808), later General Lake, was a successful general in the India campaigns. **Mr Legge**: William Legge, as Robinson notes, "brother to Lord Lewisham," and groom of the bedchamber to the young Prince of Wales.

[18] **condescendingly**: the word had a different connotation in the eighteenth century, meaning simply "to disregard one's superiority to a person; show kindness to an inferior." Our contemporary distaste for rigid demarcations of class imparts a necessary irony to the word.

After some moments of evident rumination he tremblingly drew a small letter from his pocket. I took it, and knew not what to say. It was addressed to PERDITA. I smiled, I believe rather sarcastically, and opened the *billet.* It contained only a few words, but those expressive of more than common civility: they were signed, FLORIZEL.[19]

"Well, my Lord, and what does this mean?" said I, half angry.

"Can you not guess the writer?" said Lord Malden.

"Perhaps yourself, my Lord," cried I gravely.

"Upon my honour, no," said the Viscount. "I should not have dared so to address you on so short an acquaintance."

I pressed him to tell me from whom the letter came.—He again hesitated; he seemed confused, and sorry that he had undertaken to deliver it. "I hope that I shall not forfeit your good opinion," said he, "but"—

"But what, my Lord?"

"I could not refuse,—for the letter is from the Prince of Wales."

I was astonished; I confess that I was agitated; but I was also somewhat sceptical as to the truth of Lord Malden's assertion. I returned a formal and a doubtful answer; and his Lordship shortly after took his leave.

A thousand times did I read this short but expressive letter; still I did not implicitly believe that it was written by the Prince; I rather considered it as an experiment made by Lord Malden, either on my vanity or propriety of conduct. On the next evening the Viscount repeated his visit: we had a card-party of six or seven, and the Prince of Wales was again the subject of unbounded panegyric. Lord Malden spoke of his Royal Highness's manners as the most polished and fascinating; of his temper, as the most engaging; and of his mind, the most replete with every amiable sentiment. I heard these praises, and my heart beat with conscious pride, while memory turned to the partial but delicately respectful letter which I had received on the preceding morning.

The next day Lord Malden brought me a second letter. He assured me that the Prince was most unhappy lest I should be offended at his conduct, and that he conjured me to go that night to the Oratorio,[20] where he would by some signal convince me that he was the writer of the letters, supposing I was still sceptical as to their authenticity.

I went to the Oratorio; and, on taking my seat in the balcony-box, the Prince almost instantaneously observed me. He held the printed bill before his face, and drew his hand across his forehead; still fixing his eyes on me. I was confused, and knew not what to do. My husband was with me, and I was fearful of his observing what passed. Still the Prince continued to make signs, such as moving his hand on the edge of the box as if writing, then speaking to the Duke of York, (then Bishop of Osnaburg), who also looked towards me with particular attention.

I now observed one of the gentlemen in waiting bring the Prince a glass of water: before he raised it to his lips he looked at me. So marked was his Royal Highness's conduct that many of the audience observed it; several persons in the Pit directed their gaze at the place where I sat; and, on the following day, one of the diurnal prints[21] observed that there was one passage in Dryden's Ode which seemed particularly interesting to the Prince of Wales, who

"Gazed on the fair
Who caused his care,
And sigh'd, and look'd, and sigh'd again."

However flattering it might have been to female vanity, to know that the most admired and most accomplished Prince in Europe was devotedly attached to me; however dangerous to the heart such idolatry as his Royal Highness, during many months, professed in almost daily letters, which were conveyed to me by Lord Malden, still I declined any interview with his Royal Highness. I was not insensible to all his powers of attraction; I thought him one of the most amiable of men. There was a beautiful ingenuousness in his language, a warm and enthusiastic adoration, expressed in every letter, which interested and charmed me. During the whole Spring till the theatre closed this correspondence continued; every day giving me some new assurance of inviolable affection.

After we had corresponded some months without ever speaking to each other, (for I still declined meeting

[19] **Florizel:** an author's note confesses "Those who have read *The Winter's Tale* will know the significance of these adopted names." Florizel is the Prince of Bohemia in Shakespeare's romance, who falls in love with Perdita, a highborn who has fallen on bitter circumstances. The Prince of Wales's note indicates he claims for himself the role of lover of "Perdita" Robinson.

[20] **Oratorio:** reference to an "oratorio night," when a theater offered oratorios (such as Handel's famous *Messiah*), in place of drama.

[21] **diurnal prints:** daily newspapers. Robinson was a victim of what we now call "the tabloids."

his Royal Highness, from a dread of the *éclat* which such a connection would produce, and the fear of injuring him in the opinion of his royal relatives), I received, through the hands of Lord Malden, the Prince's portrait in miniature, painted by the late Mr Meyer. This picture is now in my possession. Within the case was a small heart cut in paper, which I also have; on one side was written,*"Je ne change qu'en mourant."* On the other, *"Unalterable to my Perdita through life."*

During many months of confidential correspondence, I always offered his Royal Highness the best advice in my power; I disclaimed every sordid and interested thought; I recommended to him to be patient till he should become his own master; to wait till he knew more of my mind and manners before he engaged in a public attachment to me and, above all, to do nothing that might incur the displeasure of his Royal Highness's family. I entreated him to recollect that he was young, and led on by the impetuosity of passion; that should I consent to quit my profession and my husband, I should be thrown entirely on his mercy. I strongly pictured the temptations to which beauty would expose him; the many arts that would be practised to undermine me in his affections; the public abuse which calumny and envy would heap upon me; and the misery I should suffer, if, after I had given him every proof of confidence, he should change in his sentiments towards me. To all this I received repeated assurances of inviolable affection; and I most firmly believe that his Royal Highness meant what he professed: indeed, his soul was too ingenuous, his mind too liberal and his heart too susceptible to deceive premeditatedly, or to harbour, even for a moment the idea of deliberate deception.

At every interview with Lord Malden I perceived that he regretted the task he had undertaken; but he assured me that the Prince was almost frantic whenever he suggested a wish to decline interfering. Once I remember his Lordship's telling me that the late Duke of Cumberland had made him a visit early in the morning, at his house in Clarges-street, informing him that the Prince was most wretched on my account, and imploring him to continue his services only a short time longer. The Prince's establishment was then in agitation: at this period his Royal Highness still resided in Buckingham-house.

A proposal was now made that I should meet his Royal Highness at his apartments, in the disguise of male attire. I was accustomed to perform in that dress, and the Prince had seen me (I believe) in the character of the 'Irish Widow.' To this plan I decidedly objected. The indelicacy of such a step, as well as the danger of detection, made me shrink from the proposal. My refusal threw his Royal Highness into the most distressing agitation, as was expressed by the letter which I received on the following morning. Lord Malden again lamented that he had engaged himself in the intercourse, and declared that he had himself conceived so violent a passion for me that he was the most miserable and unfortunate of mortals.

During this period, though Mr Robinson was a stranger to my epistolary intercourse with the Prince, his conduct was entirely neglectful. He was perfectly careless respecting my fame and my repose; passed his leisure hours with the most abandoned women, and even my own servants complained of his illicit advances. I remember one, who was plain even to ugliness; she was short, ill-made, squalid, and dirty: once, on my return from a rehearsal, I found that this woman was locked with my husband in my chamber. I also knew that Mr Robinson continued his connection with a female who lodged in Maiden-lane, and who was only one of the few that proved his domestic apostacy.

His indifference naturally produced an alienation of esteem on my side, and the increasing adoration of the most enchanting of mortals hourly reconciled my mind to the idea of a separation. The unbounded assurances of lasting affection which I received from his Royal Highness in many scores of the most eloquent letters, the contempt which I experienced from my husband, and the perpetual labour which I underwent for his support, at length began to weary my fortitude. Still I was reluctant to become the theme of public animadversion, and still I remonstrated with my husband on the unkindness of his conduct.

The Narrative of Mrs Robinson closes here.

— CONTINUATION BY A FRIEND —
[MARIA ELIZABETH ROBINSON, HER DAUGHTER]

Among those persons who have at various periods attracted the attention of the public, there are few whose virtues have been so little known, or whose characters have been so unfairly estimated, as the subject of the preceding Memoir. To compress within narrow limits the numerous circumstances by which the later years of Mrs Robinson's life were chequered, will be a task of no little difficulty. The earlier periods of her existence, rendered more interesting as narrated by her own pen, have doubtless been justly appretiated by the reflecting and candid reader, whose sympathy they could not fail to awaken. That she lived not to conclude the history of a life scarcely less eventful than unfortunate, cannot but afford a subject of sincere regret.

The conflicts which shook the mind, and the passions which succeeded to each other in the breast of Mrs Robinson, at the period when her narrative closes, a crisis perhaps the most important in her life, may be more easily conceived than described. A laborious though captivating profession, the profits of which were unequal to the expenses of her establishment, and the assiduities of her illustrious lover, to whom she naturally looked for protection, combined to divide her attention and bewilder her inexperienced mind. The partiality of her royal admirer had begun to excite observation, to awaken curiosity, and to provoke the malignant passions, which, under an affected concern for decorum, assumed the guise of virtue. The daily prints teemed with hints of the favour of Mrs Robinson with "one whose manners were resistless, and whose smile was victory." These circumstances, added to the constant devoirs[22] of Lord Malden, whose attentions were as little understood as maliciously interpreted, conspired to distract a young creature, whose exposed situation, whose wavering and unformed character, rendered her but too obnoxious to a thousand errors and perils.

To terminate her correspondence with the Prince, appeared the most painful remedy that could be adopted by a heart fascinated with his accomplishments, and soothed by his professions of inviolable attachment. She was aware that, in the eye of the world, the reputation of the wife is supposed unsullied while the husband, enduring passively his dishonour, gives to her the sanction of his protection. The circles of fashion afforded more than one instance of this obliging acquiescence in matrimonial turpitude. Could Mrs Robinson have reconciled it to her own feelings to remain under the roof of her husband, whose protection she had forfeited, and to add insult to infidelity, the attentions of her illustrious admirer might have given to her popularity an additional éclat. Neither might her husband have suffered in his worldly prospects, from being to the motives of his royal visitor a little complaisantly blind. But her ingenuous nature would not permit her to render the man for whom she had once felt an affection an object of ridicule and contempt. She determined therefore to brave the world, and, for a support against its censures, to rely on the protection and friendship of him to whom she sacrificed its respect.

The managers of Drury-lane theatre suspecting that Mrs Robinson purposed, at the conclusion of the season, to withdraw from the stage, omitted no means that might tend to induce her to renew her engagements. With this view, they offered a considerable advance to her salary, while to their solicitations she returned undecisive answers. Hourly rising in a profession to which she was enthusiastically attached, the public plaudits, which her appearance never failed to excite, were too gratifying to be relinquished without regret.

During this irresolution, she was persecuted by numerous anonymous letters, which she continued to treat with derision or contempt. The correspondence between Mrs Robinson and the Prince had hitherto been merely epistolary. This intercourse had lasted several months, Mrs Robinson not having acquired sufficient courage to venture a personal interview, and bid defiance to the reproaches of the world.

At length, after many alternations of feeling, an interview with her royal lover was consented to by Mrs Robinson, and proposed, by the management of Lord Malden, to take place at his lordship's residence in Dean-street, May-fair. But the restricted situation of the Prince, controlled by a rigid tutor, rendered this project of difficult execution. A visit to Buckingham-house was then mentioned; to which Mrs Robinson positively objected as a rash attempt, abounding in peril to her august admirer. Lord Malden being again consulted, it was determined that the Prince should meet Mrs Robinson for a few moments at Kew, on the banks of the Thames, opposite to the old palace, then the summer residence of the elder princes. For an account of this incident, an extract from a letter of Mrs Robinson, written some years afterwards to a valued and since deceased friend, who during the period of these events resided in America, may not be unacceptable to the reader. The date of this letter is in 1783.

"At length an evening was fixed for this long dreaded interview. Lord Malden and myself dined at the inn on the island between Kew and Brentford. We waited the signal for crossing the river in a boat which had been engaged for the purpose. Heaven can witness how many conflicts my agitated heart endured at this most important moment! I admired the Prince; I felt grateful for his affection. He was the most engaging of created beings. I

[22] **devoirs:** acts of civility.

had corresponded with him during many months, and his eloquent letters, the exquisite sensibility which breathed through every line, his ardent professions of adoration, had combined to shake my feeble resolution. The handkerchief was waved on the opposite shore; but the signal was, by the dusk of the evening, rendered almost imperceptible. Lord Malden took my hand, I stepped into the boat, and in a few minutes we landed before the iron gates of old Kew palace. The interview was but of a moment. The Prince of Wales and the Duke of York (then Bishop of Osnaburg) were walking down the avenue. They hastened to meet us. A few words, and those scarcely articulate, were uttered by the Prince, when a noise of people approaching from the palace startled us. The moon was now rising; and the idea of being overheard, or of his Royal Highness being seen out at so unusual an hour terrified the whole group. After a few more words of the most affectionate nature uttered by the Prince, we parted, and Lord Malden and myself returned to the island. The Prince never quitted the avenue, nor the presence of the Duke of York, during the whole of this short meeting. Alas! my friend, if my mind was before influenced by esteem, it was now awakened to the most enthusiastic admiration. The rank of the Prince no longer chilled into awe that being, who now considered him as the lover and the friend. The graces of his person, the irresistible sweetness of his smile, the tenderness of his melodious yet manly voice, will be remembered by me till every vision of this changing scene shall be forgotten.

"Many and frequent were the interviews which afterwards took place at this romantic spot; our walks sometimes continued till past midnight, the Duke of York and Lord Malden were always of the party, our conversation was composed of general topics. The Prince had from his infancy been wholly secluded, and naturally took much pleasure in conversing about the busy world, its manners and pursuits, characters and scenery. Nothing could be more delightful or more rational than our midnight perambulations. I always wore a dark coloured habit; the rest of our party generally wrapped themselves in great coats to disguise them, excepting the Duke of York, who almost universally alarmed us by the display of a *buff*[23] coat, the most conspicuous colour he could have selected for an adventure of this nature. The polished and fascinating ingenuousness of his Royal Highness's manners contributed not a little to enliven our *promenades*. He sung with exquisite taste; and the tones of his voice, breaking on the silence of the night, have often appeared to my entranced senses like more than mortal melody. Often have I lamented the distance which destiny had placed between us: how would my soul have idolized such a *husband!* Alas! how often, in the ardent enthusiasm of my soul, have I formed the wish that being were *mine alone!* to whom partial millions were to look up for protection.

"The Duke of York was now on the eve of quitting the country for Hanover; the Prince was also on the point of receiving his first establishment; and the apprehension that his attachment to a married woman might injure his Royal Highness in the opinion of the world, rendered the caution which we invariably observed of the utmost importance. A considerable time elapsed in these delightful scenes of visionary happiness. The Prince's attachment seemed to increase daily, and I considered myself as the most blest of human beings. During some time we had enjoyed our meetings in the neighbourhood of Kew, and I now only looked forward to the adjusting of his Royal Highness's establishment for the public avowal of our mutual attachment.

"I had relinquished my profession. The last night of my appearance on the stage, I represented the character of Sir Harry Revel, in the comedy of 'The Miniature Picture,' written by Lady Craven; and the Irish Widow. On entering the Green-room, I informed Mr Moody, who played in the farce, that I should appear no more after that night; and, endeavouring to smile while I sung, I repeated,

'Oh joy to you all in full measure,
So wishes and prays Widow Brady!'

which were the last lines of my song in 'The Irish Widow.' This effort to conceal the emotion I felt on quitting a profession I enthusiastically loved, was of short duration; and I burst into tears on my appearance. My regret at recollecting that I was treading for the last time the boards where I had so often received the most gratifying testimonies of public approbation; where mental exertion had been emboldened by private worth; that I was flying from a happy certainty, perhaps to pursue the phantom disappointment, nearly overwhelmed my faculties, and for some time deprived me of the power of articulation. Fortunately, the person on the stage with me had to begin the scene, which allowed me time to collect myself. I went, however, mechanically dull through the business of the

[23] **buff**: dressed ox-leather, of a dull yellow color and velvety surface.

evening, and, notwithstanding the cheering expressions and applause of the audience, I was several times near fainting.

"The daily prints now indulged the malice of my enemies by the most scandalous paragraphs respecting the Prince of Wales and myself. I found it was now too late to stop the hourly augmenting torrent of abuse that was poured upon me from all quarters. Whenever I appeared in public, I was overwhelmed by the gazing of the multitude. I was frequently obliged to quit Ranelagh,[24] owing to the crowd which staring curiosity had assembled round my box; and, even in the streets of the metropolis, I scarcely ventured to enter a shop without experiencing the greatest inconvenience. Many hours have I waited till the crowd dispersed, which surrounded my carriage, in expectation of my quitting the shop. I cannot suppress a smile at the absurdity of such proceeding, when I remember that, during nearly three seasons, I was almost every night upon the stage, and that I had then been near five years with Mr Robinson at every fashionable place of entertainment. You, my dear Sir, in your quiet haunts of transatlantic simplicity, will find some difficulty in reconciling these things to your mind—these unaccountable instances of national absurdity. Yet, so it is. I am well assured, that were a being possessed of more than human endowments to visit this country, it would experience indifference, if not total neglect, while a less worthy mortal might be worshipped as the idol of its day, if whispered into notoriety by the comments of the multitude. But, thank Heaven! my heart was not formed in the mould of callous effrontery. I shuddered at the gulf before me, and felt small gratification in the knowledge of having taken a step, which many, who condemned, would have been no less willing to imitate, had they been placed in the same situation.

"Previous to my first interview with his Royal Highness, in one of his letters I was astonished to find a bond of the most solemn and binding nature, containing a promise of the sum of twenty thousand pounds, to be paid at the period of his Royal Highness's coming of age.

"This paper was signed by the Prince, and sealed with the royal arms. It was expressed in terms so liberal, so voluntary, so marked by true affection, that I had scarcely power to read it. My tears, excited by the most agonizing conflicts, obscured the letters, and nearly blotted out those sentiments, which will be impressed upon my mind till the latest period of my existence. Still, I felt shocked and mortified at the indelicate idea of entering into any pecuniary engagements with a Prince, on whose establishment I relied for the enjoyment of all that would render life desirable. I was surprised at receiving it; the idea of interest had never entered my mind: secure in the possession of his heart, I had in that delightful certainty counted all my future treasure. I had refused many splendid gifts which his Royal Highness had proposed ordering for me at Grey's and other jewellers. The Prince presented to me a few trifling ornaments, in the whole their value not exceeding one hundred guineas. Even these, on our separation, I returned to his Royal Highness through the hands of General Lake.

"The period now approached that was to destroy all the fairy visions which had filled my mind with dreams of happiness. At the moment when every thing was preparing for his Royal Highness's establishment, when I looked impatiently for the arrival of that day, in which I might behold my adored friend gracefully receiving the acclamations of his future subjects; when I might enjoy the public protection of that being for whom I gave up all, I received a letter from his Royal Highness, a cold and unkind letter—briefly informing me, that *'we must meet no more!'* . . .

"And now, my friend, suffer me to call GOD to witness, that I was unconscious why this decision had taken place in his Royal Highness's mind; only two days previous to this letter being written I had seen the Prince at Kew, and his affection appeared to be boundless as it was undiminished.

"Amazed, afflicted, beyond the power of utterance, I wrote immediately to his Royal Highness, requiring an explanation. He remained silent. Again I wrote, but received no elucidation of this most cruel and extraordinary mystery. The Prince was then at Windsor. I set out, in a small pony phaeton, wretched, and unaccompanied by any one except my postillion (a child of nine years of age). It was near dark when we quitted Hyde Park Corner. On my arrival at Hounslow, the inn-keeper informed me, that every carriage which had passed the heath for the last ten nights had been attacked and rifled. I confess the

[24] **Ranelagh:** a resort by the Thames in Chelsea, London. Opened to the public in 1742, the gardens of Ranelagh were a popular and fashionable place of entertainment. The buildings were razed in 1826, and the site purchased for the Royal Hospital.

idea of personal danger had no terrors for my mind in the state it then was, and the possibility of annihilation, divested of the crime of suicide, encouraged rather than diminished my determination of proceeding. We had scarcely reached the middle of the heath, when my horses were startled by the sudden appearance of a man rushing from the side of the road. The boy on perceiving him instantly spurred his pony, and, by a sudden bound of our light vehicle, the ruffian missed his grasp at the front rein. We now proceeded at full speed, while the footpad[25] ran endeavouring to overtake us. At length, my horses fortunately outrunning the perseverance of the assailant, we reached the first Magpie, a small inn on the heath, in safety. The alarm which, in spite of my resolution, this adventure had created, was augmented on my recollecting, for the first time, that I had then in my black stock[26] a brilliant stud of very considerable value, which could only have been possessed by the robber by strangling the wearer.

"If my heart palpitated with joy at my escape from assassination, a circumstance soon after occurred that did not tend to quiet my emotion. This was the appearance of Mr H. Meynel and Mrs A*******. My foreboding soul instantly beheld a rival, and, with jealous eagerness, interpreted the, hitherto, inexplicable conduct of the Prince, from his having frequently expressed his wish to know that lady.

"On my arrival the Prince would not see me. My agonies were now undescribable. I consulted with Lord Malden and the Duke of Dorset, whose honourable mind and truly disinterested friendship had, on many occasions, been exemplified towards me. They were both at a loss to divine any cause of this sudden change in the Prince's feelings. The Prince of Wales had hitherto assiduously sought opportunities to distinguish me more publicly than was prudent, in his Royal Highness's situation. This was in the month of August. On the fourth of the preceding June, I went, by his desire, into the Chamberlain's box at the birth night ball; the distressing observation of the circle was drawn towards the part of the box in which I sat by the marked and injudicious attentions of his Royal Highness. I had not been arrived many minutes before I witnessed a singular species of fashionable coquetry. Previous to his Highness's beginning his minuet, I perceived a woman of high rank select from the *bouquet* which she wore two rose buds, which she gave to the Prince, as he afterwards informed me, 'emblematical of herself and him,' I observed his Royal Highness immediately beckon to a nobleman who has since formed a part of his establishment, and, looking most earnestly at me, whisper a few words, at the same time presenting to him his newly acquired trophy. In a few moments Lord C. entered the Chamberlain's box, and, giving the rosebuds into my hands, informed me that he was commissioned by the Prince to do so. I placed them in my bosom, and, I confess, felt proud of the power by which I thus publicly mortified an exalted rival. His Royal Highness now avowedly distinguished me at all public places of entertainment, at the King's hunt, near Windsor, at the reviews, and at the theatres. The Prince only seemed happy in evincing his affection towards me.

"How terrible then was the change to my feelings! And I again most SOLEMNLY REPEAT, that I was totally ignorant of any JUST CAUSE for so sudden an alteration.

"My 'good-natured friends' now carefully informed me of the multitude of secret enemies who were ever employed in estranging the Prince's mind from me. So fascinating, so illustrious a lover could not fail to excite the envy of my own sex. Women of all descriptions were emulous of attracting his Royal Highness's attention. Alas! I had neither *rank* nor power to oppose such adversaries. Every engine[27] of female malice was set in motion to destroy my repose, and every petty calumny was repeated with tenfold embellishments. Tales of the most infamous and glaring falsehood were invented, and I was again assailed by pamphlets, by paragraphs, and caricatures, and all the artillery of slander, while the only being to whom I then looked up for protection, was so situated as to be unable to afford it.

"Thus perplexed, I wrote to you, my friend, and implored your advice. But you were far away; your delighted soul was absorbed in cherishing the plant of human liberty, which has since blossomed with independent splendour over your happy provinces. Eagerly did I wait for the arrival of the packet, but no answer was returned. In the anguish of my soul, I once more addressed the Prince of Wales; I complained, perhaps too vehemently, of his

[25] **footpad:** a highwayman who robs on foot.

[26] **stock:** a piece of neckwear.

[27] **engine:** device.

injustice; of the calumnies which had been by my enemies fabricated against me, of the falsehood of which he was but too sensible. I conjured him to render me justice. He did so; he wrote me a most eloquent letter, disclaiming the causes alleged by a calumniating world, and fully acquitting me of the charges which had been propagated to destroy me.

"I resided now in Cork-street, Burlington-gardens. The house, which was neat, but by no means splendid, had recently been fitted up for the reception of the Countess of Derby, on her separation from her lord. My situation now every hour became more irksome. The Prince still unkindly persisted in withdrawing himself from my society. I was now deeply involved in debt, which I despaired of ever having the power to discharge. I had quitted both my husband and my profession:—the retrospect was dreadful!

"My estrangement from the Prince was now the theme of public animadversion, while the newly invigorated shafts of my old enemies, the daily prints, were again hurled upon my defenceless head with tenfold fury.—The regrets of Mr Robinson, now that he had *lost* me, became insupportable;—he constantly wrote to me in the language of unbounded affection; nor did he fail, when we met, to express his agony at our separation, and even a wish for our reunion.

"I had, at one period, resolved on returning to my profession; but some friends whom I consulted, dreaded that the public would not suffer my reappearance on the stage. This idea intimidated me, and precluded my efforts for that independence of which my romantic credulity had robbed me. I was thus fatally induced to relinquish what would have proved an ample and honourable resource for myself and my child. My debts accumulated to near seven thousand pounds. My creditors, whose insulting illiberality could only be equalled by their unbounded impositions, hourly assailed me.

"I was, in the mean time, wholly neglected by the Prince, while the assiduities of Lord Malden daily increased. I had no other friend on whom I could rely for assistance or protection. When I say protection, I would not be understood to mean *pecuniary* assistance, Lord Malden being, at the time alluded to, even poorer than myself: the death of his lordship's grandmother, Lady Frances Coningsby, had not then placed him above the penury of his own small income.

"Lord Malden's attentions to me again exposed him to all the humiliation of former periods. The Prince assured me once more of his wishes to renew our former friendship and affection, and urged me to meet him at the house of Lord Malden in Clarges-street. I was at this period little less than frantic, deeply involved in debt, persecuted by my enemies, and perpetually reproached by my relations. I would joyfully have resigned an existence now become to me an intolerable burthen; yet my pride was not less than my sorrow, and I resolved, whatever my heart might suffer, to wear a placid countenance when I met the inquiring glances of my triumphant enemies.

"After much hesitation, by the advice of Lord Malden, I consented to meet his Royal Highness. He accosted me with every appearance of tender attachment, declaring that he had never for one moment ceased to love me—but, that I had many concealed enemies, who were exerting every effort to undermine me. We passed some hours in the most friendly and delightful conversation, and I began to flatter myself that all our differences were adjusted.—But what words can express my surprise and chagrin, when, on meeting his Royal Highness *the very next day* in Hyde Park, he turned his head to avoid seeing me, and even affected *not to know me!*

"Overwhelmed by this blow, my distress knew no limits. Yet *Heaven* can witness the truth of my assertions, even, in this moment of complete despair, when oppression bowed me to the earth, I blamed not the Prince. I did then, and ever shall, consider his mind as nobly and honourably organized, nor could I teach myself to believe, that a heart the seat of so many virtues, could possibly become inhuman and unjust. I had been taught from my infancy to believe that elevated stations are surrounded by delusive visions, which glitter but to dazzle, like an unsubstantial meteor, and flatter to betray. With legions of these phantoms it has been my fate to encounter, I have been unceasingly marked by their persecutions, and shall at length become their victim."

Here the narrative of Mrs Robinson breaks off, with some reflections to which the recital had given rise. Though diligent search has been made to elucidate the obscurity in which the preceding events are involved, but little information has been gained. All that can be learned with certainty is her final separation from the Prince of Wales in the year 1781.

The genius and engaging manners of Mrs Robinson, who was still very young, had procured her the friendship of many of the most enlightened men of this age and country: her house was the *rendezvous* of talents. While yet unconscious of the powers of her mind, which had scarcely then unfolded itself, she was honoured with the acquaintance and esteem of Sir Joshua Reynolds, Mess.

Sheridan, Burke, Henderson, Wilkes, Sir John Elliot,[28] &c. men of distinguished talents and character. But though surrounded by the wise, the witty, and the gay, her mind, naturally pensive, was still devoured by secret sorrow; neither could the blandishments of flattery, nor the soothings of friendship, extract the arrow that rankled in her heart. Involved beyond the power of extrication, she determined on quitting England, and making a tour to Paris. . . .

from THE WILD WREATH

ed. Maria Elizabeth Robinson
(1804)

The Wint'ry Day

— 1 —

Is it in mansions rich and gay,
　On downy beds, or couches warm
That NATURE owns the WINT'RY DAY,
　Or shrinks to hear the howling storm? —
　　Ah, No! —
'Tis on the bleak and barren heath,
　Where Mis'ry feels the shaft of Death,
As to the dark and freezing grave
　Her children, — not a friend to save, —
　　Unheeded go.

— 2 —

Is it in chambers silken drest,
　At tables which profusions heap:
Is it on pillows soft to rest,
　In dreams of long and balmy sleep?
　　Ah, No! —
'Tis in the rushy hut obscure,
　Where Poverty's low sons endure:
And, scarcely daring to repine,
　On a straw pallet, mute, recline,
　　O'erwhelm'd with woe!

— 3 —

Is it to flaunt in warm attire?
　To laugh, and feast, and dance and sing?
To crowd around the blazing fire?
　And make the roof with revels ring? —
　　Ah, No! —
'Tis on the prison's flinty floor,
'Tis where the deaf'ning whirlwinds roar;
'Tis when the sea-boy on the mast
　Hears the waves bounding to the blast,
　　And looks below!

— 4 —

Is it beneath the taper's ray
　The banquet's luxury to share,
And waste the midnight hour away
　With Fashion's splendid vot'ries there?
　　Ah, No! —
'Tis in the cheerless naked room
　Where Misery's victims wait their doom:
Where a fond mother famish'd dies,
　While forth a frantic father flies.
　　Man's desp'rate foe!

— 5 —

Is it to lavish fortune's store
　In vain, fantastic, empty joys!
To scatter 'round the glittering ore,
　And covet Folly's gilded toys?
　　Ah, No! —
'Tis in the silent spot obscure,
　Where, forc'd *all* sorrows to endure,
Pale GENIUS learns (OH! LESSON SAD!)
　To court the vain, and on *the bad*,
　　FALSE PRAISE BESTOW!

— 6 —

Is it where gamesters, thronging round,
　Their shining heaps of wealth display?
Where CHANCE's giddy tribes are found
　Sporting their giddy hours away?
　　Ah, No!

[28] **Sir Joshua Reynolds*** (1723–1792), the famous painter, produced over 2,000 portraits and historical paintings. His wit and charm made him popular in the social circles of London. **Edmund Burke*** (1729–1797), the famous political writer and statesman. **Henderson,** most likely refers to the actor John Henderson. **John Wilkes** (1727–1797) was a politician and journalist. Something of a demagogue, he is remembered both as a champion for political freedom and as a misogynist and a libertine.

'Tis where neglected Virtue sighs;
Where *Hope,* exhausted, silent dies;
Where *Merit* starves, by *Pride* oppress,
'Till ev'ry stream that warms the breast
Forbears to flow.

A London Summer Morning
(1804)

Who has not wak'd to list[1] the busy sounds
Of SUMMER MORNING, in the sultry smoke
Of noisy LONDON?—On the pavement hot
The sooty Chimney-boy, with dingy face
And tatter'd covering, shrilly bawls his trade,
Rousing the sleepy House-maid. At the door
The Milk-pail rattles, and the tinkling bell
Proclaims the Dustman's office; while the street
Is lost in clouds imperious. Now begins
The din of Hackney-coaches, Waggons, Carts;
While Tin-men's shops, and noisy Trunk-makers,
Knife-grinders, Coopers, squeaking Cork-cutters,
Fruit-barrows, and the hunger-giving cries
Of Vegetable-venders, fill the air.
Now ev'ry Shop displays its varied trade;
And the fresh-sprinkled pavement cools the feet
Of early walkers. At the private door
The ruddy House-maid twirls the busy mop,
Annoying the smart 'prentice, or neat girl
Tripping with band-box[2] lightly. Now the Sun
Darts burning splendor on the glitt'ring pane,
Save where the canvas awning throws a shade
On the gay merchandize. Now spruce and trim
In shops, where beauty smiles with industry,
Sits the smart damsel, while the passenger
Peeps through the window, watching ev'ry charm.
Now Pastry dainties catch the eyes minute
Of hummy insects, while the slimy snare[3]
Waits to enthral them. Now the Lamp-lighter
Mounts the slight ladder, nimbly venturous,
To trim the half-fill'd lamp; while at his feet
The Pot-boy yells discordant. All along
The sultry pavement, the Old Clothes-man cries
In tone monotonous, and sidelong views
The area for his traffic: now the bag
Is slily open'd, and the half worn-suit
(Sometimes the pilfer'd treasure of the base
Domestic spoiler) for one half its worth
Sinks in the green abyss. The porter now
Bears his huge load along the burning way;
And the poor POET wakes from busy dreams,
To paint THE SUMMER MORNING.

[1] **list:** Robinson puns on the meaning "to listen," and the listing or cataloguing of sounds and activities in the poem.

[2] **band-box:** a light cardboard package, especially for neckties or clothing.

[3] **slimy snare:** refers to birdlime or slime, a viscous, sticky substance used to catch small birds.

The Poet's Garret
(1804)

Come, sportive Fancy! Come with me, and trace
The POET'S Attic-home![1] The lofty seat
Of th' Heaven-tutor'd Nine! The airy throne
Of bold Imagination, rapture-fraught,
Above the herd of mortals!—All around,
A solemn stillness seems to guard the scene,
Nursing the brood of thought; a thriving brood,
In the rich mazes of the cultur'd brain.
Upon thy altar, an old worm-eat board,
The pannel of a broken door, or lid
Of a strong coffer, plac'd on three-legg'd stool,
Stand quires of paper, white and beautiful;
Paper, by Destiny ordain'd to be
Scrawl'd o'er and blotted, dash'd and scratch'd, and torn,
Or mark'd with lines severe, or scatter'd wide
In rage impetuous! Sonnet, Song, and Ode;
Satire, and Epigram, a[n]d smart *Charade,*
Neat Paragraph, or legendary Tale
Of short and simple metre; each by turns
Will there delight the reader.

[1] **Attic-home:** Robinson is indulging in another pun: attic is another word for garret, the highest room in a house, but it is also an adjective meaning "Greek" or "Athenian." The "attic home" of the poet implies a grounding in Greek poetry, and a high, "attic" style. **Heaven-tutor'd nine:** the nine muses who inspire learning and the arts, particularly poetry and music. According to the Greek poet Hesiod, these nine sisters are the offspring of Zeus and Mnemosyne (Memory).

On the bed
Lies an old rusty "suit of solemn black,"
Brush'd thread-bare, and with brown unglossy hue
Grown rather ancient. On the floor is seen
A pair of silken hose, whose footing bad
Shews they are travellers, but who still bear
Marks somewhat *holy*. At the scanty fire
A chop turns round, by packthread strongly held;
And on the blackened bar a vessel shines
Of batter'd pewter, just half-fill'd, and warm,
With *Whitbread's* beverage pure.[2] The kitten purs,
Anticipating dinner; while the wind
Whistles through broken panes, and drifted snow
Carpets the parapet with spotless garb
Of vestal coldness.—Now the sullen hour
(The fifth hour after noon) with dusky hand
Closes the lids of day. The farthing light
Gleams through the cobweb'd chamber, and THE BARD
Concludes his pen's hard labour. Now he eats
With appetite voracious! Nothing sad
That the costly plate, nor the napkin fine,
Nor china rich, nor sav'ry viands greet
His eye, or palate. On his lyric board
A sheet of paper serves for table cloth;
A heap of salt is serv'd (Oh! heav'nly treat,)
On *Ode Pindaric!*[3] while his tuneful Puss
Scratches his slipper, for her fragment sweet,
And sings her love-song, soft, yet mournfully.

Mocking the pillar Doric, or the roof
Of architecture Gothic, all around
The well-known ballads flit, of Grub-street[4] fame!
The casement broke gives breath celestial
To the long *"Dying Speech,"* or gently fans
The love-enflaming Sonnet. 'Round about
Small scraps of paper lie, torn vestiges
Of an unquiet fancy: here a page
Of flights poetic; here a Dedication;
A list of *Dramatis Personæ* bold,
Of heroes yet unborn, and lofty dames,
Of perishable compound "light as air,"
But sentenc'd to oblivion!
On a shelf,
Yclept[5] a mantle-piece, a phial stands,
Half-fill'd with potent spirits, clear and strong,
Which sometimes haunt the Poet's restless brain,
And fill his mind with fancies whimsical.

Poor Poet! happy art thou, thus remov'd
From pride and folly! For, in thy domain
Thou cans't command thy subjects, fill thy lines
With the all-conq'ring weapon *Heav'n* bestows
In the grey-goose's wing! which, tow'ring high,
Bears thy rich fancy to immortal fame!

[2] **Whitbread's beverage pure:** beer.

[3] **Ode Pindaric:** an ode, or exalted poetical address, after the style of the early Greek lyric poet Pindar.

[4] **Grub-street:** a street in London inhabited primarily by hack writers. Robinson pokes fun at her aspiring poet, who achieves an attic style by living in a literal attic on Grub-street, and who wields "th' all-conquering weapon Heaven bestows / On the grey goose's wing!," that is, a pen.

[5] **Yclept:** archaic form of "called."

from THE POETICAL WORKS OF THE LATE MRS. MARY ROBINSON (1806)

January, 1795

PAVEMENT slippery, people sneezing,
Lords in ermine, beggars freezing;
Titled gluttons dainties carving,
Genius in a garret starving.

Lofty mansions, warm and spacious;
Courtiers cringing and voracious;
Misers scarce the wretched heeding;
Gallant soldiers fighting, bleeding.

Wives who laugh at passive spouses;
Theatres, and meeting-houses;
Balls, where simp'ring misses languish;
Hospitals, and groans of anguish.

Arts and sciences bewailing;
Commerce drooping, credit failing;
Placemen mocking subjects loyal;
Separations, weddings royal.

Authors who can't earn a dinner;
Many a subtle rogue a winner;
Fugitives for shelter seeking;
Misers hoarding, tradesmen breaking.

Taste and talents quite deserted,
All the laws of truth perverted,
Arrogance o'er merit soaring,
Merit silently deploring

Ladies gambling night and morning,
Fools the works of genius scorning,
Ancient dames for girls mistaken,
Youthful damsels quite forsaken.

Some in luxury delighting,
More in talking than in fighting,
Lovers old, and beaux decrepid,
Lordlings empty and insipid.

Poets, painters, and musicians,
Lawyers, doctors, politicians:
Pamphlets, newspapers, and odes,
Seeking fame by different roads.

Gallant souls with empty purses,
Generals only fit for nurses,
School-boys, smit with martial spirit,
Taking place of veteran merit.

Honest men who can't get places,
Knaves who show unblushing faces,
Ruin hasten'd, peace retarded,
Candour spurn'd, and art rewarded.

from The Progress of Liberty

(1806, comp. c. 1796)

from BOOK FIRST

HAIL, Liberty sublime! hail godlike power,
Coeval[1] with the skies, to earth new born,
Thou parent of delight, thou source refined
Of human energy! Thou fountain vast
From whose immortal stream the soul of man
Imbibes celestial fervour! But for thee,
O! best and noblest attribute of God!
Who would the coil endure of mortal woe,
The frowns of fortune, or the taunts of pride,
Float with the gale, or buffet with the storm,
Who labour through the busy dream of time,
War with oppression, or resist the base!
Opposing ever, and by each opposed,
To count succeeding conflicts, and to die?
Hail, Liberty! legitimate of Heaven!
Who, on a mountain's solitary brow
First started into life, thy sire, old Time,
Thy mother, blooming, innocent and gay,
The Genius of the scene! Thy beauteous form
She gave to nature, on whose fragrant lap,
Nursed by the breath of morn, each glowing vein
Soon throbb'd with healthful streams. Thy sparkling
eyes
Snatch'd radiance from the sun! while ev'ry limb,
By custom unrestrain'd, grew firm and strong.
Thy midnight cradle, rock'd by howling winds,
Lull'd thee to wholesome rest. Thy bev'rage pure,
The wild brook gushing from the rocky steep,
And foaming, unimpeded, down the vale.
For thee no victim bled, no groan of death
Stole on the sighing gale to pitying Heaven!

. . . .

. . . On Italia's shores,[2]
On every plain, on every mountain top,
The voice of nature speaks, in mighty sounds,
To bid thee tremble! Then, O! nature, say—
Shall rich Italia's bowers, her citron shades,
Her vales prolific, mountains golden clad,
And rivers fringed with nectar-teeming groves,
Re-echo with the mighty song of praise
To empyrean[3] space, while shackled still
The man of colour dies? Shall torrid suns
Shoot downward their hot beams on misery's race,
And call forth luxuries to pamper pride,
Steep'd in the Ethiop's tears, the Ethiop's blood!
Shall the caprice of nature, the deep tint
Of sultry climes, the feature varying,
Or the uncultured mind, endure the scourge
Of sordid tyranny, or heap the stores
Of his fair fellow man, whose ruddy cheek

[1] **Coeval:** created at the same time.

[2] **Italia's shores:** ancient Rome, as well as Robinson's contemporary Europe, profitted from empire building in Africa. Robinson suggests that the freedom and dignity of Rome were compromised by the presence of slavery, just as "Italia's shores" are marred by similar inhumanities. While Portugal was a more conspicuous slave-trading nation, Italy had always had its eye on Ethiopia, as evidenced by Mussolini's 1935 invasion of that country.

[3] **empyrean:** the highest heaven, thought to be the abode of God.

Knows not the tear of pity; whose white breast
Conceals a heart, than adamant[4] more hard,
More cruel than the tiger's! Bend thy gaze,
O happy offspring of a temper'd clime,
On whom the partial hand of nature set
The stamp of bloomy tints, proportions fine,
Unmixing with the goodly outside show
The mind appropriate; bend thy pitying gaze
To Zembla's frozen sphere,[5] where in his hut,
Roof'd by the rocky steep, the savage smiles,
In conscious freedom smiles, and mocks the storm
That howls along the sky. Th' unshackled limb,
Cloth'd in the shaggy hide of uncouth bear,
Or the fleet mountain elk, bounds o'er the cliff
The free-born tenant of the desert wild.
The glow of liberty, through every vein
Bids sensate streams revolve; the dusky path
Of midnight solitudes no terror brings,
Because he fears no lord. The prowling wolf,
Whose eye-balls redden 'midst the world of gloom,
Yells fierce defiance, form'd by nature's law
To share the desert's freedom. O'er the sky
The despot darkness reigns, in sullen pride,
Half the devoted year. His ebon wing
O'ershadows the blank space: his chilling breath
Benumbs the breast of nature; on his brow,
Myriads of stars with lucid lustre gem
His boundless diadem! The savage cheek
Smiles at the potent spoiler; braves his frown;
And while the partial gloom is most opaque,
Still vaunts the mind unfetter'd! If for these
Indulgent nature breaks the bonds of woe,
Gilding the deepest solitudes of night
With the pure flame of liberty sublime;
If for the untaught sons of gelid[6] climes
Health cheers the darkest hour with vigorous age,
Shall the poor African, the passive slave,
Born in the bland effulgence of broad day,
Cherish'd by torrid splendours, while around
The plains prolific teem with honey'd stores
Of Afric's burning soil; shall such a wretch
Sink prematurely to a grave obscure,
No tear to grace his ashes? Or suspire,
To wear submission's long and goading chain,
To drink the tear, that down his swarthy cheek
Flows fast, to moisten his toil-fever'd lip,
Parch'd by the noontide blaze? Shall he endure
The frequent lash, the agonizing scourge,
The day of labour, and the night of pain;
Expose his naked limbs to burning gales;
Faint in the sun, and wither in the storm;
Traverse hot sands, imbibe the morbid breeze,
Wing'd with contagion, while his blister'd feet,
Scorch'd by the vertical and raging beam,
Pour the swift life-stream? Shall his frenzied eyes,
Oh! worst of mortal miseries! behold
The darling of his soul, his sable love,
Selected from the trembling, timid throng
By the wan tyrant, whose licentious touch
Seals the dark flat of the slave's despair!
Humanity! from thee the suppliant claims
The meed of retribution! Thy pure flame
Would light the sense opaque, and warm the spring
Of boundless ecstasy; while nature's laws
So violated, plead, immortal-tongued,
For her dark-fated children; lead them forth
From bondage infamous! Bid reason own
The dignities of man, whate'er his clime,
Estate, or colour. And, O sacred Truth!
Tell the proud lords of traffic,[7] that the breast
Thrice ebon-tinted, bears a crimson tide,
As pure, as clear as Europe's sons can boast.
Then, Liberty, extend thy thundering voice
To Afric's scorching climes, o'er seas that bound
To bear the blissful tidings, while all earth
Shall hail Humanity! the child of Heaven!

[4] **adamant:** the hardest substance thought to exist in the ancient world. Perhaps a mythic material, the ancients may have had in mind diamonds, or the hardest steel.

[5] **Zembla's frozen sphere:** Nova Zembla, a group of islands in the Arctic Ocean. Alexander Pope points to Zembla in the second epistle of his *An Essay on Man*: "Ask where's the North? At York 'tis on the Tweed, / In *Scotland* at the *Orcades*, and there / At *Greenland*, *Zembla*, or the Lord knows where."

[6] **gelid:** frozen, extremely cold.

[7] **lords of traffic:** traffic in human flesh, lords of the slave trade.

The Old Beggar

(1806; comp. c. 1799)

Do you see the old beggar who sits at yon gate,
With his beard silver'd over like snow?
Though he smiles as he meets the keen arrows of fate,
Still his bosom is wearied with woe.

— II —

Many years has he sat at the foot of the hill,
Many days seen the summer sun rise;
And at evening the traveller passes him still,
While the shadows steal over the skies.

— III —

In the bleak blast of winter he hobbles along
O'er the heath, at the dawning of day;
And the dew-drops that freeze the rude thistles among,
Are the stars that illumine his way.

— IV —

How mild is his aspect, how modest his eye,
How meekly his soul bears each wrong!
How much does he speak by his eloquent sigh,
Though no accent is heard from his tongue.

— V —

Time was, when this beggar, in martial trim dight,[1]
Was as bold as the chief of his throng;
When he march'd through the storms of the day or the night,
And still smiled as he journey'd along.

— VI —

Then his form was athletic, his eyes' vivid glance
Spoke the lustre of youth's glowing day!
And the village all mark'd, in the combat and dance,
The brave younker still valiant as gay.

— VII —

When the prize was proposed, how his footsteps would bound,
While the maid of his heart led the throng,
While the ribands that circled the May-pole around,
Waved the trophies of garlands among!

— VIII —

But love o'er his bosom triumphantly reign'd,
Love taught him in secret to pine;
Love wasted his youth, yet he never complain'd,
For the silence of love — is divine!

— IX —

The dulcet toned word, and the plaint of despair,
Are no signs of the soul-wasting smart;
'Tis the pride of affection to cherish its care,
And to count the quick throbs of the heart.

— X —

Amidst the loud din of the battle he stood,
Like a lion, undaunted and strong;
But the tear of compassion was mingled with blood,
When his sword was the first in the throng.

— XI —

When the bullet whizz'd by, and his arm bore away,
Still he shrunk not, with anguish oppress'd,
And when victory shouted the fate of the day,
Not a groan check'd the joy of his breast.

— XII —

To his dear native shore the poor wanderer hied,[2]
But he came to complete his despair:
For the maid of his soul was that morning a bride!
And a gay lordly rival was there!

— XIII —

From that hour, o'er the world he has wander'd forlorn;
But still love his companion would go;
And though deeply fond memory planted its thorn,
Still he silently cherish'd his woe.

— XIV —

See him now, while with age and with sorrow oppress'd,
He the gate opens slowly, and sighs!
See him drop the big tears on his woe-wither'd breast,
The big tears that fall fast from his eyes!

— XV —

See his habit all tatter'd, his shrivell'd cheek pale;
See his locks, waving thin in the air;
See his lip is half froze with the sharp cutting gale,
And his head, o'er the temples, all bare!

[1] **dight:** an archaism, here meaning "dressed" or "arrayed."

[2] **hied:** archaic word meaning to "hasten or strive toward."

— XVI —

His eye-beam no longer in lustre displays
The warm sunshine that visits his breast;
For deep sunk is its orbit, and darken'd its rays,
And he sighs for the grave's silent rest.

— XVII —

And his voice is grown feeble, his accent is slow,
And he sees not the distant hill's side;
And he hears not the breezes of morn as they blow,
Nor the streams that soft murmuring glide.

— XVIII —

To him all is silent, and mournful, and dim,
E'en the seasons pass dreary and slow;
For affliction has placed its cold fetters on him,
And his soul is enamour'd of woe.

— XIX —

See the tear, which, imploring, is fearful to roll,
Though in silence he bows as you stray;
'Tis the eloquent silence which speaks to the soul,
'Tis the star of his slow-setting day!

— XX —

Perchance, ere the May-blossoms cheerfully wave,
Ere the zephyrs[3] of summer soft sigh;
The sun-beams shall dance on the grass o'er his grave,
And his journey be mark'd — to the sky.

To the Poet Coleridge[1]

(1806; comp. 1800)

RAPT in the visionary theme!
Spirit divine! with thee I'll wander,
Where the blue, wavy, lucid stream,
'Mid forest glooms, shall slow meander!
With thee I'll trace the circling bounds
Of thy new Paradise extended;
And listen to the varying sounds
Of winds, and foamy torrents blended.

Now by the source which lab'ring heaves
The mystic fountain, bubbling, panting,
While Gossamer[2] its net-work weaves,
Adown the blue lawn slanting!
I'll mark thy *sunny dome,* and view
Thy *caves of ice,* thy fields of dew;
Thy ever-blooming mead, whose flower
Waves to the cold breath of the moonlight hour;
Or when the day-star, peering bright
On the grey wing of parting night;
While more than vegetating power
Throbs grateful to the burning hour,
As summer's whisper'd sighs unfold
Her million, million buds of gold;
Then will I climb the breezy bounds,
Of thy new Paradise extended,
And listen to the distant sounds
Of winds, and foamy torrents blended!

Spirit divine! with thee I'll trace
Imagination's boundless space!
With thee, beneath thy *sunny dome,*
I'll listen to the minstrel's lay,
Hymning the gradual close of day;
In *caves of ice* enchanted roam,
Where on the glittering entrance plays
The moon's-beam with its silv'ry rays;
Or, when the glassy stream,
That through the deep dell flows,
Flashes the noon's hot beam;
The noon's hot beam, that midway shows
Thy flaming temple, studded o'er
With all Peruvia's lustrous store!
There will I trace the circling bounds
Of thy new Paradise extended!
And listen to the awful sounds,
Of winds, and foamy torrents blended!

And now I'll pause to catch the moan
Of distant breezes, cavern-pent;

[3] **zephyrs:** gentle western breezes, named after the Greek deity Zephyrus, god of the west wind.

[1] In her revisitation of "thy sunny dome, / Thy caves of ice", Robinson pays tribute to S. T. Coleridge's then unpublished, later well-known poem, "Kubla Khan."* The admiration flowed in both directions, however; Coleridge once declared her "an undoubted genius."

[2] **Gossamer:** fine, filmy cobweb spun by small spiders.

Now, ere the twilight tints are flown,
Purpling the landscape, far and wide,
On the dark promontory's side
    I'll gather wild flowers, dew besprent,
And weave a crown for thee,
Genius of Heaven-taught poesy!
While, op'ning to my wond'ring eyes,
Thou bidst a new creation rise,
I'll raptured trace the circling bounds
    Of thy rich Paradise extended,
And listen to the varying sounds
    Of winds, and foaming torrents blended.

And now, with lofty tones inviting,
Thy nymph, her dulcimer swift smiting,
Shall wake me in ecstatic measures!
Far, far removed from mortal pleasures!
    In cadence rich, in cadence strong,
Proving the wondrous witcheries of song!
        I hear her voice! thy sunny dome,
    Thy caves of ice, loud repeat,
    Vibrations, madd'ning sweet,
        Calling the visionary wand'rer home.
    She sings of thee, O favour'd child
    Of minstrelsy, sublimely wild!
Of thee, whose soul can feel the tone
Which gives to airy dreams a magic all thy own!

SAPPHO

ROBERT BURNS

(1759–1796)

One might apply to Robert Burns, Voltaire's comment on the divine: "if [He] did not exist, it would be necessary to invent him." Burns was an ideal discovery for a democratic, revolutionary age, because he fulfilled the expectations of cultural primitivism: that poets be natural, rather than schooled; that they be isolated from literate culture by either place or class to be free of meretricious aesthetic norms; so that their poetry and its language would flow freely from the heart and its passions, rather than be contaminated by artifice and imitation. Born in a two-room, thatched cottage, Burns did not have to pretend to be a peasant poet. Almost entirely self-educated, Burns could only modestly compete with university-trained poets, when he attempted writing in the King's English. Thus it was a great advantage to him that scholars and antiquarians were prepared to receive a "natural" bard who would validate their philosophical theories of native genius. Fellow Scotsmen James Macpherson, Thomas Ramsay, and Robert Fergusson excited the cultural and political appetite with their songs and imitations of old Scottish heroes and heroic times; rhymsters Stephen Duck, the Thresher Poet; Mary Collier, the Poetical Washerwoman; and Henry Jones, the Poetical Shoemaker, prepared the way. Upon publication of his first volume, *Poems, Chiefly in the Scottish Dialect* (1786), Burns effaced his predecessors, receiving the moniker of "Heaven-taught Ploughman" from Henry Mackenzie, celebrated author of *The Man of Feeling* (1771).

Robert Burns was born on 25 January 1759, in the village of Alloway, Ayrshire, the first of seven children born to William Burnes (as his father spelled the family name) and Agnes Broun. His father was a hardworking but unsuccessful farmer, who saw to the education of his sons both outside the home and within, as the need arose. At the age of fifteen, Robert committed "the sin of RHYME" in eulogizing the beauty of a farmer's daughter, Nelly Kilpatrick ("Handsome Nell"). Thereafter, poetry and loving went hand-in-hand, and there was a great deal of both for the rest of Burns's life. He fathered three children in- and eight children out-of-wedlock (including two sets of twins) to five women. Burns's last child, Maxwell, was born to his wife on the day of his funeral, 25 July 1796. "There is certainly some connection between Love and Music and Poetry," Burns explained; "I never had the least thought or inclination of turning Poet till I once got heartily in love, and then rhyme and song were, in a manner, the spontaneous language of my heart." Besides "Handsome Nell," Burns's consecutive muses were Peggy Thompson, Alison Begbie, his future wife Jean Armour, "Highland" Mary Campbell, Elizabeth Paton, Margaret Chalmers, May Cameron, Mrs. Agnes McLehose, Jenny Clow, Anna Park, and Maria and Elizabeth Riddell. His literary inspirations were *The Lark*, an anthology of Scottish and English songs, which he "pored over, driving [his] cart or walking to labor, song by song, verse by verse," and the second edition of Fergusson's Scottish *Poems*, which caused him to "str[i]ng anew [his] wildly-sounding, rustic lyre with emulating vigour."

In 1785, Burns's father died, leaving him as eldest son in charge of the farm and family. The same year, Burns had his first illegitimate child by Elizabeth Paton, with whom he performed public penance for fornication in the Calvinist Mauchline kirk (church). For three successive weeks during religious services, Burns and Paton had to dress in black sackcloth—

the gown of fornication—and sit on the cutty stool, an armchair raised above the other seats, facing the pulpit. However, in "The Fornicator. A New Song," Burns asserts incorrigible innocence, rather than remorse, as his "downcast eye by chance did spy / What made my lips to water, / Those limbs so clean where I, between, / Commenc'd a Fornicator." Burns goes further in promoting sexual politics in defiance of Calvinism and the impoverishment of the proletariat in "Why should na poor folk mowe [copulate]?" Thusly, Burns makes lovemaking an act of social, political, and even existential significance: "It is the emanation of Divinity that preserves the Sons and Daughters of rustic labour from degenerating into the brutes with which they daily hold converse.—Without it, life to the poor inmates of the Cottage would be a damning gift."

Burns's *Poems, Chiefly in the Scottish Dialect* came out in three editions (1786, 1787, 1793) during his lifetime, but more of the greater and most popular poems belonged to the first edition, which vies with Smith's *Elegiac Sonnets* (1784) and the *Lyrical Ballads* (1798) of Wordsworth* and Coleridge* as one of the first influential volumes of Romantic verse. Burns's 200 or more Scottish songs and ballads, some of which he wrote, but most of which he collected assiduously during Highland and Border excursions, came out in several collections, *The Scots Musical Museum* and *Select Scottish Airs* (1792). They include his best known lyrics, "Auld Lang Syne," "O my Luve's like a red, red rose," "Ye Banks and Braes," and "Scots wha hae." David Daiches calls Burns the best songwriter Britain ever produced, praising him as "the heir of the people, of the lost authors of Scotland's folk songs, whose fragments he gathered in, like a god gathering the remnants of a shattered world to recreate them and send them abroad again with new life and meaning." Finally, however, Burns "became legendary because he was uniquely ordinary" in politics, sentiment, poetry, and human failings. As Edwin Muir comments, he was the "ordinary man for whom Scotland had been looking as it might have looked for a king; and it discovered him with greater surprise and delight than if it had found a king; for kings are more common."

from POEMS, CHIEFLY IN THE SCOTTISH DIALECT[1]

(1786–1793)

John Barleycorn. A Ballad

(1786; comp. 1785)

— I —

THERE was three kings into the east,
Three kings both great and high,
And they hae sworn a solemn oath
John Barleycorn should die.

— II —

They took a plough and plough'd him down,
Put clods upon his head,
And they hae sworn a solemn oath
John Barleycorn was dead.

— III —

But the chearful Spring came kindly on,
And show'rs began to fall;
John Barleycorn got up again,
And sore surpris'd them all.

— IV —

The sultry suns of Summer came,
And he grew thick and strong,
His head weel arm'd wi' pointed spears,
That no one should him wrong.

— V —

The sober Autumn enter'd mild,
When he grew wan and pale;
His bending joints and drooping head
Show'd he began to fail.

— VI —

His colour sicken'd more and more,
He faded into age;
And then his enemies began
To show their deadly rage.

— VII —

They've taen a weapon, long and sharp,
And cut him by the knee;
Then ty'd him fast upon a cart,
Like a rogue for forgerie.

— VIII —

They laid him down upon his back,
And cudgell'd him full sore;
They hung him up before the storm,
And turn'd him o'er and o'er.

— IX —

They filled up a darksome pit
With water to the brim,
They heaved in John Barleycorn,
There let him sink or swim.

— X —

They laid him out upon the floor,
To work him farther woe,
And still, as signs of life appear'd,
They toss'd him to and fro.

— XI —

They wasted, o'er a scorching flame,
The marrow of his bones;
But a Miller us'd him worst of all,
For he crush'd him between two stones.

— XII —

And they hae taen his very heart's blood,
And drank it round and round;
And still the more and more they drank,
Their joy did more abound.

— XIII —

John Barleycorn was a hero bold,
Of noble enterprise,
For if you do but taste his blood,
'Twill make your courage rise.

[1] First edition published by John Wilson of Kilmarnock for 600 subscribers. Burns opens his preface to the volume by saying that "The following trifles are not the production of the Poet, who, with all the advantages of learned art, and perhaps amid the elegancies and idlenesses of upper life, looks down for a rural theme, with an eye to Theocrites or Vergil." But rather: "Unacquainted with the necessary requisites for commencing Poet by rule, he sings the sentiments and manners he felt and saw in himself and his rustic compeers . . . in his and their native language." The 1786 edition contained 44 poems, songs, and epitaphs; the Edinburgh editions of 1787 and 1793 added 42 more pieces.

— XIV —

'Twill make a man forget his woe;
'Twill heighten all his joy:
'Twill make the widow's heart to sing,
Tho' the tear were in her eye.

— XV —

Then let us toast John Barleycorn,
Each man a glass in hand;
And may his great posterity
Ne'er fail in old Scotland!

To a Mouse, on Turning Her up in Her Nest, with the Plough, November, 1785.

(1786; comp. 1785)

WEE, sleeket, cowran, tim'rous *beastie,*
O, what a panic's in thy breastie!
Thou need na start awa sae hasty,
Wi' bickering brattle![1]
I wad be laith to rin an' chase thee,
Wi' murd'ring *pattle!*[2]

I'm truly sorry Man's dominion
Has broken Nature's social union,
An' justifies that ill opinion,
Which makes thee startle,
At me, thy poor, earth-born companion,
An' *fellow-mortal!*

I doubt na, whyles, but thou may *thieve;*
What then? poor beastie, thou maun live!
A *daimen-icker*[3] in a *thrave*[4]
'S a sma' request:
I'll get a blessin wi' the lave,[5]
An' never miss't!

Thy wee-bit *housie,* too, in ruin!
It's silly wa's[6] the win's are strewin!
An' naething, now, to big a new ane,
O' foggage[7] green!
An' bleak *December's winds* ensuin,[8]
Baith snell[9] an' keen!

Thou saw the fields laid bare an' wast,
An' weary *Winter* comin fast,
An' cozie here, beneath the blast,
Thou thought to dwell,
Till crash! the cruel *coulter*[10] past
Out thro' thy cell.

That wee-bit heap o' leaves an' stibble,[11]
Has cost thee monie a weary nibble!
Now thou's turn'd out, for a' thy trouble,
But house or hald,[12]
To thole[13] the Winter's *sleety dribble,*
An' *cranreuch*[14] cauld!

But Mousie, thou art no thy-lane,
In proving *foresight* may be vain:
The best laid schemes o' *Mice* an' *Men,*
Gang[15] aft agley,[16]
An' lea'e us nought but grief an' pain,
For promis'd joy!

Still, thou art blest, compar'd wi' *me!*
The *present* only toucheth thee:
But Och! I *backward* cast my e'e,
On prospects drear!
An' *forward,* tho' I canna *see,*
I *guess* an' *fear!*

[1] **brattle:** *n.* clatter; hurry; short race; noisy onset.

[2] **pattle:** *n.* small, long-handled spade used to clean the plough.

[3] **daimen-icker:** *n.* occasional ear of corn.

[4] **thrave:** *n.* two stooks of corn, hence a measure of straw.

[5] **lave:** *n.* rest, remainder, others.

[6] **wa:** *n.* wall.

[7] **foggage:** *n.* rank grass.

[8] **ensuin:** *adj.* insuing.

[9] **snell:** *adj.* keen, bitter.

[10] **coulter:** *n.* blade of the plough which makes the vertical cut.

[11] **stibble:** *n.* stubble.

[12] **hald:** *n.* hold, dwelling, refuge.

[13] **thole:** *v.* endure, suffer.

[14] **cranreuch:** *n.* hoarfrost.

[15] **gae:** *v.* go, walk; **gaun:** *pres. part.* gone; **gang:** *v.* go, depart, walk.

[16] **agley:** *adv.* awry, wrong.

Address to the Unco Guid, or the Rigidly Righteous

(1787; comp. 1786)

My Son, these maxims make a rule,
And lump them ay thegither;
The Rigid Righteous *is a fool,*
The Rigid Wise *anither:*
The cleanest corn that e'er was dight
May hae some pyles o' caff in;
So ne'er a fellow-creature slight
For random fits o' daffin.[1]

Solomon
—Eccles. ch. vii. vers. 16.

— I —

O ye wha are sae guid yoursel,
Sae pious and sae holy,
Ye've nought to do but mark and tell
Your Neebours' fauts[2] and folly!
Whase life is like a weel-gaun[3] mill,
Supply'd wi' store o' water,
The heaped happer's[4] ebbing still,
And still the clap[5] plays clatter.

— II —

Hear me, ye venerable Core,[6]
As counsel for poor mortals,
That frequent pass douce[7] Wisdom's door
For glaikit[8] Folly's portals;
I, for their thoughtless, careless sakes
Would here propone defences,
Their donsie[9] tricks, their black mistakes,
Their failings and mischances.

— III —

Ye see your state wi' theirs compar'd,
And shudder at the niffer.[10]
But cast a moment's fair regard
What maks the mighty differ;
Discount what scant occasion gave,
That purity ye pride in,
And (what's aft mair than a' the lave[11])
Your better art o' hiding.

— IV —

Think, when your castigated pulse
Gies now and then a wallop,
What ragings must his veins convulse,
That still eternal gallop:
Wi' wind and tide fair i' your tail,
Right on ye scud your sea-way;
But, in the teeth o' baith to sail,
It maks an unco[12] leeway.

— V —

See Social-life and Glee sit down,
All joyous and unthinking,
Till, quite transmugrify'd, they're grown
Debauchery and Drinking:
O would they stay to calculate
Th' eternal consequences;
Or your more dreaded h–ll to state,
D–mnation of expences!

— VI —

Ye high, exalted, virtuous Dames,
Ty'd up in godly laces,
Before ye gie poor *Frailty* names,
Suppose a change o' cases;
A dear-lov'd lad, convenience snug,
A treacherous inclination—
But, let me whisper i' your lug,[13]
Ye're aiblins[14] nae temptation.

---

[1] **daffin:** *n.* fooling, frolic, flirtation, dallying.

[2] **faut(e), fau't:** *n.* fault; (sexual) failing; want, lack; *v.* find fault with; **a' the ____ I had to:** the only fault I could find with.

[3] **gaun:** *pres. part.* gone.

[4] **happer:** *n.* hopper (of a mill).

[5] **clap:** clapper.

[6] **core:** company.

[7] **douce, douse:** *adj.* sedate, sober; prudent; kindly; **douse(ly):** *adv.* circumspectly, decorously.

[8] **glaiket:** careless, foolish.

[9] **donsie:** *adj.* hapless, unlucky; ill-tempered; unmanageable.

[10] **niffer:** *n.* an exchange; to exchange, to barter; comparison.

[11] **lave:** *n.* rest, remainder, others.

[12] **unco:** *adj.* odd, strange; *adv.* very; **uncos:** *n. pl.* strange tales.

[13] **lug:** ear.

[14] **aiblins:** *adv.* perhaps.

— VII —

Then gently scan your brother Man,
Still gentler sister Woman;
Tho' they may gang a kennin[15] wrang,
To step aside is human.
One point must still be greatly dark,
The moving *Why* they do it;
And just as lamely can ye mark,
How far perhaps they rue it.

— VIII —

Who made the heart, 'tis *He* alone
Decidedly can try us,
He knows each chord its various tone,
Each spring its various bias:
Then at the balance let's be mute,
We never can adjust it;
What's *done* we partly may compute,
But know not what's *resisted*.

from Letter to Miss Helen Craik[1]

9 Aug 1790

. . . —There is not among all the Martyrologies that ever were penned, so rueful a narrative as Johnson's Lives of the Poets. —In the comparative view of Wretches, the criterion is not, what they are doomed to suffer, but how they are formed to bear. —Take a being of our kind, give him a stronger imagination and more delicate sensibility, which will ever between them engender a more ungovernable set of Passions, than the usual lot of man; implant in him an irresistible impulse to some idle vagary, such as, arranging wild-flowers in fantastical nosegays, tracing the grasshopper to his haunt by his chirping song, watching the frisks of the little minnows in the sunny pool, or hunting after the intrigues of wanton butterflies—in short, send him adrift after some wayward pursuit which shall eternally mislead him from the paths of Lucre,[2] yet, curse him with a keener relish than any man living for the pleasures that only Lucre can bestow; lastly, fill up the measure of his woes, by bestowing on him a spurning sense of his own dignity; and you have created a wight nearly as miserable as a Poet. —

To you, Madam, I need not recount the fairy pleasures the Muse, to counterbalance this catalogue of evils, bestows on her Votaries. —Bewitching Poesy is like bewitching WOMAN: she has in all ages been accused of misleading Mankind from the counsels of Wisdom and the paths of Prudence; involving them in difficulties, baiting them with Poverty, branding them with Infamy, and plunging them in the vortex of Ruin; yet, where is the Man but must own, that all our happiness on earth is not worthy the name! that even the holy hermit's solitary prospect of paradisical bliss, is but the glitter of a northern sun rising over a frozen region! Compared with the many pleasures, the nameless raptures, we owe to the lovely QUEENS OF THE HEARTS OF MEN!!!

[15] **kennin**: *vbl. n.* (a) little, trifle.

[1] Helen Craik (1750?–1824) was a friend of Burns and a Dumfries poet, steeped in the melancholy sentimentalism inspired by Goethe's *Sorrows of Young Werther* (1774).

[2] **Lucre**: money, profits.

from Letter to [ROBERT GRAHAM of Fintry]*

Dumfries 5th Janry 1793

SIR,

I am this moment honored with your letter: with what feelings I received this other instance of your goodness,[1] I shall not pretend to describe. —

Now, to the charges which Malice & Misrepresentation have brought against me. —

It has been said, it seems, that I not only belong to, but head a disaffected party[2] in this place. —I know of no

[1] Burns's friend and patron Robert Graham, the twelfth Laird of Fintry, was a Commissioner of the Scottish Board of Excise. In 1789, with Graham's help, Burns secured a job as an Excise officer.

[2] Burns's Jacobin and Jacobite sympathies were a source of tension during his final years in Dumfries, where the political atmosphere was hostile to freedom of speech and assembly, both of which had been outlawed as part of the government's counterrevolutionary measures in response to the French Revolution. In 1792, as a gesture of solidarity with the Revolution, Burns shipped four cannon from the smuggler *Rosamund* to the French National Convention. (Burns himself had participated in the raid on the ship.) The cannon were seized by Customs at Dover, and in December 1792 Burns was denounced by an informer to the Excise Board as unpatriotic. He was later exonerated after an informal trial.

party in this place, Republican o[r] Reform, except an old party of Borough-Reform; with which I never had any thing to do.—Individuals, both Republican & Reform, we have, though not many of either; but if they have associated, it is more than I have the least knowledge of: & if there exists such an association, it must consist of such obscure, nameless beings, as precludes any possibility of my being known to them, or they to me.—

I was in the playhouse one night, when ÇA IRA[3] was called for.—I was in the middle of the Pit, & from the Pit the clamour arose.—One or two individuals with whom I occasionally associate were of the party, but I neither knew of the Plot, nor joined in the Plot; nor ever opened my lips to hiss, or huzza, that, or any other Political tune whatever.—I looked on myself as far too obscure a man to have any weight in quelling a Riot; at the same time as a character of higher respectability, than to yell in the howlings of a rabble.—This was the conduct of all the first Characters in this place; & these Characters know, & will avow, that such was my conduct.—

I never uttered any invectives against the king.[4]—His private worth, it is altogether impossible that such a man as I, can appreciate; and in his Public capacity, I always revered, & ever will, with the soundest loyalty, revere, the Monarch of Great Britain, as, to speak in Masonic,[5] the sacred KEYSTONE OF OUR ROYAL ARCH CONSTITUTION.—

As to REFORM PRINCIPLES, I look upon the British Constitution, as settled at the Revolution, to be the most glorious Constitution on earth, or that perhaps the wit of man can frame; at the same time, I think, & you know what High and distinquished Characters have for some time thought so, that we have a good deal deviated from the original principles of that Constitution; particularly, that an alarming System of Corruption has pervaded the connection between the Executive Power and the House of Commons.—This is the Truth, the Whole truth, of my Reform opinions; opinions which, before I was aware of the complection of these innovating times, I too unguardedly (now I see it) sported with: but henceforth, I seal up my lips.—However, I never dictated to, corresponded with, or had the least connection with, any political association whatever—except, that when the Magistrates & principal inhabitants of this town, met to declare their attachment to the Constitution, & their abhorrence of Riot, which declaration you would see in the Papers, I, as I thought my duty as a Subject at large, & a Citizen in particular, called upon me, subscribed the same declaratory Creed.— . . .

As to France, I was her enthusiastic votary in the beginning of the business.—When she came to shew her old avidity for conquest, in annexing Savoy, &c. to her dominions, & invading the rights of Holland, I altered my sentiments.—A tippling Ballad[6] which I made on the Prince of Brunswick's breaking up his camp, & sung one convivial evening, I shall likewise send you, sealed up, as it is not every body's reading.—This last is not worth your perusal; but lest Mrs FAME should, as she has already done, use, & even abuse, her old priviledge of lying, you shall be the master of every thing, le pour et le contre,[7] of my political writings & conduct.—

[3] "ÇA IRA": popular song of the French Revolution; the title translates as "things will work out."

[4] King George III (r. 1760–1820).

[5] Burns had become a member of the secret fraternal order of Freemasons in 1781.

[6] See "Why should na poor folk mowe."

[7] **le pour et le contre**: French for "the case for and against."

from THE MORNING CHRONICLE

(8 May 1794)

Robert Bruce's March to Bannockburn—[1]

(comp. 1793)

To its ain tune—

SCOTS, wha hae wi' WALLACE bled,
Scots, wham BRUCE has aften led,
Welcome to your gory bed,—
  Or to victorie.—

[1] Eventually subtitled "Robert Bruce's Address to His Army, Before the Battle of Bannockburn." The battle occurred on 24 June 1314. Bruce calls on his army to remember Sir William Wallace (c. 1270–1305), Scottish patriot and military leader, who led an unsuccessful insurgency against the English. In 1305, Wallace was betrayed, tried in Westminster Hall, convicted, hanged, drawn, and quartered. Bruce, who was King Robert I of Scotland (r. 1306–1329), defeated the English at Bannockburn, although his force of 30,000 was outnumbered more than three to one.

Now's the day, and now's the hour;
See the front o' battle lour;[2]
See approach proud EDWARD's power,
Chains and Slaverie.—

Wha will be a traitor-knave?
Wha can fill a coward's grave?
Wha sae base as be a Slave?
—Let him turn and flie:—

Wha for SCOTLAND's king and law,
Freedom's sword will strongly draw,
FREE-MAN stand, or FREE-MAN fa',
Let him follow me.—

By Oppression's woes and pains!
By your Sons in servile chains!
We will drain our dearest veins,
But they *shall* be free!

Lay the proud Usurpers low!
Tyrants fall in every foe!
LIBERTY's in every blow!
Let us DO—OR DIE!!!

[2] **lour:** *v.* look threateningly.

from GLASGOW MAGAZINE
(August 1795)

Song—For a' that and a' that—
(comp. 1795)

Is there, for honest Poverty
That hings his head, and a' that;
The coward-slave, we pass him by,
We dare be poor for a' that!
For a' that, and a' that,
Our toils obscure, and a' that,
The rank is but the guinea's stamp,
The Man's the gowd[1] for a' that.—

What though on hamely fare we dine,
Wear hoddin[2] grey, and a' that.
Gie fools their silks, and knaves their wine,
A Man's a Man for a' that.
For a' that, and a' that,
Their tinsel show, and a' that;
The honest man, though e'er sae poor,
Is king o' men for a' that.—

Ye see yon birkie[3] ca'd, a lord,
Wha struts, and stares, and a' that,
Though hundreds worship at his word,
He's but a coof[4] for a' that.
For a' that, and a' that,
His ribband, star and a' that,
The man of independant mind,
He looks and laughs at a' that.—

A prince can mak a belted knight,
A marquis, duke, and a' that;
But an honest man's aboon[5] his might,
Gude faith he mauna[6] fa' that!
For a' that, and a' that,
Their dignities, and a' that,
The pith o' Sense, and pride o' Worth,
Are higher rank that a' that.—

Then let us pray that come it may,
As come it will for a' that,
That Sense and Worth, o'er a' the earth
Shall bear the gree,[7] and a' that.
For a' that, and a' that,
Its comin yet for a' that,
That Man to Man the warld o'er,
Shall brothers be for a' that.—

[1] **gowd:** *n.* gold; **gowden:** *adj.* golden; **gowdie:** *n.* (golden) head.

[2] **hoddin:** *n.* coarse, grey homespun cloth of mixed black and white wool.

[3] **birkie:** *n.* lively, spry fellow.

[4] **coof, cuif:** *n.* fool, clown; lout.

[5] **aboon:** *adv.* up; *prep.* above, over.

[6] **mauna:** *auxil. v.* must not.

[7] **gree:** *n.* social degree, supremacy.

from THE SCOTS MUSICAL MUSEUM
(1787–1803)

Auld Lang Syne
(1796; comp. 1788)

SHOULD auld acquaintance be forgot
And never brought to mind?
Should auld acquaintance be forgot,
And auld lang syne![1]

— CHORUS —
For auld lang syne, my jo,
For auld lang syne,
We'll tak a cup o' kindness yet
For auld lang syne.

And surely ye'll be your pint stowp![2]
And surely I'll be mine!
And we'll tak a cup o' kindness yet,
For auld lang syne.
For auld, &c.

We twa hae run about the braes,[3]
And pou'd[4] the gowans[5] fine;
But we've wander'd mony a weary fitt,[6]
Sin auld lang syne.
For auld, &c.

We twa hae paidl'd in the burn,[7]
Frae morning sun till dine;
But seas between us braid[8] hae roar'd,
Sin auld lang syne.
For auld, &c.

And there's a hand, my trusty fiere,[9]
And gie's a hand o' thine;
And we'll tak a right gude-willie waught[10]
For auld lang syne.
For auld, &c.

[1] **lang syne:** *attrib.* ancient, long since, long ago.

[2] **stowp:** *n.* tankard, measure.

[3] **braes:** *n.* hill, hillside; high ground by a river.

[4] **pou'd:** *v.* past tense of *pull.*

[5] **gowans:** *n.* "the flower of the daisy, dandelion, hawkweed, &c."

[6] **fitt:** foot.

[7] **paidl'd:** *v.* past tense of paddle, wade; dabble, fumble impotently. **burn(ie):** *n.* water, stream; water used in brewing.

[8] **braid:** *adj.* broad

[9] **fiere:** friend.

[10] **gude-willie waught:** a good healthy swig.

Such a Parcel of Rogues in a Nation —
(1792; comp. 1792)

FAREWEEL to a' our Scotish fame,
Fareweel our ancient glory;
Fareweel even to the Scotish name,
Sae fam'd in martial story!
Now Sark rins[1] o'er the Solway sands,
And Tweed[2] rins to the ocean,
To mark whare England's province stands,
Such a parcel of rogues in a nation!

What force or guile could not subdue,
Thro' many warlike ages,
Is wrought now by a coward few,
For hireling traitors' wages.
The English steel we could disdain,
Secure in valor's station;
But English gold has been our bane,
Such a parcel of rogues in a nation!

O would, or I had seen the day
That treason thus could sell us,
My auld grey head had lien in clay,
Wi' BRUCE and loyal WALLACE![3]
But pith and power, till my last hour,
I'll mak this declaration;
We're bought and sold for English gold,
Such a parcel of rogues in a nation!

[1] **rins:** *v.* run.

[2] The Sark and Tweed Rivers form the western and eastern borders of England.

[3] See note 1 to "Robert Bruce's March to Bannockburn."

A Red Red Rose

(1796; comp. 1794)

O MY LUVE's like a red, red rose,
That's newly sprung in June;
O my Luve's like the melodie
That's sweetly play'd in tune.—

As fair art thou, my bonie lass,
So deep in luve am I;
And I will love thee still, my Dear,
Till a' the seas gang[1] dry.—

Till a' the seas gang dry, my Dear,
And the rocks melt wi' the sun:
I will love thee still, my Dear,
While the sands o' life shall run.—

And fare thee weel, my only Luve!
And fare thee weel, a while!
And I will come again, my Luve,
Tho' it were ten thousand mile!

[1]**gang:** *v.* go. **gay:** go.

from MERRY MUSES OF CALEDONIA; A COLLECTION OF FAVORITE SCOTS SONGS

(1799–1800)

The Fornicator. A New Song—

(1799; comp. 1784–1785)

Tune, Clout the Caldron

YE jovial boys who love the joys,
The blissful joys of Lovers;
Yet dare avow with dauntless brow,
When th' bony lass discovers;
I pray draw near and lend an ear,
And welcome in a Frater,[1]
For I've lately been on quarantine,
A proven Fornicator.

Before the Congregation wide
I pass'd the muster fairly,
My handsome Betsey[2] by my side,
We gat our ditty[3] rarely;
But my downcast eye by chance did spy
What made my lips to water,
Those limbs so clean where I, between,
Commenc'd a Fornicator.

With rueful face and signs of grace
I pay'd the buttock-hire,[4]
The night was dark and thro' the park
I could not but convoy her;
A parting kiss, what could I less,
My vows began to scatter,
My Betsey fell—lal de dal lal lal,
I am a Fornicator.

But for her sake this vow I make,
And solemnly I swear it,
That while I own a single crown,
She's welcome for to share it;
And my roguish boy his Mother's joy,
And the darling of his Pater,
For him I boast my pains and cost,
Although a Fornicator.

Ye wenching blades whose hireling jades[5]
Have tipt you off blue-boram,[6]
I tell ye plain, I do disdain
To rank you in the Quorum;
But a bony lass upon the grass
To teach her esse Mater,[7]
And no reward but for regard,
O that's a Fornicator.

Your warlike Kings and Heros bold,
Great Captains and Commanders;
Your mighty Cèsars fam'd of old,
And Conquering Alexanders;

[1]**Frater:** brother.

[2]**Betsey:** Elizabeth Paton. See the Introduction to Burns.

[3]**gat our ditty:** received our reproof.

[4]**buttock-hire:** fine for fornication.

[5]**jades:** *n.* mare; wench, hussy.

[6]**blue-boram:** syphilis. "Blue Boar" was a venereal bubo, or glandular swelling. The term is possibly derived from association with the licentious area near the famous Blue Boar Tavern in London.

[7]**esse Mater:** to be a mother.

In fields they fought and laurels bought
And bulwarks strong did batter,
But still they grac'd our noble list
And ranked Fornicator!!!

Green Grow the Rashes. A Fragment

(1799; comp. 1784–1785)

— CHORUS —

Green grow the rashes, O,
Green grow the rashes, O;
The sweetest hours that e'er I spend,
Are spent amang the lasses, O.

— I —

THERE's nought but care on ev'ry han',
In ev'ry hour that passes, O:
What signifies the life o' man,
An' 'twere na for the lasses, O.
Green grow, &c.

— II —

The warly[1] race may riches chase,
An' riches still may fly them, O;
An' tho' at last they catch them fast,
Their hearts can ne'er enjoy them, O.
Green grow, &c.

— III —

But gie me a canny[2] hour at e'en,
My arms about my Dearie, O;
An' warly cares, an' warly men,
May a' gae tapsalteerie,[3] O!
Green grow, &c.

— IV —

For you sae douse,[4] ye sneer at this,
Ye're nought but senseless asses, O:
The wisest Man[5] the warl' saw,
He dearly lov'd the lasses, O.
Green grow, &c.

— V —

Auld Nature swears, the lovely Dears
Her noblest work she classes, O:
Her prentice han' she try'd on man,
An' then she made the lasses, O.
Green grow, &c.

[1] **warly:** *adj.* worldly.

[2] **canny:** *adj., adv.* favorable, lucky, pleasant.

[3] **tapsalteerie:** *adj. comb.* topsy-turvy, upside down, in disorder.

[4] **douse:** sober, serious.

[5] King Solomon.

[Why should na poor folk mowe[1]]

(1799; comp. 1792)

WHEN Princes and Prelates and het[2]-headed zealots
All Europe hae set in a lowe,[3]
The poor man lies down, nor envies a crown,
And comforts himsel with a mowe.—

— CHORUS —

And why shouldna poor folk mowe, mowe, mowe,
And why shouldna poor folk mowe:
The great folk hae siller,[4] and houses and lands,
Poor bodies hae naething but mowe.—

— 2 —

When Br–nsw–ck's great Prince[5] cam a cruising to Fr–nce
Republican billies[6] to cowe,[7]
Bauld Br–nsw–ck's great Prince wad hae shawn better sense,
At hame with his Princess to mowe.—
And why should na &c.—

[1] **mowe:** *v.* copulate (with a woman); *n.* intercourse.

[2] **het:** *adj.* hot, burning; excited.

[3] **lowe:** *n.* flame; *v.* blaze, rage.

[4] **siller:** *n.* silver, wealth.

[5] **Prince:** In July 1792, the Duke of Brunswick, commander of the Prussian forces, threatened to destroy Paris if the French royal family were harmed.

[6] **billies:** *n.* craft-brother; friend, comrade, fellow, lad.

[7] **cowe:** *v.* terrify; *n.* terror, hobgoblin.

— 3 —

Out over the Rhine proud Pr–ss–a wad shine,
To *spend* his best blood he did vow;
But Frederic[8] had better ne'er forded the water,
But *spent* as he docht in[9] a mowe. —
And why &c. —

— 4 —

By sea and by shore! the Emp–r–r swore,
In Paris he'd kick up a row;
But Paris sae ready just leugh[10] at the laddie
And bade him gae tak him a mowe. —
And why &c. —

[8] Frederick II, King of Prussia (r. 1786–1797), nephew of Frederick the Great, unsuccessfully supported the monarchy during the French Revolution.

[9] **docht in:** *v.* be able, have courage (to do), dare.

[10] **leugh:** *v.* past tense of *laugh.*

— 5 —

Auld Kate[11] laid her claws on poor Stanislaus,
And Poland has bent like a bow:
May the deil in her a— ram a huge pr–ck o' brass!
And damn her in h–ll with a mowe!
And why &c. —

— 6 —

But truce with commotions and new-fangled notions,
A bumper I trust you'll allow:
Here 's George our gude king and Charlotte his
queen,[12]
And lang may they tak a gude mowe!

[11] Catherine the Great, Empress of Russia (r. 1762–1796), notorious for her amorous exploits, established her lover Stanislaw Poniatowski as King of Poland in 1764.

[12] King George III of England (r. 1760–1820) and his Queen, Charlotte Sophia of Meklenburg-Strelitz, whom he married in 1761.

MARY WOLLSTONECRAFT

(1759–1797)

The most influential feminist thinker in this period, and the leading theorist of what we now call liberal or "equality" feminism, Mary Wollstonecraft learned firsthand the ways in which her patriarchal society oppressed women. She was born on 27 April 1759, the eldest daughter of Edward John Wollstonecraft, the son of a lower-middle-class Yorkshire weaver who had prospered in Spitalfields, London, and his Irish wife, Elizabeth Dixon. Her father's laziness and increasing alcoholism caused his family status to decline, and Mary Wollstonecraft grew up with what her biographer Claire Tomalin has called "a powerful sense of grievance." Her parents favored her oldest brother Edward, who received an excellent education, became a lawyer, and inherited all his grandfather's money, refusing to help his three sisters in any significant way. Mary, although an extremely intelligent child, received only the standard education of a lower-middle-class girl: reading, writing, a little math and French, and plain sewing. At the age of 15, Mary met a more refined girl, Fanny Blood, whom she passionately loved, emulated, and helped to support economically with her sewing. At 17, she was forced to help out with the Wollstonecrafts' failing finances by becoming a "paid companion" or personal servant to the wealthy Mrs. Dawson; at 19 she was summoned home to nurse her dying mother. When her increasingly sullen, brutal father decided to marry their servant-girl after her mother's death, Mary determined to leave home forever and earn her own way in the world.

With the help of Fanny Blood and her two sisters, Wollstonecraft set up a school for girls first in Islington and then in Newington Green; such an undertaking was a typical effort on the part of respectable but "impoverished gentlewomen" to support themselves. It was here that Wollstonecraft's own education truly began: at Newington, she became acquainted with one of the leading Dissenters of the day, Dr. Richard Price, who introduced her to the writings of such radical Enlightenment thinkers as Benjamin Franklin, Thomas Jefferson, Voltaire, Condorcet, Rousseau, and Joseph Priestley. She became a convert to what was known as "natural religion": the belief that men and women can perfect themselves through the use of right reason and individual will, that God is best understood as the First Cause of a universe now governed by Natural Law, and that no hell, Trinity, or original sin exists. To advertise her school, Wollstonecraft wrote her first book, *Thoughts on the Education of Daughters* (1786), arguing that women must be educated rationally and must learn to support themselves economically; this book was too radical for the parents of her pupils, however, who wished only that their daughters gain the "accomplishments" of the average middle-class lady (namely, to read, write, sing, dance, sketch, and sew) and thus withdrew their daughters from the school. When Fanny Blood left to marry Hugh Skeys, Wollstonecraft gave up her school and became a governess to an aristocratic Irish family, Robert, Viscount Kingsborough, and Lady Caroline (the source of the portrait in her first novel of the lady who loves her lap dogs more than her children). Dismissed by Lady Caroline two years later when Sir Robert made an unwanted sexual overture toward her, Wollstonecraft described the follies of this aristocratic world, as well as her relationship with Fanny Blood, in her first, largely autobiographical novel, *Mary, A Fiction* (1788).

Penniless, alienated from her family (even her sisters resented her inability to care for them), and lonely (Fanny Blood had died in childbirth), in 1788 Wollstonecraft turned to an old friend of Richard Price, the homosexual radical bookseller and publisher, Joseph Johnson. To his lasting credit, Johnson recognized her talents, agreed to hire her as a staff writer for his pro-Jacobin *Analytical Review,* provided lodgings for her, and urged her to write for publication. Her *Original Stories from Real Life* for children, with illustrations by William Blake,* appeared in 1788, and her compilation of literary and moral texts designed to educate young girls in both public benevolence and Christian forbearance, *The Female Reader,* in 1789. At Johnson's bookshop, Wollstonecraft met all the leading radical thinkers of the period: Thomas Paine,* William Godwin,* Thomas Holcroft, Thomas Christie, William Blake,* and the painter Henri Fuseli, with whom she fell in love. In November 1790, angered at Edmund Burke's* conservative attack on the ideology of the French Revolution, she rushed her *Vindication of the Rights of Men* into print (see FRENCH REVOLUTION AND RIGHTS OF MAN). Insisting that all political authority should rest on the grounds of reason and justice alone, she demanded that every person be entitled to enjoy and dispense the fruits of his or her own labors, that inequality of rank be eliminated, and that an exaggerated respect for the opinions of "our *canonized forefathers*" be substituted with the cultivation of an independent understanding and sound judgment. In place of Burke's metaphor of the English nation as a vulnerable wife in need of virile protection, Wollstonecraft substituted the image of the nation as a benevolent family educating its children for mature independence and motivated by "natural affections" to ensure the welfare of all its members.

Since she believed that the French Revolution would quickly establish a republic that would respect the rights of every person, Wollstonecraft was appalled when the French minister of education for the new Constituent Assembly, Citizen Charles Maurice de Talleyrand-Périgord, the former Bishop of Autun, in 1791 proposed a state-supported system of public education which would prepare girls only to be housewives. She published her passionate defense of the rights of women to an equal education, to equal employment, and to the vote, *A Vindication of the Rights of Woman,* in 1792; the book was widely read and cited, and went through a second edition in the same year. Following the lead of Catherine Macaulay's *Letters on Education** (1790) which she had enthusiastically reviewed for the *Analytical Review,* Wollstonecraft called for "a REVOLUTION in female manners." She explicitly attacked her society's gender definition of the female as innately emotional, intuitive, illogical, capable of moral sentiment but not of rational understanding.

Proceeding from the rigorously logical argument that if women are held morally and legally responsible for their sins or crimes (as they were in both England and France), then they must have both souls and the capacity to think correctly or ethically. She argued that since women are capable of thinking, they must have a rational faculty which should be developed to its greatest capacity. From this philosophical position, Wollstonecraft launched her passionate plea that women be educated in the same way as men. Appealing to male as well as female readers, she argued that more highly educated women would be more virtuous, better mothers, more interesting wives and "companions," and more responsible citizens. Because she assumed that the great bulk of her readers would marry, she devoted a great deal of *A Vindication of the Rights of Woman* to describing the ideal marriage: a marriage based on mutual respect, self-esteem, affection, and compatibility; on *rational love* rather than on a fleeting erotic desire or sexual passion. (Wollstonecraft's efforts to deny her society's equation of the female with uncontrollable sexual desire and to limit the role of eroticism in marriage were in tension with her own life and fictional writings, as both *Mary* and her letters to her lovers attest, where she openly acknowledged the presence and even the value of impassioned female love and sexual desire.)

In addition to advocating a radically new, egalitarian marriage between two rational and equally respected adults, Wollstonecraft demanded even more revolutionary rights for women: the vote (which she insisted should be given to working-class men and all women); the civil and legal right to possess and distribute property; and the right to work in the most prestigious professions, including business, law, medicine, education, and politics. Above all, she demanded for all children between the ages of five and nine a state-supported, coeducational public school system that would teach reading, writing, mathematics, foreign languages, literature, history, botany, mechanics, astronomy, and general science.

Wollstonecraft also described in detail the errors and evils that followed from her society's prevailing definition of the female as the subordinate helpmate of the male. She singled out Milton's description of Eve in *Paradise Lost* and Rousseau's description of Sophy in *Émile* for particular sarcasm. Much of her *Vindication of the Rights of Woman* is devoted to a survey of the damage done to women by such representations of them as in essence submissive and sexual beings. Raised only to be desirable to men, the young women of her day were trained to become "cunning, mean and selfish," to be hypocritical flirts in public and petty tyrants to their children and servants at home. Wollstonecraft concluded *A Vindication of the Rights of Woman* with a catalogue of the female follies common in her day: superstitious belief in fortune-tellers, excessive fondness for fashion and romantic novels, mismanagement of the household, overindulgence or neglect of children. Moreover, she argued, the historical oppression or enslavement of women corrupted *men* as well, forcing them into the social role of master and thus educating them to be demanding, self-indulgent, arrogant, and tyrannical. "How can women be just or generous, when they are the slaves of injustice?" she asked rhetorically. (See RIGHTS OF WOMAN.)

In December 1792, when Fuseli rejected her love, Wollstonecraft decided to sail to Paris to witness the French Revolution firsthand. From her hotel room, she saw Louis XVI en route to his trial for treason and the beginning of the Terror. She also met and fell in love with an American entrepreneur and gambler, Gilbert Imlay, by whom she bore a daughter, christened Fanny Imlay, on 14 May 1794. Joining Imlay in Le Havre, she worked on her *Historical and Moral View of the Origin and Progress of the French Revolution* (published in 1794), while Imlay returned to England. When she followed Imlay to London in April 1795, she found him with another woman. She attempted suicide, was saved by Imlay and sent by him on a business trip to Scandinavia, accompanied only by her infant daughter Fanny and her French maid Marguerite. Her correspondence with Imlay, *Letters written during a Short Residence in Sweden, Norway, and Denmark,* was published by Johnson in 1796; her letters merge her devotion to Imlay with her extremely perceptive commentary on the political and cultural customs of the Scandinavians.

When she returned to England in September 1795, Imlay was living openly with his actress lover; in despair, Wollstonecraft jumped in rain-soaked clothes off the Putney bridge into the Thames River. She was pulled, unconscious, from the river by some watermen. This scandal—her pregnancy out of wedlock, her bastard daughter now abandoned, her lover openly living with another mistress, her two suicide attempts—was widely reported in the popular press and made it almost impossible for any woman who wished to preserve her "respectability" to identify openly with the teachings of the author of *A Vindication of the Rights of Woman.* Persuaded to live for the sake of her daughter (as is Maria, the cruelly yet legally persecuted heroine of Wollstonecraft's last and unfinished novel, *Maria, or the Wrongs of Woman,* 1797), Wollstonecraft returned a visit from the leading radical philosopher and anarchist in England, William Godwin,* in April 1796. Within three months, they had become lovers but agreed in principle not to marry and to keep separate establishments. When Mary became pregnant, they decided to marry for the sake of the child's legitimacy; on 30 August 1797, a daughter (christened Mary Wollstonecraft Godwin) was born. When Wollstonecraft failed to expel the placenta, her physician, Dr. Poignand, pulled it out with his bare hands, thereby introducing the infection that caused the puerperal fever which killed her on 10 September 1797.

Overwhelmed by grief, Godwin, in an act of homage, published in 1798 his *Memoirs of the Author of the Rights of Woman,* which included all of Wollstonecraft's love letters both to him and to Imlay, thereby branding her in the public eye as a whore and an atheist (despite her rational Christian beliefs, Godwin—himself an atheist—insisted that she had died a disbeliever). Godwin's well-meant but entirely misjudged act destroyed Wollstonecraft's reputation as a reputable feminist philosopher for the next 50 years. Nonetheless, Wollstonecraft's radical vision of the mental equality of the sexes survived throughout the next thirty years, both covertly, in the positive allusions to her work in the fiction of such authors as Jane Austen,* Susan Ferrier, and Maria Edgeworth,* and openly, in the radical feminist tracts of Mary Robinson,* Mary Hays, Frances Wright, and Priscilla Wakefield. Wollstonecraft's writings, more than those of any other eighteenth- or nineteenth-century feminist thinker, directly inspired the suffrage movements in both England and America in the later nineteenth and early twentieth centuries.

from THOUGHTS ON THE EDUCATION OF DAUGHTERS:

with Reflections on Female Conduct, in the More Important Duties of Life
(1786)

— READING —

It is an old, but a very true observation, that the human mind must ever be employed. A relish for reading, or any of the fine arts, should be cultivated very early in life; and those who reflect can tell, of what importance it is for the mind to have some resource in itself, and not to be entirely dependant on the senses for employment and amusement. If it unfortunately is so, it must submit to meanness, and often to vice, in order to gratify them. The wisest and best are too much under their influence; and the endeavouring to conquer them, when reason and virtue will not give their sanction, constitutes great part of the warfare of life. What support, then, have they who are all senses, and who are full of schemes, which terminate in temporal objects?

Reading is the most rational employment, if people seek food for the understanding, and do not read merely to remember words; or with a view to quote celebrated authors, and retail sentiments they do not understand or feel. Judicious books enlarge the mind and improve the heart, though some, by them, 'are made coxcombs whom nature meant for fools.'[1]

Those productions which give a wrong account of the human passions, and the various accidents of life, ought not to be read before the judgment is formed, or at least exercised. Such accounts are one great cause of the affectation of young women. Sensibility is described and praised, and the effects of it represented in a way so different from nature, that those who imitate it must make themselves very ridiculous. A false taste is acquired, and sensible books appear dull and insipid after those superficial performances, which obtain their full end if they can keep the mind in a continual ferment. Gallantry is made the only interesting subject with the novelist; reading, therefore, will often co-operate to make his fair admirers insignificant.

I do not mean to recommend books of an abstracted or grave cast. There are in our language many, in which instruction and amusement are blended; the Adventurer[2] is of this kind. I mention this book on account of its beautiful allegories and affecting tales, and similar ones may easily be selected. Reason strikes most forcibly when illustrated by the brilliancy of fancy. The sentiments which are scattered may be observed, and when they are relished, and the mind set to work, it may be allowed to chuse books for itself, for every thing will then instruct.

I would have every one try to form an opinion of an author themselves, though modesty may restrain them from mentioning it. Many are so anxious to have the reputation of taste, that they only praise the authors whose merit is indisputable. I am sick of hearing of the sublimity of Milton, the elegance and harmony of Pope, and the original, untaught genius of Shakespear. These cursory remarks are made by some who know nothing of nature, and could not enter into the spirit of those authors, or understand them.

A florid style mostly passes with the ignorant for fine writing; many sentences are admired that have no meaning in them, though they contain 'words of thundering sound,'[3] and others that have nothing to recommend them but sweet and musical terminations.

Books of theology are not calculated for young persons; religion is best taught by example. The Bible should be read with particular respect, and they should not be taught reading by so sacred a book; lest they might consider that as a task, which ought to be a source of the most exalted satisfaction.

It may be observed, that I recommend the mind's being put into a proper train, and then left to itself. Fixed rules cannot be given, it must depend on the nature and strength of the understanding; and those who observe it can best tell what kind of cultivation will improve it. The mind is not, cannot be created by the teacher, though it may be cultivated, and its real powers found out.

The active spirits of youth may make time glide away without intellectual enjoyments; but when the novelty of the scene is worn off, the want of them will be felt, and nothing else can fill up the void. The mind is confined to the body, and must sink into sensuality; for it has nothing to do but to provide for it, 'how it shall eat and drink, and wherewithal it shall be clothed.'[4]

All kinds of refinement have been found fault with for increasing our cares and sorrows; yet surely the contrary effect also arises from them. Taste and thought open many sources of pleasure, which do not depend on fortune.

No employment of the mind is a sufficient excuse for neglecting domestic duties, and I cannot conceive that they are incompatible. A woman may fit herself to be the companion and friend of a man of sense, and yet know how to take care of his family.

[1] Alexander Pope, *An Essay on Criticism* (1719), ll. 26–7: "Some are bewilder'd in the Maze of Schools, / And Some made *Coxcombs* Nature meant for Fools."

[2] **The Adventurer (1752–1754)**: a periodical to which Samuel Johnson regularly contributed.

[3] Oliver Goldsmith, *The Deserted Village* (1770), ll. 211–14: ". . . words of learned length, and thund'ring sound / Amazed the gazing rustics rang'd around."

[4] Matthew 6:31.

from VINDICATION OF THE RIGHTS OF WOMAN:

with Strictures on Political and Moral Subjects

(1792)

TO M. TALLEYRAND-PÉRIGORD LATE BISHOP OF AUTUN[1]

SIR,

Having read with great pleasure a pamphlet[2] which you have lately published, I dedicate this volume to you; to induce you to reconsider the subject, and maturely weigh what I have advanced respecting the rights of woman and national education: and I call with the firm tone of humanity; for my arguments, Sir, are dictated by a disinterested spirit—I plead for my sex—not for myself. Independence I have long considered as the grand blessing of life, the basis of every virtue—and independence I will ever secure by contracting my wants, though I were to live on a barren heath.

It is then an affection for the whole human race that makes my pen dart rapidly along to support what I believe to be the cause of virtue: and the same motive leads me earnestly to wish to see woman placed in a station in which she would advance, instead of retarding, the progress of those glorious principles that give a substance to morality. My opinion, indeed, respecting the rights and duties of woman, seems to flow so naturally from these simple principles, that I think it scarcely possible, but that some of the enlarged minds who formed your admirable constitution, will coincide with me.[3]

In France there is undoubtedly a more general diffusion of knowledge than in any part of the European world, and I attribute it, in a great measure, to the social intercourse which has long subsisted between the sexes. It is true, I utter my sentiments with freedom, that in France the very essence of sensuality has been extracted to regale the voluptuary, and a kind of sentimental lust has prevailed, which, together with the system of duplicity that the whole tenour of their political and civil government taught, have given a sinister sort of sagacity to the French character, properly termed finesse; from which naturally flow a polish of manners that injures the substance, by hunting sincerity out of society.—And, modesty, the fairest garb of virtue! has been more grossly insulted in France than even in England, till their women have treated as *prudish* that attention to decency, which brutes instinctively observe.

Manners and morals are so nearly allied that they have often been confounded; but, though the former should only be the natural reflection of the latter, yet, when various causes have produced factitious and corrupt manners, which are very early caught, morality becomes an empty name. The personal reserve, and sacred respect for cleanliness and delicacy in domestic life, which French women almost despise, are the graceful pillars of modesty; but, far from despising them, if the pure flame of patriotism have reached their bosoms, they should labour to improve the morals of their fellow-citizens, by teaching men, not only to respect modesty in women, but to acquire it themselves, as the only way to merit their esteem.

Contending for the rights of woman, my main argument is built on this simple principle, that if she be not prepared by education to become the companion of man, she will stop the progress of knowledge and virtue; for truth must be common to all, or it will be inefficacious with respect to its influence on general practice. And how can woman be expected to co-operate unless she know why she ought to be virtuous? unless freedom strengthen her reason till she comprehend her duty, and see in what

---

[1] The text reprinted here is from the second 1792 London edition, published the same year as the first edition and including the revisions that Wollstonecraft had not had time to make before Joseph Johnson rushed the first edition into print early in 1792.

Charles Maurice de Talleyrand-Périgord, prince de Benevent (1754–1838), was Bishop of Autun, France, from 1788 to 1791. He resigned in order to support the revolutionary French Republic, serving on the Estates General, the Constituent Assembly, and the National Assembly, and as a foreign minister and envoy. He advocated the confiscation of church property to meet government expenses and developed the plan for a new system of state-supported education.

[2] **pamphlet:** *Rapport sur l'instruction publique, fait au nom de Comité de constitution* (1791). Talleyrand called for a free public system of education for both sexes of all ages, but followed Rousseau's *Émile, ou Traité de l'Éducation* (1762) in requiring that the education of females should prepare them for a life of subservience to men.

[3] The 1791 Constitution of the new French Republic conferred citizenship only upon men over the age of 25.

manner it is connected with her real good? If children are to be educated to understand the true principle of patriotism, their mother must be a patriot; and the love of mankind, from which an orderly train of virtues spring, can only be produced by considering the moral and civil interest of mankind; but the education and situation of woman, at present, shuts her out from such investigations.

In this work I have produced many arguments, which to me were conclusive, to prove that the prevailing notion respecting a sexual character was subversive of morality, and I have contended, that to render the human body and mind more perfect, chastity must more universally prevail, and that chastity will never be respected in the male world till the person of a woman is not, as it were, idolized, when little virtue or sense embellish it with the grand traces of mental beauty, or the interesting simplicity of affection.

Consider, Sir, dispassionately, these observations—for a glimpse of this truth seemed to open before you when you observed, 'that to see one half of the human race excluded by the other from all participation of government, was a political phaenomenon that, according to abstract principles, it was impossible to explain.'[4] If so, on what does your constitution rest? If the abstract rights of man will bear discussion and explanation, those of woman, by a parity of reasoning, will not shrink from the same test: though a different opinion prevails in this country, built on the very arguments which you use to justify the oppression of woman—prescription.

Consider, I address you as a legislator, whether, when men contend for their freedom, and to be allowed to judge for themselves respecting their own happiness, it be not inconsistent and unjust to subjugate women, even though you firmly believe that you are acting in the manner best calculated to promote their happiness? Who made man the exclusive judge, if woman partake with him the gift of reason?

In this style, argue tyrants of every denomination, from the weak king to the weak father of a family; they are all eager to crush reason; yet always assert that they usurp its throne only to be useful. Do you not act a similar part, when you *force* all women, by denying them civil and political rights, to remain immured in their families groping in the dark? for surely, Sir, you will not assert, that a duty can be binding which is not founded on reason? If indeed this be their destination, arguments may be drawn from reason: and thus augustly supported, the more understanding women acquire, the more they will be attached to their duty—comprehending it—for unless they comprehend it, unless their morals be fixed on the same immutable principle as those of man, no authority can make them discharge it in a virtuous manner. They may be convenient slaves, but slavery will have its constant effect, degrading the master and the abject dependent.

But, if women are to be excluded, without having a voice, from a participation of the natural rights of mankind, prove first, to ward off the charge of injustice and inconsistency, that they want reason—else this flaw in your NEW CONSTITUTION will ever shew that man must, in some shape, act like a tyrant, and tyranny, in whatever part of society it rears its brazen front, will ever undermine morality.

I have repeatedly asserted, and produced what appeared to me irrefragable arguments drawn from matters of fact, to prove my assertion, that women cannot, by force, be confined to domestic concerns; for they will, however ignorant, intermeddle with more weighty affairs, neglecting private duties only to disturb, by cunning tricks, the orderly plans of reason which rise above their comprehension.

Besides, whilst they are only made to acquire personal accomplishments,[5] men will seek for pleasure in variety, and faithless husbands will make faithless wives; such ignorant beings, indeed, will be very excusable when, not taught to respect public good, nor allowed any civil rights, they attempt to do themselves justice by retaliation.

The box of mischief[6] thus opened in society, what is to preserve private virtue, the only security of public freedom and universal happiness?

Let there be then no coercion *established* in society, and the common law of gravity prevailing, the sexes will fall into their proper places. And, now that more equitable laws are forming your citizens, marriage may

[4] Talleyrand, *Rapport sur l'instruction publique,* p. 116.

[5] **accomplishments**: in the eighteenth century, all the skills that a well-brought-up young woman of the upper classes was supposed to acquire, namely reading, penmanship, drawing, a smattering of French and Italian, the ability to sing, dance, do fine needlework, and play the piano.

[6] **box of mischief**: in Greek mythology, the first woman Pandora, overwhelmed by curiosity, opened the forbidden box containing all the evils of humankind, thereby loosing them upon the world. Only hope remained in the box when she closed it again. Note that Wollstonecraft attributes the opening of this box to men, not women.

become more sacred: your young men may choose wives from motives of affection, and your maidens allow love to root out vanity.

The father of a family will not then weaken his constitution and debase his sentiments, by visiting the harlot, nor forget, in obeying the call of appetite, the purpose for which it was implanted. And, the mother will not neglect her children to practise the arts of coquetry, when sense and modesty secure her the friendship of her husband.

But, till men become attentive to the duty of a father, it is vain to expect women to spend that time in their nursery which they, 'wise in their generation,'[7] choose to spend at their glass; for this exertion of cunning is only an instinct of nature to enable them to obtain indirectly a little of that power of which they are unjustly denied a share: for, if women are not permitted to enjoy legitimate rights, they will render both men and themselves vicious, to obtain illicit privileges.

I wish, Sir, to set some investigations of this kind afloat in France; and should they lead to a confirmation of my principles, when your constitution is revised the Rights of Woman may be respected, if it be fully proved that reason calls for this respect, and loudly demands JUSTICE for one half of the human race.

I am, Sir,
Your's respectfully,
M. W.

— INTRODUCTION —

After considering the historic page, and viewing the living world with anxious solicitude, the most melancholy emotions of sorrowful indignation have depressed my spirits, and I have sighed when obliged to confess, that either nature has made a great difference between man and man, or that the civilization which has hitherto taken place in the world has been very partial. I have turned over various books written on the subject of education, and patiently observed the conduct of parents and the management of schools; but what has been the result?—a profound conviction that the neglected education of my fellow-creatures is the grand source of the misery I deplore; and that women, in particular, are rendered weak and wretched by a variety of concurring causes, originating from one hasty conclusion. The conduct and manners of women, in fact, evidently prove that their minds are not in a healthy state; for, like the flowers which are planted in too rich a soil, strength and usefulness are sacrificed to beauty; and the flaunting leaves, after having pleased a fastidious eye, fade, disregarded on the stalk, long before the season when they ought to have arrived at maturity.—One cause of this barren blooming I attribute to a false system of education, gathered from the books written on this subject by men who, considering females rather as women than human creatures, have been more anxious to make them alluring mistresses than affectionate wives and rational mothers; and the understanding of the sex has been so bubbled by this specious homage, that the civilized women of the present century, with a few exceptions, are only anxious to inspire love, when they ought to cherish a nobler ambition, and by their abilities and virtues exact respect.

In a treatise, therefore, on female rights and manners, the works which have been particularly written for their improvement must not be overlooked; especially when it is asserted, in direct terms, that the minds of women are enfeebled by false refinement; that the books of instruction, written by men of genius, have had the same tendency as more frivolous productions; and that, in the true style of Mahometanism,[8] they are treated as a kind of subordinate beings; and not as a part of the human species, when improveable reason is allowed to be the dignified distinction which raises men above the brute creation, and puts a natural sceptre in a feeble hand.

Yet, because I am a woman, I would not lead my readers to suppose that I mean violently to agitate the contested question respecting the equality or inferiority of the sex; but as the subject lies in my way, and I cannot pass it over without subjecting the main tendency of my reasoning to misconstruction, I shall stop a moment to deliver, in a few words, my opinion.—In the government of the physical world it is observable that the female in point of strength is, in general, inferior to the male. This is the law of nature; and it does not appear to be suspended or abrogated in favour of woman. A degree of physical superiority cannot, therefore, be denied—and it is a noble prerogative! But not content with this natural pre-eminence, men endeavour to sink us still lower, merely to render us alluring objects for a moment; and women, intoxicated by the adoration which men, under the influence of their

[7]**'wise in their generation'**: Luke 16:8, "the children of this world are in their generation wiser than the children of light."

[8]**style of Mahometanism**: reference to the widespread Christian misconception that in the religion of Islam women do not have souls.

senses, pay them, do not seek to obtain a durable interest in their hearts, or to become the friends of the fellow creatures who find amusement in their society.

I am aware of an obvious inference:—from every quarter have I heard exclamations against masculine women; but where are they to be found? If by this appellation men mean to inveigh against their ardour in hunting, shooting, and gaming, I shall most cordially join in the cry; but if it be against the imitation of manly virtues, or, more properly speaking, the attainment of those talents and virtues, the exercise of which ennobles the human character, and which raise females in the scale of animal being, when they are comprehensively termed mankind;—all those who view them with a philosophic eye must, I should think, wish with me, that they may every day grow more and more masculine.

This discussion naturally divides the subject. I shall first consider women in the grand light of human creatures, who, in common with men, are placed on this earth to unfold their faculties; and afterwards I shall more particularly point out their peculiar designation.

I wish also to steer clear of an error which many respectable writers have fallen into; for the instruction which has hitherto been addressed to women, has rather been applicable to *ladies,* if the little indirect advice, that is scattered through Sandford and Merton,[9] be excepted; but, addressing my sex in a firmer tone, I pay particular attention to those in the middle class, because they appear to be in the most natural state. Perhaps the seeds of false-refinement, immorality, and vanity, have ever been shed by the great. Weak, artificial beings, raised above the common wants and affections of their race, in a premature unnatural manner, undermine the very foundation of virtue, and spread corruption through the whole mass of society! As a class of mankind they have the strongest claim to pity; the education of the rich tends to render them vain and helpless, and the unfolding mind is not strengthened by the practice of those duties which dignify the human character.—They only live to amuse themselves, and by the same law which in nature invariably produces certain effects, they soon only afford barren amusement.

But as I purpose taking a separate view of the different ranks of society, and of the moral character of women, in each, this hint is, for the present, sufficient; and I have only alluded to the subject, because it appears to me to be the very essence of an introduction to give a cursory account of the contents of the work it introduces.

My own sex, I hope, will excuse me, if I treat them like rational creatures, instead of flattering their *fascinating* graces, and viewing them as if they were in a state of perpetual childhood, unable to stand alone. I earnestly wish to point out in what true dignity and human happiness consists—I wish to persuade women to endeavour to acquire strength, both of mind and body, and to convince them that the soft phrases, susceptibility of heart, delicacy of sentiment, and refinement of taste, are almost synonymous with epithets of weakness, and that those beings who are only the objects of pity and that kind of love, which has been termed its sister, will soon become objects of contempt.

Dismissing then those pretty feminine phrases, which the men condescendingly use to soften our slavish dependence, and despising that weak elegancy of mind, exquisite sensibility, and sweet docility of manners, supposed to be the sexual characteristics of the weaker vessel, I wish to shew that elegance is inferior to virtue, that the first object of laudable ambition is to obtain a character as a human being, regardless of the distinction of sex; and that secondary views should be brought to this simple touchstone.

This is a rough sketch of my plan; and should I express my conviction with the energetic emotions that I feel whenever I think of the subject, the dictates of experience and reflection will be felt by some of my readers. Animated by this important object, I shall disdain to cull my phrases or polish my style;—I aim at being useful, and sincerity will render me unaffected; for, wishing rather to persuade by the force of my arguments, than dazzle by the elegance of my language, I shall not waste my time in rounding periods, or in fabricating the turgid bombast of artificial feelings, which, coming from the head, never reach the heart.—I shall be employed about things, not words!—and, anxious to render my sex more respectable members of society, I shall try to avoid that flowery diction which has slided from essays into novels, and from novels into familiar letters and conversation.

These pretty superlatives, dropping glibly from the tongue, vitiate the taste, and create a kind of sickly delicacy that turns away from simple unadorned truth; and a deluge of false sentiments and overstretched feelings,

[9] **Sandford and Merton:** *The History of Sandford and Merton* (1786–1789) by Thomas Day, an extremely popular children's book heavily influenced by Rousseau's *Émile* that unfavorably contrasts the wealthy spoilt Merton to the poor honest Sandford.

stifling the natural emotions of the heart, render the domestic pleasures insipid, that ought to sweeten the exercise of those severe duties, which educate a rational and immortal being for a nobler field of action.

The education of women has, of late, been more attended to than formerly; yet they are still reckoned a frivolous sex, and ridiculed or pitied by the writers who endeavour by satire or instruction to improve them. It is acknowledged that they spend many of the first years of their lives in acquiring a smattering of accomplishments; meanwhile strength of body and mind are sacrificed to libertine notions of beauty, to the desire of establishing themselves,[10]—the only way women can rise in the world,—by marriage. And this desire making mere animals of them, when they marry they act as such children may be expected to act:—they dress; they paint, and nickname God's creatures.[11]—Surely these weak beings are only fit for a seraglio![12] Can they be expected to govern a family with judgment, or take care of the poor babes whom they bring into the world?

If then it can be fairly deduced from the present conduct of the sex, from the prevalent fondness for pleasure which takes place of ambition and those nobler passions that open and enlarge the soul; that the instruction which women have hitherto received has only tended, with the constitution of civil society, to render them insignificant objects of desire—mere propagators of fools!—if it can be proved that in aiming to accomplish them, without cultivating their understandings, they are taken out of their sphere of duties, and made ridiculous and useless when the short-lived bloom of beauty is over,[13] I presume that *rational* men will excuse me for endeavouring to persuade them to become more masculine and respectable.

[10] **libertine:** *n.* a man who is not restrained by moral law; *adj.* licentious. **establishing themselves:** gaining an establishment or comfortable home through marriage.

[11] Cf. Shakespeare, *Hamlet,* II.i.146–8: "You jig and amble, and you lisp, you nickname God's creatures and make wantonness your ignorance."

[12] **seraglio:** Turkish harem.

[13] "A lively writer, I cannot recollect his name, asks what business women turned of forty have to do in the world?" [M. W.]. Wollstonecraft may be recalling the words of the libertine Lord Merton in Frances Burney's novel *Evelina* (1778): "I don't know what the devil a woman lives for after thirty; she is only in other folks' way."

Indeed the word masculine is only a bugbear: there is little reason to fear that women will acquire too much courage or fortitude; for their apparent inferiority with respect to bodily strength, must render them, in some degree, dependent on men in the various relations of life; but why should it be increased by prejudices that give a sex to virtue, and confound simple truths with sensual reveries?

Women are, in fact, so much degraded by mistaken notions of female excellence, that I do not mean to add a paradox when I assert, that this artificial weakness produces a propensity to tyrannize, and gives birth to cunning, the natural opponent of strength, which leads them to play off those contemptible infantine airs that undermine esteem even whilst they excite desire. Let men become more chaste and modest, and if women do not grow wiser in the same ratio, it will be clear that they have weaker understandings. It seems scarcely necessary to say, that I now speak of the sex in general. Many individuals have more sense than their male relatives; and, as nothing preponderates where there is a constant struggle for an equilibrium, without it has naturally more gravity, some women govern their husbands without degrading themselves, because intellect will always govern.

— CHAPTER I —

The Rights and Involved Duties of Mankind Considered

In the present state of society it appears necessary to go back to first principles in search of the most simple truths, and to dispute with some prevailing prejudice every inch of ground. To clear my way, I must be allowed to ask some plain questions, and the answers will probably appear as unequivocal as the axioms on which reasoning is built; though, when entangled with various motives of action, they are formally contradicted, either by the words or conduct of men.

In what does man's pre-eminence over the brute creation consist? The answer is as clear as that a half is less than the whole; in Reason.

What acquirement exalts one being above another? Virtue; we spontaneously reply.

For what purpose were the passions implanted? That man by struggling with them might attain a degree of knowledge denied to the brutes; whispers Experience.

Consequently the perfection of our nature and capability of happiness, must be estimated by the degree of reason, virtue, and knowledge, that distinguish the individual, and direct the laws which bind society: and that from the exercise of reason, knowledge and virtue naturally flow, is equally undeniable, if mankind be viewed collectively.

The rights and duties of man thus simplified, it seems almost impertinent to attempt to illustrate truths that appear so incontrovertible; yet such deeply rooted prejudices have clouded reason, and such spurious qualities have assumed the name of virtues, that it is necessary to pursue the course of reason as it has been perplexed and involved in error, by various adventitious circumstances, comparing the simple axiom with casual deviations. Men, in general, seem to employ their reason to justify prejudices, which they have imbibed, they can scarcely trace how, rather than to root them out. The mind must be strong that resolutely forms its own principles; for a kind of intellectual cowardice prevails which makes many men shrink from the task, or only do it by halves. Yet the imperfect conclusions thus drawn, are frequently very plausible, because they are built on partial experience, on just, though narrow, views.

Going back to first principles, vice skulks, with all its native deformity, from close investigation; but a set of shallow reasoners are always exclaiming that these arguments prove too much, and that a measure rotten at the core may be expedient. Thus expediency is continually contrasted with simple principles, till truth is lost in a mist of words; virtue, in forms, and knowledge rendered a sounding nothing, by the specious prejudices that assume its name.

That the society is formed in the wisest manner, whose constitution is founded on the nature of man, strikes, in the abstract, every thinking being so forcibly, that it looks like presumption to endeavour to bring forward proofs; though proof must be brought, or the strong hold of prescription will never be forced by reason; yet to urge prescription as an argument to justify the depriving men (or women) of their natural rights, is one of the absurd sophisms which daily insult common sense.

The civilization of the bulk of the people of Europe is very partial; nay, it may be made a question, whether they have acquired any virtues in exchange for innocence, equivalent to the misery produced by the vices that have been plastered over unsightly ignorance, and the freedom which has been bartered for splendid slavery. The desire of dazzling by riches, the most certain pre-eminence that man can obtain, the pleasure of commanding flattering sycophants, and many other complicated low calculations of doting self-love, have all contributed to overwhelm the mass of mankind, and make liberty a convenient handle for mock patriotism. For whilst rank and titles are held of the utmost importance, before which Genius 'must hide its diminished head,'[14] it is, with a few exceptions, very unfortunate for a nation when a man of abilities, without rank or property, pushes himself forward to notice.—Alas! what unheard of misery have thousands suffered to purchase a cardinal's hat for an intriguing obscure adventurer, who longed to be ranked with princes, or lord it over them by seizing the triple crown![15]

Such, indeed, has been the wretchedness that has flowed from hereditary honours, riches, and monarchy, that men of lively sensibility have almost uttered blasphemy in order to justify the dispensations of providence. Man has been held out as independent of his power who made him, or as a lawless planet darting from its orbit to steal the celestial fire of reason; and the vengeance of heaven, lurking in the subtile flame, like Pandora's pent up mischiefs, sufficiently punished his temerity, by introducing evil into the world.

Impressed by this view of the misery and disorder which pervaded society, and fatigued with jostling against artificial fools, Rousseau became enamoured of solitude, and, being at the same time an optimist, he labours with uncommon eloquence to prove that man was naturally a solitary animal.[16] Misled by his respect for the goodness of God, who certainly—for what man of sense and feeling can doubt it!—gave life only to communicate happiness, he considers evil as positive, and the work of man; not aware that he was exalting one attribute at the expence of another, equally necessary to divine perfection.

Reared on a false hypothesis his arguments in favour of a state of nature are plausible, but unsound. I say unsound; for to assert that a state of nature is preferable to civilization, in all its possible perfection, is, in other words, to arraign supreme wisdom; and the paradoxical

---

[14] Cf. Milton, *Paradise Lost*, IV.34–35: "all the stars / Hide their diminished heads."

[15] **the triple crown**: the crown of the Roman Catholic Pope.

[16] Jean-Jacques Rousseau (1712–1778), Swiss-French philosopher, novelist, radical political theorist, and composer, was best known for the assertion in his *Social Contract* (1762) that mankind was born free but was everywhere in chains, and for his celebration of the "noble savage." Here Wollstonecraft refers to Rousseau's *Discourse on the Origin and Foundation of Human Inequality* (1755), where he describes the original state of human nature as necessarily solitary and argues that human beings inevitably grow more wicked as they grow more sociable. In his *Confessions* (1782), Rousseau describes his own love of solitude.

exclamation, that God has made all things right, and that error has been introduced by the creature, whom he formed, knowing what he formed, is as unphilosophical as impious.[17]

When that wise Being who created us and placed us here, saw the fair idea, he willed, by allowing it to be so, that the passions should unfold our reason, because he could see that present evil would produce future good. Could the helpless creature whom he called from nothing break loose from his providence, and boldly learn to know good by practising evil, without his permission? No.— How could that energetic advocate for immortality argue so inconsistently? Had mankind remained for ever in the brutal state of nature, which even his magic pen cannot paint as a state in which a single virtue took root, it would have been clear, though not to the sensitive unreflecting wanderer, that man was born to run the circle of life and death, and adorn God's garden for some purpose which could not easily be reconciled with his attributes.

But if, to crown the whole, there were to be rational creatures produced, allowed to rise in excellence by the exercise of powers implanted for that purpose; if benignity itself thought fit to call into existence a creature above the brutes,[18] who could think and improve himself, why should that inestimable gift, for a gift it was, if man was so created as to have a capacity to rise above the state in which sensation produced brutal ease, be called, in direct terms, a curse? A curse it might be reckoned, if the whole of our existence were bounded by our continuance in this world; for why should the gracious fountain of life give us passions, and the power of reflecting, only to imbitter our days and inspire us with mistaken notions of dignity? Why should he lead us from love of ourselves to the sublime emotions which the discovery of his wisdom and goodness excites, if these feelings were not set in motion to improve our nature, of which they make a part,[19] and render us capable of enjoying a more godlike portion of happiness? Firmly persuaded that no evil exists in the world that God did not design to take place, I build my belief on the perfection of God.

Rousseau exerts himself to prove that all *was* right originally: a crowd of authors that all is now right: and I, that all will *be* right.

But, true to his first position, next to a state of nature, Rousseau celebrates barbarism, and apostrophizing the shade of Fabricius,[20] he forgets that, in conquering the world, the Romans never dreamed of establishing their own liberty on a firm basis, or of extending the reign of virtue. Eager to support his system, he stigmatizes, as vicious, every effort of genius; and, uttering the apotheosis of savage virtues, he exalts those to demi-gods, who were scarcely human—the brutal Spartans, who, in defiance of justice and gratitude, sacrificed, in cold blood, the slaves who had shewn themselves heroes to rescue their oppressors.[21]

Disgusted with artificial manners and virtues, the citizen of Geneva,[22] instead of properly sifting the subject, threw away the wheat with the chaff, without waiting to inquire whether the evils which his ardent soul turned from indignantly, were the consequence of civilization or

---

[17] Rousseau's treatise on education, *Émile* (1762), begins thus: "All things are good as their Creator made them, but everything degenerates in the hands of man" (trans. William Kenrick, 1763, the translation used by Wollstonecraft).

[18] Contrary to the opinion of anatomists, who argue by analogy from the formation of the teeth, stomach, and intestines, Rousseau will not allow a man to be a carnivorous animal. And, carried away from nature by a love of system, he disputes whether man be a gregarious animal, though the long and helpless state of infancy seems to point him out as particularly impelled to pair, the first step towards herding [M. W.]. Cf. *Émile,* I.ii.286, II.iv.133–64, trans. William Kenrick (1763).

[19] What would you say to a mechanic whom you had desired to make a watch to point out the hour of the day, if, to show his ingenuity, he added wheels to make it a repeater, &c. that perplexed the simple mechanism; should he urge, to excuse himself—had you not touched a certain spring, you would have known nothing of the matter, and that he should have amused himself by making *an experiment* without doing you any harm: would you not retort fairly upon him, by insisting that if he had not added those needless wheels and springs, the accident could not have happened? [M. W.]

[20] Gaius Fabricius Luscinus (d. after 275 BC), a Roman general who criticized the effeminacy of the later Roman emperors and urged them to return to the business of conquering the world. He was known as a paragon of incorruptibility. Rousseau invokes his ghost in his first work, *A Discourse on the Sciences and the Arts* (1750), to condemn the arts.

[21] In his *History of the Peloponnesian War* (IV.80.3–4), Thucydides (c. 460–400 BC) describes how the Spartans betrayed the helots or slaves fighting for them. The Spartan generals announced that those helots who fought most bravely would be granted their freedom; they then massacred the 2,000 men who claimed this reward on the grounds that they would be the ones most likely to lead a slave revolt against Sparta.

[22] Rousseau was born in Geneva, Switzerland, and called himself *"citoyen de Genève."*

the vestiges of barbarism. He saw vice trampling on virtue, and the semblance of goodness taking place of the reality; he saw talents bent by power to sinister purposes, and never thought of tracing the gigantic mischief up to arbitrary power, up to the hereditary distinctions that clash with the mental superiority that naturally raises a man above his fellows. He did not perceive that regal power, in a few generations, introduces idiotism into the noble stem, and holds out baits to render thousands idle and vicious.

Nothing can set the regal character in a more contemptible point of view, than the various crimes that have elevated men to the supreme dignity.—Vile intrigues, unnatural crimes, and every vice that degrades our nature, have been the steps to this distinguished eminence; yet millions of men have supinely allowed the nerveless limbs of the posterity of such rapacious prowlers to rest quietly on their ensanguined thrones.[23]

What but a pestilential vapour can hover over society when its chief director is only instructed in the invention of crimes, or the stupid routine of childish ceremonies? Will men never be wise?—will they never cease to expect corn from tares, and figs from thistles?[24]

It is impossible for any man, when the most favourable circumstances concur, to acquire sufficient knowledge and strength of mind to discharge the duties of a king, entrusted with uncontrouled power; how then must they be violated when his very elevation is an insuperable bar to the attainment of either wisdom or virtue; when all the feelings of a man are stifled by flattery, and reflection shut out by pleasure! Surely it is madness to make the fate of thousands depend on the caprice of a weak fellow creature, whose very station sinks him *necessarily* below the meanest of his subjects! But one power should not be thrown down to exalt another—for all power inebriates weak man; and its abuse proves that the more equality there is established among men, the more virtue and happiness will reign in society. But this and any similar maxim deduced from simple reason, raises an outcry—the church or the state is in danger, if faith in the wisdom of antiquity is not implicit; and they who, roused by the sight of human calamity, dare to attack human authority, are reviled as despisers of God, and enemies of man. These are bitter calumnies, yet they reached one of the best of men,[25] whose ashes still preach peace, and whose memory demands a respectful pause, when subjects are discussed that lay so near his heart.—

After attacking the sacred majesty of Kings, I shall scarcely excite surprise by adding my firm persuasion that every profession, in which great subordination of rank constitutes its power, is highly injurious to morality.

A standing army, for instance, is incompatible with freedom; because subordination and rigour are the very sinews of military discipline; and despotism is necessary to give vigour to enterprizes that one will directs. A spirit inspired by romantic notions of honour, a kind of morality founded on the fashion of the age, can only be felt by a few officers, whilst the main body must be moved by command, like the waves of the sea; for the strong wind of authority pushes the crowd of subalterns forward, they scarcely know or care why, with headlong fury.

Besides, nothing can be so prejudicial to the morals of the inhabitants of country towns as the occasional residence of a set of idle superficial young men, whose only occupation is gallantry, and whose polished manners render vice more dangerous, by concealing its deformity under gay ornamental drapery. An air of fashion, which is but a badge of slavery, and proves that the soul has not a strong individual character, awes simple country people into an imitation of the vices, when they cannot catch the slippery graces, of politeness. Every corps is a chain of despots, who, submitting and tyrannizing without exercising their reason, become dead weights of vice and folly on the community. A man of rank or fortune, sure of rising by interest, has nothing to do but to pursue some extravagant freak;[26] whilst the needy *gentleman*, who is to rise, as the phrase turns, by his merit, becomes a servile parasite or vile pander.

Sailors, the naval gentlemen, come under the same description, only their vices assume a different and grosser cast. They are more positively indolent, when

[23] Could there be a greater insult offered to the rights of man than the beds of justice in France, when an infant was made the organ of the detestable Dubois [M. W.]! A **bed of justice:** (*lit de justice*) was a session held by the French monarch and parliament in which all authority rested with the Crown; during the infancy of King Louis XV, the authority of the crown was vested in Cardinal Guillaume Dubois (1656–1723).

[24] Cf. Matthew 7:16 and Luke 6:44.

[25] Dr. [Richard] Price [M. W.], (1723–1791), Dissenting (Unitarian) minister and radical political philosopher who condemned the War with the American Colonies and supported the rights of man. His *Discourse on the Love of Our Country* (1789) was attacked by Burke in his *Reflections on the Revolution in France** (1790) and defended by Wollstonecraft in her *Vindication of the Rights of Men** (1790).

[26] **freak:** whim, caprice.

not discharging the ceremonials of their station; whilst the insignificant fluttering of soldiers may be termed active idleness. More confined to the society of men, the former acquire a fondness for humour and mischievous tricks; whilst the latter, mixing frequently with well-bred women, catch a sentimental cant. — But mind is equally out of the question, whether they indulge the horse-laugh, or polite simper.

May I be allowed to extend the comparison to a profession where more mind is certainly to be found; for the clergy have superior opportunities of improvement, though subordination almost equally cramps their faculties? The blind submission imposed at college to forms of belief serves as a novitiate to the curate, who must obsequiously respect the opinion of his rector or patron, if he mean to rise in his profession. Perhaps there cannot be a more forcible contrast than between the servile dependent gait of a poor curate and the courtly mien of a bishop. And the respect and contempt they inspire render the discharge of their separate functions equally useless.

It is of great importance to observe that the character of every man is, in some degree, formed by his profession. A man of sense may only have a cast of countenance that wears off as you trace his individuality, whilst the weak, common man has scarcely ever any character, but what belongs to the body; at least, all his opinions have been so steeped in the vat consecrated by authority, that the faint spirit which the grape of his own vine yields cannot be distinguished.

Society, therefore, as it becomes more enlightened, should be very careful not to establish bodies of men who must necessarily be made foolish or vicious by the very constitution of their profession.

In the infancy of society, when men were just emerging out of barbarism, chiefs and priests, touching the most powerful springs of savage conduct, hope and fear, must have had unbounded sway. An aristocracy, of course, is naturally the first form of government. But, clashing interests soon losing their equipoise, a monarchy and hierarchy break out of the confusion of ambitious struggles, and the foundation of both is secured by feudal tenures. This appears to be the origin of monarchical and priestly power, and the dawn of civilization. But such combustible materials cannot long be pent up; and, getting vent in foreign wars and intestine[27] insurrections, the people acquire some power in the tumult, which obliges their rulers to gloss over their oppression with a shew of right. Thus, as wars, agriculture, commerce, and literature, expand the mind, despots are compelled, to make covert corruption hold fast the power which was formerly snatched by open force.[28] And this baneful lurking gangrene is most quickly spread by luxury and superstition, the sure dregs of ambition. The indolent puppet of a court first becomes a luxurious monster, or fastidious sensualist, and then makes the contagion which his unnatural state spread, the instrument of tyranny.

It is the pestiferous purple[29] which renders the progress of civilization a curse, and warps the understanding, till men of sensibility doubt whether the expansion of intellect produces a greater portion of happiness or misery. But the nature of the poison points out the antidote; and had Rousseau mounted one step higher in his investigation, or could his eye have pierced through the foggy atmosphere, which he almost disdained to breathe, his active mind would have darted forward to contemplate the perfection of man in the establishment of true civilization, instead of taking his ferocious flight back to the night of sensual ignorance.

— CHAPTER II —

The Prevailing Opinion of a Sexual Character Discussed

To account for, and excuse the tyranny of man, many ingenious arguments have been brought forward to prove, that the two sexes, in the acquirement of virtue, ought to aim at attaining a very different character: or, to speak explicitly, women are not allowed to have sufficient strength of mind to acquire what really deserves the name of virtue. Yet it should seem, allowing them to have souls, that there is but one way appointed by Providence to lead *mankind* to either virtue or happiness.

If then women are not a swarm of ephemeron[30] triflers, why should they be kept in ignorance under the specious name of innocence? Men complain, and with

[27] **intestine:** internal with regard to a country or people; civil, domestic.

[28] Men of abilities scatter seeds that grow up and have a great influence on the forming of opinion; and when once the public opinion preponderates, through the exertion of reason, the overthrow of arbitrary power is not very distant [M. W.].

[29] **purple:** the color of royalty, from the purple togas of the Roman Emperors.

[30] **ephemeron:** an insect which, in its winged state, lives only for a day.

reason, of the follies and caprices of our sex, when they do not keenly satirize our headstrong passions and groveling vices. — Behold, I should answer, the natural effect of ignorance! The mind will ever be unstable that has only prejudices to rest on, and the current will run with destructive fury when there are no barriers to break its force. Women are told from their infancy, and taught by the example of their mothers, that a little knowledge of human weakness, justly termed cunning, softness or temper, *outward* obedience, and a scrupulous attention to a puerile kind of propriety, will obtain for them the protection of man; and should they be beautiful, every thing else is needless, for, at least, twenty years of their lives.

Thus Milton describes our first frail mother; though when he tells us that women are formed for softness and sweet attractive grace, I cannot comprehend his meaning, unless, in the true Mahometan strain,[31] he meant to deprive us of souls, and insinuate that we were beings only designed by sweet attractive grace, and docile blind obedience, to gratify the senses of man when he can no longer soar on the wing of contemplation.[32]

How grossly do they insult us who thus advise us only to render ourselves gentle, domestic brutes! For instance, the winning softness so warmly, and frequently, recommended, that governs by obeying. What childish expression, and how insignificant is the being—can it be an immortal one? who will condescend to govern by such sinister methods! 'Certainly,' says Lord Bacon, 'man is of kin to the beasts by his body; and if he be not of kin to God by his spirit, he is a base and ignoble creature!'[33] Men, indeed, appear to me to act in a very unphilosophical manner when they try to secure the good conduct of women by attempting to keep them always in a state of childhood. Rousseau was more consistent when he wished to stop the progress of reason in both sexes, for if men eat of the tree of knowledge, women will come in for a taste; but, from the imperfect cultivation which their understandings now receive, they only attain a knowledge of evil.

Children, I grant, should be innocent; but when the epithet is applied to men, or women, it is but a civil term for weakness. For if it be allowed that women were destined by Providence to acquire human virtues, and by the exercise of their understandings, that stability of character which is the firmest ground to rest our future hopes upon, they must be permitted to turn to the fountain of light, and not forced to shape their course by the twinkling of a mere satellite. Milton, I grant, was of a very different opinion; for he only bends to the indefeasible right of beauty, though it would be difficult to render two passages which I now mean to contrast, consistent. But into similar inconsistencies are great men often led by their senses.

'To whom thus Eve with *perfect beauty* adorn'd.
My Author and Disposer, what thou bidst
Unargued I obey; so God ordains;
God is *thy law, thou mine*: to know no more
Is Woman's *happiest* knowledge and her *praise*.[34]

These are exactly the arguments that I have used to children; but I have added, your reason is now gaining strength, and, till it arrives at some degree of maturity, you must look up to me for advice — then you ought to *think*, and only rely on God.

Yet in the following lines Milton seems to coincide with me; when he makes Adam thus expostulate with his Maker.

'Hast thou not made me here thy substitute,
And these inferior far beneath me set?
Among *unequals* what society
Can sort, what harmony or true delight?
Which must be mutual, in proportion due
Giv'n and receiv'd; but in *disparity*
The one intense, the other still remiss
Cannot well suit with either, but soon prove
Tedious alike: of *fellowship* I speak
Such as I seek, fit to participate
All rational delight —'[35]

In treating, therefore, of the manners of women, let us, disregarding sensual arguments, trace what we should endeavour to make them in order to co-operate, if the expression be not too bold, with the supreme Being.

[31] **Mahometan strain:** Wollstonecraft invokes the erroneous Christian conception that in the religion of Islam, women do not have souls.

[32] Cf. Milton, *Paradise Lost*, IV.297–98: "For contemplation he and valour formed, / For softness she and sweet attractive grace."

[33] Francis Bacon, *Essay* (1606), XIV, "Of Atheism," p. 89.

[34] Cf. Milton, *Paradise Lost*, IV.634–38; Wollstonecraft's emphasis.

[35] Cf. Milton, *Paradise Lost*, VIII.381–92; Wollstonecraft's emphasis.

By individual education, I mean, for the sense of the word is not precisely defined, such an attention to a child as will slowly sharpen the senses, form the temper, regulate the passions as they begin to ferment, and set the understanding to work before the body arrives at maturity; so that the man may only have to proceed, not to begin, the important task of learning to think and reason.

To prevent any misconstruction, I must add, that I do not believe that a private education can work the wonders which some sanguine[36] writers have attributed to it. Men and women must be educated, in a great degree, by the opinions and manners of the society they live in. In every age there has been a stream of popular opinion that has carried all before it, and given a family character, as it were, to the century. It may then fairly be inferred, that, till society be differently constituted, much cannot be expected from education. It is, however, sufficient for my present purpose to assert, that, whatever effect circumstances have on the abilities, every being may become virtuous by the exercise of its own reason; for if but one being was created with vicious inclinations, that is positively bad, what can save us from atheism? or if we worship a God, is not that God a devil?

Consequently, the most perfect education, in my opinion, is such an exercise of the understanding as is best calculated to strengthen the body and form the heart. Or, in other words, to enable the individual to attain such habits of virtue as will render it independent. In fact, it is a farce to call any being virtuous whose virtues do not result from the exercise of its own reason. This was Rousseau's opinion respecting men.[37] I extend it to women, and confidently assert that they have been drawn out of their sphere by false refinement, and not by an endeavour to acquire masculine qualities. Still the regal homage which they receive is so intoxicating, that till the manners of the times are changed, and formed on more reasonable principles, it may be impossible to convince them that the illegitimate power, which they obtain, by degrading themselves, is a curse, and that they must return to nature and equality, if they wish to secure the placid satisfaction that unsophisticated affections impart. But for this epoch we must wait—wait, perhaps, till kings and nobles, enlightened by reason, and, preferring the real dignity of man to childish state, throw off their gaudy hereditary trappings: and if then women do not resign the arbitrary power of beauty—they will prove that they have *less* mind than man.

I may be accused of arrogance; still I must declare what I firmly believe, that all the writers who have written on the subject of female education and manners from Rousseau to Dr Gregory,[38] have contributed to render women more artificial, weak characters, than they would otherwise have been; and, consequently, more useless members of society. I might have expressed this conviction in a lower key; but I am afraid it would have been the whine of affectation, and not the faithful expression of my feelings, of the clear result, which experience and reflection have led me to draw. When I come to that division of the subject, I shall advert to the passages that I more particularly disapprove of, in the works of the authors I have just alluded to; but it is first necessary to observe, that my objection extends to the whole purport of those books, which tend, in my opinion, to degrade one half of the human species, and render women pleasing at the expence of every solid virtue.

Though, to reason on Rousseau's ground, if man did attain a degree of perfection of mind when his body arrived at maturity, it might be proper, in order to make a man and his wife *one,* that she should rely entirely on his understanding; and the graceful ivy, clasping the oak that supported it, would form a whole in which strength and beauty would be equally conspicuous. But, alas! husbands, as well as their helpmates, are often only overgrown children; nay, thanks to early debauchery, scarcely men in their outward form—and if the blind lead the blind, one need not come from heaven to tell us the consequence.

Many are the causes that, in the present corrupt state of society, contribute to enslave women by cramping their understandings and sharpening their senses. One, perhaps, that silently does more mischief than all the rest, is their disregard of order.

To do every thing in an orderly manner, is a most important precept, which women, who, generally speaking, receive only a disorderly kind of education, seldom attend to with that degree of exactness that men, who from their infancy are broken into method, observe. This negligent kind of guess-work, for what other epithet can be used to point out the random exertions of a sort of instinctive

[36] **sanguine:** hopeful, optimistic.

[37] Cf. Rousseau's *Émile,* I.i.76: "Only reason teaches us good from evil."

[38] Dr. John Gregory (1724–1773), a Scottish professor of medicine and author of *A Father's Legacy to his Daughters* (1774), one of the most influential conduct books of the period.

common sense, never brought to the test of reason? prevents their generalizing matters of fact—so they do today, what they did yesterday, merely because they did it yesterday.

This contempt of the understanding in early life has more baneful consequences than is commonly supposed; for the little knowledge which women of strong minds attain, is, from various circumstances, of a more desultory kind than the knowledge of men, and it is acquired more by sheer observations on real life, than from comparing what has been individually observed with the results of experience generalized by speculation. Led by their dependent situation and domestic employments more into society, what they learn is rather by snatches; and as learning is with them, in general, only a secondary thing, they do not pursue any one branch with that persevering ardour necessary to give vigour to the faculties, and clearness to the judgment. In the present state of society, a little learning is required to support the character of a gentleman; and boys are obliged to submit to a few years of discipline. But in the education of women, the cultivation of the understanding is always subordinate to the acquirement of some corporeal accomplishment; even while enervated by confinement and false notions of modesty, the body is prevented from attaining that grace and beauty which relaxed half-formed limbs never exhibit. Besides, in youth their faculties are not brought forward by emulation; and having no serious scientific study, if they have natural sagacity it is turned too soon on life and manners. They dwell on effects, and modifications, without tracing them back to causes; and complicated rules to adjust behaviour are a weak substitute for simple principles.

As a proof that education gives this appearance of weakness to females, we may instance the example of military men, who are, like them, sent into the world before their minds have been stored with knowledge or fortified by principles. The consequences are similar; soldiers acquire a little superficial knowledge, snatched from the muddy current of conversation, and, from continually mixing with society, they gain, what is termed a knowledge of the world; and this acquaintance with manners and customs has frequently been confounded with a knowledge of the human heart. But can the crude fruit of casual observation, never brought to the test of judgment, formed by comparing speculation and experience, deserve such a distinction? Soldiers, as well as women, practise the minor virtues with punctilious politeness. Where is then the sexual difference, when the education has been the same? All the difference that I can discern, arises from the superior advantage of liberty, which enables the former to see more of life.

It is wandering from my present subject, perhaps, to make a political remark; but, as it was produced naturally by the train of my reflections, I shall not pass it silently over.

Standing armies can never consist of resolute, robust men; they may be well disciplined machines, but they will seldom contain men under the influence of strong passions, or with very vigorous faculties. And as for any depth of understanding, I will venture to affirm, that it is as rarely to be found in the army as amongst women; and the cause, I maintain, is the same. It may be further observed, that officers are also particularly attentive to their persons, fond of dancing, crowded rooms, adventures, and ridicule.[39] Like the *fair* sex, the business of their lives is gallantry.—They were taught to please, and they only live to please. Yet they do not lose their rank in the distinction of sexes, for they are still reckoned superior to women, though in what their superiority consists, beyond what I have just mentioned, it is difficult to discover.

The great misfortune is this, that they both acquire manners before morals, and a knowledge of life before they have, from reflection, any acquaintance with the grand ideal outline of human nature. The consequence is natural; satisfied with common nature, they become a prey to prejudices, and taking all their opinions on credit, they blindly submit to authority. So that if they have any sense, it is a kind of instinctive glance, that catches proportions, and decides with respect to manners; but fails when arguments are to be pursued below the surface, or opinions analyzed.

May not the same remark be applied to women? Nay, the argument may be carried still further, for they are both thrown out of a useful station by the unnatural distinctions established in civilized life. Riches and hereditary honours have made cyphers of women to give consequence to the numerical figure; and idleness has produced a mixture of gallantry and despotism into society, which leads the very men who are the slaves of their mistresses to tyrannize over their sisters, wives, and daughters. This is only keeping them in rank and file, it is true. Strengthen the female mind by enlarging it, and there will be an end to blind

[39] Why should women be censured with petulant acrimony, because they seem to have a passion for a scarlet coat? Has not education placed them more on a level with soldiers than any other class of men? [M. W.]

obedience; but, as blind obedience is ever sought for by power, tyrants and sensualists are in the right when they endeavour to keep women in the dark, because the former only want slaves, and the latter a play-thing. The sensualist, indeed, has been the most dangerous of tyrants, and women have been duped by their lovers, as princes by their ministers, whilst dreaming that they reigned over them.

I now principally allude to Rousseau, for his character of Sophia is, undoubtedly, a captivating one, though it appears to me grossly unnatural;[40] however it is not the superstructure, but the foundation of her character, the principles on which her education was built, that I mean to attack; nay, warmly as I admire the genius of that able writer, whose opinions I shall often have occasion to cite, indignation always takes place of admiration, and the rigid frown of insulted virtue effaces the smile of complacency, which his eloquent periods are wont to raise, when I read his voluptuous reveries. Is this the man, who, in his ardour for virtue, would banish all the soft arts of peace, and almost carry us back to Spartan discipline? Is this the man who delights to paint the useful struggles of passion, the triumphs of good dispositions, and the heroic flights which carry the glowing soul out of itself?—How are these mighty sentiments lowered when he describes the pretty foot and enticing airs of his little favourite! But, for the present, I wave the subject, and, instead of severely reprehending the transient effusions of overweening sensibility, I shall only observe, that whoever has cast a benevolent eye on society, must often have been gratified by the sight of humble mutual love, not dignified by sentiment, or strengthened by a union in intellectual pursuits. The domestic trifles of the day have afforded matters for cheerful converse, and innocent caresses have softened toils which did not require great exercise of mind or stretch of thought: yet, has not the sight of this moderate felicity excited more tenderness than respect? An emotion similar to what we feel when children are playing, or animals sporting,[41] whilst the contemplation of the noble struggles of suffering merit has raised admiration, and carried our thoughts to that world where sensation will give place to reason.

Women are, therefore, to be considered either as moral beings, or so weak that they must be entirely subjected to the superior faculties of men.

Let us examine this question. Rousseau declares that a woman should never, for a moment, feel herself independent, that she should be governed by fear to exercise her *natural* cunning, and made a coquetish slave in order to render her a more alluring object of desire, a *sweeter* companion to man, whenever he chooses to relax himself. He carries the arguments, which he pretends to draw from the indications of nature, still further, and insinuates that truth and fortitude, the corner stones of all human virtue, should be cultivated with certain restrictions, because, with respect to the female character, obedience is the grand lesson which ought to be impressed with unrelenting rigour.[42]

What nonsense! when will a great man arise with sufficient strength of mind to puff away the fumes which pride and sensuality have thus spread over the subject! If women are by nature inferior to men, their virtues must be the same in quality, if not in degree, or virtue is a relative idea; consequently, their conduct should be founded on the same principles, and have the same aim.

Connected with man as daughters, wives, and mothers, their moral character may be estimated by their manner of fulfilling those simple duties; but the end, the grand end of their exertions should be to unfold their own faculties and acquire the dignity of conscious virtue. They may try to render their road pleasant; but ought never to forget, in common with man, that life yields not the felicity which can satisfy an immortal soul. I do not mean to insinuate, that either sex should be so lost in abstract reflections or distant views, as to forget the affections and duties that lie before them, and are, in truth, the means appointed to produce the fruit of life; on the contrary, I would warmly recommend them, even while I assert, that

---

[40] In Rousseau's *Émile,* Sophia is the ideal soft, obedient woman.

[41] Similar feelings has Milton's pleasing picture of paradisiacal happiness ever raised in my mind, yet, instead of envying the lovely pair, I have, with conscious dignity, or Satanic pride, turned to hell for sublimer objects [*Paradise Lost,* IV]. In the same style, when viewing some noble monument of human art, I have traced the emanation of the Deity in the order I admired, till, descending from that giddy height, I have caught myself contemplating the grandest of all human sights;—for fancy quickly placed, in some solitary recess, an outcast of fortune, rising superior to passion and discontent [M. W.].

[42] See Rousseau, *Émile,* IV.v.31–3: "What is most wanted in a woman is gentleness; formed to obey a creature so imperfect as man, a creature often vicious and always faulty, she should early learn to submit to injustice and to suffer the wrongs inflicted on her by her husband without complaint."

they afford most satisfaction when they are considered in their true, sober light.

Probably the prevailing opinion, that woman was created for man, may have taken its rise from Moses's poetical story;[43] yet, as very few, it is presumed, who have bestowed any serious thought on the subject, ever supposed that Eve was, literally speaking, one of Adam's ribs, the deduction must be allowed to fall to the ground; or, only be so far admitted as it proves that man, from the remotest antiquity, found it convenient to exert his strength to subjugate his companion, and his invention to shew that she ought to have her neck bent under the yoke, because the whole creation was only created for his convenience or pleasure.

Let it not be concluded that I wish to invert the order of things; I have already granted, that, from the constitution of their bodies, men seem to be designed by Providence to attain a greater degree of virtue. I speak collectively of the whole sex; but I see not the shadow of a reason to conclude that their virtues should differ in respect to their nature. In fact, how can they, if virtue has only one eternal standard? I must therefore, if I reason consequentially, as strenuously maintain that they have the same simple direction, as that there is a God.

It follows then that cunning should not be opposed to wisdom, little cares to great exertions, or insipid softness, varnished over with the name of gentleness, to that fortitude which grand views alone can inspire.

I shall be told that woman would then lose many of her peculiar graces, and the opinion of a well known poet might be quoted to refute my unqualified assertion. For Pope has said, in the name of the whole male sex,

'Yet ne'er so sure our passion to create,
As when she touch'd the brink of all we hate.'[44]

In what light this sally places men and women, I shall leave to the judicious to determine; meanwhile I shall content myself with observing, that I cannot discover why, unless they are mortal, females should always be degraded by being made subservient to love or lust.

To speak disrespectfully of love is, I know, high treason against sentiment and fine feelings; but I wish to speak the simple language of truth, and rather to address the head than the heart. To endeavour to reason love out of the world, would be to out Quixote Cervantes,[45] and equally offend against common sense; but an endeavour to restrain this tumultuous passion, and to prove that it should not be allowed to dethrone superior powers, or to usurp the sceptre which the understanding should ever coolly wield, appears less wild.

Youth is the season for love in both sexes; but in those days of thoughtless enjoyment provision should be made for the more important years of life, when reflection takes place of sensation. But Rousseau, and most of the male writers who have followed his steps, have warmly inculcated that the whole tendency of female education ought to be directed to one point:—to render them pleasing.

Let me reason with the supporters of this opinion who have any knowledge of human nature, do they imagine that marriage can eradicate the habitude of life? The woman who has only been taught to please will soon find that her charms are oblique sunbeams, and that they cannot have much effect on her husband's heart when they are seen every day, when the summer is passed and gone. Will she then have sufficient native energy to look into herself for comfort, and cultivate her dormant faculties? or, is it not more rational to expect that she will try to please other men; and, in the emotions raised by the expectation of new conquests, endeavour to forget the mortification her love or pride has received? When the husband ceases to be a lover—and the time will inevitably come, her desire of pleasing will then grow languid, or become a spring of bitterness; and love, perhaps, the most evanescent of all passions, gives place to jealousy or vanity.

I now speak of women who are restrained by principle or prejudice; such women, though they would shrink from an intrigue with real abhorrence, yet, nevertheless, wish to be convinced by the homage of gallantry that they are cruelly neglected by their husbands; or, days and weeks are spent in dreaming of the happiness enjoyed by congenial souls till their health is undermined and their spirits broken by discontent. How then can the great art of pleasing be such a necessary study? it is only useful to a mistress; the chaste wife, and serious mother, should only consider her power to please as the polish of her virtues, and the affection of her husband as one of the comforts

[43] Genesis 2:18–22. Moses was thought to be the author of the first five books of the Old Testament (the Pentateuch).

[44] Alexander Pope, "Of the Characters of Women: An Epistle to a Lady" (1735), ll. 51–52.

[45] In his popular novel, *Don Quixote de la Mancha* (1605), Miguel de Cervantes Saavedra mocked the rhetoric and rituals of courtly love.

that render her task less difficult and her life happier.—But, whether she be loved or neglected, her first wish should be to make herself respectable, and not to rely for all her happiness on a being subject to like infirmities with herself.

The worthy Dr Gregory fell into a similar error. I respect his heart; but entirely disapprove of his celebrated Legacy to his Daughters.

He advises them to cultivate a fondness for dress, because a fondness for dress, he asserts, is natural to them. I am unable to comprehend what either he or Rousseau mean, when they frequently use this indefinite term. If they told us that in a pre-existent state the soul was fond of dress, and brought this inclination with it into a new body, I should listen to them with a half smile, as I often do when I hear a rant about innate elegance.—But if he only meant to say that the exercise of the faculties will produce this fondness—I deny it. It is not natural; but arises, like false ambition in men, from a love of power.

Dr Gregory goes much further; he actually recommends dissimulation, and advises an innocent girl to give the lie to her feelings, and not dance with spirit, when gaiety of heart would make her feet eloquent without making her gestures immodest. In the name of truth and common sense, why should not one woman acknowledge that she can take more exercise than another? or, in other words, that she has a sound constitution; and why, to damp innocent vivacity, is she darkly to be told that men will draw conclusions which she little thinks of?—Let the libertine draw what inference he pleases; but, I hope, that no sensible mother will restrain the natural frankness of youth by instilling such indecent cautions. Out of the abundance of the heart the mouth speaketh;[46] and a wiser than Solomon hath said, that the heart should be made clean, and not trivial ceremonies observed, which it is not very difficult to fulfil with scrupulous exactness when vice reigns in the heart.[47]

Women ought to endeavour to purify their heart; but can they do so when their uncultivated understandings make them entirely dependent on their senses for employment and amusement, when no noble pursuit sets them above the little vanities of the day, or enables them to curb the wild emotions that agitate a reed over which every passing breeze has power? To gain the affections of a virtuous man is affectation necessary? Nature has given woman a weaker frame than man; but, to ensure her husband's affections, must a wife, who by the exercise of her mind and body whilst she was discharging the duties of a daughter, wife, and mother, has allowed her constitution to retain its natural strength, and her nerves a healthy tone, is she, I say, to condescend to use art and feign a sickly delicacy in order to secure her husband's affection? Weakness may excite tenderness, and gratify the arrogant pride of man; but the lordly caresses of a protector will not gratify a noble mind that pants for, and deserves to be respected. Fondness is a poor substitute for friendship!

In a seraglio, I grant, that all these arts are necessary; the epicure[48] must have his palate tickled, or he will sink into apathy; but have women so little ambition as to be satisfied with such a condition? Can they supinely dream life away in the lap of pleasure, or the languor of weariness, rather than assert their claim to pursue reasonable pleasures and render themselves conspicuous by practising the virtues which dignify mankind? Surely she has not an immortal soul who can loiter life away merely employed to adorn her person, that she may amuse the languid hours, and soften the cares of a fellow-creature who is willing to be enlivened by her smiles and tricks, when the serious business of life is over.

Besides, the woman who strengthens her body and exercises her mind will, by managing her family and practising various virtues, become the friend, and not the humble dependent of her husband; and if she, by possessing such substantial qualities, merit his regard she will not find it necessary to conceal her affection, nor to pretend to an unnatural coldness of constitution to excite her husband's passions. In fact, if we revert to history, we shall find that the women who have distinguished themselves have neither been the most beautiful nor the most gentle of their sex.

Nature, or, to speak with strict propriety, God, has made all things right; but man has sought him out many inventions to mar the work. I now allude to that part of Dr Gregory's treatise, where he advises a wife never to let her husband know the extent of her sensibility or affection.[49] Voluptuous pre-caution, and as ineffectual as absurd.—Love, from its very nature, must be transitory. To seek for a secret that would render it constant, would be

[46] Matthew 12:34.

[47] These are the words of Jesus; see Luke 11:31–41.

[48] **epicure:** gourmand, glutton.

[49] John Gregory, *A Father's Legacy to His Daughters,* 87–88.

as wild a search as for the philosopher's stone,[50] or the grand panacea: and the discovery would be equally useless, or rather pernicious, to mankind. The most holy band of society is friendship. It has been well said, by a shrewd satirist,[51] 'that rare as true love is, true friendship is still rarer.'

This is an obvious truth, and the cause not lying deep, will not elude a slight glance of inquiry.

Love, the common passion, in which chance and sensation take place of choice and reason, is, in some degree, felt by the mass of mankind; for it is not necessary to speak, at present, of the emotions that rise above or sink below love. This passion, naturally increased by suspense and difficulties, draws the mind out of its accustomed state, and exalts the affections; but the security of marriage, allowing the fever of love to subside, a healthy temperature is thought insipid, only by those who have not sufficient intellect to substitute the calm tenderness of friendship, the confidence of respect, instead of blind admiration, and the sensual emotions of fondness.

This is, must be, the course of nature—friendship or indifference inevitably succeeds love.—And this constitution seems perfectly to harmonize with the system of government which prevails in the moral world. Passions are spurs to action, and open the mind; but they sink into mere appetites, become a personal and momentary gratification, when the object is gained, and the satisfied mind rests in enjoyment. The man who had some virtue whilst he was struggling for a crown, often becomes a voluptuous tyrant when it graces his brow; and, when the lover is not lost in the husband, the dotard, a prey to childish caprices, and fond jealousies, neglects the serious duties of life, and the caresses which should excite confidence in his children are lavished on the overgrown child, his wife.

In order to fulfil the duties of life, and to be able to pursue with vigour the various employments which form the moral character, a master and mistress of a family ought not to continue to love each other with passion. I mean to say, that they ought not to indulge those emotions which disturb the order of society, and engross the thoughts that should be otherwise employed. The mind that has never been engrossed by one object wants vigour—if it can long be so, it is weak.

A mistaken education, a narrow, uncultivated mind, and many sexual prejudices, tend to make women more constant than men; but, for the present, I shall not touch on this branch of the subject. I will go still further, and advance, without dreaming of a paradox, that an unhappy marriage is often very advantageous to a family, and that the neglected wife is, in general, the best mother. And this would almost always be the consequence if the female mind were more enlarged: for, it seems to be the common dispensation of Providence, that what we gain in present enjoyment should be deducted from the treasure of life, experience; and that when we are gathering the flowers of the day and revelling in pleasure, the solid fruit of toil and wisdom should not be caught at the same time. The way lies before us, we must turn to the right or left; and he who will pass life away in bounding from one pleasure to another, must not complain if he acquire neither wisdom nor respectability of character.

Supposing, for a moment, that the soul is not immortal, and that man was only created for the present scene,—I think we should have reason to complain that love, infantine fondness, ever grew insipid and palled upon the sense. Let us eat, drink, and love, for to-morrow we die, would be, in fact, the language of reason, the morality of life; and who but a fool would part with a reality for a fleeting shadow? But, if awed by observing the improbable powers of the mind, we disdain to confine our wishes or thoughts to such a comparatively mean field of action; that only appears grand and important, as it is connected with a boundless prospect and sublime hopes, what necessity is there for falsehood in conduct, and why must the sacred majesty of truth be violated to detain a deceitful good that saps the very foundation of virtue? Why must the female mind be tainted by coquetish arts to gratify the sensualist, and prevent love from subsiding into friendship, or compassionate tenderness, when there are not qualities on which friendship can be built? Let the honest heart shew itself, and *reason* teach passion to submit to necessity; or, let the dignified pursuit of virtue and knowledge raise the mind above those emotions which rather imbitter than sweeten the cup of life, when they are not restrained within due bounds.

I do not mean to allude to the romantic passion, which is the concomitant of genius.—Who can clip its wing? But that grand passion not proportioned to the puny enjoyments of life, is only true to the sentiment, and feeds on itself. The passions which have been celebrated

[50] **philosopher's stone**: a hypothetical substance, obsessively sought by medieval alchemists, reputed to have the capacity to change base metals into gold and to produce an elixir that could prolong life indefinitely.

[51] **shrewd satirist**: La Rochefoucauld. See his *Réflexions ou sentences et maximes morales* (1678), 473.

for their durability have always been unfortunate. They have acquired strength by absence and constitutional melancholy.—The fancy has hovered round a form of beauty dimly seen—but familiarity might have turned admiration into disgust; or, at least, into indifference, and allowed the imagination leisure to start fresh game. With perfect propriety, according to this view of things, does Rousseau make the mistress of his soul, Eloisa, love St Preux, when life was fading before her; but this is no proof of the immortality of the passion.[52]

Of the same complexion is Dr Gregory's advice respecting delicacy of sentiment, which he advises a woman not to acquire, if she have determined to marry. This determination, however, perfectly consistent with his former advice, he calls *indelicate,* and earnestly persuades his daughters to conceal it, though it may govern their conduct:—as if it were indelicate to have the common appetites of human nature.

Noble morality! and consistent with the cautious prudence of a little soul that cannot extend its views beyond the present minute division of existence. If all the faculties of woman's mind are only to be cultivated as they respect her dependence on man; if, when a husband be obtained, she have arrived at her goal, and meanly proud rests satisfied with such a paltry crown, let her grovel contentedly, scarcely raised by her employments above the animal kingdom; but, if, struggling for the prize of her high calling, she looks beyond the present scene, let her cultivate her understanding without stopping to consider what character the husband may have whom she is destined to marry. Let her only determine, without being too anxious about present happiness, to acquire the qualities that ennoble a rational being, and a rough inelegant husband may shock her taste without destroying her peace of mind. She will not model her soul to suit the frailties of her companion, but to bear with them: his character may be a trial, but not an impediment to virtue.

If Dr Gregory confined his remark to romantic expectations of constant love and congenial feelings, he should have recollected that experience will banish what advice can never make us cease to wish for, when the imagination is kept alive at the expence of reason.

I own it frequently happens that women who have fostered a romantic unnatural delicacy of feeling, waste their lives in *imagining* how happy they should have been with a husband who could love them with a fervid increasing affection every day, and all day.[53] But they might as well pine married as single—and would not be a jot more unhappy with a bad husband than longing for a good one. That a proper education; or, to speak with more precision, a well stored mind, would enable a woman to support a single life with dignity, I grant; but that she should avoid cultivating her taste, lest her husband should occasionally shock it, is quitting a substance for a shadow. To say the truth, I do not know of what use is an improved taste, if the individual be not rendered more independent of the casualties of life; if new sources of enjoyment, only dependent on the solitary operations of the mind, are not opened. People of taste, married or single, without distinction, will ever be disgusted by various things that touch not less observing minds. On this conclusion the argument must not be allowed to hinge; but in the whole sum of enjoyment is taste to be denominated a blessing?

The question is, whether it procures most pain or pleasure? The answer will decide the propriety of Dr Gregory's advice, and shew how absurd and tyrannic it is thus to lay down a system of slavery; or to attempt to educate moral beings by any other rules than those deduced from pure reason, which apply to the whole species.

Gentleness of manners, forbearance and long-suffering, are such amiable Godlike qualities, that in sublime poetic strains the Deity has been invested with them; and, perhaps, no representation of his goodness so strongly fastens on the human affections as those that represent him abundant in mercy and willing to pardon. Gentleness, considered in this point of view, bears on its front all the characteristics of grandeur, combined with the winning graces of condescension; but what a different aspect it assumes when it is the submissive demeanour of dependence, the support of weakness that loves, because it wants protection; and is forbearing, because it must silently endure injuries; smiling under the lash at which it dare not snarl. Abject as this picture appears, it is the portrait of an accomplished woman, according to the received opinion of female excellence,

[52] In Rousseau's novel *Julie, ou la Nouvelle Héloïse* (1761), Julie, who has been a faithful wife to Wolmar, declares on her deathbed that her only deep and lasting passion has been for her former tutor and lover, St. Preux.

[53] For example, the herd of Novelists [M. W.]. Wollstonecraft is attacking the popular fictional romances of her day, which were similar to twentieth-century Harlequin romances.

separated by specious reasoners from human excellence. Or, they[54] kindly restore the rib, and make one moral being of a man and woman; not forgetting to give her all the 'submissive charms.'[55]

How women are to exist in that state where there is to be neither marrying nor giving in marriage,[56] we are not told. For though moralists have agreed that the tenor of life seems to prove that *man* is prepared by various circumstances for a future state, they constantly concur in advising *woman* only to provide for the present. Gentleness, docility, and a spaniel-like affection are, on this ground, consistently recommended as the cardinal virtues of the sex; and, disregarding the arbitrary economy of nature, one writer has declared that it is masculine for a woman to be melancholy. She was created to be the toy of man, his rattle, and it must jingle in his ears whenever, dismissing reason, he chooses to be amused.

To recommend gentleness, indeed, on a broad basis is strictly philosophical. A frail being should labour to be gentle. But when forbearance confounds right and wrong, it ceases to be a virtue; and, however convenient it may be found in a companion — that companion will ever be considered as an inferior, and only inspire a vapid tenderness, which easily degenerates into contempt. Still, if advice could really make a being gentle, whose natural disposition admitted not of such a fine polish, something towards the advancement of order would be attained; but if, as might quickly be demonstrated, only affectation be produced by this indiscriminate counsel, which throws a stumbling-block in the way of gradual improvement, and true melioration of temper, the sex is not much benefited by sacrificing solid virtues to the attainment of superficial graces, though for a few years they may procure the individual[']s regal sway.

As a philosopher, I read with indignation the plausible epithets which men use to soften their insults; and, as a moralist, I ask what is meant by such heterogeneous associations, as fair defects, amiable weaknesses, etc.?[57] If there be but one criterion of morals, but one archetype for man, women appear to be suspended by destiny, according to the vulgar tale of Mahomet's coffin;[58] they have neither the unerring instinct of brutes, nor are allowed to fix the eye of reason on a perfect model. They were made to be loved, and must not aim at respect, lest they should be hunted out of society as masculine.

But to view the subject in another point of view. Do passive indolent women make the best wives? Confining our discussion to the present moment of existence, let us see how such weak creatures perform their part? Do the women who, by the attainment of a few superficial accomplishments, have strengthened the prevailing prejudice, merely contribute to the happiness of their husbands? Do they display their charms merely to amuse them? And have women, who have early imbibed notions of passive obedience, sufficient character to manage a family or educate children? So far from it, that, after surveying the history of woman, I cannot help, agreeing with the severest satirist, considering the sex as the weakest as well as the most oppressed half of the species. What does history disclose but marks of inferiority, and how few women have emancipated themselves from the galling yoke of sovereign man? — So few, that the exceptions remind me of an ingenious conjecture respecting Newton: that he was probably a being of a superior order, accidently caged in a human body.[59] Following the same train of thinking, I have been led to imagine that the few extraordinary women who have rushed in eccentrical directions out of the orbit prescribed to their sex, were *male* spirits, confined by mistake in female frames. But if it be not philosophical to think of sex when the soul is mentioned, the inferiority must depend on the organs; or the heavenly fire, which is to ferment the clay, is not given in equal portions.

But avoiding, as I have hitherto done, any direct comparison of the two sexes collectively, or frankly

[54] Vide Rousseau and Swedenborg [M. W.]. Rousseau argued that man and wife comprised one moral unit; that is, a wife could not act with moral certainty by herself. Emanuel Swedenborg (1688–1772), Swedish scientist and mystic, argued that conjugality continued in heaven, where man and wife became one angel, of which the husband was the mind and the wife the desire or will.

[55] **'submissive charms'**: Cf. *Paradise Lost,* IV.497–99: "he in delight / Both of her beauty and submissive charms / Smiled with superior love."

[56] See Matthew 22:30, Mark 12:25, and Luke 20:35.

[57] Cf. *Paradise Lost,* X.891–2.

[58] **Mahomet's coffin**: according to legend, Mohammed's coffin was suspended in the center of his tomb by some magical magnetic force.

[59] Sir Isaac Newton (1642–1727), eminent physicist and mathematician, of whom the poet James Thomson, in *A Poem, sacred to the memory of Sir Isaac Newton* (1727), ll. 161–65, speculated: "can a soul / Of such extensive, deep, tremendous powers, / Enlarging still, be but a finer breath / Of spirits dancing thro' their tubes awhile, / And then for ever lost in vacant air?"

acknowledging the inferiority of woman, according to the present appearance of things, I shall only insist that men have increased that inferiority till women are almost sunk below the standard of rational creatures. Let their faculties have room to unfold, and their virtues to gain strength, and then determine where the whole sex must stand in the intellectual scale. Yet let it be remembered, that for a small number of distinguished women I do not ask a place.

It is difficult for us purblind mortals to say to what height human discoveries and improvements may arrive when the gloom of despotism subsides, which makes us stumble at every step; but, when morality shall be settled on a more solid basis, then, without being gifted with a prophetic spirit, I will venture to predict that woman will be either the friend or slave of man. We shall not, as at present, doubt whether she is a moral agent, or the link which unites man with brutes. But, should it then appear, that like the brutes they were principally created for the use of man, he will let them patiently bite the bridle, and not mock them with empty praise; or, should their rationality be proved, he will not impede their improvement merely to gratify his sensual appetites. He will not, with all the graces of rhetoric, advise them to submit implicitly their understanding to the guidance of man. He will not, when he treats of the education of women, assert that they ought never to have the free use of reason, nor would he recommend cunning and dissimulation to beings who are acquiring, in like manner as himself, the virtues of humanity.

Surely there can be but one rule of right, if morality has an eternal foundation, and whoever sacrifices virtue, strictly so called, to present convenience, or whose *duty* it is to act in such a manner, lives only for the passing day, and cannot be an accountable creature.

The poet then should have dropped his sneer when he says,

> 'If weak women go astray,
> The stars are more in fault than they.'[60]

For that they are bound by the adamantine chain of destiny is most certain, if it be proved that they are never to exercise their own reason, never to be independent, never to rise above opinion, or to feel the dignity of a rational will that only bows to God, and often forgets that the universe contains any being but itself and the model of perfection to which its ardent gaze is turned, to adore attributes that, softened into virtues, may be imitated in kind, though the degree overwhelms the enraptured mind.

If, I say, for would not impress by declamation when Reason offers her sober light, if they be really capable of acting like rational creatures, let them not be treated like slaves; or, like the brutes who are dependent on the reason of man, when they associate with him; but cultivate their minds, give them the salutary, sublime curb of principle, and let them attain conscious dignity by feeling themselves only dependent on God. Teach them, in common with man, to submit to necessity, instead of giving, to render them more pleasing, a sex to morals.

Further, should experience prove that they cannot attain the same degree of strength of mind, perseverance, and fortitude, let their virtues be the same in kind, though they may vainly struggle for the same degree; and the superiority of man will be equally clear, if not clearer; and truth, as it is a simple principle, which admits of no modification, would be common to both. Nay, the order of society as it is at present regulated would not be inverted, for woman would then only have the rank that reason assigned her, and arts could not be practised to bring the balance even, much less to turn it.

These may be termed Utopian dreams.—Thanks to that Being who impressed them on my soul, and gave me sufficient strength of mind to dare to exert my own reason, till, becoming dependent only on him for the support of my virtue, I view, with indignation, the mistaken notions that enslave my sex.

I love man as my fellow; but his scepter, real, or usurped, extends not to me, unless the reason of an individual demands my homage; and even then the submission is to reason, and not to man. In fact, the conduct of an accountable being must be regulated by the operations of its own reason; or on what foundation rests the throne of God?

It appears to me necessary to dwell on these obvious truths, because females have been insulated, as it were; and, while they have been stripped of the virtues that should clothe humanity, they have been decked with artificial graces that enable them to exercise a short-lived tyranny. Love, in their bosoms, taking place of every nobler passion, their sole ambition is to be fair, to raise emotion instead of inspiring respect; and this ignoble desire, like the servility in absolute monarchies, destroys all strength of character. Liberty is the mother of virtue, and if women be, by their very constitution, slaves, and not allowed to breathe the sharp invigorating air of freedom,

[60] Matthew Prior, "Hans Carvell," ll. 11–12.

they must ever languish like exotics, and be reckoned beautiful flaws in nature.

As to the argument respecting the subjection in which the sex has ever been held, it retorts on man. The many have always been enthralled by the few; and monsters, who scarcely have shewn any discernment of human excellence, have tyrannized over thousands of their fellow-creatures. Why have men of superior endowments submitted to such degradation? For, is it not universally acknowledged that kings, viewed collectively, have ever been inferior, in abilities and virtue, to the same number of men taken from the common mass of mankind—yet, have they not, and are they not still treated with a degree of reverence that is an insult to reason? China is not the only country where a living man has been made a God.[61] *Men* have submitted to superior strength to enjoy with impunity the pleasure of the moment—*women* have only done the same, and therefore till it is proved that the courtier, who servilely resigns the birthright of a man, is not a moral agent, it cannot be demonstrated that woman is essentially inferior to man because she has always been subjugated.

Brutal force has hitherto governed the world, and that the science of politics is in its infancy, is evident from philosophers scrupling to give the knowledge most useful to man that determinate distinction.

I shall not pursue this argument any further than to establish an obvious inference, that as sound politics diffuse liberty, mankind, including woman, will become more wise and virtuous.

—*from* CHAPTER III—
THE SAME SUBJECT CONTINUED

Bodily strength from being the distinction of heroes is now sunk into such unmerited contempt that men, as well as women, seem to think it unnecessary: the latter, as it takes from their feminine graces, and from that lovely weakness the source of their undue power; and the former, because it appears inimical to the character of a gentleman.

That they have both by departing from one extreme run into another, may easily be proved; but first it may be proper to observe, that a vulgar error has obtained a degree of credit, which has given force to a false conclusion, in which an effect has been mistaken for a cause.

People of genius have, very frequently, impaired their constitutions by study or careless inattention to their health, and the violence of their passions bearing a proportion to the vigour of their intellects, the sword's destroying the scabbard has become almost proverbial,[62] and superficial observers have inferred from thence, that men of genius have commonly weak, or, to use a more fashionable phrase, delicate constitutions. Yet the contrary, I believe, will appear to be the fact; for, on diligent inquiry, I find that strength of mind has, in most cases, been accompanied by superior strength of body,—natural soundness of constitution,—not that robust tone of nerves and vigour of muscles, which arise from bodily labour, when the mind is quiescent, or only directs the hands.

Dr Priestley has remarked, in the preface to his biographical chart, that the majority of great men have lived beyond forty-five.[63] And, considering the thoughtless manner in which they have lavished their strength, when investigating a favourite science they have wasted the lamp of life, forgetful of the midnight hour; or, when, lost in poetic dreams, fancy has peopled the scene, and the soul has been disturbed, till it shook the constitution, by the passions that meditation had raised; whose objects, the baseless fabric of a vision,[64] faded before the exhausted eye, they must have had iron frames. Shakespeare never grasped the airy dagger with a nerveless hand,[65] nor did Milton tremble when he led Satan far from the confines of his dreary prison.[66]—These were not the ravings of imbecility, the sickly effusions of distempered brains; but the exuberance of fancy, that 'in a fine phrenzy'[67] wandering, was not continually reminded of its material shackles.

I am aware that this argument would carry me further than it may be supposed I wish to go; but I follow truth, and, still adhering to my first position, I will allow that bodily strength seems to give man a natural superiority over woman; and this is the only solid basis on which the superiority of the sex can be built. But I still insist, that

[61] Chinese emperors were considered divine; the Roman Emperor Nero also proclaimed his divinity.

[62] Cf. Rousseau's *Confessions*, IV.v.86: [trans.] "It is sometimes said that the sword wears out the scabbard. That is my history."

[63] Joseph Priestley (1733–1804), *A Description of a Chart of Biography* (1765), pp. 25–26.

[64] Cf. Shakespeare, *The Tempest*, IV.i.151.

[65] Cf. Shakespeare, *Macbeth*, II.i.33–49.

[66] Cf. Milton, *Paradise Lost*, Bk. II.

[67] Cf. Shakespeare, *A Midsummer Night's Dream*, V.i.12.

not only the virtue, but the *knowledge* of the two sexes should be the same in nature, if not in degree, and that women, considered not only as moral, but rational creatures, ought to endeavour to acquire human virtues (or perfections) by the *same* means as men, instead of being educated like a fanciful kind of *half* being—one of Rousseau's wild chimeras.[68]

But, if strength of body be, with some shew of reason, the boast of men, why are women so infatuated as to be proud of a defect? Rousseau has furnished them with a plausible excuse, which could only have occurred to a man, whose imagination had been allowed to run wild, and refine on the impressions made by exquisite senses;—that they might, forsooth, have a pretext for yielding to a natural appetite without violating a romantic species of modesty, which gratifies the pride and libertinism of man.

Women, deluded by these sentiments, sometimes boast of their weakness, cunningly obtaining power by playing on the *weakness* of men; and they may well glory in their illicit sway, for, like Turkish bashaws,[69] they have more real power than their masters: but virtue is sacrificed to temporary gratifications, and the respectability of life to the triumph of an hour.

Women, as well as despots, have now, perhaps, more power than they would have if the world, divided and subdivided into kingdoms and families, were governed by laws deduced from the exercise of reason; but in obtaining it, to carry on the comparison, their character is degraded, and licentiousness spread through the whole aggregate of society. The many become pedestal to the few. I, therefore, will venture to assert, that till women are more rationally educated, the progress of human virtue and improvement in knowledge must receive continual checks. And if it be granted that woman was not created merely to gratify the appetite of man, or to be the upper servant, who provides his meals and takes care of his linen,[70] it must follow, that the first care of those mothers or fathers, who really attend to the education of females, should be, if not to strengthen the body, at least, not to destroy the constitution by mistaken notions of beauty and female excellence; nor should girls ever be allowed to imbibe the pernicious notion that a defect can, by any chemical process of reasoning, become an excellence. . . .

I have, probably, had an opportunity of observing more girls in their infancy than J. J. Rousseau—I can recollect my own feelings, and I have looked steadily around me; yet, so far from coinciding with him in opinion

[68]"Researches into abstract and speculative truths, the principles and axioms of sciences, in short, every thing which tends to generalize our ideas, is not the proper province of women; their studies should be relative to points of practice; it belongs to them to apply those principles which men have discovered; and it is their part to make observations, which direct men to the establishment of general principles. All the ideas of women, which have not the immediate tendency to points of duty, should be directed to the study of men, and to the attainment of those agreeable accomplishments which have taste for their object; for as to works of genius they are beyond their capacity, neither have they sufficient precision or power of attention to succeed in sciences which require accuracy; and as to physical knowledge, it belongs to those only who are most active, most inquisitive; who comprehend the greatest variety of objects: in short, it belongs to those who have the strongest powers, and who exercise them most, to judge of the relations between sensible beings and the laws of nature. A woman who is naturally weak, and does not carry her ideas to any great extent, knows how to judge and make a proper estimate of those movements which she sets to work, in order to aid her weakness; and these movements are the passions of men. The mechanism she employs is much more powerful than ours; for all her levers move the human heart. She must have the skill to incline us to do every thing which her sex will not enable her to do herself, and which is necessary or agreeable to her; therefore she ought to study the mind of man thoroughly, not the mind of man in general, abstractedly, but the dispositions of those men to whom she is subject, either by the laws of her country or by the force of opinion. She should learn to penetrate into their real sentiments from their conversation, their actions, their looks, and gestures. She should also have the art, by her own conversation, actions, looks, and gestures, to communicate those sentiments which are agreeable to them, without seeming to intend it. Men will argue more philosophically about the human heart; but women will read the heart of man better than they. It belongs to women, if I may be allowed the expression, to form an experimental morality, and to reduce the study of man to a system. Women have most wit, men have most genius; women observe, men reason: from the concurrence of both we derive the clearest light and the most perfect knowledge, which the human mind is, of itself, capable of attaining. In one word, from hence we acquire the most intimate acquaintance, both with ourselves and others, of which our nature is capable; and it is thus that art has a constant tendency to perfect those endowments which nature has bestowed.—The world is the book of women." Rousseau's *Émile* [trans. William Kenrick, IV.v.74–75]. I hope my readers still remember the comparison, which I have brought forward, between women and officers [M. W.].

[69]**bashaws:** pashas, Turkish military officers or provincial governors, famed for their imperiousness.

[70]**linen:** undergarments, shirts; bed linen, sheets.

respecting the first dawn of the female character, I will venture to affirm, that a girl, whose spirits have not been damped by inactivity, or innocence tainted by false shame, will always be a romp, and the doll will never excite attention unless confinement allows her no alternative. Girls and boys, in short, would play harmlessly together, if the distinction of sex was not inculcated long before nature makes any difference.—I will go further, and affirm, as an indisputable fact, that most of the women, in the circle of my observation, who have acted like rational creatures, or shewn any vigour of intellect, have accidentally been allowed to run wild—as some of the elegant formers of the fair sex would insinuate.

The baneful consequences which flow from inattention to health during infancy, and youth, extend further than is supposed—dependence of body naturally produces dependence of mind; and how can she be a good wife or mother, the greater part of whose time is employed to guard against or endure sickness? Nor can it be expected that a woman will resolutely endeavour to strengthen her constitution and abstain from enervating indulgencies, if artificial notions of beauty, and false descriptions of sensibility, have been early entangled with her motives of action. Most men are sometimes obliged to bear with bodily inconveniences, and to endure, occasionally, the inclemency of the elements; but genteel women are, literally speaking, slaves to their bodies, and glory in their subjection.

I once knew a weak woman of fashion, who was more than commonly proud of her delicacy and sensibility. She thought a distinguishing taste and puny appetite the height of all human perfection, and acted accordingly.—I have seen this weak sophisticated being neglect all the duties of life, yet recline with self-complacency on a sofa, and boast of her want of appetite as a proof of delicacy that extended to, or, perhaps, arose from, her exquisite sensibility: for it is difficult to render intelligible such ridiculous jargon.— . . .

Women are every where in this deplorable state; for, in order to preserve their innocence, as ignorance is courteously termed, truth is hidden from them, and they are made to assume an artificial character before their faculties have acquired any strength. Taught from their infancy that beauty is woman's sceptre, the mind shapes itself to the body, and, roaming round its gilt cage, only seeks to adorn its prison. Men have various employments and pursuits which engage their attention, and give a character to the opening mind; but women, confined to one, and having their thoughts constantly directed to the most insignificant part of themselves, seldom extend their views beyond the triumph of the hour. But were their understanding once emancipated from the slavery to which the pride and sensuality of man and their short-sighted desire, like that of dominion in tyrants, of present sway, has subjected them, we should probably read of their weaknesses with surprise. I must be allowed to pursue the argument a little farther.

Perhaps, if the existence of an evil being were allowed, who, in the allegorical language of scripture, went about seeking whom he should devour,[71] he could not more effectually degrade the human character than by giving a man absolute power.

This argument branches into various ramifications.—Birth, riches, and every extrinsic advantage that exalt a man above his fellows, without any mental exertion, sink him in reality below them. In proportion to his weakness, he is played upon by designing men, till the bloated monster has lost all traces of humanity. And that tribes of men, like flocks of sheep, should quietly follow such a leader, is a solecism that only a desire of present enjoyment and narrowness of understanding can solve. Educated in slavish dependence, and enervated by luxury and sloth, where shall we find men who will stand forth to assert the rights of man;—or claim the privilege of moral beings, who should have but one road to excellence? Slavery to monarchs and ministers, which the world will be long in freeing itself from, and whose deadly grasp stops the progress of the human mind, is not yet abolished.

Let not men then in the pride of power, use the same arguments that tyrannic kings and venal ministers have used, and fallaciously assert that woman ought to be subjected because she has always been so.—But, when man, governed by reasonable laws, enjoys his natural freedom, let him despise woman, if she do not share it with him; and, till that glorious period arrives, in descanting on the folly of the sex, let him not overlook his own.

Women, it is true, obtaining power by unjust means, by practising or fostering vice, evidently lose the rank which reason would assign them, and they become either abject slaves or capricious tyrants. They lose all simplicity, all dignity of mind, in acquiring power, and act as men are observed to act when they have been exalted by the same means.

It is time to effect a revolution in female manners—time to restore to them their lost dignity—and make

[71] Cf. 1 Peter 5:8.

them, as a part of the human species, labour by reforming themselves to reform the world. It is time to separate unchangeable morals from local manners.—If men be demigods—why let us serve them! And if the dignity of the female soul be as disputable as that of animals—if their reason does not afford sufficient light to direct their conduct whilst unerring instinct is denied—they are surely of all creatures the most miserable! and, bent beneath the iron hand of destiny, must submit to be a fair defect in creation. But to justify the ways of Providence[72] respecting them, by pointing out some irrefragable reason for thus making such a large portion of mankind accountable and not accountable, would puzzle the subtilest casuist.

The only solid foundation for morality appears to be the character of the supreme Being; the harmony of which arises from a balance of attributes;—and, to speak with reverence, one attribute seems to imply the *necessity* of another. He must be just, because he is wise, he must be good, because he is omnipotent. For to exalt one attribute at the expence of another equally noble and necessary, bears the stamp of the warped reason of man—the homage of passion. Man, accustomed to bow down to power in his savage state, can seldom divest himself of this barbarous prejudice, even when civilization determines how much superior mental is to bodily strength; and his reason is clouded by these crude opinions, even when he thinks of the Deity.—His omnipotence is made to swallow up, or preside over his other attributes, and those mortals are supposed to limit his power irreverently, who think that it must be regulated by his wisdom.

I disclaim that specious humility which, after investigating nature, stops at the author.—The High and Lofty One, who inhabiteth eternity, doubtless possesses many attributes of which we can form no conception; but reason tells me that they cannot clash with those I adore—and I am compelled to listen to her voice. . . .

Besides, if women be educated for dependence; that is, to act according to the will of another fallible being, and submit, right or wrong, to power, where are we to stop? Are they to be considered as vicegerents allowed to reign over a small domain, and answerable for their conduct to a higher tribunal, liable to error?

It will not be difficult to prove that such delegates will act like men subjected by fear, and make their children and servants endure their tyrannical oppression. As they submit without reason, they will, having no fixed rules to square their conduct by, be kind, or cruel, just as the whim of the moment directs; and we ought not to wonder if sometimes, galled by their heavy yoke, they take a malignant pleasure in resting it on weaker shoulders.

But, supposing a woman, trained up to obedience, be married to a sensible man, who directs her judgment without making her feel the servility of her subjection, to act with as much propriety by this reflected light as can be expected when reason is taken at second hand, yet she cannot ensure the life of her protector; he may die and leave her with a large family.

A double duty devolves on her; to educate them in the character of both father and mother; to form their principles and secure their property. But, alas! she has never thought, much less acted for herself. She has only learned to please[73] men, to depend gracefully on them; yet, encumbered with children, how is she to obtain another protector—a husband to supply the place of

[72] **fair defect:** Cf. Milton, *Paradise Lost,* X.891–2. **ways of Providence:** Cf. Milton, *Paradise Lost,* I.25–6.

[73] "In the union of the sexes, both pursue one common object, but none in the same manner. From their diversity in this particular, arises the first determinate difference between the moral relations of each. The one should be active and strong, the other passive and weak: it is necessary the one should have both the power and the will, and that the other should make little resistance.

This principle being established, it follows that woman is expressly formed to please the man: if the obligation be reciprocal also, and the man ought to please in his turn, it is not so immediately necessary: his great merit is in his power, and he pleases merely because he is strong. This, I must confess, is not one of the refined maxims of love; it is, however, one of the laws of nature, prior to love itself.

If the woman be formed to please and be subjected to man, it is her place, doubtless, to render herself agreeable to him, instead of challenging his passion. The violence of his desires depends on her charms; it is by means of these she should urge him to the exertion of those powers which nature hath given him. The most successful method of exciting them, is, to render such exertion necessary by resistance; as, in that case, self-love is added to desire, and the one triumphs in the victory which the other obliged to acquire. Hence arise the various modes of attack and defence between the sexes; the boldness of one sex and the timidity of the other; and, in a word, that bashfulness and modesty with which nature hath armed the weak, in order to subdue the strong." Rousseau's *Émile* [IV.v.3–4].

I shall make no other comment on this ingenious passage, than just to observe, that it is the philosophy of lasciviousness" [M. W.].

reason? A rational man, for we are not treading on romantic ground, though he may think her a pleasing docile creature, will not choose to marry a *family* for love, when the world contains many more pretty creatures. What is then to become of her? She either falls an easy prey to some mean fortune-hunter, who defrauds her children of their parental inheritance, and renders her miserable; or becomes the victim of discontent and blind indulgence. Unable to educate her sons, or impress them with respect; for it is not a play on words to assert, that people are never respected, though filling an important station, who are not respectable; she pines under the anguish of unavailing impotent regret. The serpent's tooth enters into her very soul, and the vices of licentious youth bring her with sorrow, if not with poverty also, to the grave.[74]

This is not an overcharged picture; on the contrary, it is a very possible case, and something similar must have fallen under every attentive eye.

I have, however, taken it for granted, that she was well-disposed, though experience shews, that the blind may as easily be led into a ditch as along the beaten road. But supposing, no very improbable conjecture, that a being only taught to please must still find her happiness in pleasing;—what an example of folly, not to say vice, will she be to her innocent daughters! The mother will be lost in the coquette, and, instead of making friends of her daughters, view them with eyes askance, for they are rivals—rivals more cruel than any other, because they invite a comparison, and drive her from the throne of beauty, who has never thought of a seat on the bench of reason.

It does not require a lively pencil, or the discriminating outline of a caricature, to sketch the domestic miseries and petty vices which such a mistress of a family diffuses. Still she only acts as a woman ought to act, brought up according to Rousseau's system. She can never be reproached for being masculine, or turning out of her sphere; nay, she may observe another of his grand rules, and, cautiously preserving her reputation free from spot, be reckoned a good kind of woman. Yet in what respect can she be termed good? She abstains, it is true, without any great struggle, from committing gross crimes; but how does she fulfil her duties? Duties!—in truth she has enough to think of to adorn her body and nurse a weak constitution.

[74] Cf. Shakespeare, *King Lear,* I.iv.297–98: "How sharper than a serpent's tooth it is / To have a thankless child!"

With respect to religion, she never presumed to judge for herself; but conformed, as a dependent creature should, to the ceremonies of the church which she was brought up in, piously believing that wiser heads than her own have settled that business:—and not to doubt is her point of perfection. She therefore pays her tythe of mint and cummin—and thanks her God that she is not as other women are.[75] These are the blessed effects of a good education! These the virtues of man's help-mate![76]

I must relieve myself by drawing a different picture. Let fancy now present a woman with a tolerable understanding, for I do not wish to leave the line of mediocrity, whose constitution, strengthened by exercise, has allowed her body to acquire its full vigour; her mind, at the same time, gradually expanding itself to comprehend the moral duties of life, and in what human virtue and dignity consist.

Formed thus by the discharge of the relative duties of her station, she marries from affection, without losing sight of prudence, and looking beyond matrimonial felicity, she secures her husband's respect before it is necessary to exert mean arts to please him and feed a dying flame, which nature doomed to expire when the object became familiar, when friendship and forbearance take place of a more ardent affection.—This is the natural death of love, and domestic peace is not destroyed by struggles to prevent its extinction. I also suppose the husband to be virtuous; or she is still more in want of independent principles.

Fate, however, breaks this tie.—She is left a widow, perhaps, without a sufficient provision; but she is not desolate! The pang of nature is felt; but after time has softened sorrow into melancholy resignation, her heart turns to her children with redoubled fondness, and anxious to provide for them, affection gives a sacred heroic cast to her maternal duties. She thinks that not only the eye sees

[75] **mint and cummin:** Cf. Matthew 23:23. **not as other women are:** Cf. Luke 18:11.

[76] "O how lovely," exclaims Rousseau speaking of Sophia, "is her ignorance! Happy is he who is destined to instruct her! She will never pretend to be the tutor of her husband, but will be content to be his pupil. Far from attempting to subject him to her taste, she will accommodate herself to his. She will be more estimable to him, than if she was learned: he will have a pleasure in instructing her." Rousseau's *Émile* [IV.v.128].

I shall content myself with simply asking, how friendship can subsist, when love expires, between the master and his pupil? [M. W.]

her virtuous efforts from whom all her comfort now must flow, and whose approbation is life; but her imagination, a little abstracted and exalted by grief, dwells on the fond hope that the eyes which her trembling hand closed, may still see how she subdues every wayward passion to fulfil the double duty of being the father as well as the mother of her children. Raised to heroism by misfortunes, she represses the first faint dawning of a natural inclination, before it ripens into love, and in the bloom of life forgets her sex—forgets the pleasure of an awakening passion, which might again have been inspired and returned. She no longer thinks of pleasing, and conscious dignity prevents her from priding herself on account of the praise which her conduct demands. Her children have her love, and her brightest hopes are beyond the grave, where her imagination often strays.

I think I see her surrounded by her children, reaping the reward of her care. The intelligent eye meets hers, whilst health and innocence smile on their chubby cheeks, and as they grow up the cares of life are lessened by their grateful attention. She lives to see the virtues which she endeavoured to plant on principles, fixed into habits, to see her children attain a strength of character sufficient to enable them to endure adversity without forgetting their mother's example.

The task of life thus fulfilled, she calmly waits for the sleep of death, and rising from the grave, may say—Behold, thou gavest me a talent—and here are five talents.[77]

I wish to sum up what I have said in a few words, for I here throw down my gauntlet, and deny the existence of sexual virtues, not excepting modesty. For man and woman, truth, if I understand the meaning of the word, must be the same; yet the fanciful female character, so prettily drawn by poets and novelists, demanding the sacrifice of truth and sincerity, virtue becomes a relative idea, having no other foundation than utility, and of that utility men pretend arbitrarily to judge, shaping it to their own convenience.

Women, I allow, may have different duties to fulfil; but they are *human* duties, and the principles that should regulate the discharge of them, I sturdily maintain, must be the same.

To become respectable, the exercise of their understanding is necessary, there is no other foundation for independence of character; I mean explicitly to say that they must only bow to the authority of reason, instead of being the *modest* slaves of opinion.

In the superior ranks of life how seldom do we meet with a man of superior abilities, or even common acquirements? The reason appears to me clear, the state they are born in was an unnatural one. The human character has ever been formed by the employments the individual, or class, pursues; and if the faculties are not sharpened by necessity, they must remain obtuse. The argument may fairly be extended to women; for, seldom occupied by serious business, the pursuit of pleasure gives that insignificancy to their character which renders the society of the *great* so insipid. The same want of firmness, produced by a similar cause, forces them both to fly from themselves to noisy pleasures, and artificial passions, till vanity takes place of every social affection, and the characteristics of humanity can scarcely be discerned. Such are the blessings of civil governments, as they are at present organized, that wealth and female softness equally tend to debase mankind, and are produced by the same cause; but allowing women to be rational creatures, they should be incited to acquire virtues which they may call their own, for how can a rational being be ennobled by any thing that is not obtained by its *own* exertions?

—*from* CHAPTER IV—

Observations on the State of Degradation to Which Woman Is Reduced by Various Causes

. . . Novels, music, poetry, and gallantry, all tend to make women the creatures of sensation, and their character is thus formed in the mould of folly during the time they are acquiring accomplishments, the only improvement they are excited, by their station in society, to acquire. This overstretched sensibility naturally relaxes the other powers of the mind, and prevents intellect from attaining that sovereignty which it ought to attain to render a rational creature useful to others, and content with its own station: for the exercise of the understanding, as life advances, is the only method pointed out by nature to calm the passions.

Satiety has a very different effect, and I have often been forcibly struck by an emphatical description of damnation:—when the spirit is represented as continually hovering with abortive eagerness round the defiled body, unable to enjoy any thing without the organs of sense. Yet, to their senses, are women made slaves,

[77] See Matthew 25:14–30.

because it is by their sensibility that they obtain present power.

And will moralists pretend to assert, that this is the condition in which one half of the human race should be encouraged to remain with listless inactivity and stupid acquiescence? Kind instructors! what were we created for? To remain, it may be said, innocent; they mean in a state of childhood.—We might as well never have been born, unless it were necessary that we should be created to enable man to acquire the noble privilege of reason, the power of discerning good from evil, whilst we lie down in the dust from whence we were taken, never to rise again.—

It would be an endless task to trace the variety of meannesses, cares, and sorrows, into which women are plunged by the prevailing opinion, that they were created rather to feel than reason, and that all the power they obtain, must be obtained by their charms and weakness:

> 'Fine by defect, and amiably weak!'[78]

And, made by this amiable weakness entirely dependent, excepting what they gain by illicit sway, on man, not only for protection, but advice, is it surprising that, neglecting the duties that reason alone points out, and shrinking from trials calculated to strengthen their minds, they only exert themselves to give their defects a graceful covering, which may serve to heighten their charms in the eye of the voluptuary, though it sink them below the scale of moral excellence? . . .

—*from* CHAPTER V—

Animadversions on Some of the Writers Who Have Rendered Women Objects of Pity, Bordering on Contempt

. . . Supposing woman to have been formed only to please, and be subject to man, the conclusion is just, she ought to sacrifice every other consideration to render herself agreeable to him: and let this brutal desire of self-preservation be the grand spring of all her actions, when it is proved to be the iron bed of fate, to fit which her character should be stretched or contracted, regardless of all moral or physical distinctions. But, if, as I think, may be demonstrated, the purposes, of even this life, viewing the whole, be subverted by practical rules built upon this ignoble base, I may be allowed to doubt whether woman were created for man: and, though the cry of irreligion, or even atheism, be raised against me, I will simply declare, that were an angel from heaven to tell me that Moses's beautiful, poetical cosmogony, and the account of the fall of man,[79] were literally true, I could not believe what my reason told me was derogatory to the character of the Supreme Being: and, having no fear of the devil before mine eyes, I venture to call this a suggestion of reason, instead of resting my weakness on the broad shoulders of the first seducer of my frail sex. . . .

—*from* CHAPTER VI—

The Effect Which an Early Association of Ideas Has upon the Character

. . . Love is, in a great degree, an arbitrary passion, and will reign, like some other stalking mischiefs, by its own authority, without deigning to reason; and it may also be easily distinguished from esteem, the foundation of friendship, because it is often excited by evanescent beauties and graces, though, to give an energy to the sentiment, something more solid must deepen their impression and set the imagination to work, to make the most fair—the first good.

Common passions are excited by common qualities.—Men look for beauty and the simper of good-humoured docility: women are captivated by easy manners; a gentleman-like man seldom fails to please them, and their thirsty ears eagerly drink the insinuating nothings of politeness, whilst they turn from the unintelligible sounds of the charmer—reason, charm he never so wisely. With respect to superficial accomplishments, the rake certainly has the advantage; and of these females can form an opinion, for it is their own ground. Rendered gay and giddy by the whole tenor of their lives, the very aspect of wisdom, or the severe graces of virtue, must have a lugubrious appearance to them; and produce a kind of restraint from which they and love, sportive child, naturally revolt. Without taste, excepting of the lighter kind, for taste is the offspring of judgment, how can they discover that true beauty and grace must arise from the play of the mind? and how can they be expected to relish in a lover what they do not, or very imperfectly, possess themselves? The sympathy that unites hearts, and invites to confidence, in them is so very faint, that it cannot take fire, and thus mount to passion. No, I repeat it, the love cherished by such minds, must have grosser fewel!

[78] Alexander Pope, "Of the Characters of Women," l. 44: "Fine by defect, and delicately weak."

[79] Genesis 3.

The inference is obvious; till women are led to exercise their understandings, they should not be satirized for their attachment to rakes,[80] or even for being rakes at heart, when it appears to be the inevitable consequence of their education. They who live to please—must find their enjoyments, their happiness, in pleasure! It is a trite, yet true remark, that we never do any thing well, unless we love it for its own sake.

Supposing, however, for a moment, that women were, in some future revolution of time, to become, what I sincerely wish them to be, even love would acquire more serious dignity, and be purified in its own fires; and virtue giving true delicacy to their affections, they would turn with disgust from a rake. Reasoning then, as well as feeling, the only province of woman, at present, they might easily guard against exteriour graces, and quickly learn to despise the sensibility that had been excited and hackneyed in the ways of women, whose trade was vice; and allurements, wanton airs. They would recollect that the flame, one must use appropriated expressions, which they wished to light up, had been exhausted by lust, and that the sated appetite, losing all relish for pure and simple pleasures, could only be roused by licentious arts or variety. What satisfaction could a woman of delicacy promise herself in a union with such a man, when the very artlessnes of her affection might appear insipid? Thus does Dryden describe the situation,

> ——— 'Where love is duty, on the female side,
> On theirs mere sensual gust, and sought with surly pride.'[81]

But one grand truth women have yet to learn, though much it imports them to act accordingly. In the choice of a husband, they should not be led astray by the qualities of a lover—for a lover the husband, even supposing him to be wise and virtuous, cannot long remain.

Were women more rationally educated, could they take a more comprehensive view of things, they would be contented to love but once in their lives; and after marriage calmly let passion subside into friendship—into that tender intimacy, which is the best refuge from care; yet is built on such pure, still affections, that idle jealousies would not be allowed to disturb the discharge of the sober duties of life, or to engross the thoughts that ought to be otherwise employed. This is a state in which many men live; but few, very few women. And the difference may easily be accounted for, without recurring to a sexual character. Men, for whom we are told women were made, have too much occupied the thoughts of women; and this association has so entangled love with all their motives of action; and, to harp a little on an old string, having been solely employed either to prepare themselves to excite love, or actually putting their lessons in practice, they cannot live without love. But, when a sense of duty, or fear of shame, obliges them to restrain this pampered desire of pleasing beyond certain lengths, too far for delicacy, it is true, though far from criminality, they obstinately determine to love, I speak of the passion, their husbands to the end of the chapter—and then acting the part which they foolishly exacted from their lovers, they become abject woers, and fond slaves.

Men of wit and fancy are often rakes; and fancy is the food of love. Such men will inspire passion. Half the sex, in its present infantine state, would pine for a Lovelace;[82] a man so witty, so graceful, and so valiant: and can they *deserve* blame for acting according to principles so constantly inculcated? They want a lover, and protector; and behold him kneeling before them—bravery prostrate to beauty! The virtues of a husband are thus thrown by love into the back ground, and gay hopes, or lively emotions, banish reflection till the day of reckoning come; and come it surely will, to turn the sprightly lover into a surly suspicious tyrant, who contemptuously insults the very weakness he fostered. Or, supposing the rake reformed, he cannot quickly get rid of old habits. When a man of abilities is first carried away by his passions, it is necessary that sentiment and taste varnish the enormities of vice, and give a zest to brutal indulgences; but when the gloss of novelty is worn off, and pleasure palls upon the sense, lasciviousness becomes barefaced, and enjoyment only the desperate effort of weakness flying from reflection as from a legion of devils. Oh! virtue, thou art not an empty name! All that life can give—thou givest!

If much comfort cannot be expected from the friendship of a reformed rake of superiour abilities, what is the consequence when he lacketh sense, as well as principles?

[80] **rake**: a man of loose habit and immoral character.

[81] John Dryden, *Fables Ancient and Modern, Translated into Verse* (1700), "Palamon and Arcite," III.230–31.

[82] **Lovelace**: the rake who rapes the virtuous Clarissa in Samuel Richardson's novel *Clarissa* (1747, 1748). In his preface, Richardson claimed he wrote this novel "To warn the Inconsiderate and Thoughtless of the one sex . . . upon that dangerous but too commonly received notion, *that a reformed Rake makes the best Husband.*"

Verily misery, in its most hideous shape. When the habits of weak people are consolidated by time, a reformation is barely possible; and actually makes the beings miserable who have not sufficient mind to be amused by innocent pleasure; like the tradesman who retires from the hurry of business, nature presents to them only a universal blank, and the restless thoughts prey on the damped spirits.[83] Their reformation, as well as his retirement, actually makes them wretched because it deprives them of all employment, by quenching the hopes and fears that set in motion their sluggish minds.

If such be the force of habit; if such be the bondage of folly, how carefully ought we to guard the mind from storing up vicious associations; and equally careful should we be to cultivate the understanding, to save the poor wight from the weak dependent state of even harmless ignorance. For it is the right use of reason alone which makes us independent of every thing—excepting the unclouded Reason—'Whose service is perfect freedom.'[84]

—*from* CHAPTER VII—

MODESTY—COMPREHENSIVELY CONSIDERED, AND NOT AS A SEXUAL VIRTUE

Modesty! Sacred offspring of sensibility and reason!—true delicacy of mind—may I unblamed presume to investigate thy nature, and trace to its cover the mild charm, that mellowing each harsh feature of a character, render what would otherwise only inspire cold admiration—lovely!—Thou that smoothest the wrinkles of wisdom, and softenest the tone of the sublimest virtues till they all melt into humanity;—thou that spreadest the ethereal cloud that, surrounding love, heightens every beauty, it half shades, breathing those coy sweets that steal into the heart, and charm the senses—modulate for me the language of persuasive reason, till I rouse my sex from the flowery bed, on which they supinely sleep life away![85]

In speaking of the association of our ideas, I have noticed two distinct modes; and in defining modesty, it appears to me equally proper to discriminate that purity of mind, which is the effect of chastity, from simplicity of character that leads us to form a just opinion of ourselves equally distant from vanity or presumption, though by no means incompatible with a lofty consciousness of our own dignity. Modesty, in the latter signification of the term, is, that soberness of mind which teaches a man not to think more highly of himself than he ought to think, and should be distinguished from humility, because humility is a kind of self-abasement.

A modest man often conceives a great plan, and tenaciously adheres to it conscious of his own strength, till success gives it a sanction that determines its character. Milton was not arrogant when he suffered a suggestion of judgment to escape him that proved a prophecy; nor was General Washington when he accepted the command of the American forces.[86] The latter has always been characterized as a modest man; but had he been merely humble, he would probably have shrunk back irresolute, afraid of trusting to himself the direction of an enterprise, on which so much depended.

A modest man is steady, an humble man timid, and a vain one presumptuous:—this is the judgment, which the observation of many characters, has led me to form. Jesus Christ was modest, Moses was humble, and Peter vain.

Thus, discriminating modesty from humility in one case, I do not mean to confound it with bashfulness in the other. Bashfulness, in fact, is so distinct from modesty, that the most bashful lass, or raw country lout,[87] often become the most impudent; for their bashfulness being merely the instinctive timidity of ignorance, custom soon changes it into assurance.

The shameless behaviour of the prostitutes, who infest the streets of this metropolis, raising alternate emotions of pity and disgust, may serve to illustrate this remark. They trample on virgin bashfulness with a sort of bravado, and glorying in their shame, become more audaciously lewd than men, however depraved, to whom this sexual quality has not been gratuitously granted, ever appear to be. But these poor ignorant wretches never had any modesty to lose, when they consigned themselves to

---

[83] I have frequently seen this exemplified in women whose beauty could no longer be repaired. They have retired from the noisy scenes of dissipation; but, unless they become methodists, the solitude of the select society of their family connections or acquaintances, has presented only a fearful void; consequently, nervous complaints, and all the vapourish train of idleness, rendered then quite as useless, and far more unhappy, than when they joined the giddy throng [M. W.].

[84] See Milton's *Paradise Lost*, III.48, and *The Book of Common Prayer* (1549), Morning Prayer, Second Collect, for Peace. These texts refer to God, not Reason.

[85] Cf. *Paradise Lost*, III.1–55.

[86] John Milton predicted his future fame in his poem "Ad Patrem" (1632?). George Washington became Commander in Chief of the American Revolutionary Army on 15 June 1775.

[87] **lout:** awkward fellow, bumpkin.

infamy; for modesty is a virtue, not a quality. No, they were only bashful, shame-faced innocents; and losing their innocence, their shame-facedness was rudely brushed off; a virtue would have left some vestiges in the mind, had it been sacrificed to passion, to make us respect the grand ruin.

Purity of mind, or that genuine delicacy, which is the only virtuous support of chastity, is near akin to that refinement of humanity, which never resides in any but cultivated minds. It is something nobler than innocence, it is the delicacy of reflection, and not the coyness of ignorance. The reserve of reason, which, like habitual cleanliness, is seldom seen in any great degree, unless the soul is active, may easily be distinguished from rustic shyness or wanton skittishness; and, so far from being incompatible with knowledge, it is its fairest fruit. . . .

I have then philosophically pursued these reflections till I inferred that those women who have most improved their reason must have the most modesty—though a dignified sedateness of deportment may have succeeded the playful, bewitching bashfulness of youth. . . .

After the foregoing remarks, it is almost superfluous to add, that I consider all those feminine airs of maturity, which succeed bashfulness, to which truth is sacrificed, to secure the heart of a husband, or rather to force him to be still a lover when nature would, had she not been interrupted in her operations, have made love give place to friendship, as immodest. The tenderness which a man will feel for the mother of his children is an excellent substitute for the ardour of unsatisfied passion; but to prolong that ardour it is indelicate, not to say immodest, for women to feign an unnatural coldness of constitution. Women as well as men ought to have the common appetites and passions of their nature, they are only brutal when unchecked by reason: but the obligation to check them is the duty of mankind, not a sexual duty. Nature, in these respects, may safely be left to herself; let women only acquire knowledge and humanity, and love will teach them modesty.[88] There is no need of falsehoods, disgusting as futile, for studied rules of behaviour only impose on shallow observers; a man of sense soon sees through, and despises the affectation.

The behaviour of young people, to each other, as men and women, is the last thing that should be thought of in education. In fact, behaviour in most circumstances is now so much thought of, that simplicity of character is rarely to be seen: yet, if men were only anxious to cultivate each virtue, and let it take root firmly in the mind, the grace resulting from it, its natural exteriour mark, would soon strip affectation of its flaunting plumes; because, fallacious as unstable, is the conduct that is not founded upon truth!

Would ye, O my sisters, really possess modesty, ye must remember that the possession of virtue, of any denomination, is incompatible with ignorance and vanity! ye must acquire that soberness of mind, which the exercise of duties, and the pursuit of knowledge, alone inspire, or ye will still remain in a doubtful dependent situation, and only be loved whilst ye are fair! The downcast eye, the rosy blush, the retiring grace, are all proper in their season; but modesty, being the child of reason, cannot long exist with the sensibility that is not tempered by reflection. Besides, when love, even innocent love, is the whole employ of your lives, your hearts will be too soft to afford modesty that tranquil retreat, where she delights to dwell, in close union with humanity.

—*from* CHAPTER VIII—

Morality Undermined by Sexual Notions of the Importance of a Good Reputation

. . . The depravity of the appetite which brings the sexes together, has had a still more fatal effect. Nature must ever be the standard of taste, the gauge of appetite—yet how grossly is nature insulted by the voluptuary. Leaving the refinements of love out of the question; nature, by making the gratification of an appetite, in this respect, as well as every other, a natural and imperious law to preserve the species, exalts the appetite, and mixes a little mind and affection with a sensual gust. The feelings of a parent mingling with an instinct merely animal, give it dignity; and the man and woman often meeting on account of the child, a mutual interest and affection is excited by the exercise of a common sympathy. Women then having necessarily some duty to fulfil, more noble than to adorn their persons, would not contentedly be the slaves of casual lust; which is now the situation of a very considerable number who are, literally speaking, standing dishes to which every glutton may have access.

---

[88] The behaviour of many newly married women has often disgusted me. They seem anxious never to let their husbands forget the privilege of marriage; and to find no pleasure in his society unless he is acting the lover. Short, indeed, must be the reign of love, when the flame is thus constantly blown up, without its receiving any solid fewel! [M. W.]

I may be told that great as this enormity is, it only affects a devoted part of the sex—devoted for the salvation of the rest. But, false as every assertion might easily be proved, that recommends the sanctioning a small evil to produce a greater good; the mischief does not stop here, for the moral character, and peace of mind, of the chaster part of the sex, is undermined by the conduct of the very women to whom they allow no refuge from guilt: whom they inexorably consign to the exercise of arts that lure their husbands from them, debauch their sons, and force them, let not modest women start, to assume, in some degree, the same character themselves. For I will venture to assert, that all the causes of female weakness, as well as depravity, which I have already enlarged on, branch out of one grand cause—want of chastity in men.

This intemperance, so prevalent, depraves the appetite to such a degree, that a wanton stimulus is necessary to rouse it; but the parental design of nature is forgotten, and the mere person, and that for a moment, alone engrosses the thoughts. So voluptuous, indeed, often grows the lustful prowler, that he refines on female softness. Something more soft than woman is then sought for; till, in Italy and Portugal, men attend the levees of equivocal beings, to sigh for more than female languor.[89]

To satisfy this genus of men, women are made systematically voluptuous, and though they may not all carry their libertinism to the same height, yet this heartless intercourse with the sex, which they allow themselves, depraves both sexes, because the taste of men is vitiated; and women, of all classes, naturally square their behaviour to gratify the taste by which they obtain pleasure and power. Women becoming, consequently, weaker, in mind and body, than they ought to be, were one of the grand ends of their being taken into the account, that of bearing and nursing children, have not sufficient strength to discharge the first duty of a mother; and sacrificing to lasciviousness the parental affection, that ennobles instinct, either destroy the embryo in the womb, or cast it off when born. Nature in every thing demands respect, and those who violate her laws seldom violate them with impunity. The weak enervated women who particularly catch the attention of libertines, are unfit to be mothers, though they may conceive; so that the rich sensualist, who has rioted among women, spreading depravity and misery, when he wishes to perpetuate his name, receives from his wife only an half-formed being that inherits both its father's and mother's weakness.

Contrasting the humanity of the present age with the barbarism of antiquity, great stress has been laid on the savage custom of exposing the children whom their parents could not maintain; whilst the man of sensibility, who thus, perhaps, complains, by his promiscuous amours produces a most destructive barrenness and contagious flagitiousness[90] of manners. Surely nature never intended that women, by satisfying an appetite, should frustrate the very purpose for which it was implanted?

I have before observed, that men ought to maintain the women whom they have seduced; this would be one means of reforming female manners, and stopping an abuse that has an equally fatal effect on population and morals. Another, no less obvious, would be to turn the attention of woman to the real virtue of chastity; for to little respect has that woman a claim, on the score of modesty, though her reputation may be white as the driven snow, who smiles on the libertine whilst she spurns the victims of his lawless appetites and their own folly.

Besides, she has a taint of the same folly, pure as she esteems herself, when she studiously adorns her person only to be seen by men, to excite respectful sighs, and all the idle homage of what is called innocent gallantry. Did women really respect virtue for its own sake, they would not seek for compensation in vanity, for the self-denial which they are obliged to practise to preserve their reputation, nor would they associate with men who set reputation at defiance.

The two sexes mutually corrupt and improve each other. This I believe to be an indisputable truth, extending it to every virtue. Chastity, modesty, public spirit, and all the noble train of virtues, on which social virtue and happiness are built, should be understood and cultivated by all mankind or they will be cultivated to little effect. And, instead of furnishing the vicious or idle with a pretext for violating some sacred duty, by terming it a sexual one, it would be wiser to shew that nature has not made any difference, for that the unchaste man doubly defeats the purpose of nature by rendering women barren, and destroying his own constitution, though he avoids the shame that pursues the crime in the other sex. These are the physical consequences, the moral are still

[89] Homosexual or "molly" clubs also existed in eighteenth-century London; see Ned Ward, *A Compleat and Humourous Account of all the Remarkable Clubs and Societies in the Cities of London and Westminster* (1749).

[90] **flagitiousness:** villainy; addiction to heinous crimes.

more alarming; for virtue is only a nominal distinction when the duties of citizens, husbands, wives, fathers, mothers, and directors of families, become merely the selfish ties of convenience.

Why then do philosophers look for public spirit? Public spirit must be nurtured by private virtue, or it will resemble the factitious sentiment which makes women careful to preserve their reputation, and men their honour. A sentiment that often exists unsupported by virtue, unsupported by that sublime morality which makes the habitual breach of one duty a breach of the whole moral law.

— *from* CHAPTER IX —
Of the Pernicious Effects Which Arise from the Unnatural Distinctions Established in Society

From the respect paid to property flow, as from a poisoned fountain, most of the evils and vices which render this world such a dreary scene to the contemplative mind. For it is in the most polished society that noisome reptiles and venomous serpents lurk under the rank herbage; and there is voluptuousness pampered by the still sultry air, which relaxes every good disposition before it ripens into virtue.

One class presses on another; for all are aiming to procure respect on account of their property: and property, once gained, will procure the respect due only to talents and virtue. Men neglect the duties incumbent on man, yet are treated like demi-gods; religion is also separated from morality by a ceremonial veil, yet men wonder that the world is almost literally speaking, a den of sharpers or oppressors.

There is a homely proverb, which speaks a shrewd truth, that whoever the devil finds idle he will employ. And what but habitual idleness can hereditary wealth and title produce? For man is so constituted that he can only attain a proper use of his faculties by exercising them, and will not exercise them unless necessity, of some kind, first set the wheels in motion. Virtue likewise can only be acquired by the discharge of relative duties; but the importance of these sacred duties will scarcely be felt by the being who is cajoled out of his humanity by the flattery of sycophants. There must be more equality established in society, or morality will never gain ground, and this virtuous equality will not rest firmly even when founded on a rock, if one half of mankind be chained to its bottom by fate, for they will be continually undermining it through ignorance or pride.

It is vain to expect virtue from women till they are, in some degree, independent of men; nay, it is vain to expect that strength of natural affection, which would make them good wives and mothers. Whilst they are absolutely dependent on their husbands they will be cunning, mean, and selfish, and the men who can be gratified by the fawning fondness of spaniel-like affection, have not much delicacy, for love is not to be bought, in any sense of the words, its silken wings are instantly shrivelled up when any thing beside a return in kind is sought. Yet whilst wealth enervates men; and women live, as it were, by their personal charms, how can we expect them to discharge those ennobling duties which equally require exertion and self-denial. Hereditary property sophisticates[91] the mind, and the unfortunate victims to it, if I may so express myself, swathed from their birth,[92] seldom exert the locomotive faculty of body or mind; and, thus viewing every thing through one medium, and that a false one, they are unable to discern in what true merit and happiness consist. False, indeed, must be the light when the drapery of situation hides the man, and makes him stalk in masquerade,[93] dragging from one scene of dissipation to another the nerveless limbs that hang with stupid listlessness, and rolling round the vacant eye which plainly tells us that there is no mind at home.

I mean, therefore, to infer that the society is not properly organized which does not compel men and women to discharge their respective duties, by making it the only way to acquire that countenance from their fellow-creatures, which every human being wishes some way to attain. The respect, consequently, which is paid to wealth and mere personal charms, is a true north-east blast, that blights the tender blossoms of affection and virtue. Nature has wisely attached affections to duties, to sweeten toil, and to give that vigour to the exertions of reason which only the heart can give. But, the affection which is put on merely because it is the appropriated

---

[91] **sophisticates**: corrupts, spoils by mixing with a baser quality.

[92] **swathed from their birth**: newborn infants were "swaddled" or wrapped in long bandages like a cocoon, preventing all movement; the bandages were changed weekly. This practice was slowly dying out in England by the late eighteenth century.

[93] **masquerade**: masquerades or masked balls, in which participants dressed in elaborate costumes of animals or humans and often spoke to each other in gibberish, were a popular form of public entertainment in the eighteenth century.

insignia[94] of a certain character, when its duties are not fulfilled, is one of the empty compliments which vice and folly are obliged to pay to virtue and the real nature of things.

To illustrate my opinion, I need only observe, that when a woman is admired for her beauty, and suffers herself to be so far intoxicated by the admiration she receives, as to neglect to discharge the indispensable duty of a mother, she sins against herself by neglecting to cultivate an affection that would equally tend to make her useful and happy. True happiness, I mean all the contentment, and virtuous satisfaction, that can be snatched in this imperfect state, must arise from well regulated affections; and an affection includes a duty. Men are not aware of the misery they cause, and the vicious weakness they cherish, by only inciting women to render themselves pleasing; they do not consider that they thus make natural and artificial duties clash, by sacrificing the comfort and respectability of a woman's life to voluptuous notions of beauty, when in nature they all harmonize.

Cold would be the heart of a husband, were he not rendered unnatural by early debauchery, who did not feel more delight at seeing his child suckled by its mother, than the most artful wanton tricks could ever raise; yet this natural way of cementing the matrimonial tie, and twisting esteem with fonder recollections, wealth leads women to spurn.[95] To preserve their beauty, and wear the flowery crown of the day, which gives them a kind of right to reign for a short time over the sex, they neglect to stamp impressions on their husbands' hearts, that would be remembered with more tenderness when the snow on the head began to chill the bosom, than even their virgin charms. The maternal solicitude of a reasonable affectionate woman is very interesting, and the chastened dignity with which a mother returns the caresses that she and her child receive from a father who has been fulfilling the serious duties of his station, is not only a respectable, but a beautiful sight. So singular, indeed, are my feelings, and I have endeavoured not to catch factitious[96] ones, that after having been fatigued with the sight of insipid grandeur and the slavish ceremonies that with cumberous pomp supplied the place of domestic affections, I have turned to some other scene to relieve my eye by resting it on the refreshing green every where scattered by nature. I have then viewed with pleasure a woman nursing her children, and discharging the duties of her station with, perhaps, merely a servant maid to take off her hands the servile part of the household business. I have seen her prepare herself and children, with only the luxury of cleanliness, to receive her husband, who returning weary home in the evening found smiling babes and a clean hearth. My heart has loitered in the midst of the group, and has even throbbed with sympathetic emotion, when the scraping of the well known foot has raised a pleasing tumult. . . .

But, to have done with these episodical observations, let me return to the more specious slavery which chains the very soul of woman, keeping her for ever under the bondage of ignorance.

The preposterous distinctions of rank, which render civilization a curse, by dividing the world between voluptuous tyrants, and cunning envious dependents, corrupt, almost equally, every class of people, because respectability is not attached to the discharge of the relative duties of life, but to the station, and when the duties are not fulfilled the affections cannot gain sufficient strength to fortify the virtue of which they are the natural reward. Still there are some loop-holes out of which a man may creep, and dare to think and act for himself; but for a woman it is an herculean task, because she has difficulties peculiar to her sex to overcome, which require almost super-human powers.

A truly benevolent legislator always endeavours to make it the interest of each individual to be virtuous; and thus private virtue becoming the cement of public happiness, an orderly whole is consolidated by the tendency of all the parts towards a common centre. But, the private or public virtue of woman is very problematical; for Rousseau, and a numerous list of male writers, insist that she should all her life be subjected to a severe restraint, that of propriety. Why subject her to propriety—blind propriety, if she be capable of acting from a nobler spring, if she be an heir of immortality? Is sugar always to be produced by vital blood? Is one half of the human species, like the poor African slaves, to be subject to prejudices that brutalize them, when principles would be a surer guard, only to sweeten the cup of man?[97] Is not

[94] **appropriated insignia:** attached or borrowed badges of rank or honor; masks.

[95] Wet-nursing, or paying another woman to breastfeed one's newborn child, was common among the upper classes in England in the eighteenth century.

[96] **factitious:** artificial; insincere.

[97] The British slave traders captured and sold Africans to the West Indian planters, who used these slaves to harvest sugarcane for export, either as refined sugar or as rum. (See SLAVERY, THE SLAVE TRADE, AND ABOLITION.)

this indirectly to deny woman reason? for a gift is a mockery, if it be unfit for use.

Women are, in common with men, rendered weak and luxurious by the relaxing pleasures which wealth procures; but added to this they are made slaves to their persons, and must render them alluring that man may lend them his reason to guide their tottering steps aright. Or should they be ambitious, they must govern their tyrants by sinister tricks, for without rights there cannot be any incumbent duties. The laws respecting woman, which I mean to discuss in a future part, make an absurd unit of a man and his wife; and then, by the easy transition of only considering him as responsible, she is reduced to a mere cypher.[98]

The being who discharges the duties of its station is independent; and, speaking of women at large, their first duty is to themselves as rational creatures, and the next, in point of importance, as citizens, is that, which includes so many, of a mother. The rank in life which dispenses with their fulfilling this duty, necessarily degrades them by making them mere dolls. Or, should they turn to something more important than merely fitting drapery upon a smooth block, their minds are only occupied by some soft platonic attachment; or, the actual management of an intrigue may keep their thoughts in motion; for when they neglect domestic duties, they have it not in their power to take the field and march and countermarch like soldiers, or wrangle in the senate to keep their faculties from rusting.

I know that, as a proof of the inferiority of the sex, Rousseau has exultingly exclaimed, How can they leave the nursery for the camp![99] And the camp has by some moralists been termed the school of the most heroic virtues; though, I think, it would puzzle a keen casuist to prove the reasonableness of the greater number of wars that have dubbed heroes. I do not mean to consider this question critically; because, having frequently viewed these freaks[100] of ambition as the first natural mode of civilization, when the ground must be torn up, and the woods cleared by fire and sword, I do not choose to call them pests; but surely the present system of war has little connection with virtue of any denomination, being rather the school of *finesse*[101] and effeminacy, than of fortitude.

Yet, if defensive war, the only justifiable war, in the present advanced state of society, where virtue can shew its face and ripen amidst the rigours which purify the air on the mountain's top, were alone to be adopted as just and glorious, the true heroism of antiquity might again animate female bosoms.—But fair and softly, gentle reader, male or female, do not alarm thyself, for though I have compared the character of a modern soldier with that of a civilized woman, I am not going to advise them to turn their distaff into a musket, though I sincerely wish to see the bayonet converted into a pruning-hook. I only recreated an imagination, fatigued by contemplating the vices and follies which all proceed from a feculent[102] stream of wealth that has muddied the pure rills of natural affection, by supposing that society will some time or other be so constituted, that man must necessarily fulfil the duties of a citizen, or be despised, and that while he was employed in any of the departments of civil life, his wife, also an active citizen, should be equally intent to manage her family, educate her children, and assist her neighbours.

But, to render her really virtuous and useful, she must not, if she discharge her civil duties, want, individually, the protection of civil laws; she must not be dependent on her husband's bounty for her subsistence during his life, or support after his death—for how can a being be generous who has nothing of its own? or virtuous, who is not free? The wife, in the present state of things, who is faithful to her husband, and neither suckles nor educates her children, scarcely deserves the name of a wife, and has no right to that of a citizen. But take away natural rights, and duties become null.

Women then must be considered as only the wanton solace of men, when they become so weak in mind and body, that they cannot exert themselves, unless to pursue some frothy pleasure, or to invent some frivolous fashion. What can be a more melancholy sight to a thinking mind, than to look into the numerous carriages that drive helter-skelter about this metropolis in a morning full of pale-faced creatures who are flying from themselves. I have

---

[98] See William Blackstone, *Commentaries on the Laws of England* (1765), I.xv.430: "By marriage, the husband and wife are one person in law: that is, the very being or legal existence of the woman is suspended during the marriage, or at least is incorporated and consolidated into that of the husband: under whose wing, protection and *cover,* she performs everything." (See RIGHTS OF WOMAN.)

[99] Rousseau, *Émile,* IV.v.13.

[100] **freaks:** whims, caprices.

[101] **finesse:** artfulness, stratagem.

[102] **feculent:** foul, fetid, containing feces.

often wished, with Dr Johnson,[103] to place some of them in a little shop with half a dozen children looking up to their languid countenances for support. I am much mistaken, if some latent vigour would not soon give health and spirit to their eyes, and some lines drawn by the exercise of reason on the blank cheeks, which before were only undulated by dimples, might restore lost dignity to the character, or rather enable it to attain the true dignity of its nature. Virtue is not to be acquired even by speculation, much less by the negative supineness that wealth naturally generates.

Besides, when poverty is more disgraceful than even vice, is not morality cut to the quick? Still to avoid misconstruction, though I consider that women in the common walks of life are called to fulfil the duties of wives and mothers, by religion and reason, I cannot help lamenting that women of a superiour cast have not a road open by which they can pursue more extensive plans of usefulness and independence. I may excite laughter, by dropping an hint, which I mean to pursue, some future time, for I really think that women ought to have representatives, instead of being arbitrarily governed without having any direct share allowed them in the deliberations of government.

But, as the whole system of representation is now, in this country, only a convenient handle for despotism, they need not complain, for they are as well represented as a numerous class of hard working mechanics, who pay for the support of royalty when they can scarcely stop their children's mouths with bread. How are they represented whose very sweat supports the splendid stud of an heir apparent, or varnishes the chariot of some female favourite who looks down on shame? Taxes on the very necessaries of life, enable an endless tribe of idle princes and princesses to pass with stupid pomp before a gaping crowd, who almost worship the very parade which costs them so dear. This is mere gothic grandeur, something like the barbarous useless parade of having sentinels on horseback at Whitehall, which I could never view without a mixture of contempt and indignation.

How strangely must the mind be sophisticated when this sort of state impresses it! But, till these monuments of folly are levelled by virtue, similar follies will leaven the whole mass. For the same character, in some degree, will prevail in the aggregate of society: and the refinements of luxury, or the vicious repinings of envious poverty, will equally banish virtue from society, considered as the characteristic of that society, or only allow it to appear as one of the stripes of the harlequin coat,[104] worn by the civilized man.

In the superiour ranks of life, every duty is done by deputies, as if duties could ever be waived, and the vain pleasures which consequent idleness forces the rich to pursue, appear so enticing to the next rank, that the numerous scramblers for wealth sacrifice every thing to tread on their heels. The most sacred trusts are then considered as sinecures, because they were procured by interest, and only sought to enable a man to keep *good company*. Women, in particular, all want to be ladies. Which is simply to have nothing to do, but listlessly to go they scarcely care where, for they cannot tell what.

But what have women to do in society? I may be asked, but to loiter with easy grace; surely you would not condemn them all to suckle fools and chronicle small beer![105] No. Women might certainly study the art of healing, and be physicians as well as nurses. And midwifery, decency seems to allot to them, though I am afraid the word midwife, in our dictionaries, will soon give place to *accoucheur*,[106] and one proof of the former delicacy of the sex be effaced from the language.

They might, also, study politics, and settle their benevolence on the broadest basis; for the reading of history will scarcely be more useful than the perusal of romances, if read as mere biography; if the character of the times, the political improvements, arts, etc. be not observed. In short, if it be not considered as the history of man; and not of particular men, who filled a niche in the temple of fame, and dropped into the black rolling stream of time, that silently sweeps all before it, into the shapeless void called—eternity.—For shape, can it be called, 'that shape hath none?'[107]

Business of various kinds, they might likewise pursue, if they were educated in a more orderly manner, which might save many from common and legal prostitution. Women would not then marry for a support, as men accept of places under government, and neglect the implied

[103] Dr. Samuel Johnson (1709–1784), renowned poet, critic, lexicographer, and conversationalist.

[104] **harlequin coat**: multicolored costume of the Arlecchino, Pierrot, or Punch, a famous comic trickster.

[105] See Shakespeare's *Othello*, II.i.160. This is Iago's definition of the activities of a praiseworthy woman.

[106] **accoucheur**: French, male midwife.

[107] Cf. *Paradise Lost*, II.667.

duties; nor would an attempt to earn their own subsistence, a most laudable one! sink them almost to the level of those poor abandoned creatures who live by prostitution. For are not milliners and mantua-makers[108] reckoned the next class? The few employments open to women, so far from being liberal, are menial; and when a superiour education enables them to take charge of the education of children as governesses, they are not treated like the tutors of sons, though even clerical tutors are not always treated in a manner calculated to render them respectable in the eyes of their pupils, to say nothing of the private comfort of the individual. But as women educated like gentlewomen, are never designed for the humiliating situation which necessity sometimes forces them to fill; these situations are considered in the light of a degradation; and they know little of the human heart, who need to be told, that nothing so painfully sharpens sensibility as such a fall in life.

Some of these women might be restrained from marrying by a proper spirit or delicacy, and others may not have had it in their power to escape in this pitiful way from servitude; is not that government then very defective, and very unmindful of the happiness of one half of its members, that does not provide for honest, independent women, by encouraging them to fill respectable stations? But in order to render their private virtue a public benefit, they must have a civil existence in the state, married or single; else we shall continually see some worthy woman, whose sensibility has been rendered painfully acute by undeserved contempt, droop like 'the lily broken down by a plow-share.'[109]

It is a melancholy truth; yet such is the blessed effect of civilization! the most respectable women are the most oppressed; and, unless they have understandings far superiour to the common run of understandings, taking in both sexes, they must, from being treated like contemptible beings, become contemptible. How many women thus waste life away the prey of discontent, who might have practised as physicians, regulated a farm, managed a shop, and stood erect, supported by their own industry, instead of hanging their heads surcharged with the dew of sensibility, that consumes the beauty to which it at first gave lustre; nay, I doubt whether pity and love are so near akin as poets feign, for I have seldom seen much compassion excited by the helplessness of females, unless they were fair; then, perhaps, pity was the soft handmaid of love, or the harbinger of lust.

How much more respectable is the woman who earns her own bread by fulfilling any duty, than the most accomplished beauty!—beauty did I say?—so sensible am I of the beauty of moral loveliness, or the harmonious propriety that attunes the passions of a well-regulated mind, that I blush at making the comparison; yet I sigh to think how few women aim at attaining this respectability by withdrawing from the giddy whirl of pleasure, or the indolent calm that stupifies the good sort of women it sucks in.

Proud of their weakness, however, they must always be protected, guarded from care, and all the rough toils that dignify the mind.—If this be the fiat of fate, if they will make themselves insignificant and contemptible, sweetly to waste 'life away,' let them not expect to be valued when their beauty fades, for it is the fate of the fairest flowers to be admired and pulled to pieces by the careless hand that plucked them. In how many ways do I wish, from the purest benevolence, to impress this truth on my sex; yet I fear that they will not listen to a truth that dear bought experience has brought home to many an agitated bosom, nor willingly resign the privileges of rank and sex for the privileges of humanity, to which those have no claim who do not discharge its duties.

Those writers are particularly useful, in my opinion, who make man feel for man, independent of the station he fills, or the drapery of factitious sentiments. I then would fain convince reasonable men of the importance of some of my remarks; and prevail on them to weigh dispassionately the whole tenor of my observations.—I appeal to their understandings; and, as a fellow-creature, claim, in the name of my sex, some interest in their hearts. I entreat them to assist to emancipate their companion, to make her a *help meet* for them!

Would men but generously snap our chains, and be content with rational fellowship instead of slavish obedience, they would find us more observant daughters, more affectionate sisters, more faithful wives, more reasonable mothers—in a word, better citizens. We should then love them with true affection, because we should learn to respect ourselves; and the peace of mind of a worthy man would not be interrupted by the idle vanity of his wife, nor the babes sent to nestle in a strange bosom, having never found a home in their mother's.

---

[108] **mantua-makers:** coat- or dressmakers.

[109] François de Salignac de La Mothe-Fénelon, *The Fortunes of Telemachus,* trans. Isaac Littlebury (1699), I.152: "As a beautiful Lilly in the midst of the Field, cut up from the Root by the Plowshare, lies down and languishes on the Ground."

— CHAPTER X —
PARENTAL AFFECTION

Parental affection is, perhaps, the blindest modification of perverse self-love; for we have not, like the French, two terms[110] to distinguish the pursuit of a natural and reasonable desire, from the ignorant calculations of weakness. Parents often love their children in the most brutal manner, and sacrifice every relative duty to promote their advancement in the world.—To promote, such is the perversity of unprincipled prejudices, the future welfare of the very beings whose present existence they imbitter by the most despotic stretch of power. Power, in fact, is ever true to its vital principle, for in every shape it would reign without controul or inquiry. Its throne is built across a dark abyss, which no eye must dare to explore, lest the baseless fabric should totter under investigation. Obedience, unconditional obedience, is the catch-word of tyrants of every description, and to render 'assurance doubly sure,'[111] one kind of despotism supports another. Tyrants would have cause to tremble if reason were to become the rule of duty in any of the relations of life, for the light might spread till perfect day appeared. And when it did appear, how would men smile at the sight of the bugbears at which they started during the night of ignorance, or the twilight of timid inquiry.

Parental affection, indeed, in many minds, is but a pretext to tyrannize where it can be done with impunity, for only good and wise men are content with the respect that will bear discussion. Convinced that they have a right to what they insist on, they do not fear reason, or dread the sifting of subjects that recur to natural justice: because they firmly believe that the more enlightened the human mind becomes the deeper root will just and simple principles take. They do not rest in expedients, or grant that what is metaphysically true can be practically false; but disdaining the shifts of the moment they calmly wait till time, sanctioning innovation, silences the hiss of selfishness or envy.

If the power of reflecting on the past, and darting the keen eye of contemplation into futurity, be the grand privilege of man, it must be granted that some people enjoy this prerogative in a very limited degree. Every thing new appears to them wrong; and not able to distinguish the possible from the monstrous, they fear where no fear should find a place, running from the light of reason, as if it were a firebrand; yet the limits of the possible have never been defined to stop the sturdy innovator's hand.

Woman, however, a slave in every situation to prejudice, seldom exerts enlightened maternal affection; for she either neglects her children, or spoils them by improper indulgence. Besides, the affection of some women for their children is, as I have before termed it, frequently very brutish; for it eradicates every spark of humanity. Justice, truth, every thing is sacrificed by these Rebekah's, and for the sake of their *own* children they violate the most sacred duties, forgetting the common relationship that binds the whole family on earth together.[112] Yet, reason seems to say, that they who suffer one duty, or affection, to swallow up the rest, have not sufficient heart or mind to fulfil that one conscientiously. It then loses the venerable aspect of a duty, and assumes the fantastic form of a whim.

As the care of children in their infancy is one of the grand duties annexed to the female character by nature, this duty would afford many forcible arguments for strengthening the female understanding, if it were properly considered.

The formation of the mind must be begun very early, and the temper, in particular, requires the most judicious attention—an attention which women cannot pay who only love their children because they are their children, and seek no further for the foundation of their duty, than in the feelings of the moment. It is this want of reason in their affections which makes women so often run into extremes, and either be the most fond or most careless and unnatural mothers.

To be a good mother—a woman must have sense, and that independence of mind which few women possess who are taught to depend entirely on their husbands. Meek wives are, in general, foolish mothers; wanting their children to love them best, and take their part, in secret, against the father, who is held up as a scarecrow. When chastisement is necessary, though they have offended the mother, the father must inflict the punishment; he must be the judge in all disputes: but I shall more fully discuss this subject when I treat of private education, I now only mean to insist, that unless the understanding of woman

[110] *L'amour propre. L'amour de soi même* [See Rousseau, *Discours sur l'inegalité*, I, note 12, pp. 252–53: "One must not confuse self-love and self-esteem . . ."] [M. W.].

[111] Cf. Shakespeare, *Macbeth*, IV.i.83.

[112] Rebekah, the wife of Isaac and the mother of Esau and Jacob, tricked her eldest son Esau out of his dying father's blessing and patrimony.

be enlarged, and her character rendered more firm, by being allowed to govern her own conduct, she will never have sufficient sense or command of temper to manage her children properly. Her parental affection, indeed, scarcely deserves the name, when it does not lead her to suckle her children, because the discharge of this duty is equally calculated to inspire maternal and filial affection: and it is the indispensable duty of men and women to fulfil the duties which give birth to affections that are the surest preservatives against vice. Natural affection, as it is termed, I believe to be a very faint tie, affections must grow out of the habitual exercise of a mutual sympathy; and what sympathy does a mother exercise who sends her babe to a nurse, and only takes it from a nurse to send it to a school?

In the exercise of their maternal feelings providence has furnished women with a natural substitute for love, when the lover becomes only a friend, and mutual confidence takes place of overstrained admiration—a child then gently twists the relaxing cord, and a mutual care produces a new mutual sympathy.—But a child, though a pledge of affection, will not enliven it, if both father and mother be content to transfer the charge to hirelings; for they who do their duty by proxy should not murmur if they miss the reward of duty—parental affection produces filial duty.

—*from* CHAPTER XI—
Duty to Parents

. . . A slavish bondage to parents cramps every faculty of the mind; and Mr Locke very judiciously observes, that 'if the mind be curbed and humbled too much in children; if their spirits be abased and broken much by too strict an hand over them; they lose all their vigour and industry.'[113] This strict hand may in some degree account for the weakness of women; for girls, from various causes, are more kept down by their parents, in every sense of the word, than boys. The duty expected from them is, like all the duties arbitrarily imposed on women, more from a sense of propriety, more out of respect for decorum, than reason; and thus taught slavishly to submit to their parents, they are prepared for the slavery of marriage. I may be told that a number of women are not slaves in the marriage state. True, but they then become tyrants; for it is not rational freedom, but a lawless kind of power resembling the authority exercised by the favourites of absolute monarchs, which they obtain by debasing means. I do not, likewise, dream of insinuating that either boys or girls are always slaves, I only insist that when they are obliged to submit to authority blindly, their faculties are weakened, and their tempers rendered imperious or abject. I also lament that parents, indolently availing themselves of a supposed privilege, damp the first faint glimmering of reason, rendering at the same time the duty, which they are so anxious to enforce, an empty name; because they will not let it rest on the only basis on which a duty can rest securely: for unless it be founded on knowledge, it cannot gain sufficient strength to resist the squalls of passion, or the silent sapping of self-love. But it is not the parents who have given the surest proof of their affection for their children, or, to speak more properly, who by fulfilling their duty, have allowed a natural parental affection to take root in their hearts, the child of exercised sympathy and reason, and not the over-weening offspring of selfish pride, who most vehemently insist on their children submitting to their will merely because it is their will. On the contrary, the parent, who sets a good example, patiently lets that example work; and it seldom fails to produce its natural effect—filial reverence.

Children cannot be taught too early to submit to reason, the true definition of that necessity, which Rousseau insisted on, without defining it; for to submit to reason is to submit to the nature of things, and to that God, who formed them so, to promote our real interest. . . .

—*from* CHAPTER XII—
On National Education

The good effects resulting from attention to private education will ever be very confined, and the parent who really puts his own hand to the plow, will always, in some degree, be disappointed, till education becomes a grand national concern. . . .

. . . in youth the seeds of every affection should be sown, and the respectful regard, which is felt for a parent, is very different from the social affections that are to constitute the happiness of life as it advances. Of these equality is the basis, and an intercourse of sentiments unclogged by that observant seriousness which prevents disputation, though it may not inforce submission. Let a child have ever such an affection for his parent, he will always languish to play and prattle with children; and the very respect he feels, for filial esteem always has a dash of fear mixed with it, will, if it do not teach him cunning, at least prevent him from pouring out the little secrets which first

[113] John Locke, *Some Thoughts Concerning Education* (1693), 45, p. 2.

open the heart to friendship and confidence, gradually leading to more expansive benevolence. Added to this, he will never acquire that frank ingenuousness of behaviour, which young people can only attain by being frequently in society where they dare to speak what they think; neither afraid of being reproved for their presumption, nor laughed at for their folly.

Forcibly impressed by the reflections which the sight of schools, as they are at present conducted, naturally suggested, I have formerly delivered my opinion rather warmly in favour of a private education; but further experience has led me to view the subject in a different light. I still, however, think schools, as they are now regulated, the hot-beds of vice and folly, and the knowledge of human nature, supposed to be attained there, merely cunning selfishness.

At school boys become gluttons and slovens, and, instead of cultivating domestic affections, very early rush into libertinism which destroys the constitution before it is formed; hardening the heart as it weakens the understanding.

I should, in fact, be averse to boarding-schools, if it were for no other reason than the unsettled state of mind which the expectation of the vacations produce. On these the children's thoughts are fixed with eager anticipating hopes, for, at least, to speak with moderation, half of the time, and when they arrive they are spent in total dissipation and beastly indulgence.

But, on the contrary, when they are brought up at home, though they may pursue a plan of study in a more orderly manner than can be adopted when near a fourth part of the year is actually spent in idleness, and as much more in regret and anticipation; yet they there acquire too high an opinion of their own importance, from being allowed to tyrannize over servants, and from the anxiety expressed by most mothers, on the score of manners, who, eager to teach the accomplishments of a gentleman, stifle, in their birth, the virtues of a man. Thus brought into company when they ought to be seriously employed, and treated like men when they are still boys, they become vain and effeminate.

The only way to avoid two extremes equally injurious to morality, would be to contrive some way of combining a public and private education. Thus to make men citizens two natural steps might be taken, which seem directly to lead to the desired point; for the domestic affections, that first open the heart to the various modifications of humanity, would be cultivated, whilst the children were nevertheless allowed to spend great part of their time, on terms of equality, with other children. . . .

. . . When, therefore, I call women slaves, I mean in a political and civil sense; for, indirectly they obtain too much power, and are debased by their exertions to obtain illicit sway.

Let an enlightened nation[114] then try what effect reason would have to bring them back to nature, and their duty; and allowing them to share the advantages of education and government with man, see whether they will become better, as they grow wiser and become free. They cannot be injured by the experiment; for it is not in the power of man to render them more insignificant than they are at present.

To render this practicable, day schools, for particular ages, should be established by government, in which boys and girls might be educated together. The school for the younger children, from five to nine years of age, ought to be absolutely free and open to all classes.[115] A sufficient number of masters should also be chosen by a select committee, in each parish, to whom any complaint of negligence, etc. might be made, if signed by six of the children's parents.

Ushers[116] would then be unnecessary; for I believe experience will ever prove that this kind of subordinate authority is particularly injurious to the morals of youth. What, indeed, can tend to deprave the character more than outward submission and inward contempt? Yet how can boys be expected to treat an usher with respect, when the master seems to consider him in the light of a servant, and almost to countenance the ridicule which becomes the chief amusement of the boys during the play hours?

But nothing of this kind could occur in an elementary day-school, where boys and girls, the rich and poor, should meet together. And to prevent any of the distinctions of vanity, they should be dressed alike, and all obliged to submit to the same discipline, or leave the school. The school-room ought to be surrounded by a large piece of ground, in which the children might be usefully exercised, for at this

---

[114] France [M. W.].

[115] Treating this part of the subject, I have borrowed some hints from a very sensible pamphlet, written by the late bishop of Autun on Public Education [M. W.].

[116] **usher:** a schoolmaster's assistant, responsible for keeping discipline.

age they should not be confined to any sedentary employment for more than an hour at a time. But these relaxations might all be rendered a part of elementary education, for many things improve and amuse the senses, when introduced as a kind of show, to the principles of which, dryly laid down, children would turn a deaf ear. For instance, botany, mechanics, and astronomy. Reading, writing, arithmetic, natural history, and some simple experiments in natural philosophy, might fill up the day; but these pursuits should never encroach on gymnastic plays in the open air. The elements of religion, history, the history of man, and politics, might also be taught by conversations, in the socratic form.[117]

After the age of nine, girls and boys, intended for domestic employments, or mechanical trades, ought to be removed to other schools, and receive instruction, in some measure appropriated to the destination of each individual, the two sexes being still together in the morning; but in the afternoon, the girls should attend a school, where plain-work, mantua-making, millinery, etc. would be their employment.

The young people of superior abilities, or fortune, might now be taught, in another school, the dead and living languages, the elements of science, and continue the study of history and politics, on a more extensive scale, which would not exclude polite literature.

Girls and boys still together? I hear some readers ask: yes. And I should not fear any other consequence than that some early attachment might take place; which, whilst it had the best effect on the moral character of the young people, might not perfectly agree with the views of the parents, for it will be a long time, I fear, before the world will be so far enlightened that parents, only anxious to render their children virtuous, shall allow them to choose companions for life themselves. . . .

To render mankind more virtuous, and happier of course, both sexes must act from the same principle; but how can that be expected when only one is allowed to see the reasonableness of it? To render also the social compact truly equitable, and in order to spread those enlightening principles, which alone can meliorate the fate of man, women must be allowed to found their virtue on knowledge, which is scarcely possible unless they be educated by the same pursuits as men. For they are now made so inferiour by ignorance and low desires, as not to deserve to be ranked with them; or, by the serpentine wrigglings of cunning they mount the tree of knowledge, and only acquire sufficient to lead men astray.

It is plain from the history of all nations, that women cannot be confined to merely domestic pursuits, for they will not fulfil family duties, unless their minds take a wider range, and whilst they are kept in ignorance they become in the same proportion the slaves of pleasure as they are the slaves of man. Nor can they be shut out of great enterprises, though the narrowness of their minds often make them mar, what they are unable to comprehend. . . .

Make them free, and they will quickly become wise and virtuous, as men become more so; for the improvement must be mutual, or the injustice which one half of the human race are obliged to submit to, retorting on their oppressors, the virtue of man will be worm-eaten by the insect whom he keeps under his feet.

Let men take their choice, man and woman were made for each other, though not to become one being; and if they will not improve women, they will deprave them!

I speak of the improvement and emancipation of the whole sex, for I know that the behaviour of a few women, who, by accident, or following a strong bent of nature, have acquired a portion of knowledge superiour to that of the rest of their sex, has often been overbearing; but there have been instances of women who, attaining knowledge, have not discarded modesty, nor have they always pedantically appeared to despise the ignorance which they laboured to disperse in their own minds. The exclamations then which any advice respecting female learning, commonly produces, especially from pretty women, often arise from envy. When they chance to see that even the lustre of their eyes, and the flippant sportiveness of refined coquetry will not always secure them attention, during a whole evening, should a woman of a more cultivated understanding endeavour to give a rational turn to the conversation, the common source of consolation is, that such women seldom get husbands. What arts have I not seen silly women use to interrupt by *flirtation,* a very significant word to describe such a manoeuvre, a rational conversation which made the men forget that they were pretty women. . . .

Indeed, if it were only on this account, the national education of women is of the utmost consequence, for what a number of human sacrifices are made to that

[117] **socratic form:** educational method based on questions and answers, derived from the method used by the Greek philosopher Socrates in Plato's *Dialogues.*

moloch[118] prejudice! And in how many ways are children destroyed by the lasciviousness of man? The want of natural affection, in many women, who are drawn from their duty by the admiration of men, and the ignorance of others, render the infancy of man a much more perilous state than that of brutes; yet men are unwilling to place women in situations proper to enable them to acquire sufficient understanding to know how even to nurse their babes.

So forcibly does this truth strike me, that I would rest the whole tendency of my reasoning upon it, for whatever tends to incapacitate the maternal character, takes woman out of her sphere.

But it is vain to expect the present race of weak mothers either to take that reasonable care of a child's body, which is necessary to lay the foundation of a good constitution, supposing that it do not suffer for the sins of its fathers; or, to manage its temper so judiciously that the child will not have, as it grows up, to throw off all that its mother, its first instructor, directly or indirectly taught; and unless the mind have uncommon vigour, womanish follies will stick to the character throughout life. The weakness of the mother will be visited on the children! And whilst women are educated to rely on their husbands for judgment, this must ever be the consequence, for there is no improving an understanding by halves, nor can any being act wisely from imitation, because in every circumstance of life there is a kind of individuality, which requires an exertion of judgment to modify general rules. The being who can think justly in one track, will soon extend its intellectual empire; and she who has sufficient judgment to manage her children, will not submit, right or wrong, to her husband, or patiently to the social laws which make a nonentity of a wife.

In public schools women, to guard against the errors of ignorance, should be taught the elements of anatomy and medicine, not only to enable them to take proper care of their own health, but to make them rational nurses of their infants, parents, and husbands; for the bills of mortality are swelled by the blunders of self-willed old women, who give nostrums[119] of their own without knowing any thing of the human frame. It is likewise proper only in a domestic view, to make women acquainted with the anatomy of the mind, by allowing the sexes to associate together in every pursuit; and by leading them to observe the progress of the human understanding in the improvement of the sciences and arts; never forgetting the science of morality, or the study of the political history of mankind.

A man has been termed a microcosm; and every family might also be called a state. States, it is true, have mostly been governed by arts that disgrace the character of man; and the want of a just constitution, and equal laws, have so perplexed the notions of the worldly wise, that they more than question the reasonableness of contending for the rights of humanity. Thus morality, polluted in the national reservoir, sends off streams of vice to corrupt the constituent parts of the body politic; but should more noble, or rather, more just principles regulate the laws, which ought to be the government of society, and not those who execute them, duty might become the rule of private conduct.

Besides, by the exercise of their bodies and minds women would acquire that mental activity so necessary in the maternal character, united with the fortitude that distinguishes steadiness of conduct from the obstinate perverseness of weakness. For it is dangerous to advise the indolent to be steady, because they instantly become rigorous, and to save themselves trouble, punish with severity faults that the patient fortitude of reason might have prevented.

But fortitude presupposes strength of mind; and is strength of mind to be acquired by indolent acquiescence? by asking advice instead of exerting the judgment? by obeying through fear, instead of practising the forbearance, which we all stand in need of ourselves?—The conclusion which I wish to draw, is obvious; make women rational creatures, and free citizens, and they will quickly become good wives, and mothers; that is—if men do not neglect the duties of husbands and fathers.

Discussing the advantages which a public and private education combined, as I have sketched, might rationally be expected to produce, I have dwelt most on such as are particularly relative to the female world, because I think the female world oppressed; yet the gangrene, which the vices engendered by oppression have produced, is not confined to the morbid part,[120] but pervades society at large: so that when I wish to see my sex become more like moral agents, my heart bounds with the anticipation of

[118] **moloch**: Moloch was a Canaanite idol to whom children were sacrificed.

[119] **bills of mortality**: weekly records of baptisms and burials kept since the Great Plague of 1603. **nostrum**: quack remedy.

[120] **morbid part**: diseased or dying part.

the general diffusion of that sublime contentment which only morality can diffuse.

— *from* CHAPTER XIII —

Some Instances of the Folly Which the Ignorance of Women Generates; with Concluding Reflections on the Moral Improvement That a Revolution in Female Manners Might Naturally Be Expected to Produce

There are many follies, in some degree, peculiar to women: sins against reason of commission as well as of omission; but all flowing from ignorance or prejudice, I shall only point out such as appear to be particularly injurious to their moral character. And in animadverting on them, I wish especially to prove, that the weakness of mind and body, which men have endeavoured, impelled by various motives, to perpetuate, prevents their discharging the peculiar duty of their sex: for when weakness of body will not permit them to suckle their children, and weakness of mind makes them spoil their tempers—is woman in a natural state? . .

— SECTION VI —

It is not necessary to inform the sagacious reader, now I enter on my concluding reflections, that the discussion of this subject merely consists in opening a few simple principles, and clearing away the rubbish which obscured them. But, as all readers are not sagacious, I must be allowed to add some explanatory remarks to bring the subject home to reason—to that sluggish reason, which supinely takes opinions on trust, and obstinately supports them to spare itself the labour of thinking.

Moralists have unanimously agreed, that unless virtue be nursed by liberty, it will never attain due strength—and what they say of man I extend to mankind, insisting that in all cases morals must be fixed on immutable principles; and, that the being cannot be termed rational or virtuous, who obeys any authority, but that of reason.

To render women truly useful members of society, I argue that they should be led, by having their undertakings cultivated on a large scale, to acquire a rational affection for their country, founded on knowledge, because it is obvious that we are little interested about what we do not understand. And to render this general knowledge of due importance, I have endeavoured to shew that private duties are never properly fulfilled unless the understanding enlarges the heart; and that public virtue is only an aggregate of private. But, the distinctions established in society undermine both, by beating out the solid gold of virtue, till it becomes only the tinsel-covering of vice; for whilst wealth renders a man more respectable than virtue, wealth will be sought before virtue; and, whilst women's persons are caressed, when a childish simper shews an absence of mind—the mind will lie fallow. Yet, true voluptuousness must proceed from the mind—for what can equal the sensations produced by mutual affection, supported by mutual respect? What are the cold, or feverish caresses of appetite, but sin embracing death, compared with the modest overflowings of a pure heart and exalted imagination? Yes, let me tell the libertine of fancy when he despises understanding in woman—that the mind, which he disregards, gives life to the enthusiastic affection from which rapture, short-lived as it is, alone can flow! And, that, without virtue, a sexual attachment must expire, like a tallow candle in the socket, creating intolerable disgust. To prove this, I need only observe, that men who have wasted great part of their lives with women, and with whom they have sought for pleasure with eager thirst, entertain the meanest opinion of the sex.—Virtue, true refiner of joy!—if foolish men were to fright thee from earth, in order to give loose to all their appetites without a check—some sensual wight of taste would scale the heavens to invite thee back, to give a zest to pleasure!

That women at present are by ignorance rendered foolish or vicious, is, I think, not to be disputed; and, that the most salutary effects tending to improve mankind might be expected from a REVOLUTION in female manners, appears, at least, with a face of probability, to rise out of the observation. For as marriage has been termed the parent of those endearing charities which draw man from the brutal herd, the corrupting intercourse that wealth, idleness, and folly, produce between the sexes, is more universally injurious to morality than all the other vices of mankind collectively considered. To adulterous lust the most sacred duties are sacrificed, because before marriage, men, by a promiscuous intimacy with women, learned to consider love as a selfish gratification—learned to separate it not only from esteem, but from the affection merely built on habit, which mixes a little humanity with it. Justice and friendship are also set at defiance, and that purity of taste is vitiated which would naturally lead a man to relish an artless display of affection rather than affected airs. But that noble simplicity of affection, which dares to appear unadorned, has few attractions for the libertine, though it be the charm, which by cementing the matrimonial tie, secures to the pledges of a warmer passion the necessary parental attention; for children will never be properly educated till friendship subsists between parents. Virtue flies from a house divided against itself—and a whole legion of devils take up their residence there.

The affection of husbands and wives cannot be pure when they have so few sentiments in common, and when so little confidence is established at home, as must be the case when their pursuits are so different. That intimacy from which tenderness should flow, will not, cannot subsist between the vicious.

Contending, therefore, that the sexual distinction which men have so warmly insisted upon, is arbitrary, I have dwelt on an observation, that several sensible men, with whom I have conversed on the subject, allowed to be well founded; and it is simply this, that the little chastity to be found amongst men, and consequent disregard of modesty, tend to degrade both sexes; and further, that the modesty of women, characterized as such, will often be only the artful veil of wantonness instead of being the natural reflection of purity, till modesty be universally respected.

From the tyranny of man, I firmly believe, the greater number of female follies proceed; and the cunning, which I allow makes at present a part of their character, I likewise have repeatedly endeavoured to prove, is produced by oppression.

Were not dissenters,[121] for instance, a class of people, with strict truth, characterized as cunning? And may I not lay some stress on this fact to prove, that when any power but reason curbs the free spirit of man, dissimulation is practised, and the various shifts of art are naturally called forth? Great attention to decorum, which was carried to a degree of scrupulosity, and all that puerile bustle about trifles and consequential solemnity, which Butler's caricature of a dissenter,[122] brings before the imagination, shaped their persons as well as their minds in the mould of prim littleness. I speak collectively, for I know how many ornaments to human nature have been enrolled amongst sectaries;[123] yet, I assert, that the same narrow prejudice for their sect, which women have for their families, prevailed in the dissenting part of the community, however worthy in other respects; and also that the same timid prudence, or headstrong efforts, often disgraced the exertions of both. Oppression thus formed many of the features of their character perfectly to coincide with that of the oppressed half of mankind; for is it not notorious that dissenters were, like women, fond of deliberating together, and asking advice of each other, till by a complication of little contrivances, some little end was brought about? A similar attention to preserve their reputation was conspicuous in the dissenting and female world, and was produced by a similar cause.

Asserting the rights which women in common with men ought to contend for, I have not attempted to extenuate their faults; but to prove them to be the natural consequence of their education and station in society. If so, it is reasonable to suppose that they will change their character, and correct their vices and follies, when they are allowed to be free in a physical, moral, and civil sense.[124]

Let woman share the rights and she will emulate the virtues of man, for she must grow more perfect when emancipated, or justify the authority that chains such a weak being to her duty.—If the latter, it will be expedient to open a fresh trade with Russia for whips,[125] a present which a father should always make to his son-in-law on his wedding day, that a husband may keep his whole family in order by the same means; and without any violation of justice reign, wielding this sceptre, sole master of his house, because he is the only being in it who has reason:—the divine, indefeasible earthly sovereignty breathed into man by the Master of the universe. Allowing this position, women have not any inherent rights to claim; and, by the same rule, their duties vanish, for rights and duties are inseparable.

Be just then, O ye men of understanding! and mark not more severely what women do amiss, than the vicious tricks of the horse or the ass for whom ye provide provender—and allow her the privileges of ignorance, to whom ye deny the rights of reason, or ye will be worse than

[121] **dissenters:** those who disagreed with or dissented from the teachings of the established Church of England.

[122] Samuel Butler portrayed a hypocritical Dissenter both in his "Hypocritical Nonconformist," in *Genuine Remains in Verse and Prose* (1759), II, p. 35, and as the protagonist of his satirical poetical romance *Hudibras* (1662–1663).

[123] **sectaries:** members of a particular religious sect or school of thought.

[124] I had further enlarged on the advantages which might reasonably be expected to result from an improvement in female manners, towards the general reformation of society; but it appeared to me that such reflections would more properly close the last volume [M. W.]. No further volumes of *Vindication of the Rights of Woman* were published.

[125] In the eighteenth century, Russians were notorious for wife-beating and for flogging convicts and peasants.

Egyptian task-masters, expecting virtue where nature has not given understanding!

Letter to Joseph Johnson[1]

Paris, December 26, 1792

I should immediately on the receipt of your letter, my dear friend, have thanked you for your punctuality, for it highly gratified me, had I not wished to wait till I could tell you that this day was not stained with blood. Indeed the prudent precautions taken by the National Convention to prevent a tumult, made me suppose that the dogs of faction would not dare to bark, much less to bite, however true to their scent; and I was not mistaken; for the citizens, who were all called out, are returning home with composed countenances, shouldering their arms. About nine o'clock this morning, the king[2] passed by my window, moving silently along (excepting now and then a few strokes on the drum, which rendered the stillness more awful) through empty streets, surrounded by the national guards, who, clustering round the carriage, seemed to deserve their name. The inhabitants flocked to their windows, but the casements were all shut, not a voice was heard, nor did I see any thing like an insulting gesture.—For the first time since I entered France, I bowed to the majesty of the people, and respected the propriety of behaviour so perfectly in unison with my own feelings. I can scarcely tell you why, but an association of ideas made the tears flow insensibly from my eyes, when I saw Louis sitting, with more dignity than I expected from his character, in a hackney coach going to meet death, where so many of his race have triumphed. My fancy instantly brought Louis XIV before me, entering the capital with all his pomp, after one of the victories most flattering to his pride, only to see the sunshine of prosperity overshadowed by the sublime gloom of misery. I have been alone ever since; and, though my mind is calm, I cannot dismiss the lively images that have filled my imagination all the day.—Nay, do not smile, but pity me; for, once or twice, lifting my eyes from the paper, I have seen eyes glare through a glass-door opposite my chair, and bloody hands shook at me. Not the distant sound of a footstep can I hear. My apartments are remote from those of the servants, the only persons who sleep with me in an immense hotel, one folding door opening after another.—I wish I had even kept the cat with me!—I want to see something alive; death in so many frightful shapes has taken hold of my fancy.—I am going to bed—and, for the first time in my life, I cannot put out the candle.

M. W.

[1] Joseph Johnson (1738–1809), editor of the *Analytical Review*, publisher and bookseller, counted among his authors most of the leading progressive thinkers of his day, including William Godwin, Joseph Priestley, Horne Tooke, Erasmus Darwin, and Maria Edgeworth. He hired Wollstonecraft as a writer for the *Analytical Review* in 1788 and sent her to Paris on 6 December 1792, to report on the French Revolution firsthand.

[2] Louis XVI's trial for treason began on 26 December 1792.

Letter to Joseph Johnson

Introductory to a Series of Letters on the Present Character of the French Nation

Paris, 15 February, 1793

My dear friend,

It is necessary perhaps for an observer of mankind, to guard as carefully the remembrance of the first impression made by a nation, as by a countenance; because we imperceptibly lose sight of the national character, when we become more intimate with individuals. It is not then useless or presumptuous to note, that, when I first entered Paris, the striking contrast of riches and poverty, elegance and slovenliness, urbanity and deceit, every where caught my eye, and saddened my soul; and these impressions are still the foundation of my remarks on the manners, which flatter the senses, more than they interest the heart, and yet excite more interest than esteem.

The whole mode of life here tends indeed to render the people frivolous, and, to borrow their favourite epithet, amiable. Ever on the wing, they are always sipping the sparkling joy on the brim of the cup, leaving satiety in the bottom for those who venture to drink deep. On all sides they trip along, buoyed up by animal spirits, and seemingly so void of care, that often, when I am walking on the *Boulevards*, it occurs to me, that they alone understand the full import of the term leisure; and they trifle their time away with such an air of contentment, I know not how to wish them wiser at the expence of their gaiety. They play before me like motes in a sunbeam,[1] enjoying

[1] Cf. Chaucer, *Canterbury Tales*, The Wyf of Bath's Tale, l. 12.

the passing ray; whilst an English head, searching for more solid happiness, loses, in the analysis of pleasure, the volatile sweets of the moment. Their chief enjoyment, it is true, rises from vanity: but it is not the vanity that engenders vexation of spirit; on the contrary, it lightens the heavy burthen of life, which reason too often weighs, merely to shift from one shoulder to the other.

Investigating the modification of the passion, as I would analyze the elements that give a form to dead matter, I shall attempt to trace to their source the causes which have combined to render this nation the most polished, in a physical sense, and probably the most superficial in the world; and I mean to follow the windings of the various streams that disembogue[2] into a terrific gulf, in which all the dignity of our nature is absorbed. For every thing has conspired to make the French the most sensual people in the world; and what can render the heart so hard, or so effectually stifle every moral emotion, as the refinements of sensuality?

The frequent repetition of the word French, appears invidious; let me then make a previous observation, which I beg you not to lose sight of, when I speak rather harshly of a land flowing with milk and honey. Remember that it is not the morals of a particular people that I would decry; for are we not all of the same stock? But I wish calmly to consider the stage of civilization in which I find the French, and, giving a sketch of their character, and unfolding the circumstances which have produced its identity, I shall endeavour to throw some light on the history of man, and on the present important subjects of discussion.

I would I could first inform you that, out of the chaos of vices and follies, prejudices and virtues, rudely jumbled together, I saw the fair form of Liberty slowly rising, and Virtue expanding her wings to shelter all her children! I should then hear the account of the barbarities that have rent the bosom of France patiently, and bless the firm hand that lopt off the rotten limbs. But, if the aristocracy of birth is levelled with the ground, only to make room for that of riches, I am afraid that the morals of the people will not be much improved by the change, or the government rendered less venal. Still it is not just to dwell on the misery produced by the present struggle, without adverting to the standing evils of the old system. I am grieved—sorely grieved—when I think of the blood that has stained the cause of freedom at Paris; but I also hear the same live stream cry aloud from the highways, through which the retreating armies passed with famine and death in their rear, and I hide my face with awe before the inscrutable ways of providence, sweeping in such various directions the besom[3] of destruction over the sons of men.

Before I came to France, I cherished, you know, an opinion, that strong virtues might exist with the polished manners produced by the progress of civilization; and I even anticipated the epoch, when, in the course of improvement, men would labour to become virtuous, without being goaded on by misery. But now, the perspective of the golden age, fading before the attentive eye of observation, almost eludes my sight; and, losing thus in part my theory of a more perfect state, start not, my friend, if I bring forward an opinion, which at the first glance seems to be levelled against the existence of God! I am not become an Atheist, I assure you, by residing at Paris: yet I begin to fear that vice, or, if you will, evil, is the grand mobile of action, and that, when the passions are justly poized, we become harmless, and in the same proportion useless.

The wants of reason are very few, and, were we to consider dispassionately the real value of most things, we should probably rest satisfied with the simple gratification of our physical necessities, and be content with negative goodness: for it is frequently, only that wanton, the Imagination, with her artful coquetry, who lures us forward, and makes us run over a rough road, pushing aside every obstacle merely to catch a disappointment.

The desire also of being useful to others, is continually damped by experience; and, if the exertions of humanity were not in some measure their own reward, who would endure misery, or struggle with care, to make some people ungrateful, and others idle?

You will call these melancholy effusions, and guess that, fatigued by the vivacity, which has all the bustling folly of childhood, without the innocence which renders ignorance charming, I am too severe in my strictures. It may be so; and I am aware that the good effects of the revolution will be last felt at Paris; where surely the soul of Epicurus[4] has long been at work to root out the simple

[2] **disembogue:** to come out of the mouth of a river into the open sea.

[3] **besom:** brush, broom.

[4] **Epicurus (341–270 BC):** Greek philosopher who argued that pleasure (which he, if not his followers, defined as serenity) is the highest and only good.

emotions of the heart, which, being natural, are always moral. Rendered cold and artificial by the selfish enjoyments of the senses, which the government fostered, is it surprising that simplicity of manners, and singleness of heart, rarely appear, to recreate me with the wild odour of nature, so passing sweet?

Seeing how deep the fibres of mischief have shot, I sometimes ask, with a doubting accent, Whether a nation can go back to the purity of manners which has hitherto been maintained unsullied only by the keen air of poverty, when, emasculated by pleasure, the luxuries of prosperity are become the wants of nature? I cannot yet give up the hope, that a fairer day is dawning on Europe, though I must hesitatingly observe, that little is to be expected from the narrow principle of commerce which seems every where to be shoving aside *the point of honour* of the *noblesse.*[5] I can look beyond the evils of the moment, and do not expect muddied water to become clear before it has had time to stand; yet, even for the moment, it is the most terrific of all sights, to see men vicious without warmth—to see the order that should be the superscription of virtue, cultivated to give security to crimes which only thoughtlessness could palliate. Disorder is, in fact, the very essence of vice, though with the wild wishes of a corrupt fancy humane emotions often kindly mix to soften their atrocity. Thus humanity, generosity, and even self-denial, sometimes render a character grand, and even useful, when hurried away by lawless passions; but what can equal the turpitude of a cold calculator who lives for himself alone, and considering his fellow-creatures merely as machines of pleasure, never forgets that honesty is the best policy? Keeping ever within the pale of the law, he crushes his thousands with impunity; but it is with that degree of management, which makes him, to borrow a significant vulgarism, a villain *in grain.* The very excess of his depravation preserves him, whilst the more respectable beast of prey, who prowls about like the lion, and roars to announce his approach, falls into a snare.

You may think it too soon to form an opinion of the future government, yet it is impossible to avoid hazarding some conjectures, when every thing whispers me, that names, not principles, are changed, and when I see that the turn of the tide has left the dregs of the old system to corrupt the new. For the same pride of office, the same desire of power are still visible; with this aggravation, that, fearing to return to obscurity after having but just acquired a relish for distinction, each hero, or philosopher, for all are dubbed with these new titles, endeavours to make hay while the sun shines; and every petty municipal officer, become the idol, or rather the tyrant of the day, stalks like a cock on a dunghil.[6]

I shall now conclude this desultory letter; which however will enable you to foresee that I shall treat more of morals than manners.

Yours—

[5] **noblesse:** nobility.

[6] Cf. Sixteenth-century proverb: "Every cock is proud on his own dunghill."

from AN HISTORICAL AND MORAL VIEW OF THE ORIGIN AND PROGRESS OF THE FRENCH REVOLUTION; AND THE EFFECT IT HAS PRODUCED IN EUROPE
(1794)

— PREFACE —

The revolution in France exhibits a scene, in the political world, not less novel and interesting than the contrast is striking between the narrow opinions of superstition, and the enlightened sentiments of masculine and improved philosophy.

To mark the prominent features of this revolution, requires a mind, not only unsophisticated by old prejudices, and the inveterate habits of degeneracy; but an amelioration of temper, produced by the exercise of the most enlarged principles of humanity.

The rapid changes, the violent, the base, and nefarious assassinations, which have clouded the vivid prospect that began to spread a ray of joy and gladness over the gloomy horizon of oppression, cannot fail to chill the sympathizing bosom, and palsy[1] intellectual vigour. To sketch these vicissitudes is a task so arduous and melancholy, that, with a heart trembling to the touches of nature, it becomes necessary to guard against the erroneous inferences of sensibility; and reason beaming on the grand

[1] **palsy:** paralyze.

theatre of political changes, can prove the only sure guide to direct us to a favourable or just conclusion.

This important conclusion, involving the happiness and exaltation of the human character, demands serious and mature consideration; as it must ultimately sink the dignity of society into contempt, and its members into greater wretchedness; or elevate it to a degree of grandeur not hitherto anticipated, but by the most enlightened statesmen and philosophers.

Contemplating then these stupendous events with the cool eye of observation, the judgement, difficult to be preserved unwrapped under the pressure of the calamitous horrours produced by desperate and enraged factions, will continually perceive that it is the uncontaminated mass of the french nation, whose minds begin to grasp the sentiments of freedom, that has secured the equilibrium of the state; often tottering on the brink of annihilation; in spite of the folly, selfishness, madness, treachery, and more fatal mock patriotism, the common result of depraved manners, the concomitant of that servility and voluptuousness which for so long a space of time has embruted[2] the higher orders of this celebrated nation.

By thus attending to circumstances, we shall be able to discern clearly that the revolution was neither produced by the abilities or intrigues of a few individuals; nor was the effect of sudden and short-lived enthusiasm; but the natural consequence of intellectual improvement, gradually proceeding to perfection in the advancement of communities, from a state of barbarism to that of polished society, till now arrived at the point when sincerity of principles seems to be hastening the overthrow of the tremendous empire of superstition and hypocrisy, erected upon the ruins of gothic[3] brutality and ignorance.

— *from* BOOK V, CHAPTER IV —

People thinking for themselves have more energy in their voice, than any government, which it is possible for human wisdom to invent; and every government not aware of this sacred truth will, at some period, be suddenly overturned. Whilst men in a savage state preserve their independence, they adopt no regular system of policy, nor ever attempt to digest their rude code of laws into a constitution, to ensure political liberty. Consequently we find in every country, after its civilization has arrived at a certain height, that the people, the moment they are displeased with their rules, begin to clamour against them; and, finally rejecting all authority but their own will, in breaking the shackles of folly or tyranny, they glut their resentment by the mischievous destruction of the works of ages, only considering them as the moments of their servitude.

From the social disposition of man, in proportion as he becomes civilized, he will mingle more and more with society. The first interest he takes in the business of his fellow-men is in that of his neighbour; next he contemplates the comfort, misery, and happiness of the nation to which he belongs, investigates the degree of wisdom and justice in the political system, under which he lives, and, striding into the regions of science, his researches embrace all human kind. Thus he is enabled to estimate the portion of evil or good which the government of his country produces, compared with that of others; and the comparison, granting him superior powers of mind, leads him to conceive a model of a more perfect form.

This spirit of inquiry first manifests itself in hamlets; when his views of improvement are confined to local advantages: but the approximation of different districts leading to further intercourse, roads of communication are opened, until a central or favourite spot becomes the vortex of men and things. Then the rising spires, pompous domes, and majestic monuments, point out the capital; the focus of information, the reservoir of genius, the school of arts, the seat of voluptuous gratification, and the hot-bed of vice and immorality.

The centrifugal rays of knowledge and science now stealing through the empire, the whole intellectual faculties of man partake of their influence, and one general sentiment governs the civil and political body. In the progress of these improvements the state undergoing a variety of changes, the happiness or misery produced occasions a diversity of opinions; and to prevent confusion, absolute governments have been tolerated by the most enlightened part of the people. But, probably, this toleration was merely the effect of the strong social feelings of men; who preferred tranquillity, and the prosperity of their country, to a resistance, which, judging from the ignorance of their fellow citizens, they believed would bring more harm than good in its train. In short, however long a combination of tyranny has retarded the progress, it has been one of the advantages of the large cities of Europe, to light up the sparks of reason, and to extend the principles of truth.

Such is the good and evil flowing from the capitals of states, that during the infancy of governments, though they tend to corrupt and enervate the mind, they accelerate

[2] **embruted**: degraded; made bestial.

[3] **gothic**: barbarous, rude, uncouth; medieval; like the Teutonic Goths.

the introduction of science, and give the tone to the national sentiments and taste.

But this influence is extremely gradual; and it requires a great length of time, for the remote corners of the empire to experience either the one, or the other of these effects. . . .

However, it appears very certain, that should a republican government be consolidated, Paris must rapidly crumble into decay. Its rise and splendour were owing chiefly, if not entirely, to the old system of government; and since the foundation of its luxury has been shaken, and it is not likely that the disparting structure will ever again rest securely on its basis, we may fairly infer, that, in proportion as the charms of solitary reflection and agricultural recreations are felt, the people, by leaving the villages and cities, will give a new complexion to the face of the country—and we may then look for a turn of mind more solid, principles more fixed, and a conduct more consistent and virtuous.

The occupations and habits of life have a wonderful influence on the forming mind; so great, that the superinductions of art stop the growth of the spontaneous shoots of nature, till it is difficult to distinguish natural from factitious[4] morals and feelings; and as the energy of thinking will always proceed, in a great measure, either from our education or manner of living, the frivolity of the french character may be accounted for, without taking refuge in the old hiding place of ignorance—occult causes.

When it is the object of education to prepare the pupil to please every body, and of course to deceive, accomplishments are the one thing needful; and the desire to be admired ever being uppermost, the passions are subjugated, or all drawn into the whirlpool of egotism.[5] This gives to each person, however different the temper, a tincture of vanity, and that weak vacillation of opinion, which is incompatible with what we term character.

Thus a frenchman, like most women, may be said to have no character distinguishable from that of the nation; unless little shades, and casual lights, be allowed to constitute an essential characteristic. What then could have been expected, when their ambition was mostly confined to dancing gracefully, entering a room with easy assurance, and smiling on and complimenting the very persons whom they meant to ridicule at the next fashionable assembly? The learning to fence with skill, it is true, was useful to a people, whose false notions of honour required that at least a drop of blood should atone for the shadow of an affront. The knack also of uttering sprightly repartees[6] became a necessary art, to supply the place of that real interest only to be nourished in the affectionate intercourse of domestic intimacy, where confidence enlarges the heart it opens. Besides, the desire of eating dish[7] at table, no matter if there were fifty, and the custom of separating immediately after the repast, destroy the social affections, reminding a stranger of the vulgar saying—'every man for himself, and God for us all.'[8] After these cursory observations, it is not going too far to advance, that the french were in some respects the most unqualified of any people in Europe to undertake the important work in which they are embarked.

Whilst pleasure was the sole object of living among the higher orders of society, it was the business of the lower to give life to their joys, and convenience to their luxury. This cast-like division,[9] by destroying all strength of character in the former, and debasing the latter to machines, taught frenchmen to be more ingenious in their contrivances for pleasure and show, than the men of any other country; whilst, with respect to the abridgment of labour in the mechanic arts, or to promote the comfort of common life, they were far behind. They had never, in fact, acquired an idea of that independent, comfortable situation, in which contentment is sought rather than happiness; because the slaves of pleasure or power can be roused only by lively emotions and extravagant hopes. Indeed they have no word in their vocabulary to express *comfort*[10]—that state of existence, in which reason renders serene and useful the days, which passion would only cheat with flying dreams of happiness.

A change of character cannot be so sudden as some sanguine calculators expect: yet by the destruction of the

[4] **superinduction:** something brought in "on the top of" something else; addition. **factitious:** artificial; insincere.

[5] **egotism:** I use this word according to the french acceptation, because we have not one to express so forcibly the same signification [M. W.]. Wollstonecraft is confused: the English word *egotism*, meaning talking too much about oneself, had been imported into French; the French word "egoism" means excessive self-love.

[6] **repartees:** witty replies.

[7] **eating dish:** consuming a great variety of foods or dishes.

[8] Proverb first recorded in J. Heywood, *A Dialogue containing the number in effect of all the Proverbs in the English Tongue* (1546).

[9] **cast-like:** like the castes or rigid class system of India.

[10] The French word *confort* meant "assistance" in the eighteenth century; the French adopted the English meaning in the nineteenth century.

rights of primogeniture, a greater degree of equality of property is sure to follow; and as Paris cannot maintain its splendour, but by the trade of luxury, which can never be carried to the same height it was formerly, the opulent having strong motives to induce them to live more in the country, they must acquire new inclinations and opinions.—As a change also of the system of education and domestic manners will be a natural consequence of the revolution, the french will insensibly rise to a dignity of character far above that of the present race; and then the fruit of their liberty, ripening gradually, will have a relish not to be expected during its crude and forced state.

The late arrangement of things seems to have been the common effect of an absolute government, a domineering priesthood, and a great inequality of fortune; and whilst it completely destroyed the most important end of society, the comfort and independence of the people, it generated the most shameful depravity and weakness of intellect; so that we have seen the french engaged in a business the most sacred to mankind, giving, by their enthusiasm, splendid examples of their fortitude at one moment, and at another, by their want of firmness and deficiency of judgment, affording the most glaring and fatal proofs of the just estimate, which all nations have formed of their character.

Men so thoroughly sophisticated,[11] it was to be supposed, would never conduct any business with steadiness and moderation: but it required a knowledge of the nation and their manners, to form a distinct idea of their disgusting conceit and wretched egotism; so far surpassing all the calculations of reason, that, perhaps, should not a faithful picture be now sketched, posterity would be at loss to account for their folly; and attribute to madness, what arose from imbecility.

The natural feelings of man seldom become so contaminated and debased as not sometimes to let escape a gleam of the generous fire, an ethereal spark of the soul; and it is these glowing emotions, in the inmost recesses of the heart, which have continued to feed feelings, that on sudden occasions manifest themselves with all their pristine purity and vigour. But, by the habitual slothfulness of rusty intellects, or the depravity of the heart, lulled into hardness on the lascivious couch of pleasure, those heavenly beams are obscured, and man appears either an hideous monster, a devouring beast; or a spiritless reptile, without dignity or humanity.

Those miserable wretches who crawl under the feet of others are seldom to be found among savages, where men accustomed to exercise and temperance are, in general, brave, hospitable, and magnanimous; and it is only as they surrender their rights, that they lose those noble qualities of the heart. The ferocity of the savage is of a distinct nature from that of the degenerate slaves of tyrants. One murders from mistaken notions of courage; yet he respects his enemy in proportion to his fortitude, and contempt of death: the other assassinates without remorse, whilst his trembling nerves betray the weakness of his affrighted soul at every appearance of danger. Among the former, men are respected according to their abilities; consequently idle drones are driven out of this society; but among the latter, men are raised to honours and employments in proportion as a talent for intrigue, the sure proof of littleness of mind, has rendered them servile. The most melancholy reflections are produced by a retrospective glance over the rise and progress of the governments of different countries, when we are compelled to remark, that flagrant follies and atrocious crimes have been more common under the governments of modern Europe, than in any of the ancient nations, if we except the jews. Sanguinary tortures, insidious poisonings, and dark assassinations, have alternately exhibited a race of monsters in human shape, the contemplation of whose ferocity chills the blood, and darkens every enlivening expectation of humanity: but we ought to observe, to reanimate the hopes of benevolence, that the perpetration of these horrid deeds has arisen from a despotism in the government, which reason is teaching us to remedy. Sometimes, it is true, restrained by an iron police, the people appear peaceable, when they are only stunned; so that we find, whenever the mob has broken loose, the fury of the populace has been shocking and calamitous. These considerations account for the contradictions in the french character, which must strike a stranger: for robberies are very rare in France, where daily frauds and sly pilfering prove, that the lower class have as little honesty as sincerity. Besides, murder and cruelty almost always show the dastardly ferocity of fear in France; whilst in England, where the spirit of liberty has prevailed, it is useful for an highwayman, demanding your money, not only to avoid barbarity, but to behave with humanity, and even complaisance.[12]

[11] **sophisticated:** corrupted, intermixed with baser qualities.

[12] **complaisance:** obligingness, deference, politeness.

Degeneracy of morals, with polished manners, produces the worst of passions, which floating through the social body, the genial current of natural feelings has been poisoned; and, committing crimes with trembling inquietude, the culprits have not only drawn on themselves the vengeance of the law, but thrown an odium on their nature, that has blackened the face of humanity. And whilst its temple has been sacrilegiously profaned by the drops of blood, which have issued from the very hearts of the sad victims of their folly; a hardness of temper, under the veil of sentiment, calling it vice, has prevented our sympathy from leading us to examine into the sources of the atrocity of our species, and obscured the true cause of disgraceful and vicious habits.

Since the existence of courts, whose aggrandisement has been conspicuous in the same degree as the miseries of the debased people have accumulated, the convenience and comfort of men have been sacrificed to the ostentatious display of pomp and ridiculous pageantry. For every order of men, from the beggar to the king, has tended to introduce that extravagance into society, which equally blasts domestic virtue and happiness. The prevailing custom of living beyond their income has had the most baneful effect on the independence of individuals of every class in England, as well as in France; so that whilst they have lived in habits of idleness, they have been drawn into excesses, which, proving ruinous, produced consequences equally pernicious to the community, and degrading to the private character. Extravagance forces the peer[13] to prostitute his talents and influence for a place, to repair his broken fortune; and the country gentleman becomes venal in the senate, to enable himself to live on a par with him, or reimburse himself for the expences of electioneering, into which he was led by sheer vanity. The professions,[14] on the same account, become equally unprincipled. The one, whose characteristic ought to be integrity, descends to chicanery; whilst another trifles with the health, of which it knows all the importance. The merchant likewise enters into speculations so closely bordering on fraudulency, that common straight forward minds can scarcely distinguish the devious art of selling any thing for a price far beyond that necessary to ensure a just profit, from sheer dishonesty, aggravated by hard-heartedness, when it is to take advantage of the necessities of the indigent.

The destructive influence of commerce, it is true, carried on by men who are eager by overgrown riches to partake of the respect paid to nobility, is felt in a variety of ways. The most pernicious, perhaps, is its producing an aristocracy of wealth, which degrades mankind, by making them only exchange savageness for tame servility, instead of acquiring the urbanity of improved reason. Commerce also, overstocking a country with people, obliges the majority to become manufacturers rather than husbandmen; and then the division of labour, solely to enrich the proprietor, renders the mind entirely inactive. The time which, a celebrated writer says, is sauntered away, in going from one part of an employment to another, is the very time that preserves the man from degenerating into a brute,[15] for every one must have observed how much more intelligent are the blacksmiths, carpenters, and masons in the country, than the journeymen in great towns; and, respecting morals, there is no making a comparison. The very gait of the man, who is his own master, is so much more steady than the slouching step of the servant of a servant, that it is unnecessary to ask which proves by his actions he has the most independence of character.

The acquiring of a fortune is likewise the least arduous road to preeminence, and the most sure; thus are whole knots of men turned into machines, to enable a keen speculator to become wealthy; and every noble principle of nature is eradicated by making a man pass his life in stretching wire, pointing a pin, heading a nail, or spreading a sheet of paper on a plain surface. Besides, it is allowed, that all associations of men render them sensual, and consequently selfish; and whilst lazy friars are driven out of their cells as stagnate bodies that corrupt society, it may admit of a doubt whether large work-shops do not contain men equally tending to impede that gradual progress of improvement, which leads to the perfection of reason, and the establishment of rational equality.

The deprivation of natural, equal, civil and political rights, reduced the most cunning of the lower orders to practice fraud, and the rest to habits of stealing, audacious robberies, and murders. And why? because the rich and poor were separated into bands of tyrants and slaves, and the retaliation of slaves is always terrible. In short, every

[13] **peer:** a member of one of the degrees of nobility in the United Kingdom; a duke, marquis, earl, viscount, or baron.

[14] **professions:** Wollstonecraft cites first the lawyers, then the doctors.

[15] See Adam Smith, *An Inquiry into the Nature and Causes of the Wealth of Nations* (1776), I.i.

sacred feeling, moral and divine, has been obliterated, and the dignity of man sullied, by a system of policy and jurisprudence as repugnant to reason, as at variance with humanity.

The only excuse that can be made for the ferocity of the parisians is then simply to observe, that they had not any confidence in the laws, which they had always found to be merely cobwebs to catch small flies. Accustomed to be punished themselves for every trifle, and often for only being in the way of the rich, or their parasites; when, in fact, had the parisians seen the execution of a noble, or priest, though convicted of crimes beyond the daring of vulgar minds?—When justice, or the law, is so partial, the day of retribution will come with the red sky of vengeance, to confound the innocent with the guilty. The mob were barbarous beyond the tiger's cruelty: for how could they trust a court that had so often deceived them, or expect to see its agents punished, when the same measures were pursuing?

Let us cast our eyes over the history of man, and we shall scarcely find a page that is not tarnished by some foul deed, or bloody transaction. Let us examine the catalogue of the vices of men in a savage state, and contrast them with those of men civilized; we shall find, that a barbarian, considered as a moral being, is an angel, compared with the refined villain of artificial life. Let us investigate the causes which have produced this degeneracy, and we shall discover, that they are those unjust plans of government, which have been formed by peculiar circumstances in every part of the globe.—Then let us coolly and impartially contemplate the improvements, which are gaining ground in the formation of principles of policy; and I flatter myself it will be allowed by every humane and considerate being, that a political system more simple than has hitherto existed would effectually check those aspiring follies, which by imitation, leading to vice, have banished from governments the very shadow of justice and magnanimity.

Thus had France grown up, and sickened on the corruption of a state diseased. But, as in medicine there is a species of complaint in the bowels which works its own cure, and, leaving the body healthy, gives an invigorated tone to the system, so there is in politics: and whilst the agitation of its regeneration continues, the excrementitious humours exuding from the contaminated body will excite a general dislike and contempt for the nation; and it is only the philosophical eye, which looks into the nature and weighs the consequences of human actions, that will be able to discern the cause, which has produced so many dreadful effects.

from LETTERS WRITTEN DURING A SHORT RESIDENCE IN SWEDEN, NORWAY, AND DENMARK

(1796; comp. 1795)

— ADVERTISEMENT —

The writing travels, or memoirs, has ever been a pleasant employment; for vanity or sensibility always renders it interesting. In writing these desultory letters, I found I could not avoid being continually the first person—'the little hero of each tale.' I tried to correct this fault, if it be one, for they were designed for publication; but in proportion as I arranged my thoughts, my letter, I found, became stiff and affected: I, therefore, determined to let my remarks and reflections flow unrestrained, as I perceived that I could not give a just description of what I saw, but by relating the effect different objects had produced on my mind and feelings, whilst the impression was still fresh.

A person has a right, I have sometimes thought, when amused by a witty or interesting egotist, to talk of himself when he can win on our attention by acquiring our affection. Whether I deserve to rank amongst this privileged number, my readers alone can judge—and I give them leave to shut the book, if they do not wish to become better acquainted with me.

My plan was simply to endeavour to give a just view of the present state of the countries I have passed through, as far as I could obtain information during so short a residence; avoiding those details which, without being very useful to travellers who follow the same route,

---

[1] These letters were written by Wollstonecraft to her lover Gilbert Imlay in 1795 and edited and published by Joseph Johnson in 1796. William Godwin, in his *Memoirs of the Author of a Vindication of the Rights of Woman* (1798), ch. 8, averred: "If ever there was a book calculated to make a man in love with its author, this appears to me to be the book."

Imlay had sent Wollstonecraft (and Fanny) to Sweden, Norway, and Denmark as his business agent to seek compensation for the loss of a treasure ship, the *Maria and Margaretha*, which he owned. The investigation into the disappearance of this ship was a delicate legal matter, since the ship had defied the British blockade on trade between neutral Scandinavia and revolutionary France.

appear very insipid to those who only accompany you in their chair.

Sweden

—*from* LETTER I—

. . . They were overflowing with civility; but to prevent their almost killing my babe with kindness, I was obliged to shorten my visit; and two or three of the girls accompanied us, bringing with them a part of whatever the house afforded to contribute towards rendering my supper more plentiful; and plentiful in fact it was, though I with difficulty did honour to some of the dishes, not relishing the quantity of sugar and spices put into every thing. At supper my host told me bluntly that I was a woman of observation, for I asked him *men's questions.*

The arrangements for my journey were quickly made; I could only have a car with post-horses, as I did not chuse to wait till a carriage could be sent for to Gothenburg. The expense of my journey, about one or two and twenty english miles, I found would not amount to more than eleven or twelve shillings, paying, he assured me, generously. I gave him a guinea and a half. But it was with the greatest difficulty that I could make him take so much, indeed any thing for my lodging and fare. He declared that it was next to robbing me, explaining how much I ought to pay on the road. However, as I was positive, he took the guinea for himself; but as a condition, insisted on accompanying me, to prevent my meeting with any trouble or imposition on the way.

I then retired to my apartment with regret. The night was so fine, that I would gladly have rambled about much longer; yet recollecting that I must rise very early, I reluctantly went to bed: but my senses had been so awake, and my imagination still continued so busy, that I fought for rest in vain. Rising before six, I scented the sweet morning air; I had long before heard the birds twittering to hail the dawning day, though it could scarcely have been allowed to have departed.

Nothing, in fact, can equal the beauty of the northern summer's evening and night; if night it may be called that only wants the glare of day, the full light, which frequently seems so impertinent; for I could write at midnight very well without a candle. I contemplated all nature at rest; the rocks, even grown darker in their appearance, looked as if they partook of the general repose, and reclined more heavily on their foundation.—What, I exclaimed, is this active principle which keeps me still awake?—Why fly my thoughts abroad when every thing around me appears at home? My child was sleeping with equal calmness—innocent and sweet as the closing flowers.—Some recollections, attached to the idea of home, mingled with reflections respecting the state of society I had been contemplating that evening, made a tear drop on the rosy cheek I had just kissed; and emotions that trembled on the brink of extacy and agony gave a poignancy to my sensations, which made me feel more alive than usual.

What are these imperious sympathies? How frequently has melancholy and even mysanthropy taken possession of me, when the world has disgusted me, and friends have proved unkind. I have then considered myself as a particle broken off from the grand mass of mankind;—I was alone, till some involuntary sympathetic emotion, like the attraction of adhesion, made me feel that I was still a part of a mighty whole, from which I could not sever myself—not, perhaps, for the reflection has been carried very far, by snapping the thread of an existence which loses its charms in proportion as the cruel experience of life stops or poisons the current of the heart. Futurity, what hast thou not to give to those who know that there is such a thing as happiness! I speak not of philosophical contentment, though pain has afforded them the strongest conviction of it. . . .

—*from* LETTER II—

. . . The swedes pique themselves on their politeness; but far from being the polish of a cultivated mind, it consists merely of tiresome forms and ceremonies. So far indeed from entering immediately into your character, and making you feel instantly at your ease, like the well-bred french, their over-acted civility is a continual restraint on all your actions. The sort of superiority which a fortune gives when there is no superiority of education, excepting what consists in the observance of senseless forms, has a contrary effect than what is intended; so that I could not help reckoning the peasantry the politest people of Sweden, who only aiming at pleasing you, never think of being admired for their behaviour.

Their tables, like their compliments, seem equally a caricature of the french. The dishes are composed, as well as theirs, of a variety of mixtures to destroy the native taste of the food without being as relishing. Spices and sugar are put into every thing, even into the bread; and the only way I can account for their partiality to high-seasoned dishes, is the constant use of salted provisions. Necessity obliges them to lay up a store of dried fish, and salted meat, for the winter; and in summer, fresh meat and fish taste insipid after them. To which may be added the constant use of spirits. Every day, before dinner and supper, even whilst the dishes are cooling on the table, men and women repair to a side-table, and to obtain an appetite, eat bread and butter, cheese, raw salmon, or anchovies, drinking a glass of brandy. Salt fish or meat then immediately follows, to give a further whet to the stomach. As the dinner advances, pardon me for taking up a few minutes to describe what, alas! has detained me two or three hours on the stretch, observing, dish after dish is changed, in endless rotation, and handed round with solemn pace to each guest: but should you happen not to like the first dishes, which was often my case, it is a gross breach of politeness to ask for part of any other till its turn comes. But have patience, and there will be eating enough. Allow me to run over the acts of a visiting day, not overlooking the interludes.

Prelude a luncheon—then a succession of fish, flesh and fowl for two hours; during which time the desert, I was sorry for the strawberries and cream, rests on the table to be impregnated by the fumes of the viands. Coffee immediately follows in the drawing-room; but does not preclude punch, ale, tea and cakes, raw salmon, etc. A supper brings up the rear, not forgetting the introductory luncheon, almost equalling in removes the dinner. A day of this kind you would imagine sufficient—but a to-morrow and a to-morrow—A never ending, still beginning feast may be bearable, perhaps, when stern winter frowns, shaking with chilling aspect his hoary locks; but during a summer, sweet as fleeting, let me, my kind strangers, escape sometimes into your fir groves, wander on the margin of your beautiful lakes, or climb your rocks to view still others in endless perspective; which, piled by more than giant's hand, scale the heavens to intercept its rays, or to receive the parting tinge of lingering day—day that, scarcely softened into twilight, allows the freshening breeze to wake, and the moon to burst forth in all her glory to glide with solemn elegance through the azure expanse. . . .

—*from* LETTER III—

. . . In fact, the situation of the servants in every respect, particularly that of the women, shews how far the swedes are from having a just conception of rational equality. They are not *termed* slaves; yet a man may strike a man with impunity because he pays him wages; though these wages are so low, that necessity must teach them to pilfer, whilst servility renders them false and boorish. Still the men stand up for the dignity of man, by oppressing the women. The most menial, and even laborious offices, are therefore left to these poor drudges. Much of this I have seen. In the winter, I am told, they take the linen down to the river, to wash it in the cold water; and though their hands, cut by the ice, are cracked and bleeding, the men, their fellow servants, will not disgrace their manhood by carrying a tub to lighten their burden.

You will not be surprised to hear that they do not wear shoes or stockings, when I inform you that their wages are seldom more than twenty or thirty shillings per annum. It is the custom, I know, to give them a new year's gift, and a present at some other period; but can it all amount to a just indemnity for their labour? The treatment of servants in most countries, I grant, is very unjust; and in England, that boasted land of freedom, it is often extremely tyrannical. I have frequently, with indignation, heard gentlemen declare that they would never allow a servant to answer them; and ladies of the most exquisite sensibility, who were continually exclaiming against the cruelty of the vulgar to the brute creation, have in my presence forgot that their attendants had human feelings, as well as forms. I do not know a more agreeable sight than to see servants part of a family. By taking an interest, generally speaking, in their concerns, you inspire them with one for yours. We must love our servants, or we shall never be sufficiently attentive to their happiness; and how can those masters be attentive to their happiness, who living above their fortunes, are more anxious to outshine their neighbours than to allow their household the innocent enjoyments they earn. . . .

Norway

—*from* LETTER V—

. . . Behold us now in Norway; and I could not avoid feeling surprise at observing the difference in the manners of the inhabitants of the two sides of the river; for every thing shews that the norwegians are more industrious and more opulent. The Swedes, for neighbours are seldom the best friends, accuse the norwegians of knavery, and they retaliate by bringing a charge of hypocrisy against the Swedes. Local circumstances probably render both unjust, speaking from their feelings, rather than reason: and is this astonishing when we consider that most writers of travels have done the same, whose works have served as materials for the compilers of universal histories. All are eager to give a national character; which is rarely just, because they do not discriminate the natural from the acquired difference. The natural, I believe, on due consideration, will be found to consist merely in the degree of vivacity or thoughtfulness, pleasure, or pain, inspired by the climate, whilst the varieties which the forms of government, including religion, produce, are much more numerous and unstable.

A people have been characterized as stupid by nature; what a paradox! because they did not consider that slaves, having no object to stimulate industry, have not their faculties sharpened by the only thing that can exercise them, self-interest. Others have been brought forward as brutes, having no aptitude for the arts and sciences, only because the progress of improvement had not reached the stage which produces them.

Those writers who have considered the history of man, or of the human mind, on a more enlarged scale, have fallen into similar errors, not reflecting that the passions are weak where the necessaries of life are too hardly or too easily obtained.

Travellers who require that every nation should resemble their native country, had better stay at home. It is, for example, absurd to blame a people for not having that degree of personal cleanliness and elegance of manners which only refinement of taste produces, and will produce every where in proportion as society attains a general polish. The most essential service, I presume, that authors could render to society, would be to promote inquiry and discussion, instead of making those dogmatical assertions which only appear calculated to gird the human mind round with imaginary circles, like the paper globe which represents the one he inhabits.

This spirit of inquiry is the characteristic of the present century, from which the succeeding will, I am persuaded, receive a great accumulation of knowledge; and doubtless its diffusion will in a great measure destroy the factitious[2] national characters which have been supposed permanent, though only rendered so by the permanency of ignorance. . . .

— *from* LETTER VI —

. . . As the norwegians do not frequently see travellers, they are very curious to know their business, and who they are — so curious that I was half tempted to adopt Dr Franklin's plan, when travelling in America, where they are equally prying, which was to write on a paper, for public inspection, my name, from whence I came, where I was going, and what was my business.[3] But if I were importuned by their curiosity, their friendly gestures gratified me. A woman, coming alone, interested them. And I know not whether my weariness gave me a look of peculiar delicacy; but they approached to assist me, and enquire after my wants, as if they were afraid to hurt, and wished to protect me. The sympathy I inspired, thus dropping down from the clouds in a strange land, affected me more than it would have done, had not my spirits been harassed by various causes — by much thinking — musing almost to madness — and even by a sort of weak melancholy that hung about my heart at parting with my daughter for the first time.

You know that as a female I am particularly attached to her — I feel more than a mother's fondness and anxiety, when I reflect on the dependent and oppressed state of her sex. I dread lest she should be forced to sacrifice her heart to her principles, or principles to her heart. With trembling hand I shall cultivate sensibility, and cherish delicacy of sentiment, lest, whilst I lend fresh blushes to the rose, I sharpen the thorns that will wound the breast I would fain guard — I dread to unfold her mind, lest it should render her unfit for the world she is to inhabit — Hapless woman! what a fate is thine!

But whither am I wandering? I only meant to tell you that the impression the kindness of the simple people made visible on my countenance increased my sensibility to a painful degree. I wished to have had a room to myself; for their attention, and rather distressing observation, embarrassed me extremely. Yet, as they would bring me eggs, and make my coffee, I found I could not leave them without hurting their feelings of hospitality.

It is customary here for the host and hostess to welcome their guests as master and mistress of the house.

My clothes, in their turn, attracted the attention of the females; and I could not help thinking of the foolish vanity which makes many women so proud of the observation of strangers as to take wonder very gratuitously for admiration. This error they are very apt to fall into; when arrived in a foreign country, the populace stare at them as they pass: yet the make of a cap, or the singularity of a gown, is often the cause of the flattering attention, which afterwards supports a fantastic superstructure of self-conceit. . . .

Denmark

— *from* LETTER XVIII —

. . . Considering Copenhagen as the capital of Denmark and Norway, I was surprised not to see so much industry

[2] **factitious:** artificial.

[3] See Benjamin Franklin, "Remarks Concerning the Savages of North America," *Two Tracts* (1748), pp. 33–34.

or taste as in Christiania.[4] Indeed from every thing I have had an opportunity of observing, the danes are the people who have made the fewest sacrifices to the graces.

The men of business are domestic tyrants, coldly immersed in their own affairs, and so ignorant of the state of other countries, that they dogmatically assert that Denmark is the happiest country in the world; the prince royal the best of all possible princes; and count Bernstorff[5] the wisest of ministers.

As for the women, they are simply notable housewives; without accomplishments, or any of the charms that adorn more advanced social life. This total ignorance may enable them to save something in their kitchens; but it is far from rendering them better parents. On the contrary, the children are spoilt; as they usually are, when left to the care of weak, indulgent mothers, who having no principle of action to regulate their feelings, become the slaves of infants, enfeebling both body and mind by false tenderness.

I am perhaps a little prejudiced, as I write from the impression of the moment; for I have been tormented today by the presence of unruly children, and made angry by some invectives thrown out against the maternal character of the unfortunate Matilda.[6] She was censured, with the most cruel insinuation, for her management of her son; though, from what I could gather, she gave proofs of good sense, as well as tenderness in her attention to him. She used to bathe him herself every morning; insisted on his being loosely clad; and would not permit his attendants to injure his digestion, by humouring his appetite. She was equally careful to prevent his acquiring haughty airs, and playing the tyrant in leading-strings. The queen dowager would not permit her to suckle him; but the next child being a daughter, and not the heir apparent of the crown, less opposition was made to her discharging the duty of a mother.

Poor Matilda! thou hast haunted me ever since my arrival; and the view I have had of the manners of the country, exciting my sympathy, has increased my respect for thy memory!

I am now fully convinced that she was the victim of the party she displaced, who would have overlooked, or encouraged, her attachment, had her lover not, aiming at being useful, attempted to overturn some established abuses before the people, ripe for the change, had sufficient spirit to support him when struggling in their behalf. Such indeed was the asperity sharpened against her, that I have heard her, even after so many years have elapsed, charged with licentiousness, not only for endeavouring to render the public amusements more elegant, but for her very charities, because she erected amongst other institutions, an hospital to receive foundlings. Disgusted with many customs which pass for virtues, though they are nothing more than observances of forms, often at the expence of truth, she probably ran into an error common to innovators, in wishing to do immediately what can only be done by time. . . .

— *from* LETTER XIX —

. . . Wealth does not appear to be sought for, amongst the danes, to obtain the elegant luxuries of life; for a want of taste is very conspicuous at Copenhagen; so much so, that I am not surprised to hear that poor Matilda offended the rigid lutherans, by aiming to refine their pleasures. The elegance which she wished to introduce, was termed lasciviousness: yet I do not find that the absence of gallantry renders the wives more chaste, or the husbands more constant. Love here seems to corrupt the morals, without polishing the manners, by banishing confidence and truth, the charm as well as cement of domestic life. A gentleman, who has resided in this city some time, assures me that he could not find language to give me an idea of the gross debaucheries into which the lower order of people fall; and the promiscuous amours of the men of the middling class with their female servants, debases both beyond measure, weakening every species of family affection.

I have every where been struck by one characteristic difference in the conduct of the two sexes; women, in general, are seduced by their superiors, and men jilted by their inferiors; rank and manners awe the one, and cunning and wantonness subjugate the other; ambition creeping into the woman's passion, and tyranny giving force to

[4] Christiania, renamed Oslo in 1925, the capital city of Norway.

[5] Count Andreas Peter von Bernstorff (1735–1797), Foreign Minister of Denmark, was succeeded as Secretary of State in 1797 by his son, Christian Günther von Bernstorff (1769–1835).

[6] Caroline Matilda (1751–1775), sister of George III of England, was married in 1766 to the mentally retarded Christian VII, King of Denmark. She became lovers with the Danish court physician, Johann Friedrich Struensee (1737–1772), who had gained sufficient influence over the king to introduce liberal reforms. In 1772, Struensee fell from favor and was executed; Matilda, who had borne Struensee's daughter, was condemned to prison but was rescued by an English warship and taken to Hanover, where she died at the age of 24.

the man's; for most men treat their mistresses as kings do their favourites: *ergo* is not man then the tyrant of the creation?

Still harping on the same subject, you will exclaim—How can I avoid it, when most of the struggles of an eventful life have been occasioned by the oppressed state of my sex: we reason deeply, when we forcibly feel.

from LETTERS TO WILLIAM GODWIN[1]

— *from* LETTER 14 —

[August 17, 1796]

I like your last—may I call it *love* letter? better than the first—and can I give you a higher proof of my esteem than to tell you, the style of my letter will whether I will or no, that it has calmed my mind—a mind that had been painfully active all the morning, haunted by old sorrows that seemed to come forward with new force to sharpen the present anguish—Well! well—it is almost gone—I mean all my unreasonable fears—and a whole train of tormentors, which you have routed—I can scarcely describe to you their ugly shapes so quickly do they vanish—and let them go, we will not bring them back by talking of them. You may see me when you please. I shall take this letter, just before dinner time, to ask you to come and dine with me, and Fanny, whom I have shut out to day. Should you be engaged come in the evening. Miss H—seldom stays late, never to supper—or to morrow—as you wish—I shall be content—You say you want soothing—will it sooth you to tell you the truth? I cannot hate you—I do not think you deserve it. Nay, more I cannot withhold my friendship from you, and will try to merit yours, that *necessity*[2] may bind you to me.

One word of my ONLY fault[3]—our imaginations have been rather differently employed—I am more of a painter than you—I like to tell the truth, my taste for the picturesque has been more cultivated—I delight to view the grand scenes of nature and the various changes of the human countenance—Beautiful as they are animated by intelligence or sympathy—My affections have been more exercised than yours, I believe, and my senses are quick, without the aid of fancy—yet tenderness always prevails, which inclines me to be angry with myself, when I do not animate and please those I [love?].

Now will you not be a good boy, and smile upon me, I dine at half past four—you ought to come and give me an appetite for my dinner, as you deprived me of one for my breakfast.

— *from* LETTER 36 —

[September 13, 1796]

Now by these presents let me assure you that you are not only in my heart, but my veins, this morning. I turn from you half abashed—yet you haunt me, and some look, word or touch thrills through my whole frame—yes, at the very moment when I am labouring to think of something, if not somebody, else. Get ye gone Intruder! though I am forced to add dear—which is a call back—

When the heart and reason accord there is no flying from voluptuous sensations, I find, do what a woman can—Can a philosopher do more?

---

[1] William Godwin (1756–1836), eminent English political philosopher and author. Began career as a Dissenting (Sandemanian) minister but gave up preaching in 1783, plagued by religious doubts. His *Enquiry Concerning Political Justice** (1793) argued that men should be guided by reason alone and, being rational and hence perfectible creatures, would by necessity come to live in harmony without laws or social institutions (such as marriage). These views are further advocated in his novels, *Adventures of Caleb Williams* (1794), *St. Leon* (1799), and *Fleetwood, or the New Man of Feeling* (1805). Inspired by her *Letters written . . . in Sweden, Norway, and Denmark,* Godwin called on Wollstonecraft; when she returned his visit in April 1796, they soon became lovers. They married on 29 March 1797; their daughter, Mary Wollstonecraft Godwin, later Shelley, was born on 30 August 1797. Overcome by grief when Wollstonecraft died 11 days later, Godwin as an act of homage gathered together all her unpublished manuscripts and published them as *Posthumous Works of the Author of a Vindication of the Rights of Woman* in 1798. His inclusion of her love letters and his biographical account of her extramarital affairs and two suicide attempts convinced the majority of the British public that Wollstonecraft was a whore and an atheist.

[2] **necessity:** alludes to Godwin's belief that human behavior obeys the same rational or scientifically provable laws of necessary causation and effect that govern physical matter; see Godwin's *Political Justice* (1793), I.364–399.

[3] **ONLY fault:** on August 17 Godwin had written, "Upon consideration I find in you one fault, & but one. You have the feelings of nature, & you have the honesty to avow them. . . . But do not let them tyrannise over you. Estimate every thing at its just value" (*Godwin and Mary,* ed. R. Wardle, 1966, p. 17).

— LETTER 63 —

[November 10, 1796]

I send you your household linen—I am not sure that I did not feel a sensation of pleasure at thus acting the part of a wife, though you have so little respect for the character. There is such a magic in affection that I have been more gratified by your clasping your hands round my arm, in company, than I could have been by all the admiration in the world, tho' I am a woman—and to mount a step higher in the scale of vanity, an author.

I shall call toward one o'clock not to deprive the world of your bright thoughts, this exhilarating day.

— *from* LETTER 160[4] —

[August 30, 1797]

Mrs. Blenkinsop tells me that I am in the most natural state, and can promise me a safe delivery—But that I must have a little patience . . . .

POSTHUMOUS PUBLICATIONS

from POSTHUMOUS WORKS OF THE AUTHOR OF A *VINDICATION OF THE RIGHTS OF WOMAN* IN FOUR VOLUMES,

ed. William Godwin
(1798)

from LETTERS TO GILBERT IMLAY[1]

— *from* LETTER II —

Neuilly, August, 1793

You can scarcely imagine with what pleasure I anticipate the day, when we are to begin almost to live together; and you would smile to hear how many plans of employment I have in my head, now that I am confident my heart has found peace in your bosom.—Cherish me with that dignified tenderness, which I have only found in you; and your own dear girl will try to keep under a quickness of feeling, that has sometimes given you pain—Yes, I will be *good*, that I may deserve to be happy; and whilst you love me, I cannot again fall into the miserable state, which rendered life a burthen almost too heavy to be borne.

But, good-night!—God bless you! Sterne says, that is equal to a kiss[2]—yet I would rather give you the kiss into the bargain, glowing with gratitude to Heaven, and affection to you. I like the word affection, because it signifies something habitual; and we are soon to meet, to try whether we have mind enough to keep our hearts warm.

Mary

I will be at the barrier[3] a little after ten o'clock to-morrow.

— *from* LETTER XXI —

Le Havre, August 19, 1794

I have only to tell you, what is sufficiently obvious, that the earnest desire I have shown to keep my place, or gain more ground in your heart, is a sure proof how necessary your affection is to my happiness.—Still I do not think it

[4] Probably the last words that Wollstonecraft wrote. Godwin noted in his *Memoirs* (p. 23) that Wollstonecraft's last words on her deathbed were "A little patience and all will be over!"

[1] Wollstonecraft's 77 letters to Gilbert Imlay, written between 1793 and 1796, were edited and published by William Godwin in his *Posthumous Works of the Author of a Vindication of the Rights of Woman* in 1798.

Gilbert Imlay (c. 1754–?1828), born in Monmouth, New Jersey; served as an officer in the American Revolution; then worked as a surveyor and real estate speculator in Kentucky. Fled to London in 1792 to avoid debts and litigation, and published a novel, *The Emigrants* (1793), celebrating the life of the frontiersman. Met Wollstonecraft in Paris at the home of Thomas Christie in 1793; they became lovers and lived together in Neuilly during the summer of 1793. Their daughter, christened Fanny Imlay although Wollstonecraft and Imlay never married, was born in Le Havre on 14 May 1794. At that time Imlay was engaged in a plot to wrest Louisiana from Spanish control and in running guns and other supplies to the new French Republic; he frequently left Wollstonecraft to undertake business trips in France and England.

[2] See Laurence Sterne, *Sentimental Journey,* Vol. II, ch. 1, "La Fille de Chambre. Paris."

[3] **the barrier**: the tollgate in the city wall of Paris where Wollstonecraft and Imlay met during the summer of 1793. Wollstonecraft later referred to her daughter Fanny Imlay as the "barrier girl."

false delicacy, or foolish pride, to wish that your attention to my happiness should arise *as much* from love, which is always rather a selfish passion, as reason — that is, I want you to promote my felicity, by seeking your own. — For, whatever pleasure it may give me to discover your generosity of soul, I would not be dependent for your affection on the very quality I most admire. No; there are qualities in your heart, which demand my affection; but, unless the attachment appears to me clearly mutual, I shall labour only to esteem your character, instead of cherishing a tenderness for your person.

I write in a hurry, because the little one, who has been sleeping a long time, begins to call for me. Poor thing! when I am sad, I lament that all my affections grow on me, till they become too strong for my peace, though they all afford me snatches of exquisite enjoyment — This for our little girl was at first very reasonable — more the effect of reason, a sense of duty, than feeling — now, she has got into my heart and imagination, and when I walk out without her, her little figure is ever dancing before me.

You too have somehow clung round my heart — I found I could not eat my dinner in the great room — and, when I took up the large knife to carve for myself, tears rushed into my eyes. — Do not however suppose that I am melancholy — for, when you are from me, I not only wonder how I can find fault with you — but how I can doubt your affection.

— *from* LETTER XXIV —

Paris, September 23, 1794

I have been playing and laughing with the little girl so long, that I cannot take up my pen to address you without emotion. Pressing her to my bosom, she looked so like you (*entre nous,*[4] your best looks, for I do not admire your commercial face) every nerve seemed to vibrate to the touch, and I began to think that there was something in the assertion of man and wife being one — for you seemed to pervade my whole frame, quickening the beat of my heart, and lending me the sympathetic tears you excited.

— *from* LETTER XXXV —

Paris, February 9, 1795

The melancholy presentiment has for some time hung on my spirits, that we were parted for ever; and the letters I received this day, by Mr. ———, convince me that it was not without foundation.[5] You allude to some other letters, which I suppose have miscarried; for most of those I have got, were only a few hasty lines, calculated to wound the tenderness the sight of the superscriptions excited.

I mean not however to complain; yet so many feelings are struggling for utterance, and agitating a heart almost bursting with anguish, that I find it very difficult to write with any degree of coherence.

You left me indisposed, though you have taken no notice of it; and the most fatiguing journey[6] I ever had, contributed to continue you. However, I recovered my health; but a neglected cold, and continual inquietude during the last two months, have reduced me to a state of weakness I never before experienced. Those who did not know that the canker-worm was at work at the core, cautioned me about suckling my child too long. — God preserve this poor child, and render her happier than her mother!

But I am wandering from my subject: indeed my head turns giddy, when I think that all the confidence I have had in the affection of others is come to this. — I did not expect this blow from you. I have done my duty to you and my child; and if I am not to have any return of affection to reward me, I have the sad consolation of knowing that I deserved a better fate. My soul is weary — I am sick at heart; and, but for this little darling, I would cease to care about a life, which is now stripped of every charm.

You see how stupid I am, uttering declamation, when I meant simply to tell you, that I consider your requesting me to come to you, as merely dictated by honour. — Indeed I scarcely understand you. — You request me to come, and then tell me, that you have not given up all thoughts of returning to this place.

When I determined to live with you, I was only governed by affection. — I would share poverty with you, but I turn with affright from the sea of trouble on which you are entering. — I have certain principles of action: I know what I look for to found my happiness on. — It is not money. — With you I wished for sufficient to procure the comforts of life — as it is, less will do. — I can still exert myself to obtain the necessaries of life for my child, and she does not want more at present. — I have two or three plans in my

[4] **entre nous**: French, between us.

[5] Imlay had informed Wollstonecraft of his intention to remain longer in London, where, unknown to her, he had begun an affair with an English actress.

[6] **fatiguing journey**: from Le Havre in the west of France to Paris in December 1794. The carriage overturned four times.

head to earn our subsistence; for do not suppose that, neglected by you, I will lie under obligations of a pecuniary kind to you! — No; I would sooner submit to menial service. — I wanted the support of your affection — that gone, all is over! — I did not think, when I complained of ——'s contemptible avidity to accumulate money, that he would have dragged you into his schemes.

I cannot write. — I inclose a fragment of a letter, written soon after your departure, and another which tenderness made me keep back when it was written. — You will see then the sentiments of a calmer, though not a more determined, moment. — Do not insult me by saying that "our being together is paramount to every other consideration!" Were it, you would not be running after a bubble, at the expence of my peace of mind.

Perhaps this is the last letter you will ever receive from me.

MARY

— *from* LETTER LV —

Göteborg, Sweden,[7] *July 3, 1795*

I grow more and more attached to my little girl — and I cherish this affection without fear, because it must be a long time before it can become bitterness of soul. — She is an interesting creature. — On shipboard, how often as I gazed at the sea, have I longed to bury my troubled bosom in the less troubled deep; asserting with Brutus, "that the virtue I had followed too far, was merely an empty name!"[8] and nothing but the sight of her — her playful smiles, which seemed to cling and twine round my heart — could have stopped me.

What peculiar misery has fallen to my share! To act up to my principles, I have laid the strictest restraint on my very thoughts — yes; not to sully the delicacy of my feelings, I have reined in my imagination; and started with affright from every sensation, (I allude to ——) that stealing with balmy sweetness into my soul, led me to scent from afar the frag[r]ance of reviving nature.

My friend, I have dearly paid for one conviction. — Love, in some minds, is an affair of sentiment, arising from the same delicacy of perception (or taste) as renders them alive to the beauties of nature, poetry, &c., alive to the charms of those evanescent graces that are, as it were, impalpable — they must be felt, they cannot be described.

Love is a want of my heart. I have examined myself lately with more care than formerly, and find, that to deaden is not to calm the mind — Aiming at tranquillity, I have almost destroyed all the energy of my soul — almost rooted out what renders it estimable — Yes, I have damped that enthusiasm of character, which converts the grossest materials into a fuel, that imperceptibly feeds hopes, which aspire above common enjoyment. Despair, since the birth of my child, has rendered me stupid — soul and body seemed to be fading away before the withering touch of disappointment.

— *from* LETTER LXXVIII —

London, Spring, 1796

You must do as you please with respect to the child. — I could wish that it might be done soon, that my name may be no more mentioned to you. It is now finished. — Convinced that you have neither regard nor friendship, I disdain to utter a reproach, though I have had reason to think, that the "forbearance" talked of, has not been very delicate. — It is however of no consequence. — I am glad you are satisfied with your own conduct.

I now solemnly assure you, that this is an eternal farewel. — Yet I flinch not from the duties which tie me to life.

That there is "sophistry" on one side or other, is certain; but now it matters not on which. On my part it has not been a question of words. Yet your understanding or mine must be strangely warped — for what you term "delicacy," appears to me to be exactly the contrary. I have no criterion for morality, and have thought in vain, if the sensations which lead you to follow an ancle or step,[9] be the sacred foundation of principle and affection. Mine has been of a very different nature, or it would not have stood the brunt of your sarcasms.

The sentiment in me is still sacred. If there be any part of me that will survive the sense of my misfortunes, it

---

[7] Imlay sent Wollstonecraft and Fanny to Sweden in June 1795 to try to claim the insurance on a lost treasure ship, the *Maria and Margaretha,* that had been running the British trade blockade against Revolutionary France. Wollstonecraft stayed at the home of Imlay's Swedish agent, Elias Backman, in Gothenburg.

[8] See Lucius Annaeus Florus, *Epitome of Roman History* (c. 27 BC), Bk. II, ch. 17. Brutus's words were quoted in Addison and Steele's *Spectator* on 5 February 1712: "O Vertue, I have worshiped thee as a Substantial Good, but I find thou art an empty Name."

[9] **ancle or step:** the ankle or footstep of his mistress.

is the purity of my affections. The impetuosity of your senses, may have led you to term mere animal desire, the source of principle; and it may give zest to some years to come.—Whether you will always think so, I shall never know.

It is strange that, in spite of all you do, something like conviction forces me to believe, that you are not what you appear to be.

I part with you in peace.

JOANNA BAILLIE

(1762–1851)

Joanna Baillie was the leading female playwright in England in this era, and perhaps the most original and highly regarded of all the dramatists of her day. As her competitor Byron* commented crudely but with admiration, "When Voltaire was asked why no woman has ever written even a tolerable tragedy? 'Ah (said the Patriarch) the composition of a tragedy requires *testicles*'.—If this be true Lord knows what Joanna Baillie does—I suppose she borrows them." (*Letters and Journals,* V.203) Byron elsewhere declared Joanna Baillie to be "our only dramatist since Otway & Southerne" and urged the Drury Lane Theater in Covent Garden to remount a production of *De Montfort* with Edward Kean, a production that took place in 1821. The opening and equally famous production of *De Montfort* was staged in 1800 at Drury Lane with Sarah Siddons as Jane de Montfort and John Philip Kemble as de Montfort.

Born on 11 September 1762, in Bothwell, Lanarkshire, Scotland, Baillie was the daughter of an Anglican clergyman, Dr. James Baillie, who became Professor of Divinity at the University of Glasgow and who instilled in her an enduring Christian faith. She received a relatively advanced education for a girl, adding to the female "accomplishments" a strong background in mathematics, partially learned from her uncle, the famous anatomist Dr. William Hunter, and from her brother, Matthew Baillie, who became a leading London physician and anatomist. In 1784, she moved to London with her mother and her sister Agnes, first keeping house for Matthew and then setting up their own modest establishment in Hampstead. Baillie began her literary career as a poet, publishing *Fugitive Verses* in 1790, but then focussed on drama, publishing 28 plays over the next 40 years (of which seven were produced in her lifetime): *A Series of Plays,* known as *Plays on the Passions,* 3 Volumes (1798–1812), *Miscellaneous Plays* (1804), *The Family Legend* (1810), and *Dramas* (1836).

In Hampstead, she became part of a female literary coterie, enjoying close friendships with Anna Barbauld,* Maria Edgeworth,* Mary Berry, and Lucy Aikin,* as well as with some of the leading male writers of the day. Sir Walter Scott* was her devoted admirer, as were William Sotheby, Samuel Rogers, and William Ellery Channing. She supported her mother (who died in 1806) and her sister on the earnings from her writings, an income "large enough to make them independent but not to afford any luxuries," said her friend Sir John Sinclair, but an income of which she nonetheless gave half to charity. She died on 23 February 1851, and was buried with her sister Agnes in a single grave beside that of Lucy Aikin in the Hampstead Cemetery.

Although Sir Walter Scott and many others claimed that Joanna Baillie was "the best dramatic writer [that Britain had produced] since the days of Shakespeare and Massinger," Baillie's plays were more often read than performed, in part because she conceived of them as "closet dramas," to be staged in smaller and more intimate theaters than existed in the England of her day. Both her *Introductory Discourse* and her dramas conceptualized a new relationship between the actor and the audience, one grounded in rational sympathy rather than in a Coleridgean "willing suspension of disbelief." Her *Introductory Discourse* to her *Plays on the Passions* constitutes the first historical statement of an aesthetic grounded on sympathy; published in 1798, it had a profound influence on Wordsworth's Preface to *Lyrical Ballads.**

Baillie begins her *Discourse* with a definition of human nature's "great master propensity" or primary motivation as "sympathetic curiosity," rather than the "self-interest" of Hobbes, Locke, Burke, and a host of other philosophers, including modern "rational choice" social scientists. Influenced by Adam Smith's *Theory of Moral Sentiments,** she argues that all human beings desire knowledge of others and experience a sense of identification with others. She assumes that the subject or self is constructed only in relation to the other selves, and that knowledge is produced, not from "objective" or detached observation but rather from empathic identification and the stories we tell of what and whom we meet, what she calls "tattling." Her epistemology thus conforms to what modern feminist philosophers have defined as "women's ways of knowing" or "standpoint theory."

Baillie's *Introductory Discourse* is specifically to *A Series of Plays: in which it is attempted to delineate The Stronger Passions of the Mind.* She further claims that the development of the individual is governed most powerfully by feelings and desires, passions which must be held in check by reason if they are not to become self-destructive. Arguing that human character is developmental, growing not from Locke's "white paper" or blank slate but from an inherent "propensity" or seed, she both anticipates William Wordsworth's notion that "fair seed-time had my soul" and argues that this growing seed takes its final shape from its interactions with its environment. Her tragedies each study the growth of a single passion that, unchecked by the rational advice of others, destroys the hero; her comedies hold that obsessive passion up to the "derision" of others, laughing its possessor back into a more moderated feeling. Significantly, in Baillie's plays, it is the male characters who are prey to unregulated passion, while the female characters are the voices of rational moderation. She thus denies the traditional gender definition of the female sex as irrational, impulsive, uncontrollable, while at the same time insisting that there is no significant sex difference between males and females.

The function of drama, Baillie asserts, is to arouse the sympathetic curiosity of the viewer so that the audience will both identify with her characters and learn from their errors. "The theater is a school," she claims, and like the other female literary critics of her day (Clara Reeve,* Elizabeth Inchbald, and Anna Barbauld*), she wishes to use literature to educate her audience to a more responsible morality. In order to do this, she recognized, drama must be probable or "natural"—it must show "the plain order of things in this everyday world," including the way that the passions develop and change *over time,* in their "infant, growing, and repressed state." We must recognize that for Baillie, what is "natural" is what is "middling and lower" class, English, and domestic. She rejects both the "artifice" of the aristocracy and the potentially disruptive "ballad-reading" of the "lowest classes of the labouring people, who are the broad foundation of society, which can never be generally moved without endangering every thing that is constructed upon it."

To achieve a "natural" or probable revelation of the human passions, Baillie used several specific techniques: the soliloquy, a focus on but one passion and one plot (with no distracting subplots or unrelated incidents); the use of processions and other social rituals or ceremonies in place of subplots to arouse audience attention but avoid distraction; and the confinement of the action to a small, intimate, often domestic space (a house, a town square). Eschewing the rhetorical excesses of satirical comedy, the amorality of witty comedy, the hypocrisies of sentimental comedy, and the contrivances (or "ambushed bush-fighting") of "busy" comedy or farce, she wrote what she called "Characteristick Comedy," a comedy devoted to the representation of the "motley world of men and women in which we live," using ordinary language and focussing on the damage done by emotional excesses.

Baillie laid claim to the highest cultural authority. Asserting, in effect, that "if I have the writing of its Drama, let who will make the laws of a nation," Baillie positioned herself as the "unacknowledged legislator" of the British nation, superior to the historian, philosopher, and poet. For the dramatist alone, she argued, can combine an abstract moral lesson with a concrete appeal to our "sympathetic curiosity," an appeal that will—in this first articulation of what we now call "reader-response" theory—produce political action, cultural ideology, and meaning itself. Although Baillie employs the literary convention of authorial modesty, she firmly asserts both the originality and the pedagogical value of her dramatic project, to reveal the growth of individual passions, from love and hatred to remorse and sexual jealousy, by writing paired plays, a tragedy and a comedy on each passion. By moving the realm of private, psychological feelings from the domestic "closet" to the public stage, Baillie implicitly asserts that the hitherto culturally marginalized "women's realm," the realm of feeling, intuition, and empathy, is in fact the basis of all human culture, and especially of political culture. Good domestic management thus becomes the model for good politics, harmonious domestic affections become the model for peaceful national and international relations.

Count Basil (1798), Baillie's examination of the passion of love, is her rejoinder to Shakespeare's *Antony and Cleopatra*: here the struggle is not between love (eros) and duty but rather between two kinds of love, one heterosexual, the other homosocial. Basil's infatuation with Victoria is, we are to assume, finally reciprocated as Victoria comes to recognize the difference between Basil's mature devotion and the hypocritical attentions of her previous lovers, and to respond judiciously to Basil's passion for her. But Basil already has another "mistress," namely war; as the play unfolds, we see that prior love unveiled as a powerful homosocial bonding between Basil and his men, and especially with his oldest and closest cousin-friend, Rosinberg. In this play, two bodies are displayed for Basil's specular desire: the "divine" body of the beautiful Victoria and the scarred body of the old soldier Geoffry. Weeping with his men over the body of Geoffry, Basil manifests his most profound relational bond, with his men. By betraying that bond, Basil destroys his own sense of selfhood: the "wounded soldier" whose mask he wears at the ball is not the rejected lover of Victoria, as he claims, but the rejecting lover of his own men, a betrayal for which he dies. Only the Countess Albini in this play is able to see the whole truth; only she has the maturity, the wisdom, and the maternal affection to understand both Victoria and Basil and to advise them well.

Joanna Baillie continued to publish poetry throughout her life. An expanded volume of *Fugitive Verses* appeared in 1840, following her celebratory verses on William Wallace, Christopher Columbus, Lady Griseld Baillie, and others in *Metrical Legends of Exalted Characters* (1821). She published numerous occasional verses, songs, and verses on sacred subjects in the magazines of her day; these were first collected together in the Longmans edition of *The Dramatic and Poetical Works of Joanna Baillie* of 1851 (available in a modern facsimile edition from Georg Olms Verlag).

from FUGITIVE VERSES

(1790)

A Winter's Day

The cock, warm roosting 'mid his feather'd mates,
Now lifts his beak and snuffs the morning air,
Stretches his neck and claps his heavy wings,
Gives three hoarse crows, and glad his task is done,
Low chuckling turns himself upon the roost,
Then nestles down again into his place.
The labouring hind[1], who, on his bed of straw
Beneath his home-made coverings, coarse but warm,
Lock'd in the kindly arms of her who spun them,
Dreams of the gain that next year's crop should bring;
Or at some fair, disposing of his wool,
Or by some lucky and unlook'd-for bargain,
Fills his skin purse with store of tempting gold;
Now wakes from sleep at the unwelcome call,
And finds himself but just the same poor man
As when he went to rest.
He hears the blast against his window beat,
And wishes to himself he were a laird,[2]
That he might lie a-bed. It may not be:
He rubs his eyes and stretches out his arms;
Heigh oh! heigh oh! he drawls with gaping mouth,
Then, most unwillingly creeps from his lair,
And without looking-glass puts on his clothes.
With rueful face he blows the smother'd fire,
And lights his candle at the reddening coal;
First sees that all be right among his cattle,
Then hies him to the barn with heavy tread,
Printing his footsteps on the new-fall'n snow.
From out the heap'd-up mow he draws his sheaves,[3]
Dislodging the poor red-breast from his shelter
Where all the live-long night he slept secure;
But now, affrighted, with uncertain flight,
Flutters round walls, and roof, to find some hole
Through which he may escape.
Then whirling o'er his head, the heavy flail
Descends with force upon the jumping sheaves,
While every rugged wall and neighbouring cot
The noise re-echoes of his sturdy strokes.

The family cares call next upon the wife
To quit her mean but comfortable bed.
And first she stirs the fire and fans the flame,
Then from her heap of sticks for winter stored
An armful brings; loud crackling as they burn,
Thick fly the red sparks upward to the roof,
While slowly mounts the smoke in wreathy clouds.
On goes the seething pot with morning cheer,
For which some little wistful folk await,
Who, peeping from the bed-clothes, spy well pleased
The cheery light that blazes on the wall,
And bawl for leave to rise.
Their busy mother knows not where to turn,
Her morning's work comes now so thick upon her.
One she must help to tie his little coat,
Unpin another's cap, or seek his shoe
Or hosen lost, confusion soon o'er-master'd!
When all is o'er, out to the door they run
With new-comb'd sleeky hair and glistening faces,
Each with some little project in his head.
His new-soled shoes one on the ice must try;
To view his well-set trap another hies,
In hopes to find some poor unwary bird
(No worthless prize) entangled in his snare;
While one, less active, with round rosy cheeks,
Spreads out his purple fingers to the fire,
And peeps most wistfully into the pot.

But let us leave the warm and cheerful house
To view the bleak and dreary scene without,
And mark the dawning of a Winter day.
The morning vapour rests upon the heights,
Lurid and red, while growing gradual shades
Of pale and sickly light spread o'er the sky
Then slowly from behind the southern hills
Enlarged and ruddy comes the rising sun,
Shooting athwart the hoary waste his beams
That gild the brow of every ridgy bank,
And deepen every valley with a shade,
The crusted window of each scatter'd cot,
The icicles that fringe the thatched roof,
The new-swept slide upon the frozen pool,
All keenly glance, new kindled with his rays;

---

[1] Hind does not perfectly express the condition of the person here intended, who is somewhat above a common labourer,—the tenant of a very small farm, which he cultivates with his own hands; a few cows, perhaps a horse, and some six or seven sheep, being all the wealth he possessed. A class of men very common in the west of Scotland, ere political economy was thought of [J. B.].

[2] **laird:** Scottish lord.

[3] **mow:** stack of hay, corn, beans. **sheaves:** bundles of hay or corn.

And e'en the rugged face of scowling Winter
Looks somewhat gay. But only for a time
He shows his glory to the brightening earth,
Then hides his face behind a sullen cloud.

The birds now quit their holes and lurking sheds,
Most mute and melancholy, where through night,
All nestling close to keep each other warm,
In downy sleep they had forgot their hardships;
But not to chant and carol in the air,
Or lightly swing upon some waving bough,
And merrily return each other's notes;
No; silently they hop from bush to bush,
Can find no seeds to stop their craving want,
Then bend their flight to the low smoking cot,
Chirp on the roof, or at the window peck,
To tell their wants to those who lodge within.
The poor lank hare flies homeward to his den,
But little burthen'd with his nightly meal
Of wither'd coleworts[4] from the farmer's garden;
A wretched scanty portion, snatch'd in fear;
And fearful creatures, forced abroad by hunger,
Are now to every enemy a prey.

The husbandman lays by his heavy flail,
And to the house returns, where for him wait
His smoking breakfast and impatient children,
Who, spoon in hand, and ready to begin,
Toward the door cast many an eager look
To see their dad come in.
Then round they sit, a cheerful company;
All quickly set to work, and with heap'd spoons
From ear to ear besmear their rosy cheeks.
The faithful dog stands by his master's side
Wagging his tail and looking in his face;
While humble puss pays court to all around,
And purs and rubs them with her furry sides,
Nor goes this little flattery unrewarded.
But the laborious sit not long at table;
The grateful father lifts his eyes to heaven
To bless his God, whose ever bounteous hand
Him and his little ones doth daily feed,
Then rises satisfied to work again.

The varied rousing sounds of industry
Are heard through all the village.
The humming wheel, the thrifty housewife's tongue,
Who scolds to keep her maidens to their work,
The wool-card's grating, most unmusical!
Issue from every house.
But hark! the sportsman from the neighbouring hedge
His thunder sends! loud bark the village curs;
Up from her cards or wheel the maiden starts
And hastens to the door; the housewife chides,
Yet runs herself to look, in spite of thrift,
And all the little town is in a stir.

Strutting before, the cock leads forth his train,
And chuckling near the barn-door 'mid the straw,
Reminds the farmer of his morning's service.
His grateful master throws a liberal handful;
They flock about it, while the hungry sparrows
Perch'd on the roof, look down with envious eye,
Then, aiming well, amidst the feeders light,
And seize upon the feast with greedy bill,
Till angry partlets[5] peck them off the field.
But at a distance, on the leafless tree,
All woe-begone, the lonely blackbird sits;
The cold north wind ruffles his glossy feathers;
Full oft he looks, but dares not make approach,
Then turns his yellow beak to peck his side
And claps his wings close to his sharpen'd breast.
The wandering fowler from behind the hedge,
Fastens his eye upon him, points his gun,
And firing wantonly, as at a mark,
Of life bereaves him in the cheerful spot
That oft hath echo'd to his summer's song.

The mid-day hour is near, the pent-up kine
Are driven from their stalls to take the air.
How stupidly they stare! and feel how strange!
They open wide their smoking mouths to low,
But scarcely can their feeble sound be heard,
Then turn and lick themselves, and step by step,
Move, dull and heavy, to their stalls again.

In scatter'd groups the little idle boys,
With purple fingers moulding in the snow
Their icy ammunition, pant for war;
And drawing up in opposite array,
Send forth a mighty shower of well-aim'd balls,
Each tiny hero tries his growing strength,
And burns to beat the foe-men off the field.
Or on the well-worn ice in eager throngs,
After short race, shoot rapidly along,
Trip up each other's heels, and on the surface

[4] **coleworts:** kale, cabbage plants.

[5] **partlets:** hens.

With studded shoes draw many a chalky line.
Untired and glowing with the healthful sport
They cease not till the sun hath run his course,
And threatening clouds, slow rising from the north,
Spread leaden darkness o'er the face of heaven;
Then by degrees they scatter to their homes,
Some with a broken head or bloody nose,
To claim their mother's pity, who, most skilful!
Cures all their troubles with a bit of bread.

The night comes on apace—
Chill blows the blast and drives the snow in wreaths;
Now every creature looks around for shelter,
And whether man or beast, all move alike
Towards their homes, and happy they who have
A house to screen them from the piercing cold!
Lo, o'er the frost a reverend form advances!
His hair white as the snow on which he treads,
His forehead mark'd with many a care-worn furrow,
Whose feeble body bending o'er a staff,
Shows still that once it was the seat of strength,
Though now it shakes like some old ruin'd tower.
Clothed indeed, but not disgraced with rags,
He still maintains that decent dignity
Which well becomes those who have served their
country.
With tottering steps he gains the cottage door;
The wife within, who hears his hollow cough,
And pattering of his stick upon the threshold,
Sends out her little boy to see who's there.
The child looks up to mark the stranger's face,
And, seeing it enlighten'd with a smile,
Holds out his tiny hand to lead him in.
Round from her work the mother turns her head,
And views them, not ill pleased.
The stranger whines not with a piteous tale,
But only asks a little to relieve
A poor old soldier's wants.
The gentle matron brings the ready chair
And bids him sit to rest his weary limbs,
And warm himself before her blazing fire.
The children, full of curiosity,
Flock round, and with their fingers in their mouths
Stand staring at him, while the stranger, pleased,
Takes up the youngest urchin on his knee.
Proud of its seat, it wags its little feet,
And prates and laughs and plays with his white locks.
But soon a change comes o'er the soldier's face;
His thoughtful mind is turn'd on other days,
When his own boys were wont to play around him,
Who now lie distant from their native land
In honourable but untimely graves:
He feels how helpless and forlorn he is,
And big, round tears course down his wither'd cheeks.
His toilsome daily labour at an end,
In comes the wearied master of the house,
And marks with satisfaction his old guest,
In the chief seat, with all the children round him.
His honest heart is fill'd with manly kindness,
He bids him stay and share their homely meal,
And take with them his quarters for the night.
The aged wanderer thankfully accepts,
And by the simple hospitable board,
Forgets the by-past hardships of the day.

When all are satisfied, about the fire
They draw their seats and form a cheerful ring.
The thrifty housewife turns her spinning-wheel;
The husband, useful even in his hour
Of ease and rest, a stocking knits, belike,
Or plaits stored rushes, which with after skill
Into a basket form'd may do good service,
With eggs or butter fill'd at fair or market.

Some idle neighbours now come dropping in,
Draw round their chairs and widen out the circle;
And every one in his own native way
Does what he can to cheer the social group.
Each tells some little story of himself,
That constant subject upon which mankind,
Whether in court or country, love to dwell.
How at a fair he saved a simple clown[6]
From being trick'd in buying of a cow;
Or laid a bet on his own horse's head
Against his neighbour's bought at twice his cost,
Which fail'd not to repay his better skill;
Or on a harvest day bound in an hour
More sheaves of corn than any of his fellows,
Though ere so stark,[7] could do in twice the time;
Or won the bridal race with savoury broose[8]
And first kiss of the bonny bride, though all
The fleetest youngsters of the parish strove
In rivalry against him.

---

[6] **clown:** peasant, countryman.

[7] **stark:** strong, robust.

[8] **savoury:** pleasant. **broose:** a race by the young men present at country weddings in the north of Scotland, the course being from the bride's former home to the bridegroom's house.

But chiefly the good man, by his own fire,
Hath privilege of being listen'd to,
Nor dares a little prattling tongue presume
Though but in play, to break upon his story.
The children sit and listen with the rest;
And should the youngest raise its lisping voice,
The careful mother, ever on the watch,
And ever pleased with what her husband says,
Gives it a gentle tap upon the fingers,
Or stops its ill-timed prattle with a kiss.
The soldier next, but not unask'd, begins
His tale of war and blood. They gaze upon him,
And almost weep to see the man so poor,
So bent and feeble, helpless and forlorn,
Who has undaunted stood the battle's brunt
While roaring cannons shook the quaking earth,
And bullets hiss'd round his defenceless head.
Thus passes quickly on the evening hour,
Till sober folks must needs retire to rest;
Then all break up, and, by their several paths,
Hie homeward, with the evening pastime cheer'd.

But long accustom'd to observe the weather,
The farmer cannot lay him down in peace
Till he has look'd to mark what bodes the night.
He lifts the latch, and moves the heavy door,
Sees wreaths of snow heap'd up on every side,
And black and dismal all above his head.
Anon the northern blast begins to rise,
He hears its hollow growling from afar,
Which, gathering strength, rolls on with doubled might,
And raves and bellows o'er his head. The trees
Like pithless saplings bend. He shuts his door,
And, thankful for the roof that covers him,
Hies him to bed.

Address to the Muses

(1790)

Ye tuneful sisters of the lyre,
Who dreams and fantasies inspire,
Who over poesy preside,
And on a lofty hill abide
Above the ken of mortal sight,
Fain would I sing of you, could I address you right.

Thus known, your power of old was sung,
And temples with your praises rung;
And when the song of battle rose,
Or kindling wine or lover's woes,
The Poet's spirit inly burn'd,
And still to you his upcast eyes were turn'd.

The youth, all wrapp'd in vision bright,
Beheld your robes of flowing white;
And knew your forms benignly grand,—
An awful but a lovely band;
And felt your inspiration strong,
And warmly pour'd his rapid lay along.

The aged bard all heavenward glow'd,
And hail'd you daughters of a God.
Though by his dimmer eyes were seen
Nor graceful form nor heavenly mien,
Full well he felt that ye were near,
And heard you in the breeze that raised his hoary hair.

Ye lighten'd up the valley's bloom,
And gave the forest deeper gloom;
The mountain peak sublimer stood,
And grander rose the mighty flood;
For then Religion lent her aid,
And o'er the mind of man your sacred empire spread.

Though rolling ages now are past,
And altars low and temples waste;
Though rites and oracles are o'er,
And Gods and heroes rule no more,
Your fading honours still remain,
And still your votaries call, a long and motley train.

They seek you not on hill or plain,
Nor court you in the sacred fane;
Nor meet you in the mid-day dream,
Upon the bank of hallow'd stream,
Yet still for inspiration sue,
And still each lifts his fervent prayer to you.

He woos you not in woodland gloom,
But in the close and shelfed room,
And seeks you in the dusty nook,
And meets you in the letter'd book;
Full well he knows you by your names,
And still with poet's faith your presence claims.

Now youthful Poet, pen in hand,
All by the side of blotted stand,
In reverie deep which none may break,

Sits rubbing of his beardless cheek,
And well his inspiration knows,
E'en by the dewy drops that trickle o'er his nose.

The tuneful sage, of riper fame,
Perceives you not in heated frame;
But at conclusion of his verse,
Which still his muttering lips rehearse,
Oft waves his hand in grateful pride,
And owns the heavenly power that did his fancy
guide.

O lovely Sisters! is it true
That they are all inspired by you,
And write by inward magic charm'd,
And high enthusiasm warm'd?
We dare not question heavenly lays,
And well, I wot, they give you all the praise.

O lovely Sisters! well it shows
How wide and far your bounty flows.
Then why from me withhold your beams?
Unvisited of vision'd dreams,
Whene'er I am at heights sublime,
Still downward am I call'd to seek some stubborn
rhyme.

No hasty lightning breaks my gloom,
Nor flashing thoughts unsought for come,
Nor fancies wake in time of need:
I labour much with little speed,
And when my studied task is done,
Too well, alas! I mark it for my own.

Yet should you never smile on me,
And rugged still my verses be,
Unpleasing to the tuneful train,
Who only prize a flowing strain,
And still the learned scorn my lays,
I'll lift my heart to you and sing your praise.

Your varied ministry of grace,
Your honour'd names and godlike race,
Your sacred caves where fountains flow
They will rehearse, who better know;
I praise you not with Grecian lyre,
Nor hail you daughters of a heathen sire.

Ye are the spirits who preside
In earth and air and ocean wide,
In rushing flood and crackling fire,
In horror dread and tumult dire,
In stilly calm and stormy wind,
And rule the answering changes in the human mind!

High on the tempest-beaten hill,
Your misty shapes ye shift at will,
The wild fantastic clouds ye form;
Your voice is in the midnight storm;
While in the dark and lonely hour
Oft starts the boldest heart, and owns your secret
power.

When lightning ceases on the waste,
And when the battle's broil is past,
When scenes of strife and blood are o'er,
And groans of death are heard no more,
Ye then renew each sound and form,
Like after echoing of the o'erpassed storm.

The shining day and nightly shade,
The cheerful plain and sunny glade,
The homeward kine, the children's play,
The busy hamlet's closing day,
Give pleasure to the peasant's heart,
Who lacks the gift his feelings to impart.

Oft when the moon looks from on high,
And black around the shadows lie,
And bright the sparkling waters gleam,
And rushes rustle by the stream,
Voices and fairy forms are known
By simple folk who wander late alone.

Ye kindle up the inward glow,
Ye strengthen every outward show,
Ye overleap the strongest bar
And join what nature sunders far,
And visit oft, in fancies wild,
The breast of learned sage and simple child.

From him who wears a monarch's crown
To the unletter'd simple clown,
All in some fitful, lonely hour
Have felt, unsought, your secret power,
And loved your inward visions well;
You add but to the bard the art to tell.

Ye mighty spirits of the song,
To whom the poet's prayers belong,
My lowly bosom to inspire
And kindle with your sacred fire,
Your wild and dizzy heights to brave,
Is boon, alas! too great for me to crave.

But O, such sense of nature bring!
As they who feel, and never sing,
Wear on their hearts; it will avail
With simple words to tell my tale;
And still contented will I be,
Though greater inspiration never fall to me.

Thunder
(1790)

SPIRIT of strength! to whom in wrath 'tis given,
To mar the earth and shake its vasty dome,
Behold the sombre robes whose gathering folds
Thy secret majesty conceal. Their skirts
Spread on mid air move slow and silently,
O'er noon-day's beam thy sultry shroud is cast,
Advancing clouds from every point of heaven,
Like hosts of gathering foes in pitchy volumes,
Grandly dilated, clothe the fields of air,
And brood aloft o'er the empurpled earth.
Spirit of strength! it is thy awful hour;
The wind of every hill is laid to rest,
And far o'er sea and land deep silence reigns.

Wild creatures of the forest homeward hie,
And in their dens with fear unwonted cower;
Pride in the lordly palace is put down,
While in his humble cot the poor man sits
With all his family round him hush'd and still,
In awful expectation. On his way
The traveller stands aghast and looks to heaven.
On the horizon's verge thy lightning gleams,
And the first utterance of thy deep voice
Is heard in reverence and holy fear.

From nearer clouds bright burst more vivid gleams,
As instantly in closing darkness lost;
Pale sheeted flashes cross the wide expanse,
While over boggy moor, or swampy plain,
A streaming cataract of flame appears,
To meet a nether fire from earth cast up,
Commingling terribly; appalling gloom
Succeeds, and lo! the rifted centre pours
A general blaze, and from the war of clouds,
Red, writhing, falls the embodied bolt of heaven.
Then swells the rolling peal, full, deep'ning, grand,
And in its strength lifts the tremendous roar,
With mingled discord, rattling, hissing, growling:
Crashing like rocky fragments downward hurl'd,
Like the upbreaking of a ruin'd world,
In awful majesty the explosion bursts
Wide and astounding o'er the trembling land.
Mountain, and cliff, repeat the dread turmoil,
And all, to man's distinctive senses known,
Is lost in the immensity of sound.
Peal after peal succeeds with waning strength,
And hush'd and deep each solemn pause between.

Upon the lofty mountain's side
The kindled forest blazes wide;
Huge fragments of the rugged steep
Are tumbled to the lashing deep;
Firm rooted in his cloven rock,
Crashing falls the stubborn oak.
The lightning keen in wasteful ire
Darts fiercely on the pointed spire,
Rending in twain the iron-knit stone,
And stately towers to earth are thrown.
No human strength may brave the storm,
Nor shelter screen the shrinking form,
Nor castle wall its fury stay,
Nor massy gate impede its way:
It visits those of low estate,
It shakes the dwellings of the great,
It looks athwart the vaulted tomb,
And glares upon the prison's gloom.
Then dungeons black in unknown light
Flash hideous on the wretches' sight,
And strangely groans the downward cell,
Where silence deep is wont to dwell.

Now eyes, to heaven up-cast, adore,
Knees bend that never bent before,
The stoutest hearts begin to fail,
And many a manly face is pale;
Benumbing fear awhile up-binds
The palsied action of their minds,
Till waked to dreadful sense they lift their eyes,
And round the stricken corse shrill shrieks of horror rise.

Now rattling hailstones, bounding as they fall
To earth, spread motley winter o'er the plain;
Receding peals sound fainter on the ear,
And roll their distant grumbling far away:
The lightning doth in paler flashes gleam,
And through the rent cloud, silver'd with his rays,
The sun on all this wild affray looks down,
As, high enthroned above all mortal ken,
A higher Power beholds the strife of men.

from A SERIES OF PLAYS: IN WHICH IT IS ATTEMPTED TO DELINEATE THE STRONGER PASSIONS OF THE MIND, EACH PASSION BEING THE SUBJECT OF A TRAGEDY AND A COMEDY

(1798)

Introductory Discourse

It is natural for a writer, who is about to submit his works to the Publick, to feel a strong inclination, by some Preliminary Address, to conciliate the favour of his reader, and dispose him, if possible, to peruse them with a favourable eye. I am well aware, however, that his endeavours are generally fruitless: in his situation our hearts revolt from all appearance of confidence, and we consider his diffidence as hypocrisy. Our own word is frequently taken for what we say of ourselves, but very rarely for what we say of our works. Were these three plays, which this small volume contains, detached pieces only, and unconnected with others that do not yet appear, I should have suppressed this inclination altogether; and have allowed my reader to begin what is before him, and to form what opinion of it his taste or his humour might direct, without any previous trespass upon his time or his patience. But they are part of an extensive design: of one which, as far as my information goes, has nothing exactly similar to it in any language: of one which a whole life time will be limited enough to accomplish; and which has, therefore, a considerable chance of being cut short by that hand which nothing can resist.

Before I explain the plan of this work, I must make a demand upon the patience of my reader, whilst I endeavour to communicate to him those ideas regarding human nature, as they in some degree affect almost every species of moral writings, but particularly the Dramatic, that induced me to attempt it; and, as far as my judgment enabled me to apply them, has directed me in the execution of it.

From that strong sympathy which most creatures, but the human above all, feel for others of their kind, nothing has become so much an object of man's curiosity as man himself. We are all conscious of this within ourselves, and so constantly do we meet with it in others, that like every circumstance of continually repeated occurrence, it thereby escapes observation. Every person, who is not deficient in intellect, is more or less occupied in tracing, amongst the individuals he converses with, the varieties of understanding and temper which constitute the characters of men; and receives great pleasure from every stroke of nature that points out to him those varieties. This is, much more than we are aware of, the occupation of children, and of grown people also, whose penetration is but lightly esteemed; and that conversation which degenerates with them into trivial and mischievous tattling, takes its rise not unfrequently from the same source that supplies the rich vein of the satirist and the wit. That eagerness so universally shewn for the conversation of the latter, plainly enough indicates how many people have been occupied in the same way with themselves. Let any one, in a large company, do or say what is strongly expressive of his peculiar character, or of some passion or humour of the moment, and it will be detected by almost every person present. How often may we see a very stupid countenance animated with a smile, when the learned and the wise have betrayed some native feature of their own minds! and how often will this be the case when they have supposed it to be concealed under a very sufficient disguise! From this constant employment of their minds, most people, I believe, without being conscious of it, have stored up in idea the greater part of those strong marked varieties of human character, which may be said to divide it into classes; and in one of those classes they involuntarily place every new person they become acquainted with.

I will readily allow that the dress and the manners of man, rather than their characters and disposition are the subjects of our common conversation, and seem chiefly to occupy the multitude. But let it be remembered that it is much easier to express our observations upon these. It is easier to communicate to another how a man wears his wig and cane, what kind of house he inhabits, and what kind of table he keeps, than from what slight traits in his words and actions we have been led to conceive certain impressions of his character: traits that will often escape the memory, when the opinions that were founded upon them remain. Besides, in communicating our ideas of the characters of others, we are often called upon to support them with more expence of reasoning than we can well afford, but our observations on the dress and appearance of men, seldom involve us in such difficulties. For these, and other reasons too tedious to mention, the generality of people appear to us more trifling than they are: and I may venture to say that, but for this sympathetick curiosity towards others of our kind, which is so strongly implanted within us, the attention we pay to the dress and the manners of men would dwindle into an employment as insipid, as examining the varieties of plants and minerals, is to one who understands not natural history.

In our ordinary intercourse with society, this sympathetick propensity of our minds is exercised upon men, under the common occurrences of life, in which we have often observed them. Here vanity and weakness put themselves forward to view, more conspicuously than the virtues: here men encounter those smaller trials, from which they are not apt to come off victorious; and here, consequently, that which is marked with the whimsical and ludicrous will strike us most forcibly, and make the strongest impression on our memory. To this sympathetick propensity of our minds, so exercised, the genuine and pure comick of every composition, whether drama, fable, story, or satire is addressed.

If man is an object of so much attention to man, engaged in the ordinary occurrences of life, how much more does he excite his curiosity and interest when placed in extraordinary situations of difficulty and distress? It cannot be any pleasure we receive from the sufferings of a fellow-creature which attracts such multitudes of people to a publick execution, though it is the horrour we conceive for such a spectacle that keeps so many more away. To see a human being bearing himself up under such circumstances, or struggling with the terrible apprehensions which such a situation impresses, must be the powerful incentive, which makes us press forward to behold what we shrink from, and wait with trembling expectation for what we dread.[1] For though few at such a spectacle can get near enough to distinguish the expression of face, or the minuter parts of a criminal's behaviour, yet from a considerable distance will they eagerly mark whether he steps firmly; whether the motions of his body denote agitation or calmness; and if the wind does but ruffle his garment, they will, even from that change upon the outline of his distant figure, read some expression connected with his dreadful situation. Though there is a greater proportion of people in whom this strong curiosity will be overcome by other dispositions and motives; though there are many more who will stay away from such a sight than will go to it; yet there are very few who will not be eager to converse with a person who has beheld it; and to learn, very minutely, every circumstance connected with it, except the very act itself of inflicting death. To lift up the roof of his dungeon, like the *Diable boiteux*,[2] and look upon a criminal the night before he suffers, in his still hours of privacy, when all that disguise, which respect for the opinion of others, the strong motive by which even the lowest and wickedest of men still continue to be moved, would present an object to the mind of every person, not withheld from it by great timidity of character, more powerfully attractive than almost any other.

Revenge, no doubt, first began amongst the savages of America that dreadful custom of sacrificing their prisoners of war. But the perpetration of such hideous cruelty could never have become a permanent national custom, but for this universal desire in the human mind to behold man in every situation, putting forth his strength against the current of adversity, scorning all bodily anguish, or struggling with those feelings of nature, which, like a beating stream, will oft'times burst through the artificial barriers of pride. Before they begin those terrible rites they treat their prisoner kindly; and it cannot be supposed that men, alternately enemies and friends to so many neighbouring tribes, in manners and appearance like themselves, should so strongly be actuated by a spirit of publick revenge. This custom, therefore, must be considered as a grand and terrible game, which every tribe plays against another; where they try not the strength of the arm, the swiftness of the feet, nor the acuteness of the eye, but the fortitude of the soul. Considered in this light, the excess of cruelty exercised upon their miserable victim, in which every hand is described as ready to inflict its portion of pain, and every head ingenious in the contrivance of it, is no longer to be wondered at. To put into his measure of misery one agony less, would be, in some degree, betraying the honour of their nation: would be doing a species of injustice to every hero of their own tribe who had already sustained it, and to those who might be called upon to do so; amongst whom each of

[1] In confirmation of this opinion I may venture to say, that of the great numbers who go to see a publick execution, there are but very few who would not run away from, and avoid it, if they happened to meet with it unexpectedly. We find people stopping to look at a procession, or any other uncommon sight, they may have fallen in with accidentally, but almost never an execution. No one goes there who has not made up his mind for the occasion; which would not be the case, if any natural love of cruelty were the cause of such assemblies [J. B.].

[2] **Diable boiteux:** French for jack-in-the-box.

these savage tormentors has his chance of being one, and has prepared himself for it from his childhood. Nay, it would be a species of injustice to the haughty victim himself, who would scorn to purchase his place amongst the heroes of his nation, at an easier price than his undaunted predecessors.

Amongst the many trials to which the human mind is subjected, that of holding intercourse, real or imaginary, with the world of spirits: of finding itself alone with a being terrifick and awful, whose nature and power are unknown, has been justly considered as one of the most severe. The workings of nature in this situation, we all know, have ever been the object of our most eager enquiry. No man wishes to see the Ghost himself, which would certainly procure him the best information on the subject, but every man wishes to see one who believes that he sees it, in all the agitation and wildness of that species of terrour. To gratify this curiosity how many people have dressed up hideous apparitions to frighten the timid and superstitious! and have done it at the risk of destroying their happiness or understanding for ever. For the instances of intellect being destroyed by this kind of trial are more numerous, perhaps, in proportion to the few who have undergone it than by any other.

How sensible are we of this strong propensity within us, when we behold any person under the pressure of great and uncommon calamity! Delicacy and respect for the afflicted will, indeed, make us turn ourselves aside from observing him, and cast down our eyes in his presence; but the first glance we direct to him will involuntarily be one of the keenest observation, how hastily soever it may be checked; and often will a returning look of enquiry mix itself by stealth with our sympathy and reserve.

But it is not in situations of difficulty and distress alone, that man becomes the object of this sympathetick curiosity; he is no less so when the evil he contends with arises in his own breast, and no outward circumstance connected with him either awakens our attention or our pity. What human creature is there, who can behold a being like himself under the violent agitation of those passions which all have, in some degree, experienced, without feeling himself most powerfully excited by the sight? I say, all have experienced; for the bravest man on earth knows what fear is as well as the coward; and will not refuse to be interested for one under the dominion of this passion, provided there be nothing in the circumstances attending it to create contempt. Anger is a passion that attracts less sympathy than any other, yet the unpleasing and distorted features of an angry man will be more eagerly gazed upon, by those who are no wise concerned with his fury or the objects of it, than the most amiable placid countenance in the world. Every eye is directed to him; every voice hushed to silence in his presence; even children will leave off their gambols as he passes, and gaze after him more eagerly than the gaudiest equipage. The wild tossings of despair; the gnashing of hatred and revenge; the yearnings of affection, and the softened mien of love; all that language of the agitated soul, which every age and nation understands, is never addressed to the dull nor inattentive.

It is not merely under the violent agitations of passion, that man so rouses and interests us; even the smallest indications of an unquiet mind, the restless eye, the muttering lip, the half-checked exclamation, and the hasty start, will set our attention as anxiously upon the watch, as the first distant flashes of a gathering storm. When some great explosion of passion bursts forth, and some consequent catastrophe happens, if we are at all acquainted with the unhappy perpetrator, how minutely will we endeavour to remember every circumstance of his past behaviour! and with what avidity will we seize upon every recollected word or gesture, that is in the smallest degree indicative of the supposed state of his mind, at the time when they took place. If we are not acquainted with him, how eagerly will we listen to similar recollections from another! Let us understand, from observation or report, that any person harbours in his breast, concealed from the world's eye, some powerful rankling passion of what kind soever it may be, we will observe every word, every motion, every look, even the distant gait of such a man, with a constancy and attention bestowed upon no other. Nay, should we meet him unexpectedly on our way, a feeling will pass across our minds as though we found ourselves in the neighbourhood of some secret and fearful thing. If invisible, would we not follow him into his lonely haunts, into his closet, into the midnight silence of his chamber? There is, perhaps, no employment which the human mind will with so much avidity pursue, as the discovery of concealed passion, as the tracing the varieties and progress of a perturbed soul.

It is to this sympathetick curiosity of our nature, exercised upon mankind in great and trying occasions, and under the influence of the stronger passions, when the grand, the generous, the terrible attract our attention far more than the base and depraved, that the high and powerfully tragick, of every composition, is addressed.

This propensity is universal. Children begin to shew it very early; it enters into many of their amusements, and that part of them too, for which they shew the keenest relish. It tempts them many times, as well as the mature in years, to be guilty of tricks, vexations, and cruelty; yet God Almighty has implanted it within us, as well as all our other propensities and passions, for wise and good purposes. It is our best and most powerful instructor. From it we are taught the proprieties and decencies of ordinary life, and are prepared for distressing and difficult situations. In examining others we know ourselves. With limbs untorn, with head unsmitten, with senses unimpaired by despair, we know what we ourselves might have been on the rack, on the scaffold, and in the most afflicting circumstances of distress. Unless when accompanied with passions of the dark and malevolent kind, we cannot well exercise this disposition without becoming more just, more merciful, more compassionate; and as the dark and malevolent passions are not the predominant inmates of the human breast, it hath produced more deeds—O many more! of kindness than of cruelty. It holds up for our example a standard of excellence, which, without its assistance, our inward consciousness of what is right and becoming might never have dictated. It teaches us, also, to respect ourselves, and our kind; for it is a poor mind, indeed, that from this employment of its faculties, learns not to dwell upon the noble view of human nature rather than the mean.

Universal, however, as this disposition undoubtedly is, with the generality of mankind it occupies itself in a passing and superficial way. Though a native trait of character or of passion is obvious to them as well as to the sage, yet to their minds it is but the visitor of a moment; they look upon it singly and unconnected: and though this disposition, even so exercised, brings instruction as well as amusement, it is chiefly by storing up in their minds those ideas to which the instructions of others refer, that it can be eminently useful. Those who reflect and reason upon what human nature holds out to their observation, are comparatively but few. No stroke of nature which engages their attention stands insulated and alone. Each presents itself to them with many varied connections; and they comprehend not merely the immediate feeling which gave rise to it, but the relation of that feeling to others which are concealed. We wonder at the changes and caprices of men; they see in them nothing but what is natural and accountable. We stare upon some dark catastrophe of passion, as the Indians did upon an eclipse of the moon; they, conceiving the track of ideas through which the impassioned mind has passed, regard it like the philosopher who foretold the phenomenon. Knowing what situation of life he is about to be thrown into, they perceive in the man, who, like Hazael,[3] says, "is thy servant a dog that he should do this thing?" the foul and ferocious murderer. A man of this contemplative character partakes, in some degree, of the entertainment of the Gods, who were supposed to look down upon this world and the inhabitants of it, as we do upon a theatrical exhibition; and if he is of a benevolent disposition, a good man struggling with, and triumphing over adversity, will be to him, also, the most delightful spectacle. But though this eagerness to observe their fellow-creatures in every situation, leads not the generality of mankind to reason and reflect; and those strokes of nature which they are so ready to remark, stand single and unconnected in their minds, yet they may be easily induced to do both: and there is no mode of instruction which they will so eagerly pursue, as that which lays open before them, in a more enlarged and connected view, than their individual observations are capable of supplying, the varieties of the human mind. Above all, to be well exercised in this study will fit a man more particularly for the most important situations of life. He will prove for it the better Judge, the better Magistrate, the better Advocate; and as a ruler or conductor of other men, under every occurring circumstance, he will find himself the better enabled to fulfil his duty, and accomplish his designs. He will perceive the natural effect of every order that he issues upon the minds of his soldiers, his subjects, or his followers; and he will deal to others judgment tempered with mercy; that is to say truly just; for justice appears to us severe only when it is imperfect.

In proportion as moral writers of every class have exercised within themselves this sympathetick propensity of our nature, and have attended to it in others, their works have been interesting and instructive. They have struck the imagination more forcibly, convinced the understanding more clearly, and more lastingly impressed the memory. If unseasoned with any reference to this, the fairy bowers of the poet, with all his gay images of delight, will be admired and forgotten; the important relations of the historian, and even the reasonings of the philosopher will make a less permanent impression.

The historian points back to the men of other ages, and from the gradually clearing mist in which they are first discovered, like the mountains of a far distant land,

[3] **Hazael:** biblical King of Damascus (c. 841–820 BC). The quotation is from 2 Kings 8:13.

the generations of the world are displayed to our mind's eye in grand and regular procession. But the transactions of men become interesting to us only as we are made acquainted with men themselves. Great and bloody battles are to us battles fought in the moon, if it is not impressed upon our minds, by some circumstances attending them, that men subject to like weaknesses and passions with ourselves, were the combatants.[4] The establishments of policy make little impression upon us, if we are left ignorant of the beings whom they affected. Even a very masterly drawn character will but slightly imprint upon our memory the great man it belongs to, if, in the account we receive of his life, those lesser circumstances are entirely neglected, which do best of all point out to us the dispositions and tempers of men. Some slight circumstance characteristick of the particular turn of a man's mind, which at first sight seems but little connected with the great events of his life, will often explain some of those events more clearly to our understanding, than the minute details of ostensible policy. A judicious selection of those circumstances which characterize the spirit of an associated mob, paltry and ludicrous as some of them may appear, will oftentimes convey to our minds a clearer idea why certain laws and privileges were demanded and agreed to, than a methodical explanation of their causes. A historian who has examined human nature himself, and likewise attends to the pleasure which developing and tracing it, does ever convey to others, will employ our understanding as well as our memory with his pages; and if this is not done, he will impose upon the latter a very difficult task, in retaining what she is concerned with alone.

In argumentative and philosophical writings, the effect which the author's reasoning produces on our minds depends not entirely on the justness of it. The images and examples that he calls to his aid, to explain and illustrate his meaning, will very much affect the attention we are able to bestow upon it, and consequently the quickness with which we shall apprehend, and the force with which it will impress us. These are selected from animated and unanimated nature, from the habits, manners, and characters of men; and though that image or example, whatever it may be in itself, which brings out his meaning most clearly, ought to be preferred before every other, yet of two equal in this respect, that which is drawn from the most interesting source will please us the most at the time, and most lastingly take hold of our minds. An argument supported with vivid and interesting illustration, will long be remembered when many equally important and clear are forgotten; and a work where many such occur will be held in higher estimation by the generality of men, than one its superior, perhaps, in acuteness, perspicuity, and good sense.

Our desire to know what men are in the closet as well as the field, by the blazing hearth, and at the social board, as well as in the council and the throne, is very imperfectly gratified by real history; romance writers, therefore, stepped boldly forth to supply the deficiency; and tale writers, and novel writers, of many descriptions, followed after. If they have not been very skilful in their delineations of nature; if they have represented men and women speaking and acting as men and women never did speak or act; if they have caricatured both our virtues and our vices; if they have given us such pure and unmixed, or such heterogeneous combinations of character as real life never presented, and yet have pleased and interested us, let it not be imputed to the dulness of man in discerning what is genuinely natural in himself. There are many inclinations belonging to us, besides this great master-propensity of which I am treating. Our love of the grand, the beautiful, the novel, and above all of the marvellous,

[4] Let two great battles be described to us with all the force and clearness of the most able pen. In the first let the most admirable exertions of military skill in the General, and the most unshaken courage in the soldiers, gain over an equal or superiour number of brave opponents a compleat and glorious victory. In the second let the General be less scientifick, and the soldiers less dauntless. Let them go into the field for a cause that is dear to them, and fight with the ardour which such motives inspire; till discouraged with the many deaths around them, and the renovated pressure of the foe, some unlooked-for circumstance, trifling in itself, strikes their imagination at once; they are visited with the terrours of nature; their national pride, the honour of soldiership is forgotten; they fly like a fearful flock. Let some beloved chief then step forth, and call upon them by the love of their country, by the memory of their valiant fathers, by every thing that kindles in the bosom of man the high and generous passions: they stop; they gather round him; and goaded by shame and indignation, returning again to the charge, with the fury of wild beasts rather than the courage of soldiers, bear down every thing before them. Which of these two battles will interest us the most? and which of them shall we remember the longest? The one will stand forth in the imagination of the reader like a rock of the desert, which points out to the far-removed traveller the country through which he has passed, when its lesser objects are obscured in the distance; whilst the other leaves no traces behind it, but in the minds of the scientifick in war [J. B.].

is very strong; and if we are richly fed with what we have a good relish for, we may be weaned to forget our native and favourite aliment. Yet we can never so far forget it, but that we will cling to, and acknowledge it again, whenever it is presented before us. In a work abounding with the marvellous and unnatural, if the author has any how stumbled upon an unsophisticated genuine stroke of nature, we will immediately perceive and be delighted with it, though we are foolish enough to admire at the same time, all the nonsense with which it is surrounded. After all the wonderful incidents, dark mysteries, and secrets revealed, which eventful novel so liberally presents to us; after the beautiful fairy ground, and even the grand and sublime scenes of nature with which descriptive novel so often enchants us: those works which most strongly characterize human nature in the middling and lower classes of society, where it is to be discovered by stronger and more unequivocal marks, will ever be the most popular. For though great pains have been taken in our higher sentimental novels to interest us in the delicacies, embarrassments, and artificial distresses of the more refined part of society, they have never been able to cope in the publick opinion with these. The one is a dressed and beautiful pleasure-ground, in which we are enchanted for a while, amongst the delicate and unknown plants of artful cultivation; the other is a rough forest of our native land; the oak, the elm, the hazle, and the bramble are there; and amidst the endless varieties of its paths we can wander for ever. Into whatever scenes the novelist may conduct us, what objects soever he may present to our view, still is our attention most sensibly awake to every touch faithful to nature; still are we upon the watch for every thing that speaks to us of ourselves.

The fair field of what is properly called poetry, is enriched with so many beauties, that in it we are often tempted to forget what we really are, and what kind of beings we belong to. Who in the enchanted regions of simile, metaphor, allegory and description, can remember the plain order of things in this every-day world? From heroes whose majestick forms rise like a lofty tower, whose eyes are lightening, whose arms are irresistible, whose course is like the storms of heaven, bold and exalted sentiments we will readily receive; and will not examine them very accurately by that rule of nature which our own breast prescribes to us. A shepherd whose sheep, with fleeces of the purest snow, browze the flowery herbage of the most beautiful vallies; whose flute is ever melodious, and whose shepherdess is ever crowned with roses; whose every care is love, will not be called very strictly to account for the loftiness and refinement of his thoughts. The fair Nymph, who sighs out her sorrows to the conscious and compassionate wilds; whose eyes gleam like the bright drops of heaven; whose loose tresses stream to the breeze, may say what she pleases with impunity. I will venture, however, to say, that amidst all this decoration and ornament, all this loftiness and refinement, let one simple trait of the human heart, one expression of passion genuine and true to nature, be introduced, and it will stand forth alone in the boldness of reality, whilst the false and unnatural around it, fades away upon every side, like the rising exhalations of the morning. With admiration, and often with enthusiasm we proceed on our way through the grand and the beautiful images, raised to our imagination by the lofty Epic muse; but what even here are those things that strike upon the heart; that we feel and remember? Neither the descriptions of war, the sound of the trumpet, the clanging of arms, the combat of heroes, nor the death of the mighty, will interest our minds like the fall of the feeble stranger, who simply expresses the anguish of his soul, at the thoughts of that far-distant home which he must never return to again, and closes his eyes amongst the ignoble and forgotten; like the timid stripling goaded by the shame of reproach, who urges his trembling steps to the fight, and falls like a tender flower before the first blast of winter. How often will some simple picture of this kind be all that remains upon our minds of the terrifick and magnificent battle, whose description we have read with admiration! How comes it that we relish so much the episodes of an heroick poem? It cannot merely be that we are pleased with a resting-place, where we enjoy the variety of contrast; for were the poem of the simple and familiar kind, and an episode after the heroick style introduced into it, ninety readers out of an hundred would pass over it altogether. Is it not that we meet such a story, so situated, with a kind of sympathetick good will, as in passing through a country of castles and of palaces, we should pop unawares upon some humble cottage, resembling the dwellings of our own native land, and gaze upon it with affection. The highest pleasures we receive from poetry, as well as from the real objects which surround us in the world, are derived from the sympathetick interest we all take in beings like ourselves; and I will even venture to say, that were the grandest scenes which can enter into the imagination of man, presented to our view, and all reference to man completely shut out from our thoughts, the objects that composed it would convey to our minds little better than dry ideas of magnitude, colour, and form; and the remembrance of them would rest upon our minds like the measurement and distances of the planets.

If the study of human nature then, is so useful to the poet, the novelist, the historian, and the philosopher, of how much greater importance must it be to the dramatick writer? To them it is a powerful auxiliary, to him it is the centre and strength of the battle. If characteristick views of human nature enliven not their pages, there are many excellencies with which they can, in some degree, make up for the deficiency, it is what we receive from them with pleasure rather than demand. But in his works no richness of invention, harmony of language, nor grandeur of sentiment will supply the place of faithfully delineated nature. The poet and the novelist may represent to you their great characters from the cradle to the tomb. They may represent them in any mood or temper, and under the influence of any passion which they see proper, without being obliged to put words into their mouths, those great betrayers of the feigned and adopted. They may relate every circumstance however trifling and minute, that serves to develope their tempers and dispositions. They tell us what kind of people they intend their men and women to be, and as such we receive them. If they are to move us with any scene of distress, every circumstance regarding the parties concerned in it, how they looked, how they moved, how they sighed, how the tears gushed from their eyes, how the very light and shadow fell upon them, is carefully described, and the few things that are given them to say along with all this assistance, must be very unnatural indeed if we refuse to sympathize with them. But the characters of the drama must speak directly for themselves. Under the influence of every passion, humour, and impression; in the artificial veilings of hypocrisy and ceremony, in the openness of freedom and confidence, and in the lonely hour of meditation they speak. He who made us hath placed within our breast a judge that judges instantaneously of every thing they say. We expect to find them creatures like ourselves; and if they are untrue to nature, we feel that we are imposed upon; as though the poet had introduced to us for brethren, creatures of a different race, beings of another world.

As in other works deficiency in characteristick truth may be compensated by excellencies of a different kind, in the drama characteristick truth will compensate every other defect. Nay, it will do what appears a contradiction; one strong genuine stroke of nature will cover a multitude of sins even against nature herself. When we meet in some scene of a good play a very fine stroke of this kind, we are apt to become so intoxicated with it, and so perfectly convinced of the author's great knowledge of the human heart, that we are unwilling to suppose that the whole of it has not been suggested by the same penetrating spirit. Many well-meaning enthusiastick criticks have given themselves a great deal of trouble in this way; and have shut their eyes most ingeniously against the fair light of nature for the very love of it. They have converted, in their great zeal, sentiments palpably false, both in regard to the character and situation of the persons who utter them, sentiments which a child or a clown would detect, into the most skilful depictments of the heart. I can think of no stronger instance to shew how powerfully this love of nature dwells within us.[5]

Formed as we are with these sympathetick propensities in regard to our own species, it is not at all wonderful that theatrical exhibition has become the grand and favourite amusement of every nation into which it has been introduced. Savages will, in the wild contortions of a dance, shape out some rude story expressive of character or passion, and such a dance will give more delight to his companions than the most artful exertions of agility. Children in their gambols will make out a mimick representation of the manners, characters, and passions of grown men and women, and such a pastime will animate and delight them much more than a treat of the daintiest sweetmeats, or the handling of the gaudiest toys. Eagerly as it is enjoyed by the rude and the young, to the polished and the ripe in years it is still the most interesting amusement. Our taste for it is durable as it is universal. Independently of those circumstances which first introduced it, the world would not have long been without it. The progress of society would soon have brought it forth; and men in the whimsical decorations of fancy would have displayed the characters and actions of their heroes, the folly

[5] It appears to me a very strong testimony of the excellence of our great national Dramatist, that so many people have been employed in finding out obscure and refined beauties, in what appear to ordinary observation his very defects. Men, it may be said, do so merely to shew their own superior penetration and ingenuity. But granting this; what could make other men listen to them, and listen so greedily too, if it were not that they have received from the works of Shakspeare, pleasure far beyond what the most perfect poetical compositions of a different character can afford [J. B.].

and absurdity of their fellow-citizens, had no Priests of Bacchus[6] ever existed.[7]

In whatever age or country the Drama might have taken its rise, tragedy would have been the first-born of its children. For every nation has its great men, and its great events upon record; and to represent their own forefathers struggling with those difficulties, and braving those dangers, of which they have heard with admiration, and the effects of which they still, perhaps, experience, would certainly have been the most animating subject for the poet, and the most interesting for his audience, even independently of the natural inclination we all so universally shew for scenes of horrour and distress, of passion and heroick exertion. Tragedy would have been the first child of the Drama, for the same reasons that have made heroick ballad, with all its battles, murders, and disasters, the earliest poetical compositions of every country.

We behold heroes and great men at a distance, unmarked by those small but distinguishing features of the mind, which give a certain individuality to such an infinite variety of similar beings, in the near and familiar intercourse of life. They appear to us from this view like distant mountains, whose dark outlines we trace in the clear horizon, but the varieties of whose roughened sides, shaded with heath and brushwood, and seamed with many a cleft, we perceive not. When accidental anecdote reveals to us any weakness or peculiarity belonging to them, we start upon it like a discovery. They are made known to us in history only, by the great events they are connected with, and the part they have taken in extraordinary or important transactions. Even in poetry and romance, with the exception of some love story interwoven with the main events of their lives, they are seldom more intimately made known to us. To Tragedy it belongs to lead them forward to our nearer regard, in all the distinguishing varieties which nearer inspection discovers; with the passions, the humours, the weaknesses, the prejudices of men. It is for her to present to us the great and magnanimous hero, who appears to our distant view as a superior being, as a God, softened down with those smaller frailties and imperfections which enable us to glory in, and claim kindred to his virtues. It is for her to exhibit to us the daring and ambitious man, planning his dark designs, and executing his bloody purposes, mark'd with those appropriate characteristicks, which distinguish him as an individual of that class; and agitated with those varied passions, which disturb the mind of man when he is engaged in the commission of such deeds. It is for her to point out to us the brave and impetuous warrior struck with those visitations of nature, which, in certain situations, will unnerve the strongest arm, and make the boldest heart tremble. It is for her to shew the tender, gentle, and unassuming mind animated with that fire which, by the provocation of circumstances, will give to the kindest

---

[6] The classical deity Bacchus, god of wine and mirth, traditionally presided over drama. **Priests of Bacchus:** playwrights.

[7] Though the progress of society would have given us the Drama, independently of the particular cause of its first commencement, the peculiar circumstances connected with its origin, have had considerable influence upon its character and style, in the ages through which it has passed even to our days, and still will continue to affect it. Homer had long preceded the dramatick poets of Greece; poetry was in a high state of cultivation when they began to write; and their style, the construction of their pieces, and the characters of their heroes were different from what they would have been, had theatrical exhibitions been the invention of an earlier age or a ruder people. Their works were represented to an audience, already accustomed to hear long poems rehearsed at their publick games, and the feasts of their gods. A play, with the principal characters of which they were previously acquainted; in which their great men and heroes, in the most beautiful language, complained of their rigorous fate, but piously submitted to the will of the Gods; in which sympathy was chiefly excited by tender and affecting sentiments; in which strong bursts of passion were few; and in which whole scenes frequently passed, without giving the actors any thing to do but to speak, was not too insipid for them. Had the Drama been the invention of a less cultivated nation, more of action and of passion would have been introduced into it. It would have been more irregular, more imperfect, more varied, more interesting. From poor beginnings it would have advanced in a progressive state; and succeeding poets, not having those polished and admired originals to look back upon, would have presented their respective contemporaries with the produce of a free and unbridled imagination. A different class of poets would most likely have been called into existence. The latent powers of men are called forth by contemplating those works in which they find any thing congenial to their own peculiar talents; and if the field, wherein they could have worked, is already enriched with a produce unsuited to their cultivation, they think not of entering it at all. Men, therefore, whose natural turn of mind led them to labour, to reason, to refine and exalt, have caught their animation from the beauties of the Grecian Drama, and they who, perhaps, ought only to have been our Criticks have become our Poets. I mean not, however, in any degree to depreciate the works of the ancients; a great deal we have gained by those beautiful compositions; and what we have lost by them it is impossible to compute. Very strong genius will sometimes break through every disadvantage of circumstances: Shakspeare has arisen in this country, and we ought not to complain [J. B.].

heart the ferocity and keenness of a tiger. It is for her to present to us the great and striking characters that are to be found amongst men, in a way which the poet, the novelist, and the historian can but imperfectly attempt. But above all, to her, and to her only it belongs to unveil to us the human mind under the dominion of those strong and fixed passions, which, seemingly unprovoked by outward circumstances, will from small beginnings brood within the breast, till all the better dispositions, all the fair gifts of nature are borne down before them. Those passions which conceal themselves from the observation of men; which cannot unbosom themselves even to the dearest friend; and can, often times, only give their fulness vent in the lonely desert, or in the darkness of midnight. For who hath followed the great man into his secret closet, or stood by the side of his nightly couch, and heard those exclamations of the soul which heaven alone may hear, that the historian should be able to inform us? and what form of story, what mode of rehearsed speech will communicate to us those feelings, whose irregular bursts, abrupt transitions, sudden pauses, and half-uttered suggestions, scorn all harmony of measured verse, all method and order of relation?

On the first part of this task her Bards have eagerly exerted their abilities: and some amongst them, taught by strong original genius to deal immediately with human nature and their own hearts, have laboured in it successfully. But in presenting to us those views of great characters, and of the human mind in difficult and trying situations which peculiarly belong to Tragedy, the far greater proportion, even of those who may be considered as respectable dramatick poets, have very much failed. From the beauty of those original dramas to which they have ever looked back with admiration, they have been tempted to prefer the embellishments of poetry to faithfully delineated nature. They have been more occupied in considering the works of the great Dramatists who have gone before them, and the effects produced by their writings, than the varieties of human character which first furnished materials for those works, or those principles in the mind of man by means of which such effects were produced. Neglecting the boundless variety of nature, certain strong outlines of character, certain bold features of passion, certain grand vicissitudes, and striking dramatick situations have been repeated from one generation to another; whilst a pompous and solemn gravity, which they have supposed to be necessary for the dignity of tragedy, has excluded almost entirely from their works those smaller touches of nature, which so well develope the mind; and by showing men in their hours of state and exertion only, they have consequently shewn them imperfectly. Thus, great and magnanimous heroes, who bear with majestick equanimity every vicissitude of fortune; who in every temptation and trial stand forth in unshaken virtue, like a rock buffeted by the waves; who encompast with the most terrible evils, in calm possession of their souls, reason upon the difficulties of their state; and, even upon the brink of destruction, pronounce long eulogiums on virtue, in the most eloquent and beautiful language, have been held forth to our view as objects of imitation and interest; as though they had entirely forgotten that it is only from creatures like ourselves that we feel, and therefore, only from creatures like ourselves that we receive the instruction of example.[8] Thus, passionate and impetuous warriors, who are proud, irritable, and vindictive, but generous, daring, and disinterested; setting their lives at a pin's fee for the good of others, but incapable of curbing their own humour of a moment to gain the whole world for themselves; who will pluck the orbs of heaven from their places, and crush the whole universe in one grasp, are called forth to kindle in our souls the generous contempt of every thing abject and base; but with an effect proportionably feeble, as the hero is made to exceed in courage and fire what the standard of humanity will agree to.[9] Thus, tender and pathetick lovers, full of the

[8] To a being perfectly free from all human infirmity our sympathy refuses to extend. Our Saviour himself, whose character is so beautiful, and so harmoniously consistent; in whom, with outward proofs of his mission less strong than those that are offered to us, I should still be compelled to believe, from being utterly unable to conceive how the idea of such a character could enter into the imagination of man, never touches the heart more nearly than when he says, "Father, let this cup pass from me." Had he been represented to us in all the unshaken strength of these tragick heroes, his disciples would have made fewer converts, and his precepts would have been listened to coldly. Plays in which heroes of this kind are held forth, and whose aim is, indeed, honourable and praise-worthy, have been admired by the cultivated and refined, but the tears of the simple, the applauses of the young and untaught have been wanting [J. B.].

[9] In all burlesque imitations of tragedy, those plays in which this hero is pre-eminent, are always exposed to bear the great brunt of the ridicule; which proves how popular they have been, and how many poets, and good ones too, have been employed upon them. That they have been so popular, however, is not owing to the intrinsick merit of the characters they represent, but their opposition to those mean and contemptible qualities belonging to human nature, of which we are most ashamed.

most gentle affections, the most amiable dispositions, and the most exquisite feelings; who present their defenceless bosoms to the storms of this rude world in all the graceful weakness of sensibility, are made to sigh out their sorrows in one unvaried strain of studied pathos, whilst this constant demand upon our feelings makes us absolutely incapable of answering it.[10] Thus, also, tyrants are represented as monsters of cruelty, unmixed with any feelings of humanity; and villains as delighting in all manner of treachery and deceit, and acting upon many occasions for the very love of villainy itself; though the perfectly wicked are as ill fitted for the purposes of warning, as the perfectly virtuous are for those of example.[11] This spirit of imitation, and attention to effect, has likewise confined them very much in their choice of situations and events to bring their great characters into action; rebellions, conspiracies, contentions for empire, and rivalships in love have alone been thought worthy of trying those heroes; and palaces and dungeons the only places magnificent or solemn enough for them to appear in.

They have, indeed, from this regard to the works of preceding authors, and great attention to the beauties of composition, and to dignity of design, enriched their plays with much striking, and sometimes sublime imagery, lofty thoughts, and virtuous sentiments; but in striving so eagerly to excell in those things that belong to tragedy in common with many other compositions, they have very much neglected those that are peculiarly her own. As far as they have been led aside from the first labours of a tragick poet by a desire to communicate more perfect moral instruction, their motive has been respectable, and they merit our esteem. But this praise-worthy end has been injured instead of promoted by their mode of pursuing it. Every species of moral writing has its own way of conveying instruction, which it can never, but with disadvantage, exchange for any other. The Drama improves us by the knowledge we acquire of our own minds, from the natural desire we have to look into the thoughts, and observe the behaviour of others. Tragedy brings to our view men placed in those elevated situations, exposed to those great trials, and engaged in those extraordinary transactions, in which few of us are called upon to act. As examples applicable to ourselves, therefore, they can but feebly effect us; it is only from the enlargement of our ideas in regard to human nature, from that admiration of virtue, and abhorrence of vice which they excite, that we can expect to be improved by them. But if they are not represented to us as real and natural characters, the lessons we are taught from their conduct and their sentiments will be no more to us than those which we receive from the pages of the poet or the moralist.

Besides, there is something in the human mind, independently of its love of applause, which inclines it to boast. This is ever the attendant of that elasticity of soul, which makes us bound up from the touch of oppression; and if there is nothing in the accompanying circumstances to create disgust, or suggest suspicions of their sincerity, (as in real life is commonly the case,) we are very apt to be carried along with the boasting of others. Let us in good earnest believe that a man is capable of achieving all that human courage can achieve, and we will suffer him to talk of impossibilities. Amidst all their pomp of words, therefore, our admiration of such heroes is readily excited, (for the understanding is more easily deceived than the heart,) but how stands our sympathy affected? As no caution nor foresight, on their own account, is ever suffered to occupy the thoughts of such bold disinterested beings, we are the more inclined to care for them, and take an interest in their fortune through the course of the play: yet, as their souls are unappalled by any thing, as pain and death are not at all regarded by them; and as we have seen them very ready to plunge their own swords into their own bosoms, on no very weighty occasion, perhaps, their death distresses us but little, and they commonly fall unwept [J. B.].

[10] Were it not, that in tragedies where these heroes preside, the same soft tones of sorrow are so often repeated in our ears, till we are perfectly tired of it, they are more fitted to interest us than any other: both because in seeing them, we own the ties of kindred between ourselves and the frail mortals we lament; and sympathize with the weakness of mortality unmixed with any thing to degrade or disgust; and also, because the misfortunes, which form the story of the play, are frequently of the more familiar and domestick kind. A king driven from his throne, will not move our sympathy so strongly, as a private man torn from the bosom of his family [J. B.].

[11] I have said nothing here in regard to female character, though in many tragedies it is brought forward as the principal one of the piece, because what I have said of the above characters is likewise applicable to it. I believe there is no man that ever lived, who has behaved in a certain manner, on a certain occasion, who has not had amongst women some corresponding spirit, who on the like occasion, and every way similarly circumstanced, would have behaved in the like manner. With some degree of softening and refinement, each class of the tragick heroes I have mentioned has its corresponding one amongst the heroines. The tender and pathetick no doubt has the most numerous, but the great and magnanimous is not without it, and the passionate and impetuous boasts of one by no means inconsiderable in numbers, and drawn sometimes to the full as passionate and impetuous as itself [J. B.].

But the last part of the task which I have mentioned as peculiarly belonging to tragedy, unveiling the human mind under the dominion of those strong and fixed passions, which seemingly unprovoked by outward circumstances, will from small beginnings brood within the breast, till all the better dispositions, all the fair gifts of nature are borne down before them, her poets in general have entirely neglected, and even her first and greatest have but imperfectly attempted. They have made use of the passions to mark their several characters, and animate their scenes, rather than to open to our view the nature and portraitures of those great disturbers of the human breast, with whom we are all, more or less, called upon to contend. With their strong and obvious features, therefore, they have been presented to us, stripped almost entirely of those less obtrusive, but not less discriminating traits, which mark them in their actual operation. To trace them in their rise and progress in the heart, seems but rarely to have been the object of any dramatist. We commonly find the characters of a tragedy affected by the passions in a transient, loose, unconnected manner; or if they are represented as under the permanent influence of the more powerful ones, they are generally introduced to our notice in the very height of their fury, when all that timidity, irresolution, distrust, and a thousand delicate traits, which make the infancy of every great passion more interesting, perhaps, than its full-blown strength, are fled. The impassioned character is generally brought into view under those irresistible attacks of their power, which it is impossible to repell; whilst those gradual steps that led him into this state, in some of which a stand might have been made against the foe, are left entirely in the shade. These passions that may be suddenly excited, and are of short duration, as anger, fear, and oftentimes jealousy, may in this manner be fully represented; but those great masters of the soul, ambition, hatred, love, every passion that is permanent in its nature, and varied in progress, if represented to us but in one stage of its course, is represented imperfectly. It is a characteristick of the more powerful passions that they will encrease and nourish themselves on very slender aliment; it is from within that they are chiefly supplied with what they feed on; and it is in contending with opposite passions and affections of the mind that we least discover their strength, not with events. But in tragedy it is events more frequently than opposite affections which are opposed to them; and those often of such force and magnitude that the passions themselves are almost obscured by the splendour and importance of the transactions to which they are attached. But besides being thus confined and mutilated, the passions have been, in the greater part of our tragedies, deprived of the very power of making themselves known. Bold and figurative language belongs peculiarly to them. Poets, admiring those bold expressions which a mind, labouring with ideas too strong to be conveyed in the ordinary forms of speech, wildly throws out, taking earth, sea, and sky, every thing great and terrible in nature to image forth the violence of its feelings, borrowed them gladly, to adorn the calm sentiments of their premeditated song. It has therefore been thought that the less animated parts of tragedy might be so embellished and enriched. In doing this, however, the passions have been robbed of their native prerogative; and in adorning with their strong figures and lofty expressions the calm speeches of the unruffled, it is found that, when they are called upon to raise their voice, the power of distinguishing themselves has been taken away. This is an injury by no means compensated, but very greatly aggravated by embellishing, in return, the speeches of passion with the ingenious conceits, and compleat similies of premeditated thought.[12] There are many other things regarding the manner in which dramatick poets have generally brought forward the passions in tragedy, to the great prejudice of that effect they are naturally fitted to produce upon the mind, which I forbear to mention, lest they should too much increase the length of this discourse; and leave an impression on the mind of my reader, that I write more on the spirit of criticism, than becomes one who is about to bring before the publick a work, with, doubtless, many faults and imperfections on its head.

From this general view, which I have endeavoured to communicate to my reader, of tragedy, and those principles in the human mind upon which the success of her efforts depends, I have been led to believe, that an attempt to write a series of tragedies, of simpler construction, less embellished with poetical decorations, less constrained by that lofty seriousness which has so generally been considered as necessary for the support of tragick dignity, and in which the chief object should be to delineate the progress of the higher passions in the human breast, each

[12] This, perhaps, more than any thing else has injured the higher scenes of tragedy. For having made such free use of bold hyperbolical language in the inferior parts, the poet when he arrives at the highly impassioned sinks into total inability: or if he will force himself to rise still higher on the wing, he flies beyond nature altogether, into the regions of bombast and nonsense [J. B.].

play exhibiting a particular passion, might not be unacceptable to the publick. And I have been the more readily induced to act upon this idea, because I am confident, that tragedy, written upon this plan, is fitted to produce stronger moral effect than upon any other. I have said that tragedy in representing to us great characters struggling with difficulties, and placed in situations of eminence and danger, in which few of us have any chance of being called upon to act, conveys its moral efficacy to our minds by the enlarged views which it gives to us of human nature, by the admiration of virtue, and execration of vice which it excites, and not by the examples it holds up for our immediate application. But in opening to us the heart of man under the influence of those passions to which all are liable, this is not the case. Those strong passions that, with small assistance from outward circumstances, work their way in the heart, till they become the tyrannical masters of it, carry on a similar operation in the breast of the Monarch, and the man of low degree. It exhibits to us the mind of man in that state when we are most curious to look into it, and is equally interesting to all. Discrimination of character is a turn of mind, tho' more common than we are aware of, which every body does not possess; but to the expressions of passion, particularly strong passion, the dullest mind is awake; and its true unsophisticated language the dullest understanding will not misinterpret. To hold up for our example those peculiarities in disposition, and modes of thinking which nature has fixed upon us, or which long and early habit has incorporated with our original selves, is almost desiring us to remove the everlasting mountains, to take away the native land-marks of the soul; but representing the passions brings before us the operation of a tempest that rages out its time and passes away. We cannot, it is true, amidst its wild uproar, listen to the voice of reason, and save ourselves from destruction; but we can foresee its coming, we can mark its rising signs, we can know the situations that will most expose us to its rage, and we can shelter our heads from the coming blast. To change a certain disposition of mind which makes us view objects in a particular light, and thereby, oftentimes, unknown to ourselves, influences our conduct and manners, is almost impossible; but in checking and subduing those visitations of the soul, whose causes and effects we are aware of, every one may make considerable progress, if he proves not entirely successful. Above all, looking back to the first rise, and tracing the progress of passion, points out to us those stages in the approach of the enemy, when he might have been combated most successfully; and where the suffering him to pass may be considered as occasioning all the misery that ensues.

Comedy presents to us men as we find them in the ordinary intercourse of the world, with all the weaknesses, follies, caprice, prejudices, and absurdities which a near and familiar view of them discovers. It is her task to exhibit them engaged in the busy turmoil of ordinary life, harassing and perplexing themselves with the endless pursuits of avarice, vanity, and pleasure; and engaged with those smaller trials of the mind, by which men are most apt to be overcome, and from which he, who could have supported with honour the attack of greater occasions, will oftentimes come off most shamefully foiled. It belongs to her to shew the varied fashions and manners of the world, as, from the spirit of vanity, caprice, and imitation, they go on in swift and endless succession; and those disagreeable or absurd peculiarities attached to particular classes and conditions in society. It is for her also to represent men under the influence of the stronger passions; and to trace the rise and progress of them in the heart, in such situations, and attended with such circumstances as take off their sublimity, and the interest we naturally take in a perturbed mind. It is hers to exhibit those terrible tyrants of the soul, whose ungovernable rage has struck us so often with dismay, like wild beasts tied to a post, who growl and paw before us, for our derision and sport. In pourtraying the characters of men she has this advantage over tragedy, that the smallest traits of nature, with the smallest circumstances which serve to bring them forth, may by her be displayed, however ludicrous and trivial in themselves, without any ceremony. And in developing the passions she enjoys a similar advantage; for they often most strongly betray themselves when touched by those small and familiar occurrences which cannot, consistently with the effect it is intended to produce, be admitted into tragedy.

As tragedy has been very much cramped in her endeavours to exalt and improve the mind, by that spirit of imitation and confinement in her successive writers, which the beauty of her earliest poets first gave rise to, so comedy has been led aside from her best purposes by a different temptation. Those endless changes in fashions and in manners, which offer such obvious and ever-new subjects of ridicule; that infinite variety of tricks and manœuvres by which the ludicrous may be produced, and curiosity and laughter excited: the admiration we so generally bestow upon satirical remark, pointed repartee, and whimsical combinations of ideas, have too often led her to forget the warmer interest we feel, and the more profitable lessons we receive from genuine representations of nature. The most interesting and instructive class of comedy, therefore, the real characteristick, has been very much neglected, whilst satirical, witty, sentimental, and, above all, busy or circumstantial comedy have usurped the exertions of the far greater proportion of Dramatick Writers.

In Satirical Comedy, sarcastick and severe reflections on the actions and manners of men, introduced with neatness, force, and poignancy of expression into a lively and well supported dialogue, of whose gay surface they are the embossed ornaments, make the most important and studied part of the work: Character is a thing talked of rather than shewn. The persons of the drama are indebted for the discovery of their peculiarities to what is said to them, rather than to any thing they are made to say or do for themselves. Much incident being unfavourable for studied and elegant dialogue, the plot is commonly simple, and the few events that compose it neither interesting nor striking. It only affords us that kind of moral instruction which an essay or a poem could as well have conveyed, and, though amusing in the closet, is but feebly attractive in the Theatre.[13]

In what I have termed Witty Comedy, every thing is light, playful, and easy. Strong decided condemnation of vice is too weighty and material to dance upon the surface of that stream, whose shallow currents sparkle in perpetual sun-beams, and cast up their bubbles to the light. Two or three persons of quick thought, and whimsical fancy, who perceive instantaneously the various connections of every passing idea, and the significations, natural or artificial, which single expressions, or particular forms of speech can possibly convey, take the lead thro' the whole, and seem to communicate their own peculiar talent to every creature in the play. The plot is most commonly feeble rather than simple, the incidents being numerous enough, but seldom striking or varied. To amuse, and only to amuse, is its aim: it pretends not to interest nor instruct. It pleases when we read, more than when we see it represented; and pleases still more when we take it up by accident, and read but a scene at a time.

Sentimental Comedy treats of those embarrassments, difficulties, and scruples, which, though sufficiently distressing to the delicate minds who entertain them, are not powerful enough to gratify the sympathetick desire we all feel to look into the heart of man in difficult and trying situations, which is the sound basis of tragedy, and are destitute of that seasoning of the lively and ludicrous, which prevents the ordinary transactions of comedy from becoming insipid. In real life, those who, from the peculiar frame of their minds, feel most of this refined distress, are not generally communicative upon the subject; and those who do feel and talk about it at the same time, if any such there be, seldom find their friends much inclined to listen to them. It is not to be supposed, then, long conversations upon the stage about small sentimental niceties, can be generally interesting. I am afraid plays of this kind, as well as works of a similar nature, in other departments of literature, have only tended to encrease amongst us a set of sentimental hypocrites; who are the same persons of this age that would have been the religious ones of another; and are daily doing morality the same kind of injury, by substituting the particular excellence which they pretend to possess, for plain simple uprightness and rectitude.

In Busy or Circumstantial Comedy, all those ingenious contrivances of lovers, guardians, governantes[14] and chamber-maids; that ambushed bushfighting amongst closets, screens, chests, easy-chairs, and toilet-tables, form a gay varied game of dexterity and invention; which, to those who have played at hide-and-seek, who have crouched down, with beating heart, in a dark corner, whilst the enemy groped near the spot; who have joined their busy school-mates in many a deep-laid plan to deceive, perplex, and torment the unhappy mortals deputed to have the charge of them, cannot be seen with indifference. Like an old hunter, who pricks up his ears at the sound of the chace, and starts away from the path of his journey, so, leaving all wisdom and criticism behind us, we follow the varied changes of the plot, and stop not for reflection. The studious man who wants a cessation from thought, the indolent man who dislikes it, and all those who, from habit or circumstances, live in a state of divorce from their own minds, are pleased with an amusement in which they have nothing to do but to open their eyes and behold; the moral tendency of it, however, is very faulty. That mockery of age and domestick authority, so constantly held forth, has a very bad effect upon the younger part of an audience;

[13] These plays are generally the work of men, whose judgement and acute observation, enable them admirably well to generalize, and apply to classes of men the remarks they have made upon individuals; yet know not how to dress up, with any natural congruity, an imaginary individual in the attributes they have assigned to those classes [J. B.].

[14] **governante:** female ruler; mistress of a household.

and that continual lying and deceit in the first characters of the piece, which is necessary for conducting the plot, has a most pernicious one.

But Characteristick Comedy, which represents to us this motley world of men and women in which we live, under those circumstances of ordinary and familiar life most favourable for the discovery of the human heart, offers to us a wide field of instruction, adapted to general application. We find in its varied scenes an exercise of the mind analogous to that which we all, less or more, find out for ourselves, amidst the mixed groupes of people whom we meet with in society; and which I have already mentioned as an exercise universally pleasing to man. As the distinctions which it is its highest aim to discriminate, are those of nature and not situation, they are judged of by all ranks of men; for a peasant will very clearly perceive in the character of a peer, those native peculiarities which belong to him as a man, though he is entirely at a loss in all that regards his manners and address as a nobleman. It illustrates to us the general remarks we have made upon men; and in it we behold, spread before us, plans of those original groundworks, upon which the general ideas we have been taught to conceive of mankind, are founded. It stands but little in need of busy plot, extraordinary incidents, witty repartee, or studied sentiments. It naturally produces for itself all that it requires; characters who are to speak for themselves, who are to be known by their own words and actions, not by the accounts that are given of them by others, cannot well be developed without considerable variety of judicious incident; a smile that is raised by some trait of undisguised nature, and a laugh that is provoked by some ludicrous effect of passion, or clashing of opposite characters, will be more pleasing to the generality of men, than either the one or the other when occasioned by a play upon words, or a whimsical combination of ideas; and to behold the operation and effects of the different propensities and weaknesses of men, will naturally call up in the mind of the spectator moral reflections more applicable, and more impressive, than all the high-sounding sentiments, with which the graver scenes of Satirical and Sentimental Comedy are so frequently interlarded. It is much to be regretted, however, that the eternal introduction of love as the grand business of the Drama, and the consequent necessity for making the chief persons in it such, in regard to age, appearance, manners, dispositions, and endowments, as are proper for interesting lovers, has occasioned so much insipid similarity in the higher characters. It is chiefly, therefore, on the second and inferiour characters, that the efforts, even of our best poets, have been exhausted; and thus we are called upon to be interested in the fortune of one man, whilst our chief attention is directed to the character of another, which produces a disunion of ideas in the mind, injurious to the general effect of the whole. From this cause, also, those characteristick varieties have been very much neglected, which men present to us in the middle stages of life; when they are too old for lovers or the confidents of lovers, and too young to be the fathers, uncles, and guardians, who are contrasted with them; but when they are still in full vigour of mind, eagerly engaged with the world, joining the activity of youth to the providence of age, and offer to our attention objects sufficiently interesting and instructive. It is to be regretted that strong contrasts of character are too often attempted, instead of those harmonious shades of it, which nature so beautifully varies, and which we so greatly delight in, whenever we clearly distinguish them. It is to be regretted that in place of those characters, which present themselves to the imagination of a writer from his general observations upon mankind, inferiour poets have so often pourtrayed with senseless minuteness the characters of particular individuals. We are pleased with the eccentricities of individuals in real life, and also in history or biography, but in fictitious writings, we regard them with suspicion; and no representation of nature, that corresponds not with some of our general ideas in regard to it, will either instruct or inform us. When the originals of such characters are known and remembered, the plays in which they are introduced are oftentimes popular; and their temporary success has induced a still inferiour class of poets to believe, that, by making men strange, and unlike the rest of the world, they have made great discoveries, and mightily enlarged the boundaries of dramatick character. They will, therefore, distinguish one man from another by some strange whim or imagination, which is ever uppermost in his thoughts, and influences every action of his life; by some singular opinion, perhaps, about politicks, fashions, or the position of the stars: by some strong unaccountable love for one thing or aversion from another; entirely forgetting, that such singularities, if they are to be found in nature, can no where be sought for, with such probability of success, as in Bedlam.[15] Above all it is to be regretted that those adventitious distinctions amongst men, of age, fortune, rank, profession, and country, are so often

[15] **Bedlam**: the Bethlehem Hospital or lunatic asylum in Spitalfields, London; a byword for madness and confusion in general.

brought forward in preference to the great original distinctions of nature; and our scenes so often filled with courtiers, lawyers, citizens, Frenchmen, &c. &c. With all the characteristicks of their respective conditions, such as they have been represented from time immemorial. This has introduced a great sameness into many of our plays, which all the changes of new fashions burlesqued, and new customs turned into ridicule, cannot conceal.

In comedy, the stronger passions, love excepted, are seldom introduced but in a passing way. We have short bursts of anger, fits of jealousy and impatience; violent passion of any continuance we seldom find. When this is attempted, however, forgetting that mode of exposing the weakness of the human mind, which peculiarly belongs to her, it is too frequently done in the serious spirit of tragedy; and this has produced so many of those serious comick plays, which so much divide and distract our attention.[16] Yet we all know from our own experience in real life, that, in certain situations, and under certain circumstances, the stronger passions are fitted to produce scenes more exquisitely comick than any other; and one well-wrought scene of this kind, will have a more powerful effect in repressing similar intemperance in the mind of a spectator, than many moral cautions, or even, perhaps, than the terrifick examples of tragedy. There are to be found, no doubt, in the works of our best dramatick writers, comick scenes descriptive of the stronger passions, but it is generally the inferiour characters of the piece who are made the subjects of them, very rarely those in whom we are much interested; and consequently the useful effect of such scenes upon the mind is very much weakened. This general appropriation of them has tempted our less-skilful Dramatists to exaggerate, and step, in further quest of the ludicrous, so much beyond the bounds of nature, that the very effect they are so anxious to produce is thereby destroyed, and all useful application of it entirely cut off; for we never apply to ourselves a false representation of nature.

But a complete exhibition of passion, with its varieties and progress in the breast of man has, I believe, scarcely ever been attempted in comedy. Even love, though the chief subject of almost every play, has been pourtrayed in a loose, scattered, and imperfect manner. The story of the lovers is acted over before us, whilst the characteristicks of that passion by which they are actuated, and which is the great master-spring of the whole, are faintly to be discovered. We are generally introduced to a lover after he has long been acquainted with his mistress, and wants but the consent of some stubborn relation, relief from some embarrassment of situation, or the clearing up some mistake or love-quarrel occasioned by malice or accident, to make him completely happy. To overcome these difficulties, he is engaged in a busy train of contrivance and exertion, in which the spirit, activity and ingenuity of the man is held forth to view, whilst the lover, comparatively speaking, is kept out of sight. But even when this is not the case; when the lover is not so busied and involved, this stage of the passion is exactly the one that is least interesting, and least instructive: not to mention as I have done already, that one stage of any passion must shew it imperfectly.

From this view of the Comick Drama I have been induced to believe, that, as companions to the forementioned tragedies, a series of comedies on a similar plan, in which bustle of plot, brilliancy of dialogue, and even the bold and striking in character, should, to the best of the authour's judgment, be kept in due subordination to nature, might likewise be acceptable to the publick. I am confident that comedy upon this plan is capable of being

[16] Such plays, however excellent the parts may be of which they are composed, can never produce the same strength and unity of effect upon our minds which we receive from plays of a simpler undivided construction. If the serious and distressing scenes make a deep impression, we do not find ourselves in a humour for the comick ones that succeed; and if the comick scenes enliven us greatly, we feel tardy and unalert in bringing back our minds to a proper tone for the serious. As in tragedy we smile at those native traits of character, or that occasional sprightliness of dialogue, which are sometimes introduced, to animate her less-interesting parts, so may we be moved by comedy; but our tears should be called forth by those gentle strokes of nature, which come at once with kindred kindness on the heart, and are quickly succeeded by smiles. Like a small summer-cloud, whose rain-drops sparkle in the sun, and which swiftly passes away, is the genuine pathetick of comedy: the gathering foreseen storm, that darkens the whole face of the sky, belongs to tragedy alone. It is often observed, I confess, that we are more apt to be affected by those scenes of distress which we meet with in comedy, than the high-wrought woes of tragedy; and I believe it is true. But this arises from the woes of tragedy being so often appropriated to high and mighty personages, and strained beyond the modesty of nature, in order to suit their great dignity; or from the softened griefs of more gentle and familiar characters being rendered feeble and tiresome with too much repetition and whining. It arises from the greater facility with which we enter into the distresses of people, more upon a level with ourselves; and whose sorrows are expressed in less studied and unnatural language [J. B.].

made as interesting, as entertaining, and superiour in moral tendency to any other. For even in ordinary life, with very slight cause to excite them, strong passions will foster themselves within the breast; and what are all the evils which vanity, folly, prejudice, or peculiarity of temper lead to, compared with those which such unquiet inmates produce? Were they confined to the exalted and the mighty, to those engaged in the great events of the world, to the inhabitants of palaces and camps, how happy comparatively would this world be! But many a miserable being, whom firm principle, timidity of character, or the fear of shame keeps back from the actual commission of crimes, is tormented in obscurity, under the dominion of those passions which set the seducer in ambush, rouse the bold spoiler to wrong, and strengthen the arm of the murderer. Though to those with whom such dangerous enemies have long found shelter, exposing them in an absurd and ridiculous light, may be shooting a finely-pointed arrow against the hardened rock; yet to those with whom they are but new, and less assured guests, this may prove a more successful mode of attack than any other.

It was the saying of a sagacious Scotchman,[17] 'let who will make the laws of a nation, if I have the writing of its ballads.' Something similar to this may be said in regard to the Drama. Its lessons reach not, indeed, to the lowest classes of the labouring people, who are the broad foundation of society, which can never be generally moved without endangering every thing that is constructed upon it, and who are our potent and formidable ballad readers; but they reach to the classes next in order to them, and who will always have over them no inconsiderable influence. The impressions made by it are communicated, at the same instant of time, to a greater number of individuals, than those made by any other species of writing; and they are strengthened in every spectator, by observing their effects upon those who surround him. From this observation, the mind of my reader will suggest of itself, what it would be unnecessary, and, perhaps, improper in me here to enlarge upon. The theatre is a school in which much good or evil may be learned. At the beginning of its career the Drama was employed to mislead and excite; and were I not unwilling to refer to transactions of the present times, I might abundantly confirm what I have said by recent examples. The authour, therefore, who aims in any degree to improve the mode of its instruction, and point to more useful lessons than it is generally employed to dispense, is certainly praiseworthy, though want of abilities may unhappily prevent him from being successful in his efforts.

This idea has prompted me to begin a work in which I am aware of many difficulties. In plays of this nature the passions must be depicted not only with their bold and prominent features, but also with those minute and delicate traits which distinguish them in an infant, growing, and repressed state; which are the most difficult of all to counterfeit, and one of which falsely imagined, will destroy the effect of a whole scene. The characters over whom they are made to usurp dominion, must be powerful and interesting, exercising them with their full measure of opposition and struggle; for the chief antagonists they contend with must be the other passions and propensities of the heart, not outward circumstances and events. Though belonging to such characters, they must still be held to view in their most baleful and unseductive light; and those qualities in the impassioned which are necessary to interest us in their fate, must not be allowed, by any lustre borrowed from them, to diminish our abhorrence of guilt. The second and even the inferiour persons of each play, as they must be kept perfectly distinct from the great impassioned one, should generally be represented in a calm unagitated state, and therefore more pains is necessary than in other dramatick works, to mark them by appropriate distinctions of character, lest they should appear altogether insipid and insignificant. As the great object here is to trace passion through all its varieties, and in every stage, many of which are marked by shades so delicate, that in much bustle of events they would be little attended to, or entirely overlooked, simplicity of plot is more necessary, than in those plays where only occasional bursts of passion are introduced, to distinguish a character, or animate a scene. But where simplicity of plot is necessary, there is very great danger of making a piece appear bare and unvaried, and nothing but great force and truth in the delineations of nature will prevent it from being tiresome.[18] Soliloquy, or those overflowings of the

[17] Andrew Fletcher of Saltoun (1655–1716), Scottish nationalist and politician who opposed both English rule in Scotland and the union of Scotland with England.

[18] To make up for this simplicity of plot, the shew and decorations of the theatre ought to be allowed, to plays written upon this plan, in their full extent. How fastidious soever some poets may be in regard to these matters, it is much better to relieve our tired-out attention with a battle, a banquet, or a procession, than an accumulation of incidents. In the latter case the mind is harassed and confused with those doubts, conjectures, and disappointments which multiplied events occasion,

perturbed soul, in which it unburthens itself of those thoughts which it cannot communicate to others, and which in certain situations is the only mode that a Dramatist can employ to open to us the mind he would display, must necessarily be often, and to considerable length, introduced. Here, indeed, as it naturally belongs to passion, it will not be so offensive as it generally is in other plays, when a calm unagitated person tells over to himself all that has befallen him, and all his future schemes of intrigue or advancement; yet to make speeches of this kind sufficiently natural and impressive, to excite no degree of weariness nor distaste, will be found to be no easy task. There are, besides these, many other difficulties peculiarly belonging to this undertaking, too minute and tedious to mention. If, fully aware of them, I have not shrunk back from the attempt, it is not from any idea that my own powers or discernment will at all times enable me to overcome them; but I am emboldened by the confidence I feel in that candour and indulgence, with which the good and enlightened do ever regard the experimental efforts of those, who wish in any degree to enlarge the sources of pleasure and instruction amongst men.

It will now be proper to say something of the particular plays which compose this volume. But, in the first place I must observe, that as I pretend not to have overcome the difficulties attached to this design, so neither from the errours and defects, which, in these pages, I have thought it necessary to point out in the works of others, do I at all pretend to be blameless. To conceive the great moral object and outline of a story; to people it with various characters, under the influence of various passions; and to strike out circumstances and situations calculated to call them into action, is a very different employment of the mind from calmly considering those propensities of our nature, to which dramatick writings are most powerfully addressed, and taking a general view upon those principles of the works of preceding authours. They are employments which cannot well occupy it at the same time; and experience has taught us, that criticks do not unfrequently write in contradiction to their own rules. If I should, therefore, sometimes appear in the foregoing remarks to have provided a stick wherewith to break mine own pate,[19] I entreat that my reader will believe I am neither confident nor boastful, and use it with gentleness.

In the two first plays [*Count Basil* and *The Tryal: A Comedy*], where love is the passion under review, their relation to the general plan may not be very obvious. Love is the chief groundwork of almost all our tragedies and comedies, and so far they are not distinguished from others. But I have endeavoured in both to give an unbroken view of the passion from its beginning, and to mark it as I went along, with those peculiar traits which distinguish its different stages of progression. I have in both these p[i]eces grafted this passion not on those open communicative impetuous characters, who have so long occupied the dramatick station of lovers, but on men of a firm, thoughtful, reserved turn of mind, with whom it commonly makes the longest stay, and maintains the hardest struggle. I should be extremely sorry if, from any thing at the conclusion of the tragedy, it should be supposed that I mean to countenance suicide, or condemn those customs whose object is the discouragement of it, by withholding from the body of the selfslain those sacred rites, and marks of respect commonly shewn to the dead. Let it be considered, that whatever I have inserted there, which can at all raise any suspicion of this kind, is put into the mouths of rude uncultivated soldiers, who are roused with the loss of a beloved leader and indignant at any idea of disgrace being at[t]ached to him. If it should seem inconsistent with the nature of this work, that in its compan[i]on the comedy, I have made strong moral principle triumph over love, let it be remembered, that without this the whole moral tendency of a play, which must end happily, would have been destroyed; and that it is not my intention to encourage the indulgence of this passion, amiable as it is, but to restrain it. The last play [*De Montfort*], the subject of which is hatred, will more clearly discover the nature and intention of my design. The rise and progress of this passion I have been obliged to give in retrospect, instead of representing it all along in its actual operation, as I could have wished to have done. But hatred is a passion of slow growth; and to have exhibited it f[r]om its beginnings would have included a longer period, than even those who are least scrupulous about the

and in a great measure unfitted for attending to the worthier parts of the piece; but in the former it enjoys a rest, a pleasing pause in its more serious occupation, from which it can return again, without any incumberance of foreign intruding ideas. The shew of a splendid procession will afford to a person of the best understanding, a pleasure in kind, though not in degree, with that which a child would receive from it. But when it is past he thinks no more of it; whereas some confusion of circumstances, some half-explained mistake, which gives him no pleasure at all when it takes place, may take off his attention afterwards from the refined beauties of a natural and characteristick dialogue [J. B.].

[19] **pate:** the top of the head.

limitation of dramatick time, would have thought allowable. I could not have introduced my chief characters upon the stage as boy, and then as men. For this passion must be kep[t] distinct from that dislike which we conceive for another when he has greatly offended us, and which is almost the constant companion of anger; and also from that eager desire to crush, and inflict suffering on him who has injured us, which constitutes revenge. This passion, as I have conceived it, is that rooted and settled aversion, which from opposition of character, aided by circumstances of little importance, grows at last into such antipathy and personal disgust as makes him who entertains it, feel, in the presence of him who is the object of it, a degree of torment and restle[s]ness which is insufferable. It is a passion, I believe less frequent than any other of the stronger passions, but in the breast where it does exist, it creates, perhaps, more misery than any other. To endeavour to interest the mind for a man under the dominion of a passion so baleful, so unamiable, may seem, perhaps, reprehensible. I therefore beg it may be considered that it is the passion and not the man which is held up to our execration; and that this and every other bad passion does more strongly evince its pernicious and dangerous nature, when we see it thus counteracting and destroying the good gifts of heaven, than when it is represented as the suitable associate in the breast of inmates as dark as itself. This remark will likewise be applicable to many of the other plays belonging to my work, that are intended to follow. A decidedly wicked character can never be interesting; and to employ such for the display of any strong passion would very much injure instead of improving the moral effect. In the breast of a bad man passion has comparatively little to combat, how then can it shew its strength? I shall say no more upon this subject, but submit myself to the judgment of my reader.

It may, perhaps, be supposed from my publishing these plays, that I have written them for the closet rather than the stage. If upon perusing them with attention, the reader is disposed to think they are better calculated for the first than the last, let him impute it to want of skill in the authour, and not to any previous design. A play, but of small poetical merit, that is suited to strike and interest the spectator, to catch the attention of him who will not, and of him who cannot read, is a more valuable and useful production than one whose elegant and harmonious pages are admired in the libraries of the tasteful and refined. To have received approbation from an audience of my countrymen, would have been more pleasing to me than any other praise. A few tears from the simple and young would have been, in my eyes, pearls of great price; and the spontaneous, untutored plaudits of the rude and uncultivated would have come to my heart as offerings of no mean value. I should, therefore, have been better pleased to have introduced them to the world from the stage than from the press. I possess, however, no likely channel to the former mode of publick introduction; and upon further reflection it appeared to me that by publishing them in this way, I have an opportunity afforded me of explaining the design of my work, and enabling the publick to judge, not only of each play by itself, but as making a part likewise of the whole; an advantage which, perhaps, does more than over-balance the splendour and effect of theatrical representation.

It may be thought that with this extensive plan before me, I should not have been in a hurry to publish, but have waited to give a larger portion of it to the publick, which would have enabled them to make a truer estimate of its merit. To bring forth only three plays of the whole, and the last without its intended companion, may seem like the haste of those vain people, who as soon as they have written a few pages of a discourse, or a few couplets of a poem, cannot be easy till every body has seen them. I do protest, in honest simplicity! it is distrust and not confidence, that has led me at this early stage of the undertaking, to bring it before the publick. To labour in uncertainty is at all times unpleasant; but to proceed in a long and difficult work with any impression upon your mind that your labour may be in vain; that the opinion you have conceived of your ability to perform it may be a delusion, a false suggestion of self-love, the fantasy of an aspiring temper, is most discouraging and cheerless. I have not proceeded so far, indeed, merely upon the strength of my own judgment; but the friends to whom I have shewn my manuscripts are partial to me, and their approbation which in the case of any indifferent person would be in my mind completely decisive, goes but a little way in relieving me from these apprehensions. To step beyond the circle of my own immediate friends in quest of opinion, from the particular temper of my mind I feel an uncommon repugnance: I can with less pain to myself bring them before the publick at once, and submit to its decision.[20] It is to my countrymen at large that I call for

[20] The first of these plays, indeed, has been shewn to two or three Gentlemen whom I have not the honour of reckoning amongst my friends. One of them, who is a man of distinguished talents, has honoured it with very flattering approbation; and, at his suggestion, one or two slight alterations in it have been made [J. B.].

assistance. If this work is fortunate enough to attract their attention, let their strictures as well as their praise come to my aid: the one will encourage me in a long and arduous undertaking, the other will teach me to improve it as I advance. For there are many errours that may be detected, and improvements that may be suggested in the prosecution of this work, which from the observations of a great variety of readers are more likely to be pointed out to me, than from those of a small number of persons, even of the best judgment. I am not possessed of that confidence in mine own powers, which enables the concealed genius, under the pressure of present discouragement, to pursue his labours in security, looking firmly forward to other more enlightened times for his reward. If my own countrymen with whom I live and converse, who look upon the same race of men, the same state of society, the same passing events with myself, receive not my offering, I presume not to look to posterity.

Before I close this discourse, let me crave the forbearance of my reader, if he has discovered in the course of it any unacknowledged use of the thoughts of other authours, which he thinks ought to have been noticed; and let me beg the same favour, if in reading the following plays, any similar neglect seems to occur. There are few writers who have sufficient originality of thought to strike out for themselves new ideas upon every occasion. When a thought presents itself to me, as suited to the purpose I am aiming at, I would neither be thought proud enough to reject it, on finding that another has used it before me, nor mean enough to make use of it without acknowledging the obligation, when I can at all guess to whom such acknowledgments are due. But I am situated where I have no library to consult; my reading through the whole of my life has been of a loose, scattered, unmethodical kind, with no determined direction, and I have not been blessed by nature with the advantages of a retentive or accurate memory. Do not, however, imagine from this, I at all wish to insinuate that I ought to be acquitted of every obligation to preceding authours; and that when a palpable similarity of thought and expression is observable between us, it is a similarity produced by accident alone, and with perfect unconsciousness on my part. I am frequently sensible, from the manner in which an idea arises to my imagination, and the readiness with which words, also, present themselves to clothe it in, that I am only making use of some dormant part of that hoard of ideas which the most indifferent memories lay up, and not the native suggestions of mine own mind. Whenever I have suspected myself of doing so, in the course of this work, I have felt a strong inclination to mark that suspicion in a note. But, besides that it might have appeared like an affectation of scrupulousness which I would avoid, there being likewise, most assuredly, many other places in it where I have done the same thing without being conscious of it, a suspicion of wishing to slur them over, and claim all the rest as unreservedly my own, would unavoidably have attached to me. If this volume should appear, to any candid and liberal critick, to merit that he should take the trouble of pointing out to me in what parts of it I seem to have made that use of other authours' writings, which according to the fair laws of literature ought to have been acknowledged,[21] I shall think myself obliged to him. I shall examine the sources he points out as having supplied my own lack of ideas; and if this book should have the good fortune to go through a second edition, I shall not fail to own my obligations to him, and the authours from whom I may have borrowed.

How little credit soever, upon perusing these plays, the reader may think me entitled to in regard to the execution of the work, he will not, I flatter myself, deny me some credit in regard to the plan. I know of no series of plays, in any language, expressly descriptive of the different passions; and I believe there are few plays existing in which the display of one strong passion is the chief business of the drama, so written that they could properly make part of such a series. I do not think that we should, from the works of various authours, be able to make a collection which would give us any thing exactly of the nature of that which is here proposed. If the reader, in perusing it, perceives that the abilities of the authour are not proportioned to the task which is imposed upon them, he will wish in the spirit of kindness rather than of censure, as I most sincerely do, that they had been more adequate to it. However, if I perform it ill, I am still confident that this (pardon me if I call it, noble) design will not be suffered to fall to the ground; some one will arise after me who will do it justice; and there is no poet, possessing genius for such a work, who will not at the same time possess that spirit of justice and of candour, which will lead him to remember me with respect.

I have now only to thank my reader, whoever he may be, who has followed me through the pages of this discourse, for having had the patience to do so. May he, in going through what follows (a wish the sincerity of which he cannot doubt) find more to reward his trouble than I dare venture to promise him; and for the pains he has already taken, and that which he intends to take for

[21] Britain had no binding copywright laws until 1844.

me, I request that he will accept of my grateful acknowledgments.

Note: Shakspeare, more than any of our poets, gives peculiar and appropriate distinction to the characters of his tragedies. The remarks I have made, in regard to the little variety of character to be met with in tragedy, apply not to him. Neither has he, as other Dramatists generally do, bestowed pains on the chief persons of his drama only, leaving the second and inferiour ones insignificant and spiritless. He never wears out our capacity to feel, by eternally pressing upon it. His tragedies are agreeably chequered with variety of scenes, enriched with good sense, nature, and vivacity, which relieve our minds from the fatigue of continued distress. If he sometimes carries this so far as to break in upon that serious tone of mind, which disposes us to listen with effect to the higher scenes of tragedy, he has done so chiefly in his historical plays, where the distresses set forth are commonly of that publick kind, which does not, at any rate, make much impression upon the feelings [J. B.].

Count Basil: A Tragedy

(1798)

PERSONS OF THE DRAMA

Men

COUNT BASIL, *a General in the Emperour's service*

COUNT ROSINBERG, *his Friend*

DUKE OF MANTUA

GAURIECIO, *his Minister*

VALTOMER
FREDERICK } *Two Officers of Basil's Troops*

GEOFFRY, *an old Soldier, very much maimed in the Wars*

MIRANDO, *a little Boy, favourite to Victoria*

Women

VICTORIA, *Daughter to the Duke of Mantua*

COUNTESS OF ALBINI, *Friend and Governess to Victoria*

ISABELLA, *a Lady attending upon Victoria*

OFFICERS, SOLDIERS, AND ATTENDANTS, MASKS, DANCERS, &C.

The Scene is in Mantua, and its environs. Time supposed to be in the Sixteenth Century, when CHARLES *the Fifth defeated* FRANCIS *the First, at the Battle of Pavia.*[1]

ACT I

— SCENE I —

An Open Street, cro[w]ded with People, who seem to be waiting in expectation of some Show.

Enter a CITIZEN.

FIRST MAN: Well friend, what tidings of the grand procession?

CIT: I left it passing by the northern gate.

SECOND MAN: I've waited long, I'm glad it comes at last.

YOUNG MAN: And does the Princess look so wondrous fair
As fame reports?

CIT: She is the fairest lady of the train,
And all the fairest beauties of the court
Are in her train.

OLD MAN: Bears she such off'rings to Saint Francis' shrine,[2]
So rich, so marvellous rich as rumour says?
'Twill drain the treasury.

CIT: Since she in all this splendid pomp, returns
Her publick thanks to the good patron Saint,
Who from his sick bed hath restor'd her father,
Thou wouldst not have her go with empty hands?
She loves magnificence.—

(Discovering among the croud Old GEOFFRY.*)*

Ha! art thou here, old remnant of the wars?
Thou art not come to see this courtly show,
Which sets the young agape?

[1] At the Battle of Pavia on 24 February 1525, the Hapsburg Emperor Charles V defeated Francis I of France, almost wiping out the French army and taking the king prisoner. This was the decisive battle of the Hapsburg-Valois wars in Italy. **Mantua:** city in northern Italy.

[2] **Saint Francis' shrine:** probably the basilica at Assisi, in northern Italy, built c. 1230 to house the relics of St. Francis of Assisi and to serve as a center for his cult.

GEOF: I came not for the show; and yet, methinks,
It were a better jest upon me still,
If thou didst truly know mine errand here.

CIT: I pri'thee say.

GEOF: What, must I tell it thee?
As o'er my ev'ning fire I musing sat
Some few days since, my mind's eye backward turn'd
Upon the various changes I have pass'd—
How in my youth with gay attire allur'd,
And all the grand accoutrements of war,
I left my peaceful home: Then my first battles,
When clashing arms, and sights of blood were new:
Then all the after chances of the war;
Ay, and that field, a well-fought field it was,
When with this arm (I speak not of it oft)

(Pointing to his empty sleeve.)

Which now thou seest is no arm of mine,
In a straight pass I stopp'd a thousand foes,
And turn'd my flying comrades to the charge;
For which good service, in his tented court,
My prince bestow'd a mark of favour on me;
Whilst his fair consort, seated by his side,
The fairest lady e'er mine eyes beheld,
Gave me what more than all besides I priz'd,
Methinks I see her still! a gracious smile;
'Twas a heart-kindling smile,—a smile of praise—
Well, musing thus on all my fortunes past,
A Neighbour drew the latchet of my door,
And full of news from town, in many words
Big with rich names, told of this grand procession.
E'en as he spoke a fancy seiz'd my soul
To see the princess pass, if in her face
I yet might trace some semblance of her mother.
This is the simple truth; laugh as thou wilt,
I came not for the show.

Enter an OFFICER.

OFFICER *to* GEOF: Make way, that the procession may have room;
Stand you aside, and let this man have place.

(Pushing GEOF. *and endeavouring to put another in his place.)*

GEOF: But that thou art the prince's officer,
I'd give thee back thy push with better blows.

OFFICER: What wilt thou not give place? the prince is near,
I will complain to him, and have thee caged.

GEOF: Yes do complain, I pray; and when thou dost,
Say that the private of the tenth brigade,
Who sav'd his army on the Danube's bank,
And since that time a private hath remain'd,
Dares, as a citizen, his right maintain
Against thy insolence. Go tell him this,
And ask him then what dungeon of his tower
He'll have me thrust into?

CIT. *to* OFFICER: This is old Geoffry of the tenth brigade.

OFFICER: I knew him not: you should have told me sooner.

(Exit, looking much ashamed.)

Martial Musick heard at a distance.

CIT: Hark, this is musick of a warlike kind.

Enter Second CITIZEN.

TO SEC. CIT: What sounds are these, good friend, which this way bear?

SEC. CIT: The Count of Basil is upon his march,
To join the Emp'rour with some chosen troops,
And doth through Mantua pass in right of Allies.

GEOF: I have heard a good report of this young soldier.

SEC. CIT: 'Tis said he disciplines his men severely,
And acts with them too much the old commander,
Which is ungracious in so young a man.

GEOF: I know he loves not ease and revelry;
He makes them soldiers at no dearer rate
Than he himself hath paid. What, dost thou think
That e'en the very meanest simple craft
May not, but with due diligence, be learn'd,
And yet the noble art of soldiership
May be attain'd by loit'ring in the sun?
Some men are born to feast, and not to fight;
Whose sluggish minds, e'en in fair honour's field,
Still on their dinner turn—
Let such pot-boiling varlets stay at home,
And wield a flesh-hook rather than a sword.
In times of easy service, true it is,
An easy, careless chief, all soldiers love;
But O! how gladly in the day of battle
Would they their jolly bottle-chief desert,
And follow such a leader as Count Basil.
So gath'ring herds, at pressing dangers' call,
Confess the master Deer.

(Musick is heard again, and nearer. Geoffry walks up and down with a military triumphant step.)

CIT: What moves thee thus?
GEOF: I've march'd to this same tune in glorious days.
My very limbs catch motion from the sound,
As they were young again.
SEC. CIT: But here they come.

Enter Count BASIL, *Officers and Soldiers in Procession, with Colours flying, and martial musick. When they have marched half way over the Stage, an Officer of the Duke's enters from the opposite side, and speaks to Count* BASIL, *upon which he gives a sign with his hand, and the martial musick ceases; soft musick is heard at a little distance, and* VICTORIA, *with a long procession of Ladies, enters from the opposite side. The General, &c. pay obeisance to her, as she passes; she stops to return it, and then goes off with her train. After which the military procession moves on, and Exeunt.*

CIT. *to* GEOF: What thinkst thou of the princess?
GEOF: She is fair,
But not so fair as her good mother was. *(Exeunt.)*

— SCENE II —

A Publick Walk on the Ramparts of the Town.

Enter COUNT ROSINBERG, VALTOMER, *and* FREDERICK.— VALTOMER *enters by the opposite side of the Stage, and meets them.*

VALT: O! what a jolly town for way-worn soldiers!
Rich steaming pots, and smell of dainty fare,
From every house salute you as you pass:
Light feats and jugglers' tricks attract the eye;
Frolick, and mirth, musick in ev'ry street;
Whilst pretty damsels, in their best attire,
Trip on in wanton groups, then look behind,
To spy the fools a-gazing after them.
FRED: But short will be the season of our ease,
For Basil is of flinty matter made,
And cannot be allur'd—
'Faith Rosinberg, I would thou didst command us;
Thou art his kinsman, of a rank as noble,
Some years his elder too; how has it been
That he should be preferr'd? I see not why.
ROS: Ah! but I see it, and allow it well;
He is too much my pride to wake my envy.
FRED: Nay, Count, it is thy foolish admiration
Which raises him to such superiour height;
And truly thou hast so infected us,
That I have felt at times an awe before him,
I know not why. 'Tis cursed folly;
Thou art as brave, of as good parts as he.
ROS: Our talents of a diff'rent nature are;
Mine for the daily intercourse of life,
And his for higher things.
FRED: Well, praise him as thou wilt; I see it not;
I'm sure I am as brave a man as he.
ROS: Yes, brave thou art, but 'tis subaltern brav'ry,
And doth respect thyself. Thou'lt bleed as well,
Give, and receive as deep an wound as he.
When Basil fights he wields a thousand swords;
For 'tis their trust in his unshaken mind,
O'erwatching all the changes of the field,
Calm and inventive midst the battle's storm,
Which makes his soldiers bold.—
There have been those, in early manhood slain,
Whose great heroick souls did yet inspire
With such a noble zeal their gen'rous troops,
That to their latest day of bearing arms,
Their grey-hair'd soldiers would all dangers brave
Of desp'rate service, claim'd with boastful pride,
For having fought beneath them in their youth.
Such men have been; of whom it may be said,
Their spirits conquer'd when their clay was cold.
VALT: Yes, I have seen in the eventful field,
When new occasion mock'd all formed art,
E'en old commanders hold experience cheap,
And look to Basil ere his chin was dark.
ROS: One fault he has, I know but only one;
His too great love of military fame
Destroys his thoughts, and makes him oft appear
Unsocial and severe.
FRED: Well, feel I not undaunted in the field?
As much enthusiastick love of glory?
Why am I not as good a man as he?
ROS: He's form'd for great occasions, thou for small.
VALT: But small occasions in the path of life
Lie thickly sown, while great are rarely scatter'd.
ROS: By which you would infer that men like Fred'rick,
Should on the whole a better figure make,
Than men of higher parts; but 'tis not so,
For some shew well, and fair applauses gain,
Where want of skill in other men is graceful.
But do not frown, good Fred'rick, no offence;
Thou canst not make a great man of thyself,
Yet wisely deign to use thy native pow'rs,
And prove an honour'd courtly gentleman.
But hush! no more of this, here Basil comes.

Enter BASIL, *who returns their salute without speaking.*

ROS: What thinkst thou, Valtomer, of Mantua's princess?

VALT: Fame prais'd her much, but hath not prais'd her more
Than on a better proof the eye consents to.
With all that grace and nobleness of mien,
She might do honour to an Emp'rour's throne;
She is too noble for a petty court.
Is it not so, my Lord?—(*To* BASIL, *who only bows assent.*)
Nay, she demeans herself with so much grace,
Such easy state, such gay magnificence,
She should be queen of revelry and show.
FRED: She's charming as the goddess of delight.
VALT: But after her, she most attracted me
Who wore the yellow scarf and walk'd the last,
For tho' Victoria is a lovely woman—
FRED: Nay, it is treason but to call her woman;
She's a divinity, and should be worshipp'd.
But on my life, since now we talk of worship,
She worshipp'd Francis with right noble gifts!
They sparkled so with gold and precious gems
Their value must be great; some thousand crowns.[3]
ROS: I would not rate them at a price so mean;
The cup alone, with precious stones beset,
Would fetch a sum as great. That olive branch
The princess bore herself, of fretted gold,
Was exquisitely wrought. I mark'd it more,
Because she held it in so white a hand.
BASIL: (*in a quick voice.*) Mark'd you her hand? I did not see her hand,
And yet she wav'd it twice.
ROS: It is a fair one, tho' you mark'd it not.
VALT: I wish some painter's eye had view'd the group,
As she and all her lovely damsels pass'd;
He would have found wherewith t'enrich his art.
ROS: I wish so too; for oft their fancied beauties
Have so much cold perfection in their parts,
'Tis plain they ne'er belong'd to flesh and blood.
This is not truth, and doth not please so well
As the varieties of lib'ral nature,
Where ev'ry kind of beauty charms the eye;
Large and small featur'd, flat, and prominent,
Ay, by the mass! and snub-nos'd beauties too.
'Faith ev'ry woman hath some 'witching charm,
If that she be not proud, or captious.
VALT: Demure, or over-wise, or giv'n to freaks.
ROS: Or giv'n to freaks! hold, hold good Valtomer!
Thou'lt leave no woman handsome under heav'n.

[3] A crown was worth five shillings in old British currency.

VALT: But I must leave you for an hour or so,
I mean to view the town if aught worth notice.
FRED: I'll go with thee, my friend.
ROS: And so will I.

(*Exeunt* VALT., FRED., *and* ROS.)

Re-enter ROSINBERG.

ROS: I have repented me, I will not go;
They will be too long absent.—(*Pauses, and looks at Basil, who remains still musing without seeing him.*)
What mighty thoughts engage my pensive friend?
BAS: O! it is admirable.
ROS: How runs thy fancy? what is admirable?
BAS: Her form, her face, her motion, ev'rything!
ROS: The princess? yes, have we not prais'd her much?
BAS: I know you prais'd her, and her off'rings too;
She might have giv'n the treasures of the east
E'er I had known it.
She came again upon my wond'ring sight—
O! didst thou mark her when she first appear'd?
Still distant, slowly moving with her train;
Her robe, and tresses floating on the wind,
Like some light figure in a morning cloud?
Then as she onward to the eye became
The more distinct, the lovelier still she grew.
That graceful bearing of her slender form;
Her roundly-spreading breast, her tow'ring neck,
Her face ting'd sweetly with the bloom of youth—
But when on near approach she tow'rds us turn'd,
Kind mercy! what a countenance was there!
And when to our salute she gently bow'd,
Didst mark that smile rise from her parting lips?
Soft swell'd her glowing cheek, her eyes smil'd too;
O! how they smil'd! 'twas like the beams of heav'n!
I felt my roused soul within me start,
Like something wak'd from sleep.
ROS: Ah! many a slumb'rer heav'n's beams do wake
To care and misery!
BAS: There's something grave and solemn in your voice
As you pronounce these words. What dost thou mean?
Thou wouldst not sound my knell?
ROS: No; not for all beneath the vaulted sky!
But to be plain, thus earnest from your lips
Her praise displeases me. To men like you
If love should come, he proves no easy guest.
BAS: What dost thou think I am beside myself,
And cannot view the fairness of perfection

With that delight which lovely beauty gives,
Without tormenting me with fruitless wishes;
Like the poor child who sees its brighten'd face,
And whimpers for the moon? Thou art not serious?
From early youth, war has my mistress been,
And tho' a rugged one, I'll constant prove,
And not forsake her now. There may be joys
Which to the strange o'erwhelming of the soul,
Visit the lover's breast beyond all others;
E'en now, how dearly do I feel there may!
But what of them? they are not made for me—
The hasty flashes of contending steel
Must serve instead of glances from my love,
And for soft breathing sighs the cannon's roar.

ROS: (*taking his hand.*) Now am I satisfied. Forgive me Basil.

BAS: I'm glad thou art, we'll talk of her no more.
Why should I vex my friend?

ROS: Thou hast not giv'n orders for the march.

BAS: I'll do it soon; thou need'st not be afraid.
To-morrow's sun shall bear us far from hence,
Never perhaps to pass these gates again.

ROS: With last night's close did you not curse this town
That would one single day your troops retard?
And now, methinks, you talk of leaving it,
As though it were the place that gave you birth;
As tho' you had around these strangers' walls
Your infant gambols play'd.

BAS: The sight of what may be but little priz'd,
Doth cause a solemn sadness in the mind,
When view'd as that we ne'er shall see again.

ROS: No, not a whit to wand'ring men like us,
No, not a whit! what custom hath endear'd
We part with sadly, tho' we prize it not;
But what is new some pow'rful charm must own,
Thus to affect the mind.

BAS: (*hastily.*) Yes, what is new, but—No, thou art impatient;
We'll let it pass—It hath no consequence.

ROS: I'm not impatient. 'Faith, I only wish
Some other route our destin'd march had been,
That still thou mightst thy glorious course pursue
With an untroubled mind.

BAS: O! wish it, wish it not! bless'd be that route!
What we have seen to-day I must remember—
I should be brutish if I could forget it.
Oft in the watchful post, or weary march,
Oft in the nightly silence of my tent,
My fixed mind shall gaze upon it still;
But it will pass before my fancy's eye,
Like some delightful vision of the soul,
To soothe, not trouble it.

ROS: What, midst the dangers of eventful war,
Still let thy mind be haunted by a woman?
Who would, perhaps, hear of thy fall in battle,
As Dutchmen read of earthquakes in Calabria,[4]
And never stop to cry alack-a-day!
For me there is but one of all the sex,
Who still shall hold her station in my breast,
Midst all the changes of inconstant fortune;
Because I'm passing sure she loves me well,
And for my sake a sleepless pillow finds
When rumour tells bad tidings of the war;
Because I know her love will never change,
Nor make me prove uneasy jealousy.

BAS: Happy art thou! who is this wond'rous woman?

ROS: It is mine own good mother, faith and truth!

BAS: (*smiling.*) Give me thy hand; I love her dearly too.
Rivals we are not, though our love is one.

ROS: And yet I might be jealous of her love,
For she bestows too much of it on thee,
Who hast no claim but to a nephew's share.

BAS: (*going.*) I'll meet thee some time hence. I must to Court.

ROS: A private conf'rence will not stay thee long.
I'll wait thy coming near the palace gate.

BAS: 'Tis to the publick Court I mean to go.

ROS: I thought you had determin'd otherwise.

BAS: Yes, but on farther thought it did appear
As though it would be failing in respect
At such a time—That look doth wrong me, Rosinberg!
For on my life, I had determin'd thus
Ere I beheld—Before we enter'd Mantua.
But wilt thou change that soldier's dusty garb,
And go with me thyself?

ROS: Yes, I will go.

(*As they are going* ROS. *stops, and looks at* BASIL.)

BAS: Why dost thou stop?

ROS: 'Tis for my wonted caution,
Which first thou gav'st me, I shall ne'er forget it.
'Twas at Vienna, on a publick day,
Thou but a youth, I then a man full form'd;

[4] **Calabria:** the extreme southwestern tip of Italy.

Thy stripling's brow grac'd with its first cockade,
Thy mighty bosom swell'd with mighty thoughts;
Thou'rt for the court, dear Rosinberg, quoth thou;
Now pray thee be not caught with some gay dame,
To laugh and ogle, and befool thyself;
It is offensive in the publick eye,
And suits not with a man of thy endowments.
So said your serious lordship to me then,
And have on like occasions often since,
In other terms repeated—
But I must go to-day without my caution.

BAS: Nay Rosinberg, I am impatient now.
Did I not say we'd talk of her no more.

ROS: Well, my good friend, God grant we keep our word!

(Exeunt.)

ACT II

— SCENE I —

A Room of State. The DUKE OF MANTUA, BASIL, ROSINBERG, *and a number of Courtiers, Attendants, &c. The* DUKE *and* BASIL *appear talking together on the front of the Stage.*

DUKE: But our opinions differ widely there;
From the position of the rival armies,
I cannot think they'll join in battle soon.

BAS: I am indeed beholden to your highness,
But tho' unwillingly, we must depart.
The foes are near, the time is critical;
A soldier's reputation is too fine
To be expos'd e'en to the smallest cloud.

DUKE: An untried soldier's is; but yours, my lord,
Nurs'd with the bloody show'rs of many a field,
And brightest sunshine of successful fortune,
A plant of such a hardy stem hath grown,
E'en Envy's sharpest blasts assail it not.
But after all, by the bless'd holy Cross!
I feel too warm an interest in the cause
To stay your progress here a single hour,
Did I not know your soldiers are fatigu'd,
And two days' rest would but renew their strength.

BAS: Your highness will be pleas'd to pardon me;
My troops are not o'ermarch'd, and one day's rest
Is all our needs require.

DUKE: Ah! hadst thou come
Unfetter'd with the duties of command,
I then had well retain'd thee for my guest,
With claims too strong, too sacred for denial;
Thy noble sire my fellow-soldier was,
Together many a rough campaign we serv'd;
I lov'd him well, and much it pleases me
A son of his beneath my roof to see.

BAS: Were I indeed free master of myself,
Strong inclination would detain me here;
No other tie were wanting.
These gracious tokens of your princely favour
I'll treasure with my best rememb'rances;
For he who shews them for my father's sake,
Doth something sacred in his kindness bear,
As tho' he shed a blessing on my head.

DUKE: Well, bear my greetings to the brave Piscaro,
And say how warmly I embrace the cause.
Your third day's march will to his presence bring
Your valiant troops: said you not so, my lord?

Enter VICTORIA, *the* COUNTESS OF ALBINI, ISABELLA, *and* LADIES.

BAS: *(who changes countenance upon seeing them.)*
Yes, I believe—I think—I know not well—
Yes, please your grace, we march by break of day.

DUKE: Nay, that I know. I ask'd you, noble count,
When you expect th' Imperial force to join.

BAS: When it shall please your grace—I crave your pardon—
I somewhat have mistaken of your words.

DUKE: You are not well? your colour changes, Count,
What is the matter?

BAS: A dizzy mist that swims before my sight—
A ringing in mine ears—'tis strange enough—
'Tis slight—'tis nothing worth—'tis gone already.

DUKE: I'm glad it is. Look to your friend, Count Rosinberg,
It may return again.—*(To* ROSINBERG, *who stands at a little distance, looking earnestly at* BASIL.—DUKE *leaves them, and joins* VICTORIA'*s party.)*

ROS: Good heavens! Basil, is it thus with thee!
Thy hand shakes too! *(taking his hand)* Would we were far from hence.

BAS: I'm well again, thou need'st not be afraid.
'Tis like enough my frame is indispos'd
With some slight weakness from our weary march.
Nay, look not on me thus, it is unkindly—
I cannot bear thine eyes.

The DUKE, *with* VICTORIA *and her* LADIES, *advance to the front of the Stage, to* BASIL.

DUKE: Victoria, welcome here the brave Count Basil.
His kinsman too, the gallant Rosinberg.
May you, and these fair ladies so prevail,
Such gentle suitors cannot plead in vain,
To make them grace my court another day.
I shall not be offended when I see
Your power surpasses mine.
VICT: Our feeble efforts will presumptuous seem
In what your highness fails.
DUKE: There's honour in th' attempt; good success to ye.—*(Duke retires, and mixes with the Courtiers at the bottom of the Stage.)*
VICT: I fear we incommoded you, my Lord,
With the slow tedious length of our procession.
E'en as I pass'd, against my heart it went
To stop your weary soldiers on their way
So long a time.—
BAS: Ah! Madam, all too short!
Time never bears such moments on his wing,
But when he flies too swiftly to be mark'd.
VICT: Ah! surely then you make too good amends
By marking now his after-progress well.
To-day must seem a weary length to him
Who is so eager to be gone to-morrow.
ROS: They must not linger who would quit these walls;
For if they do, a thousand masked foes,
Some under show of rich luxurious feasts,
Gay, sprightly pastime, and high-zested game;—
Nay, some, my gentle ladies, true it is,
The very worst and fellest of the crew,
In fair alluring shape of beauteous dames,
Do such a barrier form t'oppose their way,
As few men may o'ercome.
ISAB: From this last wicked foe should we infer
Yourself have suffer'd much?
ALB: No, Isabella, these are common words,
To please you with false notions of your pow'r.
So all men talk of ladies and of love.
VICT: 'Tis even so. If love a tyrant be,
How dare his humble chained votaries,
To tell such rude and wicked tales of him?
BAS: Because they most of lover's ills complain,
Who but affect it as a courtly grace,
Whilst he who feels is silent.
ROS: But there you wrong me; I have felt it oft.
Oft has it made me sigh at ladies' feet,
Soft ditties sing, and dismal sonnets scrawl.
ALB: In all its strange effects, most worthy Rosinberg,
Has it e'er made thee in a corner sit,
Sad, lonely, moping sit, and hold thy tongue?
ROS: No, 'faith, it never has.
ALB: Ha, ha, ha, ha! then thou hast never lov'd.
ROS: Nay, but I have, and felt its bondage too.
VICT: O! it is pedantry to call it bondage!
Love-marring wisdom, reason full of bars,
Deserve, methinks, that appellation more.
Is it not so, my Lord?—*(To BASIL.)*
BAS: O! surely Madam;
That is not bondage which the soul enthrall'd
So gladly bears, and quits not but with anguish.
Stern honour's laws, the fair report of men,
These are the fetters that enchain the mind,
But such as must not, cannot be unloos'd.
VICT: No, not unloos'd, but yet one day relax'd,
To grant a lady's suit, unus'd to sue.
ROS: Your highness deals severely with us now,
And proves indeed our freedom is but small,
Who are constrain'd, when such a lady sues,
To say it cannot be.
VICT: It cannot be! Count Basil says not so.
ROS: For that I am his friend, to save him pain
I take th'ungracious office on myself.
VICT: How ill thy face is suited to thine office!
ROS: *smiling.* Would I could suit mine office to my face,
If that would please your highness.
VICT: No, you are obstinate and perverse all,
And would not grant it if you had the pow'r.
Albini I'll retire; come Isabella.
BAS. *aside to* ROS: Ah! Rosinberg, thou hast too far presum'd;
She is offended with us.
ROS: No, she is not—
What dost thou fear? be firm and let us go.
VICT: *(pointing to a door leading to other apartments, by which she is ready to go out.)* These are apartments strangers love to see;
Some famous paintings do their walls adorn.
It leads you also to the palace court
As quickly as the way by which you came.

(Exit VICT. *led out by* ROS. *and followed by* ISAB.*)*

BAS: *(aside, looking after them.)* O! what a fool am I! where fled my thoughts?
I might as well as he, now by her side
Have held her precious hand enclos'd in mine;

As well as he, who cares not for it neither.
O! damn it, but he does! that were impossible!

ALB: You stay behind, my Lord.

BAS: Your pardon Madam; honour me so far—

(Exeunt, handing out ALBINI.*)*

— SCENE II —

A Gallery hung with Pictures. VICTORIA *discovered in conversation with* ROSINBERG, BASIL, ALBINI, *and* ISABELLA.

VICT. *to* ROS: It is indeed a work of wond'rous art.
to ISAB: You call'd Francisco here?

ISAB: He comes even now.

Enter ATTENDANT.

VICT. *to* ROS: He will conduct you to the northern gall'ry;
Its striking shades will call upon the eye,
To point its place no guide is wanted there.

(Exeunt ROS. *and* ATTENDANT.*)*

to BAS: Loves not Count Basil too this charming art?
It is an ancient painting much admir'd.

BAS: Ah! do not banish me these few short moments;
Too soon they will be gone! for ever gone!

VICT: If they are precious to you say not so,
But add to them another precious day.
A Lady asks it.

BAS: Ah, Madam! ask the life-blood from my heart!
Ask all but what a soldier may not give.

VICT: 'Tis ever thus when favours are denied,
All had been granted but the thing we beg;
And still some great unlikely substitute,
Your life, your soul, your all of earthly good,
Is proffer'd in the room of one small boon.
So keep your life-blood, gen'rous, valiant lord,
And may it long your noble heart enrich,
Until I wish it shed.

BAS: *(attempts to speak.)* Nay, frame no new excuse; I will not hear it:

(She puts out her hand as if she would shut his mouth, but at a distance from it; BAS. *runs eagerly up to her and presses it to his lips.)*

BAS: Let this sweet hand indeed its threat perform,
And make it heav'n to be for ever dumb!

*(*VICT. *looks stately and offended —* BASIL *kneels.)*

O! pardon me, I know not what I do.
Frown not, reduce me not to wretchedness,
But only grant—

VICT: What should I grant to him
Who has so oft my earnest suit deny'd?

BAS: By heav'n I'll grant it! I'll do any thing,
Say but thou art no more offended with me.

VICT: *(raising him)* Well Basil, this good promise is thy pardon.
I will not wait your noble friend's return
Since we shall meet again.—
You will perform your word!

BAS: I will perform it.

VICT: Farewell, my lord.

(Exeunt, with her LADIES.*)*

BAS: *alone:* "Farewell, my lord," O! what delightful sweetness
The musick of that voice dwells on the ear!
"Farewell, my lord!"—Ay, and then look'd she so—
The slightest glance of her bewitching eye,
Those dark blue eyes, command the inmost soul.
Well, there is yet one day of life before me,
And whatsoe'er betides I will enjoy it.
Tho' but a partial sunshine in my lot
I will converse with her, gaze on her still,
If all behind were pain and misery.
Pain! were it not the easing of all pain,
E'en in the dismal gloom of after years,
Such dear rememb'rance on the mind to wear?
Like silv'ry moon-beams on the 'nighted deep,
When heav'n's blest sun is gone!
Kind mercy! how my heart within me beat
When she so sweetly pled the cause of love!
Can she have lov'd? why shrink I at the thought?
Why should she not? no, no, it cannot be—
No man on earth is worthy of her love.
Ah! if she could, how blest a man were he!
Where rove my giddy thoughts? it must not be.
Yet might she well some gentle kindness bear;
Think of him oft, his absent fate enquire,
And, should he fall in battle, mourn his fall.
Yes, she would mourn—such love might she bestow;
And poor of soul the man who would exchange it
For warmest love of the most loving dame.
But here comes Rosinberg—have I done well?
He will not say I have.

Enter ROSINBERG.

ROS: Where is the princess?
I'm sorry I return'd not ere she went.
BAS: You'll see her still.
ROS: What, comes she forth again?
BAS: She does to-morrow.
ROS: Thou hast yielded then.
BAS: Come, Rosinberg, I'll tell thee as we go:
It was impossible I should not yield.
ROS: And has the first look of a stranger's face
So far bewitched thee?
BAS: A stranger's face!
Long has she been the inmate of my breast!
The smiling angel of my nightly dreams.
ROS: What mean you now? Your mind is raving, Basil.
BAS: I speak in sober earnest. Two years since,
When marching on the confines of this state,
We heard the distant musick of the chace,
And trampling horses near, I turn'd to look,
And saw the loveliest sight of woman's form
That ever blest mine eyes. Her fiery steed,
Struck with the strange accoutrements of war,
Became unruly, and despis'd the rein.
I gently led him with his lovely charge
Past all the ranks: she thank'd me courteously;
Then, with the few companions of her sport,
Took to the woods again. I, with my men,
Our route pursued, and met with her no more.
———————— Her name and state I knew not;
Yet, like a beauteous vision from the blest,
Her form has oft upon my mind return'd;
And tho' this day the sight had ne'er restor'd,
It ne'er had been forgotten. Gentle Rosinberg!
Be not displeas'd! I would have told thee this,
When first to-day we talk'd of Mantua's princess,
But thou wert griev'd and jealous of me then,
And so I shut my breast and said no more.
ROS: O Basil! thou are weaker than a child.
BAS: Yes, yes, my friend, but 'tis a noble weakness;
A weakness which hath greater things atchiev'd
Than all the firm, determin'd strength of reason.
By heav'n! I feel a new-born pow'r within me
Shall make me twenty-fold the man I've been
Before this fated day.
ROS: Fated indeed! but an ill-fated day,
That makes thee other than thy former self.
Yet let it work its will; it cannot change thee
To ought I shall not love.
BAS: Thanks, Rosinberg! thou art a noble heart!
I would not be the man thou couldst not love
For an Imperial Crown.

(Exeunt.)

— SCENE III —

A Small Apartment in the Palace.

Enter DUKE *and* GAURIECIO.

DUKE: The point is gain'd; my daughter is successful,
And Basil is detain'd another day.
GAUR: But does the princess know your secret aim?
DUKE: No, that had marr'd the whole: she is a woman;
Her mind, as suits the sex, too weak and narrow
To relish deep-laid schemes of policy.
Besides, so far unlike a child of mine,
She holds its subtle arts in high derision,
And will not serve us but with bandag'd eyes.
Gauriecio, could I hasty servants find,
Experienc'd, crafty, close, and unrestrain'd
By silly superstitious child-learnt fears,
What might I not effect?
GAUR: O! any thing;
The deep and piercing genius of your highness,
So ably serv'd, might e'en atchieve the empire.
DUKE: No, no, my friend, thou dost o'erprize my parts.
Yet mighty things might be — deep subtle wits
In truth are master-spirits in the world.
The brave man's courage, and the student's lore,
Are but as tools his secret ends to work,
Who hath the skill to use them.
This brave Count Basil, dost thou know him well?
Much have we gain'd but for a single day
At such a time to hold his troops detain'd;
When by that secret message of our spy,
The rival pow'rs are on the brink of action:
But might we more effect? Know'st thou this Basil?
Might he be tamper'd with?
GAUR: That were most dang'rous —
He is a man, whose sense of right and wrong
To such a high romantic pitch is wound,
And all so hot and fiery in his nature,
The slightest hint, as tho' you did suppose
Baseness and treach'ry in him, so he'll deem it,
Would be to rouse a flame that might destroy.
DUKE: But int'rest, int'rest; man's all-ruling pow'r,
Will tame the hottest spirit to your service,

And skilfully applied, mean service too.
E'en as there is an element in nature
Which when subdu'd, will on your hearth fulfil
The lowest uses of domestick wants.

GAUR: Earth-kindled fire, which from a little spark
On hidden fuel feeds its growing strength,
Till o'er the lofty fabrick it aspires
And rages out it's pow'r, may be subdu'd,
And in your base domestick service bound;
But who would madly in its wild career
The fire of heav'n arrest to boil his pot?
No, Basil will not serve your secret schemes,
Tho' you had all to give ambition strives for.
We must beware of him.

DUKE: His father was my friend, I wish'd to gain him,
But since fantastick fancies bind him thus,
The sin be on his head, I stand acquitted,
And must deceive him, even to his ruin.

GAUR: I have prepar'd Bernardo for your service;
To-night he will depart for th' Austrian camp,
And should he find them on the eve of battle,
I've bid him wait the issue of the field.
If that our secret friends victorious prove,
With th' arrow's speed he will return again;
But should fair Fortune crown Piscaro's arms,
Then shall your soothing message greet his ears;
For till our friends some sound advantage gain,
Our actions still must wear an Austrian face.

DUKE: Well hast thou school'd him. Did'st thou add withal,
That 'tis my will he garnish well his speech,
With honied words of the most dear regard,
And friendly love I bear him. This is needful;
And lest my slowness in the promis'd aid
Awake suspicion, bid him e'en rehearse
The many favours on my house bestow'd
By his Imperial master, as a theme
On which my gratitude delights to dwell.

GAUR: I have, an' please your highness.

DUKE: Then 'tis well.

GAUR: But for the yielding up that little fort
There could be no suspicion.

DUKE: My Governor I have severely punish'd
As a most daring traitor to my orders.
He cannot from his darksome dungeon tell,
Why then should they suspect?

GAUR: He must not live if Charles should prove victorious.

DUKE: He's done me service, say not so Gauriecio.

GAUR: A traitor's name he will not calmly bear,
He'll tell his tale aloud—he must not live.

DUKE: Well, if it must—we'll talk of this again.

GAUR: But while with anxious care and crafty wiles,
You would enlarge the limits of your state,
Your highness must beware lest inward broils
Bring danger near at hand: your northern subjects
E'en now are discontented and unquiet.

DUKE: What, dare the ungrateful miscreants thus return
The many favours of my princely grace?
'Tis ever thus indulgence spoils the base,
Raising up pride, and lawless turbulence,
Like noxious vapours from the fulsome marsh
When morning shines upon it—
Did I not lately, with parental care,
When dire invaders their destruction threaten'd,
Provide them all with means of their defence?
Did I not, as a mark of gracious trust,
A body of their vagrant youth select
To guard my sacred person? Till that day
An honour never yet allow'd their race.
Did I not suffer them upon their suit
T'establish manufactures in their towns?
And after all some chosen soldiers spare
To guard the blessings of interiour peace?

GUAR: Nay, please your highness, they do well allow
That when your enemies, in fell revenge,
Your former inroads threaten'd to repay,
Their ancient arms you did to them restore,
With kind permission to defend themselves.
That so far have they felt your princely grace
In drafting from their fields their goodliest youth
To be your servants. That you did vouchsafe,
On paying of a large and heavy fine,
Leave to apply the labour of their hands
As best might profit to the country's weal;
And to encourage well their infant trade
Quarter'd your troops upon them—please your grace,
All this they do most readily allow.

DUKE: They do allow it then, ungrateful varlets;
What would they have? what would they have, Gauriecio?

GAUR: Some mitigation of their grievous burdens,
Which, like an iron weight around their necks,
Do bend their care-worn faces to the earth,
Like creatures form'd upon its soil to creep,
Not stand erect, and view the sun of heav'n.

DUKE: But they beyond their proper sphere would rise;

Let them their lot fulfil as we do ours;
Society of various parts is form'd;
They are its grounds, its mud, its sediment,
And we the mantling top which crowns the whole.
Calm, steady labour is their greatest bliss,
To aim at higher things beseems them not.
To let them work in peace my care shall be,
To slacken labour is to nourish pride.
Methinks thou art a pleader for these fools;
What may this mean Gauriecio?

GAUR: They were resolv'd to lay their cause before you,
And would have found some other advocate
Less pleasing to your Grace, had I refus'd.

DUKE: Well, let them know some more convenient season
I'll think of this, and do for them as much
As suits the honour of my princely state;
Their prince's honour should be ever dear
To worthy subjects as their precious lives.

GAUR: I fear, unless you give some special promise,
They will be violent still—

DUKE: Then do it, if the wretches are so bold;
We can retract it when the times allow
'Tis of small consequence. Go see Bernardo,
And come to me again.

(Exeunt.)

GAUR. *solus*: O! happy people! whose indulgent lord
From ev'ry care, with which increasing wealth,
With all its hopes and fears, doth ever move
The human bosom, would most kindly free,
And kindly leave ye nought to do but toil!
This creature now, with all his reptile cunning,
Writhing and turning thro' a maze of wiles,
Believes his genius form'd to rule mankind,
And calls his sordid wish for territory,
That noblest passion of the soul, ambition:
Born had he been to follow some low trade,
A petty tradesman still he had remain'd,
And us'd the arts with which he rules a state,
To circumvent his brothers of the craft,
Or cheat the buyers of his paltry ware.
And yet he thinks, ha, ha, ha, ha, ha, ha!
I am the tool and servant of his will.
Well, let it be; thro' all the maze of trouble
His plots and base oppression must create,
I'll shape myself a way to higher things,
And who will say 'tis wrong?
A sordid being who expects no faith
But as self-interest binds, who would not trust
The strongest ties of nature on the soul,
Deserves no faithful service. Perverse fate!
Were I like him I would despise this dealing;
But being as I am, born low in fortune,
Yet with a mind aspiring to be great,
I must not scorn the steps which lead to it:
And if they are not right, no saint am I;
I follow nature's passion in my breast,
Which urges me to rise, in spite of fortune.

(Exit.)

—SCENE IV—

An Apartment in the Palace; VICTORIA and ISABELLA are discovered playing at Chess; the Countess ALBINI sitting by them, reading to herself.

VICT: Away with it, I will not play again;
May men no more look foolish in my presence
If thou are not a cheat, an errant cheat.

ISAB: To swear that I am false by such an oath,
Should prove me honest, since its forfeiture
Would bring your highness gain.

VICT: Thou 'rt wrong, my Isabella, simple maid,
For in the very forfeit of this oath,
There's death to all the dearest pride of women.
May man no more look foolish in my presence!

ISAB: And does your grace, hail'd by applauding crouds,
In all the graceful eloquence address'd
Of most accomplish'd, noble, courtly youths,
Prais'd in the songs of heav'n-inspired bards;
Those awkward proofs of admiration prize,
The rustick swain his village fair-one pays?

VICT: O! love will master all the pow'r of art,
Ay all! and she who never has beheld
The polish'd courtier, or the tuneful sage,
Before the glances of her conq'ring eye,
A very native simple swain become,
Has only vulgar charms.
To make the cunning artless, tame the rude,
Subdue the haughty, shake th'undaunted soul;
Yea, put a bridle in the lion's mouth,
And lead him forth as a domestick cur,
These are the triumphs of all-pow'rful beauty!
Did nought but flatt'ring words and tuneful praise,
Sighs, tender glances, and obsequious service,
Attend her presence, it were nothing worth.

I'd put a white coif o'er my braided locks,
And be a plain, good, simple, fire-side dame.
ALB: *(raising her head from her book)* And is, indeed, a plain domestick dame,
Who fills the duties of an useful state,
A being of less dignity, than she
Who vainly on her transient beauty builds
A little poor ideal tyranny?
ISAB: Ideal too!
ALB: Yes, most unreal pow'r;
For she who only finds her self-esteem
In others admiration, begs an alms,
Depends on others for her daily food,
And is the very servant of her slaves;
Tho' oftentimes, in a fantastick hour,
O'er men she may a childish pow'r exert,
Which not ennobles, but degrades her state.
VICT: You are severe, Albini, most severe:
Were human passions plac'd within the breast
But to be curb'd, subdu'd, pluck'd by the roots?
All heav'n's gifts to some good end were giv'n.
ALB: Yes, for a noble, for a gen'rous end.
VICT: Am I ungen'rous then?
ALB: O! most ungen'rous,
Who for the pleasure of a little pow'r
Would give most unavailing pain to those
Whose love you ne'er can recompense again.
E'en now, to-day, O! was it not ungen'rous
To fetter Basil with a foolish tie,
Against his will, perhaps against his duty?
VICT: What, dost thou think against his will, my friend?
ALB: Full sure I am against his reason's will.
VICT: Ah! but indeed thou must excuse me here,
For duller than a shelled crab were she,
Who could suspect her pow'r in such a mind,
And calmly leave it doubtful and unprov'd.
But wherefore dost thou look so gravely on me?
Ah! well I read those looks! methinks they say,
Your mother did not so.
ALB: Your highness reads them true, she did not so.
If foolish vanity e'er soil'd her thoughts
She kept it low, withheld its aliment;
Not pamper'd it with ev'ry motley food,
From the fond tribute of a noble heart,
To the lisp'd flatt'ry of a cunning child.
VICT: Nay, speak not thus Albini, speak not thus
Of little blue-ey'd, sweet, fair-hair'd Mirando.
He is the orphan of a hapless pair,
A loving, beautiful, but hapless pair,
Whose story is so pleasing, and so sad,
The swains have turn'd it to a plaintive lay,
And sing it as they tend their mountain sheep.
to ISAB: Besides I am the guardian of his choice,
When first I saw him dost not thou remember?
ISAB: 'Twas in the publick garden.
VICT: Even so;
Perch'd in his nurse's arms, a roughsome quean,[5]
Ill suited to the lovely charge she bore.
How steadfastly he fix'd his looks upon me,
His dark eyes shining thro' forgotten tears!
Then stretch'd his little arms, and call'd me mam!
What could I do! I took the bantling[6] home—
I could not tell the imp he had no mam!
ALB: Ah! there my child, thou hast indeed no blame.
VICT: Ay, this is kindly said, thanks sweet Albini!
Still call me child, and chide me as thou wilt.
O! would that I were such as thou couldst love!
Couldst dearly love! as thou didst love my mother.
ALB: *(pressing her to her breast)* And do I not? all perfect as she was,
I know not that she went so near my heart
As thou, with all thy faults.
VICT: And sayst thou so? would I had sooner known!
I had done any thing to give thee pleasure.
ALB: Then do so now, and put away thy faults.
VICT: No, say not faults; the freaks of thoughtless youth.
ALB: Nay, very faults they must indeed be call'd.
VICT: O! say but foibles! youthful foibles only!
ALB: Faults, faults, real faults you must confess they are.
VICT: In truth, I cannot do your sense the wrong
To think so poorly of the one you love.
ALB: I must be gone; thou hast o'ercome me now,
Another time I will not yield it so. *(Exit.)*
ISAB: The Countess is severe, she's too severe;
She once was young, tho' now advanc'd in years.
VICT: No, I deserve it all; she is most worthy.
Unlike those faded beauties of the court,
But now the wither'd stems of former flow'rs,
With all their blossoms shed; her nobler mind
Procures to her the privilege of man,
Ne'er to be old till nature's strength decays.

[5] **quean:** wench, country lass.
[6] **bantling:** infant.

Some few years hence, if I should live so long,
I'd be Albini rather than myself.
ISAB: Here comes your little pet.
VICT: I am not in the humour for him now.

Enter MIRANDO, *running up to* VICTORIA, *and taking hold of her gown, but she takes no notice of him, while he holds up his mouth to be kissed.*

ISAB *to* MIR: Thou seest the princess ca'nt be troubled with thee.
MIR: O! but she will! I'll scramble up her robe,
As naughty boys do when they climb for apples.
ISAB: Come here, sweet child; I'll kiss thee in her stead.
MIR: Nay, but I will not have a kiss of thee.
Would I were tall! O! were I but so tall!
ISAB: And how tall wouldst thou be?
MIR: Thou dost not know?
Just tall enough to reach Victoria's lips.
VICT: *(embracing him.)* O! I must bend to this, thou little urchin.
Who taught thee all this wit, this childish wit?
Who does Mirando love? *(embraces him again)*
MIR: He loves Victoria.
VICT: And wherefore loves he her?
MIR: Because she's pretty.
ISAB: Hast thou no little prate to-day Mirando?
No tale to earn a sugar-plumb withal?
MIR: Ay, that I have; I know who loves her grace.
VICT: Who is it pray? thou shalt have comfits for it.
MIR: *(looking slily at her)* It is—it is—it is the count of Maldo.
VICT: Away thou little chit, that tale is old,
And was not worth a sugar-plumb when new.
MIR: Well then, I know who loves her highness well.
VICT: Who is it then?
ISAB: Who is it naughty boy?
MIR: It is the handsome marquis of Carlatzi.
VICT: No, no, Mirando, thou art naughty still;
Thou'st twice had comfits for that tale already.
MIR: Well then, indeed, I know who loves Victoria.
VICT: And who is he?
MIR: It is Mirando's self.
VICT: Thou little imp! this story is not new,
But thou shalt have thy comfits. Let us go.
Go run before us, Boy.
MIR: Nay, but I'll shew you how Count Wolvar did,
When he conducted Isabel from Court.
VICT: How did he do?
MIR: Give me your hand: he held his body thus,
(putting himself in a ridiculous bowing posture.)
And then he whisper'd softly; then look'd so;
(ogling with his eyes affectedly.)
Then she look'd so, and smil'd to him again.
(throwing down his eyes affectedly.)
ISAB: Thou art a little knave, and must be whipp'd.

(Exeunt. MIRANDO *leading out* VICTORIA *affectedly.)*

ACT III

— SCENE I —

An Open Street, or Square

Enter ROSINBERG *and* FREDERICK, *by opposite sides of the Stage.*

FRED: So Basil, from the pressing calls of war,
Another day to rest and pastime gives.
How is it now? methinks thou art not pleas'd.
ROS: It matters little if I am or not.
FRED: Now pray thee do confess thou art asham'd.
Thou, who art wisely wont to set at nought
The noble fire of individual courage,
And call calm prudence the superiour virtue,
What sayst thou now, my candid Rosinberg?
When thy great captain, in a time like this,
Denies his weary troops one day of rest
Before the exertions of approaching battle,
Yet grants it to a pretty lady's suit?
ROS: Who told thee this? it was no friendly tale,
And no one else besides a trusty friend,
Could know his motives. Then thou wrongst me too,
For I admire, as much as thou dost, Fred'rick,
The fire of valour, e'en rash heedless valour,
But not like thee do I depreciate
That far superiour, yea that god-like talent,
Which doth direct that fire, because indeed
It is a talent nature has denied me.
FRED: Well, well, and greatly he may boast his virtue,
Who risks perhaps th'Imperial army's fate,
To please a lady's freaks—
ROS: Go, go, thou'rt prejudic'd:
A passion, which I do not chuse to name,
Has warp'd thy judgement.
FRED: No, by heav'n thou wrongst me!
I do, with most enthusiastick warmth,

True valour love; wherever he is found,
I love the hero too; but hate to see
The praises due to him so cheaply earn'd.

ROS: Then mayst thou now these gen'rous feelings prove.
Behold the man whose short and grizzly hair
In clust'ring locks, his dark brown face o'ershades;
Where now the scars of former sabre wounds,
In hon'rable companionship are seen
With the deep lines of age; whose piercing eye,
Beneath its shading eye-brow keenly darts
Its yet unquenched beams, as tho' in age
Its youthful fire had been again renew'd,
To be the guardian of its darken'd mate.
See with what vig'rous steps his upright form
He onward bears; nay, e'en that vacant sleeve,
Which droops so sadly by his better side,
Suits not ungracefully the vet'ran's mien.
This is the man, whose glorious acts in battle
We heard to-day related o'er our wine.
I go to tell the Gen'ral he is come.
Enjoy the gen'rous feelings of thy breast,
And make an old man happy. *(Exit.)*

Enter GEOFFRY.

FRED: Brave soldier, let me profit by the chance
That led me here; I've heard of thy exploits.

GEOF: Ah! then you have but heard an ancient tale,
Which has been long forgotten.

FRED: But true it is, and should not be forgotten;
Tho' Gen'rals, jealous of their soldiers' fame,
May dash it with neglect.

GEOF: There are, perhaps, who may be so ungen'rous.

FRED: Perhaps, sayst thou? in very truth there are;
How art thou else rewarded with neglect,
Whilst many a paltry fellow in thy corps
Has been promoted? it is ever thus.
Serv'd not Mardini in your company?
He was, tho' honour'd with a valiant name,
To those who knew him well, a paltry soldier.

GEOF: Your pardon, Sir, we did esteem him much,
Although inferiour to his gallant friend,
The brave Sebastian.

FRED: The brave Sebastian!
He was, as I am told, a learned coxcomb,
And lov'd a goose-quill better than a sword.
What, dost thou call him brave?
Thou, who dost bear about that war-worn trunk,
Like an old target, hack'd and rough with wounds,
Whilst, after all his mighty battles, he
Was with a smooth skin in his coffin laid,
Unblemish'd with a scar.

GEOF: His duty call'd not to such desp'rate service;
For I have fought where few alive remain'd,
And none unscath'd; where but a few remain'd,
Thus marr'd, and mangl'd. *(Shewing his wounds.)* As belike you've seen,
O'summer nights, around th'evening lamp,
Some wretched moths, wingless, and half-consum'd,
Just feebly crawling o'er their heaps of dead—
In Savoy, on a small, tho' desp'rate post,
Of full three hundred goodly, chosen men,
But twelve were left, and right dear friends were we
Forever after. They are all dead now,
I'm old and lonely—we were valiant hearts—
Fred'rick Dewalter would have stopp'd a breach
Against the devil himself. I'm lonely now.

FRED: I'm sorry for thee. Hang ungrateful chiefs!
Why art thou not promoted?

GEOF: After that battle, where my happy fate
Had led me to fulfil a glorious part,
Chaf'd with the gibing insults of a slave,
The worthless fav'rite of a great man's fav'rite,
I rashly did affront; our cautious prince,
With narrow policy dependant made,
Dar'd not, as I am told, promote me then,
And now he is asham'd, or has forgot it.

FRED: Fye, fye upon it! let him be asham'd!
Here is a trifle for thee—*(offering him money.)*

GEOF: No, good sir,
I have enough to live as poor men do.
When I'm in want I'll thankfully receive
Because I'm poor, but not because I'm brave.

FRED: You're proud, old soldier—

GEOF: No, I am not proud;
For if I were, methinks I'd be morose,
And willing to depreciate other men.

Enter ROSINBERG.

ROS: *(clapping* GEOF. *on the shoulder.)* How goes it with thee now, my good Field-marshal?

GEOF: The better that I see your honour well,
And in the humour to be merry with me.

ROS: 'Faith, by my sword, I've rightly nam'd thee too;
What is a good Field-marshal, but a man
Whose gen'rous courage and undaunted mind,
Doth marshal others on in glory's way?

Thou art not one by princely favour dubb'd,
But one of nature's making.

GEOF: You shew, my lord, such pleasant courtesy,
I know not how—

ROS: But see, the Gen'ral comes.

Enter BASIL.

ROS: *(pointing to* GEOF.*)* Behold the worthy vet'ran.

BAS: *(taking him by the hand.)* Brave, hon'rable man, your worth I know,
And greet it with a brother-soldier's love.

GEOF: *(taking away his hand in confusion.)* My Gen'ral, this is too much, too much honour.

BAS: *(taking his hand again.)* No valiant soldier, I must have it so.

GEOF: My humble state agrees not with such honour.

BAS: Confound thy state! it is no part of thee:
Let mean souls, highly rank'd, look down on thee;
As the poor dwarf, perch'd on a pedestal,
O'erlooks the giant. 'Tis not worth a thought.
Art thou not Geoffry of the tenth brigade,
Whose warlike feats child, maid, and matron know?
And oft, cross-elbow'd, o'er his nightly bowl,
The jolly toper[7] to his comrade tells.
Whose glorious feats of war, by cottage door,
The ancient soldier tracing in the sand
The many movements of the varied field,
In warlike terms to list'ning swains relate;
Whose bosoms glowing at the wond'rous tale,
First learn to scorn the hind's inglorious life.
Shame seize me if I would not rather be
The man thou art, than court-created chief,
Known only by the dates of his promotion.

GEOF: Ah! would I were, would I were young again,
To fight beneath your standard, noble gen'ral!
Methinks what I have done were but a jest,
Ay, but a jest to what I now should do,
Were I again the man that I have been.
O! I could fight!

BAS: And wouldst thou fight for me?

GEOF: Ay, to the death!

BAS: Then come brave man, and be my champion still;
The sight of thee will fire my soldiers' breasts.
Come, noble vet'ran, thou shalt fight for me.

(Exit with GEOFFRY.*)*

FRED: What does he mean to do?

ROS: We'll know ere long.

FRED: Our gen'ral bears it with a careless face
For one so wise.

ROS: A careless face! on what?

FRED: Now feign not ignorance, we know it all.
News which have spread in whispers from the court,
Since last night's messenger arriv'd from Milan.

ROS: As I'm an honest man I know it not!

FRED: 'Tis said the rival armies are so near,
A battle must immediately ensue.

ROS: It cannot be. Our gen'ral knows it not.
The Duke is of our side, an ally sworn,
And had such messenger to Mantua come,
He would have been appriz'd upon the instant.
It cannot be, it is some idle tale.

FRED: So may it prove till we have join'd them too,
Then heaven grant they may be nearer still;
For O! my soul for war and danger pants,
As doth the noble lion for his prey.
My soul delights in battle.

ROS: Upon my simple word, I'd rather see
A score of friendly fellows shaking hands,
Than all the world in arms. Hast thou no fear?

FRED: What dost thou mean?

ROS: Hast thou no fear of death?

FRED: Fear is a name for something in the mind,
But what, from inward sense I cannot tell.
I could as little anxious march to battle,
As when a boy to childish games I ran.

ROS: Then as much virtue hast thou in thy valour,
As when a child thou hadst in childish play.
The brave man is not he who feels no fear,
For that were stupid and irrational,
But he, whose noble soul its fear subdues,
And bravely dares the danger nature shrinks from.
As for your youth, whom blood and blows delight,
Away with them! there is not in the crew
One valiant spirit.—Ha! what sound is this?

(Shouting is heard without.)

FRED: The soldiers shout; I'll run and learn the cause.

ROS: But tell me first, how didst thou love the vet'ran?

FRED: He is too proud; he was displeas'd with me
Because I offer'd him a little sum.

[7] **toper:** drunkard.

ROS: What money! O! most gen'rous noble spirit!
Noble rewarder of superiour worth!
A halfpenny for Bellisarius![8]
But hark! they shout again—here comes Valtomer.

(Shouting heard without.)

Enter VALTOMER.

What does this shouting mean?
VALT: O! I have seen a sight, a glorious sight!
Thou wouldst have smil'd to see it.
ROS: How smile? methinks thine eyes are wet with tears.
VALT: *(passing the back of his hand across his eyes.)* 'Faith so they are; well, well, but I smil'd too,
You heard the shouting.
ROS *and* FRED: Yes.
VALT: O! had you seen it!
Drawn out in goodly ranks, there stood our troops;
Here, in the graceful state of manly youth,
His dark face brighten'd with a gen'rous smile,
Which to his eyes such flashing lustre gave,
As tho' his soul, like an unsheathed sword,
Had thro' them gleam'd, our noble gen'ral stood;
And to his soldiers, with heart-moving words,
The vet'ran shewing, his brave deeds rehears'd;
Who by his side stood like a storm-scath'd oak,
Beneath the shelter of some noble tree,
In the green honours of its youthful prime.
ROS: How look'd the vet'ran?
VALT: O! I cannot tell thee!
At first he bore it up with chearful looks,
As one who fain would wear his honours bravely,
And greet the soldiers with a comrade's face;
But when Count Basil, in such moving speech
Told o'er his actions past, and bad his troops
Great deeds to emulate, his count'nance chang'd;
High-heav'd his manly breast, as it had been
By inward strong emotion half convuls'd;
Trembled his nether lip; he shed some tears.
The gen'ral paus'd, the soldiers shouted loud;
Then hastily he brush'd the drops away,
And wav'd his hand, and clear'd his tear-chok'd voice,
As tho' he would some grateful answer make;
When back with double force the whelming tide
Of passion came; high o'er his hoary head
His arm he toss'd, and heedless of respect,
In Basil's bosom hid his aged face,
Sobbing aloud. From the admiring ranks
A cry arose; still louder shouts resound.
I felt a sudden tightness grasp my throat
As it would strangle me; such as I felt,
I knew it well, some twenty years ago,
When my good father shed his blessing on me.
I hate to weep, and so I came away.
ROS: *(giving* VALT. *his hand.)* And there, take thou my blessing for the tale.
Hark! how they shout again! 'tis nearer now.
This way they march.

Martial Musick heard. Enter Soldiers marching in order, bearing GEOFFRY *in triumph on their shoulders. After them enter* BASIL*; the whole preceded by a band of musick. They cross over the Stage, are joined by* ROS. &C. *and exeunt.*

— SCENE II —

Enter GAURIECIO *and a* GENTLEMAN*, talking as they enter.*

GAUR: So slight a tie as this we cannot trust.
One day her influence may detain him here,
But love a feeble agent will be found
With the ambitious.
GENT: And so you think this boyish odd conceit
Of bearing home in triumph with his troops
That aged soldier, will your purpose serve?
GAUR: Yes, I will make it serve; for tho' my prince
Is little scrupulous of right and wrong,
I have possess'd his mind, as tho' it were
A flagrant insult on his princely state
To honour thus the man he has neglected;
Which makes him relish, with a keener taste,
My purpos'd scheme. Come let us fall to work,
With all their warm heroick feelings rous'd,
We'll spirit up his troops to mutiny,
Which must retard, perhaps undo him quite.
Thanks to his childish love, which has so well
Procur'd us time to tamper with the fools.
GENT: Ah! but those feelings he has wak'd within them,
Are gen'rous feelings, and endear himself.

---

[8] **Bellisarius:** Belisarius, a great Roman general, who fought with a distinction worthy of the early Republic, during the inglorious reign of Justinian of Constantinople. Baillie refers here to the tale of his needing to beg for charity in his old age.

GAUR: It matters not; tho' gen'rous in their nature,
They yet may serve a most ungen'rous end;
And he who teaches men to think, tho' nobly,
Doth raise within their minds a busy judge
To scan his actions. Send thine agents forth,
And sound it in their ears how much Count Basil
Affects all difficult and desp'rate service,
To raise his fortunes by some daring stroke;
And to the Emp'rour hath pledg'd his word,
To make his troops all dreadful hazards brave;
For which intent he fills their simple minds
With idle tales of glory and renown;
Using their warm attachment to himself
For most unworthy ends.
This is the busy time, go forth my friend;
Mix with the soldiers now in jolly groups,
Around their ev'ning cups. There, spare no cost,

(gives him a purse.)

Observe their words, see how the poison takes,
And then return again.
GENT: I will, my lord.

(Exeunt severally.)

— SCENE III —

A Suite of grand Apartments, with their wide doors thrown open, lighted up with lamps, and filled with company in masks. Enter several MASKS, *and pass through the first apartment to the other rooms. Then enter* BASIL *in the disguise of a wounded soldier.*

BAS: *(alone.)* Now am I in the region of delight!
Within the blessed compass of these walls
She is; the gay light of those blazing lamps
Doth shine upon her, and this painted floor
Is with her footsteps press'd. E'en now perhaps
Amidst that motley rout she plays her part.
There will I go; she cannot be conceal'd,
For but the flowing of her graceful robe
Will soon betray the lovely form that wears it,
Tho' in a thousand masks. Ye homely weeds,—

(looking at his habit.)

Which half conceal, and half declare my state,
Beneath your kind disguise, O! let me prosper,
And boldly take the privilege ye give.
Follow her mazy steps, croud by her side;
Thus, near her face my list'ning ear incline,
And feel her soft breath fan my glowing cheek;
Her fair hand seize, yea press it closely too;
May it not be e'en so? by heav'n it shall!
This once, O! serve me well, and ever after
Ye shall be treasur'd like a monarch's robes;
Lodg'd in my chamber, near my pillow kept;
And oft with midnight lamp I'll visit ye,
And gazing wistfully, this night recall,
With all its past delights.—But yonder moves
A slender form, dress'd in an azure robe;
It moves not like the rest—it must be she.

(Goes hastily into another apartment, and mixes with the masks.)

Enter ROSINBERG *fantastically dressed, with a willow upon his head, and scraps of sonnets, and torn letters fluttering round his neck; pursued by a group of* MASKS *from one of the inner apartments, who hoot at him, and push him about as he enters.*

1ST MASK: Away, thou art a saucy jeering knave,
And fain wouldst make a jest of all true love.
ROS: Nay, gentle ladies, do not buffet me;
I am a right true servant of the fair;
And as this woeful chaplet on my brow,
And these tear-blotted sonnets would denote,
A poor abandon'd lover out of place;
With any mistress ready to engage,
Who will enlist me in her loving service.
Of a convenient kind my talents are,
And to all various humours may be shap'd.
2D MASK: What canst thou do?
3D MASK: Ay, what besides offending?
ROS: O! I can sigh so deeply, look so sad;
Pale out a piteous tale on bended knee;
Groan like a ghost, so very wretched be,
As would delight a tender lady's heart
But to behold.
1ST MASK: Poo, poo, insipid fool!
ROS: But should my lady brisker mettle own,
And tire of all those gentle dear delights,
Such pretty little quarrels I'd invent—
As whether such a fair-one (some dear friend!)
Whose squirrel's tail was pinch'd, or the soft maid,
With fav'rite lap-dog of a surfeit sick,
Have greatest cause of delicate distress:
Or whether—
1ST MASK: Go, thou art too bad indeed!
(aside.) How could he know I quarrell'd with the Count?
2D MASK: Wilt thou do nothing for thy lady's fame?
ROS: Yes, lovely shepherdess, on ev'ry tree,
I'll carve her name, with true-love garlands bound.

Write madrigals upon her roseate cheeks,
Odes to her eye, 'faith ev'ry wart and mole
That spots her snowy skin, shall have its sonnet!
I'll make love-posies for her thimble's edge,
Rather than please her not.

3D MASK: But for her sake what dangers wilt thou brave?

ROS: In truth, fair Nun, I stomach dangers less
Than other service, and were something loth
To storm a convent's walls for one dear glance;
But if she'll wisely manage this alone,
As maids have done, come o'er the wall herself,
And meet me fairly on the open plain,
I will engage her tender steps to aid
In all annoyance of rude briar or stone,
Or crossing rill, some half-foot wide, or so,
Which that fair lady should unaided pass,
Ye gracious powers forbid! I will defend
Against each hideous fly, whose dreadful buz—

4TH MASK: Such paltry service suits thee best indeed.
What maid of spirit would not spurn thee from her?

ROS: Yes, to recall me soon, sublime Sultana!
For I can stand the burst of female passion,
Each change of humour and affected storm;
Be scolded, frown'd upon, to exile sent,
Recall'd, caress'd, chid and disgrac'd again;
And say what maid of spirit would forego
The bliss of one to exercise it thus?
O! I can bear ill treatment like a lamb;

4TH MASK: *(beating him.)* Well, bear it then, thou hast deserv'd it well.

ROS: 'Zounds, lady! do not give such heavy blows;
I'm not your husband, as belike you guess.

5TH MASK: Come lover, I enlist thee for my swain,
Therefore good lady, do forbear your blows,
Nor thus assume my rights.

ROS: Agreed. Wilt thou a gracious mistress prove?

5TH MASK: Such as thou wouldst, such as thy genius suits;
For since of universal scope it is
All women's humour shalt thou find in me.
I'll gently soothe thee with such winning smiles—
To nothing sink thee with a scornful frown;
Teaze thee with peevish and affected fricks,[9]
Caress thee, love thee, hate thee, break thy pate;
But still between the whiles I'll careful be,
In feigned admiration of thy parts,
Thy shape, thy manners, or thy graceful mien,
To bind thy giddy soul with flatt'ry's charm:
For well thou knowst that flatt'ry ever is
The tickling spice, the pungent seas'ning,
Which makes this motley dish of monstrous scraps
So pleasing to the dainty lover's taste.
Thou canst not leave, tho' violent in extreme,
And most vexatious in her teazing moods,
Thou canst not leave the fond admiring soul
Who did declare, when calmer reason rul'd,
Thou hadst a pretty leg.

ROS: Marry, thou hast the better of me there.

5TH MASK: And more, I'll pledge to thee my honest word,
That when your noble swainship shall bestow
More faithful homage on the simple maid,
Who loves you with sincerity and truth,
Than on the changeful and capricious tyrant
Who mocking leads you like a trammell'd ass,
My studied woman's wiles I'll lay aside,
And such a one become.

ROS: Well spoke, brave lady, I will follow thee.

(follows her to the corner of the stage.)

Now on my life, these ears of mine I'd give,
To have but one look of that little face,
Where such a biting tongue doth hold its court
To keep the fools in awe. Nay, nay, unmask;
I'm sure thou hast a pair of wicked eyes,
A short and saucy nose, now prithee do.

(unmasking.)

ALB: *(unmasking.)* Well hast thou guess'd me right?

ROS: *(bowing low.)* Wild freedom chang'd to most profound respect
Doth make an aukward booby of me now.

ALB: I've join'd your frolick with a good intent,
For much I wish'd to gain your private ear.
The time is precious, and I must be short.

ROS: On me your slightest word more pow'r will have,
Most honour'd lady, than a conn'd oration.
Thou art the only one of all thy sex,
Who wearst thy years with such a winning grace,
Thou art the more admir'd the more thou fadst.

ALB: I thank your lordship for these courteous words,
But to my purpose. You are Basil's friend;
Be friendly to him then, and warn him well
This court to leave, nor be allur'd to stay,

[9] **fricks:** freaks, whims, caprices.

For if he does, there's mischief waits him here
May prove the bane of all his future days.
Remember this, I must no longer stay.
God bless your friend and you; I love you both.

(Exit.)

ROS: *(alone.)* What may this warning mean? I had my fears.
There's something hatching which I know not of.
I've lost all spirit for this masking now.

(throwing away his papers and his willow.)

Away ye scraps! I have no need of you.
I would I knew what garment Basil wears;
I watch'd him but he did escape my sight;
But I must search again and find him out. *(Exit.)*

Enter BASIL *much agitated, with his mask in his hand.*

BAS: In vain I've sought her, follow'd ev'ry form
Where aught appear'd of dignity or grace,
I've listen'd to the tone of ev'ry voice;
I've watch'd the entrance of each female mask;
My flutt'ring heart rous'd like a startled hare,
With the imagin'd rustling of her robes,
At ev'ry dame's approach. Deceitful night,
How art thou spent? where are thy promis'd joys?
How much of thee is spent! O! spiteful fate!
And yet within the compass of these walls
Somewhere she is; altho' to me she is not.
Some other eye doth gaze upon her form,
Some other ear doth listen to her voice;
Some happy fav'rite doth enjoy the bliss
My spiteful stars deny.
Disturber of my soul! what veil conceals thee?
What dev'lish spell is o'er this cursed hour?
O! heav'ns and earth, where art thou?

Enter MASK *in the dress of a female conjuror.*

MASK: Methinks thou art impatient, valiant soldier,
Thy wound doth gall thee sorely; is it so?
BAS: Away, away, I cannot fool with thee.
MASK: I have some potent drugs may ease thy smart.
Where is thy wound? is't here?

(pointing to the bandage on his arm.)

BAS: Poo, poo, begone!
Thou canst do nought — 'tis in my head, my heart —
'Tis ev'ry where, where med'cine cannot cure.

MASK: If wounded in the heart, it is a wound
Which some ungrateful fair-one hath inflicted,
And I may conjure something for thy good.
BAS: Ah! if thou couldst! what must I fool with thee?
MASK: Thou must awhile, and be examin'd too.
What kind of woman did the wicked deed?
BAS: I cannot tell thee. In her presence still
My mind in such a wild delight hath been,
I could not pause to picture out her beauty;
Yet nought of woman e'er was form'd so fair.
MASK: Art thou a soldier, and no weapon bear'st
To send her wound for wound?
BAS: Alas! she shoots from such a hopeless height,
No dart of mine hath plume to mount so far.
None but a prince may dare.
MASK: But if thou hast no hope, thou hast no love.
BAS: I love, and yet in truth I had no hope,
But that she might at least with some good will,
Some gentle pure regard, some secret kindness,
Within her dear remembrance give me place.
This was my all of hope, but it is flown,
For she regards me not; despises, scorns me;
Scorns, I must say it too, a noble heart,
That would have bled for her.

(Mask, discovering herself to be VICTORIA, *by speaking in her true voice.)*

O! no, she does not.

(Exit hastily in confusion.)

BAS: *(stands for a moment rivetted to the spot, then holds up both his hands in an extacy.)*
It is herself! it is her blessed self!
O! what a fool am I that had no power
To follow her, and urge th'advantage on.
Be gone unmanly fears! I must be bold.

(Exit after her.)

A Dance of MASKS.

Enter DUKE *and* GAURIECIO, *unmasked.*

DUKE: This revelry, methinks, goes gaily on.
The hour is late, and yet your friend returns not.
GAUR: He will return ere long — nay, there he comes.

Enter GENTLEMAN.

DUKE: Does all go well? *(going close up to him.)*
GENT: All as your grace could wish.
For now the poison works, and the stung soldiers

Rage o'er their cups, and with fire-kindled eyes
Swear vengeance on the chief who would betray
them.
That Frederick too, the discontented man
Of whom your highness was so lately told,
Swallows the bait, and does his part most bravely.
Gauriecio counsel'd well to keep him blind,
Nor with a bribe attempt him. On my soul!
He is so fiery he had spurn'd us else,
And ruin'd all the plot.

DUKE: Speak softly, friend—I'll hear it all in private.
A gay and careless face we now assume.

DUKE, GAUR. and GEN. retire into the inner apartment, appearing to laugh and talk gaily to the different MASKS as they pass them.

Re-enter VICTORIA followed by BASIL.

VICT: Forbear, my lord, these words offend mine ear.

BAS: Yet let me but this once, this once offend,
Nor thus with thy displeasure punish me;
And if my words against all prudence sin,
O! hear them, as the good of heart do list
To the wild ravings of a soul distraught.

VICT: If I indeed should listen to thy words,
They must not talk of love.

BAS: To be with thee, to speak, to hear thee speak,
To claim the soft attention of thine eye,
I'd be content to talk of any thing,
If it were possible to be with thee,
And think of ought but love.

VICT: I fear, my lord, you have too much presum'd,
On those unguarded words, which were in truth
Utter'd at unawares, with little heed,
And urge their meaning far beyond the night.

BAS: I thought, indeed, that they were kindly meant,
As tho' thy gentle breast did kindly feel
Some secret pity for my hopeless pain,
And would not pierce with scorn, ungen'rous scorn,
A heart so deeply stricken.

VICT: So far thou'st read it well.

BAS: Ha! have I well?
Thou dost not hate me then?

VICT: My father comes;
He were displeas'd if he should see thee thus.

BAS: Thou dost not hate me, then?

VICT: Away, he'll be displeas'd—I cannot say—

BAS: Well, let him come, it is thyself I fear;
For did destruction thunder o'er my head,
By the dread pow'r of heav'n I would not stir
Till thou hadst answer'd my impatient soul!
Thou does not hate me?

VICT: Nay, nay, let go thy hold—I cannot hate thee.
(breaks from him and exit.)

BAS: *(alone.)* Thou canst not hate me! no, thou canst
not hate me!
For I love thee so well, so passing well,
With such o'erflowing heart, so very dearly,
That it were sinful not to pay me back
Some small, some kind return.

Enter MIRANDO, dressed like CUPID.

MIR: Bless thee, brave soldier.

BAS: What sayst thou, pretty child? what playful fair
Has deck'd thee out in this fantastick guise?

MIR: It was Victoria's self; it was the princess.

BAS: Thou art her fav'rite then?

MIR: They say I am;
And now, between ourselves, I'll tell thee, soldier,
I think in very truth she loves me well.
Such merry little songs she teaches me—
Sly riddles too, and when I'm laid to rest
Oft times on tip-toe near my couch she steals,
And lifts the cov'ring so, to look upon me.
And often times I feign as tho' I slept;
For then her warm lips to my cheek she lays,
And pats me softly with her fair white hands;
And then I laugh, and thro' mine eye-lids peep,
And then she tickles me, and calls me cheat;
And then we do so laugh, ha, ha, ha, ha!

BAS: What, does she even so, thou happiest child?
And have those rosy cheeks been press'd so dearly?
Delicious urchin! I will kiss thee too.

(Takes him eagerly up in his arms, and kisses him.)

MIR: No, let me down, thy kisses are so rough,
So furious rough—she doth not kiss me so.

BAS: Sweet boy, where is thy chamber? by Victoria's?

MIR: Hard by her own.

BAS: Then will I come beneath thy window soon,
And, if I could, some pretty song I'd sing
To lull thee to thy rest.

MIR: O! no, thou must not; 'tis a frightful place,
It is the church-yard of the neighb'ring dome.
The princess loves it for the lofty trees,
Whose spreading branches shade her chamber
walls;
So do not I; for when 'tis dark o'nights
Goblins howl there, and ghosts rise thro' the ground.

I hear them many a time when I'm a bed,
And hide beneath the cloaths my cow'ring head.
O! is it not a frightful thing, my lord,
To sleep alone i' the dark?

BAS: Poor harmless child! thy prate is wondrous sweet.

Enter a group of MASKS.

1ST MASK: What dost thou here, thou little truant boy?
Come play thy part with us.

MASKS *place* MIRANDO *in the middle, and range themselves round him.*

SONG,—A GLEE

Child, with many a childish wile,
Timid look, and blushing smile,
Downy wings to steal thy way,
Gilded bow, and quiver gay,
Who in thy simple mien would trace
The tyrant of the human race?

Who is he whose flinty heart
Hath not felt thy flying dart?
Who is he that from the wound
Hath not pain and pleasure found?
Who is he that hath not shed
Curse and blessing on thy head?

Ah Love! our weal, our woe, our bliss, our bane,
A restless life have they who wear thy chain!
Ah Love! our weal, our woe, our bliss, our bane,
More hapless still are they who never felt thy pain.

All the MASKS *dance round* CUPID. *Then enter a band of satyrs, who frighten away* LOVE *and his votaries, and conclude the scene, dancing in a grotesque manner.*

ACT IV

— SCENE I —

The Street before BASIL'*s Lodging.*

Enter ROSINBERG *and two* OFFICERS.

ROS: *(speaking as he enters.)* Unless we find him quickly, all is lost.

1ST. OFF: His very guards, methinks, have left their post
To join the mutiny.

ROS: *(knocking very loud.)* Holla! who's there within? confound this door!
It will not ope. O! for a Giant's strength.
Holla, holla, within! will no one hear?

Enter a Porter from the house.

ROS: *(eagerly to the Porter.)* Is he return'd, is he return'd? not yet!
Thy face doth tell me so.

PORT: Not yet, my lord.

ROS: Then let him ne'er return—
Tumult, disgrace, and ruin have their way!
I'll search for him no more.

PORT: He hath been absent all the night, my lord.

ROS: I know he hath.

2D OFF: And yet 'tis possible
He may have enter'd by the secret door;
And now, perhaps, in deepest sleep entranc'd,
Is dead to ev'ry sound.

*(*ROS. *without speaking, rushes into the house, and the rest follow him.)*

Enter BASIL.

BAS: The blue air of the morning pinches keenly.
Beneath her window all the chilly night
I felt it not. Ah! night has been my day,
And the pale lamp which from her chamber gleam'd,
Has to the breeze a warmer temper lent
Than the red burning east.

Re-enter ROSINBERG, *&c. from the house.*

ROS: Himself! himself! He's here, he's here! O! Basil,
What fiend at such a time could lead thee forth?

BAS: What is the matter which disturbs you thus?

ROS: Matter that would a wiser man disturb.
Treason's abroad, thy men have mutinied.

BAS: It is not so; thy wits have mutinied,
And left their sober station in thy brain.

1ST. OFF: Indeed, my Lord, he speaks in sober earnest.
Some secret enemies have been employ'd
To fill your troops with strange imaginations;
As tho' their gen'ral would, for selfish gain,
Their gen'rous valour urge to desp'rate deeds.
All to a man, assembled on the ramparts,
Now threaten vengeance, and refuse to march.

BAS: What! think they vilely of me? threaten too!
O! most ungen'rous, most unmanly thought!

Didst thou attempt (*to* ROS.) to reason with their folly?
Folly it is; baseness it cannot be!

ROS: Yes, truly, did I reason's pow'r essay,
But as well might I reason with the storm,
And bid it cease to rage—
Their eyes look fire on him who questions them;
The hollow murmurs of their mutter'd wrath
Sound dreadful thro' the dark extended ranks,
Like subterraneous grumblings of an earthquake.
———————— The vengeful hurricane
Does not with such fantastick writhings toss
The woods green boughs, as does convulsive rage
Their forms with frantick gesture agitate.
Around the chief of hell such legions throng'd,
To bring back curse and discord on creation.

BAS: Nay, they are men, altho' impassion'd ones.
I'll to go them—

ROS: And we will stand by thee.
This sword is thine against ten thousand strong,
If it should come to this.

BAS: No, never, never!
There is no mean. I with my soldiers must
Or their commander or their victim prove.
But are my officers all staunch and faithful?

ROS: All but that devil, Fred'rick—
He, disappointed, left his former corps,
Where he, in truth, had been too long neglected,
Thinking he should all on the sudden rise,
From Basil's well-known love of valiant men;
And now, because it still must be deferr'd,
He thinks you seek from envy to depress him,
And burns to be reveng'd.

BAS: Well, well—This grieves me too—But let us go.

(*Exeunt.*)

— SCENE II —

The ramparts of the Town. The SOLDIERS *are discovered drawn up in disorderly manner, hollaing and speaking big, and clashing their arms tumultuously.*

1ST SOL: No, comrade, no, hell gape and swallow me!
If I do budge for such most dev'lish orders.

2D SOL: Huzza, brave comrades! Who says otherwise?

3D SOL: No one, huzza! confound all treach'rous leaders!

(*The* SOLDIERS *huzza and clash their arms.*)

5TH SOL: Heav'n dart its fiery light'ning on his head!
We're men, we're not cattle to be slaughter'd!

2D SOL: They who do long to caper high in air
Into a thousand bloody fragments blown,
May follow our brave gen'ral.

1ST SOL: Curse his name
I've fought for him till my strain'd nerves have crack'd!

2D SOL: We will command ourselves; for Milan comrades.

5TH SOL: Ay, ay, for Milan, valiant hearts huzza!

(*All the* SOLDIERS *cast up their caps in the air, and huzza.*)

2D SOL: Yes, comrades, tempting booty waits us there,
And easy service: keep good hearts, my soldiers
The gen'ral comes, good hearts! no flinching boys!
Look bold and fiercely; we're the masters now.

(*They all clash their arms, and put on a fierce threatening aspect to receive their General, who now enters, followed by* ROSINBERG *and* OFFICERS. BASIL *walks close along the front ranks of the Soldiers, looking at them very steadfastly, then retires a few paces back, and raising his arm, speaks with a very full loud voice.*)

BAS: How is it, soldiers, that I see you thus,
Assembled here, unsummon'd by command?

(*A confused murmur is heard amongst the* SOLDIERS; *some of them call out.*)

But we command ourselves; we wait no orders.

(*A confused noise of voices is heard, and one louder than the rest calls out.*)

Must we be butcher'd, for that we are brave?

(*A loud clamour and clashing of arms, then several voices call out.*)

Damn hidden treach'ry! we defy thy orders.
Fred'rick shall lead us now ————

(*Other voices call out.*)

We'll march where'er we list, for Milan march.

(BASIL, *waving his hand, and beckoning them to be silent, speaks with a very loud voice.*)

Yes, march where'er ye list, for Milan march.

SOL: Hear him, hear him!

(*The murmur ceases—a short pause.*)

BAS: Yes, march where'er ye list, for Milan march,
But as banditti, not as soldiers go;

For on this spot of earth I will disband,
And take from you the rank and name of soldiers.

(A great clamour amongst the ranks — some call out.)

What wear we arms for?

(Others call out.)

No, he dares not do it.

(One voice very loud.)

Disband us at thy peril, treach'rous Basil!

(Several of the SOLDIERS *brandish their arms, and threaten to attack him; the* OFFICERS *gather round* BASIL, *and draw their swords to defend him.)*

BAS: Put up your swords,[10] my friends, it must not be.
I thank your zeal, I'll deal with them alone.
ROS: What, shall we calmly stand and see thee butcher'd?
BAS: *(very earnestly.)* Put up, my friends.
*(*OFFICERS *still persist.)* What are you rebels too?
Will no one here his gen'ral's voice obey?
I do command you to put up your swords.
Retire, and at a distance wait th' event.
Obey, or henceforth be no friends of mine.

*(*OFFICERS *retire, very unwillingly.* BASIL *waves them off with his hand till they are all gone, then walks up to the front of his* SOLDIERS, *who still hold themselves in a threatening posture.)*

Soldiers, we've fought together in the field,
And bravely fought; i' the face of horrid death
At honour's call I've led you dauntless on;
Nor do I know the man of all your bands,
That ever poorly from the trial shrunk,
Or yielded to the foe contended space.
Am I the meanest then of all my troops,
That thus ye think, with base unmanly threats,
To move me now? Put up those paltry weapons;
They edgeless are to him who fears them not:
Rocks have been shaken from the solid base;
But what shall move a firm and dauntless mind?
Put up your swords, or dare the threaten'd deed—
Obey, or murder me ————

(A confused murmur — some of the SOLDIERS *call out.)*

March us to Milan, and we will obey thee.

(Others call out.)

Ay, march us there, and be our leader still.
BAS: Nay, if I am your leader, I'll command ye;
And where I do command, there shall you go,
But not to Milan. No, nor shall you deviate
E'en half a furlong from your destin'd way,
To seize the golden booty of the east.
Think not to gain, or temporize with me,
For should I this day's mutiny survive,
Much as I've lov'd you, soldiers, ye shall find me
Still more relentless in pursuit of vengeance;
Tremendous, cruel, military vengeance.
There is no mean — a desp'rate game ye play,
Therefore I say, obey, or murder me.
Do as ye will, but do it manfully.
He is a coward who doth threaten me,
The man who slays me, but an angry soldier,
Acting in passion, like the frantick son,
Who struck his sire, and wept.
*(*SOLDIERS *call out.)* It was thyself who sought to murder us.
1ST. SOL: You have unto the Emp'ror pledg'd your faith,
To lead foremost in all desp'rate service;
You have agreed to sell your soldiers' blood,
And we have shed our dearest blood for you.
BAS: Hear me, my soldiers —
2D SOL: No, hear him not, he means to cozen you.
Fred'rick will do you right —

(Endeavouring to stir up a noise and confusion amongst them.)

BAS: What cursed fiend art thou, cast out from hell
To spirit up rebellion? damned villain!

(Seizes upon 2d SOLDIER, *drags him out from the ranks, and wrests his arms from him; then takes a pistol from his side, and holds it to his head.)*

Stand there, damn'd, meddling villain, and be silent;
For if thou utt'rest but a single word,
A cough, or hem, to cross me in my speech,
I'll send thy cursed spirit from the earth,
To bellow with the damn'd!

(The SOLDIERS *keep a dead silence — after a pause,* BASIL *resumes his speech.)*

Listen to me, my soldiers —
You say that I am to the Emp'ror pledg'd

[10] **Put . . . swords:** "Keep up your bright swords, for the dew will rust them." *Othello,* I.ii.59.

To lead you foremost in all desp'rate service,
For now you call it not the path of glory,
And if in this I have offended you,
I do indeed repent me of the crime.
But new from battles, where my native troops
So bravely fought; I felt me proud at heart,
And boasted of you, boasted foolishly.
I said fair glory's palm ye would not yield
To e'er the bravest legion train'd to arms.
I swore the meanest man of all my troops
Would never shrink before an armed host,
If honour bade him stand. My royal master,
Smil'd at the ardour of my heedless words,
And promis'd, when occasion claim'd our arms,
To put them to the proof.
But ye do peace, and ease, and booty love,
Safe and ignoble service—be it so—
Forgive me that I did mistake you thus,
But do not earn with savage mutiny,
Your own destruction. We'll for Pavia march,
To join the royal army near its walls;
And there with blushing forehead will I plead,
That ye are men with warlike service worn,
Requiring ease and rest. Some other chief,
Whose cold blood boils not at the trumpet's sound,
Will in your rearward station head you then,
And so, my friends, we'll part. As for myself,
A volunteer, unheeded in the ranks,
I'll rather fight, with brave men for my fellows,
Than be the leader of a sordid band.

(A great murmur rises amongst the ranks, SOLDIERS *call out.)*

We will not part, no, no, we will not part.

(All call out together.)

We will not part, be thou our gen'ral still.
BAS: How can I be your gen'ral? ye obey
As caprice moves you; I must be obey'd
As honest men against themselves perform
A sacred oath.—
Some other chief will more indulgent prove—
You're weary grown—I've been too hard a master.
SOLDIERS: Thyself, and only thee, will we obey.
BAS: But if you follow me, yourselves ye pledge
Unto no easy service:—hardships, toils,
The hottest dangers of most dreadful fight,
Will be your portion; and when all is o'er,
Each, like his gen'ral, must contented be
Unbootied to return, a poor brave soldier.
How say ye now? I spread no tempting lure—
A better fate than this, I promise none.
SOLDIERS: We'll follow Basil.
BAS: What token of obedience will ye give?

(A deep pause.)

Soldiers, lay down your arms.

(They all lay down their arms.)

If any here are weary of the service,
Now let them quit the ranks, and they shall have
A free discharge, and passport to their homes;
And from my scanty fortune I'll make good
The well-earn'd pay their royal master owes them.
Let those who follow me their arms resume.

(They all resume their arms.)

(BASIL *holding up his hands.)* High heaven be prais'd!
I had been griev'd to part with you, my soldiers.
Here is a letter from my gracious master,
With offer of preferment in the north,
Most high preferment, which I did refuse,
For that I would not leave my gallant troops.

(Takes out a letter, and throws it amongst them.)

(A great commotion amongst the SOLDIERS*; many of them quit their ranks, and croud about him, calling out.)*

Our gallant gen'ral!

(Others call out.)

We'll spend our heart's blood for thee, noble Basil!
BAS: And so you thought me false? this bites to th' quick!
My soldiers thought me false!

(They all quit their ranks, and croud eagerly around him. BASIL *waving them off with his hands.)*

Away, away, you have disgusted me.

(SOLDIERS *retire to their ranks.)*

'Tis well—retire, and hold yourselves prepar'd
To march upon command; nor meet again
Till you are summon'd by the beat of drum.
Some secret enemy has tamper'd with you,
For yet I will not think that in these ranks,
There moves a man who wears a traitor's heart.

(The soldiers begin to march off, and musick strikes up.)

(BASIL *holding up his hand.*) Cease, cease triumphant sounds,
Which our brave fathers, men without reproach,
Rais'd in the hour of triumph; but this hour
To us no glory brings—
Then silent be your march—ere that again
Our steps to glorious strains like these shall move
A day of battle o'er our heads must pass,
And blood be shed to wash out this day's stain.

(*Exeunt* SOLDIERS, *silent and dejected.*)

Enter FREDERICK, *who starts back on seeing* BASIL *alone.*

BAS: Advance, lieutenant; wherefore shrink ye back?
I've ever seen you bear your head erect,
And front your man, tho' arm'd with frowning death.
Have you done ought the valiant should not do?
I fear you have. (FRED. *looks confused.*)
With secret art, and false insinuation,
The simple untaught soldiers to seduce
From their sworn duty, might become the base,
Become the coward well; but oh! what villain
Had the curs'd pow'r t'engage thy valiant worth
In such a work as this?
FRED: Is Basil, then, so lavish of his praise
On a neglected pitiful subaltern?
It were a libel on his royal master;
A foul reproach upon fair fortune cast,
To call me valiant:
And surely he has been too much their debtor
To mean them this rebuke.
BAS: Is nature th[e]n so sparing of her gifts,
That it is wonderful when they are found
Where fortune smiles not?
Thou art by nature brave, and so am I,
But in those distant ranks moves there not one

(*Pointing off the stage.*)

Of high ennobled soul, by nature form'd
A hero and commander, who will, yet,
In his untrophied grave forgotten lie
With meaner men? I dare be sworn there does.
FRED: What need of words? I crave of thee no favour.
I have offended against armed law,
And shrink not from my doom.
BAS: I know thee well, I know thou fear'st not death;
On scaffold or in field with dauntless breast
Thou wilt engage him: and if thy proud soul,
In sullen obstinacy scorns all grace
E'en be it so. But if with manly gratitude
Thou truly canst receive a brave man's pardon,
Thou hast it freely.
FRED: It must not be. I've been thine enemy—
I've been unjust to thee—
BAS: I know thou hast;
But thou art brave, and I forgive thee all.
FRED: My lord! my gen'ral! Oh! I cannot speak!
I cannot live and be the wretch I am!
BAS: But thou canst live, and be an honest man
From errour turn'd,—canst live and be my friend.

(*Raising* FRED. *from the ground.*)

Forbear, forbear! see where our friends advance,
They must not think thee suing for a pardon;
That would disgrace us both. Yet, ere they come,
Tell me, if that thou may'st with honour tell,
What did seduce thee from thy loyal faith?
FRED: No cunning traitor did my faith attempt,
For then I had withstood him; but of late,
I know not how—a bad and restless spirit
Has work'd within my breast, and made me wretched.
I've lent mine ear to foolish idle tales,
Of very zealous, tho' but new-made friends.
BAS: Softly, our friends approach—of this again.

(*Exeunt.*)

—SCENE III—

An Apartment in BASIL'S *lodgings. Enter* BASIL *and* ROSINBERG.

ROS: Thank heaven I am now alone with thee,
Last night I sought thee with an anxious mind,
And curs'd thine ill-tim'd absence—
There's treason in this most deceitful court,
Against thee plotting, and this morning's tumult
Hath been its damn'd effect.
BAS: Poo, poo, my friend;
The nature of man's mind too well thou know'st,
To judge as vulgar hood-wink'd statesmen do;
Who ever with their own poor wiles misled,
Believe each popular tumult or commotion,
Must be the work of deep-laid policy.
Poor, mean, mechanick souls, who little know
A few short words of energetick force,
Some pow'rful passion on the sudden rous'd,
The animating sight of something noble,
Some fond trait of the mem'ry finely wak'd,
A sound, a simple song without design,
In revolutions, tumults, wars, rebellions.
All grand events, have oft effected more
Than deepest cunning of their paltry art.

Some drunken soldier, eloquent with wine,
Who loves not fighting, hath harangu'd his mates,
For they in truth some hardships have endur'd.
Wherefore in this should we suspect the court?

ROS: Ah! there is something, friend, in Mantua's court,
Will make the blackest trait of bare-fac'd treason
Seem fair and guiltless to thy partial eye.

BAS: Nay, 'tis a weakness in thee, Rosinberg,
Which makes thy mind so jealous and distrustful.
Why should the duke be false?

ROS: Because he is a double, crafty prince—
Because I've heard it rumour'd secretly,
That he in some dark treaty is engag'd,
E'en with our master's enemy the Frank.

BAS: And so thou think'st—

ROS: Nay, hear me to the end.
Last night that good and honourable dame,
Noble Albini, with most friendly art,
From the gay clam'rous throng my steps beguil'd,
Unmask'd before me, and with earnest grace,
Entreated me, if I were Basil's friend,
To tell him hidden danger waits him here,
And warn him well fair Mantua's court to leave.
She said she lov'd thee much, and hadst thou seen
How anxiously she urg'd—

BAS: *(interrupting him.)* By heav'n and earth,
There is a ray of light breaks thro' thy tale,
And I could leap like madmen in their fricks,
So blessed is the gleam! Ah! no, no, no!
It cannot be, alas! it cannot be,
Yet didst thou say she urg'd it earnestly?
She is a woman, who avoids all share
In secret politicks; one only charge
Her int'rest claims, Victoria's guardian friend—
And she would have me hence—it must be so.
O! would it were; how saidst thou, gentle Rosinberg?
She urg'd it earnestly—how did she urge it?
Nay, pri'thee, do not stare upon me thus,
But tell me all her words—what said she else?

ROS: O Basil! I could laugh to see thy folly,
But that thy weakness doth provoke me so.
Most admirable, brave, determin'd man!
So well, so lately try'd, what art thou now?
A vain deceitful thought transports thee thus.
Thinkst thou—

BAS: I will not tell thee what I think.

ROS: But I can guess it well, and it deceives thee.
Leave this detested place, this fatal court,
Where damn'd deceitful cunning plots thy ruin.
A soldier's duty calls thee loudly hence.
The time is critical. How wilt thou feel
When they shall tell these tidings in thine ear,
That brave Piscaro, and his royal troops,
Our valiant fellows, have the en'my fought,
Whilst we, so near at hand, lay loit'ring here?

BAS: Thou dost disturb thy brain with fancied fears.
Our fortunes rest not on a point so nice
That one short day should be of all this moment;
And yet this one short day will be to me
Worth years of other time.

ROS: Nay, rather say,
A day to darken all thy days beside,
Confound the fatal beauty of that woman,
Which has bewitch'd thee so!

BAS: 'Tis most ungen'rous
To push me thus with rough unsparing hand,
Where but the slightest touch is felt so dearly.
It is unfriendly.

ROS: God knows my heart! I would not give thee pain;
But it disturbs me, Basil, vexes me,
To see thee so enthralled by a woman.
If she is fair, others are fair as she.
Some other face will like emotions raise,
When thou canst better play a lover's part;
But for the present, fye upon it, Basil!

BAS: What, is it possible thou hast beheld,
Hast tarried by her too, her converse shar'd,
Yet talkst as tho' she were a common fair-one,
Such as a man may fancy and forget?
Thou art not, sure, so dull and brutish grown;
It is not so, thou dost belie thy thoughts,
And vainly try'st to gain me with the cheat.

ROS: So thinks each lover of the maid he loves,
Yet in their lives some many maidens love.
Curse on it! leave this town, and be a soldier!

BAS: Have done, have done! why dost thou bait me thus?
Thy words become disgusting to me, Rosinberg.
What claim hast thou mine actions to controul?
I'll Mantua leave, when it is fit I should.

ROS: Then, 'faith! 'tis fitting thou shouldst leave it now;
Ay, on the instant. Is't not desperation
To stay, and hazard ruin on thy fame,
Tho' yet uncheer'd e'en by that tempting lure,
No lover breathes without? thou hast no hope.

BAS: What dost thou mean? curse on the paltry thought.
That I should count and bargain with my heart,
Upon the chances of unstinted favour,

As little souls their base-bred fancies feed?
O! were I conscious that within her breast
I held some portion of her dear regard,
Tho' pent for life within a prison's walls,
Where thro' my grate I yet might sometimes see
E'en but her shadow sporting in the sun;
Tho' plac'd by fate where some obstructing bound,
Some deep impassable, between us roll'd,
And I might yet from some high tow'ring cliff,
Perceive her distant mansion from afar,
Or mark its blue smoke rising eve and morn;
Nay, tho' within the circle of the moon
Some spell did fix her, never to return,
And I might wander in the hours of night,
And upward turn mine ever-gazing eye,
Fondly to mark upon its varied disk,
Some little spot that might her dwelling be;
My fond, my fixed heart would still adore
And own no other Love. Away, away!
How canst thou say to one who loves like me,
Thou hast no hope?

ROS: But with such hope, my friend, how stand thy fears?
Are they so well refin'd? How wilt thou bear
Ere long to hear that some high, favour'd prince
Has won her heart, her hand, has married her?
Tho' now unshackled, will it always be?

BAS: By heav'n thou dost contrive but to torment!
And hast a pleasure in the pain thou giv'st.
There is malignity in what thou say'st.

ROS: No, not malignity, but kindness, Basil,
That fain would save thee from the yawning gulph,
To which blind passion guides thy heedless steps.

BAS: Go, rather save thyself
From the weak passion which has seiz'd thy breast,
T' assume authority with sage-like brow,
And shape my actions by thine own caprice.
I can direct myself—

ROS: Yes, do thyself,
And let no artful woman do it for thee.

BAS: I scorn thy thought: it is beneath my scorn;
It is of meanness sprung—an artful woman!
O! she has all the loveliness of heav'n,
And all its goodness too!

ROS: I mean not to impute dishonest arts.
I mean not to impute—

BAS: No, 'faith, thou canst not.

ROS: What, can I not? their arts all women have.
But now of this no more; it moves thee greatly.
Yet once again, as a most loving friend,
Let me conjure thee, if thou prizest honour,
A soldier's fair repute, a hero's fame,
What noble spirits love; and well I know
Full dearly dost thou prize them, leave this place,
And give thy soldiers orders for the march.

BAS: Nay, since thou must assume it o'er me thus,
Be gen'ral, and command my soldiers too.

ROS: What hath this passion in so short a space,
O! curses on it! so far chang'd thee, Basil?
That thou dost take with such ungentle warmth,
The kindly freedom of thine ancient friend.
Methinks the beauty of a thousand maids
Would not have mov'd me thus to treat my friend,
My best, mine earliest friend!

BAS: Say kinsman rather, chance has link'd us so,
Our blood is near, our hearts are sever'd far;
No act of choice did e'er unite our souls.
Men most unlike we are, our thoughts unlike;
My breast disowns thee—thou'rt no friend of mine.

ROS: Ah! have I then so long, so dearly lov'd thee;
So often, with an elder brother's care,
Thy childish rambles tended, shar'd thy sports;
Fill'd up by stealth thy weary school-boy's task;
Taught thy young arms thine earliest feats of strength;
With boastful pride thine early rise beheld
In glory's paths, contented then to fill
A second place, so I might serve with thee;
And say'st thou now, I am no friend of thine?
Well, be it so; I am thy kinsman still,
And by that title will I save thy name
From danger of disgrace. Indulge thy will:
I'll lay me down and feign that I am sick,
And yet I shall not feign—I shall not feign,
For thy unkindness makes me sick indeed;
It will be said that Basil tarried here
To save his friend, for so they'll call me still;
Nor will dishonour fall upon thy name
For such a kindly deed.—

(BASIL *walks up and down in great agitation, then stops, covers his face with his hands, and seems to be overcome.* ROSINBERG *looks at him earnestly.*)

ROS: O! blessed heav'n, he weeps!

(*Runs up to him, and catches him in his arms.*)

O Basil! I have been too hard upon thee.
And is it possible I've mov'd thee thus?

BAS: *(in a convulsed broken voice.)* I will renounce—I'll leave—

ROS: What says my Basil?

BAS: I'll Mantua leave—I'll leave this seat of bliss—
This lovely woman—tear my heart in twain—
Cast off at once my little span of joy—
Be wretched—miserable—whate'er thou wilt—
Dost thou forgive me?

ROS: O my friend! my friend!
I love thee now more than I ever lov'd thee.
I must be cruel to thee to be kind,
Each pang I see thee feel strikes thro' my heart;
Then spare us both, call up thy noble spirit,
And meet the blow at once—thy troops are ready—
Let us depart, nor lose another hour.

*(*BASIL *shrinks from his arms, and looks at him with somewhat of an upbraiding, at the same time of a sorrowful look.)*

BAS: Nay, put me not to death upon the instant;
I'll see her once again, and then depart.

ROS: See her but once again, and thou art ruin'd.
It must not be—if thou regard'st me—

BAS: Well then, it shall not be. Thou hast no mercy!

ROS: Ah! thou wilt bless me all thine after-life
For what, to thee, seems now so merciless.

BAS: *(sitting down very dejectedly.)* Mine after life! what is mine after life?
My day is clos'd! the gloom of night is come!
A hopeless darkness settles o'er my fate.
I've seen the last look of her heav'nly eyes,
I've heard the last sounds of her blessed voice,
I've seen her fair form from my sight depart;
My doom is clos'd!

ROS: *(Hanging over him with pity and affection.)*
Alas! my friend!

BAS: In all her lovely grace she disappear'd,
Ah! little thought I never to return.

ROS: Why so desponding? think of warlike glory.
The fields of fair renown are still before thee;
Who would not burn such noble fame to earn?

BAS: What now are arms, or fair renown to me?
Strive for it those who will—and yet a while
Welcome rough war, with all thy scenes of blood,
(Starting from his seat.)
Thy roaring thunders, and thy clashing steel,
Welcome once more! what have I now to do
But play the brave man o'er again, and die?

Enter ISABELLA.

ISAB. *to* BAS: My princess bids me greet you, noble count.

BAS: *(starting.)* What dost thou say?

ROS: D——n this untimely message!

ISAB: The princess bids me greet you, noble count;
In the cool grove, hard by the southern gate,
She with her train—

BAS: What, she indeed herself?

ISAB: Herself, my lord, and she requests to see you.

BAS: Thank heav'n for this; I will be there anon.

ROS: *(taking hold of him.)* Stay, stay, and do not be a madman still.

BAS: Let go thy hold; what, must I be a brute,
A very brute to please thee? no, by heav'n!

(Breaks from him, and exit.)

ROS: *(striking his forehead.)* All lost again! black curses light upon her!

(Turning eagerly to ISAB.*)*

And so thy virtuous mistress sends thee here
To make appointments, hon'rable dame?

ISAB: Not so, my lord, you must not call it so;
The court will hunt to-morrow, and Victoria
Would have your noble gen'ral of her train.

ROS: Confound these women, and their artful snares,
Since men will be such fools!

ISAB: Yes, grumble at our empire as you will—

ROS: What, boast ye of it? empire do ye call it?
It is your shame! a short liv'd tyranny
That ends at last in hatred and contempt.

ISAB: Nay, but some women do so wisely rule,
Their subjects never from the yoke escape.

ROS: Some women do, but they are rarely found.
There is not one in all your paltry court
Hath wit enough for the ungen'rous task.
'Faith! of you all, not one, but brave Albini,
And she disdains it.—Good be with you, lady!

(Going.)

ISAB: O! would I could but touch that stubborn heart,
How dearly should he pay for this hour's storm!

(Exeunt severally.)

—SCENE IV—

A Summer Apartment in the Country, the windows of which look to a forest. Enter VICTORIA *in a hunting dress, followed by* ALBINI *and* ISABELLA, *speaking as they enter.*

VICT. *to* ALB: And so you will not share our sport to-day?
ALB: My days of frolick should ere this be o'er,
But thou, my charge, hast kept me youthful still.
I should most gladly go, but since the dawn
A heavy sickness hangs upon my heart,
I cannot hunt to-day.
VICT: I'll stay at home and nurse thee, dear Albini,
ALB: No, no, thou shalt not stay.
VICT: Nay, but I will.
I cannot follow to the cheerful horn
Whilst thou art sick at home.
ALB: Not very sick.
Rather than thou shouldst stay, my gentle child,
I'll mount my horse, and go e'en as I am.
VICT: Nay, then I'll go, and soon return again.
Meanwhile, do thou be careful of thyself.
ISAB: Hark, hark! the shrill horn calls us to the field,
Your highness hears it? *(musick without.)*
VICT: Yes, my Isabella,
I hear it, and methinks e'en at the sound
I vault already on my leathern seat,
And feel the fiery steed beneath me shake
His mantled sides, and paw the fretted earth;
Whilst I aloft, with gay equestrian grace,
The low salute of gallant lords return;
Who waiting round with eager watchful eye,
And reined steeds, the happy moment seize.
O! didst thou never hear, my Isabell,
How nobly Basil in the field becomes
His fiery courser's back?
ISAB: They say most gracefully.
ALB: What, is the valiant count not yet departed?
VICT: You would not have our gallant Basil go
When I have bade him stay? not so, Albini.
ALB: Fye! reigns that spirit still so strong within thee,
Which vainly covets all men's admiration,
And is to others cause of cruel pain?
O! would thou couldst subdue it!
VICT: My gentle friend, thou shouldst not be severe;
For now in truth I love not admiration
As I was wont to do; in truth I do not!
But yet, this once my woman's heart excuse,
For there is something strange in this man's love,
I never met before, and I must prove it.
ALB: Well, prove it then, be stricter to thyself,
And bid sweet peace of mind a sad farewell.
VICT: O no! that will not be! 'twill peace restore;
For after this, all folly of the kind
Will quite insipid and disgusting be;
And so I shall become a prudent maid,
And passing wise at last. *(musick heard without.)*
Hark, hark! again!
All good be with you! I'll return ere long.

(Exeunt VICTORIA *and* ISABELLA.*)*

ALB: *(solus.)* Ay, go, and ev'ry blessing with thee go,
My most tormenting, and most pleasing charge!
Like vapour, from the mountain stream art thou,
Which highly rises on the morning air,
And shifts its fleeting form with ev'ry breeze,
For ever varying, and for ever graceful.
Endearing, gen'rous, bountiful and kind;
Vain, fanciful, and fond of worthless praise;
Courteous and gentle, proud and magnificent;
And yet these adverse qualities in thee,
No striking contrast, nor dissonance make;
For still thy good and amiable gifts
The sober dignity of virtue wear not,
And such a 'witching mien thy follies shew,
They make a very idiot of reproof,
And smile it to disgrace—
What shall I do with thee?—it grieves me much
To hear count Basil is not yet departed.
When from the chace he comes, I'll watch his steps,
And speak to him myself—
O! I could hate her for that poor ambition
Which silly adoration only claims,
But that I well remember, in my youth
I felt the like—I did not feel it long;
I tore it soon, indignant from my breast,
As that which did degrade a noble mind. *(Exit.)*

— SCENE V —

A very beautiful Grove in the forest. Musick and horns heard afar off, whilst huntsmen and dogs appear passing over the stage, at a great distance. Enter VICTORIA *and* BASIL, *as if just alighted from their horses.*

VICT: *(speaking to attendants without.)* Lead on our horses to the further grove,
And wait us there—
(to BAS.*)* This spot so pleasing, and so fragrant is,
'Twere sacrilege with horses hoofs to wear
Its velvet turf, where little elfins dance,
And fairies sport beneath the summer's moon:
I love to tread upon it.

BAS: O! I would quit the chariot of a god
For such delightful footing!
VICT: I love this spot.
BAS: It is a spot where one would live and die.
VICT: See, thro' the twisted boughs of those high elms,
The sun-beams on the bright'ning foliage play,
And tinge the scaled bark with ruddy brown.
Is it not beautiful?
BAS: Tis passing beautiful
To see the sun-beams on the foliage play,

(In a soft voice.)

And tinge the scaled bark with ruddy brown.
VICT: And here I've stood full often, and admir'd
The graceful bending, o'er that shady pool,
Of yon green willow, whose fair sweepy boughs
So kiss their image on the glassy plain,
And bathe their leafy tresses in the stream.
BAS: And I too love to see its drooping boughs
So kiss their image on the glassy plain,
And bathe their leafy tresses in the stream.
VICT: My lord, it is uncivil in you thus
My very words with mock'ry to repeat.
BAS: Nay, pardon me, did I indeed repeat?
I meant it not; but when I hear thee speak,
So sweetly dwells thy voice upon mine ear,
My tongue e'en unawares assumes the tone;
As mothers on their lisping infants gaze,
And catch their broken words, I pri'thee pardon!
VICT: But we must leave this grove, the birds fly low,
This should forbode a storm, and yet o'erhead
The sky, bespread with little downy clouds
Of purest white, would seem to promise peace.
How beautiful those pretty snowy clouds!
BAS: Of a most dazzling brightness!
VICT: Nay, nay, a veil that tempers heaven's brightness,
Of softest, purest white.
BAS: As tho' an angel, in his upward flight,
Had left his mantle floating in mid-air.
VICT: Still most unlike a garment, small and sever'd,

(Turning round, and perceiving that he is gazing at her.)

But thou regard'st them not.
BAS: Ah! what should I regard, where should I gaze?
For in that far-shot glance, so keenly wak'd
That sweetly rising smile of admiration,
Far better do I learn how fair heav'n is,
Than if I gaz'd upon the blue serene.
VICT: Remember you have promis'd, gentle count,
No more to vex me with such foolish words.
BAS: Ah! wherefore should my tongue alone be mute?
When every look and every motion tell,
So plainly tell, and will not be forbid,
That I adore thee, love thee, worship thee!

(VICTORIA looks haughty and displeased.)

Ah! pardon me, I know not what I say.
Ah! frown not thus! I cannot see thee frown.
I'll do whate'er thou wilt, I will be silent;
But O! a reined tongue, and bursting heart,
Are hard at once to bear! will thou forgive me?
VICT: We'll think no more of it; we'll quit this spot;
I do repent me that I led thee here,
But 'twas the fav'rite path of a dear friend.
Here, many a time we wander'd, arm in arm;
We lov'd this grove, and now that he is absent,
I love to haunt it still. *(BASIL starts.)*
BAS: His fav'rite path—a friend—here arm in arm—

(Clasping his hands, and raising them to his head.)

Then there is such an one!

(Drooping his head, and looking distractedly upon the ground.)

I dream'd not of it.
VICT: *(pretending not to see him.)* That little lane with woodbine all o'ergrown,
He lov'd so well!—it is a fragrant path,
Is it not, [C]ount?
BAS: It is a gloomy one!
VICT: I have, my lord, been wont to think it cheerful.
BAS: I thought your highness meant to leave this spot.
VICT: I do, and by this lane we'll take our way;
For here he often walk'd with saunt'ring pace,
And listen'd to the wood-lark's ev'ning song;
BAS: What, must I on his very footsteps go?
Accursed be the ground on which he's trod!
VICT: And is Count Basil so uncourtly grown,
That he would curse my brother to my face?
BAS: Your brother! gracious god! is it your brother?
That dear, that loving friend of whom you spoke,
Is he indeed your brother?
VICT: He is indeed, my lord.
BAS: Then heav'n bless him! all good angels bless him!
I could weep o'er him now, shed blood for him!
I could—O! What a foolish heart have I!

(Walks up and down with a hurried step, tossing about his arms in transport, then stops short, and runs up to VICTORIA.)

Is it indeed your brother?
VICT: It is indeed: what thoughts disturb'd thee so?
BAS: I will not tell thee; foolish thoughts they were.
Heav'n bless your brother!
VICT: Ay, heav'n bless him too!
I have but he; would I had two brave brothers,
And thou wert one of them.
BAS: I would fly from thee to earth's utmost bounds,
Were I thy brother—
And yet, methinks, I would I had a sister.
VICT: And wherefore would ye?
BAS: To place her near thee,
The soft companion of thy hours to prove,
And, when far distant, sometimes talk of me.
Thou couldst not chide a gentle sister's cares.
Perhaps, when rumour from the distant war,
Uncertain tales of dreadful slaughter bore,
Thou'dst see the tear hang on her pale wan cheek.
And kindly say, how does it fare with Basil?
VICT: No more of this—indeed there must no more.
A friend's remembrance I will ever bear thee.
But see where Isabella this way comes,
I had a wish to speak with her alone.
Attend us here, for soon will we return,
And then take horse again. *(Exit.)*
BAS: *(looking after her for some time.)* See with what graceful steps she moves along,
Her lovely form in ev'ry action lovely.
If but the wind her ruffl'd garment raise,
It twists it into some light pretty fold,
Which adds new grace. Or should some small mishap,
Some tangling branch, her fair attire derange,
What would in others strange, or aukward seem,
But lends to her some wild bewitching charm.
See, yonder does she raise her lovely arm
To pluck the dangling hedge-flow'r as she goes;
And now she turns her head, as tho' she view'd
The distant landscape; now methinks she walks
With doubtful ling'ring steps—will she look back?
Ah no! yon thicket hides her from my sight.
Bless'd are the eyes that may behold her still,
Nor dread that ev'ry look shall be the last!
And yet she said she would remember me.
I will believe it; Ah! I must believe it,
Or be the saddest soul that sees the light!
But lo! a messenger, and from the army;
He brings me tidings; grant they may be good!
Till now I never fear'd what man might utter;
I dread his tale, God grant it may be good!

Enter MESSENGER.

From the army?
MESS: Yes, my lord.
BAS: What tidings brings't thou?
MESS: Th' imperial army, under brave Piscaro,
Have beat the enemy near Pavia's walls.
BAS: Ha! have they fought? and is the battle o'er?
MESS: Yes, conquer'd; ta'en the French king prisoner,
Who, like a noble, gallant gentleman,
Fought to the last, nor yielded up his sword
Till, being one amidst surrounding foes,
His arm could do no more.
BAS: What dost thou say? who is made prisoner?
What king did fight so well?
MESS: The king of France;
BAS: Thou saidst—thy words do ring so in mine ears,
I cannot catch their sense—the battle's o'er?
MESS: It is, my lord. Piscaro staid your coming,
But could no longer stay. His troops were bold,
Occasion press'd him, and they bravely fought—
They bravely fought, my lord.
BAS: I hear, I hear thee.
Accurs'd am I, that it should wring my heart
To hear they bravely fought.—
They bravely fought, whilst we lay ling'ring here;
O! what a fated blow to strike me thus!
Perdition! shame! disgrace! a damned blow!
MESS: Ten thousand of the enemy are slain;
We too have lost full many a gallant soul.
I view'd the closing armies from afar;
Their close pick'd ranks in goodly order spread,
Which seem'd alas! when that the fight was o'er,
Like the wild marshes' crop of stately reeds,
Laid with the passing storm. But woe is me!
When to the field I came, what dismal sights!
What waste of life! what heaps of bleeding slain!
BAS: Would I were laid a red, disfigur'd corse,
Amid those heaps! they fought, and we were absent!

(Walks about distractedly, then stops short.)

Who sent thee here?
MESS: Piscaro sent me to inform Count Basil
He needs not now his aid, and gives him leave
To march his tardy troops to distant quarters.
BAS: He says so, does he? well it shall be so.

(Tossing his arms distractedly.)

I will to quarters, narrow quarters go,
Where voice of war shall rouse me forth no more,

(Exit.)

MESS: I'll follow after him, he is distracted;
And yet he looks so wild I dare not do it.

Enter VICTORIA *as if frightened, followed by* ISABELLA.

VICT. *to* ISAB: Didst thou not mark him as he pass'd thee too?
ISAB: I saw him pass, but with such hasty steps,
I had no time.
VICT: I met him with a wild disorder'd air,
In furious haste; he stopp'd distractedly,
And gaz'd upon me with a mournful look,
But pass'd away, and spoke not. Who art thou?

(To the Messenger.)

I fear thou art a bearer of bad tidings.
MESS: No, rather good as I should deem it, madam,
Altho' unwelcome tidings to Count Basil.
Our army hath a glorious battle won;
Ten thousand French are slain, their monarch captive.
VICT. *to* MESS: Ah there it is! he was not in the fight.
Run after him I pray—nay, do not so—
Run to his kinsman, good Count Rosinberg,
And bid him follow him—I pray thee run!
MESS: Nay, lady, by your leave, you seem not well,
I will conduct you hence, and then I'll go.
VICT: No, no, I'm well enough, I'm very well,
Go, hie thee hence, and do thine errand swiftly.

(Exit MESSENGER.*)*

O! what a wretch am I! I am to blame!
I only am to blame!
ISAB: Nay, wherefore say so?
What have you done that others would not do?
VICT: What have I done? I've fool'd a noble heart—
I've wreck'd a brave man's honour!

(Exit, leaning upon ISABELLA.*)*

ACT V

— SCENE I —

A dark night; no moon, but a few stars glimmering; the stage represents (as much as can be discovered for the darkness) a churchyard with part of a chapel, and a wing of the ducal palace adjoining to it. Enter BASIL, *with his hat off, his hair and his dress in disorder, stepping slowly, and stopping several times to listen, as if he was afraid of meeting any one.*

BAS: No sound is here; man is at rest, and I
May near his habitations venture forth,
Like some unblessed creature of the night,
Who dares not meet his face.—Her window's dark;
No streaming light doth from her chamber beam,[11]
That I once more may on her dwelling gaze,
And bless her still. All now is dark for me!

(Pauses for some time, and looks upon the graves.)

How happy are the dead, who quietly rest
Beneath these stones! each by his kindred laid,
Still in a hallow'd neighbourship with those,
Who when alive his social converse shar'd:
And now, perhaps, some dear surviving friend,
Doth here at times the grateful visit pay,
Read with sad eyes his short memorial o'er,
And bless his mem'ry still!—
But I, like a vile outcast of my kind,
In some lone spot must lay my unburied corse,
To rot above the earth; where, if perchance
The steps of human wand'rer e'er approach,
He'll stand aghast, and flee the horrid place,
With dark imaginations frightful made,
The haunt of damned sprites. O! cursed wretch!
I' the fair and honour'd field shouldst thou have died,
Where brave friends, proudly smiling thro' their tears,
Had pointed out the spot where Basil lay!

(A light seen in VICTORIA'*s window.)*

But ha! the wonted, welcome light appears.
How bright within I see her chamber wall,
Athwart it too, a dark'ning shadow moves,
A slender woman's form; it is herself!
What means that motion of its clasped hands?
That drooping head? alas! is she in sorrow?
Alas! thou sweet enchantress of the mind,
Whose voice was gladness, and whose presence bliss,
Art thou unhappy too? I've brought thee woe;
It is for me thou weep'st! Ah! were it so,
Fall'n as I am, I yet could life endure,
In some dark den from human sight conceal'd,

---

[11] **"No streaming light . . . beam"**: "But, soft! What light through yonder window breaks? / It is the light, and Juliet is the sun." *Romeo and Juliet,* II.ii.2–3.

So, that I sometimes from my haunt might steal,
To see and love thee still. No, no, poor wretch!
She weeps thy shame, she weeps, and scorns thee too.
She moves again; e'en darkly imag'd thus,
How lovely is that form!

(Pauses, still looking at the window.)

To be so near thee, and for ever parted!
For ever lost! what art thou now to me?
Shall the departed gaze on thee again?
Shall I glide past thee in the midnight hour,
Whilst thou perceiv'st it not, and thinkst perhaps
'Tis but the mournful breeze that passes by?

(Pauses again, and gazes at the window, till the light disappears.)

'Tis gone, 'tis gone! these eyes have seen their last!
The last impression of her heavenly form!
The last sight of those walls wherein she lives,
The last blest ray of light from human dwelling!
I am no more a being of this world,
Farewell! farewell! all now is dark for me!
Come fated deed! come horrour and despair![12]
Here lies my dreadful way.

Enter GEOFFRY, *from behind a tomb.*

GEOF: O! stay, my general!
BAS: What art thou, from the grave?
GEOF: O! my brave gen'ral! do you know me not?
I am old Geoffry, the old maimed soldier
You did so nobly honour.
BAS: Then go thy way, for thou art honourable;
Thou hast no shame, thou needst not seek the dark
Like fallen, fameless men. I pray thee go!
GEOF: Nay, speak not thus, my noble general!
Ah! speak not thus! thou'rt brave, thou'rt honour'd still.
Thy soldier's fame is far too surely rais'd
To be o'erthrown with one unhappy chance.
I've heard of thy brave deeds with swelling heart,
And yet shall live to cast my cap in air
At glorious tales of thee—
BAS: Forbear, forbear! thy words but wring my soul.
GEOF: O! pardon me! I am old maimed Geoffry.
O! do not go! I've but one hand to hold thee.

[12] **"Farewell . . . despair!"**: "So farewell hope, and with hope farewell fear, / Farewell remorse: all good to me is lost." *Paradise Lost,* IV.108–109.

(Laying hold of BASIL *as he attempts to go away.* BASIL *stops, and looks round upon him with softness.)*

BAS: Two would not hold so well, old honour'd vet'ran!
What wouldst thou have me do?
GEOF: Return, my lord, for love of blessed heaven,
Seek not such desp'rate ways! where would you go?
BAS: Does Geoffry ask? where should a soldier go?
To hide disgrace? there is no place but one.

(Struggling to get free.)

Let go thy foolish hold, and force me not
To do some violence to thy hoary head—
What, wilt thou not? nay, then it must be so:

(Breaks violently from him, and exit.)

GEOF: Curs'd, feeble hand! he's gone to seek perdition!
I cannot run. O! curse that stupid hand,
He should have met me here! holla, Fernando!

Enter FERNANDO.

We've lost him, he is gone! he's broke from me!
Did I not bid thee meet me early here,
For that he has been known to haunt this place?
FER: Which way has he gone?
GEOF: Towards the forest, if I guess it right;
But do thou run with speed to Rosinberg,
And he will follow him: run swiftly, man!

(Exeunt.)

— SCENE II —

A Wood, wild and savage; an entry to a cave, very much tangled with brushwood, is seen in the background. The time represents the dawn of morning. BASIL *is discovered standing near the front of the stage in a thoughtful posture, with a couple of pistols laid by him, on a piece of projecting rock; he pauses for some time.*

BAS: *(alone.)* What shall I be a few short moments hence?
Why ask I now? who from the dead will rise
To tell me of that awful state unknown?
But be it what it may, or bliss, or torment,
Annihilation, dark and endless rest,
Or some dread thing, man's wildest range of thought
Hath never yet conceiv'd, that change I'll dare
Which makes me any thing but what I am.
I can bear scorpions' stings, tread fields of fire,
In frozen gulphs of cold eternal lie;
Be toss'd aloft through tracks of endless void,

But cannot live in shame—*(Pauses.)* O! impious thought!
Will the great God of mercy, mercy have
On all but those who are most miserable?
Will he not punish with a pitying hand
The poor fall'n, froward child? *(Pauses.)*
And shall I then against his will offend,
Because he is most good and merciful?
O! horrid baseness! what, what shall I do?
I'll think no more—it turns my dizzy brain—
It is too late to think—what must be, must be—
I cannot live, therefore I needs must die.

(Takes up the pistols, and walks up and down, looking wildly around him, then discovering the cave's mouth.)

Here is an entry to some darksome cave,
Where an uncoffin'd corse may rest in peace,
And hide its foul corruption from the earth.
The threshold is unmark'd by mortal foot,
I'll do it here.

(Enters the cave and exit: a deep silence; then the report of a pistol is heard from the cave, and soon after, Enter ROSINBERG, VALTOMER, *two* OFFICERS *and* SOLDIERS, *almost at the same moment, by different sides of the stage.)*

ROS: This way the sound did come.
VALT: How came ye, soldiers? heard ye that report?
1ST SOL: We heard it, and it seem'd to come from hence,
Which made us this way hie.
ROS: A horrid fancy darts across my mind.

(A groan heard from the cave.)

(to VALT.*)* Ha! heardst thou that?
VALT: Methinks it is the groan of one in pain.

(A second groan.)

ROS: Ha! there again!
VALT: From this cave's mouth, so dark and choak'd with weeds,
It seems to come.
ROS: I'll enter first.
1ST OFF: My Lord, the way is tangled o'er with briers;
Hard by, a few short paces to the left,
There is another mouth of easier access;
I pass'd it even now.
ROS: Then shew the way.

(Exeunt.)

—SCENE III—

The Inside of the Cave; BASIL *discovered lying on the ground, with his head raised a little upon a few stones and earth; the pistols lying beside him, and blood upon his breast. Enter* ROSINBERG, VALTOMER, *and* OFFICERS. ROSINBERG, *upon seeing* BASIL, *stops short with horrour, and remains motionless for some time.*

VALT: Great God of heav'n! what a sight is this?

*(*ROSINBERG *runs to* BASIL, *and stoops down by his side.)*

ROS: O Basil! O my friend! what hast thou done?
BAS: *(Covering his face with his hand.)* Why art thou come?
I thought to die in peace.
ROS: Thou knowst me not—I am thy Rosinberg,
Thy dearest, truest friend, thy loving kinsman;
Thou dost not say to me, Why art thou come?
BAS: Shame knows no kindred; I am fall'n, disgrac'd;
My fame is gone, I cannot look upon thee.
ROS: My Basil, noble spirit! talk not thus!
The greatest mind untoward fate may prove:
Thou art our gen'rous, valiant leader still,
Fall'n as thou art—and yet thou art not fall'n;
Who says thou art, must put his harness on,
And prove his words in blood.
BAS: Ah Rosinberg! this is no time to boast!
I once had hopes a glorious name to gain;
Too proud of heart, I did too much aspire;
The hour of trial came, and found me wanting.
Talk not of me, but let me be forgotten;—
And O! my friend! something upbraids me here,

(Laying his hand on his breast.)

For that I now remember, how oft-times,
I have usurp'd it o'er thy better worth,
Most vainly teaching where I should have learnt;
But thou wilt pardon me—
ROS: *(Taking* BASIL*'s hand, and pressing it to his breast.)* Rend not my heart in twain! O! talk not thus!
I knew thou wert superiour to myself,
And to all men beside: thou wert my pride;
I paid thee def'rence with a willing heart.
BAS: It was delusion, all delusion, Rosinberg!
I feel my weakness now, I own my pride.
Give me thy hand, my time is near the close;
Do this for me; thou know'st my love, Victoria—
ROS: O! curse that woman! she it is alone,
She has undone us all!

BAS: It doubles unto me the stroke of death
To hear thee name her thus. O! curse her not!
The fault is mine; she's gentle, good and blameless.—
Thou wilt not then my dying wish fulfil?
ROS: I will! I will! what wouldst thou have me do?
BAS: See her when I am gone, be gentle with her,
And tell her that I bless'd her in my death,
E'en in mine agonies I lov'd and bless'd her.
Wilt thou do this?—
ROS: I'll do what thou desir'st.
BAS: I thank thee Rosinberg; my time draws near.

(Raising his head a little and perceiving OFFICERS.*)*

Is there not some one here? are we alone?
ROS: *(making a sign for the* OFFICERS *to retire)* 'Tis but a sentry, to prevent intrusion.
BAS: Thou know'st this desp'rate deed from sacred rights
Hath shut me out; I am unbless'd of men,
And what I am in sight of th' awful God,
I dare not think: wilt thou, when I am gone,
A good man's prayers to gracious heav'n up send,
For an offending spirit?—Pray for me.
What thinkst thou? altho' an outcast here,
May not some heavenly mercy still be found?
ROS: Thou wilt find mercy—O! my lov'd Basil—
It cannot be that thou shouldst be rejected.
I will with bended knee—I will implore—
It choaks mine utt'rance—I will pray for thee—
BAS: This comforts me—thou art a loving friend.

(A noise without.)

ROS: *(to* OFF. *without.)* What noise is that?

Enter VALTOMER.

VALT. *to* ROS: My lord, the soldiers all insist to enter;
What shall I do? they will not be denied;
They say that they will see their noble gen'ral.
BAS: Ah, my brave fellows! do they call me so?
ROS: Then let them come.

(Enter SOLDIERS, *who gather round* BASIL, *and look mournfully upon him; he holds out his hand to them with a faint smile.)*

BAS: My gen'rous soldiers, this is kindly meant.
I'm low i' the dust; God bless you all, brave hearts!
1ST SOL: And God bless you, my noble, noble gen'ral!
We'll never follow such a leader more.
2D SOL: Ah! had you staid with us, my noble gen'ral,
We would have died for you.

*(*3D SOLDIER *endeavours next to speak, but cannot, and kneeling down by* BASIL, *covers his face with his cloak.* ROSINBERG *turns his face to the wall and weeps.)*

BAS: *(In a very faint, broken voice.)* Where art thou?—do not leave me, Rosinberg—
Come near to me—these fellows make me weep—
I have no power to weep—give me thy hand—
I love to feel thy grasp—my heart beats strangely—
It beats as tho' its breathings would be few—
Remember—
ROS: Is there aught thou wouldst desire?
BAS: Nought but a little earth to cover me,
And lay the smooth sod even with the ground—
Let no stone mark the spot—give no offence
I fain would say—what can I say to thee?

(A deep pause, after a feeble struggle, BASIL *expires.)*

1ST SOL: That motion was his last.
2D SOL: His spirit's fled.
1ST SOL: God grant it peace! it was a noble spirit!
4TH SOL: The trumpet's sound did never rouse a braver.
1ST SOL: Alas! no trumpet e'er shall rouse him more.
Until the dreadful blast that wakes the dead;
2D SOL: And when that sounds it will not wake a braver.
3D SOL: How pleasantly he shar'd our hardest toil;
Our coarsest food the daintiest fare he made.
4TH SOL: Ay, many a time i'the cold damp plains has he
With cheerful count'nance cried, good rest my hearts!
Then wrapp'd him in his cloak, and laid him down
E'en like the meanest soldier in the field.

*(*ROSINBERG *all this time continues hanging over the body, and gazing upon it.* VALTOMER *now endeavours to draw him away.)*

VALT: This is too sad, my lord.
ROS: There, seest thou how he lies? so fix'd, so pale?
Ah! what an end is this! thus lost! thus fall'n!
To be thus taken in his middle course,
Where he so nobly strove; till cursed passion
Came like a sun-stroke on his mid-day toil,
And cut the strong man down. O Basil! Basil!
VALT: Forbear, my friend, we must not sorrow here.
ROS: He was the younger brother of my soul.
VALT: Indeed, my lord, it is too sad a sight.
Time calls us, let the body be remov'd.
ROS: He was—O! he was like no other man!
VALT: *(Still endeavouring to draw him away.)*
Nay now forbear.

ROS: I lov'd him from his birth!
VALT: Time presses, let the body be remov'd.
ROS: What sayst thou?
VALT: Shall we not remove him hence?
ROS: He has forbid it, and has charg'd me well
To leave his grave unknown; for that the church
All sacred rights to the self-slain denies.
He would not give offence.
1ST SOL: What! shall our gen'ral, like a very wretch,
Be laid unhonour'd in the common ground?
No last salute to bid his soul farewell?
No warlike honours paid? it shall not be.
2D SOL: Laid thus? no, by the blessed light of heav'n!
In the most holy spot in Mantua's walls,
He shall be laid; in face of day be laid;
And tho' black priests should curse us in the teeth,
We will fire o'er him whilst our hands have power
To grasp a musket.
SEVERAL SOLDIERS: Let those who dare forbid it.
ROS: My brave companions, be it as you will.

(Spreading out his arms as if he would embrace the SOLDIERS.*—They prepare to remove the body.)*

VALT: Nay, stop a while, we will not move it now,
For see a mournful visitor appears,
And must not be denied.

Enter VICTORIA *and* ISABELLA.

VICT: I thought to find him here, where has he fled?

*(*ROSINBERG *points to the body without speaking,* VICTORIA*, shrieks out, and falls into the arms of* ISABELLA.*)*

ISAB: Ah, my sweet gentle mistress! this will kill thee.
VICT: *(recovering.)* Unloose thy hold, and let me look upon him.
O! horrid, horrid sight! my ruin'd Basil!
Is this the sad reward of all thy love?
O! I have murder'd thee!

(Kneels down by the body, and bends over it.)

These wasted streams of life! this bloody wound!

(Laying her hand upon his heart.)

Is there no breathing here? all still! all cold!
Open thine eyes, speak, be thyself again,
And I will love thee, serve thee, follow thee,
In spite of all reproach. Alas! alas!
A lifeless corse art thou for ever laid,
And dost not hear my call—
ROS: No, madam; now your pity comes too late.
VICT: Dost thou upbraid me? O! I have deserv'd it?
ROS: No, madam, no, I will not now upbraid,
But woman's grief is like a summer storm,
Short as it violent is; in gayer scenes,
Where soon thou shalt in giddy circles blaze,
And play the airy goddess of the day,
Thine eye, perchance, amidst the observing crowd,
Shall mark th' indignant face of Basil's friend,
And then it will upbraid.
VICT: No, never, never! thus it shall not be.
To the dark, shaded cloister wilt thou go,
Where sad and lonely, thro' the dismal grate
Thou'lt spy my wasted form, and then upbraid me.
ROS: Forgive me, heed me not; I'm griev'd at heart;
I'm fretted, gall'd, all things are hateful to me.
If thou didst love my friend, I will forgive thee;
I must forgive thee; with his dying breath
He bade me tell thee, that his latest thoughts
Were love to thee; in death he lov'd and blessed thee.

*(*VICTORIA *goes to throw herself upon the body, but is prevented by* VALTOMER *and* ISABELLA*, who support her in their arms, and endeavour to draw her away from it.)*

VICT: Oh! force me not away! by his cold corse
Let me lie down and weep. O! Basil, Basil!
The gallant and the brave! how hast thou lov'd me!
If there is any holy kindness in you

(To ISAB. *and* VALT.*)*

Tear me not hence.
For he lov'd me in thoughtless folly lost,
With all my faults, most worthless of his love;
And I'll love him in the low bed of death,
In horrour and decay.—
Near his lone tomb I'll spend my wretched days
In humble pray'r for his departed spirit:
Cold as his grave shall be my earthy bed,
As dark my cheerless cell. Force me not hence.
I will not go, for grief hath made me strong.

(Struggling to get loose.)

ROS: Do not withhold her, leave her sorrow free.

(They let her go, and she throws herself upon the body in an agony of grief.)

It doth subdue the sternness of my grief
To see her mourn him thus.—Yet I must curse.—
Heav'n's curses light upon her damned father,
Whose crooked policy has wrought this wreck.

ISAB: If he has done it, you are well reveng'd,
For his dark plots have been detected all.
Gauriecio, for some int'rest of his own,
His master's secret dealings with the foe
Has to Lanoy betray'd; who straight hath sent,
On the behalf of his imperial lord,
A message full of dreadful threats to Mantua.
His discontented subjects aid him not;
He must submit to the degrading terms
A haughty conq'ring power will now impose.
ROS: And art thou sure of this?
ISAB: I am, my lord.
ROS: Give me thy hand, I'm glad on't, O! I'm glad on't!
It should be so! how like a hateful ape
Detected, grinning 'midst his pilfer'd hoard
A cunning man appears, whose secret frauds
Are open'd to the day! scorn'd, hooted, mock'd!
Scorn'd by the very fools who most admir'd
His worthless art. But when a great mind falls,
The noble nature of man's gen'rous heart
Doth bear him up against the shame of ruin;
With gentle censure using but his faults
As modest means to introduce his praise;
For pity like a dewy twilight comes
To close th' oppressive splendour of his day;
And they who but admir'd him in his height,
His alter'd state lament, and love him fall'n.

(Exeunt.)

from FUGITIVE VERSES,
(Second Edition, 1840)

Lines on the Death of Sir Walter Scott[1]
(1840; comp. 1832)

THOU pleasant noble Bard, of fame far spread,
Now art thou gather'd to the mighty dead,
And the dark coffin and the girdling mould
All that of thee is perishable, hold.
Mourners and mutes and weeping friends are gone;
The pageant's closed, and thou art left alone;
The cover'd treasure of a sacred spot,
That in the course of time shall never be forgot.

Soon those who loved, admired, and honoured thee,
In death's still garner-house will gathered be;
And great their number is, who have with pride
Look'd in thy manly face, sat by thy side,
And heard thy social converse,—words of cheer,
And words of power to charm the listening ear!
At death's despotic summons will they come,
Each in his turn from many a different home:
From town and muirland,[2] cot and mansion warm,
The regal palace, and the homely farm.
Soldier and lawyer, merchant, priest and peer,
The squire, the laird of forty pounds a-year,
The crowned monarch and the simple hind,
Did all in thee a meet companion find.

For thee the peasant's wife her elbow chair,
Smiling a welcome, kindly set, and there
With fair exchange of story, saw and jest,
Thou wast to her a free and pleasant guest;
While nature, undisguised, repaid thee well
For time so spent. She and her mate could tell
Unawed, to such a man, their inmost mind;
They claim'd thee as their own, their kin, their kind.
From nature's book thou couldst extract a store,
More precious than the scholar's classic lore.

And how felt he, whose early rhymes had been
To perilous inspection given, and seen
By one whose brows were graced from every land,
With chaplets twined by many a skilful hand?
How beat his heart, as with the morning ray,
To Abbotsford he took his anxious way,
Imagining what shortly he must see,
Him in whose presence he so soon will be?
And how felt he, thy study's threshold pass'd,
When on thy real face his eyes were cast?
Thine open brow with glow of fancy heated;
Thy purring cat upon the table seated;
Thy sleeping hound that hath his easy lair
Close on the precincts of his master's chair;
The honest welcome of that sudden smile,
And outstretch'd hand, misgiving thoughts beguile.
But when thy cheerful greeting met his ear,
"Fie on thee! foolish heart, a man like this to fear!"
Thou wast to him, when blush'd the eastern sky,

[1] See Sir Walter Scott* for comments regarding the title of this work.

[2] **muirland:** moorland.

A sage of awful mien and lofty eye;
When noon-day heat called forth th' industrious bee,
Thou wast the monitor both kind and free;
But when the changeful day was at an end,
Thou wast his easy cheerful host,—his friend.

When all whose eyes have e'er beheld thy face,
Departed are to their long resting-place,
Thou wilt exist in all thy magic then,
The cherish'd, speaking friend of living men.
In torrid climes, in regions cold and bleak,
In every land and language wilt thou speak.
Within the sick man's curtain'd couch thou'lt dwell;
Within the languid prisoner's cheerless cell;
Within the seaman's cabin, where the sound
Of many leagues of water murmurs round.
The buoyant school-boy will forego his play,
In secret nook alone with thee to stray;
The sober sage wise tomes will cast aside,
An hour with thee—a pleasant hour to bide.

Men of all nations, of all creeds, all ranks,
Will owe to thee an endless meed[3] of thanks,
Which more than in thy passing, checker'd day
Of mortal life, they will delight to pay.
For who shall virtuous sympathies resign,
Or feed foul fancies from a page of thine?
No, none! thy writings as thy life are pure,
And their fair fame and influence will endure.

Not so with those where perverse skill pourtrays
Distorted, blighting passions, and displays,
Wild, maniac, selfish fiends to be admired,
As heroes with sublimest ardour fired.
Such are, to what thy faithful pen hath traced,
With all the shades of varied nature graced,
Like grim cartoons, for Flemish looms prepared,
To Titian's or Murillo's forms compared;[4]
Stately or mean, theirs still are forms of truth,
Charming unlearn'd and learned—age and youth:
Not ecstasies express'd in critic phrase,
But silent smiles of pleasure speak their praise.

When those, who now thy recent death deplore,
Lie in the dust, thought of and known no more,
As poet and romancer, thy great name
Will brightly shine with undiminish'd fame;
And future sons of fancy fondly strive
To their compatriots works like thine to give.
But of the many who on her wide sea
Shall boldly spread their sails to follow thee,
More as romancers on thy track will gain,
Than those who emulate the poet's strain.
A tale like Waverley we yet may con,
But shall we read a lay like Marmion?[5]
And fearlessly I say it, though I know
The voice of public favour says not so:
For story-telling is an art, I ween,
Which hath of old most fascinating been,
And will be ever,—strong in ready power,
To combat languor and the present hour;
And o'er these common foes will oft prevail,
When Homer's theme and Milton's song would fail.
But strong in both, there is in sooth no need
Against thy left hand for thy right to plead:
Think as we list, one truth, alas! is plain,
We ne'er shall look upon thy like again.

Thy country, bounded by her subject sea,
Adds to her fame by giving birth to thee;
In distant lands yon fancied group behold,
Where busy traders meet in quest of gold;
Motley and keen, all gather'd round a youth,
Who simply stands unconscious of the truth,
Look at him wistfully, and hark, they speak—
The Turk and Jew, Armenian and Greek,
Their rapid lips the whisper'd words betraying—
"He's from the land of Walter Scott," they're saying.
That Caledonian,[6] too, with more good will
They greet as of thy closer kindred still:
But who is he, who, standing by their side,
Raises his head with quickly-kindled pride,
As if he meant to look the others down?
Ay, he is from thine own romantic town.[7]

---

[3] **meed:** reward, gift.

[4] **cartoons . . . Flemish looms:** drawings depicting grotesque visions of hell and earth, like those of the Flemish artist Hieronymous Bosch, to be woven into tapestries. **Titian:** Italian painter (1488–1576), renowned for his elegant colors. **Murillo:** Spanish painter (1617–1682), famed as a colorist.

[5] Sir Walter Scott* (1771–1832) published the first of his historical novels depicting recent Scottish life, *Waverly*, in 1814; his lengthy poem set in Scotland's medieval past, *Marmion*, appeared in 1808.

[6] **Caledonian:** Scotsman.

[7] **own romantic town:** Abbotsford, in the Border country of Scotland, where Scott lived in a converted abbey, Melrose Abbey, until forced by debt to return to rented rooms in Edinburgh in 1826.

Thou art in time's long course a land-mark high,
A beacon blazing to the nether sky,
To which, as far and wide it shoots its rays,
Landsmen and mariners, with wistful gaze,
From ship, and shore, and mountain turn their sight,
And hail the glorious signal of the night.

Oh Dryburgh![8] often trod by pilgrim feet
Shall be thy hallow'd turf; solemn and sweet,
Will be the gentle sorrow utter'd there,
The whisper'd blessing and the quiet prayer.
Flower, herb, or leaf by children yet unborn
Will often from thy verdant turf be torn,
And kept in dear memorial of the place
Where thou art laid with a departed race;
Where every thing around, tower, turret, tree,
River, and glen, and mountain, wood and lea,
And ancient ruin, by the moonlight made
More stately with alternate light and shade,
Thy once beloved Melrose,—all speak of thee,
With mingled voices through the gale of morn,
Of evening, noon, and night, most sadly borne,
A dirge-like wailing, a mysterious moan,
That sadly seems to utter "He is gone!"

To God's forgiving mercy and his love—
To fellowship with blessed souls above—
Bright hosts redeem'd by Him whose voice of hope
Revealed th' immortal spirit's boundless scope—
We leave thee, though within its narrow cell,
Thy honour'd dust must for a season dwell—
Our friend, our bard, our brother,—fare thee well!

Hampstead, November, 1832

[8] **Dryburgh:** Scott was buried beside his wife in the old Abbey of Dryburgh.

Lines for a Friend's Album

(1840)

LINES, in addition to the treasure
Of poesy, cull'd for the pleasure
Of beau, and belle, and gentle dame,
When seated round the evening flame,
What time the social hour is waning,
And tardy coachman guests detaining,—
A courteous friend hath bid me write
Upon her Album's pages white.

But age the easy grace hath lost
That would become such pages most,
While of a quondam rhymester's skill,
Scarce aught is extant but the will;
And sober, stinted age must use
The school-girl's worn and stale excuse,
When, long her correspondent's debtor,
The apology becomes the letter.

Apologies for those who need 'em!
An Album is a thing of freedom,
Receiving all with right good will
That fortune sends from many a quill,
And then displays like scaly store
Which fisher's net brings to the shore:
The herring sheath'd in silvery green,
The whiting in its pearly sheen,
The lithe and wavy eel that glides
Athwart the mackerel's tabbied sides;
John Dory with his dolphin head,
Where amber fins like horns are spread,
And flounder, sole, and thornback, all
In turn on some observer call,
To mark each varied form and tint;
And from this simile a hint
Of some encouragement I take,
And humbly this my offering make,
Which if received with favour, truly
Will show that I have reckon'd duly
On what might homelier things commend,—
On the good nature of a friend.

To Mrs. Siddons[1]

(1840)

GIFTED of heaven! who hast, in days gone by,
Moved every heart, delighted every eye;
While age and youth, of high and low degree,
In sympathy were join'd, beholding thee,

[1] Mrs. Sarah Siddons (1755–1831) was the finest tragic actress of her time. Her great roles were Jane Shore in Nicholas Rowe's tragedy of that name; Belvidera in Thomas Otway's *Venice Preserv'd*, and Lady Macbeth. William Hazlitt wrote that "Power was seated on her brow . . . She was tragedy personified," and Sir Joshua Reynolds painted her as "the Tragic Muse."

As in the Drama's ever changing scene,
Thou heldst thy splendid state, our tragic queen!
No barriers there thy fair domains confined,
Thy sovereign sway was o'er the human mind;
And, in the triumph of that witching hour,
Thy lofty bearing well became thy power.

The impassion'd changes of thy beauteous face,
Thy stately form, and high imperial grace;
Thine arms impetuous toss'd, thy robe's wide flow,
And the dark tempest gather'd on thy brow;
What time thy flashing eye and lip of scorn
Down to the dust thy mimic foes have borne;
Remorseful musings, sunk to deep dejection,
The fix'd and yearning looks of strong affection;
The active turmoil a wrought bosom rending,
When pity, love, and honour, are contending:
They who beheld all this, right well, I ween,
A lovely, grand, and wondrous sight have seen.

Thy varied accents, rapid, fitful, slow,
Loud rage, and fear's snatch'd whisper, quick and low;
The burst of stifled love, the wail of grief,
And tones of high command, full, solemn, brief;
The change of voice, and emphasis that threw
Light on obscurity, and brought to view
Distinctions nice, when grave or comic mood,[2]
Or mingled humours, terse and new, elude
Common perception, as earth's smallest things
To size and form, the vesting hoar-frost brings,
That seem'd as if some secret voice, to clear
The ravell'd meaning, whisper'd in thine ear,
And thou hadst e'en with him communion kept,
Who hath so long in Stratford's chancel slept;[3]
Whose lines, where nature's brightest traces shine,
Alone were worthy deem'd of powers like thine;
They who have heard all this, have proved full well
Of soul-exciting sound, the mightiest spell.

But though time's lengthen'd shadows o'er thee glide,
And pomp of regal state is cast aside,
Think not the glory of thy course is spent,
There's moonlight radiance to thy evening lent,
That, to the mental world can never fade,
Till all who saw thee, in the grave are laid.
Thy graceful form still moves in nightly dreams,
And what thou wast, to the lull'd sleeper seems:
While feverish fancy oft doth fondly trace
Within her curtain'd couch thy wondrous face.
Yea; and to many a wight, bereft and lone,
In musing hours, though all to thee unknown,
Soothing his earthly course of good and ill,
With all thy potent charm, thou actest still.

And now in crowded room or rich saloon,
Thy stately presence recognized, how soon
On thee the glance of many an eye is cast,
In grateful memory of pleasures past!
Pleased to behold thee, with becoming grace,
Take, as befits thee well, an honour'd place
(Where blest by many a heart, long mayst thou stand!)
Among the virtuous matrons of our land.

[2] Those who have been happy enough to hear Mrs. Siddons read, will readily acknowledge that the discrimination and power with which she gave effect to the comic passages of Shakspeare, were nearly as remarkable and delightful as those which she displayed in passages of a grave or tragic character. It is to be regretted that only those who have heard her read, are aware of the extent or variety of her genius, which has on the stage been confined almost entirely to Tragedy; partly, I believe, from a kind of bigotry on the side of the public, which inclines it to confine poet, painter, or actor, to that department of their art in which they have first been acknowledged to excel, and partly from the cast of her features, and the majesty of her figure being peculiarly suited to Tragedy [J. B.].

[3] **Who . . . Stratford's chancel slept:** William Shakespeare, buried in Stratford-on-Avon.

POSTHUMOUS PUBLICATIONS

from THE DRAMATIC AND POETICAL WORKS OF JOANNA BAILLIE
(1851)

Lines to Agnes Baillie on Her Birthday
(1851; comp. 1828)

DEAR Agnes, gleam'd with joy and dash'd with tears,
O'er us have glided almost sixty years

Since we on Bothwell's bonny braes[1] were seen,
By those whose eyes long closed in death have been,
Two tiny imps, who scarcely stoop'd to gather
The slender harebell, or the purple heather;
No taller than the foxglove's spiky stem,
That dew of morning studs with silvery gem.
Then every butterfly that cross'd our view
With joyful shout was greeted as it flew,
And moth and lady-bird and beetle bright
In sheeny gold were each a wondrous sight.
Then as we paddled barefoot, side by side,
Among the sunny shallows of the Clyde,[2]
Minnows or spotted par with twinkling fin,
Swimming in mazy rings the pool within,
A thrill of gladness through our bosoms sent,
Seen in the power of early wonderment.

A long perspective to my mind appears,
Looking behind me to that line of years,
And yet through every stage I still can trace
Thy vision'd form, from childhood's morning grace
To woman's early bloom, changing how soon!
To the expressive glow of woman's noon;
And now to what thou art, in comely age,
Active and ardent. Let what will engage
Thy present moment, whether hopeful seeds
In garden-plat thou sow, or noxious weeds
From the fair flower remove, or ancient lore
In chronicle or legend rare explore,
Or on the parlour hearth with kitten play,
Stroking its tabby sides, or take thy way
To gain with hasty steps some cottage door,
On helpful errand to the neighbouring poor,
Active and ardent, to my fancy's eye
Thou still art young in spite of time gone by.
Though oft of patience brief and temper keen,
Well may it please me, in life's latter scene,
To think what now thou art, and long to me hast
been.

'Twas thou who woo'dst me first to look
Upon the page of printed book,
That thing by me abhorr'd, and with address
Didst win me from my thoughtless idleness,
When all too old become with bootless haste
In fitful sports the precious time to waste.
Thy love of tale and story was the stroke
At which my dormant fancy first awoke,
And ghosts and witches in my busy brain
Arose in sombre show, a motley train.
This new-found path attempting, proud was I,
Lurking approval on thy face to spy,
Or hear thee say, as grew thy roused attention,
"What! is this story all thine own invention?"

Then, as advancing through this mortal span,
Our intercourse with the mix'd world began,
Thy fairer face and sprightlier courtesy
(A truth that from my youthful vanity
Lay not conceal'd) did for the sisters twain,
Where'er we went, the greater favour gain;
While, but for thee, vex'd with its tossing tide,
I from the busy world had shrunk aside.
And now in later years, with better grace
Thou helpst me still to hold a welcome place
With those, whom nearer neighbourhood has made
The friendly cheerers of our evening shade.

With thee my humours, whether grave or gay,
Or gracious or untoward, have their way.
Silent if dull—O precious privilege!
I sit by thee; or if, cull'd from the page
Of some huge, ponderous tome, which, but thyself,
None e'er had taken from its dusty shelf,
Thou read me curious passages to speed
The winter night, I take but little heed
And thankless say "I cannot listen now,"
'Tis no offence; albeit, much do I owe
To these, thy nightly offerings of affection,
Drawn from thy ready talent for selection;
For still it seem'd in thee a natural gift
The letter'd grain from letter'd chaff to sift.
By daily use and circumstance endear'd,
Things are of value now that once appear'd
Of no account, and without notice past,
Which o'er dull life a simple cheering cast;
To hear thy morning steps the stair descending,
Thy voice with other sounds domestic blending;
After each stated nightly absence, met
To see thee by the morning table set,
Pouring from smoky spout the amber stream
Which sends from saucer'd cup its fragrant steam;
To see thee cheerly on the threshold stand,

[1] **braes:** hillsides.

[2] The Manse [the house of a Scottish Presbyterian minister] of Bothwell was at some considerable distance from the Clyde [River], but the two little girls were sometimes sent there in summer to bathe and wade about [J. B.].

On summer morn, with trowel in thy hand
For garden-work prepared; in winter's gloom
From thy cold noonday walk to see thee come,
In furry garment lapp'd, with spatter'd feet,
And by the fire resume thy wonted seat.
Ay, e'en o'er things like these, soothed age has thrown
A sober charm they did not always own:
As winter-hoarfrost makes minutest spray
Of bush or hedge-weed sparkle to the day,
In magnitude and beauty, which bereaved
Of such investment, eye had ne'er perceived.

The change of good and evil to abide,
As partners link'd, long have we side by side
Our earthly journey held, and who can say
How near the end of our united way?
By nature's course not distant; sad and 'reft
Will she remain,—the lonely pilgrim left.
If thou be taken first, who can to me
Like sister, friend, and home-companion be?
Or who, of wonted daily kindness shorn,
Shall feel such loss, or mourn as I shall mourn?
And if I should be fated first to leave
This earthly house, though gentle friends may grieve,
And he above them all, so truly proved
A friend and brother, long and justly loved,
There is no living wight, of woman born,
Who then shall mourn for me as thou wilt mourn.

Thou ardent, liberal spirit! quickly feeling
The touch of sympathy and kindly dealing
With sorrow or distress, for ever sharing
The unhoarded mite, nor for to-morrow caring,—
Accept, dear Agnes, on thy natal day,
An unadorn'd but not a careless lay.
Nor think this tribute to thy virtues paid
From tardy love proceeds, though long delay'd.
Words of affection, howsoe'er express'd,
The latest spoken still are deem'd the best:
Few are the measured rhymes I now may write;
These are, perhaps, the last I shall endite.

HELEN MARIA WILLIAMS

(1762–1827)

An ardent feminist and supporter of the ideology of the French Revolution, as well as a gifted poet, novelist, and essayist, Helen Maria Williams was best known for her firsthand accounts of the political and cultural developments in France from 1790 to 1816. The daughter of an army officer who died in 1769, she and her two sisters were educated at home in Wales by her "virtuous, amiable, and sensible mother," in the words of a close family friend, the Dissenter Dr. Andrew Kippis. Encouraged to write for publication by Dr. Kippis, in 1782 she published her first poem, the lengthy *Edwin and Eltruda,* a pathos-laden tale of two young lovers destroyed by the Wars of the Roses, in which Williams celebrates "domestic bliss" and the "uncorrupted heart" over "the conq'ring hero's meed." Initially hailed as a poet of refined sensibility, Williams developed what one critic has more perceptively defined as a "radical sensibility." She consciously extended her sympathies to the poor, the oppressed, the enslaved. Focussing on the leading political issues of the day, Williams condemned the slave trade and the corruptions of Europe's imperialist commercial activities in *Peru* (1784); in *Poems* (1786), her first collection of poetry; in *A Poem on the Bill lately passed for regulating the Slave Trade* (1788); and in *A Farewell, for Two Years, to England* (1789). Her only novel, *Julia* (1790), condemns a self-absorbed sensibility, especially in men. By indulging a Werther-like, unreciprocated passion for his wife's best friend Julia, Frederick Seymour destroys both his wife's happiness and his own life. As Williams wrote, the purpose of *Julia* is "to trace the danger arising from the uncontrouled indulgence of strong affections. . . . When disapproved by reason, and uncircumscribed by prudence, they involve even the virtuous in calamity . . ."

In 1785 she engaged the wife of a penniless French émigré, Augustin François Thomas du Fossé, to tutor her in French; this couple's account of the tyrannies of the ancien régime in France inspired her to accept their invitation to visit Paris to observe the Girondist Revolution firsthand. With her older sister, who became the wife of a French protestant minister, Athanase Coquerel, Williams sailed to Paris on 13 July 1790, arriving just in time to attend the anniversary celebration of the new Federation at the Champs de Mars. This grand fête, in which members of the aristocracy, the clergy, and the common people all intermingled in a communion of liberty, equality, and fraternity, so moved and inspired Williams that she remained convinced for the next 20 years that the French Revolution had brought genuine freedom to the people of France. Williams's eight volumes of *Letters from France* (1790–1796), describing the unfolding political events in France from July 1790 through 1795, construct a narrative in which an oppressive monarchy is gradually, if unevenly, replaced by a more just republican government. Like her close friend Mary Wollstonecraft,* Williams saw the revolution as an opportunity for women to gain greater domestic and public power. Despite her sufferings under the reign of Robespierre, the Montagnards, and the Terror they initiated (she was arrested and imprisoned in Luxembourg Palace for six months at the end of 1793 to the beginning of 1794), Williams never lost her belief that the noble ideals of the Girondists would finally prevail.

Living in Paris with another British radical, the married (but separated) John Hurford Stone, raising two nephews, and earning a modest income from her translating and writing,

Williams was famous for hosting parties at which the founding principles of the Revolution were kept alive. She initially supported Napoleon Bonaparte, convinced that he had both the soul of a poet and the capacity to unify the nation into a democratic republic. In her *Tour in Switzerland* (1798), an account of the impact of the Revolution on Swiss politics and culture, she hailed him as "the benefactor of his race converting the destructive lightning of the conqueror's sword into the benignant rays of freedom." Not until Napoleon was crowned Emperor for Life on 2 December 1804, did Williams lose faith in his leadership. Her *Narrative of the Events which have taken place in France* (1816) not only tracks the career and downfall of Napoleon after April 1815, but also the path of her own disillusion. She finally portrays the restoration of the Bourbon monarchy as "the pure effusion of real happiness" into the hearts and faces of the Parisians. Nonetheless, Williams remained convinced that in time, the French nation would arrive at a society grounded on egalitarian and benevolent human relationships. In 1817 she became a French citizen; she continued to publish poetry celebrating the virtues of political freedom and the domestic affections, including her *Poems on Various Subjects,* which appeared in 1823. After her death on 15 December 1827, her body was buried beside John Stone in Pere-Lachaise cemetery in Paris.

from PERU, A POEM IN SIX CANTOS

(1784)

— ADVERTISEMENT —

To prevent the Readers of the following Work from entertaining expectations respecting it which it would ill satisfy, it is necessary to acquaint them that the Author hath not had the presumption even to attempt a full, historical narration of the fall of the Peruvian Empire. To describe that important event with precision, and to display with just force the various causes which combined to produce it, would require all the energy of genius, all the strong colouring of the most glowing imagination. Conscious of her utter inability to execute such a design, she hath only aimed at giving a simple detail of a few incidents in that affecting and romantic History; where the unparalleled sufferings of an innocent and amiable People afford the finest subjects for true pathos, while their climate, intirely dissimilar to our own, furnishes new and ample materials for poetic description. . . .

from Canto I

— THE ARGUMENT —

General description of the country of Peru, and of its animal, and vegetable productions — the virtues of the people — character of Ataliba,[1] their Monarch — his love for Alzira — their nuptials celebrated — character of Zorai, her father — descent of the genius of Peru — prediction of the fate of that empire.

....

[1] **Ataliba:** Atahualpa (d. 1533), also known as Atabalipa, became the ruler of the empire of Quito in 1525 and, after defeating Huáscar in 1532, the Inca of Peru.

from Canto II

— THE ARGUMENT —

Pizarro, a Spanish Captain, lands with his forces—his meeting with Ataliba—its unhappy consequences—Zorai dies—Ataliba imprisoned, and strangled—Alzira's despair, and madness.

Flush'd with high hope, PIZARRO's[2] martial Band
With hostile spirit press'd Peruvia's Land:
They breathe the tones of Amity, and Guile
Veils her dark aim in Candour's open smile—
Lull'd by illusive dreams, the Monarch springs
To meet his latent Foe on Friendship's wings:
On as he moves with radiant splendours crown'd,
His subject Chiefs the golden Throne surround;
The feather'd Canopy they graceful raise,
Whose varied hues reflect the morning rays.—
And now approach'd Iberia's warlike Train,
Majestic moving o'er Peruvia's Plain.
In all the savage pomp of armour drest,
The glittering Helmet, and the nodding Crest.
Yet themes of joy PIZARRO's lips impart,
And charm with Wisdom's lore the simple heart;
Unfolding to the Monarch's wond'ring thought
All that to elder Climes inventive Art has taught.
And now he bids his swelling Spirit rise,
To Regions far beyond the circling Skies;
Presents the Page that o'er our mental Night
Pour'd the pure floods of intellectual light!—
His trembling hands the hallow'd Volume clasp—
But lo! it falls from their too-feeble grasp—
Sudden, while impious zeal each breast inspires,[3]
And raging Demons fan the rising fires,
The bloody Signal waves, the Banners play,
The unsheath'd Sabres flash a gleamy ray;
The thund'ring Cannons rend the vault around,
And the loud Trumpets pour their shrilling sound;
While fierce in sanguine rage the Sons of Spain
Rush on Peru's unarm'd defenceless Train:
The Fiends of Slaughter urg'd their dire career,
And Virtue's guardian Spirits drop'd a tear!
Mild ZORAI[4] falls amid the fatal Strife,
And pours the ling'ring drops of wasted Life—
In vain Peruvia's Chiefs undaunted stood,
Shroud their lov'd Prince, and bathe his Robes in blood,
Touch'd with heroic ardor rush around,
And high of soul receive each deathful wound;
Drag'd from his throne, and hurry'd o'er the plain,
Lo! ATALIBA swells the captive Train,
With iron grasp the frantic Prince they bear,
Nor heed th' indignant throb of wild Despair.

Deep in the lonely Dungeon's drear domain
Sad ATALIBA drag'd the galling chain;
The dank, cold bosom of the Earth he prest,
While throb'd the woes of thousands at his breast:
And now the lost ALZIRA's moan he hears,
And Passion mingles with the gushing tears.
Full soon she felt keen Sorrow's poison'd dart
Pierce her soft soul, and desolate her heart;
It's quick pulsations paus'd—and, chill'd with dread,
A livid hue her fading cheek o'erspread—
She pour'd no gushing tear, she breath'd no sigh,
Quiver'd her lip—and clos'd her languid eye—
Fainter and slower heav'd her shiv'ring breast,
Till its calm'd throbings seem'd in death to rest.
At length reviv'd, 'mid rising heaps of Slain,

[2] **Pizarro**: Francisco Pizarro (c. 1476–1541), Spanish conquistador who invaded Peru in 1532 and despite his professions of friendship to the Inca, seized, ransomed, and then treacherously executed Atahualpa. He claimed Peru for Spain, founded the capital city of Lima, and installed his half brother Hernando Pizarro as ruler of Quito, but was assassinated by a band of disaffected followers in 1541.

[3] **Sudden, while impious zeal . . .**: "Pizarro, who during a long conference, had with difficulty restrained his soldiers, eager to seize the rich spoils of which they had now so near a view, immediately gave the signal of assault. At once the martial music struck up, the cannon and muskets began to fire, the horse sallied out fiercely to the charge, the infantry rushed on, sword in hand. The Peruvians, astonished at the suddenness of an attack which they did not expect, and dismayed with the destructive effects of the firearms, fled with universal consternation on every side. Pizarro, at the head of his chosen band, advanced directly towards the Inca; and though his Nobles crowded around him with officious zeal, and fell in numbers at his feet, while they vied one with another in sacrificing their own lives, that they might cover the sacred person of their Sovereign, the Spaniards soon penetrated to the royal seat; and Pizarro seizing the Inca by the arm, dragged him to the ground, and carried him as a prisoner to his quarters."—[William] Robertson's *History of America* (1777) [H. M. W.].

[4] **Zorai**: father-in-law of the Inca; father of Alzira.

She prest with trembling step the crimson plain;
Her soul with all the force of passion fraught,
Fearless the Dungeon's dark recess has sought—
A livid paleness still her cheek o'erspreads,
The tear of mingled agony she sheds—
It quiv'ring falls on ATALIBA's chain;
He feels it thrill in every shiv'ring vein—
For murder'd ZORAI's fate the mourner weeps,
For him the flood of woe her bosom steeps—
Too-tender Spirit! check the filial tear!
A sympathy more soft, a tie more dear,
Shall claim the drops that frantic Passion sheds,
When the rude Storm its darkest Pinion spreads—
Lo! bursting the deep Cell where Misery lay,
The human Vultures seize the Dove-like Prey!—
In vain her treasur'd wealth Peruvia gave
This dearer treasure from their grasp to save—
In vain she fought to rend th' opprobrious chains
Which from her searching glance her Prince detains—
ALZIRA! lo, the ruthless Murd'rers come—
This moment seals thy ATALIBA's doom.
Ah what avails the shriek that anguish pours,
The look that Mercy's lenient aid implores!
Torn from thy clasping arms, thy throbbing breast,
The fatal cord his last, deep groan suppress—
In dire, convulsive pangs he yields his breath,
And Passion's quiv'ring flame expires in death—
In vain the livid Corse she fondly clasps,
And pours her sorrows o'er the form she grasps;
Cold is that heart, and lull'd in icy rest,
Which trembled to each woe that pierc'd her breast.
Now her soft frame, with ruthless grasp, they tear
From the lost object of her fond despair;
The swelling pang unable to sustain,
Distraction throb'd in every shiv'ring vein;
Its rising tumults seize her yielding soul,
And in her eye its frenzied glances roll—
"They come! (the mourner cried, with panting breath)
To give the lost ALZIRA rest in death—
I feel my Love, I feel the poison'd dart,
It rankles here—it quivers in my heart!—
One moment more, ye bloody forms, bestow;
'Twill heal the deep, deep wound of cureless woe—
Ah spare the weak One!—tho' my wither'd brain
Dries the calm tear, it feels the throb of pain—
Lo where afar the purple flame sheds light
On yon sad Spot—Ah hide it, pitying Night!
Slow in the breeze I see the light grass wave
That shrouds with tender tufts my Love's dark Grave:
There on its wand'ring wing, in mildness blows
The mournful Gale, or wakes his deep repose—
I'll press the cold turf to my fainting heart,
Tho' the lone Thistle points its thorny dart,
And wounds me while it drinks the tears I shed,
Those tears that oft revive its drooping head—
I weep no more—but ah! ye soft dews, shower
Your balmy freshness o'er its downy flower,
Still cherish, tho' it pierce ALZIRA's breast,
Cherish the rising plant that guards his rest—
Ah see, yon hoary form still lingers there!
Dishevell'd by rude winds his silver hair—
O'er his chill'd bosom falls the wintry rain,
I feel the big drops on my wither'd brain—
Not for himself that tear his bosom steeps,
It falls for his lost child—for me he weeps—
No more the dagger's point shall pierce thy breast,
For calm and lovely is thy silent rest;
Yet still in dust these eyes shall see thee roll,
Still the sad thought shall waste ALZIRA's Soul—
Sad Nature sickens—fades each drooping flower,—
The Blossoms languish in the rosy Bower;
The rosy Bower where once I lov'd to rove,
And shed the tear of Joy, the smile of Love:
Soft on the hanging Cliff I now can rest,
And press its pointed pillow to my breast.—
What bleeding Phantom moves along the Storm?
Dear Spirit of my Love! Ah well-known form!
Tho' the dim Moon is veil'd, his robes of light
Tinge the dark clouds, and gild the veil of Night;
Approach, my Love—Ah nearer—still more near—
Thy look, tho' pale and ghastly, wakes no fear:
ALZIRA's breast no shadowy terrors move,
For every vain alarm is lost in Love—
He weeps—o'er my full bosom streams his tear—
It chills my trembling heart, yet still 'tis dear—
Can Death's barb'd arrow yield no sweet release?
I hop'd in yon blue Sky to taste of peace—
My sorrows pierce his soul—I plunge the dart—
Those drops of blood—they issue from his heart—
To him all joyless are the Realms above:
That pale look speaks of pity, and of love—
My Love ascends!—he soars in liquid light—
Stay, tender Spirit! Cruel, stay thy flight
Ah soft descend in yonder rolling Cloud,
And veil ALZIRA in thy misty Shroud—
He hears—from azure Skies he swift descends—
With healing balms his drooping Pinion bends—
My Love has plac'd the thirsty dagger near,
And on its hallow'd point has drop'd a tear!"—
As roll'd her wand'ring glances wide around

She snatch'd a reeking Sabre from the ground;
Firmly her lifted hand the weapon press'd,
And deep she plung'd it in her panting breast:
"'Tis but a few short moments that divide
ALZIRA from her Love"—She spoke—and died—

from Canto VI

But, lo! where bursting Desolation's Night,
A scene of Glory rushes on my sight!
My tear—th' exulting drop of Rapture flows!
My swelling heart expands—my bosom glows—
A blooming Chief of India's royal Race,[5]
Whose soaring soul its high descent can trace,
The flag of Freedom rears on Chili's Plain,[6]
And leads to glorious Strife his gen'rous Train—
And see! Iberia bleeds—while Vict'ry twines
Her fairest Blossoms round Peruvia's Shrines:
The gaping wounds of earth disclose no more
The lucid silver, and the glowing ore,
A brighter glory gilds the passing hour,
While Freedom grasps the rod of lawless Power.
Lo! on the Andes' icy Steep she glows,[7]
And prints with rapid step th' eternal snows;
Or moves majestic o'er the smiling Plain,
And pours all eloquent her potent strain—
Still sacred Freedom! may thy spirit fire
The swelling bosom, may thy Flame inspire!
O may thy Eagle-Genius still ascend,
Beneath thy Crest may proud Iberia bend;
While roll'd in dust thy graceful feet beneath,
Fades her dark Laurel, and her sanguine[8] Wreath,
Bend her red Trophies, tear her Victor Plume,
And close insatiate Slaughter's yawning Tomb!
Again on soft Peruvia's od'rous breast
May Beauty blossom, and may Pleasure rest.
Ah, mild Peru! the Muse that mourn'd thy woes,
Whom bleeding Pity rob'd of dear Repose;
The Muse, whose pensive soul with anguish wrung,
Throb'd as her early Lyre she trembling strung,
Shed the weak tear, and breath'd the powerless sigh
Which soon in cold Oblivion's Shade must die;
Pants with the wish thy Deeds may rise to Fame,
Bright on some living Harp's immortal frame;
While on the string of Extasy, it pours
Thy future Triumphs o'er unnumber'd Shores.

[5] **Chief of India's Royal Race**: José Gabriel Condorcanqui, a Peruvian Indian who called himself Tupac Amaru II after his Inca ancestor, led a revolt of the Indians against the Spanish colonists in 1780, but was captured and brutally executed in 1781. The rebellion he fomented was defeated in 1783.

[6] **on Chili's Plain**: An Indian descended from the Incas, has lately obtained several victories over the Spaniards, the gold mines have been for some time shut up, and there is much reason to hope that these injured nations may recover the liberty of which they have been so cruelly deprived [H. M. W.].

[7] **Iberia**: Spain. **Andes**: high mountain range running north and south, forming the backbone of South America.

[8] **sanguine**: bloody.

from POEMS
(1786)

To Sensibility

In *Sensibility*'s lov'd praise
I tune my trembling reed;
And seek to deck her shrine with bays,
On which my heart must bleed!

No cold exemption from her pain
I ever wish'd to know;
Cheer'd with her transport, I sustain
Without complaint her woe.

Above whate'er content can give,
Above the charm of ease,
The restless hopes, and fears that live
With her, have power to please.

Where but for her, were Friendship's power
To heal the wounded heart,
To shorten sorrow's ling'ring hour,
And bid its gloom depart?

'Tis she that lights the melting eye
With looks to anguish dear;
She knows the price of ev'ry sigh,
The value of a tear.

She prompts the tender marks of love
Which words can scarce express;
The heart alone their force can prove,
And feel how much they bless.

Of every finer bliss the source!
'Tis she on love bestows

The softer grace, the boundless force
Confiding passion knows;

When to another, the fond breast
Each thought for ever gives;
When on another, leans for rest,
And in another lives!

Quick, as the trembling metal flies,
When heat or cold impels,
Her anxious heart to joy can rise,
Or sink where anguish dwells!

Yet tho' her soul must griefs sustain
Which she alone, can know;
And feel that keener sense of pain
Which sharpens every woe;

Tho' she the mourner's grief to calm,
Still shares each pang they feel,
And, like the tree distilling balm,
Bleeds, others wounds to heal;

While she, whose bosom fondly true,
Has never wish'd to range;
One alter'd look will trembling view,
And scarce can bear the change;

Tho' she, if death the bands should tear,
She vainly thought secure;
Thro' life must languish in despair
That never hopes a cure;

Tho' wounded by some vulgar mind,
Unconscious of the deed,
Who never seeks those wounds to bind
But wonders why they bleed;—

She oft will heave a secret sigh,
Will shed a lonely tear,
O'er feelings nature wrought so high,
And gave on terms so dear;

Yet who would hard INDIFFERENCE choose,
Whose breast no tears can steep?
Who, for her apathy, would lose
The sacred power to weep?

Tho' in a thousand objects, pain,
And pleasure tremble nigh,
Those objects strive to reach, in vain,
The circle of her eye.

Cold, as the fabled god appears
To the poor suppliant's grief,
Who bathes the marble form in tears,
And vainly hopes relief.

Ah *Greville!*[1] why the gifts refuse
To souls like thine allied?
No more thy nature seem to lose
No more thy softness hide.

No more invoke the playful sprite
To chill, with magic spell,
The tender feelings of delight,
And anguish sung so well;

That envied ease thy heart would prove
Were sure too dearly bought
With friendship, sympathy, and love,
And every finer thought.

A Farewell, for Two Years, to England
(1789)

Sweet Spring! while others hail thy op'ning flowers,
The first young hope of Summer's blushing hours;
Me they remind, that when her ardent ray
Shall reach the summit of our lengthen'd day,
Then, Albion![1] far from Thee, my cherish'd home,
To foreign climes my pensive steps must roam;
And twice shall Spring, dispelling Winter's gloom,
Shed o'er thy lovely vales her vernal bloom;
Twice shall thy village-maids, with chaplets gay,
And simple carols, hail returning May;
And twice shall Autumn, o'er thy cultur'd[2] plain,
Pour the rich treasures of his yellow grain;
Twice shall thy happy peasants bear along
The lavish store, and wake the harvest-song;
Ere from the bounded deep my searching eye,
Ah! land belov'd, shall thy white cliffs[3] descry.—

[1] **Greville:** Frances Greville (1726?–1789), Anglo-Irish poet, author of the "Prayer for Indifference," probably written after the death of a son in 1756.

[1] **Albion:** ancient and poetic name for England or Britain.

[2] **cultur'd:** cultivated.

[3] **white cliffs:** the white cliffs of Dover, on the southeastern coast of England, directly across the English Channel from

Where the slow Loire, on borders ever gay,
Delights to linger, in his sunny way,
Oft, while I seem to count, with musing glance,
The murm'ring waves that near his brink advance,
My wand'ring thoughts shall seek the grassy side,
Parental Thames! where rolls thy ample tide;
Where, on thy willow'd bank, methinks, appears
Engrav'd the record of my passing years;
Ah! not like thine, their course is gently led,
By zephyrs fann'd, thro' paths with verdure spread;
They flow, as urg'd by storms the mountain rill
Falls o'er the fragments of the rocky hill.
My native scenes! can aught in time, or space,
From this fond heart your lov'd remembrance chase?
Link'd to that heart by ties for ever dear,
By Joy's light smile, and Sorrow's tender tear;
By all that ere my anxious hopes employ'd,
By all my soul has suffer'd, or enjoy'd!
Still blended with those well-known scenes, arise
The varying images the past supplies;
The childish sports that fond attention drew,
And charm'd my vacant heart when life was new;
The harmless mirth, the sadness robb'd of power
To cast its shade beyond the present hour—
And that dear hope which sooth'd my youthful breast,
And show'd the op'ning world in beauty drest;
That hope which seem'd with bright unfolding rays
(Ah, vainly seem'd!) to gild my future days;
That hope which, early wrapp'd in lasting gloom,
Sunk in the cold inexorable tomb!—
And Friendship, ever powerful to controul
The keen emotions of the wounded soul,
To lift the suff'ring spirit from despair,
And bid it feel that life deserves a care.
Still each impression that my heart retains
Is link'd, dear Land! to thee by lasting chains.
She too, sweet soother of my lonely hours!
Who gilds my thorny path with fancy's flowers,
The Muse,[4] who early taught my willing heart
To feel with transport her prevailing art;
Who deign'd before my infant eyes to spread
Those dazzling visions she alone can shed;
She, who will still be found where'er I stray,
The lov'd companion of my distant way;
'Midst foreign sounds, her voice, that charms my ear,
Breath'd in my native tongue, I still shall hear;
'Midst foreign sounds, endear'd will slow the song
Whose tones, my ALBION, will to thee belong!
And when with wonder thrill'd, with mind elate,
I mark the change sublime in GALLIA's state!
Where new-born Freedom treads the banks of Seine,[5]
Hope in her eye, and Virtue in her train!
Pours day upon the dungeon's central gloom,
And leads the captive from his living tomb;
Tears the sharp iron from his loaded breast,
And bids the renovated land be blest—
My thoughts shall fondly turn to that lov'd Isle,
Where Freedom long has shed her genial smile.
Less safe in other lands the triple wall,
And massy portal, of the Gothic hall,
Than in that favour'd Isle the straw-built thatch,
Where Freedom sits, and guards the simple latch.
Yet, ALBION! while my heart to thee shall spring,
To thee its first, its best affections bring;
Yet, when I hear exulting millions pour
The shout of triumph on the GALLIC shore;
Not without sympathy my pensive mind
The bounds of human bliss enlarg'd, shall find;
Not without sympathy my glowing breast
Shall hear, on any shore, of millions blest!
Scorning those narrow souls, whate'er their clime,
Who meanly think that sympathy a crime;
Who, if one wish for human good expand
Beyond the limits of their native land,
And from the worst of ills would others free,
Deem that warm wish, my Country! guilt to thee.
Ah! why those blessings to one spot confine,
Which, when diffus'd, will not the less be thine?

France. **Loire:** the principal river of France, flowing through central and western France to the Atlantic; the Loire region is famous for its cultural heritage as well as its châteaus and agricultural richness. **Thames:** the principal river of England, flowing through southern England and London to the North Sea.

[4] **Muse:** in Greek mythology, the nine Muses, daughters of Zeus and Mnemosyne (memory), were the patron goddesses of the arts. Williams probably is referring to either Calliope or Euterpe, the Muses of epic and lyric poetry.

[5] **Gallia:** Latin and literary name for France. **Seine:** major river of northern France, flowing through Paris to the English Channel.

Ah! why repine if far those blessings spread
For which so oft thy gen'rous sons have bled?
Shall ALBION mark with scorn the lofty thought,
The love of Liberty, herself has taught?
Shall *her* brave sons, in this enlighten'd age,
Assume the bigot-frown of papal rage,[6]
Nor tolerate the vow to Freedom paid,
If diff'ring from the ritual *they* have made?
Freedom! who oft on ALBION's fost'ring breast
Has found *her* friends in stars and ermine[7] drest,
Allows that some among her chosen race
Should there the claim to partial honours trace,
And in the long-reflected lustre shine
That beams thro' Ancestry's ennobled line;
While she, with guardian wing, can well secure
From each proud wrong the undistinguish'd poor.
On GALLIA's coast, where oft the robe of state
Was trail'd by those whom Freedom's soul must hate;
Where, like a comet, rank appear'd to glow
With dangerous blaze, that threaten'd all below;
There Freedom now, with gladden'd eye, beholds
The simple vest that flows in equal folds.
And tho' on Seine's fair banks a transient storm[8]
Flung o'er the darken'd wave its angry form;
That purifying tempest now has past,
No more the trembling waters feel the blast;
The bord'ring images, confus'dly trac'd
Along the ruffled stream, to order haste;
The vernal day-spring bursts the partial gloom,
And all the landscape glows with fresher bloom.
When, far around that bright'ning scene, I view
Objects of gen'ral bliss, to GALLIA new;
Then, ALBION! shall my soul reflect with pride
Thou wert her leading star, her honour'd guide;
That, long in slav'ry sunk, when taught by thee,
She broke her fetters, and has dar'd be free;
In new-born majesty she seems to rise,
While sudden from the land oppression flies.
So, at the solemn hour of Nature's birth,
When brooding darkness veil'd the beauteous earth,
Heaven's awful mandate pierc'd the solid night,
"Let there be light," it said, "and there was light!"
Ah! when shall Reason's intellectual ray
Shed o'er the moral world more perfect day?
When shall that gloomy world appear no more
A waste, where desolating tempests roar?
Where savage Discord howls in threat'ning form,
And wild Ambition leads the mad'ning storm;
Where hideous Carnage marks his dang'rous way,
And where the screaming vulture scents his prey?—
Ah! come, blest Concord! chase, with smile serene,
The hostile passions from the human scene!
May Glory's lofty path be found afar
From agonizing groans and crimson war;
And may the ardent mind, that seeks renown,
Claim, not the martial, but the civic crown!
While pure Benevolence, with happier views
Of bright success, the gen'ral good pursues;
Ah! why, my Country! with indignant pain,
Why in thy senate did she plead in vain?
Ah! why in vain enforce the Captives' cause,[9]
And urge Humanity's eternal laws?
With fruitless zeal the tale of horror trace,
And ask redress for AFRIC's injur'd race?
Unhappy race! ah! what to them avail'd,
That touching eloquence, whose efforts fail'd?
Tho' in the senate Mercy found combin'd
All who possess the noblest pow'rs of mind,
On other themes, pre-eminently bright,
They shine, like single stars, with sep'rate light;
Here, only *here*, with intermingled rays,
In one resplendent constellation blaze;
Yes, Captive race! if all the force display'd
By glowing Genius, in Compassion's aid,
When, with that energy she boasts alone,
She made your wrongs, your ling'ring tortures known;
Bade full in view the bloody visions roll,
Shook the firm nerves, and froze the shudd'ring soul!!—
As when the sun, in piercing radiance bright,
Dispelling the low mists of doubtful light,

---

[6] **papal rage:** referring to the violent opposition of the Catholic Church (symbolized here in the person of the Pope) to the French Revolution, its political and philosophical ideals (equality, rationalism, freedom of belief), and its vengeful attack upon religion and church properties.

[7] **stars and ermine:** as used here, symbols of nobility, military honor, or high political office.

[8] **transient storm:** the violence of the early days (1789) of the French Revolution, which Williams anticipated would soon subside.

[9] **the Captives' cause:** the campaign to end the British slave trade.

Its lustre on some hideous object throws,
And all its hateful horror clearly shows—
If Genius could in Mercy's cause prevail,
When Interest presses the opposing scale,
How swift had BRITONS torn your galling chain,
And from their country wip'd its foulest stain!—
But oh, since mis'ry, in its last excess,
In vain from BRITISH honour hopes redress;
May other Lands the bright example show,
May other regions lessen human woe!
Yes, GALLIA, haste! tho' BRITAIN's sons decline
The glorious power to save, that power is thine;
Haste! since, while BRITAIN courts that dear-bought gold,
For which her virtue and her fame are sold,
And calmly calculates her trade of death,
Her groaning victims yield in pangs their breath;
Then save some portion of that suff'ring race
From ills the mind can scarce endure to trace!
Oh! whilst with mien august[10] thy Leaders scan,
And guard with jealous zeal the rights of man,
Forget not that to all kind Nature gives
Those common rights, the claim of all that lives.—
But yet my filial heart its wish must breathe
That BRITAIN first may snatch this deathless wreath;
First to the earth this act divine proclaim,
And wear the freshest palm of virtuous fame;
May I, in foreign realms, her glories hear,
Catch the lov'd sounds, and pour th' exulting tear!
And when, the destin'd hour of exile past,
My willing feet shall reach their home at last;
When, with the trembling hope Affection proves,
My eager heart shall search for those it loves,
May no sharp pang that cherish'd hope destroy,
And from my bosom tear the promis'd joy;
Shroud every object, every scene in gloom,
And lead my bleeding soul to Friendship's tomb!
But may that moment to my eyes restore
The friends whose love endears my native shore!
Ah! long may Friendship, like the western ray,
Chear the sad evening of a stormy day;
And gild my shadowy path with ling'ring light,
The last dear beam that slowly sinks in night.

[10] **mien august:** a bearing or manner inspiring admiration or reverence.

from LETTERS FROM FRANCE[1]

(1790–1796)

from Volume I

(1790)

—LETTER I—

I arrived at Paris, by a very rapid journey, the day before the Federation;[2] and when I am disposed to murmur at the evils of my destiny, I shall henceforth put this piece of good fortune into the opposite scale, and reflect how many disappointments it ought to counterbalance. Had the packet[3] which conveyed me from Brighton to Dieppe failed a few hours later; had the wind been contrary; in short, had I not reached Paris at the moment I did reach it, I should have missed the most sublime spectacle, which, perhaps, was ever represented on the theatre of this earth.

I shall send you once a week the details which I promised when we parted, though I am well aware how very imperfectly I shall be able to describe the images

[1] Williams's *Letters from France* appeared in 8 volumes with differing volume titles. Volume I bore the title *Letters written in France, in the Summer 1790, to a Friend in England. Containing Anecdotes relative to the French Revolution, and Memoirs of Mons. and Madame du F——.* (London, 1790). Volume 2 was titled *Letters from France: containing New Anecdotes relative to the French Revolution and the Present State of French Manners* (London, 1792). Volumes 3 and 4 were titled *Letters from France: containing a Great Variety of Interesting and Original Information concerning the most Important Events that have lately occurred in that Country and particularly respecting the Campaign of 1792* (London, 1794–1796). Volumes 5–8 were published under the title *Letters containing a Sketch of the Politics of France, from the Thirty-first of May 1793, till the Twenty-eighth of July 1794, and of the Scenes which have Passed in the Prisons of Paris,* Vols. 1–4 (London, 1795–1796). The 8 volumes were published in 2 volumes in a facsimile reproduction as *Letters from France,* edited by Janet Todd, by Scholars' Facsimiles & Reprints (Delmar, New York, 1975).

[2] **Federation:** the Festival of Federation, held in Paris on 14 July 1790 (the anniversary of the fall of the Bastille) to celebrate what was hoped would be a stable political compromise among the various contending social groups: among them the king, feudal aristocracy, Catholic priests, bourgeois property owners, urban laborers and artisans, and peasants. At the Festival, Louis XVI took an oath to uphold the new constitution.

[3] **packet:** a packet-boat or mail boat, usually crossing between two ports (here between **Brighton** in southern England and **Dieppe** in northern France).

which press upon my mind. It is much easier to feel what is sublime, than to paint it; and all I shall be able to give you will be a faint sketch, to which your own imagination must add colouring and spirit. The night before the Federation, by way of prelude to the solemnities of that memorable day, the Te Deum was performed at the church of Notre Dame, by a greater number of musicians than have ever been assembled together, excepting at Westminster Abbey.[4] The Overture which preceded the Te Deum was simple and majestic; the music, highly expressive, had the power of electrifying the hearers: and near the conclusion of the piece, the composer, by artful discords, produced a melancholy emotion; and then, by exciting ideas of trouble and inquietude, prepared the mind for a recitative which affected the audience in a very powerful manner, by recalling the images of that consternation and horror which prevailed in Paris on the 13th of July, 1789, the day before that on which the Bastille[5] was taken. The words were, as well as I can recollect, what follows:—"People, your enemies advance, with hostile sentiments, with menacing looks! They come to bathe their hands in your blood! Already they encompass the walls of your city! Rise, rise from the inaction in which you are plunged, seize your arms, and fly to the combat! God will combat with you!" These words were succeeded by a chorus of instruments and voices, deep and solemn, which seemed to chill the soul. But what completed the effect was, when the sound of a loud and heavy bell mixed itself with this awful concert, in imitation of the alarm-bell, which, the day before the taking of the Bastille, was rung in every church and convent in Paris; and which, it is said, produced a confusion of sounds inexpressibly horrible. At this moment the audience appeared to breathe with difficulty; every heart seemed frozen with terror: till at length the bell ceased, the music changed its tone, and another recitative announced the entire defeat of the enemy; and the whole terminated, after a flourish of drums and trumpets, with an hymn of thanksgiving to the Supreme Being.

[4]**Te Deum**: musical setting of a traditional Latin hymn beginning "Te Deum laudamus" ("We praise Thee, O God"). **Notre Dame**: Notre Dame de Paris (Our Lady of Paris), Gothic cathedral dating from the twelfth century, renamed the Temple of Reason in the later years of the revolution. **Westminster Abbey**: Gothic church in London, dating from the thirteenth century, site of the coronations and burials of the British monarchs.

[5]**Bastille**: a royal fortress and prison in Paris, regarded as a symbol of absolutism and tyranny; a crowd in search of ammunition stormed the Bastille on 14 July 1789, freeing the seven prisoners inside and precipitating the Revolution. See The French Revolution and Rights of Man.

—*from* LETTER II—

I promised to send you a description of the Federation; but it is not to be described! One must have been present, to form any judgment of a scene, the sublimity of which depended much less on its external magnificence than on the effect it produced on the minds of the spectators. "The people, sure, the people were the sight!" I may tell you of pavilions, of triumphal arches, of altars on which incense was burnt, of two hundred thousand men walking in procession; but how am I to give you an adequate idea of the behaviour of the spectators? How am I to paint the impetuous feelings of that immense, that exulting multitude? Half a million of people assembled at a spectacle, which furnished every image that can elevate the mind of man; which connected the enthusiasm of moral sentiment with the solemn pomp of religious ceremonies; which addressed itself at once to the imagination, the understanding, and the heart.

The Champ de Mars[6] was formed into an immense amphitheatre; round which were erected forty rows of seats, raised one above another with earth, on which wooden forms were placed. Twenty days labour, animated by the enthusiasm of the people, accomplished what seemed to require the toil of years. Already in the Champ de Mars the distinctions of rank were forgotten; and, inspired by the same spirit, the highest and lowest orders of citizens gloried in taking up the spade, and assisting the persons employed in a work on which the common welfare of the State depended. Ladies took the instruments of labour in their hands, and removed a little of the earth, that they might be able to boast that they also had assisted in the preparations at the Champ de Mars; and a number of old soldiers were seen voluntarily bestowing on their country the last remains of their strength. A young Abbé of my acquaintance told me, that the people beat a drum at the door of the convent where he lived, and obliged the Superior to let all the Monks come out, and work in the Champ de Mars. The Superior with great reluctance acquiesced: "Quant à moi," said the young Abbé, "je ne demandois pas mieux."[7]

[6]**Champ de Mars**: a large open area, formerly a military parade ground, near the Seine River; in 1889 the Eiffel Tower was erected there.

[7]**je ne demandois pas mieux**: "As for me, I desired nothing better" (Williams's translation).

At the upper end of the amphitheatre a pavilion was built for the reception of the King, the Queen, their attendants, and the National Assembly,[8] covered with striped tent-cloth of the national colours, and decorated with streamers of the same beloved tints, and fleurs de lys.[9] The white flag was displayed above the spot where the king was seated. In the middle of the Champ de Mars l'Autel de la Patrie was placed, on which incense was burnt by priests dressed in long white robes, with sashes of national ribbon. Several inscriptions were written on the altar; but the words visible at the greatest distance were, "La Nation, la Loi, & le Roi."[10]

At the lower end of the amphitheatre, opposite to the pavilion, three triumphal arches were erected, adorned with emblems and allegorical figures.

The procession marched to the Champ de Mars, through the central streets of Paris. At La Place de Louis Quinze, the escorts, who carried the colours, received under their banners, ranged in two lines, the National Assembly, who came from the Tuilleries.[11] When the procession passed the street where Henry the Fourth[12] was assassinated, every man paused as if by general consent: the cries of joy were suspended, and succeeded by a solemn silence. This tribute of regret, paid from the sudden impulse of feeling at such a moment, was perhaps the most honourable testimony to the virtues of that amiable Prince which his memory has yet received.

In the streets, at the windows, and on the roofs of the houses, the people, transported with joy, shouted and wept as the procession passed. Old men were seen kneeling in the streets, blessing God that they had lived to witness that happy moment. The people ran to the doors of their houses, loaded with refreshments, which they offered to the troops; and crouds of women surrounded the soldiers, and holding up their infants in their arms, and melting into tears, promised to make their children imbibe, from their earliest age, an inviolable attachment to the principles of the new constitution.

The procession entered the Champ de Mars by a long road, which thousands of people had assisted in forming, by filling up deep hollows, levelling the rising grounds, and erecting a temporary bridge across the Seine, opposite to the triumphal arches. The order of the procession was as follows:

A troop of horse, with trumpets.
A great band of music.
A detachment of grenadiers.
The electors chosen at Paris in 1789.
A band of volunteers.
The assembly of the representatives of the people.
The military committee.
Company of chaffeurs.
A band of drums.
The Presidents of sixty districts.
The Deputies of the people sent to the Federation.
The Administrators of the Municipality.
Bands of music and drums.
Battalion of children, carrying a standard, on which was written, *L'Espérance de la Patrie.*[13]
Detachment with the colours of the national guard of Paris.
Battalion of veterans.
Deputies from forty-two departments, arranged alphabetically.
The Orislamme, or grand standard of the Kings of France.
Deputies from the regular troops.
Deputies from the navy.
Deputies from forty-one departments, arranged also alphabetically.
Band of volunteer chaffeurs.
Troop of horse, with trumpets.

[8] **National Assembly**: constituent legislative body made up of members of the third estate or commons of France (the first two estates were the nobility and the clergy), who during the political crisis of 1789 declared themselves the ruling legislative body of the nation, thus defying the king and forcing a new political regime.

[9] **fleurs de lys**: French for lily flower, used as the armorial symbol of the kings of France.

[10] **l'Autel de la Patrie**: the Altar of the Nation. **La Nation, la Loi, & le Roi**: "The Nation, the Law, and the King" (Williams's translation).

[11] **the Tuilleries**: formerly a royal palace in central Paris, destroyed by fire during the siege of the Paris Commune of 1871; the formal gardens, leading to the Louvre Museum, remain.

[12] **Henry the Fourth**: born in 1553, he was King of France from 1589 to 1610, when he was stabbed to death by François Ravaillac; nevertheless, he was probably the best loved of all French kings because of his concern for the welfare of the common people.

[13] **L'Espérance de la Patrie**: "The Hope of the Country" (Williams's translation).

The procession, which was formed with eight persons abreast, entered the Champ de Mars beneath the triumphal arches, with a discharge of cannon. The deputies placed themselves round the inside of the amphitheatre. Between them and the seats of the spectators, the national guard of Paris were ranged; and the seats round the amphitheatre were filled with four hundred thousand people. The middle of the amphitheatre was crowded with an immense multitude of soldiers. The National Assembly walked towards the pavilion, where they placed themselves with the King, the Queen, the Royal Family, and their attendants; and opposite this group, rose in perspective the hills of Passy and Chaillot, covered with people. The standards, of which one was presented to each department of the kingdom, as a mark of brotherhood, by the citizens of Paris, were carried to the altar, to be consecrated by the bishop. High mass was performed, after which Mons. de la Fayette,[14] who had been appointed by the king Major-General of the Federation, ascended the altar, gave the signal, and himself took the national oath. In an instant every sword was drawn, and every arm lifted up. The King pronounced the oath, which the President of the National Assembly repeated, and the solemn words were re-echoed by six hundred thousand voices; while the Queen raised the Dauphin[15] in her arms, shewing him to the people and the army. At the moment the consecrated banners were displayed, the sun, which had been obscured by frequent showers in the course of the morning, burst forth; while the people lifted their eyes to heaven, and called upon the Deity to look down and witness the sacred engagement into which they entered. A respectful silence was succeeded by the cries, the shouts, the acclamations of the multitude: they wept, they embraced each other, and then dispersed.

You will not suspect that I was an indifferent witness of such a scene. Oh, no! this was not a time in which the distinctions of country were remembered. It was the triumph of human kind; it was man asserting the noblest privilege of his nature; and it required but the common feelings of humanity, to become in that moment a citizen of the world. For myself, I acknowledge that my heart caught with enthusiasm the general sympathy; my eyes were filled with tears: and I shall never forget the sensations of that day, "while memory holds her seat in my bosom." . . .

—*from* LETTER IV—

Before I suffered my friends at Paris to conduct me through the usual routine of convents, churches, and palaces, I requested to visit the Bastille, feeling a much stronger desire to contemplate the ruins of that building than the most perfect edifices of Paris. When we got into the carriage, our French servant called to the coachman, with an air of triumph, "A la Bastille—mais nous n'y resterons pas."[16] We drove under that porch which so many wretches have entered never to repass, and, alighting from the carriage, descended with difficulty into the dungeons, which were too low to admit of our standing upright, and so dark that we were obliged at noon-day to visit them with the light of a candle. We saw the hooks of those chains by which the prisoners were fastened round the neck, to the walls of their cells; many of which, being below the level of the water, are in a constant state of humidity; and a noxious vapour issued from them, which more than once extinguished the candle, and was so insufferable that it required a strong spirit of curiosity to tempt one to enter. Good God!—and to these regions of horror were human creatures dragged at the caprice of despotic power. What a melancholy consideration, that

> ——— "Man! proud man,
> Drest in a little brief authority,
> Plays such fantastic tricks before high heaven,
> As make the angels weep."[17]

There appears to be a greater number of these dungeons than one could have imagined the hard heart of tyranny itself would contrive; for, since the destruction of

[14] **Mons. de la Fayette**: the Marquis de La Fayette (1757–1834), French general and political leader who played an important role in the American Revolution before being elected vice president of the National Assembly and commander of the militia. He tried to mediate between the contending factions of the revolutionary period, but a year after the Festival of the Federation, on 17 July 1791, he gave the order to fire into a crowd in the Champ de Mars and lost his popular support.

[15] **the Dauphin**: title given the eldest son of the kings of France; in this case Louis XVII (1785–1795), who died in prison after the executions of his parents. It was subsequently rumored that he had been secretly released from prison and replaced by another boy, giving rise to the legend or theory of the Lost Dauphin.

[16] **A la Bastille—mais nous n'y resterons pas**: "To the Bastille—but we shall not remain there" (Williams's translation).

[17] **As make the angels weep**: Shakespeare, *Measure for Measure*, II.ii.117–122.

the building, many subterraneous cells have been discovered underneath a piece of ground which was inclosed within the walls of the Bastille, but which seemed a bank of solid earth before the horrid secrets of this prisonhouse were disclosed. Some skeletons were found in these recesses, with irons still fastened on their decaying bones.

After having visited the Bastille, we may indeed be surprised, that a nation so enlightened as the French, submitted so long to the oppressions of their government; but we must cease to wonder that their indignant spirits at length shook off the galling yoke.

Those who have contemplated the dungeons of the Bastille, without rejoicing in the French revolution, may, for aught I know, be very respectable persons, and very agreeable companions in the hours of prosperity; but if my heart were sinking with anguish, I should not fly to those persons for consolation. Sterne[18] says, that a man is incapable of loving one woman as he ought, who has not a sort of an affection for the whole sex; and as little should I look for particular sympathy from those who have no feelings of general philanthropy. If the splendor of a despotic throne can only shine like the radiance of lightning, while all around is involved in gloom and horror, in the name of heaven let its baleful lustre be extinguished for ever. May no such strong contrast of light and shade again exist in the political system of France! but may the beams of liberty, like the beams of day, shed their benign influence on the cottage of the peasant, as well as on the palace of the monarch! May Liberty, which for so many ages past has taken pleasure in softening the evils of the bleak and rugged climates of the North, in fertilizing a barren soil, in clearing the swamp, in lifting mounds against the inundations of the tempest, diffuse her blessings also on the genial land of France, and bid the husbandman rejoice under the shade of the olive and the vine! . . .

* * *

It was at this crisis,[19] it was to save themselves the shocking spectacle of their wives and infants perishing before their eyes, that the citizens of Paris flew to arms; and, impelled by such causes, fought with the daring intrepidity of men who had all that renders life of any value at stake, and who determined to die or conquer. The women too, far from indulging the fears incident to our feeble sex, in defiance of the cannon of the Bastille, ventured to bring victuals to their sons and husbands; and, with a spirit worthy of Roman matrons, encouraged them to go on. Women mounted guard in the streets, and, when any person passed, called out boldly, "Qui va là."[20] . . .

— *from* LETTER V —

. . . But let me do justice to the ladies of France. The number of those who have murmured at the loss of rank, bears a very small proportion to those who have acted with a spirit of distinguished patriotism; who, with those generous affections which belong to the female heart, have gloried in sacrificing titles, fortune, and even the personal ornaments, so dear to female vanity, for the common cause. It was the ladies who gave the example of *le don patriotique*,[21] by offering their jewels at the shrine of Liberty; and if the women of ancient Rome have gained the applause of distant ages for such actions, the women of France will also claim the admiration of posterity.

The women have certainly had a considerable share in the French revolution: for, whatever the imperious lords of the creation may fancy, the most important events which take place in this world depend a little on our influence; and we often act in human affairs like those secret springs in mechanism, by which, though invisible, great movements are regulated.

— *from* LETTER IX —

. . . Upon the whole, Liberty appears in France adorned with the freshness of youth, and is loved with the ardour of passion. In England she is seen in her matron state, and, like other ladies at that period, is beheld with sober veneration.

With respect to myself, I must acknowledge, that, in my admiration of the revolution in France, I blend the feelings of private friendship with my sympathy in public blessings; since the old constitution is connected in my mind with the image of a friend confined in the gloomy recesses of a dungeon, and pining in hopeless captivity; while, with the new constitution, I unite the soothing idea of his return to prosperity, honours, and happiness.

---

[18] **Sterne:** Laurence Sterne (1713–1768), English novelist, author of *Tristram Shandy* (1760–1766) and *A Sentimental Journey* (1768).

[19] **this crisis:** a severe bread shortage in Paris in the summer of 1789.

[20] **"Qui va là":** "Who goes there?" (Williams's translation).

[21] **le don patriotique:** "The patriotic donation" (Williams's translation).

This person is Mons. du F——, whose lady I am come to France to visit. They are friends with whom I wept in the day of their adversity, and with whom in their prosperity I have hastened to rejoice. Their history is most affecting; and when I leave the hurry of Paris, to accompany them to their Château in Normandy, I will make you acquainted with incidents as pathetic as romance itself can furnish. Adieu!

—*from* LETTER XVI—

. . . Augustin François Thomas du F[ossé], eldest son of the Baron du F——, Counsellor of the Parliament of Normandy,[22] was born on the fifteenth of July, 1750. His early years were embittered by the severity of his father, who was of a disposition that preferred the exercise of domestic tyranny to the blessings of social happiness, and chose rather to be dreaded than beloved. The endearing name of father conveyed no transport to *his* heart, which, being wrapt up in stern insensibility, was cold even to the common feelings of nature.

The Baron's austerity was not indeed confined to his son, but extended to all his dependants. Formed by nature for the support of the ancient government of France, he maintained his aristocratic rights with unrelenting severity, ruled his feudal tenures with a rod of iron, and considered the lower order of people as a set of beings whose existence was tolerated merely for the use of the nobility. The poor, he believed, were only born for suffering; and he determined, as far as in him lay, not to deprive them of their natural inheritance. On the whole, if it were the great purpose of human life to be hated, perhaps no person ever attained that end more completely than the Baron du F——.

His son discovered early a taste for literature, and received an education suitable to his rank and fortune. As he advanced in life, the treatment he experienced from his father became more and more intolerable to him, as, far from inheriting the same character, he possessed the most amiable dispositions, and the most feeling heart.

His mother, feeble alike in mind and body, submitted with the helplessness, and almost with the thoughtlessness of a child, to the imperious will of her husband. Their family was increased by two more sons and two daughters; but these children, being several years younger than Mons. du F——, were not of an age to afford him the consolations of friendship; and the young man would have found his situation intolerable, but for the sympathy of a person in whose society every evil was forgotten.

This person, his attachment to whom has tinctured the colour of his life, was the youngest of eight children, of a respectable family of Bourgeois at Rouen.[23] There is great reason to believe that her father was descended from the younger branch of a noble family of the same name, and bearing the same arms. But, unhappily, some links were wanting in this chain of honourable parentage. The claim to nobility could not be traced to the entire satisfaction of the Baron; who, though he would have dispensed with any moral qualities in favour of rank, considered obscure birth as a radical stain, which could not be wiped off by all the virtues under Heaven. He looked upon marriage as merely a convention of interest, and children as a property, of which it was reasonable for parents to make the most in their power.

The father of Mlle Monique C—— was a farmer, and died three months before the birth of this child; who, with seven other children, was educated with the utmost care by their mother, a woman of sense and virtue, beloved by all to whom she was known. It seemed as if this respectable woman had, after the death of her husband, only supported life for the sake of her infant family, from whom she was snatched by death, the moment her maternal cares became no longer necessary; her youngest daughter, Monique, having, at this period, just attained her twentieth year. Upon the death of her mother, Monique went to live with an aunt, with whom she remained only a very short time, being invited by Madame du F——, to whom she was well known, to come and live with her as an humble companion, to read to her when she was disposed to listen, and to enliven the sullen grandeur of the *château*, by her animating vivacity.

This young person had cultivated her excellent understanding by reading, and her heart stood in no need of cultivation. Mons. du F—— found in the charms of her conversation, and in the sympathy of her friendship, the most soothing consolation under the rigour of parental tyranny. Living several years beneath the same roof, he had constant opportunities of observing her disposition and character; and the passion with which she at length inspired him, was founded on the lasting basis of esteem.

---

[22] **Normandy**: region of northwestern France, bordering the English Channel.

[23] **Rouen**: major city of Normandy, on the Seine near its mouth in the English Channel, formerly seat of the provincial parliament.

If it was ever pardonable to deviate from that law, in the code of interest and etiquette, which forbids the heart to listen to its best emotions; which, stifling every generous sentiment of pure disinterested attachment, sacrifices love at the shrine of avarice or ambition; the virtues of Monique were such as might excuse this deviation. Yes, the character, the conduct of this amiable person, have nobly justified her lover's choice. How long might he have vainly sought, in the highest classes of society, a mind so elevated above the common mass! — a mind that, endowed with the most exquisite sensibility, has had sufficient firmness to sustain, with a calm and equal spirit, every transition of fortune, the most severe trials of adversity, and perhaps what is still more difficult to bear, the trial of high prosperity.

Mons. du F—— had been taught, by his early misfortunes, that domestic happiness was the first good of life. He had already found by experience, the insufficiency of rank and fortune to confer enjoyment, and he determined to seek it in the bosom of conjugal felicity. He determined to pass his life with her whose society now seemed essential not only to his happiness, but to his very existence.

At the solemn hour of midnight, the young couple went to a church, where they were met by a priest whom Mons. du F—— had made the confid[a]nt of his attachment, and by whom the marriage ceremony was performed.

Some time after, when the situation of his wife obliged Mons. du F—— to acknowledge their marriage to his mother, she assured her son that she would willingly consent to receive his wife as her daughter, but for the dread of his father's resentment. Madame du F——, with tears of regret, parted with Monique, whom she placed under the protection of her brothers: they conducted her to Caen,[24] where she was soon after delivered of a son.

The Baron du F—— was absent while these things were passing: he had been suspected of being the author of a pamphlet written against the Princes of the Blood,[25] and an order was issued to seize his papers, and conduct him to the Bastille; but he found means to escape into Holland, where he remained nearly two years. Having made his peace with the Ministry, he prepared to come home; but before he returned, Mons. du F—— received intelligence that his father, irritated almost to madness by the information of his marriage, was making application for a lettre-de-cachet,[26] in order to confine his daughter-in-law for the rest of her life; and had also obtained power to have his son seized and imprisoned. Upon this Mons. du F—— and his wife fled with precipitation to Geneva,[27] leaving their infant at nurse near Caen. The Genevois seemed to think that the unfortunate situation of these strangers gave them a claim to all the offices of friendship. After an interval of many years, I have never heard Mons. or Madame du F—— recall the kindness they received from that amiable people, without tears of tenderness and gratitude.

Meanwhile the Baron, having discovered the place of his son's retreat, obtained, in the name of the King, permission from the Cantons of Berne and Friburg to arrest them at Lausanne, where they had retired for some months. The wife of le Seigneur Baillif[28] secretly gave the young people notice of this design; and on the thirtieth of January, 1775, they had just time to make their escape, with only a few livres in their pockets, and the clothes in which they were dressed. Mons. du F——, upon his first going to Switzerland, had lent thirty louis to a friend in distress. He now, in this moment of necessity, desired to be repaid, and was promised the money within a month: mean time, he and his wife wandered from town to town, without finding any place where they could remain in security. They had spent all their small stock of money, and were almost without clothes: but, at the expiration of the appointed time, the thirty louis were paid; and with this fund Mons. and Madame du F—— determined to take shelter in the only country which could afford them a safe asylum from persecution, and immediately set off for England, travelling through Germany, and part of Holland, to avoid passing through France.

[24] **Caen:** port city in Normandy, to the west of Rouen.

[25] **Princes of the Blood:** male members of the royal family.

[26] **lettre-de-cachet:** literally, "sealed letters," letters under the private seal of the French king, often containing an order of exile or imprisonment which could not be appealed in court; although used relatively rarely, the lettres-de-cachet were much feared as symbols and instruments of royal tyranny and arbitrary power.

[27] **Geneva:** city on the southwestern tip of Lake Geneva in southwestern Switzerland, near the French border, and since the eighteenth century a major cultural and intellectual capital.

[28] **the Cantons of Berne and Friburg:** the administrative or political divisions, comparable to states, of Switzerland; those of Bern and Fribourg are in the west-central part of the country, toward the French side. **Lausanne:** city on the eastern end of Lake Geneva, formerly part of the canton of Bern. **Le Seigneur Baillif:** title of an officer of the law, comparable to a sheriff.

They embarked at Rotterdam;[29] and, after a long and gloomy passage, arrived late at night in London. An old and respectable man, who was their fellow-passenger, had the charity to procure them a lodging in a garret, and directed them where to purchase a few ready-made clothes. When they had remained in this lodging the time necessary for becoming parishioners, their banns[30] were published in the church of St. Anne, Westminster, where they were married by the Curate of the parish. They then went to the chapel of the French Ambassador, and were again married by his Chaplain; after which, Mons. du F—— told me, "Les deux époux vinrent faire maigre chère à leur petite chambre."[31]

Mons. du F—— endeavoured to obtain a situation at a school, to teach the French language; but before such a situation could be found, his wife was delivered of a girl. Not having sufficient money to hire a nurse, he attended her himself. At this period, they endured all the horrors of absolute want. Unknown and unpitied, without help or support, in a foreign country, and in the depth of a severe winter, they almost perished with cold and hunger. . . .

Oh, my dear, my ever-beloved friends! when I recollect that I am not at this moment indulging the melancholy cast of my own disposition, by painting imaginary distress: when I recollect not only that these were real sufferings, but that they were sustained by *you!* my mind is overwhelmed with its own sensations.—The paper is blotted by my tears—and I can hold my pen no longer.

— LETTER XVII —

——— "The moral world,
Which though to us it seem perplex'd, moves on
In higher order; fitted, and impell'd,
By Wisdom's finest hand, and issuing all
In universal good."[32]

Mons. and Madame du F—— were relieved from this extremity of distress at a moment so critical, and by means so unexpected, that it seemed the hand of Heaven visibly interposing in behalf of oppressed virtu[e]. Early in the morning of that fatal day when they were to leave their last sad shelter, Mons. du F—— went out, and, in the utmost distraction of mind, wandered through some of the streets in the neighbourhood. He was stopped by a gentleman whom he had known at Geneva, and who told him that he was then in search of his lodging, having a letter to deliver to him from a Genevois clergyman. Mons. du F—— opened the letter, in which he was informed by his friend, that, fearing he might be involved in difficulties, he had transmitted ten guineas to a banker in London, and intreated Mons. du F—— would accept that small relief, which was all he could afford, as a testimony of friendship. Mons. du F—— flew to the banker's, received the money as the gift of Heaven, and then, hastening to his wife and child, bade them live a little longer.

A short time after, he obtained a situation as French usher[33] at a school; and Madame du F——, when she had a little recovered her strength, put out her infant to nurse, and procured the place of French teacher at a boarding-school. They were now enabled to support their child, and to repay the generous assistance of their kind friend at Geneva.

Mons. and Madame du F—— passed two years in this situation, when they were again plunged into the deepest distress. A French jeweller was commissioned by the Baron du F—— to go to his son, and propose to him conditions of reconciliation. This man told Mons. du F—— that his father was just recovered from a severe and dangerous illness, and that his eldest daughter had lately died. These things, he said, had led him to reflect with some pain on the severity he had exercised towards his son; that the feelings of a parent were awakened in his bosom; and that, if Mons. du F—— would throw himself at his father's feet, and ask forgiveness, he would not fail to obtain it, and would be allowed a pension, on which he might live with his wife in England. In confirmation of these assurances, this man produced several letters which he had received from the Baron to that effect; who, as a farther proof of his sincerity, had given this agent seven hundred pounds to put into the hands of Mons. du F—— for the support of his wife and child during his absence. The agent told him, that he had not been able to bring the money to England, but would immediately give him three draughts upon a merchant of reputation in London with whom he had

[29] **Rotterdam:** port city in western Netherlands, near the North Sea.

[30] **banns:** proclamation or public notice given in church of an intended marriage, published so that anyone who knows of reasons why the marriage should not take place can present their objections.

[31] **"Les deux . . . à leur petite chambre":** "The new-married couple kept a fast in their little apartment" (Williams's translation).

[32] **The moral world . . . issuing all in universal good:** from *Winter*, in *The Seasons* (1746), by James Thomson (1700–1748): lines 583–87.

[33] **French usher:** assistant to the head teacher of French.

connexions in business; the first draught payable in three months, the second in six, and the third in nine.

Mons. du F—— long deliberated upon these proposals. He knew too well the vindictive spirit of his father, not to feel some dread of putting himself into his power. But his agent continued to give him the most solemn assurances of safety; and Mons. du F—— thought it was not improbable that his sister's death might have softened the mind of his father. He reflected that his marriage had disappointed those ambitious hopes of a great alliance which his father had fondly indulged, and to whom he owed at least the reparation of hastening to implore his forgiveness when he was willing to bestow it. What also weighed strongly on his mind, was the consideration that the sum which his father had offered to deposit for the use of his wife, would in case any sinister accident should befall him, afford a small provision for her and his infant.

The result of these deliberations was that Mons. du F—— determined (and who can much blame his want of prudence?) he determined to confide in a father!—to trust in that instinctive affection, which, far from being connected with any peculiar sensibility of mind, it requires only to be a parent to feel—an affection, which, not confined to the human heart, softens the ferociousness of the tiger, and speaks with a voice that is heard amidst the howlings of the desert.

Mons. du F——, after the repeated promises of his father, almost considered that suspicion which still hung upon his mind, as a crime. But, lest it might be possible that this agent was commissioned to deceive him, he endeavoured to melt him into compassion for his situation. He went to the village where his child was at nurse, and bringing her six miles in his arms, presented her to this man, telling him, that the fate of that poor infant rested upon his integrity. The man took the innocent creature in his arms, kissed her, and then returning her to her father, renewed all his former assurances. Mons. du F—— listened and believed. Alas! how difficult is it for a good heart to suspect human nature of crimes which make one blush for the species! How hard is it for a mind glowing with benevolence, to believe that the bosom of another harbours the malignity of a demon!

Mons. du F—— now fixed the time for his departure with his father's agent, who was to accompany him to Normandy. Madame du F—— saw the preparations for his journey with anguish which she could ill conceal; but she felt that the delicacy of her situation forbad her interference. It was she who had made him an alien from his family, and an exile from his country: it was for her, that, renouncing rank, fortune, friends, and connexions, all that is esteemed most valuable in life, he had suffered the last extremity of want, and now submitted to a state of drudgery and dependance. Would he not have a right to reproach her weakness, if she attempted to oppose his reconciliation with his father, and exerted that influence which she possessed over his mind, in order to detain him in a situation so remote from his former expectations? She was, therefore, sensible that the duty, the gratitude she owed her husband, now required, on her part, the absolute sacrifice of her own feelings: she suffered without complaint, and endeavoured to resign herself to the will of Heaven.

The day before his departure, Mons. du F—— went to take leave of his little girl. At this moment a dark and melancholy presage seemed to agitate his mind. He pressed the child for a long while to his bosom, and bathed it with his tears. The nurse eagerly inquired what was the matter, and assured him that the child was perfectly well. Mons. du F—— had no power to reply: he continued clasping his infant in his arms, and at length, tearing himself from her in silence, he rushed out of the house.

When the morning of his departure came, Madame du F——, addressing herself to his fellow-traveller, said to him, with a voice of supplication, "I entrust you, Sir, with my husband, with the father of my poor infant, our sole protector and support!—have compassion on the widow and the orphan!" The man, casting upon her a gloomy look, gave her a cold answer, which made her soul shrink within her. When Mons. du F—— got into the Brighthelmstone stage, he was unable to bid her farewell; but when the carriage drove off, he put his head out of the window, and continued looking after her, while she fixed her eyes on him, and might have repeated with Imogen,[34]

> "I would have broke mine eye-strings,
> Crack'd them, but to look upon him; till the
> diminution
> Of space had pointed him sharp as my needle:
> Nay, follow'd him, till he had melted from
> The smallness of a gnat to air; and then—
> Then turn'd mine eye, and wept!"

[34] **Imogen:** character in Shakespeare's *Cymbeline,* from which the following lines are taken (I.iii.17–22).

When the carriage was out of sight, she summoned all her strength, and walked with trembling steps to the school where she lived as a teacher. With much difficulty she reached the door; but her limbs could support her no longer, and she fell down senseless at the threshold. She was carried into the house, and restored to life and the sensations of misery.

—*from* LETTER XVIII

Mons. du F—— arrived at his father's *château* in Normandy, in June 1778, and was received by Mons. le Baron, and all his family, with the most affectionate cordiality. In much exultation of mind, he dispatched a letter to Madame du F——, containing this agreeable intelligence; but his letter was far from producing in her mind the effect he desired. A deep melancholy had seized her thoughts, and her foreboding heart refused to symphathise in his joy. Short, indeed, was its duration. He had not been many days at the *château,* when he perceived, with surprise and consternation, that his steps were continually watched by two servants armed with fusees.

His father now shewed him an arrét,[35] which, on the 4th of June, 1776, he had obtained from the Parliament of Rouen against his marriage. The Baron then ordered his son to accompany him to his house at Rouen, whither they went, attended by several servants. That evening, when the attendants withdrew after supper, the Baron, entirely throwing off the mask of civility and kindness which he had worn in such opposition to his nature, reproached his son, in terms of the utmost bitterness, for his past conduct, inveighed against his marriage, and, after having exhausted every expression of rage and resentment, at length suffered him to retire to his own apartment.

There the unhappy Mons. du F——, absorbed in the most gloomy reflections, lamented in vain that fatal credulity which had led him to put himself into the power of his implacable father. At the hour of midnight his meditations were interrupted by the sound of feet approaching his chamber; and in a few moments the door was thrown open, and his father, attended by a servant armed, and two *Cavaliers de Marechaussée,*[36] entered the room.

Resistance and supplication were alike unavailing. Mons. du F——'s papers were seized; a few louis d'ors, which constituted all the money he possessed, were taken from him; and he was conducted in the dead of night, July the 17th, 1778, to St. Yon, a convent used as a place of confinement near Rouen, where he was thrown into a dungeon.

A week after, his father entered the dungeon. You will perhaps conclude that his hard heart felt at length the relentings of a parent: you will at least suppose, that his imagination being haunted, and his conscience tormented, with the image of a son stretched on the floor of this subterraneous cell, he could support the idea no longer, and had hastened to give repose to his own mind by releasing his captive. Far different were the motives of his visit. He considered that such was his son's attachment to his wife, that, so long as he believed he had left her in possession of seven hundred pounds, he would find comfort from that consideration, even in the depth of his dungeon. His father, therefore, hastened to remove an error from the mind of his son, which left the measure of his woes unfilled. Nor did he choose to yield to another the office of inflicting a pang sharper than captivity; but himself informed his son, that the merchant who was to pay the seven hundred pounds to his wife, was declared a bankrupt. . . .

Mons. du F—— remained in his prison without meeting with the smallest mark of sympathy from any one of his family, though his second brother, Mons. de B——, was now eighteen years of age; an age at which the sordid considerations of interest, how much soever they may affect our conduct at a more advanced period of life, can seldom stifle those warm and generous feelings which seem to belong to youth. It might have been expected that this young man would have abhorred the prospect of possessing a fortune which was the just inheritance of his brother, and which could only be obtained by detaining that brother in perpetual captivity. Even admitting that his inexorable father prohibited his visiting the prison of his brother, his heart should have told him, that disobedience, in this instance, would have been a virtue: or, was it not sufficient to remain a passive spectator of injustice, without becoming, as he afterwards did, the agent of cruelty inflicted on a brother?

Where are the words that can convey an adequate idea of the sufferings of Madame du F—— during this period? Three weeks after her husband's departure from England, she heard the general report of the town of Rouen, that the Baron du F—— had obtained a *lettre-de-cachet*

[35] **fusees:** light muskets or firelocks, older forms of the rifle. **arrét:** an order of arrest.

[36] **Cavaliers de Marechaussée:** "Officers of justice" (Williams's translation).

against his son, and thrown him into prison. This was all she heard of her husband for the space of two years. Ignorant of the place of his confinement, uncertain if he still lived, perhaps her miseries were even more poignant than his. In the dismal solitude of a prison, his pains were alleviated by the soothing reflection that he suffered for her he loved; while that very idea was to her the most bitter aggravation of distress. Her days passed in anguish, which can only be conceived where it has been felt; and her nights were disturbed by the gloomy wanderings of fancy. Sometimes she saw him in her dreams chained to the floor of his dungeon, his bosom bathed in blood, and his countenance disfigured by death: sometimes she saw him hastening towards her, when, at the moment that he was going to embrace her, they were fiercely torn asunder. Madame du F—— was naturally of a delicate constitution; and grief of mind reduced her to such a deplorable state of weakness, that it was with infinite difficulty she performed the duties of her situation. For herself, she would have welcomed death with thankfulness; but she considered that her child now depended entirely on her labours for support: and this was a motive sufficiently powerful to prompt her to the careful preservation of her own life, though it had long become a burden. The child was three years old when her father left England; recollected him perfectly; and, whenever her mother went to visit her, used to call with eagerness for her papa. The inquiry, in the voice of her child, of, "When shall I see my dear, dear papa?" was heard by this unhappy mother with a degree of agony which it were vain indeed to describe.

—*from* LETTER XIX—

Mons. du F—— was repeatedly offered his liberty, but upon conditions which he abhorred. He was required for ever to renounce his wife; who, while she remained with her child in a distant country, was to receive from his father a small pension, as an equivalent for the pangs of disappointed affection, of disgrace and dishonour. With the indignation of offended virtue he spurned at these insulting propositions, and endeavoured to prepare his mind for the endurance of perpetual captivity.

Nor can imagination form an idea of a scene more dreadful than his prison, where he perceived with horror that the greatest number of those prisoners, who had been many years in confinement, had an appearance of frenzy in their looks, which shewed that reason had been too weak for the long struggle with calamity, and had at last yielded to despair. In the cell adjoining Mons. du F——'s, was an old man who had been confined nearly forty years. His grey beard hung down to his waist; and, during the day, he was chained by his neck to the wall. He was never allowed to leave his cell, and never spoke; but Mons. du F—— used to hear the rattling of his chains.

The prisoners, a few excepted, were generally brought from their cells at the hour of noon, and dined together. But this gloomy repast was served in uninterrupted silence. They were not suffered to utter one word; and the penalty of transgressing this rule, was a rigorous confinement of several weeks. As soon as this comfortless meal was finished, the prisoners were instantly obliged to return to their dungeons, in which they were locked up till the same hour the following day. Mons. du F——, in his damp and melancholy cell, passed two winters without fire, and suffered so severely from cold, that he was obliged to wrap himself up in the few clothes which covered his bed. Nor was he allowed any light, except that which during the short day beamed through the small grated window in the ceiling of his dungeon.

Is it not difficult to believe that these sufferings were inflicted by a father? A father!—that name which I cannot trace without emotion; which conveys all the ideas of protection, of security, of tenderness; that dear relation to which, in general, children owe their prosperity, their enjoyments, and even their virtues!—Alas, the unhappy Mons. du F—— owed nothing to *his* father, but that life, which from its earliest period his cruelty had embittered, and which he now condemned to languish in miseries that death only could heal. . . .

Mons. du F—— remained two years in prison without receiving any intelligence of his wife, on whose account he suffered the most distracting anxiety. He had reason to apprehend that her frame, which had already been enfeebled by her misfortunes, would sink beneath this additional load of misery, and that she would perhaps be rendered unable to procure that little pittance which might preserve herself and her child from want. At length one of his fellow prisoners, who was going to regain his liberty, took charge of a letter to Madame du F——, and flattered him with the hope of finding some means of transmitting to him an answer.

The letter paints so naturally the situation of his mind, that I have translated some extracts from it.

"My thoughts," he says, "are unceasingly occupied about you, and my dear little girl. I am for ever recalling the blessed moments when I had the happiness of being near you, and at that recollection my tears refuse to be controuled. How could I consent to separate myself from what was most dear to me in the world? No motive less powerful than that of seeking your welfare, and that of my child, could have determined me—and alas! I have not accomplished this end. I know too well that you have never received that sum of money which I thought I had secured for you, and for which I risked the first blessing of life. What fills my mind with the greatest horror, in the solitude of my prison, is the fear that you are suffering difficulties in a foreign country. Here I remain ignorant of your fate, and can only offer to Heaven the most ardent vows for your welfare.

"What joy would a letter from you give me! but I dare not flatter myself with the hope of such sweet consolation. All I can assure myself of is, that though separated, perhaps for ever, our souls are united by the most tender friendship and attachment. Perhaps I may not find it possible to write to you again for a long while; but be assured that no menaces, no sufferings, no dungeons, shall ever shake my fidelity to you, and that I shall love you to the last hour of my existence. I find a consolation in the reflection that it is for you I suffer. If Providence ever permits us to meet again, that moment will efface the remembrance of all my calamities. Live, my dearest wife, in that hope. I conjure you to preserve your life for my sake, and for the sake of our dear little girl! Embrace her tenderly for me, and desire her also to embrace you for her poor papa. I need not recommend my child to the care of so tender a mother; but I conjure you to inspire her mind with the deepest sense of religion. If she is born to inherit the misfortunes of her father, this will be her best source of consolation.

"Whatever offers may be made you by my father, I exhort you, never have the weakness to listen to them, but preserve your rights, and those of my dear little girl, which, perhaps, may one day be of some value. If you are still at Mrs. D——'s boarding-school, tell her that I recommend my wife and child to her compassion.—But what am I saying? I am ignorant if you are still with her, ignorant whether the dearest objects of my affection still live! But I trust that Providence has preserved you. Adieu! May God Almighty bless you, and my child! I never cease imploring him to have pity on the widow and the orphan in a land of strangers."

—*from* LETTER XX—

You, my dear friend, who have felt the tender attachments of love and friendship, and the painful anxieties which absence occasions, even amidst scenes of variety and pleasure; who understand the value at which tidings from those we love is computed in the arithmetic of the heart; who have heard with almost uncontroulable emotion the postman's rap at the door; have trembling seen the well-known hand which excited sensations that almost deprived you of power to break the seal which seemed the talisman of happiness; you can judge of the feelings of Mons. du F—— when he received, by means of the same friend who had conveyed his letter, an answer from his wife. But the person who brought the letter to his dungeon, dreading the risk of a discovery, insisted, that, after having read it, he should return it to him immediately. Mons. du F—— pressed the letter to his heart, bathed it with his tears, and implored the indulgence of keeping it at least till the next morning. He was allowed to do so, and read it till every word was imprinted on his memory; and after enjoying the sad luxury of holding it that night on his bosom, was forced the next morning to relinquish his treasure.

On the 10th of October, 1780, the Baron du F—— came to the convent, and ordered the Monks to bring his son from his dungeon to the parloir, and leave them together. With the utmost reluctance Mons. du F—— obeyed this summons, having long lost all hope of softening the obdurate heart of his father. When the Monks withdrew, the Baron began upbraiding him in the most bitter terms, for his obstinate resistance to his will, which, he informed him, had availed nothing, as he had gained his suit at law, and recovered the seven hundred pounds. Mons. du F—— replied, that the pain he felt from this intelligence would have been far more acute, had his wife been deprived, with his concurrence, of the money which was promised for her subsistence, and on the reliance of which promise he had been tempted to leave England. His father then inquired if he still persisted in his adherence to the disgraceful connexion he had formed; to which his son answered, that not merely were his affections interested, but that his honour obliged him to maintain, with inviolable fidelity, a solemn and sacred engagement. The rage of the Baron, at these words, became unbounded: he stamped the ground with his feet; he aimed a stroke at his son, who, taking advantage of this moment of frenzy, determined to attempt his escape; and, rushing out of the apartment, and avoiding that side of the convent which the Monks inhabited, he endeavoured to find his way to the garden, but missed the passage which led to it. He then flew up a stair-case, from which he heard the voice of his father calling for assistance. Finding that all the doors which he passed were shut, he continued ascending till he reached the top of the building, where, meeting with no other opening than a hole made in the sloping roof to let in light to a garret, he climbed up with much difficulty, and then putting his feet through the hole, and letting his body out by degrees, he supported himself for a moment on the roof, and deliberated on what he was about to do. But his mind was, at this crisis, wrought up to a pitch of desperation, which mocked the suggestions of fear. He quitted his hold, and, flinging himself from a height of nearly fifty feet, became insensible before he reached the ground, where he lay weltering in his blood, and to all appearance dead.

He had fallen on the high road leading from Rouen to Caen. Some people who were passing gathered round him; and one person having washed the blood from his face, instantly recognized his features, and exclaimed to the astonished crowd, that he was the eldest son of the Baron du F——. Upon examining his body, it was found that he had broken his arm, his thigh, his ancle-bone, and his heel, besides having received many violent bruises. He still remained in a state of insensibility; and, while these charitable strangers were using their efforts to restore him to life, the Monks hastened from their convent, snatched their victim from those good Samaritans who would have poured oil and wine into his wounds, and carried him to the infirmary of the convent, where he remained some weeks before he recovered his senses; after which he lay stretched upon a bed for three months, suffering agonies of pain.

His father, who had been the jailor, and almost the murderer of his son, heard of these sufferings without remorse, nor did he ever see him more. But, though he was sufficiently obdurate to hear unmoved the calamities he had inflicted on his child, though he could check the upbraidings of his own conscience, he could not silence the voice of public indignation. The report that Mons. du F—— had been found lying on the road bathed in blood, and had in that condition been dragged to the prison of St. Yon, was soon spread through the town of Rouen. Every one sympathized in the fate of this unfortunate young man, and execrated the tyranny of his unrelenting father.

The universal clamour reached the ear of his brother, Mons. de B——, who now, for the first time, out of respect to the public opinion, took a measure which his heart had never dictated during the long captivity of his brother, that of visiting him in prison. Mons. de B——'s design in these visits was merely to appease the public; for small indeed was the consolation they afforded to his brother. He did not come to bathe with his tears the bed where that unhappy young man lay stretched in pain and anguish; to lament the severity of his father; to offer him all the consolation of fraternal tenderness:—he came to warn him against indulging a hope of ever regaining his liberty—he came to pierce his soul with "hard unkindness' alter'd eye, which mocks the tear it forc'd to flow."

I will not attempt to describe the wretchedness of Madame du F——, when she heard the report of her husband's situation. Your heart will conceive what she suffered far better than I can relate it. . . .

—*from* LETTER XXI—

At length the Parliament of Rouen began to interest itself in the cause of Mons. du F——. The circumstances of his confinement were mentioned in that Assembly, and the President sent his Secretary to Mons. du F——'s prison, who had now quitted his bed, and was able to walk with the assistance of crutches. By the advice of the President, Mons. du F—— addressed some letters to the Parliament, representing his situation in the most pathetic terms, and imploring their interference in his behalf.

It is here necessary to mention, that Mons. de Bel B——, *Procureur-Genéral*[37] *de Rouen,* being intimately connected with the Baron du F——'s family, had ventured to demonstrate his friendship for the Baron, by confining his son nearly three years on his own authority, and without any *lettre-de-cachet.* And, though Mons. de Bel B well knew that every species of oppression was connived at, under the shelter of *lettres-de-cachet,* he was sensible that it was only beneath their auspices that the exercise of tyranny was permitted; and in this particular instance, not having been cruel *selon les règles,*[38] he apprehended, that if ever Mons. du F—— regained his liberty, he might be made responsible for his conduct. He therefore exerted all his influence, and with too much success, to frustrate the benevolent intention of the President of the Parliament, respecting Mons. du F——. His letters were indeed read in that Assembly, and ordered to be registered, where they still remain a record of the pusillanimity of those men who suffered the authority of Mons. de Bel B—— to overcome the voice of humanity;

[37] **Procureur-Général:** legal agent of the French state, presiding over a regional court of appeal.

[38] **selon les règles:** "according to rules" (Williams's translation).

who acknowledged the atrocity of the Baron du F——'s conduct, and yet were deaf to the supplications of his son, while, from the depth of his dungeon, he called upon them for protection and redress. . . .

The Baron du F—— perceived that, notwithstanding his machinations had prevented the Parliament of Rouen from taking any effectual measures towards liberating his son, it would be impossible to silence the murmurs of the public, while he remained confined at St. Yon. He determined, therefore, to remove him to some distant prison, where his name and family were unknown; and where, beyond the jurisdiction of the Parliament of Rouen, his groans might rise unpitied and unavenged. But the Baron, not daring, amidst the general clamour, to remove his son by force, endeavoured to draw him artfully into the snare he had prepared. . . .

Soon after this, Mons. de B——, the ambassador of the tyrant, again returned to his brother with fresh credentials, and declared to him, that if he would write to the Keeper of the Seals, desiring to be removed from St. Yon, he should, in one fortnight after his removal, be restored to liberty. Upon Mons. du F——'s asserting that he could no longer confide in the promises made him by his family, his brother, in a formal written engagement, to which he signed his name, gave him the most solemn assurance, that this promise should be fulfilled with fidelity. Mons. du F—— desired a few days for deliberation; and, during that interval, found means of consulting a magistrate of Rouen, who was his friend, and who advised him to comply with the terms that were offered, after having caused several copies of the written engagement to be taken, and certified by such of the prisoners at St. Yon as were likely to regain their freedom; a precaution necessary, lest his own copy should be torn from his hands.

Thus, having neither trusted to the affection, the mercy, or the remorse of those within whose bosoms such sentiments were extinguished; having bargained, by a written agreement, with a father and a brother, for his release from the horror of perpetual captivity, Mons. du F—— wrote the letter required.

Soon after, an order was sent from Versailles for his release from the prison of St. Yon, and with it a *lettre-de-cachet,* whereby he was exiled to Beauvais,[39] with a command not to leave that town. Mons. de B——, acting as a *Cavalier de la Marechaussée,* conducted his brother to this place of exile, and there left him. A short time after, Mons. du F—— received an intimation from that magistrate of Rouen who had interested himself in his misfortunes, that his father was on the point of obtaining another *lettre-de-cachet,* to remove him from Beauvais to some prison in the south of France, where he might never more be heard of. This gentleman added, that Mons. du F—— had not one moment to lose, and advised him immediately to attempt his escape.

Early on the morning after he received this intelligence, Mons. du F——, who had the liberty to walk about the town, fled from Beauvais. The person who brought him the letter from the magistrate, waited for him at a little distance from the town, and accompanied him on his journey. When they reached Lille[40] in Flanders, not having a passport, they were obliged to wait from eleven o'clock at night till ten the next morning, before they could obtain permission from the Governor to proceed on their journey. Mons. du F—— concluded that he was pursued, and suffered the most dreadful apprehensions of being overtaken. His companion, with some address, at length obtained a passport, and attended him as far as Ostend.[41] The wind proving contrary, he was detained two days in a state of the most distracting inquietude, and concealed himself on board the vessel in which he had taken his passage for England. At length, the wind became favourable; the vessel sailed, and arrived late in the night at Margate.[42] Mons. du F——, when he reached the English shore, knelt down, and, in a transport of joy, kissed the earth of that dear country which had twice proved his asylum.

He then inquired when the stagecoach set off for London, and was told that it went at so early an hour the next morning, that he could not go till the day after, as he must wait till his portmanteau was examined by the customhouse officers, who were now in bed. The delay of a few hours in seeing his wife and child, after such an absence, after such sufferings, was not to be endured: in a violent agitation of mind, he snatched up his portmanteau, and was going to fling it into the sea, when he was prevented by the people near him, who said, that if he would pay the fees, his portmanteau should be sent after him. He

[39] **Beauvais:** provincial capital city in northern France.

[40] **Lille:** major manufacturing city in northern France, near the border of Belgium; formerly the capital of the independent state of Flanders.

[41] **Ostend:** Oostende, port city of western Belgium, on the North Sea.

[42] **Margate:** seaport in Kent, in southeastern England.

eagerly complied with their demands, and set out for London. As he drew near, his anxiety, his impatience, his emotion increased. His present situation appeared to him like one of those delicious dreams, which sometimes visited the darkness of his dungeon, and for a while restored him, in imagination, to those he loved. Scarcely could he persuade himself that he was beyond the reach of oppression; that he was in a land of freedom; that he was hastening every moment towards his wife and child. When he entered London, his sensations became almost too strong to bear. He was in the very same place which his wife and child inhabited—but were they yet alive? were they in health? had Heaven indeed reserved for him the transport of holding them once more to his bosom, of mixing his tears with theirs? When he knocked at the door of the house where he expected to hear of Madame du F——, he had scarcely power to articulate his inquiries after her and his child. He was told that they were in health, but that Madame du F——, being in a situation six miles from London, he could not see her till the next morning. Mons. du F—— had not been in a bed for several nights, and was almost overcome with agitation and fatigue. He, however, instantly set out on foot for the habitation of his wife, announced himself to the mistress of the family, and remained in another apartment, while she, after making Madame du F—— promise that she would listen to her with calmness, told her, that there was a probability of her husband's return to England. He heard the sobs, the exclamations of his wife, at this intelligence—he could restrain no longer—he rushed into the room—he flew into her arms—he continued pressing her in silence to his bosom. She was unable to shed a tear; and it was not till after he had long endeavoured to soothe her by his tenderness, and had talked to her of her child, that she obtained relief from weeping. She then, with the most violent emotion, again and again repeated the same enquiries, and was a considerable time before she recovered any degree of composure.

All the fortune Mons. du F—— possessed when he reached London, was one half guinea; but his wife had, during his absence, saved ten guineas out of her little salary. You will easily imagine how valuable this hoard became in her estimation, when she could apply it to the precious use of relieving the necessities of her husband. Mons. du F—— went to London the next day, and hired a little garret, there, with a few books, a rush-light, and some straw in which he wrapped his legs to supply the want of fire, he recollected not the splendor to which he had once been accustomed, but the dungeon from which he had escaped. He saw his wife and child once a week; and, in those solitary moments when books failed to soothe his thoughts, he anticipated the hour in which he should again meet the objects most dear to his heart, and passed the intervals of time in philosophic resignation. His clothes being too shabby to admit of his appearing in the day, he issued from his little shed when it was dark, and endeavoured to warm himself by the exercise of walking.

Unfortunately he caught the smallpox; and his disorder rose to such a height, that his life was despaired of. In his delirium he used to recapitulate the sad story of his misfortunes; and when he saw any person near his bed-side, would call out, with the utmost vehemence, "Qu'on fasse sortir tour les François!"[43] After having been for some days in the most imminent danger, Mons. du F—— recovered from this disease.

—*from* LETTER XXII—

Six months after Mons. du F——'s return to England, his family found themselves compelled to silence the public clamours, by allowing him a small annual pension. Upon this, Madame du F—— quitted her place, and came to live with her husband and her child in an obscure lodging. Their little income received some addition by means of teaching the French language in a few private families. . . .

On the 7th of October, 1787, the Baron died, leaving, besides Mons. du F——, two other sons, and a daughter. . . .

I must here mention, that the time when Mons. du F—— was confined to his bed in the prison of St. Yon, from the consequences of his fall, his father, in order to avoid the clamours at Rouen, went for some weeks to Paris. He there [in Paris] made a will, disinheriting his eldest son. By the old laws of France, however, a father could not punish his son more than once for the same offence. . . . [T]he benignant law above-mentioned interposed to prevent farther punishment, and left the Baron without any legal right to deprive Mons. du F—— of his inheritance. His brothers, being sensible of this, wrote to inform him of his father's death, and recall him to France. He refused to go while the *lettre-de-cachet* remained in force against him. The Baron having left all his papers sealed up, which his younger sons could not open but in the presence of their brother, they obtained a revocation of

[43] **Qu'on fasse sortir tour les François!**: "Make all the French go out" (Williams's translation).

the *lettre-de-cachet,* and sent it to Mons. du F——, who immediately set off for France.

The Baron's estate amounted to about four thousand pounds a year. Willing to avoid a tedious litigation with his brothers, Mons. du F—— consented to divide with them this property. . . .

In the following summer Mons. and Madame du F—— arrived in France, at the great epocha of French liberty, on the 15th of July, 1789, the very day after that on which the Bastille was taken. It was then that Mons. du F—— felt himself in security on his native shore.—It was then that his domestic comforts were no longer embittered with the dread of being torn from his family by a separation more terrible than death itself.—It was then that he no more feared that his repose at night would be broken by the entrance of ruffians prepared to drag him to dungeons, the darkness of which was never visited by the blessed beams of day!

He immediately took possession of his *château,* and only waits for the appointment of the new Judges, to solicit the revocation of the *arret* against his marriage, and to secure the inheritance of his estate to Mademoiselle du F——, his only daughter, who is now fifteen years of age, and is that very child who was born in the bosom of adversity, and whose infancy was exposed to all the miseries of want. May she never know the afflictions of her parents, but may she inherit their virtues!

from Volume II

(1792)

To DR. MOORE,[1] in answer to a Poetical Epistle written by him, in Wales, to HELEN MARIA WILLIAMS.

While in long exile far from you I roam,
To soothe my heart with images of home,
For me, my friend, with rich poetic grace,
The landscapes of my native isle you trace;
Her cultur'd meadows, and her lavish shades,
Her winding rivers, and her verdant glades;
Far, as where frowning on the flood below,
The rough Welsh mountain lifts its craggy brow;
Where nature throws aside her softer charms,
And with sublimer views the bosom warms.

Meanwhile, my steps have stray'd where Autumn yields
A purple harvest on the sunny fields;
Where, bending with their luscious weight, recline
The loaded branches of the clust'ring vine;
There, on the Loire's sweet banks, a joyful band
Cull'd the rich produce of the fruitful land;
The youthful peasant, and the village maid,
And feeble age and childhood lent their aid.
The labours of the morning done, they haste
Where the light dinner in the field is plac'd;
Around the soup of herbs a circle make,
And all from one vast dish at once partake:
The vintage-baskets serve, revers'd, for chairs,
And the gay meal is crown'd with tuneless airs;
For each in turn must sing with all his might;
And some their carols pour in nature's spite.

Delightful land! Ah, now with gen'ral voice
Thy village sons and daughters may rejoice.
Thy happy peasant, now no more a slave,
Forbad to taste one good that nature gave,
Views with the anguish of indignant pain
The bounteous harvest spread for him in vain.
Oppression's cruel hand shall dare no more
To seize with iron gripe his scanty store;
And from his famish'd infants wring those spoils,
The hard-earned produce of his useful toils:
For now on Gallia's[2] plain the peasant knows
Those equal rights impartial Heav'n bestows.
He now, by freedom's ray illumin'd, taught
Some self-respect, some energy or thought,
Discerns the blessings that to all belong,
And lives to guard his humble shed from wrong.

Auspicious Liberty! in vain thy foes
Deride thy ardour, and thy force oppose;
In vain refuse to mark thy spreading light,
While, like the mole, they hide their heads in night;
Or hope their eloquence with taper-ray
Can dim the blaze of philosophic day;
Those reasoners who pretend that each abuse,
Sanction'd by precedent, has some blest use.

[1] **Dr. Moore:** probably Dr. John Moore, M.D. (1729–1802), physician and man of letters, author of the philosophical novel *Zeluco* (1786) and *A View of the Causes and Progress of the French Revolution* (1795).

[2] **Gallia:** Latin and literary name for France.

Does then some chemic power[3] to time belong,
Extracting, by some process, right from wrong?
Must feudal governments for ever last?
Those Gothic piles, the work of ages past;
Nor may obtrusive reason boldly scan,
Far less reform the rude mishapen plan;
The winding labyrinths, the hostile towers,
Whence danger threatens, and where horror low'rs;
The jealous draw-bridge, and the moat profound,
The lonely dungeon in the cavern'd ground;
The sullen dome above those central caves,
Where lives one tyrant, and a host of slaves?
Ah, Freedom, on this renovated shore,
That fabric frights the moral world no more!
Shook to its basis, by thy powerful spell,
Its triple walls in massy fragments fell;
While, rising from the hideous wreck, appears
The temple thy firm arm sublimely rears;
Of fair proportions, and of simple grace,
A mansion worthy of the human race.
For me, the witness of those scenes, whose birth
Forms a new era in the storied earth;
Oft while with glowing breast those scenes I view,
They lead, ah friend belov'd, my thoughts to you!
Ah, still each fine emotion they impart,
With your idea mingles in my heart;
(You, whose warm bosom, whose expanded mind,
Have shar'd this glorious triumph of mankind:
You, whom I oft have heard, with gen'rous zeal,
With all that truth can urge, or pity feel,
Refute the pompous argument that tried
The common cause of millions to deride;
With reason's force the plausive sophist hit,
Or dart on folly the quick flash of wit.)
Too swift, my friend, the moments wing'd their flight,
That gave at once instruction and delight;
That ever from your ample stores of thought
To my small stock some new accession brought.
How oft remembrance, while this bosom bleeds,
My pensive fancy to your dwelling leads;
Where, round your cheerful hearth, I weeping trace
The social circle, and my vacant place!—
When to that dwelling friendship's tie endears,
When shall I hasten with the "joy of tears"?
That joy whose keen sensation swells to pain,
And strives to utter what it feels, in vain.

[3] **chemic power**: alchemical or magical power of transmutation, by which one substance or form is changed into another.

from Volume III
(1794)

— LETTER I —

Paris, January 25, 1793

Dear Sir,

The event which has this week taken place in Paris, will no doubt furnish you with ample matter for speculation. Imagination contemplates with an overwhelming emotion that extraordinary vi[c]issitude of fortune which conducted Louis the Sixteenth[1] from the radiant palace of Versailles, to the gloomy tower of the Temple—from the first throne of Europe, to the scaffold and the block—while the feelings of the heart, which run a faster pace than the reasonings of the head, reject for a while all calculation of general good or evil, and melt in mournful sympathy over "greatness fallen from its high estate." But, when we consider the importance which this event may have in its consequences, not only to this country, but to all Europe, we lose sight of the individual sufferer, to meditate upon the destiny of mankind.

While you observe from a distance the great drama which is acting in France, I am a spectator of the representation.—I am placed near enough the scene to discern every look and every gesture of the actors, and every passion excited in the minds of the audience. I shall therefore endeavour to fill up the outline of that picture which France has presented to your contemplation since the memorable epocha of the tenth of August.[2]

That conflict which after the King's acceptance of the new constitution existed in this country between the executive and legislative powers, between the court and the people, has since the tenth of August been succeeded by a conflict far more terrible; a conflict between freedom and anarchy, knowledge and ignorance, virtue and vice.

[1] **Louis XVI**: King of France at the time of the outbreak of the French Revolution; he was forced to comply with the political changes of 1789–1791, but even after signing the new constitution of 1791 he continued to communicate with the leaders of Austria and Prussia in the hope that they would rescue him and restore the monarchy in France. He was imprisoned in the Paris **Temple** (formerly the headquarters of the Templars in Europe) on charges of treason on 10 August 1792, three years after having been forced to leave the royal residence at the palace of **Versailles**.

[2] **the tenth of August**: the date of the king's imprisonment.

While the real patriots of France, in their different conflicts with the ancient despotism, risked their lives, and shed their blood, and by their desperate valour confirmed the liberty of their country, a lot of men, who exposed not their persons to the smallest danger in the enterprise, contrived, without peril or exertion, to seize upon a considerable portion of power; and never surely in the annals of tyranny have we heard of power more shamefully abused. Those demagogues, known by the appellation of the "Commune provisoire de Paris,"[3] have, during the short period of their usurpation, committed more crimes than despotism itself would have achieved in ages. The crimes of tyrants, by exciting our abhorrence, serve to promote the cause of freedom. It was reserved for the Commune of Paris to check the generous glow of sympathy with a great and magnanimous nation, which had nobly emancipated itself from slavery, and to lead all the feelings of humanity to take part with its oppressors. Surrounding nations, who might perhaps have been animated by the example of a country which has long served as a model to the rest of Europe, have heard of the second of September,[4] and have shrunk back into the torpor of slavery. They have beheld, in the room of the pure and sublime worship of liberty, the grim idol of anarchy set up, and have seen her altar smeared with sanguinary rites. They have beheld the inhuman judges of that night wearing the municipal scarf which their polluting touch profaned, surrounded by men armed with pikes and sabres dropping with blood—while a number of blazing torches threw their glaring light on the ferocious visages of those execrable judges, who, mixing their voices with the shrieks of the dying, passed sentence with a savage mockery of justice, on victims devoted to their rage. They have beheld the infernal executioners of that night, with their arms bared for the purposes of murder, dragging forth those victims to modes of death at which nature shudders.—— Ah! ye slaughtered heroes of the immortal 14th of July, was it for this ye overthrew the towers of the Bastil[l]e, and burst open its gloomy dungeons?—was it for this, ye generous patriots, that with heroic contempt of life ye shed your blood to give liberty and happiness to your enslaved country?—Ah! had ye foreseen that the fanatics of liberty, fierce as the fanatics of superstition, would have their day of St. Bartholomew,[5] would not your victorious arms have been unnerved? Would not the sacred glow of freedom have been frozen in your veins? Ah! what is become of the delightful visions which elevated the enthusiastic heart?—What is become of the transport which beat high in every bosom, when an assembled million of the human race vowed on the altar of their country, in the name of the represented nation, inviolable fraternity and union—an eternal federation! This was indeed the golden age of the revolution.—But it is past!—the enchanting spell is broken, and the fair scenes of beauty and of order, through which imagination wandered, are transformed into the desolation of the wilderness, and clouded by the darkness of the tempest. If the genius of Liberty—profaned Liberty! does not arise in his might, and crush those violators of freedom, whose crimes have almost broken the heart of humanity, the inhabitants of Paris may indeed "wish for the wings of the dove, that they may fly away and be at rest—for there is violence and strife in the city."[6]

At the head of this band of conspirators is Robespierre[7]—gloomy and saturnine in his disposition, with a countenance of such dark aspect as seems the index of no ordinary guilt—fanatical and exaggerated in his avowed principles of liberty, possessing that species of eloquence which gives him power over the passions, and that cool determined temper which regulates the most ferocious designs with the most calm and temperate prudence. His crimes do not appear to be the result of passion, but of some deep and extraordinary malignity, and he seems formed to subvert and to destroy. . . .

[3] **Commune provisoire de Paris:** revolutionary government of Paris formed in 1792 and responsible for the storming of the Tuilleries and the arrest of the king as well as the September massacres of 1792, in which 2,000 prisoners, including royalist sympathizers, were murdered.

[4] **the second of September:** beginning of the 1792 September massacres, which went on for five days.

[5] **their day of St. Bartholomew:** massacre of French Protestants, known as Huguenots, which began as a political conspiracy on the life of the Huguenot leader, Admiral Coligny, in Paris on 24 August 1572, but quickly spread through the whole country, resulting in 70,000 deaths in all.

[6] **wish for the wings of the dove . . . for there is violence and strife in the city:** from Psalm 55: 6–9.

[7] **Robespierre:** Maximilien Robespierre (1758–1794), known as the Incorruptible, was the leading figure of the radical or Jacobin wing of the National Convention of 1792 to 1793; he pressed for the execution of Louis XVI and was the most prominent leader of the Reign of Terror instituted by the Committee of Public Safety in 1793. He was overthrown and executed in turn in July 1794.

from Volume IV

(1796)

— LETTER I —

Paris, Feb. 10, 1793

The faction of the anarchists desired that the French king should be put to death without the tedious forms of a trial. This opinion, however, was confined to the summit of the Mountain,[1] that elevated region, where, aloof from all the ordinary feelings of our nature, no one is diverted from his purpose by the weakness of humanity, or the compunction of remorse; where urbanity is considered as an aristocratical infringement of les grands principes, and mercy as a crime de leze-nation.[2]

The trial of the king was decreed by the National Convention, and the eleventh of December was fixed upon for that purpose. Lewis the sixteenth had supported his long imprisonment with fortitude; and, when he heard that the day for his trial was fixed, he said with great calmness, "Eh bien! qu'on me guillotine si on veut; je suis preparé."[3]

A short time after the taking of the Basti[l]e the king was observed reading the history of Charles the first. "Why, sire," said an attendant, "do you read that history? it will make you melancholy." "Je me mets dans l'esprit," replied the king, "qu'on jour je finirai comme lui."[4] It appears that the French queen has also chosen a model for her behaviour, in the last scene of life, from the English annals; for since her imprisonment she has been employed in reading the history of Mary queen of Scots.[5] Marie Antoinette, however, is in no danger of sharing the same fate: if she were, her haughty indignant spirit, which preferred the chance of losing empire and life to the certainty of retaining any thing less than absolute dominion, would probably meet death with becoming dignity, feeling, that "to be weak is to be miserable, doing or suffering."[6] . . .

. . . History will, indeed, condemn Lewis the sixteenth. The evidence of his guilt is clear; and the historian will fulfil his duty in passing sentence upon his memory; for the historian has not, like the judge, the prerogative to pardon. But Lewis the sixteenth will not stand alone at the bar of posterity. His judges also must appear at that tribunal; on them, also, the historian will pass sentence. He will behold the same men acting at once as accusers, party, and judge; he will behold the unfortunate monarch deprived, not only of his inviolability as a king, but of his rights as a citizen; and perhaps the irrevocable decree of posterity may reverse that of the National Convention.

The detail of the interrogation which the French king underwent at the bar of the National Convention is too well known to need repetition. — He was conducted back to the Temple about six in the evening. . . . A considerable number of horse as well as foot-guards formed the escort of the king; and the trampling of the horses' feet — the hoarse sounds of the collected multitude — the beating of drums — the frequent report of fire-arms — all conspired to excite the most solemn emotions. The long page of human history rushed upon the mind — age after age arose to memory, in sad succession, like the line of Banquo;[7] and each seemed disfigured by crimes or darkened by calamity. The past was clouded with horror — a great experiment was about to be made for the future; but it was impossible to reflect, without trembling anxiety, that the stake was human happiness, and that the issue was doubtful, while all that could be calculated with

[1] **the Mountain**: name given to the radical Jacobin deputies — who sat in the elevated benches on the left side of the hall — of the National Convention; they were opposed by the more moderate Girondists, whom they defeated in June 1793.

[2] **les grands principes . . . leze-nation**: "The great principles — High treason" (Williams's translation).

[3] **Eh bien . . . je suis preparé**: "Well! let them *guillotine* me if they will; I am prepared" (Williams's translation). Lewis is, of course, Louis the XVI.

[4] **Je me mets dans l'esprit . . . je finirai comme lui**: "I feel an impression on my mind, that one day I shall end like him" (Williams's translation).

[5] **the French queen**: Marie Antoinette (1755–1793), wife of Louis XVI and daughter of the Austrian Archduchess Maria Theresa. Unpopular because of her support of Austria and her reputation for extravagance, she worked actively in secret against the Revolution, and was executed for treason on 16 October 1793. **Mary queen of Scots**: Mary Stuart (1542–1587), child of James V of Scotland and contender (against Elizabeth I) to the throne of England; because of her Roman Catholicism and her plotting to overthrow Elizabeth with the help of a Catholic uprising and a Spanish invasion of England, she was executed on 8 February 1587.

[6] **"to be weak . . . suffering"**: *Paradise Lost*, I.157–158.

[7] **the line of Banquo**: from Shakespeare's *Macbeth* (esp. IV.i. 112–124), in which the witches show Macbeth an apparition of eight kings, Banquo's descendants.

certainty was, that millions must perish in the trial. It is asserted that the philosophers of France produced the revolution; I believe this to be an error. They, indeed, have disseminated the principles which form the basis of the new fabric of French government; but the ancient system was overthrown, not because it was unphilosophical, but because it could be upheld no longer. The revolution was the effect of imperious necessity; for, whatever permanent good may result from a change of government, the temporary evil is so certain, that every age is disposed to leave that work to a succeeding generation. The instinct of the people teaches them, that in framing a new government they can only hope, like Moses,[8] to see the promised land, but not to enter it. They may plant the seeds of general prosperity, sown with toil and trouble, and bathed in blood; but the blooming vegetation and the golden fruit belong to another race of men. . . .

—*from* LETTER V—

The destruction of the monarchy in France on the 10th of August—the horrors of the massacre of the 2d of September, and then the death of the king, finally alienated the minds of Englishmen from the French revolution; rendered popular a war,[9] which otherwise no minister would have dared to undertake; disgusted all wise, and shocked all humane men; and left to us, and all who had espoused the cause, no hope but that Heaven, which knows how to bring good out of evil, would watch over an event so interesting to the welfare of mankind as the French revolution; nor suffer the folly and vice of the agents concerned in it, to spoil the greatest and noblest enterprise ever undertaken by a nation. . . .

. . . [T]ruth changes not with the fashions of the times. It was not to be forgotten, that the English had been the first *bold experimenters* in the science of government in modern Europe—the first who carried into practical execution the calumniated principle of EQUALITY—the first people who formally brought a monarch to the scaffold—the first asserters of the neglected *rights of man*. In the common law of England, and in the commentaries of the older lawyers on it, I have found all the fundamental principles of the French declaration des droits de l'homme.[10]

But, said some, we made our revolution without bloodshed, and theirs has been a continued scene of confusion and murder. It is true, the revolution of 1688[11] was accomplished with little trouble; but it produced the wars of 1715 and 1745, in the last of which the metropolis very nearly fell into the hands of the enemy; a circumstance that would have placed a popish despot on the throne, and annihilated the liberties of England. And it is to be observed, that the revolution of 1688 was but one of many events that formed the English constitution. That system was the fruit of the labours of ages of struggle and confusion. The establishment of our liberties cost us many wars—and amidst the civil dissensions caused by the contest of principles against ancient error, our history records a sad catalogue of crimes and cruelties committed on all sides. Whoever, Madam, will examine these annals, will soon be convinced, that we have not much ground to reproach our neighbours. In France, indeed, a greater number of events have been crowded into a shorter space of time; and the enormities in France have been committed at a period, when, by means of the facility of communication, all public events are more widely and rapidly circulated than in former ages; circumstances that alter the appearance, but not the reality, of the case. We now enjoy the blessings of freedom, and have forgotten the price it cost our ancestors to obtain it. But no people ever travelled to the temple of Liberty by a path strewed with roses; nor has established tyranny ever yielded to reason and justice, till after a severe struggle. I do not pretend to justify the French, but I do not see much right that we at least have to condemn them. . . .

Whether France will finally be able to extricate herself from an intestine, as well as external war, which now assail her at once—whether she will be able to support

[8] **Moses:** at the end of his life, Moses, lawgiver to the Hebrews and their leader in the exodus from Egypt, was given a view of the Promised Land from Mount Pisgah, but was not allowed to enter it.

[9] **the death of the king:** Louis XVI was executed on 21 January 1793. **a war:** the French Revolutionary Wars, initially between France and an alliance of Austria and Prussia, were joined by Britain, Holland, and Spain (all on the Austrian side) after the king's execution.

[10] **des droits de l'homme:** of the rights of man.

[11] **the revolution of 1688:** the Glorious or Bloodless Revolution, by which the Catholic king James II was deposed from the throne of England and the Dutch Protestant rulers William and Mary were invited by Parliament to replace him as joint sovereigns, ensuring both a Protestant line of succession and the effective ascendancy of Parliament over the monarchy. **The wars of 1715 and 1745:** uprisings against the British government on the part of the Jacobites, largely Scottish supporters of the exiled Stuart family (the descendants of the deposed James II, the "**popish despot**"); the Jacobite cause was effectively crushed at the battle of Culloden in 1746.

her republic; or, fatigued with anarchy, repose herself in limited monarchy; or finally, overwhelmed by her foes, be forced to accept that constitution which they choose to give her, are points that surpass my powers to decide. Were I to conjecture, I would say, that she will succeed in maintaining her own freedom, but not in communicating it to her neighbours. But should she even be overpowered by her enemies, and should continental despots wish to load her with the most galling chains, I cannot forget, Madam, that Britain is concerned in this transaction! And this recollection cheers my mind; for a free and generous people cannot condemn twenty-five millions of men to be slaves! No: the severest sentence that England can suffer to be pronounced, even on her rival, would be, "Let France be delivered from the dominion of a ferocious mob—let her be delivered from anarchy, and restored to reason and lawful sway!" Thus, terminate how it will, I trust the French revolution will promote the good of France, and this prospect consoles me amidst the present evils. . . .

When I said that the French revolution began in wisdom, I admitted that it came afterwards into the hands of fools. But *the foundation was laid in wisdom.* I must entreat you to mark that circumstance; for if even the superstructure should fall, the foundation would remain. The BASTILLE, though honoured by Mr. Burke[12] with the title of the king's castle (a shocking satire on every humane and just prince), will never be rebuilt in France; and the declaration of the rights of man will remain eternal, as the truths it contains. In the early ages of the world, the revolutions of states, and the incursions of barbarians, often overwhelmed knowledge, and occasioned *the loss of principles:* but since the invention of printing has diffused science over Europe, and accumulated the means of extending and preserving truth, PRINCIPLES can no more be lost. Like vigorous seeds committed to the bosom of the fertile earth, accidental circumstances may prevent their vegetation for a time, but they will remain alive, and ready to spring up at the first favourable moment.

What then is the conclusion of the whole matter? This, surely, that PRINCIPLES are never to be abandoned, however unsuccessful may be the attempt to carry them into *practice.* We in England, however, have had practical experience of the good effects of right principles: our maxims of liberty have proved their intrinsic worth, by counteracting even the natural defects of our country. They have made, as Addison happily expresses, "our bleak rocks and barren mountains smile;" and on the careful preservation of these maxims depends the continuance of the blessings they have procured us. But I must conclude:

"O Liberty! expand thy vital ray,
O'er the dark globe diffuse celestial day;
Glad distant regions by thy blissful voice,
Till India's wilds and Afric's sands rejoice:
Thy spirit breathe, wide as creation's space;
Exalt, illume, inspire the human race;
As heaven's own ether thro' expansion whirl'd,
Attracts, sublimes, and animates the world."[13]

Thus wishes a worthy member of the British Senate, and such are your wishes and mine.

ADIEU.

from Volume VIII
(1796)

—*from* LETTER I—

. . . I cannot conclude this sketch of revolutionary government without observing, that we should beware of the injustice of accusing the French people of those crimes of which they are the mourners, and of which they only have been the victims. They, who have seen their fields ravaged, their vineyards stained with blood, their cities reduced to ashes; they, who have lost their fathers, their husbands, their children, their friends; they, who, far from throwing a veil over the atrocities they abhor, have proclaimed, have published them to the world—to charge that people with the enormities under which they have groaned, would be indeed to arraign the oppressed for the guilt of the oppressor. With equal candour might the English be stigmatized as a barbarous nation, because a Clive[1] has famished Asiatic provinces, or because, on the coast of Africa, the slave-merchant traffics in blood; while

[12] **Mr. Burke:** Edmund Burke (1729–1797), British political writer and statesman, author of the conservative *Reflections on the Revolution of France** (1790), a classic anti-Revolutionary text.

[13] **O Liberty! expand thy vital ray . . . Attracts, sublimes, and animates the world:** probably quoted from John Courtenay (1741–1816), British politician and author, an abolitionist and ardent supporter of the French Revolution.

[1] **Clive:** Robert, Baron Clive of Plassey (1725–1774), British soldier and first British governor of the Indian state of Bengal; who helped to strengthen British control over India.

all in the British parliament who are distinguished for genius or worth, all whose names are pronounced with honour and respect, have passed the sentence of condemnation on that detestable commerce, and, laying aside their political divisions on other points, here form *but one party, the party of humanity.* But why is humanity forced to proceed with tardy and incumbered steps? why is she thus impeded in her progress? Ah, let us, till the slave-trade no longer stains the British name, be more gentle in our censure of other nations! I know not how that partial morality can be justified, which measures right and wrong by geographical divisions; and, while it pours forth the bitterness of declamation against human crimes in France, sanctions them in Africa. I have related to you, with the detestation I have felt, the evils of that tyranny which assumed the name of revolutionary government; but the faithful historian of a slave-ship would perhaps admit, that there are horrors beyond the drowning scenes of Carrier,[2] or the guillotines of Robespierre. The wretched African, torn for ever from all he loved, and condemned to miseries which can only terminate in death, would perhaps, while chained beneath those decks where the air he breathes is contagion, and where he struggles with convulsive agony, smile at the approach of the axe which would relieve intolerable torments, or the opening planks which would bury him with his oppressors beneath the billows of the ocean. With all the feelings of an Englishwoman at my heart, a heart that glows for the real honour of my country, I pour the fervent wish that she may speedily wipe away this foul reproach; and that, while her sources of commercial wealth flow in lavish abundance from every quarter of the globe, she may reject with indignant scorn that execrable traffic of which humanity is the barter.

Upon the whole, the cause of liberty is not the less sacred, nor her charms less divine, because sanguinary monsters and sordid savages have defiled her temple, and insulted her votaries. Like Midas,[3] their uncouth ears have been deaf to her sweet sounds; and we ought not to wonder, that by such judges the coarse dialect of jacobinical jargon, like the unharmonious gratings of Marsyas's reeds, was preferred to the heavenly breathings of Apollo's lute.

But those barbarous triumphs are past, and anarchy and vandalism can return no more. The new constitution, like the spear of Romulus[4] thrown with a strong hand, will fix itself in the earth, so that no human force can root it up, and will become, like the budding wood, the object of a people's veneration.

[2] **Carrier:** Jean Baptiste Carrier (1756–1794), Jacobin leader responsible for *noyades,* or mass drownings, in the port city of Nantes; he was tried and executed himself in November 1794.

[3] **Midas:** king in Greek mythology who was given ass's ears by Apollo for preferring the flute music by Marsyas (a satyr) to the music of Apollo's lute.

[4] **Romulus:** legendary founder of Rome, the brother, and later murderer, of Remus, with whom he was raised by a she-wolf after their abandonment. A javelin thrown by Romulus from the summit of the Aventine hill in Rome stuck so firmly in the earth that no one could pull it out; it grew roots and flowered into a dogberry tree, later venerated as sacred.

from A NARRATIVE OF THE EVENTS WHICH HAVE TAKEN PLACE IN FRANCE, WITH AN ACCOUNT OF THE PRESENT STATE OF SOCIETY AND PUBLIC OPINION

(1816)

. . . Are the French people, after *all* the mazy wanderings of the Revolution, are they approaching an asylum . . . ; are they going home at last? This is indeed a momentous question. It is not made by me, as perhaps it may be by yourself, in the spirit of speculative investigation; to me it comprehends all that can awaken solicitude, all that can interest the heart; all chance of personal tranquillity towards the evening of a stormy life, and all hope of felicity for the objects most dear to me, and to whom life is opening. France is to me also the country of my friends — of persons endeared to me by the tie of common suffering. We have passed through the tempest, to use the words of M. de Boufflers, "sous la même parapluie."[1] How should I have lived so many years among the French without loving that amiable people, to apply the term in their own sense, who so well know the art of shedding a peculiar charm over social life! How much better than others they understand the secret of being happy! happy at a cheap rate, and without being too difficult, and too disdainful as we are in England, about the conditions; while they bear

[1] **sous la même parapluie:** under the same umbrella.

misfortunes with a cheerful equanimity, which if it does not deserve the proud name of philosophy, is of far more general use; the former being common property, belonging to all, and not, like the latter, the partial fortune of an enlightened few. . . .

from POEMS ON VARIOUS SUBJECTS (1823)

"To James Forbes, Esq.,[1] on his bringing me Flowers from Vaucluse, and which he had preserved by means of an ingenious process in their original beauty"

Sweet spoils of consecrated bowers,
How dear to me these chosen flowers!
I love the simplest bud that blows,
I love the meanest weed that grows:
Symbols of nature—every form
That speaks of her this heart can warm;
But ye, delicious flowers, assume
In fancy's eye a brighter bloom;
A dearer pleasure ye diffuse,
Cull'd by the fountains of Vaucluse!
For ye were nurtur'd on the sod
Where PETRARCH mourn'd, and LAURA trod;[2]
Ye grew on that inspiring ground
Where love has shed enchantment round;
Where still the tear of passion flows,
Fond tribute to a poet's woes!
Yet, cherish'd flowers, with love and fame
This wreath entwines a milder name;
Friendship, who better knows than they
The spells that smooth our length'ning way,—
Friendship the blooming off'ring bright;
When FORBES the classic fountain[3] sought,
For me he cull'd the fresh-blown flowers,
And fix'd their hues[4] with potent powers;
Their pliant forms with skillful care
He seized, and stamp'd duration there;
His gift shall ever glad the eye,—
Nor, like my verse is born to die.

[1] **James Forbes, Esq.**: possibly James Forbes (1749–1819), artist and author. A civil servant in India from 1765 to 1784, he later produced a series of volumes on Indian flora, fauna, antiquities, and culture. He travelled with his family to France in 1802, where he was detained by the government; he was released and allowed to return to England in 1804, partly on the strength of a letter from Sir Joseph Banks, botanist and President of the Royal Society. **Vaucluse**: mountainous district in southeastern France, famous for its fountain or spring, and for its association with Petrarch (see note 2), who was said to have lived there.

[2] **Petrarch**: Francesco Petrarca (1304–1374), Italian poet and humanist, who established many of the conventions of the sonnet and of European lyric poetry in general. The subject of much of his poetry was **Laura**, a real woman whom his work idealized as unattainably beautiful and disdainful.

[3] **fountain**: the fountain at Vaucluse was often compared to the Helicon, a spring symbolizing poetic inspiration in Greek mythology.

[4] **hues**: colors, but perhaps used also in the more general poetic sense of qualities.

JOHN THELWALL

(1764–1834)

The reputation of John Thelwall has benefitted from the revival of political interest in English literature of the late eighteenth and early nineteenth centuries. Virtually unread until resurrected by groundbreaking scholarship on his political role in the 1790s, John Thelwall has been assessed a lesser Samuel Taylor Coleridge in poetic accomplishment, as Coleridge is a lesser Thelwall in political activism and reputation. Coleridge claimed that "Thelwall [was] the voice of tens of thousands." William Wordsworth and Coleridge both found elements in Thelwall's verse worthy of imitation, but they especially admired his courage.

Thelwall was a Jacobin, or political radical, sympathetic to the ideals, principles, and objectives of the Revolution in France, and an outspoken member of the London Corresponding Society (LCS). (See THE FRENCH REVOLUTION AND RIGHTS OF MAN.) In 1794, he was charged with high treason and imprisoned for publicly criticizing the government for waging war against France and for disregarding the economic distress the war was causing the working and lower classes. He was acquitted seven months later. To the chagrin of authorities, the notoriety of Thelwall's persecution made him the most important radical voice in London. However, he and his family paid the price. Petty politicians, local representatives of the Home Office, and common citizens incited by authorities, harassed, antagonized, and assaulted Thelwall with impunity. Association with Thelwall became dangerous, as it proved when he visited the Wordsworths and Coleridge in their West Country retreat in 1797. A spy came to investigate the matter, and the Wordsworths lost their lease on Alfoxden House. When the weary radical retreated from public persecution to a humble farm in Llys-Wen, Wales, he found barbarous neighbors intent on driving him away with public and personal harassment. Around 1800, Thelwall resumed a public career, but as a teacher of elocution rather than as a political spokesman. In 1809 he addressed himself to cures for stammering, eventually publishing his results in "Treatment of Cases of Defective Utterance" (1814). He later became involved in parliamentary reform, but returned to elocution after failing in a new venture into political journalism.

from POEMS CHIEFLY WRITTEN IN RETIREMENT
(1801)

from Prefatory Memoir[1]

On the conclusion of the transaction with The Courier,[2] Thelwall tho unchanged in his opinions, renounced all connection with public affairs: from a conviction (however reluctantly admitted) of the state both of his own health and of the public mind. He perceived, with anguish, that, from the fury with which he was pursued, every effort he made, instead of producing the Reason he loved, only irritated to the Violence he abhorred. To that violence, indeed, every thing apparently tended. "You will drive the Reasoners from the field," he had said, repeatedly, in his Lectures, "and the assassins will rush into their places." "In the ferment of half-smothered indignation, feelings of a more gloomy complexion will be generated; and characters of a very different stamp will be called into action. Men who have neither genius nor benevolence, will succeed to those who had both; and, with no other stimulus than fury, and no other talent than hypocrisy and intrigue, will embark in projects which every friend to humanity must abhor; and which, while the free, open and manly character of the species was yet uncrushed, never could have entered the imagination."—(*See, among innumerable other passages,* THE TRIBUNE, *Vol. 1, p. 25; and Vol. 3, p. 140.*)[3]

The realization of this prophecy seemed at hand. The prospect, on all sides became abhorrent to his nature; and he determined thenceforward to lock up his sentiments in the silence of his own bosom; to concentrate his feelings in the private duties of life; and turn his attention towards making, if not a comfortable, at least, a quiet establishment, for his encreasing family.

The assistance of a few friends enabled him to stock a little farm, of about five-and-thirty acres, in the obscure and romantic village of *Llys-Wen,* in Brecknockshire; a scene once famous in Cambrian story, as one of the residences of Roderick the Great; from whose *White Palace* it derives its name.[4]

In the election of this spot, so far as it might be considered elective (for he had already devoted four months to a pedestrian excursion, in unavailing search for an elegible retreat:) Thelwall was principally influenced by the wild and picturesque scenery of the neighbourhood. For the village (embowered with orchards, and over-shadowed by grotesque mountains) is sweetly situated upon the banks of the Wye,[5] at one of the most beautiful, tho least visited, parts of that unrivalled river; and the cottage itself, thro the branches of the surrounding fruit trees, catches a *glympse*—while its alcove (elevated on the remains of an old sepulchral tumulus)[6] commands the *full view,* of one of the characteristic and more-than-crescent curves of that ever-varying stream; with its glassy pool sleeping beneath the reflected bank, its rapids above, and roaring cataracts below, bordered with plantations and pendant woods, and diversified with rocks and pastures.

Such a retreat could not but appear, to an enthusiastic imagination, as a sort of enchanted dormitory, where the agitations of political feeling might be cradled to forgetfulness, and the delicious day dreams of poesy might be renewed: and as his wife's brother (who on account of his relationship, had been hunted, by a certain Lord of the Bed-chamber, from his farms in Rutland) accompanied him in this new establishment, Thelwall flattered himself that agriculture, under the superintendance of the one, and the visitations of the Muse to the other, might secure that humble sort of subsistence to which he had determined to accommodate his desires. In the choice of this

[1] From: "Prefatory Memoir of the Life of the Author" in *Poems Chiefly Written in Retirement* (1801). Though autobiographical, it is written in the third person throughout. Thelwall stresses at the outset that "it is The Man, and not The Politician, that is here delineated. The disciple of the Muses; not The Lecturer and Leader of Popular Societies now no more" (i).

[2] *The Courier* was a London evening newspaper of high repute. Thelwall spent two weeks as its editor before public outrage required its owners to retract the agreement. This event, Thelwall says, brought his seven-year political career to an end (xxx).

[3] Thelwall published *The Tribune,* a short-lived periodical whose chief purpose was to print Thelwall's public pronouncements "as a security . . . against the audaciousness of open Perjury, and the arts of Misrepresentation" employed by the government (xxix).

[4] **Brecknockshire:** a district in southeastern Wales. **Cambrian story:** Welsh history. **Roderick the Great:** king of Wales (844–877) who fought the Danish and Saxon invaders, and is credited with unifying the greater part of Wales before he was forced into exile in Ireland by the Vikings in 877.

[5] **the Wye:** river in eastern Wales; the setting for Wordsworth's "Tintern Abbey."

[6] **tumulus:** a grave mound or barrow.

situation he was, also, further influenced by its remoteness from all political connection. For, determined himself to observe the most inviolable silence respecting his opinions, he took it for granted, that there, where they had never yet been heard of, he should be equally out of the way of all solicitations to revive the discussion, and all the animosities they had excited against him. But altho to his resolution he steadfastly adhered, in his hopes of consequent tranquility he was most woefully disappointed. Politics, hitherto unknown in that neighbourhood, were now injected, in their most acrimonious form, into the ears of the ignorant inhabitants, in order to stimulate a vulgar hostility, more harassing and more irritating than all the open oppressions of power: and the officiating clergyman of the parish seems to have thought it the duty of his function, to aggravate these hostilities, by the most pointed and inflammatory allusions from the pulpit. Thelwall's habits of living, also, so widely different from all around him—his fits of abstraction, his solitary rambles, among the woods and dingles, and, above all, the supernatural circumstances of his neither drinking CWRW, [i.e. Ale] smoaking, nor chewing tobacco, had no small tendency to encrease the animosity which the Welsh are apt enough to entertain (without other reason) against every SAXON who intrudes, as a settler, among them. . . .

To the Infant Hampden—

Written during a sleepless night. Derby. Oct. 1797

Sweet Babe! that, on thy mother's guardian breast,
Slumberest, unheedful of the autumnal blast
That rocks our lowly dwelling, nor dost dream
Of woes, or cares, or persecuting rage,
Or rending passions, or the pangs that wait
On ill-requited services, sleep on;
Sleep, and be happy!—'Tis the sole relief
This anxious mind can hope, from the dire pangs
Of deep corroding wrong, that thou, my babe!
And the sweet twain—the firstlings of my love!
As yet are blest; and that my heart's best pride,
Who, with maternal fondness, pillows thee
Beside thy Life's warm fountain, is not quite
Hopeless, or joyless; but, with matron cares,
And calm domestic Virtues, can avert
The melancholy fiend, and in your smiles
Read nameless consolations Ah! sleep on—
As yet unconscious of The Patriot's[1] name,
Or of a patriot's sorrows—of the cares
For which thy name-sire bled; and, more unblest,
Thy natural father, in his native land,
Wanders an exile; and, of all that land,
Can find no spot his home. Ill-omen'd babe!
Conceiv'd in tempests, and in tempests born!
What destiny awaits thee?—Reekless thou.[2]
Oh! blest inapprehension!—Let it last.
Sleep on, my Babe! now while the rocking wind
Pipes, mournful, length[e]ning my nocturnal plaint
With troubled symphony!—Ah! sleep, secure:
And may thy dream of Life be ne'er disturb'd
With visions such as mar thy father's peace—
Visions (Ah! that they were but such indeed!)
That shew this world a wilderness of wrongs—
A waste of troubled waters: whelming floods
Of tyrannous injustice, canopy'd
With clouds dark louring; whence the pelting storms
Of cold unkindness the rough torrents swell,
On every side resistless. There my Ark—
The scanty remnant of my delug'd joys!
Floats anchorless; while thro' the dreary round,
Fluttering on anxious pinion, the tired foot
Of persecuted Virtue cannot find
One spray on which to rest; or scarce one leaf
To cheer with promise of subsiding woe.

Maria

—A FRAGMENT—
(1801; comp. 1797)

The following thought originated in one of those infantile endearments, to which the parental heart cannot—perhaps, ought not to be insensible. It occurred, and was hastily committed to paper, during the bustle and preparation for the author's removal, with his family, from Derby to Llys-Wen. It is, perhaps, somewhat more

[1] **The Patriot's name:** John Hampden (1594–1643), opposition member of the English Parliament who opposed various taxes levied by Charles I, for which he was impeached in 1642, but escaped arrest. At the start of the Civil War, Hampden raised a regiment of foot soldiers for the Parliamentary Army, and was mortally wounded in action.

[2] **Reekless thou:** without the taint of blood or bloodshed.

tinctured with political sentiment, than is entirely consistent with the general tenour and object of this Publication: but an interest of another sort forbad its suppression. It forms a natural prologue to the Tragedy that follows;[1] and, on that account, the sensibility of the reader, whatever his opinions may happen to be, will readily excuse the insertion.

Dear is the Babe—thrice dear, to my fond heart!
For she was my first born; and she has sooth'd,
With many an infant smile, the anxious hours
Of hard captivity,[2] what time, impell'd
By tyrannous suspicion, and the thirst
Of uncontroul'd dominion, impious men
Immur'd thy patriot sons, Oh, hapless Isle!
Once deem'd the land of Freedom, now the den
Of infamous Corruption. Then how oft
Yearn'd my fond heart, and for the social bliss,
Permitted at short intervals, and rare—
Rare, and imperfect; by the watchful eyes,
And ears, and prying insolence of guards
Check'd and imbitter'd, have I heav'd the sigh
And felt the anxious wish, that yet the tongue
Disdained to utter, or the throbbing breast
To own, uncheck'd:—alive to every pang
That Nature dictates; but, not less, alive
To the strong sense of duty; to the voice
Of patriots and of martyrs, oft array'd,
At dawn or even-tide, around my couch,
With presence all inspiring, and with tongues
Awfully eloquent, that bad me think
"'Twas for Mankind I suffer'd—for the cause
For which a Hampden fought, a Sidney bled;
For which the Gracchi[3] perish'd, and for which
Each high exploit that, with unweary'd breath,
Fame, even from eldest time, still trumpets forth
Was erst achiev'd."—Ah! visions, that could rouse
Enthusiastic ardours! ye were oft
My props, my consolations: ye could turn
My bonds to trophies, my keen wrongs to boons,
My solitude to high communion;
Could make me laugh to scorn the threats of Power—
His mock tribunals, solemn pageantries,
And axe, already whetted in the pause
Of bloody expectation. Ah! how oft,
Warm'd by such thoughts, has the gaunt scaffold seem'd
A car of glorious triumph, banner'd round
With wreaths and well-earn'd trophies. Death no more
Was hideous; and the Tyrant lost his power.
But there were times when fonder thoughts prevail'd,
Soft'ning, but not abasing, the stern brow
Of Patriot-Emulation:—chiefly then
When, with a tardy pace, the wish'd for hour
Approach'd, that to a husband's, father's sight
Promis'd the social banquet. Then—ah! then,
When thro' my grated dungeon I have gaz'd,
With straining eye unmov'd, upon the gate
Thro' which the partner of my soul should pass—
And this, my only babe:—my only, then,
And still my best beloved!—ah! how high
(With what a tide of fervour thro' my breast)
Swell'd the fond passion—for Thee, babe belov'd!—
(Even in the earliest dawn of infancy,
So sweet thy promise!) and, for Her,[4] more dear
To my connubial heart, that she had giv'n
Birth to thy infant sweetness.———

[1] Thelwall refers to the sudden death of his six-year-old daughter, aggravated by the "sarcastic exultations" of his "brutal landlord" during the child's wake, and the subsequent lasting depression suffered by Thelwall and his wife (xliii).

[2] **captivity**: Thelwall was imprisoned for seven months, five of which he spent in solitary confinement, in 1794 on a charge of high treason.

[3] **Hampden**: See note 1 to "To the Infant Hampden." **Sidney**: Algernon Sidney (1622–1683), English republican leader and martyr, and cousin of Sir Philip Sidney. He fought on the Parliamentary side in the Civil War, but later opposed Cromwell's usurpation of power. In 1683 he was arrested in connection with a Whig insurrection plot, convicted of treason, and executed. **Gracchi**: Tiberius Gracchus (163–133 BC) and his brother Gaius Sempronius Gracchus (153–121 BC), Roman statesmen during the Republic who sponsored agrarian laws favoring peasant farmers and sought to limit government corruption and the power of the Senate.

[4] **Her**: Thelwall's wife, Susan Vellum Thelwall, who was his "good angel," Crabb Robinson reported, during his worst years of persecution. They married in 1791 and had four children. Mrs. Thelwall died in 1816.

MARIA EDGEWORTH

(1767–1849)

Christened "the great Maria" by Sir Walter Scott,* Maria Edgeworth was, with Frances Burney, the leading female novelist of her day (Jane Austen's success did not come until after her death), earning £11,000 from her writing. In partnership with her father, Richard Lovell Edgeworth, Maria Edgeworth was an influential exponent of educational reform, arguing effectively and in many publications for the pragmatic and rational as well as moral education of both girls and boys. She devoted much of her writing to children's literature, believing that the best way to capture the attention and to educate the young was through compelling yet pedagogically sound stories. Her six novels focussed on social injustice, on the abuses of the aristocracy, especially of Irish absentee landlords, on the evils of the class system, and on the inequities of the prevailing gender system. On the question of the rights of woman, she took the view that women should be rationally educated just as men were, but should continue to define their social roles as primarily domestic, as the educators and moral guardians of the young. Her politics were progressive rather than revolutionary; she believed in the gradual evolution of a just state under the guidance, tutelage, and control of a benevolent, rational, well-educated middle class.

Born in Oxfordshire on 1 January 1767, the eldest daughter of Richard Lovell Edgeworth and the first of his four wives (who would altogether bear him 21 children), Maria Edgeworth moved to Ireland in 1773, returned to England for her schooling (she excelled in French, Italian, and music), and finally took up her lifelong career as writer and educator in collaboration with her father in 1782. They published *Practical Education* in 1798; the enormously popular *Early Lessons* in 1801; and *Essays on Professional Education* in 1809. She also helped to mother the growing Edgeworth family and to manage the family estate in Ireland, Edgeworthtown, where she gained a firsthand knowledge of the condition of Irish peasant tenant farmers, a class existing in almost feudal servitude when she arrived. In her spare time, she wrote her fictional accounts of Irish life, *Castle Rackrent* (1800)—a humorous exposé of the Irish servant's mentality as well as of the depravities of the Irish aristocracy, whose drunkenness, gambling, duelling, and litigiousness she depicts in realistic detail. In *The Absentee* (1812) and *Ormond* (1817) she passionately denounced the poor moral and economic management of absentee Irish landlords living in Britain (a common practice in her day), contrasting them to her resident Anglo-Irish landlords who, following the principles of the conservative Edmund Burke,* attempted to secure the welfare of all the workers on their estates through a benevolent paternalism. In "The Grateful Negro," a tale for adolescents, she extended this political argument to the African slaves in the British colonies in the West Indies. Her play, *The Two Guardians* (1817), explores the connections between a sound, rational education and effective social leadership among both men and women.

Edgeworth believed passionately that women should be educated in the same way as men, to be rational, prudent, and economically independent, even as they prepared themselves for Edgeworth's highest female ideal, a companionate marriage and the role of moral and practical educator to the young, an ideal first articulated in her *Letters from Literary Ladies* (1795), and reiterated in her *Letter from a Gentleman to his Friend, upon the Birth of a Daughter, with the Answer* (1833). Her novels and novellas of English society life consistently celebrate the virtues of a sensible, modest, scrupulous heroine over the foibles of fashionable ladies or overly militant feminists. *Belinda* (1801; revised in 1810) is a powerful illustration of Wollstonecraft's arguments in *Vindication of the Rights of Woman,* as well as a parody of the Rousseauistic pedagogic experiments of Richard Edgeworth's best friend, Thomas Day. *Helen* (1834) exposes Edgeworth's ideal heroine of honesty and sympathy to the damaging maneuvers and wiles of her coquettish cousin Cecilia, showing how Helen's desire to save her cousin's reputation only entangles her in an almost inescapable web of deceit and misunderstanding. Edgeworth's numerous *Tales of Fashionable Life* (1809; 1812) catalogue the follies of contemporary upper-class women, while her novel *Patronage* (1814) analyzes the evils inherent in a hierarchical social system based on dependency rather than personal merit.

Despite her love for him, in 1802 Maria Edgeworth rejected her only offer of marriage, from the Swedish diplomat Abraham Clewberg-Edelcrantz, because she could not bear the thought of parting from her family in Ireland. Domestic affection, grounded in the education and nurturing of children, and sustained through all the years of one's life, remained her primary value. After her father's death in 1817, she continued to manage Edgeworthtown for her brother Lovell, displaying remarkable business acumen, and kept up her own writing and extensive correspondence with many of the leading literary figures of her day, including Scott,* Baillie,* Barbauld,* Inchbald, and Elizabeth Hamilton.

from Letters from Literary Ladies

(1795; comp. 1787)

No penance can absolve their guilty fame,
Nor tears, that wash out guilt, can wash out shame.

PRIOR[1]

— LETTER I —

JULIA TO CAROLINE

In vain, dear Caroline, you urge me to *think;* I profess only to *feel.*

"*Reflect upon my own feelings!* Analyze my notions of happiness! explain to you my system!"—My system! But I have no system; *that* is the very difference between us. My notions of happiness cannot be resolved into simple, fixed principles. Nor dare I even attempt to analyze them; the subtile essence would escape in the process: just punishment to the alchymist in morality!

You, Caroline, are of a more sedate, contemplative character. Philosophy becomes the rigid mistress of your life, enchanting enthusiasm the companion of mine. Suppose she lead me now and then in pursuit of a meteor; am not I happy in the chase? When one illusion vanishes, another shall appear, and, still leading me forward towards an horizon that retreats as I advance, the happy prospect of futurity shall vanish only with my existence.

"Reflect upon my feelings!" Dear Caroline, is it not enough that I do feel? All that I dread is that *apathy* which philosophers call tranquillity. You tell me, that by continually *indulging,* I shall weaken my natural sensibility; are not all the faculties of the soul improved, refined by exercise? and why shall *this* be excepted from the general law?

But I must not, you tell me, indulge my taste for romance and poetry, lest I waste that sympathy on *fiction* which *reality* so much better deserves. My dear friend, let us cherish the precious propensity to pity no matter what the object; sympathy with fiction or reality arises from the same disposition.

When the sigh of compassion rises in my bosom, when the spontaneous tear starts from my eye, what rigid moralist shall "stop the genial current of the soul;"[2] shall say to the tide of passion, *So far shalt thou go, and no farther?* Shall man presume to circumscribe that which Providence has left unbounded?

[1] **Prior:** Matthew Prior (1664–1721), English satirical poet.

[2] **"stop the genial current of the soul":** from the "Elegy Written in a Country Churchyard" (1750), by Thomas Gray (1716–1771): "Chill Penury repress'd their noble Rage, / And froze the genial Current of the Soul" (lines 51–52).

But, O Caroline! if our feelings as well as our days are numbered; if, by the immutable law of nature apathy be the sleep of passion, and languor the necessary consequence of exertion; if indeed the pleasures of life are so ill-proportioned to its duration, oh may that duration be shortened to me! Kind Heaven, let not my soul die before my body!

Yes, if at this instant my guardian genius were to appear before me, and offering me the choice of my future destiny; on the one hand, the even temper, the poised judgment, the stoical serenity of philosophy; on the other, the eager genius, the exquisite sensibility of enthusiasm: if the genius said to me "Choose"—the lot of the one is great pleasure, and great pain—great virtues and great defects—ardent hope, and severe disappointment—ecstasy and despair: the lot of the other is calm happiness unmixed with violent grief—virtue without heroism—respect without admiration—and a length of life, in which to every moment is allotted its proper portion of felicity:—Gracious genius! I should exclaim, if half my existence must be the sacrifice, take it; *enthusiasm is my choice.*

Such, my dear friend, would be my choice were I a man; as a woman, how much more readily should I determine!

What has woman to do with philosophy? Tho graces flourish not under her empire: a woman's part in life is to please, and Providence has assigned to her *success* all the pride and pleasure of her being.

Then leave us our weakness, leave us our follies; they are our best arms:—

"Leave us to trifle with more grace and ease,
Whom folly pleases and whose follies please."[3]

The moment grave sense and solid merit appear, adieu the bewitching caprice, the *"lively nonsense,"* the exquisite, yet childish susceptibility which charms, interests, captivates. Believe me, our *amiable defects* win more than our noblest virtues. Love requires sympathy, and sympathy is seldom connected with a sense of superiority. I envy none their *"painful pre-eminence."* Alas! whether it be deformity or excellence which makes us say with Richard the Third,[4]

"I am myself alone!"

it comes to much the same thing. Then let us, Caroline, content ourselves to gain in love what we lose in esteem.

Man is to be held only by the *slightest* chains; with the idea that he can break them at pleasure, he submits to them in sport; but his pride revolts against the power to which his *reason* tells him he ought to submit. What then can woman gain by reason? Can she prove by argument that she is amiable? or demonstrate that she is an angel?

Vain was the industry of the artist who, to produce the image of perfect beauty, selected from the fairest faces their most faultless features. Equally vain must be the efforts of the philosopher, who would excite the idea of mental perfection by combining an assemblage of party-coloured virtues.

Such, I had almost said, is my *system,* but I mean my *sentiments.* I am not accurate enough to compose a *system.* After all, how vain are systems, and theories, and reasonings!

We may *declaim,* but what do we really know? All is uncertainty—human prudence does nothing—fortune every thing: I leave every thing therefore to fortune; *you* leave nothing. Such is the difference between us.—and which shall be the happiest, time alone can decide.

Farewell, dear Caroline; I love you better than I thought I could love a philosopher.

Your ever affectionate
JULIA.

—LETTER II—

CAROLINE'S ANSWER TO JULIA

At the hazard of ceasing to be *"charming," "interesting," "captivating,"* I must, dear Julia, venture to reason with you, to examine your favourite doctrine of *"amiable defects,"* and, if possible, to dissipate that unjust dread of perfection which you seem to have continually before your eyes.

It is the sole object of a woman's life, you say, to *please.* Her amiable defects *please* more than her noblest virtues, her follies more than her wisdom, her caprice more than her temper, and *something,* a nameless something, which no art can imitate and no science can teach, more than all.

Art, you say, spoils the graces and corrupts the heart of woman; and at best can produce only a cold model of perfection; which, though perhaps strictly conformable to *rule,* can never touch the soul, or please the unprejudiced taste, like one simple stroke of genuine nature.

---

[3] **"Leave us to trifle with more grace and ease, / Whom folly pleases and whose follies please"**: from Pope's *Second Epistle of the Second Book of Horace Imitated* (lines 326–27).

[4] **Richard the Third:** Richard III (1452–1485), King of England from 1483 to 1485; best known as the egocentric villain of Shakespeare's tragedy *Richard III* (c. 1592).

I have often observed, dear Julia, that an inaccurate use of words produces such a strange confusion in all reasoning, that in the heat of debate, the combatants, unable to distinguish their friends from their foes, fall promiscuously on both. A skilful disputant knows well how to take advantage of this confusion, and sometimes endeavours to create it. I do not know whether I am to suspect you of such a design; but I must guard against it.

You have with great address availed yourself of the *two* ideas connected with the word *art*: first, as opposed to simplicity, it implies artifice; and next, as opposed to ignorance, it comprehends all the improvements of science, which, leading us to search for general causes, rewards us with a dominion over their dependent effects: that which instructs how to pursue the objects which we may have in view with the greatest probability of success. All men who act from general principles are so far philosophers. Their objects may be, when attained, insufficient to their happiness, or they may not previously have known all the necessary means to obtain them: but they must not therefore complain, if they do not meet with success, which they have no reason to expect.

Parrhasius,[5] in collecting the most admired excellencies from various models, to produce perfection, concluded from general principles that mankind would be pleased again with what had once excited their admiration. So far he was a philosopher: but he was disappointed of success; yes, for he was ignorant of the cause necessary to produce it. The separate features might be perfect, but they were unsuited to each other, and in their forced union he could not give to the whole countenance symmetry and an appropriate expression.

There was, as you say, a *something* wanting which his science had not taught him. He should then have set himself to examine what that *something* was, and how it was to be obtained. His want of success arose from the *insufficiency*, not the *fallacy*, of theory. Your object, dear Julia, we will suppose is "to please." If general observation and experience have taught you that slight accomplishments and a trivial character succeed more certainly in obtaining this end than higher worth and sense, you act from principle in rejecting the one and aiming at the other. You have discovered, or think you have discovered, the secret causes which produce the desired effect, and you employ them. Do not call this *instinct* or *nature*; this, also, though you scorn it, is *philosophy*.

But when you come soberly to reflect, you have a feeling in your mind that reason and cool judgment disapprove of the part you are acting.

Let us, however, distinguish between disapprobation of the *object*, and the means.

Averse as enthusiasm is to the retrograde motion of analysis, let me, my dear friend, lead you one step backward.

Why do you wish to please? I except at present from the question, the desire to please arising from a passion which requires a reciprocal return. Confined as *this* wish must be in a woman's heart to one object alone, when you say, Julia, *that the admiration of others* will be absolutely necessary to your happiness, I must suppose you mean to express only a *general* desire to please.

Then, under this limitation, let me ask you again, why do you wish to please?

Do not let a word stop you. The word *vanity* conveys to us a disagreeable idea. There seems something *selfish* in the sentiment—that all the pleasure we feel in pleasing others arises from the gratification it affords to our own *vanity*.

We refine and explain, and never can bring ourselves fairly to make a confession which we are sensible must lower us in the opinion of others, and consequently mortify the very *vanity* we would conceal. So strangely, then, do we deceive ourselves as to deny the existence of a motive which at the instant prompts the denial. But let us, dear Julia, exchange the word *vanity* for a less odious word, self-complacency; let us acknowledge that we wish to please, because the success raises our self-complacency. If you ask why raising our self-approbation gives us pleasure, I must answer that I do not know. Yet I see and feel that it does; I observe that the voice of numbers is capable of raising the highest transport, or the most fatal despair. The eye of man seems to possess a fascinating power over his fellow-creatures, to raise the blush of shame, or the glow of pride.

I look around me, and I see riches, titles, dignities, pursued with such eagerness by thousands, only as the signs of distinction. Nay, are not all these things sacrificed the moment they cease to be distinctions? The moment the prize of glory is to be won by other means, do not millions sacrifice their fortunes, their peace, their health, their lives, for *fame*? Then among the highest pleasures of human beings I must place self-approbation. With

[5] **Parrhasius**: Greek painter who flourished c. 400 BC. His works are only known through contemporary descriptions, which claimed that he was the first painter to achieve correct proportions and balance in his figures.

this belief, let us endeavour to secure it in the greatest extent, and to the longest duration.

Then, Julia, the wish to please becomes only a secondary motive, subordinate to the desire I have to secure my own self-complacency. We will examine how far they are connected.

In reflecting upon my own mind, I observe that I am flattered by the opinion of others in proportion to the opinion I have previously formed of their judgment, or I perceive that the opinion of numbers, merely as numbers, has power to give me great pleasure or great pain. I would unite both these pleasures if I could, but in general I cannot—they are incompatible. The opinion of the vulgar crowd and the enlightened individual, the applause of the highest and the lowest of mankind, cannot be obtained by the same means.

Another question then arises,—whom shall we wish to please? We must choose, and be decided in the choice.

You say that you are proud; I am prouder. You will be content with indiscriminate admiration; nothing will content me but what is *select.* As long as I have the use of my reason—as long as my heart can feel the delightful sense of a "well-earned praise"—I will fix my eye on the highest pitch of excellence, and steadily endeavour to attain it.

Conscious of her worth, and daring to assert it, I would have a woman early in life know that she is capable of filling the heart of a man of sense and merit—that she is worthy to be his companion and friend. With all the energy of her soul, with all the powers of her understanding, I would have a woman endeavour to please those whom she esteems and loves.

She runs a risk, you will say, of never meeting her equal. Hearts and understandings of a superior order are seldom met with in the world; or, when met with, it may not be her particular good-fortune to win them. True; but if ever she *wins,* she will *keep* them; and the prize appears to me well worth the pains and difficulty of attaining.

I, Julia, admire and feel enthusiasm; but I would have philosophy directed to the highest objects. I dread apathy as much as you can; and I would endeavour to prevent it, not by sacrificing half my existence, but by enjoying the whole with moderation.

You ask why exercise does not increase sensibility, and why sympathy with imaginary distress will not also increase the disposition to sympathize with what is real? Because pity should, I think, always be associated with the active desire to relieve. If it be suffered to become a *passive sensation,* it is a *useless weakness,* not a virtue. The species of reading you speak of must be hurtful, even in this respect, to the mind; as it indulges all the luxury of wo[e] in sympathy with fictitious distress, without requiring the exertion which reality demands: besides, universal experience proves to us that habit, so far from increasing sensibility, absolutely destroys it, by familiarizing it with objects of compassion.

Let me, my dear friend, appeal even to your own experience in the very instance you mention. Is there any pathetic writer in the world who could move you as much at the "twentieth reading as at the first?"[6] Speak naturally, and at the third or fourth reading you would probably say, It is very pathetic, but I have read it before. I liked it better the first time; that is to say, it *did* touch me once—I know it *ought* to touch me now; but it *does not.* Beware of this! Do not let life become *as tedious as a twice-told tale.*

Farewell, dear Julia: this is the answer of fact against eloquence, philosophy against enthusiasm. You appeal from my understanding to my heart—I appeal from the heart to the understanding of my judge; and ten years hence the decision perhaps will be in my favour.

Yours sincerely,
CAROLINE

— LETTER VII —
CAROLINE TO LORD V——,

MY LORD,

Though I am too sensible that all connexion between my unfortunate friend and her family must for some time have been dissolved, I venture now to address myself to your lordship.

On Wednesday last, about half after six o'clock in the evening, the following note was brought to me. It had been written with such a trembling hand that it was scarcely legible; but I knew the writing too well.

"If you ever loved me, Caroline, read this—do not tear it the moment you see the name of Julia: she has suffered—she is humbled. I left France with the hope of seeing you once more; but, now I am so near you, my courage fails, and my heart sinks within me. I have no friend upon earth—I deserve none; yet I cannot help wishing to see once more before I die the friend of my youth, to thank her with my last breath.

[6] **as much at the "twentieth reading as at the first"**: the phrase used by the Scottish philosopher David Hume (1711–1776) in praise of the Irish poet Thomas Parnell (1679–1718).

"But, dear Caroline, if I must not see you, write to me, if possible, one line of consolation.

"Tell me, is my father living?—do you know any thing of my children?—I dare not ask for my husband. Adieu! I am so weak that I can scarcely write—I hope I shall soon be no more. Farewell! JULIA."

I immediately determined to follow the bearer of this letter. Julia was waiting for my answer at a small inn, in a neighbouring village, at a few miles' distance. It was night when I got there: every thing was silent—all the houses were shut up, excepting one, in which we saw two or three lights glimmering through the window—this was the inn: as your lordship may imagine, it was a very miserable place. The mistress of the house seemed to be touched with pity for the stranger: she opened the door of a small room, where she said the poor lady was resting; and retired as I entered.

Upon a low matted seat beside the fire sat Lady V—; she was in black; her knees were crossed, and her white but emaciated arms flung on one side over her lap; her hands were clasped together, and her eyes fixed upon the fire; she seemed neither to hear nor see any thing round her, but, totally absorbed in her own reflections, to have sunk into insensibility. I dreaded to rouse her from this state of torpor; and I believe I stood for some moments motionless: at last I moved softly towards her—she turned her head—started up—a scarlet blush overspread her face—and she grew livid again instantly, gave a faint shriek, and sank senseless into my arms.

When she returned to herself, and found her head lying upon my shoulder, and heard my voice soothing her with all the expressions of kindness I could think of, she smiled with a look of gratitude, which I never shall forget. Like one who had been long unused to kindness, she seemed ready to pour forth all the fondness of her heart: but, as if recollecting herself better, she immediately checked her feelings—withdrew her hand from mine—thanked me—said she was quite well again—cast down her eyes, and her manner changed from tenderness to timidity. She seemed to think that she had lost all right to sympathy, and received even the common offices of humanity with surprise: her high spirit, I saw, was quite broken.

I think I never felt such sorrow as I did in contemplating Julia at this instant: she who stood before me, sitting under the sense of inferiority, I knew to be my equal—my superior; yet by fatal imprudence, by one rash step, all her great, and good, and amiable qualities were irretrievably lost to the world and to herself.

When I thought that she was a little recovered, I begged of her, if she was not too much fatigued, to let me carry her home. At these words she looked at me with surprise. Her eyes filled with tears; but without making any other reply, she suffered me to draw her arm within mine, and attempted to follow me. I did not know how feeble she was till she began to walk; it was with the utmost difficulty I supported her to the door; and by the assistance of the people of the house she was lifted into the carriage: we went very slowly. When the carriage stopped, she was seized with a universal tremor; she started when the man knocked at the door, and seemed to dread its being opened. The appearance of light and the sound of cheerful voices struck her with horror.

I could not myself help being shocked with the contrast between the dreadful situation of my friend and the happiness of the family to which I was returning.

"Oh!" said she, "what are these voices?—Whither are you taking me?—For heaven's sake do not let anybody see me!"

I assured her that she should go directly to her own apartment, and that no human being should approach her without her express permission.

Alas! it happened at this very moment that all my children came running with the utmost gayety into the hall to meet us, and the very circumstance which I had been so anxious to prevent happened—little Julia was among them. The gayety of the children suddenly ceased the moment they saw Lady V—— coming up the steps—they were struck with her melancholy air and countenance: she, leaning upon my arm, with her eyes fixed upon the ground, let me lead her in, and sank upon the first chair she came to. I made a sign to the children to retire; but the moment they began to move, Lady V—— looked up—saw her daughter—and now for the first time burst into tears. The little girl did not recollect her poor mother till she heard the sound of her voice; and then she threw her arms round her neck, crying, "Is it you, mamma?"—and all the children immediately crowded round and asked, "if this was the same Lady V— who used to play with them."

It is impossible to describe the effect these simple questions had on Julia: a variety of emotions seemed struggling in her countenance; she rose and made an attempt to break from the children, but could not—she had not strength to support herself. We carried her away, and put her to bed; she took no notice of anybody, nor did she even seem to know that I was with her: I thought she was insensible, but as I drew the curtains I heard her give a deep sigh.

I left her, and carried away her little girl, who had followed us up stairs and begged to stay with her mother but I was apprehensive that the sight of her might renew her agitation.

After I was gone, they told me that she was perfectly still, with her eyes closed; and I staid away some time, in hopes that she might sleep: however, about midnight she sent to beg to speak to me: she was very ill—she beckoned to me to sit down by her bedside—every one left the room; and when Julia saw herself alone with me, she took my hand, and in a low but calm voice she said, "I have not many hours to live—my heart is broken—I wished to see you, to thank you while it was yet in my power." She pressed my hand to her trembling lips; "Your kindness," added she, "touches me more than all the rest; but how ashamed you must be of such a friend! Oh Caroline! to die a disgrace to all who ever loved me!"

The tears trickled down her face, and choked her utterance; she wiped them away hastily. "But it is not now a time," said she, "to think of myself—can I see my daughter?" The little girl was asleep: she was awakened, and I brought her to her mother. Julia raised herself in her bed, and summoning up all her strength, "My dearest friend!" said she, putting her child's hand into mine, "when I am gone, be a mother to this child—let her know my whole history, let nothing be concealed from her. Poor girl! you will live to blush at your mother's name." She paused, and leaned back: I was going to take the child away, but she held out her arms again for her, and kissed her several times. "Farewell," said she; "I shall never see you again." The little girl burst into tears. Julia wished to say something more—she raised herself again—at last she uttered these words with energy:—"My love, *be good and happy*," she then sank down on the pillow quite exhausted—she never spoke afterward: I took her hand—it was cold—her pulse scarcely beat—her eyes rolled without meaning—in a few moments she expired.

Painful as it has been to me to recall the circumstances of her death to my imagination, I have given your lordship this exact and detailed account of my unfortunate friend's behaviour in her last moments. Whatever may have been her errors, her soul never became callous from vice. The sense of her own ill conduct was undoubtedly the immediate cause of her illness, and the remorse which had long preyed upon her mind at length brought her to the grave—

I have the honour to be,
My lord, &c.
CAROLINE

from BELINDA
(1801)

— CHAPTER XVII —

Editor's Note: In this chapter, Maria Edgeworth satirizes the militant feminism of Harriet Freke in order to support the more moderate feminism of her heroine Belinda Portman. When Belinda, an attractive young woman of sound sense, wide reading, prudence, personal modesty and a loving heart, is sent to London by her matchmaking aunt, she is presented with two negative female role models, Lady Delacour and Harriet Freke. The acknowledged leader of high society, the witty Lady Delacour exposes Belinda to the intrigues, deceptions and hidden miseries of the fashionable world, blithely compromising Belinda by borrowing money in Belinda's name from her professed suitor, Clarence Hervey, money which Belinda returns as soon as she learns of the transaction. Harriet Freke is the self-professed champion of the rights of woman who seeks to end the "slavery" of women to a false "delicacy" by having both sexes call things by their correct names. Her name, "freak," in the early nineteenth century meant not a "monstrosity" but rather "a capricious humour, a whim, a vagary" (*Oxford English Dictionary*). By wearing men's clothes, participating in a duel which seriously injures Lady Delacour, and playing cruel practical jokes on both Lady Delacour and on Juba, the black servant of the West Indian planter Mr. Vincent (also a suitor of Belinda), Harriet Freke undermines her campaign for the liberty of women. She assumes the worst aspects of masculinity—tyranny over the weak, cruelty, infidelity, physical violence—rather than fusing the best qualities of both genders, as Belinda does, following the positive example of her friends the Percivals.

[A.K.M.]

Rights of Woman

Belinda was alone, and reading, when Mrs Freke dashed into the room.

"How do, dear creature!" cried she, stepping up to her, and shaking hands with her boisterously—"How do?—Glad to see you, 'faith—Been long here? Tremendously hot today!"

She flung herself upon the sofa beside Belinda, threw her hat upon the table, and then continued speaking.

"And how d'ye go on here, poor child!—'God! I'm glad you're alone—Expected to find you encompassed by a whole host of the righteous. Give me credit for my courage in coming to deliver you out of their hands. Luttridge and I had such compassion upon you, when we heard you were close prisoner here!—I swore to set the distressed damsel free, in spite of all the dragons in Christendom—So let me carry you off in triumph in my unicorn,[1] and leave these good people to stare when they come home from their sober walk, and find you gone. There's nothing I like so much as to make *good* people stare—I hope you're of my way o'thinking—You don't look as if you were though—but I never mind young ladies' looks—always give the lie to their thoughts.—Now we talk o'looks—Never saw you look so well in my life—as handsome as an angel!—And so much the better for me.—Do you know, I've a bet of twenty guineas on your head—on your face, I mean. There's a young bride at Harrowgate, Lady H——, they're all mad about her, the men swear she's the handsomest woman in England, and I swear I know one ten times as handsome. They've dared me to make good my word, and I've pledged myself to produce my beauty at the next ball, and to pit her against their belle for any money.—Most votes carry it.—I'm willing to double my bet since I've seen you again.—Come, had not we best be off? Now don't refuse me and make speeches—you know that's all nonsense—I'll take all the blame upon myself."

Belinda, who had not been suffered to utter a word whilst Mrs Freke ran on in this strange manner, looked in unfeigned astonishment; but when she found herself seized and dragged towards the door, she drew back with a degree of gentle firmness that equally astonished Mrs Freke. With a smiling countenance, but a steady tone, she said, "that she was sorry Mrs Freke's knight-errantry should not be exerted in a better cause, for that she was neither a prisoner, nor a distressed damsel."

"And will you make me lose my bet?" cried Mrs Freke. "O, at all events you must come to the ball!—I'm down for it.—But I'll not press it now, because you're frightened out of your poor little wits, I see, at the bare thoughts of doing any thing out of rule, by these good people. Well, well! it shall be managed for you—leave that to me.—I'm used to managing for cowards.—Pray tell me—You and Lady Delacour are off, I understand?—Give ye joy!—She and I were once great friends; that is to say, I had over her 'that power which strong minds have over weak ones'; but she was too weak for me—one of those people that have neither courage to be good, nor to be bad."

"The courage to be bad," said Belinda, "I believe, indeed, that she does not possess."

Mrs Freke stared.—"Why, I heard you had quarrelled with her!"

"If I had," said Belinda, "I hope that I should still do justice to her merits. It is said that people are apt to suffer more by their friends than their enemies. I hope that will never be the case with Lady Delacour, as I confess that I have been one of her friends."

"Gad, I like your spirit—you don't want courage, I see, to fight even for your enemies. You are just the kind of girl I admire—I see you've been prejudiced against me by Lady Delacour. But whatever stories she may have trumped up, the truth of the matter is this; there's no living with her she's so jealous—so ridiculously jealous—of that lord of hers, for whom all the time she hasn't the impudence to pretend to care more than I do for the sole of my boot," said Mrs Freke, striking it with her whip, "but she hasn't the courage to give him tit for tat.—Now this is what I call weakness.—Pray, how do she and Clarence Hervey go on together?—Are they out o'the hornbook of platonics yet?"

"Mr Hervey was not in town when I left it," said Belinda.

"Was not he?—Ho! ho!—He's off then!—Ay, so I prophesied. She's not the thing for him—He has some strength of mind—some soul—above vulgar prejudices—So must a woman be to hold him. He was caught at first by her grace and beauty, and that sort of stuff; but I knew it could not last—knew she'd dilly dally with Clary, till he would turn upon his heel and leave her there."

"I fancy that you are entirely mistaken both with respect to Mr Hervey and Lady Delacour," Belinda very seriously began to say; but Mrs Freke interrupted her, and ran on—

"No! no! no! I'm not mistaken; Clarence has found her out.—She's a *very* woman—*that* he could forgive her, and so could I—But she's a *mere* woman—and that he can't forgive—no more can I."

There was a kind of drollery about Mrs Freke, which, with some people, made the odd things she said pass for wit. Humour she really possessed; and when she chose it, she could be diverting to those who like buffoonery in women. She had set her heart upon winning Belinda over

[1] **unicorn:** a carriage driven by three horses, two abreast and one in the lead.

to her party. She began by flattery of her beauty; but as she saw that this had no effect, she next tried what could be done by insinuating that she had a high opinion of her understanding, by talking to her as an esprit fort.[2]

"For my part," said she, "I own I should like a strong devil better than a weak angel."

"You forget," said Belinda, "that it is not Milton, but Satan, who says,

'Fallen spirit, to be weak is to be miserable.'"[3]

"You read, I see!—I did not know you were a reading girl.—So did I once! but I never read now. Books only spoil the originality of genius. Very well for those who can't think for themselves—But when one has made up one's opinions, there is no use in reading."

"But to *make* them up," replied Belinda, "may it not be useful?"

"Of no use upon earth to minds of a certain class.—You, who can think for yourself, should never read."

"But I read that I may think for myself."

"Only ruin your understanding, trust me. Books are full of trash—nonsense—Conversation is worth all the books in the world."

"And is there never any nonsense in conversation?"

"What have you here?" continued Mrs Freke, who did not choose to attend to this question; exclaiming as she reviewed each of the books on the table in their turns, in the summary language of presumptuous ignorance. "Smith's Theory of Moral Sentiments'—Milk and water! 'Moore's Travels'—Hasty pudding! 'La Bruyere'[4]—Nettle porridge! This is what you were at when I came in, was it not?" said she, taking up a book in which she saw Belinda's mark, 'Essay on the Inconsistency of Human Wishes'.[5] "Poor thing! who bored you with this task?"

"Mr Percival recommended it to me, as one of the best essays in the English language."

"The devil! They seem to have put you in a course of the bitters—a course of the woods might do your business better. Do you ever hunt?—Let me take you out with me some morning—You'd be quite an angel on horseback; or let me drive you out some day in my unicorn."

Belinda declined this invitation, and Mrs Freke strode away to the window to conceal her mortification, threw up the sash, and called out to her groom,

"Walk those horses about, blockhead!"—Mr Percival and Mr Vincent at this instant came into the room.

"Hail, fellow! well met," cried Mrs Freke, stretching out her hand to Mr Vincent.

It has been remarked, that an antipathy subsists between creatures, who, without being the same, have yet a strong external resemblance. Mr Percival saw this instinct rising in Mr Vincent, and smiled.

"Hail, fellow! well met, I say—Shake hands, and be friends, man!—Though I'm not in the habit of making apologies, if it will be any satisfaction to you, I beg your pardon for frightening your poor devil of a black."

Then turning towards Mr Percival, she measured him with her eye, as a person whom she longed to attack. She thought, that if Belinda's opinion of the understanding of *these Percivals* could be lowered, she should rise in her opinion: accordingly, she determined to draw Mr Percival into an argument.

"I've been talking treason, I believe, to Miss Portman," cried she, "for I've been opposing some of your opinions, Mr Percival."

"If you opposed them all, madam," said Mr Percival, "I should not think it treason."

"Vastly polite!—But I think all our politeness hypocrisy. What d'ye say to that?"

"You know that best, madam!"

"Then I'll go a step farther; for I'm determined you shall contradict me.—I think all virtue is hypocrisy."

"I need not contradict you, madam," said Mr Percival, "for the terms which you make use of contradict themselves."

---

[2] **esprit fort**: French for "strong spirit"; in English, a strong-minded person, especially a freethinker in religion.

[3] **'Fallen spirit . . . miserable'**: from Milton's *Paradise Lost*, I.157: "Fall'n Cherub, to be weak is miserable."

[4] **"Smith's Theory of Moral Sentiments"**: the *Theory of Moral Sentiments** (1759) by the Scottish economist and philosopher Adam Smith (1723–1790), a work of sophisticated ethical pragmatism grounded on human sympathy. **Moore's Travels**: the *Travels into the Inland Parts of Africa* (1738–1740), by Francis Moore (fl. 1744), a colonial agent and traveller. **La Bruyere**: Jean de La Bruyère (1645–1696), French moralist, author of *Les Caractères ou les moeurs de ce siècle* (*Characters, or the Manners of Our Times*, 1688–1696), a collection of ironic character sketches and reflections on morals.

[5] **Essay on the Inconsistency of Human Wishes**: included in *Miscellaneous Pieces in Prose* (1773) by Mrs. [Anna Letitia] Barbauld* and Dr. [John] Aikin [M. E.].

"It is my system," pursued Mrs Freke, "that shame is always the cause of the vices of women."

"It is sometimes the effect," said Mr Percival, "and, as cause and effect are reciprocal, perhaps you may, in some instances, be right."

"O! I hate qualifying arguers — Plump assertion or plump denial for me — You shan't get off so — I say, shame is the cause of all women's vices."

"False shame, I suppose you mean?" said Mr Percival.

"Mere play upon words! — All shame is false shame — We would be a great deal better without it. What say you, Miss Portman — Silent — hey? — Silence that speaks!"

"Miss Portman's blushes," said Mr Vincent, "speak *for* her."

"*Against* her," — said Mrs Freke — "Women blush because they understand."

"And you would have them understand without blushing?" said Mr Percival. "So would I; for nothing can be more different than innocence and ignorance. Female delicacy —"

"This is just the way you men spoil women," cried Mrs Freke, "by talking to them of the *delicacy of their sex*, and such stuff. This *delicacy* enslaves the pretty delicate dears."

"No; it enslaves us," said Mr Vincent.

"I hate slavery! Vive la liberté!" cried Mrs Freke — "I'm a champion for the Rights of Women."[6]

"I am an advocate for their happiness," said Mr Percival, "and for their delicacy, as I think it conduces to their happiness."

"I'm an enemy to their delicacy, as I am sure it conduces to their misery."

"You speak from experience?" said Mr Percival.

"No, from observation. — Your most delicate women are always the greatest hypocrites; and, in my opinion, no hypocrite can or ought to be happy."

"But you have not proved the hypocrisy," said Belinda. "Delicacy is not, I hope, an indisputable proof of it? — If you mean *false* delicacy —"

"To cut the matter short at once," cried Mrs Freke, "why, when a woman likes a man, does not she go and tell him so honestly?"

Belinda, surprised by this question from a woman, was too much abashed instantly to answer.

"Because she's a hypocrite. That is and must be the answer."

"No," said Mr Percival, "because, if she be a woman of sense, she knows that by such a step she would disgust the object of her affection."

"Cunning! — cunning! — cunning! — the arms of the weakest."

"Prudence! — prudence! — the arms of the strongest. Taking the best means to secure our own happiness without injuring that of others, is the best proof of sense and strength of mind, whether in man or woman. Fortunately for society, the same conduct in ladies which best secures their happiness most increases ours."

Mrs Freke beat the devil's tattoo for some moments, and then exclaimed —

"You may say what you will, but the present system of society is radically wrong: — whatever is, is wrong."[7]

"How would you improve the state of society?" asked Mr Percival calmly.

"I'm not tinker general to the world," said she.

"I am glad of it," said Mr Percival; "for I have heard that tinkers often spoil more than they mend."

"But if you want to know," said Mrs Freke, "what I would do to improve the world, I'll tell you: I'd have your sex taught to say, Horns! horns! I defy you."[8]

"This would doubtless be a great improvement," said Mr Percival; "but you would not overturn society to attain it? would you? — Should we find things much improved by tearing away what has been called the decent drapery of life?"[9]

"Drapery, if you ask me my opinion," cried Mrs Freke, "drapery, whether wet or dry, is the most confoundedly indecent thing in the world."

"That depends on *public* opinion, I allow," said Mr Percival. "The Lacedaemonian ladies, who were veiled only by public opinion, were better covered from profane eyes, than some English ladies are in wet drapery."[10]

---

[6] **Vive la liberté!**: French for "Long live liberty!," a battle cry in the late eighteenth and early nineteenth centuries. **The Rights of Women**: a reference to the *Vindication of the Rights of Woman* (1792) by Mary Wollstonecraft.*

[7] **". . . whatever is, is wrong"**: allusion to Alexander Pope's conclusion in his *Essay on Man* (1733–1734) that "Whatever is, is right" (I.294).

[8] In the 1810 revised edition of *Belinda*, this line reads as follows: "What I would do to improve the world, I'll tell you: I'd have both sexes call things by their right names."

[9] **decent drapery of life**: "But now all is to be changed. . . . All the decent drapery of life is to be rudely torn off." Burke, *Reflections on the Revolution in France.**

[10] **Lacedaemonian ladies**: the girls of ancient Sparta exercised naked together with the boys. **wet drapery**:

"I know nothing of the Lacedaemonian ladies, I took my leave of them when I was a schoolboy — girl — I should say. But, pray, what o'clock is it by you — I've sat till I'm cramped all over," cried Mrs Freke, getting up and stretching herself so violently that some part of her habiliments gave way. "Honi soit qui mal y pense!"[11] said she, bursting into a horse laugh.

Without sharing in any degree that confusion which Belinda felt for her, she strode out of the room, saying, "Miss Portman, you understand these things better than I do; come and set me to rights."

When she was in Belinda's room, she threw herself into an arm chair, and laughed immoderately.

"How I have trimmed Percival this morning!" said she.

"I am glad you think so," said Belinda; "for I really was afraid he had been too severe upon you."

"I only wish," continued Mrs Freke, "I only wish his wife had been by. Why the devil did not she make her appearance? — I suppose the prude was afraid of my demolishing and unrigging her."

"There seems to have been more danger of that for you than for any body else," said Belinda, as she assisted to set Mrs Freke's *rigging*, as she called it, to rights.

"I do, of all things, delight in hauling good people's opinions out of their musty drawers, and seeing how they look when they're all pulled to pieces before their faces. Pray, are those Lady Anne's drawers or yours?" said Mrs Freke, pointing to a chest of drawers.

"Mine."

"I'm sorry for it; for, if they were hers, to punish her for *shirking* me, by the Lord, I'd have every rag she has in the world out in the middle of the floor in ten minutes! You don't know me — I'm a terrible person when provoked — Stop at nothing!"

As Mrs Freke saw no other chance left of gaining her point with Belinda, she tried what intimidating her would do.

"I stop at nothing," repeated she, fixing her eyes upon Miss Portman, to fascinate her by terror. "Friend or foe! Peace or war! Take your choice. — Come to the ball at Harrowgate, I win my bet, and I'm your sworn friend. — Stay away, I lose my bet, and am your sworn enemy."

"It is not in my power, madam," said Belinda calmly, "to comply with your request."

"Then you'll take the consequences," cried Mrs Freke. She rushed past her, hurried down stairs, and called out,

"Bid my blockhead bring my unicorn!"

She, her unicorn, and her blockhead, were out of sight in a few minutes.

Good may be drawn from evil. Mrs Freke's conversation, though at the time it confounded Belinda, roused her, upon reflection to examine by her reason for the habits and principles which guided her conduct. She had a general feeling that they were right and necessary; but now, with the assistance of Lady Anne and Mr Percival, she established in her own understanding the exact boundaries between right and wrong. She felt a species of satisfaction and security, from seeing the demonstration of those axioms of morality, in which she had previously acquiesced. Reasoning gradually became as agreeable to her as wit; nor was her taste for wit diminished, it was only refined by this process. She now compared and judged of the value of the different species of this brilliant talent.

Mrs Freke's wit, thought she, is like a squib let off in the street by vulgar mischievous boys — The passengers start — but it is only the terror of a moment. Lady Delacour's wit is like an elegant fire work played off at a festival — The spectators applaud — but it is only the admiration of a moment. Lady Anne Percival's wit is like

"The refulgent lamp of night — "

We

"Love the mild rays, and bless the useful light."

"Miss Portman," said Mr Percival, "are not you afraid of making an enemy of Mrs Freke, by declining her invitation to Harrowgate?"

"I think her friendship more to be dreaded than her enmity," replied Belinda.

"Then you are not to be terrified by an obeah-woman?"[12] said Mr Vincent.

"Not in the least, unless she were to come in the shape of a false friend," said Belinda.

"Till lately," said Mr Vincent, "I was deceived in the character of Mrs Freke. I thought her a dashing,

Post-revolutionary French fashion, now known as the "empire style," dictated that women wear sheer fabrics that clung tightly to the breast; this drapery was often dampened to increase its cling in what today would be known as "the wet tee shirt look."

[11] **habiliments:** clothes. **Honi soit qui mal y pense:** French, "Shame on him who thinks ill (of this)" — the motto of the Order of the Garter.

[12] **obeah-woman:** a woman who practices white magic or sorcery, from the name of a form of African and Afro-Caribbean religious practice.

free-spoken, free-hearted sort of eccentric person, who would make a staunch friend, and a jolly companion. As a mistress or a wife, no man of any taste could think of her. Compare that woman now with one of our creole ladies."[13]

"But why with a creole?" said Mr Percival.

"For the sake of contrast in the first place—Our creole women are all softness, grace, delicacy—"

"And indolence," said Mr Percival.

"Their indolence is but a slight, and, in my judgment, an amiable defect; it keeps them out of mischief, and it attaches them to domestic life. The activity of a Mrs Freke would never excite their emulation, and so much the better."

"So much the better, no doubt," said Mr Percival. "But is there no other species of activity, that might excite their ambition with propriety? Without diminishing their grace, softness, or delicacy, might not they cultivate their minds? Do you think ignorance, as well as indolence, an amiable defect essential to the female character?"

"Not essential. You do not, I hope, imagine that I am so much prejudiced in favour of my countrywomen, that I can neither see nor feel the superiority in *some instances* of European cultivation? I speak only in general."

"And in general," said Lady Anne Percival, "does Mr Vincent wish to confine our sex to the bliss of ignorance?"

"If it be bliss," said Mr Vincent, "what reason would they have for complaint?"

"*If*," said Belinda; "but that is a question which you have not yet decided."

"And how can we decide it?" said Mr Vincent. "The taste and feelings of individuals must be the arbiters of their happiness."

"You leave reason quite out of the question, then," said Mr Percival, "and refer the whole to taste and feeling? So that, if the most ignorant person in the world assert that he is happier than you are, you are bound to believe him."

"Why should not I?" said Mr Vincent.

"Because," said Mr Percival, "though he can judge of his own pleasures, he cannot judge of yours; his are common to both, but yours are unknown to him.—Would you, at this instant, change places with that ploughman yonder, who is whistling as he goes for want of thought? or, would you choose to go a step higher in the bliss of ignorance, and turn savage?"

Mr Vincent laughed, and protested that he should be very unwilling to give up his title to civilised society; and that, instead of wishing to have less knowledge, he regretted that he had not more. "I am sensible," said he, "that I have many prejudices:—Miss Portman has made me ashamed of some of them."

There was a degree of candour in Mr Vincent's manner and conversation which interested every body in his favour; Belinda amongst the rest. She was perfectly at ease in Mr Vincent's company, because she considered him as a person who wished for her friendship, without having any design to engage her affections. From several hints that dropped from him, from Mr Percival, and from Lady Anne, she was persuaded that he was attached to some creole lady; and all that he said in favour of the elegant softness and delicacy of his countrywomen confirmed this opinion.

Miss Portman was not one of those young ladies who fancy that every gentleman who converses freely with them will inevitably fall a victim to the power of their charms, and who see in every man a lover, or nothing.

[13] **creole ladies:** white European women living in the West Indies.

from POPULAR TALES
(1804)

The Grateful Negro
(1804; comp. 1802)

In the island of Jamaica[1] there lived two planters, whose methods of managing their slaves were as different as possible. Mr. Jefferies considered the negroes as an inferior species, incapable of gratitude, disposed to treachery, and to be roused from their natural indolence only by force: he treated his slaves, or rather suffered his overseer to treat them, with the greatest severity.

Jefferies was not a man of a cruel, but of a thoughtless and extravagant temper. He was of such a sanguine disposition, that he always calculated upon having a fine season, and fine crops on his plantation; and never had the prudence to make allowance for unfortunate

[1] **Jamaica:** island in the West Indies, in the Caribbean Sea. In the eighteenth and nineteenth centuries, it was a British colony with a huge African slave population, most of whom were made to work on sugar plantations; there were a large number of slave rebellions until the abolition of slavery in 1833.

accidents: he required, as he said, from his overseer, produce and not excuses.

Durant, the overseer, did not scruple to use the most cruel and barbarous methods of forcing the slaves to exertions beyond their strength.[2] Complaints of his brutality, from time to time, reached his master's ears; but, though Mr. Jefferies was moved to momentary compassion, he shut his heart against conviction: he hurried away to the jovial banquet, and drowned all painful reflections in wine.

He was this year much in debt; and, therefore, being more than usually anxious about his crop, he pressed his overseer to exert himself to the utmost.

The wretched slaves, upon his plantation, thought themselves still more unfortunate, when they compared their condition with that of the negroes on the estate of Mr. Edwards. This gentleman treated his slaves with all possible humanity and kindness. He wished that there was no such thing as slavery in the world; but he was convinced, by the arguments of those who have the best means of obtaining information, that the sudden emancipation of the negroes would rather increase than diminish their miseries. His benevolence therefore confined itself within the bounds of reason. He adopted those plans for the melioration of the state of the slaves, which appeared to him the most likely to succeed, without producing any violent agitation or revolution.[3] For instance, his negroes had reasonable and fixed daily tasks; and, when these were finished, they were permitted to employ their time for their own advantage or amusement. If they chose to employ themselves longer for their master, they were paid regular wages for their extra work. This reward, for as such it was considered, operated most powerfully upon the slaves. Those who are animated by hope can perform what would seem impossibilities, to those who are under the depressing influence of fear. The wages which Mr. Edwards promised, he took care to see punctually paid.

He had an excellent overseer, of the name of Abraham Bayley; a man of a mild but steady temper, who was attached not only to his master's interests but to his virtues; and who therefore was more intent upon seconding his humane views, than upon squeezing from the labour of the negroes the utmost produce. Each negro had, near his cottage, a portion of land, called his provision-ground; and one day in the week was allowed for its cultivation.

It is common in Jamaica for the slaves to have provision-grounds, which they cultivate for their own advantage; but it too often happens that, when a good negro has successfully improved his little spot of land, when he has built himself a house, and begins to enjoy the fruits of his industry, his acquired property is seized upon by the sheriff's officer for the payment of his master's debts,[4] he is forcibly separated from his wife and children, dragged to public auction, purchased by a stranger, and perhaps sent to terminate his miserable existence in the mines of Mexico, excluded for ever from the light of heaven! and all this without any crime or imprudence on his part, real or pretended. He is punished because his master is unfortunate!

To this barbarous injustice the negroes on Mr. Edwards's plantation were never exposed. He never exceeded his income; he engaged in no wild speculations; he contracted no debts; and his slaves, therefore, were in no danger of being seized by a sheriff's officer: their property was secured to them by the prudence as well as by the generosity of their master.

One morning, as Mr. Edwards was walking in that part of his plantation which joined to Mr. Jefferies' estate, he thought he heard the voice of distress, at some distance. The lamentations grew louder and louder as he approached a cottage, which stood upon the borders of Jefferies' plantation.

This cottage belonged to a slave of the name of Caesar, the best negro in Mr. Jefferies' possession. Such had been his industry and exertion, that, notwithstanding the severe tasks imposed by Durant, the overseer, Caesar found means to cultivate his provision-ground to a degree of perfection no where else to be seen on this estate. Mr. Edwards had often admired this poor fellow's industry; and now hastened to inquire what misfortune had befallen him.

[2] **exertions beyond their strength**: Edgeworth referred her original readers to "*The Negro Slaves*—a fine drama, by Kotzebue. It is to be hoped that such horrible instances of cruelty are not now to be found in nature. Bryan Edwards, in his History of Jamaica, says that most of the planters are humane; but he allows that some facts can be cited in contradiction of this assertion" [M. E.].

[3] **without producing any violent agitation or revolution**: Edgeworth pointed here to the "History of the West Indies [1794; by Bryan Edwards (1743–1800)], from which these ideas are adopted—not stolen."

[4] **for the payment of his master's debts**: see an eloquent and pathetic passage on this subject in the History of the West Indies, vol. ii p. 153, second edition [M. E.].

When he came to the cottage, he found Caesar standing with his arms folded, and his eyes fixed upon the ground. A young and beautiful female negro was weeping bitterly, as she knelt at the feet of Durant, the overseer, who, regarding her with a sullen aspect, repeated, "He must go. I tell you, woman, he must go. What signifies all this nonsense?"

At the sight of Mr. Edwards, the overseer's countenance suddenly changed, and assumed an air of obsequious civility. The poor woman retired to the further corner of the cottage, and continued to weep. Caesar never moved. "Nothing is the matter, Sir," said Durant, "but that Caesar is going to be sold. That is what the woman is crying for. They were to be married; but we'll find Clara another husband, I tell her; and she'll get the better of her grief, you know, Sir, as I tell her, in time."

"Never! never!" said Clara.

"To whom is Caesar going to be sold; and for what sum?"

"For what can be got for him," replied Durant, laughing; "and to whoever will buy him. The sheriff's officer is here, who has seized him for debt, and must make the most of him at market."

"Poor fellow!" said Mr. Edwards; "and must he leave this cottage which he has built, and these bananas which he has planted?"

Caesar now, for the first time, looked up, and fixing his eyes upon Mr. Edwards for a moment, advanced with an intrepid rather than an imploring countenance, and said, "Will you be my master? Will you be her master? Buy both of us. You shall not repent of it. Caesar will serve you faithfully."

On hearing these words, Clara sprang forwards; and clasping her hands together, repeated, "Caesar will serve you faithfully."

Mr. Edwards was moved by their entreaties, but he left them without declaring his intentions. He went immediately to Mr. Jefferies, whom he found stretched on a sofa, drinking coffee. As soon as Mr. Edwards mentioned the occasion of his visit, and expressed his sorrow for Caesar, Jefferies exclaimed, "Yes, poor devil! I pity him from the bottom of my soul. But what can I do? I leave all those things to Durant. He says the sheriff's officer has seized him; and there's an end of the matter. You know money must be had. Besides Caesar is not worse off than any other slave sold for debt. What signifies talking about the matter, as if it were something that never happened before! Is not it a case that occurs every day in Jamaica?"

"So much the worse," replied Mr. Edwards.

"The worse for them, to be sure," said Jefferies. "But, after all, they are slaves, and used to be treated as such; and they tell me the negroes are a thousand times happier here, with us, than they ever were in their own country."

"Did the negroes tell you so themselves?"

"No; but people better informed than negroes have told me so; and, after all, slaves there must be; for indigo, and rum, and sugar we must have."

"Granting it to be physically impossible that the world should exist without rum, sugar, and indigo, why could they not be produced by freemen, as well as by slaves? If we hired negroes for labourers, instead of purchasing them for slaves, do you think they would not work as well as they do now? Does any negro, under the fear of the overseer, work harder than a Birmingham journeyman, or a Newcastle collier; who toil for themselves and their families?"

"Of that I don't pretend to judge. All I know is that the West India planters would be ruined, if they had no slaves; and I am a West India planter."

"So am I; yet I do not think they are the only people whose interest ought to be considered, in this business."

"Their interests, luckily, are protected by the laws of the land; and, though they are rich men, and white men, and freemen, they have as good a claim to their rights as the poorest black slave on any of our plantations."

"The law, in our case, seems to make the right; and the very reverse ought to be done: the right should make the law."

"Fortunately for us planters, we need not enter into such nice distinctions. You could not, if you would, abolish the trade. Slaves would be smuggled into the islands."

"What, if nobody would buy them! You know that you cannot smuggle slaves into England. The instant a slave touches English ground, he becomes free. Glorious privilege! Why should it not be extended to all her dominions? If the future importation of slaves into these islands were forbidden by law, the trade must cease. No man can either sell or possess slaves, without its being known: they cannot be smuggled, like lace or brandy."

"Well, well!" retorted Jefferies, a little impatiently, "as yet, the law is on our side. I can do nothing in this business, nor you neither."

"Yes, we can do something; we can endeavour to make our negroes as happy as possible."

"I leave the management of these people to Durant."

"That is the very thing of which they complain: forgive me for speaking to you with the frankness of an old acquaintance."

"Oh! you can't oblige me more! I love frankness of all things! To tell you the truth, I have heard complaints of Durant's severity; but I make it a principle to turn a deaf ear to them, for I know nothing can be done with these fellows without it. You are partial to negroes; but even you must allow they are a race of beings naturally inferior to us. You may in vain think of managing a black as you would a white. Do what you please for a negro, he will cheat you the first opportunity he finds. You know what their maxim is: 'God gives black men what white men forget.'"

To these common-place desultory observations, Mr. Edwards made no reply; but recurred to poor Caesar, and offered to purchase both him and Clara at the highest price the sheriff's officer could obtain for them at market. Mr. Jefferies, with the utmost politeness to his neighbour, but with the most perfect indifference to the happiness of those whom he considered a different species from himself, acceded to this proposal. "Nothing could be more reasonable," he said; "and he was happy to have it in his power to oblige a gentleman, for whom he had such a high esteem."

The bargain was quickly concluded with the sheriff's officer; for Mr. Edwards willingly paid several dollars more than the market price for the two slaves. When Caesar and Clara heard that they were not to be separated, their joy and gratitude were expressed with all the ardour and tenderness peculiar to their different characters. Clara was an Eboe, Caesar a Koromantyn Negro.[5] The Eboes are soft, languishing, and timid. The Koromantyns are frank, fearless, martial, and heroic.

Mr. Edwards carried his new slaves home with him, desired Bayley, his overseer, to mark out a provision-ground for Caesar, and to give him a cottage, which happened at this time to be vacant.

"Now, my good friend," said he to Caesar, "you may work for yourself, without fear that what you earn may be taken from you; or that you should ever be sold, to pay your master's debts. If he does not understand what I am saying," continued Mr. Edwards, turning to his overseer, "you will explain it to him."

Caesar perfectly understood all that Mr. Edwards said; but his feelings were at this instant so strong that he could not find expression for his gratitude: he stood like one stupified! Kindness was new to him; it overpowered his manly heart; and, at hearing the words "my good friend," the tears gushed from his eyes. Tears which no torture could have extorted! Gratitude swelled in his bosom; and he longed to be alone, that he might freely yield to his emotions.

He was glad when the conch-shell sounded, to call the negroes to their daily labour, that he might relieve the sensations of his soul by bodily exertion. He performed his task in silence; and an inattentive observer might have thought him sullen.

In fact, he was impatient for the day to be over, that he might get rid of a heavy load which weighed upon his mind.

The cruelties practised by Durant, the overseer of Jefferies' plantation, had exasperated the slaves under his dominion.

They were all leagued together in a conspiracy, which was kept profoundly secret. Their object was to extirpate every white man, woman, and child in the island. Their plans were laid with consummate art; and the negroes were urged to execute them by all the courage of despair.

The confederacy extended to all the negroes in the island of Jamaica, excepting those on the plantation of Mr. Edwards. To them no hint of the dreadful secret had yet been given; their countrymen, knowing the attachment they felt to their master, dared not trust them with these projects of vengeance. Hector,[6] the negro who was at the head of the conspirators, was the particular friend of Caesar, and had imparted to him all his designs. These friends were bound to each other by the strongest ties. Their slavery and their sufferings began in the same hour: they were both brought from their own country in the same ship. This circumstance alone forms, amongst the negroes, a bond of connexion not easily to be dissolved. But the friendship of Caesar and Hector commenced even before they were united by the sympathy of misfortune; they were both of the same nation, both Koromantyns. In Africa, they had both been accustomed to command; for they had signalized themselves by superior fortitude and courage. They respected each other for excelling in all

[5] **Eboe:** an alternate spelling for Ibo, or Igbo, a people from what is now southeast Nigeria, an area controlled by the British under colonialism. **Koromantyn:** alternate spelling of Kormantin, an English slave trade port in present-day Ghana, established 1638.

[6] **Hector:** like Caesar, a classical name suggesting the heroic nobility of the character, even under slavery; Hector was the leader of the Trojan forces during the war against Greece.

which they had been taught to consider as virtuous: and with them revenge was a virtue!

Revenge was the ruling passion of Hector: in Caesar's mind, it was rather a principle instilled by education. The one considered it as a duty, the other felt it as a pleasure. Hector's sense of injury was acute in the extreme; he knew not how to forgive. Caesar's sensibility was yet more alive to kindness than to insult. Hector would sacrifice his life to extirpate an enemy. Caesar would devote himself for the defence of a friend; and Caesar now considered a white man as his friend.

He was now placed in a painful situation. All his former friendships, all the solemn promises, by which he was bound to his companions in misfortune, forbade him to indulge that delightful feeling of gratitude and affection, which, for the first time, he experienced for one of that race of beings whom he had hitherto considered as detestable tyrants! objects of implacable and just revenge!

Caesar was most impatient to have an interview with Hector, that he might communicate his new sentiments, and dissuade him from those schemes of destruction which he meditated. At midnight, when all the slaves except himself were asleep, he left his cottage, and went to Jefferies' plantation, to the hut in which Hector slept. Even in his dreams, Hector breathed vengeance. "Spare none! Sons of Africa, spare none!" were the words he uttered in his sleep, as Caesar approached the mat on which he lay. The moon shone full upon him. Caesar contemplated the countenance of his friend, fierce even in sleep. "Spare none! Oh, yes! There is one that must be spared. There is one for whose sake all must be spared!"

He wakened Hector by this exclamation: "Of what were you dreaming?" said Caesar.

"Of that which, sleeping or waking, fills my soul! Revenge! Why did you waken me from my dream? It was delightful! The whites were weltering in their blood! But, silence! We may be overheard!"

"No; every one sleeps, but ourselves," replied Caesar. "I could not sleep — without speaking to you on — a subject that weighs upon my mind. You have seen Mr. Edwards?"

"Yes. He that is now your master."

"He that is now my benefactor! My friend!"

"Friend! Can you call a white man friend?" cried Hector, starting up with a look of astonishment and indignation.

"Yes;" replied Caesar, with firmness. "And you would speak, ay, and would feel as I do, Hector, if you knew this white man! Oh, how unlike he is to all of his race, that we have ever seen! Do not turn from me with so much disdain! Hear me with patience, my friend!"

"I cannot," replied Hector, "listen with patience to one who, between the rising and the setting sun, can forget all his resolutions, all his promises! who, by a few soft words, can be so wrought upon as to forget all the insults, all the injuries he has received from this accursed race; and can even call a white man friend!"

Caesar, unmoved by Hector's anger, continued to speak of Mr. Edwards with the warmest expressions of gratitude; and finished by declaring he would sooner forfeit his life than rebel against such a master. He conjured Hector to desist from executing his designs; but all was in vain. Hector sat with his elbows fixed upon his knees, leaning his head upon his hands, in gloomy silence.

Caesar's mind was divided, between love for his friend and gratitude to his master: the conflict was violent and painful. Gratitude at last prevailed: he repeated his declaration, that he would rather die than continue in a conspiracy against his benefactor!

Hector refused to except him from the general doom. "Betray us if you will!" cried he. "Betray our secrets to him whom you call your benefactor: to him whom a few hours have made your friend! To him sacrifice the friend of your youth, the companion of your better days, of your better self! Yes, Caesar, deliver me over to the tormentors: I can endure more than they can inflict. I shall expire without a sigh, without a groan. Why do you linger here, Caesar? Why do you hesitate? Hasten this moment to your master; claim your reward for delivering into his power hundreds of your countrymen! Why do you hesitate? Away! The coward's friendship can be of use to none. Who can value his gratitude? Who can fear his revenge?"

Hector raised his voice so high, as he pronounced these words, that he wakened Durant, the overseer, who slept in the next house. They heard him call out suddenly, to inquire who was there; and Caesar had but just time to make his escape, before Durant appeared. He searched Hector's cottage; but, finding no one, again retired to rest. This man's tyranny made him constantly suspicious: he dreaded that the slaves should combine against him; and he endeavoured to prevent them, by every threat and every strategem he could devise, from conversing with each other.

They had, however, taken their measures, hitherto, so secretly, that he had not the slightest idea of the conspiracy which was forming in the island. Their schemes were not yet ripe for execution; but the appointed time approached. Hector, when he coolly reflected on what had passed between him and Caesar, could not help admiring the frankness and courage with which he had avowed his change of sentiments. By this avowal, Caesar had in fact exposed his own life to the most imminent danger, from the vengeance of the conspirators; who might be tempted to assassinate him who had their lives in his power. Notwithstanding the contempt with which, in the first moment of passion, he had treated his friend, he was extremely anxious that he should not break off all connexion with the conspirators. He knew that Caesar possessed both intrepidity and eloquence; and that his opposition to their schemes would perhaps entirely frustrate their whole design. He therefore determined to use every possible means to bend him to their purposes.

He resolved to have recourse to one of those persons who, amongst the negroes, are considered as sorceresses.[7] Esther, an old Koromantyn negress, had obtained by her skill in poisonous herbs, and her knowledge of venomous reptiles, a high reputation amongst her countrymen. She soon taught them to believe her to be possessed of supernatural powers; and she then worked their imagination to what pitch and purpose she pleased.

She was the chief instigator of this intended rebellion. It was she who had stimulated the revengeful temper of Hector almost to phrenzy. She now promised him that her arts should be exerted over his friend; and it was not

---

[7] The enlightened inhabitants of Europe may, perhaps, smile at the superstitious credulity of the negroes, who regard those ignorant beings called *Obeah* people, with the most profound respect and dread; who believe that they hold in their hands the power of good and evil fortune, of health and sickness, of life and death. The instances which are related of their power over the minds of their countrymen, are so wonderful that none but the most unquestionable authority could make us think them credible. The following passage, from Edwards' History of the West Indies, is inserted, to give an idea of this strange infatuation.

"In the year 1760, when a very formidable insurrection of the Koromantyn or Gold Coast negroes broke out, in the parish of St. Mary, and spread through almost every other district of the island, an old Koromantyn negro, the chief instigator and oracle of the insurgents in that parish, who had administered the fetish, or solemn oath, to the conspirators, and furnished them with a magical preparation, which was to render them invulnerable, was fortunately apprehended, convicted, and hung up, with all his feathers and trumperies about him; and his execution struck the insurgents with a general panic, from which they never afterwards recovered. The examinations, which were taken at that period, first opened the eyes of the public to the very dangerous tendency of the *Obeah* practices; and gave birth to the law, which was then enacted, for their suppression and punishment; but neither the terror of this law, the strict investigation which has since been made after the professors of *Obi*, nor the many examples of those who from time to time have been hanged or transported, have hitherto produced the desired effect. A gentleman, on his returning to Jamaica in the year 1775, found that a great many of his negroes had died during his absence; and that, of such as remained alive, at least one half were debilitated, bloated, and in a very deplorable condition. The mortality continued after his arrival: and two or three were frequently buried in one day; others were taken ill, and began to decline under the same symptoms. Every means were tried, by medicine and the most careful nursing, to preserve the lives of the feeblest; but, in spite of all his endeavours, this depopulation went on for a twelvemonth longer, with more or less intermission, and without his being able to ascertain the real cause; though the *Obeah* practice was strongly suspected, as well by himself as by the doctor, and other white persons upon the plantation; as it was known to have been very common in that part of the island, and particularly among the negroes of the *Popaw* or *Popo* country. Still, he was unable to verify his suspicions; because the patients constantly denied their having any thing to do with persons of that order, or any knowledge of them. At length, a negress, who had been ill for some time, came and informed him that, feeling it was impossible for her to live much longer, she thought herself bound in duty, before she died, to impart a very great secret, and acquaint him with the true cause of her disorder; in hopes that the disclosure might prove the means of stopping that mischief, which had already swept away such a number of her fellow slaves. She proceeded to say that her stepmother, a woman of the *Popo* country, above eighty years old, but still hale and active, had put *Obi upon her,* as she had upon those who had lately died: and that the old woman had practised *Obi* for as many years past as she could remember. The other negroes of the plantation no sooner heard of this impeachment than they ran in a body to their master, and confirmed the truth of it. Upon this he repaired directly, with six white servants, to the old woman's house; and, forcing open the door, observed the whole inside of the roof, which was of thatch, and every crevice of the wall, stuck with the implements of her trade; consisting of rags, feathers, bones of cats, and a thousand other articles. The house was instantly pulled down; and, with the whole of its contents, committed to the flames, amidst the general acclamations of all his other negroes. From the moment of her departure, his negroes seemed all to be animated with new spirits; and the malady spread no further among them. The total of his losses, in the course of about fifteen years preceding the discovery, and imputable solely to the *Obeah practice,* he estimates, at least, at one hundred negroes" [M. E.].

long before he felt their influence. Caesar soon perceived an extraordinary change in the countenance and manner of his beloved Clara. A melancholy hung over her, and she refused to impart to him the cause of her dejection. Caesar was indefatigable in his exertions to cultivate and embellish the ground near his cottage, in hopes of making it an agreeable habitation for her; but she seemed to take no interest in any thing. She would stand beside him immoveable, in a deep reverie; and, when he inquired whether she was ill, she would answer no, and endeavour to assume an air of gaiety: but this cheerfulnes was transient; she soon relapsed into despondency. At length, she endeavoured to avoid her lover; as if she feared his farther inquiries.

Unable to endure this state of suspense, he one evening, resolved to bring her to an explanation. "Clara," said he, "you once loved me: I have done nothing, have I, to forfeit your confidence?"

"I once loved you!" said she, raising her languid eyes, and looking at him with reproachful tenderness; "and can you doubt my constancy? Oh, Caesar, you little know what is passing in my heart! You are the cause of my melancholy!"

She paused, and hesitated; as if afraid that she had said too much: but Caesar urged her with so much vehemence, and so much tenderness, to open to him her whole soul, that, at last, she could not resist his eloquence. She reluctantly revealed to him that secret of which she could not think without horror. She informed him that, unless he complied with what was required of him by the sorceress Esther, he was devoted to die. What it was that Esther required of him Clara knew not: she knew nothing of the conspiracy. The timidity of her character was ill-suited to such a project; and every thing relating to it had been concealed from her with the utmost care.

When she explained to Caesar the cause of her dejection, his natural courage resisted these superstitious fears; and he endeavoured to raise Clara's spirits. He endeavoured in vain: she fell at his feet, and with tears, and the most tender supplications, conjured him to avert the wrath of the sorceress by obeying her commands whatever they might be!

"Clara," replied he, "you know not what you ask!"

"I ask you to save your life!" said she. "I ask you, for my sake, to save your life, while yet it is in your power!"

"But would you, to save my life, Clara, make me the worst of criminals? Would you make me the murderer of my benefactor?"

Clara started with horror!

"Do you recollect the day, the moment, when we were on the point of being separated for ever, Clara? Do you remember the white man's coming to my cottage? Do you remember his look of benevolence? his voice of compassion? Do you remember his generosity? Oh! Clara, would you make me the murderer of this man?"

"Heaven forbid!" said Clara. "This cannot be the will of the sorceress!"

"It is!" said Caesar. "But she shall not succeed, even though she speaks with the voice of Clara. Urge me no farther; my resolution is fixed. I should be unworthy of your love if I were capable of treachery and ingratitude."

"But, is there no means of averting the wrath of Esther?" said Clara. "Your life— "

"Think, first, of my honour," interrupted Caesar. "Your fears deprive you of reason. Return to this sorceress, and tell her that I dread not her wrath. My hands shall never be imbrued in the blood of my benefactor. Clara! Can you forget his look, when he told us that we should never more be separated?"

"It went to my heart," said Clara, bursting into tears. "Cruel, cruel Esther! Why do you command us to destroy such a generous master?"

The conch sounded to summon the negroes to their morning's work. It happened, this day, that Mr. Edwards, who was continually intent upon increasing the comforts and happiness of his slaves, sent his carpenter, while Caesar was absent, to fit up the inside of his cottage; and, when Caesar returned from work, he found his master pruning the branches of a tamarind tree, that overhung the thatch. "How comes it, Caesar," said he, "that you have not pruned these branches?"

Caesar had no knife. "Here is mine for you," said Mr. Edwards. "It is very sharp," added he, smiling; "but I am not one of those masters who are afraid to trust their negroes with sharp knives."

These words were spoken with perfect simplicity: Mr. Edwards had no suspicion, at this time, of what was passing in the negro's mind. Caesar received the knife without uttering a syllable; but no sooner was Mr. Edwards out of sight, than he knelt down, and, in a transport of gratitude, swore that, with this knife, he would stab himself to the heart, sooner than betray his master!

The principle of gratitude conquered every other sensation. The mind of Caesar was not insensible to the charms of freedom: he knew the negro conspirators had so taken their measures that there was the greatest probability of their success. His heart beat high at the idea of recovering his liberty; but he was not to be seduced from his duty, not even by this delightful hope; nor was he to be intimidated by the dreadful certainty that his former friends and countrymen, considering him as a deserter from their cause, would become his bitterest enemies. The loss of Hector's esteem and affection was deeply felt by Caesar. Since the night that the decisive conversation, relative to Mr. Edwards, passed, Hector and he had never exchanged a syllable.

This visit proved the cause of much suffering to Hector, and to several of the slaves on Jefferies' plantation. We mentioned that Durant had been awakened by the raised voice of Hector. Though he could not find any one in the cottage, yet his suspicions were not dissipated; and an accident nearly brought the whole conspiracy to light. Durant had ordered one of the negroes to watch a boiler of sugar: the slave was overcome by the heat, and fainted. He had scarcely recovered his senses when the overseer came up, and found that the sugar had fermented, by having remained a few minutes too long in the boiler. He flew into a violent passion, and ordered that the negro should receive fifty lashes. His victim bore them without uttering a groan; but, when his punishment was over, and when he thought the overseer was gone, he exclaimed, "It will soon be our turn!"

Durant was not out of hearing. He turned suddenly, and observed that the negro looked at Hector, when he pronounced these words; and this confirmed the suspicion that Hector was carrying on some conspiracy. He immediately had recourse to that brutality which he considered as the only means of governing black men: Hector and three other negroes were lashed unmercifully; but no confessions could be extorted.

Mr. Jefferies might perhaps have forbidden such violence to be used, if he had not been at the time carousing with a party of jovial West Indians; who thought of nothing but indulging their appetites in all the luxuries that art and nature could supply. The sufferings, which had been indured by many of the wretched negroes, to furnish out this magnificent entertainment, were never once thought of by these selfish epicures. Yet, so false are the general estimates of character, that all these gentlemen passed for men of great feeling and generosity! The human mind, in certain situations, becomes so accustomed to ideas of tyranny and cruelty, that they no longer appear extraordinary or detestable: they rather seem part of the necessary and immutable order of things.

Mr. Jefferies was stopped, as he passed from his dining-room into his drawing-room, by a little negro child, of about five years old, who was crying bitterly. He was the son of one of the slaves, who were at the moment under the torturer's hand. "Poor little devil!" said Mr. Jefferies, who was more than half intoxicated. "Take him away; and tell Durant, some of ye, to pardon his father—if he can."

The child ran, eagerly, to announce his father's pardon; but he soon returned, crying more violently than before. Durant would not hear the boy; and it was now no longer possible to appeal to Mr. Jefferies, for he was in the midst of an assembly of fair ladies; and no servant belonging to the house dared to interrupt the festivities of the evening. The three men, who were so severely flogged to extort from them confessions, were perfectly innocent: they knew nothing of the confederacy; but the rebels seized the moment when their minds were exasperated by this cruelty and injustice, and they easily persuaded them to join the league. The hopes of revenging themselves upon the overseer was a motive sufficient to make them brave death in any shape.

Another incident, which happened a few days before the time destined for the revolt of the slaves, determined numbers who had been undecided. Mrs. Jefferies was a languid beauty: or rather a languid fine lady who had been a beauty, and who spent all that part of the day which was not devoted to the pleasures of the table, or in reclining on a couch, in dress. She was one day extended on a sofa, fanned by four slaves, two at her head and two at her feet, when news was brought that a large chest, directed to her, was just arrived from London.

This chest contained various articles of dress of the newest fashions. The Jamaica ladies carry their ideas of magnificence to a high pitch: they willingly give a hundred guineas for a gown, which they perhaps wear but once or twice. In the elegance and variety of her ornaments, Mrs. Jefferies was not exceeded by any lady in the island, except by one who had lately received a cargo from England. She now expected to outshine her competitor, and desired that the chest should be unpacked in her presence.

In taking out one of the gowns, it caught on a nail in the lid, and was torn. The lady, roused from her natural indolence by this disappointment to her vanity, instantly ordered that the unfortunate female slave should be severely chastised. The woman was the wife of Hector; and this fresh injury worked up his temper, naturally vindictive, to the highest point. He ardently longed for the moment when he might satiate his vengeance.

The plan the negroes had laid was to set fire to the canes, at one and the same time, on every plantation; and, when the white inhabitants of the island should run to put out the fire, the blacks were to seize this moment of confusion and consternation to fall upon them, and make a general massacre. The time when this scheme was to be carried into execution was not known to Caesar; for the conspirators had changed their day, as soon as Hector told them that his friend was no longer one of the confederacy. They dreaded he should betray them; and it was determined that he and Clara should both be destroyed, unless they could be prevailed upon to join the conspiracy.

Hector wished to save his friend; but the desire of vengeance overcame every other feeling. He resolved, however, to make an attempt, for the last time, to change Caesar's resolution.

For this purpose, Esther was the person he employed: she was to work upon his mind by means of Clara. On returning to her cottage one night, she found, suspended from the thatch, one of those strange fantastic charms, with which the Indian sorceresses terrify those whom they have proscribed. Clara, unable to conquer her terror, repaired again to Esther, who received her first in mysterious silence; but, after she had implored her forgiveness for the past, and with all possible humility conjured her to grant her future protection, the sorceress deigned to speak. Her commands were that Clara should prevail upon her lover to meet her, on this awful spot, the ensuing night.

Little suspecting what was going forward on the plantation of Jefferies, Mr. Edwards that evening gave his slaves a holiday. He and his family came out at sunset, when the fresh breeze had sprung up, and seated themselves under a spreading palm-tree, to enjoy the pleasing spectacle of this negro festival. His negroes were all well clad, their turbans were of the gayest colours, and their merry countenances suited the gaiety of their dress. While some were dancing, and some playing on the tambourine, others appeared amongst the distant trees, bringing baskets of avocado pears, grapes, and pineapples, the produce of their own provision-grounds; and others were employed in spreading their clean trenchers, or the calabashes, which served for plates and dishes. The negroes continued to dance and divert themselves till late in the evening. When they separated and retired to rest, Caesar, recollecting his promise to Clara, repaired secretly to the habitation of the sorceress. It was situated in the recess of a thick wood. When he arrived there, he found the door fastened; and he was obliged to wait some time before it was opened by Esther.

The first object he beheld was his beloved Clara, stretched on the ground, apparently a corpse! The sorceress had thrown her into a trance, by a preparation of deadly nightshade. The hag burst into an infernal laugh, when she beheld the despair that was painted in Caesar's countenance! — "Wretch!" cried she; "you have defied my power: behold its victim!"

Caesar, in a transport of rage, seized her by the throat: but his fury was soon checked.

"Destroy me," said the fiend, "and you destroy your Clara. She is not dead; but she lies in the sleep of death, into which she has been thrown by magic art, and from which no power, but mine, can restore her to the light of life. Yes! look at her, pale and motionless! Never will she rise from the earth, unless, within one hour, you obey my commands. I have administered to Hector and his companions the solemn fetish oath, at the sound of which every negro in Africa trembles! You know my object."

"Fiend, I do!" replied Caesar, eyeing her sternly; "but, while I have life, it shall never be accomplished."

"Look yonder!" cried she, pointing to the moon; "in a few minutes that moon will set: at that hour Hector and his friends will appear. They come armed! armed with weapons which I shall steep in poison for their enemies. Themselves I will render invulnerable. Look again!" continued she, "if my dim eyes mistake not, yonder they come. Rash man, you die if they cross my threshold."

"I wish for death," said Caesar. "Clara is dead!"

"But you can restore her to life by a single word."

Caesar, at this moment, seemed to hesitate.

"Consider! Your heroism is vain," continued Esther. "You will have the knives of fifty of the conspirators in your bosom, if you do not join them; and, after you have fallen, the death of your master is inevitable. Here is the bowl of poison, in which the negro knives are to be steeped. Your friends, your former friends, your countrymen, will be in arms in a few minutes; and they will bear down every thing before them! Victory! Wealth! Freedom! and Revenge! will be theirs!"

Caesar appeared to be more and more agitated. His eyes were fixed upon Clara. The conflict in his mind was violent; but his sense of gratitude and duty could not be shaken by hope, fear, or ambition: nor could it be vanquished by love. He determined, however, to appear to yield. As if struck with panic, at the approach of the confederate negroes, he suddenly turned to the sorceress, and said, in a tone of feigned submission, "It is in vain to struggle with fate. Let my knife, too, be dipped in your magic poison."

The sorceress clapped her hands, with infernal joy in her countenance. She bade him instantly give her his knife, that she might plunge it to the hilt in the bowl of poison; to which she turned with savage impatience. His knife was left in his cottage; and, under pretence of going in search of it, he escaped. Esther promised to prepare Hector, and all his companions, to receive him with their ancient cordiality, on his return. Caesar ran with the utmost speed along a by-path out of the wood, met none of the rebels, reached his master's house, scaled the wall of his bed-chamber, got in at the window, and wakened him, exclaiming, "Arm! Arm yourself, my dear master! Arm all your slaves! They will fight for you, and die for you; as I will the first. The Koromantyn yell of war will be heard in Jefferies' plantation this night! Arm! Arm yourself, my dear master, and let us surround the rebel leaders while it is yet time. I will lead you to the place where they are all assembled, on condition that their chief, who is my friend, shall be pardoned."

Mr. Edwards armed himself and the negroes on his plantation, as well as the whites: they were all equally attached to him. He followed Caesar into the recesses of the wood.

They proceeded with all possible rapidity, but in perfect silence, till they reached Esther's habitation; which they surrounded completely, before they were perceived by the conspirators.

Mr. Edwards looked through a hole in the wall; and, by the blue flame of a caldron, over which the sorceress was stretching her shrivelled hands, he saw Hector and five stout negroes standing, intent upon her incantations. These negroes held their knives in their hands, ready to dip them into the bowl of poison. It was proposed, by one of the whites, to set fire immediately to the hut; and thus to force the rebels to surrender. The advice was followed; but Mr. Edwards charged his people to spare their prisoners. The moment the rebels saw that the thatch of the hut was in flames, they set up the Koromantyn yell of war, and rushed out with frantic desperation.

"Yield! You are pardoned, Hector," cried Mr. Edwards, in a loud voice.

"You are pardoned, my friend!" repeated Caesar.

Hector, incapable at this instant of listening to any thing but revenge, sprang forwards, and plunged his knife into the bosom of Caesar. The faithful servant staggered back a few paces: his master caught him in his arms. "I die content," said he. "Bury me with Clara."

He swooned from loss of blood, as they were carrying him home; but, when his wound was examined, it was found not to be mortal. As he recovered from his swoon, he stared wildly round him, trying to recollect where he was, and what had happened. He thought that he was still in a dream, when he saw his beloved Clara standing beside him. The opiate, which the pretended sorceress had administered to her, had ceased to operate; she wakened from her trance just at the time the Koromantyn yell commenced. Caesar's joy!—We must leave that to the imagination.

In the mean time, what became of the rebel negroes, and Mr. Edwards?

The taking the chief conspirators prisoners did not prevent the negroes, upon Jefferies' plantation, from insurrection. The moment they heard the war-whoop, the signal agreed upon, they rose in a body; and, before they could be prevented, either by the whites on the estate, or by Mr. Edwards's adherents, they had set fire to the overseer's house, and to the canes. The overseer was the principal object of their vengeance: he died in tortures, inflicted by the hands of those who had suffered most by his cruelties. Mr. Edwards, however, quelled the insurgents before rebellion spread to any other estates in the island. The influence of his character, and the effect of his eloquence upon the minds of the people, were astonishing: nothing but his interference could have prevented the total destruction of Mr. Jefferies and his family, who, as it was computed, lost this night upwards of fifty thousand pounds. He was never afterward able to recover his losses, or to shake off his constant fear of a fresh insurrection among his slaves. At length, he and his lady returned to England; where they were obliged to live in obscurity and indigence. They had no consolation, in their misfortunes, but that of railing at the treachery of the whole race of slaves.—Our readers, we hope, will think that at least one exception may be made, in favour of THE GRATEFUL NEGRO.

AMELIA ALDERSON OPIE

(1769–1853)

A close friend of Mary Wollstonecraft,* William Godwin* (who without success proposed to her), Elizabeth Inchbald, and Thomas Holcroft, Amelia Alderson imbibed her republican, pro-Jacobin principles from her father, the Dissenting Unitarian minister James Alderson, M.D. After her mother's death in 1784, Amelia at 15 took over the running of her father's busy, elegant social circle at Lowestoft, in Norwich, where she was encouraged to write poetry and dramatic pieces for recitation. In 1794, she attended Horne Tooke's trial for sedition in London, sitting on the anti-government side. In May 1798, she married the ambitious, successful portrait painter John Opie and moved to London, where she began her writing career in earnest. She specialized in what she called "Tales," novellas which explored the difficulties of contemporary women's lives from a distinctively feminist viewpoint. Her most famous and widely reprinted tale, *The Father and Daughter* (1801), challenged her society's conception of the guilt and irredeemable condition of the "fallen woman." In her most popular novel, *Adeline Mowbray* (1804), she drew on the life and writings of Wollstonecraft, Godwin, and Mary Hays to explore in depth and with great complexity the options available to a woman who does not wish, in principle, to marry yet at the same time experiences passionate love and sexual desire. The ending of this revolutionary novel suggests that an all-female, interracial, and mixed-class "family of choice" may be a preferable alternative to the traditional patriarchal family. Her *Simple Tales,* in four volumes, appeared in 1806; *Tales of Real Life,* in three volumes, in 1813; *New Tales,* in four volumes, in 1818; and *Tales of the Heart* in 1820. She published three volumes of poetry: *Poems* in 1802; *The Warrior's Return and Other Poems,* 1808; and *Lays of the Dead* in 1833; as well as several novels, most notably *Valentine's Eve* (1816).

After her husband's death in 1807, Amelia Opie returned to Norwich, where she nursed her ailing father until his death in 1825. Here she became increasingly friendly with the Quaker family of Joseph John Gurney; in 1825, she was formally received into the Society of Friends and as a matter of principle gave up writing fiction, refusing to finish her half-written tale, *The Painter and his Wife,* for which she had been promised a thousand pounds. As she wrote to Gurney's sister, Mrs. Fry, on 6 December 1823, "I have *felt* the sacrifice but I do not *repent* of it." Amelia Opie devoted the remainder of her life to charitable activities, working to reform the management of workhouses, prisons, and hospitals, and ministering to the poor. She confined her writing to religious and moral tracts: *Illustrations of Lying in all its Branches* appeared in 1825, *Detraction Displayed* in 1828. She ardently opposed the slave trade, joining the Anti-Slavery Society in Norwich, campaigning vigorously for abolition, and attending the anti-slavery convention in London in 1840 as the delegate from Norwich (she appears in Benjamin Haydon's painting of the delegates, now in the National Portrait Gallery in London). Her first widely reprinted and influential abolitionist poem, "The Negro Boy's Tale," appeared in 1802, her second, "The Black Man's Lament, or How to Make Sugar" in 1826. (See SLAVERY, THE SLAVE TRADE, AND ABOLITION.)

Widely admired for her vivacity, sense of humor, unfailing benevolence, and physical vigor, Amelia Opie lived to be 84, the center of a wide circle of admiring literary and Quaker friends.

from POEMS
(1802)

Consumption

Consumption,[1] fairest of Death's craving brood!
But, ah! most treacherous too! thou smiling fate,
Hence! I conjure thee, hence from those I love!
For on the heart's best feelings thou canst play
A dread variety of hopes and fears.
Thy flattering hand paints the poor victim's cheek
With roses emulous of health's rich glow,
And to the sinking eye such lustre gives
As fills the eager glance of joy and love.
Thy long-devoted prey by thee is decked
With bright attractions ne'er till then its own,
As victims were of old with flowers adorned
Before they bled in pagan sacrifice: . . . .
And as the schoolboy, whose expected sport
Adown some favourite stream or well-known walk
Thick gathering clouds and falling rains prevent,
If he of sunshine see one partial beam,
Fancies (fond dreamer!) general splendor near, . . .
So anxious friends thy beauteous seemings watch,
As o'er thy victim's restless couch they hang,
And hail them pledges that all danger's past; . . .
Pledges as sure as to the Patriarch's eye
Was the bright arch of ever-mingling hues:
But, in that very moment, (treacherous power!)
Upon security Death softly steals,
And on thy conquest lays his icy hand,
Smiling amidst the beauty thou hast made.

Ye who have watched beside a fading friend,
Unconscious that the cheek's luxuriant red
Bloomed like the nightshade[2] with unwholesome
 beauty,
And that the bright dilated eye but owed,
Like mouldering wood, its lustre to decay, ...
Ye who have wept, then smiled amidst your tears,
And checked forebodings which ill-founded
 seemed, . . .
Ye who have hoped even in death's dread presence,
And then been summoned, O heart-freezing call!
Affection's last sad duties to perform,
And hear upon the narrow dwelling's lid
The first earth thrown, (sound deadliest to the soul! . . .
For, strange delusion! then, and then alone,
Hope seems for ever fled, and separation,
The final separation, to begin) . . . .
Ye who have felt all this . . . . will on my verse
Drop, as you read, a sympathetic tear,
And, sighing, own the mournful picture just.

[1] **consumption:** common older name for tuberculosis of the lungs, a contagious, wasting disease common in Europe and America up to the mid-twentieth century.

[2] **nightshade:** deadly nightshade or belladonna, a plant with purplish red, bell-shaped flowers and small black poisonous berries, traditionally used in cosmetics to artificially dilate the pupils of the eye.

The Orphan Boy's Tale
(1802)

Stay, lady, stay, for mercy's sake,
And hear a helpless orphan's tale!
Ah! sure my looks must pity wake, . . .
'Tis want that makes my cheek so pale.
Yet I was once a mother's pride,
And my brave father's hope and joy;
But in the Nile's proud fight[1] he died,
And I am now an ORPHAN BOY.
Poor foolish child! how pleased was I,
When news of Nelson's victory came,
Along the crowded streets to fly
And see the lighted windows flame!
To force me home my mother sought;
She could not bear to see my joy;
For with my father's life 'twas bought,
And made me a poor ORPHAN BOY.

The people's shouts were long and loud;
My mother, shuddering, closed her ears;
'Rejoice! rejoice!' still cried the crowd;
My mother answered with her tears.
'Why are you crying thus,' said I,
'While others laugh and shout with joy?'

[1] **Nile's proud fight:** the British naval victory over the French fleet at Abu Qir (in the Nile River delta) in August 1798, also called the Battle of the Nile. The British forces were under the command of Admiral Horatio Nelson (1758–1805).

She kissed me, ... and, with such a sigh!
She called me her poor Orphan Boy.
'What is an orphan boy?' I said, ...
When suddenly she gasped for breath,
And her eyes closed; . . . . I shrieked for aid, ...
But, ah! her eyes were closed in death.
My hardships since I will not tell:
But, now no more a parent's joy,
Ah! lady, ... I have learnt too well
What 'tis to be an Orphan Boy.

Oh! were I by your bounty fed!
Nay, gentle lady, do not chide, ...
Trust me, I mean to earn my bread;
The sailor's orphan boy has pride.
Lady, you weep! . . . . Ha? . . . . this to me?
You'll give me clothing, food, employ? . . . .
Look down, dear parents! look, and see
Your happy happy Orphan Boy.

Lines Respectfully Inscribed to the Society for the Relief of Persons Imprisoned for Small Debts

(1802)

What are the deeds that fill the historic page,
And most the plaudits of the world engage?
What actions most attract the eyes of Fame,
And from her voice the loudest paeans claim?
The conqueror's deeds, ... the awful works of death, . . .
For them the trophied bust, the flatterer's breath.
He, he alone a nation's praise enjoys,
Whose noble daring dazzles, but destroys;
While the blest deeds performed by Pity's hand
Nor praise nor notice from the world command:
Her useful charities to virtue dear,
Lost in the blaze of victories, disappear;
E'en the blest Howard's, long the boast of fame,
To Abercrombie's[1] shines a second name.
So, when the traveller various countries seeks,
Not the smooth-flowing stream his praise bespeaks,
Which, as it humbly fills its narrow bound,
Diffuses verdure, plenty, health, around:
Unseen by him, perhaps, its waters glide;
He seeks the foaming cataract's lofty tide;
And while, creating wonder, awe, delight,
The frantic torrent sparkles to the sight,
He sees, admiring, the dread flood expand
That scatters waste and havoc o'er the land.

But though I Valour's offspring love to praise,
To Pity's humbler sons shall flow my lays.[2]
To me the warrior's brightest wreath appears
Steeped in the orphan's, parent's, widow's, tears.
More blest, to me, one deed of Christian love,
Than all the feats which British prowess prove:
More dear than e'en our greatest chief, to me,
Are those combined to set the debtor free, ...
Those who the victim of misfortune's hour
To useful labour, and his home, restore, ...
Snatch him from indolence, from noxious air,
From vile associates, from his own despair,
Destructive habits, misery's baleful gloom,
An useless life, and an untimely tomb.

Blest men! to you, howe'er you shrink from fame,
Belongs the patriot's prostituted name.
If Rome to him a civic garland gave,
Who of one citizen the life could save,
What should your grateful country give to you?
What to your patriot services is due?
From you Society true aid derives;
Your timely bounty saves unnumbered lives;
You countless children to her breast restore;
Your soothing kindness makes the murmuring poor
Their rage at fortune's partial smiles repress, ...
Since wealth in you appears the power to bless.
But what on you could public praise bestow?
From your own hearts your best reward must flow:
And when, by fashion led, you chance to stray
Where busy triflers bow to Pleasure's sway,
As the phosphoric flame, though always bright,
Shines in pure air with most refulgent light, ...

[1] **Howard:** John Howard (1726–1790), English humanitarian prison reformer. **Abercrombie:** probably Sir Ralph Abercromby (1734–1801), British general who was a victorious commander in chief in the West Indies from 1795 to 1797 and led the successful land campaign against Napoleon in Egypt in 1801.

[2] **lays:** short lyric poems or songs.

So still for you, to whose benignant hearts
The sense of conscious worth pure joy imparts,
Pleasure's bright rose shall seem fresh sweets to shed,
And its soft blush assume a livelier red.

But hail to all who others' sufferings feel,
And ills they pity nobly strive to heal!
Whether they rear the felon's orphan child,
Or sooth the stranger from his home exiled,
Or helpless foundlings to their care receive,
Or bid the captive debtor cease to grieve, ...
Or, urged by justice to the virtuous deed,
The cause of Afric's injured offspring plead; . . . .
Theirs is the greatest bliss on earth we find;
Bliss nought can harm . . . . a self-approving mind:
And when around them death's dark night shall
 gloom,
Theirs be the day that beams beyond the tomb!

WILLIAM WORDSWORTH

(1770–1850)

In countering the skepticism of a friend on the poetic genius of then unknown William Wordsworth, Samuel Taylor Coleridge* remarked in 1797 that Wordsworth "strides so far before you, he dwindles in the distance." He risked a further comparison: "since Milton no man has *manifested* himself equal to him." Eighty years later, the Victorian poet-critic Matthew Arnold assessed the poetry of what he called Wordsworth's Great Decade (1797–1807) as second in importance only to Shakespeare and Milton. Such estimations have generally held.

William Wordsworth was born 7 April 1770 to a middle-class family of Cockermouth, a northern market town in the English Lake District. William was the second eldest of four boys; junior to him by twenty months was his only sister and lifelong companion, Dorothy. They recalled having a divine childhood in their rustic environs of hills, valleys, lakes, and shepherds' farms, until their mother's death in 1778. Their father then sent William to a grammar school in a neighboring village of Hawkshead, where he boarded with villagers, and sent Dorothy to live with relatives in the midlands of England. The separation between Dorothy and her brothers was to last ten years.

Following grammar school, William attended Cambridge University with the financial assistance of uncles, but his academic performance was a disappointment. Feeling that he "was not for that hour / Nor for that place" (*Prelude* III), young Wordsworth succumbed to the distractions of the French Revolution and British debate over French politics. Rather than studying for comprehensive exams the summer prior to his senior year, Wordsworth joined the troop of British adventurers touring Revolutionary France in 1790. He witnessed the first anniversary of Bastille Day as a citizen of the world: "'twas a time when Europe was rejoiced, / France standing on the top of golden hours, / And human nature seeming born again" (*Prelude* VI). After graduating, Wordsworth returned to France, where his life became complicated with political and sexual romance.

Michel Beaupuy, a nobleman-general in the thirty-second regiment of the revolutionary army, and Annette Vallon, a twenty-four-year-old woman from a royalist family, provided the poles for Wordsworth's revolutionary education. While Beaupuy held heady conversations with Wordsworth about shaping a new world order on republican principles, Wordsworth's love for Annette Vallon led to fatherhood. Meantime, the leaders of France's infant republic were growing paranoid over counterrevolutionary forces. The "land wax'd mad," Wordsworth recalls, and the September massacres of 1792 commenced. Thousands of heads rolled off the block in Paris and provincial towns in a spree of political cleansing. In October Wordsworth left France to make arrangements for domesticating in England, but a declaration of war between his homeland and France in February 1793 prevented his return. His daughter, Anne-Caroline, had been born to Annette in December 1792.

The next few years of Wordsworth's life are tantalizingly obscure. Biographical speculation pictures a distressed young man haunting London's radical circles, perhaps risking his safety in editing a journal sympathetic to Jacobin ideals, perhaps risking a return to France the winter of 1793 to be with Annette and their child. Wordsworth admits to having a mental breakdown of sorts over the war, the dire course of events in France, his shattered ideals, and remorse for his love affair. In 1795, after inheriting £900 from a tubercular friend he had nursed, Wordsworth established a household with Dorothy in the West Country of England, where he might convalesce and write. In June 1797, poet Samuel Taylor Coleridge entered the Wordsworths' lives like a whirlwind to transform an able but derivative poet into a confident visionary. The Wordsworths moved from Racedown to Alfoxden, a gentleman's estate in the vicinity of Coleridge's residence, to be nearer his vital inspiration.

Rightly described as a creative symbiosis, the relationship of Wordsworth and Coleridge stimulated a poetic dialogue of radical originality. *Lyrical Ballads* (1798) contained the first fruits. Although Coleridge's chief contributions to the volume—*The Rime of the Ancyent Marinere* and "The Nightingale"—are hardly negligible, Wordsworth's nature lyrics, his ballads of social concern, and *Lines Written a Few Miles above Tintern Abbey* were the poems in which contemporaries felt "the spirit of the age" (Hazlitt*). However, just as Coleridge's meddlesome Man from Porlock ruined the poetic vision of "Kubla Khan" (cf. "Of the Fragment of Kubla Khan"*), so neighborhood politics ruined this creative moment. The friends had invited one radical too many, specifically the notorious John Thelwall,* to visit a neighborhood wrought with anxiety over a French invasion via the Bristol Channel. They were spied upon by government agents, and their distressed landlord refused to renew their lease. This *annus mirabilis* of poetic achievement ended in late summer 1798 with the composition of *Lines Written a Few Miles above Tintern Abbey, On Revisiting the Banks of the Wye during A Tour, July 13, 1798.* Dorothy was the poet's companion on this eventful walking tour, dated, some believe intentionally, to recall the fall of the Bastille on 14 July 1789 and related biographical matter.

The Wordsworths now consented to accompany Coleridge on an educational venture to Germany, where they would prepare to become capable translators of German literature for a lucrative English market, and where Coleridge might study philosophy and natural science. Out of economic necessity, the friends separated shortly after arriving in Germany. William and Dorothy moved to Goslar, an inexpensive, but isolated and culturally vacant, village in the Harz Mountains, where they lived reclusively through the coldest winter of the century, and Coleridge departed for the more exciting intellectual and social life of university towns.

Having ample time to brood upon the ambitious poetic plans that he and Coleridge had dreamed about, but which he felt incapable of working on independently, Wordsworth wrote some depressing lyrics on the loss of loved ones (the Matthew and the Lucy poems) and began an experimental autobiography to prove to himself that he had been chosen from childhood to be a great poet. Wordsworth developed a formal innovation which he called a "Spot of Time," an epiphany that rises from a precise description of mundane experience to a psychological moment of visionary insight. Composed and revised obsessively over the next thirty years, *The Prelude; or, Growth of a Poet's Mind* (1850) as the autobiography came to be called, weaves such moments into a "meditative history" of imagination's development from "the twilight of memorable life" to the visionary experiences of manhood.

Shortly after returning to England in 1799, the Wordsworths settled in Grasmere, a lakeside village nestled among the hills of the Lake District. William published the second edition of *Lyrical Ballads* in two volumes within a year. It includes the great lyrics written in Germany and several important narrative poems, especially *Michael,* which celebrate the political and moral values of rustic life in northern England. The second edition also contains a preface which synthesizes current psychological, cultural, aesthetic, and political thought into a poetic manifesto arguing for a new poetic diction—"the language really used by men"; a new psychology of poetic creation—"all good poetry is the spontaneous overflow of powerful feelings in a mind that has thought long and deeply"; and an exalted representational status for the poet as a "man talking to men."

Wordsworth's most prolific period now commenced. His sense of poetic mission clarified. In a "spousal" verse "Speaking of nothing more than what we are," he planned to show, "How exquisitely the individual Mind / . . . to the external world / Is fitted; and how exquisitely too / . . . / The external world is fitted to the mind; / And the creation . . . / . . . which they with blended might / Accomplish: this is my great argument" ("Prospectus" to *The Recluse*). Wordsworth also spoke out in patriotic sonnets during this still tumultuous and dangerous political time. Seeking to arouse his countrymen to withstand the real threat of Napoleon's forces to England, Wordsworth chided—"The world is too much with us"; he appealed to national pride—"We must be free or die, who speak the tongue / That Shakespeare spake; the faith and morals hold / Which Milton held"; he belittled the enemy as sycophants kneeling at their tyrant's throne—"Ye Men of prostrate mind!"; with the model of Milton on his mind, he called out for strength—"Milton! thou shoulds't be living at this hour: / England hath need of thee"; he enlisted in the Grasmere volunteers and announced an imagined victory, should French forces be foolish enough to invade—"The breath of Heaven has drifted them like snow, / And left them lying in the silent sun, / Never to rise again!"

During a short-lived peace between England and France in 1802, Wordsworth visited with Annette Vallon and Caroline to separate honorably and amicably before marrying the woman he now loved, Mary Hutchinson. Wordsworth became beset with vocational anxiety. Nature was losing its inspirational value. "Whither is fled the visionary gleam / Where is it now, the glory and the dream?" he asked at the conclusion of a modest, short poem in 1802. Unhappily married and in a funk over his own vocational doldrums, Coleridge felt compelled to respond. Understanding too well the dependence of poetic inspiration upon an inner state or condition of joy, Coleridge took the occasion to relate the wedding metaphor of Wordsworth's epic project to a truth and warning about intimate relationships: "Ours is her [nature's] wedding garment / Ours her shroud," Coleridge argues in *Dejection: An Ode,* by which he meant that the inspiration Wordsworth had once received from nature was but a projection of his own joy, which apparently had passed. The latter seven stanzas of *Ode,* later entitled *Ode: Intimations of Immortality from Recollections of Early Childhood,* became Wordsworth's response to Coleridge's challenge to creative longevity. While Wordsworth's *Ode* contains wonderful and famous passages of poetry and is arguably the greatest short poem of the nineteenth century, its argument is singular: memories of vertiginous psychological experiences of childhood are now reinterpreted by the poet as "intimations" of "immortality," and thus, he need not regret the loss of nature's inspiration and spiritual meaning. The poet's next crisis tested this newly discovered "faith that looks through death." Recollecting the forgetting of immortal moments could not lessen Wordsworth's grief over the death of his mariner brother John, who went down with his vessel during a violent storm off the coast of England in 1805. The poems that conclude Wordsworth's Great Decade bring to a full circle the formal and thematic experiments of *Lyrical Ballads.* In ironic contrast with the credal lyrics of his youth, the poet now sings a dirge in "Elegiac

Stanzas" for the loss of his early hallowing of nature with "the light that never was on sea or land." Companion poems, "The Solitary Reaper," "Stepping Westward," and *Ode to Duty*, describe the poet's discovery of an alternative solace now heard, sometimes by chance, in the human voice.

Wordsworth lived for 43 years beyond his "great decade." With the publication of his long philosophical poem, *The Excursion* (1814), Wordsworth's poetic reputation solidified. Acquisition of a government sinecure as Collector of Stamps in 1813, an intermittent but influential voice on issues and elections of national importance, and appointment as the nation's poet laureate in 1843, indicate that Wordsworth achieved the national stature he sought as a younger man. However, his apostasy to liberalism and his position on reform were disappointing to youthful admirers. In "To Wordsworth," Percy Shelley* grieves over a poet who no longer sang in "honoured poverty . . . / Songs consecrate to truth and liberty." Upon Wordsworth's death, the *Democratic Review* bluntly encouraged no tears for a "salaried slave of Aristocracy and pensioned parasite of monarchy." Charles Dickens's obituary in *Household Words* denounced Wordsworth's poetry as irrelevant to the urgent social concerns of mid-century England.

But while Wordsworth's reputation once suffered for political reasons, today it could not be higher. To paraphrase a comment from the Preface to *Lyrical Ballads*, Wordsworth's poetry successfully created the taste by which it is now judged.

from EUROPEAN MAGAZINE

Sonnet on Seeing Miss Helen Maria Williams Weep at a Tale of Distress[1]

(1787; comp. 1787)

She wept.—Life's purple tide began to flow
In languid streams through every thrilling vein;
Dim were my swimming eyes—my pulse beat slow,
And my full heart was swelled to dear delicious pain.
Life left my loaded heart, and closing eye;
A sigh recalled the wanderer to my breast;
Dear was the pause of life, and dear the sigh
That called the wanderer home, and home to rest.
That tear proclaims—in thee each virtue dwells,
And bright will shine in misery's midnight hour;
As the soft star of dewy evening tells
What radiant fires were drowned by day's malignant
power,
That only wait the darkness of the night
To cheer the wandering wretch with hospitable light.

[1] Wordsworth's first published poem. Appeared in the *European Magazine*, March 1787, over the name Axiologus, which translates "Words-Worth." See Helen Maria Williams.*

from LYRICAL BALLADS[1]

with A Few Other Poems
(1798, 1800)

Lines Written at a Small Distance from My House, and Sent by My Little Boy to the Person to whom They Are Addressed[2]

(1798; comp. 1798)

It is the first mild day of March:
Each minute sweeter than before,
The red-breast sings from the tall larch
That stands beside our door.

There is a blessing in the air,
Which seems a sense of joy to yield
To the bare trees, and mountains bare,
And grass in the green field.

My Sister! ('tis a wish of mine)
Now that our morning meal is done,
Make haste, your morning task resign;
Come forth and feel the sun.

Edward will come with you, and pray,
Put on with speed your woodland dress,
And bring no book, for this one day
We'll give to idleness.

No joyless forms shall regulate
Our living Calendar:
We from to-day, my friend, will date
The opening of the year.

Love, now an universal birth,
From heart to heart is stealing,
From earth to man, from man to earth,
—It is the hour of feeling.

One moment now may give us more
Than fifty years of reason;[3]
Our minds shall drink at every pore
The spirit of the season.

Some silent laws our hearts may make,
Which they shall long obey;
We for the year to come may take
Our temper from to-day.

And from the blessed power that rolls
About, below, above;
We'll frame the measure of our souls,
They shall be tuned to love.

Then come, my sister! come, I pray,
With speed put on your woodland dress,
And bring no book; for this one day
We'll give to idleness.

Simon Lee, the Old Huntsman, with an Incident in Which He Was Concerned

(1798; comp. 1798)

In the sweet shire of Cardigan,[1]
Not far from pleasant Ivor-hall,
An old man dwells, a little man,
I've heard he once was tall.
Of years he has upon his back,

---

[1] Published anonymously by Wordsworth and Samuel Taylor Coleridge in 1798. The edition of 1798 included 23 poems, four of which were Coleridge's—*Rime of the Ancyent Marinere,* which opened the volume; "The Foster Mother's Tale"; "The Dungeon"; and "The Nightingale, a Conversational Poem." In the "Advertisement" to *1798,* Wordsworth wrote that "The majority of the following poems are to be considered as experiments. They were written chiefly with a view to ascertain how far the language of conversation in the middle and lower classes is adapted to the purposes of poetic pleasure." He also requested that the reader not let "pre-established codes of decision" interfere with the pleasure the experimental poems might impart. The two-volume edition of 1800 included an additional 37 poems, all except one of which were Wordsworth's. Coleridge's "Love" replaced Wordsworth's "The Convict" from the first edition.

[2] The little boy of the title is Basil Montague, Wordsworth's ward at Alfoxden. Also, see note 1 to "The Thorn." The "Person . . . addressed" is the poet's sister, Dorothy Wordsworth. The poem was later given the short title, "To My Sister."

[3] **Than fifty . . . reason:** "Than years of toiling reason": later variant.

[1] Cardigan is in central Wales.

No doubt, a burthen weighty;
He says he is three score and ten,
But others say he's eighty.

A long blue livery-coat[2] has he,
That's fair behind, and fair before;
Yet, meet him where you will, you see
At once that he is poor.
Full five and twenty years he lived
A running huntsman merry;
And, though he has but one eye left,
His cheek is like a cherry.

No man like him the horn could sound,
And no man was so full of glee;
To say the least, four counties round
Had heard of Simon Lee;
His master's dead; and no one now
Dwells in the hall of Ivor;
Men, dogs, and horses, all are dead;
He is the sole survivor.

His hunting feats have him bereft
Of his right eye, as you may see:
And then, what limbs those feats have left
To poor old Simon Lee!
He has no son, he has no child,
His wife, an aged woman,
Lives with him, near the waterfall,
Upon the village common.

And he is lean and he is sick,
His little body's half awry,
His ancles they are swoln and thick;
His legs are thin and dry.
When he was young he little knew
Of husbandry or tillage;
And now he's forced to work, though weak,
—The weakest in the village.

He all the country could outrun,
Could leave both man and horse behind;
And often, ere the race was done,
He reeled and was stone-blind.
And still there's something in the world
At which his heart rejoices;
For when the chiming hounds are out,
He dearly loves their voices!

Old Ruth works out of doors with him,
And does what Simon cannot do;
For she, not over stout of limb,
Is stouter of the two.
And though you with your utmost skill
From labour could not wean them,
Alas! 'tis very little, all
Which they can do between them.

Beside their moss-grown hut of clay,
Not twenty paces from the door,
A scrap of land they have, but they
Are poorest of the poor.
This scrap of land he from the heath
Enclosed when he was stronger;
But what avails the land to them,
Which they can till no longer?

Few months of life has he in store,
As he to you will tell,
For still, the more he works, the more
His poor old ancles swell.
My gentle reader, I perceive
How patiently you've waited,
And I'm afraid that you expect
Some tale will be related.

O reader! had you in your mind
Such stores as silent thought can bring,
O gentle reader! you would find
A tale in every thing.
What more I have to say is short,
I hope you'll kindly take it;
It is no tale; but should you think,
Perhaps a tale you'll make it.

One summer-day I chanced to see
This old man doing all he could
About the root of an old tree,
A stump of rotten wood.
The mattock totter'd in his hand;
So vain was his endeavour
That at the root of the old tree
He might have worked for ever.

"You're overtasked, good Simon Lee,
Give me your tool" to him I said;
And at the word right gladly he
Received my proffer'd aid.
I struck, and with a single blow

[2] **livery-coat:** uniform worn by male servants of a family. Wordsworth later revealed that Simon Lee was employed by the St. Albyn family, who formerly owned Alfoxden.

The tangled root I sever'd,
At which the poor old man so long
And vainly had endeavour'd.

The tears into his eyes were brought,
And thanks and praises seemed to run
So fast out of his heart, I thought
They never would have done.
—I've heard of hearts unkind, kind deeds
With coldness still returning.
Alas! the gratitude of men
Has oftner left me mourning.

We Are Seven
(1798; comp. 1798)

A simple child, dear brother Jim,[1]
That lightly draws its breath,
And feels its life in every limb,
What should it know of death?

I met a little cottage girl,
She was eight years old, she said;
Her hair was thick with many a curl
That cluster'd round her head.

She had a rustic, woodland air,
And she was wildly clad;
Her eyes were fair, and very fair,
—Her beauty made me glad.

"Sisters and brothers, little maid,
How many may you be?"
"How many? seven in all," she said,
And wondering looked at me.

"And where are they, I pray you tell?"
She answered, "Seven are we,
And two of us at Conway[2] dwell,
And two are gone to sea.

Two of us in the church-yard lie,
My sister and my brother,
And in the church-yard cottage, I
Dwell near them with my mother."

"You say that two at Conway dwell,
And two are gone to sea,
Yet you are seven; I pray you tell
Sweet Maid, how this may be?"

Then did the little Maid reply,
"Seven boys and girls are we;
Two of us in the church-yard lie,
Beneath the church-yard tree."

"You run about, my little maid,
Your limbs they are alive;
If two are in the church-yard laid,
Then ye are only five."

"Their graves are green, they may be seen,"
The little Maid replied,
"Twelve steps or more from my mother's door,
And they are side by side.

My stockings there I often knit,
My 'kerchief there I hem;
And there upon the ground I sit—
I sit and sing to them.

And often after sunset, Sir,
When it is light and fair,
I take my little porringer,
And eat my supper there.

The first that died was little Jane;
In bed she moaning lay,
Till God released her of her pain,
And then she went away.

So in the church-yard she was laid,
And all the summer dry,
Together round her grave we played,
My brother John and I.

And when the ground was white with snow,
And I could run and slide,
My brother John was forced to go,
And he lies by her side."

"How many are you then," said I,
"If they two are in Heaven?"
The little Maiden did reply,
"O Master! we are seven."

"But they are dead; those two are dead!
Their spirits are in heaven!"
'Twas throwing words away; for still
The little Maid would have her will,
And said, "Nay, we are seven!"

[1] James Tobin, a friend.

[2] Conway: seaport in Wales.

Lines Written in Early Spring
(1798; comp. 1798)

I heard a thousand blended notes,
While in a grove I sate reclined,
In that sweet mood when pleasant thoughts
Bring sad thoughts to the mind.

To her fair works did nature link
The human soul that through me ran;
And much it griev'd my heart to think
What man has made of man.

Through primrose-tufts, in that sweet bower,
The periwinkle trail'd its wreathes;
And 'tis my faith that every flower
Enjoys the air it breathes.[1]

The birds around me hopp'd and play'd:
Their thoughts I cannot measure,
But the least motion which they made,
It seem'd a thrill of pleasure.

The budding twigs spread out their fan,
To catch the breezy air;
And I must think, do all I can,
That there was pleasure there.

If I these thoughts may not prevent,
If such be of my creed the plan,
Have I not reason to lament
What man has made of man?[2]

[1] See Darwin's *The Loves of the Plants* (1789)* for current speculation on the emotional and psychological lives of plants.

[2] The final stanza was revised to read: "If this belief from Heaven be sent, / If such be Nature's holy plan, / Have I not reason to lament / What man has made of man?"

The Thorn[1]
(1798; comp. 1798)

— I —

There is a thorn; it looks so old,
In truth you'd find it hard to say,
How it could ever have been young,
It looks so old and grey.
Not higher than a two-years' child,
It stands erect this aged thorn;
No leaves it has, no thorny points;
It is a mass of knotted joints,
A wretched thing forlorn.
It stands erect, and like a stone
With lichens[2] it is overgrown.

— II —

Like a rock or stone, it is o'ergrown
With lichens to the very top,
And hung with heavy tufts of moss,
A melancholy crop:
Up from the earth these mosses creep,
And this poor thorn they clasp it round
So close, you'd say that they were bent
With plain and manifest intent,
To drag it to the ground;
And all had joined in one endeavour
To bury this poor thorn for ever.

— III —

High on a mountain's highest ridge,
Where oft the stormy winter gale
Cuts like a scythe, while through the clouds
It sweeps from vale to vale;
Not five yards from the mountain-path,
This thorn you on your left espy;
And to the left, three yards beyond,
You see a little muddy pond
Of water, never dry;

[1] Wordsworth says in the 1798 "Advertisement" that "The poem of the Thorn, as the reader will soon discover, is not supposed to be spoken in the author's own person: the character of the locquacious narrator will sufficiently shew itself in the course of the story." Although Dorothy Wordsworth writes in her Journal that William was inspired by a "stunted thorn" in the vicinity of their residence, the thorn tree or bush in England generally refers to the Hawthorn or White-thorn (OED). A Note to the poem in the 1800 edition addresses criticism of the poem's verbal repetition: "There is a numerous class of readers who imagine that the same words cannot be repeated without tautology: this is a great error: virtual tautology is much oftener produced by using different words when the meaning is exactly the same. Words, a Poet's words more particularly, ought to be weighed in the balance of feeling, and not measured by the space which they occupy upon paper."

[2] **lichen:** fungus or algae that form a scaly crust that climbs the tree.

I've measured it from side to side:
'Tis three feet long, and two feet wide.

— IV —

And close beside this aged thorn,
There is a fresh and lovely sight,
A beauteous heap, a hill of moss,
Just half a foot in height.
All lovely colours there you see,
All colours that were ever seen,
And mossy network too is there,
As if by hand of lady fair
The work had woven been,
And cups, the darlings of the eye,
So deep is their vermilion dye.

— V —

Ah me! what lovely tints are there!
Of olive-green and scarlet bright,
In spikes, in branches, and in stars,
Green, red, and pearly white.
This heap of earth o'ergrown with moss,
Which close beside the thorn you see,
So fresh in all its beauteous dyes,
Is like an infant's grave in size
As like as like can be:
But never, never any where,
An infant's grave was half so fair.

— VI —

Now would you see this aged thorn,
This pond and beauteous hill of moss,
You must take care and chuse your time
The mountain when to cross.
For oft there sits, between the heap
That's like an infant's grave in size,
And that same pond of which I spoke,
A woman in a scarlet cloak,
And to herself she cries,
"Oh misery! oh misery!
Oh woe is me! oh misery!"

— VII —

At all time of the day and night
This wretched woman thither goes,
And she is known to every star,
And every wind that blows;
And there beside the thorn she sits
When the blue day-light's in the skies,
And when the whirlwind's on the hill,
Or frosty air is keen and still,
And to herself she cries,
"Oh misery! oh misery!
Oh woe is me! oh misery!"

— VIII —

"Now wherefore thus, by day and night,[3]
In rain, in tempest, and in snow,
Thus to the dreary mountain-top
Does this poor woman go?
And why sits she beside the thorn
When the blue day-light's in the sky,
Or when the whirlwind's on the hill,
Or frosty air is keen and still,
And wherefore does she cry?—
Oh wherefore? wherefore? tell me why
Does she repeat that doleful cry?"

— IX —

I cannot tell; I wish I could;
For the true reason no one knows,
But if you'd gladly view the spot,
The spot to which she goes;
The heap that's like an infant's grave,
The pond—and thorn, so old and grey,
Pass by her door—'tis seldom shut—
And if you see her in her hut,
Then to the spot away!—
I never heard of such as dare
Approach the spot when she is there.

— X —

"But wherefore to the mountain-top
Can this unhappy woman go,
Whatever star is in the skies,
Whatever wind may blow?"
Nay rack your brain—'tis all in vain,
I'll tell you every thing I know;
But to the thorn, and to the pond
Which is a little step beyond,
I wish that you would go:
Perhaps when you are at the place
You something of her tale may trace.

[3] This is the first of three interruptions by an unspecified interlocutor.

— XI —

I'll give you the best help I can:
Before you up the mountain go,
Up to the dreary mountain-top,
I'll tell you all I know.
'Tis now some two and twenty years,
Since she (her name is Martha Ray)[4]
Gave with a maiden's true good will
Her company to Stephen Hill;
And she was blithe and gay,
And she was happy, happy still
Whene'er she thought of Stephen Hill.

— XII —

And they had fix'd the wedding-day,
The morning that must wed them both;
But Stephen to another maid
Had sworn another oath;
And with this other maid to church
Unthinking Stephen went—
Poor Martha! on that woful day
A cruel, cruel fire, they say,
Into her bones was sent:
It dried her body like a cinder,
And almost turn'd her brain to tinder.

— XIII —

They say, full six months after this,
While yet the summer-leaves were green,
She to the mountain-top would go,
And there was often seen.
'Tis said, a child was in her womb,
As now to any eye was plain;
She was with child, and she was mad,
Yet often she was sober sad
From her exceeding pain.
Oh me! ten thousand times I'd rather
That he had died, that cruel father!

— XIV —

Sad case for such a brain to hold
Communion with a stirring child!
Sad case, as you may think, for one
Who had a brain so wild!
Last Christmas when we talked of this,
Old Farmer Simpson did maintain,
That in her womb the infant wrought
About its mother's heart, and brought
Her senses back again:
And when at last her time drew near,
Her looks were calm, her senses clear.

— XV —

No more I know, I wish I did,
And I would tell it all to you;
For what became of this poor child
There's none that ever knew:
And if a child was born or no,
There's no one that could ever tell;[5]
And if 'twas born alive or dead,
There's no one knows, as I have said,
But some remember well,
That Martha Ray about this time
Would up the mountain often climb.

— XVI —

And all that winter, when at night
The wind blew from the mountain-peak,
'Twas worth your while, though in the dark,
The church-yard path to seek:
For many a time and oft were heard
Cries coming from the mountain-head,
Some plainly living voices were,
And others, I've heard many swear,
Were voices of the dead:
I cannot think, whate'er they say,
They had to do with Martha Ray.

— XVII —

But that she goes to this old thorn,
The thorn which I've described to you,
And there sits in a scarlet cloak,
I will be sworn is true.
For one day with my telescope,

[4] A Martha Ray had been shot by a rejected lover, the Rev. James Hackman, in the lobby of a playhouse in April 1779. Basil Montague (1770–1851), the father of the child William and Dorothy were caring for at Alfoxden, was the natural son of Martha Ray and the fourth Earl of Sandwich. See note 1 to "Lines Written at a Small Distance from My House."

[5] Helen Darbishire reports finding a Scots ballad transcribed in Wordsworth's notebook which contains the lines: "Ah there she's leaned her back to a thorn / . . . / And there she has her baby born. / . . . / She has houked a grave ayont the sun, / . . . / And there she has buried the sweet babe in."

To view the ocean wide and bright,
When to this country first I came,[6]
Ere I had heard of Martha's name,
I climbed the mountain's height:
A storm came on, and I could see
No object higher than my knee.

— XVIII —

'Twas mist and rain, and storm and rain,
No screen, no fence could I discover,
And then the wind! in faith, it was
A wind full ten times over.
I looked around, I thought I saw
A jutting crag, and off I ran,
Head-foremost, through the driving rain,
The shelter of the crag to gain,
And, as I am a man,
Instead of jutting crag, I found
A woman seated on the ground.

— XIX —

I did not speak—I saw her face,
Her face it was enough for me;
I turned about and heard her cry,
"O misery! O misery!"
And there she sits, until the moon
Through half the clear blue sky will go,
And when the little breezes make
The waters of the pond to shake,
As all the country know,
She shudders and you hear her cry,
"Oh misery! oh misery!"

— XX —

"But what's the thorn? and what's the pond?
And what's the hill of moss to her?
And what's the creeping breeze that comes
The little pond to stir?"
I cannot tell; but some will say
She hanged her baby on the tree,
Some say she drowned it in the pond,
Which is a little step beyond,
But all and each agree,
The little babe was buried there,
Beneath that hill of moss so fair.

— XXI —

I've heard the scarlet moss is red
With drops of that poor infant's blood;
But kill a new-born infant thus!
I do not think she could.
Some say, if to the pond you go,
And fix on it a steady view,
The shadow of a babe you trace,
A baby and a baby's face,
And that it looks at you;
Whene'er you look on it, 'tis plain
The baby looks at you again.

— XXII —

And some had sworn an oath that she
Should be to public justice brought;
And for the little infant's bones
With spades they would have sought.
But then the beauteous hill of moss
Before their eyes began to stir;
And for full fifty yards around,
The grass it shook upon the ground;
But all do still aver
The little babe is buried there,
Beneath that hill of moss so fair.

— XXIII —

I cannot tell how this may be,
But plain it is, the thorn is bound
With heavy tufts of moss, that strive
To drag it to the ground.
And this I know, full many a time,
When she was on the mountain high,
By day, and in the silent night,
When all the stars shone clear and bright,
That I have heard her cry,
"O misery! oh misery!
O woe is me! oh misery!"

[6] The 1800 note to the poem identifies the narrator as a superstitious type, exemplified here as a "Captain of a small trading vessel . . . who being past the middle age of life, had retired upon an annuity . . . to some village or country town of which he was not a native. . . . Such men having little to do become credulous and talkative from indolence; and . . . prone to superstition." "Superstitious men," Wordsworth goes on to say, "are almost always men of slow faculties and deep feelings; their minds are not loose, but adhesive. . . . "

Expostulation and Reply
(1798; comp. 1798)

"Why, William, on that old grey stone,
Thus for the length of half a day,
Why, William, sit you thus alone,
And dream your time away?

Where are your books? that light bequeath'd
To beings else forlorn and blind!
Up! Up! and drink the spirit breath'd
From dead men to their kind.

You look round on your mother earth,
As if she for no purpose bore you;
As if you were her first-born birth,
And none had lived before you!"

One morning thus, by Esthwaite lake,
When life was sweet I knew not why,
To me my good friend Matthew spake,
And thus I made reply.

"The eye it cannot chuse but see,
We cannot bid the ear be still;
Our bodies feel, where'er they be,
Against, or with our will.

Nor less I deem that there are powers,
Which of themselves our minds impress,
That we can feed this mind of ours,
In a wise passiveness.

Think you, mid all this mighty sum
Of things for ever speaking,
That nothing of itself will come,
But we must still be seeking?

—Then ask not wherefore, here, alone,
Conversing as I may,
I sit upon this old grey stone,
And dream my time away."

The Tables Turned; An Evening Scene, on the Same Subject
(1798; comp. 1798)

Up! up! my friend, and clear your looks,
Why all this toil and trouble?
Up! up! my friend, and quit your books,
Or surely you'll grow double.

The sun, above the mountain's head,
A freshening lustre mellow
Through all the long green fields has spread,
His first sweet evening yellow.

Books! 'tis a dull and endless strife,
Come, hear the woodland linnet,
How sweet his music; on my life
There's more of wisdom in it.

And hark! how blithe the throstle sings!
And he is no mean preacher;
Come forth into the light of things,
Let Nature be your teacher.

She has a world of ready wealth,
Our minds and hearts to bless—
Spontaneous wisdom breathed by health,
Truth breathed by chearfulness.

One impulse from a vernal wood
May teach you more of man;
Of moral evil and of good,
Than all the sages can.

Sweet is the lore which nature brings;
Our meddling intellect
Mishapes the beauteous forms of things;
—We murder to dissect.

Enough of science and of art;
Close up these barren leaves;
Come forth, and bring with you a heart
That watches and receives.

Lines Written a Few Miles above Tintern Abbey, On Revisiting the Banks of the WYE during a Tour, July 13, 1798[1]
(1798; comp. 1798)

Five years have passed; five summers, with the length
Of five long winters! and again I hear

[1] Wordsworth's 1800 note to the poem reads: "I have not ventured to call this Poem an Ode; but it was written with a hope

These waters, rolling from their mountain-springs
With a sweet inland murmur.[2]—Once again
Do I behold these steep and lofty cliffs,
Which on a wild secluded scene impress
Thoughts of more deep seclusion; and connect
The landscape with the quiet of the sky.[3]
The day is come when I again repose
Here, under this dark sycamore, and view
These plots of cottage-ground, these orchard-tufts,
Which, at this season, with their unripe fruits,
Among the woods and copses lose themselves,
Nor, with their green and simple hue, disturb
The wild green landscape. Once again I see
These hedge-rows, hardly hedge-rows, little lines
Of sportive wood run wild; these pastoral farms
Green to the very door; and wreathes of smoke
Sent up, in silence, from among the trees,
With some uncertain notice, as might seem,
Of vagrant dwellers in the houseless woods,
Or of some hermit's cave, where by his fire
The hermit sits alone.

Though absent long,
These forms of beauty have not been to me,
As is a landscape to a blind man's eye:
But oft, in lonely rooms, and mid the din
Of towns and cities, I have owed to them,
In hours of weariness, sensations sweet,
Felt in the blood, and felt along the heart,
And passing even into my purer mind
With tranquil restoration:—feelings too
Of unremembered pleasure; such, perhaps,
As may have had no trivial influence
On that best portion of a good man's life;
His little, nameless, unremembered acts
Of kindness and of love. Nor less, I trust,
To them I may have owed another gift,
Of aspect more sublime; that blessed mood,
In which the burthen of the mystery,
In which the heavy and the weary weight
Of all this unintelligible world
Is lighten'd:—that serene and blessed mood,
In which the affections gently lead us on,
Until, the breath of this corporeal frame,
And even the motion of our human blood
Almost suspended, we are laid asleep
In body, and become a living soul:
While with an eye made quiet by the power
Of harmony, and the deep power of joy,
We see into the life of things.

If this
Be but a vain belief, yet, oh! how oft,
In darkness, and amid the many shapes
Of joyless day-light; when the fretful stir
Unprofitable, and the fever of the world,
Have hung upon the beatings of my heart,
How oft, in spirit, have I turned to thee
O sylvan Wye! Thou wanderer through the woods,
How often has my spirit turned to thee!

And now, with gleams of half-extinguish'd thought,
With many recognitions dim and faint,
And somewhat of a sad perplexity,
The picture of the mind revives again:
While here I stand, not only with the sense
Of present pleasure, but with pleasing thoughts
That in this moment there is life and food
For future years. And so I dare to hope
Though changed, no doubt, from what I was, when first
I came among these hills; when like a roe
I bounded o'er the mountains, by the sides
Of the deep rivers, and the lonely streams,
Wherever nature led; more like a man
Flying from something that he dreads, than one
Who sought the thing he loved. For nature then
(The coarser pleasures of my boyish days,
And their glad animal movements all gone by,)
To me was all in all.—I cannot paint
What then I was. The sounding cataract
Haunted me like a passion: the tall rock,
The mountain, and the deep and gloomy wood,
Their colours and their forms, were then to me
An appetite: a feeling and a love,
That had no need of a remoter charm,
By thought supplied, or any interest

---

that in the transitions, and the impassioned music of the versification, would be found the principal requisites of that species of composition."

[2] The river is not affected by the tides a few miles above Tintern. [W.W.]

[3] "Many of the furnaces, on the banks of the river, consume charcoal, which is manufactured on the spot; and the smoke, which is frequently seen issuing from the sides of the hills; and spreading its thin veil over a part of them, beautifully breaks their lines, and unites them with the sky." From William Gilpin's *Observations on the River Wye* (1782),* a work that did much to promote the concept of the *picturesque* as an aesthetic term for scenery with attributes of roughness and irregularity. (See Aesthetic Theory and Literary Criticism.)

Unborrowed from the eye.—That time is past,
And all its aching joys are now no more,
And all its dizzy raptures. Not for this
Faint I, nor mourn nor murmur: other gifts
Have followed, for such loss, I would believe,
Abundant recompence. For I have learned
To look on nature, not as in the hour
Of thoughtless youth, but hearing oftentimes
The still, sad music of humanity,
Not harsh nor grating, though of ample power
To chasten and subdue. And I have felt
A presence that disturbs me with the joy
Of elevated thoughts; a sense sublime
Of something far more deeply interfused,
Whose dwelling is the light of setting suns,
And the round ocean, and the living air,
And the blue sky, and in the mind of man,
A motion and a spirit, that impels
All thinking things, all objects of all thought,
And rolls through all things. Therefore am I still
A lover of the meadows and the woods,
And mountains; and of all that we behold
From this green earth; of all the mighty world
Of eye and ear, both what they half-create,[4]
And what perceive; well pleased to recognize
In nature and the language of the sense,
The anchor of my purest thoughts, the nurse,
The guide, the guardian of my heart, and soul
Of all my moral being.

Nor, perchance,
If I were not thus taught, should I the more
Suffer my genial spirits to decay:
For thou art with me, here, upon the banks
Of this fair river; thou, my dearest Friend,
My dear, dear Friend, and in thy voice I catch
The language of my former heart, and read
My former pleasures in the shooting lights
Of thy wild eyes. Oh! yet a little while
May I behold in thee what I was once,
My dear, dear Sister! And this prayer I make,
Knowing that Nature never did betray
The heart that loved her; 'tis her privilege,
Through all the years of this our life, to lead
From joy to joy: for she can so inform
The mind that is within us, so impress
With quietness and beauty, and so feed
With lofty thoughts, that neither evil tongues,
Rash judgments, nor the sneers of selfish men,
Nor greetings where no kindness is, nor all
The dreary intercourse of daily life,
Shall e'er prevail against us, or disturb
Our chearful faith that all which we behold
Is full of blessings. Therefore let the moon
Shine on thee in thy solitary walk;
And let the misty mountain winds be free
To blow against thee: and in after years,
When these wild ecstasies shall be matured
Into a sober pleasure, when thy mind
Shall be a mansion for all lovely forms,
Thy memory be as a dwelling-place
For all sweet sounds and harmonies; Oh! then,
If solitude, or fear, or pain, or grief,
Should be thy portion, with what healing thoughts
Of tender joy wilt thou remember me,
And these my exhortations! Nor, perchance,
If I should be, where I no more can hear
Thy voice, nor catch from thy wild eyes these gleams
Of past existence, wilt thou then forget
That on the banks of this delightful stream
We stood together; and that I, so long
A worshipper of Nature, hither came,
Unwearied in that service: rather say
With warmer love, oh! with far deeper zeal
Of holier love. Nor wilt thou then forget,
That after many wanderings, many years
Of absence, these steep woods and lofty cliffs,
And this green pastoral landscape, were to me
More dear, both for themselves, and for thy sake.

[4] This line has a close resemblance to an admirable line of Young, the exact expression of which I cannot recollect. [W.W.]

from LYRICAL BALLADS

(Second Edition, 1800)

—*from* PREFACE[1] —

The first volume of these Poems has already been submitted to general perusal. It was published, as an experiment which, I hoped, might be of some use to ascertain, how far, by fitting to metrical arrangement a selection of the

[1] Composed in 1800; lengthened significantly for the 1802 edition of *Lyrical Ballads, with Pastoral and Other Poems*; improved in 1836. The text provided here is 1800, with the addition of an italicized passage from 1802 on "What is a Poet?"

real language of men in a state of vivid sensation, that sort of pleasure and that quantity of pleasure may be imparted, which a Poet may rationally endeavour to impart.

I had formed no very inaccurate estimate of the probable effect of those Poems: I flattered myself that they who should be pleased with them would read them with more than common pleasure: and on the other hand I was well aware that by those who should dislike them they would be read with more than common dislike. The result has differed from my expectation in this only, that I have pleased a greater number, than I ventured to hope I should please.

For the sake of variety and from a consciousness of my own weakness I was induced to request the assistance of a Friend, who furnished me with the Poems of the ANCIENT MARINER, the FOSTER-MOTHER'S TALE, the NIGHTINGALE, the DUNGEON, and the Poem entitled LOVE. I should not, however, have requested this assistance, had I not believed that the poems of my Friend[2] would in a great measure have the same tendency as my own, and that, though there would be found a difference, there would be found no discordance in the colours of our style; as our opinions on the subject of poetry do almost entirely coincide.

Several of my Friends are anxious for the success of these Poems from a belief, that if the views, with which they were composed, were indeed realized, a class of Poetry would be produced, well adapted to interest mankind permanently, and not unimportant in the multiplicity and in the quality of its moral relations: and on this account they have advised me to prefix a systematic defence of the theory, upon which the poems were written. But I was unwilling to undertake the task, because I knew that on this occasion the Reader would look coldly upon my arguments, since I might be suspected of having been principally influenced by the selfish and foolish hope of *reasoning* him into an approbation of these particular Poems: and I was still more unwilling to undertake the task, because adequately to display my opinions and fully to enforce my arguments would require a space wholly disproportionate to the nature of a preface. For to treat the subject with the clearness and coherence, of which I believe it susceptible, it would be necessary to give a full account of the present state of the public taste in this country, and to determine how far this taste is healthy or depraved; which again could not be determined, without pointing out, in what manner language and the human mind act and react on each other, and without retracing the revolutions not of literature alone but likewise of society itself. I have therefore altogether declined to enter regularly upon this defence; yet I am sensible, that there would be some impropriety in abruptly obtruding upon the Public, without a few words of introduction, Poems so materially different from those, upon which general approbation is at present bestowed.

It is supposed, that by the act of writing in verse an Author makes a formal engagement that he will gratify certain known habits of association, that he not only thus apprizes the Reader that certain classes of ideas and expressions will be found in his book, but that others will be carefully excluded. This exponent or symbol held forth by metrical language must in different areas of literature have excited very different expectations: for example, in the age of Catullus Terence and Lucretius, and that of Statius or Claudian, and in our own country, in the age of Shakespeare and Beaumont and Fletcher, and that of Donne and Cowley, or Dryden, or Pope. I will not take upon me to determine the exact import of the promise which by the act of writing in verse an Author in the present day makes to his Reader; but I am certain it will appear to many persons that I have not fulfilled the terms of an engagement thus voluntarily contracted. I hope therefore the Reader will not censure me, if I attempt to state what I have proposed to myself to perform, and also, (as far as the limits of a preface will permit) to explain some of the chief reasons which have determined me in the choice of my purpose: that at least he may be spared any unpleasant feeling of disappointment, and that I myself may be protected from the most dishonorable accusation which can be brought against an Author, namely that of an indolence which prevents him from endeavouring to ascertain what is his duty, or, when his duty is ascertained prevents him from performing it.

The principal object then which I proposed to myself in these Poems was to make the incidents of common life interesting by tracing in them, truly though not ostentatiously, the primary laws of our nature: chiefly as far as regards the manner in which we associate ideas in a state of excitement.[3] Low and rustic life was generally chosen because in that situation the essential passions of the heart find a better soil in which they can attain their maturity,

[2] The friend is Coleridge.

[3] Wordsworth relies heavily throughout on Hartley's associationist psychology. See Hartley* and SCIENCE AND NATURE.

are less under restraint, and speak a plainer and more emphatic language; because in that situation our elementary feelings exist in a state of greater simplicity and consequently may be more accurately contemplated and more forcibly communicated; because the manners of rural life germinate from those elementary feelings; and from the necessary character of rural occupations are more easily comprehended; and are more durable; and lastly, because in that situation the passions of men are incorporated with the beautiful and permanent forms of nature. The language too of these men is adopted (purified indeed from what appear to be its real defects, from all lasting and rational causes of dislike or disgust) because such men hourly communicate with the best objects from which the best part of language is originally derived; and because, from their rank in society and the sameness and narrow circle of their intercourse, being less under the action of social vanity they convey their feelings and notions in simple and unelaborated expressions. Accordingly such a language arising out of repeated experience and regular feelings is a more permanent and a far more philosophical language than that which is frequently substituted for it by Poets, who think that they are conferring honour upon themselves and their art in proportion as they separate themselves from the sympathies of men, and indulge in arbitrary and capricious habits of expression in order to furnish food for fickle tastes and fickle appetites of their own creation.[4]

I cannot be insensible of the present outcry against the triviality and meanness both of thought and language, which some of my contemporaries have occasionally introduced into their metrical compositions; and I acknowledge that this defect where it exists, is more dishonorable to the Writer's own character than false refinement or arbitrary innovation, though I should contend at the same time that it is far less pernicious in the sum of its consequences. From such verses the Poems in these volumes will be found distinguished at least by one mark of difference, that each of them had a worthy *purpose.* Not that I mean to say, that I always began to write with a distinct purpose formally conceived; but I believe that my habits of meditation have so formed my feelings, as that my descriptions of such objects as strongly excite those feelings will be found to carry along with them a *purpose.* If in this opinion I am mistaken I can have little right to the name of a Poet. For all good poetry is the spontaneous overflow of powerful feelings; but though this be true, Poems to which any value can be attached, were never produced on any variety of subjects but by a man who being possessed of more than usual organic sensibility had also thought long and deeply. For our continued influxes of feeling are modified and directed by our thoughts, which are indeed the representatives of all our past feelings; and as by contemplating the relation of these general representatives to each other, we discover what is really important to men, so by the repetition and continuance of this act feelings connected with important subjects will be nourished, till at length, if we be originally possessed of much organic sensibility, such habits of mind will be produced that by obeying blindly and mechanically the impulses of those habits we shall describe objects and utter sentiments of such a nature and in such connection with each other, that the understanding of the being to whom we address ourselves, if he be in a healthful state of association, must necessarily be in some degree enlightened, his taste exalted, and his affections ameliorated. . . .

I will not suffer a sense of false modesty to prevent me from asserting, that I point my Reader's attention to this mark of distinction far less for the sake of these particular Poems than from the general importance of the subject. The subject is indeed important! For the human mind is capable of excitement without the application of gross and violent stimulants and he must have a very faint perception of its beauty and dignity who does not know this, and who does not further know that one being is elevated above another in proportion as he possesses this capability. It has therefore appeared to me that to endeavour to produce or enlarge this capability is one of the best services in which, at any period, a Writer can be engaged; but this service, excellent at all times, is especially so at the present day. For a multitude of causes unknown to former times are now acting with a combined force to blunt the discriminating powers of the mind, and unfitting it for all voluntary exertion to reduce it to a state of almost savage torpor. The most effective of these causes are the great national events which are daily taking place, and the encreasing accumulation of men in cities,[5] where the uniformity of their occupations produces a craving for extraordinary incident which the rapid communication of intelligence hourly gratifies. To this tendency of life and

[4] It is worth while here to observe that the affecting parts of Chaucer are almost always expressed in language pure and universally intelligible even to this day. [W.W.]

[5] See SOCIETY AND POLITICAL ECONOMY.

manners the literature and theatrical exhibitions of the country have conformed themselves. The invaluable works of our elder writers, I had almost said the works of Shakespear and Milton, are driven into neglect by frantic novels, sickly and stupid German Tragedies, and deluges of idle and extravagant stories in verse.—When I think upon this degrading thirst after outrageous stimulation I am almost ashamed to have spoken of the feeble effort with which I have endeavoured to counteract it; and reflecting upon the magnitude of the general evil, I should be oppressed with no dishonorable melancholy, had I not a deep impression of certain inherent and indestructible qualities of the human mind, and likewise of certain powers in the great and permanent objects that act upon it which are equally inherent and indestructible; and did I not further add to this impression a belief that the time is approaching when the evil will be systematically opposed by men of greater powers and with far more distinguished success.

Having dwelt thus long on the subjects and aim of these Poems, I shall request the Reader's permission to apprize him of a few circumstances relating to their *style*, in order, among other reasons, that I may not be censured for not having performed what I never attempted. Except in a very few instances the Reader will find no personifications of abstract ideas in these volumes, not that I mean to censure such personifications: they may be well fitted for certain sorts of composition, but in these Poems I propose to myself to imitate, and, as far as possible, to adopt the very language of men, and I do not find that such personifications make any regular or natural part of that language. I wish to keep my Reader in the company of flesh and blood, persuaded that by so doing I shall interest him. Not but that I believe that others who pursue a different track may interest him likewise: I do not interfere with their claim, I only wish to prefer a different claim of my own. There will also be found in these volumes little of what is usually called poetic diction; I have taken as much pains to avoid it as others ordinarily take to produce it; this I have done for the reason already alleged, to bring my language near to the language of men, and further, because the pleasure which I have proposed to myself to impart is of a kind very different from that which is supposed by many persons to be the proper object of poetry. I do not know how without being culpably particular I can give my Reader a more exact notion of the style in which I wished these poems to be written than by informing him that I have at all times endeavoured to look steadily at my subject, consequently I hope it will be found that there is in these Poems little falsehood of description, and that my ideas are expressed in language fitted to their respective importance. Something I must have gained by this practice, as it is friendly to one property of all good poetry, namely good sense; but it has necessarily cut me off from a large portion of phrases and figures of speech which from father to son have long been regarded as the common inheritance of Poets. I have also thought it expedient to restrict myself still further, having abstained from the use of many expressions, in themselves proper and beautiful, but which have been foolishly repeated by bad Poets till such feelings of disgust are connected with them as it is scarcely possible by any art of association to overpower.

If in a Poem there should be found a series of lines, or even a single line, in which the language, though naturally arranged and according to the strict laws of metre, does not differ from that of prose, there is a numerous class of critics who, when they stumble upon these prosaisms as they call them, imagine that they have made a notable discovery, and exult over the Poet as over a man ignorant of his own profession. Now these men would establish a canon of criticism which the Reader will conclude he must utterly reject if he wishes to be pleased with these volumes. And it would be a most easy task to prove to him that not only the language of a large portion of every good poem, even of the most elevated character, must necessarily, except with reference to the metre, in no respect differ from that of good prose, but likewise that some of the most interesting parts of the best poems will be found to be strictly the language of prose when prose is well written. The truth of this assertion might be demonstrated by innumerable passages from almost all the poetical writings, even of Milton himself. I have not space for much quotation; but, to illustrate the subject in a general manner, I will here adduce a short composition of Gray,[6] who was at the head of those who by their reasonings have attempted to widen the space of separation betwixt Prose and Metrical composition, and was more than any other man curiously elaborate in the structure of his own poetic diction.

> In vain to me the smiling mornings shine,
> And reddening Phoebus lifts his golden fire:
> The birds in vain their amorous descant join,
> Or chearful fields resume their green attire:

[6] Thomas Gray (1716–1771), author of the very important *Elegy written in a Country Churchyard* (1751) and "Sonnet on the Death of West" (1775), which Wordsworth here critiques.

These ears alas! for other notes repine;
A different object do these eyes require;
My lonely anguish melts no heart but mine;
And in my breast the imperfect joys expire;
Yet Morning smiles the busy race to cheer,
And new-born pleasure brings to happier men;
The fields to all their wonted tribute bear;
To warm their little loves the birds complain.
I fruitless mourn to him that cannot hear
And weep the more because I weep in vain.

It will easily be perceived that the only part of this Sonnet which is of any value is the lines printed in Italics: it is equally obvious that except in the rhyme, and in the use of the single word "fruitless" for fruitlessly, which is so far a defect, the language of these lines does in no respect differ from that of prose.

Is there then, it will be asked, no essential difference between the language of prose and metrical composition? I answer that there neither is nor can be any essential difference. We are fond of tracing the resemblance between Poetry and Painting, and, accordingly, we call them Sisters: but where shall we find bonds of connection sufficiently strict to typify the affinity betwixt metrical and prose composition? They both speak by and to the same organs; the bodies in which both of them are clothed may be said to be of the same substance, their affections are kindred and almost identical, not necessarily differing even in degree; Poetry[7] sheds no tears "such as Angels weep," but natural and human tears; she can boast of no celestial Ichor that distinguishes her vital juices from those of prose; the same human blood circulates through the veins of them both.

If it be affirmed that rhyme and metrical arrangement of themselves constitute a distinction which overturns what I have been saying on the strict affinity of metrical language with that of prose, and paves the way for other distinctions which the mind voluntarily admits, I answer that[8]

. . . the language of such Poetry as I am recommending is, as far as is possible, a selection of the language really spoken by men; that this selection, wherever it is made with true taste and feeling, will of itself form a distinction far greater than would at first be imagined, and will entirely separate the composition from the vulgarity and meanness of ordinary life; and, if metre be superadded thereto, I believe that a dissimilitude will be produced altogether sufficient for the gratification of a rational mind. What other distinction would we have? Whence is it to come? And where is it to exist? Not, surely, where the Poet speaks through the mouths of his characters: it cannot be necessary here, either for elevation of style, or any of its supposed ornaments: for, if the Poet's subject be judiciously chosen, it will naturally, and upon fit occasion, lead him to passions the language of which, if selected truly and judiciously, must necessarily be dignified and variegated, and alive with metaphors and figures. I forbear to speak of an incongruity which would shock the intelligent Reader, should the Poet interweave any foreign splendour of his own with that which the passion naturally suggests: it is sufficient to say that such addition is unnecessary. And, surely, it is more probable that those passages, which with propriety abound with metaphors and figures, will have their due effect, if, upon other occasions where the passions are of a milder character, the style also be subdued and temperate.

But, as the pleasure which I hope to give by the Poems I now present to the Reader must depend entirely on just notions upon this subject, and, as it is in itself of the highest importance to our taste and moral feelings, I cannot content myself with these detached remarks. And if, in what I am about to say, it shall appear to some that my labour is unnecessary, and that I am like a man fighting a battle without enemies, I would remind such persons, that, whatever may be the language outwardly holden by men, a practical faith in the opinions which I am wishing to establish is almost unknown. If my conclusions are admitted, and carried as far as they must be carried if admitted at all, our judgments concerning the works of the greatest Poets both ancient and modern will be far different from what they are at present, both when we praise, and when we censure: and our moral feelings influencing, and influenced by these judgments will, I believe, be corrected and purified.

Taking up the subject, then, upon general grounds, I ask what is meant by the word Poet? What is a Poet? To whom does he address himself? And what language is to be expected from him? He is a man speaking to men: a man, it is true, endued with more lively sensibility, more enthusiasm and tenderness, who has a greater knowledge of human nature, and a more comprehensive soul, than are supposed to be common among mankind; a man pleased with his own passions and volitions, and who rejoices more than other men in the spirit of life that is in him; delighting to contemplate similar volitions and passions as manifested in the goings-on of the Universe, and habitually impelled to create them where he does not find them. To these qualities he has

---

[7] I here use the word "Poetry" (though against my own judgment) as opposed to the word Prose, and synonomous with metrical composition. But much confusion has been introduced into criticism by this contradistinction of Poetry and Prose, instead of the more philosophical one of Poetry and Science. The only strict antithesis to Prose is Metre [W.W.].

[8] After "I answer that" begins the extended passage in italics on "What is a Poet?" See note 1. The passage from the 1802 text ends with "inform the Reader" on page 579.

added a disposition to be affected more than other men by absent things as if they were present; an ability of conjuring up in himself passions, which are indeed far from being the same as those produced by real events, yet (especially in those parts of the general sympathy which are pleasing and delightful) do more nearly resemble the passions produced by real events, than anything which, from the motions of their own minds merely, other men are accustomed to feel in themselves; whence, and from practice, he has acquired a greater readiness and power in expressing what he thinks and feels, and especially those thoughts and feelings which, by his own choice, or from the structure of his own mind, arise in him without immediate external excitement.

But, whatever portion of this faculty we may suppose even the greatest Poet to possess, there cannot be a doubt but that the language which it will suggest to him, must, in liveliness and truth, fall far short of that which is uttered by men in real life, under the actual pressure of those passions, certain shadows of which the Poet thus produces, or feels to be produced, in himself. However exalted a notion we would wish to cherish of the character of a Poet it is obvious, that, while he describes and imitates passions, his situation is altogether slavish and mechanical, compared with the freedom and power of real and substantial action and suffering. So that it will be the wish of the Poet to bring his feelings near to those of the persons whose feelings he describes, nay, for short spaces of time perhaps, to let himself slip into an entire delusion, and even confound and identify his own feelings with theirs; modifying only the language which is thus suggested to him, by a consideration that he describes for a particular purpose, that of giving pleasure. Here, then, he will apply the principle on which I have so much insisted, namely, that of selection; on this he will depend for removing what would otherwise be painful or disgusting in the passion; he will feel that there is no necessity to trick out or to elevate nature: and, the more industriously he applies this principle, the deeper will be his faith that no words, which his fancy or imagination can suggest, will be to be compared with those which are the emanations of reality and truth.

But it may be said by those who do not object to the general spirit of these remarks, that, as it is impossible for the Poet to produce upon all occasions language as exquisitely fitted for the passion as that which the real passion itself suggests, it is proper that he should consider himself as in the situation of a translator, who deems himself justified when he substitutes excellences of another kind for those which are unattainable by him; and endeavours occasionally to surpass his original, in order to make some amends for the general inferiority to which he feels that he must submit. But this would be to encourage idleness and unmanly despair. Further, it is the language of men who speak of what they do not understand; who talk of Poetry as of a matter of amusement and idle pleasure; who will converse with us as gravely about a taste *for Poetry, as they express it, as if it were a thing as indifferent as a taste for Rope-dancing, or Frontiniac or Sherry. Aristotle, I have been told, hath said, that Poetry is the most philosophic of all writing: it is so: its object is truth, not individual and local, but general, and operative; not standing upon external testimony, but carried alive into the heart by passion; truth which is its own testimony, which gives strength and divinity to the tribunal to which it appeals, and receives them from the same tribunal. Poetry is the image of man and nature. The obstacles which stand in the way of the fidelity of the Biographer and Historian, and of their consequent utility, are incalculably greater than those which are to be encountered by the Poet who has an adequate notion of the dignity of his art. The Poet writes under one restriction only, namely, that of the necessity of giving immediate pleasure to a human Being possessed of that information which may be expected from him, not as a lawyer, a physician, a mariner, an astronomer or a natural philosopher, but as a Man. Except this one restriction, there is no object standing between the Poet and the image of things; between this, and the Biographer and Historian there are a thousand.*

Nor let this necessity of producing immediate pleasure be considered as a degradation of the Poet's art. It is far otherwise. It is an acknowledgment of the beauty of the universe, an acknowledgment the more sincere, because it is not formal, but indirect; it is a task light and easy to him who looks at the world in the spirit of love: further, it is a homage paid to the native and naked dignity of man, to the grand elementary principle of pleasure, by which he knows, and feels, and lives, and moves. We have no sympathy but what is propagated by pleasure: I would not be misunderstood; but wherever we sympathize with pain it will be found that the sympathy is produced and carried on by subtle combinations with pleasure. We have no knowledge, that is, no general principles drawn from the contemplation of particular facts, but what has been built up by pleasure, and exists in us by pleasure alone. The Man of Science, the Chemist and Mathematician, whatever difficulties and disgusts they may have had to struggle with, know and feel this. However painful may be the objects with which the Anatomist's knowledge is connected, he feels that his knowledge is pleasure; and where he has no pleasure he has no knowledge. What then does the Poet? He considers man and the objects that surround him as acting and re-acting upon each other, so as to produce an infinite complexity of pain and pleasure; he considers man in his own nature and in his ordinary life as contemplating this with a certain quantity of immediate knowledge, with certain convictions, intuitions, and deductions which by habit become of the nature of intuitions; he considers him as looking upon this complex scene of ideas and sensations, and finding every where objects that immediately excite in him sympathies which, from the necessities of his nature, are accompanied by an overbalance of enjoyment.

To this knowledge which all men carry about with them, and to these sympathies in which without any other discipline than that of our daily life we are fitted to take delight, the Poet principally directs his attention. He considers man and nature as essentially adapted to each other, and the mind of man as naturally the mirror of the fairest and most interesting qualities of nature. And thus the Poet, prompted by this feeling of pleasure which accompanies him through the whole course of his studies, converses with general nature with affections akin to those, which, through labour and length of time, the Man of Science has raised up in himself, by conversing with those particular parts of nature which are the objects of his studies. The knowledge both of the Poet and the Man of Science is pleasure; but the knowledge of the one cleaves to us as a necessary part of our existence, our natural and unalienable inheritance; the other is a personal and individual acquisition, slow to come to us, and by no habitual and direct sympathy connecting us with our fellow-beings. The Man of Science seeks truth as a remote and unknown benefactor; he cherishes and loves it in his solitude: the Poet, singing a song in which all human beings join with him, rejoices in the presence of truth as our visible friend and hourly companion. Poetry is the breath and finer spirit of all knowledge: it is the impassioned expression which is in the countenance of all Science. Emphatically may it be said of the Poet, as Shakespeare hath said of man, "that he looks before and after." He is the rock of defence of human nature; an upholder and preserver, carrying every where with him relationship and love. In spite of difference of soil and climate, of language and manners, of laws and customs, in spite of things silently gone out of mind and things violently destroyed, the Poet binds together by passion and knowledge the vast empire of human society, as it is spread over the whole earth, and over all time. The objects of the Poet's thoughts are every where; though the eyes and senses of man are, it is true, his favorite guides, yet he will follow wheresoever he can find an atmosphere of sensation in which to move his wings. Poetry is the first and last of all knowledge—it is as immortal as the heart of man. If the labours of men of Science should ever create any material revolution, direct or indirect, in our condition, and in the impressions which we habitually receive, the Poet will sleep then no more than at present, but he will be ready to follow the steps of the Man of Science, not only in those general indirect effects, but he will be at his side, carrying sensation into the midst of the objects of the Science itself. The remotest discoveries of the Chemist, the Botanist, or Mineralogist, will be as proper objects of the Poet's art as any upon which it can be employed, if the time should ever come when these things shall be familiar to us, and the relations under which they are contemplated by the followers of these respective Sciences shall be manifestly and palpably material to us as enjoying and suffering beings. If the time should ever come when what is now called Science, thus familiarized to men, shall be ready to put on, as it were, a form of flesh and blood, the Poet will lend his divine spirit to aid the transfiguration, and will welcome the Being thus produced, as a dear and genuine inmate of the household of man.—It is not, then, to be supposed that any one, who holds that sublime notion of Poetry which I have attempted to convey, will break in upon the sanctity and truth of his pictures by transitory and accidental ornaments, and endeavour to excite admiration of himself by arts, the necessity of which must manifestly depend upon the assumed meanness of his subject.

What I have thus far said applies to Poetry in general; but especially to those parts of composition where the Poet speaks through the mouths of his characters; and upon this point it appears to have such weight that I will conclude, there are few persons of good sense, who would not allow that the dramatic parts of composition are defective, in proportion as they deviate from the real language of nature, and are coloured by a diction of the Poet's own, either peculiar to him as an individual Poet, or belonging simply to Poets in general, to a body of men who, from the circumstance of their compositions being in metre, it is expected will employ a particular language.

It is not, then, in the dramatic parts of composition that we look for this distinction of language; but still it may be proper and necessary where the Poet speaks to us in his own person and character. To this I answer by referring my Reader to the description which I have before given of a Poet. Among the qualities which I have enumerated as principally conducing to form a Poet, is implied nothing differing in kind from other men, but only in degree. The sum of what I have there said is, that the Poet is chiefly distinguished from other men by a greater promptness to think and feel without immediate external excitement, and a greater power in expressing such thoughts and feelings as are produced in him in that manner. But these passions and thoughts and feelings are the general passions and thoughts and feelings of men. And with what are they connected? Undoubtedly with our moral sentiments and animal sensations, and with the causes which excite these; with the operations of the elements and the appearances of the visible universe; with storm and sun-shine, with the revolutions of the seasons, with cold and heat, with loss of friends and kindred, with injuries and resentments, gratitude and hope, with fear and sorrow. These, and the like, are the sensations and objects which the Poet describes, as they are the sensations of other men, and the objects which interest them. The Poet thinks and feels in the spirit of the passions of men. How, then, can his language differ in any material degree from that of all other men who feel vividly and see clearly? It might be proved *that it is impossible. But supposing that this were not the case, the Poet might then be allowed to use a peculiar language when expressing his feelings for his own gratification, or that of men like himself. But Poets do not write for Poets alone, but for men. Unless therefore we are advocates for that admiration which depends upon ignorance, and that pleasure which arises from hearing what we do not understand, the Poet must descend from this supposed height, and, in order to excite rational sympathy, he must express himself as other men express themselves. To this it may be added, that while he is only selecting from the real language of men, or, which amounts to the same thing, composing accurately in the spirit of such selection, he is treading upon safe ground, and we know what we are to expect from him. Our feelings are the same with respect to metre; for, as it may be proper to inform the Reader,* the distinction of rhyme and metre is regular and uniform, and not, like that which is produced by what is usually called poetic diction, arbitrary and subject to infinite caprices upon which no calculation whatever can be made. In the one case the Reader is utterly at the mercy of the Poet respecting what imagery or diction he may choose to connect with the passion, whereas in the other the metre obeys certain laws, to which the Poet and Reader both willingly submit because they are certain, and because no interference is made by them with the passion but such as the concurring testimony of ages has shewn to heighten and improve the pleasure which co-exists with it. . . .

But I might point out various causes why, when the style is manly, and the subject of some importance, words metrically arranged will long continue to impart such a pleasure to mankind as he who is sensible of the extent of that pleasure will be desirous to impart. The end of Poetry is to produce excitement in coexistence with an overbalance of pleasure. Now, by the supposition, excitement is an unusual and irregular state of the mind; ideas and feelings do not in that state succeed each other in accustomed order. But if the words by which this excitement is produced are in themselves powerful, or the images and feelings have an undue proportion of pain connected with them, there is some danger that the excitement may be carried beyond its proper bounds. Now the co-presence of something regular, something to which the mind has been accustomed when in an unexcited or a less excited state, cannot but have great efficacy in tempering and restraining the passion by an intertexture of ordinary feeling. This may be illustrated by appealing to the Reader's own experience of the reluctance with which he comes to the re-perusal of the distressful parts of Clarissa Harlowe, or the Gamester.[9] While Shakespeare's writings, in the most pathetic scenes, never act upon us as pathetic beyond the bounds of pleasure—an effect which is in a great degree to be ascribed to small, but continual and regular impulses of pleasurable surprise from the metrical arrangement. . . .

If I had undertaken a systematic defence of the theory upon which these poems are written, it would have been my duty to develope the various causes upon which the pleasure received from metrical language depends. Among the chief of these causes is to be reckoned a principle which must be well known to those who have made any of the Arts the object of accurate reflection; I mean the pleasure which the mind derives from the perception of similitude in dissimilitude. This principle is the great spring of the activity of our minds and their chief feeder. From this principle the direction of the sexual appetite, and all the passions connected with it take their origin: It is the life of our ordinary conversation; and upon the accuracy with which similitude in dissimilitude, and dissimilitude in similitude are perceived, depend our taste and our moral feelings. It would not have been a useless employment to have applied this principle to the consideration of metre, and to have shown that metre is hence enabled to afford much pleasure, and to have pointed out in what manner that pleasure is produced. But my limits will not permit me to enter upon this subject, and I must content myself with a general summary.

I have said that Poetry is the spontaneous overflow of powerful feelings: it takes its origin from emotion recollected in tranquillity: the emotion is contemplated till by a species of reaction the tranquillity gradually disappears, and an emotion, similar to that which was before the subject of contemplation, is gradually produced, and does itself actually exist in the mind. In this mood successful composition generally begins, and in a mood similar to this it is carried on; but the emotion, of whatever kind and in whatever degree, from various causes is qualified by various pleasures, so that in describing any passions whatsoever, which are voluntarily described, the mind will upon the whole be in a state of enjoyment. Now if Nature be thus cautious in preserving in a state of enjoyment a being thus employed, the Poet ought to profit by the lesson thus held forth to him, and ought especially to take care, that whatever passions he communicates to his Reader, those passions, if his Reader's mind be sound and vigorous, should always be accompanied with an overbalance of pleasure. Now the music of harmonious metrical language, the sense of difficulty overcome, and the blind association of pleasure which has been previously received from works of rhyme or metre of the same or similar construction, all these imperceptibly make up a complex feeling of delight, which is of the most important use in tempering the painful feeling which will always be found intermingled with powerful descriptions of the deeper passions. This effect is always produced in pathetic and impassioned poetry; while in lighter compositions the ease and gracefulness with which the Poet

---

[9] **Clarissa Harlowe:** *Clarissa: or The History of a Young Lady* (1748–1749), an epistolary novel by Samuel Richardson (1689–1761). **Gamester:** *The Gamester* (1753), a play by Edward Moore (1712–1757).

manages his numbers are themselves confessedly a principal source of the gratification of the Reader. I might perhaps include all which it is *necessary* to say upon this subject by affirming what few persons will deny, that of two descriptions either of passions, manners, or characters, each of them equally well executed, the one in prose and the other in verse, the verse will be read a hundred times where the prose is read once. We see that Pope by the power of verse alone, has contrived to render the plainest common sense interesting, and even frequently to invest it with the appearance of passion. In consequence of these convictions I related in metre the Tale of GOODY BLAKE and HARRY GILL, which is one of the rudest of this collection. I wished to draw attention to the truth that the power of the human imagination is sufficient to produce such changes even in our physical nature as might almost appear miraculous. The truth is an important one; the fact (for it is a *fact*)[10] is a valuable illustration of it. And I have the satisfaction of knowing that it has been communicated to many hundreds of people who would never have heard of it, had it not been narrated as a Ballad, and in a more impressive metre than is usual in Ballads. . . .

Long as I have detained my Reader, I hope he will permit me to caution him against a mode of false criticism which has been applied to Poetry in which the language closely resembles that of life and nature. Such verses have been triumphed over in parodies of which Dr. Johnson's Stanza is a fair specimen.

"I put my hat upon my head,
And walk'd into the Strand,
And there I met another man
Whose hat was in his hand."

Immediately under these lines I will place one of the most justly admired stanzas of the "*Babes* in the Wood."[11]

"These pretty Babes with hand in hand
Went wandering up and down;
But never more they saw the Man
Approaching from the Town."

In both of these stanzas the words, and the order of the words, in no respect differ from the most unimpassioned conversation. There are words in both, for example, "the Strand," and "the Town," connected with none but the most familiar ideas; yet the one stanza we admit as admirable, and the other as a fair example of the superlatively contemptible. Whence arises this difference? Not from the metre, not from the language, not from the order of the words; but the *matter* expressed in Dr. Johnson's stanza is contemptible. The proper method of treating trivial and simple verses to which Dr. Johnson's stanza would be a fair parallelism is not to say this is a bad kind of poetry, or this is not poetry, but this wants sense; it is neither interesting in itself, nor can *lead* to any thing interesting; the images neither originate in that sane state of feeling which arises out of thought, nor can excite thought or feeling in the Reader. This is the only sensible manner of dealing with such verses: Why trouble yourself about the species till you have previously decided upon the genus? Why take pains to prove that an Ape is not a Newton when it is self-evident that he is not a man.

I have one request to make of my Reader, which is, that in judging these Poems he would decide by his own feelings genuinely, and not by reflection upon what will probably be the judgment of others. How common is it to hear a person say, "I myself do not object to this style of composition or this or that expression, but to such and such classes of people it will appear mean or ludicrous." This mode of criticism so destructive of all sound unadulterated judgment is almost universal: I have therefore to request that the Reader would abide independently by his own feelings, and that if he finds himself affected he would not suffer such conjectures to interfere with his pleasure. . . .

[10] "(for it is a fact)": Wordsworth based "Goody Blake and Henry Gill" and other experimental ballads on case studies of aberrant psychology in Erasmus Darwin's *Zoonomia* (1794).

[11] **Babes in the Wood**: *The Children in the Wood*, also known as the story of *Babes in the Wood*, an old ballad found in Thomas Percy's (1729–1811) important and influential collection, *Reliques of Ancient English Poetry* (3 vols., 1765).

'There Was a Boy'

(1800; comp. 1798)

There was a Boy,[1] ye knew him well, ye Cliffs
And Islands of Winander! many a time,
At evening, when the stars had just begun
To move along the edges of the hills,

[1] This autobiographical poem is also included in *Prelude*, V, to contrast the educative influence of nature versus formal schooling on the human imagination. See notes to the *Two-Part Prelude*.

Rising or setting, would he stand alone,
Beneath the trees, or by the glimmering lake,
And there, with fingers interwoven, both hands
Press'd closely palm to palm and to his mouth
Uplifted, he, as through an instrument,
Blew mimic hootings to the silent owls
That they might answer him. And they would shout
Across the wat'ry vale and shout again,
Responsive to his call, with quivering peals,
And long halloos, and screams, and echoes loud
Redoubled and redoubled, a wild scene
Of mirth and jocund din. And, when it chanced
That pauses of deep silence mock'd his skill,
Then, sometimes, in that silence, while he hung
Listening, a gentle shock of mild surprize
Has carried far into his heart the voice
Of mountain torrents, or the visible scene
Would enter unawares into his mind
With all its solemn imagery, its rocks,
Its woods, and that uncertain heaven, receiv'd
Into the bosom of the steady lake.
Fair are the woods, and beauteous is the spot,
The vale where he was born: the Church-yard hangs
Upon a slope above the village school,
And there along that bank when I have pass'd
At evening, I believe, that near his grave
A full half-hour together I have stood
Mute—for he died when he was ten years old.

'Strange Fits of Passion I Have Known'

(1800; comp. 1798)

Strange fits of passion I have known,[1]
And I will dare to tell,
But in the lover's ear alone,
What once to me befel.

When she I lov'd, was strong and gay
And like a rose in June,
I to her cottage bent my way,
Beneath the evening moon.

Upon the moon I fix'd my eye,
All over the wide lea;
My horse trudg'd on, and we drew nigh
Those paths so dear to me.

And now we reach'd the orchard-plot,
And, as we climb'd the hill,
Towards the roof of Lucy's cot
The moon descended still.

In one of those sweet dreams I slept,
Kind Nature's gentlest boon!
And, all the while, my eyes I kept
On the descending moon.

My horse mov'd on; hoof after hoof
He rais'd and never stopp'd:
When down behind the cottage roof
At once the planet dropp'd.

What fond and wayward thoughts will slide
Into a Lover's head—
"O mercy!" to myself I cried,
"If Lucy should be dead!"

[1] "Strange fits of passion," "She dwelt among th' untrodden ways," "A slumber did my spirit seal," and "Three years she grew in sun and shower" are traditionally grouped with the later poem, "I travell'd among unknown Men" (from *Poems in Two Volumes*) as the Lucy poems.

Song

(1800; comp. 1798)

She dwelt among th' untrodden ways
Beside the springs of Dove,
A Maid whom there were none to praise
And very few to love.

A Violet by a mossy Stone
Half-hidden from the Eye!
—Fair as a star when only one
Is shining in the sky!

She *liv'd* unknown, and few could know
When Lucy ceas'd to be;
But she is in her Grave, and oh!
The difference to me.

'A Slumber Did My Spirit Seal'

(1800; comp. 1798)

A slumber did my spirit seal,
I had no human fears:

She seem'd a thing that could not feel
  The touch of earthly years.

No motion has she now, no force;
  She neither hears nor sees;
Roll'd round in earth's diurnal course
  With rocks and stones and trees!

Lucy Gray
(1800; comp. 1798–1799)

Oft had I heard of Lucy Gray,
And when I cross'd the Wild,
I chanc'd to see at break of day
The solitary Child.

No mate, no comrade Lucy knew:
She dwelt on a wide Moor,
The sweetest Thing that ever grew
Beside a human door!

You yet may spy the Fawn at play,
The Hare upon the Green:
But the sweet face of Lucy Gray
Will never more be seen.

"To-night will be a stormy night,
You to the Town must go,
And take a lantern, Child, to light
Your Mother thro' the snow."

"That, Father! will I gladly do,
'Tis scarcely afternoon—
The Minster-clock has just struck two,
And yonder is the Moon."

At this the Father rais'd his hook
And snapp'd a faggot-band;
He plied his work, and Lucy took
The lantern in her hand.

Not blither is the mountain roe,
With many a wanton stroke
Her feet disperse the powd'ry snow
That rises up like smoke.

The storm came on before its time,
She wander'd up and down
And many a hill did Lucy climb
But never reach'd the Town.

The wretched Parents all that night
Went shouting far and wide;
But there was neither sound nor sight
To serve them for a guide.

At day-break on a hill they stood
That overlook'd the Moor;
And thence they saw the Bridge of wood
A furlong from their door.

And now they homeward turn'd, and cry'd
"In Heaven we all shall meet!"
When in the snow the Mother spied
The print of Lucy's feet.

Then downward from the steep hill's edge
They track'd the foot-marks small;
And through the broken hawthorn-hedge,
And by the long stone-wall;

And then an open field they cross'd,
The marks were still the same;
They track'd them on, nor ever lost,
And to the Bridge they came.

They follow'd from the snowy bank
The foot-marks, one by one,
Into the middle of the plank
—And further there were none.

Yet some maintain that to this day
She is a living Child,
That you may see sweet Lucy Gray
Upon the lonesome Wild.

O'er rough and smooth she trips along,
And never looks behind;
And sings a solitary song
That whistles in the wind.

The Two April Mornings
(1800; comp. 1798–1799)

We walk'd along, while bright and red
Uprose the morning sun,
And Mathew stopp'd, he look'd, and said,
"The will of God be done!"

A village Schoolmaster was he,
With hair of glittering grey;
As blithe a man as you could see
On a spring holiday.

And on that morning, through the grass,
And by the steaming rills,

We travell'd merrily to pass
A day among the hills.

"Our work," said I, "was well begun;
Then, from thy breast what thought,
Beneath so beautiful a sun,
So sad a sigh has brought?"

A second time did Mathew stop,
And fixing still his eye
Upon the eastern mountain-top
To me he made reply.

"Yon cloud with that long purple cleft
Brings fresh into my mind
A day like this which I have left
Full thirty years behind.

And on that slope of springing corn
The self-same crimson hue
Fell from the sky that April morn,
The same which now I view!

With rod and line my silent sport
I plied by Derwent's wave,
And, coming to the church, stopp'd short
Beside my Daughter's grave.

Nine summers had she scarcely seen,
The pride of all the vale;
And then she sang!—she would have been
A very nightingale.—

Six feet in earth my Emma lay,
And yet I lov'd her more,
For so it seem'd, than till that day
I e'er had lov'd before.

And, turning from her grave, I met
Beside the church-yard Yew
A blooming Girl, whose hair was wet
With points of morning dew.

A basket on her head she bare,
Her brow was smooth and white,
To see a Child so very fair,
It was a pure delight!

No fountain from its rocky cave
E'er tripp'd with foot so free,
She seem'd as happy as a wave
That dances on the sea.

There came from me a sigh of pain
Which I could ill confine;
I look'd at her and look'd again;
—And did not wish her mine."

Mathew is in his grave, yet now
Methinks I see him stand,
As at that moment, with his bough
Of wilding in his hand.—

The Fountain

—A CONVERSATION—

(1800; comp. 1798–1799)

We talk'd with open heart, and tongue
Affectionate and true,
A pair of Friends, though I was young,
And Mathew seventy-two.

We lay beneath a spreading oak,
Beside a mossy seat,
And from the turf a fountain broke,
And gurgled at our feet.

Now, Mathew, let us try to match
This water's pleasant tune
With some old Border-song, or catch
That suits a summer's noon.

Or of the Church-clock and the chimes
Sing here beneath the shade,
That half-mad thing of witty rhymes
Which you last April made!

In silence Mathew lay, and eyed
The spring beneath the tree;
And thus the dear old Man replied,
The grey-hair'd Man of glee.

"Down to the vale this water steers,
How merrily it goes!
'Twill murmur on a thousand years,
And flow as now it flows.

And here, on this delightful day,
I cannot chuse but think
How oft, a vigorous Man, I lay
Beside this Fountain's brink.

My eyes are dim with childish tears,
My heart is idly stirr'd,
For the same sound is in my ears
Which in those days I heard.

Thus fares it still in our decay:
And yet the wiser mind
Mourns less for what age takes away
Than what it leaves behind.

The blackbird in the summer trees,
The lark upon the hill,
Let loose their carols when they please,
Are quiet when they will.

With Nature never do *they* wage
A foolish strife; they see
A happy youth, and their old age
Is beautiful and free:

But we are press'd by heavy laws,
And often, glad no more,
We wear a face of joy, because
We have been glad of yore.

If there is one who need bemoan
His kindred laid in earth,
The houshold hearts that were his own,
It is the man of mirth.

My days, my Friend, are almost gone,
My life has been approv'd,
And many love me, but by none
Am I enough belov'd."

"Now both himself and me he wrongs,
The man who thus complains!
I live and sing my idle songs
Upon these happy plains,

And, Mathew, for thy Children dead
I'll be a son to thee."
At this he grasp'd his hands[1], and said,
"Alas! that cannot be."

We rose up from the fountain-side,
And down the smooth descent
Of the green sheep-track did we glide,
And through the wood we went,

And, ere we came to Leonard's Rock,
He sang those witty rhymes
About the crazy old Church-clock
And the bewilder'd chimes.

[1] **his hands**: revised in 1815 to "my hand."

Nutting
(1800; comp. 1798)

——————— It seems a day,
One of those heavenly days which cannot die,
When forth I sallied from our cottage-door,[1]
And with a wallet o'er my shoulder slung,
A nutting crook in hand, I turn'd my steps
Towards the distant woods, a Figure quaint,
Trick'd out in proud disguise of Beggar's weeds,
Put on for the occasion, by advice
And exhortation of my frugal Dame.
Motley accoutrement! of power to smile
At thorns, and brakes, and brambles, and, in truth,
More ragged than need was. Among the woods,
And o'er the pathless rocks, I forc'd my way
Until, at length, I came to one dear nook
Unvisited, where not a broken bough
Droop'd with its wither'd leaves, ungracious sign
Of devastation, but the hazels rose
Tall and erect, with milk-white clusters hung,
A virgin scene!—A little while I stood,
Breathing with such suppression of the heart
As joy delights in; and with wise restraint
Voluptuous, fearless of a rival, eyed
The banquet, or beneath the trees I sate
Among the flowers, and with the flowers I play'd;
A temper known to those, who, after long
And weary expectation, have been bless'd
With sudden happiness beyond all hope.—
—Perhaps it was a bower beneath whose leaves
The violets of five seasons reappear
And fade, unseen by any human eye,
Where fairy water-breaks do murmur on
For ever, and I saw the sparkling foam,
And with my cheek on one of those green stones
That, fleec'd with moss, beneath the shady trees
Lay round me scatter'd like a flock of sheep,
I heard the murmur and the murmuring sound,
In that sweet mood when pleasure loves to pay
Tribute to ease, and, of its joy secure,
The heart luxuriates with indifferent things,
Wasting its kindliness on stocks and stones,

[1] The house at which I was boarding during the time I was at school. [W.W.]

And on the vacant air.—Then up I rose,
And dragg'd to earth both branch and bough, with crash
And merciless ravage, and the shady nook
Of hazels, and the green and mossy bower,
Deform'd and sullied, patiently gave up
Their quiet being; and unless I now
Confound my present feelings with the past,
Even then, when from the bower I turn'd away,
Exulting, rich beyond the wealth of kings—
I felt a sense of pain when I beheld
The silent trees and the intruding sky.—

Then, dearest Maiden! move along these shades
In gentleness of heart; with gentle hand
Touch,—for there is a Spirit in the woods.

'Three Years She Grew in Sun and Shower'

(1800; comp. 1799)

Three years she grew in sun and shower,
Then Nature said, "A lovelier flower
On earth was never sown;
This Child I to myself will take,
She shall be mine, and I will make
A Lady of my own.

Myself will to my darling be
Both law and impulse, and with me
The Girl in rock and plain,
In earth and heaven, in glade and bower,
Shall feel an overseeing power
To kindle or restrain.

She shall be sportive as the fawn
That wild with glee across the lawn
Or up the mountain springs;
And hers shall be the breathing balm
And hers the silence and the calm
Of mute insensate things.

The floating clouds their state shall lend
To her, for her the willow bend,
Nor shall she fail to see
Even in the motions of the storm
A beauty that shall mould her form
By silent sympathy.

The stars of midnight shall be dear
To her, and she shall lean her ear
In many a secret place
Where rivulets dance their wayward round,
And beauty born of murmuring sound
Shall pass into her face.

And vital feelings of delight
Shall rear her form to stately height,
Her virgin bosom swell;
Such thoughts to Lucy I will give
While she and I together live
Here in this happy dell."

Thus Nature spake—The work was done—
How soon my Lucy's race was run!
She died and left to me
This heath, this calm and quiet scene,
The memory of what has been,
And never more will be.—

Michael, a Pastoral Poem[1]

(1800; comp. 1800)

If from the public way you turn your steps
Up the tumultuous brook of Green-head Gill,
You will suppose that with an upright path
Your feet must struggle; in such bold ascent
The pastoral Mountains front you, face to face.
But, courage! for beside that boisterous Brook
The Mountains have all open'd out themselves,
And made a hidden valley of their own.
No habitation there is seen; but such
As journey thither find themselves alone
With a few sheep, with rocks and stones, and kites
That overhead are sailing in the Sky.
It is in truth an utter solitude,
Nor should I have made mention of this Dell
But for one object which you might pass by,
Might see and notice not. Beside the brook
There is a straggling Heap of unhewn stones;
And to that place a Story appertains,

[1] On the political purpose of the poem, see letter to Charles James Fox, following.

Which, though it be ungarnish'd with events,
Is not unfit, I deem, for the fire-side
Or for the summer shade. It was the first,
The earliest of those Tales that spake to me
Of Shepherds, dwellers in the Vallies, men
Whom I already lov'd, not verily
For their own sakes, but for the fields and hills
Where was their occupation and abode.
And hence this Tale, while I was yet a boy
Careless of books, yet having felt the power
Of Nature, by the gentle agency
Of natural objects led me on to feel
For passions that were not my own, and think
At random and imperfectly indeed
On man, the heart of man, and human life.
Therefore, although it be a history
Homely and rude, I will relate the same
For the delight of a few natural hearts,
And with yet fonder feeling, for the sake
Of youthful Poets, who among these Hills
Will be my second Self when I am gone.

Upon the Forest-side in Grasmere Vale
There dwelt a Shepherd, Michael was his name,
An old man, stout of heart, and strong of limb.
His bodily frame had been from youth to age
Of an unusual strength: his mind was keen,
Intense and frugal, apt for all affairs,
And in his Shepherd's calling he was prompt
And watchful more than ordinary men.
Hence he had learn'd the meaning of all winds,
Of blasts of every tone, and often-times
When others heeded not, He heard the South
Make subterraneous music, like the noise
Of Bagpipers on distant Highland Hills.
The Shepherd, at such warning, of his flock
Bethought him, and he to himself would say,
"The Winds are now devising work for me!"
And truly at all times the storm, that drives
The Traveller to a shelter, summon'd him
Up to the mountains: he had been alone
Amid the heart of many thousand mists
That came to him and left him on the heights.
So liv'd he till his eightieth year was pass'd.
And grossly that man errs, who should suppose
That the green Valleys, and the Streams and Rocks
Were things indifferent to the Shepherd's thoughts.
Fields where with chearful spirits he had breath'd
The common air; the hills, which he so oft
Had climb'd with vigorous steps; which had impress'd
So many incidents upon his mind
Of hardship, skill or courage, joy or fear;
Which like a book preserv'd the memory
Of the dumb animals, whom he had sav'd,
Had fed or shelter'd, linking to such acts,
So grateful in themselves, the certainty
Of honorable gains; these fields, these hills
Which were his living Being even more
Than his own Blood—what could they less? had lay'd
Strong hold on his Affections, were to him
A pleasurable feeling of blind love,
The pleasure which there is in life itself.

He had not pass'd his days in singleness.
He had a Wife, a comely Matron, old
Though younger than himself full twenty years.
She was a Woman of a stirring life
Whose heart was in her house: two wheels she had
Of antique form, this large for spinning wool,
That small for flax, and if one wheel had rest,
It was because the other was at work.
The Pair had but one Inmate in their house,
An only Child, who had been born to them
When Michael telling o'er his years began
To deem that he was old, in shepherd's phrase,
With one foot in the grave. This only Son
With two brave Sheep-dogs tried in many a storm,
The one of an inestimable worth,
Made all their Household. I may truly say,
That they were as a proverb in the vale
For endless industry. When day was gone,
And from their occupations out of doors
The Son and Father were come home, even then
Their labour did not cease, unless when all
Turn'd to their cleanly Supper-board, and there
Each with a mess of pottage and skimm'd milk,
Sate round their Basket pil'd with oaten cake
And their plain home-made cheese. Yet when their
Meal
Was ended, LUKE (for so the Son was nam'd)
And his old Father both betook themselves
To such convenient work, as might employ
Their hands by the fire-side; perhaps to card
Wool for the Housewife's spindle, or repair
Some injury done to sickle, flail, or scythe
Or other implement of house or field.

Down from the ceiling by the chimney's edge
Which in our antient uncouth country style
Did with a huge Projection overbrow

Large space beneath, as duly as the light
Of day grew dim, the Housewife hung a Lamp,
An aged utensil, which had perform'd
Service beyond all others of its kind.
Early at evening did it burn and late,
Surviving Comrade of uncounted Hours
Which going by from year to year had found
And left the Couple neither gay perhaps
Nor chearful, yet with objects and with hopes
Living a life of eager industry.
And now when Luke was in his eighteenth year
There by the light of this old Lamp they sate,
Father and Son, while late into the night
The Housewife plied her own peculiar work,
Making the Cottage through the silent hours
Murmur as with the sound of summer flies.
Not with a waste of words, but for the sake
Of pleasure, which I know that I shall give
To many living now, I of this Lamp
Speak thus minutely: for there are no few
Whose memories will bear witness to my Tale.
The Light was famous in its neighbourhood
And was a public Symbol of the life,
The thrifty Pair had liv'd. For as it chanc'd
Their Cottage on a plot of rising ground
Stood single, with large prospect North and South,
High into Easedale, up to Dunmal-Raise,
And Westward to the Village near the Lake.
And from this constant light so regular
And so far seen, the House itself by all
Who dwelt within the limits of the Vale,
Both old and young, was nam'd The Evening Star.

Thus living on through such a length of years
The Shepherd if he lov'd himself must needs
Have lov'd his Helpmate; but to Michael's heart
This Son of his old age was yet more dear—
Effect which might perhaps have been produc'd
By that instinctive tenderness, the same
Blind Spirit, which is in the blood of all,
Or that a child more than all other gifts
Brings hope with it, and forward-looking thoughts
And stirrings of inquietude, when they
By tendency of nature needs must fail.
From such and other causes to the thoughts
Of the old Man his only Son was now
The dearest object that he knew on earth.
Exceeding was the Love he bare to him,
His Heart and his Heart's Joy! For oftentimes
Old Michael, while he was a Babe in arms,
Had done him female service, not alone
For dalliance and delight, as is the use
Of Fathers, but with patient mind enforc'd
To acts of tenderness; and he had rock'd
His cradle with a woman's gentle hand.

And in a later time ere yet the Boy
Had put on Boy's attire, did Michael love,
Albeit of a stern unbending mind,
To have the young one in his sight, when he
Had work by his own door, or when he sate
With sheep before him on his Shepherd's stool
Beneath that large old Oak, which near their door
Stood, and from its enormous breadth of shade
Chosen for the Shearer's covert from the sun
Thence in our rustic dialect was call'd
The Clipping[2] Tree, a name which yet it bears.
There while they two were sitting in the shade
With others round them, earnest all and blithe,
Would Michael exercise his heart with looks
Of fond correction and reproof bestow'd
Upon the Child, if he disturb'd the sheep
By catching at their legs, or with his shouts
Scar'd them, while they lay still beneath the Shears.

And when by Heaven's good grace the Boy grew up
A healthy Lad, and carried in his cheek
Two steady roses that were five years old,
Then Michael from a winter coppice cut
With his own hands a sapling, which he hoop'd
With iron, making it throughout in all
Due requisites a perfect Shepherd's Staff,
And gave it to the Boy; wherewith equipp'd
He as a Watchman oftentimes was plac'd
At gate or gap to stem or turn the Flock,
And to his office prematurely call'd
There stood the Urchin, as you will divine
Something between a hindrance and a help,
And for this cause not always I believe
Receiving from his Father hire of praise
Though nought was left undone, which staff or voice
Or looks or threatening gestures could perform.
But soon as Luke, now ten years old, could stand
Against the mountain blasts, and to the Heights,
Not fearing toil, nor length of weary ways,

[2] Clipping is the word used in the North of England for shearing. [W.W.]

He with his Father daily went, and they
Were as companions, why should I relate
That objects which the Shepherd lov'd before
Were dearer now? That from the Boy there came
Feelings and emanations, things which were
Light to the sun, and music to the wind,
And that the Old Man's Heart seem'd born again.

Thus in his Father's sight the Boy grew up,
And now when he had reach'd his eighteenth year,
He was his comfort and his daily hope.
While this good household thus were living on
From day to day, to Michael's ear there came
Distressful tidings. Long before the time
Of which I speak, the Shepherd had been bound
In surety for his Brother's Son, a man
Of an industrious life and ample means,
But unforeseen misfortunes suddenly
Had press'd upon him, and old Michael now
Was summon'd to discharge the forfeiture,
A grievous penalty, but little less
Than half his substance. This unlook'd-for claim
At the first hearing for a moment took
More hope out of his life than he supposed
That any old man ever could have lost.
As soon as he had gather'd so much strength
That he could look his trouble in the face,
It seem'd that his sole refuge was to sell
A portion of his patrimonial fields.
Such was his first resolve; he thought again
And his heart fail'd him. "Isabel," said he,
Two evenings after he had heard the news,
"I have been toiling more than seventy years,
And in the open sunshine of God's love
Have we all lived, yet if these fields of ours
Should pass into a Stranger's hand, I think
That I could not lie quiet in my grave.
Our lot is a hard lot; the sun itself
Has scarcely been more diligent than I,
And I have lived to be a fool at last
To my own family. An evil Man
That was, and made an evil choice, if he
Were false to us; and if he were not false
There are ten thousand to whom loss like this
Had been no sorrow. I forgive him—but
'Twere better to be dumb than to talk thus.
When I began, my purpose was to speak
Of remedies and of a chearful hope.
Our Luke shall leave us, Isabel; the land
Shall not go from us, and it shall be free,
He shall possess it free as is the wind
That passes over it. We have, thou knowest,
Another kinsman, he will be our friend
In this distress. He is a prosperous man,
Thriving in trade, and Luke to him shall go
And with his Kinsman's help and his own thrift
He quickly will repair this loss, and then
May come again to us. If here he stay
What can be done? Where every one is poor
What can be gain'd?" At this the old man paus'd,
And Isabel sate silent, for her mind
Was busy, looking back into past times.
There's Richard Bateman, thought she to herself,
He was a parish Boy[3]—At the church door
They made a gathering for him, shillings, pence,
And halfpennies, wherewith the Neighbours bought
A Basket which they fill'd with Pedlar's wares,
And with this Basket on his arm the Lad
Went up to London, found a Master there
Who out of many chose the trusty Boy
To go and overlook his merchandise
Beyond the seas, where he grew wondrous rich,
And left estates and monies to the poor,
And at his birth-place built a Chapel, floor'd
With marble which he sent from foreign Lands.
These thoughts and many others of like sort
Pass'd quickly through the mind of Isabel
And her face brighten'd. The Old Man was glad
And thus resumed. "Well! Isabel, this scheme
These two days has been meat and drink to me.
Far more than we have lost is left us yet.
—We have enough—I wish indeed that I
Were younger, but this hope is a good hope.
—Make ready Luke's best garments, of the best
Buy for him more, and let us send him forth
To-morrow, or the next day, or to-night,
—If he could go the Boy should go to-night."

Here Michael ceased, and to the fields went forth
With a light heart. The Housewife for five days
Was restless morn and night, and all day long
Wrought on with her best fingers to prepare
Things needful for the journey of her Son.

---

[3] **parish Boy:** a parish was a governmental district with responsibility for executing the Poor-law. A parish Boy was one who had received such relief.

But Isabel was glad when Sunday came
To stop her in her work: for, when she lay
By Michael's side, she for the two last nights
Heard him, how he was troubled in his sleep;
And when they rose at morning she could see
That all his hopes were gone. That day at noon
She said to Luke while they two by themselves
Were sitting at the door, "Thou must not go,
We have no other Child but thee to lose,
None to remember—do not go away,
For if thou leave thy Father he will die."
The Lad made answer with a jocund voice,
And Isabel when she had told her fears
Recover'd heart. That evening her best fare
Did she bring forth, and all together sate
Like happy people round a Christmas fire.

Next morning Isabel resumed her work,
And all the ensuing week the house appear'd
As cheerful as a grove in spring: at length
The expected letter from their Kinsman came
With kind assurances that he would do
His utmost for the welfare of the Boy,
To which requests were added that forthwith
He might be sent to him. Ten times or more
The letter was read over, Isabel
Went forth to shew it to the neighbours round,
Nor was there at that time on English Land
A prouder heart than Luke's. When Isabel
Had to her house returned, the Old Man said,
"He shall depart tomorrow." To this word
The Housewife answered, talking much of things
Which, if at such short notice he should go,
Would surely be forgotten. But at length
She gave consent, and Michael was at ease.

Near the tumultuous brook of Green-head Gill
In that deep Valley Michael had designed
To build a Sheep-fold and, before he heard
The tidings of his melancholy loss,
For this same purpose he had gathered up
A heap of stones, which close to the brook side
Lay thrown together, ready for the work.
With Luke that evening thitherward he walk'd;
And soon as they had reach'd the place he stopp'd
And thus the old man spake to him. "My Son,
To-morrow thou wilt leave me; with full heart
I look upon thee, for thou art the same
That wert a promise to me ere thy birth,
And all thy life hast been my daily joy.
I will relate to thee some little part
Of our two histories; 'twill do thee good
When thou art from me, even if I should speak
Of things thou canst not know of.—After thou
First cam'st into the world, as it befalls
To new-born infants, thou didst sleep away
Two days, and blessings from thy Father's tongue
Then fell upon thee. Day by day pass'd on,
And still I lov'd thee with encreasing love.
Never to living ear came sweeter sounds
Than when I heard thee by our own fire-side
First uttering without words a natural tune,
When thou, a feeding babe, didst in thy joy
Sing at thy Mother's breast. Month follow'd month,
And in the open fields my life was pass'd
And in the mountains, else I think that thou
Hadst been brought up upon thy father's knees.
—But we were playmates, Luke; among these hills,
As well thou know'st, in us the old and young
Have play'd together, nor with me didst thou
Lack any pleasure which a boy can know."
Luke had a manly heart; but at these words
He sobb'd aloud; the Old Man grasp'd his hand,
And said, "Nay do not take it so—I see
That these are things of which I need not speak.
—Even to the utmost I have been to thee
A kind and a good Father: and herein
I but repay a gift which I myself
Receiv'd at others' hands, for, though now old
Beyond the common life of man, I still
Remember them who lov'd me in my youth.
Both of them sleep together: here they liv'd
As all their Forefathers had done, and when
At length their time was come they were not loth
To give their bodies to the family mold.
I wish'd that thou should'st live the life they liv'd.
But 'tis a long time to look back, my Son,
And see so little gain from sixty years.
These fields were burthen'd when they came to me,
'Till I was forty years of age, not more
Than half of my inheritance was mine.
I toil'd and toil'd; God bless'd me in my work
And 'till these three weeks past the land was free,
—It looks as if it never could endure
Another master. Heaven forgive me, Luke,
If I judge ill for thee, but it seems good
That thou should'st go." At this the Old Man paus'd,

Then, pointing to the stones near which they stood,
Thus after a short silence he resumed.
"This was a work for us, and now, my Son,
It is a work for me. But lay one stone,
Here lay it for me, Luke, with thine own hands.
I for the purpose brought thee to this place.
Nay, Boy, be of good hope:—we both may live
To see a better day: at eighty four
I still am strong and stout,—do thou thy part,
I will do mine.—I will begin again
With many tasks that were resigned to thee,
Up to the heights and in among the storms
Will I without thee go again, and do
All works which I was wont to do alone,
Before I knew thy face—Heaven bless thee, Boy,
Thy heart these two weeks has been beating fast
With many hopes—it should be so—yes—yes—
I knew that thou could'st never have a wish
To leave me, Luke,—thou hast been bound to me
Only by links of love, when thou art gone
What will be left to us!—But I forget
My purposes. Lay now the corner stone
As I requested, and hereafter, Luke,
When thou art gone away, should evil men
Be thy companions, let this Sheep-fold be
Thy anchor and thy shield; amid all fear
And all temptation let it be to thee
An emblem of the life thy Fathers liv'd,
Who, being innocent, did for that cause
Bestir them in good deeds. Now fare thee well:
When thou return'st thou in this place wilt see
A work which is not here, a covenant
'Twill be between us——but whatever fate
Befall thee, I shall love thee to the last,
And bear thy memory with me to the grave."

The Shepherd ended here; and Luke stoop'd down,
And as his Father had requested, laid
The first stone of the Sheep-fold; at the sight
The Old Man's grief broke from him, to his heart
He press'd his Son, he kissed him and wept:
And to the House together they return'd.
Next morning, as had been resolv'd, the Boy
Began his journey, and when he had reach'd
The public Way, he put on a bold face;
And all the Neighbours as he pass'd their doors
Came forth with wishes and with farewell prayers,
That follow'd him 'till he was out of sight.
A good report did from their Kinsman come
Of Luke and his well doing; and the Boy
Wrote loving letters full of wondrous news,
Which, as the Housewife phras'd it, were throughout
The prettiest letters that were ever seen.
Both parents read them with rejoicing hearts.
So, many months pass'd on: and once again
The shepherd went about his daily work
With confident and cheerful thoughts; and now
Sometimes when he could find a leisure hour
He to that valley took his way, and there
Wrought at the sheep-fold. Meantime, Luke began
To slacken in his duty, and at length
He in the dissolute city gave himself
To evil courses: ignominy and shame
Fell on him, so that he was driven at last
To seek a hiding-place beyond the seas.

There is a comfort in the strength of love;
'Twill make a thing endurable, which else
Would break the heart:—old Michael found it so.
I have convers'd with more than one who well
Remember the Old Man and what he was
Years after he had heard this heavy news.
His bodily frame had been from youth to age
Of an unusual strength. Among the rocks
He went, and still look'd up upon the sun,
And listen'd to the wind; and as before
Perform'd all kinds of labour for his sheep,
And for the land his small inheritance.
And to that hollow Dell from time to time
Did he repair, to build the Fold of which
His flock had need. 'Tis not forgotten yet
The pity which was then in every heart
For the Old Man—and 'tis believ'd by all
That many and many a day he thither went,
And never lifted up a single stone.
There, by the Sheep-fold, sometimes was he seen
Sitting alone, with that his faithful Dog,
Then old, beside him, lying at his feet.
The length of full seven years from time to time
He at the building of this sheep-fold wrought,
And left the work unfinished when he died.

Three years, or little more, did Isabel
Survive her Husband: at her death the estate
Was sold, and went into a Stranger's hand.
The Cottage which was nam'd The Evening Star
Is gone, the ploughshare has been through the ground

On which it stood; great changes have been wrought
In all the neighbourhood, yet the Oak is left
That grew beside their Door; and the remains
Of the unfinished Sheep-fold may be seen
Beside the boisterous brook of Green-head Gill.

from Letter to Charles James Fox[1]

Grasmere, Westmoreland January 14th 1801

SIR,

. . . It appears to me that the most calamitous effect, which has followed the measures which have lately been pursued in this country, is a rapid decay of the domestic affections among the lower orders of society. This effect the present Rulers of this country are not conscious of, or they disregard it. For many years past, the tendency of society amongst almost all the nations of Europe has been to produce it. But recently, by the spreading of manufactures[2] through every part of the country, by the heavy taxes upon postage, by workhouses, Houses of Industry, and the invention of Soup-shops &c. &c. superadded to the encreasing disproportion between the price of labour and that of the necessaries of life, the bond of domestic feeling among the poor, as far as the influence of these things has extended, have been weakened, and in innumerable instances entirely destroyed. The evil would be the less to be regretted, if these institutions were regarded only as palliatives to a disease; but the vanity and pride of their promoters are so subtly interwoven with them, that they are deemed great discoveries and blessings to humanity. In the mean time parents are separated from their children, and children from their parents; the wife no longer prepares with her own hands a meal for her husband, the produce of his labour; there is little doing in his house in which his affections can be interested, and but little left in it which he can love. I have two neighbours, a man and his wife, both upwards of eighty years of age; they live alone; the husband has been confined to his bed many months and has never had, nor till within these few weeks has ever needed, any body to attend to him but his wife. She has recently been seized with a lameness which has often prevented her from being able to carry him his food to his bed; the neighbours fetch water for her from the well, and do other kind offices for them both, but her infirmities encrease. She told my Servant two days ago that she was afraid they must both be boarded out among some other Poor of the parish (they have long been supported by the parish) but she said, it was hard, having kept house together so long, to come to this, and she was sure that "it would burst her heart." I mention this fact to shew how deeply the spirit of independence is, even yet, rooted in some parts of the country. These people could not express themselves in this way without an almost sublime conviction of the blessings of independent domestic life. If it is true, as I believe, that this spirit is rapidly disappearing, no greater curse can befal a land.

I earnestly entreat your pardon for having detained you so long. In the two Poems, "The Brothers" and "Michael" I have attempted to draw a picture of the domestic affections as I know they exist amongst a class of men who are now almost confined to the North of England. They are small independent *proprietors* of land here called statesmen, men of respectable education who daily labour on their own little properties. The domestic affections will always be strong amongst men who live in a country not crowded with population, if these men are placed above poverty. But if they are proprietors of small estates, which have descended to them from their ancestors, the power which these affections will acquire amongst such men is inconceivable by those who have only had an opportunity of observing hired labourers, farmers, and the manufacturing Poor. Their little tract of land serves as a kind of permanent rallying point for their domestic feelings, as a tablet upon which they are written which makes them objects of memory in a thousand instances when they would otherwise be forgotten. It is a fountain fitted to the nature of social man from which supplies of affection, as pure as his heart was intended for, are daily drawn. This class of men is rapidly disappearing. You, Sir, have a consciousness, upon which every good man will congratulate you, that the whole of your public conduct has in one way or other been directed to the preservation of this class of men, and those who hold similar situations. You have felt that the most sacred of all property is the property of the Poor. The two poems which I have mentioned were written with a view to shew that men who do not wear fine cloaths can feel deeply. . . .

[1] Whig statesman, orator, and Member of Parliament, Fox was one of several prominent figures to whom Wordsworth sent complimentary copies of *Lyrical Ballads* (1800). See Burke's *Reflections** for family and property values Wordsworth here espouses.

[2] **manufactures:** Factories. See SOCIETY AND POLITICAL ECONOMY.

from POEMS IN TWO VOLUMES
(1807)

from Volume One

'She Was a Phantom of Delight'
(1807; comp. 1803–1804)

She was a Phantom of delight
When first she gleam'd upon my sight;
A lovely Apparition, sent
To be a moment's ornament;
Her eyes as stars of Twilight fair;
Like Twilight's, too, her dusky hair;
But all things else about her drawn
From May-time and the chearful Dawn;
A dancing Shape, an Image gay,
To haunt, to startle, and way-lay.

I saw her upon nearer view,
A Spirit, yet a Woman too!
Her household motions light and free,
And steps of virgin liberty;
A countenance in which did meet
Sweet records, promises as sweet;
A Creature not too bright or good
For human nature's daily food;
For transient sorrows, simple wiles,
Praise, blame, love, kisses, tears, and smiles.

And now I see with eye serene
The very pulse of the machine;
A Being breathing thoughtful breath;
A Traveller betwixt life and death;
The reason firm, the temperate will,
Endurance, foresight, strength and skill;
A perfect Woman; nobly plann'd,
To warn, to comfort, and command;
And yet a Spirit still, and bright
With something of an angel light.[1]

[1] **angel light:** revised to "angelic light" in 1845.

I Travell'd among Unknown Men
(1807; comp. 1801)

I travell'd among unknown Men,
In Lands beyond the Sea;
Nor England! did I know till then
What love I bore to thee.

'Tis past, that melancholy dream!
Nor will I quit thy shore
A second time; for still I seem
To love thee more and more.

Among thy mountains did I feel
The joy of my desire;
And She I cherish'd turn'd her wheel
Beside an English fire.

Thy mornings shew'd—thy nights conceal'd
The bowers where Lucy play'd;
And thine is, too, the last green field
Which Lucy's eyes survey'd!

Resolution and Independence[1]
(1807; comp. 1802)

There was a roaring in the wind all night;
The rain came heavily and fell in floods;
But now the sun is rising calm and bright;
The birds are singing in the distant woods;
Over his own sweet voice the Stock-dove broods;
The Jay makes answer as the Magpie chatters;
And all the air is fill'd with pleasant noise of waters.

All things that love the sun are out of doors;
The sky rejoices in the morning's birth;
The grass is bright with rain-drops; on the moors
The Hare is running races in her mirth;
And with her feet she from the plashy earth
Raises a mist; which, glittering in the sun,
Runs with her all the way, wherever she doth run.

[1] See Dorothy Wordsworth's *Grasmere Journal* (3 October 1800).*

I was a Traveller then upon the moor;
I saw the Hare that rac'd about with joy;
I heard the woods, and distant waters, roar;
Or heard them not, as happy as a Boy:
The pleasant season did my heart employ:
My old remembrances went from me wholly;
And all the ways of men, so vain and melancholy.

But, as it sometimes chanceth, from the might
Of joy in minds that can no farther go,
As high as we have mounted in delight
In our dejection do we sink as low,
To me that morning did it happen so;
And fears, and fancies, thick upon me came;
Dim sadness, and blind thoughts I knew not nor could name.

I heard the Sky-lark singing in the sky;
And I bethought me of the playful Hare:
Even such a happy Child of earth am I;
Even as these blissful Creatures do I fare;
Far from the world I walk, and from all care;
But there may come another day to me,
Solitude, pain of heart, distress, and poverty.

My whole life I have liv'd in pleasant thought,
As if life's business were a summer mood;
As if all needful things would come unsought
To genial faith, still rich in genial good;
But how can He expect that others should
Build for him, sow for him, and at his call
Love him, who for himself will take no heed at all?

I thought of Chatterton,[2] the marvellous Boy,
The sleepless Soul that perish'd in its pride;
Of Him[3] who walk'd in glory and in joy
Behind his plough,[4] upon the mountain-side:
By our own spirits are we deified;
We Poets in our youth begin in gladness;
But thereof comes in the end despondency and madness.

Now, whether it were by peculiar grace,
A leading from above, a something given,
Yet it befel, that, in this lonely place,
When up and down my fancy thus was driven,
And I with these untoward thoughts had striven,
I saw a Man before me unawares:
The oldest Man he seem'd that ever wore grey hairs.

My course I stopped as soon as I espied
The Old Man in that naked wilderness:
Close by a Pond, upon the further side,
He stood alone: a minute's space I guess
I watch'd him, he continuing motionless:
To the Pool's further margin then I drew;
He being all the while before me full in view.[5]

As a huge Stone is sometimes seen to lie
Couch'd on the bald top of an eminence;
Wonder to all who do the same espy
By what means it could thither come, and whence;
So that it seems a thing endued with sense:
Like a Sea-beast crawl'd forth, which on a shelf
Of rock or sand reposeth, there to sun itself.

Such seem'd this Man, not all alive nor dead,
Nor all asleep; in his extreme old age:
His body was bent double, feet and head
Coming together in their[6] pilgrimage;
As if some dire constraint of pain, or rage
Of sickness felt by him in times long past,
A more than human weight upon his frame had cast.

Himself he propp'd, his body, limbs, and face,
Upon a long grey Staff of shaven wood:
And, still as I drew near with gentle pace,
Beside the little pond or moorish flood
Motionless as a Cloud the Old Man stood;
That heareth not the loud winds when they call;
And moveth altogether, if it move at all.

At length, himself unsettling, he the Pond
Stirred with his Staff, and fixedly did look
Upon the muddy water, which he conn'd,
As if he had been reading in a book:
And now such freedom as I could I took;
And, drawing to his side, to him did say,
"This morning gives us promise of a glorious day."

[2] **Chatterton**: Thomas Chatterton (1752–1770), author of *Excellent Ballade of Charitie,* which has the same stanzaic form as Wordsworth's poem. Apparently in despair over poverty, Chatterton committed suicide with arsenic in 1770, the year of Wordsworth's birth.

[3] **Him**: Robert Burns,* the "heaven taught Ploughman," also known for his dissolute life.

[4] **Behind his plough . . .** : revised to "following his plough along the mountainside" in 1820.

[5] **My course . . . full in view**: ll. 57–63 were omitted in 1820.

[6] **their**: changed to "life's" in 1820.

A gentle answer did the Old Man make,
In courteous speech which forth he slowly drew:
And him with further words I thus bespake,
"What kind of work is that which you pursue?
This is a lonesome place for one like you."
He answer'd me with pleasure and surprize;
And there was, while he spake, a fire about his eyes.

His words came feebly, from a feeble chest,
Yet each in solemn order follow'd each,
With something of a lofty utterance drest;
Choice word, and measured phrase; above the reach
Of ordinary men; a stately speech!
Such as grave Livers do in Scotland use,
Religious men, who give to God and Man their dues.

He told me that he to this Pond had come
To gather Leeches, being old and poor:
Employment hazardous and wearisome!
And he had many hardships to endure:
From Pond to Pond he roam'd, from moor to moor,
Housing, with God's good help, by choice or chance:
And in this way he gain'd an honest maintenance.

The Old Man still stood talking by my side;
But now his voice to me was like a stream
Scarce heard; nor word from word could I divide;
And the whole Body of the man did seem
Like one whom I had met with in a dream;
Or like a Man from some far region sent,
To give me human strength, and strong admonishment.

My former thoughts return'd: the fear that kills;
The hope that is unwilling to be fed;
Cold, pain, and labour, and all fleshly ills;
And mighty Poets in their misery dead.
And now, not knowing what the Old Man had said,
My question eagerly did I renew,
"How is it that you live, and what is it you do?"

He with a smile did then his words repeat;
And said, that, gathering Leeches, far and wide
He travelled; stirring thus about his feet
The waters of the Ponds where they abide.
"Once I could meet with them on every side;
But they have dwindled long by slow decay;
Yet still I persevere, and find them where I may."

While he was talking thus, the lonely place,
The Old Man's shape, and speech, all troubled me:
In my mind's eye I seem'd to see him pace
About the weary moors continually,
Wandering about alone and silently.
While I these thoughts within myself pursued,
He, having made a pause, the same discourse renewed.

And soon with this he other matter blended,
Chearfully uttered, with demeanour kind,
But stately in the main; and, when he ended,
I could have laugh'd myself to scorn, to find
In that decrepit Man so firm a mind.
"God," said I, "be my help and stay secure;
I'll think of the Leech-gatherer on the lonely moor."

Prefatory Sonnet[1]

(1807; comp. 1802)

Nuns fret not at their Convent's narrow room;
And Hermits are contented with their Cells;
And Students with their pensive Citadels:
Maids at the Wheel, the Weaver at his Loom,
Sit blithe and happy; Bees that soar for bloom,
High as the highest Peak of Furness Fells,[2]
Will murmur by the hour in Foxglove bells:
In truth, the prison, unto which we doom
Ourselves, no prison is: and hence to me,
In sundry moods, 'twas pastime to be bound
Within the Sonnet's scanty plot of ground:
Pleas'd if some Souls (for such there needs must be)
Who have felt the weight of too much liberty,
Should find short solace there, as I have found.

'With Ships the Sea Was Sprinkled Far and Nigh'

(1807; comp. 1802–1804)

With Ships the sea was sprinkled far and nigh,
Like stars in heaven, and joyously it showed;
Some lying fast at anchor in the road,

[1] Commonly titled "Nuns fret not at their Convent's narrow room," this sonnet introduces two groups of sonnets: "Part the First. Miscellaneous Sonnets" and "Part the Second. Sonnets Dedicated to Liberty." The sonnets are numbered rather than titled, thus it has become conventional to use their first lines as titles.

[2] **Furness Fells:** hills west of Lake Windermere, in the Lake District.

Some veering up and down, one knew not why.
A goodly Vessel did I then espy
Come like a Giant from a haven broad;
And lustily along the Bay she strode,
Her tackling[1] rich, and of apparel high.
This Ship was nought to me, nor I to her,
Yet I pursued her with a Lover's look;
This Ship to all the rest did I prefer:
When will she turn, and whither? She will brook
No tarrying; where she comes the winds must stir:
On went She, and due north her journey took.

Composed upon Westminster Bridge, Sept. 3, 1803[1†]

(1807, comp. 1802)

Earth has not any thing to shew more fair:
Dull would he be of soul who could pass by
A sight so touching in it's majesty:
This City now doth like a garment wear
The beauty of the morning; silent, bare,
Ships, towers, domes, theatres, and temples lie
Open unto the fields, and to the sky;
All bright and glittering in the smokeless air.
Never did sun more beautifully steep
In his first splendor valley, rock, or hill;
Ne'er saw I, never felt, a calm so deep!
The river glideth at his own sweet will:
Dear God! the very houses seem asleep;
And all that mighty heart is lying still!

'The World Is Too Much with Us; Late and Soon'

(1807; comp. 1802–1804)

The world is too much with us; late and soon,
Getting and spending, we lay waste our powers:
Little we see in nature that is ours;
We have given our hearts away, a sordid boon!
This Sea that bares her bosom to the moon;
The Winds that will be howling at all hours
And are up-gathered now like sleeping flowers;
For this, for every thing, we are out of tune;
It moves us not. Great God! I'd rather be
A Pagan suckled in a creed outworn;
So might I, standing on this pleasant lea,
Have glimpses that would make me less forlorn;
Have sight of Proteus[1] coming from the sea;
Or hear old Triton[2] blow his wreathed horn.

'It Is a Beauteous Evening, Calm and Free'

(1807; comp. 1802)

It is a beauteous Evening, calm and free,
The holy time is quiet as a Nun
Breathless with adoration; the broad sun
Is sinking down in its tranquillity;
The gentleness of heaven is on the Sea:
Listen! the mighty Being is awake
And doth with his eternal motion make
A sound like thunder—everlastingly.
Dear Child! dear Girl![1†] that walkest with me here,
If thou appear'st untouch'd by solemn thought,
Thy nature is not therefore less divine:
Thou liest in Abraham's bosom all the year;
And worshipp'st at the Temple's inner shrine,[2†]
God being with thee when we know it not.

[1] **tackling:** ship's gear, especially that used to apply tension to its sails with cables, blocks, and pulleys.

[1†] **1803:** the date was changed to 1802 in 1838. The composition dates were probably July–September 1802.

[1] **Proteus:** "minor sea-god, herdsman of the flocks of the sea, seals, etc. In Homer . . . servant of Poseidon, who has the power to take all manner of shapes, but if held till he resumes the true one, will answer questions" (*Oxford Classical Dictionary*, 2nd. ed).

[2] **Triton:** the merman of Greek mythology who plays a conch.

[1†] **dear Girl!:** Anne-Caroline, the French daughter of Wordsworth and Annette Vallon. See the introduction to Wordsworth.

[2†] Luke 16:22. "And it came to pass, that the beggar died, and was carried into Abraham's bosom . . ." The "Temple's inner shrine" is probably a reference to the Holy of Holies, the innermost enclosure where the Ark of the Covenant and the mercy-seat are located. See Exodus 25:8–22.

Composed by the Sea-side, near Calais,[1] August, 1802
(1807; comp. 1802)

Fair Star of Evening, Splendor of the West,
Star of my Country! on the horizon's brink
Thou hangest, stooping, as might seem, to sink
On England's bosom; yet well pleas'd to rest,
Meanwhile, and be to her a glorious crest
Conspicuous to the Nations. Thou, I think,
Should'st be my Country's emblem; and should'st wink,
Bright Star! with laughter on her banners, drest
In thy fresh beauty. There! that dusky spot
Beneath thee, it is England; there it lies.
Blessings be on you both! one hope, one lot,
One life, one glory! I, with many a fear
For my dear Country, many heartfelt sighs,
Among Men who do not love her linger here.

Calais, August, 1802[1†]
(1803/1807; comp. 1802)

Is it a Reed that's shaken by the wind,[2†]
Or what is it that ye go forth to see?
Lords, Lawyers, Statesmen, Squires of low degree,
Men known, and men unknown, Sick, Lame, and Blind,
Post forward all, like Creatures of one kind,
With first-fruit offerings crowd to bend the knee
In France, before the new-born Majesty.[3†]
'Tis ever thus. Ye Men of prostrate mind!
A seemly reverence may be paid to power;
But that's a loyal virtue, never sown
In haste, nor springing with a transient shower:
When truth, when sense, when liberty were flown
What hardship had it been to wait an hour?
Shame on you, feeble Heads, to slavery prone!

[1] Calais, France, is the seaport town opposite Dover, England.

[1†] First published 13 January 1803 in the *Morning Post.*

[2†] Matthew 11:7. "And as they departed, Jesus began to say unto the multitudes concerning John, 'What went ye out into the wilderness to see? A reed shaken with the wind?'"

[3†] **Majesty:** Napoleon, who was made Consul for life on 2 August 1802. (See THE FRENCH REVOLUTION AND RIGHTS OF MAN.)

'I Griev'd for Buonaparte'[1]
(1802/1807; comp. 1802)

I griev'd for Buonaparte, with a vain
And an unthinking grief! the vital blood
Of that Man's mind what can it be? What food
Fed his first hopes? What knowledge could *He* gain?
'Tis not in battles that from youth we train
The Governor who must be wise and good,
And temper with the sternness of the brain
Thoughts motherly, and meek as womanhood.
Wisdom doth live with children round her knees:
Books, leisure, perfect freedom, and the talk
Man holds with week-day man in the hourly walk
Of the mind's business: these are the degrees
By which true Sway doth mount; this is the stalk
True Power doth grow on; and her rights are these.

On the Extinction of the Venetian Republic[1†]
(1807; comp. 1802–1807)

Once did She hold the gorgeous East in fee;
And was the safeguard of the West: the worth
Of Venice did not fall below her birth,
Venice, the eldest Child of Liberty.[2†]
She was a Maiden City, bright and free;
No guile seduced, no force could violate;
And when She took unto herself a Mate

[1] First published in the *Morning Post,* September 1802 and January 1803.

[1†] Napoleon conquered Venice 16 May 1797.

[2†] The navy of Venice defeated the German emperor in 1177. In the next century Venice captured Constantinople, thereby protecting Europe temporarily from Turkish invasion from the south.

She must espouse the everlasting Sea.[3†]
And what if she had seen those glories fade,
Those titles vanish, and that strength decay,
Yet shall some tribute of regret be paid
When her long life hath reach'd its final day:
Men are we, and must grieve when even the Shade
Of that which once was great is pass'd away.

To Toussaint L'ouverture[1]

(1803/1807; comp. 1802)

Toussaint,[2] the most unhappy Man of Men!
Whether the rural Milk-maid by her Cow
Sing in thy hearing, or thou liest now
Alone in some deep dungeon's earless den,
O miserable Chieftain! where and when
Wilt thou find patience? Yet die not; do thou
Wear rather in thy bonds a chearful brow:
Though fallen Thyself, never to rise again,
Live, and take comfort. Thou hast left behind
Powers that will work for thee; air, earth, and skies;
There's not a breathing of the common wind
That will forget thee; thou hast great allies;
Thy friends are exultations, agonies,
And love, and Man's unconquerable mind.

September 1st, 1802[1†]

(1803/1807; comp. 1802)

We had a fellow-Passenger who came
From Calais with us, gaudy in array,
A Negro Woman like a Lady gay,
Yet silent as a woman fearing blame;
Dejected, meek, yea pitiably tame,
She sate, from notice turning not away,
But on our proffer'd kindness still did lay
A weight of languid speech, or at the same
Was silent, motionless in eyes and face.
She was a Negro Woman driv'n from France,
Rejected like all others of that race,
Not one of whom may now find footing there;
This the poor Out-cast did to us declare,
Nor murmur'd at the unfeeling Ordinance.[2†]

Written in London, September, 1802

(1807; comp. 1802)

O Friend! I know not which way I must look
For comfort, being, as I am, opprest,
To think that now our Life is only drest
For shew; mean handywork of craftsman, cook,
Or groom![1] We must run glittering like a Brook
In the open sunshine, or we are unblest:
The wealthiest man among us is the best:
No grandeur now in nature or in book
Delights us. Rapine, avarice, expence,
This is idolatry; and these we adore:
Plain living and high thinking are no more:
The homely beauty of the good old cause[2]
Is gone; our peace, our fearful innocence,
And pure religion breathing household laws.

[3†] Following the naval victory of 1177, the Pope gave a ring to the Doge of Venice and bade him wed the Adriatic Sea in an annual ceremony on Ascension Day to symbolize Venice's sovereignty.

[1] First published 2 February 1803 in *Morning Post.*

[2] **Toussaint**: the son of a black slave and governor of Haiti. In 1802, he was arrested and imprisoned in Paris for resisting Napoleon's attempt to reinstitute slavery on the island. He died in prison in 1803.

[1†] First published 11 February 1803 in *Morning Post* with the title "The Banished Negroes."

[2†] Wordsworth's headnote to the poem in 1827 explained: "Among the capricious acts of Tyranny that disgraced these times, was the chasing of all Negroes from France by decree of the Government: we had a Fellow-passenger who was one of the expelled."

[1] **groom**: one who takes care of horses.

[2] **the good old cause**: reference to the Puritan rebellion of 1642. The phrase is also used in Dryden's *Absalom and Achitophel* (1.82): "The Good old Cause reviv'd, a Plot requires."

London, 1802
(1807; comp. 1802)

Milton! thou should'st be living at this hour:
England hath need of thee: she is a fen
Of stagnant waters: altar, sword, and pen,
Fireside, the heroic wealth of hall and bower,
Have forfeited their ancient English dower
Of inward happiness. We are selfish men;
Oh! raise us up, return to us again;
And give us manners, virtue, freedom, power.
Thy soul was like a Star and dwelt apart:
Thou hadst a voice whose sound was like the sea;
Pure as the naked heavens, majestic, free,
So didst thou travel on life's common way,
In chearful godliness; and yet thy heart
The lowliest duties on itself did lay.

'It Is Not to Be Thought'[1]
(1803/1807; comp. 1802)

It is not to be thought of that the Flood
Of British freedom, which to the open Sea
Of the world's praise from dark antiquity
Hath flowed, "with pomp of waters, unwithstood,"[2]
Road by which all might come and go that would,
And bear out freights of worth to foreign lands;
That this most famous Stream in Bogs and Sands
Should perish; and to evil and to good
Be lost for ever. In our Halls is hung
Armoury of the invincible Knights of old:
We must be free or die, who speak the tongue
That Shakespeare spake; the faith and morals hold
Which Milton held. In every thing we are sprung
Of Earth's first blood, have titles manifold.

[1] First published 16 April 1803 in *Morning Post.*

[2] From the Elizabethan poet, Samuel Daniels's, *Civil Wars* (1595).

from POEMS IN TWO VOLUMES

from Volume Two

The Solitary Reaper[1]
(1807; comp. 1805)

Behold her, single in the field,
Yon solitary Highland Lass!
Reaping and singing by herself;
Stop here, or gently pass!
Alone she cuts, and binds the grain,
And sings a melancholy strain;
O listen! for the Vale profound
Is overflowing with the sound.

No Nightingale did ever chaunt
So sweetly to reposing bands
Of Travellers in some shady haunt,
Among Arabian Sands:
No sweeter voice was ever heard
In spring-time from the Cuckoo-bird,
Breaking the silence of the seas
Among the farthest Hebrides.[2]

Will no one tell me what she sings?
Perhaps the plaintive numbers flow
For old, unhappy, far-off things
And battles long ago:
Or is it some more humble lay,
Familiar matter of today?
Some natural sorrow, loss, or pain,
That has been, and may be again!

[1] Wordsworth included the following note in *Poems* (1807): "This poem was suggested by a beautiful sentence in a MS. [manuscript] Tour in Scotland written by a friend, the last line being taken from it *verbatim.*" The manuscript became Thomas Wilkinson's *Tours to the British Mountains* (1824). The "beautiful sentence" is: "Passed a female who was reaping alone: she sung in Erse as she bended over her sickle; the sweetest human voice I ever heard: her strains were tenderly melancholy, and felt delicious, long after they were heard no more."

[2] Islands off the Western coast of Scotland.

Whate'er the theme, the Maiden sang
As if her song could have no ending;
I saw her singing at her work,
And o'er the sickle bending;
I listen'd till I had my fill:
And, as I mounted up the hill,
The music in my heart I bore,
Long after it was heard no more.

Stepping Westward
(1807; comp. 1805)

While my Fellow-traveller and I were walking by the side of Loch Ketterine, one fine evening after sun-set, in our road to a Hut where in the course of our Tour we had been hospitably entertained some weeks before, we met, in one of the loneliest parts of that solitary region, two well-dressed Women, one of whom said to us, by way of greeting, "What you are stepping westward?"

....

"What you are stepping westward?" — *"Yea."*
— 'Twould be a wildish destiny,
If we, who thus together roam
In a strange Land, and far from home,
Were in this place the guests of Chance:
Yet who would stop, or fear to advance,
Though home or shelter he had none,
With such a Sky to lead him on?

The dewy ground was dark and cold;
Behind, all gloomy to behold;
And stepping westward seem'd to be
A kind of *heavenly* destiny;
I liked the greeting; 'twas a sound
Of something without place or bound;
And seem'd to give me spiritual right
To travel through that region bright.

The voice was soft, and she who spake
Was walking by her native Lake:
The salutation had to me
The very sound of courtesy:
It's power was felt; and while my eye
Was fixed upon the glowing sky,
The echo of the voice enwrought
A human sweetness with the thought
Of traveling through the world that lay
Before me in my endless way.

To a Butterfly[1]
(1807; comp. 1802)

Stay near me — do not take thy flight!
A little longer stay in sight!
Much converse do I find in Thee,
Historian of my Infancy!
Float near me; do not yet depart!
Dead times revive in thee:
Thou bring'st, gay Creature as thou art!
A solemn image to my heart,
My Father's Family!

Oh! pleasant, pleasant were the days,
The time, when in our childish plays
My Sister Emmeline[2] and I
Together chaced the Butterfly!
A very hunter did I rush
Upon the prey: — with leaps and springs
I follow'd on from brake to bush;
But She, God love her! feared to brush
The dust from off its wings.

'My Heart Leaps Up When I Behold'
(1807; comp. 1802)

My heart leaps up when I behold
    A Rainbow in the sky:
So was it when my life began;
So is it now I am a Man;
So be it when I shall grow old,
    Or let me die!
The Child is Father of the Man;
And I could wish my days to be
Bound each to each by natural piety.

[1] The first of six poems included here from the volume section entitled "Moods of My Own Mind."

[2] *Dorothy* appears in several manuscripts instead of Emmeline. See Dorothy Wordsworth's *Grasmere Journal* (14 Mar 1802).*

'I Wandered Lonely as a Cloud'

(1807; comp. 1804–1807)

I wandered lonely as a Cloud[1]
That floats on high o'er Vales and Hills,
When all at once I saw a crowd
A host of dancing[2] Daffodils;
Along the Lake, beneath the trees,
Ten thousand dancing[3] in the breeze.[4]

The waves beside them danced, but they
Outdid the sparkling waves in glee:—
A Poet could not but be gay
In such a laughing company:
I gaz'd—and gaz'd—but little thought
What wealth the shew to me had brought:

For oft when on my couch I lie
In vacant or in pensive mood,
They flash upon that inward eye
Which is the bliss of solitude,
And then my heart with pleasure fills,
And dances with the Daffodils.

The Sparrow's Nest

(1807; comp. 1802)

Look, five blue eggs are gleaming there!
Few visions have I seen more fair,
Nor many prospects of delight
More pleasing than that simple sight![1†]
I started, seeming to espy
The home and shelter'd bed,
The Sparrow's dwelling, which, hard by
My Father's House, in wet or dry,
My Sister Emmeline and I
Together visited.

She look'd at it as if she fear'd it;
Still wishing, dreading to be near it:
Such heart was in her, being then
A little Prattler among men.
The Blessing of my later years
Was with me when a Boy;
She gave me eyes, she gave me ears;
And humble cares, and delicate fears;
A heart, the fountain of sweet tears;
And love, and thought, and joy.

To the Cuckoo

(1807; comp. 1802)

O blithe New-comer! I have heard,
I hear thee and rejoice:
O Cuckoo! shall I call thee Bird,
Or but a wandering Voice?

While I am lying on the grass
I hear thy restless shout:
From hill to hill it seems to pass,
About, and all about![1]

To me, no Babbler with a tale
Of sunshine and of flowers,
Thou tellest, Cuckoo! in the vale
Of visionary hours.

Thrice welcome, Darling of the Spring!
Even yet thou art to me
No Bird; but an invisible Thing,
A voice, a mystery.

---

[1] See Dorothy Wordsworth's *Grasmere Journal* (15 April 1802).*

[2] **dancing:** revised to "golden" in 1815.

[3] **Ten thousand dancing:** revised to "fluttering and dancing" in 1815.

[4] Between lines 6–7, Wordsworth inserted the following stanza in 1815:

"Continuous as the stars that shine
And twinkle on the milky way,
They stretched in never-ending line
Along the margin of a bay:
Ten thousand saw I at a glance,
Tossing their heads in sprightly dance."

[1†] The 1815 text reads: "Behold within the leafy shade / Those bright blue eggs together laid. / On me the chance-discovered sight / Gleamed like a vision of delight."

[1] Lines five through eight went through significant revisions in future editions. The final text reads: "While I am lying on the grass / Thy twofold shout I hear, / From hill to hill it seems to pass, / At once far off, and near." (1845–?)

The same whom in my School-boy days
I listen'd to; that Cry
Which made me look a thousand ways;
In bush, and tree, and sky.

To seek thee did I often rove
Through woods and on the green;
And thou wert still a hope, a love;
Still long'd for, never seen!

And I can listen to thee yet;
Can lie upon the plain
And listen, till I do beget
That golden time again.

O blessed Bird! the earth we pace
Again appears to be
An unsubstantial, faery place;
That is fit home for Thee!

To a Butterfly

(1807; comp. 1802)

I've watch'd you now a full half hour,
Self-pois'd upon that yellow flower;
And, little Butterfly! indeed
I know not if you sleep, or feed.
How motionless! not frozen seas
More motionless! and then
What joy awaits you, when the breeze
Hath found you out among the trees,
And calls you forth again!

This plot of Orchard-ground is ours;
My trees they are, my Sister's flowers;
Stop here whenever you are weary,
And rest[1] as in a sanctuary!
Come often to us, fear no wrong;
Sit near us on the bough!
We'll talk of sunshine and of song;
And summer days, when we were young,
Sweet childish days, that were as long
As twenty days are now!

[1]**Stop . . . rest:** revised in 1815 to read, "Here rest your wings when they are weary / Here lodge."

Elegiac Stanzas[1]

(1807; comp. 1806)

Suggested by a Picture of PEELE CASTLE, in a Storm, painted by Sir George Beaumont.

I was thy Neighbour once, thou rugged Pile![2]
Four summer weeks I dwelt in sight of thee:
I saw thee every day; and all the while
Thy Form was sleeping on a glassy sea.

So pure the sky, so quiet was the air!
So like, so very like, was day to day!
Whene'er I look'd, thy Image still was there;
It trembled, but it never pass'd away.

How perfect was the calm! it seem'd no sleep;
No mood, which season takes away, or brings:
I could have fancied that the mighty Deep
Was even the gentlest of all gentle Things.

Ah! THEN, if mine had been the Painter's hand,
To express what then I saw; and add the gleam,
The light that never was, on sea or land,
The consecration, and the Poet's dream;

I would have planted thee, thou hoary Pile!
Amid a world how different from this!
Beside a sea that could not cease to smile;
On tranquil land, beneath a sky of bliss:

Thou shouldst have seem'd a treasure-house, a mine
Of peaceful years; a chronicle of heaven:—
Of all the sunbeams that did ever shine
The very sweetest had to thee been given.

[1]Dedicated to the memory of John Wordsworth, Wordsworth's mariner brother and captain of the East Indian Company's (EIC) merchant vessel, *Earl of Abergavenny*, which sank in a storm off the coast of England, killing John Wordsworth and many others. The Wordsworth family was much concerned with rumors and innuendoes of John's irresponsibility, incompetence, and possible inebriation, all of which were finally dissolved after a public hearing into the matter. (See SOCIETY AND POLITICAL ECONOMY for discussion of the EIC.)

[2]**Pile:** the mouldering castle, in the vicinity of which the poet lived in his youth, and also the image in the painting, which the poet here addresses.

A Picture had it been of lasting ease,
Elysian quiet, without toil or strife;
No motion but the moving tide, a breeze,
Or merely silent Nature's breathing life.

Such, in the fond delusion of my heart,
Such Picture would I at that time have made:
And seen the soul of truth in every part;
A faith, a trust, that could not be betray'd.

So once it would have been,—'tis so no more;
I have submitted to a new controul:
A power is gone, which nothing can restore;
A deep distress hath humaniz'd my Soul.

Not for a moment could I now behold
A smiling sea and be what I have been:
The feeling of my loss will ne'er be old;
This, which I know, I speak with mind serene.

Then, Beaumont, Friend! who would have been the
Friend,
If he had lived, of Him whom I deplore,
This Work of thine I blame not, but commend;
This sea in anger, and that dismal shore.

Oh 'tis a passionate Work!—yet wise and well;
Well chosen is the spirit that is here;
That Hulk[3] which labours in the deadly swell,
This rueful sky, this pageantry of fear!

And this huge Castle, standing here sublime,
I love to see the look with which it braves,
Cased in the unfeeling armour of old time,
The light'ning, the fierce wind, and trampling waves.

Farewell, farewell the Heart that lives alone,
Hous'd in a dream, at distance from the Kind!
Such happiness, wherever it be known,
Is to be pitied; for 'tis surely blind.

But welcome fortitude, and patient chear,
And frequent sights of what is to be borne!
Such sights, or worse, as are before me here.—
Not without hope we suffer and we mourn.

[3] **Hulk:** a large cargo or passenger vessel.

Ode

(1807; comp. 1802–1804)

Paulò majora canamus.[1]

There was a time when meadow, grove, and stream,
The earth, and every common sight,
To me did seem
Apparell'd in celestial light,
The glory and the freshness of a dream.
It is not now as it has been of yore;—
Turn wheresoe'er I may,
By night or day,
The things which I have seen I now can see no more.

The Rainbow comes and goes,
And lovely is the Rose,
The Moon doth with delight
Look round her when the heavens are bare;
Waters on a starry night
Are beautiful and fair;
The sunshine is a glorious birth;
But yet I know, where'er I go,
That there hath pass'd away a glory from the earth.

Now, while the Birds thus sing a joyous song,
And while the young Lambs bound
As to the tabor's sound,
To me alone there came a thought of grief:
A timely utterance gave that thought relief,
And I again am strong.
The Cataracts blow their trumpets from the steep,
No more shall grief of mine the season wrong;
I hear the Echoes through the mountains throng,
The Winds come to me from the fields of sleep,
And all the earth is gay,
Land and sea
Give themselves up to jollity,
And with the heart of May

[1] **Paulò majora canamus:** translates "Let us sing a little higher." Verse paragraphs one through four (ll. 1–57) were written in 1802, prompting Coleridge's *Dejection: An Ode.** The remainder of the poem was composed in 1804. In the 1815 edition of Wordsworth's works, the title was changed to *Ode: Intimations of Immortality from Recollections of Early Childhood,* and its epigraph became the last three lines of "My heart leaps up."*

Doth every Beast keep holiday,
Thou Child of Joy,
Shout round me, let me hear thy shouts, thou happy
Shepherd Boy!

Ye blessed Creatures, I have heard the call
Ye to each other make; I see
The heavens laugh with you in your jubilee;
My heart is at your festival,
My head hath it's coronal,
The fullness of your bliss, I feel—I feel it all.
Oh evil day! if I were sullen
While the Earth herself is adorning,
This sweet May-morning,
And the Children are pulling,
On every side,
In a thousand vallies far and wide,
Fresh flowers; while the sun shines warm,
And the Babe leaps up on his mother's arm:—
I hear, I hear, with joy I hear!
—But there's a Tree, of many one,
A single Field which I have look'd upon,
Both of them speak of something that is gone:
The Pansy at my feet
Doth the same tale repeat:
Whither is fled the visionary gleam?
Where is it now, the glory and the dream?

Our birth is but a sleep and a forgetting:
The Soul that rises with us, our life's Star,
Hath had elsewhere it's setting,
And cometh from afar:
Not in entire forgetfulness,
And not in utter nakedness,
But trailing clouds of glory do we come
From God, who is our home:
Heaven lies about us in our infancy!
Shades of the prison-house begin to close
Upon the growing Boy,
But He beholds the light, and whence it flows,
He sees it in his joy;
The Youth, who daily farther from the East
Must travel, still is Nature's Priest,
And by the vision splendid
Is on his way attended;
At length the Man perceives it die away,
And fade into the light of common day.

Earth fills her lap with pleasures of her own;
Yearnings she hath in her own natural kind,
And, even with something of a Mother's mind,
And no unworthy aim,
The homely Nurse doth all she can
To make her Foster-child, her Inmate Man,
Forget the glories he hath known,
And that imperial palace whence he came.

Behold the Child among his new-born blisses,
A four year's Darling of a pigmy size!
See, where mid work of his own hand he lies,
Fretted by sallies of his Mother's kisses,
With light upon him from his Father's eyes!
See, at his feet, some little plan or chart,
Some fragment from his dream of human life,
Shap'd by himself with newly-learned art;
A wedding or a festival,
A mourning or a funeral;
And this hath now his heart,
And unto this he frames his song:
Then will he fit his tongue
To dialogues of business, love, or strife;
But it will not be long
Ere this be thrown aside,
And with new joy and pride
The little Actor cons another part,
Filling from time to time his "humorous stage"
With all the Persons, down to palsied Age,
That Life brings with her in her Equipage;
As if his whole vocation
Were endless imitation.

Thou, whose exterior semblance doth belie
Thy Soul's immensity;
Thou best Philosopher, who yet dost keep
Thy heritage, thou Eye among the blind,
That, deaf and silent, read'st the eternal deep,
Haunted for ever by the eternal mind,—
Mighty Prophet! Seer blest!
On whom those truths do rest,
Which we are toiling all our lives to find;[2]
Thou, over whom thy Immortality
Broods like the Day, a Master o'er a Slave,
A Presence which is not to be put by;
To whom the grave
Is but a lonely bed without the sense or sight
Of day or the warm light,

[2] The line, "In darkness lost, the darkness of the grave," was added between lines 116–117 in 1820.

A place of thought where we in waiting lie;[3]
Thou little Child, yet glorious in the might
Of untam'd pleasures, on thy Being's height,[4]
Why with such earnest pains dost thou provoke
The Years to bring the inevitable yoke,
Thus blindly with thy blessedness at strife?
Full soon thy Soul shall have her earthly freight,
And custom lie upon thee with a weight,
Heavy as frost, and deep almost as life!

O joy! that in our embers
Is something that doth live,
That nature yet remembers
What was so fugitive!
The thought of our past years in me doth breed
Perpetual benedictions: not indeed
For that which is most worthy to be blest;
Delight and liberty, the simple creed
Of Childhood, whether fluttering or at rest,
With new-born hope for ever in his breast:[5] —
Not for these I raise
The song of thanks and praise;
But for those obstinate questionings
Of sense and outward things,
Fallings from us, vanishings;
Blank misgivings of a Creature
Moving about in worlds not realiz'd,
High instincts, before which our mortal Nature
Did tremble like a guilty Thing surpriz'd:
But for those first affections,
Those shadowy recollections,
Which, be they what they may,
Are yet the fountain light of all our day,
Are yet a master light of all our seeing;
Uphold us, cherish us, and make[6]
Our noisy years seem moments in the being
Of the eternal Silence: truths that wake,
To perish never;
Which neither listlessness, nor mad endeavour,
Nor Man nor Boy,
Nor all that is at enmity with joy,
Can utterly abolish or destroy!
Hence, in a season of calm weather,
Though inland far we be,
Our Souls have sight of that immortal sea
Which brought us hither,
Can in a moment travel thither,
And see the Children sport upon the shore,
And hear the mighty waters rolling evermore.

Then, sing ye Birds, sing, sing a joyous song!
And let the young Lambs bound
As to the tabor's sound!
We in thought will join your throng,
Ye that pipe and ye that play,
Ye that through your hearts to day
Feel the gladness of the May!
What though the radiance which was once so bright
Be now for ever taken from my sight,
Though nothing can bring back the hour
Of splendour in the grass, of glory in the flower;
We will grieve not, rather find
Strength in what remains behind,
In the primal sympathy
Which having been must ever be,
In the soothing thoughts that spring
Out of human suffering,
In the faith that looks through death,
In years that bring the philosophic mind.

And oh ye Fountains, Meadows, Hills, and Groves,
Think not of any severing of our loves!
Yet in my heart of hearts I feel your might;
I only have relinquish'd one delight
To live beneath your more habitual sway.
I love the Brooks which down their channels fret,
Even more than when I tripp'd lightly as they;
The innocent brightness of a new-born Day
Is lovely yet;
The Clouds that gather round the setting sun
Do take a sober colouring from an eye
That hath kept watch o'er man's mortality;
Another race hath been, and other palms are won.
Thanks to the human heart by which we live,
Thanks to its tenderness, its joys, and fears,
To me the meanest flower that blows can give
Thoughts that do often lie too deep for tears.

[3] Lines 120 through 123 were deleted in 1820.

[4] This line was revised to "Of heaven-born freedom, on thy Being's height" in 1815.

[5] Lines 140–141 revised to "Of childhood, whether busy or at rest / With new-fledged hope still fluttering in his breast." *New-fledged* means newly feathered with reference to a young bird.

[6] Line 156 revised to "Uphold us—cherish—and have power to make."

from Letter to Mary Wordsworth[1]

[Hindwell—Saturday August 11th, 1810]

. . . Every day every hour every moment makes me feel more deeply how blessed we are in each other, how purely how faithfully how ardently, and how tenderly we love each other; I put this last word last because, though I am persuaded that a deep affection is not uncommon in married life, yet I am confident that a lively, gushing, thought-employing, spirit-stirring, passion of love, is very rare even among good people. I will say more upon this when we meet, grounded upon recent observation of the condition of others. We have been parted my sweet Mary too long, but we have not been parted in vain, for wherever I go I am admonished how blessed, and almost peculiar a lot mine is. . . .

On friday Morning, I was called a little after three, having had two hours feverish sleep, got on the top of the Coach, it began to rain before we were out of Birming: and rained for two hours and a half; my umbrella & coat however protected me pretty well; when we were half way to Worcester the weather cleared up and I had a pleasant ride through a fine Country to that City, which stands charmingly upon the Severn, at no great distance from the Malvern hills. These hills which are a fine object brought Joseph Cottle[2] to my mind, and dearest Dorothy, who had travelled this way when she came from Newcastle to meet me at Bristol whence we journeyd to Racedown;[3] but though much endeared to me on this latter account, I looked at them with a trembling which I cannot describe when I thought that *you* had not seen them, but *might* have seen, if you had but taken the road through Bristol when you left Racedown; in which case I should certainly have accompanied you as far as Bristol; or further, perhaps: and then I thought, that you would not have taken the coach at Bristol, but that you would have walked on Northwards with me at your side, till unable to part from each other we might have come in sight of those hills which skirt the road for so many miles, and thus continuing our journey (for we should have moved on at small expense) I fancied that we should have seen so deeply into each others hearts, and been so fondly locked in each others arms, that we should have braved the worst and parted no more. Under that tree, I thought as I passed along we might have rested, of that stream might have drank, in that thicket we might have hidden ourselves from the sun, and from the eyes of the passenger; and thus did I feed on the thought of bliss that might have been, which would have [been] intolerable from the force of regret had I not felt the happiness which waits me when I see you again. O Mary I love you with a passion of love which grows till I tremble to think of its strength; your children and the care which they require must fortunately steal between you and the solitude and the longings of absence—when I am moving about in travelling I am less unhappy than when stationary, but then I am at every moment, I will not say reminded of you, for you never I think are out of my mind 3 minutes together however I am engaged, but I am every moment seized with a longing wish that you might see the objects which interest me as I pass along, and not having you at my side my pleasure is so imperfect that after a short look I had rather not see the objects at all. . . .

As to Politics the old opposition seem confident they shall come in, but nothing is yet decided. It is clear the Prince Regent[4] is most averse to them; but I fear they will be forced upon him. In fact the country is in a deplorable state; and if firmness be not shewn by the government, with descretion also, disturbances wide & frightful are inevitable. The Prince is neither respected nor love[d] by any class of Men. By the bye I forgot to mention that from Lord Mulgraves we went to Lady Crewes, and there I had the honour of being introduced to the Princess Regent, an empty honour, for her R. H.—— was at some distance from me, and I had no conversation with her. She is a fat unwieldy Woman, but has rather a handsome & pleasing Countenance, with an expression of hilarity that is not however free from Coarseness. This was a large Assembly, saw few pretty women, and many most disgusting objects; one I encountered of a tolerable face & features, but in her

[1] Wordsworth's letters to his wife Mary Hutchinson Wordsworth came to light in 1977 and were first published as *The Love Letters of William and Mary Wordsworth*, ed. Beth Darlington (Cornell University Press, 1981).

[2] Joseph Cottle of Bristol published *Lyrical Ballads* (1798). The Malvern Hills brought Cottle to mind because of his own volume of poems, *Malvern Hills* (1798).

[3] Wordsworth refers to his move to Racedown Lodge in 1795 with his sister, after their ten-year separation. See the introductions to William Wordsworth and Dorothy Wordsworth.

[4] The Prince of Wales became Prince Regent in February 1811, after the insanity of his father George III was conceded.

native bosom so huge & tremendous, that had you seen her enter a room in that condition I am sure the soul of modest womenhood in you would have shrunk almost as with horror. Her Breasts were like two great hay-cocks or rather hay stacks, protruding themselves upon the Spectator, and yet no body seemed to notice them—

But to come to something more interesting. It now wants only 20 minutes of four. Just as was concluding the last page I received a Message from Lord Lonsdale[5] in answer to my note that he would be glad to see me at 12. I posted away immediately. He shook me by the hand and received me very kindly. I began with enquiries after his Family, then thanked him for his Letter, and for Giving me this opportunity of seeing him.—I beg[ged] leave to state in addition to the unfavorable circumstances in my course of life, mentioned in my first Letter, that had appeared to me to justify the representation I had made to him, was to be reckoned a calamity which had befallen our family in the person of my Brother Captain Wordsworth, who, he would recollect, had lost his life by Shipwreck. I said that My Brother had entirely sympathized with my literary pursuits, and encouraged me to give myself entirely to that way of Life, with assurance that [if] I stood in need of assistance, and he proved fortunate, it should ever be ready for me.—I requested also permission to supply what appeared to me deficient in my second Letter—, deficient I mean in the expression; I had thrown myself in the mere form of words more upon his Lordships recollection of me, I said, than I had a right to do. I wished to give him no unnecessary trouble, and if I could procure knowledge of any thing that was likely to suit me I certainly should not be so wanting to my own interests as to omit making an immediate application. Of course all this was soon cleared. I then said that by way of giving him a general Idea of what might suit me I would mention the place of Distributor of Stamps,[6] now holden by a Relative of mine at Applebye; I had endeavoured to learn the emolument of it, but could not speak accurately, but I thought that place should it prove vacant would suit me,—but I adverted to it merely as a General guide for his Lordship in this service to be done to me. He then said, that I must be aware that all his influence of this kind depended upon the Government which was now in an unsettled state. To which I replied that I was sorry for the condition of the Country in this respect; but I hope such arrangements would be made, as would not exclude his Lordship from that influence which his family and character entitled him to.—He then very amicably entered into conversation on indifferent topics for at least twenty minutes, chiefly relating to Persons & things in Cumberland & Westmoreland; he leading the Conversation; and when I took my leave he shook me by the hand; and said "I shall not be unmindful of you":—Tell me if you are satisfied with this. I am, & know not what more I could have done. His Lordship told me that he had this morning received a Letter from Mr Southey, requesting his exertion to procure him a place recently vacant by the Death of a Frenchman of the Name of Dutens. It is that of Historiographer to the King, or some thing of that kind. . . .

Thy faithful Husband W. W.

[5] Sir William Lowther, Lord Lonsdale, was probably the largest landowner in the North of England and held great political influence as a result. Wordsworth's father had worked for Lord Lonsdale's cousin, Sir James Lowther, Earl of Lonsdale.

[6] Wordsworth implored Lonsdale for a government sinecure because of his growing family and responsibilities and, as he alluded to above, the investment the family lost when John Wordsworth's vessel sank. Four adults and five children now made up the Wordsworth household. By 1813, Lonsdale was able to provide Wordsworth with an appointment as Distributor of Stamps, which required that he supervise the collection of revenues for the stamped paper used in legal transactions. The appointment paid something less than £400 per year. See the dedication to *The Excursion*.*

from Letter to Mary, 3–4 June 1812

Wednesday aftern[oon] 2. o clock.

MY DEAREST MARY,

. . . I received very expeditiously your sweet Letter from Hereford; That very evening, viz Tuesday, I had been reading at Lamb's the Tintern abbey,[1] and repeated a 100 times to my self the passage "O Sylvan Wye thou Wanderer through the woods," thinking of past times, & Dorothy, dear Dorothy, and you my Darling. The weather has been good & therefore I trust you have had a delightful Tour without any untoward accident; oh that I could have been with you. I long to be with you, I feel nightly and daily, waking & asleep the neccessity of my not prolonging our separation; and I have the happiness of saying, that I can now look forward with some confidence as to the Time. . . .

[1] The residence of Mary and Charles Lamb* in London. The reference is to *Lines Written a Few Miles above Tintern Abbey*.*

How I long, (again must I say) to be with thee; every hour of absence now is a grievous loss, because we have been parted sufficiently to feel how profoundly in soul & body we love each other; and to be taught what a sublime treasure we possess in each others love. — I am happy to say that my health has been much better, and could I manage myself as to exertion, I should be strong & well, for every cause but one; which injures me, though upon the whole I never was before so well, or had so little to complain of in that respect. But I feel every day & hour that herein I shall fare worse, the fever of thought & longing & affection & desire is strengthening in me, and I am sure will be beginning to make me wakeful and to consume me. Last night I *suffered*, and this morning I tremble with sensations that almost overpower me. I think of you by the waters & under the shades of the Wye, and the visions of nature & the music of [ ] raptures of love, the love I felt for thee [ ] not venture to *tell* what he felt [ ] which inspired me as an honoured & cherished [ ] and lastly as a [ ] as an expecting Bride [ ] Husband seated for ever on the [ ] as a Father, and a long tried sharer of [ ] pleasures, — each and all of these [ ] existence have passed through my mind, [ ] over again my past self, & thy past self also, [?participating] every sentiment of thy heart & being, as far as Nature would allow what thou hast been, from the hour of our first walks near Penrith till our last parting at Chester, and till thy wanderings upon Wye, & till this very moment when I am writing, & Thou most probably art thinking of me and losing all sense of the motion of the horse that bears thee, in the tenderness & strength of thy conceptions and wishes, & remembrances. Oh my beloved — but I ought not to trust myself to this senseless & visible sheet of paper; speak for me to thyself, find the evidence of what is passing within me in *thy* heart, in thy mind, in thy steps as they touch the green grass, in thy limbs as they are stretched upon the soft earth; in thy own involuntary sighs & ejaculations, in the trembling of thy hands, in the tottering of thy knees, in the blessings which thy lips pronounce, find it in thy lips themselves, & such kisses as I often give to the empty air, and in the aching of thy bosom, and let a voice speak for me in every thing within thee & without thee. Here I stop & wherefore, — Oh what an age seems it till we shall be again together under the shade of the green trees, by the rippling of the waters, and in that hour — which thou lovest the most the silence the vacancy & the impenetrable gloom of night. Happy Chamber that has been so enriched with the sweet prayers of thy pure bosom; with what gratitude shall I behold it! Ah Mary I must turn my pen from this course. . . .

from THE EXCURSION, *being a portion of* THE RECLUSE, A POEM[1]

(1814; comp. 1797–1814)

To The Right Honourable William, Earl of Lonsdale, K. G.[2] &C. &C.

Oft, through thy fair domains, illustrious Peer!
In youth I roamed, on youthful pleasures bent;
And mused in rocky cell or sylvan tent,
Beside swift-flowing Lowther's current clear.
— Now by thy care befriended, I appear
Before thee, LONSDALE, and this Work present,
A token (may it prove a monument!)
Of high respect and gratitude sincere.
Gladly would I have waited till my task
Had reached its close; but Life is insecure,
And Hope full oft fallacious as a dream:
Therefore, for what is here produced I ask
Thy favour; trusting that thou wilt not deem
The Offering, though imperfect, premature.

WILLIAM WORDSWORTH
Rydal Mount, Westmorland,
July 29, 1814.

— *from* PREFACE —

. . . It may be proper to state whence the Poem, of which The Excursion is a part, derives its Title of THE RECLUSE.[3]

[1] *The Excursion,* a poem of nine Books and over 9,000 lines, is the longest, most influential work Wordsworth published during his lifetime.

[2] See note 6 to letter to Mary Wordsworth (11 August 1810).

[3] Wordsworth says earlier in the preface that *The Excursion* is "the second part of a long and laborious Work, which is to consist of three parts." That Work is *The Recluse.* Part First, Book First, of *The Recluse* is *Home at Grasmere,* which remained unpublished until 1888. The second Part is *The Excursion.* It is unclear how or if *The Prelude* was to fit in to the final work, but the point is moot, for *The Recluse* itself was never completed.

—Several years ago, when the Author retired to his native Mountains, with the hope of being enabled to construct a literary Work that might live, it was a reasonable thing that he should take a review of his own Mind, and examine how far Nature and Education had qualified him for such employment. As subsidiary to this preparation, he undertook to record, in Verse, the origin and progress of his own powers, as far as he was acquainted with them. That Work,[4] addressed to a dear Friend, most distinguished for his knowledge and genius, and to whom the Author's Intellect is deeply indebted, has been long finished; and the result of the investigation which gave rise to it was a determination to compose a philosophical Poem, containing views of Man, Nature, and Society; and to be entitled, The Recluse; as having for its principal subject the sensations and opinions of a Poet living in retirement.—The preparatory Poem is biographical, and conducts the history of the Author's mind to the point when he was emboldened to hope that his faculties were sufficiently matured for entering upon the arduous labour which he had proposed to himself; and the two Works have the same kind of relation to each other, if he may so express himself, as the Anti-chapel has to the body of a gothic Church. Continuing this allusion, he may be permitted to add, that his minor Pieces, which have been long before the Public, when they shall be properly arranged, will be found by the attentive Reader to have such connection with the main Work as may give them claim to be likened to the little Cells, Oratories, and sepulchral Recesses, ordinarily included in those Edifices.

The Author would not have deemed himself justified in saying, upon this occasion, so much of performances either unfinished, or unpublished, if he had not thought that the labour bestowed by him upon what he has heretofore and now laid before the Public, entitled him to candid attention for such a statement as he thinks necessary to throw light upon his endeavours to please, and he would hope, to benefit his countrymen.—Nothing further need be added, than that the first and third parts of the Recluse will consist chiefly of meditations in the Author's own Person; and that in the intermediate part (The Excursion) the intervention of Characters speaking is employed, and something of a dramatic form adopted.

It is not the Author's intention formally to announce a system: it was more animating to him to proceed in a different course; and if he shall succeed in conveying to the mind clear thoughts, lively images, and strong feelings, the Reader will have no difficulty in extracting the system for himself. And in the mean time the following passage, taken from the conclusion of the first Book of the Recluse, may be acceptable as a kind of *Prospectus* of the design and scope of the whole Poem.[5]

"On Man, on Nature, and on Human Life
Musing in Solitude, I oft perceive
Fair trains of imagery before me rise,
Accompanied by feelings of delight
Pure, or with no unpleasing sadness mixed;
And I am conscious of affecting thoughts
And dear remembrances, whose presence soothes
Or elevates the Mind, intent to weigh
The good and evil of our mortal state.
—To these emotions, whencesoe'er they come,
Whether from breath of outward circumstance,
Or from the Soul—an impulse to herself,
I would give utterance in numerous Verse.
—Of Truth, of Grandeur, Beauty, Love, and Hope—
And melancholy Fear subdued by Faith;
Of blessed consolations in distress;
Of moral strength, and intellectual power;
Of joy in widest commonalty spread;
Of the individual Mind that keeps her own
Inviolate retirement, subject there
To Conscience only, and the law supreme
Of that Intelligence which governs all;
I sing:—"fit audience let me find though few!"[6]

So prayed, more gaining than he asked, the Bard,
Holiest of Men.—Urania, I shall need
Thy guidance, or a greater Muse, if such
Descend to earth or dwell in highest heaven!
For I must tread on shadowy ground, must sink
Deep—and, aloft ascending, breathe in worlds
To which the heaven of heavens is but a veil.
All strength—all terror, single or in bands,
That ever was put forth in personal form;
Jehovah—with his thunder, and the choir

[4] "That Work" and "the preparatory Poem" mentioned later refer to *The Prelude,* completed in 1804, revised incessantly thereafter, and left unpublished until Wordsworth's death in 1850. The "dear Friend" is Samuel Taylor Coleridge.*

[5] The "Prospectus" is the revised, concluding verse paragraph of *Home at Grasmere* (1800–1806?).

[6] Milton's *Paradise Lost,* VII.30–31: "still govern thou my song, / Urania, and fit audience find, though few."

Of shouting Angels, and the empyreal thrones,
I pass them, unalarmed. Not Chaos, not
The darkest pit of lowest Erebus,[7]
Nor aught of blinder vacancy — scooped out
By help of dreams, can breed such fear and awe
As fall upon us often when we look
Into our Minds, into the Mind of Man,
My haunt, and the main region of my Song.
— Beauty — a living Presence of the earth,
Surpassing the most fair ideal Forms
Which craft of delicate Spirits hath composed
From earth's materials — waits upon my steps;
Pitches her tents before me as I move,
An hourly neighbour. Paradise, and groves
Elysian, Fortunate Fields — like those of old
Sought in the Atlantic Main, why should they be
A history only of departed things,
Or a mere fiction of what never was?
For the discerning intellect of Man,
When wedded to this goodly universe
In love and holy passion, shall find these
A simple produce of the common day.
— I, long before the blissful hour arrives,
Would chaunt, in lonely peace, the spousal verse
Of this great consummation: — and, by words
Which speak of nothing more than what we are,
Would I arouse the sensual from their sleep
Of Death, and win the vacant and the vain
To noble raptures; while my voice proclaims
How exquisitely the individual Mind
(And the progressive powers perhaps no less
Of the whole species) to the external World
Is fitted: — and how exquisitely, too,
Theme this but little heard of among Men,
The external World is fitted to the Mind;
And the creation (by no lower name
Can it be called) which they with blended might
Accomplish: — this is our high argument.
— Such grateful haunts foregoing, if I oft
Must turn elsewhere — to travel near the tribes
And fellowships of men, and see ill sights
Of madding passions mutually inflamed;
Must hear Humanity in fields and groves
Pipe solitary anguish; or must hang
Brooding above the fierce confederate storm
Of sorrow, barricadoed evermore
Within the walls of Cities; may these sounds
Have their authentic comment, — that, even these
Hearing, I be not downcast or forlorn!
— Come thou prophetic Spirit, that inspir'st
The human Soul of universal earth,
Dreaming on things to come; and dost possess
A metropolitan Temple in the hearts
Of mighty Poets; upon me bestow
A gift of genuine insight; that my Song
With star-like virtue in its place may shine;
Shedding benignant influence, — and secure,
Itself, from all malevolent effect
Of those mutations that extend their sway
Throughout the nether sphere! — And if with this
I mix more lowly matter; with the thing
Contemplated, describe the Mind and Man
Contemplating; and who, and what he was,
The transitory Being that beheld
This Vision, — when and where, and how he lived; —
Be not this labour useless. If such theme
May sort with highest objects, then, dread Power,
Whose gracious favour is the primal source
Of all illumination, may my Life
Express the image of a better time,
More wise desires, and simpler manners; — nurse
My Heart in genuine freedom: — all pure thoughts
Be with me; — so shall thy unfailing love
Guide, and support, and cheer me to the end!"

Book First,[8] The Wanderer

'TWAS summer, and the sun had mounted high:
Southward, the landscape indistinctly glared
Through a pale steam; but all the northern downs,
In clearest air ascending, shew'd far off

[7] **Chaos:** "this wild abyss, / The womb of Nature and perhaps her grave, / Of neither sea, nor shore, nor air, nor fire, / But all these in their pregnant causes mixed / Confus'dly" (*Paradise Lost,* II.910–14). **Erebus:** the underworld.

[8] This first Book is composed of two early manuscript poems now referred to as "The Pedlar" and "Ruined Cottage," which were Wordsworth's first attempts at *The Recluse* in 1797–1798.

A surface dappled o'er with shadows, flung
From many a brooding cloud; far as the sight
Could reach, those many shadows lay in spots
Determined and unmoved, with steady beams
Of bright and pleasant sunshine interposed.
Pleasant to him who on the soft cool moss
Extends his careless limbs along the front
Of some huge cave, whose rocky ceiling casts
A twilight of its own, an ample shade,
Where the wren warbles; while the dreaming Man,
Half conscious of the soothing melody,
With side-long eye looks out upon the scene,
By that impending covert made more soft,
More low and distant! Other lot was mine;
Yet with good hope that soon I should obtain
As grateful resting-place, and livelier joy.
Across a bare wide Common I was toiling
With languid feet, which by the slippery ground
Were baffled; nor could my weak arm disperse
The host of insects gathering round my face,
And ever with me as I paced along.

Upon that open level stood a Grove,
The wished-for Port to which my steps were bound.
Thither I came, and there—amid the gloom
Spread by a brotherhood of lofty elms—
Appeared a roofless Hut; four naked walls
That stared upon each other! I looked round,
And to my wish and to my hope espied
Him whom I sought; a Man of reverend age,
But stout and hale, for travel unimpaired.
There was he seen upon the Cottage bench,
Recumbent in the shade, as if asleep;
An iron-pointed staff lay at his side.

Him had I marked the day before—alone
And in the middle of the public way
Stationed, as if to rest himself, with face
Turned tow'rds the sun then setting, while that staff
Afforded to his Figure, as he stood,
Detained for contemplation or repose,
Graceful support; the countenance of the Man
Was hidden from my view, and he himself
Unrecognized; but, stricken by the sight,
With slacken'd footsteps I advanced, and soon
A glad congratulation we exchanged
At such unthought-of meeting.—For the night
We parted, nothing willingly; and now
He by appointment waited for me here,
Beneath the shelter of these clustering elms.

We were tried Friends: I from my Childhood up
Had known him.—In a little Town obscure,
A market-village, seated in a tract
Of mountains, where my school-day time was pass'd,
One room he owned, the fifth part of a house,
A place to which he drew, from time to time,
And found a kind of home or harbour there.

He loved me; from a swarm of rosy Boys
Singled out me, as he in sport would say,
For my grave looks—too thoughtful for my years.
As I grew up it was my best delight
To be his chosen Comrade. Many a time,
On holidays, we wandered through the woods,
A pair of random travellers; we sate—
We walked; he pleas'd me with his sweet discourse
Of things which he had seen; and often touch'd
Abstrusest matter, reasonings of the mind
Turned inward; or at my request he sang
Old songs—the product of his native hills;
A skilful distribution of sweet sounds,
Feeding the soul, and eagerly imbibed
As cool refreshing Water, by the care
Of the industrious husbandman, diffused
Through a parched meadow-ground, in time of
drought.
Still deeper welcome found his pure discourse:
How precious when in riper days I learn'd
To weigh with care his words, and to rejoice
In the plain presence of his dignity!

Oh! many are the Poets that are sown
By Nature; Men endowed with highest gifts,
The vision and the faculty divine,
Yet wanting the accomplishment of Verse,
(Which in the docile season of their youth
It was denied them to acquire, through lack
Of culture and the inspiring aid of books,
Or haply by a temper too severe,
Or a nice backwardness afraid of shame),
Nor having e'er, as life advanced, been led
By circumstance to take unto the height
The measure of themselves, these favored Beings,
All but a scattered few, live out their time,
Husbanding that which they possess within,
And go to the grave, unthought of. Strongest minds
Are often those of whom the noisy world
Hears least; else surely this Man had not left
His graces unrevealed and unproclaimed.
But, as the mind was filled with inward light,

So not without distinction had he lived,
Beloved and honoured — far as he was known.
And some small portion of his eloquent speech,
And something that may serve to set in view
The feeling pleasures of his loneliness,
The doings, observations, which his mind
Had dealt with — I will here record in verse;
Which, if with truth it correspond, and sink
Or rise, as venerable Nature leads,
The high and tender Muses shall accept
With gracious smile, deliberately pleased,
And listening Time reward with sacred praise.

Among the hills of Athol he was born:
There, on a small hereditary Farm,
An unproductive slip of rugged ground,
His Father dwelt; and died in poverty;
While He, whose lowly fortune I retrace,
The youngest of three sons, was yet a babe,
A little One — unconscious of their loss.
But ere he had outgrown his infant days
His widowed Mother, for a second Mate,
Espoused the Teacher of the Village School;
Who on her offspring zealously bestowed
Needful instruction; not alone in arts
Which to his humble duties appertained,
But in the lore of right and wrong, the rule
Of human kindness, in the peaceful ways
Of honesty, and holiness severe.
A virtuous Household though exceeding poor!
Pure Livers were they all, austere and grave,
And fearing God; the very Children taught
Stern self-repect, a reverence for God's word,
And an habitual piety, maintained
With strictness scarcely known on English ground.

From his sixth year, the Boy of whom I speak,
In summer, tended cattle on the Hills;
But, through the inclement and the perilous days
Of long-continuing winter, he repaired
To his Step-father's School, that stood alone,
Sole Building on a mountain's dreary edge,
Far from the sight of City spire, or sound
Of Minster clock! From that bleak Tenement
He, many an evening to his distant home
In solitude returning, saw the Hills
Grow larger in the darkness, all alone
Beheld the stars come out above his head,
And travelled through the wood, with no one near
To whom he might confess the things he saw.
So the foundations of his mind were laid.
In such communion, not from terror free,
While yet a Child, and long before his time,
He had perceived the presence and the power
Of greatness; and deep feelings had impress'd
Great objects on his mind, with portraiture
And colour so distinct, that on his mind
They lay like substances, and almost seemed
To haunt the bodily sense. He had received
(Vigorous in native genius as he was)
A precious gift; for, as he grew in years,
With these impressions would he still compare
All his remembrances, thoughts, shapes, and forms;
And, being still unsatisfied with aught
Of dimmer character, he thence attained
An active power to fasten images
Upon his brain; and on their pictured lines
Intensely brooded, even till they acquired
The liveliness of dreams. Nor did he fail,
While yet a Child, with a Child's eagerness
Incessantly to turn his ear and eye
On all things which the moving seasons brought
To feed such appetite: nor this alone
Appeased his yearning: — in the after day
Of Boyhood, many an hour in caves forlorn,
And 'mid the hollow depths of naked crags
He sate, and even in their fix'd lineaments,
Or from the power of a peculiar eye,
Or by creative feeling overborne,
Or by predominance of thought oppress'd,
Even in their fix'd and steady lineaments
He traced an ebbing and a flowing mind,
Expression ever varying!

Thus informed,
He had small need of books; for many a Tale
Traditionary, round the mountains hung,
And many a Legend, peopling the dark woods,
Nourished Imagination in her growth,
And gave the Mind that apprehensive power
By which she is made quick to recognize
The moral properties and scope of things.
But eagerly he read, and read again,
Whate'er the Minister's old Shelf supplied;
The life and death of Martyrs, who sustained,
With will inflexible, those fearful pangs
Triumphantly displayed in records left
Of Persecution, and the Covenant — Times
Whose echo rings through Scotland to this hour!
And there by lucky hap had been preserved

A straggling volume, torn and incomplete,
That left half-told the preternatural tale,
Romance of Giants, chronicle of Fiends
Profuse in garniture of wooden cuts
Strange and uncouth, dire faces, figures dire,
Sharp-knee'd, sharp-elbowed, and lean-ankled too,
With long and ghostly shanks—forms which once
seen
Could never be forgotten!
In his heart
Where Fear sate thus, a cherished visitant,
Was wanting yet the pure delight of love
By sound diffused, or by the breathing air,
Or by the silent looks of happy things,
Or flowing from the universal face
Of earth and sky. But he had felt the power
Of Nature, and already was prepared,
By his intense conceptions, to receive
Deeply the lesson deep of love which he,
Whom Nature, by whatever means, has taught
To feel intensely, cannot but receive.

From early childhood, even, as hath been said.
From his sixth year, he had been sent abroad
In summer to tend herds: such was his task
Thenceforward 'till the later day of youth.
O then what soul was his, when, on the tops
Of the high mountains, he beheld the sun
Rise up, and bathe the world in light! He looked—
Ocean and earth, the solid frame of earth
And ocean's liquid mass, beneath him lay
In gladness and deep joy. The clouds were touch'd
And in their silent faces did he read
Unutterable love. Sound needed none,
Nor any voice of joy; his spirit drank
The spectacle; sensation, soul, and form
All melted into him; they swallowed up
His animal being; in them did he live,
And by them did he live; they were his life.
In such access of mind, in such high hour
Of visitation from the living God,
Thought was not; in enjoyment it expired.
No thanks he breathed, he proferred no request;
Rapt into still communion that transcends
The imperfect offices of prayer and praise,
His mind was a thanksgiving to the power
That made him; it was blessedness and love!

A Herdsman on the lonely mountain tops,
Such intercourse was his, and in this sort
Was his existence oftentimes *possessed.*
Oh then how beautiful, how bright appeared
The written Promise! He had early learned
To reverence the Volume which displays
The mystery, the life which cannot die:
But in the mountains did he *feel* his faith;
There did he see the writing;—all things there
Breathed immortality, revolving life
And greatness still revolving; infinite;
There littleness was not; the least of things
Seemed infinite; and there his spirit shaped
Her prospects, nor did he believe,—he *saw.*
What wonder if his being thus became
Sublime and comprehensive! Low desires,
Low thoughts had there no place; yet was his heart
Lowly; for he was meek in gratitude,
Oft as he called those extacies to mind,
And whence they flowed; and from them he acquired
Wisdom, which works through patience; thence he
learned
In many a calmer hour of sober thought
To look on Nature with a humble heart,
Self-questioned where it did not understand,
And with a superstitious eye of love.

So passed the time; yet to a neighbouring town
He duly went with what small overplus
His earnings might supply, and brought away
The Book which most had tempted his desires
While at the Stall he read. Among the hills
He gazed upon that mighty Orb of Song
The divine Milton. Lore of different kind,
The annual savings of a toilsome life,
His Step-father supplied; books that explain
The purer elements of truth involved
In lines and numbers, and, by charm severe,
(Especially perceived where nature droops
And feeling is suppressed,) preserve the mind
Busy in solitude and poverty.
These occupations oftentimes deceived
The listless hours, while in the hollow vale,
Hollow and green, he lay on the green turf
In pensive idleness. What could he do
With blind endeavours, in that lonesome life,
Thus thirsting daily? Yet still uppermost
Nature was at his heart as if he felt,
Though yet he knew not how, a wasting power
In all things which from her sweet influence
Might tend to wean him. Therefore with her hues,

Her forms, and with the spirit of her forms,
He clothed the nakedness of austere truth.
While yet he lingered in the rudiments
Of science, and among her simplest laws,
His triangles — they were the stars of heaven,
The silent stars! Oft did he take delight
To measure th' altitude of some tall crag
Which is the eagle's birth-place, or some peak
Familiar with forgotten years, that shews
Inscribed, as with the silence of the thought,
Upon it's bleak and visionary sides,
The history of many a winter storm, —
Or obscure records of the path of fire.

And thus, before his eighteenth year was told,
Accumulated feelings pressed his heart
With an increasing weight; he was o'erpower'd
By Nature, by the turbulence subdued
Of his own mind; by mystery and hope,
And the first virgin passion of a soul
Communing with the glorious Universe.
Full often wished he that the winds might rage
When they were silent; far more fondly now
Than in his earlier season did he love
Tempestuous nights — the conflict and the sounds
That live in darkness: — from his intellect
And from the stillness of abstracted thought
He asked repose; and I have heard him say
That often, failing at this time to gain
The peace required, he scanned the laws of light
Amid the roar of torrents, where they send
From hollow clefts up to the clearer air
A cloud of mist, which in the sunshine frames
A lasting tablet — for the observer's eye
Varying it's rainbow hues. But vainly thus,
And vainly by all other means, he strove
To mitigate the fever of his heart.

In dreams, in study, and in ardent thought,
Thus, even from Childhood upward, was he reared;
For intellectual progress wanting much,
Doubtless, of needful help — yet gaining more;
And every moral feeling of his soul
Strengthened and braced, by breathing in content
The keen, the wholesome air of poverty,
And drinking from the well of homely life.
— But, from past liberty, and tried restraints,
He now was summoned to select the course
Of humble industry which promised best
To yield him no unworthy maintenance.
The Mother strove to make her Son perceive
With what advantage he might teach a School
In the adjoining Village; but the Youth,
Who of this service made a short essay,
Found that the wanderings of his thought were then
A misery to him; that he must resign
A task he was unable to perform.

That stern yet kindly spirit, Who constrains
The Savoyard[9] to quit his naked rocks,
The free-born Swiss to leave his narrow vales,
(Spirit attached to regions mountainous
Like their own stedfast clouds) — did now impel
His restless Mind to look abroad with hope.
— An irksome drudgery seems it to plod on,
Through dusty ways, in storm, from door to door,
A vagrant Merchant bent beneath his load!
Yet do such Travellers find their own delight;
And their hard service, deemed debasing now,
Gained merited respect in simpler times;
When Squire, and Priest, and they who round them dwelt
In rustic sequestration,[10] all, dependant
Upon the Pedlar's toil — supplied their wants,
Or pleased their fancies, with the wares he brought.
Not ignorant was the Youth that still no few
Of his adventurous Countrymen were led
By perseverance in this Track of life
To competence and ease; — for him it bore
Attractions manifold; — and this he chose.
He asked his Mother's blessing; and, with tears
Thanking his second Father, asked from him
Paternal blessings. The good Pair bestowed
Their farewell benediction, but with hearts
Foreboding evil. From his native hills
He wandered far; much did he see of Men,
Their manners, their enjoyments, and pursuits,
Their passions, and their feelings; chiefly those
Essential and eternal in the heart,
Which, mid the simpler forms of rural life,
Exist more simple in their elements,
And speak a plainer language. In the woods,
A lone Enthusiast, and among the fields,
Itinerant in this labour, he had passed
The better portion of his time; and there

[9] **Savoyard:** one from the Alpine region of Savoy in south-eastern France.

[10] **sequestration:** separation or seclusion.

Spontaneously had his affections thriven
Upon the bounties of the year, and felt
The liberty of Nature; there he kept
In solitude and solitary thought
His mind in a just equipoise of love.
Serene it was, unclouded by the cares
Of ordinary life; unvexed, unwarped
By partial bondage. In his steady course
No piteous revolutions had he felt,
No wild varieties of joy and grief.
Unoccupied by sorrow of it's own
His heart lay open; and, by Nature tuned
And constant disposition of his thoughts
To sympathy with Man, he was alive
To all that was enjoyed where'er he went;
And all that was endured; for in himself
Happy, and quiet in his chearfulness,
He had no painful pressure from without
That made him turn aside from wretchedness
With coward fears. He could *afford* to suffer
With those whom he saw suffer.[11] Hence it came
That in our best experience he was rich,
And in the wisdom of our daily life.
For hence, minutely, in his various rounds,
He had observed the progress and decay
Of many minds, of minds and bodies too:
The History of many Families;
How they had prospered; how they were o'erthrown
By passion or mischance; or such misrule
Among the unthinking masters of the earth
As makes the nations groan.—This active course,
Chosen in youth, through manhood he pursued,
Till due provision for his modest wants
Had been obtained;—and, thereupon, resolved
To pass the remnant of his days—untasked
With needless services,—from hardship free.
His Calling laid aside, he lived at ease:
But still he loved to pace the public roads
And the wild paths; and, when the summer's warmth
Invited him, would often leave his home
And journey far, revisiting those scenes
Which to his memory were most endeared.
—Vigorous in health, of hopeful spirits, untouched
By worldly-mindedness or anxious care;
Observant, studious, thoughtful, and refreshed
By knowledge gathered up from day to day;—
Thus had he lived a long and innocent life.

The Scottish Church, both on himself and those
With whom from childhood he grew up, had held
The strong hand of her purity; and still
Had watched him with an unrelenting eye.
This he remembered in his riper age
With gratitude, and reverential thoughts.
But by the native vigour of his mind,
By his habitual wanderings out of doors,
By loneliness, and goodness, and kind works,
Whate'er in docile childhood or in youth
He had imbibed of fear or darker thought
Was melted all away: so true was this
That sometimes his religion seemed to me
Self-taught, as of a dreamer in the woods;
Who to the model of his own pure heart
Framed his belief, as grace divine inspired,
Or human reason dictated with awe.
—And surely never did there live on earth
A Man of kindlier nature. The rough sports
And teazing ways of Children vexed not him,
Nor could he bid them from his presence, tired
With questions and importunate demands:
Indulgent listener was he to the tongue
Of garrulous age; nor did the sick man's tale,
To his fraternal sympathy addressed,
Obtain reluctant hearing.

Plain his garb
Such as might suit a rustic sire, prepared
For sabbath duties; yet he was a Man
Whom no one could have passed without remark.
Active and nervous was his gait; his limbs
And his whole figure breathed intelligence.
Time had compressed the freshness of his cheek
Into a narrower circle of deep red
But had not tamed his eye; that under brows
Shaggy and grey had meanings which it brought
From years of youth; which, like a Being made
Of many Beings, he had wondrous skill
To blend with knowledge of the years to come,
Human, or such as lie beyond the grave.

So was He framed; and such his course of life
Who now, with no Appendage but a Staff,
The prized memorial of relinquish'd toils,
Upon that Cottage bench reposed his limbs,
Screened from the sun. Supine the Wanderer lay,

[11]*The Tempest*, I.ii.5–6: "O, I have suffer'd / With those that I saw suffer."

His eyes as if in drowsiness half shut,
The shadows of the breezy elms above
Dappling his face. He had not heard my steps
As I approached; and near him did I stand
Unnotic'd in the shade, some minutes' space.
At length I hailed him, seeing that his hat
Was moist with water-drops, as if the brim
Had newly scooped a running stream. He rose,
And ere the pleasant greeting that ensued
Was ended, "'Tis," said I, "a burning day;
My lips are parched with thirst, but you, I guess,
Have somewhere found relief." He, at the word,
Pointing towards a sweet-briar, bade me climb
The fence hard by, where that aspiring shrub
Looked out upon the road. It was a plot
Of garden-ground run wild, it's matted weeds
Marked with the steps of those, whom, as they pass'd,
The gooseberry trees that shot in long lank slips,
Or currants hanging from their leafless stems
In scanty strings, had tempted to o'erleap
The broken wall. I looked around, and there,
Where two tall hedge-rows of thick alder boughs
Joined in a cold damp nook, espied a Well
Shrouded with willow-flowers and plumy fern.
My thirst I slaked, and from the chearless spot
Withdrawing, straightway to the shade returned
Where sate the Old Man on the Cottage bench;
And, while, beside him, with uncovered head,
I yet was standing, freely to respire,
And cool my temples in the fanning air,
Thus did he speak. "I see around me here
Things which you cannot see: we die, my Friend,
Nor we alone, but that which each man loved
And prized in his peculiar nook of earth
Dies with him, or is changed; and very soon
Even of the good is no memorial left.
—The Poets, in their elegies and songs
Lamenting the departed, call the groves,
They call upon the hills and streams to mourn,
And senseless rocks; nor idly; for they speak,
In these their invocations, with a voice
Obedient to the strong creative power
Of human passion. Sympathies there are
More tranquil, yet perhaps of kindred birth,
That steal upon the meditative mind,
And grow with thought. Beside yon Spring I stood,
And eyed its waters till we seemed to feel
One sadness, they and I. For them a bond
Of brotherhood is broken: time has been
When, every day, the touch of human hand
Dislodged the natural sleep that binds them up
In mortal stillness; and they minister'd
To human comfort. As I stooped to drink,
Upon the slimy foot-stone I espied
The useless fragment of a wooden bowl,
Green with the moss of years; a pensive sight
That moved my heart!—recalling former days
When I could never pass that road but She
Who lived within these walls, at my approach,
A Daughter's welcome gave me; and I loved her
As my own child. O Sir! the good die first,
And they whose hearts are dry as summer dust
Burn to the socket. Many a Passenger
Hath blessed poor Margaret for her gentle looks,
When she upheld the cool refreshment drawn
From that forsaken Spring; and no one came
But he was welcome; no one went away
But that it seemed she loved him. She is dead,
The light extinguished of her lonely Hut,
The Hut itself abandoned to decay,
And She forgotten in the quiet grave!

"I speak," continued he, "of One whose stock
Of virtues bloom'd beneath this lowly roof.
She was a Woman of a steady mind,
Tender and deep in her excess of love,
Not speaking much, pleased rather with the joy
Of her own thoughts: by some especial care
Her temper had been framed, as if to make
A Being—who by adding love to peace
Might live on earth a life of happiness.
Her wedded Partner lacked not on his side
The humble worth that satisfied her heart:
Frugal, affectionate, sober, and withal
Keenly industrious. She with pride would tell
That he was often seated at his loom,
In summer, ere the Mower was abroad
Among the dewy grass,—in early spring,
Ere the last Star had vanished.—They who passed
At evening, from behind the garden fence
Might hear his busy spade, which he would ply,
After his daily work, until the light
Had failed, and every leaf and flower were lost
In the dark hedges. So their days were spent
In peace and comfort; and a pretty Boy
Was their best hope,—next to the God in Heaven.

Not twenty years ago, but you I think
Can scarcely bear it now in mind, there came

Two blighting seasons when the fields were left
With half a harvest. It pleased heaven to add
A worse affliction in the plague of war;
This happy Land was stricken to the heart!
A Wanderer then among the Cottages
I, with my freight of winter raiment, saw
The hardships of that season; many rich
Sank down, as in a dream, among the poor;
And of the poor did many cease to be
And their place knew them not. Meanwhile abridg'd
Of daily comforts, gladly reconciled
To numerous self-denials, Margaret
Went struggling on through those calamitous years
With chearful hope: but ere the second autumn
Her life's true Help-mate on a sick-bed lay,
Smitten with perilous fever. In disease
He lingered long; and when his strength return'd,
He found the little he had stored, to meet
The hour of accident or crippling age,
Was all consumed. Two children had they now,
One newly born. As I have said, it was
A time of trouble; shoals of Artisans
Were from their daily labour turn'd adrift
To seek their bread from public charity,
They, and their wives and children—happier far
Could they have lived as do the little birds
That peck along the hedges, or the Kite
That makes his dwelling on the mountain Rocks!

A sad reverse it was for Him who long
Had filled with plenty, and possess'd in peace,
This lonely Cottage. At his door he stood,
And whistled many a snatch of merry tunes
That had no mirth in them; or with his knife
Carved uncouth figures on the heads of sticks—
Then, not less idly, sought, through every nook
In house or garden, any casual work
Of use or ornament; and with a strange,
Amusing, yet uneasy novelty,
He blended, where he might, the various tasks
Of summer, autumn, winter, and of spring.
But this endured not; his good humour soon
Became a weight in which no pleasure was:
And poverty brought on a petted mood
And a sore temper: day by day he drooped,
And he would leave his work—and to the Town,
Without an errand, would direct his steps,
Or wander here and there among the fields.
One while he would speak lightly of his Babes,
And with a cruel tongue: at other times
He toss'd them with a false unnatural joy:
And 'twas a rueful thing to see the looks
Of the poor innocent children. "Every smile,"
Said Margaret to me, here beneath these trees,
"Made my heart bleed."

At this the Wanderer paused;
And, looking up to those enormous Elms,
He said, "'Tis now the hour of deepest noon.—
At this still season of repose and peace,
This hour, when all things which are not at rest
Are chearful; while this multitude of flies
Is filling all the air with melody;
Why should a tear be in an Old Man's eye?
Why should we thus, with an untoward mind,
And in the weakness of humanity,
From natural wisdom turn our hearts away,
To natural comfort shut our eyes and ears,
And, feeding on disquiet, thus disturb
The calm of nature with our restless thoughts?"

He spake with somewhat of a solemn tone:
But, when he ended, there was in his face
Such easy chearfulness, a look so mild,
That for a little time it stole away
All recollection, and that simple Tale
Passed from my mind like a forgotten sound.
A while on trivial things we held discourse,
To me soon tasteless. In my own despite
I thought of that poor Woman as of one
Whom I had known and loved. He had rehearsed
Her homely Tale with such familiar power,
With such an active countenance, an eye
So busy, that the things of which he spake
Seemed present; and, attention now relax'd,
There was a heart-felt chillness in my veins.—
I rose; and, turning from the breezy shade,
Went forth into the open air, and stood
To drink the comfort of the warmer sun.
Long time I had not staid, ere, looking round
Upon that tranquil Ruin, I return'd,
And begged of the Old Man that, for my sake,
He would resume his story.—

He replied,
"It were a wantonness, and would demand
Severe reproof, if we were Men whose hearts
Could hold vain dalliance with the misery
Even of the dead; contented thence to draw
A momentary pleasure, never marked
By reason, barren of all future good.

But we have known that there is often found
In mournful thoughts, and always might be found,
A power to virtue friendly; were't not so,
I am a Dreamer among men, indeed
An idle Dreamer! 'Tis a common Tale,
An ordinary sorrow of Man's life,
A tale of silent suffering, hardly clothed
In bodily form.—But, without further bidding,
I will proceed.—
While thus it fared with them,
To whom this Cottage, till those hapless years,
Had been a blessed home, it was my chance
To travel in a Country far remote.
And glad I was, when, halting by yon gate
That leads from the green lane, once more I saw
These lofty elm-trees. Long I did not rest:
With many pleasant thoughts I chear'd my way
O'er the flat Common.—Having reached the door
I knock'd,—and, when I entered with the hope
Of usual greeting, Margaret looked at me
A little while; then turn'd her head away
Speechless,—and sitting down upon a chair
Wept bitterly. I wist not what to do,
Or how to speak to her. Poor Wretch! at last
She rose from off her seat, and then,—O Sir!
I cannot *tell* how she pronounced my name.—
With fervent love, and with a face of grief
Unutterably helpless, and a look
That seemed to cling upon me, she enquired
If I had seen her Husband. As she spake
A strange surprize and fear came to my heart,
Nor had I power to answer ere she told
That he had disappear'd—not two months gone.
He left his House: two wretched days had pass'd,
And on the third, as wistfully she rais'd
Her head from off her pillow, to look forth,
Like one in trouble, for returning light,
Within her chamber-casement she espied
A folded paper, lying as if placed
To meet her waking eyes. This tremblingly
She open'd—found no writing, but therein
Pieces of money carefully enclosed,
Silver and gold.—"I shuddered at the sight,"
Said Margaret, "for I knew it was his hand
Which placed it there: and ere that day was ended,
That long and anxious day! I learned from One
Sent hither by my Husband to impart
The heavy news,—that he had joined a Troop
Of Soldiers, going to a distant Land.
—He left me thus—he could not gather heart
To take a farewell of me; for he fear'd
That I should follow with my Babes, and sink
Beneath the misery of that wandering Life."

This Tale did Margaret tell with many tears:
And when she ended I had little power
To give her comfort, and was glad to take
Such words of hope from her own mouth as served
To chear us both:—but long we had not talked
Ere we built up a pile of better thoughts,
And with a brighter eye she look'd around
As if she had been shedding tears of joy.
We parted.—'Twas the time of early spring;
I left her busy with her garden tools;
And well remember, o'er that fence she looked,
And, while I paced along the foot-way path,
Called out, and sent a blessing after me,
With tender chearfulness; and with a voice
That seem'd the very sound of happy thoughts.

I roved o'er many a hill and many a dale,
With my accustomed load; in heat and cold,
Through many a wood, and many an open ground,
In sunshine and in shade, in wet and fair,
Drooping, or blithe of heart, as might befal;
My best companions now the driving winds,
And now the "trotting brooks"[12] and whispering trees,
And now the music of my own sad steps,
With many a short-lived thought that pass'd between,
And disappeared.—I journey'd back this way
Towards the wane of Summer; when the wheat
Was yellow; and the soft and bladed grass
Springing afresh had o'er the hay-field spread
Its tender verdure. At the door arrived,
I found that she was absent. In the shade,
Where now we sit, I waited her return.
Her Cottage, then a chearful Object, wore
Its customary look,—only, I thought,
The honeysuckle, crowding round the porch,
Hung down in heavier tufts: and that bright weed,
The yellow stone-crop, suffered to take root
Along the window's edge, profusely grew,
Blinding the lower panes. I turned aside,

[12] **trotting brooks:** Robert Burns, "To William Simpson": "The Muse, nae poet ever fand her, / Till by himsel he learn'd to wander, / Adown some trottin burn's [brook's] meander, / An' no think lang . . ."

And strolled into her garden. It appeared
To lag behind the season, and had lost
Its pride of neatness. From the border lines
Composed of daisy and resplendent thrift,
Flowers straggling forth had on those paths encroached
Which they were used to deck:—Carnations, once
Prized for surpassing beauty, and no less
For the peculiar pains they had required,
Declined their languid heads—without support.
The cumbrous bind-weed, with its wreaths and bells,
Had twined about her two small rows of pease,
And dragged them to the earth.—Ere this an hour
Was wasted.—Back I turned my restless steps,
And, as I walked before the door, it chanced
A Stranger passed; and, guessing whom I sought,
He said that she was used to ramble far.—
The sun was sinking in the west; and now
I sate with sad impatience. From within
Her solitary Infant cried aloud;
Then, like a blast that dies away self-stilled,
The voice was silent. From the bench I rose;
But neither could divert nor soothe my thoughts.
The spot, though fair, was very desolate—
The longer I remained more desolate.
And, looking round, I saw the corner stones,
Till then unnotic'd, on either side the door
With dull red stains discolour'd, and stuck o'er
With tufts and hairs of wool, as if the Sheep,
That fed upon the Common, thither came
Familiarly; and found a couching-place
Even at her threshold. Deeper shadows fell
From these tall elms;—the Cottage-clock struck eight;—
I turned, and saw her distant a few steps.
Her face was pale and thin, her figure too
Was changed. As she unlocked the door, she said,
"It grieves me you have waited here so long,
But, in good truth, I've wandered much of late,
And, sometimes,—to my shame I speak, have need
Of my best prayers to bring me back again."
While on the board she spread our evening meal
She told me,—interrupting not the work
Which gave employment to her listless hands,
That she had parted with her elder Child;
To a kind Master on a distant farm
Now happily apprenticed—"I perceive
You look at me, and you have cause; to-day
I have been travelling far; and many days
About the fields I wander, knowing this
Only, that what I seek I cannot find.
And so I waste my time: for I am changed;
And to myself, said she, have done much wrong
And to this helpless Infant. I have slept
Weeping, and weeping I have waked; my tears
Have flowed as if my body were not such
As others are; and I could never die.
But I am now in mind and in my heart
More easy; and I hope," said she, "that heaven
Will give me patience to endure the things
Which I behold at home." It would have grieved
Your very soul to see her; Sir, I feel
The story linger in my heart: I fear
'Tis long and tedious; but my spirit clings
To that poor Woman:—so familiarly
Do I perceive her manner, and her look,
And presence, and so deeply do I feel
Her goodness, that, not seldom, in my walks
A momentary trance comes over me;
And to myself I seem to muse on One
By sorrow laid asleep;—or borne away,
A human being destined to awake
To human life, or something very near
To human life, when he shall come again
For whom she suffered. Yes, it would have grieved
Your very soul to see her: evermore
Her eyelids drooped, her eyes were downward cast;
And, when she at her table gave me food,
She did not look at me. Her voice was low,
Her body was subdued. In every act
Pertaining to her house affairs, appeared
The careless stillness of a thinking mind
Self-occupied; to which all outward things
Are like an idle matter. Still she sighed,
But yet no motion of the breast was seen,
No heaving of the heart. While by the fire
We sate together, sighs came on my ear,
I knew not how, and hardly whence they came.

Ere my departure to her care I gave,
For her Son's use, some tokens of regard,
Which with a look of welcome She received;
And I exhorted her to have her trust
In God's good love, and seek his help by prayer.
I took my staff, and when I kissed her babe
The tears stood in her eyes. I left her then
With the best hope and comfort I could give;
She thanked me for my wish;—but for my hope

Methought she did not thank me.
I returned,
And took my rounds along this road again
Ere on its sunny bank the primrose flower
Peeped forth, to give an earnest of the Spring.
I found her sad and drooping; she had learned
No tidings of her Husband; if he lived
She knew not that he lived; if he were dead
She knew not he was dead. She seem'd the same
In person and appearance; but her House
Bespake a sleepy hand of negligence.
The floor was neither dry nor neat, the hearth
Was comfortless, and her small lot of books,
Which, in the Cottage window, heretofore
Had been piled up against the corner panes
In seemly order, now, with straggling leaves
Lay scattered here and there, open or shut,
As they had chanced to fall. Her Infant Babe
Had from its Mother caught the trick of grief,
And sighed among its playthings. Once again
I turned towards the garden gate, and saw,
More plainly still, that poverty and grief
Were now come nearer to her: weeds defaced
The harden'd soil, and knots of wither'd grass;
No ridges there appeared of clear black mold,
No winter greenness; of her herbs and flowers,
It seemed the better part were gnawed away
Or trampled into earth; a chain of straw,
Which had been twined about the slender stem
Of a young apple-tree, lay at its root;
The bark was nibbled round by truant Sheep.
—Margaret stood near, her Infant in her arms,
And, noting that my eye was on the tree,
She said, "I fear it will be dead and gone
Ere Robert come again." Towards the House
Together we returned; and she enquired
If I had any hope:—but for her Babe
And for her little orphan Boy, she said,
She had no wish to live, that she must die
Of sorrow. Yet I saw the idle loom
Still in its place; his Sunday garments hung
Upon the self-same nail; his very staff
Stood undisturbed behind the door. And when,
In bleak December, I retraced this way,
She told me that her little Babe was dead,
And she was left alone. She now, released
From her maternal cares, had taken up
The employment common through these Wilds, and gain'd
By spinning hemp a pittance for herself;
And for this end had hired a neighbour's Boy
To give her needful help. That very time
Most willingly she put her work aside,
And walked with me along the miry road
Heedless how far; and, in such piteous sort
That any heart had ached to hear her, begged
That, wheresoe'er I went, I still would ask
For him whom she had lost. We parted then,
Our final parting; for from that time forth
Did many seasons pass ere I return'd
Into this tract again.
Nine tedious years;
From their first separation, nine long years,
She lingered in unquiet widowhood;
A Wife and Widow. Needs must it have been
A sore heart-wasting! I have heard, my Friend,
That in yon arbour oftentimes she sate
Alone, through half the vacant Sabbath-day,
And if a dog passed by she still would quit
The shade, and look abroad. On this old Bench
For hours she sate; and evermore her eye
Was busy in the distance, shaping things
That made her heart beat quick. You see that path,
Now faint,—the grass has crept o'er its grey line;
There, to and fro, she paced through many a day
Of the warm summer, from a belt of hemp
That girt her waist, spinning the long drawn thread
With backward steps. Yet ever as there pass'd
A man whose garments shewed the Soldiers red,
Or crippled Mendicant in Sailor's garb,
The little Child who sate to turn the wheel
Ceas'd from his task; and she with faultering voice
Made many a fond enquiry; and when they,
Whose presence gave no comfort, were gone by,
Her heart was still more sad. And by yon gate,
That bars the Traveller's road, she often stood,
And when a stranger Horseman came the latch
Would lift, and in his face look wistfully;
Most happy, if, from aught discovered there
Of tender feeling, she might dare repeat
The same sad question. Meanwhile her poor Hut
Sank to decay: for he was gone—whose hand,
At the first nipping of October frost,
Closed up each chink, and with fresh bands of straw
Chequered the green-grown thatch. And so she lived
Through the long winter, reckless and alone;
Until her House by frost, and thaw, and rain,
Was sapped; and while she slept the nightly damps

Did chill her breast; and in the stormy day
Her tattered clothes were ruffled by the wind;
Even at the side of her own fire. Yet still
She loved this wretched spot, nor would for worlds
Have parted hence; and still that length of road,
And this rude bench, one torturing hope endeared,
Fast rooted at her heart: and here, my Friend,
In sickness she remained; and here she died,
Last human Tenant of these ruined Walls."

The Old Man ceased: he saw that I was moved;
From that low Bench, rising instinctively
I turn'd aside in weakness, nor had power
To thank him for the Tale which he had told.
I stood, and leaning o'er the Garden wall,
Reviewed that Woman's sufferings; and it seemed
To comfort me while with a Brother's love
I bless'd her—in the impotence of grief.
At length towards the Cottage I returned
Fondly,—and traced, with interest more mild,
That secret spirit of humanity
Which, mid the calm oblivious tendencies
Of Nature, mid her plants, and weeds, and flowers,
And silent overgrowings, still survived.
The Old Man, noting this, resumed, and said,
"My Friend! enough to sorrow you have given,
The purposes of wisdom ask no more;
Be wise and chearful; and no longer read
The forms of things with an unworthy eye.
She sleeps in the calm earth, and peace is here.
I well remember that those very plumes,
Those weeds, and the high spear-grass on that wall,
By mist and silent rain-drops silver'd o'er,
As once I passed, did to my heart convey
So still an image of tranquillity,
So calm and still, and looked so beautiful
Amid the uneasy thoughts which filled my mind,
That what we feel of sorrow and despair
From ruin and from change, and all the grief
The passing shews of Being leave behind,
Appeared an idle dream, that could not live
Where meditation was. I turned away
And walked along my road in happiness."

He ceased. Ere long the sun declining shot
A slant and mellow radiance, which began
To fall upon us, while beneath the trees
We sate on that low Bench: and now we felt,
Admonished thus, the sweet hour coming on.
A linnet warbled from those lofty elms,
A thrush sang loud, and other melodies,
At distance heard, peopled the milder air.
The Old Man rose, and, with a sprightly mien
Of hopeful preparation, grasped his Staff:
Together casting then a farewell look
Upon those silent walls, we left the Shade;
And, ere the Stars were visible, had reached
A Village Inn,—our Evening resting-place.

from POEMS[1]
(1815–1849/50)

A Night-Piece[2]
(1815; comp. 1798)

—The sky is overcast
With a continuous cloud of texture close,
Heavy and wan, all whitened by the Moon,
Which through that veil is indistinctly seen,
A dull, contracted circle, yielding light
So feebly spread, that not a shadow falls,
Chequering the ground—from rock, plant, tree, or
tower.
At length a pleasant instantaneous gleam
Startles the pensive traveller while he treads
His lonesome path, with unobserving eye
Bent earthwards; he looks up—the clouds are split
Asunder,—and above his head he sees
The clear Moon, and the glory of the heavens.
There, in a black-blue vault she sails along,
Followed by multitudes of stars, that, small
And sharp, and bright, along the dark abyss
Drive as she drives: how fast they wheel away,
Yet vanish not!—the wind is in the tree,
But they are silent;—still they roll along
Immeasurably distant; and the vault,
Built round by those white clouds, enormous clouds,
Still deepens its unfathomable depth.
At length the Vision closes; and the mind,

[1] Wordsworth's collected works were variously titled *Poems by William Wordsworth* (1815) or *Poetical Works of William Wordsworth* (1827, 1832, 1836–1837, 1849–1850).

[2] See Dorothy Wordsworth's *Alfoxden Journal* (25 January 1798).*

Not undisturbed by the delight it feels,
Which slowly settles into peaceful calm,
Is left to muse upon the solemn scene.

'Surprised by Joy—Impatient as the Wind'

(1815; comp. 1813–1814)

Surprised by joy—impatient as the Wind
I turned to share the transport—Oh! with whom
But Thee,[1] deep buried in the silent tomb,
That spot which no vicissitude can find?
Love, faithful love, recalled thee to my mind—
But how could I forget thee? Through what power,
Even for the least division of an hour,
Have I been so beguiled as to be blind
To my most grievous loss!—That thought's return
Was the worst pang that sorrow ever bore,
Save one, one only, when I stood forlorn,
Knowing my heart's best treasure was no more;
That neither present time, nor years unborn
Could to my sight that heavenly face restore.

Extempore Effusion upon the Death of James Hogg[1†]

(1836; comp. 1835)

When first, descending from the moorlands,
I saw the Stream of Yarrow glide
Along a bare and open valley,
The Ettrick Shepherd was my guide.

When last along its banks I wandered,
Through groves that had begun to shed
Their golden leaves upon the pathways,
My steps the Border-minstrel led.[2]

The mighty Minstrel breathes no longer,
'Mid mouldering ruins low he lies;
And death upon the braes of Yarrow,
Has closed the Shepherd-poet's eyes:

Nor has the rolling year twice measured,
From sign to sign, its stedfast course,
Since every mortal power of Coleridge
Was frozen at its marvellous source;

The rapt One, of the godlike forehead,
The heaven-eyed creature sleeps in earth:
And Lamb, the frolic and the gentle,
Has vanished from his lonely hearth.

Like clouds that rake the mountain-summits,
Or waves that own no curbing hand,
How fast has brother followed brother,
From sunshine to the sunless land!

Yet I, whose lids from infant slumber
Were earlier raised, remain to hear
A timid voice, that asks in whispers,
'Who next will drop and disappear?'

Our haughty life is crowned with darkness,
Like London with its own black wreath,
On which with thee, O Crabbe! forth-looking,
I gazed from Hampstead's breezy heath.

As if but yesterday departed,
Thou too art gone before; but why,
O'er ripe fruit, seasonably gathered,
Should frail survivors heave a sigh?

Mourn rather for that holy Spirit,
Sweet as the spring, as ocean deep;
For Her who, ere her summer faded,
Has sunk into a breathless sleep.

No more of old romantic sorrows,
For slaughtered Youth or love-lorn Maid!
With sharper grief is Yarrow smitten,
And Ettrick mourns with her their Poet dead.

[1] l. 3: "Thee" is Wordsworth's daughter Catharine, who died on 4 June 1812, at the age of three.

[1†] First published in the *Athenaeum* (12 December 1835). James Hogg ("The Ettrick Shepherd") died 21 November 1835. He is best known as the author of *Private Memoirs and Confessions of a Justified Sinner* (1824). The poets and friends commemorated in the poem are Walter Scott,* d. 21 September 1832; Coleridge,* d. 25 July 1834; Charles Lamb,* d. 27 December 1834; George Crabbe, d. 3 February 1832; and Felicia Hemans,* d. 16 May 1835.

[2] **Border-minstrel:** Scott.*

'So Fair, So Sweet, Withal So Sensitive'

(1845; comp. 1844)

So fair, so sweet, withal so sensitive,
Would that the little Flowers were born to live,
Conscious of half the pleasure which they give;

That to this mountain-daisy's self were known
The beauty of its star-shaped shadow, thrown
On the smooth surface of this naked stone!

And what if hence a bold desire should mount
High as the Sun, that he could take account
Of all that issues from his glorious fount!

So might he ken how by his sovereign aid
These delicate companionships are made;
And how he rules the pomp of light and shade;

And were the Sister-power that shines by night
So privileged, what a countenance of delight
Would through the clouds break forth on human sight!

Fond fancies! wheresoe'er shall turn thine eye
On earth, air, ocean, or the starry sky,
Converse with Nature in pure sympathy;

All vain desires, all lawless wishes quelled,
Be Thou to love and praise alike impelled,
Whatever boon is granted or withheld.

On the Projected Kendal and Windermere Railway

(1845; comp. 1844)

Is then 'no nook of English ground secure
From rash assault?'[1] Schemes of retirement sown
In youth, and 'mid the busy world kept pure
As when their earliest flowers of hope were blown,
Must perish;—how can they this blight endure?
And must he too the ruthless change bemoan
Who scorns a false utilitarian lure
'Mid his paternal fields at random thrown?
Baffle the threat, bright Scene, from Orrest-head[2]
Given to the pausing traveller's rapturous glance:
Plead for thy peace, thou beautiful romance
Of nature; and, if human hearts be dead,
Speak, passing winds; ye torrents, with your strong
And constant voice, protest against the wrong.

[1] The degree and kind of attachment which many of the yeomanry feel to their small inheritances can scarcely be over-rated. Near the house of one of them stands a magnificent tree, which a neighbour of the owner advised him to fell for profit's sake. 'Fell it!' exclaimed the yeoman, 'I had rather fall on my knees and worship it.' It happens, I believe, that the intended railway would pass through this little property, and I hope that an apology for the answer will not be thought necessary by one who enters into the strength of the feeling—W.

[2] **Orrest-head**: a height north of Windermere which commands a magnificent view of the lake and its surroundings.

POSTHUMOUS PUBLICATIONS

from THE PRELUDE; OR, GROWTH OF A POET'S MIND

(1799; 1805; 1850)[1]

The Two-Part Prelude of 1799

(1973; comp. 1798–1799)

— [FIRST PART] —

Was it for this[2]
That one, the fairest of all rivers, loved
To blend his murmurs with my nurse's song,
And from his alder shades and rocky falls,
And from his fords and shallows, sent a voice
That flowed along my dreams? For this didst thou,
O Derwent,[3] travelling over the green plains
Near my 'sweet birthplace',[4] didst thou, beauteous
stream,
Make ceaseless music through the night and day,
Which with its steady cadence tempering
Our human waywardness, composed my thoughts
To more than infant softness, giving me
Among the fretful dwellings of mankind
A knowledge, a dim earnest, of the calm
Which Nature breathes among the fields and groves?
Beloved Derwent, fairest of all streams,
Was it for this that I, a four years' child,
A naked boy, among thy silent pools
Made one long bathing of a summer's day,
Basked in the sun, or plunged into thy streams,
Alternate, all a summer's day, or coursed
Over the sandy fields, and dashed the flowers
Of yellow grunsel; or, when crag and hill,
The woods, and distant Skiddaw's[5] lofty height,
Were bronzed with a deep radiance, stood alone
A naked savage in the thunder-shower?

And afterwards ('twas in a later day,
Though early), when upon the mountain slope
The frost and breath of frosty wind had snapped
The last autumnal crocus, 'twas my joy
To wander half the night among the cliffs
And the smooth hollows where the woodcocks ran
Along the moonlight turf. In thought and wish
That time, my shoulder all with springes[6] hung,

---

[1] *The Prelude* is Wordsworth's masterpiece, although left unpublished during his lifetime because the poet was reticent to publish an autobiographical poem of 14 Books and over 9,000 lines. Although preserved in many manuscripts, the sections included here represent the poem's three principal surviving forms, the earliest version of 1799; the first, fully developed poem of 1805; and the much-revised, published form of 1850. *The Prelude*'s complicated textual history is described lucidly and succinctly by Jonathan Wordsworth, M. H. Abrams, and Stephen Gill in their edition of *The Prelude, 1799, 1805, 1850* (1979).

The parts of the autobiographical epic anthologized here represent the three major formative influences on the development of the poet's imagination: Nature, represented in *Prelude* (1799); Books, in *Prelude* (1805), Book V; and History, specifically, the French Revolution, and its effect on the youthful idealists of Great Britain, from Books VI–X (1805). The selections conclude with parallel passages from Books XIII (1805) and XIV (1850) on the transcendental and creative powers Wordsworth claims for his mature Imagination.

Prelude (1799) offers the reader a complete and dramatic poem of Wordsworth's earliest narrative experiments with the awakening and early growth of imagination in its fearful, loving, and mysterious interactions with nature. Begun during Wordsworth's residence in Germany (1798–1799) and completed in this first form after returning to England, *Prelude* (1799) provides the substance for Books I–II of the 1805 and 1850 versions, except for the climactic episodes of Part One, the three experiences which the poet says "cannot here / Be regularly classed," or organized according to the categories of "danger or desire," "hope and fear"—the drowned-man episode (ll. 258–87) and the two experiences specifically designated by the poet as "Spots of Time," being lost as child (ll. 296–327) and waiting to return home the Christmas season of his father's death (ll. 330–74). When Wordsworth expanded the poem, the drowned-man episode was transferred to Book V in both the 1805 and 1850 versions, and the two Spots of Time were relocated to Book XI of the 1805 version and Book XII of the 1850 version of the poem.

[2] "[T]his" is left unspecified, but probably refers to the unpromising creative situation the poet found himself in while residing in Goslar, Germany, in the severe winter of 1798–1799.

[3] **Derwent:** a stream that flowed outside of Wordsworth's backyard in his parental home at Cockermouth.

[4] **'sweet birthplace':** phrase from Coleridge's "Frost at Midnight."*

[5] **Skiddaw:** peak just over 3,000 feet in height located nine miles outside of Cockermouth.

[6] **springes:** traps or snares for catching woodcocks. *Hamlet*, I.iii.115: "Ay, springes to catch woodcocks."

I was a fell destroyer. Gentle powers,
Who give us happiness and call it peace,
When scudding on from snare to snare I plied
My anxious visitation, hurrying on,
Still hurrying, hurrying onward, how my heart
Panted; among the scattered yew-trees and the crags
That looked upon me, how my bosom beat
With expectation! Sometimes strong desire
Resistless overpowered me, and the bird
Which was the captive of another's toils
Became my prey; and when the deed was done[7]
I heard among the solitary hills
Low breathings coming after me, and sounds
Of undistinguishable motion, steps
Almost as silent as the turf they trod.

Nor less in springtime, when on southern banks
The shining sun had from his knot of leaves
Decoyed the primrose flower, and when the vales
And woods were warm, was I a rover then
In the high places, on the lonesome peaks,
Among the mountains and the winds. Though mean
And though inglorious were my views, the end
Was not ignoble. Oh, when I have hung
Above the raven's nest, by knots of grass
Or half-inch fissures in the slipp'ry rock
But ill sustained, and almost, as it seemed,
Suspended by the blast which blew amain,
Shouldering the naked crag, oh, at that time,
While on the perilous ridge I hung alone,
With what strange utterance did the loud dry wind
Blow through my ears; the sky seemed not a sky
Of earth, and with what motion moved the clouds!

The mind of man is fashioned and built up
Even as a strain of music. I believe
That there are spirits which, when they would form
A favored being, from his very dawn
Of infancy do open out the clouds
As at the touch of lightning, seeking him
With gentle visitation—quiet powers,
Retired, and seldom recognized, yet kind,
And to the very meanest not unknown—
With me, though rarely, in my boyish days
They communed. Others too there are, who use,
Yet haply aiming at the self-same end,
Severer interventions, ministry
More palpable—and of their school was I.

They guided me: one evening led by them
I went alone into a shepherd's boat,
A skiff, that to a willow-tree was tied
Within a rocky cave, its usual home.
The moon was up, the lake was shining clear
Among the hoary mountains; from the shore
I pushed, and struck the oars, and struck again
In cadence, and my little boat moved on
Just like a man who walks with stately step
Though bent on speed. It was an act of stealth
And troubled pleasure. Not without the voice
Of mountain echoes did my boat move on,
Leaving behind her still on either side
Small circles glittering idly in the moon,
Until they melted all into one track
Of sparkling light. A rocky steep uprose
Above the cavern of the willow-tree,
And now, as suited one who proudly rowed
With his best skill, I fixed a steady view
Upon the top of that same craggy ridge,
The bound of the horizon—for behind
Was nothing but the stars and the grey sky.
She was an elfin pinnace;[8] twenty times
I dipped my oars into the silent lake,
And as I rose upon the stroke my boat
Went heaving through the water like a swan—
When from behind that rocky steep, till then
The bound of the horizon, a huge cliff,
As if with voluntary power instinct,
Upreared its head. I struck, and struck again,
And, growing still in stature, the huge cliff
Rose up between me and the stars, and still,
With measured motion, like a living thing,
Strode after me. With trembling hands I turned,
And through the silent water stole my way
Back to the cavern of the willow-tree.
There in her mooring-place I left my bark,
And through the meadows homeward went with grave
And serious thoughts; and after I had seen
That spectacle, for many days my brain
Worked with a dim and undetermined sense
Of unknown modes of being. In my thoughts
There was a darkness—call it solitude,
Or blank desertion—no familiar shapes

[7] *Macbeth,* I.vii.1–2: "If it were done when 'tis done, then 'twere well / It were done quickly."

[8] **pinnace:** a small ship or ship's boat, generally used as a tender to a larger vessel; obsolete: mistress (cf. OED).

Of hourly objects, images of trees,
Of sea or sky, no colours of green fields,
But huge and mighty forms that do not live
Like living men moved slowly through my mind
By day, and were the trouble of my dreams.

Ah, not in vain ye beings of the hills,
And ye that walk the woods and open heaths
By moon or star-light, thus, from my first dawn
Of childhood, did ye love to intertwine
The passions that build up our human soul
Not with the mean and vulgar works of man,
But with high objects, with eternal things,
With life and Nature, purifying thus
The elements of feeling and of thought,
And sanctifying by such discipline
Both pain and fear, until we recognise
A grandeur in the beatings of the heart.
Nor was this fellowship vouchsafed to me
With stinted kindness. In November days,
When vapours rolling down the valleys made
A lonely scene more lonesome, among woods
At noon, and 'mid the calm of summer nights
When by the margin of the trembling lake
Beneath the gloomy hills I homeward went
In solitude, such intercourse was mine.

And in the frosty season, when the sun
Was set, and visible for many a mile
The cottage windows through the twilight blazed,
I heeded not the summons. Clear and loud
The village clock tolled six; I wheeled about
Proud and exulting, like an untired horse
That cares not for its home. All shod with steel
We hissed along the polished ice in games
Confederate, imitative of the chace
And woodland pleasures, the resounding horn,
The pack loud bellowing, and the hunted hare.
So through the darkness and the cold we flew,
And not a voice was idle. With the din,
Meanwhile, the precipices rang aloud;
The leafless trees and every icy crag
Tinkled like iron; while the distant hills
Into the tumult sent an alien sound
Of melancholy, not unnoticed; while the stars,
Eastward, were sparkling clear, and in the west
The orange sky of evening died away.

Not seldom from the uproar I retired
Into a silent bay, or sportively
Glanced sideway, leaving the tumultuous throng,
To cut across the shadow of a star
That gleamed upon the ice. And oftentimes
When we had given our bodies to the wind,
And all the shadowy banks on either side
Came sweeping through the darkness, spinning still
The rapid line of motion, then at once
Have I, reclining back upon my heels
Stopped short—yet still the solitary cliffs
Wheeled by me, even as if the earth had rolled
With visible motion her diurnal round.
Behind me did they stretch in solemn train,
Feebler and feebler, and I stood and watched
Till all was tranquil as a summer sea.

Ye powers of earth, ye genii of the springs,
And ye that have your voices in the clouds,
And ye that are familiars of the lakes
And of the standing pools, I may not think
A vulgar hope was yours when ye employed
Such ministry—when ye through many a year
Thus, by the agency of boyish sports,
On caves and trees, upon the woods and hills,
Impressed upon all forms the characters
Of danger or desire, and thus did make
The surface of the universal earth
With meanings of delight, of hope and fear,
Work like a sea.

Not uselessly employed,
I might pursue this theme through every change
Of exercise and sport to which the year
Did summon us in its delightful round.
We were a noisy crew; the sun in heaven
Beheld not vales more beautiful than ours,
Nor saw a race in happiness and joy
More worthy of the fields where they were sown.
I would record with no reluctant voice
Our home amusements by the warm peat fire
At evening, when with pencil and with slate,
In square divisions parcelled out, and all
With crosses and with cyphers scribbled o'er,
We schemed and puzzled, head opposed to head,
In strife too humble to be named in verse;
Or round the naked table, snow-white deal,[9]
Cherry, or maple, sate in close array,
And to the combat—lu or whist[10]—led on

[9] **deal:** fir or pine wood.

[10] **lu or whist:** card games.

A thick-ribbed army, not as in the world
Discarded and ungratefully thrown by
Even for the very service they had wrought,
But husbanded through many a long campaign.
Oh, with what echoes on the board they fell—
Ironic diamonds, hearts of sable hue,
Queens gleaming through their splendour's last decay,
Knaves wrapt in one assimilating gloom,
And kings indignant at the shame incurred
By royal visages.[11] Meanwhile abroad
The heavy rain was falling, or the frost
Raged bitterly with keen and silent tooth,
And, interrupting the impassioned game,
Oft from the neighbouring lake the splitting ice,
While it sank down towards the water, sent
Among the meadows and the hills its long
And frequent yellings, imitative some
Of wolves that howl along the Bothnic main.

Nor with less willing heart would I rehearse
The woods of autumn, and their hidden bowers
With milk-white clusters hung; the rod and line—
True symbol of the foolishness of hope—
Which with its strong enchantment led me on
By rocks and pools, where never summer star
Impressed its shadow, to forlorn cascades
Among the windings of the mountain-brooks;
The kite in sultry calms from some high hill
Sent up, ascending thence till it was lost
Among the fleecy clouds—in gusty days
Launched from the lower grounds, and suddenly
Dashed headlong and rejected by the storm.
All these, and more, with rival claims demand
Grateful acknowledgement. It were a song
Venial, and such as—if I rightly judge—
I might protract unblamed, but I perceive
That much is overlooked, and we should ill
Attain our object if, from delicate fears
Of breaking in upon the unity
Of this my argument, I should omit
To speak of such effects as cannot here
Be regularly classed, yet tend no less
To the same point, the growth of mental power
And love of Nature's works.

Ere I had seen
Eight summers—and 'twas in the very week
When I was first transplanted to thy vale,
Beloved Hawkshead,[12] when thy paths, thy shores
And brooks, were like a dream of novelty
To my half-infant mind—I chanced to cross
One of those open fields which, shaped like ears,
Make green peninsulas on Esthwaite's lake.
Twilight was coming on, yet through the gloom
I saw distinctly on the opposite shore,
Beneath a tree and close by the lake side,
A heap of garments, as if left by one
Who there was bathing. Half an hour I watched
And no one owned them; meanwhile the calm lake
Grew dark with all the shadows on its breast,
And now and then a leaping fish disturbed
The breathless stillness. The succeeding day
There came a company, and in their boat
Sounded with iron hooks and with long poles.
At length the dead man, 'mid that beauteous scene
Of trees and hills and water, bolt upright
Rose with his ghastly face. I might advert
To numerous accidents in flood or field,[13]
Quarry or moor, or 'mid the winter snows,
Distresses and disasters, tragic facts
Of rural history, that impressed my mind
With images to which in following years
Far other feelings were attached—with forms
That yet exist with independent life,
And, like their archetypes, know no decay.

There are in our existence spots of time
Which with distinct preeminence retain
A fructifying[14] virtue, whence, depressed
By trivial occupations and the round
Of ordinary intercourse, our minds—
Especially the imaginative power—
Are nourished and invisibly repaired,
Such moments chiefly seem to have their date
In our first childhood. I remember well
('Tis of an early season that I speak,
The twilight of rememberable life),

[11] Lines 221 through 225 are usually associated with Pope's game of ombre in *Rape of the Lock*. Read in the context of the 1790s, these lines suggest the contemporary experience of the aristocracy and continental monarchies, especially in France.

[12] Wordsworth left for the village of Hawkshead to study at its Grammar School shortly after his mother died. See the section Introduction.

[13] Cf. *Othello*, I.iii.134–35: "Wherein I spake of most disastrous chances, / Of moving accidents by flood and field."

[14] **fructifying**: making fruitful or productive.

While I was yet an urchin, one who scarce
Could hold a bridle, with ambitious hopes
I mounted, and we rode towards the hills.
We were a pair of horsemen: honest James[15]
Was with me, my encourager and guide.
We had not travelled long ere some mischance
Disjoined me from my comrade, and, through fear
Dismounting, down the rough and stony moor
I led my horse, and stumbling on, at length
Came to a bottom where in former times
A man, the murderer of his wife, was hung
In irons. Mouldered was the gibbet-mast;
The bones were gone, the iron and the wood;
Only a long green ridge of turf remained
Whose shape was like a grave. I left the spot,
And reascending the bare slope I saw
A naked pool that lay beneath the hills,
The beacon on the summit, and more near
A girl who bore a pitcher on her head
And seemed with difficult steps to force her way
Against the blowing wind. It was in truth
An ordinary sight, but I should need
Colours and words that are unknown to man
To paint the visionary dreariness
Which, while I looked all round for my lost guide,
Did at that time invest the naked pool,
The beacon on the lonely eminence,
The woman and her garments vexed and tossed
By the strong wind.

Nor less I recollect—
Long after, though my childhood had not ceased—
Another scene which left a kindred power
Implanted in my mind. One Christmas-time,
The day before the holidays began,
Feverish, and tired, and restless, I went forth
Into the fields, impatient for the sight
Of those three horses which should bear us home,
My brothers and myself. There was a crag,
An eminence, which from the meeting-point
Of two highways ascending overlooked
At least a long half-mile of those two roads,
By each of which the expected steeds might come—
The choice uncertain. Thither I repaired
Up to the highest summit. 'Twas a day
Stormy, and rough, and wild, and on the grass
I sate half sheltered by a naked wall.
Upon my right hand was a single sheep,
A whistling hawthorn on my left, and there,
Those two companions at my side, I watched
With eyes intensely straining, as the mist
Gave intermitting prospects of the wood
And plain beneath. Ere I to school returned
That dreary time, ere I had been ten days
A dweller in my father's house, he died,
And I and my two brothers, orphans then,
Followed his body to the grave. The event,
With all the sorrow which it brought, appeared
A chastisement; and when I called to mind
That day so lately passed, when from the crag
I looked in such anxiety of hope,
With trite reflections of morality,
Yet with the deepest passion, I bowed low
To God who thus corrected my desires.
And afterwards the wind and sleety rain,
And all the business of the elements,
The single sheep, and the one blasted tree,
And the bleak music of that old stone wall,
The noise of wood and water, and the mist
Which on the line of each of those two roads
Advanced in such indisputable shapes—[16]
All these were spectacles and sounds to which
I often would repair, and thence would drink
As at a fountain. And I do not doubt
That in this later time, when storm and rain
Beat on my roof at midnight, or by day
When I am in the woods, unknown to me
The workings of my spirit thence are brought.

Nor, sedulous as I have been to trace
How Nature by collateral interest,
And by extrinsic passion, peopled first
My mind with forms or beautiful or grand
And made me love them, may I well forget
How other pleasures have been mine, and joys
Of subtler origin—how I have felt
Not seldom, even in that tempestuous time,
Those hallowed and pure motions of the sense[17]
Which seem in their simplicity to own

[15] **James:** most likely a family servant.

[16] **indisputable shapes:** Ernest de Selincourt points out the allusion to *Hamlet*, I.iv.43–44: "Thou comst in such a questionable shape / That I will speak with thee."

[17] J. C. Maxwell points out the allusion to *Measure for Measure*, I.iv.59: "The wanton stings and motions of the sense."

An intellectual charm, that calm delight
Which, if I err not, surely must belong
To those first-born affinities that fit
Our new existence to existing things,
And, in our dawn of being, constitute
The bond of union betwixt life and joy.

Yes, I remember when the changeful earth
And twice five seasons on my mind had stamped
The faces of the moving year, even then,
A child, I held unconscious intercourse
With the eternal beauty, drinking in
A pure organic pleasure from the lines
Of curling mist, or from the level plain
Of waters coloured by the steady clouds.
The sands of Westmoreland, the creeks and bays
Of Cumbria's rocky limits, they can tell
How when the sea threw off his evening shade
And to the shepherd's hut beneath the crags
Did send sweet notice of the rising moon,
How I have stood, to images like these
A stranger, linking with the spectacle
No body of associated forms,
And bringing with me no peculiar sense
Of quietness or peace—yet I have stood
Even while my eye has moved o'er three long leagues
Of shining water, gathering, as it seemed,
Through the wide surface of that field of light
New pleasure, like a bee among the flowers.

Thus often in those fits of vulgar joy
Which through all seasons on a child's pursuits
Are prompt attendants, 'mid that giddy bliss
Which like a tempest works along the blood
And is forgotten, even then I felt
Gleams like the flashing of a shield. The earth
And common face of Nature spake to me
Rememberable things—sometimes, 'tis true,
By quaint associations, yet not vain
Nor profitless, if haply they impressed
Collateral objects and appearances,
Albeit lifeless then, and doomed to sleep
Until maturer seasons called them forth
To impregnate and to elevate the mind.
And if the vulgar joy by its own weight
Wearied itself out of the memory,
The scenes which were a witness of that joy
Remained, in their substantial lineaments
Depicted on the brain, and to the eye
Were visible, a daily sight. And thus
By the impressive agency of fear,
By pleasure and repeated happiness—
So frequently repeated—and by force
Of obscure feelings representative
Of joys that were forgotten, these same scenes,
So beauteous and majestic in themselves,
Though yet the day was distant, did at length
Become habitually dear, and all
Their hues and forms were by invisible links
Allied to the affections.[18]

I began
My story early, feeling, as I fear,
The weakness of a human love for days
Disowned by memory—ere the birth of spring
Planting my snowdrops[19] among winter snows.
Nor will it seem to thee, my friend,[20] so prompt
In sympathy, that I have lengthened out
With fond and feeble tongue a tedious tale.
Meanwhile my hope has been that I might fetch
Reproaches from my former years, whose power
May spur me on, in manhood now mature,
To honourable toil. Yet should it be
That this is but an impotent desire—
That I by such inquiry am not taught
To understand myself, nor thou to know
With better knowledge how the heart was framed
Of him thou lovest—need I dread from thee
Harsh judgements if I am so loth to quit
Those recollected hours that have the charm
Of visionary things, and lovely forms
And sweet sensations, that throw back our life
And make our infancy a visible scene
On which the sun is shining?

—[SECOND PART]—

Thus far, my friend, have we retraced the way
Through which I travelled when I first began
To love the woods and fields; the passion yet
Was in its birth, sustained, as might befal,
By nourishment that came unsought—for still
From week to week, from month to month, we lived

---

[18] Lines 418 through 442 are influenced by David Hartley's* theory of associationism.

[19] **snowdrops:** an early-flowering bulbous plant with a white flower.

[20] **my friend:** Coleridge, to whom the poem is addressed in all of its forms.

A round of tumult. Duly were our games
Prolonged in summer till the daylight failed:
No chair remained before the doors, the bench
And threshold steps were empty, fast asleep
The labourer and the old man who had sate
A later lingerer, yet the revelry
Continued and the loud uproar. At last,
When all the ground was dark and the huge clouds
Were edged with twinkling stars, to bed we went
With weary joints and with a beating mind.
Ah, is there one who ever has been young
And needs a monitory voice to tame
The pride of virtue and of intellect?
And is there one, the wisest and the best
Of all mankind, who does not sometimes wish
For things which cannot be, who would not give,
If so he might, to duty and to truth
The eagerness of infantine desire?
A tranquillizing spirit presses now
On my corporeal frame, so wide appears
The vacancy between me and those days,
Which yet have such self-presence in my heart
That sometimes when I think of them I seem
Two consciousnesses—conscious of myself,
And of some other being.
A grey stone
Of native rock, left midway in the square
Of our small market-village, was the home
And centre of these joys; and when, returned
After long absence thither I repaired,
I found that it was split and gone to build
A smart assembly-room that perked and flared
With wash and rough-cast, elbowing the ground
Which had been ours. But let the fiddle scream,
And be ye happy! Yet I know, my friends,
That more than one of you will think with me
Of those soft starry nights, and that old dame
From whom the stone was named, who there had sate
And watched her table with its huckster's wares,
Assiduous, for the length of sixty years.

We ran a boisterous race, the year span round
With giddy motion; but the time approached
That brought with it a regular desire
For calmer pleasures—when the beauteous scenes
Of Nature were collaterally attached
To every scheme of holiday delight,
And every boyish sport, less grateful else
And languidly pursued. When summer came
It was the pastime of our afternoons
To beat along the plain of Windermere
With rival oars; and the selected bourn[1]
Was now an island musical with birds
That sang for ever, now a sister isle
Beneath the oak's umbrageous[2] covert, sown
With lilies-of-the-valley like a field,
And now a third small island where remained
An old stone table and one mouldered cave—
A hermit's history. In such a race,
So ended, disappointment could be none,
Uneasiness, or pain, or jealousy;
We rested in the shade, all pleased alike,
Conquered or conqueror. Thus our selfishness
Was mellowed down, and thus the pride of strength
And the vainglory of superior skill
Were interfused with objects which subdued
And tempered them, and gradually produced
A quiet independence of the heart.
And to my friend who knows me I may add,
Unapprehensive of reproof, that hence
Ensued a diffidence and modesty,
And I was taught to feel—perhaps too much—
The self-sufficing power of solitude.

No delicate viands sapped our bodily strength:
More than we wished we knew the blessing then
Of vigorous hunger, for our daily meals
Were frugal, Sabine[3] fare—and then, exclude
A little weekly stipend, and we lived
Through three divisions of the quartered year
In pennyless poverty. But now, to school
Returned from the half-yearly holidays,
We came with purses more profusely filled,
Allowance which abundantly sufficed
To gratify the palate with repasts
More costly than the dame of whom I spake,
That ancient woman, and her board, supplied.
Hence inroads into distant vales, and long
Excursions far away among the hills,
Hence rustic dinners on the cool green ground—
Or in the woods, or by a river-side
Or fountain—festive banquets, that provoked

[1] **bourn:** destination.

[2] **umbrageous:** shady.

[3] **Sabine:** related to the Sabini, an ancient people who dwelt in the Appenines and are known for their bravery, simple morality, and strong religious feelings.

The languid action of a natural scene
By pleasure of corporeal appetite.
  Nor is my aim neglected if I tell
How twice in the long length of those half-years
We from our funds perhaps with bolder hand
Drew largely, anxious for one day at least
To feel the motion of the galloping steed;
And with the good old innkeeper, in truth
I needs must say, that sometimes we have used
Sly subterfuge, for the intended bound
Of the day's journey was too distant far
For any cautious man: a structure famed
Beyond its neighbourhood, the antique walls
Of a large abbey, with its fractured arch,
Belfry, and images, and living trees—
A holy scene. Along the smooth green turf
Our horses grazed. In more than inland peace,
Left by the winds that overpass the vale,
In that sequestered ruin trees and towers—
Both silent and both motionless alike—
Hear all day long the murmuring sea that beats
Incessantly upon a craggy shore.
  Our steeds remounted, and the summons given,
With whip and spur we by the chantry flew
In uncouth race, and left the cross-legged knight
And the stone abbot, and that single wren
Which one day sang so sweetly in the nave
Of the old church that, though from recent showers
The earth was comfortless, and, touched by faint
Internal breezes, from the roofless walls
The shuddering ivy dripped large drops, yet still
So sweetly 'mid the gloom the invisible bird
Sang to itself that there I could have made
My dwelling-place, and lived for ever there,
To hear such music. Through the walls we flew
And down the valley, and, a circuit made
In wantonness of heart, through rough and smooth
We scampered homeward. O, ye rocks and streams,
And that still spirit of the evening air,
Even in this joyous time I sometimes felt
Your presence, when, with slackened step, we
  breathed
Along the sides of the steep hills, or when,
Lightened by gleams of moonlight from the sea,
We beat with thundering hoofs the level sand.
  There was a row of ancient trees, since fallen,
That on the margin of a jutting land
Stood near the lake of Coniston, and made,
With its long boughs above the water stretched,
A gloom through which a boat might sail along
As in a cloister. An old hall was near,
Grotesque and beautiful, its gavel-end[4]
And huge round chimneys to the top o'ergrown
With fields of ivy. Thither we repaired—
'Twas even a custom with us—to the shore,
And to that cool piazza. They who dwelt
In the neglected mansion-house supplied
Fresh butter, tea-kettle and earthernware,
And chafing-dish with smoking coals; and so
Beneath the trees we sate in our small boat,
And in the covert eat our delicate meal
Upon the calm smooth lake. It was a joy
Worthy the heart of one who is full grown
To rest beneath those horizontal boughs
And mark the radiance of the setting sun,
Himself unseen, reposing on the top
Of the high eastern hills. And there I said,
That beauteous sight before me, there I said
(Then first beginning in my thoughts to mark
That sense of dim similitude which links
Our moral feelings with external forms)
That in whatever region I should close
My mortal life I would remember you,
Fair scenes—that dying I would think on you,
My soul would send a longing look to you,
Even as that setting sun, while all the vale
Could nowhere catch one faint memorial gleam,
Yet with the last remains of his last light
Still lingered, and a farewell lustre threw
On the dear mountain-tops where first he rose.
'Twas then my fourteenth summer, and these words
Were uttered in a casual access
Of sentiment, a momentary trance
That far outran the habit of my mind.
  Upon the eastern shore of Windermere
Above the crescent of a pleasant bay
There was an inn, no homely-featured shed,
Brother of the surrounding cottages,
But 'twas a splendid place, the door beset
With chaises, grooms, and liveries, and within
Decanters, glasses and the blood-red wine.
In ancient times, or ere the hall was built
On the large island, had the dwelling been
More worthy of a poet's love, a hut

[4] gavel-end: gable end.

Proud of its one bright fire and sycamore shade;
But though the rhymes were gone which once
inscribed
The threshold, and large golden characters
On the blue-frosted signboard had usurped
The place of the old lion, in contempt
And mockery of the rustic painter's hand,
Yet to this hour the spot to me is dear
With all its foolish pomp. The garden lay
Upon a slope surmounted by the plain
Of a small bowling-green; beneath us stood
A grove, with gleams of water through the trees
And over the tree-tops — nor did we want
Refreshment, strawberries and mellow cream —
And there through half an afternoon we played
On the smooth platform, and the shouts we sent
Made all the mountains ring. But ere the fall
Of night, when in our pinnace we returned
Over the dusky lake, and to the beach
Of some small island steered our course, with one,
The minstrel of our troop, and left him there,
And rowed off gently, while he blew his flute
Alone upon the rock, oh, then the calm
And dead still water lay upon my mind
Even with a weight of pleasure, and the sky,
Never before so beautiful, sank down
Into my heart and held me like a dream.

Thus day by day my sympathies increased,
And thus the common range of visible things
Grew dear to me: already I began
To love the sun, a boy I loved the sun
Not as I since have loved him — as a pledge
And surety of my earthly life, a light
Which while I view I feel I am alive —
But for this cause, that I had seen him lay
His beauty on the morning hills, had seen
The western mountain touch his setting orb
In many a thoughtless hour, when from excess
Of happiness my blood appeared to flow
With its own pleasure, and I breathed with joy.
And from like feelings, humble though intense,
To patriotic and domestic love
Analogous, the moon to me was dear:
For I would dream away my purposes
Standing to look upon her, while she hung
Midway between the hills as if she knew
No other region but belonged to thee,
Yea, appertained by a peculiar right
To thee and thy grey huts, my native vale.

Those incidental charms which first attached
My heart to rural objects, day by day
Grew weaker, and I hasten on to tell
How Nature, intervenient till this time
And secondary, now at length was sought
For her own sake. But who shall parcel out
His intellect by geometric rules,
Split like a province into round and square?
Who knows the individual hour in which
His habits were first sown even as a seed?
Who that shall point as with a wand, and say
'This portion of the river of my mind
Came from yon fountain'? Thou, my friend, art one
More deeply read in thy own thoughts, no slave
Of that false secondary power[5] by which
In weakness we create distinctions, then
Believe our puny boundaries are things
Which we perceive, and not which we have made.
To thee, unblinded by these outward shews,
The unity of all has been revealed;
And thou wilt doubt with me, less aptly skilled
Than many are to class the cabinet
Of their sensations, and in voluble phrase
Run through the history and birth of each
As of a single independent thing.
Hard task[6] to analyse a soul, in which
Not only general habits and desires,
But each most obvious and particular thought —
Not in a mystical and idle sense,
But in the words of reason deeply weighed —
Hath no beginning.

Blessed the infant babe —
For my best conjectures I would trace
The progress of our being — blest the babe
Nursed in his mother's arms, the babe who sleeps
Upon his mother's breast, who, when his soul
Claims manifest kindred with an earthly soul,
Doth gather passion from his mother's eye.
Such feelings pass into his torpid life
Like an awakening breeze, and hence his mind,
Even in the first trial of its powers,
Is prompt and watchful, eager to combine
In one appearance all the elements
And parts of the same object, else detached

[5] **false secondary power:** reason.

[6] *Paradise Lost,* V.564: "Sad task and hard."

And loth to coalesce.[7] Thus day by day
Subjected to the discipline of love,
His organs and recipient faculties
Are quickened, are more vigorous; his mind spreads,
Tenacious of the forms which it receives.
In one beloved presence — nay and more,
In that most apprehensive habitude[8]
And those sensations which have been derived
From this beloved presence — there exists
A virtue which irradiates and exalts
All objects through all intercourse of sense.
No outcast he, bewildered and depressed;
Along his infant veins are interfused
The gravitation and the filial bond
Of Nature that connect him with the world.
Emphatically such a being lives,
An inmate of this *active* universe.
From Nature largely he receives, nor so
Is satisfied, but largely gives again;
For feeling has to him imparted strength,
And — powerful in all sentiments of grief,
Of exultation, fear and joy — his mind,
Even as an agent of the one great mind,
Creates, creator and receiver both,
Working but in alliance with the works
Which it beholds. Such, verily, is the first
Poetic spirit of our human life —
By uniform control of after years
In most abated and suppressed, in some
Through every change of growth or of decay
Preeminent till death.

From early days,
Beginning not long after that first time
In which, a babe, by intercourse of touch
I held mute dialogues with my mother's heart,
I have endeavoured to display the means
Whereby this infant sensibility,
Great birthright of our being, was in me
Augmented and sustained. Yet is a path
More difficult before me, and I fear
That in its broken windings we shall need
The chamois' sinews and the eagle's wing.
For now a trouble came into my mind
From obscure causes: I was left alone
Seeking this visible world, nor knowing why.
The props of my affections were removed,
And yet the building stood, as if sustained
By its own spirit. All that I beheld
Was dear to me, and from this cause it came
That now to Nature's finer influxes
My mind lay open — to that more exact
And intimate communion which our hearts
Maintain with the minuter properties
Of objects which already are beloved,
And of those only.

Many are the joys
Of youth, but oh, what happiness to live
When every hour brings palpable access
Of knowledge, when all knowledge is delight,
And sorrow is not there. The seasons came,
And every season brought a countless store
Of modes and temporary qualities
Which but for this most watchful power of love
Had been neglected, left a register
Of permanent relations else unknown.
Hence life, and change, and beauty, solitude
More active even than 'best society',[9]
Society made sweet as solitude
By silent inobtrusive sympathies,
And gentle agitations of the mind
From manifold distinctions, difference
Perceived in things where to the common eye
No difference is, and hence, from the same source,
Sublimer joy. For I would walk alone
In storm and tempest, or in starlight nights
Beneath the quiet heavens, and at that time
Would feel whate'er there is of power in sound
To breathe an elevated mood, by form
Or image unprofaned; and I would stand
Beneath some rock, listening to sounds that are
The ghostly language of the ancient earth,
Or make their dim abode in distant winds.
Thence did I drink the visionary power.
I deem not profitless these fleeting moods

[7] **coalesce:** an important word in Hartley's associationist psychology, in which it refers to the mental process by which ideas of sensations aggregate and synthesize into higher, intellectual ideas. *Coalescence* is thus a primary engine in "All that great *Apparatus* for carrying us from Body to Mind, and from self-love to the pure Love of God, which the Doctrine of Association opens to View" (*Observations on Man*, II. 387).

[8] **habitude:** customary behavior or propensity.

[9] Cf. *Paradise Lost*, IX.249: "For solitude sometimes is best society."

Of shadowy exaltation, not for this,
That they are kindred to our purer mind
And intellectual life, but that the soul—
Remembering how she felt, but what she felt
Remembering not—retains an obscure sense
Of possible sublimity, to which
With growing faculties she doth aspire,
With faculties still growing, feeling still
That whatsoever point they gain they still
Have something to pursue.

And not alone
In grandeur and in tumult, but no less
In tranquil scenes, that universal power
And fitness in the latent qualities
And essences of things, by which the mind
Is moved with feelings of delight, to me
Came strengthened with a superadded soul,
A virtue not its own. My morning walks
Were early: oft before the hours of school
I travelled round our little lake, five miles
Of pleasant wandering—happy time, more dear
For this, that one was by my side, a friend
Then passionately loved. With heart how full
Will he peruse these lines, this page—perhaps
A blank to other men—for many years
Have since flowed in between us, and, our minds
Both silent to each other, at this time
We live as if those hours had never been.
Nor seldom did I lift our cottage latch
Far earlier, and before the vernal thrush
Was audible, among the hills I sate
Alone upon some jutting eminence
At the first hour of morning, when the vale
Lay quiet in an utter solitude.
How shall I trace the history, where seek
The origin of what I then have felt?
Oft in those moments such a holy calm
Did overspread my soul that I forgot
The agency of sight, and what I saw
Appeared like something in myself, a dream,
A prospect in my mind.

'Twere long to tell
What spring and autumn, what the winter snows,
And what the summer shade, what day and night,
The evening and the morning, what my dreams
And what my waking thoughts, supplied to nurse
That spirit of religious love in which
I walked with Nature. But let this at least
Be not forgotten, that I still retained
My first creative sensibility,
That by the regular action of the world
My soul was unsubdued. A plastic power[10]
Abode with me, a forming hand, at times
Rebellious, acting in a devious mood,
A local spirit of its own, at war
With general tendency, but for the most
Subservient strictly to the external things
With which it communed. An auxiliar light
Came from my mind, which on the setting sun
Bestowed new splendour, the melodious birds,
The gentle breezes, foundations that ran on
Murmuring so sweetly in themselves, obeyed
A like dominion, and the midnight storm
Grew darker in the presence of my eye.
Hence my obeisance, my devotion hence,
And *hence* my transport.

Nor should this, perchance,
Pass unrecorded, that I still had loved
The exercise and produce of a toil
Than analytic industry to me
More pleasing, and whose character I deem
Is more poetic, as resembling more
Creative agency—I mean to speak
Of that interminable building reared
By observation of affinities
In objects where no brotherhood exists
To common minds. My seventeenth year was come,
And, whether from this habit rooted now
So deeply in my mind, or from excess
Of the great social principle of life
Coercing all things into sympathy,
To unorganic natures I transferred
My own enjoyments, or, the power of truth
Coming in revelation, I conversed
With things that really are, I at this time
Saw blessings spread around me like a sea.
Thus did my days pass on, and now at length
From Nature and her overflowing soul
I had received so much that all my thoughts
Were steeped in feeling. I was only then
Contented when with bliss ineffable
I felt the sentiment of being spread
O'er all that moves, and all that seemeth still,

[10] **plastic power**: power to form, shape, or model.

O'er all that, lost beyond the reach of thought
And human knowledge, to the human eye
Invisible, yet liveth to the heart
O'er all that leaps, and runs, and shouts, and sings,
Or beats the gladsome[11] air, o'er all that glides
Beneath the wave, yea, in the wave itself
And mighty depth of waters. Wonder not
If such my transports were, for in all things
I saw one life, and felt that it was joy;
One song they sang and it was audible—
Most audible then when the fleshly ear,
O'ercome by grosser prelude of that strain,
Forgot its functions and slept undisturbed.
  If this be error, and another faith
Find easier access to the pious mind,
Yet were I grossly destitute of all
Those human sentiments which make this earth
So dear if I should fail with grateful voice
To speak of you, ye mountains, and ye lakes
And sounding cataracts, ye mists and winds
That dwell among the hills where I was born.
If in my youth I have been pure in heart,
If, mingling with the world, I am content
With my own modest pleasures, and have lived
With God and Nature communing, removed
From little enmities and low desires,
The gift is yours; if in these times of fear,
This melancholy waste of hopes o'erthrown,[12]
If, 'mid indifference and apathy
And wicked exultation, when good men
On every side fall off we know not how
To selfishness, disguised in gentle names
Of peace and quiet and domestic love[13]—
Yet mingled, not unwillingly, with sneers
On visionary minds—if, in this time
Of dereliction and dismay, I yet
Despair not of our nature, but retain
A more than Roman confidence, a faith
That fails not, in all sorrow my support,
The blessing of my life, the gift is yours
Ye mountains, thine O Nature. Thou hast fed
My lofty speculations, and in thee
For this uneasy heart of ours I find
A never-failing principle of joy
And purest passion.
                    Thou, my friend, wast reared
In the great city, 'mid far other scenes,[14]
But we by different roads at length have gained
The self-same bourne. And from this cause to thee
I speak unapprehensive of contempt,
The insinuated scoff of coward tongues,
And all that silent language which so oft
In conversation betwixt man and man
Blots from the human countenance all trace
Of beauty and of love. For thou has sought
The truth in solitude, and thou art one
The most intense of Nature's worshippers,
In many things my brother, chiefly here
In this my deep devotion. Fare thee well:
Health and the quiet of a healthful mind
Attend thee, seeking oft the haunts of men—
But yet more often living with thyself,
And for thyself—so haply shall thy days
Be many, and a blessing to mankind.[15]

from THE PRELUDE
(1926; comp. 1805)

—*from* BOOK FIFTH—

Books

Even in the steadiest mood of reason, when
All sorrow for thy transitory pains
Goes out, it grieves me for thy state, O Man,
Thou paramount Creature! and thy race, while ye
Shall sojourn on this planet, not for woes
Which thou endur'st, that weight, albeit huge,
I charm away; but for those palms atchiev'd
Through length of time, by study and hard thought,
The honours of thy high endowments, there

[11] **gladsome:** joyful; causing gladness.

[12] **melancholy . . . o'erthrown:** disenchantment with the progress of the French Revolution and destruction of millenial hopes for human regeneration.

[13] **good men . . . domestic love:** Cf. Thewall's "Prefatory Memoir,"* for an example.

[14] Coleridge's "Frost at Midnight": "For I was reared / In the great city, pent 'mid cloisters dim." The great city is London.

[15] Coleridge was off to London to do work as a political journalist in early 1800.

My sadness finds its fuel. Hitherto,
In progress through this Verse, my mind hath look'd
Upon the speaking face of earth and heaven
As her prime Teacher, intercourse with man
Establish'd by the sovereign Intellect,
Who through that bodily Image hath diffus'd
A soul divine which we participate,
A deathless spirit. Thou also, Man, hast wrought,
For commerce of thy nature with itself,
Things worthy of unconquerable life;
And yet we feel, we cannot chuse but feel
That these must perish. Tremblings of the heart
It gives, to think that the immortal being
No more shall need such garments; and yet Man,
As long as he shall be the Child of Earth,
Might almost 'weep to have'[1] what he may lose,
Nor be himself extinguish'd, but survive
Abject, depress'd, forlorn, disconsolate.
A thought is with me sometimes, and I say,
Should earth by inward throes be wrench'd throughout,
Or fire be sent from far to wither all
Her pleasant habitations, and dry up
Old Ocean in his bed left sing'd and bare,
Yet would the living Presence still subsist
Victorious; and composure would ensue,
And kindlings like the morning; presage sure,
Though slow, perhaps, of a returning day.
But all the meditations of mankind,
Yea, all the adamantine holds of truth,
By reason built, or passion, which itself
Is highest reason in a soul sublime;
The consecrated works of Bard and Sage,
Sensuous or intellectual, wrought by men,
Twin labourers and heirs of the same hopes,
Where would they be? Oh! why hath not the mind
Some element to stamp her image on
In nature somewhat nearer to her own?
Why, gifted with such powers to send abroad
Her spirit, must it lodge in shrines so frail?

One day, when in the hearing of a Friend,
I had given utterance to thoughts like these,
He answer'd with a smile that, in plain truth
'Twas going far to seek disquietude;
But on the front of his reproof, confess'd
That he, at sundry seasons, had himself
Yielded to kindred hauntings. And forthwith
Added, that once upon a summer's noon,
While he was sitting in a rocky cave
By the sea-side, perusing, as it chanced,
The famous History of the Errant Knight
Recorded by Cervantes,[2] these same thoughts
Came to him; and to height unusual rose
While listlessly he sate, and having closed
The Book, had turned his eyes towards the Sea.
On Poetry and geometric Truth,
The knowledge that endures, upon these two,
And their high privilege of lasting life,
Exempt from all internal injury,
He mused: upon these chiefly: and at length,
His senses yielding to the sultry air,
Sleep seiz'd him, and he pass'd into a dream.
He saw before him an Arabian Waste,
A Desart; and he fancied that himself
Was sitting there in the wide wilderness,
Alone, upon the sands. Distress of mind
Was growing in him when, behold! at once
To his great joy a Man was at his side,
Upon a dromedary,[3] mounted high.
He seem'd an Arab of the Bedouin Tribes,[4]
A Lance he bore, and underneath one arm
A Stone; and, in the opposite hand, a Shell
Of a surpassing brightness. Much rejoic'd
The dreaming Man that he should have a Guide
To lead him through the Desart; and he thought,
While questioning himself what this strange freight
Which the Newcomer carried through the Waste
Could mean, the Arab told him that the Stone,
To give it in the language of the Dream,
Was Euclid's Elements; 'and this,' said he,
'This other,' pointing to the Shell, 'this Book
Is something of more worth.' And, at the word,
The Stranger, said my Friend continuing,

[1] Shakespeare's Sonnet 64: "This thought is as a death, which cannot choose / But weep to have that which it fears to lose."

[2] Miguel de Cervantes Saavedra (1547–1616), author of the satirical romance *Don Quixote de la Mancha* (1605, 1615), to which reference is here made.

[3] **dromedary**: one-humped camel and common beast of burden.

[4] **Bedouin Tribes**: nomadic Arab tribes of the deserts of North Africa, Arabia, and Syria.

Stretch'd forth the Shell towards me, with command
That I should hold it to my ear; I did so,
And heard that instant in an unknown Tongue,
Which yet I understood, articulate sounds,
A loud prophetic blast of harmony,
An Ode, in passion utter'd, which foretold
Destruction to the Children of the Earth,
By deluge now at hand. No sooner ceas'd
The Song, but with calm look, the Arab said
That all was true; that it was even so
As had been spoken; and that he himself
Was going then to bury those two Books:
The one that held acquaintance with the stars
And wedded man to man by purest bond
Of nature, undisturbed by space or time;
Th' other that was a God, yea many Gods,
Had voices more than all the winds, and was
A joy, a consolation, and a hope.
My friend continued, 'strange as it may seem,
I wonder'd not, although I plainly saw
The one to be a Stone, th' other a Shell,
Nor doubted once but that they both were Books,
Having a perfect faith in all that pass'd.
A wish was now ingender'd in my fear
To cleave unto this Man, and I begg'd leave
To share his errand with him. On he pass'd
Not heeding me; I follow'd, and took note
That he look'd often backward with wild look,
Grasping his twofold treasure to his side.
—Upon a Dromedary, Lance in rest,
He rode, I keeping pace with him, and now
I fancied that he was the very Knight
Whose Tale Cervantes tells, yet not the Knight,
But was an Arab of the Desart, too;
Of these was neither, and was both at once.
His countenance, meanwhile, grew more disturb'd,
And, looking backwards when he look'd, I saw
A glittering light, and ask'd him whence it came.
'It is,' said he, 'the waters of the deep
Gathering upon us,' quickening then his pace
He left me: I call'd after him aloud;
He heeded not; but with his twofold charge
Beneath his arm, before me full in view
I saw him riding o'er the Desart Sands,
With the fleet waters of the drowning world
In chase of him, whereat I wak'd in terror,
And saw the Sea before me; and the Book,
In which I had been reading, at my side.

Full often, taking from the world of sleep
This Arab Phantom, which my Friend beheld,
This Semi-Quixote, I to him have given
A substance, fancied him a living man,
A gentle Dweller in the Desart, craz'd
By love and feeling and internal thought,
Protracted among endless solitudes;
Have shap'd him, in the oppression of his brain,
Wandering upon this quest, and thus equipp'd.
And I have scarcely pitied him; have felt
A reverence for a Being thus employ'd;
And thought that in the blind and awful lair
Of such a madness, reason did lie couch'd.
Enow there are on earth to take in charge
Their Wives, their Children, and their virgin Loves,
Or whatsoever else the heart holds dear;
Enow to think of these; yea, will I say,
In sober contemplation of the approach
Of such great overthrow, made manifest
By certain evidence, that I, methinks,
Could share that Maniac's anxiousness, could go
Upon like errand. Oftentimes, at least,
Me hath such deep entrancement half-possess'd,
When I have held a volume in my hand
Poor earthly casket of immortal Verse!
Shakespeare, or Milton, Labourers divine!

. . . .

I am sad
At thought of raptures, now for ever flown,
Even unto tears, I sometimes could be sad
To think of, to read over, many a page,
Poems withal of name, which at that time
Did never fail to entrance me, and are now
Dead in my eyes as is a theatre
Fresh emptied of spectators. Thirteen years
Or haply less, I might have seen, when first
My ears began to open to the charm
Of words in tuneful order, found them sweet
For *their own sakes*, a passion and a power;
And phrases pleas'd me, chosen for delight,
For pomp, or love. Oft in the public roads,
Yet unfrequented, while the morning light
Was yellowing the hill-tops, with that dear Friend[5]

---

[5]**dear Friend:** John Fleming; see also *Two-Part Prelude,* II.382–383.

The same whom I have mention'd heretofore,
I went abroad, and for the better part
Of two delightful hours we stroll'd along
By the still borders of the misty Lake,
Repeating favourite verses with one voice,
Or conning more; as happy as the birds
That round us chaunted. Well might we be glad,
Lifted above the ground by airy fancies
More bright than madness or the dreams of wine,
And, though full oft the objects of our love
Were false, and in their splendour overwrought,
Yet, surely, at such time no vulgar power
Was working in us, nothing less, in truth,
Than that most noble attribute of man,
Though yet untutor'd and inordinate,
That wish for something loftier, more adorn'd,
Than is the common aspect, daily garb
Of human life. What wonder then if sounds
Of exultation echoed through the groves!
For images, and sentiments, and words,
And everything with which we had to do
In that delicious world of poesy,
Kept holiday; a never-ending show,
With music, incense, festival, and flowers!

Here must I pause: this only will I add,
From heart-experience, and in humblest sense
Of modesty, that he, who, in his youth
A wanderer among the woods and fields,
With living Nature hath been intimate,
Not only in that raw unpractis'd time
Is stirr'd to ecstasy, as others are,
By glittering verse; but, he doth furthermore,
In measure only dealt out to himself,
Receive enduring touches of deep joy
From the great Nature that exists in works
Of mighty Poets. Visionary Power
Attends upon the motions of the winds
Embodied in the mystery of words.
There darkness makes abode, and all the host
Of shadowy things do work their changes there,
As in a mansion like their proper home;
Even forms and substances are circumfused
By that transparent veil with light divine;
And through the turnings intricate of Verse,
Present themselves as objects recognis'd,
In flashes, and with a glory scarce their own.

. . . .

—*from* BOOK SIXTH[1]—

Cambridge and the Alps

—[ALPINE TOUR AND CROSSING]—

'Tis not my present purpose to retrace
That variegated journey step by step:
A march it was of military speed,
And earth did change her images and forms
Before us, fast as clouds are chang'd in Heaven.
Day after day, up early and down late,
From vale to vale, from hill to hill we went
From Province on to Province did we pass,
Keen Hunters in a chace of fourteen weeks
Eager as birds of prey, or as a Ship
Upon the stretch when winds are blowing fair.
Sweet coverts did we cross of pastoral life,
Enticing Vallies, greeted them, and left
Too soon, while yet the very flash and gleam
Of salutation were not pass'd away.
Oh! sorrow for the Youth who could have seen
Unchasten'd, unsubdu'd, unaw'd, unrais'd
To patriarchal dignity of mind,
And pure simplicity of wish and will,
Those sanctified abodes of peaceful Man.
My heart leap'd[2] up when first I did look down
On that which was first seen of those deep haunts,
A green recess, an aboriginal vale
Quiet, and lorded over and possess'd
By naked huts, wood-built, and sown like tents
Or Indian cabins over the fresh lawns,
And by the river side. That day we first
Beheld the summit of Mont Blanc[3] and griev'd
To have a soulless image on the eye

---

[1] Book VI recounts a walking tour Wordsworth took through the Alps the summer of 1790. The poet and a boyhood friend, Robert Jones, landed at Calais, France, on 13 July 1790, a day before the anniversary of the fall of the Bastille (14 July 1789). They would traverse over 1,500 miles, mainly on foot, through France, Switzerland, Italy, and Germany before returning to England in mid-October, or just prior to the start of Wordsworth's final term at Cambridge University. He graduated B.A., without distinction, in January 1791.

[2] See "My heart leaps up" from *Poems in Two Volumes.**

[3] **Mont Blanc:** highest mountain in the Alps at 15,781 feet. Near the French-Italian border.

Which had usurp'd upon a living thought
That never more could be: the wondrous Vale
Of Chamouny did, on the following dawn,
With its dumb cataracts and streams of ice,
A motionless array of mighty waves,
Five rivers broad and vast, make rich amends,
And reconcil'd us to realities.
There small birds warble from the leafy trees,
The Eagle soareth in the element;
There doth the Reaper bind the yellow sheaf,
The Maiden spread the haycock in the sun,
While Winter like a tamed Lion walks
Descending from the mountain to make sport
Among the cottages by beds of flowers.

Whate'er in this wide circuit we beheld,
Or heard, was fitted to our unripe state
Of intellect and heart. By simple strains
Of feeling, the pure breath of real life,
We were not left untouch'd. With such a book
Before our eyes, we could not chuse but read
A frequent lesson of sound tenderness,
The universal reason of mankind,
The truth of Young and Old. Nor, side by side
Pacing, two brother Pilgrims, or alone
Each with his humour, could we fail to abound
(Craft this which hath been hinted at before)
In dreams and fictions pensively compos'd,
Dejection taken up for pleasure's sake,
And gilded sympathies; the willow wreath,
Even among those solitudes sublime,
And sober posies of funereal flowers,
Cull'd from the gardens of the Lady Sorrow,
Did sweeten many a meditative hour.

Yet still in me, mingling with these delights
Was something of stern mood, an under-thirst
Of vigour, never utterly asleep.
Far different dejection once was mine,
A deep and genuine sadness then I felt;
The circumstances I will here relate
Even as they were. Upturning with a Band
Of Travellers, from the Valais we had clomb
Along the road that leads to Italy;
A length of hours, making of these our Guides
Did we advance, and having reach'd an Inn
Among the mountains, we together ate
Our noon's repast, from which the Travellers rose,
Leaving us at the Board. Ere long we follow'd,
Descending by the beaten road that led
Right to a rivulet's edge, and there broke off.
The only track now visible was one
Upon the further side, right opposite,
And up a lofty Mountain. This we took
After a little scruple, and short pause,
And climb'd with eagerness, though not, at length
Without surprise, and some anxiety
On finding that we did not overtake
Our Comrades gone before. By fortunate chance,
While every moment now encreas'd our doubts,
A Peasant met us, and from him we learn'd
That to the place which had perplex'd us first
We must descend, and there should find the road
Which in the stony channel of the Stream
Lay a few steps, and then along its Banks;
And further, that thenceforward all our course
Was downwards, with the current of that Stream.
Hard of belief, we question'd him again,
And all the answers which the Man return'd
To our inquiries, in their sense and substance,
Translated by the feelings which we had
Ended in this; *that we had cross'd the Alps.*

Imagination! lifting up itself
Before the eye and progress of my Song[4]
Like an unfather'd vapour; here that Power,
In all the might of its endowments, came
Athwart me; I was lost as in a cloud,
Halted, without a struggle to break through.
And now recovering, to my Soul I say
I recognise thy glory; in such strength
Of usurpation, in such visitings
Of awful promise, when the light of sense
Goes out in flashes that have shewn to us
The invisible world, doth Greatness make abode.
There harbours whether we be young or old.
Our destiny, our nature, and our home
Is with infinitude, and only there;
With hope it is, hope that can never die,
Effort, and expectation, and desire,
And something evermore about to be.
The mind beneath such banners militant
Thinks not of spoils or trophies, nor of aught
That may attest its prowess, blest in thoughts
That are their own perfection and reward,

[4] **my Song:** the poem presently being composed.

Strong in itself, and in the access of joy
Which hides it like the overflowing Nile.

The dull and heavy slackening that ensued
Upon those tidings by the Peasant given
Was soon dislodg'd; downwards we hurried fast,
And enter'd with the road which we had miss'd
Into a narrow chasm; the brook and road
Were fellow-travellers in this gloomy Pass,
And with them did we journey several hours
At a slow step. The immeasurable height
Of woods decaying, never to be decay'd,
The stationary blasts of water-falls,
And every where along the hollow rent
Winds thwarting winds, bewilder'd and forlorn,
The torrents shooting from the clear blue sky,
The rocks that mutter'd close upon our ears,
Black drizzling crags that spake by the way-side
As if a voice were in them, the sick sight
And giddy prospect of the raving stream,
The unfetter'd clouds, and region of the Heavens,
Tumult and peace, the darkness and the light
Were all like workings of one mind, the features
Of the same face, blossoms upon one tree,
Characters of the great Apocalypse,
The types and symbols of Eternity,
Of first and last, and midst, and without end.

That night our lodging was an Alpine House,
An Inn, or Hospital, as they are nam'd,
Standing in that same valley by itself,
And close upon the confluence of two Streams;
A dreary Mansion, large beyond all need,
With high and spacious rooms, deafen'd and stunn'd
By noise of waters, making innocent Sleep
Lie melancholy among weary bones.

. . . .

— *from* BOOK SEVENTH[1] —

Residence in London

. . . .

But foolishness, and madness in parade,
Though most at home in this their dear domain,
Are scatter'd everywhere, no rarities,
Even to the rudest novice of the Schools.
O Friend! one feeling was there which belong'd
To this great City, by exclusive right;
How often in the overflowing Streets,
Have I gone forward with the Crowd, and said
Unto myself, the face of every one
That passes by me is a mystery.
Thus have I look'd, nor ceas'd to look, oppress'd
By thoughts of what, and whither, when and how,
Until the shapes before my eyes became
A second-sight procession, such as glides
Over still mountains, or appears in dreams;
And all the ballast of familiar life,
The present, and the past; hope, fear; all stays,
All laws of acting, thinking, speaking man
Went from me, neither knowing me, nor known.
And once, far-travell'd in such mood, beyond
The reach of common indications, lost
Amid the moving pageant, 'twas my chance
Abruptly to be smitten with the view
Of a blind Beggar, who, with upright face,
Stood propp'd against a Wall, upon his Chest
Wearing a written paper, to explain
The story of the Man, and who he was.
My mind did at this spectacle turn round
As with the might of waters, and it seem'd
To me that in this Label was a type,
Or emblem, of the utmost that we know,
Both of ourselves and of the universe;
And, on the shape of the unmoving man,
His fixèd face and sightless eyes, I look'd
As if admonish'd from another world.

Though rear'd upon the base of outward things,
These, chiefly, are such structures as the mind
Builds for itself. Scenes different there are,
Full-form'd, which take, with small internal help,
Possession of the faculties; the peace
Of night, for instance, the solemnity
Of nature's intermediate hours of rest,
When the great tide of human life stands still,
The business of the day to come unborn,
Of that gone by, lock'd up as in the grave;
The calmness, beauty, of the spectacle,
Sky, stillness, moonshine, empty streets, and sounds
Unfrequent as in desarts; at late hours
Of winter evenings when unwholesome rains
Are falling hard, with people yet astir,

---

[1] Wordsworth travelled about in England and Wales after graduation until leaving again for France in November 1791. He spent several months in London (mid-January through late May).

The feeble salutation from the voice
Of some unhappy Woman, now and then
Heard as we pass; when no one looks about,
Nothing is listen'd to. But these, I fear,
Are falsely catalogu'd, things that are, are not,
Even as we give them welcome, or assist,
Are prompt, or are remiss. What say you then,
To times, when half the City shall break out
Full of one passion, vengeance, rage, or fear,
To executions, to a Street on fire,
Mobs, riots, or rejoicings? From these sights
Take one, an annual Festival, the Fair
Holden where Martyrs suffer'd in past time,
And named of Saint Bartholomew,[2] there see
A work that's finish'd to our hands, that lays,
If any spectacle on earth can do,
The whole creative powers of man asleep!
For once the Muse's help will we implore,
And she shall lodge us, wafted on her wings,
Above the press and danger of the Crowd,
Upon some Showman's platform: what a hell
For eyes and ears! what anarchy and din
Barbarian and infernal! 'tis a dream,
Monstrous in colour, motion, shape, sight, sound.
Below, the open space, through every nook
Of the wide area, twinkles, is alive
With heads; the midway region and above
Is throng'd with staring pictures, and huge scrolls,
Dumb proclamations of the prodigies;
And chattering monkeys dangling from their poles,
And children whirling in their roundabouts;[3]
With those that stretch the neck, and strain the eyes,
And crack the voice in rivalship, the crowd
Inviting; with buffoons against buffoons
Grimacing, writhing, screaming; him who grinds
The hurdy-gurdy, at the fiddle weaves;
Rattles the salt-box, thumps the kettle-drum,
And him who at the trumpet puffs his cheeks,
The silver-collar'd Negro with his timbrel,
Equestrians, Tumblers, Women, Girls, and Boys,
Blue-breech'd, pink-vested, and with towering plumes.
—All moveables of wonder from all parts,
Are here, Albinos, painted Indians, Dwarfs,
The Horse of Knowledge, and the learned Pig,[4]
The Stone-eater, the Man that swallows fire,
Giants, Ventriloquists, the Invisible Girl,
The Bust that speaks, and moves its goggling eyes,
The Wax-work, Clock-work, all the marvellous craft
Of modern Merlins, wild Beasts, Puppet-shows,
All out-o'-th'-way, far-fetch'd, perverted things,
All freaks of Nature, all Promethean thoughts
Of Man; his dulness, madness, and their feats,
All jumbled up together to make up
This Parliament of Monsters. Tents and Booths
Meanwhile, as if the whole were one vast Mill,
Are vomiting, receiving, on all sides,
Men, Women, three-years' Children, Babes in arms.

Oh, blank confusion! and a type not false
Of what the mighty City is itself
To all except a Straggler here and there,
To the whole Swarm of its inhabitants;
An undistinguishable world to men,
The slaves unrespited of low pursuits,
Living amid the same perpetual flow
Of trivial objects, melted and reduced
To one identity, by differences
That have no law, no meaning, and no end;
Oppression under which even highest minds
Must labour, whence the strongest are not free;
But though the picture weary out the eye,
By nature an unmanageable sight,
It is not wholly so to him who looks
In steadiness, who hath among least things
An under-sense of greatest; sees the parts
As parts, but with a feeling of the whole.
This, of all acquisitions first, awaits
On sundry and most widely different modes
Of education; nor with least delight
On that through which I pass'd. Attention comes,
And comprehensiveness and memory,
From early converse with the works of God
Among all regions; chiefly where appear
Most obviously simplicity and power.
By influence habitual to the mind
The mountain's outline and its steady form
Gives a pure grandeur, and its presence shapes

[2] **Saint Bartholomew:** the largest London street fair, held August 24 at Smithfield.

[3] **roundabouts:** merry-go-rounds.

[4] **The Horse . . . Pig:** animals trained to answer questions with some responsive movement. J. Wordsworth relates that "Toby the Sapient Pig" made his debut in 1817, with an act of spelling, reading, playing cards, and even reading people's thoughts.

The measure and the prospect of the soul
To majesty; such virtue have the forms
Perennial of the ancient hills; nor less
The changeful language of their countenances
Gives movement to the thoughts, and multitude,
With order and relation. This, if still,
As hitherto, with freedom I may speak,
And the same perfect openness of mind,
Not violating any just restraint,
As I would hope, of real modesty,
This did I feel in that vast receptacle.
The Spirit of Nature was upon me here;
The Soul of Beauty and enduring life
Was present as a habit, and diffused,
Through meagre lines and colours, and the press
Of self-destroying, transitory things
Composure and ennobling Harmony.

— *from* BOOK EIGHTH —

Retrospect. — Love of Nature Leading to Love of Mankind

[HELVELLYN FAIR]

What sounds are those, Helvellyn,[1] which are heard
Up to thy summit? Through the depth of air
Ascending, as if distance had the power
To make the sounds more audible: what Crowd
Is yon, assembled in the gay green Field?
Crowd seems it, solitary Hill! to thee,
Though but a little Family of Men,
Twice twenty, with their Children and their Wives,
And here and there a Stranger interspers'd.
It is a summer festival, a Fair,
Such as, on this side now, and now on that,
Repeated through his tributary Vales,
Helvellyn, in the silence of his rest,
Sees annually, if storms be not abroad,
And mists have left him an unshrouded head.
Delightful day it is for all who dwell
In this secluded Glen, and eagerly
They give it welcome. Long ere heat of noon
Behold the cattle are driven down; the sheep
That have for traffic been cull'd out are penn'd
In cotes[2] that stand together on the Plain
Ranged side by side; the chaffering[3] is begun.
The Heifer lows uneasy at the voice
Of a new Master, bleat the Flocks aloud;
Booths are there none; a Stall or two is here,
A lame Man, or a blind, the one to beg,
The other to make music; hither, too,
From far, with Basket, slung upon her arm,
Of Hawker's Wares, books, pictures, combs, and pins,
Some aged Woman finds her way again,
Year after year a punctual Visitant!
The Showman with his Freight upon his Back,
And once, perchance, in lapse of many years
Prouder Itinerant, Mountebank,[4] or He
Whose Wonders in a cover'd Wain lie hid.
But One is here, the loveliest of them all,
Some sweet Lass of the Valley, looking out
For gains, and who that sees her would not buy?
Fruits of her Father's Orchard, apples, pears,
(On that day only to such office stooping)
She carries in her Basket, and walks round
Among the crowd, half pleas'd with, half ashamed
Of her new calling, blushing restlessly.
The Children now are rich, the old Man now
Is generous; so gaiety prevails
Which all partake of, Young and Old. Immense
Is the Recess, the circumambient World
Magnificent, by which they are embraced.
They move about upon the soft green field:
How little They, they and their doings seem,
Their herds and flocks about them, they themselves,
And all that they can further or obstruct!
Through utter weakness pitiably dear
As tender Infants are: and yet how great!
For all things serve them; them the Morning light
Loves as it glistens on the silent rocks,
And them the silent Rocks, which now from high
Look down upon them; the reposing Clouds,
The lurking Brooks from their invisible haunts,
And Old Helvellyn, conscious of the stir,
And the blue Sky that roofs their calm abode.

[1] **Helvellyn:** a peak of 3,118 feet near Grasmere, Wordsworth's residence in the Lake District. The Grasmere Fair is held in September.

[2] **cotes:** shelters for sheep.

[3] **chaffering:** bargaining or haggling.

[4] **Mountebank:** an itenerant quack who from an elevated platform appealed to his audience by means of stories, tricks, juggling, and the like. (OED)

With deep devotion, Nature, did I feel
In that great City what I owed to thee,
High thoughts of God and Man, and love of Man,
Triumphant over all those loathsome sights
Of wretchedness and vice; a watchful eye,
Which with the outside of our human life
Not satisfied, must read the inner mind;
For I already had been taught to love
My Fellow-beings, to such habits train'd
Among the woods and mountains, where I found
In thee a gracious Guide, to lead me forth
Beyond the bosom of my Family,
My Friends and youthful Playmates. 'Twas thy power
That rais'd the first complacency in me,
And noticeable kindliness of heart,
Love human to the Creature in himself
As he appear'd, a stranger in my path,
Before my eyes a Brother of this world;
Thou first didst with those motions of delight
Inspire me.—I remember, far from home
Once having stray'd, while yet a very Child,
I saw a sight, and with what joy and love!
It was a day of exhalations, spread
Upon the mountains, mists and steam-like fogs
Redounding everywhere, not vehement,
But calm and mild, gentle and beautiful,
With gleams of sunshine on the eyelet spots
And loop-holes of the hills, wherever seen,
Hidden by quiet process, and as soon
Unfolded, to be huddled up again:
Along a narrow Valley and profound
I journey'd, when, aloft above my head,
Emerging from the silvery vapours, lo!
A Shepherd and his Dog! in open day:
Girt round with mists they stood and look'd about
From that enclosure small, inhabitants
Of an aerial Island floating on,
As seem'd, with that Abode in which they were,
A little pendant area of grey rocks,
By the soft wind breath'd forward. With delight
As bland almost, one Evening I beheld,
And at as early age (the spectacle
Is common, but by me was then first seen)
A Shepherd in the bottom of a Vale
Towards the centre standing, who with voice,
And hand waved to and fro as need required
Gave signal to his Dog, thus teaching him
To chace along the mazes of steep crags
The Flock he could not see: and so the Brute
Dear Creature! with a Man's intelligence
Advancing, or retreating on his steps,
Through every pervious strait,[5] to right or left,
Thridded a way unbaffled; while the Flock
Fled upwards from the terror of his Bark
Through rocks and seams of turf with liquid gold
Irradiate, that deep farewell light by which
The setting sun proclaims the love he bears
To mountain regions.

. . . .

—*from* BOOK NINTH[1]—

Residence in France

As oftentimes a River, it might seem,
Yielding in part to old remembrances,
Part sway'd by fear to tread an onward road
That leads direct to the devouring sea
Turns, and will measure back his course, far back,
Towards the very regions which he cross'd
In his first outset; so have we long time
Made motions retrograde, in like pursuit
Detain'd. But now we start afresh; I feel
An impulse to precipitate my Verse.
Fair greetings to this shapeless eagerness,
Whene'er it comes, needful in work so long,
Thrice needful to the argument which now
Awaits us; Oh! how much unlike the past!
One which though bright the promise, will be found
Ere far we shall advance, ungenial, hard
To treat of, and forbidding in itself.

. . . .

Through Paris lay my readiest path, and there
I sojourn'd a few days, and visited

---

[5] **pervious strait:** a narrow way or opening through boulders, rocks, or other landscape obstacles.

[1] Wordsworth spent November 1791 through December 1792 in France. He toured sites of recent political importance in Paris for several weeks, but most of his time was spent in Orleans and Blois (December 1791 through October 1792). Wordsworth's opening welcome to the surge of creativity that will be required to deal with the thematic reversals to come bears comparison with *Paradise Lost*, IX.1–47, the introduction to The Fall of Man. The COMPREHENSIVE CHRONOLOGY and the section on THE FRENCH REVOLUTION AND RIGHTS OF MAN will assist in contextualizing Wordsworth's experience in Revolutionary France.

In haste each spot of old and recent fame
The latter chiefly, from the Field of Mars
Down to the Suburbs of St. Anthony,
And from Mont Martyr southward, to the Dome
Of Geneviève. In both her clamorous Halls,
The National Synod and the Jacobins[2]
I saw the revolutionary Power
Toss like a Ship at anchor, rock'd by storms;
The Arcades I traversed in the Palace huge
Of Orleans, coasted round and round the line
Of Tavern, Brothel, Gaming-house, and Shop,
Great rendezvous of worst and best, the walk
Of all who had a purpose, or had not;
I star'd and listen'd with a stranger's ears
To Hawkers and Haranguers, hubbub wild!
And hissing Factionists with ardent eyes,
In knots, or pairs, or single, ant-like swarms
Of Builders and Subverters, every face
That hope or apprehension could put on,
Joy, anger, and vexation in the midst
Of gaiety and dissolute idleness.

Where silent zephyrs sported with the dust
Of the Bastile, I sate in the open sun,
And from the rubbish gather'd up a stone
And pocketed the relick in the guise
Of an Enthusiast, yet, in honest truth
Though not without some strong incumbrences;
And glad, (could living man be otherwise)
I look'd for something that I could not find,
Affecting more emotion than I felt,
For 'tis most certain that the utmost force
Of all these various objects which may shew
The temper of my mind as then it was
Seem'd less to recompense the Traveller's pains,
Less mov'd me, gave me less delight than did
Among other sights, the Magdalene of le Brun,[3]
A Beauty exquisitely wrought, fair face
And rueful, with its ever-flowing tears.

But hence to my more permanent residence
I hasten; there, by novelties in speech
Domestic manners, customs, gestures, looks,
And all the attire of ordinary life,
Attention was at first engross'd; and thus,
Amused and satisfied, I scarcely felt
The shock of these concussions, unconcerned,
Tranquil, almost, and careless as a flower
Glassed in a Green-house, or a Parlour shrub
When every bush and tree, the country through,
Is shaking to the roots; indifference this
Which may seem strange; but I was unprepared
With needful knowledge, had abruptly pass'd
Into a theatre of which the stage
Was busy with an action far advanced.
Like others I had read, and eagerly
Sometimes, the master Pamphlets of the day;
Nor wanted such half-insight as grew wild
Upon that meagre soil, help'd out by Talk
And public News; but having never chanced
To see a regular Chronicle which might shew,
(If any such indeed existed then)
Whence the main Organs of the Public Power
Had sprung, their transmigrations when and how
Accomplish'd, giving thus unto events
A form and body, all things were to me
Loose and disjointed, and the affections left
Without a vital interest. At that time,
Moreover, the first storm was overblown,
And the strong hand of outward violence
Lock'd up in quiet. For myself, I fear
Now in connection with so great a Theme
To speak (as I must be compell'd to do)
Of one so unimportant: a short time
I loiter'd, and frequented night by night
Routs, card-tables, the formal haunts of Men,
Whom in the City privilege of birth

[2] The fall of the Bastille was commemorated at the Field of Mars. A huge altar was constructed for the first anniversary, and here King Louis XVI swore fidelity to the French Constitution, but by July 1791 the King had fled and the altar held a petition asking for his deposition. The Suburbs of St. Anthony was the revolutionary working class community abutting the Bastille. Mont Martyr was the site of revolutionary meeting halls in the north of Paris. The Dome of St. Genevieve was a church the National Assembly chose as a burial place, much like Westminster Abbey in London, for burying revolutionary heroes and inspirations to the Revolution, such as Voltaire and Rousseau. The National Assembly or Synod met at the Riding Hall in the Rue de Rivoli. The Jacobin Club met in the library of the convent of the Dominicans near the Rue St. Honore. Ironically, the revolutionary Jacobins took their name from the Dominicans, who were also called Jacobins because St. Jacques was the name of their earliest convent in Paris (AD 1218). (De Selincourt)

[3] **Magdalene of le Brun:** a painting of Mary Magdalene by Charles Le Brun (1616–1690), then a tourist attraction, now in the Louvre.

Sequester'd from the rest, societies
Where, through punctilios of elegance
And deeper causes, all discourse, alike
Of good and evil in the time, was shunn'd
With studious care; but 'twas not long ere this
Proved tedious, and I gradually withdrew
Into a noisier world; and thus did soon
Become a Patriot, and my heart was all
Given to the People, and my love was theirs.

. . . .

Meantime, day by day, the roads
(While I consorted with these Royalists)
Were crowded with the bravest Youth of France,
And all the promptest of her Spirits, link'd
In gallant Soldiership, and posting on
To meet the War upon her Frontier Bounds.[4]
Yet at this very moment do tears start
Into mine eyes; I do not say I weep,
I wept not then, but tears have dimm'd my sight,
In memory of the farewells of that time,
Domestic severings, female fortitude
At dearest separation, patriot love
And self-devotion, and terrestrial hope
Encourag'd with a martyr's confidence;
Even files of Strangers merely, seen but once,
And for a moment, men from far with sound
Of music, martial tunes, and banners spread
Entering the City, here and there a face
Or person singled out among the rest,
Yet still a Stranger and belov'd as such,
Even by these passing spectacles my heart
Was oftentimes uplifted, and they seem'd
Like arguments from Heaven, that 'twas a cause
Good, and which no one could stand up against
Who was not lost, abandon'd, selfish, proud,
Mean, miserable, wilfully deprav'd,
Hater perverse of equity and truth.

Among that band of Officers was one
Already hinted at, of other mold,
A Patriot,[5] thence rejected by the rest
And with an oriental loathing spurn'd,
As of a different Cast. A meeker Man
Than this liv'd never, or a more benign
Meek, though enthusiastic to the height
Of highest expectation. Injuries
Made him more gracious, and his nature then
Did breathe its sweetness out most sensibly
As aromatic flowers on alpine turf
When foot hath crush'd them. He thro' the events
Of that great change wander'd in perfect faith,
As through a Book, an old Romance or Tale
Of Fairy, or some dream of actions wrought
Behind the summer clouds. By birth he rank'd
With the most noble, but unto the poor
Among mankind he was in service bound
As by some tie invisible, oaths profess'd
To a religious Order. Man he lov'd
As Man; and to the mean and the obscure
And all the homely in their homely works
Transferr'd a courtesy which had no air
Of condescension, but did rather seem
A passion and a gallantry, like that
Which he, a Soldier, in his idler day
Had pay'd to Woman . . .

. . . .

Along the very Loire, with festivals
Resounding at all hours, and innocent yet
Of civil slaughter was our frequent walk
Or in wide Forests of the neighbourhood,
High woods and over-arch'd with open space
On every side, and footing many a mile,
Inwoven roots and moss smooth as the sea,
A solemn region. Often in such place
From earnest dialogues I slipp'd in thought
And let remembrance steal to other times
When Hermits from their sheds and caves forth
  stray'd
Walk'd by themselves, so met in shades like these,
And if a devious Traveller was heard
Approaching from a distance, as might chance,
With speed and echoes loud of trampling hoofs
From the hard floor reverberated, then
It was Angelica thundering through the woods
Upon her Palfrey, or that gentler Maid
Erminia, fugitive as fair as She.[6]
Sometimes I saw, methought, a pair of Knights
Joust underneath the trees, that, as in storm,
Did rock above their heads; anon the din

[4] **Frontier Bounds:** on the Austrian border, because France declared war against Austria in April 1792.

[5] **A Patriot:** Michel Beaupuy. See the introduction.

[6] **Angelica:** the heroine of Ariosto's *Orlando Furioso,* who causes the madness of Orlando. **Erminia:** the heroine of Tasso's *Jerusalem Delivered.*

Of boisterous merriment and music's roar,
With sudden Proclamation, burst from haunt
Of Satyrs in some viewless glade, with dance
Rejoicing o'er a Female in the midst,
A mortal Beauty, their unhappy Thrall;
The width of those huge Forests, unto me
A novel scene, did often in this way
Master my fancy, while I wander'd on
With that revered Companion. And sometimes
When to a Convent in a meadow green
By a brook-side we came, a roofless Pile,
And not by reverential touch of Time
Dismantled, but by violence abrupt,
In spite of those heart-bracing colloquies,
In spite of real fervour, and of that
Less genuine and wrought up within myself
I could not but bewail a wrong so harsh,
And for the matin Bell to sound no more
Griev'd, and the evening Taper, and the Cross
High on the topmost Pinnacle, a sign
Admonitory to the Traveller
First seen above the woods.

. . . .

. . . And when we chanc'd
One day to meet a hunger-bitten Girl,
Who crept along, fitting her languid self
Unto a Heifer's motion, by a cord
Tied to her arm, and picking thus from the lane
Its sustenance, while the Girl with her two hands
Was busy knitting, in a heartless mood
Of solitude, and at the sight my Friend
In agitation said, ''Tis against *that*
Which we are fighting,' I with him believed
Devoutly that a spirit was abroad
Which could not be withstood, that poverty
At least like this, would in a little time
Be found no more, that we should see the earth
Unthwarted in her wish to recompense
The industrious, and the lowly Child of Toil,
All institutes for ever blotted out
That legalized exclusion, empty pomp
Abolish'd, sensual state and cruel power
Whether by edict of the one or few,
And finally, as sum and crown of all,
Should see the People having a strong hand
In making their own Laws, whence better days
To all mankind. . . .

. . . .

—*from* BOOK TENTH—

Residence in France and French Revolution

. . . .

This was the time in which enflam'd with hope,
To Paris I returned.[1] Again I rang'd
More eagerly than I had done before
Through the wide City, and in progress pass'd
The Prison where the unhappy Monarch lay,
Associate with his Children and his Wife
In bondage; and the Palace lately storm'd
With roar of cannon, and a numerous Host.
I crossed (a black and empty area then)
The Square of the Carousel, few weeks back
Heap'd up with dead and dying, upon these
And other sights looking as doth a man
Upon a volume whose contents he knows
Are memorable, but from him lock'd up,
Being written in a tongue he cannot read,
So that he questions the mute leaves with pain
And half upbraids their silence. But that night
When on my bed I lay, I was most mov'd

[1] After arranging for a surrogate father to represent him at the baptism of the child he and Annette Vallon were expecting, Wordsworth left Orleans for Paris in late October 1792. He left, he says, because he was running out of money. Wordsworth alludes to his romantic experience with Annette Vallon in a narrative of two French lovers in Book IX entitled Vaudracour and Julia, but the fact of his love affair and child did not come to light until 1921 in George McLean Harper's *Wordsworth's French Daughter.* For the tale Wordsworth probably adapted to his biographical purpose see Helen Maria Williams's tale of the du Fossés, *Letters from France.** By this time in the Revolution, the king was imprisoned, and Prussian and Austrian allies had invaded France and won a battle at Verdun. In retaliation, Marat, Danton, and Robespierre organized the September Massacres (September 2–6), during which some 3,000 prisoners and suspected Royalists were removed from prison and summarily executed in the streets by guillotine; and, after the revolutionary army defeated the allied invaders at Valmy, a republic was declared on September 22. (See THE FRENCH REVOLUTION AND RIGHTS OF MAN and Helen Maria Williams, *Letters from France,* for a contemporary account of these same events.)

And felt most deeply in what world I was;
My room was high and lonely, near the roof
Of a large Mansion or Hotel, a spot
That would have pleased me in more quiet times,
Nor was it wholly without pleasure then.
With unextinguish'd taper I kept watch,
Reading at intervals; the fear gone by
Press'd on me almost like a fear to come;
I thought of those September Massacres,
Divided from me by a little month,
And felt and touch'd them, a substantial dread;
The rest was conjured up from tragic fictions,
And mournful Calendars of true history,
Remembrances and dim admonishments.
'The horse is taught his manage, and the wind
Of heaven wheels round and treads in his own steps,
Year follows year, the tide returns again,
Day follows day, all things have second birth;
The earthquake is not satisfied at once.'
And in such way I wrought upon myself,
Until I seem'd to hear a voice that cried,
To the whole City, 'Sleep no more.'[2] To this
Add comments of a calmer mind, from which
I could not gather full security,
But at the best it seem'd a place of fear
Unfit for the repose which night requires,
Defenceless as a wood where tigers roam.

Betimes next morning to the Palace Walk
Of Orleans I repair'd and entering there
Was greeted, among divers other notes,
By voices of the Hawkers in the crowd
Bawling, *Denunciation of the crimes*
Of Maximilian Robespierre, the speech
Which in their hands they carried was the same
Which had been recently pronounced, the day
When Robespierre, well knowing for what mark
Some words of indirect reproof had been
Intended, rose in hardihood, and dared
The Man who had an ill surmise of him
To bring his charge in openness, whereat
When a dead pause ensued, and no one stirr'd,
In silence of all present, from his seat
Louvet walked singly through the avenue
And took his station in the Tribune, saying,
'I, Robespierre, accuse thee!'[3] 'Tis well known
What was the issue of that charge, and how
Louvet was left alone without support
Of his irresolute Friends; but these are things
Of which I speak, only as they were storm
Or sunshine to my individual mind,
No further. . . .

. . . .

When to my native Land
(After a whole year's absence) I return'd[4]
I found the air yet busy with the stir
Of a contention which had been rais'd up
Against the Traffickers in Negro blood,[5]
An effort, which though baffled, nevertheless
Had call'd back old forgotten principles
Dismiss'd from service, had diffus'd some truths
And more of virtuous feeling through the heart
Of the English People. And no few of those
So numerous (little less in verity
Than a whole Nation crying with one voice)
Who had been cross'd in this their just intent
And righteous hope, thereby were well prepared
To let that journey sleep awhile, and join
Whatever other Caravan appear'd
To travel forward towards Liberty
With more success. For me that strife had ne'er
Fasten'd on my affections, nor did now
Its unsuccessful issue much excite
My sorrow, having laid this faith to heart,
That, if France prosper'd, good Men would not long
Pay fruitless worship to humanity,
And this most rotten branch of human shame,
Object, as seem'd, of a superfluous pains
Would fall together with its parent tree.

Such was my then belief, that there was one,
And only one solicitude for all;
And now the strength of Britain was put forth

[2]*Macbeth,* II.ii.34–35: "Methought I heard a voice cry, 'Sleep no more! / Macbeth does murder sleep.' The innocent sleep, / . . ."

[3]**Louvet:** a member of the Girondist party or faction, Louvet made his courageous but futile charge against Robespierre on 29 October 1792.

[4]Wordsworth arrived in England in late November or early December 1792.

[5]See SLAVERY, THE SLAVE TRADE, AND ABOLITION.

In league with the confederated Host,[6]
Not in my single self alone I found,
But in the minds of all ingenuous Youth,
Change and subversion from this hour. No shock
Given to my moral nature had I known
Down to that very moment; neither lapse
Nor turn of sentiment that might be nam'd
A revolution, save at this one time,
All else was progress on the self-same path
On which with a diversity of pace
I had been travelling; this a stride at once
Into another region. True it is,
'Twas not conceal'd with what ungracious eyes
Our native Rulers from the very first
Had look'd upon regenerated France
Nor had I doubted that this day would come.
But in such contemplation I had thought
Of general interests only, beyond this
Had [never] once foretasted the event.
Now had I other business for I felt
The ravage of this most unnatural strife
In my own heart; there lay it like a weight
At enmity with all the tenderest springs
Of my enjoyments. I, who with the breeze
Had play'd, a green leaf on the blessed tree
Of my beloved country; nor had wish'd
For happier fortune than to wither there,
Now from my pleasant station was cut off,
And toss'd about in whirlwinds. I rejoiced,
Yea, afterwards, truth most painful to record!
Exulted in the triumph of my soul
When Englishmen by thousands were o'erthrown,
Left without glory on the Field, or driven,
Brave hearts, to shameful flight. It was a grief,
Grief call it not, 'twas anything but that,
A conflict of sensations without name,
Of which he only who may love the sight
Of a Village Steeple as I do can judge
When in the Congregation, bending all
To their great Father, prayers were offer'd up,
Or praises for our Country's Victories,
And 'mid the simple worshippers, perchance,
I only, like an uninvited Guest
Whom no one own'd sate silent, shall I add,
Fed on the day of vengeance yet to come?
. . . .

In France, the Men who for their desperate ends
Had pluck'd up mercy by the roots were glad
Of this new enemy. Tyrants, strong before
In devilish pleas were ten times stronger now,
And thus beset with Foes on every side
The goaded Land wax'd mad; the crimes of few
Spread into madness of the many, blasts
From hell came sanctified like airs from heaven;
The sternness of the Just, the faith of those
Who doubted not that Providence had times
Of anger and of vengeance,—theirs who throned
The human understanding paramount
And made of that their God, the hopes of those
Who were content to barter short-lived pangs
For a paradise of ages, the blind rage
Of insolent tempers, the light vanity
Of intermeddlers, steady purposes
Of the suspicious, slips of the indiscreet,
And all the accidents of life were press'd
Into one service, busy with one work;
The Senate was heart-stricken, not a voice
Uplifted, none to oppose or mitigate;
Domestic carnage now filled all the year
With Feast-days; the old Man from the chimney-nook,
The Maiden from the bosom of her Love,
The Mother from the Cradle of her Babe,
The Warrior from the Field, all perish'd, all,
Friends, enemies, of all parties, ages, ranks,
Head after head, and never heads enough
For those that bade them fall:[7] they found their joy,
They made it, ever thirsty as a Child,
If light desires of innocent little Ones
May with such heinous appetites be match'd,
Having a toy, a wind-mill, though the air
Do of itself blow fresh, and make the vane
Spin in his eyesight, he is not content
But with the plaything at arm's length he sets
His front against the blast, and runs amain,
To make it whirl the faster.
. . . .

[6] France declared war on England on 1 February 1793. England then prepared to ally with the Austrian and Prussian forces.

[7] October–December 1793, 15,000 were beheaded in Nantes alone.

It was a lamentable time for man
Whether a hope had e'er been his or not,
A woeful time for them whose hopes did still
Outlast the shock; most woeful for those few,
They had the deepest feeling of the grief,
Who still were flattered, and had trust in man.
Meanwhile, the Invaders fared as they deserv'd;
The Herculean Commonwealth had put forth her arms
And throttled with an infant Godhead's might
The snakes about her cradle; that was well
And as it should be, yet no cure for those
Whose souls were sick with pain of what would be
Hereafter brought in charge against mankind;
Most melancholy at that time, O Friend!
Were my day-thoughts, my dreams were miserable;
Through months, through years, long after the last beat
Of those atrocities (I speak bare truth,
As if to thee alone in private talk)
I scarcely had one night of quiet sleep
Such ghastly visions had I of despair
And tyranny, and implements of death,
And long orations which in dreams I pleaded
Before unjust Tribunals, with a voice
Labouring, a brain confounded, and a sense
Of treachery and desertion in the place
The holiest that I know of, my own soul.

. . . .

. . . I must return
To my own History. It hath been told
That I was led to take an eager part
In arguments of civil polity
Abruptly, and indeed before my time:
I had approach'd, like other Youth, the Shield
Of human nature from the golden side
And would have fought, even to the death, to attest
The quality of the metal which I saw.
What there is best in individual Man,
Of wise in passion, and sublime in power,
What there is strong and pure in household love,
Benevolent in small societies,
And great in large ones also, when call'd forth
By great occasions, these were things of which
I something knew, yet even these themselves,
Felt deeply, were not thoroughly understood
By Reason; nay, far from it, they were yet,
As cause was given me afterwards to learn,
Not proof against the injuries of the day,
Lodged only at the Sanctuary's door,
Not safe within its bosom. Thus prepared,
And with such general insight into evil,
And of the bounds which sever it from good,
As books and common intercourse with life
Must needs have given; to the noviciate mind,
When the world travels in a beaten road,
Guide faithful as is needed, I began
To think with fervour upon management
Of Nations, what it is and ought to be,
And how their worth depended on their Laws
And on the Constitution of the State.

O pleasant exercise of hope and joy!
For great were the auxiliars which then stood
Upon our side, we who were strong in love;
Bliss was it in that dawn to be alive,
But to be young was very heaven: O times,
In which the meagre, stale, forbidding ways
Of custom, law, and statute took at once
The attraction of a Country in Romance;
When Reason seem'd the most to assert her rights
When most intent on making of herself
A prime Enchanter to assist the work,
Which then was going forwards in her name.
Not favour'd spots alone, but the whole earth
The beauty wore of promise, that which sets,
To take an image which was felt, no doubt,
Among the bowers of paradise itself,
The budding rose above the rose full blown.
What temper at the prospect did not wake
To happiness unthought of? The inert
Were rouz'd, and lively natures rapt away:
They who had fed their childhood upon dreams,
The Play-fellows of Fancy, who had made
All powers of swiftness, subtlety, and strength
Their ministers, used to stir in lordly wise
Among the grandest objects of the sense,
And deal with whatsoever they found there
As if they had within some lurking right
To wield it; they too, who, of gentle mood,
Had watch'd all gentle motions, and to these
Had fitted their own thoughts, schemers more mild,
And in the region of their peaceful selves,
Did now find helpers to their hearts' desire,
And stuff at hand, plastic as they could wish,
Were call'd upon to exercise their skill,
Not in Utopia, subterraneous Fields,
Or some secreted Island, Heaven knows where,
But in the very world which is the world

Of all of us, the place in which, in the end,
We find our happiness, or not at all.

Why should I not confess that earth was then
To me what an inheritance new-fallen
Seems, when the first time visited, to one
Who thither comes to find in it his home?
He walks about and looks upon the place
With cordial transport, moulds it, and remoulds,
And is half pleased with things that are amiss,
'Twill be such joy to see them disappear.

An active partisan, I thus convoked
From every object pleasant circumstance
To suit my ends; I moved among mankind
With genial feelings still predominant;
When erring, erring on the better part,
And in the kinder spirit; placable,
Indulgent oft-times to the worst desires
As on one side not uninform'd that men
See as it hath been taught them, and that time
Gives rights to error; on the other hand
That throwing off oppression must be work
As well of licence as of liberty;
And above all, for this was more than all,
Not caring if the wind did now and then
Blow keen upon an eminence that gave
Prospect so large into futurity,
In brief, a child of nature, as at first,
Diffusing only those affections wider
That from the cradle had grown up with me,
And losing, in no other way than light
Is lost in light, the weak in the more strong.

In the main outline, such, it might be said,
Was my condition, till with open war
Britain opposed the Liberties of France;

. . . .

This was the time when all things tending fast
To depravation, the Philosophy
That promised to abstract the hopes of man
Out of his feelings, to be fix'd thenceforth
For ever in a purer element
Found ready welcome.[8] Tempting region that
For Zeal to enter and refresh herself,
Where passions had the privilege to work,
And never hear the sound of their own names;
But, speaking more in charity, the dream
Was flattering to the young ingenuous mind
Pleas'd with extremes, and not the least with that
Which makes the human Reason's naked self
The object of its fervour. What delight!
How glorious! in self-knowledge and self-rule,
To look through all the frailties of the world,
And, with a resolute mastery shaking off
The accidents of nature, time, and place,
That make up the weak being of the past,
Build social freedom on its only basis,
The freedom of the individual mind,
Which, to the blind restraint of general laws
Superior, magisterially adopts
One guide, the light of circumstances, flash'd
Upon an independent intellect.

. . . .

Enough, no doubt, the advocates themselves
Of ancient institutions had perform'd
To bring disgrace upon their very names,
Disgrace of which custom and written law
And sundry moral sentiments as props
And emanations of those institutes
Too justly bore a part. A veil had been
Uplifted; why deceive ourselves? 'Twas so,
'Twas even so, and sorrow for the Man
Who either had not eyes wherewith to see,
Or seeing hath forgotten. Let this pass,
Suffice it that a shock had then been given
To old opinions; and the minds of all men
Had felt it; that my mind was both let loose,
Let loose and goaded. After what hath been
Already said of patriotic love,
And hinted at in other sentiments
We need not linger long upon this theme.
This only may be said, that from the first
Having two natures in me, joy the one
The other melancholy, and withal
A happy man, and therefore bold to look
On painful things, slow, somewhat, too, and stern
In temperament, I took the knife in hand
And stopping not at parts less sensitive,
Endeavoured with my best of skill to probe
The living body of society
Even to the heart; I push'd without remorse
My speculations forward; yea, set foot
On Nature's holiest places. Time may come
When some dramatic Story may afford
Shapes livelier to convey to thee, my Friend,

[8] The reference is to the philosophy of Godwin's *Enquiry Concerning Political Justice.**

What then I learn'd, or think I learn'd, of truth,
And the errors into which I was betray'd
By present objects, and by reasoning false
From the beginning, inasmuch as drawn
Out of a heart which had been turn'd aside
From nature by external accidents,
And which was thus confounded more and more,
Misguiding and misguided. Thus I fared,
Dragging all passions, notions, shapes of faith,
Like culprits to the bar, suspiciously
Calling the mind to establish in plain day
Her titles and her honours, now believing,
Now disbelieving, endlessly perplex'd
With impulse, motive, right and wrong, the ground
Of moral obligation, what the rule
And what the sanction, till, demanding *proof*,
And seeking it in everything, I lost
All feeling of conviction, and, in fine,
Sick, wearied out with contrarieties,
Yielded up moral questions in despair,
And for my future studies, as the sole
Employment of the enquiring faculty,
Turn'd towards mathematics, and their clear
And solid evidence — Ah! then it was
That Thou, most precious Friend! about this time
First known to me, didst lend a living help
To regulate my Soul, and then it was
That the belovèd Woman[9] in whose sight
Those days were pass'd, now speaking in a voice
Of sudden admonition, like a brook
That does but cross a lonely road, and now
Seen, heard and felt, and caught at every turn,
Companion never lost through many a league,
Maintain'd for me a saving intercourse
With my true self; for, though impair'd and chang'd
Much, as it seem'd, I was no further chang'd
Than as a clouded, not a waning moon:
She, in the midst of all, preserv'd me still
A Poet, made me seek beneath that name
My office upon earth, and nowhere else,
And lastly, Nature's Self, by human love
Assisted, through the weary labyrinth
Conducted me again to open day,
Revived the feelings of my earlier life,
Gave me that strength and knowledge full of peace,
Enlarged, and never more to be disturb'd,
Which through the steps of our degeneracy,
All degradation of this age, hath still
Upheld me, and upholds me at this day
In the catastrophe (for so they dream,
And nothing less), when finally, to close
And rivet up the gains of France, a Pope
Is summon'd in to crown an Emperor;[10]
This last opprobrium, when we see the dog
Returning to his vomit,[11] when the sun
That rose in splendour, was alive, and moved
In exultation among living clouds
Hath put his function and his glory off,
And, turned into a gewgaw, a machine,
Sets like an opera phantom.

. . . .

[9] **belovèd Woman:** the poet's sister, Dorothy Wordsworth.*

[10] The reference is to Napoleon's coronation, during which Napoleon crowned himself in the presence of Pius VII to symbolize that he did not owe his power to the Church of Rome. Wordsworth apparently either did not know or thought the detail irrelevant. The coronation occurred November 1804.

[11] II Peter 2.22: "But it is happened unto them according to the true proverb, the dog is turned to his own vomit again; and the sow that was washed to her wallowing in the mire."

from BOOK THIRTEENTH[1]
(1805)

Conclusion

In one of these excursions, travelling then
Through Wales on foot, and with a youthful Friend,
I left Bethkelet's huts at couching-time,
And westward took my way to see the sun
Rise from the top of Snowdon.[2] Having reach'd
The Cottage at the Mountain's foot, we there
Rouz'd up the Shepherd, who by ancient right
Of office is the Stranger's usual Guide;
And after short refreshment sallied forth.

It was a Summer's night, a close warm night,
Wan, dull and glaring, with a dripping mist
Low-hung and thick that cover'd all the sky,
Half threatening storm and rain; but on we went
Uncheck'd, being full of heart and having faith
In our tried Pilot. Little could we see
Hemm'd round on every side with fog and damp,
And, after ordinary Travellers' chat
With our Conductor, silently we sank
Each into commerce with his private thoughts:
Thus did we breast the ascent, and by myself
Was nothing either seen or heard the while
Which took me from my musings, save that once
The Shepherd's Cur did to his own great joy
Unearth a Hedgehog in the mountain crags
Round which he made a barking turbulent.
This small adventure, for even such it seem'd
In that wild place and at the dead of night,
Being over and forgotten, on we wound
In silence as before. With forehead bent
Earthward, as if in opposition set
Against an enemy, I panted up
With eager pace, and no less eager thoughts.
Thus might we wear perhaps an hour away,
Ascending at loose distance each from each,
And I, as chanced, the foremost of the Band;

from BOOK FOURTEENTH
(1850)

Conclusion

In one of those excursions (may they ne'er
Fade from remembrance!) through the Northern tracts
Of Cambria ranging with a youthful friend,
I left Bethgelert's huts at couching-time,
And westward took my way, to see the sun
Rise from the top of Snowdon. To the door
Of a rude cottage at the mountain's base
We came, and roused the shepherd who attends
The adventurous stranger's steps, a trusty guide;
Then, cheered by short refreshment, sallied forth.

It was a close, warm, breezeless summer night,
Wan, dull, and glaring, with a dripping fog
Low-hung and thick that covered all the sky;
But, undiscouraged, we began to climb
The mountain-side. The mist soon girt us round,
And, after ordinary travellers' talk
With our conductor, pensively we sank
Each into commerce with his private thoughts:
Thus did we breast the ascent, and by myself
Was nothing either seen or heard that checked
Those musings or diverted, save that once
The shepherd's lurcher, who, among the crags,
Had to his joy unearthed a hedgehog, teased
His coiled-up prey with barkings turbulent.
This small adventure, for even such it seemed
In that wild place and at the dead of night,
Being over and forgotten, on we wound
In silence as before. With forehead bent
Earthward, as if in opposition set
Against an enemy, I panted up
With eager pace, and no less eager thoughts.
Thus might we wear a midnight hour away,
Ascending at loose distance each from each,
And I, as chanced, the foremost of the band;

---

[1] There is a lasting controversy in Wordsworth studies over the relative merits of the two finished forms of *The Prelude,* the thirteen-book poem of 1805 and the fourteen-book poem of 1850. Those who favor the 1850 text argue that Wordsworth spent a great deal of his life revising the 1850 text for publication. Those who prefer the earlier version argue that the poet revised away his poetical and political radicalism in the process and thus the 1805 poem better represents the poet in his youth. The parallel texts presented here offer the reader an opportunity to consider the matter in a comparison of the climactic experience of this poem on the "Growth of a Poet's Mind."

[2] **Snowdon:** a mountain in Wales. Wordsworth made the climb in 1791.

(1805) *(Continued)*

When at my feet the ground appear'd to brighten,
And with a step or two seem'd brighter still;
Nor had I time to ask the cause of this,
For instantly a Light upon the turf
Fell like a flash: I looked about, and lo!
The Moon stood naked in the Heavens, at height
Immense above my head, and on the shore
I found myself of a huge sea of mist,
Which, meek and silent, rested at my feet:
A hundred hills their dusky backs upheaved
All over this still Ocean, and beyond,
Far, far beyond, the vapours shot themselves,
In headlands, tongues, and promontory shapes,
Into the Sea, the real Sea, that seem'd
To dwindle, and give up its majesty,
Usurp'd upon as far as sight could reach.
Meanwhile, the Moon look'd down upon this shew
In single glory, and we stood, the mist
Touching our very feet; and from the shore
At distance not the third part of a mile
Was a blue chasm; a fracture in the vapour,
A deep and gloomy breathing-place through which
Mounted the roar of waters, torrents, streams
Innumerable, roaring with one voice.
The universal spectacle throughout
Was shaped for admiration and delight,
Grand in itself alone, but in that breach
Through which the homeless voice of waters rose,
That dark deep thoroughfare had Nature lodg'd
The Soul, the Imagination of the whole.

A meditation rose in me that night
Upon the lonely Mountain when the scene
Had pass'd away, and it appear'd to me
The perfect image of a mighty Mind,
Of one that feeds upon infinity,
That is exalted by an under-presence,
The sense of God, or whatsoe'er is dim
Or vast in its own being, above all
One function of such mind had Nature there
Exhibited by putting forth, and that
With circumstance most awful and sublime,
That domination which she oftentimes
Exerts upon the outward face of things,
So moulds them, and endues, abstracts, combines,
Or by abrupt and unhabitual influence
Doth make one object so impress itself
Upon all others, and pervade them so
That even the grossest minds must see and hear
And cannot chuse but feel. The Power which these

(1850) *(Continued)*

When at my feet the ground appeared to brighten,
And with a step or two seemed brighter still;
Nor was time given to ask or learn the cause,
For instantly a light upon the turf
Fell like a flash, and lo! as I looked up,
The Moon hung naked in a firmament
Of azure without cloud, and at my feet
Rested a silent sea of hoary mist.
A hundred hills their dusky backs upheaved
All over this still ocean; and beyond,
Far, far beyond, the solid vapours stretched,
In headlands, tongues, and promontory shapes,
Into the main Atlantic, that appeared
To dwindle, and give up his majesty,
Usurped upon far as the sight could reach.
Not so the ethereal vault; encroachment none
Was there, nor loss; only the inferior stars
Had disappeared, or shed a fainter light
In the clear presence of the full-orbed Moon,
Who, from her sovereign elevation, gazed
Upon the billowy ocean, as it lay
All meek and silent, save that through a rift—
Not distant from the shore whereon we stood,
A fixed, abysmal, gloomy, breathing-place—
Mounted the roar of waters, torrents, streams
Innumerable, roaring with one voice!
Heard over earth and sea, and, in that hour,
For so it seemed, felt by the starry heavens.

When into air had partially dissolved
That vision, given to spirits of the night
And three chance human wanderers, in calm thought
Reflected, it appeared to me the type
Of a majestic intellect, its acts
And its possessions, what it has and craves,
What in itself it is, and would become.
There I beheld the emblem of a mind
That feeds upon infinity, that broods
Over the dark abyss, intent to hear
Its voices issuing forth to silent light
In one continuous stream; a mind sustained
By recognitions of transcendent power,
In sense conducting to ideal form,
In soul of more than mortal privilege.
One function, above all, of such a mind
Had Nature shadowed there, by putting forth,
'Mid circumstances awful and sublime,
That mutual domination which she loves
To exert upon the face of outward things,
So moulded, joined, abstracted, so endowed

(1805) (*Continued*)

Acknowledge when thus moved, which Nature thus
Thrusts forth upon the senses, is the express
Resemblance, in the fulness of its strength
Made visible, a genuine Counterpart
And Brother of the glorious faculty
Which higher minds bear with them as their own.
That is the very spirit in which they deal
With all the objects of the universe;
They from their native selves can send abroad
Like transformation, for themselves create
A like existence, and, whene'er it is
Created for them, catch it by an instinct;
Them the enduring and the transient both
Serve to exalt; they build up greatest things
From least suggestions, ever on the watch,
Willing to work and to be wrought upon,
They need not extraordinary calls
To rouze them, in a world of life they live,
By sensible impressions not enthrall'd,
But quicken'd, rouz'd, and made thereby more fit
To hold communion with the invisible world.
Such minds are truly from the Deity,
For they are Powers; and hence the highest bliss
That can be known is theirs, the consciousness
Of whom they are habitually infused
Through every image, and through every thought,
And all impressions; hence religion, faith
And endless occupation for the soul
Whether discursive or intuitive;
Hence sovereignty within and peace at will
Emotion which best foresight need not fear
Most worthy then of trust when most intense.
Hence chearfulness in every act of life
Hence truth in moral judgements and delight
That fails not in the external universe.

(1850) (*Continued*)

With interchangeable supremacy,
That men, least sensitive, see, hear, perceive,
And cannot choose but feel. The power, which all
Acknowledge when thus moved, which Nature thus
To bodily sense exhibits, is the express
Resemblance of that glorious faculty
That higher minds bear with them as their own.
This is the very spirit in which they deal
With the whole compass of the universe:
They from their native selves can send abroad
Kindred mutations; for themselves create
A like existence; and, whene'er it dawns
Created for them, catch it, or are caught
By its inevitable mastery,
Like angels stopped upon the wing by sound
Of harmony from Heaven's remotest spheres.
Them the enduring and the transient both
Serve to exalt; they build up greatest things
From least suggestions; ever on the watch,
Willing to work and to be wrought upon,
They need not extraordinary calls
To rouse them; in a world of life they live,
By sensible impressions not enthralled,
But by their quickening impulse made more prompt
To hold fit converse with the spiritual world,
And with the generations of mankind
Spread over time, past, present, and to come,
Age after age, till Time shall be no more.
Such minds are truly from the Deity,
For they are Powers; and hence the highest bliss
That flesh can know is theirs — the consciousness
Of Whom they are, habitually infused
Through every image and through every thought,
And all affections by communion raised
From earth to heaven, from human to divine;
Hence endless occupation for the Soul,
Whether discursive or intuitive;
Hence cheerfulness for acts of daily life,
Emotions which best foresight need not fear,
Most worthy then of trust when most intense.
Hence, amid ills that vex and wrongs that crush
Our hearts — if here the words of Holy Writ
May with fit reverence be applied — that peace
Which passeth understanding, that repose
In moral judgments which from this pure source
Must come, or will by man be sought in vain.

[Here ends parallel texts]

(1805) (Continued)

Oh! who is he that hath his whole life long
Preserved, enlarged this freedom in himself?
For this alone is genuine Liberty.
Witness, ye Solitudes! where I received
My earliest visitations, careless then
Of what was given me, and where now I roam,
A meditative, oft a suffering Man,
And yet, I trust, with undiminish'd powers,
Witness, whatever falls my better mind,
Revolving with the accidents of life,
May have sustain'd, that, howsoe'er misled,
I never, in the quest of right and wrong,
Did tamper with myself from private aims;
Nor was in any of my hopes the dupe
Of selfish passions; nor did wilfully
Yield ever to mean cares and low pursuits;
But rather did with jealousy shrink back
From every combination that might aid
The tendency, too potent in itself,
Of habit to enslave the mind, I mean
Oppress it by the laws of vulgar sense,
And substitute a universe of death,
The falsest of all worlds, in place of that
Which is divine and true. To fear and love,
To love as first and chief, for there fear ends,
Be this ascribed; to early intercourse,
In presence of sublime and lovely Forms,
With the adverse principles of pain and joy,
Evil as one is rashly named by those
Who know not what they say. From love, for here
Do we begin and end, all grandeur comes,
All truth and beauty, from pervading love,
That gone, we are as dust. Behold the fields
In balmy spring-time, full of rising flowers
And happy creatures; see that Pair, the Lamb
And the Lamb's Mother, and their tender ways
Shall touch thee to the heart; in some green bower
Rest, and be not alone, but have thou there
The One who is thy choice of all the world,
There linger, lull'd and lost, and rapt away,
Be happy to thy fill; thou call'st this love
And so it is, but there is higher love
Than this, a love that comes into the heart
With awe and a diffusive sentiment;
Thy love is human merely; this proceeds
More from the brooding Soul, and is divine.

This love more intellectual cannot be
Without Imagination, which, in truth,
Is but another name for absolute strength
And clearest insight, amplitude of mind,
And reason in her most exalted mood.
This faculty hath been the moving soul
Of our long labour: we have traced the stream
From darkness, and the very place of birth
In its blind cavern, whence is faintly heard
The sound of waters; follow'd it to light
And open day, accompanied its course
Among the ways of Nature, afterwards
Lost sight of it, bewilder'd and engulph'd,
Then given it greeting, as it rose once more
With strength, reflecting in its solemn breast
The works of man and face of human life,
And lastly, from its progress have we drawn
The feeling of life endless, the great thought
By which we live, Infinity and God.

. . . .

And now, O Friend! this history is brought
To its appointed close: the discipline
And consummation of the Poet's mind
In everything that stood most prominent
Have faithfully been pictured; we have reach'd
The time (which was our object from the first)
When we may, not presumptuously, I hope,
Suppose my powers so far confirmed, and such
My knowledge, as to make me capable
Of building up a work that should endure.
Yet much hath been omitted, as need was;
Of Books how much! and even of the other wealth
That is collected among woods and fields,
Far more: for Nature's secondary grace,
That outward illustration which is hers,
Hath hitherto been barely touch'd upon,
The charm more superficial, and yet sweet
Which from her works finds way, contemplated
As they hold forth a genuine counterpart
And softening mirror of the moral world.

. . . .

Oh! yet a few short years of useful life,
And all will be complete, thy race be run,
Thy monument of glory will be raised.
Then, though, too weak to tread the ways of truth,
This Age fall back to old idolatry,
Though men return to servitude as fast
As the tide ebbs, to ignominy and shame
By Nations sink together, we shall still
Find solace in the knowledge which we have,
Bless'd with true happiness if we may be

United helpers forward of a day
Of firmer trust, joint-labourers in a work
(Should Providence such grace to us vouchsafe)
Of their redemption, surely yet to come.
Prophets of Nature, we to them will speak
A lasting inspiration, sanctified
By reason and by truth; what we have loved,
Others will love; and we may teach them how;
Instruct them how the mind of man becomes
A thousand times more beautiful than the earth
On which he dwells, above this Frame of things
(Which, 'mid all revolutions in the hopes
And fears of men, doth still remain unchanged)
In beauty exalted, as it is itself
Of substance and of fabric more divine.

from HOME AT GRASMERE[1]

(1888; comp. 1800–1832)

from Ms. D.

. . . .

On Nature's invitation do I come,
By Reason sanctioned. Can the choice mislead
That made the calmest, fairest spot of earth,
With all its unappropriated good,
My own; and not mine only, for with me
Entrenched—say rather, peacefully embowered—
Under yon Orchard, in yon humble Cot,
A younger orphan of a Home extinct,
The only Daughter of my Parents dwells.
Aye, think on that, my Heart, and cease to stir;
Pause upon that, and let the breathing frame
No longer breathe, but all be satisfied.
Oh, if such silence be not thanks to God
For what hath been bestowed, then where, where then
Shall gratitude find rest? Mine eyes did ne'er
Fix on a lovely object, nor my mind
Take pleasure in the midst of happy thoughts,
But either She whom now I have, who now
Divides with me this loved Abode, was there
Or not far off. Where'er my footsteps turned,
Her Voice was like a hidden Bird that sang;
The thought of her was like a flash of light
Or an *unseen* companionship, a breath
Or fragrance independent of the wind;
In all my goings, in the new and old
Of all my meditations, and in this
Favorite of all, in this the most of all.
What Being, therefore, since the birth of Man
Had ever more abundant cause to speak
Thanks, and if favours of the heavenly Muse
Make him more thankful, then to call on verse
To aid him and in song resound his joy?
The boon is absolute; surpassing grace
To me hath been vouchsafed; among the bowers
Of blissful Eden this was neither given
Nor could be given—possession of the good
Which had been sighed for, ancient thought fulfilled,
And dear Imaginations realized
Up to their highest measure, yea, and more.
Embrace me then, ye Hills, and close me in;
Now in the clear and open day I feel
Your guardianship; I take it to my heart;
'Tis like the solemn shelter of the night.
But I would call thee beautiful, for mild
And soft and gay and beautiful thou art,
Dear Valley, having in thy face a smile
Though peaceful, full of gladness. Thou art pleased,
Pleased with thy crags and woody steeps, thy Lake,
Its one green Island and its winding shores,
The multitude of little rocky hills,
Thy Church and Cottages of mountain stone—
Clustered like stars, some few, but single most,
And lurking dimly in their shy retreats,
Or glancing at each other chearful looks,
Like separated stars with clouds between.
What want we? Have we not perpetual streams,
Warm woods and sunny hills, and fresh green fields,
And mountains not less green, and flocks and herds,
And thickets full of songsters, and the voice
Of lordly birds—an unexpected sound
Heard now and then from morn to latest eve

[1] A poem of over 1,000 lines, the first draft of *Home at Grasmere* was composed between 1800–1806. *Ms. D.* is the revised version, most likely largely revised by 1832. The poem was intended to be a part of *The Recluse* project, but left incomplete and unpublished during Wordsworth's lifetime. MacMillan's published it in 1888 with the title *The Recluse: Book First, Part First, Home at Grasmere.* Last re-edited in 1977.

Admonishing the man who walks below
Of solitude and silence in the sky?
These have we, and a thousand nooks of earth
Have also these; but *no* where else is found—
No where (or is it fancy?) can be found—
The one sensation that is here; 'tis here,
Here as it found its way into my heart
In childhood, here as it abides by day,
By night, here only; or in chosen minds
That take it with them hence, where'er they go.
'Tis (but I cannot name it), 'tis the sense
Of majesty and beauty and repose,
A blended holiness of earth and sky,
Something that makes this individual Spot,
This small Abiding-place of many Men,
A termination and a last retreat,
A Centre, come from wheresoe'er you will,
A Whole without dependence or defect,
Made for itself and happy in itself,
Perfect Contentment, Unity entire.

DOROTHY WORDSWORTH

(1771–1855)

Dorothy Wordsworth wrote letters of biographical interest, about 170 printed pages of journals of natural description and daily life, an occasional poem, and a few children's stories. Embarrassed at thoughts of publication, Dorothy sought fulfillment in the emotional and vocational support she provided her brother, William Wordsworth, including the language and images he occasionally appropriated from her journals for his poetry. Her journals are also valued by contemporary readers for their exquisite rendering of nature's singular beauties.

Dorothy Wordsworth was born Christmas Day, 1771, the fourth child in a family of four brothers. She was twenty months younger than William, the brother closest to her in age. The Wordsworth children shared a happy childhood in their northern Lake District home in the village of Cockermouth, until their mother's death in 1778. Their father decided he could not raise his children because he travelled often on legal business. He dissolved his household, sending Dorothy to the town of Halifax in central England for rearing by maternal grandparents and sending William and his younger brothers to a famous grammar school in the neighboring village of Hawkshead.

Dorothy did not see her brothers again for a decade. Though brothers and father spent the Christmas holidays at the family home, she was excluded, which biographers aptly describe as a hurtful mystery. Dorothy's response was to fantasize a "Tower of Joy" to share with her girlhood friend Jane Pollard. The first reunion of the Wordsworth children occurred in the summer of 1787, when William and Dorothy rediscovered their mutual affection.

During intermittent visits over the next five years, William's solicitude for Dorothy evolved into plans for living together. Even William's fathering a child out-of-wedlock during his residence in revolutionary France failed to alter the direction of their lives. Essentially impoverished, but blessed with rich friends and few wants, William and Dorothy rented for nominal rates several grand homes in the West Country of England: first a gentleman's country estate called Racedown (1795) and then the vast Alfoxden House and grounds in the vicinity of the Bristol Channel (1797–1798). Dorothy sauntered about the "sylvan Coombs" with William and friend Samuel Taylor Coleridge,* gathering material for her nature journals while William and Coleridge wrote *Lyrical Ballads* (1798). Their domestic behavior, however, was atypical. Hospitality toward friends who were political radicals, moonlight ramblings in search of poetic images, and investigations into the origin and progress of streams to establish accurate metaphors were interpreted by fearful neighbors during these heated political times as acts of intelligence-gathering for a French invasion by sea. Their lease was not renewed. The Alfoxden period (1797–1798) ended for William and Dorothy with a walking tour in Wales during which William composed *Lines Written a Few Miles above Tintern Abbey,* his visionary poem of love for nature and of hopes for his "dear, / Dear sister."

After a horrible winter idling in Germany where they travelled on behalf of Coleridge's vocational ambitions, the Wordsworths returned to England, confirmed in chauvinism and single-minded in their desire to establish a permanent residence in the area of their birth. They rented Dove Cottage, a modest dwelling of country stone in the Lake District village of Grasmere, which William described as "a home / Within a home, what was to be, and soon, / Our love within a love" (*Home at Grasmere*).

Dorothy returned to her journal writing in the spring, with greater attention to animate life—"The little birds busy making love and pecking blossoms and bits of moss off the trees, they flutter about and about and thrid the trees as I lie under them" (5 June 1800). Life progressed happily for several productive years. When William married Mary Hutchinson, the sweetheart of his youth, Dorothy was understandably anxious over the prospect of being displaced; however, she was readily and happily absorbed into her brother's extended family. As children came, Aunt Dorothy became increasingly useful.

After a serious illness in 1835, Dorothy's generous life of sacrifice effectively ended. Her remaining twenty years were lived in bleak and often querulous states of consciousness under the faithful and loving care of William and his family. Dying in 1855, she survived her brother by five years.

Floating Island at Hawkshead, An Incident in the Schemes of Nature[1]

(1842; comp. 182?)

Harmonious Powers with Nature work
On sky, earth, river, lake, and sea:
Sunshine and storm, whirlwind and breeze
All in one duteous task agree.

Once did I see a slip of earth,
By throbbing waves long undermined,
Loosed from its hold;—*how* no one knew
But all might see it float, obedient to the wind.

Might see it, from the verdant shore
Dissevered float upon the Lake,
Float, with its crest of trees adorned
On which the warbling birds their pastime take.

Food, shelter, safety there they find
There berries ripen, flowerets bloom;
There insects live their lives—and die:
A peopled *world* it is;—in size a tiny room.

And thus through many seasons' space
This little Island may survive
But Nature, though we mark her not,
Will take away—may cease to give.

Perchance when you are wandering forth
Upon some vacant sunny day
Without an object, hope, or fear,
Thither your eyes may turn—the Isle is passed away.

Buried beneath the glittering Lake!
Its place no longer to be found,
Yet the lost fragments shall remain,
To fertilize some other ground.

[1] First appeared in William Wordsworth's *Poems* (1842) with the headnote: "These lines are by the Author of the Address to the Wind, &c. published heretofore along with my poems." The Floating Island is at the southern end of Derwent Water, one of the larger lakes in the Lake District of northern England.

POSTHUMOUS PUBLICATIONS

from THE JOURNALS OF DOROTHY WORDSWORTH
(1941)

from The Alfoxden Journal[1]
(comp. 1798)

ALFOXDEN, *20th January 1798.* The green paths down the hillsides are channels for streams. The young wheat is streaked by silver lines of water running between the ridges, the sheep are gathered together on the slopes. After the wet dark days, the country seems more populous. It peoples itself in the sunbeams. The garden, mimic of spring, is gay with flowers. The purple-starred hepatica spreads itself in the sun, and the clustering snow-drops put forth their white heads, at first upright, ribbed with green, and like a rosebud; when completely opened, hanging their heads downwards, but slowly lengthening their slender stems. The slanting woods of an unvarying brown, showing the light through the thin net-work of their upper boughs. Upon the highest ridge of that round hill covered with planted oaks, the shafts of the trees show in the light like the columns of a ruin.

21st. Walked on the hill-tops—a warm day. Sate under the firs in the park. The tops of the beeches of a brown-red, or crimson. Those oaks, fanned by the sea breeze, thick with feathery sea-green moss, as a grove not stripped of its leaves. Moss cups more proper than acorns for fairy goblets.

22nd. Walked through the wood to Holford. The ivy twisting round the oaks like bristled serpents. The day cold—a warm shelter in the hollies, capriciously bearing berries. Query: Are the male and female flowers on separate trees?

23rd. Bright sunshine, went out at 3 o'clock. The sea perfectly calm blue, streaked with deeper colour by the clouds, and tongues or points of sand; on our return of a gloomy red. The sun gone down. The crescent moon, Jupiter, and Venus. The sound of the sea[2] distinctly heard on the tops of the hills, which we could never hear in summer. We attribute this partly to the bareness of the trees, but chiefly to the absence of the singing of birds, the hum of insects, that noiseless noise which lives in the summer air. The villages marked out by beautiful beds of smoke. The turf fading into the mountain road. The scarlet flowers of the moss.

24th. Walked between half-past three and half-past five. The evening cold and clear. The sea of a sober grey, streaked by the deeper grey clouds. The half dead sound of the near sheep-bell, in the hollow of the sloping coombe,[3] exquisitely soothing.

25th. Went to Poole's[4] after tea. The sky spread over with one continuous cloud, whitened by the light of the moon, which, though her dim shape was seen, did not throw forth so strong a light as to chequer the earth with shadows. At once the clouds seemed to cleave asunder, and left her in the centre of a black-blue vault. She sailed along, followed by multitudes of stars, small, and bright, and sharp. Their brightness seemed concentrated, (half-moon).[5]

26th. Walked upon the hill-tops; followed the sheep tracks till we overlooked the larger coombe. Sat in the sunshine. The distant sheep-bells, the sound of the stream; the woodman winding along the half-marked road with his laden pony; locks of wool still spangled with the dewdrops; the blue-grey sea, shaded with immense masses of cloud, not streaked; the sheep glittering in the sunshine. Returned through the wood. The trees skirting the wood, being exposed more directly to the action of the

[1] The manuscript of the Alfoxden Journal disappeared sometime after William Knight published a first, but incomplete, edition of the Journals in 1897, which left out what he considered to be "trivial" details. The only surviving manuscript is in William Wordsworth's hand but contains only the opening sentences of the first entry, which he transcribed into his Alfoxden Notebook. Alfoxden is the name of the estate where the Wordsworths lived from midsummer 1797 to 25 June 1798. It is located in the southwest county of Somerset, England.

[2] **sea:** the Bristol Channel.

[3] **coombe:** a hollow or valley on the flank of a hill.

[4] **Poole:** Thomas Poole (1765–1837), tanner, friend, and neighbor of Coleridge's from the nearby town of Stowey.

[5] See William Wordsworth's "A Night-Piece" for a poetic rendering—almost verbatim—of Dorothy's lunar description.

sea breeze, stripped of the net-work of their upper boughs, which are stiff and erect, like black skeletons; the ground strewed with the red berries of the holly. Set forward before two o'clock. Returned a little after four.

27th. Walked from seven o'clock till half-past eight. Upon the whole an uninteresting evening. Only once while we were in the wood the moon burst through the invisible veil which enveloped her, the shadows of the oaks blackened, and their lines became more strongly marked. The withered leaves were coloured with a deeper yellow, a brighter gloss spotted the hollies; again her form became dimmer; the sky flat, unmarked by distances, a white thin cloud. The manufacturer's dog makes a strange, uncouth howl, which it continues many minutes after there is no noise near it but that of the brook. It howls at the murmur of the village stream.

30th. William called me into the garden to observe a singular appearance about the moon. A perfect rainbow, within the bow one star, only of colours more vivid. The semi-circle soon became a complete circle, and in the course of three or four minutes the whole faded away. Walked to the blacksmith's and the baker's; an uninteresting evening.

31st. Set forward to Stowey at half-past five. A violent storm in the wood; sheltered under the hollies. When we left home the moon immensely large, the sky scattered over with clouds. These soon closed in, contracting the dimensions of the moon without concealing her. The sound of the pattering shower, and the gusts of wind, very grand. Left the wood when nothing remained of the storm but the driving wind, and a few scattering drops of rain. Presently all clear, Venus first showing herself between the struggling clouds; afterwards Jupiter appeared. The hawthorn hedges, black and pointed, glittering with millions of diamond drops; the hollies shining with broader patches of light. The road to the village of Holford glittered like another stream. On our return, the wind high—a violent storm of hail and rain at the Castle of Comfort.[6] All the Heavens seemed in one perpetual motion when the rain ceased; the moon appearing, now half veiled, and now retired behind heavy clouds, the stars still moving, the roads very dirty.

[6] **Castle of Comfort:** a public house.

1st February. About two hours before dinner, set forward towards Mr Bartholemew's.[7] The wind blew so keen in our faces that we felt ourselves inclined to seek the covert of the wood. There we had a warm shelter, gathered a burthen of large rotten boughs blown down by the wind of the preceding night. The sun shone clear, but all at once a heavy blackness hung over the sea. The trees almost *roared,* and the ground seemed in motion with the multitudes of dancing leaves, which made a rustling sound, distinct from that of the trees. Still the asses pastured in quietness under the hollies, undisturbed by these forerunners of the storm. The wind beat furiously against us as we returned. Full moon. She rose in uncommon majesty over the sea, slowly ascending through the clouds. Sat with the window open an hour in the moonlight.

2nd. Walked through the wood, and on to the Downs before dinner; a warm pleasant air. The sun shone, but was often obscured by straggling clouds. The redbreasts made a ceaseless song in the woods. The wind rose very high in the evening. The room smoked so that we were obliged to quit it. Young lambs in a green pasture in the Coombe, thick legs, large heads, black staring eyes.

3rd. A mild morning, the windows open at breakfast, the redbreasts singing in the garden. Walked with Coleridge over the hills. The sea at first obscured by vapour; that vapour afterwards slid in one mighty mass along the sea-shore; the islands and one point of land clear beyond it. The distant country (which was purple in the clear dull air), overhung by straggling clouds that sailed over it, appeared like the darker clouds, which are often seen at a great distance apparently motionless, while the nearer ones pass quickly over them, driven by the lower winds. I never saw such a union of earth, sky, and sea. The clouds beneath our feet spread themselves to the water, and the clouds of the sky almost joined them. Gathered sticks in the wood; a perfect stillness. The redbreasts sang upon the leafless boughs. Of a great number of sheep in the field, only one standing. Returned to dinner at five o'clock. The moonlight still and warm as a summer's night at nine o'clock.

4th. Walked a great part of the way to Stowey with Coleridge. The morning warm and sunny. The young lasses seen on the hill-tops, in the villages and roads, in

[7] **Mr. Bartholomew:** John Bartholomew sublet Alfoxden to the Wordsworths.

their summer holiday clothes — pink petticoats and blue. Mothers with their children in arms, and the little ones that could just walk, tottering by their side. Midges or small flies spinning in the sunshine; the songs of the lark and redbreast; daisies upon the turf; the hazels in blossom; honeysuckles budding. I saw one solitary strawberry flower under a hedge. The furze gay with blossom. The moss rubbed from the pailings by the sheep, that leave locks of wool, and the red marks with which they are spotted, upon the wood.

. . .

8th. Went up the Park, and over the tops of the hills, till we came to a new and very delicious pathway, which conducted us to the Coombe. Sat a considerable time upon the heath. Its surface restless and glittering with the motion of the scattered piles of withered grass, and the waving of the spiders' threads. On our return the mist still hanging over the sea, but the opposite coast clear, and the rocky cliffs distinguishable. In the deep Coombe, as we stood upon the sunless hill, we saw miles of grass, light and glittering, and the insects passing.

. . .

17th. A deep snow upon the ground. Wm and Coleridge walked to Mr Bartholemew's, and to Stowey. Wm returned, and we walked through the wood into the Coombe to fetch some eggs. The sun shone bright and clear. A deep stillness in the thickest part of the wood, undisturbed except by the occasional dropping of the snow from the holly boughs; no other sound but that of the water, and the slender notes of a redbreast, which sang at intervals on the outskirts of the southern side of the wood. There the bright green moss was bare at the roots of the trees, and the little birds were upon it. The whole appearance of the wood was enchanting; and each tree, taken singly, was beautiful. The branches of the hollies pendent with their white burden, but still showing their bright red berries, and their glossy green leaves. The bare branches of the oaks thickened by the snow.

. . .

24th. Went to the hill-top. Sat a considerable time overlooking the country towards the sea. The air blew pleasantly round us. The landscape mildly interesting. The Welsh hills capped by a huge range of tumultuous white clouds. The sea, spotted with white, of a bluish grey in general, and streaked with darker lines. The near shores clear; scattered farm houses, half-concealed by green mossy orchards, fresh straw lying at the doors; hay-stacks in the fields. Brown fallows, the springing wheat, like a shade of green over the brown earth, and the choice meadow plots, full of sheep and lambs, of a soft and vivid green; a few wreaths of blue smoke, spreading along the ground; the oaks and beeches in the hedges retaining their yellow leaves; the distant prospect on the land side, islanded with sunshine; the sea, like a basin full to the margin; the dark fresh-ploughed fields; the turnips of a lively rough green. Returned through the wood.

25th. I lay down in the morning, though the whole day was very pleasant, and the evening fine. We did not walk.

26th. Coleridge came in the morning, and Mr and Mrs Crewkshank; walked with Coleridge nearly to Stowey after dinner. A very clear afternoon. We lay sidelong upon the turf, and gazed on the landscape till it melted into more than natural loveliness. The sea very uniform, of a pale greyish blue, only one distant bay, bright and blue as a sky; had there been a vessel sailing up it, a perfect image of delight. Walked to the top of a high hill to see a fortification. Again sat down to feed upon the prospect; a magnificent scene, *curiously* spread out for even minute inspection, though so extensive that the mind is afraid to calculate its bounds. A winter prospect shows every cottage, every farm, and the forms of distant trees, such as in summer have no distinguishing mark. On our return, Jupiter and Venus before us. While the twilight still overpowered the light of the moon, we were reminded that she was shining bright above our heads, by our faint shadows going before us. We had seen her on the tops of the hills, melting into the blue sky. Poole called while we were absent.

27th. I walked to Stowey in the evening. Wm and Basil[8] went with me through the wood. The prospect bright, yet *mildly* beautiful. The sea big and white, swelled to the very shores, but round and high in the middle. Coleridge returned with me, as far as the wood. A very bright moonlight night. Venus almost like another moon. Lost to us at Alfoxden long before she goes down the large white sea.

. . .

1st March. We rose early. A thick fog obscured the distant prospect entirely, but the shapes of the nearer

[8] **Basil:** Basil Montague, the then five-year-old child of William's friend by the same name, whom the Wordsworths cared for from 1795 until they departed Alfoxden in 1798.

trees and the dome of the wood dimly seen and dilated. It cleared away between ten and eleven. The shapes of the mist, slowly moving along, exquisitely beautiful; passing over the sheep they almost seemed to have more of life than those quiet creatures. The unseen birds singing in the mist.

. . .

10th. Coleridge, Wm, and I walked in the evening to the top of the hill. We all passed the morning in sauntering about the park and gardens, the children playing about, the old man at the top of the hill gathering furze; interesting groups of human creatures, the young frisking and dancing in the sun, the elder quietly drinking in the life and soul of the sun and air.

. . .

24th. Coleridge, the Chesters, and Ellen Cruikshank[9] called. We walked with them through the wood. Went in the evening into the Coombe to get eggs; returned through the wood, and walked in the park. A duller night than last night: a sort of white shade over the blue sky. The stars dim. The spring continues to advance very slowly, no green trees, the hedges leafless; nothing green but the brambles that still retain their old leaves, the evergreens, and the palms, which indeed are not absolutely green. Some brambles I observed to-day budding afresh, and those have shed their old leaves. The crooked arm of the old oak tree points upwards to the moon.

. . .

2nd. A very high wind. Coleridge came to avoid the smoke; stayed all night. We walked in the wood, and sat under the trees. The half of the wood perfectly still, while the wind was making a loud noise behind us. The still trees only gently bowed their heads, as if listening to the wind. The hollies in the thick wood unshaken by the blast; only, when it came with a greater force, shaken by the rain drops falling from the bare oaks above.

. . .

15th. Set forward after breakfast to Crookham, and returned to dinner at three o'clock. A fine cloudy morning. Walked about the squire's grounds. Quaint waterfalls about, about which Nature was very successfully striving to make beautiful what art had deformed—ruins, hermitages, etc. etc. In spite of all these things, the dell romantic and beautiful, though everywhere planted with unnaturalised trees. Happily we cannot shape the huge hills, or carve out the valleys according to our fancy.

[9] **the Chesters, and Ellen Cruikshank:** Coleridge's friends and neighbors.

. . .

from The Grasmere Journals

(comp. 1800–1803[1])

[14 May to 22 December 1800]

May 14 1800 [Wednesday]. Wm & John[2] set off into Yorkshire after dinner at ½ past 2 o'clock—cold pork in their pockets. I left them at the turning of the Low-wood bay under the trees. My heart was so full that I could hardly speak to W when I gave him a farewell kiss. I sate a long time upon a stone at the margin of the lake, & after a flood of tears my heart was easier. The lake looked to me I knew not why dull and melancholy, the weltering on the shores seemed a heavy sound. I walked as long as I could amongst the stones of the shore. The wood rich in flowers. A beautiful yellow, palish yellow flower, that looked thick round & double, & smelt very sweet—I supposed it was a ranunculus—Crowfoot, the grassy-leaved Rabbit-toothed white flower, strawberries, Geranium—scentless violet, anemones two kinds, orchises, primroses. The heckberry very beautiful as a low shrub. The crab coming out. Met a blind man driving a very large beautiful Bull & a cow—he walked with two sticks. Came home by Clappersgate. The valley very green, many sweet views up to Rydale head when I could juggle away the fine houses, but they disturbed me even more than when I have been happier—one beautiful view of the Bridge, without Sir Michaels.[3] Sate down very often, tho' it was cold. I resolved to write a journal of the time till W & J return, & I set about keeping my resolve because I will not quarrel with myself, & because I shall give Wm Pleasure by it

[1] The Grasmere Journals survive in manuscript. They were last edited by Pamela Woof (1993). The Wordsworths moved to Dove Cottage in the Lake District village of Grasmere in December 1799.

[2] William and brother John (1772–1805). John lived with William and Dorothy at Dove Cottage from January to September 1800.

[3] The seat of Sir Michael le Fleming.

when he comes home again. At Rydale a woman of the village, stout & well-dressed, begged a halfpenny—she had never she said done it before—but these hard times!—Arrived at home with a bad head-ach, set some slips of privett.[4] The evening cold had a fire—my face now flame-coloured. It is nine o'clock, I shall soon go to bed. A young woman begged at the door—she had come from Manchester on Sunday morn with two shillings & a slip of paper which she supposed a Bank note—it was a cheat. She had buried her husband & three children within a year & a half—All in one grave—burying very dear—paupers all put in one place—20 shillings paid for as much ground as will bury a man—a grave stone to be put over it or the right will be lost—11/6 each time the ground is opened. Oh! that I had a letter from William! . . .

. . .

Wednesday 3rd September. Coleridge Wm & John went from home to go upon Helvellyn[5] with Mr Simpson. They set out after breakfast. I accompanied them up near the Blacksmith's. A fine coolish morning. I ironed till ½ past three—now very hot. I then went to a funeral at John Dawsons.[6] About 10 men & 4 women. Bread cheese & ale—they talked sensibly & chearfully about common things. The dead person 56 years of age buried by the parish—the coffin was neatly lettered & painted black & covered with a decent cloth. They set the corpse down at the door & while we stood within the threshold the men with their hats off sang with decent & solemn countenances a verse of a funeral psalm. The corpse was then borne down the hill & they sang till they had got past the Town-end. I was affected to tears while we stood in the house, the coffin lying before me. There were no near kindred, no children. When we got out of the dark house the sun was shining & the prospect looked so divinely beautiful as I never saw it. It seemed more sacred than I had ever seen it, & yet more allied to human life. The green fields, neighbours of the churchyard, were green as possible & with the brightness of the sunshine looked quite Gay. I thought she was going to a quiet spot & I could not help weeping very much. When we came to the bridge they began to sing again & stopped during 4 lines before they entered the church-yard. The priest met us—he did not look as a man ought to do on such an occasion—I had seen him half drunk the day before in a pot-house. Before we came with the corpse one of the company observed he wondered what sort of cue 'our Parson would be in.' NB it was the day after the Fair. I had not finished ironing till 7 o'clock. The wind was now high & I did not walk—writing my journal now at 8 o clock. Wm & John came home at 10 o clock. . . .

. . .

[Friday 3rd October] . . . When Wm & I returned from accompanying Jones we met an old man almost double, he had on a coat thrown over his shoulders above his waistcoat & coat. Under this he carried a bundle & had an apron on & a night cap. His face was interesting. He had Dark eyes & a long nose—John who afterwards met him at Wythburn took him for a Jew. He was of Scotch parents but had been born in the army. He had had a wife '& a good woman & it pleased God to bless us with ten children'—all these were dead but one of whom he had not heard for many years, a Sailor—his trade was to gather leeches[7] but now leeches are scarce & he had not strength for it—he lived by begging & was making his way to Carlisle where he should buy a few godly books to sell. He said leeches were very scarce partly owing to this dry season, but many years they have been scarce—he supposed it owing to their being much sought after, that they did not breed fast, & were of slow growth. Leeches were formerly 2/6 100; they are now 30/. He had been hurt in driving a cart his leg broke his body driven over his skull fractured—he felt no pain till he recovered from his first insensibility. It was then 'late in the evening—when the light was just going away.'[8] . . .

. . .

Saturday 11th. A fine October morning—sat in the house working all the morning. Wm composing—Sally Ashburner[9] learning to mark. After Dinner we walked up Greenhead Gill in search of a Sheepfold.[10] We went by

[4] **privett:** a flowering shrub.

[5] Lake District peak. Mr. Simpson is the Reverend Joseph Simpson, Vicar of the church at Wythburn.

[6] Neighbor's farm. The funeral was for a Susan Shacklock, a pauper.

[7] Leeches were aquatic bloodsucking worms used for the medicinal purpose of bloodletting. William Wordsworth indicates that this meeting with the Leech Gatherer inspired "Resolution and Independence."*

[8] Dorothy records the man's actual words.

[9] **Sally Ashburner:** daughter of the Wordsworths' neighbor Thomas Ashburner.

[10] **Sheepfold:** the setting and inspiration for William's poem "Michael."*

Mr Ollifs & through his woods. It was a delightful day & the views looked excessively chearful & beautiful chiefly that from Mr Oliff's field where our house is to be built. The Colours of the mountains soft & rich, with orange fern—The Cattle pasturing upon the hilltops Kites sailing as in the sky above our heads—Sheep bleating & in lines & chains & patterns scattered over the mountains. They come down & feed on the little green islands in the beds of the torrents & so may be swept away. The Sheepfold is falling away it is built nearly in the form of a heart unequally divided. Look down the brook & see the drops rise upwards & sparkle in the air, at the little falls, the higher sparkles the tallest. We walked along the turf of the mountain till we came to a Cattle track—made by the cattle which come upon the hills. We drank tea at Mr Simpson's returned at about nine—a fine mild night. . . .

[MARCH 1802]

Wednesday [3rd]. I was so unlucky as to propose to rewrite The Pedlar.[11] Wm got to work & was worn to death, we did not walk I wrote in the afternoon.

Thursday [4th]. Before we had quite finished Breakfast Calvert's[12] man brought the horses for Wm. We had a deal to do to shave—pens to make—poems to put in order for writing, to settle the dress pack up &c & The man came before the pens were made & he was obliged to leave me with only two—Since he has left me (at ½ past 11) it is now 2 I have been putting the Drawers into order, laid by his clothes which we had thrown here & there & everywhere, filed two months' newspapers & got my dinner 2 boiled Eggs & 2 apple tarts. I have set Molly on to clear the garden a little, & I myself have helped. I transplanted some snowdrops—The Bees are busy—Wm has a rich bright day—It was hard frost in the night—The Robins are singing sweetly—Now for my walk. I *will* be busy, I *will* look well & be well when he comes back to me. O the Darling! here is one of his bitten apples! I can hardly find in my heart to throw it into the fire. I must wash myself, then off—I walked round the two Lakes crossed the stepping stones at Rydale Foot. Sate down where we always sit I was full of thoughts about my darling. Blessings on him. I came home at the foot of our own lake under Loughrigg. They are making sad ravages in the woods—Benson's Wood is going & the wood above the River. The wind has blown down a small fir tree on the Rock that terminates John's path—I suppose the wind of Wednesday night. I read German after my return till tea time. After tea I worked & read the LB, enchanted with the Idiot Boy. Wrote to Wm then went to Bed. It snowed when I went to Bed. . . .

Sunday Morning [14th]. William had slept badly—he got up at 9 o clock, but before he rose he had finished the Beggar Boys—& while we were at Breakfast that is (for I had Breakfasted) he, with his Basin of Broth before him untouched & a little plate of Bread & butter he wrote the Poem to a Butterfly!—He ate not a morsel, nor put on his stockings but sate with his shirt neck unbuttoned, & his waistcoat open while he did it. The thought first came upon him as we were talking about the pleasure we both always feel at the sight of a Butterfly. I told him that I used to chase them a little but that I was afraid of brushing the dust off their wings, & did not catch them—He told me how they used to kill all the white ones when he went to school because they were frenchmen.[13] Mr Simpson came in just as he was finishing the Poem. After he was gone I wrote it down & the other poems & I read them all over to him. . . . We dined & then Wm went to bed. I lay upon the fur gown before the fire but I could not sleep—I lay there a long time—it is now half past 5 I am going to write letters. I began to write to Mrs Rawson—William rose without having slept we sate comfortably by the fire till he began to try to alter the butterfly, & tired himself he went to bed tired.

Thursday [18th]. A very fine morning the Sun shone but it was far colder than yesterday. I felt myself weak, & William charged me not to go to Mrs Lloyds—I seemed indeed, to myself unfit for it but when he was gone I thought I would get the visit over if I could—so I ate a Beef-steak thinking it would strengthen me so it did, & I went off—I had a very pleasant walk. Rydale vale was full of life & motion. The wind blew briskly & the lake was covered all over with Bright silver waves that were there each the twinkling of an eye, then others rose up & took their place as fast as they went away. The Rocks glittered in the sunshine, the crows & the Ravens were busy, & the thrushes & little Birds sang—I went through the fields, & sate ½ an hour afraid to pass a Cow. The Cow looked at me & I looked at the cow & whenever I stirred the cow gave over eating. I was not very much tired when I

[11] **The Pedlar**: the first part of William Wordsworth's *Excursion** dealing with the narrator's youth.

[12] The servant of William Calvert, a school friend of William Wordsworth.

[13] See William Wordsworth's "To a Butterfly."*

reached Lloyds, I walked in the garden. Charles is all for Agriculture. Mrs Ll in her kindest way. A parcel came in from Birmingham, with Lamb's[14] play for us & for C. They came with me as far as Rydale. As we came along Ambleside vale in the twilight—it was a grave evening—there was something in the air that compelled me to serious thought—the hills were large, closed in by the sky. It was nearly dark when I parted from the Lloyds that is, night was come on & the moon was overcast. But as I climbed Moss the moon came out from behind a Mountain Mass of Black Clouds—O the unutterable darkness of the sky & the Earth below the Moon! & the glorious brightness of the moon itself! There was a vivid sparkling streak of light at this end of Rydale water but the rest was very dark & Loughrigg fell & Silver How were white & bright as if they were covered with hoar frost. The moon retired again & appeared & disappeared several times before I reached home. Once there was no moonlight to be seen but upon the Island house & the promontory of the Island where it stands, 'That needs must be a holy place' &c—&c. I had many many exquisite feelings when I saw this lowly Building in the waters among the dark & lofty hills, with that bright soft light upon it—it made me more than half a poet. I was tired when I reached home I could not sit down to reading & tried to write verses but alas! I gave up expecting William & went soon to bed. Fletcher's carts came home late. . . .

[APRIL 1802]

Thursday 15th. It was a threatening misty morning—but mild. We set off after dinner from Eusemere . . . The wind was furious & we thought we must have returned. We first rested in the large Boat-house, then under a furze Bush opposite Mr Clarksons, saw the plough going in the field. The wind seized our breath the Lake was rough. There was a Boat by itself floating in the middle of the Bay below Water Millock—We rested again in the Water Millock lane. The hawthorns are black & green, the birches here & there greenish but there is yet more of purple to be seen on the Twigs. We got over into a field to avoid some cows—people working, a few primroses by the roadside, woodsorrel flowers, the anemone, scentless violets, strawberries, & that starry yellow flower which Mrs C[oleridge] calls pile wort. When we were in the woods beyond Gowbarrow park we saw a few daffodils close to the water side,[15] we fancied that the lake had floated the seeds ashore & that the little colony had so sprung up—But as we went along there were more & yet more & at last under the boughs of the trees, we saw that there was a long belt of them along the shore, about the breadth of a country turnpike road. I never saw daffodils so beautiful they grew among the mossy stones about & about them, some rested their heads upon these stones as on a pillow for weariness & the rest tossed & reeled & danced & seemed as if they verily laughed with the wind that blew upon them over the Lake, they looked so gay ever glancing ever changing. This wind blew directly over the Lake to them. There was here & there a little knot & a few stragglers a few yards higher up but they were so few as not to disturb the simplicity & unity & life of that one busy highway—We rested again & again. The Bays were stormy & we heard the waves at different distances & in the middle of the water like the Sea—Rain came on. . . .

[MAY 1802]

Tuesday May 4th. William had slept pretty well & though he went to bed nervous & jaded in the extreme he rose refreshed. I wrote the Leech Gatherer for him which he had begun the night before & of which he wrote several stanzas in bed this Monday morning. It was very hot, we called at Mr Simpson's door as we passed but did not go in. We rested several times by the way, read & repeated the Leech gatherer. We were almost melted before we were at the top of the hill. We saw Coleridge on the Wytheburn Side of the water, he crossed the Beck to us. Mr Simpson was fishing there. William & I ate a Luncheon, then went on towards the Waterfall. It is a glorious wild solitude under that lofty purple crag. It stood upright by itself. Its own self & its shadow below, one mass—all else was sunshine. We went on further. A Bird at the top of the crags was flying round & round & looked in thinness & transparency, shape & motion, like a moth. We climbed the hill but looked in vain for a shade except at the foot of the great waterfall, & there we did not like to stay on account of the loose stones above our heads. We came down & rested upon a moss covered Rock, rising out of the bed of the River. There we lay ate our dinner & stayed there till about 4 o clock or later—Wm & C repeated & read verses. I drank a little Brandy & water & was in Heaven. The Stags horn is very beautiful & fresh springing upon the fells.

[14] Charles Lamb's* play *John Woodvil* (1802), originally titled *Pride's Cure.*

[15] See William Wordsworth's "I Wandered Lonely as a Cloud" for the poem based on Dorothy's description of daffodils.

Mountain ashes, green. We drank tea at a farm house. The woman had not a pleasant countenance, but was civil enough. She had a pretty Boy a year old whom she suckled. We parted from Coleridge at Sara's Crag after having looked at the letters which C carved in the morning. I kissed them all. Wm deepened the T with C's penknife. We sate afterwards on the wall, seeing the sun go down & the reflections in the still water. C looked well & parted from us chearfully, hopping up upon the Side stones. On the Rays we met a woman with 2 little girls one in her arms the other about 4 years old walking by her side, a pretty little thing, but half starved. She had on a pair of slippers that had belonged to some gentlemans child, down at the heels, but it was not easy to keep them on—but, poor thing! young as she was, she walked carefully with them. Alas too young for such cares & such travels—The Mother when we accosted her told us that her Husband had left her & gone off with another woman & how she *'pursued'* them. Then her fury kindled & her eyes rolled about. She changed again to tears. She was a Cockermouth woman—30 years of age a child at Cockermouth when I was—I was moved & gave her a shilling, I believe 6^{d} more than I ought to have given. We had the Crescent moon with the 'auld moon in her arms'[16]—We rested often:—always upon the Bridges. Reached home at about 10 o clock. The Lloyds had been here in our absence. We went soon to bed. I repeated verses to William while he was in bed—he was soothed & I left him. 'This is the Spot'[17] over & over again. . . .

[OCTOBER 1802]

On Monday 4th October 1802, my Brother William was married to Mary Hutchinson. I slept a good deal of the night & rose fresh & well in the morning—at a little after 8 o clock I saw them go down the avenue towards the Church. William had parted from me up stairs. I gave him the wedding ring—with how deep a blessing! I took it from my forefinger where I had worn it the whole of the night before—he slipped it again onto my finger and blessed me fervently. When they were absent my dear little Sara prepared the breakfast. I kept myself as quiet as I could, but when I saw the two men[18] running up the walk, coming to tell us it was over, I could stand it no longer & threw myself on the bed where I lay in stillness, neither hearing or seeing any thing, till Sara[19] came upstairs to me & said 'They are coming'. This forced me from the bed where I lay & I moved I knew not how straight forward, faster than my strength could carry me till I met my beloved William & fell upon his bosom. He & John Hutchinson led me to the house & there I stayed to welcome my dear Mary. As soon as we had breakfasted we departed. It rained when we set off. Poor Mary was much agitated when she parted from her Brothers & Sisters & her home. Nothing particular occurred till we reached Kirby. We had sunshine & showers, pleasant talk, love & chearfulness. We were obliged to stay two hours at K. while the horses were feeding. We wrote a few lines to Sara & then walked out, the sun shone & we went to the Church-yard, after we had put a Letter into the Post office for the York Herald. We sauntered about & read the Grave-stones. There was one to the memory of 5 Children, who had all died within 5 years, & the longest lived had only lived 4 years. There was another Stone erected to the memory of an unfortunate woman (as we supposed, by a stranger). The verses engraved upon it expressed that she had been neglected by her Relations & counselled the Readers of those words to look within & recollect their own frailties. . . .

[16] Quote from epigraph to Coleridge's *Dejection: An Ode.**

[17] **'This is the Spot'**: line from an unpublished poem.

[18] **the two men**: Mary Hutchinson's brothers, Thomas and John, who served as witnesses at the wedding.

[19] **Sara**: Sara Hutchinson, sister of the poet's wife, who remained behind to make the wedding breakfast.

from THE COLLECTED POEMS
(1987)

Irregular Verses[1]
(1978/1987; comp. 1829)

Ah Julia![2] ask a Christmas rhyme
Of me who in the golden time
Of careless, hopeful, happy youth
Ne'er strove to decorate the truth,

[1] First printed in its entirety in *The Wordsworth Circle* (1978), along with the following poem, "Thoughts on My Sick-bed," and collected by the same editor, Susan M. Levin, as "Appendix One: The Collected Poems of Dorothy Wordsworth," in *Dorothy Wordsworth and Romanticism* (1987).

[2] Julia was Dorothy's goddaughter and daughter of Jane Pollard Marshall, the Friend (l. 6) of the poem.

Contented to lay bare my heart
To one dear Friend, who had her part
In all the love and all the care
And every joy that harboured there.
—To her I told in simple prose
Each girlish vision, as it rose
Before an active busy brain
That needed neither spur nor rein,
That still enjoyed the present hour
Yet for the *future* raised a tower
Of bliss more exquisite and pure
Bliss that (so deemed we) should endure
Maxims of caution, prudent fears
Vexed not the projects of those years
Simplicity our steadfast theme,
No works of Art adorned our scheme.—
A cottage in a verdant dell,
A foaming stream, a crystall Well,
A garden stored with fruit and flowers
And sunny seats and shady bowers,
A file of hives for humming bees
Under a row of stately trees
And, sheltering all this faery ground,
A belt of hills must wrap it round,
Not stern or mountainous, or bare,
Nor lacking herbs to scent the air;
Nor antient trees, nor scattered rocks,
And pastured by the blameless flocks
That print their green tracks to invite
Our wanderings to the topmost height.

Such was the spot I fondly framed
When life was new, and hope untamed:
There with my one dear Friend would dwell,
Nor wish for aught beyond the dell.
Alas! the cottage fled in air,
The streamlet never flowed:
—Yet did those visions pass away
So gently that they seemed to stay,
Though in our riper years we each pursued a different way.

—We parted, sorrowful; by duty led;
My Friend, ere long a happy Wife
Was seen with dignity to tread
The paths of usefulness, in active life;
And such her course through later days;
The same her honour and her praise;
As thou canst witness, thou dear Maid,
One of the Darlings of her care;
Thy *Mother* was that Friend who still repaid
Frank confidence with unshaken truth:
This was the glory of her youth,
A brighter gem than shines in prince's diadem.

You ask why in that jocund time
Why did I not in jingling rhyme
Display those pleasant guileless dreams
That furnished still exhaustless themes?
—I *reverenced* the Poet's skill,
And *might have* nursed a mounting Will
To imitate the tender Lays
Of them who sang in Nature's praise;
But bashfulness, a struggling shame
A fear that elder heads might blame
—Or something worse—a lurking pride
Whispering my playmates would deride
Stifled ambition, checked the aim
If e'er by chance "the numbers came"
—Nay even the mild maternal smile,
That oft-times would repress, beguile
The over-confidence of youth,
Even that dear smile, to own the truth,
Was dreaded by a fond self-love;
"'Twill glance on me—and to reprove
Or," (sorest wrong in childhood's school)
"Will *point* the sting of ridicule."
And now, dear Girl, I hear you ask
Is this your lightsome, chearful task?
You tell us tales of forty years,
Of hopes extinct, of childish fears,
Why cast among us thoughts of sadness
When we are seeking mirth and gladness?
Nay, ill those words befit the Maid
Who pleaded for my Christmas rhyme
Mirthful she is; but placid—staid—
Her heart beats to no giddy chime
Though it with Chearfulness keep time
For Chearfulness, a willing guest,
Finds ever in her tranquil breast
A fostering home, a welcome rest.
And well she knows that, casting *thought* away,
We lose the best part of our day;
That joys of youth remembered when our youth is past
Are joys that to the end of life will last;

And if this poor memorial strain,
Breathed from the depth of years gone by,
Should touch her Mother's heart with tender pain,

Or call a tear into her loving eye,
She will not check the tear or still the rising sigh.
—The happiest heart is given to sadness;
The saddest heart feels deepest gladness.

Thou dost not ask, thou dost not need
A verse from me; nor wilt thou heed
A greeting masked in laboured rhyme
From one whose heart has still kept time
With every pulse of thine

Thoughts on My Sick-Bed

(1978/1987; comp. 1832)

And has the remnant of my life
Been pilfered of this sunny Spring?
And have its own prelusive sounds
Touched in my heart no echoing string?

Ah! say not so—the hidden life
Couchant within this feeble frame
Hath been enriched by kindred gifts,
That, undesired, unsought-for, came

With joyful heart in youthful days
When fresh each season in its Round
I welcomed the earliest Celandine
Glittering upon the mossy ground;

With busy eyes I pierced the lane
In quest of known and *un*known things,
—The primrose a lamp on its fortress rock,
The silent butterfly spreading its wings,

The violet betrayed by its noiseless breath,
The daffodil dancing in the breeze,
The carolling thrush, on his naked perch,
Towering above the budding trees.

Our cottage-hearth no longer our home,
Companions of Nature were we,
The Stirring, the Still, the Loquacious, the Mute—
To all we gave our sympathy.

Yet never in those careless days
When spring-time in rock, field, or bower
Was but a fountain of earthly hope
A promise of fruits & the *splendid* flower.

No! then I never felt a bliss
That might with *that* compare
Which, piercing to my couch of rest,
Came on the vernal air.

When loving Friends an offering brought,
The first flowers of the year,
Culled from the precincts of our home,
From nooks to Memory dear.

With some sad thoughts the work was done,
Unprompted and unbidden,
But joy it brought to my *hidden* life,
To consciousness no longer hidden.

I felt a Power unfelt before,
Controlling weakness, languor, pain;
It bore me to the Terrace walk
I trod the Hills again;—

No prisoner in this lonely room,
I *saw* the green Banks of the Wye,
Recalling thy prophetic words,[1]
Bard, Brother, Friend from infancy!

No need of motion, or of strength,
Or even the breathing air;
—I thought of Nature's loveliest scenes;
And with Memory I was there.

---

[1] Reference to William Wordsworth, "Lines Written a Few Miles above Tintern Abbey," ll. 111 ff.

WALTER SCOTT

(1771–1832)

Walter Scott relates in his "Memoir" that composing romances with a boyhood friend established his artistic direction for life:

> These legends [of the Scottish Border], in which the martial and the miraculous always predominated, we rehearsed to each other during our walks. . . . Whole holidays were spent in this singular pastime, which continued for two or three years, and had, I believe, no small effect in directing the turn of my imagination to the chivalrous and romantic in poetry and prose.

The son of a middle-class family of Edinburgh, Scott began his literary education listening to his grandmother's tales of clans from the Border region of Scotland and England, which included heroic lore of his own family ancestry. Scott studied at Edinburgh University in preparation for working in his father's law firm, but his enthusiasm for literature and antiquity prevailed. He began his literary career with the anonymous publication of a translation from the German of *The Chase and William and Helen* (1796). Like Robert Burns,* who was presently engaged in a similar endeavor, Scott traversed the Border country collecting manuscripts, listening to peasants sing old ballads, and then revised, completed, or improved the songs for publication in *Minstrelsy of the Scottish Border* (1802). Scott's original compositions, *The Lay of the Last Minstrel* (1805) and *Marmion* (1808), achieved immediate and spectacular success. He continued to publish in verse until the rise of Lord Byron's* star with *Childe Harold* (1812) and the Oriental Tales. Then, bested by Byron, Scott became, and continued for the remainder of his life, the novelist of chivalry and romance, and here made his mark on literary history as the inventor of the historical novel. While Maria Edgeworth's* *Castle Rackrent* (1800) is the first regional novel in English as well as the first to use local dialects, Scott magnified and enriched local settings in the context of vast narratives that feature scores of common people caught up in the great events of history. The *Edinburgh Review* said of the immediate impact of *Waverley* (1814), Scott's first experiment with historical fiction: "The unexpected newness of the thing, the profusion of original characters, the Scotch language, Scotch scenery, Scotch men and women, the simplicity of the writing, and the graphic force of the descriptions, all struck us with an electric shock of delight." *Waverley* (1814)—the namesake of the series—*Guy Mannering* (1815), *Rob Roy* (1817), *The Heart of Midlothian* (1818), *The Bride of Lammermoor* (1819), *Ivanhoe* (1819), and 20 other romances established their author as the most popular novelist of his day and one of the most imitated. Novelists in England: Dickens, Thackeray, George Eliot; on the Continent: Balzac, Hugo, Manzoni; and in America: Cooper, Hawthorne, and Melville, followed Scott in attempting historical fiction.

from MINSTRELSY OF THE SCOTTISH BORDER
(1802–1803)

Lord Randal

— I —

'O where hae[1] ye been, Lord Randal, my son?
O where hae ye been, my handsome young man?'
'I hae been to the wild wood; mother, make my bed soon,
For I'm weary wi' hunting, and fain wald[2] lie down.'

— II —

'Where gat[3] ye your dinner, Lord Randal, my son?
Where gat ye your dinner, my handsome young man?'
'I din'd wi' my true-love; mother, make my bed soon,
For I'm weary wi' hunting, and fain wald lie down.'

— III —

'What gat ye to[4] your dinner, Lord Randal, my son?
What gat ye to your dinner, my handsome young man?'
'I gat eels boil'd in broo[5]; mother, make my bed soon,
For I'm weary wi' hunting, and fain wald lie down.'

— IV —

'What became of your bloodhounds, Lord Randal, my son?
What became of your bloodhounds, my handsome young man?'
'O they swell'd and they died; mother, make my bed soon,
For I'm weary wi' hunting, and fain wald lie down.'

— V —

'O I fear ye are poison'd, Lord Randal, my son!
O I fear ye are poison'd, my handsome young man!'
'O yes! I am poison'd; mother, make my bed soon,
For I'm sick at the heart, and I fain wald lie down.'

[1] **hae:** have.
[2] **fain wald:** eagerly would.
[3] **gat:** got or had.
[4] **What gat ye to:** what did you have for.
[5] **broo:** broth.

from THE LAY OF THE LAST MINSTREL
(1805)

from Canto Sixth[1]

— I —

Breathes there the man, with soul so dead,
Who never to himself hath said,
This is my own, my native land!
Whose heart hath ne'er within him burn'd,
As home his footsteps he hath turn'd,
From wandering on a foreign strand!
If such there breathe, go, mark him well;
For him no Minstrel raptures swell;
High though his titles, proud his name,
Boundless his wealth as wish can claim;
Despite those titles, power, and pelf,[2]
The wretch, concentred all in self,
Living, shall forfeit fair renown,
And, doubly dying, shall go down
To the vile dust, from whence he sprung,
Unwept, unhonour'd, and unsung.

— II —

O Caledonia![3] stern and wild,
Meet nurse for a poetic child!
Land of brown heath and shaggy wood,

[1] The poem, set in the mid-16th Century, is narrated by a fictional ancient minstrel, the last of his kind, and based on an old Border legend of the goblin Gilpin Horner. The lady of Branksome Hall is 'Anne, Duchess of Buccleuch and Monmouth, representative of the ancient Lords of Buccleuch, and widow of the unfortunate James, Duke of Monmouth, who was beheaded in 1685' [W. S.].
[2] **pelf:** ill-gotten wealth, plunder.
[3] **Caledonia:** Scotland.

Land of the mountain and the flood,
Land of my sires! what mortal hand
Can e'er untie the filial band,
That knits me to thy rugged strand!
Still as I view each well-known scene,
Think what is now, and what hath been,
Seems as, to me, of all bereft,
Sole friends thy woods and streams were left;
And thus I love them better still,
Even in extremity of ill.
By Yarrow's stream still let me stray,
Though none should guide my feeble way;
Still feel the breeze down Ettrick break,
Although it chill my wither'd cheek;
Still lay my head by Teviot[4] Stone,
Though there, forgotten and alone,
The Bard may draw his parting groan.

— III —

Not scorn'd like me, to Branksome Hall[5]
The Minstrels came at festive call;
Trooping they came, from near and far,
The jovial priests of mirth and war;
Alike for feast and fight prepar'd,
Battle and banquet both they shar'd.
Of late, before each martial clan,
They blew their death-note in the van,
But now, for every merry mate,
Rose the portcullis' iron grate;
They sound the pipe, they strike the string,
They dance, they revel, and they sing,
Till the rude turrets shake and ring.

— X —

. . . .

And first stept forth old Albert Græme,
The Minstrel of that ancient name:[6]
Was none who struck the harp so well
Within the Land Debateable;
Well friended, too, his hardy kin,
Whoever lost, were sure to win;
They sought the beeves that made their broth,
In Scotland and in England both.
In homely guise, as nature bade,
His simple song the Borderer said.

— XI —

ALBERT GRAEME

It was an English ladye bright,
　　(The sun shines fair on Carlisle wall,)
And she would marry a Scottish knight,
　　For Love will still be lord of all.
Blithely they saw the rising sun,
　　When he shone fair on Carlisle wall;
But they were sad ere day was done,
　　Though Love was still the lord of all.

Her sire gave brooch and jewel fine,
　　Where the sun shines fair on Carlisle wall;
Her brother gave but a flask of wine,
　　For ire that Love was lord of all.

For she had lands, both meadow and lea,[7]
　　Where the sun shines fair on Carlisle wall;
And he swore her death ere he would see
　　A Scottish knight the lord of all!

[4] **Yarrow . . . Teviot**: rivers in southern Scotland. **Ettrick**: a forest in southern Scotland. Scott lived in the region.

[5] **Branksome Hall**: the seat of the Buccleuchs, an old aristocratic Scottish family around whom the action of the poem takes place.

[6] **The Minstrel of that ancient name**: John Grahame, second son of *Malice*, Earl of *Monteith*, commonly surnamed *John with the Bright Sword*, upon some displeasure risen against him at court, retired with many of his clan and kindred into the English Borders, in the reign of King Henry the Fourth, where they seated themselves; and many of their posterity have continued there ever since. Mr. Sandford, speaking of them, says (which indeed was applicable to most of the Borderers on both sides): 'They were all stark moss-troopers, and arrant thieves: Both to England and Scotland outlawed: yet sometimes connived at, because they gave intelligence forth of Scotland, and would raise 400 horse at any time upon a raid of the English into Scotland. A saying is recorded of a mother to her son (which is now become proverbial), *Ride, Rowley, hough 's i' the pot*: that is, the last piece of beef was in the pot, and therefore it was high time for him to go and fetch more.' *History of Cumberland*, introd.

The residence of the Graemes being chiefly in the Debatable Land, so called because it was claimed by both kingdoms, their depredations extended both to England and Scotland with impunity; for as both wardens accounted them the proper subjects of their own prince, neither inclined to demand reparation for their excesses from the opposite officers, which would have been an acknowledgment of his jurisdiction over them. [W. S.]

[7] **lea**: pasture.

— XII —

That wine she had not tasted well,
(The sun shines fair on Carlisle wall,)
When dead in her true love's arms she fell,
For Love was still the lord of all!

He pierc'd her brother to the heart,
Where the sun shines fair on Carlisle wall:
So perish all would true love part,
That Love may still be lord of all!

And then he took the cross divine,
(Where the sun shines fair on Carlisle wall,)
And died for her sake in Palestine;
So Love was still the lord of all.

Now all ye lovers that faithful prove,
(The sun shines fair on Carlisle wall,)
Pray for their souls who died for love,
For Love shall still be lord of all!

— XIII —

As ended Albert's simple lay,
Arose a bard of loftier port;
For sonnet, rhyme, and roundelay,
Renown'd in haughty Henry's court:
There rung thy harp, unrivall'd long,
Fitztraver of the silver song!
The gentle Surrey loved his lyre —[8]
Who has not heard of Surrey's fame?
His was the hero's soul of fire,
And his the bard's immortal name,
And his was love, exalted high
By all the glow of chivalry.

— XVI —

FITZTRAVER[9]

'Twas All-soul's eve, and Surrey's heart beat high;
He heard the midnight bell with anxious start,
Which told the mystic hour, approaching nigh,
When wise Cornelius promis'd, by his art,
To show to him the ladye of his heart,
Albeit betwixt them roar'd the ocean grim;
Yet so the sage had hight[10] to play his part,
That he should see her form in life and limb,
And mark, if still she lov'd, and still she thought of him.

— XVII —

Dark was the vaulted room of gramarye,[11]
To which the wizard led the gallant Knight,
Save that before a mirror, huge and high,
A hallow'd taper shed a glimmering light
On mystic implements of magic might;
On cross, and character,[12] and talisman,
And almagest,[13] and altar, nothing bright:
For fitful was the lustre, pale and wan,
As watchlight by the bed of some departing man.

— XVIII —

But soon, within that mirror huge and high,
Was seen a self-emitted light to gleam;
And forms upon its breast the Earl 'gan spy,[14]
Cloudy and indistinct, as feverish dream;
Till, slow arranging, and defin'd, they seem
To form a lordly and a lofty room,
Part lighted by a lamp with silver beam,
Plac'd by a couch of Agra's[15] silken loom,
And part by moonshine pale, and part was hid in gloom.

---

[8] **The gentle Surrey loved his lyre:** the gallant and unfortunate Henry Howard, Earl of Surrey, was unquestionably the most accomplished cavalier of his time; and his sonnets display beauties which would do honor to a more polished age. He was beheaded on Tower-hill in 1546; a victim to the mean jealousy of Henry VIII., who could not bear so brilliant a character near his throne. [W. S.]

[9] The song of the supposed bard is founded on an incident said to have happened to the Earl in his travels. Cornelius Agrippa, the celebrated alchemist, showed him, in a looking-glass, the lovely Geraldine, to whose service he had devoted his pen and his sword. The vision represented her as indisposed, and reclining upon a couch, reading her lover's verses by the light of a waxen taper. [W. S.]

[10] **hight:** promised.

[11] **gramarye:** magic.

[12] **character:** magical lettering.

[13] **almagest:** an early medieval treatise on some branch of knowledge.

[14] **'gan:** began to.

[15] **Agra:** a province in north-central India known for its fine textiles (and later as the site of the Taj Mahal).

— XIX —

Fair all the pageant: but how passing fair
    The slender form which lay on couch of Ind!
O'er her white bosom stray'd her hazel hair;
    Pale her dear cheek, as if for love she pin'd;
All in her night-robe loose she lay reclin'd,
    And pensive read from tablet eburnine[16]
Some strain that seem'd her inmost soul to find:
    That favour'd strain was Surrey's raptur'd line,
That fair and lovely form, the Lady Geraldine.

— XX —

Slow roll'd the clouds upon the lovely form,
    And swept the goodly vision all away—
So royal envy roll'd the murky storm
    O'er my beloved Master's glorious day.
Thou jealous, ruthless tyrant![17] Heaven repay
    On thee, and on thy children's latest line,
The wild caprice of thy despotic sway,
    The gory bridal bed, the plunder'd shrine,
The murder'd Surrey's blood, the tears of Geraldine!

— XXI —

Both Scots, and Southern chiefs, prolong
Applauses of Fitztraver's song;
These hated Henry's name as death,
And those still held the ancient faith.[18]
Then, from his seat, with lofty air,
Rose Harold, bard of brave St. Clair;
St. Clair, who, feasting high at Home,
Had with that lord to battle come.
Harold was born where restless seas
Howl round the storm-swept Orcades;[19]
Where erst St. Clairs held princely sway
O'er isle and islet, strait and bay;—
Still nods their palace to its fall,
Thy pride and sorrow, fair Kirkwall![20]
Thence oft he mark'd fierce Pentland rave,
As if grim Odin[21] rode her wave;
And watch'd the whilst,[22] with visage pale,
And throbbing heart, the struggling sail;
For all of wonderful and wild
Had rapture for the lonely child.

— XXIII —

HAROLD

O listen, listen, ladies gay!
    No haughty feat of arms I tell;
Soft is the note, and sad the lay,
    That mourns the lovely Rosabelle.[23]

—'Moor, moor the barge, ye gallant crew!
    And, gentle ladye, deign to stay!
Rest thee in Castle Ravensheuch,[24]
    Nor tempt the stormy firth to-day.

'The blackening wave is edg'd with white:
    To inch and rock the sea-mews[25] fly;
The fishers have heard the Water-Sprite,
    Whose screams forebode that wreck is nigh.

'Last night the gifted Seer did view
    A wet shroud swathed round ladye gay;
Then stay thee, Fair, in Ravensheuch:
    Why cross the gloomy firth to-day?'

''Tis not because Lord Lindesay's heir
    To-night at Roslin leads the ball,
But that my ladye-mother there
    Sits lonely in her castle-hall.

---

[16] **eburnine**: ivory, or ivory-colored.

[17] **tyrant**: Henry VIII.

[18] **the ancient faith**: Roman Catholicism, against which Henry VIII rebelled by creating the Church of England in 1534.

[19] **Orcades**: the Orkney Islands, off the northeast coast of Scotland.

[20] **Kirkwall**: the Castle of Kirkwall was built by the St. Clairs while Earls of Orkney. It was dismantled by the Earl of Caithness about 1615, having been garrisoned against the government by Robert Stewart, natural son to the Earl of Orkney. [W. S.]

[21] **Odin**: the king of the gods in Norse mythology.

[22] **the whilst**: meanwhile.

[23] **Rosabelle**: this was a family name in the house of St. Clair. Henry St. Clair, the second of the line, married Rosabelle, fourth daughter of the Earl of Stratherne. [W. S.]

[24] **Castle Ravensheuch**: a large and strong castle, situated betwixt Kirkaldy and Dysart, on a steep crag, washed by the Frith of Forth. It was conferred on Sir William St. Clair, as a slight compensation for the earldom of Orkney, by a charter of King James III., dated in 1471. [W. S.]

[25] **inch**: island. **sea-mews**: seagulls.

''Tis not because the ring they ride,[26]
And Lindesay at the ring rides well,
But that my sire the wine will chide,
If 'tis not fill'd by Rosabelle.'

O'er Roslin all that dreary night
A wondrous blaze was seen to gleam;
'Twas broader than the watch-fire's light,
And redder than the bright moonbeam.

It glar'd on Roslin's castled rock,
It ruddied all the copse-wood glen;
'Twas seen from Dryden's groves of oak,
And seen from cavern'd Hawthornden.

Seem'd all on fire that chapel proud
Where Roslin's chiefs uncoffin'd lie,
Each Baron, for a sable shroud,
Sheath'd in his iron panoply.

Seem'd all on fire within, around,
Deep sacristy and altar's pale;
Shone every pillar foliage-bound,
And glimmer'd all the dead men's mail.

Blaz'd battlement and pinnet[27] high,
Blaz'd every rose-carved buttress fair—
So still they blaze when fate is nigh
The lordly line of high St. Clair.

There are twenty of Roslin's barons bold
Lie buried within that proud chapelle;
Each one the holy vault doth hold—
But the sea holds lovely Rosabelle!

And each St. Clair was buried there,
With candle, with book, and with knell;
But the sea-caves rung, and the wild winds sung,
The dirge of lovely Rosabelle.

— XXIV —

So sweet was Harold's piteous lay,
Scarce mark'd the guests the darken'd hall,
Though, long before the sinking day,
A wondrous shade involv'd[28] them all:
It was not eddying mist or fog,
Drain'd by the sun from fen or bog;
Of no eclipse had sages told;
And yet, as it came on apace,[29]
Each one could scarce his neighbour's face,
Could scarce his own stretch'd hand behold.
A secret horror check'd the feast,
And chill'd the soul of every guest;
Even the high Dame stood half aghast—
She knew some evil on the blast;
The elvish page[30] fell to the ground,
And, shuddering, mutter'd, 'Found! found! found!'

— XXV —

Then sudden, through the darken'd air,
A flash of lightning came;
So broad, so bright, so red the glare,
The castle seem'd on flame.
Glanc'd every rafter of the hall,
Glanc'd every shield upon the wall;
Each trophied beam, each sculptur'd stone,
Were instant seen, and instant gone;
Full through the guests' bedazzled band
Resistless flash'd the levin-brand,[31]
And fill'd the hall with smouldering smoke,
As on the elvish page it broke.
It broke, with thunder long and loud,
Dismay'd the brave, appall'd the proud,—
From sea to sea the larum rung;
On Berwick wall, and at Carlisle withal,
To arms the startled warders sprung.
When ended was the dreadful roar,
The elvish dwarf was seen no more!

— XXVI —

Some heard a voice in Branksome Hall,
Some saw a sight, not seen by all;
That dreadful voice was heard by some,
Cry, with loud summons, 'GYLBIN, COME!'
And on the spot where burst the brand,
Just where the page had flung him down,
Some saw an arm, and some a hand,
And some the waving of a gown.
The guests in silence pray'd and shook,
And terror dimm'd each lofty look.

---

[26] **the ring they ride:** knights would play at catching suspended rings on their lances as they galloped at full speed.

[27] **pinnet:** pennant.

[28] **involv'd:** wrapped around, surrounded.

[29] **apace:** quickly.

[30] **the elvish page:** Gilpin Horner.

[31] **resistless:** unstoppable (*lit.*, irresistible). **levin-brand:** lightning bolt.

But none of all the astonish'd train
Was so dismay'd as Deloraine;
His blood did freeze, his brain did burn,
'Twas fear'd his mind would ne'er return;
For he was speechless, ghastly, wan,
Like him of whom the story ran,
Who spoke the spectre-hound in Man.[32]
At length, by fits, he darkly told,
With broken hint, and shuddering cold,
That he had seen, right certainly,
A shape with amice wrapp'd around,
With a wrought Spanish baldric[33] *bound,*
Like pilgrim from beyond the sea;
And knew—but how it matter'd not—
It was the wizard, Michael Scott.

— XXVII —

The anxious crowd, with horror pale,
All trembling heard the wondrous tale
. . . .

— XXVIII —

Nought of the bridal will I tell,
Which after in short space befell;
Nor how brave sons and daughters fair
Bless'd Tevoit's Flower, and Cranstoun's heir;[34]
After such dreadful scene, 'twere vain
To wake the note of mirth again.
More meet it were to mark the day
Of penitence, and prayer divine,
When pilgrim-chiefs, in sad array,
Sought Melrose' holy shrine.

— XXIX —

With naked foot, and sackcloth[35] vest,
And arms enfolded on his breast,
Did every pilgrim go;
The standers-by might hear uneath,[36]
Footstep, or voice, or high-drawn breath,
Through all the lengthen'd row:
No lordly look, nor martial stride;
Gone was their glory, sunk their pride,
Forgotten their renown;
Silent and slow, like ghosts they glide
To the high altar's hallow'd side,
And there they knelt them down:
Above the suppliant chieftains wave
The banners of departed brave;
Beneath the letter'd stones were laid

[32] **Who spoke . . . in Man:** The ancient castle of Peel-town in the Isle of Man is surrounded by four churches, now ruinous. They say that an apparition, called, in the Mankish language, the *Mauthe Doog*, in the shape of a large black spaniel, with curled shaggy hair, was used to haunt Peel-castle; and has been frequently seen in every room, but particularly in the guard-chamber, where, as soon as candles were lighted, it came and lay down before the fire, in presence of all the soldiers, who, at length, by being so much accustomed to the sight of it, lost great part of the terror they were seized with at its first appearance. But though they endured the shock of such a guest when all together in a body, none cared to be left alone with it. It being the custom, therefore, for one of the soldiers to lock the gates of the castle at a certain hour, and carry the keys to the captain to whose apartment . . . the way led through the church, they agreed among themselves, that whoever was to succeed the ensuing night his fellow in this errand, should accompany him that went first, and by this means no man would be exposed singly to the danger. One night a fellow, being drunk, laughed at the simplicity of his companions; and though it was not his turn to go with the keys, would needs take that office upon him, to testify his courage. All the soldiers endeavored to dissuade him; but the more they said, the more resolute he seemed, and swore that he desired nothing more than that the *Mauthe Doog* would follow him as it had done the others; for he would try if it were dog or devil. After having talked in a very reprobate manner for some time, he snatched up the keys, and went out of the guard-room. In some time after his departure, a great noise was heard, but nobody had the boldness to see what occasioned it, till, the adventurer returning, they demanded the knowledge of him; but as loud and noisy as he had been at leaving them, he was now become sober and silent enough; for he was never heard to speak more; and though all the time he lived, which was three days, he was entreated by all who came near him, either to speak, or, if he could not do that, to make some signs, by which they might understand what had happened to him, yet nothing intelligible could be got from him, only that, by the distortion of his limbs and features, it might be guessed that he died in agonies more than is common in a natural death [W. S.].

[33] **amice:** a shawl-like liturgical vestment worn about the neck and shoulders. **baldric:** an ornamental belt worn diagonally over the shoulder and across the chest.

[34] **Tevoit's Flower, and Cranstoun's heir:** Margaret and Lord Cranstoun.

[35] **sackcloth:** material worn traditionally in mourning.

[36] **uneath:** scarcely.

The ashes of their fathers dead;
From many a garnish'd niche around,
Stern saints and tortur'd martyrs frown'd

— XXX —

And slow up the dim aisle afar,
With sable cowl and scapular,[37]
And snow-white stoles, in order due,
The holy Fathers, two and two,
    In long procession came;
Taper and host, and book they bare,
And holy banner, flourish'd fair
    With the Redeemer's name.
Above the prostrate pilgrim band
The mitred Abbot stretch'd his hand,
    And bless'd them as they kneel'd;
With holy cross he sign'd them all,
And pray'd they might be sage in hall,
    And fortunate in field.
Then mass was sung, and prayers were said,
And solemn requiem for the dead;
And bells toll'd out their mighty peal,
For the departed spirit's weal;
And ever in the office close
The hymn of intercession rose;
And far the echoing aisles prolong
The awful burthen of the song,—
    DIES IRAE DIES ILLA,
    SOLVET SAECLUM IN FAVILLA,—[38]
While the pealing organ rung.
    Were it meet with sacred strain
    To close my lay, so light and vain,
Thus the holy Fathers sung:

[37] **scapular:** the outer garment of a monk's habit.

[38] **Dies irae, etc:** "A famous medieval hymn on the Last Judgment, probably the composition of Thomas of Celano (in the Abruzzi), who died c. 1255. It is derived from the vulgate version of Joel 2:31 ['The sun shall be turned into darkness, and the moon into blood, before the great and the terrible day of the Lord come'], and is used by Roman Catholics in the Mass for the Dead and on All Souls' Day" (*Brewer's Dictionary of Phrase and Fable*). The Latin of the hymn translates, "Day of wrath, that terrible day, when the age crumbles to ashes . . ."

— XXXI —

HYMN FOR THE DEAD

That day of wrath, that dreadful day,
When heaven and earth shall pass away,
What power shall be the sinner's stay?
How shall he meet that dreadful day?

When, shriveling like a parched scroll,
The flaming heavens together roll;
When louder yet, and yet more dread,
Swells the high trump[39] that wakes the dead;

Oh! on that day, that wrathful day,
When man to judgment wakes from clay,
Be THOU the trembling sinner's stay,
Though heaven and earth shall pass away!

HUSH'D is the harp: the Minstrel gone.
And did he wander forth alone?
Alone, in indigence and age,
To linger out his pilgrimage?
No; close beneath proud Newark's tower,
Arose the Minstrel's lowly bower;
A simple hut; but there was seen
The little garden hedged with green,
The cheerful hearth, and lattice[40] clean.
There shelter'd wanderers, by the blaze,
Oft heard the tale of other days;
For much he lov'd to ope his door,
And give the aid he begg'd before.
So pass'd the winter's day; but still,
When summer smil'd on sweet Bow hill,
And July's eve, with balmy breath,
Wav'd the blue-bells on Newark heath;
When throstles sung in Hareheadshaw,
And corn was green on Carterhaugh,
And flourish'd broad Blackandro's oak,
The aged Harper's soul awoke!
Then would he sing achievements high,
And circumstance of chivalry,
Till the rapt traveller would stay,
Forgetful of the closing day;
And noble youths, the strain to hear,
Forsook the hunting of the deer;
And Yarrow, as he roll'd along,
Bore burden to the Minstrel's song.

[39] **trump:** trumpet.

[40] **lattice:** lattice window.

from Marmion[1]

(1808)

from CANTO V

— XI —

The Queen sits lone in Lithgow pile,
And weeps the weary day
The war against her native soil,
Her Monarch's[2] risk in battle broil: —
And in gay Holy-Rood,[3] the while,
Dame Heron rises with a smile
Upon the harp to play.
Fair was her rounded arm, as o'er
The strings her fingers flew;
And as she touch'd and tuned them all,
Ever her bosom's rise and fall
Was plainer given to view;
For, all for heat, was laid aside
Her wimple, and her hood untied.
And first she pitch'd her voice to sing,
Then glanced her dark eye on the King,
And then around the silent ring;
And laugh'd, and blush'd, and oft did say
Her pretty oath, by Yea, and Nay,
She could not, would not, durst not play!
At length, upon the harp, with glee,
Mingled with arch simplicity,
A soft, yet lively, air she rung,
While thus the wily lady sung:

— XII —

LOCHINVAR

O, young Lochinvar is come out of the west,
Through all the wide Border[4] his steed was the best;
And save his good broadsword he weapons had none,
He rode all unarm'd, and he rode all alone.
So faithful in love, and so dauntless in war,
There never was knight like the young Lochinvar.

[1] Lord Marmion, the principal character of the present romance, is entirely a fictitious personage. In earlier times, indeed, the family of Marmion, Lords of Fontenay, in Normandy, was highly distinguished. Robert de Marmion, Lord of Fontenay, a distinguished follower of the Conqueror, obtained a grant of the castle and town of Tamworth, and also of the manor of Scrivelby, in Lincolnshire. One or both of these noble possessions was held by the honorable service of being the royal champion, as the ancestors of Marmion had formerly been to the Dukes of Normandy. But after the castle and demesne of Tamworth had passed through four successive barons from Robert, the family became extinct in the person of Philip de Marmion, who died in 20th Edward I. without issue male. He was succeeded in his castle of Tamworth by Alexander de Freville, who married Mazera, his granddaughter. Baldwin de Freville, Alexander's descendant, in the reign of Richard I., by the supposed tenure of his castle of Tamworth, claimed the office of royal champion, and to do the service appertaining; namely, on the day of coronation to ride, completely armed, upon a barbed horse, into Westminster Hall, and there to challenge the combat against any who would gainsay the king's title. But this office was adjudged to Sir John Dymoke, to whom the manor of Scrivelby had descended by another of the co-heiresses of Robert de Marmion; and it remains in that family, whose representative is Hereditary Champion of England at the present day. The family and possessions of Freville have merged in the Earls of Ferrars. I have not, therefore, created a new family, but only revived the titles of an old one in an imaginary personage. [W. S.]

[2] **Queen:** Margaret, daughter of Henry VII of England. **Lithgow pile:** Linlithgow Palace, west of Edinburgh. The situation of Linlithgow Palace is eminently beautiful. It stands on a promontory of some elevation, which advances almost into the midst of the lake. The form is that of a square court, composed of buildings of four stories high, with towers at the angles. The fronts within the square, and the windows, are highly ornamented, and the size of the rooms, as well as the width and character of the staircases, are upon a magnificent scale. One banquet-room is ninety-four feet long, thirty feet wide, and thirty-three feet high, with a gallery for music. The king's wardrobe, or dressing-room, looking to the west, projects over the walls, so as to have a delicious prospect on three sides, and is one of the most enviable boudoirs we have ever seen [W. S.].

[3] **Holy-Rood:** King James's castle in Edinburgh, where Dame Heron is a guest (while the Queen is at Linlithgow). It has been already noticed that King James's acquaintance with Lady Heron of Ford did not commence until he marched into England. Our historians impute to the king's infatuated passion the delays which led to the fatal defeat of Flodden. The author of *The Genealogy of the Heron Family* endeavors, with laudable anxiety, to clear the Lady Ford from this scandal: that she came and went, however, between the armies of James and Surrey, is certain [W. S.]. The "Surrey" referred to in Scott's note is Thomas Howard I, Earl of Surrey (1443–1524), who led the English forces in their victory over the Scots at Flodden Field.

[4] **Border:** the Borderlands of Scotland and England.

He staid not for brake,[5] and he stopp'd not for stone,
He swam the Eske[6] river where ford there was none;
But ere he alighted at Netherby gate,
The bride had consented, the gallant came late:
For a laggard in love, and a dastard in war,
Was to wed the fair Ellen of brave Lochinvar.

So boldly he enter'd the Netherby Hall,
Among bride's-men, and kinsmen, and brothers, and all:
Then spoke the bride's father, his hand on his sword,
(For the poor craven bridegroom said never a word,)
'O come ye in peace here, or come ye in war,
Or to dance at our bridal, young Lord Lochinvar?'

'I long woo'd your daughter, my suit you denied:—
Love swells like the Solway,[7] but ebbs like its tide—
And now am I come, with this lost love of mine,
To lead but one measure, drink one cup of wine.
There are maidens in Scotland more lovely by far,
That would gladly be bride to the young Lochinvar.'

The bride kiss'd the goblet: the knight took it up,
He quaff'd off the wine, and he threw down the cup.
She look'd down to blush, and she look'd up to sigh,
With a smile on her lips, and a tear in her eye.
He took her soft hand, ere her mother could bar,—
'Now tread we a measure!' said young Lochinvar.

So stately his form, and so lovely her face,
That never a hall such a galliard[8] did grace;
While her mother did fret, and her father did fume,
And the bridegroom stood dangling his bonnet and plume;
And the bride-maidens whisper'd, ''Twere better by far,
To have match'd our fair cousin with young Lochinvar.'

One touch to her hand, and one word in her ear,
When they reach'd the hall-door, and the charger stood near;
So light to the croupe[9] the fair lady he swung,
So light to the saddle before her he sprung!
'She is won! we are gone, over bank, bush, and scaur;[10]
They'll have fleet steeds that follow,' quoth young Lochinvar.

There was mounting[11] 'mong Graemes of the Netherby clan;
Forsters, Fenwicks, and Musgraves, they rode and they ran:
There was racing and chasing on Cannobie Lee,
But the lost bride of Netherby ne'er did they see.
So daring in love, and so dauntless in war,
Have ye e'er heard of gallant like young Lochinvar?—

— XIII —

The Monarch o'er the siren hung
And beat the measure as she sung;
And, pressing closer, and more near,
He whisper'd praises in her ear.
In loud applause the courtiers vied;
And ladies wink'd, and spoke aside.

. . . .

[5] **brake:** rough, broken, or marshy land, thickly overgrown.

[6] **Eske river:** a river southeast of Edinburgh.

[7] **Solway:** the Solway Firth, at the southwest border of Scotland, is known for its extraordinary spring tides, depicted in Scott's *Redgauntlet*.

[8] **galliard:** a dance popular in the sixteenth century.

[9] **croupe:** the back of a horse (*lit.*, the top hindquarters).

[10] **scaur:** a rock, steep rocky peak, or bare place on a mountainside.

[11] **mounting:** mounting of forces (on horseback).

SAMUEL TAYLOR COLERIDGE

(1772–1834)

During a period of frustration over practical matters impinging on vocational aspirations, Coleridge remarked that "*all things* appear little—all the knowledge, that can be acquired, child's play—the universe itself—what but an immense heap of little things?" At the time, fall 1797, the young poet-philosopher sought the metaphysical meaning of life, but complained that he could "contemplate nothing but parts, & parts are all *little*—!" He concluded with a statement that can serve as the intellectual thrust of his life's writing on politics, religion, aesthetics, and literature: "My mind feels as if it ached to behold & know something *great*—something *one & indivisible*." Coleridge set out to discern the "one," or first principles of every field he explored.

Samuel Taylor Coleridge was the youngest of ten sons and a daughter born to an impoverished clergyman and his ambitious wife. Samuel was their most gifted child. In a series of delightful autobiographical letters, he boasts of entrancing the old women of his home village with his memory and precocious understanding at the age of eight; of pronouncing his father's description of the grandeur of the physical universe less wonderful than worlds he could imagine, his mind having been "habituated *to the Vast*" by fairy tales; of a prescience that awoke him from sleep knowing his father had died that very moment; and of a wit capable of dazzling the sophisticates of London's coffeehouses and taverns where he "drank, & talked & disputed," at the age of nine, "as if [he] had been a man." The other side of the coin was anxiety over living up to such promise. A pithy statement Coleridge scribbled in one of his notebooks states the case: "Doing nothing ends in being nothing."

Coleridge also made a mark as a *wunderkind* in Christ's Hospital, the London Grammar School for gifted children of the poor, but then his transition to university life was unsuccessful. Feeling insufficiently appreciated by the faculty at Cambridge University, miserably in debt for squandering money on dormitory furnishings and on enthusiastic carousing, and more engrossed in the revolutionary politics of the 1790s, Coleridge left without a degree. He befriended Robert Southey,* a comparably disillusioned undergraduate from Oxford. Together they planned an emigration to America, where they would found an egalitarian utopia on Pennsylvania's Susquehanna River. They betrothed a pair of attractive sisters and proselytized for émigrés to form a viable community they would call Pantisocracy.

Thinking of first principles, Coleridge defined the "leading Idea of Pantisocracy" as making "men *necessarily* virtuous by removing all Motives to Evil—all possible Temptations." The greatest motive to evil, William Godwin taught in *Enquiry Concerning Political Justice* (1793),* was personal property, so the Pantisocrats would practice communal ownership. Southey eventually lost interest in the scheme, but Coleridge kept his promise to wed Sara Fricker and to conduct on the homefront "the bloodless fight / Of Science, Freedom, and the Truth in Christ."

Coleridge wrote some fine poems inspired by love, social commitment, and contempt for intellectual adversaries, most notably "The Eolian Harp" and "Reflections on Having Left a Place of Retirement." Besides writing a number of politically inspired poems of uneven quality, Coleridge commenced an aggressive campaign to solicit subscriptions for *The*

Watchman, a short-lived miscellany of news, political analyses, reviews, and poetry that would bring his "bloodless fight" to print against aristocrats and democrats, who had lately adopted atheism as the latest religious fashion from Revolutionary France.

However, economic and vocational anxieties now came upon Coleridge with a vengeance. Sara was pregnant with their first child, Hartley (b. September 1796), and Coleridge was justifiably concerned about his paternal adequacy. Images of failure beset him: "the phantasms of a Wife broken-hearted, & a hunger-bitten baby." He took laudanum (grains of opium mixed with alcohol) for anxiety, rheumatic pains of the neck and back, and psychosomatic ailments of blisters and facial swelling. A devoted friend and businessman, Thomas Poole, helped Coleridge with economic assistance and a domestic relocation to his village of Stowey, while a second relationship with the rising poet and political radical, William Wordsworth, revived dormant aspirations. Coleridge's physical ailments and anxiety subsided.

Coleridge had never given himself wholly to becoming a poet, partly because he did not conceive of vocation narrowly, but neither could he afford to rely on poetry, for income. Producing timely essays on politics, literature, and religion for the London press both paid him well and provided satisfying intellectual engagement with the times. But for now, while ranging the Quantock Hills overlooking the Bristol Channel in the daily company of William and Dorothy Wordsworth, Coleridge concentrated fully on poetry, and the results were astonishing. Coleridge wrote several groups of immensely influential poems, inspired Wordsworth to develop works in his own inimitable vein, and developed ideas on literature as permanently significant for literary studies as his poetry. Coleridge's production between 1797 and 1798, the *annus mirabilis* of this seminal literary relationship, includes *Rime of the Ancyent Marinere,* "Kubla Khan," *Christabel* (Part One), "This Lime-Tree Bower My Prison," "Frost at Midnight," and "The Nightingale." The combined results of the poetic relationship of Coleridge and Wordsworth were published anonymously as *Lyrical Ballads, with a Few Other Poems* (1798), a volume that many literary historians consider to be the opening statement of Romanticism in England.

Due now to some unexpectedly good fortune, Coleridge's economic anxieties ended when he accepted a lifetime annuity of £150 from the brothers of the Wedgwood pottery family. The purpose of this philanthropic act was to free Coleridge of mundane concerns so he might dedicate his genius to the improvement of society. How this was to be fulfilled was up to him. Coleridge ventured the idea of studying in Germany to the Wordsworths, where William and Dorothy could learn German in preparation for doing some profitable work as translators, and where Coleridge could read philosophy and religion with the world-renowned faculty of the University of Göttingen.

Coleridge left his family for eighteen months, which could be expected to place a strain upon a marriage under the best of circumstances, but the death of his infant son, Berkeley, in his absence was fatal. His friendship with the Wordsworths also suffered because they could not afford to reside with him. Residence abroad did serve its intellectual purpose however. Coleridge renewed himself intellectually and came back enthused about preparing a biography of the German man-of-letters, Gotthold Ephraim Lessing. The point of such a project, Coleridge said, was to convey under a "better name, than my own ever will be, opinions, which I deem of the highes[t] importance." Even more importantly, Coleridge found in Lessing's varied literary life a model for his own. After a year or so of writing political essays for the London *Morning Post* and *Courier,* however, Coleridge tired of parliamentary reporting and reflecting on Napoleon and French politics. In July 1800, he relocated with his family to Keswick, Cumberland, some fifteen miles from the residence of the Wordsworths in Grasmere. He hoped to settle down to a worthy project perhaps with the benefit of another *annus mirabilis.*

In passing along his change of address to a friend, Coleridge facetiously referred to himself as a "Gentleman-poet and Philosopher in a mist." This bemused detachment toward his vocational identity introduces one of the darker periods of Coleridge's biography. Instead of moving ahead with his Life of Lessing, Coleridge sought to revive the poetic magic of 1797 to 1798. He completed a second part to *Christabel,* and superintended through the press a second, two-volume, edition of *Lyrical Ballads,* that would feature the many lyric and narrative poems Wordsworth had written in Germany and Grasmere. At first it seemed that Wordsworth would find a place for *Christabel* in the new edition, but not only did Wordsworth decide against its publication, he also moved *Ancyent Marinere* out of its place of honor in the volume and noted the poem's "great flaws." Coleridge respected Wordsworth's decision to exclude *Christabel* and remained silent on the critique, but he was demoralized. He also lacked support and comfort at home. Sara Coleridge had grown increasingly distressed with her husband's instability and compared him unfavorably with her brother-in-law, whose poetry was a commercial success and who was also a good father.

The conjugal chill that afflicted his marriage caused Coleridge to seek love outside the home. His hopeless love for Sara Hutchinson, the sister of Wordsworth's future wife, inspired his great *Dejection: An Ode,* but to little avail, for Coleridge acceded to devaluations of his poetry: "If I die," he wrote William Godwin, "and the Booksellers will give you any thing for my Life, be sure to say—'Wordsworth descended on him, like the [Know Thyself] from Heaven; by shewing to him what true Poetry was, he made him know, that he himself was no Poet'." Coleridge's self-abasement is deplorable, but his assessment is quite understandable. Though *Dejection: An Ode* (1802) follows this declaration by about a year, and though he continued to write excellent verse throughout his life, Coleridge meant to say that he could not compete favorably with Wordsworth.

Partly in search of better health, but also to escape his marriage and his declining vocational aspirations, Coleridge moved to the Mediterranean island of Malta from 1804 to 1806, where he served as secretary to the British High Commissioner, Alexander Ball, and travelled throughout Italy. He returned to England in August 1806 more deeply addicted to opium, in worse health, and without having accomplished much more than the duties of his position. He finally returned to his family in November to separate from his wife. In London from 1807 on, Coleridge lectured and published. His friendship with the Wordsworths suffered a devastating break in 1810, when Coleridge learned that they had openly criticized him for complicity in his own demise. Not yet medically understood, drug addiction seemed a matter of will rather than physical dependency. Coleridge's "Pains of Sleep," written in 1802, but published in the extraordinary volume of 1816, *Christabel; Kubla Khan, A Vision; The Pains of Sleep* manages to make art out of his misery and painful self-disclosure: "To be beloved is all I need, / And whom I love, I love indeed."

Over the next decade, Coleridge lectured on modern literature, Shakespeare, Milton, education, and philosophy; he continued with journalism in the London *Courier* and a second, more ambitious journalistic venture, called *The Friend;* he provided welcomed guidance to the learned or educated classes on their cultural and political responsibilities to British society; and finally he provided a respected critique of the parliamentary monarchy of Great Britain in *On the Constitution of Church and State.* Most importantly, he published in 1817 *Biographia Literaria: or Biographical Sketches of My Literary Life and Opinions,* a two-volume narrative of his life, times, ideas on religion, philosophy, politics, and literature, with special emphasis on applying "philosophical principles, to poetry and criticism." *Biographia* includes brilliant speculations on poetic genius, some unfortunate and unnecessary passages of plagiarism from Schelling and other philosophers Coleridge had studied in Germany, a cryptic but inspiring definition of primary and secondary imagination also derivative from German aesthetics, and some delightful biographical narration of his early experience as poet and political activist. Above all, *Biographia* contains the greatest practical criticism of poetry in English in its florid passages on Shakespeare and in its fastidious analysis of the defects and strengths of Wordsworth's verse.

In 1816, a Dr. James Gillman invited Coleridge to reside permanently with him in his Highgate apartment, where he might assist in controlling Coleridge's addiction. Over an eighteen-year period, Coleridge's residence at Highgate became a mecca for intellectuals from home and abroad. His inspired conversation helped to attract visitors, prevent loneliness, and give some vent to an inexhaustible supply of intellectual energy that never ceased to flow.

Letter to Robert Southey, 18 September 1794

Sept 18th 10 o clock Thursday Morning

Well, my dear Southey! I am at last arrived at Jesus [College]. My God! how tumultuous are the movements of my Heart—Since I quitted this room what and how important Events have been evolved! America! Southey! Miss Fricker!—Yes—Southey—you are right—Even Love is the creature of strong Motive—I certainly love her. I think of her incessantly & with unspeakable tenderness—with that inward melting away of Soul that symptomatizes it.

Pantisocracy[1]—O I shall have such a scheme of it! My head, my heart are all alive—I have drawn up my arguments in battle array—they shall have the *Tactician* Excellence of the Mathematician with the Enthusiasm of the Poet—The Head shall be the Mass—the Heart the fiery Spirit, that fills, informs, and agitates the whole—Harwood!—Pish! I say nothing of him—

SHAD[2] GOES WITH US. HE IS MY BROTHER! I am longing to be with you—Make Edith my Sister—Surely, Southey! we shall be frendotatoi meta frendous. Most friendly where all are friends. She must therefore be more emphatically my Sister.

Brookes & Berdmore, as I suspected, have spread my Opinions in mangled forms at Cambridge—Caldwell the most excellent, the most pantisocratic of Aristocrats, has been laughing at me—Up I arose terrible in Reasoning—he fled from me—because 'he could not answer for his own Sanity sitting so near a madman of Genius!' He told me, that the Strength of my Imagination had intoxicated my Reason—and that the acuteness of my Reason had given a directing Influence to my Imagination.—Four months ago the Remark would not have been more elegant than Just—. Now it is Nothing. . . .

. . . I am almost ashamed to write the following—it is so inferior—Ashamed! No—Southey—God knows my heart—I am *delighted* to feel you superior to me in Genius as in Virtue.

[1] See introduction for background on the pantisocratic scheme.

[2] **Shad:** the servant of Southey's aunt.

No more my Visionary Soul shall dwell
On Joys, that were! No more endure to weigh
The Shame and Anguish of the evil Day,
Wisely forgetful! O'er the Ocean swell
Sublime of Hope I seek the cottag'd Dell,
Where Virtue calm with careless step may stray,
And dancing to the moonlight Roundelay
The Wizard Passions weave an holy Spell.
Eyes that have ach'd with Sorrow! ye shall weep
Tears of doubt-mingled Joy, like theirs who start
From Precipices of distemper'd Sleep,
On which the fierce-eyed Fiends their Revels k[eep,]
And see the rising Sun, & feel it dart
New Rays of Pleasance trembling to the Heart.[3]

from Conciones ad Populum; or Addresses to the People[1]

[February 1795]

— *from* INTRODUCTORY ADDRESS —

When the Wind is fair and the Planks of the Vessel sound, we may safely trust every thing to the management of professional Mariners: in a Tempest and on board a crazy Bark, all must contribute their Quota of Exertion. The Stripling is not exempted from it by his Youth, nor the Passenger by his Inexperience. Even so, in the present agitations of the public mind, every one ought to consider his intellectual faculties as in a state of immediate requisition. All may benefit Society in some degree. The exigences of the Times do not permit us to stay for the maturest years, lest the opportunity be lost, while we are waiting for an increase of power.

Companies resembling the present will, from a variety of circumstances, consist *chiefly* of the zealous Advocates for Freedom. It will therefore be our endeavour, not so much to excite the torpid, as to regulate the feelings of the ardent; and above all, to evince the necessity of *bottoming* on fixed Principles, that so we may not be the unstable Patriots of Passion or Accident, nor hurried away by names of which we have not sifted the meaning, and by tenets of which we have not examined the consequences. The Times are trying; and in order to be prepared against their difficulties, we should have acquired a prompt facility of adverting in all our doubts to some grand and comprehensive Truth. In a deep and strong Soil must that Tree fix its Roots, the height of which, is to "reach to Heaven, and the Sight of it to the ends of all the Earth."[2]

The Example of France is indeed a "Warning to Britain." A Nation wading to their Rights through Blood, and marking the track of Freedom by Devastation! Yet let us not embattle our Feelings against our Reason. Let us not indulge our malignant Passions under the mask of Humanity. Instead of railing with infuriate declamation against these excesses, we shall be more profitably employed in developing the sources of them. French Freedom is the Beacon, which while it guides to Equality, should shew us the Dangers that throng the road.

The Annals of the French Revolution have recorded in Letters of Blood, that the Knowledge of the Few cannot counteract the Ignorance of the Many; that the Light of Philosophy, when it is confined to a small Minority, points out the Possessors as the Victims, rather than the Illuminators, of the Multitude. The Patriots of France either hastened into the dangerous and gigantic Error of making certain Evil the means of contingent Good, or were sacrificed by the Mob, with whose prejudices and ferocity their unbending Virtue forbade them to assimilate. Like Sampson, the People were strong—like Sampson, the People were blind. Those two massy Pillars of Oppression's Temple, the Monarchy and Aristocracy,

With horrible Convulsion to and fro
They tugg'd, they shook—till down they came and drew
The whole Roof after them with burst of Thunder
Upon the heads of all who sat beneath,
Lords, Ladies, Captains, Counsellors, and Priests,
Their choice Nobility!

MILTON SAM AGON[3]

[3] This poem, later titled "Pantisocracy," was first published in *Life and Correspondence of Robert Southey* (1849).

[1] Includes the revised text of two or three lectures delivered at Bristol in 1795. The Introductory Address was delivered and earlier published as "A Moral and Political Lecture" (1795). It would be helpful to review the COMPREHENSIVE CHRONOLOGY for the political and martial events preceding this essay.

[2] **"reach to Heaven . . . Earth"**: Daniel 4.11: "The tree grew, and was strong, and the height thereof reached unto heaven, and the sight thereof to the end of all the earth."

[3] *Samson Agonistes*, ll. 1649–1654, with minor variations.

There was not a Tyrant in Europe, who did not tremble on his Throne. Freedom herself heard the Crash aghast!—

The Girondists, who were the first republicans in power, were men of enlarged views and great literary attainments; but they seem to have been deficient in that vigour and daring activity, which circumstances made necessary. Men of genius are rarely either prompt in action or consistent in general conduct: their early habits have been those of contemplative indolence; and the day-dreams, with which they have been accustomed to amuse their solitude, adapt them for splendid speculation, not temperate and practicable counsels. Brissot,[4] the leader of the Gironde party, is entitled to the character of a virtuous man, and an eloquent speaker; but he was rather a sublime visionary, than a quick-eyed politician; and his excellences equally with his faults rendered him unfit for the helm, in the stormy hour of Revolution. Robespierre,[5] who displaced him, possessed a glowing ardor that still remembered the *end*, and a cool ferocity that never either overlooked, or scrupled, the *means*. What that *end* was, is not known: that it was a wicked one, has by no means been proved. I rather think, that the distant prospect, to which he was travelling, appeared to him grand and beautiful; but that he fixed his eye on it with such intense eagerness as to neglect the foulness of the road. If however his first intentions were pure, his subsequent enormities yield us a melancholy proof, that it is not the character of the possessor which directs the power, but the power which shapes and depraves the character of the possessor. In Robespierre, its influence was assisted by the properties of his disposition.—Enthusiasm, even in the gentlest temper, will frequently generate sensations of an unkindly order. If we clearly perceive any one thing to be of vast and infinite importance to ourselves and all mankind, our first feelings impel us to turn with angry contempt from those, who doubt and oppose it. The ardor of undisciplined benevolence seduces us into malignity: and whenever our hearts are warm, and our objects great and excellent, intolerance is the sin that does most easily beset us. But this enthusiasm in Robespierre was blended with gloom, and suspiciousness, and inordinate vanity. His dark imagination was still brooding over supposed plots against freedom—to prevent tyranny he became a Tyrant—and having realized the evils which he suspected, a wild and dreadful Tyrant.—Those loud-tongued adulators, the mob, overpowered the lone-whispered denunciations of conscience—he despotized in all the pomp of Patriotism, and masqueraded on the bloody stage of Revolution, a Caligula[6] with the cap of Liberty on his head. . . .

Revolutions are sudden to the unthinking only. Political Disturbances happen not without their warning Harbingers. Strange Rumblings and confused Noises still precede these earthquakes and hurricanes of the moral World. The process of Revolution in France has been dreadful, and should incite us to examine with an anxious eye the motives and manners of those, whose conduct and opinions seem calculated to forward a similar event in our own country. The oppositionists to "things as they are,"[7] are divided into many and different classes. To delineate them with an unflattering accuracy may be a delicate, but it is a necessary Task, in order that we may enlighten, or at least beware of, the misguided Men who have enlisted under the banners of Liberty, from no principles or with bad ones: whether they be those, who

> admire they know not what,
> And know not whom, but as one leads the other:

or whether those,

> Whose end is private Hate, not help to Freedom,
> Adverse and turbulent when she would lead
> To Virtue.[8]

The majority of Democrats[9] appear to me to have attained that portion of knowledge in politics, which Infidels possess in religion. I would by no means be supposed

[4] **Brissot**: Jean-Pierre Brissot (1754–1793), executed by guillotine October 1793.

[5] **Robespierre**: Maximilien de Robespierre (1758–1794), the most powerful member of the Committee of Public Safety and strategist of the Reign of Terror, who was overthrown and guillotined on 27 July 1794, by members of the Convention fearing for their own safety.

[6] **Caligula**: emperor of Rome (37–42), renowned for brutality.

[7] **"things as they are"**: title of a novel by William Godwin,* *Things as they are: or the Adventures of Caleb Williams* (1794), designed to show "the tyranny and perfidiousness exercised by the powerful members of the community against those who are less privileged. . . ."

[8] Cf. Milton's *Samson Agonistes*.

[9] **Democrats**: political radicals, such as Thomas Paine* and his disciples, who sympathized with revolution to achieve the Rights of Man, and who wanted peace with France and political recognition of the French Republic. They went with their hair unpowdered to distinguish themselves from Aristocrats.

to imply, that the objections of both are equally unfounded, but that they both attribute to the system which they reject, all the evils existing under it; and that both contemplating truth and justice "in the nakedness of abstraction,"[10] condemn constitutions and dispensations without having sufficiently examined the natures, circumstances, and capacities of their recipients.

The first Class among the professed Friends of Liberty is composed of Men, who unaccustomed to the labour of thorough investigation, and not particularly oppressed by the Burthen of State, are yet impelled by their feelings to disapprove of its grosser depravities, and prepared to give an indolent Vote in favour of Reform. Their sensibilities unbraced by the co-operation of fixed Principles, they offer no sacrifices to the divinity of active Virtue. Their political Opinions depend with weathercock uncertainty on the winds of rumour, that blow from France. On the report of French victories they blaze into Republicanism, at a tale of French excesses they darken into Aristocrats; and seek for shelter among those despicable adherents to fraud and tyranny, who ironically style themselves Constitutionalists.— These *dough-baked*[11] *Patriots* are not however useless. This oscillation of political opinion will retard the day of Revolution, and it will operate as a preventive to its excesses. Indecisiveness of character, though the effect of timidity, is almost always associated with benevolence.

Wilder features characterize the second class. Sufficiently possessed of natural sense to despise the Priest, and of natural feeling to hate the Oppressor, they listen only to the inflammatory harangues of some mad-headed Enthusiast, and imbibe from them Poison, not Food; Rage, not Liberty. Unillumined by Philosophy, and stimulated to a lust of revenge by aggravated wrongs, they would make the Altar of Freedom stream with blood, while the grass grew in the desolated halls of Justice. These men are the rude materials from which a detestable Minister manufactures conspiracies. Among these men he sends a brood of sly political monsters, in the character of sanguinary Demagogues, and like Satan of old, "the Tempter ere the Accuser,"[12] ensnares a few into Treason, that he may alarm the whole into Slavery. He, who has dark purposes to serve, must use dark means—light would discover, reason would expose him: he must endeavour to shut out both—or if this prove impracticable, make them appear frightful by giving them frightful names: for farther than Names the Vulgar enquire not. Religion and Reason are but poor substitutes for "Church and Constitution;" and the sable-vested Instigators of the Birmingham riots[13] well knew, that a Syllogism could not disarm a drunken Incendiary of his Firebrand, or a Demonstration *helmet* a Philosopher's head against a Brickbat. But in the principles, which this Apostate has, by his emissaries, sown among a few blind zealots for Freedom, he has digged a pit into which he himself may perhaps be doomed to fall. We contemplate those principles with horror. Yet they possess a kind of wild Justice well calculated to spread them among the grossly ignorant. To unenlightened minds, there are terrible charms in the idea of Retribution, however savagely it be inculcated. The Groans of the Oppressors make fearful yet pleasant music to the ear of him, whose mind is darkness, and into whose soul the iron has entered. . . .

There are a third class among the friends of Freedom, who possess not the wavering character of the first description, nor the ferocity last delineated. They pursue the interests of Freedom steadily, but with narrow and self-centering views: they anticipate with exultation the abolition of privileged orders, and of Acts that persecute by exclusion from the right of citizenship. They are prepared to join in digging up the rubbish of mouldering Establishments, and stripping off the tawdry pageantry of Governments. Whatever is above them they are most willing to drag down; but every proposed alteration, that would elevate the ranks of our poorer brethren, they regard with suspicious jealousy, as the dreams of the visionary; as if there were any thing in the superiority of Lord to Gentleman, so mortifying in the barrier, so fatal to happiness in the consequences, as the more real distinction of master and servant, of rich man and of poor. Wherein am I made worse by my ennobled neighbour? Do the childish titles of Aristocracy detract from my domestic comforts, or prevent my intellectual acquisitions? But those institutions of

[10] **"nakedness of abstraction"**: from Burke's *Reflections on the Revolution in France,** "in all the nakedness and solitude of metaphysical abstraction."

[11] **dough-baked**: "deficient, esp. in intellect and sense" (*OED*).

[12] Cf. Milton, *Paradise Lost,* IV.9–10: "Satan, now first inflamed with rage, came down; / The tempter ere th'accuser of mankind."

[13] **Birmingham riots**: riots against religious dissenters and political radicals encouraged by the authorities of "Church and King." In July 1791, a Birmingham mob had burned down the laboratory and home of the eminent scientist and Unitarian minister, Joseph Priestley.

Society which should condemn me to the necessity of twelve hours daily toil, would make my *soul* a slave, and sink the *rational* being in the mere animal. It is a mockery of our fellow creatures' wrongs to call them equal in rights, when by the bitter compulsion of their wants we make them inferior to us in all that can soften the heart, or dignify the understanding. Let us not say that this is the work of time—that it is impracticable at present, unless we each in our individual capacities do strenuously and perseveringly endeavour to diffuse among our domestics those comforts and that illumination which far beyond all political ordinances are the true equalizers of men.

We turn with pleasure to the contemplation of that small but glorious band, whom we may truly distinguish by the name of thinking and disinterested Patriots. These are the men who have encouraged the sympathetic passions till they have become irresistible habits, and made their duty a necessary part of their self-interest, by the long-continued cultivation of that moral taste which derives our most exquisite pleasures from the contemplation of possible perfection, and proportionate pain from the perception of existing *depravation.* Accustomed to regard all the affairs of man as a process, they never hurry and they never pause. Theirs is not that twilight of political knowledge which gives us just light enough to place one foot before the other; as they advance the scene still opens upon them, and they press right onward with a vast and various landscape of existence around them. Calmness and energy mark all their actions. Convinced that vice originates not in the man, but in the surrounding circumstances; not in the heart, but in the understanding; he is hopeless concerning no one—to correct a vice or generate a virtuous conduct he pollutes not his hands with the scourge of coercion; but by endeavouring to alter the circumstances would remove, or by strengthening the intellect, disarms, the temptation. The unhappy children of vice and folly, whose tempers are adverse to their own happiness as well as to the happiness of others, will at times awaken a natural pang; but he looks forward with gladdened heart to that glorious period when Justice shall have established the universal fraternity of Love. These soul-ennobling views bestow the virtues which they anticipate. He whose mind is habitually impress with them soars above the present state of humanity, and may be justly said to dwell in the presence of the Most High. . . .

That general Illumination should precede Revolution, is a truth as obvious, as that the Vessel should be cleansed before we fill it with a pure Liquor. But the mode of diffusing it is not discoverable with equal facility. We certainly should never attempt to make Proselytes by appeals to the *selfish feelings*—and consequently, should plead *for* the Oppressed, not *to* them. The Author of an essay on political Justice considers private Societies as the sphere of real utility—that (each one illuminating those immediately beneath him,) Truth by a gradual descent may at last reach the lowest order. But this is rather plausible than just or practicable. Society as at present constituted does not resemble a chain that ascends in a continuity of Links.—There are three ranks possessing an intercourse with each other: these are well comprized in the superscription of a Perfumer's advertisement, which I lately saw—"the Nobility, Gentry, and People of Dress." But alas! between the Parlour and the Kitchen, the Tap and the Coffee-Room—there is a gulph that may not be passed. He would appear to me to have adopted the best as well as the most benevolent mode of diffusing Truth, who uniting the zeal of the Methodist with the views of the Philosopher, should be *personally* among the Poor, and teach them their *Duties* in order that he may render them susceptible of their *Rights.*

Yet by what means can the lower Classes be made to learn their Duties, and urged to practise them? The human Race may perhaps possess the capability of all excellence; and Truth, I doubt not, is omnipotent to a mind already disciplined for its reception; but assuredly the over-worked Labourer, skulking into an Ale-house, is not likely to exemplify the one, or prove the other. In that barbarous tumult of inimical Interests, which the present state of Society exhibits, *Religion* appears to offer the only means universally *efficient.* The perfectness of future Men is indeed a benevolent tenet, and may operate on a few Visionaries, whose studious habits supply them with employment, and seclude them from temptation. But a distant prospect, which we are never to reach, will seldom quicken our footsteps, however lovely it may appear; and a Blessing, which not ourselves but *posterity* are destined to enjoy, will scarcely influence the actions of *any*—still less of the ignorant, the prejudiced, and the selfish.

"Go, preach the GOSPEL to the Poor."[14] By its Simplicity it will meet their comprehension, by its Benevolence soften their affections, by its Precepts it will direct their conduct, by the vastness of its Motives ensure their

[14] A conflation of Mark 16:15 and esp. Luke 4:18: Jesus opened the scroll of Isaiah and read: "The Spirit of the Lord is upon me, because he hath anointed me to preach the gospel to the poor."

obedience. The situation of the Poor is perilous: they are indeed both

from within and from without
Unarm'd to all Temptations.[15]

Prudential reasonings will in general be powerless with them. For the incitements of this world are weak in proportion as we are wretched—

The World is not *my* Friend, nor the World's Law.
The World has got no Law to make *me* rich.[16]

They too, who live *from Hand to Mouth,* will most frequently become improvident. Possessing no *stock* of happiness they eagerly seize the gratifications of the moment, and snatch the froth from the wave as it passes by them. Nor is the desolate state of their families a restraining motive, unsoftened as they are by education, and benumbed into selfishness by the torpedo touch of extreme Want. Domestic affections depend on association. We love an object if, as often as we see or recollect it, an agreeable sensation arises in our minds. But alas! how should *he* glow with the charities of Father and Husband, who gaining scarcely more, than his own necessities demand, must have been accustomed to regard his wife and children, not as the Soothers of finished labour, but as Rivals for the insufficient meal! In a man so circumstanced the Tyranny of the *Present* can be overpowered only by the tenfold mightiness of the *Future.* Religion will cheer his gloom with her promises, and by habituating his mind to anticipate an infinitely great Revolution hereafter, may prepare it even for the sudden reception of a less degree of amelioration in this World.

But if we hope to instruct others, we should familiarize our own minds to some fixed and determinate principles of action. The World is a vast labyrinth, in which almost every one is running a different way, and almost every one manifesting hatred to those who do not run the same way. A few indeed stand motionless, and not seeking to lead themselves or others out of the maze laugh at the failures of their brethren. Yet with little reason: for more grossly than the most bewildered wanderer does *he* err, who never aims to go right. It is more honourable to the Head, as well as to the heart, to be misled by our eagerness in the pursuit of Truth, than to be safe from blundering by contempt of it. The happiness of Mankind is the *end* of Virtue, and Truth is the Knowledge of the *means;* which he will never seriously attempt to discover, who has not habitually interested himself in the welfare of others. The searcher after Truth must love and be beloved; for general Benevolence is a necessary motive to constancy of pursuit; and this general Benevolence is begotten and rendered permanent by social and domestic affections. Let us beware of that proud Philosophy, which affects to inculcate Philanthropy while it denounces every home-born feeling, by which it is produced and nurtured. The paternal and filial duties discipline the Heart and prepare it for the love of all Mankind. The intensity of private attachments encourages, not prevents, universal Benevolence. The nearer we approach to the Sun, the more intense his heat: yet what corner of the system does he not cheer and vivify? . . .

A system of fundamental Reform will scarcely be effected by massacres mechanized into Revolution. Yet rejected intreaty leads in its consequences to fierce coercion. And much as we deprecate the event, we have reason to conjecture that throughout all Europe it may not be far distant. The folly of the rulers of mankind grows daily more wild and ruinous: Oppression is grievous—the oppressed feel and are restless. Such things *may* happen. We cannot therefore inculcate on the minds of each other too often or with too great earnestness the necessity of cultivating benevolent affections. We should be cautious how we indulge the feelings even of virtuous indignation. Indignation is the handsome brother of Anger and Hatred. The Temple of Despotism, like that of Tescalipoca, the Mexican Deity, is built of human skulls, and cemented with human blood;—let us beware that we be not transported into revenge while we are levelling the loathsome Pile; lest when we erect the edifice of Freedom we but vary the stile of Architecture, not change the materials. Let us not wantonly offend even the prejudices of our weaker brethren, nor by ill-timed and vehement declarations of opinion excite in them malignant feelings towards us. The energies of mind are wasted in these intemperate effusions. Those materials of projectile force, which now carelessly scattered explode with an offensive and useless noise, directed by wisdom and union might heave Rocks from their base,—or perhaps (dismissing the metaphor) might produce the desired effect without the convulsion.

For this "subdued sobriety" of temper a practical faith in the doctrine of philosophical necessity seems the only preparative. That vice is the effect of error and the

[15] Cf. Milton, *Paradise Lost,* IV.63–65: "other Powers as great / Fell not, but stand unshaken, from within / Or from without, to all temptations armed."

[16] *Romeo and Juliet,* V. i.72–73: "The world is not thy friend, nor the world's law, / The world affords no law to make thee rich."

offspring of surrounding circumstances, the object therefore of condolence not of anger, is a proposition easily understood, and as easily demonstrated. But to make it spread from the understanding to the affections, to call it into action, not only in the great exertions of Patriotism, but in the daily and hourly occurrences of social life, requires the most watchful attentions of the most energetic mind. It is not enough that we have once swallowed these Truths—we must feed on them, as insects on a leaf, till the whole heart be coloured by their qualities, and shew its food in every the minutest fibre.

Finally, in the Words of an Apostle,

Watch ye! Stand fast in the principles of which ye have been convinced! Quit yourselves like Men! Be strong! Yet let all things be done in the spirit of Love.[17]

from Bristol Lectures

—*from* LECTURE SIX[1]—

(June 1796)

. . . Drunkenness, Prostitution, Rapine, Beggary and Diseases—Can we walk the Streets of a City without observing them in all their most loathsome forms? Add to these Irreligion. The smoakes that rise from our crowded Towns hide from us the face of Heaven. In the country, the Love and Power of the great Invisible are everywhere perspicuous, and by degrees we become partakers of that which we are accustomed to contemplate. The Beautiful and the Good are miniatured on the Heart of the Contemplator as the surrounding Landscape on a Convex Mirror. But in Cities God is everywhere removed from our Sight and Man obtruded upon us—not Man, the work of God, but the debased offspring of Luxury and Want. At every step some Instance of bloated Depravity, or squallid wretchedness meets us till at last we have doubts of providential Benevolence—and selfish Man accuses God for Miseries, which, if he had been employing himself as God and Nature ordained, he would not have been present to behold.

I address myself to those who acknowledge the Scriptures as their rule of Life and depend for eternal happiness on their obedience to them. In these Scriptures Christians are ordered to keep themselves unspotted from the World. Now can a conscientious man make himself the Instrument of upholding and increasing those Enormities, which make the World a contradistinction to the kingdom of God? If he be a Commercial Man, can he be always sincere? Can he always prevent a spirit of selfishness? and is [he] not guilty of tempting God by placing himself in a situation so full of danger? Let him look around his shop? Does nothing in it come from the desolate plains of Indostan? From what motives did Lord Clive murder his million and justify it to all but his own conscience? From what motives did the late rice-contracting Governor famish a million and gain from the Company the Title of Saviour of India?[2] Was it not that wicked as they were they increased and preserved the commercial Intercourse? It has been openly asserted that our commercial intercourse with the East Indies has been the occasion of the loss of eight million Lives—in return for which most foul and heart-inslaving Guilt we receive gold, diamonds, silks, muslins & callicoes for fine Ladies and Prostitutes, Tea to make a pernicious Beverage, Porcelain to drink it from, and salt-petre for the making of gunpowder with which we may murder the poor Inhabitants who supply all these things. Not one thing necessary or even useful do we receive in return for the horrible guilt in which we have involved ourselves. Africa and the West India Islands, on these fearful subjects I shall observe nothing at present. I hang my head when I think of them, they leave an indelible stain on our national character—all the waters of the Ocean cannot purify, all the perfumes of Araby cannot sweeten it. But the continuance of these abominations depends on the will of those who consume

[17] Cf. St. Paul, 1 Corinthians 16:13–14: "Watch ye, stand fast in the faith, quit you like men, be strong. / Let all your things be done with charity."

[1] The sixth in a series of lectures on politics and religion, delivered to raise money for the Pantisocratic scheme. Lecture Six was delivered either Tuesday, 9 June or Friday, 12 June 1796. The Prospectus to the series, "Six Lectures on Revealed Religion its' Corruptions and Political Views," states that the lectures are intended for "two Classes of Men—Christians and Infidels / to the former, that they may be able to give a reason for the hope that it [sic] is in them—to the latter that they may not determine against Christianity from arguments applicable to its' Corruptions only." The topic of the sixth lecture is "the grand political Views of Christianity—that far beyond all other Religions, and even sects of Philosophy, it is the Friend of Civil Freedom—The probable State of Society & Government if all men were Christians."

[2] **Saviour of India**: Warren Hastings, governor of Bengal, India. (See SOCIETY AND POLITICAL ECONOMY.)

the produce of the Trade.[3] And is not he more particularly the Consumer who administers to others the means of providing themselves with these pestilent Luxuries? And can a Christian justify himself? God is not to be mocked! Family connections, and the necessity of a maintenance are no excuses! "He that loveth Father or Mother more than me is not worthy of me, and he that loveth Son or Daughter more than me is not worthy of me—and taketh not his Cross, is not worthy of me."[4] I appeal to common sense whether or no every motive by which these men excuse themselves might not have been urged by the Apostles—and with much greater reason!

I have asserted that Jesus Christ forbids to his disciples all property—and teaches us that accumulation was incompatible with their Salvation! An assertion so novel may require proof [Apologize for the (?)] In Matthew VI. 25–33 the most plausible defences of accumulation are declared to be of no avail. "Therefore take no thought what shall we eat and what shall we drink? or Wherewithal shall we be clothed? But seek ye first the Kingdom of God and his Righteousness—and all these things shall be added unto you. Take therefore no thought for the morrow."! Now this positive Precept of our Saviour either means that we are to be idle and expect miraculous subsistence, or it means, that we are to gain our daily bread by our daily Labor and not accumulate from any prudential Fears of Tomorrow. But it does not mean the former—for St. Paul II Thess. III. 11–12. forbids Christians to depend upon any person for their livelihood. ["]Them that work not at all we command and exhort by the Lord Jesus Christ that with quietness they work and eat their own Bread.["] Therefore it means the latter. In Matt: XIX 16–24, our saviour declares that all other virtues however rigidly practised, are rendered vain by accumulation—for the young man said unto him "All the commandments I have kept from my Youth upward—what lack I yet?" Jesus said unto him—"If thou wilt be perfect go and sell that thou hast and distribute it among them who have none—and follow me." But when the young man heard that saying, he went away sorrowful: for he had great possessions. Then said Jesus unto his Disciples. "It is easier for a Camel to go through the Eye of a Needle, than for a rich man to enter the kingdom of God."

Now it is absurd to suppose that Jesus meant any particular sum by Riches. Wealth is a comparative Word. The day labourer thinks the man with 100£ a year a rich man; but if Property were an allowable Institution, so severe a sentence could not have been passed on rich men—since it would include all but the very poor. If great Wealth be meant, why are the very rich thus dangerously situated above all others? They have temptations to Vice arising from superfluities, but have not the Poor as great arising from Want?[5] But if we understand by Riches comparative Wealth the meaning is clear and conveys a sublime Truth. That as long as anyone possesses more than another, Luxury, Envy, Rapine, Government & Priesthood will be the necessary consequence, and prevent the Kingdom of God—that is the progressiveness of the moral World. Our Saviour by no means authorizes an Equalization of Property, which in the first place is impracticable for how are we to equalize? Measuring will not do it—one soil is better than another—and where is the scale to adjust the differences, and balance Quality with Quantity? and secondly, if it were practicable, it would answer no end, for this Equalisation could not continue for a year, and while it continued, it would only narrow the Theatre, and exclude the actors. While I possess anything exclusively mine, the selfish Passions will have full play, and our Hearts will never learn that great Truth that the good of the Whole etc. We find in the twelfth of Luke that our Lord refused to authorize a division of Inheritance, and in the subsequent verses forbids all property, and orders men to depend for their subsistence upon their Labor. And in Luke the 20th 21.22 they asked Jesus—"Is it lawful for us to give Tribute unto Caesar or no? And he said unto them—Shew me a penny whose Image and Superscription hath it? They answered and said Caesar's And he said unto them—render unto Caesar the Things that are Caesars, and unto God the Things that are God's." A wise Sentence. That we use money is a proof that we possess individual property, and Commerce and Manufactures, and while these evils continue, your own vices will make a government necessary, and it is fit that you maintain that government. Emperor and King are but the lord lieutenants of conquered Souls—secondaries and vicegerents who govern not with their own right but with power delegated to them by our Avarice and appetites! Let us exert over our own hearts a virtuous despotism, and lead our own Passions in triumph, and then we shall want neither Monarch nor General. If we would have no Nero without,

[3] See SLAVERY, THE SLAVE TRADE, AND ABOLITION. Coleridge lectured on the slave trade 16 June 1795.

[4] Cf. Matthew 10: 37–38. "He that loveth father or mother more than me is not worthy of me: and he that loveth son or daughter more than me is not worthy of me. / And he that taketh not his cross, and followeth after me is not worthy of me."

[5] See also Godwin* on Property.

we must place a Caesar within us, and that Caesar must be Religion! That I have given no fanciful Interpretation of these passages is evident from hence—that the Apostles and immediate Converts of Christ understood them in the same manner. In Acts II. 44. 45. we read "And all that believed were together, & had all things in common—and sold their possessions & goods and parted them to all men, as every man had need." But this part of the Christian Doctrine, which is indeed almost the whole of it, soon was corrupted, and that it would do so was foretold. Luke 13 v. 18.21. contains two prophetic similitudes. "It is like a grain of mustard seed and it grew and waxed a great Tree,["] and ["]it is like a very little leaven which a woman took and hid in three measures of Meal till the whole was leavened!" It is natural for seeds which at length rise to great Trees to lie long in the ground before their vegetation is perceptible and to increase very slowly for a considerable Length of Time—a small Quantity of Leaven also enclosed within a great bulk of meal must of necessity operate very slowly and a cold unfavourable season would restrain the vegetative [. . .]

from POEMS[1]

(1796)

Effusion XXXV[2]

(1796; comp. 1795)

Composed August 20th, 1795, at Clevedon, Somersetshire

My pensive Sara[3]! thy soft cheek reclin'd
Thus on mine arm, most soothing sweet it is
To sit beside our cot, our cot[4] o'er grown
With white-flower'd Jasmin, and the broad-leav'd Myrtle,
(Meet emblems they of Innocence and Love!)
And watch the clouds, that late were rich with light,
Slow-sad'ning round, and mark the star of eve
Serenely brilliant (such should Wisdom be)
Shine opposite! How exquisite the scents
Snatch'd from yon bean-field! and the world *so* hush'd!
The stilly murmur of the distant Sea
Tells us of Silence. And that simplest Lute[5]
Plac'd length-ways in the clasping casement, hark!
How by the desultory breeze caress'd,
Like some coy Maid half-yielding to her Lover,
It pours such sweet upbraidings, as must needs
Tempt to repeat the wrong! And now its strings
Boldlier swept, the long sequacious notes
Over delicious surges sink and rise,
Such a soft floating witchery of sound
As twilight Elfins make, when they at eve
Voyage on gentle gales from Faery Land,
Where *Melodies* round honey-dropping flowers
Footless and wild, like birds of Paradise,
Nor pause nor perch, hov'ring on untam'd wing.

And thus, my Love! as on the midway slope
Of yonder hill I stretch my limbs at noon
Whilst thro' my half-clos'd eyelids I behold
The sunbeams dance, like diamonds, on the main,
And tranquil muse upon tranquillity;
Full many a thought uncall'd and undetain'd,
And many idle flitting phantasies,
Traverse my indolent and passive brain
As wild and various, as the random gales
That swell or flutter on this subject Lute!
And what if all of animated nature
Be but organic Harps diversly fram'd,
That tremble into thought, as o'er them sweeps,
Plastic and vast, one intellectual Breeze,
At once the Soul of each, and God of all?
But thy more serious eye a mild reproof
Darts, O beloved Woman! nor such thoughts
Dim and unhallow'd dost thou not reject,
And biddest me walk humbly with my God.

[1] Includes four poems by Charles Lamb and forty-seven by Coleridge, mostly "Effusions," "in defiance of Churchill's line 'Effusion on effusion *pour* away.'" Coleridge indirectly defines effusions as short poems that "do not possess that *oneness* of thought which I deem indispensible in a Sonnet." The volume also includes Coleridge's long religious poem *Religious Musings*.

[2] Later entitled "The Aeolian Harp." See *Poetical Works* (1828)* for the final text.

[3] **Sara:** Sara Fricker, whom Coleridge engaged to marry in August, the month of the poem's composition. They wed 4 October 1795.

[4] **Cot:** cottage.

[5] **that simplest Lute:** an aeolian harp, a "stringed instrument adapted to produce musical sounds on exposure to a current of air" (*OED*).

Meek Daughter in the Family of Christ,
Well hast thou said and holily disprais'd
These shapings of the unregenerate mind,
Bubbles that glitter as they rise and break
On vain Philosophy's aye-babbling spring.
For never guiltless may I speak of Him,
Th' INCOMPREHENSIBLE! save when with awe
I praise him, and with Faith that inly *feels*,
Who with his saving mercies healed me,
A sinful and most miserable man
Wilder'd and dark, and gave me to possess
PEACE, and this COT, and THEE, heart-honor'd Maid!

from THE WATCHMAN[1]

from Remonstrance to the French Legislators[2]

(27 April 1796)

Guardians of the LIBERTY of Europe! the Individual, who has devoted his Joys and his Sorrows to the Interests of the whole, partakes of the importance of the object which he has accustomed himself to contemplate. He addresses you therefore with that dignity with which his subject invests him: for he speaks in the name of HUMAN KIND. When America emancipated herself from the oppressive capriciousness of her old and doting Foster-Mother, we beheld an instructive speculation on the probable *Loss and Gain* of unprotected and untributary Independence; and considered the Congress as a respectable body of Tradesmen, deeply versed in the ledgers of Commerce, who well understood their own worldly concerns, and adventurously improved them. France presented a more interesting spectacle. Her great men with a profound philosophy investigated the interests common to all intellectual beings, and legislated for the WORLD. The lovers of Mankind were every where fired and exalted by their example: each heart proudly expatriated itself, and we heard with transport of the victories of Frenchmen, as the victories of Human Nature. But the effects of Despotism could not be instantly removed with the cause: and the vices, and the Ignorance, and the Terrors of the multitude conspired to subject them to the tyranny of a bloody and fanatic faction. The fortune of France prevailed; and a Government has been established, which without counteracting the progressiveness, gratifies the more importunate frailties, of our present nature. To give stability to such a Constitution, it is needful only that its effects should be experienced. Peace therefore is necessary.

At this season, when all the creative powers of nature are in action, and all things animated and inanimate inspire the human heart with joy and kindliness, at this season, your executive Department have transmitted a paper, which, they knew would be the signal for recommencing the horrors of War. Legislators of France! if you had been nursed amid the insolent splendour of hereditary prosperity, ignorant of misery and unsympathizing with the miserable, I should not dare repeat to you the common-place pleadings of humanity.—But *you* are from among your countrymen.

> But *you* were nurs'd upon the self-same hills,
> Fed the same flocks by fountains, shades, or rills.[3]

You ought to tremble and weep beneath the stern necessity, that should command you to issue the mandate for the death even of *one* man—alas! what if for the death of perhaps half-a-MILLION? Permit me then to examine whether or no this necessity existed.—The Directory assign as their motives for rejecting his Britannic Majesty's overtures, first, their doubts respecting the sincerity of the English Court, and secondly, "the constitutional act, which does not permit it to consent to any alienation of that which according to the existing laws, constitutes the Territory of the Republic."—The Directory doubts the sincerity of the English Court, because Mr. Wickham who transmitted the overture, was not himself authorized to negociate.—If a disposition favourable to Peace had been discovered in the French Government, a man of greater name and dignity than the Minister to the Swiss Cantons, would have been appointed to treat with the August Legislature of France; but it ought not to have been expected, that the English Court should send a special messenger of high rank on an uncertain errand. To enquire concerning the intentions of the French Government, Mr. Wickham

[1] *The Watchman* was a political newspaper Coleridge published from March to May 1796. Its motto was: "THAT ALL MAY KNOW THE TRUTH; AND THAT THE TRUTH MAY MAKE US FREE."

[2] Written in response to France's rejection of England's overture to begin peace negotiations.

[3] Cf. Milton's *Lycidas*, ll. 23–24: "For we were nurst upon the self-same hill, / Fed the same flock, by fountain, shade, and rill."

was well qualified by his being on the spot with the French Ambassador. . . .

But, Legislators of France! if your system be true, a few years only of Peace would so increase your population and multiply your resources, as to place you beyond all danger of attack. The Tyrants of Europe will be ineffectually employed in preventing the irresistible influence of your example on their own subjects.—Let only your magnificent promises be performed, and we shall have no reason to doubt the Almightiness of Truth. That which in Theory has been ridiculed, must necessarily excite imitation, if realized: for why has it been ridiculed except that the despairing children of this world think it too excellent to be practicable? "Let us (says Condorcet[4]) be cautious not to despair of the human race. Let us dare to foresee in the ages that will succeed us, a knowledge and a happiness of which we can only form a vague and undetermined idea. Let us count on the *perfectibility* with which nature has endowed us; and on the strength of the human genius, from which long experience gives us a right to expect prodigies." These are the revolutionary measures which Wisdom prescribes—not the intrigues of your Emissaries, not the terror of your arms.

If however you persevere in your intentions, will your soldiers fight with the same enthusiasm for the Ambition as they have done for the Liberty of their Country? Will they not by degrees amid the stern discipline of arms and the horrors of War, forget the proud duties of *Citizens*, and become callous to the softer claims of domestic life? May not some future Dumourier find a more pliant Army? May not the distresses of the poor drive them to Anarchy? May not the rising generation, who have only *heard* of the evils of Despotism but have *felt* the horrors of a revolutionary Republic, imbibe sentiments favourable to Royalty? Will not the multitude of discontented men make *such* regulations necessary for the preservation of your Freedom, as in themselves destroy Freedom? Have not some of your supposed Patriots already deemed it expedient to limit the liberty of the Press? Legislators of France! in the name of Posterity we adjure you to consider, that misused success is soon followed by adversity, and that the adversity of France may lead, in its train of consequences, [to] the slavery of all Europe!

[4] **Condorcet:** Marquis de Condorcet (1743–1794), French philosophe. The passage quoted is from *Outlines of an Historical View of the Progress of the Human Mind* (1795). See also Godwin* and Malthus* on the perfectibility debate.

from POEMS
(1797)

Reflections on Having Left a Place of Retirement[1]
(comp. 1795)

Sermoni propriora.—Hor.

Low was our pretty Cot: our tallest Rose
Peep'd at the chamber-window. We could hear
At silent noon, and eve, and early morn,
The Sea's faint murmur. In the open air
Our Myrtles blossom'd; and across the porch
Thick Jasmins twined: the little landscape round
Was green and woody, and refresh'd the eye.
It was a spot which you might aptly call
The Valley of Seclusion! Once I saw
(Hallowing his Sabbath-day by quietness)
A wealthy son of Commerce saunter by,
Bristowa's[2] citizen: methought, it calm'd
His thirst of idle gold, and made him muse
With wiser feelings: for he paus'd, and look'd
With a pleas'd sadness, and gaz'd all around,
Then eyed our Cottage, and gaz'd round again,
And sigh'd, and said, *it was a blessed place.*
And we *were* bless'd. Oft with patient ear
Long-listening to the viewless sky-lark's note
(Viewless, or haply for a moment seen
Gleaming on sunny wing) in whisper'd tones
I've said to my Belovéd, 'Such, sweet Girl!
The inobtrusive song of Happiness,
Unearthly minstrelsy! then only heard
When the Soul seeks to hear; when all is hush'd,
And the Heart listens!'

But the time, when first
From that low Dell, steep up the stony Mount

[1] The original title of the poem when it appeared in the *Monthly Magazine*, October 1796, was "Reflections on entering into active life. A Poem which affects not to be Poetry." It received its familiar title in *Poems* (1797), to which was added the motto *Sermoni propriora*, translated by Coleridge in a letter, "Properer for a Sermon."

[2] **Bristowa's:** Bristol's.

I climb'd with perilous toil and reach'd the top,
Oh! what a goodly scene! *Here* the bleak mount,
The bare bleak mountain speckled thin with sheep;
Grey clouds, that shadowing spot the sunny fields;
And river, now with bushy rocks o'er-brow'd,
Now winding bright and full, with naked banks;
And seats, and lawns, the Abbey and the wood,
And cots, and hamlets, and faint city-spire;
The Channel *there,* the Islands and white sails,
Dim coasts, and cloud-like hills, and shoreless
  Ocean—
It seem'd like Omnipresence! God, methought,
Had built him there a Temple: the whole World
Seem'd *imag'd* in its vast circumference:
No *wish* profan'd my overwhelméd heart.
Blest hour! It was a luxury,—to be!

Ah! quiet Dell! dear Cot, and Mount sublime!
I was constrain'd to quit you. Was it right,
While my unnumber'd brethren toil'd and bled,
That I should dream away the trusted hours
On rose-leaf beds, pampering the coward heart
With feelings all too delicate for use?
Sweet is the tear that from some Howard's[3] eye
Drops on the cheek of one he lifts from earth:
And he that works me good with unmov'd face,
Does it but half: he chills me while he aids,
My benefactor, not my brother man!
Yet even this, this cold beneficence
Praise, praise it, O my Soul! oft as thou scann'st
The sluggard Pity's vision-weaving tribe!
Who sigh for Wretchedness, yet shun the Wretched,
Nursing in some delicious solitude
Their slothful loves and dainty sympathies!
I therefore go, and join head, heart, and hand,
Active and firm, to fight the bloodless fight
Of Science, Freedom, and the Truth in Christ.

Yet oft when after honourable toil
Rests the tir'd mind, and waking loves to dream,
My spirit shall revisit thee, dear Cot!
Thy Jasmin and thy window-peeping Rose,
And Myrtles fearless of the mild sea-air.
And I shall sigh fond wishes—sweet Abode!
Ah!—had none greater! And that all had such!
It might be so—but the time is not yet.
Speed it, O Father! Let thy Kingdom come!

[3] **Howard:** John Howard (1726–1790), philanthropist and prison reformer. Published *The State of the Prisons in England and Wales, and an account of some foreign prisons and hospitals* (1777) and a work on lazarettos, or hospitals that treat contagious illnesses (1778).

from FEARS IN SOLITUDE[1]
(1798)

Fears in Solitude

Written in 1798, during the Alarm of an Invasion
(comp. April 1798)

A green and silent spot amid the hills!
A small and silent dell!—O'er stiller place
No singing sky-lark ever pois'd himself!
The hills are heathy, save that swelling slope,
Which hath a gay and gorgeous covering on,
All golden with the never-bloomless furze,
Which now blooms most profusely; but the dell,
Bath'd by the mist, is fresh and delicate,
As vernal corn field, or the unripe flax,
When thro' its half-transparent stalks, at eve,
The level sunshine glimmers with green light.
O 'tis a quiet spirit-healing nook,
Which all, methinks, would love; but chiefly he,
The humble man, who in his youthful years
Knew just so much of folly as had made
His early manhood more securely wise:
Here he might lie on fern or wither'd heath,
While from the singing lark (that slings unseen
The minstrelsy which solitude loves best)
And from the sun, and from the breezy air,
Sweet influences trembled o'er his frame;
And he with many feelings, many thoughts,
Made up a meditative joy, and found
Religious meanings in the forms of nature!

[1] Published with "France, an Ode" and "Frost at Midnight." Twelve hundred Frenchmen attempted an invasion of the English coast near Fishguard in February 1797. Though the invasion was unsuccessful, panic spread when word got out that the planned landing site had been the coast of Stowey and that Bristol had been its principal target. The population remained anxious and watchful thereafter.

And so, his senses gradually wrapp'd
In a half-sleep, he dreams of better worlds,
And dreaming hears thee still, O singing lark!
That singest like an angel in the clouds.

My God! it is a melancholy thing
For such a man, who would full fain preserve
His soul in calmness, yet perforce must feel
For all his human brethren — O my God,
It is indeed a melancholy thing,
And weighs upon the heart, that he must think
What uproar and what strife may now be stirring
This way or that way o'er these silent hills —
Invasion, and the thunder and the shout,
And all the crash of onset; fear and rage
And undetermined conflict — even now,
Ev'n now, perchance, and in his native Isle,
Carnage and screams beneath this blessed sun!
We have offended, O my countrymen!
We have offended very grievously,
And have been tyrannous. From east to west
A groan of accusation pierces heaven!
The wretched plead against us, multitudes
Countless and vehement, the sons of God,
Our brethren! like a cloud that travels on,
Steam'd up from Cairo's swamps of pestilence,
Ev'n so, my countrymen! have we gone forth
And borne to distant tribes slavery and pangs,
And, deadlier far, our vices, whose deep taint
With slow perdition murders the whole man,
His body and his soul! Meanwhile, at home,
We have been drinking with a riotous-thirst
Pollutions from the brimming cup of wealth,
A selfish, lewd, effeminated race,
Contemptuous of all honourable rule,
Yet bartering freedom, and the poor man's life,
For gold, as at a market! The sweet words
Of christian promise, words that even yet
Might stem destruction, were they wisely preach'd,
Are mutter'd o'er my men, whose tones proclaim,
How flat and wearisome they feel their trade.
Rank scoffers some, but most too indolent,
To deem them falsehoods, or to *know* their truth.
O blasphemous! the book of life is made
A superstitious instrument, on which
We gabble o'er the oaths we mean to break,
For all must swear — all, and in every place,
College and wharf, council and justice-court,
All, all must swear, the briber and the brib'd,
Merchant and lawyer, senator and priest,
The rich, the poor, the old man, and the young,
All, all make up one scheme of perjury,
That faith doth reel; the very name of God
Sounds like a juggler's charm; and bold with joy,
Forth from his dark and lonely hiding-place
(Portentous fight) the owlet, ATHEISM,
Sailing on obscene wings athwart the noon,
Drops his blue-fringed lids, and holds them close,
And, hooting at the glorious sun in heaven,
Cries out, "where is it?"
Thankless too for peace,
(Peace long preserv'd by fleets and perilous seas)
Secure from actual warfare, we have lov'd
To swell the war-whoop, passionate for war!
Alas! for ages ignorant of all
It's ghastlier workings (famine or blue plague,
Battle, or siege, or flight thro' wintry snows)
We, this whole people, have been clamorous
For war and bloodshed, animating sports,
The which we pay for, as a thing to talk of,
Spectators and not combatants! no guess
Anticipative of a wrong unfelt,
No speculation on contingency,
However dim and vague, too vague and dim
To yield a justifying cause: and forth
(Stuff'd out with big preamble, holy names,
And adjurations of the God in heaven)
We send our mandates for the certain death
Of thousands and ten thousands! Boys and girls,
And women that would groan to see a child
Pull off an insect's leg, all read of war,
The best amusement for our morning meal!
The poor wretch, who has learnt his only prayers
From curses, who knows scarcely words enough
To ask a blessing of his heavenly Father,
Becomes a fluent phraseman, absolute
And technical in victories and defeats,
And all our dainty terms for fratricide,
Terms which we trundle smoothly o'er our tongues
Like mere abstractions, empty sounds to which
We join no feeling and attach no form,
As if the soldier died without a wound;
As if the fibres of this godlike frame
Were gor'd without a pang: as if the wretch,
Who fell in battle doing bloody deeds,
Pass'd off to heaven, *translated* and not kill'd;
As tho' he had no wife to pine for him,
No God to judge him! — Therefore evil days

Are coming on us, O my countrymen!
And what if all-avenging Providence,
Strong and retributive, should make us know
The meaning of our words, force us to feel
The desolation and the agony
Of our fierce doings?—
Spare us yet a while,
Father and God! O spare us yet a while!
O let not English women drag their flight
Fainting beneath the burden of their babes,
Of the sweet infants, that but yesterday
Laugh'd at the breast! Sons, brothers, husbands, all
Who ever gaz'd with fondness on the forms,
Which grew up with you round the same fire side,
And all who ever heard the sabbath bells
Without the infidel's scorn, make yourselves pure!
Stand forth! be men! repel an impious foe,
Impious and false, a light yet cruel race,
That laugh away all virtue, mingling mirth
With deeds of murder; and still promising
Freedom, themselves too sensual to be free
Poison life's amities, and cheat the heart
Of Faith and quiet Hope, and all that soothes
And all that lifts the spirit! Stand we forth;
Render them back upon th' insulted ocean,
And let them toss as idly on it's waves,
As the vile sea-weeds, which some mountain blast
Swept from our shores! And O! may we return
Not with a drunken triumph, but with fear,
Repenting of the wrongs, with which we stung
So fierce a foe to frenzy!
I have told,
O Britons! O my brethren! I have told
Most bitter truth, but without bitterness.
Nor deem my zeal or factious or mistim'd;
For never can true courage dwell with them,
Who, playing tricks with conscience, dare not look
At their own vices. We have been too long
Dupes of a deep delusion! Some, belike,
Groaning with restless enmity, expect
All change from change of constituted power:
As if a government had been a robe,
On which our vice and wretchedness were tagg'd
Like fancy-points and fringes, with the robe
Pull'd off at pleasure. Fondly these attach
A radical causation to a few
Poor drudges of chastising Providence,
Who borrow all their hues and qualities
From our own folly and rank wickedness,
Which gave them birth, and nurse them. Others, meanwhile,
Dote with a mad idolatry; and all,
Who will not fall before their images,
And yield them worship, they are enemies
Ev'n of their country!—Such have I been deem'd.
But, O dear Britain! O my mother Isle!
Needs must thou prove a name most dear and holy
To me, a son, a brother, and a friend,
A husband and a father! who revere
All bonds of natural love, and find them all
Within the limits of thy rocky shores.
O native Britain! O my mother Isle!
How should'st thou prove aught else but dear and holy
To me, who from thy lakes and mountain-hills,
Thy clouds, thy quiet dales, thy rocks, and seas,
Have drunk in all my intellectual life,
All sweet sensations, all ennobling thoughts,
All adoration of the God in nature,
All lovely and all honourable things,
Whatever makes this mortal spirit feel
The joy and greatness of it's future being?
There lives nor form nor feeling in my soul
Unborrow'd from my country! O divine
And beauteous island, thou hast been my sole
And most magnificent temple, in the which
I walk with awe, and sing my stately songs,
Loving the God that made me!—
May my fears,
My filial fears, be vain! and may the vaunts
And menace of the vengeful enemy
Pass like the gust, that roar'd and died away
In the distant tree, which heard, and only heard;
In this low dell bow'd not the delicate grass.
But now the gentle dew-fall sends abroad
The fruitlike perfume of the golden furze:
The light has left the summit of the hill,
Tho' still a sunny gleam lies beautiful
On the long-ivied beacon.—Now, farewell,
Farewell, awhile, O soft and silent spot!
On the green sheep-track, up the heathy hill,
Homeward I wind my way; and lo! recall'd
From bodings, that have well nigh wearied me,
I find myself upon the brow, and pause
Startled! And after longly sojourning

In such a quiet and surrounded scene,
This burst of prospect, here the shadowy main,
Dim-tinted, there the mighty majesty
Of that huge amphitheatre of rich
And elmy fields, seems like society,
Conversing with the mind, and giving it
A livelier impulse, and a dance of thought;
And now, beloved STOWEY! I behold
Thy church-tower, and (methinks) the four huge elms
Clust'ring, which mark the mansion of my friend;
And close behind them, hidden from my view,
Is my own lowly cottage, where my babe
And my babe's mother dwell in peace! With light
And quicken'd footsteps thitherward I tend,
Rememb'ring thee, O green and silent dell!
And grateful, that by nature's quietness
And solitary musings all my heart
Is soften'd, and made worthy to indulge
Love, and the thoughts that yearn for human kind.

Nether Stowey, April 20th, 1798.

Frost at Midnight

(1798; comp. 1798)

The Frost performs it's secret ministry,
Unhelp'd by any wind. The owlet's cry
Came loud—and hark, again! loud as before.
The inmates of my cottage, all at rest,
Have left me to that solitude, which suits
Abstruser musings: save that at my side
My cradled infant[1] slumbers peacefully.
'Tis calm indeed! so calm, that it disturbs
And vexes meditation with it's strange
And extreme silentness. Sea, hill, and wood,
This populous village! Sea, and hill, and wood,
With all the numberless goings on of life,
Inaudible as dreams! The thin blue flame
Lies on my low-burnt fire, and quivers not:
Only that film,[2] which flutter'd on the grate,
Still flutters there, the sole unquiet thing,
Methinks, it's motion in this hush of nature
Gives it dim sympathies with me, who live,
Making it a companionable form,[3]
With which I can hold commune. Idle thought!
But still the living spirit in our frame,
That loves not to behold a lifeless thing,
Transfuses into all it's own delights
It's own volition, sometimes with deep faith,
And sometimes with fantastic playfulness.
Ah me! amus'd by no such curious toys
Of the self-watching subtilizing mind,
How often in my early school-boy days,[4]
With most believing superstitious wish
Presageful have I gaz'd upon the bars,
To watch the *stranger* there! and oft belike,
With unclos'd lids, already had I dreamt
Of my sweet birthplace,[5] and the old church-tower,
Whose bells, the poor man's only music, rang
From morn to evening, all the hot fair-day,
So sweetly, that they stirr'd and haunted me
With a wild pleasure, falling on mine ear
Most like articulate sounds of things to come!
So gaz'd I, till the soothing things, I dreamt,
Lull'd me to sleep, and sleep prolong'd my dreams!
And so I brooded all the following morn,
Aw'd by the stern preceptor's face, mine eye
Fix'd with mock study on my swimming book:[6]
Save if the door half-open'd, and I snatch'd
A hasty glance, and still my heart leapt up,
For still I hop'd to see the *stranger's* face,
Townsman, or aunt, or sister, more belov'd,[7]
My play-mate when we both were cloth'd alike!

---

[1] **cradled infant:** Hartley Coleridge (b. 19 September 1796).

[2] **Only that film:** in all parts of the kingdom these films are called *strangers,* and supposed to portend the arrival of some absent friend. [S.T.C.]

[3] Lines 20–29 are replaced by the following lines in the poem's final version: "Whose puny flaps and freaks the idling spirit / By its own moods interprets, everywhere / Echo or mirror seeking of itself, / And makes a toy of Thought. But O! how oft, / How oft, at school, with most believing mind."

[4] **school-boy days:** Coleridge attended Christ's Hospital, the London grammar school for the talented children of the poor.

[5] **sweet birthplace:** the village of Ottery St. Mary, from which Coleridge departed for Christ's Hospital after the death of his father in 1781.

[6] **"eye / . . . swimming book":** see Charlotte Smith, *The Emigrants,** II.46, "swimming eye."

[7] **sister:** Anne (Nancy), five years older than Samuel. She died in 1791.

Dear babe, that sleepest cradled by my side,
Whose gentle breathings, heard in this dead calm,
Fill up the interspersed vacancies
And momentary pauses of the thought!
My babe so beautiful! it fills my heart
With tender gladness, thus to look at thee,
And think, that thou shalt learn far other lore,
And in far other scenes! For I was rear'd
In the great city, pent mid cloisters dim,
And saw nought lovely but the sky and stars.
But *thou*, my babe! Shalt wander, like a breeze,
By lakes and sandy shores, beneath the crags
Of ancient mountain, and beneath the clouds,
Which image in their bulk both lakes and shores
And mountain crags: so shalt thou see and hear
The lovely shapes and sounds intelligible
Of that eternal language, which thy God
Utters, who from eternity doth teach
Himself in all, and all things in himself.
Great universal Teacher! he shall mould
Thy spirit, and by giving make it ask.

Therefore all seasons shall be sweet to thee,
Whether the summer clothe the general earth
With greenness, or the redbreasts sit and sing
Betwixt the tufts of snow on the bare branch
Of mossy apple-tree, while all the thatch
Smokes in the sun-thaw: whether the eave-drops fall
Heard only in the trances of the blast,
Or whether the secret ministery of cold
Shall hang them up in silent icicles,
Quietly shining to the quiet moon,[8]
Like those, my babe! which, ere to-morrow's warmth
Have capp'd their sharp keen points with pendulous drops,
Will catch thine eye, and with their novelty
Suspend thy little soul; then make thee shout,
And stretch and flutter from thy mother's arms
As thou would'st fly for very eagerness.

[8] The final version of the poem ends with this line.

from LYRICAL BALLADS[1]
(1798)

The Rime of the Ancyent Marinere[2]

IN SEVEN PARTS
(comp. 1797–1798)

— ARGUMENT —

How a Ship having passed the Line was driven by Storms to the cold Country towards the South Pole; and how

[1] For information regarding the volume, see note to *Lyrical Ballads* under W. Wordsworth.

[2] *Ancyent Marinere* is the lead poem of *Lyrical Ballads* (1798), and Wordsworth's *Lines Composed a Few Miles above Tintern Abbey* is the concluding poem. Robert Southey,* Coleridge's brother-in-law, wrote of *Ancyent Marinere* in *The Critical Review* (October 1798) that many stanzas are "laboriously beautiful; but in connection they are absurd or unintelligible." Dr. Charles Burney wrote in *The Monthly Review* (June 1799) that it was "a rhapsody of unintelligible wildness and incoherence." A reviewer in the *British Critic* (October 1799) was less severe, but still troubled by a "confusion of images." Coleridge changed the title for the 1800 edition to *The Ancient Mariner: A Poet's Reverie* and either normalized the spelling or provided modern equivalents for archaic words. However, Wordsworth removed *Ancyent Marinere* from the position of honor in 1800, because he believed that the poem's obscurities and archaisms hurt sales. Coleridge revised the poem and added a marginal gloss when he republished *Ancient Mariner* in *Sibylline Leaves* (1817)* for the first time under his own name.

Wordsworth says in his 1800 "Note to the *Ancient Mariner*" that he has included the poem, despite its defects and the wish of his friend that it be "suppressed" for the criticism it drew, because of its unique beauties: "The Poem of my Friend has indeed great defects; first that the principal person has no distinct character, either in his profession of Mariner, or as a human being who having been long under the controul of supernatural impressions might be supposed himself to partake of something supernatural: secondly, that he does not act, but is continually acted upon: thirdly, that the events having no necessary connection do not produce each other; and lastly, that the imagery is somewhat too laboriously accumulated. Yet the Poem contains many delicate touches of passion, . . ; a great number of the stanzas present beautiful images, and are expressed with unusual felicity of language; and the versification . . . is harmonious and artfully varied, . . ." [W.W.].

from thence she made her course to the tropical Latitude of the Great Pacific Ocean; and of the strange things that befell; and in what manner the Ancyent Marinere came back to his own Country.

....

— I —

It is an ancyent Marinere,
And he stoppeth one of three:
'By thy long grey beard and thy glittering eye
'Now wherefore stoppest me?

'The Bridegroom's doors are open'd wide
'And I am next of kin;
'The Guests are met, the Feast is set,—
'May'st hear the merry din.

But still he holds the wedding-guest—
There was a Ship, quoth he—
'Nay, if thou'st got a laughsome tale,
'Marinere! come with me.'

He holds him with his skinny hand,
Quoth he, there was a Ship—
'Now get thee hence, thou grey-beard Loon!
'Or my Staff shall make thee skip.

He holds him with his glittering eye—
The wedding guest stood still
And listens like a three year's child;
The Marinere hath his will.

The wedding-guest sate on a stone,
He cannot chuse but hear:
And thus spake on that ancyent man,
The bright-eyed Marinere.

The Ship was cheer'd, the Harbour clear'd—
Merrily did we drop
Below the Kirk,[3] below the Hill,
Below the Light-house top.

The Sun came up upon the left,
Out of the Sea came he:
And he shone bright, and on the right
Went down into the Sea.

Higher and higher every day,
Till over the mast at noon—
The wedding-guest here beat his breast,
For he heard the loud bassoon.

The Bride hath pac'd into the Hall,
Red as a rose is she;
Nodding their heads before her goes
The merry Minstralsy.

The wedding-guest he beat his breast,
Yet he cannot chuse but hear:
And thus spake on that ancyent Man,
The bright-eyed Marinere.

Listen, Stranger! Storm and Wind,
A Wind and Tempest strong!
For days and weeks it play'd us freaks—
Like Chaff we drove along.

Listen, Stranger! Mist and Snow,
And it grew wond'rous cauld:
And Ice mast-high came floating by
As green as Emerauld.

And thro' the drifts the snowy clifts
Did send a dismal sheen;
Ne shapes of men ne beasts we ken—
The Ice was all between.

The Ice was here, the Ice was there,
The Ice was all around:
It crack'd and growl'd, and roar'd and howl'd—
Like noises of a swound.[4]

At length did cross an Albatross,[5]
Thorough the Fog it came;
And an it were a Christian Soul,
We hail'd it in God's name.

The Marineres gave it biscuit-worms,[6]
And round and round it flew:
The Ice did split with a Thunder-fit;
The Helmsman steer'd us thro'.

And a good south wind sprung up behind,
The Albatross did follow;
And every day for food or play
Came to the Marinere's hollo!

---

[3] **Kirk:** Scottish for *church*.

[4] **swound:** fainting fit, swoon.

[5] **Albatross:** a large, web-footed bird, with a hooked beak and long, narrow wings, generally found in the southern hemisphere. The wingspan of the Wandering Albatross is eleven feet.

[6] **biscuit-worms:** literally, worms bred from the biscuits.

In mist or cloud on mast or shroud
It perch'd for vespers nine,
Whiles all the night thro' fog-smoke white
Glimmer'd the white moon-shine.

'God save thee, ancyent Marinere!
'From the fiends that plague thee thus—
'Why look'st thou so?'—with my cross bow
I shot the Albatross.

— II —

The Sun came up upon the right,
Out of the Sea came he;
And broad as a weft[7] upon the left
Went down into the Sea.

And the good south wind still blew behind,
But no sweet Bird did follow
Ne any day for food or play
Came to the Marinere's hollo!

And I had done an hellish thing
And it would work 'em woe:
For all averr'd, I had kill'd the Bird
That made the Breeze to blow.

Ne dim ne red, like God's own head,
The glorious Sun uprist:
Then all averr'd, I had kill'd the Bird
That brought the fog and mist.
'Twas right, said they, such birds to slay
That bring the fog and mist.

The breezes blew, the white foam flew,
The furrow follow'd free:
We were the first that ever burst
Into that silent Sea.

Down dropt the breeze, the Sails dropt down,
'Twas sad as sad could be
And we did speak only to break
The silence of the Sea.

All in a hot and copper sky
The bloody sun at noon,
Right up above the mast did stand,
No bigger than the moon.

Day after day, day after day,
We stuck, ne breath ne motion,
As idle as a painted Ship
Upon a painted Ocean.

Water, water, every where
And all the boards did shrink;
Water, water, every where
Ne any drop to drink.

The very deeps did rot: O Christ!
That ever this should be!
Yea, slimy things did crawl with legs
Upon the slimy Sea.

About, about, in reel and rout[8]
The Death-fires danc'd at night;
The water, like a witch's oils,
Burnt green and blue and white.

And some in dreams assured were
Of the Spirit that plagued us so:
Nine fathom[9] deep he had follow'd us
From the Land of Mist and Snow.

And every tongue thro' utter drouth
Was wither'd at the root;
We could not speak no more than if
We had been choked with soot.

Ah wel-a-day! what evil looks
Had I from old and young;
Instead of the Cross the Albatross
About my neck was hung.

— III —

I saw a something in the Sky
No bigger than my fist;
At first it seem'd a little speck
And then it seem'd a mist:
It mov'd and mov'd, and took at last
A certain shape, I wist.

A speck, a mist, a shape, I wist!
And still it ner'd and ner'd;
And, an it dodg'd a water-sprite,
It plung'd and tack'd and veer'd.

With throat unslack'd, with black lips bak'd
Ne could we laugh, ne wail:
Then while thro' drouth all dumb they stood
I bit my arm and suck'd the blood
And cry'd, A sail! a sail!

---

[7] **weft:** nautical term to mean a cloth used to signal distress at sea (Lowes).

[8] **reel:** Scottish dance. **rout:** Scottish word for clamor.

[9] **fathom:** six feet.

With throat unslack'd,[10] with black lips bak'd
  Agape they hear'd me call:
Gramercy! they for joy did grin
And all at once their breath drew in
  As they were drinking all.

She doth not tack from side to side—
  Hither to work us weal
Withouten wind, withouten tide
  She steddies with upright keel.[11]

The western wave was all a flame,
  The day was well nigh done!
Almost upon the western wave
  Rested the broad bright Sun;
When that strange shape drove suddenly
  Betwixt us and the Sun.

And strait the Sun was fleck'd with bars
  (Heaven's mother send us grace)
As if thro' a dungeon grate he peer'd
  With broad and burning face.

Alas! (thought I, and my heart beat loud)
  How fast she neres and neres!
Are those *her* Sails that glance in the Sun
  Like restless gossameres?[12]

Are these *her* naked ribs, which fleck'd
  The sun that did behind them peer?
And are these two all, all the crew,
  That woman and her fleshless Pheere?[13]

His bones were black with many a crack,
  All black and bare, I ween;[14]
Jet-black and bare, save where with rust
Of mouldy damps and charnel crust
  They're patch'd with purple and green.

Her lips are red, *her* looks are free,
  Her locks are yellow as gold:
Her skin is as white as leprosy,
And she is far liker Death than he;
  Her flesh makes the still air cold.

[10] **unslack'd:** unquenched.

[11] **keel:** the backbone of the ship's frame, extending the length of the vessel.

[12] **gossameres:** sheer, gauzy fabric.

[13] *Pheere* was changed to *mate* in 1800.

[14] **ween:** think.

The naked Hulk alongside came
  And the Twain were playing dice;
'The Game is done! I've won, I've won!'
  Quoth she, and whistled thrice.

A gust of wind sterte up behind
  And whistled thro' his bones;
Thro' the holes of his eyes and the hole of his mouth
  Half-whistles and half-groans.

With never a whisper in the Sea
  Off darts the Spectre-ship;
While clombe above the Eastern bar
The horned Moon, with one bright Star
  Almost atween the tips.

One after one by the horned Moon
  (Listen, O Stranger! to me)
Each turn'd his face with a ghastly pang
  And curs'd me with his ee.[15]

Four times fifty living men,
  With never a sigh or groan,
With heavy thump, a lifeless lump
  They dropp'd down one by one.

Their souls did from their bodies fly,—
  They fled to bliss or woe;
And every soul it pass'd me by,
  Like the whiz of my Cross-bow.

—IV—

'I fear thee, ancyent Marinere!
  'I fear thy skinny hand;
'And thou art long and lank and brown
  'As is the ribb'd Sea-sand.

'I fear thee and thy glittering eye
  'And thy skinny hand so brown—
Fear not, fear not, thou wedding guest!
  This body dropt not down.

Alone, alone, all all alone
  Alone on the wide wide Sea;
And Christ would take no pity on
  My soul in agony.

The many men so beautiful,
  And they all dead did lie!
And a million million slimy things
Liv'd on—and so did I.

[15] **ee:** eye.

I look'd upon the rotting Sea,
And drew my eyes away;
I look'd upon the eldritch[16] deck,
And there the dead men lay.

I look'd to Heaven, and try'd to pray;
But or ever a prayer had gusht,
A wicked whisper came and made
My heart as dry as dust.

I clos'd my lids and kept them close,
Till the balls like pulses beat;
For the sky and the sea, and the sea and the sky
Lay like a load on my weary eye,
And the dead were at my feet.

The cold sweat melted from their limbs,
Ne rot, ne reek did they;
The look with which they look'd on me,
Had never pass'd away.

An orphan's curse would drag to Hell
A spirit from on high:
But O! more horrible than that
Is the curse in a dead man's eye!
Seven days, seven nights I saw that curse,
And yet I could not die.

The moving Moon went up the sky
And no where did abide:
Softly she was going up
And a star or two beside.

Her beams bemock'd the sultry main
Like morning frosts yspread;
But where the ship's huge shadow lay,
The charmed water burnt alway
A still and awful red.

Beyond the shadow of the ship
I watch'd the water-snakes:
They mov'd in tracks of shining white;
And when they rear'd, the elfish light
Fell off in hoary flakes.

Within the shadow of the ship
I watch'd their rich attire:
Blue, glossy green, and velvet black
They coil'd and swam; and every track
Was a flash of golden fire.

[16] **eldritch**: ghastly, hideous.

O happy living things! no tongue
Their beauty might declare:
A spring of love gusht from my heart,
And I bless'd them unaware!
Sure my kind saint took pity on me,
And I bless'd them unaware.

The self-same moment I could pray;
And from my neck so free
The Albatross fell off, and sank
Like lead into the sea.

— V —

O sleep, it is a gentle thing
Belov'd from pole to pole!
To Mary-queen the praise be yeven
She sent the gentle sleep from heaven
That slid into my soul.

The silly[17] buckets on the deck
That had so long remain'd,
I dreamt that they were fill'd with dew
And when I awoke it rain'd.

My lips were wet, my throat was cold,
My garments all were dank;
Sure I had drunken in my dreams
And still my body drank.

I mov'd and could not feel my limbs,
I was so light, almost
I thought that I had died in sleep,
And was a blessed Ghost.

The roaring wind! it roar'd far off,
It did not come anear;
But with its sound it shook the sails
That were so thin and sere.

The upper air bursts into life,
And a hundred fire-flags sheen[18]
To and fro they are hurried about;
And to and fro, and in and out
The stars dance on between.

The coming wind doth roar more loud;
The sails do sigh, like sedge:
The rain pours down from one black cloud
And the Moon is at its edge.

[17] **silly**: common, simple.

[18] **sheen**: shone.

Hark! hark! the thick black cloud is cleft,
    And the Moon is at its side:
Like waters shot from some high crag,
The lightning falls with never a jag
    A river steep and wide.

The strong wind reach'd the ship: it roar'd
    And dropp'd down, like a stone!
Beneath the lightning and the moon
    The dead men gave a groan.

They groan'd, they stirr'd, they all uprose,
    Ne spake, ne mov'd their eyes:
It had been strange, even in a dream
    To have seen those dead men rise.

The helmsman steerd, the ship mov'd on;
    Yet never a breeze up-blew;
The Marineres all 'gan work the ropes,
    Where they were wont to do:
They rais'd their limbs like lifeless tools—
    We were a ghastly crew.

The body of my brother's son
    Stood by me knee to knee:
The body and I pull'd at one rope,
    But he said nought to me—
And I quak'd to think of my own voice
    How frightful it would be!

The day-light dawn'd—they dropp'd their arms,
    And cluster'd round the mast:
Sweet sounds rose slowly thro' their mouths
    And from their bodies pass'd.

Around, around, flew each sweet sound,
    Then darted to the sun:
Slowly the sounds came back again
    Now mix'd, now one by one.

Sometimes a dropping from the sky
    I heard the Lavrock[19] sing;
Sometimes all little birds that are
How they seem'd to fill the sea and air
    With their sweet jargoning,[20]

And now 'twas like all instruments,
    Now like a lonely flute;
And now it is an angel's song
    That makes the heavens be mute.

It ceas'd: yet still the sails made on
    A pleasant noise till noon,
A noise like of a hidden brook
    In the leafy month of June,
That to the sleeping woods all night
    Singeth a quiet tune.

Listen, O listen, thou Wedding-guest!
    'Marinere! thou hast thy will:
'For that, which comes out of thine eye, doth make
    'My body and soul to be still.'

Never sadder tale was told
    To a man of woman born:
Sadder and wiser thou wedding-guest!
    Thou'lt rise to morrow morn.

Never sadder tale was heard
    By a man of woman born:
The Marineres all return'd to work
    As silent as beforne.

The Marineres all 'gan pull the ropes,
    But look at me they n'old:[21]
Thought I, I am as thin as air—
    They cannot me behold.

Till noon we silently sail'd on
    Yet never a breeze did breathe:
Slowly and smoothly went the ship
    Mov'd onward from beneath.

Under the keel nine fathom deep
    From the land of mist and snow
The spirit slid: and it was He
    That made the Ship to go.
The sails at noon left off their tune
    And the Ship stood still also.

The sun right up above the mast
    Had fix'd her to the ocean:
But in a minute she 'gan stir
    With a short uneasy motion—
Backwards and forwards half her length
    With a short uneasy motion.

Then, like a pawing horse let go,
    She made a sudden bound:
It flung the blood into my head,
    And I fell into a swound.

[19] **Lavrock:** skylark.

[20] **jargoning:** twittering.

[21] **n'old:** could not.

How long in that same fit I lay,
  I have not to declare;
But ere my living life return'd,
I heard and in my soul discern'd
  Two voices in the air,

'Is it he?' quoth one, 'Is this the man?
  'By him who died on cross,
'With his cruel bow he lay'd full low
  'The harmless Albatross.

'The spirit who 'bideth by himself
  'In the land of mist and snow,
'He lov'd the bird that lov'd the man
  'Who shot him with his bow.

The other was a softer voice,
  As soft as honey-dew:
Quoth he the man hath penance done,
  And penance more will do.

— VI —

FIRST VOICE

'But tell me, tell me! speak again,
  'Thy soft response renewing—
'What makes that ship drive on so fast?
  'What is the Ocean doing?

SECOND VOICE

'Still as a Slave before his Lord,
  'The Ocean hath no blast:
'His great bright eye most silently
  'Up to the moon is cast—

'If he may know which way to go,
  'For she guides him smooth or grim.
'See, brother, see! how graciously
  'She looketh down on him.

FIRST VOICE

'But why drives on that ship so fast
  'Withouten wave or wind?

SECOND VOICE

'The air is cut away before,
  'And closes from behind.

'Fly, brother, fly! more high, more high,
  'Or we shall be belated:
'For slow and slow that ship will go,
  'When the Marinere's trance is abated.'

I woke, and we were sailing on
  As in a gentle weather:
'Twas night, calm night, the moon was high;
  The dead men stood together.

All stood together on the deck,
  For a charnel-dungeon[22] fitter:
All fix'd on me their stony eyes
  That in the moon did glitter.

The pang, the curse, with which they died,
  Had never pass'd away:
I could not draw my een from theirs
  Ne turn them up to pray.

And in its time the spell was snapt,
  And I could move my een:
I look'd far-forth, but little saw
  Of what might else be seen.

Like one, that on a lonely road
  Doth walk in fear and dread,
And having once turn'd round, walks on
  And turns no more his head:
Because he knows, a frightful fiend
  Doth close behind him tread.

But soon there breath'd a wind on me,
  Ne sound ne motion made:
Its path was not upon the sea
  In ripple or in shade.

It rais'd my hair, it fann'd my cheek,
  Like a meadow-gale of spring—
It mingled strangely with my fears,
  Yet it felt like a welcoming.

Swiftly, swiftly flew the ship,
  Yet she sail'd softly too:
Sweetly, sweetly blew the breeze—
  On me alone it blew.

O dream of joy! is this indeed
  The light-house top I see?
Is this the Hill? Is this the Kirk?
  Is this mine own countrée?

We drifted o'er the Harbour-bar,
  And I with sobs did pray—
'O let me be awake, my God!
  'Or let me sleep alway!'

---

22 **charnel-dungeon:** room for dead bodies.

The harbour-bay was clear as glass,
  So smoothly it was strewn!
And on the bay the moon light lay,
  And the shadow of the moon.

The moonlight bay was white all o'er,
  Till rising from the same,
Full many shapes, that shadows were,
  Like as of torches came.

A little distance from the prow[23]
  Those dark-red shadows were;
But soon I saw that my own flesh
  Was red as in a glare.

I turn'd my head in fear and dread,
  And by the holy rood,[24]
The bodies had advanc'd, and now
  Before the mast they stood.

They lifted up their stiff right arms,
  They held them strait and tight;
And each right-arm burnt like a torch,
  A torch that's borne upright.
Their stony eye-balls glitter'd on
  In the red and smoky light.

I pray'd and turn'd my head away
  Forth looking as before.
There was no breeze upon the bay,
  No wave against the shore.

The rock shone bright, the kirk no less
  That stands above the rock:
The moonlight steep'd in silentness
  The steady weathercock.

And the bay was white with silent light,
  Till rising from the same
Full many shapes, that shadows were,
  In crimson colours came.

A little distance from the prow
  Those crimson shadows were:
I turn'd my eyes upon the deck—
  O Christ! what saw I there?

Each corse lay flat, lifeless and flat;
  And by the Holy rood
A man all light, a seraph-man,
  On every corse there stood.

This seraph-band, each wav'd his hand:
  It was a heavenly sight:
They stood as signals to the land,
  Each one a lovely light:

This seraph-band, each wav'd his hand,
  No voice did they impart—
No voice; but O! the silence sank,
  Like music on my heart.

Eftsones[25] I heard the dash of oars,
  I heard the pilot's cheer:
My head was turn'd perforce away
  And I saw a boat appear.

Then vanish'd all the lovely lights;
  The bodies rose anew:
With silent pace, each to his place,
  Came back the ghastly crew.
The wind, that shade nor motion made,
  On me alone it blew.

The pilot, and the pilot's boy
  I heard them coming fast:
Dear Lord in Heaven! it was a joy,
  The dead men could not blast.

I saw a third—I heard his voice:
  It is the Hermit good!
He singeth loud his godly hymns
  That he makes in the wood.
He'll shrieve[26] my soul, he'll wash away
  The Albatross's blood.

— VII —

This Hermit good lives in that wood
  Which slopes down to the Sea.
How loudly his sweet voice he rears!
He loves to talk with Marineres
  That come from a far Contrée.

He kneels at morn and noon and eve—
  He hath a cushion plump:
It is the moss, that wholly hides
  The rotted old Oak-stump.

The Skiff-boat ne'rd: I heard them talk,
  'Why, this is strange, I trow!
'Where are those lights so many and fair
  'That signal made but now?

[23] **prow:** the forward part of a ship, i.e., the bow.
[24] **holy rood:** cross, or crucifix on which Christ died.
[25] **Eftsones:** but soon.
[26] **shrieve:** confess and provide absolution.

'Strange, by my faith! the hermit said—
'And they answer'd not our cheer.
'The planks look warp'd, and see those sails
'How thin they are and sere!
'I never saw aught like to them
'Unless perchance it were

'The skeletons of leaves that lag
'My forest brook along:
'When the Ivy-tod[27] is heavy with snow,
'And the owlet whoops to the wolf below
'That eats the she-wolf's young.

'Dear Lord! it has a fiendish look—
(The Pilot made reply)
'I am a-fear'd.—'Push on, push on!
'Said the Hermit cheerily.

The Boat came closer to the Ship,
But I ne spake ne stirr'd!
The Boat came close beneath the Ship,
And strait a sound was heard!

Under the water it rumbled on,
Still louder and more dread:
It reach'd the Ship, it split the bay;
The Ship went down like lead.

Stunn'd by that loud and dreadful sound,
Which sky and ocean smote:
Like one that hath been seven days drown'd
My body lay afloat:
But, swift as dreams, myself I found
Within the Pilot's boat.

Upon the whirl, where sank the Ship,
The boat spun round and round:
And all was still, save that the hill
Was telling of the sound.

I mov'd my lips: the Pilot shriek'd
And fell down in a fit.
The Holy Hermit rais'd his eyes
And pray'd where he did sit.

I took the oars: the Pilot's boy,
Who now doth crazy go,
Laugh'd loud and long, and all the while
His eyes went to and fro,
'Ha! ha!' quoth he—'full plain I see,
'The devil knows how to row.'

And now all in mine own Countrée
I stood on the firm land!
The Hermit stepp'd forth from the boat,
And scarcely he could stand.

'O shrieve me, shrieve me, holy Man!
The Hermit cross'd his brow—
'Say quick,' quoth he, 'I bid thee say
'What manner man art thou?

Forthwith this frame of mine was wrench'd
With a woeful agony,
Which forc'd me to begin my tale
And then it left me free.

Since then at an uncertain hour,
Now oftimes and now fewer,
That anguish comes and makes me tell
My ghastly aventure.

I pass, like night, from land to land;
I have strange power of speech;
The moment that his face I see
I know the man that must hear me;
To him my tale I teach.

What loud uproar bursts from that door!
The Wedding-guests are there;
But in the Garden-bower the Bride
And Bride-maids singing are:
And hark the little Vesper-bell
Which biddeth me to prayer.

O Wedding-guest! this soul hath been
Alone on a wide wide sea:
So lonely 'twas, that God himself
Scarce seemed there to be.

O sweeter than the Marriage-feast,
'Tis sweeter far to me
To walk together to the Kirk
With a goodly company.

To walk together to the Kirk
And all together pray,
While each to his great father bends,
Old men, and babes, and loving friends,
And Youths, and Maidens gay.

Farewell, farewell! but this I tell
To thee, thou wedding-guest!
He prayeth well who loveth well
Both man and bird and beast.

[27] **Ivy-tod:** bushy clump of ivy.

He prayeth best who loveth best,
All things both great and small:
For the dear God, who loveth us,
He made and loveth all.

The Marinere, whose eye is bright,
Whose beard with age is hoar,
Is gone; and now the wedding-guest
Turn'd from the bridegroom's door.

He went, like one that hath been stunn'd
And is of sense forlorn:
A sadder and a wiser man
He rose the morrow morn.

The Nightingale

A Conversational Poem,
Written in April, 1798
(1798)

No cloud, no relique of the sunken day
Distinguishes the West, no long thing slip
Of sullen Light, no obscure trembling hues.
Come, we will rest on this old mossy Bridge!
You see the glimmer of the stream beneath,
But hear no murmuring: it flows silently
O'er its soft bed of verdure. All is still,
A balmy night! and tho' the stars be dim,
Yet let us think upon the vernal showers
That gladden the green earth, and we shall find
A pleasure in the dimness of the stars.
And hark! the Nightingale begins its song,
"Most musical, most melancholy"[1] Bird!
A melancholy Bird? O idle thought!
In nature there is nothing melancholy.
—But some night-wandering Man, whose heart was pierc'd
With the remembrance of a grievous wrong,
Or slow distemper or neglected love,
(And so, poor Wretch! fill'd all things with himself
And made all gentle sounds tell back the tale
Of his own sorrows) he and such as he
First nam'd these notes a melancholy strain;
And many a poet echoes the conceit,
Poet, who hath been building up the rhyme
When he had better far have stretch'd his limbs
Beside a brook in mossy forest-dell
By sun or moonlight, to the influxes
Of shapes and sounds and shifting elements
Surrendering his whole spirit, of his song
And of his fame forgetful! so his fame
Should share in nature's immortality,
A venerable thing! and so his song
Should make all nature lovelier, and itself
Be lov'd, like nature!—But 'twill not be so;
And youths and maidens most poetical
Who lose the deep'ning twilights of the spring
In ball-rooms and hot theatres, they still
Full of meek sympathy must heave their sighs
O'er Philomela's pity-pleading strains.[2]
My Friend, and my Friend's Sister![3] we have learnt
A different lore: we may not thus profane
Nature's sweet voices always full of love
And joyance! 'Tis the merry Nightingale
That crowds, and hurries, and precipitates
With fast thick warble his delicious notes,
As he were fearful, that an April night
Would be too short for him to utter forth
His love-chant, and disburthen his full soul
Of all its music! And I know a grove
Of large extent, hard by a castle huge
Which the great lord inhabits not: and so
This grove is wild with tangling underwood,
And the trim walks are broken up, and grass,
Thin grass and king-cups grow within the paths.
But never elsewhere in one place I knew
So many Nightingales: and far and near
In wood and thicket over the wide grove
They answer and provoke each other's songs—
With skirmish and capricious passagings,

[1] Cf. Milton's *Il Penseroso* (1645), ll. 61–62: "Sweet bird that shunn'st the noise of folly / Most musical, most melancholy!"

[2] Philomela, daughter of Pandion, king of Athens, was raped by her sister Procne's husband, Tereus, king of Thrace. Tereus cut out Philomela's tongue to prevent her telling, but she successfully informed Procne by weaving her story on a piece of embroidery. Procne avenged her sister by feeding Tereus the flesh of their child Itys in a meal. When Tereus realized what had happened, he pursued the women but the gods transformed all of them into birds. Procne became the swallow, Tereus, the hoopoe, and Philomela, the nightingale, although the latter two are sometimes reversed in legend.

[3] **My Friend, and . . . Sister:** William and Dorothy Wordsworth.

And murmurs musical and swift jug jug
And one low piping sound more sweet than all—
Stirring the air with such an harmony,
That should you close your eyes, you might almost
Forget it was not day! On moonlight bushes,
Whose dewy leafits are but half disclos'd,
You may perchance behold them on the twigs,
Their bright, bright eyes, their eyes both bright and
 full,
Glistning, while many a glow-worm in the shade
Lights up her love-torch.

A most gentle maid[4]
Who dwelleth in her hospitable home
Hard by the Castle, and at latest eve,
(Even like a Lady vow'd and dedicate
To something more than nature in the grove)
Glides thro' the pathways; she knows all their notes,
That gentle Maid! and oft, a moment's space,
What time the moon was lost behind a cloud,
Hath heard a pause of silence: till the Moon
Emerging, hath awaken'd earth and sky
With one sensation, and those wakeful Birds
Have all burst forth in choral minstrelsy,
As if one quick and sudden Gale had swept
An hundred airy harps! And she hath watch'd
Many a Nightingale perch giddily
On blosmy twig still swinging from the breeze,
And to that motion tune his wanton song,
Like tipsy Joy that reels with tossing head.

Farewell, O Warbler! till to-morrow eve,
And you, my friends! farewell, a short farewell!
We have been loitering long and pleasantly,
And now for our dear homes.—That strain again!
Full fain it would delay me!—My dear Babe,[5]
Who, capable of no articulate sound,
Mars all things with his imitative lisp,
How he would place his hand beside his ear,
His little hand, the small forefinger up,
And bid us listen! And I deem it wise
To make him Nature's playmate. He knows well
The evening star: and once when he awoke
In most distressful mood (some inward pain
Had made up that strange thing, an infant's dream)
I hurried with him to our orchard plot,
And he beholds the moon, and hush'd at once
Suspends his sobs, and laughs most silently,
While his fair eyes that swam with undropt tears
Did glitter in the yellow moon-beam! Well—
It is a father's tale. But if that Heaven
Should give me life, his childhood shall grow up
Familiar with these songs, that with the night
He may associate Joy! Once more farewell,
Sweet Nightingale! once more, my friends! farewell.

[4]**a most gentle maid**: possibly Ellen Cruikshank, the sister of John Cruikshank, a friend of Coleridge's.

[5]**My dear Babe**: Coleridge's son, Hartley.

from THE MORNING POST

On the French Constitution. IV[1]

(31 December 1799)

A Legislative Assembly, the elected Representatives of a mighty nation, is attacked and dissolved by a military faction. The Leaders of this faction assume the Supreme Power with all its Royal patronage and emoluments, and, not content with this, create moreover four or five hundred places with high salaries under the titles of Senate, Legislature, and Tribunate; partly to reward their immediate creatures, and partly from the same motives with which puppet-shewmen are hired by cut-purses, viz. to amuse the crowd while they are picking their pockets. These enormities they modestly submit to the suffrages of the Great Nation, "proclaim them at the head of the military," and begging, like the mendicant in Gil Blas, with levelled musquets, crave the Great Nation to call them a Constitution, and, as the last act of its indefeasible sovereignty, to vote itself enslaved for ever! The eighteenth century is now at its close—a century venerable for its discoveries, terrific in its events! This impudent offer of

[1]In November, Napoleon provided military assistance to Abbe Sieyes, a Director of the revolutionary government who proposed a new constitution that would divide executive authority among three consuls. The coup against the legislators was successful, but Napoleon altered the Constitution of the year VIII to provide for the rule of one. In December Napoleon assumed the office of First Consul, effectively ending the Revolution. The French later approved the new Constitution by a vote of 3,011,077 to 1,567. The *Morning Post* was a London daily published by Coleridge's friend Daniel Stuart. Founded in 1722, it amalgamated with the *Daily Telegraph* in 1937.

these mountebank Liberticides—was it to mortify human pride, that *this* is doomed to be the *last* incident of such a century? Is it to deaden the extravagance of human hope, that the general acceptance of it will probably be the *first* incident of the new age? Alas, poor human nature! Or rather, indeed, alas, poor Gallic nature! For Γραιοι αει παιδες: the French are always children, and it is an infirmity of benevolence to wish, or dread aught concerning them. . . .

It were wasting our readers' attention to direct it particularly to the other branches of the Legislature, the hundred Tribunes who are to talk and do nothing, and the three hundred Legislators whom the Constitution orders to be silent. What a ludicrous purgatory for three hundred Frenchmen! The shamelessness of calling that a Legislature which can neither propose nor reason, and whose acts are annullable *ad arbitrium*,[2] can only be equalled by the exquisite absurdity involved in the very notion of splitting the intellectual faculties, and subdividing the business of Thought, almost as curiously as that of a pin manufactory. However, all these different law-manufacturers are well salaried; yet not so as to place them out of the temptation of corruption. Even the Chief Consul must find it necessary to bribe high to secure his re-election, by influence, by promises, and not improbably by taking the pay of foreign Governments. Indeed, never was a Government framed which lay so open to corruption, both in itself and from external powers! There exists no appearance of a preventive, in a nominal Legislature, for which no property is requisite, in which no talent can be exerted, and where no popularity can be gained. The whole Constitution betrays a rooted contempt of the people, and a distrust of human virtue in general, yet leaves to none, whom it invests with power, any of those common assistants to well doing which the most virtuous man does not profess to deem useless. It has indeed divisions and sub-divisions even to superfluity; but how, under any circumstances these could be a check on each other, or on the Consulate, no where appears. It is indeed mere fraud and mockery. Checks and counterpoises can only be produced by real diversity of interests, of interests existing independent of legislative functions; but these chambers are all alike filled with the creatures of the Dictator, by him chosen, feeding on his stipends, and acting under his controul. But it cannot last: for to what body of men or species of interest can it appeal for love or protection? The property, the talent, the popular spirit, the prejudices of the Royalist, the Priest, and the Jacobin, are all injured, insulted, trodden under foot by it. And what are idle promises of individual liberty in a Constitution which recognises in the Chief Consul the right of suspending it *ad arbitrium*, and which does not recognise in the nation that which is worth a thousand Tribunates, that without which no nation can be free or happy under the wisest Government, the LIBERTY OF THE PRESS?

[2] **ad arbitrium:** at will, at pleasure.

from ANNUAL ANTHOLOGY

This Lime-Tree Bower My Prison[1]

(1800; comp. 1797)

In the June of 1797, some long-expected Friends paid a visit to the author's cottage; and on the morning of their arrival, he met with an accident, which disabled him from walking during the whole time of their stay. One evening, when they had left him for a few hours, he composed the following lines in the garden-bower.

Well, they are gone, and here must I remain,
This lime-tree bower my prison! I have lost
Beauties and feelings, such as would have been
Most sweet to my remembrance even when age
Had dimmed mine eyes to blindness! They, meanwhile,
Friends, whom I never more may meet again,
On springy heath, along the hill-top edge,
Wander in gladness, and wind down, perchance,
To that still roaring dell, of which I told;
The roaring dell, o'erwooded, narrow, deep,
And only speckled by the mid-day sun;
Where its slim trunk the ash from rock to rock
Flings arching like a bridge;—that branchless ash,
Unsunned and damp, whose few poor yellow leaves
Ne'er tremble in the gale, yet tremble still,
Fanned by the water-fall! and there my friends

[1] The text included here is that of 1834, because the 1800 text was unavailable. Variants between the early and late texts identified in *Coleridge: Poetical Works* (1912) are minor, except where indicated. The original title read, "This Lime-Tree Bower my Prison. A Poem Addressed to Charles Lamb, of the India House, London."

Behold the dark green file of long lank weeds,
That all at once (a most fantastic sight!)
Still nod and drip beneath the dripping edge
Of the blue clay-stone.
Now, my friends emerge
Beneath the wide wide Heaven—and view again
The many-steepled tract magnificent
Of hilly fields and meadows, and the sea,
With some fair bark, perhaps, whose sails light up
The slip of smooth clear blue betwixt two Isles
Of purple shadow! Yes! they wander on
In gladness all; but thou, methinks, most glad,
My gentle-hearted Charles! for thou hast pined
And hungered after Nature, many a year,
In the great City pent, winning thy way
With sad yet patient soul, through evil and pain
And strange calamity![2] Ah! slowly sink
Behind the western ridge, thou glorious sun!
Shine in the slant beams of the sinking orb,
Ye purple heath-flowers! richlier burn, ye clouds!
Live in the yellow light, ye distant groves!
And kindle, thou blue ocean! So my Friend
Struck with deep joy may stand, as I have stood,
Silent with swimming sense; yea, gazing round
On the wide landscape, gaze till all doth seem
Less gross than bodily; and of such hues[3]
As veil the Almighty Spirit, when yet he makes
Spirits perceive his presence.
A delight
Comes sudden on my heart, and I am glad
As I myself were there! Nor in this bower,
This little lime-tree bower, have I not marked
Much that has soothed me. Pale beneath the blaze
Hung the transparent foliage; and I watched
Some broad and sunny leaf, and loved to see
The shadow of the leaf and stem above
Dappling its sunshine! And that walnut-tree
Was richly tinged, and a deep radiance lay
Full on the ancient ivy, which usurps
Those fronting elms, and now, with blackest mass
Makes their dark branches gleam a lighter hue
Through the late twilight: and though now the bat
Wheels silent by, and not a swallow twitters,
Yet still the solitary humble bee
Sings in the bean-flower! Henceforth I shall know
That Nature ne'er deserts the wise and pure;
No plot so narrow, be but Nature there,
No waste so vacant, but may well employ
Each faculty of sense, and keep the heart
Awake to Love and Beauty! and sometimes
'Tis well to be bereft of promised good,
That we may lift the Soul, and contemplate
With lively joy the joys we cannot share.
My gentle-hearted Charles! when the last rook
Beat its straight path along the dusky air
Homewards, I blest it! deeming, its black wing
(Now a dim speck, now vanishing in light)
Had crossed the mighty orb's dilated glory,
While thou stood'st gazing; or when all was still,
Flew creeking o'er thy head, and had a charm
For thee, my gentle-hearted Charles, to whom
No sound is dissonant which tells of Life.

[2] Charles Lamb's* sister, Mary Lamb, murdered their mother in a fit of insanity in 1796.

[3] Following l. 41 and in lieu of l. 42, the 1800 text reads, "Less gross than bodily, a living thing / Which acts upon the mind and with such hues / As cloathe the Almighty Spirit, when he makes."

from Letter to Thomas Poole[1]

March 31, 1800

. . . You charge me with prostration in regard to Wordsworth. Have I affirmed anything miraculous of W.? Is it impossible that a greater poet than any since Milton may appear in our days? Have there any *great* poets appeared since him? . . . Future greatness! Is it not an awful thing, my dearest Poole? What if you had known Milton at the age of thirty, and believed all you now know of him?—What if you should meet in the letters of any then living man, expressions concerning the young Milton *totidem verbis*[2] the same as mine of Wordsworth, would it not convey to you a most delicious sensation? Would it not be an assurance to you that your admiration of the *Paradise Lost* was no superstition, no shadow of flesh and bloodless abstraction, but that the *Man* was even so, that the greatness was incarnate and personal? Wherein blame I you,

[1] Coleridge's neighbor at Stowey, friend, ardent admirer, and sometimes economic support.

[2] **totidem verbis:** in so many words.

my best friend? Only in being borne down by other men's rash opinions concerning W. You yourself, for yourself, judged wisely. . . .

from Letter to William Godwin[1]

Greta Hall, Keswick Wednesday, March 25, 1801

DEAR GODWIN

I fear, your Tragedy[2] will find me in a very unfit state of mind to sit in Judgement on it. I have been, during the last 3 months, undergoing a process of intellectual *exsiccation*.[3] In my long Illness I had compelled into hours of Delight many a sleepless, painful hour of Darkness by chasing down metaphysical Game—and since then I have continued the Hunt, till I found myself unaware at the Root of Pure Mathematics—and up that tall smooth Tree, whose few poor Branches are all at it's very summit, am I climbing by pure adhesive strength of arms and thighs—still slipping down, still renewing my ascent.—You would not know me—! all sounds of similitude keep at such a distance from each other in my mind, that I have *forgotten* how to make a rhyme—I look at the Mountains (that visible God Almighty that looks in at all my windows) I look at the Mountains only for the Curves of their outlines; the Stars, as I behold them, form themselves into Triangles—and my hands are scarred with scratches from a Cat, whose back I was rubbing in the Dark in order to see whether the sparks from it were refrangible by a Prism. The Poet is dead in me—my imagination (or rather the Somewhat that had been imaginative) lies, like a Cold Snuff on the circular Rim of a Brass Candle-stick, without even a stink of Tallow to remind you that it was once cloathed & mitred with Flame. That is past by!—I was once a Volume of Gold Leaf, rising & riding on every breath of Fancy—but I have beaten myself back into weight & density, & now I sink in quicksilver, yea, remain squat and square on the earth amid the hurricane, that makes Oaks and Straws join in one Dance, fifty yards high in the Element.

However, I will do what I can—Taste & Feeling have I none, but what I have, give I unto thee.—But I repeat, that I am unfit to decide on any but works of severe Logic. . . .

Have you seen the second Volume of the Lyrical Ballads, & the Preface prefixed to the First?—I should judge of a man's Heart, and Intellect precisely according to the degree & intensity of the admiration, with which he read those poems—Perhaps, instead of Heart I should have said Taste, but when I think of The Brothers, of Ruth, and of Michael, I recur to the expression, & am enforced to say *Heart*. If I die, and the Booksellers will give you any thing for my Life, be sure to say—'Wordsworth descended on him, like the *Γνῶθι σεαυτόν*[4] from Heaven; by shewing to him what true Poetry was, he made him know, that he himself was no Poet.'

God bless you
& S. T. COLERIDGE

[1] See Godwin.*

[2] **your Tragedy:** *Abbas, King of Persia.*

[3] **exsiccation:** dehydration.

from THE MORNING POST
(1802)

"LATE, late yestreen I saw the New Moon,
With the Old Moon in her arms;
And I fear, I fear, my master dear,
We shall have a deadly storm."

BALLAD OF SIR PATRICK SPENCE

Dejection: An Ode, Written April 4, 1802

WELL! if the Bard was weather-wise, who made
The grand Old Ballad of Sir PATRICK SPENCE,
This night, so tranquil now, will not go hence
Unrous'd by winds, that ply a busier trade
Than those, which mould yon clouds in lazy flakes,
Or this dull sobbing draft, that drones and rakes
Upon the strings of this Aeolian lute,
Which better far were mute.
For lo! the New Moon, winter-bright!
And overspread with phantom light,
(With swimming phantom light o'erspread,
But rimm'd and circled by a silver thread)
I see the Old Moon in her lap, foretelling
The coming on of rain and squally blast:

[4] Greek for "Know thyself."

And O! that even now the gust were swelling,
And the slant night-show'r driving loud and fast!
Those sounds which oft have rais'd me, while they aw'd,
And sent my soul abroad,
Might now perhaps their wonted impulse give,
Might startle this dull pain, and make it move and live!

— II —

A grief without a pang, void, dark, and drear,
A stifled, drowsy, unimpassion'd grief,
Which finds no nat'ral outlet, no relief
In word, or sigh, or tear—
O EDMUND![1] in this wan and heartless mood,
To other thoughts by yonder throstle woo'd,
All this long eve, so balmy and serene,
Have I been gazing on the Western sky,
And its peculiar tint of yellow-green:
And still I gaze—and with how blank an eye!
And those thin clouds above, in flakes and bars,
That give away their motion to the stars;
Those stars, that glide behind them, or between,
Now sparkling, now bedimm'd, but always seen;
Yon crescent moon, as fix'd as if it grew,
In its own cloudless, starless lake of blue,
A boat becalm'd! a lovely sky-canoe!
I see them all, so excellently fair—
I *see*, not *feel*, how beautiful they are!

— III —

My genial spirits fail,
And what can these avail,
To lift the smoth'ring weight from off my breast!
It were a vain endeavour,
Tho' I should gaze for ever
On that green light that lingers in the west:
I may not hope from outward forms to win
The passion and the life, whose fountains are within!

— IV —

O EDMUND! we receive but what we give,
And in *our* life alone does Nature live:
Ours is her wedding-garment, ours her shroud!
And would we aught behold, of higher worth,
Than that inanimate cold world, *allow'd*
To the poor loveless ever-anxious crowd,
Ah from the soul itself must issue forth,
A light, a glory, a fair luminous cloud
Enveloping the earth—
And from the soul itself must there be sent
A sweet and potent voice, of its own birth,
Of all sweet sounds the life and element!
O pure of heart! Thou need'st not ask of me
What this strong music in the soul may be?
What, and wherein it doth exist,
This light, this glory, this fair luminous mist,
This beautiful and beauty-making pow'r?
Joy, virtuous EDMUND! joy, that ne'er was given,
Save to the pure, and in their purest hour,
Joy, EDMUND! is the spirit and the pow'r,
Which wedding Nature to us gives in dow'r
A new earth and new Heaven,
Undream'd of by the sensual and the proud—
Joy is the sweet voice, Joy the luminous cloud—
We, we ourselves rejoice!
And thence flows all that charms or ear or light,
All melodies the echoes of that voice
All colours a suffusion from that light.

— V —

Yes, dearest EDMUND, yes!
There was a time when, tho' my path was rough,
This joy within me dallied with distress,
And all misfortunes were but as the stuff
Whence fancy made me dreams of happiness:
For hope grew round me, like the twining vine,
And fruits and foliage, not my own, seem'd mine.
But now afflictions bow me down to earth:
Nor care I, that they rob me of my mirth,
But O! each visitation
Suspends what nature gave me at my birth,
My shaping spirit of imagination.[2]

[1] William Wordsworth.

[2] The 1817 text continues this stanza with the lines: "For not to think of what I needs must feel, / But to be still and patient, all I can; / And haply by abstruse research to steal / From my own nature all the natural Man— / This was my sole resource, my only plan; / Till that which suits a part infects the whole, / And now is almost grown the habit of my Soul." See *Biographia Literaria*, I,* also published in 1817, for the origin of this inclination.

—VIII[3]—

O wherefore did I let it haunt my mind,
    This dark distressful dream?[4]
I turn from it and listen to the wind
    Which long has rav'd unnotic'd. What a scream
Of agony, by torture, lengthen'd out,
That lute sent forth! O wind, that rav'st without,
    Bare crag, or mountain tairn,[5] or blasted tree,
Or pine-grove, whither woodman never clomb,
Or lonely house, long held the witches' home,
    Methinks were fitter instruments for thee,
Mad Lutanist! who, in this month of show'rs,
Of dark-brown gardens, and of peeping flow'rs,
Mak'st devil's yule, with worse than wintry song,
The blossoms, buds, and tim'rous leaves among.
    Thou Actor, perfect in all tragic sounds!
        Thou mighty Poet, ev'n to frenzy bold!
What tell'st thou now about?
'Tis of the rushing of an host in rout,
    With many groans of men with smarting wounds—
        At once they groan with pain, and shudder with the cold!
But hush! there is a pause of deepest silence!
    And all that noise, as of a rushing crowd,
        With groans and tremulous shudderings—all is over!
    It tells another tale, with sounds less deep and loud—
            A tale of less affright,
        And temper'd with delight,
    As EDMUND's self had fram'd the tender lay—[6]
        'Tis of a little child,
        Upon a lonesome wild,
Not far from home; but she has lost her way—
And now moans low, in utter grief and fear;
And now screams loud, and hopes to make her mother *hear!*

—IX—

'Tis midnight, and small thoughts have I of sleep;
Full seldom may my friend such vigils keep!
Visit him, gentle Sleep, with wings of healing,
    And may this storm be but a mountain birth,[7]
May all the stars hang bright above his dwelling,
    Silent, as tho' they *watch'd* the sleeping earth!
        With light heart may he rise,
        Gay fancy, cheerful eyes,
And sing his lofty song, and teach me to rejoice!
O EDMUND, friend of my devoutest choice,
O rais'd from anxious dread and busy care,
By the immenseness of the good and fair
Which thou see'st ev'ry where
Joy lifts thy spirit, joy attunes thy voice,
To thee do all things live from pole to pole,
Their life the eddying of thy living soul!
O simple spirit, guided from above,
O lofty Poet, full of light and love,
Brother and friend of my devoutest choice,
Thus may'st thou ever evermore rejoice!

ΕΣΤΗΣΕ.[8]

[3] A line of asterisks and a note to this poem states: "The sixth and seventh Stanzas omitted."

[4] 1817 variant to ll. 88–89: "Hence, viper thoughts, that coil around my mind, / Reality's dark dream!"

[5] Tairn, a small lake, generally, if not always, applied to the lakes up in the mountains, and which are the feeders of those in the vallies. This address to the wind will not appear extravagant to those who have heard it at night, in a mountainous country. [S.T.C.]

[6] Wordsworth's "Lucy Gray."*

[7] Cf. Horace's *The Art of Poetry*: "What will this boaster produce in keeping with such mouthing? Mountains will labour, to birth will come a laughter-rousing mouse! How much better he who makes no foolish effort."

[8] Greek letters, "STC," the author's initials.

from THE MORNING POST

from Once a Jacobin Always a Jacobin[1]

(21 October 1802)

. . . What *is* a Jacobin? Perhaps the best answer to this question would be, that it is a term of abuse, the convenient watch-word of a faction. Of course, it has either no

[1] By this time in the French Revolution, Napoleon had himself appointed Consul for life (May 1802) and France had recently invaded Switzerland (October 1802) to assure a government friendly to France. Former sympathizers with the Revolution were deeply shaken by both events, and *Jacobinism* became a label of embarrassment, ridicule, and even shame.

meaning, or a very vague one: for definite terms are unmanageable things, and the passions of men do not readily gather round them. Party rage, and fanatical aversion, have their birth place, and natural abode, in floating and obscure generalities, and seldom or never burst forth, except from clouds and vapours. Thunder and lightning from a clear blue sky has been deemed a miracle in all ages. But though we should find it difficult to determine, what a Jacobin *is*, we may however easily conjecture, what the different sects of Anti-Jacobins have meant by the word.

The base and venal creatures, and the blind and furious bigots, of the late Ministry, comprehended under that word all, who from whatever cause opposed the late war, and the late Ministry, and whom they hate for this opposition with such mortal hatred, as is usual with bigots alarmed, and detected culprits. *"Once a Jacobin, always a Jacobin,"* signifies no more in the minds of these men, than *"such a one is a man, whom I shall never cease to hate."* With other men, honest and less violent Anti-Jacobins, the word implies a man, whose affections have been warmly and deeply interested in the cause of general freedom, who has hoped all good and honourable things both *of*, and *for*, mankind. In this sense of the word, Jacobin, the adage would affirm, that no man can ever become altogether an apostate to Liberty, who has at any time been sincerely and fervently attached to it. His hopes will burn like the Greek fire, hard to be extinguished, and easily rekindling. Even when he despairs of the cause, he will yet *wish*, that it had been successful. And even when private interests have warped his public character, his convictions will remain, and his wishes often rise up in rebellion against his outward actions and public avowals. Thus interpreted, the assertion, *"Once a Jacobin, always a Jacobin,"* is so favourable a representation of human nature, that we are willing, too willing perhaps, to admit it even without proof.

There is yet a third class of Anti-Jacobins, and of this class we profess ourselves to be, who use the word, *Jacobin*, as they use the word, *Whig*, and both words only for want of better; who confess, that Jacobin is too often a word of vague abuse, but believe, that there are certain definite ideas, hitherto not expressed in any single word, which may be attached to this word; and who in consequence uniformly use the word, Jacobin, with certain definite ideas attached to it, those ideas, and no other. A Jacobin, in *our* sense of the term, is one who believes, and is disposed to act on the belief, that all, or the greater part of, the happiness or misery, virtue or vice, of mankind, depends on forms of government; who admits no form of government as either good or rightful, which does not flow directly and formally from the persons governed; who—considering life, health, moral and intellectual improvement, and liberty both of person and conscience, as blessings which governments are bound as far as possible to increase and secure to every inhabitant, whether he has or has not any fixed property, and moreover as blessings of infinitely greater value to each individual, than the preservation of property can be to any individual—does consequently and consistently hold, that every inhabitant, who has attained the age of reason, has a natural and inalienable right to an *equal* share of power in the choice of the governors. In other words, the Jacobin affirms that no legislature can be rightful or good, which did not proceed from universal suffrage. In the power, and under the controul, of a legislature so chosen, he places all and every thing, with the exception of the natural rights of man, and the means appointed for the preservation and exercise of these rights, by a direct vote of the nation itself—that is to say, by a CONSTITUTION. Finally, the Jacobin deems it both justifiable and expedient to effect these requisite changes in faulty governments, by absolute revolutions, and considers no violences as properly rebellious or criminal, which are the *means* of giving to a nation the power of declaring and enforcing its sovereign will.

In brief, therefore, a Jacobin's Creed is this: 1. A government is the organ, by which form and publicity are given to the sovereign will of the people; and by which that will is enforced and exercised. 2. A government is likewise the instrument and means of purifying and regulating the national will by its public discussions, and by direct institutions for the comforts and instruction of the people. 3. Every native of a country has an equal right to that quantity of property, which is necessary for the sustenance of his life, and health. 4. All property beyond this, not being itself a right, can confer no right. Superior wisdom, with superior virtue, would indeed confer a right of superior power; but who is to decide on the possession? Not the person himself, who makes the claim: and if the people, then the right is given, and not inherent. Votes, therefore, *cannot* be *weighed* in this way, and they *must not* be weighed in any other way, and nothing remains possible, but that they must be *numbered*. No form of electing representatives is rightful, but that of universal suffrage. Every individual has a *right* to elect, and a capability of being elected. 5. The legislature has an absolute power over all other property, but that of article 3: unless the people shall have declared otherwise in the constitution. 6. All governments not constituted on these principles are unjust Governments. 7. The people have a right to overturn them, in whatever way it is possible; and any means necessary to this end become, *ipso facto,* right means. 8. It is the right and duty of each individual, living under that Government, as far as in him lies, to impel and enable the people to exercise these rights. . . .

from THE FRIEND[1]

from Nos. 5 & 6 [Genius and Novelty]

(14–21 September 1809)

. . . I am fully aware, that what I am writing and have written (in these latter paragraphs at least) will expose me to the Censure of some, as bewildering myself and Readers with Metaphysics; to the Ridicule of others as a Schoolboy declaimer on old and worn-out Truisms or exploded Fancies; and to the Objection of most as obscure. The last real or supposed defect requires and will receive a particular answer in a following Number, preparatory to the disquisition on the elements of our moral and intellectual faculties. Of the two former, I shall take the present opportunity of declaring my sentiments: especially as I have already received a hint that my "idol, MILTON, has represented Metaphysics as the subjects which the bad Spirits in Hell delight in discussing."[2] And truly, if I had exerted my subtlety and invention in persuading myself and others that we are but living machines, and that (as one of the late followers of Hobbes and Hartley has expressed the system) the Assassin and his Dagger are equally fit objects of moral esteem and abhorrence; or if with a Writer of wider influence and higher authority, I had reduced all Virtue to a selfish prudence eked out by Superstition (for assuredly, a creed which takes its central point in conscious selfishness, whatever be the forms or names that act on the selfish passion, a Ghost or a Constable, can have but a distant relationship to that Religion, which places its' Essence in our loving our Neighbour as ourselves, and God above all) I know not, by what arguments I could repel the sarcasm. But what are my Metaphysics, but the referring of the Mind to its' own Consciousness for Truths indispensible to its' own Happiness? To what purposes do I, or am I about, to employ them? To perplex our clearest notions and living moral instincts? To deaden the feelings of Will and free Power, to extinguish the Light of Love and of Conscience, to make myself and others Worth-less, Soul-less, God-less? No! To expose the Folly and the Legerdemain[3] of those who have thus abused the blessed machine of Language; to support all old and venerable Truths; and by them to support, to kindle, to project the Spirit; to make the Reason spread Light over our Feelings, to make our Feelings, with their vital warmth, actualize our Reason;—these are my objects, these are my subjects, and are these the Metaphysics which the bad Spirits in Hell delight in?

But how shall I avert the scorn of those Critics who laugh at the oldness of my Topics, Evil and Good, Necessity and Arbitrement, Immortality and the ultimate Aim. By what shall I regain their favour? My Themes must be *new,* a French Constitution; a Balloon; a change of Ministry; a fresh Batch of Kings on the Continent, or of Peers in our happier Island; or who had the best of it of two parliamentary Gladiators, and whose Speech, on the subject of Europe bleeding at a thousand wounds, or our own Country struggling for herself and all human nature, was cheered by the greatest number of *Laughs, loud Laughs, and very loud Laughs,* (which, carefully marked by italics, form most conspicuous and strange parentheses in the Newspaper Reports). Or if I must be philosophical, the last chemical discoveries, provided I do not trouble my Reader with the Principle which gives them their highest Interest, and the character of intellectual grandeur to the Discoverer; or the last shower of stones, and that they were supposed, by certain Philosophers, to have been projected from some Volcano in the Moon, taking care, however, not to add any of their cramp reasons for their Opinion! Something new, however, it must be, quite new and quite out of themselves: for whatever is within them, whatever is deep within them, must be as old as the first dawn of human Reason. But to find no contradiction in the union of old and new, to contemplate the ANCIENT OF DAYS with feelings as fresh as if they then sprang forth at

[1] Published by Coleridge in twenty-seven numbers between 1 June 1809 and 15 March 1810 in part to compete with *Cobbett's Weekly Political Register* by providing readers with fixed principles rather than partisan reporting for making their own judgments on the events of the day. Coleridge collected his essays into volumes of *The Friend* in 1812 and 1818.

[2] Reference to Milton's devils delighting in metaphysical disquisition. *Paradise Lost,* II.555–69.

[3] **Legerdemain:** sleight of hand; deceit.

his own fiat, this characterizes the minds that feel the Riddle of the World, and may help to unravel it! To carry on the feelings of Childhood into the powers of Manhood, to combine the Child's sense of wonder and novelty with the Appearances which every day for perhaps forty years had rendered familiar,

With Sun and Moon and Stars throughout the year,
And Man and Woman—[4]

this is the character and privilege of Genius, and one of the marks which distinguish Genius from Talents. And so to represent familiar objects as to awaken the minds of others to a like freshness of sensation concerning them (that constant accompaniment of mental, no less than of bodily convalescence)—to the same modest questioning of a self-discovered and intelligent ignorance, which, like the deep and massy Foundations of a Roman Bridge, forms half of the whole Structure (*prudens interrogatio dimidium scientiæ,*[5] says Lord Bacon)—this is the prime merit of Genius, and its' most unequivocal mode of manifestation. Who has not a thousand times, seen it snow upon water? Who has not seen it with a new feeling, since he has read Burns's comparison of sensual pleasure

To snow that falls upon a river,
A moment white—then gone for ever![6]

In Philosophy equally as in Poetry, Genius produces the strongest impressions of novelty, while it rescues the stalest and most admitted Truths from the Impotence caused by the very circumstance of their universal admission. Extremes meet—a proverb, by the bye, to collect and explain all the instances and exemplifications of which, would employ a Life. Truths, of all others the most awful and mysterious, yet being at the same time of universal interest, are too often considered as so true that they lose all the powers of Truth, and lie bed-ridden in the Dormitory of the Soul, side by side with the most despised and exploded Errors. . . .

But God created Man in his own Image; to be the Image of his own Eternity and Infinity created he Man. He gave us Reason and with Reason Ideas of its own formation and underived from material Nature, self-consciousness, Principles, and above all, the Law of Conscience, which in the power of an holy and omnipotent Being *commands* us to attribute Reality—among the numerous Ideas[7] mathematical or philosophical, which the Reason by the necessity of its own excellence, creates for itself—to those, (and those only) without which the Conscience would be baseless and contradictory; namely, to the Ideas of Soul, the Free Will, Immortality, and God. To God as the Reality of the Conscience and the Source of all Obligation; to Free Will, as the power of the human being to maintain the Obedience, which God through the Conscience has commanded, against all the might of Nature; and to the immortality of the Soul as a State in which the weal and woe of man shall be proportioned to his moral Worth. . . .[8]

[4] Cf. Milton's Sonnet XXII.

[5] **prudens . . . scientiae:** "wise interrogating is half a knowledge."

[6] Cf. Robert Burns's *Tam O'Shanter,* ll. 61–62: "Or like the snow falls in the river— / A moment white, then melts for ever."

[7] The essay ends here in the 14 September issue and continues with "mathematical or philosophical" to the end in the 21 September issue.

[8] This essay revised is XV in *The Friend* (1812).

from No. 8. [Luther and Rousseau]

(5 October 1809)

Shall we succeed better or worse with the next pair, in this our new Dance of Death, or rather of the Shadows which we have brought forth—two by two—from the historic Ark? In our first couple[1] we have at least secured an honourable retreat, and though we failed as to the *Agents,* we have maintained a fair analogy in the *Actions* and the Objects. But the heroic LUTHER, a Giant awaking in his strength! and the crazy ROUSSEAU,[2] the Dreamer of love-sick Tales, and the Spinner of speculative Cobwebs; shy of light as the Mole, but as quick-eared too for every whisper of the public opinion; the Teacher of stoic *Pride* in his Principles, yet the Victim of morbid *Vanity* in his Feel-

[1] A comparison between Erasmus and Voltaire, much to the latter's disadvantage.

[2] Martin Luther (1483–1546), inspired leader of the Protestant Reformation in Germany, and Jean-Jacques Rousseau (1712–1778), tempestuous inspiration for many of the ideas and literary forms associated with Romanticism—primitivism, egalitarianism, the return to nature, the glories of childhood, confessional writing, etc.

ings and Conduct! from what point of Likeness can we commence the Comparison between a Luther and a Rousseau? And truly had I been seeking for Characters that taken, as they really existed, closely resemble each other, and this too to our first apprehensions, and according to the common rules of biographical comparison, I could scarcely have made a more unlucky choice: unless I had desired that my Parallel of the German "Son of Thunder" and the Visionary of Geneva, should sit on the same bench with honest Fluellin's of Alexander the Great and Harry of Monmouth. Still, however, the same analogy would hold as in my former instance: the effects produced on their several Ages by Luther and Rousseau, were commensurate with each other, and were produced in both cases by (what their Contemporaries felt as) serious and vehement eloquence, and an elevated tone of moral feeling: and Luther, not less than Rousseau, was actuated by an almost superstitious hatred of Superstition, and a turbulent prejudice against Prejudices. In the relation too which their Writings severally bore to those of Erasmus and Voltaire, and the way in which the latter co-operated with them to the same general end, each finding its' own class of Admirers and Proselytes, the Parallel is complete. I cannot, however, rest here! Spite of the apparent incongruities, I am disposed to plead for a resemblance in the Men themselves, for that similarity in their *radical* natures, which I abandoned all pretence and desire of shewing in the instances of Voltaire and Erasmus. But then my Readers must think of Luther not as he really was, but as he might have been, if he had been born in the Age and under the Circumstances of the Swiss Philosopher. For this purpose I must strip him of many advantages which he derived from his own Times, and must contemplate him in his natural weaknesses as well as in his original strength. Each referred all things to his own Ideal. The Ideal was indeed widely different in the one and in the other: and this was not the least of Luther's many advantages, or (to use a favourite phrase of his own) not one of his least favours of preventing Grace. Happily for him he had derived his standard from a common measure already received by the Good and Wise: I mean the inspired Writings, the study of which Erasmus had previously restored among the Learned. To know that we are in sympathy with others, moderates our feelings as well as strengthens our convictions: and for the mind, which opposes itself to the faith of the multitude, it is more especially desirable, that there should exist an object out of itself, on which it may fix its attention, and thus balance its own energies.

Rousseau, on the contrary, in the inauspicious Spirit of his Age and Birth-place,[3] had slipped the Cable of his Faith, and steered by the Compass of unaided Reason, ignorant of the hidden Currents that were bearing him out of his Course, and too proud to consult the faithful Charts prized and held sacred by his Forefathers. But the strange influences of his bodily temperament on his understanding; his constitutional Melancholy pampered into a morbid excess by solitude; his wild Dreams of suspicion; his hypochondriacal Fancies of hosts of conspirators all leagued against him and his cause; and headed by some arch-enemy, to whose machinations he attributed every trifling mishap (all as much the creatures of his imagination, as if instead of Men he had conceived them to be infernal Spirits and Beings preternatural)—these, or at least the predisposition to them, existed in the ground-work of his Nature: they were parts of Rousseau himself. And what corresponding in *kind* to these, not to speak of *degree,* can we detect in the Character of his supposed Parallel? This difficulty will suggest itself at the first thought, to those who derive all their knowledge of Luther from the meagre biography met with in "The Lives of eminent Reformers," or even from the ecclesiastical Histories of Mosheim or Milner: for a Life of Luther, in extent and style of execution proportioned to the grandeur and interest of the Subject, a Life of the *Man* Luther, as well as of Luther the *Theologian,* is still a desideratum in English Literature, though perhaps there is no Subject for which so many unused materials are extant, both printed and in manuscript.

Whoever has sojourned in Eisenach, will assuredly have visited the WARTEBURG, interesting by so many historical Associations, which stands on a high rock, about two miles to the south from the City Gate. To this Castle Luther was taken on his return from the imperial Diet, where Charles the fifth had pronounced the ban upon him, and limited his safe convoy to one and twenty days. . . .

[3] Infidelity was so common in Geneva about that Time, that Voltaire in one of his Letters exults, that in this, Calvin's own City, some half dozen only of the most ignorant believed in Christianity under any form. This was, no doubt, one of Voltaire's usual lies of exaggeration: it is not however to be denied, that here, and throughout Switzerland, he and the dark Master in whose service he employed himself, had ample grounds of triumph [S.T.C.].

To this friendly Imprisonment the Reformation owes many of Luther's most important labours. In this Place he wrote his Works against auricular Confession, against Jacob Latronum, the tract on the abuse of Masses, that against clerical and monastic Vows, composed his Exposition of the 22, 27, and 68 Psalms, finished his Declaration of the Magnificat, began to write his Church Homilies, and translated the New Testament. Here too, and during this time, he is said to have hurled his inkstand at the Devil, the black spot from which yet remains on the stone wall of the room he studied in; which, surely, no one will have visited the Warteburg without having had pointed out to him by the good Catholic who is, or at least some few years ago was, the Warden of the Castle. He must have been either a very supercilious or a very incurious Traveller if he did not, for the gratification of his Guide at least, inform himself by means of his Penknife, that the said marvellous blot bids defiance to all the toils of the scrubbing Brush, and is to remain a sign for ever; and with this advantage over most of its kindred, that being capable of a double interpretation, it is equally flattering to the Protestant and the Papist, and is regarded by the wonder-loving Zealots of both Parties, with equal Faith.

Whether the great Man ever did throw his inkstand at his Satanic Majesty, whether he ever boasted of the Exploit, and himself declared the dark blotch on his Study Wall in the Warteburg, to be the result and relict of this Author-like hand-grenado (happily for mankind he used his inkstand at other times to better purpose, and with more effective hostility against the Arch-fiend), I leave to my Readers own Judgement; on condition, however, that he has previously perused Luther's Table Talk, and other Writings of the same stamp, of some of his most illustrious Contemporaries, which contain facts still more strange and whimsical, related by themselves and of themselves, and accompanied with solemn protestations of the Truth of their statements. Luther's Table Talk, which to a truly philosophic mind, will not be less interesting than Rousseau's Confessions, I have not myself the means of consulting at present, and cannot therefore say, whether this ink-pot Adventure is, or is not, told or referred to in it; but many considerations inclined me to give credit to the Story. . . .

Had Luther been himself a Prince, he could not have desired better treatment than he received during his eight months stay in the Warteburg; and in consequence of a more luxurious diet than he had been accustomed to, he was plagued with temptations both from the "Flesh and the Devil." It is evident from his Letters[4] that he suffered under great irritability of his nervous System, the common effect of deranged Digestion in men of sedentary habits, who are at the same time intense thinkers: and this irritability added to, and revivifying the impressions made upon him in early life, and fostered by the theological Systems of his Manhood, is abundantly sufficient to explain all his Apparitions and all his nightly combats with evil Spirits. I see nothing improbable in the supposition, that in one of those unconscious half sleeps, or rather those rapid alternations of the sleeping with the half waking state, which is the *true witching-time,*

———————— "the season
Wherein the spirits hold their wont to walk"[5]

the fruitful matrix of Ghosts—I see nothing improbable, that in some one of those momentary Slumbers, into which the suspension of all Thought in the perplexity of intense thinking so often passes; Luther should have had a full view of the Room in which he was sitting, of his writing Table and all the Implements of Study, as they really existed, and at the same time a brain-image of the Devil, vivid enough to have acquired apparent *Outness*, and a distance regulated by the proportion of its distinctness to that of the objects really impressed on the outward senses.

I will endeavour to make my meaning more clear to those of my Readers, who are fortunate enough to find it obscure in consequence of their own good health and unshattered nerves. The Window of my Library at Keswick is opposite to the Fire-place, and looks out on the very large Garden that occupies the whole slope of the Hill on which the House stands. Consequently, the rays of Light transmitted *through* the Glass, (i.e. the Rays from the Garden, the opposite Mountains, and the Bridge, River, Lake, and Vale interjacent) and the rays reflected *from* it, (of the Fire-place, &c.) enter the eye at the same moment. At the coming on of Evening, it was my frequent amusement to watch the image or reflection of the Fire, that seemed

---

[4] I can scarcely conceive a more delightful Volume than might be made from Luther's Letters, especially from those that were written from the Warteburg, if they were translated in the simple, sinewy, idiomatic, *hearty* mother-tongue of the original. A difficult task I admit—and scarcely possible for any man, however great his Talents in other respects, whose favourite reading has not lain among the English Writers from Edward the sixth to Charles the first. [S.T.C.]

[5] Cf. *Hamlet*, I.iv.5–6: "it draws near the season / Wherein the spirit held his wont to walk."

burning in the bushes or between the trees in different parts of the Garden or the Fields beyond it, according as there was more or less Light; and which still arranged itself among the real objects of Vision, with a distance and magnitude proportioned to its greater or less faintness. For still as the darkness encreased, the Image of the Fire lessened and grew nearer and more distinct; till the twilight had deepened into perfect night, when all outward objects being excluded, the window became a perfect Looking-glass: save only that my Books on the side shelves of the Room were lettered, as it were, on their Backs with Stars, more or fewer as the sky was more or less clouded (the rays of the stars being at that time the only ones transmitted.) Now substitute the Phantom from the brain for the Images of *reflected* light (the Fire for instance) and the Forms of the room and its furniture for the *transmitted* rays, and you have a fair resemblance of an Apparition, and a just conception of the manner in which it is seen together with real objects. As I shall devote some future Numbers to the Subject of Dreams, Visions, Ghosts, Witchcraft, &c. in which I shall first give, and then endeavour to explain the most interesting and best attested fact of each, which has come within my knowledge, either from Books or from personal Testimony, I defer till then the explanation of the mode in which our Thoughts, in states of morbid Slumber, become at times perfectly *dramatic* (for in certain sorts of dreams the dullest Wight becomes a Shakespeare) and by what Law the form of the Vision appears to talk to us its own thoughts in a voice as audible as the shape is visible; and this too oftentimes in connected trains, and sometimes even with a concentration of Power which may easily impose on the soundest judgements, uninstructed in the *Optics* and *Acoustics* of the inner sense, for Revelations and gifts of Prescience. I will only remark, in aid of the present case, that it would appear incredible to Persons not accustomed to these subtle notices of self observation, what small and remote resemblances, what mere *hints* of likeness from some real external object, (especially if the shape be aided by colour) will suffice to make a vivid thought consubstantiate with the real object, and derive from it an outward perceptibility. Even when we are broad awake, if we are in anxious expectation, how often will not the most confused sounds of nature be heard by us as articulate sounds? for instance, the babbling of a brook will appear, for a moment, the voice of a Friend, for whom we are waiting, calling out our own names, &c. A short meditation, therefore, on this Law of the imagination, that a Likeness in part tends to become a likeness of the whole, will make it not only conceivable but probable, that the Inkstand itself, and the dark-coloured Stone on the Wall, which Luther perhaps had never till then noticed, might have a considerable influence in the production of the Fiend, and of the hostile act with which his obtrusive visit was repelled.

If this Christian Hercules, this heroic Cleanser of the Augean Stable[6] of Apostacy, had been born and educated in the present or the preceding Generation, he would, doubtless, have held himself for a Man of Genius and original Power. But with this faith alone he would scarcely have removed the Mountains which he did remove. The Darkness and Superstition of the Age, which required such a Reformer, had moulded his mind for the reception of ideas concerning himself, better suited to inspire the strength and enthusiasm necessary for the task of Reformation, ideas more in sympathy with the spirits whom he was to influence. He deemed himself gifted with supernatural influxes, an especial Servant of Heaven, a chosen Warrior, fighting as the General of a small but faithful troop, against an Army of evil Beings headed by the Prince of the Air. These were no metaphorical Beings in his Apprehension. He was a Poet indeed, as great a Poet as ever lived in any Age or Country; but his poetic images were so vivid, that they mastered the Poet's own mind! He was *possessed* with them, as with substances distinct from himself: LUTHER did not *write,* he *acted* Poems. The Bible was a spiritual indeed, but not a *figurative* Armoury in his belief: it was the magazine of his warlike stores, and from thence he was to arm himself, and supply both Shield, and Sword, and Javelin, to the Elect. Methinks I see him sitting, the heroic Student, in his Chamber in the Warteburg, with his midnight Lamp before him, seen by the late Traveller in the distant Plain of *Bischofsroda,* as a Star on the Mountain! Below it lies the Hebrew Bible open, on which he gazes, his brow pressing on his palm, brooding over some obscure Text, which he desires to make plain to the simple Boor and to the humble Artizan, and to transfer its' whole force into their own natural and living Tongue. And he himself does not understand it! Thick Darkness lies on the original Text: he counts the Letters, he calls up the Roots of each separate Word, and questions them as the familiar Spirits of an Oracle. In vain thick Darkness continues to cover it! not a ray of meaning dawns through it. With sullen and angry Hope he

[6] **Augean Stable**: reference to Augeas, legendary king of Elis, who left his stables uncleaned for thirty years.

reached for the VULGATE, his old and sworn enemy, the treacherous confederate of the Roman Antichrist, which he so gladly, when he can, rebukes for idolatrous Falsehoods, which had dared place

> "Within the sanctuary itself their shrines,
> Abominations!" ——————[7]

Now—O thought of humiliation—he must entreat its aid. See! there has the sly Spirit of Apostacy worked-in a phrase, which favours the doctrine of Purgatory, the intercession of Saints, or the efficacy of Prayers for the Dead. And what is worst of all, the interpretation is plausible. The original Hebrew might be forced into this meaning: and no other meaning seems to lie *in* it, none to hover *above* it in the heights of Allegory, none to lurk *beneath* it even in the depths of Cabala![8] This is the work of the Tempter! it is a cloud of Darkness conjured up between the Truth of the sacred Letters and the eyes of his Understanding, by the malice of the Evil One, and for a trial of his Faith! Must he then at length confess, must he subscribe the name of LUTHER to an Exposition which consecrates a Weapon for the hand of the idolatrous Hierarchy? Never! never!

There still remains one auxiliary in reserve, the translation of the Seventy.[9] The Alexandrine Greeks, anterior to the Church itself, could intend no support to its corruptions—the Septuagent will have profaned the Altar of Truth with no incense for the Nostrils of the universal Bishop to snuff up. And here again his hopes are baffled! Exactly at this perplexed Passage had the Greek Translator given his Understanding a Holiday, and made his Pen supply its place. O honoured Luther! as easily mightest thou convert the whole City of Rome, with the Pope and the conclave of Cardinals inclusive, as strike a spark of Light from the Words, and *nothing-but-Words*, of the Alexandrine Version. Disappointed, despondent, enraged, ceasing to *think*, yet continuing his brain on the stretch, in solicitation of a Thought, and gradually giving himself up to angry Fancies, to recollections of past persecutions, to uneasy Fears and inward Defiances, and floating Images of the evil Being, their supposed personal Author, he sinks, without perceiving it, into a Trance of Slumber: during which his brain retains its' waking energies, excepting that what would have been mere *Thoughts* before, now (the action and counterweight of his outward senses and their impressions being withdrawn) shape and condense themselves into *Things*, into Realities! Repeatedly half-wakening, and his eyelids as often re-closing, the objects which really surround him form the place and scenery of his Dream. All at once he sees the Arch-fiend coming forth on the Wall of the Room, from the very spot perhaps, on which his Eyes had been fixed vacantly during the perplexed moments of his former Meditation: the Ink-stand, which he had at the same time been using, becomes associated with it: and in that struggle of Rage, which in these distempered Dreams almost constantly precedes the helpless Terror by the pain of which we are finally awakened, he *imagines* that he hurls it at the Intruder, or not improbably in the first instant of awakening, while yet both his imagination and his eyes are possessed by the Dream, he *actually* hurls it! Some weeks after, perhaps, during which interval he had often mused on the incident, undetermined whether to deem it a Visitation of Satan to him in the body or out of the body, he discovers the dark spot on his Wall, and receives it as a sign and pledge vouchsafed to him of the Event having actually taken place.

Such was Luther under the influences of the Age and Country in and for which he was born. Conceive him a Citizen of Geneva, and a Contemporary of Voltaire; suppose the French Language his Mother-tongue, and the political and moral Philosophy of English Free-thinkers remodelled by *Parisian Fort Esprits*,[10] to have been the objects of his Study;—conceive this change of Circumstances, and Luther will no longer dream of Fiends or of Antichrist—but will he have no Dreams in their place? His melancholy will have changed its' Drapery; but will it find no new Costume wherewith to cloath itself? His impetuous temperament, his deep-working mind, his busy and vivid Imagination—would they not have been a *trouble* to him in a World, where nothing was to be altered, where nothing was to obey his Power, to cease to be that, which it had been, in order to realize his pre-conceptions of what ought to be? His Sensibility, which found Objects for itself, and shadows of human suffering in the harmless Brute, and even the Flowers which he trod upon—might it not naturally, in an unspiritualized Age, have wept and trembled, and dissolved over scenes of earthly Passion, and the

[7] *Paradise Lost*, I.387–90: "yea, often placed / Within his sanctuary itself their shrines, / Abomination; and with cursed things / His holy rites, and solemn feasts profaned."

[8] Occult rabbinical interpretation of the Scriptures, developed between the ninth and thirteenth centuries.

[9] Greek translation of the Old Testament from the third century, BC. According to legend, 70 to 72 Jewish scholars completed the task in 72 days.

[10] **Parisian Fort Esprits:** French philosophes.

struggles of Love with Duty? His Pity, that so easily passed into Rage, would it not have found in the inequalities of Mankind, in the oppressions of Governments, and the miseries of the governed, an entire instead of a divided Object? And might not a perfect Constitution, a Government of Pure Reason, a renovation of the social Contract, have easily supplied the place of the reign of Christ in the new Jerusalem, of the restoration of the visible Church, and the Union of all Men by one Faith in one Charity? Henceforward, then, we will conceive his Reason employed in building up anew the Edifice of *earthly* Society, and his Imagination as pledging itself for the possible realization of the Structure. We will lose the great Reformer, who was born in an Age which needed him, in the Philosopher of Geneva, who was doomed to misapply his Energies to materials the properties of which he misunderstood, and happy only that he did not live to witness the direful effects of his System.[11]

[11] This essay became *The Landing Place,* Essay ii, of *The Friend* (1812).

CHRISTABEL; KUBLA KHAN, A VISION; THE PAINS OF SLEEP[1]

(1816)

— PREFACE —

The first part of the following poem was written in the year one thousand seven hundred and ninety seven, at Stowey in the county of Somerset. The second part, after my return from Germany, in the year one thousand eight hundred, at Keswick, Cumberland. Since the latter date, my poetic powers have been, till very lately, in a state of suspended animation. But as, in my very first conception of the tale, I had the whole present to my mind, with the wholeness, no less than with the liveliness of a vision; I trust that I shall be able to embody in verse the three parts yet to come, in the course of the present year.

It is probable, that if the poem had been finished at either of the former periods, or if even the first and second part had been published in the year 1800, the impression of its originality would have been much greater than I dare at present expect. But for this, I have only my own indolence to blame. The dates are mentioned for the exclusive purpose of precluding charges of plagiarism or servile imitation from myself. For there is among us a set of critics, who seem to hold, that every possible thought and image is traditional; who have no notion that there are such things as fountains in the world, small as well as great; and who would therefore charitably derive every rill, they behold flowing, from a perforation made in some other man's tank. I am confident however, that as far as the present poem is concerned, the celebrated poets whose writings I might be suspected of having imitated,[2] either in particular passages, or in the tone and the spirit of the whole, would be among the first to vindicate me from the charge, and who, on any striking coincidence, would permit me to address them in this doggrel version of two monkish Latin hexameters:

'Tis mine and it is likewise your's,
But an if this will not do;
Let it be mine, good friend! for I
Am the poorer of the two.

I have only to add, that the metre of the Christabel is not, properly speaking, irregular, though it may seem so from its being founded on a new principle: namely, that of counting in each line the accents, not the syllables. Though the latter may vary from seven to twelve, yet in each line the accents will be found to be only four. Nevertheless this occasional variation in the number of syllables is not introduced wantonly, or for the mere ends of convenience, but in correspondence with some transition in the nature of the imagery or passion.

[1] The *Christabel* volume went through three editions in 1816.

Christabel[3]

(1816; comp. 1797–1800)

— PART I —

'Tis the middle of night by the castle clock,
And the owls have awaken'd the crowing cock;
Tu—whit!———Tu—whoo!
And hark, again! the crowing cock,
How drowsily it crew.

[2] Especially Walter Scott,* whose *The Lay of the Last Minstrel** (1805) employed the metrical system Coleridge describes. In 1801, Scott heard Coleridge recite *Christabel* in manuscript. The other celebrated poet is Lord Byron,* who heard the poem in 1811 and imitated its metrics in *Siege of Corinth* (1816).

[3] Coleridge intended *Christabel* for the second edition of *Lyrical Ballads* (1800), but Wordsworth decided against it. The poem remained unpublished, though circulated in manuscript, until 1816.

Sir Leoline, the Baron rich,
Hath a toothless mastiff bitch;
From her kennel beneath the rock
She makes answer to the clock,
Four for the quarters, and twelve for the hour;
Ever and aye, moonshine or shower,
Sixteen short howls, not over loud;
Some say, she sees my lady's shroud.

Is the night chilly and dark?
The night is chilly, but not dark.
The thin gray cloud is spread on high,
It covers but not hides the sky.
The moon is behind, and at the full;
And yet she looks both small and dull.
The night is chill, the cloud is gray:
'Tis a month before the month of May,
And the Spring comes slowly up this way.

The lovely lady, Christabel,
Whom her father loves so well,
What makes her in the wood so late,
A furlong from the castle gate?
She had dreams all yesternight
Of her own betrothed knight;
Dreams, that made her moan and leap,
As on her bed she lay in sleep;
And she in the midnight wood will pray
For the weal of her lover that's far away.

She stole along, she nothing spoke,
The breezes they were still also;
And nought was green upon the oak,
But moss and rarest misletoe:
She kneels beneath the huge oak tree,
And in silence prayeth she.

The lady leaps up suddenly,
The lovely lady, Christabel!
It moan'd as near, as near can be,
But what it is, she cannot tell.—
On the other side it seems to be,
Of the huge, broad-breasted, old oak tree.

The night is chill; the forest bare;
Is it the wind that moaneth bleak?
There is not wind enough in the air
To move away the ringlet curl
From the lovely lady's cheek—
There is not wind enough to twirl
The one red leaf, the last of its clan,
That dances as often as dance it can,
Hanging so light, and hanging so high,
On the topmost twig that looks up at the sky.

Hush, beating heart of Christabel!
Jesu, Maria, shield her well!
She folded her arms beneath her cloak,
And stole to the other side of the oak.
What sees she there?

There she sees a damsel bright,
Drest in a silken robe of white;
Her neck, her feet, her arms were bare,
And the jewels disorder'd in her hair.
I guess, 'twas frightful there to see
A lady so richly clad as she—
Beautiful exceedingly!

Mary mother, save me now!
(Said Christabel,) And who art thou?

The lady strange made answer meet,
And her voice was faint and sweet:—
Have pity on my sore distress,
I scarce can speak for weariness.
Stretch forth thy hand, and have no fear,
Said Christabel, How cam'st thou here?
And the lady, whose voice was faint and sweet,
Did thus pursue her answer meet:—

My sire is of a noble line,
And my name is Geraldine.
Five warriors seiz'd me yestermorn,
Me, even me, a maid forlorn:
They chok'd my cries with force and fright,
And tied me on a palfrey white.
The palfrey was as fleet as wind,
And they rode furiously behind.
They spurr'd amain, their steeds were white;
And once we cross'd the shade of night.
As sure as Heaven shall rescue me,
I have no thought what men they be;
Nor do I know how long it is
(For I have lain in fits, I wis)
Since one, the tallest of the five,
Took me from the palfrey's back,
A weary woman, scarce alive.
Some mutter'd words his comrades spoke:
He plac'd me underneath this oak,
He swore they would return with haste;
Whither they went I cannot tell—
I thought I heard, some minutes past,

Sounds as of a castle bell.
Stretch forth thy hand (thus ended she),
And help a wretched maid to flee.

Then Christabel stretch'd forth her hand
And comforted fair Geraldine,
Saying, that she should command
The service of Sir Leoline;
And straight be convoy'd, free from thrall,
Back to her noble father's hall.
So up she rose, and forth they pass'd,
With hurrying steps, yet nothing fast;
Her lucky stars the lady blest,
And Christabel she sweetly said—
All our household are at rest,
Each one sleeping in his bed;
Sir Leoline is weak in health,
And may not well awaken'd be;
So to my room we'll creep in stealth,
And you to-night must sleep with me.

They cross'd the moat, and Christabel
Took the key that fitted well;
A little door she open'd straight,
All in the middle of the gate;
The gate that was iron'd within and without,
Where an army in battle array had march'd out.
The lady sank, belike thro' pain,
And Christabel with might and main
Lifted her up, a weary weight,
Over the threshold of the gate:
Then the lady rose again,
And mov'd, as she were not in pain.

So free from danger, free from fear,
They cross'd the court: right glad they were.
And Christabel devoutly cried,
To the lady by her side,
Praise we the Virgin all divine
Who hath rescued thee from thy distress!
Alas, alas! said Geraldine,
I cannot speak for weariness.
So free from danger, free from fear,
They cross'd the court: right glad they were
Outside her kennel, the mastiff old
Lay fast asleep, in moonshine cold.
The mastiff old did not awake,
Yet she an angry moan did make!
And what can ail the mastiff bitch?
Never till now she utter'd yell
Beneath the eye of Christabel.
Perhaps it is the owlet's scritch:
For what can ail the mastiff bitch?

They pass'd the hall, that echoes still,
Pass as lightly as you will!
The brands were flat, the brands were dying,
Amid their own white ashes lying;
But when the lady pass'd, there came
A tongue of light, a fit of flame;
And Christabel saw the lady's eye,
And nothing else saw she thereby,
Save the boss of the shield of Sir Leoline tall,
Which hung in a murky old nitch in the wall.
O softly tread, said Christabel,
My father seldom sleepeth well.

Sweet Christabel her feet she bares,
And they are creeping up the stairs;
Now in glimmer, and now in gloom,
And now they pass the Baron's room,
As still as death with stifled breath!
And now have reach'd her chamber door;
And now with eager feet press down
The rushes of her chamber floor.

The moon shines dim in the open air,
And not a moonbeam enters here.
But they without its light can see
The chamber carv'd so curiously,
Carv'd with figures strange and sweet,
All made out of the carver's brain,
For a lady's chamber meet:
The lamp with twofold silver chain
Is fasten'd to an angel's feet.

The silver lamp burns dead and dim;
But Christabel the lamp will trim.
She trimm'd the lamp, and made it bright,
And left it swinging to and fro,
While Geraldine, in wretched plight,
Sank down upon the floor below.

O weary lady, Geraldine,
I pray you, drink this cordial wine!
It is a wine of virtuous powers;
My mother made it of wild flowers.

And will your mother pity me,
Who am a maiden most forlorn?
Christabel answer'd—Woe is me!
She died the hour that I was born.
I have heard the gray-hair'd friar tell,
How on her death-bed she did say,

That she should hear the castle bell
Strike twelve upon my wedding day.
O mother dear! that thou wert here!
I would, said Geraldine, she were!

But soon with alter'd voice, said she—
"Off, wandering mother! Peak and pine!
I have power to bid thee flee."
Alas! what ails poor Geraldine?
Why stares she with unsettled eye?
Can she the bodiless dead espy?
And why with hollow voice cries she,
"Off, woman, off! this hour is mine—
Though thou her guardian spirit be,
Off, woman, off! 'tis given to me."

Then Christabel knelt by the lady's side,
And rais'd to heaven her eyes so blue—
Alas! said she, this ghastly ride—
Dear lady! it hath wilder'd you!
The lady wip'd her moist cold brow,
And faintly said, "'Tis over now!"

Again the wild-flower wine she drank:
Her fair large eyes 'gan glitter bright,
And from the floor whereon she sank,
The lofty lady stood upright:
She was most beautiful to see,
Like a lady of a far countrée.

And thus the lofty lady spake—
All they, who live in the upper sky,
Do love you, holy Christabel!
And you love them, and for their sake
And for the good which me befel,
Even I in my degree will try,
Fair maiden, to requite you well.
But now unrobe yourself; for I
Must pray, ere yet in bed I lie.

Quoth Christabel, so let it be!
And as the lady bade, did she.
Her gentle limbs did she undress,
And lay down in her loveliness.

But thro' her brain of weal and woe
So many thoughts mov'd to and fro,
That vain it were her lids to close;
So half-way from the bed she rose,
And on her elbow did recline
To look at the lady Geraldine.

Beneath the lamp the lady bow'd,
And slowly roll'd her eyes around;
Then drawing in her breath aloud,
Like one that shudder'd, she unbound
The cincture from beneath her breast:
Her silken robe, and inner vest,
Dropt to her feet, and full in view,
Behold! her bosom and half her side—
A sight to dream of, not to tell!
And she is to sleep by Christabel.

She took two paces, and a stride,
And lay down by the maiden's side:
And in her arms the maid she took,
Ah wel-a-day!
And with low voice and doleful look
These words did say:
In the touch of this bosom there worketh a spell,
Which is lord of thy utterance, Christabel!
Thou knowest to-night, and wilt know to-morrow
This mark of my shame, this seal of my sorrow;
But vainly thou warrest,
For this is alone in
Thy power to declare,
That in the dim forest
Thou heard'st a low moaning,
And found'st a bright lady, surpassingly fair:
And didst bring her home with thee in love and in charity,
To shield her and shelter her from the damp air.

—THE CONCLUSION TO PART THE FIRST—

It was a lovely sight to see
The lady Christabel, when she
Was praying at the old oak tree.
Amid the jagged shadows
Of mossy leafless boughs,
Kneeling in the moonlight,
To make her gentle vows;
Her slender palms together prest,
Heaving sometimes on her breast;
Her face resign'd to bliss or bale—
Her face, oh call it fair not pale,
And both blue eyes more bright than clear,
Each about to have a tear.

With open eyes (ah woe is me!)
Asleep, and dreaming fearfully,

Fearfully dreaming, yet I wis,
Dreaming that alone, which is—
O sorrow and shame! Can this be she,
The lady, who knelt at the old oak tree?
And lo! the worker of these harms,
That holds the maiden in her arms,
Seems to slumber still and mild,
As a mother with her child.

A star hath set, a star hath risen,
O Geraldine! since arms of thine
Have been the lovely lady's prison.
O Geraldine! one hour was thine—
Thou'st had thy will! By tairn and rill,
The night-birds all that hour were still.
But now they are jubilant anew,
From cliff and tower, tu—whoo! tu—whoo!
Tu—whoo! tu—whoo! from wood and fell!

And see! the lady Christabel
Gathers herself from out her trance;
Her limbs relax, her countenance
Grows sad and soft; the smooth thin lids
Close o'er her eyes; and tears she sheds—
Large tears that leave the lashes bright!
And oft the while she seems to smile
As infants at a sudden light!

Yea, she doth smile, and she doth weep,
Like a youthful hermitess,
Beauteous in a wilderness,
Who, praying always, prays in sleep.
And, if she move unquietly,
Perchance, 'tis but the blood so free,
Comes back and tingles in her feet.
No doubt, she hath a vision sweet.
What if her guardian spirit 'twere
What if she knew her mother near?
But this she knows, in joys and woes,
That saints will aid if men will call:
For the blue sky bends over all!

— PART II —

Each matin bell, the Baron saith,
Knells us back to a world of death.
These words Sir Leoline first said,
When he rose and found his lady dead:
These words Sir Leoline will say
Many a morn to his dying day.
And hence the custom and law began,
That still at dawn the sacristan,
Who duly pulls the heavy bell,
Five and forty beads must tell
Between each stroke—a warning knell,
Which not a soul can choose but hear
From Bratha Head to Wyn'dermere.

Saith Bracy the bard, So let it knell!
And let the drowsy sacristan
Still count as slowly as he can!
There is no lack of such, I ween
As well fill up the space between.
In Langdale Pike and Witch's Lair,
And Dungeon-ghyll so foully rent,
With ropes of rock and bells of air
Three sinful sextons' ghosts are pent,
Who all give back, one after t'other,
The death-note to their living brother;
And oft too, by the knell offended,
Just as their one! two! three! is ended,
The devil mocks the doleful tale
With a merry peal from Borrowdale.[4]

The air is still! thro' mist and cloud
That merry peal comes ringing loud;
And Geraldine shakes off her dread,
And rises lightly from the bed;
Puts on her silken vestments white,
And tricks her hair in lovely plight,
And nothing doubting of her spell
Awakens the lady Christabel.
"Sleep you, sweet lady Christabel?
I trust that you have rested well."

And Christabel awoke and spied
The same who lay down by her side—
O rather say, the same whom she
Rais'd up beneath the old oak tree!
Nay, fairer yet! and yet more fair!
For she belike hath drunken deep
Of all the blessedness of sleep!
And while she spake, her looks, her air
Such gentle thankfulness declare,
That (so it seem'd) her girded vests

---

[4] Langdale Pike, Witch's Lair, Dungeon-ghyll, and Borrowdale are all places in the English Lake District within the vicinity of Coleridge's home in Keswick and the Wordsworth residence at Grasmere.

Grew tight beneath her heaving breasts.
"Sure I have sinn'd!" said Christabel,
"Now heaven be prais'd if all be well!"
And in low faltering tones, yet sweet,
Did she the lofty lady greet
With such perplexity of mind
As dreams too lively leave behind.

So quickly she rose, and quickly array'd
Her maiden limbs, and having pray'd
That He, who on the cross did groan,
Might wash away her sins unknown,
She forthwith led fair Geraldine
To meet her sire, Sir Leoline.

The lovely maid and the lady tall
Are pacing both into the hall,
And pacing on thro' page and groom
Enter the Baron's presence room.

The Baron rose, and while he prest
His gentle daughter to his breast,
With cheerful wonder in his eyes
The lady Geraldine espies,
And gave such welcome to the same,
As might beseem so bright a dame!

But when he heard the lady's tale,
And when she told her father's name,
Why wax'd Sir Leoline so pale,
Murmuring o'er the name again,
Lord Roland de Vaux of Tryermaine?

Alas! they had been friends in youth
But whispering tongues can poison truth;
And constancy lives in realms above;
And life is thorny; and youth is vain;
And to be wroth with one we love,
Doth work like madness in the brain.
And thus it chanc'd, as I divine,
With Roland and Sir Leoline.
Each spake words of high disdain
And insult to his heart's best brother:
They parted — ne'er to meet again!
But never either found another
To free the hollow heart from paining —
They stood aloof, the scars remaining,
Like cliffs which had been rent asunder;
A dreary sea now flows between,
But neither heat, nor frost, nor thunder,
Shall wholly do away, I ween,
The marks of that which once hath been.

Sir Leoline, a moment's space,
Stood gazing on the damsel's face;
And the youthful Lord of Tryermaine
Came back upon his heart again.

O then the Baron forgot his age,
His noble heart swell'd high with rage;
He swore by the wounds in Jesu's side,
He would proclaim it far and wide
With trump and solemn heraldry,
That they, who thus had wrong'd the dame,
Were base as spotted infamy!
"And if they dare deny the same,
My herald shall appoint a week,
And let the recreant traitors seek
My tournay court — that there and then
I may dislodge their reptile souls
From the bodies and forms of men!"
He spake: his eye in lightning rolls!
For the lady was ruthlessly seiz'd; and he kenn'd
In the beautiful lady the child of his friend!

And now the tears were on his face,
And fondly in his arms he took
Fair Geraldine, who met th' embrace,
Prolonging it with joyous look.
Which when she view'd, a vision fell
Upon the soul of Christabel,
The vision of fear, the touch and pain!
She shrunk and shudder'd, and saw again
(Ah, woe is me! Was it for thee,
Thou gentle maid! such sights to see?)
Again she saw that bosom old,
Again she felt that bosom cold,
And drew in her breath with a hissing sound:
Whereat the Knight turn'd wildly round,
And nothing saw, but his own sweet maid
With eyes uprais'd, as one that pray'd.

The touch, the sight, had pass'd away,
And in its stead that vision blest,
Which comforted her after-rest,
While in the lady's arms she lay,
Had put a rapture in her breast,
And on her lips and o'er her eyes
Spread smiles like light!
With new surprise,
"What ails then my beloved child?"
The Baron said — His daughter mild
Made answer, "All will yet be well!"
I ween, she had no power to tell

Aught else: so mighty was the spell.
Yet he, who saw this Geraldine,
Had deem'd her sure a thing divine,
Such sorrow with such grace she blended,
As if she fear'd, she had offended
Sweet Christabel, that gentle maid!
And with such lowly tones she pray'd,
She might be sent without delay
Home to her father's mansion.
"Nay!
Nay, by my soul!" said Leoline.
"Ho! Bracy the bard, the charge be thine!
Go thou, with music sweet and loud,
And take two steeds with trappings proud,
And take the youth whom thou lov'st best
To bear thy harp, and learn thy song,
And clothe you both in solemn vest,
And over the mountains haste along,
Lest wand'ring folk, that are abroad,
Detain you on the valley road.

And when he has cross'd the Irthing flood,
My merry bard! he hastes, he hastes
Up Knorren Moor, thro' Halegarth Wood,
And reaches soon that castle good
Which stands and threatens Scotland's wastes.

Bard Bracy! bard Bracy! your horses are fleet,
Ye must ride up the hall, your music so sweet,
More loud than your horses' echoing feet!
And loud and loud to Lord Roland call,
Thy daughter is safe in Langdale hall!
Thy beautiful daughter is safe and free—
Sir Leoline greets thee thus thro' me.
He bids thee come without delay
With all thy numerous array;
And take thy lovely daughter home,
And he will meet thee on the way
With all his numerous array
White with their panting palfreys' foam,
And, by mine honour! I will say,
That I repent me of the day
When I spake words of fierce disdain
To Roland de Vaux of Tryermaine!—
—For since that evil hour hath flown,
Many a summer's sun have shone;
Yet ne'er found I a friend again
Like Roland de Vaux of Tryermaine."

The lady fell, and clasped his knees,
Her face uprais'd, her eyes o'erflowing;
And Bracy replied, with faltering voice,
His gracious hail on all bestowing:—
Thy words, thou sire of Christabel,
Are sweeter than my harp can tell;
Yet might I gain a boon of thee,
This day my journey should not be,
So strange a dream hath come to me:
That I had vow'd with music loud
To clear yon wood from thing unblest,
Warn'd by a vision in my rest!
For in my sleep I saw that dove,
That gentle bird, whom thou dost love,
And call'st by thy own daughter's name—
Sir Leoline! I saw the same,
Fluttering, and uttering fearful moan,
Among the green herbs in the forest alone.
Which when I saw and when I heard,
I wonder'd what might ail the bird:
For nothing near it could I see,
Save the grass and green herbs underneath the old tree.

And in my dream, methought, I went
To search out what might there be found;
And what the sweet bird's trouble meant,
That thus lay fluttering on the ground.
I went and peer'd, and could descry
No cause for her distressful cry;
But yet for her dear lady's sake
I stoop'd, methought the dove to take,
When lo! I saw a bright green snake
Coil'd around its wings and neck.
Green as the herbs on which it couch'd,
Close by the dove's its head it crouch'd;
And with the dove it heaves and stirs,
Swelling its neck as she swell'd hers!
I woke; it was the midnight hour,
The clock was echoing in the tower;
But tho' my slumber was gone by,
This dream it would not pass away—
It seems to live upon my eye!
And thence I vow'd this self-same day,
With music strong and saintly song
To wander thro' the forest bare,
Lest aught unholy loiter there.

Thus Bracy said: the Baron, the while,
Half-listening heard him with a smile;
Then turn'd to Lady Geraldine,
His eyes made up of wonder and love;

And said in courtly accents fine,
Sweet maid, Lord Roland's beauteous dove,
With arms more strong than harp or song,
Thy sire and I will crush the snake!
He kiss'd her forehead as he spake,
And Geraldine in maiden wise,
Casting down her large bright eyes,
With blushing cheek and courtesy fine
She turn'd her from Sir Leoline;
Softly gathering up her train,
That o'er her right arm fell again;
And folded her arms across her chest,
And couch'd her head upon her breast,
And look'd askance at Christabel—
Jesu, Maria, shield her well!

A snake's small eye blinks dull and shy,
And the lady's eyes they shrunk in her head,
Each shrunk up to a serpent's eye,
And with somewhat of malice, and more of dread
At Christabel she look'd askance!—
One moment—and the sight was fled!
But Christabel in dizzy trance,
Stumbling on the unsteady ground—
Shudder'd aloud, with a hissing sound;
And Geraldine again turn'd round,
And like a thing, that sought relief,
Full of wonder and full of grief,
She roll'd her large bright eyes divine
Wildly on Sir Leoline.

The maid, alas! her thoughts are gone,
She nothing sees—no sight but one!
The maid, devoid of guile and sin,
I know not how, in fearful wise
So deeply had she drunken in
That look, those shrunken serpent eyes,
That all her features were resign'd
To this sole image in her mind:
And passively did imitate
That look of dull and treacherous hate.
And thus she stood, in dizzy trance,
Still picturing that look askance,
With forc'd unconscious sympathy
Full before her father's view—
As far as such a look could be,
In eyes so innocent and blue!

But when the trance was o'er, the maid
Paus'd awhile, and inly pray'd,
Then falling at her father's feet,
"By my mother's soul do I entreat
That thou this woman send away!"
She said; and more she could not say,
For what she knew she could not tell,
O'er-master'd by the mighty spell.

Why is thy cheek so wan and wild,
Sir Leoline? Thy only child
Lies at thy feet, thy joy, thy pride,
So fair, so innocent, so mild;
The same, for whom thy lady died!
O by the pangs of her dear mother
Think thou no evil of thy child!
For her, and thee, and for no other,
She pray'd the moment, ere she died;
Pray'd that the babe for whom she died,
Might prove her dear lord's joy and pride!
 That prayer her deadly pangs beguil'd,
  Sir Leoline!
 And would'st thou wrong thy only child,
  Her child and thine?
Within the Baron's heart and brain
If thoughts, like these, had any share,
They only swell'd his rage and pain,
And did but work confusion there.
His heart was cleft with pain and rage,
His cheeks they quiver'd, his eyes were wild,
Dishonour'd thus in his old age;
Dishonour'd by his only child,
And all his hospitality
To th' insulted daughter of his friend
By more than woman's jealousy,
Brought thus to a disgraceful end—
He roll'd his eye with stern regard
Upon the gentle minstrel bard,
And said in tones abrupt, austere—
Why, Bracy! dost thou loiter here?
I bade thee hence! The bard obey'd;
And turning from his own sweet maid,
The aged knight, Sir Leoline,
Led forth the lady Geraldine!

—THE CONCLUSION TO PART THE SECOND—

A little child, a limber elf,
Singing, dancing to itself,
A fairy thing with red round cheeks
That always finds, and never seeks,
Makes such a vision to the sight
As fills a father's eyes with light;
And pleasures flow in so thick and fast
Upon his heart, that he at last

Must needs express his love's excess
With words of unmeant bitterness.
Perhaps 'tis pretty to force together
Thoughts so all unlike each other;
To mutter and mock a broken charm,
To dally with wrong that does no harm.
Perhaps 'tis tender too and pretty
At each wild word to feel within,
A sweet recoil of love and pity.
And what, if in a world of sin
(O sorrow and shame should this be true!)
Such giddiness of heart and brain
Comes seldom save from rage and pain,
So talks as it's most used to do.

Kubla Khan: or, A Vision in a Dream

(1816; comp. 1797)

Of the Fragment of Kubla Khan

The following fragment is here published at the request of a poet of great and deserved celebrity,[1] and as far as the Author's own opinions are concerned, rather as a psychological curiosity, than on the ground of any supposed *poetic* merits.

In the summer of the year 1797, the Author, then in ill health, had retired to a lonely farmhouse between Porlock and Linton, on the Exmoor confines of Somerset and Devonshire. In consequence of a slight indisposition, an anodyne had been prescribed, from the effects of which he fell asleep in his chair at the moment that he was reading the following sentence, or words of the same substance, in "Purchas's Pilgrimage:" "Here the Khan Kubla commanded a palace to be built, and a stately garden thereunto. And thus ten miles of fertile ground were inclosed with a wall." The author continued for about three hours in a profound sleep, at least of the external senses, during which time he has the most vivid confidence, that he could not have composed less than from two to three hundred lines; if that indeed can be called composition in which all the images rose up before him as *things*,[2] with a parallel production of the correspondent expressions, without any sensation or consciousness of effort. On awaking he appeared to himself to have a distinct recollection of the whole, and taking his pen, ink, and paper, instantly and eagerly wrote down the lines that are here preserved. At this moment he was unfortunately called out by a person on business from Porlock, and detained by him above an hour, and on his return to his room, found to his no small surprise and mortification, that though he still retained some vague and dim recollection of the general purpose of the vision, yet, with the exception of some eight or ten scattered lines and images, all the rest had passed away like the images on the surface of a stream into which a stone has been cast, but, alas! without the after restoration of the latter:

> Then all the charm
> Is broken—all that phantom-world so fair
> Vanishes, and a thousand circlets spread,
> And each mis-shape the other. Stay awhile,
> Poor youth! who scarcely dar'st lift up thine eyes—
> The stream will soon renew its smoothness, soon
> The visions will return! And lo, he stays,
> And soon the fragments dim of lovely forms
> Come trembling back, unite, and now once more
> The pool becomes a mirror.[3]

Yet from the still surviving recollections in his mind, the Author has frequently purposed to finish for himself what had been originally, as it were, given to him. *Σαμεζον αδιον ασω*:[4] but the to-morrow is yet to come.

As a contrast to this vision, I have annexed a fragment of a very different character, describing with equal fidelity the dream of pain and disease.[5]

....

In Xanadu did Kubla Khan
A stately pleasure-dome decree:
Where Alph, the sacred river, ran
Through caverns measureless to man
Down to a sunless sea.
So twice five miles of fertile ground
With walls and towers were girdled round;
And here were gardens bright with sinuous rills
Where blossom'd many an incense-bearing tree;

[1] **a poet . . . celebrity:** Lord Byron.*

[2] See *The Friend,* No. 8, on Luther's Dreams.*

[3] Cf. Coleridge's "The Picture; or, The Lover's Resolution," ll. 91–100.

[4] Cf. Theocritus, *Idyls:* "I shall sing a sweeter song on a later day."

[5] Reference to "The Pains of Sleep," which follows "Kubla Khan."

And here were forests ancient as the hills,
And folding[1] sunny spots of greenery.

But oh that deep romantic chasm which slanted
Down the green hill athwart a cedarn cover!
A savage place! as holy and inchanted
As e'er beneath a waning moon was haunted
By woman wailing for her demon-lover!
And from this chasm, with ceaseless turmoil seething,
As if this earth in fast thick pants were breathing,
A mighty fountain momently was forced:
Amid whose swift half-intermitted Burst
Huge fragments vaulted like rebounding hail,
Or chaffy grain beneath the thresher's flail:
And mid these dancing rocks at once and ever
It flung up momently the sacred river.
Five miles meandering with a mazy motion
Through wood and dale the sacred river ran,
Then reached the caverns measureless to man,
And sank in tumult to a lifeless ocean:
And 'mid this tumult Kubla heard from far
Ancestral voices prophesying war!

The shadow of the dome of pleasure
Floated midway on the waves;
Where was heard the mingled measure
From the fountain and the caves.
It was a miracle of rare device,
A sunny pleasure-dome with caves of ice!

A damsel with a dulcimer
In a vision once I saw:
It was an Abyssinian maid
And on her dulcimer she play'd,
Singing of Mount Abora.
Could I revive within me
Her symphony and song,
To such a deep delight 'twould win me,
That with music loud and long,
I would build that dome in air,
That sunny dome! those caves of ice!
And all who heard should see them there,
And all should cry, Beware! Beware!
His flashing eyes, his floating hair!
Weave a circle round him thrice,
And close your eyes with holy dread:
For he on honey-dew hath fed,
And drank[2] the milk of Paradise.

[1] Changed to enfolding in future editions.

[2] Changed to drunk in 1834 text.

The Pains of Sleep

(1816; comp. 1803)

Ere on my bed my limbs I lay,
It hath not been my use to pray
With moving lips or bended knees;
But silently, by slow degrees,
My spirit I to Love compose,
In humble Trust mine eye-lids close,
With reverential resignation,
No wish conceived, no thought expressed!
Only a *sense* of supplication,
A sense o'er all my soul imprest
That I am weak, yet not unblest,
Since in me, round me, every where
Eternal Strength and Wisdom are.

But yester-night I pray'd aloud
In anguish and in agony,
Up-starting from the fiendish crowd
Of shapes and thoughts that tortured me:
A lurid light, a trampling throng,
Sense of intolerable wrong,
And whom I scorn'd, those only strong!
Thirst of revenge, the powerless will
Still baffled, and yet burning still!
Desire with loathing strangely mixed
On wild or hateful objects fixed.
Fantastic passions! mad'ning brawl!
And shame and terror over all!
Deeds to be hid which were not hid,
Which all confused I could not know,
Whether I suffered, or I did:
For all seemed guilt, remorse or woe,
My own or others still the same
Life-stifling fear, soul-stifling shame!

So two nights passed: the night's dismay
Sadden'd and stunn'd the coming day.
Sleep, the wide blessing, seemed to me
Distemper's worst calamity.
The third night, when my own loud scream
Had waked me from the fiendish dream,
O'ercome with sufferings strange and wild,
I wept as I had been a child;
And having thus by tears subdued
My anguish to a milder mood,
Such punishments, I said, were due
To natures deepliest stain'd with sin:

For aye entempesting anew
Th'unfathomable hell within
The horror of their deeds to view,
To know and loathe, yet wish and do!
Such griefs with such men well agree,
But wherefore, wherefore fall on me?
To be beloved is all I need,
And whom I love, I love indeed.

from THE STATESMAN'S MANUAL, OR, THE BIBLE THE BEST GUIDE TO POLITICAL SKILL AND FORESIGHT[1]

(1816)

[Philosophy, Revolution and the Bible]

. . . The true origin of human events is so little susceptible of that kind of evidence which can *compel* our belief; so many are the disturbing forces which in every cycle or ellipse of changes modify the motion given by the first projection; and every age has, or imagines it has, its own circumstances which render past experience no longer applicable to the present case; that there will never be wanting answers, and explanations, and specious flatteries of hope to persuade a people and its government, that the history of the past is inapplicable to *their* case. And no wonder, if we read history for the facts instead of reading it for the sake of the general principles, which are to the facts as the root and sap of a tree to its leaves: and no wonder, if history so read should find a dangerous rival in novels, nay, if the latter should be preferred to the former on the score even of probability. I well remember, that when the examples of former Jacobins, as Julius Caesar, Cromwell, and the like, were adduced in France and England at the commencement of the French Consulate, it was ridiculed as pedantry and pedant's ignorance to fear a repetition of usurpation and military despotism at the close of the ENLIGHTENED EIGHTEENTH CENTURY! . . . I have known men, who with significant nods and the pitying contempt of smiles, have denied all influence to the corruptions of moral and political philosophy, and with much solemnity have proceeded to solve the riddle of the French Revolution by ANECDOTES! Yet it would not be difficult, by an unbroken chain of historic facts, to demonstrate that the most important changes in the commercial relations of the world had their origin in the closets or lonely walks of uninterested theorists;—that the mighty epochs of commerce, that have changed the face of empires; nay, the most important of those discoveries and improvements in the mechanic arts, which have numerically increased our population beyond what the wisest statesmen of Elizabeth's reign deemed possible, and again doubled this population virtually,[2] the most important, I say, of those inventions that in their results

—best uphold
War by her two main nerves, iron and gold;[3]

had their origin not in the cabinets of statesmen, or in the practical insight of men of business, but in the closets of uninterested theorists, in the visions of recluse genius. To the immense majority of men, even in civilized countries, speculative philosophy has ever been, and must ever remain, a terra incognita. Yet it is not the less true, that all the *epoch-forming* Revolutions of the Christian world, the revolutions of religion and with them the civil, social, and domestic habits of the nations concerned, have coincided with the rise and fall of metaphysical systems. So few are the minds that really govern the machine of society, and so incomparably more numerous and more important are the indirect consequences of things than their foreseen and direct effects.

It is with nations as with individuals. In tranquil moods and peaceable times we are quite *practical*. Facts only and cool common sense are then in fashion. But let the winds of passion swell, and straitway men begin to generalize; to connect by remotest analogies; to express the most universal positions of reason in the most glowing figures of fancy; in short, to feel particular truths and mere facts, as poor, cold, narrow, and incommensurate with their feelings.

The Apostle of the Gentiles[4] quoted from a Greek comic poet. Let it not then be condemned as unseasonable

[1] The first of two Lay Sermons designed to assist the educated classes in governing in accordance with religious principles.

[2] See Malthus.*

[3] Cf. Milton's Sonnet XVII.

[4] **The Apostle of the Gentiles:** the Apostle Paul (5?–?67).

or out of place, if I remind you that in the intuitive knowledge of this truth, and with his wonted fidelity to nature, our own great poet[5] has placed the greater number of his profoundest maxims and general truths, both political and moral, not in the mouths of men at ease, but of men under the influence of passion, when the mighty thoughts overmaster and become the tyrants of the mind that has brought them forth. In his Lear, Othello, Macbeth, Hamlet, principles of deepest insight and widest interest fly off like sparks from the glowing iron under the loud anvil. It seems a paradox only to the unthinking, and it is a fact that none, but the unread in history, will deny, that in periods of popular tumult and innovation the more abstract a notion is, the more readily has it been found to combine, the closer has appeared its affinity, with the feelings of a people and with all their immediate impulses of action. At the commencement of the French revolution, in the remotest villages every tongue was employed in echoing and enforcing the almost geometrical abstractions of the physiocratic politicians and economists. The public roads were crowded with armed enthusiasts disputing on the inalienable sovereignty of the people, the imprescriptible laws of the pure reason, and the universal constitution, which, as rising out of the nature and rights of man as man, all nations alike were under the obligation of adopting. Turn over the fugitive writings, that are still extant, of the age of Luther; peruse the pamphlets and loose sheets that came out in flights during the reign of Charles the First and the Republic;[6] and you will find in these one continued comment on the aphorism of Lord Chancellor Bacon[7] (a man assuredly sufficiently acquainted with the extent of secret and personal influence) that the knowledge of the speculative principles of men in general between the age of twenty and thirty, is the one great source of political prophecy. And Sir Philip Sidney[8] regarded the adoption of one set of principles in the Netherlands, as a proof of the divine agency and the fountain of all the events and successes of that revolution.

A calm and detailed examination of the facts justifies me to my own mind in hazarding the bold assertion, that the fearful blunders of the late dread revolution, and all the calamitous mistakes of its opponents from its commencement even to the aera of loftier principles and wiser measures (an aera, that began with, and ought to be named from, the war of the Spanish and Portuguese insurgents)[9] every failure with all its gloomy results may be unanswerably deduced from the neglect of some maxim or other that had been established by clear reasoning and plain facts in the writings of Thucydides, Tacitus, Machiavel, Bacon, or Harrington.[10] These are red-letter names even in the almanacks of worldly wisdom: and yet I dare challenge all the critical benches of infidelity to point out any one important truth, any one efficient, practical direction or warning, which did not pre-exist, and for the most part in a sounder, more intelligible, and more comprehensive form in the Bible.

In addition to this, the Hebrew legislator, and the other inspired poets, prophets, historians and moralists of the Jewish church have two immense advantages in their favor. First, their particular rules and prescripts flow directly and visibly from universal principles, as from a fountain: they flow from principles and ideas that are not so properly said to be confirmed by reason as to be reason itself! Principles, in act and procession, disjoined from which, and from the emotions that inevitably accompany the actual intuition of their truth, the widest maxims of prudence are like arms without hearts, muscles without nerves. Secondly, from the very nature of these principles, as taught in the Bible, they are understood in exact proportion as they are believed and felt. The regulator is never separated from the main spring. For the words of the apostle are literally and philosophically true: WE (that is, the human race) LIVE BY FAITH. . . . This primal act of faith is enunciated in the word, GOD: a faith not derived

[5] **our own great poet:** Shakespeare.

[6] The beheading of Charles I in 1649 was followed by the Puritan Commonwealth of Oliver Cromwell.

[7] **Lord Chancellor Bacon:** Francis Bacon (1561–1626), Lord Chancellor from 1618 until charged with taking bribes in 1621, disqualified from Parliament, and excluded from court.

[8] **Sir Philip Sidney:** poet, statesman, and soldier (1554–1586). Had his greatest military success in the Netherlands in a surprise attack on the town of Axel.

[9] Napoleon's forces occupied Portugal from 1807 to 1808, arousing an insurgency throughout the Iberian Peninsula.

[10] **Thucydides:** Athenian historian (c. 460–c. 395 BC) who brilliantly analyzed Athens's unsuccessful war against Sparta. **Tacitus:** Cornelius Tacitus (c. AD 55–?115): the greatest historian of Rome, who had great influence in seventeenth-century England. **Machiavel:** Niccolò Machiavelli (1469–1527): Florentine political philosopher who wrote *The Art of War* (1517–1520) and *The Prince* (1513). **Harrington:** James Harrington (1611–1677): attendant to Charles I during his incarceration (1647–1648) and author of works espousing government by commonwealth, *The Commonwealth of Oceana* (1656).

from experience, but its ground and source, and without which the fleeting *chaos of facts* would no more form experience, that the dust of the grave can of itself make a living man. The imperative and oracular form of the inspired Scripture is the form of reason itself in all things purely rational and moral. . . .

[The Bible and Universal Truths]

The great PRINCIPLES of our religion, the sublime IDEAS spoken out everywhere in the Old and New Testament, resemble the fixed stars, which appear of the same size to the naked as to the armed eye; the magnitude of which the telescope may rather seem to diminish than to increase. At the annunciation of *principles*, of *ideas*, the soul of man awakes, and starts up, as an exile in a far distant land at the unexpected sounds of his native language, when after long years of absence, and almost of oblivion, he is suddenly addressed in his own mother-tongue. He weeps for joy, and embraces the speaker as his brother. How else can we explain the fact so honorable to Great Britain, that the poorest amongst us will content with as much enthusiasm as the richest for the rights of property? These rights are the spheres and necessary conditions of free agency. But free agency contains the idea of the free will; and in this he intuitively knows the sublimity, and the infinite hopes, fears, and capabilities of his own nature. On what other ground but the cognateness of ideas and principles to man as man, does the nameless soldier rush to the combat in defence of the liberties or the honor of his country?—Even men wofully neglectful of the precepts of religion will shed their blood for its truth.

Alas!—the main hindrance to the use of the Scriptures, as your Manual, lies in the notion that you are already acquainted with its contents. Something *new* must be presented to you, wholly new and wholly out of yourselves; for whatever is within us must be as old as the first dawn of human reason. Truths of all others the most awful and mysterious and at the same time of universal interest, are considered as so true as to lose all the powers of truth, and lie bed-ridden in the dormitory of the soul, side by side, with the most despised and exploded errors. But it should not be so with you! The pride of education, the sense of consistency should preclude the objection: for would you not be ashamed to apply it to the works of Tacitus, or of Shakespear? Above all, the rank which you hold, the influence you possess, the powers you may be called to wield, give a special unfitness to this frivolous craving for novelty. To find no contradiction in the union of old and new, to contemplate the ANCIENT OF DAYS, his words and his works, with a feeling as fresh as if they were now first springing forth at his fiat—this characterizes the minds that feel the riddle of the world and may help to unravel it! This, most of all things, will raise you above the mass of mankind, and therefore will best entitle and qualify you to guide and controul them! You say, you are already familiar with the Scriptures. With the *words*, perhaps, but in any other sense you might as wisely boast of your familiar acquaintance with the rays of the sun, and under that pretence turn away your eyes from the light of Heaven . . .

[The Bible and Imagination]

But do you require some one or more particular passage from the Bible, that may at once illustrate and exemplify its applicability to the changes and fortunes of empires? Of the numerous chapters that relate to the Jewish tribes, their enemies and allies, before and after their division into two kingdoms, it would be more difficult to state a single one, from which some guiding light might *not* be struck. And in nothing is Scriptural history more strongly contrasted with the histories of highest note in the present age than in its freedom from the hollowness of abstractions. While the latter present a shadow-fight of Things and Quantities, the former gives us the history of Men, and balances the important influence of individual Minds with the previous state of the national morals and manners, in which, as constituting a specific susceptibility, it presents to us the true cause both of the Influence itself, and of the Weal or Woe that were its Consequents. How should it be otherwise? The histories and political economy of the present and preceding century partake in the general contagion of its mechanic philosophy, and are the *product* of an unenlivened generalizing Understanding. In the Scriptures they are the living *educts* of the Imagination; of that reconciling and mediatory power, which incorporating the Reason in Images of the Sense, and organizing (as it were) the flux of the Senses by the permanence of self-circling energies of the Reason, gives birth to a system of symbols, harmonious in themselves, and consubstantial with the truths, of which they are the *conductors*. These are the Wheels which Ezekiel beheld, when the hand of the Lord was upon him, and he saw visions of God as he sate among the captives by the river of Chebar. *Whithersoever the Spirit was to go, the wheels went, and thither was their spirit to go: for the spirit of the living creature was in the wheels also.* The truths and the symbols that represent them move in conjunction and form the living chariot that bears up (for *us*) the throne of the Divine Humanity. Hence, by a derivative, indeed, but not a divided, influence, and though in a secondary yet in more than a metaphorical sense, the Sacred Book is worthily intitled *the* WORD OF GOD. Hence too, its contents present to us the stream of time continuous as Life and a symbol of Eternity, inasmuch as the Past and the Future are virtually contained in the Present. According therefore to our relative position on its banks the Sacred History becomes prophetic, the Sacred Prophecies historical, while the power and substance of both inhere in its Laws, its Promises, and its Comminations.[1] In the Scriptures therefore both Facts and Persons must of necessity have a two-fold significance, a past and a future, a temporary and a perpetual, a particular and a universal application. They must be at once Portraits and Ideals:

Eheu! paupertina philosophia in paupertinam religionem ducit:—A hunger-bitten and idea-less philosophy naturally produces a starveling and comfortless religion. It is among the miseries of the present age that it recognizes no medium between *Literal* and *Metaphorical*. Faith is either to be buried in the dead letter, or its name and honors usurped by a counterfeit product of the mechanical understanding, which in the blindness of self-complacency confounds SYMBOLS with ALLEGORIES. Now an Allegory is but a translation of abstract notions into a picture-language which is itself nothing but an abstraction from objects of the senses; the principal being more worthless even than its phantom proxy, both alike unsubstantial, and the former shapeless to boot. On the other hand a Symbol (ὁ ἔστιν ἄει ταυτηγόρικον)[2] is characterized by a translucence of the Special in the Individual or of the General in the Especial or of the Universal in the General. Above all by the translucence of the Eternal through and in the Temporal. It always partakes of the Reality which it renders intelligible; and while it enunciates the whole, abides itself as a living part in that Unity, of which it is the representative. The other are but empty echoes which the fancy arbitrarily associates with apparitions of matter, less beautiful but not less shadowy than the sloping orchard or hill-side pasture-field seen in the transparent lake below. Alas! for the flocks that are to be led forth to such pastures! *"It shall even be as when the hungry dreameth, and behold! he eateth; but he waketh and his soul is empty: or as when the thirsty dreameth, and behold he drinketh; but he awaketh and is faint!"* (ISAIAH xxix.8.) O! that we would seek for the bread which was given from heaven, that we should eat thereof and be strengthened! O that we would draw at the well at which the flocks of our forefathers had living water drawn for them, even that water which, instead of mocking the thirst of him to whom it is given, becomes a well within himself springing up to life everlasting! . . .

[1] **Comminations:** threat of divine power or punishment.

[2] Has been translated as "which is always tautegorical," or capable of expressing the same thing with a difference.

from SIBYLLINE LEAVES: A COLLECTION OF POEMS[1]
(1817)

The Rime of the Ancient Mariner[2]
(comp. 1797–1798)

Facile credo, plures esse Naturas invisibiles quam visibiles in rerum universitate. Sed horum omnium familiam quis nobis enarrabit? et gradus et cognationes et discrimina et

[1] Coleridge explains in the preface that the title is "in allusion to the fragmentary and widely scattered state in which [his poems] have been long suffered to remain." The poems included above, which were collected in *Sibylline Leaves,* are: "Effusion XXXV," retitled as "Eolian Harp"; "Reflections on Having Left a Place of Retirement"; "Fears in Solitude"; "Frost at Midnight"; *Rime of the Ancyent Marinere,* here in its revised form with the addition of the famous gloss; "The Nightingale"; "This Lime-Tree Bower My Prison"; and "Dejection: An Ode." Sibyls were prophetic females whose ecstatic utterances were transformed into Greek hexameter verse. The Cumaean Sibyl wrote on palm leaves. Collections of Sibylline verse were made, lost, and re-created. "The influence of Jewish and Christian interpolations . . . combined with the prophecy of the Cumaean Sibyl in Vergil's *Fourth Eclogue* to give to all the Sibyls a position in Christian literature and art similar to that accorded the Old Testament prophets" (*Oxford Classical Dictionary,* 2nd ed.). See also *Aeneid,* VI.42–76.

[2] Published in *Sibylline Leaves* here for the first time under the author's name and with the marginal gloss, which may have been composed as early as 1800 to 1805.

singulorum munera? Quid agunt? quæ loca habitant? Harum rerum notitiam semper ambivit ingenium humanum, nunquam attigit. Juvat, interea, non diffiteor, quandoque in animo, tanquam in Tabulâ, majoris et melioris mundi imaginem contemplari: ne mens assuefecta hodiernię vitæ minutiis se contrahat nimis, & tota subsidat in pusillas cogitationes. Sed veritati interea invigilandum est, modusque servandus, ut certa ab incertis, diem a nocte, distinguamus.[3]

T. BURNET: *Archæol, Phil.* p. 68.

....

An ancient Mariner meeteth three Gallants bidden to a wedding-feast, and detaineth one.

It is an ancient Mariner,
And he stoppeth one of three.
"By thy long grey beard and glittering
    eye,
Now wherefore stopp'st thou me?

The Bridegroom's doors are open'd wide,
And I am next of kin;
The guests are met, the feast is set:
May'st hear the merry din."

He holds him with his skinny hand,
"There was a ship," quoth he.
"Hold off! unhand me, grey-beard loon!"
Eftsoons his hand dropt he.

The wedding-guest is spell-bound by the eye of the old sea-faring man, and constrained to hear his tale.

He holds him with his glittering eye—
The wedding-guest stood still,
And listens like a three years child:
The Mariner hath his will.

The wedding-guest sat on a stone:
He can not chuse but hear;
And thus spake on that ancient man,
The bright-eyed mariner.

The ship was cheer'd, the harbour
    clear'd,
Merrily did we drop
Below the kirk,[4] below the hill,
Below the light-house top.

The Mariner tells how the ship sailed southward with a good wind and fair weather, till it reached the line.

The Sun came up upon the left,
Out of the sea came he;
And he shone bright, and on the right
Went down into the sea.

Higher and higher every day,
Till over the mast at noon—
The Wedding-Guest here beat his breast,
For he heard the loud bassoon.

The wedding-guest heareth the bridal music; but the mariner continueth his tale.

The bride hath paced into the hall,
Red as a rose is she;
Nodding their heads before her goes
The merry minstrelsy.

The Wedding-Guest he beat his breast,
Yet he can not chuse but hear;
And thus spake on that ancient man,
The bright-eyed Mariner.

The ship drawn by a storm toward the south pole.

And now the STORM-BLAST came, and he
Was tyrannous and strong:
He struck with his o'ertaking wings,
And chased us south along.

With sloping masts and dipping prow,
As who pursued with yell and blow
Still treads the shadow of his foe
And forward bends his head,
The ship drove fast, loud roar'd the
    blast,
And southward aye we fled.

And now there came both mist and
    snow,
And it grew wonderous cold:
And ice, mast-high, came floating by,
As green as emerald.

The land of ice, and of fearful sounds, where no living thing was to be seen.

And through the drifts the snowy clift
Did send a dismal sheen:
Nor shapes of men nor beasts we ken—
The ice was all between.

[3] "I can easily believe that there are more invisible creatures in the universe than visible ones. But who will tell us what family each belongs to, what their ranks and relationships are, and what their respective distinguishing characters may be? What do they do? Where do they live? Human wit has always circled around a knowledge of these things without ever attaining it. But I do not doubt that it is beneficial sometimes to contemplate in the mind, as in a picture, the image of a grander and better world; for if the mind grows used to the trivia of daily life, it may dwindle too much and decline altogether into worthless thoughts. Meanwhile, however, we must be on the watch for the truth, keeping a sense of proportion so that we can tell what is certain from what is uncertain and day from night."

[4] **kirk:** church.

The ice was here, the ice was there,
The ice was all around:
It cracked and growled, and roar'd and
howl'd,
Like noises in a swound![5]

Till a great sea-bird, called the Albatross, came through the snow-fog, and was received with great joy and hospitality.

At length did cross an Albatross:
Thorough the fog it came;
As if it had been a Christian soul,
We hailed it in God's name.

It ate the food it ne'er had eat,
And round and round it flew.
The ice did split with a thunder-fit;
The helmsman steer'd us through!

And lo! the Albatross proveth a bird of good omen, and followeth the ship as it returned northward, through fog and floating ice.

And a good south wind sprung up
behind;
The Albatross did follow,
And every day, for food or play,
Came to the Mariner's hollo!

In mist or cloud, on mast or shroud,
It perch'd for vespers nine;
Whiles all the night, through fog-smoke
white,
Glimmered the white Moon-shine.

The ancient Mariner inhospitably killeth the pious bird of good omen.

"God save thee, ancient Mariner!
From the fiends, that plague thee thus!—
Why look'st thou so?"—With my cross-
bow
I shot the ALBATROSS!

—PART THE SECOND—

The Sun now rose upon the right:
Out of the sea came he,
Still hid in mist, and on the left
Went down into the sea.

And the good south wind still blew
behind,
But no sweet bird did follow,
Nor any day for food or play
Came to the mariners' hollo!

His ship-mates cry out against the ancient Mariner, for killing the bird of good luck.

And I had done an hellish thing,
And it would work 'em woe:
For all averred, I had killed the bird
That made the breeze to blow.
Ah wretch! said they, the bird to slay'
That made the breeze to blow!

But when the fog cleared off, they justify the same and thus make themselves accomplices in the crime.

Nor dim nor red, like God's own head,
The glorious Sun uprist:
Then all averred, I had killed the bird
That brought the fog and mist.
'Twas right, said they, such birds to slay,
That bring the fog and mist.

The fair breeze continues; the ship enters the Pacific Ocean and sails northward, even till it reaches the Line.

The fair breeze blew, the white foam
flew
The furrow[6] stream'd off free:
We were the first that ever burst
Into that silent sea.

The ship hath been suddenly becalmed.

Down dropt the breeze, the sails dropt
down,
'Twas sad as sad could be;
And we did speak only to break
The silence of the sea!

All in a hot and copper sky,
The bloody Sun, at noon,
Right up above the mast did stand,
No bigger than the Moon.

Day after day, day after day,
We stuck, nor breath nor motion,
As idle as a painted ship
Upon a painted ocean.

And the Albatross begins to be avenged.

Water, water, every where,
And all the boards did shrink;
Water water, every where,
Nor any drop to drink.

The very deep did rot: O Christ!
That ever this should be!
Yea, slimy things did crawl with legs
Upon the slimy sea.

About, about, in reel and rout
The death-fires danced at night;
The water, like a witch's oils,
Burnt green, and blue and white.

[5] **swound:** fainting fit.

[6] In the former edition the line was, "The furrow follow'd free;" but I had not been long on board a ship, before I perceived that this was the image as seen by a spectator from the shore, or from another vessel. From the ship itself the *Wake* appears like a brook flowing off from the stern. [S.T.C.]

A spirit had followed them; one of the invisible inhabitants of this planet, neither departed souls nor angels; concerning whom the learned Jew, Josephus, and the Platonic Constantinopolitan, Michael Psellus, may be consulted. They are very numerous, and there is no climate or element without one or more.

And some in dreams assured were
Of the spirit that plagued us so:
Nine fathom deep he had followed us
From the land of mist and snow.

And every tongue, through utter
    drought,
Was wither'd at the root;
We could not speak, no more than if
We had been choak'd with soot.

The ship-mates, in their sore distress, would fain throw the whole guilt on the ancient Mariner: in sign whereof they hang the dead sea-bird round his neck.

Ah! well a-day! what evil looks
Had I from old and young!
Instead of the cross, the Albatross
About my neck was hung.

— PART THE THIRD —

The ancient Mariner beholdeth a sign in the element afar off.

There passed a weary time. Each throat
Was parched, and glazed each eye.
A weary time! a weary time!
How glazed each weary eye!
When looking westward, I beheld
A something in the sky.

At first it seem'd a little speck,
And then it seem'd a mist:
It moved and moved, and took at last
A certain shape, I wist.

A speck, a mist, a shape, I wist!
And still it near'd and near'd:
And as if it dodged a water-sprite,
It plunged and tack'd and veer'd.

At its nearer approach, it seemeth him to be a ship; and at a dear ransom he freeth his speech from the bonds of thirst.

With throat unslack'd,[7] with black lips
    baked,
We could nor laugh nor wail;
Through utter drought all dumb we
    stood!
I bit my arm, I sucked the blood,
And cried, A sail! a sail!

With throat unslacked, with black lips
    baked,
Agape they heard me call:

A flash of joy.

Gramercy! they for joy did grin,
And all at once their breath drew in,
As they were drinking all.

And horror follows. For can it be a *ship* that comes onward without wind or tide?

See! see! (I cried) she tacks no more!
Hither to work us weal;
Without a breeze, without a tide,
She steddies with upright keel!

The western wave was all a-flame.
The day was well nigh done!
Almost upon the western wave
Rested the broad bright Sun;
When that strange shape drove suddenly
Betwixt us and the Sun.

It seemeth him but the skeleton of a ship.

And straight the Sun was flecked with
    bars,
(Heaven's Mother send us grace!)
As if through a dungeon-grate he peer'd,
With broad and burning face.

Alas! (thought I, and my heart beat loud)
How fast she nears and nears!
Are those *her* sails that glance in the Sun,
Like restless gossameres![8]

And its ribs are seen as bars on the face of the setting Sun. The spectre-woman and her death-mate, and no other on board the skeleton-ship

Are those *her* ribs through which the
    Sun
Did peer, as through a grate?
And is that Woman all her crew?
Is that a DEATH? and are there two?
Is DEATH that woman's mate?

Like vessel, like crew!

Her lips were red, *her* looks were free,
Her locks were yellow as gold:
Her skin was as white as leprosy,
The Night-Mair LIFE-IN-DEATH was
    she,
Who thicks man's blood with cold.

DEATH, and LIFE-IN-DEATH have diced for the ship's crew, and she (the latter) winneth the ancient Mariner.

The naked hulk alongside came,
And the twain were casting dice;
"The game is done! I've, I've won!"
Quoth she, and whistles thrice.

A gust of wind sterte up behind
And whistled through his bones;
Through the holes of his eyes and the
    hole of his mouth,
Half whistles and half groans.

The Sun's rim dips; the stars rush out:
At one stride comes the dark;
With far-heard whisper, o'er the sea,
Off shot the spectre-bark.

[7] **unslack'd:** unquenched.

[8] **gossameres:** sheer, gauzy fabric.

We listen'd and look'd sideways up!
Fear at my heart, as at a cup,
My life-blood seem'd to sip!
The stars were dim, and thick the night,
The steersman's face by his lamp gleam'd
white;
From the sails the dews did drip—
Till clombe above the eastern bar
The horned Moon, with one bright star
Within the nether tip.

At the rising of the Moon,

One after one, by the star-dogg'd Moon
Too quick for groan or sigh,
Each turn'd his face with a ghastly pang,
And curs'd me with his eye.

One after another,

Four times fifty living men,
(And I heard nor sigh nor groan)
With heavy thump, a lifeless lump,
They dropped down one by one.

His ship-mates drop down dead;

The souls did from their bodies fly,—
They fled to bliss or woe!
And every soul, it passed me by,
Like the whiz of my CROSS-BOW!

But LIFE-IN-DEATH begins her work on the ancient Mariner.

— PART THE FOURTH —

"I FEAR thee, ancient Mariner!
I fear thy skinny hand!
And thou art long, and lank, and brown,
As is the ribbed sea-sand.[9]

The wedding-guest feareth that a spirit is talking to him;

I fear thee and thy glittering eye,
And thy skinny hand, so brown."—
Fear not, fear not, thou Wedding-Guest!
This body dropt not down.

But the ancient Mariner assureth him of his bodily life, and proceedeth to relate his horrible penance.

Alone, alone, all, all alone,
Alone on a wide wide sea!
And never a saint took pity on
My soul in agony.

The many men, so beautiful!
And they all dead did lie:
And a thousand thousand slimy things
Liv'd on; and so did I.

He despiseth the creatures of the calm,

I look'd upon the rotting sea,
And drew my eyes away;
I look'd upon the rotting deck,
And there the dead men lay.

And envieth that *they* should live, and so many lie dead.

I look'd to Heaven, and tried to pray;
But or ever a prayer had gusht,
A wicked whisper came, and made
My heart as dry as dust.

I closed my lids, and kept them close,
And the balls like pulses beat;
For the sky and the sea, and the sea and
the sky
Lay, like a cloud, on my weary eye,
And the dead were at my feet.

The cold sweat melted from their limbs,
Nor rot nor reek did they:
The look with which they look'd on me
Had never pass'd away.

But the curse liveth for him in the eye of the dead men.

An orphan's curse would drag to Hell
A spirit from on high;
But oh! more horrible than that
Is the curse in a dead man's eye!
Seven days, seven nights, I saw that
curse,
And yet I could not die.

The moving Moon went up the sky,
And no where did abide:
Softly she was going up,
And a star or two beside—

In his loneliness and fixedness, he yearneth towards the journeying Moon, and the stars that still sojourn, yet still move onward; and every where the blue sky belongs to them, and is their appointed rest, and their native country, and their own natural homes, which they enter unannounced, as lords that are certainly expected, and yet there is a silent joy at their arrival.

Her beams bemock'd the sultry main,
Like April hoar-frost spread;
But where the ship's huge shadow lay,
The charmed water burnt alway
A still and awful red.

Beyond the shadow of the ship,
I watch'd the water-snakes:
They moved in tracks of shining
white,
And when they reared, the elfish light
Fell off in hoary flakes.

By the light of the Moon he beholdeth God's creatures of the great calm.

Within the shadow of the ship
I watch'd their rich attire:
Blue, glossy green, and velvet black,
They coiled and swam; and every
track
Was a flash of golden fire.

[9]For the two last lines of this stanza, I am indebted to Mr. WORDSWORTH. It was on a delightful walk from Nether Stowey to Dulverton, with him and his sister, in the Autumn of 1797, that this Poem was planned, and in part composed. [S.T.C.]

Their beauty and their happiness.

O happy living things! no tongue
Their beauty might declare:
A spring of love gusht from my heart,
And I blessed them unaware!

He blesseth them in his heart.

Sure my kind saint took pity on me,
And I blessed them unaware.

The spell begins to break.

The self same moment I could pray;
And from my neck so free
The Albatross fell off, and sank
Like lead into the sea.

— PART THE FIFTH —

Oh SLEEP! it is a gentle thing,
Belov'd from pole to pole!
To Mary Queen the praise be given!
She sent the gentle sleep from Heaven,
That slid into my soul.

By grace of the holy Mother, the ancient Mariner is refreshed with rain.

The silly buckets on the deck,
That had so long remained,
I dreamt that they were filled with dew;
And when I awoke, it rained.

My lips were wet, my throat was cold,
My garments all were dank;
Sure I had drunken in my dreams,
And still my body drank.

I moved, and could not feel my limbs:
I was so light — almost
I thought that I had died in sleep,
And was a blessed ghost.

He heareth sounds, and seeth strange sights and commotions in the sky and the element.

And soon I heard a roaring wind:
It did not come anear;
But with its sound it shook the sails,
That were so thin and sere.

The upper air burst into life!
And a hundred fire-flags sheen,
To and fro they were hurried about;
And to and fro, and in and out,
The wan stars danced between.

And the coming wind did roar more
loud,
And the sails did sigh like sedge;
And the rain pour'd down from one
black cloud;
The Moon was at its edge.

The thick black cloud was cleft, and still
The Moon was at its side:
Like waters shot from some high crag,
The lightning fell with never a jag,
A river steep and wide.

The bodies of the ship's crew are inspirited, and the ship moves on;

The loud wind never reached the ship,
Yet now the ship moved on!
Beneath the lightning and the Moon
The dead men gave a groan.

They groan'd, they stirr'd, they all
uprose,
Nor spake, nor moved their eyes;
It had been strange, even in a dream,
To have seen those dead men rise.

The helmsman steered, the ship moved
on;
Yet never a breeze up blew;
The mariners all 'gan work the ropes,
Where they were wont to do:
They raised their limbs like lifeless
tools —
We were a ghastly crew.

The body of my brother's son
Stood by me, knee to knee:
The body and I pulled at one rope,
But he said nought to me.

But not by the souls of the men, nor by dæmons of earth or middle air, but by a blessed troop of angelic spirits, sent down by the invocation of the guardian saint.

"I fear thee, ancient Mariner!"
Be calm, thou Wedding-Guest!
'Twas not those souls that fled in pain,
Which to their corses came again,
But a troop of spirits blest:

For when it dawned — they dropped
their arms,
And clustered round the mast;
Sweet sounds rose slowly through their
mouths,
And from their bodies passed.

Around, around, flew each sweet sound,
Then darted to the Sun;
Slowly the sounds came back again,
Now mixed, now one by one.

Sometimes a-dropping from the sky
I heard the sky-lark sing;
Sometimes all little birds that are,
How they seem'd to fill the sea and air
With their sweet jargoning![10]

[10] **jargoning:** twittering.

And now 'twas like all instruments,
Now like a lonely flute;
And now it is an angel's song,
That makes the Heavens be mute.

It ceased; yet still the sails made on
A pleasant noise till noon,
A noise like of a hidden brook
In the leafy month of June,
That to the sleeping woods all night
Singeth a quiet tune.

Till noon we quietly sailed on,
Yet never a breeze did breathe:
Slowly and smoothly went the ship,
Moved onward from beneath.

The lonesome spirit from the south-pole carries on the ship as far as the line, in obedience to the angelic troop, but still requireth vengeance.

Under the keel nine fathom deep,
From the land of mist and snow,
The spirit slid: and it was he
That made the ship to go.
The sails at noon left off their tune,
And the ship stood still also.

The Sun, right up above the mast,
Had fixt her to the ocean;
But in a minute she 'gan stir,
With a short uneasy motion—
Backwards and forwards half her length,
With a short uneasy motion.

Then like a pawing horse let go,
She made a sudden bound:
It flung the blood into my head,
And I fell down in a swound.

The Polar-Spirit's fellow-dæmons, the invisible inhabitants of the element, take part in his wrong; and two of them relate, one to the other, that penance long and heavy for the ancient Mariner hath been accorded to the Polar Spirit, who returneth southward.

How long in that same fit I lay,
I have not to declare;
But ere my living life returned,
I heard and in my soul discerned
Two VOICES in the air.

"Is it he?" quoth one, "Is this the man?
By him who died on cross,
With his cruel bow he laid full low,
The harmless Albatross.

The spirit who bideth by himself
In the land of mist and snow,
He loved the bird that loved the man
Who shot him with his bow."

The other was a softer voice,
As soft as honey-dew:
Quoth he, "The man hath penance done,
And penance more will do."

— PART THE SIXTH —

FIRST VOICE

But tell me, tell me! speak again,
Thy soft response renewing—
What makes that ship drive on so fast?
What is the OCEAN doing?

SECOND VOICE

Still as a slave before his lord,
The OCEAN hath no blast;
His great bright eye most silently
Up to the Moon is cast—

If he may know which way to go;
For she guides him smooth or grim.
See, brother, see! how graciously
She looketh down on him.

FIRST VOICE

The Mariner hath been cast into a trance; for the angelic power causeth the vessel to drive northward, faster than human life could endure.

But why drives on that ship so fast,
Without or wave or wind?

SECOND VOICE

The air is cut away before,
And closes from behind.

Fly, brother, fly! more high, more high!
Or we shall be belated:
For slow and slow that ship will go,
When the Mariner's trance is abated."

The supernatural motion is retarded; the Mariner awakes, and his penance begins anew.

I woke, and we were sailing on
As in a gentle weather:
'Twas night, calm night, the Moon was high;
The dead men stood together.

All stood together on the deck,
For a charnel-dungeon[11] fitter:
All fixed on me their stony eyes,
That in the Moon did glitter.

The pang, the curse, with which they died,

[11] **charnel-dungeon**: a building or room where the bones and bodies of the dead are kept.

Had never passed away:
I could not draw my eyes from theirs,
Nor turn them up to pray.

The curse is finally expiated.

And now this spell was snapt: once more
I viewed the ocean green,
And looked far forth, yet little saw
Of what had else been seen—

Like one, that on a lonesome road
Doth walk in fear and dread,
And having once turn'd round, walks on,
And turns no more his head;
Because he knows, a frightful fiend
Doth close behind him tread.

But soon there breathed a wind on me,
Nor sound nor motion made:
Its path was not upon the sea,
In ripple or in shade.

It raised my hair, it fanned my cheek
Like a meadow-gale of spring—
It mingled strangely with my fears,
Yet it felt like a welcoming.

Swiftly, swiftly flew the ship,
Yet she sailed softly too:
Sweetly, sweetly blew the breeze—
On me alone it blew.

And the ancient Mariner beholdeth his native country.

Oh! dream of joy! is this indeed
The light-house top I see?
Is this the hill? is this the kirk?
Is this mine own countree?

We drifted o'er the harbour-bar,
And I with sobs did pray—
O let me be awake, my God!
Or let me sleep alway.

The harbour-bay was clear as glass,
So smoothly it was strewn!
And on the bay the moonlight lay,
And the shadow of the moon.

The rock shone bright, the kirk no less,
That stands above the rock:
The moonlight steeped in silentness
The steady weathercock.

The angelic spirits leave the dead bodies,

And the bay was white with silent light,
Till rising from the same,
Full many shapes, that shadows were,
In crimson colours came.

And appear in their own forms of light.

A little distance from the prow[12]
Those crimson shadows were:
I turned my eyes upon the deck—
Oh, Christ! what saw I there!

Each corse lay flat, lifeless and flat,
And, by the holy rood!
A man all light, a seraph-man,
On every corse there stood.

This seraph-band, each waved his hand:
It was a heavenly sight!
They stood as signals to the land,
Each one a lovely light:

This seraph-band, each waved his hand,
No voice did they impart—
No voice, but oh! the silence sank
Like music on my heart.

But soon I heard the dash of oars,
I heard the Pilot's cheer;
My head was turn'd perforce away,
And I saw a boat appear.

The Pilot, and the Pilot's boy,
I heard them coming fast:
Dear Lord in Heaven! it was a joy
The dead man could not blast.

I saw a third—I heard his voice:
It is the Hermit good!
He singeth loud his godly hymns
That he makes in the wood.
He'll shrieve[13] my soul, he'll wash away
The Albatross's blood.

—PART THE SEVENTH—

The Hermit of the Wood,

This Hermit good lives in that wood
Which slopes down to the sea.
How loudly his sweet voice he rears!
He loves to talk with marineres
That come from a far countree.

He kneels at morn, and noon and eve—
He hath a cushion plump:
It is the moss that wholly hides
The rotted old oak-stump.

[12] **prow:** the forward part of a ship, i.e., the bow.

[13] **shrieve:** confess and provide absolution.

The Skiff-boat near'd: I heard them talk,
"Why this is strange, I trow!
Where are those lights so many and fair,
That signal made but now?"

Approacheth the ship with wonder.

"Strange, by my faith!" the Hermit said—
"And they answered not our cheer!
The planks look warped! and see those sails,
How thin they are and sere!
I never saw ought like to them,
Unless perchance it were
The skeletons of leaves that lag
My forest-brook along:
When the ivy-tod is heavy with snow,
And the owlet whoops to the wolf below,
That eats the she-wolf's young."

Dear Lord! it hath a fiendish look—
(The Pilot made reply)
I am a-feared—Push on, push on!
Said the Hermit cheerily.

The boat came closer to the ship,
But I nor spake nor stirred;
The boat came close beneath the ship,
And straight a sound was heard.

The ship suddenly sinketh.

Under the water it rumbled on,
Still louder and more dread:
It reach'd the ship, it split the bay;
The ship went down like lead.

The ancient Mariner is saved in the Pilot's boat.

Stunned by that loud and dreadful sound,
Which sky and ocean smote,
Like one that hath been seven days drown'd,
My body lay afloat;
But swift as dreams, myself I found
Within the Pilot's boat.

Upon the whirl, where sank the ship,
The boat spun round and round;
And all was still, save that the hill
Was telling of the sound.

I moved my lips—the Pilot shrieked
And fell down in a fit;
The holy Hermit raised his eyes,
And prayed where he did sit.

I took the oars: the Pilot's boy,
Who now doth crazy go,
Laughed loud and long, and all the while
His eyes went to and fro.
"Ha! ha!" quoth he, "full plain I see,
The Devil knows how to row."

And now, all in my own countree,
I stood on the firm land!
The Hermit stepped forth from the boat,
And scarcely he could stand.

The ancient Mariner earnestly entreateth the Hermit to shrieve him; and the penance of life falls on him.

"O shrieve me, shrieve me, holy man!"
The Hermit cross'd his brow.
"Say quick," quoth he, "I bid thee say—
What manner of man art thou?"

Forthwith this frame of mine was wrench'd
With a woeful agony,
Which forced me to begin my tale;
And then it left me free.

And ever and anon throughout his future life an agony constraineth him to travel from land to land,

Since then, at an uncertain hour,
That agony returns;
And till my ghastly tale is told,
This heart within me burns.

I pass, like night, from land to land;
I have strange power of speech;
That moment that his face I see,
I know the man that must hear me:
To him my tale I teach.

What loud uproar bursts from that door!
The wedding-guests are there;
But in the garden-bower the bride
And bride-maids singing are;
And hark the little vesper bell,
Which biddeth me to prayer!

O Wedding-Guest! this soul hath been
Alone on a wide wide sea:
So lonely 'twas, that God himself
Scarce seemed there to be.

O sweeter than the marriage-feast,
'Tis sweeter far to me,
To walk together to the kirk
With a goodly company!—

To walk together to the kirk,
And all together pray,
While each to his great Father bends,
Old men, and babes, and loving friends,
And youths and maidens gay!

And to teach by his own example, love and reverence to all things that God made and loveth.

Farewell, farewell! but this I tell
To thee, thou Wedding-Guest!
He prayeth well, who loveth well
Both man and bird and beast.

He prayeth best, who loveth best
All things both great and small;
For the dear God who loveth us,
He made and loveth all."

The Mariner, whose eye is bright,
Whose beard with age is hoar,
Is gone; and now the Wedding-Guest
Turned from the bridegroom's door.

He went like one that hath been stunned,
And is of sense forlorn:
A sadder and a wiser man,
He rose the morrow morn.

To a Gentleman

(1817; comp. 1807)

Composed on the night after his recitation of a Poem on the Growth of an Individual Mind.[1]

Friend of the Wise! and Teacher of the Good!
Into my heart have I received that Lay
More than historic, that prophetic Lay
Wherein (high theme by thee first sung aright)
Of the foundations and the building up
Of the Human Spirit, thou hast dared to tell
What may be told, to th' understanding mind
Revealable; and what within the mind
By vital Breathings, like the secret soul
Of vernal growth, oft quickens in the Heart
Thoughts all too deep for words!—
Theme hard as high!
Of smiles spontaneous, and mysterious fears
(The first-born they of Reason and twin-birth)
Of tides obedient to external force,
And currents self-determined, as might seem,
Or by some inner Power; of moments awful,
Now in thy inner life, and now abroad,
When Power stream'd from thee, and thy soul received
The light reflected, as a light bestow'd—
Of Fancies fair, and milder hours of youth,
Hyblean[2] murmurs of Poetic Thought
Industrious in its Joy, in Vales and Glens
Native or outland, Lakes and famous Hills!
Or on the lonely High-road, when the Stars
Were rising; or by secret Mountain-streams,
The Guides and the Companions of thy way!

Of more than Fancy, of the Social Sense
Distending wide, and Man belov'd as Man,
Where France in all her Towns lay vibrating
Even as a Bark becalm'd beneath the Burst
Of Heaven's immediate Thunder, when no cloud
Is visible, or shadow on the Main.
For thou wert there, thine own brows garlanded,
Amid the tremor of a realm aglow,
Amid a mighty nation jubilant,
When from the general Heart of Human kind
Hope sprang forth like a full-born Deity!
—Of that dear Hope afflicted and struck down,
So summon'd homeward, thenceforth calm and sure
From the dread Watch-Tower of man's absolute Self,
With light unwaning on her eyes, to look
Far on—herself a glory to behold,
The Angel of the vision! Then (last strain)
Of Duty, chosen Laws controlling choice,
Action and Joy!—An orphic song indeed,
A song divine of high and passionate thoughts,
To their own Music chaunted!
O great Bard!
Ere yet that last strain dying awed the air,
With stedfast eye I view'd thee in the choir
Of ever-enduring men. The truly Great
Have all one age, and from one visible space
Shed influence! They, both in power and act,
Are permanent, and Time is not with *them*,
Save as it worketh *for* them, they *in* it.
Nor less a sacred Roll, than those of old,
And to be placed, as they, with gradual fame
Among the Archives of Mankind, thy work

[1] The poem referred to is William Wordsworth's *Prelude*,* which he read aloud to Coleridge over a two-week period in late December to early January 1806–1807.

[2] **Hyblean:** from Hybla, a mountain in Sicily, renowned for its flowers and famous for its honey.

Makes audible a linked lay of Truth,
Of Truth profound a sweet continuous lay,
Not learnt, but native, her own natural notes!
Ah! as I listen'd with a heart forlorn
The pulses of my Being beat anew:
And even as Life returns upon the Drown'd,
Life's joy rekindling rous'd a throng of Pains—
Keen Pangs of Love, awakening as a babe
Turbulent, with an outcry in the heart;
And Fears self-will'd, that shunn'd the eye of Hope;
And Hope that scarce would know itself from Fear;
Sense of past Youth, and Manhood come in vain,
And Genius given, and Knowledge won in vain;
And all which I had cull'd in Wood-walks wild,
And all which patient toil had rear'd, and all,
Commune with *thee* had open'd out—but Flowers
Strew'd on my corse, and borne upon my Bier,
In the same Coffin, for the self-same Grave!

That way no more! and ill beseems it me,
Who came a welcomer in Herald's Guise,
Singing of Glory, and Futurity,
To wander back on such unhealthful road,
Plucking the poisons of self-harm! And ill
Such Intertwine beseems triumphal wreaths
Strew'd before *thy* advancing!

Nor do thou,
Sage Bard! impair the memory of that hour
Of thy communion with my nobler mind
By Pity or Grief, already felt too long!
Nor let my words import more blame than needs.
The tumult rose and ceas'd: for Peace is nigh
Where wisdom's voice has found a listening heart.
Amid the howl of more than wintry storms,
The Halcyon[3] hears the voice of vernal Hours
Already on the wing!

Eve following Eve,
Dear tranquil time, when the sweet sense of Home
Is sweetest! moments for their own sake hail'd
And more desired, more precious for thy song,
In silence listening, like a devout child,
My soul lay passive, by thy various strain
Driven, as in surges now beneath the stars,
With momentary Stars of my own birth,
Fair constellated[4] Foam, still darting off
Into the darkness; now a tranquil sea,
Outspread and bright, yet swelling to the Moon.

And when—O Friend! my comforter and guide!
Strong in thy self, and powerful to give strength!—
Thy long sustained Song finally closed,
And thy deep voice had ceased—yet thou thyself
Wert still before my eyes, and round us both
That happy vision of beloved Faces—
Scarce conscious, and yet conscious of its close
I sate, my being blended in one thought
(Thought was it? or Aspiration? or Resolve?)
Absorb'd, yet hanging still upon the sound—
And when I rose, I found myself in prayer.

The Visionary Hope
(1817; comp. 1810?)

Sad lot, TO HAVE NO HOPE! Tho' lowly kneeling,
He fain would frame a prayer within his breast,
Would fain intreat for some sweet breath of healing,
That his sick body might have ease and rest;
He strove in vain! the dull sighs from his chest
Against his will the stifling load revealing.
Tho' Nature forc'd; tho' like some captive guest,
Some royal prisoner at his conqueror's feast,
An alien's restless mood but half concealing,
The sternness on his gentle brow confest
Sickness within and miserable feeling:
Tho' obscure pangs made curses of his dreams,
And dreaded sleep, each night repell'd in vain,
Each night was scatter'd by its own loud screams:
Yet never could his heart command, tho' fain,
One deep full wish to be no more in pain.

That HOPE, which was his inward bliss and boast,
Which wan'd and died, yet ever near him stood,
Tho' chang'd in nature, wander where he wou'd—

[3] **Halcyon:** a fabled bird, usually identified as the kingfisher, which has power to calm the seas on which it nests during the winter solstice.

[4] "A beautiful white cloud of Foam at momentary intervals coursed by the side of the Vessel with a Roar, and little stars of flame danced and sparkled and went out in it: and every now and then light detachments of this white cloud-like foam darted off from the vessel's side, each with its own small constellation, over the Sea, and scoured out of sight like a Tartar Troop over a Wilderness."—*The Friend*, p. 220. [S.T.C.]

For Love's Despair is but Hope's pining Ghost!
For this one hope he makes his hourly moan,
He wishes and *can* wish for this alone!
Pierc'd, as with light from Heaven, before its gleams
(So the love-stricken visionary deems)
Disease would vanish, like a summer shower,
Whose dews fling sunshine from the noon-tide bower!
Or let it stay! yet this one Hope should give
Such strength that he would bless his pains and live.

from BIOGRAPHIA LITERARIA

or, Biographical Sketches of My Literary Life and Opinions[1]

(1817)

—*from* CHAPTER 1—

[The Motives of the Present Work]

It has been my lot to have had my name introduced both in conversation, and in print, more frequently than I find it easy to explain, whether I consider the fewness, unimportance, and limited circulation of my writings, or the retirement and distance, in which I have lived, both from the literary and political world. Most often it has been connected with some charge, which I could not acknowledge, or some principle which I had never entertained. Nevertheless, had I had no other motive, or incitement, the reader would not have been troubled with this exculpation. What my additional purposes were, will be seen in the following pages. It will be found, that the least of what I have written concerns myself personally. I have used the narration chiefly for the purpose of giving a continuity to the work, in part for the sake of the miscellaneous reflections suggested to me by particular events, but still more as introductory to the statement of my principles in politics, religion, and philosophy, and the application of the rules, deduced from philosophical principles, to poetry and criticism. But of the objects, which I proposed to myself, it was not the least important to effect, as far as possible, a settlement of the long continued controversy concerning the true nature of poetic diction: and at the same time to define with the utmost impartiality the real *poetic* character of the poet,[2] by whose writings this controversy was first kindled, and has been since fuelled and fanned.

In 1794, when I had barely passed the verge of manhood, I published a small volume of juvenile poems.[3] They were received with a degree of favour, which, young as I was, I well knew, was bestowed on them not so much for any positive merit, as because they were considered buds of hope, and promises of better works to come. The critics of that day, the most flattering, equally with the severest, concurred in objecting to them, obscurity, a general turgidness of diction, and a profusion of new coined double epithets. The first is the fault which a writer is the least able to detect in his own compositions: and my mind was not then sufficiently disciplined to receive the authority of others, as a substitute for my own conviction. Satisfied that the thoughts, such as they were, could not have been expressed otherwise, or at least more perspicuously, I forgot to enquire, whether the thoughts themselves did not demand a degree of attention unsuitable to the nature and objects of poetry. This remark however applies chiefly, though not exclusively to the *Religious Musings*. The remainder of the charge I admitted to its full extent, and not without sincere acknowledgements to both my private and public censors for their friendly admonitions. In the after editions, I pruned the double epithets with no sparing hand, and used my best efforts to tame the swell and glitter both of thought and diction; though in truth, these parasite plants of youthful poetry had insinuated themselves into my longer poems with such intricacy of union, that I was often obliged to omit disentangling the weed, from the fear of snapping the flower. From that period to the date of the present work I have published nothing, with my name, which could by any possibility have come before the board of anonymous criticism. Even the three or four poems, printed with the works of a friend, as far as they were censured at all, were charged with the same or similar defects, though I am persuaded not with equal justice: with an excess of ornament, in addition to strained and elaborate diction. (*Vide* [see] the criticisms on the 'Ancient Mariner,' in the Monthly and Critical Reviews* of the first volume of the Lyrical Ballads.) May I be permitted to add, that, even at the early period of my juvenile poems, I saw and admitted the superiority of an austerer, and more natural style, with an

[1] Published in two volumes the same week in 1817 as *Sibylline Leaves*. See Introduction for more information.

[2] **the poet:** W. Wordsworth.

[3] **volume of . . . poems:** *Poems* (1796).*

insight not less clear, than I at present possess. My judgement was stronger, than were my powers of realizing its dictates; and the faults of my language, though indeed partly owing to a wrong choice of subjects, and the desire of giving a poetic colouring to abstract and metaphysical truths, in which a new world then seemed to open upon me, did yet, in part likewise, originate in unfeigned diffidence of my own comparative talent.—During several years of my youth and early manhood, I reverenced those, who had reintroduced the manly simplicity of the Grecian, and of our own elder poets, with such enthusiasm, as made the hope seem presumptuous of writing successfully in the same style. Perhaps a similar process has happened to others; but my earliest poems were marked by an ease and simplicity, which I have studied, perhaps with inferior success, to impress on my later compositions.

At school I enjoyed the inestimable advantage of a very sensible, though at the same time, a very severe master. He[4] early moulded my taste to the preference of Demosthenes to Cicero, of Homer and Theocritus to Virgil, and again of Virgil to Ovid. He habituated me to compare Lucretius, (in such extracts as I then read), Terence, and above all the chaster poems of Catullus, not only with the Roman poets of the, so-called, Silver and Brazen Ages; but with even those of the Augustan era: and on grounds of plain sense and universal logic to see and assert the superiority of the former, in the truth and nativeness, both of their thoughts and diction. At the same time that we were studying the Greek tragic poets, he made us read Shakespeare and Milton as lessons: and they were the lessons too, which required most time and trouble to *bring up*, so as to escape his censure. I learnt from him, that poetry, even that of the loftiest, and, seemingly, that of the wildest odes, had a logic of its own, as severe as that of science; and more difficult, because more subtle, more complex, and dependent on more, and more fugitive causes. In the truly great poets, he would say, there is a reason assignable, not only for every word, but for the position of every word; and I well remember, that availing himself of the synonyms to the Homer of Didymus, he made us attempt to show, with regard to each, why it would not have answered the same purpose; and wherein consisted the peculiar fitness of the word in the original text.

In our own English compositions (at least for the last three years of our school education) he showed no mercy to phrase, metaphor, or image, unsupported by a sound sense, or where the same sense might have been conveyed with equal force and dignity in plainer words. Lute, harp, and lyre, muse, muses, and inspirations, Pegasus, Parnassus, and Hipocrene, were all an abomination to him. In fancy I can almost hear him now, exclaiming 'Harp? Harp? Lyre? Pen and ink, boy, you mean! Muse, boy, Muse? your Nurse's daughter, you mean! Pierian spring? Oh 'aye! the cloister-pump, I suppose!' . . .

Be this as it may, there was one custom of our master's, which I cannot pass over in silence, because I think it imitable and worthy of imitation. He would often permit our theme exercises, under some pretext of want of time, to accumulate, till each lad had four or five to be looked over. Then placing the whole number abreast on his desk, he would ask the writer, why this or that sentence might not have found as appropriate a place under this or that other thesis: and if no satisfying answer could be returned, and two faults of the same kind were found in one exercise, the irrevocable verdict followed, the exercise was torn up, and another on the same subject to be produced, in addition to the tasks of the day. The reader will, I trust, excuse this tribute of recollection to a man, whose severities, even now, not seldom furnish the dreams, by which the blind fancy would fain interpret to the mind the painful sensations of distempered sleep; but neither lessen nor dim the deep sense of my moral and intellectual obligations. He sent us to the university excellent Latin and Greek scholars, and tolerable Hebraists. Yet our classical knowledge was the least of the good gifts, which we derived from his zealous and conscientious tutorage. He is now gone to his final reward, full of years, and full of honours, even of those honours, which were dearest to his heart, as gratefully bestowed by that school, and still binding him to the interests of that school, in which he had been himself educated, and to which during his whole life he was a dedicated thing. . . .

I had just entered on my seventeenth year, when the sonnets of Mr Bowles,[5] twenty in number, and just then published in a quarto pamphlet, were first made known and presented to me, by a schoolfellow who had quitted us for the university, and who, during the whole time that he was in our first form (or in our school language a Grecian) had been my patron and protector. I refer to Dr

[4] **He:** the Revd James Boyer, many years Head Master of the Grammar School, Christ's Hospital. [S.T.C.]

[5] **Mr Bowles**: William Lisle Bowles (1762–1850), whose *Fourteen Sonnets* (1789), greatly impressed the youthful Coleridge.

Middleton, the truly learned, and every way excellent Bishop of Calcutta . . .

. . . My obligations to Mr Bowles were indeed important, and for radical good. At a very premature age, even before my fifteenth year, I had bewildered myself in metaphysics, and in theological controversy. Nothing else pleased me. History, and particular facts, lost all interest in my mind. Poetry (though for a schoolboy of that age, I was above par in English versification, and had already produced two or three compositions which, I may venture to say, without reference to my age, were somewhat above mediocrity, and which had gained me more credit, than the sound, good sense of my old master was at all pleased with) poetry itself, yea novels and romances, became insipid to me. In my friendless wanderings on our *leave-days*,[6] (for I was an orphan, and had scarce any connections in London) highly was I delighted, if any passenger, especially if he were dressed in black, would enter into conversation with me. For I soon found the means of directing it to my favourite subjects

> Of providence, fore-knowledge, will, and fate,
> Fix'd fate, free will, fore-knowledge absolute,
> And found no end in wandering mazes lost.[7]

This preposterous pursuit was, beyond doubt, injurious, both to my natural powers, and to the progress of my education. It would perhaps have been destructive, had it been continued; but from this I was auspiciously withdrawn, partly indeed by an accidental introduction to an amiable family, chiefly however, by the genial influence of a style of poetry, so tender, and yet so manly, so natural and real, and yet so dignified, and harmonious, as the sonnets, etc. of Mr Bowles! Well were it for me perhaps, had I never relapsed into the same mental disease; if I had continued to pluck the flower and reap the harvest from the cultivated surface, instead of delving in the unwholesome quicksilver mines of metaphysic depths. But if in after time I have sought a refuge from bodily pain and mismanaged sensibility in abstruse researches, which exercised the strength and subtlety of the understanding without awakening the feelings of the heart; still there was a long and blessed interval, during which my natural faculties were allowed to expand, and my original tendencies to develop themselves: my fancy, and the love of nature, and the sense of beauty in forms and sounds.

The second advantage, which I owe to my early perusal, and admiration of these poems (to which let me add, though known to me at a somewhat later period, the Lewesdon Hill of Mr Crowe) bears more immediately on my present subject. Among those with whom I conversed, there were, of course, very many who had formed their taste, and their notions of poetry, from the writings of Mr Pope[8] and his followers: or to speak more generally, in that school of French poetry, condensed and invigorated by English understanding, which had predominated from the last century. I was not blind to the merits of this school, yet as from inexperience of the world, and consequent want of sympathy with the general subjects of these poems, they gave me little pleasure, I doubtless undervalued the kind, and with the presumption of youth withheld from its masters the legitimate name of poets. I saw, that the excellence of this kind consisted in just and acute observations on men and manners in an artificial state of society, as its matter and substance: and in the logic of wit, conveyed in smooth and strong epigrammatic couplets, as its form. Even when the subject was addressed to the fancy, or the intellect, as in the Rape of the Lock, or the Essay on Man; nay, when it was a consecutive narration, as in that astonishing product of matchless talent and ingenuity, Pope's Translation of the Iliad; still a point was looked for at the end of each second line, and the whole was as it were a sorites, or, if I may exchange a logical for a grammatical metaphor, a *conjunction disjunctive,* of epigrams. Meantime the matter and diction seemed to me characterized not so much by poetic thoughts, as by thoughts translated into the language of poetry. On this last point, I had occasion to render my own thoughts gradually more and more plain to myself, by frequent amicable disputes concerning Darwin's[9] Botanic Garden, which, for some years, was greatly extolled, not only by the reading public in general, but even by those, whose genius and natural robustness of understanding enabled them afterwards to act foremost in dissipating these 'painted mists' that occasionally rise from the marshes at

[6] The Christ's Hospital phrase, not for holidays altogether, but for those on which the boys are permitted to go beyond the precincts of the school. [S.T.C.]

[7] Cf. *Paradise Lost,* ll. 557–62: "Others [devils] apart sat on a hill retired, / In thoughts more elevate, and reasoned high / Of providence, foreknowledge, will, and fate, / Fixed fate, free will, foreknowledge absolute, / And found no end, in wand'ring mazes lost."

[8] **Mr. Pope:** Alexander Pope (1688–1744).

[9] **Darwin:** Erasmus Darwin.*

the foot of Parnassus. During my first Cambridge vacation, I assisted a friend in a contribution for a literary society in Devonshire: and in this I remember to have compared Darwin's work to the Russian palace of ice, glittering, cold and transitory. . . . I had continually to adduce the metre and diction of the Greek poets from Homer to Theocritus inclusive; and still more of our elder English poets from Chaucer to Milton. Nor was this all. But as it was my constant reply to authorities brought against me from later poets of great name, that no authority could avail in opposition to truth, nature, logic, and the laws of universal grammar; actuated too by my former passion for metaphysical investigations; I laboured at a solid foundation, on which permanently to ground my opinions, in the component faculties of the human mind itself, and their comparative dignity and importance. According to the faculty or source, from which the pleasure given by any poem or passage was derived, I estimated the merit of such poem or passage. As the result of all my reading and meditation, I abstracted two critical aphorisms, deeming them to comprise the conditions and criteria of poetic style; first, that not the poem which we have *read,* but that to which we *return,* with the greatest pleasure, possesses the genuine power, and claims the name of *essential poetry.* Second, that whatever lines can be translated into other words of the same language, without diminution of their significance, either in sense, or association, or in any worthy feeling, are so far vicious in their diction. Be it however observed, that I excluded from the list of worthy feelings, the pleasure derived from mere novelty, in the reader, and the desire of exciting wonderment at his powers in the author. . . .

— *from* CHAPTER 4 —

[*LYRICAL BALLADS* AND PREFACE; WORDSWORTH]

. . . During the last year of my residence at Cambridge, I became acquainted with Mr Wordsworth's first publication entitled 'Descriptive Sketches';[1] and seldom, if ever, was the emergence of an original poetic genius above the literary horizon more evidently announced. In the form, style, and manner of the whole poem, and in the structure of the particular lines and periods, there is an harshness and acerbity connected and combined with words and images all a-glow, which might recall those products of the vegetable world, where gorgeous blossoms rise out of the hard and thorny rind and shell, within which the rich fruit was elaborating. The language was not only peculiar and strong, but at times knotty and contorted, as by its own impatient strength; while the novelty and struggling crowd of images acting in conjunction with the difficulties of the style, demanded always a greater closeness of attention, than poetry, (at all events, than descriptive poetry) has a right to claim. It not seldom therefore justified the complaint of obscurity. In the following extract I have sometimes fancied, that I saw an emblem of the poem itself, and of the author's genius as it was then displayed.

'Tis storm; and hid in mist from hour to hour,
All day the floods a deepening murmur pour;
The sky is veiled, and every cheerful sight:
Dark is the region as with coming night;
And yet what frequent bursts of overpowering light!
Triumphant on the bosom of the storm,
Glances the fire-clad eagle's wheeling form;
Eastward, in long perspective glittering, shine
The wood-crowned cliffs that o'er the lake recline;
Wide o'er the Alps a hundred streams unfold,
At once to pillars turn'd that flame with gold;
Behind his sail the peasant strives to shun
The West, that burns like one dilated sun,
Where in a mighty crucible expire
The mountains, glowing hot, like coals of fire.[2]

. . . I was in my twenty-fourth year, when I had the happiness of knowing Mr Wordsworth personally, and while memory lasts, I shall hardly forget the sudden effect produced on my mind, by his recitation of a manuscript poem, which still remains unpublished, but of which the stanza, and tone of style, were the same as those of the 'Female Vagrant' as originally printed in the first volume of the 'Lyrical Ballads.' There was here, no mark of strained thought, or forced diction, no crowd or turbulence of imagery, and, as the poet hath himself well described in his lines 'on revisiting the Wye,' manly reflection, and human associations had given both variety, and an additional interest to natural objects, which in the passion and appetite of the first love they had seemed to him neither to need or permit. The occasional obscurities, which had risen from an imperfect control over the resources of his native language, had almost wholly disappeared, together with that

[1] **Descriptive Sketches:** Coleridge quotes the revised text of 1815 rather than the lines he read in 1793, the year of the poem's first publication.

[2] See Introduction to SCIENCE AND NATURE for more on the place and importance of imagination in nineteenth-century thought.

worse defect of arbitrary and illogical phrases, at once hackneyed, and fantastic, which hold so distinguished a place in the technique of ordinary poetry, and will, more or less, alloy the earlier poems of the truest genius, unless the attention has been specifically directed to their worthlessness and incongruity. I did not perceive anything particular in the mere style of the poem alluded to during its recitation, except indeed such difference as was not separable from the thought and manner; and the Spenserian stanza, which always, more or less, recalls to the reader's mind Spenser's own style, would doubtless have authorized in my then opinion a more frequent descent to the phrases of ordinary life, than could without an ill effect have been hazarded in the heroic couplet. It was not however the freedom from false taste, whether as to common defects, or to those more properly his own, which made so unusual an impression on my feelings immediately, and subsequently on my judgement. It was the union of deep feeling with profound thought; the fine balance of truth in observing with the imaginative faculty in modifying the objects observed; and above all the original gift of spreading the tone, the atmosphere, and with it the depth and height of the ideal world around forms, incidents, and situations, of which, for the common view, custom had bedimmed all the lustre, had dried up the sparkle and the dewdrops. . . .

This excellence, which in all Mr Wordsworth's writings is more or less predominant, and which constitutes the character of his mind, I no sooner felt, than I sought to understand. Repeated meditations led me first to suspect, (and a more intimate analysis of the human faculties, their appropriate marks, functions, and effects matured my conjecture into full conviction) that fancy and imagination were two distinct and widely different faculties, instead of being, according to the general belief, either two names with one meaning, or at furthest, the lower and higher degree of one and the same power. It is not, I own, easy to conceive a more apposite translation of the Greek *phantasia*, than the Latin *imaginatio*; but it is equally true that in all societies there exists an instinct of growth, a certain collective, unconscious good sense working progressively to desynonymize those words originally of the same meaning, which the conflux of dialects had supplied to the more homogeneous languages, as the Greek and German: and which the same cause, joined with accidents of translation from original works of different countries, occasion in mixed languages like our own. The first and most important point to be proved is, that two conceptions perfectly distinct are confused under one and the same word, and (this done) to appropriate that word exclusively to one meaning, and the synonym (should there be one) to the other. But if (as will be often the case in the arts and sciences) no synonym exists, we must either invent or borrow a word. In the present instance the appropriation had already begun, and been legitimated in the derivative adjective: Milton had a highly *imaginative*, Cowley and very *fanciful* mind. If therefore I should succeed in establishing the actual existences of two faculties generally different, the nomenclature would be at once determined. To the faculty by which I had characterized Milton, we should confine the term *imagination*; while the other would be contra-distinguished as *fancy*. Now were it once fully ascertained, that this division is no less grounded in nature, than that of delirium from mania, or Otway's

> Lutes, lobsters, seas of milk, and ships of amber,

from Shakespeare's

> What! have his daughters brought him to this pass?

or from the preceding apostrophe to the elements; the theory of the fine arts, and of poetry in particular, could not, I thought, but derive some additional and important light. It would in its immediate effects furnish a torch of guidance to the philosophical critic; and ultimately to the poet himself. In energetic minds, truth soon changes by domestication into power; and from directing in the discrimination and appraisal of the product, becomes influencive in the production. To admire on principle, is the only way to imitate without loss of originality. . . .

—*from* CHAPTER 13—
[Imagination]

On the imagination, or esemplastic power[1]

. . . The IMAGINATION then I consider either as primary, or secondary. The primary IMAGINATION I hold to be the living Power and prime Agent of all human Perception, and as a repetition in the finite mind of the eternal act of

[1] **esemplastic power:** in Chapter 10, Coleridge introduces this neologism from Greek words that translate, "to shape into one; because, having to convey a new sense, I thought that a new term would both aid the recollection of my meaning, and prevent its being confounded with the usual import of the word, imagination."

creation in the infinite I AM. The secondary I consider as an echo of the former, co-existing with the conscious will, yet still as identical with the primary in the *kind* of its agency, and differing only in *degree*, and in the *mode* of its operation. It dissolves, diffuses, dissipates, in order to re-create; or where this process is rendered impossible, yet still at all events it struggles to idealize and to unify. It is essentially *vital*, even as all objects (as objects) are essentially fixed and dead.

FANCY, on the contrary, has no other counters to play with, but fixities and definites. The Fancy is indeed no other than a mode of Memory emancipated from the order of time and space; and blended with, and modified by that empirical phenomenon of the will, which we express by the word CHOICE. But equally with the ordinary memory it must receive all its materials ready made from the law of association. . . .

— CHAPTER 14 —

[*LYRICAL BALLADS* AND POETIC CONTROVERSY]

During the first year that Mr. Wordsworth and I were neighbours, our conversations turned frequently on the two cardinal points of poetry, the power of exciting the sympathy of the reader by a faithful adherence to the truth of nature, and the power of giving the interest of novelty by the modifying colours of imagination. The sudden charm, which accidents of light and shade, which moon-light or sun-set diffused over a known and familiar landscape, appeared to represent the practicability of combining both. These are the poetry of nature. The thought suggested itself (to which of us I do not recollect) that a series of poems might be composed of two sorts. In the one, the incidents and agents were to be, in part at least, supernatural; and the excellence aimed at was to consist in the interesting of the affections by the dramatic truth of such emotions, as would naturally accompany such situations, supposing them real. And real in *this* sense they have been to every human being who, from whatever source of delusion, has at any time believed himself under supernatural agency. For the second class, subjects were to be chosen from ordinary life; the characters and incidents were to be such, as will be found in every village and its vicinity, where there is a meditative and feeling mind to seek after them, or to notice them, when they present themselves.

In this idea originated the plan of the "Lyrical Ballads;" in which it was agreed, that my endeavours should be directed to persons and characters supernatural, or at least romantic; yet so as to transfer from our inward nature a human interest and a semblance of truth sufficient to procure for these shadows of imagination that willing suspension of disbelief for the moment, which constitutes poetic faith. Mr. Wordsworth, on the other hand, was to propose to himself as his object, to give the charm of novelty to things of every day, and to excite a feeling analogous to the supernatural, by awakening the mind's attention from the lethargy of custom, and directing it to the loveliness and the wonders of the world before us; an inexhaustible treasure, but for which in consequence of the film of familiarity and selfish solicitude we have eyes, yet see not, ears that hear not, and hearts that neither feel nor understand.

With this view I wrote the "Ancient Mariner," and was preparing among other poems, the "Dark Ladie," and the "Christabel," in which I should have more nearly realized my ideal, than I had done in my first attempt. But Mr. Wordsworth's industry had proved so much more successful, and the number of his poems so much greater, that my compositions, instead of forming a balance, appeared rather an interpolation of heterogeneous matter. Mr. Wordsworth added two or three poems written in his own character, in the impassioned, lofty, and sustained diction, which is characteristic of his genius. In this form the "Lyrical Ballads" were published; and were presented by him, as an *experiment*, whether subjects, which from their nature rejected the usual ornaments and extra-colloquial style of poems in general, might not be so managed in the language of ordinary life as to produce the pleasurable interest, which it is the peculiar business of poetry to impart. To the second edition he added a preface of considerable length; in which notwithstanding some passages of apparently a contrary import, he was understood to contend for the extension of this style to poetry of all kinds, and to reject as vicious and indefensible all phrases and forms of style that were not included in what he (unfortunately, I think, adopting an equivocal expression) called the language of *real* life. From this preface, prefixed to poems in which it was impossible to deny the presence of original genius, however mistaken its direction might be deemed, arose the whole long continued controversy. For from the conjunction of perceived power with supposed heresy I explain the inveteracy and in some instances, I grieve to say, the acrimonious passions, with which the controversy has been conducted by the assailants.[1]

---

[1] See, for example, Francis Jeffrey's review of Wordsworth's *Excursion* (1814)* in AESTHETIC THEORY AND LITERARY CRITICISM.

Had Mr. Wordsworth's poems been the silly, the childish things, which they were for a long time described as being; had they been really distinguished from the compositions of other poets merely by meanness of language and inanity of thought; had they indeed contained nothing more than what is found in the parodies and pretended imitations of them; they must have sunk at once, a dead weight, into the slough of oblivion, and have dragged the preface along with them. But year after year increased the number of Mr. Wordsworth's admirers. They were found too not in the lower classes of the reading public, but chiefly among young men of strong sensibility and meditative minds; and their admiration (inflamed perhaps in some degree by opposition) was distinguished by its intensity, I might almost say, by its *religious* fervour. These facts, and the intellectual energy of the author, which was more or less consciously felt, where it was outwardly and even boisterously denied, meeting with sentiments of aversion to his opinions, and of alarm at their consequences, produced an eddy of criticism, which would of itself have borne up the poems by the violence, with which it whirled them round and round. With many parts of this preface in the sense attributed to them and which the words undoubtedly seem to authorise, I never concurred; but on the contrary objected to them as erroneous in principle, and as contradictory (in appearance at least) both to other parts of the same preface, and to the author's own practice in the greater number of the poems themselves. Mr. Wordsworth in his recent collection has, I find, degraded this prefatory disquisition to the end of his second volume, to be read or not at the reader's choice. But he has not, as far as I can discover, announced any change in his poetic creed. At all events, considering it as the source of a controversy, in which I have been honored more, than I deserve, by the frequent conjunction of my name with his, I think it expedient to declare once for all, in what points I coincide with his opinions, and in what points I altogether differ. But in order to render myself intelligible I must previously, in as few words as possible, explain my ideas, first, of a POEM; and secondly, of POETRY itself, in *kind*, and in *essence*.

The office of philosophical *disquisition* consists in just *distinction*; while it is the priviledge of the philosopher to preserve himself constantly aware, that distinction is not division. In order to obtain adequate notions of any truth, we must intellectually separate its distinguishable parts; and this is the technical *process* of philosophy. But having so done, we must then restore them in our conceptions to the unity, in which they actually co-exist; and this is the *result* of philosophy. A poem contains the same elements as a prose composition; the difference therefore must consist in a different combination of them, in consequence of a different object proposed. According to the difference of the object will be the difference of the combination. It is possible, that the object may be merely to facilitate the recollection of any given facts or observations by artificial arrangement; and the composition will be a poem, merely because it is distinguished from prose by metre, or by rhyme, or by both conjointly. In this, the lowest sense, a man might attribute the name of a poem to the well known enumeration of the days in the several months;

Thirty days hath September,
April, June, and November, &c.

and others of the same class and purpose. And as a particular pleasure is found in anticipating the recurrence of sounds and quantities, all compositions that have this charm superadded, whatever be their contents, *may* be entitled poems.

So much for the superficial *form*. A difference of object and contents supplies an additional ground of distinction. The immediate purpose may be the communication of truths; either of truth absolute and demonstrable, as in works of science; or of facts experienced and recorded, as in history. Pleasure, and that of the highest and most permanent kind, may *result* from the *attainment* of the end; but it is not itself the immediate end. In other works the communication of pleasure may be the immediate purpose; and though truth, either moral or intellectual, ought to be the *ultimate* end, yet this will distinguish the character of the author, not the class to which the work belongs. Blest indeed is that state of society, in which the immediate purpose would be baffled by the perversion of the proper ultimate end; in which no charm of diction or imagery could exempt the Bathyllus even of an Anacreon, or the Alexis of Virgil,[2] from disgust and aversion!

But the communication of pleasure may be the immediate object of a work not metrically composed; and that object may have been in a high degree attained, as in novels and romances. Would then the mere superaddition of metre, with or without rhyme, entitle *these* to the name of poems? The answer is, that nothing can permanently please, which does not contain in itself the reason why it

[2] The reference is to poets and poems of homosexual love. "Bathyllus" was loved by Anacreon; "Alexis" by Corydon in Virgil's *Eclogue* 2.

is so, and not otherwise. If metre be superadded, all other parts must be made consonant with it. They must be such, as to justify the perpetual and distinct attention to each part, which an exact correspondent recurrence of accent and sound are calculated to excite. The final definition then, so deduced, may be thus worded. A poem is that species of composition, which is opposed to works of science, by proposing for its *immediate* object pleasure, not truth; and from all other species (having *this* object in common with it) it is discriminated by proposing to itself such delight from the *whole,* as is compatible with a distinct gratification from each component *part.*

Controversy is not seldom excited in consequence of the disputants attaching each a different meaning to the same word; and in few instances has this been more striking, than in disputes concerning the present subject. If a man chooses to call every composition a poem, which is rhyme, or measure, or both, I must leave his opinion uncontroverted. The distinction is at least competent to characterize the writer's intention. If it were subjoined, that the whole is likewise entertaining or affecting, as a tale, or as a series of interesting reflections, I of course admit this as another fit ingredient of a poem, and an additional merit. But if the definition sought for be that of a *legitimate* poem, I answer, it must be one, the parts of which mutually support and explain each other; all in their proportion harmonizing with, and supporting the purpose and known influences of metrical arrangement. The philosophic critics of all ages coincide with the ultimate judgement of all countries, in equally denying the praises of a just poem, on the one hand, to a series of striking lines or distichs, each of which absorbing the whole attention of the reader to itself disjoins it from its context, and makes it a separate whole, instead of an harmonizing part; and on the other hand, to an unsustained composition, from which the reader collects rapidly the general result unattracted by the component parts. The reader should be carried forward, not merely or chiefly by the mechanical impulse of curiosity, or by a restless desire to arrive at the final solution; but by the pleasureable activity of mind excited by the attractions of the journey itself. Like the motion of a serpent, which the Egyptians made the emblem of intellectual power; or like the path of sound through the air; at every step he pauses and half recedes, and from the retrogressive movement collects the force which again carries him onward. Precipitandus est *liber* spiritus,[3] says Petronius Arbiter most happily. The epithet, *liber,* here balances the preceding verb; and it is not easy to conceive more meaning condensed in fewer words.

But if this should be admitted as a satisfactory character of a poem, we have still to seek for a definition of poetry. The writings of PLATO, and Bishop TAYLOR, and the Theoria Sacra of BURNET,[4] furnish undeniable proofs that poetry of the highest kind may exist without metre, and even without the contradistinguishing objects of a poem. The first chapter of Isaiah (indeed a very large proportion of the whole book) is poetry in the most emphatic sense; yet it would be not less irrational than strange to assert, that pleasure, and not truth, was the immediate object of the prophet. In short, whatever *specific* import we attach to the word, poetry, there will be found involved in it, as a necessary consequence, that a poem of any length neither can be, or ought to be, all poetry. Yet if an harmonious whole is to be produced, the remaining parts must be preserved *in keeping* with the poetry; and this can be no otherwise effected than by such a studied selection and artificial arrangement, as will partake of *one,* though not a *peculiar,* property of poetry. And this again can be no other than the property of exciting a more continuous and equal attention, than the language of prose aims at, whether colloquial or written.

My own conclusions on the nature of poetry, in the strictest use of the word, have been in part anticipated in the preceding disquisition on the fancy and imagination. What is poetry? is so nearly the same question with, what is a poet? that the answer to the one is involved in the solution of the other. For it is a distinction resulting from the poetic genius itself, which sustains and modifies the images, thoughts, and emotions of the poet's own mind. The poet, described in *ideal* perfection, brings the whole soul of man into activity, with the subordination of its faculties to each other, according to their relative worth and dignity. He diffuses a tone, and spirit of unity, that blends, and (as it were) *fuses,* each into each, by that synthetic and magical power, to which we have exclusively appropriated the name of imagination. This power, first put in action by the will and understanding, and retained under their irremissive, though gentle and unnoticed,

[3] **Precipitandus . . . spiritus:** "the free spirit must be hurried onward."

[4] **Bishop Taylor:** Jeremy Taylor (1613–1667), author of *The Rule and Exercises of Holy Living* (1650), *The Rule and Exercises of Holy Dying* (1651), both renowned for splendour of style. **Theoria Sacra of Burnet:** Thomas Burnet (1635?–1715), author of *The Sacred Theory of the Earth* (2 vols., 1684–1690), admired for its many sonorous passages.

controul (*laxis effertur habenis*)[5] reveals itself in the balance or reconciliation of opposite or discordant qualities: of sameness, with difference; of the general, with the concrete; the idea, with the image; the individual, with the representative; the sense of novelty and freshness, with old and familiar objects; a more than usual state of emotion, with more than usual order; judgement ever awake and steady self-possession, with enthusiasm and feeling profound or vehement; and while it blends and harmonizes the natural and the artificial, still subordinates art to nature; the manner to the matter; and our admiration of the poet to our sympathy with the poetry. "Doubtless," as Sir John Davies observes of the soul (and his words may with slight alteration be applied, and even more appropriately to the poetic IMAGINATION.)

Doubtless this could not be, but that she turns
Bodies to spirit by sublimation strange,
As fire converts to fire the things it burns,
As we our food into our nature change.

From their gross matter she abstracts their forms,
And draws a kind of quintessence from things;
Which to her proper nature she transforms
To bear them light, on her celestial wings.

Thus does she, when from individual states
She doth abstract the universal kinds;
Which then re-clothed in divers names and fates
Steal access through our senses to our minds.[6]

— CHAPTER 17 —

[POETIC LANGUAGE]

As far then as Mr Wordsworth in his preface contended, and most ably contended, for a reformation in our poetic diction, as far as he has evinced the truth of passion, and the *dramatic* propriety of those figures and metaphors in the original poets, which stript of their justifying reasons, and converted into mere artifices of connection or ornament, constitute the characteristic falsity in the poetic style of the moderns; and as far as he has, with equal acuteness and clearness, pointed out the process in which this change was effected, and the resemblances between that state into which the reader's mind is thrown by the pleasureable confusion of thought from an unaccustomed train of words and images; and that state which is induced by the natural language of empassioned feeling; he undertook a useful task, and deserves all praise, both for the attempt and for the execution. . . .

My own differences from certain supposed parts of Mr Wordsworth's theory ground themselves on the assumption, that his words had been rightly interpreted, as purporting that the proper diction for poetry in general consists altogether in a language taken, with due exceptions, from the mouths of men in real life, a language which actually constitutes the natural conversation of men under the influence of natural feelings. My objection is, first, that in *any* sense this rule is applicable only to *certain* classes of poetry; secondly, that even to these classes it is not applicable, except in such a sense, as hath never by any one (as far as I know or have read) been denied or doubted; and lastly, that as far as, and in that degree in which it is *practicable,* yet as a *rule* it is useless, if not injurious, and therefore either need not, or ought not to be practised. The poet informs his reader, that he had generally chosen *low and rustic* life; but not *as* low and rustic, or in order to repeat that pleasure of doubtful moral effect, which persons of elevated rank and of superior refinement oftentimes derive from a happy *imitation* of the rude unpolished manners and discourse of their inferiors. . . . *He* chose low and rustic life, "because in that condition the essential passions of the heart find a better soil, in which they can attain their maturity, are less under restraint, and speak a plainer and more emphatic language; because in that condition of life our elementary feelings co-exist in a state of greater simplicity, and consequently may be more accurately contemplated, and more forcibly communicated; because the manners of rural life germinate from those elementary feelings; and from the necessary character of rural occupations are more easily comprehended, and are more durable; and lastly, because in that condition the passions of men are incorporated with the beautiful and permanent forms of nature."

Now it is clear to me, that in the most interesting of the poems, in which the author is more or less dramatic, as the "Brothers," "Michael," "Ruth," the "Mad Mother," &c. the persons introduced are by no means taken *from low or rustic life* in the common acceptation of those words; and it is not less clear, that the sentiments and language, as far as they can be conceived to have been really transferred from the minds and conversation of such persons, are attributable to causes and circumstances not necessarily connected with "their occupations and abode." The thoughts, feelings, language, and manners of the shepherd-farmers in the vales of Cumberland and Westmoreland, as far as they are actually adopted in those poems, may be accounted for from causes, which will and do

[5] **laxis effertur habenis**: "carried on with slackened reins."

[6] Cf. John Davies (1570–1626), *Nosce Teipsum: Of the Soule of Man and the Immortalitie Thereof* (1599).

produce the same results in *every* state of life, whether in town or country. As the two principal I rank that INDEPENDENCE, which raises a man above servitude, or daily toil for the profit of others, yet not above the necessity of industry and a frugal simplicity of domestic life; and the accompanying unambitious, but solid and religious EDUCATION, which has rendered few books familiar, but the bible, and the liturgy or hymn book. To this latter cause, indeed, which is so far *accidental,* that it is the blessing of particular countries and a particular age, not the product of particular places or employments, the poet owes the shew of probability, that his personages might really feel, think, and talk with any tolerable resemblance to his representation. . . .

. . . I adopt with full faith the principle of Aristotle, that poetry as poetry is essentially *ideal,* that it avoids and excludes all *accident;* that its apparent individualities of rank, character, or occupation must be *representative* of a class; and that the *persons* of poetry must be clothed with *generic* attributes, with the *common* attributes of the class; not with such as one gifted individual might *possibly* possess, but such as from his situation it is most probable before-hand, that he *would* possess.[1] If my premises are right, and my deductions legitimate, it follows that there can be no *poetic* medium between the swains of Theocritus and those of an imaginary golden age. . . .

If then I am compelled to doubt the theory, by which the choice of *characters* was to be directed, not only *a priori,* from grounds of reason, but both from the few instances in which the poet himself *need* be supposed to have been governed by it, and from the comparative inferiority of those instances; still more must I hesitate in my assent to the sentence which immediately follows the former citation; and which I can neither admit as particular fact, or as general rule. "The language too of these men is adopted (purified indeed from what appear to be its real defects, from all lasting and rational causes of dislike or disgust) because such men hourly communicate with the best objects from which the best part of language is originally derived; and because, from their rank in society, and the sameness and narrow circle of their intercourse, being less under the action of social vanity, they convey their feelings and notions in simple and unelaborated expressions." To this I reply; that a rustic's language, purified from all provincialism and grossness, and so far re-constructed as to be made consistent with the rules of grammar (which are in essence no other than the laws of universal logic, applied to Psychological materials) will not differ from the language of any other man of common-sense, however learned or refined he may be, except as far as the notions, which the rustic has to convey, are fewer and more indiscriminate. . . .

As little can I agree with the assertion, that from the objects with which the rustic hourly communicates, the best part of language is formed. For first, if to communicate with an object implies such an acquaintance with it, as renders it capable of being discriminately reflected on; the distinct knowledge of an uneducated rustic would furnish a very scanty vocabulary. The few things, and modes of action, requisite for his bodily conveniences, would alone be individualized; while all the rest of nature would be expressed by a small number of confused, general terms. Secondly, I deny that the words and combinations of words derived from the objects, with which the rustic is familiar, whether with distinct or confused knowledge, can be justly said to form the *best* part of language. It is more than probable, that many classes of the brute creation possess discriminating sounds, by which they can convey to each other notices of such objects as concern their food, shelter, or safety. Yet we hesitate to call the aggregate of such sounds a language, otherwise than metaphorically. The best part of human language, properly so called, is derived from reflection on the acts of the mind itself. It is formed by a voluntary appropriation of fixed symbols to internal acts, to processes and results of imagination, the greater part of which have no place in the consciousness of uneducated man; though in civilized society, by imitation and passive remembrance of what they hear from their religious instructors and other superiors, the most uneducated share in the harvest which they neither sowed or reaped. If the history of the phrases in hourly currency among our peasants were traced, a person not previously aware of the fact would be surprized at finding so large a number, which three or four centuries ago were the exclusive property of the universities and the schools; and at the commencement of the Reformation had been transferred from the school to the pulpit, and thus gradually passed into common life. The extreme difficulty, and often the impossibility, of finding words for the simplest moral and intellectual processes in the languages of uncivilized tribes has proved perhaps the weightiest obstacle to the progress of our most zealous and adroit missionaries. Yet these tribes

[1] Cf. Aristotle's *Poetics,* 9.1.4, and Samuel Johnson's *Rasselas* (1759), chap. X, for the classical and neoclassical background of S.T.C.'s comment. (See AESTHETIC THEORY.)

are surrounded by the same nature, as our peasants are; but in still more impressive forms; and they are, moreover, obliged to *particularize* many more of them. When therefore Mr. Wordsworth adds, "accordingly such a language" (meaning, as before, the language of rustic life purified from provincialism) "arising out of repeated experience and regular feelings is a more permanent, and a far more philosophical language, than that which is frequently substituted for it by poets, who think they are conferring honor upon themselves and their art in proportion as they indulge in arbitrary and capricious habits of expression;" it may be answered, that the language, which he has in view, can be attributed to rustics with no greater right, than the style of Hooker or Bacon or Tom Brown or Sir Roger L'Estrange. Doubtless, if what is peculiar to each were omitted in each, the result must needs be the same. Further, that the poet, who uses an illogical diction, or a style fitted to excite only the low and changeable pleasure of wonder by means of groundless novelty, substitutes a language of *folly* and *vanity*, not for that of the *rustic*, but for that of *good sense* and *natural feeling*.

Here let me be permitted to remind the reader, that the positions, which I controvert, are contained in the sentences—*"a selection of the* REAL *language of men;"*—*"the language of these men* (i.e. men in low and rustic life) *I propose to myself to imitate, and as far as possible, to adopt the very language of men." "Between the language of prose and that of metrical composition, there neither is, nor can be any essential difference."* It is against these exclusively, that my opposition is directed.

I object, in the very first instance, to an equivocation in the use of the word "real." Every man's language varies, according to the extent of his knowledge, the activity of his faculties, and the depth or quickness of his feelings. Every man's language has, first, its *individualities*; secondly, the common properties of the *class* to which he belongs; and thirdly, words and phrases of *universal* use. The language of Hooker, Bacon, Bishop Taylor, and Burke, differ from the common language of the learned class only by the superior number and novelty of the thoughts and relations which they had to convey. The language of Algernon Sidney differs not at all from that, which every well educated gentleman would wish to write, and (with due allowances for the undeliberateness, and less connected train, of thinking natural and proper to conversation) such as he would wish to talk. Neither one or the other differ half as much from the general language of cultivated society, as the language of Mr. Wordsworth's homeliest composition differs from that of a common peasant. For "real" therefore, we must substitute *ordinary*, or *lingua communis*. And this, we have proved, is no more to be found in the phraseology of low and rustic life, than in that of any other class. Omit the peculiarities of each, and the result of course must be common to all. . . .

Neither is the case rendered at all more tenable by the addition of the words, *"in a state of excitement."* For the nature of a man's words, when he is strongly affected by joy, grief, or anger, must necessarily depend on the number and quality of the general truths, conceptions and images, and of the words expressing them, with which his mind had been previously stored. For the property of passion is not to *create*; but to set in increased activity. At least, whatever new connections of thoughts or images, or (which is equally, if not more than equally, the appropriate effect of strong excitement) whatever generalizations of truth or experience, the heat of passion may produce; yet the terms of their conveyance must have pre-existed in his former conversations, and are only collected and crowded together by the unusual stimulation. . . .

---

from LECTURES[1]

(1818)

—*from* LECTURE 11—
[On Education][2]

In the education of children, love is first to be instilled, and out of love obedience is to be educed. Then impulse and power should be given to the intellect, and the ends of a moral being be exhibited. For this object thus much is effected by works of imagination;—that they carry the mind out of self, and show the possible of the good and the great in the human character. The height, whatever it

---

[1] Coleridge delivered a series of fourteen lectures "On the Principles of Judgement, Culture, and European Literature" in the Great Room of the London Philosophical Society between January and March 1818.

[2] The eleventh in the series of lectures. The syllabus included the complete list of topics: "On the Arabian Nights, Entertainments, and on the *romantic* Use of the Supernatural in Poetry, and in Works of Fiction not poetical. On the Conditions and Regulations under which such Books may be employed advantageously in the earlier Periods of Education." The text of this lecture is derived from Coleridge's notes as edited by H. N. Coleridge in *The Literary Remains of Samuel Taylor Coleridge*, 4 vols. (1836–1839).

may be, of the imaginative standard will do no harm; we are commanded to imitate one who is inimitable. We should address ourselves to those faculties in a child's mind, which are first awakened by nature, and consequently first admit of cultivation, that is to say, the memory and the imagination. The comparing power, the judgement, is not at that age active, and ought not to be forcibly excited, as is too frequently and mistakenly done in the modern systems of education, which can only lead to selfish views, debtor and creditor principles of virtue, and an inflated sense of merit. In the imagination of man exist the seeds of all moral and scientific improvement; chemistry was first alchemy, and out of astrology sprang astronomy. In the childhood of those sciences the imagination opened a way, and furnished materials, on which the ratiocinative powers in a maturer state operated with success. The imagination is the distinguishing characteristic of man as a progressive being; and I repeat that it ought to be carefully guided and strengthened as the indispensable means and instrument of continued amelioration and refinement. Men of genius and goodness are generally restless in their minds in the present, and this, because they are by a law of their nature unremittingly regarding themselves in the future, and contemplating the possible of moral and intellectual advance towards perfection. Thus we live by hope and faith; thus we are for the most part able to realize what we will, and thus we accomplish the end of our being. The contemplation of futurity inspires humility of soul in our judgement of the present.

I think the memory of children cannot, in reason, be too much stored with the objects and facts of natural history. God opens the images of nature, like the leaves of a book, before the eyes of his creature, Man — and teaches him all that is grand and beautiful in the foaming cataract, the glassy lake, and the floating mist.

The common modern novel, in which there is no imagination, but a miserable struggle to excite and gratify mere curiosity, ought, in my judgment, to be wholly forbidden to children. Novel-reading of this sort is especially injurious to the growth of the imagination, the judgment, and the morals, especially to the latter, because it excites mere feelings without at the same time ministering an impulse to action. Women are good novelists, but indifferent poets; and this because they rarely or never thoroughly distinguish between fact and fiction. In the jumble of the two lies the secret of the modern novel, which is the *medium aliquid* between them, having just so much of fiction as to obscure the fact, and so much of fact as to render the fiction insipid. The perusal of a fashionable lady's novel is to me very much like looking at the scenery and decorations of a theatre by broad daylight. The source of the common fondness for novels of this sort rests in that dislike of vacancy and that love of sloth, which are inherent in the human mind; they afford excitement without producing reaction. By reaction I mean an activity of the intellectual faculties, which shows itself in consequent reasoning and observation, and originates action and conduct according to a principle. Thus, the act of thinking presents two sides for contemplation, — that of external causality, in which the train of thought may be considered as the result of outward impressions, of accidental combinations, of fancy, or the associations of the memory, — and on the other hand, that of internal causality, or of the energy of the will on the mind itself. Thought, therefore, might thus be regarded as passive or active; and the same faculties may in a popular sense be expressed as perception or observation, fancy or imagination, memory or recollection.

— *from* LECTURE 13[1] —
[ON POESY OR ART]

Man communicates by articulation of Sounds, and paramountly by the memory in the Ear — Nature by the impression of Surfaces and Bounds on the Eye, and thro' the Eye gives significance and appropriation, and thus the conditions of Memory (or the capability of being remembered) to Sounds, smells, &c. Now *Art* (I use the word collectively for Music, Painting, Statuary and Architecture) is the Mediatress, the reconciliator of Man and Nature. —

The primary Art is *Writing,* primary if we regard the purpose, abstracted from the different modes of realizing it — the *steps,* of which the instances are still presented to us in the lower degrees of civilization — gesticulation and rosaries or Wampum, in the lowest — picture Language — Hieroglyphics — and finally, Alphabetic / These all alike consist in the *translation,* as it were, of Man into Nature — the use of the visible in place of the Audible. The (so called) Music of Savage Tribes as little deserves the name

[1] The thirteenth in the series of lectures. The syllabus announced its topics would include: "On Colour, Sound, and Form, in Nature, as connected with POESY: the word 'Poesy' used as the *generic* or class term, including Poetry, Music, Painting, Statuary, and ideal Architecture, as its Species. The reciprocal Relations of Poetry and Philosophy to each other; and of both to Religion, and the Moral Sense." The lecture was given its short title, "On Poesy or Art," in *Literary Remains.*

of Art to the Understanding, as the Ear warrants it for Music—. Its lowest step is a mere expression of Passion by the sounds which the Passion itself necessitates—its highest, a voluntary re-production of those Sounds, in the absence of the occasioning Causes, so as to give the pleasure of *Contrast*—ex. gr. the various outcries of Battle in the song of Triumph, & Security.

Poetry likewise is purely *human*—all its materials are *from* the mind, and all the products are *for* the mind. It is the Apotheosis of the former state—viz. Order and Passion—*N.b.* how by excitement of the Associative Power Passion itself imitates Order, and the *order* resulting produces a pleasurable *Passion* (whence Metre) and thus elevates the Mind by making its feelings the Objects of its reflection / and how recalling the Sights and Sounds that had accompanied the occasions of the original passion it impregnates them with an interest not their own by means of the Passions, and yet tempers the passion by the calming power which all *distinct* images exert on the human soul. (This *illustrated.*)

In this way Poetry is the Preparation for Art: inasmuch as it avails itself of the forms of Nature to recall, to express, and to modify the thoughts and feelings of the mind—still however thro' the medium of *articulate Speech,* which is so peculiarly human that in all languages it is the ordinary phrase by which Man and Nature are contradistinguished—it is the original force of the word *brute*—and even now mute, and dumb do not convey the absence of sound, but the absence of articulate Sounds.

As soon as the human mind is intelligibly addressed by any outward medium, exclusive of articulate Speech, so soon does *Art* commence. But please to observe, that I have layed stress on the words, *human mind*—excluding thereby all results common to Man and all sentient creatures—and consequently, confining it to the effect produced by the congruity of the animal impression with the reflective Powers of the mind—so that not the Thing presented, but that which is *re*-presented, by the Thing, is the source of the Pleasure.—In this sense Nature itself is to a religious Observer the Art of God—and for the same cause Art itself might be defined, as of a middle nature between a Thought and a Thing, or, as before, the union and reconciliation of that which is Nature with that which is exclusively Human.—Exemplify this by a good Portrait, which becomes more and more like in proportion to its excellence as a Work of Art—While a real *Copy,* a Fac Simile, ends in shocking us.—

Taking therefore *mute* as opposed not to sound but to articulate Speech, the oldest definition of Painting is in fact the true and the best definition of the Fine Arts in general—*muta Poesis*—*mute* Poesy—and of course, *Poesy*—/—(and as all Languages perfect themselves by a gradual process of desynonymizing words originally equivalent, as Propriety, Property—I, Me—Mister, Master—&c / I have cherished the wish, to use the word, Poesy, as the generic or common term, distinguishing that species of Poesy, which is not *muta* Poesis, by its usual name, *Poetry* /) while of all the other species, which collectively form the *Fine Arts,* there would remain this as the common definition—that they all, like Poetry, are to express intellectual purposes, Thoughts, Conceptions, Sentiments that have their origin in the human Mind, but not, as Poetry, by means of articulate Speech, but as Nature, or the divine Art, does, by form, color magnitude, Sound, and proportion, silently or musically.—

Well—it may be said—but who has ever thought otherwise. We all know, that Art is the imitatress of Nature.—And doubtless, the Truths, I hope to convey, would be barren Truisms, if all men meant the same by the words, *imitate* and *nature.* But it would be flattering mankind at large, to presume that this is the Fact. First, imitate—The impression on the wax is not an imitation but a *Copy* of the Seal—the Seal itself is an Imitation / But farther—in order to form a philosophic conception, we must seek for the *kind*—as the *heat* in Ice—invisible Light—&c—but for practical purposes, we must have reference to the degree.

It is sufficient that philosophically we understand that in all Imitation two elements must exist, and not only exist but must be perceived as existing—Likeness and unlikeness, or Sameness and Difference. All Imitation in the Fine Arts is the union of Disparate Things.—Wax Image—Statues—Bronze—Pictures—the Artist may take his point where he likes—provided that the effect desired is produced—namely, that there should be a Likeness in Difference & a union of the two—*Tragic Dance.*

So Nature—i.e. natura naturata[2]—& hence the natural Question / What *all* and every thing?—No, but the Beautiful.—And what is the Beautiful?—The definition is at once undermined.— / If the Artist painfully *copies* nature, what an idle rivalry! If he proceeds from a Form, that answers to the notion of Beauty, namely, the many seen as

[2] **natura naturata:** nature as phenomena. A concept borrowed from the German philosopher Friedrich Wilhelm Joseph von Schelling (1775–1854).

one[3]—what an emptiness, an unreality—as in Cypriani[4]—The *essence* must be mastered—the natura naturans,[5] & this presupposes *a bond* between *Nature* in this higher sense and the soul of Man—.— . . . .

The wisdom in Nature distinguished from Man by the coinstantaneity[6] of the Plan & the Execution, the Thought and the Production—In nature there is no reflex act—but the same powers without reflection, and consequently without Morality. (Hence *Man* the *Head* of the visible Creation—*Genesis*.) Every step antecedent to full consciousness found in Nature—so to place them as for some one effect, totalized & fitted to the limits of a human Mind, as to elicit and as it were superinduce *into* the forms the reflection, to which they approximate—this is the Mystery of Genius in the Fine Arts—Dare I say that the Genius must act on the feeling, that *Body* is but a striving to become Mind—that it is *mind*, in its essence—?

As in every work of Art the Conscious is so impressed on the Unconscious, as to appear *in* it (ex. gr. Letters on a Tomb compared with Figures constituting a Tomb)—so is the Man of Genius the Link that combines the two—but for that reason, he must partake of both—Hence, there is in Genius itself an unconscious activity—nay, that is *the* Genius in the man of Genius.—

This is the true Exposition of the Rule, that the Artist must first *eloign*[7] himself from Nature in order to return to her with full effect.—Why this?—Because—if he began by mere painful copying, he would produce Masks only, not forms breathing Life—he must out of his own mind create forms according to the several Laws of the Intellect, in order to produce in himself that co-ordination of Freedom & Law, that involution of the Obedience in the Prescript, and of the Prescript in the impulse to obey, which assimilates him to Nature—enables him to understand her—. He absents himself from her only in his own Spirit, which has the same ground with Nature, to learn her unspoken language, in its main radicals, before he approaches to her endless compositions of those radicals—Not to acquire cold notions, lifeless technical Rules, but living and life-producing Ideas, which contain their own evidence / and in that evidence the certainty that they are essentially one with the germinal causes in Nature, his Consciousness being the focus and mirror of both—for this does he for a time abandon the external *real*, in order to return to it with a full sympathy with its internal & actual—. Of all, we see, hear, or touch, the substance is and must be in ourselves—and therefore there is no alternative *in reason* between the dreary (& thank heaven! almost impossible) belief that every thing around us is but a phantom, or that the Life which is in us is in them likewise—and that to know is to *resemble*. When we speak of Objects out of ourselves, even as within ourselves to learn is, according to Plato, only to *recollect*.[8]—The only effective Answer to which (that I have been fortunate enough to meet with) is that which Mr Pope has consecrated for future use in the Line—

And Coxcombs vanquish Berkley with a Grin.[9]

To that within the thing, active thro' Form and Figure as by symbols [?discoursing / discovering / discerning] *Natur-geist*[10] must the Artist imitate, as we unconsciously imitate those we love—So only can he produce any work truly *natural*, in the Object, and truly *human* in the Effect.—The Idea that puts the forms together, can not be itself form—It is above Form, is its Essence, the Universal in the Individual, Individuality itself—the Glance and the Exponent of the indwelling Power—

Each thing, that lives, has its moment of *self-exposition*, and each period of *each* thing—if we remove the disturbing forces of accident—and this is the business of ideal Art.—Childhood—Youth—Age—Man—Woman /—And each thing, that appears not to live, has its possible position & relation to Life / & so it is in Nature—where she cannot *be*, she *prophecies* in the tree-like forms of ores &c /

Difference of Form as proceeding and Shape as superinduced[11]—the latter either the Death or the imprisonment of the Thing; the former, its self-witnessing, and self-effected sphere of agency—

Art would or should be the Abridgment of Nature. Now the Fullness of Nature is without character as Water

[3] **Beauty . . . one:** Coleridge earlier defines Beauty as "Multëity in Unity" in "On the Principles of Genial Criticism."

[4] **Cypriani:** Giovanni Battista Cipriani (1727–1785), Italian painter whose work was then much in vogue in London.

[5] **natura naturans:** nature as active or creative. Also from Schelling.

[6] **coinstantaneity:** simultaneous occurrence.

[7] **eloign:** remove.

[8] Reference from Plato's *Phaedo*.

[9] Cf. *An Essay on Satire* (1754) by John Brown (1715–1766), not Alexander Pope. "Berkley" is George Berkeley (1685–1753), philosopher noted for his theory of philosophical idealism.

[10] **Natur-geist:** nature spirit.

[11] **superinduced:** brought on in addition.

is purest when without taste, smell or color—but this is the Highest, the Apex, not the whole—& Art is to give *the whole* ad hominem / hence each step of Nature has its Ideal, & hence too the possibility of a climax up to the perfect Form, of harmonized Chaos—

To the idea of Life Victory or Strife is necessary—As Virtue not in the absence of vicious Impulses but in the overcoming of them / so Beauty not in the absence of the Passions, but on the contrary—it is heightened by the sight of what is conquered—this in the [? figure / fugue], or out by contrast . . .

—*from* LECTURE 14[1]—
[ON STYLE AND POLITICS]

. . . After the Revolution, the spirit of the nation became much more commercial, than it had been before; a learned body, or clerisy,[2] as such, gradually disappeared, and literature in general began to be addressed to the common miscellaneous public. That public had become accustomed to, and required, a strong stimulus; and to meet the requisitions of the public taste, a style was produced which by combining triteness of thought with singularity and excess of manner of expression, was calculated at once to soothe ignorance and to flatter vanity. The thought was carefully kept down to the immediate apprehension of the commonest understanding, and the dress was as anxiously arranged for the purpose of making the thought appear something very profound. The essence of this style consisted in a mock antithesis, that is, an opposition of mere sounds, in a rage for personification, the abstract made animate, far-fetched metaphors, strange phrases, metrical scraps, in every thing, in short, but genuine prose. Style is, of course, nothing else but the art of conveying the meaning appropriately and with perspicuity, whatever that meaning may be, and one criterion of style is that it shall not be translateable without injury to the meaning. Johnson's[3] style has pleased many from the very fault of being perpetually translateable; he creates an impression of cleverness by never saying any thing in a common way. The best specimen of this manner is in Junius,[4] because his antithesis is less merely verbal than Johnson's. Gibbon's[5] manner is the worst of all; it has every fault of which this peculiar style is capable. Tacitus is an example of it in Latin; in coming from Cicero you feel the *falsetto* immediately.

In order to form a good style, the primary rule and condition is, not to attempt to express ourselves in language before we thoroughly know our own meaning;—when a man perfectly understands himself, appropriate diction will generally be at his command either in writing or speaking. In such cases the thoughts and the words are associated. In the next place preciseness in the use of terms is required, and the test is whether you can translate the phrase adequately into simpler terms, regard being had to the feeling of the whole passage. Try this upon Shakspeare, or Milton, and see if you can substitute other simpler words in any given passage without a violation of the meaning or tone. The source of bad writing is the desire to be something more than a man of sense,—the straining to be thought a genius; and it is just the same in speech making. If men would only say what they have to say in plain terms, how much more eloquent they would be! Another rule is to avoid converting mere abstractions into persons. I believe you will very rarely find in any great writer before the Revolution the possessive case of an inanimate noun used in prose instead of the dependent case, as "the watch's hand," for "the hand of the watch." The possessive or Saxon genitive was confined to persons, or at least to animated subjects. And I cannot conclude this Lecture without insisting on the importance of accuracy of style as being near akin to veracity and truthful habits of mind; he who thinks loosely will write loosely, and, perhaps, there is some moral inconvenience in the common forms of our grammars which give children so many obscure terms for material distinctions. Let me also exhort you to careful examination of what you read, if it be worth any perusal at all; such examination will be a safeguard from fanaticism, the universal origin of which is in the contemplation of phenomena without investigation into their causes. . . .

[1] Delivered 13 March 1818. The syllabus listed the topics of the lecture as: "On the Corruptions of the English Language since the reign of Queen Anne, in our Style of writing Prose. A few easy Rules for the Attainment of a manly, unaffected, and pure Language, in our genuine Mother-Tongue, whether for the purposes of Writing, Oratory, or Conversation. . . ."

[2] **clerisy:** Coleridge's neologism. See *The Statesman's Manual** for a fuller discussion.

[3] **Johnson:** Samuel Johnson (1709–1784), generally considered to be one of the great prose stylists of eighteenth-century letters.

[4] **Junius:** pseudonym for the author of witty letters of political criticism published in the *Public Examiner* from 1769 to 1772.

[5] **Gibbon:** Edward Gibbon (1737–1794), author of *The History of the Decline and Fall of the Roman Empire,* 6 vols. (1776–1788).

from POETICAL WORKS
(1828)

The Eolian Harp[1]
(comp. 1795)

Composed at Clevedon, Somersetshire

My pensive Sara! thy soft cheek reclined
Thus on mine arm, most soothing sweet it is
To sit beside our cot, our cot o'ergrown
With white-flowered jasmin, and the broad-leaved
  myrtle,
(Meet emblems they of Innocence and Love!)
And watch the clouds, that late were rich with light,
Slow saddening round, and mark the star of eve
Serenely brilliant (such should wisdom be)
Shine opposite! How exquisite the scents
Snatched from yon bean-field! and the world so
  hushed!
The stilly murmur of the distant sea
Tells us of silence.

  And that simplest lute,
Placed length-ways in the clasping casement, hark!
How by the desultory breeze caressed,
Like some coy maid half yielding to her lover,
It pours such sweet upbraiding, as must needs
Tempt to repeat the wrong! And now, its strings
Boldlier swept, the long sequacious notes
Over delicious surges sink and rise,
Such a soft floating witchery of sound
As twilight Elfins make, when they at eve
Voyage on gentle gales from Fairy-Land,
Where Melodies round honey-dropping flowers,
Footless and wild, like birds of Paradise,
Nor pause, nor perch, hovering on untamed wing!
O the one life within us and abroad,
Which meets all motion and becomes its soul,
A light in sound, a sound-like power in light
Rhythm in all thought, and joyance every where—
Methinks, it should have been impossible
Not to love all things in a world so filled;
Where the breeze warbles, and the mute still air
Is Music slumbering on her instrument.

  And thus, my love! as on the midway slope
Of yonder hill I stretch my limbs at noon,
Whilst through my half-closed eye-lids I behold
The sunbeams dance, like diamonds, on the main,
And tranquil muse upon tranquillity;
Full many a thought uncalled and undetained,
And many idle flitting phantasies,
Traverse my indolent and passive brain,
As wild and various as the random gales
That swell and flutter on this subject lute!

  And what if all of animated nature
Be but organic harps diversely framed,
That tremble into thought, as o'er them sweeps
Plastic and vast, one intellectual breeze,
At once the Soul of each, and God of All?

  But thy more serious eye a mild reproof
Darts, O beloved woman! nor such thoughts
Dim and unhallowed dost thou not reject,
And biddest me walk humbly with my God.
Meek daughter in the family of Christ!
Well hast thou said and holily dispraised
These shapings of the unregenerate mind;
Bubbles that glitter as they rise and break
On vain Philosophy's aye-babbling spring.
For never guiltless may I speak of him,
The Incomprehensible! save when with awe
I praise him, and with Faith that inly feels;
Who with his saving mercies healed me,
A sinful and most miserable man,
Wildered, and dark, and gave me to possess
Peace, and this cot, and thee, heart-honour'd Maid!

[1] See "Effusion XXXV" in *Poems* (1796)* for the first published form of this work and background. The title was changed to "Eolian Harp" in *Sibylline Leaves* (1817), but lines 26 to 33 were first included in 1828.

Work without Hope
(1828; comp. 1825)

Lines composed 21st February 1825

All Nature seems at work. Slugs[1] leave their lair—
The bees are stirring—birds are on the wing—
And Winter slumbering in the open air,

[1] **Slugs:** snails.

Wears on his smiling face a dream of Spring!
And I the while, the sole unbusy thing,
Nor honey make, nor pair, nor build, nor sing.

Yet well I ken the banks where amaranths blow,
Have traced the fount whence streams of nectar flow.
Bloom, O ye amaranths! bloom for whom ye may,
For me ye bloom not! Glide, rich streams, away!
With lips unbrightened, wreathless brow, I stroll:
And would you learn the spells that drowse my soul?
Work without Hope draws nectar in a sieve,
And Hope without an object cannot live.

Constancy to an Ideal Object

(1828; comp. 1804–1807?, 1823?, 1826?)

Since all that beat about in Nature's range,
Or veer or vanish; why should'st thou remain
The only constant in a world of change,
O yearning Thought! that liv'st but in the brain?
Call to the Hours, that in the distance play,
The faery people of the future day—
Fond Thought! not one of all that shining swarm
Will breathe on thee with life-enkindling breath,
Till when, like strangers shelt'ring from a storm,
Hope and Despair meet in the porch of Death!
Yet still thou haunt'st me; and though well I see,
She is not thou, and only thou art she,
Still, still as though some dear embodied Good,
Some living Love before my eyes there stood
With answering look a ready ear to lend,
I mourn to thee and say—'Ah! loveliest friend!
That this the meed[1] of all my toils might be,
To have a home, an English home, and thee!'
Vain repetition! Home and Thou are one.
The peacefull'st cot, the moon shall shine upon,
Lulled by the thrush and wakened by the lark,
Without thee were but a becalméd bark,
Whose Helmsman on an ocean waste and wide
Sits mute and pale his mouldering helm beside.

And art thou nothing? Such thou art, as when
The woodman winding westward up the glen
At wintry dawn, where o'er the sheep-track's maze
The viewless snow-mist weaves a glist'ning haze,
Sees full before him, gliding without tread,
An image with a glory round its head;
The enamoured rustic worships its fair hues,
Nor knows he makes the shadow, he pursues!

[1] **meed:** an earned gift or reward.

from ON THE CONSTITUTION OF CHURCH & STATE, ACCORDING TO THE IDEA OF EACH

(1829; 2nd edition 1830)[1]

—*from* CHAPTER I—

[THE BRITISH CONSTITUTION AS IDEA]

. . . Just so is it with the constitution.[2] Ask any of our politicians what is meant by the constitution, and it is ten to one that he will give you a false explanation, *ex. gr.* that it is the body of our laws, or that it is the Bill of Rights; or perhaps, if he have read Tom Payne,[3] he may tell you, that we have not yet got one; and yet not an hour may have elapsed, since you heard the same individual denouncing, and possibly with good reason, this or that code of laws, the excise and revenue laws, or those for including pheasants,[4] or those for excluding Catholics, as altogether unconstitutional: and such and such acts of parliament as gross outrages on the constitution. Mr. Peel,[5] who is rather remarkable for groundless and unlucky concessions, owned that the present Bill breaks in on the constitution of 1688: and, A.D. 1689, a very imposing minority of the then House of Lords, with

[1] First published in December 1829. The text here is from the revised edition of 1830.

[2] I do not say, with the idea: for the constitution itself is an IDEA. This will sound like a paradox or a sneer to those with whom an Idea is but another word for *a fancy*, a something unreal; but not to those who in the ideas contemplate the most real of all realities, and of all operative powers the most *actual*. [S.T.C.]

[3] **Tom Payne:** Thomas Paine, author of *The Rights of Man* (1791).*

[4] Allusion to Game Laws prohibiting hunting on private or crown land unless entitled or licensed. They were progressively extended (1817, 1828) and rigorously enforced during periods of food shortage.

[5] **Mr. Peel:** Sir Robert Peel (1788–1850), leader of the House of Commons.

a decisive majority in the Lower House of Convocation, denounced the constitution of 1688, as breaking in on the English Constitution.

But a Constitution is an idea arising out of the idea of a state; and because our whole history from Alfred[6] onward demonstrates the continued influence of such an idea, or ultimate aim, on the minds of our fore-fathers, in their characters and functions as public men; alike in what they resisted and in what they claimed; in the institutions and forms of polity which they established, and with regard to those, against which they more or less successfully contended; and because the result has been a progressive, though not always a direct, or equable advance in the gradual realization of the idea; and that it is actually, though even because it is an *idea* it cannot be *adequately*, represented in a correspondent scheme of means really existing; we speak, and have a right to speak, of the idea itself, as actually existing, *i.e.*, as a *principle*, existing in the only way in which a principle can exist — in the minds and consciences of the persons, whose duties it prescribes, and whose rights it determines. In the same sense that the sciences of arithmetic and of geometry, that mind, that life itself, have reality; the constitution has real existence, and does not the less exist in reality, because it both *is*, and *exists as*, an IDEA.

— *from* CHAPTER V —
[THE CLERISY]

After these introductory preparations, I can have no difficulty in setting forth the right idea of a national church as in the language of Elizabeth the *third* great venerable estate of the realm. The first being the estate of the landowners or possessors of fixed property, consisting of the two classes of the Barons and the Franklins; the second comprising the merchants, the manufacturers, free artizans, and the distributive class. To comprehend, therefore, this third estate, in whom the reserved nationalty was vested, we must first ascertain the end, or national purpose, for which it was reserved.

Now, as in the former state, the permanency of the nation was provided for; and in the second estate its progressiveness, and personal freedom; while in the king the cohesion by interdependence, and the unity of the country, were established; there remains for the third estate only that interest, which is the ground, the necessary antecedent condition, of both the former. Now these depend on a continuing and progressive civilization. But civilization is itself but a mixed good, if not far more a corrupting influence, the hectic of disease, not the bloom of health, and a nation so distinguished more fitly to be called a varnished than a polished people; where this civilization is not grounded in *cultivation*, in the harmonious developement of those qualities and faculties that characterise our *humanity*. We must be men in order to be citizens.

The Nationalty, therefore, was reserved for the support and maintenance of a permanent class or order, with the following duties. A certain smaller number were to remain at the fountain heads of the humanities, in cultivating and enlarging the knowledge already possessed, and in watching over the interests of physical and moral science; being, likewise, the instructors of such as constituted, or were to constitute, the remaining more numerous classes of the order. This latter and far more numerous body were to be distributed throughout the country, so as not to leave even the smallest integral part or division without a resident guide, guardian, and instructor; the objects and final intention of the whole order being these — to preserve the stores, to guard the treasures, of past civilization, and thus to bind the present with the past; to perfect and add to the same, and thus to connect the present with the future; but especially to diffuse through the whole community, and to every native entitled to its laws and rights, that quantity and quality of knowledge which was indispensable both for the understanding of those rights, and for the performance of the duties correspondent. Finally, to secure for the nation, if not a superiority over the neighbouring states, yet an equality at least, in that character of general civilization, which equally with, or rather more than, fleets, armies, and revenue, forms the ground of its defensive and offensive power. The object of the two former estates of the realm, which conjointly form the STATE, was to reconcile the interests of permanence with that of progression — law with liberty. The object of the National Church, the third remaining estate of the realm, was to secure and improve that civilization, without which the nation could be neither permanent nor progressive.

That in all ages, individuals who have directed their meditations and their studies to the nobler characters of our nature, to the cultivation of those powers and instincts which constitute the man, at least separate him

---

[6] **Alfred:** Alfred (the Great) (848–890), king of the West Saxons.

from the animal, and distinguish the nobler from the animal part of his own being, will be led by the *supernatural* in themselves to the contemplation of a power which is likewise super-*human*; that science, and especially moral science, will lead to religion, and remain blended with it—this, I say, will, in all ages, be the course of things. That in the earlier ages, and in the dawn of civility, there will be a twilight in which science and religion give light, but a light refracted through the dense and the dark, a superstition—this is what we learn from history, and what philosophy would have taught us to expect. But we affirm, that in the spiritual purpose of the word, and as understood in reference to a future state, and to the abiding essential interest of the individual as a person, and not as the citizen, neighbour, or subject, religion may be an indispensable ally, but is not the essential constitutive end of that national institute, which is unfortunately, at least improperly, styled a church—a name which, in its best sense is exclusively appropriate to the church of Christ. If this latter be ecclesia, the communion of such as are called out of the world, *i.e.* in reference to the especial ends and purposes of that communion; this other might more expressively have been entitled *enclesia,* or an order of men, chosen in and of the realm, and constituting an estate of that realm. And in fact, such was the original and proper sense of the more appropriately named CLERGY. It comprehended the learned of all names, and the CLERK was the synonyme of the man of learning. Nor can any fact more strikingly illustrate the conviction entertained by our ancestors, respecting the intimate connexion of this clergy with the peace and weal of the nation, than the privilege formerly recognized by our laws, in the well-known phrase, "benefit of clergy."

Deeply do I feel, for clearly do I see, the importance of my Theme. And had I equal confidence in my ability to awaken the same interest in the minds of others, I should dismiss as affronting to my readers all apprehension of being charged with prolixity, while I am labouring to compress in two or three brief Chapters, the principal sides and aspects of a subject so large and multilateral as to require a volume for its full exposition. With what success will be seen in what follows, commencing with the Churchmen, or (a far apter and less objectionable designation,) the National CLERISY.

THE CLERISY of the nation, or national church, in its primary acceptation and original intention comprehended the learned of all denominations;—the sages and professors of the law and jurisprudence; of medicine and physiology; of music; of military and civil architecture; of the physical sciences; with the mathematical as the common *organ* of the preceding; in short, all the so called liberal arts and sciences, the possession and application of which constitute the civilization of a country, as well as the Theological. The last was, indeed, placed at the head of all; and of good right did it claim the precedence. But why? Because under the name of Theology, or Divinity, were contained the interpretation of languages; the conservation and tradition of past events; the momentous epochs, and revolutions of the race and nation; the continuation of the records; logic, ethics, and the determination of ethical science, in application to the rights and duties of men in all their various relations, social and civil; and lastly, the ground-knowledge, the prima scientia[1] as it was named,—PHILOSOPHY, or the doctrine and discipline of *ideas.*

Theology formed only a part of the objects, the Theologians formed only a portion of the clerks or clergy of the national church. The theological order had precedency indeed, and deservedly; but not because its members were priests, whose office was to conciliate the invisible powers, and to superintend the interests that survive the grave; not as being exclusively, or even principally, sacerdotal or templar, which, when it did occur, is to be considered as an accident of the age, a mis-growth of ignorance and oppression, a falsification of the constitutive principle, not a constituent part of the same. No! The Theologians took the lead, because the SCIENCE of Theology was the root and the trunk of the knowledges that civilized man, because it gave unity and the circulating sap of life to all other sciences, by virtue of which alone they could be contemplated as forming, collectively, the living tree of knowledge. It had the precedency, because, under the name theology, were comprised all the main aids, instruments, and materials of NATIONAL EDUCATION, the *nisus formativus*[2] of the body politic, the shaping and informing spirit, which *educing,* i.e. eliciting, the latent *man* in all the natives of the soil, *trains them up* to citizens of the country, free subjects of the realm. And lastly, because to divinity belong those fundamental truths, which are the common ground-work of our civil and our religious duties, not less indispensable to a right view of our temporal concerns, than to a rational faith

[1] **prima scientia:** first knowledge.

[2] **nisus formativus:** formative impulse.

respecting our immortal well-being. (Not without celestial observations, can even terrestrial charts be accurately constructed.) And of especial importance is it to the objects here contemplated, that only by the vital warmth diffused by these truths throughout the MANY, and by the guiding light from the philosophy, which is the basis of *divinity*, possessed by the FEW, can either the community or its rulers fully comprehend, or rightly appreciate, the permanent *distinction*, and the occasional *contrast*, between cultivation and civilization; or be made to understand this most valuable of the lessons taught by history, and exemplified alike in her oldest and her most recent records—that a nation can never be a too cultivated, but may easily become an over-civilized race.

Reason[1]

(1830)

['Finally, what is Reason? You have often asked me: and this is my answer':—]

....

Whene'er the mist, that stands 'twixt God and thee,
Defecates[2] to a pure transparency,
That intercepts no light and adds no stain—
There Reason is, and then begins her reign!

But alas!

—'tu stesso, ti fai grosso
Col falso immaginar, si che non vedi
Cio che vedresti, se l'avessi scosso.'[3]

Dante, *Paradiso*, Canto i.

[1] First published as conclusion of *Church & State*.

[2] Defecates: clarifies.

[3] Cf. *Paradiso*, ll. 88–90. "With false imagination thou thyself / Makest Dull; so that thou seest not the thing / Which thou hadst seen, had that been shaken off" (Trans. Henry Francis Cary, 1814).

from POETICAL WORKS

(1834)

Phantom or Fact

(1834; comp. 1830?)

—A DIALOGUE IN VERSE—

AUTHOR

A LOVELY form there sate beside my bed,
And such a feeding calm its presence shed,
A tender love so pure from earthly leaven,
That I unnethe[1] the fancy might control,
'Twas my own spirit newly come from heaven,
Wooing its gentle way into my soul!
But ah! the change—It had not stirr'd, and yet—
Alas! that change how fain would I forget!
That shrinking back, like one that had mistook!
That weary, wandering, disavowing look!
'Twas all another, feature, look, and frame,
And still, methought, I knew, it was the same!

FRIEND

This riddling tale, to what does it belong?
Is't history? vision? or an idle song?
Or rather say at once, within what space
Of time this wild disastrous change took place?

AUTHOR

Call it a moment's work (and such it seems)
This tale 's a fragment from the life of dreams;
But say, that years matur'd the silent strife,
And 'tis a record from the dream of life.

[1] unnethe: uncompelled.

Self-Knowledge

(1834; comp. 1832)

—E coelo descendit γνῶθι σεαυτόν.—JUVENAL, xi.27.[1]

....

Γνῶθι σεαυτόν![2]—and is this the prime
And heaven-sprung adage of the olden time!—
Say, canst thou make thyself?—Learn first that trade;—
Haply thou mayst know what thyself had made.
What hast thou, Man, that thou dar'st call thine own?—
What is there in thee, Man, that can be known?—
Dark fluxion, all unfixable by thought,
A phantom dim of past and future wrought,
Vain sister of the worm,—life, death, soul, clod—
Ignore thyself, and strive to know thy God!

Ne Plus Ultra[1]

(1834)

Sole Positive of Night!
Antipathist of Light!
Fate's only essence! primal scorpion rod—
The one permitted opposite of God!—
Condensèd blackness and abysmal storm
Compacted to one sceptre
Arms the Grasp enorm—
The Intercepter—
The Substance that still casts the shadow Death!—
The Dragon foul and fell—
The unrevealable,
And hidden one, whose breath
Gives wind and fuel to the fires of Hell!
Ah! sole despair
Of both th' eternities in Heaven!
Sole interdict of all-bedewing prayer,
The all-compassionate!
Save to the Lampads Seven[2]
Reveal'd to none of all th' Angelic State,
Save to the Lampads Seven,
That watch the throne of Heaven!

Epitaph

(1834; comp. 1833)

Stop, Christian passer-by!—Stop, child of God,
And read with gentle breast. Beneath this sod
A poet lies, or that which once seem'd he.
O, lift one thought in prayer for S. T. C.;
That he who many a year with toil of breath
Found death in life, may here find life in death![1]
Mercy for praise—to be forgiven for fame
He ask'd, and hoped, through Christ. Do thou the same!

---

[1] "From heaven descended Know Thyself." See Coleridge's letter to William Godwin [25 March 1801].*

[2] Know thyself!

[1] Ne Plus Ultra: no more beyond.

[2] Cf. Revelation 4:5. "From the throne came flashes of lightning and peals of thunder. Burning before the throne were seven flaming torches, the seven spirits of God, and in front of it stretched what looked like a sea of glass or a sheet of ice."

[1] See *Ancient Mariner* (1817), l. 93.

JANE AUSTEN

(1775–1817)

The finest female novelist of this historical period, perhaps the finest novelist of the time, Jane Austen was not well known in her day. Her reputation is the product of a Victorian and early twentieth-century recognition of the subtleties of her ironic wit and rhetorical craft, together with an endorsement of what were thought to be her conservative sympathies with the gentry class. Only since the 1980s have the feminist dimensions of her thought and writing been identified and critically evaluated. Jane Austen read and shared Mary Wollstonecraft's conviction that women were potentially as rational as men; that women should be educated to exercise sound judgment based on accurate observation of the social and natural world around them; that the ideal marriage is based not on sexual passion but rather on rational love: mutual esteem, compatibility, and enduring friendship; and that domestic affection and responsibility provide the paradigm for just and benevolent national and international relations. Neither a political conservative nor a radical feminist, Austen in her fiction and letters takes up the position of the *moderate* feminist, solidly progressive in her measured examinations both of the failures of patriarchy and of the landed gentry class and of the potential for moral and intellectual equality between the sexes.

Educated primarily at home at the Steventon Rectory in Hampshire by her Anglican clergyman father, the Rev. George Austen, Jane Austen read widely the fiction and history of her day. She began writing for her family's amusement at an early age—her comic defense of the Stuarts, "The History of England," in 1791; her humorous self-portrait as Charlotte in "The Female Philosopher" in 1793, *Lady Susan* in 1793 to 1794, among many other pieces. First drafts of *Pride and Prejudice, Northanger Abbey,* and *Sense and Sensibility* were finished by 1798. When she couldn't find a publisher for her novels, she set them aside for several years. She moved to Bath in 1801 when her father retired; after his death in 1805, she took up permanent residence with her mother and sister Cassandra in a comfortable but small cottage in the country town of Chawton, in Hampshire. She received only two proposals of marriage, the first on 2 December 1802, from Harris Bigg-Wither, which she at first accepted but after a sleepless night, rejected; the second, six years later, from Edward Bridges, the model for Captain Benwick in *Persuasion,* which she also rejected. Recent critics have speculated that Austen preferred the career of writer to that of wife, mother, and gentry hostess.

Living under severe financial constraints on an allowance from her brother Edward and her mother's and sister's small annuities, Austen was acutely aware of the plight of the impoverished gentlewoman, a familiar figure in her fiction. To help with the family expenses, she revised her earlier novels and wrote three more, working without a room of her own in the family sitting room at Chawton. After publishing *Sense and Sensibility* at her own expense in 1811, she found publishers for three more novels, receiving modest sums for them: £110 for *Pride and Prejudice* (1813), £100 for *Mansfield Park* (1814), £150 for *Emma* (1816), and £140 for a second edition of *Sense and Sensibility* in 1813. *Northanger Abbey* and *Persuasion* were published posthumously and *Sanditon* remained unfinished at her death. Her "Plan of a Novel" (written from 1815 to 1816) burlesques the tendencies of her female contemporaries to write implausible stories with black-or-white characters, and to use fiction as an occasion for lengthy lectures on economic, political, religious, or pedagogical issues. As in *Lady Susan*, Jane Austen preferred to make her moral and social criticisms ironically, by letting her characters, realistically rendered, speak for themselves.

Jane Austen's letters illustrate her acute recognition of the perilous condition of middle-class women in her day. They were given only an inferior education in the "accomplishments," forced to marry incompatible husbands, overburdened by frequent pregnancies, and were entirely dependent on fathers, husbands, or brothers for their economic support, without alternative means of "respectable" employment (in *Emma*, Jane Fairfax compares the governess trade to the slave trade). While she ardently supported Britain's claims in the wars against France and Spain (her favorite brothers served in the British navy), she was critical of the social disruption brought on by Britain's imperialist projects. Her novels and letters subtly condemn slavery and the slave trade (in both the title and the plot of *Mansfield Park* she alludes to the 1772 Judgement of Lord Mansfield that legally abolished slavery, but not the slave trade, in England), absentee landlordism in both Ireland and the West Indies, the need for a standing army, and the needless sacrifice of young men in foreign wars. She was acutely aware of the errors of patriarchy. Both her fiction and her letters portray in detail the amorality, irresponsibility, and selfish greed of men from the aristocracy, landed gentry, and professional classes. Influenced by the ideals of the American and French Revolutions, she envisioned for both men and women a more egalitarian and gender-free society in which the best attributes of the industrious middle classes would prevail: good breeding combined with sound management of the family estate.

from Letter to Cassandra Austen

[27 October 1798]

Steventon: Saturday October 27

My dear Cassandra

Your letter was a most agreeable surprise to me to-day, and I have taken a long sheet of paper to show my gratitude. . . .

Whilst my mother and Mr. Lyford[1] were together I went to Mrs. Ryder's and bought what I intended to buy, but not in much perfection. There were no narrow braces for children and scarcely any notting silk;[2] but Miss Wood, as usual, is going to town very soon, and will lay in a fresh stock. I gave 2*s.* 3*d.* a yard for my flannel, and I fancy it is not very good, but it is so disgraceful and contemptible an article in itself that its being comparatively good or bad is of little importance. I bought some Japan ink likewise, and next week shall begin my operations on my hat, on which you know my principal hopes of happiness depend. . . .

Mrs. Hall, of Sherborne, was brought to bed yesterday of a dead child, some weeks before she expected,

[1] **Mr. Lyford:** the doctor who attended Jane Austen's mother.

[2] **narrow braces:** suspenders. **notting silk:** silk thread used to make knotting—fancywork produced by twisting and looping thread into knots to form designs.

owing to a fright. I suppose she happened unawares to look at her husband. . . .

. . . My dear itty Dordy's[3] remembrance of me is very pleasing to me—foolishly pleasing, because I know it will be over so soon. My attachment to him will be more durable. I shall think with tenderness and delight on his beautiful and smiling countenance and interesting manners till a few years have turned him into an ungovernable, ungracious fellow. . . .

Yours ever,
J. A.

To the Memory of Mrs. Lefroy[1]
(16 December 1808)

1

The day returns again, my natal day;
 What mix'd emotions in my mind arise!
Beloved Friend; four years have passed away
 Since thou wert snatched for ever from our eyes.

2

The day commemorative of my birth,
 Bestowing life, and light, and hope to me,
Brings back the hour which was thy last on earth.
 O! bitter pang of torturing memory!

3

Angelic woman! past my power to praise
 In language meet thy talents, temper, mind,
Thy solid worth, thy captivating grace,
 Thou friend and ornament of human kind.

4

But come, fond Fancy, thou indulgent power;
 Hope is desponding, chill, severe, to thee:
Bless thou this little portion of an hour;
 Let me behold her as she used to be.

5

I see her here with all her smiles benign,
 Her looks of eager love, her accents sweet,
That voice and countenance almost divine,
 Expression, harmony, alike complete.

6

Listen! It is not sound alone, 'tis sense,
 'Tis genius, taste, and tenderness of soul:
'Tis genuine warmth of heart without pretence,
 And purity of mind that crowns the whole.

7

She speaks! 'Tis eloquence, that grace of tongue,
 So rare, so lovely, never misapplied
By her, to palliate vice, or deck a wrong:
 She speaks and argues but on virtue's side.

8

Hers is the energy of soul sincere;
 Her Christian spirit, ignorant to feign,
Seeks but to comfort, heal, enlighten, cheer,
 Confer a pleasure or prevent a pain.

9

Can aught enhance such goodness? yes, to me
 Her partial favour from my earliest years
Consummates all: ah! give me but to see
 Her smile of love! The vision disappears.

10

'Tis past and gone. We meet no more below.
 Short is the cheat of Fancy o'er the tomb.
Oh! might I hope to equal bliss to go,
 To meet thee, angel, in thy future home.

11

Fain would I feel an union with thy fate:
 Fain would I seek to draw an omen fair
From this connection in our earthly date.
 Indulge the harmless weakness. Reason, spare.

[3] **My dear itty Dordy:** Austen's nephew George (1795–1867).

[1] **Mrs. Lefroy:** Anne Lefroy (1749–1804), a friend of Austen's, who died as a result of falling from a horse.

from Letter to Anna Austen[1]

(9 September 1814)

Chawton Sept: 9.

MY DEAR ANNA

We have been very much amused by your 3 books, but I have a good many criticisms to make—more than you will like. . . . —You are now collecting your People delightfully, getting them exactly into such a spot as is the delight of my life;—3 or 4 Families in a Country Village is the very thing to work on—& I hope you will write a great deal more, & make full use of them while they are so very favourably arranged. You are but *now* coming to the heart & beauty of your book; till the heroine grows up, the fun must be imperfect—but I expect a great deal of entertainment from the next 3 or 4 books, & I hope you will not resent these remarks by sending me no more. . . .

Yrs affec^{ly}

J. AUSTEN

from Letter to J. Edward Austen[1]

(16 December 1816)

Chawton, Monday Dec: 16.

MY DEAR EDWARD

One reason for my writing to you now, is that I may have the pleasure of directing to you Esqre.—*I give you Joy of having left Winchester*. . . .

. . . —*Uncle Henry*[2] writes very superior Sermons.—You and I must try to get hold of one or two, & put them into our Novels;—it would be a fine help to a volume; & we could make our Heroine read it aloud of a Sunday Evening, . . . —By the bye, my dear Edward, I am quite concerned for the loss your Mother mentions in her Letter; two Chapters & a half to be missing is monstrous! It is well that I have not been at Steventon lately, & therefore cannot be suspected of purloining them;—two strong twigs & a half towards a Nest of my own, would have been something.—I do not think however that any theft of that sort would be really very useful to me. What should I do with your strong, manly, spirited Sketches, full of Variety and Glow?—How could I possibly join them on to the little bit (two Inches wide) of Ivory on which I work with so fine a Brush, as produces little effect after much labour? . . .

Yours affec^{ly}

J. AUSTEN

[1] **Anna Austen**: Jane Austen's niece, Jane Anna Elizabeth Austen (1793–1872), who made an unsuccessful attempt at authorship.

[1] **J. Edward Austen**: Austen's nephew, James Edward Austen-Leigh (1798–1874), an aspiring novelist in his youth, and later author of a *Memoir of Jane Austen* (1870).

[2] **Uncle Henry**: Austen's brother, Henry Thomas Austen (1771–1850), a failed businessman and, from 1816, curate of Bentley.

POSTHUMOUS PUBLICATIONS

Lady Susan

(1871; comp. 1794–1795)

This work was composed in 1794–95.

— LETTER 1 —

Lady Susan Vernon to Mr. Vernon

Langford, December

MY DEAR BROTHER

I can no longer refuse myself the pleasure of profitting by your kind invitation when we last parted, of spending some weeks with you at Churchill, and therefore if quite convenient to you and Mrs. Vernon to receive me at present, I shall hope within a few days to be introduced to a Sister whom I have so long desired to be acquainted with. My kind friends here are most affectionately urgent with me to prolong my stay, but their hospitable and chearful dispositions lead them too much into society for my present situation and state of mind; and I impatiently look forward to the hour when I shall be admitted into your delightful retirement. I long to be made known to your dear little Children, in whose hearts I shall be very eager to secure an interest. I shall soon have occasion for all my fortitude, as I am on the point of separation from my own daughter. The long illness of her dear Father prevented my paying her that attention which Duty and affection equally dictated, and I have but too much reason to fear that the Governess to whose care I consigned her, was unequal to the charge. I have therefore resolved on placing her at one of the best Private Schools in Town, where I shall have an opportunity of leaving her myself, in my way to you. I am determined you see, not to be denied admittance at Churchill. It would indeed give me most painful sensations to know that it were not in your power to receive me.

Yr most obliged and affec: Sister
S. VERNON.

— LETTER 2 —

Lady Susan to Mrs. Johnson

You were mistaken my dear Alicia, in supposing me fixed at this place for the rest of the winter. It greives me to say how greatly you were mistaken, for I have seldom spent three months more agreably than those which have just flown away. At present nothing goes smoothly. The Females of the Family are united against me. You foretold how it would be, when I first came to Langford; and Manwaring is so uncommonly pleasing that I was not without apprehensions myself. I remember saying to myself as I drove to the House, 'I like this Man; pray Heaven no harm come of it!' But I was determined to be discreet, to bear in mind my being only four months a widow, and to be as quiet as possible,—and I have been so; My dear Creature, I have admitted no one's attentions but Manwaring's, I have avoided all general flirtation whatever, I have distinguished no Creature besides of all the Numbers resorting hither, except Sir James Martin, on whom I bestowed a little notice in order to detach him from Miss Manwaring. But if the World could know my motive *there*, they would honour me. I have been called an unkind Mother, but it was the sacred impulse of maternal affection, it was the advantage of my Daughter that led me on; and if that Daughter were not the greatest simpleton on Earth, I might have been rewarded for my Exertions as I ought.—Sir James did make proposals to me for Frederica —but Frederica, who was born to be the torment of my life, chose to set herself so violently against the match, that I thought it better to lay aside the scheme for the present. I have more than once repented that I did not marry him myself, and were he but one degree less contemptibly weak I certainly should, but I must own myself rather romantic in that respect, and that Riches only, will not satisfy me. The event of all this is very provoking. Sir James is gone, Maria highly incensed, and Mrs. Manwaring insupportably jealous; so jealous in short, and so enraged against me, that in the fury of her temper I should not be surprised at her appealing to her Guardian if she had the liberty of addressing him—but there your Husband stands my friend, and the kindest, most amiable action of his Life was his throwing her off forever on her Marriage. Keep up his resentment therefore I charge you. We are now in a sad state; no house was ever more altered; the whole family are at war, and Manwaring scarcely dares speak to me. It is time for me to be gone; I have therefore determined on leaving them, and shall spend I hope a comfortable day with you in Town within this week. If I am as little in favour with Mr. Johnson as ever, you must come to me at No. 10 Wigmore Street—but I hope this may not be the case, for as Mr. Johnson with all his faults is a Man to whom that great word 'Respectable' is always given, and I am known to be so intimate with his wife, his slighting me has an awkward Look. I take Town in my way to that insupportable spot, a Country Village, for I am really going to Churchill. Forgive me my dear friend, it is my last resource. Were there another place in England open to me, I would prefer it. Charles Vernon is my aversion, and I am afraid of his wife. At Churchill however I must remain till I have something better in view. My young Lady accompanies me to Town, where I shall deposit her under the care of Miss Summers in Wigmore Street, till she becomes a little more reasonable. She will make good connections there, as the Girls are all of the best Families. The price is immense, and much beyond what I can ever attempt to pay.

Adeiu. I will send you a line, as soon as I arrive in Town.—

Yours Ever,
S. VERNON.

— LETTER 3 —

Mrs. Vernon to Lady De Courcy

Churchill

MY DEAR MOTHER

I am very sorry to tell you that it will not be in our power to keep our promise of spending the Christmas with you;

and we are prevented that happiness by a circumstance which is not likely to make us any amends. Lady Susan in a letter to her Brother, has declared her intention of visiting us almost immediately—and as such a visit is in all probability an affair of convenience, it is impossible to conjecture it's length. I was by no means prepared for such an event, nor can I now account for her Ladyship's conduct. Langford appeared so exactly the place for her in every respect, as well from the elegant and expensive stile of Living there, as from her particular attachment to Mrs. Manwaring, that I was very far from expecting so speedy a distinction, tho' I always imagined from her increasing friendship for us since her Husband's death, that we should at some future period be obliged to receive her. Mr. Vernon I think was a great deal too kind to her, when he was in Staffordshire. Her behaviour to him, independent of her general Character, has been so inexcusably artful and ungenerous since our Marriage was first in agitation, that no one less amiable and mild than himself could have overlooked it at all; and tho' as his Brother's widow and in narrow circumstances it was proper to render her pecuniary assistance, I cannot help thinking his pressing invitation to her to visit us at Churchill perfectly unnecessary. Disposed however as he always is to think the best of every one, her display of Greif, and professions of regret, and general resolutions of prudence were sufficient to soften his heart, and make him really confide in her sincerity. But as for myself, I am still unconvinced; and plausibly as her Ladyship has now written, I cannot make up my mind, till I better understand her real meaning in coming to us. You may guess therefore my dear Madam, with what feelings I look forward to her arrival. She will have occasion for all those attractive Powers for which she is celebrated, to gain any share of my regard; and I shall certainly endeavour to guard myself against their influence, if not accompanied by something more substantial. She expresses a most eager desire of being acquainted with me, and makes very gracious mention of my children, but I am not quite weak enough to suppose a woman who has behaved with inattention if not unkindness to her own child, should be attached to any of mine. Miss Vernon is to be placed at a school in Town before her Mother comes to us, which I am glad of, for her sake and my own. It must be to her advantage to be separated from her Mother: and a girl of sixteen who has received so wretched an education would not be a very desirable companion here. Reginald has long wished I know to see this captivating Lady Susan, and we shall depend on his joining our party soon. I am glad to hear that my Father continues so well, and am, with best Love &c.,

CATH. VERNON

— LETTER 4 —

Mr. De Courcy to Mrs. Vernon

Parklands

MY DEAR SISTER

I congratulate you and Mr. Vernon on being about to receive into your family, the most accomplished Coquette in England. As a very distinguished Flirt, I have been always taught to consider her; but it has lately fallen in my way to hear some particulars of her conduct at Langford, which prove that she does not confine herself to that sort of honest flirtation which satisfies most people, but aspires to the more delicious gratification of making a whole family miserable. By her behaviour to Mr. Manwaring, she gave jealousy and wretchedness to his wife, and by her attentions to a young man previously attached to Mr. Manwaring's sister, deprived an amiable girl of her Lover. I learnt all this from a Mr. Smith now in this neighbourhood—(I have dined with him at Hurst and Wilford)—who is just come from Langford, where he was a fortnight in the house with her Ladyship, and who is therefore well qualified to make the communication.

What a Woman she must be! I long to see her, and shall certainly accept your kind invitation, that I may form some idea of those bewitching powers which can do so much—engaging at the same time and in the same house the affections of two Men who were neither of them at liberty to bestow them—and all this, without the charm of Youth. I am glad to find that Miss Vernon does not come with her Mother to Churchill, as she has not even Manners to recommend her, and according to Mr. Smith's account, is equally dull and proud. Where Pride and Stupidity unite, there can be no dissimulation worthy notice, and Miss Vernon shall be consigned to unrelenting contempt; but by all that I can gather, Lady Susan possesses a degree of captivating Deceit which must be pleasing to witness and detect. I shall be with you very soon, and am

your affec. Brother
R. DE COURCY.

— LETTER 5 —

Lady Susan to Mrs. Johnson.

Churchill

I received your note my dear Alicia, just before I left Town, and rejoice to be assured that Mr. Johnson suspected nothing of your engagement the evening before; it is undoubtedly better to deceive him entirely; since he will be stubborn, he must be tricked. I arrived here in safety, and have no reason to complain of my reception from Mr. Vernon; but I confess myself not equally satisfied with the behaviour of his Lady. She is perfectly well bred indeed, and has the air of a woman of fashion, but her Manners are not such as can persuade me of her being prepossessed in my favour. I wanted her to be delighted at seeing me—I was as amiable as possible on the occasion—but all in vain—she does not like me. To be sure, when we consider that I *did* take some pains to prevent my Brother-in-law's marrying her, this want of cordiality is not very surprising—and yet it shews an illiberal and vindictive spirit to resent a project which influenced me six years ago, and which never succeeded at last. I am sometimes half disposed to repent that I did not let Charles buy Vernon Castle when we were obliged to sell it, but it was a trying circumstance, especially as the sale took place exactly at the time of his marriage—and everybody ought to respect the delicacy of those feelings, which could not endure that my Husband's Dignity should be lessened by his younger brother's having possession of the Family Estate. Could Matters have been so arranged as to prevent the necessity of our leaving the Castle, could we have lived with Charles and kept him single, I should have been very far from persuading my husband to dispose of it elsewhere; but Charles was then on the point of marrying Miss De Courcy, and the event has justified me. Here are Children in abundance, and what benefit could have accrued to me from his purchasing Vernon? My having prevented it, may perhaps have given his wife an unfavourable impression—but where there is a disposition to dislike a motive will never be wanting; and as to money-matters, it has not with-held him from being very useful to me. I really have a regard for him, he is so easily imposed on!

The house is a good one, the Furniture fashionable, and everything announces plenty and elegance. Charles is very rich I am sure; when a Man has once got his name in a Banking House he rolls in money. But they do not know what to do with their fortune, keep very little company, and never go to Town but on business. We shall be as stupid as possible. I mean to win my Sister-in-law's heart through her Children; I know all their names already, and am going to attach myself with the greatest sensibility to one in particular, a young Frederic, whom I take on my lap and sigh over for his dear Uncle's sake.

Poor Manwaring!—I need not tell you how much I miss him—how perpetually he is in my Thoughts. I found a dismal letter from him on my arrival here, full of complaints of his wife and sister, and lamentations on the cruelty of his fate. I passed off the letter as his wife's, to the Vernons, and when I write to him, it must be under cover to you.

Yours Ever,
S. V.

— LETTER 6 —

Mrs. Vernon to Mr. De Courcy

Churchill

Well my dear Reginald, I have seen this dangerous creature, and must give you some description of her, tho' I hope you will soon be able to form your own judgement. She is really excessively pretty. However you may chuse to question the allurements of a Lady no longer young, I must for my own part declare that I have seldom seen so lovely a Woman as Lady Susan. She is delicately fair, with fine grey eyes and dark eyelashes; and from her appearance one would not suppose her more than five and twenty, tho' she must in fact be ten years older. I was certainly not disposed to admire her, tho' always hearing she was beautiful; but I cannot help feeling that she possesses an uncommon union of Symmetry, Brilliancy and Grace. Her address to me was so gentle, frank and even affectionate, that if I had not known how much she has always disliked me for marrying Mr. Vernon, and that we had never met before, I should have imagined her an attached friend. One is apt I beleive to connect assurance of manner with coquetry, and to expect that an impudent address will necessarily attend an impudent mind; at least I was myself prepared for an improper degree of confidence in Lady Susan; but her Countenance is absolutely sweet, and her voice and manner winningly mild. I am sorry it is so, for what is this but Deceit? Unfortunately one knows her too well. She is clever and agreable, has all that knowledge of the world which makes conversation easy, and talks very well, with a happy command of Language, which is too often used I beleive to make Black appear White. She has already almost persuaded me of her being warmly attached to her daughter, tho' I have so long been convinced of the contrary. She speaks of her with so much tenderness and anxiety, lamenting so bitterly the neglect of her education, which she represents however as wholly unavoidable, that I am forced to recollect how many successive Springs her Ladyship spent in Town, while her daughter was left in Staffordshire to the care of servants or a Governess very little better, to prevent my beleiving whatever she says.

If her manners have so great an influence on my resentful heart, you may guess how much more strongly they operate on Mr. Vernon's generous temper. I wish I could be as well satisfied as he is, that it was really her choice to leave Langford for Churchill; and if she had not staid three months there before she discovered that her friends' manner of Living did not suit her situation or feelings, I might have beleived that concern for the loss of such a Husband as Mr. Vernon, to whom her own behaviour was far from unexceptionable, might for a time make her wish for retirement. But I cannot forget the length of her visit to the Manwarings, and when I reflect on the different mode of Life which she led with them, from that to which she must now submit, I can only suppose that the wish of establishing her reputation by following, tho' late, the path of propriety, occasioned her removal from a family where she must in reality have been particularly happy. Your friend Mr. Smith's story however cannot be quite true, as she corresponds regularly with Mrs. Manwaring; at any rate it must be exaggerated; it is scarcely possible that two men should be so grossly deceived by her at once.

Yrs &c.

CATH. VERNON.

— LETTER 7 —

Lady Susan to Mrs. Johnson

Churchill

MY DEAR ALICIA

You are very good in taking notice of Frederica, and I am grateful for it as a mark of your friendship; but as I cannot have a doubt of the warmth of that friendship, I am far from exacting so heavy a sacrifice. She is a stupid girl, and has nothing to recommend her. I would not therefore on any account have you encumber one moment of your precious time by sending her to Edward Street, especially as every visit is so many hours deducted from the grand affair of Education, which I really wish to be attended to, while she remains with Miss Summers. I want her to play and sing with some portion of Taste, and a good deal of assurance, as she has *my* hand and arm, and a tolerable voice. *I* was so much indulged in my infant years that I was never obliged to attend to anything, and consequently am without those accomplishments which are now necessary to finish a pretty Woman. Not that I am an advocate for the prevailing fashion of acquiring a perfect knowledge in all the Languages Arts and Sciences; it is throwing time away; to be Mistress of French, Italian, German, Music, Singing, Drawing &c. will gain a Woman some applause, but will not add one Lover to her list. Grace and Manner after all are of the greatest importance. I do not mean therefore that Frederica's acquirements should be more than superficial, and I flatter myself that she will not remain long enough at school to understand anything thoroughly. I hope to see her the wife of Sir James within a twelvemonth. You know on what I ground my hope, and it is certainly a good foundation, for School must be very humiliating to a girl of Frederica's age; and by the bye, you had better not invite her any more on that account, as I wish her to find her situation as unpleasant as possible. I am sure of Sir James at any time, and could make him renew his application by a Line. I shall trouble you meanwhile to prevent his forming any other attachment when he comes to Town; ask him to your House occasionally, and talk to him about Frederica that he may not forget her.

Upon the whole I commend my own conduct in this affair extremely, and regard it as a very happy mixture of circumspection and tenderness. Some Mothers would have insisted on their daughter's accepting so great an offer on the first overture, but I could not answer it to myself to force Frederica into a marriage from which her heart revolted; and instead of adopting so harsh a measure, merely propose to make it her own choice by rendering her thoroughly uncomfortable till she does accept him. But enough of this tiresome girl.

You may well wonder how I contrive to pass my time here—and for the first week, it was most insufferably dull. Now however, we begin to mend; our party is enlarged by Mrs. Vernon's brother, a handsome young Man, who promises me some amusement. There is something about him that rather interests me, a sort of sauciness, of familiarity which I shall teach him to correct. He is lively and seems clever, and when I have inspired him with greater respect for me than his sister's kind offices have implanted, he may be an agreable Flirt. There is exquisite pleasure in subduing an insolent spirit, in making a person predetermined to dislike, acknowledge one's superiority. I have disconcerted him already by my calm reserve; and it shall be my endeavour to humble the Pride of these self-important De Courcies still lower, to convince Mrs. Vernon that her sisterly cautions have been bestowed in vain, and to persuade Reginald that she has scandalously belied me. This project will serve at least to amuse me, and prevent my feeling so acutely this dreadful separation from You and all whom I love. Adeiu.

Yours Ever
S. Vernon

— LETTER 8 —

Mrs. Vernon to Lady De Courcy

....

Churchill

My dear Mother

You must not expect Reginald back again for some time. He desires me to tell you that the present open weather induces him to accept Mr. Vernon's invitation to prolong his stay in Sussex that they may have some hunting together. He means to send for his Horses immediately, and it is impossible to say when you may see him in Kent. I will not disguise my sentiments on this change from you my dear Madam, tho' I think you had better not communicate them to my Father, whose excessive anxiety about Reginald would subject him to an alarm which might seriously affect his health and spirits. Lady Susan has certainly contrived in the space of a fortnight to make my Brother like her. In short, I am persuaded that his continuing here beyond the time originally fixed for his return, is occasioned as much by a degree of fascination towards her, as by the wish of hunting with Mr. Vernon, and of course I cannot receive that pleasure from the length of his visit which my Brother's company would otherwise give me. I am indeed provoked at the artifice of this unprincipled Woman. What stronger proof of her dangerous abilities can be given, than this perversion of Reginald's Judgement, which when he entered the house was so decidedly against her? In his last letter he actually gave me some particulars of her behaviour at Langford, such as he received from a Gentleman who knew her perfectly well, which if true must raise abhorrence against her, and which Reginald himself was entirely disposed to credit. His opinion of her I am sure, was as low as of any Woman in England, and when he first came it was evident that he considered her as one entitled neither to Delicacy nor respect, and that he felt she would be delighted with the attentions of any Man inclined to flirt with her.

Her behaviour I confess has been calculated to do away such an idea, I have not detected the smallest impropriety in it,—nothing of vanity, of pretension, of Levity—and she is altogether so attractive, that I should not wonder at his being delighted with her, had he known nothing of her previous to this personal acquaintance; but against reason, against conviction, to be so well pleased with her as I am sure he is, does really astonish me. His admiration was at first very strong, but no more than was natural; and I did not wonder at his being struck by the gentleness and delicacy of her Manners; but when he has mentioned her of late, it has been in terms of more extraordinary praise, and yesterday he actually said, that he could not be surprised at any effect produced on the heart of Man by such Loveliness and such Abilities; and when I lamented in reply the badness of her disposition, he observed that whatever might have been her errors, they were to be imputed to her neglected Education and early Marriage, and that she was altogether a wonderful Woman.

This tendency to excuse her conduct, or to forget it in the warmth of admiration vexes me; and if I did not know that Reginald is too much at home at Churchill to need an invitation for lengthening his visit, I should regret Mr. Vernon's giving him any.

Lady Susan's intentions are of course those of absolute coquetry, or a desire of universal admiration. I cannot for a moment imagine that she has anything more serious in veiw, but it mortifies me to see a young Man of Reginald's sense duped by her at all. I am &c.

Cath. Vernon.

— LETTER 9 —

Mrs. Johnson to Lady Susan

....

Edward Street

My dearest Friend

I congratulate you on Mr. De Courcy's arrival, and advise you by all means to marry him; his Father's Estate is we know considerable, and I beleive certainly entailed.[1] Sir Reginald is very infirm, and not likely to stand in your way long. I hear the young Man well spoken of, and tho' no one can really deserve you my dearest Susan, Mr. De Courcy may be worth having. Manwaring will storm of course, but you may easily pacify him. Besides, the most scrupulous point of honour could not require you to wait for *his* emancipation. I have seen Sir James, — he came to Town for a few days last week, and called several times in Edward Street. I talked to him about you and your daughter, and he is so far from having forgotten you, that I am sure he would marry either of you with pleasure. I gave him hopes of Frederica's relenting, and told him a great deal of her improvements. I scolded him for making Love to Maria Manwaring; he protested that he had been only in joke, and we both laughed heartily at her disappointment, and in short were very agreable. He is as silly as ever. — Yours faithfully

ALICIA

— LETTER 10 —

Lady Susan to Mrs. Johnson

Churchill

I am much obliged to you my dear Friend, for your advice respecting Mr. De Courcy, which I know was given with the fullest conviction of it's expediency, tho' I am not quite determined on following it. I cannot easily resolve on anything so serious as Marriage, especially as I am not at present in want of money, and might perhaps till the old Gentleman's death, be very little benefited by the match. It is true that I am vain enough to beleive it within my reach. I have made him sensible of my power, and can now enjoy the pleasure of triumphing over a Mind prepared to dislike me, and prejudiced against all my past actions. His sister too, is I hope convinced how little the ungenerous representations of any one to the disadvantage of another will avail, when opposed to the immediate influence of Intellect and Manner. I see plainly that she is uneasy at my progress in the good opinion of her Brother, and conclude that nothing will be wanting on her part to counteract me; but having once made him doubt the justice of her opinion of me, I think I may defy her.

It has been delightful to me to watch his advances towards intimacy, especially to observe his altered manner in consequence of my repressing by the calm dignity of my deportment, his insolent approach to direct familiarity. My conduct has been equally guarded from the first, and I never behaved less like a Coquette in the whole course of my Life, tho' perhaps my desire of dominion was never more decided. I have subdued him entirely by sentiment and serious conversation, and made him I may venture to say at least *half* in Love with me, without the semblance of the most common-place flirtation. Mrs. Vernon's consciousness of deserving every sort of revenge that it can be in my power to inflict, for her ill-offices, could alone enable her to perceive that I am actuated by any design in behaviour so gentle and unpretending. Let her think and act as she chuses however; I have never yet found that the advice of a Sister could prevent a young Man's being in love if he chose it. We are advancing now towards some kind of confidence, and in short are likely to be engaged in a kind of platonic friendship. On *my* side, you may be sure of it's never being more, for if I were not already as much attached to another person as I can be to any one, I should make a point of not bestowing my affection on a Man who had dared to think so meanly of me.

Reginald has a good figure, and is not unworthy the praise you have heard given him, but is still greatly inferior to our friend at Langford. He is less polished, less insinuating than Manwaring, and is comparatively deficient in the power of saying those delightful things which put one in good humour with oneself and all the world. He is quite agreable enough however, to afford me amusement, and to make many of those hours pass very pleasantly which would be otherwise spent in endeavouring to overcome my sister-in-law's reserve, and listening to her Husband's insipid talk.

Your account of Sir James is most satisfactory, and I mean to give Miss Frederica a hint of my intentions very soon. — Yours &c.

S. VERNON

— LETTER 11 —

Mrs. Vernon to Lady De Courcy

I really grow quite uneasy my dearest Mother about Reginald, from witnessing the very rapid increase of Lady

[1] **entailed:** a landed estate which by law cannot be sold or divided but must be inherited by the oldest and nearest male kin in the next generation.

Susan's influence. They are now on terms of the most particular friendship, frequently engaged in long conversations together, and she has contrived by the most artful coquetry to subdue his Judgement to her own purposes. It is impossible to see the intimacy between them, so very soon established, without some alarm, tho' I can hardly suppose that Lady Susan's views extend to marriage. I wish you could get Reginald home again, under any plausible pretence. He is not at all disposed to leave us, and I have given him as many hints of my Father's precarious state of health, as common decency will allow me to do in my own house. Her power over him must now be boundless, as she has entirely effaced all his former ill-opinion, and persuaded him not merely to forget, but to justify her conduct. Mr. Smith's account of her proceedings at Langford, where he accused her of having made Mr. Manwaring and a young Man engaged to Miss Manwaring distractedly in love with her, which Reginald firmly beleived when he came to Churchill, is now he is persuaded only a scandalous invention. He has told me so in a warmth of manner which spoke his regret at having ever believed the contrary himself.

How sincerely do I greive that she ever entered this house! I always looked forward to her coming with uneasiness—but very far was it, from originating in anxiety for Reginald. I expected a most disagreable companion to myself, but could not imagine that my Brother would be in the smallest danger of being captivated by a Woman with whose principles he was so well acquainted, and whose character he so heartily despised. If you can get him away, it will be a good thing.

Yrs affectly
CATH. VERNON.

— LETTER 12 —

Sir Reginald De Courcy to his Son

....

Parklands

I know that young Men in general do not admit of any enquiry even from their nearest relations, into affairs of the heart; but I hope my dear Reginald that you will be superior to such as allow nothing for a Father's anxiety, and think themselves privileged to refuse him their confidence and slight his advice. You must be sensible that as an only son and the representative of an ancient Family, your conduct in Life is most interesting to your connections. In the very important concern of Marriage especially, there is everything at stake; your own happiness, that of your Parents, and the credit of your name. I do not suppose that you would deliberately form an absolute engagement of that nature without acquainting your Mother and myself, or at least without being convinced that we should approve your choice; but I cannot help fearing that you may be drawn in by the Lady who has lately attached you, to a Marriage, which the whole of your Family, far and near, must highly reprobate.

Lady Susan's age is itself a material objection, but her want of character is one so much more serious, that the difference of even twelve years becomes in comparison of small account. Were you not blinded by a sort of fascination, it would be ridiculous in me to repeat the instances of great misconduct on her side, so very generally known. Her neglect of her husband, her encouragement of other Men, her extravagance and dissipation were so gross and notorious, that no one could be ignorant of them at the time, nor can now have forgotten them. To our Family, she has always been represented in softened colours by the benevolence of Mr. Charles Vernon; and yet in spite of his generous endeavours to excuse her, we know that she did, from the most selfish motives, take all possible pains to prevent his marrying Catherine.

My Years and increasing Infirmities make me very desirous my dear Reginald, of seeing you settled in the world. To the Fortune of your wife, the goodness of my own, will make me indifferent; but her family and character must be equally unexceptionable. When your choice is so fixed as that no objection can be made to either, I can promise you a ready and chearful consent; but it is my Duty to oppose a Match, which deep Art only could render probable, and must in the end make wretched.

It is possible that her behaviour may arise only from Vanity, or a wish of gaining the admiration of a Man whom she must imagine to be particularly prejudiced against her; but it is more likely that she should aim at something farther. She is poor, and may naturally seek an alliance which may be advantageous to herself. You know your own rights, and that it is out of my power to prevent your inheriting the family Estate. My Ability of distressing you during my Life, would be a species of revenge to which I should hardly stoop under any circumstances. I honestly tell you my Sentiments and Intentions. I do not wish to work on your Fears, but on your Sense and Affection. It would destroy every comfort of my Life, to know that you were married to Lady Susan Vernon. It would be the death of that honest Pride with which I have hitherto considered my son, I should blush to see him, to hear of him, to think of him.

I may perhaps do no good, but that of relieving my own mind, by this Letter; but I felt it my Duty to tell you that your partiality for Lady Susan is no secret to your friends, and to warn you against her. I should be glad to hear your reasons for disbeleiving Mr. Smith's intelligence; you had no doubt of it's authenticity a month ago.

If you can give me your assurance of having no design beyond enjoying the conversation of a clever woman for a short period, and of yeilding admiration only to her Beauty and Abilities without being blinded by them to her faults, you will restore me to happiness; but if you cannot do this, explain to me at least what has occasioned so great an alteration in your opinion of her.

I am &c.
REGINALD DE COURCY

— LETTER 13 —

Lady De Courcy to Mrs. Vernon

....

Parklands

MY DEAR CATHERINE,

Unluckily I was confined to my room when your last letter came, by a cold which affected my eyes so much as to prevent my reading it myself, so I could not refuse your Father when he offered to read it to me, by which means he became acquainted to my great vexation with all your fears about your Brother. I had intended to write to Reginald myself, as soon as my eyes would let me, to point out as well as I could the danger of an intimate acquaintance with so artful a woman as Lady Susan, to a young Man of his age and high expectations. I meant moreover to have reminded him of our being quite alone now, and very much in need of him to keep up our spirits these long winter evenings. Whether it would have done any good, can never be settled now; but I am excessively vexed that Sir Reginald should know anything of a matter which we foresaw would make him so uneasy. He caught all your fears the moment he had read your Letter, and I am sure has not had the business out of his head since; he wrote by the same post to Reginald, a long letter full of it all, and particularly asking for an explanation of what he may have heard from Lady Susan to contradict the late shocking reports. His answer came this morning, which I shall enclose to you, as I think you will like to see it; I wish it was more satisfactory, but it seems written with such a determination to think well of Lady Susan, that his assurances as to Marriage &c., do not set my heart at ease. I say all I can however to satisfy your Father, and he is certainly less uneasy since Reginald's letter. How provoking it is my dear Catherine, that this unwelcome Guest of yours, should not only prevent our meeting this Christmas, but be the occasion of so much vexation and trouble. Kiss the dear Children for me. Your affec: Mother

C. DE COURCY

— LETTER 14 —

Mr. De Courcy to Sir Reginald

....

Churchill

MY DEAR SIR

I have this moment received your Letter, which has given me more astonishment than I ever felt before. I am to thank my Sister I suppose, for having represented me in such a light as to injure me in your opinion, and give you all this alarm. I know not why she should chuse to make herself and her family uneasy by apprehending an Event, which no one but herself I can affirm, would ever have thought possible. To impute such a design to Lady Susan would be taking from her every claim to that excellent understanding which her bitterest Enemies have never denied her; and equally low must sink my pretensions to common sense, if I am suspected of matrimonial veiws in my behaviour to her. Our difference of age must be an insuperable objection, and I entreat you my dear Sir to quiet your mind, and no longer harbour a suspicion which cannot be more injurious to your own peace than to our Understandings.

I can have no *view* in remaining with Lady Susan than to enjoy for a short time (as you have yourself expressed it) the conversation of a Woman of high mental powers. If Mrs. Vernon would allow something to my affection for herself and her husband in the length of my visit, she would do more justice to us all; but my Sister is unhappily prejudiced beyond the hope of conviction against Lady Susan. From an attachment to her husband which in itself does honour to both, she cannot forgive those endeavours at preventing their union, which have been attributed to selfishness in Lady Susan. But in this case, as well as in many others, the World has most grossly injured that

Lady, by supposing the worst, where the motives of her conduct have been doubtful.

Lady Susan had heard something so materially to the disadvantage of my Sister, as to persuade her that the happiness of Mr. Vernon, to whom she was always much attached, would be absolutely destroyed by the Marriage. And this circumstance while it explains the true motive of Lady Susan's conduct, and removes all the blame which has been so lavished on her, may also convince us how little the general report of any one ought to be credited, since no character however upright, can escape the malevolence of slander. If my Sister in the security of retirement, with as little opportunity as inclination to do Evil, could not avoid Censure, we must not rashly condemn those who living in the World and surrounded with temptation, should be accused of Errors which they are known to have the power of committing.

I blame myself severely for having so easily believed the scandalous tales invented by Charles Smith to the prejudice of Lady Susan, as I am now convinced how greatly they have traduced her. As to Mrs. Manwaring's jealousy, it was totally his own invention; and his account of her attaching Miss Manwaring's Lover was scarcely better founded. Sir James Martin had been drawn in by that young Lady to pay her some attention, and as he is a Man of fortune, it was easy to see that *her* veiws extended to Marriage. It is well known that Miss Manwaring is absolutely on the catch for a husband, and no one therefore can pity her, for losing by the superior attractions of another woman, the chance of being able to make a worthy Man completely miserable. Lady Susan was far from intending such a conquest, and on finding how warmly Miss Manwaring resented her Lover's defection, determined, in spite of Mr. and Mrs. Manwaring's most earnest entreaties, to leave the family. I have reason to imagine that she did receive serious Proposals from Sir James, but her removing from Langford immediately on the discovery of his attachment, must acquit her on that article, with every Mind of common candour.[2] You will, I am sure my dear Sir, feel the truth of this reasoning, and will hereby learn to do justice to the character of a very injured Woman.

I know that Lady Susan in coming to Churchill was governed only by the most honourable and amiable intentions. Her prudence and economy are exemplary, her regard for Mr. Vernon equal even to *his* deserts, and her wish of obtaining my sister's good opinion merits a better return than it has received. As a Mother she is unexceptionable. Her solid affection for her Child is shewn by placing her in hands, where her Education will be properly attended to; but because she has not the blind and weak partiality of most Mothers, she is accused of wanting Maternal Tenderness. Every person of Sense however will know how to value and commend her well directed affection, and will join me in wishing that Frederica Vernon may prove more worthy than she has yet done, of her Mother's tender care.

I have now my dear Sir, written my real sentiments of Lady Susan; you will know from this Letter, how highly I admire her Abilities, and esteem her character; but if you are not equally convinced by my full and solemn assurance that your fears have been most idly created, you will deeply mortify and distress me. — I am &c.

R. De Courcy

— LETTER 15 —

Mrs. Vernon to Lady De Courcy

Churchill

My dear Mother

I return you Reginald's letter, and rejoice with all my heart that my Father is made easy by it. Tell him so, with my congratulations; but between ourselves, I must own it has only convinced me of my Brother's having no *present* intention of marrying Lady Susan — not that he is in no danger of doing so three months hence. He gives a very plausible account of her behaviour at Langford, I wish it may be true, but his intelligence must come from herself, and I am less disposed to beleive it, than to lament the degree of intimacy subsisting between them, implied by the discussion of such a subject.

I am sorry to have incurred his displeasure, but can expect nothing better while he is so very eager in Lady Susan's justification. He is very severe against me indeed, and yet I hope I have not been hasty in my judgement of her. Poor Woman! tho' I have reasons enough for my dislike, I can not help pitying her at present as she is in real distress, and with too much cause. She had this morning a letter from the Lady with whom she has placed her daughter, to request that Miss Vernon might be immediately

[2] **common candour:** ordinary disinterested judgment.

removed, as she had been detected in an attempt to run away. Why, or whither she intended to go, does not appear; but as her situation seems to have been unexceptionable, it is a sad thing and of course highly afflicting to Lady Susan.

Frederica must be as much as sixteen, and ought to know better, but from what her Mother insinuates I am afraid she is a perverse girl. She has been sadly neglected however, and her Mother ought to remember it.

Mr. Vernon set off for Town as soon as she had determined what should be done. He is if possible to prevail on Miss Summers to let Frederica continue with her, and if he cannot succeed, to bring her to Churchill for the present, till some other situation can be found for her. Her Ladyship is comforting herself meanwhile by strolling along the Shrubbery with Reginald, calling forth all his tender feelings I suppose on this distressing occasion. She has been talking a great deal about it to me, she talks vastly well, I am afraid of being ungenerous or I should say she talks *too* well to feel so very deeply. But I will not look for Faults. She may be Reginald's Wife. Heaven forbid it!—but why should I be quicker sighted than anybody else? Mr. Vernon declares that he never saw deeper distress than hers, on the receipt of the Letter—and is his Judgement inferior to mine?

She was very unwilling that Frederica should be allowed to come to Churchill, and justly enough, as it seems a sort of reward to Behaviour deserving very differently. But it was impossible to take her any where else, and she is not to remain here long.

'It will be absolutely necessary,' said she, 'as you my dear Sister must be sensible, to treat my daughter with some severity while she is here;—a most painful necessity, but I will endeavour to submit to it. I am afraid I have been often too indulgent, but my poor Frederica's temper could never bear opposition well. You must support and encourage me—You must urge the necessity of reproof, if you see me too lenient.'

All this sounds very reasonably. Reginald is so incensed against the poor silly Girl! Surely it is not to Lady Susan's credit that he should be so bitter against her daughter; his idea of her must be drawn from the Mother's description.

Well, whatever may be his fate, we have the comfort of knowing that we have done our utmost to save him. We must commit the event to an Higher Power. Yours Ever &c.

CATH. VERNON

—LETTER 16—

Lady Susan to Mrs. Johnson

Churchill

Never my dearest Alicia, was I so provoked in my life as by a Letter this morning from Miss Summers. That horrid girl of mine has been trying to run away.—I had not a notion of her being such a little Devil before; she seemed to have all the Vernon Milkiness; but on receiving the letter in which I declared my intentions about Sir James, she actually attempted to elope; at least, I cannot otherwise account for her doing it. She meant I suppose to go to the Clarkes in Staffordshire, for she has no other acquaintance. But she *shall* be punished, she *shall* have him. I have sent Charles to Town to make matters up if he can, for I do not by any means want her here. If Miss Summers will not keep her, you must find me out another school, unless we can get her married immediately. Miss S. writes word that she could not get the young Lady to assign any cause for her extraordinary conduct, which confirms me in my own private explanation of it.

Frederica is too shy I think, and too much in awe of me, to tell tales; but if the mildness of her Uncle *should* get anything from her, I am not afraid. I trust I shall be able to make my story as good as her's. If I am vain of anything, it is of my eloquence. Consideration and Esteem as surely follow command of Language, as Admiration waits on Beauty. And here I have opportunity enough for the exercise of my Talent, as the chief of my time is spent in Conversation. Reginald is never easy unless we are by ourselves, and when the weather is tolerable, we pace the shrubbery for hours together. I like him on the whole very well, he is clever and has a good deal to say, but he is sometimes impertinent and troublesome. There is a sort of ridiculous delicacy about him which requires the fullest explanation of whatever he may have heard to my disadvantage, and is never satisfied till he thinks he has ascertained the beginning and end of everything.

This is *one* sort of Love—but I confess it does not particularly recommend itself to me. I infinitely prefer the tender and liberal spirit of Manwaring, which impressed with the deepest conviction of my merit, is satisfied that whatever I do must be right; and look with a degree of contempt on the inquisitive and doubting Fancies of that Heart which seems always debating on the reasonableness of it's

Emotions. Manwaring is indeed beyond compare superior to Reginald—superior in everything but the power of being with me. Poor fellow! he is quite distracted by Jealousy, which I am not sorry for, as I know no better support of Love. He has been teizing me to allow of his coming into this country, and lodging somewhere near me *incog.*[3] but I forbid anything of the kind. Those women are inexcusable who forget what is due to themselves and the opinion of the World.

S. Vernon

—LETTER 17—

Mrs. Vernon to Lady De Courcy

Churchill

My dear Mother

Mr. Vernon returned on Thursday night, bringing his neice with him. Lady Susan had received a line from him by that day's post informing her that Miss Summers had absolutely refused to allow of Miss Vernon's continuance in her Academy. We were therefore prepared for her arrival, and expected them impatiently the whole evening. They came while we were at Tea, and I never saw any creature look so frightened in my life as Frederica when she entered the room.

Lady Susan who had been shedding tears before and shewing great agitation at the idea of the meeting, received her with perfect self-command, and without betraying the least tenderness of spirit. She hardly spoke to her, and on Frederica's bursting into tears as soon as we were seated, took her out of the room and did not return for some time; when she did, her eyes looked very red, and she was as much agitated as before. We saw no more of her daughter.

Poor Reginald was beyond measure concerned to see his fair friend in such distress, and watched her with so much tender solicitude that I, who occasionally caught her observing his countenance with exultation, was quite out of patience. This pathetic representation[4] lasted the whole evening, and so ostentatious and artful a display had entirely convinced me that she did in fact feel nothing.

I am more angry with her than ever since I have seen her daughter. The poor girl looks so unhappy that my heart aches for her. Lady Susan is surely too severe, because Frederica does not seem to have the sort of temper to make severity necessary. She looks perfectly timid, dejected and penitent.

She is very pretty, tho' not so handsome as her Mother, nor at all like her. Her complexion is delicate, but neither so fair, nor so blooming as Lady Susan's—and she has quite the Vernon cast of countenance, the oval face and mild dark eyes, and there is peculiar sweetness in her look when she speaks either to her Uncle or me, for as we behave kindly to her, we have of course engaged her gratitude. Her Mother has insinuated that her temper is untractable, but I never saw a face less indicative of any evil disposition than her's; and from what I now see of the behaviour of each to the other, the invariable severity of Lady Susan, and the silent dejection of Frederica, I am led to beleive as heretofore that the former has no real Love for her daughter and has never done her justice, or treated her affectionately.

I have not yet been able to have any conversation with my neice; she is shy, and I think I can see that some pains are taken to prevent her being much with me. Nothing satisfactory transpires as to her reason for running away. Her kindhearted Uncle you may be sure, was too fearful of distressing her, to ask many questions as they travelled. I wish it had been possible for me to fetch her instead of him; I think I should have discovered the truth in the course of a Thirty mile Journey.

The small Pianoforté has been removed within these few days at Lady Susan's request, into her Dressing room, and Frederica spends great part of the day there; *practising* it is called, but I seldom hear any noise when I pass that way. What she does with herself there I do not know, there are plenty of books in the room, but it is not every girl who has been running wild the first fifteen years of her life, that can or will read. Poor Creature! the prospect from her window is not very instructive, for that room overlooks the Lawn you know with the Shrubbery on one side, where she may see her Mother walking for an hour together, in earnest conversation with Reginald. A girl of Frederica's age must be childish indeed, if such things do not strike her. Is it not inexcusable to give such an example to a daughter? Yet Reginald still thinks

[3] **incog:** incognito. Latin: unknown, concealed under a disguised or assumed character.

[4] **pathetic representation:** performance of pathos or deep feeling.

Lady Susan the best of Mothers—still condemns Frederica as a worthless girl! He is convinced that her attempt to run away, proceeded from no justifiable cause, and had no provocation. I am sure I cannot say that it *had*, but while Miss Summers declares that Miss Vernon shewed no sign of Obstinacy or Perverseness during her whole stay in Wigmore Street till she was detected in this scheme, I cannot so readily credit what Lady Susan has made him and wants to make me beleive, that it was merely an impatience of restraint, and a desire of escaping from the tuition of Masters which brought on the plan of an elopement. Oh! Reginald, how is your Judgement enslaved! He scarcely dares even allow her to be handsome, and when I speak of her beauty, replies only that her eyes have no Brilliancy.

Sometimes he is sure that she is deficient in Understanding, and at others that her temper only is in fault. In short when a person is always to deceive, it is impossible to be consistent. Lady Susan finds it necessary for her own justification that Frederica should be to blame, and probably has sometimes judged it expedient to accuse her of ill-nature and sometimes to lament her want of sense. Reginald is only repeating after her Ladyship.

I am &c.
CATH. VERNON

— LETTER 18 —

From the same to the same

Churchill

MY DEAR MADAM

I am very glad to find that my description of Frederica Vernon has interested you, for I do beleive her truly deserving of our regard, and when I have communicated a notion that has recently struck me, your kind impression in her favour will I am sure be heightened. I cannot help fancying that she is growing partial to my brother, I so very often see her eyes fixed on his face with a remarkable expression of pensive admiration! He is certainly very handsome—and yet more—there is an openness in his manner that must be highly prepossessing, and I am sure she feels it so. Thoughtful and pensive in general her countenance always brightens with a smile when Reginald says anything amusing; and let the subject be ever so serious that he may be conversing on, I am much mistaken if a syllable of his uttering, escape her.

I want to make *him* sensible of all this, for we know the power of gratitude on such a heart as his; and could Frederica's artless affection detach him from her Mother, we might bless the day which brought her to Churchill. I think my dear Madam, you would not disapprove of her as a Daughter. She is extremely young to be sure, has had a wretched Education and a dreadful example of Levity in her Mother; but yet I can pronounce her disposition to be excellent, and her natural abilities very good.

Tho' totally without accomplishment, she is by no means so ignorant as one might expect to find her, being fond of books and spending the cheif of her time in reading. Her Mother leaves her more to herself now than she *did*, and I have her with me as much as possible, and have taken great pains to overcome her timidity. We are very good friends, and though she never opens her lips before her Mother, she talks enough when alone with me, to make it clear that if properly treated by Lady Susan she would always appear to much greater advantage. There cannot be a more gentle, affectionate heart, or more obliging manners, when acting without restraint. Her little Cousins are all very fond of her.

Yrs affectly
CATH. VERNON

— LETTER 19 —

Lady Susan to Mrs. Johnson

Churchill

You will be eager I know to hear something farther of Frederica, and perhaps may think me negligent for not writing before. She arrived with her Uncle last Thursday fortnight, when of course I lost no time in demanding the reason of her behaviour, and soon found myself to have been perfectly right in attributing it to my own letter. The purport of it frightened her so thoroughly that with a mixture of true girlish perverseness and folly, without considering that she could not escape from my authority by running away from Wigmore Street, she resolved on getting out of the house, and proceeding directly by the stage to her friends the Clarkes, and had really got as far as the length of two streets in her journey, when she was fortunately miss'd, pursued, and overtaken.

Such was the first distinguished exploit of Miss Frederica Susanna Vernon, and if we consider that it was atchieved at the tender age of sixteen we shall have room for the most flattering prognostics of her future renown. I am excessively provoked however at the parade of propriety which prevented Miss Summers from keeping the girl; and it seems so extraordinary a peice of nicety, considering what are my daughter's family connections, that I can only suppose the Lady to be governed by the fear of never getting her money. Be that as it may however, Frederica is returned on my hands, and having now nothing else to employ her, is busy in pursueing the plan of Romance begun at Langford. She is actually falling in love with Reginald De Courcy. To disobey her Mother by refusing an unexceptionable offer is not enough; her affections must likewise be given without her Mother's approbation. I never saw a girl of her age, bid fairer to be the sport of Mankind. Her feelings are tolerably lively, and she is so charmingly artless in their display, as to afford the most reasonable hope of her being ridiculed and despised by every Man who sees her.

Artlessness will never do in Love matters, and that girl is born a simpleton who has it either by nature or affectation. I am not yet certain that Reginald sees what she is about; nor is it of much consequence; she is now an object of indifference to him, she would be one of contempt were he to understand her Emotions. Her beauty is much admired by the Vernons but it has no effect on *him*. She is in high favour with her Aunt altogether—because she is so little like myself of course. She is exactly the companion for Mrs. Vernon, who dearly loves to be first, and to have all the sense and all the wit of the Conversation to herself; Frederica will never eclipse her. When she first came, I was at some pains to prevent her seeing much of her Aunt, but I have since relaxed, as I beleive I may depend on her observing the rules I have laid down for their discourse.

But do not imagine that with all this Lenity, I have for a moment given up my plan of her marriage; No, I am unalterably fixed on that point, though I have not yet quite resolved on the manner of bringing it about. I should not chuse to have the business brought forward here, and canvassed by the wise heads of Mr. and Mrs. Vernon; and I cannot just now afford to go to Town. Miss Frederica therefore must wait a little.

Yours Ever
S. VERNON

LETTER 20

Mrs Vernon to Lady De Courcy

Churchill

We have a very unexpected Guest with us at present, my dear Mother. He arrived yesterday. I heard a carriage at the door as I was sitting with my children while they dined, and supposing I should be wanted left the Nursery soon afterwards and was half way down stairs, when Frederica as pale as ashes came running up, and rushed by me into her own room. I instantly followed, and asked her what was the matter. 'Oh!' cried she, 'he is come, Sir James is come—and what am I to do?' This was no explanation; I begged her to tell me what she meant. At that moment we were interrupted by a knock at the door; it was Reginald, who came by Lady Susan's direction to call Frederica down. 'It is Mr. De Courcy,' said she, colouring violently, 'Mama has sent for me, and I must go.'

We all three went down together, and I saw my Brother examining the terrified face of Frederica with surprise. In the breakfast room we found Lady Susan and a young Man of genteel appearance, whom she introduced to me by the name of Sir James Martin, the very person, as you may remember, whom it was said she had been at pains to detach from Miss Manwaring. But the conquest it seems was not designed for herself, or she has since transferred it to her daughter, for Sir James is now desperately in love with Frederica, and with full encouragement from Mama. The poor girl however I am sure dislikes him; and tho' his person and address are very well, he appears both to Mr. Vernon and me a very weak young Man.

Frederica looked so shy, so confused, when we entered the room, that I felt for her exceedingly. Lady Susan behaved with great attention to her Visitor, and yet I thought I could perceive that she had no particular pleasure in seeing him. Sir James talked a good deal, and made many civil excuses to me for the liberty he had taken in coming to Churchill, mixing more frequent laughter with his discourse than the subject required; said many things over and over again, and told Lady Susan three times that he had seen Mrs. Johnson a few Evenings before. He now and then addressed Frederica, but more frequently her Mother. The poor girl sat all this time without opening her lips; her eyes cast down, and her colour varying every instant, while Reginald observed all that passed, in perfect silence.

At length Lady Susan, weary I believe of her situation, proposed walking, and we left the two Gentlemen together to put on our Pelisses.[5]

As we went upstairs Lady Susan begged permission to attend me for a few moments in my Dressing room, as she was anxious to speak with me in private. I led her thither accordingly, and as soon as the door was closed she said, 'I was never more surprised in my life than by Sir James's arrival, and the suddenness of it requires some apology to *You* my dear Sister, tho' to *me* as a Mother, it is highly flattering. He is so warmly attached to my daughter that he could exist no longer without seeing her. Sir James is a young Man of an amiable disposition, and excellent character; a little too much of the *Rattle*[6] perhaps, but a year or two will rectify *that,* and he is in other respects so very eligible a Match for Frederica that I have always observed his attachment with the greatest pleasure, and am persuaded that you and my Brother will give the alliance your hearty approbation. I have never before mentioned the likelihood of it's taking place to any one, because I thought that while Frederica continued at school, it had better not be known to exist; but now, as I am convinced that Frederica is too old ever to submit to school confinement, and have therefore begun to consider her union with Sir James as not very distant, I had intended within a few days to acquaint yourself and Mr. Vernon with the whole business. I am sure my dear Sister, you will excuse my remaining silent on it so long, and agree with me that such circumstances, while they continue from any cause in suspence, cannot be too cautiously concealed. When you have the happiness of bestowing your sweet little Catherine some years hence on a Man, who in connection and character is alike unexceptionable, you will know what I feel now; tho' Thank Heaven! you cannot have all my reasons for rejoicing in such an Event. Catherine will be amply provided for, and not like my Frederica endebted to a fortunate Establishment for the comforts of Life.'

She concluded by demanding my congratulations. I gave them somewhat awkwardly I beleive; for in fact, the sudden disclosure of so important a matter took from me the power of speaking with any clearness. She thanked me however most affectionately for my kind concern in the welfare of herself and her daughter, and then said,

'I am not apt to deal in professions, my dear Mrs. Vernon, and I never had the convenient talent of affecting sensations foreign to my heart; and therefore I trust you will beleive me when I declare that much as I had heard in your praise before I knew you, I had no idea that I should ever love you as I now do; and I must farther say that your friendship towards me is more particularly gratifying, because I have reason to beleive that some attempts were made to prejudice you against me. I only wish that They—whoever they are—to whom I am endebted for such kind intentions, could see the terms on which we now are together, and understand the real affection we feel for each other! But I will not detain you any longer. God bless you, for your goodness to me and my girl, and continue to you all your present happiness.'

What can one say of such a Woman, my dear Mother?—such earnestness, such solemnity of expression! and yet I cannot help suspecting the truth of everything she said.

As for Reginald, I beleive he does not know what to make of the matter. When Sir James first came, he appeared all astonishment and perplexity. The folly of the young Man, and the confusion of Frederica entirely engrossed him; and tho' a little private discourse with Lady Susan has since had it's effect, he is still hurt I am sure at her allowing of such a Man's attentions to her daughter.

Sir James invited himself with great composure to remain here a few days; hoped we would not think it odd, was aware of it's being very impertinent, but he took the liberty of a relation, and concluded by wishing with a laugh, that he might be really one soon. Even Lady Susan seemed a little disconcerted by this forwardness;—in her heart I am persuaded, she sincerely wishes him gone.

But something must be done for this poor Girl, if her feelings are such as both her Uncle and I beleive them to be. She must not be sacrificed to Policy or Ambition, she must not be even left to suffer from the dread of it. The Girl, whose heart can distinguish Reginald De Courcy, deserves, however he may slight her, a better fate than to be Sir James Martin's wife. As soon as I can get her alone, I will discover the real Truth, but she seems to wish to avoid me. I hope this does not proceed from anything wrong, and that I shall not find out I have thought too well of her. Her behaviour before Sir James certainly

[5] **Pelisse:** a long mantle or cloak of silk, velvet or cloth, often lined with fur, worn by women.

[6] **rattle:** an empty-headed noisy person.

speaks the greatest consciousness[7] and Embarrassment; but I see nothing in it more like Encouragement.

Adieu my dear Madam,

Yrs &c.
CATH. VERNON

— LETTER 21 —

Miss Vernon to Mr. De Courcy

SIR,

I hope you will excuse this liberty, I am forced upon it by the greatest distress, or I should be ashamed to trouble you. I am very miserable about Sir James Martin, and have no other way in the world of helping myself but by writing to you, for I am forbidden ever speaking to my Uncle or Aunt on the subject; and this being the case, I am afraid my applying to you will appear no better than equivocation, and as if I attended only to the letter and not the spirit of Mama's commands, but if *you* do not take my part, and persuade her to break it off, I shall be half-distracted, for I cannot bear him. No human Being but *you* could have any chance of prevailing with her. If you will therefore have the unspeakable great kindness of taking my part with her, and persuading her to send Sir James away, I shall be more obliged to you than it is possible for me to express. I always disliked him from the first, it is not a sudden fancy I assure you Sir, I always thought him silly and impertinent and disagreeable, and now he is grown worse than ever. I would rather work for my bread than marry him. I do not know how to apologise enough for this Letter, I know it is taking so great a liberty, I am aware how dreadfully angry it will make Mama, but I must run the risk. I am Sir, your most Humble Servant

F. S. V.

— LETTER 22 —

Lady Susan to Mrs. Johnson

Churchill

This is insufferable! My dearest friend, I was never so enraged before, and must releive myself by writing to you, who I know will enter into all my feelings. Who should come on Tuesday but Sir James Martin? Guess my astonishment and vexation—for as you well know, I never wished him to be seen at Churchill. What a pity that you should not have known his intentions! Not content with coming, he actually invited himself to remain here a few days. I could have poisoned him; I made the best of it however, and told my story with great success to Mrs. Vernon who, whatever might be her real sentiments, said nothing in opposition to mine. I made a point also of Frederica's behaving civilly to Sir James, and gave her to understand that I was absolutely determined on her marrying him. She said something of her misery, but that was all. I have for some time been more particularly resolved on the Match, from seeing the rapid increase of her affection for Reginald, and from not feeling perfectly secure that a knowledge of *that* affection might not in the end awaken a return. Contemptible as a regard founded only on compassion, must make them both, in my eyes, I felt by no means assured that such might not be the consequence. It is true that Reginald had not in any degree grown cool towards me; but yet he had lately mentioned Frederica spontaneously and unnecessarily, and once had said something in praise of her person.

He was all astonishment at the appearance of my visitor; and at first observed Sir James with an attention which I was pleased to see not unmixed with jealousy; but unluckily it was impossible for me really to torment him, as Sir James tho' extremely gallant to me, very soon made the whole party understand that his heart was devoted to my daughter.

I had no great difficulty in convincing De Courcy when we were alone, that I was perfectly justified, all things considered, in desiring the match; and the whole business seemed most comfortably arranged. They could none of them help perceiving that Sir James was no Solomon,[8] but I had positively forbidden Frederica's complaining to Charles Vernon or his wife, and they had therefore no pretence for Interference, though my impertinent Sister I beleive wanted only opportunity for doing so.

Everything however was going on calmly and quietly; and tho' I counted the hours of Sir James's stay, my mind was entirely satisfied with the posture of affairs. Guess then what I must feel at the sudden disturbance of

[7] **consciousness:** acute self-awareness.

[8] **Solomon:** one who resembles the Old Testament King Solomon, famed for his wisdom and justice.

all my schemes, and that too from a quarter, whence I had least reason to apprehend it. Reginald came this morning into my Dressing room, with a very unusual solemnity of countenance, and after some preface informed me in so many words, that he wished to reason with me on the Impropriety and Unkindness of allowing Sir James Martin to address my Daughter, contrary to *her* inclination. I was all amazement. When I found that he was not to be laughed out of his design, I calmly required an explanation, and begged to know by what he was impelled, and by whom commissioned to reprimand me. He then told me, mixing in his speech a few insolent compliments and illtimed expressions of Tenderness to which I listened with perfect indifference, that my daughter had acquainted him with some circumstances concerning herself, Sir James, and me, which gave him great uneasiness.

In short, I found that she had in the first place actually written to him, to request his interference, and that on receiving her Letter he had conversed with her on the subject of it, in order to understand the particulars and assure himself of her real wishes!

I have not a doubt but that the girl took this opportunity of making downright Love to him; I am convinced of it, from the manner in which he spoke of her. Much good, may such Love do him! I shall ever despise the Man who can be gratified by the Passion, which he never wished to inspire, nor solicited the avowal of. I shall always detest them both. He can have no true regard for me, or he would not have listened to her; And she, with her little rebellious heart and indelicate feelings to throw herself into the protection of a young Man with whom she had scarcely ever exchanged two words before. I am equally confounded at *her* Impudence and *his* Credulity. How dared he believe what she told him in my disfavour! Ought he not to have felt assured that I must have unanswerable Motives for all that I had done! Where was his reliance on my Sense or Goodness then; where the resentment which true Love would have dictated against the person defaming me, that person, too, a Chit,[9] a Child, without Talent or Education, whom he had been always taught to despise?

I was calm for some time, but the greatest degree of Forbearance may be overcome; and I hope I was afterwards sufficiently keen. He endeavoured, long endeavoured to soften my resentment, but that woman is a fool indeed who while insulted by accusation, can be worked on by compliments. At length he left me, as deeply provoked as myself, and he shewed his anger *more.* I was quite cool, but he gave way to the most violent indignation. I may therefore expect it will sooner subside; and perhaps his may be vanished for ever, while mine will be found still fresh and implacable.

He is now shut up in his apartment, whither I heard him go, on leaving mine. How unpleasant, one would think, must his reflections be! But some people's feelings are incomprehensible. I have not yet tranquillized myself enough to see Frederica. *She* shall not soon forget the occurrences of this day. She shall find that she has poured forth her tender Tale of Love in vain, and exposed herself forever to the contempt of the whole world, and the severest Resentment of her injured Mother.

Yrs affec:ly
S. VERNON

— LETTER 23 —

Mrs. Vernon to Lady De Courcy

Churchill

Let me congratulate you, my dearest Mother. The affair which has given us so much anxiety is drawing to a happy conclusion. Our prospect is most delightful; and since matters have now taken so favourable a turn, I am quite sorry that I ever imparted my apprehensions to you; for the pleasure of learning that the danger is over, is perhaps dearly purchased by all that you have previously suffered.

I am so much agitated by Delight that I can scarcely hold a pen, but am determined to send you a few lines by James, that you may have some explanation of what must so greatly astonish you, as that Reginald should be returning to Parklands.

I was sitting about half an hour ago with Sir James in the Breakfast parlour, when my Brother called me out of the room. I instantly saw that something was the matter; his complexion raised, and he spoke with great emotion. You know his eager manner, my dear Madam, when his mind is interested.

'Catherine,' said he, 'I am going home today. I am sorry to leave you, but I must go. It is a great while since I have seen my Father and Mother. I am going to send James forward with my Hunters immediately, if you have

[9] **Chit:** a very young child, animal or plant; a whelp or sprout.

any Letter therefore he can take it. I shall not be at home myself till Wednesday or Thursday, as I shall go through London, where I have business. But before I leave you,' he continued, speaking in a lower voice and with still greater energy, 'I must warn you of one thing. Do not let Frederica Vernon be made unhappy by that Martin. He wants to marry her—her Mother promotes the Match—but *she* cannot endure the idea of it. Be assured that I speak from the fullest conviction of the Truth of what I say. I *know* that Frederica is made wretched by Sir James' continuing here. She is a sweet girl, and deserves a better fate. Send him away immediately. *He* is only a fool—but what her Mother can mean, Heaven only knows! Good bye,' he added shaking my hand with earnestness—'I do not know when you will see me again. But remember what I tell you of Frederica; you *must* make it your business to see justice done her. She is an amiable girl, and has a very superior Mind to what we have ever given her credit for.'

He then left me and ran upstairs. I would not try to stop him, for I knew what his feelings must be; the nature of mine as I listened to him, I need not attempt to describe. For a minute or two I remained in the same spot, over-powered by wonder—of a most agreeable sort indeed; yet it required some consideration to be tranquilly happy.

In about ten minutes after my return to the parlour, Lady Susan entered the room. I concluded of course that she and Reginald had been quarrelling, and looked with anxious curiosity for a confirmation of my beleif in her face. Mistress of Deceit however she appeared perfectly unconcerned, and after chatting on indifferent subjects for a short time, said to me, 'I find from Wilson that we are going to lose Mr. De Courcy. Is it true that he leaves Churchill this morning?' I replied that it was. 'He told us nothing of all this last night,' said she laughing, 'or even this morning at Breakfast. But perhaps he did not know it himself. Young Men are often hasty in their resolutions—and not more sudden in forming, than unsteady in keeping them. I should not be surprised if he were to change his mind at last, and not go.'

She soon afterwards left the room. I trust however my dear Mother, that we have no reason to fear an alteration of his present plan; things have gone too far. They must have quarrelled, and about Frederica too. Her calmness astonishes me. What delight will be yours in seeing him again, in seeing him still worthy your Esteem, still capable of forming your Happiness!

When I next write, I shall be able I hope to tell you that Sir James is gone, Lady Susan vanquished, and Frederica at peace. We have much to do, but it shall be done. I am all impatience to know how this astonishing change was effected. I finish as I began, with the warmest congratulations.

Yrs Ever,
CATH. *VERNON*

— LETTER 24 —

From the same to the same

....

Churchill

Little did I imagine my dear Mother, when I sent off my last letter, that the delightful perturbation of spirits I was then in, would undergo so speedy, so melancholy a reverse! I never can sufficiently regret that I wrote to you at all. Yet who could have foreseen what has happened? My dear Mother, every hope which but two hours ago made me so happy, is vanished. The quarrel between Lady Susan and Reginald is made up, and we are all as we were before. One point only is gained; Sir James Martin is dismissed. What are we now to look forward to? I am indeed disappointed. Reginald was all but gone; his horse was ordered, and almost brought to the door! Who would not have felt safe?

For half an hour I was in momentary expectation of his departure. After I had sent off my Letter to you, I went to Mr. Vernon and sat with him in his room, talking over the whole matter. I then determined to look for Frederica, whom I had not seen since breakfast. I met her on the stairs and saw that she was crying.

'My dear Aunt,' said she, 'he is going, Mr. De Courcy is going, and it is all my fault. I am afraid you will be angry, but indeed I had no idea it would end so.'

'My Love,' replied I, 'do not think it necessary to apologize to me on that account. I shall feel myself under an obligation to anyone who is the means of sending my brother home; because, (recollecting myself) I know my Father wants very much to see him. But what is it that *you* have done to occasion all this?'

She blushed deeply as she answered, 'I was so unhappy about Sir James that I could not help—I have done something very wrong I know—but you have not an idea of the misery I have been in, and Mama had ordered me never to speak to you or my Uncle about it,—and—' 'You therefore spoke to my Brother, to engage *his* interference;' said I, wishing to save her the explanation. 'No—but I wrote to him. I did indeed. I got up this morning before it was light—I was two hours about it—and when my Letter was done, I thought I never should have courage to give it. After breakfast however, as I was going to my own room I met him in the passage, and then as I knew that everything must depend on that moment, I forced myself to give it. He was so good as to take it immediately; I dared not look at him—and ran away directly. I was in such a fright that I could hardly breathe. My dear Aunt, you do not know how miserable I have been.'

'Frederica,' said I, 'you ought to have told *me* all your distresses. You would have found in me a friend always ready to assist you. Do you think that your Uncle and I should not have espoused your cause as warmly as my Brother?'

'Indeed I did not doubt your goodness,' said she, colouring again, 'but I thought that Mr. De Courcy could do anything with my Mother; but I was mistaken; they have had a dreadful quarrel about it, and he is going. Mama will never forgive me, and I shall be worse off than ever.' 'No you shall not,' replied I.—'In such a point as this, your Mother's prohibition ought not to have prevented your speaking to me on the subject. She has no right to make you unhappy, and she shall *not* do it. Your applying however to Reginald can be productive only of Good to all parties. I beleive it is best as it is. Depend upon it that you shall not be made unhappy any longer.'

At that moment, how great was my astonishment at seeing Reginald come out of Lady Susan's Dressing room. My heart misgave me instantly. His confusion on seeing me was very evident. Frederica immediately disappeared. 'Are you going?' said I. 'You will find Mr. Vernon in his own room.' 'No Catherine', replied he. 'I am *not* going. Will you let me speak to you a moment?'

We went into my room. 'I find,' continued he, his confusion increasing as he spoke, 'that I have been acting with my usual foolish impetuosity. I have entirely misunderstood Lady Susan, and was on the point of leaving the house under a false impression of her conduct. There has been some very great mistake—we have been all mistaken I fancy. Frederica does not know her Mother—Lady Susan means nothing but her Good—but Frederica will not make a friend of her. Lady Susan therefore does not always know what will make her daughter happy. Besides *I* could have no right to interfere—Miss Vernon was mistaken in applying to me. In short Catherine, everything has gone wrong—but it is now all happily settled. Lady Susan I beleive wishes to speak to you about it, if you are at leisure.'

'Certainly,' replied I, deeply sighing at the recital of so lame a story. I made no remarks however, for words would have been in vain. Reginald was glad to get away, and I went to Lady Susan; curious indeed to hear her account of it.

'Did not I tell you,' said she with a smile, 'that your Brother would not leave us after all?' 'You did indeed,' replied I very gravely, 'but I flattered myself that you would be mistaken.' 'I should not have hazarded such an opinion,' returned she, 'if it had not at that moment occurred to me, that his resolution of going might be occasioned by a Conversation in which we had been this morning engaged, and which had ended very much to his Dissatisfaction from our not rightly understanding each other's meaning. This idea struck me at the moment, and I instantly determined that an accidental dispute in which I might probably be as much to blame as himself, should not deprive you of your Brother. If you remember, I left the room almost immediately. I was resolved to lose no time in clearing up these mistakes as far as I could. The case was this. Frederica had set herself violently against marrying Sir James'—'And can your Ladyship wonder that she should?' cried I with some warmth. 'Frederica has an excellent Understanding, and Sir James has none.' 'I am at least very far from regretting it, my dear Sister,' said she; 'on the contrary, I am grateful for so favourable a sign of my Daughter's sense. Sir James is certainly under par—(his boyish manners make him appear the worse)—and had Frederica possessed the penetration, the abilities, which I could have wished in my daughter, or had I even known her to possess so much as she does, I should not have been anxious for the match.' 'It is odd that you alone should be ignorant of your Daughter's sense.' 'Frederica never does justice to herself; her manners are shy and childish. She is besides afraid of me; she scarcely loves me. During her poor Father's life she was a spoilt child; the severity which it has since been necessary for me to shew, has entirely alienated her affection; neither has she any of that Brilliancy of Intellect, that Genius, or Vigour of Mind which will force itself forward.' 'Say rather that she has been unfortunate in her Education.' 'Heaven knows my dearest Mrs. Vernon, how fully I am aware of *that*; but I would wish to forget every circumstance that might throw blame on the memory of one, whose name is sacred with me.'

Here she pretended to cry. I was out of patience with her. 'But what,' said I, 'was your Ladyship going to tell me about your disagreement with my Brother?' 'It originated in an action of my Daughter's, which equally marks her want of Judgement, and the unfortunate Dread of me I have been mentioning. She wrote to Mr. De Courcy.' 'I know she did. You had forbidden her speaking to

Mr. Vernon or to me on the cause of her distress; what could she do therefore but apply to my Brother?' 'Good God!'—she exclaimed, 'what an opinion must you have of me! Can you possibly suppose that I was aware of her unhappiness? that it was my object to make my own child miserable, and that I had forbidden her speaking to you on the subject from a fear of your interrupting the Diabolical scheme? Do you think me destitute of every honest, every natural feeling? Am I capable of consigning her to everlasting Misery, whose welfare it is my first Earthly Duty to promote?' 'The idea is horrible. What then was your intention when you insisted on her silence?' 'Of what use my dear Sister, could be any application to you, however the affair might stand? Why should I subject you to entreaties, which I refused to attend to myself? Neither for your sake, for hers, nor for my own, could such a thing be desireable. Where my own resolution was taken, I could not wish for the interference, however friendly, of another person. I was mistaken, it is true, but I beleived myself to be right.' 'But what was this mistake, to which your Ladyship so often alludes? From whence arose so astonishing a misapprehension of your Daughter's feelings? Did not you know that she disliked Sir James?' 'I knew that he was not absolutely the Man she would have chosen. But I was persuaded that her objections to him did not arise from any perception of his Deficiency. You must not question me however my dear Sister, too minutely on this point'—continued she, taking me affectionately by the hand. 'I honestly own that there is something to conceal. Frederica makes me very unhappy. Her applying to Mr. De Courcy hurt me particularly.' 'What is it that you mean to infer' said I, 'by this appearance of mystery? If you think your daughter at all attached to Reginald, her objecting to Sir James could not less deserve to be attended to, than if the cause of her objecting had been a consciousness of his folly. And why should your Ladyship at any rate quarrel with my brother for an interference which you must know, it was not in his nature to refuse, when urged in such a manner?'

'His disposition you know is warm, and he came to expostulate with me, his compassion all alive for this ill-used Girl, this Heroine in distress! We misunderstood each other. He beleived me more to blame than I really was; I considered his interference as less excusable than I now find it. I have a real regard for him, and was beyond expression mortified to find it as I thought so ill bestowed. We were both warm, and of course both to blame. His resolution of leaving Churchill is consistent with his general eagerness; when I understood his intention however, and at the same time began to think that we had perhaps been equally mistaken in each other's meaning, I resolved to have an explanation before it were too late. For any Member of your Family I must always feel a degree of affection, and I own it would have sensibly hurt me, if my acquaintance with Mr. De Courcy had ended so gloomily. I have now only to say farther, that as I am convinced of Frederica's having a reasonable dislike to Sir James, I shall instantly inform him that he must give up all hope of her. I reproach myself for having ever, tho' so innocently, made her unhappy on that score. She shall have all the retribution in my power to make; if she value her own happiness as much as I do, if she judge wisely and command herself as she ought, she may now be easy. Escuse me, my dearest Sister, for thus trespassing on your time, but I owed it to my own Character; and after this explanation I trust I am in no danger of sinking in your opinion.'

I could have said 'Not much indeed,'—but I left her almost in silence. It was the greatest stretch of Forbearance I could practise. I could not have stopped myself, had I begun. Her assurance, her Deceit—but I will not allow myself to dwell on them; they will strike you sufficiently. My heart sickens within me.

As soon as I was tolerably composed, I returned to the Parlour. Sir James's carriage was at the door, and he, merry as usual, soon afterwards took his leave. How easily does her Ladyship encourage, or dismiss a Lover!

In spite of this release, Frederica still looks unhappy, still fearful perhaps of her Mother's anger, and tho' dreading my Brother's departure jealous, it may be, of his staying. I see how closely she observes him and Lady Susan. Poor Girl, I have now no hope for her. There is not a chance of her affection being returned. He thinks very differently of her, from what he used to do, he does her some justice, but his reconciliation with her Mother precludes every dearer hope.

Prepare my dear Madam, for the worst. The probability of their marrying is surely heightened. He is more securely her's than ever. When that wretched Event takes place, Frederica must wholly belong to us.

I am thankful that my last Letter will precede this by so little, as every moment that you can be saved from feeling a Joy which leads only to disappointment is of consequence.

Yrs Ever,
CATH. VERNON

— LETTER 25 —

Lady Susan to Mrs. Johnson

Churchill

I call on you dear Alicia, for congratulations. I am again myself; — gay and triumphant. When I wrote to you the other day, I was in truth in high irritation, and with ample cause. Nay, I know not whether I ought to be quite tranquil now, for I have had more trouble in restoring peace than I ever intended to submit to. This Reginald has a proud spirit of his own! — a spirit too, resulting from a fancied sense of superior Integrity which is peculiarly insolent. I shall not easily forgive him I assure you. He was actually on the point of leaving Churchill! I had scarcely concluded my last, when Wilson brought me word of it. I found therefore that something must be done, for I did not chuse to have my character at the mercy of a Man whose passions were so violent and resentful. It would have been trifling with my reputation, to allow of his departing with such an impression in my disfavour; in this light, condescension was necessary.

I sent Wilson to say that I desired to speak with him before he went. He came immediately. The angry emotions which had marked every feature when we last parted, were partially subdued. He seemed astonished at the summons, and looked as if half wishing and half fearing to be softened by what I might say.

If my Countenance expressed what I aimed at, it was composed and dignified — and yet with a degree of pensiveness which might convince him that I was not quite happy. 'I beg your pardon Sir, for the liberty I have taken in sending to you,' said I; 'but as I have just learnt your intention of leaving this place to-day, I feel it my duty to entreat that you will not on my account shorten your visit here, even an hour. I am perfectly aware that after what has passed between us, it would ill suit the feelings of either to remain longer in the same house. So very great, so total a change from the intimacy of Friendship, must render any future intercourse the severest punishment; and your resolution of quitting Churchill is undoubtedly in unison with our situation and with those lively feelings which I know you to possess. But at the same time, it is not for me to suffer such a sacrifice, as it must be, to leave Relations to whom you are so much attached and are so dear. My remaining here cannot give that pleasure to Mr. and Mrs. Vernon which your society must; and my visit has already perhaps been too long. My removal therefore, which must at any rate take place soon, may with perfect convenience be hastened; and I make it my particular request that I may not in any way be instrumental in separating a family so affectionately attached to each other. Where *I* go is of no consequence to anyone; of very little to myself; but *you* are of importance to all your connections.' Here I concluded, and I hope you will be satisfied with my speech. It's effect on Reginald justifies some portion of vanity, for it was no less favourable than instantaneous. Oh! how delightful it was, to watch the variations of his Countenance while I spoke, to see the struggle between returning Tenderness and the remains of Displeasure. There is something agreable in feelings so easily worked on. Not that I would envy him their possession, nor would for the world have such myself, but they are very convenient when one wishes to influence the passions of another. And yet this Reginald, whom a very few words from me softened at once into the utmost submission, and rendered more tractable, more attached, more devoted than ever, would have left me in the first angry swelling of his proud heart, without deigning to seek an explanation!

Humbled as he now is, I cannot forgive him such an instance of Pride; and am doubtful whether I ought not to punish him, by dismissing him at once after this our reconciliation, or by marrying and teizing him for ever. But these measures are each too violent to be adopted without some deliberation. At present my Thoughts are fluctuating between various schemes. I have many things to compass. I must punish Frederica, and pretty severely too, for her application to Reginald; I must punish him for receiving it so favourably, and for the rest of his conduct. I must torment my Sister-in-law for the insolent triumph of her Look and Manner since Sir James has been dismissed — for in reconciling Reginald to me, I was not able to save that ill-fated young Man — and I must make myself amends for the humiliations to which I have stooped within these few days. To effect all this I have various plans. I have also an idea of being soon in Town, and whatever may be my determination as to the rest, I shall probably put *that* project in execution — for London will be always the fairest field of action, however my veiws may be directed, and at any rate, I shall there be rewarded by your society and a little Dissipation for a ten weeks' penance at Churchill.

I believe I owe it to my own Character, to complete the match between my daughter and Sir James, after having so long intended it. Let me know your opinion on this point. Flexibility of Mind, a Disposition easily biassed[10] by others, is an attribute which you know I am not very desirous of obtaining; nor has Frederica any claim to the indulgence of her whims, at the expense of her Mother's inclination. Her idle Love for Reginald too; it is surely my duty to discourage such romantic nonsense. All things considered therefore, it seems encumbent on me to take her to Town, and marry her immediately to Sir James.

When my own will is effected, contrary to his, I shall have some credit in being on good terms with Reginald, which at present in fact I have not, for tho' he is still in my power, I have given up the very article by which our quarrel was produced, and at best, the honour of victory is doubtful.

Send me your opinion on all these matters, my dear Alicia, and let me know whether you can get Lodgings to suit me within a short distance of you.

Yr most attached
S. VERNON

— LETTER 26 —

Mrs. Johnson to Lady Susan

....

Edward Street

I am gratified by your reference, and this is my advice; that you come to Town yourself without loss of time, but that you leave Frederica behind. It would surely be much more to the purpose to get yourself well established by marrying Mr. De Courcy, than to irritate him and the rest of his family, by making her marry Sir James. You should think more of yourself, and less of your Daughter. She is not of a disposition to do you credit in the World, and seems precisely in her proper place, at Churchill with the Vernons; but *you* are fitted for Society, and it is shameful to have you exiled from it. Leave Frederica therefore to punish herself for the plague she has given you, by indulging that romantic tender-heartedness which will always ensure her misery enough; and come yourself to Town, as soon as you can.

I have another reason for urging this.

Manwaring came to town last week, and has contrived, in spite of Mr. Johnson, to make opportunities of seeing me. He is absolutely miserable about you, and jealous to such a degree of De Courcy, that it would be highly unadvisable for them to meet at present; and yet if you do not allow him to see you here, I cannot answer for his not committing some great imprudence — such as going to Churchill for instance, which would be dreadful. Besides, if you take my advice, and resolve to marry De Courcy, it will be indispensably necessary for you to get Manwaring out of the way, and you only can have influence enough to send him back to his wife.

I have still another motive for your coming. Mr. Johnson leaves London next Tuesday. He is going for his health to Bath, where if the waters are favourable to his constitution and my wishes, he will be laid up with the gout many weeks. During his absence we shall be able to chuse our own society, and have true enjoyment. I would ask you to Edward Street but that he once forced from me a kind of promise never to invite you to my house. Nothing but my being in the utmost distress for Money, could have extorted it from me. I can get you however a very nice Drawingroom-apartment in Upper Seymour Street, and we may be always together, there or here, for I consider my promise to Mr. Johnson as comprehending only (at least in his absence) your not sleeping in the House.

Poor Manwaring gives me such histories of his wife's jealousy! — Silly Woman, to expect constancy from so charming a Man! But she was always silly; intolerably so, in marrying him at all. She, the Heiress of a large Fortune, he without a shilling! *One* title I know she might have had, besides Baronets. Her folly in forming the connection was so great, that tho' Mr Johnson was her Guardian and I do not in general share his feelings, I never can forgive her.

Adeiu, *Yours,* ALICIA.

— LETTER 27 —

Mrs. Vernon to Lady De Courcy

....

Churchill

This Letter my dear Mother, will be brought you by Reginald. His long visit is about to be concluded at last, but I fear the separation takes place too late to do us any good. *She* is going to Town, to see her particular friend, Mrs. Johnson. It was at first her intention that Frederica should accompany her for the benefit of Masters, but we overruled her there. Frederica was wretched in the idea of going, and I could not bear to have her at the mercy of her Mother. Not all the Masters in London could compensate

[10] **biassed:** influenced.

for the ruin of her comfort. I should have feared too for her health, and for everything in short but her Principles; *there* I beleive she is not to be injured, even by her Mother, or all her Mother's friends; but with those friends (a very bad set I doubt not) she must have mixed, or have been left in total solitude, and I can hardly tell which would have been worse for her. If she is with her Mother moreover, she must alas! in all probability, be with Reginald—and that would be the greatest evil of all.

Here we shall in time be at peace. Our regular employments, our Books and conversation, with Exercise, the Children, and every domestic pleasure in my power to procure her, will, I trust, gradually overcome this youthful attachment. I should not have a doubt of it, were she slighted for any other woman in the world, than her own Mother.

How long Lady Susan will be in Town, or whether she returns here again, I know not. I could not be cordial in my invitation; but if she chuses to come, no want of cordiality on my part will keep her away.

I could not help asking Reginald if he intended being in Town this winter, as soon as I found that her Ladyship's steps would be bent thither; and tho' he professed himself quite undetermined, there was a something in his Look and voice as he spoke, which contradicted his words. I have done with Lamentation. I look upon the Event as so far decided, that I resign myself to it in despair. If he leaves you soon for London, everything will be concluded.

Yours affec:ly
CATH. VERNON

— LETTER 28 —

Mrs. Johnson to Lady Susan.

Edward Street

MY DEAREST FRIEND,

I write in the greatest distress; the most unfortunate event has just taken place. Mr. Johnson has hit on the most effectual manner of plaguing us all. He had heard I imagine by some means or other, that you were soon to be in London, and immediately contrived to have such an attack of the Gout, as must at least delay his journey to Bath, if not wholly prevent it. I am persuaded the Gout is brought on, or kept off at pleasure; it was the same, when I wanted to join the Hamiltons to the Lakes; and three years ago when *I* had a fancy for Bath, nothing could induce him to have a Gouty symptom.

I have received yours, and have engaged the Lodgings in consequence. I am pleased to find that my Letter had so much effect on you, and that De Courcy is certainly your own. Let me hear from you as soon as you arrive, and in particular tell me what you mean to do with Manwaring. It is impossible to say when I shall be able to see you. My confinement must be great. It is such an abominable trick, to be ill here, instead of at Bath, that I can scarcely command myself at all. At Bath, his old Aunts would have nursed him, but here it all falls upon me—and he bears pain with such patience that I have not the common excuse for losing my temper.

Yrs Ever,
ALICIA

— LETTER 29 —

Lady Susan to Mrs. Johnson

Upper Seymour Street

MY DEAR ALICIA

There needed not this last fit of the Gout to make me detest Mr Johnson; but now the extent of my aversion is not to be estimated. To have you confined, a Nurse in his apartment! My dear Alicia, of what a mistake were you guilty in marrying a Man of his age!—just old enough to be formal, ungovernable and to have the Gout—too old to be agreable, and too young to die.

I arrived last night about five, and had scarcely swallowed my dinner when Manwaring made his appearance. I will not dissemble what real pleasure his sight afforded me, nor how strongly I felt the contrast between his person and manners, and those of Reginald, to the infinite disadvantage of the latter. For an hour or two, I was even stagger'd in my resolution of marrying him—and though this was too idle and nonsensical an idea to remain long on my mind, I do not feel very eager for the conclusion of my Marriage, or look forward with much impatience to the time when Reginald according to our agreement is to be in Town. I shall probably put off his arrival, under some pretence or other. He must not come till Manwaring is gone.

I am still doubtful at times, as to Marriage. If the old Man would die, I might not hesitate; but a state of dependance on the caprice of Sir Reginald, will not suit the freedom of my spirit; and if I resolve to wait for that event, I shall have excuse enough at present, in having been scarcely ten months a Widow.

I have not given Manwaring any hint of my intention—or allowed him to consider my acquaintance with Reginald as more than the commonest flirtation; and he is tolerably appeased. Adeiu till we meet. I am enchanted with my Lodgings.

Yrs Ever,
S. VERNON

— LETTER 30 —

Lady Susan to Mr. De Courcy

....

Upper Seymour Street

I have received your Letter; and tho' I do not attempt to conceal that I am gratified by your impatience for the hour of meeting, I yet feel myself under the necessity of delaying that hour beyond the time originally fixed. Do not think me unkind for such an exercise of my power, or accuse me of Instability, without first hearing my reasons. In the course of my journey from Churchill, I had ample leisure for reflection on the present state of our affairs, and every review has served to convince me that they require a delicacy and cautiousness of conduct, to which we have hitherto been too little attentive. We have been hurried on by our feelings to a degree of Precipitance which ill accords with the claims of our Friends, or the opinion of the World. We have been unguarded in forming this hasty Engagement; but we must not complete the imprudence by ratifying it, while there is so much reason to fear the Connection would be opposed by those Friends on whom you depend.

It is not for us to blame any expectation on your Father's side of your marrying to advantage; where possessions are so extensive as those of your Family, the wish of increasing them, if not strictly reasonable, is too common to excite surprise or resentment. He has a right to require a woman of fortune in his daughter-in-law, and I am sometimes quarreling with myself for suffering you to form a connection so imprudent. But the influence of reason is often acknowledged too late by those who feel like me.

I have now been but a few months a widow; and however little endebted to my Husband's memory for any happiness derived from him during an Union of some years, I cannot forget that the indelicacy of so early a second marriage, must subject me to the censure of the World, and incur what would be still more insupportable, the displeasure of Mr. Vernon. I might perhaps harden myself in time against the injustice of general reproach; but the loss of *his* valued Esteem, I am as you well know, ill fitted to endure; and when to this, may be added the consciousness of having injured you with your Family, how am I to support myself. With feelings so poignant as mine, the conviction of having divided the son from his Parents, would make me, even with *you*, the most miserable of Beings.

It will surely therefore be advisable to delay our Union, to delay it till appearances are more promising, till affairs have taken a more favourable turn. To assist us in such a resolution, I feel that absence will be necessary. We must not meet. Cruel as this sentence may appear, the necessity of pronouncing it, which can alone reconcile it to myself, will be evident to you when you have considered our situation in the light in which I have found myself imperiously obliged to place it. You may be, you must be well assured that nothing but the strongest conviction of Duty, could induce me to wound my own feelings by urging a lengthened separation; and of Insensibility to yours, you will hardly suspect me. Again therefore I say that we ought not, we must not yet meet. By a removal for some Months from each other, we shall tranquillize the sisterly fears of Mrs. Vernon, who, accustomed herself to the enjoyment of riches, considers Fortune as necessary every where, and whose Sensibilities are not of a nature to comprehend ours.

Let me hear from you soon, very soon. Tell me that you submit to my Arguments, and do not reproach me for using such. I cannot bear reproaches. My spirits are not so high as to need being repressed. I must endeavour to seek amusement abroad, and fortunately many of my Friends are in town—among them, the Manwarings. You know how sincerely I regard both Husband and wife.

I am ever, Faithfully Yours
S. VERNON

— LETTER 31 —

Lady Susan to Mrs. Johnson

....

Upper Seymour Street

MY DEAR FRIEND,

That tormenting creature Reginald is here. My Letter, which was intended to keep him longer in the Country, has hastened him to Town. Much as I wish him away however, I cannot help being pleased with such a proof of attachment. He is devoted to me, heart and soul. He will carry this note himself, which is to serve as an Introduction to you, with whom he longs to be acquainted. Allow him to spend the Evening with you, that I may be in no danger of his returning here. I have told him that I am not quite well, and must be alone—and should he call again there might be confusion, for it is impossible to be sure of servants. Keep him therefore I entreat you in Edward Street. You will not find him a heavy companion, and I allow you to flirt with him as much as you like. At the same time do not forget my real interest; say all that you can to convince him that I shall be quite wretched if he remain here; you know my reasons—Propriety and so forth. I would urge them more myself, but that I am impatient to be rid of him, as Manwaring comes within half an hour. Adeiu.

S. V.

— LETTER 32 —

Mrs. Johnson to Lady Susan

Edward Street

My dear Creature,

I am in agonies, and know not what to do, nor what *you* can do. Mr. De Courcy arrived, just when he should not. Mrs. Manwaring had that instant entered the House, and forced herself into her Guardian's presence, tho' I did not know a syllable of it till afterwards, for I was out when both she and Reginald came, or I would have sent him away at all events; but *she* was shut up with Mr. Johnson, while *he* waited in the Drawing room for me. She arrived yesterday in pursuit of her Husband; but perhaps you know this already from himself. She came to this house to entreat my Husband's interference, and before I could be aware of it, everything that you could wish to be concealed, was known to him; and unluckily she had wormed out of Manwaring's servant that he had visited you every day since your being in Town, and had just watched him to your door herself! What could I do? Facts are such horrid things! All is by this time known to De Courcy, who is now alone with Mr. Johnson. Do not accuse me; indeed, it was impossible to prevent it. Mr. Johnson has for some time suspected De Courcy of intending to marry you, and would speak with him alone, as soon as he knew him to be in the House.

That detestable Mrs. Manwaring, who for your comfort, has fretted herself thinner and uglier than ever, is still here, and they have been all closeted together. What can be done? If Manwaring is now with you, he had better be gone. At any rate I hope he will plague his wife more than ever. With anxious wishes,

Yrs faithfully
Alicia

— LETTER 33 —

Lady Susan to Mrs. Johnson

Upper Seymour Street

This Eclaircissement[11] is rather provoking. How unlucky that you should have been from home! I thought myself sure of you at seven. I am undismayed however. Do not torment yourself with fears on my account. Depend upon it, I can make my own story good with Reginald. Manwaring is just gone; he brought me the news of his wife's arrival. Silly Woman! what does she expect by such Manoeuvres? Yet, I wish she had staid quietly at Langford.

Reginald will be a little enraged at first, but by Tomorrow's Dinner, everything will be well again.

Adeiu
S. V.

— LETTER 34 —

Mr. De Courcy to Lady Susan

Hotel

I write only to bid you Farewell. The spell is removed. I see you as you are. Since we parted yesterday, I have received from indisputable authority, such an history of you as must bring the most mortifying conviction of the Imposition I have been under, and the absolute necessity of an immediate and eternal separation from you. You cannot doubt to what I allude; Langford—Langford—that word will be sufficient. I received my information in Mr. Johnson's house, from Mrs. Manwaring herself.

[11] **Eclaircissement:** French: a clearing up of what is unknown or misunderstood, an explanation.

You know how I have loved you, you can intimately judge of my present feelings; but I am not so weak as to find indulgence in describing them to a woman who will glory in having excited their anguish, but whose affection they have never been able to gain.

R. DE COURCY

— LETTER 35 —

Lady Susan to Mr. De Courcy

Upper Seymour Street

I will not attempt to describe my astonishment on reading the note, this moment received from you. I am bewilder'd in my endeavours to form some rational conjecture of what Mrs. Manwaring can have told you, to occasion so extraordinary a change in your sentiments. Have I not explained everything to you with respect to myself which could bear a doubtful meaning, and which the ill-nature of the World had interpreted to my Discredit? What can you *now* have heard to stagger your Esteem for me? Have I ever had a concealment from you? Reginald, you agitate me beyond expression. I cannot suppose that the old story of Mrs. Manwaring's jealousy can be revived again, or at least, be *listened* to again. Come to me immediately, and explain what is at present absolutely incomprehensible. Believe me, the single word of *Langford* is not of such potent intelligence, as to supersede the necessity of more. If we *are* to part, it will at least be handsome to take your personal Leave. But I have little heart to jest; in truth, I am serious enough—for to be sunk, tho' but an hour, in your opinion, is an humiliation to which I know not how to submit. I shall count every moment till your arrival.

S. V.

— LETTER 36 —

Mr. De Courcy to Lady Susan

Hotel

Why would you write to me? Why do you require particulars? But since it must be so, I am obliged to declare that all the accounts of your misconduct during the life and since the death of Mr. Vernon which had reached me in common with the World in general, and gained my entire beleif before I saw you, but which you by the exertion of your perverted Abilities had made me resolve to disallow, have been unanswerably proved to me. Nay, more, I am assured that a connection, of which I had never before entertained a thought, has for some time existed, and still continues to exist between you and the Man, whose family you robbed of it's Peace, in return for the hospitality with which you were received into it! That you have corresponded with him ever since your leaving Langford—not with his wife—but with him—and he now visits you every day. Can you, dare you deny it? and all this at the time when I was an encouraged, an accepted Lover! From what have I not escaped! I have only to be grateful. Far from me be all complaint, and every sigh of regret. My own Folly has endangered me, my Preservation I owe to the kindness, the Integrity of another. But the unfortunate Mrs. Manwaring, whose agonies while she related the past, seemed to threaten her reason—how is *she* to be consoled?

After such a discovery as this, you will scarcely affect farther wonder at my meaning in bidding you Adeiu. My Understanding is at length restored, and teaches me no less to abhor the Artifices which had subdued me, than to despise myself for the weakness, on which their strength was founded.

R. DE COURCY

— LETTER 37 —

Lady Susan to Mr. De Courcy

Upper Seymour Street

I am satisfied—and will trouble you no more when these few Lines are dismissed. The Engagement which you were eager to form a fortnight ago, is no longer compatible with your veiws, and I rejoice to find that the prudent advice of your Parents has not been given in vain. Your restoration to Peace will, I doubt not, speedily follow this act of filial Obedience, and I flatter myself with the hope of surviving *my* share in this disappointment.

S. V.

— LETTER 38 —

Mrs. Johnson to Lady Susan

Edward Street

I am greived, tho' I cannot be astonished at your rupture with Mr. De Courcy; he had just informed Mr. Johnson of it by letter. He leaves London he says to-day. Be assured that I partake in all your feelings, and do not be angry if I say that our intercourse even by Letter must soon be given up. It makes me miserable—but Mr. Johnson vows that if I persist in the connection, he will settle in the country for the rest of his life—and you know it is impossible to submit to such an extremity while any other alternative remains.

You have heard of course that the Manwarings are to part; I am afraid Mrs. M. will come home to us again. But she is still so fond of her Husband and frets so much about him that perhaps she may not live long.

Miss Manwaring is just come to Town to be with her Aunt, and they say, that she declares she will have Sir James Martin before she leaves London again. If I were you, I would certainly get him myself. I had almost forgot to give you my opinion of De Courcy, I am really delighted with him, he is full as handsome I think as Manwaring, and with such an open, goodhumoured Countenance that one cannot help loving him at first sight. Mr. Johnson and he are the greatest friends in the World. Adeiu, my dearest Susan. I wish matters did not go so perversely. That unlucky visit to Langford! But I dare say you did all for the best, and there is no defying Destiny.

Yr sincerely attached
Alicia

— LETTER 39 —

Lady Susan to Mrs. Johnson

Upper Seymour Street

My dear Alicia

I yeild to the necessity which parts us. Under such circumstances you could not act otherwise. Our friendship cannot be impaired by it; and in happier times, when your situation is as independant as mine, it will unite us again in the same Intimacy as ever. For this I shall impatiently wait; and meanwhile can safely assure you that I never was more at ease, or better satisfied with myself and everything about me, than at the present hour. Your Husband I abhor—Reginald I despise—and I am secure of never seeing either again. Have I not reason to rejoice? Manwaring is more devoted to me than ever; and were he at liberty, I doubt if I could resist even Matrimony offered by *him*. This Event, if his wife live with you, it may be in your power to hasten. The violence of her feelings, which must wear her out, may be easily kept in irritation. I rely on your friendship for this. I am now satisfied that I never could have brought myself to marry Reginald; and am equally determined that Frederica never *shall*. To-morrow I shall fetch her from Churchill, and let Maria Manwaring tremble for the consequence. Frederica shall be Sir James's wife before she quits my house. *She* may whimper, and the Vernons may storm; I regard them not. I am tired of submitting my will to the Caprices of others—of resigning my own Judgement in deference to those, to whom I owe no Duty, and for whom I feel no respect. I have given up too much—have been too easily worked on; but Frederica shall now find the difference.

Adeiu, dearest of Friends. May the next Gouty Attack be more favourable. And may you always regard me as unalterably yours

S. Vernon

— LETTER 40 —

Lady De Courcy to Mrs. Vernon

Parklands

My dear Catherine

I have charming news for you, and if I had not sent off my Letter this morning, you might have been spared the vexation of knowing of Reginald's being gone to Town, for he is returned, Reginald is returned, not to ask our consent to his marrying Lady Susan, but to tell us that they are parted forever! He has been only an hour in the House, and I have not been able to learn particulars, for he is so very low, that I have not the heart to ask questions; but I hope we shall soon know all. This is the most joyful hour he has ever given us, since the day of his birth. Nothing is wanting but to have you here, and it is our particular wish and entreaty that you would come to us as soon as you can. You have owed us a visit many long weeks. I hope nothing will make it inconvenient to Mr. Vernon, and pray bring all my Grand Children, and your dear Neice is included of course; I long to see her. It has been a sad heavy winter hitherto, without Reginald, and seeing nobody from Churchill; I never found the season so dreary before, but this happy meeting will make us young again. Frederica runs much in my thoughts, and when Reginald has recovered his usual good spirits, (as I trust he soon will) we will try to rob him of his heart once more, and I am full of hopes of seeing their hands joined at no great distance.

Yr affec: Mother
C. De Courcy

— LETTER 41 —

Mrs. Vernon to Lady De Courcy

Churchill

My dear Madam

Your Letter has surprised me beyond measure. Can it be true that they are really separated—and for ever? I should be overjoyed if I dared depend on it, but after all that I have seen, how can one be secure? And Reginald really with you! My surprise is the greater, because on Wednesday, the very day of his coming to Parklands, we had a most unexpected and unwelcome visit from Lady Susan, looking all chearfulness and good humour, and seeming more as if she were to marry him when she got back to Town, than as if parted from him for ever. She staid nearly two hours, was as affectionate and agreable as ever, and not a syllable, not a hint was dropped of any Disagreement or coolness between them. I asked her whether she had seen my Brother since his arrival in Town—not as you may suppose with any doubt of the fact—but merely to see how she looked. She immediately answered without any embarrassment that he had been kind enough to call on her on Monday, but she believed he had already returned home—which I was very far from crediting.

Your kind invitation is accepted by us with pleasure, and on Thursday next, we and our little ones will be with you. Pray Heaven! Reginald may not be in Town again by that time!

I wish we could bring dear Frederica too, but I am sorry to add that her Mother's errand hither was to fetch her away; and miserable as it made the poor Girl, it was impossible to detain her. I was thoroughly unwilling to let her go, and so was her Uncle; and all that could be urged, we *did* urge. But Lady Susan declared that as she was now about to fix herself in Town for several Months, she could not be easy if her Daughter were not with her, for Masters &c. Her Manner, to be sure, was very kind and proper—and Mr. Vernon beleives that Frederica will now be treated with affection. I wish I could think so too!

The poor girl's heart was almost broke at taking leave of us. I charged her to write to me very often, and to remember that if she were in any distress, we should be always her friends. I took care to see her alone, that I might say all this, and I hope made her a little more comfortable. But I shall not be easy till I can go to Town and judge of her situation myself.

I wish there were a better prospect than now appears, of the Match, which the conclusion of your Letter declares your expectation of. At present it is not very likely.

Yrs &c.
Cath. Vernon

— CONCLUSION —

This Correspondence, by a meeting between some of the Parties and a separation between the others, could not, to the great detriment of the Post office Revenue, be continued longer. Very little assistance to the State could be derived from the Epistolary Intercourse of Mrs. Vernon and her neice, for the former soon perceived by the stile of Frederica's Letters, that they were written under her Mother's inspection, and therefore deferring all particular enquiry till she could make it personally in Town, ceased writing minutely or often.

Having learnt enough in the meanwhile from her openhearted Brother, of what had passed between him and Lady Susan to sink the latter lower than ever in her opinion, she was proportionably more anxious to get Frederica removed from such a Mother, and placed under her own care; and tho' with little hope of success, was resolved to leave nothing unattempted that might offer a chance of obtaining her Sister-in-law's consent to it. Her anxiety on the subject made her press for an early visit to London; and Mr. Vernon who, as it must have already appeared, lived only to do whatever he was desired, soon found some accomodating Business to call him thither. With a heart full of the Matter, Mrs. Vernon waited on Lady Susan, shortly after her arrival in Town; and she was met with such an easy and chearful affection as made her almost turn from her with horror. No remembrance of

Reginald, no consciousness of Guilt, gave one look of embarrassment. She was in excellent spirits, and seemed eager to shew at once, by every possible attention to her Brother and Sister, her sense of their kindness, and her pleasure in their society.

Frederica was no more altered than Lady Susan; the same restrained Manners, the same timid Look in the presence of her Mother as heretofore, assured her Aunt of her situation's being uncomfortable, and confirmed her in the plan of altering it. No unkindness however on the part of Lady Susan appeared. Persecution on the subject of Sir James was entirely at an end—his name merely mentioned to say that he was not in London; and in all her conversation she was solicitous only for the welfare and improvement of her Daughter, acknowledging in terms of grateful delight that Frederica was now growing every day more and more what a Parent could desire.

Mrs. Vernon surprised and incredulous, knew not what to suspect, and without any change in her own veiws, only feared greater difficulty in accomplishing them. The first hope of anything better was derived from Lady Susan's asking her whether she thought Frederica looked quite as well as she had done at Churchill, as she must confess herself to have sometimes an anxious doubt of London's perfectly agreeing with her.

Mrs. Vernon encouraging the doubt, directly proposed her Neice's returning with them into the country. Lady Susan was unable to express her sense of such kindness; yet knew not from a variety of reasons how to part with her Daughter; and as, though her own plans were not yet wholly fixed, she trusted it would ere long be in her power to take Frederica into the country herself, concluded by declining entirely to profit by such unexampled attention. Mrs. Vernon however persevered in the offer of it, and though Lady Susan continued to resist, her resistance in the course of a few days seemed somewhat less formidable.

The lucky alarm of an Influenza, decided what might not have been decided quite so soon. Lady Susan's maternal fears were then too much awakened for her to think of anything but Frederica's removal from the risk of infection. Above all Disorders in the World, she most dreaded the influenza for her daughter's constitution. Frederica returned to Churchill with her Uncle and Aunt, and three weeks afterwards Lady Susan announced her being married to Sir James Martin.

Mrs. Vernon was then convinced of what she had only suspected before, that she might have spared herself all the trouble of urging a removal, which Lady Susan had doubtless resolved on from the first. Frederica's visit was nominally for six weeks; but her Mother, though inviting her to return in one or two affectionate Letters, was very ready to oblige the whole Party by consenting to a prolongation of her stay, and in the course of two months ceased to write of her absence, and in the course of two more, to write to her at all.

Frederica was therefore fixed in the family of her Uncle and Aunt, till such time as Reginald De Courcy could be talked, flattered and finessed[12] into an affection for her—which, allowing leisure for the conquest of his attachment to her Mother, for his abjuring all future attachments and detesting the Sex, might be reasonably looked for in the course of a Twelvemonth. Three Months might have done it in general, but Reginald's feelings were no less lasting than lively.

Whether Lady Susan was, or was not happy in her second Choice—I do not see how it can ever be ascertained—for who would take her assurance of it, on either side of the question? The World must judge from Probability. She had nothing against her, but her Husband, and her Conscience.

Sir James may seem to have drawn an harder Lot than mere Folly merited. I leave him therefore to all the Pity that anybody can give him. For myself, I confess that *I* can pity only Miss Manwaring, who coming to Town and putting herself to an expence in Cloathes, which impoverished her for two years, on purpose to secure him, was defrauded of her due by a Woman ten years older than herself.

---

[12] **finessed:** skillfully maneuvered or conducted by artifice.

CHARLES LAMB

(1775–1834)

Charles Lamb wrote that the motto of his life was "Contented with little yet wishing for more." It is a genial understatement. His aged father's mind was unsound. Charles himself was briefly committed to a private asylum for depression over unrequited love. His older sister Mary murdered their mother in a fit of insanity. Against the advice of a "remotely human" brother, who believed she should be institutionalized, Charles assumed responsibility for his sister's welfare. They lived together except when relapses made temporary confinements necessary. After the first confinement, Charles saw that she would remain "perpetually on the brink of madness." When the symptoms came on, brother and sister would walk arm-in-arm to the asylum carrying her straitjacket. Yet they were not morose, and could even appreciate the humor that others might enjoy at their expense: "I am very nervous and she most so at those times when I am: so that a merry friend, adverting to the noble consolation we were able to afford each other, denominated us not unaptly *Gum Boil* and *Tooth Ache*: for they used to say that a Gum Boil is a great relief to a Tooth Ache."

Lamb worked as a bookkeeper for the East India Company. (See SOCIETY AND POLITICAL ECONOMY.) Things might have gone differently had Lamb attended the university after graduating from Christ's Hospital, the London grammar school for exceptional children from impoverished families. But Lamb failed to attain the requisite academic rank for advanced education because he stammered. Friends, including his lifelong companion and hero, Samuel Taylor Coleridge, went to Oxford and Cambridge. At the age of fourteen, Lamb went to work as a clerk for a countinghouse. By the time of his retirement more than thirty years later, he commented, "I had grown to my desk, as it were; and the wood had entered my soul."

Nevertheless, the Lambs' intellectual and social life was never wooden. Charles's critical and familiar essays made him interesting to the London literati, and he was entertaining company for a circle of friends—William* and Dorothy Wordsworth,* Leigh Hunt, William Hazlitt,* Robert Southey,* et al—at his weekly whist parties. He was a shameless punster, and a harmless or devastating wit (depending on the occasion), who became increasingly whimsical with drink.

The richest vein of Lamb's humor was directed at self and loved ones. When his unfortunate play, *Mr. H——*, was hissed off the stage, Henry Crabb Robinson reports that "Lamb joined [in] and was probably the loudest hisser in the house" so that no one would suspect that he was the author. When one of his early sonnets was rejected for publication, he exclaimed: "Damn the age: I will write for Antiquity!"

Although he had early published several poems and essays, some in collaboration with his sister's literary adaptions for children—*Tales from Shakespear* (1807), *The Adventures of Ulysses* (1808), and *Mrs. Leicester's School* (1809)—Lamb's literary reputation begins with *Specimens of English Dramatic Poets who lived about the time of Shakespeare* (1808), his remarkable anthology that rediscovered the Elizabethan age for his time. In 1818, Lamb's essays and poems were collected in two volumes, which aroused an interest in his work. In 1820, "Recollections of the South-Sea House" appeared in the *London Magazine* under the pseudonym Elia. The essay was well received, and Lamb was contracted to contribute a series.

The distinguishing characteristic of Lamb's Elia prose is a warmth of tone and a generosity of spirit in reminiscing on common pain, troubles, triumphs, and joy.

In 1825, Lamb received an early retirement from the East India House, but rather than increasing his literary output, free time proved a distraction. "I could scarcely trust myself with myself," he wrote. "It was like passing out of Time into Eternity." Five weeks after the death of his beloved Coleridge, Lamb fell returning from a tavern. He banged his face, complications related to erysipelas (St. Anthony's Fire) developed, and days later he passed away, "faintly murmuring the names of friends." Though Lamb had made financial provision for his sister, his care was indispensible. Mary was required to spend her final years in confinement.

from BLANK VERSE
(1798)

Written on Christmas Day, 1797

I am a widow'd thing, now thou art gone![1]
Now thou art gone, my own familiar friend,
Companion, sister, help-mate, counsellor!
Alas! that honour'd mind, whose sweet reproof
And meekest wisdom in times past have smooth'd
The unfilial harshness of my foolish speech,
And made me loving to my parents old,
(Why is this so, ah God! why is this so?)
That honour'd mind become a fearful blank,
Her senses lock'd up, and herself kept out
From human sight or converse, while so many
Of the foolish sort are left to roam at large,
Doing all acts of folly, and sin, and shame?
Thy paths are mystery!
Yet I will not think,
Sweet friend, but we shall one day meet, and live
In quietness, and die so, fearing God.
Or if not, and these false suggestions be
A fit of the weak nature, loth to part
With what it lov'd so long, and held so dear;
If thou art to be taken, and I left
(More sinning, yet unpunish'd, save in thee),
It is the will of God, and we are clay
In the potter's hands; and, at the worst, are made
From absolute nothing, vessels of disgrace,
Till, his most righteous purpose wrought in us,
Our purified spirits find their perfect rest.

[1] Reference to Mary Lamb's temporary confinement following the matricide.

The Old Familiar Faces
(1798; comp. 1798)

Where are they gone, the old familiar faces?

I had a mother, but she died, and left me,
Died prematurely in a day of horrors—
All, all are gone, the old familiar faces.

I have had playmates, I have had companions,
In my days of childhood, in my joyful school-days,
All, all are gone, the old familiar faces.

I have been laughing, I have been carousing,
Drinking late, sitting late, with my bosom cronies,
All, all are gone, the old familiar faces.

I loved a love once, fairest among women;[1]
Closed are her doors on me, I must not see her—
All, all are gone, the old familiar faces.

I have a friend,[2] a kinder friend has no man;
Like an ingrate, I left my friend abruptly;
Left him, to muse on the old familiar faces.

[1] Lamb's sweetheart Ann Simmons.

[2] Poet Charles Lloyd (1775–1839).

Ghost-like, I paced round the haunts of my
childhood.
Earth seemed a desart I was bound to traverse,
Seeking to find the old familiar faces.

Friend of my bosom,[3] thou more than a brother,
Why wert not thou born in my father's dwelling?
So might we talk of the old familiar faces—

How some they have died, and some they have left
me,
And some are taken from me;[4] all are departed;
All, all are gone, the old familiar faces.

from ELIA
(1823)

Dream-Children[1]
A Reverie

Children love to listen to stories about their elders, when *they* were children; to stretch their imagination to the conception of a traditionary great-uncle, or grandame, whom they never saw. It was in this spirit that my little ones crept about me the other evening to hear about their great-grandmother Field,[2] who lived in a great house in Norfolk (a hundred times bigger than that in which they and papa lived) which had been the scene—so at least it was generally believed in that part of the country—of the tragic incidents which they had lately become familiar with from the ballad of the Children in the Wood.[3] Certain it is that the whole story of the children and their cruel uncle was to be seen fairly carved out in wood upon the chimney-piece of the great hall, the whole story down to the Robin Redbreasts, till a foolish rich person pulled it down to set up a marble one of modern invention in its stead, with no story upon it. Here Alice put out one of her dear mother's looks, too tender to be called upbraiding. Then I went on to say, how religious and how good their great-grandmother Field was, how beloved and respected by every body, though she was not indeed the mistress of this great house, but had only the charge of it (and yet in some respects she might be said to be the mistress of it too) committed to her by the owner, who preferred living in a newer and more fashionable mansion which he had purchased somewhere in the adjoining county; but still she lived in it in a manner as if it had been her own, and kept up the dignity of the great house in a sort while she lived, which afterwards came to decay, and was nearly pulled down, and all its old ornaments stripped and carried away to the owner's other house, where they were set up, and looked as awkward as if some one were to carry away the old tombs they had seen lately at the Abbey, and stick them up in Lady C.'s tawdry gilt drawing-room. Here John smiled, as much as to say, "that would be foolish indeed." And then I told how, when she came to die, her funeral was attended by a concourse of all the poor, and some of the gentry too, of the neighbourhood for many miles round, to show their respect for her memory, because she had been such a good and religious woman: so good indeed that she knew all the Psaltery[4] by heart, ay, and a great part of the Testament besides. Here little Alice spread her hands. Then I told what a tall, upright, graceful person their great-grandmother Field once was; and how in her youth she was esteemed the best dancer—here Alice's little right foot played an involuntary movement, till, upon my looking grave, it desisted—the best dancer, I was saying, in the county, till a cruel disease, called a cancer, came, and bowed her down with pain; but it could never bend her good spirits, or make them stoop, but they were still upright, because she was so good and religious. Then I told how she was used to sleep by herself in a lone chamber of the great lone house; and how she believed that an apparition of two infants was to be seen at midnight gliding up and down the great staircase near where she slept, but she said "those innocents would do her no harm;" and how frightened I used to be, though in those days I had my maid to sleep with me, because I was never half so good or religious as she—and yet I never saw the infants. Here John expanded all his eye-brows and tried to look

[3] Coleridge.

[4] Refers to Mary Lamb's second psychotic break and reinstitutionalization in January 1798.

[1] First published in 1822.

[2] **great-grandmother Field**: Lamb's grandmother, Mary Field.

[3] A ballad included in Thomas Percy's collection *Reliques of Ancient English Poetry* (1765). Also known as the story of the Babes in the Wood.

[4] **Psaltery**: psalter book containing the Psalms.

courageous. Then I told how good she was to all her grand-children, having us to the great-house in the holydays, where I in particular used to spend many hours by myself, in gazing upon the old busts of the Twelve Caesars, that had been Emperors of Rome, till the old marble heads would seem to live again, or I to be turned into marble with them; how I never could be tired with roaming about that huge mansion, with its vast empty rooms, with their worn-out hangings, fluttering tapestry, and carved oaken pannels, with the gilding almost rubbed out — sometimes in the spacious old-fashioned gardens, which I had almost to myself, unless when now and then a solitary gardening man would cross me — and how the nectarines and peaches hung upon the walls, without my ever offering to pluck them, because they were forbidden fruit, unless now and then, — and because I had more pleasure in strolling about among the old melancholy-looking yew trees, or the firs, and picking up the red berries, and the fir apples, which were good for nothing but to look at — or in lying about upon the fresh grass, with all the fine garden smells around me — or basking in the orangery, till I could almost fancy myself ripening too along with the oranges and the limes in that grateful warmth — or in watching the dace that darted to and fro in the fish-pond, at the bottom of the garden, with here and there a great sulky pike hanging midway down the water in a silent state, as if it mocked at their impertinent friskings, — I had more pleasure in these busy-idle diversions than in all the sweet flavours of peaches, nectarines, oranges, and such like common baits of children. Here John slyly deposited back upon the plate a bunch of grapes, which, not unobserved by Alice, he had meditated dividing with her, and both seemed willing to relinquish them for the present as irrelevant. Then in somewhat a more heightened tone, I told how, though their great-grandmother Field loved all her grand-children, yet in an especial manner she might be said to love their uncle, John L——,[5] because he was so handsome and spirited a youth, and a king to the rest of us; and, instead of moping about in solitary corners, like some of us, he would mount the most mettlesome horse he could get, when but an imp no bigger than themselves, and make it carry him half over the county in a morning, and join the hunters when there were any out — and yet he loved the old great house and gardens too, but had too much spirit to be always pent up within their boundaries — and how their uncle grew up to man's estate as brave as he was handsome, to the admiration of every body, but of their great-grandmother Field most especially; and how he used to carry me upon his back when I was a lame-footed boy — for he was a good bit older than me — many a mile when I could not walk for pain; — and how in after life he became lame-footed too, and I did not always (I fear) make allowances enough for him when he was impatient, and in pain, nor remember sufficiently how considerate he had been to me when I was lame-footed; and how when he died, though he had not been dead an hour, it seemed as if he had died a great while ago, such a distance there is betwixt life and death; and how I bore his death as I thought pretty well at first, but afterwards it haunted and haunted me; and though I did not cry or take it to heart as some do, and as I think he would have done if I had died, yet I missed him all day long, and knew not till then how much I had loved him. I missed his kindness, and I missed his crossness, and wished him to be alive again, to be quarrelling with him (for we quarreled sometimes), rather than not have him again, and was as uneasy without him, as he their poor uncle must have been when the doctor took off his limb. Here the children fell a crying, and asked if their little mourning which they had on was not for uncle John, and they looked up, and prayed me not to go on about their uncle, but to tell them some stories about their pretty dead mother. Then I told how for seven long years, in hope sometimes, sometimes in despair, yet persisting ever, I courted the fair Alice W——n[6], and, as much as children could understand, I explained to them what coyness, and difficulty, and denial meant in maidens — when suddenly, turning to Alice, the soul of the first Alice looked out at her eyes with such a reality of re-presentment, that I became in doubt which of them stood there before me, or whose that bright hair was; and while I stood gazing, both the children gradually grew fainter to my view, receding, and still receding till nothing at last but two mournful features were seen in the uttermost distance, which, without speech, strangely impressed upon me the effects of speech; "We are not of Alice, nor of thee, nor are we children at all. The children of Alice called Bartrum father.[7] We are nothing; less than nothing,

[5] **John L——:** John Lamb.

[6] **Alice W——n:** Alice Winterton, a feigned name; possibly referring to Ann Simmons.

[7] **Bartrum:** Ann Simmons married a London merchant named Bartram.

and dreams. We are only what might have been, and must wait upon the tedious shores of Lethe millions of ages before we have existence, and a name"[8]—and immediately awaking, I found myself quietly seated in my bachelor arm-chair, where I had fallen asleep, with the faithful Bridget unchanged by my side—but John L. (or James Elia) was gone for ever.

from THE LAST ESSAYS OF ELIA
(1833, 1835)

The Superannuated Man[1]

Sera tamen respexit
Libertas.
VIRGIL

A Clerk I was in London gay.
O'KEEFE

If peradventure, Reader, it has been thy lot to waste the golden years of thy life—thy shining youth—in the irksome confinement of an office; to have thy prison days prolonged through middle age down to decrepitude and silver hairs, without hope of release or respite; to have lived to forget that there are such things as holidays, or to remember them but as the prerogatives of childhood; then, and then only, will you be able to appreciate my deliverance.

It is now six and thirty years since I took my seat at the desk in Mincing-lane. Melancholy was the transition at fourteen from the abundant play-time, and the frequently-intervening vacations of school days, to the eight, nine, and sometimes ten hours' a-day attendance at a counting-house. But time partially reconciles us to anything. I gradually became content—doggedly contented, as wild animals in cages.

It is true I had my Sundays to myself; but Sundays, admirable as the institution of them is for purposes of worship, are for that very reason the very worst adapted for days of unbending and recreation. In particular, there is a gloom for me attendant upon a city Sunday, a weight in the air. I miss the cheerful cries of London, the music, and the ballad-singers—the buzz and stirring murmur of the streets. Those eternal bells depress me. The closed shops repel me. Prints, pictures, all the glittering and endless succession of knacks and gewgaws, and ostentatiously displayed wares of tradesmen, which make a week-day saunter through the less busy parts of the metropolis so delightful—are shut out. No book-stalls deliciously to idle over—No busy faces to recreate the idle man who contemplates them ever passing by—the very face of business a charm by contrast to his temporary relaxation from it. Nothing to be seen but unhappy countenances—or half-happy at best—of emancipated 'prentices and little tradesfolks, with here and there a servant maid that has got leave to go out, who, slaving all the week, with the habit has lost almost the capacity of enjoying a free hour; and livelily expressing the hollowness of a day's pleasuring. The very strollers in the fields on that day look anything but comfortable.

But besides Sundays I had a day at Easter, and a day at Christmas, with a full week in the summer to go and air myself in my native fields of Hertfordshire. This last was a great indulgence; and the prospect of its recurrence, I believe, alone kept me up through the year, and made my durance tolerable. But when the week came round, did the glittering phantom of the distance keep touch with me? or rather was it not a series of seven uneasy days, spent in restless pursuit of pleasure, and a wearisome anxiety to find out how to make the most of them? Where was the quiet, where the promised rest? Before I had a taste of it, it was vanished. I was at the desk again, counting upon the fifty-one tedious weeks that must intervene before such another snatch would come. Still the prospect of its coming threw something of an illumination upon the darker side of my captivity. Without it, as I have said, I could scarcely have sustained my thraldom.

Independently of the rigours of attendance, I have ever been haunted with a sense (perhaps a mere caprice) of incapacity for business. This, during my latter years, had increased to such a degree, that it was visible in all the lines of my countenance. My health and my good spirits flagged. I had perpetually a dread of some crisis, to

[8] Refers to the ancient Greek and Roman doctrine of reincarnation, according to which the spirits of previous lives, about to be reincarnated, are made to drink from the waters of Lethe (the river of forgetfulness in the classical underworld) in order to forget their former existence. See *Aeneid,* VI.748–51.

[1] Lamb retired from East India House in March 1825. The first epigraph cites Virgil's *Eclogues,* I.27: "Freedom, though late, turned and looked on me." The second epigraph, mistakenly attributed to farce writer John O'Keefe (1747–1833), is actually taken from the younger George Colman's *Inkle and Yarico* (1787).

which I should be found unequal. Besides my daylight servitude, I served over again all night in my sleep, and would awake with terrors of imaginary false entries, errors in my accounts, and the like. I was fifty years of age, and no prospect of emancipation presented itself. I had grown to my desk, as it were; and the wood had entered into my soul.

My fellows in the office would sometimes rally me upon the trouble legible in my countenance; but I did not know that it had raised the suspicions of any of my employers, when, on the 5th of last month, a day ever to be remembered by me, L——, the junior partner in the firm, calling me on one side, directly taxed me with my bad looks, and frankly inquired the cause of them. So taxed, I honestly made confession of my infirmity, and added that I was afraid I should eventually be obliged to resign his service. He spoke some words of course to hearten me, and there the matter rested. A whole week I remained labouring under the impression that I had acted imprudently in my disclosure; that I had foolishly given a handle against myself, and had been anticipating my own dismissal. A week passed in this manner, the most anxious one, I verily believe, in my whole life, when on the evening of the 12th of April, just as I was about quitting my desk to go home (it might be about eight o'clock) I received an awful summons to attend the presence of the whole assembled firm in the formidable back parlour. I thought, now my time is surely come, I have done for myself, I am going to be told that they have no longer occasion for me. L——, I could see, smiled at the terror I was in, which was a little relief to me,—when to my utter astonishment B——, the eldest partner, began a formal harangue to me on the length of my services, my very meritorious conduct during the whole of the time (the deuce, thought I, how did he find out that? I protest I never had the confidence to think as much). He went on to descant on the expediency of retiring at a certain time of life (how my heart panted!) and asking me a few questions as to the amount of my own property, of which I have a little, ended with a proposal, to which his three partners nodded a grave assent, that I should accept from the house, which I had served so well, a pension for life to the amount of two-thirds of my accustomed salary—a magnificent offer! I do not know what I answered between surprise and gratitude, but it was understood that I accepted their proposal, and I was told that I was free from that hour to leave their service. I stammered out a bow, and at just ten minutes after eight I went home—for ever. This noble benefit—gratitude forbids me to conceal their names—I owe to the kindness of the most munificent firm in the world—the house of Boldero, Merryweather, Bosanquet, and Lacy.

Esto perpetua![2]

For the first day or two I felt stunned, overwhelmed. I could only apprehend my felicity; I was too confused to taste it sincerely. I wandered about, thinking I was happy, and knowing that I was not. I was in the condition of a prisoner in the old Bastile, suddenly let loose after a forty years' confinement. I could scarce trust myself with myself. It was like passing out of Time into Eternity—for it is a sort of Eternity for a man to have his Time all to himself. It seemed to me that I had more time on my hands than I could ever manage. From a poor man, poor in Time, I was suddenly lifted up into a vast revenue; I could see no end of my possessions; I wanted some steward, or judicious bailiff, to manage my estates in Time for me. And here let me caution persons grown old in active business, not lightly, nor without weighing their own resources, to forego their customary employment all at once, for there may be danger in it. I feel it by myself, but I know that my resources are sufficient; and now that those first giddy raptures have subsided, I have a quiet home-feeling of the blessedness of my condition. I am in no hurry. Having all holidays, I am as though I had none. If Time hung heavy upon me, I could walk it away; but I do *not* walk all day long, as I used to do in those old transient holidays, thirty miles a day, to make the most of them. If Time were troublesome, I could read it away, but I do *not* read in that violent measure, with which, having no Time my own but candlelight Time, I used to weary out my head and eyesight in by-gone winters. I walk, read or scribble (as now) just when the fit seizes me. I no longer hunt after pleasure; I let it come to me. I am like the man

——That's born, and has his years come to him,[3]
In some green desart.

"Years," you will say! "what is this superannuated simpleton calculating upon? He has already told us, he is past fifty."

I have indeed lived nominally fifty years, but deduct out of them the hours which I have lived to other people, and not to myself, and you will find me still a young

---

[2] **Esto perpetua!**: "May it endure forever!"

[3] Cf. *The Mayor of Queenborough,* I.i.333–34, by Thomas Middleton (1580–1627).

fellow. For *that* is the only true Time, which a man can properly call his own, that which he has all to himself; the rest, though in some sense he may be said to live it, is other people's time, not his. The remnant of my poor days, long or short, is at least multiplied for me three-fold. My ten next years, if I stretch so far, will be as long as any preceding thirty. 'Tis a fair rule-of-three sum.

Among the strange fantasies which beset me at the commencement of my freedom, and of which all traces are not yet gone, one was, that a vast tract of time had intervened since I quitted the Counting House. I could not conceive of it as an affair of yesterday. The partners, and the clerks, with whom I had for so many years, and for so many hours in each day of the year, been closely associated—being suddenly removed from them—they seemed as dead to me. There is a fine passage, which may serve to illustrate this fancy, in a Tragedy by Sir Robert Howard, speaking of a friend's death:

——'Twas but just now he went away;
I have not since had time to shed a tear;
And yet the distance does the same appear
As if he had been a thousand years from me.
Time takes no measure in Eternity.[4]

To dissipate this awkward feeling, I have been fain to go among them once or twice since; to visit my old desk-fellows—my co-brethren of the quill—that I had left below in the state militant. Not all the kindness with which they received me could quite restore to me that pleasant familiarity, which I had heretofore enjoyed among them. We cracked some of our old jokes, but methought they went off but faintly. My old desk; the peg where I hung my hat, were appropriated to another. I knew it must be, but I could not take it kindly. D—— take me, if I did not feel some remorse—beast, if I had not,—at quitting my old compeers, the faithful partners of my toils for six and thirty years, that smoothed for me with their jokes and conundrums the ruggedness of my professional road. Had it been so rugged then after all? or was I a coward simply? Well, it is too late to repent; and I also know, that these suggestions are a common fallacy of the mind on such occasions. But my heart smote me. I had violently broken the bands betwixt us. It was at least not courteous. I shall be some time before I get quite reconciled to the separation. Farewell, old cronies, yet not for long, for again and again I will come among ye, if I shall have your leave. Farewell Ch——, dry, sarcastic, and friendly! Do——, mild, slow to move, and gentlemanly! Pl——, officious to do, and to volunteer, good services! —and thou, thou dreary pile, fit mansion for a Gresham or a Whittington[5] of old, stately House of Merchants; with thy labyrinthine passages, and light-excluding, pent-up offices, where candles for one half the year supplied the place of the sun's light; unhealthy contributor to my weal, stern fosterer of my living, farewell! In thee remain, and not in the obscure collection of some wandering bookseller, my "works!" There let them rest, as I do from my labours, piled on thy massy shelves, more MSS. in folio than ever Aquinas[6] left, and full as useful! My mantle I bequeath among ye.

A fortnight has passed since the date of my first communication. At that period I was approaching to tranquillity, but had not reached it. I boasted of a calm indeed, but it was comparative only. Something of the first flutter was left; an unsettling sense of novelty; the dazzle to weak eyes of unaccustomed light. I missed my old chains, forsooth, as if they had been some necessary part of my apparel. I was a poor Carthusian,[7] from strict cellular discipline suddenly by some revolution returned upon the world. I am now as if I had never been other than my own master. It is natural to me to go where I please, to do what I please. I find myself at eleven o'clock in the day in Bond-street,[8] and it seems to me that I have been sauntering there at that very hour for years past. I digress into Soho, to explore a book-stall. Methinks I have been thirty years a collector. There is nothing strange nor new in it. I find myself before a fine picture in a morning. Was it ever otherwise? What is become of Fish-street Hill? Where is Fenchurch-street? Stones of old Mincing-lane, which I have worn with my daily pilgrimage for six and thirty years, to the footsteps of what toil-worn clerk are your everlasting flints now vocal? I indent the gayer flags of Pall Mall. It is Change time, and I

[4] Cf. *The Vestal Virgin* (1665).

[5] **Gresham**: financier Sir Thomas Gresham (1519–1579) founded the Royal Exchange. **Whittington**: Sir Richard Whittington (c. 1358–1423) was three times Mayor of London.

[6] **Aquinas**: Italian theologian and philosopher Thomas Aquinas (1225–1274).

[7] **Carthusian**: a strict monastic order founded in France in 1084; here, student at Christ's Hospital.

[8] The following place-names are all London neighborhoods that Lamb frequented.

am strangely among the Elgin marbles.[9] It was no hyperbole when I ventured to compare the change in my condition to a passing into another world. Time stands still in a manner to me. I have lost all distinction of season. I do not know the day of the week, or of the month. Each day used to be individually felt by me in its reference to the foreign post days; in its distance from, or propinquity to, the next Sunday. I had my Wednesday feelings, my Saturday nights' sensations. The genius of each day was upon me distinctly during the whole of it, affecting my appetite, spirits, &c. The phantom of the next day, with the dreary five to follow, sate as a load upon my poor Sabbath recreations. What charm has washed that Ethiop[10] white? What is gone of Black Monday? All days are the same. Sunday itself—that unfortunate failure of a holyday as it too often proved, what with my sense of its fugitiveness, and over-care to get the greatest quantity of pleasure out of it—is melted down into a week day. I can spare to go to church now, without grudging the huge cantle[11] which it used to seem to cut out of the holyday. I have Time for everything. I can visit a sick friend. I can interrupt the man of much occupation when he is busiest. I can insult over him with an invitation to take a day's pleasure with me to Windsor this fine May-morning. It is Lucretian pleasure[12] to behold the poor drudges, whom I have left behind in the world, carking and caring; like horses in a mill, drudging on in the same eternal round—and what is it all for? A man can never have too much Time to himself, nor too little to do. Had I a little son, I would christen him NOTHING-TO-DO; he should do nothing. Man, I verily believe, is out of his element as long as he is operative. I am altogether for the life contemplative. Will no kindly earthquake come and swallow up those accursed cotton mills? Take me that lumber of a desk there, and bowl it down

As low as to the fiends.[13]

I am no longer ******, clerk to the Firm of &c. I am Retired Leisure. I am to be met with in trim gardens. I am already come to be known by my vacant face and careless gesture, perambulating at no fixed pace, nor with any settled purpose. I walk about; not to and from. They tell me, a certain *cum dignitate*[14] air, that has been buried so long with my other good parts, has begun to shoot forth in my person. I grow into gentility perceptibly. When I take up a newspaper, it is to read the state of the opera. *Opus operatum est.*[15] I have done all that I came into this world to do. I have worked task work, and have the rest of the day to myself.

---

[9] **Elgin marbles**: outstanding relics of classical Greek sculpture brought to the British Museum by Lord Elgin (1766–1841).

[10] **Ethiop**: Ethiopian. Cf. Jeremiah 13:23: "Can the Ethiopian change his skin, or the leopard his spots?"

[11] **cantle**: slice.

[12] **Lucretian pleasure**: reference to the opening lines of Book 2 of Lucretius's *De Rerum Natura:* "How sweet it is, when whirlwinds roil great ocean, To watch from land, the danger of another . . ."

[13] Cf. *Hamlet,* II.iii.519.

[14] **cum dignitate**: dignified; adapted from Cicero's phrase *otium cum dignitate,* "leisure with dignity."

[15] **Opus operatum est**: "my work is done"; playing upon "opera." Latin: works.

SYDNEY OWENSON, LADY MORGAN

(1776–1859)

An enthusiastic advocate of Irish culture, language, and literature, Sydney Owenson was the daughter of an English Methodist, Jane Hill, and an Irish actor, Robert Owenson. A frequent and enthralled visitor to the Irish theaters and music halls where her father performed, she became a lifelong devotee of Irish music and poetry and of Shakespeare. After her mother's death in 1791, she was sent to the finest Protestant finishing school for girls in Ireland, Madame Terson's School in Clontarf, where she learned the French which she frequently used in her later writings. Vivacious, articulate, and amusing, she was taken up by the aristocratic families of her schoolmates. When she graduated, she became by necessity —which she called the muse of women writers—first a governess and then a poet and novelist. Her first volume, *Poems,* appeared in 1801. Her first novel, *St. Clair,* which depicts a young girl of intense sensibility enthusing over the Irish past, was published in 1803. Her next novel, *The Novice of St. Dominick* (1805), followed Jane Porter and Walter Scott into the realm of historical fiction, narrating the story of a girl disguised as a troubadour who encounters numerous adventures in sixteenth-century France before she finds her true love.

Sydney Owenson's best-known novel, *The Wild Irish Girl,* appeared in 1806 and made her famous. An epistolary account of the travels of Horatio M., the son of an absentee British landowner, through his father's Irish territories, *The Wild Irish Girl* systematically explodes the prejudices of its anti-Irish protagonist. At the same time, Horatio is introduced to and overcome by the glories of the sublime Irish landscape and the beauties of the Irish literary tradition. These are here voiced by the ravishing Irish princess and bard, Glorvina, whose father, the Prince of Innismore (i.e., Ireland), finally consents to the marriage of Glorvina and Horatio. After this novel made Sydney Owenson a national heroine at a time when Catholic Ireland was struggling for emancipation from Protestant English domination, she appeared everywhere in public as "the wild Irish girl," wearing Glorvina's Celtic brooch and traditional bardic garb. She continued to write for money: her second collection of poems, *The Lay of an Irish Harp,* appeared in 1807; her novelistic account of a strong-willed and learned woman, *Ida of Athens,* in 1809, and her critique of the British colonization of India, *The Missionary,* in 1809. She was sought out by the members of the nationalistic Irish aristocracy, two of whom, Lord and Lady Abercorn, became her particular patrons and finally found her a congenial husband, the physician Charles Morgan, for whom they also obtained a knighthood.

As Lady Morgan, Sydney Owenson returned to her successful career as a celebrant of all things Irish. In her novels *O'Donnel* (1814), *Florence McCarthy* (1818), and *The O'Briens and the O'Flahertys* (1827), she firmly condemned the British oppression of Ireland and America, and articulated her support for revolutionary France. After travelling extensively in France in 1816, she published a journal of her impressions of post-Napoleonic France, *France* (1817), a subject to which she returned 13 years later, after a second tour, in *France in 1829* (1830). She also visited Italy with her husband, meeting the leading Italian nationalists and cultural heroes, of which she gives a detailed account in her *Italy* (1821); this trip also inspired her hagiographic account of the Italian painter Salvator Rosa, *The Life and Times of Salvator Rosa* (1824). In 1837 she received a pension from the Irish government for her "services to the world of letters," the first woman to be so honored. Although her British critics frequently satirized her as a frivolous and self-indulgent Irish enthusiast, she and Maria Edgeworth* did more than anyone else in this period to expose the deplorable living conditions of the Irish peasants under the absentee landlord system. Further, they stimulated a new and enduring European appreciation for the richness of an Irish literary tradition that was dying out under the Anglo-Irish ascendency.

from The Wild Irish Girl
(1806)

—*from* LETTER VII—

. . . 'And is this, madam,' said I, 'the original ancient Irish harp?'

'Not exactly, for I have strung it with gut instead of wire, merely for the gratification of my own ear; but it is, however, precisely the same form as that preserved in the Irish university, which belonged to one of the most celebrated of our heroes, Brian Boru; for the warrior and the bard often united in the character of our kings, and they sang the triumphs of those departed chiefs whose feats they emulated.

'You see,' she added, with a smile, while my eager glance pursued the kindling animation of her countenance as she spoke,—'you see, that in all which concerns my national music, I speak with national enthusiasm; and much indeed do we stand indebted to the most charming of all the sciences for the eminence it has obtained for us; for in *music only* do *you* English allow us poor Irish any superiority; and therefore your King, who made the *harp* the armorial bearing of Ireland, perpetuated our former musical celebrity beyond the power of time or prejudice to destroy it.'

Not for the world would I have annihilated the triumph which this fancied superiority seemed to give to this patriotic little being, by telling her, that we thought as little of the music of her country, as of every thing else which related to it; and that all we knew of the style of its melodies reached us through the false medium of comic airs, sung by some popular actor, who, in coincidence with his author, caricatures those national traits he attempts to delineate.

I therefore simply told her, that, though I doubted not the former musical celebrity of her country, yet that I perceived the *bardic* order in Wales seemed to have survived the tuneful race of *Erin*; while every little Cambrian village had its harper, I had not yet met one of the profession in Ireland.

She waved her hand with a melancholy air, and replied—'The rapid decline of the Sons of Song, once the pride of our country, is indeed very evident; and the tones of that tender and expressive instrument, the parent of those which now survive them in happier countries, no longer vibrate in our own; for of course you are not ignorant that the importation of Irish bards and Irish instruments into Wales,[1] by *Griffith ap Conan*, formed an epoch in Welsh music, and awakened there a genius of style in composition, which still breathes a kindred spirit to that whence it derived its being—and that even the invention of Scottish music is given to Ireland.[2] . . .

'Our national music,' she returned, 'like our national character, admits of no medium in sentiment; it either sinks our spirit to despondency by its heart-breaking pathos, or elevates it to wildness by its exhilarating animation.

'For my own part, I confess myself the victim of its magic—an Irish planxty[3] cheers me into maddening vivacity; an Irish lamentation depresses me into a sadness of melancholy emotion, to which the energy of despair might be deemed comparative felicity.'

Imagine how I felt while she spoke—but you cannot conceive the feelings, unless you beheld and heard the object who inspired them—unless you watched the

[1] Cardoc (of Lhancarvan,) without any of that illiberal partiality, so common with national writers, assures us that the Irish devised all the instruments, tunes, and measures, in use among the Welch. *Cambrensis* is even more copious in its praise, when he peremptorily declares that the Irish, above any other nation, is incomparably skilled in symphonal music.—*Walker's Hist. Mem. of the Irish Bards.* [L. M.]

[2] See Doctor Campbell, Phi. Surv. Letter 44; and Walker's Hist. of Irish Bards, p. 131, 132. [L. M.]

[3] **planxty**: a harp tune of a sportive and animated character.

kindling animation of her countenance and the varying hue of that mutable complexion, which seemed to ebb and flow with every sentiment she expressed; and while the tones of her round and sighing voice were modulated to each expression it harmonized.

After a moment's pause, she continued:

'This susceptibility to the influence of my country's music, discovered itself at a period of my existence, when no associating sentiment of the heart could have called it into being; for I have often wept in convulsive emotion at an air, before the sad story it accompanied was understood: but now—now—that feeling is matured, and associations are awakened.—Oh! you cannot judge—cannot feel—for you have no national music; and your country is the happiest under heaven!'

Her voice faltered as she spoke—her fingers seemed unconsciously to stray over the chords of the harp—her eyes, her tearful, beautiful eyes, were thrown up to heaven, and her voice, 'low and mournful as the song of the tomb,' sighed over the chords of her national lyre, as she faintly murmured Campbell's beautiful poem to the ancient Irish air of *Erin go Brach!*[4]

And is there on earth a being so cold, so icy, so insensible, as to have made a comment, even a flattering one, when this song of the soul ceased to breathe! God knows, how little I was inclined or empowered to make the faintest eulogium, or disturb the sacred silence which succeeded to her music's dying murmur. On the contrary, I sat silent and motionless, my eyes covered with my hand: when at last I withdrew it, I found her ardent glance fixed on me with a smile of such expression, seeming to say,—but who dares to translate the language of the soul, which such eyes only can express?

We both arose at the same moment, and walked in silence towards the window. Beyond the mass of ruins which spread in desolate confusion below, the ocean, calm and unruffled, expanded its awful waters almost to apparent infinitude; while a body of dark sullen clouds, tinged with the partial beam of a meridian sun, floated above the summits of those savage cliffs, which skirt this bold and rocky coast, the tall spectral figure of Father John, leaning on a broken column, appeared the very impersonation of philosophy moralizing on the instability of all human greatness.

What a sublime assemblage of images!

'How consonant,' thought I, gazing at Glorvina, 'to the tone of our present feelings!' Glorvina bowed her head affirmatively, as though my lips had given utterance to the reflection.

How, think you, I felt, on this involuntary acknowledgement of a mutual intelligence?

Be that as it may, my eyes, too faithful I fear to my feelings, covered the face on which they were passionately rivetted, with blushes.

At that moment Glorvina was summoned to dinner by a servant, for she only is permitted to dine with the Prince, as being of royal descent. The vision dissolved—she was again the proud Milesian Princess, and I the poor wandering *artist*—the eleemosynary[5] guest of her hospitable father.

The priest and I dined *tête-à-tête*[6], and, for the first time, he had all the conversation to himself . . . I thought only of Glorvina, and understood not one word.

Again I beheld her gracefully bending over her harp—again caught the melody of her song, and the sentiment it conveyed; and entered fully, as I listened, into the idea of the Greek painter, who drew *Love,* not with a bow and arrow, but a lyre.

I could not avoid mentioning with admiration her great musical powers.

'Yes,' said the Priest, 'she inherits them from her mother, who obtained the appellation of *Glorvina,* from the sweetness of her voice, by which our little friend was baptized at her mother's request.[7]

Adieu! Glorvina has been confined in her father's room during the whole of the evening—to this circumstance you are indebted for my long letter.

Adieu!
H.M.

[4] **Erin go brach!**: "Ireland forever!" The reference is to the Scottish poet Thomas Campbell (1777–1834), whose "Exile of Erin" was an enormously popular poem that was frequently set to music.

[5] **eleemosynary**: dependent on charity.

[6] **tête-à-tête**: French: one-on-one.

[7] To derive an appellation from some ancient quality or talent is still very common in the interior parts of Ireland. The author's grandmother was known in the neighbourhood where she resided (in the county of Mayo) by the appellative of *Clarseach na Callagh,* or, *The Villa Harp;* for the superiority of her musical abilities. *Glor-bhin* (pronounced *vin*) is literally 'sweet voice.' [L. M.]

from THE LAY OF AN IRISH HARP; OR METRICAL FRAGMENTS

(1807)

The Irish Harp[1]

— FRAGMENT I —

"Voice of the days of old, let me hear you.—Awake the soul of song."

OSSIAN[2]

[1] With an enthusiasm incidental to my natural and national character, I visited the western part of the province of Connaught in the autumn of 1805, full of many an evident expectation that promised to my feelings, and my taste, a *festival* of national enjoyment. The result of this interesting little pilgrimage has already been given to the world in the story of the "Wild Irish Girl," and in a collection of *Irish Melodies*, learned among those who still *"hum'd the Song of other times."* But the hope I had long cherished of hearing the *Irish Harp* played in perfection was not only far from being realized, but infinitely disappointed. That encouragement so nutritive to genius, so indispensably necessary to perseverance, no longer stimulates the Irish bard to excellence, nor rewards him when it is attained; and the decline of that tender and impressive instrument, once so dear to Irish enthusiasm, is as visibly rapid, as it is obviously unimpeded by any effort of national pride or national affection. [L. M.]

[2] **Ossian**: the name commonly given to Oisin, a legendary Gaelic warrior and bard. In 1762, James Macpherson, a Scots poet, published a collection of prose fragments, entitled *Fingal, an Ancient Epic Poem, in Six Books*, which purported to be his faithful translation of an epic by Ossian, the son of Fingal, dating from a remote period of early Scottish history. This "epic" was everywhere hailed by Scots nationalists (including Adam Smith, David Hume, and Hugh Blair) as evidence of their historical cultural superiority to the British. After Macpherson's death, in 1805, a committee chaired by the novelist Henry Mackenzie documented that Macpherson had fabricated the epic by adding his own passages to existing Gaelic poems; nonetheless, the enormous popularity of the poem continued. Morgan quotes an oft-repeated refrain supposedly spoken by the bard Ossian himself.

I

Why sleeps the Harp of Erin's pride?
Why with'ring droops its Shamrock[3] wreath?
Why has that song of sweetness died
Which Erin's Harp alone can breathe?

II

Oh! 'twas the simplest, wildest thing!
The sighs of *Eve* that faintest flow
O'er airy lyres, did never fling
So sweet, so sad, a song of woe.

III

And yet its sadness seem'd to borrow
From love, or joy, a mystic spell;
'Twas doubtful still if *bliss* or *sorrow*
From its melting lapses fell.

IV

For if amidst its tone's soft languish
A note of love or joy e'er stream'd,
'Twas the plaint of love-sick anguish,
And still the "joy of grief" it seem'd.

V

'Tis said *oppression* taught the lay
To him—(of all the "sons of song"
That bask'd in Erin's brighter day)
The *last* of the inspir'd throng;

VI

That not in sumptuous hall, or bow'r,
To victor chiefs, on tented plain,
To festive souls, in festal hour,
Did he (sad bard!) pour forth the strain.

VII

Oh no! for he, oppress, pursued,[4]
Wild, wand'ring, doubtful of his course,
With tears his silent Harp bedew'd,
That drew from *Erin's* woes their source.

[3] **Erin**: Ireland. **Shamrock**: three-leaf clover, national emblem of Ireland.

[4] **he, oppress, pursued . . .** : the persecution begun by the Danes against the Irish bards finished in almost the total extirpation of that sacred order in the reign of Elizabeth [L. M.].

VIII

It was beneath th'impervious gloom
Of some dark forest's deepest dell,
'Twas at some *patriot hero's tomb*,
Or on the drear heath where *he* fell.

IX

It was beneath the loneliest cave
That roofs the brow of misery,
Or stems the ocean's wildest wave,
Or mocks the sea-blast's keenest sigh.

X

It was through night's most spectral hours,
When reigns the spirit of *dismay*,
And *terror* views demoniac pow'rs
Flit ghastly round in dread array.

XI

Such was the time, and such the place,
The bard respir'd[5] *his* song of woe,
To those, who had of Erin's race
Surviv'd their freedom's vital blow.

XII

Oh, what a lay the minstrel breath'd!
How many bleeding hearts around,
In suff'ring sympathy enwreath'd,
Hung desponding o'er the sound!

XIII

For still his Harp's wild plaintive tones
Gave back their sorrows keener still,
Breath'd *sadder* sighs, heav'd *deeper* moans,
And wilder wak'd *despair's* wild thrill.

XIV

For still he sung the ills that flow
From dire oppression's ruthless fang,
And deepen'd every patriot woe,
And sharpen'd every patriot pang.

[5] **respir'd:** breathed again, after distress or trouble.

XV

Yet, ere he ceas'd, a prophet's fire
Sublim'd[6] his lay, and louder rung
The deep-ton'd music of his lyre,
And *Erin go brach*[7] he boldly sung.

To Signor Alphonso Pilligrini, LL.D.

Professor of Italian and Spanish, Trinity College, Dublin.
(1807)

— FRAGMENT XVI —

(Written on the north-west coast of CONNAUGHT, at the seat of Sir M. C——N, Bart.)

I

The castle[1] lies low, whose *towers* frown'd so high,
And the landscape is awful and bold;
The mountains around lift their heads to the sky,
And the woods many ages have told.

II

And the world's greatest *ocean* still dashes its wave
'Gainst the coast that is savagely wild:
Midst the castle's grey ruins there still yawns a cave
Where the sun's cheering light never smil'd.[2]

[6] **Sublim'd:** raised to an elevated state; transmuted into something higher, nobler, as heat transmutes solids into gases or vapour.

[7] **Erin go brach:** Ireland for ever!—a national exclamation, and, in less felicitous times, the rallying point to which many an Irish heart revolted from the influence of despair. [L. M.]

[1] **castle:** Longford Castle, founded by the O'Dowels, and purchased by the C____n family in the reign of Elizabeth [1558–1603]. It was a place of considerable strength, but its ruins now strew the earth, and are scarcely discernible amidst the vegetation with which they are covered. [L. M.]

[2] **a cave . . . smil'd:** these caves were accidentally discovered a few months back. [L. M.]

III

And steep is the precipice,[3] horrid to view,
That rears o'er the ocean its crest:
They say that no bird to its summit e'er flew,[4]
And its base 'neath the waves seems to rest.

IV

And the blast that awakes on *Columbia's* far shore[5]
Unimpeded here breathes its last sigh,
And the rocks round whose brow th'Atlantic winds roar
The spent storms of Columbia defy.

V

Nor is there a spot midst this scene of romance
Obscur'd by *oblivion's* dark veil,
Nor is there a fragment that rivets the glance
But some charm from *tradition* can steal.

VI

For many a pilgrim has pillow'd his head
In that CELL that now moulders away,
And many a brave chief and *warrior* has bled
Near these walls[6] that now fall to decay.

VII

In that spot, by the thistle and long grass o'ergrown,
That breathes round a desolate gloom
When the blasts through the old abbey's[7] grey ruins moan,
Lies the pilgrim and warrior's tomb.

VIII

But the little *enthusiast* who boasts THEE her friend,
And who strays midst this world of romance,
Where *nature* such scenes e'en to fancy can lend
As ne'er floated on fancy's rapt glance;

IX

Who roams midst this landscape, so awful and wild,
Who hangs on th'Atlantic's deep roar,
Who visits the cave where the sun never smil'd,
And wanders the desolate shore;

X

Who sighs o'er the *tomb* where the warrior's laid low,
Where the rough thistle waves its lone head,
Where the blasts o'er the old abbey's grey ruins flow,
And a requiem breathe over the dead;

XI

Yes, th'enthusiast e'en here, midst these scenes drear and wild,
The *gentlest of spirits* has found.
And many a bosom "ethereally mild,"
By the sweet ties of sympathy bound.

XII

And that *polish* of manner which only can flow
From the soul that is warm and refin'd,
And those *heart-born* endearments which shed their soft glow
O'er the *stronger* endowments of mind.

XIII

Then, oh! tell me, dear friend,[8] what has place, what has scene,
To do with the *heart* or the *soul?*
For like *theirs, sure thine own gen'rous bosom* had been
The same 'neath the *line* or the *pole.*

---

[3] **precipice:** the precipice of ALT-BO—— of which *Shakespeare's* exquisite description of the ". . . . Cliff whose high and bending head / Look'd dreadfully down the roaring deep," [*King Lear,* IV.i.76–77, misquoted] will give the most adequate idea. [L. M.]

[4] **no bird . . . e'er flew:** "The shrill-tun'd lark so high / Cannot be seen or heard." LEAR, Act IV.[vi. 58–59, misquoted]. [L. M.]

[5] **Columbia:** a north-east point of the North American coast [Cape Columbia, Northwest Territories, Canada] lies exactly opposite to these shores, without the intervention of any land [L. M.].

[6] **these walls:** a small chapel, whose almost unimpaired walls are hung with a crucifix, and the richly carved heads of many of the saints. [L. M.]

[7] **the old abbey:** the abbey of Drumard [L. M.].

[8] **dear friend:** of this solicitous friend of my maturer life, and attentive perceptor of my earliest days, it may be truly said that he is "Homme de tous les pais / Comme les savants sont de tous les temps." [French: He is a man of all countries as the wise are of all times.] There are few countries whose language and literature have not contributed to enrich his mind; while his heart, in the most benevolent and liberal sense of the term, has ever proved itself a *citizen of the world!* [L. M.].

The Swan Quill[1]
(1807)

— FRAGMENT XXXVI —

To * * * * * * * * * *

I

The quill that now traces the thought of my heart,
And speeds the soft wand'rer to thine,
From the pinion of love, by thy hand's erring dart,
Was sever'd, and then became mine.[2]

II

"Preserve it," thou saidst, "for it shatter'd the breast
Which once glow'd with love's purest fire;
And it fell as the *mistress* and *mother* caress'd
In love's transport, the offspring and sire."

III

Then thou toldst me the tale, and I wept o'er the quill,
Where already thy tear had been shed;
"And oh!" I exclaim'd, "may its point ever thrill
O'er the nerve where soft pity is bred."

IV

From that point may the fanciful sorrow still flow
Which, *though* fancied, ne'er misses the heart;
Be *it* sacred alone to the delicate woe
Which *genius* and *feeling* impart."

V

But little I dream'd the first trace it imprest
With a sorrow *not* fancied should flow,
And that, that *real* sorrow should spring from *my* heart,
And that *thou* shouldst awaken that woe.

VI

For they tell me, alone and unfriended thou'rt left
On the pillow of sickness to languish;
By absence, by fate, of the fond friend bereft
Who could *feel* for, and *solace,* thy anguish.

VII

May this quill then convey *one* fond truth to thy heart,
And its languid pulsation elate;
That still in each suff'ring *that friend* takes a part,
And *shares,* as she *mourns* for thy fate.

VIII

Then fancy thou viewest that tear of the soul
Which thy destiny draws to her eye,
And believe that no sigh from *thy* bosom e'er stole
But she gave thee as *heart-felt* a sigh.

IX

For sweet is the solace that lurks in the tear
Which flows from the eye that we love;
And what is the suff'ring, oh! what is the care
That *sympathy* cannot remove?

X

Oh! then speed thy return, and thy sweet cure receive,
Which *affection* and *friendship* present,
From her who by *pity* was taught to forgive,
And who *feels,* where she ought to *resent.*[3]

[1] "I aimed my fowling-piece," said the friend from whom I received the quill, "at some birds that floated on the lake; but its contents were unfortunately lodged in the breast of a swan which lay sheltered amongst the reeds on the shore. I flew to the spot, and found the mate hovering near his wounded love; and two cygnets fluttering beneath the wings from which this quill dropped." [L. M.]

[2] In traditional Irish poetry, the Swan is an emblem of Ireland [L. M.].

[3] In allusion to a petite brouillerie [French: little misunderstanding], which occasioned the absence of the friend to whom this fragment is addressed [L. M.].

from France
(1817)

— PARISIAN SOCIETY —

The society of Paris, after the second restoration of the Bourbons,[1] appearing half in *shade* and half in *relief,* is not inaptly imaged by that condition of the moon, in which,

[1] **the Bourbons:** the Bourbon dynasty, led by Louis XVIII (1755–1824), was restored to the throne of France in 1814. Cf. THE FRENCH REVOLUTION AND RIGHTS OF MAN and the COMPREHENSIVE CHRONOLOGY.

although her whole orb be visible, the effulgence of her light proceeds only from a part. While the *royaliste pur* and the *royaliste exagéré*[2] buz, and bustle, and flutter on the scene, warmed into animation by the rays of princely protection, or of royal favour; all who cannot claim these distinguishing epithets, "preserve the noiseless tenor of their way," and (to borrow a phrase of Cowley) "lead a life, as it were, by stealth."

This unclassed, but suspected order, generally under the *surveillance* of the police, and often little better than prisoners to their own porters and valets, have, by some fatal experiences, been broken into circumspection; and, in general society, are cautious not to risk opinions, which might unavailingly incur the penalty of exile, or perhaps of death. A certain tone of pleasant *équivoque*, however, pervades their conversation; an ambushed raillery, which well supplies the place of bitter invective, or of whining complaint. How often, and how willingly, have I hastened to one of their *"petits comités sous la rose,"*[3] from some catacomb circle, where each monumental member spoke in his turn, or was called to order, if he infringed on the prescribed *regularity* of the conversation!—With what pleasure have I flown to some forbidden ground, where, in the hallowed circle of amity and confidence, *wit* and *genius* exercised their proscribed witcheries; where talents, which were even then, under various forms, delighting the world, and pursuing their golden course to immortality, reserved some of their brightest beams to illumine the passing moments of private intercourse; and where names were re-echoed, destined to live for ever, and already traced in the luminous rolls of splendid celebrity! This, indeed, was a society, often "dream'd of in my philosophy,"[4] but never counted upon in my expectations. These were hours over which weariness held no jurisdiction; and every sand in the glass turned to gold, as it fell.

The society of Paris, taken as a whole, and including all parties and factions, is infinitely superior in point of taste, acquirement, and courtesy, to that of the capital of any other nation. Paris, the elysium of men of letters, has always been the resort of foreigners of literary, scientific and political eminence; and princes and potentates, who have influenced the destinies of nations, are seen mingling in her circles with the more valuable characters of Europe; whose works and names are destined to reach posterity, when titles of higher sound shall be forgotten. . . .

— THE PARISIANS OUT OF DOORS —

The street-population of Paris seemed, indeed, always to me, to be characterized by great temperance, mildness, gaiety, and activity, and to be peculiarly governed by a spirit of innocent, though luxurious enjoyment, evidently influenced by their climate. They are perpetually buying or selling fruit and flowers; . . . Cakes are baking, soup is bubbling, sweetmeats are vending in every quarter, in the open streets, over little stoves, and under temporary sheds. Learned monkies, popular orators, humorous story-tellers, excellent fiddle-players, and tolerable ballad-singers, present continual amusement and recreation to those, who cannot pay for more expensive and luxurious *"feasts of reason."* . . .

The street-population of Paris have scarcely time to *brood and be wicked*; they are working, talking, laughing, listening, recreating, and enjoying,

> "From night till morn,
> From morn till dewy eve."[5]

They may, perhaps, be deemed frivolous—but they are not vicious—they doubtless commit many follies, but they unquestionably are guilty of few crimes.

From the *multitudinous* population which swarms in the fine evenings of summer, on Sundays and holidays, through the numerous public walks and gardens of Paris, an impression is given to the mind of the English stranger, of a dissipated and light headed people, insensible to the sober interests of home, for whom domestic privacy has no enjoyment, and the close drawn circle of family ties no charm. But it is an error inherent to the narrowness of the human mind, to make its own habits the standard of excellence, the supreme point of wisdom, to others; and thus overlooking the necessity and fitness which govern different customs in different countries, to forget that climate, soil, and remote institutions produce that variety in manners over the surface of the earth, which diversifies the existence of its various inhabitants. . . .

[2] **royaliste pur . . . exagéré**: French: the pure or hereditary royalist and the amplified or newly ennobled royalist.

[3] **équivoque**: French: equivocation, double talk. **petits . . . rose**: little meetings or conversational gatherings "under the rose," i.e., under the surveillance of those loyal to the king.

[4] **"dream'd of in my philosophy"**: *Hamlet*, I.v.166–167: "There are more things in heaven and earth, Horatio, / Than are dreamt of in your philosophy."

[5] **"From night . . . eve"**: *Paradise Lost*, I.742–743: "From morn / To noon he fell, from noon to dewy eve."

— DOMESTIC SERVITUDE —

Modern servitude in France, less dignified and respectable than in more primitive times, is still softened by many indulgences, and rendered more tolerable by the mutual good-will which usually exists between the master and the domestic. The health and comfort of the servants in France are much more attended to than in any part of Great Britain. They are not confined, the greater portion of the day, under ground, in *unwholesome vaults*, dignified by the name of kitchen and offices. The French *office* is on the ground-floor; or, frequently, every *étage* has its little kitchen, where the *chef-de-cuisine* and the *garçon d'office* only inhabit; all the rest of the domestics occupy the *anti-room*, which is too near the apartment of the superior of the family, to admit of boisterous mirth, or coarse impropriety. . . .

There is no contrast more shocking and violent, in English society, than that presented by the situation of master and servants, during the hours of social intercourse of fashionable London. For the one, the air is perfumed with roses, and the chill atmosphere of winter expelled by every artificial contrivance; and comfort, enjoyment, and accomodation, are studiously accumulated. For the other, all hardship, suffering, and endurance. Exposed for hours to all the inclemency of the season, in listless idleness, or in vicious excess (the necessary and inevitable alleviation of their degraded situation), this large and useless class of persons gratify the ostentation of their masters, at the expense of health, and of every better feeling and higher consideration. . . .

from France in 1829

(1830)

— CURIOSITY SHOPS — NAPOLEON IN 1829 —

Paris, says a witty French writer, abounds in those shops, which "sell every thing that is useless." I know nothing more amusing than to go through a course of these repositories. It is reading history in tangible forms. Every antiquated article is a page in the story of other days. The mirror of Marie de Medicis, or the cabinet of Madame de Pompadour,[1] gives a sketch of the progress of the arts, which comes home to the apprehension more strikingly than a volume of Vitruvius.[2] I find every thing that I want in these delightful *magazins*,[3] except the money to buy their whole contents.

Amidst the infinite variety of these collections, there is one feature common to all, and which struck me forcibly: I mean the busts and engravings of Napoleon, and of all his dynasty; — not hidden in the old closets, or concealed behind less mysterious objects, and only offered to the notice of the initiated, — but openly exposed in the windows, and at the doors, to be haggled for, like a second-hand clock, or any other *meuble d'occasion*.[4]

This bespeaks a vast change in public opinion, and in the whole order of things in France. Ten or twelve years back, the very name of Bonaparte had treason in its echo; and the *"celui,"*[5] substituted for imperial titles, and for a name now immortal, was more emphatic and perilous, a thousand times, than the present open allusions made to the government of the Emperor, whose reign, character, and acts, are as freely canvassed as those of Charles the Bold, Charles the Simple, or even Charles the Tenth, himself. Every one, in 1829, speaks out upon all subjects; nothing is sacred from public discussion except *la Charte*;[6] and that, too, must eventually submit to popular invasion, when a happier day shall come, as come it must, in which new combinations, more suited to the happiness of society, shall be irresistibly demanded.

---

[1] **Marie de Medicis**: wife of Henry IV of France. **Madame de Pompadour**: Mistress of Louis XV of France.

[2] **Vitruvius**: Marcus Vitruvius Pollio, first-century BC Roman architect and engineer; author of ten-volume treatise on architecture.

[3] **magazins**: French: stores, shops.

[4] **mueble d'occasion**: piece of second hand furniture.

[5] **"celui"**: French: the one.

[6] **Charles the Bold**: Carolingian dynasty, last Duke of Burgundy (1433–1477). **Charles the Simple**: Charles III of France (879–929). **Charles the Tenth**: King of France (r. 1824–1830), reigning at this time (1757–1836). **La Charte**: the July Ordinances imposed by Charles X in his attempt to restore the ancien regime of pre-revolutionary France; they provoked the July Revolution of 1830 which forced him to abdicate.

LUCY AIKIN

(1781–1864)

Widely known during her lifetime as one of England's leading Whig (or liberal) historians—she published Memoirs of the Courts of Queen Elizabeth (1818), James I (1822), and Charles I (1833)—Lucy Aikin was the daughter of the distinguished physician John Aikin and the niece of the poet and literary critic Anna Letitia Aikin Barbauld.* In their homes she learned Latin, French, and Italian, together with the progressive scientific and unitarian religious views that influenced all her work. She published her first literary work, *Epistles on Women,* in 1810, followed by her only novel, *Lorimer,* in 1814. She spent her adult life in Hampstead, living first with her mother and then with a niece, Anna Letitia Le Breton. She was a close friend of Joanna Baillie,* next to whom she is buried in Hampstead Cemetery, and by her own account she knew "almost every literary woman of celebrity" of her day. She carried on a long-term correspondence with the unitarian minister, Rev. William Ellery Channing of Boston, to whom she vigorously expressed her defense of political liberty, criticisms of the Church of England, and commitment to the higher arts of civilization.

Epistles on Women is Aikin's answer to Alexander Pope's misogynist representation of women in the second of his *Moral Essays,* "Epistle to a Lady." Here Pope endorses the view that "Most Women have no Characters at all" and insists that "every Woman is at heart a Rake." Imitating Pope's Juvenalian heroic couplets, Lucy Aikin offers an alternative account of the character or nature of the female sex. Her introduction must be read as a masterpiece of feminine irony: apparently denying "the absurd idea that the two sexes ever can be, or ever ought to be, placed in all respects on a footing of equality," she nonetheless asserts that there is "no talent, no virtue . . . not an endowment, or propensity, or mental quality of any kind" that the female cannot possess. Men may have a superior physical strength that enables them to perform certain public tasks (warfare, physical labor, etc.) that women cannot do, but women are capable of every mental and moral achievement of "common human nature." The Great Truth which her poem proclaims, in a clear echo of Mary Wollstonecraft's *Vindication of the Rights of Woman,** is the *identity* in mental and moral capacities of the two sexes and the benefits to be gained by both when women are accorded the status of "partnership" with men.

After denouncing her society's construction of woman as nothing more than "a plaything and a slave," Aikin's first Epistle rewrites the story of the Creation and Fall from a feminist perspective, asserting the "primary equality" of Eve with Adam. Indeed, Aikin suggests, Eve is superior to Adam because she has a "stepdame" Nature while Adam is unmothered, unnursed, joyless, a "moping idiot." Strategically omitting the Genesis account of Eve's creation from Adam's rib, Aikin presents Eve as having imbibed sympathy from her mother and hence as capable of *civilizing* Adam, as the one who awakes Adam's soul and inspires his speech. The Fall, in Aikin's rewriting of the Biblical and Miltonic myths, is caused not by a serpent who tempts Eve but rather by *men,* by the "savage blood" spilt by Cain in his rivalry with Abel.

Demonstrating her claim to learning and intellectual authority through her wide range of references and footnotes to history, geography, anthropology, and the Latin and Greek classics, Aikin describes in the second Epistle the condition of women throughout the known world, in both "primitive" and "civilized" societies. Everywhere, the primary equality of women has been denied and women reduced to "female servitude" and "homely misery." Parodying Rousseau's celebration of the noble savage, she portrays untaught Savage Man as "half-humanized: the monster-man" who drags "the bleeding victim bride away." Only Maternal Love can save human beings from lawless brutality, through sympathy and "the generous intercourse of equal love" that creates "respect, decorum, friendship"—for Aikin the hallmarks of civilization itself.

Aikin's third Epistle tracks the development of Western culture from Antiquity through the Middle Ages, focussing on the civilizing influence of women throughout and attributing the decline of Rome to male lust and greed. "Souls have no sex," she claims, celebrating the great female matrons and martyrs of the past. Her final Epistle turns to modern Europe, invoking the Celtic ideal of sexual equality against Turkish harems, Indian practices of suttee, and French promiscuity. Her goal is to redefine the feminine gender or ideal woman as one notable for learning, able to sustain a companionate marriage, and capable of nurturing her children emotionally, mentally, and morally. This poem, an affirmation of women's capacities and a denunciation of the historical oppression of the female sex, is appropriately dedicated to a female muse, Aikin's sister-in-law, Anna Wakefield Aikin.

Epistles on Women, Exemplifying Their Character and Condition in Various Ages and Nations

(1810)

(Editor's Note: The 1810 publication of *Epistles on Women* carried the following dedication.) "To Mrs. Charles Rochemont Aikin, the following epistles, originally addressed to her by the sole appellation of friend, are now inscribed, together with the remaining contents of this volume, by her affectionate friend and sister Lucy Aikin."

—*from* INTRODUCTION—

The poetical epistles occupying the principal part of this volume are presented to the public with all the diffidence and anxiety of a literary novice conscious of a bold and arduous undertaking. As I am not, however, aware of any circumstances in my own case which peculiarly appeal to the indulgence of the reader, I shall decline any further exposure of feelings purely personal, and proceed to the proper business of this introduction, ... to offer such preliminary remarks on the plan of the work as may be necessary to prevent misapprehension.

Let me in the first place disclaim entirely the absurd idea that the two sexes ever can be, or ever ought to be, placed in all respects on a footing of equality. Man when he abuses his power may justly be considered as a tyrant; but his power itself is no tyranny, being founded not on usurpation, but on certain unalterable necessities; . . . . sanctioned, not by prescription alone, but by the fundamental laws of human nature. As long as the bodily constitution of the species shall remain the same, man must in general assume those public and active offices of life which confer authority, whilst to woman will usually be allotted such domestic and private ones as imply a certain degree of subordination.

Nothing therefore could, in my opinion, be more foolish than the attempt to engage our sex in a struggle for stations that they are physically unable properly to fill; for power of which they must always want the means to possess themselves. No! instead of aspiring to be inferior men, let us content ourselves with becoming noble women: . . . . but let not sex be carried into every thing. Let the impartial voice of History testify for us, that, when permitted, we have been the worthy associates of the best efforts of the best of men; let the daily observation of mankind bear witness, that no talent, no virtue, is masculine alone; no fault or folly exclusively feminine; . . . . that there is not an endowment, or propensity, or mental quality of any kind, which may not be derived from her father to the daughter, to the son from his mother. These positions once established, and carried into their consequences, will do every thing for woman. Perceiving that any shaft aimed at her, must strike in its recoil upon some vulnerable part of common human nature, the Juvenals and Popes[1] of future ages will abstain from making her the butt of scorn or malice. Feeling with gratitude of what her heart and mind are capable, the scholars, the sages, and the patriots of coming days will treat her as a sister and a friend.

The politic father will not then leave as a "legacy" to his daughters the injunction to conceal their wit, their learning, and even their good sense, in deference to the *"natural malignity"* with which most men regard every woman of a sound understanding and cultivated mind; nor will even the reputation of our great Milton[2] himself secure him from the charge of a blasphemous presumption in making his Eve address to Adam the acknowledgement, "God is thy head, thou mine;" and in the assertion that the first human pair were formed, "He for God only, she for God in him."

To mark the effect of various codes, institutions, and states of manners, on the virtue and happiness of man, and the concomitant and proportional elevation or depression of woman in the scale of existence, is the general plan of this work. The historical and biographical authorities from which its facts and many of its sentiments are derived, will easily be recognised by the literary reader, who will know how to estimate my correctness and fidelity: for the use of other readers a few notes are subjoined.

With respect to arrangement, I may remark, that as a strictly chronological one was incompatible with the design of tracing the progress of human society not in one country alone, but in many, I have judged it most advisable to form to myself such an one as seemed best adapted to my own peculiar purposes, moral and poetical. We have no records of any early people in a ruder state than some savage tribes of the present day; and it would be in vain to seek amongst the ancient writers for such distinct and accurate delineations of the customs of Lotophagi and Troglodytes as we now possess of the life and manners of New Hollanders, American Indians and Hottentots.[3] From these latter, therefore, my first descriptions have been borrowed. Of the tribes of ancient Germany, indeed, we possess an unrivaled portraiture; but in the age of Tacitus[4] most of them had already risen far above the lowest stage of human society; and the progenitors of the noblest nations of modern Europe ought not to be classed with families of men whose name has perished from the earth, or wandering hordes of which we do not yet know whether or not they contain a living seed of future greatness.

In the way of explanation I have little more to add. I make no specific claims for my sex. Convinced that it is rather to the policy, or the generosity, of man, than to his justice that we ought to appeal, I have simply endeavoured to point out, that between the two partners of human life, not only the strongest family likeness, but the most complete identity of interest subsists: so that it is impossible for man to degrade his companion without degrading himself, or to elevate her without receiving a proportional accession of dignity and happiness. This is the chief "moral of my song;"[5] on this point all my examples are brought to bear. I regard it as the Great Truth to the support of which my pen has devoted itself; and whoever shall rise from the perusal of these epistles deeply impressed with its importance, will afford me the success dearest to my heart, ... the hope of having served, in some small degree, the best interests of the human race. . . .

---

[1] **Juvenal:** Roman poet of the 1st century AD, author of sixteen poetic satires. His work was admired and imitated by poets of later ages, especially the neoclassical writers of the eighteenth century. **Pope:** Alexander Pope (1688–1744), poet and man of letters, whose *Moral Essays* and verse epistles imitate the meter and subject matter of Juvenalian satire.

[2] **Milton:** John Milton (1608–1674), English poet; see his *Paradise Lost* (1667–1674), iv. 637, 299.

[3] **Lotophagi:** "lotus eaters," a mythical island race who try to lure Odysseus and his men into a life of forgetful indolence. See Homer, *Odyssey*, 9.82–97. **Troglodytes:** primitive cave-dwellers, possibly of Ethiopian origin. **New Hollanders:** Australian aborigines. (The Dutch colonized Australia in the seventeenth century.) **Hottentots:** a southwest African tribe.

[4] **Tacitus:** Roman historian, born around AD 55, chronicler of the latter days of the Empire.

[5] **"moral of my song":** Spenser, *The Faerie Queene:* "Fierce wars and faithful loves shall moralize my song," Introduction, I.9.

— EPISTLE I —

Argument of Epistle I

Subject proposed — the fame of man extended over every period of life — that of woman transient as the beauty on which it is founded — Man renders her a trifler, then despises her, and makes war upon the sex with Juvenal and Pope. A more impartial view of the subject to be attempted. Weakness of woman, and her consequent subserviency. General view of various states of society undertaken. Birth of Eve — Angels prophesy the doom of the sex — description of Adam before he sees her — a joyless, hopeless, indolent creature. Meeting of Adam and Eve — Change produced in both — their mutual happiness and primary equality. Reflections. Conclusion.

Hear, O my friend, my Anna, nor disdain
My sober lyre and moralizing strain!
I sing the Fate of Woman: . . . . Man to man
Adds praise, and glory lights his mortal span;
Creation's lord, he shines from youth to age,
The blooming warrior or the bearded sage;
But she, frail offspring of an April morn,
Poor helpless passenger from love to scorn,
While dimpled youth her sprightly cheek adorns
Blooms a sweet rose, a rose amid the thorns;
A few short hours, with faded charms to earth
She sinks, and leaves no vestige of her birth.
E'en while the youth, in love and rapture warm,
Sighs as he hangs upon her beauteous form,
Careless and cold he views the beauteous mind,
For virtue, bliss, eternity designed.
"Banish, my fair," he cries, "those studious looks;
Oh! what should beauty learn from crabbed books?
Sweetly to speak and sweetly smile be thine;
Beware, nor change that dimple to a line!"

Well pleased she hears, vain triumph lights her eyes;
Well pleased, in prattle and in smiles complies;
But eyes, alas! grow dim, and roses fade,
And man contemns the trifler he has made.
The glass reversed by magic power of Spleen,
A wrinkled idiot now the fair is seen;
Then with the sex his headlong rage must cope.
And stab with Juvenal, or sting with Pope.
Be mine, while Truth with calm and artless grace
Lifts her clear mirror to the female face.
With steadier hand the pencil's task to guide,
And win a blush from Man's relenting pride.
No Amazon, in frowns and terror drest,
I poise the spear, or nod the threatening crest,
Defy the law, arraign the social plan,
Throw down the gauntlet in the face of man,
And, rashly bold, divided empire claim,
Unborrowed honours, and an equal's name:
No, Heaven forbid! I touch no sacred thing,
But bow to Right Divine in man and king;
Nature endows him with superior force,
Superior wisdom then I grant, of course;
For who gainsays the despot in his might,
Or when was ever weakness in the right?
With passive reference too I hail the law,
Formed to secure the strong, the weak to awe,
Impartial guardian of unerring sway,
Set up by man for woman to obey.
In vain we pout or argue, rail or chide,
He mocks our idle wrath and checks our pride;
Resign we then the club and lion's skin,
And be our sex content to knit and spin;
To bow inglorious to a master's rule,
And good and bad obey, and wise and fool;
Here a meek drudge, a listless captive there,
For gold now bartered, now as cheap as air;
Prize of the coward rich or lawless brave,
Scorned and caressed, a plaything and a slave,
Yet taught with spaniel soul to kiss the rod,
And worship man as delegate of God.

Ah! what is human life? a narrow span
Eked out with cares and pains to us and man;
A bloody scroll that vice and folly stain,
That blushing Nature blots with tears in vain,
That frowning Wisdom reads with tone severe,
While Pity shudders with averted ear.
Yet will I dare its varying modes to trace
Through many a distant tribe and vanisht race;
The sketch perchance shall touch the ingenuous heart,
And hint its moral with a pleasing art.
Aid me, Historic Muse! unfold thy store
Of rich, or various, never-cloying lore;
Thence Fancy flies with new-born visions fraught,
There old Experience lends his hoards to Thought.

When slumbering Adam pressed the lonely earth, . . .
Unconscious parent of a wondrous birth. . . .
As forth to light the infant-woman sprung,
By pitying angels thus her doom was sung:

"Ah! fairest creature! born to changeful skies,
To bliss and agony, to smiles and sighs:
Beauty's frail child, to thee, though doomed to bear
By far the heavier half of human care,
Deceitful Nature's stepdame-love assigned
A form more fragile, and a tenderer mind;
More copious tears from Pity's briny springs,
And, trembling Sympathy! thy finest strings:
While ruder man she prompts, in pride of power,
To bruise, to slay, to ravage, to devour;
On prostrate weakness turn his gory steel,
And point the wounds not all thy tears can heal.
Poor victim! stern the mandate of thy birth,
Ah dote not, smile not, on the things of earth!
Subdue thyself; those rapturous flutterings still!
Armed with meek courage and a patient will,
With thoughtful eye pursue thy destined way,
Adore thy God, and hope a brighter day!"
In solemn notes thus flowed the prescient strain.
But flowed on Eve's unpractised ear in vain;
In smiling wonder fixt, the new-born bride
Drank the sweet gale, the glowing landscape eyed,
And murmured untried sounds, and gazed on every side.
With look benign the boding angels view
The fearless innocent, and wave adieu:
"Too well thy daughters shall our strain believe;
Too short thy dream of bliss, ill-fated Eve."

Prophetic spirits! that with ken sublime
Sweep the long windings of the flood of time,
Joyless and stern, your deep-toned numbers dwell
On rocks, on whirlpools, and the foaming swell,
But pass unmarked the skiffs that gaily glide
With songs and streamers down the dimpling tide:
Else rapturous notes had floated on the wind,
And hailed the stranger born to bless her kind,
To bear from heaven to earth the golden ties,
Bind willing man, and draw him to the skies.

See where the world's new master roams along,
Vainly intelligent and idly strong;
Mark his long listless step and torpid air,
His brow of densest gloom and fixt infantile stare!
Those sullen lips no mother's lips have prest,
Nor drawn, sweet labour! at her kindly breast;
No mother's voice has touched that slumbering ear,
Nor glistening eye beguiled him of a tear;
Love nursed not him with sweet endearing wiles,
Nor woman taught the sympathy of smiles;
Vacant and sad his rayless glances roll,
Nor hope nor joy illumes his darkling soul;
Ah! hapless world that such a wretch obeys!
Ah! joyless Adam, though a world he sways!

But see! . . . . they meet, ... they gaze, ... the new-born pair; . . . .
Mark now the wakening youth, the wondering fair:
Sure a new soul that moping idiot warms,
Dilates his stature, and his mien informs!
A brighter crimson tints his glowing cheek;
His broad eye kindles, and his glances speak.
So roll the clouds from some vast mountain's head,
Melt into mist, and down the valleys spread;
His crags and caves the bursting sunbeams light,
And burn and blaze upon his topmost height;
Broad in full day he lifts his towering crest,
And fire celestial sparkles from his breast.
Eve too, how changed! . . . . No more with baby grace
The smile runs dimpling o'er her trackless face,
As painted meads invite her roving glance,
Or birds with liquid trill her ear intrance:
With downcast look she stands, abasht and meek,
Now pale, now rosy red, her varying cheek;
Now first her fluttering bosom heaves a sigh,
Now first a tear stands trembling in her eye;
For hark! the youth, as love and nature teach,
Breathes his full bosom, and breaks forth in *speech*:
His quivering lips the winged accents part,
And pierce, how swift! to Eve's unguarded heart.

Now rose complete the mighty Maker's plan,
And Eden opened in the heart of Man;
Kindled by Hope, by gentle Love refined,
Sweet converse cheered him, and a kindred mind;
Nor deem that He, beneficent and just,
In woman's hand who lodged this sacred trust,
For man alone her conscious soul informed,
For man alone her tenderer bosom warmed;
Denied to her the cup of joy to sip,
But bade her raise it to his greedy lip,
Poor instrument of bliss, and tool of ease,
Born but to serve, existing but to please: . . . .
No; . . . . hand in hand the happy creatures trod,
Alike the children of no partial God;
Equal they trod till want and guilt arose,
Till savage blood was spilt, and man had foes:
Ah! days of happiness, ... with tearful eye

I see you gleam, and fade, and hurry by:
Why should my strain the darkening theme pursue?
Be husht, my plaintive lyre! my listening friend, adieu!

— EPISTLE II —

Argument of Epistle II

The subject resumed. Sketch of savage life in general—The sex oppressed by slaves and barbarians, but held in honour by the good and the brave.—New Holland—brutality of the inhabitants—their courtship. North American Indians—one of their women describes her wretched condition and destroys her female infant. Hardening effect of want on the human mind. Transition to Otaheite—Licentious manners of those islanders—Infanticide. Address to maternal affection—exemplified in the hind—fawns destroyed by the stag. Coast of Guinea—a native sells his son for a slave—agony of the mother—her speech. Pastoral life—Chaldee astronomers—King David. Tartars—removal of a Tartar camp—their gaiety and happy mediocrity of condition relative to the gifts of nature—yet no refined affection between the sexes—female captives and women sent in tribute preferred to the natives—No perfect Arcadia to be found on earth—Caffres[1] and Hottentots sprightly and harmless—but all pastoral and hunting tribes deficient in mental cultivation—hence the weaker sex held by all in some kind of subjection.

....

Once more my Muse uplifts her drooping eye,
Checks the weak murmur and restrains the sigh;
Once more, my friend, incline thy candid ear,
And grace my numbers with a smile and tear.
Not mine the art in solemn garb to dress
The shadowy forms of *delicate distress*,
With baleful charms to call from Fancy's bower
Vain shapes of dread to haunt the lonely hoar;
In feverish dreams to feed the pampered thought
With heavenly bliss . . . . . on earth how vainly sought!
Fan with rash breath the passions' smouldering fire,
Whet the keen wish, the thrilling hope inspire,
Woo the young soul its blossoms to unfold,
Then leave it chilled with more than wintry cold.

No; . . . . rude of hand, with bolder lines I trace
The rugged features of a coarser race:
Fierce on thy view the savage world shall glare,
And all the ills of wretched woman there;
Unknown to her fond love's romantic glow,
The graceful throbs of sentimental woe,
The play of passions and the feelings' strife
That weave the web of finely-chequered life.
But thou possest, unspoiled by tyrant art,
Of the large empire of a generous heart,
Thou wilt not scorn plain nature's rudest strain,
Nor *homely* misery claim thy sighs in vain.

Come then, my friend; my devious way pursue;
Pierce every clime, and search all ages through;
Stretch wide and wider yet thy liberal mind,
And grasp the sisterhood of womankind:
With mingling anger mark, and conscious pride,
The sex by whom exalted or decried;
Crusht by the savage, fettered by the slave,
But served, but honoured, by the good and brave.

With daring keel attend yon convict train
To new-found deserts of the Southern Main;[2]
Beasts of strange gait there roam the trackless earth,
And monstrous compounds struggle into birth;
A younger world it seems, abortive, crude,
Where untaught Nature sports her fancies rude,
By slow gradations rears her infant plan,
And shows, half-humanized, the monster-man.
Mark the grim ruffian roll his crafty glance,
And crouching, slow, his tiger-step advance,
With brandisht club surprise his human prey,
And drag the bleeding victim bride away,
While shouts triumphant wake the orgies dire,
And Rage and Terror trim the nuptial fire.[3]
E'en such is Savage Man, of beasts the worst,
In want, in guilt, in lawless rapine nurst.
To the dumb tribes that plod their even life
Unbruised by tyranny, unvext by strife,
Instincts and appetites kind Nature gave,

[1] **New Holland**: Australia. **Otaheite**: former name for Tahiti. **Chaldee**: Babylonian, native of "Chaldea" (II. 184). **Caffres**: specifically, a South African tribe of Bantu stock, but also generally "savages" or primitive people.

[2] **Southern Main**: the south seas; Oceania.

[3] "The courtship" of the savages of New Holland" consists in watching the lady's retirement, and then knocking her down with repeated blows of a club or wooden sword; after which the truly matrimonial victim is led streaming with blood to her future husband's party, where a scene ensues too shocking to relate." [David] Collins's Hist. of the Colony in New Holland. [L.A.]

These just supplying what the others crave;
The human brute the headlong passions rule,
While infant Reason flies the moody fool,
Hope, Fear, and Memory play their busy part
And mingle all their chaos in his heart;
Hence Vengeance fires, hence Envy's stings infest,
Hence Superstition goads his timorous breast.
O! not for him life's healthful current flows;
An equal stream that murmurs as it goes;
As rage and torpor hold alternate rule,
It roars a flood, or stagnates in a pool.
Whose sterile brink no buds of fragrance cheer
By love or pity nurtured with a tear.

What wonder then, the Western wilds among
Where the red Indian's hunter-bow is strung,
(Nature's tough son, whose adamantine frame
No pleasures soften and no tortures tame)
If, fiercely pondering in her gloomy mind
The desperate ills that scowl on womankind,
The maddening mother gripes the infant slave,
And forces back the worthless life she gave?[4]
"Swift, swift," she cries, "receive thy last release;
Die, little wretch; die once and be at peace!
Why shouldst thou live, in toil, and pain, and strife,
To curse the names of mother and of wife?
To see at large thy lordly master roam,
The beasts his portion and the woods his home,
Whilst thou, infirm, the sheltering hut must seek,
Poorly dependent, timorously weak,
There hush thy babe, with patient love carest,
And tearful clasp him to thy milkless breast
Hungry and faint, while feasting on his way
Thy reckless hunter wastes the jocund day?
Or, harder task, his rapid courses share,
With patient back the galling burden bear,
While he treads light, and smacks the knotted thong,
And goads with taunts his staggering troop along?
Enough; . . . . 'tis love, dear babe, that stops thy
breath;
'Tis mercy lulls thee to the sleep of death:
Ah! would for me, by like indulgent doom,
A mother's hand had raised the early tomb!
O'er these poor bones the moons had rolled in vain,
And brought nor stripes nor famine, toil nor pain;
I had not sought in agony the wild,
Nor, wretched, frantic mother! killed my child."
Want hardens man; by fierce extremes the smart
Inflames and chills and indurates his heart,
Arms his relentless hand with brutal force,
And drives o'er female necks his furious course.

Not such his mind where Nature, partial queen,
With lavish plenty heaps the bounteous scene;
In laughing isles with broad bananas crowned,
Where tufted cocoas shade the flowery ground;
Here, here at least, where dancing seasons shed
Unfading garlands on his sleeping head,
Love melts to love, and man's ingenuous mind
Feels nature's kindness prompt him to be kind;
He acts no tyranny, he knows no strife,
One harmless holiday his easy life.
Ah cheated hopes! . . . . see Lawless Love invade
The withering scene, and poison every shade;
Embruted nations couch beneath his yoke,

[4] "In all unpolished nations, it is true, the functions in domestic economy which fall naturally to the share of the women, are so many, that they are subjected to hard labour, and must bear more than their full portion of the common burden. But in America their condition is so peculiarly grievous, and their depression so complete, that servitude is a name too mild to describe their wretched state. A wife, amongst most tribes, is no better than a beast of burden, destined to every office of labour and fatigue. While the men loiter out the day in sloth, or spend it in amusement, the women are condemned to incessant toil. Tasks are imposed upon them without pity, and services are received without complacency or gratitude.

"Every circumstance reminds the women of this mortifying inferiority. They must approach their lords with reverence, they must regard them as more exalted beings, and are not permitted to eat in their presence."

"There are many districts in America where this dominion is so grievous, and so sensibly felt, that some women, in a wild emotion of maternal tenderness, have destroyed their female children in their infancy, in order to deliver them from that intolerable bondage to which they knew they were doomed." [William] Robertson's Hist. of America [1777], vol. ii. p. 105.

Hearne describes the women of the Northern tribes which he visited, as wading through the snow encumbered with heavy burdens, while the men, themselves carrying nothing, urged them on with blows and threats. He mentions other particulars, also illustrative of the wretched condition of the American females, too numerous and too horrid for poetical narration.

Certainly Rousseau did not consult the interests of the weaker sex in his preference of savage life to civilized. [L.A.]

And infant gore on his dire altars smoke!
Lost Otaheite! . . . . Breathe one parting sigh,
Then swift, my friend, we turn the bashful eye.[5]

Thrice holy Power, whose fostering, bland embrace
Shields the frail scions of each transient race,
To whom fair Nature trusts the teeming birth
That fills the air, that crowds the peopled earth,
Maternal Love! thy watchful glances roll
From zone to zone, from pole to distant pole;
Cheer the long patience of the brooding hen,
Soothe the she-fox that trembles in her den,
'Mid Greenland ice-caves warm the female bear,
And rouse the tigress from her sultry lair.
At thy command, what zeal, what arduour, fires
The softer sex! a mightier soul inspires: . . . .
Lost to themselves, our melting eyes behold
Prudent, the simple, and the timid, bold.
All own thy sway, save where, on Simoom[6] wing
Triumphant sailing o'er the blasted spring,
(Weather in Otaheitan groves accurst,
Or Europe's polisht scenes the fiend be nurst)
Unhallowed Love bids Nature's self depart,
And makes a desert of the female heart.
But O! how oft, their tender bosoms torn
By countless shafts, thy noblest votaries mourn!
See the soft hind forsake the dewy lawns
To shroud in thicket-shades her tender fawns;
Fearless for them confront the growling foe,
And aim with hoof and head the desperate blow;
Freely for them with new-born courage face
The howling horrors of the deathful chase:
Ah! fond in vain, see fired by furious heat
The jealous stag invade her soft retreat,
Wanton in rage her pleading anguish scorn,
And gore his offspring with relentless horn.

Hark to that shriek! from Afric's palmy shore
The yell rolls mingling with the billows' roar:
Grovelling in dust the frantic mother lies; . . . .
"My son, my son, O spare my son!" she cries:
"Sell not thy child! Yon dreary ocean crost,
To thee, to me, to all forever lost,
The white man's slave, no swift-returning oar
Shall homeward urge the wretched captive more,
No tidings reach: . . . Who then with kindly care
Shall tend our age, and leafy beds prepare?
Who climb for us the cocoa's scaly side,
Or drain the juicy palm? . . . . who skim the tide,
Or bold in woods with pointed javelin roam,
And bear to us the savoury booty home?
Save thine own flesh! . . . . we must not, will not part. . . .
O save this bleeding, bursting, mother's heart!"

Ah fruitless agony! ah slighted prayer!
That bids the husband and the father, spare!
On to the mart the sable tyrant drives
His flocks of children and his herds of wives:
For toys, for drams, their kindred blood is sold,
And broken female hearts are paid with gold;
Exulting Avarice gripes his struggling prize,
The savage tenders, and the christian . . . . *buys*.[7]

Shrinkst thou, my startled friend, with feeling tear,
From tints too lively, numbers too sincere?
Swift wouldst thou fly to some unspotted scene
Where love and nature rule the blue serene?
Hail, Pastoral Life, to thy calm scenes belong
The lore of sages and the poet's song;
Nurse of rude man, in whose soft lap reclined,
Art, science, dawn upon his wakening mind,
And passion's tender strains, and sentiment refined!

Where cloudless heavens o'erarch Chaldea's plain,
Stretched by his nightly flock, the vacant swain,
His upturned gaze as sportful fancy warmed,
With ready crook the sand-drawn monsters formed;
Thence learn'd, Astronomy, thy studious eye,
To track yon orbs, to sweep yon pathless sky.
While still young David roamed the pastoral wild,
The harp, the song, his ardent soul beguiled,
And now to heaven upsoared the ethereal flame,
Now blazed some humble charmer's rustic fame.
E'en now, by Freedom led, see gay Content
Stoop from above, to shepherd-wanderers sent;
See o'er the green expanse of pathless plain

[5] It is supposed that two-thirds of the children born in Otaheite are immediately murdered. For the particulars of that dreadful licentiousness which is the consequence of the complete indolence of these islanders, and the countless and nameless evils and enormities which are *its* consequence, see Transactions of the [Church] Missionary Society, vol. i. [L.A.]

[6] Simoom: windstorm, in Asia Minor.

[7] These lines were written before the late glorious abolition [in 1807]: but there are still Christian nations to whom they apply with full force. [L.A.]

The sunburnt Tartars urge the tented wain;
How gay the living prospect! far and wide
Spread flocks and herds, and shouting herdsmen ride;
And hark! from youths and maids, a mingled throng,
How full, how joyous, bursts the choral song!

Free are these tribes and blest; a churlish soil
They till not, bowed by tyranny and toil;
Nor troll the deep for life's precarious stay;
Nor, beastlike, roam the tangled woods for prey;
Their lot, with sober kindness, gives to share
Labour with plenty, and with freedom, care:
Yet seek not here the boon, all boons above,
The generous intercourse of equal love;
A homely drudge, the Tartar matron knows
No eye that kindles and no heart that glows;
For foreign charms the faithless husband burns,
And clasps in loathed embrace, which fear returns,
The captive wife or tributary maid
By conquest snatched, or lawless terror paid.[8]

No! . . . . vain the search, ... of warm poetic birth,
Arcadian blossoms scorn the fields of earth;
No lovelorn swains, to tender griefs a prey,
Sigh, sing, and languish through the livelong day;
No rapturous husband and enamoured wife,
To live and love their only care in life,
With crook and scrip on flowery banks reclined
Breathe the warm heart and share the answering
    mind:
The sprightly Caffre o'er the moonlight meads
In jovial dance his dusky partner leads,
And vacant Hottentots, short labour done,
Toy, pipe, and carol, in the evening sun;
But the high promptings of the conscious soul
The weak that elevate, the strong control,
Respect, decorum, friendship, ties that bind
To woman's form the homage of the mind,
Heaven's nobler gifts, to riper ages lent,
Disdain the hunter's cave, the shepherd's tent,
And *lawless* man, or cold, or fierce, or rude,
Proves every mode of female servitude.

— EPISTLE III —

Argument of Epistle III

Dawn of civilization, freedom, and the virtues. Troy taken — captives — Andromache. Spartans — character of their women — remarks. Athens — Phryne — Aspasia — degradation of the married women. Rome — present degraded state of both sexes — women in a condition approaching freedom, follow and imitate the course of the men with whom they are connected, as his shadow, the traveller. Ancient Rome — its female deities — Sabine women — mother and wife of Coriolanus. Cornelia. Portia. Arria. Corruption of manners in Rome — its conquest by the barbarians. Another scene of virtue and glory unfolded by the promulgation of christianity — its favourable effect on the condition of women — their zeal in its defence equal to that of men — Female martyrs. Marriage rendered indissoluble — belief of a reunion in a future state. Rise of superstition — monastic institutions. Convent. Saints Theresa, Clara, and Catharine of Siena. Conclusion.

....

Ye heaven-taught bards, who first for human woe
Bade human tears to melting numbers flow;
Ye godlike sages, who with plastic hand
Moulded rude man, and arts and cities planned:
Ye holy patriots, whose protecting name
Still lives, and issuing from the trump of fame
Fans sacred Freedom's everlasting flame,
All hail! . . . . by you sublimed, the expanding heart
First learned the bliss its blessings to impart:
The fierce barbarian checked his headlong course,
And bent to Wisdom's hand his yielded force:
Each loftier Virtue bowed to meet the brave,
And clasped, a freeman, whom she scorned, a slave;
And smiling round, the daughter, mother, wife,
Fed the dear charities of social life.

Bright as the welcome orb that wakes to chase
The polar Night from Earth's reviving face. . . .
(Grim Power that shakes the meteor from his hair,
While shaggy prowlers in the fitful glare

[8] An annual tribute of women was exacted by the Tartars, or Huns, from the Chinese; and even the daughters, genuine or adopted, of the eastern emperors were claimed in marriage by the Tanjous as a bond of union between the nations. "The situation of these unhappy victims is described," says Gibbon, "in the verses of a Chinese princess, who laments that she had been condemned by her parents to a distant exile, under a barbarian husband; who complains that sour milk was her only drink, raw flesh her only food, a tent her only palace; and who expresses, in a strain of pathetic simplicity, the natural wish that she were transformed into a bird, to fly back to her dear country, the object of her tender and perpetual regret." Decline and Fall, vol. iv. p. 363, 8 vol. edition. [L.A.] **Tanjous:** unidentified; possibly a tribe from Tanjore (now Thanjavur) in Tamil Nadu, India.

Roam with rude yells along the mountains drear,
Ravening and yet undisciplined to fear)
Behold, my friend, with pleased and anxious gaze
Fair Reason's day-star light her gradual blaze;
Pant up the steepness of her high career,
And win by toil the empire of the sphere;
While with slow hand the ungenial shades withdrawn,
Vapours and tempests struggle with the dawn.

Mark the last hour of Ilium, ... work divine!
Sunk her proud towers, and sunk each holy shrine:
Slaughter has done his work: the manly brave
Sighed as they fell, despairing of a grave.
Yet, weep not them! behold yon captive train;
Houseless and bound they strew the smoking plain;
Matrons and maids, gray sires and babes are there,
Shrill wails and frantic screams, deep groans and
dumb despair.
Hark! 'tis the lost Andromache that shrieks,[1]
Her loose locks rent, and bruised her bleeding cheeks:
Home the proud victor bears his beauteous prize;
For death, for death she sues with fruitless cries.
Ah! might she wait that kind, that last release,
And drain the dregs of bitterness in peace!
But no; . . . . she bears the vengeful brand of strife,
Fires the loose rover, stings the jealous wife;
What scorn, what rage, the wretched captive waits,
Envied and hated for the love she hates!
The rest, a mingled, nameless, feeble throng,
The savage squadrons drive with taunts along,
Destined to whirl with pain the slavish mill;
Bear ponderous logs, and sparkling goblets fill
To hostile Gods; explore the distant spring,
And faint with heat the cooling burthen bring;
In housewife tasks the midnight hours employ,
And lave those feet that spurned the dust of Troy.[2]

[1] **Ilium**: Troy. **Andromache**: the devoted wife of Hector, Trojan hero; taken as a spoil of war and bride by the Greek Neoptolemus, whose father Achilles had slain Hector; her story is related by Homer in the *Iliad*.

[2] One of the most pathetic passages of Homer thus paints the situation of a female captive: "As when a woman weeps / Her husband fall'n in battle for her sake, / And for his children's sake, before the gate / Of his own city; sinking to his side / She close infolds him with a last embrace, / And gazing on him as he pants and dies, / Shrieks at the sight; meantime the ruthless foe / Smiting her shoulders with the spear, to toil / Command her and to bondage far away, / And her cheek fades with horror at the sound." *Odyssey*. viii.523—[trans. William] Cowper. [L.A.]

These were the days, while yet the scourge and chain
Quivered and clanked in wild War's demon train,
When Honour first his calm firm phalanx ranged:
Fury to Valour, men to heroes changed:
And mark! emerging from the gulf of night,
What towering phantom strikes our wondering sight?
Fierce with strange joy she stands, the battle won,
Elate and tearless o'er her slaughtered son.
"He died for Sparta, died unknown to fear,
His wounds all honest, and his shield his bier;
And shall I weep?" Stern daughters of the brave,
Thus maids and matrons hailed the Spartan's grave;
By turns they caught, they lit, the hero-flame,
And scorned the Woman's for the Patriot's name;
Unmoved, unconquered, bowed to fate's decree,
And taught in chains the lesson . . . . to be free.[3]
Souls of gigantic mould, they fill our gaze
With pigmy wonder and despairing praise: . . . .
Thus when, 'mid western wilds, the delver's toil
Reared the huge mammoth from the quaking soil,
Columbia's swains in mute amazement eyed
And heaved the monstrous frame from side to side;[4]
Saw bones on bones in mouldering ruin lie,
And owned the relics of a world gone by: . . . .
Yet self-same clay our limbs of frailty formed,
And hearts like ours those dreadless bosoms warmed;
But war, and blood, and Danger's gorgon face,
Froze into stone the unconquerable race.

Graced by the sword, the chisel, and the pen,
Athens! illustrious seat of far-famed men,
Receive my homage! Hark! what shouts arise
As Phryne gilds the pomp of sacrifice!
To Beauty's Queen the graceful dance they twine,
Trill the warm hymn, and dress the flowery shrine;
Priestess of love she fills the eager gaze,
And fires and shares the worship that she pays.
Haste, sculptor, haste! that form, that heavenly face
Catch ere they fade, and fix the mortal grace;
Phryne in gold shall deck the sacred fane,
And Pallas' virgin image frown in vain.

[3] A captive Lacedaemonian woman, being asked by her master what she understood, replied, "How to be free." And on his afterwards requiring of her something unworthy, she put herself to death. Valerius Maximus. [L.A.]

[4] Archaeological excavations in Columbia, a poetic name for America, in the early nineteenth century had uncovered the skeleton of a dinosaur.

Rise, bright Aspasia,[5] too! thy tainted name
Sails down secure through infamy to fame;
Statesmen and bards and heroes bend the knee,
Nor blushes Socrates to learn of thee.
Thy wives, proud Athens! fettered and debased,
Listlessly duteous, negatively chaste,
O vapid summary of a slavish lot!
They sew and spin, they die and are forgot.
Cease, headlong Muse! resign the dangerous theme,
Perish the glory that defies esteem!
Inspire thy trump at Virtue's call alone,
And blush to blazon whom She scorns to own.

Mark where seven hills uprear yon stately scene,
And reedy Tiber lingering winds between:
Ah mournful view! ah check to human pride!
There Glory's ghost and Empire's phantom glide:
Shrunk art thou, mighty Rome; the ivy crawls,
The vineyard flaunts, within thy spacious walls;
Still, still, Destruction plies his iron mace,
And fanes and arches totter to their base:
Thy sons . . . . O traitors to their fathers' fame!
O last of men, and Romans but in name!
See where they creep with still and listless tread,
While cowls, not helmets, veil the inglorious head.
If then, sad partner of her country's shame,
To nobler promptings deaf, the Latian dame
Nor honour's law nor nuptial faith can bind,
Vagrant and light of eye, of air, of mind, ...
Whom now a vile gallant's obsequious cares
Engage, now mass, processions, penance, prayers, ...
Think not 'twas always thus: . . . . what generous view,
What noble aim that noble men pursue,
Has never woman shared? As o'er the plain
The sun-drawn shadow tracks the wandering swain,
Treads in his footsteps, counterfeits his gait,
Erect or stooping, eager or sedate;
Courses before, behind, in mimic race,
Turns as he turns, and hunts him pace by pace; . . . .
Thus, to the sex when milder laws ordain
A lighter fetter and a longer chain,
Since freedom, fame, and lettered life began,
Has faithful woman tracked the course of man.
Strains his firm step for Glory's dazzling height,
Panting she follows with a proud delight;
Led by the sage, with pausing foot she roves
By classic fountains and religious groves;
In Pleasure's path if strays her treacherous guide,
By fate compelled, she deviates at his side, ...
Yet seeks with tardier tread the downward way,
Averted eyes, and timorous, faint delay.
In mystic fable thus, together trod
The dire Bellona and the Warrior God;
The golden Archer and chaste Huntress' queen
With deaths alternate strewed the sickening scene;
And Jove-born Pallas shared the Thunderer's state,
The shield of horror and the nod of fate.[6]

The indignant Muse for yon polluted ground
Shall chase the vampire forms that flit around;
Restore the scene with one commanding glance;
Awake old Rome, and bid her shades advance:
A sad but glorious pageant! . . . . First are borne
Her sculptured deities, and seem to mourn;
Dian and Vesta, powers of awful mien,
And in her purer garb the Paphian Queen;[7]
Here smiles the Appeaser of the angry spouse,[8]
There *distaffed* Pallas knits her thoughtful brows;
Imperial Juno rears her head on high,
Unspotted guardian of the nuptial tie.
See then advance with wild disordered charms
The matron Sabines[9] . . . . prize of lawless arms. . . .
Such as they rushed athwart the clanging fight,
Bold in their fears and strong in nature's right:
Each lifts her babe; the babe, 'mid vengeful strife,

[5] **Phryne**: a golden statue of Phryne the courtesan was placed by the Athenians in one of their temples amongst the images of their deities [L. A.]. **Pallas' virgin**: Athena, the virgin goddess of wisdom. **Aspasia**: Greek courtesan (470?–410 BC) noted for her beauty, wit, and learning; consort of Pericles.

[6] **Bellona**: Roman goddess of war; consort of Mars, the god of War. **chaste Huntress**: Diana, the virgin goddess of the moon. **Pallas**: Athena/Minerva, supposedly born from the brow of Jove or Jupiter, the Thunderer.

[7] **Vesta**: the Roman goddess of the hearth, or domesticity. **Paphian Queen**: Venus, the goddess of love.

[8] **Appeaser . . . the angry spouse**: whenever a disagreement arose between a husband and wife, they repaired to the shrine of the Goddess Viriplaca (the appeaser of husbands); and there, having alternately spoken what they thought proper, they laid aside their contention, and returned in peace. Val. Max. [L.A.]

[9] **Sabines**: ancient people of central Italy, frequently at war with the Romans; according to legend, the followers of Romulus raped (or seized) the Sabine women when they could not find wives among their own people. "The Rape of the Sabine Women" was a popular subject of painting in the eighteenth century. (See works by Poussin and Delacroix.)

Lisps to his grandsire for his father's life;
The vanquisht grandsire clasps the blooming boy;
Rage sinks in tears, in smiles, in shouting joy;
Peace joins their hands, Love mingles race with race,
And Woman triumphs in the wide embrace.

I see her rise, the chaste polluted fair,
And claim the death of honour in despair.
Rome's Saviour wakes[10] . . . . "By that ennobled shade,
By this pure blood, and by this reeking blade,
Vengeance I swear!" . . . . Heaven blessed the generous rage
That lit the splendours of a brightening age;
The patriot spark from dying honour springs,
And female virtue buys . . . . the flight of Kings.

And who are they that lead yon suppliant train?
Mother and wife, when Latium's fertile plain
Fierce Velseians trod, the rebel's armed hate
They soothed, and soothing saved the tottering state:
Rome crowned the sex . . . . a high and graceful meed. . . .
And bade yon temple consecrate the deed.[11]

Hail! who thy sons to Glory's altar led,
And boldly called her lightnings on their head:
What though they fell? the pure ethereal flame
Touched but the life, and spared the nobler fame.
Lift thy proud head, and proudly tell their tale;
Cornelia, mother of the Gracchi, hail!
See there the ghost of noble Portia glide,
Cato to lead, and Brutus at her side![12]
Souls have no sex; sublimed by Virtue's lore
Alike they scorn the earth and try to soar;
Buoyant alike on daring wing they rise
As Emulation nerves them for the skies.
See Pætus' wife,[13] by strong affection manned,
Taste the sharp steel and give it to his hand:
But what avails? On Rome's exhausted soil
Nor patriots' fattening blood, nor heroes' toil,
One plant, one stem, of generous growth may rear
To grace the dark December of her year.
Whelmed in the flood of vice, one putrid heap,
Rank, sex, age, race, are hurried to the deep;
Low-bending sycophant and upstart knave,
Athlete and mime, loose dame and minion slave.
Wild in the frighted rear the crowds recoil,
Urged by the barbarous brood of war and spoil;
Nearer and nearer yet, with harpy rush
They sweep; they pounce, they violate, they crush;
Flap their triumphant wings o'er grovelling Rome,
And roost in Glory's desolated home.
Scared at the portent, see the phantom train
Veil their wreathed brows; then, rising in disdain,
With thunders borne upon the howling wind,
Leave Rome and all her infamy behind.

Is frighted Virtue then for ever fled
To veil in heaven her scorned and houseless head,
While Vice and Misery lord it here below
O'er God's waste scene of bliss and beauty? No!
Virtue, pure essence mingled with the whole,
Its subtle, viewless, all-inspiring soul, ...
Virtue, the mental world's pervading fire,
Unquenched remains, or nature must expire.
Now fresh and strong in renovated rays

[10] "Brutus adest, tandemque animo sua nomina fallit: / Fixaque semanimi corpore tela rapit. / Stillantemque tenens generoso sanguine cultrum, / Edidit impavidos ore minante sonos: / Per tibi ego hunc juro fortem castumque cruorem, / Perque tuos Manes, qui mihi numen erunt: / Tarquinium poenas profugá cum stirpe daturum." Ovid. Fast. [L.A.]

Translation by Sir James George Frazer: "Brutus came, and then at last belied his name; for from the half-dead body he snatched the weapon stuck in it, and holding the knife, that dripped with noble blood, he fearless spoke these words of menace: "By this brave blood and chaste, and by thy ghost, who shall be god to me I swear to be avenged on Tarquin and on his banished brood" (Ovid, *Fasti* II:837–843).

[11] **bade yon temple . . . deed:** the Roman Senate caused a temple to *Female Fortune* to be erected on the spot where the wife and mother of Coriolanus met him, and prevailed upon him to return. Some new privileges were also granted to the women on that occasion. [L.A.]

[12] **Cornelia:** daughter of Scipio Africanus, wife of Tiberius Sempronius Gracchus, and mother of the Gracchi; devoted herself to raising her sons for heroic military careers; model of Roman motherhood. **Portia:** Porcia, daughter of Cato Uticensis and wife of Marcus Brutus, murderer of Caesar; ardent supporter of Republican liberties; stabbed self before Brutus to show him that it was not so hard to die for the cause of freedom.

[13] **Paetus' wife:** Arria (d. 42 AD), wife of Caecina Paetus, who was condemned to death for his role in a conspiracy against the emperor Claudius. Determined not to survive her husband, Arria stabbed herself and handed the dagger to her husband with the remark, "Paetus, it doesn't hurt" [*D.N.B.*].

She flings on eastern hills the glorious blaze;
Now, wrapt in richer lustre, slopes her beams
Tranquil and sweet along the western streams;
Now, with faint twinkling of a single star,
She greets the guideless pilgrim from afar;
And red with anger now, a dreadful form,
She glares in lightning through the howling storm.

From Juda's rocks[14] the sacred light expands,
And beams and broadens into distant lands;
Heaven's thunder speaks, the mighty bolt is hurled;
Pride, bite the dust! and quake, thou guilty world!
But, O ye weak, beneath a master's rod
Trembling and prostrate, own a helping God!
Ardent in faith, through bonds and toil and loss
Bear the glad tidings, triumph in the cross!
Away with woman's fears! proud man shall own
As proud a mate on Virtue's loftiest throne;
On to the death in joy . . . . for Jesus' sake
Writhed on the rack, or blackening at the stake,
Scorn the vain splendours of the world below,
And soar to bliss that only martyrs know![15]
Now comrades, equals, in the toilsome strife,
Partners of glory and coheirs of life,
See sex to sex with port sublimer turn.
And steadier flames and holier ardours burn;
At God's pure altar pledged, the nuptial band
Turns to a lifelong vow, and dreads no severing hand;
E'en death, they deem, (once sped the second blow
That social lays the sad survivor low,
Shrowds the dissolving forms in kindred gloom,
Mingles in dust and marries in the tomb,)
With stronger, purer, closer ties shall bind
The blest communion of the immortal mind,
Free the winged soul to larger bliss above,
And ope the heaven of everlasting love.

O faith, O hope divine! ordained to flow
A stream of comfort through the vales of woe!
Rise, mystic dove! explore on venturous wing
The wastes of winter and the wilds of spring;
Bear back thine olive from the emerging strand,
Restore the virtues, and redeem the land:
Rebel no more, again repentant man
Shall own, shall bless, the mighty Maker's plan;
Heaven's warmest beam salute his second birth,
And one wide Eden round the peopled earth.
Vain hope! the wretch, or slave or tyrant born,
Who looked with terror up, or down with scorn,
Untaught to hope in that all-seeing mind
Unbounded love with boundless power combined,
Self-judged, self-doomed, a timorous outcast trod,
Nor dared to claim a father in his God:
Hence, Superstition, spleenful, doting, blind,
Thy mystic horrors shake his palsied mind;
Hence, as thy baleful spells in misty gloom
Wrap the fair earth and dim her orient bloom,
'Wildered, the maniac eyes a fancied waste,
And starves 'mid banquets that he dares not taste.
The yawning cloister shows its living grave,
Receives the trembler, and confirms him . . . . slave.
And thee, O woman, formed with smiling mien
To temper man, and gild the social scene, ...
Bid home-born blessings, home-born virtues rise,
And light the sunbeam in a husband's eyes, ...
Thy dearest bliss the sound of infant mirth,
His heart thy chief inheritance on earth, ...
Thee too, as fades around heaven's blessed light,
And age to age rolls on a darker night,
With steely gripe the exulting hag invades,
And drags relentless to her sullen shades.
O hear the sighs that break the sluggish air
Mixt with the convent hymn, the convent prayer,
The languid lip-devotion of despair!

---

[14] **Juda**: Judah, southernmost of two kingdoms remaining after the division of the kingdom of the Jews that occurred under Rehoboam; continually at war with the northern kingdom of Israel. In the Bible, Judah (931–586 BC), whose capital was Jerusalem and whose dynasty was the house of David, is portrayed as more loyal to God than is Israel.

[15] "Viros cum Mucio, vel cum Aquilio, aut Regulo comparo? *Pueri* et *Mulierculae* nostrae cruces et tormenta, feras, et omnes suppliciorum terriculas inspiratâ patientiâ doloris illudunt." Minucius Felix.

Do I compare our men with Mucius or Aquilius, or Regulus? Even our *Boys and Women,* with an inspired patience of suffering, deride crosses and racks, wild beasts, and all the terrors of punishment. [L.A.]

Minucius Felix, native of the Roman province of Africa, lived between mid-second and mid-third century AD; hailed the martyrdoms of the early Christians in his *Octavius.* **Mucius:** Gaius Mucius Scaevola, heroic Roman warrior who held his hand in fire to demonstrate his imperviousness to pain. **Aquilius:** Manius Aquilius, consul who crushed a slave revolt in Sicily (101 BC), but was later tortured to death by Mithridates, who poured molten gold down his throat. **Regulus:** Marcus Atilius Regulus, defeated the Carthaginians (256 BC), but was tortured to death when he returned with a peace treaty.

But ne'er could cloister rule or midnight bell,
Penance, or fast, in dank and lonesome cell,
Break the mind's spring, or stupefy to rest
The master-passion of an ardent breast.
In that dim cell the rapt Theresa lies
Ingulft and lost in speechless ecstasies;
All-powerful Love has lit the holy flame,
The fewel altered, but the fire the same.[16]

Her fearful nuns see dark-browed Clara school,
And tight and tighter strain her rigid rule:
Claims not the Thirst of Sway his lion's part
E'en in that pale ascetic's bloodless heart?[17]

Hail, lofty Catharine, visionary maid!
Carest by princes, by a pope obeyed;
Nor blush to own, though dead to all below,
A brave ambition and a patriot glow.[18]

But cease! of amorous worship, bigot pride,
Distorted virtue, talent misapplied,
No more: . . . . with anxious heart and straining mind
Long have I scanned the annals of the kind;
Here let me pause, o'erwearied and opprest;
Thou, my calm friend, thou moralize the rest.

— EPISTLE IV —

Argument of Epistle IV

Recurrence to the subject — many varieties of female condition still unnoticed — ancient German women — inhabitants of the Haram — Hindoo widow — fascinating French woman — English mother. Survey of a Turkish haram — mean and childish character of the women, haughty yet contemptible one of the men — fatal effects of polygamy — Man cannot degrade the female sex without degrading the whole race. Ancient Germans — their women free and honoured — hence the valour of the men, the virtue of both sexes, the success of their resistance to Rome. Chivalry personified and depicted — his valour — his devotion to the ladies, his pure and romantic love — his lady described as endowed with all virtues and graces, but found to be a visionary being, only existing in the Fairy land of Spenser — contrasted by the giddy and unprincipled women introduced into the French court by Francis I. Gallantry, the parasite and treacherous corruptor of the sex — Man always suffers by degrading woman — public freedom dependent on domestic virtue. Switzerland virtuous when first made free — virtuous still, though oppress by France — Swiss women died fighting for their country. France not pure enough for freedom, yet had some heroines — Cordé — Roland. Transition to England — address to the author's female companions — survey of its female characters from the earliest times. Boadicca — Ethelfleda. Revival of letters gives consequence to women — Sir Thomas More and his daughter — Lady Jane Grey — Queen Elizabeth — Mrs. Hutchinson — Lady Russell. Enumeration concluded — Exhortation to Englishmen to look with favour on the mental improvement of females —

[16] Saint Theresa, born in Old Castile in 1515; a nun, and one of the most enthusiastic of devotees. She thus describes her feelings in a Life of herself: "In this representation which I made to place myself near to Christ, there would come suddenly upon me, without either expectation or preparation on my part, such an evident feeling of the presence of God, as that I could by no means doubt, but that either he was within me, or else I all engulfed in him. This was not in the manner of a vision, but I think they call it Mystical Theology; and it suspends the soul in such sort, that she seems to be wholly out of herself. The will is in the act of loving, the memory seems to be in a manner lost, the understanding in my opinion discourses not; and although it be not lost, yet it works not, as I was saying, but remains as it were amazed to consider how much it understands." [L.A.]

[17] Saint Clara, a celebrated abbess, born at Assisi in 1193. She put herself under the direction of St. Francis d'Assisi, and by his assistance founded a convent of which she became abbess. Her whole life appears to have been employed in the work of enforcing cloister discipline; but rigid as was the *rule* she imposed upon her nuns, Clara went far beyond it in the austerities she practised upon herself. Pope Innocent IV visited this abbess in her last moments, and soothed her departing spirit by the assurance that her *rule* should never in after times be mitigated. [L.A.]

[18] "Saint Catharine of Sienna was born in the city whence she takes her name in 1347. She vowed virginity at eight years of age, and soon after assumed the Dominican habit. She became famous for her revelations; and being ingenious, a good writer for her age, and distinguished for piety and charity, her influence was considerable. She went to Avignon to procure a reconciliation between the Florentines and Pope Gregory XI, who had excommunicated them; and by her eloquence she persuaded that pontiff to restore the papal seat to Rome after it had been seventy years at Avignon. Gregory however lived to repent of the step, and on his deathbed exhorted all persons present not to credit visions of private persons, acknowledging that he himself had been deceived by an enthusiast, and foresaw that it would produce evil consequences to the church. In the schism that succeeded, Catharine adhered to Urban VI. She died in 1380, and was canonized by Pope Pius II in 1461. There is extant of hers a volume of "Italian letters," written to popes, princes, cardinals, &c., besides several devotional pieces." General Biography. [L.A.]

to English women to improve and principle their minds, and by their merit induce the men to treat them as friends. Valediction.

....

Fain would I greet my gentle friend again;
Yet how renew, or where conclude, the strain?
Still as I gaze what mingled throngs appear!
What varying accents rush upon my ear!
Stern, awful, chaste, in savage freedom bred,
Here, German matrons shout o'er Varus dead;[1]
There, languid beauties, 'mid a haram's gloom,
In jealous bickerings pine away their bloom;
Here, well-dissembling, with a decent pride,
The victim-widow laves in Ganges' tide,
Clasps the loathed corse, invites the dreaded flame,
And dies in anguish, not to live with shame.
I turn, and meet the animated glance
Shot by the dames of gay seductive France;
Then melting catch the gaze, so fond, so mild,
Some English mother bends upon her child.
A thought, a look, a line, the meanest ask
To swell my growing tale, and lengthen out my task.

A glorious task! were mine the godlike power,
By Genius snatched in some propitious hour,
To bid the fleeting airy forms be still,
Or move, or change, obedient to my will;
Then fix the groupe, and pour in living light
Its vivid picture on the enraptured sight,
And bid it speak, in forceful tones and clear,
To Truth and Feeling just, to Fancy dear.
It may not be: . . . . my fainter sketch shall glide
Like dim reflections on an evening tide;
My task like hers, the soft Corinthian maid,
To trace a tintless shadow of a shade![2]
But to *that* shade fond fancy would supply
The bloom, the grace, the all-expressive eye;
Still would she gaze, till swam her cheated sight,
And the true lover blessed her wild delight.
Me such bright dreams delude not: . . . . thoughtful, cold,
The fading lines I languidly behold;
But thou, my friend, assert the generous part,
O praise, O foster, with a partial heart!
So shall the power my happier pencil guide,
And Friendship grant me what the Muse denied.

Come, pierce with me the Haram's jealous walls:
I see, I see, the soul-degraded thralls!
With childlike smile, one glittering dame surveys
Her splendid *caftan* and her diamonds' blaze;
One spreads the *henna*; one with sable dye
Wakes the dim lustre of her languid eye;[3]
Some seek the bath: . . . . O life, are these thy joys?
These all thy cares? How the dull prospect cloys!
Yet turn not from the view; deign first to scan
That lordly thing, the Asiatic Man.
O speaking lesson! marked with grateful awe;
Self is his God, his wildest will is law;
Him Beauty serves, all emulous to bless;
Yet where his envied, dear-bought happiness?
'Tis his, ... each proud, each manly virtue wreckt,
Truth, science, freedom lost in base neglect, ...
A pampered slave, in lazy state to sit
Shut from the sun of reason and of wit,
By senses cloyed of sensual bliss bereft,
And a dull drug his only refuge left.
One equal sole companion, skilled to blend
In one dear name the mistress and the friend,
Was Nature's boon; but when insatiate Man
Grasps wider joys, and scorns her sacred plan,
Farewell life's loveliest charm, farewell the glow
Affection casts upon the scene below;
Farewell each finer art, each softer grace,
All that adorns and all that lifts the race!
Woman no more, a deed-inspiring mate,
Shall fan the kindling glories of the state;
Suspicion's evil eye, with dire control,
Blights all the fairest blossoms of her soul,
And bids each rankling thorn, each poisonous weed,
A hostile crop, by righteous doom succeed.

[1] **Varus dead:** Publius Quintilius Varus (d. 9 AD), Roman general; appointed governor of Germany by Augustus; led three Roman legions against German uprising where they were massacred by the troops of Arminius; Varus then committed suicide.

[2] **To trace . . . shade!:** in classical legend, the origin of painting is attributed to a young woman of Corinth who, seeing the shadow of her beloved on the wall, traced the outline of his head.

[3] **caftan:** the caftan is an upper robe of rich materials worn by the Turkish ladies. **henna:** or alkanet, is a drug employed by them to tinge red the ends of the fingers and the inside of the hand. They increase the apparent lustre of the eye by introducing, within the edge of the eyelid, crude antimony in powder [L.A.].

Man, stamp the moral on thy haughty mind:
Degrade the sex, and thou degrad'st the kind![4]

Mark the bold contrast! hail, my friend, with me
The generous son of German liberty:
Barbarian? Yes: To spread the winged sail
Of venturous Commerce to the speeding gale,
To urge his ploughshare o'er the conquered soil,
And earn from Culture's hand the meed of toil,
As yet he knew not; nurst amid alarms,
His care was freedom, his rude trade was arms:
But this he knew; to woman's feeling heart
Its best its dearest tribute to impart;
Not the cheap falsehoods of a flattering strain,
Not idle gauds, vain incense to the vain;
But such high fellowship, such honoured life
As throws a glory round the exulting wife,
Seats her revered, sublime, on Virtue's throne,
Judge of his honour, guardian of her own.[5]
Dear was to him the birthright of the free;
More welcome death than her captivity;
And *hence* his valour's rude but vigorous stroke
Stunned Rome, and snapped her vainly-fitted yoke;[6]
(So swells Araxes[7] foaming in his pride,
So wrecks the insulting Spanner of his tide;)
And still he lives along the warning page
Of piercing Tacitus:[8] . . . Prophetic Sage!
With awe, with envy, with a patriot dread,
He saw the Western Genius lift his head;
Marked his large limbs to bracing hardship bared,
His stubborn mind for worst extremes prepared;
Marked the chaste virtues of his frugal home,
And read the destinies of stooping Rome.[9]

From Elbe and Weser,[10] or some unknown North
Derived, what bold yet courteous form rides forth
To view? At all points armed, with lance in rest,
Gilded his spurs, and plumed his haughty crest;
One steel-clad arm uprears a silver shield,
"Such is my faith!" upon its burnish't field
The motto quaint; its fond device, a heart
That burns and bleeds with Cupid's fiery dart.
Claspt to his mailed breast he bears a glove,
Dear parting token of his lady-love:
At speed he comes; he 'lights, he bends the knee
Proud where she sits. . . . It is, 'tis Chivalry! . . . .
Love's gallant martyr! Honour's generous child!
Thy bright extravagance, thy darings wild,
O who may think by pedant rules to try
That owns a woman's heart, a poet's eye;
An eye by Glory's dazzling glance controled,
A coward heart that dotes upon the bold?

---

[4] The following passage is cited in confirmation of the sentiments here expressed, from Mr. Southey's noble and eloquent introduction to his translation of The Chronicle of the Cid. "The continuance of polygamy was his (Mahommed's) great and ruinous error: where this pernicious custom is established, there will be neither connubial, nor paternal, nor brotherly affection; and hence the unnatural murders with which Asiatic history abounds. The Mahommedan imprisons his wives, and sometimes knows not the faces of his own children; he believes that despotism must be necessary in the state, because he knows it to be necessary at home: thus the domestic tyrant becomes the contented slave, and the atrocity of the ruler and the patience of the people proceed from the same cause. It is the inevitable tendency of polygamy to degrade both sexes: wherever it prevails, the intercourse between them is merely sexual. Women are only instructed in wantonness, sensuality becomes the characteristic of whole nations, and humanity is disgraced by crimes the most loathsome and detestable. This is the primary and general cause of that despotism and degradation which are universal throughout the East." &c. [L.A.]

[5] "These too (the women) are the most respected witnesses, the most liberal applauders of every man's conduct. The warriors come and show their wounds to their mothers and wives, who are not shocked at counting, and even requiring them." Tacit. de Morib. vii. [Tacitus, *Germania,* 7] Aikin's translation. [L.A.]

[6] "Tradition relates, that armies beginning to give way have been brought again to the charge by the females, through the earnestness of their supplications, the interposition of their bodies, and the pictures they have drawn of impending slavery, ... a calamity which these people bear with more impatience for their women than for themselves; so that those states who have been obliged to give among their hostages the daughters of noble families, are most effectually bound to fidelity." Ibid. viii. [L.A.]

[7] **Araxes:** modern Aras, turbulent river in Turkey; in Greco-Roman times, the major trade route from the Caspian to Asia Minor.

[8] **Tacitus:** Cornelius Tacitus (c. 55–after 115 AD), greatest Roman historian, author of *Germania, Annals,* and *Histories* of the Roman Emperors.

[9] "May the nations retain and perpetuate, if not an affection for us, at least an animosity against each other! since, while the fate of the empire is thus urgent, fortune can bestow no higher benefit upon us than the discord of our enemies." [Tacitus], Ibid, xxxiii. et pass. [L.A.]

[10] **Elbe and Weser:** rivers flowing through Czechoslovakia, northern and central Germany.

How dear the contrast! he, whose haughty brow
Scowls on the pride of man, nor deigns to bow;
Stung by a look, who challenges the strife
Where angry comrades stake the bauble, life;
Humble and suppliant bows her scorn to meet,
And soothes himself to meekness at her feet:
Then, at a word, again her own true knight
Tilts for her fame, or combats in her right.

Courts, tourneys, camps, high dames, a dazzling train,
A masque of glory, danced before his brain;
He lived in trance, and so the enchantment wrought
That 'mid the high illusions of his thought
Passion grew worship, and his heart a shrine
Where Beauty reigned all awful and divine;
Where steadfast, pure, Love burned a sacred flame;
Long years it burned, unquenchably the same,
Fed but on looks, and fanned with suppliant breath,
To her whose smile was life, whose frown was death.
But she, his Goddess; how may fancy trace
Her bright perfections and amazing grace?
Methinks I see a sweet and holy band,
A wreath of hovering Virtues, hand in hand
The new Pandora bless,[11] and on her head
In one rich dower their mingled treasury shed.
Majestic Honour, first, with matron care
Forms her high gait, and dignifies her air;
But chasing Pride, sweet Modesty the while
On her cheek blushes, Cheerfulness her smile
Blends with the blush, and innocently free
She learns the look, the tone, of Courtesy.
A thousand Graces in harmonious play
Throned in her eyes assert alternate sway;
With frank Benevolence they glance around,
Or dewed by Pity bend upon the ground,
Now seek the skies, by soaring Faith inspired,
Now beam with pure Serenity retired.

But say, this paragon, this matchless fair,
Trod she this care-crazed earth? No; . . . . born of air,
A flitting dream, a rainbow of the mind,
The tempting glory leaves my grasp behind;
Formed for no rugged clime, no barbarous age,
She blooms in Fairy land the grace of Spenser's page.[12]

Not such the dames with revelry and sport
Who tripped the wanton maze of Gallia's court,
By love and Francis[13] lured in evil hour
From hearths domestic and the sheltering bower.
New to the discipline of good and ill,
Unformed of manners, impotent of will,
What thirst of empire seized the giddy train!
Man bowed obsequious, and deferred the rein;
(So Mars on Venus smiled in courts above,

[11] **Pandora**: in Greek mythology, the first woman on earth, endowed with every "feminine" charm, including curiosity and deceit, which led her to open the forbidden box of human evils, thus releasing misery upon humanity. Only Hope remained in her box, to console suffering humans.

[12] On the obscure and much controverted subject of chivalry, I find it necessary in this place to hazard a few observations. Several circumstances convince me, and especially some striking facts in the history of Alboin king of the Lombards, and in that of the northern pirates, that a truly chivalrous spirit of honour and generosity had been introduced into the commerce of warriors with each other, in all the relations of peace and war, long before the refinements of gallantry, or even a tolerable decency of behaviour towards the weaker sex, came to be considered as incumbent on the brave and the noble. I also find that even during those ages when the spirit of chivalry is supposed to have been at its height, and when a very romantic kind of gallantry did in fact prevail, in the times, for instance, commemorated by the narrative Froissart, when, for their ladies' love, a party of young knights took a solemn vow to keep one of their eyes blinded with a silken patch till they should have achieved some signal deed of arms, ... manners were still gross, and morals extremely corrupt. In France, the nuptial tie, seldom cemented by mutual preference and inclination, has in no age been sufficient to restrain the wanderings of the imagination, or preserve the innocency of domestic life. In Spain, an absurd spirit of jealous rigour long fostered in both sexes the taste for clandestine amours; and the Spanish or Portuguese author of Amadis de Gaul, accounted the most moral as well as popular work of its kind, has represented his adorable and peerless Oriana herself as more fortunate in the constancy of her lover, but not more discreet in her loves, than the hapless Dido of ancient story. In England and the northern parts of the continent, if morals were somewhat more pure during these ages than in the south, manners were still more coarse. I am compelled to infer, that it was not till knight errantry, ceasing to exist in reality, had become a frame for the poetic fictions of a dignified and learned age, that it assumed the pure and lofty character which delights us in the beautiful coinage of Spenser's brain, stamped with the impress of all the Virtues, and superscribed with the titles of a Maiden Queen. [see Edmund Spenser, *The Faerie Queene* (1596)] [L.A.].

[13] **Gallia**: France. **Francis**: Francis I (1494–1547), king of France; noted for liberality, patronage of the arts, and submission to the political influence of his numerous mistresses.

So crouched in all the loyalty of love,)
Ah! feigned humility to scorn allied,
That stoops to conquer, flatters to deride!
Learn, thoughtless woman, learn his arts to scan,
And dread that fearful portent . . . . kneeling Man!
Dread the gay form whom now, her favourite birth,
Some smiling mischief trusts upon the earth
Veiled in a scented cloud; . . . . it melts, and see
Come dancing forth the phantom Gallantry.
His are the lowly bow, the adoring air,
The attentive eye that dwells upon the fair;
His the soft tone to grace a tender tale,
And his the flattering sighs that more prevail;
His the whole art of love: . . . . but all is art,
For kindly Nature never warmed his heart;
No hardy knight with wrong-redressing brand
He roams on Honour's pilgrimage the land;
No awful champion vowed to Virtue's aid
He flings his buckler o'er the trembling maid;
No high enthusiast to his peerless love
He plights pure vows and registered above; . . . .
Canker of Innocence! he lives at ease,
His only care his wanton self to please:
Hymen's dear tie, for him a sordid league
Knit by Ambition, Avarice, or Intrigue,
He scorns, he tramples, and insulting bears
To other shrines his incense and his prayers;
There, skilled in perfidy, he hangs to view
A hundred fopperies Passion never knew. . . .
Liveries that love by telegraph convey,[14]
Lines traced in blood, and quaint acrostic lay. . . .
Poor trifles all; . . . but trifles poor as these
Cheat the cold heart, the vagrant fancy seize,
From sober love, from faithful duty wean,
And sell to fear and sin the fancied queen.
Thus woman sinks, withdrawn each thin pretence,
The dupe of Vanity, the slave of Sense:
The light seducer, with brief rapture fraught,
Smiles on her prostrate dignity of thought,
And boasts his deeper wiles, his keener art,
Lord of the fond, confiding, female heart.
Vain boast, as profligate! he too shall find,
The sex dishonoured, Honour scorns the kind;
For never yet with cap and oaken crown,

[14] The emblematical meaning given to different colours, once so familiar to the gallant and the fair, is here alluded to [L.A.]

Symbol of joy and charter of renown,
Has man-exalting Freedom deigned to grace
A spurious rabble and adulterous race,
Steept in corruption, destined to be base.
Pure was the heart of Switzerland, when Tell[15]
Aimed the avenging shaft, and cried "Rebel!"

Pure was the self-devoted blood that dyed
The mangled breast of her bold Winkelreid;
Pure were the mountain homes whence foaming out
The patriot-torrent rushed, and gave the rout,
Where rose the pile of bones to tell mankind
"This monument the Spoiler left behind."[16]
Nor Virtue yet had fled her rock-built bower
When Gaul's intruding Demon, drunk with power,
Burst on that paradise: appalled he found
A Spartan fortitude embattled round;
Rapt by a fine despair, the maid, the wife,
Charged by their heroes' side and fired the strife. . . .
The strife victorious; . . . . but oppress, betrayed,
Fell the brave patriot few . . . . no friend to aid.
Then, spotless victims of a doom severe,
They died upon their murdered country's bier;
Died not in vain, ... to stamp on that proud name
The weight of vengeance and the curse of shame.[17]

Plant thy bright eagles o'er each prostrate realm,
Audacious France! and headlong from his helm
Each dozing steersman dash, ... but hope not thou,
Amid the plundered baubles of thy brow,
To twine a wreath from Freedom's sacred tree:
It blooms with virtue, but it dies with thee.

[15] **Tell:** William Tell, legendary Swiss patriot who inspired rebellion against Austrian bailiff Gessler—who had forced Tell to shoot an apple off the head of his son with an arrow and then imprisoned him—in 1308 which led to unification of the cantons of Switzerland.

[16] **"This monument . . . behind.":** the pile of bones was at Morat, where the duke of Burgundy was defeated by the Swiss. It was at the battle of Sempach that Arnold Winkelreid, recommending his family to that country for which he devoted himself, rushed upon a wedge of Austrian spears, and, burying as many of them as he could grasp, in his own body, thereby made a passage for the Swiss, who could not before bring their shorter weapons to bear upon the enemy; through which they advanced and slaughtered the invaders [L.A.]

[17] After the last struggle of the democratic Cantons against the hordes of France, many females were found among the slain [L.A.]

Once we had hope. When Tyranny and Wrong
Had stung thy patient bosom deep and long,
To vengeance roused, a generous short-lived red
Flushed o'er thy cheek, and all the wanton fled:
And failed thy daughters then? No, by thy hand,
Devoted brave Cordé![18] No, pure Roland!
No, by thy high "Appeal," thy parting breath,
Thy sage's fortitude, thy patriot's death![19]

But blest the land where ages glide away,
And not a single heroine starts to day:
'Tis angry skies must nurse that daring form,
As billows rock the Petrel[20] of the Storm:
Domestic virtue, femininely frail,
Courts the pure azure and the summer gale,
A brooding Halcyon,[21] on her island-nest
Lulled on old Neptune's pleased pacific breast.[22]
Such lot is ours, so rests our rock-bound isle,
A soft asylum reared in ocean's smile.
Thither fond Fancy flies, with busy care
Decks forth the scene, and paints it fresh and fair;
Soft Memory comes, adds every touching grace,
The form familiar, and the well-known face;
Quick beats my heart, mine eyes with rapture stream,
And truth and daylight burst upon my dream.

Rapt while I stand, my weary wanderings past,
Like some poor exile, welcomed home at last,
You, you I hail, dear playmates, who with me
Led the blind game, or wove the dance of glee;
(Fond mothers now, who watch with tenderer joy
Your tottering girl, or prompt your lisping boy;)
And rapt, inspired, beyond the trick of art,
Trace English manners with an English heart.
But not alone one fleeting speck of time
Shall flash in my contemporary rhyme;
Our sex's honour, and our country's weal,
Past or to come, this patriot breast must feel;
O'er the long lapse of years these eyes must roll,
And all its mazes agitate my soul:
For who that marks along the valley gleam
The silver waves of some majestic stream,
Served by a hundred rills, that winds along
Pride of the land and theme of poet's song,
Burns not, enamoured of the scene, to climb
Some airy mount, contemplative, sublime,
Whence all its sweeps, its whole expanding course,
Trackt from its small and weed-entangled source
To that wide rush of waves that spreads the plain
Where mists o'erhang its marriage with the main,
With eagle-ken in fleet succession caught,
May fill at once the hunger of his thought?

Like Ceres maddening on her car-borne way,
Her virgin daughter snatcht in face of day,
The fierce Bonduca, brave and injured queen,
In fire and carnage wraps the blasted scene,
And bids her barbarous wrongs, her vengeful rage,
Tell the dark story of the Roman age.[23]
Roused at her call, yon rude and frantic band
Yell round their Mona's violated strand,
Dire with funereal weeds and streaming hair,
And lurid torches tost with angry glare:
The chilled invader bows his pallid face,
And deprecates the Furies of the place.[24]

[18] **Cordé**: Charlotte Corday (1768–1793), fervent supporter of ideals of French Revolution; assassinated Marat, leader of the Montagnards, on 13 July 1793; guillotined 17 July 1793.

[19] Madame Roland's "Appeal to impartial Posterity," containing memoirs of her own life, is here alluded to; and her apostrophe to the statue of Liberty, on passing it in her way to the guillotine, "O Liberty, how many horrors are perpetrated in thy name!" Her noble fortitude during her imprisonment was also conspicuous [L.A.]

The home of Jeanne Manon Phlipon, Madame Roland (1754–1793), served as the headquarters for the Republicans and Girondists during the early years of the French Revolution (1791–1793); after the downfall of the Girondists, she was arrested, tried before the Revolutionary Tribunal, condemned, and guillotined on 8 November 1793.

[20] **petrel**: small seagull.

[21] **Halcyon**: kingfisher, anciently fabled to breed in a nest floating at sea.

[22] **Neptune**: classical god of the sea. **pacific**: peaceful, calm.

[23] **Like Ceres . . . Roman age**: the outrages and insults inflicted upon Boadicia and her daughters by the Romans, and the sanguinary vengeance taken by her upon the Roman colonies, are sufficiently known to every reader of early British history [L.A.].

Ceres: Roman goddess of grain and fertility. **Bonduca**: Boadicia, Boudicca; queen of the Iceni, the ancient Britons; defeated by the Romans; took poison in 62 AD.

[24] When Suetonius Paulinus landed his army on the island of Mona, "there stood along the beach," says Tacitus, "a thick and mingled crowd of men and arms; the women running up and down like Furies with funereal garb, dishevelled hair, uplifted

Hail, Ethelfleda! On his Alfred's child
The parting Genius gazed, and fondly smiled;
Wise in the council, dauntless in the fight,
She streaks the gloom and sheds a troubled light,
A beacon fire, whose fitful gleams display
The raging Dane, and England's evil day.[25]

But few our Amazons. While Egypt bleeds,
And Syrian echoes ring of Richard's deeds,
Edwards and Henries with victorious lance
Bear down the lily in the field of France,
And York and Lancaster with rival hate
Shake at the deep foundations of the state,
(Bred of intestine fires, the earthquake's shock
So strews the forest, splits the solid rock,)
Our timorous mothers, from invading strife
Wrapt in a meek monotony of life,
Humbly content to pace with duteous round
Their little world, ... the dear domestic ground, ...
Wards of protecting Man, nor dared to claim,
Nor dared to wish, the dangerous meed of fame,
Till, snatcht in triumph from his ancient tomb,
The lamp of Learning blazed upon the gloom,
And wide around to kindling hope revealed
The bloodless contests of a nobler field,
And courteous Wisdom to the bashful throng
Waved his pure hand, and beckoned them along.

Thou gav'st the call, O England's martyred sage!
O More! the grief and glory of thy age!
Bounteous as Nature's self, thy heart assigned
Its own large charter to a daughter's mind;[26]
Spread with adventurous hand its swelling sails
Free to the breath of Greek and Roman gales,
And heaped its freight with riches, dug or wrought
In mines of science and in looms of thought.
Splendid example! fame that shall not fade!
Large debt, in gratitude how fondly paid!
She, she it was, when that stern tyrant's breath
Doomed thy firm virtue to the axe of death,
Burst the mute throng to snatch a last farewell,
And pale and shrieking on thy bosom fell;
Weeping who clasped thy knees, and felt it sweet
To kiss in dust thy consecrated feet;
Called thy soul back, that winged her flight above,
And drew thy latest looks of sorrowing love.

Rise, gentle Grey! forth from the sainted dead
Lift the meek honours of thy victim-head!
Mockt with no pageant-rule, no vain renown,
Take thy due homage, take thy lasting crown!
O ripe in suffering, fair in spotless truth!
The fruits of Virtue with the flowers of Youth
Shall wreath thy brow, and Learning to thy hand

torches; whilst the Druids around, hurling forth dire imprecations, their hands raised to heaven, so affrighted the soldiers with the strangeness of their appearance, that they stood as if stupefied, affording a motionless body to the weapons of the enemy." Annal. xiv. 30 [L.A.]

[25] "In all these noble toils for the defence and security of his dominions, Edward (the elder) was greatly assisted by his sister Ethelfleda, widow of Ethered governor of Mercia. This heroic princess (who inherited more of the spirit of the great Alfred than any of his children), despising the humble cares and trifling amusements of her own sex, commanded armies, gained victories, built cities, and performed exploits which would have done honour to the greatest princes. Having governed Mercia eight years after the death of her husband, she died AD 920, and Edward took the government of that country into his own hand." [Robert] Henry's Hist. of Britain [1788], vol. iii. p. 93. [L.A.]

[26] Sir Thomas More [1478–1535] is highly commended by Erasmus for making his daughters partakers in all the benefits of a learned education. His favourite daughter, Margaret, wife of William Roper, esq. "became a mistress of the Greek and Latin languages, of arithmetic, and the sciences then generally taught, and of various musical instruments. She wrote with elegance both in English and Latin. In the latter her style was so pure, that cardinal Pole could scarcely be brought to believe that her compositions were the work of a female."

"Her reverence and affection for her father were unbounded. After his head had been exposed during fourteen days upon London bridge, she found means to procure it, and, preserving it carefully in a leaden box, gave directions that it should be placed in her arms when she was buried; which was accordingly done." The scene particularly referred to is thus related. After receiving sentence Sir Thomas More was conveyed to the Tower. "At the Tower-wharf, his favourite daughter, Mrs. Roper, was waiting to take her last farewell of him. At his approach, she burst through the throng, fell on her knees before her father, and, closely embracing him, could only utter, 'My father, oh my father!' He tenderly returned her embrace, and, exhorting her to patience, parted from her. She soon in a passion of grief again burst through the crowd, and clung round his neck in speechless anguish. His firmness was now overcome; tears flowed plentifully down his cheeks, till with a final kiss she left him." General Biography [ed. Richmond Mangnall], 1805. [L.A.]

Yield his large scroll, thy sceptre of command,
While Wisdom hears thy parting accents mild,
And cries, "Behold me honoured in my child!"[27]

The dread Eliza bids. Wake, O my strain!
Wake the long triumph of the Maiden Reign:[28]
Here Faction, vanquisht terror of the land,
Suppliant to kiss the chastenings of her hand;
(The fiend of Rome with imprecating eye
Fang-drawn and chained, and idly muttering by,)
Reviving France with fixt and awful air
Watching her glance, and grateful Henry there:
Here refuged Belgia from the tyrant's frown
Creeps to her knees, and lifts the proffered crown;
There gloomy Philip eyes a hostile main,
And o'er his foiled Armada mourns in vain.
High o'er her head the golden censer swings
That wafts all sweetness to the sense of kings;
Her dulcet voice each hymning Muse applies,
And the graced mortal half assumes the skies.
But mark pale Mary's vengeful spectre gleam
Clouding the pomp, and dash her glorious dream,
Brand her base envy, blaze each treacherous art,
And bare the meanness of her selfish heart;
Stung to the soul, her gallant Essex chide
Her captious favour and exacting pride,
Then bow his neck to death, ... and seem to cry,
"Relentless Mistress, see, despair, and die!"
Yet, O Britannia! on thy glory's car
The brightest gem shall flame that Maiden Star,
Queen of the' ascendant, whose propitious ray
Wisdom and wit, and arts and arms obey;
Blest orb, that flashed on Spenser's dazzling sight
Long meteor-streams and trails of fairy-light;
Twinkled on Shakespeare's lowly lot, and shed
A smile of love on Bacon's boyish head:
Now gleams the lode-star of our northern skies,
And points our galaxy to distant eyes.

But thou, pure partner of man's noblest cause,
Take, generous Hutchinson, this heart's applause:
'Twas thine to stem a foul and angry tide,
A high-souled helpmate at the patriot's side;
Then cast, sad relict! on an angry shore,
All wreckt, all lost, the gallant struggle o'er,
Yet, greatly constant to a husband's trust,
True to the joyful memory of the just,
Chide back thy tears, uplift thy mourning head,
And live, the high historian of the dead;
Knock at thy children's breasts, and cry with pride,
"Thus lived our patriot, thus our martyr died!"[29]
So virtuous Russell burst the shades of life,
And shone a heroine, for she loved, a wife.
"Grant me but her!" the noble culprit cried,
No friend, no advocate, I ask beside."
Secure in conscious fortitude she rose,
A present aid, ... and checked her gushing woes
And ruled her trembling hand, ... while all around

[27] A more illustrious instance than that afforded by lady Jane Grey [1537–1554], of the power of learning and philosophy to fortify and tranquillize a youthful and feminine mind under the severest trials, is nowhere to be found. Her dying confession of her fault in not refusing with sufficient steadiness the crown that had been forced upon her, and the willingness she expressed to expiate that fault by death, sufficiently evince her just and magnanimous way of thinking. [L.A.]

[28] Elizabeth I (1533–1603), queen of England and Ireland (1558–1603), never married, hence known as "Virgin Queen." Sustained Protestant claim to English throne and foiled Roman Catholic efforts to crown Mary Queen of Scots; sustained peace treaty with Henry III of France; aided Protestants in the Netherlands (Belgia); defeated Spanish Armada of Philip II in 1588; executed her rival Mary Queen of Scots in 1587 and her favorite, Robert Devereux, third Earl of Essex, in 1601, after he conspired against her. Reigned during English Renaissance of literature and humanistic learning, led by Edmund Spenser, William Shakespeare, and Francis Bacon.

[29] The admirable Memoirs of Colonel Hutchinson, by his widow [Anne Hutchinson, 1591–1643, American poet and Puritan], ought to be known to every reader capable of being warmed to a noble emulation. The work is inscribed to her children, and is introduced by a kind of dirge, in which after mentioning that some mourners, who have doted on "mortal excellencies," are only to be consoled by removing every thing that may "with their remembrance renew their grief," she proceeds: "But I that am under a command (of her husband at his death) not to grieve at the common rate of desolate women, while I am studying which way to moderate my woe, and if it were possible to augment my love, can for the present find out none more just to your deare father nor consolatory to myselfe then the preservation of his memory, which I need not guild with such flattering commendations as the higher preachers doe equally give to the truly and titularly honourable; a naked undrest narrative, speaking the simple truth of him, will deck him with more substantiall glorie, than all the panegyricks the best pens could ever consecrate to the best men." [L.A.]

A thrill of anguish ran, and mingled cries resound.
Vain every hope; the murderous doom is sped,
And Charles and vengeance claim his forfeit head.
But not from life, from only life to part,
Could wring a murmur from that patriot heart;
One dear companion of the darksome way
His eyes require, and mourn her lonely stay:
"Farewell, farewell!" he cries, "I look my last,
And now 'tis o'er; . . . . death's bitterness is past!"[30]

Such were the dames who grace our storied page:
Life's guiding lamp they hand from age to age,[31]
Assert their sex beyond the loftiest pen,
And live on tongues and reign in hearts of men.
Enough, indulgent Muse! evoke no more
The blissful phantoms from their silent shore,
Nor give again my curious eye to range
O'er times, o'er realms, remote and rude and strange;
Yet O be present still! but meek, subdued,
In sober, wistful, contemplative mood:
Her trusted stores while faithful Memory brings,
And Judgement ponders o'er the sum of things,
Aid my full heart, obtest[32] the mingled throng,
And point the varied moral of my song.

Sons of fair Albion, tender, brave, sincere,
(Be this the strain) an earnest suppliant hear!
Feel that when heaven, evolved its perfect plan,
Crowned with its last best gift transported Man,
It formed no creature of ignoble strain,
Of heart unteachable, obtuse of brain;
(Such had not filled the solitary void,
Nor such his soul's new sympathies employed,)
But one all eloquent of eye, of mien;
Intensely human; exquisitely keen
To feel, to know: Be generous then, unbind
Your barbarous shackles, loose the female mind;
Aid its new flights, instruct its wavering wing,
And guide its thirst to Wisdom's purest spring:
Sincere as generous, with fraternal heart
Spurn the dark satirist's unmanly part;
Scorn too the flatterer's, in the medium wise,
Nor feed those follies that yourselves despise.

For you, bright daughters of a land renowned,
By Genius blest, by glorious Freedom crowned;
Safe in a polisht privacy, content
To grace, not shun, the lot that Nature lent,
Be yours the joys of home, affection's charms,
And infants clinging with caressing arms:
Yours too the boon, of Taste's whole garden free,
To pluck at will her bright Hesperian tree,
Uncheckt the wreath of each fair Muse assume,
And fill your lap with amaranthine bloom.[33]
Press eager on; of this great art possest,
To seize the good, to follow still the best,
Ply the pale lamp, explore the breathing page,
And catch the soul of each immortal age.
Strikes the pure bard his old romantic lyre?
Let high Belphoebe warm, let Amoret sweet inspire:[34]
Does History speak? drink in her loftiest tone,
And be Cornelia's[35] virtues all your own.
Thus self-endowed, thus armed for every state,
Improve, excel, surmount, subdue, your fate!
So shall at length enlightened Man efface
That slavish stigma scared on half the race,
His rude forefathers' shame; and pleased confess,
'Tis yours to elevate, 'tis yours to bless;
Your interest one with his; your hopes the same;
Fair peace in life, in death undying fame,

[30] The history of lord William Russell and his lady,—her attendance upon him at his trial,—his expression after parting with her,—and the other traits illustrative of their heroic affection and excelling virtues, are too familiarly known to need repetition. [L.A.]

Lord William Russell (1639–1683), known as "the Patriot," was executed in 1683 by King Charles II for his supposed participation in the Rye House Plot; William III later vindicated his innocence. His wife Rachel Wriothesley (1636–1723), Lady Russell, was tireless in her efforts to save his life and restore his good name.

[31] **Life's guiding lamp . . . :** "Vitai lampada tradunt" [they pass on the lamps of life]. Lucretius. [L. A.]

[32] **obtest:** adjure, beg earnestly, supplicate.

[33] **Hesperian:** western isles, where the sun sets; in classical myth, the blessed isles. **amaranthine:** purple flower; in classical mythology, a fadeless, immortal flower.

[34] It ought always to be remembered for the honour of Spenser, that no poet has given such pure and perfect, such noble, lovely, and at the same time various drafts of female characters. His Belphoebe, his Amoret, his Canace, his Britomart and his Pastora, are a gallery of portraits, all beautiful, but each in a different style from all the rest. [L.A.]

These female characters appear in Edmund Spenser's *The Faerie Queene* (1596).

[35] **Cornelia:** mother of the Gracchi, model of Roman motherhood. (See Epistle III, note 12.)

And bliss in worlds beyond, the species' general aim.
"Rise," shall he cry, "O Woman, rise! be free!
My life's associate, now partake with me:
Rouse thy keen energies, expand thy soul,
And see, and feel, and comprehend the whole;
My deepest thoughts, intelligent, divide;
When right confirm me, and when erring guide;
Soothe all my cares, in all my virtues blend,
And be, my sister, be at length my friend."

Anna, farewell! O spirit richly fraught
With all that feeds the noble growth of thought!
(For not the Roman, not the Attic store,
Nor poets' song, nor reverend sages' lore,
To thee a Wakefield's[36] liberal love denied,
His child and friend, his pupil and his pride,)
Whose life of female loveliness shall teach
The finisht charm that precept fails to reach; . . . .
Born to delight, instructed to excel,
My judge, my sister, take this heart's farewell!

[36] **Wakefield**: Gilbert Wakefield (1756–1801), the father of Anna Wakefield Aikin, to whom this poem is dedicated; classical scholar; taught at Warrington Academy with Lucy Aikin's aunt and uncle, Anna and Rochemont Barbauld; known for his editions of Bion, Moschus, the *Georgics*, Horace, Lucretius and Greek plays, as well as for his critical commentaries on the Scriptures, *Silva Critica* (1789).

JANE TAYLOR

(1783–1824)

A prolific writer of children's verse and moral tales, Jane Taylor was the youngest daughter of the engraver and Dissenting minister Isaac Taylor and Ann Martin, a woman who refused to become "a mere plod" as a wife and followed her daughters Jane and Ann into authorship with seven books of religious and moral advice, published between 1814 and 1825. Born in London on 23 September 1783, Jane Taylor moved with her parents in 1786 to Lavenham, Suffolk, to Cochester in 1796, and to Ongar in Devon in 1811. In Lavenham, she lived on the same street with the impoverished spinners employed by the wool trade, and developed an intense sympathy for the sufferings of the poor. A child noted for her rich fantasy-life and constant "castle-building" or storytelling, she was trained in her father's profession of engraving in order to be able to support herself. Educated at home by her father, who believed that all his children should have a solid grounding in mathematics, science, and nonconformist theology, she imbibed a love of literature from her mother, who because she was almost deaf, would read aloud at all family meals in order not to be shut out of the social gathering. After a failed attempt to establish a school for girls in London with her sister, Ann Taylor Gilbert, in 1810, Jane Taylor returned to Ongar and devoted herself to writing, engraving, and charitable works. She taught Sunday School in her father's Independent Church, as well as writing and mathematics to the children of the local parish, and established a Ladies' Society for the relief of the poor. She died of breast cancer in 1824.

Jane Taylor began her career as a writer at the age of 19 by publishing a didactic tale in *Minor's Pocket Book*; she continued to publish moral essays, stories, and verse, under the signature of Q. Q., in *Youth's Magazine*, an Evangelical magazine for young people which she edited from 1816 to 1822. *Original Poems for Infant Minds*, written by Jane and Ann Taylor and Adelaide O'Keefe, appeared from 1804 to 1805; they received a phenomenal £15 for this first effort. Translated into German, Dutch, and Russian, this volume ran into over 50 editions in England alone. Jane and Ann Taylor's extraordinary success as writers for children was confirmed by their *Rhymes for the Nursery* (1806), for which Jane wrote what became one of the best known poems in the English language, "Twinkle, twinkle, little star," and *Hymns for Infant Minds* (1810), both of which went into well over 100 editions each in England and America. *Hymns for Infant Minds* earned £150 in 1810 alone, the equivalent of a well-paid clergyman's or schoolmaster's salary.

Jane Taylor's penetrating poetic satires on class snobbery and social injustice appeared in her *Essays in Rhyme* (1816). A staunch believer in a middle-class domestic ideology which teaches that a woman must serve her husband and her god, her novel *Display* (1814) celebrated the vain Elizabeth's recognition that a true religious spirit requires her to accept her husband's foolishness and her own loss of social rank. Elizabeth, a "female in name only," for whom "to speak, to move, to weep, or to smile, were . . . so many maneuvers, which she was practising for *effect*, and to attract attention" learns from the "real" female Emily, who "possessed the grace of SIMPLICITY," that "only religion will cure the love of—DISPLAY." Never married, Jane Taylor believed that a single woman's mission was "to care for the things of the lord," in her case through her "ministry of the press."

from RHYMES FOR THE NURSERY

(1806)

The Star

Twinkle, twinkle, little star,
How I wonder what you are!
Up above the sky so high,
Like a diamond in the sky.

When the blazing sun is gone,
When he nothing shines upon,
Then you show your little light,
Twinkle, twinkle, all the night.

Then the trav'ller in the dark,
Thanks you for your tiny spark:
He could not see which way to go,
If you did not twinkle so.

In the dark blue sky you keep,
And often through my curtains peep,
For you never shut your eye
Till the sun is in the sky.

As your bright and tiny spark
Lights the trav'ller in the dark,
Though I know not what you are,
Twinkle, twinkle, little star.

from ESSAYS IN RHYME, ON MORALS AND MANNERS

(1816)

from Prejudice

In yonder red-brick mansion, tight and square,
Just at the town's commencement, lives the mayor.
Some yards of shining gravel, fenc'd with box,[1]
Lead to the painted portal—where one knocks:
There, in the left-hand parlour, all in state,
Sit he and she, on either side the grate.
But though their goods and chattels,[2] sound and new,
Bespeak the owners *very well to do,*
His worship's wig and morning suit, betray
Slight indications of an humbler day.

That long, low shop, where still the name appears,
Some doors below, they kept for forty years:
And there, with various fortunes, smooth and rough,
They sold tobacco, coffee, tea, and snuff.
There labell'd draw'rs display their spicy row,—
Clove, mace, and nutmeg: from the ceiling low
Dangle long *twelves* and *eights,* and slender rush,
Mix'd with the varied forms of *genus brush;*[3]
Cask, firkin, bag, and barrel, crowd the floor,
And piles of country cheeses guard the door.
The frugal dames came in from far and near,
To buy their ounces and their quarterns here.[4]
Hard was the toil, the profits slow to count;
And yet the mole-hill was at last a mount:
Those petty gains were hoarded day by day,
With little cost, (nor chick nor child had they);
Till, long proceeding on the saving plan,
He found himself *a warm, fore-handed man;*[5]
And being now arrived at life's decline,
Both he and she, they formed the bold design,
(Although it touch'd their prudence to the quick)
To turn their savings into stone and brick.
How many a cup of tea and pinch of snuff,
There must have been consumed to make enough!

At length, with paint and paper, bright and gay,
The box[6] was finish'd, and they went away.
But when their faces were no longer seen
Amongst the canisters of *black* and *green,*
—Those well known faces, all the country round—
'Twas said that had they levell'd to the ground

[1] **box:** small evergreen tree or shrub, boxwood.

[2] **chattels:** moveable possessions.

[3] **twelves and eights:** things sold in packages of twelve or eight, i.e., candles. **rush:** dried, long-stemmed river plant, used for lighting candles; rushlight. **genus brush:** Latin: the brush family.

[4] **firkin:** a small cask (a quarter of a barrel) for holding liquids, fish, butter, etc. **quartern:** a quarter of anything, specifically a quarter-loaf of bread.

[5] **warm:** comfortably settled, securely established. **fore-handed:** looking to the forehand; prudent, thrifty; hence well-to-do.

[6] **box:** house, shaped like a square box.

The two old walnut trees before the door,
The customers would not have missed *them* more.
Now, like a pair of parrots in a cage,
They live, and civic honours crown their age:
Thrice, since the Whitsuntide[7] they settled there,
Seven years ago, has he been chosen mayor;
And now you'd scarcely know they were the same;
Conscious he struts, of power, and wealth, and fame,
Proud in official dignity, the dame,
And extra stateliness of dress and mien,
During the mayor'lty, is plainly seen;
With nicer care bestow'd to puff and pin
The august lappet[8] that contains her chin.

Such is her life; and like the wise and great,
The mind has journey'd hand in hand with fate:
Her thoughts, unused to take a longer flight
Than from the left-hand counter to the right,
With little change, are vacillating still,
Between his worship's glory and the till.
The few ideas that travel, slow and dull,
Across the sandy desert of her skull,
Still the same course must follow, to and fro,
As first they travers'd three-score years ago;
From whence, not all the world could turn them back,
Or lead them out upon another track.
What once was right or wrong, or high or low
In her opinion, always must be so:—
You might, perhaps, with reasons new and pat,
Have made *Columbus* think the world was flat,
Or, when of thought and controversy weary,
Have got *Sir Isaac*[9] to deny his theory;
But not the powers of argument combin'd,
Could make this dear good woman change her mind,
Or give her intellect the slightest clue
To that vast world of things she never knew.
Were but her brain dissected, it would show
Her stiff opinions fastened in a row;
Rang'd duly, side by side, without a gap,
Much like the plaiting on her Sunday cap.

It is not worth our while, but if it were,
We all could undertake to laugh at *her*;
Since vulgar prejudice, the lowest kind,
Of course, has full possession of her mind;
Here, therefore, let us leave her, and inquire
Wherein it differs as it rises higher.
—As for the few who claim distinction here,
The little gentry of our narrow sphere,
Who occupy a safe enclosure, made
Completely inaccessible to trade—
Where, should a foot plebeian pass the bound,
'Tis like a trespass on *Tom Tickler's ground*;[10]—
Wide as the distance that we choose to make
For pride, precedence, and for custom's sake,
Yet, philosophic eyes (though passing fine)
Could scarcely ascertain the bound'ry line;
So that, if any should be found at all,
The diff'rence must be infinitely small.
The powder'd matron, who for many a year
Has held her mimic routs and parties here;
(Exchanging just the counter, scales, and till,
For cups of coffee, scandal, and quadrille)[11]
Could boast nor range of thought, nor views of life,
Much more extended than our grocer's wife.
Although her notions may be better drest,
They are but vulgar notions at the best;
—Mere petrifactions, formed as time runs by,
Hard and unmalleable, and dull and dry,
Ne'er placed in reason's crucible—in short,
Opinions made by habit, not by thought.

Then let inquiry rise, with sudden flight,
To reason's utmost intellectual height;
Where native powers, with culture high combin'd,
Present the choicest specimen of mind.

[7] **Whitsuntide:** the season following Whit ("white") Sunday, the seventh Sunday after Easter, a Christian festival day commemorating the descent of the Holy Spirit upon the Apostles on the Day of Pentecost.

[8] **mien:** facial expression. **lappet:** flap or fold of a garment.

[9] **Columbus:** Christopher Columbus (1451–1506), Italian sailor and explorer who by sailing due west, reached the Americas in 1492. **Sir Isaac:** Sir Issac Newton (1642–1727), mathematician and physicist, discoverer of the laws of gravity and thermodynamics.

[10] **Tom Tickler's ground:** a children's game, in which one of the players is 'Tom Tiddler,' his territory being marked by a line drawn on the ground. The other players run over this line, crying "We're on Tom Tiddler's ground, picking up gold and silver." Hence, any place where money is "picked up" or acquired readily.

[11] **routs:** large evening parties or receptions, much in vogue among the upper classes in the eighteenth and nineteenth centuries, here being imitated or mimicked by the bourgeoisie. **quadrille:** card game played by four persons.

—Those minds that stand from all mankind aloof,
To smile at folly, or dispense reproof;
Enlarged, excursive, reason soars away,
And breaks the shackles that confine its sway:
Their keen, dissecting, penetrating view,
Searches poor human nature through and through;
But while they notice all the forms absurd,
That prejudice assumes among the herd,
And every nicer variation see,
—*Theirs* lies in thinking that themselves are free.

There is a science reason cannot teach;
It lies beyond the depth her line can reach;
It is but taught by Heaven's imparted grace,—
The feet of Jesus is the only place;
And they who mental riches largely share,
But seldom stoop to seek their wisdom there.
'Not many mighty' in His train appear;
The simple poor adorn it best;—and here,
While prejudice the mental sight impairs
Of vulgar minds,—'tis like a *beam* in theirs.[12]

. . . .

Accomplishment[1]
(1816)

How is it that masters, and science, and art,
One spark of intelligence fail to impart,
Unless in that chemical union combin'd,
Of which the result, in one word, is a *mind?*

A youth may have studied, and travelled abroad,
May sing like *Apollo,* and paint like a *Claude,*[2]
And speak all the languages under the pole,
And have every gift in the world, but a soul.

That drapery wrought by the leisurely fair,
Call'd *patchwork,*[3] may well to such genius compare;
Wherein every tint of the rainbow appears,
And stars to adorn it are forc'd from their spheres.

There glows a bright pattern (a sprig or a spot)
'Twixt clusters of roses full-blown and red hot;
Here magnified tulips divided in three,
Alternately shaded with sections of tree.

But when all is finish'd, this labour of years,
A mass unharmonious, unmeaning appears;
'Tis showy, but void of intelligent grace;
It is not a landscape, it is not a face.

'Tis thus Education (so call'd in our schools)
With costly materials, and capital tools,
Sits down to her work, and at last she produces,
Exactly the job that her customer chooses.

See French and Italian spread out on her lap;
Then Dancing springs up, and skips into a gap;
Next Drawing and all its varieties come,
Sew'd down in their place by her finger and thumb.

And then, for completing her fanciful robes,
Geography, Music, the use of the Globes,
&c. &c. which, match as they will,
Are sewn into shape and set down in the bill.

Thus Science distorted, and torn into bits,
Art tortur'd, and frighten'd half out of her wits,
In portions and patches, some light and some shady,
Are stitch'd up together, and make a young lady.

A Pair
(1816)

There was a youth—but woe is me!
I quite forget his name, and he
Without some label round his neck,
Is like one pea among a peck.
Go search the country up and down,
Port, city, village, parish, town,
And, saving just the face and name,

---

[12] **'Not many mighty':** Cf. Apocryphya 6:6. **mental sight . . . beam:** Cf. Matthew 7:2–3: "And why beholdest thou the mote that is in thy brother's eye, but considerest not the beam that is in thine own eye?"

[1] Taylor is referring not only to human achievement in general but specifically to the "female accomplishments" (see Wollstonecraft, *Vindication of the Rights of Woman,** note 5).

[2] **Apollo:** the Greek god of music. **Claude:** Claude Lorrain (1600–1682), professional name Claude Gellée, frequently shortened to Claude, French landscape painter famed for his depictions of idealised classical Italian landscapes, the painter of "the beautiful" in landscape. (See AESTHETIC THEORY.)

[3] **patchwork:** work consisting of small pieces of cloth sewn together by the edges, so as to make a bedspread, tea-cosy, cushion, etc.

You shall behold the very same,
Wherever pleasure's train resorts,
From the Land's-End to *Johnny Groats'*;
And thousands such have swell'd the herd,
From *William*, down to *George* the Third.[1]

To life he started—thanks to fate,
In contact with a good estate:
Provided thus, and quite at ease,
He takes for granted all he sees;
Ne'er sends a thought, nor lifts an eye,
To ask what am I? where? and why?—
All that is no affair of his,
Somehow he came—and there he is!
Without such prosing,[2] stupid stuff,
Alive and well, and that's enough.

Thoughts! why, if all that crawl like trains
Of caterpillars through his brains,
With every syllable let fall,
Bon mot,[3] and compliment, and all,
Were melted down in furnace fire,
I doubt if shred of golden wire,
To make, amongst it all would linger,
A ring for *Tom Thumb's*[4] little finger.
Yet, think not that he comes below
The modern, average ratio—
The current coin of fashion's mint—
The common, ball-room-going stint.[5]
Of trifling cost his stock in trade is,
Whose business is to please the ladies;
Or who to honours may aspire,
Of a town beau or country squire.

The cant[6] of fashion and of vice
To learn, slight effort will suffice;
And he was furnish'd with that knowledge,
Even *before* he went to college.
And thus, without the toil of thought,
Favour and flattery may be bought.
No need to win the laurel, now,
For lady's smile or vassal's bow;
To lie exposed in patriot camp,
Or study by the midnight lamp.

Nature and art might vainly strive
To keep his intellect alive.
—'Twould not have forc'd an exclamation,
Worthy a note of admiration,
If he had been on Gibeon's hill,
And seen the sun and moon stand still.[7]
What prodigy was ever known,
To raise the pitch of fashion's tone!
Or make it yield, by any chance,
That studied air of *nonchalance*,
Which after all, however grac'd,
Is apathy, and want of taste.

The *vulgar* every station fill,
St. Giles' or *James's*[8]—which you will;
Spruce drapers in their masters shops,
Rank with right honorable fops;[9]
No real distinction marks the kinds—
The *raw material* of their minds.
But *mind* claims rank that cannot yield
To blazon'd arms[10] and crested shield:
Above the need and reach it stands,
Of diamond stars from royal hands;
Nor waits the nod of courtly state,
To bid it be, or not be great.

---

[1] **Land's-End**: the southwesternmost tip of the United Kingdom, in Cornwall. **Johnny Groats**: John o' Groats, the northernmost tip of the United Kingdom, in Scotland. **William**: William the Conqueror (1027–1087), the first king of England. **George the Third**: the reigning king of England in 1816 (1738–1820), although his son (the future George IV) had assumed the regency in 1811 when his father became permanently deranged.

[2] **prosing**: writing or speaking in a prosy, dull, or tiresome way.

[3] **bon mot**: French: a clever or witty saying.

[4] **Tom Thumb**: a dwarf or pygmy in popular British folklore.

[5] **stint**: allotted amount.

[6] **cant**: peculiar language or jargon of a class, sect, or subject; affected phraseology.

[7] Reference to Joshua's triumphant battle against the Canaanites (see Joshua 9–10).

[8] **St. Giles' or James's**: coach stations, ranging from those used by highwaymen (St. Giles, near Charing Cross) to those patronized by aristocrats (James, near Belgravia).

[9] **spruce**: trim, dapper. **drapers**: assistant salesmen in cloth stores. **fops**: persons who are excessively or foolishly concerned with dress or appearance; dandies.

[10] **blazon'd arms**: the coats-of-arms of nobility.

The regions where it wings its way,
Are set with brighter stars than they:
With calm contempt it thence looks down
On fortune's favour or its frown;
Looks down on those, who vainly try,
By strange inversion of the eye,
From that poor mole-hill where they sit,
To cast a downward look on it:
As robin, from his pear-tree height,
Looks *down* upon the eagle's flight.

Before our youth had learnt his letters,
They taught him to despise his betters;
And if *some* things have been forgot,
That lesson certainly has not.
The haunts his genius chiefly graces,
Are tables,[11] stables, taverns, races;—
The things of which he most afraid is,
Are tradesmen's bills, and learned ladies:
He deems the first a grievous bore,
But loathes the latter even more
Than solitude or rainy weather,
Unless they happen both together.

Soft his existence rolls away,
To-morrow plenteous as to day:
He lives, enjoys, and lives anew,—
And when he dies,—what shall we do!

Down a close street, whose darksome shops display,
Old clothes and iron on both sides the way;
Loathsome and wretched, whence the eye in pain,
Averted turns, nor seeks to view again;
Where lowest dregs of human nature dwell,
More loathsome than the rags and rust they sell;—
A pale mechanic rents an attic floor;
By many a shatter'd stair you gain the door:
'Tis one poor room, whose blacken'd walls are hung
With dust that settled there when he was young.
The rusty grate two massy bricks displays,
To fill the sides and make a frugal blaze.
The door unhing'd, the window patch'd and broke;
The panes obscur'd by half a century's smoke:
There stands the bench at which his life is spent;
Worn, groov'd, and bor'd,[12] and worm-devour'd, and bent:
Where daily, undisturb'd by foes or friends,
In one unvaried attitude he bends.
His tools, long practis'd, seem to understand
Scarce less their functions, than his own right hand.
With these he drives his craft with patient skill;
Year after year would find him at it still:
The noisy world around is changing all,
War follows peace, and kingdoms rise and fall;
France rages now, and Spain, and now the Turk;
Now victory sounds;—but there he sits at work!
A man might see him so, then bid adieu,—
Make a long voyage to China or Peru;
There traffic, settle, build; at length might come,
Alter'd, and old, and weather-beaten home,
And find him on the same square foot of floor,
On which he left him twenty years before.
—The self same bench, and attitude, and stool,
The same quick movement of his cunning tool;
The very distance 'twixt his knees and chin,
As though he had but stepp'd just out and in.

Such is his fate—and yet you might descry
A latent spark of meaning in his eye.
—That crowded shelf beside his bench, contains
One old, worn, volume that employs his brains:
With algebraic lore its page is spread,
Where *a* and *b* contend with *x* and *z*:—
Sold by some *student* from an Oxford hall,
—Bought by the pound upon a broker's stall.
On this it is his sole delight to pore,
Early and late, when working time is o'er:
But oft he stops, bewilder'd and perplex'd,
At some hard problem in the learned text;
Pressing his hand upon his puzzled brain,
At what the dullest school-boy could explain.

From needful sleep the precious hour he saves,
To give his thirsty mind the stream it craves:
There, with his slender rush beside him plac'd,
He drinks the knowledge in with greedy haste.
At early morning, when the frosty air
Brightens Orion and the northern Bear,
His distant window mid the dusky row,
Shews a dim light to passenger below.
—A light more dim is flashing on his mind,

[11] **tables:** gaming tables.

[12] **bor'd:** pierced with holes.

That shows its darkness, and its views confin'd.
Had science shone around his early days,
How had his soul expanded in the blaze!
But penury bound him, and his mind in vain
Struggles and writhes beneath her iron chain.

—At length the taper fades, and distant cry
Of early sweep[13] bespeaks the morning nigh:
Slowly it breaks,—and that rejoicing ray,
That wakes the healthful country into day,
Tips the green hills, slants o'er the level plain,
Reddens the pool, and stream, and cottage pane,
And field, and garden, park, and stately hall,—
Now darts obliquely on his wretched wall.
He knows the wonted signal; shuts his book,
Slowly consigns it to its dusty nook;
Looks out awhile, with fixt and absent stare,
On crowded roofs, seen through the foggy air;
—Stirs up the embers, takes his sickly draught,
Sighs at his fortunes, and resumes his craft.

Recreation
(1816)

—We took our work, and went, you see,
To take an early cup of tea.
We did so now and then, to pay
The friendly debt, and so did they.
Not that our friendship burnt so bright
That all the world could see the light;
'Twas of the ordinary *genus,*[1]
And little love was lost between us:
We lov'd, I think, about as true
As such near neighbours mostly do.

At first, we all were somewhat dry;
Mamma felt cold, and so did I:
Indeed, that room, sit where you will,
Has draught enough to turn a mill.
'I hope you're warm,' says Mrs. G.
'O, quite so,' says mamma, *says she;*
'I'll take my shawl off by and by.'—
'This room is always warm,' *says I.*

At last the tea came up, and so,
With that, our tongues began to go.
Now, in that house you're sure of knowing
The smallest scrap of news that's going;
We find it *there* the wisest way
To take some care of what we say.

—Says she, 'there's dreadful doings still
In that affair about the *will,*
For now the folks in Brewer's Street
Don't speak to *James's,* when they meet.
Poor Mrs. *Sam* sits all alone,
And frets herself to skin and bone.
For months she manag'd, she declares,
All the old gentleman's affairs;
And always let him have his way,
And never left him night nor day;
Waited and watch'd his every look,
And gave him every drop he took.
Dear Mrs. *Sam,* it was too bad!
He might have left her all he had.'

'Pray ma'am,' says I, 'has poor Miss A.
Been left as *handsome* as they say?'
'My dear,' says she, ''tis no such thing,
She'd nothing but a mourning ring.
But is it not *uncommon* mean
To wear that rusty bombazeen!'[2]
'She had,' says I, 'the very same
Three years ago, for—what's his name?'—
'The Duke of *Brunswick,*—very true,
And has not bought a thread of new,
I'm positive,' said Mrs. G.—
So then we laugh'd, and drank our tea.

—'So,' says mamma, 'I find it's true
What Captain P. intends to do;
To hire that house, or else to buy—'
'Close to the tan-yard,[3] ma'am,' says I;
'Upon my word it's very strange,
I wish they mayn't repent the change!'
'My dear,' says she, ''tis very well
You know, if *they* can bear the smell.'

[13] **sweep:** a chimney sweep, usually a young boy.

[1] **genus:** Latin: class or kind.

[2] **mourning ring:** ring worn as a memorial of a deceased person. **bombazeen:** cheap black cotton-worsted material, much used for mourning clothes.

[3] **tan-yard:** tanning factory, where raw hides are converted into leather; notable for the foul smell of the tannin.

'Miss F.' says I, 'is said to be
A sweet young woman, is not she?'
'O, excellent! I hear,' she cried;
'O, truly so!' mamma replied.
'How old should you suppose her, pray?
She's older than she looks, they say.'
'Really,' says I, 'she seems to me
Not more than twenty-two or three.'

'O, then you're wrong,' says Mrs. G.
'Their upper servant told our *Jane*,
She'll not see twenty-nine again.'
'Indeed, so old! I wonder why
She does not marry, then,' says I;
'So many thousands to bestow,
And such a beauty, too, you know.'
'A beauty! O, my dear Miss B.
You must be joking now,' says she;
Her *figure's* rather pretty,'—'Ah!
That's what *I* say,' replied mamma.

'Miss F.' says I, 'I've understood,
Spends all her time in doing good:
The people say her coming down
Is quite a blessing to the town.'
At that our hostess fetch'd a sigh,
And shook her head; and so, says I,
'It's very kind of her, I'm sure,
To be so generous to the poor.'
'No doubt,' says she, ''tis very true;
Perhaps there may be *reasons* too:—
You know some people like to pass
For *patrons* with the lower class.'

And here I break my story's thread,
Just to remark, that what she said,
Although I took the other part,
Went like a cordial to my heart.

Some inuendos more had pass'd,
Till out the scandal came at last.
'Come then, I'll tell you something more,'
Says she,—'Eliza, shut the door.—
I would not trust a creature here,
For all the world, but you, my dear.
Perhaps it's false—I wish it may,
—But let it go no further, pray!'
'O,' says mamma, 'You need not fear,
We never mention what we hear.'
And so, we drew our chairs the nearer,
And whispering, lest the child should hear her,
She told a tale, at least too *long*
To be repeated in a song;
We, panting every breath between,
With curiosity and spleen.[4]
And how we did enjoy the sport!
And echo every faint report,
And answer every candid doubt,
And turn her motives inside out,
And holes in all her virtues pick,
Till we were sated, almost sick.

—Thus having brought it to a close,
In great good-humour, we arose.
Indeed, 'twas more than time to go,
Our boy had been an hour below.
So, warmly pressing Mrs. G.
To fix a day to come to tea,
We muffled up in cloke and plaid,
And trotted home behind the lad.

POSTHUMOUS PUBLICATIONS

from POETICAL REMAINS
(1832)

To Mad. De Staël[1]
(comp. 1822)

Written after reading "Corine ou L'Italie."

O WOMAN, greatly gifted! why
Wert thou not gifted from on high?
What had that noble genius done—
That knew all hearts—all things, but *one*,

---

[4] **spleen:** sudden depression, irritability, melancholy.

[1] **Mad. de Staël:** Anne Louise Germaine Necker de Staël, Baron de Staël-Holstein (1766–1817), distinguished Swiss-French author and radical intellectual, famous for hosting a salon in Paris and, after she was exiled from France by Napoleon, in Copet, on the shore of Lake Geneva. Her novel *Corinne or Italy* (1807) created the character of an inspired and triumphant Italian female poet, Corinne, who finally succumbs to a passionate love, only to be abandoned by the English gentleman she adores.

—Had that been known? O, would it might
Be whispered, here she took her flight!
Where, where is that fine spirit hurled,
That seemed unmeet for either world?

While o'er thy magic page I bend,
I know thee—claim thee for my friend:
With thee a secret converse hold,
And see my inmost thoughts unfold.
Each notion crude, defined—expressed;
And certain, what I vaguely guessed.
And hast thou taught, with cruel skill,
The art to suffer better still:—
Grief's finest secret to explore,
Though understood too well before?
Ah well, I'd thank thee if I might;
Although so wrong, thou art so right!
While I condemn, my heart replies,
And deeper feelings sympathize.

Thy view of life—that painful view,
How false it is!—and yet how true!
"Life without love—a cheerless strife;
Yet love so rarely given to life."
And why must truth and virtue, why,
This mighty claim of love deny?
—What was this earth, so full, so fair?—
A cheerless desert, bleak, and bare—
God knew it was—till love was there.
Say, has the heart a glance at bliss—
One—till it glance or gaze at this?
Ah no! unblessed, unsoothed the lot,
Fair though it seem, that knows it not!
'T is true!—and to the truth replies
A thousand joyless hearts and eyes;—
Eyes beamless—hearts that do not break—
They cannot—but that always ache;
And slowly wither, day by day,
Till life at last is dried away.

"Love or Religion;" yes, she knew,
Life has no choice but 'twixt the two:
But when she sought *that* balm to find,
She guessed and groped; but still was blind.
Aloft she flew, yet failed to see
Aught but an earthly deity.
The humble Christian's holy love,
O, how it calmly soars above
These storms of passion!—Yes, too much
I've felt her talent's magic touch.
Return, my soul, to that retreat
From sin and wo—thy Savior's feet!
There learn an art she never knew,
The heart's own empire to subdue:—
A large, but willing sacrifice.
All to resign that He denies;—
To him in meek submission bend;
Own Him an all-sufficient friend;
Here, and in holy worlds above,
My portion—and my only love!

September 23, 1822

THOMAS DE QUINCEY

(1785–1859)

The great bulk of Thomas De Quincey's literary production — some 215 journalistic essays, dream rhapsodies, and major autobiographical works — were published after 1830, many well into the Victorian period (c. 1830–1901): *Recollections of the Lake Poets* (1834–1839), *Suspira de Produndis* (1845), *The English Mail Coach* (1849). His most famous literary production, however, was *Confessions of an English Opium-Eater,* which appeared anonymously in two issues of the *London Magazine* in 1821 and then in book form the following year. De Quincey claimed that the hero of *Confessions* is opium; its subject is the author's early life and his experience in altered states of consciousness induced by the drug. If style is the man, *Confessions* is appropriately brilliant, self-indulgent, and strange.

As the son of a wealthy Manchester merchant, who died early but left his large family financially secure, De Quincey was educated for the University, and matriculated at Worcester College, Oxford, in 1803, already an accomplished scholar of classical languages and literature. Unfortunately, by that time De Quincey had misspent three years. Because of his astonishing precocity for languages and prodigious intelligence, he was well-prepared for Oxford at the age of fifteen, but his mother sent him to Manchester Grammar School to mark time so that he might be more competitive for a scholarship. Thomas wrote an unavailing letter to her before fleeing school to drift through Wales and then loiter in London for over a year as a penniless vagrant: "I ask whether a person can be happy, . . . who is in a situation which deprives him of *health,* of *society,* of *amusement,* of *congeniality of pursuits,* and which, to complete the precious picture, admits of no *variety.*" Of course De Quincey found none of these during his vagabondage, but rather intense physical suffering and lasting memories of marginal beings leading nominal existences.

De Quincey was discovered by friends and became reconciled with his family, but his experience at Oxford turned out to be similar to that at Manchester and led to the same end. He claimed that in two years he probably did not speak over one hundred words aloud, and disappeared without a degree because he was displeased that he was not permitted to answer examination questions in Greek. He returned to London, made the acquaintance of prominent writers, and became a disciple of the Lake poets, especially Wordsworth* and Coleridge.* So enamoured of Wordsworth did De Quincey become, that he moved to the Lake District in 1809 to inhabit the Wordsworth residence at Dove Cottage after the family moved to larger quarters. In 1816, De Quincey married Margaret Simpson, who had borne him a child out of wedlock, and now took up writing in earnest to support a growing family. To be nearer the markets employing him, De Quincey and his family left Grasmere for London, where he worked for the *London Magazine,* and then for Edinburgh to reside from 1828 on, in the employ of *Blackwood's Magazine,* the *Edinburgh Literary Gazette,* and *Tait's Edinburgh Magazine.* De Quincey began the supervision of a collected edition of his works, *Selections Grave and Gay,* in 1853, and finally earned a respectable profit when he sold his interest in the edition to his co-editor, James Hogg, for over £800 in 1858.

De Quincey once described his life as being composed of "subtle links of suffering." Sir Leslie Stephen (1832–1904) represented it biographically as "an operation which for want of a better term we must describe as living, but which would be more fitly described by some mode of speech indicating an existence on the borders of dreamland and reality." *Confessions* offers the reader both versions.

from Confessions of an English Opium-Eater[1]

(1822)

—*from* PRELIMINARY CONFESSIONS—

. . . I have often been asked, how I first came to be a regular opium-eater; and have suffered, very unjustly, in the opinion of my acquaintance, from being reputed to have brought upon myself all the sufferings which I shall have to record, by a long course of indulgence in this practice purely for the sake of creating an artificial state of pleasurable excitement. This, however, is a misrepresentation of my case. True it is, that for nearly ten years I did occasionally take opium, for the sake of the exquisite pleasure it gave me: but, so long as I took it with this view, I was effectually protected from all material bad consequences, by the necessity of interposing long intervals between the several acts of indulgence, in order to renew the pleasurable sensations. It was not for the purpose of creating pleasure, but of mitigating pain in the severest degree, that I first began to use opium as an article of daily diet.[2] In the twenty-eighth year of my age, a most painful affection of the stomach, which I had first experienced about ten years before, attacked me in great strength. This affection had originally been caused by extremities of hunger, suffered in my boyish days. During the season of hope and redundant happiness which succeeded (that is, from eighteen to twenty-four) it had slumbered: for the three following years it had revived at intervals: and now, under unfavourable circumstances, from depression of spirits, it attacked me with a violence that yielded to no remedies but opium. As the youthful sufferings, which first produced this derangement of the stomach, were interesting in themselves, and in the circumstances that attended them, I shall here briefly retrace them. . . . [3]

Soon after this, I contrived, by means which I must omit for want of room, to transfer myself to London. And now began the latter and fiercer stage of my long sufferings; without using a disproportionate expression I might say, of my agony. For I now suffered, for upwards of sixteen weeks, the physical anguish of hunger in various degrees of intensity; but as bitter, perhaps, as ever any human being can have suffered who has survived it. I would not needlessly harass my reader's feelings by a detail of all that I endured: for extremities such as these, under any circumstances of heaviest misconduct or guilt, cannot be contemplated, even in description, without a rueful pity that is painful to the natural goodness of the human heart. Let it suffice, at least on this occasion, to say, that a few fragments of bread from the breakfast-table of one individual (who supposed me to be ill, but did not know of my being in utter want), and these at uncertain intervals, constituted my whole support. During the former part of my sufferings (that is, generally in Wales, and always for the first two months in London) I was houseless, and very seldom slept under a roof. To this constant exposure to the open air I ascribe it mainly, that I did not sink under my torments. Latterly, however, when colder and more inclement weather came on, and when, from the length of my sufferings, I had begun to sink into a more languishing condition, it was, no doubt, fortunate for me, that the same person to whose breakfast-table I had access, allowed me to sleep in a large unoccupied house, of which he was tenant. Unoccupied, I call it, for there was no household or establishment in it; nor any furniture, indeed, except a table, and a few chairs. But I found, on taking possession of my new quarters, that the house already contained one single inmate, a poor friendless child, apparently ten years old; but she seemed hunger-bitten; and sufferings of that sort often make children look older than they are. From this forlorn child I learned, that she had slept and lived there alone, for some time before I came: and great joy the poor creature expressed, when she found that I was, in future, to be her companion through the hours of darkness. The house was large; and, from the want of furniture, the noise of the rats made a prodigious echoing on the spacious stair-case and hall; and, amidst

[1] Published anonymously in London.

[2] See SOCIETY AND POLITICAL ECONOMY for discussion of widespread use of opium for medicinal purposes.

[3] De Quincey provides from this point on a narrative of his residence at Oxford University and his travels in Wales after leaving the University.

the real fleshly ills of cold, and, I fear, hunger, the forsaken child had found leisure to suffer still more (it appeared) from the self-created one of ghosts. I promised her protection against all ghosts whatsoever: but, alas! I could offer her no other assistance. We lay upon the floor, with a bundle of cursed law papers for a pillow: but with no other covering than a sort of large horseman's cloak: afterwards, however, we discovered, in a garret, an old sofa-cover, a small piece of rug, and some fragments of other articles, which added a little to our warmth. The poor child crept close to me for warmth, and for security against her ghostly enemies. When I was not more than usually ill, I took her into my arms, so that, in general, she was tolerably warm, and often slept when I could not: for, during the last two months of my sufferings, I slept much in the day-time, and was apt to fall into transient dozings at all hours. But my sleep distressed me more than my watching: for, besides the tumultuousness of my dreams (which were only not so awful as those which I shall have to describe hereafter as produced by opium), my sleep was never more than what is called *dog-sleep*; so that I could hear myself moaning, and was often, as it seemed to me, wakened suddenly by my own voice; and, about this time, a hideous sensation began to haunt me as soon as I fell into a slumber, which has since returned upon me, at different periods of my life, viz. a sort of twitching (I know not where, but apparently about the region of the stomach), which compelled me violently to throw out my feet for the sake of relieving it. This sensation coming on as soon as I began to sleep, and the effort to relieve it constantly awaking me, at length I slept only from exhaustion; and from increasing weakness (as I said before) I was constantly falling asleep, and constantly awaking. Meantime, the master of the house sometimes came in upon us suddenly, and very early, sometimes not till ten o'clock, sometimes not at all. He was in constant fear of bailiffs: improving on the plan of Cromwell, every night he slept in a different quarter of London; and I observed that he never failed to examine, through a private window, the appearance of those who knocked at the door, before he would allow it to be opened. He breakfasted alone: indeed, his tea equipage would hardly have admitted of his hazarding an invitation to a second person—any more than the quantity of esculent *matériel,* which, for the most part, was little more than a roll, or a few biscuits, which he had bought on his road from the place where he had slept. Or, if he *had* asked a party, as I once learnedly and facetiously observed to him—the several members of it must have *stood* in the relation to each other (not *sat* in any relation whatever) of succession, as the meta-physicians have it, and not of co-existence; in the relation of the parts of time, and not of the parts of space. During his breakfast, I generally contrived a reason for lounging in; and, with an air of as much indifference as I could assume, took up such fragments as he had left—sometimes, indeed, there were none at all. In doing this, I committed no robbery except upon the man himself, who was thus obliged (I believe) now and then to send out at noon for an extra biscuit; for, as to the poor child, *she* was never admitted into his study (if I may give that name to his chief depositary of parchments, law writings, &c.); that room was to her the Blue-beard[4] room of the house, being regularly locked on his departure to dinner, about six o'clock, which usually was his final departure for the night. Whether this child were an illegitimate daughter of Mr. ——, or only a servant, I could not ascertain; she did not herself know; but certainly she was treated altogether as a menial servant. No sooner did Mr. —— make his appearance, than she went below stairs, brushed his shoes, coat, &c.; and, except when she was summoned to run an errand, she never emerged from the dismal Tartarus[5] of the kitchens, &c. to the upper air, until my welcome knock at night called up her little trembling footsteps to the front door. Of her life during the day-time, however, I knew little but what I gathered from her own account at night; for, as soon as the hours of business commenced, I saw that my absence would be acceptable; and, in general, therefore, I went off, and sat in the parks, or elsewhere, until night-fall.

But who, and what, meantime, was the master of the house himself? Reader, he was one of those anomalous practitioners in lower departments of the law, who—what shall I say?—who, on prudential reasons, or from necessity, deny themselves all indulgence in the luxury of too delicate a conscience: (a periphrasis which might be abridged considerably, but *that* I leave to the reader's taste:) in many walks of life, a conscience is a more expensive encumbrance, than a wife or a carriage; and just as people talk of "laying down" their carriages, so I suppose my friend, Mr. —— had "laid down" his conscience for a time; meaning, doubtless, to resume it as soon as he could

[4] **Blue-beard:** from *Blue Beard,* the French tale of a wealthy man with a blue beard, who kept his murdered wives in a locked room.

[5] **Tartarus:** one of the gloomiest regions of hell, where the most evil were punished.

afford it. The inner economy of such a man's daily life would present a most strange picture, if I could allow myself to amuse the reader at his expense. Even with my limited opportunities for observing what went on, I saw many scenes of London intrigues, and complex chicanery, "cycle and epicycle, orb in orb," at which I sometimes smile to this day—and at which I smiled then, in spite of my misery. My situation, however, at that time, gave me little experience, in my own person, of any qualities in Mr. ——'s character but such as did him honour; and of his whole strange composition, I must forget every thing but that towards me he was obliging, and, to the extent of his power, generous.

That power was not, indeed, very extensive; however, in common with the rats, I sat rent free; and, as Dr. Johnson[6] has recorded, that he never but once in his life had as much wall-fruit as he could eat, so let me be grateful, that on that single occasion I had as large a choice of apartments in a London mansion as I could possibly desire. Except the Blue-beard room, which the poor child believed to be haunted, all others, from the attics to the cellars, were at our service; "the world was all before us;"[7] and we pitched our tent for the night in any spot we chose. This house I have already described as a large one; it stands in a conspicuous situation, and in a well-known part of London. Many of my readers will have passed it, I doubt not, within a few hours of reading this. For myself, I never fail to visit it when business draws me to London; about ten o'clock, this very night, August 15, 1821, being my birth-day,—I turned aside from my evening walk, down Oxford-street, purposely to take a glance at it: it is now occupied by a respectable family; and, by the lights in the front drawing-room, I observed a domestic party, assembled perhaps at tea, and apparently cheerful and gay. Marvellous contrast in my eyes to the darkness—cold—silence—and desolation of that same house eighteen years ago, when its nightly occupants were one famishing scholar,[8] and a neglected child.—Her, by the bye, in after years, I vainly endeavoured to trace. Apart from her situation, she was not what would be called an interesting child: she was neither pretty, nor quick in understanding, nor remarkably pleasing in manners. But, thank God! even in those years I needed not the embellishments of novel-accessaries to conciliate my affections; plain human nature, in its humblest and most homely apparel, was enough for me: and I loved the child because she was my partner in wretchedness. If she is now living, she is probably a mother, with children of her own; but, as I have said, I could never trace her.

This I regret, but another person there was at that time, whom I have since sought to trace with far deeper earnestness, and with far deeper sorrow at my failure. This person was a young woman, and one of that unhappy class who subsist upon the wages of prostitution. I feel no shame, nor have any reason to feel it, in avowing, that I was then on familiar and friendly terms with many women in that unfortunate condition. The reader needs neither smile at this avowal, nor frown. For, not to remind my classical readers of the old Latin proverb—*"Sine Cerere,"* &c.,[9] it may well be supposed that in the existing state of my purse, my connexion with such women could not have been an impure one. But the truth is, that at no time of my life have I been a person to hold myself polluted by the touch or approach of any creature that wore a human shape: on the contrary, from my very earliest youth it has been my pride to converse familiarly, *more Socratico,*[10] with all human beings, man, woman, and child, that chance might fling in my way: a practice which is friendly to the knowledge of human nature, to good feelings, and to that frankness of address which becomes a man who would be thought a philosopher. For a philosopher should not see with the eyes of the poor limitary creature, calling himself a man of the world, and filled with narrow and self-regarding prejudices of birth and education, but should look upon himself as a Catholic[11] creature, and as standing in an equal relation to high and low—to educated and uneducated, to the guilty and the innocent. Being myself at that time of necessity a peripatetic, or a walker of the streets, I naturally fell in more frequently with those female peripatetics who are technically called street-walkers. Many of these women had occasionally taken my part against watchmen who wished to drive me off the steps of houses where I was sitting. But one

[6] **Dr. Johnson:** Samuel Johnson (1709–1784), preeminent man of letters.

[7] Cf. *Paradise Lost,* XII.646–47: "The world was all before them [Adam and Eve], where to choose / Their place of rest, and Providence their guide."

[8] **one famishing scholar:** De Quincey earlier describes himself as an unusually capable Greek scholar.

[9] **"Sine Cerere," &c.:** without food and wine Venus withers. Terence, *Eunuchus,* IV. v. 6.

[10] **more Socratico:** in the Socratic manner.

[11] **Catholic:** having broad and universal interests.

amongst them, the one on whose account I have at all introduced this subject—yet no! let me not class thee, oh noble-minded Ann ——, with that order of women; let me find, if it be possible, some gentler name to designate the condition of her to whose bounty and compassion, ministering to my necessities when all the world had forsaken me, I owe it that I am at this time alive.—For many weeks I had walked at nights with this poor friendless girl up and down Oxford-street, or had rested with her on steps and under the shelter of porticos. She could not be so old as myself: she told me, indeed, that she had not completed her sixteenth year. By such questions as my interest about her prompted, I had gradually drawn forth her simple history. Hers was a case of ordinary occurrence (as I have since had reason to think), and one in which, if London beneficence had better adapted its arrangements to meet it, the power of the law might oftener be interposed to protect, and to avenge. But the stream of London charity flows in a channel which, though deep and mighty, is yet noiseless and underground; not obvious or readily accessible to poor houseless wanderers: and it cannot be denied that the outside air and frame-work of London society is harsh, cruel, and repulsive. In any case, however, I saw that part of her injuries might easily have been redressed; and I urged her often and earnestly to lay her complaint before a magistrate: friendless as she was, I assured her that she would meet with immediate attention; and that English justice, which was no respecter of persons, would speedily and amply avenge her on the brutal ruffian who had plundered her little property. She promised me often that she would; but she delayed taking the steps I pointed out from time to time: for she was timid and dejected to a degree which showed how deeply sorrow had taken hold of her young heart: and perhaps she thought justly that the most upright judge, and the most righteous tribunals, could do nothing to repair her heaviest wrongs. Something, however, would perhaps have been done: for it had been settled between us at length, but unhappily on the very last time but one that I was ever to see her, that in a day or two we should go together before a magistrate, and that I should speak on her behalf. This little service it was destined, however, that I should never realise. Meantime, that which she rendered to me, and which was greater than I could ever have repaid her, was this:—One night, when we were pacing slowly along Oxford-street, and after a day when I had felt more than usually ill and faint, I requested her to turn off with me into Soho-square: thither we went; and we sat down on the steps of a house, which, to this hour, I never pass without a pang of grief, and an inner act of homage to the spirit of that unhappy girl, in memory of the noble action which she there performed. Suddenly, as we sat, I grew much worse: I had been leaning my head against her bosom; and all at once I sank from her arms and fell backwards on the steps. From the sensations I then had, I felt an inner conviction of the liveliest kind that without some powerful and reviving stimulus, I should either have died on the spot—or should at least have sunk to a point of exhaustion from which all re-ascent under my friendless circumstances would soon have become hopeless. Then it was, at this crisis of my fate, that my poor orphan companion—who had herself met with little but injuries in this world—stretched out a saving hand to me. Uttering a cry of terror, but without a moment's delay, she ran off into Oxford-street, and in less time than could be imagined, returned to me with a glass of port wine and spices, that acted upon my empty stomach (which at that time would have rejected all solid food) with an instantaneous power of restoration: and for this glass the generous girl without a murmur paid out of her own humble purse at a time—be it remembered!—when she had scarcely wherewithal to purchase the bare necessaries of life, and when she could have no reason to expect that I should ever be able to reimburse her.—Oh! youthful benefactress! how often in succeeding years, standing in solitary places, and thinking of thee with grief of heart and perfect love, how often have I wished that, as in ancient times the curse of a father was believed to have a supernatural power, and to pursue its object with a fatal necessity of self-fulfilment,—even so the benediction of a heart oppressed with gratitude, might have a like prerogative; might have power given to it from above to chase—to haunt—to way-lay—to overtake—to pursue thee into the central darkness of a London brothel, or (if it were possible) into the darkness of the grave[12]—there to awaken thee with an authentic message of peace and forgiveness, and of final reconciliation!

I do not often weep: for not only do my thoughts on subjects connected with the chief interests of man daily, nay hourly, descend a thousand fathoms "too deep for

[12] **"to haunt . . . darkness of the grave"**: Wordsworth, "She Was a Phantom of Delight,"* l. 10: "To haunt, to startle, and way-lay"; and "Ode"* l. 117 (variant): "In darkness lost, the darkness of the grave."

tears;"[13] not only does the sternness of my habits of thought present an antagonism to the feelings which prompt tears—wanting of necessity to those who, being protected usually by their levity from any tendency to meditative sorrow, would by that same levity be made incapable of resisting it on any casual access of such feelings:—but also, I believe that all minds which have contemplated such objects as deeply as I have done, must, for their own protection from utter despondency, have early encouraged and cherished some tranquillizing belief as to the future balances and the hieroglyphic meanings of human sufferings. On these accounts, I am cheerful to this hour; and, as I have said, I do not often weep. Yet some feelings, though not deeper or more passionate, are more tender than others; and often, when I walk at this time in Oxford-street by dreamy lamp-light, and hear those airs played on a barrel-organ which years ago solaced me and my dear companion (as I must always call her), I shed tears, and muse with myself at the mysterious dispensation which so suddenly and so critically separated us for ever. . . . [14]

— PART II —

So then, Oxford-street, stony-hearted step-mother! thou that listenest to the sighs of orphans, and drinkest the tears of children, at length I was dismissed from thee: the time was come at last that I no more should pace in anguish thy never-ending terraces; no more should dream, and wake in captivity to the pangs of hunger. Successors, too many, to myself and Ann, have, doubtless, since trodden in our footsteps,—inheritors of our calamities: other orphans than Ann have sighed: tears have been shed by other children: and thou, Oxford-street, hast since, doubtless, echoed to the groans of innumerable hearts. For myself, however, the storm which I had outlived seemed to have been the pledge of a long fair-weather; the premature sufferings which I had paid down, to have been accepted as a ransom for many years to come, as a price of long immunity from sorrow: and if again I walked in London, a solitary and contemplative man (as oftentimes I did), I walked for the most part in serenity and peace of mind. And, although it is true that the calamities of my noviciate in London had struck root so deeply in my bodily constitution that afterwards they shot up and flourished afresh, and grew into a noxious umbrage that has overshadowed and darkened my latter years, yet these second assaults of suffering were met with a fortitude more confirmed, with the resources of a maturer intellect, and with alleviations from sympathising affection—how deep and tender!

Thus, however, with whatsoever alleviations, years that were far asunder were bound together by subtle links of suffering derived from a common root. And herein I notice an instance of the short-sightedness of human desires, that oftentimes on moonlight nights, during my first mournful abode in London, my consolation was (if such it could be thought) to gaze from Oxford-street up every avenue in succession which pierces through the heart of Marylebone to the fields and the woods; and *that*, said I, travelling with my eyes up the long vistas which lay part in light and part in shade, "*that* is the road to the north, and therefore to ——, and if I had the wings of a dove, *that* way I would fly for comfort."[15] Thus I said, and thus I wished, in my blindness; yet, even in that very northern region it was, even in that very valley, nay, in that very house to which my erroneous wishes pointed, that this second birth of my sufferings began; and that they again threatened to besiege the citadel of life and hope. There it was, that for years I was persecuted by visions as ugly, and as ghastly phantoms as ever haunted the couch of an Orestes:[16] and in this unhappier than he, that sleep, which comes to all as a respite and a restoration, and to him especially, as a blessed balm for his wounded heart and his haunted brain, visited me as my bitterest scourge. Thus blind was I in my desires; yet, if a veil interposes between the dimsightedness of man and his future calamities, the same veil hides from him their alleviations; and a grief which had not been feared is met by consolations which had not been hoped. I, therefore, who participated, as it were, in the troubles of Orestes (excepting only in his

[13] **"too deep for tears;":** Wordsworth, "Ode"* l. 206: "Thoughts that do often lie too deep for tears."

[14] **separated . . . for ever:** De Quincey goes on to describe his separation from Ann when he left London in pursuit of a note of credit from a friend at Eton. He left without learning Ann's surname, and could not find her after a series of disappointments delayed his return.

[15] **that way . . . comfort:** north to Grasmere and Dove Cottage, where the Wordsworths resided and where De Quincey was living when he composed *Confessions.*

[16] **Orestes:** the son of Agamemnon and brother of Electra, who murders his mother Clytemnestra and her lover for killing his father, and is then pursued by Furies or Eumenides until his acquittal through the assistance of Athena, Goddess of Wisdom. From *The Oresteia,* a trilogy of plays by Aeschylus.

agitated conscience), participated no less in all his supports: my Eumenides, like his, were at my bed-feet, and stared in upon me through the curtains: but, watching by my pillow, or defrauding herself of sleep to bear me company through the heavy watches of the night sat my Electra: for thou, beloved M.,[17] dear companion of my later years, thou wast my Electra! and neither in nobility of mind nor in long-suffering affection, wouldst permit that a Grecian sister should excel an English wife. For thou thoughtest not much to stoop to humble offices of kindness, and to servile ministrations of tenderest affection;—to wipe away for years the unwholesome dews upon the forehead, or to refresh the lips when parched and baked with fever; nor, even when thy own peaceful slumbers had by long sympathy become infected with the spectacle of my dread contest with phantoms and shadowy enemies that oftentimes bade me "sleep no more!"[18]—not even then, didst thou utter a complaint or any murmur, nor withdraw thy angelic smiles, nor shrink from thy service of love more than Electra did of old. For she too, though she was a Grecian woman, and the daughter of the king of men, yet wept sometimes, and hid her face[19] in her robe.

But these troubles are past: and thou wilt read these records of a period so dolorous to us both as the legend of some hideous dream that can return no more. Meantime, I am again in London: and again I pace the terraces of Oxford-street by night: and oftentimes, when I am oppressed by anxieties that demand all my philosophy and the comfort of thy presence to support, and yet remember that I am separated from thee by three hundred miles, and the length of three dreary months,—I look up the streets that run northwards from Oxford-street, upon moonlight nights, and recollect my youthful ejaculation of anguish;—and remembering that thou art sitting alone in that same valley, and mistress of that very house to which my heart turned in its blindness nineteen years ago, I think that, though blind indeed, and scattered to the winds of late, the promptings of my heart may yet have had reference to a remoter time, and may be justified if read in another meaning:—and, if I could allow myself to descend again to the impotent wishes of childhood, I should again say to myself, as I look to the north, "Oh, that I had the wings of a dove—"[20] and with how just a confidence in thy good and gracious nature might I add the other half of my early ejaculation—"And *that* way I would fly for comfort."

— THE PLEASURES OF OPIUM —

It is so long since I first took opium, that if it had been a trifling incident in my life, I might have forgotten its date: but cardinal events are not to be forgotten; and from circumstances connected with it, I remember that it must be referred to the autumn of 1804. During that season I was in London, having come thither for the first time since my entrance at college. And my introduction to opium arose in the following way. From an early age I had been accustomed to wash my head in cold water at least once a day: being suddenly seized with tooth-ache, I attributed it to some relaxation caused by an accidental intermission of that practice; jumped out of bed; plunged my head into a basin of cold water; and with hair thus wetted went to sleep. The next morning, as I need hardly say, I awoke with excruciating rheumatic pains of the head and face, from which I had hardly any respite for about twenty days. On the twenty-first day, I think it was, and on a Sunday, that I went out into the streets; rather to run away, if possible, from my torments, than with any distinct purpose. By accident I met a college acquaintance who recommended opium. Opium! dread agent of unimaginable pleasure and pain! I had heard of it as I had of manna or of ambrosia, but no further: how unmeaning a sound was it at that time! what solemn chords does it now strike upon my heart! what heart-quaking vibrations of sad and happy remembrances! Reverting for a moment to these, I feel a mystic importance attached to the minutest circumstances connected with the place and the time, and the man (if man he was) that first laid open to me the

[17] **M.**: Margaret, a Grasmere farmer's daughter whom De Quincey married in 1816 and by whom he had eight children.

[18] Cf. *Macbeth,* II.ii.34–36: "Methought I heard a voice cry 'Sleep no more! / Macbeth does murder sleep.'"

[19] The scholar will know that throughout this passage I refer to the early scenes of the Orestes; one of the most beautiful exhibitions of the domestic affections which even the dramas of Euripedes can furnish. To the English reader, it may be necessary to say, that the situation at the opening of the drama is that of a brother attended only by his sister during the demoniacal possession of a suffering conscience (or, in the mythology of the play, haunted by the furies), and in circumstances of immediate danger from enemies, and of desertion or cold regard from nominal friends. [T.D.Q.]

[20] **"wings of a dove"**: Byron, "For years fleetaway with the wings of a dove." "The First Kiss of Love," l. 26.

Paradise of Opium-eaters.[21] It was a Sunday afternoon, wet and cheerless: and a duller spectacle this earth of ours has not to show than a rainy Sunday in London. My road homewards lay through Oxford-street; and near "the *stately* Pantheon,"[22] (as Mr. Wordsworth has obligingly called it) I saw a druggist's shop. The druggist, unconscious minister of celestial pleasures! — as if in sympathy with the rainy Sunday, looked dull and stupid, just as any mortal druggist might be expected to look on a Sunday: and, when I asked for the tincture of opium,[23] he gave it to me as any other man might do: and furthermore, out of my shilling, returned me what seemed to be real copper half-pence, taken out of a real wooden drawer. Nevertheless, in spite of such indications of humanity, he has ever since existed in my mind as the beatific vision of an immortal druggist, sent down to earth on a special mission to myself. And it confirms me in this way of considering him, that, when I next came up to London, I sought him near the stately Pantheon, and found him not: and thus to me, who knew not his name (if indeed he had one) he seemed rather to have vanished from Oxford-street than to have removed in any bodily fashion. The reader may choose to think of him as, possibly, no more than a sublunary druggist: it may be so: but my faith is better: I believe him to have evanesced, or evaporated. So unwillingly would I connect any mortal remembrances with that hour, and place, and creature, that first brought me acquainted with the celestial drug.

Arrived at my lodgings, it may be supposed that I lost not a moment in taking the quantity prescribed. I was necessarily ignorant of the whole art and mystery of opium-taking: and, what I took, I took under every disadvantage. But I took it: — and in an hour, oh! heavens! what a revulsion! what an upheaving, from its lowest depths, of the inner spirit! what an apocalypse of the world within me! That my pains had vanished, was now a trifle in my eyes: — this negative effect was swallowed up in the immensity of those positive effects which had opened before me — in the abyss of divine enjoyment thus suddenly revealed. Here was a panacea — a *φαρμαχον νήπενθες*[24] for all human woes: here was the secret of happiness, about which philosophers had disputed for so many ages, at once discovered: happiness might now be bought for a penny, and carried in the waistcoat pocket: portable ecstasies might be had corked up in a pint bottle: and peace of mind could be sent down in gallons by the mail coach. But, if I talk in this way, the reader will think I am laughing: and I can assure him, that nobody will laugh long who deals much with opium: its pleasures even are of a grave and solemn complexion; and in his happiest state, the opium-eater cannot present himself in the character of *l'Allegro*: even then, he speaks and thinks as becomes *Il Penseroso*.[25] Nevertheless, I have a very reprehensible way of jesting at times in the midst of my own misery: and, unless when I am checked by some more powerful feelings, I am afraid I shall be guilty of this indecent practice even in these annals of suffering or enjoyment. The reader must allow a little to my infirm nature in this respect: and with a few indulgences of that sort, I shall endeavour to be as grave, if not drowsy, as fits a theme like opium, so anti-mercurial as it really is, and so drowsy as it is falsely reputed.

And, first, one word with respect to its bodily effects: for upon all that has been hitherto written on the subject of opium, whether by travellers in Turkey (who may plead their privilege of lying as an old immemorial right), or by professors of medicine, writing *ex cathedrâ*,[26] — I have but one emphatic criticism to pronounce — Lies! lies! lies! I remember once, in passing a book-stall, to have caught these words from a page of some satiric author: — "By this time I became convinced that the London newspapers spoke truth at least twice a week, viz. on Tuesday and Saturday, and might safely be depended upon for —— the list of bankrupts." In like manner, I do by no means deny that some truths have been delivered to the world in regard to opium: thus it has been repeatedly affirmed by the learned, that opium is a dusky brown in colour; and this, take notice, I grant: secondly, that it is rather dear; which also I grant: for in my time, East-India opium has been three guineas a pound, and Turkey eight:[27] and, thirdly, that if you eat a good deal of it, most probably you must —— do what is particularly

[21] **Opium-eaters:** De Quincey's neologism.

[22] **stately Pantheon:** concert hall.

[23] **tincture of opium:** laudanum; crude opium mixed with alcohol, commonly prescribed for many ailments. (See SOCIETY AND POLITICAL ECONOMY.)

[24] Cf. Homer's *Odyssey*, IV.220–22: "an anodyne, mild magic of forgetfulness. / Whoever drank this mixture in the wine bowl / would be incapable of tears that day" (trans. Robert Fitzgerald).

[25] **l'Allegro . . . Il Penseroso:** titles of Milton's poems on the cheerful man and the pensive man.

[26] **ex cathedrâ:** from a position of authority.

[27] A guinea equals 1 pound 3 shillings. There are 20 shillings in a pound.

disagreeable to any man of regular habits, viz. die.[28] These weighty propositions are, all and singular, true: I cannot gainsay them: and truth ever was, and will be, commendable. But in these three theorems, I believe we have exhausted the stock of knowledge as yet accumulated by man on the subject of opium. And therefore, worthy doctors, as there seems to be room for further discoveries, stand aside, and allow me to come forward and lecture on this matter.

First, then, it is not so much affirmed as taken for granted, by all who ever mention opium, formally or incidentally, that it does, or can, produce intoxication. Now, reader, assure yourself, *meo periculo,*[29] that no quantity of opium ever did, or could intoxicate. As to the tincture of opium (commonly called laudanum) *that* might certainly intoxicate if a man could bear to take enough of it; but why? because it contains so much proof spirit,[30] and not because it contains so much opium. But crude opium, I affirm peremptorily, is incapable of producing any state of body at all resembling that which is produced by alcohol: and not in *degree* only incapable, but even in *kind*: it is not in the quantity of its effects merely, but in the quality, that it differs altogether. The pleasure given by wine is always mounting, and tending to a crisis, after which it declines: that from opium, when once generated, is stationary for eight or ten hours: the first, to borrow a technical distinction from medicine, is a case of acute—the second, of chronic pleasure: the one is a flame, the other a steady and equable glow. [But the main distinction lies in this, that whereas wine disorders the mental faculties, opium, on the contrary (if taken in a proper manner), introduces amongst them the most exquisite order, legislation, and harmony.] Wine robs a man of his self-possession: opium greatly invigorates it. Wine unsettles and clouds the judgment, and gives a preternatural brightness, and a vivid exaltation to the contempts and the admirations, the loves and the hatreds, of the drinker: opium, on the contrary, communicates serenity and equipoise to all the faculties, active or passive: and with respect to the temper and moral feelings in general, it gives simply that sort of vital warmth which is approved by the judgment, and which would probably always accompany a bodily constitution of primeval or antediluvian[31] health. Thus, for instance, opium, like wine, gives an expansion to the heart and the benevolent affections: but then, with this remarkable difference, that in the sudden development of kind-heartedness which accompanies inebriation, there is always more or less of a maudlin character, which exposes it to the contempt of the bystander. Men shake hands, swear eternal friendship, and shed tears—no mortal knows why: and the sensual creature is clearly uppermost. But the expansion of the benigner feelings, incident to opium, is no febrile[32] access, but a healthy restoration to that state which the mind would naturally recover upon the removal of any deep-seated irritation of pain that had disturbed and quarrelled with the impulses of a heart originally just and good. True it is, that even wine, up to a certain point, and with certain men, rather tends to exalt and to steady the intellect: I myself, who have never been a great wine-drinker, used to find that half a dozen glasses of wine advantageously affected the faculties—brightened and intensified the consciousness—and gave to the mind a feeling of being "ponderibus librata suis:"[33] and certainly it is most absurdly said, in popular language, of any man, that he is *disguised* in liquor: for, on the contrary, most men are disguised by sobriety; and it is when they are drinking (as some old gentleman says in Athenaeus), that men *εαντοὺς ἐμφανίζουσιν οἵτινες εἰσίν*[34]—display themselves in their true complexion of character; which surely is not disguising themselves. But still, wine constantly leads a man to the brink of absurdity and extravagance; and, beyond a certain point, it is sure to volatilize and to disperse the intellectual energies: whereas opium always seems to compose what had been agitated, and to concentrate what had been distracted. In short, to sum up all in one word, a man who is inebriated, or tending to inebriation, is, and feels that he is, in a condition which calls up into supremacy the merely human, too often the brutal, part of his nature: but the opium-eater (I speak of him who is not suffering from any disease, or other remote effects of opium,) feels that the diviner part of his nature is paramount; that is, the moral affections are in a state of cloudless serenity; and over all is the great light of the majestic intellect. . . .

[28] Of this, however, the learned appear latterly to have doubted: for in a pirated edition of Buchan's *Domestic Medicine,* which I once saw in the hands of a farmer's wife who was studying it for the benefit of her health, the doctor was made to say—'Be particularly careful never to take above five-and-twenty *ounces* of laudanum at once;' the true rending being probably five and twenty *drops,* which are held equal to about one grain of crude opium. [T.D.Q.]

[29] **meo periculo**: at my peril.

[30] **proof spirit**: alcohol.

[31] **antidiluvian**: before the Flood of Genesis.

[32] **febrile**: feverish.

[33] **ponderibus librata suis**: freed of its burdens.

[34] The translation follows in De Quincey's sentence.

. . . Certainly, opium is classed under the head of narcotics; and some such effect it may produce in the end: but the primary effects of opium are always, and in the highest degree, to excite and stimulate the system: this first stage of its action always lasted with me, during my noviciate, for upwards of eight hours; so that it must be the fault of the opium-eater himself if he does not so time his exhibition of the dose (to speak medically) as that the whole weight of its narcotic influence may descend upon his sleep. Turkish opium-eaters, it seems, are absurd enough to sit, like so many equestrian statues, on logs of wood as stupid as themselves. But that the reader may judge of the degree in which opium is likely to stupify the faculties of an Englishman, I shall (by way of treating the question illustratively, rather than argumentatively) describe the way in which I myself often passed an opium evening in London, during the period between 1804 and 1812. It will be seen, that at least opium did not move me to seek solitude, and much less to seek inactivity, or the torpid state of self-involution ascribed to the Turks. I give this account at the risk of being pronounced a crazy enthusiast or visionary: but I regard *that* little: I must desire my reader to bear in mind, that I was a hard student, and at severe studies for all the rest of my time: and certainly I had a right occasionally to relaxations as well as other people: these, however, I allowed myself but seldom.

The late Duke of —— used to say, "Next Friday, by the blessing of Heaven, I purpose to be drunk:" and in like manner I used to fix beforehand how often, within a given time, and when, I would commit a debauch of opium. This was seldom more than once in three weeks: for at that time I could not have ventured to call every day (as I did afterwards) for *"a glass of laudanun negus, warm, and without sugar."* No: as I have said, I seldom drank laudanum, at that time, more than once in three weeks: this was usually on a Tuesday or a Saturday night; my reason for which was this. In those days Grassini[35] sang at the Opera: and her voice was delightful to me beyond all that I had ever heard. I know not what may be the state of the Opera-house now, having never been within its walls for seven or eight years, but at that time it was by much the most pleasant place of public resort in London for passing an evening. Five shillings admitted one to the gallery, which was subject to far less annoyance than the pit of the theatres: the orchestra was distinguished by its sweet and melodious grandeur from all English orchestras, the composition of which, I confess, is not acceptable to my ear, from the predominance of the clangorous instruments, and the absolute tyranny of the violin. The choruses were divine to hear: and when Grassini appeared in some interlude, as she often did, and poured forth her passionate soul as Andromache, at the tomb of Hector, &c. I question whether any Turk, of all that ever entered the paradise of opium-eaters, can have had half the pleasure I had. But, indeed, I honour the Barbarians too much by supposing them capable of any pleasures approaching to the intellectual ones of an Englishman. For music is an intellectual or a sensual pleasure, according to the temperament of him who hears it. And, by the by, with the exception of the fine extravaganza on that subject in Twelfth Night, I do not recollect more than one thing said adequately on the subject of music in all literature: it is a passage in the *Religio Medici*[36] of Sir T. Brown; and, though chiefly remarkable for its sublimity, has also a philosophic value, inasmuch as it points to the true theory of musical effects. The mistake of most people is to suppose that it is by the ear they communicate with music, and, therefore, that they are purely passive to its effects. But this is not so: it is by the reaction of the mind upon the notices of the ear, (the *matter* coming by the senses, the *form* from the mind,) that the pleasure is constructed: and therefore it is that people of equally good ear differ so much in this point from one another. Now opium, by greatly increasing the activity of the mind generally, increases, of necessity, that particular mode of its activity by which we are able to construct out of the raw material of organic sound an elaborate intellectual pleasure. But, says a friend, a succession of musical sounds is to me like a collection of Arabic characters: I can attach no ideas to them. Ideas! my good sir? there is no occasion for them: all that class of ideas, which can be available in such a case, has a language of representative feelings. But this is a subject foreign to my present purposes: it is sufficient to say, that a chorus, &c. of elaborate harmony, displayed before me, as in a piece of arras work, the whole of my past life—not as if recalled by an act of memory, but as if present and incarnated in the music: no longer painful to dwell upon: but the detail of its incidents removed, or blended in some hazy abstraction; and its passions exalted, spiritualized, and sublimed. All this

[35] **Grassini:** Josephina Grassini (1773–1850).

[36] I have not the book at this moment to consult: but I think the passage begins—"And even that tavern music, which makes one man merry, another mad, in me strikes a deep fit of devotion," &c. [T.D.Q.]

was to be had for five shillings. And over and above the music of the stage and the orchestra, I had all around me, in the intervals of the performance, the music of the Italian language talked by Italian women: for the gallery was usually crowded with Italians: and I listened with a pleasure such as that with which Weld the traveller lay and listened, in Canada, to the sweet laughter of Indian women; for the less you understand of a language, the more sensible you are to the melody or harshness of its sounds: for such a purpose, therefore, it was an advantage to me that I was a poor Italian scholar, reading it but little, and not speaking it at all, nor understanding a tenth part of what I heard spoken.

These were my Opera pleasures: but another pleasure I had which, as it could be had only on a Saturday night, occasionally struggled with my love of the Opera; for, at that time, Tuesday and Saturday were the regular Opera nights. On this subject I am afraid I shall be rather obscure, but, I can assure the reader, not at all more so than Marinus in his life of Proclus, or many other biographers and auto-biographers of fair reputation. This pleasure, I have said, was to be had only on a Saturday night. What then was Saturday night to me more than any other night? I had no labours that I rested from; no wages to receive: what needed I to care for Saturday night, more than as it was a summons to hear Grassini? True, most logical reader: what you say is unanswerable. And yet so it was and is, that, whereas different men throw their feelings into different channels, and most are apt to show their interest in the concerns of the poor, chiefly by sympathy, expressed in some shape or other, with their distresses and sorrows, I, at that time, was disposed to express my interest by sympathising with their pleasures. The pains of poverty I had lately seen too much of; more than I wished to remember: but the pleasures of the poor, their consolations of spirit, and their reposes from bodily toil, can never become oppressive to contemplate. Now Saturday night is the season for the chief, regular, and periodic return of rest to the poor: in this point the most hostile sects unite, and acknowledge a common link of brotherhood: almost all Christendom rests from its labours. It is a rest introductory to another rest: and divided by a whole day and two nights from the renewal of toil. On this account I feel always, on a Saturday night, as though I also were released from some yoke of labour, had some wages to receive, and some luxury of repose to enjoy. For the sake, therefore, of witnessing, upon as large a scale as possible, a spectacle with which my sympathy was so entire, I used often, on Saturday nights, after I had taken opium, to wander forth, without much regarding the direction or the distance, to all the markets, and other parts of London, to which the poor resort on a Saturday night, for laying out their wages. Many a family party, consisting of a man, his wife, and sometimes one or two of his children, have I listened to, as they stood consulting on their ways and means, or the strength of their exchequer, or the price of household articles. Gradually I became familiar with their wishes, their difficulties, and their opinions. Sometimes there might be heard murmurs of discontent: but far oftener expressions on the countenance, or uttered in words, of patience, hope, and tranquillity. And taken generally, I must say, that, in this point at least, the poor are far more philosophic than the rich—that they show a more ready and cheerful submission to what they consider as irremediable evils, or irreparable losses. Whenever I saw occasion, or could do it without appearing to be intrusive, I joined their parties; and gave my opinion upon the matter in discussion, which, if not always judicious, was always received indulgently. If wages were a little higher, or expected to be so, or the quartern loaf a little lower, or it was reported that onions and butter were expected to fall, I was glad: yet, if the contrary were true, I drew from opium some means of consoling myself. For opium (like the bee, that extracts its materials indiscriminately from roses and from the soot of chimneys) can overrule all feelings into a compliance with the master key. Some of these rambles led me to great distances: for an opium-eater is too happy to observe the motion of time. And sometimes in my attempts to steer homewards, upon nautical principles, by fixing my eye on the polestar, and seeking ambitiously for a northwest passage, instead of circumnavigating all the capes and headlands I had doubled in my outward voyage, I came suddenly upon such knotty problems of alleys, such enigmatical entries, and such sphinx's riddles of streets without thoroughfares, as must, I conceive, baffle the audacity of porters, and confound the intellects of hackney-coachmen. I could almost have believed, at times, that I must be the first discoverer of some of these *terrae incognitae*,[37] and doubted, whether they had yet been laid down in the modern charts of London. For all this, however, I paid a heavy price in distant years, when the human face tyrannized over my dreams, and the perplexities of my steps in London came back and haunted my sleep, with the feeling of

[37] **terrae incognitae**: unknown lands.

perplexities moral or intellectual, that brought confusion to the reason, or anguish and remorse to the conscience.

Thus I have shown that opium does not, of necessity, produce inactivity or torpor; but that, on the contrary, it often led me into markets and theatres. Yet, in candour, I will admit that markets and theatres are not the appropriate haunts of the opium-eater, when in the divinest state incident to his enjoyment. In that state, crowds become an oppression to him; music even, too sensual and gross. He naturally seeks solitude and silence, as indispensable conditions of those trances, or profoundest reveries, which are the crown and consummation of what opium can do for human nature. I, whose disease it was to meditate too much, and to observe too little, and who, upon my first entrance at college, was nearly falling into a deep melancholy, from brooding too much on the sufferings which I had witnessed in London, was sufficiently aware of the tendencies of my own thoughts to do all I could to counteract them.—I was, indeed, like a person who, according to the old legend, had entered the cave of Trophonius:[38] and the remedies I sought were to force myself into society, and to keep my understanding in continual activity upon matters of science. But for these remedies, I should certainly have become hypochondriacally melancholy. In after years, however, when my cheerfulness was more fully re-established, I yielded to my natural inclination for a solitary life. And, at that time, I often fell into these reveries upon taking opium; and more than once it has happened to me, on a summer night, when I have been at an open window, in a room from which I could overlook the sea at a mile below me, and could command a view of the great town of L——, at about the same distance, that I have sat, from sun-set to sun-rise, motionless, and without wishing to move.

I shall be charged with mysticism, Behmenism, quietism, &c. but *that* shall not alarm me. Sir H. Vane,[39] the younger, was one of our wisest men: and let my readers see if he, in his philosophical works, be half as unmystical as I am.—I say, then, that it has often struck me that the scene itself was somewhat typical of what took place in such a reverie. The town of L—— represented the earth, with its sorrows and its graves left behind, yet not out of sight, nor wholly forgotten. The ocean, in everlasting but gentle agitation, and brooded over by a dove-like calm, might not unfitly typify the mind and the mood which then swayed it. For it seemed to me as if then first I stood at a distance, and aloof from the uproar of life; as if the tumult, the fever, and the strife,[40] were suspended; a respite granted from the secret burthens of the heart; a sabbath of repose; a resting from human labours. Here were the hopes which blossom in the paths of life, reconciled with the peace which is in the grave; motions of the intellect as unwearied as the heavens, yet for all anxieties a halcyon calm: a tranquillity that seemed no product of inertia, but as if resulting from mighty and equal antagonisms; infinite activities, infinite repose.

Oh! just, subtle, and mighty opium! that to the hearts of poor and rich alike, for the wounds that will never heal, and for "the pangs that tempt the spirit to rebel,"[41] bringest an assuaging balm; eloquent opium! that with thy potent rhetoric stealest away the purposes of wrath; and to the guilty man, for one night givest back the hopes of his youth, and hands washed pure from blood; and to the proud man, a brief oblivion for

Wrongs unredress'd, and insults unavenged;[42]

that summonest to the chancery of dreams, for the triumphs of suffering innocence, false witnesses; and confoundest perjury; and dost reverse the sentences of unrighteous judges:—thou buildst upon the bosom of darkness, out of the fantastic imagery of the brain, cities and temples, beyond the art of Phidias and Praxiteles—beyond the splendour of Babylon and Hekatómpylos:[43] and "from the anarchy of dreaming sleep,"[44] callest into sunny light the faces of long-buried beauties, and the blessed household countenances, cleansed from the "dishonours of the grave."[45] Thou only givest these gifts to man; and thou hast the keys of Paradise, oh, just, subtle, and mighty opium! . . .

---

[38] **Trophonius:** oracular god who provides revelations underground after the inquirer performs elaborate rituals.

[39] **Behmenism:** from Jacob Boehme (1575–1624), German peasant and mystic. **Sir H. Vane:** Henry Vane, Puritan statesman (1613–1662).

[40] **"tumult, the fever, and the strife":** Keats, *Ode to a Nightingale:* "The weariness, the fever, and the fret," l. 23.

[41] Cf. Wordsworth, Dedication to *The White Doe of Rylstone,* 36.

[42] Cf. Wordsworth, *The Excursion,* 3.374.

[43] **Phidias and Praxiteles . . . Babylon and Hekatómpylos:** Grecian sculptors and wondrous Egyptian cities.

[44] Cf. *The Excursion,* 4.87.

[45] Cf. I Corinthians 15:43: "It [the body at death] is sown in dishonour; it is raised in glory: it is sown in weakness; it is raised in power."

—*from* INTRODUCTION TO THE PAINS OF OPIUM—

If any man, poor or rich, were to say that he would tell us what had been the happiest day in his life, and the why, and the wherefore, I suppose that we should all cry out—Hear him! Hear him!—As to the happiest *day,* that must be very difficult for any wise man to name; because any event, that could occupy so distinguished a place in a man's retrospect of his life, or be entitled to have shed a special felicity on any one day, ought to be of such an enduring character, as that (accidents apart) it should have continued to shed the same felicity, or one not distinguishably less, on many years together. To the happiest *lustrum,* however, or even to the happiest *year,* it may be allowed to any man to point without discountenance from wisdom. This year, in my case, reader, was the one which we have now reached; though it stood, I confess, as a parenthesis between years of a gloomier character. It was a year of brilliant water (to speak after the manner of jewellers), set as it were, and insulated, in the gloom and cloudy melancholy of opium. Strange as it may sound, I had a little before this time descended suddenly, and without any considerable effort, from 320 grains of opium (i.e. eight[46] thousand drops of laudanum) per day, to forty grains, or one eighth part. Instantaneously, and as if by magic, the cloud of profoundest melancholy which rested upon my brain, like some black vapours that I have seen roll away from the summits of mountains, drew off in one day (*νυχθημεζον*);[47] passed off with its murky banners as simultaneously as a ship that has been stranded, and is floated off by a spring tide—

> That moveth altogether, if it move at all.[48]

Now, then, I was again happy: I now took only 1000 drops of laudanum per day: and what was that? A latter spring had come to close up the season of youth: my brain performed its functions as healthily as ever before: I read Kant[49] again; and again I understood him, or fancied that I did. Again my feelings of pleasure expanded themselves to all around me: and if any man from Oxford or Cambridge, or from neither, had been announced to me in my unpretending cottage, I should have welcomed him with as sumptuous a reception as so poor a man could offer. Whatever else was wanting to a wise man's happiness,—of laudanum I would have given him as much as he wished, and in a golden cup. And, by the way, now that I speak of giving laudanum away, I remember, about this time, a little incident, which I mention, because, trifling as it was, the reader will soon meet it again in my dreams, which it influenced more fearfully than could be imagined. One day a Malay knocked at my door. What business a Malay could have to transact amongst English mountains, I cannot conjecture: but possibly he was on his road to a sea-port about forty miles distant.

The servant who opened the door to him was a young girl born and bred amongst the mountains, who had never seen an Asiatic dress of any sort: his turban, therefore, confounded her not a little: and, as it turned out, that his attainments in English were exactly of the same extent as hers in the Malay, there seemed to be an impassable gulf fixed between all communication of ideas, if either party had happened to possess any. In this dilemma, the girl, recollecting the reputed learning of her master (and, doubtless, giving me credit for a knowledge of all the languages of the earth, besides, perhaps, a few of the lunar ones), came and gave me to understand that there was a sort of demon below, whom she clearly imagined that my art could exorcise from the house. I did not immediately go down: but, when I did, the group which presented itself, arranged as it was by accident, though not very elaborate, took hold of my fancy and my eye in a way that none of the statuesque attitudes exhibited in the ballets at the Opera House, though so ostentatiously complex, had ever done. In a cottage kitchen, but panelled on the wall with dark wood that from age and rubbing resembled oak, and looking more like a rustic hall of entrance than a kitchen, stood the Malay—his turban and loose trowsers of dingy white relieved upon the dark panelling: he had placed himself nearer to the girl than she seemed to relish; though her native spirit of mountain intrepidity contended with the feeling of simple awe which her countenance expressed as she gazed upon the

[46] I here reckon twenty-five drops of laudanum as equivalent to one grain of opium, which, I believe, is the common estimate. However, as both may be considered variable quantities (the crude opium varying much in strength, and the tincture still more), I suppose that no infinitesimal accuracy can be had in such a calculation. Tea-spoons vary as much in size as opium in strength. Small ones hold about 100 drops: so that 8000 drops are about eighty times a tea-spoonful. [T.D.Q.]

[47] a night and a day.

[48] Cf. Wordsworth, "Resolution and Independence,"* l. 84: "And moveth altogether, if it move at all."

[49] **Kant:** Immanuel Kant (1724–1804), philosopher.

tiger-cat before her. And a more striking picture there could not be imagined, than the beautiful English face of the girl, and its exquisite fairness, together with her erect and independent attitude, contrasted with the sallow and bilious skin of the Malay, enamelled or veneered with mahogany, by marine air, his small, fierce, restless eyes, thin lips, slavish gestures and adorations. Half-hidden by the ferocious looking Malay, was a little child from a neighbouring cottage who had crept in after him, and was now in the act of reverting its head, and gazing upwards at the turban and the fiery eyes beneath it, whilst with one hand he caught at the dress of the young woman for protection. My knowledge of the Oriental tongues is not remarkably extensive, being indeed confined to two words—the Arabic word for barley, and the Turkish for opium (madjoon), which I have learnt from Anastasius. And, as I had neither a Malay dictionary, nor even Adelung's *Mithridates*,[50] which might have helped me to a few words, I addressed him in some lines from the Iliad; considering that, of such languages as I possessed, Greek, in point of longitude, came geographically nearest to an Oriental one. He worshipped me in a most devout manner, and replied in what I suppose was Malay. In this way I saved my reputation with my neighbours: for the Malay had no means of betraying the secret. He lay down upon the floor for about an hour, and then pursued his journey. On his departure, I presented him with a piece of opium. To him, as an Orientalist, I concluded that opium must be familiar: and the expression of his face convinced me that it was. Nevertheless, I was struck with some little consternation when I saw him suddenly raise his hand to his mouth, and (in the school-boy phrase) bolt the whole, divided into three pieces, at one mouthful. The quantity was enough to kill three dragoons and their horses: and I felt some alarm for the poor creature: but what could be done? I had given him the opium in compassion for his solitary life, on recollecting that if he had travelled on foot from London, it must be nearly three weeks since he could have exchanged a thought with any human being. I could not think of violating the laws of hospitality, by having him seized and drenched with an emetic, and thus frightening him into a notion that we were going to sacrifice him to some English idol. No: there was clearly no help for it:—he took his leave: and for some days I felt anxious: but as I never heard of any Malay being found dead, I became convinced that he was used[51] to opium: and that I must have done him the service I designed, by giving him one night of respite from the pains of wandering.

This incident I have digressed to mention, because this Malay (partly from the picturesque exhibition he assisted to frame, partly from the anxiety I connected with his image for some days) fastened afterwards upon my dreams, and brought other Malays with him worse than himself, that ran "a-muck"[52] at me, and led me into a world of troubles.—But to quit this episode, and to return to my intercalary year[53] of happiness. I have said already, that on a subject so important to us all as happiness, we should listen with pleasure to any man's experience or experiments, even though he were but a plough-boy, who cannot be supposed to have ploughed very deep into such an intractable soil as that of human pains and pleasures, or to have conducted his researches upon any very enlightened principles. But I, who have taken happiness, both in a solid and a liquid shape, both boiled and unboiled, both East India and Turkey—who have conducted my experiments upon this interesting subject with a sort of galvanic battery—and have, for the general benefit of the world, inoculated myself, as it were, with the poison of 8000 drops of laudanum per day (just, for the same reason, as a French surgeon inoculated himself lately with cancer—an English one, twenty years ago, with plague—and a third, I know not of what nation, with hydrophobia),—*I* (it will be admitted) must surely know what happiness is,

[50] **Anastasius:** a novel by Thomas Hope (1770–1831), published in 1819. **Mithridates:** treatise on Oriental languages by J. C. Adelung (1732–1806).

[51] This, however, is not a necessary conclusion: the varieties of effect produced by opium on different constitutions are infinite. A London magistrate (Harriott's *Struggles through Life*, vol. iii. p. 391, third edition,) has recorded that, on the first occasion of his trying laudanum for the gout, he took *forty* drops, the next night *sixty*, and on the fifth night *eighty*, without any effect whatever: and this at an advanced age. I have an anecdote from a country surgeon, however, which sinks Mr. Harriott's case into a trifle; and in my projected medical treatise on opium, which I will publish, provided the College of Surgeons will pay me for enlightening their benighted understandings upon this subject, I will relate it: but it is far too good a story to be published gratis. [T.D.Q.]

[52] See the common accounts in any Eastern traveller or voyager of the frantic excesses committed by Malays who have taken opium, or are reduced to desperation by ill luck at gambling. [T.D.Q.]

[53] **intercalary year:** period of time added to the calendar to make the calendar year correspond to the solar year.

if any body does. And, therefore, I will here lay down an analysis of happiness; and as the most interesting mode of communicating it, I will give it, not didactically, but wrapt up and involved in a picture of one evening, as I spent every evening during the intercalary year when laudanum, though taken daily, was to me no more than the elixir of pleasure. This done, I shall quit the subject of happiness altogether, and pass to a very different one—the *pains of opium.*

Let there be a cottage, standing in a valley, 18 miles from any town—no spacious valley, but about two miles long, by three quarters of a mile in average width; the benefit of which provision is, that all the families resident within its circuit will compose, as it were, one larger household personally familiar to your eye, and more or less interesting to your affections. Let the mountains be real mountains, between 3 and 4000 feet high; and the cottage, a real cottage; not (as a witty author has it) "a cottage with a double coach-house:" let it be, in fact (for I must abide by the actual scene), a white cottage, embowered with flowering shrubs, so chosen as to unfold a succession of flowers upon the walls, and clustering round the windows through all the months of spring, summer, and autumn—beginning, in fact, with May roses, and ending with jasmine. Let it, however, *not* be spring, nor summer, nor autumn—but winter, in his sternest shape. This is a most important point in the science of happiness. And I am surprised to see people overlook it, and think it matter of congratulation that winter is going; or, if coming, is not likely to be a severe one. On the contrary, I put up a petition annually, for as much snow, hail, frost, or storm, of one kind or other, as the skies can possibly afford us. Surely every body is aware of the divine pleasures which attend a winter fire-side: candles at four o'clock, warm hearth-rugs, tea, a fair tea-maker, shutters closed, curtains flowing in ample draperies on the floor, whilst the wind and rain are raging audibly without,

> And at the doors and windows seem to call,
> As heav'n and earth they would together mell;
> Yet the least entrance find they none at all;
> Whence sweeter grows our rest secure in massy hall.
>
> *Castle of Indolence.*[54]

. . .

[54] Misquoted from James Thompson (1700–1748), I.384–87: "At doors and windows, threatening, seemed to call / The demons of the tempest, growling fell; / Yet the least entrance found they none at all; / Whence sweeter grew our sleep, secure in massy hall."

—*from* THE PAINS OF OPIUM—

I now pass to what is the main subject of these latter confessions, to the history and journal of what took place in my dreams; for these were the immediate and proximate cause of my acutest suffering.

The first notice I had of any important change going on in this part of my physical economy, was from the re-awakening of a state of eye generally incident to childhood, or exacted states of irritability. I know not whether my reader is aware that many children, perhaps most, have a power of painting, as it were, upon the darkness, all sorts of phantoms; in some, that power is simply a mechanic affection of the eye; others have a voluntary, or a semi-voluntary power to dismiss or to summon them; or, as a child once said to me when I questioned him on this matter, "I can tell them to go, and they go; but sometimes they come, when I don't tell them to come." Whereupon I told him that he had almost as unlimited a command over apparitions, as a Roman centurion over his soldiers.[55]—In the middle of 1817, I think it was, that this faculty became positively distressing to me: at night, when I lay awake in bed, vast processions passed along in mournful pomp; friezes of never-ending stories, that to my feelings were as sad and solemn as if they were stories drawn from times before OEdipus or Priam—before Tyre—before Memphis. And, at the same time, a corresponding change took place in my dreams; a theatre seemed suddenly opened and lighted up within my brain, which presented nightly spectacles of more than earthly splendour. And the four following facts may be mentioned, as noticeable at this time:

1. That, as the creative state of the eye increased, a sympathy seemed to arise between the waking and the dreaming states of the brain in one point—that whatsoever I happened to call up and to trace by a voluntary act upon the darkness was very apt to transfer itself to my dreams; so that I feared to exercise this faculty; for, as Midas turned all things to gold, that yet baffled his hopes and defrauded his human desires, so whatsoever things capable of being visually represented I did but think of in the darkness, immediately shaped themselves into phantoms of the eye; and, by a process apparently no less inevitable, when thus once traced in faint and visionary colours, like writings in sympathetic ink, they were drawn

[55] "**Roman centurion over his soldiers**": Cf. Matthew, 8:9: "I say to this man, Go, and he goeth; and to another, Come, and he cometh."

out by the fierce chemistry of my dreams, into insufferable splendour that fretted my heart.

2. For this, and all other changes in my dreams, were accompanied by deep-seated anxiety and gloomy melancholy, such as are wholly incommunicable by words. I seemed every night to descend, not metaphorically, but literally to descend, into chasms and sunless abysses, depths below depths, from which it seemed hopeless that I could ever reascend. Nor did I, by waking, feel that I *had* reascended. This I do not dwell upon; because the state of gloom which attended these gorgeous spectacles, amounting at least to utter darkness, as of some suicidal despondency, cannot be approached by words.

3. The sense of space, and in the end, the sense of time, were both powerfully affected. Buildings, landscapes, &c. were exhibited in proportions so vast as the bodily eye is not fitted to receive. Space swelled, and was amplified to an extent of unutterable infinity. This, however, did not disturb me so much as the vast expansion of time; I sometimes seemed to have lived for 70 or 100 years in one night; nay, sometimes had feelings representative of a millennium passed in that time, or, however, of a duration far beyond the limits of any human experience.

4. The minutest incidents of childhood, or forgotten scenes of later years, were often revived: I could not be said to recollect them; for if I had been told of them when waking, I should not have been able to acknowledge them as parts of my past experience. But placed as they were before me, in dreams like intuitions, and clothed in all their evanescent circumstances and accompanying feelings, I *recognised* them instantaneously. I was once told by a near relative of mine, that having in her childhood fallen into a river, and being on the very verge of death but for the critical assistance which reached her, she saw in a moment her whole life, in its minutest incidents, arrayed before her simultaneously as in a mirror; and she had a faculty developed as suddenly for comprehending the whole and every part. This, from some opium experiences of mine, I can believe; I have, indeed, seen the same thing asserted twice in modern books, and accompanied by a remark which I am convinced is true; viz. that the dread book of account, which the Scriptures speak of, is, in fact, the mind itself of each individual. Of this, at least, I feel assured, that there is no such thing as *forgetting* possible to the mind; a thousand accidents may, and will interpose a veil between our present consciousness and the secret inscriptions on the mind; accidents of the same sort will also rend away this veil; but alike, whether veiled or unveiled, the inscription remains for ever; just as the stars seem to withdraw before the common light of day, whereas, in fact, we all know that it is the light which is drawn over them as a veil—and that they are waiting to be revealed, when the obscuring daylight shall have withdrawn. . . .

Many years ago, when I was looking over Piranesi's Antiquities of Rome, Mr. Coleridge, who was standing by, described to me a set of plates by that artist, called his *Dreams,*[56] and which record the scenery of his own visions during the delirium of a fever. Some of them (I describe only from memory of Mr. Coleridge's account) represented vast Gothic halls: on the floor of which stood all sorts of engines and machinery, wheels, cables, pulleys, levers, catapults, &c. &c. expressive of enormous power put forth, and resistance overcome. Creeping along the sides of the walls, you perceived a staircase; and upon it, groping his way upwards, was Piranesi himself: follow the stairs a little further, and you perceive it come to a sudden abrupt termination, without any balustrade, and allowing no step onwards to him who had reached the extremity, except into the depths below. Whatever is to become of poor Piranesi, you suppose, at least, that his labours must in some way terminate here. But raise your eyes, and behold a second flight of stairs still higher: on which again Piranesi is perceived, but this time standing on the very brink of the abyss. Again elevate your eye, and a still more aerial flight of stairs is beheld: and again is poor Piranesi busy on his aspiring labours: and so on, until the unfinished stairs and Piranesi both are lost in the upper gloom of the hall.—With the same power of endless growth and self-reproduction did my architecture proceed in dreams. In the early stage of my malady, the splendours of my dreams were indeed chiefly architectural:[57] and I beheld such pomp of cities and palaces as was never yet beheld by the waking eye, unless in the clouds. . . .

To my architecture succeeded dreams of lakes—and silvery expanses of water:—these haunted me so much, that I feared (though possibly it will appear ludicrous to a medical man) that some dropsical state or tendency of the brain might thus be making itself (to use a metaphysical word) *objective;* and the sentient organ *project* itself as its own object.—For two months I suffered greatly in my head—a part of my bodily structure which had hitherto

[56] **Piranesi . . . Dreams:** Giovanni Battista Piranesi (1720–1778), Italian architect and painter. De Quincey refers to his *Carceri d'Invensione* (1745, 1761).

[57] **"splendours . . . architectural":** Cf. Coleridge's "Kubla Khan."*

been so clear from all touch or taint of weakness (physically, I mean), that I used to say of it, as the last Lord Orford said of his stomach, that it seemed likely to survive the rest of my person.—Till now I had never felt a headach even, or any the slightest pain, except rheumatic pains caused by my own folly. However, I got over this attack, though it must have been verging on something very dangerous.

The waters now changed their character,—from translucent lakes, shining like mirrors, they now became seas and oceans. And now came a tremendous change, which, unfolding itself slowly like a scroll, through many months, promised an abiding torment; and, in fact, it never left me until the winding up of my case. Hitherto the human face had mixed often in my dreams, but not despotically, nor with any special power of tormenting. But now that which I have called the tyranny of the human face began to unfold itself. Perhaps some part of my London life might be answerable for this. Be that as it may, now it was that upon the rocking waters of the ocean the human face began to appear: the sea appeared paved with innumerable faces, upturned to the heavens: faces, imploring, wrathful, despairing, surged upwards by thousands, by myriads, by generations, by centuries:—my agitation was infinite,—my mind tossed—and surged with the ocean.

May, 1818

The Malay has been a fearful enemy for months. I have been every night, through his means, transported into Asiatic scenes. I know not whether others share in my feelings on this point; but I have often thought that if I were compelled to forego England, and to live in China, and among Chinese manners and modes of life and scenery, I should go mad. The causes of my horror lie deep; and some of them must be common to others. Southern Asia, in general, is the seat of awful images and associations. As the cradle of the human race, it would alone have a dim and reverential feeling connected with it. But there are other reasons. No man can pretend that the wild, barbarous, and capricious superstitions of Africa, or of savage tribes elsewhere, affect him in the way that he is affected by the ancient, monumental, cruel, and elaborate religions of Indostan, &c. The mere antiquity of Asiatic things, of their institutions, histories, modes of faith, &c. is so impressive, that to me the vast age of the race and name overpowers the sense of youth in the individual. A young Chinese seems to me an antediluvian man renewed. Even Englishmen, though not bred in any knowledge of such institutions, cannot but shudder at the mystic sublimity of *castes* that have flowed apart, and refused to mix, through such immemorial tracts of time; nor can any man fail to be awed by the names of the Ganges, or the Euphrates. It contributes much to these feelings, that southern Asia is, and has been for thousands of years, the part of the earth most swarming with human life; the great *officina gentium*.[58] Man is a weed in those regions. The vast empires also, into which the enormous population of Asia has always been cast, give a further sublimity to the feelings associated with all Oriental names or images. In China, over and above what it has in common with the rest of southern Asia, I am terrified by the modes of life, by the manners, and the barrier of utter abhorrence, and want of sympathy, placed between us by feelings deeper than I can analyze. I could sooner live with lunatics, or brute animals. All this, and much more than I can say, or have time to say, the reader must enter into before he can comprehend the unimaginable horror which these dreams of Oriental imagery, and mythological tortures, impressed upon me. Under the connecting feeling of tropical heat and vertical sun-lights, I brought together all creatures, birds, beasts, reptiles, all trees and plants, usages and appearances, that are found in all tropical regions, and assembled them together in China or Indostan. From kindred feelings, I soon brought Egypt and all her gods under the same law. I was stared at, hooted at, grinned at, chattered at, by monkeys, by paroquets, by cockatoos. I ran into pagodas: and was fixed, for centuries, at the summit, or in secret rooms; I was the idol; I was the priest; I was worshipped; I was sacrificed. I fled from the wrath of Brama through all the forests of Asia: Vishnu hated me: Seeva laid wait for me. I came suddenly upon Isis and Osiris: I had done a deed, they said, which the ibis[59] and the crocodile trembled at. I was buried, for a thousand years, in stone coffins, with mummies and sphinxes, in narrow chambers at the heart of eternal pyramids. I was kissed, with cancerous kisses, by crocodiles; and laid, confounded with all unutterable slimy things, amongst reeds and Nilotic mud.

I thus give the reader some slight abstraction of my Oriental dreams, which always filled me with such

[58] **officina gentium**: the workshop of nations.

[59] **Brama** [sic] . . . **Vishnu** . . . **Seeva** [sic]: the divine triad of Brahmanism. **Isis and Osiris**: Egyptian gods. Isis is the wife of Osiris, the god of fertility. **ibis**: long-billed wading bird.

amazement at the monstrous scenery, that horror seemed absorbed, for a while, in sheer astonishment. Sooner or later, came a reflux of feeling that swallowed up the astonishment, and left me, not so much in terror, as in hatred and abomination of what I saw. Over every form, and threat, and punishment, and dim sightless incarceration, brooded a sense of eternity and infinity that drove me into an oppression as of madness. Into these dreams only, it was, with one or two slight exceptions, that any circumstances of physical horror entered. All before had been moral and spiritual terrors. But here the main agents were ugly birds, or snakes, or crocodiles; especially the last. The cursed crocodile became to me the object of more horror than almost all the rest! I was compelled to live with him; and (as was always the case almost in my dreams) for centuries. I escaped sometimes, and found myself in Chinese houses, with cane tables, &c. All the feet of the tables, sofas, &c. soon became instinct with life: the abominable head of the crocodile, and his leering eyes, looked out at me, multiplied into a thousand repetitions: and I stood loathing and fascinated. And so often did this hideous reptile haunt my dreams, that many times the very same dream was broken up in the very same way: I heard gentle voices speaking to me (I hear every thing when I am sleeping); and instantly I awoke: it was broad noon; and my children were standing, hand in hand, at my bed-side; come to show me their coloured shoes, or new frocks, or to let me see them dressed for going out. I protest that so awful was the transition from the damned crocodile, and the other unutterable monsters and abortions of my dreams, to the sight of innocent *human* natures and of infancy, that, in the mighty and sudden revulsion of mind, I wept, and could not forbear it, as I kissed their faces.

June, 1819

I have had occasion to remark, at various periods of my life, that the deaths of those whom we love, and indeed the contemplation of death generally, is (*cateris paribus*)[60] more affecting in summer than in any other season of the year. And the reasons are these three, I think: first, that the visible heavens in summer appear far higher, more distant, and (if such a solecism may be excused) more infinite; the clouds, by which chiefly the eye expounds the distance of the blue pavilion stretched over our heads, are in summer more voluminous, massed, and accumulated in far grander and more towering piles: secondly, the light and the appearances of the declining and the setting sun are much more fitted to be types and characters of the Infinite: and, thirdly, (which is the main reason) the exuberant and riotous prodigality of life naturally forces the mind more powerfully upon the antagonist thought of death, and the wintry sterility of the grave. For it may be observed, generally, that wherever two thoughts stand related to each other by a law of antagonism, and exist, as it were, by mutual repulsion, they are apt to suggest each other. On these accounts it is that I find it impossible to banish the thought of death when I am walking alone in the endless days of summer; and any particular death, if not more affecting, at least haunts my mind more obstinately and besiegingly in that season. Perhaps this cause, and a slight incident which I omit, might have been the immediate occasions of the following dream; to which, however, a predisposition must always have existed in my mind; but having been once roused, it never left me, and split into a thousand fantastic varieties, which often suddenly reunited, and composed again the original dream.

I thought that it was a Sunday morning in May, that it was Easter Sunday, and as yet very early in the morning. I was standing, as it seemed to me, at the door of my own cottage. Right before me lay the very scene which could really be commanded from that situation, but exalted, as was usual, and solemnized by the power of dreams. There were the same mountains, and the same lovely valley at their feet; but the mountains were raised to more than Alpine height, and there was interspace far larger between them of meadows and forest lawns; the hedges were rich with white roses; and no living creature was to be seen, excepting that in the green churchyard there were cattle tranquilly reposing upon the verdant graves, and particularly round about the grave of a child whom I had tenderly loved, just as I had really beheld them, a little before sun-rise in the same summer, when that child died. I gazed upon the well-known scene, and I said aloud (as I thought) to myself, "It yet wants much of sun-rise; and it is Easter Sunday; and that is the day on which they celebrate the first-fruits of resurrection. I will walk abroad; old griefs shall be forgotten to-day; for the air is cool and still, and the hills are high, and stretch away to heaven; and the forest-glades are as quiet as the churchyard; and, with the dew, I can wash the fever from my forehead, and then I shall be unhappy no longer." And I turned, as if to open my garden gate; and immediately I saw upon the left

[60] **cateris paribus:** other things being equal.

a scene far different; but which yet the power of dreams had reconciled into harmony with the other. The scene was an Oriental one; and there also it was Easter Sunday, and very early in the morning. And at a vast distance were visible, as a stain upon the horizon, the domes and cupolas of a great city—an image or faint abstraction, caught perhaps in childhood from some picture of Jerusalem. And not a bow-shot from me, upon a stone, and shaded by Judean palms, there sat a woman; and I looked; and it was—Ann! She fixed her eyes upon me earnestly; and I said to her at length: "So then I have found you at last." I waited: but she answered me not a word. Her face was the same as when I saw it last, and yet again how different! Seventeen years ago, when the lamp-light fell upon her face, as for the last time I kissed her lips (lips, Ann, that to me were not polluted), her eyes were streaming with tears: the tears were now wiped away; she seemed more beautiful than she was at that time, but in all other points the same, and not older. Her looks were tranquil, but with unusual solemnity of expression; and I now gazed upon her with some awe, but suddenly her countenance grew dim, and, turning to the mountains, I perceived vapours rolling between us; in a moment, all had vanished; thick darkness came on; and, in the twinkling of an eye, I was far away from mountains, and by lamp-light in Oxford-street, walking again with Ann—just as we walked seventeen years before, when we were both children.

As a final specimen, I cite one of a different character, from 1820.

The dream commenced with a music which now I often heard in dreams—a music of preparation and of awakening suspense; a music like the opening of the Coronation Anthem, and which, like *that,* gave the feeling of a vast march—of infinite cavalcades filing off—and the tread of innumerable armies. The morning was come of a mighty day—a day of crisis and of final hope for human nature, then suffering some mysterious eclipse, and labouring in some dread extremity. Somewhere, I knew not where—somehow, I knew not how—by some beings, I knew not whom—a battle, a strife, an agony, was conducting,—was evolving like a great drama, or piece of music; with which my sympathy was the more insupportable from my confusion as to its place, its cause, its nature, and its possible issue. I, as is usual in dreams (where, of necessity, we make ourselves central to every movement), had the power, and yet had not the power, to decide it. I had the power, if I could raise myself, to will it; and yet again had not the power, for the weight of twenty Atlantics was upon me, or the oppression of inexpiable guilt. "Deeper than ever plummet sounded,"[61] I lay inactive. Then, like a chorus, the passion deepened. Some greater interest was at stake; some mightier cause than ever yet the sword had pleaded, or trumpet had proclaimed. Then came sudden alarms: hurryings to and fro: trepidations of innumerable fugitives, I knew not whether from the good cause or the bad: darkness and lights: tempest and human faces: and at last, with the sense that all was lost, female forms, and the features that were worth all the world to me, and but a moment allowed,—and clasped hands, and heart-breaking partings, and then—everlasting farewells! and with a sigh, such as the caves of hell sighed when the incestuous mother uttered the abhorred name of death,[62] the sound was reverberated—everlasting farewells! and again, and yet again reverberated—everlasting farewells!

And I awoke in struggles, and cried aloud—"I will sleep no more!" . . .[63]

from LONDON MAGAZINE
(1823)

Notes from the Pocket-Book of a Late Opium-Eater

[ON THE KNOCKING AT THE GATE IN MACBETH]

From my boyish days I had always felt a great perplexity on one point in *Macbeth.* It was this:—The knocking at the gate which succeeds to the murder of Duncan[1] produced to my feelings an effect for which I never could account. The effect was that it reflected back upon the murderer a peculiar awfulness and a depth of solemnity;

[61] Cf. Shakespeare, *The Tempest,* V.i.56–57: "deeper than did ever plummet sound / I'll drown my book." **Plummet,** or **plumb**: a weight suspended from a line used to measure the depth of water.

[62] **"incestuous mother . . . death"**: Sin, made pregnant by her father, Satan, describes the birth of their offspring, Death, in *Paradise Lost,* II.760–814.

[63] See note 17.

[1] **the murder of Duncan**: the knocking is to be heard during the conclusion of II.ii and opening of II.iii.

yet, however obstinately I endeavoured with my understanding to comprehend this, for many years I never could see *why* it should produce such an effect.

Here I pause for one moment, to exhort the reader never to pay any attention to his understanding when it stands in opposition to any other faculty of his mind. The mere understanding, however useful and indispensable, is the meanest faculty in the human mind, and the most to be distrusted; and yet the great majority of people trust to nothing else, — which may do for ordinary life, but not for philosophical purposes. Of this out of ten thousand instances that I might produce I will cite one. Ask of any person whatsoever who is not previously prepared for the demand by a knowledge of the perspective to draw in the rudest way the commonest appearance which depends upon the laws of that science, — as, for instance, to represent the effect of two walls standing at right angles to each other, or the appearance of the houses on each side of a street as seen by a person looking down the street from one extremity. Now, in all cases, unless the person has happened to observe in pictures how it is that artists produce these effects, he will be utterly unable to make the smallest approximation to it. Yet why? For he has actually seen the effect every day of his life. The reason is that he allows his understanding to overrule his eyes. His understanding, which includes no intuitive knowledge of the laws of vision, can furnish him with no reason why a line which is known and can be proved to be a horizontal line should not *appear* a horizontal line: a line that made any angle with the perpendicular less than a right angle would seem to him to indicate that his houses were all tumbling down together. Accordingly, he makes the line of his houses a horizontal line, and fails, of course, to produce the effect demanded. Here, then, is one instance out of many in which not only the understanding is allowed to overrule the eyes, but where the understanding is positively allowed to obliterate the eyes, as it were; for not only does the man believe the evidence of his understanding in opposition to that of his eyes, but (what is monstrous) the idiot is not aware that his eyes ever gave such evidence. He does not know that he has seen (and therefore *quoad*[2] his consciousness has *not* seen) that which he *has* seen every day of his life.

But to return from this digression. My understanding could furnish no reason why the knocking at the gate in Macbeth should produce any effect, direct or reflected. In fact, my understanding said positively that it could *not* produce any effect. But I knew better; I felt that it did; and I waited and clung to the problem until further knowledge should enable me to solve it. At length, in 1812, Mr. Williams made his *début* on the stage of Ratcliffe Highway, and executed those unparalleled murders which have procured for him such a brilliant and undying reputation. On which murders, by the way, I must observe that in one respect they have had an ill effect, by making the connoisseur in murder very fastidious in his taste, and dissatisfied by anything that has been since done in that line. All other murders look pale by the deep crimson of his; and, as an amateur once said to me in a querulous tone, "There has been absolutely nothing *doing* since his time, or nothing that's worth speaking of." But this is wrong; for it is unreasonable to expect all men to be great artists, and born with the genius of Mr. Williams. Now, it will be remembered that in the first of these murders (that of the Marrs) the same incident (of a knocking at the door soon after the work of extermination was complete) did actually occur which the genius of Shakspere has invented; and all good judges, and the most eminent dilettanti, acknowledged the felicity of Shakspere's suggestion as soon as it was actually realized. Here, then, was a fresh proof that I was right in relying on my own feeling, in opposition to my understanding; and I again set myself to study the problem. At length I solved it to my own satisfaction; and my solution is this: — Murder, in ordinary cases, where the sympathy is wholly directed to the case of the murdered person, is an incident of coarse and vulgar horror; and for this reason, — that it flings the interest exclusively upon the natural but ignoble instinct by which we cleave to life: an instinct which, as being indispensable to the primal law of self-preservation, is the same in kind (though different in degree) amongst all living creatures. This instinct, therefore, because it annihilates all distinctions, and degrades the greatest of men to the level of "the poor beetle that we tread on,"[3] exhibits human nature in its most abject and humiliating attitude. Such an attitude would little suit the purposes of the poet. What then must he do? He must throw the interest on the murderer. Our sympathy must be with *him* (of course I mean a sympathy of comprehension, a sympathy by which we enter into his

[2] **quoad:** with respect to.

[3] Cf. Shakespeare, *Measure for Measure,* III.i.79–81: "And the poor beetle, that we tread upon, / In corporal sufferance finds a pang as great / As when a giant dies."

feelings, and are made to understand them,—not a sympathy of pity or approbation). In the murdered person, all strife of thought, all flux and reflux of passion and of purpose, are crushed by one overwhelming panic; the fear of instant death smites him "with its petrific mace." But in the murderer, such a murderer as a poet will condescend to, there must be raging some great storm of passion,—jealousy, ambition, vengeance, hatred,—which will create a hell within him;[4] and into this hell we are to look.

In *Macbeth,* for the sake of gratifying his own enormous and teeming faculty of creation, Shakspere has introduced two murderers: and, as usual in his hands, they are remarkably discriminated: but,—though in Macbeth the strife of mind is greater than in his wife, the tiger spirit not so awake, and his feelings caught chiefly by contagion from her,—yet, as both were finally involved in the guilt of murder, the murderous mind of necessity is finally to be presumed in both. This was to be expressed; and, on its own account, as well as to make it a more proportionable antagonist to the unoffending nature of their victim, "the gracious Duncan," and adequately to expound "the deep damnation of his taking off," this was to be expressed with peculiar energy. We were to be made to feel that the human nature,—*i.e.* the divine nature of love and mercy, spread through the hearts of all creatures, and seldom utterly withdrawn from man,—was gone, vanished, extinct, and that the fiendish nature had taken its place. And, as this effect is marvellously accomplished in the *dialogues* and *soliloquies* themselves, so it is finally consummated by the expedient under consideration; and it is to this that I now solicit the reader's attention. If the reader has ever witnessed a wife, daughter, or sister in a fainting fit, he may chance to have observed that the most affecting moment in such a spectacle is *that* in which a sigh and a stirring announce the recommencement of suspended life. Or, if the reader has ever been present in a vast metropolis on the day when some great national idol was carried in funeral pomp to his grave, and, chancing to walk near the course through which it passed, has felt powerfully, in the silence and desertion of the streets, and in the stagnation of ordinary business, the deep interest which at that moment was possessing the heart of man,—if all at once he should hear the death-like stillness broken up by the sound of wheels rattling away from the scene, and making known that the transitory vision was dissolved, he will be aware that at no moment was his sense of the complete suspension and pause in ordinary human concerns so full and affecting as at that moment when the suspension ceases, and the goings-on of human life are suddenly resumed. All action in any direction is best expounded, measured, and made apprehensible, by reaction. Now, apply this to the case in *Macbeth.* Here, as I have said, the retiring of the human heart and the entrance of the fiendish heart was to be expressed and made sensible. Another world has stept in; and the murderers are taken out of the region of human things, human purposes, human desires. They are transfigured: Lady Macbeth is "unsexed"; Macbeth has forgot that he was born of woman; both are conformed to the image of devils; and the world of devils is suddenly revealed. But how shall this be conveyed and made palpable? In order that a new world may step in, this world must for a time disappear. The murderers and the murder must be insulated—cut off by an immeasurable gulf from the ordinary tide and succession of human affairs—locked up and sequestered in some deep recess; we must be made sensible that the world of ordinary life is suddenly arrested, laid asleep, tranced, racked into a dread armistice; time must be annihilated, relation to things without abolished; and all must pass self-withdrawn into a deep syncope and suspension of earthly passion.[5] Hence it is that, when the deed is done, when the work of darkness is perfect, then the world of darkness passes away like a pageantry in the clouds: the knocking at the gate is heard, and it makes known audibly that the reaction has commenced; the human has made its reflux upon the fiendish; the pulses of life are beginning to beat again; and the re-establishment of the goings-on of the world in which we live first makes us profoundly sensible of the awful parenthesis that had suspended them.

O mighty poet! Thy works are not as those of other men, simply and merely great works of art, but are also like the phenomena of nature, like the sun and the sea, the stars and the flowers, like frost and snow, rain and dew, hail-storm and thunder, which are to be studied with entire submission of our own faculties, and in the perfect faith that in them there can be no too much or too little, nothing useless or inert, but that, the farther we press in our discoveries, the more we shall see proofs of design and self-supporting arrangement where the careless eye had seen nothing but accident!

---

[4] **"a hell within him"**: *Paradise Lost*: "Which way I fly is hell; myself am hell," IV. 75.

[5] Cf. Wordsworth's "There Was a Boy"* for a comparable psychological event.

MARY PRINCE

(c. 1788–after 1833)

The first slave narrative written by a woman (that we are aware of), *The History of Mary Prince, A West Indian Slave, Related by Herself* (published in 1831) tells a harrowing tale of the physical and emotional cruelty experienced by a healthy young black girl living in Bermuda in the early nineteenth century. Mary Prince was born about 1788 on a farm in Brackish Pond, Devonshire parish, in Bermuda, a West Indian archipelago that had been declared a colony of the British crown in 1684. Its major industries were shipbuilding and salting; the center of the Bermudian salt industry was located on Turks Island, 200 miles northeast of Bermuda Island in the remote Caicos group. The first black slaves were brought to the Bermudas in 1616; their descendants—who became expert divers and sugarcane growers—and subsequent slaves kidnapped from Africa formed the backbone of the labor force in Bermuda.

Mary Prince's outspoken verbal attacks on her abusive masters Captain and Mrs. I—— and Mr. and Mrs. D—— may have been inspired by her knowledge of the successful slave rebellion only 200 miles away, in San Domingo, led by Toussaint L'Ouverture in 1791. Her desire to gain her own freedom inspired her attempts first to move to Antigua, an island known for its liberal attitudes to freed blacks, where she hoped to purchase her freedom, and then to England, where she knew she would be legally free, since slavery had been outlawed in Great Britain by the Mansfield Judgment of 1772. (See SLAVERY, THE SLAVE TRADE, AND ABOLITION.)

Mary Prince's account of the conditions of slavery and the myriad physical and sexual atrocities that she and her slave companions endured was published in London in 1831 by the *Anti-Slavery Reporter,* the in-house journal of the Anti-Slavery Society. This journal was dedicated to revealing the actual conditions of life in the slave-owning British colonies. Since the Anti-Slavery Society was also committed to the inculcation of Christianity among slaves and former slaves, its secretary and editor, Thomas Pringle, doubtless encouraged Mary Prince's insistence on her original innocence, her unwilling sexual corruption (which the text implies rather than graphically details), and her conversion to Methodist Christianity. Her account was transcribed by another devout Methodist, Susanna Strickland Moodie, who also bore witness to her numerous beating scars. When Prince's narrative appeared, it was virulently attacked in *Blackwood's* by James Macqueen, the editor of the *Glasgow Courier* and a powerful foe of emancipation, as well as by an Anglican missionary, James Curtin. Both denounced Prince as a liar, a woman of loose morals, and an agitator who did not represent the view of the majority of black slaves. Two court cases ensued: Prince sued Macqueen's publisher, Thomas Cadell, for libel; and Prince's former owner James Wood sued *her* publisher, Thomas Pringle, for libel. Prince and Pringle won their cases, since their antagonists could not produce West Indian witnesses to buttress their claims that the abuse Prince described had *not* occurred.

from The History of Mary Prince, a West Indian Slave

Related by Herself
(1831)

I was born at Brackish-Pond, in Bermuda, on a farm belonging to Mr. Charles Myners. My mother was a household slave; and my father, whose name was Prince, was a sawyer belonging to Mr. Trimmingham, a shipbuilder at Crow-Lane. When I was an infant, old Mr. Myners died, and there was a division of the slaves and other property among the family. I was bought along with my mother by old Captain Darrel, and given to his grandchild, little Miss Betsey Williams. Captain Williams, Mr. Darrel's son-in-law, was master of a vessel which traded to several places in America and the West Indies, and he was seldom at home long together.

Mrs. Williams was a kind-hearted good woman, and she treated all her slaves well. She had only one daughter, Miss Betsey, for whom I was purchased, and who was about my own age. I was made quite a pet of by Miss Betsey, and loved her very much. She used to lead me about by the hand, and call me her little nigger. This was the happiest period of my life; for I was too young to understand rightly my condition as a slave, and too thoughtless and full of spirits to look forward to the days of toil and sorrow.

My mother was a household slave in the same family. I was under her own care, and my little brothers and sisters were my play-fellows and companions. My mother had several fine children after she came to Mrs. Williams, —three girls and two boys. The tasks given out to us children were light, and we used to play together with Miss Betsey, with as much freedom almost as if she had been our sister.

My master, however, was a very harsh, selfish man; and we always dreaded his return from sea. His wife was herself much afraid of him; and, during his stay at home, seldom dared to shew her usual kindness to the slaves. He often left her, in the most distressed circumstances, to reside in other female society, at some place in the West Indies of which I have forgot the name. My poor mistress bore his ill-treatment with great patience, and all her slaves loved and pitied her. I was truly attached to her, and, next to my own mother, loved her better than any creature in the world. My obedience to her commands was cheerfully given: it sprung solely from the affection I felt for her, and not from fear of the power which the white people's law had given her over me.

I had scarcely reached my twelfth year when my mistress became too poor to keep so many of us at home; and she hired me out to Mrs. Pruden, a lady who lived about five miles off, in the adjoining parish, in a large house near the sea. I cried bitterly at parting with my dear mistress and Miss Betsey, and when I kissed my mother and brothers and sisters, I thought my young heart would break, it pained me so. But there was no help; I was forced to go. Good Mrs. Williams comforted me by saying that I should still be near the home I was about to quit, and might come over and see her and my kindred whenever I could obtain leave of absence from Mrs. Pruden. A few hours after this I was taken to a strange house, and found myself among strange people. This separation seemed a sore trial to me then; but oh! 'twas light, light to the trials I have since endured!—'twas nothing—nothing to be mentioned with them; but I was a child then, and it was according to my strength.

I knew that Mrs. Williams could no longer maintain me; that she was fain[1] to part with me for my food and clothing; and I tried to submit myself to the change. My new mistress was a passionate woman; but yet she did not treat me very unkindly. I do not remember her striking me but once, and that was for going to see Mrs. Williams when I heard she was sick, and staying longer than she had given me leave to do. All my employment at this time was nursing a sweet baby, little Master Daniel; and I grew so fond of my nursling that it was my greatest delight to walk out with him by the sea-shore, accompanied by his brother and sister, Miss Fanny and Master James.—Dear Miss Fanny! She was a sweet, kind young lady, and so fond of me that she wished me to learn all that she knew herself; and her method of teaching me was as follows:—Directly she had said her lessons to her grandmamma, she used to come running to me, and make me repeat them one by one after her; and in a few months I was able not only to say my letters but to spell many small words. But this happy state was not to last long. Those days were too pleasant to last. My heart always softens when I think of them.

At this time Mrs. Williams died. I was told suddenly of her death, and my grief was so great that, forgetting I had the baby in my arms, I ran away directly to my poor

[1] **fain:** obliged.

mistress's house; but reached it only in time to see the corpse carried out. Oh, that was a day of sorrow—a heavy day! All the slaves cried. My mother cried and lamented her sore; and I (foolish creature!) vainly entreated them to bring my dear mistress back to life. I knew nothing rightly about death then, and it seemed a hard thing to bear. When I thought about my mistress I felt as if the world was all gone wrong; and for many days and weeks I could think of nothing else. I returned to Mrs. Pruden's; but my sorrow was too great to be comforted, for my own dear mistress was always in my mind. Whether in the house or abroad, my thoughts were always talking to me about her.

I staid at Mrs. Pruden's about three months after this; I was then sent back to Mr. Williams to be sold. Oh, that was a sad sad time! I recollect the day well. Mrs. Pruden came to me and said, 'Mary, you will have to go home directly; your master is going to be married, and he means to sell you and two of your sisters to raise money for the wedding.' Hearing this I burst out a crying,—though I was then far from being sensible of the full weight of my misfortune, or of the misery that waited for me. Besides, I did not like to leave Mrs. Pruden, and the dear baby, who had grown very fond of me. For some time I could scarcely believe that Mrs. Pruden was in earnest, till I received orders for my immediate return.—Dear Miss Fanny! how she cried at parting with me, whilst I kissed and hugged the baby, thinking I should never see him again. I left Mrs. Pruden's, and walked home with a heart full of sorrow. The idea of being sold away from my mother and Miss Betsey was so frightful, that I dared not trust myself to think about it. We had been bought of Mrs. Myners, as I have mentioned, by Miss Betsey's grandfather, and given to her, so that we were by right *her* property, and I never thought we should be separated or sold away from her.

When I reached the house, I went in directly to Miss Betsey. I found her in great distress; and she cried out as soon as she saw me, 'Oh, Mary! my father is going to sell you all to raise money to marry that wicked woman. You are *my* slaves, and he has no right to sell you; but it is all to please her.' She then told me that my mother was living with her father's sister at a house close by, and I went there to see her. It was a sorrowful meeting; and we lamented with a great and sore crying our unfortunate situation. 'Here comes one of my poor piccaninnies!' she said, the moment I came in, 'one of the poor slave-brood who are to be sold to-morrow.'

Oh dear! I cannot bear to think of that day,—it is too much.—It recalls the great grief that filled my heart, and the woeful thoughts that passed to and fro through my mind, whilst listening to the pitiful words of my poor mother, weeping for the loss of her children. I wish I could find words to tell you all I then felt and suffered. The great God above alone knows the thoughts of the poor slave's heart, and the bitter pains which follow such separations as these. All that we love taken away from us—oh, it is sad, sad! and sore to be borne!—I got no sleep that night for thinking of the morrow; and dear Miss Betsey was scarcely less distressed. She could not bear to part with her old playmates and she cried sore and would not be pacified.

The black morning at length came; it came too soon for my poor mother and us. Whilst she was putting on us the new osnaburgs[2] in which we were to be sold, she said, in a sorrowful voice, (I shall never forget it!) 'See, I am *shrouding* my poor children; what a task for a mother!'—She then called Miss Betsey to take leave of us. 'I am going to carry my little chickens to market,' (these were her very words) 'take your last look of them; may be you will see them no more.' 'Oh, my poor slaves! my own slaves!' said dear Miss Betsey, 'you belong to me; and it grieves my heart to part with you.'—Miss Betsey kissed us all, and, when she left us, my mother called the rest of the slaves to bid us good bye. One of them, a woman named Moll, came with her infant in her arms, 'Ay!' said my mother, seeing her turn away and look at her child with the tears in her eyes, 'your turn will come next.' The slaves could say nothing to comfort us; they could only weep and lament with us. When I left my dear little brothers and the house in which I had been brought up, I thought my heart would burst.

Our mother, weeping as she went, called me away with the children Hannah and Dinah, and we took the road that led to Hamble Town, which we reached about four o'clock in the afternoon. We followed my mother to the market place, where she placed us in a row against a large house, with our backs to the wall and our arms folded across our breasts. I, as the eldest, stood first, Hannah next to me, then Dinah; and our mother stood beside, crying over us. My heart throbbed with grief and terror so violently, that I pressed my hands quite tightly across my breast, but I could not keep it still, and it continued to

[2] **osnaburgs:** coarse linen sack dresses.

leap as though it would burst out of my body. But who cared for that? Did one of the many bystanders, who were looking at us so carelessly, think of the pain that wrung the hearts of the negro woman and her young ones? No, no! They were not all bad, I dare say, but slavery hardens white people's hearts towards the blacks; and many of them were not slow to make their remarks upon us aloud, without regard to our grief—though their light words fell like cayenne on the fresh wounds of our hearts. Oh those white people have small hearts who can only feel for themselves.

At length the vendue master,[3] who was to offer us for sale like sheep or cattle, arrived, and asked my mother which was the eldest. She said nothing, but pointed to me. He took me by the hand, and led me out into the middle of the street, and, turning me slowly round, exposed me to the view of those who attended the vendue. I was soon surrounded by strange men, who examined and handled me in the same manner that a butcher would a calf or a lamb he was about to purchase, and who talked about my shape and size in like words—as if I could no more understand their meaning than the dumb beasts. I was then put up for sale. The bidding commenced at a few pounds, and gradually rose to fifty-seven,[4] when I was knocked down to the highest bidder; and the people who stood by said that I had fetched a great sum for so young a slave.

I then saw my sisters led forth, and sold to different owners; so that we had not the sad satisfaction of being partners in bondage. When the sale was over, my mother hugged and kissed us, and mourned over us, begging of us to keep up a good heart, and do our duty to our new masters. It was a sad parting; one went one way, one another, and our poor mammy went home with nothing.[5]

My new master was a Captain I——, who lived at Spanish Point. After parting with my mother and sisters, I followed him to his store, and he gave me into the charge of his son, a lad about my own age, Master Benjy, who took me to my new home. I did not know where I was going, or what my new master would do with me. My heart was quite broken with grief, and my thoughts went back continually to those from whom I had been so suddenly parted. 'Oh, my mother! my mother!' I kept saying to myself, 'Oh, my mammy and my sisters and my brothers, shall I never see you again!'

Oh, the trials! the trials! they make the salt water come into my eyes when I think of the days in which I was afflicted—the times that are gone; when I mourned and grieved with a young heart for those whom I loved.

It was night when I reached my new home. The house was large, and built at the bottom of a very high hill; but I could not see much of it that night. I saw too much of it afterwards. The stones and the timber were the

[3] **vendue master:** auctioneer at a public slave sale or auction.

[4] **fifty-seven [pounds]:** Bermuda currency; about 38 pounds sterling.

[5] **our poor mammy . . . nothing:** let the reader compare the above affecting account, taken down from the mouth of this negro woman, with the following description of a vendue of slaves at the Cape of Good Hope, published by me in 1826, from the letter of a friend,—and mark their similarity in several characteristic circumstances. The resemblance is easily accounted for: slavery wherever it prevails produces similar effects.—'Having heard that there was to be a sale of cattle, farm stock, &c. by auction, at a Veld-Cornet's in the vicinity, we halted our waggon one day for the purpose of procuring a fresh spann of oxen. Among the stock of the farm sold, was a female slave and her three children. The two oldest children were girls, the one about thirteen years of age, and the other about eleven; the youngest was a boy. The whole family were exhibited together, but they were sold separately, and to different purchasers. The farmers examined them as if they had been so many head of cattle. While the sale was going on, the mother and her children were exhibited on a table, that they might be seen by the company, which was very large. There could not have been a finer subject for an able painter than this unhappy group. The tears, the anxiety, the anguish of the mother, while she met the gaze of the multitude, eyed the different countenances of the bidders, or cast a heart-rending look upon the children; and the simplicity and touching sorrow of the young ones, while they clung to their distracted parent, wiping their eyes, and half concealing their faces,—contrasted with the marked insensibility and jocular countenances of the spectators and purchasers,—furnished a striking commentary on the miseries of slavery, and its debasing effects upon the hearts of its abettors. While the woman was in this distressed situation she was asked, "Can you feed sheep?" Her reply was so indistinct that it escaped me; but it was probably in the negative, for her purchaser rejoined, in a loud and harsh voice, "Then I will teach you with the sjamboc," (a whip made of the rhinoceros' hide.) The mother and her three children were sold to three separate purchasers; and they were literally torn from each other.' [Thomas Pringle, Editor]

best things in it; they were not so hard as the hearts of the owners.[6]

Before I entered the house, two slave women, hired from another owner, who were at work in the yard, spoke to me, and asked who I belonged to? I replied, 'I am come to live here.' 'Poor child, poor child!' they both said; 'you must keep a good heart, if you are to live here.'—When I went in, I stood up crying in a corner. Mrs. I—— came and took off my hat, a little black silk hat Miss Pruden made for me, and said in a rough voice, 'You are not come here to stand up in corners and cry, you are come here to work.' She then put a child into my arms, and, tired as I was, I was forced instantly to take up my old occupation of a nurse.—I could not bear to look at my mistress, her countenance was so stern. She was a stout tall woman with a very dark complexion, and her brows were always drawn together into a frown. I thought of the words of the two slave women when I saw Mrs. I——, and heard the harsh sound of her voice.

The person I took the most notice of that night was a French Black called Hetty, whom my master took in privateering[7] from another vessel, and made his slave. She was the most active woman I ever saw, and she was tasked to her utmost. A few minutes after my arrival she came in from milking the cows, and put the sweet-potatoes on for supper. She then fetched home the sheep, and penned them in the fold; drove home the cattle, and staked them about the pond side;[8] fed and rubbed down my master's horse, and gave the hog and the fed cow[9] their suppers; prepared the beds, and undressed the children, and laid them to sleep. I liked to look at her and watch all her doings, for her's was the only friendly face I had as yet seen, and I felt glad that she was there. She gave me my supper of potatoes and milk, and a blanket to sleep upon, which she spread for me in the passage before the door of Mrs. I——'s chamber.

I got a sad fright, that night. I was just going to sleep, when I heard a noise in my mistress's room; and she presently called out to inquire if some work was finished that she had ordered Hetty to do. 'No, Ma'am, not yet,' was Hetty's answer from below. On hearing this, my master started up from his bed, and just as he was, in his shirt, ran down stairs with a long cow-skin[10] in his hand. I heard immediately after, the cracking of the thong, and the house rang to the shrieks of poor Hetty, who kept crying out, 'Oh, Massa! Massa! me dead. Massa! have mercy upon me—don't kill me outright.'—This was a sad beginning for me. I sat up upon my blanket, trembling with terror, like a frightened hound, and thinking that my turn would come next. At length the house became still, and I forgot for a little while all my sorrows by falling fast asleep.

The next morning my mistress set about instructing me in my tasks. She taught me to do all sorts of household work; to wash and bake, pick cotton and wool, and wash floors, and cook. And she taught me (how can I ever forget it!) more things than these; she caused me to know the exact difference between the smart of the rope, the cart-whip, and the cow-skin, when applied to my naked body by her own cruel hand. And there was scarcely any punishment more dreadful than the blows I received on my face and head from her hard heavy fist. She was a fearful woman, and a savage mistress to her slaves. . . .

. . . I was licked, and flogged, and pinched by her pitiless fingers in the neck and arms, exactly as they were. To strip me naked—to hang me up by the wrists and lay my flesh open with the cow-skin, was an ordinary punishment for even a slight offence. My mistress often robbed me too of the hours that belong to sleep. She used to sit up very late, frequently even until morning; and I had then to stand at a bench and wash during the greater part of the night, or pick wool and cotton and often I have dropped down overcome by sleep and fatigue, till roused from a state of stupor by the whip, and forced to start up to my tasks.

Poor Hetty, my fellow slave, was very kind to me, and I used to call her my Aunt; but she led a most miserable life, and her death was hastened (at least the slaves all believed and said so,) by the dreadful chastisement she received from my master during her pregnancy. It happened as follows. One of the cows had dragged the rope

[6] These strong expressions, and all of a similar character in this little narrative, are given verbatim as uttered by Mary Prince. [Thomas Pringle, Editor]

[7] **privateering:** capture of merchant ships owned by a nation at war with Britain; piracy.

[8] **staked . . . side:** the cattle on a small plantation in Bermuda are, it seems, often thus staked or tethered, both night and day, in situations where grass abounds. [Thomas Pringle, Editor]

[9] **fed cow:** a cow fed or raised for slaughter.

[10] **long cow-skin:** a thong of hard twisted cowhide used as a whip.

away from the stake to which Hetty had fastened it, and got loose. My master flew into a terrible passion, and ordered the poor creature to be stripped quite naked, notwithstanding her pregnancy, and to be tied up to a tree in the yard. He then flogged her as hard as he could lick, both with the whip and cow-skin, till she was all over streaming with blood. He rested, and then beat her again and again. Her shrieks were terrible. The consequence was that poor Hetty was brought to bed before her time, and was delivered after severe labour of a dead child. She appeared to recover after her confinement, so far that she was repeatedly flogged by both master and mistress afterwards; but her former strength never returned to her. Ere long her body and limbs swelled to a great size; and she lay on a mat in the kitchen, till the water burst out of her body and she died. All the slaves said that death was a good thing for poor Hetty; but I cried very much for her death. The manner of it filled me with horror. I could not bear to think about it; yet it was always present to my mind for many a day.

After Hetty died all her labours fell upon me, in addition to my own. I had now to milk eleven cows every morning before sunrise, sitting among the damp weeds; to take care of the cattle as well as the children; and to do the work of the house. There was no end to my toils—no end to my blows. I lay down at night and rose up in the morning in fear and sorrow; and often wished that like poor Hetty I could escape from this cruel bondage and be at rest in the grave. But the hand of that God whom then I knew not, was stretched over me; and I was mercifully preserved for better things. It was then, however, my heavy lot to weep, weep, weep, and that for years; to pass from one misery to another, and from one cruel master to a worse. . . .

For five years after this I remained in his house, and almost daily received the same harsh treatment. At length he put me on board a sloop, and to my great joy sent me away to Turk's Island. I was not permitted to see my mother or father, or poor sisters and brothers, to say good bye, though going away to a strange land, and might never see them again. Oh the Buckra people[11] who keep slaves think that black people are like cattle, without natural affection. But my heart tells me it is far otherwise. . . .

When we went ashore at the Grand Quay, the captain sent me to the house of my new master, Mr. D——, to whom Captain I—— had sold me. Grand Quay is a small town upon a sandbank; the houses low and built of wood. Such was my new master's. The first person I saw, on my arrival, was Mr. D——, a stout sulky looking man, who carried me through the hall to show me to his wife and children. Next day I was put up by the vendue master to know how much I was worth, and I was valued at one hundred pounds currency.[12]

My new master was one of the owners or holders of the salt ponds, and he received a certain sum for every slave that worked upon his premises, whether they were young or old. This sum was allowed him out of the profits arising from the salt works. I was immediately sent to work in the salt water with the rest of the slaves. This work was perfectly new to me. I was given a half barrel and a shovel, and had to stand up to my knees in the water, from four o'clock in the morning till nine, when we were given some Indian corn boiled in water, which we were obliged to swallow as fast as we could for fear the rain should come on and melt the salt. We were then called again to our tasks, and worked through the heat of the day; the sun flaming upon our heads like fire, and raising salt blisters in those parts which were not completely covered. Our feet and legs, from standing in the salt water for so many hours, soon became full of dreadful boils, which eat down in some cases to the very bone, afflicting the sufferers with great torment. We came home at twelve; ate our corn soup, called *blawly*, as fast as we could, and went back to our employment till dark at night. We then shovelled up the salt in large heaps, and went down to the sea, where we washed the pickle from our limbs, and cleaned the barrows and shovels from the salt. When we returned to the house, our master gave us each our allowance of raw Indian corn, which we pounded in a mortar and boiled in water for our suppers.

We slept in a long shed, divided into narrow slips, like the stalls used for cattle. Boards fixed upon stakes driven into the ground, without mat or covering, were our only beds. On Sundays, after we had washed the salt bags, and done other work required of us, we went into the bush and cut the long soft grass, of which we made trusses[13] for our legs and feet to rest upon, for they were so full of the salt boils that we could get no rest lying upon the bare boards.

[11] **Buckra people:** white people.

[12] **one hundred pounds:** Bermuda currency, about 67 pounds sterling. Mary Prince's value almost doubled since she was first sold.

[13] **trusses:** bundles of hay or straw.

Though we worked from morning till night, there was no satisfying Mr. D——. I hoped, when I left Capt. I——, that I should have been better off, but I found it was but going from one butcher to another. There was this difference between them: my former master used to beat me while raging and foaming with passion; Mr. D—— was usually quite calm. He would stand by and give orders for a slave to be cruelly whipped, and assist in the punishment, without moving a muscle of his face; walking about and taking snuff with the greatest composure. Nothing could touch his hard heart——neither sighs, nor tears, nor prayers, nor streaming blood; he was deaf to our cries, and careless of our sufferings.—Mr. D—— has often stripped me naked, hung me up by the wrists, and beat me with the cow-skin, with his own hand, till my body was raw with gashes. Yet there was nothing very remarkable in this; for it might serve as a sample of the common usage of the slaves on that horrible island.

Owing to the boils in my feet, I was unable to wheel the barrow fast through the sand, which got into the sores, and made me stumble at every step; and my master, having no pity for my sufferings from this cause, rendered them far more intolerable, by chastising me for not being able to move so fast as he wished me. Another of our employments was to row a little way off from the shore in a boat, and dive for large stones to build a wall round our master's house. This was very hard work; and the great waves breaking over us continually, made us often so giddy that we lost our footing, and were in danger of being drowned.

Ah, poor me!—my tasks were never ended. Sick or well, it was work—work—work!—After the diving season was over, we were sent to the South Creek, with large bills,[14] to cut up mangoes to burn lime with. Whilst one party of slaves were thus employed, another were sent to the other side of the island to break up coral out of the sea.

When we were ill, let our complaint be what it might, the only medicine given to us was a great bowl of hot salt water, with salt mixed with it, which made us very sick. If we could not keep up with the rest of the gang of slaves, we were put in the stocks, and severely flogged the next morning. Yet, not the less, our master expected, after we had thus been kept from our rest, and our limbs rendered stiff and sore with ill usage, that we should still go through the ordinary tasks of the day all the same.—Sometimes we had to work all night, measuring salt to load a vessel; or turning a machine to draw water out of the sea for the salt-making. Then we had no sleep—no rest—but were forced to work as fast as we could, and go on again all next day the same as usual. Work—work—work—Oh that Turk's Island was a horrible place! The people in England, I am sure, have never found out what is carried on there. Cruel, horrible place!

Mr. D—— had a slave called old Daniel, whom he used to treat in the most cruel manner. Poor Daniel was lame in the hip, and could not keep up with the rest of the slaves; and our master would order him to be stripped and laid down on the ground, and have him beaten with a rod of rough briar till his skin was quite red and raw. He would then call for a bucket of salt, and fling upon the raw flesh till the man writhed on the ground like a worm, and screamed aloud with agony. This poor man's wounds were never healed, and I have often seen them full of maggots, which increased his torments to an intolerable degree. He was an object of pity and terror to the whole gang of slaves, and in his wretched case we saw, each of us, our own lot, if we should live to be as old.

Oh the horrors of slavery!—How the thought of it pains my heart! But the truth ought to be told of it; and what my eyes have seen I think it is my duty to relate; for few people in England know what slavery is. I have been a slave—I have felt what a slave feels, and I know what a slave knows; and I would have all the good people in England to know it too, that they may break our chains, and set us free. . . .

I had seen my poor mother during the time I was a slave in Turk's Island. One Sunday morning I was on the beach with some of the slaves, and we saw a sloop come in loaded with slaves to work in the salt water. We got a boat and went aboard. When I came upon the deck I asked the black people, 'Is there any one here for me?' 'Yes,' they said, 'your mother.' I thought they said this in jest—I could scarcely believe them for joy; but when I saw my poor mammy my joy was turned to sorrow, for she had gone from her senses. 'Mammy,' I said, 'is this you?' She did not know me. 'Mammy,' I said, 'what's the matter?' She began to talk foolishly and said that she had been under the vessel's bottom. They had been overtaken by a violent storm at sea. My poor mother had never been on the sea before, and she was so ill, that she lost her senses, and it was long before she came quite to herself again. She had a sweet child with her—a little sister I had never seen, about four years of age, called Rebecca. I took her on

[14] **bill:** implement having a long blade with a concave edge, used for pruning, cutting wood, etc.

shore with me, for I felt I should love her directly; and I kept her with me a week. Poor little thing! her's has been a sad life, and continues so to this day. My mother worked for some years on the island, but was taken back to Bermuda some time before my master carried me again thither. . . .[15]

I was several years the slave of Mr. D—— after I returned to my native place. Here I worked in the grounds. My work was planting and hoeing sweet-potatoes, Indian corn, plaintains, bananas, cabbages, pumpkins, onions, &c. I did all the household work, and attended upon a horse and cow besides,—going also upon all errands. I had to curry the horse—to clean and feed him—and sometimes to ride him a little. I had more than enough to do—but still it was not so very bad as Turk's Island.

My old master often got drunk, and then he would get in a fury with his daughter, and beat her till she was not fit to be seen. I remember on one occasion, I had gone to fetch water, and when I was coming up the hill I heard a great screaming; I ran as fast as I could to the house, put down the water, and went into the chamber, where I found my master beating Miss D—— dreadfully. I strove with all my strength to get her away from him; for she was all black and blue with bruises. He had beat her with his fist, and almost killed her. The people gave me credit for getting her away. He turned round and began to lick me. Then I said, 'Sir, this is not Turk's Island.' I can't repeat his answer, the words were too wicked—too bad to say. He wanted to treat me the same in Bermuda as he had done in Turk's Island.

He had an ugly fashion of stripping himself quite naked and ordering me then to wash him in a tub of water. This was worse to me than all the licks. Sometimes when he called me to wash him I would not come, my eyes were so full of shame. He would then come to beat me. One time I had plates and knives in my hand, and I dropped both plates and knives, and some of the plates were broken. He struck me so severely for this, that at last I defended myself, for I thought it was high time to do so. I then told him I would not live longer with him, for he was a very indecent man—very spiteful, and too indecent; with no shame for his servants, no shame for his own flesh. So I went away to a neighbouring house and sat down and cried till the next morning, when I went home again, not knowing what else to do.

After that I was hired to work at Cedar Hills, and every Saturday night I paid the money to my master. I had plenty of work to do there—plenty of washing; but yet I made myself pretty comfortable. I earned two dollars and a quarter a week, which is twenty pence a day.

During the time I worked there, I heard that Mr. John Wood was going to Antigua. I felt a great wish to go there, and I went to Mr. D——, and asked him to let me go in Mr. Wood's service. Mr. Wood did not then want to purchase me; it was my own fault that I came under him, I was so anxious to go. It was ordained to be, I suppose; God led me there. The truth is, I did not wish to be any longer the slave of my indecent master.

Mr. Wood took me with him to Antigua, to the town of St. John's, where he lived. This was about fifteen years ago. He did not then know whether I was to be sold; but Mrs. Wood found that I could work, and she wanted to buy me. Her husband then wrote to my master to inquire whether I was to be sold? Mr. D—— wrote in reply, 'that I should not be sold to any one that would treat me ill.' It was strange he should say this, when he had treated me so ill himself. So I was purchased by Mr. Wood for 300 dollars (or £100 Bermuda currency).

My work there was to attend the chambers and nurse the child, and to go down to the pond and wash clothes. But I soon fell ill of the rheumatism, and grew so very lame that I was forced to walk with a stick. I got the Saint Anthony's fire,[16] also, in my left leg, and became quite a cripple. No one cared much to come near me, and I was ill a long long time; for several months I could not lift the limb. I had to lie in a little old out-house, that was swarming with bugs and other vermin, which tormented me greatly; but I had no other place to lie in. I got the rheumatism by catching cold at the pond side, from washing in the fresh water; in the salt water I never got cold. The person who lived in next yard, (a Mrs. Greene,) could not bear to hear my cries and groans. She was kind,

[15] **My mother . . . thither:** of the subsequent lot of her relatives she can tell but little. She says, her father died while she and her mother were at Turk's Island; and that he had been long dead and buried before any of his children in Bermuda knew of it, they being slaves on other estates. Her mother died after Mary went to Antigua. Of the fate of the rest of her kindred, seven brothers and three sisters, she knows nothing further than this—that the eldest sister, who had several children to her master, was taken by him to Trinidad; and that the youngest, Rebecca, is still alive, and in slavery in Bermuda. Mary herself is now about forty-three years of age. [Thomas Pringle, Editor]

[16] **Saint Anthony's fire:** erysipelas; fever accompanied by inflammation of the skin.

and used to send an old slave woman to help me, who sometimes brought me a little soup. When the doctor found I was so ill, he said I must be put into a bath of hot water. The old slave got the bark of some bush that was good for pains, which she boiled in the hot water, and every night she came and put me into the bath, and did what she could for me; I don't know what I should have done, or what would have become of me, had it not been for her.—My mistress, it is true, did send me a little food; but no one from our family came near me but the cook, who used to shove my food in at the door, and say, 'Molly, Molly, there's your dinner." My mistress did not care to take any trouble about me; and if the Lord had not put it into the hearts of the neighbours to be kind to me, I must, I really think, have lain and died.

It was a long time before I got well enough to work in the house. . . .

When we moved from the middle of the town to the Point, I used to be in the house and do all the work and mind the children, though still very ill with the rheumatism. Every week I had to wash two large bundles of clothes, as much as a boy could help me to lift; but I could give no satisfaction. My mistress was always abusing and fretting after me. It is not possible to tell all her ill language.—One day she followed me foot after foot scolding and rating[17] me. I bore in silence a great deal of ill words: at last my heart was quite full, and I told her that she ought not to use me so;—that when I was ill I might have lain and died for what she cared; and no one would then come near me to nurse me, because they were afraid of my mistress. This was a great affront. She called her husband and told him what I had said. He flew into a passion: but did not beat me then; he only abused and swore at me; and then gave me a note and bade me go and look for an owner. Not that he meant to sell me; but he did this to please his wife and to frighten me. I went to Adam White, a cooper, a free black who had money, and asked him to buy me. He went directly to Mr. Wood, but was informed that I was not to be sold. The next day my master whipped me.

Another time (about five years ago) my mistress got vexed with me because I fell sick and I could not keep on with my work. She complained to her husband, and he sent me off again to look for an owner. I went to a Mr. Burchell, showed him the note, and asked him to buy me for my own benefit; for I had saved about 100 dollars, and hoped with a little help, to purchase my freedom. He accordingly went to my master:—'Mr. Wood,' he said, 'Molly has brought me a note that she wants an owner. If you intend to sell her, I may as well buy her as another.' My master put him off and said that he did not mean to sell me. I was very sorry at this, for I had no comfort with Mrs. Wood, and I wished greatly to get my freedom.

The way in which I made my money was this.—When my master and mistress went from home, as they sometimes did, and left me to take care of the house and premises, I had a good deal of time to myself and made the most of it. I took in washing, and sold coffee and yams and other provisions to the captains of ships. I did not sit still idling during the absence of my owners; for I wanted, by all honest means, to earn money to buy my freedom. Sometimes I bought a hog cheap on board ship, and sold it for double the money on shore; and I also earned a good deal by selling coffee. By this means I by degrees acquired a little cash. A gentleman also lent me some to help to buy my freedom—but when I could not get free he got it back again. His name was Captain Abbot. . . .

While we were at Date Hill Christmas came; and the slave woman who had the care of the place (which then belonged to Mr. Roberts the marshal), asked me to go with her to her husband's house, to a Methodist meeting for prayer, at a plantation called Winthorps. I went; and they were the first prayers I ever understood. One woman prayed; and then they all sung a hymn; then there was another prayer and another hymn; and then they all spoke by turns of their own griefs as sinners. The husband of the woman I went with was a black driver. His name was Henry. He confessed that he had treated the slaves very cruelly; but said that he was compelled to obey the orders of his master. He prayed them all to forgive him, and he prayed that God would forgive him. He said it was a horrid thing for a ranger[18] to have sometimes to beat his own wife or sister; but he must do so if ordered by his master.

I felt sorry for my sins also. I cried the whole night, but I was too much ashamed to speak. I prayed God to forgive me. This meeting had a great impression on my mind, and led my spirit to the Moravian church;[19] so that

[17] **rating**: chiding, angrily scolding, berating.

[18] **ranger**: the head slave of an estate; responsible for disciplining the other slaves.

[19] **Moravian church**: evangelical Christian communion, also known as United Brethren, founded in 1457 in Bohemia by the followers of John Huss; especially active in missionary work, especially under the direction of August Gottlieb Spangenberg

when I got back to town, I went and prayed to have my name put down in the Missionaries' book; and I followed the church earnestly every opportunity. I did not then tell my mistress about it; for I knew that she would not give me leave to go. But I felt I *must* go. Whenever I carried the children their lunch at school, I ran round and went to hear the teachers.

The Moravian ladies (Mrs. Richter, Mrs. Olufsen, and Mrs. Sauter) taught me to read in the class; and I got on very fast. In this class there were all sorts of people, old and young, grey headed folks and children; but most of them were free people. After we had done spelling, we tried to read in the Bible. After the reading was over, the missionary gave out a hymn for us to sing. I dearly loved to go to the church, it was so solemn. I never knew rightly that I had much sin till I went there. When I found out that I was a great sinner, I was very sorely grieved, and very much frightened. I used to pray God to pardon my sins for Christ's sake, and forgive me for every thing I had done amiss; and when I went home to my work, I always thought about what I had heard from the missionaries, and wished to be good that I might go to heaven. After a while I was admitted a candidate for the holy Communion.—I had been baptized long before this, in August 1817, by the Rev. Mr. Curtin, of the English Church, after I had been taught to repeat the Creed and the Lord's Prayer. I wished at that time to attend a Sunday School taught by Mr. Curtin, but he would not receive me without a written note from my master, granting his permission. I did not ask my owner's permission, from the belief that it would be refused; so that I got no farther instruction at that time from the English Church.[20]

Some time after I began to attend the Moravian Church, I met with Daniel James, afterwards my dear husband. He was a carpenter and cooper to his trade; an honest, hard-working, decent black man, and a widower. He had purchased his freedom of his mistress, old Mrs. Baker, with money he had earned whilst a slave. When he asked me to marry him, I took time to consider the matter over with myself, and would not say yes till he went to church with me and joined the Moravians. He was very industrious after he bought his freedom; and he had hired a comfortable house, and had convenient things about him. We were joined in marriage, about Christmas 1826, in the Moravian Chapel at Spring Gardens, by the Rev. Mr. Olufsen. We could not be married in the English Church. English marriage is not allowed to slaves; and no free man can marry a slave woman.

When Mr. Wood heard of my marriage, he flew into a great rage, and sent for Daniel, who was helping to build a house for his old mistress. Mr. Wood asked him who gave him a right to marry a slave of his? My husband said, 'Sir, I am a free man, and thought I had a right to choose a wife; but if I had known Molly was not allowed to have a husband, I should not have asked her to marry me.' Mrs. Wood was more vexed about my marriage than her husband. She could not forgive me for getting married, but stirred up Mr. Wood to flog me dreadfully with his horsewhip. I thought it very hard to be whipped at my time of life for getting a husband—I told her so. She said that she would not have nigger men about the yards and premises, or allow a nigger man's clothes to be washed in the same tub where hers were washed. She was fearful, I think, that I should lose her time, in order to wash and do things for my husband: but I had then no time to wash for myself; I was obliged to put out my own clothes, though I was always at the wash-tub.

I had not much happiness in my marriage, owing to my being a slave. It made my husband sad to see me so ill-treated. Mrs. Wood was always abusing me about him. She did not lick me herself, but she got her husband to do it for her, whilst she fretted the flesh off my bones. Yet for all this she would not sell me. She sold five slaves whilst I was with her; but though she was always finding fault with me, she would not part with me. However, Mr. Wood afterwards allowed Daniel to have a place to live in our yard, which we were very thankful for.

After this, I fell ill again with the rheumatism, and was sick a long time; but whether sick or well, I had my work to do. About this time I asked my master and mistress to let me buy my own freedom. With the help of

---

who became the founder of the Moravian Church in America in 1735. The Moravians stress the subjective aspects of religion, employing emotional hymns and complex part-singing in their services, and emphasizing conduct rather than doctrine in their teachings.

[20] She possesses a copy of Mrs. Trimmer's 'Charity School Spelling Book,' presented to her by the Rev. Mr. Curtin, and dated August 30, 1817. In this book her name is written 'Mary, Princess of Wales'—an appellation which, she says, was given her by her owners. It is a common practice for the colonists to give ridiculous names of this description to their slaves; being, in fact, one of the numberless modes of expressing the habitual contempt with which they regard the negro race.—In printing this narrative we have retained Mary's paternal name of Prince. [Thomas Pringle, Editor]

Mr. Burchell, I could have found the means to pay Mr. Wood; for it was agreed that I should afterwards serve Mr. Burchell a while, for the cash he was to advance for me. I was earnest in the request to my owners; but their hearts were hard — too hard to consent. Mrs. Wood was very angry — she grew quite outrageous — she called me a black devil, and asked me who had put freedom into my head. 'To be free is very sweet,' I said: but she took good care to keep me a slave. I saw her change colour, and I left the room.

About this time my master and mistress were going to England to put their son in school, and bring their daughters home; and they took me with them to take care of the child. I was willing to come to England: I thought that by going there I should probably get cured of my rheumatism, and should return with my master and mistress, quite well, to my husband. My husband was willing for me to come away, for he had heard that my master would free me, — and I also hoped this might prove true; but it was all a false report. . . .

When we drew near to England, the rheumatism seized all my limbs worse than ever, and my body was dreadfully swelled. When we landed at the Tower,[21] I shewed my flesh to my mistress, but she took no great notice of it. We were obliged to stop at the tavern till my master got a house; and a day or two after, my mistress sent me down into the wash-house to learn to wash in the English way. In the West Indies we wash with cold water — in England with hot. I told my mistress I was afraid that putting my hands first into the hot water and then into the cold, would increase the pain in my limbs. The doctor had told my mistress long before I came from the West Indies, that I was a sickly body and the washing did not agree with me. But Mrs. Wood would not release me from the tub, so I was forced to do as I could. I grew worse, and could not stand to wash. I was then forced to sit down with the tub before me, and often through pain and weakness was reduced to kneel or to sit down on the floor, to finish my task. When I complained to my mistress of this, she only got into a passion as usual, and said washing in hot water could not hurt any one; — that I was lazy and insolent, and wanted to be free of my work; but that she would make me do it. I thought her very hard on me, and my heart rose up within me. However I kept still at that time, and went down again to wash the child's things; but the English washerwomen who were at work there, when they saw that I was so ill, had pity upon me and washed them for me. . . .

My master quarrelled with me another time, about one of our great washings, his wife having stirred him up to do so. He said he would compel me to do the whole of the washing given out to me, or if I again refused, he would take a short course with me: he would either send me down to the brig in the river, to carry me back to Antigua, or he would turn me at once out of doors, and let me provide for myself. I said I would willingly go back, if he would let me purchase my own freedom. But this enraged him more than all the rest: he cursed and swore at me dreadfully, and said he would never sell my freedom — if I wished to be free, I was free in England, and I might go and try what freedom would do for me, and be d——d. My heart was very sore with this treatment, but I had to go on. I continued to do my work, and did all I could to give satisfaction, but all would not do.

Shortly after, the cook left them, and then matters went on ten times worse. I always washed the child's clothes without being commanded to do it, and any thing else that was wanted in the family; though still I was very sick — very sick indeed. When the great washing came round, which was every two months, my mistress got together again a great many heavy things, such as bed-ticks, bed-coverlets, &c. for me to wash. I told her I was too ill to wash such heavy things that day. She said, she supposed I thought myself a free woman, but I was not; and if I did not do it directly I should be instantly turned out of doors. I stood a long time before I could answer, for I did not know well what to do. I knew that I was free in England, but I did not know where to go, or how to get my living; and therefore, I did not like to leave the house. But Mr. Wood said he would send for a constable to thrust me out; and at last I took courage and resolved that I would not be longer thus treated, but would go and trust to Providence. This was the fourth time they had threatened to turn me out, and, go where I might, I was determined now to take them at their word; though I thought it very hard, after I had lived with them for thirteen years, and worked for them like a horse, to be driven out in this way, like a beggar. My only fault was being sick, and therefore unable to please my mistress, who thought she never could get work enough out of her slaves; and I told them so: but they only abused me and drove me out. This took place from two to three months, I think, after we came to England.

[21] **the Tower**: Tower of London, ancient fortress on the north bank of the Thames River where many English royalty and nobility were imprisoned and executed.

When I came away, I went to the man (one Mash) who used to black the shoes of the family, and asked his wife to get somebody to go with me to Hatton Garden to the Moravian Missionaries: these were the only persons I knew in England. The woman sent a young girl with me to the mission house, and I saw there a gentleman called Mr. Moore. I told him my whole story, and how my owners had treated me, and asked him to take in my tru[n]k with what few clothes I had. The missionaries were very kind to me—they were sorry for my destitute situation, and gave me leave to bring my things to be placed under their care. They were very good people, and they told me to come to the church. . . .

And so I came out, and went and carried my trunk to the Moravians. I then returned back to Mash the shoe-black's house, and begged his wife to take me in. I had a little West Indian money in my trunk; and they got it changed for me. This helped to support me for a little while. The man's wife was very kind to me. I was very sick, and she boiled nourishing things up for me. She also sent for a doctor to see me, and sent me medicine, which did me good, though I was ill for a long time with the rheumatic pains. I lived a good many months with these poor people, and they nursed me, and did all that lay in their power to serve me. The man was well acquainted with my situation, as he used to go to and fro to Mr. Wood's house to clean shoes and knives; and he and his wife were sorry for me.

About this time, a woman of the name of Hill told me of the Anti-Slavery Society, and went with me to their office, to inquire if they could do any thing to get me my freedom, and send me back to the West Indies. The gentlemen of the Society took me to a lawyer, who examined very strictly into my case; but told me that the laws of England could do nothing to make me free in Antigua. However they did all they could for me: they gave me a little money from time to time to keep me from want; and some of them went to Mr. Wood to try to persuade him to let me return a free woman to my husband; but though they offered him, as I have learned, a large sum for my freedom, he was sulky and obstinate, and would not consent to let me go free. . . .

At last I went into the service of Mr. and Mrs. Pringle, where I have been ever since, and am as comfortable as I can be while separated from my dear husband, and away from my own country and all old friends and connections. My dear mistress teaches me daily to read the word of God, and takes great pains to make me understand it. I enjoy the great privilege of being enabled to attend church three times on the Sunday; and I have met with many kind friends since I have been here, both clergymen and others. . . .

I still live in the hope that God will find a way to give me my liberty, and give me back to my husband. I endeavour to keep down my fretting, and to leave all to Him, for he knows what is good for me better than I know myself. Yet, I must confess, I find it a hard and heavy task to do so.

I am often much vexed, and I feel great sorrow when I hear some people in this country say, that the slaves do not need better usage, and do not want to be free.[22] They believe the foreign people,[23] who deceive them, and say slaves are happy. I say, Not so. How can slaves be happy when they have the halter round their neck and the whip upon their back? and are disgraced and thought no more of than beasts?—and are separated from their mothers, and husbands, and children, and sisters, just as cattle are sold and separated? Is it happiness for a driver in the field to take down his wife or sister or child, and strip them, and whip them in such a disgraceful manner?—women that have had children exposed in the open field to shame! There is no modesty or decency shown by the owner to his slaves; men, women, and children are exposed alike. Since I have been here I have often wondered how English people can go out into the West Indies and act in such a beastly manner. But when they go to the West Indies, they forget God and all feeling of shame, I think, since they can see and do such things. They tie up slaves like hogs—moor[24] them up like cattle, and they lick them, so as hogs, or cattle, or horses never were flogged;—and yet they come home and say, and make some good people believe, that slaves don't want to get out of slavery. But they put a cloak about the truth. It is not so. All slaves want to be free—to be free is very sweet. I will say the truth to English people who may read this history that my good friend, Miss S——, is now writing down for me. I have been a slave myself—I know what slaves feel—I can tell by myself what other slaves feel, and by what they have told me. The man that says slaves be quite happy in slavery—that they don't want to be free—that man is either ignorant or a lying person. I

[22] The whole of this paragraph especially, is given as nearly as was possible in Mary's precise words. [Thomas Pringle, Editor]

[23] **foreign people**: she means West Indians. [Thomas Pringle, Editor]

[24] **moor**: a West Indian phrase: to fasten or tie up. [Thomas Pringle, Editor]

never heard a slave say so. I never heard a Buckra man say so, till I heard tell of it in England. Such people ought to be ashamed of themselves. They can't do without slaves, they say. What's the reason they can't do without slaves as well as in England? No slaves here—no whips—no stocks—no punishment, except for wicked people. They hire servants in England; and if they don't like them, they send them away: they can't lick them. Let them work ever so hard in England, they are far better off than slaves. If they get a bad master, they give warning and go hire to another. They have their liberty. That's just what *we* want. We don't mind hard work, if we had proper treatment, and proper wages like English servants, and proper time given in the week to keep us from breaking the Sabbath. But they won't give it; they will have work—work—work, night and day, sick or well, till we are quite done up; and we must not speak up nor look amiss, however much we be abused. And then when we are quite done up, who cares for us, more than for a lame horse? This is slavery. I tell it to let English people know the truth; and I hope they will never leave off to pray God, and call loud to the great King of England, till all the poor blacks be given free, and slavery done up for evermore.

GEORGE GORDON, LORD BYRON

(1788–1824)

George Gordon, the sixth Lord Byron, was the most famous poet of Europe and one of the great personalities of an age replete with titans—Napoleon, Lafayette, Kosciusko, Metternich, Washington, Franklin, Catherine the Great, the Duke of Wellington. His continental reputation especially was enormous. The great German writer and intellect Johann Wolfgang von Goethe (1749–1832) claimed that Byron was "the greatest talent of our century" for being "neither antique nor romantic, but like the present day itself." The brilliant French novelist Stendhal (1788–1842) wanted to weep and kiss Byron's hand in adulation when they met.

Public fascination with Byron at home was due to his being a handsome renegade of the aristocratic class who wrote dashing Oriental romances and defiant confessional poetry. However, except for the Shelleys, very few, if any, of Byron's major literary contemporaries respected him as man or artist. Keats's charge against Byron in *The Fall of Hyperion** as a "careless Hectorer in proud bad verse" succinctly stated the case. Today, a wider biographical and poetic tolerance offsets the criticism of Byron's respected peers; we have come to confirm the judgment of Byron's European readers in finding a unique expression of the consciousness and moods of early modernity in his verse, especially a romantic irony born of teleological uncertainty. His death on behalf of Grecian independence seals the legend of one whose contradictions bespeak the times.

George Gordon was the only son of Captain John "Mad Jack" Byron (1756–1791) and his second wife Catherine Gordon (1765–1811). There was nobility in Byron's blood from both sides of the family. The ancestral line on his father's side could be traced to followers of William the Conqueror; his mother's line went back to James I of Scotland. After squandering his wife's fortune, "Mad Jack" fled to France to escape creditors shortly after his son's birth, where it seems he committed suicide. Catherine moved with her son back to her father's home in Aberdeen, Scotland. His father dead, Byron inherited the family seat at Newstead Abbey, Nottinghamshire, when his granduncle, William "the Wicked Lord" Byron, died in 1798. Byron attended the Harrow School from 1801 to 1805, where he lived up to the headmaster Dr. Joseph Drury's initial assessment that "a wild mountain colt had been submitted to my management," and then Trinity College, Cambridge, where his "violent, though *pure* love and passion," for a choirboy, John Edleston, marked him for life. He left before taking a degree, proving to be his profligate father's son in amassing a debt of over £12,000 before reaching his majority, or legal age, in 1809.

After an extended gentleman's tour of Europe and the Mediterranean that began in July 1809, Byron returned home in July 1811 prepared to assume his seat in the House of Lords. He immediately began to espouse causes guaranteed to be ill-received by his peers. Byron's maiden speech against the death penalty for frame-breaking—the destruction of technological innovations that were causing unemployment—was judged by Lord Holland to be "full of fancy, wit, and invective, but not exempt from affectation . . . , nor at all suited to our common notions of Parliamentary eloquence." Byron's second speech supported Irish Catholic rights.

The very year of these parliamentary lead balloons, Byron became the darling of British society with the publication of *Childe Harold, Cantos I and II* (1812). He noted: "I awoke one morning and found myself famous." A thin disguise for his poet, Harold is introduced as the "shameless wight" of a noble but mouldering family line, who at first finds favor with little else but "concubines and carnal companie, / And flaunting wassailers of high and low degree." When satiated with debauchery and tormented by a love for an unidentified one who "could never be his," he leaves "sick at heart" for adventures abroad. Byron's notes to this travelogue in Spenserian stanzas assure the reader that Harold's tour, family, and romantic torments were his own.

Byron married Annabella Milbanke in January 1815 to normalize his life, to ward off annoying female suitors, to gain her dowry, and perhaps to quell his passion for his half-sister, Augusta Leigh. Annabella naively believed that she might domesticate her husband. The newlyweds had a daughter, Augusta Ada, within the year, but then Lady Byron left with their infant for her father's house in January 1816, and within two weeks Byron received a proposal of separation. Rumors of Byron's past and perhaps continuing incest with Augusta Leigh spread rapidly. Women scattered when he entered a room. Surprised and embittered by these domestic and social reversals, Byron signed the separation papers and left England for good in April 1816, as Matthew Arnold later described, "trailing the pageant of his bleeding heart across Europe."

Byron spent his first summer abroad in Switzerland with the kindred spirits of the notorious Shelley party and with his travelling physician, John William Polidori (1795–1821). Percy Shelley* had recently abandoned his pregnant wife Harriet and their child to elope with Mary Wollstonecraft Godwin,* the 16-year-old daughter of the deceased Mary Wollstonecraft* and William Godwin.* The couple was accompanied by Mary's 15-year-old half-sister, Claire Clairmont, who had initiated a sexual liaison with Byron shortly before he left England. In daily company, the poets wrote prolifically, Mary began *Frankenstein* (1818), Polidori wrote *The Vampyre* (1819), and Claire became pregnant with Allegra (b. January 1817). Byron recalled being "half mad" with "metaphysics, mountains, lakes, love inextinguishable and thoughts unutterable, and the nightmare of my own delinquencies." Percy Shelley returned to England with the manuscripts of Byron's third canto of *Childe Harold*, which is partly reflective of "metaphysics, mountains, lakes," but more expressive of the moral malaise and political frustrations of post-revolutionary European liberals. A second volume, *The Prisoner of Chillon and Other Poems* (1816), offered both inspirational poems of political resistance against repression and lyrics of disappointed love for Lady Byron and permissible longings for Augusta. Byron reserved his "love inextinguishable and thoughts unutterable" for his developing psychodrama, *Manfred*.

Byron distilled his romantic madness, metaphysics, forbidden longings, and guilt into his play's aristocratic hero. Manfred epitomizes the Byronic Hero, a sullen mixture of misanthropy, arrogance, world-weariness, and fierce independence, obsessed with a conscience tortured for unspeakable, even undefineable, sins. Textual clues reveal that Manfred and his sister Astarte had an incestuous relationship, but it is equally apparent that the cause of his torment transcends social taboo. The literary progenitors of this new character type have been identified as the Wandering Jew, Milton's Satan, Marlowe's Dr. Faustus, and Goethe's Faust, but Byron's biographical self provides the distinguishing uniqueness.

After Shelley and company departed Switzerland, Byron left Geneva for Venice. Always brilliantly descriptive of manners and personality, Byron's letters to friends in England wittily flaunt the sensuousity of his Italian life. After claiming to make promiscuous love to more than a hundred women from all classes and stations in life during the Venetian carnival of 1817, Byron wrote in a charmingly risque lyric that he "would go no more a roving," for "the sword outwears its sheath, / And the soul wears out the breast." He now settled for playing the *cavalier servante,* or socially approved lover, to the young wife of an older man. The woman was Teresa, the 17-year-old daughter of Count Gamba of Ravenna and the wife of the 60-year-old Count Guiccioli. Byron rented a magnificent apartment in the Guiccioli Palace to be with Teresa daily, where he bragged of regulating his love according to the "strictest adultery."

Byron's next and greatest poetic enterprise begins by exploiting the inherent humor and hypocrisy of incompatible relationships. Byron said that *Don Juan* was "meant to be a little quietly facetious upon everything," that is, every ethical and moral problem caused by the institutional repressions of Church, education, marriage, and law. No knowledgeable contemporary reader is likely to have missed the biographical allusions of *Don Juan:* that Juan's mother, Donna Inez, and first lover, Donna Julia, are much like Lady Byron; that Juan's father is a good representative of the paternal scoundrels of the Byron line; and that Juan's upbringing and sexual initiation are reminiscent of Byron's vulnerability to beautiful, shrewd, and hypocritical women from his childhood on.

Byron boasted that *Don Juan* was unique. In early 1819, he wrote to his publisher John Murray: "You have so many *'divine'* poems, is it nothing to have written a *Human* one?" Later he wrote to friend Douglas Kinnaird of the opening cantos: "It may be profligate but is it not *life,* is it not *the thing?* Could any man have written it who has not lived in the world?—and [f]ooled in a post-chaise?—in a hackney coach?—in a gondola?—against a wall?—in a court carriage?—in a vis a vis—on a table?—and under it?" Cantos of *Don Juan* came out incrementally for the remainder of Byron's life, increasingly reflecting the political frustrations and imminent nihilism of a reactionary and war-weary Europe. The narrator himself says that he laughs to prevent crying and only the poet's death stopped his laughter.

Although Byron published all cantos of *Don Juan* (1819–1824) anonymously, he was widely known as the author. British society was displeased. A review of the opening Cantos in *Blackwood's Magazine* derided the poem as "filthy and impious." Robert Southey later generalized as well as intensified the attack:

> The school which they [Byron, Shelley, etc.] have set up may properly be called the Satanic School; for though their productions breathe the spirit of Belial in their lascivious parts, and the spirit of Moloch in those loathsome images of atrocities and horror which they delight to represent, they are more especially characterized by a satanic spirit of pride and audacious impiety, which still betrays the wretched feeling of hopelessness wherewith it is allied.

Because of Murray's fear of legal reprisal, Byron's mocking "Dedication" of *Don Juan* to Southey did not appear in 1819. However, Southey's attack on Byron inspired *The Vision of Judgment* (1822), which criticizes the Poet Laureate as a political apostate and sycophant, who had supported the ideals of the French Revolution in his youth, but who now sings in praise of a mentally incompetent monarch.

Besides hypocrisy, thoughts of liberty also aroused Byron. He found an entree into clandestine Italian politics through the Gamba family after the Count and Countess Guiccoli separated and Teresa moved back to her family home in Ravenna. Teresa's father and brother were Carbonari, or members of the secret revolutionary society devoted to overthrowing the Austrian forces occupying northern Italy, placed there and in all countries contiguous to France by the Quadruple Alliance of Britain, Austria, Russia, and Prussia to protect Europe against future French aggression. The Carbonari insurrection failed, and Byron languished in domesticity for several years before taking up the cause of Greek independence.

In 1820, Byron wrote cynically and prophetically of his susceptibility to liberal causes:

> When a man hath no freedom to fight for at home,
> Let him combat for that of his neighbours;
> Let him think of the glories of Greece and of Rome,
> And get knock'd in the head for his labours.
>
> To do good to mankind is the chivalrous plan,
> And is always as nobly requited;
> Then battle for freedom wherever you can,
> And, if not shot or hang'd, you'll get knighted.

In August 1823, Byron set sail for the island of Cephalonia in a vessel he rented with a cargo of medical supplies and arms he had purchased to support the Greek uprising against the Turks. The Greek forces and strategy being in a state of confusion, Byron remained at Cephalonia until December. After a harrowing sea voyage fleeing from the Turks, he reached Missolonghi in January "prepar[ed] for active operations." Prince Alexander Mavrocordatos, Greek patriot and later Prime Minister, asked Byron to lead a forthcoming assault of several thousand Greeks against the Turkish forces at Lepanto. By February, however, Byron became unaccountably convulsive and vertiginous. After developing a rheumatic fever following exposure to rain, Byron's condition worsened. He died without experiencing military action on Easter Sunday, 18 April 1824, amidst a great thunderstorm. The Greeks cried out, "The great man is gone!" for, as one in attendance explained, Byron had been "the hope of a whole nation and the admiration of the civilized world."

One of Byron's last requests was that his "body [not] be hacked, or be sent to England. Here let my bones moulder. —Lay me in the first corner without pomp or nonsense." None of his wishes were honored, except the last, but in England. He received a crude autopsy, which failed to discern the cause of death. Except for his lungs, which remained in the San Spiridione chapel in Missolonghi, Byron's containerized remains received a distinguished military farewell as their vessel departed for England. Towns throughout Greece held memorial services, and eventually built statues and renamed streets in Byron's honor. However, Byron's "worldwide reputation for immorality among English-speaking people," kept him out of Poet's Corner, Westminster Abbey, until 1968, when due was finally paid to Byron's poetic immortality with a marble floor slab.

from Parliamentary Speeches in the House of Lords
(1812)

Debate on the Frame Work Bill,[1] in the House of Lords, February 27, 1812.

The order of the day for the second reading of this Bill being read,

LORD BYRON rose, and (for the first time) addressed their Lordships as follows:

MY LORDS, the subject now submitted to your Lordships for the first time, though new to the House, is by no means new to the country. I believe it had occupied the serious thoughts of all descriptions of persons, long before its introduction to the notice of that legislature, whose interference alone could be of real service. As a person in some degree connected with the suffering county, though a stranger not only to this House in general, but to almost every individual whose attention I presume to solicit, I must claim some portion of your Lordships' indulgence, whilst I offer a few observations on a question in which I confess myself deeply interested.

To enter into any detail of the riots would be superfluous: the House is already aware that every outrage short of actual bloodshed, has been perpetrated, and that the proprietors of the Frames obnoxious to the rioters, and all persons supposed to be connected with them, have been liable to insult and violence. During the short time I recently passed in Nottinghamshire, not twelve hours elapsed without some fresh act of violence; and on the day I left the county I was informed that forty Frames had been broken the preceding evening, as usual, without resistance and without detection.

Such was then the state of that county, and such I have reason to believe it to be at this moment. But whilst these outrages must be admitted to exist to an alarming extent, it cannot be denied that they have arisen from circumstances of the most unparalleled distress: The perseverance of these miserable men in their proceedings, tends to prove that nothing but absolute want could have driven a large, and once honest and industrious, body of the people, into the commission of excesses so hazardous to themselves, their families, and the community. At the time to which I allude, the town and county were burthened with large detachments of the military; the police was in motion, the magistrates assembled, yet all the movements, civil and military, had led to—nothing. Not a single instance had occurred of the apprehension of any real delinquent actually taken in the fact, against whom there existed legal evidence sufficient for conviction. But the police, however useless, were by no means idle: several notorious delinquents had been detected; men, liable to conviction, on the clearest evidence, of the capital crime of Poverty; men, who had been nefariously guilty of lawfully begetting several children, whom, thanks to the times! they were unable to maintain. Considerable injury has been done to the proprietors of the improved Frames. These machines were to them an advantage, inasmuch as they superseded the necessity of employing a number of workmen, who were left in consequence to starve. By the adoption of one species of Frame in particular, one man performed the work of many, and the superfluous labourers were thrown out of employment. Yet it is to be observed, that the work thus executed was inferior in quality; not marketable at home, and merely hurried over with a view to exportation. It was called, in the cant of the trade, by the name of "Spider work." The rejected workmen, in the blindness of their ignorance, instead of rejoicing at these improvements in arts so beneficial to mankind, conceived themselves to be sacrificed to improvements in mechanism. In the foolishness of their hearts they imagined, that the maintenance and well doing of the industrious poor, were objects of greater consequence than the enrichment of a few individuals by any improvement, in the implements of trade, which threw the workmen out of employment, and rendered the labourer unworthy of his hire. And it must be confessed that although the adoption of the enlarged machinery in that state of our commerce which the country once boasted, might have been beneficial to the master without being detrimental to the servant; yet, in the present situation of our manufactures, rotting in warehouses, without a prospect of exportation, with the demand for work and

[1] **Frame Work Bill:** in Nov. 1811 the unemployed stocking weavers of Nottingham (also known as "Luddites"), some of them near the point of starvation, began rioting and breaking the mechanized weaving frames that were costing them their jobs. The militia were called in, but were unable to stop the violence. The government then responded with the Tory-sponsored Frame Work Bill, which specified the death penalty for frame-breaking.

workmen equally diminished; Frames of this description tend materially to aggravate the distress and discontent of the disappointed sufferers. But the real cause of these distresses and consequent disturbances lies deeper. When we are told that these men are leagued together not only for the destruction of their own comfort, but of their very means of subsistence, can we forget that it is the bitter policy, the destructive warfare of the last eighteen years,[2] which has destroyed their comfort, your comfort, all men's comfort? That policy, which, originating with "great statesmen now no more," has survived the dead to become a curse on the living, unto the third and fourth generation! These men never destroyed their looms till they were become useless, worse than useless; till they were become actual impediments to their exertions in obtaining their daily bread. Can you, then, wonder that in times like these, when bankruptcy, convicted fraud, and imputed felony are found in a station not far beneath that of your Lordships, the lowest, though once most useful portion of the people, should forget their duty in their distresses, and become only less guilty than one of their representatives? But while the exalted offender can find means to baffle the law, new capital punishments must be devised, new snares of death must be spread for the wretched mechanic, who is famished into guilt. These men were willing to dig, but the spade was in other hands: they were not ashamed to beg, but there was none to relieve them: their own means of subsistence were cut off, all other employments pre-occupied, and their excesses, however to be deplored and condemned, can hardly be subject of surprise. . . .

At present the county suffers from the double infliction of an idle military and a starving population. In what state of apathy have we been plunged so long, that now for the first time the House has been officially apprized of these disturbances? All this has been transacting within 130 miles of London, and yet we, "good easy men, have deemed full sure our greatness was a ripening,"[3] and have sat down to enjoy our foreign triumphs in the midst of domestic calamity. But all the cities you have taken, all the armies which have retreated before your leaders, are but paltry subjects of self congratulation, if your land divides against itself, and your dragoons and your executioners must be let loose against your fellow citizens. — You call these men a mob, desperate, dangerous, and ignorant; and seem to think that the only way to quiet the "Bellua multorum capitum"[4] is to lop off a few of its superfluous heads. But even a mob may be better reduced to reason by a mixture of conciliation and firmness, than by additional irritation and redoubled penalties. Are we aware of our obligations to a mob? It is the mob that labour in your fields and serve in your houses, — that man your navy, and recruit your army, — that have enabled you to defy all the world, and can also defy you when neglect and calamity have driven them to despair. You may call the people a mob; but do not forget, that a mob too often speaks the sentiments of the people. And here I must remark, with what alacrity you are accustomed to fly to the succour of your distressed allies, leaving the distressed of your own country to the care of Providence or — the Parish. When the Portuguese suffered under the retreat of the French,[5] every arm was stretched out, every hand was opened, from the rich man's largess to the widow's mite, all was bestowed to enable them to rebuild their villages and replenish their granaries. And at this moment, when thousands of misguided but most unfortunate fellow-countrymen are struggling with the extremes of hardships and hunger, as your charity began abroad it should end at home. . . .

Sure I am from what I have heard, and from what I have seen, that to pass the Bill under all the existing circumstances, without enquiry, without deliberation, would only be to add injustice to irritation, and barbarity to neglect. The framers of such a Bill must be content to inherit the honours of that Athenian lawgiver whose edicts were said to be written not in ink but in blood. But suppose it past; suppose one of these men, as I have seen them, — meagre with famine, sullen with despair, careless of a life which your Lordships are perhaps about to value at something less than the price of a stocking-frame — suppose this man surrounded by the children for whom he is unable to procure bread at the hazard of his existence, about to be torn for ever from a family which he lately supported in peaceful industry, and which it is not his fault

[2] **the destructive warfare . . . years:** the Napoleonic Wars.

[3] **"good easy men . . . ripening":** Shakespeare, *King Henry VIII*: "And, when he thinks, good easy man, full surely / his greatness is a-ripening, nips his root, / And then he falls" (III.ii.357–359).

[4] **Bellua multorum capitum:** many-headed monster.

[5] **When the Portuguese . . . the French:** in August to September of 1808.

that he can no longer so support—suppose this man, and there are ten thousand such from whom you may select your victims, dragged into court, to be tried for this new offence, by this new law; still, there are two things wanting to convict and condemn him; and these are, in my opinion,—Twelve Butchers for a Jury, and a Jefferies for a Judge![6]

Childe[1] Harold's Pilgrimage

A Romaunt[2]

(1812; comp. 1809–1810)

L'univers est une espèce de livre, dont on n'a lu que la première page quand on n'a vu que son pays. J'en ai feuilleté un assez grand nombre, que j'ai trouvé également mauvaises. Cet examen ne m'a point été infructueux. Je haïssais ma patrie. Toutes les impertinences des peuples divers, parmi lesquels j'ai vécu, m'ont réconcilié avec elle. Quand je n'aurais tiré d'autre bénéfice de mes voyages que celui-là, je n'en regretterais ni les frais, ni les fatigues.

Le Cosmopolite

—PREFACE [TO CANTOS I–II]—

The following poem was written, for the most part, amidst the scenes which it attempts to describe. It was begun in Albania; and the parts relative to Spain and Portugal were composed from the author's observations in those countries. Thus much it may be necessary to state for the correctness of the descriptions. The scenes attempted to be sketched are in Spain, Portugal, Epirus, Acarnania,[3] and Greece. There for the present the poem stops: its reception will determine whether the author may venture to conduct his readers to the capital of the East, through Ionia and Phrygia:[4] these two cantos are merely experimental.

A fictitious character is introduced for the sake of giving some connexion to the piece; which, however, no pretension to regularity. It has been suggested to me by friends, on whose opinions I set a high value, that in this fictitious character, 'Childe Harold', I may incur the suspicion of having intended some real personage: this I beg leave, once for all, to disclaim—Harold is the child of imagination, for the purpose I have stated. In some very trivial particulars, and those merely local, there might be grounds for such a notion; but in the main points, I should hope, none whatever.

It is almost superfluous to mention that the appellation 'Childe', as 'Childe Waters', 'Childe Childers', etc. is used as more consonant with the old structure of versification which I have adopted. The 'Good Night', in the beginning of the first canto, was suggested by 'Lord Maxwell's Good Night', in the Border Minstrelsy,[5] edited by Mr. Scott.

With the different poems which have been published on Spanish subjects, there may be found some slight coincidence in the first part, which treats of the Peninsula, but it can only be casual; as, with the exception of a few concluding stanzas, the whole of this poem was written in Levant.[6]

The stanza of Spenser, according to one of our most successful poets, admits of every variety. Dr. Beattie[7] makes the following observation: 'Not long ago I began a poem in the style and stanza of Spenser, in which I propose to give full scope to my inclination, and be either

[6] **Jeffries:** reference to the "hanging judge" George Jeffreys (1645–1689), notorious for his injustice and brutality.

[1] **Childe:** medieval term for a youth of noble birth.

[2] **romaunt:** a verse romance. The epigraph, from *The Citizen of the World* (1753) by Fougeret de Monbron, translates: "The universe is a kind of book of which you have read but one page when you have seen only your own country. I have leafed through a sufficient number to have found them equally bad. This study has not been unprofitable for me. I hated my country. All the peculiarities of the different people among whom I have lived have reconciled me to it. Even if I should have gained no other benefit from my voyages than that one, I should never regret the pains, and the fatigues" (McGann).

[3] **Epirus, Acarnania:** Epirus was an area northwest of Greece, in what is now Albania; Acarnania is a region on the northwest coast of Greece, just south of Epirus.

[4] **Ionia and Phrygia:** Ionia comprises the islands along the west coast of Greece; Phrygia refers to the northwest coast of Asia Minor—the location of Troy, and what is now northwest Turkey.

[5] **the Border Minstrelsy:** Walter Scott's* collection *Minstrelsy of the Scottish Border* appeared in 1802 to 1803.

[6] **Levant:** the eastern Mediterranean.

[7] **Dr. Beattie:** James Beattie (1735–1803), Scottish poet and professor of moral philosophy, is best known for his unfinished poem *The Minstrel* (1771–1774).

droll or pathetic, descriptive or sentimental, tender or satirical, as the humour strikes me; for, if I mistake not, the measure which I have adopted admits equally of all these kinds of composition.'—Strengthened in my opinion by such authority, and by the example of some in the highest order of Italian poets, I shall make no apology for attempts at similar variations in the following composition; satisfied that, if they are unsuccessful, their failure must be in the execution, rather than in the design sanctioned by the practice of Ariosto, Thomson,[8] and Beattie.

— ADDITION TO THE PREFACE — (1813)

. . . I now leave 'Childe Harold' to live his day, such as he is; it has been more agreeable, and certainly more easy, to have drawn an amiable character. It had been easy to varnish over his faults, to make him do more and express less, but he never was intended as an example, further than to show that early perversion of mind and morals leads to satiety of past pleasures and disappointment in new ones, and that even the beauties of nature, and the stimulus of travel (except ambition, the most powerful of all excitements) are lost on a soul so constituted, or rather misdirected. Had I proceeded with the Poem, this character would have deepened as he drew to the close; for the outline which I once meant to fill up for him was, with some exceptions, the sketch of a modern Timon, perhaps a poetical Zeluco.[9]

from CANTO I

1

Oh, thou! in Hellas[1] deem'd of heav'nly birth,
Muse! form'd or fabled at the minstrel's will!
Since sham'd full oft by later lyres on earth,
Mine dares not call thee from thy sacred hill:
Yet there I've wander'd by thy vaunted rill;
Yes! sigh'd o'er Delphi's long-deserted shrine,[2]
Where, save that feeble fountain, all is still;
Nor mote my shell awake the weary Nine
To grace so plain a tale—this lowly lay[3] of mine.

2

Whilome in Albion's isle there dwelt a youth,
Who ne[4] in virtue's ways did take delight;
But spent his days in riot most uncouth,
And vex'd with mirth the drowsy ear of Night.
Ah, me! in sooth he was a shameless wight,[5]
Sore given to revel and ungodly glee;
Few earthly things found favour in his sight
Save concubines and carnal companie,
And flaunting wassailers[6] of high and low degree.

3

Childe Harold was he hight:[7]—but whence his name
And lineage long, it suits me not to say;
Suffice it, that perchance they were of fame,
And had been glorious in another day:
But one sad losel soils a name for aye,[8]
However mighty in the olden time;
Nor all that heralds rake from coffin'd clay,
Nor florid prose, nor honied lies of rhyme
Can blazon evil deeds, or consecrate a crime.

4

Childe Harold bask'd him in the noon-tide sun,
Disporting there like any other fly;
Nor deem'd before his little day was done
One blast might chill him into misery.
But long ere scarce a third of his pass'd by,
Worse than adversity the Childe befell;

---

[8] **Ariosto, Thomson:** Italian poet Ludovico Ariosto (1474–1533), author of *Orlando Furioso* (1516), and James Thomson (1700–1748), author of *The Castle of Indolence* (1748), in Spenserian stanzas.

[9] **Timon:** the disillusioned, embittered and misanthropic protagonist of Shakespeare's *Timon of Athens*. **Zeluco:** the villainous protagonist of the 1789 Gothic novel of the same name by John Moore.

[1] **Hellas:** Greece.

[2] **Delphi's . . . shrine:** the cave from which the oracle of Apollo issued her prophecies.

[3] **mote:** might (Spenserian). **the weary nine:** the Muses. **lay:** song.

[4] **Whilome**—once upon a time (Spenserian). **ne:** not.

[5] **sooth:** truth. **wight:** creature, person (Spenserian).

[6] **wassailers:** revelers.

[7] **hight:** named (Spenserian).

[8] **losel:** a worthless person. **aye:** always.

He felt the fulness of satiety:
Then loath'd he in his native land to dwell,
Which seem'd to him more lone than Eremite's[9] sad cell.

5

For he through Sin's long labyrinth had run,
Nor made atonement when he did amiss,
Had sigh'd to many though he lov'd but one,
And that lov'd one, alas! could ne'er be his.
Ah, happy she! to 'scape from him whose kiss
Had been pollution unto aught so chaste;
Who soon had left her charms for vulgar bliss,
And spoil'd her goodly lands to gild his waste,
Nor calm domestic peace had ever deign'd to taste.

6

And now Childe Harold was sore sick at heart,
And from his fellow bacchanals[10] would flee;
'Tis said, at times the sullen tear would start,
But Pride congeal'd the drop within his ee:
Apart he stalk'd in joyless reverie,
And from his native land resolv'd to go,
And visit scorching climes beyond the sea;
With pleasure drugg'd he almost long'd for woe,
And e'en for change of scene would seek the shades below.

7

The Childe departed from his father's hall:
It was a vast and venerable pile;[11]
So old, it seemed only not to fall,
Yet strength was pillar'd in each massy aisle.
Monastic dome! condemn'd to uses vile!
Where Superstition once had made her den
Now Paphian[12] girls were known to sing and smile;
And monks might deem their time was come agen,
If ancient tales say true, nor wrong these holy men.

8

Yet oft-times in his maddest mirthful mood
Strange pangs would flash along Childe Harold's brow,
As if the memory of some deadly feud
Or disappointed passion lurk'd below:
But this none knew, nor haply car'd to know;
For his was not that open, artless soul
That feels relief by bidding sorrow flow,
Nor sought he friend to counsel or condole,
Whate'er his grief mote be, which he could not control.

9

And none did love him—though to hall and bower
He gather'd revellers from far and near,
He knew them flatt'rers of the festal hour;
The heartless parasites of present cheer.
Yea! none did love him—not his lemans[13] dear—
But pomp and power alone are woman's care,
And where these are light Eros finds a feere;
Maidens, like moths, are ever caught by glare,
And Mammon wins his way where Seraphs[14] might despair.

10

Childe Harold had a mother—not forgot,
Though parting from that mother he did shun;
A sister whom he lov'd, but saw her not
Before his weary pilgrimage begun:
If friends he had, he bade adieu to none.
Yet deem not thence his breast a breast of steel;
Ye, who have known what 'tis to doat upon
A few dear objects, will in sadness feel
Such partings break the heart they fondly hope to heal.

. . . .

[9] **Eremite:** a Christian hermit.

[10] **bacchanals:** devotees of Bacchus, the god of wine and fertility, worshipped in orgiastic rites.

[11] **pile:** ruin.

[12] **Paphian:** the city of Paphos, in Cyprus, was the center for the worship of Aphrodite, goddess of love.

[13] **lemans:** mistresses (archaic).

[14] **Mammon:** material wealth. **Seraphs:** the highest order of angels.

49

On yon long, level plain, at distance crown'd
With crags, whereon those Moorish turrets rest,
Wide scatter'd hoof-marks dint the wounded ground;[15]
And, scath'd by fire, the green sward's darken'd vest
Tells that the foe was Andalusia's guest:
Here was the camp, the watch-flame, and the host,
Here the bold peasant storm'd the dragon's nest;
Still does he mark it with triumphant boast,
And points to yonder cliffs, which oft were won and lost.

50

And whomsoe'er along the path you meet
Bears in his cap the badge of crimson hue,[16]
Which tells you whom to shun and whom to greet:
Woe to the man that walks in public view
Without of loyalty this token true:
Sharp is the knife, and sudden is the stroke;
And sorely would the Gallic foeman rue,
If subtle poniards,[17] wrapt beneath the cloke,
Could blunt the sabre's edge, or clear the cannon's smoke.

51

At every turn Morena's dusky height
Sustains aloft the battery's iron load;
And, far as mortal eye can compass sight,
The mountain-howitzer, the broken road,
The bristling palisade, the fosse o'er-flow'd,
The station'd bands, the never-vacant watch,
The magazine in rocky durance stow'd,
The holster'd steed beneath the shed of thatch,
The ball-pil'd pyramid, the ever-blazing match,

[15]**Moorish turrets:** Refers to the city of Granada, last refuge of the Moorish occupation of Spain (1238–1492), and the seat of the palace of Alhambra. **wounded ground:** The French invaded the Sierra Morena (Spain's southern plain) in 1808, but the city of Jaen — the "dragon's nest — was recaptured by the Spanish in July of that same year. The following stanzas describe the battles.

[16]**badge of crimson hue:** "The red cockade, with *Fenando Septimo* in the centre." [L.B.]

[17]**poniards:** daggers.

52

Portend the deeds to come: — but he whose nod
Has tumbled feebler despots from their sway
A moment pauseth ere he lifts the rod;
A little moment deigneth to delay:
Soon will his legions sweep through these their way;
The West must own the Scourger of the world.
Ah! Spain! how sad will be thy reckoning-day,
When soars Gaul's Vulture, with his wings unfurl'd,
And thou shalt view thy sons in crowds to Hades hurl'd.

53

And must they fall? the young, the proud, the brave,
To swell one bloated Chief's unwholesome reign?
No step between submission and a grave?
The rise of rapine and the fall of Spain?
And doth the Power that man adores ordain
Their doom, nor heed the suppliant's appeal?
Is all that desperate Valour acts in vain?
And Counsel sage, and patriotic Zeal,
The Veteran's skill, Youth's fire, and Manhood's heart of steel?

54

Is it for this the Spanish maid, arous'd,
Hangs on the willow her unstrung guitar,
And, all unsex'd, the Anlace[18] hath espous'd,
Sung the loud song, and dar'd the deed of war?
And she, whom once the semblance of a scar
Appall'd, an owlet's 'larum[19] chill'd with dread,
Now views the column-scattering bay'net jar,
The falchion[20] flash, and o'er the yet warm dead
Stalks with Minerva's step where Mars might quake to tread.

55

Ye who shall marvel when you hear her tale,
Oh! had you known her in her softer hour,
Mark'd her black eye that mocks her coal-black veil,

[18]**Anlace:** a two-edged dagger.

[19]**'larum:** alarm.

[20]**falchion:** sword.

Heard her light, lively tones in Lady's bower,
Seen her long locks that foil the painter's power,
Her fairy form, with more than female grace,
Scarce would you deem that Saragoza's tower
Beheld her smile in Danger's Gorgon[21] face,
Thin the clos'd ranks, and lead in Glory's fearful chase.

56

Her lover sinks—she sheds no ill-tim'd tear;
Her chief is slain—she fills his fatal post;
Her fellows flee—she checks their base career;
The foe retires—she heads the sallying host:
Who can appease like her a lover's ghost?
Who can avenge so well a leader's fall?
What maid retrieve when man's flush'd hope is lost?
Who hang so fiercely on the flying Gaul,
Foil'd by a woman's hand, before a batter'd wall?[22]

57

Yet are Spain's maids no race of Amazons,
But form'd for all the witching arts of love:
Though thus in arms they emulate her sons,
And in the horrid phalanx dare to move,
'Tis but the tender fierceness of the dove
Pecking the hand that hovers o'er her mate:
In softness as in firmness far above
Remoter females, fam'd for sickening prate;
Her mind is nobler sure, her charms perchance as great.

58

The seal Love's dimpling finger hath impress'd
Denotes how soft that chin which bears his touch:
Her lips, whose kisses pout to leave their nest,
Bid man be valiant ere he merit such:
Her glance how wildly beautiful! how much
Hath Phoebus[23] woo'd in vain to spoil her cheek,
Which glows yet smoother from his amorous clutch!

Who round the North for paler dames would seek?
How poor their forms appear! how languid, wan, and weak!

59

Match me, ye climes! which poets love to laud;
Match me, ye harams of the land! where now
I strike my strain, far distant, to applaud
Beauties that ev'n a cynic must avow;
Match me those Houries,[24] whom ye scarce allow
To taste the gale lest Love should ride the wind,
With Spain's dark-glancing daughters—deign to know,
There your wise Prophet's paradise we find,
His black-eyed maids of Heaven, angelically kind.

60

Oh, thou Parnassus![25] whom I now survey,
Not in the phrenzy of a dreamer's eye,
Not in the fabled landscape of a lay,
But soaring snow-clad through thy native sky,
In the wild pomp of mountain majesty!
What marvel if I thus essay to sing?
The humblest of thy pilgrims passing by
Would gladly woo thine Echoes with his string,
Though from thy heights no more one Muse will wave her wing.

61

Oft have I dream'd of Thee! whose glorious name
Who knows not, knows not man's divinest lore:
And now I view thee, 'tis, alas! with shame
That I in feeblest accents must adore.
When I recount thy worshippers of yore
I tremble, and can only bend the knee;
Nor raise my voice, nor vainly dare to soar,
But gaze beneath thy cloudy canopy
In silent joy to think at last I look on Thee!

---

[21] **Gorgon:** the Medusa.

[22] "Such were the exploits of the Maid of Saragoza. When the author was at Seville she walked daily in the Prado, decorated with medals and orders, by command of the Junta." [L.B.]

[23] **Phoebus:** Apollo, the sun.

[24] **Houries:** a nymph of the Mohammaden paradise; a voluptuous woman.

[25] **Parnassus:** mountain sacred to the muses, and thus associated with poetic inspiration, but literally the location of these next stanzas. Parnassus is an 8,060 feet mountain of Southern Greece. Its modern name is Lia Kourz.

62

Happier in this than mightiest bards have been,
Whose fate to distant homes confin'd their lot,
Shall I unmov'd behold the hallow'd scene,
Which others rave of, though they know it not?
Though here no more Apollo haunts his grot,
And thou, the Muses' seat, art now their grave,
Some gentle Spirit still pervades the spot,
Sighs in the gale, keeps silence in the cave,
And glides with glassy foot o'er yon melodious Wave.

63

Of thee hereafter.—Ev'n amidst my strain
I turn'd aside to pay my homage here;
Forgot the land, the sons, the maids of Spain;
Her fate, to every freeborn bosom dear,
And hail'd thee, not perchance without a tear.
Now to my theme—but from thy holy haunt
Let me some remnant, some memorial bear;
Yield me one leaf of Daphne's deathless plant,[26]
Nor let thy votary's hope be deem'd an idle vaunt.

. . . .

85

Adieu, fair Cadiz![27] yea, a long adieu!
Who may forget how well thy walls have stood?
When all were changing thou alone wert true,
First to be free and last to be subdued:
And if amidst a scene, a shock so rude,
Some native blood was seen thy streets to dye;
A traitor only fell beneath the feud:
Here all were noble, save Nobility;
None hugg'd a Conqueror's chain, save fallen
Chivalry!

86

Such be the sons of Spain, and strange her fate!
They fight for freedom who were never free,
A Kingless people for a nerveless state;
Her vassals combat when their chieftains flee,
True to the veriest slaves of Treachery:
Fond of a land which gave them nought but life,
Pride points the path that leads to Liberty;
Back to the struggle, baffled in the strife,
War, war is still the cry, 'War even to the knife!'

87

Ye, who would more of Spain and Spaniards know,
Go, read whate'er is writ of bloodiest strife:
Whate'er keen Vengeance urg'd on foreign foe
Can act, is acting there against man's life:
From flashing scimitar to secret knife,
War mouldeth there each weapon to his need—
So may he guard the sister and the wife,
So may he make each curst oppressor bleed,
So may such foes deserve the most remorseless deed!

88

Flows there a tear of pity for the dead?
Look o'er the ravage of the reeking plain;
Look on the hands with female slaughter red;
Then to the dogs resign the unburied slain,
Then to the vulture let each corse remain;
Albeit unworthy of the prey-bird's maw,
Let their bleach'd bones, and blood's unbleaching
stain,
Long mark the battle-field with hideous awe:
Thus only may our sons conceive the scenes we saw!

. . . .

from CANTO II
(1812; comp. 1809–1810)

1

Come, blue-eyed maid of heaven!—but thou, alas!
Didst never yet one mortal song inspire—
Goddess of Wisdom![1] here thy temple was,
And is, despite of war and wasting fire,[2]
And years, that bade thy worship to expire:
But worse than steel, and flame, and ages slow,
Is the dread sceptre and dominion dire
Of men[3] who never felt the sacred glow.
That thoughts of thee and thine on polish'd breasts
bestow.

[26] **Daphne's deathless plant:** the laurel, into which the nymph Daphne was transformed to escape the pursuit of Apollo, was used to crown poets (thus the term "poet laureate").

[27] **Cadiz:** a port city near the southern tip of Spain.

[1] **Goddess of wisdom:** Athena. Harold is in Greece.

[2] **wasting fire:** "part of the Acropolis was destroyed by the explosion of a magazine during the Venetian siege". [L.B.]

[3] **men:** the Turks. At this time Greece was under Ottoman rule.

2

Ancient of days! august Athena! where,
Where are thy men of might? thy grand in soul?
Gone — glimmering through the dream of things that were:
First in the race that led to Glory's goal,
They won, and pass'd away — is this the whole?
A school-boy's tale, the wonder of an hour!
The warrior's weapon and the sophist's stole
Are sought in vain, and o'er each mouldering tower,
Dim with the mist of years, grey flits the shade of power.

. . . .

83

This must he feel, the true-born son of Greece,
If Greece one true-born patriot still can boast:
Not such as prate of war, but skulk in peace,
The bondman's peace, who sighs for all he lost,
Yet with smooth smile his tyrant can accost,
And wield the slavish sickle, not the sword:
Ah! Greece! they love thee least who owe thee most;
Their birth, their blood, and that sublime record
Of hero sires, who shame thy now degenerate horde!

84

When riseth Lacedemon's hardihood,
When Thebes Epaminondas[4] rears again,
When Athens' children are with hearts endued,
When Grecian mothers shall give birth to men,
Then may'st thou be restored; but not till then.
A thousand years scarce serve to form a state;
An hour may lay it in the dust: and when
Can man its shatter'd splendour renovate,
Recall its virtues back, and vanquish Time and Fate?

85

And yet how lovely in thine age of woe,
Land of lost gods and godlike men! art thou!
Thy vales of ever-green, thy hills of snow
Proclaim thee Nature's varied favourite now:
Thy fanes, thy temples to thy surface bow,
Commingling slowly with heroic earth,
Broke by the share of every rustic plough:
So perish monuments of mortal birth,
So perish all in turn, save well-recorded Worth;

86

Save where some solitary column mourns
Above its prostrate brethren of the cave;
Save where Tritonia's[5] airy shrine adorns
Colonna's cliff, and gleams along the wave;
Save o'er some warrior's half-forgotten grave,
Where the grey stones and unmolested grass
Ages, but not oblivion, feebly brave,
While strangers only not regardless pass,
Lingering like me, perchance, to gaze, and sigh 'Alas!'

87

Yet are thy skies as blue, thy crags as wild;
Sweet are thy groves, and verdant are thy fields,
Thine olive ripe as when Minerva smil'd,
And still his honied wealth Hymettus[6] yields;
There the blithe bee his fragrant fortress builds,
The freeborn wanderer of thy mountain-air;
Apollo still thy long, long summer gilds,
Still in his beam Mendeli's[7] marbles glare;
Art, Glory, Freedom fail, but Nature still is fair.

88

Where'er we tread 'tis haunted, holy ground;
No earth of thine is lost in vulgar mould,
But one vast realm of wonder spreads around,
And all the Muse's tales seem truly told,
Till the sense aches with gazing to behold
The scenes our earliest dreams have dwelt upon:
Each hill and dale, each deepening glen and wold[8]

---

[4] **Lacedemon**: Sparta, proverbial for the hardiness of its lifestyle. **Epaminondas**: statesman and general of Thebes (d. 362 BC) who was a hero of the Peloponnesian War (431–404 BC), known for his noble character.

[5] **cave**: "Of Mount Pentelicus, from whence the marble was dug that constructed the public edifices of Athens. The modern name is Mount Mendeli. An immense cave formed by the quarries still remains, and will till the end of time" [L.B.]. **Tritonia**: Athena.

[6] **Minerva**: Roman name for Athena. **Hymettus**: a mountain in Attica, famous for its honey.

[7] **Mendeli**: possibly Mendae, on the west coast of Pellene, famous for its wine.

[8] **wold**: an upland plain.

Defies the power which crush'd thy temples gone:
Age shakes Athena's tower, but spares gray
Marathon.[9]

89

The sun, the soil, but not the slave, the same;
Unchanged in all except its foreign lord—
Preserves alike its bounds and boundless fame
The Battle-field, where Persia's victim horde
First bowed beneath the brunt of Hellas' sword,
As on the morn to distant Glory dear,
When Marathon became a magic word;
Which utter'd, to the hearer's eye appear
The camp, the host, the fight, the conqueror's career,

90

The flying Mede,[10] his shaftless broken bow;
The fiery Greek, his red pursuing spear;
Mountains above, Earth's, Ocean's plain below;
Death in the front, Destruction in the rear!
Such was the scene—what now remaineth here?
What sacred trophy marks the hallow'd ground,
Recording Freedom's smile and Asia's tear?
The rifled urn, the violated mound,
The dust thy courser's hoof, rude stranger! spurns
around.

91

Yet to the remnants of thy splendour past
Shall pilgrims, pensive, but unwearied, throng;
Long shall the voyager, with th' Ionian[11] blast,
Hail the bright clime of battle and of song;
Long shall thine annals and immortal tongue
Fill with thy fame the youth of many a shore;
Boast of the aged! lesson of the young!
Which sages venerate and bards adore,
As Pallas[12] and the Muse unveil their awful lore.

92

The parted bosom clings to wonted home,
If aught that's kindred cheer the welcome hearth;
He that is lonely hither let him roam,
And gaze complacent on congenial earth.
Greece is no lightsome land of social mirth;
But he whom Sadness sootheth may abide,
And scarce regret the region of this birth,
When wandering slow by Delphi's sacred side,
Or gazing o'er the plains where Greek and Persian
died.

93

Let such approach this consecrated land,
And pass in peace along the magic waste:
But spare its relics—let no busy hand[13]
Deface the scenes, already how defac'd!
Nor for such purpose were these altars plac'd:
Revere the remnants nations once rever'd:
So may our country's name be undisgrac'd,
So may'st thou prosper where thy youth was rear'd,
By every honest joy of love and life endear'd!

94

For thee, who thus in too protracted song
Hast sooth'd thine idlesse[14] with inglorious lays,
Soon shall thy voice be lost amid the throng
Of louder minstrels in these later days:
To such resign the strife for fading bays—
Ill may such contest now the spirit move
Which heeds nor keen reproach nor partial praise;
Since cold each kinder heart that might approve,
And none are left to please when none are left to love.

[9] **Marathon:** a plain northeast of Athens, site of the famous victory of the Athenians over the Persians in 490 BC.

[10] **Mede:** Persian.

[11] **Ionian:** the Ionian Islands are off the west coast of Greece.

[12] **Pallas:** title of Athena.

[13] **busy hand:** Thomas Bruce, seventh Earl of Elgin (1766–1841), who, while a British envoy to the Ottoman Sultan, arranged for the conveyance (1803–1812) of priceless Athenian statuary (afterward known as the "Elgin Marbles") from the Acropolis to the British Museum. Byron makes a reference in Canto II, Stanza 9, to Elgin's vessel the *Mentor* going down with ancient statuary off the coast of Cerigo in 1803. The cargo was later recovered.

[14] **idlesse:** pseudo-antique for "idleness."

95

Thou too art gone, thou lov'd and lovely one![15]
Whom youth and youth's affection bound to me;
Who did for me what none beside have done,
Nor shrank from one albeit unworthy thee.
What is my being? thou hast ceas'd to be!
Nor stayed to welcome here thy wanderer home,
Who mourns o'er hours which we no more shall
see —
Would they had never been, or were to come!
Would he had ne'er return'd to find fresh cause to
roam!

96

Oh! ever loving, lovely, and belov'd!
How selfish Sorrow ponders on the past,
And clings to thoughts now better far remov'd!
But Time shall tear thy shadow from me last.
All thou could'st have of mine, stern Death! thou
hast;
The parent, friend, and now the more than friend:
Ne'er yet for one thine arrows flew so fast,
And grief with grief continuing still be blend,
Hath snatch'd the little joy that life had yet to lend.

97

Then must I plunge again into the crowd,
And follow all that Peace disdains to seek?
Where Revel calls, and Laughter, vainly loud,
False to the heart, distorts the hollow cheek,
To leave the flagging spirit doubly weak;
Still o'er the features, which perforce they cheer,
To feign the pleasure or conceal the pique,
Smiles form the channel of a future tear,
Or raise the writhing lip with ill-dissembled sneer.

98

What is the worst of woes that wait on age?
What stamps the wrinkle deeper on the brow?
To view each lov'd one blotted from life's page,
And be alone on earth, as I am now.
Before the Chastener humbly let me bow:
O'er hearts divided and o'er hopes destroy'd,

[15] **thou lov'd and lovely one:** Byron leaves the referent unidentified, but scholars believe that he is John Edleston, a choirboy at Trinity Chapel at Cambridge when Byron was a student there. Edleston had recently died in May 1811.

Roll on, vain days! full reckless may ye flow,
Since Time hath reft whate'er my soul enjoy'd,
And with the ills of Eld[16] mine earlier years alloy'd.

Song

Ζώη μοῦ, σάς ἀγαπῶ[1]

Athens, 1810

(1812)

1

Maid of Athens,[2] ere we part,
Give, oh, give me back my heart!
Or, since that has left my breast,
Keep it now, and take the rest!
Hear my vow before I go,
Ζώη μοῦ, σάς ἀγαπῶ.

2

By those tresses unconfin'd,
Woo'd by each Aegean[3] wind;
By those lids whose jetty fringe
Kiss thy soft cheeks' blooming tinge;
By those wild eyes like the roe,
Ζώη μοῦ, σάς ἀγαπῶ.

3

By that lip I long to taste;
By that zone-encircl'd waist;
By all the token-flowers that tell
What words can never speak so well;
By Love's alternate joy and woe,
Ζώη μοῦ, σάς ἀγαπῶ.

[16] **Eld:** personification for one who is aged.

[1] Byron's note to the epigraph and refrain reads: "*Zoe mou, sas agapo*, . . . a Romaic [modern Greek] expression of tenderness: if I translate it I shall affront the gentlemen, as it may seem I supposed they could not; and if I do not I may affront the ladies. For fear of any misconstruction on the part of the latter I shall do so, begging pardon of the learned. It means, 'My life, I love you!' which sounds very prettily in all languages. . . ." [L.B.]

[2] Teresa Macri, the twelve-year-old daughter of the family Byron lodged with in Athens.

[3] **Aegean:** the sea to the east of the Greek mainland, between Greece and Turkey.

4

Maid of Athens! I am gone:
Think of me, sweet! when alone.
Though I fly to Istambol,
Athens holds my heart and soul:
Can I cease to love thee? No!
Ζώη μοῦ, σάς ἀγαπῶ.

Ode to Napoleon Buonaparte[1]

(1814; comp. 1814)

Expende Annibalem: — quot libras in duce summo
Invenies? —

Juvenal, Sat. x [147–8]

The Emperor Nepos was acknowledged by the *Senate,* by the *Italians,* and by the Provincials of *Gaul;* his moral virtues, and military talents, were loudly celebrated; and those who derived any private benefit from his government, announced in prophetic strains the restoration of public felicity.

* * * * * * * * * * * *
* * * * * * * * * * * *

By this shameful abdiction, he protracted his life a few years, in a very ambiguous state, between an Emperor and an Exile, till——[2]

Gibbon's Decline and Fall [chap. 36]

....

1

'Tis done — but yesterday a King!
And arm'd with Kings to strive —
And now thou art a nameless thing
So abject — yet alive!
Is this the man of thousand thrones,
Who strew'd our Earth with hostile bones,
And can he thus survive?
Since he, miscall'd the Morning Star,[3]
Nor man nor fiend hath fall'n so far.

2

Ill-minded man! why scourge thy kind
Who bow'd so low the knee?
By gazing on thyself grown blind,
Thou taught'st the rest to see.
With might unquestion'd, — power to save —
Thine only gift hath been the grave
To those that worshipp'd thee;
Nor till thy fall could mortals guess
Ambition's less than littleness!

3

Thanks for that lesson — it will teach
To after-warriors more
Than high Philosophy can preach,
And vainly preached before.
That spell upon the minds of men
Breaks never to unite again,
That led them to adore
Those Pagod[4] things of sabre-sway,
With fronts of brass, and feet of clay.

4

The triumph, and the vanity,
The rapture of the strife —
The earthquake voice of Victory,
To thee the breath of life;
The sword, the sceptre, and that sway
Which man seem'd made but to obey,
Wherewith renown was rife —
All quell'd! — Dark Spirit! what must be
The madness of thy memory!

[1] Published anonymously. Napoleon abdicated on April 6, and was confined on the Isle of Elba, off the coast of Tuscany. (See THE FRENCH REVOLUTION AND RIGHTS OF MAN.) The Latin epigraph translates, "Put Hannibal in the scales; how much weight will you find in that greatest of commanders?" (McGann).

[2] Julius Nepos, emperor of the Western Roman empire from 474 to 480 AD, was deposed by his general Orestes in 475 and fled into exile, but continued to be recognized as emperor in Gaul and in the East. Byron's quote from Gibbons continues, "till he was assassinated at Sabna . . ." (III.36.519, Everyman's edition, 1993).

[3] **the Morning Star:** Lucifer, who led the rebellion in heaven to become Satan after the fall.

[4] **Pagod:** one reverenced superstitiously, a heathen deity or idol.

5

The Desolator desolate!
The Victor overthrown!
The Arbiter of other's fate
A Suppliant for his own!
Is it some yet imperial hope
That with such change can calmly cope?
Or dread of death alone?
To die a prince—or live a slave—
Thy choice is most ignobly brave!

6

He[5] who of old would rend the oak,
Dreamed not of the rebound;
Chained by the trunk he vainly broke—
Alone—how looked he round?
Thou in the sternness of thy strength
An equal deed hast done at length,
And darker fate hast found:
He fell, the forest-prowlers' prey;
But thou must eat thy heart away!

7

The Roman,[6] when his burning heart
Was slaked with blood of Rome,
Threw down the dagger—dared depart,
In savage grandeur, home.—
He dared depart in utter scorn
Of men that such a yoke had borne,
Yet left him such a doom!
His only glory was that hour
Of self-upheld abandon'd power.

8

The Spaniard,[7] when the lust of sway
Had lost its quickening spell,
Cast crowns for rosaries away,
An empire for a cell;
A strict accountant of his beads,
A subtle disputant on creeds,
His dotage trifled well:
Yet better had he neither known
A bigot's shrine, nor despot's throne.

9

But thou—from thy reluctant hand
The thunderbolt is wrung—
Too late thou leav'st the high command
To which thy weakness clung;
All Evil Spirit as thou art,
It is enough to grieve the heart,
To see thine own unstrung;
To think that God's fair world hath been
The footstool of a thing so mean;

10

And Earth hath spilt her blood for him,
Who thus can hoard his own!
And Monarchs bowed the trembling limb,
And thanked him for a throne!
Fair Freedom! we may hold thee dear,
When thus thy mightiest foes their fear
In humblest guise have shown.
Oh! ne'er may tyrant leave behind
A brighter name to lure mankind!

11

Thine evil deeds are writ in gore,
Nor written thus in vain—
Thy triumphs tell of fame no more,
Or deepen every stain—
If thou hadst died as honour dies,

[5] **He:** probably Milon of Crotona, a celebrated Greek wrestler of late 6th century BC, who, while trying to split apart a tree, got caught in the cleft and was eaten alive by wolves (the "forest-prowlers" of line 53).

[6] **The Roman:** Sulla (I) Felix, Lucius Cornelius (born c. 138 BC), great and clever Roman warrior, who massacred his way into the dictatorship of Rome in 81 BC, only to leave two years later because he believed a prophecy that he would die at the height of his power. He died a year later in 78 BC.

[7] **The Spaniard:** Charles V (1500–1558), distinguished warrior, devout Catholic, king of Spain (as Charles I), and emperor of the Holy Roman Empire, formally abdicated his throne in 1558 after having resigned his responsibilities and territories over the course of three years. His humble retirement home was affixed to a monastery.

Some new Napoleon might arise,
  To shame the world again—
But who would soar the solar height,
  To set in such a starless night?

12

Weigh'd in the balance, hero dust
  Is vile as vulgar clay;
Thy scales, Mortality! are just
  To all that pass away;
But yet methought the living great
Some higher sparks should animate,
  To dazzle and dismay;
Nor deem'd Contempt could thus make mirth
Of these, the Conquerors of the earth.

13

And she,[8] proud Austria's mournful flower,
  Thy still imperial bride;
How bears her breast the torturing hour?
  Still clings she to thy side?
Must she too bend, must she too share
Thy late repentance, long despair,
  Thou throneless Homicide?
If still she loves thee, hoard that gem,
'Tis worth thy vanished diadem!

14

Then haste thee to thy sullen Isle,[9]
  And gaze upon the sea;
That element may meet thy smile,
  It ne'er was ruled by thee!
Or trace with thine all idle hand
In loitering mood upon the sand
  That Earth is now as free!
That Corinth's pedagogue[10] hath now
Transferred his bye word to thy brow.

15

Thou Timour![11] in his captive's cage
  What thoughts will there be thine,
While brooding in thy prisoned rage?
  But one—'The world *was* mine';
Unless, like he of Babylon,[12]
All sense is with thy sceptre gone,
  Life will not long confine
That spirit poured so widely forth—
So long obeyed—so little worth!

16

Or like the thief of fire[13] from heaven,
  Wilt thou withstand the shock?
And share with him, the unforgiven,
  His vulture and his rock!
Foredoomed by God—by man accurst,
And that last act, though not thy worst,
  The very Fiend's arch mock;[14]
He in his fall preserv'd his pride,
And if a mortal, had as proudly died!

Letter [to Lady Byron][1]

February 8th. 1816

All I can say seems useless—and all I could say—might be no less unavailing—yet I still cling to the wreck of my hopes—before they sink forever.——Were you then *never*

[8] **she**: Princess Marie Louise of Austria (1791–1847), who became Napoleon's second wife in 1810.

[9] **Isle**: Elba. See Comprehensive Chronology for the succession of events Byron refers to.

[10] **Corinth's pedagogue**: Dionysius, son of the great tyrant, Dionysius I, attempted to bring sophistication and learning to his empire of Syracuse, yet Plato was unsuccessful in making him a philosopher-king. His difficulties in battle against Dion and then rebel Syracusans brought him to his political end. He was transported to Corinth and became a "famous object lesson on the fate of tyrants" (*Oxford Classical Dictionary*).

[11] **Timour**: Timur, also known as Tamburlaine (1336–1405), the Scythian shepherd/robber who conquered much of Asia Minor, and invaded Russia and India. In Marlowe's play *Tamburlaine the Great* (pub. 1590), Tamburlaine leads his captive, Turkish emperor Bajazet, in a cage.

[12] **he of Babylon**: King Nebuchadnezzar (c. 630–562 BC). The allusion is to the Book of Daniel, Chapter 4, where Nebuchadnezzar is depicted as going mad and eating grass.

[13] **the thief of fire**: Prometheus.

[14] **The very Fiend's arch mock**: Cf. *Othello* IV.i.70–73: (Iago) "your case is better. / O 'tis the spite of hell, the fiend's arch-mock, / To lip a wanton in a secure couch, / And to suppose her chaste!" The "Fiend" is Satan, who retains his pride and his defiance of God's monarchy after his Fall.

[1] On Jan. 15, Byron's wife, Annabella Milbanke, took their five-week-old daughter Augusta Ada and went to live with her parents. Byron never saw her or Augusta Ada again.

happy with me?—did you never at any time or times express yourself so?—have no marks of affection—of the warmest & most reciprocal attachment passed between us?—or did in fact hardly a day go down without some such on one side and generally on both?—do not mistake me—[two lines crossed out] I have not denied my state of mind—but you know it's causes—& were those deviations from calmness never followed by acknowledgement & repentance?—was not the last which occurred more particularly so?—& had I not—had we not—the days before & on the day when we parted—every reason to believe that we loved each other—that we were to meet again—were not your letters kind?—had I not acknowledged to you all my faults & follies—& assured you that some had not—& would not be repeated?—I do not require these questions to be answered to me—but to your own heart.——The day before I received your father's letter—I had fixed a day for rejoining you—if I did not write lately—Augusta[2] did—and as you had been my proxy in correspondence with her—so did I imagine—she might be the same for me to you.—Upon your letter to me—this day—I surely may remark—that it's expressions imply a treatment which I am incapable of inflicting—& you of imputing to me—if aware of their latitude—& the extent of the inferences to be drawn from them.—This is not just——but I have no reproaches—nor the wish to find cause for them.——Will you see me?—when & where you please—in whose presence you please:—the interview shall pledge you to nothing—& I will say & do nothing to agitate either—it is torture to correspond thus—& there are things to be settled & said which cannot be written.——You say "it is my disposition to deem what I *have worthless*"—did I deem *you* so?—did I ever so express myself to you—or of you—to others?——You are much changed within these twenty days or you would never have thus poisoned your own better feelings—and trampled upon mine.——

ever yrs. most truly & affectionately
B

[2] **Augusta:** Byron's half-sister, Augusta Leigh.

from POEMS 1816

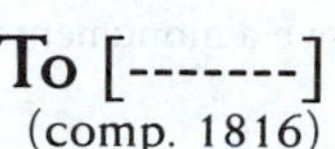

To [-------][1]

(comp. 1816)

1

When all around grew drear and dark,
And reason half withheld her ray—
And hope but shed a dying spark
Which more misled my lonely way;

2

In that deep midnight of the mind,
And that internal strife of heart,
When dreading to be deemed too kind,
The weak despair—the cold depart;

3

When fortune changed—and love fled far,
And hatred's shafts flew thick and fast,
Thou wert the solitary star
Which rose and set not to the last.

4

Oh! blest be thine unbroken light!
That watched me as a seraph's[2] eye,
And stood between me and the night,
For ever shining sweetly nigh.

5

And when the cloud upon us came,
Which strove to blacken o'er thy ray—
Then purer spread its gentle flame,
And dashed the darkness all away.

6

Still may thy spirit dwell on mine,
And teach it what to brave or brook—
There's more in one soft word of thine,
Than in the world's defied rebuke.

[1] Savvy readers would infer that the subject of this poem was Byron's half-sister, Augusta Leigh, because rumors of incestuous relations between them were rampant. The poem led off this small volume of eleven poems, published in June, six weeks after Byron had left England for good.

[2] **seraph:** the highest grade of angel in the celestial hierarchy.

7

Thou stood'st, as stands a lovely tree,
  That still unbroke, but gently bent,
Still waves with fond fidelity
  Its boughs above a monument.

8

The winds might rend—the skies might pour,
  But there thou wert—and still wouldst be
Devoted in the stormiest hour
  To shed thy weeping leaves o'er me.

9

But thou and thine shall know no blight,
  Whatever fate on me may fall;
For heaven in sunshine will requite
  The kind—and thee the most of all.

10

Then let the ties of baffled love
  Be broken—thine will never break;
Thy heart can feel—but will not move,
  Thy soul, though soft, will never shake.

11

And these, when all was lost beside—
  Were found and still are fixed in thee—
And bearing still a breast so tried,
  Earth is no desart—ev'n to me.

When We Two Parted[1]

(1816; comp. 1815)

1

When we two parted
  In silence and tears,
Half broken-hearted
  To sever for years,
Pale grew thy cheek and cold,
  Colder thy kiss;
Truly that hour foretold
  Sorrow to this.

2

The dew of the morning
  Sunk chill on my brow—
It felt like the warning
  Of what I feel now.
Thy vows are all broken,
  And light is thy fame;
I hear thy name spoken,
  And share in its shame.

3

They name thee before me,
  A knell to mine ear;
A shudder comes o'er me—
  Why wert thou so dear?
They know not I knew thee,
  Who knew thee too well:—
Long, long shall I rue thee,
  Too deeply to tell.

4

In secret we met—
  In silence I grieve,
That thy heart could forget,
  Thy spirit deceive.
If I should meet thee
  After long years,
How should I greet thee!—
  With silence and tears.

Fare Thee Well[1]

(1816; comp. 1816)

Alas! they had been friends in Youth;
But whispering tongues can poison truth;
And constancy lives in realms above:
And Life is thorny; and youth is vain:
And to be wroth with one we love,
Doth work like madness in the brain:

* * * * * * * * * * * *

[1] Byron's audience would speculate, as we, upon the subject of this poem: Lady Caroline Lamb, Lady Wedderburn, Lady Byron, whether one, several, or all in part.

[1] Readers would have been certain that the subject of this poem was Lady Byron. She and Byron had separated in March 1816. Coleridge's *Christabel* had been recently published with "Kubla Khan" and "The Pains of Sleep" in May and June of 1816.

But never either found another
To free the hollow heart from paining—
They stood aloof, the scars remaining,
Like cliffs, which had been rent asunder;
A dreary sea now flows between,
But neither heat, nor frost, nor thunder
Shall wholly do away, I ween,
The marks of that which once hath been.

Coleridge's *Christabel* [408–13, 419–26].

Fare thee well! and if for ever—
  Still for ever, fare *thee well*—
Even though unforgiving, never
  'Gainst thee shall my heart rebel.—
Would that breast were bared before thee
  Where thy head so oft hath lain,
While that placid sleep came o'er thee
  Which thou ne'er can'st know again:
Would that breast by thee glanc'd over,
  Every inmost thought could show!
Then, thou would'st at last discover
  'Twas not well to spurn it so—
Though the world for this commend thee—
  Though it smile upon the blow,
Even its praises must offend thee,
  Founded on another's woe—
Though my many faults defaced me,
  Could no other arm be found
Than the one which once embraced me,
  To inflict a cureless wound!
Yet—oh, yet—thyself deceive not—
  Love may sink by slow decay,
But by sudden wrench, believe not,
  Hearts can thus be torn away;
Still thine own its life retaineth—
  Still must mine—though bleeding—beat,
And the undying thought which paineth
  Is—that we no more may meet.—
These are words of deeper sorrow
  Than the wail above the dead,
Both shall live—but every morrow
  Wake us from a widowed bed.—
And when thou wouldst solace gather—
  When our child's[2] first accents flow—
Wilt thou teach her to say—'Father!'
  Though his care she must forego?
When her little hands shall press thee—
  When her lip to thine is prest—
Think of him whose prayer shall bless thee—
  Think of him thy love had bless'd.
Should her lineaments resemble
  Those thou never more may'st see—
Then thy heart will softly tremble
  With a pulse yet true to me.—
All my faults—perchance thou knowest—
  All my madness—none can know;
All my hopes—where'er thou goest—
  Wither—yet with *thee* they go.—
Every feeling hath been shaken,
  Pride—which not a world could bow—
Bows to thee—by thee forsaken
  Even my soul forsakes me now.—
But 'tis done—all words are idle—
  Words from me are vainer still;
But the thoughts we cannot bridle
  Force their way without the will.—
Fare thee well!—thus disunited—
  Torn from every nearer tie—
Seared in heart—and lone—and blighted—
  More than this, I scarce can die.

[2] **our child:** Augusta Ada Byron, born 10 December 1815.

Childe Harold's Pilgrimage

from CANTO III
(1816; comp. 1816)

Afin que cette application vous forçât à penser à autre chose. Il n'y a en vérité de remède que celui-là et le temps. *Lettre du Roi de Prusse à D'Alembert, Sept. 7, 1776.*[1]

1

Is thy face like thy mother's, my fair child!
Ada! sole daughter of my house and heart?
When last I saw thy young blue eyes they smiled,

[1] The French epigraph reads: "So that this employment would force you to think of other things. There is in truth but this remedy and time." Letter from the king of Prussia to D'Alembert, 7 September 1776.

And then we parted, — not as now we part,
But with a hope. —
Awaking with a start,
The waters heave around me; and on high
The winds lift up their voices: I depart,
Whither I know not; but the hour's gone by,
When Albion's[2] lessening shores could grieve or glad mine eye.

2

Once more upon the waters! yet once more!
And the waves bound beneath me as a steed
That knows his rider. Welcome, to their roar!
Swift be their guidance, wheresoe'er it lead!
Though the strain'd mast should quiver as a reed,
And the rent canvas fluttering strew the gale,
Still must I on; for I am as a weed,
Flung from the rock, on Ocean's foam, to sail
Where'er the surge may sweep, or tempest's breath prevail.

3

In my youth's summer I did sing of One,
The wandering outlaw of his own dark mind;
Again I seize the theme then but begun,
And bear it with me, as the rushing wind
Bears the cloud onwards: in that Tale I find
The furrows of long thought, and dried-up tears,
Which, ebbing, leave a sterile track behind,
O'er which all heavily the journeying years
Plod the last sands of life, — where not a flower appears.

4

Since my young days of passion — joy, or pain,
Perchance my heart and harp have lost a string,
And both may jar: it may be, that in vain
I would essay,[3] as I have sung to sing.
Yet, though a dreary strain, to this I cling;
So that it wean me from the weary dream
Of selfish grief or gladness — so it fling
Forgetfulness around me — it shall seem
To me, though to none else, a not ungrateful theme.

5

He, who grown aged in this world of woe,
In deeds, not years, piercing the depths of life,
So that no wonder waits him; nor below
Can love, or sorrow, fame, ambition, strife,
Cut to his heart again with the keen knife
Of silent, sharp endurance: he can tell
Why thought seeks refuge in lone caves, yet rife
With airy images, and shapes which dwell
Still unimpair'd, though old, in the soul's haunted cell.

6

'Tis to create, and in creating live
A being more intense, that we endow
With form our fancy, gaining as we give
The life we image, even as I do now.
What am I? Nothing; but not so art thou,
Soul of my thought! with whom I traverse earth,
Invisible but gazing, as I glow
Mix'd with thy spirit, blended with thy birth,
And feeling still with thee in my crush'd feeling's dearth.

7

Yet must I think less wildly: — I *have* thought
Too long and darkly, till my brain became,
In its own eddy boiling and o'erwrought,
A whirling gulf of phantasy and flame:
And thus, untaught in youth my heart to tame,
My springs of life were poison'd. 'Tis too late!
Yet am I chang'd; though still enough the same
In strength to bear what time can not abate,
And feed on bitter fruits without accusing Fate.

8

Something too much of this: — but now 'tis past,
And the spell closes with its silent seal.
Long absent Harold re-appears at last;
He of the breast which fain no more would feel,
Wrung with the wounds which kill not, but ne'er heal;
Yet Time, who changes all, had altered him
In soul and aspect as in age: years steal
Fire from the mind as vigour from the limb;
And life's enchanted cup but sparkles near the brim.

---

[2] **Ada:** Byron's daughter by Lady Byron, b. 10 December 1815. **Albion:** England.

[3] **essay:** to attempt.

9

His had been quaff'd too quickly, and he found
The dregs were wormwood;[4] but he fill'd again,
And from a purer fount, on holier ground,
And deem'd its spring perpetual; but in vain!
Still round him clung invisibly a chain
Which gall'd for ever, fettering though unseen,
And heavy though it clank'd not; worn with pain,
Which pined although it spoke not, and grew keen,
Entering with every step, he took, through many a scene.

10

Secure in guarded coldness, he had mix'd
Again in fancied safety with his kind,
And deem'd his spirit now so firmly fix'd
And sheath'd with an invulnerable mind,
That, if no joy, no sorrow lurk'd behind;
And he, as one, might midst the many stand
Unheeded, searching through the crowd to find
Fit speculation! such as in strange land
He found in wonder-works of God and Nature's hand.

11

But who can view the ripened rose, nor seek
To wear it? who can curiously behold
The smoothness and the sheen of beauty's cheek,
Nor feel the heart can never all grow old?
Who can contemplate Fame through clouds unfold
The star which rises o'er her steep, nor climb?
Harold, once more within the vortex, roll'd
On with the giddy circle, chasing Time,
Yet with a nobler aim than in his youth's fond prime.

12

But soon he knew himself the most unfit
Of men to herd with Man; with whom he held
Little in common; untaught to submit
His thoughts to others, though his soul was quell'd
In youth by his own thoughts; still uncompell'd,
He would not yield dominion of his mind
To spirits against whom his own rebell'd;
Proud though in desolation; which could find
A life within itself, to breathe without mankind.

[4] **quaff:** to drink heartily. **wormwood:** a bitter substance.

13

Where rose the mountains, there to him were friends;
Where roll'd the ocean, thereon was his home;
Where a blue sky, and glowing clime, extends,
He had the passion and the power to roam;
The desert, forest, cavern, breaker's foam,
Were unto him companionship; they spake
A mutual language, clearer than the tome
Of his land's tongue, which he would oft forsake
For Nature's pages glass'd by sunbeams on the lake.

14

Like the Chaldean,[5] he could watch the stars,
Till he had peopled them with beings bright
As their own beams; and earth, and earth-born jars,
And human frailties, were forgotten quite:
Could he have kept his spirit to that flight
He had been happy; but this clay will sink
Its spark immortal, envying it the light
To which it mounts, as if to break the link
That keeps us from yon heaven which woos us to its brink.

15

But in Man's dwellings he became a thing
Restless and worn, and stern and wearisome,
Droop'd as a wild-born falcon with clipt wing,
To whom the boundless air alone were home:
Then came his fit again, which to o'ercome,
As eagerly the barr'd-up bird will beat
His breast and beak against his wiry dome
Till the blood tinge his plumage, so the heat
Of his impeded soul would through his bosom eat.

16

Self-exiled Harold wanders forth again,
With nought of hope left, but with less of gloom;
The very knowledge that he lived in vain,
That all was over on this side the tomb,

[5] **Chaldean:** possibly Julianus "the Chaldaean," who composed the Chaldaen Oracles (*Oxford Classical Dictionary*). Generally, Chaldeans were an ancient people of Babylonia noted for occult and astrological learning.

Had made Despair a smilingness assume,
Which, though 'twere wild,—as on the plundered wreck
When mariners would madly meet their doom
With draughts intemperate on the sinking deck,—
Did yet inspire a cheer, which he forbore to check.

17

Stop!—for thy tread is on an Empire's dust!
An Earthquake's spoil is sepulchred below!
Is the spot mark'd with no colossal bust?
Nor column trophied for triumphal show?
None; but the moral's truth tells simpler so,
As the ground was before, thus let it be;—
How that red rain hath made the harvest grow!
And is this all the world has gained by thee,
Thou first and last of fields! king-making Victory?

18

And Harold stands upon this place of skulls,
The grave of France, the deadly Waterloo!
How in an hour the power which gave annuls
Its gifts, transferring fame as fleeting too!
In 'pride of place'[6] here last the eagle flew,
Then tore with bloody talon the rent plain,
Pierced by the shaft of banded nations through;
Ambition's life and labours all were vain;
He wears the shattered links of the world's broken chain.

19

Fit retribution! Gaul may champ the bit
And foam in fetters;—but is Earth more free?
Did nations combat to make *One* submit;
Or league to teach all kings true sovereignty?
What! shall reviving Thraldom again be
The patched-up idol of enlightened days?
Shall we, who struck the Lion down, shall we
Pay the Wolf homage? proffering lowly gaze
And servile knees to thrones? No; *prove* before ye praise!

20

If not, o'er one fallen despot boast no more!
In vain fair cheeks were furrowed with hot tears
For Europe's flowers long rooted up before
The trampler of her vineyards; in vain years
Of death, depopulation, bondage, fears,
Have all been borne, and broken by the accord
Of roused-up millions: all that most endears
Glory, is when the myrtle wreathes a sword
Such as Harmodius[7] drew on Athens' tyrant lord.

21

There was a sound of revelry by night,[8]
And Belgium's capital had gathered then
Her Beauty and her Chivalry, and bright
The lamps shone o'er fair women and brave men;
A thousand hearts beat happily; and when
Music arose with its voluptuous swell,
Soft eyes look'd love to eyes which spake again,
And all went merry as a marriage-bell;
But hush! hark! a deep sound strikes like a rising knell!

22

Did ye not hear it?—No; 'twas but the wind,
Or the car rattling o'er the stony street;
On with the dance! let joy be unconfined;
No sleep till morn, when Youth and Pleasure meet
To chase the glowing Hours with flying feet—
But, hark!—that heavy sound breaks in once more,

---

[6] **'pride of place'**: A term of falconry, meaning the highest pitch of flight.—See *Macbeth*, etc. (Byron's note). The eagle is a reference to Napoleon; the "shaft of banded nations" are the allied forces. A contemporary cartoon of the Battle of Waterloo in the British Museum shows Napoleon, crown flying off, his sceptre broken and falling, riding a wounded imperial eagle above the battle, and exclaiming: "Run my boys your Emperor leads the way—My dear Eagle only conduct me safe to Paris this time as you did from Moscow & Leipsig & I"ll never trouble you again—Oh d—d that Wellington." See The French Revolution and Rights of Man and the Comprehensive Chronology.

[7] **Harmodius**: in 514 BC took the life of the Athenian tyrant Hipparchus with a dagger concealed in a myrtle branch. Since antiquity, the myrtle has been the symbol of love (because sacred to Aphrodite), immortality (for being ever green), and, in contrast with laurel, which was the symbol of victory after bloody battles, the myrtle signified a bloodless victory.

[8] **. . . revelry by night**: reference to a well-known ball given in Brussels by the Duchess of Richmond on the eve of the Battle of Quatre-bras, 15 June 1815, between Napoleon's forces and the allied Prussian and British forces. Napoleon was defeated at the Battle of Waterloo, 18 June 1815.

As if the clouds its echo would repeat;
And nearer, clearer, deadlier than before!
Arm! Arm! and out—it is—the cannon's opening roar!

23

Within a windowed niche of that high hall
Sate Brunswick's fated chieftain;[9] he did hear
That sound the first amidst the festival,
And caught its tone with Death's prophetic ear;
And when they smiled because he deem'd it near,
His heart more truly knew that peal too well
Which stretch'd his father on a bloody bier,[10]
And roused the vengeance blood alone could quell:
He rush'd into the field, and, foremost fighting, fell.

24

Ah! then and there was hurrying to and fro,
And gathering tears, and tremblings of distress,
And cheeks all pale, which but an hour ago
Blush'd at the praise of their own loveliness;
And there were sudden partings, such as press
The life from out young hearts, and choking sighs
Which ne'er might be repeated; who could guess
If ever more should meet those mutual eyes,
Since upon nights so sweet such awful morn could rise?

25

And there was mounting in hot haste: the steed,
The mustering squadron, and the clattering car,[11]
Went pouring forward in impetuous speed,
And swiftly forming in the ranks of war;
And the deep thunder peal on peal afar;
And near, the beat of the alarming drum
Roused up the soldier ere the morning star;
While throng'd the citizens with terror dumb,
Or whispering, with white lips—'The foe! They come! they come!'

26

And wild and high the 'Cameron's gathering'[12] rose!
The war-note of Lochiel, which Albyn's hills
Have heard, and heard, too, have her Saxon foes:—
How in the noon of night that pibroch[13] thrills,
Savage and shrill! But with the breath which fills
Their mountain-pipe, so fill the mountaineers
With the fierce native daring which instils
The stirring memory of a thousand years,
And Evan's, Donald's fame rings in each clansman's ears!

27

And Ardennes[14] waves above them her green leaves,
Dewy with nature's tear-drops, as they pass,
Grieving, if aught inanimate e'er grieves,
Over the unreturning brave,—alas!
Ere evening to be trodden like the grass
Which now beneath them, but above shall grow
In its next verdure, when this fiery mass
Of living valour, rolling on the foe
And burning with high hope, shall moulder cold and low.

28

Last noon beheld them full of lusty life,
Last eve in Beauty's circle proudly gay,
The midnight brought the signal-sound of strife,
The morn the marshalling in arms,—the day
Battle's magnificently-stern array!
The thunder-clouds close o'er it, which when rent
The earth is covered thick with other clay,
Which her own clay shall cover, heaped and pent,
Rider and horse,—friend, foe,—in one red burial blent!

---

[9] **Brunswick's fated chieftain:** Frederick William, the German Duke of Brunswick (1771–1815) was killed at Quatre-Bras.

[10] **stretched . . . bloody bier:** Frederick's father had been killed in the crushing defeat suffered by Prussian forces at the Battle of Auerstadt in October 1806.

[11] **car:** carriage.

[12] **'Cameron's gathering':** the war song of the Scottish Cameron Clan. Past chiefs, Evan fought for James II in 1689 against Cromwell, and Donald had fought for James Stuart, the Young Pretender, in the mid-eighteenth century.

[13] **pibroch:** war song for the bagpipe.

[14] **Ardennes:** the forested plateau of northern France, southeastern Belgium, and Luxembourg, where important battles of twentieth-century wars also occurred, especially the Battle of the Bulge of World War II.

29

Their praise is hymn'd by loftier harps than mine,
Yet one I would select from that proud throng,
Partly because they blend me with his line,
And partly that I did his sire some wrong,
And partly that bright names will hallow song;
And his was of the bravest, and when shower'd
The death-bolts deadliest the thinn'd files along,
Even where the thickest of war's tempest lower'd,
They reach'd no nobler breast than thine, young, gallant Howard![15]

30

There have been tears and breaking hearts for thee,
And mine were nothing, had I such to give;
But when I stood beneath the fresh green tree,
Which living waves where thou didst cease to live,
And saw around me the wide field revive
With fruits and fertile promise, and the Spring
Come forth her work of gladness to contrive,
With all her reckless birds upon the wing,
I turn'd from all she brought to those she could not bring.

31

I turn'd to thee, to thousands, of whom each
And one as all a ghastly gap did make
In his own kind and kindred, whom to teach
Forgetfulness were mercy for their sake;
The Archangel's trump,[16] not Glory's, must awake
Those whom they thirst for; though the sound of Fame
May for a moment soothe, it cannot slake
The fever of vain longing, and the name
So honoured but assumes a stronger, bitterer claim.

32

They mourn, but smile at length; and, smiling, mourn:
The tree will wither long before it fall;
The hull drives on, though mast and sail be torn;
The roof-tree sinks, but moulders on the hall
In massy hoariness; the ruined wall
Stands when its wind-worn battlements are gone;
The bars survive the captive they enthral;
The day drags through though storms keep out the sun;
And thus the heart will break, yet brokenly live on:

33

Even as a broken mirror, which the glass
In every fragment multiplies; and makes
A thousand images of one that was,
The same, and still the more, the more it breaks;
And thus the heart will do which not forsakes,
Living in shattered guise, and still, and cold,
And bloodless, with its sleepless sorrow aches,
Yet withers on till all without is old,
Shewing no visible sign, for such things are untold.

34

There is a very life in our despair,
Vitality of poison,—a quick root
Which feeds these deadly branches; for it were
As nothing did we die; but Life will suit
Itself to Sorrow's most detested fruit,
Like to the apples on the Dead Sea's shore,[17]
All ashes to the taste: Did man compute
Existence by enjoyment, and count o'er
Such hours 'gainst years of life,—say, would he name three-score?

35

The Psalmist[18] numbered out the years of man:
They are enough; and if thy tale be *true*,

[15] **Howard:** Frederick Howard (1785–1815), Byron's cousin, was killed at Waterloo. With reference to line 256, Byron had satirized Howard's father, the Earl of Carlisle, in *English Bards and Scotch Reviewers* (ll. 725ff), for writing dull verse: "So dull in youth, so drivelling in his age, / His scenes alone had damned our sinking stage" (ll. 734–35).

[16] **Archangel's trump:** the trumpet of the Apocalypse, which would raise the dead; cf. Corinthians 15:52.

[17] **the apples . . . shore:** "The (Fabled) apples on the brink of the lake Asphaltes were said to be fair without, and within ashes." [L.B.]

[18] **Psalmist:** Cf. Psalms 90:10: "The days of our years are threescore years and ten; and if by reason of strength they be fourscore years, yet is their strength labour and sorrow; for it is soon cut off, and we fly away."

Thou, who didst grudge him even that fleeting
span,
More than enough, thou fatal Waterloo!
Millions of tongues record thee, and anew
Their children's lips shall echo them, and say—
'Here, where the sword united nations drew,
Our countrymen were warring on that day!'
And this is much, and all which will not pass away.

36

There sunk the greatest, nor the worst of men,
Whose spirit antithetically mixt
One moment of the mightiest, and again
On little objects with like firmness fixt,
Extreme in all things! hadst thou been betwixt,
Thy throne had still been thine, or never been;
For daring made thy rise as fall: thou seek'st
Even now to re-assume the imperial mien,
And shake again the world, the Thunderer of the
scene!

37

Conqueror and captive of the earth art thou!
She trembles at thee still, and thy wild name
Was ne'er more bruited in men's minds than now
That thou art nothing, save the jest of Fame,
Who wooed thee once, thy vassal, and became
The flatterer of thy fierceness, till thou wert
A god unto thyself; nor less the same
To the astounded kingdoms all inert,
Who deem'd thee for a time whate'er thou didst
assert.

38

Oh, more or less than man—in high or low,
Battling with nations, flying from the field;
Now making monarchs' necks thy footstool, now
More than thy meanest soldier taught to yield;
An empire thou couldst crush, command, rebuild,
But govern not thy pettiest passion, nor,
However deeply in men's spirits skill'd,
Look through thine own, nor curb the lust of war,
Nor learn that tempted Fate will leave the loftiest star.

39

Yet well thy soul hath brook'd the turning tide
With that untaught innate philosophy,
Which, be it wisdom, coldness, or deep pride,
Is gall and wormwood to an enemy.
When the whole host of hatred stood hard by,
To watch and mock thee shrinking, thou hast
smiled
With a sedate and all-enduring eye;—
When Fortune fled her spoil'd and favourite child,
He stood unbowed beneath the ills upon him piled.

40

Sager than in thy fortunes; for in them
Ambition steel'd thee on too far to show
That just habitual scorn which could contemn
Men and their thoughts; 'twas wise to feel, not so
To wear it ever on thy lip and brow,
And spurn the instruments thou wert to use
Till they were turn'd unto thine overthrow:
'Tis but a worthless world to win or lose;
So hath it proved to thee, and all such lot who
choose.

41

If, like a tower upon a headlong rock,
Thou hadst been made to stand or fall alone,
Such scorn of man had help'd to brave the shock;
But men's thoughts were the steps which paved thy
throne,
Their admiration thy best weapon shone;
The part of Philip's son was thine, not then
(Unless aside thy purple had been thrown)
Like stern Diogenes[19] to mock at men;
For sceptred cynics earth were far too wide a den.

42

But quiet to quick bosoms is a hell,
And *there* hath been thy bane; there is a fire
And motion of the soul which will not dwell
In its own narrow being, but aspire
Beyond the fitting medium of desire;
And, but once kindled, quenchless evermore,
Preys upon high adventure, nor can tire
Of aught but rest; a fever at the core,
Fatal to him who bears, to all who ever bore.

[19] **Philip's son:** Alexander the Great (356–323 BC). **Diogenes:** the Greek Cynic philosopher (d. c. 320 BC) who was said to have gone through the streets with a lantern, looking for an honest man.

43

This makes the madmen who have made men mad
By their contagion; Conquerors and Kings,
Founders of sects and systems, to whom add
Sophists,[20] Bards, Statesmen, all unquiet things
Which stir too strongly the soul's secret springs,
And are themselves the fools to those they fool;
Envied, yet how unenviable! what stings
Are theirs! One breast laid open were a school
Which would unteach mankind the lust to shine or rule:

44

Their breath is agitation, and their life
A storm whereon they ride, to sink at last,
And yet so nurs'd and bigotted to strife,
That should their days, surviving perils past,
Melt to calm twilight, they feel overcast
With sorrow and supineness, and so die;
Even as a flame unfed, which runs to waste
With its own flickering, or a sword laid by
Which eats into itself, and rusts ingloriously.

45

He who ascends to mountain-tops, shall find
The loftiest peaks most wrapt in clouds and snow;
He who surpasses or subdues mankind,
Must look down on the hate of those below.
Though high *above* the sun of glory glow,
And far *beneath* the earth and ocean spread,
Round him are icy rocks, and loudly blow
Contending tempests on his naked head,
And thus reward the toils which to those summits led.

46

Away with these! true Wisdom's world will be
Within its own creation, or in thine,
Maternal Nature! for who teems like thee,
Thus on the banks of thy majestic Rhine?
There Harold gazes on a work divine,
A blending of all beauties; streams and dells,
Fruit, foliage, crag, wood, cornfield, mountain, vine,
And chiefless castles breathing stern farewells
From gray but leafy walls, where Ruin greenly dwells.

[20] **Sophists:** philosophers and thinkers. Sophists were hired teachers of philosophy and rhetoric in Athens c. mid-fifteenth century BC.

47

And there they stand, as stands a lofty mind,
Worn, but unstooping to the baser crowd,
All tenantless, save to the crannying wind,
Or holding dark communion with the cloud.
There was a day when they were young and proud,
Banners on high, and battles pass'd below;
But they who fought are in a bloody shroud,
And those which waved are shredless dust ere now,
And the bleak battlements shall bear no future blow.

48

Beneath these battlements, within those walls,
Power dwelt amidst her passions; in proud state
Each robber chief upheld his armed halls,
Doing his evil will, nor less elate
Than mightier heroes of a longer date.
What want these outlaws conquerors should have
But History's purchased page to call them great?
A wider space, an ornamented grave?
Their hopes were not less warm, their souls were full as brave.

49

In their baronial feuds and single fields,
What deeds of prowess unrecorded died!
And Love, which lent a blazon to their shields,
With emblems well devised by amorous pride,
Through all the mail of iron hearts would glide;
But still their flame was fierceness, and drew on
Keen contest and destruction near allied,
And many a tower for some fair mischief won,
Saw the discoloured Rhine beneath its ruin run.

50

But Thou, exulting and abounding river!
Making thy waves a blessing as they flow
Through banks whose beauty would endure for ever
Could man but leave thy bright creation so,
Nor its fair promise from the surface mow
With the sharp scythe of conflict,—then to see
Thy valley of sweet waters, were to know
Earth paved like Heaven; and to seem such to me
Even now what wants thy stream?—that it should Lethe[21] be.

[21] **Lethe:** the river of forgetfulness in the classical underworld.

51

A thousand battles have assail'd thy banks,
But these and half their fame have pass'd away,
And Slaughter heap'd on high his weltering ranks;
Their very graves are gone, and what are they?
Thy tide wash'd down the blood of yesterday,
And all was stainless, and on thy clear stream
Glass'd with its dancing light the sunny ray;
But o'er the blackened memory's blighting dream
Thy waves would vainly roll, all sweeping as they seem.

52

Thus Harold inly said, and pass'd along,
Yet not insensibly to all which here
Awoke the jocund birds to early song
In glens which might have made even exile dear:
Though on his brow were graven lines austere,
And tranquil sternness which had ta'en the place
Of feelings fierier far but less severe,
Joy was not always absent from his face,
But o'er it in such scenes would steal with transient trace.

53

Nor was all love shut from him, though his days
Of passion had consumed themselves to dust.
It is in vain that we would coldly gaze
On such as smile upon us; the heart must
Leap kindly back to kindness, though disgust
Hath wean'd it from all worldlings: thus he felt,
For there was soft remembrance, and sweet trust
In one fond breast, to which his own would melt,
And in its tenderer hour on that his bosom dwelt.

54

And he had learn'd to love,—I know not why,
For this in such as him seems strange of mood,—
The helpless looks of blooming infancy,
Even in its earliest nurture; what subdued,
To change like this, a mind so far imbued
With scorn of man, it little boots[22] to know;
But thus it was; and though in solitude
Small power the nipp'd affections have to grow,
In him this glowed when all beside had ceased to glow.

[22] **boots:** helps.

55

And there was one soft breast, as hath been said,
Which unto his was bound by stronger ties
Than the church links withal; and, though unwed,
That love was pure, and, far above disguise,
Had stood the test of mortal enmities
Still undivided, and cemented more
By peril, dreaded most in female eyes;
But this was firm, and from a foreign shore
Well to that heart might his these absent greetings pour!

1

The castled crag of Drachenfels[23]
Frowns o'er the wide and winding Rhine,
Whose breast of waters broadly swells
Between the banks which bear the vine,
And hills all rich with blossomed trees,
And fields which promise corn and wine,
And scattered cities crowning these,
Whose far white walls along them shine,
Have strewed a scene, which I should see
With double joy wert *thou*[24] with me!

2

And peasant girls, with deep blue eyes,
And hands which offer early flowers,
Walk smiling o'er this paradise;
Above, the frequent feudal towers
Through green leaves lift their walls of grey,
And many a rock which steeply lours,
And noble arch in proud decay,
Look o'er this vale of vintage-bowers;
But one thing want these banks of Rhine,—
Thy gentle hand to clasp in mine!

3

I send the lilies given to me;
Though long before thy hand they touch,
I know that they must withered be,
But yet reject them not as such;
For I have cherish'd them as dear,
Because they yet may meet thine eye,
And guide thy soul to mine even here,

[23] **Drachenfels:** castle on the hills above the Rhine River.

[24] **thou:** it is possible that Byron's reference to his half-sister Augusta would be recognized by his readers.

When thou behold'st them drooping nigh,
And knowst them gathered by the Rhine,
And offered from my heart to thine!

4

The river nobly foams and flows,
The charm of this enchanted ground,
And all its thousand turns disclose
Some fresher beauty varying round;
The haughtiest breast its wish might bound
Through life to dwell delighted here;
Nor could on earth a spot be found
To nature and to me so dear,
Could thy dear eyes in following mine
Still sweeten more these banks of Rhine!

56

By Coblentz,[25] on a rise of gentle ground,
There is a small and simple pyramid,
Crowning the summit of the verdant mound;
Beneath its base are heroes' ashes hid,
Our enemy's,—but let not that forbid
Honour to Marceau![26] o'er whose early tomb
Tears, big tears, gush'd from the rough soldier's lid,
Lamenting and yet envying such a doom,
Falling for France, whose rights he battled to resume.

57

Brief, brave, and glorious was his young career,—
His mourners were two hosts, his friends and foes;
And fitly may the stranger lingering here
Pray for his gallant spirit's bright repose;
For he was Freedom's champion, one of those,
The few in number, who had not o'erstept
The charter to chastise which she bestows
On such as wield her weapons; he had kept
The whiteness of his soul, and thus men o'er him
wept.

58

Here Ehrenbreitstein,[27] with her shattered wall
Black with the miner's blast, upon her height
Yet shows of what she was, when shell and ball
Rebounding idly on her strength did light;
A tower of victory! from whence the flight
Of baffled foes was watch'd along the plain:
But Peace destroy'd what War could never blight,
And laid those proud roofs bare to Summer's rain—
On which the iron shower for years had pour'd in
vain.

59

Adieu to thee, fair Rhine! How long delighted
The stranger fain would linger on his way!
Thine is a scene alike where souls united
Or lonely Contemplation thus might stray;
And could the ceaseless vultures cease to prey
On self-condemning bosoms, it were here,
Where Nature, nor too sombre nor too gay,
Wild but not rude, awful yet not austere,
Is to the mellow Earth as Autumn to the year.

60

Adieu to thee again! a vain adieu!
There can be no farewell to scene like thine;
The mind is coloured by thy every hue;
And if reluctantly the eyes resign
Their cherish'd gaze upon thee, lovely Rhine!
'Tis with the thankful glance of parting praise;
More mighty spots may rise—more glaring shine,
But none unite in one attaching maze
The brilliant, fair, and soft,—the glories of old days,

61

The negligently grand, the fruitful bloom
Of coming ripeness, the white city's sheen,
The rolling stream, the precipice's gloom,
The forest's growth, and Gothic walls between,
The wild rocks shaped as they had turrets been
In mockery of man's art; and these withal

[25] **Coblentz:** a town on the Rhine about 30 miles southeast of Bonn.

[26] **Marceau:** François Séverin Marceau-Desgraviers (1769–1796), French general who distinguished himself in fighting along the Rhine, where he died.

[27] **Ehrenbreitstein:** "'the broad Stone of Honour,' one of the strongest fortresses in Europe, was dismantled and blown up by the French at the truce of Leoben" [1797] [L.B.]. The castle was actually destroyed by the French in 1801.

A race of faces happy as the scene,
Whose fertile bounties here extend to all,
Still springing o'er thy banks, though Empires near them fall.

62

But these recede. Above me are the Alps,
The palaces of Nature, whose vast walls
Have pinnacled in clouds their snowy scalps,
And throned Eternity in icy halls
Of cold sublimity, where forms and falls
The avalanche — the thunderbolt of snow!
All which expands the spirit, yet appals,
Gather around these summits, as to show
How Earth may pierce to Heaven, yet leave vain man below.

. . . .

68

Lake Leman[28] woos me with its crystal face,
The mirror where the stars and mountains view
The stillness of their aspect in each trace
Its clear depth yields of their far height and hue:
There is too much of man here, to look through
With a fit mind the might which I behold;
But soon in me shall Loneliness renew
Thoughts hid, but not less cherish'd than of old,
Ere mingling with the herd had penn'd me in their fold.

69

To fly from, need not be to hate, mankind;
All are not fit with them to stir and toil,
Nor is it discontent to keep the mind
Deep in its fountain, lest it overboil
In the hot throng, where we become the spoil
Of our infection, till too late and long
We may deplore and struggle with the coil,
In wretched interchange of wrong for wrong
'Midst a contentious world, striving where none are strong.

70

There, in a moment, we may plunge our years
In fatal penitence, and in the blight
Of our own soul, turn all our blood to tears,
And colour things to come with hues of Night;
The race of life becomes a hopeless flight
To those that walk in darkness: on the sea,
The boldest steer but where their ports invite,
But there are wanderers o'er Eternity
Whose bark drives on and on, and anchored ne'er shall be.

71

Is it not better, then, to be alone,
And love Earth only for its earthly sake?
By the blue rushing of the arrowy Rhone,[29]
Or the pure bosom of its nursing lake,
Which feeds it as a mother who doth make
A fair but froward infant her own care,
Kissing its cries away as these awake; —
Is it not better thus our lives to wear,
Than join the crushing crowd, doom'd to inflict or bear?

72

I live not in myself, but I become
Portion of that around me; and to me,
High mountains are a feeling, but the hum
Of human cities torture: I can see
Nothing to loathe in nature, save to be
A link reluctant in a fleshly chain,
Class'd among creatures, when the soul can flee,
And with the sky, the peak, the heaving plain
Of ocean, or the stars, mingle, and not in vain.

73

And thus I am absorb'd, and this is life:
I look upon the peopled desert past,
As on a place of agony and strife,
Where, for some sin, to Sorrow I was cast,
To act and suffer, but remount at last
With a fresh pinion;[30] which I feel to spring,
Though young, yet waxing vigorous, as the blast
Which it would cope with, on delighted wing,
Spurning the clay-cold bonds which round our being cling.

[28] **Lake Leman**: also known as Lake Geneva.

[29] **Rhone**: one of the rivers draining into (and out of) Lake Geneva.

[30] **pinion**: wing.

74

And when, at length, the mind shall be all free
From what it hates in this degraded form,
Reft of its carnal life, save what shall be
Existent happier in the fly and worm,—
When elements to elements conform,
And dust is as it should be, shall I not
Feel all I see, less dazzling, but more warm?
The bodiless thought? the Spirit of each spot?
Of which, even now, I share at times the immortal lot?

75

Are not the mountains, waves, and skies, a part
Of me and of my soul, as I of them?
Is not the love of these deep in my heart
With a pure passion? should I not contemn
All objects, if compared with these? and stem
A tide of suffering, rather than forego
Such feelings for the hard and worldly phlegm
Of those whose eyes are only turn'd below,
Gazing upon the ground, with thoughts which dare not glow?

76

But this is not my theme; and I return
To that which is immediate, and require
Those who find contemplation in the urn,
To look on One, whose dust was once all fire,
A native of the land where I respire
The clear air for a while—a passing guest,
Where he became a being,—whose desire
Was to be glorious; 'twas a foolish quest,
The which to gain and keep, he sacrificed all rest.

77

Here the self-torturing sophist, wild Rousseau,[31]
The apostle of affliction, he who threw
Enchantment over passion, and from woe
Wrung overwhelming eloquence, first drew
The breath which made him wretched; yet he knew
How to make madness beautiful, and cast
O'er erring deeds and thoughts, a heavenly hue
Of words, like sunbeams, dazzling as they past
The eyes, which o'er them shed tears feelingly and fast.

78

His love was passion's essence—as a tree
On fire by lightning; with ethereal flame
Kindled he was, and blasted; for to be
Thus, and enamoured, were in him the same.
But his was not the love of living dame,
Nor of the dead who rise upon our dreams,
But of ideal beauty, which became
In him existence, and o'erflowing teems
Along his burning page, distempered though it seems.

79

This breathed itself to life in Júlie, *this*
Invested her with all that's wild and sweet;
This hallowed, too, the memorable kiss
Which every morn his fevered lip would greet,
From hers,[32] who but with friendship his would meet;
But to that gentle touch, through brain and breast
Flash'd the thrill'd spirit's love-devouring heat;
In that absorbing sigh perchance more blest,
Than vulgar minds may be with all they seek possest.

80

His life was one long war with self-sought foes,
Or friends by him self-banish'd; for his mind
Had grown Suspicion's sanctuary, and chose
For its own cruel sacrifice, the kind,
'Gainst whom he raged with fury strange and blind.
But he was phrenzied,—wherefore, who may know?

[31] **Rousseau**: French writer and philosopher Jean-Jacques Rousseau (1712–1778), born in Geneva, whose epistolary novel *Julie, ou la nouvelle Héloïse* (1761), was also set in the area.

[32] **hers**: this refers to the account in his [Rousseau's] 'Confessions' of his passion for the Comtesse d'Houdetot . . . and his long walk every morning for the sake of the single kiss which was the common salutation of French acquaintance. Rousseau's description of his feelings on this occasion may be considered as the most passionate, yet not impure description and expression of love that ever kindled into words; which after all must be felt, from their very force, to be inadequate to the delineation: a painting can give no sufficient idea of the ocean. [L.B.]

Since cause might be which skill could never find;
But he was phrenzied by disease or woe,
To that worst pitch of all, which wears a reasoning show.

81

For then he was inspired, and from him came,
As from the Pythian's mystic cave of yore,[33]
Those oracles which set the world in flame,
Nor ceased to burn till kingdoms were no more:
Did he not this for France? which lay before
Bowed to the inborn tyranny of years?
Broken and trembling, to the yoke she bore,
Till by the voice of him and his compeers,
Roused up to too much wrath which follows o'ergrown fears?

82

They made themselves a fearful monument!
The wreck of old opinions — things which grew
Breathed from the birth of time: the veil they rent,
And what behind it lay, all earth shall view.
But good with ill they also overthrew,
Leaving but ruins, wherewith to rebuild
Upon the same foundation, and renew
Dungeons and thrones, which the same hour re-fill'd,
As heretofore, because ambition was self-will'd.

83

But this will not endure, nor be endured!
Mankind have felt their strength, and made it felt.
They might have used it better, but, allured
By their new vigour, sternly have they dealt
On one another; pity ceased to melt
With her once natural charities. But they,
Who in oppression's darkness caved had dwelt,
They were not eagles, nourish'd with the day;
What marvel then, at times, if they mistook their prey?

84

What deep wounds ever closed without a scar?
The heart's bleed longest, and but heal to wear
That which disfigures it; and they who war
With their own hopes, and have been vanquish'd, bear
Silence, but not submission: in his lair
Fix'd Passion holds his breath, until the hour
Which shall atone for years; none need despair:
It came, it cometh, and will come, — the power
To punish or forgive — in *one* we shall be slower.

85

Clear, placid Leman! thy contrasted lake,
With the wild world I dwelt in, is a thing
Which warns me, with its stillness, to forsake
Earth's troubled waters for a purer spring.
This quiet sail is as a noiseless wing
To waft me from distraction; once I loved
Torn ocean's roar, but thy soft murmuring
Sounds sweet as if a sister's voice reproved,
That I with stern delights should e'er have been so moved.

86

It is the hush of night, and all between
Thy margin and the mountains, dusk, yet clear,
Mellowed and mingling, yet distinctly seen,
Save darken'd Jura,[34] whose capt heights appear
Precipitously steep; and drawing near,
There breathes a living fragrance from the shore,
Of flowers yet fresh with childhood; on the ear
Drops the light drip of the suspended oar,
Or chirps the grasshopper one good-night carol more;

87

He is an evening reveller, who makes
His life an infancy, and sings his fill;
At intervals, some bird from out the brakes,
Starts into voice a moment, then is still.
There seems a floating whisper on the hill,
But that is fancy, for the starlight dews
All silently their tears of love instil,
Weeping themselves away, till they infuse
Deep into Nature's breast the spirit of her hues.

88

Ye stars! which are the poetry of heaven!
If in your bright leaves we would read the fate

[33] **Pythian's mystic cave . . . :** the oracle of Apollo at Delphi.

[34] **Jura:** mountain range northwest of Lake Geneva.

Of men and empires,—'tis to be forgiven,
That in our aspirations to be great,
Our destinies o'erleap their mortal state,
And claim a kindred with you; for ye are
A beauty and a mystery, and create
In us such love and reverence from afar,
That fortune, fame, power, life, have named themselves a star.

89

All heaven and earth are still—though not in sleep,
But breathless, as we grow when feeling most;
And silent, as we stand in thoughts too deep:—
All heaven and earth are still: From the high host
Of stars, to the lull'd lake and mountain-coast,
All is concentered in a life intense,
Where not a beam, nor air, nor leaf is lost,
But hath a part of being, and a sense
Of that which is of all Creator and defence.

90

Then stirs the feeling infinite, so felt
In solitude, where we are *least* alone;
A truth, which through our being then doth melt
And purifies from self: it is a tone,
The soul and source of music, which makes known
Eternal harmony, and sheds a charm,
Like to the fabled Cytherea's zone,[35]
Binding all things with beauty;—'twould disarm
The spectre Death, had he substantial power to harm.

91

Not vainly did the early Persian make
His altar[36] the high places and the peak
Of earth-o'ergazing mountains, and thus take
A fit and unwall'd temple, there to seek
The Spirit, in whose honour shrines are weak,
Uprear'd of human hands. Come, and compare
Columns and idol-dwellings, Goth or Greek,
With Nature's realms of worship, earth and air,
Nor fix on fond abodes to circumscribe thy prayer!

92

The sky is changed!—and such a change! Oh night,
And storm, and darkness, ye are wondrous strong,
Yet lovely in your strength, as is the light
Of a dark eye in woman! Far along,
From peak to peak, the rattling crags among
Leaps the live thunder! Not from one lone cloud,
But every mountain now hath found a tongue,
And Jura answers, through her misty shroud,
Back to the joyous Alps, who call to her aloud!

93

And this is in the night:—Most glorious night!
Thou wert not sent for slumber! let me be
A sharer in thy fierce and far delight,—
A portion of the tempest and of thee!
How the lit lake shines, a phosphoric sea,
And the big rain comes dancing to the earth!
And now again 'tis black,—and now, the glee
Of the loud hills shakes with its mountain-mirth,
As if they did rejoice o'er a young earthquake's birth.

94

Now, where the swift Rhone cleaves his way between
Heights which appear as lovers who have parted
In hate, whose mining depths so intervene,
That they can meet no more, though broken-hearted;
Though in their souls, which thus each other thwarted,
Love was the very root of the fond rage
Which blighted their life's bloom, and then departed:—
Itself expired, but leaving them an age
Of years all winters,—war within themselves to wage.

95

Now, where the quick Rhone thus hath cleft his way,
The mightiest of the storms hath ta'en his stand:
For here, not one, but many, make their play,
And fling their thunder-bolts from hand to hand,
Flashing and cast around: of all the band,
The brightest through these parted hills hath fork'd

---

[35] **Cytherea's zone:** Venus's mantle aroused love in those who wore it.

[36] **His altar:** reference to the Zoroastrian religion, which held that there were two spirits ruling the universe, Ahura-Mazda, the spirit of light and good, and Ahriman, the spirit of evil and darkness.

His lightnings,—as if he did understand,
That in such gaps as desolation work'd,
There the hot shaft should blast whatever therein
lurk'd.

96

Sky, mountains, river, winds, lake, lightnings! ye!
With night, and clouds, and thunder, and a soul
To make these felt and feeling, well may be
Things that have made me watchful; the far roll
Of your departing voices, is the knoll
Of what in me is sleepless,—if I rest.
But where of ye, oh tempests! is the goal?
Are ye like those within the human breast?
Or do ye find, at length, like eagles, some high nest?

97

Could I embody and unbosom now
That which is most within me,—could I wreak
My thoughts upon expression, and thus throw
Soul, heart, mind, passions, feelings, strong or
weak,
All that I would have sought, and all I seek,
Bear, know, feel, and yet breathe—into *one* word,
And that one word were Lightning, I would speak;
But as it is, I live and die unheard,
With a most voiceless thought, sheathing it as a
sword.

98

The morn is up again, the dewy morn,
With breath all incense, and with cheek all bloom,
Laughing the clouds away with playful scorn,
And living as if earth contain'd no tomb,—
And glowing into day: we may resume
The march of our existence: and thus I,
Still on thy shores, fair Leman! may find room
And food for meditation, nor pass by
Much, that may give us pause, if pondered fittingly.

99

Clarens![37] sweet Clarens, birth-place of deep Love!
Thine air is the young breath of passionate
thought;
Thy trees take root in Love; the snows above
The very Glaciers have his colours caught,
And sun-set into rose-hues sees them wrought
By rays which sleep there lovingly: the rocks,
The permanent crags, tell here of Love, who
sought
In them a refuge from the worldly shocks,
Which stir and sting the soul with hope that woos,
then mocks.

100

Clarens! by heavenly feet thy paths are trod,—
Undying Love's, who here ascends a throne
To which the steps are mountains; where the god
Is a pervading life and light,—so shown
Not on those summits solely, nor alone
In the still cave and forest: o'er the flower
His eye is sparkling, and his breath hath blown,
His soft and summer breath, whose tender power
Passes the strength of storms in their most desolate
hour.

101

All things are here of *him*; from the black pines,
Which are his shade on high, and the loud roar
Of torrents, where he listeneth, to the vines
Which slope his green path downward to the
shore,
Where the bowed waters meet him, and adore,
Kissing his feet with murmurs; and the wood,
The covert of old trees, with trunks all hoar,
But light leaves, young as joy, stands where it
stood,
Offering to him, and his, a populous solitude,

102

A populous solitude of bees and birds,
And fairy-form'd and many-coloured things,
Who worship him with notes more sweet than
words,
And innocently open their glad wings,
Fearless and full of life: the gush of springs,
And fall of lofty fountains, and the bend
Of stirring branches, and the bud which brings
The swiftest thought of beauty, here extend,
Mingling, and made by Love, unto one mighty end.

103

He who hath loved not, here would learn that lore,
And make his heart a spirit; he who knows
That tender mystery, will love the more,
For this is Love's recess, where vain men's woes,

[37] **Clarens:** Rousseau immortalized the village of Clarens and its environs in *Héloïse*.

And the world's waste, have driven him far from those,
For 'tis his nature to advance or die;
He stands not still, but or decays, or grows
Into a boundless blessing, which may vie
With the immortal lights, in its eternity!

104

'Twas not for fiction chose Rousseau this spot,
Peopling it with affections; but he found
It was the scene which passion must allot
To the mind's purified beings; 'twas the ground
Where early Love his Psyche's zone unbound,[38]
And hallowed it with loveliness: 'tis lone,
And wonderful, and deep, and hath a sound,
And sense, and sight of sweetness; here the Rhone
Hath spread himself a couch, the Alps have rear'd a throne.

105

Lausanne! and Ferney! ye have been the abodes
Of names[39] which unto you bequeath'd a name;
Mortals, who sought and found, by dangerous roads,
A path to perpetuity of fame:
They were gigantic minds, and their steep aim,
Was, Titan-like, on daring doubts to pile
Thoughts which should call down thunder, and the flame
Of Heaven, again assail'd, if Heaven the while
On man and man's research could deign do more than smile.

106

The one[40] was fire and fickleness, a child,
Most mutable in wishes, but in mind,
A wit as various,—gay, grave, sage, or wild,—
Historian, board, philosopher, combined;
He multiplied himself among mankind,
The Proteus[41] of their talents: But his own
Breathed most in ridicule,—which, as the wind,
Blew where it listed, laying all things prone,—
Now to o'erthrow a fool, and now to shake a throne.

107

The other,[42] deep and slow, exhausting thought,
And hiving wisdom with each studious year,
In meditation dwelt, with learning wrought,
And shaped his weapon with an edge severe,
Sapping a solemn creed with solemn sneer;
The lord of irony,—that master-spell,
Which stung his foes to wrath, which grew from fear,
And doom'd him to the zealot's ready Hell,
Which answers to all doubts so eloquently well.

108

Yet, peace be with their ashes,—for by them,
If merited, the penalty is paid;
It is not ours to judge,—far less condemn;
The hour must come when such things shall be made
Known unto all,—or hope and dread allay'd
By slumber, on one pillow,—in the dust,
Which, thus much we are sure, must lie decay'd;
And when it shall revive, as is our trust,
'Twill be to be forgiven, or suffer what is just.

109

But let me quit man's works, again to read
His Maker's, spread around me, and suspend
This page, which from my reveries feed,
Until it seems prolonging without end.
The clouds above me to the white Alps tend,
And I must pierce them, and survey whate'er
May be permitted, as my steps I bend
To their most great and growing region, where
The earth to her embrace compels the powers of air.

110

Italia! too, Italia! looking on thee,
Full flashes on the soul the light of ages,
Since the fierce Carthaginian[43] almost won thee,

---

[38] **Where . . . unbound:** allusion to the love of Cupid and the goddess Psyche.

[39] **Lausanne! . . . names . . . :** "Voltaire and Gibbon" [L.B.].

[40] **the one:** Voltaire.

[41] **Proteus:** a Greek sea god fabled for his ability to change form.

[42] **The other:** Gibbon.

[43] **the fierce Carthaginian:** reference to Hannibal's invasion of Italy (over the Alps) in 218 BC, and his subsequent devastating campaign against the Romans.

To the last halo of the chiefs and sages,
Who glorify thy consecrated pages;
Thou wert the throne and grave of empires; still,
The fount at which the panting mind assuages
Her thirst of knowledge, quaffing there her fill,
Flows from the eternal source of Rome's imperial hill.

111

Thus far I have proceeded in a theme
Renewed with no kind auspices:—to feel
We are not what we have been, and to deem
We are not what we should be,—and to steel
The heart against itself; and to conceal,
With a proud caution, love, or hate, or aught,—
Passion or feeling, purpose, grief or zeal,—
Which is the tyrant spirit of our thought,
Is a stern task of soul:—No matter,—it is taught.

112

And for these words, thus woven into song,
It may be that they are a harmless wile,—[44]
The colouring of the scenes which fleet along,
Which I would seize, in passing, to beguile
My breast, or that of others, for a while.
Fame is the thirst of youth,—but I am not
So young as to regard men's frown or smile,
As loss or guerdon[45] of a glorious lot;
I stood and stand alone,—remembered or forgot.

113

I have not loved the world, nor the world me;
I have not flattered its rank breath, nor bow'd
To its idolatries a patient knee,—
Nor coin'd my cheek to smiles,—nor cried aloud
In worship of an echo; in the crowd
They could not deem me one of such; I stood
Among them, but not of them; in a shroud
Of thoughts which were not their thoughts, and still could,
Had I not filed my mind, which thus itself subdued.

114

I have not loved the world, nor the world me,—
But let us part fair foes; I do believe,
Though I have found them not, that there may be
Words which are things,—hopes which will not deceive,
And virtues which are merciful, nor weave
Snares for the failing: I would also deem
O'er others' griefs that some sincerely grieve;
That two, or one, are almost what they seem,—
That goodness is no name, and happiness no dream.

115

My daughter! with thy name this song begun—
My daughter! with thy name thus much shall end—
I see thee not,—I hear thee not,—but none
Can be so wrapt in thee; thou art the friend
To whom the shadows of far years extend:
Albeit my brow thou never should'st behold,
My voice shall with thy future visions blend,
And reach into thy heart,—when mine is cold,—
A token and a tone, even from thy father's mould.

116

To aid thy mind's development,—to watch
Thy dawn of little joys,—to sit and see
Almost thy very growth,—to view thee catch
Knowledge of objects,—wonders yet to thee!
To hold thee lightly on a gentle knee,
And print on thy soft cheek a parent's kiss,—
This, it should seem, was not reserv'd for me;
Yet this was in my nature:—as it is,
I know not what is there, yet something like to this.

117

Yet, though dull Hate as duty should be taught,
I know that thou wilt love me; though my name
Should be shut from thee, as a spell still fraught
With desolation,—and a broken claim:
Though the grave closed between us,—'twere the same,
I know that thou wilt love me; though to drain
My blood from out thy being, were an aim,
And an attainment,—all would be in vain,—
Still thou would'st love me, still that more than life retain.

118

The child of love,—though born in bitterness,
And nurtured in convulsion,—of thy sire
These were the elements,—and thine no less.
As yet such are around thee,—but thy fire
Shall be more tempered, and thy hope far higher.

[44] **wile:** trick.
[45] **guerdon:** reward.

Sweet by thy cradled slumbers! O'er the sea,
And from the mountains where I now respire,
Fain would I waft such blessing upon thee,
As, with a sigh, I deem thou might'st have been to me!

from THE PRISONER OF CHILLON AND OTHER POEMS
(1816)

Sonnet on Chillon[1]
(comp. 1816)

Eternal spirit of the chainless mind!
Brightest in dungeons, Liberty! thou art,
For there thy habitation is the heart—
The heart which love of thee alone can bind;
And when thy sons to fetters are consigned—
To fetters, and the damp vault's dayless gloom,
Their country conquers with their martyrdom,
And Freedom's fame finds wings on every wind.
Chillon! thy prison is a holy place,
And thy sad floor an altar—for 'twas trod,
Until his very steps have left a trace
Worn, as if thy cold pavement were a sod,
By Bonnivard![2]—May none those marks efface!
For they appeal from tyranny to God.

Stanzas to ——
(1816; comp. 1816)

I

Though the day of my destiny's over,
And the star of my fate hath declined,
Thy soft heart refused to discover
The faults which so many could find;
Though thy soul with my grief was acquainted,
It shrunk not to share it with me,
And the love which my spirit hath painted
It never hath found but in *thee*.

II

Then when nature around me is smiling
The last smile which answers to mine,
I do not believe it beguiling
Because it reminds me of thine;
And when winds are at war with the ocean,
As the breasts I believed in with me,
If their billows excite an emotion
It is that they bear me from *thee*.

III

Though the rock of my last hope is shiver'd,
And its fragments are sunk in the wave,
Though I feel that my soul is deliver'd
To pain—it shall not be its slave.
There is many a pang to pursue me:
They may crush, but they shall not contemn—
They may torture, but shall not subdue me—
'Tis of *thee* that I think—not of them.

IV

Though human, thou didst not deceive me,
Though woman, thou didst not forsake,
Though loved, thou forborest to grieve me,
Though slander'd, thou never could'st shake,—
Though trusted, thou didst not disclaim me,
Though parted, it was not to fly,
Though watchful, 'twas not to defame me,
Nor, mute, that the world might belie.

V

Yet I blame not the world, nor despise it,
Nor the war of the many with one—
If my soul was not fitted to prize it
'Twas folly not sooner to shun:
And if dearly that error hath cost me,
And more than I once could foresee,
I have found that, whatever it lost me,
It could not deprive me of *thee*.

VI

From the wreck of the past, which hath perish'd,
Thus much I at least may recall,
It hath taught me that what I most cherish'd
Deserved to be dearest of all:
In the desert a fountain is springing,
In the wide waste there still is a tree,
And a bird in the solitude singing,
Which speaks to my spirit of *thee*.

[1] Chillon Castle.

[2] Swiss republican patriot and scholar François de Bonnivard was held prisoner from 1530 to 1536 by the Duke of Savoy. After his release Bonnivard became a national hero.

Darkness

(1816; comp. 1816)

I had a dream, which was not all a dream.
The bright sun was extinguish'd, and the stars
Did wander darkling in the eternal space,
Rayless, and pathless, and the icy earth
Swung blind and blackening in the moonless air;
Morn came, and went—and came, and brought no
  day,
And men forgot their passions in the dread
Of this their desolation; and all hearts
Were chill'd into a selfish prayer for light:
And they did live by watchfires—and the thrones,
The palaces of crowned kings—the huts,
The habitations of all things which dwell,
Were burnt for beacons; cities were consumed,
And men were gathered round their blazing homes
To look once more into each other's face;
Happy were those who dwelt within the eye
Of the volcanos, and their mountain-torch:
A fearful hope was all the world contain'd;
Forests were set on fire—but hour by hour
They fell and faded—and the crackling trunks
Extinguish'd with a crash—and all was black.
The brows of men by the despairing light
Wore an unearthly aspect, as by fits
The flashes fell upon them; some lay down
And hid their eyes and wept; and some did rest
Their chins upon their clenched hands, and smiled;
And others hurried to and fro, and fed
Their funeral piles with fuel, and looked up
With mad disquietude on the dull sky,
The pall of a past world; and then again
With curses cast them down upon the dust,
And gnash'd their teeth and howl'd: the wild birds
  shriek'd,
And, terrified, did flutter on the ground,
And flap their useless wings; the wildest brutes
Came tame and tremulous; and vipers crawl'd
And twined themselves among the multitude,
Hissing, but stingless—they were slain for food:
And War, which for a moment was no more,
Did glut himself again;—a meal was bought
With blood, and each sate sullenly apart
Gorging himself in gloom: no love was left;
All earth was but one thought—and that was death,
Immediate and inglorious; and the pang
Of famine fed upon all entrails—men
Died, and their bones were tombless as their flesh;
The meagre by the meagre were devoured,
Even dogs assail'd their masters, all save one,
And he was faithful to a corse, and kept
The birds and beasts and famish'd men at bay,
Till hunger clung them, or the dropping dead
Lured their lank jaws; himself sought out no food,
But with a piteous and perpetual moan
And a quick desolate cry, licking the hand
Which answered not with a caress—he died.
The crowd was famish'd by degrees; but two
Of an enormous city did survive,
And they were enemies; they met beside
The dying embers of an altar-place
Where had been heap'd a mass of holy things
For an unholy usage; they raked up,
And shivering scraped with their cold skeleton hands
The feeble ashes, and their feeble breath
Blew for a little life, and made a flame
Which was a mockery; then they lifted up
Their eyes as it grew lighter, and beheld
Each other's aspects—saw, and shriek'd, and died—
Even of their mutual hideousness they died,
Unknowing who he was upon whose brow
Famine had written Fiend. The world was void,
The populous and the powerful—was a lump,
Seasonless, herbless, treeless, manless, lifeless—
A lump of death—a chaos of hard clay.
The rivers, lakes, and ocean all stood still,
And nothing stirred within their silent depths;
Ships sailorless lay rotting on the sea,
And their masts fell down piecemeal; as they dropp'd
They slept on the abyss without a surge—
The waves were dead; the tides were in their grave,
The moon their mistress had expired before;
The winds were withered in the stagnant air,
And the clouds perish'd; Darkness had no need
Of aid from them—She was the universe.[1]

[1] Cf. Alexander Pope's *Dunciad*, IV.627–656, closing with: "Lo! thy dread Empire, CHAOS! is restored; / Light dies before thy uncreating word: / Thy hand, great Anarch! lets the 'curtain fall; / And universal darkness buries all." (1743)

[A Fragment]

(1816; comp. 1816)

A dreary shroud around us—and invest
With sad remembrancers our hours of rest.
The absent are the dead,—for they are cold,
And ne'er can be what once we did behold—
And they are changed—and cheerless—or if yet
The unforgotten do not all forget—
Since thus divided—equal must it be
If the deep barrier be of earth or sea—
It may be both,—but one day end it must
In the dark union of insensate dust.
The underearth inhabitants—are they
But mingled millions decomposed to clay—
The ashes of a thousand Ages spread
Wherever Man has trodden or shall tread—
Or do they in their silent cities dwell
Each in his incommunicative cell—
Or have they their own language—and a sense
Of breathless being—darkened and intense—
As midnight in her solitude—Oh Earth!
Where are the past—and wherefore had they birth?
The dead are thy inheritors—and we
But bubbles on thy surface:—and the key
Of thy profundity is in the grave,
The portal of thy universal cave—
Where I would walk in Spirit—and behold
Our elements resolved to things untold,
And fathom hidden wonders—and explore
The essence of great bosoms now no more.

Prometheus

(1816; comp. 1816)

1

Titan![1] To whose immortal eyes
The sufferings of mortality,
Seen in their sad reality,
Were not as things that gods despise;
What was thy pity's recompense?
A silent suffering, and intense;
The rock, the vulture, and the chain,
All that the proud can feel of pain,
The agony they do not show,
The suffocating sense of woe,
Which speaks but in its loneliness,
And then is jealous lest the sky
Should have a listener, nor will sigh
Until its voice is echoless.

2

Titan! to thee the strife was given
Between the suffering and the will,
Which torture where they cannot kill;
And the inexorable Heaven,
And the deaf tyranny of Fate,
The ruling principle of Hate,
Which for its pleasure doth create
The things it may annihilate,
Refused thee even the boon to die:
The wretched gift eternity
Was thine—and thou hast borne it well.
All that the Thunderer[2] wrung from thee
Was but the menace which flung back
On him the torments of thy rack;[3]
The fate thou didst so well foresee
But would not to appease him tell;
And in thy Silence was his Sentence,
And in his Soul a vain repentance,
And evil dread so ill dissembled
That in his hand the lightnings trembled.

3

Thy Godlike crime was to be kind,
To render with thy precepts less
The sum of human wretchedness,
And strengthen Man with his own mind;
But baffled as thou wert from high,
Still in thy patient energy,
In the endurance, and repulse
Of thine impenetrable Spirit,
Which Earth and Heaven could not convulse,
A mighty lesson we inherit:

[1] **Titan:** Prometheus stole fire from the Olympian gods and gave it to man, for which Jupiter punished him by chaining him to Mt. Caucasus, where an eagle fed perpetually on his liver.

[2] **the Thunderer:** Jupiter.

[3] **rack:** instrument of torture, literally, a torture device on which the victim was stretched.

Thou art a symbol and a sign
To Mortals of their fate and force;
Like thee, Man is in part divine,
A troubled stream from a pure source;
And Man in portions can foresee
His own funereal destiny;
His wretchedness, and his resistance,
And his sad unallied existence:
To which his Spirit may oppose
Itself—an equal to all woes,
And a firm will, and a deep sense,
Which even in torture can descry
Its own concentred[4] recompense,
Triumphant where it dares defy,
And making Death a Victory.

from Letter to Augusta Leigh

[Diodati—Geneva Sept. 8th. 1816][1]

My dearest Augusta

By two opportunities of private conveyance—I have sent answers to your letter delivered by Mr. H[obhouse].——S[crope][2] is on his return to England—& may probably arrive before this.—He is charged with a few packets of seals—necklaces—balls &c.—& I know not what—formed of Chrystals—Agates—and other stones—*all of & from* Mont Blanc[3] bought & brought by me on & from the spot—expressly for you to divide among yourself and the children—including also your niece Ada, for whom I selected a ball (of Granite—a soft substance by the way—but the only one there) wherewithall to roll & play—when she is old enough—and mischievous enough—and moreover a Chrystal necklace—and anything else you may like to add for her—the Love!——The rest are for you—& the Nursery—but particularly Georgiana[4]—who has sent me a very nice letter.—I hope Scrope will carry them all safely—as he promised——There are seals & all kinds of fooleries—pray—like them—for they come from a very curious place (nothing like it hardly in all I ever saw)—to say nothing of the giver.——And so—Lady B[yron] has been "kind to you" you tell me—"very kind"—umph—it is as well she should be kind to some of us—and I am glad she has the heart & the discernment to be still *your* friend—you was ever so to her.—I heard the other day—that she was very unwell—I was shocked enough—and sorry enough—God knows—but never mind;—H[obhouse] tells me however that she is *not* ill—that she *had* been indisposed—but is better & well to do.—this is a relief.——As for me I am in good health—& fair—though very unequal—spirits—but for all that—she—or rather—the Separation[5]—has broken my heart—I feel as if an Elephant had trodden on it—I am convinced I shall never get over it—but I try.—I had enough before I ever knew her and more than enough—but time & agitation had done something for me; but this last wreck has affected me very differently,—if it were *acutely*—it would not signify—but it is not that,—I breathe lead.——While the storm lasted & you were all pressing & comforting me with condemnation in Piccadilly[6]—it was bad enough—& violent enough—but it is worse now.—I have neither strength nor spirits—nor inclination to carry me through anything which will clear my brain or lighten my heart.—I mean to cross the Alps at the end of this month—and go—God knows where—by Dalmatia—up to the Arnauts[7] again—if nothing better can be done;—I have still a world before me—this—or the next.——H[obhouse] has told me all the strange stories in circulation of me & mine;—*not* true,—I have been in some danger on the lake[8]—(near Meillerie) but nothing to speak of; and as to all these "mistresses"—Lord help me—I have had but one.—Now—don't scold—but what could I do?—a

[4] **concentred:** drawn to a center, focussed, concentrated.

[1] In June of 1816, Byron had leased the Villa Diodati, two miles east of Geneva, where Milton had once stayed.

[2] **Mr. H[obhouse] . . . S[crope]:** Byron's friends John Cam Hobhouse and Scrope Davies.

[3] **Mont Blanc:** the highest peak of the Alps, about 50 miles south of where Byron was staying on Lake Geneva.

[4] **Georgiana:** Augusta's eldest daughter, and Byron's favorite.

[5] **the Separation:** Lady Byron left her husband with their child in January 1816.

[6] **Piccadilly:** Byron and his wife had taken an apartment in London's Piccadilly district soon after their wedding, and Byron stayed there after the separation.

[7] **Dalmatia:** an area on the east coast of the Adriatic, in what is now Croatia. **Arnauts:** Albanians.

[8] **I have been in some danger on the lake:** reference to his sailing expeditions on Lake Geneva, in the company of Shelley and alone.

foolish girl[9]—in spite of all I could say or do—would come after me—or rather went before me—for I found her here—and I have had all the plague possible to persuade her to go back again—but at last she went.—Now—dearest—I do most truly tell thee—that I could not help this—that I did all I could to prevent it—& have at last put an end to it.—I am not in love—nor have any love left for any,—but I could not exactly play the Stoic with a woman—who had scrambled eight hundred miles to unphilosophize me—besides I had been regaled of late with so many "two courses and a *desert*" (Alas!) of aversion—that I was fain to take a little love (if pressed particularly) by way of novelty.——And now you know all that I know of that matter—& it is over. Pray—write—I have heard nothing since your last—at least a month or five weeks ago.——I go out very little—except into the *air*—and on journeys—and on the water—and to Coppet—where Me. de Stael[10] has been particularly kind & friendly towards me—& (I hear) fought battles without number in my very indifferent cause.—It has (they say) made quite as much noise on this as the other side of "La Manche"[11]—Heaven knows why—but I seem destined to set people by the ears.——Don't hate me—but believe me ever

yrs. most affectly.
B

Alpine Journal
18–29 September 1816
[for Augusta Leigh]

Clarens. Septr. 18th. 1816

Yesterday September 17th. 1816—I set out (with H[obhouse]) on an excursion of some days to the Mountains.—I shall keep a short journal of each day's progress for my Sister Augusta—

SEPT. 17TH

Rose at 5.—left Diodati about seven—in one of the country carriages—(a Charaban)—our servants on horseback—weather very fine—the Lake calm and clear—Mont Blanc—and the Aiguille of Argentière both very distinct—the borders of the Lake beautiful—reached Lausanne before Sunset—stopped & slept at Ouchy.—H[obhouse] went to dine with a Mr. Okeden—I remained at our Caravansera[1] (though invited to the house of H's friend—too lazy or tired—or something else to go) and wrote a letter to Augusta—Went to bed at nine—sheets damp—swore and stripped them off & flung them—Heaven knows where—wrapt myself up in the blankets—and slept like a Child of a month's existence—till 5 o Clock of

SEPTR. 18TH

Called by Berger (my Courier who acts as Valet for a day or two—the learned Fletcher[2] being left in charge of Chattels at Diodati) got up—H[obhouse] walked on before—a mile from Lausanne—the road overflowed by the lake—got on horseback & rode—till within a mile of Vevey—the Colt young but went very well—overtook H. & resumed the carriage which is an open one—stopped at Vevey two hours (the second time I have visited it) walked to the Church—view from the Churchyard superb—within it General Ludlow[3] (the Regicide's) monument—black marble—long inscription—Latin—but simple—particularly the latter part—in which his wife (Margaret de Thomas) records her long—her tried—and unshaken affection—he was an Exile *two and thirty years*—one of the King's (Charles's) Judges—a fine fellow.—I remember reading his memoirs in January 1815 (at Halnaby[4]—) the first part of them very amusing—the latter less so,—I little thought at the time of their perusal by me of seeing his tomb—near him Broughton (who read King Charles's sentence to Charles Stuart)—is

[9] **a foolish girl**: Claire Clairmont, Mary Shelley's half-sister, with whom Byron had a liaison in 1816. In January 1817 she bore his daughter, whom she called Alba (Mary Shelley's nickname for Byron was "Albe"). The name was later changed to Allegra.

[10] **Me. de Stael**: French writer Anne Louise Germaine de Staël (1766–1817), who wrote one of the first studies of Romantic literature, *De l'Allemagne* (1810).

[11] **"La Manche"**: the French name for the English Channel.

[1] **Caravansera**: caravan.

[2] **Fletcher**: Byron's valet.

[3] **General Ludlow**: Parliamentary leader Edmund Ludlow (c. 1617–1692) signed the death warrant for King Charles I.

[4] **Halnaby**: Byron and Lady Byron spent their honeymoon at Halnaby Hall in Yorkshire.

buried with a *queer* and rather *canting*—but still a Republican epitaph——Ludlow's house shown—it retains still his inscription "Omne Solum forte patria"[5]—Walked down to the Lake side—servants—Carriage—saddle horses—all set off and left us plantes la by some mistake—and we walked on after them towards Clarens—H[obhouse] ran on before and overtook them at last—arrived the second time (1st time was by water) at Clarens beautiful Clarens!—went to Chillon through Scenery worthy of I know not whom—went over the Castle of Chillon[6] again—on our return met an English party in a carriage—a lady in it fast asleep!—fast asleep in the most anti-narcotic spot in the world—excellent—I remember at Chamouni—in the very eyes of Mont Blanc—hearing another woman—English also—exclaim to her party—"did you ever see any thing more *rural*"—as if it was Highgate or Hampstead—or Brompton—or Hayes.[7]—"*Rural*" quotha!—Rocks—pines—torrents—Glaciers—Clouds—and Summits of eternal snow far above them—and "*Rural!*" I did not know the thus exclaiming fair one—but she was a—very good kind of a woman.——After a slight & short dinner—we visited the Chateau de Clarens—an English woman has rented it recently—(it was not let when I saw it first) the roses are gone with their Summer—the family out—but the servants desired us to walk over the interior—saw on the table of the saloon—Blair's sermons[8]—and somebody else's (I forgot who's—) sermons—and a set of noisy children—saw all worth seeing and then descended to the "Bosquet de Julie" &c. &c.—our Guide full of *Rousseau*—whom he is eternally confounding with St. Preux[9]—and mixing the man and the book—on the steps of a cottage in the village—I saw a young paysanne[10]—beautiful as Julie herself—went again as far as Chillon to revisit the little torrent from the hill behind it—Sunset—reflected in the lake—have to get up at 5 tomorrow to cross the mountains on horseback—carriage to be sent round—lodged at my old Cottage—hospitable & comfortable—tired with a longish ride—on the Colt—and the subsequent jolting of the Charaban—and my scramble in the hot sun—shall go to bed—thinking of you dearest Augusta.——Mem.[11]—The Corporal who showed the wonders of Chillon was as drunk as Blucher[12]—and (to my mind) as great a man.—He was *deaf* also—and thinking every one else so—roared out the legends of the Castle so fearfully that H[obhouse] got out of humour—however we saw all things from the Gallows to the Dungeon (the *Potence* & the *Cachets*) and returned to Clarens with more freedom than belonged to the 15th. Century.——At Clarens——the only book (except the Bible) a translation of "Cecilia"[13] (Miss Burney's *Cecilia*) and the owner of the Cottage had also called her dog (a fat Pug *ten* years old—and hideous as *Tip*)[14] after Cecilia's (or rather Delville's) dog—Fidde—

SEPTR. 19TH

Rose at 5—ordered the carriage round.—Crossed the mountains to Montbovon on horseback—and on Mules—and by dint of scrambling on foot also,—the whole route beautiful as a *Dream* and now to me almost as indistinct,—I am so tired—for though healthy I have not the strength I possessed but a few years ago.—At Mont Davant we breakfasted—afterwards on a steep ascent—dismounted—tumbled down & cut a finger open—the baggage also got loose and fell down a ravine, till stopped by a large tree—swore—recovered baggage—horse tired & dropping—mounted Mule—at the approach of the summit of Dent Jamant—dismounted again with H. & all the party.—Arrived at a lake in the very nipple of the bosom of the Mountain.—left our quadrupeds with a Shepherd—& ascended further—came to some snow in patches—upon which my forehead's perspiration fell like rain making the same dints as in a sieve—the chill of the

[5] **"Omne Solum forte patria"**: The precise meaning of this Latin phrase is unclear due to its equivocal and condensed syntax; two possibilities are: "The whole foundation [of the house lies] in a strong country," or "The nation is the entire firm foundation [of the house]."

[6] **Castle of Chillon**: see note to "Sonnet on Chillon," above.

[7] **Highgate . . . Hayes**: towns which at that time were on the outskirts of London.

[8] **Blair's sermons**: reference to Scottish clergyman and poet Robert Blair (1699–1746).

[9] **"Bosquet de Julie"**: *trans.* "Julie's woods". **St. Preux**: Julie's tutor and lover in Rousseau's novel.

[10] **paysanne**: peasant woman.

[11] **Mem**: memo.

[12] **Blucher**: Gebhard Leberecht von Blücher (1742–1819) was Commander of the Prussian forces who aided Wellington in the defeat of Napoleon at Waterloo.

[13] **"Cecilia"**: a very successful novel (pub. 1782) by Frances Burney (1752–1840).

[14] **Tip**: Augusta's dog.

wind & the snow turned me giddy—but I scrambled on & upwards—*H.* went to the highest *pinnacle*—I did not—but paused within a few yards (at an opening of the Cliff)—in coming down the Guide tumbled three times—I fell a laughing & tumbled too—the descent luckily soft though steep & slippery—H. also fell—but nobody hurt. The whole of the Mountain superb—the shepherd on a very steep & high cliff playing upon his *pipe*—very different from Arcadia[15]—(where I saw the pastors with a long Musquet instead of a Crook—and pistols in their Girdles)—our Swiss Shepherd's pipe was sweet—& his time agreeable—saw a cow strayed—told that they often break their necks on & over the crags—descended to Montbovon—pretty scraggy village with a wild river—and a wooden bridge.—H. went to fish—caught one—our carriage not come—our horses—mules &c. knocked up—ourselves fatigued—(but so much the better—I shall sleep). The view from the highest point of today's journey comprized on one side the greatest part of Lake Leman—on the other—the valleys & mountains of the Canton Fribourg—and an immense plain with the Lakes of Neufchatel & Morat—and all which the borders of these and of the Lake of Geneva inherit—we had both sides of the Jura[16] before us in one point of view, with Alps in plenty.—In passing a ravine—the Guide recommended strenuously a quickening of pace—as the stones fall with great rapidity & occasional damage—the advice is excellent—but like most good advice impracticable—the road being so rough in this precise point—that neither mules nor mankind—nor horses—can make any violent progress.—Passed without any fractures or menace thereof.—The music of the Cows' bells (for their wealth like the Patriarchs[17] is cattle) in the pastures (which reach to a height far above any mountains in Britain—) and the Shepherds' shouting to us from crag to crag & playing on their reeds where the steeps appeared almost inaccessible, with the surrounding scenery—realized all that I have ever heard or imagined of a pastoral existence—much more so than Greece or Asia Minor—for there we are a little too much of the sabre & musquet order—and if there is a Crook in one hand, you are sure to see a gun in the other—but this was pure and unmixed—solitary—savage and patriarchal—the effect I cannot describe—as we went they played the "Ranz des Vaches" and other airs[18] by way of farewell.—I have lately repeopled my mind with Nature.

SEPTR. 20TH

Up at 6—off at 8—the whole of this days journey at an average of between from two thousand seven hundred to three thousand feet above the level of the Sea. This valley the longest—narrowest—& considered one of the finest of the Alps—little traversed by travellers—saw the Bridge of La Roche—the bed of the river very low & deep between immense rocks & rapid as anger—a man & mule said to have tumbled over without damage—(the mule was lucky at any rate—unless I knew the *man* I should be loth to pronounce *him* fortunate).—The people looked free & happy and *rich* (which last implies neither of the former) the cows superb—a Bull nearly leapt into the Charaban—"agreeable companion in a postchaise"—Goats & Sheep very thriving—a mountain with enormous Glaciers to the right—the Kletsgerberg—further on—the Hockthorn—nice names—so soft—Hockthorn I believe very lofty & craggy—patched with snow only—no Glaciers on it—but some good epaulettes of clouds.—Past the boundaries—out of Vaud—& into Bern Canton—French exchanged for a bad German—the district famous for Cheese—liberty—property—& no taxes.—H. went to fish—caught none—strolled to river—saw a boy [and] a kid—kid followed him like a dog—kid could not get over a fence & bleated piteously—tried myself to help kid—but nearly overset both self & kid into the river.—Arrived here about six in the evening—nine o clock—going to bed—H. in next room—knocked his head against the door—and exclaimed of course against doors—not tired today—but hope to sleep nevertheless—women gabbling below—read a French translation of Schiller[19]—Good Night—Dearest Augusta.——

SEPTR. 21ST

Off early—the valley of Simmenthal as before—entrance to the plain of Thoun very narrow—high rocks—wooded to the top—river—new mountains—with fine Glaciers—Lake of Thoun—extensive plain with a girdle

---

[15] **Arcadia:** a district in the central Pelopponesus (in Greece) fabled for its bucolic beauty.

[16] **Jura:** the mountain range northwest of Lake Geneva.

[17] **Patriarchs:** the Patriarchs of the Bible (Abraham, Isaac, and Jacob).

[18] **airs:** songs.

[19] **Schiller:** German Romantic poet, playwright, and critic Johann Christoph Friedrich von Schiller (1759–1805).

of Alps—walked down to the Chateau de Schadau—view along the lake—crossed the river in a boat rowed by women—*women* [went?] right for the first time in my recollection.—Thoun a pretty town—the whole day's journey Alpine & proud.—

SEPTR. 22D

Left Thoun in a boat which carried us the length of the lake in three hours—the lake small—but the banks fine—rocks down to the water's edge.—Landed at Neuhause—passed Interlachen—entered upon a range of scenes beyond all description—or previous conception.—Passed a rock—inscription—2 brothers—one murdered the other—just the place fit for it.—After a variety of windings came to an enormous rock—Girl with fruit—very pretty—blue eyes—good teeth—very fair—long but good features—reminded me of Fy.[20] bought some of her pears—and patted her upon the cheek—the expression of her face very mild—but good—and not at all coquettish.—Arrived at the foot of the Mountain (the Yung-frau—i.e. the Maiden) Glaciers—torrents—one of these torrents *nine hundred feet* in height of visible descent—lodge at the Curate's—set out to see the Valley—heard an Avalanche fall—like thunder—saw Glacier—enormous—Storm came on—thunder—lightning—hail—all in perfection—and beautiful—I was on horseback—Guide wanted to carry my cane—I was going to give it him when I recollected that it was a Swordstick and I thought that the lightning might be attracted towards him—kept it myself—a good deal encumbered with it & my cloak—as it was too heavy for a whip—and the horse was stupid—& stood still every other peal. Got in—not very wet—the Cloak being staunch—H. wet through—H. took refuge in cottage—sent man—umbrella—& cloak (from the Curate's when I arrived—) after him.—Swiss Curate's house—very good indeed—much better than most English Vicarages—it is immediately opposite the torrent I spoke of—the torrent is in shape curving over the rock—like the *tail* of a white horse streaming in the wind—such as it might be conceived would be that of the "*pale* horse" on which *Death* is mounted in the Apocalypse.[21]—It is neither mist nor water but a something between both—it's immense height (nine hundred feet) gives it a wave—a curve—a spreading here—a condensation there—wonderful—& indescribable.—I think upon the whole—that this day has been better than any of this present excursion.—

SEPTR. 23D

Before ascending the mountain—went to the torrent (7 in the morning) again—the Sun upon it forming a *rainbow* of the lower part of all colours—but principally purple and gold—the bow moving as you move—I never saw anything like this—it is only in the Sunshine.——Ascended the Wengren [sic] Mountain.——at noon reached a valley near the summit—left the horses—took off my coat & went to the summit—7000 feet (English feet) above the level of the *sea*—and about 5000 above the valley we left in the morning—on one side our view comprized the *Yung frau* with all her glaciers—then the *Dent d'Argent*—shining like truth—then the *little Giant* (the Kleiner Elgher) & the great Giant (the Grosser Elgher) and last not least—the Wetterhorn.—The height of the Yung frau is 13000 feet above the sea—and 11000 above the valley—she is the highest of this range,—heard the Avalanches falling every five minutes nearly—as if God was pelting the Devil down from Heaven with snow balls—from where we stood on the *Wengren* [sic] Alp—we had all these in view on one side—on the other the clouds rose from the opposite valley curling up perpendicular precipices—like the foam of the Ocean of Hell during a Springtide—it was white & sulphery—and immeasurably deep in appearance—the side we ascended was (of course) not of so precipitous a nature—but on arriving at the summit we looked down the other side upon a boiling sea of cloud—dashing against the crags on which we stood (these crags on one side quite perpendicular);—staid a quarter of an hour—began to descend—quite clear from cloud on that side of the mountain—in passing the masses of snow—I made a snowball & pelted H. with it—got down to our horses again—eat something—remounted—heard the Avalanches still—came to a morass—H. dismounted—H. got well over—I tried to pass my horse over—the horse sunk up [to] the chin—& of course he & I were in the mud together—bemired all over—but not hurt—laughed & rode on.—Arrived at the Grindenwald—dined—mounted again & rode to the higher Glacier—twilight—but distinct—very fine Glacier—like a *frozen hurricane*—Starlight—beautiful—but a devil of a path—never mind—got safe in—a little lightning—but the whole of the day as fine in point of

[20] **Fy:** possibly Fanny (Frances) Webster, the wife of Byron's friend James Webster.

[21] **Apocalypse:** cf. Revelation 6:8: "And I looked, and behold a pale horse: and his name that sat on him was Death, and Hell followed with him."

weather—as the day on which Paradise was made.—Passed *whole woods of withered pines—all withered*—trunks stripped & barkless—branches lifeless—done by a single winter—their appearance reminded me of me & my family.—

SEPTR. 24TH

Set out at seven—up at five—passed the black Glacier—the Mountain Wetterhorn on the right—crossed the Scheideck mountain—came to the Rose Glacier—said to be the largest & finest in Switzerland.—*I* think the Bossons Glacier at Chamouni—as fine—H. does not—came to the Reichenback waterfall—two hundred feet high—halted to rest the horses—arrived in the valley of Oberhasli—rain came on—drenched a little—only 4 hours rain however in 8 days—came to Lake of Brientz—then to town of Brientz—changed—H. hurt his head against door.—In the evening four Swiss Peasant Girls of Oberhasli came & sang the airs of their country—two of the voices beautiful—the tunes also—they sing too that *Tyrolese air* & song which you love—Augusta—because I love it—& I love because you love it—they are still singing—Dearest—you do not know how I should have liked this—were you with me—the airs are so wild & original & at the same time of great sweetness.—The singing is over—but below stairs I hear the notes of a Fiddle which bode no good to my nights rest.—The Lord help us!—I shall go down & see the dancing.—

SEPTR. 25TH

The whole town of Brientz were apparently gathered together in the rooms below—pretty music—& excellent Waltzing—none but peasants—the dancing much better than in England—the English can't Waltz—never could—nor ever will.—One man with his pipe in his mouth—but danced as well as the others—some other dances in pairs—and in fours—and very good.—I went to bed but the revelry continued below late & early.—Brientz but a village.——Rose early.—Embarked on the Lake of Brientz.—Rowed by women in a long boat—one very young & very pretty—seated myself by her—& began to row also—presently we put to shore & another woman jumped in—it seems it is the custom here for the boats to be *manned by women*—for of five men & three women in our bark—all the women took an oar—and but one man. ——Got to Interlachen in three hours—pretty Lake—not so large as that of Thoun.—Dined at Interlachen—Girl gave me some flowers—& made me a speech in German—of which I know nothing—I do not know whether the speech was pretty but as the woman was—I hope so. —Saw another—very pretty too—and *tall* which I prefer—I hate short women—for more reasons than one.—Reembarked on the Lake of Thoun—fell asleep part of the way—sent our horses round—found people on the shore blowing up a rock with gunpowder—they blew it up near our boat—only telling us a minute before—mere stupidity—but they might have broke our noddles.—Got to Thoun in the Evening—the weather has been tolerable the whole day—but as the wild part of our tour is finished, it don't matter to us—in all the desirable part—we have been most lucky in warmth & clearness of Atmosphere—for which "Praise we the Lord."——

SEPTR. 26TH

Being out of the mountains my journal must be as flat as my journey.——From Thoun to Bern good road—hedges—villages—industry—prosperity—and all sorts of tokens of insipid civilization.——From Bern to Fribourg.—Different Canton—Catholics—passed a field of Battle—Swiss beat the French—in one of the late wars against the French Republic.—Bought a dog—a very ugly dog—but *"tres mechant"*.[22] this was his great recommendation in the owner's eyes & mine—for I mean him to watch the carriage—he hath no tail—& is called "Mutz"—which signifies *"Short-tail"*—he is apparently of the Shepherd dog genus!—The greater part of this tour has been on horseback—on foot—and on mule;—the Filly (which is one of two young horses I bought of the Baron de Vincy) carried me very well—she is young and as quiet as anything of her sex can be—very goodtempered—and perpetually neighing—when she wants any thing—which is every five minutes—I have called her *Biche*—because her manners are not unlike a little dog's—but she is a very tame—pretty childish quadruped.—

SEPTR. 28TH [27TH]

Saw the tree planted in honour of the battle of Morat[23]—340 years old—a good deal decayed.—Left Fribourg—but first saw the Cathedral—high tower—overtook the baggage of the Nuns of La Trappe who are removing to

---

[22] **French Republic:** The French had invaded Switzerland in 1798 to establish the Helvetic Republic. The Congress of Vienna restored the Swiss Republic. **tres mechant:** very unpleasant.

[23] **battle of Morat:** the bloodiest battle of three between the Swiss and Charles the Bold, Duke of Burgundy, in 1476.

Normandy from their late abode in the Canton of Fribourg — afterwards a coach with a quantity of Nuns in it — Nuns old — proceeded along the banks of the Lake of Neufchatel — very pleasing & soft — but not so mountainous — at least the Jura not appearing so — after the Bernese Alps — reached Yverdun in the dusk — a long line of large trees on the border of the lake — fine & sombre — the Auberge nearly full — with a German Princess & suite — got rooms — we hope to reach Diodati the day after tomorrow — and I wish for a letter from you my own dearest Sis — May your sleep be soft and your dreams of me. — I am going to bed — good night. —

SEPTR. 29TH [28TH]

Passed through a fine & flourishing country — but not mountainous — in the evening reached Aubonne (the entrance & bridge something like that of Durham) which commands by far the fairest view of the Lake of Geneva — twilight — the Moon on the Lake — a grove on the height — and of very noble trees. — Here Tavernier[24] (the Eastern traveller) bought (or built) the Chateau because the site resembled and equalled that of *Erivan* (a frontier city of Persia) here he finished his voyages — and I this little excursion — for I am within a few hours of Diodati — & have little more to see — & no more to say. — In the weather for this tour (of 13 days) I have been very fortunate — fortunate in a companion (Mr. H[obhous]e) fortunate in our prospects — and exempt from even the little petty accidents & delays which often render journeys in a less wild country — disappointing. — I was disposed to be pleased — I am a lover of Nature — and an Admirer of Beauty — I can bear fatigue — & welcome privation — and have seen some of the noblest views in the world. — But in all this — the recollections of bitterness — & more especially of recent & more home desolation — which must accompany me through life — have preyed upon me here — and neither the music of the Shepherd — the crashing of the Avalanche — nor the torrent — the mountain — the Glacier — the Forest — nor the Cloud — have for one moment — lightened the weight upon my heart — nor enabled me to lose my own wretched identity in the majesty & the power and the Glory — around — above — & beneath me. — I am past reproaches — and there is a time for all things — I am past the wish of vengeance — and I know of none like for what I have suffered — but the hour will come — when what I feel must be felt — & the —— but enough. —— To you — dearest Augusta — I send — and *for* you — I have kept this record of what I have seen & felt. — Love me as you are beloved by me. ——

[24] **Tavernier:** French traveller and author Jean-Baptiste Tavernier (1605–1689) journeyed to Turkey, Persia, Central Asia, and the East Indies.

Manfred, a Dramatic Poem

(1817; comp. 1816–1817)

'There are more things in heaven and earth, Horatio,
Than are dreamt of in your philosophy.'[1]

— DRAMATIS PERSONAE —

MANFRED	WITCH OF THE ALPS
CHAMOIS HUNTER	ARIMANES
ABBOT OF ST. MAURICE	NEMESIS
MANUEL	THE DESTINIES
HERMAN	SPIRITS, &C.

(The Scene of the Drama is amongst the Higher Alps — partly in the Castle of Manfred, and partly in the Mountains.)

ACT I

— SCENE I —

(MANFRED *alone — Scene, a Gothic gallery — Time, Midnight.*)

MAN: The lamp must be replenish'd, but even then
It will not burn so long as I must watch:
My slumbers — if I slumber — are not sleep,
But a continuance of enduring thought,
Which then I can resist not: in my heart
There is a vigil, and these eyes but close
To look within; and yet I live, and bear
The aspect and the form of breathing men.
But grief should be the instructor of the wise;
Sorrow is knowledge: they who know the most
Must mourn the deepest o'er the fatal truth,
The Tree of Knowledge is not that of Life.
Philosophy and science, and the springs
Of wonder, and the wisdom of the world,
I have essayed, and in my mind there is
A power to make these subject to itself —
But they avail not: I have done men good,

[1] Cf. *Hamlet*, I.v.166–67.

And I have met with good even among men—
But this avail'd not: I have had my foes,
And none have baffled, many fallen before me—
But this avail'd not:—Good, or evil, life,
Powers, passions, all I see in other beings,
Have been to me as rain unto the sands,
Since that all-nameless hour. I have no dread,
And feel the curse to have no natural fear,
Nor fluttering throb, that beats with hopes or
  wishes,
Or lurking love of something on the earth.—
Now to my task.—
      Mysterious Agency!
Ye spirits of the unbounded Universe!
Whom I have sought in darkness and in light—
Ye, who do compass earth about, and dwell
In subtler essence—ye, to whom the tops
Of mountains inaccessible are haunts,
And earth's and ocean's caves familiar things—
I call upon ye by the written charm
Which gives me power upon you—Rise! appear!

(A pause)

They come not yet.—Now by the voice of him
Who is the first among you—by this sign,
Which makes you tremble—by the claims of him
Who is undying,—Rise! appear!—Appear!

(A pause)

If it be so.—Spirits of earth and air,
Ye shall not thus elude me: by a power,
Deeper than all yet urged, a tyrant-spell,
Which had its birth-place in a star condemn'd,
The burning wreck of a demolish'd world,
A wandering hell in the eternal space;
By the strong curse which is upon my soul,
The thought which is within me and around me,
I do compel ye to my will.—Appear!

(A star is seen at the darker end of the gallery; it is stationary; and a voice is heard singing.)

FIRST SPIRIT:

Mortal! to thy bidding bow'd,
From my mansion in the cloud,
Which the breath of twilight builds,
And the summer's sun-set gilds
With the azure and vermilion,
Which is mix'd for my pavilion;
Though thy quest may be forbidden,
On a star-beam I have ridden;
To thine adjuration bow'd,
Mortal—be thy wish avow'd!

(Voice of the SECOND SPIRIT*)*

Mont Blanc[2] is the monarch of mountains,
  They crowned him long ago
On a throne of rocks, in a robe of clouds,
  With a diadem of snow.
Around his waist are forests braced,
  The Avalanche in his hand;
But ere it fall, that thundering ball
  Must pause for my command.
The Glacier's cold and restless mass
  Moves onward day by day;
But I am he who bids it pass,
  Or with its ice delay.
I am the spirit of the place,
  Could make the mountain bow
And quiver to his cavern'd base—
  And what with me wouldst *Thou*?

(Voice of the THIRD SPIRIT*)*

In the blue depth of the waters,
  Where the wave hath no strife,
Where the wind is a stranger,
  And the sea-snake hath life,
Where the Mermaid is decking
  Her green hair with shells;
Like the storm on the surface
  Came the sound of thy spells;
O'er my calm Hall of Coral
  The deep echo roll'd—
To the Spirit of Ocean
  Thy wishes unfold!

FOURTH SPIRIT:

Where the slumbering earthquake
  Lies pillow'd on fire,
And the lakes of bitumen[3]
  Rise boilingly higher;
Where the roots of the Andes
  Strike deep in the earth,
As their summits to heaven
  Shoot soaringly forth;
I have quitted my birth-place,
  Thy bidding to bide—

[2] **Mont Blanc:** the highest peak in the Alps at 15,771 feet.

[3] **bitumen:** pitch.

Thy spell hath subdued me,
Thy will be my guide!

FIFTH SPIRIT:
I am the Rider of the wind,
The Stirrer of the storm;
The hurricane I left behind
Is yet with lightning warm;
To speed to thee, o'er shore and sea
I swept upon the blast:
The fleet I met sailed well, and yet
'Twill sink ere night be past.

SIXTH SPIRIT:
My dwelling is the shadow of the night,
Why doth thy magic torture me with light?

SEVENTH SPIRIT:
The star which rules thy destiny,
Was ruled, ere earth began, by me:
It was a world as fresh and fair
As e'er revolved round sun in air;
Its course was free and regular,
Space bosom'd not a lovelier star.
The hour arrived—and it became
A wandering mass of shapeless flame,
A pathless comet, and a curse,
The menace of the universe;
Still rolling on with innate force,
Without a sphere, without a course,
A bright deformity on high,
The monster of the upper sky!
And thou! beneath its influence born—
Thou worm! whom I obey and scorn—
Forced by a power (which is not thine,
And lent thee but to make thee mine)
For this brief moment to descend,
Where these weak spirits round thee bend
And parley with a thing like thee—
What wouldst thou, Child of Clay! with me?

THE SEVEN SPIRITS:
Earth, ocean, air, night, mountains, winds, thy star,
Are at thy beck and bidding, Child of Clay!
Before thee at thy quest their spirits are—
What wouldst thou with us, son of mortals—
say?

MAN: Forgetfulness—
FIRST SPIRIT: Of what—of whom—and why?
MAN: Of that which is within me; read it there—
Ye know it, and I cannot utter it.
SPIRIT: We can but give thee that which we possess:
Ask of us subjects, sovereignty, the power
O'er earth, the whole, or portion, or a sign
Which shall control the elements, whereof
We are the dominators, each and all,
These shall be thine.
MAN: Oblivion, self-oblivion—
Can ye not wring from out the hidden realms
Ye offer so profusely what I ask?
SPIRIT: It is not in our essence, in our skill;
But—thou mayst die.
MAN: Will death bestow it on me?
SPIRIT: We are immortal, and do not forget;
We are eternal; and to us the past
Is, as the future, present. Art thou answered?
MAN: Ye mock me—but the power which brought ye
here
Hath made you mine. Slaves, scoff not at my will!
The mind, the spirit, the Promethean spark,
The lightning of my being, is as bright,
Pervading, and far-darting as your own,
And shall not yield to yours, though coop'd in clay!
Answer, or I will teach ye what I am.
SPIRIT: We answer as we answered; our reply
Is even in thine own words.
MAN: Why say ye so?
SPIRIT: If, as thou say'st, thine essence be as ours,
We have replied in telling thee, the thing
Mortals call death hath nought to do with us.
MAN: I then have call'd ye from your realms in vain;
Ye cannot, or ye will not, aid me.
SPIRIT: Say;
What we possess we offer; it is thine:
Bethink ere thou dismiss us, ask again—
Kingdom, and sway, and strength, and length of
days—
MAN: Accursed! what have I to do with days?
They are too long already.—Hence—begone!
SPIRIT: Yet pause: being here, our will would do thee
service;
Bethink thee, is there then no other gift
Which we can make not worthless in thine eyes?
MAN: No, none: yet stay—one moment, ere we
part—
I would behold ye face to face. I hear
Your voices, sweet and melancholy sounds,
As music on the waters;[4] and I see
The steady aspect of a clear large star;

[4] Cf. *The Tempest,* I.ii.391: "This music crept by me upon the waters."

But nothing more. Approach me as ye are,
Or one, or all, in your accustom'd forms.

SPIRIT: We have no forms beyond the elements
Of which we are the mind and principle:
But choose a form—in that we will appear.

MAN: I have no choice; there is no form on earth
Hideous or beautiful to me. Let him,
Who is most powerful of ye, take such aspect
As unto him may seem most fitting.—Come!

SEVENTH SPIRIT: (*appearing in the shape of a beautiful female figure*). Behold!

MAN: Oh God! if it be thus, and *thou*
Art not a madness and a mockery,
I yet might be most happy.—I will clasp thee,
And we again will be—

(*The figure vanishes.*)

My heart is crush'd!

(MANFRED *falls senseless.*) (*A voice is heard in the Incantation which follows.*)

When the moon is on the wave,
And the glow-worm in the grass,
And the meteor on the grave,
And the wisp on the morass;[5]
When the falling stars are shooting,
And the answer'd owls are hooting,
And the silent leaves are still
In the shadow of the hill,
Shall my soul be upon thine,
With a power and with a sign.

Though thy slumber may be deep,
Yet thy spirit shall not sleep,
There are shades which will not vanish,
There are thoughts thou canst not banish;
By a power to thee unknown,
Thou canst never be alone;
Thou art wrapt as with a shroud,
Thou art gathered in a cloud;
And for ever shalt thou dwell
In the spirit of this spell.

Though thou seest me not pass by,
Thou shalt feel me with thine eye
As a thing that, though unseen,
Must be near thee, and hath been;
And when in that secret dread
Thou hast turn'd around thy head,
Thou shalt marvel I am not
As thy shadow on the spot,
And the power which thou dost feel
Shall be what thou must conceal.

And a magic voice and verse
Hath baptized thee with a curse;
And a spirit of the air
Hath begirt thee with a snare;
In the wind there is a voice
Shall forbid thee to rejoice;
And to thee shall Night deny
All the quiet of her sky;
And the day shall have a sun,
Which shall make thee wish it done.

From thy false tears I did distil
An essence which hath strength to kill;
From thy own heart I then did wring
The black blood in its blackest spring;
From thy own smile I snatch'd the snake,
For there it coil'd as in a brake;
From thy own lip I drew the charm
Which gave all these their chiefest harm;
In proving every poison known,
I found the strongest was thine own.

By thy cold breast and serpent smile,
By thy unfathom'd gulfs of guile,
By that most seeming virtuous eye,
By thy shut soul's hypocrisy;
By the perfection of thine art
Which pass'd for human thine own heart;
By thy delight in others' pain,
And by thy brotherhood of Cain,
I call upon thee! and compel
Thyself to be thy proper Hell![6]

And on thy head I pour the vial
Which doth devote thee to this trial;
Nor to slumber, nor to die,
Shall be in thy destiny;
Though thy death shall still seem near
To thy wish, but as a fear;
Lo! the spell now works around thee,

[5] **wisp**: will-o'-the-wisp. **morass**: swamp.

[6] Cf. *Paradise Lost*, IV.75: "Which way I fly is hell; myself am hell. . . ."

And the clankless chain hath bound thee;
O'er thy heart and brain together
Hath the word been pass'd—now wither!

—SCENE II—

*(The Mountain of the Jungfrau.—Time, Morning.—*MANFRED *alone upon the Cliffs.)*

MAN: The spirits I have raised abandon me—
The spells which I have studied baffle me—
The remedy I reck'd of tortured me;
I lean no more on super-human aid,
It hath no power upon the past, and for
The future, till the past be gulf'd in darkness,
It is not of my search.—My mother Earth!
And thou fresh breaking Day, and you, ye Mountains,
Why are ye beautiful? I cannot love ye.
And thou, the bright eye of the universe,
That openest over all, and unto all
Art a delight—thou shin'st not on my heart.[7]
And you, ye crags, upon whose extreme edge
I stand, and on the torrent's brink beneath
Behold the tall pines dwindled as to shrubs
In dizziness of distance; when a leap,
A stir, a motion, even a breath, would bring
My breast upon its rocky bosom's bed
To rest for ever—wherefore do I pause?
I feel the impulse—yet I do not plunge;
I see the peril—yet do not recede;
And my brain reels—and yet my foot is firm:
There is a power upon me which withholds
And makes it my fatality to live;
If it be life to wear within myself
This barrenness of spirit, and to be
My own soul's sepulchre, for I have ceased
To justify my deeds unto myself—
The last infirmity[8] of evil. Ay,
Thou winged and cloud-cleaving minister,

(An eagle passes.)

Whose happy flight is highest into heaven,
Well may'st thou swoop so near me—I should be
Thy prey, and gorge thine eaglets; thou art gone
Where the eye cannot follow thee; but thine
Yet pierces downward, onward, or above
With a pervading vision.—Beautiful!
How beautiful is all this visible world!
How glorious in its action and itself;[9]
But we, who name ourselves its sovereigns, we,
Half dust, half deity, alike unfit
To sink or soar, with our mix'd essence make
A conflict of its elements, and breathe
The breath of degradation and of pride,
Contending with low wants and lofty will
Till our mortality predominates,
And men are—what they name not to themselves,
And trust not to each other. Hark! the note,

(The Shepherd's pipe in the distance is heard.)

The natural music of the mountain reed—
For here the patriarchal days are not
A pastoral fable—pipes in the liberal air,
Mix'd with the sweet bells of the sauntering herd;
My soul would drink those echoes.—Oh, that I were
The viewless spirit of a lovely sound,
A living voice, a breathing harmony,
A bodiless enjoyment—born and dying
With the blest tone which made me!

(Enter from below a CHAMOIS[10] HUNTER.*)*

CHAMOIS HUNTER: Even so
This way the chamois leapt: her nimble feet
Have baffled me; my gains to-day will scarce
Repay my break-neck travail.—What is here?
Who seems not of my trade, and yet hath reach'd
A height which none even of our mountaineers,
Save our best hunters, may attain: his garb
Is goodly, his mien manly, and his air
Proud as a free-born peasant's, at this distance.—
I will approach him nearer.

MAN. *(not perceiving the other)*: To be thus—
Grey-hair'd with anguish, like these blasted pines,

---

[7] Cf. *Paradise Lost,* IV.35–37: "to thee I call, / . . . and add thy name / O sun, to tell thee how I hate thy beams. . . ."

[8] Cf. Milton, *Lycidas,* 70–72: "*Fame* is the spur that the clear spirit doth raise / (That last infirmity of noble mind) / To scorn delights, and live laborious days."

[9] Cf. *Hamlet,* II.ii.315ff: "What a piece of work is man! . . . How infinite in faculty, in form and moving! How express and admirable in action! . . . And yet, to me, what is this quintessence of dust?"

[10] **chamois:** a hoofed mammal, like an antelope, that lives in the mountainous regions of Europe.

Wrecks of a single winter, barkless, branchless,
A blighted trunk upon a cursed root,
Which but supplies a feeling to decay—
And to be thus, eternally but thus,
Having been otherwise! Now furrow'd o'er
With wrinkles, plough'd by moments, not by years;
And hours—all tortured into ages—hours
Which I outlive!—Ye toppling crags of ice!
Ye avalanches, whom a breath draws down
In mountainous o'erwhelming, come and crush
me—
I hear ye momently above, beneath,
Crash with a frequent conflict; but ye pass,
And only fall on things which still would live;
On the young flourishing forest, or the hut
And hamlet of the harmless villager.

C. HUN: The mists begin to rise from up the valley;
I'll warn him to descend, or he may chance
To lose at once his way and life together.

MAN: The mists boil up around the glaciers; clouds
Rise curling fast beneath me, white and sulphury,
Like foam from the roused ocean of deep Hell,
Whose every wave breaks on a living shore,
Heaped with the damn'd like pebbles.—I am
giddy.

C. HUN: I must approach him cautiously; if near,
A sudden step will startle him, and he
Seems tottering already.

MAN: Mountains have fallen,
Leaving a gap in the clouds, and with the shock
Rocking their Alpine brethren; filling up
The ripe green valleys with destruction's splinters;
Damming the rivers with a sudden dash,
Which crush'd the waters into mist, and made
Their fountains find another channel—thus,
Thus, in its old age, did Mount Rosenberg[11]—
Why stood I not beneath it?

C. HUN: Friend! have a care,
Your next step may be fatal!—for the love
Of him who made you, stand not on that brink!

MAN. *(not hearing him)*: Such would have been for me a
fitting tomb;
My bones had then been quiet in their depth;
They had not then been strewn upon the rocks
For the wind's pastime—as thus—thus they shall
be—
In this one plunge.—Farewell, ye opening heavens!
Look not upon me thus reproachfully—
Ye were not meant for me—Earth! take these atoms!

(As MANFRED *is in act to spring from the cliff, the* CHAMOIS HUNTER *seizes and retains him with a sudden grasp.)*

C. HUN: Hold, madman!—though aweary of thy life,
Stain not our pure vales with thy guilty blood.—
Away with me—I will not quit my hold.

MAN: I am most sick at heart—nay, grasp me not—
I am all feebleness—the mountains whirl
Spinning around me—I grow blind—What art
thou?

C. HUN: I'll answer that anon.—Away with me
The clouds grow thicker—there—now lean on
me—
Place your foot here—here, take this staff, and
cling
A moment to that shrub—now give me your hand,
And hold fast by my girdle—softly—well—
The Chalet will be gained within an hour—
Come on, we'll quickly find a surer footing,
And something like a pathway, which the torrent
Hath wash'd since winter.—Come, 'tis bravely
done—
You should have been a hunter.—Follow me.

(As they descend the rocks with difficulty, the scene closes.)

ACT II

—SCENE I—

(A Cottage amongst the Bernese[12] Alps.)

(MANFRED and the CHAMOIS HUNTER.)

C. HUN: No, no—yet pause—thou must not yet go
forth:
Thy mind and body are alike unfit
To trust each other, for some hours, at least;
When thou art better, I will be thy guide—
But whither?

MAN: It imports not: I do know
My route full well, and need no further guidance.

[11] **Mount Rosenberg:** in 1806, a landslide from a Mt. Rossberg buried four villages (McGann).

[12] **Bernese:** the city of Bern is located in northwest Switzerland.

C. HUN: Thy garb and gait bespeak thee of high
lineage—
One of the many chiefs, whose castled crags
Look o'er the lower valleys—which of these
May call thee Lord? I only know their portals;[13]
My way of life leads me but rarely down
To bask by the huge hearths of those old halls,
Carousing with the vassals; but the paths,
Which step from out our mountains to their doors,
I know from childhood—which of these is thine?

MAN: No matter.

C. HUN: Well, sir, pardon me the question,
And be of better cheer. Come, taste my wine;
'Tis of an ancient vintage; many a day
'T has thawed my veins among our glaciers, now
Let it do thus for thine—Come, pledge me fairly.

MAN: Away, away! there's blood upon the brim!
Will it then never—never sink in the earth?

C. HUN: What dost thou mean? thy senses wander
from thee.

MAN: I say 'tis blood—my blood![14] the pure warm
stream
Which ran in the veins of my fathers, and in ours
When we were in our youth, and had one heart,
And loved each other as we should not love,
And this was shed: but still it rises up,
Colouring the clouds, that shut me out from
heaven,
Where thou art not—and I shall never be.

C. HUN: Man of strange words, and some half-
maddening sin,
Which makes thee people vacancy, whate'er
Thy dread and sufferance be, there's comfort yet—
The aid of holy men, and heavenly patience—

MAN: Patience and patience! Hence—that word was
made
For brutes of burthen, not for birds of prey;
Preach it to mortals of a dust like thine,—
I am not of thine order.

C. HUN: Thanks to heaven!
I would not be of thine for the free fame
Of William Tell;[15] but whatsoe'er thine ill,
It must be borne, and these wild starts are useless.

MAN: Do I not bear it?—Look on me—I live.

C. HUN: This is convulsion, and no healthful life.

MAN: I tell thee, man! I have lived many years,
Many long years, but they are nothing now
To those which I must number: ages—ages—
Space and eternity—and consciousness,
With the fierce thirst of death—and still unslaked!

C. HUN: Why, on thy brow the seal of middle age
Hath scarce been set; I am thine elder far.

MAN: Think'st thou existence doth depend on time?
It doth; but actions are our epochs: mine
Have made my days and nights imperishable,
Endless, and all alike, as sands on the shore,
Innumerable atoms, and one desart,
Barren and cold, on which the wild waves break,
But nothing rests, save carcases and wrecks,
Rocks, and the salt-surf weeds of bitterness.

C. HUN: Alas! he's mad—but yet I must not leave
him.

MAN: I would I were—for then the things I see
Would be but a distempered dream.

C. HUN: What is it
That thou dost see, or think thou look'st upon?

MAN: Myself, and thee—a peasant of the Alps—
Thy humble virtues, hospitable home,
And spirit patient, pious, proud and free;
Thy self-respect, grafted on innocent thoughts;
Thy days of health, and nights of sleep; thy toils,
By danger dignified, yet guiltless; hopes
Of cheerful old age and a quiet grave,
With cross and garland over its green turf,
And thy grandchildren's love for epitaph;
This do I see—and then I look within—
It matters not—my soul was scorch'd already!

C. HUN: And would'st thou then exchange thy lot for
mine?

MAN: No, friend! I would not wrong thee, nor
exchange
My lot with living being: I can bear—
However wretchedly, 'tis still to bear—

[13] **portal:** an entrance or gate.

[14] Cf. Matthew, 27–28: "Drink ye all of it; For this is my blood of the new testament."

[15] **William Tell:** the legendary Swiss patriot and hero who resisted the rule of the Austrians in Switzerland in the late thirteenth to early fourteenth centuries. As punishment, Tell was forced to shoot an apple off his son's head.

In life what others could not brook to dream,
But perish in their slumber.

C. HUN: And with this—
This cautious feeling for another's pain,
Canst thou be black with evil?—say not so.
Can one of gentle thoughts have wreak'd revenge
Upon his enemies?

MAN: Oh! no, no, no!
My injuries came down on those who loved me—
On those whom I best loved: I never quell'd
An enemy, save in my just defence—
My wrongs were all on those I should have cherished—
But my embrace was fatal.

C. HUN: Heaven give thee rest!
And penitence restore thee to thyself;
My prayers shall be for thee.

MAN: I need them not,
But can endure thy pity. I depart—
'Tis time—farewell!—Here's gold, and thanks for thee—
No words—it is thy due.—Follow me not—
I know my path—the mountain peril's past:—
And once again, I charge thee, follow not!

(Exit MANFRED.*)*

— SCENE II —

(A lower Valley in the Alps—A Cataract)

(Enter MANFRED.*)*

It is not noon—the sunbow's rays still arch
The torrent with the many hues of heaven,
And roll the sheeted silver's waving column
O'er the crag's headlong perpendicular,
And fling its lines of foaming light along,
And to and fro, like the pale courser's tail,
The Giant steed, to be bestrode by Death,
As told in the Apocalypse.[16] No eyes
But mine now drink this sight of loveliness;
I should be sole in this sweet solitude,
And with the Spirit of the place divide
The homage of these waters.—I will call her.

*(*MANFRED *takes some of the water into the palm of his hand, and flings it in the air, muttering the adjuration. After a pause, the* WITCH OF THE ALPS *rises beneath the arch of the sunbow of the torrent.)*

MAN: Beautiful Spirit! with thy hair of light,
And dazzling eyes of glory, in whose form
The charms of Earth's least-mortal daughters grow
To an unearthly stature, in an essence
Of purer elements; while the hues of youth,—
Carnation'd like a sleeping infant's cheek,
Rock'd by the beating of her mother's heart,
Or the rose tints, which summer's twilight leaves
Upon the lofty glacier's virgin snow,
The blush of earth embracing with her heaven,—
Tinge thy celestial aspect, and make tame
The beauties of the sunbow which bends o'er thee.
Beautiful Spirit! in thy calm clear brow,
Wherein is glass'd serenity of soul,
Which of itself shows immortality,
I read that thou wilt pardon to a Son
Of Earth, whom the abstruser powers permit
At times to commune with them—if that he
Avail him of his spells—to call thee thus,
And gaze on thee a moment.

WITCH: Son of Earth!
I know thee, and the powers which give thee power;
I know thee for a man of many thoughts,
And deeds of good and ill, extreme in both,
Fatal and fated in thy sufferings.
I have expected this—what wouldst thou with me?

MAN: To look upon thy beauty—nothing further.
The face of the earth hath madden'd me, and I
Take refuge in her mysteries, and pierce
To the abodes of those who govern her—
But they can nothing aid me. I have sought
From them what they could not bestow, and now
I search no further.

WITCH: What could be the quest
Which is not in the power of the most powerful,
The rulers of the invisible?

MAN: A boon;
But why should I repeat it? 'twere in vain.

WITCH: I know not that; let thy lips utter it.

MAN: Well, though it torture me, 'tis but the same;
My pang shall find a voice. From my youth upwards
My spirit walk'd not with the souls of men,
Nor look'd upon the earth with human eyes;
The thirst of their ambition was not mine,
The aim of their existence was not mine;
My joys, my griefs, my passions, and my powers,

[16] Cf. *Alpine Journal,* n. 21, above.

Made me a stranger; though I wore the form,
I had no sympathy with breathing flesh,
Nor midst the creatures of clay that girded me
Was there but one who—but of her anon.
I said, with men, and with the thoughts of men,
I held but slight communion; but instead,
My joy was in the Wilderness, to breathe
The difficult air of the iced mountain's top,
Where the birds dare not build, nor insect's wing
Flit o'er the herbless granite; or to plunge
Into the torrent, and to roll along
On the swift whirl of the new breaking wave
Of river-stream, or ocean, in their flow.
In these my early strength exulted; or
To follow through the night the moving moon,
The stars and their developement; or catch
The dazzling lightnings till my eyes grew dim;
Or to look, list'ning, on the scattered leaves,
While Autumn winds were at their evening song.
These were my pastimes, and to be alone;
For if the beings, of whom I was one,—
Hating to be so,—cross'd me in my path,
I felt myself degraded back to them,
And was all clay again. And then I dived,
In my lone wanderings, to the caves of death,
Searching its cause in its effect; and drew
From wither'd bones, and skulls, and heap'd up
  dust,
Conclusions most forbidden. Then I pass'd
The nights of years in sciences untaught,
Save in the old-time; and with time and toil,
And terrible ordeal, and such penance
As in itself hath power upon the air,
And spirits that do compass air and earth,
Space, and the peopled infinite, I made
Mine eyes familiar with Eternity,
Such as, before me, did the Magi, and
He who from out their fountain dwellings raised
Eros and Anteros,[17] at Gadara,
As I do thee;—and with my knowledge grew
The thirst of knowledge, and the power and joy
Of this most bright intelligence, until—

WITCH: Proceed.

MAN: Oh! I but thus prolonged my words,
Boasting these idle attributes, because
As I approach the core of my heart's grief—
But to my task. I have not named to thee
Father or mother, mistress, friend, or being,
With whom I wore the chain of human ties;
If I had such, they seem'd not such to me—
Yet there was one—

WITCH: Spare not thyself—proceed.

MAN: She was like me in lineaments—her eyes,
Her hair, her features, all, to the very tone
Even of her voice, they said were like to mine;
But soften'd all, and temper'd into beauty;
She had the same lone thoughts and wanderings,
The quest of hidden knowledge, and a mind
To comprehend the universe: nor these
Alone, but with them gentler powers than mine,
Pity, and smiles, and tears—which I had not;
And tenderness—but that I had for her;
Humility—and that I never had.
Her faults were mine—her virtues were her own—
I loved her, and destroy'd her!

WITCH: With thy hand?

MAN: Not with my hand, but heart—which broke
  her heart—
It gazed on mine, and withered. I have shed
Blood, but not hers—and yet her blood was shed—
I saw—and could not staunch it.[18]

WITCH: And for this—
A being of the race thou dost despise,
The order which thine own would rise above,
Mingling with us and ours, thou dost forego
The gifts of our great knowledge, and shrink'st back
To recreant[19] mortality—Away!

MAN: Daughter of Air! I tell thee, since that hour—
But words are breath—look on me in my sleep,
Or watch my watchings—Come and sit by me!
My solitude is solitude no more,
But peopled with the Furies;[20]—I have gnash'd

[17] **Magi:** priestly class among the ancient Medes and Persians whose doctrines included belief in astrology. **He who . . . :** The neo-Platonist philosopher Iamblicus (c. 250–c. 325), who wrote *De mysteriis,* a defense of ritualistic magic, was said to have raised the spirits of the gods Eros and his brother Anteros from fountains in Syria.

[18] **staunch it:** to stop the flow; cf. William Cowper, "[To] staunch the bleedings of a broken heart" ("Retirement," l. 322).

[19] **recreant:** cowardly.

[20] **Furies:** the Greek deities of vengeance.

My teeth in darkness till returning morn,
Then cursed myself till sunset;—I have pray'd
For madness as a blessing—'tis denied me.
I have affronted death—but in the war
Of elements the waters shrunk from me,
And fatal things pass'd harmless—the cold hand
Of an all-pitiless demon held me back,
Back by a single hair, which would not break.
In phantasy, imagination, all
The affluence of my soul—which one day was
A Croesus[21] in creation—I plunged deep,
But, like an ebbing wave, it dash'd me back
Into the gulf of my unfathom'd thought.
I plunged amidst mankind—Forgetfulness
I sought in all, save where 'tis to be found,
And that I have to learn—my sciences,
My long pursued and super-human art,
Is mortal here—I dwell in my despair—
And live—and live for ever.

WITCH: It may be
That I can aid thee.

MAN: To do this thy power
Must wake the dead, or lay me low with them.
Do so—in any shape—in any hour—
With any torture—so it be the last.

WITCH: That is not in my province; but if thou
Wilt swear obedience to my will, and do
My bidding, it may help thee to thy wishes.[22]

MAN: I will not swear—Obey! and whom? the spirits
Whose presence I command, and be the slave
Of those who served me—Never!

WITCH: Is this all?
Hast thou no gentler answer—Yet bethink thee,
And pause ere thou rejectest.

MAN: I have said it.

WITCH: Enough!—I may retire then—say!

MAN: Retire!

(The WITCH *disappears.)*

MAN: *(alone).* We are the fools of time and terror: Days
Steal on us and steal from us; yet we live,
Loathing our life, and dreading still to die.
In all the days of this detested yoke—
This heaving burthen, this accursed breath—
This vital weight upon the struggling heart,
Which sinks with sorrow, or beats quick with pain,
Or joy that ends in agony or faintness—
In all the days of past and future, for
In life there is no present, we can number
How few—how less than few—wherein the soul
Forbears to pant for death, and yet draws back
As from a stream in winter, though the chill
Be but a moment's. I have one resource
Still in my science—I can call the dead,
And ask them what it is we dread to be:
The sternest answer can but be the Grave,
And that is nothing—if they answer not—
The buried Prophet answered to the Hag
Of Endor; and the Spartan Monarch drew
From the Byzantine maid's unsleeping spirit
An answer and his destiny—he slew
That which he loved, unknowing what he slew,
And died unpardon'd—though he call'd in aid
The Phyxian Jove, and in Phigalia roused
The Arcadian Evocators to compel
The indignant shadow to depose her wrath,
Or fix her term of vengeance—she replied
In words of dubious import, but fulfill'd.[23]

If I had never lived, that which I love
Had still been living; had I never loved,
That which I love would still be beautiful—
Happy and giving happiness. What is she?
What is she now?—a sufferer for my sins—
A thing I dare not think upon—or nothing.
Within few hours I shall not call in vain—
Yet in this hour I dread the thing I dare:
Until this hour I never shrunk to gaze
On spirit, good or evil—now I tremble,
And feel a strange cold thaw upon my heart,
But I can act even what I most abhor,
And champion human fears.—The night
approaches.

(Exit.)

[21] **Croesus:** the last king of Lydia in Asia Minor (rg. 560–546 BC), whose name became proverbial for wealth.

[22] Cf. Matthew 4:9: "All these things will I give thee, if thou wilt fall down and worship me."

[23] **The buried Prophet . . . fulfill'd:** at King Saul's bidding, the Witch of Endor raised the prophet Samuel from the dead; cf. 1 Samuel 28:7, ff. Pausanias, king of Sparta, mistakenly killed his mistress Cleonice. When he requests forgiveness of her spirit, she tells him his troubles will end when he returns to Sparta. He is killed when he returns.

— SCENE III —

(The Summit of the Jungfrau[24] *Mountain.)*

(Enter FIRST DESTINY.)

The moon is rising broad, and round, and bright;
And here on snows, where never human foot
Of common mortal trod, we nightly tread,
And leave no traces; o'er the savage sea,
The glassy ocean of the mountain ice,
We skim its rugged breakers, which put on
The aspect of a tumbling tempest's foam,
Frozen in a moment — a dead whirlpool's image;
And this most steep fantastic pinnacle,
The fretwork of some earthquake — where the clouds
Pause to repose themselves in passing by —
Is sacred to our revels, or our vigils;
Here do I wait my sisters, on our way
To the Hall of Arimanes,[25] for to-night
Is our great festival — 'tis strange they come not.

(A Voice without, singing.)

The Captive Usurper,
Hurl'd down from the throne,
Lay buried in torpor,
Forgotten and lone;
I broke through his slumbers,
I shivered his chain,
I leagued him with numbers —
He's Tyrant again!
With the blood of a million he'll answer my care,
With a nation's destruction — his flight and despair.

(Second Voice, without.)

The ship sail'd on, the ship sail'd fast,
But I left not a sail, and I left not a mast;
There is not a plank of the hull or the deck,
And there is not a wretch to lament o'er his wreck;
Save one, whom I held, as he swam, by the hair,
And he was a subject well worthy my care;
A traitor on land, and a pirate at sea —
But I saved him to wreak further havoc for me!

(FIRST DESTINY, *answering.*)

The city lies sleeping;
The morn, to deplore it,
May dawn on it weeping:
Sullenly, slowly,
The black plague flew o'er it —
Thousands lie lowly;
Tens of thousands shall perish —
The living shall fly from
The sick they should cherish;
But nothing can vanquish
The touch that they die from.
Sorrow and anguish,
And evil and dread,
Envelope a nation —
The blest are the dead,
Who see not the sight
Of their own desolation. —
This work of a night —
This wreck of a realm — this deed of my doing —
For ages I've done, and shall still be renewing!

(Enter the SECOND *and* THIRD DESTINIES.*)*

(The Three.)

Our hands contain the hearts of men,
Our footsteps are their graves;
We only give to take again
The spirits of our slaves!

FIRST DES: Welcome! — Where's Nemesis?[26]
SECOND DES: At some great work;
But what I know not, for my hands were full.
THIRD DES: Behold she cometh.

(Enter NEMESIS.*)*

FIRST DES: Say, where hast thou been? —
My sisters and thyself are slow to-night.
NEM: I was detain'd repairing shattered thrones,
Marrying fools, restoring dynasties,
Avenging men upon their enemies,
And making them repent their own revenge;
Goading the wise to madness; from the dull
Shaping out oracles to rule the world
Afresh, for they were waxing out of date,
And mortals dared to ponder for themselves,

[24] **Jungfrau:** a mountain in south-central Switzerland, so named for its perceived resemblance to a young woman reclining.

[25] **Arimanes:** reference to Ahriman, the spirit of evil and darkness in the Zoroastrian religion.

[26] **Nemesis:** the Greek goddess of retribution especially for human presumptuousness.

To weigh kings in the balance, and to speak
Of freedom, the forbidden fruit.[27] — Away!
We have outstaid the hour — mount we our clouds!

(Exeunt.)

— SCENE IV —

(The Hall of Arimanes — Arimanes on his Throne, a Globe of Fire, surrounded by the Spirits.)

(Hymn of the SPIRITS*)*

Hail to our Master! — Prince of Earth and Air! —
Who walks the clouds and waters — in his hand
The sceptre of the elements, which tear
Themselves to chaos at his high command!
He breatheth — and a tempest shakes the sea;
He speaketh — and the clouds reply in thunder;
He gazeth — from his glance the sunbeams flee;
He moveth — earthquakes rend the world asunder.
Beneath his footsteps the volcanos rise;
His shadow is the Pestilence; his path
The comets herald through the crackling skies;
And planets turn to ashes at his wrath.
To him War offers daily sacrifice;
To him Death pays his tribute; Life is his,
With all its infinite of agonies —
And his the spirit of whatever is!

(Enter the DESTINIES *and* NEMESIS.*)*

FIRST DES: Glory to Arimanes! on the earth
His power increaseth — both my sisters did
His bidding, nor did I neglect my duty!
SECOND DES: Glory to Arimanes! we who bow
The necks of men, bow down before his thrown!
THIRD DES: Glory to Arimanes! — we await
His nod!
NEM: Sovereign of Sovereigns! we are thine,
And all that liveth, more or less, is ours,
And most things wholly so; still to increase
Our power increasing thine, demands our care,
And we are vigilant — Thy late commands
Have been fulfilled to the utmost.

(Enter MANFRED.*)*

A SPIRIT: What is here?
A mortal! — Thou most rash and fatal wretch,
Bow down and worship!
SECOND SPIRIT: I do know the man —
A Magian of great power, and fearful skill!
THIRD SPIRIT: Bow down and worship, slave! — What, know'st thou not
Thine and our Sovereign? — Tremble, and obey!
ALL THE SPIRITS: Prostrate thyself, and thy condemned clay,
Child of the Earth! or dread the worst.
MAN: I know it;
And yet ye see I kneel not.
FOURTH SPIRIT: 'Twill be taught thee.
MAN: 'Tis taught already; — many a night on the earth,
On the bare ground, have I bow'd down my face,
And strew'd my head with ashes;[28] I have known
The fulness of humiliation, for
I sunk before my vain despair, and knelt
To my own desolation.
FIFTH SPIRIT: Dost thou dare
Refuse to Arimanes on his throne
What the whole earth accords, beholding not
The terror of his Glory — Crouch! I say.
MAN: Bid *him* bow down to that which is above him,
The overruling Infinite — the Maker
Who made him not for worship — let him kneel,
And we will kneel together.
THE SPIRITS: Crush the worm!
Tear him in pieces! —
FIRST DES: Hence! Avaunt![29] — he's mine.
Prince of the Powers invisible! This man
Is of no common order, as his port
And presence here denote; his sufferings
Have been of an immortal nature, like
Our own; his knowledge and his powers and will,
As far as is compatible with clay,
Which clogs the etherial essence, have been such
As clay hath seldom borne; his aspirations
Have been beyond the dwellers of the earth,
And they have only taught him what we know —

[27] Cf. *Paradise Lost*, IX.904: "the sacred fruit forbidd'n."

[28] **And strew'd . . . ashes:** reference to the Roman Catholic rite of rubbing the forehead with ashes on Ash Wednesday to recall Genesis 3:19: "for dust thou art, and unto dust shalt thou return."

[29] **Avaunt!:** be gone!

That knowledge is not happiness, and science
But an exchange of ignorance for that
Which is another kind of ignorance.
This is not all—the passions, attributes
Of earth and heaven, from which no power, nor
being,
Nor breath from the worm upwards is exempt,
Have pierced his heart; and in their consequence
Made him a thing, which I, who pity not,
Yet pardon those who pity. He is mine,
And thine, it may be—be it so, or not,
No other Spirit in this region hath
A soul like his—or power upon his soul.

NEM: What doth he here then?

FIRST DES: Let *him* answer that.

MAN: Ye know what I have known; and without
power
I could not be amongst ye: but there are
Powers deeper still beyond—I come in quest
Of such, to answer unto what I seek.

NEM: What wouldst *thou*?

MAN: Thou canst not reply to me.
Call up the dead—my question is for them.

NEM: Great Arimanes, doth thy will avouch
The wishes of this mortal?

ARI: Yea.

NEM: Whom would'st thou
Uncharnel?[30]

MAN: One without a tomb—call up
Astarte.

NEM: Shadow! or Spirit!
Whatever thou art,
Which still doth inherit
The whole or a part
Of the form of thy birth,
Of the mould of thy clay,
Which returned to the earth,
Re-appear to the day!
Bear what thou borest,
The heart and the form,
And the aspect thou worest
Redeem from the worm.
Appear!—Appear!—Appear!
Who sent thee there requires thee here!

(The Phantom of ASTARTE *rises and stands in the midst.)*

MAN: Can this be death? there's bloom upon her
cheek;
But now I see it is no living hue,
But a strange hectic—like the unnatural red
Which Autumn plants upon the perish'd leaf.
It is the same! Oh, God! that I should dread
To look upon the same—Astarte!—No,
I cannot speak to her—but bid her speak—
Forgive me or condemn me.

NEM: By the power which hath broken
The grave which enthrall'd thee,
Speak to him who hath spoken,
Or those who have call'd thee!

MAN: She is silent,
And in that silence I am more than answered.

NEM: My power extends no further. Prince of air!
It rests with thee alone—command her voice.

ARI: Spirit—obey this sceptre!

NEM: Silent still!
She is not of our order, but belongs
To the other powers. Mortal! thy quest is vain,
And we are baffled also.

MAN: Hear me, hear me—
Astarte! my beloved! speak to me:
I have so much endured—so much endure—
Look on me! the grave hath not changed thee more
Than I am changed for thee. Thou lovedst me
Too much, as I loved thee: we were not made
To torture thus each other, though it were
The deadliest sin to love as we have loved.
Say that thou loath'st me not—that I do bear
This punishment for both—that thou wilt be
One of the blessed—and that I shall die,
For hitherto all hateful things conspire
To bind me in existence—in a life
Which makes me shrink from immortality—
A future like the past. I cannot rest.
I know not what I ask, nor what I seek:
I feel but what thou art—and what I am;
And I would hear yet once before I perish
The voice which was my music—Speak to me!
For I have call'd on thee in the still night,
Startled the slumbering birds from the hush'd
boughs,
And woke the mountain wolves, and made the
caves
Acquainted with thy vainly echoed name,

[30] **Uncharnel:** raise from the charnel house, or room for corpses and remains of the dead.

Which answered me — many things answered me —
Spirits and men — but thou wert silent all.
Yet speak to me! I have outwatch'd the stars,
And gazed o'er heaven in vain in search of thee.
Speak to me! I have wandered o'er the earth
And never found thy likeness — Speak to me!
Look on the fiends around — they feel for me:
I fear them not, and feel for thee alone —
Speak to me! though it be in wrath, — but say —
I reck not what — but let me hear thee once —
This once — once more!

PHANTOM OF ASTARTE: Manfred!

MAN: Say on, say on —
I live but in the sound — it is thy voice!

PHAN: Manfred! To-morrow ends thine earthly ills.
Farewell!

MAN: Yet one word more — am I forgiven?

PHAN: Farewell!

MAN: Say, shall we meet again?

PHAN: Farewell!

MAN: One word for mercy! Say, thou lovest me.

PHAN: Manfred!

(The Spirit of ASTARTE *disappears.)*

NEM: She's gone, and will not be recall'd;
Her words will be fulfill'd. Return to the earth.

A SPIRIT: He is convulsed — This is to be a mortal
And seek the things beyond mortality.

ANOTHER SPIRIT: Yet, see, he mastereth himself, and makes
His torture tributary to his will.
Had he been one of us, he would have made
An awful[31] spirit.

NEM: Hast thou further question
Of our great sovereign, or his worshippers?

MAN: None.

NEM: Then for a time farewell.

MAN: We meet then —
Where? On the earth?

NEM: That will be seen hereafter.

MAN: Even as thou wilt: and for the grace accorded
I now depart a debtor. Fare ye well!

(Exit MANFRED.*)*

(Scene closes.)

[31] **awful**: awe-inspiring.

ACT III

— SCENE I —

(A Hall in the Castle of Manfred.)

*(*MANFRED *and* HERMAN*)*

MAN: What is the hour?

HER: It wants but one till sunset,
And promises a lovely twilight.

MAN: Say,
Are all things so disposed of in the tower
As I directed?

HER: All, my lord, are ready;
Here is the key and casket.

MAN: It is well:
Thou mayst retire.

(Exit HERMAN.*)*

MAN: *(alone).* There is a calm upon me —
Inexplicable stillness! which till now
Did not belong to what I knew of life.
If that I did not know philosophy
To be of all our vanities the motliest,
The merest word that ever fool'd the ear
From out the schoolman's jargon, I should deem
The golden secret, the sought 'Kalon,'[32] found,
And seated in my soul. It will not last,
But it is well to have known it, though but once:
It hath enlarged my thoughts with a new sense,
And I within my tablets would note down
That there is such a feeling. Who is there?

(Re-enter HERMAN.*)*

My lord, the abbot of St. Maurice craves
To greet your presence.

(Enter the ABBOT OF ST. MAURICE.*)*

ABBOT: Peace be with Count Manfred!

MAN: Thanks, holy father! welcome to these walls;
Thy presence honours them, and blesseth those
Who dwell within them.

ABBOT: Would it were so, Count! —
But I would fain confer with thee alone.

MAN: Herman, retire. What would my reverend guest?

(Exit HERMAN.*)*

[32] **Kalon**: *Greek*: beautiful.

ABBOT: Thus, without prelude:—Age and zeal, my office,
And good intent, must plead my privilege;
Our near, though not acquainted neighbourhood,
May also be my herald. Rumours strange,
And of unholy nature, are abroad,
And busy with thy name; a noble name
For centuries; may he who bears it now
Transmit it unimpair'd!
MAN: Proceed,—I listen.
ABBOT: 'Tis said thou holdest converse with the things
Which are forbidden to the search of man;
That with the dwellers of the dark abodes,
The many evil and unheavenly spirits
Which walk the valley of the shade of death,[33]
Thou communest. I know that with mankind,
Thy fellows in creation, thou dost rarely
Exchange thy thoughts, and that thy solitude
Is as an anchorite's,[34] were it but holy.
MAN: And what are they who do avouch these things?
ABBOT: My pious brethren—the scared peasantry—
Even thy own vassals—who do look on thee
With most unquiet eyes. Thy life's in peril.
MAN: Take it.
ABBOT: I come to save, and not destroy—
I would not pry into thy secret soul;
But if these things be sooth,[35] there still is time
For penitence and pity: reconcile thee
With the true church, and through the church to heaven.
MAN: I hear thee. This is my reply; whate'er
I may have been, or am, doth rest between
Heaven and myself.—I shall not choose a mortal
To be my mediator. Have I sinn'd
Against your ordinances? prove and punish!
ABBOT: My son! I did not speak of punishment,
But penitence and pardon;—with thyself
The choice of such remains—and for the last,
Our institutions and our strong belief
Have given me power to smooth the path from sin
To higher hope and better thoughts; the first
I leave to heaven—'Vengeance is mine alone!'[36]
So saith the Lord, and with all humbleness
His servant echoes back the awful word.
MAN: Old man! there is no power in holy men,
Nor charm in prayer—nor purifying form
Of penitence—nor outward look—nor fast—
Nor agony—nor, greater than all these,
The innate tortures of that deep despair,
Which is remorse without the fear of hell,
But all in all sufficient to itself
Would make a hell of heaven[37]—can exorcise
From out the unbounded spirit, the quick sense
Of its own sins, wrongs, sufferance, and revenge
Upon itself; there is no future pang
Can deal that justice on the self-condemn'd
He deals on his own soul.
ABBOT: All this is well;
For this will pass away, and be succeeded
By an auspicious hope, which shall look up
With calm assurance to that blessed place,
Which all who seek may win, whatever be
Their earthly errors, so they be atoned:
And the commencement of atonement is
The sense of its necessity.—Say on—
And all our church can teach thee shall be taught;
And all we can absolve thee, shall be pardon'd.
MAN: When Rome's sixth Emperor[38] was near his last,
The victim of a self-inflicted wound,
To shun the torments of a public death
From senates once his slaves, a certain soldier,
With show of loyal pity, would have staunch'd
The gushing throat with his officious robe;
The dying Roman thrust him back and said—
Some empire still in his expiring glance,
'It is too late—is this fidelity?'
ABBOT: And what of this?
MAN: I answer with the Roman—
'It is too late!'
ABBOT: It never can be so,
To reconcile thyself with thy own soul,
And thy own soul with heaven. Hast thou no hope?
'Tis strange—even those who do despair above,

[33] Cf. Psalms 23:4: "Yea, though I walk through the valley of the shadow of death, I will fear no evil."

[34] **anchorite:** Christian hermit.

[35] **sooth:** truth, or true.

[36] Cf. Romans 12:19. "Vengeance is mine; I will repay, saith the Lord."

[37] Cf. *Paradise Lost*, I.254–55: "The mind is its own place, and in itself / Can make a heav'n of hell, a hell of heav'n."

[38] **Rome's sixth Emperor:** reference to Nero.

Yet shape themselves some phantasy on earth,
To which frail twig they cling, like drowning men.
MAN: Ay—father! I have had those earthly visions
And noble aspirations in my youth,
To make my own the mind of other men,
The enlightener of nations; and to rise
I knew not whither—it might be to fall;
But fall, even as the mountain-cataract,
Which having leapt from its more dazzling height,
Even in the foaming strength of its abyss,
(Which casts up misty columns that become
Clouds raining from the re-ascended skies)
Lies low but mighty still.—But this is past,
My thoughts mistook themselves.
ABBOT: And wherefore so?
MAN: I could not tame my nature down; for he
Must serve who fain would sway—and soothe—
and sue—
And watch all time—and pry into all place—
And be a living lie—who would become
A mighty thing amongst the mean, and such
The mass are; I disdained to mingle with
A herd, though to be leader—and of wolves.
The lion is alone, and so am I.
ABBOT: And why not live and act with other men?
MAN: Because my nature was averse from life;
And yet not cruel; for I would not make,
But find a desolation:—like the wind,
The red-hot breath of the most lone Simoom,[39]
Which dwells but in the desart, and sweeps o'er
The barren sands which bear no shrubs to blast,
And revels o'er their wild and arid waves,
And seeketh not, so that it is not sought,
But being met is deadly; such hath been
The course of my existence; but there came
Things in my path which are no more.
ABBOT: Alas!
I 'gin to fear that thou art past all aid
From me and from my calling; yet so young,
I still would—
MAN: Look on me! there is an order
Of mortals on the earth, who do become
Old in their youth, and die ere middle age,
Without the violence of warlike death;
Some perishing of pleasure—some of study—
Some worn with toil—some of mere weariness—
Some of disease—and some insanity—
And some of withered, or of broken hearts;
For this last is a malady which slays
More than are numbered in the lists of Fate,
Taking all shapes, and bearing many names.
Look upon me! for even of all these things
Have I partaken; and of all these things,
One were enough; then wonder not that I
Am what I am, but that I ever was,
Or, having been, that I am still on earth.
ABBOT: Yet, hear me still—
MAN: Old man! I do respect
Thine order, and revere thine years; I deem
Thy purpose pious, but it is in vain:
Think me not churlish; I would spare thyself,
Far more than me, in shunning at this time
All further colloquy—and so—farewell.

(Exit MANFRED.*)*

ABBOT: This should have been a noble creature: he
Hath all the energy which would have made
A goodly frame of glorious elements,
Had they been wisely mingled; as it is,
It is an awful chaos—light and darkness—
And mind and dust—and passions and pure
thoughts,
Mix'd, and contending without end or order,
All dormant or destructive: he will perish,
And yet he must not, I will try once more,
For such are worth redemption; and my duty
Is to dare all things for a righteous end.
I'll follow him—but cautiously, though surely.

(Exit ABBOT.*)*

—SCENE II—

(Another Chamber)

(MANFRED *and* HERMAN)

HER: My Lord, you bade me wait on you at sunset:
He sinks behind the mountain.
MAN: Doth he so?
I will look on him.

(MANFRED *advances to the Window of the Hall.)*

Glorious Orb! the idol
Of early nature, and the vigorous race

[39] **Simoom:** hot, dry desert wind.

Of undiseased mankind, the giant sons[40]
Of the embrace of angels, with a sex
More beautiful than they, which did draw down
The erring spirits who can ne'er return.—
Most glorious orb! that wert a worship, ere
The mystery of thy making was reveal'd!
Thou earliest minister of the Almighty,
Which gladden'd, on their mountain tops, the hearts
Of the Chaldean shepherds, till they pour'd
Themselves in orisons![41] Thou material God!
And representative of the Unknown—
Who chose thee for his shadow! Thou chief star!
Centre of many stars! which mak'st our earth
Endurable, and temperest the hues
And hearts of all who walk within thy rays!
Sire of the seasons! Monarch of the climes,
And those who dwell in them! for near or far,
Our inborn spirits have a tint of thee,
Even as our outward aspects;—thou dost rise,
And shine, and set in glory. Fare thee well!
I ne'er shall see thee more. As my first glance
Of love and wonder was for thee, then take
My latest look: thou wilt not beam on one
To whom the gifts of life and warmth have been
Of a more fatal nature. He is gone:
I follow.

(Exit MANFRED.*)*

— SCENE III —

(The Mountains.—The Castle of Manfred at some distance.—A Terrace before a Tower.—Time, Twilight.)

(HERMAN, MANUEL, *and other Dependants of* MANFRED.*)*

HER: 'Tis strange enough; night after night, for years,
He hath pursued long vigils in this tower,
Without a witness. I have been within it,—
So have we all been oft-times; but from it,
Or its contents, it were impossible
To draw conclusions absolute, of aught
His studies tend to. To be sure, there is
One chamber where none enter; I would give
The fee of what I have to come these three years,
To pore upon its mysteries.

MANUEL: 'Twere dangerous;
Content thyself with what thou knowest already.

HER: Ah! Manuel! thou art elderly and wise,
And could'st say much; thou hast dwelt within the castle—
How many years is't?

MANUEL: Ere Count Manfred's birth,
I served his father, whom he nought resembles.

HER: There be more sons in like predicament.
But wherein do they differ?

MANUEL: I speak not
Of features or of form, but mind and habits:
Count Sigismund was proud,—but gay and free,—
A warrior and a reveller; he dwelt not
With books and solitude, nor made the night
A gloomy vigil, but a festal time,
Merrier than day; he did not walk the rocks
And forests like a wolf, nor turn aside
From men and their delights.

HER: Beshrew[42] the hour,
But those were jocund times! I would that such
Would visit the old walls again; they look
As if they had forgotten them.

MANUEL: These walls
Must change their chieftain first. Oh! I have seen
Some strange things in them, Herman.

HER: Come, be friendly;
Relate me some to while away our watch:
I've heard thee darkly speak of an event
Which happened hereabouts, by this same tower.

MANUEL: That was a night indeed; I do remember
'Twas twilight, as it may be now, and such
Another evening;—yon red cloud, which rests
On Eigher's[43] pinnacle, so rested then,—
So like that it might be the same; the wind
Was faint and gusty, and the mountain snows
Began to glitter with the climbing moon;
Count Manfred was, as now, within his tower,—
How occupied, we knew not, but with him
The sole companion of his wanderings
And watchings—her, whom of all earthly things

---

[40] Cf. Genesis 6:4. "There were giants in the earth in those days."

[41] **orisons**: prayers.

[42] **Beshrew**: curse.

[43] **Eigher**: mountain near the Jungfrau in south-central Switzerland.

That lived, the only thing he seem'd to love,—
As he, indeed, by blood was bound to do,
The lady Astarte, his—
Hush! who comes here?

(Enter the ABBOT.*)*

ABBOT: Where is your master?
HER: Yonder, in the tower.
ABBOT: I must speak with him.
MANUEL: 'Tis impossible;
He is most private, and must not be thus
Intruded on.
ABBOT: Upon myself I take
The forfeit of my fault, if fault there be—
But I must see him.
HER: Thou has seen him once
This eve already.
ABBOT: Sirrah! I command thee,
Knock, and apprize the Count of my approach.
HER: We dare not.
ABBOT: Then it seems I must be herald
Of my own purpose.
MANUEL: Reverend father, stop—
I pray you pause.
ABBOT: Why so?
MANUEL: But step this way,
And I will tell you further.

(Exeunt.)

— SCENE IV —

(Interior of the Tower)

*(*MANFRED *alone.)*

MAN: The stars are forth, the moon above the tops
Of the snow-shining mountains.—Beautiful!
I linger yet with Nature, for the night
Hath been to me a more familiar face
Than that of man; and in her starry shade
Of dim and solitary loveliness,
I learn'd the language of another world.
I do remember me, that in my youth,
When I was wandering,—upon such a night
I stood within the Coliseum's[44] wall,
'Midst the chief relics of almighty Rome;
The trees which grew along the broken arches
Waved dark in the blue midnight, and the stars
Shone through the rents of ruin; from afar
The watchdog bayed beyond the Tiber; and
More near from out the Caesars' palace[45] came
The owl's long cry, and, interruptedly,
Of distant sentinels the fitful song
Begun and died upon the gentle wind.
Some cypresses beyond the time-worn breach
Appeared to skirt the horizon, yet they stood
Within a bowshot—where the Caesars dwelt,
And dwell the tuneless birds of night; amidst
A grove which springs through levell'd battlements,
And twines its roots with the imperial hearths,
Ivy usurps the laurel's place of growth;—
But the gladiators' bloody Circus[46] stands,
A noble wreck in ruinous perfection!
While Caesar's chambers, and the Augustan halls,
Grovel on earth in indistinct decay.—
And thou didst shine, thou rolling moon, upon
All this, and cast a wide and tender light,
Which soften'd down the hoar austerity
Of rugged desolation, and fill'd up,
As 'twere, anew, the gaps of centuries;
Leaving that beautiful which still was so,
And making that which was not, till the place
Became religion, and the heart ran o'er
With silent worship of the great of old!—
The dead, but sceptred sovereigns, who still rule
Our spirits from their urns.—
'Twas such a night!
'Tis strange that I recall it at this time;
But I have found our thoughts take wildest flight
Even at the moment when they should array
Themselves in pensive order.

(Enter the ABBOT.*)*

ABBOT: My good Lord!
I crave a second grace for this approach;
But yet let not my humble zeal offend
By its abruptness—all it hath of ill
Recoils on me; its good in the effect

[44] **Coliseum**: the central ampitheater of ancient Rome.

[45] **Tiber**: the river that runs through Rome. **Caesars' palace**: the palace that housed, at various times and with various additions, Tiberius, Gaius, Nero, Domitian, and Hadrian, and was located on the Palatine Hill.

[46] **Circus**: the Circus Maximus, between the Palatine and Aventine Hills.

May light upon your head—could I say *heart*—
Could I touch *that,* with words or prayers, I should
Recall a noble spirit which hath wandered,
But is not yet all lost.

MAN: Thou know'st me not;
My days are numbered, and my deeds recorded:
Retire, or 'twill be dangerous—Away!

ABBOT: Thou dost not mean to menace me?

MAN: Not I;
I simply tell thee peril is at hand,
And would preserve thee.

ABBOT: What dost mean?

MAN: Look there!
What dost thou see?

ABBOT: Nothing.

MAN: Look there, I say,
And steadfastly;—now tell me what thou seest?

ABBOT: That which should shake me,—but I fear it not—
I see a dusk and awful figure rise
Like an infernal god from out the earth;
His face wrapt in a mantle, and his form
Robed as with angry clouds; he stands between
Thyself and me—but I do fear him not.

MAN: Thou hast no cause—he shall not harm thee—but
His sight may shock thine old limbs into palsy.
I say to thee—Retire!

ABBOT: And, I reply—
Never—till I have battled with this fiend—
What doth he here?

MAN: Why—ay—what doth he here?
I did not send for him,—he is unbidden.

ABBOT: Alas! lost mortal! what with guests like these
Hast thou to do? I tremble for thy sake;
Why doth he gaze on thee, and thou on him?
Ah! he unveils his aspect; on his brow
The thunder-scars are graven; from his eye
Glares forth the immortality of hell[47]—
Avaunt!—

MAN: Pronounce—what is thy mission?

SPIRIT: Come!

ABBOT: What art thou, unknown being? answer!—speak!

SPIRIT: The genius[48] of this mortal.—Come! 'tis time.

MAN: I am prepared for all things, but deny
The power which summons me. Who sent thee here?

SPIRIT: Thou'lt know anon—Come! come!

MAN: I have commanded
Things of an essence greater far than thine,
And striven with thy masters. Get thee hence!

SPIRIT: Mortal! thine hour is come—Away! I say.

MAN: I knew, and know my hour is come, but not
To render up my soul to such as thee:
Away! I'll die as I have lived—alone.

SPIRIT: Then I must summon up my brethren.—Rise!

(Other Spirits rise up.)

ABBOT: Avaunt! ye evil ones!—Avaunt! I say,—
Ye have no power where piety hath power,
And I do charge ye in the name—

SPIRIT: Old man!
We know ourselves, our mission, and thine order;
Waste not thy holy words on idle uses,
It were in vain; this man is forfeited.
Once more I summon him—Away! away!

MAN: I do defy ye,—though I feel my soul
Is ebbing from me, yet I do defy ye;
Nor will I hence, while I have earthly breath
To breathe my scorn upon ye—earthly strength
To wrestle, though with spirits; what ye take
Shall be ta'en limb by limb.

SPIRIT: Reluctant mortal!
Is this the Magian who would so pervade
The world invisible, and make himself
Almost our equal?—Can it be that thou
Art thus in love with life? the very life
Which made thee wretched!

MAN: Thou false fiend, thou liest!
My life is in its last hour,—*that* I know,
Nor would redeem a moment of that hour;
I do not combat against death, but thee
And thy surrounding angels; my past power
Was purchased by no compact with thy crew,
But by superior science—penance—daring—

[47] **"thunder-scars are graven . . . immortality of hell":** *Paradise Lost:* "but his face / Deep scars of thunder had intrenched, and care / Sat on his faded cheek" I.600–602.

[48] **genius:** guardian spirit.

And length of watching—strength of mind—and skill
In knowledge of our fathers—when the earth
Saw men and spirits walking side by side,
And gave ye no supremacy: I stand
Upon my strength—I do defy—deny—
Spurn back, and scorn ye!—

SPIRIT: But thy many crimes
Have made thee—

MAN: What are they to such as thee?
Must crimes be punish'd but by other crimes,
And greater criminals?—Back to thy hell!
Thou hast no power upon me, *that* I feel;
Thou never shalt possess me, *that* I know:
What I have done is done; I bear within
A torture which could nothing gain from thine:
The mind which is immortal makes itself
Requital for its good or evil thoughts—
Is its own origin of ill and end—
And its own place and time—its innate sense,
When stripp'd of this mortality, derives
No colour from the fleeting things without,
But is absorb'd in sufferance or in joy,
Born from the knowledge of its own desert.
Thou didst not tempt me, and thou couldst not tempt me;
I have not been thy dupe, nor am thy prey—
But was my own destroyer, and will be
My own hereafter.—Back, ye baffled fiends!
The hand of death is on me—but not yours!

(The Demons disappear.)

ABBOT: Alas! how pale thou art—thy lips are white—
And thy breast heaves—and in thy gasping throat
The accents rattle—Give thy prayers to heaven—
Pray—albeit but in thought,—but die not thus.

MAN: 'Tis over—my dull eyes can fix thee not;
But all things swim around me, and the earth
Heaves as it were beneath me. Fare thee well—
Give me thy hand.

ABBOT: Cold—cold—even to the heart—
But yet one prayer—alas! how fares it with thee?—

MAN: Old man! 'tis not so difficult to die.

(MANFRED expires.)

ABBOT: He's gone—his soul hath ta'en its earthless flight—
Whither? I dread to think—but he is gone.

from Letter to Thomas Moore

Venice, February 28th, 1817

You will, perhaps, complain as much of the frequency of my letters now, as you were wont to do of their rarity. I think this is the fourth within as many moons. I feel anxious to hear from you, even more than usual, because your last indicated that you were unwell. At present, I am on the invalid regimen myself. The Carnival[1]—that is, the latter part of it—and sitting up late o'nights, had knocked me up a little. But it is over,—and it is now Lent, with all its abstinence and Sacred Music.

The mumming closed with a masked ball at the Fenice,[2] where I went, as also to most of the ridottos, etc., etc.; and, though I did not dissipate much upon the whole, yet I find "the sword wearing out the scabbard," though I have but just turned the corner of twenty-nine.

So we'll go no more a roving
So late into the night,
Though the heart be still as loving,
And the moon be still as bright.

For the sword outwears its sheath,
And the soul wears out the breast,
And the heart must pause to breathe,
And Love itself have rest.

Though the night was made for loving,
And the day returns too soon,
Yet we'll go no more a roving
By the light of the moon.

. . .

I believe I told you that the E[dinburgh] R[eview][3] had attacked me, in an article on Coleridge (I have not seen it)—*"Et tu, Jeffrey?"*—"there is nothing but roguery

[1] **Carnival:** in the Roman Catholic calendar, the period between the Feast of the Epiphany (Jan. 6) and Ash Wednesday, and in Venice a time of great festivity and merrymaking.

[2] **Fenice:** *Teatro La Fenice,* Venice's grandest theatre and opera house.

[3] **E[dinburgh] R[eview]:** the leading English literary periodical of the day, edited by Francis Jeffrey (1773–1850). The *Edinburgh* was Whig in its political sympathies, the *Quarterly,* Tory.

in villanous man."[4] But I absolve him of all attacks, present and future; for I think he had already pushed his clemency in my behoof to the utmost, and I shall always think well of him. I only wonder he did not begin before, as my domestic destruction was a fine opening for all the world, of which all, who could, did well to avail themselves.

If I live ten years longer, you will see, however, that it is not over with me — I don't mean in literature, for that is nothing; and it may seem odd enough to say, I do not think it my vocation. But you will see that I will do something or other — the times and fortune permitting — that, "like the cosmogony, or creation of the world, will puzzle the philosophers of all ages."[5] But I doubt whether my constitution will hold out. I have, at intervals, exorcised it most devilishly. . . .

Childe Harold's Pilgrimage

from CANTO IV

(1818; comp. 1817–1818)

. . . With regard to the conduct of the last canto, there will be found less of the pilgrim than in any of the preceding, and that little slightly, if at all, separated from the author speaking in his own person. The fact is, that I had become weary of drawing a line which every one seemed determined not to perceive: like the Chinese in Goldsmith's 'Citizen of the World', whom nobody would believe to be a Chinese, it was in vain that I asserted, and imagined, that I had drawn a distinction between the author and the pilgrim; and the very anxiety to preserve this difference, and disappointment at finding it unavailing, so far crushed my efforts in the composition, that I determined to abandon it altogether — and have done so.[1] The opinions which have been, or may be, formed on that subject, are *now* a matter of indifference; the work is to depend on itself, and not on the writer; and the author, who has no resources in his own mind beyond the reputation, transient or permanent, which is to arise from his literary efforts, deserves the fate of authors. . . .

1

I stood in Venice, on the Bridge of Sighs;[2]
A palace and a prison on each hand:
I saw from out the wave her structures rise
As from the stroke of the enchanter's wand:
A thousand years their cloudy wings expand
Around me, and a dying Glory smiles
O'er the far times, when many a subject land
Look'd to the winged Lion's[3] marble piles,
Where Venice sate in state, thron'd on her hundred isles!

2

She looks a sea Cybele,[4] fresh from ocean,
Rising with her tiara of proud towers
At airy distance, with majestic motion,
A ruler of the waters and their powers:
And such she was; — her daughters had their dowers
From spoils of nations, and the exhaustless East
Pour'd in her lap all gems in sparkling showers.
In purple was she robed, and of her feast
Monarchs partook, and deem'd their dignity increas'd.

---

[4] **"there is nothing . . .":** cf. *I Henry IV*, II.iv.124ff: "There is nothing but roguery to be found in a villanous man."

[5] **"like the cosmogony . . . ages":** cf. Goldsmith's *The Vicar of Wakefield*, Chapter 14.

[1] **Goldsmith's 'Citizen . . . World':** Anglo-Irish poet and novelist Oliver Goldsmith (1730?–1774), author of *The Vicar of Wakefield* (1766); published *The Citizen of the World* in 1762. Byron is addressing friend John Hobhouse in this prefatory letter.

[2] **Bridge of Sighs:** "The Bridge of Sighs (*il ponte dei Sospiri*) divides the Doge's Palace from the state prison. — It is roofed and *divided* by a wall into two passages — By the one — the prisoner was conveyed to judgment — by the other he returned to death, being generally strangled in an adjoining chamber". [L.B.]

[3] **winged Lion:** the emblem of St. Mark, patron saint of Venice. In the fifteenth century the Republic of Venice (1697–1797) was the preeminent mercantile and military power in Europe. Venice remained a major cultural center throughout the eighteenth century.

[4] **Cybele:** in Greek mythology, mother of the gods during the reign of the Titans.

3

In Venice Tasso's[5] echoes are no more,
And silent rows the songless gondolier;
Her palaces are crumbling to the shore,
And music meets not always now the ear:
Those days are gone—but Beauty still is here.
States fall, arts fade—but Nature doth not die,
Nor yet forget how Venice once was dear,
The pleasant place of all festivity,
The revel of the earth, the masque[6] of Italy!

. . . .

18

I lov'd her from my boyhood—she to me
Was as a fairy city of the heart,
Rising like water-columns from the sea,
Of joy the sojourn, and of wealth the mart;
And Otway, Radcliffe, Schiller, Shakespeare's art,[7]
Had stamp'd her image in me, and even so,
Although I found her thus, we did not part,
Perchance even dearer in her day of woe,
Than when she was a boast, a marvel, and a show.

19

I can repeople with the past—and of
The present there is still for eye and thought,
And meditation chasten'd down, enough;
And more, it may be, than I hoped or sought;
And of the happiest moments which were wrought
Within the web of my existence, some
From thee, fair Venice! have their colours caught:
There are some feelings Time can not benumb,
Nor Torture shake, or mine would now be cold and
dumb.

20

But from their nature will the tannen grow
Loftiest on loftiest and least shelter'd rocks,
Rooted in barrenness, where nought below
Of soil supports them 'gainst the Alpine shocks
Of eddying storms; yet springs the trunk, and
mocks
The howling tempest, till its height and frame
Are worthy of the mountains from whose blocks
Of bleak, grey, granite, into life it came,
And grew a giant tree;—the mind may grow the
same.

21

Existence may be borne, and the deep root
Of life and sufferance make its firm abode
In bare and desolated bosoms: mute
The camel labours with the heaviest load,
And the wolf dies in silence,—not bestow'd
In vain should such example be; if they,
Things of ignoble or of savage mood,
Endure and shrink not, we of nobler clay
May temper it to bear,—it is but for a day.

22

All suffering doth destroy, or is destroy'd,
Even by the sufferer; and, in each event
Ends:—Some, with hope replenish'd and rebuoy'd,
Return to whence they came—with like intent,
And weave their web again; some, bow'd and bent,
Wax gray and ghastly, withering ere their time,
And perish with the reed on which they leant;
Some seek devotion, toil, war, good or crime,
According as their souls were form'd to sink or climb:

23

But ever and anon of griefs subdued
There comes a token like a scorpion's sting,
Scarce seen, but with fresh bitterness imbued;
And slight withal may be the things which bring
Back on the heart the weight which it would fling
Aside for ever: it may be a sound—
A tone of music,—summer's eve—or spring,
A flower—the wind—the ocean—which shall
wound,
Striking the electric chain wherewith we are darkly
bound;

24

And how and why we know not, nor can trace
Home to its cloud this lightning of the mind,
But feel the shock renew'd, nor can efface
The blight and blackening which it leaves behind,

[5] **Tasso:** poet Torquato Tasso (1544–1595), author of *Gerusalemme Liberata* (1581).

[6] **masque:** short allegorical dramatic performance, including music, dancing, and sometimes poetry.

[7] **And Otway . . . Shakespeare's art:** *Venice Preserved; Mysteries of Udolpho; the Ghost-Seer, or Armenian; The Merchant of Venice; Othello* [L.B.].

Which out of things familiar, undesign'd,
When least we deem of such, calls up to view
The spectres whom no exorcism can bind,
The cold—the changed—perchance the dead—and anew,
The mourn'd, the loved, the lost—too many!—yet how few!

25

But my soul wanders; I demand it back
To meditate amongst decay, and stand
A ruin amidst ruins; there to track
Fall'n states and buried greatness, o'er a land
Which *was* the mightiest in its old command,
And *is* the loveliest, and must ever be
The master-mould of Nature's heavenly hand,
Wherein were cast the heroic and the free,
The beautiful, the brave—the lords of earth and sea,

26

The commonwealth of kings, the men of Rome!
And even since, and now, fair Italy!
Thou art the garden of the world, the home
Of all Art yields, and Nature can decree;
Even in thy desart, what is like to thee?
Thy very weeds are beautiful, thy waste
More rich than other climes' fertility;
Thy wreck a glory, and thy ruin graced
With an immaculate charm which can not be defaced.

. . . .

128

Arches on arches! as it were that Rome,
Collecting the chief trophies of her line,
Would build up all her triumphs in one dome,
Her Coliseum[8] stands; the moonbeams shine
As 'twere its natural torches, for divine
Should be the light which streams here, to illume
This long-explored but still exhaustless mine
Of contemplation; and the azure gloom
Of an Italian night, where the deep skies assume

129

Hues which have words, and speak to ye of heaven,
Floats o'er this vast and wondrous monument,
And shadows forth its glory. There is given
Unto the things of earth, which time hath bent,
A spirit's feeling, and where he hath leant
His hand, but broke his scythe, there is a power
And magic in the ruined battlement,
For which the palace of the present hour
Must yield its pomp, and wait till ages are its dower.

130

Oh Time! the beautifier of the dead,
Adorner of the ruin, comforter
And only healer when the heart hath bled—
Time! the corrector where our judgments err,
The test of truth, love,—sole philosopher,
For all beside are sophists, from thy thrift,
Which never loses though it doth defer—
Time, the avenger! unto thee I lift
My hands, and eyes, and heart, and crave for thee a gift:

131

Amidst this wreck, where thou hast made a shrine
And temple more divinely desolate,
Among thy mightier offerings here are mine,
Ruins of years—though few, yet full of fate:—
If thou hast ever seen me too elate,
Hear me not; but if calmly I have borne
Good, and reserved my pride against the hate
Which shall not whelm me, let me not have worn
This iron in my soul in vain—shall *they* not mourn?

132

And thou, who never yet of human wrong
Left'st the unbalanced scale, great Nemesis!
Here, where the ancient paid thee homage long—
Thou, who didst call the Furies from the abyss,
And round Orestes[9] bade them howl and hiss
For that unnatural retribution—just,
Had it but been from hands less near—in this
Thy former realm, I call thee from the dust!
Dost thou not hear my heart?—Awake! thou shalt, and must.

---

[8] **Coliseum:** the Roman ampitheater, and site of gladiatorial contests.

[9] **Nemesis:** Greek goddess of vengeance. **Furies:** also divinities associated with vengeance retribution. **Orestes:** son of Agamemnon, persecuted by the Furies for the murder of his mother Clytemnestra.

133

It is not that I may not have incurr'd
For my ancestral faults or mine the wound
I bleed withal, and, had it been conferr'd
With a just weapon, it had flowed unbound;
But now my blood shall not sink in the ground;
To thee I do devote it—*thou* shalt take
The vengeance, which shall yet be sought and found,
Which if *I* have not taken for the sake—
But let that pass—I sleep, but thou shalt yet awake.

134

And if my voice break forth, 'tis not that now
I shrink from what is suffered: let him speak
Who hath beheld decline upon my brow,
Or seen my mind's convulsion leave it weak;
But in this page a record will I seek.
Not in the air shall these my words disperse,
Though I be ashes; a far hour shall wreak
The deep prophetic fullness of this verse,
And pile on human heads the mountain of my curse!

135

That curse shall be Forgiveness.—Have I not—
Hear me, my mother Earth! behold it, Heaven!—
Have I not had to wrestle with my lot?
Have I not suffered things to be forgiven?
Have I not had my brain seared, my heart riven,
Hopes sapp'd, name blighted, Life's life lied away?
And only not to desperation driven,
Because not altogether of such clay
As rots into the souls of those whom I survey.

136

From mighty wrongs to petty perfidy
Have I not seen what human things could do?
From the loud roar of foaming calumny
To the small whisper of the as paltry few,
And subtler venom of the reptile crew,
The Janus[10] glance of whose significant eye,
Learning to lie with silence, would *seem* true,
And without utterance, save the shrug or sigh,
Deal round to happy fools its speechless obloquy.

[10] **Janus:** ancient Roman deity with two faces, one facing forward, the other backward.

137

But I have lived, and have not lived in vain:
My mind may lose its force, my blood its fire,
And my frame perish even in conquering pain,
But there is that within me which shall tire
Torture and Time, and breathe when I expire;
Something unearthly, which they deem not of,
Like the remembered tone of a mute lyre,
Shall on their softened spirits sink, and move
In hearts all rocky now the late remorse of love.

138

The seal is set.—Now welcome, thou dread power
Nameless, yet thus omnipotent, which here
Walk'st in the shadow of the midnight hour
With a deep awe, yet all distinct from fear;
Thy haunts are ever where the dead walls rear
Their ivy mantles, and the solemn scene
Derives from thee a sense so deep and clear
That we become a part of what has been,
And grow unto the spot, all-seeing but unseen.

139

And here the buzz of eager nations ran,
In murmured pity, or loud-roared applause,
As man was slaughtered by his fellow man.
And wherefore slaughtered? wherefore, but because
Such were the bloody Circus' genial laws,
And the imperial pleasure.—Wherefore not?
What matters where we fall to fill the maws
Of worms—on battle-plains or listed spot?[11]
Both are but theatres where the chief actors rot.

140

I see before me the Gladiator lie:
He leans upon his hand—his manly brow
Consents to death, but conquers agony,
And his drooped head sinks gradually low—
And through his side the last drops, ebbing slow
From the red gash, fall heavy, one by one,
Like the first of a thunder-shower; and now
The arena swims around him—he is gone,
Ere ceased the inhuman shout which hail'd the wretch who won.

[11] **listed spot:** from "list," an arena of combat.

141

He heard it, but he heeded not—his eyes
Were with his heart, and that was far away;
He reck'd not of the life he lost nor prize,
But where his rude hut by the Danube lay
There were his young barbarians all at play,
There was their Dacian[12] mother—he, their sire,
Butcher'd to make a Roman holiday—
All this rush'd with his blood—Shall he expire
And unavenged?—Arise! ye Goths, and glut your ire!

142

But here, where Murder breathed her bloody
stream;
And here, where buzzing nations choked the ways,
And roar'd or murmur'd like a mountain stream
Dashing or winding as its torrent strays;
Here, where the Roman million's blame or praise
Was death or life, the playthings of a crowd,
My voice sounds much—and fall the stars' faint
rays
On the arena void—seats crush'd—walls bow'd—
And galleries, where my steps seem echoes strangely
loud.

143

A ruin—yet what ruin! from its mass
Walls, palaces, half-cities, have been reared;
Yet oft the enormous skeleton ye pass
And marvel where the spoil could have appeared,
Hath it indeed been plundered, or but cleared?
Alas! developed, opens the decay,
When the colossal fabric's form is neared:
It will not bear the brightness of the day,
Which streams too much on all years, man, have reft
away.

144

But when the rising moon begins to climb
Its topmost arch, and gently pauses there;
When the stars twinkle through the loops of time,
And the low night-breeze waves along the air
The garland-forest, which the grey walls wear,
Like laurels on the bald first Caesar's head;
When the light shines serene but doth not glare,
Then in this magic circle raise the dead:
Heroes have trod this spot—'tis on their dust ye
tread.

145

'While stands the Coliseum, Rome shall stand;
When falls the Coliseum, Rome shall fall;
And when Rome falls—the World.'[13] From our
own land
Thus spake the pilgrims o'er this mighty wall
In Saxon times, which we are wont to call
Ancient; and these three mortal things are still
On their foundations, and unaltered all;
Rome and her Ruin past Redemption's skill,
The World, the same wide den—of thieves, or what
ye will.

. . . .

164

But where is he, the Pilgrim[14] of my song,
The being who upheld it through the past?
Methinks he cometh late and tarries long.
He is no more—these breathings are his last;
His wanderings done, his visions ebbing fast,
And he himself as nothing:—if he was
Aught but a phantasy, and could be class'd
With forms which live and suffer—let that pass—
His shadow fades away into Destruction's mass,

165

Which gathers shadow, substance, life, and all
That we inherit in its mortal shroud,
And spreads the dim and universal pall
Through which all things grow phantoms; and
the cloud
Between us sinks and all which ever glowed,
Till Glory's self is twilight, and displays
A melancholy halo scarce allowed
To hover on the verge of darkness; rays
Sadder than saddest night, for they distract the gaze,

[12] **Dacia:** province in the Roman empire in the loop of the lower Danube River, in what is now Romania.

[13] **"While stands the Coliseum . . .":** quoted by Gibbon in *Decline and Fall of the Roman Empire* from Bede's *Ecclesiastical History of the English People.*

[14] **Pilgrim:** Childe Harold.

166

And send us prying into the abyss,
To gather what we shall be when the frame
Shall be resolv'd to something less than this
Its wretched essence; and to dream of fame,
And wipe the dust from off the idle name
We never more shall hear,—but never more,
Oh, happier thought! can we be made the same:
It is enough in sooth that *once* we bore
These fardels[15] of the heart—the heart whose sweat was gore.

. . . .

175

But I forget.—My pilgrim's shrine is won,
And he and I must part,—so let it be,—
His task and mine alike are nearly done;
Yet once more let us look upon the sea;
The midland ocean breaks on him and me,
And from the Alban Mount[16] we now behold
Our friend of youth, that ocean, which when we
Beheld it last by Calpe's rock unfold
Those waves, we followed on till the dark Euxine roll'd

176

Upon the blue Symplegades:[17] long years—
Long, though not very many, since have done
Their work on both; some suffering and some tears
Have left us nearly where we had begun:
Yet not in vain our mortal race hath run,
We have had our reward—and it is here;
That we can yet feel gladden'd by the sun,
And reap from earth, sea, joy almost as dear
As if there were no man to trouble what is clear.

177

Oh! that the Desert were my dwelling place,
With one fair Spirit for my minister,
That I might all forget the human race,
And, hating no one, love but only her!
Ye Elements!—in whose ennobling stir
I feel myself exalted—Can ye not
Accord me such a being? Do I err
In deeming such inhabit many a spot?
Though with them to converse can rarely be our lot.

178

There is a pleasure in the pathless woods,
There is a rapture on the lonely shore,
There is society, where none intrudes,
By the deep Sea, and music in its roar:
I love not Man the less, but Nature more,
From these our interviews, in which I steal
From all I may be, or have been before,
To mingle with the Universe, and feel
What I can ne'er express, yet can not all conceal.

179

Roll on, thou deep and dark blue ocean—roll!
Ten thousand fleets sweep over thee in vain;
Man marks the earth with ruin—his control
Stops with the shore;—upon the watery plain
The wrecks are all thy deed, nor doth remain
A shadow of man's ravage, save his own,
When, for a moment, like a drop of rain,
He sinks into thy depths with bubbling groan,
Without a grave, unknell'd, uncoffin'd, and unknown.

180

His steps are not upon thy paths,—thy fields
Are not a spoil for him,—thou dost arise
And shake him from thee; the vile strength he wields
For earth's destruction thou dost all despise,
Spurning him from thy bosom to the skies,
And send'st him, shivering in thy playful spray
And howling, to his Gods, where haply lies
His petty hope in some near port or bay,
And dashest him again on earth:—there let him lay.

181

The armaments which thunderstrike the walls
Of rock-built cities, bidding nations quake,
And monarchs tremble in their capitals,
The oak leviathans, whose huge ribs make
Their clay creator the vain title take
Of lord of thee, and arbiter of war;

---

[15] **fardels:** burdens.

[16] **Alban Mount:** the highest peak of the Alban Hills, 13 miles southeast of Rome. Gibraltar is Calpe's rock.

[17] **Symplegades:** islands between the Black and Bosporus Seas.

These are thy toys, and, as the snowy flake,
They melt into thy yeast of waves, which mar
Alike the Armada's pride, or spoils of Trafalgar.[18]

182

Thy shores are empires, changed in all save thee—
Assyria, Greece, Rome, Carthage, what are they?
Thy waters washed them power while they were free,
And many a tyrant since; their shores obey
The stranger, slave, or savage; their decay
Has dried up realms to desarts:—not so thou,
Unchangeable save to thy wild waves' play—
Time writes no wrinkle on thine azure brow—
Such as creation's dawn beheld, thou rollest now.

183

Thou glorious mirror, where the Almighty's form
Glasses itself in tempests; in all time,
Calm or convuls'd—in breeze, or gale, or storm,
Icing the pole, or in the torrid clime
Dark-heaving;—boundless, endless, and sublime—
The image of Eternity—the throne
Of the Invisible, even from out thy slime
The monsters of the deep are made; each zone
Obeys thee; thou goest forth, dread, fathomless, alone.

184

And I have loved thee, Ocean! and my joy
Of youthful sports was on thy breast to be
Borne, like thy bubbles, onward: from a boy
I wantoned with thy breakers—they to me
Were a delight; and if the freshening sea
Made them a terror—'twas a pleasing fear,
For I was as it were a child of thee,
And trusted to thy billows far and near,
And laid my hand upon thy mane—as I do here.

185

My task is done—my song hath ceased—my theme
Has died into an echo; it is fit
The spell should break of this protracted dream.
The torch shall be extinguish'd which hath lit
My midnight lamp—and what is writ, is writ,—
Would it were worthier! but I am not now
That which I have been—and my visions flit
Less palpably before me—and the glow
Which in my spirit dwelt, is fluttering, faint, and low.

186

Farewell! a word that must be, and hath been—
A sound which makes us linger;—yet—farewell!
Ye! who have traced the Pilgrim to the scene
Which is his last, if in your memories dwell
A thought which once was his, if on ye swell
A single recollection, not in vain
He wore his sandal-shoon, and scallop-shell;[19]
Farewell! with *him* alone may rest the pain,
If such there were—with *you*, the moral of his strain!

from Letter to John Murray[1]

Venice April 6 1819

Dear Sir—

The Second Canto of Don Juan was sent on Saturday last by post in 4 packets—two of 4—& two of three sheets each—containing in all two hundred & seventeen stanzas octave measure.—But I will permit no curtailments except those mentioned about Castlereagh & the two *"Bobs"* in the introduction.[2]—You sha'n't make *Canticles* of my Cantos. The poem will please if it is lively—if it is stupid it will fail—but I will have none of your damned cutting & slashing.—If you please you may publish *anonymously*[;] it will perhaps be better;—but I will battle my way

[18] **Armada:** after sustaining heavy damage by the English Navy in 1588, the ships of the Spanish Armada were then buffetted by storms off the coasts of Scotland and Ireland. **Trafalgar:** "The Gale of wind which succeeded the battle of Trafalgar [1805] destroyed the greater part (if not all) of the prizes—nineteen sail of the line—taken on that memorable day" [L.B.].

[19] **sandal-shoon:** sandals. **scallop-shell:** pilgrim's badge.

[1] **John Murray:** the publisher of *Don Juan,* Cantos I and II.

[2] **Castlereagh . . . introduction:** reference to risqué comments Byron made in his dedication to *Don Juan,* which were suppressed, as was the entire dedication. The dedication first appeared in 1832.

against them all — like a Porcupine. — So you and Mr. Foscolo &c. want me to undertake what you call a "great work" an Epic poem I suppose or some such pyramid. — I'll try no such thing — I hate tasks — and then "seven or eight years!" God send us all well this day three months — let alone years — if one's years can't be better employed than in sweating poesy — a man had better be a ditcher. — And works too! — is Childe Harold nothing? you have so many *"divine"* poems, is it nothing to have written a *Human* one? without any of your worn out machinery. — Why — man — I could have spun the thought of the four cantos of that poem into twenty — had I wanted to book-make — & it's passion into as many modern tragedies — since you want *length* you shall have enough of *Juan* for I'll make 50 cantos. — And Foscolo too! why does *he* not do something more than the letters of Ortis — and a tragedy — and pamphlets — he has good fifteen years more at his command than I have — what has he done all that time? — proved his Genius doubtless — but not fixed it's fame — nor done his utmost. — Besides I mean to write my best work in *Italian* — & it will take me nine years more thoroughly to master the language — & then if my fancy exists & I exist too — I will try what I *can* do *really*. — As to the Estimation of the English which you talk of, let them calculate what it is worth — before they insult me with their insolent condescension. — I have not written for their pleasure; — if they are pleased — it is that they chose to be so, — I have never flattered their opinions — nor their pride — nor will I. — Neither will I make "Ladies books" "al dilettar le femine e la plebe"[3] — I have written from the fullness of my mind, from passion — from impulse — from many motives — but not for their "sweet voices."[4] — I know the precise worth of popular applause — for few Scribblers have had more of it — and if I chose to swerve into their paths — I could retain it or resume it — or increase it — but I neither love ye — nor fear ye — and though I buy with ye — and sell with ye — and talk with ye — I will neither eat with ye — drink with ye — nor pray with ye.[5] — They made me without my search a species of popular Idol — they — without reason or judgement beyond the caprice of their Good pleasure — threw down the Image from it's pedestal — it was not broken with the fall — and they would it seems again replace it — but they shall not. You ask about my health — about the beginning of the year — I was in a state of great exhaustion — attended by such debility of Stomach — that nothing remained upon it — and I was obliged to reform my "way of life" which was conducting me from the "yellow leaf"[6] to the Ground with all deliberate speed. — I am better in health and morals — and very much yrs. ever,

[scrawl]

Don Juan[1]

(1819; comp. 1818–1819)

— CANTO I —

1

I want a hero: an uncommon want,
  When every year and month sends forth a new
    one,
Till, after cloying the gazettes with cant,
  The age discovers he is not the true one;
Of such as these I should not care to vaunt,
  I'll therefore take our ancient friend Don Juan,
We all have seen him in the pantomime[2]
Sent to the devil, somewhat ere his time.

2

Vernon, the butcher Cumberland, Wolfe, Hawke,
  Prince Ferdinand, Granby, Burgoyne, Keppel,
    Howe,

[3] **"al dilettar le femine e la plebe":** *trans.* for the pleasure of women and plebians.

[4] **"sweet voices":** cf. *Coriolanus,* II.iii.119–21: "Most sweet voices! / Better it is to die, better to starve, / Than crave the hire which first we do deserve."

[5] **. . . I buy with ye . . . pray with ye:** cf. *Merchant of Venice,* I.iii.36ff: "I will buy with you, sell with you, talk with you, walk with you, and so following; but I will not eat with you, drink with you, nor pray with you."

[6] **yellow leaf:** *Macbeth,* "my way of life / Is fall'n into the sere, the yellow leaf" V.iii. 22–23.

[1] Published anonymously and without the publisher's name on 15 July 1819. Also published without the dedication to Robert Southey. See *Works of Lord Byron* (1832) below for "Dedication."

[2] **in the pantomime:** Popular plays, pantomimes, and musicals portrayed Don Juan as a cruel seducer, who usually went to hell.

Evil and good, have had their tithe of talk,
  And fill'd their sign-posts[3] then, like Wellesley now;
Each in their turn like Banquo's monarchs stalk,
  Followers of fame, 'nine farrow'[4] of that sow:
France, too, had Buonaparté and Dumourier
Recorded in the Moniteur and Courier.[5]

3

Barnave, Brissot, Condorcet, Mirabeau,
  Petion, Clootz, Danton, Marat, La Fayette,
Were French, and famous people, as we know;
  And there were others, scarce forgotten yet,
Joubert, Hoche, Marceau, Lannes, Dessaix, Moreau,
  With many of the military set,
Exceedingly remarkable at times,
But not at all adapted to my rhymes.[6]

4

Nelson[7] was once Britannia's god of war,
  And still should be so, but the tide is turn'd;
There's no more to be said of Trafalgar,
  'Tis with our hero quietly inurn'd;
Because the army's grown more popular,
  At which the naval people are concern'd;
Besides, the Prince is all for the land-service,
Forgetting Duncan, Nelson, Howe, and Jervis.[8]

5

Brave men were living before Agamemnon[9]
  And since, exceeding valorous and sage,
A good deal like him too, though quite the same none;
  But then they shone not on the poet's page,
And so have been forgotten:—I condemn none,
  But can't find any in the present age
Fit for my poem (that is, for my new one);
So, as I said, I'll take my friend Don Juan.

6

Most epic poets plunge in 'medias res',[10]
  (Horace makes this the heroic turnpike road)
And then your hero tells, whene'er you please,
  What went before—by way of episode,
While seated after dinner at his ease,
  Beside his mistress in some soft abode,
Palace, or garden, paradise, or cavern,
Which serves the happy couple for a tavern.

7

That is the usual method, but not mine—
  My way is to begin with the beginning;
The regularity of my design
  Forbids all wandering as the worst of sinning,
And therefore I shall open with a line
  (Although it cost me half an hour in spinning)
Narrating somewhat of Don Juan's father,
And also of his mother, if you'd rather.

8

In Seville was he born, a pleasant city,
  Famous for oranges and women—he
Who has not seen it will be much to pity,
  So says the proverb—and I quite agree;
Of all the Spanish towns is none more pretty,
  Cadiz perhaps—but that you soon may see:—
Don Juan's parents lived beside the river,
A noble stream, and call'd the Guadalquivir.

9

His father's name was Jóse—*Don*, of course,
  A true Hidalgo,[11] free from every stain
Of Moor or Hebrew blood, he traced his source
  Through the most Gothic gentlemen of Spain;

---

[3] **sign-posts:** reference to streets, squares, or other public place-names identifying the hero, and dedicated to his honor and memory.

[4] **Banquo's monarchs . . . 'nine farrow':** cf. *Macbeth*, IV.i. 122–23 and IV.i.65.

[5] **the Moniteur and Courier:** newspapers of that day.

[6] Stanzas 2 to 3 list remembered and unremembered British and French military and revolutionary heroes.

[7] **Nelson:** Admiral Viscount Horatio Nelson (1758–1805) is the great naval hero who destroyed Napoleon's fleet at Trafalgar in 1805, thereby assuring the allies' supremacy of the seas. Nelson died during the battle.

[8] **Duncan . . . Jervis:** all naval heroes.

[9] **Agamemnon:** Commander in chief of the Greeks in the Trojan War.

[10] **in 'medias res':** *trans.* "in the middle of things."

[11] **Hidalgo:** a member of the minor nobility of Spain.

A better cavalier ne'er mounted horse,
Or, being mounted, e'er got down again,
Than Jóse, who begot our hero, who
Begot—but that's to come——Well, to renew:

10

His mother was a learned lady, famed
For every branch of every science known—
In every christian language ever named,
With virtues equall'd by her wit alone,
She made the cleverest people quite ashamed,
And even the good with inward envy groan,
Finding themselves so very much exceeded
In their own way by all the things that she did.

11

Her memory was a mine: she knew by heart
All Calderon and greater part of Lopé,[12]
So that if any actor miss'd his part
She could have served him for the prompter's copy;
For her Feinagle's were an useless art,[13]
And he himself obliged to shut up shop—he
Could never make a memory so fine as
That which adorn'd the brain of Donna Inez.

12

Her favourite science was the mathematical,
Her noblest virtue was her magnanimity,
Her wit (she sometimes tried at wit) was Attic[14] all,
Her serious sayings darken'd to sublimity;
In short, in all things she was fairly what I call
A prodigy—her morning dress was dimity,
Her evening silk, or, in the summer, muslin,
And other stuffs, with which I won't stay puzzling.

13

She knew the Latin—that is, 'the Lord's prayer',
And Greek—the alphabet—I'm nearly sure;
She read some French romances here and there,
Although her mode of speaking was not pure;
For native Spanish she had no great care,
At least her conversation was obscure;
Her thoughts were theorems, her words a problem,
As if she deem'd that mystery would ennoble 'em.

14

She liked the English and the Hebrew tongue,
And said there was analogy between 'em;
She proved it somehow out of sacred song,
But I must leave the proofs to those who've seen 'em,
But this I heard her say, and can't be wrong,
And all may think which way their judgements lean 'em,
''Tis strange—the Hebrew noun which means "I am",
The English always use to govern d——n.'

15

Some women use their tongues—she look'd a lecture,
Each eye a sermon, and her brow a homily,
An all-in-all-sufficient self-director,
Like the lamented late Sir Samuel Romilly,
The Law's expounder, and the State's corrector,
Whose suicide was almost an anomaly—
One sad example more, that 'All is vanity',[15]—
(The jury brought their verdict in 'Insanity').

16

In short, she was a walking calculation,
Miss Edgeworth's novels stepping from their covers,
Or Mrs Trimmer's books on education,
Or 'Coelebs' Wife' set out in search of lovers,
Morality's prim personification,
In which not Envy's self a flaw discovers,
To others' share let 'female errors fall',[16]
For she had not even one—the worst of all.

---

[12] **Calderon:** Calderon de la Barca (1600–1681), dramatist and priest. **Lopé:** Lope de la Vega (1562–1635), father of the Spanish drama.

[13] **Feinagle's . . . art:** Gregor von Feinagle had developed popular schemes for improving the memory.

[14] **Attic:** Greek, sophisticated.

[15] **Sir Samuel Romilly:** lawyer who represented Lady Byron in separation proceedings; he committed suicide after his wife's death in 1818. **"All is vanity":** Ecclesiastes 1:2: "Vanity of vanities, saith the Preacher, vanity of vanities; all is vanity."

[16] **Miss Edgeworth's novels . . . 'Coelebs' Wife':** reference to women authors Maria Edgeworth,* Sarah Trimmer, and Hannah More* (*Coelebs in Search of a Wife* [1800]). **'female errors fall':** cf. Alexander Pope's *Rape of the Lock* (1714), II.17–18: "If to her share some female errors fall, / Look on her face, and you'll forget 'em all."

17

Oh! she was perfect past all parallel—
    Of any modern female saint's comparison;
So far beyond the cunning powers of hell,
    Her guardian angel had given up his garrison;
Even her minutest motions went as well
    As those of the best time-piece made by Harrison:
In virtues nothing earthly could surpass her,
Save thine 'incomparable oil', Macassar![17]

18

Perfect she was, but as perfection is
    Insipid in this naughty world of ours,
Where our first parents never learn'd to kiss
    Till they were exiled from their earlier bowers,
Where all was peace, and innocence, and bliss,
    (I wonder how they got through the twelve hours)
Don Jóse, like a lineal son of Eve,
Went plucking various fruit without her leave.

19

He was a mortal of the careless kind,
    With no great love for learning, or the learn'd,
Who chose to go where'er he had a mind,
    And never dream'd his lady was concern'd;
The world, as usual, wickedly inclined
    To see a kingdom or a house o'erturn'd,
Whisper'd he had a mistress, some said *two*,
But for domestic quarrels *one* will do.

20

Now Donna Inez had, with all her merit,
    A great opinion of her own good qualities;
Neglect, indeed, requires a saint to bear it,
    And so, indeed, she was in her moralities;
But then she had a devil of a spirit,
    And sometimes mix'd up fancies with realities,
And let few opportunities escape
Of getting her liege lord into a scrape.

21

This was an easy matter with a man
    Oft in the wrong, and never on his guard;
And even the wisest, do the best they can,
    Have moments, hours, and days, so unprepared
That you might 'brain them with their lady's fan';[18]
    And sometimes ladies hit exceeding hard,
And fans turn into falchions[19] in fair hands,
And why and wherefore no one understands.

22

'Tis pity learned virgins ever wed
    With persons of no sort of education,
Or gentlemen, who, though well-born and -bred,
    Grow tired of scientific conversation:
I don't choose to say much upon this head,
    I'm a plain man, and in a single station,
But—Oh! ye lords of ladies intellectual,
Inform us truly, have they not hen-peck'd you all?

23

Don Jóse and his lady quarrell'd—*why*,
    Not any of the many could divine,
Though several thousand people chose to try,
    'Twas surely no concern of theirs nor mine;
I loathe that low vice curiosity,
    But if there's any thing in which I shine
'Tis in arranging all my friends' affairs
Not having, of my own, domestic cares.

24

And so I interfered, and with the best
    Intentions, but their treatment was not kind;
I think the foolish people were possess'd,
    For neither of them could I ever find,
Although their porter afterwards confess'd—
    But that's no matter, and the worst's behind,
For little Juan o'er me threw, down stairs,
A pail of housemaid's water[20] unawares.

25

A little curly-headed, good-for-nothing,
    And mischief-making monkey from his birth;
His parents ne'er agreed except in doting
    Upon the most unquiet imp on earth;
Instead of quarrelling, had they been but both in
    Their senses, they'd have sent young master forth

[17] **Harrison:** John Harrison was an English watchmaker. **'incomparable oil':** hair oil from the Island of Macassar.

[18] **'brain them . . . fan':** Cf. *1 Henry IV,* II.iii.20–21: "'Zounds, an I were now by this rascal, I could brain him with his lady's fan."

[19] **falchion:** short, broad sword.

[20] **housemaid's water:** possibly, urine.

To school, or had him soundly whipp'd at home,
To teach him manners for the time to come.

26

Don Jóse and the Donna Inez led
For some time an unhappy sort of life,
Wishing each other, not divorced, but dead;
They lived respectably as man and wife,
Their conduct was exceedingly well-bred,
And gave no outward signs of inward strife,
Until at length the smother'd fire broke out,
And put the business past all kind of doubt.

27

For Inez call'd some druggists and physicians,
And tried to prove her loving lord was *mad*,
But as he had some lucid intermissions,
She next decided he was only *bad*;
Yet when they ask'd her for her depositions,
No sort of explanation could be had,
Save that her duty both to man and God
Required this conduct—which seem'd very odd.

28

She kept a journal, where his faults were noted,
And open'd certain trunks of books and letters,
All which might, if occasion served, be quoted;
And then she had all Seville for abettors,
Besides her good old grandmother (who doted);
The hearers of her case became repeaters,
Then advocates, inquisitors, and judges,
Some for amusement, others for old grudges.

29

And then this best and meekest woman bore
With such serenity her husband's woes,
Just as the Spartan ladies did of yore,
Who saw their spouses kill'd, and nobly chose
Never to say a word about them more—
Calmly she heard each calumny that rose,
And saw *his* agonies with such sublimity,
That all the world exclaim'd, 'What magnanimity!'

30

No doubt, this patience, when the world is damning us,
Is philosophic in our former friends;
'Tis also pleasant to be deem'd magnanimous,
The more so in obtaining our own ends;
And what the lawyers call a *'malus animus'*,[21]
Conduct like this by no means comprehends:
Revenge in person's certainly no virtue,
But then 'tis not *my* fault, if *others* hurt you.

31

And if our quarrels should rip up old stories,
And help them with a lie or two additional,
I'm not to blame, as you well know, no more is
Any one else—they were become traditional;
Besides, their resurrection aids our glories
By contrast, which is what we just were wishing all:
And science profits by this resurrection—
Dead scandals form good subjects for dissection.

32

Their friends had tried at reconciliation,
Then their relations, who made matters worse;
('Twere hard to say upon a like occasion
To whom it may be best to have recourse—
I can't say much for friend or yet relation):
The lawyers did their utmost for divorce,
But scarce a fee was paid on either side
Before, unluckily, Don Jóse died.

33

He died: and most unluckily, because,
According to all hints I could collect
From counsel learned in those kinds of laws,
(Although their talk's obscure and circumspect)
His death contrived to spoil a charming cause;
A thousand pities also with respect
To public feeling, which on this occasion
Was manifested in a great sensation.

34

But ah! he died; and buried with him lay
The public feeling and the lawyers' fees:
His house was sold, his servants sent away,
A Jew took one of his two mistresses,
A priest the other—at least so they say:
I ask'd the doctors after his disease,
He died of the slow fever call'd the tertian,[22]
And left his widow to her own aversion.

---

[21] **'malus animus'**: malicious intent.
[22] **tertian**: form of malaria.

35

Yet Jóse was an honourable man,
  That I must say, who knew him very well;
Therefore his frailties I'll no further scan,[23]
  Indeed there were not many more to tell;
And if his passions now and then outran
  Discretion, and were not so peaceable
As Numa's (who was also named Pompilius),[24]
He had been ill brought up, and was born bilious.

36

Whate'er might be his worthlessness or worth,
  Poor fellow! he had many things to wound him,
Let's own, since it can do no good on earth;
  It was a trying moment that which found him
Standing alone beside his desolate hearth,
  Where all his household gods lay shiver'd round
    him;
No choice was left his feelings or his pride
Save death or Doctors' Commons[25]—so he died.

37

Dying intestate, Juan was sole heir
  To a chancery suit, and messuages, and lands,[26]
Which, with a long minority and care,
  Promised to turn out well in proper hands:
Inez became sole guardian, which was fair,
  And answer'd but to nature's just demands;
An only son left with an only mother
Is brought up much more wisely than another.

38

Sagest of women, even of widows, she
  Resolved that Juan should be quite a paragon,
And worthy of the noblest pedigree:
  (His sire was of Castile, his dam from Arragon).
Then for accomplishments of chivalry,
  In case our lord the king should go to war again,
He learn'd the arts of riding, fencing, gunnery,
And how to scale a fortress—or a nunnery.

39

But that which Donna Inez most desired,
  And saw into herself each day before all
The learned tutors whom for him she hired,
  Was, that his breeding should be strictly moral;
Much into all his studies she inquired,
  And so they were submitted first to her, all,
Arts, sciences, no branch was made a mystery
To Juan's eyes, excepting natural history.

40

The languages, especially the dead,
  The sciences, and most of all the abstruse,
The arts, at least all such as could be said
  To be the most remote from common use,
In all these he was much and deeply read;
  But not a page of any thing that's loose,
Or hints continuation of the species,
Was ever suffer'd, lest he should grow vicious.

41

His classic studies made a little puzzle,
  Because of filthy loves of gods and goddesses,
Who in the earlier ages made a bustle,
  But never put on pantaloons or bodices;
His reverend tutors had at times a tussle,
  And for their Aeneids, Iliads, and Odysseys,
Were forced to make an odd sort of apology,
For Donna Inez dreaded the mythology.

42

Ovid's a rake, as half his verses show him,
  Anacreon's morals are a still worse sample,
Catullus scarcely has a decent poem,
  I don't think Sappho's Ode a good example,
Although Longinus tells us there is no hymn
  Where the sublime soars forth on wings more
    ample;
But Virgil's songs are pure, except that horrid one
Beginning with *'Formosum Pastor Corydon'*.

43

Lucretius' irreligion is too strong
  For early stomachs, to prove wholesome food;

---

[23] **his frailties . . . scan:** cf. Thomas Gray, *Elegy Written in a Country Churchyard* (1751), 125–26: "No farther seek his merits to disclose, / Or draw his frailties from their dread abode."

[24] **Pompilius:** legendary second king of Rome, known for wisdom and piety.

[25] **Doctors' Commons:** the College or Association of Doctors of Civil Law in London.

[26] **Dying intestate . . . lands:** his father having died without a will (intestate), Juan inherits a house with its adjoining building and lands (messuages) in litigation.

I can't help thinking Juvenal was wrong,
Although no doubt his real intent was good,
For speaking out so plainly in his song,
So much indeed as to be downright rude;
And then what proper person can be partial
To all those nauseous epigrams of Martial?[27]

44

Juan was taught from out the best edition,
Expurgated by learned men, who place,
Judiciously, from out the schoolboy's vision,
The grosser parts; but fearful to deface
Too much their modest bard by this omission,
And pitying sore his mutilated case,
They only add them all in an appendix,
Which saves, in fact, the trouble of an index;

45

For there we have them all at one fell swoop,
Instead of being scatter'd through the pages;
They stand forth marshall'd in a handsome troop,
To meet the ingenuous youth of future ages,
Till some less rigid editor shall stoop
To call them back into their separate cages,
Instead of standing staring altogether,
Like garden gods—and not so decent either.

46

The Missal too (it was the family Missal)
Was ornamented in a sort of way
Which ancient mass-books often are, and this all
Kinds of grotesques illumined; and how they,
Who saw those figures on the margin kiss all,
Could turn their optics to the text and pray
Is more than I know—but Don Juan's mother
Kept this herself, and gave her son another.

47

Sermons he read, and lectures he endured,
And homilies, and lives of all the saints;
To Jerome and to Chrysostom inured,
He did not take such studies for restraints;
But how faith is acquired, and then insured,
So well not one of the aforesaid paints
As Saint Augustine in his fine Confessions,
Which make the reader envy his transgressions.[28]

48

This, too, was a seal'd book to little Juan—
I can't but say that his mamma was right,
If such an education was the true one.
She scarcely trusted him from out her sight;
Her maids were old, and if she took a new one
You might be sure she was a perfect fright,
She did this during even her husband's life—
I recommend as much to every wife.

49

Young Juan wax'd in goodliness and grace;
At six a charming child, and at eleven
With all the promise of as fine a face
As e'er to man's maturer growth was given:
He studied steadily, and grew apace,
And seem'd, at least, in the right road to heaven,
For half his days were pass'd at church, the other
Between his tutors, confessor, and mother.

50

At six, I said, he was a charming child,
At twelve he was a fine, but quiet boy;
Although in infancy a little wild,
They tamed him down amongst them; to destroy
His natural spirit not in vain they toil'd,
At least it seem'd so; and his mother's joy
Was to declare how sage, and still, and steady,
Her young philosopher was grown already.

---

[27] Stanzas 42 to 43: These classical Greek (Anacreon, Sappho) and Roman (Ovid, Catullus, Juvenal, Martial) poets wrote erotic poetry; a Greek literary theorist known as Longinus praised the power of Sappho's Ode in his first-century treatise *On the Sublime;* the Roman poet Lucretius wrote in his philosophical poem *De Rerum Natura* that the universe can be accounted for as a product of chance rather than as an act of divine creation; Virgil's *Bucolics,* Eclogue II, deals with homoerotic love. Translation of line 336: Handsome Shepherd Corydon.

[28] **To Jerome and to Chrysostom . . . :** the early Christian fathers, Saints Jerome and John Chrysostom led ascetic lives. **As Saint Augustine . . . transgressions:** in his *Confessions,* Saint Augustine describes his youth as morally debauched.

51

I had my doubts, perhaps I have them still,
But what I say is neither here nor there:
I knew his father well, and have some skill
In character—but it would not be fair
From sire to son to augur good or ill:
He and his wife were an ill-sorted pair—
But scandal's my aversion—I protest
Against all evil speaking, even in jest.

52

For my part I say nothing—nothing—but
This I will say—my reasons are my own—
That if I had an only son to put
To school (as God be praised that I have none)
'Tis not with Donna Inez I would shut
Him up to learn his catechism alone,
No—no—I'd send him out betimes to college,
For there it was I pick'd up my own knowledge.

53

For there one learns—'tis not for me to boast,
Though I acquired—but I pass over *that,*
As well as all the Greek I since have lost:
I say that there's the place—but *'Verbum sat'*,[29]
I think I pick'd up too, as well as most,
Knowledge of matters—but no matter *what*—
I never married—but, I think, I know
That sons should not be educated so.

54

Young Juan now was sixteen years of age,
Tall, handsome, slender, but well knit; he seem'd
Active, though not so sprightly, as a page;
And every body but his mother deem'd
Him almost man; but she flew in a rage,
And bit her lips (for else she might have scream'd),
If any said so, for to be precocious
Was in her eyes a thing the most atrocious.

55

Amongst her numerous acquaintance, all
Selected for discretion and devotion,
There was the Donna Julia, whom to call
Pretty were but to give a feeble notion
Of many charms in her as natural
As sweetness to the flower, or salt to ocean,
Her zone to Venus, or his bow to Cupid,
(But this last simile is trite and stupid).

56

The darkness of her oriental eye
Accorded with her Moorish origin;[30]
(Her blood was not all Spanish, by the by:
In Spain, you know, this is a sort of sin).
When proud Grenada fell, and, forced to fly,
Boabdil[31] wept, of Donna Julia's kin
Some went to Africa, some staid in Spain,
Her great great grandmamma chose to remain.

57

She married (I forget the pedigree)
With an Hidalgo, who transmitted down
His blood less noble than such blood should be;
At such alliances his sires would frown,
In that point so precise in each degree
That they bred *in and in,* as might be shown,
Marrying their cousins—nay, their aunts, and nieces,
Which always spoils the breed, if it increases.

58

This heathenish cross restored the breed again,
Ruin'd its blood, but much improved its flesh;
For, from a root the ugliest in Old Spain
Sprung up a branch as beautiful as fresh;
The sons no more were short, the daughters plain:
But there's a rumour which I fain would hush,
'Tis said that Donna Julia's grandmamma
Produced her Don more heirs at love than law.

59

However this might be, the race went on
Improving still through every generation,
Until it centr'd in an only son,
Who left an only daughter; my narration

[29] **'Verbum sat'**: *trans.* A word [to the wise] is sufficient.

[30] **her Moorish origin**: the Moors were Africans of Berber and Arab descent who ruled much of southern Spain (Granada) from the eighth century until driven out by Ferdinand in 1492.

[31] **Boabdil**: the last Moorish prince.

May have suggested that this single one
  Could be but Julia (whom on this occasion
I shall have much to speak about), and she
Was married, charming, chaste, and twenty-three.

60

Her eye (I'm very fond of handsome eyes)
  Was large and dark, suppressing half its fire
Until she spoke, then through its soft disguise
  Flash'd an expression more of pride than ire,
And love than either; and there would arise
  A something in them which was not desire,
But would have been, perhaps, but for the soul
Which struggled through and chasten'd down the
    whole.

61

Her glossy hair was cluster'd o'er a brow
  Bright with intelligence, and fair and smooth;
Her eyebrow's shape was like the aerial bow,
  Her cheek all purple with the beam of youth,
Mounting, at times, to a transparent glow,
  As if her veins ran lightning; she, in sooth,
Possess'd an air and grace by no means common:
Her stature tall — I hate a dumpy woman.

62

Wedded she was some years, and to a man
  Of fifty, and such husbands are in plenty;
And yet, I think, instead of such a ONE
  'Twere better to have TWO of five and twenty,
Especially in countries near the sun:
  And now I think on't, 'mi vien in mente',[32]
Ladies even of the most uneasy virtue
Prefer a spouse whose age is short of thirty.

63

'Tis a sad thing, I cannot choose but say,
  And all the fault of that indecent sun,
Who cannot leave alone our helpless clay,
  But will keep baking, broiling, burning on,
That howsoever people fast and pray
  The flesh is frail, and so the soul undone:
What men call gallantry, and gods adultery,
Is much more common where the climate's sultry.

[32] **I think on't, 'mi vien in mente':** the English and Italian mean essentially the same thing.

64

Happy the nations of the moral north!
  Where all is virtue, and the winter season
Sends sin, without a rag on, shivering forth;
  ('Twas snow that brought St Anthony to reason);[33]
Where juries cast up what a wife is worth
  By laying whate'er sum, in mulct,[34] they please on
The lover, who must pay a handsome price,
Because it is a marketable vice.

65

Alfonso was the name of Julia's lord,
  A man well looking for his years, and who
Was neither much beloved, nor yet abhorr'd;
  They lived together as most people do,
Suffering each other's foibles by accord,
  And not exactly either *one* or *two*;
Yet he was jealous, though he did not show it,
For jealousy dislikes the world to know it.

66

Julia was — yet I never could see why —
  With Donna Inez quite a favourite friend;
Between their tastes there was small sympathy,
  For not a line had Julia ever penn'd:
Some people whisper (but, no doubt, they lie,
  For malice still imputes some private end)
That Inez had, ere Don Alfonso's marriage,
Forgot with him her very prudent carriage;

67

And that still keeping up the old connection,
  Which time had lately render'd much more chaste,
She took his lady also in affection,
  And certainly this course was much the best:
She flatter'd Julia with her sage protection,
  And complimented Don Alfonso's taste;
And if she could not (who can?) silence scandal,
At least she left it a more slender handle.

68

I can't tell whether Julia saw the affair
  With other people's eyes, or if her own

[33] **'Twas snow . . . reason:** mistaken reference to St. Anthony. Should be to St. Francis, who curbed his passions with cold and snow.

[34] **in mulct:** as a fine or penalty.

Discoveries made, but none could be aware
Of this, at least no symptom e'er was shown;
Perhaps she did not know, or did not care,
Indifferent from the first, or callous grown:
I'm really puzzled what to think or say,
She kept her counsel in so close a way.

69

Juan she saw, and, as a pretty child,
Caress'd him often, such a thing might be
Quite innocently done, and harmless styled,
When she had twenty years, and thirteen he;
But I am not so sure I should have smiled
When he was sixteen, Julia twenty-three,
These few short years make wondrous alterations,
Particularly amongst sun-burnt nations.

70

Whate'er the cause might be, they had become
Changed; for the dame grew distant, the youth shy,
Their looks cast down, their greetings almost dumb,
And much embarrassment in either eye;
There surely will be little doubt with some
That Donna Julia knew the reason why,
But as for Juan, he had no more notion
Than he who never saw the sea of ocean.

71

Yet Julia's very coldness still was kind,
And tremulously gentle her small hand
Withdrew itself from his, but left behind
A little pressure, thrilling, and so bland
And slight, so very slight, that to the mind
'Twas but a doubt; but ne'er magician's wand
Wrought change with all Armida's[35] fairy art
Like what this light touch left on Juan's heart.

72

And if she met him, though she smiled no more,
She look'd a sadness sweeter than her smile,
As if her heart had deeper thoughts in store
She must not own, but cherish'd more the while,
For that compression in its burning core;
Even innocence itself has many a wile,
And will not dare to trust itself with truth,
And love is taught hypocrisy from youth.

73

But passion most dissembles yet betrays
Even by its darkness; as the blackest sky
Foretells the heaviest tempest, it displays
Its workings through the vainly guarded eye,
And in whatever aspect it arrays
Itself, 'tis still the same hypocrisy;
Coldness or anger, even disdain or hate,
Are masks it often wears, and still too late.

74

Then there were sighs, the deeper for suppression,
And stolen glances, sweeter for the theft,
And burning blushes, though for no transgression,
Tremblings when met, and restlessness when left;
All these are little preludes to possession,
Of which young Passion cannot be bereft,
And merely tend to show how greatly Love is
Embarrass'd at first starting with a novice.

75

Poor Julia's heart was in an awkward state;
She felt it going, and resolved to make
The noblest efforts for herself and mate,
For honour's, pride's, religion's, virtue's sake;
Her resolutions were most truly great,
And almost might have made a Tarquin[36] quake;
She pray'd the Virgin Mary for her grace,
As being the best judge of a lady's case.

76

She vow'd she never would see Juan more,
And next day paid a visit to his mother,
And look'd extremely at the opening door,
Which, by the Virgin's grace, let in another;
Grateful she was, and yet a little sore—
Again it opens, it can be no other,
'Tis surely Juan now—No! I'm afraid
That night the Virgin was no further pray'd.

[35] **Armida**: sorceress in Italian poet Torquato Tasso's *Jerusalem Delivered* (1580–1581).

[36] **Tarquin**: name of a family of Roman kings, some noted for cruelty.

77

She now determined that a virtuous woman
  Should rather face and overcome temptation,
That flight was base and dastardly, and no man
  Should ever give her heart the least sensation;
That is to say, a thought beyond the common
  Preference, that we must feel upon occasion,
For people who are pleasanter than others,
But then they only seem so many brothers.

78

And even if by chance—and who can tell?
  The devil's so very sly—she should discover
That all within was not so very well,
  And, if still free, that such or such a lover
Might please perhaps, a virtuous wife can quell
  Such thoughts, and be the better when they're
    over;
And if the man should ask, 'tis but denial:
I recommend young ladies to make trial.

79

And then there are such things as love divine,
  Bright and immaculate, unmix'd and pure,
Such as the angels think so very fine,
  And matrons, who would be no less secure,
Platonic, perfect, 'just such love as mine':
  Thus Julia said—and thought so, to be sure,
And so I'd have her think, were I the man
On whom her reveries celestial ran.

80

Such love is innocent, and may exist
  Between young persons without any danger,
A hand may first, and then a lip be kist;
  For my part, to such doings I'm a stranger,
But *hear* these freedoms form the utmost list
  Of all o'er which such love may be a ranger:
If people go beyond, 'tis quite a crime,
But not my fault—I tell them all in time.

81

Love, then, but love within its proper limits,
  Was Julia's innocent determination
In young Don Juan's favour, and to him its
  Exertion might be useful on occasion;
And, lighted at too pure a shrine to dim its
  Etherial lustre, with what sweet persuasion
He might be taught, by love and her together—
I really don't know what, nor Julia either.

82

Fraught with this fine intention, and well fenced
  In mail of proof—her purity of soul,
She, for the future of her strength convinced,
  And that her honour was a rock, or mole,
Exceeding sagely from that hour dispensed
  With any kind of troublesome control;
But whether Julia to the task was equal
Is that which must be mentioned in the sequel.

83

Her plan she deem'd both innocent and feasible,
  And, surely, with a stripling of sixteen
Not scandal's fangs could fix on much that's seizable,
  Or if they did so, satisfied to mean
Nothing but what was good, her breast was
    peaceable—
  A quiet conscience makes one so serene!
Christians have burnt each other, quite persuaded
That all the Apostles would have done as they did.

84

And if in the mean time her husband died,
  But heaven forbid that such a thought should cross
Her brain, though in a dream! (and then she sigh'd)
  Never could she survive that common loss;
But just suppose that moment should betide,
  I only say suppose it—*inter nos*—[37]
(This should be *entre nous*, for Julia thought
In French, but then the rhyme would go for nought).

85

I only say suppose this supposition:
  Juan being then grown up to man's estate
Would fully suit a widow of condition,
  Even seven years hence it would not be too late;
And in the interim (to pursue this vision)
  The mischief, after all, could not be great,
For he would learn the rudiments of love,
I mean the seraph way of those above.

[37] **inter nos:** *trans.* between us.

86

So much for Julia. Now we'll turn to Juan,
Poor little fellow! he had no idea
Of his own case, and never hit the true one;
In feelings quick as Ovid's Miss Medea,[38]
He puzzled over what he found a new one,
But not as yet imagined it could be a
Thing quite in course, and not at all alarming,
Which, with a little patience, might grow charming.

87

Silent and pensive, idle, restless, slow,
His home deserted for the lonely wood,
Tormented with a wound he could not know,
His, like all deep grief, plunged in solitude:
I'm fond myself of solitude or so,
But then, I beg it may be understood,
By solitude I mean a sultan's, not
A hermit's, with a haram for a grot.

88

'Oh Love! in such a wilderness as this,
Where transport and security entwine,
Here is the empire of thy perfect bliss,
And here thou art a god indeed divine.'
The bard I quote from does not sing amiss,
With the exception of the second line,
For that same twining 'transport and security'
Are twisted to a phrase of some obscurity.

89

The poet meant, no doubt, and thus appeals
To the good sense and senses of mankind,
The very thing which every body feels,
As all have found on trial, or may find,
That no one likes to be disturb'd at meals
Or love.—I won't say more about 'entwined'
Or 'transport', as we knew all that before,
But beg 'Security' will bolt the door.

90

Young Juan wander'd by the glassy brooks
Thinking unutterable things; he threw
Himself at length within the leafy nooks
Where the wild branch of the cork forest grew;
There poets find materials for their books,
And every now and then we read them through,
So that their plan and prosody are eligible,
Unless, like Wordsworth, they prove unintelligible.

91

He, Juan, (and not Wordsworth) so pursued
His self-communion with his own high soul,
Until his mighty heart, in its great mood,
Had mitigated part, though not the whole
Of its disease; he did the best he could
With things not very subject to control,
And turn'd, without perceiving his condition,
Like Coleridge, into a metaphysician.

92

He thought about himself, and the whole earth,
Of man the wonderful, and of the stars,
And how the deuce they ever could have birth;
And then he thought of earthquakes, and of wars,
How many miles the moon might have in girth,
Of air-balloons, and of the many bars
To perfect knowledge of the boundless skies;
And then he thought of Donna Julia's eyes.

93

In thoughts like these true wisdom may discern
Longings sublime, and aspirations high,
Which some are born with, but the most part learn
To plague themselves withal, they know not why:
'Twas strange that one so young should thus concern
His brain about the action of the sky;
If *you* think 'twas philosophy that this did,
I can't help thinking puberty assisted.

94

He pored upon the leaves, and on the flowers,
And heard a voice in all the winds; and then
He thought of wood nymphs and immortal bowers,
And how the goddesses came down to men:
He miss'd the pathway, he forgot the hours,
And when he look'd upon his watch again,
He found how much old Time had been a winner—
He also found that he had lost his dinner.

[38] **Ovid's Miss Medea:** Medea is smitten with a burning passion at first sight for Jason of the Argonauts in Ovid's *Metamorphoses,* VII.

95

Sometimes he turn'd to gaze upon his book,
Boscan, or Garcilasso;[39]—by the wind
Even as the page is rustled while we look,
So by the poesy of his own mind
Over the mystic leaf his soul was shook,
As if 'twere one whereon magicians bind
Their spells, and give them to the passing gale,
According to some good old woman's tale.

96

Thus would he while his lonely hours away
Dissatisfied, nor knowing what he wanted;
Nor glowing reverie, nor poet's lay,
Could yield his spirit that for which it panted,
A bosom whereon he his head might lay,
And hear the heart beat with the love it granted,
With——several other things, which I forget,
Or which, at least, I need not mention yet.

97

Those lonely walks, and lengthening reveries,
Could not escape the gentle Julia's eyes;
She saw that Juan was not at his ease;
But that which chiefly may, and must surprise,
Is, that the Donna Inez did not tease
Her only son with question or surmise;
Whether it was she did not see, or would not,
Or, like all very clever people, could not.

98

This may seem strange, but yet 'tis very common;
For instance—gentlemen, whose ladies take
Leave to o'erstep the written rights of woman,
And break the——Which commandment is't they break?[40]
(I have forgot the number, and think no man
Should rashly quote, for fear of a mistake)
I say, when these same gentlemen are jealous,
They make some blunder, which their ladies tell us.

99

A real husband always is suspicious,
But still no less suspects in the wrong place,
Jealous of some one who had no such wishes,
Or pandering blindly to his own disgrace
By harbouring some dear friend extremely vicious;
The last indeed's infallibly the case:
And when the spouse and friend are gone off wholly,
He wonders at their vice, and not his folly.

100

Thus parents also are at times short-sighted;
Though watchful as the lynx, they ne'er discover,
The while the wicked world beholds delighted,
Young Hopeful's mistress, or Miss Fanny's lover,
Till some confounded escapade has blighted
The plan of twenty years, and all is over;
And then the mother cries, the father swears,
And wonders why the devil he got heirs.

101

But Inez was so anxious, and so clear
Of sight, that I must think, on this occasion,
She had some other motive much more near
For leaving Juan to this new temptation,
But what that motive was, I shan't say here;
Perhaps to finish Juan's education,
Perhaps to open Don Alfonso's eyes,
In case he thought his wife too great a prize.

102

It was upon a day, a summer's day;—
Summer's indeed a very dangerous season,
And so is spring about the end of May;
The sun, no doubt, is the prevailing reason;
But whatsoe'er the cause is, one may say,
And stand convicted of more truth than treason,
That there are months which nature grows more merry in,
March has its hares, and May must have its heroine.

103

'Twas on a summer's day—the sixth of June:—
I like to be particular in dates,
Not only of the age, and year, but moon;
They are a sort of post-house, where the Fates
Change horses, making history change its tune,
Then spur away o'er empires and o'er states,

[39] Boscan . . . Garcilasso: sixteenth-century Spanish poets known for their works on romantic love.

[40] Cf. Exodus 20:14: "Thou shalt not commit adultery," the sixth Commandment.

Leaving at last not much besides chronology,
Excepting the post-obits[41] of theology.

104

'Twas on the sixth of June, about the hour
Of half-past six—perhaps still nearer seven,
When Julia sate within as pretty a bower
As e'er held houri in that heathenish heaven
Described by Mahomet, and Anacreon Moore,[42]
To whom the lyre and laurels have been given,
With all the trophies of triumphant song—
He won them well, and may he wear them long!

105

She sate, but not alone; I know not well
How this same interview had taken place,
And even if I knew, I should not tell—
People should hold their tongues in any case;
No matter how or why the thing befell,
But there were she and Juan, face to face—
When two such faces are so, 'twould be wise,
But very difficult, to shut their eyes.

106

How beautiful she look'd! her conscious heart
Glow'd in her cheek, and yet she felt no wrong.
Oh Love! how perfect is thy mystic art,
Strengthening the weak, and trampling on the strong,
How self-deceitful is the sagest part
Of mortals whom thy lure hath led along—
The precipice she stood on was immense,
So was her creed in her own innocence.

107

She thought of her own strength, and Juan's youth,
And of the folly of all prudish fears,
Victorious virtue, and domestic truth,
And then of Don Alfonso's fifty years;

[41] **post-obits:** that which takes place after death.

[42] **houri:** the Koran's voluptuous virgins of paradise. **Anacreon Moore:** Thomas Moore (1779–1852) had written and translated works of Oriental romance, as well as the lyrics of the Greek poet Anacreon. He became famous with the publication of his immensely popular oriental tales, *Lalla Rookh* (1817).

I wish these last had not occurr'd, in sooth,
Because that number rarely much endears,
And through all climes, the snowy and the sunny,
Sounds ill in love, whate'er it may in money.

108

When people say, 'I've told you *fifty* times,'
They mean to scold, and very often do;
When poets say, 'I've written *fifty* rhymes,'
They make you dread that they'll recite them too;
In gangs of *fifty*, thieves commit their crimes;
At *fifty* love for love is rare, 'tis true,
But then, no doubt, it equally as true is,
A good deal may be bought for *fifty* Louis.

109

Julia had honour, virtue, truth, and love,
For Don Alfonso; and she inly swore,
By all the vows below to powers above,
She never would disgrace the ring she wore,
Nor leave a wish which wisdom might reprove;
And while she ponder'd this, besides much more,
One hand on Juan's carelessly was thrown,
Quite by mistake—she thought it was her own;

110

Unconsciously she lean'd upon the other,
Which play'd within the tangles of her hair;
And to contend with thoughts she could not smother,
She seem'd by the distraction of her air.
'Twas surely very wrong in Juan's mother
To leave together this imprudent pair,
She who for many years had watch'd her son so—
I'm very certain *mine* would not have done so.

111

The hand which still held Juan's, by degrees
Gently, but palpably confirm'd its grasp,
And if it said 'detain me, if you please';
Yet there's no doubt she only meant to clasp
His fingers with a pure Platonic squeeze;
She would have shrunk as from a toad, or asp,[43]
Had she imagined such a thing could rouse
A feeling dangerous to a prudent spouse.

[43] **asp:** poisonous snake, such as the cobra.

112

I cannot know what Juan thought of this,
But what he did, is much what you would do;
His young lip thank'd it with a grateful kiss,
And then, abash'd at its own joy, withdrew
In deep despair, lest he had done amiss,
Love is so very timid when 'tis new:
She blush'd, and frown'd not, but she strove to speak,
And held her tongue, her voice was grown so weak.

113

The sun set, and up rose the yellow moon:
The devil's in the moon for mischief; they
Who call'd her CHASTE, methinks, began too soon
Their nomenclature; there is not a day,
The longest, not the twenty-first of June,
Sees half the business in a wicked way
On which three single hours of moonshine smile—
And then she looks so modest all the while.

114

There is a dangerous silence in that hour,
A stillness, which leaves room for the full soul
To open all itself, without the power
Of calling wholly back its self-control;
The silver light which, hallowing tree and tower,
Sheds beauty and deep softness o'er the whole,
Breathes also to the heart, and o'er it throws
A loving languor, which is not repose.

115

And Julia sate with Juan, half embraced
And half retiring from the glowing arm,
Which trembled like the bosom where 'twas placed;
Yet still she must have thought there was no harm,
Or else 'twere easy to withdraw her waist;
But then the situation had its charm,
And then——God knows what next—I can't go on;
I'm almost sorry that I e'er begun.

116

Oh Plato! Plato! you have paved the way,
With your confounded fantasies, to more
Immoral conduct by the fancied sway
Your system feigns o'er the controlless core
Of human hearts, than all the long array
Of poets and romancers:—You're a bore,
A charlatan, a coxcomb—and have been,
At best, no better than a go-between.

117

And Julia's voice was lost, except in sighs,
Until too late for useful conversation;
The tears were gushing from her gentle eyes,
I wish, indeed, they had not had occasion,
But who, alas! can love, and then be wise?
Not that remorse did not oppose temptation,
A little still she strove, and much repented,
And whispering 'I will ne'er consent'—consented.

118

'Tis said that Xerxes[44] offer'd a reward
To those who could invent him a new pleasure;
Methinks, the requisition's rather hard,
And must have cost his majesty a treasure:
For my part, I'm a moderate-minded bard,
Fond of a little love (which I call leisure);
I care not for new pleasures, as the old
Are quite enough for me, so they but hold.

119

Oh Pleasure! you're indeed a pleasant thing,
Although one must be damn'd for you, no doubt;
I make a resolution every spring
Of reformation, ere the year run out,
But, somehow, this my vestal vow[45] takes wing,
Yet still, I trust, it may be kept throughout:
I'm very sorry, very much ashamed,
And mean, next winter, to be quite reclaim'd.

120

Here my chaste Muse a liberty must take—
Start not! still chaster reader—she'll be nice hence-
Forward, and there is no great cause to quake;
This liberty is a poetic licence,
Which some irregularity may make
In the design, and as I have a high sense
Of Aristotle and the Rules,[46] 'tis fit
To beg his pardon when I err a bit.

[44] **Xerxes:** King of Persia (486–465 BC).

[45] **vestal vow:** vow of chastity.

[46] **Rules:** reference to the "rules" of Aristotle's *Poetics*—the unities of time, place, and action.

121

This licence is to hope the reader will
Suppose from June the sixth (the fatal day,
Without those epoch my poetic skill
For want of facts would all be thrown away),
But keeping Julia and Don Juan still
In sight, that several months have pass'd; we'll say
'Twas in November, but I'm not so sure
About the day — the era's more obscure.

122

We'll talk of that anon. — 'Tis sweet to hear
At midnight on the blue and moonlit deep
The song and oar of Adria's[47] gondolier,
By distance mellow'd, o'er the waters sweep;
'Tis sweet to see the evening star appear;
'Tis sweet to listen as the nightwinds creep
From leaf to leaf; 'tis sweet to view on high
The rainbow, based on ocean, span the sky.

123

'Tis sweet to hear the watchdog's honest bark
Bay deep-mouth'd welcome as we draw near home;
'Tis sweet to know there is an eye will mark
Our coming, and look brighter when we come;
'Tis sweet to be awaken'd by the lark,
Or lull'd by falling waters; sweet the hum
Of bees, the voice of girls, the song of birds,
The lisp of children, and their earliest words.

124

Sweet is the vintage, when the showering grapes
In Bacchanal profusion reel to earth
Purple and gushing: sweet are our escapes
From civic revelry to rural mirth;
Sweet to the miser are his glittering heaps,
Sweet to the father is his first-born's birth,
Sweet is revenge — especially to women,
Pillage to soldiers, prize-money to seamen.

125

Sweet is a legacy, and passing sweet
The unexpected death of some old lady
Or gentleman of seventy years complete,
Who've made 'us youth' wait too — too long already
For an estate, or cash, or country-seat,
Still breaking, but with stamina so steady,
That all the Israelites are fit to mob its
Next owner for their double-damn'd post-obits.[48]

126

'Tis sweet to win, no matter how, one's laurels
By blood or ink; 'tis sweet to put an end
To strife; 'tis sometimes sweet to have our quarrels,
Particularly with a tiresome friend;
Sweet is old wine in bottles, ale in barrels;
Dear is the helpless creature we defend
Against the world; and dear the schoolboy spot
We ne'er forget, though there we are forgot.

127

But sweeter still than this, than these, than all,
Is first and passionate love — it stands alone,
Like Adam's recollection of his fall;
The tree of knowledge has been pluck'd — all's known —
And life yields nothing further to recall
Worthy of this ambrosial sin, so shown,
No doubt in fable, as the unforgiven
Fire which Prometheus filch'd for us from heaven.

128

Man's a strange animal, and makes strange use
Of his own nature, and the various arts,
And likes particularly to produce
Some new experiment to show his parts;
This is the age of oddities let loose,
Where different talents find their different marts;
You'd best begin with truth, and when you've lost your
Labour, there's a sure market for imposture.

129

What opposite discoveries we have seen!
(Signs of true genius, and of empty pockets)
One makes new noses, one a guillotine,
One breaks your bones, one sets them in their sockets;

[47] **Adria:** Venice.

[48] **double-damn'd post-obits:** debt placed upon an estate to be repaid by the heir upon receiving the inheritance.

But vaccination certainly has been
A kind antithesis to Congreve's rockets,
With which the doctor paid off an old pox
By borrowing a new one from an ox.[49]

130

Bread has been made (indifferent) from potatoes;
And galvanism[50] has set some corpses grinning,
But has not answer'd like the apparatus
Of the Humane Society's beginning,
By which men are unsuffocated gratis:
What wondrous new machines have late been spinning![51]
I said the small-pox has gone out of late,
Perhaps it may be followed by the great.[52]

131

'Tis said the great came from America;
Perhaps it may set out on its return;
The population there so spreads, they say,
'Tis grown high time to thin it in its turn,
With war, or plague, or famine, any way,
So that civilization they may learn,
And which in ravage the more loathesome evil is,
Their real lues,[53] or our pseudo-syphilis.

132

This is the patent-age of new inventions
For killing bodies, and for saving souls,
All propagated with the best intentions;
Sir Humphrey Davy's lantern,[54] by which coals
Are safely mined for in the mode he mentions,
Timbuctoo travels, voyages to the Poles,
Are ways to benefit mankind, as true,
Perhaps, as shooting them at Waterloo.

133

Man's a phenomenon, one knows not what,
And wonderful beyond all wondrous measure;
'Tis pity though, in this sublime world, that
Pleasure's a sin, and sometimes sin's a pleasure;
Few mortals know what end they would be at,
But whether glory, power, or love, or treasure,
The path is through perplexing ways, and when
The goal is gain'd, we die, you know—and then——

134

What then?—I do not know, no more do you—
And so good night.—Return we to our story:
'Twas in November, when fine days are few,
And the far mountains wax a little hoary,
And clap a white cape on their mantles blue;
And the sea dashes round the promontory,
And the loud breaker boils against the rock,
And sober suns must set at five o'clock.

135

'Twas, as the watchmen say, a cloudy night;
No moon, no stars, the wind was low or loud
By gusts, and many a sparkling hearth was bright
With the piled wood, round which the family crowd;
There's something cheerful in that sort of light,
Even as a summer sky's without a cloud:
I'm fond of fire, and crickets, and all that,
A lobster-salad, and champaigne, and chat.

136

'Twas midnight—Donna Julia was in bed,
Sleeping, most probably,—when at her door
Arose a clatter might awake the dead,
If they had never been awoke before,
And that they have been so we all have read,
And are to be so, at the least, once more—
The door was fasten'd, but with voice and fist
First knocks were heard, then 'Madam—Madam—hist!'

---

[49] **Congreve's rockets:** artillery rockets created by British inventor Sir William Congreve (1772–1828) which were first fired from special boats on Boulogne in 1806 and used to great effect at the Battle of Leipzig in 1813. **the doctor . . . an ox:** Edward Jenner (1749–1823) discovered the vaccine for the highly contagious skin disease of smallpox. This vaccine came from the virus of the skin infection of cattle (cowpox).

[50] **galvanism:** see introduction to SCIENCE AND NATURE.

[51] **machines . . . spinning:** reference to spinning machines. See Byron's "Parliamentary Speech on Frame-Breaking."*

[52] **the great:** syphilis, the Great Pox.

[53] **lues:** syphilis, plague. Byron is also summarizing in this stanza the dire prediction of Malthus's *First Essay on Population.**

[54] **Sir Humphrey Davy:** (1778–1829) inventor of the safety lantern for miners.

137

'For God's sake, Madam—Madam—here's my master,
With more than half the city at his back—
Was ever heard of such a curst disaster!
'Tis not my fault—I kept good watch—Alack!
Do, pray undo the bolt a little faster—
They're on the stair just now, and in a crack
Will all be here; perhaps he yet may fly—
Surely the window's not so *very* high!'

138

By this time Don Alfonso was arrived,
With torches, friends, and servants in great number;
The major part of them had long been wived,
And therefore paused not to disturb the slumber
Of any wicked woman, who contrived
By stealth her husband's temples to encumber:[55]
Examples of this kind are so contagious,
Were *one* not punish'd, *all* would be outrageous.

139

I can't tell how, or why, or what suspicion
Could enter into Don Alfonso's head;
But for a cavalier of his condition
It surely was exceedingly ill-bred,
Without a word of previous admonition,
To hold a levee round his lady's bed,
And summon lackeys, arm'd with fire and sword,
To prove himself the thing he most abhorr'd.

140

Poor Donna Julia! starting as from sleep,
(Mind—that I do not say—she had not slept)
Began at once to scream, and yawn, and weep;
Her maid Antonia, who was an adept,
Contrived to fling the bed-clothes in a heap,
As if she had just now from out them crept:
I can't tell why she should take all this trouble
To prove her mistress had been sleeping double.

141

But Julia mistress, and Antonia maid,
Appear'd like two poor harmless women, who
Of goblins, but still more of men afraid,
Had thought one man might be deterr'd by two,
And therefore side by side were gently laid,
Until the hours of absence should run through,
And truant husband should return, and say,
'My dear, I was the first who came away.'

142

Now Julia found at length a voice, and cried,
'In heaven's name, Don Alfonso, what d'ye mean?
Has madness seized you? would that I had died
Ere such a monster's victim I had been!
What may this midnight violence betide,
A sudden fit of drunkenness or spleen?
Dare you suspect me, whom the thought would kill?
Search, then, the room!'—Alfonso said, 'I will.'

143

He search'd, *they* search'd, and rummaged every where,
Closet and clothes'-press, chest and window-seat,
And found much linen, lace, and several pair
Of stockings, slippers, brushes, combs, complete,
With other articles of ladies fair,
To keep them beautiful, or leave them neat:
Arras they prick'd and curtains with their swords,
And wounded several shutters, and some boards.

144

Under the bed they search'd, and there they found—
No matter what—it was not that they sought;
They open'd windows, gazing if the ground
Had signs or footmarks, but the earth said nought;
And then they stared each other's faces round:
'Tis odd, not one of all these seekers thought,
And seems to me almost a sort of blunder,
Of looking *in* the bed as well as under.

145

During this inquisition Julia's tongue
Was not asleep—'Yes, search and search,' she cried,
'Insult on insult heap, and wrong on wrong!
It was for this that I became a bride!
For this in silence I have suffer'd long
A husband like Alfonso at my side;
But now I'll bear no more, nor here remain,
If there be law, or lawyers, in all Spain.

[55] **her husband's . . . encumber:** husbands with unfaithful wives were said to grow horns, or to be cuckolded.

146

'Yes, Don Alfonso! husband now no more,
If ever you indeed deserved the name,
Is't worthy of your years?—you have threescore,
Fifty, or sixty—it is all the same—
Is't wise or fitting causeless to explore
For facts against a virtuous woman's fame?
Ungrateful, perjured, barbarous Don Alfonso,
How dare you think your lady would go on so?

147

'Is it for this I have disdain'd to hold
The common privileges of my sex?
That I have chosen a confessor so old
And deaf, that any other it would vex,
And never once he has had cause to scold,
But found my very innocence perplex
So much, he always doubted I was married—
How sorry you will be when I've miscarried!

148

'Was it for this that no Cortejo[56] ere
I yet have chosen from out the youth of Seville?
Is it for this I scarce went any where,
Except to bull-fights, mass, play, rout, and revel?
Is it for this, whate'er my suitors were,
I favour'd none—nay, was almost uncivil?
Is it for this that General Count O'Reilly,
Who took Algiers, declares I used him vilely?

149

'Did not the Italian Musico Cazzani
Sing at my heart six months at least in vain?
Did not his countryman, Count Corniani,
Call me the only virtuous wife in Spain?
Were there not also Russians, English, many?
The Count Strongstroganoff I put in pain,
And Lord Mount Coffeehouse, the Irish peer,
Who kill'd himself for love (with wine) last year.

150

'Have I not had two bishops at my feet?
The Duke of Ichar, and Don Fernan Nunez,
And is it thus a faithful wife you treat?
I wonder in what quarter now the moon is:
I praise your vast forbearance not to beat
Me also, since the time so opportune is—
Oh, valiant man! with sword drawn and cock'd trigger,
Now, tell me, don't you cut a pretty figure?

151

'Was it for this you took your sudden journey,
Under pretence of business indispensible
With that sublime of rascals your attorney,
Whom I see standing there, and looking sensible
Of having play'd the fool? though both I spurn, he
Deserves the worst, his conduct's less defensible,
Because, no doubt, 'twas for his dirty fee,
And not from any love to you nor me.

152

'If he comes here to take a deposition,
By all means let the gentleman proceed;
You've made the apartment in a fit condition:—
There's pen and ink for you, sir, when you need—
Let every thing be noted with precision,
I would not you for nothing should be fee'd—
But, as my maid's undrest, pray turn your spies out.'
'Oh!' sobb'd Antonia, 'I could tear their eyes out.'

153

'There is the closet, there the toilet, there
The ante-chamber—search them under, over:
There is the sofa, there the great arm-chair,
The chimney—which would really hold a lover.
I wish to sleep, and beg you will take care
And make no further noise, till you discover
The secret cavern of this lurking treasure—
And when 'tis found, let me, too, have that pleasure.

154

'And now, Hidalgo! now that you have thrown
Doubt upon me, confusion over all,
Pray have the courtesy to make it known
Who is the man you search for? how d'ye call
Him? what's his lineage? let him but be shown—
I hope he's young and handsome—is he tall?
Tell me—and be assured, that since you stain
My honour thus, it shall not be in vain.

155

'At least, perhaps, he has not sixty years,
At that age he would be too old for slaughter,
Or for so young a husband's jealous fears—

[56] **Cortejo:** the acknowledged lover of a married woman, comparable to the Italian *cavalier servante.*

(Antonia! let me have a glass of water)
I am ashamed of having shed these tears,
They are unworthy of my father's daughter;
My mother dream'd not in my natal hour
That I should fall into a monster's power.

156

'Perhaps 'tis of Antonia you are jealous,
You saw that she was sleeping by my side
When you broke in upon us with your fellows:
Look where you please—we've nothing, sir, to hide;
Only another time, I trust, you'll tell us,
Or for the sake of decency abide
A moment at the door, that we may be
Drest to receive so much good company.

157

'And now, sir, I have done, and say no more;
The little I have said may serve to show
The guileless heart in silence may grieve o'er
The wrongs to whose exposure it is slow:
I leave you to your conscience as before,
'Twill one day ask you *why* you used me so?
God grant you feel not then the bitterest grief!
Antonia! Where's my pocket-handkerchief?'

158

She ceased, and turn'd upon her pillow; pale
She lay, her dark eyes flashing through their tears,
Like skies that rain and lighten; as a veil,
Waved and o'ershading her wan cheek, appears
Her streaming hair; the black curls strive, but fail,
To hide the glossy shoulder, which uprears
Its snow through all;—her soft lips lie apart,
And louder than her breathing beats her heart.

159

The Senhor Don Alfonso stood confused;
Antonia bustled round the ransack'd room,
And, turning up her nose, with looks abused
Her master, and his myrmidons, of whom
Not one, except the attorney, was amused;
He, like Achates,[57] faithful to the tomb,
So there were quarrels, cared not for the cause,
Knowing they must be settled by the laws.

[57] **Achates:** Aeneas's faithful companion in Virgil's *Aenead*.

160

With prying snub-nose, and small eyes, he stood,
Following Antonia's motions here and there,
With much suspicion in his attitude;
For reputations he had little care;
So that a suit or action were made good,
Small pity had he for the young and fair,
And ne'er believed in negatives, till these
Were proved by competent false witnesses.

161

But Don Alfonso stood with downcast looks,
And, truth to say, he made a foolish figure;
When, after searching in five hundred nooks,
And treating a young wife with so much rigour,
He gain'd no point, except some self-rebukes,
Added to those his lady with such vigour
Had pour'd upon him for the last half-hour,
Quick, thick, and heavy—as a thunder-shower.

162

At first he tried to hammer an excuse,
To which the sole reply were tears, and sobs,
And indications of hysterics, whose
Prologue is always certain throes, and throbs,
Gasps, and whatever else the owners choose:—
Alfonso saw his wife, and thought of Job's;[58]
He saw too, in perspective, her relations,
And then he tried to muster all his patience.

163

He stood in act to speak, or rather stammer,
But sage Antonia cut him short before
The anvil of his speech received the hammer,
With 'Pray sir, leave the room, and say no more,
Or madam dies.'—Alfonso mutter'd 'D——n her,'
But nothing else, the time of words was o'er;
He cast a rueful look or two, and did,
He knew not wherefore, that which he was bid.

164

With him retired his '*posse comitatus*',[59]
The attorney last, who linger'd near the door,

[58] Cf. Job 2:9: "Then said his wife unto him, Dost thou still retain thine integrity? curse God, and die."

[59] '**posse comitatus**': body of men empowered by one with legal authority to protect the peace.

Reluctantly, still tarrying there as late as
 Antonia let him — not a little sore
At this most strange and unexplain'd '*hiatus*'[60]
 In Don Alfonso's facts, which just now wore
An awkward look; as he revolved the case
The door was fasten'd in his legal face.

165

No sooner was it bolted, than — Oh shame!
 Oh sin! Oh sorrow! and Oh womankind!
How can you do such things and keep your fame,
 Unless this world, and t'other too, be blind?
Nothing so dear as an unfilch'd good name!
 But to proceed — for there is more behind:
With much heart-felt reluctance be it said,
Young Juan slipp'd, half-smother'd, from the bed.

166

He had been hid — I don't pretend to say
 How, nor can I indeed describe the where —
Young, slender, and pack'd easily, he lay,
 No doubt, in little compass, round or square;
But pity him I neither must nor may
 His suffocation by that pretty pair;
'Twere better, sure, to die so, than be shut
With maudlin Clarence in his Malmsey butt.[61]

167

And, secondly, I pity not, because
 He had no business to commit a sin,
Forbid by heavenly, fined by human laws,
 At least 'twas rather early to begin;
But at sixteen the conscience rarely gnaws
 So much as when we call our old debts in
At sixty years, and draw the accompts of evil,
And find a deuced balance with the devil.

168

Of his position I can give no notion:
 'Tis written in the Hebrew Chronicle,[62]
How the physicians, leaving pill and potion,
 Prescribed, by way of blister, a young belle,
When old King David's blood grew dull in motion,
 And that the medicine answer'd very well;
Perhaps 'twas in a different way applied,
For David lived, but Juan nearly died.

169

What's to be done? Alfonso will be back
 The moment he has sent his fools away.
Antonia's skill was put upon the rack,
 But no device could be brought into play —
And how to parry the renew'd attack?
 Besides, it wanted but few hours of day:
Antonia puzzled; Julia did not speak,
But press'd her bloodless lip to Juan's cheek.

170

He turn'd his lip to hers, and with his hand
 Call'd back the tangles of her wandering hair;
Even then their love they could not all command,
 And half forgot their danger and despair:
Antonia's patience now was at a stand —
 'Come, come, 'tis no time now for fooling there,'
She whisper'd, in great wrath — 'I must deposit
This pretty gentleman within the closet:

171

'Pray, keep your nonsense for some luckier night —
 Who can have put my master in this mood?
What will become on't? — I'm in such a fright,
 The devil's in the urchin, and no good —
Is this a time for giggling? this a plight?
 Why, don't you know that it may end in blood?
You'll lose your life, and I shall lose my place,
My mistress, all, for that half-girlish face.

172

'Had it but been for a stout cavalier
 Of twenty-five or thirty — (Come, make haste)
But for a child, what piece of work is here!
 I really, madam, wonder at your taste —
(Come, sir, get in) — my master must be near.
 There, for the present, at the least he's fast,
And, if we can but till the morning keep
Our counsel — (Juan, mind, you must not sleep).'

173

Now, Don Alfonso entering, but alone,
 Closed the oration of the trusty maid:
She loiter'd, and he told her to be gone,
 An order somewhat sullenly obey'd;

[60] **'hiatus'**: break or interruption.

[61] **Malmsey butt**: cf. *Richard III*, I.iv. where murderers speak of drowning the Duke of Clarence in the malmsey-butt [wine cask].

[62] **The Hebrew Chronicle**: I Kings I: 1–3.

However, present remedy was none,
And no great good seem'd answer'd if she staid:
Regarding both with slow and sidelong view,
She snuff'd the candle, curtsied, and withdrew.

174

Alfonso paused a minute—then begun
Some strange excuses for his late proceeding;
He would not justify what he had done,
To say the best, it was extreme ill-breeding;
But there were ample reasons for it, none
Of which he specified in this his pleading:
His speech was a fine sample, on the whole,
Of rhetoric, which the learn'd call *'rigmarole'*.

175

Julia said nought; though all the while there rose
A ready answer, which at once enables
A matron, who her husband's foible knows,
By a few timely words to turn the tables,
Which if it does not silence still must pose,
Even if it should comprise a pack of fables;
'Tis to retort with firmness, and when he
Suspects with *one*, do you reproach with *three*.

176

Julia, in fact, had tolerable grounds,
Alfonso's loves with Inez were well known;
But whether 'twas that one's own guilt confounds,
But that can't be, as has been often shown,
A lady with apologies abounds;
It might be that her silence sprang alone
From delicacy to Don Juan's ear,
To whom she knew his mother's fame was dear.

177

There might be one more motive, which makes two;
Alfonso ne'er to Juan had alluded,
Mention'd his jealousy, but never who
Had been the happy lover, he concluded,
Conceal'd amongst his premises; 'tis true,
His mind the more o'er this its mystery brooded;
To speak of Inez now were, one may say,
Like throwing Juan in Alfonso's way.

178

A hint, in tender cases, is enough;
Silence is best, besides there is a *tact*
(That modern phrase appears to me sad stuff,
But it will serve to keep my verse compact)
Which keeps, when push'd by questions rather rough,
A lady always distant from the fact—
The charming creatures lie with such a grace,
There's nothing so becoming to the face.

179

They blush, and we believe them; at least I
Have always done so; 'tis of no great use,
In any case, attempting a reply,
For then their eloquence grows quite profuse;
And when at length they're out of breath, they sigh,
And cast their languid eyes down, and let loose
A tear or two, and then we make it up;
And then—and then—and then—sit down and sup.

180

Alfonso closed his speech, and begg'd her pardon,
Which Julia half withheld, and then half granted,
And laid conditions, he thought, very hard on,
Denying several little things he wanted:
He stood like Adam lingering near his garden,
With useless penitence perplex'd and haunted,
Beseeching she no further would refuse,
When lo! he stumbled o'er a pair of shoes.

181

A pair of shoes!—what then? not much, if they
Are such a fit with lady's feet, but these
(No one can tell how much I grieve to say)
Were masculine; to see them, and to seize,
Was but a moment's act.—Ah! Well-a-day!
My teeth begin to chatter, my veins freeze—
Alfonso first examined well their fashion,
And then flew out into another passion.

182

He left the room for his relinquish'd sword,
And Julia instant to the closet flew.
'Fly, Juan, fly! for heaven's sake—not a word—
The door is open—you may yet slip through
The passage you so often have explored—
Here is the garden-key—Fly—fly—Adieu!
Haste—haste!—I hear Alfonso's hurrying feet—
Day has not broke—there's no one in the street.'

183

None can say that this was not good advice,
The only mischief was, it came too late;
Of all experience 'tis the usual price,
A sort of income-tax laid on by fate:

Juan had reach'd the room-door in a trice,
 And might have done so by the garden-gate,
But met Alfonso in his dressing-gown,
Who threaten'd death — so Juan knock'd him down.

184

Dire was the scuffle, and out went the light,
 Antonia cried out 'Rape!' and Julia 'Fire!'
But not a servant stirr'd to aid the fight.
 Alfonso, pommell'd to his heart's desire,
Swore lustily he'd be revenged this night;
 And Juan, too, blasphemed an octave higher,
His blood was up; though young, he was a Tartar,
And not at all disposed to prove a martyr.

185

Alfonso's sword had dropp'd ere he could draw it,
 And they continued battling hand to hand,
For Juan very luckily ne'er saw it;
 His temper not being under great command,
If at that moment he had chanced to claw it,
 Alfonso's days had not been in the land
Much longer. — Think of husbands', lovers' lives!
And how ye may be doubly widows — wives!

186

Alfonso grappled to detain the foe,
 And Juan throttled him to get away,
And blood ('twas from the nose) began to flow;
 At last, as they more faintly wrestling lay,
Juan contrived to give an awkward blow,
 And then his only garment quite gave way;
He fled, like Joseph, leaving it; but there,[63]
I doubt, all likeness ends between the pair.

187

Lights came at length, and men, and maids, who found
 An awkward spectacle their eyes before;
Antonia in hysterics, Julia swoon'd,
 Alfonso leaning, breathless, by the door;
Some half-torn drapery scatter'd on the ground,
 Some blood, and several footsteps, but no more:
Juan the gate gain'd, turn'd the key about,
And liking not the inside, lock'd the out.

188

Here ends this canto. — Need I sing, or say,
 How Juan, naked, favour'd by the night,
Who favours what she should not, found his way,
 And reach'd his home in an unseemly plight?
The pleasant scandal which arose next day,
 The nine days' wonder which was brought to light,
And how Alfonso sued for a divorce,
Were in the English newspapers, of course.

189

If you would like to see the whole proceedings,
 The depositions, and the cause at full,
The names of all the witnesses, the pleadings
 Of counsel to nonsuit, or to annul,
There's more than one edition, and the readings
 Are various, but they none of them are dull,
The best is that in shorthand ta'en by Gurney,[64]
Who to Madrid on purpose made a journey.

190

But Donna Inez, to divert the train
 Of one of the most circulating scandals
That had for centuries been known in Spain,
 Since Roderic's Goths, or older Genseric's Vandals,[65]
First vow'd (and never had she vow'd in vain)
 To Virgin Mary several pounds of candles;
And then, by the advice of some old ladies,
She sent her son to be embark'd at Cadiz.

191

She had resolved that he should travel through
 All European climes, by land or sea,
To mend his former morals, or get new,
 Especially in France and Italy,
(At least this is the thing most people do).
 Julia was sent into a nunnery,
And there, perhaps, her feelings may be better
Shown in the following copy of her letter:

[63] **He fled . . . there:** cf. Genesis 39:12–15: Joseph ran from Potiphar's wife when she physically attempted to seduce him, leaving his coat of many colors in her hands.

[64] **Gurney:** William Gurney, Parliamentary reporter and journalist.

[65] **Goths . . . Vandals:** Germanic barbarian tribes, the latter of which invaded Spain in the fourth and fifth centuries and sacked Rome.

192

'They tell me 'tis decided; you depart:
'Tis wise—'tis well, but not the less a pain;
I have no further claim on your young heart,
Mine was the victim, and would be again;
To love too much has been the only art
I used;—I write in haste, and if a stain
Be on this sheet, 'tis not what it appears,
My eyeballs burn and throb, but have no tears.

193

'I loved, I love you, for that love have lost
State, station, heaven, mankind's, my own esteem,
And yet can not regret what it hath cost,
So dear is still the memory of that dream;
Yet, if I name my guilt, 'tis not to boast,
None can deem harshlier of me than I deem:
I trace this scrawl because I cannot rest—
I've nothing to reproach, nor to request.

194

'Man's love is of his life a thing apart,
'Tis woman's whole existence; man may range
The court, camp, church, the vessel, and the mart,
Sword, gown, gain, glory, offer in exchange
Pride, fame, ambition, to fill up his heart,
And few there are whom these can not estrange;
Man has all these resources, we but one,
To love again, and be again undone.

195

'My breast has been all weakness, is so yet;
I struggle, but cannot collect my mind;
My blood still rushes where my spirit's set,
As roll the waves before the settled wind;
My brain is feminine, nor can forget—
To all, except your image, madly blind;
As turns the needle trembling to the pole
It ne'er can reach, so turns to you, my soul.

196

'You will proceed in beauty, and in pride,
Beloved and loving many; all is o'er
For me on earth, except some years to hide
My shame and sorrow deep in my heart's core;
These I could bear, but cannot cast aside
The passion which still rends it as before,
And so farewell—forgive me, love me—No,
That word is idle now—but let it go.

197

'I have no more to say, but linger still,
And dare not set my seal upon this sheet,
And yet I may as well the task fulfil,
My misery can scarce be more complete:
I had not lived till now, could sorrow kill;
Death flies the wretch who fain the blow would
meet,
And I must even survive this last adieu,
And bear with life, to love and pray for you!'

198

This note was written upon gilt-edged paper
With a neat crow-quill, rather hard, but new;
Her small white fingers scarce could reach the taper,
But trembled as magnetic needles do,
And yet she did not let one tear escape her;
The seal a sunflower; *'Elle vous suit partout'*,
The motto, cut upon a white cornelian,[66]
The wax was superfine, its hue vermilion.

199

This was Don Juan's earliest scrape; but whether
I shall proceed with his adventures is
Dependent on the public altogether;
We'll see, however, what they say to this,
Their favour in an author's cap's a feather,
And no great mischief's done by their caprice;
And if their approbation we experience,
Perhaps they'll have some more about a year hence.

200

My poem's epic, and is meant to be
Divided in twelve books; each book containing,
With love, and war, a heavy gale at sea,
A list of ships, and captains, and kings reigning,
New characters; the episodes are three:
A panorama view of hell's in training,
After the style of Virgil and of Homer,
So that my name of Epic's no misnomer.

201

All these things will be specified in time,
With strict regard to Aristotle's rules,
The *vade mecum*[67] of the true sublime,

---

[66] **'Elle vous suit partout'**: *trans.* She follows you everywhere. **a white cornelian**: a piece of quartz.

[67] **vade mecum**: reference book.

Which makes so many poets, and some fools;
Prose poets like blank-verse, I'm fond of rhyme,
Good workmen never quarrel with their tools;
I've got new mythological machinery,
And very handsome supernatural scenery.

202

There's only one slight difference between
Me and my epic brethren gone before,
And here the advantage is my own, I ween;
(Not that I have not several merits more,
But this will more peculiarly be seen)
They so embellish, that 'tis quite a bore
Their labyrinth of fables to thread through,
Whereas this story's actually true.

203

If any person doubt it, I appeal
To history, tradition, and to facts,
To newspapers, whose truth all know and feel,
To plays in five, and operas in three acts;
All these confirm my statement a good deal,
But that which more completely faith exacts
Is, that myself, and several now in Seville,
Saw Juan's last elopement with the devil.

204

If ever I should condescend to prose,
I'll write poetical commandments, which
Shall supersede beyond all doubt all those
That went before; in these I shall enrich
My text with many things that no one knows,
And carry precept to the highest pitch:
I'll call the work 'Longinus o'er a Bottle,
Or, Every Poet his *own* Aristotle'.

205

Thou shalt believe in Milton, Dryden, Pope;[68]
Thou shalt not set up Wordsworth, Coleridge,
Southey;
Because the first is crazed beyond all hope,
The second drunk, the third so quaint and
mouthey:
With Crabbe it may be difficult to cope,
And Campbell's Hippocrene is somewhat drouthy:
Thou shalt not steal from Samuel Rogers, nor
Commit—flirtation with the muse of Moore.

206

Thou shalt not covet Mr Sotheby's Muse,
His Pegasus, nor any thing that's his;
Thou shalt not bear false witness like 'the Blues',[69]
(There's one, at least, is very fond of this);
Thou shalt not write, in short, but what I choose:
This is true criticism, and you may kiss—
Exactly as you please, or not, the rod,
But if you don't, I'll lay it on, by G—d!

207

If any person should presume to assert
This story is not moral, first, I pray,
That they will not cry out before they're hurt,
Then that they'll read it o'er again, and say,
(But, doubtless, nobody will be so pert)
That this is not a moral tale, though gay;
Besides, in canto twelfth, I mean to show
The very place where wicked people go.

208

If, after all, there should be some so blind
To their own good this warning to despise,
Led by some tortuosity of mind,
Not to believe my verse and their own eyes,
And cry that they 'the moral cannot find',
I tell him, if a clergyman, he lies;
Should captains the remark or critics make,
They also lie too—under a mistake.

209

The public approbation I expect,
And beg they'll take my word about the moral,
Which I with their amusement will connect,
(So children cutting teeth receive a coral);
Meantime, they'll doubtless please to recollect
My epical pretensions to the laurel:

[68] **Milton, Dryden, Pope**: these authors represent the Classical and Neoclassical tradition in British verse; Byron's major contemporaries, Wordsworth,* Coleridge,* and Southey* represent the new Romantic impulse in poetry. Crabbe, Rogers, Moore, and Sotheby are lesser contemporaries.

[69] **'the Blues'**: Bluestockings. See introduction to the RIGHTS OF WOMAN.

For fear some prudish readers should grow skittish,
I've bribed my grandmother's review — the British.

210

I sent it in a letter to the editor,
Who thank'd me duly by return of post —
I'm for a handsome article his creditor;
Yet if my gentle Muse he please to roast,
And break a promise after having made it her,
Denying the receipt of what it cost,
And smear his page with gall instead of honey,
All I can say is — that he had the money.

211

I think that with this holy new alliance
I may ensure the public, and defy
All other magazines of art or science,
Daily, or monthly, or three monthly; I
Have not essay'd to multiply their clients,
Because they tell me 'twere in vain to try,
And that the Edinburgh Review and Quarterly
Treat a dissenting author very martyrly.

212

'Non ego hoc ferrem calida juventâ
Consule Planco',[70] Horace said, and so
Say I; by which quotation there is meant a
Hint that some six or seven good years ago
(Long ere I dreamt of dating from the Brenta)
I was most ready to return a blow,
And would not brook at all this sort of thing
In my hot youth — when George the Third was King.

213

But now at thirty years my hair is gray —
(I wonder what it will be like at forty?
I thought of a peruke[71] the other day)
My heart is not much greener; and, in short, I
Have squander'd my whole summer while 'twas May,
And feel no more the spirit to retort; I
Have spent my life, both interest and principal,
And deem not, what I deem'd, my soul invincible.

214

No more — no more — Oh! never more on me
The freshness of the heart can fall like dew,
Which out of all the lovely things we see
Extracts emotions beautiful and new,
Hived in our bosoms like the bag o' the bee:
Think'st thou the honey with those objects grew?
Alas! 'twas not in them, but in thy power
To double even the sweetness of a flower.

215

No more — no more — Oh! never more, my heart,
Canst thou be my sole world, my universe!
Once all in all, but now a thing apart,
Thou canst not be my blessing or my curse:
The illusion's gone for ever, and thou art
Insensible, I trust, but none the worse,
And in thy stead I've got a deal of judgement,
Though heaven knows how it ever found a lodgement.

216

My days of love are over, me no more
The charms of maid, wife, and still less of widow,
Can make the fool of which they made before,
In short, I must not lead the life I did do;
The credulous hope of mutual minds is o'er,
The copious use of claret is forbid too,
So for a good old-gentlemanly vice,
I think I must take up with avarice.

217

Ambition was my idol, which was broken
Before the shrines of Sorrow and of Pleasure;
And the two last have left me many a token
O'er which reflection may be made at leisure:
Now, like Friar Bacon's brazen head, I've spoken,
'Time is, Time was, Time's past', a chymic[72] treasure
Is glittering youth, which I have spent betimes —
My heart in passion, and my head on rhymes.

218

What is the end of fame? 'tis but to fill
A certain portion of uncertain paper:

[70] **'Non ego . . . Planco'**: Byron translates the Latin in the last two lines of the stanza: "except to change the Consulship of Planco for the reign of George III."

[71] **peruke**: a man's wig.

[72] **'Time is . . . past'**: quote from Elizabethan dramatist, drunkard, and debtor, Robert Greene's *Friar Bacon, and Friar Bongay* (1594). **chymic**: magical.

Some liken it to climbing up a hill,
Whose summit, like all hills', is lost in vapour;
For this men write, speak, preach, and heroes kill,
And bards burn what they call their 'midnight taper',
To have, when the original is dust,
A name, a wretched picture, and worse bust.

219

What are the hopes of man? old Egypt's King
Cheops erected the first pyramid
And largest, thinking it was just the thing
To keep his memory whole, and mummy hid;
But somebody or other rummaging,
Burglariously broke his coffin's lid:
Let not a monument give you or me hopes,
Since not a pinch of dust remains of Cheops.

220

But I being fond of true philosophy,
Say very often to myself, 'Alas!
All things that have been born were born to die,
And flesh (which Death mows down to hay) is grass;
You've pass'd your youth not so unpleasantly,
And if you had it o'er again—'twould pass—
So thank your stars that matters are no worse,
And read your Bible, sir, and mind your purse.'

221

But for the present, gentle reader! and
Still gentler purchaser! the bard—that's I—
Must, with permission, shake you by the hand,
And so your humble servant, and good bye!
We meet again, if we should understand
Each other, and if not, I shall not try
Your patience further than by this short sample—
'Twere well if others follow'd my example.

222

'Go, little book, from this my solitude!
I cast thee on the waters, go thy ways!
And if, as I believe, thy vein be good,
The world will find thee after many days.'
When Southey's read, and Wordsworth understood,
I can't help putting in my claim to praise—
The four first rhymes are Southey's every line:
For God's sake, reader! take them not for mine.

—*from* CANTO II—

1

Oh ye! who teach the ingenuous youth of nations,
Holland, France, England, Germany, or Spain,
I pray ye flog them upon all occasions,
It mends their morals, never mind the pain:
The best of mothers and of educations
In Juan's case were but employ'd in vain,
Since in a way, that's rather of the oddest, he
Became divested of his native modesty.

2

Had he but been placed at a public school,
In the third form, or even in the fourth,
His daily task had kept his fancy cool,
At least, had he been nurtured in the north;
Spain may prove an exception to the rule,
But then exceptions always prove its worth—
A lad of sixteen causing a divorce
Puzzled his tutors very much, of course.

3

I can't say that it puzzles me at all,
If all things be consider'd: first, there was
His lady-mother, mathematical,
A——never mind; his tutor, an old ass;
A pretty woman—(that's quite natural,
Or else the thing had hardly come to pass);
A husband rather old, not much in unity
With his young wife—a time, and opportunity.

4

Well—well, the world must turn upon its axis,
And all mankind turn with it, heads or tails,
And live and die, make love and pay our taxes,
And as the veering wind shifts, shift our sails;
The king commands us, and the doctor quacks us,
The priest instructs, and so our life exhales,
A little breath, love, wine, ambition, fame,
Fighting, devotion, dust,—perhaps a name.

. . . .

8

But to our tale: the Donna Inez sent
Her son to Cadiz only to embark;
To stay there had not answer'd her intent,
But why?—we leave the reader in the dark—

'Twas for a voyage that the young man was meant,
As if a Spanish ship were Noah's ark,
To wean him from the wickedness of earth,
And send him like a dove of promise forth.

9

Don Juan bade his valet pack his things
According to direction, then received
A lecture and some money: for four springs
He was to travel; and though Inez grieved,
(As every kind of parting has its stings)
She hoped he would improve—perhaps believed:
A letter, too, she gave (he never read it)
Of good advice—and two or three of credit.

10

In the mean time, to pass her hours away,
Brave Inez now set up a Sunday school
For naughty children, who would rather play
(Like truant rogues) the devil, or the fool;
Infants of three years old were taught that day,
Dunces were whipt, or set upon a stool:
The great success of Juan's education,
Spurr'd her to teach another generation.

11

Juan embark'd—the ship got under way,
The wind was fair, the water passing rough;
A devil of a sea rolls in that bay,
As I, who've cross'd it oft, know well enough;
And, standing upon deck, the dashing spray
Flies in one's face, and makes it weather-tough:
And there he stood to take, and take again,
His first—perhaps his last—farewell of Spain.

12

I can't but say it is an awkward sight
To see one's native land receding through
The growing waters; it unmans one quite,
Especially when life is rather new:
I recollect Great Britain's coast looks white,
But almost every other country's blue,
When gazing on them, mystified by distance,
We enter on our nautical existence.

13

So Juan stood, bewilder'd, on the deck:
The wind sung, cordage strain'd, and sailors swore,
And the ship creak'd, the town became a speck,
From which away so fair and fast they bore.
The best of remedies is a beef-steak
Against sea-sickness; try it, sir, before
You sneer, and I assure you this is true,
For I have found it answer—so may you.

14

Don Juan stood, and, gazing from the stern,
Beheld his native Spain receding far:
First partings form a lesson hard to learn,
Even nations feel this when they go to war;
There is a sort of unexprest concern,
A kind of shock that sets one's heart ajar:
At leaving even the most unpleasant people
And places, one keeps looking at the steeple.

15

But Juan had got many things to leave,
His mother, and a mistress, and no wife,
So that he had much better cause to grieve
Than many persons more advanced in life;
And if we now and then a sigh must heave
At quitting even those we quit in strife,
No doubt we weep for those the heart endears—
That is, till deeper griefs congeal our tears.

16

So Juan wept, as wept the captive Jews
By Babel's waters, still remembering Sion:
I'd weep, but mine is not a weeping Muse,
And such light griefs are not a thing to die on;
Young men should travel, if but to amuse
Themselves; and the next time their servants tie on
Behind their carriages their new portmanteau,
Perhaps it may be lined with this my canto.

17

And Juan wept, and much he sigh'd and thought,
While his salt tears dropp'd into the salt sea,
'Sweets to the sweet;'[1] (I like so much to quote;
You must excuse this extract, 'tis where she,

[1] **'Sweets to the sweet'**: cf. *Hamlet,* V.i.265: "Sweets to the sweet; farewell!"

The Queen of Denmark, for Ophelia brought
  Flowers to the grave); and, sobbing often, he
Reflected on his present situation,
And seriously resolved on reformation.

18

'Farewell, my Spain! a long farewell!' he cried,
  'Perhaps I may revisit thee no more,
But die, as many an exiled heart hath died,
  Of its own thirst to see again thy shore:
Farewell, where Guadalquivir's waters glide!
  Farewell, my mother! and, since all is o'er,
Farewell, too dearest Julia!'—(here he drew
Her letter out again, and read it through).

19

'And oh! if e'er I should forget, I swear—
  But that's impossible, and cannot be—
Sooner shall this blue ocean melt to air,
  Sooner shall earth resolve itself to sea,
Than I resign thine image, Oh! my fair!
  Or think of any thing excepting thee;
A mind diseased no remedy can physic—'
(Here the ship gave a lurch, and he grew sea-sick.)

20

'Sooner shall heaven kiss earth'—(here he fell sicker)
  'Oh, Julia! what is every other woe?—
(For God's sake let me have a glass of liquor,
  Pedro, Battista, help me down below).
Julia, my love!—(you rascal, Pedro, quicker)—
  Oh Julia!—(this curst vessel pitches so)—
Beloved Julia, hear me still beseeching!'
(Here he grew inarticulate with reaching.)[2]

21

He felt that chilling heaviness of heart,
  Or rather stomach, which, alas! attends,
Beyond the best apothecary's art,
  The loss of love, the treachery of friends,
Or death of those we doat on, when a part
  Of us dies with them as each fond hope ends:
No doubt he would have been much more pathetic,
But the sea acted as a strong emetic.

. . . .

[2] **reaching:** retching, heaving.

52

Then rose from sea to sky the wild farewell,[3]
  Then shriek'd the timid, and stood still the brave,
Then some leap'd overboard with dreadful yell,
  As eager to anticipate their grave;
And the sea yawn'd around her like a hell,
  And down she suck'd with her the whirling wave,
Like one who grapples with his enemy,
And strives to strangle him before he die.

53

And first one universal shriek there rush'd,
  Louder than the loud ocean, like a crash
Of echoing thunder; and then all was hush'd,
  Save the wild wind and the remorseless dash
Of billows; but at intervals there gush'd,
  Accompanied with a convulsive splash,
A solitary shriek, the bubbling cry
Of some strong swimmer in his agony.

54

The boats, as stated, had got off before,
  And in them crowded several of the crew;
And yet their present hope was hardly more
  Than what it had been, for so strong it blew
There was slight chance of reaching any shore;
  And then they were too many, though so few—
Nine in the cutter, thirty in the boat,
Were counted in them when they got afloat.

55

All the rest perish'd; near two hundred souls
  Had left their bodies; and, what's worse, alas!
When over Catholics the ocean rolls,
  They must wait several weeks before a mass
Takes off one peck of purgatorial coals,[4]
  Because, till people know what's come to pass,
They won't lay out their money on the dead—
It costs three francs for every mass that's said.

[3] **Then rose . . . farewell:** the vessel sank, overcome by storm and filled with taking in water.

[4] **purgatorial coals:** reference to Purgatory, the region in the afterlife between Heaven and Hell where souls go until purged and purified of sin. Survivors can help the departed in their atonement through prayer and offering masses in their memory.

56

Juan got into the long-boat, and there
Contrived to help Pedrillo[5] to a place;
It seem'd as if they had exchanged their care,
For Juan wore the magisterial face
Which courage gives, while poor Pedrillo's pair
Of eyes were crying for their owner's case:
Battista, though, (a name call'd shortly Tita)
Was lost by getting at some aqua-vita.

57

Pedro, his valet, too, he tried to save,
But the same cause, conducive to his loss,
Left him so drunk, he jump'd into the wave
As o'er the cutter's edge he tried to cross,
And so he found a wine-and-watery grave;
They could not rescue him although so close,
Because the sea ran higher every minute,
And for the boat—the crew kept crowding in it.

58

A small old spaniel,—which had been Don Jóse's,
His father's, whom he loved, as ye may think,
For on such things the memory reposes
With tenderness,—stood howling on the brink,
Knowing, (dogs have such intellectual noses!)
No doubt, the vessel was about to sink;
And Juan caught him up, and ere he stepp'd
Off, threw him in, then after him he leap'd.

59

He also stuff'd his money where he could
About his person, and Pedrillo's too,
Who let him do, in fact, whate'er he would,
Not knowing what himself to say, or do,
As every rising wave his dread renew'd;
And Juan, trusting they might still get through,
And deeming there were remedies for any ill,
Thus re-embark'd his tutor and his spaniel.

60

'Twas a rough night, and blew so stiffly yet,
That the sail was becalm'd between the seas,
Though on the wave's high top too much to set,
They dared not take it in for all the breeze;
Each sea curl'd o'er the stern, and kept them wet,
And made them bale without a moment's ease,
So that themselves as well as hopes were damp'd,
And the poor little cutter quickly swamp'd.

61

Nine souls more went in her: the long-boat still
Kept above water, with an oar for mast,
Two blankets stitch'd together, answering ill
Instead of sail, were to the oar made fast:
Though every wave roll'd menacing to fill,
And present peril all before surpass'd,
They grieved for those who perish'd with the cutter,
And also for the biscuit casks and butter.

. . . .

67

But man is a carnivorous production,
And must have meals, at least one meal a day;
He cannot live, like woodcocks, upon suction,
But, like the shark and tiger, must have prey,
Although his anatomical construction
Bears vegetables in a grumbling way,
Your labouring people think beyond all question,
Beef, veal, and mutton, better for digestion.

68

And thus it was with this our hapless crew,
For on the third day there came on a calm,
And though at first their strength it might renew,
And lying on their weariness like balm,
Lull'd them like turtles sleeping on the blue
Of ocean, when they woke they felt a qualm,
And fell all ravenously on their provision,
Instead of hoarding it with due precision.

69

The consequence was easily foreseen—
They ate up all they had, and drank their wine,
In spite of all remonstrances, and then
On what, in fact, next day were they to dine?
They hoped the wind would rise, these foolish men!
And carry them to shore; these hopes were fine,
But as they had but one oar, and that brittle,
It would have been more wise to save their victual.

70

The fourth day came, but not a breath of air,
And Ocean slumber'd like an unwean'd child:
The fifth day, and their boat lay floating there,
The sea and sky were blue, and clear, and mild—

[5] **Pedrillo:** Juan's tutor.

With their one oar (I wish they had had a pair)
    What could they do? and hunger's rage grew wild:
So Juan's spaniel, spite of his entreating,
Was kill'd, and portion'd out for present eating.

71

On the sixth day they fed upon his hide,
    And Juan, who had still refused, because
The creature was his father's dog that died,
    Now feeling all the vulture in his jaws,
With some remorse received (though first denied)
    As a great favour one of the fore-paws,
Which he divided with Pedrillo, who
Devour'd it, longing for the other too.

72

The seventh day, and no wind—the burning sun
    Blister'd and scorch'd, and, stagnant on the sea,
They lay like carcases; and hope was none,
    Save in the breeze that came not; savagely
They glared upon each other—all was done,
    Water, and wine, and food,—and you might see
The longings of the cannibal arise
(Although they spoke not) in their wolfish eyes.

73

At length one whisper'd his campanion, who
    Whisper'd another, and thus it went round,
And then into a hoarser murmur grew,
    An ominous, and wild, and desperate sound,
And when his comrade's thought each sufferer knew,
    'Twas but his own, suppress'd till now, he found:
And out they spoke of lots for flesh and blood,
And who should die to be his fellow's food.

74

But ere they came to this, they that day shared
    Some leathern caps, and what remain'd of shoes;
And then they look'd around them, and despair'd,
    And none to be the sacrifice would choose;
At length the lots were torn up, and prepared,
    But of materials that much shock the Muse—
Having no paper, for the want of better,
They took by force from Juan Julia's letter.

75

The lots were made, and mark'd, and mix'd, and handed,
    In silent horror, and their distribution
Lull'd even the savage hunger which demanded,
    Like the Promethean vulture, this pollution;
None in particular had sought or plann'd it,
    'Twas nature gnaw'd them to this resolution,
By which none were permitted to be neuter—
And the lot fell on Juan's luckless tutor.

76

He but requested to be bled to death:
    The surgeon had his instruments, and bled
Pedrillo, and so gently ebb'd his breath,
    You hardly could perceive when he was dead.
He died as born, a Catholic in faith,
    Like most in the belief in which they're bred,
And first a little crucifix he kiss'd,
And then held out his jugular and wrist.

77

The surgeon, as there was no other fee,
    Had his first choice of morsels for his pains;
But being thirstiest at the moment, he
    Preferr'd a draught from the fast-flowing veins:
Part was divided, part thrown in the sea,
    And such things as the entrails and the brains
Regaled two sharks, who follow'd o'er the billow—
The sailors ate the rest of poor Pedrillo.

78

The sailors ate him, all save three or four,
    Who were not quite so fond of animal food;
To these were added Juan, who, before
    Refusing his own spaniel, hardly could
Feel now his appetite increased much more;
    'Twas not to be expected that he should,
Even in extremity of their disaster,
Dine with them on his pastor and his master.

79

'Twas better that he did not; for, in fact,
    The consequence was awful in the extreme;
For they, who were most ravenous in the act,
    Went raging mad—Lord! how they did blaspheme!
And foam and roll, with strange convulsions rack'd,
    Drinking salt-water like a mountain-stream,
Tearing and grinning, howling, screeching, swearing,
And, with hyaena laughter, died despairing.

80

Their numbers were much thinn'd by this infliction,
And all the rest were thin enough, heaven knows;
And some of them had lost their recollection,
Happier than they who still perceived their woes;
But others ponder'd on a new dissection,
As if not warn'd sufficiently by those
Who had already perish'd, suffering madly,
For having used their appetites so sadly.

81

And next they thought upon the master's mate,
As fattest; but he saved himself, because,
Besides being much averse from such a fate,
There were some other reasons; the first was,
He had been rather indisposed of late,
And that which chiefly proved his saving clause,
Was a small present made to him at Cadiz,
By general subscription of the ladies.

82

Of poor Pedrillo something still remain'd,
But was used sparingly,—some were afraid,
And others still their appetites constrain'd,
Or but at times a little supper made;
All except Juan, who throughout abstain'd,
Chewing a piece of bamboo, and some lead:
At length they caught two boobies, and a noddy,[6]
And then they left off eating the dead body.

83

And if Pedrillo's fate should shocking be,
Remember Ugolino condescends
To eat the head of his arch-enemy[7]
The moment after he politely ends
His tale; if foes be food in hell, at sea
'Tis surely fair to dine upon our friends,
When shipwreck's short allowance grows too scanty,
Without being much more horrible than Dante.

[6] **boobies . . . noddy:** sea birds.

[7] **Remember . . . arch-enemy:** reference to Dante's *Inferno*, XXXIII.76–68: Count Ugolino's "eyes narrowed to slits when he was done, / And he seized the skull again between his teeth / grinding it as a mastiff grinds a bone."

84

And the same night there fell a shower of rain,
For which their mouths gaped, like the cracks of earth
When dried to summer dust; till taught by pain,
Men really know not what good water's worth;
If you had been in Turkey or in Spain,
Or with a famish'd boat's-crew had your berth,
Or in the desert heard the camel's bell,
You'd wish yourself where Truth is—in a well.

. . . .

97

As morning broke the light wind died away,
When he who had the watch sung out and swore,
If 'twas not land that rose with the sun's ray
He wish'd that land he never might see more;
And the rest rubb'd their eyes, and saw a bay,
Or thought they saw, and shaped their course for shore,
For shore it was, and gradually grew
Distinct, and high, and palpable to view.

98

And then of these some part burst into tears,
And others, looking with a stupid stare,
Could not yet separate their hopes from fears,
And seem'd as if they had no further care;
While a few pray'd—(the first time for some years)—
And at the bottom of the boat three were
Asleep; they shook them by the hand and head,
And tried to awaken them, but found them dead.

99

The day before, fast sleeping on the water,
They found a turtle of the hawk's-bill kind,
And by good fortune gliding softly, caught her,
Which yielded a day's life, and to their mind
Proved even still a more nutritious matter,
Because it left encouragement behind:
They thought that in such perils, more than chance
Had sent them this for their deliverance.

100

The land appear'd a high and rocky coast,
And higher grew the mountains as they drew,
Set by a current, toward it: they were lost
In various conjectures, for none knew

To what part of the earth they had been tost,
  So changeable had been the winds that blew;
Some thought it was Mount Aetna, some the highlands
Of Candia, Cyprus, Rhodes, or other islands.

101

Meantime the current, with a rising gale,
  Still set them onwards to the welcome shore,
Like Charon's bark of spectres, dull and pale:
  Their living freight was now reduced to four,
And three dead, whom their strength could not avail
  To heave into the deep with those before,
Though the two sharks still follow'd them, and dash'd
The spray into their faces as they splash'd.

102

Famine, despair, cold, thirst, and heat, had done
  Their work on them by turns, and thinn'd them to
Such things a mother had not known her son
  Amidst the skeletons of that gaunt crew;
By night chill'd, by day scorch'd, thus one by one
  They perish'd, until wither'd to these few,
But chiefly by a species of self-slaughter,
In washing down Pedrillo with salt water.

103

As they drew nigh the land, which now was seen
  Unequal in its aspect here and there,
They felt the freshness of its growing green,
  That waved in forest-tops, and smooth'd the air,
And fell upon their glazed eyes like a screen
  From glistening waves, and skies so hot and bare—
Lovely seem'd any object that should sweep
Away the vast, salt, dread, eternal deep.

104

The shore look'd wild, without a trace of man,
  And girt by formidable waves; but they
Were made for land, and thus their course they ran,
  Though right ahead the roaring breakers lay:
A reef between them also now began
  To show its boiling surf and bounding spray,
But finding no place for their landing better,
They ran the boat for shore, and overset her.

105

But in his native stream, the Guadalquivir,
  Juan to lave his youthful limbs was wont;
And having learnt to swim in that sweet river,
  Had often turn'd the art to some account:
A better swimmer you could scarce see ever,
  He could, perhaps, have pass'd the Hellespont,
As once (a feat on which ourselves we prided)
Leander, Mr Ekenhead, and I did.[8]

106

So here, though faint, emaciated, and stark,
  He buoy'd his boyish limbs, and strove to ply
With the quick wave, and gain, ere it was dark,
  The beach which lay before him, high and dry:
The greatest danger here was from a shark,
  That carried off his neighbour by the thigh;
As for the other two they could not swim,
So nobody arrived on shore but him.

107

Nor yet had he arrived but for the oar,
  Which, providentially for him, was wash'd
Just as his feeble arms could strike no more,
  And the hard wave o'erwhelm'd him as 'twas dash'd
Within his grasp; he clung to it, and sore
  The waters beat while he thereto was lash'd;
At last, with swimming, wading, scrambling, he
Roll'd on the beach, half senseless, from the sea:

108

There, breathless, with his digging nails he clung
  Fast to the sand, lest the returning wave,
From whose reluctant roar his life he wrung,
  Should suck him back to her insatiate grave:
And there he lay, full length, where he was flung,
  Before the entrance of a cliff-worn cave,
With just enough of life to feel its pain,
And deem that it was saved, perhaps, in vain.

109

With slow and staggering effort he arose,
  But sunk again upon his bleeding knee
And quivering hand; and then he look'd for those
  Who long had been his mates upon the sea,
But none of them appear'd to share his woes,
  Save one, a corpse from out the famish'd three,
Who died two days before, and now had found
An unknown barren beach for burial ground.

[8] Byron himself swam the Hellespont in 1810.

110

And as he gazed, his dizzy brain spun fast,
And down he sunk; and as he sunk, the sand
Swam round and round, and all his senses pass'd:
He fell upon his side, and his stretch'd hand
Droop'd dripping on the oar, (their jury-mast)
And, like a wither'd lily, on the land
His slender frame and pallid aspect lay,
As fair a thing as e'er was form'd of clay.

111

How long in his damp trance young Juan lay
He knew not, for the earth was gone for him,
And Time had nothing more of night nor day
For his congealing blood, and senses dim;
And how this heavy faintness pass'd away
He knew not, till each painful pulse and limb,
And tingling vein, seem'd throbbing back to life,
For Death, though vanquish'd, still retired with strife.

112

His eyes he open'd, shut, again unclosed,
For all was doubt and dizziness; methought
He still was in the boat, and had but dozed,
And felt again with his despair o'erwrought,
And wish'd it death in which he had reposed,
And then once more his feelings back were brought,
And slowly by his swimming eyes was seen
A lovely female face of seventeen.

113

'Twas bending close o'er his, and the small mouth
Seem'd almost prying into his for breath;
And chafing him, the soft warm hand of youth
Recall'd his answering spirits back from death;
And, bathing his chill temples, tried to soothe
Each pulse to animation, till beneath
Its gentle touch and trembling care, a sigh
To these kind efforts made a low reply.

114

Then was the cordial pour'd, and mantle flung
Around his scarce-clad limbs; and the fair arm
Raised higher the faint head which o'er it hung;
And her transparent cheek, all pure and warm,
Pillow'd his death-like forehead; then she wrung
His dewy curls, long drench'd by every storm;
And watch'd with eagerness each throb that drew
A sigh from his heaved bosom—and hers, too.

115

And lifting him with care into the cave,
The gentle girl, and her attendant,—one
Young, yet her elder, and of brow less grave,
And more robust of figure,—then begun
To kindle fire, and as the new flames gave
Light to the rocks that roof'd them, which the sun
Had never seen, the maid, or whatsoe'er
She was, appear'd distinct, and tall, and fair.

116

Her brow was overhung with coins of gold,
That sparkled o'er the auburn of her hair,
Her clustering hair, whose longer locks were roll'd
In braids behind, and though her stature were
Even of the highest for a female mould,
They nearly reach'd her heel; and in her air
There was a something which bespoke command,
As one who was a lady in the land.

117

Her hair, I said, was auburn; but her eyes
Were black as death, their lashes the same hue,
Of downcast length, in whose silk shadow lies
Deepest attraction, for when to the view
Forth from its raven fringe the full glance flies,
Ne'er with such force the swiftest arrow flew;
'Tis as the snake late coil'd, who pours his length,
And hurls at once his venom and his strength.

118

Her brow was white and low, her cheek's pure dye
Like twilight rosy still with the set sun;
Short upper lip—sweet lips! that make us sigh
Ever to have seen such; for she was one
Fit for the model of a statuary,
(A race of mere impostors, when all's done—
I've seen much finer women, ripe and real,
Than all the nonsense of their stone ideal).

119

I'll tell you why I say so, for 'tis just
One should not rail without a decent cause:
There was an Irish lady, to whose bust
I ne'er saw justice done, and yet she was

A frequent model; and if e'er she must
  Yield to stern Time and Nature's wrinkling laws,
They will destroy a face which mortal thought
Ne'er compass'd, nor less mortal chisel wrought.

120

And such was she, the lady of the cave:
  Her dress was very different from the Spanish,
Simpler, and yet of colours not so grave;
  For, as you know, the Spanish women banish
Bright hues when out of doors, and yet, while wave
  Around them (what I hope will never vanish)
The basquīna and the mantilla,[9] they
Seem at the same time mystical and gay.

121

But with our damsel this was not the case:
  Her dress was many-colour'd, finely spun;
Her locks curl'd negligently round her face,
  But through them gold and gems profusely shone;
Her girdle sparkled, and the richest lace
  Flow'd in her veil, and many a precious stone
Flash'd on her little hand; but, what was shocking,
Her small snow feet had slippers, but no stocking.

122

The other female's dress was not unlike,
  But of inferior materials; she
Had not so many ornaments to strike,
  Her hair had silver only, bound to be
Her dowry; and her veil, in form alike,
  Was coarser; and her air, though firm, less free;
Her hair was thicker, but less long; her eyes
As black, but quicker, and of smaller size.

123

And these two tended him, and cheer'd him both
  With food and raiment, and those soft attentions,
Which are (as I must own) of female growth,
  And have ten thousand delicate inventions:
They made a most superior mess of broth,
  A thing which poesy but seldom mentions,
But the best dish that e'er was cook'd since Homer's
Achilles order'd dinner for new comers.[10]

124

I'll tell you who they were, this female pair,
  Lest they should seem princesses in disguise;
Besides, I hate all mystery, and that air
  Of clap-trap, which your recent poets prize;
And so, in short, the girls they really were
  They shall appear before your curious eyes,
Mistress and maid; the first was only daughter
Of an old man, who lived upon the water.

125

A fisherman he had been in his youth,
  And still a sort of fisherman was he;
But other speculations were, in sooth,
  Added to his connection with the sea,
Perhaps not so respectable, in truth:
  A little smuggling, and some piracy,
Left him, at last, the sole of many masters
Of an ill-gotten million of piastres.

126

A fisher, therefore, was he—though of men,
  Like Peter the Apostle,—and he fish'd
For wandering merchant vessels, now and then,
  And sometimes caught as many as he wish'd;
The cargoes he confiscated, and gain
  He sought in the slave-market too, and dish'd
Full many a morsel for that Turkish trade,
By which, no doubt, a good deal may be made.

127

He was a Greek, and on his isle had built
  (One of the wild and smaller Cyclades)
A very handsome house from out his guilt,
  And there he lived exceedingly at ease;
Heaven knows what cash he got, or blood he spilt,
  A sad old fellow was he, if you please,
But this I know, it was a spacious building,
Full of barbaric carving, paint, and gilding.

128

He had an only daughter, call'd Haidee,
  The greatest heiress of the Eastern Isles;
Besides, so very beautiful was she,
  Her dowry was as nothing to her smiles:
Still in her teens, and like a lovely tree
  She grew to womanhood, and between whiles
Rejected several suitors, just to learn
How to accept a better in his turn.

---

[9] **basquīna:** outer petticoat. **mantilla:** a lace scarf worn over the head and shoulders.

[10] Cf. *Iliad,* IX.205 ff.

129

And walking out upon the beach, below
The cliff, towards sunset, on that day she found,
Insensible,—not dead, but nearly so,—
Don Juan, almost famish'd, and half drown'd;
But being naked, she was shock'd, you know,
Yet deem'd herself in common pity bound,
As far as in her lay, 'to take him in,
A stranger' dying, with so white a skin.

130

But taking him into her father's house
Was not exactly the best way to save,
But like conveying to the cat the mouse,
Or people in a trance into their grave;
Because the good old man had so much 'νους',[11]
Unlike the honest Arab thieves so brave,
He would have hospitably cured the stranger,
And sold him instantly when out of danger.

131

And therefore, with her maid, she thought it best
(A virgin always on her maid relies)
To place him in the cave for present rest:
And when, at last, he open'd his black eyes,
Their charity increased about their guest;
And their compassion grew to such a size,
It open'd half the turnpike-gates to heaven—
(St Paul says 'tis the toll which must be given).[12]

. . . .

135

Young Juan slept all dreamless:—but the maid,
Who smooth'd his pillow, as she left the den
Look'd back upon him, and a moment staid,
And turn'd, believing that he call'd again.
He slumber'd; yet she thought, at least she said,
(The heart will slip even as the tongue and pen)
He had pronounced her name—but she forgot
That at this moment Juan knew it not.

136

And pensive to her father's house she went,
Enjoining silence strict to Zoe, who
Better than her knew what, in fact, she meant,
She being wiser by a year or two:
A year or two's an age when rightly spent,
And Zoe spent hers, as most women do,
In gaining all that useful sort of knowledge
Which is acquired in nature's good old college.

137

The morn broke, and found Juan slumbering still
Fast in his cave, and nothing clash'd upon
His rest; the rushing of the neighbouring rill,
And the young beams of the excluded sun,
Troubled him not, and he might sleep his fill;
And need he had of slumber yet, for none
Had suffer'd more—his hardships were comparative
To those related in my grand-dad's Narrative.[13]

138

Not so Haidee; she sadly toss'd and tumbled,
And started from her sleep, and, turning o'er,
Dream'd of a thousand wrecks, o'er which she stumbled,
And handsome corpses strew'd upon the shore;
And woke her maid so early that she grumbled,
And call'd her father's old slaves up, who swore
In several oaths—Armenian, Turk, and Greek,—
They knew not what to think of such a freak.

139

But up she got, and up she made them get,
With some pretence about the sun, that makes
Sweet skies just when he rises, or is set;
And 'tis, no doubt, a sight to see when breaks
Bright Phoebus, while the mountains still are wet
With mist, and every bird with him awakes,
And night is flung off like a mourning suit
Worn for a husband, or some other brute.

140

I say, the sun is a most glorious sight,
I've seen him rise full oft, indeed of late

[11] **'νους':** spirit.

[12] **St. Paul . . . given:** cf. St. Paul's letter to the Colossians 3:14: "And above all these things put on charity, which is the bond of perfectness."

[13] **My grand-dad's Narrative:** reference to *A Narrative of the Honourable John Byron* (1786).

I have sate up on purpose all the night,
  Which hastens, as physicians say, one's fate;
And so all ye, who would be in the right
  In health and purse, begin your day to date
From day-break, and when coffin'd at fourscore,
Engrave upon the plate, you rose at four.

141

And Haidee met the morning face to face;
  Her own was freshest, though a feverish flush
Had dyed it with the headlong blood, whose race
  From heart to cheek is curb'd into a blush,
Like to a torrent which a mountain's base,
  That overpowers some alpine river's rush,
Checks to a lake, whose waves in circles spread;
Or the Red Sea—but the sea is not red.

142

And down the cliff the island virgin came,
  And near the cave her quick light footsteps drew,
While the sun smiled on her with his first flame,
  And young Aurora kiss'd her lips with dew,
Taking her for sister; just the same
  Mistake you would have made on seeing the two,
Although the mortal, quite as fresh and fair,
Had all the advantage too of not being air.

143

And when into the cavern Haidee stepp'd
  All timidly, yet rapidly, she saw
That like an infant Juan sweetly slept;
  And then she stopp'd, and stood as if in awe,
(For sleep is awful) and on tiptoe crept
  And wrapt him closer, lest the air, too raw,
Should reach his blood, then o'er him still as death
Bent, with hush'd lips, that drank his scarce-drawn
  breath.

144

And thus like to an angel o'er the dying
  Who die in righteousness, she lean'd; and there
All tranquilly the shipwreck'd boy was lying,
  As o'er him lay the calm and stirless air:
But Zoe the meantime some eggs was frying,
  Since, after all, no doubt the youthful pair
Must breakfast, and betimes—lest they should ask it,
She drew out her provision from the basket.

145

She knew that the best feelings must have victual,
  And that a shipwreck'd youth would hungry be;
Besides, being less in love, she yawn'd a little,
  And felt her veins chill'd by the neighbouring sea;
And so, she cook'd their breakfast to a tittle;
  I can't say that she gave them any tea,
But there were eggs, fruit, coffee, bread, fish, honey,
With Scio wine,—and all for love, not money.

146

And Zoe, when the eggs were ready, and
  The coffee made, would fain have waken'd Juan;
But Haidee stopp'd her with her quick small hand,
  And without word, a sign her finger drew on
Her lip, which Zoe needs must understand;
  And, the first breakfast spoilt, prepared a new one,
Because her mistress would not let her break
That sleep which seem'd as it would ne'er awake.

147

For still he lay, and on his thin worn cheek
  A purple hectic play'd like dying day
On the snow-tops of distant hills; the streak
  Of sufferance yet upon his forehead lay,
Where the blue veins look'd shadowy, shrunk, and
  weak;
  And his black curls were dewy with the spray,
Which weigh'd upon them yet, all damp and salt,
Mix'd with the stony vapours of the vault.

148

And she bent o'er him, and he lay beneath,
  Hush'd as the babe upon its mother's breast,
Droop'd as the willow when no winds can breathe,
  Lull'd like the depth of ocean when at rest,
Fair as the crowning rose of the whole wreath,
  Soft as the callow cygnet[14] in its nest;
In short, he was a very pretty fellow,
Although his woes had turn'd him rather yellow.

149

He woke and gazed, and would have slept again,
  But the fair face which met his eyes forbade

[14] cygnet: young swan.

Those eyes to close, though weariness and pain
Had further sleep a further pleasure made;
For woman's face was never form'd in vain
For Juan, so that even when he pray'd
He turn'd from grisly saints, and martyrs hairy,
To the sweet portraits of the Virgin Mary.

150

And thus upon his elbow he arose,
And look'd upon the lady, in whose cheek
The pale contended with the purple rose,
As with an effort she began to speak;
Her eyes were eloquent, her words would pose,
Although she told him, in good modern Greek,
With an Ionian accent, low and sweet,
That he was faint, and must not talk, but eat.

151

Now Juan could not understand a word,
Being no Grecian; but he had an ear,
And her voice was the warble of a bird,
So soft, so sweet, so delicately clear,
That finer, simpler music ne'er was heard;
The sort of sound we echo with a tear,
Without knowing why—an overpowering tone,
Whence Melody descends as from a throne.

152

And Juan gazed as one who is awoke
By a distant organ, doubting if he be
Not yet a dreamer, till the spell is broke
By the watchman, or some such reality,
Or by one's early valet's cursed knock;
At least it is a heavy sound to me,
Who like a morning slumber—for the night
Shows stars and women in a better light.

153

And Juan, too, was help'd out from his dream
Or sleep, or whatsoe'er it was, by feeling
A most prodigious appetite: the steam
Of Zoe's cookery no doubt was stealing
Upon his senses, and the kindling beam
Of the new fire, which Zoe kept up, kneeling,
To stir her viands, made him quite awake
And long for food, but chiefly a beef-steak.
. . . .

158

He ate, and he was well supplied; and she,
Who watch'd him like a mother, would have fed
Him past all bounds, because she smiled to see
Such appetite in one she had deem'd dead:
But Zoe, being older than Haidee,
Knew (by tradition, for she ne'er had read)
That famish'd people must be slowly nurst,
And fed by spoonfuls, else they always burst.

159

And so she took the liberty to state,
Rather by deeds than words, because the case
Was urgent, that the gentleman, whose fate
Had made her mistress quit her bed to trace
The sea-shore at this hour, must leave his plate,
Unless he wish'd to die upon the place—
She snatch'd it, and refused another morsel,
Saying, he had gorged enough to make a horse ill.

160

Next they—he being naked, save a tatter'd
Pair of scarce decent trousers—went to work,
And in the fire his recent rags they scatter'd,
And dress'd him, for the present, like a Turk,
Or Greek—that is, although it not much matter'd,
Omitting turban, slippers, pistols, dirk,[15]—
They furnish'd him, entire except some stitches,
With a clean shirt, and very spacious breeches.

161

And then fair Haidee tried her tongue at speaking,
But not a word could Juan comprehend,
Although he listen'd so that the young Greek in
Her earnestness would ne'er have made an end;
And, as he interrupted not, went eking
Her speech out to her protégé and friend,
Till pausing at the last her breath to take,
She saw he did not understand Romaic.[16]

162

And then she had recourse to nods, and signs,
And smiles, and sparkles of the speaking eye,

---

[15] **dirk:** dagger.

[16] **Romaic:** vernacular Greek.

And read (the only book she could) the lines
    Of his fair face, and found, by sympathy,
The answer eloquent, where the soul shines
    And darts in one quick glance a long reply;
And thus in every look she saw exprest
A world of words, and things at which she guess'd.

163

And now, by dint of fingers and of eyes,
    And words repeated after her, he took
A lesson in her tongue; but by surmise,
    No doubt, less of her language than her look:
As he who studies fervently the skies
    Turns oftener to the stars than to his book,
Thus Juan learn'd his alpha beta better
From Haidee's glance than any graven letter.

164

'Tis pleasing to be school'd in a strange tongue
    By female lips and eyes—that is, I mean,
When both the teacher and the taught are young,
    As was the case, at least, where I have been;
They smile so when one's right, and when one's
        wrong
    They smile still more, and then there intervene
Pressure of hands, perhaps even a chaste kiss;—
I learn'd the little that I know by this:

165

That is, some words of Spanish, Turk, and Greek,
    Italian not at all, having no teachers;
Much English I cannot pretend to speak,
    Learning that language chiefly from its preachers,
Barrow, South, Tillotson, whom every week
    I study, also Blair,[17] the highest reachers
Of eloquence in piety and prose—
I hate your poets, so read none of those.

166

As for the ladies, I have nought to say,
    A wanderer from the British world of fashion,
Where I, like other 'dogs, have had my day,'
    Like other men too, may have had my passion—
But that, like other things, has pass'd away,
    And all her fools whom I *could* lay the lash on:
Foes, friends, men, women, now are nought to me
But dreams of what has been, no more to be.[18]

167

Return we to Don Juan. He begun
    To hear new words, and to repeat them; but
Some feelings, universal as the sun,
    Were such as could not in his breast be shut
More than within the bosom of a nun:
    He was in love,—as you would be, no doubt,
With a young benefactress—so was she,
Just in the way we very often see.

168

And every day by day-break—rather early
    For Juan, who was somewhat fond of rest—
She came into the cave, but it was merely
    To see her bird reposing in his nest;
And she would softly stir his locks so curly,
    Without disturbing her yet slumbering guest,
Breathing all gently o'er his cheek and mouth,
As o'er a bed of roses the sweet south.

169

And every morn his colour freshlier came,
    And every day help'd on his convalescence;
'Twas well, because health in the human frame
    Is pleasant, besides being true love's essence,
For health and idleness to passion's flame
    Are oil and gunpowder; and some good lessons
Are also learnt from Ceres and from Bacchus,[19]
Without whom Venus will not long attack us.

[17] **Barrow, South, Tillotson . . . Blair:** Isaac Barrow (1630–1677), master of Trinity College and author of *Exposition of the Creed, Decalogue and Sacraments* (1669) and *The Pope's Supremacy* (1680); Robert South (1634–1716), preacher at the court of Charles II and author of *Animadversions* (1690), known for his vicious wit; John Tillotson (1630–1694), Archbishop of Canterbury, known for his brief and lucid sermons; Hugh Blair (1718–1800), professor of rhetoric at Edinburgh and author of the immensely influential *Lectures on Rhetoric and Belles Lettres* (1784).

[18] **what has been, no more to be:** Wordsworth, "The memory of what has been, / And never more will be," from "Three Years She Grew in Sun and Shower,"* ll. 41–42.

[19] **Ceres:** fertility goddess associated with grain or food. **Bacchus:** fertility god, associated with wine and orgiastic rites. **Venus:** goddess of love.

170

While Venus fills the heart (without heart really
Love, though good always, is not quite so good)
Ceres presents a plate of vermicelli,—
For love must be sustain'd like flesh and blood,—
While Bacchus pours out wine, or hands a jelly:
Eggs, oysters too, are amatory food;
But who is their purveyor from above
Heaven knows,—it may be Neptune, Pan, or Jove.[20]

171

When Juan woke he found some good things ready,
A bath, a breakfast, and the finest eyes
That ever made a youthful heart less steady,
Besides her maid's, as pretty for their size;
But I have spoken of all this already—
And repetition's tiresome and unwise,—
Well—Juan, after bathing in the sea,
Came always back to coffee and Haidee.

172

Both were so young, and one so innocent,
That bathing pass'd for nothing; Juan seem'd
To her, as 'twere, the kind of being sent,
Of whom these two years she had nightly dream'd,
A something to be loved, a creature meant
To be her happiness, and whom she deem'd
To render happy; all who joy would win
Must share it,—Happiness was born a twin.

173

It was such pleasure to behold him, such
Enlargement of existence to partake
Nature with him, to thrill beneath his touch,
To watch him slumbering, and to see him wake:
To live with him for ever were too much;
But then the thought of parting made her quake:
He was her own, her ocean-treasure, cast
Like a rich wreck—her first love, and her last.

174

And thus a moon roll'd on, and fair Haidee
Paid daily visits to her boy, and took
Such plentiful precautions, that still he
Remain'd unknown within his craggy nook;
At last her father's prows put out to sea,
For certain merchantmen upon the look,
Not as of yore to carry off an Io,
But three Ragusan vessels, bound for Scio.[21]

175

Then came her freedom, for she had no mother,
So that, her father being at sea, she was
Free as a married woman, or such other
Female, as where she likes may freely pass,
Without even the incumbrance of a brother,
The freest she that ever gazed on glass:
I speak of christian lands in this comparison,
Where wives, at least, are seldom kept in garrison.

176

Now she prolong'd her visits and her talk
(For they must talk), and he had learnt to say
So much as to propose to take a walk,—
For little had he wander'd since the day
On which, like a young flower snapp'd from the stalk,
Drooping and dewy on the beach he lay,—
And thus they walk'd out in the afternoon,
And saw the sun set opposite the moon.

177

It was a wild and breaker-beaten coast,
With cliffs above, and a broad sandy shore,
Guarded by shoals and rocks as by an host,
With here and there a creek, whose aspect wore
A better welcome to the tempest-tost;
And rarely ceased the haughty billow's roar,
Save on the dead long summer days, which make
The outstretch'd ocean glitter like a lake.

178

And the small ripple spilt upon the beach
Scarcely o'erpass'd the cream of your champaigne,
When o'er the brim the sparkling bumpers reach,
That spring-dew of the spirit! the heart's rain!

[20] **Neptune:** god of the sea. **Pan:** god of flocks and shepherds, who dwells in the environs of mountains and caves. **Jove:** god of heaven.

[21] **Io:** the priestess of Hera, who was kidnapped either by Phoenicians or Egyptians; Ragusa is a city of southeastern Sicily; it is also Italian for Dubrovnik, a city on the Adriatic shore of the Ilyrrian Peninsula, and capital of the former Yugoslavia; Scio is an Aegean Island.

Few things surpass old wine; and they may preach
Who please,—the more because they preach in vain,—
Let us have wine and woman, mirth and laughter,
Sermons and soda water the day after.

179

Man, being reasonable, must get drunk;
The best of life is but intoxication:
Glory, the grape, love, gold, in these are sunk
The hopes of all men, and of every nation;
Without their sap, how branchless were the trunk
Of life's strange tree, so fruitful on occasion:
But to return,—Get very drunk; and when
You wake with head-ache, you shall see what then.

180

Ring for your valet—bid him quickly bring
Some hock[22] and soda-water, then you'll know
A pleasure worthy Xerxes the great king;
For not the blest sherbet, sublimed with snow,
Nor the first sparkle of the desert-spring,
Nor Burgundy in all its sunset glow,
After long travel, ennui, love, or slaughter,
Vie with that draught of hock and soda-water.

181

The coast—I think it was the coast that I
Was just describing—Yes, it *was* the coast—
Lay at this period quiet as the sky,
The sands untumbled, the blue waves untost,
And all was stillness, save the sea-bird's cry,
And dolphin's leap, and little billow crost
By some low rock or shelve, that made it fret
Against the boundary it scarcely wet.

182

And forth they wandered, her sire being gone,
As I have said, upon an expedition;
And mother, brother, guardian, she had none,
Save Zoe, who, although with due precision
She waited on her lady with the sun,
Thought daily service was her only mission,
Bringing warm water, wreathing her long tresses,
And asking now and then for cast-off dresses.

[22] **hock:** white Rhine wine.

183

It was the cooling hour, just when the rounded
Red sun sinks down behind the azure hill,
Which then seems as if the whole earth is bounded,
Circling all nature, hush'd, and dim, and still,
With the far mountain-crescent half surrounded
On one side, and the deep sea calm and chill
Upon the other, and the rosy sky,
With one star sparkling through it like an eye.

184

And thus they wander'd forth, and hand in hand,
Over the shining pebbles and the shells,
Glided along the smooth and harden'd sand,
And in the worn and wild receptacles
Work'd by the storms, yet work'd as it were plann'd,
In hollow halls, with sparry roofs and cells,
They turn'd to rest; and, each clasp'd by an arm,
Yielded to the deep twilight's purple charm.

185

They look'd up to the sky, whose floating glow
Spread like a rosy ocean, vast and bright;
They gazed upon the glittering sea below,
Whence the broad moon rose circling into sight;
They heard the wave's splash, and the wind so low,
And saw each other's dark eyes darting light
Into each other—and, beholding this,
Their lips drew near, and clung into a kiss;

186

A long, long kiss, a kiss of youth, and love,
And beauty, all concentrating like rays
Into one focus, kindled from above;
Such kisses as belong to early days,
Where heart, and soul, and sense, in concert move,
And the blood's lava, and the pulse a blaze,
Each kiss a heart-quake,—for a kiss's strength,
I think, it must be reckon'd by its length.

187

By length I mean duration; theirs endured
Heaven knows how long—no doubt they never reckon'd;
And if they had, they could not have secured
The sum of their sensations to a second:
They had not spoken; but they felt allured,
As if their souls and lips each other beckon'd,

Which, being join'd, like swarming bees they clung—
Their hearts the flowers from whence the honey
sprung.

188

They were alone, but not alone as they
Who shut in chambers think it loneliness;
The silent ocean, and the starlight bay,
The twilight glow, which momently grew less,
The voiceless sands, and dropping caves, that lay
Around them, made them to each other press,
As if there were no life beneath the sky
Save theirs, and that their life could never die.

189

They fear'd no eyes nor ears on that lone beach,
They felt no terrors from the night, they were
All in all to each other: though their speech
Was broken words, they *thought* a language
there,—
And all the burning tongues the passions teach
Found in one sigh the best interpreter
Of nature's oracle—first love,—that all
Which Eve has left her daughters since her fall.

190

Haidee spoke not of scruples, ask'd no vows,
Nor offer'd any; she had never heard
Of plight and promises to be a spouse,
Or perils by a loving maid incurr'd;
She was all which pure ignorance allows,
And flew to her young mate like a young bird;
And, never having dreamt of falsehood, she
Had not one word to say of constancy.

191

She loved, and was beloved—she adored,
And she was worshipp'd; after nature's fashion,
Their intense souls, into each other pour'd,
If souls could die, had perish'd in that passion,—
But by degrees their senses were restored,
Again to be o'ercome, again to dash on;
And, beating 'gainst *his* bosom, Haidee's heart
Felt as if never more to beat apart.

192

Alas! they were so young, so beautiful,
So lonely, loving, helpless, and the hour
Was that in which the heart is always full
And, having o'er itself no further power,
Prompts deeds eternity can not annul,
But pays off moments in an endless shower
Of hell-fire—all prepared for people giving
Pleasure or pain to one another living.

193

Alas! for Juan and Haidee! they were
So loving and so lovely—till then never,
Excepting our first parents, such a pair
Had run the risk of being damn'd for ever;
And Haidee, being devout as well as fair,
Had, doubtless, heard about the Stygian river,
And hell and purgatory—but forgot
Just in the very crisis she should not.

194

They look upon each other, and their eyes
Gleam in the moonlight; and her white arm clasps
Round Juan's head, and his around her lies
Half buried in the tresses which it grasps;
She sits upon his knee, and drinks his sighs,
He hers, until they end in broken gasps;
And thus they form a group that's quite antique,
Half naked, loving, natural, and Greek.

195

And when those deep and burning moments pass'd,
And Juan sunk to sleep within her arms,
She slept not, but all tenderly, though fast,
Sustain'd his head upon her bosom's charms;
And now and then her eye to heaven is cast,
And then on the pale cheek her breast now warms,
Pillow'd on her o'erflowing heart, which pants
With all it granted, and with all it grants.

196

An infant when it gazes on a light,
A child the moment when it drains the breast,
A devotee when soars the Host[23] in sight,
An Arab with a stranger for a guest,
A sailor when the prize has struck in fight,
A miser filling his most hoarded chest,

[23] **Host:** the moment during the Catholic Mass when the wafer representing the body of Christ is raised to heaven.

Feel rapture; but not such true joy are reaping
As they who watch o'er what they love while sleeping.

197

For there it lies so tranquil, so beloved,
All that it hath of life with us is living;
So gentle, stirless, helpless, and unmoved,
And all unconscious of the joy 'tis giving;
All it hath felt, inflicted, pass'd, and proved,
Hush'd into depths beyond the watcher's diving;
There lies the thing we love with all its errors
And all its charms, like death without its terrors.

198

The lady watch'd her lover—and that hour
Of Love's, and Night's, and Ocean's solitude,
O'erflow'd her soul with their united power;
Amidst the barren sand and rocks so rude
She and her wave-worn love had made their bower,
Where nought upon their passion could intrude,
And all the stars that crowded the blue space
Saw nothing happier than her glowing face.

199

Alas! the love of women! it is known
To be a lovely and a fearful thing;
For all of theirs upon that die is thrown,
And if 'tis lost, life hath no more to bring
To them but mockeries of the past alone,
And their revenge is as the tiger's spring,
Deadly, and quick, and crushing; yet, as real
Torture is theirs, what they inflict they feel.

200

They are right; for man, to man so oft unjust,
Is always so to women; one sole bond
Awaits them, treachery is all their trust;
Taught to conceal, their bursting hearts despond
Over their idol, till some wealthier lust
Buys them in marriage—and what rests beyond?
A thankless husband, next a faithless lover,
Then dressing, nursing, praying, and all's over.

201

Some take a lover, some take drams or prayers,
Some mind their household, others dissipation,
Some run away, and but exchange their cares,
Losing the advantage of a virtuous station;
Few changes e'er can better their affairs,
Theirs being an unnatural situation,
From the dull palace to the dirty hovel:
Some play the devil, and then write a novel.[24]

202

Haidee was Nature's bride, and knew not this;
Haidee was Passion's child, born where the sun
Showers triple light, and scorches even the kiss
Of his gazelle-eyed daughters; she was one
Made but to love, to feel that she was his
Who was her chosen: what was said or done
Elsewhere was nothing—She had nought to fear,
Hope, care, nor love beyond, her heart beat *here*.

203

And oh! that quickening of the heart, that beat!
How much it costs us! yet each rising throb
Is in its cause as its effect so sweet,
That Wisdom, ever on the watch to rob
Joy of its alchymy, and to repeat
Fine truths; even Conscience, too, has a tough job
To make us understand each good old maxim,
So good—I wonder Castlereagh[25] don't tax 'em.

204

And now 'twas done—on the lone shore were plighted
Their hearts; the stars, their nuptial torches, shed
Beauty upon the beautiful they lighted:
Ocean their witness, and the cave their bed,
By their own feelings hallow'd and united,
Their priest was Solitude, and they were wed:
And they were happy, for to their young eyes
Each was an angel, and earth paradise.

. . . .

208

But Juan! had he quite forgotten Julia?
And should he have forgotten her so soon?
I can't but say it seems to me most truly a
Perplexing question; but, no doubt, the moon
Does these things for us, and whenever newly a
Strong palpitation rises, 'tis her boon,
Else how the devil is it that fresh features
Have such a charm for us poor human creatures?

---

[24] **Some play . . . novel:** readers would have known that Byron's former lover, Lady Caroline Lamb, had written of him and their affair in *Glenarvon* (1816), at the end of which Glenarvon (Byron) is literally sent to Hell.

[25] **Castlereagh:** Robert Stewart, Viscount Castlereagh, a Tory politician Byron abhorred.

209

I hate inconstancy—I loathe, detest,
Abhor, condemn, abjure the mortal made
Of such quicksilver clay that in his breast
No permanent foundation can be laid;
Love, constant love, has been my constant guest,
And yet last night, being at a masquerade,
I saw the prettiest creature, fresh from Milan,
Which gave me some sensations like a villain.

210

But soon Philosophy came to my aid,
And whisper'd 'think of every sacred tie!'
'I will, my dear Philosophy!' I said,
'But then her teeth, and then, Oh heaven! her eye!
I'll just inquire if she be wife or maid,
Or neither—out of curiosity.'
'Stop!' cried Philosophy, with air so Grecian,
(Though she was masqued then as a fair Venetian).

211

'Stop!' so I stopp'd.—But to return: that which
Men call inconstancy is nothing more
Than admiration due where nature's rich
Profusion with young beauty covers o'er
Some favour'd object; and as in the niche
A lovely statue we almost adore,
This sort of adoration of the real
Is but a heightening of the 'beau ideal.'

212

'Tis the perception of the beautiful,
A fine extension of the faculties,
Platonic, universal, wonderful,
Drawn from the stars, and filter'd through the skies,
Without which life would be extremely dull;
In short, it is the use of our own eyes,
With one or two small senses added, just
To hint that flesh is form'd of fiery dust.

213

Yet 'tis a painful feeling, and unwilling,
For surely if we always could perceive
In the same object graces quite as killing
As when she rose upon us like an Eve,
'Twould save us many a heart-ache, many a shilling,
(For we must get them any how, or grieve)
Whereas if one sole lady pleased for ever,
How pleasant for the heart, as well as liver!

214

The heart is like the sky, a part of heaven,
But changes night and day too, like the sky;
Now o'er it clouds and thunder must be driven,
And darkness and destruction as on high:
But when it hath been scorch'd, and pierced, and riven,
Its storms expire in water-drops; the eye
Pours forth at last the heart's blood turn'd to tears,
Which make the English climate of our years.

215

The liver is the lazaret[26] of bile,
But very rarely executes its function,
For the first passion stays there such a while,
That all the rest creep in and form a junction,
Like knots of vipers on a dunghill's soil,
Rage, fear, hate, jealousy, revenge, compunction,
So that all mischiefs spring up from this entrail,
Like earthquakes from the hidden fire call'd 'central.'

216

In the mean time, without proceeding more
In this anatomy, I've finish'd now
Two hundred and odd stanzas as before,
That being about the number I'll allow
Each canto of the twelve, or twenty-four;
And, laying down my pen, I make my bow,
Leaving Don Juan and Haidee to plead
For them and theirs with all who deign to read.

from Letter to Augusta Leigh

Ravenna. July 26th. 1819

My dearest Augusta—

I am at too great a distance to scold you—but I *will* ask you—whether *your* letter of the *1st.* July *is an answer* to the letter I wrote you before I quitted Venice?—What? is it come to *this?*—Have you no memory? or no heart?—You *had* both—and I *have* both—at least for *you.*——I write this presuming that you received *that* letter—is it that you fear? do not be afraid of the post—the World has it's own affairs without thinking of *ours* and you may write safely—if you do—address as usual to *Venice.*—My house is not in St. Marc's but on the Grand Canal—

[26] **lazaret:** hospital for contagious diseases.

within sight of the Rialto Bridge.——I do not like at all this pain in your side and always think of your mother's constitution—you must always be to me the first consideration in the World.—Shall I come to *you?*—or would a warm climate do you good?—if so say the word—and I will provide you & your whole family (including that precious baggage your Husband) with the means of making an agreeable journey—you need not fear about *me*—I am much altered—and should be little trouble to you—nor would I give you more of my company than you like. ——I confess after three years and a half—and *such* years! and *such a year* as preceded those three years! it would be a relief to see you again—and if it would be so to you—I will come to you.——Pray—answer me—and recollect that I will do as you like in everything—even to returning to England—which is *not* the pleasantest of residences were *you* out of it.——I write from Ravenna—I came here on account of a Countess Guiccioli—a Girl of Twenty married to a very rich old man of Sixty—about a year ago;—with her last Winter I had a *liaison* according to the good old Italian custom—she miscarried in May—and sent for me here—and here I have been these two months.—She is pretty—a great Coquette—extremely vain—excessively affected—clever enough—without the smallest principle—with a good deal of imagination and some passion;—She had set her heart on carrying me off from Venice out of vanity—and succeeded—and having made herself the subject of general conversation has greatly contributed to her recovery.—Her husband is one of the richest Nobles of Ravenna—threescore years of age—this is his third wife.——You may suppose what *esteem* I entertain for *her*—perhaps it is about equal on both sides.—I have my saddle-horses here and there is good riding in the forest—with these—and my carriage which is here also—and the Sea—and my books—and the lady—the time passes—I am very fond of riding and always *was out* of England—but I hate your Hyde Park—and your turnpike roads—& must have forests—downs—or deserts to expatiate in—I detest *knowing* the road—one is to go,—and being interrupted by your damned fingerposts, or a blackguard roaring for twopence at a turnpike.——I send you a sonnet which this faithful Lady had made for the nuptials of one of her relations in which she swears the most *alarming constancey* to her husband—is not this good? you may suppose my *face* when she showed it to me—I could not help laughing—one of *our* laughs.——All this is very absurd—but you see that I have good morals at bottom.——She is an Equestrian too—but a bore in her rides—for she can't guide her horse—and he runs after mine—and tries to bite him—and then she begins screaming in a high hat and Sky-blue habit—making a most absurd figure—and embarrassing me and both our grooms—who have the devil's own work to keep her from tumbling—or having her clothes torn off by the trees and thickets of the Pine forest.——I fell a little in love with her intimate friend—a certain Geltruda—(that is *Gertrude*) who is very young & seems very well disposed to be perfidious—but alas!—*her* husband is jealous—and the G. also detected me in an illicit squeezing of hands, the consequence of which was that the friend was whisked off to Bologna for a few days—and since her return I have never been able to see her but twice—with a dragon of a mother in law—and a barbarous husband by her side—besides my own dear precious *Amica*—who hates all flirting but her own.—But I have a Priest who befriends me—and the Gertrude says a good deal with her great black eyes, so that perhaps—but Alas! I mean to give up these things altogether.——I have now given you some account of my present state—the Guide-book will tell you about Ravenna—I can't tell how long or short may be my stay—write to me—love me—as ever

yrs. most affectly.
B

P.S.—*This* affair is *not* in the least expensive—being all in the wealthy line—but troublesome—for the lady is imperious—and exigeante—however there are hopes that we may quarrel—when we do you shall hear. . .

from Letter to Douglas Kinnaird[1]

Venice. Octr. 26th. 1818 [1819]

MY DEAR DOUGLAS—

My late expenditure has arisen from living at a distance from Venice and being obliged to keep up two establishments, from frequent journeys—and buying some furniture and books as well as a horse or two—and not from any renewal of the EPICUREAN system as you suspect. I have been faithful to my honest liaison with Countess

[1] **Douglas Kinnaird:** Byron's longtime friend, literary agent, and banker in London.

Guiccioli—and I can assure you that *She* has never cost me directly or indirectly a sixpence—indeed the circumstances of herself and family render this no merit.—I never offered her but one present—a broach of brilliants—and she sent it back to me with her *own hair* in it (I shall *not* say of *what part* but *that* is an Italian custom) and a note to say that she was not in the habit of receiving presents of that value—but hoped that I would not consider her sending it back as an affront—nor the value diminished by the enclosure.—I have not had a whore this half-year—confining myself to the strictest adultery. . . . —As to "Don Juan"—confess—confess—you dog—and be candid—that it is the sublime of *that there* sort of writing—it may be bawdy—but is it not good English?—it may be profligate—but is it not *life,* is it not *the thing?*—Could any man have written it—who has not lived in the world?—and tooled in a post-chaise? in a hackney coach? in a Gondola? against a wall? in a court carriage? in a vis a vis?—on a table?—and under it?—I have written about a hundred stanzas of a third Canto—but it is damned modest—the outcry has frightened me.—I had such projects for the Don—but the *Cant* is so much stronger than *Cunt*—now a days,—that the benefit of experience in a man who had well weighed the worth of both monosyllables—must be lost to despairing posterity.—After all what stuff this outcry is—Lalla Rookh and Little—are more dangerous than my burlesque poem can be—Moore has been here—we got tipsy together—and were very amicable—he is gone on to Rome—I put my life (in M.S.) into his hands—(*not* for publication) you—or any body else may see it—at his return.—It only comes up to 1816.——He is a noble fellow—and looks quite fresh and poetical—nine years (the age of a poem's education) my Senior—he looks younger—this comes of marriage and being settled in the Country. I want to go to South America—I have written to Hobhouse all about it.—I wrote to my wife—three months ago—under care to Murray—has she got the letter—or is the letter got into Blackwood's magazine?——You ask after my Christmas pye—Remit it any how—*Circulars* is the best—you are right about *income*—I must have it all—how the devil do I know that I may live a year or a month?—I wish I knew that I might regulate my spending in more ways than one.—As it is one always thinks that there is but a span.—A man may as well break or be damned for a large sum as a small one—I should be loth to pay the devil or any other creditor more than sixpence in the pound.—

[scrawl for signature]

from Don Juan [III–IV]

(1821; comp. 1819–1820)

—*from* CANTO III—

. . .

1

Hail, Muse! *et cetera.*—We left Juan sleeping,
Pillow'd upon a fair and happy breast,
And watch'd by eyes that never yet knew weeping,
And loved by a young heart, too deeply blest
To feel the poison through her spirit creeping,
Or know who rested there; a foe to rest
Had soil'd the current of her sinless years,
And turn'd her pure heart's purest blood to tears.

2

Oh, Love! what is it in this world of ours
Which makes it fatal to be loved? Ah why
With cypress branches[1] hast thou wreathed thy bowers,
And made thy best interpreter a sigh?
As those who dote on odours pluck the flowers,
And place them on their breast—but place to die—
Thus the frail beings we would fondly cherish
Are laid within our bosoms but to perish.

3

In her first passion woman loves her lover,
In all the others all she loves is love,
Which grows a habit she can ne'er get over,
And fits her loosely—like an easy glove,
As you may find, whene'er you like to prove her.
One man alone at first her heart can move;
She then prefers him in the plural number,
Not finding that the additions much encumber.

4

I know not if the fault be men's or theirs;
But one thing's pretty sure; a woman planted—
(Unless at once she plunge for life in prayers)—
After a decent time must be gallanted;[2]

[1] **cypress branches:** symbol of death.
[2] **gallanted:** wooed.

Although, no doubt, her first of love affairs
 Is that to which her heart is wholly granted;
Yet there are some, they say, who have had *none*,
 But those who have ne'er end with only *one*.

5

'Tis melancholy, and a fearful sign
 Of human frailty, folly, also crime,
That love and marriage rarely can combine,
 Although they both are born in the same clime;
Marriage from love, like vinegar from wine—
 A sad, sour, sober beverage—by time
Is sharpen'd from its high celestial flavour
Down to a very homely household savour.

6

There's something of antipathy, as 'twere,
 Between their present and their future state;
A kind of flattery that's hardly fair
 Is used until the truth arrives too late—
Yet what can people do, except despair?
 The same things change their names at such a rate;
For instance—passion in a lover's glorious,
But in a husband is pronounced uxorious.

7

Men grow ashamed of being so very fond,
 They sometimes also get a little tired
(But that, of course, is rare), and then despond:
 The same things cannot always be admired,
Yet 'tis 'so nominated in the bond',
 That both are tied till one shall have expired.
Sad thought! to lose the spouse that was adorning
Our days, and put one's servants into mourning.

8

There's doubtless something in domestic doings,
 Which forms, in fact, true love's antithesis;
Romances paint at full length people's wooings,
 But only give a bust of marriages;
For no one cares for matrimonial cooings,
 There's nothing wrong in a connubial kiss:
Think you, if Laura had been Petrarch's wife,
He would have written sonnets all his life?

9

All tragedies are finish'd by a death,
 All comedies are ended by a marriage;
The future states of both are left to faith,
 For authors fear description might disparage
The worlds to come of both, or fall beneath,
 And then both worlds would punish their
  miscarriage;
So leaving each their priest and prayer-book ready,
They say no more of Death or of the Lady.

10

The only two that in my recollection
 Have sung of heaven and hell, or marriage, are
Dante and Milton, and of both the affection
 Was hapless in their nuptials, for some bar
Of fault or temper ruin'd the connection
 (Such things, in fact, it don't ask much to mar);
But Dante's Beatrice and Milton's Eve
Were not drawn from their spouses, you conceive.

11

Some persons say that Dante meant theology
 By Beatrice, and not a mistress—I,
Although my opinion may require apology,
 Deem this a commentator's phantasy,
Unless indeed it was from his own knowledge he
 Decided thus, and show'd good reason why;
I think that Dante's more abstruse ecstatics
Meant to personify the mathematics.

12

Haidée and Juan were not married, but
 The fault was theirs, not mine: it is not fair,
Chaste reader, then, in any way to put
 The blame on me, unless you wish they were;
Then if you'd have them wedded, please to shut
 The book which treats of this erroneous pair,
Before the consequences grow too awful;
'Tis dangerous to read of loves unlawful.

13

Yet they were happy,—happy in the illicit
 Indulgence of their innocent desires;
But more imprudent grown with every visit,
 Haidée forgot the island was her sire's;
When we have what we like, 'tis hard to miss it,
 At least in the beginning, ere one tires;
Thus she came often, not a moment losing,
Whilst her piratical papa was cruising.

14

Let not his mode of raising cash seem strange,
 Although he fleeced the flags of every nation,

For into a prime minister but change
  His title, and 'tis nothing but taxation;
But he, more modest, took an humbler range
  Of life, and in an honester vocation
Pursued o'er the high seas his watery journey,
And merely practised as a sea-attorney.

15

The good old gentleman had been detain'd
  By winds and waves, and some important captures;
And, in the hope of more, at sea remain'd,
  Although a squall or two had damp'd his raptures,
By swamping one of the prizes; he had chain'd
  His prisoners, dividing them like chapters
In number'd lots; they all had cuffs and collars,
And averaged each from ten to a hundred dollars.

. . . .

19

Then having settled his marine affairs,
  Dispatching single cruisers here and there,
His vessel having need of some repairs,
  He shaped his course to where his daughter fair
Continued still her hospitable cares;
  But that part of the coast being shoal and bare,
And rough with reefs which ran out many a mile,
His port lay on the other side o' the isle.

20

And there he went ashore without delay,
  Having no custom-house nor quarantine
To ask him awkward questions on the way
  About the time and place where he had been:
He left his ship to be hove down next day,
  With orders to the people to careen;[3]
So that all hands were busy beyond measure,
In getting out goods, ballast, guns, and treasure.

21

Arriving at the summit of a hill
  Which overlook'd the white walls of his home,
He stopp'd.—What singular emotions fill
  Their bosoms who have been induced to roam!
With fluttering doubts if all be well or ill—
  With love for many, and with fears for some;
All feelings which o'erleap the years long lost,
And bring our hearts back to their starting-post.

22

The approach of home to husbands and to sires,
  After long travelling by land or water,
Most naturally some small doubt inspires—
  A female family's a serious matter;
(None trusts the sex more, or so much admires—
  But they hate flattery, so I never flatter);
Wives in their husbands' absences grow subtler,
And daughters sometimes run off with the butler.

23

An honest gentleman at his return
  May not have the good fortune of Ulysses;
Not all lone matrons for their husbands mourn,[4]
  Or show the same dislike to suitors' kisses;
The odds are that he finds a handsome urn
  To his memory, and two or three young misses
Born to some friend, who holds his wife and riches,
And that his Argus[5] bites him by—the breeches.

24

If single, probably his plighted fair
  Has in his absence wedded some rich miser;
But all the better, for the happy pair
  May quarrel, and the lady growing wiser,
He may resume his amatory care
  As 'cavalier servente', or despise her;
And that his sorrow may not be a dumb one,
Write odes on the Inconstancy of Woman.

25

And oh! ye gentlemen who have already
  Some chaste *liaison* of the kind—I mean
An honest friendship with a married lady—
  The only thing of this sort ever seen
To last—of all connections the most steady,
  And the true Hymen,[6] (the first's but a screen)—
Yet for all that keep not too long away,
I've known the absent wrong'd four times a-day.

[3] **hove:** to empty of contents. **careen:** to cause a ship to list, or lean to one side, so that it might be repaired.

[4] **Not all . . . mourn:** reference to Ulysses's faithful wife Penelope, who rejected many suitors during his absence of twenty years.

[5] **Argus:** Ulysses's faithful dog, who died of joy when his master returned.

[6] **Hymen:** the god of marriage; the tissue covering the entrance to the vagina.

26

Lambro, our sea-solicitor, who had
Much less experience of dry land than ocean,
On seeing his own chimney-smoke, felt glad;
But not knowing metaphysics, had no notion
Of the true reason of his not being sad,
Or that of any other strong emotion;
He loved his child, and would have wept the loss of her,
But knew the cause no more than a philosopher.

27

He saw his white walls shining in the sun,
His garden trees all shadowy and green;
He heard his rivulet's light bubbling run,
The distant dog-bark; and perceived between
The umbrage of the wood so cool and dun
The moving figures, and the sparkling sheen
Of arms (in the East all arm)—and various dyes
Of colour'd garbs, as bright as butterflies.

28

And as the spot where they appear he nears,
Surprised at these unwonted signs of idling,
He hears—alas! no music of the spheres,
But an unhallow'd, earthly sound of fiddling!
A melody which made him doubt his ears,
The cause being past his guessing or unriddling;
A pipe, too, and a drum, and shortly after,
A most unoriental roar of laughter.

. . . .

35

Here was no lack of innocent diversion
For the imagination or the senses,
Song, dance, wine, music, stories from the Persian,
All pretty pastimes in which no offence is;
But Lambro saw all these things with aversion,
Perceiving in his absence such expenses,
Dreading that climax of all human ills,
The inflammation of his weekly bills.

36

Ah! what is man? what perils still environ
The happiest mortals even after dinner—
A day of gold from out an age of iron
Is all that life allows the luckiest sinner;
Pleasure (whene'er she sings, at least) 's a siren,
That lures to flay alive the young beginner;
Lambro's reception at his people's banquet
Was such as fire accords to a wet blanket.

37

He—being a man who seldom used a word
Too much, and wishing gladly to surprise
(In general he surprised men with the sword)
His daughter—had not sent before to advise
Of his arrival, so that no one stirr'd;
And long he paused to re-assure his eyes,
In fact much more astonish'd than delighted,
To find so much good company invited.

38

He did not know (Alas! how men will lie)
That a report (especially the Greeks)
Avouch'd his death (such people never die),
And put his house in mourning several weeks,
But now their eyes and also lips were dry;
The bloom too had return'd to Haidée's cheeks.
Her tears too being return'd into their fount,
She now kept house upon her own account.

39

Hence all this rice, meat, dancing, wine, and fiddling,
Which turn'd the isle into a place of pleasure;
The servants all were getting drunk or idling,
A life which made them happy beyond measure.
Her father's hospitality seem'd middling,
Compared with what Haidée did with his treasure;
'Twas wonderful how things went on improving,
While she had not one hour to spare from loving.

40

Perhaps you think in stumbling on this feast
He flew into a passion, and in fact
There was no mighty reason to be pleased;
Perhaps you prophesy some sudden act,
The whip, the rack, or dungeon at the least,
To teach his people to be more exact,
And that, proceeding at a very high rate,
He show'd the royal *penchants* of a pirate.

41

You're wrong.—He was the mildest manner'd man
That ever scuttled ship or cut a throat;
With such true breeding of a gentleman,
You never could divine his real thought;

No courtier could, and scarcely woman can
    Gird more deceit within a petticoat;
Pity he loved adventurous life's variety,
He was so great a loss to good society.

42

Advancing to the nearest dinner tray,
    Tapping the shoulder of the nighest guest,
With a peculiar smile, which, by the way,
    Boded no good, whatever it express'd,
He ask'd the meaning of this holiday;
    The vinous[7] Greek to whom he had address'd
His question, much too merry to divine
The questioner, fill'd up a glass of wine,

43

And without turning his facetious head,
    Over his shoulder, with a Bacchant air,
Presented the o'erflowing cup, and said,
    'Talking's dry work, I have no time to spare.'
A second hiccup'd, 'Our old master's dead,
    You'd better ask our mistress who's his heir.'
'Our mistress!' quoth a third: 'Our mistress!—pooh!—
You mean our master—not the old but new.

44

These rascals, being new comers, knew not whom
    They thus address'd—and Lambro's visage fell—
And o'er his eye a momentary gloom
    Pass'd, but he strove quite courteously to quell
The expression, and endeavouring to resume
    His smile, requested one of them to tell
The name and quality of his new patron,
Who seem'd to have turn'd Haidée into a matron.

45

'I know not,' quoth the fellow, 'who or what
    He is, nor whence he came—and little care;
But this I know, that this roast capon's fat,
    And that good wine ne'er wash'd down better fare;
And if you are not satisfied with that,
    Direct your questions to my neighbour there;
He'll answer all for better or for worse,
For none likes more to hear himself converse.'

[7] **vinous**: intoxicated with wine.

46

I said that Lambro was a man of patience,
    And certainly he show'd the best of breeding,
Which scarce even France, the paragon of nations,
    E'er saw her most polite of sons exceeding;
He bore these sneers against his near relations,
    His own anxiety, his heart too bleeding,
The insults too of every servile glutton,
Who all the time were eating up his mutton.

47

Now in a person used to much command—
    To bid men come, and go, and come again—
To see his orders done too out of hand—
    Whether the word was death, or but the chain
It may seem strange to find his manners bland;
    Yet such things are, which I can not explain,
Though doubtless he who can command himself
Is good to govern—almost as a Guelf.[8]

48

Not that he was not sometimes rash or so,
    But never in his real and serious mood;
Then calm, concentrated, and still, and slow,
    He lay coil'd like the boa in the wood;
With him it never was a word and blow,
    His angry word once o'er, he shed no blood,
But in his silence there was much to rue,
And his *one* blow left little work for *two*.

49

He ask'd no further questions, and proceeded
    On to the house, but by a private way,
So that the few who met him hardly heeded,
    So little they expected him that day;
If love paternal in his bosom pleaded
    For Haidée's sake, is more than I can say,
But certainly to one deem'd dead returning,
This revel seem'd a curious mode of mourning.

[8] **Guelf**: medieval Italian political faction that sided with the pope and city states against the Germans and the Ghibellines; also an ancient German ducal family and possible reference to the family line of George III, the Hanovers and royal family of England from 1714 to 1901 (McGann).

50

If all the dead could now return to life,
(Which God forbid!) or some, or a great many,
For instance, if a husband or his wife
(Nuptial examples are as good as any),
No doubt whate'er might be their former strife,
The present weather would be much more rainy—
Tears shed into the grave of the connection
Would share most probably its resurrection.

51

He enter'd in the house no more his home,
A thing to human feelings the most trying,
And harder for the heart to overcome,
Perhaps, than even the mental pangs of dying;
To find our hearthstone turn'd into a tomb,
And round its once warm precincts palely lying
The ashes of our hopes, is a deep grief,
Beyond a single gentleman's belief.

52

He enter'd in the house—his home no more,
For without hearts there is no home;—and felt
The solitude of passing his own door
Without a welcome; *there* he long had dwelt,
There his few peaceful days Time had swept o'er,
There his worn bosom and keen eye would melt
Over the innocence of that sweet child,
His only shrine of feelings undefiled.

53

He was a man of a strange temperament,
Of mild demeanour though of savage mood,
Moderate in all his habits, and content
With temperance in pleasure, as in food,
Quick to perceive, and strong to bear, and meant
For something better, if not wholly good;
His country's wrongs and his despair to save her
Had stung him from a slave to an enslaver.

54

The love of power, and rapid gain of gold,
The hardness by long habitude produced,
The dangerous life in which he had grown old,
The mercy he had granted oft abused,
The sights he was accustom'd to behold,
The wild seas, and wild men with whom he
cruised,
Had cost his enemies a long repentance,
And made him a good friend, but bad acquaintance.

55

But something of the spirit of old Greece
Flash'd o'er his soul a few heroic rays,
Such as lit onward to the Golden Fleece
His predecessors in the Colchian days;[9]
'Tis true he had no ardent love for peace—
Alas! his country show'd no path to praise:
Hate to the world and war with every nation
He waged, in vengeance of her degradation.

56

Still o'er his mind the influence of the clime
Shed its Ionian elegance, which show'd
Its power unconsciously full many a time,—
A taste seen in the choice of his abode,
A love of music and of scenes sublime,
A pleasure in the gentle stream that flow'd
Past him in crystal, and a joy in flowers,
Bedew'd his spirit in his calmer hours.

57

But whatsoe'er he had of love reposed
On that beloved daughter; she had been
The only thing which kept his heart unclosed
Amidst the savage deeds he had done and seen;
A lonely pure affection unopposed:
There wanted but the loss of this to wean
His feelings from all milk of human kindness,
And turn him like the Cyclops[10] mad with blindness.

. . . .

61

Old Lambro pass'd unseen a private gate,
And stood within his hall at eventide;
Meantime the lady and her lover sate
At wassail in their beauty and their pride:
An ivory inlaid table spread with state
Before them, and fair slaves on every side;
Gems, gold, and silver, form'd the service mostly,
Mother of pearl and coral the less costly.

---

[9] **Such as . . . days:** Jason and the Argonauts stole the ram with golden fleece, owned by the king of Colchis.

[10] **Cyclops:** cf. *Odyssey*, IX.298–364. Polyphemous, the one-eyed giant who went berserk when Odysseus put out his eye.

62

The dinner made about a hundred dishes;
  Lamb and pistachio nuts—in short, all meats,
And saffron soups, and sweetbreads; and the fishes
  Were of the finest that e'er flounced in nets,
Drest to a Sybarite's most pamper'd wishes;
  The beverage was various sherbets
Of raisin, orange, and pomegranate juice,
Squeezed through the rind, which makes it best for use.

63

These were ranged round, each in its crystal ewer,
  And fruits, and date-bread loaves closed the repast,
And Mocha's berry, from Arabia pure,
  In small fine China cups, came in at last;
Gold cups of filigree made to secure
  The hand from burning underneath them placed,
Cloves, cinnamon, and saffron too were boil'd
Up with the coffee, which (I think) they spoil'd.

64

The hangings of the room were tapestry, made
  Of velvet panels, each of different hue,
And thick with damask flowers of silk inlaid;
  And round them ran a yellow border too;
The upper border, richly wrought, display'd,
  Embroider'd delicately o'er with blue,
Soft Persian sentences, in lilac letters,
From poets, or the moralists their betters.

65

These oriental writings on the wall,
  Quite common in those countries, are a kind
Of monitors adapted to recall,
  Like skulls at Memphian banquets, to the mind
The words which shook Belshazzar in his hall,[11]
  And took his kingdom from him: You will find,
Though sages may pour out their wisdom's treasure,
There is no sterner moralist than pleasure.

66

A beauty at the season's close grown hectic,
  A genius who has drunk himself to death,
A rake turn'd methodistic or eclectic—
  (For that's the name they like to pray beneath)—
But most, an alderman struck apoplectic,
  Are things that really take away the breath
And show that late hours, wine, and love are able
To do not much less damage than the table.

67

Haidée and Juan carpeted their feet
  On crimson satin, border'd with pale blue;
Their sofa occupied three parts complete
  Of the apartment—and appear'd quite new;
The velvet cushions—(for a throne more meet)—
  Were scarlet, from whose glowing centre grew
A sun emboss'd in gold, whose rays of tissue,
Meridian-like, were seen all light to issue.

68

Crystal and marble, plate and porcelain,
  Had done their work of splendour; Indian mats
And Persian carpets, which the heart bled to stain,
  Over the floors were spread; gazelles and cats,
And dwarfs and blacks, and such like things, that gain
  Their bread as ministers and favourites—(that's
To say, by degradation)—mingled there
As plentiful as in a court or fair.

69

There was no want of lofty mirrors, and
  The tables, most of ebony inlaid
With mother of pearl or ivory, stood at hand,
  Or were of tortoise-shell or rare woods made,
Fretted with gold or silver:—by command
  The greater part of these were ready spread
With viands and sherbets in ice—and wine—
Kept for all comers, at all hours to dine.

70

Of all the dresses I select Haidée's:
  She wore two jelicks[12]—one was of pale yellow;
Of azure, pink, and white was her chemise—
  'Neath which her breast heaved like a little billow;
With buttons form'd of pearls as large as peas,
  All gold and crimson shone her jelick's fellow,
And the striped white gauze baracan[13] that bound her,
Like fleecy clouds about the moon, flow'd round her.

---

[11] **Like skulls . . . hall:** Herodotus Book II, Section 78 describes the Egyptian custom: "when the banquet is ended, a servant carries round to the several guests . . . a wooden image of a corpse to remind all of their mortality." (McGann)

[12] **jelick:** a vest or bodice worn by Turkish women.

[13] **baracan:** coarse blanket or garment.

71

One large gold bracelet clasp'd each lovely arm,
  Lockless—so pliable from the pure gold
That the hand stretch'd and shut it without harm,
  The limb which it adorn'd its only mould;
So beautiful—its very shape would charm,
  And clinging as if loth to lose its hold,
The purest ore enclosed the whitest skin
That e'er by precious metal was held in.

72

Around, as princess of her father's land,
  A like gold bar above her instep roll'd[14]
Announced her rank; twelve rings were on her hand;
  Her hair was starr'd with gems; her veil's fine fold
Below her breast was fasten'd with a band
  Of lavish pearls, whose worth could scarce be told;
Her orange silk full Turkish trousers furl'd
About the prettiest ankle in the world.

73

Her hair's long auburn waves down to her heel
  Flow'd like an Alpine torrent which the sun
Dyes with his morning light,—and would conceal
  Her person if allow'd at large to run,
And still they seem resentfully to feel
  The silken fillet's curb, and sought to shun
Their bonds whene'er some Zephyr caught began
To offer his young pinion as her fan.

74

Round her she made an atmosphere of life,
  The very air seem'd lighter from her eyes,
They were so soft and beautiful, and rife
  With all we can imagine of the skies,
And pure as Psyche ere she grew a wife—
  Too pure even for the purest human ties;
Her overpowering presence made you feel
It would not be idolatry to kneel.

75

Her eyelashes, though dark as night, were tinged
  (It is the country's custom), but in vain;
For those large black eyes were so blackly fringed,
  The glossy rebels mock'd the jetty stain,
And in their native beauty stood avenged:
  Her nails were touch'd with henna; but again
The power of art was turn'd to nothing, for
They could not look more rosy than before.

76

The henna should be deeply dyed to make
  The skin relieved appear more fairly fair;
She had no need of this, day ne'er will break
  On mountain tops more heavenly white than her:
The eye might doubt if it were well awake,
  She was so like a vision; I might err,
But Shakespeare also says 'tis very silly,
'To gild refined gold, or paint the lily'.[15]

77

Juan had on a shawl of black and gold,
  But a white baracan, and so transparent
The sparkling gems beneath you might behold,
  Like small stars through the milky way apparent;
His turban, furl'd in many a graceful fold,
  An emerald aigrette with Haidée's hair in't[16]
Surmounted as its clasp—a glowing crescent,
Whose rays shone ever trembling, but incessant.

78

And now they were diverted by their suite,
  Dwarfs, dancing girls, black eunuchs, and a poet,
Which made their new establishment complete;
  The last was of great fame, and liked to show it:
His verses rarely wanted their due feet—
  And for his theme—he seldom sung below it,
He being paid to satirize or flatter,
As the psalm says, 'inditing a good matter.'

79

He praised the present, and abused the past,
  Reversing the good custom of old days,
An eastern antijacobin at last
  He turn'd, preferring pudding to *no* praise—

[14] **gold bar . . . roll'd:** "The bar of gold above the instep is a mark of sovereign rank in the women of the families of the deys [rulers of Tunis or Tripoli], and is worn as such by their female relatives." [L.B.]

[15] **'To gild . . . lily':** cf. *King John*, IV.ii.11: "To gild refined gold, to paint the lily."

[16] **An emerald . . . in't:** head ornament with a tuft of plumes, especially the tail feathers of an egret.

For some few years his lot had been o'ercast
By his seeming independent in his lays,
But now he sung the Sultan and the Pacha
With truth like Southey and with verse like Crashaw.[17]

80

He was a man who had seen many changes,
And always changed as true as any needle;
His polar star being one which rather ranges,
And not the fix'd—he knew the way to wheedle:
So vile, he 'scaped the doom which oft avenges;
And being fluent (save indeed when fee'd ill),
He lied with such a fervour of intention—
There was no doubt he earn'd his laureate pension.

. . . .

84

He had travell'd 'mongst the Arabs, Turks, and Franks,
And knew the self-loves of the different nations;
And having lived with people of all ranks,
Had something ready upon most occasions—
Which got him a few presents and some thanks.
He varied with some skill his adulations;
To 'do at Rome as Romans do', a piece
Of conduct was which he observed in Greece.

85

Thus, usually, when he was ask'd to sing,
He gave the different nations something national;
'Twas all the same to him—'God save the king,'
Or *'Ça ira'*,[18] according to the fashion all;
His music made increment of any thing,
From the high lyric down to the low rational:
If Pindar sang horse-races, what should hinder
Himself from being as pliable as Pindar?

86

In France, for instance, he would write a chanson;
In England, a six canto quarto tale;
In Spain, he'd make a ballad or romance on
The last war—much the same in Portugal;
In Germany, the Pegasus he'd prance on
Would be old Goethe's—(see what says de Staël)
In Italy, he'd ape the 'Trecentisti';[19]
In Greece, he'd sing some sort of hymn like this t'ye:

1

The isles of Greece, the isles of Greece!
Where burning Sappho loved and sung,
Where grew the arts of war and peace,—
Where Delos rose, and Phoebus sprung![20]
Eternal summer gilds them yet,
But all, except their sun, is set.

2

The Scian and the Teian muse,[21]
The hero's harp, the lover's lute,
Have found the fame your shores refuse;
Their place of birth alone is mute
To sounds which echo further west
Than your sires' 'Islands of the Blest'.

3

The mountains look on Marathon—
And Marathon looks on the sea;
And musing there an hour alone,
I dream'd that Greece might still be free;
For standing on the Persian's grave,
I could not deem myself a slave.[22]

4

A king sate on the rocky brow
Which looks o'er sea-born Salamis;
And ships, by thousands, lay below,
And men in nations;—all were his!
He counted them at break of day—
And when the sun set where were they?[23]

[17] **With truth . . . Crashaw:** Byron refers to Robert Southey's laureateship as an apostasy from the revolutionary ideals of his youth. Richard Crashaw's (1612/13–1649) religious verse is known for its baroque style or stylistic ornateness.

[18] **'Ça ira':** anthem of the French Revolution, "It will go on."

[19] **'Trecentisti':** poets of the 1300s.

[20] **Where Delos . . . sprung:** Delos was called out of the sea by Poseidon's trumpet. It was a floating island until Zeus chained it to the floor of the sea to be the home of [Phoebus] Apollo.

[21] **The Scian . . . muse:** Scian refers to Homer, Teian to Anacreon.

[22] **I dream'd . . . slave:** in the Battle of Marathon (490 BC) the Athenians became the first Greeks to defeat the Persians.

[23] **A king . . . they:** the navy of Xerxes, king of Persia, was defeated at Salamis by Themistocles and the Greek fleet in 480 BC.

5

And where are they? and where art thou,
My country? On thy voiceless shore
The heroic lay is tuneless now—
The heroic bosom beats no more!
And must thy lyre, so long divine,
Degenerate into hands like mine?

6

'Tis something, in the dearth of fame,
Though link'd among a fetter'd race,
To feel at least a patriot's shame,
Even as I sing, suffuse my face;
For what is left the poet here?
For Greeks a blush—for Greece a tear.

7

Must *we* but weep o'er days more blest?
Must *we* but blush?—Our fathers bled.
Earth! render back from out thy breast
A remnant of our Spartan dead!
Of the three hundred grant but three,
To make a new Thermopylae![24]

8

What, silent still? and silent all?
Ah! no;—the voices of the dead
Sound like a distant torrent's fall,
And answer, 'Let one living head,
But one arise,—we come, we come!'
'Tis but the living who are dumb.

9

In vain—in vain: strike other chords;
Fill high the cup with Samian wine!
Leave battles to the Turkish hordes,
And shed the blood of Scio's vine!
Hark! rising to the ignoble call—
How answers each bold bacchanal!

10

You have the Pyrrhic dance as yet,
Where is the Pyrrhic phalanx gone?[25]
Of two such lessons, why forget
The nobler and the manlier one?
You have the letters Cadmus gave—[26]
Think ye he meant them for a slave?

11

Fill high the bowl with Samian wine!
We will not think of themes like these!
It made Anacreon's song divine:
He served—but served Polycrates[27]—
A tyrant; but our masters then
Were still, at least, our countrymen.

12

The tyrant of the Chersonese
Was freedom's best and bravest friend;
That tyrant was Miltiades![28]
Oh! that the present hour would lend
Another despot of the kind!
Such chains as his were sure to bind.

13

Fill high the bowl with Samian wine!
On Suli's rock, and Parga's shore,
Exists the remnant of a line[29]
Such as the Doric mothers bore;
And there, perhaps, some seed is sown,
The Heracleidan blood might own.[30]

---

[24] **Thermopylae**: site of the famous battle where the Persians vanquished the heroic Spartans in 480 BC.

[25] **Pyrrhic dance . . . Pyrrhic phalanx**: victory dance named after Pyrrhus (319–272 BC), king of Epirus, but here employed by Byron to contrast a dance for a pyrrhic victory, i.e., one with more losses than gains, with the battle formation of the phalanx.

[26] **letters Cadmus gave**: Mythology: Cadmus introduced writing into Greece. At the advice of Athena, he also planted dragon's teeth and armed warriors arose as the harvest, five of which became the ancestors of the Spartoi (sown men).

[27] **Polycrates**: tyrant of Samos, summoned Anacreon to his court to teach his son music. Anacreon's lyrics dwell on pleasure.

[28] **Miltiades**: ruled as king over the Thracian Chersonese; won an important victory against the Persians at Marathon.

[29] **remnant of a line**: Spartans.

[30] **the Doric . . . own**: the Dorians were the last of the northern invaders of Greece who brought little to Mycenean culture other than the iron sword; however, Heracles was a mythical Dorian hero, whose sons formed the Heracleidan line.

14

Trust not for freedom to the Franks[31]—
They have a king who buys and sells:
In native swords, and native ranks,
The only hope of courage dwells;
But Turkish force, and Latin fraud,
Would break your shield, however broad.

15

Fill high the bowl with Samian wine!
Our virgins dance beneath the shade—
I see their glorious black eyes shine;
But gazing on each glowing maid,
My own the burning tear-drop laves,
To think such breasts must suckle slaves.

16

Place me on Sunium's marbled steep,
Where nothing, save the waves and I,
May hear our mutual murmurs sweep;
There, swan-like, le me sing and die:
A land of slaves shall ne'er be mine—
Dash down yon cup of Samian wine!

87

Thus sung, or would, or could, or should have sung,
The modern Greek, in tolerable verse;
If not like Orpheus quite, when Greece was young,
Yet in these times he might have done much worse:
His strain display'd some feeling—right or wrong;
And feeling, in a poet, is the source
Of others' feeling; but they are such liars,
And take all colours—like the hands of dyers.

88

But words are things, and a small drop of ink,
Falling like dew, upon a thought, produces
That which makes thousands, perhaps millions, think;
'Tis strange, the shortest letter which man uses
Instead of speech, may form a lasting link
Of ages; to what straits old Time reduces
Frail man, when paper—even a rag like this,
Survives himself, his tomb, and all that's his.

[31] **Franks**: Western Europeans generally, but perhaps the French specifically.

89

And when his bones are dust, his grave a blank,
His station, generation, even his nation,
Become a thing, or nothing, save to rank
In chronological commemoration,
Some dull MS[32] oblivion long has sank,
Or graven stone found in a barrack's station
In digging the foundation of a closet,
May turn his name up, as a rare deposit.

. . . .

96

But let me to my story: I must own,
If I have any fault, it is digression;
Leaving my people to proceed alone,
While I soliloquize beyond expression;
But these are my addresses from the throne,
Which put off business to the ensuing session:
Forgetting each omission is a loss to
The world, not quite so great as Ariosto.

97

I know that what our neighbours call *'longueurs'*,[33]
(We've not so good a *word*, but have the *thing*
In that complete perfection which ensures
An epic from Bob Southey every spring—)
Form not the true temptation which allures
The reader; but 'twould not be hard to bring
Some fine examples of the *épopée*,[34]
To prove it grand ingredient is *ennui*.

98

We learn from Horace, Homer sometimes sleeps;
We feel without him: Wordsworth sometimes
wakes,
To show with what complacency he creeps,
With his dear *'Waggoners'*, around his lakes;
He wishes for 'a boat' to sail the deeps—[35]
Of ocean?—No, of air; and then he makes
Another outcry for 'a little boat,'
And drivels seas to set it well afloat.

[32] **MS**: manuscript.

[33] **'longueurs'**: literally, *length*, but meant to imply tediousness.

[34] **épopée**: epic.

[35] **'Waggoners' . . . deeps**: in 1819, Wordsworth published *The Waggoner* and *Peter Bell*, which begins with a fanciful prologue about "a little Boat, / Shaped like the crescent-moon."

99

If he must fain sweep o'er the etherial plain,
And Pegasus runs restive in his 'waggon',
Could he not beg the loan of Charles's Wain?[36]
Or pray Medea for a single dragon?
Or if too classic for his vulgar brain,
He fear'd his neck to venture such a nag on,
And he must needs mount nearer to the moon,
Could not the blockhead ask for a balloon?

100

'Pedlars', and 'boats', and 'waggons'! Oh! ye shades
Of Pope and Dryden, are we come to this?
That trash of such sort not alone evades
Contempt, but from the bathos' vast abyss
Floats scumlike uppermost, and these Jack Cades[37]
Of sense and song above your graves may hiss—
The 'little boatman' and his 'Peter Bell'
Can sneer at him who drew 'Achitophel'![38]

101

T' our tale.—The feast was over, the slaves gone,
The dwarfs and dancing girls had all retired;
The Arab lore and poet's song were done,
And every sound of revelry expired;
The lady and her lover, left alone,
The rosy flood of twilight's sky admired;—
Ave Maria![39] o'er the earth and sea,
That heavenliest hour of Heaven is worthiest thee!

102

Ave Maria! blessed be the hour!
The time, the clime, the spot, where I so oft
Have felt that moment in its fullest power
Sink o'er the earth so beautiful and soft,
While swung the deep bell in the distant tower,
Or the faint dying day-hymn stole aloft,
And not a breath crept through the rosy air,
And yet the forest leaves seem'd stirr'd with prayer.

103

Ave Maria! 'tis the hour of prayer!
Ave Maria! 'tis the hour of love!
Ave Maria! may our spirits dare
Look up to thine and to thy Son's above!
Ave Maria! oh that face so fair!
Those downcast eyes beneath the Almighty dove—
What though 'tis but a pictured image strike—
That painting is no idol, 'tis too like.

104

Some kinder casuists are pleased to say,
In nameless print—that I have no devotion;
But set those persons down with me to pray,
And you shall see who has the properest notion
Of getting into Heaven the shortest way;
My altars are the mountains and the ocean,
Earth, air, stars—all that springs from the great Whole,
Who hath produced, and will receive the soul.

. . . .

107

Oh Hesperus![40] thou bringest all good things—
Home to the weary, to the hungry cheer,
To the young bird the parent's brooding wings,
The welcome stall to the o'erlabour'd steer;
Whate'er of peace about our hearthstone clings,
Whate'er our household gods protect of dear,
Are gather'd round us by thy look of rest;
Thou bring'st the child, too, to the mother's breast.

. . . .

—*from* CANTO IV—

1

Nothing so difficult as a beginning
In poesy, unless perhaps the end;
For oftentimes when Pegasus seems winning
The race, he sprains a wing, and down we tend,
Like Lucifer when hurl'd from heaven for sinning;
Our sin the same, and hard as his to mend,
Being pride, which leads the mind to soar too far,
Till our own weakness shows us what we are.

[36] **Charles Wain:** the constellation Ursa Major (the Big Dipper) was once called Charles's Wagon. Medea is drawn away by a chariot pulled by Dragons in Euripides's *Medea.*

[37] **Jack Cade:** led a popular revolt against Henry VI in 1450, called the Jack Cade Rebellion. He appears as a character in Shakespeare's *Henry VI.*

[38] **'Achitophel':** pro-royalist allegory by John Dryden, *Absalom and Achitophel* (1681).

[39] **Ave Maria!:** cf. Luke 1:28–42: "Hail Mary." Also the title of a prayer.

[40] **Hesperus:** Venus, appearing as the evening star.

2

But Time, which brings all beings to their level,
  And sharp Adversity, will teach at last
Man,—and, as we would hope,—perhaps the devil,
  That neither of their intellects are vast:
While youth's hot wishes in our red veins revel,
  We know not this—the blood flows on too fast;
But as the torrent widens towards the ocean,
We ponder deeply on each past emotion.

3

As boy, I thought myself a clever fellow,
  And wish'd that others held the same opinion;
They took it up when my days grew more mellow,
  And other minds acknowledged my dominion:
Now my sere fancy 'falls into the yellow
  Leaf'[1], and imagination droops her pinion,
And the sad truth which hovers o'er my desk
Turns what was once romantic to burlesque.

4

And if I laugh at any mortal thing,
  'Tis that I may not weep; and if I weep,
'Tis that our nature cannot always bring
  Itself to apathy, for we must steep
Our hearts first in the depths of Lethe's spring
  Ere what we least wish to behold will sleep:
Thetis baptized her mortal son in Styx,
A mortal mother would on Lethe fix.[2]

5

Some have accused me of a strange design
  Against the creed and morals of the land,
And trace it in this poem every line:
  I don't pretend that I quite understand
My own meaning when I would be *very* fine;
  But the fact is that I have nothing plann'd,
Unless it were to be a moment merry,
A novel word in my vocabulary.

6

To the kind reader of our sober clime
  This way of writing will appear exotic;
Pulci was sire of the half-serious rhyme,
  Who sang when chivalry was more Quixotic,
And revell'd in the fancies of the time,
  True knights, chaste dames, huge giants, kings despotic;
But all these, save the last, being obsolete,
I chose a modern subject as more meet.

7

How I have treated it, I do not know;
  Perhaps no better than they have treated me
Who have imputed such designs as show
  Not what they saw, but what they wish'd to see;
But if it gives them pleasure, be it so,
  This is a liberal age, and thoughts are free:
Meantime Apollo plucks me by the ear,
And tells me to resume my story here.

8

Young Juan and his lady-love were left
  To their own hearts' most sweet society;
Even Time the pitiless in sorrow cleft
  With his rude scythe such gentle bosoms; he
Sigh'd to behold them of their hours bereft
  Though foe to love; and yet they could not be
Meant to grow old, but die in happy spring,
Before one charm or hope had taken wing.

9

Their faces were not made for wrinkles, their
  Pure blood to stagnate, their great hearts to fail;
The blank grey was not made to blast their hair,
  But like the climes that know nor snow nor hail
They were all summer: lightning might assail
  And shiver them to ashes, but to trail
A long and snake-like life of dull decay
Was not for them—they had too little clay.

10

They were alone once more; for them to be
  Thus was another Eden; they were never
Weary, unless when separate: the tree
  Cut from its forest root of years—the river
Damm'd from its fountain—the child from the knee
  And breast maternal wean'd at once for ever,

[1] **'falls into the yellow leaf'**: cf. *Macbeth*, V.iii.22–23: "My way of life / Is fallen into the sear, the yellow leaf."

[2] **Thetis baptized . . . Styx**: Thetis, the mother of Achilles, sought to make him immortal by dipping him into the River Styx. Lethe is the river of forgetfulness.

Would wither less than these two torn apart;
Alas! there is no instinct like the heart—

11

The heart—which may be broken: happy they!
Thrice fortunate! who of that fragile mould,
The precious porcelain of human clay,
Break with the first fall: they can ne'er behold
The long year link'd with heavy day on day,
And all which must be borne, and never told;
While life's strange principle will often lie
Deepest in those who long the most to die.

12

'Whom the gods love die young' was said of yore,
And many deaths do they escape by this:
The death of friends, and that which slays even more—
The death of friendship, love, youth, all that is,
Except mere breath; and since the silent shore
Awaits at last even those whom longest miss
The old archer's shafts, perhaps the early grave
Which men weep over may be meant to save.

13

Haidée and Juan thought not of the dead.
The heavens and earth, and air, seem'd made for them:
They found no fault with Time, save that he fled;
They saw not in themselves aught to condemn:
Each was the other's mirror, and but read
Joy sparkling in their dark eyes like a gem,
And knew such brightness was but the reflection
Of their exchanging glances of affection.

14

The gentle pressure, and the thrilling touch,
The least glance better understood than words,
Which still said all, and ne'er could say too much;
A language, too, but like to that of birds,
Known but to them, at least appearing such
As but to lovers a true sense affords;
Sweet playful phrases, which would seem absurd
To those who have ceased to hear such, or ne'er heard:

15

All these were theirs, for they were children still,
And children still they should have ever been;
They were not made in the real world to fill
A busy character in the dull scene,
But like two beings born from out a rill,
A nymph and her beloved, all unseen
To pass their lives in fountains and on flowers,
And never know the weight of human hours.

16

Moons changing had roll'd on, and changeless found
Those their bright rise had lighted to such joys
As rarely they beheld throughout their round;
And these were not of the vain kind which cloys,
For theirs were buoyant spirits, never bound
By the mere senses; and that which destroys
Most love, possession, unto them appear'd
A thing which each endearment more endear'd.

17

Oh beautiful! and rare as beautiful!
But theirs was love in which the mind delights
To lose itself, when the old world grows dull,
And we are sick of its hack sounds and sights,
Intrigues, adventures of the common school,
Its petty passions, marriages, and flights,
Where Hymen's torch but brands one strumpet more,
Whose husband only knows her not a wh—re.

18

Hard words; harsh truth; a truth which many know.
Enough.—The faithful and the fairy pair,
Who never found a single hour too slow,
What was it made them thus exempt from care?
Young innate feelings all have felt below
Which perish in the rest, but in them were
Inherent; what we mortals call romantic,
And always envy, though we deem it frantic.

19

This is in others a factitious state,
An opium dream of too much youth and reading,
But was in them their nature, or their fate:
No novels e'er had set their young hearts bleeding,
For Haidée's knowledge was by no means great,
And Juan was a boy of saintly breeding;
So that there was no reason for their loves
More than for those of nightingales or doves.

20

They gazed upon the sunset; 'tis an hour
Dear unto all, but dearest to *their* eyes,

For it had made them what they were: the power
Of love had first o'erwhelm'd them from such skies,
When happiness had been their only dower,
And twilight saw them link'd in passion's ties;
Charm'd with each other, all things charm'd that brought
The past still welcome as the present thought.

21

I know not why, but in that hour to-night,
Even as they gazed, a sudden tremor came,
And swept, as 'twere, across their heart's delight,
Like the wind o'er a harp-string, or a flame,
When one is shook in sound, and one in sight;
And thus some boding flash'd through either frame,
And call'd from Juan's breast a faint low sigh,
While one new tear arose in Haidée's eye.

22

That large black prophet eye seem'd to dilate
And follow far the disappearing sun,
As if their last day of a happy date
With his broad, bright, and dropping orb were gone;
Juan gazed on her as to ask his fate—
He felt a grief, but knowing cause for none,
His glance inquired of hers for some excuse
For feelings causeless, or at least abstruse.

23

She turn'd to him, and smiled, but in that sort
Which makes not others smile; then turn'd aside:
Whatever feeling shook her, it seem'd short,
And master'd by her wisdom or her pride;
When Juan spoke, too—it might be in sport—
Of this their mutual feeling, she replied—
'If it should be so,—but—it cannot be—
Or I at least shall not survive to see.'

24

Juan would question further, but she press'd
His lip to hers, and silenced him with this,
And then dismiss'd the omen from her breast,
Defying augury with that fond kiss;
And no doubt of all methods 'tis the best:
Some people prefer wine—'tis not amiss;
I have tried both; so those who would a part take
May choose between the headache and the heartache.

25

One of the two, according to your choice,
Woman or wine, you'll have to undergo;
Both maladies are taxes on our joys:
But which to choose, I really hardly know;
And if I had to give a casting voice,
For both sides I could many reasons show,
And then decide, without great wrong to either,
It were much better to have both than neither.

26

Juan and Haidée gazed upon each other
With swimming looks of speechless tenderness,
Which mix'd all feelings, friend, child, lover, brother,
All that the best can mingle and express
When two pure hearts are pour'd in one another,
And love too much, and yet can not love less;
But almost sanctify the sweet excess
By the immortal wish and power to bless.

27

Mix'd in each other's arms, and heart in heart,
Why did they not then die?—they had lived too long
Should an hour come to bid them breathe apart;
Years could but bring them cruel things or wrong,
The world was not for them, nor the world's art
For beings passionate as Sappho's song;
Love was born *with* them, *in* them, so intense,
It was their very spirit—not a sense.

28

They should have lived together deep in woods,
Unseen as sings the nightingale; they were
Unfit to mix in these thick solitudes
Call'd social, haunts of Hate, and Vice, and Care:
How lonely every freeborn creature broods!
The sweetest song-birds nestle in a pair;
The eagle soars alone; the gull and crow
Flock o'er their carrion, just like men below.

29

Now pillow'd cheek to cheek, in loving sleep,
Haidée and Juan their siesta took,
A gentle slumber, but it was not deep,
For ever and anon a something shook
Juan, and shuddering o'er his frame would creep;
And Haidée's sweet lips murmur'd like a brook
A wordless music, and her face so fair
Stirr'd with her dream as rose-leaves with the air;

30

Or as the stirring of a deep clear stream
Within an Alpine hollow, when the wind
Walks o'er it, was she shaken by the dream,
The mystical usurper of the mind—
O'erpowering us to be whate'er may seem
Good to the soul which we no more can bind;
Strange state of being! (for 'tis still to be)
Senseless to feel, and with seal'd eyes to see.

31

She dream'd of being alone on the sea-shore,
Chain'd to a rock; she knew not how, but stir
She could not from the spot, and the loud roar
Grew, and each wave rose roughly, threatening her;
And o'er her upper lip they seem'd to pour,
Until she sobb'd for breath, and soon they were
Foaming o'er her lone head, so fierce and high—
Each broke to drown her, yet she could not die.

32

Anon—she was released, and then she stray'd
O'er the sharp shingles with her bleeding feet,
And stumbled almost every step she made;
And something roll'd before her in a sheet,
Which she must still pursue howe'er afraid;
'Twas white and indistinct, nor stopp'd to meet
Her glance nor grasp, for still she gazed and grasp'd,
And ran, but it escaped her as she clasp'd.

33

The dream changed; in a cave she stood, its walls
Were hung with marble icicles; the work
Of ages on its water-fretted halls,
Where waves might wash, and seals might breed and lurk;
Her hair was dripping, and the very balls
Of her black eyes seemed turn'd to tears, and murk
The sharp rocks look'd below each drop they caught,
Which froze to marble as it fell, she thought.

34

And wet, and cold, and lifeless at her feet,
Pale as the foam that froth'd on his dead brow,
Which she essay'd in vain to clear, (how sweet
Were once her cares, how idle seem'd they now!)
Lay Juan, nor could aught renew the beat
Of his quench'd heart; and the sea dirges low
Rang in her sad ears like a mermaid's song,
And that brief dream appear'd a life too long.

35

And gazing on the dead, she thought his face
Faded, or alter'd into something new—
Like to her father's features, till each trace
More like and like to Lambro's aspect grew—
With all his keen worn look and Grecian grace;
And starting, she awoke, and what to view?
Oh! Powers of Heaven! what dark eye meets she there?
'Tis—'tis her father's—fix'd upon the pair!

36

Then shrieking, she arose, and shrieking fell,
With joy and sorrow, hope and fear, to see
Him whom she deem'd a habitant where dwell
The ocean-buried, risen from death, to be
Perchance the death of one she loved too well:
Dear as her father had been to Haidée,
It was a moment of that awful kind—
I have seen such—but must not call to mind.

37

Up Juan sprung to Haidée's bitter shriek,
And caught her falling, and from off the wall
Snatch'd down his sabre, in hot haste to wreak
Vengeance on him who was the cause of all:
Then Lambro, who till now forbore to speak,
Smiled scornfully, and said, 'Within my call,
A thousand scimitars await the word;
Put up, young man, put up your silly sword.'

38

And Haidée clung around him; 'Juan, 'tis—
'Tis Lambro—'tis my father! Kneel with me—
He will forgive us—yes—it must be—yes.
Oh! dearest father, in this agony
Of pleasure and of pain—even while I kiss
Thy garment's hem with transport, can it be
That doubt should mingle with my filial joy?
Deal with me as thou wilt, but spare this boy.'

39

High and inscrutable the old man stood,
Calm in his voice, and calm within his eye—
Not always signs with him of calmest mood:
He look'd upon her, but gave no reply;

Then turn'd to Juan, in whose cheek the blood
  Oft came and went, as there resolved to die;
In arms, at least, he stood, in act to spring
On the first foe whom Lambro's call might bring.

40

'Young man, your sword,' so Lambro once more said:
  Juan replied, 'Not while this arm is free.'
The old man's cheek grew pale, but not with dread,
  And drawing from his belt a pistol, he
Replied, 'Your blood be then on your own head.'
  Then look'd close at the flint, as if to see
'Twas fresh—for he had lately used the lock—
And next proceeded quietly to cock.

41

It has a strange quick jar upon the ear,
  That cocking of a pistol, when you know
A moment more will bring the sight to bear
  Upon your person, twelve yards off, or so;
A gentlemanly distance, not too near,
  If you have got a former friend for foe;
But after being fired at once or twice,
The ear becomes more Irish, and less nice.

42

Lambro presented, and one instant more
  Had stopp'd this Canto, and Don Juan's breath,
When Haidée threw herself her boy before;
  Stern as her sire: 'On me,' she cried, 'let death
Descend—the fault is mine; this fatal shore
  He found—but sought not. I have pledged my
    faith;
I love him—I will die with him: I knew
Your nature's firmness—know your daughter's too.'

43

A minute past, and she had been all tears,
  And tenderness, and infancy: but now
She stood as one who champion'd human fears—
  Pale, statue-like, and stern, she woo'd the blow;
And tall beyond her sex, and their compeers,
  She drew up to her height, as if to show
A fairer mark; and with a fix'd eye scann'd
Her father's face—but never stopp'd his hand.

44

He gazed on her, and she on him; 'twas strange
  How like they look'd! the expression was the same;
Serenely savage, with a little change
  In the large dark eye's mutual-darted flame;
For she too was as one who could avenge,
  If cause should be—a lioness, though tame:
Her father's blood before her father's face
Boil'd up, and proved her truly of his race.

45

I said they were alike, their features and
  Their stature differing but in sex and years;
Even to the delicacy of their hand
  There was resemblance, such as true blood wears;
And now to see them, thus divided, stand
  In fix'd ferocity, when joyous tears,
And sweet sensations, should have welcomed both,
Show what the passions are in their full growth.

46

The father paused a moment, then withdrew
  His weapon, and replaced it; but stood still,
And looking on her, as to look her through,
  'Not *I*,' he said, 'have sought this stranger's ill;
Not *I* have made this desolation: few
  Would bear such outrage, and forbear to kill;
But I must do my duty—how thou hast
Done thine, the present vouches for the past.

47

'Let him disarm; or, by my father's head,
  His own shall roll before you like a ball!'
He raised his whistle, as the word he said,
  And blew; another answer'd to the call,
And rushing in disorderly, though led,
  And arm'd from boot to turban, one and all,
Some twenty of his train came, rank on rank;
He gave the word, 'Arrest or slay the Frank.'

48

Then, with a sudden movement, he withdrew
  His daughter; while compress'd within his clasp,
'Twixt her and Juan interposed the crew;
  In vain she struggled in her father's grasp—
His arms were like a serpent's coil: then flew
  Upon their prey, as darts an angry asp,
The file of pirates; save the foremost, who
Had fallen, with his right shoulder half cut through.

49

The second had his cheek laid open; but
  The third, a wary, cool old sworder, took

The blows upon his cutlass, and then put
His own well in; so well, ere you could look,
His man was floor'd, and helpless at his foot,
With the blood running like a little brook
From two smart sabre gashes, deep and red—
One on the arm, the other on the head.

50

And then they bound him where he fell, and bore
Juan from the apartment: with a sign
Old Lambro bade them take him to the shore,
Where lay some ships which were to sail at nine.
They laid him in a boat, and plied the oar
Until they reach'd some galliots, placed in line;
On board of one of these, and under hatches,
They stow'd him, with strict orders to the watches.

51

The world is full of strange vicissitudes,
And here was one exceedingly unpleasant:
A gentleman so rich in the world's goods,
Handsome and young, enjoying all the present,
Just at the very time when he least broods
On such a thing is suddenly to sea sent,
Wounded and chain'd, so that he cannot move,
And all because a lady fell in love.

. . . .

58

The last sight which she saw was Juan's gore,
And he himself o'ermaster'd and cut down;
His blood was running on the very floor
Where late he trod, her beautiful, her own;
Thus much she view'd an instant and no more,—
Her struggles ceased with one convulsive groan;
On her sire's arm, which until now scarce held
Her writhing, fell she like a cedar fell'd.

59

A vein had burst, and her sweet lips' pure dyes
Were dabbled with the deep blood which ran o'er;
And her head droop'd as when the lily lies
O'ercharged with rain: her summon'd handmaids bore
Their lady to her couch with gushing eyes;
Of herbs and cordials they produced their store,
But she defied all means they could employ,
Like one life could not hold, nor death destroy.

60

Days lay she in that state unchanged, though chill
With nothing livid, still her lips were red;
She had no pulse, but death seem'd absent still;
No hideous sign proclaim'd her surely dead;
Corruption came not in each mind to kill
All hope; to look upon her sweet face bred
New thoughts of life, for it seem'd full of soul,
She had so much, earth could not claim the whole.

. . . .

64

Her handmaids tended, but she heeded not;
Her father watch'd, she turn'd her eyes away;
She recognized no being, and no spot
However dear or cherish'd in their day;
They changed from room to room, but all forgot,
Gentle, but without memory she lay;
At length those eyes, which they would fain be weaning
Back to old thoughts, wax'd full of fearful meaning.

65

And then a slave bethought her of a harp;
The harper came, and tuned his instrument;
At the first notes, irregular and sharp,
On him her flashing eyes a moment bent,
Then to the wall she turn'd as if to warp
Her thoughts from sorrow through her heart re-sent,
And he begun a long low island song
Of ancient days, ere tyranny grew strong.

66

Anon her thin wan fingers beat the wall
In time to his old tune; he changed the theme,
And sung of love; the fierce name struck through all
Her recollection; on her flash'd the dream
Of what she was, and is, if ye could call
To be so being; in a gushing stream
The tears rush'd forth from her o'erclouded brain,
Like mountain mists at length dissolved in rain.

67

Short solace, vain relief!—thought came too quick,
And whirl'd her brain to madness; she arose
As one who ne'er had dwelt among the sick,
And flew at all she met, as on her foes;

But no one ever heard her speak or shriek,
Although her paroxysm drew towards its close:
Hers was a phrensy which disdain'd to rave,
Even when they smote her, in the hope to save.

68

Yet she betray'd at times a gleam of sense;
Nothing could make her meet her father's face,
Though on all other things with looks intense
She gazed, but none she ever could retrace;
Food she refused, and raiment; no pretence
Avail'd for either; neither change of place,
Nor time, nor skill, nor remedy, could give her
Senses to sleep—the power seem'd gone for ever.

69

Twelve days and nights she wither'd thus; at last,
Without a groan, or sigh, or glance, to show
A parting pang, the spirit from her past:
And they who watch'd her nearest could not know
The very instant, till the change that cast
Her sweet face into shadow, dull and slow,
Glazed o'er her eyes—the beautiful, the black—
Oh! to possess such lustre—and then lack!

70

She died, but not alone; she held within
A second principle of life, which might
Have dawned a fair and sinless child of sin;
But closed its little being without light,
And went down to the grave unborn, wherein
Blossom and bough lie wither'd with one blight;
In vain the dews of Heaven descend above
The bleeding flower and blasted fruit of love.

71

Thus lived—thus died she; never more on her
Shall sorrow light, or shame. She was not made
Through years or moons the inner weight to bear,
Which colder hearts endure till they are laid
By age in earth; her days and pleasures were
Brief, but delightful—such as had not staid
Long with her destiny; but she sleeps well
By the sea shore, whereon she loved to dwell.

72

That isle is now all desolate and bare,
Its dwellings down, its tenants past away;
None but her own and father's grave is there,
And nothing outward tells of human clay;
Ye could not know where lies a thing so fair,
No stone is there to show, no tongue to say
What was; no dirge, except the hollow sea's,
Mourns o'er the beauty of the Cyclades.

73

But many a Greek maid in a loving song
Sighs o'er her name; and many an islander
With her sire's story makes the night less long;
Valour was his, and beauty dwelt with her;
If she loved rashly, her life paid for wrong—
A heavy price must all pay who thus err,
In some shape; let none think to fly the danger,
For soon or late Love is his own avenger.

74

But let me change this theme, which grows too sad,
And lay this sheet of sorrows on the shelf;
I don't much like describing people mad,
For fear of seeming rather touch'd myself—
Besides I've no more on this head to add;
And as my Muse is a capricious elf,
We'll put about, and try another tack
With Juan, left half-kill'd some stanzas back.

75

Wounded and fetter'd, 'cabin'd, cribb'd, confined',
Some days and nights elapsed before that he
Could altogether call the past to mind;
And when he did, he found himself at sea,
Sailing six knots an hour before the wind;
The shores of Ilion lay beneath their lee—
Another time he might have liked to see 'em,
But now was not much pleased with Cape Sigaeum.

from Detached Thoughts

(1821–1822)[1]

(79)

My first dash into poetry, was as early as 1800.——It was the ebullition of a passion for my first Cousin Margaret Parker (daughter and grand-daughter of the two Admirals

[1] A journal of reminiscences written in Ravenna and Pisa.

Parker) one of the most beautiful of Evanescent beings.— I have long forgotten the verses—but it would be difficult for me to forget her——Her dark eyes!—her long eyelashes! her completely Greek cast of face and figure!— I was then about twelve—She rather older—perhaps a year.——She died about a year or two afterwards—in consequence of a fall which injured her spine and induced consumption.—Her Sister Augusta—(by some thought still more beautiful) died of the same malady—and it was indeed in attending her that Margaret met with the accident which occasioned her own death.—My Sister told me that when she went to see her shortly before her death —upon accidentally mentioning my name—Margaret coloured through the paleness of mortality to the eyes— to the great astonishment of my Sister—who (residing with her Grand-mother Lady Holderness—saw at that time but little of me for family reasons) knew nothing of our attachment—nor could conceive why my name should affect her at such a time.——I knew nothing of her illness—(being at Harrow and in the country) till she was gone.——Some years after I made an attempt at an Elegy.—A very dull one.—I do not recollect scarcely anything equal to the *transparent* beauty of my cousin—or to the sweetness of her temper—during the short period of our intimacy——she looked as if she had been made out of a rainbow—all beauty and peace.—My passion had it's effects upon me—I could not sleep—I could not eat—I could not rest—and although I had reason to know that she loved me—it was the torture of my life— to think of the time which must elapse before we could meet again—being usually about *twelve hours*—of separation!——But I was a fool then—and am not much wiser now.

(80)

My passions were developed very early—so early— that few would believe me—if I were to state the period —and the facts which accompanied it.—Perhaps this was one of the reasons which caused the anticipated melancholy of my thoughts—having anticipated life.— My earlier poems are the thoughts of one at least ten years older than the age at which they were written,—I don't mean for their solidity—but their Experience—the two first Cantos of C[hild]e H[arold]e were completed at twenty two—and they were written as if by a man— older than I shall probably ever be.—

(83)

Like Sylla—I have always believed that all things depend upon Fortune & nothing upon ourselves.—I am not aware of any one thought or action worthy of being called good to myself or others—which is not to be attributed to the Good Goddess—*Fortune!*—

(91)

My School friendships were with *me passions* (for I was always violent) but I do not know that there is one which has endured (to be sure some have been cut short by death) till now—that with Lord Clare[2] began one of the earliest and lasted longest—being only interrupted by distance—that I know of.—I never hear the word *"Clare"* without a beating of the heart—even *now,* & I write it— with the feelings of 1803–4–5—ad infinitum.—

(95)

If I had to live over again—I do not know what I would change in my life—unless it were *for—not to have lived at all*[.] All history and experience—and the rest— teaches us that the good and evil are pretty equally balanced in this existence—and that what is most to be desired is an easy passage out of it.——What can it give us but *years?* & those have little of good but their ending.—

---

from Don Juan [VI–XIV][1]

(1823)

—*from* CANTO IX—

1

Oh, Wellington![2] (or 'Vilainton'—for Fame
    Sounds the heroic syllables both ways;
France could not even conquer your great name,
    But punned it down to this facetious phrase—

---

[2] **Lord Clare:** John Fitzgibbon, second Earl of Clare.

[1] Cantos VI to XIV were published in three increments in 1823: VI to VIII in July, IX to XI in August, and XII to XIV in December. All were published by the radical publisher John Hunt, brother of Leigh Hunt, because John Murray, the publisher of Cantos I to V, found the new cantos "outrageously shocking" and became fearful for his political safety. His fears were not groundless. John Hunt was being prosecuted for publishing Byron's *Vision of Judgment* in 1822.

[2] **Wellington:** Arthur Wellesley, first Duke of Wellington, great hero of the Battle of Waterloo, 18 June 1815. Later became Prime Minister (1828–1839) and Secretary of State for Foreign Affairs (1834–1835).

Beating or beaten she will laugh the same)—
You have obtained great pensions and much praise;
Glory like yours should any dare gainsay,
Humanity would rise, and thunder 'Nay!'

2

I don't think that you used Kinnaird quite well
In Marinêt's affair—in fact 'twas shabby,[3]
And like some other things won't do to tell
Upon your tomb in Westminster's old abbey.
Upon the rest 'tis not worth while to dwell,
Such tales being for the tea hours of some tabby;
But though your years as *man* tend fast to zero,
In fact your Grace is still but a *young Hero.*

3

Though Britain owes (and pays you too) so much,
Yet Europe doubtless owes you greatly more:
You have repaired Legitimacy's crutch,[4]—
A prop not quite so certain as before:
The Spanish, and the French, as well as Dutch,
Have seen, and felt, how strongly you *restore;*
And Waterloo has made the world your debtor—
(I wish your bards would sing it rather better).

4

You are 'the best of cut-throats':—do not start;[5]
The phrase is Shakespeare's, and not misapplied:—
War's a brain-spattering, windpipe-slitting art,
Unless her cause by Right be sanctified.
If you have acted *once* a generous part,
The World, not the World's masters, will decide,
And I shall be delighted to learn who,
Save you and yours, have gained by Waterloo?

5

I am no flatterer—you've supped full of flattery:
They say you like it too—'tis no great wonder:
He whose whole life has been assault and battery,
At last may get a little tired of thunder;
And swallowing eulogy much more than satire, he
May like being praised for every lucky blunder;
Called 'Saviour of the Nations'—not yet saved,
And Europes' Liberator—still enslaved.

6

I've done. Now go and dine from off the plate
Presented by the Prince of the Brazils,
And send the sentinel before your gate
A slice or two from your luxurious meals:
He fought, but has not fed so well of late.
Some hunger too they say the people feels:—
There is no doubt that you deserve your ration,
But pray give back a little to the nation.

7

I don't mean to reflect—a man so great as
You, my Lord Duke! is far above reflection.
The high Roman fashion too of Cincinnatus,[6]
With modern history has but small connection:
Though as an Irishman you love potatoes,
You need not take them under your direction;
And half a million for your Sabine farm[7]
Is rather dear!—I'm sure I mean no harm.

8

Great men have always scorned great recompenses:
Epaminondas[8] saved his Thebes, and died,
Not leaving even his funeral expenses:
George Washington had thanks and nought beside,
Except the all-cloudless Glory (which few men's is)
To free his country: Pitt[9] too had his pride,
And, as a high-soul'd Minister of State, is
Renowned for ruining Great Britain gratis.

---

[3] **I don't think . . . shabby:** a Lord Kinnaird had warned Wellington that a Frenchman by the name of Marinet would attempt to assassinate him, but because Kinnaird refused to identify his source of information Wellington accused him of treason.

[4] **repaired Legitimacy's crutch:** the Bourbon monarchy had been restored in France. See the COMPREHENSIVE CHRONOLOGY.

[5] **'the best of cut-throats':** cf. *Macbeth,* III.iv.17: "Thou art the best o' th' cut-throats".

[6] **Cincinnatus:** Roman general remembered for his courage and patriotism.

[7] **half a million . . . farm:** Wellington's endowment as duke was £500,000. Sabine is a region of central Italy associated with the farms of the poet Horace, who received one from Augustus in patronage, and of Cincinnatus, who gave up his farm to serve in Rome.

[8] **Epaminondas:** Theban general who waged successful battles against the Spartans with imaginative military tactics.

[9] **Pitt:** William Pitt the Younger (1759–1806), twice Prime Minister (1783–1801; 1804–1806).

9

Never had mortal Man such opportunity,
 Except Napoleon, or abused it more:
You might have freed fall'n Europe from the Unity
 Of Tyrants, and been blest from shore to shore:
And *now*—What *is* your fame? Shall the Muse tune it
 ye?
Now—that the rabble's first vain shouts are o'er?
Go, hear it in your famished Country's cries!
Behold the World! and curse your victories!

10

As these new Cantos touch on warlike feats,
 To *you* the unflattering Muse deigns to inscribe
Truths that you will not read in the Gazettes,
 But which, 'tis time to teach the hireling tribe
Who fatten on their Country's gore and debts,
 Must be recited, and—without a bribe.
You *did great* things; but not being *great* in mind,
Have left *undone* the *greatest*—and mankind.

11

Death laughs—Go ponder o'er the skeleton
 With which men image out the unknown thing
That hides the past world, like to a set sun
 Which still elsewhere may rouse a brighter
 spring,—
Death laughs at all you weep for:—look upon
 This hourly dread of all, whose *threatened sting*
Turns life to terror, even though in its sheath!
Mark! how its lipless mouth grins without breath!

12

Mark! how it laughs and scorns at all you are!
 And yet *was* what you are: from *ear* to *ear*
It *laughs not*—there is now no fleshy bar
 So called; the Antic long hath ceased to *hear*,
But still he *smiles*; and whether near or far
 He strips from man that mantle (far more dear
Than even the tailor's) his incarnate skin,
White, black, or copper—the dead bones will grin.

13

And thus Death laughs,—it is sad merriment,
 But still it *is* so; and with such example
Why should not Life be equally content,
 With his Superior, in a smile to trample
Upon the nothings which are daily spent
 Like bubbles on an ocean much less ample
Than the eternal deluge, which devours
Suns as rays—worlds like atoms—years like hours?

14

'To be or not to be! that is the question,'
 Says Shakespeare, who just now is much in fashion
I am neither Alexander nor Hephaestion,[10]
 Nor ever had for *abstract* fame much passion;
But would much rather have a sound digestion,
 Than Buonaparte's cancer:—could I dash on
Through fifty victories to shame or fame,
Without a stomach—what were a good name?

15

'Oh dura ilia messorum!'[11]—'Oh
 Ye rigid guts of reapers!'—I translate
For the great benefit of those who know
 What Indigestion is—that inward fate
Which makes all Styx through one small liver flow.
 A peasant's sweat is worth his Lord's estate:
Let *this* one toil for bread—*that* rack for rent,
He who sleeps best, may be the most content.

16

'To be or not to be?'—Ere I decide,
 I should be glad to know that which *is being*?
'Tis true we speculate both far and wide,
 And deem, because we *see*, we are *all-seeing*:
For my part, I'll enlist on neither side,
 Until I see both sides for once agreeing.
For me, I sometimes think that Life is Death,
Rather than Life a mere affair of breath.

17

'Que sçais-je?'[12] was the motto of Montaigne,
 As also of the first Academicians:
That all is dubious which Man may attain,
 Was one of their most favourite positions.

---

[10] **Hephaestion**: Alexander's closest friend.

[11] **'Oh dura ilia messorum!'**: cf. Horace, *Epodes* III. (Translation follows in the same stanza.)

[12] **'Que sçais-je?'**: *trans.* 'What do know?' Montaigne (1533–1592), French essayist and moralist, whose *Essais* (1580–1588) established the form of the modern essay and whose *Apologie de Ramond Sebond* introduced an attack on reason that inspired a critique that carried on through the eighteenth century.

There's no such thing as certainty, that's plain
As any of Mortality's Conditions:
So little do we know what we're about in
This world, I doubt if doubt itself be doubting.

18

It is a pleasant voyage perhaps to float,
Like Pyrrho, on a sea of speculation,[13]
But what if carrying sail capsize the boat?
Your wise men don't know much of navigation;
And swimming long in the abyss of thought
Is apt to tire: a calm and shallow station
Well nigh the shore, where one stoops down and
gathers
Some pretty shell, is best for moderate bathers.

19

'But Heaven,' as Cassio says, 'is above all,—[14]
No more of this then,—let us pray!' We have
Souls to save, since Eve's slip and Adam's fall,
Which tumbled all mankind into the grave,
Besides fish, beasts, and birds. 'The Sparrow's fall[15]
Is special providence,' though how *it* gave
Offence, we know not; probably it perched
Upon the tree which Eve so fondly searched.

20

Oh, ye immortal Gods! what is Theogony?
Oh, thou too mortal Man! what is Philanthropy?
Oh, World! which was and is, what is Cosmogony?
Some people have accused me of Misanthropy;
And yet I know no more than the mahogany
That forms this desk, of what they mean;
—*Lykanthropy*[16]
I comprehend, for without transformation
Men become wolves on any slight occasion.

21

But I, the mildest, meekest of mankind,
Like Moses, or Melancthon,[17] who have ne'er
Done any thing exceedingly unkind,—
And (though I could not now and then forbear
Following the bent of body or of mind)
Have always had a tendency to spare,—
Why do they call me misanthrope? Because
They hate me, not I them:—And here we'll pause.

22

'Tis time we should proceed with our good poem,
For I maintain that it is really good,
Not only in the body, but the proem,[18]
However little both are understood
Just now,—but by and by the Truth will show 'em
Herself in her sublimest attitude:
And till she doth, I fain must be content
To share her Beauty and her Banishment.

23

Our Hero (and, I trust, kind reader! yours)—
Was left upon his way to the chief City
Of the immortal Peter's polished boors,[19]
Who still have shown themselves more brave than
witty.
I know its mighty Empire now allures
Much flattery—even Voltaire's, and that's a pity.
For me, I deem an absolute Autocrat
Not a Barbarian, but much worse than that.

24

And I will war, at least in words (and—should
My chance so happen—deeds) with all who war
With Thought;—and of Thought's foes by far most
rude,
Tyrants and Sycophants have been and are.
I know not who may conquer: if I could
Have such a prescience, it should be no bar

[13] **Like Pyrrho . . . speculation**: Pyrrhon (c. 365–60–275–70 BC), the founder of Greek scepticism, who believed that no positive knowledge is possible.

[14] **'But Heaven . . . above all'**: cf. *Othello*, II.iii.105–15: "Well, [God's] above all; and there be souls must be saved, and there be souls must not be saved. / . . . / Let's have no more of this; let's to our affairs."

[15] **'The Sparrow's fall'**: cf. *Hamlet*, V.II.230–31: "There's a special providence in the fall of a sparrow."

[16] **Theogony**: any work on the origin of gods. **Cosmogony**: on the origin of the universe. **Lykanthropy**: the ability to assume the characteristics of a wolf, as a werewolf.

[17] **Melancthon**: friend of Martin Luther.

[18] **proem**: introduction or preface.

[19] **Our Hero . . . boors**: Juan is on his way to St. Petersburg, to report on a Russian victory against the Turks in the Battle of Ismail (1790). Juan had fought well for the Russians.

To this my plain, sworn, downright detestation
Of every despotism in every nation.

25

It is not that I adulate the people:
Without *me,* there are Demagogues enough,
And Infidels, to pull down every steeple
And set up in their stead some proper stuff.
Whether they may sow Scepticism to reap Hell,
As is the Christian dogma rather rough,
I do not know;—I wish men to be free
As much from mobs as kings—from you as me.

26

The consequence is, being of no party,
I shall offend all parties:—never mind!
My words, at least, are more sincere and hearty
Than if I sought to sail before the wind.
He who has nought to gain can have small art: he
Who neither wishes to be bound nor bind,
May still expatiate freely, as will I,
Nor give my voice to Slavery's Jackall cry.

27

That's an appropriate simile, *that Jackall;*—
I've heard them in the Ephesian ruins howl
By night, as do that mercenary pack all,
Power's base purveyors, who for pickings prowl,
And scent the prey their masters would attack all.
However, the poor Jackalls are less foul
(As being the brave Lions' keen providers)
Than human Insects, catering for Spiders.

28

Raise but an arm! 'twill brush their web away,
And without *that,* their poison and their claws
Are useless. Mind, good People! what I say—
(Or rather Peoples)—*go on* without pause!
The web of these Tarantulas each day
Increases, till you shall make common cause:
None, save the Spanish Fly and Attic Bee,
As yet are strongly stinging to be free.

. . . .

—*from* CANTO XIII—

1

I now mean to be serious;—it is time,
Since laughter now-a-days is deemed too serious.
A jest at Vice by Virtue's called a crime,
And critically held as deleterious:
Besides, the sad's a source of the sublime,
Although when long a little apt to weary us;
And therefore shall my lay soar high and solemn
As an old temple dwindled to a column.

2

The Lady Adeline Amundeville—
('Tis an old Norman name, and to be found
In pedigrees by those who wander still
Along the last fields of that Gothic ground)—
Was high-born, wealthy by her father's will,
And beauteous, even where beauties most abound,
In Britain—which of course true patriots find
The goodliest soil of Body and of Mind.

3

I'll not gainsay them; it is not my cue;
I leave them to their taste, no doubt the best:
An eye's an eye, and whether black or blue,
Is no great matter, so 'tis in request:
'Tis nonsense to dispute about a hue—
The kindest may be taken as a test.
The fair sex should be always fair, and no man,
Till thirty, should perceive there's a plain woman.

4

And after that serene and somewhat dull
Epoch, that awkward corner turned for days
More quiet, when our Moon's no more at full,
We may presume to criticise or praise;
Because indifference begins to lull
Our passions, and we walk in Wisdom's ways;
Also because the figure and the face
Hint, that 'tis time to give the younger place.

5

I know that some would fain postpone this era,
Reluctant as all placemen to resign
Their post; but theirs is merely a chimera,
For they have passed life's equinoctial line:
But then they have their claret and madeira
To irrigate the dryness of decline;
And County Meetings and the Parliament,
And debt, and what not, for their solace sent.

6

And is there not Religion, and Reform,
Peace, War, the taxes, and what's called the
'Nation?'

The struggle to be Pilots in a storm?
    The landed and the monied speculation?
The joys of mutual hate, to keep them warm,
    Instead of love, that mere hallucination?
Now hatred is by far the longest pleasure;
Men love in haste, but they detest at leisure.

7

Rough Johnson, the great moralist, professed,
    Right honestly, 'he liked an honest hater'—[1]
The only truth that yet has been confest
    Within these latest thousand years or later.
Perhaps the fine old fellow spoke in jest:—
    For my part, I am but a mere spectator,
And gaze where'er the palace or the hovel is,
Much in the mode of Goethe's Mephistopheles,[2]

8

But neither love nor hate in much excess;
    Though 'twas not once so. If I sneer sometimes,
It is because I cannot well do less,
    And now and then it also suits my rhymes.
I should be very willing to redress
    Men's wrongs, and rather check than punish
        crimes,
Had not Cervantes in that too true tale
Of Quixote, shown how all such efforts fail.

9

Of all tales 'tis the saddest—and more sad,
    Because it makes us smile: his hero's right,
And still pursues the right;—to curb the bad,
    His only object, and 'gainst odds to fight,
His guerdon: 'tis his virtue makes him mad!
    But his adventures form a sorry sight;—
A sorrier still is the great moral taught
By that real Epic unto all who have thought.

10

Redressing injury, revenging wrong,
    To aid the damsel and destroy the caitiff;[3]
Opposing singly the united strong,
    From foreign yoke to free the hapless native;—
Alas! Must noblest views, like an old song,
    Be for mere Fancy's sport a theme creative?
A jest, a riddle, Fame through thin and thick sought?
And Socrates himself but Wisdom's Quixote?

11

Cervantes smiled Spain's Chivalry away;
    A single laugh demolished the right arm
Of his own country;—seldom since that day
    Has Spain had heroes. While Romance could
        charm,
The world gave ground before her bright array;
    And therefore have his volumes done such harm,
That all their glory, as a composition,
Was dearly purchased by his land's perdition.

12

I'm 'at my old Lunes'[4]—digression, and forget
    The Lady Adeline Amundeville;
The fair most fatal Juan ever met,
    Although she was not evil, nor meant ill;
But Destiny and Passion spread the net,
    (Fate is a good excuse for our own will)
And caught them;—what do they *not* catch,
        methinks?
But I'm not Oedipus, and life's a Sphinx.

13

I tell the tale as it is told, nor dare
    To venture a solution: *'Davus sum!'*[5]
And now I will proceed upon the pair.
    Sweet Adeline, amidst the gay world's hum,
Was the Queen-Bee, the glass of all that's fair;
    Whose charms made all men speak, and women
        dumb.
The last's a miracle, and such was reckoned,
And since that time there has not been a second.

14

Chaste was she, to detraction's desperation,
    And wedded unto one she had loved well;

[1] **'he liked an honest hater'**: cf. James Boswell's *Life of Samuel Johnson* (1791).

[2] **Mephistopheles**: the devil's name in Goethe's poetic drama *Faust* (1808, 1832).

[3] **caitiff**: coward.

[4] **'at my old Lunes'**: cf. letter from Samuel Johnson to Mrs. Thrale, 14 November: "My master is in his old lunes and so am I." A lune is a fit or frenzy.

[5] **'Davus sum!'**: a proverb from Terence: "Davus sum, non Oedipus," [I am Davus, not Oedipus], Davus being a name frequently given to Roman slaves in the comedies of Plautus and Terence (*Oxford Latin Dictionary*).

A man known in the councils of the nation,
Cool, and quite English; imperturbable,
Though apt to act with fire upon occasion;
Proud of himself and her, the world could tell
Nought against either, and both seemed secure—
She in her virtue, he in his hauteur.[6]

15

It chanced some diplomatical relations,
Arising out of business, often brought
Himself and Juan in their mutual stations
Into close contact. Though reserved, nor caught
By specious seeming, Juan's youth, and patience,
And talent, on his haughty spirit wrought,
And formed a basis of esteem, which ends
In making men what Courtesy calls friends.

16

And thus Lord Henry, who was cautious as
Reserve and pride could make him, and full slow
In judging men—when once his judgment was
Determined, right or wrong, on friend or foe,
Had all the pertinacity pride has,
Which knows no ebb to its imperious flow,
And loves or hates, disdaining to be guided,
Because its own good pleasure hath decided.

17

His friendship therefore, and no less aversions,
Though oft well founded, which confirmed but more
His prepossessions, like the laws of Persians
And Medes, would ne'er revoke what went before.
His feelings had not those strange fits, like tertians,[7]
Of common likings, which make some deplore
What they should laugh at—the mere ague still
Of Men's regard, the fever or the chill.

18

''Tis not in mortals to command success;
But *do you more,* Sempronius—*don't* deserve it;'[8]
And take my word, you won't have any less:
Be wary, watch the time, and always serve it;
Give gently way, when there's too great a press;
And for your conscience, only learn to nerve it,—
For, like a racer or a boxer training,
'Twill make, if proved, vast efforts without paining.

19

Lord Henry also liked to be superior,
As most men do, the little or the great;
The very lowest find out an inferior,
At least they think so, to exert their state
Upon: for there are very few things wearier
Than solitary Pride's oppressive weight,
Which mortals generously would divide,
By bidding others carry while they ride.

20

In birth, in rank, in fortune likewise equal
O'er Juan he could no distinction claim;
In years he had the advantage of time's sequel;
And, as he thought, in country much the same—
Because bold Britons have a tongue and free quill,
At which all modern nations vainly aim;
And the Lord Henry was a great debater,
So that few members kept the House up later.

21

These were advantages: and then he thought—
It was his foible, but by no means sinister—
That few or none more than himself had caught
Court mysteries, having been himself a minister:
He liked to teach that which he had been taught,
And greatly shone whenever there had been a stir;
And reconciled all qualities which grace man,
Always a Patriot, and sometimes a Placeman.

22

He liked the gentle Spaniard for his gravity;
He almost honoured him for his docility,
Because, though young, he acquiesced with suavity,
Or contradicted but with proud humility.
He knew the world, and would not see depravity
In faults which sometimes show the soil's fertility,
If that the weeds o'erlive not the first crop,—
For then they are very difficult to stop.

23

And then he talked with him about Madrid,
Constantinople, and such distant places;

[6] **hauteur:** *trans.* arrogance.

[7] **tertians:** form of malaria.

[8] **'Tis not . . . deserve it':** cf. Joseph Addison's *Cato*, I.ii. (McGann).

Where people always did as they were bid,
  Or did what they should not with foreign graces.
Of coursers also spake they: Henry rid
  Well, like most Englishmen, and loved the races;
And Juan, like a true-born Andalusian,
Could back a horse, as despots ride a Russian.

24

And thus acquaintance grew, at noble routs,
  And diplomatic dinners, or at other—
For Juan stood well both with Ins and Outs,
  As in Freemasonry[9] a higher brother.
Upon his talent Henry had no doubts,
  His manner showed him sprung from a high
    mother;
And all men like to show their hospitality
To him whose breeding marches with his quality.

25

At Blank-Blank Square;—for we will break no squares
  By naming streets: since men are so censorious,
And apt to sow an author's wheat with tares,[10]
  Reaping allusions private and inglorious,
Where none were dreamt of, unto love's affairs,
  Which were, or are, or are to be notorious,
That therefore do I previously declare,
Lord Henry's mansion was in Blank-Blank Square.

26

Also there bin another pious reason
  For making squares and streets anonymous;
Which is, that there is scarce a single season
  Which doth not shake some very splendid house
With some slight heart-quake of domestic treason—
  A topic Scandal doth delight to rouse:
Such I might stumble over unawares,
Unless I knew the very chastest Squares.

27

'Tis true, I might have chosen Piccadilly,
  A place where peccadillos are unknown;
But I have motives, whether wise or silly,
  For letting that pure sanctuary alone.
Therefore I name not square, street, place, until I
  Find one where nothing naughty can be shown,
A vestal shrine of innocence of heart:
Such are——but I have lost the London Chart.

28

At Henry's mansion then, in Blank-Blank Square,
  Was Juan a *recherché*,[11] welcome guest,
As many other noble Scions were;
  And some who had but talent for their crest;
Or wealth, which is a passport every where;
  Or even mere fashion, which indeed's the best
Recommendation;—and to be well drest
Will very often supersede the rest.

29

And since 'there's safety in a multitude
  Of counsellors,' as Solomon has said,[12]
Or some one for him, in some sage, grave mood;—
  Indeed we see the daily proof displayed
In Senates, at the Bar, in wordy feud,
  Where'er collective wisdom can parade,
Which is the only cause that we can guess
Of Britain's present wealth and happiness;—

30

But as 'there's safety grafted in the number
  Of Counsellors' for men,—thus for the sex
A large acquaintance lets not Virtue slumber;
  Or should it shake, the choice will more perplex—
Variety itself will more encumber.
  'Midst many rocks we guard more against wrecks;
And thus with women: howsoe'er it shock some's
Self-love, there's safety in a crowd of coxcombs.

31

But Adeline had not the least occasion
  For such a shield, which leaves but little merit
To virtue proper, or good education.
  Her chief resource was in her own high spirit,
Which judged mankind at their due estimation;
  And for coquetry, she disdained to wear it:
Secure of admiration, its impression
Was faint, as of an every-day possession.

---

[9] **Freemasonry:** secret fraternity.

[10] **tares:** weeds. Cf. Matthew 13:25: "his enemy came and sowed tares among the wheat."

[11] **recherché:** sought after.

[12] **'there's safety . . . counsellors':** cf. Proverbs 11:14: "in the multitude of counsellors there is safety."

32

To all she was polite without parade;
To some she showed attention of that kind
Which flatters, but is flattery conveyed
In such a sort as cannot leave behind
A trace unworthy either wife or maid;—
A gentle, genial courtesy of mind,
To those who were or passed for meritorious,
Just to console sad Glory for being glorious;

33

Which is in all respects, save now and then,
A dull and desolate appendage. Gaze
Upon the Shades of those distinguished men,
Who were or are the puppet-shows of praise,
The praise of persecution. Gaze again
On the most favoured; and amidst the blaze
Of sunset halos o'er the laurel-browed,
What can ye recognize?—A gilded cloud.

from Don Juan, [XV–XVI]

(1824; comp. 1824)

—*from* CANTO XV—

1

Ah!—What should follow slips from my reflection:
Whatever follows ne'ertheless may be
As apropos of hope or retrospection,
As though the lurking thought had follow'd free.
All present life is but an Interjection,
An 'Oh!' or 'Ah!' of joy or misery,
Or a 'Ha! ha!' or 'Bah!'—a yawn, or 'Pooh!'
Of which perhaps the latter is most true.

2

But, more or less, the whole's a syncopé
Or a singultus[1]—emblems of Emotion,
The grand Antithesis to great Ennui,
Wherewith we break our bubbles on the ocean,
That Watery Outline of Eternity,
Or miniature at least, as is my notion,
Which ministers unto the soul's delight,
In seeing matters which are out of sight.

3

But all are better than the sigh suppress,
Corroding in the cavern of the heart,
Making the countenance a masque of rest,
And turning human nature to an art.
Few men dare show their thoughts of worst or best;
Dissimulation always sets apart
A corner for herself; and therefore Fiction
Is that which passes with least contradiction.

4

Ah! who can tell? Or rather, who can not
Remember, without telling, passion's errors?
The drainer of oblivion, even the sot,
Hath got blue devils[2] for his morning mirrors:
What though on Lethe's stream he seem to float,
He cannot sink his tremors or his terrors;
The ruby glass that shakes within his hand,
Leaves a sad sediment of Time's worst sand.

5

And as for Love—Oh, Love!—We will proceed.
The Lady Adeline Amundeville,
A pretty name as one would wish to read,
Must perch harmonious on my tuneful quill.
There's music in the sighing of a reed;
There's music in the gushing of a rill;
There's music in all things, if men had ears:
Their Earth is but an echo of the spheres.[3]

6

The Lady Adeline, right honourable,
And honour'd, ran a risk of growing less so;
For few of the soft sex are very stable
In their resolves—alas! that I should say so!
They differ as wine differs from its label,
When once decanted;—I presume to guess so,
But will not swear: yet both upon occasion,
Till old, may undergo adulteration.

[1] **syncopé:** a swoon. **singultus:** sob.

[2] **blue devils:** the blues, the condition of being downcast.

[3] **Earth . . . spheres:** planets in the Ptolemaic system of astronomy were believed to create harmonious sounds as they vibrated and moved through the heavens, thus music of the spheres is natural and perfect.

7

But Adeline was of the purest vintage,
  The unmingled essence of the grape; and yet
Bright as a new Napoleon[4] from its mintage,
  Or glorious as a diamond richly set;
A page where Time should hesitate to print age,
  And for which Nature might forego her debt—
Sole creditor whose process doth involve in't
The luck of finding every body solvent.

. . . .

11

Some parts of Juan's history, which Rumour,
  That live Gazette, had scatter'd to disfigure,
She had heard; but women hear with more good
  humour
  Such aberrations than we men of rigour.
Besides, his conduct, since in England, grew more
  Strict, and his mind assumed a manlier vigour;
Because he had, like Alcibiades,[5]
The art of living in all climes with ease.

12

His manner was perhaps the more seductive,
  Because he ne'er seem'd anxious to seduce;
Nothing affected, studied, or constructive
  Of coxcombry or conquest: no abuse
Of his attractions marr'd the fair perspective,
  To indicate a Cupidon broke loose,
And seem to say, 'resist us if you can'—
Which makes a dandy while it spoils a man.

13

They are wrong—that's not the way to set about it;
  As, if they told the truth, could well be shown.
But right or wrong, Don Juan was without it;
  In fact, his manner was his own alone:
Sincere he was—at least you could not doubt it,
  In listening merely to his voice's tone.
The Devil hath not in all his quiver's choice
An arrow for the heart like a sweet voice.

[4] **Napoleon:** a twenty-franc gold coin.

[5] **Alcibiades:** Athenian general and statesman.

14

By Nature soft, his whole address held off
  Suspicion: though not timid, his regard
Was such as rather seem'd to keep aloof,
  To shield himself, than put you on your guard:
Perhaps 'twas hardly quite assured enough,
  But Modesty's at times its own reward,
Like Virtue; and the absence of pretension
Will go much further than there's need to mention.

15

Serene, accomplish'd, cheerful but not loud;
  Insinuating without insinuation;
Observant of the foibles of the crowd,
  Yet ne'er betraying this in conversation;
Proud with the proud, yet courteously proud,
  So as to make them feel he knew his station
And theirs:—without a struggle for priority,
He neither brook'd nor claim'd superiority.

16

That is, with men: with women he was what
  They pleased to make or take him for; and their
Imagination's quite enough for that:
  So that the outline's tolerably fair,
They fill the canvass up—and 'verbum sat.'
  If once their phantasies be brought to bear
Upon an object, whether sad or playful,
They can transfigure brighter than a Raphael.

17

Adeline, no deep judge of character,
  Was apt to add a colouring from her own.
'Tis thus the good will amiably err,
  And eke the wise, as has been often shown.
Experience is the chief philosopher,
  But saddest when his science is well known:
And persecuted sages teach the schools
Their folly in forgetting there are fools.

. . . .

38

Had Adeline read Malthus?[6] I can't tell;
  I wish she had: his book's the eleventh
    commandment,

[6] See Society and Political Economy and Malthus.*

Which says, 'thou shalt not marry,' unless *well*:
This he (as far as I can understand) meant:
'Tis not my purpose on his views to dwell,
Nor canvass what 'so eminent a hand' meant;
But *certes* it conducts to lives ascetic,
Or turning marriage into arithmetic.

39

But Adeline, who probably presumed
That Juan had enough of maintenance,
Or *separate* maintenance, in case 'twas doom'd—
As on the whole it is an even chance
That bridegrooms, after they are fairly *groom'd*,
May retrograde a little in the dance
Of marriage—(which might form a painter's fame,
Like Holbein's 'Dance of Death'[7]—but 'tis the same);—

40

But Adeline determined Juan's wedding
In her own mind, and that's enough for woman.
But then, with whom? There was the sage Miss Reading,
Miss Raw, Miss Flaw, Miss Showman, and Miss Knowman,
And the two fair co-heiresses Giltbedding.
She deemed his merits something more than common:
All these were unobjectionable matches,
And might go on, if well wound up, like watches.

41

There was Miss Millpond, smooth as summer's sea,
That usual paragon, an only daughter,
Who seem'd the cream of equanimity,
Till skimm'd—and then there was some milk and water,
With a slight shade of Blue[8] too it might be,
Beneath the surface; but what did it matter?
Love's riotous, but marriage should have quiet,
And being consumptive, live on a milk diet.

42

And then there was the Miss Audacia Shoestring,
A dashing demoiselle[9] of good estate,
Whose heart was fix'd upon a star or bluestring;
But whether English Dukes grew rare of late,
Or that she had not harp'd upon the true string,
By which such sirens can attract our great,
She took up with some foreign younger brother,
A Russ or Turk—the one's as good as t'other.

43

And then there was—but why should I go on,
Unless the ladies should go off?—there was
Indeed a certain fair and fairy one,
Of the best class, and better than her class,—
Aurora Raby, a young star who shone
O'er life, too sweet an image for such glass,
A lovely being, scarcely form'd or moulded,
A Rose with all its sweetest leaves yet folded;

44

Rich, noble, but an orphan; left an only
Child to the care of guardians good and kind;
But still her aspect had an air so lonely!
Blood is not water; and where shall we find
Feelings of youth like those which overthrown lie
By death, when we are left, alas! behind,
To feel, in friendless palaces, a home
Is wanting, and our best ties in the tomb?

45

Early in years, and yet more infantine
In figure, she had something of sublime
In eyes which sadly shone, as seraphs' shine.
All youth—but with an aspect beyond time;
Radiant and grave—as pitying man's decline;
Mournful—but mournful of another's crime,
She look'd as if she sat by Eden's door,
And grieved for those who could return no more.

46

She was a Catholic too, sincere, austere,
As far as her own gentle heart allow'd,
And deem'd that fallen worship far more dear
Perhaps because 'twas fallen: her sires were proud

[7] **'Dance of Death'**: Hans Holbein's (1497–1543) series of woodcuts, *The Dance of Death*, was extremely popular and influential in nineteenth-century England.

[8] **Blue**: reference to Bluestockings, or women intellectuals (See RIGHTS OF WOMAN).

[9] **demoiselle**: young woman.

Of deeds and days when they had fill'd the ear
Of nations, and had never bent or bow'd
To novel power; and as she was the last,
She held their old faith and old feelings fast.

47

She gazed upon a world she scarcely knew
As seeking not to know it; silent, lone,
As grows a flower, thus quietly she grew,
And kept her heart serene within its zone.
There was awe in the homage which she drew;
Her spirit seem'd as seated on a throne
Apart from the surrounding world, and strong
In its own strength—most strange in one so young!

48

Now it so happen'd, in the catalogue
Of Adeline, Aurora was omitted,
Although her birth and wealth had given her vogue
Beyond the charmers we have already cited;
Her beauty also seem'd to form no clog
Against her being mention'd as well fitted,
By many virtues, to be worth the trouble
Of single gentlemen who would be double.

49

And this omission, like that of the bust
Of Brutus at the pageant of Tiberius,[10]
Made Juan wonder, as no doubt the must.
This he express'd half smiling and half serious;
When Adeline replied with some disgust,
And with an air, to say the least, imperious,
She marvell'd 'what he saw in such a baby
As that prim, silent, cold Aurora Raby?'

50

Juan rejoined—'She was a Catholic,
And therefore fittest, as of his persuasion;
Since he was sure his mother would fall sick,
And the Pope thunder excommunication,
If——' But here Adeline, who seem'd to pique
Herself extremely on the inoculation
Of others with her own opinions, stated—
As usual—the same reason which she late did.

[10]**And this omission . . . bust:** "The Caesar's pageant, shorn of Brutus' bust, / Did but of Rome's best Son remind her more" (*Childe Harold's Pilgrimage*, IV.525–26).

51

And wherefore not? A reasonable reason,
If good, is none the worse for repetition;
If bad, the best way's certainly to teaze on
And amplify: you lose much by concision,
Whereas insisting in or out of season
Convinces all men, even a politician;
Or—what is just the same—it wearies out.
So the end's gain'd, what signifies the route?

52

Why Adeline had this slight prejudice—
For prejudice it was—against a creature
As pure as sanctity itself from vice,
With all the added charm of form and feature,
For me appears a question far too nice,
Since Adeline was liberal by Nature;
But Nature's Nature, and has more caprices
Than I have time, or will, to take to pieces.

53

Perhaps she did not like the quiet way
With which Aurora on those baubles look'd,
Which charm most people in their earlier day:
For there are few things by mankind less brook'd,
And womankind too, if we so may say,
Than finding thus their genius stand rebuked,
Like 'Anthony's by Caesar,' by the few[11]
Who look upon them as they ought to do.

54

It was not envy—Adeline had none;
Her place was far beyond it, and her mind.
It was not scorn—which could not light on one
Whose greatest *fault* was leaving few to find.
It was not jealousy, I think: but shun
Following the 'Ignes Fatui'[12] of mankind.
It was not——but 'tis easier far, alas!
To say what it was not, than what it was.

[11]**their genius stand . . . few:** cf. *Macbeth*, III.i.56–57: "My genius is rebuk'd, as, it is said, / Mark Antony's was by Caesar."

[12]**'Ignes Fatui':** *trans.* "Foolish fires"; the phosphorescent lights that hover over swampy areas giving the illusion of fire; hence, that which misleads or deludes with brightness.

55

Little Aurora deem'd she was the theme
Of such discussion. She was there a guest,
A beauteous ripple of the brilliant stream
Of rank and youth, though purer than the rest,
Which flow'd on for a moment in the beam
Time sheds a moment o'er each sparkling crest.
Had she known this, she would have calmly smiled—
She had so much, or little, of the child.

56

The dashing and proud air of Adeline
Imposed not upon her: she saw her blaze
Much as she would have seen a glowworm shine,
Then turn'd unto the stars for loftier rays.
Juan was something she could not divine,
Being no Sibyl in the new world's ways;
Yet she was nothing dazzled by the meteor,
Because she did not pin her faith on feature.

57

His fame too,—for he had that kind of fame
Which sometimes plays the deuce with womankind,
A heterogeneous mass of glorious blame,
Half virtues and whole vices being combined;
Faults which attract because they are not tame;
Follies trick'd out so brightly that they blind:—
These seals upon her wax made no impression,
Such was her coldness or her self-possession.

58

Juan knew nought of such a character—
High, yet resembling not his lost Haidée;
Yet each was radiant in her proper sphere:
The Island girl, bred up by the lone sea,
More warm, as lovely, and not less sincere,
Was Nature's all: Aurora could not be
Nor would be thus;—the difference in them
Was such as lies between a flower and gem.

59

Having wound up with this sublime comparison,
Methinks we may proceed upon our narrative,
And, as my friend Scott says, 'I sound my Warison';[13]
Scott, the superlative of my comparative—
Scott, who can paint your Christian knight or Saracen,
Serf, Lord, Man, with such skill as none would share it, if
There had not been one Shakespeare and Voltaire,
Of one or both of whom he seems the heir.

60

I say, in my slight way I may proceed
To play upon the surface of Humanity.
I write the world, nor care if the world read,
At least for this I cannot spare its vanity.
My Muse hath bred, and still perhaps may breed
More foes by this same scroll: when I began it, I
Thought that it might turn out so—*now* I *know* it,
But still I am, or was, a pretty poet

. . . .

—CANTO XVI—

1

The antique Persians taught three useful things,
To draw the bow, to ride, and speak the truth.
This was the mode of Cyrus,[1] best of kings—
A mode adopted since by modern youth.
Bows have they, generally with two strings;
Horses they ride without remorse or ruth;
At speaking truth perhaps they are less clever,
But draw the long bow better now than ever.

2

The cause of this effect, or this defect,—
'For this effect defective comes by cause,'—[2]
Is what I have not leisure to inspect;
But this I must say in my own applause,
Of all the Muses that I recollect,
Whate'er may be her follies or her flaws
In some things, mine's beyond all contradiction
The most sincere that ever dealt in fiction.

3

And as she treats all things, and ne'er retreats
From any thing, this Epic will contain

---

[13] 'I sound my Warison': from *Lay of the Last Minstrel,* IV.24.

[1] **Cyrus**: Cyrus I, founder of the Persian Empire (559–529 BC), admired as a model king by the Greeks for the wisdom and tolerance he practiced toward peoples he conquered.

[2] 'For this effect . . . cause': cf. *Hamlet,* II.ii.103.

A wilderness of the most rare conceits,
  Which you might elsewhere hope to find in vain,
'Tis true there be some bitters with the sweets,
  Yet mixed so slightly that you can't complain,
But wonder they so few are, since my tale is
  'De rebus cunctis et quibûsdam aliis'.[3]

4

But of all truths which she has told, the most
  True is that which she is about to tell.
I said it was a story of a ghost—
  What then? I only know it so befell.
Have you explored the limits of the coast,
  Where all the dwellers of the earth must dwell?
'Tis time to strike such puny doubters dumb as
The sceptics who would not believe Columbus.

5

Some people would impose now with authority,
  Turpin's or Monmouth Geoffry's Chronicle;[4]
Men whose historical superiority
  Is always greatest at a miracle.
But Saint Augustine has the great priority,
  Who bids all men believe the impossible,
Because 'tis so. Who nibble, scribble, quibble, he
Quiets at once with *'quia* impossibile'.[5]

6

And therefore, mortals, cavil not at all;
  Believe:—if 'tis improbable, you *must*;
And if it is impossible, you *shall*:
  'Tis always best to take things upon trust.
I do not speak profanely, to recall
  Those holier mysteries, which the wise and just
Receive as gospel, and which grow more rooted,
As all truths must, the more they are disputed.

7

I merely mean to say what Johnson[6] said,
  That in the course of some six thousand years,
All nations have believed that from the dead
  A visitant at intervals appears;
And what is strangest upon this strange head,
  Is, that whatever bar the reason rears
'Gainst such belief, there's something stronger still
In its behalf, let those deny who will.

8

The dinner and the soirée too were done,
  The supper too discussed, the dames admired,
The banqueteers had dropped off one by one—
  The song was silent, and the dance expired:
The last thin petticoats were vanished, gone
  Like fleecy clouds into the sky retired,
And nothing brighter gleamed through the saloon
Than dying tapers—and the peeping moon.

9

The evaporation of a joyous day
  Is like the last glass of champagne, without
The foam which made its virgin bumper[7] gay;
  Or like a system coupled with a doubt;
Or like a soda bottle when its spray
  Has sparkled and let half its spirit out;
Or like a billow left by storms behind,
Without the animation of the wind;

10

Or like an opiate which brings troubled rest,
  Or none; or like—like nothing that I know
Except itself;—such is the human breast;
  A thing, of which similitudes can show
No real likeness,—like the old Tyrian vest
  Dyed purple, none at present can tell how,
If from a shell-fish or from cochineal.[8]
So perish every tyrant's robe piece-meal!

[3] **'De rebus . . . aliis':** *trans.* concerning all things and some other things: amalgamation from the titles of two works by Thomas Aquinas, *De Omnibus* and *De Quibusdam Aliis.*

[4] **Monmouth Geoffrey:** Geoffrey of Monmouth, Bishop of St. Asaph (1152), wrote *Historia Regum Britanniae* (c. 1136), which did much to establish Arthurian legend. **Turpin:** historian who wrote earlier on religious history.

[5] **'quia impossibile':** allusion to the comment of Tertullian (150 BC) (not Augustine) from *The Body of Christ* that 'I believe because it is impossible.'

[6] **Johnson:** Samuel Johnson (1709–1784), preeminent man-of-letters of the eighteenth century, from *Rasselas,* Chap. XXX: "There is no people, rude or learned, among whom apparitions of the dead are not related and believed."

[7] **virgin bumper:** glass when filled to the brim.

[8] **like the old Tyrian vest . . . cochineal:** Tyrian purple and Cochineal are dyes made from mollusks and from the bodies of tropical female insects.

11

But next to dressing for a rout or ball,
  Undressing is a woe; our robe de chambre
May sit like that of Nessus and recall[9]
  Thoughts quite as yellow, but less clear than amber.
Titus exclaimed, 'I've lost a day!'[10] Of all
  The nights and days most people can remember,
(I have had of both, some not to be disdained)
I wish they'd state how many they have gained.

12

And Juan, on retiring for the night,
  Felt restless, and perplexed, and compromised;
He thought Aurora Raby's eyes more bright
  Than Adeline (such is advice) advised;
If he had known exactly his own plight,
  He probably would have philosophized;
A great resource to all, and ne'er denied
Till wanted; therefore Juan only sighed.

13

He sighed;—the next resource is the full moon,
  Where all sighs are deposited; and now
It happened luckily, the chaste orb shone
  As clear as such a climate will allow;
And Juan's mind was in the proper tone
  To hail her with the apostrophe—'Oh, Thou!'
Of amatory egotism the *Tuism*,[11]
Which further to explain would be a truism.

14

But lover, poet, or astronomer,
  Shepherd, or swain, whoever may behold,
Feel some abstraction when they gaze on her:
  Great thoughts we catch from thence (besides a cold
Sometimes, unless my feelings rather err);
  Deep secrets to her rolling light are told;
The ocean's tides and mortal's brains she sways,
And also hearts, if there be truth in lays.

15

Juan felt somewhat pensive, and disposed
  For contemplation rather than his pillow:
The Gothic chamber, where he was enclosed,
  Let in the rippling sound of the lake's billow,
With all the mystery by midnight caused;
  Below his window waved (of course) a willow;[12]
And he stood gazing out on the cascade
That flashed and after darkened in the shade.

16

Upon his table or his toilet,—*which*
  Of these is not exactly ascertained—
(I state this, for I am cautious to a pitch
  Of nicety, where a fact is to be gained)
A lamp burned high, while he leant from a niche,
  Where many a gothic ornament remained,
In chiselled stone and painted glass, and all
That time has left our father of their Hall.

17

Then, as the night was clear though cold, he threw
  His chamber door wide open—and went forth
Into a gallery, of a sombre hue,
  Long, furnished with old pictures of great worth,
Of knights and dames heroic and chaste too,
  As doubtless should be people of high birth.
But by dim lights the portraits of the dead
Have something ghastly, desolate, and dread.

18

The frowns of the grim knights and pictured saint
  Look living in the moon; and as you turn
Backward and forward to the echoes faint
  Of your own footsteps—voices from the urn
Appear to wake, and shadows wild and quaint
  Start from the frames which fence their aspects stern,
As if to ask how you can dare to keep
A vigil there, where all but death should sleep.

---

[9] **Undressing is a woe . . . :** Hercules killed the centaur Nessus with a poison arrow for attempting to rape his wife. She later dipped Hercules's shirt in Nessus's blood to assure his fidelity, but the poison so inflicted his limbs with pain that he ripped away his flesh with the garment.

[10] **'I've lost a day!':** according to the biographer Suetonious (AD c. 70–c. 140), the emperor Titus lamented spending a day without doing some good for his subjects.

[11] **Tuism:** form of expression using the pronoun "Thou." In ethics, a concern for the other.

[12] **willow:** tree associated with spirits and witches.

19

And the pale smile of Beauties in the grave,
The charms of other days, in starlight gleams
Glimmer on high; their buried locks still wave
Along the canvas; their eyes glance like dreams
On ours, or spars within some dusky cave,
But death is imaged in their shadowy beams
A picture is the past; even ere its frame
Be gilt, who sate hath ceased to be the same.

20

As Juan mused on mutability,
Or on his mistress — terms synonymous —
No sound except the echo of his sigh
Or step ran sadly through that antique house,
When suddenly he heard, or thought so, nigh,
A supernatural agent — or a mouse,
Whose little nibbling rustle will embarrass
Most people as it plays along the arras.[13]

21

It was no mouse, but lo! a monk, arrayed
In cowl and beads and dusky garb, appeared,
Now in the moonlight, and now lapsed in shade,
With steps that trod as heavy, yet unheard;
His garments only a slight murmur made;
He moved as shadowy as the sisters weird,[14]
But slowly; and as he passed Juan by,
Glanced, without pausing, on him a bright eye.

22

Juan was petrified; he had heard a hint
Of such a spirit in these halls of old,
But thought, like most men, there was nothing in't
Beyond the rumour which such spots unfold,
Coined from surviving superstition's mint,
Which passes ghosts in currency like gold,
But rarely seen, like gold compared with paper.
And *did* he see this? or was it a vapour?

23

Once, twice, thrice passed, repassed — the thing of air,
Or earth beneath, or heaven, or t'other place;
And Juan gazed upon it with a stare,
Yet could not speak or move; but, on its base
As stands a statue, stood: he felt his hair
Twine like a knot of snakes around his face;
He taxed his tongue for words, which were not granted,
To ask the reverend person what he wanted.

24

The third time, after a still longer pause,
The shadow passed away — but where? the hall
Was long, and thus far there was no great cause
To think his vanishing unnatural:
Doors there were many, through which, by the laws
Of physics, bodies whether short or tall
Might come or go; but Juan could not state
Through which the spectre seemed to evaporate.

25

He stood — how long he knew not, but it seemed
An age, — expectant, powerless, with his eyes
Strained on the spot where first the figure gleamed;
Then by degrees recalled his energies,
And would have passed the whole off as a dream,
But could not wake; he was, he did surmise,
Waking already, and returned at length
Back to his chamber, shorn of half his strength.

26

All there was as he left it: still his taper
Burnt, and not *blue*, as modest tapers use,
Receiving sprites with sympathetic vapour;
He rubbed his eyes, and they did not refuse
Their office; he took up an old newspaper;
The paper was right easy to peruse;
He read an article the king attacking,
And a long eulogy of 'Patent Blacking.'[15]

27

This savoured of this world; but his hand shook —
He shut his door, and after having read
A paragraph, I think about Horne Tooke,[16]
Undrest, and rather slowly went to bed.

[13] **arras:** hanging tapestry.

[14] **sisters weird:** the witches from *Macbeth*.

[15] **'Patent Blacking':** shoe coloring protected by patent.

[16] **Horne Tooke:** John Horne Tooke (1736–1812), philologist and political radical once imprisoned for high treason, but later acquitted.

There couched all snugly on his pillow's nook,
With what he had seen his phantasy he fed,
And though it was no opiate, slumber crept
Upon him by degrees, and so he slept.

28

He woke betimes; and, as may be supposed,
Pondered upon his visitant or vision,
And whether it ought not to be disclosed,
At risk of being quizzed for superstition.
The more he thought, the more his mind was posed;
In the mean time, his valet, whose precision
Was great, because his master brooked no less,
Knocked to inform him it was time to dress.

29

He dressed; and like young people, he was wont
To take some trouble with his toilet, but
This morning rather spent less time upon't;
Aside his very mirror soon was put;
His curls fell negligently o'er his front,
His clothes were not curbed to their usual cut,
His very neckcloth's Gordian knot[17] was tied
Almost an hair's breadth too much on one side.

30

And when he walked down into the saloon,[18]
He sate him pensive o'er a dish of tea,
Which he perhaps had not discovered soon,
Had it not happened scalding hot to be,
Which made him have recourse unto his spoon;
So much distrait he was, that all could see
That something *was* the matter—Adeline
The first—but *what* she could not well divine.

31

She looked, and saw him pale, and turned as pale
Herself; then hastily looked down, and muttered
Something, but what's not stated in my tale.
Lord Henry said, his muffin was ill buttered;
The Duchess of Fitz-Fulke played with her veil,
And looked at Juan hard, but nothing uttered.
Aurora Raby, with her large dark eyes,
Surveyed him with a kind of calm surprise.

[17] **Gordian knot:** a complicated knot, so-named after the legendary knot of Gordius, of which an oracle proclaimed that whoever untied it would rule Asia.

[18] **saloon:** large reception room.

32

But seeing him all cold and silent still,
And every body wondering more or less,
Fair Adeline enquired, 'If he were ill?'
He started, and said, 'Yes—no—rather—yes.'
The family physician had great skill,
And being present, now began to express
His readiness to feel his pulse and tell
The cause, but Juan said, 'He was quite well.'

33

'Quite well; yes; no.'—These answers were mysterious,
And yet his looks appeared to sanction both,
However they might savour of delirious;
Something like illness of a sudden growth
Weighed on his spirit, though by no means serious.
But for the rest, as he himself seemed loth
To state the case, it might be ta'en for granted
It was not the physician that he wanted.

34

Lord Henry, who had now discussed his chocolate,
Also the muffin whereof he complained,
Said, Juan had not got his usual look elate,
At which he marvelled, since it had not rained;
Then asked her Grace what news were of the Duke of late?
Her Grace replied, *his* Grace was rather pained
With some slight, light, hereditary twinges
Of gout, which rusts aristocratic hinges.

35

Then Henry turned to Juan and addressed
A few words of condolence on his state:
'You look,' quoth he, 'as if you had had your rest
Broke in upon by the Black Friar of late.'
'What Friar?' said Juan; and he did his best
To put the question with an air sedate,
Or careless; but the effort was not valid
To hinder him from growing still more pallid.

36

'Oh! have you never heard of the Black Friar?
The spirit of these walls?'—'In truth not I.'
'Why Fame—but Fame you know's sometimes a liar—
Tells an odd story, of which by the bye:
Whether with time the spectre has grown shyer,
Or that our sires had a more gifted eye

For such sights, though the tale is half believed,
The Friar of late has not been oft perceived.

37

'The last time was——' 'I pray,' said Adeline,—
(Who watched the changes of Don Juan's brow,
And from its context thought she could divine
Connections stronger than he chose to avow
With this same legend)—'if you but design
To jest, you'll choose some other theme just now,
Because the present tale has oft been told,
And is not much improved by growing old.'

38

'Jest!' quoth Milor, 'Why, Adeline, you know
That we ourselves—'twas in the Honey Moon—
Saw——' 'Well, no matter, 'twas so long ago;
But, come, I'll set your story to a tune.'
Graceful as Dian when she draws her bow,
She seized her harp, whose strings were kindled soon
As touched, and plaintively began to play
The air of "Twas a Friar of Orders Grey.'

39

'But add the words,' cried Henry, 'which you made;
For Adeline is half a poetess,'
Turning round to the rest, he smiling said.
Of course the others could not but express
In courtesy their wish to see displayed
By one *three* talents, for there were no less—
The voice, the words, the harper's skill, at once
Could hardly be united by a dunce.

40

After some fascinating hesitation,—
The charming of these charmers, who seem bound,
I can't tell why, to this dissimulation,—
Fair Adeline, with eyes fixed on the ground
At first, then kindling into animation,
Added her sweet voice to the lyric sound,
And sang with much simplicity,—a merit
Not the less precious, that we seldom hear it.

1

Beware! beware! of the Black Friar,
Who sitteth by Norman stone,
For he mutters his prayer in the midnight air,
And his mass of the days that are gone.
When the Lord of the Hill, Amundeville,
Made Norman Church his prey,
And expelled the friars, one friar still
Would not be driven away.

2

Though he came in his might, with King Henry's right,
To turn church lands to lay,
With sword in hand, and torch to light
Their walls, if they said nay,
A monk remained, unchased, unchained,
And he did not seem formed of clay,
For he's seen in the porch, and he's seen in the church,
Though he is not seen by day.

3

And whether for good, or whether for ill,
It is not mine to say;
But still to the house of Amundeville
He abideth night and day.
By the marriage bed of their lords, 'tis said,
He flits on the bridal eve;
And 'tis held as faith, to their bed of death,
He comes—but not to grieve.

4

When an heir is born, he is heard to mourn,
And when aught is to befall
That ancient line, in the pale moonshine
He walks from hall to hall.
His form you may trace, but not his face,
'Tis shadowed by his cowl;
But his eyes may be seen from the folds between,
And they seem of a parted soul.

5

But beware! beware! of the Black Friar,
He still retains his sway,
For he is yet the church's heir
Who ever may be the lay.
Amundeville is lord by day,
But the monk is lord by night.
Nor wine nor wassail could raise a vassal
To question that friar's right.

6

Say nought to him as he walks the hall,
And he'll say nought to you;

He sweeps along in his dusky pall,
As o'er the grass the dew.
Then Grammercy![19] for the Black Friar;
Heaven sain[20] him! fair or foul,
And whatsoe'er may be his prayer,
Let ours be for his soul.

41

The lady's voice ceased, and the thrilling wires
Died from the touch that kindled them to sound;
And the pause followed, which when song expires,
Pervades a moment those who listen round;
And then of course the circle much admires,
Nor less applauds as in politeness bound,
The tones, the feeling, and the execution,
To the performer's diffident confusion.

42

Fair Adeline, though in a careless way,
As if she rated such accomplishment
As the mere pastime of an idle day,
Pursued an instant for her own content,
Would now and then as 'twere *without* display,
Yet *with* display in fact, at times relent
To such performances with haughty smile,
To show she *could,* if it were worth her while.

43

Now this (but we will whisper it aside)
Was—pardon the pedantic illustration—
Trampling on Plato's pride with greater pride,
As did the Cynic on some like occasion;
Deeming the sage would be much mortified,
Or thrown into a philosophic passion,
For a spoilt carpet—but the 'Attic Bee'
Was much consoled by his own repartee.[21]

44

Thus Adeline would throw into the shade,
(By doing easily whene'er she chose,
What dilettanti do with vast parade)
Their sort of *half profession:* for it grows
To something like this when too oft displayed,
And that it is so, every body knows,
Who have heard Miss That or This, or Lady T'other,
Show off—to please their company or mother.

45

Oh! the long evenings of duets and trios!
The admirations and the speculations;
The 'Mamma Mia's!' and the 'Amor Mio's!'
The 'Tanti palpiti's' on such occasions:
The 'Lasciami's,' and quavering 'Addio's!'[22]
Amongst our own most musical of nations;
With 'Tu mi chamas's' from Portingale,[23]
To soothe our ears, lest Italy should fail.

46

In Babylon's bravuras—as the home
Heart-ballads of Green Erin or Grey Highlands,
That bring Lochaber[24] back to eyes that roam
O'er far Atlantic continents or islands,
The calentures[25] of music which o'ercome
All mountaineers with dreams that they are nigh lands,
No more to be beheld but in such visions,—
Was Adeline well versed, as compositions.

47

She also had a twilight tinge of *'Blue,'*[26]
Could write rhymes, and compose more than she wrote;
Made epigrams occasionally too
Upon her friends, as every body ought.

[19] **Grammercy!**: expression meaning 'heaven have mercy.'

[20] **sain**: bless or protect from evil influence.

[21] **the 'Attic Bee' . . . repartee**: In a note, Byron explains his meaning: "I think it *was* a carpet on which Diogenes [the Cynic] trod, with—'Thus I trample on the pride of Plato!'—'With greater pride,' the other replied" (McGann). Plato is the "Attic Bee."

[22] **'Mamma Mia's!' . . . 'Amor Mio's!' . . . 'Tanti palpiti's . . . 'Lasciami's'**: "My mothers," "My loves," "So many heartbeats," "Farewells," "Good-byes."

[23] **'Tu mi chamas's'**: *trans.* "You call me [still your life]": a Portuguese song once translated by Byron.

[24] **Heart-ballads . . . Lochaber**: ballads that bring Ireland and Scotland to mind.

[25] **calentures**: fevers.

[26] **'Blue'**: Bluestocking, a female intellectual (see Rights of Woman).

But still from that sublimer azure hue,
So much the present dye, she was remote,
Was weak enough to deem Pope[27] a great poet,
And what was worse, was not ashamed to show it.

48

Aurora—since we are touching upon taste,
Which now-a-days is the thermometer
By whose degrees all characters are classed—
Was more Shakespearian, if I do not err.
The worlds beyond this world's perplexing waste
Had more of her existence, for in her
There was a depth of feeling to embrace
Thoughts, boundless, deep, but silent too as Space.

49

Not so her gracious, graceful, graceless Grace,
The full grown Hebe[28] of Fitz-Fulke, whose mind,
If she had any, was upon her face,
And that was of a fascinating kind.
A little turn for mischief you might trace
Also thereon,—but that's not much; we find
Few females without some such gentle leaven,
For fear we should suppose us quite in heaven.

50

I have not heard she was at all poetic,
Though once she was seen reading the 'Bath Guide',[29]
And 'Hayley's Triumphs,'[30] which she deemed pathetic,
Because, she said, *her temper* had been tried
So much, the bard had really been prophetic
Of what she had gone through with,—since a bride.
But of all verse, what most insured her praise
Were sonnets to herself, or 'Bouts rimés'.[31]

51

'Twere difficult to say what was the object
Of Adeline, in bringing this same lay
To bear on what appeared to her the subject
Of Juan's nervous feelings on that day.
Perhaps she merely had the simple project
To laugh him out of his supposed dismay;
Perhaps she might wish to confirm him in it,
Though why I cannot say—at least this minute.

52

But so far the immediate effect
Was to restore him to his self propriety,
A thing quite necessary to the elect,
Who wish to take the tone of their society:
In which you cannot be too circumspect,
Whether the mode be persiflage[32] or piety,
But wear the newest mantle of hypocrisy,
On pain of much displeasing the Gynocracy.[33]

53

And therefore Juan now began to rally
His spirits, and without more explanation,
To jest upon such themes in many a sally.
Her Grace too also seized the same occasion,
With various similar remarks to tally,
But wished for a still more detailed narration
Of this same mystic Friar's curious doings,
About the present family's deaths and wooings.

54

Of these few could say more than has been said;
They passed as such things do, for superstition
With some, while others, who held more in dread
The theme, half credited the strange tradition;
And much was talked on all sides on that head;
But Juan, when cross-questioned on the vision,
Which some supposed (though he had not avowed it)
Had stirred him, answered in a way to cloud it.

[27] **Pope**: Alexander Pope (1688–1744), Byron's favorite neoclassical poet but derided by Romantic contemporaries.

[28] **Hebe**: the beautiful cup-bearer of the gods.

[29] **'Bath Guide'**: *New Bath Guide* (1766), social satire of the squire Blunderhead family of Bath, by Christopher Anstey (1724–1805).

[30] **'Hayley's Triumphs'**: Byron wrote of William Hayley's *The Triumphs of Temper* (1781) and *The Triumphs of Music* (1804) that they were "Forever feeble and forever tame."

[31] **'Bouts rimés'**: parlor game, whereby one was given a list of words that were to form the end-rhymes of a poem to be created on the spot.

[32] **persiflage**: teasing, light-hearted banter.

[33] **Gynocracy**: government by women.

55

And then, the mid-day having worn to one,
The company prepared to separate;
Some to their several pastimes, or to none,
Some wondering 'twas so early, some so late.
There was a goodly match too, to be run
Between some greyhounds on my Lord's estate,
And a young race-horse of old pedigree,
Matched for the spring, whom several went to see.

56

There was a picture dealer who had brought
A special Titian,[34] warranted original,
So precious that it was not to be bought,
Though princes the possessor were besieging all.
The king himself had cheapened it, but thought
The Civil List (he deigns to accept, obliging all
His subjects by his gracious acceptation)
Too scanty, in these times of low taxation.

57

But as Lord Henry was a connoisseur,—
The friend of artists, if not arts,—the owner,
With motives the most classical and pure,
So that he would have been the very donor,
Rather than seller, had his wants been fewer,
So much he deemed his patronage an honour,
Had brought the Capo d'opera,[35] not for sale,
But for his judgement,—never known to fail.

58

Bricklayer of Babel, called an architect,
Brought to survey these grey walls, which though so thick,
Might have from time acquired some slight defect;
Who, after rummaging the Abbey through thick
And thin, produced a plan whereby to erect
New buildings of correctest conformation,
And throw down old, which he called *restoration*.

59

The cost would be a trifle—an 'old song'
Set to some thousands ('tis the usual burthen
Of that same tune, when people hum it long)—
The price would speedily repay its worth in
An edifice no less sublime than strong,
By which Lord Henry's good taste would go forth in
Its glory, through all ages shining sunny,
For Gothic daring shown in English money.

60

There were two lawyers busy on a mortgage
Lord Henry wished to raise for a new purchase;
Also a lawsuit upon tenures burgage,[36]
And one on tithes, which sure are Discord's torches,
Kindling Religion till she throws down *her* gage,[37]
'Untying' squires 'to fight against the churches';[38]
There was a prize ox, a prize pig, and ploughman,
For Henry was a sort of Sabine showman.

61

There were two poachers caught in a steel trap
Ready for jail, their place of convalescence;
There was a country girl in a close cap
And scarlet cloak (I hate the sight to see, since—
Since—since—in youth, I had the sad mishap—
But luckily I have paid few parish fees[39] since)
That scarlet cloak, alas! unclosed with Rigour,
Presents the problem of a double figure.

62

A reel within a bottle is a mystery,
One can't tell how it e'er got in or out,
Therefore the present piece of natural history,
I leave to those who are fond of solving doubt,
And merely state, though not for the consistory,
Lord Henry was a justice, and that Scout
The constable, beneath a warrant's banner,
Had bagged this poacher upon Nature's manor.

[34] **a special Titian:** a painting by the great and prolific Venetian artist, Titian (c. 1487–1576).

[35] **Capo d'opera:** masterpiece.

[36] **tenures burgage:** 1768 Blackstone: "Tenure in burgage is . . . where the king or other person is lord of an antient borough, in which the tenements are held by a rent certain." [*OED*, refers to Sir William Blackstone's *Commentaries on the Laws of England* (1765–1769)].

[37] **gage:** a pledge (usually a glove thrown on the ground) to do battle, a challenge.

[38] **'Untying' . . . churches':** cf. *Macbeth*, IV.i.52–53: "Though you untie the winds and let them fight / Against the churches."

[39] **paid . . . fees:** in child support.

63

Now Justices of Peace must judge all pieces
Of mischief of all kinds, and keep the game
And morals of the country from caprices
Of those who have not a licence for the same;
And of all things, excepting tithes and leases,
Perhaps these are most difficult to tame:
Preserving partridges and pretty wenches
Are puzzles to the most precautious benches.

64

The present culprit was extremely pale,
Pale as if painted so; her cheek being red
By nature, as in higher dames less hale
'Tis white, at least when they just rise from bed.
Perhaps she was ashamed of seeming frail,
Poor soul! for she was country born and bred,
And knew no better in her immorality
Than to wax white—for blushes are for quality.

65

Her black, bright, downcast, wet espiegle[40] eye,
Had gathered a large tear into its corner,
Which the poor thing at times essayed to dry,
For she was not a sentimental mourner,
Parading all her sensibility,
Nor insolent enough to scorn the scorner,
But stood in trembling, patient tribulation,
To be called up for her examination.

66

Of course these groups were scattered here and there,
Not nigh the gay saloon of ladies gent.
The lawyers in the study; and in air
The prize pigs, ploughmen, poachers; the men sent
From town, viz, architect and dealer, were
Both busy (as a general in his tent
Writing dispatches) in their several stations,
Exulting in their brilliant lucubrations.

67

But this poor girl was left in the great hall,
While Scout, the parish guardian of the frail,
Discussed (he hated beer yclept the 'small')[41]
A mighty mug of *moral* double ale:
She waited until Justice could recall
Its kind attentions to their proper pale,
To name a thing in nomenclature rather
Perplexing for most virgins—a child's father.

68

You see here was enough of occupation
For the Lord Henry, linked with dogs and horses.
There was much bustle too and preparation
Below stairs on the score of second courses,
Because, as suits their rank and situation,
Those who in countries have great land resources,
Have 'public days,' when all men may carouse,
Though not exactly what's called 'open house.'

69

But once a week or fortnight, *un*invited
(Thus we translate a *general invitation*)
All country gentlemen, esquired or knighted,
May drop in without cards, and take their station
At the full board, and sit alike delighted
With fashionable wines and conversation;
And as the Isthmus of the grand connection,
Talk o'er themselves, the past and next election.

70

Lord Henry was a great electioneerer,
Burrowing for boroughs like a rat or rabbit.
But county contests cost him rather dearer,
Because the neighbouring Scotch Earl of
Giftgabbit
Had English influence, in the self-same sphere here;
His son, the Honourable Dick Dicedrabbit,
Was member for the 'other Interest' (meaning
The same self-interest, with a different leaning).

71

Courteous and cautious therefore in his county,
He was all things to all men, and dispensed
To some civility, to others bounty,
And promises to all—which last commenced
To gather to a somewhat large amount, he
Not calculating how much they condensed;
But what with keeping some, and breaking others,
His word had the same value as another's.

72

A friend to freedom and freeholders—yet
No less a friend to government—he held,

---

[40] **espiègle**: frolicsome, roguish.

[41] **beer . . . 'small'**: weak beer.

That he exactly the just medium hit
 'Twixt place and patriotism — albeit compelled,
Such was his Sovereign's pleasure (though unfit,
 He added modestly, when rebels railed)
To hold some sinecures he wished abolished,
But that with them all law would be demolished.

73

He was 'free to confess' — (whence comes this phrase?
 Is't English? No — 'tis only parliamentary)
That innovation's spirit now-a-days
 Had made more progress than for the last century.
He would not tread a factious path to praise,
 Though for the public weal disposed to venture
  high;
As for his place, he could but say this of it,
That the fatigue was greater than the profit.

74

Heaven, and his friends, knew that a private life
 Had ever been his sole and whole ambition;
But could he quit his king in times of strife
 Which threatened the whole country with
  perdition?
When demagogues would with a butcher's knife
 Cut through and (oh! damnable incision!)
The Gordian or the Geordi-an knot,[42] whose strings
Have tied together Commons, Lords, and Kings.

75

Sooner 'come place into the civil list
 And champion him to the utmost'[43] — he would
  keep it,
Till duly disappointed or dismissed:
 Profit he cared not for, let others reap it;
But should the day come when place ceased to exist,
 The country would have far more cause to weep it,
For how could it go on? Explain who can!
He gloried in the name of Englishman.

76

He was as independent — aye, much more —
 Than those who were not paid for independence,
As common soldiers, or a common —— Shore,[44]
 Have in their several arts or parts ascendence
O'er the irregulars in lust or gore,
 Who do not give professional attendance.
Thus on the mob all statesmen are as eager
To prove their pride, as footmen to a beggar.

77

All this (save the last stanza) Henry said,
 And thought. I say no more — I've said too much;
For all of us have either heard or read
 Of — or *upon* the hustings[45] — some slight such
Hints from the independent heart or head
 Of the official candidate. I'll touch
No more on this — the dinner bell hath rung,
And grace is said; the grace I *should* have *sung* —

78

But I'm too late, and therefore must make play.
 'Twas a great banquet, such as Albion old
Was wont to boast — as if a glutton's tray
 Were something very glorious to behold.
But 'twas a public feast and public day, —
 Quite full, right dull, guests hot, and dishes cold,
Great plenty, much formality, small cheer,
And every body out of their own sphere.

79

The squires familiarly formal, and
 My lords and ladies proudly condescending;
The very servants puzzling how to hand
 Their plates — without it might be too much
  bending
From their high places by the sideboard's stand —
 Yet like their masters fearful of offending.
For any deviation from the graces
Might cost both men and master too — their *places*.

80

There were some hunters bold, and coursers keen,
 Whose hounds ne'er erred, nor greyhounds
  deigned to lurch;

[42] **Geordi-an Knot:** reference to King George III.

[43] **'come . . . utmost':** cf. *Macbeth*, III.i.71–72: "Rather than so, come fate into the list / And champion me to th' utterance!"

[44] **—— Shore:** wooden plank or beam used as a temporary support. McGann suggests a possible reference to the mistress of Edward IV, Jane Shore.

[45] **hustings:** platform upon which Parliamentary candidates addressed the electorate.

Some deadly shots too, Septembrizers,[46] seen
    Earliest to rise, and last to quit the search
Of the poor partridge through his stubble screen.
    There were some massy members of the church,
Takers of tithes, and makers of good matches,
And several who sung fewer psalms than catches.[47]

81

There were some country wags too,—and, alas!
    Some exiles from the town, who had been driven
To gaze, instead of pavement, upon grass,
    And rise at nine in lieu of long eleven.
And lo! upon that day it came to pass,
    I sate next that o'erwhelming son of heaven,
The very powerful Parson, Peter Pith,
The loudest wit I e'er was deafened with.

82

I knew him in his livelier London days,
    A brilliant diner out, though but a curate,
And not a joke he cut but earned its praise,
    Until preferment, coming at a sure rate,
(Oh, Providence! how wondrous are thy ways,
    Who would suppose thy gifts sometimes
        obdurate?)
Gave him, to lay the devil who looks o'er Lincoln,[48]
A fat fen vicarage, and nought to think on.

83

His jokes were sermons, and his sermons jokes;
    But both were thrown away amongst the fens;
For wit hath no great friend in aguish folks.
    No longer ready ears and short-hand pens
Imbibed the gay *bon mot*, or happy hoax:
    The poor priest was reduced to common sense,
Or to coarse efforts very loud and long,
To hammer a coarse laugh from the thick throng.

84

There *is* a difference, says the song, 'between
    A beggar and a queen,' or *was* (of late
The latter worse used of the two we've seen—
    But we'll say nothing of affairs of state)
A difference "twixt a bishop and a dean,'
    A difference between crockery ware and plate,
As between English beef and Spartan broth—
And yet great heroes have been bred by both.

85

But of all nature's discrepancies, none
    Upon the whole is greater than the difference
Beheld between the country and the town,
    Of which the latter merits every preference
From those who have few resources of their own,
    And only think, or act, or feel with reference
To some small plan of interest or ambition—
Both which are limited to no condition.

86

But 'en avant!'[49] The light loves languish o'er
    Long banquets and too many guests, although
A slight repast makes people love much more,
    Bacchus and Ceres[50] being, as we know,
Even from our grammar upwards, friends of yore
    With vivifying Venus, who doth owe
To these the invention of champagne and truffles:
Temperance delights her, but long fasting ruffles.

87

Dully past o'er the dinner of the day;
    And Juan took his place, he knew not where,
Confused, in the confusion, and distrait,
    And sitting as if nailed upon his chair;
Though knives and forks clanged round as in a fray,
    He seemed unconscious of all passing there,
Till some one, with a groan, exprest a wish
(Unheeded twice) to have a fin of fish.

88

On which, at the *third* asking of the banns,
    He started; and perceiving smiles around
Broadening to grins, he coloured more than once,
    And hastily—as nothing can confound

---

[46] **Septembrizers**: the hunting season begins in September. Septembrists were the French revolutionists responsible for the September Massacres in Paris, 3 to 7 September 1792.

[47] **catches**: playful songs for three or four voices in which the second and subsequent singers repeat the lines sung by the preceding singer who goes forward with the next line. A round.

[48] **devil . . . Lincoln**: the gargoyle looking over St. Hugh's chapel of Lincoln Cathedral.

[49] **'en avant!'**: forward!

[50] **Bacchus . . . Ceres**: See note 17, Canto II.

A wise man more than laughter from a dunce—
Inflicted on the dish a deadly wound,
And with such hurry, that ere he could curb it,
He had paid his neighbour's prayer with half a turbot.

89

This was no bad mistake, as it occurred,
The supplicator being an amateur;
But others, who were left with scarce a third,
Were angry—as they well might, to be sure.
They wondered how a young man so absurd
Lord Henry at his table should endure;
And this, and his not knowing how much oats
Had fallen last market, cost his host three votes.

90

They little knew, or might have sympathized,
That he the night before had seen a ghost;
A prologue which but slightly harmonized
With the substantial company engrossed
By Matter, and so much materialized,
That one scarce knew at what to marvel most
Of two things—how (the question rather odd is)
Such bodies could have souls, or souls such bodies.

91

But what confused him more than smile or stare
From all the 'squires and 'squiresses around,
Who wondered at the abstraction of his air,
Especially as he had been renowned
For some vivacity among the fair,
Even in the country circle's narrow bound—
(For little things upon my Lord's estate
Were good small-talk for others still less great)—

92

Was, that he caught Aurora's eye on his,
And something like a smile upon her cheek.
Now this he really rather took amiss:
In those who rarely smile, their smiles bespeak
A strong external motive; and in this
Smile of Aurora's there was nought to pique
Or hope, or love, with any of the wiles
Which some pretend to trace in ladies' smiles.

93

'Twas a mere quiet smile of contemplation,
Indicative of some surprise and pity;
And Juan grew carnation[51] with vexation,
Which was not very wise and still less witty,
Since he had gained at least her observation,
A most important outwork of the city—
As Juan should have known, had not his senses
By last night's ghost been driven from their defences.

94

But what was bad, she did not blush in turn,
Nor seem embarrassed—quite the contrary;
Her aspect was as usual, still—*not* stern—
And she withdrew, but cast not down, her eye,
Yet grew a little pale—with what? concern?
I know not; but her colour ne'er was high—
Though sometimes faintly flushed—and always clear,
As deep seas in a Sunny Atmosphere.

95

But Adeline was occupied by fame
This day; and watching, witching, condescending
To the consumers of fish, fowl and game,
And dignity with courtesy so blending,
As all must blend whose part it is to aim
(Especially as the sixth year[52] is ending)
At their lord's, son's, or similar connection's
Safe conduct through the rocks of re-elections.

96

Though this was most expedient on the whole,
And usual—Juan, when he cast a glance
On Adeline while playing her grand role,
Which she went through as though it were a dance,
(Betraying only now and then her soul
By a look scarce perceptibly askance
Of weariness or scorn) began to feel
Some doubt how much of Adeline was *real*;

97

So well she acted, all and every part
By turns—with that vivacious versatility,

[51] **carnation:** rosy pink.

[52] **the sixth year:** the final year of Lord Henry's Parliamentary term.

Which many people take for want of heart.
They err—'tis merely what is called mobility,[53]
A thing of temperament and not of art,
Though seeming so, from its supposed facility;
And false—though true; for surely they're sincerest,
Who are strongly acted on by what is nearest.

98

This makes your actors, artists, and romancers,
Heroes sometimes, though seldom—sages never;
But speakers, bards, diplomatists, and dancers,
Little that's great, but much of what is clever;
Most orators, but very few financiers,
Though all Exchequer Chancellors endeavour,
Of late years, to dispense with Cocker's rigours,[54]
And grow quite figurative with their figures.

99

The poets of arithmetic are they
Who, though they prove not two and two to be
Five, as they would do in a modest way,
Have plainly made it out that four are three,
Judging by what they take, and what they pay.
The Sinking Fund's[55] unfathomable sea,
That most unliquidating liquid, leaves
The debt unsunk, yet sinks all it receives.

100

While Adeline dispensed her airs and graces,
The fair Fitz-Fulke seemed very much at ease;
Though too well bred to quiz men to their faces,
Her laughing blue eyes with a glance could seize
The ridicules of people in all places—
That honey of your fashionable bees—
And store it up for mischievous enjoyment;
And this at present was her kind employment.

101

However, the day closed, as days must close;
The evening also waned—and coffee came.
Each carriage was announced, and ladies rose,
And curtseying off, as curtsies country dame,
Retired: with most unfashionable bows
Their docile esquires also did the same,
Delighted with the dinner and their host,
But with the Lady Adeline the most.

102

Some praised her beauty; others her great grace;
The warmth of her politeness, whose sincerity
Was obvious in each feature of her face,
Whose traits were radiant with the rays of verity.
Yes; *she* was truly worthy *her* high place!
No one could envy her deserved prosperity;
And then her dress—what beautiful simplicity
Draperied her form with curious felicity!

103

Meanwhile sweet Adeline deserved their praises,
By an impartial indemnification
For all her past exertion and soft phrases,
In a most edifying conversation,
Which turned upon their late guests' miens and faces,
And families, even to the last relation;
Their hideous wives, their horrid selves and dresses,
And truculent distortion of their tresses.

104

True, *she* said little—'twas the rest that broke
Forth into universal epigram;
But then 'twas to the purpose what she spoke:
Like Addison's 'faint praise,' so wont to damn,[56]
Her own but served to set off every joke,
As music chimes in with a melodrame.[57]
How sweet the task to shield an absent friend!
I ask but this of mine, to——*not* defend.

105

There were but two exceptions to this keen
Skirmish of wits o'er the departed; one,
Aurora, with her pure and placid mien;
And Juan too, in general behind none

[53] **mobility:** French: *mobilité*—changeableness, instability of character.

[54] **Cocker's rigours:** standard textbook *Arithmetic* (1677) by Edward Cocker (1631–1675).

[55] **Sinking Fund:** fund collected to pay off a corporate debt.

[56] **'faint praise' . . . damn:** Pope on Joseph Addison in *Epistle to Dr. Arbuthnot* (1734): "Damn with faint praise, assent with civil leer, / And, without sneering, teach the rest to sneer" (201–202).

[57] **melodrame:** melodrama.

In gay remark on what he had heard or seen,
Sate silent now, his usual spirits gone:
In vain he heard the others rail or rally,
He would not join them in a single sally.

106

'Tis true he saw Aurora look as though
She approved his silence; she perhaps mistook
Its motive for that charity we owe
But seldom pay the absent, nor would look
Further; it might or it might not be so.
But Juan, sitting silent in his nook,
Observing little in his reverie,
Yet saw this much, which he was glad to see.

107

The ghost at least had done him this much good,
In making him as silent as a ghost,
If in the circumstances which ensued
He gained esteem where it was worth the most.
And certainly Aurora had renewed
In him some feelings he had lately lost
Or hardened; feelings which, perhaps ideal,
Are so divine, that I must deem them real:—

108

The love of higher things and better days;
The unbounded hope, and heavenly ignorance
Of what is called the world, and the world's ways;
The moments when we gather from a glance
More joy than from all future pride or praise,
Which kindle manhood, but can ne'er entrance
The heart in an existence of its own,
Of which another's bosom is the zone.

109

Who would not sigh *Αι αι ταν Κυθερειαν*![58]
That *hath* a memory, or that *had* a heart?
Alas! *her* star must wane like that of Dian;[59]
Ray fades on ray, as years on years depart.
Anacreon[60] only had the soul to tie an
Unwithering myrtle[61] round the unblunted dart
Of Eros; but though thou hast played us many tricks,
Still we respect thee, 'Alma Venus Genetrix'![62]

110

And full of sentiments, sublime as billows
Heaving between this world and worlds beyond,
Don Juan, when the midnight hour of pillows
Arrived, retired to his; but to despond
Rather than rest. Instead of poppies, willows
Waved o'er his couch; he meditated, fond
Of those sweet bitter thoughts which banish sleep,
And make the worldling sneer, the youngling weep.

111

The night was as before: he was undrest,
Saving his night gown, which is an undress;
Completely 'sans culotte,'[63] and without vest;
In short, he hardly could be clothed with less;
But apprehensive of his spectral guest,
He sate, with feelings awkward to express,
(By those who have not had such visitations)
Expectant of the ghost's fresh operations.

112

And not in vain he listened—Hush! what's that?
I see—I see—Ah, no!—'tis not—yet 'tis—
Ye powers! it is the—the—the Pooh! the cat!
The devil may take that stealthy pace of his!
So like a spiritual pit-a-pat,
Or tiptoe of an amatory Miss,
Gliding the first time to a rendezvous,
And dreading the chaste echoes of her shoe.

113

Again—what is't? The wind? No, no,—this time
It is the sable Friar as before,
With awful footsteps regular as rhyme,
Or (as rhymes may be in these days) much more.

[58] Cf. Bion's "Lament for Adonis": "Ah, Ah, for Cytherea."

[59] **Dian**: moon goddess and goddess of women.

[60] **Anacreon**: Greek lyric poet who celebrated love and wine.

[61] **myrtle**: evergreen plant sacred to Aphrodite and thus emblematic of love.

[62] **'Alma Venus Genetrix'**: opening lines of Lucretius's *De Rerum Natura*: "Hail fertile Venus."

[63] **'sans culotte'**: *Lit.* "without breeches"; common name for French revolutionists, because they wore trousers instead of the knee breeches worn by the aristocracy.

Again, through shadows of the night sublime,
When deep sleep fell on men, and the world wore
The starry darkness round her like a girdle
Spangled with gems—the monk made his blood
curdle.

114

A noise like to wet fingers drawn on glass,
Which sets the teeth on edge; and a slight clatter
Like showers which on the midnight gusts will pass,
Sounding like very supernatural water,
Came over Juan's ear, which throbbed, alas!
For immaterialism's a serious matter;
So that even those whose faith is the most great
In souls immortal, shun them *tête-à-tête*.

115

Were his eyes open?—Yes! and his mouth too.
Surprise has this effect—to make one dumb,
Yet leave the gate which Eloquence slips through
As wide as if a long speech were to come.
Nigh and more nigh the awful echoes drew,
Tremendous to a mortal tympanum:
His eyes were open, and (as was before
Stated) his mouth. What opened next?—the door.

116

It opened with a most infernal creak,
Like that of Hell. 'Lasciate ogni speranza
Voi che entrate!'[64] The hinge seemed to speak,
Dreadful as Dante's Rima,[65] or this stanza;
Or—but all words upon such themes are weak;
A single shade's sufficient to entrance a
Hero—for what is substance to a Spirit?
Or how is't *matter* trembles to come near it?

117

The door flew wide, not swiftly—but, as fly
The sea-gulls, with a steady, sober flight—
And then swung back; nor close—but stood awry,
Half letting in long shadows on the light,
Which still in Juan's candlesticks burned high,
For he had two, both tolerably bright,
And in the door-way, darkening Darkness, stood
The sable Friar in his solemn hood.

118

Don Juan shook, as erst he had been shaken
The night before; but being sick of shaking,
He first inclined to think he had been mistaken,
And then to be ashamed of such mistaking;
His own internal ghost began to awaken
Within him, and to quell his corporal quaking—
Hinting that soul and body on the whole
Were odds against a disembodied soul.

119

And then his dread grew wrath, and his wrath fierce;
And he arose, advanced—the shade retreated;
But Juan, eager now the truth to pierce,
Followed, his veins no longer cold, but heated,
Resolved to thrust the mystery carte and tierce.[66]
At whatsoever risk of being defeated:
The ghost stopped, menaced, then retired, until
He reached the ancient wall, then stood stone still.

120

Juan put forth one arm—Eternal Powers!
It touched no soul, nor body, but the wall,
On which the moonbeams fell in silvery showers
Chequered with all the tracery of the hall;
He shuddered, as no doubt the bravest cowers
When he can't tell what 'tis that doth appal.
How odd, a single hobgoblin's non-entity
Should cause more fear than a whole host's identity!

121

But still the shade remained; the blue eyes glared,
And rather variably for stony death;
Yet one thing rather good the grave had spared,
The ghost had a remarkably sweet breath.
A straggling curl showed he had been fair-haired;
A red lip, with two rows of pearls beneath,
Gleamed forth, as through the casement's ivy shroud
The moon peeped, just escaped from a grey cloud.

[64] **'Lasciate . . . entrate!'**: the inscription over the Gates of Hell in Dante's *Inferno*: "Abandon every hope, you who enter here" (Canto III.9).

[65] **Dante's Rima**: the rhyme scheme of the *Divine Comedy* is terza rima.

[66] **carte and tierce**: the third and fourth positions in fencing.

122

And Juan, puzzled, but still curious, thrust
His other arm forth—Wonder upon wonder!
It pressed upon a hard but glowing bust,
Which beat as if there was a warm heart under.
He found, as people on most trials must,
That he had made at first a silly blunder,
And that in his confusion he had caught
Only the wall, instead of what he sought.

123

The ghost, if ghost it were, seemed a sweet soul
As ever lurked beneath a holy hood:
A dimpled chin, a neck of ivory, stole
Forth into something much like flesh and blood;
Back fell the sable frock and dreary cowl,
And they revealed—alas! that ere they should!
In full, voluptuous, but *not o'er*grown bulk,
The phantom of her frolic Grace—Fitz-Fulke![67]

POSTHUMOUS PUBLICATIONS

from MORNING CHRONICLE
(1824)

On this day I complete my thirty sixth year

January 22nd 1824
Messalonghi

1

'T is time this heart should be unmoved
Since others it hath ceased to move,
Yet though I cannot be beloved
Still let me love.

2

My days are in the yellow leaf
The flowers and fruits of love are gone—
The worm, the canker and the grief
Are mine alone.

3

The fire that on my bosom preys
Is lone as some Volcanic Isle,
No torch is kindled at its blaze
A funeral pile!

4

The hope, the fear, the jealous care
The exalted portion of the pain
And power of Love I cannot share
But wear the chain.

5

But 't is not *thus*—and 't is not *here*
Such thoughts should shake my soul, nor *now*
Where glory decks the hero's bier
Or binds his brow.

6

The Sword—the Banner—and the Field
Glory and Greece around us see!
The Spartan borne upon his shield
Was not more free!

7

Awake! (*not* Greece—She *is* awake!)
Awake my spirit—think through *whom*
Thy Life blood tracks its parent lake
And then strike home!

8

Tread those reviving passions down
Unworthy Manhood;—unto thee
Indifferent should the smile or frown
Of Beauty be.

9

If thou regret'st thy youth, why *live?*
The Land of honourable Death
Is here—up to the Field! and give
Away thy Breath.

[67] Byron reveals in Stanza 14, the final stanza of the unfinished Canto XVII, written in 1824 and published in 1903, that both Juan and Adeline looked weary at the breakfast table the following morning.

10

Seek out — less often sought than found,
A Soldier's Grave — for thee the best;
Then look around and choose thy ground
And take thy Rest.

from THE WORKS OF LORD BYRON

With his letters and Journals, and his Life [by Thomas Moore]
(1832–1833)

from Dedication [to Don Juan]

(1832–1833; comp. 1819)

— DEDICATION —

1

Bob Southey! You're a poet — poet Laureate,[1]
And representative of all the race;
Although 'tis true you turn'd out a Tory at
Last, — yours has lately been a common case: —
And now, my epic renegade! what are ye at,
With all the Lakers[2] in and out of place?
A nest of tuneful persons, to my eye
Like four and twenty blackbirds in a pie;

2

'Which pie being open'd, they began to sing' —
(This old song and new simile holds good)
'A dainty dish to set before the King,'
Or Regent,[3] who admires such kind of food.
And Coleridge, too, has lately taken wing,
But, like a hawk encumber'd with his hood,
Explaining metaphysics to the nation —
I wish he would explain his Explanation.

3

You, Bob! are rather insolent, you know,
At being disappointed in your wish
To supersede all warblers here below,
And be the only Blackbird in the dish;
And then you overstrain yourself, or so,
And tumble downward like the flying fish
Gasping on deck, because you soar too high, Bob,
And fall, for lack of moisture, quite adry, Bob![4]

4

And Wordsworth, in a rather long 'Excursion',[5]
(I think the quarto holds five hundred pages)
Has given a sample from the vasty version
Of his new system to perplex the sages;
'Tis poetry — at least by his assertion,
And may appear so when the dogstar[6] rages;
And he who understands it would be able
To add a story to the Tower of Babel.

5

You, Gentlemen! by dint of long seclusion
From better company have kept your own
At Keswick,[7] and through still continued fusion
Of one another's minds at last have grown
To deem as a most logical conclusion
That Poesy has wreaths for you alone;
There is a narrowness in such a notion
Which makes me wish you'd change your lakes for
ocean.

---

[1] Byron acceded to publisher John Murray's wish in 1819 that the Dedication be suppressed. Murray feared a libel suit; however, Byron rationalized the suppression as a gentlemanly act because attacking anonymously was more befitting "Scoundrels and renegadoes" like Robert Southey.* Byron at first despised the Poet Laureate for turning on the revolutionary ideals of his youth in now serving a despicable monarch, and later for his attack on Byron and company in his preface to *A Vision of Judgment* (1821), written in commemoration of the death of George III. In rejoinder, Byron wrote his biting satire, *The Vision of Judgment* (1822).

[2] **Lakers:** Wordsworth,* Coleridge,* and Southey* especially, all of whose poetry is associated with the English Lake District.

[3] **Regent:** because of the mental instability of George III, his son had been serving as Prince Regent from 1811 until his father's death in January 1820.

[4] **adry, Bob!:** "Dry bob" was slang for sexual intercourse without the male ejaculating.

[5] **'Excursion':** published in 1814. See William Wordsworth.

[6] **dogstar:** Sirius, brightest star in the sky, and part of the constellation Canis Major.

[7] **Keswick:** the town of Southey's home in the Lake District.

6

I would not imitate the petty thought,
Nor coin my self-love to so base a vice,
For all the glory your conversion brought,
Since gold alone should not have been its price.
You have your salary — was't for that you wrought?
And Wordsworth has his place in the Excise.[8]
You're shabby fellows — true — but poets still,
And duly seated on the immortal hill.

7

Your bays may hide the baldness of your brows,
Perhaps some virtuous blushes — let them go,
To you I envy neither fruit nor boughs —
And for the fame you would engross below
The field is universal, and allows
Scope to all such as feel the inherent glow —
Scott, Rogers, Campbell, Moore, and Crabbe,[9] will try
'Gainst you the question with posterity.

8

For me who, wandering with pedestrian Muses,
Contend not with you on the winged steed,[10]
I wish your fate may yield ye, when she chooses,
The fame you envy, and the skill you need;
And recollect a poet nothing loses
In giving to his brethren their full meed
Of merit, and complaint of present days
Is not the *certain* path to future praise.

9

He that reserves his laurels for posterity
(Who does not often claim the bright reversion?)
Has generally no great crop to spare it, he
Being only injured by his own assertion;
And although here and there some glorious rarity
Arise, like Titan from the sea's immersion,[11]
The major part of such appellants go
To — God knows where — for no one else can know.

10

If, fallen in evil days on evil tongues,[12]
Milton appeal'd to the Avenger, Time,
If Time, the Avenger, execrates his wrongs,
And makes the word *'Miltonic'* mean *'sublime'*,
He deign'd not to belie his soul in songs,
Nor turn his very talent to a crime —
He did not loathe the sire to laud the son,
But closed the tyrant-hater he begun.

11

Think'st thou, could he, the blind Old Man,[13] arise
Like Samuel from the grave, to freeze once more
The blood of monarchs with his prophecies,[14]
Or be alive again — again all hoar
With time and trials, and those helpless eyes
And heartless daughters,[15] worn, and pale, and poor,
Would *he* adore a sultan? *he* obey
The intellectual eunuch Castlereagh?[16]

12

Cold-blooded, smooth-faced, placid miscreant!
Dabbling its sleek young hands in Erin's gore,[17]

---

[8] **place in the Excise:** Wordsworth held the sinecure of Distributor of Stamps for Westmorland County, i.e., a tax collector.

[9] **Scott . . . Crabbe:** contemporary poets of both romantic and neoclassical temperaments.

[10] **winged steed:** Pegasus, winged horse of inspiration.

[11] **Titan:** Oceanus, god of the Ocean.

[12] **fallen . . . evil tongues:** referring to his political constancy as a radical during the conservative Restoration period, Milton writes in *Paradise Lost*, VII.25–26: "More safe I sing with mortal voice, unchanged / To hoarse or mute, though fall'n on evil days, / On evil days though fall'n, and evil tongues; / In darkness, and with dangers compassed round, / And solitude."

[13] **blind Old Man:** Milton was blind when composing *Paradise Lost.*

[14] **prophecies:** reference to I Samuel 28:13–20, esp. 19–20: "the Lord will also deliver Israel with thee into the hand of the Philistines: and to morrow shalt thou and thy sons be with me . . . Then Saul fell straightway all along on the earth, and was sore afraid, because of the words of Samuel."

[15] **heartless daughters:** Milton's daughters supposedly took financial advantage of him in his old age and blindness.

[16] **eunuch Castlereagh:** Robert Stewart, Viscount Castlereagh (1769–1822), foreign minister in the Tory government from 1812 until his suicide in 1822. He was instrumental in establishing the Quadruple Alliance of Britain, Austria, Russia, and Prussia at the Congress of Vienna and in restoring the Bourbon dynasty to the French throne after the fall of Napoleon.

[17] **Cold-blooded . . . gore:** Castlereagh, an Irish peer, served as the chief secretary for Ireland (1799–1801) following

And thus for wider carnage taught to pant,
   Transferr'd to gorge upon a sister-shore;
The vulgarest tool that tyranny could want,
   With just enough of talent, and no more,
To lengthen fetters by another fix'd,
And offer poison long already mix'd.

13

An orator of such set trash of phrase
   Ineffably, legitimately vile,
That even its grossest flatterers dare not praise,
   Nor foes—all nations—condescend to smile:
Not even a *sprightly* blunder's spark can blaze
   From that Ixion grindstone's ceaseless toil,[18]
That turns and turns, to give the world a notion
Of endless torments, and perpetual motion.

14

A bungler even in its disgusting trade,
   And botching, patching, leaving still behind
Something of which its masters are afraid,
   States to be curb'd, and thoughts to be confined,
Conspiracy or Congress to be made—
   Cobbling at manacles for all mankind—
A tinkering slavemaker, who mends old chains,
With God and man's abhorrence for its gains.

15

If we may judge of matter by the mind,
   Emasculated to the marrow, *It*
Hath but two objects—how to serve, and bind,
   Deeming the chain it wears even men may fit;
Eutropius[19] of its many masters—blind
   To worth as freedom, wisdom as to wit—
Fearless, because *no* feeling dwells in ice,
Its very courage stagnates to a vice.

16

Where shall I turn me not to *view* its bonds?
   For I will never *feel* them—Italy!
Thy late reviving Roman soul desponds
   Beneath the lie this state-thing breathed o'er thee,[20]
Thy clanking chain, and Erin's yet green wounds,
   Have voices—tongues to cry aloud for me.
Europe has slaves, allies, kings, armies still,
And Southey lives to sing them very ill.

17

Meantime, Sir Laureate, I proceed to dedicate
   In honest, simple verse, this song to you;
And if in flattering strains I do not predicate,
   'Tis that I still retain my 'buff and blue'.[21]
My politics, as yet, are all to educate,
   Apostasy's so fashionable too,
To keep *one* creed's a task grown quite Herculean,
Is it not so, my Tory ultra-Julian?[22]

---

the bloody Irish Rebellion of 1798. (See THE FRENCH REVOLUTION AND RIGHTS OF MAN.)

[18] **Ixion grindstone's . . . toil:** for attempting to woo Hera, Zeus's wife, Ixion was chained to a wheel that rotated eternally.

[19] **Eutropius:** minister in the court of the Emperor Arcadius and the most influential man in the East from 395 AD until overthrown by political rivals in 399 AD, after becoming the first eunuch to hold the office of consul.

[20] **Beneath the lie . . . o'er thee:** The Congress of Vienna assured that Europe would be protected against future French imperialism by placing states bordering France under the control of the Quadruple Alliance. In these arrangements, northern Italy fell under Austrian control.

[21] **'buff and blue':** colors of the liberal Whig Club.

[22] **ultra-Julian:** reference to Julian the Apostate (332–363 AD), who was raised as Christian, but became enamored of the classics and the gods of Greece and Rome. Professed his paganism (and religious tolerance) after becoming emperor.

PERCY BYSSHE SHELLEY

(1792–1822)

The family of Percy Bysshe Shelley was among the thousand or so near the top of the oligarchical pyramid of England. Bysshe Shelley, the poet's grandfather, amassed a fortune through several marriages and became a baronet in 1806. Percy's father Timothy (later Sir Timothy) was a Member of Parliament in the House of Commons. Percy, as the oldest son of a family of five sisters and a much younger brother, was in line for a baronetcy, which is a kind of hereditary knighthood. Fittingly, he was educated at Syon House Academy and Eton College (1802–1810). Shelley, however, proved to be more the child of the radical 1790s than a scion of England's conservative ruling class. Not only was he incapable of conforming to traditional institutions, his behavior, politics, and art were devoted to dismantling them.

Shelley led an unorthodox and wildly colorful life. Personal eccentricities, iconoclasm, and effeminacy made him a favorite victim of bullies at Syon and Eton, where he was known as Mad Shelley for his volatile temper and later as the Eton Atheist. Within six months of matriculating at University College, Oxford, Shelley and classmate Thomas Jefferson Hogg were expelled for the "contumacious conduct" of distributing their pamphlet, *The Necessity of Atheism* (1811), throughout the University and to Anglican bishops of the Kingdom. (*Necessity* has the distinction of being one of the earliest admissions of atheism to be printed in England.) Shelley's outraged father failed to convince him to recant. Several months later, Shelley eloped to Scotland with Harriet Westbrook, the 16-year-old daughter of a prosperous London merchant, and the split with his father grew wider. Shelley agreed to an annuity of £200 in return for renouncing his inheritance. In the summer of 1814, he took a further step toward public ostracism in abandoning his pregnant wife and their first child to elope with Mary Godwin, the 16-year-old daughter of Mary Wollstonecraft* (d. 1797) and his intellectual hero, William Godwin.* Percy invited Harriet to join himself, Mary, and Mary's 15-year-old stepsister, Jane (Claire) Clairmont, on a tour of the Continent, but Harriet refused to play the role of "sister" to Percy and his new lover. After the death of his grandfather in 1815, Shelley's annual income was increased to £1000, £200 of which went to Harriet, and a great deal of which made its way to Godwin, who was now mollified by this turn in his fortune. In 1816, the Shelley ménage, including an infant son, spent a fateful summer with Lord Byron* in Geneva. Moved by the natural grandeur of the Swiss Alps, Percy meditated upon the relationship of the creative mind to nature in *Mont Blanc*; in *Hymn to Intellectual Beauty*, he dwelt on inspiration evoked internally by recollecting ecstatic experiences of beauty. Mary conceived *Frankenstein* in response to the challenge of a ghost-story contest suggested by Byron; Byron began the drama *Manfred*; and Claire became pregnant by Byron. Speaking as the voice of respectable British society, then poet laureate Robert Southey* condemned the "league of incest" abroad.

Life darkened considerably for Shelley after returning to England. He was troubled by the part his relationship with Mary may have played in the recent suicide of Mary's half-sister, Fanny Imlay. Pregnant with another man's child, Harriet also committed suicide by drowning. Although Percy and Mary married shortly thereafter, the courts refused Shelley custody of Ianthe and Charles, his children by Harriet, in favor of Harriet's family. The embittered Shelleys left England permanently in 1818 for the "Paradise of exiles, Italy!" (*Julian and Maddalo*). They again joined their kindred spirit Lord Byron, who had remained abroad for comparably compelling reasons: a scandalous divorce and well-founded rumors of incest and a child by his half-sister. The lovelight in the Shelley marriage waned after the death of their two children in 1818 and 1819, brought on by Percy's insistence on nomadic wandering. Their daughter Clara died in Venice. William's death in Rome finally drove Mary to a state of deep depression.

Despite domestic tragedy, a foundering marriage, and despair over his ideals, Shelley experienced his most prolific period. *Julian and Maddalo, Prometheus Unbound, The Cenci* (written between acts of *Prometheus*), "Ode to the West Wind," *The Mask of Anarchy,* "Stanzas Written in Dejection," Odes "To a Skylark" and "To Liberty," numerous shorter poems, and some penetrating political prose were all composed between late 1818 and 1820. In the meantime, having a third child, Percy Florence, did not repair the Shelley marriage, and Percy again experienced infatuation for a young woman in distress. He found Teresa Viviani, the daughter of the governor of Pisa, immured in a nunnery and wrote ecstatically of his platonic love in *Epipsychidion* (1821), i.e., "soul out of my soul." He had never been one of the monogamous "sect, / Whose doctrine is, that each one should select / Out of the crowd a mistress or a friend, / And all the rest though fair and wise, commend / To cold oblivion." Rather, he has believed that "True Love in this differs from gold and clay, / That to divide is not to take away."

Shelley's political aspirations were comparably idealistic. He admitted to "a passion for reforming the world" and early on attempted to incite revolution with futile political acts, such as floating his broadside of 1812, *A Declaration of Rights,* off to Ireland in bottles and above the sea in air balloons. Shelley also attempted to sell his poems expensively to "squeeze money out of the rich," so that he might sell his political pamphlets cheaply. Shortly after his first marriage, he travelled to Ireland with Harriet to arouse the spirit of nationalism among the Catholic peasantry. He spent some time making public speeches and posting broadsides. He published *An Address to the Irish People* (1812) and dreamed of dwelling "in some antique feudal castle whose mouldering turrets are fit emblems of decaying inequality and oppression, which the ivy shall wave its green banners above like Liberty." He also espoused in a series of pamphlets and in excursive *Notes* to *Queen Mab* (1813), the behavior he was to practice through life: vegetarianism, free love, and free speech. He scorned institutional religion and anthropomorphic sentiments about the deity and made Free Will the casualty of philosophical Necessity. (See SCIENCE AND NATURE):

> The advocates of free will assert that the will has the power of refusing to be determined by the strongest motive: but the strongest motive is that which, overcoming all others, ultimately prevails; this assertion therefore amounts to a denial of the will being ultimately determined by that motive which does determine it, which is absurd.

Intellectual arrogance was restricted to Shelley's prose. Rather than providing closure, the language and imagery of Shelley's poetry provoke a sense of the indeterminacy of history, knowledge, and being.

Abhorring didactic poetry but committed to the Renaissance ideal that poetry should "instruct and delight," Shelley composed his great lyric drama *Prometheus Unbound* (1820) to "familiarise the highly refined imagination of the more select classes of poetical readers with beautiful idealisms of moral excellence." The chief political idea Shelley wished to implant is a secularized version of the millennial anarchy promised by Milton's God in *Paradise Lost* (1667), when Christ His "regal scepter shalt lay by," and "God shall be all in all" (III.339–41). Shelley challenges his reader to muse seriously on the possibility that man may find himself, if he would only will it, "Sceptreless, free, uncircumscribed, . . . / Equal, unclassed, tribeless, and nationless, / Exempt from awe, worship, degree, the king / Over himself." But though an argument for the achievement of a millennial moment might be made "refutation-tight / As far as words go," as Shelley writes in *Julian and Maddalo,* he does not hesitate to cast doubt on its feasibility until mankind experiences an imaginative and spiritual regeneration.

Shelley's faith in the humanist position that language constructs our perceptual reality is the subject of *Defence of Poetry.* The poet's friend Thomas Love Peacock (1785–1866) had argued humorously—but with sufficient point—in his essay "The Four Ages of Poetry" that the best minds of society must give up poetry as the thing of a child for the adult concerns of economics and social science. Shelley responds that the schemes of modern reformers are misguided because vacuous. Could one seriously believe with Benthamite liberals, for example, that *counting* the greatest good for the greatest number is the way to a higher social morality? "We have more moral, political, and historical wisdom than we know how to reduce into practice; we have more scientific and economic knowledge than can be accommodated to the just distribution of the produce which it multiplies," Shelley argues: "we want the poetry of life." If the "great secret of morals is Love," defined by Shelley as "an identification of ourselves with the beautiful which exists in thought, action, or person, not our own," poetry increases our ability to love by exercising the sympathetic capacity of imagination. Poetic metaphor underwrites the laws of society as language becomes reality. Poets thus effect even more than they know. Infused with "the spirit of the age," or "the influence which is moved not, but moves," they become "the unacknowledged legislators of the world."

Although Shelley acknowledged that his aspirations for politics, life, and his art were beyond immediate human possibility, he was more attracted to death than inclined to accommodation. Reviewing *Alastor* (1816) in *Blackwood's Magazine,* John Gibson Lockhart noted that "Mr. Shelley's imagination is enamoured of dreams of death; and he loves to strike his harp among the tombs." Shelley drowned during a summer squall on the Bay of Spezia. Together with a boat boy and a friend, Edward Williams, Shelley was sailing home after a visit to Livorno. Although setting out late on a threatening afternoon was imprudent, and seems suspicious behavior for one allured by death, Shelley was too generous to endanger others consciously. Because of the strictures of quarantine, Byron and the romantic adventurer Edward John Trelawney conducted a ceremonious cremation on the beach, during which, Trelawney reports, "more wine was poured over Shelley's dead body than he had consumed during his life." The flames reduced to powder everything but a few scraps of bone and Shelley's heart, which, Trelawney reports, "remained entire." Shelley's ashes were buried in the Protestant Cemetary in Rome near the remains of his beloved "Wilmouse" (son William).

At the time of his death, Shelley was working on the enigmatic *Triumph of Life,* which ends with a truncated response to the question "Then, what is Life?" Mary Shelley assured her husband's posthumous literary life by collecting, editing, and brilliantly annotating his works in several important editions (1824, 1839).

from ALASTOR; OR, THE SPIRIT OF SOLITUDE[1]

and Other Poems

(1816)

—PREFACE—

The poem entitled "ALASTOR," may be considered as allegorical of one of the most interesting situations of the human mind. It represents a youth of uncorrupted feelings and adventurous genius led forth by an imagination inflamed and purified through familiarity with all that is excellent and majestic, to the contemplation of the universe. He drinks deep of the fountains of knowledge, and is still insatiate. The magnificence and beauty of the external world sinks profoundly into the frame of his conceptions, and affords to their modifications a variety not to be exhausted. So long as it is possible for his desires to point towards objects thus infinite and unmeasured, he is joyous, and tranquil, and self-possessed. But the period arrives when these objects cease to suffice. His mind is at length suddenly awakened and thirsts for intercourse with an intelligence similar to itself. He images to himself the Being whom he loves. Conversant with speculations of the sublimest and most perfect natures, the vision in which he embodies his own imaginations unites all of wonderful, or wise, or beautiful, which the poet, the philosopher, or the lover could depicture. The intellectual faculties, the imagination, the functions of sense, have their respective requisitions on the sympathy of corresponding powers in other human beings. The Poet is represented as uniting these requisitions, and attaching them to a single image. He seeks in vain for a prototype of his conception. Blasted by his disappointment, he descends to an untimely grave.

The picture is not barren of instruction to actual men. The Poet's self-centred seclusion was avenged by the furies of an irresistible passion pursuing him to speedy ruin. But that Power which strikes the luminaries of the world with sudden darkness and extinction, by awakening them to too exquisite a perception of its influences, dooms to a slow and poisonous decay those meaner spirits that dare to abjure its dominion. Their destiny is more abject and inglorious as their delinquency is more contemptible and pernicious. They who, deluded by no generous error, instigated by no sacred thirst of doubtful knowledge, duped by no illustrious superstition, loving nothing on this earth, and cherishing no hopes beyond, yet keep aloof from sympathies with their kind, rejoicing neither in human joy nor mourning with human grief; these, and such as they, have their apportioned curse. They languish, because none feel with them their common nature. They are morally dead. They are neither friends, nor lovers, nor fathers, nor citizens of the world, nor benefactors of their country. Among those who attempt to exist without human sympathy, the pure and tender-hearted perish through the intensity and passion of their search after its communities, when the vacancy of their spirit suddenly makes itself felt. All else, selfish, blind, and torpid, are those unforeseeing multitudes who constitute, together with their own, the lasting misery and loneliness of the world. Those who love not their fellow-beings live unfruitful lives, and prepare for their old age a miserable grave.

> "The good die first,
> And those whose hearts are dry as summer dust,
> Burn to the socket!"[2]

December 14, 1815.

[1] Published in London. The other poems numbered ten.

[2] Cf. W. Wordsworth, *The Excursion,** I.500–502: "the good die first, / And they whose hearts are dry as summer dust / Burn to the socket." **socket:** the part of the candlestick that holds the candle.

Alastor; or, The Spirit of Solitude

(comp. 1815)

Nondum amabam, et amare amabam, quaerebam quid amarem, amans amare. — Confess. St. August.[3]

Earth, ocean, air, beloved brotherhood!
If our great Mother has imbued my soul
With aught of natural piety[4] to feel
Your love, and recompense the boon with mine;
If dewy morn, and odorous noon, and even,
With sunset and its gorgeous ministers,
And solemn midnight's tingling silentness;
If autumn's hollow sighs in the sere wood,
And winter robing with pure snow and crowns
Of starry ice the grey grass and bare boughs;
If spring's voluptuous pantings when she breathes
Her first sweet kisses, have been dear to me;
If no bright bird, insect, or gentle beast
I consciously have injured, but still loved
And cherished these my kindred; then forgive
This boast, beloved brethren, and withdraw
No portion of your wonted favour now!
Mother of this unfathomable world!
Favour my solemn song, for I have loved
Thee ever, and thee only; I have watched
Thy shadow, and the darkness of thy steps,
And my heart ever gazes on the depth
Of thy deep mysteries. I have made my bed
In charnels and on coffins, where black death
Keeps record of the trophies won from thee.
Hoping to still these obstinate questionings[5]
Of thee and thine, by forcing some lone ghost,
Thy messenger, to render up the tale
Of what we are. In lone and silent hours,
When night makes a weird sound of its own stillness,
Like an inspired and desperate alchymist
Staking his very life on some dark hope,
Have I mixed awful talk and asking looks
With my most innocent love, until strange tears
Uniting with those breathless kisses, made
Such magic as compels the charmed night
To render up thy charge: . . . and, though ne'er yet
Thou hast unveil'd thy inmost sanctuary,
Enough from incommunicable dream,
And twilight phantasms, and deep noonday thought,
Has shone within me, that serenely now
And moveless, as a long-forgotten lyre
Suspended in the solitary dome
Of some mysterious and deserted fane,[6]
I wait thy breath, Great Parent, that my strain
May modulate with murmurs of the air,
And motions of the forests and the sea,
And voice of living beings, and woven hymns
Of night and day, and the deep heart[7] of man.

There was a Poet whose untimely tomb
No human hands with pious reverence reared,
But the charmed eddies of autumnal winds
Built o'er his mouldering bones a pyramid
Of mouldering leaves in the waste wilderness: —
A lovely youth, — no mourning maiden decked
With weeping flowers, or votive cypress wreath,
The lone couch of his everlasting sleep: —
Gentle, and brave, and generous, — no lorn[8] bard
Breathed o'er his dark fate one melodious sigh:
He lived, he died, he sung, in solitude.
Strangers have wept to hear his passionate notes,
And virgins, as unknown he past, have pined
And wasted for fond love of his wild eyes.
The fire of those soft orbs has ceased to burn,
And Silence, too enamoured of that voice,
Locks its mute music in her rugged cell.

By solemn vision, and bright silver dream,
His infancy was nurtured. Every sight
And sound from the vast earth and ambient air,

---

[3] Cf. St. Augustine's *Confessions* 3.1: "Not yet did I love, yet I loved to love, seeking what I might love, loving to love."

[4] **natural piety**: Cf. W. Wordsworth's "My heart leaps up when I behold"*: "And I could wish my days to be / Bound each to each by natural piety."

[5] **obstinate questionings**: Cf. W. Wordsworth's *Ode*: "Obstinate questionings / Of sense and outward things," ll. 144–45.

[6] **fane**: temple.

[7] **the deep heart**: W. Wordsworth's "There Was a Boy": "a gentle shock of mild surprize / Has carried far into his heart the voice / Of mountain torrents."

[8] **cypress wreath**: funeral wreath of cypress, the tree associated with death by the Romans because when cut, it never grows back. **lorn**: forlorn.

Sent to his heart its choicest impulses.[9]
The fountains of divine philosophy
Fled not his thirsting lips, and all of great
Or good, or lovely, which the sacred past
In truth or fable consecrates, he felt
And knew. When early youth had past, he left
His cold fireside and alienated home
To seek strange truths in undiscovered lands.
Many a wide waste and tangled wilderness
Has lured his fearless steps; and he has bought
With his sweet voice and eyes, from savage men,
His rest and food. Nature's most secret steps
He like her shadow has pursued, where'er
The red volcano overcanopies
Its fields of snow and pinnacles of ice
With burning smoke, or where bitumen lakes[10]
On black bare pointed islets ever beat
With sluggish surge, or where the secret caves
Rugged and dark, winding among the springs
Of fire and poison, inaccessible
To avarice or pride, their starry domes
Of diamond and of gold expand above
Numberless and immeasurable halls,
Frequent with crystal column, and clear shrines
Of pearl, and thrones radiant with chrysolite.
Nor had that scene of ampler majesty
Than gems or gold, the varying roof of heaven
And the green earth lost in his heart its claims
To love and wonder; he would linger long
In lonesome vales, making the wild his home,
Until the doves and squirrels would partake
From his innocuous hand his bloodless food,
Lured by the gentle meaning of his looks,
And the wild antelope, that starts whene'er
The dry leaf rustles in the brake,[11] suspend
Her timid steps to gaze upon a form
More graceful than her own.

His wandering step
Obedient to high thoughts, has visited
The awful ruins of the days of old:
Athens, and Tyre, and Balbec, and the waste
Where stood Jerusalem, the fallen towers
Of Babylon, the eternal pyramids,
Memphis and Thebes,[12] and whatsoe'er of strange
Sculptured on alabaster obelisk,
Or jasper tomb, or mutilated sphynx,
Dark Æthiopia[13] in her desert hills
Conceals. Among the ruined temples there,
Stupendous columns, and wild images
Of more than man, where marble daemons watch
The Zodiac's brazen mystery,[14] and dead men
Hang their mute thoughts on the mute walls around,
He lingered, poring on memorials
Of the world's youth, through the long burning day
Gazed on those speechless shapes, nor, when the
moon
Filled the mysterious halls with floating shades
Suspended he that task, but ever gazed
And gazed, till meaning on his vacant mind
Flashed like strong inspiration, and he saw
The thrilling secrets of the birth of time.

Meanwhile an Arab maiden brought his food,
Her daily portion, from her father's tent,
And spread her matting for his couch, and stole
From duties and repose to tend his steps:—
Enamoured, yet not daring for deep awe
To speak her love:—and watched his nightly sleep,
Sleepless herself, to gaze upon his lips
Parted in slumber, whence the regular breath
Of innocent dreams arose: then, when red morn
Made paler the pale moon, to her cold home
Wildered, and wan, and panting, she returned.

The Poet wandering on, through Arabie
And Persia, and the wild Carmanian waste,[15]
And o'er the aërial mountains which pour down

[9] **ambient**: surrounding encircling. **impulses**: Wordsworth, "A Poet's Epitaph": "And impulses of deeper birth / Have come to him in solitude" ll. 47–48.

[10] **bitumen lakes**: "a kind of mineral pitch found in Palestine and Babylon, used as mortar" (*OED*).

[11] **brake**: an area overgrown with brush and undergrowth.

[12] **Athens . . . Thebes**: Athens, Greece; Tyre, capital of Phoenicia after eleventh century BC; Balbec or Baalbek, former Heliopolis, also in Phoenicia; Jerusalem, founded c. 4000 BC; Babylon, capital of ancient Babylonia, capital c. 1750 BC; Memphis, ancient Egyptian city; Thebes, Egyptian city that flourished 2200–1800 BC; Thebes was also a Grecian city that flourished 400 BC.

[13] **Æthiopia**: country in northeast Africa; modern-day Ethiopia.

[14] **Zodiac's brazen mystery**: The Zodiac is represented in a temple dedicated to Isis in Dendera, Egypt.

[15] **Carmanian waste**: desert in Persia; present-day Iran.

Indus and Oxus[16] from their icy caves,
In joy and exultation held his way;
Till in the vale of Cashmire,[17] far within
Its loneliest dell, where odorous plants entwine
Beneath the hollow rocks a natural bower,
Beside a sparkling rivulet he stretched
His languid limbs. A vision on his sleep
There came, a dream of hopes that never yet
Had flushed his cheek. He dreamed a veiled maid
Sate near him, talking in low solemn tones.
Her voice was like the voice of his own soul
Heard in the calm of thought; its music long,
Like woven sounds of streams and breezes, held
His inmost sense suspended in its web
Of many-coloured woof and shifting hues.
Knowledge and truth and virtue were her theme,
And lofty hopes of divine liberty,
Thoughts the most dear to him, and poesy,
Herself a poet. Soon the solemn mood
Of her pure mind kindled through all her frame
A permeating fire: wild numbers[18] then
She raised, with voice stifled in tremulous sobs
Subdued by its own pathos: her fair hands
Were bare alone, sweeping from some strange harp
Strange symphony, and in their branching veins
The eloquent blood told an ineffable tale.
The beating of her heart was heard to fill
The pauses of her music, and her breath
Tumultuously accorded with those fits
Of intermitted song. Sudden she rose,
As if her heart impatiently endured
Its bursting burthen: at the sound he turned,
And saw by the warm light of their own life
Her glowing limbs beneath the sinuous veil
Of woven wind, her outspread arms now bare,
Her dark locks floating in the breath of night,
Her beamy bending eyes, her parted lips
Outstretched, and pale, and quivering eagerly.
His strong heart sunk and sickened with excess
Of love. He reared his shuddering limbs and quelled
His gasping breath, and spread his arms to meet
Her panting bosom: . . . she drew back a while,
Then, yielding to the irresistible joy,
With frantic gesture and short breathless cry
Folded his frame in her dissolving arms.
Now blackness veiled his dizzy eyes, and night
Involved and swallowed up the vision; sleep,
Like a dark flood suspended in its course,
Rolled back its impulse on his vacant brain.

Roused by the shock he started from his trance—
The cold white light of morning, the blue moon
Low in the west, the clear and garish hills,
The distinct valley and the vacant woods,
Spread round him where he stood. Whither have fled[19]
The hues of heaven that canopied his bower
Of yesternight? The sounds that soothed his sleep,
The mystery and the majesty of Earth,
The joy, the exultation? His wan eyes
Gaze on the empty scene as vacantly
As ocean's moon looks on the moon in heaven.
The spirit of sweet human love has sent
A vision to the sleep of him who spurned
Her choicest gifts. He eagerly pursues
Beyond the realms of dream that fleeting shade;
He overleaps the bounds. Alas! alas!
Were limbs, and breath, and being intertwined
Thus treacherously? Lost, lost, for ever lost,
In the wide pathless desart of dim sleep,
That beautiful shape! Does the dark gate of death
Conduct to thy mysterious paradise,
O Sleep? Does the bright arch of rainbow clouds,
And pendent[20] mountains seen in the calm lake,
Lead only to a black and watery depth,
While death's blue vault, with loathliest vapours hung,
Where every shade which the foul grave exhales
Hides its dead eye from the detested day,
Conduct, O Sleep, to thy delightful realms?
This doubt with sudden tide flowed on his heart,
The insatiate hope which it awakened, stung
His brain even like despair.
While day-light held
The sky, the Poet kept mute conference
With his still soul. At night the passion came,
Like the fierce fiend of a distempered dream,
And shook him from his rest, and led him forth
Into the darkness.—As an eagle grasped

[16] **Indus and Oxus:** rivers that originate in the Hindu Kush Mountains.

[17] **Cashmire:** a region of northwest India and northeast Pakistan.

[18] **numbers:** metrical feet of poetry.

[19] **Whither have fled . . . :** Cf. W. Wordsworth's *Ode*, l. 56: "Whither is fled the visionary gleam?"

[20] **pendent:** overhanging.

In folds of the green serpent, feels her breast
Burn with the poison, and precipitates
Through night and day, tempest, and calm, and cloud,
Frantic with dizzying anguish, her blind flight
O'er the wide aëry wilderness: thus driven
By the bright shadow of that lovely dream,
Beneath the cold glare of the desolate night,
Through tangled swamps and deep precipitous dells,
Startling with careless step the moon-light snake,
He fled. Red morning dawned upon his flight,
Shedding the mockery of its vital hues
Upon his cheek of death. He wandered on
Till vast Aornos seen from Petra's steep
Hung o'er the low horizon like a cloud;
Through Balk, and where the desolated tombs
Of Parthian kings scatter to every wind
Their wasting dust, wildly he wandered on,[21]
Day after day, a weary waste of hours,
Bearing within his life the brooding care
That ever fed on its decaying flame.
And now his limbs were lean; his scattered hair
Sered by the autumn of strange suffering
Sung dirges in the wind; his listless hand
Hung like dead bone within its withered skin;
Life, and the lustre that consumed it, shone
As in a furnace burning secretly
From his dark eyes alone. The cottagers,
Who ministered with human charity
His human wants, beheld with wondering awe
Their fleeting visitant. The mountaineer,
Encountering on some dizzy precipice
That spectral form, deemed that the Spirit of wind
With lightning eyes, and eager breath, and feet
Disturbing not the drifted snow, had paused
In its career: the infant would conceal
His troubled visage in his mother's robe
In terror at the glare of those wild eyes,
To remember their strange light in many a dream
Of after-times; but youthful maidens, taught
By nature, would interpret half the woe
That wasted him, would call him with false names
Brother, and friend, would press his pallid hand
At parting, and watch, dim through tears, the path
Of his departure from their father's door.

At length upon the lone Chorasmian[22] shore
He paused, a wide and melancholy waste
Of putrid marshes. A strong impulse urged
His steps to the sea-shore. A swan was there,
Beside a sluggish stream among the reeds.
It rose as he approached, and with strong wings
Scaling the upward sky, bent its bright course
High over the immeasurable main.[23]
His eyes pursued its flight.—"Thou hast a home,
Beautiful bird; thou voyagest to thine home,
Where thy sweet mate will twine her downy neck
With thine, and welcome thy return with eyes
Bright in the lustre of their own fond joy.
And what am I that I should linger here,
With voice far sweeter than thy dying notes,
Spirit more vast than thine, frame more attuned
To beauty, wasting these surpassing powers
In the deaf air, to the blind earth, and heaven
That echoes not my thoughts?" A gloomy smile
Of desperate hope wrinkled his quivering lips.
For sleep, he knew, kept most relentlessly
Its precious charge, and silent death exposed,
Faithless perhaps as sleep, a shadowy lure,
With doubtful smile mocking its own strange charms.

Startled by his own thoughts he looked around.
There was no fair fiend near him, not a sight
Or sound of awe but in his own deep mind.
A little shallop floating near the shore
Caught the impatient wandering of his gaze.
It had been long abandoned, for its sides
Gaped wide with many a rift, and its frail joints
Swayed with the undulations of the tide.
A restless impulse urged him to embark
And meet lone Death on the drear ocean's waste;
For well he knew that mighty Shadow loves
The slimy caverns of the populous deep.

The day was fair and sunny; sea and sky
Drank its inspiring radiance, and the wind
Swept strongly from the shore, blackening the waves.
Following his eager soul, the wanderer
Leaped in the boat, he spread his cloak aloft

[21] **Aornos:** a mountain. **Petra:** an ancient city of Edom in modern Jordan, discovered in 1812 ("the rose-red city"). **Balk** or **Balkh:** an ancient city in modern Afghanistan. **Parthia:** an ancient country that was located in the northeast region of modern Iran, and part of the Assyrian and Persian empires.

[22] **Chorasmian:** Aral Sea, the fourth largest inland body of water in the world at 24,700 square miles.

[23] **main:** the sea.

On the bare mast, and took his lonely seat,
And felt the boat speed o'er the tranquil sea
Like a torn cloud before the hurricane.

As one that in a silver vision floats
Obedient to the sweep of odorous winds
Upon resplendent clouds, so rapidly
Along the dark and ruffled waters fled
The straining boat. — A whirlwind swept it on,
With fierce gusts and precipitating force,
Through the white ridges of the chafed[24] sea.
The waves arose. Higher and higher still
Their fierce necks writhed beneath the tempest's
scourge
Like serpents struggling in a vulture's grasp.
Calm and rejoicing in the fearful war
Of wave running on wave, and blast on blast
Descending, and black flood on whirlpool driven
With dark obliterating course, he sate:
As if their genii were the ministers
Appointed to conduct him to the light
Of those beloved eyes, the Poet sate
Holding the steady helm. Evening came on,
The beams of sunset hung their rainbow hues
High 'mid the shifting domes of sheeted spray
That canopied his path o'er the waste deep;
Twilight, ascending slowly from the east,
Entwin'd in duskier wreaths her braided locks
O'er the fair front and radiant eyes of day;
Night followed, clad with stars. On every side
More horribly the multitudinous streams
Of ocean's mountainous waste to mutual war
Rushed in dark tumult thundering, as to mock
The calm and spangled sky. The little boat
Still fled before the storm; still fled, like foam
Down the steep cataract of a wintry river;
Now pausing on the edge of the riven wave;
Now leaving far behind the bursting mass
That fell, convulsing ocean. Safely fled—
As if that frail and wasted human form,
Had been an elemental god.
At midnight
The moon arose: and lo! the etherial cliffs
Of Caucasus, whose icy summits shone
Among the stars like sunlight, and around
Whose cavern'd base the whirlpools and the waves
Bursting and eddying irresistibly
Rage and resound for ever. — Who shall save?—
The boat fled on, — the boiling torrent drove, —
The crags closed round with black and jagged arms,
The shattered mountain overhung the sea,
And faster still, beyond all human speed,
Suspended on the sweep of the smooth wave,
The little boat was driven. A cavern there
Yawned, and amid its slant and winding depths
Ingulphed the rushing sea. The boat fled on
With unrelaxing speed. — "Vision and Love!"
The Poet cried aloud, "I have beheld
The path of thy departure. Sleep and death
Shall not divide us long!"
The boat pursued
The winding of the cavern. Day-light shone
At length upon that gloomy river's flow;
Now, where the fiercest war among the waves
Is calm, on the unfathomable stream
The boat moved slowly. Where the mountain, riven,
Exposed those black depths to the azure sky,
Ere yet the flood's enormous volume fell
Even to the base of Caucasus, with sound
That shook the everlasting rocks, the mass
Filled with one whirlpool all that ample chasm;
Stair above stair the eddying waters rose,
Circling immeasurably fast, and laved
With alternating dash the knarled roots
Of mighty trees, that stretched their giant arms
In darkness over it. I' the midst was left,
Reflecting, yet distorting every cloud,
A pool of treacherous and tremendous calm.
Seized by the sway of the ascending stream,
With dizzy swiftness, round, and round, and round,
Ridge after ridge the straining boat arose,
Till on the verge of the extremest curve,
Where, through an opening of the rocky bank,
The waters overflow, and a smooth spot
Of glassy quiet mid those battling tides
Is left, the boat paused shuddering. — Shall it sink
Down the abyss? Shall the reverting stress
Of that resistless gulph embosom it?
Now shall it fall? — A wandering stream of wind,
Breathed from the west, has caught the expanded sail,
And lo! with gentle motion, between banks
Of mossy slope, and on a placid stream,
Beneath a woven grove it sails, and, hark!
The ghastly torrent mingles its far roar,
With the breeze murmuring in the musical woods.

[24] **chafed:** angered, vexed.

Where the embowering trees recede, and leave
A little space of green expanse, the cove
Is closed by meeting banks, whose yellow flowers[25]
For ever gaze on their own drooping eyes,
Reflected in the crystal calm. The wave
Of the boat's motion marred their pensive task,
Which nought but vagrant bird, or wanton wind,
Or falling spear-grass, or their own decay
Had e'er disturbed before. The Poet longed
To deck with their bright hues his withered hair,
But on his heart its solitude returned,
And he forbore. Not the strong impulse hid
In those flushed cheeks, bent eyes, and shadowy
    frame,
Had yet performed its ministry: it hung
Upon his life, as lightning in a cloud
Gleams, hovering ere it vanish, ere the floods
Of night close over it.
                The noonday sun
Now shone upon the forest, one vast mass
Of mingling shade, whose brown magnificence
A narrow vale embosoms. There, huge caves,
Scooped in the dark base of their aëry rocks
Mocking its moans, respond and roar for ever.
The meeting boughs and implicated leaves
Wove twilight o'er the Poet's path, as led
By love, or dream, or god, or mightier Death,
He sought in Nature's dearest haunt, some bank,
Her cradle, and his sepulchre. More dark
And dark the shades accumulate. The oak,
Expanding its immense and knotty arms,
Embraces the light beech. The pyramids
Of the tall cedar overarching, frame
Most solemn domes within, and far below.
Like clouds suspended in an emerald sky,
The ash and the acacia floating hang
Tremulous and pale. Like restless serpents, clothed
In rainbow and in fire, the parasites,
Starred with ten thousand blossoms, flow around
The grey trunks, and, as gamesome infants' eyes,
With gentle meanings, and most innocent wiles,
Fold their beams round the hearts of those that love,
These twine their tendrils with the wedded boughs
Uniting their close union; the woven leaves
Make net-work of the dark blue light of day,
And the night's noontide clearness, mutable
As shapes in the weird clouds. Soft mossy lawns
Beneath these canopies extend their swells,
Fragrant with perfumed herbs, and eyed with blooms
Minute yet beautiful. One darkest glen
Sends from its woods of musk-rose, twined with
    jasmine,
A soul-dissolving odour, to invite
To some more lovely mystery. Through the dell,
Silence and Twilight here, twin-sisters, keep
Their noonday watch, and sail among the shades,
Like vaporous shapes half seen; beyond, a well,
Dark, gleaming, and of most translucent wave,
Images all the woven boughs above,
And each depending leaf, and every speck
Of azure sky, darting between their chasms;
Nor aught else in the liquid mirror laves
Its portraiture, but some inconstant star
Between one foliaged lattice twinkling fair,
Or, painted bird, sleeping beneath the moon,
Or gorgeous insect floating motionless,
Unconscious of the day, ere yet his wings
Have spread their glories to the gaze of noon.

  Hither the Poet came. His eyes beheld
Their own wan light through the reflected lines
Of his thin hair, distinct in the dark depth
Of that still fountain; as the human heart,
Gazing in dreams over the gloomy grave,
Sees its own treacherous likeness there. He heard
The motion of the leaves, the grass that sprung
Startled and glanced and trembled even to feel
An unaccustomed presence, and the sound
Of the sweet brook that from the secret springs
Of that dark fountain rose. A Spirit seemed
To stand beside him—clothed in no bright robes
Of shadowy silver or enshrining light,
Borrowed from aught the visible world affords
Of grace, or majesty, or mystery;—
But, undulating woods, and silent well,
And leaping rivulet, and evening gloom
Now deepening the dark shades, for speech assuming
Held commune with him, as if he and it
Were all that was,—only . . . when his regard
Was raised by intense pensiveness, . . . two eyes,
Two starry eyes, hung in the gloom of thought,
And seemed with their serene and azure smiles
To beckon him.

[25] **yellow flowers:** the narcissus, which suggests the legend of Narcissus, the youth who fell in love with his image in a pool of water and was transformed into the flower.

Obedient to the light
That shone within his soul, he went, pursuing
The windings of the dell.—The rivulet
Wanton and wild, through many a green ravine
Beneath the forest flowed. Sometimes it fell
Among the moss with hollow harmony
Dark and profound. Now on the polished stones
It danced; like childhood laughing as it went:
Then, through the plain in tranquil wanderings crept,
Reflecting every herb and drooping bud
That overhung its quietness.—"O stream!
Whose source is inaccessibly profound,
Whither do thy mysterious waters tend?
Thou imagest my life. Thy darksome stillness,
Thy dazzling waves, thy loud and hollow gulphs,
Thy searchless fountain, and invisible course
Have each their type in me: and the wide sky,
And measureless ocean may declare as soon
What oozy cavern or what wandering cloud
Contains thy waters, as the universe
Tell where these living thoughts reside, when stretched
Upon thy flowers my bloodless limbs shall waste
I' the passing wind!"

Beside the grassy shore
Of the small stream he went; he did impress
On the green moss his tremulous step, that caught
Strong shuddering from his burning limbs. As one
Roused by some joyous madness from the couch
Of fever, he did move; yet, not like him,
Forgetful of the grave, where, when the flame
Of his frail exultation shall be spent,
He must descend. With rapid steps he went
Beneath the shade of trees, beside the flow
Of the wild babbling rivulet; and now
The forest's solemn canopies were changed
For the uniform and lightsome evening sky.
Grey rocks did peep from the spare moss, and stemmed
The struggling brook: tall spires of windlestrae[26]
Threw their thin shadows down the rugged slope,
And nought but knarled roots of antient pines
Branchless and blasted, clenched with grasping roots
The unwilling soil. A gradual change was here,
Yet ghastly. For, as fast years flow away,
The smooth brow gathers, and the hair grows thin
And white, and where irradiate dewy eyes
Had shone, gleam stony orbs:—so from his steps
Bright flowers departed, and the beautiful shade
Of the green groves, with all their odorous winds
And musical motions. Calm, he still pursued
The stream, that with a larger volume now
Rolled through the labyrinthine dell, and there
Fretted a path through its descending curves
With its wintry speed. On every side now rose
Rocks, which, in unimaginable forms,
Lifted their black and barren pinnacles
In the light of evening, and its precipice
Obscuring the ravine, disclosed above,
Mid toppling stones, black gulphs and yawning caves,
Whose windings gave ten thousand various tongues
To the loud stream. Lo! where the pass expands
Its stony jaws, the abrupt mountain breaks,
And seems, with its accumulated crags,
To overhang the world: for wide expand
Beneath the wan stars and descending moon
Islanded seas, blue mountains, mighty streams,
Dim tracts and vast, robed in the lustrous gloom
Of leaden-coloured even, and fiery hills
Mingling their flames with twilight, on the verge
Of the remote horizon. The near scene,
In naked and severe simplicity,
Made contrast with the universe. A pine,
Rock-rooted, stretched athwart the vacancy
Its swinging boughs, to each inconstant blast
Yielding one only response, at each pause
In most familiar cadence, with the howl
The thunder and the hiss of homeless streams
Mingling its solemn song, whilst the broad river,
Foaming and hurrying o'er its rugged path,
Fell into that immeasurable void
Scattering its waters to the passing winds.

Yet the grey precipice and solemn pine
And torrent, were not all;—one silent nook
Was there. Even on the edge of that vast mountain,
Upheld by knotty roots and fallen rocks,
It overlooked in its serenity
The dark earth, and the bending vault of stars.
It was a tranquil spot, that seemed to smile
Even in the lap of horror. Ivy clasped
The fissured stones with its entwining arms,
And did embower with leaves for ever green,
And berries dark, the smooth and even space
Of its inviolated floor, and here
The children of the autumnal whirlwind bore,

[26] **windlestrae:** dry stalks.

In wanton sport, those bright leaves, whose decay,
Red, yellow, or etherially pale,
Rivals the pride of summer. 'Tis the haunt
Of every gentle wind, whose breath can teach
The wilds to love tranquillity. One step,
One human step alone, has ever broken
The stillness of its solitude:—one voice
Alone inspired its echoes,—even that voice
Which hither came, floating among the winds,
And led the loveliest among human forms
To make their wild haunts the depository
Of all the grace and beauty that endued
Its motions, render up its majesty,
Scatter its music on the unfeeling storm,
And to the damp leaves and the blue cavern mould,
Nurses of rainbow flowers and branching moss,
Commit the colours of that varying cheek,
That snowy breast, those dark and drooping eyes.

The dim and horned moon[27] hung low, and poured
A sea of lustre on the horizon's verge
That overflowed its mountains. Yellow mist
Filled the unbounded atmosphere, and drank
Wan moonlight even to fulness: not a star
Shone, not a sound was heard; the very winds,
Danger's grim playmates, on that precipice
Slept, clasped in his embrace.—O, storm of death!
Whose sightless speed divides this sullen night:
And thou, colossal Skeleton, that, still
Guiding its irresistible career
In thy devastating omnipotence,
Art king of this frail world, from the red field
Of slaughter, from the reeking hospital,
The patriot's sacred couch, the snowy bed
Of innocence, the scaffold and the throne,
A mighty voice invokes thee. Ruin calls
His brother Death. A rare and regal prey
He hath prepared, prowling around the world;
Glutted with which thou mayst repose, and men
Go to their graves like flowers or creeping worms,
Nor ever more offer at thy dark shrine
The unheeded tribute of a broken heart.

When on the threshold of the green recess
The wanderer's footsteps fell, he knew that death
Was on him. Yet a little, ere it fled,
Did he resign his high and holy soul
To images of the majestic past,
That paused within his passive being now,
Like winds that bear sweet music, when they breathe
Through some dim latticed chamber. He did place
His pale lean hand upon the rugged trunk
Of the old pine. Upon an ivied stone
Reclined his languid head, his limbs did rest,
Diffused and motionless, on the smooth brink
Of that obscurest chasm;—and thus he lay,
Surrendering to their final impulses
The hovering powers of life. Hope and despair,
The torturers, slept; no mortal pain or fear
Marred his repose, the influxes of sense,
And his own being unalloyed by pain,
Yet feebler and more feeble, calmly fed
The stream of thought, till he lay breathing there
At peace, and faintly smiling:—his last sight
Was the great moon, which o'er the western line
Of the wide world her mighty horn suspended,
With whose dun[28] beams inwoven darkness seemed
To mingle. Now upon the jagged hills
It rests, and still as the divided frame
Of the vast meteor sunk, the Poet's blood,
That ever beat in mystic sympathy
With nature's ebb and flow, grew feebler still:
And when two lessening points of light alone
Gleamed through the darkness, the alternate gasp
Of his faint respiration scarce did stir
The stagnate night:—till the minutest ray
Was quenched, the pulse yet lingered in his heart.
It paused—it fluttered. But when heaven remained
Utterly black, the murky shades involved
An image, silent, cold, and motionless,
As their own voiceless earth and vacant air.
Even as a vapour fed with golden beams
That ministered on sunlight, ere the west
Eclipses it, was now that wonderous frame—
No sense, no motion, no divinity—
A fragile lute, on whose harmonious strings
The breath of heaven did wander—a bright stream
Once fed with many-voiced waves—a dream
Of youth, which night and time have quenched
for ever,
Still, dark, and dry, and unremembered now.

[27] **horned moon:** crescent moon.

[28] **dun:** brownish gray.

O, for Medea's wondrous alchemy,[29]
Which wheresoe'er it fell made the earth gleam
With bright flowers, and the wintry boughs exhale
From vernal blooms fresh fragrance! O, that God,
Profuse of poisons, would concede the chalice
Which but one living man has drained, who now,
Vessel of deathless wrath, a slave that feels
No proud exemption in the blighting curse
He bears, over the world wanders for ever,
Lone as incarnate death![30] O, that the dream
Of dark magician in his visioned cave,
Raking the cinders of a crucible
For life and power, even when his feeble hand
Shakes in its last decay, were the true law
Of this so lovely world! But thou art fled
Like some frail exhalation; which the dawn
Robes in its golden beams,—ah! thou hast fled!
The brave, the gentle, and the beautiful,
The child of grace and genius. Heartless things
Are done and said i' the world, and many worms
And beasts and men live on, and mighty Earth
From sea and mountain, city and wilderness,
In vesper low or joyous orison,
Lifts still its solemn voice:—but thou art fled—
Thou canst no longer know or love the shapes
Of this phantasmal scene, who have to thee
Been purest ministers, who are, alas!
Now thou art not. Upon those pallid lips
So sweet even in their silence, on those eyes
That image sleep in death, upon that form
Yet safe from the worm's outrage, let no tear
Be shed—not even in thought. Nor, when those hues
Are gone, and those divinest lineaments,
Worn by the senseless wind, shall live alone
In the frail pauses of this simple strain,
Let not high verse, mourning the memory
Of that which is no more, or painting's woe
Or sculpture, speak in feeble imagery
Their own cold powers. Art and eloquence,
And all the shews o' the world are frail and vain
To weep a loss that turns their lights to shade.
It is a woe too "deep for tears,"[31] when all
Is reft at once, when some surpassing Spirit,
Whose light adorned the world around it, leaves
Those who remain behind, not sobs or groans,
The passionate tumult of a clinging hope;
But pale despair and cold tranquillity,
Nature's vast frame, the web of human things,
Birth and the grave, that are not as they were.

To Wordsworth

(1816; comp. 1814–1815?)

POET of Nature, thou hast wept to know
That things depart which never may return:
Childhood and youth, friendship and love's first glow,
Have fled like sweet dreams, leaving thee to mourn.
These common woes I feel. One loss is mine
Which thou too feel'st, yet I alone deplore.
Thou wert as a lone star, whose light did shine
On some frail bark in winter's midnight roar:
Thou hast like to a rock-built refuge stood
Above the blind and battling multitude:
In honoured poverty thy voice did weave
Songs consecrate to truth and liberty,—
Deserting these, thou leavest me to grieve,
Thus having been, that thou should cease to be.[1]

Feelings of a Republican on the Fall of Bonaparte

(1816; comp. 1814–1815?)

I hated thee, fallen tyrant! I did groan
To think that a most unambitious slave,
Like thee, should dance and revel on the grave
Of Liberty. Thou mightst have built thy throne
Where it had stood even now: thou didst prefer

[29] **Medea's wondrous alchemy:** Medea's potion rejuvenated Aeson, the aged father of Jason, and caused fresh growth wherever it spilled. Cf. Ovid, *Metamorphoses,* VII.

[30] **He bears . . . death!:** the Wandering Jew.

[31] **too "deep for tears":** Cf. W. Wordsworth's *Ode,* l. 206: "Thoughts that do often lie too deep for tears."

[1] The language and imagery of light, mourning, ocean, embattled refuge, and permanent loss suggest a dialogic interplay with Wordsworth's *Elegiac Stanzas,** *Ode,** and Lucy poems, especially "Three Years She Grew."*

A frail and bloody pomp which Time has swept
In fragments towards Oblivion. Massacre,—
For this I prayed,—would on thy sleep have crept,
Treason and Slavery, Rapine, Fear, and Lust,
And stifled thee, their minister. I know
Too late, since thou and France are in the dust,
That Virtue owns a more eternal foe
Than Force or Fraud: old Custom, legal Crime,
And bloody Faith, the foulest birth of Time.

from HISTORY OF A SIX WEEKS' TOUR

(1817)

Mont Blanc[1] Lines Written in the Vale of Chamouni

(comp. 1816)

I

The everlasting universe of things
Flows through the mind, and rolls its rapid waves,
Now dark—now glittering—now reflecting gloom—
Now lending splendour, where from secret springs
The source of human thought its tribute brings
Of waters,—with a sound but half its own,
Such as a feeble brook will oft assume
In the wild woods, among the mountains lone,
Where waterfalls around it leap for ever,
Where woods and winds contend, and a vast river
Over its rocks ceaselessly bursts and raves.

II

Thus thou, Ravine of Arve[2]—dark, deep Ravine—
Thou many-coloured, many-voiced vale,
Over whose pines, and crags, and caverns sail
Fast cloud-shadows and sunbeams: awful scene,
Where Power in likeness of the Arve comes down
From the ice-gulfs that gird his secret throne,
Bursting through these dark mountains like the flame
Of lightning through the tempest;—thou dost lie,
Thy giant brood of pines around thee clinging,
Children of elder time, in whose devotion
The chainless winds still come and ever came
To drink their odours, and their mighty swinging
To hear—an old and solemn harmony;
Thine earthly rainbows stretched across the sweep
Of the aethereal waterfall, whose veil
Robes some unsculptured image; the strange sleep
Which when the voices of the desert fail
Wraps all in its own deep eternity;—
Thy caverns echoing to the Arve's commotion,
A loud, lone sound no other sound can tame;
Thou art pervaded with that ceaseless motion,
Thou art the path of that unresting sound—
Dizzy Ravine! and when I gaze on thee
I seem as in a trance sublime and strange
To muse on my own separate fantasy,
My own, my human mind, which passively
Now renders and receives fast influencings,
Holding an unremitting interchange
With the clear universe of things around;
One legion of wild thoughts, whose wandering wings
Now float above thy darkness, and now rest
Where that or thou art no unbidden guest,
In the still cave of the witch Poesy,
Seeking among the shadows that pass by
Ghosts of all things that are, some shade of thee,
Some phantom, some faint image; till the breast
From which they fled recalls them, thou art there!

III

Some say that gleams of a remoter world
Visit the soul in sleep,—that death is slumber,
And that its shapes the busy thoughts outnumber
Of those who wake and live.—I look on high;
Has some unknown omnipotence unfurled

[1] Shelley's note to the poem reads: "It was composed under the immediate impression of the deep and powerful feelings excited by the objects which it attempts to describe; and, as an undisciplined overflowing of the soul, rests its claim to approbation on an attempt to imitate the untamable wildness and inaccessible solemnity from which those feelings sprang." *History of a Six Weeks' Tour* is the combined journal of Mary and Percy that provides a record of their travels through postwar France, Germany, and Switzerland. Mont Blanc is the highest mountain of the Alps (15,771 feet), located in France on the border with Italy, near Switzerland.

[2] **Ravine of Arve:** ravine of the River Arve, which originates in the Vale of Chamouni.

The veil of life and death? or do I lie
In dream, and does the mightier world of sleep
Spread far around and inaccessibly
Its circles? For the very spirit fails,
Driven like a homeless cloud from steep to steep
That vanishes among the viewless gales!
Far, far above, piercing the infinite sky,
Mont Blanc appears, —still, snowy, and serene—
Its subject mountains their unearthly forms
Pile around it, ice and rock; broad vales between
Of frozen floods, unfathomable deeps,
Blue as the overhanging heaven, that spread
And wind among the accumulated steeps;
A desert peopled by the storms alone,
Save when the eagle brings some hunter's bone,
And the wolf tracks her there—how hideously
Its shapes are heaped around! rude, bare, and high,
Ghastly, and scarred, and riven.—Is this the scene
Where the old Earthquake-daemon taught her young
Ruin? Were these their toys? or did a sea
Of fire envelop once this silent snow?
None can reply—all seems eternal now.
The wilderness has a mysterious tongue
Which teaches awful doubt, or faith so mild,
So solemn, so serene, that man may be,
But for such faith, with nature reconciled;
Thou hast a voice, great Mountain, to repeal
Large codes of fraud and woe; not understood
By all, but which the wise, and great, and good
Interpret, or make felt, or deeply feel.

IV

The fields, the lakes, the forests, and the streams,
Ocean, and all the living things that dwell
Within the daedal earth: lightning, and rain,
Earthquake, and fiery flood, and hurricane,
The torpor of the year when feeble dreams
Visit the hidden buds, or dreamless sleep
Holds every future leaf and flower;—the bound
With which from that detested trance they leap;
The works and ways of man, their death and birth,
And that of him and all that his may be;
All things that move and breathe with toil and sound
Are born and die; revolve, subside, and swell.
Power dwells apart in its tranquillity,
Remote, serene, and inaccessible:
And *this*, the naked countenance of earth,
On which I gaze, even these primaeval mountains
Teach the adverting mind. The glaciers creep
Like snakes that watch their prey, from their far
fountains,
Slow rolling on; there, many a precipice,
Frost and the Sun in scorn of mortal power
Have piled: dome, pyramid, and pinnacle,
A city of death, distinct with many a tower
And wall impregnable of beaming ice.
Yet not a city, but a flood of ruin
Is there, that from the boundaries of the sky
Rolls its perpetual stream; vast pines are strewing
Its destined path, or in the mangled soil
Branchless and shattered stand; the rocks, drawn
down
From yon remotest waste, have overthrown
The limits of the dead and living world,
Never to be reclaimed. The dwelling-place
Of insects, beasts, and birds, becomes its spoil
Their food and their retreat for ever gone,
So much of life and joy is lost. The race
Of man flies far in dread; his work and dwelling
Vanish, like smoke before the tempest's stream,
And their place is not known. Below, vast caves
Shine in the rushing torrents' restless gleam,
Which from those secret chasms in tumult welling
Meet in the vale, and one majestic River,
The breath and blood of distant lands, for ever
Rolls its loud waters to the ocean-waves,
Breathes its swift vapours to the circling air.

V

Mont Blanc yet gleams on high:—the power is there,
The still and solemn power of many sights,
And many sounds, and much of life and death.
In the calm darkness of the moonless nights,
In the lone glare of day, the snows descend
Upon that Mountain; none beholds them there,
Nor when the flakes burn in the sinking sun,
Or the star-beams dart through them:—Winds
contend
Silently there, and heap the snow with breath
Rapid and strong, but silently! Its home
The voiceless lightning in these solitudes
Keeps innocently, and like vapour broods
Over the snow. The secret Strength of things
Which governs thought, and to the infinite dome
Of Heaven is as a law, inhabits thee!
And what were thou, and earth, and stars, and sea,
If to the human mind's imaginings
Silence and solitude were vacancy?

from THE EXAMINER
(1817–1818)

Hymn to Intellectual Beauty[1]
(1817; comp. 1816)

1

The awful shadow of some unseen Power
Floats though unseen amongst us,—visiting
This various world with as inconstant wing
As summer winds that creep from flower to flower.—
Like moonbeams that behind some piny mountain shower,
It visits with inconstant glance
Each human heart and countenance;
Like hues and harmonies of evening,—
Like clouds in starlight widely spread,—
Like memory of music fled,—
Like aught that for its grace may be
Dear, and yet dearer for its mystery.

2

Spirit of BEAUTY, that doth consecrate
With thine own hues all thou dost shine upon
Of human thought or form,—where art thou gone?
Why dost thou pass away and leave our state,
This dim vast vale of tears, vacant and desolate?
Ask why the sunlight not forever
Weaves rainbows o'er yon mountain river,
Why aught should fail and fade that once is shewn,
Why fear and dream and death and birth
Cast on the daylight of this earth
Such gloom,—why man has such a scope
For love and hate, despondency and hope?

3

No voice from some sublimer world hath ever
To sage or poet these responses given—
Therefore the name of God and ghosts and Heaven,
Remain the records of their vain endeavour,
Frail spells—whose uttered charm might not avail to sever,
From all we hear and all we see,
Doubt, chance, and mutability.
Thy light alone—like mist o'er mountains driven,
Or music by the night wind sent
Through strings of some still instrument,
Or moonlight on a midnight stream,
Gives grace and truth to life's unquiet dream.

4

Love, Hope, and Self-esteem, like clouds depart
And come, for some uncertain moments lent.
Man were immortal, and omnipotent,
Didst thou, unknown and awful as thou art,
Keep with thy glorious train firm state within his heart.
Thou messenger of sympathies,
That wax and wane in lovers' eyes—
Thou—that to human thought art nourishment,
Like darkness to a dying flame!
Depart not as thy shadow came,
Depart not—lest the grave should be,
Like life and fear, a dark reality.

5

While yet a boy I sought for ghosts, and sped
Through many a listening chamber, cave and ruin,
And starlight wood, with fearful steps pursuing
Hopes of high talk with the departed dead.
I called on poisonous names with which our youth is fed;
I was not heard—I saw them not—
When musing deeply on the lot
Of life, at that sweet time when winds are wooing
All vital things that wake to bring
News of buds and blossoming,—
Sudden, thy shadow fell on me;
I shrieked, and clasped my hands in extacy!

6

I vowed that I would dedicate my powers
To thee and thine—have I not kept the vow?
With beating heart and streaming eyes, even now
I call the phantoms of a thousand hours
Each from his voiceless grave: they have in visioned bowers
Of studious zeal or love's delight

[1] Published in John and Leigh Hunt's radical weekly newspaper, *The Examiner*, January 1817. Revised and published in *Rosalind and Helen* (1819).

Outwatched with me the envious night—
They know that never joy illumed my brow
Unlinked with hope that thou wouldst free
This world from its dark slavery,
That thou—O awful LOVELINESS,
Wouldst give whate'er these words cannot express.

7

The day becomes more solemn and serene
When noon is past—there is a harmony
In autumn, and a lustre in its sky,
Which through the summer is not heard or seen,
As if it could not be, as if it had not been!
Thus let thy power, which like the truth
Of nature on my passive youth
Descended, to my onward life supply
Its calm—to one who worships thee,
And every form containing thee,
Whom, SPIRIT fair, thy spells did bind
To fear[2] himself, and love all human kind.

Ozymandias[1]

(1818; comp. 1817)

I met a traveller from an antique land
Who said: Two vast and trunkless legs of stone
Stand in the desert . . . Near them, on the sand,
Half sunk, a shattered visage lies, whose frown,
And wrinkled lip, and sneer of cold command,
Tell that its sculptor well those passions read
Which yet survive, stamped on these lifeless things,
The hand that mocked them, and the heart that fed:
And on the pedestal these words appear:
'My name is Ozymandias, king of kings:
Look on my works, ye Mighty, and despair!'
Nothing beside remains. Round the decay
Of that colossal wreck, boundless and bare
The lone and level sands stretch far away.

[2] **fear:** have "a mingled feeling of dread and reverence" (*OED*).

[1] Published January 1818. Also republished with *Rosalind and Helen* (1819).

THE CENCI

A Tragedy, in Five Acts[1]

(1819)

—*from* PREFACE—

A manuscript was communicated to me during my travels in Italy which was copied from the archives of the Cenci Palace at Rome, and contains a detailed account of the horrors which ended in the extinction of one of the noblest and richest families of that city during the Pontificate of Clement VIII,[2] in the year, 1599. The story is, that an old man having spent his life in debauchery and wickedness, conceived at length an implacable hatred towards his children; which shewed itself towards one daughter under the form of an incestuous passion, aggravated by every circumstance of cruelty and violence. This daughter, after long and vain attempts to escape from what she considered a perpetual contamination both of body and mind, at length plotted with her mother-in-law and brother to murder their common tyrant. The young maiden who was urged to this tremendous deed by an impulse which overpowered its horror, was evidently a most gentle and amiable being, a creature formed to adorn and be admired, and thus violently thwarted from her nature by the necessity of circumstance and opinion. The deed was quickly discovered and in spite of the most earnest prayers made to the Pope by the highest persons in Rome the criminals were put to death. The old man had during his life repeatedly bought his pardon from the Pope for capital crimes of the most enormous and unspeakable kind, at the price of a hundred thousand crowns;[3] the death therefore of his victims can scarcely be accounted for by the love of justice. The Pope, among other motives for severity, probably felt that whoever killed the Count Cenci deprived his treasury of a certain and copious source of revenue. The Papal Government formerly took the most extraordinary precautions against the publicity of facts which offer so tragical a demonstration of its own wickedness and weakness; so that the communication of

[1] First published by Shelley in Rome, 1819, and in London, 1820.

[2] **Pontificate of Clement VIII:** Pope (1592–1605) of the Roman Catholic Church during the period of the Italian Renaissance.

[3] **a hundred thousand crowns:** 50,000 British pounds.

the M. S. [MSS.] had become, until very lately, a matter of some difficulty. Such a story, if told so as to present to the reader all the feelings of those who once acted it, their hopes and fears, their confidences and misgivings, their various interests, passions and opinions acting upon and with each other, yet all conspiring to one tremendous end, would be as a light to make apparent some of the most dark and secret caverns of the human heart.

On my arrival at Rome I found that the story of the Cenci was a subject not to be mentioned in Italian society without awakening a deep and breathless interest; and that the feelings of the company never failed to incline to a romantic pity for the wrongs, and a passionate exculpation of the horrible deed to which they urged her, who has been mingled two centuries with the common dust. All ranks of people knew the outlines of this history, and participated in the overwhelming interest which it seems to have the magic of exciting in the human heart. I had a copy of Guido's[4] picture of Beatrice which is preserved in the Colonna Palace, and my servant instantly recognized it as the portrait of *La Cenci*.

This national and universal interest which the story produces and has produced for two centuries and among all ranks of people in a great City, where the imagination is kept for ever active and awake, first suggested to me the conception of its fitness for a dramatic purpose. In fact it is a tragedy which has already received from its capacity of awakening and sustaining the sympathy of men, approbation and success. Nothing remained as I imagined, but to clothe it to the apprehensions of my countrymen in such language and action as would bring it home to their hearts. The deepest and the sublimest tragic compositions, King Lear and the two plays in which the tale of Ædipus is told, were stories which already existed in tradition, as matters of popular belief and interest, before Shakspeare and Sophocles made them familiar to the sympathy of all succeeding generations of mankind.

This story of the Cenci is indeed eminently fearful and monstrous: any thing like a dry exhibition of it on the stage would be insupportable. The person who would treat such a subject must increase the ideal, and diminish the actual horror of the events, so that the pleasure which arises from the poetry which exists in these tempestuous sufferings and crimes may mitigate the pain of the contemplation of the moral deformity from which they spring. There must also be nothing attempted to make the exhibition subservient to what is vulgarly termed a moral purpose. The highest moral purpose aimed at in the highest species of the drama, is the teaching the human heart, through its sympathies and antipathies, the knowledge of itself; in proportion to the possession of which knowledge, every human being is wise, just, sincere, tolerant and kind. If dogmas can do more, it is well: but a drama is no fit place for the enforcement of them. Undoubtedly, no person can be truly dishonoured by the act of another; and the fit return to make to the most enormous injuries is kindness and forbearance, and a resolution to convert the injurer from his dark passions by peace and love. Revenge, retaliation, atonement, are pernicious mistakes. If Beatrice had thought in this manner she would have been wiser and better; but she would never have been a tragic character: the few whom such an exhibition would have interested, could never have been sufficiently interested for a dramatic purpose, from the want of finding sympathy in their interest among the mass who surround them. It is in the restless and anatomizing casuistry[5] with which men seek the justification of Beatrice, yet feel that she has done what needs justification; it is in the superstitious horror with which they contemplate alike her wrongs and their revenge; that the dramatic character of what she did and suffered, consists.

I have endeavoured as nearly as possible to represent the characters as they probably were, and have sought to avoid the error of making them actuated by my own conceptions of right or wrong, false or true thus under a thin veil converting names and actions of the sixteenth century into cold impersonations of my own mind. They are represented as Catholics, and as Catholics deeply tinged with religion. To a Protestant apprehension there will appear something unnatural in the earnest and perpetual sentiment of the relations between God and man which pervade the tragedy of the Cenci. It will especially be startled at the combination of an undoubting persuasion of the truth of the popular religion with a cool and determined perseverance in enormous guilt. But religion in Italy is not, as in protestant countries, a cloak to be worn on particular days; or a passport which those who do not wish to be railed at carry with them to exhibit; or a gloomy passion for penetrating the impenetrable mysteries of our

[4] **Guido:** Guido Reni, whom Shelley mistakenly believes to have painted the portrait of Beatrice Cenci, who murdered her father, Count Francesco Cenci, in 1599. The painting of Beatrice Cenci is now in the Corsini Palace in Rome.

[5] **casuistry:** faulty reasoning intended to mislead.

being, which terrifies its possessor at the darkness of the abyss to the brink of which it has conducted him. Religion coexists, as it were, in the mind of an Italian Catholic with a faith in that of which all men have the most certain knowledge. It is interwoven with the whole fabric of life. It is adoration, faith, submission, penitence, blind admiration; not a rule for moral conduct. It has no necessary connexion with any one virtue. The most atrocious villain may be rigidly devout, and without any shock to established faith, confess himself to be so. Religion pervades intensely the whole frame of society, and is according to the temper of the mind which it inhabits, a passion, a persuasion, an excuse, a refuge; never a check. Cenci himself built a chapel in the court of his Palace, and dedicated it to St. Thomas the Apostle, and established masses for the peace of his soul. Thus in the first scene of the fourth act Lucretia's design in exposing herself to the consequences of an expostulation with Cenci after having administered the opiate, was to induce him by a feigned tale to confess himself before death; this being esteemed by Catholics as essential to salvation; and she only relinquishes her purpose when she perceives that her perseverance would expose Beatrice to new outrages.

I have avoided with great care in writing this play the introduction of what is commonly called mere poetry, and I imagine there will scarcely be found a detached simile or a single isolated description, unless Beatrice's description of the chasm appointed for her father's murder should be judged to be of that nature.

In a dramatic composition the imagery and the passion should interpenetrate one another, the former being reserved simply for the full developement and illustration of the latter. Imagination is as the immortal God which should assume flesh for the redemption of mortal passion. It is thus that the most remote and the most familiar imagery may alike be fit for dramatic purposes when employed in the illustration of strong feeling, which raises what is low, and levels to the apprehension that which is lofty, casting over all the shadow of its own greatness. In other respects I have written more carelessly; that is, without an over-fastidious and learned choice of words. In this respect I entirely agree with those modern critics who assert that in order to move men to true sympathy we must use the familiar language of men.[6] And that our great ancestors the antient English poets are the writers, a study of whom might incite us to do that for our own age which they have done for theirs. But it must be the real language of men in general and not that of any particular class to whose society the writer happens to belong.[7] So much for what I have attempted; I need not be assured that success is a very different matter; particularly for one whose attention has but newly been awakened to the study of dramatic literature.[8]

I endeavoured whilst at Rome to observe such monuments of this story as might be accessible to a stranger. The portrait of Beatrice at the Colonna Palace is most admirable as a work of art: it was taken by Guido during her confinement in prison. But it is most interesting as a just representation of one of the loveliest specimens of the workmanship of Nature. There is a fixed and pale composure upon the features: she seems sad and stricken down in spirit, yet the despair thus expressed is lightened by the patience of gentleness. Her head is bound with folds of white drapery from which the yellow strings of her golden hair escape, and fall about her neck. The moulding of her face is exquisitely delicate; the eye brows are distinct and arched: the lips have that permanent meaning of imagination and sensibility which suffering has not repressed and which it seems as if death scarcely could extinguish. Her forehead is large and clear; her eyes which we are told were remarkable for their vivacity, are swollen with weeping and lustreless, but beautifully tender and serene. In the whole mien there is a simplicity and dignity which united with her exquisite loveliness and deep sorrow are inexpressibly pathetic. Beatrice Cenci appears to have been one of those rare persons in whom energy and gentleness dwell together without destroying one another: her nature was simple and profound. The crimes and miseries in which she was an actor and a sufferer are as the mask and the mantle in which circumstances clothed her for her impersonation on the scene of the world.

The Cenci Palace is of great extent; and though in part modernized, there yet remains a vast and gloomy pile

[6] **modern critics . . . language of men:** See W. Wordsworth's preface to *Lyrical Ballads* (1800)* on poetic diction and the "language really used by men."

[7] **men in general . . . belong:** Shelley implicitly accepts Coleridge's criticism of Wordsworth in *Biographia Literaria* (1816),* chapter 17, that diction should be generic rather than unique to an individual or a social class.

[8] **success . . . dramatic literature:** Shelley's play was not performed publicly in England until 1922.

of feudal architecture in the same state as during the dreadful scenes which are the subject of this tragedy. The Palace is situated in an obscure corner of Rome, near the quarter of the Jews, and from the upper windows you see the immense ruins of Mount Palatine half hidden under their profuse overgrowth of trees. There is a court in one part of the palace (perhaps that in which Cenci built the Chapel to St. Thomas), supported by granite columns and adorned with antique friezes of fine workmanship and built up, according to the antient Italian fashion, with balcony over balcony of open work. One of the gates of the palace formed of immense stones and leading through a passage, dark and lofty and opening into gloomy subterranean chambers, struck me particularly.

Of the Castle of Petrella, I could obtain no further information than that which is to be found in the manuscript.

The Cenci

— DRAMATIS PERSONAE —

COUNT FRANCESCO CENCI
GIACOMO, BERNARDO } *his sons*
CARDINAL CAMILLO
ORSINO, *a prelate*
SAVELLA, *the Pope's Legate*
OLIMPIO, MARZIO } *Assassins*
ANDREA, *servant to Cenci*
Nobles - Judges - Guards - Servants
LUCRETIA, *Wife of Cenci, and step-mother of his children*
BEATRICE, *his daughter*

(The Scene lies principally in Rome, but changes during the fourth Act to Petrella a castle among the Apulia Apennines.)
(TIME: *During the Pontificate of Clement VIII.)*

ACT 1

— SCENE I —

(An apartment in the Cenci Palace.)
(Enter COUNT CENCI, *and* CARDINAL CAMILLO.*)*

CAMILLO: That matter of the murder is hushed up
If you consent to yield his Holiness
Your fief that lies beyond the Pincian gate.[9] —
It needed all my interest in the conclave
To bend him to this point: he said that you
Bought perilous impunity with your gold;
That crimes like yours if once or twice compounded
Enriched the Church, and respited from hell
An erring soul which might repent and live: —
But that the glory and the interest
Of the high throne he fills, little consist
With making it a daily mart of guilt
So manifold and hideous as the deeds
Which you scarce hide from men's revolted eyes.

CENCI: The third of my possessions — let it go!
Aye, I once heard the nephew of the Pope
Had sent his architect to view the ground,
Meaning to build a villa on my vines
The next time I compounded[10] with his uncle:
I little thought he should outwit me so!
Henceforth no witness — not the lamp — shall see
That which the vassal threatened to divulge
Whose throat is choked with dust for his reward.
The deed he saw could not have rated higher
That his most worthless life: — it angers me!
Respited from Hell! — So may the Devil
Respite their souls from Heaven. No doubt Pope Clement,
And his most charitable nephews, pray
That the apostle Peter and the saints
Will grant for their sake that I long enjoy
Strength, wealth, and pride, and lust, and length of days
Wherein to act the deeds which are the stewards
Of their revenue. — But much yet remains
To which they shew no title.

CAMILLO: Oh, Count Cenci!
So much that thou migh'st honourably live
And reconcile thyself with thine own heart
And with thy God, and with the offended world.
How hideously look deeds of lust and blood
Thro' those snow white and venerable hairs! —
Your children should be sitting round you now,
But that you fear to read upon their looks
The shame and misery you have written there.
Where is your wife? Where is your gentle daughter?

---

[9] **fief . . . gate:** an estate outside of the gate at the Via Veneto.

[10] **compounded:** came to some agreement with.

Methinks her sweet looks, which make all things
 else
Beauteous and glad, might kill the fiend within you.
Why is she barred from all society
But her own strange and uncomplaining wrongs?
Talk with me, Count,—you know I mean you well.
I stood beside your dark and fiery youth
Watching its bold and bad career, as men
Watch meteors, but it vanished not—I marked
Your desperate and remorseless manhood; now
Do I behold you in dishonoured age
Charged with a thousand unrepented crimes.
Yet I have ever hoped you would amend,
And in that hope have saved your life three times.

CENCI: For which Aldobrandino[11] owes you now
My fief beyond the Pincian.—Cardinal,
One thing, I pray you, recollect henceforth,
And so we shall converse with less restraint.
A man you knew spoke of my wife and daughter—
He was accustomed to frequent my house;
So the next day *his* wife and daughter came
And asked if I had seen him; and I smiled:
I think they never saw him any more.

CAMILLO: Thou execrable man, beware!—

CENCI: Of thee?
Nay this is idle:—We should know each other.
As to my character for what men call crime
Seeing I please my senses as I list,
And vindicate that right with force or guile,
It is a public matter, and I care not
If I discuss it with you. I may speak
Alike to you and my own conscious heart—
For you give out that you have half reformed me,
Therefore strong vanity will keep you silent
If fear should not; both will, I do not doubt.
All men delight in sensual luxury,
All men enjoy revenge; and most exult
Over the tortures they can never feel—
Flattering their secret peace with other's pain.
But I delight in nothing else. I love
The sight of agony, and the sense of joy,
When this shall be another's, and that mine.
And I have no remorse and little fear,
Which are, I think, the checks of other men.
This mood has grown upon me, untill now
Any design my captious fancy makes

[11] **Aldobrandino**: the Pope's family name.

The picture of its wish, and it forms none
But such as men like you would start to know,
Is as my natural food and rest debarred
Untill it be accomplished

CAMILLO: Art thou not
Most miserable?

CENCI: Why, miserable?—
No.—I am what your theologians call
Hardened;—which they must be in impudence,
So to revile a man's peculiar taste.
True, I was happier than I am, while yet
Manhood remained to act the thing I thought;
While lust was sweeter than revenge; and now
Invention palls:—Aye, we must all grow old—
But that there yet remains a deed to act
Whose horror might make sharp an appetite
Duller than mine—I' d do,—I know not what.
When I was young I thought of nothing else
But pleasure; and I fed on honey sweets:
Men, by St. Thomas! cannot live like bees
And I grew tired:—yet, till I killed a foe,
And heard his groans, and heard his childrens
 groans,
Knew I not what delight was else on earth,
Which now delights me little. I the rather
Look on such pangs as terror ill conceals,
The dry fixed eye ball; the pale quivering lip,
Which tell me that the spirit weeps within
Tears bitterer than the bloody sweat of Christ.
I rarely kill the body which preserves,
Like a strong prison, the soul within my power,
Wherein I feed it with the breath of fear
For hourly pain.

CAMILLO: Hell's most abandoned fiend
Did never, in the drunkenness of guilt,
Speak to his heart as now you speak to me,
I thank my God that I believe you not.

(Enter ANDREA.*)*

ANDREA: My Lord, a gentleman from Salamanca
Would speak with you.

CENCI: Bid him attend me in the grand saloon.

(Exit ANDREA.*)*

CAMILLO: Farewell; and I will pray
Almighty God that thy false, impious words
Tempt not his spirit to abandon thee.

(Exit CAMILLO.*)*

CENCI: The third of my possessions! I must use
Close husbandry, or gold, the old man's sword,
Falls from my withered hand. But yesterday
There came an order from the Pope to make
Fourfold provision for my cursed sons;
Whom I have sent from Rome to Salamanca,
Hoping some accident might cut them off;
And meaning if I could to starve them there.
I pray thee, God, send some quick death upon
them!
Bernardo and my wife could not be worse
If dead and damned: — then, as to Beatrice —

(looking around him suspiciously)

I think they cannot hear me at that door;
What if they should? And yet I need not speak
Though the heart triumphs with itself in words.
O, thou most silent air, that shall not hear
What now I think! Thou, pavement, which I tread
Towards her chamber, — let your echoes talk
Of my imperious step scorning surprise,
But not of my intent! — Andrea!

(Enter ANDREA.*)*

ANDREA: My lord?
CENCI: Bid Beatrice attend me in her chamber
This evening: — no, at midnight and alone.

(Exeunt.)

— SCENE II —

(A garden of the Cenci Palace.)
(Enter BEATRICE *and* ORSINO, *as in conversation.)*

BEATRICE: Pervert not truth,
Orsino. You remember where we held
That conversation, — nay, we see the spot
Even from this cypress, — two long years are past
Since, on an April midnight, underneath
The moon-light ruins of mount Palatine,
I did confess to you my secret mind.
ORSINO: You said you loved me then.
BEATRICE: You are a Priest,
Speak to me not of love.
ORSINO: I may obtain
The dispensation of the Pope to marry.
Because I am a Priest do you believe
Your image, as the hunter some struck deer,
Follows me not whether I wake or sleep?
BEATRICE: As I have said, speak to me not of love;
Had you a dispensation I have not;
Nor will I leave this home of misery
Whilst my poor Bernard, and that gentle lady
To whom I owe life, and these virtuous thoughts,
Must suffer what I still have strength to share.
Alas, Orsino! All the love that once
I felt for you, is turned to bitter pain.
Ours was a youthful contract, which you first
Broke, by assuming vows no Pope will loose.
And yet I love you still, but holily,
Even as a sister or a spirit might;
And so I swear a cold fidelity.
And it is well perhaps we shall not marry.
You have a sly, equivocating vein
That suits me not. — Ah, wretched that I am!
Where shall I turn? Even now you look on me
As you were not my friend, and as if you
Discovered that I thought so, with false smiles
Making my true suspicion seem your wrong.
Ah! No, forgive me; sorrow makes me seem
Sterner than else my nature might have been;
I have a weight of melancholy thoughts,
And they forbode, — but what can they forbode
Worse than I now endure?
ORSINO: All will be well.
Is the petition yet prepared? You know
My zeal for all you wish, sweet Beatrice;
Doubt not but I will use my utmost skill
So that the Pope attend to your complaint.
BEATRICE: Your zeal for all I wish; — Ah me, you are
cold!
Your utmost skill . . . speak but one word . . . *(aside)*
Alas!
Weak and deserted creature that I am,
Here I stand bickering with my only friend!

(to ORSINO*)*

This night my father gives a sumptuous feast,
Orsino; he has heard some happy news
From Salamanca, from my brothers there,
And with this outward shew of love he mocks
His inward hate. 'Tis bold hypocrisy
For he would gladlier celebrate their deaths,
Which I have heard him pray for on his knees:
Great God! that such a father should be mine!
But there is mighty preparation made,
And all our kin, the Cenci, will be there,
And all the chief nobility of Rome.

And he has bidden me and my pale Mother
Attire ourselves in festival array.
Poor lady! She expects some happy change
In his dark spirit from this act; I none.
At supper I will give you the petition:
'Till when—farewell.

ORSINO: Farewell.

(Exit BEATRICE.)

I know the Pope
Will ne'er absolve me from my priestly vow
But by absolving me from the revenue
Of many a wealthy see,[12] and, Beatrice,
I think to win thee at an easier rate.
Nor shall he read her eloquent petition:
He might bestow her on some poor relation
Of his sixth cousin, as he did her sister,
And I should be debarred from all access.
Then as to what she suffers from her father,
In all this there is much exaggeration:—
Old men are testy and will have their way;
A man may stab his enemy, or his slave,
And live a free life as to wine or women,
And with a peevish temper may return
To a dull home, and rate[13] his wife and children;
Daughters and wives call this, foul tyranny.
I shall be well content if on my conscience
There rest no heavier sin than what they suffer
From the devices of my love—A net
From which she shall escape not. Yet I fear
Her subtle mind, her awe-inspiring gaze,
Whose beams anatomize me nerve by nerve
And lay me bare, and make me blush to see
My hidden thoughts.—Ah, no! A friendless girl
Who clings to me, as to her only hope:—
I were a fool, not less than if a panther
Were panic-stricken by the Antelope's eye
If she escape me.

(Exit.)

—SCENE III—

(A magnificent Hall in the Cenci Palace.)

(A Banquet. Enter CENCI, LUCRETIA, BEATRICE, ORSINO, CAMILLO, NOBLES.)

CENCI: Welcome, my friends and Kinsmen; welcome ye,
Princes and Cardinals, pillars of the church,
Whose presence honours our festivity.
I have too long lived like an Anchorite,[14]
And in my absence from your merry meetings
An evil word is gone abroad of me;
But I do hope that you, my noble friends,
When you have shared the entertainment here,
And heard the pious cause for which 'tis given,
And we have pledged a health or two together,
Will think me flesh and blood as well as you;
Sinful indeed, for Adam made all so,
But tender-hearted, meek and pitiful.

1. GUEST: In truth, my Lord, you seem too light of heart,
Too sprightly and companionable a man,
To act the deeds that rumour pins on you.

(to his companion)

I never saw such blithe and open cheer
In any eye!

2. GUEST: Some most desired event,
In which we all demand a common joy,
Has brought us hither; let us hear it, Count.

CENCI: It is indeed a most desired event.
If when a parent from a parent's heart
Lifts from this earth to the great father of all
A prayer, both when he lays him down to sleep,
And when he rises up from dreaming it;
One supplication, one desire, one hope,
That he would grant a wish for his two sons
Even all that he demands in their regard—
And suddenly beyond his dearest hope,
It is accomplished, he should then rejoice,
And call his friends and kinsmen to a feast,
And task their love to grace his merriment,
Then honour me thus far—for I am he.

BEATRICE: *(to* LUCRETIA*)* Great God! How horrible!
Some dreadful ill
Must have befallen my brothers.

LUCRETIA: Fear not, Child,
He speaks too frankly.

BEATRICE: Ah! My blood runs cold.
I fear that wicked laughter round his eye
Which wrinkles up the skin even to the hair.

[12] **see:** official seat, or jurisdiction, of a bishop.

[13] **rate:** berate.

[14] **Anchorite:** religious recluse.

CENCI: Here are the letters brought from Salamanca;
Beatrice, read them to your mother. God!
I thank thee! In one night didst thou perform,
By ways inscrutable, the thing I sought.
My disobedient and rebellious sons
Are dead!—Why dead!—What means this change of cheer?
You hear me not, I tell you they are dead;
And they will need no food or raiment more:
The tapers that did light them the dark way
Are their last cost. The Pope, I think, will not
Expect I should maintain them in their coffins.
Rejoice with me—my heart is wondrous glad.

BEATRICE: (LUCRETIA *sinks, half fainting;* BEATRICE *supports her.*)
It is not true!—Dear lady, pray look up.
Had it been true, there is a God in Heaven,
He would not live to boast of such a boon.
Unnatural man, thou knowest that it is false.

CENCI: Aye, as the word of God; whom here I call
To witness that I speak the sober truth;—
And whose most favouring Providence was shewn
Even in the manner of their deaths. For Rocco
Was kneeling at the mass, with sixteen others,
When the Church fell and crushed him to a mummy,
The rest escaped unhurt. Cristofano
Was stabbed in error by a jealous man,
Whilst she he loved was sleeping with his rival;
All in the self same hour of the same night;
Which shews that Heaven has special care of me.
I beg those friends who love me, that they mark
The day a feast upon their calenders.
It was the twenty seventh of December:
Aye, read the letters if you doubt my oath.

(*The assembly appears confused; several of the guests rise.*)

1. GUEST: Oh, horrible! I will depart.—

2. GUEST: And I.—

3. GUEST: No, stay!
I do believe it is some jest; tho' faith!
'Tis mocking us somewhat too solemnly.
I think his son has married the Infanta,[15]
Or found a mine of gold in El dorado;[16]
'Tis but to season some such news; stay, stay!
I see 'tis only raillery by his smile.

CENCI: (*filling a bowl of wine, and lifting it up*)
Oh, thou bright wine whose purple splendor leaps
And bubbles gaily in this golden bowl
Under the lamp light, as my spirits do,
To hear the death of my accursed sons!
Could I believe thou wert their mingled blood,
Then would I taste thee like a sacrament,
And pledge with thee the mighty Devil in Hell,
Who, if a father's curses, as men say,
Climb with swift wings after their children's souls,
And drag them from the very throne of Heaven,
Now triumphs in my triumph!—But thou art
Superfluous; I have drunken deep of joy
And I will taste no other wine to night.
Here, Andrea! Bear the bowl around.

A GUEST: (*rising*) Thou wretch!
Will none among this noble company
Check the abandoned villain?

CAMILLO: For God's sake
Let me dismiss the guests! You are insane,
Some ill will come of this.

2 GUEST: Seize, silence him!

1. GUEST: I will!

3. GUEST: And I!

CENCI: (*addressing those who rise with a threatening gesture*)
Who moves? Who speaks?

(*turning to the Company*)

'tis nothing,
Enjoy yourselves.—Beware! For my revenge
Is as the sealed commission of a king
That kills, and none dare name the murderer.

(*The Banquet is broken up; several of the Guests are departing.*)

BEATRICE: I do entreat you, go not, noble guests;
What although tyranny, and impious hate
Stand sheltered by a father's hoary hair?
What, if 'tis he who clothed us in these limbs
Who tortures them, and triumphs? What, if we,
The desolate and the dead, were his own flesh,
His children and his wife, whom he is bound
To love and shelter? Shall we therefore find
No refuge in this merciless wide world?
Oh, think what deep wrongs must have blotted out
First love, then reverence in a child's prone mind
Till it thus vanquish shame and fear! O, think
I have borne much, and kissed the sacred hand

[15] **Infanta:** the daughter of a Spanish king.

[16] **El Dorado:** City of Gold reputed to be somewhere in South America. See Voltaire's *Candide* (1759).

Which crushed us to the earth, and thought its stroke
Was perhaps some paternal chastisement!
Have excused much, doubted; and when no doubt
Remained, have sought by patience, love and tears
To soften him, and when this could not be
I have knelt down through the long sleepless nights
And lifted up to God, the father of all,
Passionate prayers: and when these were not heard
I have still borne,—until I meet you here,
Princes and kinsmen, at this hideous feast
Given at my brothers' deaths. Two yet remain,
His wife remains and I, whom if ye save not,
Ye may soon share such merriment again
As fathers make over their children's graves.
Oh! Prince Colonna,[17] thou art our near kinsman,
Cardinal, thou art the Pope's chamberlain,
Camillo, thou art chief justiciary,
Take us away!

CENCI: *(He has been conversing with* CAMILLO *during the first part of* BEATRICE'*s speech; he hears the conclusion, and now advances.)*
I hope my good friends here
Will think of their own daughters—or perhaps
Of their own throats—before they lend an ear
To this wild girl.

BEATRICE: *(not noticing the words of* CENCI.*)*
Dare not one look on me?
None answer? Can one tyrant overbear
The sense of many best and wisest men?
Or is it that I sue not in some form
Of scrupulous law, that ye deny my suit?
Oh, God! That I were buried with my brothers!
And that the flowers of this departed spring
Were fading on my grave! And that my father
Were celebrating now one feast for all!

CAMILLO: A bitter wish for one so young and gentle;
Can we do nothing?—

COLONNA: Nothing that I see.
Count Cenci were a dangerous enemy:
Yet I would second any one.

A CARDINAL: And I.

CENCI: Retire to your chamber, insolent girl!

BEATRICE: Retire thou impious man! Aye hide thyself
Where never eye can look upon thee more!
Wouldst thou have honour and obedience
Who art a torturer? Father, never dream
Though thou mayst overbear this company,
But ill must come of ill.—Frown not on me!
Haste hide thyself, lest with avenging looks
My brothers' ghosts should hunt thee from thy seat!
Cover thy face from every living eye,
And start if thou but hear a human step:
Seek out some dark and silent corner, there,
Bow thy white head before offended God,
And we will kneel around, and fervently
Pray that he pity both ourselves and thee.

CENCI: My friends, I do lament this insane girl
Has spoilt the mirth of our festivity.
Good night, farewell; I will not make you longer
Spectators of our dull domestic quarrels.
Another time.—

(Exeunt all but CENCI *and* BEATRICE.*)*

My brain is swimming round;
Give me a bowl of wine!
(to BEATRICE*)* Thou painted viper!
Beast that thou art! Fair and yet terrible!
I know a charm shall make thee meek and tame,
Now get thee from my sight!

(Exit BEATRICE.*)*

Here, Andrea,
Fill up this goblet with Greek wine. I said
I would not drink this evening; but I must;
For, strange to say, I feel my spirits fail
With thinking what I have decreed to do.—

(drinking the wine)

Be thou the resolution of quick youth
Within my veins, and manhood's purpose stern,
And age's firm, cold, subtle villainy;
As if thou wert indeed my children's blood
Which I did thirst to drink! The charm works well;
It must be done; it shall be done, I swear!

(Exit.)

ACT II

—SCENE I—

(An apartment in the Cenci Palace.)
(Enter LUCRETIA *and* BERNARDO.*)*

LUCRETIA: Weep not, my gentle boy; he struck but me
Who have borne deeper wrongs. In truth, if he

[17] **Colonna:** powerful rival and family.

Had killed me, he had done a kinder deed.
O, God Almighty, do thou look upon us,
We have no other friend but only thee!
Yet weep not; though I love you as my own
I am not your true mother.

BERNARDO: Oh more, more,
Than ever mother was to any child,
That have you been to me! Had he not been
My father, do you think that I should weep?

LUCRETIA: Alas! Poor boy, what else could'st thou have done?

(Enter BEATRICE.*)*

BEATRICE: *(in a hurried voice)*
Did he pass this way? Have you seen him, brother?
Ah! No, that is his step upon the stairs;
'Tis nearer now; his hand is on the door;
Mother, if I to thee have ever been
A duteous child, now save me! Thou, great God,
Whose image upon earth a father is,
Dost thou indeed abandon me! He comes;
The door is opening now; I see his face;
He frowns on others, but he smiles on me,
Even as he did after the feast last night.

(Enter a Servant.)

Almighty God, how merciful thou art!
'Tis but Orsino's servant.—Well, what news?

SERVANT: My master bids me say, the Holy Father
Has sent back your petition thus unopened.

(giving a paper)

And he demands at what hour 'twere secure
To visit you again?

LUCRETIA: At the Ave Mary.

(Exit Servant.)

So, daughter, our last hope has failed; Ah me!
How pale you look; you tremble, and you stand
Wrapped in some fixed and fearful meditation,
As if one thought were over strong for you:
Your eyes have a chill glare; O, dearest child!
Are you gone mad? If not, pray speak to me.

BEATRICE: You see I am not mad; I speak to you.

LUCRETIA: You talked of some thing that your father did
After that dreadful feast? Could it be worse
Than when he smiled, and cried, My sons are dead!
And every one looked in his neighbour's face
To see if others were as white as he?
At the first word he spoke I felt the blood
Rush to my heart, and fell into a trance;
And when it past I sat all weak and wild;
Whilst you alone stood up, and with strong words
Checked his unnatural pride; and I could see
The devil was rebuked that lives in him.
Until this hour thus you have ever stood
Between us and your father's moody wrath
Like a protecting presence: your firm mind
Has been our only refuge and defence:
What can have thus subdued it? What can now
Have given you that cold melancholy look,
Succeeding to your unaccustomed fear?

BEATRICE: What is it that you say? I was just thinking
'Twere better not to struggle any more.
Men, like my father, have been dark and bloody,
Yet never—O! Before worse comes of it
'Twere wise to die: it ends in that at last.

LUCRETIA: Oh, talk not so, dear child! Tell me at once
What did your father do or say to you?
He stayed not after that accursed feast
One moment in your chamber.—Speak to me.

BERNARDO: Oh, sister, sister, prithee, speak to us!

BEATRICE: *(speaking very slowly with a forced calmness)*
It was one word, Mother, one little word;
One look, one smile. *(wildly)*
Oh! He has trampled me
Under his feet, and made the blood stream down
My pallid cheeks. And he has given us all
Ditch water, and the fever-stricken flesh
Of buffaloes, and bade us eat or starve,
And we have eaten.—He has made me look
On my beloved Bernardo, when the rust
Of heavy chains has gangrened his sweet limbs,
And I have never yet despaired—but now!
What would I say?

(recovering herself)

Ah! No, 'tis nothing new.
The sufferings we all share have made me wild:
He only struck and cursed me as he passed;
He said, he looked, he did;—nothing at all
Beyond his wont, yet it disordered me.
Alas! I am forgetful of my duty,
I should preserve my senses for your sake.

LUCRETIA: Nay, Beatrice; have courage my sweet girl.
If any one despairs it should be I
Who loved him once, and now must live with him

Till God in pity call for him or me.
For you may, like your sister, find some husband,
And smile, years hence, with children round your knees;
Whilst I, then dead, and all this hideous coil
Shall be remembered only as a dream.

BEATRICE: Talk not to me, dear lady, of a husband.
Did you not nurse me when my mother died?
Did you not shield me and that dearest boy?
And had we any other friend but you
In infancy, with gentle words and looks,
To win our father not to murder us?
And shall I now desert you? May the ghost
Of my dead Mother plead against my soul
If I abandon her who filled the place
She left, with more, even, than a mother's love!

BERNARDO: And I am of my sister's mind. Indeed
I would not leave you in this wretchedness,
Even though the Pope should make me free to live
In some blithe place, like others of my age,
With sports, and delicate food, and the fresh air.
Oh, never think that I will leave you, Mother!

LUCRETIA: My dear, dear children!

(Enter CENCI, *suddenly.)*

CENCI: What, Beatrice here!
Come hither!

(She shrinks back, and covers her face.)

Nay hide not your face, 'tis fair;
Look up! Why, yesternight you dared to look
With disobedient insolence upon me,
Bending a stern and an inquiring brow
On what I meant; whilst I then sought to hide
That which I came to tell you—but in vain.

BEATRICE: *(wildly, staggering towards the door)*
Oh, that the earth would gape! Hide me, oh God!

CENCI: Then it was I whose inarticulate words
Fell from my lips, and who with tottering steps
Fled from your presence, as you now from mine.
Stay, I command you—from this day and hour
Never again, I think, with fearless eye,
And brow superior, and unaltered cheek,
And that lip made for tenderness or scorn,
Shalt thou strike dumb the meanest of mankind;
Me least of all. Now get thee to thy chamber!
Thou too, loathed image of thy cursed mother,

(to BERNARDO*)*

Thy milky, meek face makes me sick with hate!

(Exeunt BEATRICE *and* BERNARDO.*)*

(aside) So much has past between us as must make
Me bold, her fearful.—'Tis an awful thing
To touch such mischief as I now conceive:
So men sit shivering on the dewy bank,
And try the chill stream with their feet, once in . . .
How the delighted spirit pants for joy!

LUCRETIA: *(advancing timidly towards him)*
Oh, husband! Pray forgive poor Beatrice,
She meant not any ill.

CENCI: Nor you perhaps?
Nor that young imp, whom you have taught by rote
Parricide with his alphabet? Nor Giacomo?
Nor those two most unnatural sons, who stirred
Enmity up against me with the Pope?
Whom in one night merciful God cut off:
Innocent lambs! They thought not any ill.
You were not here conspiring? You said nothing
Of how I might be dungeoned as a madman;
Or be condemned to death for some offence,
And you would be the witnesses?—This failing,
How just it were to hire assassins, or
Put sudden poison in my evening drink?
Or smother me when overcome by wine?
Seeing we had no other judge but God,
And he had sentenced me, and there were none
But you to be the executioners
Of his decree enregistered in heaven?
Oh, no! You said not this?

LUCRETIA: So help me God,
I never thought the things you charge me with!

CENCI: If you dare speak that wicked lie again
I'll kill you. What! It was not by your counsel
That Beatrice disturbed the feast last night?
You did not hope to stir some enemies
Against me, and escape, and laugh to scorn
What every nerve of you now trembles at?
You judged that men were bolder than they are;
Few dare to stand between their grave and me.

LUCRETIA: Look not so dreadfully! By my salvation
I knew not aught that Beatrice designed;
Nor do I think she designed any thing
Until she heard you talk of her dead brothers.

CENCI: Blaspheming liar! You are damned for this!
But I will take you where you may persuade
The stones you tread on to deliver you:
For men shall there be none but those who dare

All things — not question that which I command.
On Wednesday next I shall set out: you know
That savage rock, the Castle of Petrella,
'Tis safely walled, and moated round about:
Its dungeons underground, and its thick towers
Never told tales; though they have heard and seen
What might make dumb things speak. — Why do you linger?
Make speediest preparation for the journey!

(*Exit* LUCRETIA.)

The all beholding sun yet shines; I hear
A busy stir of men about the streets;
I see the bright sky through the window panes:
It is a garish, broad, and peering day;
Loud, light, suspicious, full of eyes and ears,
And every little corner, nook and hole
Is penetrated with the insolent light.
Come darkness! Yet, what is the day to me?
And wherefore should I wish for night, who do
A deed which shall confound both night and day?
'Tis she shall grope through a bewildering mist
Of horror: if there be a sun in heaven
She shall not dare to look upon its beams;
Nor feel its warmth. Let her then wish for night;
The act I think shall soon extinguish all
For me: I bear a darker deadlier gloom
Than the earth's shade, or interlunar air,
Or constellations quenched in murkiest cloud,
In which I walk secure and unbeheld
Towards my purpose. — Would that it were done!

(*Exit.*)

— SCENE II —

(*A chamber in the Vatican.*)

(*Enter* CAMILLO *and* GIACOMO, *in conversation.*)

CAMILLO: There is an obsolete and doubtful law
By which you might obtain a bare provision
Of food and clothing —

GIACOMO: Nothing more? Alas!
Bare must be the provision which strict law
Awards, and aged, sullen avarice pays.
Why did my father not apprentice me
To some mechanic trade? I should have then
Been trained in no highborn necessities
Which I could meet not by my daily toil.
The eldest son of a rich nobleman
Is heir to all his incapacities;
He has wide wants, and narrow powers. If you,
Cardinal Camillo, were reduced at once
From thrice-driven beds of down, and delicate food,
An hundred servants, and six palaces,
To that which nature doth indeed require? —

CAMILLO: Nay, there is reason in your plea; 'twere hard.

GIACOMO: 'Tis hard for a firm man to bear: but I
Have a dear wife, a lady of high birth,
Whose dowry in ill hour I lent my father
Without a bond or witness to the deed:
And children, who inherit her fine senses,
The fairest creatures in this breathing world;
And she and they reproach me not. Cardinal,
Do you not think the Pope would interpose
And stretch authority beyond the law?

CAMILLO: Though your peculiar case is hard, I know
The Pope will not divert the course of law.
After that impious feast the other night
I spoke with him, and urged him then to check
Your father's cruel hand; he frowned and said,
'Children are disobedient, and they sting
Their father's hearts to madness and despair
Requiting years of care with contumely.
I pity the Count Cenci from my heart;
His outraged love perhaps awakened hate,
And thus he is exasperated to ill.
In the great war between the old and young
I, who have white hairs and a tottering body,
Will keep at least blameless neutrality.'

(*Enter* ORSINO.)

You, my good lord Orsino, heard those words.

ORSINO: What words?

GIACOMO: Alas, repeat them not again!
There then is no redress for me, at least
None but that which I may atchieve myself,
Since I am driven to the brink. — But, say,
My innocent sister and my only brother
Are dying underneath my father's eye.
The memorable torturers of this land,
Galeaz Visconti, Borgia, Ezzelin,[18]

---

[18] **Galeaz Visconti:** Gian Galeazzo Visconti (1351–1402), most powerful, ambitious, and wealthy prince of the Visconti family, political rulers of Milan for centuries. **Borgia:** Cesare Borgia (1476–1507), son of Pope Alexander VI and duke of

Never inflicted on their meanest slave
What these endure; shall they have no protection?
CAMILLO: Why, if they would petition to the Pope
I see not how he could refuse it—yet
He holds it of most dangerous example
In aught to weaken the paternal power,
Being, as 'twere the shadow of his own.
I pray you now excuse me. I have business
That will not bear delay.

(Exit CAMILLO.*)*

GIACOMO: But you, Orsino,
Have the petition wherefore not present it?
ORSINO: I have presented it, and backed it with
My earnest prayers, and urgent interest;
It was returned unanswered. I doubt not
But that the strange and execrable deeds
Alledged in it—in truth they might well baffle
Any belief—have turned the Pope's displeasure
Upon the accusers from the criminal:
So I should guess from what Camillo said.
GIACOMO: My friend, that palace-walking devil Gold
Has whispered silence to his Holiness:
And we are left, as scorpions ringed with fire,
What should we do but strike ourselves to death?[19]
For he who is our murderous persecutor
Is shielded by a father's holy name,
Or I would—

(Stops abruptly.)

ORSINO: What? Fear not to speak your thought.
Words are but holy as the deeds they cover:
A priest who has forsworn the God he serves;
A judge who makes the truth weep at his decree;
A friend who should weave counsel, as I now,
But as the mantle of some selfish guile;
A father who is all a tyrant seems,
Were the prophaner for his sacred name.
GIACOMO: Ask me not what I think; the unwilling brain
Feigns often what it would not; and we trust

Valentinois and Cattanei, known for personal violence, ferocity, and unscrupulousness in battles of conquest. **Ezzelin:** Eccelino da Romano (1194–1259), Ghibelline leader excommunicated by Pope Gregory IX for cruelty and object of a crusade by Pope Alexander IV. Also, sometimes called *the tyrant.*

[19] **scorpions . . . death:** allusion to the belief that scorpions encircled by fire will commit suicide by stinging themselves to death.

Imagination with such phantasies
As the tongue dares not fashion into words,
Which have no words, their horror makes them dim
To the mind's eye.—My heart denied itself
To think what you demand.
ORSINO: But a friend's bosom
Is as the inmost cave of our own mind
Where we sit shut from the wide gaze of day,
And from the all-communicating air.
You look what I suspected—
GIACOMO: Spare me now!
I am as one lost in a midnight wood
Who dares not ask some harmless passenger
The path across the wilderness, lest he,
As my thoughts are, should be—a murderer.
I know you are my friend, and all I dare
Speak to my soul that will I trust with thee.
But now my heart is heavy and would take
Lone counsel from a night of sleepless care.
Pardon me, that I say farewell—farewell!
I would that to my own suspected self
I could address a word so full of peace.
ORSINO: Farewell!—Be your thoughts better or more bold.

(Exit GIACOMO.*)*

I had disposed the Cardinal Camillo
To feed his hope with cold encouragement:
It fortunately serves my close designs
That 'tis a trick of this same family
To analyse their own and other minds.
Such self-anatomy shall teach the will
Dangerous secrets: for it tempts our powers,
Knowing what must be thought, and may be done,
Into the depth of darkest purposes:
So Cenci fell into the pit; even I,
Since Beatrice unveiled me to myself,
And made me shrink from what I cannot shun,
Shew a poor figure to my own esteem,
To which I grow half reconciled. I'll do
As little mischief as I can; that thought
Shall fee the accuser conscience.

(after a pause)

Now what harm
If Cenci should be murdered?—Yet, if murdered,
Wherefore by me? And what if I could take
The profit, yet omit the sin and peril
In such an action? Of all earthly things
I fear a man whose blows outspeed his words;

And such is Cenci: and while Cenci lives
His daughter's dowry were a secret grave
If a priest wins her.—Oh, fair Beatrice!
Would that I loved thee not, or loving thee
Could but despise danger and gold and all
That frowns between my wish and its effect,
Or smiles beyond it! There is no escape . . .
Her bright form kneels beside me at the altar,
And follows me to the resort of men,
And fills my slumber with tumultuous dreams,
So when I wake my blood seems liquid fire;
And if I strike my damp and dizzy head
My hot palm scorches it: her very name,
But spoken by a stranger, makes my heart
Sicken and pant; and thus unprofitably
I clasp the phantom of unfelt delights
Till weak imagination half possesses
The self created shadow. Yet much longer
Will I not nurse this life of feverous hours:
From the unravelled hopes of Giacomo
I must work out my own dear purposes.
I see, as from a tower, the end of all:
Her father dead; her brother bound to me
By a dark secret, surer than the grave;
Her mother scared and unexpostulating
From the dread manner of her wish atchieved:
And she!—Once more take courage my faint heart;
What dares a friendless maiden matched with thee?
I have such foresight as assures success:
Some unbeheld divinity doth ever,
When dread events are near, stir up men's minds
To black suggestions; and he prospers best,
Not who becomes the instrument of ill,
But who can flatter the dark spirit, that makes
Its empire and its prey of other hearts
Till it become his slave . . . as I will do.

(Exit.)

ACT III

— SCENE I —

(An apartment in the Cenci Palace.)
(LUCRETIA, to her enter BEATRICE.)

BEATRICE: *(She enters staggering, and speaks wildly.)*
Reach me that handkerchief!—My brain is hurt;
My eyes are full of blood; just wipe them for me . . .
I see but indistinctly . . .

LUCRETIA: My sweet child,
You have no wound; 'tis only a cold dew
That starts from your dear brow . . . Alas! Alas!
What has befallen?

BEATRICE: How comes this hair undone?
Its wandering strings must be what blind me so,
And yet I tied it fast.—O, horrible!
The pavement sinks under my feet! The walls
Spin round! I see a woman weeping there,
And standing calm and motionless, whilst I
Slide giddily as the world reels . . . My God!
The beautiful blue heaven is flecked with blood!
The sunshine on the floor is black! The air
Is changed to vapours such as the dead breathe
In charnel pits! Pah! I am choked! There creeps
A clinging, black, contaminating mist
About me . . . 'tis substantial, heavy, thick,
I cannot pluck it from me, for it glues
My fingers and my limbs to one another,
And eats into my sinews, and dissolves
My flesh to a pollution, poisoning
The subtle, pure, and inmost spirit of life!
My God! I never knew what the mad felt
Before; for I am mad beyond all doubt!

(more wildly)

No, I am dead! These putrefying limbs
Shut round and sepulchre the panting soul
Which would burst forth into the wandering air!

(a pause)

What hideous thought was that I had even now?
'Tis gone; and yet its burthen remains here
O'er these dull eyes . . . upon this weary heart!
O, world! O, life! O, day! O, misery!

LUCRETIA: What ails thee, my poor child? She answers not:
Her spirit apprehends the sense of pain,
But not its cause; suffering has dried away
The source from which it sprung . . .

BEATRICE: *(franticly)* Like Parricide . . .
Misery has killed its father: yet its father
Never like mine . . . O, God! What thing am I?

LUCRETIA: My dearest child, what has your father done?

BEATRICE: *(doubtfully)*
Who art thou questioner? I have no father.

(aside)

She is the madhouse nurse who tends on me,
It is a piteous office.

(to LUCRETIA, in a slow, subdued voice)

Do you know
I thought I was that wretched Beatrice
Men speak of, whom her father sometimes hales[20]
From hall to hall by the entangled hair;
At others, pens up naked in damp cells
Where scaly reptiles crawl, and starves her there,
Till she will eat strange flesh. This woful story
So did I overact in my sick dreams,
That I imagined . . . no, it cannot be!
Horrible things have been in this wild world,
Prodigious mixtures, and confusions strange
Of good and ill; and worse have been conceived
Than ever there was found a heart to do.
But never fancy imaged such a deed
As . . .

(Pauses, suddenly recollecting herself.)

Who art thou? Swear to me, ere I die
With fearful expectation, that indeed
Thou art not what thou seemest . . . Mother!

LUCRETIA: Oh!
My sweet child, know you . . .

BEATRICE: Yet speak it not:
For then if this be truth, that other too
Must be a truth, a firm enduring truth,
Linked with each lasting circumstance of life,
Never to change, never to pass away.
Why so it is. This is the Cenci palace;
Thou art Lucretia; I am Beatrice.
I have talked some wild words, but will no more.
Mother, come near me: from this point of time,
I am . . .

(Her voice dies away faintly.)

LUCRETIA: Alas! What has befallen thee, child?
What has thy father done?

BEATRICE: What have I done?
Am I not innocent? Is it my crime
That one with white hair, and imperious brow,
Who tortured me from my forgotten years,
As parents only dare, should call himself
My father, yet should be!—Oh, what am I?
What name, what place, what memory shall be mine?
What retrospects, outliving even despair?

LUCRETIA: He is a violent tyrant, surely, child:
We know that death alone can make us free;
His death or ours. But what can he have done
Of deadlier outrage or worse injury?
Thou art unlike thyself; thine eyes shoot forth
A wandering and strange spirit. Speak to me,
Unlock those pallid hands whose fingers twine
With one another.

BEATRICE: 'Tis the restless life
Tortured within them. If I try to speak
I shall go mad. Aye, something must be done;
What, yet I know not . . . something which shall make
The thing that I have suffered but a shadow
In the dread lightning which avenges it;
Brief, rapid, irreversible, destroying
The consequence of what it cannot cure.
Some such thing is to be endured or done:
When I know what, I shall be still and calm,
And never any thing will move me more
But now!—Oh blood, which art my father's blood,
Circling thro' these contaminated veins
If thou, poured forth on the polluted earth,
Could wash away the crime, and punishment
By which I suffer . . . no, that cannot be!
Many might doubt there were a God above
Who sees and permits evil, and so die:
That faith no agony shall obscure in me.

LUCRETIA: It must indeed have been some bitter wrong;
Yet what, I dare not guess: Oh, my lost child,
Hide not in proud impenetrable grief
Thy sufferings from my fear.

BEATRICE: I hide them not.
What are the words which you would have me speak?
I, who can feign no image in my mind
Of that which has transformed me. I, whose thought
Is like a ghost shrouded and folded up
In its own formless horror. Of all words,
That minister to mortal intercourse,
Which wouldst thou hear? For there is none to tell
My misery: if another ever knew
Aught like to it, she died as I will die.
And left it, as I must, without a name.
Death! Death! Our law and our religion call thee
A punishment and a reward . . . Oh, which
Have I deserved?

[20] **hales:** forces.

LUCRETIA: The peace of innocence;
Till in your season you be called to heaven.
Whate'er you may have suffered, you have done
No evil. Death must be the punishment
Of crime, or the reward of trampling down
The thorns which God has strewed upon the path
Which leads to immortality.

BEATRICE: Aye, death . . .
The punishment of crime. I pray thee, God,
Let me not be bewildered while I judge.
If I must live day after day, and keep
These limbs, the unworthy temple of thy spirit,
As a foul den from which what thou abhorrest
May mock thee, unavenged . . . it shall not be!
Self murder . . . no that might be no escape,
For thy decree yawns like a Hell between
Our will and it: — O! In this mortal world
There is no vindication and no law
Which can adjudge and execute the doom
Of that through which I suffer.

(Enter ORSINO.*)*

(She approaches him solemnly.) Welcome, Friend!
I have to tell you that, since last we met,
I have endured a wrong so great and strange,
That neither life or death can give me rest.
Ask me not what it is, for there are deeds
Which have no form, sufferings which have no
tongue.

ORSINO: And what is he who has thus injured you?

BEATRICE: The man they call my father: a dread name.

ORSINO: It cannot be . . .

BEATRICE: What it can be, or not,
Forbear to think. It is, and it has been;
Advise me how it shall not be again.
I thought to die; but a religious awe
Restrains me, and the dread lest death itself
Might be no refuge from the consciousness
Of what is yet unexpiated. Oh, speak!

ORSINO: Accuse him of the deed, and let the law
Avenge thee.

BEATRICE: Oh, ice-hearted counsellor!
If I could find a word that might make known
The crime of my destroyer; and that done
My tongue should like a knife tear out the secret
Which cankers my heart's core; aye, lay all bare
So that my unpolluted fame should be
With vilest gossips a stale mouthed story;
A mock, a bye-word, an astonishment: —
If this were done, which never shall be done,
Think of the offender's gold, his dreaded hate,
And the strange horror of the accuser's tale,
Baffling belief, and overpowering speech;
Scarce whispered, unimaginable, wrapt
In hideous hints . . . Oh, most assured redress!

ORSINO: You will endure it then?

BEATRICE: Endure? — Orsino,
It seems your counsel is small profit.

(Turns from him, and speaks half to herself.)

Aye,
All must be suddenly resolved and done.
What is this undistinguishable mist
Of thoughts, which rise, like shadow after shadow,
Darkening each other?

ORSINO: Should the offender live?
Triumph in his misdeed? and make, by use,
His crime, whate'er it is, dreadful no doubt,
Thine element; until thou mayest become
Utterly lost; subdued even to the hue
Of that which thou permittest?

BEATRICE: *(to herself)* Mighty death!
Thou double visaged shadow! Only judge!
Rightfullest arbiter!

(She retires absorbed in thought.)

LUCRETIA: If the lightning
Of God has e'er descended to avenge . . .

ORSINO: Blaspheme not! His high Providence
commits
Its glory on this earth, and their own wrongs
Into the hands of men; if they neglect
To punish crime . . .

LUCRETIA: But if one, like this wretch,
Should mock with gold, opinion law and power?
If there be no appeal to that which makes
The guiltiest tremble? If because our wrongs,
For that they are, unnatural, strange and monstrous,
Exceed all measure of belief? Oh, God!
If, for the very reasons which should make
Redress most swift and sure, our injurer triumphs?
And we the victims, bear worse punishment
Than that appointed for their torturer?

ORSINO: Think not
But that there is redress where there is wrong,
So we be bold enough to seize it.

LUCRETIA: How?
If there were any way to make all sure,

I know not . . . but I think it might be good
To . . .
ORSINO: Why, his late outrage to Beatrice;
For it is such, as I but faintly guess,
As makes remorse dishonour, and leaves her
Only one duty, how she may avenge:
You, but one refuge from ills ill endured;
Me, but one counsel . . .
LUCRETIA: For we cannot hope
That aid, or retribution, or resource
Will arise thence, where every other one
Might find them with less need.

(BEATRICE *advances.*)

ORSINO: Then . . .
BEATRICE: Peace, Orsino!
And, honoured Lady, while I speak, I pray,
That you put off, as garments overworn,
Forbearance and respect, remorse and fear,
And all the fit restraints of daily life,
Which have been borne from childhood, but which now
Would be a mockery to my holier plea.
As I have said, I have endured a wrong,
Which, though it be expressionless, is such
As asks atonement; both for what is past,
And lest I be reserved, day after day,
To load with crimes an overburthened soul,
And be . . . what ye can dream not. I have prayed
To God, and I have talked with my own heart,
And have unravelled my entangled will,
And have at length determined what is right.
Art thou my friend Orsino? False or true?
Pledge thy salvation ere I speak.
ORSINO: I swear
To dedicate my cunning, and my strength
My silence, and whatever else is mine,
To thy commands.
LUCRETIA: You think we should devise
His death?
BEATRICE: And execute what is devised,
And suddenly. We must be brief and bold.
ORSINO: And yet most cautious.
LUCRETIA: For the jealous laws
Would punish us with death and infamy
For that which it became themselves to do.
BEATRICE: Be cautious as ye may, but prompt. Orsino,
What are the means?
ORSINO: I know two dull, fierce outlaws,
Who think man's spirit as a worm's, and they
Would trample out, for any slight caprice,
The meanest or the noblest life. This mood
Is marketable here in Rome. They sell
What we now want.
LUCRETIA: To morrow before dawn,
Cenci will take us to that lonely rock,
Petrella, in the Apulian Apennines.[21]
If he arrive there . . .
BEATRICE: He must not arrive.
ORSINO: Will it be dark before you reach the tower?
LUCRETIA: The sun will scarce be set.
BEATRICE: But I remember
Two miles on this side of the fort, the road
Crosses a deep ravine; 'tis rough and narrow,
And winds with short turns down the precipice;
And in its depth there is a mighty rock,
Which has, from unimaginable years,
Sustained itself with terror and with toil
Over a gulph, and with the agony
With which it clings seems slowly coming down;
Even as a wretched soul hour after hour,
Clings to the mass of life; yet clinging, leans;
And leaning, makes more dark the dread abyss
In which it fears to fall: beneath this crag
Huge as despair, as if in weariness,
The melancholy mountain yawns . . . below,
You hear but see not an impetuous torrent
Raging among the caverns, and a bridge
Crosses the chasm; and high above there grow,
With intersecting trunks, from crag to crag,
Cedars, and yews, and pines; whose tangled hair
Is matted in one solid roof of shade
By the dark ivy's twine. At noon day here
'Tis twilight, and at sunset blackest night.
ORSINO: Before you reach that bridge make some excuse
For spurring on your mules, or loitering
Until . . .
BEATRICE: What sound is that?
LUCRETIA: Hark! No, it cannot be a servant's step;
It must be Cenci, unexpectedly
Returned . . . Make some excuse for being here.

[21] **Apulian Apennines:** mountains in southeast Italy.

BEATRICE: (*to* ORSINO, *as she goes out*)
That step we hear approach must never pass
The bridge of which we spoke.

(*Exeunt* LUCRETIA *and* BEATRICE.)

ORSINO: What shall I do?
Cenci must find me here, and I must bear
The imperious inquisition of his looks
As to what brought me hither: let me mask
Mine own in some inane and vacant smile.

(*Enter* GIACOMO, *in a hurried manner.*)

How! Have you ventured thither? know you then
That Cenci is from home?
GIACOMO: I sought him here;
And now must wait till he returns.
ORSINO: Great God!
Weigh you the danger of this rashness?
GIACOMO: Aye!
Does my destroyer know his danger? We
Are now no more, as once, parent and child,
But man to man; the oppressor to the oppressed;
The slanderer to the slandered; foe to foe:
He has cast Nature off, which was his shield,
And Nature casts him off, who is her shame;
And I spurn both. Is it a father's throat
Which I will shake, and say, I ask not gold;
I ask not happy years; nor memories
Of tranquil childhood; nor home-sheltered love;
Though all these hast thou torn from me, and more;
But only my fair fame; only one hoard
Of peace, which I thought hidden from thy hate,
Under the penury heaped on me by thee,
Or I will . . . God can understand and pardon,
Why should I speak with man?
ORSINO: Be calm, dear friend.
GIACOMO: Well, I will calmly tell you what he did.
This old Francesco Cenci, as you know,
Borrowed the dowry of my wife from me,
And then denied the loan; and left me so
In poverty, the which I sought to mend
By holding a poor office in the state.
It had been promised to me, and already
I bought new clothing for my ragged babes,
And my wife smiled; and my heart knew repose.
When Cenci's intercession, as I found,
Conferred this office on a wretch, whom thus
He paid for vilest service. I returned
With this ill news, and we sate sad together
Solacing our despondency with tears
Of such affection and unbroken faith
As temper life's worst bitterness; when he,
As he is wont, came to upbraid and curse,
Mocking our poverty, and telling us
Such was God's scourge for disobedient sons.
And then, that I might strike him dumb with shame,
I spoke of my wife's dowry; but he coined
A brief yet specious tale, how I had wasted
The sum in secret riot; and he saw
My wife was touched, and he went smiling forth.
And when I knew the impression he had made,
And felt my wife insult with silent scorn
My ardent truth, and look averse and cold,
I went forth too: but soon returned again;
Yet not so soon but that my wife had taught
My children her harsh thoughts, and they all cried,
'Give us clothes, father! Give us better food!
What you in one night squander were enough
For months!' I looked, and saw that home was hell.
And to that hell will I return no more
Until mine enemy has rendered up
Atonement, or, as he gave life to me
I will, reversing nature's law . . .
ORSINO: Trust me,
The compensation which thou seekest here
Will be denied.
GIACOMO: Then . . . Are you not my friend?
Did you not hint at the alternative,
Upon the brink of which you see I stand,
The other day when we conversed together?
My wrongs were then less. That word parricide,
Although I am resolved, haunts me like fear.
ORSINO: It must be fear itself, for the bare word
Is hollow mockery. Mark, how wisest God
Draws to one point the threads of a just doom,
So sanctifying it: what you devise
Is, as it were, accomplished.
GIACOMO: Is he dead?
ORSINO: His grave is ready. Know that since we met
Cenci has done an outrage to his daughter.
GIACOMO: What outrage?
ORSINO: That she speaks not, but you may
Conceive such half conjectures as I do,
From her fixed paleness, and the lofty grief
Of her stern brow bent on the idle air,
And her severe unmodulated voice,

Drowning both tenderness and dread; and last
From this; that whilst her step-mother and I,
Bewildered in our horror, talked together
With obscure hints; both self-misunderstood
And darkly guessing, stumbling, in our talk,
Over the truth, and yet to its revenge,
She interrupted us, and with a look
Which told before she spoke it, he must die . . .

GIACOMO: It is enough. My doubts are well appeased;
There is a higher reason for the act
Than mine; there is a holier judge than me,
A more unblamed avenger. Beatrice,
Who in the gentleness of thy sweet youth
Hast never trodden on a worm, or bruised
A living flower, but thou hast pitied it
With needless tears! Fair sister, thou in whom
Men wondered how such loveliness and wisdom
Did not destroy each other! Is there made
Ravage of thee? O, heart, I ask no more
Justification! Shall I wait, Orsino,
Till he return, and stab him at the door?

ORSINO: Not so; some accident might interpose
To rescue him from what is now most sure;
And you are unprovided where to fly,
How to excuse or to conceal. Nay, listen:
All is contrived; success is so assured
That . . .

(Enter BEATRICE.*)*

BEATRICE: 'Tis my brother's voice! You know me not?

GIACOMO: My sister, my lost sister!

BEATRICE: Lost indeed!
I see Orsino has talked with you, and
That you conjecture things too horrible
To speak, yet far less than the truth. Now, stay not,
He might return: yet kiss me; I shall know
That then thou hast consented to his death.
Farewell, Farewell! Let piety to God,
Brotherly love, justice and clemency,
And all things that make tender hardest hearts
Make thine hard, brother. Answer not . . . farewell.

(Exeunt severally.)

— SCENE II —

(A mean apartment in GIACOMO*'s house.)*
*(*GIACOMO*, alone.)*

GIACOMO: 'Tis midnight, and Orsino comes not yet.

(Thunder, and the sound of a storm.)

What! can the everlasting elements
Feel with a worm like man? If so the shaft
Of mercy-winged lightning would not fall
On stones and trees. My wife and children sleep:
They are now living in unmeaning dreams:
But I must wake, still doubting if that deed
Be just which was most necessary. O,
Thou unreplenished lamp! whose narrow fire
Is shaken by the wind, and on whose edge
Devouring darkness hovers! Thou small flame,
Which, as a dying pulse rises and falls,
Still flickerest up and down, how very soon,
Did I not feed thee, wouldst thou fail and be
As thou hadst never been! So wastes and sinks
Even now, perhaps, the life that kindled mine:
But that no power can fill with vital oil
That broken lamp of flesh. Ha! 'tis the blood
Which fed these veins that ebbs till all is cold:
It is the form that moulded mine that sinks
Into the white and yellow spasms of death:
It is the soul by which mine was arrayed
In God's immortal likeness which now stands
Naked before Heaven's judgement seat!

(A bell strikes.)

One! Two!
The hours crawl on; and when my hairs are white
My son will then perhaps be waiting thus,
Tortured between just hate and vain remorse;
Chiding the tardy messenger of news
Like those which I expect. I almost wish
He be not dead, although my wrongs are great;
Yet . . . 'tis Orsino's step . . .

(Enter ORSINO.*)*

Speak!

ORSINO: I am come
To say he has escaped.

GIACOMO: Escaped!

ORSINO: And safe
Within Petrella. He past by the spot
Appointed for the deed an hour too soon.

GIACOMO: Are we the fools of such contingencies?
And do we waste in blind misgivings thus
The hours when we should act? Then wind and thunder,
Which seemed to howl his knell, is the loud laughter

With which Heaven mocks our weakness! I henceforth
Will ne'er repent of aught designed or done
But my repentance.

ORSINO: See, the lamp is out.

GIACOMO: If no remorse is ours when the dim air
Has drank this innocent flame, why should we quail
When Cenci's life, that light by which ill spirits
See the worst deeds they prompt, shall sink for ever?
No, I am hardened.

ORSINO: Why, what need of this?
Who feared the pale intrusion of remorse
In a just deed? Altho' our first plan failed
Doubt not but he will soon be laid to rest.
But light the lamp; let us not talk i' the dark.

GIACOMO: *(lighting the lamp)*
And yet once quenched I cannot thus relume
My father's life: do you not think his ghost
Might plead that argument with God?

ORSINO: Once gone
You cannot now recall your sister's peace;
Your own extinguished years of youth and hope;
Nor your wife's bitter words; nor all the taunts
Which, from the prosperous, weak misfortune takes;
Nor your dead mother; nor . . .

GIACOMO: O, speak no more!
I am resolved, although this very hand
Must quench the life that animated it.

ORSINO: There is no need of that. Listen: you know
Olimpio, the castellan[22] of Petrella
In old Colonna's time; him whom your father
Degraded from his post? And Marzio,
That desperate wretch, whom he deprived last year
Of a reward of blood, well earned and due?

GIACOMO: I knew Olimpio; and they say he hated
Old Cenci so, that in his silent rage
His lips grew white only to see him pass.
Of Marzio I know nothing.

ORSINO: Marzio's hate
Matches Olimpio's. I have sent these men,
But in your name, and as at your request,
To talk with Beatrice and Lucretia.

GIACOMO: Only to talk?

ORSINO: The moments which even now
Pass onward to morrow's midnight hour
May memorize[23] their flight with death: ere then
They must have talked, and may perhaps have done,
And made an end . . .

GIACOMO: Listen! What sound is that?

ORSINO: The housedog moans, and the beams crack: nought else.

GIACOMO: It is my wife complaining in her sleep:
I doubt not she is saying bitter things
Of me; and all my children round her dreaming
That I deny them sustenance.

ORSINO: Whilst he
Who truly took it from them, and who fills
Their hungry rest with bitterness, now sleeps
Lapped in bad pleasures, and triumphantly
Mocks thee in visions of successful hate
Too like the truth of day.

GIACOMO: If e'er he wakes
Again, I will not trust to hireling hands . . .

ORSINO: Why, that were well. I must be gone; good night!
When next we meet . . .

GIACOMO: May all be done—and all
Forgotten—Oh, that I had never been!

(Exeunt.)

ACT IV

— SCENE I —

(An apartment in the Castle of Petrella.)
(Enter CENCI.*)*

CENCI: She comes not; yet I left her even now
Vanquished and faint. She knows the penalty
Of her delay: yet what if threats are vain?
Am I now not within Petrella's moat?
Or fear I still the eyes and ears of Rome?
Might I not drag her by the golden hair?
Stamp on her? Keep her sleepless till her brain
Be overworn? Tame her with chains and famine?
Less would suffice. Yet so to leave undone
What I most seek! No, 'tis her stubborn will

[22] **castellan:** the keeper of a castle.

[23] **memorize:** cause to be remembered.

Which by its own consent shall stoop as low
As that which drags it down.

(Enter LUCRETIA.*)*

Thou loathed wretch!
Hide thee from my abhorrence; Fly, begone!
Yet stay! Bid Beatrice come hither.

LUCRETIA: Oh,
Husband! I pray for thine own wretched sake
Heed what thou dost. A man who walks like thee
Thro' crimes, and thro' the danger of his crimes,
Each hour may stumble o'er a sudden grave.
And thou art old; thy hairs are hoary gray;
As thou wouldst save thyself from death and hell,
Pity thy daughter; give her to some friend
In marriage: so that she may tempt thee not
To hatred, or worse thoughts, if worse there be.

CENCI: What! like her sister who has found a home
To mock my hate from with prosperity?
Strange ruin shall destroy both her and thee
And all that yet remain. My death may be
Rapid, her destiny outspeeds it. Go,
Bid her come hither, and before my mood
Be changed, lest I should drag her by the hair.

LUCRETIA: She sent me to thee, husband. At thy presence
She fell, as thou dost know, into a trance;
And in that trance she heard a voice which said,
'Cenci must die! Let him confess himself!
Even now the accusing Angel waits to hear
If God, to punish his enormous crimes,
Harden his dying heart!'

CENCI: Why—such things are . . .
No doubt divine revealings may be made.
'Tis plain I have been favoured from above,
For when I cursed my sons they died.—
Aye . . . so . . .
As to the right or wrong thats talk . . . repentance . . .
Repentance is an easy moment's work
And more depends on God than me. Well . . . well . . .
I must give up the greater point, which was
To poison and corrupt her soul.

(A pause; LUCRETIA *approaches anxiously, and then shrinks back as he speaks.)*

One, two;
Aye . . . Rocco and Cristofano my curse
Strangled: and Giacomo, I think, will find
Life a worse Hell than that beyond the grave:
Beatrice shall, if there be skill in hate
Die in despair, blaspheming: to Bernardo,
He is so innocent, I will bequeath
The memory of these deeds, and make his youth
The sepulchre of hope, where evil thoughts
Shall grow like weeds on a neglected tomb.
When all is done, out in the wide Campagna,
I will pile up my silver and my gold;
My costly robes, paintings and tapestries;
My parchments and all records of my wealth,
And make a bonfire in my joy, and leave
Of my possessions nothing but my name;
Which shall be an inheritance to strip
Its wearer bare as infamy. That done,
My soul, which is a scourge, will I resign
Into the hands of him who wielded it;
Be it for its own punishment or theirs,
He will not ask it of me till the lash
Be broken in its last and deepest wound;
Untill its hate be all inflicted. Yet,
Lest death outspeed my purpose, let me make
Short work and sure . . . *(going)*

LUCRETIA: *(Stops him.)* Oh, stay! It was a feint:
She had no vision, and she heard no voice.
I said it but to awe thee.

CENCI: That is well.
Vile palterer[24] with the sacred truth of God,
Be thy soul choked with that blaspheming lie!
For Beatrice worse terrors are in store
To bend her to my will.

LUCRETIA: Oh! to what will?
What cruel sufferings more than she has known
Canst thou inflict?

CENCI: Andrea! Go call my daughter,
And if she comes not tell her that I come.
What sufferings? I will drag her, step by step,
Thro' infamies unheard of among men:
She shall stand shelterless in the broad noon
Of public scorn, for acts blazoned abroad,
One among which shall be . . . What? Canst thou guess?
She shall become, (for what she most abhors
Shall have a fascination to entrap
Her loathing will), to her own conscious self

[24] **palterer:** trifler.

All she appears to others; and when dead,
As she shall die unshrived[25] and unforgiven,
A rebel to her father and her God,
Her corpse shall be abandoned to the hounds;
Her name shall be the terror of the earth;
Her spirit shall approach the throne of God
Plague spotted with my curses. I will make
Body and soul a monstrous lump of ruin.

(Enter ANDREA.*)*

ANDREA: The lady Beatrice . . .
CENCI: Speak, pale slave! What
Said she?
ANDREA: My Lord, 'twas what she looked; she said:
Go tell my father that I see the gulph
Of Hell between us two, which he may pass,
I will not.

(Exit ANDREA.*)*

CENCI: Go thou quick, Lucretia,
Tell her to come; yet let her understand
Her coming is consent; and say, moreover,
That if she come not I will curse her.

(Exit LUCRETIA.*)*

Ha!
With what but a father's curse doth God
Panic-strike armed victory, and make pale
Cities in their prosperity? The world's Father
Must grant a parent's prayer against his child
Be he who asks even what men call me.
Will not the deaths of her rebellious brothers
Awe her before I speak? For I on them
Did imprecate[26] quick ruin, and it came.

(Enter LUCRETIA.*)*

Well, what? Speak, wretch!
LUCRETIA: She said, I cannot come;
Go tell my father that I see a torrent
Of his own blood raging between us.
CENCI: *(kneeling)* God!
Hear me! If this most specious mass of flesh,
Which thou hast made my daughter; this my blood,
This particle of my divided being;
Or rather, this my bane and my disease,
Whose sight infects and poisons me; this devil
Which sprung from me as from a hell, was meant
To aught good use; if her bright loveliness
Was kindled to illumine this dark world;
If nursed by thy selectest dew of love
Such virtues blossom in her as should make
The peace of life, I pray thee for my sake,
As thou the common God and Father art
Of her, and me, and all; reverse that doom!
Earth, in the name of God, let her food be
Poison, untill she be encrusted round
With leprous stains! Heaven, rain upon her head
The blistering drops of the Maremma's[27] dew,
Till she be speckled like a toad; parch up
Those love-enkindled lips, warp those fine limbs
To loathed lameness! All beholding sun,
Strike in thine envy those life darting eyes
With thine own blinding beams!
LUCRETIA: Peace! Peace!
For thine own sake unsay those dreadful words.
When high God grants he punishes such prayers.
CENCI: *(leaping up, and throwing his right hand towards Heaven)*
He does his will, I mine! This in addition,
That if she have a child . . .
LUCRETIA: Horrible thought!
CENCI: That if she ever have a child; and thou,
Quick Nature! I adjure thee by thy God,
That thou be fruitful in her, and encrease
And multiply, fulfilling his command,
And my deep imprecation! May it be
A hideous likeness of herself, that as
From a distorting mirror, she may see
Her image mixed with what she most abhors,
Smiling upon her from her nursing breast.
And that the child may from its infancy
Grow, day by day, more wicked and deformed,
Turning her mother's love to misery:
And that both she and it may live until
It shall repay her care and pain with hate,
Or what may else be more unnatural.
So he may hunt her thro' the clamorous scoffs
Of the loud world to a dishonoured grave.
Shall I revoke this curse? Go, bid her come,
Before my words are chronicled in heaven.

[25] **unshrived:** without the benefit of confession and absolution.

[26] **imprecate:** invoke a curse upon.

[27] **Maremma:** swamp near Pisa.

(Exit LUCRETIA.*)*

I do not feel as if I were a man,
But like a fiend appointed to chastise
The offences of some unremembered world.
My blood is running up and down my veins;
A fearful pleasure makes it prick and tingle:
I feel a giddy sickness of strange awe;
My heart is beating with an expectation
Of horrid joy.

(Enter LUCRETIA.*)*

What? Speak!

LUCRETIA: She bids thee curse;
And if thy curses, as they cannot do,
Could kill her soul . . .

CENCI: She would not come. 'Tis well,
I can do both: first take what I demand,
And then extort concession. To thy chamber!
Fly ere I spurn thee: and beware this night
That thou cross not my footsteps. It were safer
To come between the tiger and his prey.

(Exit LUCRETIA.*)*

It must be late; mine eyes grow weary dim
With unaccustomed heaviness of sleep.
Conscience! Oh, thou most insolent of lies!
They say that sleep, that healing dew of heaven,
Steeps not in balm the foldings of the brain
Which thinks thee an imposter. I will go
First to belie thee with an hour of rest,
Which will be deep and calm, I feel: and then . . .
O, multitudinous Hell, the fiends will shake
Thine arches with the laughter of their joy!
There shall be lamentation heard in Heaven
As o'er an angel fallen; and upon Earth
All good shall droop and sicken, and ill things
Shall with a spirit of unnatural life
Stir and be quickened . . . even as I am now.

(Exit.)

— SCENE II —

(Before the Castle of Petrella.)

(Enter BEATRICE *and* LUCRETIA *above on the ramparts.)*

BEATRICE: They come not yet.

LUCRETIA: 'Tis scarce midnight.

BEATRICE: How slow
Behind the course of thought, even sick with speed.
Lags leaden-footed time!

LUCRETIA: The minutes pass . . .
If he should wake before the deed is done?

BEATRICE: O, Mother! He must never wake again.
What thou hast said persuades me that our act
Will but dislodge a spirit of deep hell
Out of a human form.

LUCRETIA: 'Tis true he spoke
Of death and judgement with strange confidence
For one so wicked; as a man believing
In God, yet recking not of good or ill.
And yet to die without confession! . . .

BEATRICE: Oh!
Believe that heaven is merciful and just,
And will not add our dread necessity
To the amount of his offences.

(Enter OLIMPIO *and* MARZIO, *below.)*

LUCRETIA: See,
They come.

BEATRICE: All mortal things must hasten thus
To their dark end. Let us go down.

(Exeunt LUCRETIA *and* BEATRICE *from above.)*

OLIMPIO: How feel you to this work?

MARZIO: As one who thinks
A thousand crowns excellent market price
For an old murderer's life. Your cheeks are pale.

OLIMPIO: It is the white reflexion of your own,
Which you call pale.

MARZIO: Is that their natural hue?

OLIMPIO: Or 'tis my hate and the deferred desire
To wreak it, which extinguishes their blood.

MARZIO: You are inclined then to this business?

OLIMPIO: Aye.
If one should bribe me with a thousand crowns
To kill a serpent which had stung my child,
I could not be more willing.

(Enter BEATRICE *and* LUCRETIA, *below.)*

Noble ladies!

BEATRICE: Are ye resolved?

OLIMPIO: Is he asleep?

MARZIO: Is all
Quiet?

LUCRETIA: I mixed an opiate with his drink:
He sleeps so soundly . . .

BEATRICE: That his death will be
But as a change of sin-chastising dreams,
A dark continuance of the Hell within him,

Which God extinguish! But ye are resolved?
Ye know it is a high and holy deed?
OLIMPIO: We are resolved.
MARZIO: As to the how this act
Be warranted, it rests with you.
BEATRICE: Well, follow!
OLIMPIO: Hush! Hark! What noise is that?
MARZIO: Ha! some one comes!
BEATRICE: Ye conscience-stricken cravens,[28] rock to rest
Your baby hearts. It is the iron gate,
Which ye left open, swinging to the wind,
That enters whistling as in scorn. Come, follow!
And be your steps like mine, light, quick and bold.

(Exeunt.)

— SCENE III —

(An apartment in the Castle.)
(Enter BEATRICE *and* LUCRETIA.*)*

LUCRETIA: They are about it now.
BEATRICE: Nay, it is done.
LUCRETIA: I have not heard him groan.
BEATRICE: He will not groan.
LUCRETIA: What sound is that?
BEATRICE: List! 'tis the tread of feet
About his bed.
LUCRETIA: My God!
If he be now a cold stiff corpse . . .
BEATRICE: O, fear not
What may be done, but what is left undone:
The act seals all.

(Enter OLIMPIO *and* MARZIO.*)*

Is it accomplished?
MARZIO: What?
OLIMPIO: Did you not call?
BEATRICE: When?
OLIMPIO: Now.
BEATRICE: I ask if all is over?
OLIMPIO: We dare not kill an old and sleeping man;
His thin grey hair, his stern and reverent brow,
His veined hands crossed on his heaving breast,
And the calm innocent sleep in which he lay,
Quelled me. Indeed, indeed, I cannot do it.
MARZIO: But I was bolder; for I chid Olimpio,
And bade him bear his wrongs to his own grave
And leave me the reward. And now my knife
Touched the loose wrinkled throat, when the old man
Stirred in his sleep, and said, 'God! hear, O, hear,
A father's curse! What art thou not our father?'
And then he laughed. I knew it was the ghost
Of my dead father speaking through his lips,
And could not kill him.
BEATRICE: Miserable slaves!
Where, if ye dare not kill a sleeping man,
Found ye the boldness to return to me
With such a deed undone? Base palterers!
Cowards and traitors! Why, the very conscience
Which ye would sell for gold and for revenge
Is an equivocation: it sleeps over
A thousand daily acts disgracing men;
And when a deed where mercy insults heaven . . .
Why do I talk?

(snatching a dagger from one of them and raising it)

Hadst thou a tongue to say,
She murdered her own father, I must do it!
But never dream ye shall outlive him long!
OLIMPIO: Stop, for God's sake!
MARZIO: I will go back and kill him.
OLIMPIO: Give me the weapon, we must do thy will.
BEATRICE: Take it! Depart! Return!

(Exeunt OLIMPIO *and* MARZIO.*)*

How pale thou art!
We do but that which 'twere a deadly crime
To leave undone.
LUCRETIA: Would it were done!
BEATRICE: Even whilst
That doubt is passing through your mind, the world
Is conscious of a change. Darkness and hell
Have swallowed up the vapour they sent forth
To blacken the sweet light of life. My breath
Comes, methinks, lighter and the gellyed blood
Runs freely thro' my veins. Hark!

(Enter OLIMPIO *and* MARZIO.*)*

He is . . .
OLIMPIO: Dead!
MARZIO: We strangled him that there might be no blood;
And then we threw his heavy corpse i' the garden
Under the balcony; 'twill seem it fell.
BEATRICE: *(giving them a bag of coin)*
Here take this gold, and hasten to your homes.

[28] **cravens:** cowards.

And, Marzio, because thou wast only awed
By that which made me tremble, wear thou this!

(Clothes him in a rich mantle.)

It was the mantle which my grandfather
Wore in his high prosperity, and men
Envied his state: so may they envy thine.
Thou wert a weapon in the hand of God
To a just use. Live long and thrive! And, mark,
If thou hast crimes, repent: this deed is none.

(A horn is sounded.)

LUCRETIA: Hark, 'tis the castle horn; my God! it sounds
Like the last trump.[29]
BEATRICE: Some tedious guest is coming.
LUCRETIA: The drawbridge is let down; there is a tramp
Of horses in the court; fly, hide yourselves!

(Exeunt OLIMPIO and MARZIO.)

BEATRICE: Let us retire to counterfeit deep rest;
I scarcely need to counterfeit it now:
The spirit which doth reign within these limbs
Seems strangely undisturbed. I could even sleep
Fearless and calm: all ill is surely past.

(Exeunt.)

— SCENE IV —

(Another apartment in the Castle.)
(Enter on one side the Legate SAVELLA introduced by a servant, and on the other LUCRETIA and BERNARDO.)

SAVELLA: Lady, my duty to his Holiness
Be my excuse that thus unseasonably
I break upon your rest. I must speak with
Count Cenci; doth he sleep?
LUCRETIA: *(in a hurried and confused manner)*
I think he sleeps;
Yet wake him not, I pray, spare me awhile,
He is a wicked and wrathful man;
Should he be roused out of his sleep to night,
Which is, I know, a hell of angry dreams,
It were not well; indeed it were not well.
Wait till day break. . . .
(aside) O, I am deadly sick!
SAVELLA: I grieve thus to distress you, but the Count
Must answer charges of the gravest import,
And suddenly; such my commission is.
LUCRETIA: *(with increased agitation)*
I dare not rouse him: I know none who dare . . .
'Twere perilous; . . . you might as safely waken
A serpent; or a corpse in which some fiend
Were laid to sleep.
SAVELLA: Lady, my moments here
Are counted. I must rouse him from his sleep,
Since none else dare.
LUCRETIA: *(aside)* O, terror! O, despair!
(to BERNARDO) Bernardo, conduct you the Lord Legate to
Your father's chamber.

(Exeunt SAVELLA and BERNARDO.)
(Enter BEATRICE.)

BEATRICE: 'Tis a messenger
Come to arrest the culprit who now stands
Before the throne of unappealable God.
Both Earth and Heaven, consenting arbiters,
Acquit our deed.
LUCRETIA: Oh, agony of fear!
Would that he yet might live! Even now I heard
The legate's followers whisper as they passed
They had a warrant for his instant death.
All was prepared by unforbidden means
Which we must pay so dearly, having done.
Even now they search the tower, and find the body;
Now they suspect the truth; now they consult
Before they come to tax us with the fact;
O, horrible, 'tis all discovered!
BEATRICE: Mother,
What is done wisely, is done well. Be bold
As thou art just. 'Tis like a truant child
To fear that others know what thou hast done,
Even from thine own strong consciousness, and thus
Write on unsteady eyes and altered cheeks
All thou wouldst hide. Be faithful to thyself,
And fear no other witness but thy fear.
For if, as cannot be, some circumstance
Should rise in accusation, we can blind
Suspicion with such cheap astonishment,
Or overbear it with such guiltless pride,
As murderers cannot feign. The deed is done,

[29] **trump**: trumpet. The angel Gabriel's trumpet will blow to announce the Last Judgment.

And what may follow now regards not me.
I am as universal as the light;
Free as the earth-surrounding air; as firm
As the world's centre. Consequence, to me,
Is as the wind which strikes the solid rock
But shakes it not.

(a cry within and tumult)

Murder! Murder! Murder!

(Enter BERNARDO *and* SAVELLA.*)*

SAVELLA: *(to his followers)*
Go, search the castle round; sound the alarm;
Look to the gates that none escape!

BEATRICE: What now?

BERNARDO: I know not what to say . . . my father's dead.

BEATRICE: How; dead! he only sleeps; you mistake, brother.
His sleep is very calm, very like death;
'Tis wonderful how well a tyrant sleeps.
He is not dead?

BERNARDO: Dead; murdered.

LUCRETIA: *(with extreme agitation)* Oh, no, no,
He is not murdered though he may be dead;
I have alone the keys of those apartments.

SAVELLA: Ha! Is it so?

BEATRICE: My Lord, I pray excuse us;
We will retire; my mother is not well:
She seems quite overcome with this strange horror.

(Exeunt LUCRETIA *and* BEATRICE.*)*

SAVELLA: Can you suspect who may have murdered him?

BERNARDO: I know not what to think.

SAVELLA: Can you name any
Who had an interest in his death?

BERNARDO: Alas!
I can name none who had not, and those most
Who most lament that such a deed is done;
My mother, and my sister, and myself.

SAVELLA: 'Tis strange! There were clear marks of violence.
I found the old man's body in the moonlight
Hanging beneath the window of his chamber
Among the branches of a pine: he could not
Have fallen there, for all his limbs lay heaped
And effortless; 'tis true there was no blood . . .
Favour me, Sir; it much imports your house
That all should be made clear; to tell the ladies
That I request their presence.

(Exit BERNARDO.*)*
(Enter Guards bringing in MARZIO.*)*

GUARD: We have one.

OFFICER: My Lord, we found this ruffian and another
Lurking among the rocks; there is no doubt
But that they are the murderers of Count Cenci:
Each had a bag of coin; this fellow wore
A gold-inwoven robe, which shining bright
Under the dark rocks to the glimmering moon
Betrayed them to our notice: the other fell
Desperately fighting.

SAVELLA: What does he confess?

OFFICER: He keeps firm silence; but these lines found on him
May speak.

SAVELLA: Their language is at least sincere.

(Reads.)

TO THE LADY BEATRICE.

'That the atonement of what my nature
Sickens to conjecture may soon arrive,
I send thee, at thy brother's desire, those
Who will speak and do more than I dare
Write . . . Thy devoted servant,
ORSINO.'

(Enter LUCRETIA, BEATRICE *and* BERNARDO.*)*

Knowest thou this writing, Lady?

BEATRICE: No.

SAVELLA: Nor thou?

LUCRETIA: *(Her conduct throughout the scene is marked by extreme agitation.)*
Where was it found? What is it? It should be
Orsino's hand! It speaks of that strange horror
Which never yet found utterance, but which made
Between that hapless child and her dead father
A gulph of obscure hatred.

SAVELLA: Is it so?
Is it true, Lady, that thy father did
Such outrages as to awaken in thee
Unfilial hate?

BEATRICE: Not hate, 'twas more than hate:
This is most true, yet wherefore question me?

SAVELLA: There is a deed demanding question done;
Thou hast a secret which will answer not.

BEATRICE: What sayest? My Lord, your words are bold and rash.
SAVELLA: I do arrest all present in the name
Of the Pope's Holiness. You must to Rome.
LUCRETIA: O, not to Rome! Indeed we are not guilty.
BEATRICE: Guilty! Who dares talk of guilt? My Lord,
I am more innocent of parricide
Than is a child born fatherless . . . Dear Mother,
Your gentleness and patience are no shield
For this keen judging world, this two edged lie,
Which seems, but is not. What! will human laws,
Rather will ye who are their ministers,
Bar all access to retribution first,
And then, when heaven doth interpose to do
What ye neglect, arming familiar things
To the redress of an unwonted[30] crime,
Make ye the victims who demanded it
Culprits? 'Tis ye are culprits! That poor wretch
Who stands so pale, and trembling, and amazed,
If it be true he murdered Cenci, was
A sword in the right hand of justest God,
Wherefore should I have wielded it? Unless
The crimes which mortal tongue dare never name
God therefore scruples to avenge.
SAVELLA: You own
That you desired his death?
BEATRICE: It would have been
A crime no less than his, if for one moment
That fierce desire had faded in my heart.
'Tis true I did believe, and hope, and pray,
Aye, I even knew . . . for God is wise and just,
That some strange sudden death hung over him.
'Tis true that this did happen, and most true
There was no other rest for me on earth,
No other hope in Heaven . . . now what of this?
SAVELLA: Strange thoughts beget strange deeds; and here are both:
I judge thee not.
BEATRICE: And yet, if you arrest me,
You are the judge and executioner
Of that which is the life of life: the breath
Of accusation kills an innocent name,
And leaves for lame acquittal the poor life
Which is a mask without it. 'Tis most false
That I am guilty of foul parricide;
Although I must rejoice, for justest cause,
That other hands have sent my father's soul
To ask the mercy he denied to me.
Now leave us free: stain not a noble house
With vague surmises of rejected crime;
Add to our sufferings and your own neglect
No heavier sum: let them have been enough:
Leave us the wreck we have.
SAVELLA: I dare not, Lady.
I pray that you prepare yourselves for Rome:
There the Pope's further pleasure will be known.
LUCRETIA: O, not to Rome! O, take us not to Rome!
BEATRICE: Why not to Rome, dear mother? There as here
Our innocence is as an armed heel
To trample accusation. God is there
As here, and with his shadow ever clothes
The innocent, the injured and the weak;
And such are we. Cheer up, dear Lady, lean
On me; collect your wandering thoughts. My Lord,
As soon as you have taken some refreshment,
And had all such examinations made
Upon the spot, as may be necessary
To the full understanding of this matter,
We shall be ready. Mother; will you come?
LUCRETIA: Ha! they will bind us to the rack, and wrest
Self-accusation from our agony!
Will Giacomo be there? Orsino? Marzio?
All present; all confronted; all demanding
Each from the others countenance the thing
Which is in every heart! O, misery!

(She faints, and is borne out.)

SAVELLA: She faints: an ill appearance this.
BEATRICE: My Lord,
She knows not yet the uses of the world.
She fears that power is as a beast which grasps
And loosens not: a snake whose look transmutes
All things to guilt which is its nutriment.
She cannot know how well the supine slaves
Of blind authority read the truth of things
When written on a brow of guilelessness:
She sees not yet triumphant Innocence
Stand at the judgement-seat of mortal man,
A judge and an accuser of the wrong
Which drags it there. Prepare yourself, My Lord;
Our suite[31] will join yours in the court below.

(Exeunt.)

[30] **unwonted:** unusual.

[31] **suite:** staff of attendants.

ACT V

— SCENE I —

(An apartment in ORSINO*'s Palace.)*
(Enter ORSINO *and* GIACOMO.*)*

GIACOMO: Do evil deeds thus quickly come to end?
O, that the vain remorse which must chastise
Crimes done, had but as loud a voice to warn
As its keen sting is mortal to avenge!
O, that the hour when present had cast off
The mantle of its mystery, and shewn
The ghastly form with which it now returns
When its scared game is roused, cheering the hounds
Of conscience to their prey! Alas! Alas!
It was a wicked thought, a piteous deed,
To kill an old and hoary-headed father.

ORSINO: It has turned out unluckily, in truth.

GIACOMO: To violate the sacred doors of sleep;
To cheat kind nature of the placid death
Which she prepares for overwearied age;
To drag from Heaven an unrepentant soul
Which might have quenched in reconciling prayers
A life of burning crimes . . .

ORSINO: You cannot say
I urged you to the deed.

GIACOMO: O, had I never
Found in thy smooth and ready countenance
The mirror of my darkest thoughts; hadst thou
Never with hints and questions made me look
Upon the monster of my thought, until
It grew familiar to desire . . .

ORSINO: 'Tis thus
Men cast the blame of their unprosperous acts
Upon the abettors of their own resolve;
Or any thing but their weak, guilty selves.
And yet, confess the truth, it is the peril
In which you stand that gives you this pale sickness
Of penitence; Confess 'tis fear disguised
From its own shame that takes the mantle now
Of thin remorse. What if we yet were safe?

GIACOMO: How can that be? Already Beatrice,
Lucretia and the murderer are in prison.
I doubt not officers are, whilst we speak,
Sent to arrest us.

ORSINO: I have all prepared
For instant flight. We can escape even now,
So we take fleet occasion by the hair.

GIACOMO: Rather expire in tortures, as I may.
What! will you cast by self-accusing flight
Assured conviction upon Beatrice?
She, who alone in this unnatural work,
Stands like God's angel ministered upon
By fiends; avenging such a nameless wrong
As turns black parricide to piety;
Whilst we for basest ends . . . I fear, Orsino,
While I consider all your words and looks,
Comparing them with your proposal now,
That you must be a villain. For what end
Could you engage in such a perilous crime,
Training me on with hints, and signs, and smiles,
Even to this gulph? Thou art no liar? No,
Thou art a lie! Traitor and murderer!
Coward and slave! But, no, defend thyself;

(drawing)

Let the sword speak what the indignant tongue
Disdains to brand thee with.

ORSINO: Put up your weapon.
Is it the desperation of your fear
Makes you thus rash and sudden with a friend,
Now ruined for your sake? If honest anger
Have moved you, know, that what I just proposed
Was but to try you. As for me, I think,
Thankless affection led me to this point,
From which, if my firm temper could repent,
I cannot now recede. Even whilst we speak
The ministers of justice wait below:
They grant me these brief moments. Now if you
Have any word of melancholy comfort
To speak to your pale wife, 'twere best to pass
Out at the postern,[32] and avoid them so.

GIACOMO: O, generous friend! How canst thou pardon me?
Would that my life could purchase thine!

ORSINO: That wish
Now comes a day too late. Haste; fare thee well!
Hear'st thou not steps along the corridor?

(Exit GIACOMO.*)*

I'm sorry for it; but the guards are waiting
At his own gate, and such was my contrivance
That I might rid me both of him and them.
I thought to act a solemn comedy
Upon the painted scene of this new world,
And to attain my own peculiar ends

---

[32] **postern:** rear gate of a castle.

By some such plot of mingled good and ill
As others weave; but there arose a Power
Which graspt and snapped the threads of my device
And turned it to a net of ruin . . . Ha!

(A shout is heard.)

Is that my name I hear proclaimed abroad?
But I will pass, wrapt in a vile disguise;
Rags on my back, and a false innocence
Upon my face, thro' the misdeeming crowd
Which judges by what seems. 'Tis easy then
For a new name and for a country new,
And a new life, fashioned on old desires,
To change the honours of abandoned Rome.
And these must be the masks of that within,
Which must remain unaltered . . . Oh, I fear
That what is past will never let me rest!
Why, when none else is conscious, but myself,
Of my misdeeds, should my own heart's contempt
Trouble me? Have I not the power to fly
My own reproaches? Shall I be the slave
Of . . . what? A word? which those of this false
  world
Employ against each other, not themselves;
As men wear daggers not for self offence.
But if I am mistaken, where shall I
Find the disguise to hide me from myself,
As now I skulk from every other eye?

(Exit.)

—SCENE II—

(A Hall of Justice.)
(CAMILLO, *Judges etc. are discovered seated;* MARZIO *is led in.)*

1. JUDGE: Accused, do you persist in your denial?
I ask you, are you innocent, or guilty?
I demand who were the participators
In your offence? Speak truth and the whole truth.
MARZIO: My God! I did not kill him; I know nothing;
Olimpio sold the robe to me from which
You would infer my guilt.
2. JUDGE: Away with him!
1. JUDGE: Dare you, with lips yet white from the
  rack's[33] kiss
Speak false? Is it so soft a questioner,
That you would bandy lover's talk with it
Till it wind out your life and soul? Away!
MARZIO: Spare me! O, spare! I will confess.
1. JUDGE: Then speak.
MARZIO: I strangled him in his sleep.
1. JUDGE: Who urged you to it?
MARZIO: His own son Giacomo, and the young
  prelate
Orsino sent me to Petrella; there
The ladies Beatrice and Lucretia
Tempted me with a thousand crowns, and I
And my companion forthwith murdered him.
Now let me die.
2. JUDGE: This sounds as bad as truth. Guards, there,
Lead forth the prisoners!

(Enter LUCRETIA, BEATRICE *and* GIACOMO, *guarded.)*

Look upon this man;
When did you see him last?
BEATRICE: We never saw him.
MARZIO: You know me too well, Lady Beatrice.
BEATRICE: I know thee! How? where? when?
MARZIO: You know 'twas I
Whom you did urge with menaces and bribes
To kill your father. When the thing was done
You clothed me in a robe of woven gold
And bade me thrive: how I have thriven, you see.
You, my Lord Giacomo, Lady Lucretia,
You know that what I speak is true.

*(*BEATRICE *advances towards him; he covers his face, and shrinks back.)*

O, dart
The terrible resentment of those eyes
On the dead earth! Turn them away from me!
They wound: 'twas torture forced the truth. My
  Lords,
Having said this let me be led to death.
BEATRICE: Poor wretch, I pity thee: yet stay awhile.
CAMILLO: Guards, lead him not away.
BEATRICE: Cardinal Camillo,
You have a good repute for gentleness
And wisdom: can it be that you sit here
To countenance a wicked farce like this?
When some obscure, and trembling slave is dragged
From sufferings which might shake the sternest
  heart
And bade to answer, not as he believes,
But as those may suspect or do desire
Whose questions thence suggest their own reply:
And that in peril of such hideous torments

[33] rack: instrument of torture.

As merciful God spares even the damned. Speak now
The thing you surely know, which is that you,
If your fine frame were stretched upon that wheel,
And you were told: Confess that you did poison
Your little nephew; that fair blue-eyed child
Who was the loadstar of your life: and though
All see, since his most swift and piteous death,
That day and night, and heaven and earth, and time,
And all the things hoped for or done therein
Are changed to you, through your exceeding grief,
Yet you would say I confess any thing.
And beg from your tormentors, like that slave,
The refuge of dishonourable death.
I pray thee, Cardinal, that thou assert
My innocence.

CAMILLO: *(Much moved)* What shall we think, my lords?
Shame on these tears! I thought the heart was frozen
Which is their fountain. I would pledge my soul
That she is guiltless.

JUDGE: Yet she must be tortured.

CAMILLO: I would as soon have tortured mine own nephew:
(If he now lived he would be just her age;
His hair, too, was her colour, and his eyes
Like her's in shape, but blue and not so deep)
As that most perfect image of God's love
That ever came sorrowing upon the earth.
She is as pure as speechless infancy!

JUDGE: Well, be her purity on your head, my Lord,
If you forbid the rack. His Holiness
Enjoined us to pursue this monstrous crime
By the severest forms of law; nay even
To stretch a point against the criminals.
The prisoners stand accused of parricide
Upon such evidence as justifies
Torture.

BEATRICE: What evidence? This man's?

JUDGE: Even so.

BEATRICE: *(to MARZIO)* Come near. And who art thou thus chosen forth
Out of the multitude of living men
To kill the innocent?

MARZIO: I am Marzio,
Thy father's vassal.

BEATRICE: Fix thine eyes on mine;
Answer to what I ask.

(turning to the Judges)

I prithee mark
His countenance: unlike bold calumny
Which sometimes dares not speak the thing it looks,
He dares not look the thing he speaks, but bends
His gaze on the blind earth.

(to MARZIO)

What! wilt thou say
That I did murder my own father?

MARZIO: Oh!
Spare me! My brain swims round . . . I cannot speak . . .
It was that horrid torture forced the truth.
Take me away! Let her not look on me!
I am a guilty miserable wretch;
I have said all I know; now, let me die!

BEATRICE: My Lords, if by my nature I had been
So stern, as to have planned the crime alledged,
Which your suspicions dictate to this slave,
And the rack makes him utter, do you think
I should have left this two edged instrument
Of my misdeed; this man, this bloody knife
With my own name engraven on the heft,
Lying unsheathed amid' a world of foes,
For my own death? That with such horrible need
For deepest silence, I should have neglected
So trivial a precaution, as the making
His tomb the keeper of a secret written
On a thief's memory? What is his poor life?
What are a thousand lives? A parricide
Had trampled them like dust; and, see, he lives!

(turning to MARZIO)

And thou . . .

MARZIO: Oh, spare me! Speak to me no more!
That stern yet piteous look, those solemn tones,
Wound worse than torture.

(to the Judges)

I have told it all;
For pity's sake lead me away to death.

CAMILLO: Guards, lead him nearer the lady Beatrice,
He shrinks from her regard like autumn's leaf
From the keen breath of the serenest north.

BEATRICE: Oh, thou who tremblest on the giddy verge
Of life and death, pause ere thou answerest me;
So mayest thou answer God with less dismay:

What evil have we done thee? I, alas!
Have lived but on this earth a few sad years
And so my lot was ordered, that a father
First turned the moments of awakening life
To drops, each poisoning youth's sweet hope; and
then
Stabbed with one blow my everlasting soul;
And my untainted fame; and even that peace
Which sleeps within the core of the heart's heart;
But the wound was not mortal; so my hate
Became the only worship I could lift
To our great father, who in pity and love,
Armed thee, as thou dost say, to cut him off;
And thus his wrong becomes my accusation;
And art thou the accuser? If thou hopest
Mercy in heaven, shew justice upon earth:
Worse than a bloody hand is a hard heart.
If thou hast done murders, made thy life's path
Over the trampled laws of God and man,
Rush not before thy Judge, and say: 'My maker,
I have done this and more; for there was one
Who was most pure and innocent on earth;
And because she endured what never any
Guilty or innocent endured before:
Because her wrongs could not be told, not thought;
Because thy hand at length did rescue her;
I with my words killed her and all her kin.
Think, I adjure you, what it is to slay
The reverence living in the minds of men
Towards our ancient house, and stainless fame!
Think what it is to strangle infant pity,
Cradled in the belief of guileless looks,
Till it become a crime to suffer. Think
What 'tis to blot with infamy and blood
All that which shews like innocence, and is,
Hear me, great God! I swear, most innocent,
So that the world lose all discrimination
Between the sly, fierce, wild regard of guilt,
And that which now compels thee to reply
To what I ask: Am I, or am I not
A parricide?

MARZIO: Thou art not!

JUDGE: What is this?

MARZIO: I here declare those whom I did accuse
Are innocent. 'Tis I alone am guilty.

JUDGE: Drag him away to torments; let them be
Subtle and long drawn out, to tear the folds
Of the heart's inmost cell. Unbind him not
Till he confess.

MARZIO: Torture me as ye will:
A keener pain has wrung a higher truth
From my last breath. She is most innocent!
Bloodhounds, not men, glut yourselves well with me;
I will not give you that fine piece of nature
To rend and ruin.

(Exit MARZIO, *guarded.)*

CAMILLO: What say ye now, my Lords?

JUDGE: Let tortures strain the truth till it be white
As snow thrice sifted by the frozen wind.

CAMILLO: Yet stained with blood.

JUDGE: *(to* BEATRICE*)* Know you this paper, Lady?

BEATRICE: Entrap me not with questions. Who stands
here
As my accuser? Ha! wilt thou be he,
Who art my judge? Accuser, witness, judge,
What, all in one? Here is Orsino's name;
Where is Orsino? Let his eye meet mine.
What means this scrawl? Alas! Ye know not what,
And therefore on the chance that it may be
Some evil, will ye kill us?

(Enter an officer.)

OFFICER: Marzio's dead.

JUDGE: What did he say?

OFFICER: Nothing. As soon as we
Had bound him on the wheel, he smiled on us,
As one who baffles a deep adversary;
And holding his breath, died.

JUDGE: There remains nothing
But to apply the question to those prisoners,
Who yet remain stubborn.

CAMILLO: I overrule
Further proceedings, and in the behalf
Of these most innocent and noble persons
Will use my interest with the Holy Father.

JUDGE: Let the Pope's pleasure then be done.
Meanwhile
Conduct these culprits each to separate cells;
And be the engines[34] ready: for this night
If the Pope's resolution be as grave,
Pious and just as once, I'll wring the truth
Out of those nerves and sinews, groan by groan.

(Exeunt.)

[34] **engines:** the rack and other instruments of torture.

— SCENE III —

(The cell of a prison.)

*(*BEATRICE *is discovered asleep on a couch; enter* BERNARDO.*)*

BERNARDO: How gently slumber rests upon her face,
Like the last thoughts of some day sweetly spent
Closing in night and dreams, and so prolonged.
After such torments as she bore last night,
How light and soft her breathing comes. Ay, me!
Methinks that I shall never sleep again.
But I must shake the heavenly dew of rest
From this sweet folded flower, thus . . . wake! awake!
What, sister, canst thou sleep?

BEATRICE: *(awaking)* I was just dreaming
That we were all in Paradise. Thou knowest
This cell seems like a kind of Paradise
After our father's presence.

BERNARDO: Dear, dear sister,
Would that thy dream were not a dream! O, God!
How shall I tell?

BEATRICE: What wouldst thou tell, sweet brother?

BERNARDO: Look not so calm and happy, or even whilst
I stand considering what I have to say
My heart will break.

BEATRICE: See now, thou mak'st me weep:
How very friendless thou would'st be, dear child,
If I were dead. Say what thou hast to say.

BERNARDO: They have confessed; they could endure no more
The tortures . . .

BEATRICE: Ha! What was there to confess?
They must have told some weak and wicked lie
To flatter their tormentors. Have they said
That they were guilty? O, white innocence,
That thou shouldst wear the mask of guilt to hide
Thine awful and serenest countenance
From those who know thee not!

(Enter JUDGE *with* LUCRETIA *and* GIACOMO, *guarded.)*

Ignoble[35] hearts!
For some brief spasms of pain, which are at least
As mortal as the limbs through which they pass,
Are centuries of high splendour laid in dust?
And that eternal honour which should live
Sunlike, above the reek of mortal fame,
Changed to a mockery and a bye-word? What!
Will you give up these bodies to be dragged
At horse's heels, so that our hair should sweep
The footsteps of the vain and senseless crowd,
Who, that they may make our calamity
Their worship and their spectacle, will leave
The churches and the theatres as void
As their own hearts? Shall the light multitude
Fling, at their choice, curses or faded pity,
Sad funeral flowers to deck a living corpse,
Upon us as we pass to pass away,
And leave . . . what memory of our having been?
Infamy, blood, terror, despair? O thou,
Who wert a mother to the parentless
Kill not thy child! Let not her wrongs kill thee!
Brother, lie down with me upon the rack,
And let us each be silent as a corpse;
It soon will be as soft as any grave.
'Tis but the falsehood it can wring from fear
Makes the rack cruel.

GIACOMO: They will tear the truth
Even from thee at last, those cruel pains:
For pity's sake say thou art guilty now.

LUCRETIA: O, speak the truth! Let us all quickly die;
And after death, God is our judge, not they;
He will have mercy on us.

BERNARDO: If indeed
It can be true, say so, dear sister mine;
And then the Pope will surely pardon you,
And all be well.

JUDGE: Confess, or I will warp
Your limbs with such keen tortures . . .

BEATRICE: Tortures! Turn
The rack henceforth into a spinning wheel!
Torture your dog, that he may tell when last
He lapped the blood his master shed . . . not me!
My pangs are of the mind, and of the heart,
And of the soul; aye, of the inmost soul,
Which weeps within tears as of burning gall
To see, in this ill world where none are true,
My kindred false to their deserted selves.
And with considering all the wretched life
Which I have lived, and its now wretched end,
And the small justice shewn by Heaven and Earth
To me or mine; and what a tyrant thou art,
And what slaves these; and what a world we make,
The oppressor and the oppressed . . . such pangs compel

[35] **Ignoble:** dishonorable.

My answer. What is it thou wouldst with me?
JUDGE: Art thou not guilty of thy father's death?
BEATRICE: Or wilt thou rather tax high judging God
That he permitted such an act as that
Which I have suffered, and which he beheld;
Made it unutterable, and took from it
All refuge, all revenge, all consequence,
But that which thou hast called my father's death?
Which is or is not what men call a crime,
Which either I have done, or have not done;
Say what ye will. I shall deny no more.
If ye desire it thus, thus let it be,
And so an end of all. Now do your will;
No other pains shall force another word.
JUDGE: She is convicted, but has not confessed.
Be it enough. Until their final sentence
Let none have converse with them. You, young Lord,
Linger not here!
BEATRICE: O, tear him not away!
JUDGE: Guards do your duty.
BERNARDO: (*embracing* BEATRICE) Oh! would ye divide
Body from soul?
OFFICER: That is the headsman's business.

(*Exeunt all but* LUCRETIA, BEATRICE *and* GIACOMO.)

GIACOMO: Have I confessed? Is it all over now?
No hope! No refuge! O, weak, wicked tongue
Which hast destroyed me would that thou hadst been
Cut out and thrown to dogs first? To have killed
My father first, and then betrayed my sister;
Aye, thee! the one thing innocent and pure
In this black guilty world, to that which I
So well deserve! My wife! my little ones!
Destitute, helpless and I . . . . Father! God!
Canst thou forgive even the unforgiving,
When their full hearts break thus, thus!

(*Covers his face and weeps.*)

LUCRETIA: O, my child!
To what a dreadful end are we all come!
Why did I yield? Why did I not sustain
Those torments? Oh, that I were all dissolved
Into these fast and unavailing tears,
Which flow and feel not!
BEATRICE: What 'twas weak to do,
'Tis weaker to lament, once being done;
Take cheer! The God who knew my wrong, and made
Our speedy act the angel of his wrath,
Seems, and but seems to have abandoned us.
Let us not think that we shall die for this.
Brother, sit near me; give me your firm hand,
You had a manly heart. Bear up! Bear up!
O, dearest Lady, put your gentle head
Upon my lap, and try to sleep awhile:
Your eyes look pale, hollow and overworn,
With heaviness of watching and slow grief.
Come, I will sing you some low, sleepy tune,
Not cheerful, nor yet sad; some dull old thing,
Some outworn and unused monotony,
Such as our country gossips sing and spin,
Till they almost forget they live: lie down!
So, that will do. Have I forgot the words?
Faith! They are sadder than I thought they were.

— SONG —

False friend, wilt thou smile or weep
When my life is laid asleep?
Little cares for a smile or a tear,
The clay-cold corpse upon the bier!
Farewell! Heighho!
What is this whispers low?
There is a snake in thy smile, my dear;
And bitter poison within thy tear.

Sweet sleep, were death like to thee,
Or if thou couldst mortal be,
I would close these eyes of pain;
When to wake? Never again.
O, World! Farewell!
Listen to the passing bell!
It says, thou and I must part,
With a light and a heavy heart.

(*The scene closes.*)

— SCENE IV —

(*A Hall of the Prison.*)
(*Enter* CAMILLO *and* BERNARDO.)

CAMILLO: The Pope is stern; not to be moved or bent.
He looked as calm and keen as is the engine
Which tortures and which kills, exempt itself
From aught that it inflicts; a marble form,

A rite, a law, a custom: not a man.
He frowned, as if to frown had been the trick
Of his machinery, on the advocates
Presenting the defences, which he tore
And threw behind, muttering with hoarse, harsh
voice:
'Which among ye defended their old father
Killed in his sleep?' Then to another: 'Thou
Dost this in virtue of thy place; 'tis well.'
He turned to me then, looking deprecation,
And said these three words, coldly: 'They must die.'

BERNARDO: And yet you left him not?

CAMILLO: I urged him still;
Pleading, as I could guess, the devilish wrong
Which prompted your unnatural parent's death.
And he replied. 'Paolo Santa Croce
Murdered his mother yester evening,
And he is fled. Parricide grows so rife
That soon, for some just cause no doubt, the young
Will strangle us all, dozing in our chairs.
Authority, and power, and hoary hair
Are grown crimes capital. You are my nephew,
You come to ask their pardon; stay a moment;
Here is their sentence; never see me more
Till, to the letter, it be all fulfilled.'

BERNARDO: O, God, not so! I did believe indeed
That all you said was but sad preparation
For happy news. O, there are words and looks
To bend the sternest purpose! Once I knew them,
Now I forget them at my dearest need.
What think you if I seek him out, and bathe
His feet and robe with hot and bitter tears?
Importune him with prayers, vexing his brain
With my perpetual cries, until in rage
He strike me with his pastoral cross, and trample
Upon my prostrate head, so that my blood
May stain the senseless dust on which he treads,
And remorse waken mercy? I will do it!
O, wait till I return!

(Rushes out.)

CAMILLO: Alas! poor boy!
A wreck-devoted seaman thus might pray
To the deaf sea.

(Enter LUCRETIA, BEATRICE *and* GIACOMO, *guarded.)*

BEATRICE: I hardly dare to fear
That thou bring'st other news than a just pardon.

CAMILLO: May God in heaven be less inexorable
To the Pope's prayers, than he has been to mine.
Here is the sentence and the warrant.

BEATRICE: *(wildly)* Oh,
My God! Can it be possible I have
To die so suddenly? So young to go
Under the obscure, cold, rotting, wormy ground!
To be nailed down into a narrow place;
To see no more sweet sunshine; hear no more
Blithe voice of living thing; muse not again
Upon familiar thoughts, sad, yet thus lost
How fearful! to be nothing! Or to be . . .
What? O, where am I? Let me not go mad!
Sweet Heaven, forgive weak thoughts! If there
should be
No God, no Heaven, no Earth in the void world;
The wide, grey, lampless, deep, unpeopled world!
If all things then should be . . . my father's spirit
His eye, his voice, his touch surrounding me;
The atmosphere and breath of my dead life!
If sometimes, as a shape more like himself,
Even the form which tortured me on earth,
Masked in grey hairs and wrinkles, he should come
And wind me in his hellish arms, and fix
His eyes on mine, and drag me down, down, down!
For was he not alone omnipotent
On Earth, and ever present? Even tho' dead,
Does not his spirit live in all that breathe,
And work for me and mine still the same ruin,
Scorn, pain, despair? Who ever yet returned
To teach the laws of death's untrodden realm?
Unjust perhaps as those which drive us now,
O, whither, whither?

LUCRETIA: Trust in God's sweet love,
The tender promises of Christ: ere night
Think we shall be in Paradise.[36]

BEATRICE: 'Tis past!
Whatever comes my heart shall sink no more.
And yet, I know not why, your words strike chill:
How tedious, false and cold seem all things. I
Have met with much injustice in this world;
No difference has been made by God or man,
Or any power moulding my wretched lot,

[36] **we shall be in Paradise:** Luke 24:43. "And Jesus said unto him, Verily I say unto thee, Today shalt thou be with me in paradise."

'Twixt good or evil, as regarded me.
I am cut off from the only world I know,
From light, and life, and love, in youth's sweet
prime.
You do well telling me to trust in God,
I hope I do trust in him. In whom else
Can any trust? And yet my heart is cold.

(During the latter speeches GIACOMO *has retired conversing with* CAMILLO, *who now goes out;* GIACOMO *advances.)*

GIACOMO: Know you not, Mother . . . Sister, know
you not?
Bernardo even now is gone to implore
The Pope to grant our pardon.
LUCRETIA: Child, perhaps
It will be granted. We may all then live
To make these woes a tale for distant years:
O, what a thought! It gushes to my heart
Like the warm blood.
BEATRICE: Yet both will soon be cold.
O, trample out that thought! Worse than despair,
Worse than the bitterness of death, is hope:
It is the only ill which can find place
Upon the giddy, sharp and narrow hour
Tottering beneath us. Plead with the swift frost
That it should spare the eldest flower of spring:
Plead with awakening Earthquake, o'er whose
couch
Even now a city stands, strong, fair and free;
Now stench and blackness yawns, like death. O,
plead
With famine, or wind-walking Pestilence,
Blind lightning, or the deaf sea, not with man!
Cruel, cold, formal man; righteous in words,
In deeds a Cain. No, Mother, we must die:
Since such is the reward of innocent lives;
Such the alleviation of worst wrongs.
And whilst our murderers live, and hard, cold men,
Smiling and slow, walk thro' a world of tears
To death as to life's sleep; 'twere just the grave
Were some strange joy for us. Come, obscure
Death,
And wind me in thine all-embracing arms!
Like a fond mother hide me in thy bosom,
And rock me to the sleep from which none wake.
Live ye, who live, subject to one another
As we were once, who now . . .

*(*BERNARDO *rushes in.)*

BERNARDO: Oh, horrible!
That tears, that looks, that hope poured forth in
prayer,
Even till the heart is vacant and despairs,
Should all be vain! The ministers of death
Are waiting round the doors. I thought I saw
Blood on the face of one . . . what if 'twere fancy?
Soon the heart's blood of all I love on earth
Will sprinkle him, and he will wipe it off
As if 'twere only rain. O, life! O, world!
Cover me! let me be no more! To see
That perfect mirror of pure innocence
Wherein I gazed, and grew happy and good,
Shivered to dust! To see thee, Beatrice,
Who made all lovely thou didst look upon . . .
Thee, light of life . . . dead, dark! while I say, sister,
To hear I have no sister; and thou, Mother,
Whose love was a bond to all our loves . . .
Dead! The sweet bond broken!

(Enter CAMILLO *and Guards.)*

They come! Let me
Kiss those warm lips before their crimson leaves
Are blighted . . . white . . . cold. Say farewell,
before
Death chokes that gentle voice! O, let me hear
You speak!
BEATRICE: Farewell, my tender brother. Think
Of our sad fate with gentleness, as now:
And let mild, pitying thoughts lighten for thee
Thy sorrow's load. Err not in harsh despair,
But tears and patience. One thing more, my child,
For thine own sake be constant to the love
Thou bearest us; and to the faith that I,
Tho' wrapt in a strange cloud of crime and shame,
Lived ever holy and unstained. And tho'
Ill tongues shall wound me, and our common name
Be as a mark stamped on thine innocent brow
For men to point at as they pass, do thou
Forbear, and never think a thought unkind
Of those, who perhaps love thee in their graves.
So mayest thou die as I do; fear and pain
Being subdued. Farewell! Farewell! Farewell!
BERNARDO: I cannot say, farewell!
CAMILLO: O, Lady Beatrice!
BEATRICE: Give yourself no unnecessry pain,
My dear Lord Cardinal. Here, Mother, tie
My girdle for me, and bind up this hair
In any simple knot; aye, that does well.

And yours I see is coming down. How often
Have we done this for one another; now
We shall not do it any more. My Lord,
We are quite ready. Well, 'tis very well.

from PROMETHEUS UNBOUND, A LYRICAL DRAMA IN FOUR ACTS WITH OTHER POEMS
(1820)

Ode to the West Wind
(1820; comp. 1819)

I

O wild West Wind, thou breath of Autumn's being,
Thou, from whose unseen presence the leaves dead
Are driven, like ghosts from an enchanter fleeing,

Yellow, and black, and pale, and hectic[1] red,
Pestilence-stricken multitudes: O Thou,
Who chariotest to their dark wintry bed

The winged seeds, where they lie cold and low,
Each like a corpse within its grave, until
Thine azure sister of the Spring shall blow

Her clarion o'er the dreaming earth, and fill
(Driving sweet buds like flocks to feed in air)
With living hues and odours plain and hill:

Wild Spirit, which art moving everywhere;
Destroyer and Preserver; hear, O hear!

II

Thou on whose stream, 'mid the steep sky's
commotion,
Loose clouds like Earth's decaying leaves are shed,
Shook from the tangled boughs of Heaven and
Ocean,

Angels of rain and lightning: there are spread
On the blue surface of thine aery surge,
Like the bright hair uplifted from the head

Of some fierce Maenad,[2] even from the dim verge
Of the horizon to the zenith's height,
The locks of the approaching storm. Thou Dirge[3]

Of the dying year, to which this closing night
Will be the dome of a vast sepulchre,
Vaulted with all thy congregated might

Of vapours, from whose solid atmosphere
Black rain and fire and hail will burst: O hear!

III

Thou who didst waken from his summer dreams
The blue Mediterranean, where he lay,
Lulled by the coil of his chrystalline streams,

Beside a pumice isle in Baiae's bay,[4]
And saw in sleep old palaces and towers
Quivering within the wave's intenser day,

All overgrown with azure moss and flowers
So sweet, the sense faints picturing them! Thou
For whose path the Atlantic's level powers

Cleave themselves into chasms, while far below
The sea-blooms and the oozy woods which wear
The sapless foliage of the ocean, know

Thy voice, and suddenly grow grey with fear,
And tremble and despoil[5] themselves: O hear!

IV

If I were a dead leaf thou mightest bear;
If I were a swift cloud to fly with thee;
A wave to pant beneath thy power, and share

The impulse of thy strength, only less free
Than thou, O Uncontrollable! If even
I were as in my boyhood, and could be

The comrade of thy wanderings over Heaven,
As then, when to outstrip thy skiey speed
Scarce seemed a vision; I would ne'er have striven

As thus with thee in prayer in my sore need.
Oh! lift me as a wave, a leaf, a cloud!
I fall upon the thorns of life! I bleed!

[1] **hectic:** consumptive, feverish.

[2] **Maenad:** priestesses of Dionysus, god of fertility and wine, who work themselves into drunken frenzy during festivals.

[3] **Dirge:** funeral hymn.

[4] **pumice . . . bay:** porous volcanic rock. The isle in the Bay of Baiae was an ancient summer resort near Naples.

[5] **despoil:** to strip of value or worth.

A heavy weight of hours has chained and bowed
One too like thee: tameless, and swift, and proud.

V

Make me thy lyre, even as the forest is:
What if my leaves are falling like its own!
The tumult of thy mighty harmonies

Will take from both a deep, autumnal tone,
Sweet though in sadness. Be thou, Spirit fierce,
My spirit! Be thou me, impetuous one!

Drive my dead thoughts over the universe
Like withered leaves to quicken a new birth!
And, by the incantation of this verse,

Scatter, as from an unextinguished hearth
Ashes and sparks, my words among mankind!
Be through my lips to unawakened Earth

The trumpet of a prophecy! O Wind,
If Winter comes, can Spring be far behind?

Prometheus Unbound

A Lyrical Drama in Four Acts
(1820; comp. 1818–1819)

Audisne haec amphiarae, sub terram abdite?[1]

— PREFACE —

The Greek tragic writers, in selecting as their subject any portion of their national history or mythology, employed in their treatment of it a certain arbitrary discretion. They by no means conceived themselves bound to adhere to the common interpretation or to imitate in story as in title their rivals and predecessors. Such a system would have amounted to a resignation of those claims to preference over their competitors which incited the composition. The Agamemnonian story was exhibited on the Athenian theatre with as many variations as dramas.

I have presumed to employ a similar licence. The *Prometheus Unbound* of Aeschylus supposed the reconciliation of Jupiter with his victim as the price of the disclosure of the danger threatened to his empire by the consummation of his marriage with Thetis. Thetis, according to this view of the subject, was given in marriage to Peleus, and Prometheus, by the permission of Jupiter, delivered from his captivity by Hercules. Had I framed my story on this model, I should have done no more than have attempted to restore the lost drama of Aeschylus; an ambition which, if my preference to this mode of treating the subject had incited me to cherish, the recollection of the high comparison such an attempt would challenge might well abate. But, in truth, I was averse from a catastrophe so feeble as that of reconciling the Champion with the Oppressor of mankind. The moral interest of the fable, which is so powerfully sustained by the sufferings and endurance of Prometheus, would be annihilated if we could conceive of him as unsaying his high language and quailing before his successful and perfidious adversary. The only imaginary being resembling in any degree Prometheus, is Satan; and Prometheus is, in my judgement, a more poetical character than Satan, because, in addition to courage, and majesty, and firm and patient opposition to omnipotent force, he is susceptible of being described as exempt from the taints of ambition, envy, revenge, and a desire for personal aggrandisement, which, in the Hero of *Paradise Lost*, interfere with the interest. The character of Satan engenders in the mind a pernicious casuistry which leads us to weigh his faults with his wrongs, and to excuse the former because the latter exceed all measure. In the minds of those who consider that magnificent fiction with a religious feeling it engenders something worse. But Prometheus is, as it were, the type of the highest perfection of moral and intellectual nature, impelled by the purest and the truest motives to the best and noblest ends.

This Poem was chiefly written upon the mountainous ruins of the Baths of Caracalla, among the flowery glades, and thickets of odoriferous blossoming trees, which are extended in ever winding labyrinths upon its immense platforms and dizzy arches suspended in the air. The bright blue sky of Rome, and the effect of the vigorous awakening spring in that divinest climate, and the new life with which it drenches the spirits even to intoxication, were the inspiration of this drama.

The imagery which I have employed will be found, in many instances, to have been drawn from the operations of the human mind, or from those external actions by which they are expressed. This is unusual in modern poetry, although Dante and Shakespeare are full of instances of the same kind: Dante indeed more than any other poet,

[1] Cf. Cicero: "Do you hear this, O Amphiaraus, concealed under the Earth?"

and with greater success. But the Greek poets, as writers to whom no resource of awakening the sympathy of their contemporaries was unknown, were in the habitual use of this power; and it is the study of their works (since a higher merit would probably be denied me) to which I am willing that my readers should impute this singularity.

One word is due in candour to the degree in which the study of contemporary writings may have tinged my composition, for such has been a topic of censure with regard to poems far more popular, and indeed more deservedly popular, than mine. It is impossible that any one who inhabits the same age with such writers as those who stand in the foremost ranks of our own, can conscientiously assure himself that his language and tone of thought may not have been modified by the study of the productions of those extraordinary intellects. It is true, that, not the spirit of their genius, but the forms in which it has manifested itself, are due less to the peculiarities of their own minds than to the peculiarity of the moral and intellectual condition of the minds among which they have been produced. Thus a number of writers possess the form, whilst they want the spirit of those whom, it is alleged, they imitate; because the former is the endowment of the age in which they live, and the latter must be the uncommunicated lightning of their own mind.

The peculiar style of intense and comprehensive imagery which distinguishes the modern literature of England, has not been, as a general power, the product of the imitation of any particular writer. The mass of capabilities remains at every period materially the same; the circumstances which awaken it to action perpetually change. If England were divided into forty republics, each equal in population and extent to Athens, there is no reason to suppose but that, under institutions not more perfect than those of Athens, each would produce philosophers and poets equal to those who (if we except Shakespeare) have never been surpassed. We owe the great writers of the golden age of our literature to that fervid awakening of the public mind which shook to dust the oldest and most oppressive form of the Christian religion. We owe Milton to the progress and development of the same spirit: the sacred Milton was, let it ever be remembered, a republican, and a bold inquirer into morals and religion. The great writers of our own age are, we have reason to suppose, the companions and forerunners of some unimagined change in our social condition or the opinions which cement it. The cloud of mind is discharging its collected lightning, and the equilibrium between institutions and opinions is now restoring, or is about to be restored.

As to imitation, poetry is a mimetic art. It creates, but it creates by combination and representation. Poetical abstractions are beautiful and new, not because the portions of which they are composed had no previous existence in the mind of man or in nature, but because the whole produced by their combination has some intelligible and beautiful analogy with those sources of emotion and thought, and with the contemporary condition of them: one great poet is a masterpiece of nature which another not only ought to study but must study. He might as wisely and as easily determine that his mind should no longer be the mirror of all that is lovely in the visible universe, as exclude from his contemplation the beautiful which exists in the writings of a great contemporary. The pretence of doing it would be a presumption in any but the greatest; the effect, even in him, would be strained, unnatural, and ineffectual. A poet is the combined product of such internal powers as modify the nature of others; and of such external influences as excite and sustain these powers; he is not one, but both. Every man's mind is, in this respect, modified by all the objects of nature and art; by every word and every suggestion which he ever admitted to act upon his consciousness; it is the mirror upon which all forms are reflected, and in which they compose one form. Poets, not otherwise than philosophers, painters, sculptors, and musicians, are, in one sense, the creators, and, in another, the creations, of their age. From this subjection the loftiest do not escape. There is a similarity between Homer and Hesiod, between Aeschylus and Euripides, between Virgil and Horace, between Dante and Petrarch, between Shakespeare and Fletcher, between Dryden and Pope;[2] each has a generic resemblance under which their specific distinctions are

---

[2] Homer (eighth century BC?), Greek epic poet and author of *The Iliad* and *The Odyssey*; Hesiod (eighth century BC), lesser Greek epic poet and author of *Theogony* and *Works and Days*; Aeschylus (525–456 BC), Athenian tragic poet and author of the *Oresteia* (*Agamemnon, Choephoroe, Eumenides*); Euripides (480–406 BC), lesser Greek tragedian and author of *Medea* and *Alcestis*; Virgil (70–19 BC), Roman epic poet and author of *Aenead*; Horace (95–8 BC), Latin poet and author of *Epistles, Satires*, and a critical treatise *Ars Poetica*; Dante (1265–1321), Florentine epic poet and author of *the Divine Comedy*; Petrarch (1304–1374), Italian poet, humanist, and especially sonneteer; Shakespeare (1564–1616), English dramatist and greatest of English writers; Fletcher (1579–1625), dramatist and contemporary of Shakespeare; Dryden (1631–1700), English dramatist and satirist; Pope (1688–1744), English poet, satirist, and translator of Homer.

arranged. If this similarity be the result of imitation, I am willing to confess that I have imitated.

Let this opportunity be conceded to me of acknowledging that I have, what a Scotch philosopher characteristically terms, 'a passion for reforming the world:' what passion incited him to write and publish his book, he omits to explain. For my part I had rather be damned with Plato and Lord Bacon, than go to Heaven with Paley and Malthus.[3] But it is a mistake to suppose that I dedicate my poetical compositions solely to the direct enforcement of reform, or that I consider them in any degree as containing a reasoned system on the theory of human life. Didactic poetry is my abhorrence; nothing can be equally well expressed in prose that is not tedious and supererogatory[4] in verse. My purpose has hitherto been simply to familiarise the highly refined imagination of the more select classes of poetical readers with beautiful idealisms of moral excellence; aware that until the mind can love, and admire, and trust, and hope, and endure, reasoned principles of moral conduct are seeds cast upon the highway of life which the unconscious passenger tramples into dust, although they would bear the harvest of his happiness. Should I live to accomplish what I purpose, that is, produce a systematical history of what appear to me to be the genuine elements of human society, let not the advocates of injustice and superstition flatter themselves that I should take Aeschylus rather than Plato as my model.

The having spoken of myself with unaffected freedom will need little apology with the candid; and let the uncandid consider that they injure me less than their own hearts and minds by misrepresentation. Whatever talents a person may possess to amuse and instruct others, be they ever so inconsiderable, he is yet bound to exert them: if his attempt be ineffectual, let the punishment of an unaccomplished purpose have been sufficient; let none trouble themselves to heap the dust of oblivion upon his efforts; the pile they raise will betray his grave which might otherwise have been unknown.

[3]Francis Bacon (1561–1626), great English political figure and man of letters, renowned especially for the style of his prose; William Paley (1743–1805), theologian and author of *Moral and Political Philosophy* (1785), *Evidences of Christianity* (1794), and *Natural Theology* (1802), which opens with the analogy of a watch found on the heath permitting the inference that "as the watch must have had a maker" so must the natural world; Thomas Malthus* (1766–1834), see *First Essay on Population* (1798) in SOCIETY AND POLITICAL ECONOMY.

[4]**supererogatory**: superfluous.

DRAMATIS PERSONAE

PROMETHEUS	HERCULES
DEMOGORGON	THE PHANTASM OF JUPITER
JUPITER	THE SPIRIT OF THE EARTH
THE EARTH	THE SPIRIT OF THE MOON
OCEAN	SPIRITS OF THE HOURS
APOLLO	SPIRITS
MERCURY	ECHOES
ASIA } *Oceanides*	FAUNS
PANTHEA } *Oceanides*	FURIES
IONE } *Oceanides*	

ACT I

(SCENE—*A Ravine of Icy Rocks in the Indian Caucasus.* PROMETHEUS *is discovered bound to the Precipice.* PANTHEA *and* IONE *are seated at his feet. Time, night. During the Scene, morning slowly breaks.*)

PROMETHEUS: Monarch of Gods and Daemons,[5] and
    all Spirits
But One, who throng those bright and rolling
    worlds
Which Thou and I alone of living things
Behold with sleepless eyes! regard this Earth
Made multitudinous with thy slaves, whom thou
Requitest for knee-worship, prayer, and praise,
And toil, and hecatombs[6] of broken hearts,
With fear and self-contempt and barren hope.
Whilst me, who am thy foe, eyeless in hate,
Hast thou made reign and triumph, to thy scorn,
O'er mine own misery and thy vain revenge.
Three thousand years of sleep-unsheltered hours,
And moments aye divided by keen pangs
Till they seemed years, torture and solitude,
Scorn and despair,—these are mine empire:—
More glorious far than that which thou surveyest
From thine unenvied throne, O Mighty God!
Almighty, had I deigned to share the shame
Of thine ill tyranny, and hung not here
Nailed to this wall of eagle-baffling mountain,
Black, wintry, dead, unmeasured; without herb,
Insect, or beast, or shape or sound of life.
Ah me! alas, pain, pain ever, for ever!

[5]**Daemons**: intermediate beings between gods and mankind.

[6]**hecatombs**: any large scale sacrifice; in ancient Greece, 100 oxen per hecatomb.

No change, no pause, no hope! Yet I endure.
I ask the Earth, have not the mountains felt?
I ask yon Heaven, the all-beholding Sun,
Has it not seen? The Sea, in storm or calm,
Heaven's ever-changing Shadow, spread below,
Have its deaf waves not heard my agony?
Ah me! alas, pain, pain ever, for ever!

The crawling glaciers pierce me with the spears
Of their moon-freezing crystals, the bright chains
Eat with their burning cold into my bones.
Heaven's wingèd hound, polluting from thy lips
His beak in poison not his own, tears up
My heart; and shapeless sights come wandering by,
The ghastly people of the realm of dream,
Mocking me: and the Earthquake-fiends are charged
To wrench the rivets from my quivering wounds
When the rocks split and close again behind:
While from their loud abysses howling throng
The genii of the storm, urging the rage
Of whirlwind, and afflict me with keen hail.
And yet to me welcome is day and night,
Whether one breaks the hoar frost of the morn,
Or starry, dim, and slow, the other climbs
The leaden-coloured east; for then they lead
The wingless, crawling hours, one among whom
—As some dark Priest hales the reluctant victim
Shall drag thee, cruel King, to kiss the blood
From these pale feet, which then might trample
 thee
If they disdained not such a prostrate slave.
Disdain! Ah no! I pity thee. What ruin
Will hunt thee undefended through wide Heaven!
How will thy soul, cloven to its depth with terror,
Gape like a hell within! I speak in grief,
Not exultation, for I hate no more,
As then ere misery made me wise. The curse
Once breathed on thee I would recall. Ye
 Mountains,
Whose many-voiced Echoes, through the mist
Of cataracts, flung the thunder of that spell!
Ye icy Springs, stagnant with wrinkling frost,
Which vibrated to hear me, and then crept
Shuddering through India! Thou serenest Air,
Through which the Sun walks burning without
 beams!
And ye swift Whirlwinds, who on poisèd wings
Hung mute and moveless o'er yon hushed abyss,
As thunder, louder than your own, made rock
The orbèd world! If then my words had power,
Though I am changed so that aught evil wish
Is dead within; although no memory be
Of what is hate, let them not lose it now!
What was that curse? for ye all heard me speak.

FIRST VOICE (*from the Mountains*):
Thrice three hundred thousand years
 O'er the Earthquake's couch we stood:
Oft, as men convulsed with fears,
 We trembled in our multitude.

SECOND VOICE (*from the Springs*):
Thunderbolts had parched our water,
 We had been stained with bitter blood,
And had run mute, 'mid shrieks of slaughter,
 Thro' a city and a solitude.

THIRD VOICE (*from the Air*):
I had clothed, since Earth uprose,
 Its wastes in colours not their own,
And oft had my serene repose
 Been cloven by many a rending groan.

FOURTH VOICE (*from the Whirlwinds*):
We had soared beneath these mountains
 Unresting ages; nor had thunder,
Nor yon volcano's flaming fountains,
 Nor any power above or under
 Ever made us mute with wonder.

FIRST VOICE:
But never bowed our snowy crest
As at the voice of thine unrest.

SECOND VOICE:
Never such a sound before
To the Indian waves we bore.
A pilot asleep on the howling sea
Leaped up from the deck in agony,
And heard, and cried, 'Ah, woe is me!'
And died as mad as the wild waves be.

THIRD VOICE:
By such dread words from Earth to Heaven
My still realm was never riven:
When its wound was closed, there stood
Darkness o'er the day like blood.

FOURTH VOICE:
And we shrank back: for dreams of ruin
To frozen caves our flight pursuing
Made us keep silence—thus—and thus—
Though silence is as hell to us.

THE EARTH: The tongueless Caverns of the craggy
 hills
Cried, 'Misery!' then; the hollow Heaven replied,

'Misery!' And the Ocean's purple waves,
Climbing the land, howled to the lashing winds,
And the pale nations heard it, 'Misery!'

PROMETHEUS: I heard a sound of voices: not the voice
Which I gave forth. Mother, thy sons and thou
Scorn him, without whose all-enduring will
Beneath the fierce omnipotence of Jove,
Both they and thou had vanished, like thin mist
Unrolled on the morning wind. Know ye not me,
The Titan? He who made his agony
The barrier to your else all-conquering foe?
Oh, rock-embosomed lawns, and snow-fed streams,
Now seen athwart frore[7] vapours, deep below,
Through whose o'ershadowing woods I wandered once
With Asia, drinking life from her loved eyes;
Why scorns the spirit which informs ye, now
To commune with me? me alone, who checked,
As one who checks a fiend-drawn charioteer,
The falsehood and the force of him who reigns
Supreme, and with the groans of pining slaves
Fills your dim glens and liquid wildernesses:
Why answer ye not, still? Brethren!

THE EARTH: They dare not.

PROMETHEUS: Who dares? for I would hear that curse again.
Ha, what an awful whisper rises up!
'Tis scarce like sound: it tingles through the frame
As lightning tingles, hovering ere it strike.
Speak, Spirit! from thine inorganic voice
I only know that thou art moving near
And love. How cursed I him?

THE EARTH: How canst thou hear
Who knowest not the language of the dead?

PROMETHEUS: Thou art a living spirit; speak as they.

THE EARTH: I dare not speak like life, lest Heaven's fell King
Should hear, and link me to some wheel of pain
More torturing than the one whereon I roll.
Subtle thou art and good, and though the Gods
Hear not this voice, yet thou art more than God,
Being wise and kind: earnestly hearken now.

PROMETHEUS: Obscurely through my brain, like shadows dim,
Sweep awful thoughts, rapid and thick. I feel
Faint, like one mingled in entwining love;
Yet 'tis not pleasure.

THE EARTH: No, thou canst not hear:
Thou art immortal, and this tongue is known
Only to those who die.

PROMETHEUS: And what art thou,
O, melancholy Voice?

THE EARTH: I am the Earth,
Thy mother; she within whose stony veins,
To the last fibre of the loftiest tree
Whose thin leaves trembled in the frozen air,
Joy ran, as blood within a living frame,
When thou didst from her bosom, like a cloud
Of glory, arise, a spirit of keen joy!
And at thy voice her pining sons uplifted
Their prostrate brows from the polluting dust,
And our almighty Tyrant with fierce dread
Grew pale, until his thunder chained thee here.
Then, see those million worlds which burn and roll
Around us: their inhabitants beheld
My spherèd light wane in wide Heaven; the sea
Was lifted by strange tempest, and new fire
From earthquake-rifted mountains of bright snow
Shook its portentous hair beneath Heaven's frown;
Lightning and Inundation vexed the plains;
Blue thistles bloomed in cities; foodless toads
Within voluptuous chambers panting crawled:
When Plague had fallen on man, and beast, and worm,
And Famine; and black blight on herb and tree;
And in the corn, and vines, and meadow-grass,
Teemed ineradicable poisonous weeds
Draining their growth, for my wan breast was dry
With grief; and the thin air, my breath was stained
With the contagion of a mother's hate
Breathed on her child's destroyer; ay, I heard
Thy curse, the which, if thou rememberest not,
Yet my innumerable seas and streams,
Mountains, and caves, and winds, and yon wide air,
And the inarticulate people of the dead,
Preserve, a treasured spell. We meditate
In secret joy and hope those dreadful words,
But dare not speak them.

PROMETHEUS: Venerable mother!
All else who live and suffer take from thee
Some comfort; flowers, and fruits, and happy sounds,
And love, though fleeting; these may not be mine.
But mine own words, I pray, deny me not.

[7] **frore**: frosty.

THE EARTH: They shall be told. Ere Babylon was dust,
The Magus Zoroaster,[8] my dead child,
Met his own image walking in the garden.
That apparition, sole of men, he saw.
For know there are two worlds of life and death:
One that which thou beholdest; but the other
Is underneath the grave, where do inhabit
The shadows of all forms that think and live
Till death unite them and they part no more;
Dreams and the light imaginings of men,
And all that faith creates or love desires,
Terrible, strange, sublime and beauteous shapes.
There thou art, and dost hang, a writhing shade,
'Mid whirlwind-peopled mountains; all the gods
Are there, and all the powers of nameless worlds,
Vast, sceptred phantoms; heroes, men, and beasts;
And Demogorgon, a tremendous gloom;
And he, the supreme Tyrant, on his throne
Of burning gold. Son, one of these shall utter
The curse which all remember. Call at will
Thine own ghost, or the ghost of Jupiter,
Hades or Typhon, or what mightier Gods
From all-prolific Evil, since thy ruin
Have sprung, and trampled on my prostrate sons.
Ask, and they must reply: so the revenge
Of the Supreme may sweep through vacant shades,
As rainy wind through the abandoned gate
Of a fallen palace.

PROMETHEUS: Mother, let not aught
Of that which may be evil, pass again
My lips, or those of aught resembling me.
Phantasm of Jupiter, arise, appear!

IONE:

My wings are folded o'er mine ears:
My wings are crossèd o'er mine eyes:
Yet through their silver shade appears,
And through their lulling plumes arise,
A Shape, a throng of sounds;
May it be no ill to thee
O thou of many wounds!
Near whom, for our sweet sister's sake,
Ever thus we watch and wake.

PANTHEA:

The sound is of whirlwind underground,
Earthquake, and fire, and mountains cloven;
The shape is awful like the sound,
Clothed in dark purple, star-inwoven.
A sceptre of pale gold
To stay steps proud, o'er the slow cloud
His veinèd hand doth hold.
Cruel he looks, but calm and strong,
Like one who does, not suffers wrong.

PHANTASM OF JUPITER: Why have the secret powers of this strange world
Driven me, a frail and empty phantom, hither
On direst storms? What unaccustomed sounds
Are hovering on my lips, unlike the voice
With which our pallid race hold ghastly talk
In darkness? And, proud sufferer, who art thou?

PROMETHEUS: Tremendous Image, as thou art must be
He whom thou shadowest forth. I am his foe,
The Titan. Speak the words which I would hear,
Although no thought inform thine empty voice.

THE EARTH: Listen! And though your echoes must be mute,
Gray mountains, and old woods, and haunted springs,
Prophetic caves, and isle-surrounding streams,
Rejoice to hear what yet ye cannot speak.

PHANTASM: A spirit seizes me and speaks within:
It tears me as fire tears a thunder-cloud.

PANTHEA: See, how he lifts his mighty looks, the Heaven
Darkens above.

IONE: He speaks! O shelter me!

PROMETHEUS: I see the curse on gestures proud and cold,
And looks of firm defiance, and calm hate,
And such despair as mocks itself with smiles,
Written as on a scroll: yet speak: Oh, speak!

PHANTASM:

Fiend, I defy thee! with a calm, fixed mind,
All that thou canst inflict I bid thee do;
Foul Tyrant both of Gods and Human-kind,
One only being shalt thou not subdue.
Rain then thy plagues upon me here,
Ghastly disease, and frenzying fear;
And let alternate frost and fire
Eat into me, and be thine ire

[8] **Magus Zoroaster:** possibly a Persian who lived in the sixth century BC and found the Magian religion, which held that there are two spirits or forces in the world, Ahura-Mazda, the spirit of light and good, and Ahriman, the spirit of darkness and evil.

Lightning, and cutting hail, and legioned forms
Of furies, driving by upon the wounding storms.
 Ay, do thy worst. Thou art omnipotent.
  O'er all things but thyself I gave thee power,
 And my own will. Be thy swift mischiefs sent
  To blast mankind, from yon ethereal tower.
 Let thy malignant spirit move
 In darkness over those I love:
 On me and mine I imprecate[9]
 The utmost torture of thy hate;
And thus devote to sleepless agony,
This undeclining head while thou must reign on high.
 But thou, who art the God and Lord: O, thou,
  Who fillest with thy soul this world of woe,
 To whom all things of Earth and Heaven do bow
  In fear and worship: all-prevailing foe!
 I curse thee! let a sufferer's curse
 Clasp thee, his torturer, like remorse;
 Till thine Infinity shall be
 A robe of envenomed agony;
And thine Omnipotence a crown of pain,
To cling like burning gold round thy dissolving brain.
 Heap on thy soul, by virtue of this Curse,
  Ill deeds, then be thou damned, beholding good;
 Both infinite as is the universe,
  And thou, and thy self-torturing solitude.
 An awful image of calm power
 Though now thou sittest, let the hour
 Come, when thou must appear to be
 That which thou art internally;
And after many a false and fruitless crime
Scorn track thy lagging fall through boundless space and time.

PROMETHEUS: Were these my words, O Parent?

THE EARTH: They were thine.

PROMETHEUS: It doth repent me: words are quick and vain;
Grief for awhile is blind, and so was mine.
I wish no living thing to suffer pain.

THE EARTH:
 Misery, Oh misery to me,
 That Jove at length should vanquish thee.
 Wail, howl aloud, Land and Sea,
 The Earth's rent heart shall answer ye.
Howl, Spirits of the living and the dead,
Your refuge, your defence lies fallen and vanquishèd.

FIRST ECHO:
 Lies fallen and vanquishèd!

SECOND ECHO:
 Fallen and vanquishèd!

IONE:
 Fear not: 'tis but some passing spasm,
  The Titan is unvanquished still.
 But see, where through the azure chasm
  Of yon forked and snowy hill
 Trampling the slant winds on high
  With golden-sandalled feet, that glow
 Under plumes of purple dye,
 Like rose-ensanguined ivory,
  A Shape comes now,
 Stretching on high from his right hand
 A serpent-cinctured wand.[10]

PANTHEA: 'Tis Jove's world-wandering herald, Mercury.

IONE:
 And who are those with hydra[11] tresses
  And iron wings that climb the wind,
 Whom the frowning God represses
  Like vapours steaming up behind,
 Clanging loud, an endless crowd—

PANTHEA:
 These are Jove's tempest-walking hounds,
Whom he gluts with groans and blood,
When charioted on sulphurous cloud
 He bursts Heaven's bounds.

IONE:
 Are they now led, from the thin dead
 On new pangs to be fed?

PANTHEA:
 The Titan looks as ever, firm, not proud.

FIRST FURY: Ha! I scent life!

---

[9] **imprecate:** call for a curse upon.

[10] **serpent-cinctured wand:** wand encircled with a serpent form.

[11] **hydra:** snakelike, from the creature with many heads that grew two more for each cut off.

SECOND FURY: Let me but look into his eyes!
THIRD FURY: The hope of torturing him smells like a
heap
Of corpses, to a death-bird after battle.
FIRST FURY: Darest thou delay, O Herald! take cheer,
Hounds
Of Hell: what if the Son of Maia[12] soon
Should make us food and sport—who can please
long
The Omnipotent?
MERCURY: Back to your towers of iron,
And gnash, beside the streams of fire and wail,
Your foodless teeth. Geryon, arise! and Gorgon,
Chimaera, and thou Sphinx,[13] subtlest of fiends
Who ministered to Thebes Heaven's poisoned wine,
Unnatural love, and more unnatural hate:
These shall perform your task.
FIRST FURY: Oh, mercy! mercy!
We die with our desire: drive us not back!
MERCURY: Crouch then in silence.
Awful Sufferer!
To thee unwilling, most unwillingly
I come, by the great Father's will driven down,
To execute a doom of new revenge.
Alas! I pity thee, and hate myself
That I can do no more: aye from thy sight
Returning, for a season, Heaven seems Hell,
So thy worn form pursues me night and day,
Smiling reproach. Wise art thou, firm and good,
But vainly wouldst stand forth alone in strife
Against the Omnipotent; as yon clear lamps
That measure and divide the weary years
From which there is no refuge, long have taught
And long must teach. Even now thy Torturer arms
With the strange might of unimagined pains
The powers who scheme slow agonies in Hell,
And my commission is to lead them here,
Or what more subtle, foul, or savage fiends
People the abyss, and leave them to their task.
Be it not so! there is a secret known
To thee, and to none else of living things,
Which may transfer the sceptre of wide Heaven,
The fear of which perplexes the Supreme:
Clothe it in words, and bid it clasp his throne
In intercession; bend thy soul in prayer,
And like a suppliant in some gorgeous fane,
Let the will kneel within thy haughty heart:
For benefits and meek submission tame
The fiercest and the mightiest.
PROMETHEUS: Evil minds
Change good to their own nature. I gave all
He has; and in return he chains me here
Years, ages, night and day: whether the Sun
Split my parched skin, or in the moony night
The crystal-wingèd snow cling round my hair:
Whilst my belovèd race is trampled down
By his thought-executing ministers.
Such is the tyrant's recompense: 'tis just:
He who is evil can receive no good;
And for a world bestowed, or a friend lost,
He can feel hate, fear, shame; not gratitude:
He but requites me for his own misdeed.
Kindness to such is keen reproach, which breaks
With bitter stings the light sleep of Revenge.
Submission, thou dost know I cannot try:
For what submission but that fatal word,
The death-seal of mankind's captivity,
Like the Sicilian's hair-suspended sword,[14]
Which trembles o'er his crown, would he accept,
Or could I yield? Which yet I will not yield.
Let others flatter Crime, where it sits throned
In brief Omnipotence: secure are they:
For Justice, when triumphant, will weep down
Pity, not punishment, on her own wrongs,
Too much avenged by those who err. I wait,
Enduring thus, the retributive hour
Which since we spake is even nearer now.
But hark, the hell-hounds clamour: fear delay:
Behold! Heaven lowers under thy Father's frown.

[12] **Maia:** the most beautiful of the seven sisters and mother of Hermes or Mercury, the herald of the gods.

[13] **Geryon:** monster with three heads. **Gorgon:** three frightful sisters with snakes for hair. **Chimaera:** female fire-breathing monster with the shape of a lion in the fore part, a goat in the middle, and a dragon at the tail end. **Sphinx:** female monster with the shape of a lion and woman, who ate Thebans who failed to solve her riddle.

[14] **hair-suspended sword:** reference to the Sword of Damocles. Damocles envied the elder Dionysius his wealth and power, until he exchanged places with the tyrant and felt the precariousness of Dionysius's position emblemized by a sword hanging over his head by a single horsehair.

MERCURY: Oh, that we might be spared: I to inflict
And thou to suffer! Once more answer me:
Thou knowest not the period of Jove's power?
PROMETHEUS: I know but this, that it must come.
MERCURY: Alas!
Thou canst not count thy years to come of pain?
PROMETHEUS: They last while Jove must reign: nor more, nor less
Do I desire or fear.
MERCURY: Yet pause, and plunge
Into Eternity, where recorded time,
Even all that we imagine, age on age,
Seems but a point, and the reluctant mind
Flags wearily in its unending flight,
Till it sink, dizzy, blind, lost, shelterless;
Perchance it has not numbered the slow years
Which thou must spend in torture, unreprieved?
PROMETHEUS: Perchance no thought can count them, yet they pass.
MERCURY: If thou might'st dwell among the Gods the while
Lapped in voluptuous joy?
PROMETHEUS: I would not quit
This bleak ravine, these unrepentant pains.
MERCURY: Alas! I wonder at, yet pity thee.
PROMETHEUS: Pity the self-despising slaves of Heaven,
Not me, within whose mind sits peace serene,
As light in the sun, throned: how vain is talk!
Call up the fiends.
IONE: O, sister, look! White fire
Has cloven to the roots yon huge snow-loaded cedar;
How fearfully God's thunder howls behind!
MERCURY: I must obey his words and thine: alas!
Most heavily remorse hangs at my heart!
PANTHEA: See where the child of Heaven, with wingèd feet,
Runs down the slanted sunlight of the dawn.
IONE: Dear sister, close thy plumes over thine eyes
Lest thou behold and die: they come: they come
Blackening the birth of day with countless wings,
And hollow underneath, like death.
FIRST FURY: Prometheus!
SECOND FURY: Immortal Titan!
THIRD FURY: Champion of Heaven's slaves!
PROMETHEUS: He whom some dreadful voice invokes is here,
Prometheus, the chained Titan. Horrible forms,
What and who are ye? Never yet there came
Phantasms so foul through monster-teeming Hell
From the all-miscreative brain of Jove;
Whilst I behold such execrable shapes,
Methinks I grow like what I contemplate,
And laugh and stare in loathsome sympathy.
FIRST FURY: We are the ministers of pain, and fear,
And disappointment, and mistrust, and hate,
And clinging crime; and as lean dogs pursue
Through wood and lake some struck and sobbing fawn,
We track all things that weep, and bleed, and live,
When the great King betrays them to our will.
PROMETHEUS: Oh! many fearful natures in one name,
I know ye; and these lakes and echoes know
The darkness and the clangour of your wings.
But why more hideous than your loathèd selves
Gather ye up in legions from the deep?
SECOND FURY: We knew not that: Sisters, rejoice, rejoice!
PROMETHEUS: Can aught exult in its deformity?
SECOND FURY: The beauty of delight makes lovers glad,
Gazing on one another: so are we.
As from the rose which the pale priestess kneels
To gather for her festal crown of flowers
The aëreal crimson falls, flushing her cheek,
So from our victim's destined agony
The shade which is our form invests us round,
Else we are shapeless as our mother Night.
PROMETHEUS: I laugh your power, and his who sent you here,
To lowest scorn. Pour forth the cup of pain.
FIRST FURY: Thou thinkest we will rend thee bone from bone,
And nerve from nerve, working like fire within?
PROMETHEUS: Pain is my element, as hate is thine;
Ye rend me now: I care not.
SECOND FURY: Dost imagine
We will but laugh into thy lidless eyes?
PROMETHEUS: I weigh not what ye do, but what ye suffer,
Being evil. Cruel was the power which called
You, or aught else so wretched, into light.
THIRD FURY: Thou think'st we will live through thee, one by one,
Like animal life, and though we can obscure not
The soul which burns within, that we will dwell
Beside it, like a vain loud multitude
Vexing the self-content of wisest men:
That we will be dread thought beneath thy brain,

And foul desire round thine astonished heart,
And blood within thy labyrinthine veins
Crawling like agony?

PROMETHEUS: Why, ye are thus now;
Yet am I king over myself, and rule
The torturing and conflicting throngs within,
As Jove rules you when Hell grows mutinous.

CHORUS OF FURIES:
From the ends of the earth, from the ends of the earth,
Where the night has its grave and the morning its birth,
Come, come, come!
Oh, ye who shake hills with the scream of your mirth,
When cities sink howling in ruin; and ye
Who with wingless footsteps trample the sea,
And close upon Shipwreck and Famine's track,
Sit chattering with joy on the foodless wreck;
Come, come, come!
Leave the bed, low, cold, and red,
Strewed beneath a nation dead;
Leave the hatred, as in ashes
Fire is left for future burning:
It will burst in bloodier flashes
When ye stir it, soon returning:
Leave the self-contempt implanted
In young spirits, sense-enchanted,
Misery's yet unkindled fuel:
Leave Hell's secrets half unchanted
To the maniac dreamer; cruel
More than ye can be with hate
Is he with fear.
Come, come, come!
We are steaming up from Hell's wide gate
And we burthen the blast of the atmosphere,
But vainly we toil till ye come here.

IONE: Sister, I hear the thunder of new wings.

PANTHEA: These solid mountains quiver with the sound
Even as the tremulous air: their shadows make
The space within my plumes more black than night.

FIRST FURY:
Your call was as a wingèd car
Driven on whirlwinds fast and far;
It rapped us from red gulfs of war.

SECOND FURY:
From wide cities, famine-wasted;

THIRD FURY:
Groans half heard, and blood untasted;

FOURTH FURY:
Kingly conclaves stern and cold,
Where blood with gold is bought and sold;

FIFTH FURY:
From the furnace, white and hot,
In which—

A FURY:
Speak not: whisper not:
I know all that ye would tell,
But to speak might break the spell
Which must bend the Invincible,
The stern of thought;
He yet defies the deepest power of Hell.

A FURY:
Tear the veil!

ANOTHER FURY:
It is torn.

CHORUS:
The pale stars of the morn
Shine on a misery, dire to be borne.
Dost thou faint, mighty Titan? We laugh thee to scorn.
Dost thou boast the clear knowledge thou waken'dst for man?
Then was kindled within him a thirst which outran
Those perishing waters; a thirst of fierce fever,
Hope, love, doubt, desire, which consume him for ever.
One came forth of gentle worth
Smiling on the sanguine earth;
His words outlived him, like swift poison
Withering up truth, peace, and pity.
Look! where round the wide horizon
Many a million-peopled city
Vomits smoke in the bright air.
Hark that outcry of despair!
'Tis his mild and gentle ghost
Wailing for the faith he kindled:
Look again, the flames almost
To a glow-worm's lamp have dwindled:
The survivors round the embers
Gather in dread.
Joy, joy, joy!
Past ages crowd on thee, but each one remembers,
And the future is dark, and the present is spread
Like a pillow of thorns for thy slumberless head.

SEMICHORUS I:
Drops of bloody agony flow
From his white and quivering brow.
Grant a little respite now:
See a disenchanted nation
Springs like day from desolation;
To Truth its state is dedicate,
And Freedom leads it forth, her mate;
A legioned bank of linkèd brothers
Whom Love calls children—

SEMICHORUS II:
'Tis another's:
See how kindred murder kin:
'Tis the vintage-time for death and sin:
Blood, like new wine, bubbles within:
Till Despair smothers
The struggling world, which slaves and tyrants win.

(All the FURIES *vanish, except one.)*

IONE: Hark, sister! what a low yet dreadful groan
Quite unsuppressed is tearing up the heart
Of the good Titan, as storms tear the deep,
And beasts hear the sea moan in inland caves.
Darest thou observe how the fiends torture him?
PANTHEA: Alas! I looked forth twice, but will no more.
IONE: What didst thou see?
PANTHEA: A woful sight: a youth
With patient looks nailed to a crucifix.
IONE: What next?
PANTHEA: The heaven around, the earth below
Was peopled with thick shapes of human death,
All horrible, and wrought by human hands,
And some appeared the work of human hearts,
For men were slowly killed by frowns and smiles:
And other sights too foul to speak and live
Were wandering by. Let us not tempt worse fear
By looking forth: those groans are grief enough.
FURY: Behold an emblem: those who do endure
Deep wrongs for man, and scorn, and chains, but heap
Thousandfold torment on themselves and him.
PROMETHEUS: Remit the anguish of that lighted stare;
Close those wan lips, let that thorn-wounded brow[15]
Stream not with blood; it mingles with thy tears!
Fix, fix those tortured orbs in peace and death,
So thy sick throes shake not that crucifix,
So those pale fingers play not with thy gore.
O, horrible! Thy name I will not speak,
It hath become a curse. I see, I see
The wise, the mild, the lofty, and the just,
Whom thy slaves hate for being like to thee,
Some hunted by foul lies from their heart's home,
An early-chosen, late-lamented home;
As hooded ounces cling to the driven hind;[16]
Some linked to corpses in unwholesome cells:
Some—Hear I not the multitude laugh loud?—
Impaled in lingering fire: and mighty realms
Float by my feet, like sea-uprooted isles,
Whose sons are kneaded down in common blood
By the red light of their own burning homes.
FURY: Blood thou canst see, and fire; and canst hear groans;
Worse things, unheard, unseen, remain behind.
PROMETHEUS: Worse?
FURY: In each human heart terror survives
The ravin it has gorged: the loftiest fear
All that they would disdain to think were true:
Hypocrisy and custom make their minds
The fanes of many a worship, now outworn.
They dare not devise good for man's estate,
And yet they know not that they do not dare.
The good want power, but to weep barren tears.
The powerful goodness want: worse need for them.
The wise want love; and those who love want wisdom;
And all best things are thus confused to ill.
Many are strong and rich, and would be just,
But live among their suffering fellow-men
As if none felt: they know not what they do.[17]
PROMETHEUS: Thy words are like a cloud of wingèd snakes;
And yet I pity those they torture not.
FURY: Thou pitiest them? I speak no more!

(Vanishes.)

[15] **thorn-wounded brow**: reference to the wounded head of Christ, on which was implanted a crown of thorns during his Passion to mock his claims to sovereignty.

[16] **hooded ounces . . . hind**: leopards in pursuit of a female deer.

[17] **As if . . . do**: paraphrase of Christ's words of forgiveness towards his executioners: "Father, forgive them; for they know not what they do." Luke 23:34.

PROMETHEUS: Ah woe!
Ah woe! Alas! pain, pain ever, for ever!
I close my tearless eyes, but see more clear
Thy works within my woe-illumèd mind,
Thou subtle tyrant! Peace is in the grave.
The grave hides all things beautiful and good:
I am a God and cannot find it there,
Nor would I seek it: for, though dread revenge,
This is defeat, fierce king, not victory.
The sights with which thou torturest gird my soul
With new endurance, till the hour arrives
When they shall be no types of things which are.

PANTHEA: Alas! what sawest thou more?

PROMETHEUS: There are two woes:
To speak, and to behold; thou spare me one.
Names are there, Nature's sacred watchwords, they
Were borne aloft in bright emblazonry;
The nations thronged around, and cried aloud,
As with one voice, Truth, liberty, and love!
Suddenly fierce confusion fell from heaven
Among them: there was strife, deceit, and fear:
Tyrants rushed in, and did divide the spoil.
This was the shadow of the truth I saw.

THE EARTH: I felt thy torture, son; with such mixed joy
As pain and virtue give. To cheer thy state
I bid ascend those subtle and fair spirits,
Whose homes are the dim caves of human thought,
And who inhabit, as birds wing the wind,
Its world-surrounding aether: they behold
Beyond that twilight realm, as in a glass,
The future: may they speak comfort to thee!

PANTHEA: Look, sister, where a troop of spirits gather,
Like flocks of clouds in spring's delightful weather,
Thronging in the blue air!

IONE: And see! more come,
Like fountain-vapours when the winds are dumb,
That climb up the ravine in scattered lines.
And, hark! is it the music of the pines?
Is it the lake? Is it the waterfall?

PANTHEA: 'Tis something sadder, sweeter far than all.

CHORUS OF SPIRITS:
From unremembered ages we
Gentle guides and guardians be
Of heaven-oppressed mortality;
And we breathe, and sicken not,
The atmosphere of human thought:
Be it dim, and dank, and gray,
Like a storm-extinguished day,
Travelled o'er by dying gleams;
Be it bright as all between
Cloudless skies and windless streams,
Silent, liquid, and serene;
As the birds within the wind,
As the fish within the wave,
As the thoughts of man's own mind
Float through all above the grave;
We make there our liquid lair,
Voyaging cloudlike and unpent
Through the boundless element:
Thence we bear the prophecy
Which begins and ends in thee!

IONE: More yet come, one by one: the air around them
Looks radiant as the air around a star.

FIRST SPIRIT:
On a battle-trumpet's blast
I fled hither, fast, fast, fast,
'Mid the darkness upward cast.
From the dust of creeds outworn,
From the tyrant's banner torn,
Gathering 'round me, onward borne,
There was mingled many a cry—
Freedom! Hope! Death! Victory!
Till they faded through the sky;
And one sound, above, around,
One sound beneath, around, above,
Was moving; 'twas the soul of Love;
'Twas the hope, the prophecy,
Which begins and ends in thee.

SECOND SPIRIT:
A rainbow's arch stood on the sea,
Which rocked beneath, immovably;
And the triumphant storm did flee,
Like a conqueror, swift and proud,
Between, with many a captive cloud,
A shapeless, dark and rapid crowd,
Each by lightning riven in half:
I heard the thunder hoarsely laugh:
Mighty fleets were strewn like chaff
And spread beneath a hell of death
O'er the white waters. I alit
On a great ship lightning-split,
And speeded hither on the sigh
Of one who gave an enemy
His plank, then plunged aside to die.

THIRD SPIRIT:

I sate beside a sage's bed,
And the lamp was burning red
Near the book where he had fed,
When a Dream with plumes of flame,
To his pillow hovering came,
And I knew it was the same
Which had kindled long ago
Pity, eloquence, and woe;
And the world awhile below
Wore the shade, its lustre made.
It has borne me here as fleet
As Desire's lightning feet:
I must ride it back ere morrow,
Or the sage will wake in sorrow.

FOURTH SPIRIT:

On a poet's lips I slept
Dreaming like a love-adept
In the sound his breathing kept;
Nor seeks nor finds he mortal blisses,
But feeds on the aëreal kisses
Of shapes that haunt thought's wildernesses.
He will watch from dawn to gloom
The lake-reflected sun illume
The yellow bees in the ivy-bloom,
Nor heed nor see, what things they be;
But from these create he can
Forms more real than living man,
Nurslings of immortality!
One of these awakened me,
And I sped to succour thee.

IONE:

Behold'st thou not two shapes from the east and west
Come, as two doves to one beloved nest,
Twin nurslings of the all-sustaining air
On swift still wings glide down the atmosphere?
And, hark! their sweet, sad voices! 'tis despair
Mingled with love and then dissolved in sound.

PANTHEA: Canst thou speak, sister? all my words are drowned.

IONE: Their beauty gives me voice. See how they float
On their sustaining wings of skiey grain,
Orange and azure deepening into gold:
Their soft smiles light the air like a star's fire.

CHORUS OF SPIRITS:

Hast thou beheld the form of Love?

FIFTH SPIRIT:

As over wide dominions
I sped, like some swift cloud that wings the wide air's wildernesses,
That planet-crested shape swept by on lightning-braided pinions,[18]
Scattering the liquid joy of life from his ambrosial tresses:
His footsteps paved the world with light; but as I passed 'twas fading,
And hollow Ruin yawned behind: great sages bound in madness,
And headless patriots, and pale youths who perished, unupbraiding,
Gleamed in the night. I wandered o'er, till thou, O King of sadness,
Turned by thy smile the worst I saw to recollected gladness.

SIXTH SPIRIT:

Ah, sister! Desolation is a delicate thing:
It walks not on the earth, it floats not on the air,
But treads with lulling footstep, and fans with silent wing
The tender hopes which in their hearts the best and gentlest bear;
Who, soothed to false repose by the fanning plumes above
And the music-stirring motion of its soft and busy feet,
Dream visions of aëreal joy, and call the monster, Love,
And wake, and find the shadow Pain, as he whom now we greet.

CHORUS:

Though Ruin now Love's shadow be,
Following him, destroyingly,
On Death's white and wingèd steed,
Which the fleetest cannot flee,
Trampling down both flower and weed,
Man and beast, and foul and fair,
Like a tempest through the air;

[18] **pinions:** wings.

Thou shalt quell this horseman grim,
Woundless though in heart or limb.

PROMETHEUS: Spirits! how know ye this shall be?

CHORUS:
In the atmosphere we breathe,
As buds grow red when the snow-storms flee,
From Spring gathering up beneath,
Whose mild winds shake the elder brake,
And the wandering herdsmen know
That the white-thorn soon will blow:
Wisdom, Justice, Love, and Peace,
When they struggle to increase,
Are to us as soft winds be
To shepherd boys, the prophecy
Which begins and ends in thee.

IONE: Where are the Spirits fled?

PANTHEA: Only a sense
Remains of them, like the omnipotence
Of music, when the inspired voice and lute
Languish, ere yet the responses are mute,
Which through the deep and labyrinthine soul,
Like echoes through long caverns, wind and roll.

PROMETHEUS: How fair these airborn shapes! and yet I feel
Most vain all hope but love; and thou art far,
Asia! who, when my being overflowed,
Wert like a golden chalice to bright wine
Which else had sunk into the thirsty dust.
All things are still: alas! how heavily
This quiet morning weighs upon my heart;
Though I should dream I could even sleep with grief
If slumber were denied not. I would fain
Be what it is my destiny to be,
The saviour and the strength of suffering man,
Or sink into the original gulf of things:
There is no agony, and no solace left;
Earth can console, Heaven can torment no more.

PANTHEA: Hast thou forgotten one who watches thee
The cold dark night, and never sleeps but when
The shadow of thy spirit falls on her?

PROMETHEUS: I said all hope was vain but love: thou lovest.

PANTHEA: Deeply in truth; but the eastern star looks white,
And Asia waits in that far Indian vale,
The scene of her sad exile; rugged once
And desolate and frozen, like this ravine;
But now invested with fair flowers and herbs,
And haunted by sweet airs and sounds, which flow
Among the woods and waters, from the aether
Of her transforming presence, which would fade
If it were mingled not with thine. Farewell!

ACT II

—SCENE I—

(Morning. A lovely Vale in the Indian Caucasus. ASIA *alone.)*

ASIA: From all the blasts of heaven thou hast descended:
Yes, like a spirit, like a thought, which makes
Unwonted tears throng to the horny eyes,[19]
And beatings haunt the desolated heart,
Which should have learnt repose: thou hast descended
Cradled in tempests; thou dost wake, O Spring!
O child of many winds! As suddenly
Thou comest as the memory of a dream,
Which now is sad because it hath been sweet;
Like genius, or like joy which riseth up
As from the earth, clothing with golden clouds
The desert of our life.
This is the season, this the day, the hour;
At sunrise thou shouldst come, sweet sister mine,
Too long desired, too long delaying, come!
How like death-worms the wingless moments crawl!
The point of one white star is quivering still
Deep in the orange light of widening morn
Beyond the purple mountains: through a chasm
Of wind-divided mist the darker lake
Reflects it: now it wanes: it gleams again
As the waves fade, and as the burning threads
Of woven cloud unravel in pale air:
'Tis lost! and through yon peaks of cloud-like snow
The roseate sunlight quivers: hear I not
The Aeolian music of her sea-green plumes
Winnowing the crimson dawn?

(PANTHEA *enters.*)

I feel, I see
Those eyes which burn through smiles that fade in tears,
Like stars half quenched in mists of silver dew.

---

[19] **horny eyes:** dull and semi-opaque like horn (*OED*).

Belovèd and most beautiful, who wearest
The shadow of that soul by which I live,
How late thou art! the spherèd sun had climbed
The sea; my heart was sick with hope, before
The printless air felt thy belated plumes.

PANTHEA: Pardon, great Sister! but my wings were faint
With the delight of a remembered dream,
As are the noontide plumes of summer winds
Satiate with sweet flowers. I was wont to sleep
Peacefully, and awake refreshed and calm
Before the sacred Titan's fall, and thy
Unhappy love, had made, through use and pity,
Both love and woe familiar to my heart
As they had grown to thine: erewhile I slept
Under the glaucous[20] caverns of old Ocean
Within dim bowers of green and purple moss,
Our young Ione's soft and milky arms
Locked then, as now, behind my dark, moist hair,
While my shut eyes and cheek were pressed within
The folded depth of her life-breathing bosom:
But not as now, since I am made the wind
Which fails beneath the music that I bear
Of thy most wordless converse; since dissolved
Into the sense with which love talks, my rest
Was troubled and yet sweet; my waking hours
Too full of care and pain.

ASIA: Lift up thine eyes,
And let me read thy dream.

PANTHEA: As I have said
With our sea-sister at his feet I slept.
The mountain mists, condensing at our voice
Under the moon, had spread their snowy flakes,
From the keen ice shielding our linkèd sleep.
Then two dreams came. One, I remember not.
But in the other his pale wound-worn limbs
Fell from Prometheus, and the azure night
Grew radiant with the glory of that form
Which lives unchanged within, and his voice fell
Like music which makes giddy the dim brain,
Faint with intoxication of keen joy:
'Sister of her whose footsteps pave the world
With loveliness—more fair than aught but her,
Whose shadow thou art—lift thine eyes on me.'
I lifted them: the overpowering light
Of that immortal shape was shadowed o'er
By love; which, from his soft and flowing limbs,
And passion-parted lips, and keen, faint eyes,
Steamed forth like vaporous fire; an atmosphere
Which wrapped me in its all-dissolving power,
As the warm aether of the morning sun
Wraps ere it drinks some cloud of wandering dew.
I saw not, heard not, moved not, only felt
His presence flow and mingle through my blood
Till it became his life, and his grew mine,
And I was thus absorbed, until it passed,
And like the vapours when the sun sinks down,
Gathering again in drops upon the pines,
And tremulous as they, in the deep night
My being was condensed; and as the rays
Of thought were slowly gathered, I could hear
His voice, whose accents lingered ere they died
Like footsteps of weak melody: thy name
Among the many sounds alone I heard
Of what might be articulate; though still
I listened through the night when sound was none.
Ione wakened then, and said to me:
'Canst thou divine what troubles me to-night?
I always knew what I desired before,
Nor ever found delight to wish in vain.
But now I cannot tell thee what I seek;
I know not; something sweet, since it is sweet
Even to desire; it is thy sport, false sister;
Thou hast discovered some enchantment old,
Whose spells have stolen my spirit as I slept
And mingled it with thine: for when just now
We kissed, I felt within thy parted lips
The sweet air that sustained me, and the warmth
Of the life-blood, for loss of which I faint,
Quivered between our intertwining arms.'
I answered not, for the Eastern star grew pale,
But fled to thee.

ASIA: Thou speakest, but thy words
Are as the air: I feel them not: Oh, lift
Thine eyes, that I may read his written soul!

PANTHEA: I lift them though they droop beneath the load
Of that they would express: what canst thou see
But thine own fairest shadow imaged there?

ASIA: Thine eyes are like the deep, blue, boundless heaven
Contracted to two circles underneath
Their long, fine lashes; dark, far, measureless,
Orb within orb, and line through line inwoven.

[20] glaucous: grayish or bluish-green.

PANTHEA: Why lookest thou as if a spirit passed?
ASIA: There is a change: beyond their inmost depth
I see a shade, a shape: 'tis He, arrayed
In the soft light of his own smiles, which spread
Like radiance from the cloud-surrounded moon.
Prometheus, it is thine! depart not yet!
Say not those smiles that we shall meet again
Within that bright pavilion which their beams
Shall build o'er the waste world? The dream is told.
What shape is that between us? Its rude hair
Roughens the wind that lifts it, its regard
Is wild and quick, yet 'tis a thing of air,
For through its gray robe gleams the golden dew
Whose stars the noon has quenched not.
DREAM: Follow! Follow!
PANTHEA: It is mine other dream.
ASIA: It disappears.
PANTHEA: It passes now into my mind. Methought
As we sate here, the flower-infolding buds
Burst on yon lightning-blasted almond-tree,
When swift from the white Scythian[21] wilderness
A wind swept forth wrinkling the Earth with frost:
I looked, and all the blossoms were blown down;
But on each leaf was stamped, as the blue bells
Of Hyacinth tell Apollo's written grief,
O, FOLLOW, FOLLOW!
ASIA: As you speak, your words
Fill, pause by pause, my own forgotten sleep
With shapes. Methought among these lawns together
We wandered, underneath the young gray dawn,
And multitudes of dense white fleecy clouds
Were wandering in thick flocks along the mountains
Shepherded by the slow, unwilling wind;
And the white dew on the new-bladed grass,
Just piercing the dark earth, hung silently;
And there was more which I remember not:
But on the shadows of the morning clouds,
Athwart the purple mountain slope, was written
FOLLOW, O, FOLLOW! as they vanished by;
And on each herb, from which Heaven's dew had fallen,
The like was stamped, as with a withering fire;
A wind arose among the pines; it shook
The clinging music from their boughs, and then
Low, sweet, faint sounds, like the farewell of ghosts,
Were heard: O, FOLLOW, FOLLOW, FOLLOW ME!
And then I said: 'Panthea, look on me.'
But in the depth of those belovèd eyes
Still I saw, FOLLOW, FOLLOW!
ECHO: Follow, follow!
PANTHEA: The crags, this clear spring morning, mock our voices
As they were spirit-tongued.
ASIA: It is some being
Around the crags. What fine clear sounds! O, list!
ECHOES (*unseen*):
Echoes we: listen!
We cannot stay:
As dew-stars glisten
Then fade away—
Child of Ocean!
ASIA: Hark! Spirits speak. The liquid responses
Of their aëreal tongues yet sound.
PANTHEA: I hear.
ECHOES:
O, follow, follow,
As our voice recedeth
Through the caverns hollow,
Where the forest spreadeth;
(*More distant.*)
O, follow, follow!
Through the caverns hollow,
As the song floats thou pursue,
Where the wild bee never flew,
Through the noontide darkness deep,
By the odour-breathing sleep
Of faint night flowers, and the waves
At the fountain-lighted caves,
While our music, wild and sweet,
Mocks thy gently falling feet,
Child of Ocean!
ASIA: Shall we pursue the sound? It grows more faint
And distant.
PANTHEA: List! the strain floats nearer now.
ECHOES:
In the world unknown
Sleeps a voice unspoken;
By thy step alone
Can its rest be broken,
Child of Ocean!

[21] **Scythian:** from Scythia, an ancient region of Asia and southeastern Europe.

ASIA: How the notes sink upon the ebbing wind!

ECHOES:

O, follow, follow!
Through the caverns hollow,
As the song floats thou pursue,
By the woodland noontide dew;
By the forest, lakes, and fountains,
Through the many-folded mountains;
To the rents, and gulfs, and chasms,
Where the Earth reposed from spasms,
On the day when He and thou
Parted, to commingle now;
Child of Ocean!

ASIA: Come, sweet Panthea, link thy hand in mine,
And follow, ere the voices fade away.

— SCENE II —

(A Forest, intermingled with Rocks and Caverns. ASIA *and* PANTHEA *pass into it. Two young Fauns*[22] *are sitting on a Rock listening.)*

SEMICHORUS I. OF SPIRITS:

The path through which that lovely twain
Have passed, by cedar, pine, and yew.
And each dark tree that ever grew,
Is curtained out from Heaven's wide blue;
Nor sun, nor moon, nor wind, nor rain,
Can pierce its interwoven bowers,
Nor aught, save where some cloud of dew,
Drifted along the earth-creeping breeze,
Between the trunks of the hoar trees,
Hangs each a pearl in the pale flowers
Of the green laurel, blown anew;
And bends, and then fades silently,
One frail and fair anemone:
Or when some star of many a one
That climbs and wanders through steep night,
Has found the cleft through which alone
Beams fall from high those depths upon
Ere it is borne away, away,
By the swift Heavens that cannot stay,
It scatters drops of golden light,
Like lines of rain that ne'er unite:
And the gloom divine is all around,
And underneath is the mossy ground.

[22] Faun: rural deity with horns with the body of a man to the waist, and goat-like legs and hooves; satyr.

SEMICHORUS II:

There the voluptuous nightingales,
Are awake through all the broad noonday.
When one with bliss or sadness fails,
And through the windless ivy-boughs,
Sick with sweet love, droops dying away
On its mate's music-panting bosom;
Another from the swinging blossom,
Watching to catch the languid close
Of the last strain, then lifts on high
The wings of the weak melody,
'Till some new strain of feeling bear
The song, and all the woods are mute;
When there is heard through the dim air
The rush of wings, and rising there
Like many a lake-surrounded flute,
Sounds overflow the listener's brain
So sweet, that joy is almost pain.

SEMICHORUS I:

There those enchanted eddies play
Of echoes, music-tongued, which draw,
By Demogorgon's mighty law,
With melting rapture, or sweet awe,
All spirits on that secret way;
As inland boats are driven to Ocean
Down streams made strong with mountain-thaw:
And first there comes a gentle sound
To those in talk or slumber bound,
And wakes the destined soft emotion,—
Attracts, impels them; those who saw
Say from the breathing earth behind
There steams a plume-uplifting wind
Which drives them on their path, while they
Believe their own swift wings and feet
The sweet desires within obey:
And so they float upon their way,
Until, still sweet, but loud and strong,
The storm of sound is driven along,
Sucked up and hurrying: as they fleet
Behind, its gathering billows meet
And to the fatal mountain bear
Like clouds amid the yielding air.

FIRST FAUN: Canst thou imagine where those spirits live
Which make such delicate music in the woods?
We haunt within the least frequented caves
And closest coverts, and we know these wilds,
Yet never meet them, though we hear them oft:
Where may they hide themselves?

SECOND FAUN: 'Tis hard to tell:
I have heard those more skilled in spirits say,
The bubbles, which the enchantment of the sun
Sucks from the pale faint water-flowers that pave
The oozy bottom of clear lakes and pools,
Are the pavilions where such dwell and float
Under the green and golden atmosphere
Which noontide kindles through the woven leaves;
And when these burst, and the thin fiery air,
The which they breathed within those lucent[23] domes,
Ascends to flow like meteors through the night,
They ride on them, and rein their headlong speed,
And bow their burning crests, and glide in fire
Under the waters of the earth again.

FIRST FAUN: If such live thus, have others other lives,
Under pink blossoms or within the bells
Of meadow flowers, or folded violets deep,
Or on their dying odours, when they die,
Or in the sunlight of the spherèd dew?

SECOND FAUN: Ay, many more which we may well divine.
But, should we stay to speak, noontide would come,
And thwart Silenus[24] find his goats undrawn,
And grudge to sing those wise and lovely songs
Of Fate, and Chance, and God, and Chaos old,
And Love, and the chained Titan's woful doom,
And how he shall be loosed, and make the earth
One brotherhood: delightful strains which cheer
Our solitary twilights, and which charm
To silence the unenvying nightingales.

— SCENE III —

(A Pinnacle of Rock among Mountains. ASIA *and* PANTHEA.*)*

PANTHEA: Hither the sound has borne us—to the realm
Of Demogorgon, and the mighty portal,
Like a volcano's meteor-breathing chasm,
Whence the oracular vapour is hurled up
Which lonely men drink wandering in their youth,
And call truth, virtue, love, genius, or joy,
That maddening wine of life, whose dregs they drain
To deep intoxication; and uplift,
Like Maenads who cry loud, Evoe! Evoe![25]
The voice which is contagion to the world.

ASIA: Fit throne for such a Power! Magnificent!
How glorious art thou, Earth! And if thou be
The shadow of some spirit lovelier still,
Though evil stain its work, and it should be
Like its creation, weak yet beautiful,
I could fall down and worship that and thee.
Even now my heart adoreth: Wonderful!
Look, sister, ere the vapour dim thy brain:
Beneath is a wide plain of billowy mist,
As a lake, paving in the morning sky,
With azure waves which burst in silver light,
Some Indian vale. Behold it, rolling on
Under the curdling winds, and islanding
The peak whereon we stand, midway, around,
Encinctured by the dark and blooming forests,
Dim twilight-lawns, and stream-illumèd caves,
And wind-enchanted shapes of wandering mist;
And far on high the keen sky-cleaving mountains
From icy spires of sun-like radiance fling
The dawn, as lifted Ocean's dazzling spray,
From some Atlantic islet scattered up,
Spangles the wind with lamp-like water-drops.
The vale is girdled with their walls, a howl
Of cataracts from their thaw-cloven ravines,
Satiates the listening wind, continuous, vast,
Awful as silence. Hark! the rushing snow!
The sun-awakened avalanche! whose mass,
Thrice sifted by the storm, had gathered there
Flake after flake, in heaven-defying minds
As thought by thought is piled, till some great truth
Is loosened, and the nations echo round,
Shaken to their roots, as do the mountains now.

PANTHEA: Look how the gusty sea of mist is breaking
In crimson foam, even at our feet! it rises
As Ocean at the enchantment of the moon
Round foodless men wrecked on some oozy isle.

ASIA: The fragments of the cloud are scattered up;
The wind that lifts them disentwines my hair;
Its billows now sweep o'er mine eyes; my brain
Grows dizzy; see'st thou shapes within the mist?

[23] **lucent:** luminous.

[24] **Silenus:** an older Satyr-like god who accompanies Dionysius. He is generally drunk, riding an ass or supported by Satyrs. When drunk and asleep, he is under the control of mortals to speak prophecy and to sing when surrounded by flowers.

[25] **Maenads . . . Evoe! Evoe!:** See note 2 to *Ode to the West Wind.* Maenads would shout "Evoe!" in their frenzies.

PANTHEA: A countenance with beckoning smiles: there burns
An azure fire within its golden locks!
Another and another: hark! they speak!

Song of Spirits

To the deep, to the deep,
Down, down!
Through the shade of sleep,
Through the cloudy strife
Of Death and of Life;
Through the veil and the bar
Of things which seem and are
Even to the steps of the remotest throne,
Down, down!

While the sound whirls around,
Down, down!
As the fawn draws the hound,
As the lightning the vapour,
As a weak moth the taper;
Death, despair; love, sorrow;
Time both; to-day, to-morrow;
As steel obeys the spirit of the stone,
Down, down!

Through the gray, void abysm,
Down, down!
Where the air is no prism,
And the moon and stars are not,
And the cavern-crags wear not
The radiance of Heaven,
Nor the gloom to Earth given,
Where there is One pervading, One alone,
Down, down!

In the depth of the deep,
Down, down!
Like veiled lightning asleep,
Like the spark nursed in embers,
The last look Love remembers,
Like a diamond, which shines
On the dark wealth of mines,
A spell is treasured but for thee alone.
Down, down!

We have bound thee, we guide thee;
Down, down!
With the bright form beside thee;
Resist not the weakness,
Such strength is in meekness
That the Eternal, the Immortal,
Must unloose through life's portal
The snake-like Doom coiled underneath his throne
By that alone.

— SCENE IV —

(*The Cave of* DEMOGORGON. ASIA *and* PANTHEA.)

PANTHEA: What veilèd form sits on that ebon throne?
ASIA: The veil has fallen.
PANTHEA: I see a mighty darkness
Filling the seat of power, and rays of gloom
Dart round, as light from the meridian sun.
—Ungazed upon and shapeless; neither limb,
Nor form, nor outline; yet we feel it is
A living Spirit.
DEMOGORGON: Ask what thou wouldst know.
ASIA: What canst thou tell?
DEMOGORGON: All things thou dar'st demand.
ASIA: Who made the living world?
DEMOGORGON: God.
ASIA: Who made all
That it contains? thought, passion, reason, will,
Imagination?
DEMOGORGON: God: Almighty God.
ASIA: Who made that sense which, when the winds of Spring
In rarest visitation, or the voice
Of one belovèd heard in youth alone,
Fills the faint eyes with falling tears which dim
The radiant looks of unbewailing flowers,
And leaves this peopled earth a solitude
When it returns no more?
DEMOGORGON: Merciful God.
ASIA: And who made terror, madness, crime, remorse,
Which from the links of the great chain of things,
To every thought within the mind of man
Sway and drag heavily, and each one reels
Under the load towards the pit of death;
Abandoned hope, and love that turns to hate;
And self-contempt, bitterer to drink than blood;
Pain, whose unheeded and familiar speech
Is howling, and keen shrieks, day after day;
And Hell, or the sharp fear of Hell?
DEMOGORGON: He reigns.
ASIA: Utter his name: a world pining in pain
Asks but his name: curses shall drag him down.
DEMOGORGON: He reigns.
ASIA: I feel, I know it: who?
DEMOGORGON: He reigns.

ASIA: Who reigns? There was the Heaven and Earth at first,
And Light and Love; then Saturn, from whose throne
Time fell, an envious shadow: such the state
Of the earth's primal spirits beneath his sway,
As the calm joy of flowers and living leaves
Before the wind or sun has withered them
And semivital worms; but he refused
The birthright of their being, knowledge, power,
The skill which wields the elements, the thought
Which pierces this dim universe like light,
Self-empire, and the majesty of love;
For thirst of which they fainted. Then Prometheus
Gave wisdom, which is strength, to Jupiter,
And with this law alone, 'Let man be free,'
Clothed him with the dominion of wide Heaven.
To know nor faith, nor love, nor law; to be
Omnipotent but friendless is to reign;
And Jove now reigned; for on the race of man
First famine, and then toil, and then disease,
Strife, wounds, and ghastly death unseen before,
Fell; and the unseasonable seasons drove
With alternating shafts of frost and fire,
Their shelterless, pale tribes to mountain caves:
And in their desert hearts fierce wants he sent,
And mad disquietudes, and shadows idle
Of unreal good, which levied mutual war,
So ruining the lair wherein they raged.
Prometheus saw, and waked the legioned hopes
Which sleep within folded Elysian flowers,
Nepenthe, Moly, Amaranth, fadeless blooms,
That they might hide with thin and rainbow wings
The shape of Death; and Love he sent to bind
The disunited tendrils of that vine
Which bears the wine of life, the human heart;
And he tamed fire which, like some beast of prey,
Most terrible, but lovely, played beneath
The frown of man; and tortured to his will
Iron and gold, the slaves and signs of power,
And gems and poisons, and all subtlest forms
Hidden beneath the mountains and the waves.
He gave man speech, and speech created thought,
Which is the measure of the universe;
And Science struck the thrones of earth and heaven,
Which shook, but fell not; and the harmonious mind
Poured itself forth in all-prophetic song;
And music lifted up the listening spirit
Until it walked, exempt from mortal care.
Godlike, o'er the clear billows of sweet sound;
And human hands first mimicked and then mocked,
With moulded limbs more lovely than its own,
The human form, till marble grew divine;
And mothers, gazing, drank the love men see
Reflected in their race, behold, and perish.
He told the hidden power of herbs and springs,
And Disease drank and slept. Death grew like sleep.
He taught the implicated orbits woven
Of the wide-wandering stars; and how the sun
Changes his lair, and by what secret spell
The pale moon is transformed, when her broad eye
Gazes not on the interlunar sea:
He taught to rule, as life directs the limbs,
The tempest-wingèd chariots of the Ocean,
And the Celt knew the Indian. Cities then
Were built, and through their snow-like columns flowed
The warm winds, and the azure aether shone,
And the blue sea and shadowy hills were seen.
Such, the alleviations of his state,
Prometheus gave to man, for which he hangs
Withering in destined pain: but who rains down
Evil, the immedicable plague, which, while
Man looks on his creation like a God
And sees that it is glorious, drives him on,
The wreck of his own will, the scorn of earth,
The outcast, the abandoned, the alone?
Not Jove: while yet his frown shook Heaven, ay, when
His adversary from adamantine chains
Cursed him, he trembled like a slave. Declare
Who is his master? Is he too a slave?

DEMOGORGON: All spirits are enslaved which serve things evil:
Thou knowest if Jupiter be such or no.

ASIA: Whom calledst thou God?

DEMOGORGON: I spoke but as ye speak,
For Jove is the supreme of living things.

ASIA: Who is the master of the slave?

DEMOGORGON: If the abysm
Could vomit forth its secrets. . . . But a voice
Is wanting, the deep truth is imageless;
For what would it avail to bid thee gaze
On the revolving world? What to bid speak
Fate, Time, Occasion, Chance, and Change? To these
All things are subject but eternal Love.

ASIA: So much I asked before, and my heart gave
The response thou hast given; and of such truths

Each to itself must be the oracle.
One more demand; and do thou answer me
As mine own soul would answer, did it know
That which I ask. Prometheus shall arise
Henceforth the sun of this rejoicing world:
When shall the destined hour arrive?

DEMOGORGON: Behold!

ASIA: The rocks are cloven, and through the purple night
I see cars drawn by rainbow-wingèd steeds
Which trample the dim winds: in each there stands
A wild-eyed charioteer urging their flight.
Some look behind, as fiends pursued them there,
And yet I see no shapes but the keen stars:
Others, with burning eyes, lean forth, and drink
With eager lips the wind of their own speed,
As if the thing they loved fled on before,
And now, even now, they clasped it. Their bright locks
Stream like a comet's flashing hair: they all
Sweep onward.

DEMOGORGON: These are the immortal Hours,
Of whom thou didst demand. One waits for thee.

ASIA: A spirit with a dreadful countenance
Checks its dark chariot by the craggy gulf.
Unlike thy brethren, ghastly charioteer,
Who art thou? Whither wouldst thou bear me? Speak!

SPIRIT: I am the shadow of a destiny
More dread than is my aspect: ere yon planet
Has set, the darkness which ascends with me
Shall wrap in lasting night heaven's kingless throne.

ASIA: What meanest thou?

PANTHEA: That terrible shadow floats
Up from its throne, as may the lurid smoke
Of earthquake-ruined cities o'er the sea.
Lo! it ascends the car; the coursers fly
Terrified: watch its path among the stars
Blackening the night!

ASIA: Thus I am answered: strange!

PANTHEA: See, near the verge, another chariot stays;
An ivory shell inlaid with crimson fire,
Which comes and goes within its sculptured rim
Of delicate strange tracery; the young spirit
That guides it has the dove-like eyes of hope;
How its soft smiles attract the soul! as light
Lures wingèd insects through the lampless air.

SPIRIT:

My coursers are fed with the lightning,
They drink of the whirlwind's stream,
And when the red morning is bright'ning
They bathe in the fresh sunbeam;
They have strength for their swiftness I deem,
Then ascend with me, daughter of Ocean.
I desire: and their speed makes night kindle;
I fear: they outstrip the Typhoon;
Ere the cloud piled on Atlas can dwindle
We encircle the earth and the moon:
We shall rest from long labours at noon:
Then ascend with me, daughter of Ocean.

— SCENE V —

(*The Car pauses within a Cloud on the top of a snowy Mountain.* ASIA, PANTHEA, *and the* SPIRIT OF THE HOUR.)

SPIRIT:

On the brink of the night and the morning
My coursers are wont to respire;[26]
But the Earth has just whispered a warning
That their flight must be swifter than fire:
They shall drink the hot speed of desire!

ASIA: Thou breathest on their nostrils, but my breath
Would give them swifter speed.

SPIRIT: Alas! it could not.

PANTHEA: Oh Spirit! pause, and tell whence is the light
Which fills this cloud? the sun is yet unrisen.

SPIRIT: The sun will rise not until noon. Apollo
Is held in heaven by wonder; and the light
Which fills this vapour, as the aëreal hue
Of fountain-gazing roses fills the water,
Flows from thy mighty sister.

PANTHEA: Yes, I feel—

ASIA: What is it with thee, sister? Thou art pale.

PANTHEA: How thou art changed! I dare not look on thee;
I feel but see thee not. I scarce endure
The radiance of thy beauty. Some good change
Is working in the elements, which suffer
Thy presence thus unveiled. The Nereids[27] tell
That on the day when the clear hyaline[28]
Was cloven at thine uprise, and thou didst stand

---

[26] **respire:** breathe, or catch one's breath after exertion.

[27] **Nereids:** the fifty daughters of Nereus, the god of the Aegean Sea.

[28] **clear hyaline:** glassy surface of a calm sea.

Within a veinèd shell, which floated on
Over the calm floor of the crystal sea,
Among the Ægean isles, and by the shores
Which bear thy name; love, like the atmosphere
Of the sun's fire filling the living world,
Burst from thee, and illumined earth and heaven
And the deep ocean and the sunless caves
And all that dwells within them; till grief cast
Eclipse upon the soul from which it came:
Such art thou now; nor is it I alone,
Thy sister, thy companion, thine own chosen one,
But the whole world which seeks thy sympathy.
Hearest thou not sounds i' the air which speak the
love
Of all articulate beings? Feelest thou not
The inanimate winds enamoured of thee? List!

(Music.)

ASIA: Thy words are sweeter than aught else but his
Whose echoes they are: yet all love is sweet,
Given or returned. Common as light is love,
And its familiar voice wearies not ever.
Like the wide heaven, the all-sustaining air,
It makes the reptile equal to the God:
They who inspire it most are fortunate,
As I am now; but those who feel it most
Are happier still, after long sufferings,
As I shall soon become.

PANTHEA: List! Spirits speak.

VOICE IN THE AIR, SINGING:

Life of Life! thy lips enkindle
With their love the breath between them;
And thy smiles before they dwindle
Make the cold air fire; then screen them
In those looks, where whoso gazes
Faints, entangled in their mazes.

Child of Light! thy limbs are burning
Through the vest which seems to hide
them;
As the radiant lines of morning
Through the clouds ere they divide them;
And this atmosphere divinest
Shrouds thee wheresoe'er thou shinest.

Fair are others; none beholds thee,
But thy voice sounds low and tender
Like the fairest, for it folds thee
From the sight, that liquid splendour,
And all feel, yet see thee never,
As I feel now, lost for ever!

Lamp of Earth! where'er thou movest
Its dim shapes are clad with brightness,
And the souls of whom thou lovest
Walk upon the winds with lightness,
Till they fail, as I am failing,
Dizzy, lost, yet unbewailing!

ASIA:

My soul is an enchanted boat,
Which, like a sleeping swan, doth float
Upon the silver waves of thy sweet singing;
And thine doth like an angel sit
Beside a helm conducting it,
Whilst all the winds with melody are ringing.
It seems to float ever, for ever,
Upon that many-winding river,
Between mountains, woods, abysses,
A paradise of wildernesses!
Till, like one in slumber bound,
Borne to the ocean, I float down, around,
Into a sea profound, of ever-spreading sound:

Meanwhile thy spirit lifts its pinions
In music's most serene dominions;
Catching the winds that fan that happy heaven.
And we sail on, away, afar,
Without a course, without a star,
But, by the instinct of sweet music driven;
Till through Elysian garden islets
By thee, most beautiful of pilots,
Where never mortal pinnace glided,
The boat of my desire is guided:
Realms where the air we breathe is love,
Which in the winds and on the waves doth
move,
Harmonizing this earth with what we feel
above.

We have passed Age's icy caves,
And Manhood's dark and tossing waves,
And Youth's smooth ocean, smiling to betray:
Beyond the glassy gulfs we flee
Of shadow-peopled Infancy,
Through Death and Birth, to a diviner day;
A paradise of vaulted bowers,
Lit by downward-gazing flowers,
And watery paths that wind between
Wildernesses calm and green,
Peopled by shapes too bright to see,
And rest, having beheld, somewhat like thee;
Which walk upon the sea, and chant
melodiously!

ACT III

— SCENE I —

(*Heaven.* JUPITER *on his Throne;* THETIS *and the other Deities assembled.*)

JUPITER: Ye congregated powers of heaven, who share
The glory and the strength of him ye serve,
Rejoice! henceforth I am omnipotent.
All else had been subdued to me; alone
The soul of man, like unextinguished fire,
Yet burns towards heaven with fierce reproach, and doubt,
And lamentation, and reluctant prayer,
Hurling up insurrection, which might make
Our antique empire insecure, though built
On eldest faith, and hell's coeval,[29] fear;
And though my curses through the pendulous[30] air,
Like snow on herbless peaks, fall flake by flake,
And cling to it; though under my wrath's night
It climbs the crags of life, step after step,
Which wound it, as ice wounds unsandalled feet,
It yet remains supreme o'er misery,
Aspiring, unrepressed, yet soon to fall:
Even now have I begotten a strange wonder,
That fatal child, the terror of the earth,
Who waits but till the destined hour arrive,
Bearing from Demogorgon's vacant throne
The dreadful might of ever-living limbs
Which clothed that awful spirit unbeheld,
To redescend, and trample out the spark.
Pour forth heaven's wine, Idaean Ganymede,[31]
And let it fill the Daedal[32] cups like fire,
And from the flower-inwoven soil divine
Ye all-triumphant harmonies arise,
As dew from earth under the twilight stars:
Drink! be the nectar circling through your veins
The soul of joy, ye ever-living Gods,
Till exultation burst in one wide voice
Like music from Elysian winds.
And thou
Ascend beside me, veilèd in the light
Of the desire which makes thee one with me,
Thetis, bright image of eternity!
When thou didst cry, 'Insufferable might!
God! Spare me! I sustain not the quick flames,
The penetrating presence; all my being,
Like him whom the Numidian seps[33] did thaw
Into a dew with poison, is dissolved,
Sinking through its foundations:' even then
Two mighty spirits, mingling, made a third
Mightier than either, which, unbodied now,
Between us floats, felt, although unbeheld,
Waiting the incarnation, which ascends,
(Hear ye the thunder of the fiery wheels
Griding[34] the winds?) from Demogorgon's throne.
Victory! victory! Feel'st thou not, O world,
The earthquake of his chariot thundering up
Olympus?

(*The Car of the* HOUR *arrives.* DEMOGORGON *descends, and moves towards the Throne of* JUPITER.)

Awful shape, what art thou? Speak!

DEMOGORGON: Eternity. Demand no direr name.
Descend, and follow me down the abyss.
I am thy child, as thou wert Saturn's child;
Mightier than thee: and we must dwell together
Henceforth in darkness. Lift thy lightnings not.
The tyranny of heaven none may retain,
Or reassume, or hold, succeeding thee:
Yet if thou wilt, as 'tis the destiny
Of trodden worms to writhe till they are dead,
Put forth thy might.

JUPITER: Detested prodigy!
Even thus beneath the deep Titanian prisons
I trample thee! thou lingerest?
Mercy! mercy!
No pity, no release, no respite! Oh,
That thou wouldst make mine enemy my judge,
Even where he hangs, seared by my long revenge,
On Caucasus! he would not doom me thus.
Gentle, and just, and dreadless, is he not

[29] **coeval**: existing during the same period of time.

[30] **pendulous**: wavering.

[31] **Idaean Ganymede**: a beautiful boy, in some accounts, carried off Mt. Ida by an eagle sent from Zeus to be his cupbearer.

[32] **Daedal**: intricately adorned, as if by the mythological craftsman, Daedalus, who created both a famous wooden cow and then the labyrinth for the mother of the monster Minataur.

[33] **Numidia**: formerly a country in north Africa. **Seps**: poisonous snake of the desert in Numidia.

[34] **Griding**: piercing, wounding.

The monarch of the world? What then art thou?
No refuge! no appeal!
Sink with me then,
We two will sink on the wide waves of ruin,
Even as a vulture and a snake outspent
Drop, twisted in inextricable fight,
Into a shoreless sea. Let hell unlock
Its mounded oceans of tempestuous fire,
And whelm on them into the bottomless void
This desolated world, and thee, and me,
The conqueror and the conquered, and the wreck
Of that for which they combated.
Ai! Ai!
The elements obey me not. I sink
Dizzily down, ever, for ever, down.
And, like a cloud, mine enemy above
Darkens my fall with victory! Ai, Ai!

— SCENE II —

(The Mouth of a great River in the Island Atlantis. OCEAN *is discovered reclining near the Shore;* APOLLO *stands beside him.)*

OCEAN: He fell, thou sayest, beneath his conqueror's frown?
APOLLO: Ay, when the strife was ended which made dim
The orb I rule, and shook the solid stars,
The terrors of his eye illumined heaven
With sanguine light, through the thick ragged skirts
Of the victorious darkness, as he fell:
Like the last glare of day's red agony,
Which, from a rent among the fiery clouds,
Burns far along the tempest-wrinkled deep.
OCEAN: He sunk to the abyss? To the dark void?
APOLLO: An eagle so caught in some bursting cloud
On Caucasus, his thunder-baffled wings
Entangled in the whirlwind, and his eyes
Which gazed on the undazzling sun, now blinded
By the white lightning, while the ponderous hail
Beats on his struggling form, which sinks at length
Prone, and the aëreal ice clings over it.
OCEAN: Henceforth the fields of heaven-reflecting sea
Which are my realm, will heave, unstained with blood,
Beneath the uplifting winds, like plains of corn
Swayed by the summer air, my streams will flow
Round many-peopled continents, and round
Fortunate isles; and from their glassy thrones
Blue Proteus[35] and his humid nymphs shall mark
The shadow of fair ships, as mortals see
The floating bark of the light-laden moon
With that white star, its sightless pilot's crest,
Borne down the rapid sunset's ebbing sea;
Tracking their path no more by blood and groans,
And desolation, and the mingled voice
Of slavery and command; but by the light
Of wave-reflected flowers, and floating odours,
And music soft, and mild, free, gentle voices,
And sweetest music, such as spirits love.
APOLLO: And I shall gaze not on the deeds which make
My mind obscure with sorrow, as eclipse
Darkens the sphere I guide; but list, I hear
The small, clear, silver lute of the young Spirit
That sits i' the morning star.
OCEAN: Thou must away;
Thy steeds will pause at even, till when farewell:
The loud deep calls me home even now to feed it
With azure calm out of the emerald urns
Which stand for ever full beside my throne.
Behold the Nereids under the green sea,
Their wavering limbs borne on the wind-like stream,
Their white arms lifted o'er their streaming hair
With garlands pied and starry sea-flower crowns,
Hastening to grace their mighty sister's joy.

(A sound of waves is heard.)

It is the unpastured sea hungering for calm.
Peace, monster; I come now. Farewell.
APOLLO: Farewell.

— SCENE III —

(Caucasus. PROMETHEUS, HERCULES, IONE, *the* EARTH, SPIRITS, ASIA, *and* PANTHEA, *borne in the Car with the* SPIRIT OF THE HOUR. HERCULES *unbinds* PROMETHEUS, *who descends.)*

HERCULES: Most glorious among Spirits, thus doth strength
To wisdom, courage, and long-suffering love,

[35]**Proteus:** minor sea god; servant to Poseidon and keeper of the herds of the sea.

And thee, who art the form they animate,
Minister like a slave.

PROMETHEUS: Thy gentle words
Are sweeter even than freedom long desired
And long delayed.
Asia, thou light of life,
Shadow of beauty unbeheld: and ye,
Fair sister nymphs, who made long years of pain
Sweet to remember, through your love and care:
Henceforth we will not part. There is a cave,
All overgrown with trailing odorous plants,
Which curtain out the day with leaves and flowers,
And paved with veinèd emerald, and a fountain
Leaps in the midst with an awakening sound.
From its curved roof the mountain's frozen tears
Like snow, or silver, or long diamond spires,
Hang downward, raining forth a doubtful light:
And there is heard the ever-moving air,
Whispering without from tree to tree, and birds,
And bees; and all around are mossy seats,
And the rough walls are clothed with long soft grass;
A simple dwelling, which shall be our own,
Where we will sit and talk of time and change,
As the world ebbs and flows, ourselves unchanged.[36]
What can hide man from mutability?
And if ye sigh, then I will smile; and thou,
Ione, shalt chant fragments of sea-music,
Until I weep, when ye shall smile away
The tears she brought, which yet were sweet to shed.
We will entangle buds and flowers and beams
Which twinkle on the fountain's brim, and make
Strange combinations out of common things,
Like human babes in their brief innocence;
And we will search, with looks and words of love,
For hidden thoughts, each lovelier than the last,
Our unexhausted spirits; and like lutes
Touched by the skill of the enamoured wind,
Weave harmonies divine, yet ever new,
From difference sweet where discord cannot be;
And hither come, sped on the charmèd winds,
Which meet from all the points of heaven, as bees
From every flower aëreal Enna feeds,
At their known island-homes in Himera,[37]
The echoes of the human world, which tell
Of the low voice of love, almost unheard,
And dove-eyed pity's murmured pain, and music,
Itself the echo of the heart, and all
That tempers or improves man's life, now free;
And lovely apparitions,—dim at first,
Then radiant, as the mind, arising bright
From the embrace of beauty (whence the forms
Of which these are the phantoms) casts on them
The gathered rays which are reality—
Shall visit us, the progeny immortal
Of Painting, Sculpture, and rapt Poesy,
And arts, though unimagined, yet to be.
The wandering voices and the shadows these
Of all that man becomes, the mediators
Of that best worship love, by him and us
Given and returned; swift shapes and sounds, which grow
More fair and soft as man grows wise and kind,
And, veil by veil, evil and error fall:
Such virtue has the cave and place around.

(*Turning to the* SPIRIT OF THE HOUR.)

For thee, fair Spirit, one toil remains. Ione,
Give her that curvèd shell, which Proteus old
Made Asia's nuptial boon, breathing within it
A voice to be accomplished, and which thou
Didst hide in grass under the hollow rock.

IONE: Thou most desired Hour, more loved and lovely
Than all thy sisters, this is the mystic shell;
See the pale azure fading into silver
Lining it with a soft yet glowing light:
Looks it not like lulled music sleeping there?

SPIRIT: It seems in truth the fairest shell of Ocean:
Its sound must be at once both sweet and strange.

PROMETHEUS: Go, borne over the cities of mankind
On whirlwind-footed coursers: once again
Outspeed the sun around the orbèd world;
And as thy chariot cleaves the kindling air,
Thou breathe into the many-folded shell,

[36] **we will sit . . . ourselves unchanged:** *King Lear,* V.iii.8–19: "We two alone will sing like birds i' th' cage" and talk with rogues of "Who loses and who wins; who's in, who's out. . . ."

[37] **Enna:** known for its flowery groves and worship of Demeter. Pluto carried off Prosperpine from one of its meadows. **Himera:** formerly on the north coast of Sicily.

Loosening its mighty music; it shall be
As thunder mingled with clear echoes: then
Return; and thou shalt dwell beside our cave.
And thou, O, Mother Earth!—

THE EARTH: I hear, I feel;
Thy lips are on me, and their touch runs down
Even to the adamantine central gloom
Along these marble nerves; 'tis life, 'tis joy,
And through my withered, old, and icy frame
The warmth of an immortal youth shoots down
Circling. Henceforth the many children fair
Folded in my sustaining arms; all plants,
And creeping forms, and insects rainbow-winged,
And birds, and beasts, and fish, and human shapes,
Which drew disease and pain from my wan bosom,
Draining the poison of despair, shall take
And interchange sweet nutriment; to me
Shall they become like sister-antelopes
By one fair dam, snow-white and swift as wind,
Nursed among lilies near a brimming stream.
The dew-mists of my sunless sleep shall float
Under the stars like balm: night-folded flowers
Shall suck unwithering hues in their repose:
And men and beasts in happy dreams shall gather
Strength for the coming day, and all its joy:
And death shall be the last embrace of her
Who takes the life she gave, even as a mother
Folding her child, says, 'Leave me not again.'

ASIA: Oh, mother! wherefore speak the name of death?
Cease they to love, and move, and breathe, and speak,
Who die?

THE EARTH: It would avail not to reply:
Thou art immortal, and this tongue is known
But to the uncommunicating dead.
Death is the veil which those who live call life:
They sleep, and it is lifted: and meanwhile
In mild variety the seasons mild
With rainbow-skirted showers, and odorous winds,
And long blue meteors cleansing the dull night,
And the life-kindling shafts of the keen sun's
All-piercing bow, and the dew-mingled rain
Of the calm moonbeams, a soft influence mild,
Shall clothe the forests and the fields, ay, even
The crag-built deserts of the barren deep,
With ever-living leaves, and fruits, and flowers.
And thou! There is a cavern where my spirit
Was panted forth in anguish whilst thy pain
Made my heart mad, and those who did inhale it
Became mad too, and built a temple there,
And spoke, and were oracular, and lured
The erring nations round to mutual war,
And faithless faith, such as Jove kept with thee;
Which breath now rises, as amongst tall weeds
A violet's exhalation, and it fills
With a serener light and crimson air
Intense, yet soft, the rocks and woods around;
It feeds the quick growth of the serpent vine,
And the dark linkèd ivy tangling wild,
And budding, blown, or odour-faded blooms
Which star the winds with points of coloured light,
As they rain through them, and bright golden globes
Of fruit, suspended in their own green heaven,
And through their veinèd leaves and amber stems
The flowers whose purple and translucid bowls
Stand ever mantling with aëreal dew,
The drink of spirits: and it circles round,
Like the soft waving wings of noonday dreams,
Inspiring calm and happy thoughts, like mine,
Now thou art thus restored. This cave is thine.
Arise! Appear!

(A SPIRIT *rises in the likeness of a winged child.*)

This is my torch-bearer;
Who let his lamp out in old time with gazing
On eyes from which he kindled it anew
With love, which is as fire, sweet daughter mine,
For such is that within thine own. Run, wayward,
And guide this company beyond the peak
Of Bacchic Nysa, Maenad-haunted mountain,
And beyond Indus and its tribute rivers,
Trampling the torrent streams and glassy lakes
With feet unwet, unwearied, undelaying,
And up the green ravine, across the vale,
Beside the windless and crystalline pool,
Where ever lies, on unerasing waves,
The image of a temple, built above,
Distinct with column, arch, and architrave,[38]
And palm-like capital, and over-wrought,
And populous with most living imagery,

[38] **architrave:** architectural term for the lower part of an entablature, or section of a building that extends between the roof and supporting columns.

Praxitelean[39] shapes, whose marble smiles
Fill the hushed air with everlasting love.
It is deserted now, but once it bore
Thy name, Prometheus; there the emulous youths
Bore to thy honour through the divine gloom
The lamp which was thine emblem; even as those
Who bear the untransmitted torch of hope
Into the grave, across the night of life,
As thou hast borne it most triumphantly
To this far goal of Time. Depart, farewell.
Beside that temple is the destined cave.

SCENE IV

(A Forest. In the Background a Cave. PROMETHEUS, ASIA, PANTHEA, IONE, *and the* SPIRIT OF THE EARTH.*)*

IONE: Sister, it is not earthly: how it glides
Under the leaves! how on its head there burns
A light, like a green star, whose emerald beams
Are twined with its fair hair! how, as it moves,
The splendour drops in flakes upon the grass!
Knowest thou it?
PANTHEA: It is the delicate spirit
That guides the earth through heaven. From afar
The populous constellations call that light
The loveliest of the planets; and sometimes
It floats along the spray of the salt sea,
Or makes its chariot of a foggy cloud,
Or walks through fields or cities while men sleep,
Or o'er the mountain tops, or down the rivers,
Or through the green waste wilderness, as now,
Wondering at all it sees. Before Jove reigned
It loved our sister Asia, and it came
Each leisure hour to drink the liquid light
Out of her eyes, for which it said it thirsted
As one bit by a dipsas,[40] and with her
It made its childish confidence, and told her
All it had known or seen, for it saw much,
Yet idly reasoned what it saw; and called her—
For whence it sprung it knew not, nor do I—
Mother, dear mother.
THE SPIRIT OF THE EARTH *(running to* ASIA*)*: Mother,
dearest mother;
May I then talk with thee as I was wont?
May I then hide my eyes in thy soft arms,
After thy looks have made them tired of joy?
May I then play beside thee the long noons,
When work is none in the bright silent air?
ASIA: I love thee, gentlest being, and henceforth
Can cherish thee unenvied: speak, I pray:
Thy simple talk once solaced, now delights.
SPIRIT OF THE EARTH: Mother, I am grown wiser,
though a child
Cannot be wise like thee, within this day;
And happier too; happier and wiser both.
Thou knowest that toads, and snakes, and loathly
worms,
And venomous and malicious beasts, and boughs
That bore ill berries in the woods, were ever
An hindrance to my walks o'er the green world:
And that, among the haunts of humankind,
Hard-featured men, or with proud, angry looks,
Or cold, staid gait, or false and hollow smiles,
Or the dull sneer of self-loved ignorance,
Or other such foul masks, with which ill thoughts
Hide that fair being whom we spirits call man;
And women too, ugliest of all things evil,
(Though fair, even in a world where thou art fair,
When good and kind, free and sincere like thee),
When false or frowning made me sick at heart
To pass them, though they slept, and I unseen.
Well, my path lately lay through a great city
Into the woody hills surrounding it:
A sentinel was sleeping at the gate:
When there was heard a sound, so loud, it shook
The towers amid the moonlight, yet more sweet
Than any voice but thine, sweetest of all;
A long, long sound, as it would never end:
And all the inhabitants leaped suddenly
Out of their rest, and gathered in the streets,
Looking in wonder up to Heaven, while yet
The music pealed along. I hid myself
Within a fountain in the public square,
Where I lay like the reflex of the moon
Seen in a wave under green leaves; and soon
Those ugly human shapes and visages
Of which I spoke as having wrought me pain,
Passed floating through the air, and fading still
Into the winds that scattered them; and those
From whom they passed seemed mild and lovely
forms
After some foul disguise had fallen, and all

[39] **Praxitelean:** from the great Greek sculptor of the fourth century BC.

[40] **dipsas:** poisonous snake whose bite creates a terrible thirst.

Were somewhat changed, and after brief surprise
And greetings of delighted wonder, all
Went to their sleep again: and when the dawn
Came, wouldst thou think that toads, and snakes,
and efts,[41]
Could e'er be beautiful? yet so they were,
And that with little change of shape or hue:
All things had put their evil nature off:
I cannot tell my joy, when o'er a lake
Upon a drooping bough with nightshade twined,
I saw two azure halcyons[42] clinging downward
And thinning one bright bunch of amber berries,
With quick long beaks, and in the deep there lay
Those lovely forms imaged as in a sky;
So, with my thoughts full of these happy changes,
We meet again, the happiest change of all.

ASIA: And never will we part, till thy chaste sister
Who guides the frozen and inconstant moon
Will look on thy more warm and equal light
Till her heart thaw like flakes of April snow
And love thee.

SPIRIT OF THE EARTH: What; as Asia loves
Prometheus?

ASIA: Peace, wanton, thou art yet not old enough.
Think ye by gazing on each other's eyes
To multiply your lovely selves, and fill
With spherèd fires the interlunar[43] air?

SPIRIT OF THE EARTH: Nay, mother, while my sister
trims her lamp
'Tis hard I should go darkling.

ASIA: Listen; look!

(*The* SPIRIT OF THE HOUR *enters.*)

PROMETHEUS: We feel what thou hast heard and seen:
yet speak.

SPIRIT OF THE HOUR: Soon as the sound had ceased
whose thunder filled
The abysses of the sky and the wide earth,
There was a change: the impalpable thin air
And the all-circling sunlight were transformed,
As if the sense of love dissolved in them
Had folded itself round the spherèd world.
My vision then grew clear, and I could see
Into the mysteries of the universe:
Dizzy as with delight I floated down,
Winnowing the lightsome air with languid plumes,
My coursers sought their birthplace in the sun,
Where they henceforth will live exempt from toil,
Pasturing flowers of vegetable fire;
And where my moonlike car will stand within
A temple, gazed upon by Phidian[44] forms
Of thee, and Asia, and the Earth, and me,
And you fair nymphs looking the love we feel,—
In memory of the tidings it has borne,—
Beneath a dome fretted with graven flowers,
Poised on twelve columns of resplendent stone,
And open to the bright and liquid sky.
Yoked to it by an amphisbaenic[45] snake
The likeness of those wingèd steeds will mock
The flight from which they find repose. Alas,
Whither has wandered now my partial tongue
When all remains untold which ye would hear?
As I have said, I floated to the earth:
It was, as it is still, the pain of bliss
To move, to breathe, to be; I wandering went
Among the haunts and dwellings of mankind,
And first was disappointed not to see
Such mighty change as I had felt within
Expressed in outward things; but soon I looked,
And behold, thrones were kingless, and men walked
One with the other even as spirits do,
None fawned, none trampled; hate, disdain, or fear,
Self-love or self-contempt, on human brows
No more inscribed, as o'er the gate of hell,
'All hope abandon ye who enter here;'[46]
None frowned, none trembled, none with eager fear
Gazed on another's eye of cold command,
Until the subject of a tyrant's will
Became, worse fate, the abject of his own,
Which spurred him, like an outspent horse, to death.
None wrought his lips in truth-entangling lines
Which smiled the lie his tongue disdained to speak;
None, with firm sneer, trod out in his own heart

[41] **efts:** lizards.

[42] **halcyons:** kingfishers.

[43] **interlunar:** of the four-day period when the moon is not visible.

[44] **Phidias:** the most famous sculptor and architect of ancient Greece, having designed the Parthenon and the statue of Athena within.

[45] **amphisbaenic snake:** serpent with a head at each end of its body.

[46] **'All hope . . . here':** written above the gate of hell in Dante's *Inferno* (III.9).

The sparks of love and hope till there remained
Those bitter ashes, a soul self-consumed,
And the wretch crept a vampire among men,
Infecting all with his own hideous ill;
None talked that common, false, cold, hollow talk
Which makes the heart deny the *yes* it breathes,
Yet question that unmeant hypocrisy
With such a self-mistrust as has no name.
And women, too, frank, beautiful, and kind
As the free heaven which rains fresh light and dew
On the wide earth, past; gentle radiant forms,
From custom's evil taint exempt and pure;
Speaking the wisdom once they could not think,
Looking emotions once they feared to feel,
And changed to all which once they dared not be,
Yet being now, made earth like heaven; nor pride,
Nor jealousy, nor envy, nor ill shame,
The bitterest of those drops of treasured gall,
Spoilt the sweet taste of the nepenthe,[47] love.

Thrones, altars, judgement-seats, and prisons; wherein,
And beside which, by wretched men were borne
Sceptres, tiaras, swords, and chains, and tomes
Of reasoned wrong, glozed[48] on by ignorance,
Were like those monstrous and barbaric shapes,
The ghosts of a no-more-remembered fame,
Which, from their unworn obelisks, look forth
In triumph o'er the palaces and tombs
Of those who were their conquerors: mouldering round,
These imaged to the pride of kings and priests
A dark yet mighty faith, a power as wide
As is the world it wasted, and are now
But an astonishment; even so the tools
And emblems of its last captivity,
Amid the dwellings of the peopled earth,
Stand, not o'erthrown, but unregarded now.
And those foul shapes, abhorred by god and man,—
Which, under many a name and many a form
Strange, savage, ghastly, dark and execrable,
Were Jupiter, the tyrant of the world;
And which the nations, panic-stricken, served
With blood, and hearts broken by long hope, and love
Dragged to his altars soiled and garlandless,
And slain amid men's unreclaiming tears,
Flattering the thing they feared, which fear was hate,—
Frown, mouldering fast, o'er their abandoned shrines:
The painted veil, by those who were, called life,
Which mimicked, as with colours idly spread,
All men believed or hoped, is torn aside;
The loathsome mask has fallen, the man remains
Sceptreless, free, uncircumscribed, but man
Equal, unclassed, tribeless, and nationless,
Exempt from awe, worship, degree, the king
Over himself; just, gentle, wise: but man
Passionless?——no, yet free from guilt or pain,
Which were, for his will made or suffered them,
Nor yet exempt, though ruling them like slaves,
From chance, and death, and mutability,
The clogs of that which else might oversoar
The loftiest star of unascended heaven,
Pinnacled dim in the intense inane.

ACT IV

(SCENE—*A Part of the Forest near the Cave of* PROMETHEUS. PANTHEA *and* IONE *are sleeping: they awaken gradually during the first Song.*)

VOICE OF UNSEEN SPIRITS:

The pale stars are gone!
For the sun, their swift shepherd,
To their folds them compelling,
In the depths of the dawn,
Hastes, in meteor-eclipsing array, and they flee
Beyond his blue dwelling,
As fawns flee the leopard.
But where are ye?

(*A Train of dark Forms and Shadows passes by confusedly, singing.*)

Here, oh, here:
We bear the bier[49]
Of the Father of many a cancelled year

[47] **nepenthe:** drug that causes forgetfulness.
[48] **glozed:** flattered.

[49] **bier:** stand upon which a coffin is placed.

Spectres we
Of the dead Hours be,
We bear Time to his tomb in eternity.

Strew, oh, strew
Hair, not yew!
Wet the dusty pall with tears, not dew!
Be the faded flowers
Of Death's bare bowers
Spread on the corpse of the King of Hours!

Haste, oh, haste!
As shades are chased,
Trembling, by day, from heaven's blue waste.
We melt away,
Like dissolving spray,
From the children of a diviner day,
With the lullaby
Of winds that die
On the bosom of their own harmony!

IONE:
What dark forms were they?

PANTHEA:
The past Hours weak and gray,
With the spoil which their toil
Raked together
From the conquest but One could foil.

IONE:
Have they passed?

PANTHEA:
They have passed;
They outspeeded the blast,
While 'tis said, they are fled:

IONE:
Whither, oh, whither?

PANTHEA:
To the dark, to the past, to the dead.

VOICE OF UNSEEN SPIRITS:
Bright clouds float in heaven,
Dew-stars gleam on earth,
Waves assemble on ocean,
They are gathered and driven
By the storm of delight, by the panic of glee!
They shake with emotion,
They dance in their mirth.
But where are ye?

The pine boughs are singing
Old songs with new gladness,
The billows and fountains
Fresh music are flinging,
Like the notes of a spirit from land and from sea;
The storms mock the mountains
With the thunder of gladness.
But where are ye?

IONE:
What charioteers are these?

PANTHEA:
Where are their chariots?

SEMICHORUS OF HOURS:
The voice of the Spirits of Air and of Earth
Have drawn back the figured curtain of sleep
Which covered our being and darkened our birth
In the deep.

A VOICE:
In the deep?

SEMICHORUS II:
Oh, below the deep.

SEMICHORUS I:
An hundred ages we had been kept
Cradled in visions of hate and care,
And each one who waked as his brother slept,
Found the truth—

SEMICHORUS II:
Worse than his visions were!

SEMICHORUS I:
We have heard the lute of Hope in sleep;
We have known the voice of Love in dreams;
We have felt the wand of Power, and leap—

SEMICHORUS II:
As the billows leap in the morning beams!

CHORUS:
Weave the dance on the floor of the breeze,
Pierce with song heaven's silent light,
Enchant the day that too swiftly flees,
To check its flight ere the cave of Night.

Once the hungry Hours were hounds
Which chased the day like a bleeding dear,
And it limped and stumbled with many wounds
Through the nightly dells of the desert year.

But now, oh weave the mystic measure
Of music, and dance, and shapes of light,
Let the Hours, and the spirits of might and pleasure,
Like the clouds and sunbeams, unite.

A VOICE:

Unite!

PANTHEA: See, where the Spirits of the human mind
Wrapped in sweet sounds, as in bright veils, approach.

CHORUS OF SPIRITS:

We join the throng
Of the dance and the song,
By the whirlwind of gladness borne along;
As the flying-fish leap
From the Indian deep,
And mix with the sea-birds, half asleep.

CHORUS OF HOURS:

Whence come ye, so wild and so fleet,
For sandals of lightning are on your feet,
And your wings are soft and swift as thought,
And your eyes are as love which is veilèd not?

CHORUS OF SPIRITS: Dramatic representation of the mind

We come from the mind
Of human kind
Which was late so dusk, and obscene, and blind,
Now 'tis an ocean
Of clear emotion,
A heaven of serene and mighty motion.

From that deep abyss
Of wonder and bliss,
Whose caverns are crystal palaces;
From those skiey towers
Where Thought's crowned powers
Sit watching your dance, ye happy Hours!

From the dim recesses
Of woven caresses,
Where lovers catch ye by your loose tresses
From the azure isles,
Where sweet Wisdom smiles,
Delaying your ships with her siren wiles.

From the temples high
Of Man's ear and eye,
Roofed over Sculpture and Poesy;
From the murmurings
Of the unsealed springs
Where Science bedews her Daedal wings.

Years after years,
Through blood, and tears,
And a thick hell of hatreds, and hopes, and fears;
We waded and flew,
And the islets were few
Where the bud-blighted flowers of happiness grew.

Our feet now, every palm,
Are sandalled with calm,
And the dew of our wings is a rain of balm;
And, beyond our eyes,
The human love lies
Which makes all it gazes on Paradise.

CHORUS OF SPIRITS AND HOURS:

Then weave the web of the mystic measure;
From the depths of the sky and the ends of the earth,
Come, swift Spirits of might and of pleasure,
Fill the dance and the music of mirth,
As the waves of a thousand streams rush by
To an ocean of splendour and harmony!

CHORUS OF SPIRITS:

Our spoil is won,
Our task is done,
We are free to dive, or soar, or run;
Beyond and around,
Or within the bound
Which clips the world with darkness round.

We'll pass the eyes
Of the starry skies
Into the hoar deep to colonize:
Death, Chaos, and Night,
From the sound of our flight,
Shall flee, like mist from a tempest's might.

And Earth, Air, and Light,
And the Spirit of Might,
Which drives round the stars in their fiery flight;
And Love, Thought, and Breath,
The powers that quell Death,
Wherever we soar shall assemble beneath.

And our singing shall build
In the void's loose field
A world for the Spirit of Wisdom to wield;
We will take our plan
From the new world of man,
And our work shall be called the Promethean.

CHORUS OF HOURS:

Break the dance, and scatter the song;
Let some depart, and some remain.

SEMICHORUS I:
We, beyond heaven, are driven along:

SEMICHORUS II:
Us the enchantments of earth retain:

SEMICHORUS I:
Ceaseless, and rapid, and fierce, and free,
With the Spirits which build a new earth and sea,
And a heaven where yet heaven could never be.

SEMICHORUS II:
Solemn, and slow, and serene, and bright,
Leading the Day and outspeeding the Night,
With the powers of a world of perfect light.

SEMICHORUS I:
We whirl, singing loud, round the gathering sphere,
Till the trees, and the beasts, and the clouds appear
From its chaos made calm by love, not fear.

SEMICHORUS II:
We encircle the ocean and mountains of earth,
And the happy forms of its death and birth
Change to the music of our sweet mirth.

CHORUS OF HOURS AND SPIRITS:
Break the dance, and scatter the song,
Let some depart, and some remain,
Wherever we fly we lead along
In leashes, like starbeams, soft yet strong,
The clouds that are heavy with love's sweet rain.

PANTHEA: Ha! they are gone!

IONE: Yet feel you no delight
From the past sweetness?

PANTHEA: As the bare green hill
When some soft cloud vanishes into rain,
Laughs with a thousand drops of sunny water
To the unpavilioned sky!

IONE: Even whilst we speak
New notes arise. What is that awful sound?

PANTHEA: 'Tis the deep music of the rolling world
Kindling within the strings of the waved air
Aeolian modulations.

IONE: Listen, too,
How every pause is filled with under-notes,
Clear, silver, icy, keen, awakening tones,
Which pierce the sense, and live within the soul,
As the sharp stars pierce winter's crystal air
And gaze upon themselves within the sea.

PANTHEA: But see where through two openings in the forest
Which hanging branches overcanopy,
And where two runnels of a rivulet,
Between the close moss violet-inwoven,
Have made their path of melody, like sisters
Who part with sighs that they may meet in smiles,
Turning their dear disunion to an isle
Of lovely grief, a wood of sweet sad thoughts;
Two visions of strange radiance float upon
The ocean-like enchantment of strong sound,
Which flows intenser, keener, deeper yet
Under the ground and through the windless air.

IONE: I see a chariot like that thinnest boat,
In which the Mother of the Months is borne
By ebbing light into her western cave,
When she upsprings from interlunar dreams;
O'er which is curved an orblike canopy
Of gentle darkness, and the hills and woods,
Distinctly seen through that dusk aery veil,
Regard like shapes in an enchanter's glass;
Its wheels are solid clouds, azure and gold,
Such as the genii of the thunderstorm
Pile on the floor of the illumined sea
When the sun rushes under it; they roll
And move and grow as with an inward wind;
Within it sits a wingèd infant, white
Its countenance, like the whiteness of bright snow,
Its plumes are as feathers of sunny frost,
Its limbs gleam white, through the wind-flowing folds
Of its white robe, woof of ethereal pearl.
Its hair is white, the brightness of white light
Scattered in strings; yet its two eyes are heavens
Of liquid darkness, which the Deity
Within seems pouring, as a storm is poured
From jaggèd clouds, out of their arrowy lashes,
Tempering the cold and radiant air around,
With fire that is not brightness; in its hand
It sways a quivering moonbeam, from whose point
A guiding power directs the chariot's prow
Over its wheelèd clouds, which as they roll
Over the grass, and flowers, and waves, wake sounds,
Sweet as a singing rain of silver dew.

PANTHEA: And from the other opening in the wood
Rushes, with loud and whirlwind harmony,
A sphere, which is as many thousand spheres,
Solid as crystal, yet through all its mass
Flow, as through empty space, music and light:

Ten thousand orbs involving and involved,
Purple and azure, white, and green, and golden,
Sphere within sphere; and every space between
Peopled with unimaginable shapes,
Such as ghosts dream dwell in the lampless deep,
Yet each inter-transpicuous, and they whirl
Over each other with a thousand motions,
Upon a thousand sightless axles spinning,
And with the force of self-destroying swiftness,
Intensely, slowly, solemnly roll on,
Kindling with mingled sounds, and many tones,
Intelligible words and music wild.
With mighty whirl the multitudinous orb
Grinds the bright brook into an azure mist
Of elemental subtlety, like light;
And the wild odour of the forest flowers,
The music of the living grass and air,
The emerald light of leaf-entangled beams
Round its intense yet self-conflicting speed,
Seem kneaded into one aëreal mass
Which drowns the sense. Within the orb itself,
Pillowed upon its alabaster arms,
Like to a child o'erwearied with sweet toil,
On its own folded wings, and wavy hair,
The Spirit of the Earth is laid asleep,
And you can see its little lips are moving,
Amid the changing light of their own smiles,
Like one who talks of what he loves in dream.

IONE: 'Tis only mocking the orb's harmony.

PANTHEA: And from a star upon its forehead, shoot,
Like swords of azure fire, or golden spears
With tyrant-quelling myrtle overtwined,
Embleming heaven and earth united now,
Vast beams like spokes of some invisible wheel
Which whirl as the orb whirls, swifter than
thought,
Filling the abyss with sun-like lightenings,
And perpendicular now, and now transverse,
Pierce the dark soil, and as they pierce and pass,
Make bare the secrets of the earth's deep heart;
Infinite mines of adamant and gold,
Valueless stones, and unimagined gems,
And caverns on crystalline columns poised
With vegetable silver overspread;
Wells of unfathomed fire, and water springs
Whence the great sea, even as a child is fed,
Whose vapours clothe earth's monarch mountain-
tops
With kingly, ermine snow. The beams flash on
And make appear the melancholy ruins
Of cancelled cycles; anchors, beaks of ships;
Planks turned to marble; quivers, helms, and spears,
And gorgon-headed targes,[50] and the wheels
Of scythèd chariots,[51] and the emblazonry
Of trophies, standards, and armorial beasts,
Round which death laughed, sepulchred emblems
Of dead destruction, ruin within ruin!
The wrecks beside of many a city vast,
Whose population which the earth grew over
Was mortal, but not human; see, they lie,
Their monstrous works, and uncouth skeletons,
Their statues, homes and fanes; prodigious shapes
Huddled in gray annihilation, split,
Jammed in the hard, black deep; and over these,
The anatomies of unknown wingèd things,
And fishes which were isles of living scale,
And serpents, bony chains, twisted around
The iron crags, or within heaps of dust
To which the tortuous strength of their last pangs
Had crushed the iron crags; and over these
The jaggèd alligator, and the might
Of earth-convulsing behemoth, which once
Were monarch beasts, and on the slimy shores,
And weed-overgrown continents of earth,
Increased and multiplied like summer worms
On an abandoned corpse, till the blue globe
Wrapped deluge round it like a cloak, and they
Yelled, gasped, and were abolished; or some God
Whose throne was in a comet, passed, and cried,
'Be not!' And like my words they were no more.

THE EARTH:
The joy, the triumph, the delight, the madness!
The boundless, overflowing, bursting gladness,
The vaporous exultation not to be confined!
Ha! ha! the animation of delight
Which wraps me, like an atmosphere of light,
And bears me as a cloud is borne by its own wind.

THE MOON:
Brother mine, calm wanderer,
Happy globe of land and air,
Some Spirit is darted like a beam from thee,

[50] **gorgon-headed targes:** shields embossed with Gorgon heads, or women with hair of snakes.

[51] **scythèd chariots:** chariot with blades extending from the axles.

Which penetrates my frozen frame,
And passes with the warmth of flame,
With love, and odour, and deep melody
Through me, through me!

THE EARTH:

Ha! ha! the caverns of my hollow mountains,
My cloven fire-crags, sound-exulting fountains
Laugh with a vast and inextinguishable laughter.
The oceans, and the deserts, and the abysses,
And the deep air's unmeasured wildernesses,
Answer from all their clouds and billows, echoing after.

They cry aloud as I do. Sceptred curse,
Who all our green and azure universe
Threatenedst to muffle round with black destruction, sending
A solid cloud to rain hot thunderstones,
And splinter and knead down my children's bones,
All I bring forth, to one void mass battering and blending,—

Until each crag-like tower, and storied column,
Palace, and obelisk, and temple solemn,
My imperial mountains crowned with cloud, and snow, and fire;
My sea-like forests, every blade and blossom
Which finds a grave or cradle in my bosom,
Were stamped by thy strong hate into a lifeless mire:

How art thou sunk, withdrawn, covered, drunk up
By thirsty nothing, as the brackish cup
Drained by a desert-troop, a little drop for all;
And from beneath, around, within, above,
Filling thy void annihilation, love
Burst in like light on caves cloven by the thunder-ball.

THE MOON:

The snow upon my lifeless mountains
Is loosened into living fountains,
My solid oceans flow, and sing, and shine:
A spirit from my heart bursts forth,
It clothes with unexpected birth
My cold bare bosom: Oh! it must be thine
On mine, on mine!

Gazing on thee I feel, I know
Green stalks burst forth, and bright flowers grow,
And living shapes upon my bosom move:
Music is in the sea and air,
Wingèd clouds soar here and there,
Dark with the rain new buds are dreaming of:
'Tis love, all love!

THE EARTH:

It interpenetrates my granite mass,
Through tangled roots and trodden clay doth pass
Into the utmost leaves and delicatest flowers;
Upon the winds, among the clouds 'tis spread,
It wakes a life in the forgotten dead,
They breathe a spirit up from their obscurest bowers.

And like a storm bursting its cloudy prison
With thunder, and with whirlwind, has arisen
Out of the lampless caves of unimagined being:
With earthquake shock and swiftness making shiver
Thought's stagnant chaos, unremoved for ever,
Till hate, and fear, and pain, light-vanquished shadows, fleeing,

Leave Man, who was a many-sided mirror,
Which could distort to many a shape of error,
This true fair world of things, a sea reflecting love;
Which over all his kind, as the sun's heaven
Gliding o'er ocean, smooth, serene, and even,
Darting from starry depths radiance and life, doth move:

Leave Man, even as a leprous child is left,
Who follows a sick beast to some warm cleft
Of rocks, through which the might of healing springs is poured;
Then when it wanders home with rosy smile,
Unconscious, and its mother fears awhile
It is a spirit, then, weeps on her child restored.

Man, oh, not men! a chain of linkèd thought,
Of love and might to be divided not,
Compelling the elements with adamantine stress;
As the sun rules, even with a tyrant's gaze,
The unquiet republic of the maze
Of planets, struggling fierce towards heaven's free wilderness.

Man, one harmonious soul of many a soul,
Whose nature is its own divine control,

Where all things flow to all, as rivers to the sea;
Familiar acts are beautiful through love;
Labour, and pain, and grief, in life's green grove
Sport like tame beasts, none knew how gentle they could be!

His will, with all mean passions, bad delights,
And selfish cares, its trembling satellites,
A spirit ill to guide, but mighty to obey,
Is as a tempest-wingèd ship, whose helm
Love rules, through waves which dare not overwhelm,
Forcing life's wildest shores to own its sovereign sway.

All things confess his strength. Through the cold mass
Of marble and of colour his dreams pass;
Bright threads whence mothers weave the robes their children wear;
Language is a perpetual Orphic song,
Which rules with Daedal harmony a throng
Of thoughts and forms, which else senseless and shapeless were.

The lightning is his slave; heaven's utmost deep
Gives up her stars, and like a flock of sheep
They pass before his eye, are numbered, and roll on!
The tempest is his steed, he strides the air;
And the abyss shouts from her depth laid bare,
Heaven, hast thou secrets? Man unveils me; I have none.

THE MOON:

The shadow of white death has passed
From my path in heaven at last,
A clinging shroud of solid frost and sleep;
And through my newly-woven bowers,
Wander happy paramours,
Less mighty, but as mild as those who keep
Thy vales more deep.

THE EARTH:

As the dissolving warmth of dawn may fold
A half unfrozen dew-globe, green, and gold,
And crystalline, till it becomes a wingèd mist,
And wanders up the vault of the blue day,
Outlives the noon, and on the sun's last ray
Hangs o'er the sea, a fleece of fire and amethyst.

THE MOON:

Thou art folded, thou art lying
In the light which is undying
Of thine own joy, and heaven's smile divine;
All suns and constellations shower
On thee a light, a life, a power
Which doth array thy sphere; thou pourest thine
On mine, on mine!

THE EARTH:

I spin beneath my pyramid of night,
Which points into the heavens dreaming delight,
Murmuring victorious joy in my enchanted sleep;
As a youth lulled in love-dreams faintly sighing,
Under the shadow of his beauty lying,
Which round his rest a watch of light and warmth doth keep.

THE MOON:

As in the soft and sweet eclipse,
When soul meets soul on lovers' lips,
High hearts are calm, and brightest eyes are dull;
So when thy shadow falls on me,
Then am I mute and still, by thee
Covered; of thy love, Orb most beautiful,
Full, oh, too full!

Thou art speeding round the sun
Brightest world of many a one;
Green and azure sphere which shinest
With a light which is divinest
Among all the lamps of Heaven
To whom life and light is given;
I, thy crystal paramour[52]
Borne beside thee by a power
Like the polar Paradise,
Magnet-like of lovers' eyes;
I, a most enamoured maiden
Whose weak brain is overladen
With the pleasure of her love,

[52] **paramour**: lover.

Maniac-like around thee move
Gazing, an insatiate bride,
On thy form from every side
Like a Maenad, round the cup
Which Agave[53] lifted up
In the weird Cadmaean[54] forest.
Brother, wheresoe'er thou soarest
I must hurry, whirl and follow
Through the heavens wide and hollow,
Sheltered by the warm embrace
Of thy soul from hungry space,
Drinking from thy sense and sight
Beauty, majesty, and might,
As a lover or a chameleon
Grows like what it looks upon,
As a violet's gentle eye
Gazes on the azure sky
Until its hue grows like what it beholds,
As a gray and watery mist
Glows like solid amethyst
Athwart the western mountain it enfolds,
When the sunset sleeps
Upon its snow—

THE EARTH:

And the weak day weeps
That it should be so.
Oh, gentle Moon, the voice of thy delight
Falls on me like thy clear and tender light
Soothing the seaman, borne the summer night,
Through isles for ever calm;
Oh, gentle Moon, thy crystal accents pierce
The caverns of my pride's deep universe,
Charming the tiger joy, whose tramplings fierce
Made wounds which need thy balm.

PANTHEA: I rise as from a bath of sparkling water,
A bath of azure light, among dark rocks,
Out of the stream of sound.

IONE: Ah me! sweet sister,
The stream of sound has ebbed away from us,
And you pretend to rise out of its wave,
Because your words fall like the clear, soft dew
Shaken from a bathing wood-nymph's limbs and hair.

PANTHEA: Peace! peace! A mighty Power, which is as darkness,
Is rising out of Earth, and from the sky
Is showered like night, and from within the air
Bursts, like eclipse which had been gathered up
Into the pores of sunlight: the bright visions,
Wherein the singing spirits rode and shone,
Gleam like pale meteors through a watery night.

IONE: There is a sense of words upon mine ear.

PANTHEA: An universal sound like words: Oh, list!

DEMOGORGON:

Thou, Earth, calm empire of a happy soul,
Sphere of divinest shapes and harmonies
Beautiful orb! gathering as thou dost roll
The love which paves thy path along the skies:

THE EARTH:

I hear: I am as a drop of dew that dies.

DEMOGORGON:

Thou, Moon, which gazest on the nightly Earth
With wonder, as it gazes upon thee;
Whilst each to men, and beasts, and the swift birth
Of birds, is beauty, love, calm, harmony:

THE MOON:

I hear: I am a leaf shaken by thee!

DEMOGORGON:

Ye Kings of suns and stars, Daemons and Gods,
Aetherial Dominations, who possess
Elysian, windless, fortunate abodes
Beyond Heaven's constellated wilderness:

A VOICE FROM ABOVE:

Our great Republic hears, we are blest, and bless.

DEMOGORGON:

Ye happy Dead, whom beams of brightest verse
Are clouds to hide, not colours to portray,
Whether your nature is that universe
Which once ye saw and suffered—

A VOICE FROM BENEATH:

Or as they
Whom we have left, we change and pass away.

DEMOGORGON:

Ye elemental Genii, who have homes
From man's high mind even to the central stone

[53] **Agave:** daughter of Cadmus who became a maenad.

[54] **Cadmaean forest:** forest of Cadmus, legendary founder of Thebes.

Of sullen lead; from heaven's star-fretted domes
To the dull weed some sea-worm battens on:

A CONFUSED VOICE:
We hear: thy words waken Oblivion.

DEMOGORGON:
Spirits, whose homes are flesh: ye beasts and birds,
Ye worms, and fish; ye living leaves and buds;
Lightning and wind; and ye untameable herds,
Meteors and mists, which throng air's solitudes:—

A VOICE:
Thy voice to us is wind among still woods.

DEMOGORGON:
Man, who wert once a despot and a slave;
A dupe and a deceiver; a decay;
A traveller from the cradle to the grave
Through the dim night of this immortal day:

ALL:
Speak: thy strong words may never pass away.

DEMOGORGON:
This is the day, which down the void abysm
At the Earth-born's spell yawns for Heaven's despotism,
And Conquest is dragged captive through the deep:
Love, from its awful throne of patient power
In the wise heart, from the last giddy hour
Of dread endurance, from the slippery, steep,
And narrow verge of crag-like agony, springs
And folds over the world its healing wings.

Gentleness, Virtue, Wisdom, and Endurance,
These are the seals of that most firm assurance
Which bars the pit over Destruction's strength;
And if, with infirm hand, Eternity,
Mother of many acts and hours, should free
The serpent that would clasp her with his length;
These are the spells by which to reassume
An empire o'er the disentangled doom.

To suffer woes which Hope thinks infinite;
To forgive wrongs darker than death or night;
To defy Power, which seems omnipotent;
To love, and bear; to hope till Hope creates
From its own wreck the thing it contemplates;
Neither to change, nor falter, nor repent;
This, like thy glory, Titan, is to be
Good, great and joyous, beautiful and free;
This is alone Life, Joy, Empire, and Victory.

To a Skylark

(1820; comp. 1820)

Hail to thee, blithe Spirit!
Bird thou never wert,
That from Heaven, or near it,
Pourest thy full heart
In profuse strains of unpremeditated art.[1]

Higher still and higher
From the earth thou springest
Like a cloud of fire;
The blue deep thou wingest,
And singing still dost soar, and soaring ever singest.

In the golden lightning
Of the sunken sun,
O'er which clouds are bright'ning,
Thou dost float and run;
Like an unbodied joy whose race is just begun.

The pale purple even
Melts around thy flight;
Like a star of Heaven,
In the broad daylight
Thou art unseen, but yet I hear thy shrill delight,

Keen as are the arrows
Of that silver sphere,
Whose intense lamp narrows
In the white dawn clear
Until we hardly see—we feel that it is there.

All the earth and air
With thy voice is loud,
As, when night is bare,
From one lonely cloud
The moon rains out her beams, and Heaven is overflowed.

[1] **unpremeditated art:** Cf. Milton, *Paradise Lost,* IX.21–24: the poet's "celestial patroness, . . . inspires / Easy [his] unpremeditated verse."

What thou art we know not;
What is most like thee?
From rainbow clouds there flow not
Drops so bright to see
As from thy presence showers a rain of melody.

Like a Poet hidden
In the light of thought,
Singing hymns unbidden,
Till the world is wrought
To sympathy with hopes and fears it heeded not:

Like a high-born maiden
In a palace-tower,
Soothing her love-laden
Soul in secret hour
With music sweet as love, which overflows her bower:

Like a glow-worm golden
In a dell of dew,
Scattering unbeholden
Its aëreal hue
Among the flowers and grass, which screen it from the view!

Like a rose embowered
In its own green leaves,
By warm winds deflowered,
Till the scent it gives
Makes faint with too much sweet those heavy-wingèd thieves:

Sound of vernal[2] showers
On the twinkling grass,
Rain-awakened flowers,
All that ever was
Joyous, and clear, and fresh, thy music doth surpass:

Teach us, Spirit or Bird,
What sweet thoughts are thine:
I have never heard
Praise of love or wine
That panted forth a flood of rapture so divine.

Chorus Hymeneal,[3]
Or triumphal chant,
Matched with thine would be all
But an empty vaunt,[4]
A thing wherein we feel there is some hidden want.

What objects are the fountains
Of thy happy strain?
What fields, or waves, or mountains?
What shapes of sky or plain?
What love of thine own kind? what ignorance of pain?

With thy clear keen joyance
Languor cannot be:
Shadow of annoyance
Never came near thee:
Thou lovest — but ne'er knew love's sad satiety.

Waking or asleep,
Thou of death must deem
Things more true and deep
Than we mortals dream,
Or how could thy notes flow in such a crystal stream?

We look before and after,
And pine for what is not:
Our sincerest laughter
With some pain is fraught;
Our sweetest songs are those that tell of saddest thought.

Yet if we could scorn
Hate, and pride, and fear;
If we were things born
Not to shed a tear,
I know not how thy joy we ever should come near.

Better than all measures
Of delightful sound,
Better than all treasures
That in books are found,
Thy skill to poet were, thou scorner of the ground!

Teach me half the gladness
That thy brain must know,
Such harmonious madness
From my lips would flow[5]
The world should listen then — as I am listening now.

---

[2] **vernal:** springtime.

[3] **Chorus Hymeneal:** wedding hymn.

[4] **vaunt:** boast.

[5] Cf. Coleridge, "Kubla Khan" (42ff): "Could I revive within me / Her symphony and song, / To such deep delight 'twould win me . . ."

Adonais

An Elegy on the Death of John Keats, Author of Endymion, Hyperion Etc.[1]
(1821; comp. 1821)

Ἀστὴρ πρὶν μὲν ἔλαμπες ἐνὶ ζωοῖσιν Ἑῷος·
γῦν δὲ θανὼν λάμπεις Ἕσπερος ἐν φθιμένοις.

PLATO[2]

— PREFACE —

Φάρμακον ἦλθε, Βίων, ποτὶ σὸν στόμα, φάρμακον εἶδες.
πῶς τευ τοῖς χεύλεσσι ποτέδραμε, κοὐκ ἐγλυκάνθη;
τίς δὲ βροτὸς τοσσοῦτον ἀνάμερος, ἢ κεράσαι τοι,
ἢ δοῦναι λαλέοντι το φάρμακον; ἔκφυγεν ᾠδάν.

MOSCHUS, EPITAPH. BION.[3]

It is my intention to subjoin to the London edition of this poem, a criticism upon the claims of its lamented object to be classed among the writers of the highest genius who have adorned our age. My known repugnance to the narrow principles of taste on which several of his earlier compositions were modelled, prove, at least that I am an impartial judge. I consider the fragment of *Hyperion*,* as second to nothing that was ever produced by a writer of the same years.

John Keats, died at Rome of a consumption, in his twenty-fourth year, on the —— of —— 1821; and was buried in the romantic and lonely cemetery of the protestants in that city, under the pyramid which is the tomb of Cestius, and the massy walls and towers, now mouldering and desolate, which formed the circuit of antient Rome. The cemetery is an open space among the ruins covered in winter with violets and daisies. It might make one in love with death, to think that one should be buried in so sweet a place.

The genius of the lamented person to whose memory I have dedicated these unworthy verses, was not less delicate and fragile than it was beautiful; and where cankerworms abound, what wonder if its young flower was blighted in the bud? The savage criticism on his *Endymion*, which appeared in the *Quarterly Review*,[4] produced the most violent effect on his susceptible mind; the agitation thus originated ended in the rupture of a blood-vessel in the lungs; a rapid consumption ensued, and the succeeding acknowledgements from more candid critics, of the true greatness of his powers, were ineffectual to heal the wound thus wantonly inflicted.

It may be well said, that these wretched men know not what they do.[5] They scatter their insults and their slanders without heed as to whether the poisoned shaft lights on a heart made callous by many blows, or one, like Keats's composed of more penetrable stuff. One of their associates, is, to my knowledge, a most base and unprincipled calumniator. As to *Endymion*, was it a poem, whatever might be its defects, to be treated contemptuously by those who had celebrated, with various degrees of complacency and panegyric, *Paris*, and *Woman*, and a *Syrian Tale*, and Mrs. Lefanu, and Mr. Barrett, and Mr. Howard Payne, and a long list of the illustrious obscure? Are these the men, who in their venal good nature, presumed to draw a parallel between the Rev. Mr. Milman and Lord Byron?[6] What gnat did they strain at here, after having swallowed all those camels? Against what woman taken in adultery, dares the foremost of these literary prostitutes to cast his opprobrious stone?[7] Miserable man! you, one of the meanest, have wantonly defaced one of the noblest specimens of the workmanship of God. Nor shall it be

[1] Printed at Pisa, Italy, in 1821. First London edition was published in 1829.

[2] *Trans.* by Shelley: "Thou wert the morning star among the living, / Ere thy fair light had fled— / Now, having died, thou are as Hesperus, giving / New splendour to the dead." Plato's *Aster* (Star) has also been translated: "Morning star, you shone among the living; and now in death you shine, evening star, on the dead." Aster was a youth beloved by Plato. See note 7 to *Triumph of Life*.

[3] *Trans.* by Andrew Lang: "Poison came, Bion, to thy mouth—thou didst know poison. To such lips as thine did it come, and was not sweetened? What mortal was so cruel that could mix poison for thee, or who could give thee the venom that heard thy voice? Surely he had no music in his soul."

[4] See the introduction to John Keats for a summary of the critical/political assault on Keats's poetry.

[5] **these . . . men know not what they do:** Cf. Luke 23:34. See note 17 to *Prometheus Unbound*.

[6] Except for Shelley's mention, Barret, Lefanu, Payne, Milman, et al. are forgotten.

[7] Cf. Matthew 23:24: "Ye blind guides, which strain at a gnat, and swallow a camel." John 8:7: "He that is without sin among you, let him first cast a stone at her." **opprobrious:** shameful.

your excuse, that, murderer as you are, you have spoken daggers, but used none.[8]

The circumstances of the closing scene of poor Keats's life were not made known to me until the Elegy was ready for the press. I am given to understand that the wound which his sensitive spirit had received from the criticism of *Endymion,* was exasperated by the bitter sense of unrequited benefits; the poor fellow seems to have been hooted from the stage of life, no less by those on whom he had wasted the promise of his genius, than those on whom he had lavished his fortune and his care. He was accompanied to Rome, and attended in his last illness by Mr. Severn,[9] a young artist of the highest promise, who, I have been informed "almost risked his own life, and sacrificed every prospect to unwearied attendance upon his dying friend." Had I known these circumstances before the completion of my poem, I should have been tempted to add my feeble tribute of applause to the more solid recompense which the virtuous man finds in the recollection of his own motives. Mr. Severn can dispense with a reward from "such stuff as dreams are made of."[10] His conduct is a golden augury of the success of his future career—may the unextinguished Spirit of his illustrious friend animate the creations of his pencil, and plead against Oblivion for his name!

1

I weep for Adonais—he is dead!
O, weep for Adonais! though our tears
Thaw not the frost which binds so dear a head!
And thou, sad Hour, selected from all years
To mourn our loss, rouse thy obscure compeers,
And teach them thine own sorrow, say: with me
Died Adonais; till the Future dares
Forget the Past, his fate and fame shall be
An echo and a light unto eternity!

2

Where wert thou mighty Mother, when he lay,
When thy Son lay, pierced by the shaft which flies
In darkness? where was lorn Urania[11]
When Adonais died? With veiled eyes,
'Mid listening Echoes, in her Paradise
She sate, while one, with soft enamoured breath,
Rekindled all the fading melodies,
With which, like flowers that mock the corse beneath,
He had adorned and hid the coming bulk of death.

3

O, weep for Adonais—he is dead!
Wake, melancholy Mother, wake and weep!
Yet wherefore? Quench within their burning bed
Thy fiery tears, and let thy loud heart keep
Like his, a mute and uncomplaining sleep;
For he is gone, where all things wise and fair
Descend;—oh, dream not that the amorous Deep
Will yet restore him to the vital air;
Death feeds on his mute voice, and laughs at our despair.

4

Most musical of mourners, weep again!
Lament anew, Urania!—He died,[12]
Who was the Sire of an immortal strain,
Blind, old, and lonely, when his country's pride,
The priest, the slave, and the liberticide,
Trampled and mocked with many a loathed rite
Of lust and blood; he went, unterrified,
Into the gulph of death; but his clear Sprite
Yet reigns o'er earth; the third among the sons of light.[13]

5

Most musical of mourners, weep anew!
Not all to that bright station dared to climb;
And happier they their happiness who knew,
Whose tapers yet burn through that night of time
In which suns perished; others more sublime,
Struck by the envious wrath of man or God,

[8] **You have spoken . . . none:** Cf. *Hamlet,* III.ii.381: "I will speak daggers to her, but use none."

[9] **Mr. Severn:** Joseph Severn (1793–1879), painter and devoted friend of Keats. See his letter on Keats's death below.

[10] **"such stuff . . . made of":** Cf. Shakespeare, *The Tempest,* IV.i.156–57: "We are such stuff / As dreams are made on."

[11] **lorn Urania:** forlorn Urania, the "mighty Mother."

[12] **He died:** Reference to John Milton (1608–1674), Latin Secretary for the Cromwell government and author of *Paradise Lost,* the muse for which is Urania.

[13] **the third . . . light:** the third great epic poet after Homer and Dante.

Have sunk, extinct in their refulgent[14] prime;
And some yet live, treading the thorny road,
Which leads, through toil and hate, to Fame's serene
abode.

6

But now, thy youngest, dearest one, has perished
The nursling of thy widowhood, who grew,
Like a pale flower by some sad maiden cherished,
And fed with true love tears, instead of dew;
Most musical of mourners, weep anew!
Thy extreme hope, the loveliest and the last,
The bloom, whose petals nipt before they blew
Died on the promise of the fruit, is waste;
The broken lily lies—the storm is overpast.

7

To that high Capital,[15] where kingly Death
Keeps his pale court in beauty and decay,
He came; and bought, with price of purest breath,
A grave among the eternal.—Come away!
Haste, while the vault of blue Italian day
Is yet his fitting charnel-roof! while still
He lies, as if in dewy sleep he lay;
Awake him not! surely he takes his fill
Of deep and liquid rest, forgetful of all ill.

8

He will awake no more, oh, never more!—
Within the twilight chamber spreads apace,
The shadow of white Death, and at the door
Invisible Corruption waits to trace
His extreme way to her dim dwelling-place;
The eternal Hunger sits, but pity and awe
Soothe her pale rage, nor dares she to deface
So fair a prey, till darkness, and the law
Of mortal change, shall fill the grave which is her
maw.[16]

9

O, weep for Adonais!—The quick Dreams,
The passion-winged Ministers of thought,
Who were his flocks, whom near the living streams
Of his young spirit he fed, and whom he taught
The love which was its music, wander not,—
Wander no more, from kindling brain to brain,
But droop there, whence they sprung; and mourn
their lot
Round the cold heart, where, after their sweet pain,
They ne'er will gather strength, or find a home again.

10

And one with trembling hands clasps his cold
head,
And fans him with her moonlight wings, and cries;
"Our love, our hope, our sorrow, is not dead;
See, on the silken fringe of his faint eyes,
Like dew upon a sleeping flower, there lies
A tear some Dream has loosened from his brain."
Lost Angel of a ruined Paradise!
She knew not 'twas her own; as with no stain
She faded, like a cloud which had outwept its rain.

11

One from a lucid urn of starry dew
Washed his light limbs as if embalming them;
Another clipt her profuse locks, and threw
The wreath upon him, like an anadem,[17]
Which frozen tears instead of pearls begem;
Another in her wilful grief would break
Her bow and winged reeds, as if to stem
A greater loss with one which was more weak;
And dull the barbed fire against his frozen cheek.

12

Another Splendour on his mouth alit,
That mouth, whence it was wont to draw the
breath
Which gave it strength to pierce the guarded wit,
And pass into the panting heart beneath
With lightning and with music: the damp death
Quenched its caress upon his icy lips;
And, as a dying meteor stains a wreath
Of moonlight vapour, which the cold night clips,[18]
It flushed through his pale limbs, and past to its
eclipse.

13

And others came . . . Desires and Adorations,
Winged Persuasions and veiled Destinies,

[14] **refulgent:** shining brilliantly.

[15] **that high Capital:** Rome.

[16] This line was later changed to: "Of change, shall o'er his sleep the mortal curtain draw."

[17] **anadem:** head wreath.

[18] **clips:** embraces, clasps.

Splendours, and Glooms, and glimmering
Incarnations
Of hopes and fears, and twilight Phantasies;
And Sorrow, with her family of Sighs,
And Pleasure, blind with tears, led by the gleam
Of her own dying smile instead of eyes,
Came in slow pomp;—the moving pomp might
seem
Like pageantry of mist on an autumnal stream.

14

All he had loved, and moulded into thought,
From shape, and hue, and odour, and sweet sound,
Lamented Adonais. Morning sought
Her eastern watchtower, and her hair unbound,
Wet with the tears which should adorn the ground,
Dimmed the aerial eyes that kindle day;
Afar the melancholy thunder moaned,
Pale Ocean in unquiet slumber lay,
And the wild winds flew round, sobbing in their dis-
may.

15

Lost Echo sits amid the voiceless mountains,
And feeds her grief with his remembered lay,
And will no more reply to winds or fountains,
Or amorous birds perched on the young green
spray,
Or herdsman's horn, or bell at closing day;
Since she can mimic not his lips, more dear
Than those for whose disdain she pined away
Into a shadow of all sounds:—a drear
Murmur, between their songs, is all the woodmen
hear.

16

Grief made the young Spring wild, and she threw
down
Her kindling buds, as if she Autumn were,
Or they dead leaves; since her delight is flown
For whom should she have waked the sullen year?
To Phoebus was not Hyacinth so dear
Nor to himself Narcissus,[19] as to both
Thou Adonais: wan they stand and sere
Amid the drooping comrades of their youth,
With dew all turned to tears; odour, to sighing ruth.[20]

17

Thy spirit's sister, the lorn nightingale
Mourns not her mate with such melodious pain;
Not so the eagle, who like thee could scale
Heaven, and could nourish in the sun's domain
Her mighty youth with morning, doth complain,
Soaring and screaming round her empty nest,
As Albion wails for thee: the curse of Cain[21]
Light on his head who pierced thy innocent breast,
And scared the angel soul that was its earthly guest!

18

Ah woe is me! Winter is come and gone,
But grief returns with the revolving year;
The airs and streams renew their joyous tone;
The ants, the bees, the swallows reappear;
Fresh leaves and flowers deck the dead Seasons'
bier;
The amorous birds now pair in every brake,
And build their mossy homes in field and brere;[22]
And the green lizard, and the golden snake,
Like unimprisoned flames, out of their trance awake.

19

Through wood and stream and field and hill and
Ocean
A quickening life from the Earth's heart has burst
As it has ever done, with change and motion,
From the great morning of the world when first
God dawned on Chaos; in its steam immersed
The lamps of Heaven flash with a softer light;
All baser things pant with life's sacred thirst;
Diffuse themselves; and spend in love's delight,
The beauty and the joy of their renewed might.

---

[19] **Hyacinth . . . Narcissus:** Both young men Hyacinth and Narcissus became flowers upon their deaths. Hyacinth was killed by Zephyrus for not returning his love; Narcissus metamorphosed into a flower for unceasingly gazing upon his reflection in a pond.

[20] **sere:** dry; **drooping comrades:** later changed to "faint companions"; **ruth:** compassion.

[21] **Albion:** England. **curse of Cain:** to be "a fugitive and a vagabond in the earth" for slaying his brother, Abel, but also marked by God to prevent his slaying by vengeful others. Genesis 4:12–15.

[22] **brere:** original form of brier (heather).

20

The leprous corpse touched by this spirit tender
Exhales itself in flowers of gentle breath;
Like incarnations of the stars, when splendour
Is changed to fragrance, they illumine death
And mock the merry worm that wakes beneath;
Nought we know, dies. Shall that alone which
knows
Be as a sword consumed before the sheath
By sightless lightning?—th'intense atom glows
A moment, then is quenched in a most cold repose.

21

Alas! that all we loved of him should be,
But for our grief, as if it had not been,
And grief itself be mortal! Woe is me!
Whence are we, and why are we? of what scene
The actors or spectators? Great and mean
Meet massed in death, who lends what life must
borrow.
As long as skies are blue, and fields are green,
Evening must usher night, night urge the morrow,
Month follow month with woe, and year wake year to
sorrow.

22

He will awake no more, oh, never more!
"Wake thou," cried Misery, "childless Mother, rise
Out of thy sleep, and slake,[23] in thy heart's core,
A wound more fierce than his with tears and sighs."
And all the Dreams that watched Urania's eyes,
And all the Echoes whom their sister's song
Had held in holy silence, cried: "Arise!"
Swift as a Thought by the snake Memory stung,
From her ambrosial rest the fading Splendour sprung.

23

She rose like an autumnal Night, that springs
Out of the East, and follows wild and drear
The golden Day, which, on eternal wings,
Even as a ghost abandoning a bier,
Had left the Earth a corpse. Sorrow and fear
So struck, so roused, so rapt Urania;
So saddened round her like an atmosphere
Of stormy mist; so swept her on her way
Even to the mournful place where Adonais lay.

[23] **slake:** quench.

24

Out of her secret Paradise she sped,
Through camps and cities rough with stone, and
steel,
And human hearts, which to her aery tread
Yielding not, wounded the invisible
Palms of her tender feet where'er they fell:
And barbed tongues, and thoughts more sharp
than they
Rent the soft Form they never could repel,
Whose sacred blood, like the young tears of May,
Paved with eternal flowers that undeserving way.

25

In the death chamber for a moment Death
Shamed by the presence of that living Might
Blushed to annihilation, and the breath
Revisited those lips, and life's pale light
Flashed through those limbs, so late her dear
delight.
"Leave me not wild and drear and comfortless,
As silent lightning leaves the starless night!
Leave me not!" cried Urania: her distress
Roused Death: Death rose and smiled, and met her
vain caress.

26

"Stay yet awhile! speak to me once again;
Kiss me, so long but as a kiss may live;
And in my heartless breast and burning brain
That word, that kiss shall all thoughts else survive
With food of saddest memory kept alive,
Now thou art dead, as if it were a part
Of thee, my Adonais! I would give
All that I am to be as thou now art!
But I am chained to Time, and cannot thence depart!

27

"Oh gentle child, beautiful as thou wert,
Why didst thou leave the trodden paths of men
Too soon, and with weak hands though mighty
heart
Dare the unpastured dragon in his den?
Defenceless as thou wert, oh where was then
Wisdom the mirrored shield, or scorn the spear?[24]

[24] **the mirrored shield . . . spear:** Armed with a sickle from Hermes and a mirror from Athena, Perseus decapitated the

Or hadst thou waited the full cycle, when
Thy spirit should have filled its crescent sphere,
The monsters of life's waste had fled from thee like
deer.

28

"The herded wolves, bold only to pursue;
The obscene ravens, clamorous o'er the dead;
The vultures to the conqueror's banner true
Who feed where Desolation first has fed,
And whose wings rain contagion;—how they fled,
When like Apollo, from his golden bow,
The Pythian of the age one arrow sped
And smiled!—The spoilers tempt no second blow,
They fawn on the proud feet that spurn them as they
go.[25]

29

"The sun comes forth, and many reptiles spawn;
He sets, and each ephemeral insect then
Is gathered into death without a dawn,
And the immortal stars awake again;
So is it in the world of living men:
A godlike mind soars forth, in its delight
Making earth bare and veiling heaven, and when
It sinks, the swarms that dimmed or shared its light
Leave to its kindred lamps the spirit's awful night."

30

Thus ceased she: and the mountain shepherds
came
Their garlands sere, their magic mantles rent;
The Pilgrim of Eternity,[26] whose fame
Over his living head like Heaven is bent,
An early but enduring monument,
Came, veiling all the lightnings of his song
In sorrow; from her wilds Ierne[27] sent
The sweetest lyrist of her saddest wrong,
And love taught grief to fall like music from his
tongue.

31

Midst others of less note, came one frail Form,
A phantom among men; companionless
As the last cloud of an expiring storm
Whose thunder is its knell; he, as I guess,
Had gazed on Nature's naked loveliness,
Actaeon-like,[28] and now he fled astray
With feeble steps o'er the world's wilderness,
And his own thoughts, along that rugged way,
Pursued, like raging hounds, their father and their
prey.

32

A pardlike[29] Spirit beautiful and swift—
A Love in desolation masked;—a Power
Girt round with weakness;—it can scarce uplift
The weight of the superincumbent hour;[30]
It is a dying lamp, a falling shower,
A breaking billow;—even whilst we speak
Is it not broken? On the withering flower
The killing sun smiles brightly: on a cheek
The life can burn in blood, even while the heart may
break.

33

His head was bound with pansies overblown,
And faded violets, white, and pied, and blue;
And a light spear topped with a cypress cone,
Round whose rude shaft dark ivy tresses grew
Yet dripping with the forest's noonday dew,
Vibrated, as the ever-beating heart
Shook the weak hand that grasped it; of that crew
He came the last, neglected and apart;
A herd-abandoned deer struck by the hunter's dart.

Medusa while she lay asleep by looking at her in the mirror, because looking directly at the monster would have turned him into stone.

[25] **Pythian . . . arrow:** reference to Apollo, whose earliest adventure was killing Python with an arrow. Suggests Lord Byron,* who struck back at hostile critics in his verse and won them over with his great popularity, though he spurned his public. **as they go:** later changed to "lying low."

[26] **Pilgrim of Eternity:** Byron.

[27] **Ierne:** Ireland, who sent Thomas Moore (1801–1834), the poet of *Irish Melodies.*

[28] **Actaeon:** a famous hunter, who came upon Diana bathing naked in the woods. She transformed him into a stag and he was pursued by his hounds and killed.

[29] **pardlike:** leopard-like.

[30] **superincumbent:** lying or resting above or on.

34

All stood aloof, and at his partial[31] moan
Smiled through their tears; well knew that gentle band
Who in another's fate now wept his own;
As in the accents of an unknown land,
He sung new sorrow; sad Urania scanned
The Stranger's mien, and murmured: "who art thou?"
He answered not, but with a sudden hand
Made bare his branded and ensanguined brow,
Which was like Cain's or Christ's—Oh! that it should be so!

35

What softer voice is hushed over the dead?
Athwart what brow is that dark mantle thrown?
What form leans sadly o'er the white death-bed,
In mockery of monumental stone,
The heavy heart heaving without a moan?
If it be He,[32] who, gentlest of the wise,
Taught, soothed, loved, honoured the departed one;
Let me not vex, with inharmonious sighs
The silence of that heart's accepted sacrifice.

36

Our Adonais has drunk poison—oh!
What deaf and viperous murderer could crown
Life's early cup with such a draught of woe?
The nameless worm would now itself disown:
It felt, yet could escape the magic tone
Whose prelude held all envy, hate, and wrong,
But what was howling in one breast alone,
Silent with expectation of the song,
Whose master's hand is cold, whose silver lyre unstrung.

37

Live thou, whose infamy is not thy fame!
Live! fear no heavier chastisement from me,
Thou noteless blot on a remembered name!
But be thyself, and know thyself to be!
And ever at thy season be thou free
To spill the venom when thy fangs o'erflow:
Remorse and Self-contempt shall cling to thee;
Hot Shame shall burn upon thy secret brow,
And like a beaten hound tremble thou shalt—as now.

38

Nor let us weep that our delight is fled
Far from these carrion kites[33] that scream below;
He wakes or sleeps with the enduring dead;
Thou canst not soar where he is sitting now.—
Dust to the dust! but the pure spirit shall flow
Back to the burning fountain whence it came,
A portion of the Eternal, which must glow
Through time and change, unquenchably the same,
Whilst thy cold embers choke the sordid hearth of shame.

39

Peace, peace! he is not dead, he doth not sleep—
He hath awakened from the dream of life—
'Tis we, who lost in stormy visions, keep
With phantoms an unprofitable strife,
And in mad trance, strike with our spirit's knife
Invulnerable nothings.—*We decay*
Like corpses in a charnel; fear and grief
Convulse us and consume us day by day,
And cold hopes swarm like worms within our living clay.

40

He has outsoared the shadow of our night;
Envy and calumny and hate and pain,
And that unrest which men miscall delight,
Can touch him not and torture not again;
From the contagion of the world's slow stain
He is secure, and now can never mourn
A heart grown cold, a head grown grey in vain;
Nor, when the spirit's self has ceased to burn,
With sparkless ashes load an unlamented urn.

41

He lives, he wakes—'tis Death is dead, not he;
Mourn not for Adonais.—Thou young Dawn
Turn all thy dew to splendour, for from thee
The spirit thou lamentest is not gone;
Ye caverns and ye forests, cease to moan!

[31] **partial:** revealing self-interest or bias.

[32] **He:** Leigh Hunt, Keats's friend and poetic mentor.

[33] **carrion kites:** hawks who will eat carrion, or dead flesh.

Cease ye faint flowers and fountains, and thou Air
Which like a mourning veil thy scarf hadst thrown
O'er the abandoned Earth, now leave it bare
Even to the joyous stars which smile on its despair!

42

He is made one with Nature: there is heard
His voice in all her music, from the moan
Of thunder, to the song of night's sweet bird;
He is a presence to be felt and known
In darkness and in light, from herb and stone,
Spreading itself where'er that Power may move
Which has withdrawn his being to its own;
Which wields the world with never wearied love,
Sustains it from beneath, and kindles it above.

43

He is a portion of the loveliness
Which once he made more lovely: he doth bear
His part, while the one Spirit's plastic stress
Sweeps through the dull dense world, compelling there,
All new successions to the forms they wear;
Torturing th'unwilling dross that checks it's flight
To it's own likeness, as each mass may bear;
And bursting in it's beauty and its might
From trees and beasts and men into the Heaven's light.

44

The splendours of the firmament of time
May be eclipsed, but are extinguished not;
Like stars to their appointed height they climb
And death is a low mist which cannot blot
The brightness it may veil. When lofty thought
Lifts a young heart above its mortal lair,
And love and life contend in it, for what
Shall be its earthly doom, the dead live there
And move like winds of light on dark and stormy air.

45

The inheritors of unfulfilled renown
Rose from their thrones, built beyond mortal thought,
Far in the Unapparent. Chatterton
Rose pale, his solemn agony had not
Yet faded from him; Sidney, as he fought
And as he fell and as he lived and loved
Sublimely mild, a Spirit without spot,
Arose; and Lucan, by his death approved:
Oblivion as they rose shrank like a thing reproved.[34]

46

And many more, whose names on Earth are dark
But whose transmitted effluence cannot die
So long as fire outlives the parent spark,
Rose, robed in dazzling immortality.
"Thou art become as one of us," they cry,
"It was for thee yon kingless sphere has long
Swung blind in unascended majesty,
Silent alone amid an Heaven of song.
Assume thy winged throne, thou Vesper[35] of our throng!"

47

Who mourns for Adonais? oh come forth
Fond wretch! and know thyself and him aright.
Clasp with thy panting soul the pendulous[36] Earth;
As from a centre, dart thy spirit's light
Beyond all worlds, until its spacious might
Satiate the void circumference: then shrink
Even to a point within our day and night;
And keep thy heart light lest it make thee sink
When hope has kindled hope, and lured thee to the brink.

48

Or go to Rome, which is the sepulchre
O, not of him, but of our joy: 'tis nought
That ages, empires, and religions there
Lie buried in the ravage they have wrought;
For such as he can lend,—they borrow not
Glory from those who made the world their prey;
And he is gathered to the kings of thought
Who waged contention with their time's decay,
And of the past are all that cannot pass away.

---

[34] **Chatterton . . . Lucan:** Thomas Chatterton (1752–1780) was a famous boy-poet who committed suicide; Sir Philip Sidney (1554–1586) was a soldier-poet, who died nobly in battle. Lucan (AD 39–65) was a Roman poet, who committed suicide after a failed plot against Nero.

[35] **Vesper:** evening star.

[36] **pendulous:** suspended so that it can swing and sway; hanging loosely.

49

Go thou to Rome,—at once the Paradise,
The grave, the city, and the wilderness;
And where its wrecks like shattered mountains rise,
And flowering weeds, and fragrant copses dress
The bones of Desolation's nakedness
Pass, till the Spirit of the spot shall lead
Thy footsteps to a slope of green access
Where, like an infant's smile, over the dead,
A light of laughing flowers along the grass is spread.[37]

50

And grey walls moulder round, on which dull Time
Feeds, like slow fire upon a hoary brand;
And one keen pyramid with wedge sublime,
Pavilioning the dust of him who planned
This refuge for his memory, doth stand
Like flame transformed to marble; and beneath,
A field is spread, on which a newer band
Have pitched in Heaven's smile their camp of death
Welcoming him we lose with scarce extinguished breath.

51

Here pause: these graves are all too young as yet
To have out grown the sorrow which consigned
Its charge to each; and if the seal is set,
Here, on one fountain of a mourning mind,
Break it not thou! too surely shalt thou find
Thine own well full, if thou returnest home,
Of tears and gall. From the world's bitter wind
Seek shelter in the shadow of the tomb.
What Adonais is, why fear we to become?

52

The One remains, the many change and pass;
Heaven's light forever shines, Earth's shadows fly;
Life, like a dome of many-coloured glass,
Stains the white radiance of Eternity,
Until Death tramples it to fragments.—Die,
If thou wouldst be with that which thou dost seek!
Follow where all is fled!—Rome's azure sky,
Flowers, ruins, statues, music, words, are weak
The glory they transfuse[38] with fitting truth to speak.

53

Why linger, why turn back, why shrink, my Heart?
Thy hopes are gone before; from all things here
They have departed; thou shouldst now depart!
A light is past from the revolving year,
And man, and woman; and what still is dear
Attracts to crush, repels to make thee wither.
The soft sky smiles,—the low wind whispers near:
'Tis Adonais calls! oh, hasten thither,
No more let Life divide what Death can join together.

54

That Light whose smile kindles the Universe,
That Beauty in which all things work and move,
That Benediction which the eclipsing Curse
Of birth can quench not, that sustaining Love
Which through the web of being blindly wove
By man and beast and earth and air and sea,
Burns bright or dim, as each are mirrors of
The fire for which all thirst; now beams on me,
Consuming the last clouds of cold mortality.

55

The breath whose might I have invoked in song
Descends on me; my spirit's bark is driven,
Far from the shore, far from the trembling throng
Whose sails were never to the tempest given;
The massy earth and sphered skies are riven![39]
I am borne darkly, fearfully, afar:
Whilst burning through the inmost veil of Heaven,
The soul of Adonais, like a star,
Beacons from the abode where the Eternal are.

[37] **like an infant's smile . . . spread:** Shelley's son William was also buried at the Protestant Cemetary in Rome, where Keats was laid not far off. See introduction to Percy Shelley.

[38] **transfuse:** cause to flow from one receptacle to another.

[39] **The breath . . . skies are riven:** Shelley alludes in those lines to his works and their imagery: "Ode to the West Wind," "Alastor," *Julian and Maddalo.*

POSTHUMOUS PUBLICATIONS

from POSTHUMOUS POEMS OF PERCY BYSSHE SHELLEY[1]
(1824)

Stanzas
Written in Dejection, Near Naples
(comp. 1818)

The sun is warm, the sky is clear,
 The waves are dancing fast and bright,
Blue isles and snowy mountains wear
 The purple noon's transparent light,
Around its unexpanded buds;
 Like many a voice of one delight,
The winds, the birds, the ocean floods,
The City's voice itself, is soft like Solitude's.

I see the Deep's untrampled floor
 With green and purple seaweeds strown;
I see the waves upon the shore,
 Like light dissolved in star-showers, thrown:
 I sit upon the sands alone,—
The lightning of the noontide ocean
 Is flashing round me, and a tone
Arises from its measured motion,
How sweet! did any heart now share in my emotion.

Alas! I have nor hope nor health,
 Nor peace within nor calm around,
Nor that content surpassing wealth
 The sage in meditation found,
 And walked with inward glory crowned—
Nor fame, nor power, nor love, nor leisure.
 Others I see whom these surround—
Smiling they live and call life pleasure;—
To me that cup has been dealt in another measure.

Yet now despair itself is mild,
 Even as the winds and waters are;
I could lie down like a tired child,
 And weep away the life of care
 Which I have borne and yet must bear,
Till death like sleep might steal on me,
 And I might feel in the warm air
My cheek grow cold, and hear the sea
Breathe o'er my dying brain its last monotony.

Some might lament that I were cold,
 As I, when this sweet day is gone,
Which my lost heart, too soon grown old,
 Insults with this untimely moan;
They might lament—for I am one
 Whom men love not,—and yet regret,
 Unlike this day, which, when the sun
Shall on its stainless glory set,
Will linger, though enjoyed, like joy in memory yet.

from Julian and Maddalo;[1] A Conversation
(1824; comp. 1819)

The meadows with fresh streams, the bees with thyme,
The goats with the green leaves of budding spring,
Are saturated not—nor Love with tears.

VIRGIL'S *Gallus*.

Count Maddalo[2] is a Venetian nobleman of antient family and of great fortune, who, without mixing much in the society of his countrymen, resides chiefly at his magnificent palace in that city. He is a person of the most consummate genius, and capable, if he would direct his energies to such an end, of becoming the redeemer of his degraded country. But it is his weakness to be proud: he derives, from a comparison of his own extraordinary mind with the dwarfish intellects that surround him, an intense apprehension of the nothingness of human life. His passions and his powers are incomparably greater than those of other men; and, instead of the latter having been

[1] Edited by Mary Shelley in 1824 and published by the radical publishers John and Henry Hunt. Of the 500 volumes printed, 309 were sold and 191 destroyed by Sir Timothy Shelley, Shelley's father and Mary's benefactor after the death of Shelley.

[1] The text included here is that established by Donald Reiman from the author's manuscript in the Pierpont Morgan Library.

[2] **Maddalo:** reputed to be Lord Byron and Julian, Shelley.

employed in curbing the former, they have mutually lent each other strength. His ambition preys upon itself, for want of objects which it can consider worthy of exertion. I say that Maddalo is proud, because I can find no other word to express the concentered and impatient feelings which consume him; but it is on his own hopes and affections only that he seems to trample, for in social life no human being can be more gentle, patient, and unassuming than Maddalo. He is cheerful, frank, and witty. His more serious conversation is a sort of intoxication; men are held by it as by a spell. He has travelled much; and there is an inexpressible charm in his relation of his adventures in different countries.

Julian is an Englishman of good family, passionately attached to those philosophical notions which assert the power of man over his own mind, and the immense improvements of which, by the extinction of certain moral superstitions, human society may be yet susceptible. Without concealing the evil in the world, he is for ever speculating how good may be made superior. He is a complete infidel, and a scoffer at all things reputed holy; and Maddalo takes a wicked pleasure in drawing out his taunts against religion. What Maddalo thinks on these matters is not exactly known. Julian, in spite of his heterodox opinions, is conjectured by his friends to possess some good qualities. How far this is possible the pious reader will determine. Julian is rather serious.

Of the Maniac I can give no information. He seems by his own account to have been disappointed in love. He was evidently a very cultivated and amiable person when in his right senses. His story, told at length, might be like many other stories of the same kind: the unconnected exclamations of his agony will perhaps be found a sufficient comment for the text of every heart.

I rode one evening with Count Maddalo
Upon the bank of land which breaks the flow
Of Adria towards Venice:[3]—a bare strand
Of hillocks, heaped from ever-shifting sand,
Matted with thistles and amphibious weeds,
Such as from earth's embrace the salt ooze breeds,
Is this;—an uninhabitable sea-side
Which the lone fisher, when his nets are dried,
Abandons; and no other object breaks
The waste, but one dwarf tree and some few stakes
Broken and unrepaired, and the tide makes
A narrow space of level sand thereon,—
Where 'twas our wont to ride while day went down.
This ride was my delight.—I love all waste
And solitary places; where we taste
The pleasure of believing what we see
Is boundless, as we wish our souls to be:
And such was this wide ocean, and this shore
More barren than its billows;—and yet more
Than all, with a remembered friend I love
To ride as then I rode;—for the winds drove
The living spray along the sunny air
Into our faces; the blue heavens were bare,
Stripped to their depths by the awakening North;
And, from the waves, sound like delight broke forth
Harmonizing with solitude, and sent
Into our hearts aërial merriment . . .
So, as we rode, we talked; and the swift thought,
Winging itself with laughter, lingered not,
But flew from brain to brain,—such glee was ours—
Charged with light memories of remembered hours,
None slow enough for sadness: till we came
Homeward, which always makes the spirit tame.
This day had been cheerful but cold, and now
The sun was sinking, and the wind also.
Our talk grew somewhat serious, as may be
Talk interrupted with such raillery
As mocks itself, because it cannot scorn
The thoughts it would extinguish:—'twas forlorn
Yet pleasing, such as once, so poets tell,
The devils held within the dales of Hell
Concerning God, freewill and destiny:[4]
Of all that earth has been or yet may be,
All that vain men imagine or believe,
Or hope can paint or suffering may atchieve,
We descanted,[5] and I (for ever still
Is it not wise to make the best of ill?)
Argued against despondency, but pride
Made my companion take the darker side.
The sense that he was greater than his kind
Had struck, methinks, his eagle spirit blind

[3] **bank of land:** Reference to the Lido. **Adria:** Adriatic Sea.

[4] **The devils . . . destiny:** Allusion to Milton's *Paradise Lost*, II.557–61, where the philosophical devils discoursed in Satan's absence on metaphysical matters—"providence, foreknowledge, will, and fate, / Fixed fate, free will, foreknowledge absolute, / And found no end, in wand'ring mazes lost."

[5] **descanted:** discussed at length on a particular theme; secondary meaning, sung melodiously.

By gazing on its own exceeding light.
—Meanwhile the sun paused ere it should alight,
Over the horizon of the mountains;—Oh,
How beautiful is sunset, when the glow
Of Heaven descends upon a land like thee,
Thou Paradise of exiles, Italy!
Thy mountains, seas and vineyards and the towers
Of cities they encircle!—it was ours
To stand on thee, beholding it; and then
Just where we had dismounted, the Count's men
Were waiting for us with the gondola.—
As those who pause on some delightful way
Though bent on pleasant pilgrimage, we stood
Looking upon the evening and the flood
Which lay between the city and the shore
Paved with the image of the sky . . . the hoar
And aery Alps towards the North appeared
Through mist, an heaven-sustaining bulwark reared
Between the East and West; and half the sky
Was roofed with clouds of rich emblazonry
Dark purple at the zenith, which still grew
Down the steep West into a wondrous hue
Brighter than burning gold, even to the rent
Where the swift sun yet paused in his descent
Among the many folded hills: they were
Those famous Euganean hills, which bear
As seen from Lido through the harbour piles
The likeness of a clump of peaked isles—
And then—as if the Earth and Sea had been
Dissolved into one lake of fire, were seen
Those mountains towering as from waves of flame
Around the vaporous sun, from which there came
The inmost purple spirit of light, and made
Their very peaks transparent. "Ere it fade,"
Said my Companion, "I will shew you soon
A better station"—so, o'er the lagune
We glided, and from that funereal bark
I leaned, and saw the City, and could mark
How from their many isles, in evening's gleam,
Its temples and its palaces did seem
Like fabrics of enchantment piled to Heaven.
I was about to speak, when—"We are even
Now at the point I meant," said Maddalo,
And bade the gondolieri cease to row.
"Look, Julian, on the West, and listen well
If you hear not a deep and heavy bell."
I looked, and saw between us and the sun
A building on an island; such a one
As age to age might add, for uses vile,
A windowless, deformed and dreary pile;
And on the top an open tower, where hung
A bell, which in the radiance swayed and swung,
We could just hear its hoarse and iron tongue:
The broad sun sunk behind it, and it tolled
In strong and black relief.—"What we behold
Shall be the madhouse and its belfry tower,"
Said Maddalo, "and ever at this hour
Those who may cross the water, hear that bell
Which calls the maniacs each one from his cell
To vespers."—"As much skill as need to pray
In thanks or hope for their dark lot have they
To their stern maker," I replied. "O ho!
You talk as in years past," said Maddalo.
"'Tis strange men change not. You were ever still
Among Christ's flock a perilous infidel,
A wolf for the meek lambs—if you can't swim
Beware of Providence." I looked on him,
But the gay smile had faded in his eye.
"And such,"—he cried, "is our mortality
And this must be the emblem and the sign
Of what should be eternal and divine!—
And like that black and dreary bell, the soul,
Hung in a heaven-illumined tower, must toll
Our thoughts and our desires to meet below
Round the rent heart and pray—as madmen do
For what? they know not,—till the night of death
As sunset that strange vision, severeth
Our memory from itself, and us from all
We sought and yet were baffled!" I recall
The sense of what he said, although I mar
The force of his expressions. The broad star
Of day meanwhile had sunk behind the hill
And the black bell became invisible
And the red tower looked grey, and all between
The churches, ships and palaces were seen
Huddled in gloom;—into the purple sea
The orange hues of heaven sunk silently.
We hardly spoke, and soon the gondola
Conveyed me to my lodging by the way.

The following morn was rainy, cold and dim:
Ere Maddalo arose, I called on him,
And whilst I waited with his child I played;
A lovelier toy sweet Nature never made,
A serious, subtle, wild, yet gentle being,
Graceful without design and unforeseeing,
With eyes—oh speak not of her eyes!—which seem
Twin mirrors of Italian Heaven, yet gleam
With such deep meaning, as we never see

But in the human countenance: with me
She was a special favourite: I had nursed
Her fine and feeble limbs when she came first
To this bleak world; and she yet seemed to know
On second sight her antient playfellow,
Less changed than she was by six months or so;
For after her first shyness was worn out
We sate there, rolling billiard balls about.
When the Count entered—salutations past—
"The word you spoke last night might well have cast
A darkness on my spirit—if man be
The passive thing you say, I should not see
Much harm in the religions and old saws
(Though I may never own[6] such leaden laws)
Which break a teachless nature to the yoke:
Mine is another faith"—thus much I spoke
And noting he replied not, added: "See
This lovely child, blithe, innocent and free;
She spends a happy time with little care
While we to such sick thoughts subjected are
As came on you last night—it is our will
That thus enchains us to permitted ill—
We might be otherwise—we might be all
We dream of happy, high, majestical.
Where is the love, beauty and truth we seek
But in our mind? and if we were not weak
Should we be less in deed than in desire?"
"Ay, if we were not weak—and we aspire
How vainly to be strong!" said Maddalo;
"You talk Utopia." "It remains to know,"
I then rejoined, "and those who try may find
How strong the chains are which our spirit bind;
Brittle perchance as straw . . . We are assured
Much may be conquered, much may be endured
Of what degrades and crushes us. We know
That we have power over ourselves to do
And suffer—what, we know not till we try;
But something nobler than to live and die—
So taught those kings of old philosophy
Who reigned, before Religion made men blind;
And those who suffer with their suffering kind
Yet feel their faith, religion." "My dear friend,"
Said Maddalo, "my judgement will not bend
To your opinion, though I think you might
Make such a system refutation-tight
As far as words go. I knew one like you
Who to this city came some months ago
With whom I argued in this sort, and he
Is now gone mad,—and so he answered me,—
Poor fellow! but if you would like to go
We'll visit him, and his wild talk will show
How vain are such aspiring theories."
"I hope to prove the induction otherwise,
And that a want of that true theory, still,
Which seeks a 'soul of goodness'[7] in things ill
Or in himself or others has thus bowed
His being—there are some by nature proud,
Who patient in all else demand but this:
To love and be beloved with gentleness;
And being scorned, what wonder if they die
Some living death? this is not destiny
But man's own wilful ill." As thus I spoke
Servants announced the gondola, and we
Through the fast-falling rain and high-wrought sea
Sailed to the island where the madhouse stands.
We disembarked. The clap of tortured hands,
Fierce yells and howlings and lamentings keen,
And laughter where complaint had merrier been,
Moans, shrieks and curses and blaspheming prayers
Accosted us. We climbed the oozy stairs
Into an old courtyard. I heard on high,
Then, fragments of most touching melody,
But looking up saw not the singer there—
Through the black bars in the tempestuous air
I saw, like weeds on a wrecked palace growing,
Long tangled locks flung wildly forth, and flowing,
Of those who on a sudden were beguiled
Into strange silence, and looked forth and smiled
Hearing sweet sounds.—Then I: "Methinks there were
A cure of these with patience and kind care,
If music can thus move . . . but what is he
Whom we seek here?" "Of his sad history
I know but this," said Maddalo: "he came
To Venice a dejected man, and fame
Said he was wealthy, or he had been so;
Some thought the loss of fortune wrought him woe;
But he was ever talking in such sort
As you do—far more sadly—he seemed hurt,
Even as a man with his peculiar wrong,
To hear but of the oppression of the strong,
Or those absurd deceits (I think with you

[6] **own:** acknowledge or to accept as one's own.

[7] Cf. Shakespeare, *King Henry V*, IV.i.4: "There is some soul of goodness in things evil."

In some respects, you know) which carry through
The excellent impostors of this Earth
When they outface detection—he had worth,
Poor fellow! but a humourist in his way"—
"Alas, what drove him mad?" "I cannot say;
A Lady came with him from France, and when
She left him and returned, he wandered then
About yon lonely isles of desart sand
Till he grew wild—he had no cash or land
Remaining,—the police had brought him here—
Some fancy took him and he would not bear
Removal; so I fitted up for him
Those rooms beside the sea, to please his whim,
And sent him busts and books and urns for flowers,
Which had adorned his life in happier hours,
And instruments of music—you may guess
A stranger could do little more or less
For one so gentle and unfortunate;
And those are his sweet strains which charm the
    weight
From madmen's chains, and make this Hell appear
A heaven of sacred silence, hushed to hear."—
"Nay, this was kind of you—he had no claim,
As the world says"—"None—but the very same
Which I on all mankind were I as he
Fallen to such deep reverse;—his melody
Is interrupted now—we hear the din
Of madmen, shriek on shriek again begin;
Let us now visit him; after this strain
He ever communes with himself again,
And sees nor hears not any." Having said
These words we called the keeper, and he led
To an apartment opening on the sea—
There the poor wretch was sitting mournfully
Near a piano, his pale fingers twined
One with the other, and the ooze and wind
Rushed through an open casement, and did sway
His hair, and starred it with the brackish spray;
His head was leaning on a music book,
And he was muttering, and his lean limbs shook;
His lips were pressed against a folded leaf
In hue too beautiful for health, and grief
Smiled in their motions as they lay apart—
As one who wrought from his own fervid heart
The eloquence of passion, soon he raised
His sad meek face and eyes lustrous and glazed
And spoke—sometimes as one who wrote and
    thought
His words might move some heart that heeded not
If sent to distant lands; and then as one
Reproaching deeds never to be undone
With wondering self-compassion; then his speech
Was lost in grief, and then his words came each
Unmodulated, cold, expressionless;
But that from one jarred accent you might guess
It was despair made them so uniform:
And all the while the loud and gusty storm
Hissed through the window, and we stood behind
Stealing his accents from the envious wind
Unseen. I yet remember what he said
Distinctly: such impression his words made.

. . . .

                "O Thou, my spirit's mate
Who, for thou art compassionate and wise,
Wouldst pity me from thy most gentle eyes
If this sad writing thou shouldst ever see—
My secret groans must be unheard by thee,
Thou wouldst weep tears bitter as blood to know
Thy lost friend's incommunicable woe.

. . . .

                "I must remove
A veil from my pent mind. 'Tis torn aside!
O, pallid as death's dedicated bride,
Thou mockery which art sitting by my side,
Am I not wan like thee? at the grave's call
I haste, invited to thy wedding ball
To greet the ghastly paramour, for whom
Thou hast deserted me . . . and made the tomb
Thy bridal bed . . . But I beside your feet
Will lie and watch ye from my winding sheet—
Thus . . . wide awake, though dead . . . yet stay, o stay!
Go not so soon—I know not what I say—
Hear but my reasons . . . I am mad, I fear,
My fancy is o'erwrought . . . thou art not here . . .
Pale art thou, 'tis most true . . . but thou art gone,
Thy work is finished . . . I am left alone!—

. . . .

"That you had never seen me—never heard
My voice, and more than all had ne'er endured
The deep pollution of my loathed embrace—
That your eyes ne'er had lied love in my face—
That, like some maniac monk, I had torn out
The nerves of manhood by their bleeding root
With mine own quivering fingers, so that ne'er
Our hearts had for a moment mingled there
To disunite in horror—these were not
With thee, like some suppressed and hideous thought

Which flits athwart our musings, but can find
No rest within a pure and gentle mind . . .
Thou sealedst them with many a bare broad word,
And cearedst[8] my memory o'er them,—for I heard
And can forget not . . . they were ministered
One after one, those curses. Mix them up
Like self-destroying poisons in one cup,
And they will make one blessing which thou ne'er
Didst imprecate for, on me,—death.

. . . .

"How vain
Are words! I thought never to speak again,
Not even in secret,—not to my own heart—
But from my lips the unwilling accents start
And from my pen the words flow as I write,
Dazzling my eyes with scalding tears . . . my sight
Is dim to see that charactered in vain
On this unfeeling leaf which burns the brain
And eats into it . . . blotting all things fair
And wise and good which time had written there.

"Those who inflict must suffer, for they see
The work of their own hearts and this must be
Our chastisement or recompense—O child!
I would that thine were like to be more mild
For both our wretched sakes . . . for thine the most
Who feelest already all that thou hast lost
Without the power to wish it thine again;
And as slow years pass, a funereal train
Each with the ghost of some lost hope or friend
Following it like its shadow, wilt thou bend
No thought on my dead memory?

"Alas, love,
Fear me not . . . against thee I would not move
A finger in despite. Do I not live
That thou mayst have less bitter cause to grieve?
I give thee tears for scorn and love for hate,
And that thy lot may be less desolate
Than his on whom thou tramplest, I refrain
From that sweet sleep which medicines all pain.
Then, when thou speakest of me, never say,
'He could forgive not.' Here I cast away
All human passions, all revenge, all pride;
I think, speak, act no ill; I do but hide
Under these words like embers, every spark
Of that which has consumed me—quick and dark
The grave is yawning . . . as its roof shall cover
My limbs with dust and worms under and over
So let Oblivion hide this grief . . . the air
Closes upon my accents, as despair
Upon my heart—let death upon despair!"

He ceased, and overcome leant back awhile,
Then rising, with a melancholy smile
Went to a sofa, and lay down, and slept
A heavy sleep, and in his dreams he wept
And muttered some familiar name, and we
Wept without shame in his society.
I think I never was impressed so much;
The man who were not, must have lacked a touch
Of human nature . . . then we lingered not,
Although our argument was quite forgot,
But calling the attendants, went to dine
At Maddalo's; yet neither cheer nor wine
Could give us spirits, for we talked of him
And nothing else, till daylight made stars dim;
And we agreed his was some dreadful ill
Wrought on him boldly, yet unspeakable
By a dear friend; some deadly change in love
Of one vowed deeply which he dreamed not of;
For whose sake he, it seemed, had fixed a blot
Of falshood on his mind which flourished not
But in the light of all-beholding truth;
And having stamped this canker on his youth
She had abandoned him—and how much more
Might be his woe, we guessed not—he had store
Of friends and fortune once, as we could guess
From his nice habits and his gentleness;
These were now lost . . . it were a grief indeed
If he had changed one unsustaining reed
For all that such a man might else adorn.
The colours of his mind seemed yet unworn;
For the wild language of his grief was high,
Such as in measure were called poetry;
And I remember one remark which then
Maddalo made. He said: "Most wretched men
Are cradled into poetry by wrong,
They learn in suffering what they teach in song."

If I had been an unconnected man
I, from this moment, should have formed some plan
Never to leave sweet Venice,—for to me
It was delight to ride by the lone sea;

[8] **cearedst:** Glossed by Reiman as "Wrapped in waxed cloth, embalmed; previous editors have changed the word to 'seardst.'" **sear:** brand, scorch.

And then, the town is silent—one may write
Or read in gondolas by day or night,
Having the little brazen lamp alight,
Unseen, uninterrupted; books are there,
Pictures, and casts from all those statues fair
Which were twin-born with poetry, and all
We seek in towns, with little to recall
Regrets for the green country. I might sit
In Maddalo's great palace, and his wit
And subtle talk would cheer the winter night
And make me know myself, and the firelight
Would flash upon our faces, till the day
Might dawn and make me wonder at my stay:
But I had friends in London too: the chief
Attraction here, was that I sought relief
From the deep tenderness that maniac wrought
Within me—'twas perhaps an idle thought,
But I imagined that if day by day
I watched him, and but seldom went away,
And studied all the beatings of his heart
With zeal, as men study some stubborn art
For their own good, and could by patience find
An entrance to the caverns of his mind,
I might reclaim him from his dark estate:
In friendships I had been most fortunate—
Yet never saw I one whom I would call
More willingly my friend; and this was all
Accomplished not; such dreams of baseless good
Oft come and go in crowds or solitude
And leave no trace—but what I now designed
Made for long years impression on my mind.
The following morning, urged by my affairs,
I left bright Venice.

After many years
And many changes I returned; the name
Of Venice, and its aspect, was the same;
But Maddalo was travelling far away
Among the mountains of Armenia.
His dog was dead. His child had now become
A woman; such as it has been my doom
To meet with few, a wonder of this earth,
Where there is little of transcendent worth,
Like one of Shakespeare's women: kindly she
And with a manner beyond courtesy
Received her father's friend; and when I asked
Of the lorn maniac, she her memory tasked
And told as she had heard the mournful tale:
"That the poor sufferer's health began to fail
Two years from my departure, but that then
The Lady who had left him, came again.
Her mien had been imperious, but she now
Looked meek—perhaps remorse had brought her low.
Her coming made him better, and they stayed
Together at my father's—for I played
As I remember with the lady's shawl—
I might be six years old—but after all
She left him" . . . "Why, her heart must have been
tough:
How did it end?" "And was not this enough?
They met—they parted"—"Child, is there no more?"
"Something within that interval which bore
The stamp of *why* they parted, *how* they met:
Yet if thine aged eyes disdain to wet
Those wrinkled cheeks with youth's remembered tears,
Ask me no more, but let the silent years
Be closed and ceared over their memory
As yon mute marble where their corpses lie."
I urged and questioned still, she told me how
All happened—but the cold world shall not know.

To ———
(1824; comp. 1821)

Music, when soft voices die,
Vibrates in the memory—
Odours, when sweet violets sicken,
Live within the sense they quicken.

Rose leaves, when the rose is dead,
Are heaped for the belovèd's bed;
And so thy thoughts, when thou art gone,
Love itself shall slumber on.

Lines: 'When the Lamp Is Shattered'
(1824; comp. 1822)

When the lamp is shattered
The light in the dust lies dead—
When the cloud is scattered
The rainbow's glory is shed.
When the lute is broken,

Sweet tones are remembered not;
When the lips have spoken,
Loved accents are soon forgot.

As music and splendour
Survive not the lamp and the lute,
The heart's echoes render
No song when the spirit is mute:—
No song but sad dirges,
Like the wind through a ruined cell,
Or the mournful surges
That ring the dead seaman's knell.

When hearts have once mingled
Love first leaves the well-built nest;
The weak one is singled
To endure what it once possest.
O Love! who bewailest
The frailty of all things here,
Why choose you the frailest
For your cradle, your home, and your bier?

Its passions will rock thee
As the storms rock the ravens on high;
Bright reason will mock thee,
Like the sun from a wintry sky.
From thy nest every rafter
Will rot, and thine eagle home
Leave thee naked to laughter,
When leaves fall and cold winds come.

The Triumph of Life[1]

(1824; comp. 1822)

Swift as a spirit hastening to his task
Of glory and of good, the Sun sprang forth
Rejoicing in his splendour, and the mask

Of darkness fell from the awakened Earth.
The smokeless altars of the mountain snows
Flamed above crimson clouds, and at the birth

Of light, the Ocean's orison arose
To which the birds tempered their matin lay.[2]
All flowers in field or forest which unclose

Their trembling eyelids to the kiss of day,
Swinging their censers in the element,
With orient incense lit by the new ray

Burned slow and inconsumably, and sent
Their odorous sighs up to the smiling air,
And in succession due, did Continent,

Isle, Ocean, and all things that in them wear
The form and character of mortal mould
Rise as the Sun their father rose, to bear

Their portion of the toil which he of old
Took as his own and then imposed on them;
But I, whom thoughts which must remain untold

Had kept as wakeful as the stars that gem
The cone of night, now they were laid asleep,
Stretched my faint limbs beneath the hoary stem

Which an old chestnut flung athwart the steep
Of a green Apennine: before me fled
The night; behind me rose the day; the Deep

Was at my feet, and Heaven above my head
When a strange trance over my fancy grew
Which was not slumber, for the shade it spread

Was so transparent that the scene came through
As clear as when a veil of light is drawn
O'er evening hills they glimmer; and I knew

That I had felt the freshness of that dawn,
Bathed in the same cold dew my brow and hair
And sate as thus upon that slope of lawn

Under the self same bough, and heard as there
The birds, the fountains and the Ocean hold
Sweet talk in music through the enamoured air.
And then a Vision on my brain was rolled. . . .

As in that trance of wondrous thought I lay
This was the tenour of my waking dream.
Methought I sate beside a public way

[1] Donald H. Reiman, in consultation with G. M. Matthews, established the present text in 1971.

[2] **orison:** prayer. **matin:** pertaining to the early part of the day. Together, connotation of morning prayer of Roman Catholicism.

Thick strewn with summer dust, and a great stream
Of people there was hurrying to and fro
Numerous as gnats upon the evening gleam,

All hastening onward, yet none seemed to know
Whither he went, or whence he came, or why
He made one of the multitude, yet so

Was borne amid the crowd as through the sky
One of the million leaves of summer's bier.—
Old age and youth, manhood and infancy,

Mixed in one mighty torrent did appear,
Some flying from the thing they feared and some
Seeking the object of another's fear,

And others as with steps towards the tomb
Pored on the trodden worms that crawled beneath,
And others mournfully within the gloom

Of their own shadow walked, and called it death . . .
And some fled from it as it were a ghost,
Half fainting in the affliction of vain breath.

But more with motions which each other crost
Pursued or shunned the shadows the clouds threw
Or birds within the noonday ether lost,

Upon that path where flowers never grew;
And weary with vain toil and faint for thirst
Heard not the fountains whose melodious dew

Out of their mossy cells forever burst
Nor felt the breeze which from the forest told
Of grassy paths, and wood lawns interpersed

With overarching elms and caverns cold,
And violet banks where sweet dreams brood, but they
Pursued their serious folly as of old. . . .

And as I gazed methought that in the way
The throng grew wilder, as the woods of June
When the South wind shakes the extinguished day.—

And a cold glare, intenser than the noon
But icy cold, obscured with [ ][3] light
The Sun as he the stars. Like the young Moon

When on the sunlit limits of the night
Her white shell trembles amid crimson air
And whilst the sleeping tempest gathers might

Doth, as a herald of its coming, bear
The ghost of her dead Mother, whose dim form
Bends in dark ether from her infant's chair,

So came a chariot on the silent storm
Of its own rushing splendour, and a Shape
So sate within as one whom years deform

Beneath a dusky hood and double cape
Crouching within the shadow of a tomb,
And o'er what seemed the head a cloud like crape[4]

Was bent, a dun and faint etherial gloom
Tempering the light; upon the chariot's beam
A Janus-visaged[5] Shadow did assume

The guidance of that wonder-winged team.
The Shapes which drew it in thick lightnings
Were lost: I heard alone on the air's soft stream

The music of their ever moving wings.
All the four faces of that charioteer
Had their eyes banded . . . little profit brings

Speed in the van and blindness in the rear,
Nor then avail the beams that quench the Sun
Or that these banded eyes could pierce the sphere

Of all that is, has been, or will be done.—
So ill was the car guided, but it past
With solemn speed majestically on . . .

The crowd gave way, and I arose aghast,
Or seemed to rise, so mighty was the trance,
And saw like clouds upon the thunder blast

The million with fierce song and maniac dance
Raging around; such seemed the jubilee
As when to greet some conqueror's advance

Imperial Rome poured forth her living sea
From senatehouse and prison and theatre
When Freedom left those who upon the free

[3] [ ]: Most editors follow Mary Shelley in placing *blinding* where the poet left a blank.

[4] **crape:** light, soft fabric, worn in black when mourning.

[5] **Janus:** an old Italian deity with two or four faces looking either backwards and forwards, or in all directions.

Had bound a yoke which soon they stooped to bear.
Nor wanted here the just similitude
Of a triumphal pageant, for where'er

The chariot rolled a captive multitude
Was driven; all those who had grown old in power
Or misery,—all who have their age subdued,

By action or by suffering, and whose hour
Was drained to its last sand in weal or woe,
So that the trunk survived both fruit and flower;

All those whose fame or infamy must grow
Till the great winter lay the form and name
Of their own earth with them forever low—

All but the sacred few who could not tame
Their spirits to the Conqueror, but as soon
As they had touched the world with living flame

Fled back like eagles to their native noon,
Or those who put aside the diadem
Of earthly thrones or gems, till the last one

Were there; for they of Athens and Jerusalem
Were neither mid the mighty captives seen
Nor mid the ribald crowd that followed them

Or fled before. . . . Swift, fierce and obscene
The wild dance maddens in the van, and those
Who lead it, fleet as shadows on the green,

Outspeed the chariot and without repose
Mix with each other in tempestuous measure
To savage music. . . . Wilder as it grows,

They, tortured by the agonizing pleasure,
Convulsed and on the rapid whirlwinds spun
Of that fierce spirit, whose unholy leisure

Was soothed by mischief since the world begun,
Throw back their heads and loose their streaming hair,
And in their dance round her who dims the Sun

Maidens and youths fling their wild arms in air
As their feet twinkle; now recede and now
Bending within each other's atmosphere

Kindle invisibly; and as they glow
Like moths by light attracted and repelled,
Oft to new bright destruction come and go,

Till like two clouds into one vale impelled
That shake the mountains when their lightnings mingle
And die in rain,—the fiery band which held

Their natures, snaps . . . ere the shock cease to tingle
One falls and then another in the path
Senseless, nor is the desolation single,

Yet ere I can say *where* the chariot hath
Past over them; nor other trace I find
But as of foam after the Ocean's wrath

Is spent upon the desert shore.—Behind,
Old men, a[nd] women foully disarrayed
Shake their grey hair in the insulting wind,

Limp in the dance and strain with limbs decayed
To reach the car of light which leaves them still
Farther behind and deeper in the shade.

But not the less with impotence of will
They wheel, though ghastly shadows interpose
Round them and round each other, and fulfill

Their work and to the dust whence they arose
Sink and corruption veils them as they lie—
And frost in these performs what fire in those.

Struck to the heart by this sad pageantry,
Half to myself I said, "And what is this?
Whose shape is that within the car? & why"—

I would have added—"is all here amiss?"
But a voice answered . . "Life" . . . I turned and knew
(O Heaven have mercy on such wretchedness!)

That what I thought was an old root which grew
To strange distortion out of the hill side
Was indeed one of that deluded crew,

And that the grass which methought hung so wide
And white, was but his thin discoloured hair,
And that the holes it vainly sought to hide

Were or had been eyes.—"If thou canst forbear
To join the dance, which I had well forborne,"
Said the grim Feature, of my thought aware,

"I will tell all that which to this deep scorn
Led me and my companions, and relate
The progress of the pageant since the morn;

"If thirst of knowledge doth not thus abate,
Follow it even to the night, but I
Am weary" . . . Then like one who with the weight

Of his own words is staggered, wearily
He paused, and ere he could resume, I cried,
"First who art thou?" . . . "Before thy memory

"I feared, loved, hated, suffered, did, and died,
And if the spark with which Heaven lit my spirit
Earth had with purer nutriment supplied

"Corruption would not now thus much inherit
Of what was once Rousseau—nor this disguise
Stained that within which still disdains to wear it.—

"If I have been extinguished, yet there rise
A thousand beacons from the spark I bore."—
"And who are those chained to the car?" "The Wise,

"The great, the unforgotten: they who wore
Mitres and helms and crowns, or wreathes of light,
Signs of thought's empire over thought; their lore

"Taught them not this—to know themselves; their might
Could not repress the mutiny within,
And for the morn of truth they feigned, deep night

"Caught them ere evening." "Who is he with chin
Upon his breast and hands crost on his chain?"
"The Child of a fierce hour; he sought to win

"The world, and lost all it did contain
Of greatness, in its hope destroyed; and more
Of fame and peace than Virtue's self can gain

"Without the opportunity which bore
Him on its eagle's pinion to the peak
From which a thousand climbers have before

"Fall'n as Napoleon fell."—I felt my cheek
Alter to see the great form pass away
Whose grasp had left the giant world so weak

That every pigmy kicked it as it lay—
And much I grieved to think how power and will
In opposition rule our mortal day—

And why God made irreconcilable
Good and the means of good; and for despair
I half disdained mine eye's desire to fill

With the spent vision of the times that were
And scarce have ceased to be . . "Dost thou behold,"
Said then my guide, "those spoilers spoiled, Voltaire,

"Frederic, and Kant, Catherine, and Leopold,[6]
Chained hoary anarchs, demagogue and sage
Whose name the fresh world thinks already old—

"For in the battle Life and they did wage
She remained conqueror—I was overcome
By my own heart alone, which neither age

"Nor tears nor infamy nor now the tomb
Could temper to its object."—"Let them pass"—
I cried—"the world and its mysterious doom

"Is not so much more glorious than it was
That I desire to worship those who drew
New figures on its false and fragile glass

"As the old faded."—"Figures ever new
Rise on the bubble, paint them how you may;
We have but thrown, as those before us threw,

"Our shadows on it as it past away.
But mark, how chained to the triumphal chair
The mighty phantoms of an elder day—

"All that is mortal of great Plato there
Expiates the joy and woe his master knew not;
That star that ruled his doom was far too fair[7]—

"And Life, where long that flower of Heaven grew not,
Conquered the heart by love which gold or pain
Or age or sloth or slavery could subdue not—

"And near [ ] walk the [ ] twain.[8]
The tutor and his pupil, whom Dominion
Followed as tame as vulture in a chain.—

"The world was darkened beneath either pinion
Of him whom from the flock of conquerors
Fame singled as her thunderbearing minion;

"The other long outlived both woes and wars,
Throned in new thoughts of men, and still had kept
The jealous keys of truth's eternal doors

"If Bacon's spirit [ ] had not leapt
Like lightning out of darkness;[9] he compelled
The Proteus shape of Nature's as it slept

[6]**Voltaire:** French satirist (1694–1778) and leading figure of the Enlightenment. **Frederic:** King Frederick II of Prussia (1712–1786). **Kant:** Immanuel Kant (1724–1804), professor of logic and metaphysics at Konigsberg and leading philosopher of the age. **Catherine:** Catherine the Great of Russia (1729–1796). **Leopold:** Leopold II (1747–1792) of Austria.

[7]**That star . . . fair:** See the epigraph to *Adonais.*

[8]**[ ] . . . twain:** Mary Shelley included *him* for the first blank, which most editors have accepted. The second blank was left thus. The *twain* are Aristotle and Alexander the Great.

[9]**If Bacon's spirit . . . darkness:** In *The Advancement of Learning* (1605) Francis Bacon (1561–1626) introduced the scientific method as the way to gain knowledge and control of the natural

"To wake and to unbar the caves that held
The treasure of the secrets of its reign—
See the great bards of old who inly quelled

"The passions which they sung, as by their strain
May well be known: their living melody
Tempers its own contagion to the vein

"Of those who are infected with it—I
Have suffered what I wrote, or viler pain!—

"And so my words were seeds of misery—
Even as the deeds of others."—"Not as theirs,"
I said—he pointed to a company

In which I recognized amid the heirs
Of Caesar's crime from him to Constantine.
The Anarchs old whose force and murderous snares

Had founded many a sceptre bearing line
And spread the plague of blood and gold abroad,
And Gregory and John and men divine[10]

Who rose like shadows between Man and god
Till that eclipse, still hanging under Heaven,
Was worshipped by the world o'er which they strode

For the true Sun it quenched.—"Their power was given
But to destroy," replied the leader—"I
Am one of those who have created, even

"If it be but a world of agony."—
"Whence camest thou and whither goest thou?
How did thy course begin," I said, "and why?

"Mine eyes are sick of this perpetual flow
Of people, and my heart of one sad thought.—
Speak." "Whence I came, partly I seem to know,

"And how and by what paths I have been brought
To this dread pass, methinks even thou mayst guess;
Why this should be my mind can compass not;

"Whither the conqueror hurries me still less.
But follow thou, and from spectator turn
Actor or victim in this wretchedness,

"And what thou wouldst be taught I then may learn
From thee.—Now listen . . . In the April prime
When all the forest tops began to burn

"With kindling green, touched by the azure clime
Of the young year, I found myself asleep
Under a mountain, which from unknown time

"Had yawned into a cavern high and deep,
And from it came a gentle rivulet
Whose water like clear air in its calm sweep

"Bent the soft grass and kept for ever wet
The stems of the sweet flowers, and filled the grove
With sound which all who hear must needs forget

"All pleasure and all pain, all hate and love,
Which they had known before that hour of rest:
A sleeping mother then would dream not of

"The only child who died upon her breast
At eventide, a king would mourn no more
The crown of which his brow was dispossest

"When the sun lingered o'er the Ocean floor
To gild his rival's new prosperity.—
Thou wouldst forget thus vainly to deplore

"Ills, which if ills, can find no cure from thee,
The thought of which no other sleep will quell
Nor other music blot from memory—

"So sweet and deep is the oblivious spell.—
Whether my life had been before that sleep
The Heaven which I imagine, or a Hell

"Like this harsh world in which I wake to weep,
I know not. I arose and for a space
The scene of woods and waters seemed to keep,

"Though it was now broad day, a gentle trace
Of light diviner than the common Sun
Sheds on the common Earth, but all the place

"Was filled with many sounds woven into one
Oblivious melody, confusing sense
Amid the gliding waves and shadows dun;

"And as I looked the bright omnipresence
Of morning through the orient cavern flowed,
And the Sun's image radiantly intense

"Burned on the waters of the well that glowed
Like gold, and threaded all the forest maze
With winding paths of emerald fire—there stood

"Amid the sun, as he amid the blaze
Of his own glory, on the vibrating
Floor of the fountain, paved with flashing rays,

"A shape all light, which with one hand did fling
Dew on the earth, as if she were the Dawn
Whose invisible rain forever seemed to sing

world as opposed to the ways to gaining knowledge espoused by humanists, scholastics, and occultists.

[10] **Gregory and John:** names of popes.

"A silver music on the mossy lawn,
And still before her on the dusky grass
Iris[11] her many coloured scarf had drawn.—

"In her right hand she bore a chrystal glass
Mantling with bright Nepenthe;[12]—the fierce splendour
Fell from her as she moved under the mass

"Of the deep cavern, and with palms so tender
Their tread broke not the mirror of its billow,
Glided along the river, and did bend her

"Head under the dark boughs, till like a willow
Her fair hair swept the bosom of the stream
That whispered with delight to be their pillow.—

"As one enamoured is upborne in dream
O'er lily-paven lakes mid silver mist
To wondrous music, so this shape might seem

"Partly to tread the waves with feet which kist
The dancing foam, partly to glide along
The airs that roughened the moist amethyst,[13]

"Or the slant morning beams that fell among
The trees, or the soft shadows of the trees;
And her feet ever to the ceaseless song

"Of leaves and winds and waves and birds and bees
And falling drops moved in a measure new
Yet sweet, as on the summer evening breeze

"Up from the lake a shape of golden dew
Between two rocks, athwart the rising moon,
Dances i' the wind where eagle never flew.—

"And still her feet, no less than the sweet tune
To which they moved, seemed as they moved, to blot
The thoughts of him who gazed on them, and soon

"All that was seemed as if it had been not,
As if the gazer's mind was strewn beneath
Her feet like embers, and she, thought by thought,

"Trampled its fires into the dust of death,
As Day upon the threshold of the east
Treads out the lamps of night, until the breath

"Of darkness reillumines even the least
Of heaven's living eyes—like day she came,
Making the night a dream; and ere she ceased

"To move, as one between desire and shame
Suspended, I said—'If, as it doth seem,
Thou comest from the realm without a name,

"'Into this valley of perpetual dream,
Shew whence I came, and where I am, and why—
Pass not away upon the passing stream.'

"'Arise and quench thy thirst,' was her reply.
And as a shut lily, stricken by the wand
Of dewy morning's vital alchemy,

"I rose; and, bending at her sweet command,
Touched with faint lips the cup she raised,
And suddenly my brain became as sand

"Where the first wave had more than half erased
The track of deer on desert Labrador,
Whilst the fierce wolf from which they fled amazed

"Leaves his stamp visibly upon the shore
Until the second bursts—so on my sight
Burst a new Vision never seen before.—

"And the fair shape waned in the coming light
As veil by veil the silent splendour drops
From Lucifer,[14] amid the chrysolite

"Of sunrise ere it strike the mountain tops—
And as the presence of that fairest planet
Although unseen is felt by one who hopes

"That his day's path may end as he began it
In that star's smile, whose light is like the scent
Of a jonquil[15] when evening breezes fan it,

"Or the soft notes in which his dear lament
The Brescian[16] shepherd breathes, or the caress
That turned his weary slumber to content.—

"So knew I in that light's severe excess
The presence of that shape which on the stream
Moved, as I moved along the wilderness,

"More dimly than a day appearing dream,
The ghost of a forgotten form of sleep,
A light from Heaven whose half extinguished beam

[11] **Iris:** the messenger of the gods and personified as a rainbow.

[12] **Nepenthe:** drug that causes forgetfulness and eliminates sorrow; possibly opium.

[13] **amethyst:** transparent quartz, generally purple or violet.

[14] **Lucifer:** *lit.* the light bearer. The archangel who led the revolt against God, causing the fall of the angels into Hell.

[15] **jonquil:** plant with fragrant yellow flowers.

[16] **Brescia:** a city in northern Italy.

"Through the sick day in which we wake to weep
Glimmers, forever sought, forever lost.—
So did that shape its obscure tenour keep

"Beside my path, as silent as a ghost;
But the new Vision, and its cold bright car,
With savage music, stunning music, crost

"The forest, and as if from some dread war
Triumphantly returning, the loud million
Fiercely extolled the fortune of her star.—

"A moving arch of victory the vermilion
And green and azure plumes of Iris had
Built high over her wind-winged pavilion,

"And underneath ætherial glory clad
The wilderness, and far before her flew
The tempest of the splendour which forbade

"Shadow to fall from leaf or stone;—the crew
Seemed in that light like atomies[17] that dance
Within a sunbeam.—Some upon the new

"Embroidery of flowers that did enhance
The grassy vesture of the desart, played,
Forgetful of the chariot's swift advance;

"Others stood gazing till within the shade
Of the great mountain its light left them dim.—
Others outspeeded it, and others made

"Circles around it like the clouds that swim
Round the high moon in a bright sea of air,
And more did follow, with exulting hymn,

"The chariot and the captives fettered there,
But all like bubbles on an eddying flood
Fell into the same track at last and were

"Borne onward.—I among the multitude
Was swept; me sweetest flowers delayed not long,
Me not the shadow nor the solitude,

"Me not the falling stream's Lethean[18] song,
Me, not the phantom of that early form
Which moved upon its motion,—but among

"The thickest billows of the living storm
I plunged, and bared my bosom to the clime
Of that cold light, whose airs too soon deform.—

"Before the chariot had begun to climb
The opposing steep of that mysterious dell,
Behold a wonder worthy of the rhyme

"Of him who from the lowest depths of Hell
Through every Paradise and through all glory
Love led serene, and who returned to tell

"In words of hate and awe the wondrous story
How all things are transfigured, except Love;[19]
For deaf as is a sea which wrath makes hoary

"The world can hear not the sweet notes that move
The sphere whose light is melody to lovers—
A wonder worthy of his rhyme—the grove

"Grew dense with shadows to its inmost covers,
The earth was grey with phantoms, and the air
Was peopled with dim forms, as when there hovers

"A flock of vampire-bats before the glare
Of the tropic sun, bringing ere evening
Strange night upon some Indian isle,—thus were

"Phantoms diffused around, and some did fling
Shadows of shadows, yet unlike themselves,
Behind them, some like eaglets on the wing

"Were lost in the white blaze, others like elves
Danced in a thousand unimagined shapes
Upon the sunny streams and grassy shelves;

"And others sate chattering like restless apes
On vulgar paws and voluble like fire.
Some made a cradle of the ermined capes

"Of kingly mantles, some upon the tiar[20]
Of pontiffs sate like vultures, others played
Within the crown which girt with empire

"A baby's or an idiot's brow, and made
Their nests in it; the old anatomies
Sate hatching their bare brood under the shade

"Of demon wings, and laughed from their dead
eyes
To reassume the delegated power
Arrayed in which these worms did monarchize

[17] **atomies:** particles.

[18] **Lethean:** from Lethe, the river of the underworld, whose waters provide forgetfulness for the dead.

[19] **Of him . . . Love:** synopsis of Dante's *Divine Comedy.*

[20] **tiar:** crown.

"Who make this earth their charnel.[21]—Others more
Humble, like falcons sate upon the fist
Of common men, and round their heads did soar,

"Or like small gnats and flies, as thick as mist
On evening marshes, thronged about the brow
Of lawyer, statesman, priest and theorist,

"And others like discoloured flakes of snow
On fairest bosoms and the sunniest hair
Fell, and were melted by the youthful glow

"Which they extinguished; for like tears, they were
A veil to those from whose faint lids they rained
In drops of sorrow.—I became aware

"Of whence those forms proceeded which thus stained
The track in which we moved; after brief space
From every form the beauty slowly waned,

"From every firmest limb and fairest face
The strength and freshness fell like dust, and left
The action and the shape without the grace

"Of life; the marble brow of youth was cleft
With care, and in the eyes where once hope shone
Desire like a lioness bereft

"Of its last cub, glared ere it died; each one
Of that great crowd sent forth incessantly
These shadows, numerous as the dead leaves blown

"In Autumn evening from a poplar tree—
Each, like himself and like each other were,
At first, but soon distorted, seemed to be

"Obscure clouds moulded by the casual air;
And of this stuff the car's creative ray
Wrought all the busy phantoms that were there

"As the sun shapes the clouds—thus, on the way
Mask after mask fell from the countenance
And form of all, and long before the day

"Was old, the joy which waked like Heaven's glance
The sleepers in the oblivious valley, died,
And some grew weary of the ghastly dance

"And fell, as I have fallen by the way side,
Those soonest from whose forms most shadows past
And least of strength and beauty did abide."—

"Then, what is Life?" I said . . . the cripple cast
His eye upon the car which now had rolled
Onward, as if that look must be the last,

And answered. . . . "Happy those for whom the fold
Of[22]

[21] **charnel**: house for bones and remains of the dead.

[22] Here the manuscript ends. Mary Shelley's edition of 1824 has the poem close with line 544 thusly: "Then, what is life? I cried."—Some editors have followed her in closing the poem and reading *said* as *cried*.

from KEEPSAKE FOR 1829
(1829)

Essay on Love[1]
(comp. 1818)

What is love? Ask him who lives, what is life? Ask him who adores, what is God?

I know not the internal constitution of other men, nor even yours whom I now address. I see that in some external attributes they resemble me, but when misled by that appearance I have thought to appeal to something in common and unburden my inmost soul to them, I have found my language misunderstood like one in a distant and savage land. The more opportunities they have afforded me for experience, the wider has appeared the interval between us, and to a greater distance have the points of sympathy been withdrawn. With a spirit ill fitted to sustain such proof, trembling and feeble through its tenderness, I have everywhere sought sympathy and found only repulse and disappointment.

Thou demandest, What is Love? It is that powerful attraction towards all that we conceive, or fear, or hope beyond ourselves, when we find within our own thoughts the chasm of an insufficient void and seek to awaken in all things that are a community with what we experience within ourselves. If we reason, we would be understood; if we imagine, we would that the airy children of our brain were born anew within another's; if we feel, we would that another's nerves should vibrate to our own, that the beams of their eyes should kindle at once and mix and

[1] first published by Mary Shelley in the gift book *Keepsake.*

melt into our own, that lips of motionless ice should not reply to lips quivering and burning with the heart's best blood. This is Love. This is the bond and the sanction which connects not only man with man but with everything which exists. We are born into the world, and there is something within us which, from the instant that we live, more and more thirsts after its likeness. It is probably in correspondence with this law that the infant drains milk from the bosom of its mother; this propensity develops itself with the development of our nature. We dimly see within our intellectual nature a miniature as it were of our entire self, yet deprived of all that we condemn or despise, the ideal prototype of every thing excellent or lovely that we are capable of conceiving as belonging to the nature of man. Not only the portrait of our external being but an assemblage of the minutest particles of which our nature is composed;[2] a mirror whose surface reflects only the forms of purity and brightness; a soul within our soul that describes a circle around its proper paradise which pain, and sorrow, and evil dare not overleap. To this we eagerly refer all sensations, thirsting that they should resemble or correspond with it. The discovery of its anti-type; the meeting with an understanding capable of clearly estimating our own; an imagination which should enter into and seize upon the subtle and delicate peculiarities which we have delighted to cherish and unfold in secret; with a frame whose nerves, like the chords of two exquisite lyres, strung to the accompaniment of one delightful voice, vibrate with the vibrations of our own; and of a combination of all these in such proportion as the type within demands; this is the invisible and unattainable point to which Love tends; and to attain which, it urges forth the powers of man to arrest the faintest shadow of that without the possession of which there is no rest nor respite to the heart over which it rules. Hence in solitude, or in that deserted state when we are surrounded by human beings, and yet they sympathize not with us, we love the flowers, the grass, and the waters, and the sky. In the motion of the very leaves of spring, in the blue air, there is then found a secret correspondence with our heart. There is eloquence in the tongueless wind, and a melody in the flowing brooks and the rustling of the reeds beside them, which by their inconceivable relation to something within the soul, awaken the spirits to a dance of breathless rapture, and bring tears of mysterious tenderness to the eyes, like the enthusiasm of patriotic success, or the voice of one beloved singing to you alone. Sterne says that, if he were in a desert, he would love some cypress. So soon as this want or power is dead, man becomes the living sepulchre of himself, and what yet survives is the mere husk of what once he was.[3]

[2] "These words are ineffectual and metaphorical. Most words are so—No help!" [P.B.S.]

[3] Although Shelley indicates that this idea is from (Laurence) Sterne, the source is still unidentified.

from THE ATHENAEUM[1]

(1832)

Similes for Two Political Characters of 1819[2]

(comp. 1819)

I

As from an ancestral oak
  Two empty ravens sound their clarion,
Yell by yell, and croak by croak,
When they scent the noonday smoke
    Of fresh human carrion:—

II

As two gibbering night-birds flit
  From their bowers of deadly yew
Through the night to frighten it,
When the moon is in a fit,
    And the stars are none, or few:—

III

As a shark and dog-fish wait
  Under an Atlantic isle,
For the negro-ship, whose freight
Is the theme of their debate,
    Wrinkling their red gills the while—

[1] *The Athenaeum* (1828–1921) was a literary review that sought to be critical rather than political in editorial policy.

[2] The two political characters are Viscount Castlereagh, the foreign secretary, and Viscount Sidmouth, the home secretary, both notorious for ultra-conservatism.

IV

Are ye, two vultures sick for battle,
Two scorpions under one wet stone,
Two bloodless wolves whose dry throats rattle,
Two crows perched on the murrained[3] cattle,
Two vipers tangled into one.

With a Guitar, to Jane[1]

(comp. 1822)

Ariel to Miranda[2]:—Take
This slave of Music, for the sake
Of him who is the slave of thee,
And teach it all the harmony
In which thou canst, and only thou,
Make the delighted spirit glow,
Till joy denies itself again,
And, too intense, is turned to pain;
For by permission and command
Of thine own Prince Ferdinand,
Poor Ariel sends this silent token
Of more than ever can be spoken;
Your guardian spirit, Ariel, who,
From life to life, must still pursue
Your happiness;—for thus alone
Can Ariel ever find his own.
From Prospero's enchanted cell,
As the mighty verses tell,
To the throne of Naples, he
Lit you o'er the trackless sea,
Flitting on, your prow before,
Like a living meteor.
When you die, the silent Moon,
In her interlunar swoon,
Is not sadder in her cell
Than deserted Ariel.
When you live again on earth,
Like an unseen star of birth,
Ariel guides you o'er the sea
Of life from your nativity.
Many changes have been run
Since Ferdinand and you begun
Your course of love, and Ariel still
Has tracked your steps, and served your will;
Now, in humbler, happier lot,
This is all remembered not;
And now, alas! the poor sprite is
Imprisoned, for some fault of his,
In a body like a grave;—
From you he only dares to crave,
For his service and his sorrow,
A smile to-day, a song to-morrow.
The artist who this idol wrought,
To echo all harmonious thought,
Felled a tree, while on the steep
The woods were in their winter sleep,
Rocked in that repose divine
On the wind-swept Apennine;
And dreaming, some of Autumn past,
And some of Spring approaching fast,
And some of April buds and showers,
And some of songs in July bowers,
And all of love; and so this tree,—
O that such our death may be!—
Died in sleep, and felt no pain,
To live in happier form again:
From which, beneath Heaven's fairest star,
The artist wrought this loved Guitar,
And taught it justly to reply,
To all who question skilfully,
In language gentle as thine own;
Whispering in enamoured tone
Sweet oracles of woods and dells,
And summer winds in sylvan cells;
For it had learned all harmonies
Of the plains and of the skies,
Of the forests and the mountains,
And the many-voicèd fountains;
The clearest echoes of the hills,
The softest notes of falling rills,
The melodies of birds and bees,
The murmuring of summer seas,
And pattering rain, and breathing dew,
And airs of evening; and it knew

---

[3] **murrained:** seriously diseased.

[1] Addressed to Jane Williams, wife of Edward Williams. The Williams were friends of the Shelleys. Edward Williams drowned with Shelley in the Gulf of Spezia.

[2] **Ariel . . . Miranda:** The allusions are to characters of Shakespeare's *The Tempest*: Jane is Miranda, Shelley is Ariel, Edward Williams is Prince Ferdinand (line 10).

That seldom-heard mysterious sound,
Which, driven on its diurnal round,
As it floats through boundless day,
Our world enkindles on its way.—
All this it knows, but will not tell
To those who cannot question well
The Spirit that inhabits it;
It talks according to the wit
Of its companions; and no more
Is heard than has been felt before,
By those who tempt it to betray
These secrets of an elder day:
But, sweetly as its answers will
Flatter hands of perfect skill,
It keeps its highest, holiest tone
For our belovèd Jane alone.

To Jane: 'The Keen Stars Were Twinkling'

(1832; comp. 1822)

I

The keen stars were twinkling,
And the fair moon was rising among them,
Dear Jane!
The guitar was tinkling,
But the notes were not sweet till you sung them
Again.

II

As the moon's soft splendour
O'er the faint cold starlight of Heaven
Is thrown,
So your voice most tender
To the strings without soul had then given
Its own.

III

The stars will awaken,
Though the moon sleep a full hour later,
To-night;
No leaf will be shaken
Whilst the dews of your melody scatter
Delight.

IV

Though the sound overpowers,
Sing again, with your dear voice revealing
A tone
Of some world far from ours,
Where music and moonlight and feeling
Are one.

from THE POETICAL WORKS OF PERCY BYSSHE SHELLEY[1]

(1839)

Sonnet: England in 1819

(comp. 1819)

An old, mad, blind, despised, and dying king,[2]—
Princes, the dregs of their dull race, who flow
Through public scorn,—mud from a muddy
spring,—
Rulers who neither see, nor feel, nor know,
But leech-like to their fainting country cling,
Till they drop, blind in blood, without a blow,—
A people starved and stabbed in the untilled field,—
An army, which liberticide and prey
Makes as a two-edged sword to all who wield,—
Golden and sanguine laws which tempt and slay;
Religion Christless, Godless—a book sealed;
A Senate,—Time's worst statute unrepealed,—
Are graves, from which a glorious Phantom may
Burst, to illumine our tempestuous day.

Song to the Men of England

(1839; comp. 1819)

I

Men of England, wherefore plough
For the lords who lay ye low?

[1] The first collected edition of Shelley's works, edited by Mary Shelley.

[2] George III, who had been declared insane in 1811, died in 1820.

Wherefore weave with toil and care
The rich robes your tyrants wear?

II

Wherefore feed, and clothe, and save,
From the cradle to the grave,
Those ungrateful drones who would
Drain your sweat — nay, drink your blood?

III

Wherefore, Bees of England, forge
Many a weapon, chain, and scourge,
That these stingless drones may spoil
The forced produce of your toil?

IV

Have ye leisure, comfort, calm,
Shelter, food, love's gentle balm?
Or what is it ye buy so dear
With your pain and with your fear?

V

The seed ye sow, another reaps;
The wealth ye find, another keeps;
The robes ye weave, another wears;
The arms ye forge, another bears.

VI

Sow seed, — but let no tyrant reap;
Find wealth, — let no impostor heap;
Weave robes, — let not the idle wear;
Forge arms, in your defence to bear.

VII

Shrink to your cellars, holes, and cells;
In halls ye deck another dwells.
Why shake the chains ye wrought?
  Ye see
The steel ye tempered glance on ye.

VIII

With plough and spade, and hoe and loom,
Trace your grave, and build your tomb,
And weave your winding-sheet, till fair
England be your sepulchre.

from ESSAYS, LETTERS FROM ABROAD, TRANSLATIONS AND FRAGMENTS

(1840)

from A Defence of Poetry

or Remarks Suggested by an Essay Entitled "The Four Ages of Poetry"[1]

(comp. 1821)

According to one mode of regarding those two classes of mental action, which are called reason and imagination, the former may be considered as mind contemplating the relations borne by one thought to another, however produced; and the latter, as mind acting upon those thoughts so as to colour them with its own light, and composing from them, as from elements, other thoughts, each containing within itself the principle of its own integrity. The one is the τὸ ποιειν, or the principle of synthesis, and has for its objects those forms which are common to universal nature and existence itself; the other is the τὸ λογιζειν, or principle of analysis, and its action regards the relations of things, simply as relations; considering thoughts, not in their integral unity, but as the algebraical representations which conduct to certain general results. Reason is the enumeration of quantities already known; imagination is the perception of the value of those quantities, both separately and as a whole. Reason respects the differences, and imagination the similitudes of things. Reason is to Imagination as the instrument to the agent, as the body to the spirit, as the shadow to the substance.

Poetry, in a general sense, may be defined to be "the expression of the Imagination": and poetry is connate with the origin of man. Man is an instrument over which a series of external and internal impressions are driven, like the alternations of an ever-changing wind over an Aeolian Lyre, which move it by their motion to ever-changing melody. But there is a principle within the human being, and perhaps within all sentient beings, which acts otherwise than

[1] Shelley's *Defence* is a response to friend Thomas Love Peacock's "The Four Ages of Poetry," published in the *Literary Miscellany* of the London publishers, C. and J. Ollier, in 1820. See section introduction for background.

in the lyre, and produces not melody, alone, but harmony, by an internal adjustment of the sounds or motions thus excited to the impressions which excite them. It is as if the lyre could accommodate its chords to the motions of that which strikes them, in a determined proportion of sound; even as the musician can accommodate his voice to the sound of the lyre. A child at play by itself will express its delight by its voice and motions; and every inflexion of tone and every gesture will bear exact relation to a corresponding antitype in the pleasurable impressions which awakened it; it will be the reflected image of that impression; and as the lyre trembles and sounds after the wind has died away, so the child seeks, by prolonging in its voice and motions the duration of the effect, to prolong also a consciousness of the cause. In relation to the objects which delight a child, these expressions are, what poetry is to higher objects. The savage (for the savage is to ages what the child is to years) expresses the emotions produced in him by surrounding objects in a similar manner; and language and gesture, together with plastic or pictorial imitation, become the image of the combined effect of those objects, and of his apprehension of them. Man in society, with all his passions and his pleasures, next becomes the object of the passions and pleasures of man; an additional class of emotions produces an augmented treasure of expressions; and language, gesture, and the imitative arts, become at once the representation and the medium, the pencil and the picture, the chisel and the statue, the chord and the harmony. The social sympathies, or those laws from which as from its elements society results, begin to develope themselves from the moment that two human beings coexist; the future is contained within the present as the plant within the seed; and equality, diversity, unity, contrast, mutual dependence, become the principles alone capable of affording the motives according to which the will of a social being is determined to action, inasmuch as he is social; and constitute pleasure in sensation, virtue in sentiment, beauty in art, truth in reasoning, and love in the intercourse of kind. Hence men, even in the infancy of society, observe a certain order in their words and actions, distinct from that of the objects and the impressions represented by them, all expression being subject to the laws of that from which it proceeds. But let us dismiss those more general considerations which might involve an enquiry into the principles of society itself, and restrict our view to the manner in which the imagination is expressed upon its forms.

In the youth of the world, men dance and sing and imitate natural objects, observing in these actions, as in all others, a certain rhythm or order. And, although all men observe a similar, they observe not the same order, in the motions of the dance, in the melody of the song, in the combinations of language, in the series of their imitations of natural objects. For there is a certain order or rhythm belonging to each of these classes of mimetic representation, from which the hearer and the spectator receive an intenser and purer pleasure than from any other: the sense of an approximation to this order has been called taste, by modern writers. Every man in the infancy of art, observes an order which approximates more or less closely to that from which this highest delight results: but the diversity is not sufficiently marked, as that its gradations should be sensible, except in those instances where the predominance of this faculty of approximation to the beautiful (for so we may be permitted to name the relation between this highest pleasure and its cause) is very great. Those in whom it exists in excess are poets, in the most universal sense of the word; and the pleasure resulting from the manner in which they express the influence of society or nature upon their own minds, communicates itself to others, and gathers a sort of reduplication from that community. Their language is vitally metaphorical; that is, it marks the before unapprehended relations of things, and perpetuates their apprehension, until the words which represent them, become through time signs for portions of classes of thoughts instead of pictures of integral thoughts; and then if no new poets should arise to create afresh the associations which have been thus disorganized, language will be dead to all the nobler purposes of human intercourse. These similitudes or relations are finely said by Lord Bacon to be "the same footsteps of nature impressed upon the various subjects of the world"[2] —and he considers the faculty which perceives them as the storehouse of axioms common to all knowledge. In the infancy of society every author is necessarily a poet, because language itself is poetry; and to be a poet is to apprehend the true and the beautiful, in a word the good which exists in the relation, subsisting, first between existence and perception, and secondly between perception and expression. Every original language near to its source

[2] **"the same footsteps . . . the world"**: Cf. Francis Bacon's *The Advancement of Learning* (1605).

is in itself the chaos of a cyclic poem: the copiousness of lexicography and the distinctions of grammar are the works of a later age, and are merely the catalogue and the form of the creations of Poetry.

But Poets, or those who imagine and express this indestructible order, are not only the authors of language and of music, of the dance and architecture and statuary and painting: they are the institutors of laws, and the founders of civil society and the inventors of the arts of life and the teachers, who draw into a certain propinquity with the beautiful and the true that partial apprehension of the agencies of the invisible world which is called religion. Hence all original religions are allegorical, or susceptible of allegory, and like Janus have a double face of false and true. Poets, according to the circumstances of the age and nation in which they appeared, were called in the earlier epochs of the world legislators or prophets: a poet essentially comprises and unites both these characters. For he not only beholds intensely the present as it is, and discovers those laws according to which present things ought to be ordered, but he beholds the future in the present, and his thoughts are the germs of the flower and the fruit of latest time. Not that I assert poets to be prophets in the gross sense of the word, or that they can foretell the form as surely as they foreknow the spirit of events: such is the pretence of superstition which would make poetry an attribute of prophecy, rather than prophecy an attribute of poetry. A Poet participates in the eternal, the infinite, and the one; as far as relates to his conceptions, time and place and number are not. The grammatical forms which express the moods of time, and the difference of persons and the distinction of place are convertible with respect to the highest poetry without injuring it as poetry, and the choruses of Aeschylus, and the book of Job, and Dante's Paradise would afford, more than any other writings, examples of this fact, if the limits of this essay did not forbid citation. The creations of sculpture, painting, and music, are illustrations still more decisive.

cause + effect.

Language, colour, form, and religious and civil habits of action are all the instruments and materials of poetry; they may be called poetry by that figure of speech which considers the effect as a synonime of the cause. But poetry in a more restricted sense expresses those arrangements of language, and especially metrical language, which are created by that imperial faculty, whose throne is curtained within the invisible nature of man. And this springs from the nature itself of language, which is a more direct representation of the actions and passions of our internal being, and is susceptible of more various and delicate combinations, than colour, form, or motion, and is more plastic and obedient to the controul of that faculty of which it is the creation. For language is arbitrarily produced by the Imagination and has relation to thoughts alone; but all other materials, instruments and conditions of art, have relations among each other, which limit and interpose between conception and expression. The former is as a mirror which reflects, the latter as a cloud which enfeebles, the light of which both are mediums of communication. Hence the fame of sculptors, painters and musicians, although the intrinsic powers of the great masters of these arts, may yield in no degree to that of those who have employed language as the hieroglyphic of their thoughts, has never equalled that of poets in the restricted sense of the term; as two performers of equal skill will produce unequal effects from a guitar and a harp. The fame of legislators and founders of religions, so long as their institutions last, alone seems to exceed that of poets in the restricted sense; but it can scarcely be a question whether, if we deduct the celebrity which their flattery of the gross opinions of the vulgar usually conciliates, together with that which belonged to them in their higher character of poets, any excess will remain.

We have thus circumscribed the meaning of the word Poetry within the limits of that art which is the most familiar and the most perfect expression of the faculty itself. It is necessary however to make the circle still narrower, and to determine the distinction between measured and unmeasured language; for the popular division into prose and verse is inadmissible in accurate philosophy.

Sounds as well as thoughts have relation both between each other and towards that which they represent, and a perception of the order of those relations has always been found connected with a perception of the order of the relations of thoughts. Hence the language of poets has ever affected a certain uniform and harmonious recurrence of sound, without which it were not poetry, and which is scarcely less indispensable to the communication of its influence, than the words themselves, without reference to that peculiar order. Hence the vanity of translation; it were as wise to cast a violet into a crucible that you might discover the formal principle of its colour and odour, as seek to transfuse from one language into another the creations of a poet. The plant must spring again from its seed or it will bear no flower—and this is the burthen of the curse of Babel.

An observation of the regular mode of the recurrence of this harmony in the language of poetical minds, together with its relation to music, produced metre, or a certain system of traditional forms of harmony of language. Yet it is by no means essential that a poet should accommodate his language to this traditional form, so that the harmony which is its spirit, be observed. The practise is indeed convenient and popular, and to be preferred, especially in such composition as includes much form and action: but every great poet must inevitably innovate upon the example of his predecessors in the exact structure of his peculiar versification. The distinction between poets and prose writers is a vulgar error. The distinction between philosophers and poets has been anticipated. Plato was essentially a poet—the truth and splendour of his imagery and the melody of his language is the most intense that it is possible to conceive. He rejected the measure of the epic, dramatic, and lyrical forms, because he sought to kindle a harmony in thoughts divested of shape and action, and he forbore to invent any regular plan of rhythm which would include, under determinate forms, the varied pauses of his style. Cicero sought to imitate the cadence of his periods but with little success. Lord Bacon was a poet. His language has a sweet and majestic rhythm, which satisfies the sense, no less than the almost superhuman wisdom of his philosophy satisfies the intellect; it is a strain which distends, and then bursts the circumference of the hearer's mind, and pours itself forth together with it into the universal element with which it has perpetual sympathy. All the authors of revolutions in opinion are not only necessarily poets as they are inventors, nor even as their words unveil the permanent analogy of things by images which participate in the life of truth; but as their periods are harmonious and rhythmical and contain in themselves the elements of verse; being the echo of the eternal music. Nor are those supreme poets, who have employed traditional forms of rhythm on account of the form and action of their subjects, less capable of perceiving and teaching the truth of things, than those who have omitted that form. Shakespeare, Dante and Milton (to confine ourselves to modern writers) are philosophers of the very loftiest power.

A poem is the very image of life expressed in its eternal truth. There is this difference between a story and a poem, that a story is a catalogue of detached facts, which have no other bond of connexion than time, place, circumstance, cause and effect; the other is the creation of the actions according to the unchangeable forms of human nature, as existing in the mind of the creator, which is itself the image of all other minds. The one is partial, and applies only to a definite period of time, and a certain combination of events which can never again recur; the other is universal, and contains within itself the germ of a relation to whatever motives or actions have place in the possible varieties of human nature. Time, which destroys the beauty and the use of the story of particular facts, stript of the poetry which should invest them, augments that of Poetry, and for ever developes new and wonderful applications of the eternal truth which it contains. Hence epitomes[3] have been called the moths of just history; they eat out the poetry of it. The story of particular facts is as a mirror which obscures and distorts that which should be beautiful: Poetry is a mirror which makes beautiful that which is distorted.

The parts of a composition may be poetical, without the composition as a whole being a poem. A single sentence may be considered as a whole though it be found in a series of unassimilated portions; a single word even may be a spark of inextinguishable thought. And thus all the great historians, Herodotus, Plutarch, Livy, were poets;[4] and although the plan of these writers, especially that of Livy, restrained them from developing this faculty in its highest degree, they make copious and ample amends for their subjection, by filling all the interstices of their subjects with living images.

Having determined what is poetry, and who are poets, let us proceed to estimate its effects upon society.

Poetry is ever accompanied with pleasure: all spirits on which it falls, open themselves to receive the wisdom which is mingled with its delight. In the infancy of the world, neither poets themselves nor their auditors are fully aware of the excellence of poetry: for it acts in a divine and unapprehended manner, beyond and above consciousness; and it is reserved for future generations to

---

[3] **epitomes**: abstracts or abridgements. The idea following is from Bacon's *Advancement of Learning*: "As for the corruptions and moths of history, which are epitomes, the use of them deserveth to be banished" (II.ii.4). Noted by Reiman.

[4] **Herodotus**: Greek historian and Father of History (c. 480–c. 425 BC), for being the first to systematically collect and assess materials. **Plutarch**: Greek biographer (AD c. 50–c. 125) wrote *Parallel Lives*, which established the tradition of biography based upon moral anecdotes. **Livy**: Titus Livius (59 BC–?AD 17), wrote the history of Rome from its origin to 9 BC in 142 volumes.

contemplate and measure the mighty cause and effect in all the strength and splendour of their union. Even in modern times, no living poet ever arrived at the fulness of his fame; the jury which sits in judgement upon a poet, belonging as he does to all time, must be composed of his peers: it must be impanelled by Time from the selectest of the wise of many generations. A Poet is a nightingale, who sits in darkness and sings to cheer its own solitude with sweet sounds; his auditors are as men entranced by the melody of an unseen musician, who feel that they are moved and softened, yet know not whence or why. The poems of Homer and his contemporaries were the delight of infant Greece; they were the elements of that social system which is the column upon which all succeeding civilization has reposed. Homer embodied the ideal perfection of his age in human character; nor can we doubt that those who read his verses were awakened to an ambition of becoming like to Achilles, Hector and Ulysses:[5] the truth and beauty of friendship, patriotism and persevering devotion to an object, were unveiled to the depths in these immortal creations: the sentiments of the auditors must have been refined and enlarged by a sympathy with such great and lovely impersonations, until from admiring they imitated, and from imitation they identified themselves with the objects of their admiration. Nor let it be objected, that these characters are remote from moral perfection, and that they can by no means be considered as edifying patterns for general imitation. Every epoch under names more or less specious has deified its peculiar errors; Revenge is the naked Idol of the worship of a semi-barbarous age; and Self-deceit is the veiled Image of unknown evil before which luxury and satiety lie prostrate. But a poet considers the vices of his contemporaries as the temporary dress in which his creations must be arrayed, and which cover without concealing the eternal proportions of their beauty. An epic or dramatic personage is understood to wear them around his soul, as he may the antient armour or the modern uniform around his body; whilst it is easy to conceive a dress more graceful than either. The beauty of the internal nature cannot be so far concealed by its accidental vesture, but that the spirit of its form shall communicate itself to the very disguise, and indicate the shape it hides from the manner in which it is worn. A majestic form and graceful motions will express themselves through the most barbarous and tasteless costume. Few poets of the highest class have chosen to exhibit the beauty of their conceptions in its naked truth and splendour; and it is doubtful whether the alloy of costume, habit, etc., be not necessary to temper this planetary music for mortal ears.

The whole objection however of the immorality of poetry rests upon a misconception of the manner in which poetry acts to produce the moral improvement of man. Ethical science arranges the elements which poetry has created, and propounds schemes and proposes examples of civil and domestic life: nor is it for want of admirable doctrines that men hate, and despise, and censure, and deceive, and subjugate one another. But Poetry acts in another and diviner manner. It awakens and enlarges the mind itself by rendering the receptable of a thousand unapprehended combinations of thought. Poetry lifts the veil from the hidden beauty of the world, and makes familiar objects be as if they were not familiar; it reproduces all that it represents, and the impersonations clothed in its Elysian light stand thenceforward in the minds of those who have once contemplated them, as memorials of that gentle and exalted content which extends itself over all thoughts and actions with which it coexists. The great secret of morals is Love; or a going out of our own nature, and an identification of ourselves with the beautiful which exists in thought, action, or person, not our own. A man, to be greatly good, must imagine intensely and comprehensively; he must put himself in the place of another and of many others; the pains and pleasures of his species must become his own. The great instrument of moral good is the imagination; and poetry administers to the effect by acting upon the cause. Poetry enlarges the circumference of the imagination by replenishing it with thoughts of ever new delight, which have the power of attracting and assimilating to their own nature all other thoughts, and which form new intervals and interstices whose void for ever craves fresh food. Poetry strengthens that faculty which is the organ of the moral nature of man, in the same manner as exercise strengthens a limb. A Poet therefore would do ill to embody his own conceptions of right and wrong, which are usually those of his place and time, in his poetical creations, which participate in neither. By this assumption of the inferior office of interpreting the effect, in which perhaps after all he might acquit himself but imperfectly, he would resign the glory in a participation in the cause. There was little danger

[5] Achilles and Hector are the Greek and Trojan heroes of Homer's epic of the Trojan War, *The Iliad*. **Ulysses:** (also Odysseus) Greek hero of *The Odyssey*, an epic of the hero's return from that war. Today it is argued that Homer is a composite of poets, rather than an individual bard.

that Homer, or any of the eternal poets, should have so far misunderstood themselves as to have abdicated this throne of their widest dominion. Those in whom the poetical faculty, though great, is less intense, as Euripides, Lucan, Tasso, Spenser,[6] have frequently affected a moral aim, and the effect of their poetry is diminished in exact proportion to the degree in which they compel us to advert to this purpose.

Homer and the cyclic poets were followed at a certain interval by the dramatic and lyrical Poets of Athens, who flourished contemporaneously with all that is most perfect in the kindred expressions of the poetical faculty; architecture, painting, music, the dance, sculpture, philosophy, and we may add the forms of civil life. For although the scheme of Athenian society was deformed by many imperfections which the poetry existing in Chivalry and Christianity have erased from the habits and institutions of modern Europe; yet never at any other period has so much energy, beauty, and virtue, been developed; never was blind strength and stubborn form so disciplined and rendered subject to the will of man, or that will less repugnant to the dictates of the beautiful and the true, as during the century which preceded the death of Socrates. Of no other epoch in the history of our species have we records and fragments stamped so visibly with the image of the divinity in man. But it is Poetry alone, in form, in action, or in language, which has rendered this epoch memorable above all others, and the storehouse of examples to everlasting time. For written poetry existed at that epoch simultaneously with the other arts, and it is an idle enquiry to demand which gave and which received the light, which all as from a common focus have scattered over the darkest periods of succeeding time. We know no more of cause and effect than a constant conjunction of events: Poetry is ever found to coexist with whatever other arts contribute to the happiness and perfection of man. I appeal to what has already been established to distinguish between the cause and the effect.

It was at the period here adverted to, that the Drama had its birth; and however a succeeding writer may have equalled or surpassed those few great specimens of the Athenian drama which have been preserved to us, it is indisputable that the art itself never was understood or practised according to the true philosophy of it, as at Athens. For the Athenians employed language, actions, music, painting, the dance, and religious institutions, to produce a common effect in the representation of the highest idealisms of passion and of power; each division in the art was made perfect in its kind by artists of the most consummate skill, and was disciplined into a beautiful proportion and unity one towards another. On the modern stage a few only of the elements capable of expressing the image of the poet's conception are employed at once. We have tragedy without music and dancing; and music and dancing without the highest impersonations of which they are the fit accompaniment, and both without religion and solemnity. Religious institution has indeed been usually banished from the stage. Our system of divesting the actor's face of a mask, on which the many expressions appropriated to his dramatic character might be moulded into one permanent and unchanging expression, is favourable only to a partial and inharmonious effect; it is fit for nothing but a monologue, where all the attention may be directed to some great master of ideal mimicry. The modern practice of blending comedy with tragedy, though liable to great abuse in point of practise, is undoubtedly an extension of the dramatic circle; but the comedy should be as in King Lear, universal, ideal, and sublime. It is perhaps the intervention of this principle which determines the balance in favour of King Lear against the Oedipus Tyrannus or the Agamemnon, or, if you will the trilogies with which they are connected; unless the intense power of the choral poetry, especially that of the latter, should be considered as restoring the equilibrium. King Lear, if it can sustain this comparison, may be judged to be the most perfect specimen of the dramatic art existing in the world; in spite of the narrow conditions to which the poet was subjected by the ignorance of the philosophy of the Drama which has prevailed in modern Europe. Calderon[7] in his religious Autos has attempted to fulfil some of the high conditions of dramatic representation neglected by Shakespeare; such as the establishing a relation between the drama and religion, and the accommodating them to music and dancing; but he omits the observation of conditions still more important, and more is lost than gained by a substitution of the rigidly-defined and ever-repeated idealisms of a distorted superstition

[6] **Euripides:** Greek tragedian (480–406 BC). **Lucan:** Roman epic poet (AD 39–65). **Tasso:** Torquato Tasso (1544–1595), Italian poet. **Spenser:** Edmund Spenser (c. 1552–1599), English poet of *The Faerie Queene.*

[7] **Calderon:** Calderon de la Barca (1600–1681), great Spanish dramatist. The reference is to his religious dramas, *Autos Sacramentales.*

for the living impersonations of the truth of human passion. . . .

The poetry of Dante may be considered as the bridge thrown over the stream of time, which unites the modern and antient world. The distorted notions of invisible things which Dante and his rival Milton have idealized, are merely the mask and the mantle in which these great poets walk through eternity enveloped and disguised. It is a difficult question to determine how far they were conscious of the distinction which must have subsisted in their minds between their own creeds and that of the people. Dante at least appears to wish to mark the full extent of it by placing Riphæus, whom Virgil calls *justissimus unus*,[8] in Paradise, and observing a most heretical caprice in his distribution of rewards and punishments. And Milton's poem contains within itself a philosophical refutation of that system of which, by a strange and natural antithesis, it has been a chief popular support. Nothing can exceed the energy and magnificence of the character of Satan as expressed in Paradise Lost. It is a mistake to suppose that he could ever have been intended for the popular personification of evil. Implacable hate, patient cunning, and a sleepless refinement of device to inflict the extremest anguish on an enemy, these things are evil; and although venial in a slave are not to be forgiven in a tyrant; although redeemed by much that ennobles his defeat in one subdued, are marked by all that dishonours his conquest in the victor. Milton's Devil as a moral being is as far superior to his God as one who perseveres in some purpose which he has conceived to be excellent in spite of adversity and torture, is to one who in the cold security of undoubted triumph inflicts the most horrible revenge upon his enemy, not from any mistaken notion of inducing him to repent of a perseverance in enmity, but with the alleged design of exasperating him to deserve new torments. Milton has so far violated the popular creed (if this shall be judged to be a violation) as to have alleged no superiority of moral virtue to his God over his Devil. And this bold neglect of a direct moral purpose is the most decisive proof of the supremacy of Milton's genius. He mingled as it were the elements of human nature, as colours upon a single pallet, and arranged them into the composition of his great picture according to the laws of epic truth; that is, according to the laws of that principle by which a series of actions of the external universe and of intelligent and ethical beings is calculated to excite the sympathy of succeeding generations of mankind. The Divina Commedia and Paradise Lost have conferred upon modern mythology a systematic form; and when change and time shall have added one more superstition to the mass of those which have arisen and decayed upon the earth, commentators will be learnedly employed in elucidating the religion of ancestral Europe, only not utterly forgotten because it will have been stamped with the eternity of genius. . . .

Dante and Milton were both deeply penetrated with the antient religion of the civilized world; and its spirit exists in their poetry probably in the same proportion as its forms survived in the unreformed worship of modern Europe. The one preceded and the other followed the Reformation at almost equal intervals. Dante was the first religious reformer, and Luther surpassed him rather in the rudeness and acrimony, than in the boldness of his censures of papal usurpation. Dante was the first awakener of entranced Europe; he created a language in itself music and persuasion out of a chaos of inharmonious barbarisms. He was the congregator of those great spirits who presided over the resurrection of learning; the Lucifer of that starry flock which in the thirteenth century shone forth from republican Italy, as from a heaven, into the darkness of the benighted world. His very words are instinct with spirit; each is as a spark, a burning atom of inextinguishable thought; and many yet lie covered in the ashes of their birth, and pregnant with a lightning which has yet found no conductor. All high poetry is infinite; it is as the first acorn, which contained all oaks potentially. Veil after veil may be undrawn, and the inmost naked beauty of the meaning never exposed. A great Poem is a fountain for ever overflowing with the waters of wisdom and delight; and after one person and one age has exhausted all its divine effluence which their peculiar relations enable them to share, another and yet another succeeds, and new relations are ever developed, the source of an unforeseen and an unconceived delight.

The age immediately succeeding to that of Dante, Petrarch, and Boccaccio, was characterized by a revival of painting, sculpture, music, and architecture. Chaucer caught the sacred inspiration, and the superstructure of English literature is based upon the materials of Italian invention.

But let us not be betrayed from a defence into a critical history of Poetry and its influence on Society. Be it enough to have pointed out the effects of poets, in the large and true sense of the word, upon their own and all succeeding times and to revert to the partial instances

[8] **justissimus unus:** *trans.* the one most just.

cited as illustrations of an opinion the reverse of that attempted to be established in the Four Ages of Poetry.

But poets have been challenged to resign the civic crown to reasoners and mechanists on another plea. It is admitted that the exercise of the imagination is most delightful, but it is alleged that that of reason is more useful. Let us examine as the grounds of this distinction, what is here meant by Utility. Pleasure or good in a general sense, is that which the consciousness of a sensitive and intelligent being seeks, and in which when found it acquiesces. There are two kinds of pleasure, one durable, universal, and permanent; the other transitory and particular. Utility may either express the means of producing the former or the latter. In the former sense, whatever strengthens and purifies the affections, enlarges the imagination, and adds spirit to sense, is useful. But the meaning in which the Author of the Four Ages of Poetry seems to have employed the word utility is the narrower one of banishing the importunity of the wants of our animal nature, the surrounding men with security of life, the dispersing the grosser delusions of superstition, and the conciliating such a degree of mutual forbearance among men as may consist with the motives of personal advantage.

Undoubtedly the promoters of utility in this limited sense, have their appointed office in society. They follow the footsteps of poets, and copy the sketches of their creations into the book of common life. They make space, and give time. Their exertions are of the highest value so long as they confine their administration of the concerns of the inferior powers of our nature within the limits due to the superior ones. But whilst the sceptic destroys gross superstitions, let him spare to deface, as some of the French writers have defaced, the eternal truths charactered upon the imaginations of men. Whilst the mechanist abridges, and the political oeconomist combines, labour, let them beware that their speculations, for want of correspondence with those first principles which belong to the imagination, do not tend, as they have in modern England, to exasperate at once the extremes of luxury and want. They have exemplified the saying, "To him that hath, more shall be given; and from him that hath not, the little that he hath shall be taken away."[9] The rich have become richer, and the poor have become poorer; and the vessel of the state is driven between the Scylla and Charybdis[10] of anarchy and despotism. Such are the effects which must ever flow from an unmitigated exercise of the calculating faculty.[11]

It is difficult to define pleasure in its highest sense; the definition involving a number of apparent paradoxes. For, from an inexplicable defect of harmony in the constitution of human nature, the pain of the inferior is frequently connected with the pleasures of the superior portions of our being. Sorrow, terror, anguish, despair itself are often the chosen expressions of an approximation to the highest good. Our sympathy in tragic fiction depends on this principle; tragedy delights by affording a shadow of the pleasure which exists in pain. This is the source also of the melancholy which is inseparable from the sweetest melody. The pleasure that is in sorrow is sweeter than the pleasure of pleasure itself. And hence the saying, "It is better to go to the house of mourning, than to the house of mirth."[12] Not that this highest species of pleasure is necessarily linked with pain. The delight of love and friendship, the extacy of the admiration of nature, the joy of the perception and still more of the creation of poetry is often wholly unalloyed.

The production and assurance of pleasure in this highest sense is true utility. Those who produce and preserve this pleasure are Poets or poetical philosophers.

The exertions of Locke, Hume, Gibbon, Voltaire, Rousseau, and their disciples, in favour of oppressed and deluded humanity, are entitled to the gratitude of mankind. Yet it is easy to calculate the degree of moral and intellectual improvement which the world would have exhibited, had they never lived. A little more nonsense would have been talked for a century or two; and perhaps a few more men, women, and children, burnt as

[9] **"To him that hath . . . taken away":** a comment of Christ's represented in the Gospels of Matthew (25:29), Mark (4:25), and Luke (8:18 and 19:26), but this seems to be Shelley's own translation.

[10] **between the Scylla and Charybdis:** two rocks between Sicily and Italy. The man-eating monster Scylla dwelt in a cave on the one nearest Italy; Charybdis, who swallowed the sea and threw it up again three times daily, dwelt under a tree on the opposing rock nearest Sicily. (See Homer's *Odyssey*, XII.73–110.) Between both is a position of inescapable danger.

[11] See SOCIETY AND POLITICAL ECONOMY and the introduction to Percy Shelley for a discussion of utility and the social evil Shelley is here describing.

[12] **"It is better . . . mirth.":** Cf. Ecclesiastes or, The Preacher 7:2: "It is better to go to the house of mourning, than to go to the house of feasting: for that *is* the end of all men, and the living will lay *it* to his heart."

heretics. We might not at this moment have been congratulating each other on the abolition of the Inquisition in Spain.[13] But it exceeds all imagination to conceive what would have been the moral condition of the world if neither Dante, Petrarch, Boccaccio, Chaucer, Shakespeare, Calderon, Lord Bacon, nor Milton, had ever existed; if Raphael and Michael Angelo had never been born; if the Hebrew poetry had never been translated; if a revival of the study of Greek literature had never taken place; if no monuments of antient sculpture had been handed down to us; and if the poetry of the religion of the antient world had been extinguished together with its belief. The human mind could never, except by the intervention of these excitements, have been awakened to the invention of the grosser sciences, and that application of analytical reasoning to the aberrations of society, which it is now attempted to exalt over the direct expression of the inventive and creative faculty itself.

We have more moral, political and historical wisdom, than we know how to reduce into practise; we have more scientific and oeconomical knowledge than can be accommodated to the just distribution of the produce which it multiplies. The poetry in these systems of thought, is concealed by the accumulation of facts and calculating processes. There is no want of knowledge respecting what is wisest and best in morals, government, and political oeconomy, or at least, what is wiser and better than what men now practise and endure. But we let "*I dare not* wait upon *I would*, like the poor cat i' the adage."[14] We want the creative faculty to imagine that which we know; we want the generous impulse to act that which we imagine; we want the poetry of life: our calculations have outrun conception; we have eaten more than we can digest. The cultivation of those sciences which have enlarged the limits of the empire of man over the external world, has, for want of the poetical faculty, proportionally circumscribed those of the internal world; and man, having enslaved the elements, remains himself a slave. To what but a cultivation of the mechanical arts in a degree disproportioned to the presence of the creative faculty, which is the basis of all knowledge, is to be attributed the abuse of all invention for abridging and combining labour, to the exasperation of the inequality of mankind? From what other cause has it arisen that the discoveries which should have lightened, have added a weight to the curse imposed on Adam? Poetry, and the principle of Self, of which money is the visible incarnation, are the God and the Mammon[15] of the world.

The functions of the poetical faculty are two-fold; by one it creates new materials of knowledge, and power and pleasure; by the other it engenders in the mind a desire to reproduce and arrange them according to a certain rhythm and order which may be called the beautiful and the good. The cultivation of poetry is never more to be desired than at periods when, from an excess of the selfish and calculating principle, the accumulation of the materials of external life exceed the quantity of the power of assimilating them to the internal laws of human nature. The body has then become too unwieldy for that which animates it.

Poetry is indeed something divine. It is at once the centre and circumference of knowledge; it is that which comprehends all science, and that to which all science must be referred. It is at the same time the root and blossom of all other systems of thought: it is that from which all spring, and that which adorns all; and that which, if blighted, denies the fruit and the seed, and withholds from the barren world the nourishment and the succession of the scions of the tree of life. It is the perfect and consummate surface and bloom of things; it is as the odour and the colour of the rose to the texture of the elements which compose it, as the form and the splendour of unfaded beauty to the secrets of anatomy and corruption. What were Virtue, Love, Patriotism, Friendship &c.—what were the scenery of this beautiful Universe which we inhabit—what were our consolations on this side of the grave—and what were our aspirations beyond it—if Poetry did not ascend to bring light and fire from those eternal regions where the owl-winged faculty of calculation dare not ever soar? Poetry is not like reasoning, a power to be exerted according to the determination of the will. A man cannot say, "I will compose poetry." The greatest poet even cannot say it: for the mind in creation is as a fading coal which some invisible influence, like an inconstant wind, awakens to transitory brightness: this

[13] **Inquisition in Spain:** a tribunal of the Catholic Church to suppress heresy. Begun in 1480, abolished in 1808 by Bonaparte, restored by Ferdinand VII in 1814, and abolished again with the Liberal revolution of 1820. It was temporarily restored in 1823, but finally abolished in 1834. Shelley, of course, refers to the abolition of 1820.

[14] **"I dare not . . . adage":** Cf. *Macbeth*, I.vii.44–45.

[15] **Mammon:** New Testament's false god of money and worldly goods (Matthew 6:24; Luke 16:9, 11, 13).

power arises from within, like the colour of a flower which fades and changes as it is developed, and the conscious portions of our natures are unprophetic either of its approach or its departure. Could this influence be durable in its original purity and force, it is impossible to predict the greatness of the results: but when composition begins, inspiration is already on the decline, and the most glorious poetry that has ever been communicated to the world is probably a feeble shadow of the original conception of the poet. I appeal to the greatest Poets of the present day, whether it be not an error to assert that the finest passages of poetry are produced by labour and study. The toil and the delay recommended by critics can be justly interpreted to mean no more than a careful observation of the inspired moments, and an artificial connexion of the spaces between their suggestions by the intertexture of conventional expressions; a necessity only imposed by a limitedness of the poetical faculty itself. For Milton conceived the Paradise Lost as a whole before he executed it in portions. We have his own authority also for the Muse having "dictated" to him the "unpremeditated song,"[16] and let this be an answer to those who would allege the fifty-six various readings of the first line of the Orlando Furioso.[17] Compositions so produced are to poetry what mosaic is to painting. This instinct and intuition of the poetical faculty is still more observable in the plastic and pictorial arts: a great statue or picture grows under the power of the artist as a child in the mother's womb, and the very mind which directs the hands in formation is incapable of accounting to itself for the origin, the gradations, or the media of the process.

Poetry is the record of the best and happiest moments of the happiest and best minds. We are aware of evanescent visitations of thought and feeling sometimes associated with place or person, sometimes regarding our own mind alone, and always arising unforeseen and departing unbidden, but elevating and delightful beyond all expression: so that even in the desire and the regret they leave, there cannot but be pleasure, participating as it does in the nature of its object. It is as it were the interpenetration of a diviner nature through our own; but its footsteps are like those of a wind over a sea, which the coming calm erases, and whose traces remain only as on the wrinkled sand which paves it. These and corresponding conditions of being are experienced principally by those of the most delicate sensibility and the most enlarged imagination; and the state of mind produced by them is at war with every base desire. The enthusiasm of virtue, love, patriotism, and friendship is essentially linked with these emotions; and whilst they last, self appears as what it is, an atom to a Universe. Poets are not only subject to these experiences as spirits of the most refined organization, but they can colour all that they combine with the evanescent hues of this etherial world; a word, a trait in the representation of a scene or a passion, will touch the enchanted chord, and reanimate, in those who have ever experienced these emotions, the sleeping, the cold, the buried image of the past. Poetry thus makes immortal all that is best and most beautiful in the world; it arrests the vanishing apparitions which haunt the interlunations of life, and veiling them or in language or in form sends them forth among mankind, bearing sweet news of kindred joy to those with whom their sisters abide—abide, because there is no portal of expression from the caverns of the spirit which they inhabit into the universe of things. Poetry redeems from decay the visitations of the divinity in man.

Poetry turns all things to loveliness; it exalts the beauty of that which is most beautiful, and it adds beauty to that which is most deformed: it marries exultation and horror, grief and pleasure, eternity and change; it subdues to union under its light yoke all irreconcilable things. It transmutes all that it touches, and every form moving within the radiance of its presence is changed by wondrous sympathy to an incarnation of the spirit which it breathes; its secret alchemy turns to potable gold the poisonous waters which flow from death through life; it strips the veil of familiarity from the world, and lays bare the naked and sleeping beauty which is the spirit of its forms.

All things exist as they are perceived: at least in relation to the percipient. "The mind is its own place, and of itself can make a heaven of hell, a hell of heaven."[18] But poetry defeats the curse which binds us to be subjected to the accident of surrounding impressions. And whether it spreads its own figured curtain or withdraws life's dark veil from before the scene of things, it equally creates for

[16] **"dictated . . . song":** Cf. *Paradise Lost,* IX.21–24. See note 1 to "To a Skylark" above.

[17] **Orlando Furioso:** a poem by Ariosto (1532) on the battle between Christians and Saracens for control of Europe.

[18] **"The mind . . . heaven.":** Shelley significantly misquotes *Paradise Lost,* II.254–55: "The mind is its own place, and *in* [not *of*] itself / Can make a heav'n of hell, a hell of heav'n."

us a being within our being. It makes us the inhabitants of a world to which the familiar world is a chaos. It reproduces the common universe of which we are portions and percipients, and it purges from our inward sight the film of familiarity which obscures from us the wonder of our being. It compels us to feel that which we perceive, and to imagine that which we know. It creates anew the universe after it has been annihilated in our minds by the recurrence of impressions blunted by reiteration. It justifies that bold and true word of Tasso—*Non merita nome di creatore, se non Iddio ed il Poeta.*[19]

A Poet, as he is the author to others of the highest wisdom, pleasure, virtue and glory, so he ought personally to be the happiest, the best, the wisest, and the most illustrious of men. As to his glory, let Time be challenged to declare whether the fame of any other institutor of human life be comparable to that of a poet. That he is the wisest, the happiest, and the best, inasmuch as he is a poet, is equally incontrovertible: the greatest poets have been men of the most spotless virtue, of the most consummate prudence, and, if we could look into the interior of their lives, the most fortunate of men: and the exceptions, as they regard those who possessed the poetic faculty in a high yet inferior degree, will be found on consideration to confirm rather than destroy the rule. Let us for a moment stoop to the arbitration of popular breath, and usurping and uniting in our own persons the incompatible characters of accuser, witness, judge and executioner, let us decide without trial, testimony, or form, that certain motives of those who are "there sitting where we dare not soar"[20] are reprehensible. Let us assume that Homer was a drunkard, that Virgil was a flatterer, that Horace was a coward, that Tasso was a madman, that Lord Bacon was a peculator, that Raphael was a libertine, that Spenser was a poet laureate. It is inconsistent with this division of our subject to cite living poets, but Posterity has done ample justice to the great names now referred to. Their errors have been weighed and found to have been dust in the balance; if their sins "were as scarlet, they are now white as snow"; they have been washed in the blood of the mediator and the redeemer Time. Observe in what a ludicrous chaos the imputations of real or fictitious crime have been confused in the contemporary calumnies against poetry and poets; consider how little is, as it appears—or appears, as it is; look to your own motives, and judge not, lest ye be judged.

Poetry, as has been said, in this respect differs from logic, that it is not subject to the controul of the active power of the mind, and that its birth and recurrence has no necessary connexion with consciousness or will. It is presumptuous to determine that these are the necessary conditions of all mental causation, when mental effects are experienced insusceptible of being referred to them. The frequent recurrence of the poetical power, it is obvious to suppose, may produce in the mind an habit of order and harmony correlative with its own nature and with its effects upon other minds. But in the intervals of inspiration, and they may be frequent without being durable, a poet becomes a man, and is abandoned to the sudden reflux of the influences under which others habitually live. But as he is more delicately organized than other men, and sensible to pain and pleasure, both his own and that of others, in a degree unknown to them, he will avoid the one and pursue the other with an ardour proportioned to this difference. And he renders himself obnoxious to calumny, when he neglects to observe the circumstances under which these objects of universal pursuit and flight have disguised themselves in one another's garments.

But there is nothing necessarily evil in this error, and thus cruelty, envy, revenge, avarice, and the passions purely evil, have never formed any portion of the popular imputations on the lives of poets.

I have thought it most favourable to the cause of truth to set down these remarks according to the order in which they were suggested to my mind by a consideration of the subject itself, instead of following that of the treatise that excited me to make them public. Thus although devoid of the formality of a polemical reply; if the view they contain be just, they will be found to involve a refutation of the Four Ages of Poetry, so far at least as regards the first division of the subject. I can readily conjecture what should have moved the gall of the learned and intelligent author of that paper; I confess myself like him unwilling to be stunned by the Theseids of the hoarse Codri of the day. Bavius and Maevius[21] undoubtedly are, as they ever were, insufferable persons. But it belongs to a philosophical critic to distinguish rather than confound.

---

[19] *Trans.* "No one merits the name of Creator but God and the Poet."

[20] **"there . . . soar"**: Cf. *Paradise Lost,* IV.829–30: "Ye knew me once no mate / For you, there sitting where ye durst not soar" (Satan).

[21] **Bavius and Maevius**: dull writers satirized by Virgil and Juvenal.

The first part of these remarks has related to Poetry in its elements and principles; and it has been shewn, as well as the narrow limits assigned them would permit, that what is called poetry, in a restricted sense, has a common source with all other forms of order and of beauty according to which the materials of human life are susceptible of being arranged, and which is poetry in an universal sense.

The second part will have for its object an application of these principles to the present state of the cultivation of Poetry, and a defence of the attempt to idealize the modern forms of manners and opinion, and compel them into a subordination to the imaginative and creative faculty. For the literature of England, an energetic developement of which has ever preceded or accompanied a great and free developement of the national will, has arisen as it were from a new birth. In spite of the low-thoughted envy which would undervalue contemporary merit, our own will be a memorable age in intellectual achievements, and we live among such philosophers and poets as surpass beyond comparison any who have appeared since the last national struggle for civil and religious liberty. The most unfailing herald, companion, and follower of the awakening of a great people to work a beneficial change in opinion or institution, is Poetry. At such periods there is an accumulation of the power of communicating and receiving intense and impassioned conceptions respecting man and nature. The persons in whom this power resides, may often, as far as regards many portions of their nature, have little apparent correspondence with that spirit of good of which they are the ministers. But even whilst they deny and abjure, they are yet compelled to serve, the Power which is seated upon the throne of their own soul. It is impossible to read the compositions of the most celebrated writers of the present day without being startled with the electric life which burns within their words. They measure the circumference and sound the depths of human nature with a comprehensive and all-penetrating spirit, and they are themselves perhaps the most sincerely astonished at its manifestations, for it is less their spirit than the spirit of the age. Poets are the hierophants[22] of an unapprehended inspiration, the mirrors of the gigantic shadows which futurity casts upon the present, the words which express what they understand not; the trumpets which sing to battle, and feel not what they inspire: the influence which is moved not, but moves. Poets are the unacknowledged legislators of the World.

[22] **hierophants:** interpreters of sacred mysteries; ministers of revelation.

FELICIA DOROTHEA BROWNE HEMANS

(1793–1835)

Felicia Hemans was the most popular poet in England between 1820 and 1835, second only — if that — to Byron* (who did not welcome the competition, recommending that she "knit blue stockings instead of wearing them," *Byron's Letters and Journals,* VII:182). Her nineteen volumes of poetry and two dramas sold thousands of copies; her tragedy, *The Vespers of Palermo,* was produced at Covent Garden in 1823 and in Edinburgh, with Sarah Siddons, the following year. She regularly contributed to the annual gift books and keepsakes of her day, earning enough to support five sons single-handedly. Her poetry was especially well received in America where she was offered an annual salary of $1,500 to accept the sinecure of a nominal editorship of a literary magazine. Although she died in 1835, her popularity continued unabated through the nineteenth century; she led all other poets in her appearances in American and British anthologies of poetry in this period, outdistancing even Tennyson. Through World War II, her poems — particularly "Casabianca," "The Homes of England," and "The Graves of a Household" — were memorized by almost every British and American schoolchild and were regularly recited in elocution competitions.

Born on 25 September 1793, in Liverpool, she spent a happy childhood in North Wales where she learned Latin and modern languages at home from a tutor, and was known as a child prodigy for her phenomenal memory. After her father's emigration to Quebec, effectively abandoning his wife and six children, she began writing poetry to help defray household expenses. Her first volume of poetry was published when she was 14, initiating a deep-rooted connection in her psyche between male desertion and female literary creativity. Rejecting Percy Shelley's requests for a "correspondence," she published her second volume of poetry, *The Domestic Affections, and Other Poems* in 1812. That same year she married Captain Alfred Hemans of the Fourth or King's Own Regiment, a survivor of the Peninsular Campaign who was a man "by no means destitute of advantages, either of person or education" (Hughes, I.11). Within the next six years she produced five sons and four more volumes of poetry, including her celebrations of heroic military valor, *Tales and Historic Scenes* (published in 1819) and *Songs of the Cid* (published in 1822). Shortly before the birth of his last son in 1819, Captain Hemans set sail for Italy, either for reasons of health (the public explanation) or because of a profound domestic "incompatibility" (as friends and later biographers surmised). Felicia Hemans never saw her husband again, and while she never complained of him, resolutely upholding the decorum of the proper lady and devoted wife, she referred to their separation as *"une grand chagrin"* (a great mortification).

Thereafter, her mother raised Hemans's sons while Felicia wrote to earn the family income, publishing a volume a year, including plays, poems, essays, and literary criticism. Her most successful volumes were *The Siege of Valencia* (1823); *Lays of Many Lands* (1826) which included "The Forest Sanctuary," her own favorite poem; *Songs of the Affections* (1830); and above all, *Records of Woman* (1828). She won numerous prizes and was widely celebrated, praised by Wordsworth,* and befriended by several other successful female writers, most notably Maria Jane Jewsbury and Joanna Baillie.* But Felicia Hemans was devastated by her mother's death in 1827, going into a physical decline which brought on her early death at the age of 41.

Throughout her writing, Hemans reveals the tensions between her society's definition of the Proper Lady or "true woman" as the devoted daughter, wife, and mother, and her own experience of domestic disintegration. Overtly celebrating the primacy of the home and the domestic affections as the source of enduring human fulfillment, her poetry nonetheless records all the ways in which the values of hearth and home are betrayed: by men who prefer fame and fortune to love, by men who reject their female lovers for another, by men who follow a chivalric code of honor that willingly sacrifices the good of the family to the needs of the state. By inhabiting and advocating the private sphere or domestic ideology assigned to the feminine gender, Hemans shows all the ways in which that sphere fails to support the women and children it supposedly protects. The recurrent figure of her poetry—the filled circle of the happy family—is repeatedly emptied out, reduced to "nought," while patterns of exile, displacement, and the estranged heart come to predominate.

The Siege of Valencia stages the conflict between the values of the private feminine realm—maternal love—and the public masculine realm—chivalric honor or heroism—only to reveal their mutual destruction. At stake in this play is the control both of language and of nature. Gonzalez, embracing a Judaeo-Christian code of duty, writes the sacrifice of his sons as Abraham's willingness to sacrifice Isaac: a heroic "steadfastness." His devotion to his city is endorsed by his "heroic child," Ximena, who reenacts the script for the female warrior of the medieval epic romance *El Cid.* The Catholic Church, represented here by Father Hernandez, further insists upon the sacred necessity for the deaths of Alphonse and Carlos to preserve a Christian city from falling into the hands of the heathen Muslims. But Elmina rewrites the story of Abraham and Isaac as cruelty, as child abuse, as infanticide, an act that redefines the word "Father" to mean *only* "steadfast." Her narrative of the maternal devotion that is universal or *natural* and that would save her sons' lives no matter what the social cost is subtly endorsed by Hemans's undermining of her opponents: Ximena dies of a heart broken for domestic love; Hernandez has murdered his own son in battle; the city of Valencia will fall in three days anyway; and Gonzalez receives his death wound in his futile effort to save his sons. Despite the *deus ex machina,* the arrival of the troops of the king of Castile, that ends the play, the final stage image is one of "desolation." When the state sacrifices its own children, all civilized values collapse and only Elmina is left to say the last word, a word that memorializes a "love" forever lost.

from TALES AND HISTORIC SCENES IN VERSE
(1819)

The Widow of Crescentius
(1819)

In the reign of Otho III, Emperor of Germany, the Romans, excited by their Consul, Crescentius, who ardently desired to restore the ancient glory of the Republic, made a bold attempt to shake off the Saxon yoke, and the authority of the Popes, whose vices rendered them objects of universal contempt. The Consul was besieged by Otho in the Mole of Hadrian, which long afterwards continued to be called the Tower of Crescentius. Otho, after many unavailing attacks upon this fortress, at last entered into negotiations; and, pledging his imperial word to respect the life of Crescentius, and the rights of the Roman citizens, the unfortunate leader was betrayed into his power, and immediately beheaded, with many of his partisans. Stephania, his widow, concealing her affliction and her resentment for the insults to which she had been exposed, secretly resolved to revenge her husband and herself. On the return of Otho from a pilgrimage to Mount Gargano, which, perhaps, a feeling of remorse had induced him to undertake, she found means to be introduced to him, and to gain his confidence; and a poison administered by her was soon afterwards the cause of his painful death." (See SISMONDI, *History of the Italian Republics*, vol. i.)[1]

"L'orage peut briser en un moment les fleurs qui
tiennent encore la tête levée."[2]

MAD. DE STAËL

'Midst Tivoli's[3] luxuriant glades,
Bright-foaming falls, and olive shades,
Where dwelt, in days departed long,
The sons of battle and of song,
No tree, no shrub its foliage rears,
But o'er the wrecks of other years,
Temples and domes, which long have been
The soil of that enchanted scene.

There the wild fig-tree and the vine
O'er Hadrian's mouldering villa twine;
The cypress, in funereal grace,
Usurps the vanished column's place;
O'er fallen shrine and ruined frieze
The wall-flower rustles in the breeze;
Acanthus-leaves the marble hide
They once adorned in sculptured pride;
And nature hath resumed her throne
O'er the vast works of ages flown.

Was it for this that many a pile,
Pride of Ilissus and of Nile,
To Anio's banks the image lent
Of each imperial monument?[4]
Now Athens weeps her shattered fanes,
Thy temples, Egypt, strew thy plains;
And the proud fabrics Hadrian reared
From Tibur's vale have disappeared.
We need no prescient sibyl there
The doom of grandeur to declare;
Each stone, where weeds and ivy climb
Reveals some oracle of Time;
Each relic utters Fate's decree,
The future as the past shall be.

Halls of the dead! in Tibur's vale,
Who now shall tell your lofty tale?
Who trace the high patrician's dome,
The bard's retreat, the hero's home?
When moss-clad wrecks alone record
There dwelt the world's departed lord!
In scenes where verdure's rich array
Still sheds young beauty o'er decay,
And sunshine on each glowing hill,
'Midst ruins finds a dwelling still.

Sunk is thy palace—but thy tomb,
Hadrian[5] hath shared a prouder doom,
Though vanished with the days of old
Its pillars of Corinthian mould;
And the fair forms by sculpture wrought,
Each bodying some immortal thought,
Which o'er that temple of the dead,
Serene but solemn beauty shed,

[1] **Epitaph**: Johannes Crescentius Nomentanus (d. 998 AD), scion of a family of leaders of the Roman aristocracy in the tenth century, assumed the title of patrician and dominated Rome and the papacy. He opposed the Holy Roman Emperor Otto III and Pope Gregory V and raised John XVI as the antipope; he was defeated by Otto III at the Castle of Sant'Angelo (April 998) and executed. **Sismondi**: Jean-Charles-Léonard Simonde de Sismondi (1773–1842), *Histoire des Republiques italiennes du moyen age* (Paris, 1807–1818); first English translation, *Italian Republics, or the origin, progress and fall of Italian freedom* (Paris: Galignani, 1832; 1841).

[2] French, *trans.* "A thunderstorm can destroy in a moment those flowers whose heads are raised."

[3] **Tivoli**: ancient Tibur, city overlooking Rome, famed for its waterfalls and gardens, site of the Roman emperor Hadrian's summer villa.

[4] **Ilissus**: river near Athens, Greece. **Nile**: river in Egypt. **Anio**: Aniene, river that flows through Tivoli into Tiber River, in Rome. **imperial monument**: "The gardens and buildings of Hadrian's villa were copies of the most celebrated scenes and edifices in his dominions—the Lycaeum, the Academia, the Prytaneum of Athens, the Temple of Serapis at Alexandra, the Vale of Tempe, &c." [F. H.].

[5] "The Mausoleum of Hadrian, now the castle of St. Angelo, was first converted into a citadel by Belisarius, in his successful defense of Rome against the Goths. ... In the middle ages, the Moles Hadriana was made a permanent fortress by the Roman government, and bastions, outworks, &c. were added to the original edifice, which had been stripped of its marble covering, its Corinthian pillars, and the brazen cone which crowned its summit" [F. H.].

Have found, like glory's self, a grave
In Time's abyss, or Tiber's wave:
Yet dreams more lofty, and more fair,
Than art's bold hand hath imaged e'er,
High thoughts of many a mighty mind,
Expanding when all else declined,
In twilight years, when only they
Recalled the radiance passed away,
Have made that ancient pile their home,
Fortress of freedom and of Rome.

There he, who strove in evil days
Again to kindle glory's rays,
Whose spirit sought a path of light,
For those dim ages far too bright,—
Crescentius long maintained the strife
Which closed but with its martyr's life,
And left th' imperial tomb a name,
A heritage of holier fame,
There closed De Brescia's[6] mission high,
From thence the patriot came to die;
And thou, whose Roman soul the last,
Spoke with the voice of ages past,
Whose thoughts so long from earth had fled,
To mingle with the glorious dead,
That 'midst the world's degenerate race
They vainly sought a dwelling-place,
Within that house of death didst brood
O'er visions to thy ruin wooed.
Yet, worthy of a brighter lot,
Rienzi,[7] be thy faults forgot!
For thou, when all around thee lay
Chained in the slumbers of decay—
So sunk each heart, that mortal eye
Had scarce a *tear* for liberty—
Alone, amidst the darkness there,
Couldst gaze on Rome—yet not despair!

'Tis morn, and Nature's richest dyes
Are floating o'er Italian skies;
Tints of transparent lustre shine
Along the snow-clad Apennine;
The clouds have left Soracte's height,
And yellow Tiber winds in light,
Where tombs and fallen fanes have strewed
The wide Campagna's[8] solitude,
'Tis sad amidst that scene to trace
Those relics of a vanished race;
Yet o'er the ravaged path of time—
Such glory sheds that brilliant clime,
Where Nature still, though empires fall,
Holds her triumphant festival—
E'en Desolation wears a smile,
Where skies and sunbeams laugh the while;
And heaven's own light, earth's richest bloom,
Array the ruin and the tomb.

But she, who from yon convent tower
Breathes the pure freshness of the hour;
She, whose rich flow of raven hair
Streams wildly on the morning air,
Heeds not how fair the scene below,
Robed in Italia's brightest glow.
Though throned 'midst Latium's classic plains
Th' Eternal City's towers and fanes,
And they, the Pleiades of earth,
The seven proud hills of Empire's birth,
Lie spread beneath: not now her glance
Roves o'er that vast sublime expanse,
Inspired, and bright with hope, 'tis thrown
On Adrian's[9] massy tomb alone:
There, from the storm, when Freedom fled,
His faithful few Crescentius led;

[6] **De Brescia**: "Arnold de Brescia, the undaunted and eloquent champion of Roman liberty, after unremitting efforts to restore the ancient constitution of the republic, was put to death in the year 1155 by Adrian IV" [F. H.]. Arnaldo da Brescia (1100?–1155), Italian political reformer: combated corruption of clergy; led a popular revolt against the Bishop of Brescia; was condemned by Second Lateran Council; exiled, betrayed by Frederick I, and executed at Rome (1155).

[7] **Rienzi**: Cola di Rienzo (Niccolo Gabrini, 1313–1354), Italian patriot, called "last of the Romans," led revolution in Rome (1347) against aristocracy; instituted constitutional government; opposed by Pope and finally even by followers offended by his dictatorial rule; murdered in a riot (8 October 1354).

[8] **Apennines**: mountain range running north-south along entire peninsula of Italy. **Soracte**: isolated mountain, 2,267 feet high, in central Italy. **Campagna**: plains in central Italy.

[9] **Latium**: ancient name for Italy. **Eternal City**: Rome. **Pleiades**: seven stars in constellation Taurus; in classical myth, seven daughters of Atlas and Pleione, changed into stars. Rome is built on seven hills surrounding the Tiber River. **Adrian**: Hadrian (76–138), Emperor of Rome (117–138); his monumental mausoleum, Castel Sant'Angelo, is now the Papal garrison in Rome.

While she, his anxious bride, who now
Bends o'er the scene her youthful brow,
Sought refuge in the hallowed fane,
Which then could shelter, not in vain.

But now the lofty strife is o'er,
And Liberty shall weep no more.
At length imperial Otho's voice
Bids her devoted sons rejoice;
And he, who battled to restore
The glories and the rights of yore,
Whose accents, like the clarion's sound,
Could burst the dead repose around,
Again his native Rome shall see,
The sceptred city of the free!
And young Stephania waits the hour
When leaves her lord his fortress tower,
Her ardent heart with joy elate,
That seems beyond the reach of fate;
Her mien, like creature from above,
All vivified with hope and love.

Fair is her form, and in her eye
Lives all the soul of Italy!
A meaning lofty and inspired,
As by her native day-star fired;
Such wild and high expression, fraught
With glances of impassioned thought,
As fancy sheds, in visions bright,
O'er priestess of the God of Light!
And the dark locks that lend her face
A youthful and luxuriant grace,
Wave o'er her cheek, whose kindling dyes
Seem from the fire within to rise,
But deepened by the burning heaven
To her own land of sunbeams given.
Italian art that fervid glow
Would o'er ideal beauty throw,
And with such ardent life express
Her high-wrought dreams of loveliness,—
Dreams which, surviving Empire's fall,
The shade of glory still recall.

But see!—the banner of the brave
O'er Adrian's tomb hath ceased to wave.
'Tis lowered—and now Stephania's eye
Can well the martial train descry,
Who, issuing from that ancient dome,
Pour through the crowded street of Rome.
Now from her watch-tower on the height,
With step as fabled wood-nymph's light,
She flies—and swift her way pursues,
Through the lone convent's avenues.
Dark cypress groves, and fields o'erspread
With records of the conquering dead.
And paths which track a glowing waste,
She traverses in breathless haste;
And by the tombs where dust is shrined,
Once tenanted by loftiest mind,
Still passing on, hath reached the gate
Of Rome, the proud, the desolate!
Thronged are the streets, and, still renewed,
Rush on the gathering multitude.

Is it their high-souled chief to greet
That thus the Roman thousands meet?
With names that bid their thoughts ascend,
Crescentius, thine in song to blend;
And of triumphal days gone by
Recall the inspiring pageantry?
—There is an air of breathless dread,
An eager glance, a hurrying tread;
And now a fearful silence round,
And now a fitful murmuring sound,
'Midst the pale crowds, that almost seem
Phantoms of some tumultuous dream.
Quick is each step, and wild each mien,
Portentous of some awful scene.
Bride of Crescentius! as the throng
Bore thee with whelming force along,
How did thine anxious heart beat high,
Till rose suspense to agony!—
Too brief suspense, that soon shall close,
And leave thy heart to deeper woes.

Who 'midst yon guarded precinct stands,
With fearless mien, but fettered hands?
The ministers of death are nigh,
Yet a calm grandeur lights his eye;
And in his glance there lives a mind
Which was not formed for chains to bind,
But cast in such heroic mould
As theirs, the ascendant ones of old.
Crescentius! freedom's daring son,
Is this the guerdon thou hast won?
O worthy to have lived and died
In the bright days of Latium's pride!
Thus must the beam of glory close
O'er the seven hills again that rose,

When at thy voice, to burst the yoke,
The soul of Rome indignant woke?
Vain dream! the sacred shields are gone,
Sunk is the crowning city's[10] throne:
Th' illusions, that around her cast
Their guardian spells, have long been past.
Thy life hath been a short-star's ray,
Shed o'er her midnight of decay;
Thy death at freedom's ruined shrine
Must rivet every chain—but thine.

Calm is his aspect, and his eye
Now fixed upon the deep-blue sky,
Now on those wrecks of ages fled,
Around in desolation spread—
Arch, temple, column, worn and gray,
Recording triumphs passed away;
Works of the mighty and the free,
Whose steps on earth no more shall be,
Though their bright course hath left a trace
Nor years nor sorrows can efface.

Why changes now the patriot's mien,
Erewhile so loftily serene?
Thus can approaching death control
The might of that commanding soul?
No!—Heard ye not that thrilling cry
Which told of bitterest agony?
He heard it, and at once, subdued,
Hath sunk the hero's fortitude.
He heard it, and his heart too well
Whence rose that voice of woe can tell;
And 'midst the gazing throngs around
One well-known form his glance hath found—
One fondly loving and beloved,
In grief, in peril, faithful proved.
Yes, in the wildness of despair,
She, his devoted bride, is there.
Pale, breathless, through the crowd she flies,
The light of frenzy in her eyes:
But ere her arms can clasp the form,
Which life ere long must cease to warm,
Ere on his agonizing breast
Her heart can heave, her head can rest,
Checked in her course by ruthless hands,
Mute, motionless, at once she stands;
With bloodless cheek and vacant glance,
Frozen and fixed in horror's trance;
Spell-bound, as every sense were fled,
And thought o'erwhelmed, and feeling dead.
And the light waving of her hair,
And veil, far floating on the air,
Alone, in that dread moment, show
She is no sculptured form of woe.

The scene of grief and death is o'er,
The patriot's heart shall throb no more:
But *hers*—so vainly formed to prove
The pure devotedness of love,
And draw from fond affection's eye
All thought sublime, all feeling high;
When consciousness again shall wake,
Hath now no refuge—but to break.
The spirit long inured to pain
May smile at fate in calm disdain;
Survive its darkest hour, and rise
In more majestic energies.
But in the glow of vernal pride,
If each warm hope *at once* hath died,
Then sinks the mind, a blighted flower,
Dead to the sunbeam and the shower;
A broken gem, whose inborn light
Is scattered—ne'er to reunite.

—PART II—

Hast thou a scene that is not spread
With records of thy glory fled?
A monument that doth not tell
The tale of liberty's farewell?
Italia! thou are but a grave
Where flowers luxuriate o'er the brave,
And nature gives her treasures birth
O'er all that hath been great on earth.
Yet smile thy heavens as once they smiled,
When thou wert freedom's favored child:
Though fane and tomb alike are low,
Time hath not dimmed thy sunbeam's glow;
And robed in that exulting ray,
Thou seem'st to triumph o'er decay.
Oh yet, though by thy sorrows bent,
In nature's pomp magnificent;
What marvel if, when all was lost,

[10] **sacred shields**: the buckler or brazen shield, and eleven copies thereof, supposedly received from heaven by Numa Pompilius, the second king of Rome (715–673 BC), consecrated to the Muses and kept in the temple of Mars, to protect Rome from the plague. **crowning city**: Tyre; see Isaiah 23.

Still on thy bright, enchanted coast,
Though many an omen warned him thence,
Lingered the lord of eloquence?[11]
Still gazing on the lovely sky,
Whose radiance wooed him — but to die:
Like him, *who* would not linger there,
Where heaven, earth, ocean, all are fair?
Who 'midst thy glowing scenes could dwell,
Nor bid awhile his griefs farewell?
Hath not thy pure and genial air
Balm for all sadness but despair?[12]
No! there are pangs, whose deep-worn trace
Not all thy magic can efface!
Hearts, by unkindness wrung, may learn
The world and all its gifts to spurn;
Time may steal on with silent tread,
And dry the tear that mourns the dead,
May change fond love, subdue regret,
And teach e'en vengeance to forget:
But thou, Remorse! there is no charm,
Thy sting, avenger, to disarm!
Vain are bright suns and laughing skies
To soothe thy victim's agonies;
The heart once made thy burning throne,
Still, while it beats, is thine alone.

In vain for Otho's joyless eye
Smile the fair scenes of Italy,
As through her landscapes' rich array
Th' imperial pilgrim bends his way.
Thy form, Crescentius, on his sight
Rises when nature laughs in light,
Glides round him at the midnight hour,
Is present in his festal bower,
With awful voice and frowning mien,
By all but him unheard, unseen.
Oh! thus to shadows of the grave
Be every tyrant still a slave!

Where through Gargano's[13] woody dells,
O'er bending oaks the north wind swells,
A sainted hermit's lowly tomb
Is bosomed in umbrageous gloom,
In shades that saw him live and die
Beneath their waving canopy.
'Twas his, as legends tell, to share
The converse of immortals there;
Around that dweller of the wild
There "bright appearances"[14] have smiled,
And angel-wings, at eve, have been
Gleaming the shadowy boughs between.
And oft from that secluded bower
Hath breathed, at midnight's calmer hour,
A swell of viewless harps, a sound
Of warbled anthems pealing round.
Oh, none but voices of the sky
Might wake that thrilling harmony,
Whose tones, whose very echoes made
An Eden of the lonely shade!
Years have gone by; the hermit sleeps
Amidst Gargano's woods and steeps;
Ivy and flowers have half o'ergrown,
And veiled his low sepulchral stone:
Yet still the spot is holy, still
Celestial footsteps haunt the hill;
And oft the awe-struck mountaineer
Aërial vesper-hymns may hear,
Around those forest precincts float,
Soft, solemn, clear, but still remote.
Oft will Affliction breathe her plaint
To that rude shrine's departed saint,
And deem that spirits of the blest
There shed sweet influence o'er her breast.

And thither Otho now repairs,
To soothe his soul with vows and prayers;
And if for him, on holy ground,
The lost one, Peace, may yet be found,
'Midst rocks and forests by the bed,
Where calmly sleep the sainted dead,
She dwells, remote from heedless eye,
With Nature's lonely majesty.

Vain, vain the search — his troubled breast
Nor vow nor penance lulls to rest;
The weary pilgrimage is o'er,
The hopes that cheered it are no more.
Then sinks his soul, and day by day,
Youth's buoyant energies decay.

[11] **lord of eloquence**: Marcus Tullius Cicero (106–43 BC), famous Roman orator, rhetorician, philosopher, and poet.

[12] **Balm . . . despair?**: Reference to Milton, *Paradise Lost*, IV:156.

[13] **Gargano**: Mount Gargano, in Apulia, in north-central Italy.

[14] **"bright appearances"**: Cf. Milton, *Paradise Lost*, XI:329.

The light of health his eye hath flown,
The glow that tinged his cheek is gone.
Joyless as one on whom is laid
Some baleful spell that bids him fade,
Extending its mysterious power
O'er every scene, o'er every hour:
E'en thus *he* withers; and to him,
Italia's brilliant skies are dim.
He withers—in that glorious clime
Where Nature laughs in scorn of Time;
And suns, that shed on all below
Their full and vivifying glow,
From him alone their power withhold,
And leave his heart in darkness cold.
Earth blooms around him, heaven is fair,
He only seems to perish there.

Yet, sometimes will a transient smile
Play o'er his faded cheek awhile,
When breathes his minstrel boy a strain
Of power to lull all earthly pain;
So wildly sweet, its notes might seem
The ethereal music of a dream,
A spirit's voice from worlds unknown,
Deep thrilling power in every tone!
Sweet is that lay, and yet its flow
Hath language only given to woe;
And if at times its wakening swell
Some tale of glory seems to tell,
Soon the proud notes of triumph die,
Lost in a dirge's harmony.
Oh! many a pang the heart hath proved,
Hath deeply suffered, fondly loved,
Ere the sad strain could catch from thence
Such deep impassioned eloquence!—
Yes! gaze on him, that minstrel boy—
He is no child of hope and joy;
Though few his years, yet have they been
Such as leave traces on the mien,
And o'er the roses of our prime
Breathe other blights than those of time.

Yet seems his spirit wild and proud,
By grief unsoftened and unbowed.
Oh! there are sorrows which impart
A sternness foreign to the heart,
And rushing with an earthquake's power,
That makes a desert in an hour;
Rouse the dread passions in their course,
As tempests wake the billows' force!—
'Tis sad, on youthful Guido's face,[15]
The stamp of woes like these to trace.
Oh! where can ruins awe mankind,
Dark as the ruins of the mind?

His mien is lofty, but his gaze
Too well a wandering soul betrays:
His full dark eye at times is bright
With strange and momentary light,
Whose quick uncertain flashes throw
O'er his pale cheek a hectic glow:
And oft his features and his air
A shade of troubled mystery wear,
A glance of hurried wildness, fraught
With some unfathomable thought.
Whate'er that thought, still unexpressed,
Dwells that sad secret in his breast;
The pride his haughty brow reveals,
All other passions well conceals.
He breathes each wounded feeling's tone,
In music's eloquence alone;
His soul's deep voice is only poured
Through his full song and swelling chord.
He seeks no friend, but shuns the train
Of courtiers with a proud disdain;
And, save when Otho bids his lay
Its half unearthly power essay,
In hall or bower the heart to thrill,
His haunts are wild and lonely still.
Far distant from the heedless throng,
He roves old Tiber's banks along,
Where Empire's desolate remains
Lie scattered o'er the silent plains;
Or, lingering 'midst each ruined shrine
That strews the desert Palatine,[16]
With mournful, yet commanding mien,
Like the sad genius of the scene,
Entranced in awful thought appears
To commune with departed years.
Or at the dead of night, when Rome
Seems of heroic shades the home;

[15] **Guido . . . swelling chord,** ll. 435–456: the Widow's alias and disguise may allude to Guido d'Arezzo (995?–1050), Benedictine monk and musician, reputed inventor of the medieval "great scale" or gamut and the hexachord; author of several works on theory of music.

[16] **Palatine:** chief of the seven hills of Rome, site of the oldest settlement and of the palace of the Emperor Domitian.

When Tiber's murmuring voice recalls
The mighty to their ancient halls;
When hushed is every meaner sound,
And the deep moonlight-calm around
Leaves to the solemn scene alone
The majesty of ages flown,—
A pilgrim to each hero's tomb,
He wanders through the sacred gloom;
And, 'midst those dwellings of decay,
At times will breathe so sad a lay,
So wild a grandeur in each tone,
'Tis like a dirge for empires gone!

Awake thy pealing harp again,
But breathe a more exulting strain,
Young Guido! for awhile forgot
Be the dark secrets of thy lot,
And rouse the inspiring soul of song
To speed the banquet's hour along!—
The feast is spread, the music's call
Is echoing through the royal hall,
And banners wave and trophies shine
O'er stately guests in glittering line;
And Otho seeks awhile to chase
The thoughts he never can erase,
And bid the voice, whose murmurs deep
Rise like a spirit on his sleep—
The still small voice of conscience—die,
Lost in the din of revelry.

On his pale brow dejection lowers,
But that shall yield to festal hours:
A gloom is in his faded eye,
But that from music's power shall fly:
His wasted cheek is wan with care,
But mirth shall spread fresh crimson there.
Wake, Guido! wake thy numbers high,
Strike the bold chord exultingly!
And pour upon the enraptured ear
Such strains as warriors love to hear!
Let the rich mantling[17] goblet flow,
And banish all resembling woe;
And, if a thought intrude, of power
To mar the bright convivial hour,
Still must its influence lurk unseen,
And cloud the heart—but not the mien!

Away, vain dream!—on Otho's brow,
Still darker lower the shadows now;
Changed are his features, now o'erspread
With the cold paleness of the dead;
Now crimsoned with a hectic dye,
The burning flush of agony!
His lip is quivering, and his breast
Heaves with convulsive pangs oppressed;
Now his dim eye seems fixed and glazed,
And now to heaven in anguish raised;
And as, with unavailing aid,
Around him throng his guests dismayed,
He sinks—while scarce his struggling breath
Hath power to falter—"This is death!"

Then rushed that haughty child of song,
Dark Guido, through the awe-struck throng;
Filled with a strange delirious light,
His kindling eye shone wildly bright,
And on the sufferer's mien awhile
Gazing with stern vindictive smile,
A feverish glow of triumph dyed
His burning cheek, while thus he cried:—
"Yes! these are death-pangs—on thy brow
Is set the seal of vengeance now!
Oh! well was mixed the deadly draught,
And long and deeply hast thou quaffed;
And bitter as thy pangs may be,
They are but guerdons meet from me!
Yet, these are but a moment's throes,
Howe'er intense, they soon shall close.
Soon shalt thou yield thy fleeting breath,
My life hath been a lingering death;
Since one dark hour of woe and crime,
A blood-spot on the page of time!

"Deemest thou my mind of reason void?
It is not frenzied,—but destroyed!
Ay! view the wreck with shuddering thought,—
That work of ruin thou hast wrought!

"The secret of thy doom to tell,
My name alone suffices well!
Stephania!—once a hero's bride!
Otho! thou knowest the rest—*he died.*
Yes! trusting to a monarch's word,
The Roman fell, untried, unheard!
And thou, whose every pledge was vain,
How couldst *thou* trust in aught again?

"He died, and I was changed—my soul,
A lonely wanderer, spurned control.

[17] **mantling:** embossed, as with heraldic scrollwork.

From peace, and light, and glory hurled,
The outcast of a purer world,
I saw each brighter hope o'erthrown,
And lived for one dread task alone.
The task is closed, fulfilled the vow,
The hand of death is on thee now.
Betrayer! in thy turn betrayed,
The debt of blood shall soon be paid!
Thine hour is come—the time hath been
My heart had shrunk from such a scene;
That feeling long is past—my fate
Hath made me stern as desolate.

"Ye that around me shuddering stand,
Ye chiefs and princes of the land!
Mourn ye a guilty monarch's doom?
Ye wept not o'er the patriot's tomb!
He sleeps unhonored—yet be mine
To share his low, neglected shrine.
His soul with freedom finds a home,
His grave is that of glory—Rome!
Are not the great of old with her,
That city of the sepulchre?
Lead me to death! and let me share
The slumbers of the mighty there!"

The day departs—that fearful day
Fades in calm loveliness away:
From purple heavens its lingering beam
Seems melting into Tiber's stream,
And softly tints each Roman hill
With glowing light, as clear and still,
As if, unstained by crime or woe,
Its hours had passed in silent flow.
The day sets calmly—it hath been
Marked with a strange and awful scene:
One guilty bosom throbs no more,
And Otho's pangs and life are o'er.
And thou, ere yet another sun
His burning race hath brightly run,
Released from anguish by thy foes,
Daughter of Rome! shalt find repose.—
Yes, on thy country's lovely sky
Fix yet once more thy parting eye!
A few short hours—and all shall be
The silent and the past for thee.

Oh! thus with tempests of a day
We struggle, and we pass away,
Like the wild billows as they sweep,
Leaving no vestige on the deep!
And o'er thy dark and lowly bed
The sons of future days shall tread,
The pangs, the conflicts, of thy lot
By them unknown, by thee forgot.

The Wife of Asdrubal

(1819)

"This governor, who had braved death when it was at a distance, and protested that the sun should never see him survive Carthage—this fierce Asdrubal was so mean-spirited as to come alone, and privately throw himself at the conqueror's feet. The general, pleased to see his proud rival humbled, granted his life, and kept him to grace his triumph. The Carthaginians in the citadel no sooner understood that their commander had abandoned the place, than they threw open the gates, and put the proconsul in possession of Byrsa. The Romans had now no enemy to contend with but the nine hundred deserters, who, being reduced to despair, retired into the temple of Esculapius, which was a second citadel within the first: there the proconsul attacked them; and these unhappy wretches, finding there was no way to escape, set fire to the temple. As the flames spread, they retreated from one part to another, till they got to the roof of the building: there Asdrubal's wife appeared in her best apparel, as if the day of her death had been a day of triumph; and after having uttered the most bitter imprecations against her husband, whom she saw standing below with Emilianus,—'Base coward!' said she, 'the mean things thou hast done to save thy life shall not avail thee; thou shalt die this instant, at least in thy two children.' Having thus spoken, she drew out a dagger, stabbed them both, and while they were yet struggling for life, threw them from the top of the temple, and leaped down after them into the flames."—*Ancient Universal History*.[1]

[1] Asdrubal (Hasdrubal, lived second century BC), general of Carthage, major classical city on northern African coast; fought Romans in Third Punic War at Nepheris and Carthage, but surrendered to Scipio Aemilianus after siege of Carthage (148–146 BC) and graced Scipio's triumphal procession in Rome. His wife and children preferred death to capture (see Polybius 38:1–2). **Ancient Universal History:** William Fordyce Mavor, *Universal*

The sun sets brightly—but a ruddier glow
O'er Afric's heaven the flames of Carthage throw;
Her walls have sunk, and pyramids of fire
In lurid splendour from her domes aspire;
Swayed by the wind, they wave—while glares the sky
As when the desert's red simoom[2] is nigh;
The sculptured altar, and the pillared hall,
Shine out in dreadful brightness ere they fall,
Far o'er the seas the light of ruin streams,
Rock, wave, and isle are crimsoned by its beams;
While captive thousands, bound in Roman chains,
Gaze in mute horror on their burning fanes;
And shouts of triumph, echoing far around,
Swell from the victors' tents with ivy crowned.[3]
But mark! from yon fair temple's loftiest height
What towering form bursts wildly on the sight,
All regal in magnificent attire,
And sternly beauteous in terrific ire?

She might be deemed a Pythia[4] in the hour
Of dread communion and delirious power;
A being more than earthly, in whose eye
There dwells a strange and fierce ascendancy.
The flames are gathering round—intensely bright,
Full on her features glares their meteor-light;
But a wild courage sits triumphant there,
The stormy grandeur of a proud despair;
A daring spirit, in its woes elate,
Mightier than death, untameable by fate.
The dark profusion of her locks unbound,
Waves like a warrior's floating plumage round;
Flushed is her cheek, inspired her haughty mien,
She seems the avenging goddess of the scene.
Are those *her* infants, that with suppliant cry
Cling round her, shrinking as the flame draws nigh,
Clasp with their feeble hands her gorgeous vest,
And fain would rush for shelter to her breast?
Is that a mother's glance, where stern disdain,
And passion, awfully vindictive, reign?

Fixed is her eye on Asdrubal, who stands,
Ignobly safe amidst the conquering bands;
On him who left her to that burning tomb,
Alone to share her children's martyrdom;
Who, when his country perished, fled the strife,
And knelt to win the worthless boon of life.
"Live, traitor, live!" she cries, "since dear to thee,
E'en in thy fetters, can existence be!
Scorned and dishonoured live!—with blasted name,
The Romans triumph not to grace, but shame.
O slave in spirit! bitter be thy chain
With tenfold anguish to avenge my pain!
Still may the manes[5] of thy children rise
To chase calm slumber from thy wearied eyes;
Still may their voices on the haunted air
In fearful whispers tell thee to despair,
Till vain remorse thy withered heart consume,
Scourged by relentless shadows of the tomb!
E'en now my sons shall die—and thou, their sire,
In bondage safe, shalt yet in them expire.
Think'st thou I love them not?—'Twas thine to fly—
'Tis mine with these to suffer and die.
Behold their fate!—the arms that cannot save
Have been their cradle, and shall be their grave."
Bright in her hand the lifted dagger gleams,
Swift from her children's hearts the life-blood streams;
With frantic laugh she clasps them to the breast
Whose woes and passions soon shall be at rest;
Lifts one appealing, frenzied glance on high,
Then deep 'midst rolling flames is lost to mortal eye.

History, Ancient and Modern, from the earliest records of time, to the general peace of 1801 (London, 1802–1804, 25 Vols.).

[2] **simoom:** hot desert wind, in northern Africa.

[3] **fanes:** temples. **tents . . . crowned:** It was a Roman custom to adorn the tents of victors with ivy [F. H.].

[4] **Pythia:** the priestess of Apollo's most famous oracle, at Delphi; Apollo's oracular messages were uttered in unintelligible sounds by the priestess while in a frenzied trance and then translated into coherent verse by an attendant priest.

[5] **manes:** household gods; in ancient Rome, specifically the deified spirits of one's ancestors; hence, shades of departed persons, demanding either reverence or propitiation by revenge.

THE SIEGE OF VALENCIA

A Dramatic Poem

(1823)

Judicio ha dado esta no vista hazanna
Del valor que en los siglos venideros
Tendrán los Hijos de la fuerte Espanna,
Hijos de tal padres herederos.

Hallò sola en Numancia todo quanto
Debe con justo titulo cantarse,
Y lo que puede dar materia al canto.

CERVANTES, *NUMANCIA*[1]

— ADVERTISEMENT —

The history of Spain records two instances of the severe and self-devoting heroism, which forms the subject of the following dramatic poem. The first of these occurred at the siege of Tarifa, which was defended, in 1294, for Sancho, King of Castile, during the rebellion of his brother, Don Juan, by Guzman, surnamed the Good.[2] The second is related of Alonso Lopez de Texeda, who, until his garrison had been utterly disabled by pestilence, maintained the city of Zamora for the children of Don Pedro the Cruel, against the forces of Henrique of Trastamara.[3]

Impressive as were the circumstances which distinguished both these memorable sieges, it appeared to the author of the following pages that a deeper interest, as well as a stronger colour of nationality, might be imparted to the scenes in which she has feebly attempted "to describe high passions and high actions," by connecting a religious feeling with the patriotism and high-minded loyalty which had thus been proved "faithful unto death," and by surrounding her ideal *dramatis personae* with recollections derived from the heroic legends of Spanish chivalry. She has, for this reason, employed the agency of imaginary characters, and fixed upon Valencia del Cid[4] as the scene to give them.

"A local habitation and a name."[5]

DRAMATIS PERSONAE

ALVAR GONZALEZ	*Governor of Valencia*
ALPHONSO, CARLOS	*His Sons*
HERNANDEZ	*A Priest*
ABDULLAH	*A Moorish Prince, Chief of the Army besieging Valencia*
GARCIAS	*A Spanish Knight*
ELMINA	*Wife to Gonzalez*
XIMENA	*Her Daughter*
THERESA	*An Attendant*

Citizens, Soldiers, Attendants, &c.

— SCENE I —

(Room in a Palace of Valencia.— XIMENA *singing to a Lute.)*

BALLAD

"Thou hast not been with a festal throng
At the pouring of the wine;
Men bear not from the hall of song
A mien so dark as thine!

---

[1] *trans.* "Justice has given no greater vision of the bravery that, in future centuries, the sons of mighty Spain will inherit, the sons of the fathers who left this legacy. In Numancia did he [the poet] find that which alone could justify the name of bravery—and that which gave him the matter for this song." **Cervantes:** Miguel de Cervantes Saavedra (1547–1616), Spanish novelist and dramatist, author of *Don Quixote* (1605, 1615); *Numancia* is one of his 40 plays, and is based on the following historical event. In 133 AD, the Numancians of northern Spain committed mass suicide rather than fall into the hands of their Roman conquerors.

[2] **Don Juan . . . the Good:** See [Manuel José] Quintana's *Vidas de Espanoles Celebres* [1807–1833], p. 53 [F. H.].

[3] **the second . . . Trastamara:** See the preface to [Robert] Southey's *Chronicle of the Cid* [1808] [F. H.].

[4] **Valencia del Cid:** reference to "el Cid Campeador" (Spanish-Arabic, "lord conqueror"), the popular name of Rodrigo Diaz de Bivar (1040?–1099), Spanish soldier and national hero. Under kings Ferdinand I and Sancho II of Castile, el Cid fought successfully against the Moors; he married Ximena, daughter of Count Oviedo. Distrusted and banished by Sancho's successor, King Alphonso VI of Castile (c. 1081), he entered service of Moorish rulers of Zaragosa (a course not unusual among Castilian nobles of his time, in accord with the rights of a free lord in feudal society); fought against Christians and Moors alike. Conquered the city of Valencia in 1094 and ruled until killed by the North African Berber king Almoravides in 1099. His widow Ximena surrendered Valencia to the Moors in 1102, after a three-year siege. The exploits of el Cid were much romanticized in the Spanish national epic *Poema del Cid* (c. 1140).

[5] **"A local habitation and a name":** cf. Shakespeare, *A Midsummer Night's Dream,* V.i.17.

There's blood upon thy shield,
There's dust upon thy plume,
Thou hast brought from some disastrous field
That brow of wrath and gloom!"

"And is there blood upon my shield?
Maiden, it well may be!
We have sent the streams, from our battle-field,
All darken'd to the sea!
We have given the founts a stain,
'Midst their woods of ancient pine;
And the ground is wet—but not with rain,
Deep dyed—but not with wine!

"The ground is wet—but not with rain—
We have been in war array,
And the noblest blood of Christian Spain
Hath bathed her soil to-day.
I have seen the strong man die,
And the stripling meet his fate,
Where the mountain-winds go sounding by,
In the Roncesvalles' Strait.[6]

"In the gloomy Roncesvalles' Strait
There are helms and lances cleft;
And they that moved at morn elate
On a bed of heath are left!
There's many a fair young face
Which the war-steed hath gone o'er;
At many a board there is kept a place
For those that come no more!"

"Alas! for love, for woman's breast,
If woe like this must be!
Hast thou seen a youth with an eagle crest,
And a white plume waving free?
With his proud quick-flashing eye,
And his mien of knightly state?
Doth he come from where the swords flash'd high,
In the Roncesvalles' Strait?"

"In the gloomy Roncesvalles' Strait
I saw, and mark'd him well;
For nobly on his steed he sate,
When the pride of manhood fell!
But it is not *youth* which turns
From the field of spears again;
For the boy's high heart too wildly burns,
Till it rests amidst the slain!"

"Thou canst not say that *he* lies low,
The lovely and the brave?
Oh! none could look on his joyous brow,
And think upon the grave!
Dark, dark perchance the day,
Hath been with valour's fate;
But *he* is on his homeward way,
From the Roncesvalles' Strait!"

"There is dust upon his joyous brow,
And o'er his graceful head,
And the war-horse will not wake him now,
Though it browse his greensward bed!
I have seen the stripling die,
And the strong man meet his fate,
Where the mountain-winds go sounding by,
In the Roncesvalles' Strait!"

(ELMINA *enters.*)

ELM: Your songs are not as those of other days,
Mine own Ximena! Where is now the young
And buoyant spirit of the morn, which once
Breathed in your spring-like melodies, and woke
Joy's echo from all hearts?

XIM: My mother, this
Is not the free air of our mountain-wilds;
And these are not the halls wherein my voice
First pour'd those gladd'ning strains.

ELM: Alas! thy heart
(I see it well) doth sicken for the pure
Free-wand'ring breezes of the joyous hills,
Where thy young brothers, o'er the rock and heath,
Bound in glad boyhood, e'en as torrent streams
Leap brightly from the heights. Had we not been
Within these walls, thus suddenly begirt,
Thou shouldst have track'd ere now, with step as light,
Their wild-wood paths.

XIM: I would not but have shared
These hours of woe and peril, though the deep
And solemn feelings wak'ning at their voice,
Claim all the wrought-up spirit to themselves,
And will not blend with mirth. The storm doth hush
All floating whispery sounds, all bird-notes wild
O' th' summer-forest, filling earth and heaven
With its own awful music. And 'tis well!
Should not a hero's child be train'd to hear

[6] **Roncesvalles' Strait:** a mountain pass in the Pyrenees; the great medieval hero Roland was killed here in 778 AD.

The trumpet's blast unstartled, and to look
In the fix'd face of death without dismay?

ELM: Woe! woe! that aught so gentle and so young
Should thus be call'd to stand i' the tempest's path,
And bear the token and the hue of death
On a bright soul so soon! I had not shrunk
From mine own lot; but thou, my child, shouldst move,
As a light breeze of heaven, through summer-bowers,
And not o'er foaming billows. We are fall'n
On dark and evil days![7]

XIM: Ay, days, that wake
All to their tasks!—Youth may not loiter now
In the green walks of spring; and womanhood
Is summon'd unto conflicts, heretofore
The lot of warrior-souls. Strength is born
In the deep silence of long-suffering hearts;
Not amidst joy.

ELM: Hast thou some secret woe
That thus thou speak'st?

XIM: What sorrow should be mine,
Unknown to thee?

ELM: Alas! the baleful air
Wherewith the pestilence in darkness walks
Through the devoted city, like a blight
Amidst the rose-tints of thy cheek hath fall'n,
And wrought an early withering!—Thou hast cross'd
The paths of death, and minister'd to those
O'er whom his shadow rested, till thine eye
Hath changed its glancing sunbeam for a still,
Deep, solemn radiance, and thy brow hath caught
A wild and high expression, which at times
Fades into desolate calmness, most unlike
What youth's bright mien should wear. My gentle child!
I look on thee in fear!

XIM: Thou hast no cause
To fear for me. When the wild clash of steel,
And the deep tambour, and the heavy step
Of armed men, break on our morning dreams!
When, hour by hour, the noble and the brave
Are falling round us, and we deem it much
To give them funeral-rites, and call them blest
If the good sword, in its own stormy hour,
Hath done its work upon them, ere disease
Had chill'd their fiery blood;—it is no time
For the light mien wherewith, in happier hours,
We trode the woodland mazes, when young leaves
Were whisp'ring in the gale.—My father comes—
Oh! speak of me no more. I would not shade
His princely aspect with a thought less high
Than his proud duties claim.

(GONZALEZ *enters*.)

ELM: My noble lord!
Welcome from this day's toil!—It is the hour
Whose shadows, as they deepen, bring repose
Unto all weary men; and wilt not thou
Free thy mail'd bosom from the corslet's weight,
To rest at fall of eve?

GON: There may be rest
For the tired peasant, when the vesper-bell
Doth send him to his cabin, and beneath
His vine and olive he may sit at eve,
Watching his children's sport: but unto *him*
Who keeps the watch-place on the mountain-height,
When Heaven lets loose the storms that chasten realms
—Who speaks of rest?

XIM: My father, shall I fill
The wine-cup for thy lips, or bring the lute
Whose sounds thou lovest?

GON: If there be strains of power
To rouse a spirit, which in triumphant scorn
May cast off nature's feebleness, and hold
Its proud career unshackled, dashing down
Tears and fond thoughts to earth; give voice to those!
I have need of such, Ximena!—we must hear
No melting music now!

XIM: I know all high
Heroic ditties of the elder-time,
Sung by the mountain-Christians, in the holds
Of th' everlasting hills, whose snows yet bear
The print of Freedom's step; and all wild strains
Wherein the dark serranos[8] teach the rocks,

[7] **fall'n . . . evil days:** cf. Milton, *Paradise Lost,* VII:25–26: "though fall'n on evil days / On evil days though fall'n, and evil tongues."

[8] **serranos:** mountain Christians, those natives of Spain, who, under their prince, Pelayo, took refuge amongst the mountains of the northern provinces, where they maintained their

And the pine-forests, deeply to resound
The praise of later champions. Wouldst thou hear
The war-song of thine ancestor, the Cid?

GON: Ay, speak of him; for in that name is power,
Such as might rescue kingdoms! Speak of him!
We are his children! They that can look back
I' th' annals of their house on such a name,
How should *they* take dishonour by the hand.
And o'er the threshold of their father's halls
First lead her as a guest?

ELM: Oh, why is this?
How my heart sinks!

GON: It must not fail thee *yet*,
Daughter of heroes! — thine inheritance
Is strength to meet all conflicts. Thou canst number
In thy long line of glorious ancestry
Men, the bright offering of whose blood hath made
The ground it bathed e'en as an altar, whence
High thoughts shall rise for ever. Bore they not,
'Midst flame and sword, their witness of the Cross,
With its victorious inspiration girt
As with a conqueror's robe, till th' infidel,
O'erawed, shrank back before them? — Ay, the earth
Doth call them martyrs, but *their* agonies
Were of a moment, tortures whose brief aim
Was to destroy, within whose powers and scope
Lay nought but dust. — And earth doth call them martyrs!
Why, Heaven but claim'd their blood, their lives, and not
The things which grow as tendrils round their hearts;
No, not their children!

ELM: Mean'st thou? — know'st thou aught? —
I cannot utter it — My sons! my sons!
Is it of them? — Oh! wouldst thou speak of them?

GON: A mother's heart divineth but too well!

ELM: Speak, I adjure thee! — I can bear it all. —
Where are my children?

GON: In the Moorish camp
Whose lines have girt the city.

XIM: But they live?
— All is not lost, my mother!

ELM: Say, they live.

GON: Elmina, still they live.

ELM: But captives! — They
Whom my fond heart had imaged to itself
Bounding from cliff to cliff amidst the wilds
Where the rock-eagle seem'd not more secure
In its rejoicing freedom! — And my boys
Are captives with the Moor! — Oh! how was this?

GON: Alas! our brave Alphonso, in the pride
Of boyish daring, left our mountain-halls,
With his young brother, eager to behold
The face of noble war. Thence on their way
Were the rash wanderers captured.

ELM: 'Tis enough.
— And when shall they be ransom'd?

GON: There is ask'd
A ransom far too high.

ELM: What! have we wealth
Which might redeem a monarch, and our sons
The while wear fetters? — Take thou all for them,
And we will cast our worthless grandeur from us,
As 'twere a cumbrous robe! — Why *thou* art one,
To whose high nature pomp hath ever been
But as the plumage to a warrior's helm,
Worn or thrown off as lightly. And for me,
Thou know'st not how serenely I could take
The peasant's lot upon me, so my heart,
Amidst its deep affections undisturb'd,
May dwell in silence.

XIM: Father! doubt thou not
But we will bind ourselves to poverty,
With glad devotedness, if this, but this,
May win them back. — Distrust us not, my father!
We can bear all things.

GON: Can ye bear disgrace?

XIM: We were not born for this.

GON: No, thou say'st well!
Hold to that lofty faith. — My wife, my child!
Hath earth no treasures richer than the gems
Torn from her secret caverns? — If by them
Chains may be riven, then let the captive spring
Rejoicing to the light! — But he, for whom
Freedom and life may but be worn with shame,
Hath nought to do, save fearlessly to fix
His stedfast look on the majestic heavens,
And proudly die!

ELM: Gonzalez, *who* must die?

GON. *(hurriedly)*: They on whose lives a fearful price is set,
But to be paid by treason! — Is't enough?
Or must I yet seek words?

---

religion and liberty, whilst the rest of the country was overrun by the Moors [F. H.].

ELM: That look saith more!—
Thou canst not mean—
GON: I do!—why dwells there not
Power in a glance to speak it?—They must die!
They—must their names be told—*Our sons* must die
Unless I yield the city!
XIM: Oh! look up!
My mother, sink not thus!—Until the grave
Shut from our sight its victims, there is hope.
ELM. *(in a low voice)*: Whose knell was in the breeze?—No, no, not *theirs!*
Whose was the blessed voice that spoke of hope?
—And there is hope!—I will not be subdued—
I will not hear a whisper of despair!
For nature is all-powerful, and her breath
Moves like a quickening spirit o'er the depths
Within a father's heart.—Thou too, Gonzalez,
Wilt tell me there is hope!
GON. *(solemnly)*: Hope but in Him
Who bade the patriarch[9] lay his fair young son
Bound on the shrine of sacrifice, and when
The bright steel quiver'd in the father's hand
Just raised to strike, sent forth his awful voice
Through the still clouds, and on the breathless air
Commanding to withhold!—Earth has no hope:
It rests with Him.
ELM: *Thou* canst not tell me this!
Thou father of my sons, within whose hands
Doth lie thy children's fate.
GON: If there have been
Men in whose bosoms nature's voice hath made
Its accents as the solitary sound
Of an o'erpowering torrent, silencing
Th' austere and yet divine remonstrances
Whisper'd by faith and honour, lift thy hands,
And, to that Heaven which arms the brave with strength,
Pray, that the father of thy sons may ne'er
Be thus found wanting!
ELM: Then their doom is seal'd!—
Thou wilt not save thy children?
GON: Hast thou cause
Wife of my youth! to deem it lies within
The bounds of possible things, that I should link
My name to that word—*traitor?*—They that sleep
On their proud battle-fields, thy sires and mine,
Died not for this!
ELM: Oh, cold and hard of heart!
Thou shouldst be born for empire, since thy soul
Thus lightly from all human bonds can free
Its haughty flight!—Men! men! too much is yours
Of vantage; ye that with a sound, a breath,
A shadow, thus can fill the desolate space
Of rooted up affections, o'er whose void
Our yearning hearts must wither!—So it is,
Dominion must be won!—Nay, leave me not—
My heart is bursting, and I *must* be heard!
Heaven hath given power to mortal agony,
As to the elements in their hour of might
And mastery o'er creation!—Who shall dare
To mock that fearful strength!—I *must* be heard!
Give me my sons!
GON: That they may live to hide
With covering hands th' indignant flush of shame
On their young brows, when men shall speak of him
They call'd their father!—Was the oath, whereby,
On th' altar of my faith, I bound myself,
With an unswerving spirit to maintain
This free and Christian city for my God,
And for my king, a writing traced on sand?
That passionate tears should wash it from the earth,
Or e'en the life-drops of a bleeding heart
Efface it, as a billow sweeps away
The last light vessel's wake?—Then never more
Let man's deep vows be trusted!—though enforced
By all th' appeals of high remembrances,
And silent claims o' th' sepulchres, wherein
His fathers with their stainless glory sleep,
On their good swords! Think'st thou *I* feel no pangs?
He that hath given me sons doth know the heart
Whose treasure he recalls.—Of this no more.
'Tis vain. I tell thee that th' inviolate cross
Still from our ancient temples, must look up
Through the blue heavens of Spain, though at its foot
I perish, with my race. Thou *darest* not ask
That I, the son of warriors—men who died
To fix it on that proud supremacy—
Should tear the sign of our victorious faith,
From its high place of sunbeams, for the Moor
In impious joy to trample!

---

[9] **patriarch:** reference to the story of Abraham and Isaac. Genesis 22:1–18.

ELM: Scorn me not
In mine extreme of misery!—Thou art strong—
Thy heart is not as mine.—My brain grows wild;
I know not what I ask!—And yet 'twere but
Anticipating fate—since it must fall,
That cross *must* fall at last! There is no power,
No hope within this city of the grave,
To keep its place on high. Her sultry air
Breathes heavily of death, her warriors sink
Beneath their ancient banners, ere the Moor
Hath bent his bow against them; for the shaft
Of pestilence flies more swiftly to its mark,
Than th' arrow of the desert. Even the skies
O'erhang the desolate splendour of her domes
With an ill omen's aspect, shaping forth,
From the dull clouds, wild menacing forms and
signs
Foreboding ruin. *Man* might be withstood,
But who shall cope with famine and disease
When leagued with armed foes?—Where now the
aid,
Where the long-promised lances, of Castile?
—We are forsaken in our utmost need—
By Heaven and earth forsaken!

GON: If this be
(And yet I will not deem it), we must fall
As men that in severe devotedness
Have chosen their part, and bound themselves to
death,
Through high conviction that their suffering land,
By the free blood of martyrdom alone,
Shall call deliverance down.

ELM: Oh! I have stood
Beside thee through the beating storms of life,
With the true heart of unrepining love,
As the poor peasant's mate doth cheerily,
In the parch'd vineyard, or the harvest-field,
Bearing her part, sustain with him the heat
And burden of the day;—But now the hour,
The heavy hour is come, when human strength
Sinks down, a toil-worn pilgrim, in the dust,
Owning that woe is mightier!—Spare me yet
This bitter cup, my husband!—Let not her,
The mother of the lovely, sit and mourn
In her unpeopled home, a broken stem,
O'er its fallen roses dying!

GON: Urge me not,
Thou that through all sharp conflicts hast been
found
Worthy a brave man's love!—oh, urge me not
To guilt, which through the midst of blinding tears,
In its own hues thou seest not!—Death may scarce
Bring aught like this!

ELM: All, all thy gentle race,
The beautiful beings that around thee grew,
Creatures of sunshine! Wilt thou doom them all?
—She too, thy daughter—doth her smile unmark'd
Pass from thee, with its radiance, day by day?
Shadows are gathering round her—seest thou not
The misty dimness of the spoiler's breath
Hangs o'er her beauty, and the face which made
The summer of our hearts, now doth but send,
With every glance, deep bodings through the soul,
Telling of early fate.

GON: I see a change
Far nobler on her brow!—She is as one,
Who, at the trumpet's sudden call, hath risen
From the gay banquet, and in scorn cast down
The wine-cup, and the garland, and the lute
Of festal hours, for the good spear and helm,
Beseeming sterner tasks.—Her eye hath lost
The beam which laugh'd upon th' awakening heart,
E'en as morn breaks o'er earth. But far within
Its full dark orb, a light hath sprung, whose source
Lies deeper in the soul.—And let the torch
Which but illumed the glittering pageant, fade!
The altar-flame, i' th' sanctuary's recess,
Burns quenchless, being of heaven!—She hath put
on
Courage, and faith, and generous constancy,
Even as a breastplate.—Ay, men look on her,
As she goes forth, serenely to her tasks,
Binding the warrior's wounds, and bearing fresh
Cool draughts to fever'd lips; they look on her,
Thus moving in her beautiful array
Of gentle fortitude, and bless the fair
Majestic vision, and unmurmuring turn
Unto their heavy toils.

ELM: And seest thou not
In that high faith and strong collectedness,
A fearful inspiration?—*They* have cause
To tremble, who behold th' unearthly light
Of high, and, it may be, prophetic thought,
Investing youth with grandeur!—From the grave
It rises, on whose shadowy brink thy child
Waits but a father's hand to snatch her back
Into the laughing sunshine.—Kneel with me,
Ximena, kneel beside me, and implore

That which a deeper, more prevailing voice
Than ours doth ask, and will not be denied,
— His children's lives!

XIM: Alas! this may not be,
Mother! — I cannot. *[Exit* XIMENA.*]*

GON: My heroic child!
— A terrible sacrifice thou claim'st, O God!
From creatures in whose agonizing hearts
Nature is strong as death!

ELM: Is't thus in thine?
Away! — what time is given thee to resolve
On — what I cannot utter? — Speak! thou know'st
Too well what I would say.

GON: Until — ask not!
The time is brief.

ELM: Thou said'st — I heard not right —

GON: The time is brief.

ELM: What! must we burst all ties
Wherewith the thrilling chords of life are twined;
And, for this task's fulfilment, can it be
That man in his cold heartlessness, hath dared,
To number and to mete us forth the sands
Of hours, nay, moments? — Why, the sentenced wretch,
He on whose soul there rests a brother's blood
Pour'd forth in slumber, is allow'd more time
To wean his turbulent passions from the world
His presence doth pollute! — It is not thus!
We must have time to school us.

GON: We have but
To bow the head in silence, when Heaven's voice
Calls back the things we love.

ELM: Love! love! — there are soft smiles and gentle words,
And there are faces, skilful to put on
The look we trust in — and 'tis mockery all!
— A faithless mist, a desert-vapour, wearing
The brightness of clear waters, thus to cheat
The thirst that semblance kindled! — There is none,
In all this cold and hollow world, no fount
Of deep, strong, deathless love, save that within
A mother's heart. — It is but pride, wherewith
To his fair son the father's eye doth turn,
Watching his growth. Ay, on the boy he looks,
The bright glad creature springing in his path,
But as the heir of his great name, the young
And stately tree, whose rising strength erelong
Shall bear his trophies well. — And this is love!
This is *man's* love! — What marvel? — *you* ne'er made
Your breast the pillow of his infancy,
While to the fulness of your heart's glad heavings
His fair cheek rose and fell; and his bright hair
Waved softly to your breath! — *You* ne'er kept watch
Beside him, till the last pale star had set,
And morn, all dazzling, as in triumph, broke
On your dim weary eye; not *yours* the face
Which, early faded through fond care for him,
Hung o'er his sleep, and, duly as heaven's light,
Was there to greet his wak'ning! *You* ne'er smooth'd
His couch, ne'er sung him to his rosy rest,
Caught his least whisper, when his voice from yours
Had learn'd soft utterance; press'd your lip to his,
When fever parch'd it; hush'd his wayward cries,
With patient, vigilant, never-wearied love!
No! these are *woman's* tasks! — In these her youth,
And bloom of cheek, and buoyancy of heart,
Steal from her all unmark'd! — My boys! my boys!
Hath vain affection borne with all for this?
— Why were ye given me?

GON: Is there strength in man
Thus to endure? That thou couldst read, through all
Its depths of silent agony, the heart
Thy voice of woe doth rend!

ELM: Thy heart — *thy* heart! — Away! it feels not *now!*
But an hour comes to tame the mighty man
Unto the infant's weakness; nor shall Heaven
Spare you that bitter chastening! — May you live
To be alone, when loneliness doth seem
Most heavy to sustain! — For me, my voice
Of prayer and fruitless weeping shall be soon
With all forgotten sounds; my quiet place
Low with my lovely ones, and we shall sleep,
Though kings lead armies o'er us, we shall sleep,
Wrapt in earth's covering mantle! — you the while
Shall sit within your vast, forsaken halls,
And hear the wild and melancholy winds
Moan through their drooping banners, never more
To wave above your race. Ay, then call up
Shadows — dim phantoms from ancestral tombs,
But all, all — *glorious* — conquerors, chieftains, kings,
To people that cold void! — And when the strength
From your right arm hath melted, when the blast
Of the shrill clarion gives your heart no more

A fiery wakening; if at last you pine
For the glad voices, and the bounding steps,
Once through your home re-echoing, and the clasp
Of twining arms, and all the joyous light
Of eyes that laugh'd with youth, and made your board
A place of sunshine;—when those days are come,
Then, in your utter desolation, turn
To the cold world, the smiling, faithless world,
Which hath swept past you long, and bid it quench
Your soul's deep thirst with *fame!* immortal *fame!*
Fame to the sick of heart!—a gorgeous robe,
A crown of victory, unto him that dies
I' th' burning waste, for water!

GON: This from *thee!*
Now the last drop of bitterness is pour'd.
Elmina—I forgive thee!

(Exit ELMINA.*)*

Aid me, Heaven!
From whom alone is power!—Oh! thou hast set
Duties, so stern of aspect, in my path,
They almost, to my startled gaze, assume
The hue of things less hallow'd! Men have sunk
Unblamed beneath such trials! Doth not He
Who made us know the limits of our strength?
My wife! my sons! Away! I must not pause
To give my heart one moment's mastery thus!

(Exit GONZALEZ.*)*

—SCENE II—

(The Aisle of a Gothic Church.)

(HERNANDEZ, GARCIAS, *and others.)*

HER: The rites are closed. Now, valiant men depart,
Each to his place—I may not say, of rest—
Your faithful vigils for your sons may win
What must not be your own. Ye are as those
Who sow, in peril and in care, the seed
Of the fair tree, beneath whose stately shade
They may not sit. But bless'd be those who toil
For after-days!—All high and holy thoughts
Be with you, warriors, through the lingering hours
Of the night-watch!

GAR: Ay, father! we have need
Of high and holy thoughts, wherewith to fence
Our hearts against despair. Yet have I been
From youth a son of war. The stars have look'd
A thousand times upon my couch of heath,
Spread 'midst the wild sierras, by some stream
Whose dark-red waves look'd e'en as though their source
Lay not in rocky caverns, but the veins
Of noble hearts; while many a knightly crest
Roll'd with them to the deep. And, in the years
Of my long exile and captivity,
With the fierce Arab I have watch'd beneath
The still, pale shadow of some lonely palm,
At midnight in the desert; while the wind
Swell'd with the lion's roar, and heavily
The fearfulness and might of solitude
Press'd on my weary heart.

HER. *(thoughtfully)*: Thou little know'st
Of what is solitude!—I tell thee, those
For whom—in earth's remotest nook, howe'er
Divided from their path by chain on chain
Of mighty mountains, and the amplitude
Of rolling seas—there beats one human heart,
There breathes one being, unto whom their name
Comes with a thrilling and a gladd'ning sound
Heard o'er the din of life, are not alone!
Not on the deep, nor in the wild, alone;
For there is that on earth with which they hold
A brotherhood of soul!—Call *him* alone,
Who stands shut out from this!—and let not those
Whose homes are bright with sunshine and with love,
Put on the insolence of happiness,
Glorying in that proud lot!—A lonely hour
Is on its way to each, to all; for Death
Knows no companionship.

GAR: I have look'd on Death
In field, and storm, and flood. But never yet
Hath aught weigh'd down my spirit to a mood
Of sadness, dreaming o'er dark auguries,
Like this, our watch by midnight. Fearful things
Are gathering round us. Death upon the earth,
Omens in heaven!—The summer skies put forth
No clear bright stars above us, but at times,
Catching some comet's fiery hue of wrath,
Marshall their clouds to armies, traversing
Heaven with the rush of meteor-steeds, th' array
Of spears and banners, tossing like the pines
Of Pyrenean forests, when the storm
Doth sweep the mountains.

HER: Ay, last night I too
Kept vigil, gazing on the angry heavens;
And I beheld the meeting and the shock
Of those wild hosts i' th' air, when, as they closed,
A red and sultry mist, like that which mantles
The thunder's path, fell o'er them. Then were flung
Through the dull glare, broad cloudy banners forth,
And chariots seem'd to whirl, and steeds to sink,
Bearing down crested warriors. But all this
Was dim and shadowy;—then swift darkness rush'd
Down on the unearthly battle, as the deep
Swept o'er the Egyptian's armament.[10]—I look'd—
And all that fiery field of plumes and spears
Was blotted from heaven's face!—I look'd again—
And from the brooding mass of cloud leap'd forth
One meteor-sword, which o'er the reddening sea
Shook with strange motion, such as earthquakes
give
Unto a rocking citadel!—I beheld,
And yet my spirit sunk not.

GAR: Neither deem
That mine hath blench'd. But these are sights and
sounds
To awe the firmest.—Know'st thou what we hear
At midnight from the walls?—Were't but the deep
Barbaric horn, or Moorish tambour's peal,
Thence might the warrior's heart catch impulses
Quickening its fiery currents. But our ears
Are pierced by other tones. We hear the knell
For brave men in their noon of strength cut down,
And the shrill wail of woman, and the dirge
Faint swelling through the streets. Then e'en the air
Hath strange and fitful murmurs of lament,
As if the viewless watchers of the land
Sigh'd on its hollow breezes!—To my soul,
The torrent rush of battle, with its din
Of trampling steeds and ringing panoply,
Were, after these faint sounds of drooping woe,
As the free sky's glad music unto him
Who leaves a couch of sickness.

HER. (*with solemnity*): If to plunge
In the mid-waves of combat, as they bear
Chargers and spearmen onwards; and to make
A reckless bosom's front the buoyant mark,
On that wild current, for ten thousand arrows;
If *thus* to dare were valour's noblest aim,
Lightly might fame be won! But there are things
Which ask a spirit of more exalted pitch,
And courage temper'd with a holier fire!
Well may'st thou say that these are fearful times,
Therefore be firm, be patient!—There is strength,
And a fierce instinct, e'en in common souls,
To bear up manhood with a stormy joy,
When red swords meet in lightning!—But our task
Is more and nobler!—We have to endure,
And to keep watch, and to arouse a land,
And to defend an altar!—If we fall,
So that our blood make but the millionth part
Of Spain's great ransom, we may count it joy
To die upon her bosom, and beneath
The banner of her faith!—Think but on this,
And gird your hearts with silent fortitude,
Suffering, yet hoping all things—Fare ye well.

GAR: Father, farewell.

(*Exeunt* GARCIAS *and his followers.*)

HER: These men have earthly ties
And bondage on their natures! To the cause
Of God, and Spain's revenge, they bring but half
Their energies and hopes. But he whom Heaven
Hath call'd to be th' awakener of a land,
Should have his soul's affections all absorb'd
In that majestic purpose, and press on
To its fulfilment, as a mountain-born
And mighty stream, with all its vassal-rills,
Sweeps proudly to the ocean, pausing not
To dally with the flowers. Hark! What quick step
Comes hurrying through the gloom at this dead
hour?

(ELMINA *enters.*)

ELM: Are not all hours as one to misery? Why
Should *she* take note of time, for whom the day
And night have lost their blessed attributes
Of sunshine and repose?

HER: I know thy griefs;
But there are trials for the noble heart,
Wherein its own deep fountains must supply
All it can hope of comfort. Pity's voice
Comes with vain sweetness to th' unheeding ear

[10] **the Egyptian's armament:** the Egyptian forces, drowned while crossing the Red Sea. Exodus 14:26–31.

Of anguish, e'en as music heard afar
On the green shore, by him who perishes
'Midst rocks and eddying waters.

ELM: Think thou not
I sought thee but for pity. I am come
For that which grief is priv'leged to demand
With an imperious claim, from all whose form,
Whose human form, doth seal them unto suffering!
Father! I ask thine *aid*.

HER: There is no aid
For thee or for thy children, but with Him
Whose presence is around us in the cloud,
As in the shining and the glorious light.

ELM: There is no aid!—art thou a man of God?
Art thou a man of sorrow?—for the world
Doth call thee such—and hast thou not been taught
By God and sorrow?—mighty as they are,
To own the claims of misery?

HER: Is there power
With me to save thy sons?—implore of Heaven!

ELM: Doth not Heaven work its purposes by man?
I tell thee *thou* canst save them! Art thou not
Gonzalez' counsellor? Unto him thy words
Are e'en as oracles—

HER: And therefore?—Speak!
The noble daughter of Pelayo's line
Hath nought to ask, unworthy of the name
Which is a nation's heritage. Dost thou shrink?

ELM: Have pity on me, father! I must speak
That, from the thought of which but yesterday
I had recoil'd in scorn!—But this is past.
Oh! we grow humble in our agonies,
And to the dust—their birthplace—bow the heads
That wore the crown of glory!—I am weak—
My chastening is far more than I can bear.

HER: These are no times for weakness. On our hills
The ancient cedars, in their gather'd might,
Are battling with the tempest; and the flower
Which cannot meet its driving blast must die.
—But thou hast drawn thy nurture from a stem
Unwont to bend or break.—Lift thy proud head,
Daughter of Spain!—What would'st thou with thy lord?

ELM: Look not upon me thus!—I have no power
To tell thee. Take thy keen disdainful eye
Off from my soul!—What! am I sunk to this?
I, whose blood sprung from heroes!—How my sons
Will scorn the mother that would bring disgrace
On their majestic line!—My sons! my sons!
—Now is all else forgotten!—I had once
A babe that in the early spring-time lay
Sickening upon my bosom, till at last,
When earth's young flowers were opening to the sun,
Death sunk on his meek eyelid, and I deem'd
All sorrow light to mine!—But now the fate
Of all my children seems to brood above me
In the dark thunder-clouds!—Oh! I have power
And voice unfaltering now to speak my prayer
And my last lingering hope, that thou should'st win
The father to relent, to save his sons!

HER: By yielding up the city?

ELM: Rather say
By meeting that which gathers close upon us
Perchance one day the sooner!—Is't not so?
Must we not yield at last?—How long shall man
Array his single breast against disease,
And famine, and the sword?

HER: How long?—While he
Who shadows forth his power more gloriously
In the high deeds and sufferings of the soul,
Than in the circling heavens, with all their stars,
Or the far-sounding deep, doth send abroad
A spirit, which takes affliction for its mate,
In the good cause, with solemn joy!—How long?
—And who art *thou*, that, in the littleness
Of thine own selfish purpose, would'st set bounds
To the free current of all noble thought
And generous action, bidding its bright waves
Be stay'd, and flow no further?—But the Power
Whose interdict is laid on seas and orbs,
To chain them in from wandering, hath assign'd
No limits unto that which man's high strength
Shall, through its aid, achieve!

ELM: Oh! there are times,
When *all* that hopeless courage can achieve
But sheds a mournful beauty o'er the fate
Of those who die in vain.

HER: *Who* dies in vain
Upon his country's war-fields, and within
The shadow of her altars!—Feeble heart!
I tell thee that the voice of noble blood,
Thus pour'd for faith and freedom, hath a tone

Which, from the night of ages, from the gulf
Of death, shall burst, and make its high appeal
Sound unto earth and heaven! Ay, let the land,
Whose sons, through centuries of woe hath striven,
And perish'd by her temples, sink awhile,
Borne down in conflict! — But immortal seed
Deep, by heroic suffering, hath been sown
On all her ancient hills; and generous hope
Knows that the soil, in its good time, shall yet
Bring forth a glorious harvest! — Earth receives
Not one red drop from faithful hearts in vain.

ELM: Then it must be! — And ye will make those lives,
Those young bright lives, an offering — to retard
Our doom one day!

HER: The mantle of that day
May wrap the fate of Spain!

ELM: What led me here?
Why did I turn to *thee* in my despair?
Love hath no ties upon thee; what had I
To hope from *thee*, thou lone and childless man!
Go to thy silent home! — there no young voice
Shall bid thee welcome, no light footstep spring
Forth at the sound of thine! — What knows thy heart?

HER: Woman! how darest thou taunt me with my woes?
Thy children too shall perish, and I say
It shall be well! — Why takest thou thought for them?
Wearing thy heart, and wasting down thy life
Unto its dregs, and making night thy time
Of care yet more intense, and casting health,
Unprized, to melt away, i' th' bitter cup
Thou minglest for thyself? — Why, what hath earth
To pay thee back for this? Shall they not live
(If the sword spare them now) to prove how soon
All love may be forgotten? — Years of thought,
Long faithful watchings, looks of tenderness,
That changed not, though to change be this world's law —
Shall they not flush thy cheek with shame, whose blood
Marks, e'en like branding iron? — to thy sick heart
Make death a want, as sleep to weariness?
Doth not all hope end thus? — or e'en at best,
Will they not leave thee? — far from thee seek room
For the o'erflowings of their fiery souls,
On life's wide ocean? — Give the bounding steed,
Or the wing'd bark to youth, that his free course
May be o'er hills and seas; and weep thou not
In thy forsaken home, for the bright world
Lies all before him, and be sure he wastes
No thought on thee!

ELM: Not so! it is not so!
Thou dost but torture me! — *My* sons are kind,
And brave, and gentle.

HER: Others too have worn
The semblance of all good. Nay, stay thee yet;
I will be calm, and thou shalt learn how earth,
The fruitful in all agonies, hath woes
Which far outweigh thine own.

ELM: It may not be!
Whose grief is like a mother's for her sons?

HER: *My* son lay stretch'd upon his battle-bier,
And there were hands wrung o'er him which had caught
Their hue from his young blood!

ELM: What tale is this?

HER: Read you no records in this mien, of things
Whose traces on man's aspect are not such
As the breeze leaves on water? — Lofty birth,
War, peril, power? — Affliction's hand is strong,
If it erase the haughty characters
They grave so deep! — I have not always been
That which I am. The name I bore is not
Of those which perish! — I was once a chief —
A warrior — nor as now, a lonely man!
I was a father!

ELM: Then thy heart can *feel!*
Thou wilt have pity!

HER: Should I pity *thee?*
Thy sons will perish gloriously — their blood —

ELM: Their blood! my children's blood! — Thou speak'st as 'twere
Of casting down a wine-cup, in the mirth
And wantonness of feasting! — My fair boys!
— Man! hast *thou* been a father?

HER: Let them die!
Let them die *now*, thy children! so thy heart
Shall wear their beautiful image all undimm'd
Within it, to the last! Nor shalt thou learn
The bitter lesson, of what worthless dust
Are framed the idols, whose false glory binds
Earth's fetter on our souls! — Thou think'st it much
To mourn the early dead; but there are tears
Heavy with deeper anguish! We endow

Those whom we love, in our fond passionate
 blindness,
With power upon our souls, too absolute
To be a mortal's trust! Within their hands
We lay the flaming sword, whose stroke alone
Can reach our hearts, and *they* are merciful,
As they are strong, that wield it not to pierce us!
—Ay, fear them, fear the loved!—Had I but wept
O'er my son's grave, or o'er a babe's, where tears
Are as spring dew-drops, glittering in the sun,
And brightening the young verdure, *I* might still
Have loved and trusted!
ELM. (*disdainfully*): But he fell in war!
And hath not glory medicine in her cup
For the brief pangs of nature?
HER: Glory!—Peace,
And listen!—By my side the stripling grew,
Last of my line. I rear'd him to take joy
I' th' blaze of arms, as eagles train their young
To look upon the day-king!—His quick blood
Even to his boyish cheek would mantle up,
When the heavens rang with trumpets, and his eye
Flash with the spirit of a race whose deeds—
—But this availeth not!—Yet he *was* brave.
I've seen him clear himself a path in fight
As lightning through a forest, and his plume
Waved like a torch, above the battle-storm,
The soldier's guide, when princely crests had sunk,
And banners were struck down.—Around my steps
Floated his fame, like music, and I lived
But in the lofty sound. But when my heart
In one frail ark had ventured all, when most
He seem'd to stand between my soul and heaven,
—Then came the thunder-stroke!
ELM: 'Tis ever thus!
And the unquiet and foreboding sense
That thus 'twill ever be, doth link itself
Darkly with all deep love!—He died?
HER: Not so!
—Death! Death!—Why, earth should be a paradise,
To make that name so fearful!—Had he died,
With his young fame about him for a shroud,
I had not learn'd the might of agony,
To bring proud natures low!—No! he fell off—
—Why do I tell thee this,—What right hast *thou*
To learn how pass'd the glory from my house?
Yet listen!—He forsook me!—He, that was
As mine own soul, forsook me! trampled o'er
The ashes of his sires!—ay, leagued himself
E'en with the infidel, the curse of Spain;
And, for the dark eye of a Moorish maid,
Abjured his faith, his God!—Now, talk of death!
ELM: Oh! I can pity thee—
HER: There's more to hear.
I braced the corslet o'er my heart's deep wound,
And cast my troubled spirit on the tide
Of war and high events, whose stormy waves
Might bear it up from sinking;—
ELM: And ye met
No more?
HER: Be still!—We did!—we met *once* more.
God had his own high purpose to fulfil,
Or think'st thou that the sun in his bright heaven
Had look'd upon such things?—We met *once more.*
That was an hour to leave its lightning-mark
Sear'd upon brain and bosom! There had been
Combat on Ebro's[11] banks, and when the day
Sank in red clouds, it faded from a field
Still held by Moorish lances. Night closed round—
A night of sultry darkness, in the shadow
Of whose broad wing, e'en unto death, I strove
Long with a turban'd champion; but my sword
Was heavy with God's vengeance—and prevail'd.
He fell—my heart exulted—and I stood
In gloomy triumph o'er him. Nature gave
No sign of horror, for 'twas Heaven's decree!
He strove to speak—but I had done the work
Of wrath too well;—yet in his last deep moan
A dreadful something of familiar sound
Came o'er my shuddering sense. The moon look'd
 forth,
And I beheld—speak not!—twas he—my son!
My boy lay dying there! He raised one glance,
And knew me—for he sought with feeble hand
To cover his glazed eyes. A darker veil
Sank o'er them soon.—I will not have thy look
Fix'd on me thus!—Away!
ELM: Thou hast seen this,
Thou hast *done* this—and yet thou liv'st?
HER: I live!
And know'st thou wherefore?—On my soul there
 fell
A horror of great darkness, which shut out

[11] **Ebro:** river in northeastern Spain.

All earth, and heaven, and hope. I cast away
The spear and helm, and made the cloister's shade
The home of my despair. But a deep voice
Came to me through the gloom, and sent its tones
Far through my bosom's depths. And I awoke,
Ay, as the mountain-cedar doth shake off
Its weight of wintry snow, e'en so I shook
Despondence from my soul, and knew myself
Seal'd by that blood wherewith my hands were dyed,
And set apart, and fearfully mark'd out
Unto a mighty task!—To rouse the soul
Of Spain as from the dead; and to lift up
The cross, her sign of victory, on the hills,
Gathering her sons to battle!—And my voice
Must be as freedom's trumpet on the winds,
From Roncesvalles to the blue sea-waves
Where Calpe[12] looks on Afric; till the land
Have fill'd her cup of vengeance!—Ask me *now*
To yield the Christian city, that its fanes
May rear the minaret in the face of Heaven!—
But death shall have a bloodier vintage-feast
Ere that day come!

ELM: I ask thee this no more,
For I am hopeless now.—But yet one boon—
Hear me, by all thy woes!—Thy voice hath power
Through the wide city—here I cannot rest:—
Aid me to pass the gates!

HER: And wherefore?

ELM: Thou,
That *wert* a father, and art now—alone!
Canst *thou* ask "wherefore?"—Ask the wretch
whose sands
Have not an hour to run, whose failing limbs
Have but one earthly journey to perform,
Why, on his pathway to the place of death,
Ay, when the very axe is glistening cold
Upon his dizzy sight, his pale, parch'd lip
Implores a cup of water?—Why, the stroke
Which trembles o'er him in itself shall bring
Oblivion of all wants, yet who denies
Nature's last prayer?—I tell thee that the thirst
Which burns my spirit up is agony
To be endured no more!—And I *must* look
Upon my children's faces, I must hear
Their voices, ere they perish!—But hath Heaven
Decreed that they *must* perish?—Who shall say
If in yon Moslem camp there beats no heart
Which prayers and tears may melt?

HER: There!—with the Moor!
Let him fill up the measure of his guilt!
—'Tis madness all!—How would'st thou pass th'
array
Of armed foes?

ELM: Oh! free doth sorrow pass,
Free and unquestion'd, through a suffering world![13]

HER: This must not be. Enough of woe is laid
E'en now upon thy lord's heroic soul,
For man to bear, unsinking. Press thou not
Too heavily th' o'erburthen'd heart.—Away!
Bow down the knee, and send thy prayers for
strength
Up to Heaven's gate.—Farewell!

(*Exit* HERNANDEZ.)

ELM: Are all men thus?
—Why, were't not better they should fall e'en now
Than live to shut their hearts, in haughty scorn,
Against the sufferer's pleadings!—But no, no!
Who can be like *this* man, that slew his son,
Yet wears his life still proudly, and a soul
Untamed upon his brow?

(*After a pause.*)

There's one, whose arms
Have borne my children in their infancy,
And on whose knees they sported, and whose hand
Hath led them oft—a vassal of their sire's;
And I will seek him: he may lend me aid,
When all beside pass on.

Dirge, Heard Without

Thou to thy rest art gone,
High heart! and what are we,
While o'er our heads the storm sweeps on,
That we should mourn for thee?

[12] **Calpe**: a town on a cape south of Valencia.

[13] **Oh! free . . . suffering world!**: "Frey geht das Unglück durch die ganze Erde." Schiller, *Death of Wallenstein*, act iv. sc. 2 [F. H.].

Free grave and peaceful bier
To the buried son of Spain!
To those that live, the lance and spear,
And well if not the chain!

Be *theirs* to weep the dead,
As they sit beneath their vines,
Whose flowery land hath borne no tread
Of spoilers o'er its shrines!

Thou hast thrown off the load
Which we must yet sustain,
And pour our blood where *thine* hath flow'd,
Too blest if not in vain!

We give thee holy rite,
Slow knell, and chaunted strain!
—For those that fall to-morrow night,
May be left no funeral-train.

Again, when trumpets wake,
We must brace our armour on;
But a deeper note *thy* sleep must break—
—Thou to thy rest art gone!

Happier in *this* than all,
That, now thy race is run,
Upon thy name no stain may fall,
Thy work hath well been done!

ELM: "Thy work hath well been done!"—so thou
may'st rest!
—There is a solemn lesson in those words—
But now I may not pause.

(Exit ELMINA.*)*

—SCENE III—

(A Street in the City.)

(HERNANDEZ—GONZALEZ.)

HER: Would they not hear?
GON: They heard, as one that stands
By the cold grave which hath but newly closed
O'er his last friend doth hear some passer-by
Bid him be comforted!—Their hearts have died
Within them!—We must perish, not as those
That fall when battle's voice doth shake the hills,
And peal through heaven's great arch, but silently,
And with a wasting of the spirit down,
A quenching, day by day, of some bright spark,
Which lit us on our toils!—Reproach me not;
My soul is darken'd with a heavy cloud—
—Yet fear not I shall yield!
HER: Breathe not the word,
Save in proud scorn!—Each bitter day o'erpass'd
By slow endurance, is a triumph won
For Spain's red cross.[14] And be of trusting heart!
A few brief hours, and those that turn'd away
In cold despondence, shrinking from your voice,
May crowd around their leader, and demand
To be array'd for battle. We must watch
For the swift impulse, and await its time,
As the bark waits the ocean's. You have chosen
To kindle up their souls, an hour, perchance,
When they were weary; they had cast aside
Their arms to slumber; or a knell, just then,
With its deep hollow tone, had made the blood
Creep shuddering through their veins; or they had
caught
A glimpse of some new meteor, and shaped forth
Strange omens from its blaze.
GON: Alas! the cause
Lies deeper in their misery!—I have seen,
In my night's course through this beleaguer'd city,
Things whose remembrance doth not pass away
As vapours from the mountains.—There were
some,
That sat beside their dead, with eyes wherein
Grief had ta'en place of sight, and shut out all
But its own ghastly object. To my voice
Some answer'd with a fierce and bitter laugh,
As men whose agonies were made to pass
The bounds of sufferance, by some reckless word,
Dropt from the light of spirit.—Others lay
—Why should I tell thee, father! how despair
Can bring the lofty brow of manhood down
Unto the very dust?—And yet for this,
Fear not that I embrace my doom—Oh God!
That 'twere *my* doom alone!—with less of fix'd
And solemn fortitude.—Lead on, prepare
The holiest rites of faith, that I by them
Once more may consecrate my sword, my life;

[14] **Spain's red cross:** the Christian forces.

— But what are these? — Who hath not dearer lives
Twined with his own? — I shall be lonely soon —
Childless! — Heaven wills it so. Let us begone.
Perchance before the shrine my heart may beat
With a less troubled motion.

(Exeunt GONZALEZ *and* HERNANDEZ.*)*

— SCENE IV —

(A Tent in the Moorish Camp.)
(ABDULLAH — ALPHONSO — CARLOS.)

ABD: These are bold words: but hast thou look'd on death,
Fair stripling? — On thy cheek and sunny brow
Scarce fifteen summers of their laughing course
Have left light traces. If thy shaft hath pierced
The ibex of the mountains, if thy step
Hath climb'd some eagle's nest, and thou hast made
His nest thy spoil, 'tis much! — And fear'st thou not
The leader of the mighty?

ALPH: I have been
Rear'd amongst fearless men, and 'midst the rocks
And the wild hills, whereon my fathers fought
And won their battles. There are glorious tales
Told of their deeds, and I have learn'd them all.
How should I fear thee, Moor?

ABD: So, thou hast seen
Fields, where the combat's roar hath died away
Into the whispering breeze, and where wild flowers
Bloom o'er forgotten graves! — But know'st thou aught
Of those, where sword from crossing sword strikes fire,
And leaders are borne down, and rushing steeds
Trample the life from out the mighty hearts
That ruled the storm so late? — Speak not of death
Till thou hast look'd on such.

ALPH: I was not born
A shepherd's son, to dwell with pipe and crook,
And peasant men, amidst the lowly vales;
Instead of ringing clarions, and bright spears,
And crested knights! — I am of princely race;
And, if my father would have heard my suit,
I tell thee, infidel, that long ere now,
I should have seen how lances meet, and swords
Do the field's work.

ABD: Boy! — know'st thou there are sights
A thousand times more fearful? — Men may die
Full proudly, when the skies and mountains ring
To battle-horn and tecbir.[15] But not all
So pass away in glory. There are those,
'Midst the dead silence of pale multitudes,
Led forth in fetters — dost thou mark me, boy?
To take their last look of th' all gladdening sun,
And bow, perchance, the stately head of youth
Unto the death of shame! — Hadst thou seen this ——

ALPH. *(to Carlos)*: Sweet brother, God is with us — fear thou not!
We have had heroes for our sires: — this man
Should not behold us tremble.

ABD: There are means
To tame the loftiest natures. Yet, again
I ask thee, wilt thou, from beneath the walls
Sue to thy sire for life? — or would'st thou die
With this thy brother?

ALPH: Moslem! — on the hills,
Around my father's castle, I have heard
The mountain-peasants, as they dress'd the vines,
Or drove the goats, by rock and torrent, home,
Singing their ancient songs; and these were all
Of the Cid Campeador; and how his sword
Tizona,[16] clear'd its way through turban'd hosts,
And captured Afric's kings, and how he won
Valencia from the Moor[17] — I will not shame
The blood we draw from him!

---

[15] **tecbir**: the war cry of the Moors and Arabs [F. H.].

[16] **Campeador**: conqueror. **Tizona**: Tizona, the firebrand. The name of the Cid's favourite sword, taken in battle from the Moorish king Bucar [F. H.].

[17] **how he won . . . Moor**: Valencia, which has been repeatedly besieged and taken by the armies of different nations, remained in the possession of the Moors for a hundred and seventy years after the Cid's death. It was regained from them by King Don Jayme of Aragon, surnamed the Conqueror; after whose success I have ventured to suppose it governed by a descendant of the Campeador [F. H.].

(A Moorish soldier enters.)

SOL: Valencia's lord
Sends messengers, my chief.

ABD: Conduct them hither.

(The soldier goes out and re-enters with ELMINA, *disguised, and an attendant.)*

CAR. *(springing forward to the attendant)*: Oh!
take me hence, Diego! take me hence
With thee, that I may see my mother's face
At morning when I wake. Here dark-brow'd men
Frown strangely, with their cruel eyes, upon us.
Take me with thee, for thou art good and kind,
And well I know thou lov'st me, my Diego!

ABD: Peace, boy!—What tidings, Christian, from thy lord?
Is he grown humbler?—doth he set the lives
Of these fair nurslings at a city's worth?

ALPH. *(rushing forward impatiently)*: Say not he
doth!—Yet wherefore art thou here?
If it be so, I could weep burning tears
For very shame! If this *can* be, return!
Tell him, of all his wealth, his battle-spoils,
I will but ask a war-horse and a sword,
And that beside him in the mountain-chase,
And in his halls, and at his stately feasts,
My place shall be no more!—but, no!—I wrong,
I wrong my father! Moor, believe it not,
He is a champion of the cross and Spain,
Sprung from the Cid!—and I, too, I can die
As a warrior's high-born child!

ELM: Alas, alas!
And would'st thou die, thus early die, fair boy?
What hath life done to thee, that thou should'st cast
Its flower away, in very scorn of heart,
Ere yet the blight be come?

ALPH: That voice doth sound—

ABD: Stranger, who art thou?—this is mockery! speak!

ELM. *(throwing off a mantle and helmet, and embracing her sons)*: My boys! whom I have rear'd through many hours
Of silent joys and sorrows, and deep thoughts
Untold and unimagined; let me die
With you, now I have held you to my heart,
And seen once more the faces, in whose light
My soul hath lived for years!

CAR: Sweet mother! now
Thou shalt not leave us more.

ABD: Enough of this!
Woman! what seek'st thou here? How hast thou dared
To front the mighty thus amidst his hosts?

ELM: Think'st thou there dwells no courage but in breasts
That set their mail against the ringing spears,
When helmets are struck down? Thou little know'st
Of nature's marvels. Chief, my heart is nerved
To make its way through things which warrior men,
Ay, they that master death by field or flood,[18]
Would look on, ere they braved!—I have no thought,
No sense of fear! Thou'rt mighty! but a soul
Wound up like mine is mightier, in the power
Of that one feeling pour'd through all its depths,
Than monarchs with their hosts! Am I not come
To die with these my children?

ABD: Doth thy faith
Bid thee do this, fond Christian? Hast thou not
The means to save them?

ELM: I have prayers, and tears,
And agonies!—and he, my God; the God
Whose hand, or soon or late, doth find its hour
To bow the crested head—hath made these things
Most powerful in a world where all must learn
That one deep language, by the storm call'd forth
From the bruis'd reeds of earth! For thee, perchance,
Affliction's chastening lesson hath not yet
Been laid upon thy heart, and thou may'st love
To see the creatures, by its might brought low,
Humbled before thee.

(She throws herself at his feet.)

Conqueror, I can kneel!
I, that drew birth from princes, bow myself
E'en to thy feet! Call in thy chiefs, thy slaves,

[18] **field or flood:** cf. *Othello*, I.iii.134–35: "Wherein I spoke of most disastrous chances; / Of moving accidents by flood and field."

If this will swell thy triumph, to behold
The blood of kings, of heroes, thus abased!
Do this, but spare my sons!
ALPH. *(attempting to raise her)*: Thou should'st not kneel
Unto this infidel! Rise, rise, my mother!
This sight doth shame our house!
ABD: Thou daring boy!
They that in arms have taught thy father's land
How chains are worn, shall school that haughty
  mien
Unto another language.
ELM: Peace, my son!
Have pity on my heart!—Oh, pardon, chief!
He is of noble blood. Hear, hear me yet!
Are there no lives through which the shafts of
  Heaven
May reach your soul? He that loves aught on earth,
Dares far too much, if he be merciless!
Is it for those, whose frail mortality
Must one day strive alone with God and death,
To shut their souls against th' appealing voice
Of nature, in her anguish?—warrior, man,
To you, too, ay, and haply with your hosts,
By thousands and ten thousands marshall'd round,
And your strong armour on, shall come that stroke
Which the lance wards not!—where shall your
  high heart
Find refuge then, if in the day of might
Woe hath lain prostrate, bleeding at your feet,
And you have pitied not?
ABD: These are vain words.
ELM: Have you no children?—fear you not to bring
The lightning on their heads?—In your own land
Doth no fond mother, from the tents beneath
Your native palms, look o'er the deserts out,
To greet your homeward step?—You have not yet
Forgot so utterly her patient love;—
For is not woman's in all climes the same?
That you should scorn *my* prayer!—O Heaven! his
  eye
Doth wear no mercy!
ABD: Then it mocks you not.
I have swept o'er the mountains of your land,
Leaving my traces, as the visitings
Of storms upon them! Shall I now be stay'd?
Know, unto me it were as light a thing
In this my course, to quench your children's lives,
As, journeying through a forest, to break off
The young wild branches that obstruct the way
With their green sprays and leaves.
ELM: Are there such hearts
Amongst thy works, O God?
ABD: Kneel not to me.
Kneel to your lord! on his resolves doth hang
His children's doom. He may be lightly won
By a few bursts of passionate tears and words.
ELM: *(rising indignantly)*: Speak not of noble
  men!—He bears a soul
Stronger than love or death.
ALPH. *(with exultation)*: I knew 'twas thus!
He could not fail!
ELM: There is no mercy, none,
On this cold earth!—To strive with such a world,
Hearts should be void of love!—We will go hence,
My children! we are summon'd. Lay your heads,
In their young radiant beauty, once again
To rest upon this bosom. He that dwells
Beyond the clouds which press us darkly round,
Will yet have pity, and before his face
We three will stand together! Moslem! now
Let the stroke fall at once!
ABD: 'Tis thine own will.
These might e'en yet be spared.
ELM: *Thou* wilt not spare!
And he beneath whose eye their childhood grew,
And in whose paths they sported, and whose ear
From their first lisping accents caught the sound
Of that word—*Father*—once a name of love—
Is——Men shall call him *steadfast*.
ABD: Hath the blast
Of sudden trumpets ne'er at dead of night,
When the land's watchers fear'd no hostile step,
Startled the slumberers from their dreamy world,
In cities, whose heroic lords have been
Steadfast as thine?
ELM: There's meaning in thine eye,
More than thy words.
ABD. *(pointing to the city)*: Look to yon towers and walls!
Think you no hearts within their limits pine,
Weary of hopeless warfare, and prepared
To burst the feeble links which bind them still
Unto endurance?
ELM: Thou hast said too well.
But what of this?
ABD: Then there are those, to whom
The prophet's armies not as foes would pass

Yon gates, but as deliverers. Might they not
In some still hour, when weariness takes rest,
Be won to welcome us?—Your children's steps
May yet bound lightly through their father's halls!

ALPH. *(indignantly)*: Thou treacherous Moor!

ELM: Let me not thus be tried
Beyond all strength, oh, Heaven!

ABD: Now, 'tis for *thee*,
Thou Christian mother! on thy sons to pass
The sentence—life or death!—the price is set
On their young blood, and rests within thy hands.

ALPH: Mother! thou tremblest!

ABD: Hath thy heart resolved?

ELM. *(covering her face with her hands)*: My boy's
proud eye is on me, and the things
Which rush in stormy darkness through my soul,
Shrink from his glance. I cannot answer *here*.

ABD: Come forth. We'll commune elsewhere.

CAR. *(to his mother)*: Wilt thou go?
Oh! let me follow thee!

ELM: Mine own fair child!
Now that thine eyes have pour'd once more on mine
The light of their young smile, and thy sweet voice
Hath sent its gentle music through my soul,
And I have felt the twining of thine arms—
How shall I leave thee?

ABD: Leave him, as 'twere but
For a brief slumber, to behold his face
At morning, with the sun's.

ALPH: Thou hast no look
For me, my mother!

ELM: Oh! that I should live
To say, I *dare* not look on thee!—Farewell,
My first-born, fare thee well!

ALPH: Yet, yet beware!
It were a grief more heavy on thy soul,
That I should blush for thee, than o'er my grave
That thou should'st proudly weep!

ABD: Away! we trifle here. The night wanes fast.
Come forth!

ELM: One more embrace! My sons, farewell!

(Exeunt ABDULLAH *with* ELMINA *and her Attendant.)*

ALPH: Hear me yet once, my mother!—Art thou gone?
But one word more!

(He rushes out, followed by CARLOS.)

—SCENE V—

(The Garden of a Palace in Valencia.)

(XIMENA, THERESA.)

THER: Stay yet awhile. A purer air doth rove
Here through the myrtles whispering, and the limes,
And shaking sweetness from the orange boughs,
Than waits you in the city.

XIM: There are those
In their last need, and on their bed of death,
At which no hand doth minister but mine
That wait me in the city. Let us hence.

THER: You have been wont to love the music made
By founts, and rustling foliage, and soft winds,
Breathing of citron-groves. And will you turn
From these to scenes of death?

XIM: To me the voice
Of summer, whispering through young flowers and
leaves,
Now speaks too deep a language! and of all
Its dreamy and mysterious melodies,
The breathing soul is sadness!—I have felt
That summons through my spirit, after which
The hues of earth are changed, and all her sounds
Seem fraught with secret warnings.—There is
cause
That I should bend my footsteps to the scenes
Where Death is busy, taming warrior-hearts,
And pouring winter through the fiery blood,
And fett'ring the strong arm!—For now no sigh
In the dull air, nor floating cloud in heaven,
No, not the lightest murmur of a leaf,
But of his angel's silent coming bears
Some token to my soul.—But nought of this
Unto my mother!—These are awful hours!
And on their heavy steps afflictions crowd
With such dark pressure, there is left no room
For one grief more.

THER: Sweet lady, talk not thus!
Your eye this morn doth wear a calmer light,
There's more of life in its clear trem'lous ray
Than I have mark'd of late. Nay, go not yet;
Rest by this fountain, where the laurels dip
Their glossy leaves. A fresher gale doth spring
From the transparent waters, dashing round
Their silvery spray, with a sweet voice of coolness,
O'er the pale glistening marble. 'Twill call up
Faint bloom, if but a moment's, to your cheek.

Rest here, ere you go forth, and I will sing
The melody you love.

(THERESA *sings*.)

Why is the Spanish maiden's grave
So far from her own bright land?
The sunny flowers that o'er it wave
Were sown by no kindred hand.

'Tis not the orange-bough that sends
Its breath on the sultry air,
'Tis not the myrtle-stem that bends
To the breeze of evening there!

But the rose of Sharon's eastern bloom
By the silent dwelling fades,
And none but strangers pass the tomb
Which the palm of Judah shades.

The lowly Cross, with flowers o'ergrown,
Marks well that place of rest;
But who hath graved, on its mossy stone,
A sword, a helm, a crest?

These are the trophies of a chief,
A lord of the axe and spear!
—Some blossom pluck'd, some faded leaf,
Should grace a maiden's bier!

Scorn not her tomb—deny not her
The honours of the brave!
O'er that forsaken sepulchre,
Banner and plume might wave.

She bound the steel, in battle tried,
Her fearless heart above,
And stood with brave men, side by side,
In the strength and faith of love!

That strength prevail'd—that faith was bless'd!
True was the javelin thrown,
Yet pierced it not her warrior's breast:
She met it with her own!

And nobly won, where heroes fell
In arms for the holy shrine,
A death which saved what she loved so well,
And a grave in Palestine.

Then let the rose of Sharon spread
Its breast to the glowing air,
And the palm of Judah lift its head,
Green and immortal there!

And let yon grey stone, undefaced,
With its trophy mark the scene,
Telling the pilgrim of the waste,
Where Love and Death have been.

XIM: Those notes were wont to make my heart beat quick,
As at a voice of victory; but to-day
The spirit of the song is changed, and seems
All mournful. Oh! that, ere my early grave
Shuts out the sunbeam, I might hear one peal
Of the Castilian trumpet, ringing forth
Beneath my father's banner!—In that sound
Were life to you, sweet brothers!—But for me—
Come on—our tasks await us. They who know
Their hours are number'd out, have little time
To give the vague and slumberous languor way,
Which doth steal o'er them in the breath of flowers,
And whisper of soft winds.

(ELMINA *enters hurriedly*.)

ELM: The air will calm my spirit, ere yet I meet
His eye, which must be met.—Thou here, Ximena!

(*She starts back on seeing* XIMENA.)

XIM: Alas! my mother! In that hurrying step
And troubled glance I read——
ELM. (*wildly*): Thou read'st it not!
Why, who would live, if unto mortal eye
The things lay glaring, which within our hearts
We treasure up for God's?—Thou read'st it not!
I say, thou canst not!—There's not one on earth
Shall know the thoughts, which for themselves have made
And kept dark places in the very breast
Whereon he hath laid his slumber, till the hour
When the graves open!
XIM: Mother! what is this?
Alas! your eye is wandering, and your cheek
Flush'd, as with fever! To your woes the night
Hath brought no rest.
ELM: Rest!—who should rest?—not he
That holds one earthly blessing to his heart
Nearer than life!—No! if this world have aught
Of bright or precious, let not him who calls
Such things his own, take rest!—Dark spirits keep watch,
And they to whom fair honour, chivalrous fame,
Were as heaven's air, the vital element

Wherein they breathed, may wake, and find their souls
Made marks for human scorn!—Will they bear on
With life struck down, and thus disrobed of all
Its glorious drapery?—Who shall tell us this?
—Will *he* so bear it?

XIM: Mother! let us kneel
And blend our hearts in prayer!—What else is left
To mortals when the dark hour's might is on them?
—Leave us, Theresa.—Grief like this doth find
Its balm in solitude.

(*Exit* THERESA.)

My mother! peace
Is heaven's benignant answer to the cry
Of wounded spirits. Wilt thou kneel with me?

ELM: Away! 'tis but for souls unstain'd, to wear
Heaven's tranquil image on their depths.—The stream
Of my dark thoughts, all broken by the storm,
Reflects but clouds and lightnings!—Didst thou speak
Of peace?—'tis fled from earth!—but there is joy!
Wild, troubled joy! And who shall know, my child!
It is not happiness?—Why, our own hearts
Will keep the secret close!—Joy, joy! if but
To leave this desolate city, with its dull
Slow knells and dirges, and to breathe again
Th' untainted mountain-air!—But hush! the trees,
The flowers, the waters, must hear nought of this!
They are full of voices, and will whisper things——
—We'll speak of it no more.

XIM: Oh! pitying Heaven!
This grief doth shake her reason!

ELM. (*starting*): Hark! a step!
'Tis—tis thy father's!—come away—not now—
He must not see us now!

XIM: Why should this be?

(GONZALEZ *enters, and detains* ELMINA.)

GON: Elmina, dost thou shun me?—Have we not,
E'en from the hopeful and the sunny time
When youth was as a glory round our brows,
Held on through life together?—And is this,
When eve is gathering round us, with the gloom
Of stormy clouds, a time to part our steps
Upon the darkening wild?

ELM. (*coldly*): There needs not this.
Why should'st thou think I shunn'd thee?

GON: Should the love
That shone o'er many years, th' unfading love,
Whose only change hath been from gladd'ning smiles
To mingling sorrows and sustaining strength,
Thus lightly be forgotten?

ELM: Speak'st *thou* thus?
—I have knelt before thee with that very plea,
When it avail'd me not!—But there are things
Whose very breathings from the soul erase
All record of past love, save the chill sense,
Th' unquiet memory of its wasted faith,
And vain devotedness!—Ay! they that fix
Affection's perfect trust on aught of earth,
Have many a dream to start from!

GON: This is but
The wildness and the bitterness of grief,
Ere yet the unsettled heart hath closed its long
Impatient conflicts with a mightier power,
Which makes all conflict vain.

——Hark! was there not
A sound of distant trumpets, far beyond
The Moorish tents, and of another tone
Than th' Afric horn, Ximena?

XIM: Oh, my father!
I know that horn too well.—'Tis but the wind,
Which, with a sudden rising, bears its deep
And savage war-note from us, wafting it
O'er the far hills.

GON: Alas! this woe must be!
I do not shake my spirit from its height,
So startling it with hope!—But the dread hour
Shall be met bravely still. I can keep down
Yet for a little while—and Heaven will ask
No more—the passionate workings of my heart
—And thine—Elmina?

ELM: 'Tis—I am prepared.
I *have* prepared for all.

GON: Oh, well I knew
Thou would'st not fail me!—Not in vain my soul,
Upon thy faith and courage, hath built up
Unshaken trust.

ELM. (*wildly*): Away!—thou know'st me not!
Man dares too far, his rashness would invest
This our mortality with an attribute
Too high and awful, boasting that he knows
One human heart!

GON: These are wild words, but yet
I will not doubt thee!—Hast thou not been found
Noble in all things, pouring thy soul's light
Undimm'd o'er every trial?—And, as our fates,
So must our names be, undivided!—Thine,
I' th' record of a warrior's life, shall find
Its place of stainless honour.—By his side—
ELM: May this be borne?—How much of agony
Hath the heart room for?—Speak to me in wrath
—I can endure it!—But no gentle words!
No words of love! no praise!—Thy sword might
slay,
And be merciful!
GON: Wherefore art thou thus?
Elmina, my beloved!
ELM: No more of love!
—Have I not said there's that within my heart,
Whereon it falls as living fire would fall
Upon an unclosed wound?
GON: Nay, lift thine eyes,
That I may read *their* meaning!
ELM: Never more
With a free soul—What have I said?—'twas
nought!
Take thou no heed! The words of wretchedness
Admit not scrutiny. Would'st thou mark the speech
Of troubled dreams?
GON: I have seen thee in the hour
Of thy deep spirit's joy, and when the breath
Of grief hung chilling round thee; in all change,
Bright health and drooping sickness; hope and fear;
Youth and decline; but never yet, Elmina,
Ne'er hath thine eye till now shrunk back perturb'd
With shame or dread, from mine!
ELM: Thy glance doth search
A wounded heart too deeply.
GON: Hast thou there
Aught to conceal?
ELM: Who hath not?
GON: Till this hour
Thou never hadst!—Yet hear me!—by the free
And unattainted fame which wraps the dust
Of thine heroic fathers—
ELM: This to me!
—Bring your inspiring war-notes, and your sounds
Of festal music round a dying man!
Will his heart echo them?—But if thy words
Were spells, to call up, with each lofty tone,
The grave's most awful spirits, they would stand
Powerless, before my anguish!
GON: Then, by her,
Who there looks on thee in the purity
Of her devoted youth, and o'er whose name
No blight must fall, and whose pale cheek must
ne'er
Burn with that deeper tinge, caught painfully
From the quick feeling of dishonour.—Speak!
Unfold this mystery!—By thy sons—
ELM: My sons!
And canst *thou* name them?
GON: Proudly!—Better far
They died with all the promise of their youth,
And the fair honour of their house upon them,
Than that, with manhood's high and passionate
soul,
To fearful strength unfolded, they should live,
Barr'd from the lists of crested chivalry,
And pining, in the silence of a woe,
Which from the heart shuts daylight—o'er the
shame
Of those who gave them birth!—But *thou* could'st
ne'er
Forget their lofty claims!
ELM. (*wildly*): 'Twas but for them!
'Twas for them only!—Who shall dare arraign
Madness of crime?—And He who made us, knows
There are dark moments of all hearts and lives,
Which bear down reason!
GON: Thou, whom I have loved
With such high trust as o'er our nature threw
A glory scarce allow'd;—what hast thou done?
—Ximena, go thou hence!
ELM: No, no! my child!
There's pity in thy look!—All other eyes
Are full of wrath and scorn!—Oh! leave me not!
GON: That I should live to see thee thus abased!
—Yet speak?—What hast thou done?
ELM: Look to the gate!
Thou'rt worn with toil—but take no rest to-night!
The western gate!—Its watchers have been won—
The Christian city hath been bought and sold!—
They will admit the Moor!
GON: They have been won!
Brave men and tried so long!—Whose work was
this?

ELM: Think'st thou all hearts like thine?—Can mothers stand
To see their children perish?
GON: Then the guilt
Was thine?
ELM: Shall mortal dare to call it guilt?
I tell thee, Heaven, which made all holy things,
Made nought more holy than the boundless love
Which fills a mother's heart!—I say, 'tis woe
Enough, with such an aching tenderness,
To love aught earthly!—and in vain! in vain!
—We are press'd down too sorely!
GON. (*in a low desponding voice*): Now my life
Is struck to worthless ashes!—In my soul
Suspicion hath ta'en root. The nobleness
Henceforth is blotted from all human brows;
And fearful power, a dark and troublous gift,
Almost like prophecy, is pour'd upon me,
To read the guilty secrets in each eye
That once look'd bright with truth!
—Why, then, I have gain'd
What men call wisdom!—A new sense, to which
All tales that speak of high fidelity,
And holy courage, and proud honour, tried,
Search'd, and found steadfast, even to martyrdom,
Are food for mockery!—Why should I not cast
From my thinn'd locks the wearing helm at once,
And in the heavy sickness of my soul
Throw the sword down for ever?—Is there aught
In all this world of gilded hollowness,
Now the bright hues drop off its loveliest things,
Worth striving for again?
XIM: Father! look up!
Turn unto me, thy child!
GON: Thy face is fair;
And hath been unto me, in other days,
As morning to the journeyer of the deep;
But now—'tis too like hers!
ELM. (*falling at his feet*): Woe, shame and woe,
Are on me in their might!—forgive, forgive!
GON. (*starting up*): Doth the Moor deem that *I* have part, or share,
Or counsel in this vileness?—Stay me not!
Let go thy hold—'tis powerless on me now—
I linger there, while treason is at work!

(*Exit* GONZALEZ.)

ELM: Ximena, dost *thou* scorn me?
XIM: I have found
In mine own heart too much of feebleness,
Hid, beneath many foldings, from all eyes
But His whom nought can blind, to dare do aught
But pity thee, dear mother!
ELM: Blessings light
On thy fair head, my gentle child, for this!
Thou kind and merciful!—My soul is faint—
Worn with long strife!—Is there aught else to do,
Or suffer, ere we die?—Oh God! my sons!
—I have betray'd them!—All their innocent blood
Is on my soul!
XIM: How shall I comfort thee?
—Oh! hark! what sounds come deepening on the wind,
So full of solemn hope!

(*A procession of Nuns passes across the Scene, bearing relics, and chanting.*)

Chant

A sword is on the land!
He that bears down young tree and glorious flower,
Death is gone forth, he walks the wind in power!
Where is the warrior's hand?
Our steps are in the shadows of the grave,
Hear us, we perish! Father, hear and save!

If, in the days of song,
The days of gladness, we have call'd on thee,
When mirthful voices range from sea to sea,
And joyous hearts were strong;
Now that alike the feeble and the brave
Must cry, "We perish!"—Father, hear and save!

The days of song are fled!
The winds come loaded, wafting dirge-notes by,
But they that linger soon unmourn'd must die;—
The dead weep not the dead!—
Wilt thou forsake us 'midst the stormy wave?
We sink, we perish!—Father, hear and save!

Helmet and lance are dust!
Is not the strong man wither'd from our eye?
The arm struck down that held our banners high?—
Thine is our spirits' trust!
Look through the gath'ring shadows of the grave!
Do we not perish?—Father, hear and save!

(HERNANDEZ *enters.*)

ELM: Why com'st thou, man of vengeance?—
What have I
To do with thee?—Am I not bow'd enough?—
Thou art no mourner's comforter!
HER: Thy lord
Hath sent me unto thee. Till this day's task
Be closed, thou daughter of the feeble heart!
He bids thee seek him not, but lay thy ways
Before Heaven's altar, and in penitence
Make thy soul's peace with God.
ELM: Till this day's task
Be closed!—there is strange triumph in thine
eyes—
Is it that I have fall'n from that high place
Whereon I stood in fame?—But I can feel
A wild and bitter pride in thus being past
The power of thy dark glance!—My spirit now
Is wound about by one sole mighty grief;
Thy scorn hath lost its sting. Thou may'st
reproach—
HER: I come not to reproach thee. Heaven doth work
By many agencies; and in its hour
There is no insect which the summer breeze
From the green leaf shakes trembling, but may serve
Its deep unsearchable purposes, as well
As the great ocean, or th' eternal fires
Pent in earth's caves!—Thou hast but speeded that,
Which, in th' infatuate blindness of thy heart,
Thou would'st have trampled o'er all holy ties
But to avert one day!
ELM: My senses fail—
Thou said'st—speak yet again—I could not catch
The meaning of thy words.
HER: E'en now thy lord
Hath sent our foes defiance. On the walls
He stands in conference with the boastful Moor,
And awful strength is with him. Through the blood
Which this day must be pour'd in sacrifice
Shall Spain be free. On all her olive-hills
Shall men set up the battle-sign of fire,
And round its blaze, at midnight, keep the sense
Of vengeance wakeful in each other's hearts
E'en with thy children's tale!
XIM: Peace, father! peace!
Behold she sinks!—the storm hath done its work
Upon the broken reed. Oh! lend thine aid
To bear her hence.

(They lead her away.)

—SCENE VI—

(A Street in Valencia. Several Groups of Citizens and Soldiers, many of them lying on the steps of a church. Arms scattered on the ground around them.)

AN OLD CIT: The air is sultry, as with thunder-clouds.
I left my desolate home, that I might breathe
More freely in heaven's face, but my heart feels
With this hot gloom o'erburden'd. I have now
No sons to tend me. Which of you, kind friends,
Will bring the old man water from the fount,
To moisten his parch'd lip?

(A citizen goes out.)

2D CIT: This wasting siege,
Good Father Lopez, hath gone hard with you!
'Tis sad to hear no voices through the house,
Once peopled with fair sons!
3D CIT: Why, better thus,
Than to be haunted with their famish'd cries,
E'en in your very dreams!
OLD CIT: Heaven's will be done!
These are dark times! I have not been alone
In my affliction.
3D CIT. *(with bitterness)*: Why, we have but this thought
Left for our gloomy comfort!—And tis well!
Ay, let the balance be awhile struck even
Between the noble's palace and the hut,
Where the worn peasant sickens!—They that bear
The humble dead unhonour'd to their homes,
Pass now i' th' streets no lordly bridal train
With its exulting music; and the wretch
Who on the marble steps of some proud hall
Flings himself down to die, in his last need
And agony of famine, doth behold
No scornful guests, with their long purple robes,
To the banquet sweeping by. Why, this is just!
These are the days when pomp is made to feel
Its human mould!
4TH CIT: Heard you last night the sound
Of Saint Iago's bell?—How sullenly
From the great tower it peal'd!
5TH CIT: Ay, and tis said
No mortal hand was near when so it seem'd
To shake the midnight streets.
OLD CIT: Too well I know
The sound of coming fate!—'Tis ever thus
When Death is on his way to make it night

In the Cid's ancient house.[19] — Oh! there are things
In this strange world of which we've all to learn
When its dark bounds are pass'd. — Yon bell,
untouch'd
(Save by the hands we see not), still doth speak —
When of that line some stately head is mark'd, —
With a wild hollow peal, at dead of night,
Rocking Valencia's towers. I've heard it oft,
Nor known its warning false.

4TH CIT: And will our chief
Buy with the price of his fair children's blood
A few more days of pining wretchedness
For this forsaken city?

OLD CIT: Doubt it not!
— But with that ransom he may purchase still
Deliverance for the land! — And yet 'tis sad
To think that such a race, with all its fame,
Should pass away! — For she, his daughter too,
Moves upon earth as some bright thing whose time
To sojourn there is short.

5TH CIT: Then woe for us
When she is gone! — Her voice — the very sound
Of her soft step was comfort, as she moved
Through the still house of mourning! — Who like
her
Shall give us hope again?

OLD CIT: Be still! — she comes,
And with a mien how changed! — A hurrying step,
And a flush'd cheek! — What may this bode? — Be
still!

(XIMENA *enters, with Attendants carrying a Banner.*)

XIM: Men of Valencia! in an hour like this,
What do ye here?

A CIT: We die!

XIM: Brave men die *now*
Girt for the toil, as travellers suddenly
By the dark night o'ertaken on their way!
These days require such death! — It is too much
Of luxury for our wild and angry times,
To fold the mantle round us, and to sink
From life, as flowers that shut up silently,
When the sun's heat doth scorch them! Hear ye
not?

A CIT: Lady! what would'st thou with us?

XIM: Rise and arm!
E'en now the children of your chief are led
Forth by the Moor to perish! — Shall this be,
Shall the high sound of such a name be hush'd,
I' th' land to which for ages it hath been
A battle-word, as 'twere some passing note
Of shepherd-music? — Must this work be done,
And ye lie pining here, as men in whom
The pulse which God hath made for noble thought
Can so be thrill'd no longer?

CIT: 'Tis e'en so!
Sickness, and toil, and grief, have breathed upon us,
Our hearts beat faint and low.

XIM: Are ye so poor
Of soul, my countrymen! that ye can draw
Strength from no deeper source than that which
sends
The red blood mantling through the joyous veins,
And gives the fleet step wings? — Why, how have
age
And sens'tive womanhood ere now endured,
Through pangs of searching fire, in some proud
cause,
Blessing that agony? Think ye the Power
Which bore them nobly up, as if to teach
The torturer where eternal Heaven had set
Bounds to his sway, was earthy, of this earth —
This dull mortality? — Nay, then look on me!
Death's touch hath mark'd me, and I stand amongst
you,
As one whose place, i' th' sunshine of your world,
Shall soon be left to fill! — I say, the breath
Of th' incense, floating through yon fane, shall
scarce
Pass from your path before me! But even now,
I've that within me, kindling through the dust,
Which from all time hath made high deeds its voice
And token to the nations; — Look on me!
Why hath Heaven pour'd forth courage, as a flame
Wasting the womanish heart, which must be still'd
Yet sooner for its swift consuming brightness,
If not to shame your doubt, and your despair,
And your soul's torpor? — Yet, arise and arm!
It may not be too late.

A CIT: Why, what are we,
To cope with hosts? — Thus faint, and worn, and
few,
O'ernumber'd and forsaken, is't for us
To stand against the mighty?

[19] **The sound . . . house:** It was a Spanish tradition, that the great bell of the cathedral of Saragossa always tolled spontaneously before a King of Spain died [F. H.].

XIM: And for whom
Hath He, who shakes the mighty with a breath
From their high places, made the fearfulness,
And ever-wakeful presence of his power,
To the pale startled earth most manifest,
But for the weak?—Was't for the helm'd and crown'd
That suns were stay'd at noonday?—Stormy seas
As a rill parted?—Mail'd archangels sent
To wither up the strength of kings with death?
—I tell you, if these marvels have been done,
'Twas for the wearied and th' oppress'd of men.
They needed such!—And generous faith hath power
By her prevailing spirit, e'en yet to work
Deliverances, whose tale shall live with those
Of the great elder-time!—Be of good heart!
Who is forsaken?—He that gives the thought
A place within his breast!—'Tis not for you.
—Know ye this banner?

CITS. (*murmuring to each other*): Is she not inspired?
Doth not Heaven call us by her fervent voice?

XIM: Know ye this banner?

CIT: 'Tis the Cid's.

XIM: The Cid's!
Who breathes that name but in th' exulting tone
Which the heart rings to?—Why, the very wind,
As it swells out the noble standard's fold,
Hath a triumphant sound!—The Cid's!—it moved
Even as a sign of victory through the land,
From the free skies ne'er stooping to a foe!

OLD CIT: Can ye still pause, my brethren? Oh! that youth
Through this worn frame were kindling once again!

XIM: Ye linger still? Upon this very air,
He that was born in happy hour[20] for Spain,
Pour'd forth his conquering spirit! 'Twas the breeze
From your own mountains which came down to wave
This banner of his battles, as it droop'd
Above the champion's deathbed. Nor even then
Its tale of glory closed. They made no moan
O'er the dead hero, and no dirge was sung,[21]
But the deep tambour and shrill horn of war
Told when the mighty pass'd! They wrapt him not
With the pale shroud, but braced the warrior's form
In war array, and on his barbed steed,
As for a triumph, rear'd him; marching forth
In the hush'd midnight from Valencia's walls,
Beleaguer'd then, as now. All silently
The stately funeral moved. But who was he
That follow'd, charging on the tall white horse,
And with the solemn standard, broad and pale,
Waving in sheets of snowlight? And the cross,
The bloody cross, far-blazing from his shield,
And the fierce meteor-sword? They fled, they fled,
The kings of Afric, with their countless hosts,
Were dust in his red path. The scimitar
Was shiver'd as a reed;—for in that hour
The warrior-saint that keeps the watch for Spain,
Was arm'd betimes. And o'er that fiery field
The Cid's high banner stream'd all joyously,
For still its lord was there.

CITS. (*rising tumultuously*): Even unto death
Again it shall be follow'd!

XIM: Will he see
The noble stem hewn down, the beacon-light
Which from his house for ages o'er the land
Hath shone through cloud and storm, thus quench'd at once?
Will he not aid his children in the hour
Of this their utmost peril?—Awful power
Is with the holy dead, and there are times
When the tomb hath no chain they cannot burst!
Is it a thing forgotten how he woke
From its deep rest of old, remembering Spain
In her great danger? At the night's mid-watch
How Leon[22] started, when the sound was heard
That shook her dark and hollow-echoing streets,
As with the heavy tramp of steel-clad men,
By thousands marching through. For he had risen!
The Campeador was on his march again,

[20] **He . . . hour:** "El que en buen hora nasco;" he that was born in happy hour. An appellation given to the Cid in the ancient chronicles [F. H.].

[21] **O'er the dead hero . . . sung:** For this, and the subsequent allusions to Spanish legends, see *The Romances, and Chronicle of the Cid* [F. H.].

[22] **Leon:** city in northwestern Spain.

And in his arms, and follow'd by his hosts
Of shadowy spearmen. He had left the world
From which we are dimly parted, and gone forth,
And call'd his buried warriors from their sleep,
Gathering them round him to deliver Spain;
For Afric was upon her. Morning broke,
Day rush'd through clouds of battle; but at eve
Our God had triumph'd, and the rescued land
Sent up a shout of victory from the field,
That rock'd her ancient mountains.

THE CITS: Arm! to arms!
On to our chief! We have strength within us yet
To die with our blood roused! Now, be the word
For the Cid's house!

(They begin to arm themselves.)

XIM: Ye know his battle song?
The old rude strain wherewith his bands went forth
To strike down Paynim swords!

(She sings.)

The Cid's Battle Song

The Moor is on his way,
With the tambour peal and the tecbir-shout,
And the horn o'er the blue seas ringing out,
He hath marshall'd his dark array!

Shout through the vine-clad land!
That her sons on all their hills may hear,
And sharpen the point of the red wolf-spear,
And the sword for the brave man's hand!

(The CITIZENS *join in the song, while they continue arming themselves.)*

Banners are in the field!
The chief must rise from his joyous board,
And turn from the feast ere the wine be pour'd,
And take up his father's shield!

The Moor is on his way!
Let the peasant leave his olive-ground,
And the goats roam wild through the pine-woods round!
There is nobler work to-day!

Send forth the trumpet's call!
Till the bridegroom cast the goblet down,
And the marriage-robe, and the flowery crown,
And arm in the banquet-hall!

And stay the funeral train:
Bid the chanted mass be hush'd awhile,
And the bier laid down in the holy aisle,
And the mourners girt for Spain.

(They take up the banner and follow XIMENA *out. Their voices are heard gradually dying away at a distance.)*

Ere night must swords be red!
It is not an hour for knells and tears,
But for helmets braced, and serried spears!
To-morrow for the dead!

The Cid is in array!
His steed is barded,[23] his plume waves high,
His banner is up in the sunny sky,
Now, joy for the Cross to-day!

— SCENE VII —

(The Walls of the City. The Plains beneath, with the Moorish Camp and Army.)

(GONZALEZ — GARCIAS — HERNANDEZ.)

(A wild sound of Moorish Music heard from below.)

HER: What notes are these in their deep mournfulness
So strangely wild?

GAR: 'Tis the shrill melody
Of the Moor's ancient death-song. Well I know
The rude barbaric sound; but, till this hour,
It seem'd not fearful. — Now, a shuddering chill
Comes o'er me with its tones. — Lo! from yon tent
They lead the noble boys!

HER: The young, and pure,
And beautiful victims! — 'Tis on things like these
We cast our hearts in wild idolatry,
Sowing the winds with hope! — Yet this is well,
Thus brightly crown'd with life's most gorgeous flowers,
And all unblemish'd, earth should offer up
Her treasures unto Heaven!

GAR. *(to* GONZALEZ*)*: My chief, the Moor
Hath led your children forth.

GON. *(starting)*: Are my sons there?
I knew they could not perish; for yon Heaven

[23] **barded:** caparisoned for battle [F. H.].

Would ne'er behold it!—Where is he that said
I was no more a father?—They look changed—
Pallid and worn, as from a prison-house!
Or is't mine eye sees dimly?—But their steps
Seem heavy, as with pain.—I hear the clank—
Oh God! their limbs are fetter'd!

ABD. (*coming forward beneath the walls*): Christian! look
Once more upon thy children. There is yet
One moment for the trembling of the sword;
Their doom is still with thee.

GON: Why should this man
So mock us with the semblance of our kind?
—Moor! Moor! thou dost too daringly provoke,
In thy bold cruelty, th' all-judging One,
Who visits for such things!—Hast thou no sense
Of thy frail nature?—'Twill be taught thee yet,
And darkly shall the anguish of my soul,
Darkly and heavily, pour itself on thine,
When thou shalt cry for mercy from the dust,
And be denied!

ABD: Nay, is it not thyself,
That hast no mercy and no love within thee?
These are thy sons, the nurslings of thy house;
Speak! must they live or die?

GON. (*in violent emotion*): Is it Heaven's will
To try the dust it kindles for a day,
With infinite agony!—How have I drawn
This chastening on my head!—They bloom'd around me,
And my heart grew too fearless in its joy,
Glorying in their bright promise!—If we fall,
Is there no pardon for our feebleness?

(HERNANDEZ, *without speaking, holds up a cross before him*.)

ABD: Speak!

GON. (*snatching the cross, and lifting it up*): Let the earth be shaken through its depths,
But *this* must triumph!

ABD. (*coldly*): Be it as thou wilt.
—Unsheath the scimitar!

(*To his guards*.)

GAR. (*to* GONZALEZ): Away, my chief!
This is your place no longer. There are things
No human heart, though battle-proof as yours,
Unmadden'd may sustain.

GON: Be still! I have now
No place on earth but this!

ALPH. (*from beneath*): Men! give me way,
That I may speak forth once before I die!

GAR: The princely boy!—how gallantly his brow
Wears its high nature in the face of death!

ALPH: Father!

GON: My son! my son!—Mine eldest-born!

ALPH: Stay but upon the ramparts! Fear thou not
—There is good courage in me: oh! my father!
I will not shame thee!—only let me fall
Knowing thine eye looks proudly on thy child,
So shall my heart have strength.

GON: Would, would to God,
That I might die for thee, my noble boy!
Alphonso, my fair son!

ALPH: Could I have lived,
I might have been a warrior!—Now, farewell!
But look upon me still!—I will not blench
When the keen sabre flashes—Mark me well!
Mine eyelids shall not quiver as it falls,
So thou wilt look upon me!

GAR. (*to* GONZALEZ): Nay, my lord!
We must begone!—Thou *canst* not bear it!

GON: Peace!
—Who hath told *thee* how much man's heart can bear?
—Lend me thine arm—my brain whirls fearfully—
How thick the shades close round!—my boy! my boy!
Where art thou in this gloom?

GAR: Let us go hence!
This is a dreadful moment!

GON: Hush!—what saidst thou?
Now let me look on him!—Dost *thou* see aught
Through the dull mist which wraps us?

GAR: I behold—
O! for a thousand Spaniards! to rush down—

GON: Thou seest—My heart stands still to hear thee speak!
—There seems a fearful hush upon the air,
As 'twere the dead of night!

GAR: The hosts have closed
Around the spot in stillness. Through the spears,
Ranged thick and motionless, I see him not;
—But now—

GON: He bade me keep mine eye upon him,
And all is darkness round me!—Now?

GAR: A sword,
A sword, springs upward, like a lightning burst,
Through the dark serried mass!—Its cold blue glare
Is wavering to and fro—'tis vanish'd—hark!

GON: I heard it, yes!—I heard the dull dead sound
That heavily broke the silence!—Didst thou speak?
—I lost thy words—come nearer!

GAR: 'Twas—'tis past!—
The sword fell *then!*

HER. (*with exultation*): Flow forth, thou noble blood!
Fount of Spain's ransom and deliverance, flow
Uncheck'd and brightly forth!—Thou kingly stream!
Blood of our heroes! blood of martyrdom!
Which through so many warrior-hearts hast pour'd
Thy fiery currents, and hast made our hills
Free, by thine own free offering!—Bathe the land,
But there thou shalt not sink!—Our very air
Shall take thy colouring, and our loaded skies
O'er th' infidel hang dark and ominous,
With battle-hues of thee!—And thy deep voice
Rising above them to the judgment-seat
Shall call a burst of gather'd vengeance down,
To sweep th' oppressor from us!—For thy wave
Hath made his guilt run o'er!

GON. (*endeavouring to rouse himself*): 'Tis all a dream!
There is not one—no hand on earth could harm
That fair boy's graceful head!—Why look you thus?

ABD. (*pointing to* CARLOS): Christian! e'en yet thou hast a son!

GON: E'en yet!

GAR: My father! take me from these fearful men!
Wilt thou not save me, father?

GON. (*attempting to unsheath his sword*): Is the strength
From mine arm shiver'd?—Garcias, follow me!

GAR: Whither, my chief?

GON: Why, we can die as well
On yonder plain,—ay, a spear's thrust will do
The little that our misery doth require,
Sooner than e'en this anguish! Life is best
Thrown from us in such moments.

(*Voices heard at a distance.*)

HER: Hush! what strain
Floats on the wind?

GAR: 'Tis the Cid's battle-song!
What marvel hath been wrought?

(*Voices approaching heard in chorus.*)

The Moor is on his way!
With the tambour peal and the tecbir-shout,
And the horn o'er the blue seas ringing out;
He hath marshall'd his dark array!

(XIMENA *enters, followed by the* CITIZENS, *with the Banner.*)

XIM: Is it too late?—My father, these are men
Through life and death prepared to follow thee
Beneath this banner!—Is their zeal too late?
—Oh! there's a fearful history on thy brow!
What hast thou seen?

GAR: It is not *all* too late.

XIM: My brothers!

HER: All is well.
(*To* GARCIAS.) Hush! would'st thou chill
That which hath sprung within them, as a flame
From th' altar-embers mounts in sudden brightness?
I say, 'tis not too late, ye men of Spain!
On to the rescue!

XIM: Bless me, O my father!
And I will hence, to aid thee with my prayers,
Sending my spirit with thee through the storm
Lit up by flashing swords!

GON. (*falling upon her neck*): Hath aught been spared?
Am I not all bereft?—Thou 'rt left me still!
Mine own, my loveliest one, thou 'rt left me still!
Farewell!—thy father's blessing, and thy God's,
Be with thee, my Ximena!

XIM: Fare thee well!
If e'er thy steps turn homeward from the field,
The voice is hush'd that still hath welcomed thee,
Think of me in thy victory!

HER: Peace! no more!
This is no time to melt our nature down
To a soft stream of tears!—Be of strong heart!
Give me the banner! Swell the song again!

THE CITS: Ere night must swords be red!
It is not an hour for knells and tears,
But for helmets braced and serried spears!
—To-morrow for the dead!

(*Exeunt omnes.*)

— SCENE VIII —

(Before the Altar of a Church.)

(ELMINA *rises from the steps of the Altar.*)

ELM: The clouds are fearful that o'erhang thy ways,
Oh, thou mysterious Heaven! — It cannot be
That I have drawn the vials of thy wrath,
To burst upon me through the lifting up
Of a proud heart, elate in happiness!
No! in my day's full noon, for me life's flowers
But wreath'd a cup of trembling; and the love,
The boundless love, my spirit was form'd to bear,
Hath ever, in its place of silence, been
A trouble and a shadow, tinging thought
With hues too deep for joy! — I never look'd
On my fair children, in their buoyant mirth
Or sunny sleep, when all the gentle air
Seem'd glowing with their quiet blessedness,
But o'er my soul there came a shudd'ring sense
Of earth, and its pale changes; ev'n like that
Which vaguely mingles with our glorious dreams —
A restless and disturbing consciousness
That the bright things must fade! — How have I shrunk
From the dull murmur of th' unquiet voice,
With its low tokens of mortality,
Till my heart fainted 'midst their smiles! — their smiles!
— Where are those glad looks now? — Could they go down,
With all their joyous light, that seem'd not earth's,
To the cold grave? — My children! — righteous Heaven!
There floats a dark remembrance o'er my brain
Of one who told me, with relentless eye,
That *this* should be the hour!

(XIMENA *enters.*)

XIM: They are gone forth
Unto the rescue! — strong in heart and hope,
Faithful, though few! — My mother, let thy prayers
Call on the land's good saints to lift once more
The sword and cross that sweep the field for Spain,
As in old battle; so thine arms e'en yet
May clasp thy sons! — For me, my part is done!
The flame which dimly might have linger'd yet
A little while, hath gather'd all its rays
Brightly to sink at once; and it is well!
The shadows are around me; to thy heart
Fold me, that I may die.

ELM: My child! — What dream
Is on thy soul? — Even now thine aspect wears
Life's brightest inspiration!

XIM: Death's!

ELM: Away!
Thine eye hath starry clearness; and thy cheek
Doth glow beneath it with a richer hue
Than tinged its earliest flower!

XIM: It well may be!
There are far deeper and far warmer hues
Than those which draw their colouring from the founts
Of youth, or health, or hope.

ELM: Nay, speak not thus!
There's that about thee shining which would send
E'en through *my* heart a sunny glow of joy,
Were't not for these sad words. The dim cold air
And solemn light, which wrap these tombs and shrines
As a pale gleaming shroud, seem kindled up
With a young spirit of ethereal hope
Caught from thy mien! — Oh no! this is not death!

XIM: Why should not He, whose touch dissolves our chain,
Put on his robes of beauty when he comes
As a deliverer? — He hath many forms,
They should not all be fearful! — If his call
Be but our gathering to that distant land
For whose sweet waters we have pined with thirst,
Why should not its prophetic sense be borne
Into the heart's deep stillness, with a breath
Of summer-winds, a voice of melody,
Solemn, yet lovely? — Mother, I depart! —
Be it thy comfort, in the after-days,
That thou hast seen me thus!

ELM: Distract me not
With such wild fears! Can I bear on with life
When thou art gone? — Thy voice, thy step, thy smile,
Pass'd from my path? — Alas! even now thine eye
Is changed — thy cheek is fading!

XIM: Ay, the clouds
Of the dim hour are gathering o'er my sight,
And yet I fear not, for the God of Help

Comes in that quiet darkness!—It may soothe
Thy woes, my mother! if I tell thee now
With what glad calmness I behold the veil
Falling between me and the world, wherein
My heart so ill hath rested.

ELM: Thine!

XIM: Rejoice
For her, that, when the garland of her life
Was blighted, and the springs of hope were dried,
Received her summons hence: and had no time,
Bearing the canker at th' impatient heart,
To wither, sorrowing for that gift of Heaven,
Which lent one moment of existence light,
That dimm'd the rest for ever!

ELM: How is this?
My child, what mean'st thou?

XIM: Mother! I have loved,
And been beloved!—the sunbeam of an hour,
Which gave life's hidden treasures to mine eye,
As they lay shining in their secret founts,
Went out and left them colourless.—'Tis past—
And what remains on earth?—the rainbow mist,
Through which I gazed, hath melted, and my sight
Is clear'd to look on all things as they are!—
But this is far too mournful!—Life's dark gift
Hath fall'n too early and too cold upon me!—
Therefore I would go hence!

ELM: And thou hast loved
Unknown——

XIM: Oh! pardon, pardon that I veil'd
My thoughts from thee!—But thou hadst woes enough,
And mine came o'er me when thy soul had need
Of more than mortal strength!—For I had scarce
Given the deep consciousness that I was loved
A treasure's place within my secret heart,
When earth's brief joy went from me!
'Twas at morn
I saw the warriors to their field go forth,
And he—my chosen—was there amongst the rest,
With his young, glorious brow!—I look'd again—
The strife grew dark beneath me—but his plume
Waved free above the lances. Yet again
It had gone down! and steeds were trampling o'er
The spot to which mine eyes were riveted,
Till blinded by th' intenseness of their gaze!—
And then—at last—I hurried to the gate,
And met him there!—I met him!—on his shield,
And with his cloven helm, and shiver'd sword,
And dark hair steep'd in blood!—They bore him past—
Mother!—I saw his face!—Oh! such a death
Works fearful changes on the fair of earth,
The pride of woman's eye!

ELM: Sweet daughter, peace!
Wake not the dark remembrance; for thy frame——

XIM: There will be peace ere long. I shut my heart,
Even as a tomb, o'er that lone silent grief,
That I might spare it thee!—But now the hour
Is come when that which would have pierced thy soul
Shall be its healing balm. Oh! weep thou not,
Save with a gentle sorrow!

ELM: Must it be?
Art thou indeed to leave me?

XIM. (*exultingly*): Be thou glad!
I say, rejoice above thy favour'd child!
Joy, for the soldier when his field is fought,
Joy, for the peasant when his vintage-task
Is closed at eve!—But most of all for her,
Who, when her life had changed its glittering robes
For the dull garb of sorrow, which doth cling
So heavily around the journeyers on,
Cast down its weight—and slept!

ELM: Alas! thine eye
Is wandering—yet how brightly!—Is this death,
Or some high wondrous vision?—Speak, my child!
How is it with thee now?

XIM. (*wildly*): I see it still!
'Tis floating like a glorious cloud on high,
My father's banner!—Hear'st thou not a sound?
The trumpet of Castile?[24]—Praise, praise to Heaven!
—Now may the weary rest!—Be still!—Who calls
The night so fearful?——

(*She dies.*)

ELM: No! she is not dead!—
Ximena!—speak to me!—Oh yet a tone

[24] **Castile:** (Christian) Spain.

From that sweet voice, that I may gather in
One more remembrance of its lovely sound,
Ere the deep silence fall!—What, is all hush'd?—
No, no!—it cannot be!—How should we bear
The dark misgivings of our souls, if Heaven
Left not such beings with us?—But is this
Her wonted look?—too sad a quiet lies
On its dim fearful beauty!—Speak, Ximena!
Speak!—my heart dies within me!—she is gone,
With all her blessed smiles!—my child! my child!
Where art thou?—Where is that which answer'd me,
From thy soft-shining eyes?—Hush! doth she move?
—One light lock seem'd to tremble on her brow,
As a pulse throbb'd beneath;—'twas but the voice
Of my despair that stirr'd it!—She is gone!

(She throws herself on the body. GONZALEZ *enters, alone, and wounded.)*

ELM. *(rising as he approaches):* I must not *now*
be scorn'd!—No, not a look,
A whisper of reproach!—Behold my woe!—
Thou canst not scorn me now!

GON: Hast thou heard *all*?

ELM: Thy daughter on my bosom laid her head,
And pass'd away to rest.—Behold her there,
Even such as death hath made her.[25]

GON. *(bending over* XIMENA'S *body):* Thou art gone
A little while before me, oh, my child!
Why should the traveller weep to part with those
That scarce an hour will reach their promised land,
Ere he too cast his pilgrim staff away,
And spread his couch beside them?

ELM: Must it be
Henceforth enough that *once* a thing so fair
Had its bright place amongst us?—Is this all
Left for the years to come?—We will not stay!
Earth's chain each hour grows weaker.

GON. *(still gazing upon* XIMENA*):* And thou 'rt laid
To slumber in the shadow, blessed child!
Of a yet stainless altar, and beside
A sainted warrior's tomb!—Oh, fitting place
For thee to yield thy pure heroic soul
Back unto him that gave it!—And thy cheek
Yet smiles in its bright paleness!

ELM: Hadst thou seen
The look with which she pass'd!

GON. *(still bending over her):* Why, 'tis almost
Like joy to view thy beautiful repose!
The faded image of that perfect calm
Floats, e'en as long-forgotten music, back
Into my weary heart!—No dark wild spot
On *thy* clear brow doth tell of bloody hands
That quench'd young life by violence!—We've seen
Too much of horror, in one crowded hour,
To weep for aught so gently gather'd hence!
—Oh! *man* leaves other traces!

ELM. *(suddenly starting):* It returns
On my bewilder'd soul?—Went ye not forth
Unto the rescue?—And thou 'rt here alone!
—Where are my sons?

GON. *(solemnly):* We were too late!

ELM: Too late!
Hast thou nought else to tell me?

GON: I brought back
From that last field the banner of my sires,
And my own death-wound.

ELM: Thine!

GON: Another hour
Shall hush its throbs for ever. I go hence,
And with me—

ELM: No!—Man *could* not lift his hands—
—Where hast thou left thy sons?

GON: I *have* no sons.

ELM: What hast thou said?

GON: That now there lives not one
To wear the glory of mine ancient house,
When I am gone to rest.

ELM. *(throwing herself on the ground, and speaking in a low hurried voice):* In one brief hour, all gone!—and *such* a death!
—I see their blood gush forth!—their graceful heads—
—Take the dark vision from me, oh, my God!
And such a death for *them!*—I was not there!
They were but mine in beauty and in joy,
Not in that mortal anguish!—All, all gone!
—Why should I struggle more?—What *is* this Power,
Against whose might, on all sides pressing us,

[25] **Even such . . . her:** "La voilà, telle que la morte nous l'a faite!" [Jacques Bénigne] Bossuet, [*Recueil d'*] *Oraisons Funèbres* [1689; 1815] [F. H.]: *trans.* "See what death has done to us."

We strive with fierce impatience, which but lays
Our own frail spirits prostrate?

(After a long pause.)

Now I know
Thy hand, my God!—and they are soonest crush'd
That most withstand it!—I resist no more.

(She rises.)

A light, a light springs up from grief and death,
Which with its solemn radiance doth reveal
Why we have thus been tried!

GON: Then I may still
Fix my last look on thee, in holy love,
Parting, but yet with hope!

ELM. *(falling at his feet)*: Canst thou forgive?
—Oh, I have driven the arrow to thy heart,
That should have buried it within mine own,
And borne the pang in silence!—I have cast
Thy life's fair honour, in my wild despair,
As an unvalued gem upon the waves,
Whence thou hast snatch'd it back, to bear from earth,
All stainless, on thy breast.—Well hast thou done—
But I—canst thou forgive?

GON: Within this hour
I've stood upon that verge whence mortals fall,
And learn'd how 'tis with one whose sight grows dim,
And whose foot trembles on the gulf's dark side,
—Death purifies all feeling—We will part
In pity and in love.

ELM: Death!—And thou too
Art on thy way!—Oh, joy for thee, high heart!
Glory and joy for thee!—The day is closed,
And well and nobly hast thou borne thyself
Through its long battle-toils, though many swords
Have enter'd thine own soul!—But on my head
Recoil the fierce invokings of despair,
And I am left far distanced in the race,
The lonely one of earth!—Ay, this is just.
I am not worthy that upon my breast
In this, thine hour of vict'ry, thou should'st yield
Thy spirit unto God!

GON: Thou art! thou art!
Oh! a life's love, a heart's long faithfulness,
Even in the presence of eternal things,
Wearing their chasten'd beauty all undimm'd,
Assert their lofty claims; and these are not
For one dark hour to cancel!—We are here,
Before that altar which received the vows
Of our unbroken youth, and meet it is
For such a witness, in the sight of Heaven,
And in the face of death, whose shadowy arm
Comes dim between us, to record th' exchange
Of our tried hearts' forgiveness.—Who are they,
That in one path have journey'd, needing not
Forgiveness at its close?

(A CITIZEN enters hastily.)

CIT: The Moors! the Moors!

GON: How! is the city storm'd?
O righteous Heaven! for this I look'd not yet!
Hath all been done in vain? Why, then, 'tis time
For prayer, and then to rest!

CIT: The sun shall set,
And not a Christian voice be left for prayer,
To-night, within Valencia. Round our walls
The paynim host is gathering for th' assault,
And we have none to guard them.

GON: Then my place
Is here no longer. I had hoped to die
E'en by the altar and the sepulchre
Of my brave sires; but this was not to be!
Give me my sword again, and lead me hence
Back to the ramparts. I have yet an hour,
And it hath still high duties. Now, my wife!
Thou mother of my children—of the dead—
Whom I name unto thee in steadfast hope—
Farewell!

ELM: No, *not* farewell! My soul hath risen
To mate itself with thine; and by thy side,
Amidst the hurling lances, I will stand,
As one on whom a brave man's love hath been
Wasted not utterly.

GON: I thank thee, Heaven!
That I have tasted of the awful joy
Which thou hast given, to temper hours like this
With a deep sense of thee, and of thine ends
In these dread visitings!

(To ELMINA.) We will not part,
But with the spirit's parting.

ELM: One farewell
To her, that, mantled with sad loveliness,
Doth slumber at our feet! My blessed child!

Oh! in thy heart's affliction thou wert strong,
And holy courage did pervade thy woe,
As light the troubled waters! Be at peace!
Thou whose bright spirit made itself the soul
Of all that were around thee! And thy life
E'en then was struck and withering at the core!
Farewell! thy parting look hath on me fallen,
E'en as a gleam of heaven, and I am now
More like what thou hast been. My soul is hush'd,
For a still sense of purer worlds hath sunk
And settled on its depths with that last smile
Which from thine eye shone forth. Thou hast not lived
In vain—my child, farewell!

GON: Surely for thee
Death had no sting, Ximena! We are blest,
To learn one secret of the shadowy pass,
From such an aspect's calmness. Yet once more
I kiss thy pale young cheek, my broken flower!
In token of th' undying love and hope
Whose land is far away.

(Exeunt.)

—SCENE IX—

(The Walls of the City.)

(HERNANDEZ.—*A few Citizens gathered round him.)*

HER: Why, men have cast the treasures, which their lives
Had been worn down in gathering, on the pyre,
Ay, at their household hearths have lit the brand,
Even from that shrine of quiet love to bear
The flame which gave their temples and their homes,
In ashes, to the winds! They have done this,
Making a blasted void where once the sun
Look'd upon lovely dwellings; and from earth
Razing all record that on such a spot
Childhood hath sprung, age faded, misery wept,
And frail humanity knelt before her God;
They have done *this*, in their free nobleness,
Rather than see the spoiler's tread pollute
Their holy places. Praise, high praise be theirs,
Who have left man such lessons! And these things,
Made your own hills their witnesses! The sky,
Whose arch bends o'er you, and the seas, wherein
Your rivers pour their gold, rejoicing saw
The altar, and the birthplace, and the tomb,
And all memorials of man's heart and faith,
Thus proudly honour'd! Be ye not outdone
By the departed! Though the godless foe
Be close upon us, we have power to snatch
The spoils of victory from him. Be but strong!
A few bright torches and brief moments yet
Shall baffle his flush'd hope, and we may die,
Laughing him unto scorn. Rise, follow me,
And thou, Valencia! triumph in thy fate,
The ruin, not the yoke, and make thy towers
A beacon unto Spain!

CITS: We'll follow thee!
Alas! for our fair city, and the homes
Wherein we rear'd our children! But away!
The Moor shall plant no crescent o'er our fanes!

VOICE *(from a Tower on the Walls)*: Succours!—
Castile! Castile!

CITS. *(rushing to the spot)*: It is even so!
Now blessing be to Heaven, for we are saved!—
Castile! Castile!

VOICE *(from the Tower)*: Line after line of spears,
Lance after lance, upon th' horizon's verge,
Like festal lights from cities bursting up,
Doth skirt the plain. In faith, a noble host!

ANOTHER VOICE: The Moor hath turn'd him from our walls, to front
Th' advancing might of Spain!

CITS. *(shouting)*: Castile! Castile!

(GONZALEZ *enters, supported by* ELMINA *and a Citizen.)*

GON: What shouts of joy are these?

HER: Hail! chieftain, hail!
Thus, even in death, 'tis given thee to receive
The conqueror's crown! Behold our God hath heard,
And arm'd himself with vengeance! Lo! they come!
The lances of Castile!

GON: I knew, I knew
Thou would'st not utterly, my God, forsake
Thy servant in his need! My blood and tears
Have not sunk vainly to th' attesting earth!
Praise to thee, thanks and praise, that I have lived
To see this hour!

ELM: And I, too, bless thy name,
Though thou hast proved me unto agony!
O God!—thou God of chastening!

VOICE (*from the Tower*): They move on!
I see the royal banner in the air,
With its emblazon'd towers!

GON: Go, bring ye forth
The banner of the Cid, and plant it here,
To stream above me, for an answering sign
That the good cross doth hold its lofty place
Within Valencia still! What see ye now?

HER: I see a kingdom's might upon its path,
Moving, in terrible magnificence,
Unto revenge and victory! With the flash
Of knightly swords, up-springing from the ranks,
As meteors from a still and gloomy deep,
And with the waving of ten thousand plumes,
Like a land's harvest in the autumn-wind,
And with fierce light, which is not of the sun,
But flung from sheets of steel—it comes, it comes,
The vengeance of our God!

GON: I hear it now,
The heavy tread of mail-clad multitudes,
Like thunder showers upon the forest paths.

HER: Ay, earth knows well the omen of that sound,
And she hath echoes, like a sepulchre's,
Pent in her secret hollows, to respond
Unto the step of death!

GON: Hark! how the wind
Swells proudly with the battle-march of Spain!
Now the heart feels its power!—A little while
Grant me to live, my God! What pause is this?

HER: A deep and dreadful one!—the serried files
Level their spears for combat; now the hosts
Look on each other in their brooding wrath,
Silent, and face to face.

VOICES HEARD WITHOUT, CHANTING:

Calm on the bosom of thy God,
Fair spirit! rest thee now!
E'en while with ours thy footsteps trode
His seal was on thy brow.

Dust, to its narrow house beneath!
Soul, to its place on high!
They that have seen thy look in death,
No more may fear to die.

ELM. (*to* GONZALEZ): It is the death-hymn o'er
thy daughter's bier!
But I am calm; and e'en like gentle winds,
That music, through the stillness of my heart,
Sends mournful peace.

GON: Oh! well those solemn tones
Accord with such an hour, for all her life
Breath'd of a hero's soul!

(*A sound of trumpets and shouting from the plain.*)

HER: Now, now they close! Hark! what a dull dead
sound
Is in the Moorish war-shout!—I have known
Such tones prophetic oft.—The shock is given—
Lo! they have placed their shields before their
hearts,
And lower'd their lances with the streamers on,
And on their steeds bent forward!—God for Spain!
The first bright sparks of battle have been struck
From spear to spear, across the gleaming field!—
There is no sight on which the blue sky looks
To match with this!—'Tis not the gallant crests,
Nor banners with their glorious blazonry;
The very nature and high soul of man
Doth now reveal itself!

GON: Oh, raise me up,
That I may look upon the noble scene!—
It will not be!—That this dull mist would pass
A moment from my sight!—Whence rose that
shout,
As in fierce triumph?

HER. (*clasping his hands*): Must I look on this?
The banner sinks—'tis taken!

GON: Whose?

HER: Castile's!

GON: Oh, God of Battles!

ELM: Calm thy noble heart!
Thou wilt not pass away without thy meed.
Nay, rest thee on my bosom.

HER: Cheer thee yet!
Our knights have spurr'd to rescue—There is now
A whirl, a mingling of all terrible things,
Yet more appalling than the fierce distinctness
Wherewith they moved before!—I see tall plumes
All wildly tossing o'er the battle's tide,
Sway'd by the wrathful motion, and the press
Of desperate men, as cedar-boughs by storms.
Many a white streamer there is dyed with blood,
Many a false corslet broken, many a shield
Pierced through!—Now, shout for Santiago, shout!
Lo! javelins with a moment's brightness cleave
The thickening dust, and barbed steeds go down
With their helm'd riders!—Who, but One, can tell

How spirits part amidst that fearful rush
And trampling on of furious multitudes?
GON: Thou'rt silent!—See'st thou more?—My soul
grows dark.
HER: And dark and troubled, as an angry sea,
Dashing some gallant armament in scorn
Against its rocks, is all on which I gaze!—
I can but tell thee how tall spears are cross'd,
And lances seem to shiver, and proud helms
To lighten with the stroke!—But round the spot,
Where, like a storm-fell'd mast, our standard sank,
The heart of battle burns.
GON: Where is that spot?
HER: It is beneath the lonely tuft of palms,
That lift their green heads o'er the tumult still,
In calm and stately grace.
GON: *There* didst thou say?
Then God is with us, and we *must* prevail!
For on that spot they died!—My children's blood
Calls on th' avenger thence!
ELM: They perish'd there!
—And the bright locks that waved so joyously
To the free winds, lay trampled and defiled
Even on that place of death!—Oh, Merciful!
Hush the dark thought within me!
HER. (*with sudden exultation*): Who is he,
On the white steed, and with the castled helm,
And the gold-broider'd mantle, which doth float
E'en like a sunny cloud above the fight,
And the pale cross, which from his breast-plate
gleams
With star-like radiance?
GON. (*eagerly*): Didst thou say the cross?
HER: On his mail'd bosom shines a broad white cross,
And his long plumage through the dark'ning air
Streams like a snow-wreath.
GON: That should be—
HER: The king!
—Was it not told us how he sent, of late,
To the Cid's tomb, e'en for the silver cross,
Which he who slumbers there was wont to bind
O'er his brave heart in fight?[26]

GON. (*springing up joyfully*): My king! my king!
Now all good saints for Spain!—My noble king!
And thou art there!—That I might look once more
Upon thy face!—But yet I thank thee, Heaven!
That thou hast sent him, from my dying hands
Thus to receive his city!

(*He sinks back into* ELMINA'S *arms.*)

HER: He hath clear'd
A pathway 'midst the combat, and the light
Follows his charge through yon close living mass,
E'en as a gleam on some proud vessel's wake
Along the stormy waters!—'Tis redeem'd—
The castled banner!—It is flung once more
In joy and glory, to the sweeping winds!
—There seems a wavering through the paynim
hosts—
Castile doth press them sore—Now, now rejoice!
GON: What hast thou seen?
HER: Abdullah falls! He falls!
The man of blood!—the spoiler!—he hath sunk
In our king's path!—Well hath that royal sword
Avenged thy cause, Gonzalez!
They give way,
The Crescent's van[27] is broken!—On the hills
And the dark pine-woods may the infidel
Call vainly, in his agony of fear,
To cover him from vengeance!—Lo! they fly!
They of the forest and the wilderness
Are scatter'd, e'en as leaves upon the wind!
Woe to the sons of Afric!—Let the plains,
And the vine-mountains, and Hesperian seas,
Take their dead unto them!—that blood shall wash
Our soil from stains of bondage.
GON. (*attempting to raise himself*): Set me free!
Come with me forth, for I must greet my king,
After his battle-field!
HER: Oh, blest in death!
Chosen of Heaven, farewell!—Look on the Cross,
And part from earth in peace!
GON: Now, charge once more!
God is with Spain, and Santiago's sword
Is reddening all the air!—Shout forth "Castile!"
The day is ours!—I go; but fear ye not!

[26] **he sent . . . in fight:** This circumstance is recorded of King Don Alfonso, the last of that name. He sent to the Cid's tomb for the cross which that warrior was accustomed to wear upon his breast when he went to battle, and had it made into one for himself; "Because of the faith which he had, that through it he should obtain the victory." [Robert] Southey's *Chronicle of the Cid* [F. H.].

[27] **Crescent's van:** Moorish army.

For Afric's lance is broken, and my sons
Have won their first good field!

(He dies.)

ELM: Look on me yet!
Speak one farewell, my husband! — must thy voice
Enter my soul no more! — Thine eye is fix'd —
Now is my life uprooted, — And' tis well.

(A sound of triumphant music is heard, and many Castilian Knights and Soldiers enter.)

A CIT: Hush your triumphal sounds, although ye come
E'en as deliverers! — But the noble dead,
And those that mourn them, claim from human hearts
Deep silent reverence.
ELM. *(rising proudly)*: No, swell forth, Castile!
Thy trumpet-music, till the seas and heavens,
And the deep hills, give every stormy note
Echoes to ring through Spain! — How, know ye not
That all array'd for triumph, crown'd and robed
With the strong spirit which hath saved the land,
E'en now a conqueror to his rest is gone?
— Fear not to break that sleep, but let the wind
Swell on with victory's shout! — *He* will not hear —
Hath earth a sound more sad?
HER: Lift ye the dead,
And bear him with the banner of his race
Waving above him proudly, as it waved
O'er the Cid's battles, to the tomb wherein
His warrior-sires are gather'd.

(They raise the body.)

ELM: Ay, 'tis thus
Thou should'st be honour'd! — And I follow thee
With an unfaltering and a lofty step,
To that last home of glory. She that wears
In her deep heart the memory of thy love,
Shall thence draw strength for all things, till the God
Whose hand around her hath unpeopled earth,
Looking upon her still and chasten'd soul,
Call it once more to thine!
(To the Castilians.) Awake, I say,
Tambour and trumpet, wake! — And let the land
Through all her mountains hear your funeral peal
— So should a hero pass to his repose.

(Exeunt omnes.)

from THE LEAGUE OF THE ALPS AND OTHER POEMS
(Boston, 1826)

The Landing of the Pilgrim Fathers
(1826)

"Look now abroad! Another race has till'd
Those populous borders — wide the wood recedes,
And towns shoot up, and fertile realms are till'd;
The land is full of harvests and green meads."[1]

BRYANT

The breaking waves dash'd high
On a stern and rock-bound coast,
And the woods, against a stormy sky,
Their giant branches toss'd;

And the heavy night hung dark,
The hills and waters o'er,
When a band of exiles moor'd their bark
On the wild New-England shore.

Not as the conqueror comes,
They, the true-hearted, came;
Not with the roll of the stirring drums,
And the trumpet that sings of fame;

Not as the flying come,
In silence and in fear, —
They shook the depths of the desert gloom,
With their hymns of lofty cheer.

Amidst the storm they sang,
And the stars heard and the sea!
And the sounding aisles of the dim woods rang
To the anthem of the free!

The ocean eagle soar'd
From his nest by the white wave's foam,
And the rocking pines of the forest roar'd —
This was their welcome home!

[1] From "The Ages" (1822), st. 32, lines 1 to 4, by William Cullen Bryant (1794–1878), American poet.

There were men with hoary hair,
  Amidst that pilgrim band—
Why had *they* come to wither there,
  Away from their childhood's land?

There was woman's fearless eye,
  Lit by her deep love's truth;
There was manhood's brow serenely high,
  And the fiery heart of youth.

What sought they thus afar?
  Bright jewels of the mine?
The wealth of seas, the spoils of war?
  —They sought a faith's pure shrine!

Ay, call it holy ground,
  The soil where first they trod!
They have left unstain'd what there they found—
  Freedom to worship God!

The Graves of a Household
(1826)

They grew in beauty, side by side,
  They fill'd one home with glee—
Their graves are sever'd far and wide,
  By mount, and stream, and sea.

The same fond mother bent at night
  O'er each fair sleeping brow;
She had each folded flower in sight—
  Where are those dreamers now?

One, 'midst the forest of the West,
  By a dark stream is laid—
The Indian knows his place of rest,
  Far in the cedar shade.

The sea, the blue lone sea, hath one,
  He lies where pearls lie deep—
He was the loved of all, yet none
  O'er his low bed may weep.

One sleeps where southern vines are drest,
  Above the noble slain;
He wrapt his colours round his breast,
  On a blood-red field of Spain.

And one—o'er *her* the myrtle showers
  Its leaves, by soft winds fann'd;
She faded 'midst Italian flowers,
  The last of that bright band.

And parted thus they rest, who play'd
  Beneath the same green tree;
Whose voices mingled as they pray'd
  Around one parent knee!

They that with smiles lit up the hall,
  And cheer'd with song the hearth—
Alas! for love! if *thou* wert all,
  And nought beyond, Oh earth!

To the Poet Wordsworth
(1826)

Thine is a strain to read among the hills,
  The old and full of voices—by the source
Of some free stream, whose gladdening presence fills
  The solitude with sound; for in its course
Even such is thy deep song, that seems a part
Of those high scenes, a fountain from their heart.

Or its calm spirit fitly may be taken
  To the still breast, in sunny garden-bowers,
Where summer winds each tree's low tones awaken,
  And bud and bell with changes mark the hours.
There let thy thoughts be with me, while the day
Sinks with a golden and serene decay.

Or by some hearth where happy faces meet,
  When night hath hush'd the woods with all their
    birds,
There, from some gentle voice, that lay were sweet
  As antique music, link'd with household words.
While, in pleased murmurs, woman's lip might move,
And the raised eye of childhood shine in love.

Or where the shadows of dark solemn yews
  Brood silently o'er some lone burial-ground,
Thy verse hath power that brightly might diffuse
  A breath, a kindling, as of spring, around,
From its own glow of hope and courage high,
And steadfast faith's victorious constancy.

True bard and holy!—thou art e'en as one
  Who, by some secret gift of soul or eye,
In every spot beneath the smiling sun,
  Sees where the springs of living waters lie—
Unseen awhile they sleep—till, touch'd by thee,
Bright, healthful waves flow forth, to each glad
    wanderer free!

Casabianca[1]
(1826)

The boy stood on the burning deck,
Whence all but him had fled;
The flame that lit the battle's wreck
Shone round him o'er the dead.

Yet beautiful and bright he stood,
As born to rule the storm;
A creature of heroic blood,
A proud, though child-like form.

The flames roll'd on — he would not go,
Without his father's word;
That father, faint in death below,
His voice no longer heard.

He call'd aloud: — "Say, father, say
If yet my task is done?"
He knew not that the chieftain lay
Unconscious of his son.

"Speak, father!" once again he cried,
"If I may yet be gone!"
— And but the booming shots replied,
And fast the flames roll'd on.

Upon his brow he felt their breath,
And in his waving hair;
And look'd from that lone post of death,
In still, yet brave despair.

And shouted but once more aloud,
"My father! must I stay?"
While o'er him fast, through sail and shroud,
The wreathing fires made way.

They wrapt the ship in splendor wild,
They caught the flag on high,
And stream'd above the gallant child,
Like banners in the sky.

There came a burst of thunder-sound —
The boy — oh! where was he?
— Ask of the winds that far around
With fragments strew'd the sea!

With mast, and helm, and pennon fair,
That well had borne their part —
But the noblest thing that perish'd there
Was that young faithful heart.

[1] Young Casabianca, a boy about thirteen years old, son to the Admiral of the Orient, remained at his post (in the Battle of the Nile) after the ship had taken fire, and all the guns had been abandoned; and perished in the explosion of the vessel, when the flames had reached the powder [F. H.]. Giacomo Casabianca was in fact only ten years old at the Battle of the Nile on 1 August 1798, in which his father Louis de Casabianca, Admiral of the French ship *Orient,* was killed. This battle was Admiral Lord Nelson's greatest naval victory, before the Battle of Trafalgar, over Napoleon.

Evening Prayer, at a Girls' School
(1826)

"Now in thy youth, beseech of Him,
Who giveth, upbraiding not,
That His light in thy heart become not dim,
And his love be unforgot;
And thy God, in the darkest of days, will be
Greenness, and beauty, and strength to thee."[1]

BERNARD BARTON

Hush! 'tis a holy hour — the quiet room
Seems like a temple, while yon soft lamp sheds
A faint and starry radiance, through the gloom
And the sweet stillness, down on bright young heads,
With all their clust'ring locks, untouch'd by care,
And bow'd, as flowers are bow'd with night–in prayer.

Gaze on, — 'tis lovely! — childhood's lip and cheek,
Mantling beneath its earnest brow of thought: —
Gaze — yet what seest thou in those fair, and meek,
And fragile things, as but for sunshine wrought? —
Thou seest what grief must nurture for the sky,
What death must fashion for eternity!

O! joyous creatures, that will sink to rest,
Lightly, when those pure orisons are done,
As birds with slumber's honey-dew opprest,
Midst the dim folded leaves, at set of sun —

[1] Motto is from Bernard Barton (1784–1849), Quaker poet.

Lift up your hearts!—though yet no sorrow lies
Dark in the summer-heaven of those clear eyes;

Though fresh within your breasts th' untroubled springs
Of hope make melody where'er ye tread;
And o'er your sleep bright shadows, from the wings
Of spirits visiting but youth, be spread;
Yet in those flute-like voices, mingling low,
Is woman's tenderness—how soon her woe!

Her lot is on you—silent tears to weep,
And patient smiles to wear through suffering's hour,
And sumless riches, from Affection's deep,
To pour on broken reeds—a wasted shower!
And to make idols, and to find them clay,
And to bewail that worship—therefore pray!

Her lot is on you—to be found untired,
Watching the stars out by the bed of pain,
With a pale cheek, and yet a brow inspired,
And a true heart of hope, though hope be vain.
Meekly to bear with wrong, to cheer decay,
And oh! to love through all things—therefore pray!

And take the thought of this calm vesper time,
With its low murmuring sounds and silvery light,
On through the dark days fading from their prime,
As a sweet dew to keep your souls from blight.
Earth will forsake—oh! happy to have given
Th' unbroken heart's first fragrance unto Heaven!

from Letter to Maria Jane Jewsbury[1]

(1826)

"The inclosed lines,[2] an effusion of deep and sincere admiration, will give you some idea of the enjoyment, and, I hope I may say, advantage, which you have been the means of imparting, by so kindly entrusting me with your precious copy of Wordsworth's Miscellaneous Poems.[3] It has opened to me such a treasure of thought and feeling, that I shall always associate your name with some of my pleasantest recollections, as having introduced me to the knowledge of what I can only regret should have been so long a 'Yarrow unvisited.'[4] I would not write to you sooner, because I wished to tell you that I had really *studied* these poems, and they have been the daily food of my mind ever since I borrowed them. There is hardly any scene of a happy, though serious, domestic life, or any mood of a reflective mind, with the spirit of which some one or other of them does not beautifully harmonize. This author is the true *Poet of Home,* and of all the lofty feelings which have their root in the soil of home affections. His fine sonnets to Liberty, and indeed, all his pieces which have any reference to political interest, remind me of the spirit in which Schiller has conceived the character of William Tell, a calm, single hearted herdsman of the hills, breaking forth into fiery and indignant eloquence, when the sanctity of his hearth is invaded.[5] Then, what power Wordsworth condenses into single lines, like Lord Byron's 'curdling a long life into one hour.'

The still sad music of humanity.—

The river glideth at his own sweet will—

Over his own sweet voice the stock-dove broods.—[6]

And a thousand others, which we must sometime, (and I hope not a very distant one,) talk over together. Many of these lines quite haunt me, and I have a strange feeling, as if I must have known them in my childhood, they come over me so like old melodies. I can hardly speak of *favorites* among so many things that delight me, but I think 'The Narrow Glen,' the lines on 'Corra Linn,' the 'Song for the Feast of Brougham Castle,' 'Yarrow visited,' and 'The

[1] Maria Jane Jewsbury (1800–1833), poet, essayist, and fiction writer; she dedicated her collected poems, *Lays of Leisure Hours* (1829), to her dear friend Felicia Hemans; married Rev. William Fletcher in 1832; sailed with him to India where she died the following year at Poona of cholera.

[2] **"The inclosed lines"**: Felicia Hemans's poem, "To the Poet Wordsworth."*

[3] Reference to William Wordsworth's *Miscellaneous Poems,* published in two volumes in 1815.

[4] **'Yarrow unvisited'**: Wordsworth's "Yarrow Unvisited" appeared in *Poems in Two Volumes* (1807).

[5] **Schiller**: J. S. Friedrich von Schiller (1759–1805), German dramatist, poet, and literary theorist. *Wilhelm Tell* (1804) was his most popular work.

[6] The quoted lines are from, respectively, Byron's "The Dream,"* line 26; Wordsworth's "Tintern Abbey,"* line 91; Wordsworth's "Composed upon Westminster Bridge,"* line 12; and Wordsworth's "Resolution and Independence,"* line 5.

Cuckoo,'[7] are among those which take hold of imagination the soonest, and recur most frequently to memory.

. . . I know not how I can have so long omitted to mention the 'Ecclesiastical Sketches,'[8] which I have read, and do constantly read with deep interest. Their beauty grows upon you and develops as you study it, like that of the old pictures by the Italian masters. My sister, who shares the feelings with which I write, desires I will not fail to ask if you can throw any light for us on the piece of 'The Danish Boy.' Its poetry is beautiful, but the subject requires explanation; does it refer to any wild mountain legend of the 'Land of Lakes?'[9] I had many more things to say respecting all that I have thought and felt during the perusal of these works, but my interruptions, consisting of morning visits from the Bishop down to the tailor of the diocese, (which latter guest, to the mother of five boys, is by no means an unimportant one), have been incessant, to say nothing of the boys themselves. My mother being unwell, and my sister engaged, all the duties of politeness have devolved upon me for the day. . . .

Your sincere friend,
F. HEMANS.

Letter to an unknown female correspondent
(comp. 1828)

"No indeed, my dear—there is *no* enjoyment to compare with the happiness of gladdening hearth and home for others—it is woman's own true sphere; . . . I cannot therefore regret your usefulness, though I should rejoice if it allowed you to pay me more frequent visits. . . . I am not at all well just now; I believe it is owing to the great fatigue I have had of late with my boys; and this time of the year makes one so long for the far away—do not you think so? If my sister were near me now, I should lay my head down upon her shoulder and cry 'like a tired child.' How very foolish——would think me! and rightly too! so do not betray my weakness! . . ."

[7] The correct titles of Wordsworth's poems are as follows: "Glen-Almain; or, the Narrow Glen"; "Composed at Cora Linn, in sight of Wallace's Tower"; "Song at the Feast of Brougham Castle"; "Yarrow Visited, September 1814," and "To the Cuckoo."

[8] Wordsworth's *Ecclesiastical Sketches* (1822) were augmented and republished as *Ecclesiastical Sonnets* in 1837. "The Danish Boy" was published in 1800.

[9] 'Land of Lakes': the Lake District in Cumbria, England, sometimes called Lakeland.

from RECORDS OF WOMAN: WITH OTHER POEMS
(1828)

The Bride of the Greek Isle[1]

Fear!—I'm a Greek, and how should I fear death?
A slave, and wherefore should I dread my freedom?

I will not live degraded.

Sardanapalus[2]

I

Come from the woods with the citron-flowers,
Come with your lyres for the festal hours,
Maids of bright Scio! They came, and the breeze
Bore their sweet songs o'er the Grecian seas;—
They came, and Eudora stood rob'd and crown'd,
The bride of the morn, with her train around.
Jewels flash'd out from her braided hair,
Like starry dews midst the roses there;
Pearls on her bosom quivering shone,
Heav'd by her heart thro' its golden zone;
But a brow, as those gems of the ocean pale,
Gleam'd from beneath her transparent veil;
Changeful and faint was her fair cheek's hue,
Tho' clear as a flower which the light looks through;
And the glance of her dark resplendent eye,
For the aspect of woman at times too high,
Lay floating in mists, which the troubled stream
Of the soul sent up o'er its fervid beam.

[1] Founded on a circumstance related in the second series of the *Curiosities of Literature,* and forming part of a picture in the "Painted Biography" there described [F. H.].

[2] Motto comes from Lord Byron, *Sardanapalus* (1821), I.ii.527–8, 676; the first two lines are spoken by the female Greek slave Myrrha, the last by King Sardanapalus.

She look'd on the vine at her father's door,
Like one that is leaving his native shore;
She hung o'er the myrtle once call'd her own,
As it greenly wav'd by the threshold stone;
She turn'd—and her mother's gaze brought back
Each hue of her childhood's faded track.
Oh! hush the song, and let her tears
Flow to the dream of her early years!
Holy and pure are the drops that fall
When the young bride goes from her father's hall;
She goes unto love yet untried and new,
She parts from love which hath still been true;
Mute be the song and the choral strain,
Till her heart's deep well-spring is clear again!
She wept on her mother's faithful breast,
Like a babe that sobs itself to rest;
She wept—yet laid her hand awhile
In *his* that waited her dawning smile,
Her soul's affianced, nor cherish'd less
For the gush of nature's tenderness!
She lifted her graceful head at last—
The choking swell of her heart was past;
And her lovely thoughts from their cells found way
In the sudden flow of a plaintive lay.[3]

The Bride's Farewell

Why do I weep?—to leave the vine
  Whose clusters o'er me bend,—
The myrtle—yet, oh! call it mine!—
  The flowers I lov'd to tend.
A thousand thoughts of all things dear,
  Like shadows o'er me sweep,
I leave my sunny childhood here,—
  Oh, therefore let me weep!

I leave thee, sister! we have play'd
  Thro' many a joyous hour,
Where the silvery green of the olive shade
  Hung dim o'er fount and bower.
Yes, thou and I, by stream, by shore,
  In song, in prayer, in sleep,
Have been as we may be no more,—
  Kind sister, let me weep!

I leave thee, father! Eve's bright moon
  Must now light other feet,
With the gather'd grapes, and the lyre in tune,
  Thy homeward step to greet.
Thou in whose voice, to bless thy child,
  Lay tones of love so deep,
Whose eye o'er all my youth hath smiled—
  I leave thee! let me weep!

Mother! I leave thee! on thy breast
  Pouring out joy and wo,
I have found that holy place of rest
  Still changeless,—yet I go!
Lips, that have lulled me with your strain,
  Eyes, that have watch'd my sleep!
Will earth give love like *yours* again?
  Sweet mother! let me weep!

And like a slight young tree, that throws
The weight of rain from its drooping boughs,
Once more she wept. But a changeful thing
Is the human heart, as a mountain spring,
That works it[s] way, thro' the torrent's foam,
To the bright pool near it, the lily's home!
It is well!—the cloud, on her soul that lay,
Hath melted in glittering drops away.
Wake again, mingle, sweet flute and lyre!
She turns to her lover, she leaves her sire.
Mother! on earth it must still be so,
Thou rearest the lovely to see them go!

They are moving onward, the bridal throng,
Ye may track their way by the swells of song;
Ye may catch thro' the foliage their white robes' gleam,
Like a swan midst the reeds of a shadowy stream.
Their arms bear up garlands, their gliding tread
Is over the deep-vein'd violet's bed;
They have light leaves around them, blue skies above,
An arch for the triumph of youth and love!

II

Still and sweet was the home that stood
In the flowering depths of a Grecian wood,
With the soft green light o'er its low roof spread,
As if from the glow of an emerald shed,
Pouring thro' lime-leaves that mingled on high,
Asleep in the silence of noon's clear sky.
Citrons amidst their dark foliage glow'd,
Making a gleam round the lone abode;
Laurels o'erhung it, whose faintest shiver
Scatter'd out rays like a glancing river;

---

[3] **her lovely thoughts . . . lay:** A Greek Bride, on leaving her father's house, takes leave of her friends and relatives frequently in extemporaneous verse [F. H.].

Stars of the jasmine its pillars crown'd,
Vine-stalks its lattice and walls had bound,
And brightly before it a fountain's play
Flung showers thro' a thicket of glossy bay,
To a cypress which rose in that flashing rain,
Like one tall shaft of some fallen fane.

And thither Ianthis had brought his bride,
And the guests were met by that fountain-side;
They lifted the veil from Eudora's face,
It smiled out softly in pensive grace,
With lips of love, and a brow serene,
Meet for the soul of the deep wood-scene.—
Bring wine, bring odours!—the board is spread—
Bring roses! a chaplet for every head!
The wine-cups foam'd, and the rose was shower'd
On the young and fair from the world embower'd;
The sun looked not on them in that sweet shade,
The winds amid scented boughs were laid;
But there came by fits, thro' some wavy tree,
A sound and a gleam of the moaning sea.

Hush! be still!—was that no more
Than the murmur from the shore?
Silence!—did thick rain-drops beat
On the grass like trampling feet?—
Fling down the goblet, and draw the sword!
The groves are filled with a pirate-horde!
Thro' the dim olives their sabres shine;—
Now must the red blood stream for wine!

The youths from the banquet to battle sprang,
The woods with the shriek of the maidens rang;
Under the golden-fruited boughs
There were flashing poniards, and dark'ning brows,
Footsteps, o'er garland and lyre that fled,
And the dying soon on a greensward bed.

Eudora, Eudora! *thou* dost not fly!—
She saw but Ianthis before her lie,
With the blood from his breast in a gushing flow,
Like a child's large tears in its hour of wo,
And a gathering film in his lifted eye,
That sought his young bride out mournfully.—
She knelt down beside him, her arms she wound,
Like tendrils, his drooping neck around,
As if the passion of that fond grasp
Might chain in life with its ivy-clasp.
But they tore her thence in her wild despair,
The sea's fierce rovers—they left him there;
They left to the fountain a dark-red vein,
And on the wet violets a pile of slain,
And a hush of fear thro' the summer-grove,—
So clos'd the triumph of youth and love!

III

Gloomy lay the shore that night,
When the moon, with sleeping light,
Bath'd each purple Sciote hill,
Gloomy lay the shore, and still.
O'er the wave no gay guitar
Sent its floating music far;
No glad sound of dancing feet
Woke, the starry hours to greet.
But a voice of mortal wo,
In its changes wild or low,
Thro' the midnight's blue repose,
From the sea-beat rocks arose,
As Eudora's mother stood
Gazing o'er th' Egean flood,
With a fix'd and straining eye—
Oh! was the spoilers' vessel nigh?
Yes! there, becalm'd in silent sleep,
Dark and alone on a breathless deep,
On a sea of molten silver, dark,
Brooding it frown'd that evil bark!
There its broad pennon a shadow cast,
Moveless and black from the tall, still mast,
And the heavy sound of its flapping sail,
Idly and vainly wooed the gale.
Hush'd was all else:—Had ocean's breast
Rock'd e'en Eudora that hour to rest?

To rest?—the waves tremble!—what piercing cry
Bursts from the heart of the ship on high?
What light through the heavens, in a sudden spire,
Shoots from the deck up? Fire! 'tis fire!
There are wild forms hurrying to and fro,
Seen darkly clear on that lurid glow;
There are shout, and signal-gun, and call,
And the dashing of water,—but fruitless all!
Man may not fetter, nor ocean tame
The might and wrath of the rushing flame!
It hath twined the mast like a glittering snake,
That coils up a tree from a dusky brake;
It hath touch'd the sails, and their canvass rolls
Away from its breath into shrivell'd scrolls;
It hath taken the flag's high place in air,
And redden'd the stars with its wavy glare;
And sent out bright arrows, and soar'd in glee,
To a burning mount midst the moonlight sea.
The swimmers are plunging from stern and prow—
Eudora, Eudora! where, where art thou?

The slave and his master alike are gone.—
Mother! who stands on the deck alone?
The child of thy bosom!—and lo! a brand
Blazing up high in her lifted hand!
And her veil flung back, and her free dark hair
Sway'd by the flames as they rock and flare;
And her fragile form to its loftiest height
Dilated, as if by the spirit's might,
And her eye with an eagle-gladness fraught,—
Oh! could this work be of woman wrought?
Yes! 'twas her deed!—by that haughty smile
It was hers—She hath kindled her funeral pile!
Never might shame on that bright head be,
Her blood was the Greek's, and hath made her free.

Proudly she stands, like an Indian bride
On the pyre with the holy dead beside;
But a shriek from her mother hath caught her ear,
As the flames to her marriage-robe draw near,
And starting, she spreads her pale arms in vain
To the form they must never infold again.

One moment more, and her hands are clasp'd,
Fallen is the torch they had wildly grasp'd,
Her sinking knee unto Heaven is bow'd,
And her last look rais'd thro' the smoke's dim shroud,
And her lips as in prayer for her pardon move:—
Now the night gathers o'er youth and love!

Properzia Rossi[1]

(1828)

——Tell me no more, no more
Of my soul's lofty gifts! Are they not vain
To quench its haunting thirst for happiness?
Have I not lov'd, and striven, and fail'd to bind
One true heart unto me, whereon my own
Might find a resting-place, a home for all
Its burden of affections? I depart,
Unknown, tho' Fame goes with me; I must leave
The earth unknown. Yet it may be that death
Shall give my name a power to win such tears
As would have made life precious.

I

One dream of passion and of beauty more!
And in its bright fulfilment let me pour
My soul away! Let earth retain a trace
Of that which lit my being, tho' its race
Might have been loftier far.—Yet one more dream!
From my deep spirit one victorious gleam
Ere I depart! For thee alone, for thee!
May this last work, this farewell triumph be,—
Thou, lov'd so vainly! I would leave enshrined
Something immortal of my heart and mind,
That yet may speak to thee when I am gone,
Shaking thine inmost bosom with a tone
Of lost affection;—something that may prove
What she hath been, whose melancholy love
On thee was lavish'd; silent pang and tear,
And fervent song, that gush'd when none were near,
And dream by night, and weary thought by day,
Stealing the brightness from her life away,—
While thou——Awake! not yet within me die,
Under the burden and the agony
Of this vain tenderness,—my spirit, wake!
Ev'n for thy sorrowful affection's sake,
Live! in thy work breathe out!—that he may yet,
Feeling sad mastery there, perchance regret
Thine unrequited gift.

II

It comes,—the power
Within me born, flows back; my fruitless dower
That could not win me love. Yet once again
I greet it proudly, with its rushing train
Of glorious images:—they throng—they press—
A sudden joy lights up my loneliness,—
I shall not perish all!

The bright work grows
Beneath my hand, unfolding, as a rose,
Leaf after leaf, to beauty; line by line,
I fix my thought, heart, soul, to burn, to shine,
Thro' the pale marble's veins. It grows—and now

[1] Properzia Rossi, a celebrated female sculptor of Bologna, possessed also of talents for poetry and music, died in consequence of an unrequited attachment. A painting by Ducis, represents her showing her last work, a basso-relievo of Ariadne, to a Roman Knight, the object of her affection, who regards it with indifference [F. H.]. **Properzia de' Rossi** (c. 1490–1530) learned her craft from her father, Francesco de' Rossi (Cecco di Salviati), who assisted Primaticcio in decorating Fontainebleau. She began her career as a painter of miniatures and progressed to sculpture, at which she excelled. **Ducis:** Louis Ducis (1773–1847), French painter.

I give my own life's history to thy brow,
Forsaken Ariadne! thou shalt wear
My form, my lineaments; but oh! more fair,
Touch'd into lovelier being by the glow
Which in me dwells, as by the summer-light
All things are glorified. From thee my wo
Shall yet look beautiful to meet his sight,
When I am pass'd away. Thou art the mould
Wherein I pour the fervent thoughts, th' untold,
The self-consuming! Speak to him of me,
Thou, the deserted by the lonely sea,
With the soft sadness of thine earnest eye,
Speak to him, lorn one, deeply, mournfully,
Of all my love and grief! Oh! could I throw
Into thy frame a voice, a sweet, and low,
And thrilling voice of song! — when he came nigh,
To send the passion of its melody
Thro' his pierced bosom — on its tones to bear
My life's deep feeling, as the southern air
Wafts the faint myrtle's breath, — to rise, to swell,
To sink away in accents of farewell,
Winning but one, *one* gush of tears, whose flow
Surely my parted spirit yet might know,
If love be strong as death!

III

Now fair thou art,
Thou form, whose life is of my burning heart!
Yet all the vision that within me wrought,
I cannot make thee! Oh! I might have given
Birth to creations of far nobler thought,
I might have kindled, with the fire of heaven,
Things not of such as die! But I have been
Too much alone; a heart, whereon to lean,
With all these deep affections that o'erflow
My aching soul, and find no shore below,
An eye to be my star, a voice to bring
Hope o'er my path, like sounds that breathe of spring,
These are denied me — dreamt of still in vain, —
Therefore my brief aspirings from the chain,
Are ever but as some wild fitful song,
Rising triumphantly, to die ere long
In dirge-like echoes.

IV

Yet the world will see
Little of this, my parting work, in thee,
Thou shalt have fame! Oh, mockery! give the reed
From storms a shelter, — give the drooping vine
Something round which its tendrils may entwine, —
Give the parch'd flower a rain-drop, and the meed
Of love's kind words to woman! Worthless fame!
That in *his* bosom wins not for my name
Th' abiding place it asked! Yet how my heart,
In its own fairy world of song and art,
Once beat for praise! — Are those high longings o'er?
That which I have been can I be no more? —
Never, oh! never more; tho' still thy sky
Be blue as then, my glorious Italy!
And tho' the music, whose rich breathings fill
Thine air with soul, be wandering past me still,
And tho' the mantle of thy sunlight streams
Unchang'd on forms instinct with poet-dreams;
Never, oh! never more! Where'er I move,
The shadow of this broken-hearted love
Is on me and around! Too well *they* know,
Whose life is all within, too soon and well,
When there the blight hath settled; — but I go
Under the silent wings of Peace to dwell;
From the slow wasting, from the lonely pain,
The inward burning of those words, *"in vain,"*
Sear'd on the heart — I go. 'Twill soon be past.
Sunshine, and song, and bright Italian heaven,
And thou, oh! thou, on whom my spirit cast
Unvalued wealth, — who know'st not what was given
In that devotedness, — the sad, and deep,
And unrepaid — farewell! If I could weep
Once, only once, belov'd one! on thy breast,
Pouring my heart forth ere I sink to rest!
But that were happiness, and unto me
Earth's gift is *fame.* Yet I was form'd to be
So richly blest! With thee to watch the sky,
Speaking not, feeling but that thou wert nigh;
With thee to listen, while the tones of song
Swept ev'n as part of our sweet air along,
To listen silently; — with thee to gaze
On forms, the deified of olden days, —
This had been joy enough; — and hour by hour,
From its glad well-springs drinking life and power,
How had my spirit soar'd, and made its fame
A glory for thy brow! — Dreams, dreams! — the fire
Burns faint within me. Yet I leave my name —
As a deep thrill may linger on the lyre
When its full chords are hush'd — awhile to live,
And one day haply in thy heart revive
Sad thoughts of me: — I leave it, with a sound,

A spell o'er memory, mournfully profound,
I leave it, on my country's air to dwell,—
Say proudly yet—*"Twas hers who lov'd me well!"*

The Indian City[1]
(1828)

What deep wounds ever clos'd without a scar?
The heart's bleed longest, and but heal to wear
That which disfigures it.[2]

Childe Harold

I

Royal in splendour went down the day
On the plain where an Indian city lay,
With its crown of domes o'er the forest high,
Red as if fused in the burning sky,
And its deep groves pierced by the rays which made
A bright stream's way thro' each long arcade,
Till the pillar'd vaults of the Banian[3] stood,
Like torch-lit aisles midst the solemn wood,
And the plantain glitter'd with leaves of gold,
As a tree midst the genii-gardens old,
And the cypress lifted a blazing spire,
And the stems of the cocoas were shafts of fire.
Many a white pagoda's gleam
Slept lovely round upon lake and stream,
Broken alone by the lotus-flowers,
As they caught the glow of the sun's last hours,
Like rosy wine in their cups, and shed
Its glory forth on their crystal bed.
Many a graceful Hindoo maid,
With the water-vase from the palmy shade,
Came gliding light as the desert's roe,
Down marble steps to the tanks below;
And a cool sweet plashing was ever heard,
As the molten glass of the wave was stirr'd;
And a murmur, thrilling the scented air,
Told where the Bramin bow'd in prayer.

There wandered a noble Moslem boy
Thro' the scene of beauty in breathless joy;
He gazed where the stately city rose
Like a pageant of clouds in its red repose;
He turn'd where birds thro' the gorgeous gloom
Of the woods went glancing on starry plume;
He track'd the brink of the shining lake,
By the tall canes feather'd in tuft and brake,
Till the path he chose, in its mazes wound
To the very heart of the holy ground.

And there lay the water, as if enshrin'd
In a rocky urn from the sun and wind,
Bearing the hues of the grove on high,
Far down thro' its dark still purity.
The flood beyond, to the fiery west
Spread out like a metal-mirror's breast,
But that lone bay, in its dimness deep,
Seem'd made for the swimmer's joyous leap,
For the stag athirst from the noontide chase,
For all free things of the wild-wood's race.

Like a falcon's glance on the wide blue sky,
Was the kindling flash of the boy's glad eye,
Like a sea-bird's flight to the foaming wave
From the shadowy bank was the bound he gave;
Dashing the spray-drops, cold and white,
O'er the glossy leaves in his young delight,
And bowing his locks to the waters clear—
Alas! he dreamt not that fate was near.

His mother look'd from her tent the while,
O'er heaven and earth with a quiet smile:
She, on her way unto Mecca's fane,
Had staid the march of her pilgrim-train,
Calmly to linger a few brief hours,
In the Bramin city's glorious bowers;
For the pomp of the forest, the wave's bright fall,
The red gold of sunset—she lov'd them all.

II

The moon rose clear in the splendour given
To the deep-blue night of an Indian heaven;
The boy from the high-arch'd woods came back—
Oh! what had he met in his lonely track?
The serpent's glance, thro' the long reeds bright?
The arrowy spring of the tiger's might?
No!—yet as one by a conflict worn,
With his graceful hair all soil'd and torn,
And a gloom on the lids of his darken'd eye,

[1] From a tale in [James] Forbes' *Oriental Memoirs* (1813) [F. H.].

[2] Motto is from Byron's *Childe Harold*, III.788–90.*

[3] **Banian:** banyan tree or Indian fig tree, the branches of which drop shoots to the ground that take root and support their parent branches.

And a gash on his bosom—he came to die!
He look'd for the face to his young heart sweet,
And found it, and sank at his mother's feet.

"Speak to me!—whence doth the swift blood run?
What hath befall'n thee, my child, my son?"
The mist of death on his brow lay pale,
But his voice just linger'd to breathe the tale,
Murmuring faintly of wrongs and scorn,
And wounds from the children of Brahma born:
This was the doom for a Moslem found
With foot profane on their holy ground;
This was for sullying the pure waves free
Unto them alone—'twas their God's decree.

A change came o'er his wandering look—
The mother shriek'd not then, nor shook:
Breathless she knelt in her son's young blood,
Rending her mantle to staunch its flood;
But it rush'd like a river which none may stay,
Bearing a flower to the deep away.
That which our love to the earth would chain,
Fearfully striving with Heaven in vain,
That which fades from us, while yet we hold,
Clasp'd to our bosoms, its mortal mould,
Was fleeting before her, afar and fast;
One moment—the soul from the face had pass'd!

Are there no words for that common wo?
—Ask of the thousands, its depths that know!
The boy had breathed, in his dreaming rest,
Like a low-voiced dove, on her gentle breast;
He had stood, when she sorrow'd, beside her knee
Painfully stilling his quick heart's glee;
He had kiss'd from her cheek the widow's tears,
With the loving lip of his infant years;
He had smil'd o'er her path like a bright spring-day—
Now in his blood on the earth he lay,
Murder'd!—Alas! and we love so well
In a world where anguish like this can dwell!

She bow'd down mutely o'er her dead—
They that stood round her watch'd in dread;
They watch'd—she knew not they were by—
Her soul sat veil'd in its agony.
On the silent lip she press'd no kiss,
Too stern was the grasp of her pangs for this;
She shed no tear as her face bent low,
O'er the shining hair of the lifeless brow;
She look'd but into the half-shut eye,
With a gaze that found there no reply,
And shrieking, mantled her head from sight,
And fell, struck down by her sorrow's might!

And what deep change, what work of power,
Was wrought on her secret soul that hour?
How rose the lonely one?—She rose
Like a prophetess from dark repose!
And proudly flung from her face the veil,
And shook the hair from her forehead pale,
And 'midst her wondering handmaids stood,
With the sudden glance of a dauntless mood.
Ay, lifting up to the midnight sky
A brow in its regal passion high,
With a close and rigid grasp she press'd
The blood-stain'd robe to her heaving breast,
And said—"Not yet—not yet I weep,
Not yet my spirit shall sink or sleep,
Not till yon city, in ruins rent,
Be piled for its victim's monument.
—Cover his dust! bear it on before!
It shall visit those temple-gates once more."

And away in the train of the dead she turn'd,
The strength of her step was the heart that burn'd;
And the Bramin groves in the starlight smil'd,
As the mother pass'd with her slaughter'd child.

III

Hark! a wild sound of the desert's horn
Thro' the woods round the Indian city borne,
A peal of the cymbal and tambour afar—
War! 'tis the gathering of Moslem war!
The Bramin look'd from the leaguer'd towers—
He saw the wild archer amidst his bowers;
And the lake that flash'd through the plantain shade,
As the light of the lances along it play'd;
And the canes that shook as if winds were high,
When the fiery steed of the waste swept by;
And the camp as it lay, like a billowy sea,
Wide round the sheltering Banian tree.

There stood one tent from the rest apart—
That was the place of a wounded heart.
—Oh! deep is a wounded heart, and strong
A voice that cries against mighty wrong;
And full of death, as a hot wind's blight,
Doth the ire of a crush'd affection light!

Maimuna from realm to realm had pass'd,
And her tale had rung like a trumpet's blast;
There had been words from her pale lips pour'd,

Each one a spell to unsheath the sword.
The Tartar had sprung from his steed to hear,
And the dark chief of Araby grasp'd his spear,
Till a chain of long lances begirt the wall,
And a vow was recorded that doom'd its fall.

Back with the dust of her son she came,
When her voice had kindled that lightning flame;
She came in the might of a queenly foe,
Banner, and javelin, and bended bow;
But a deeper power on her forehead sate—
There sought the warrior his star of fate;
Her eye's wild flash through the tented line
Was hail'd as a spirit and a sign,
And the faintest tone from her lip was caught,
As a Sybil's breath of prophetic thought.

Vain, bitter glory!—the gift of grief,
That lights up vengeance to find relief,
Transient and faithless!—it cannot fill
So the deep void of the heart, nor still
The yearning left by a broken tie,
That haunted fever of which we die!

Sickening she turn'd from her sad renown,
As a king in death might reject his crown;
Slowly the strength of the walls gave way—
She wither'd faster, from day to day.
All the proud sounds of that banner'd plain,
To stay the flight of her soul were vain;
Like an eagle caged, it had striven, and worn
The frail dust ne'er for such conflicts born,
Till the bars were rent, and the hour was come
For its fearful rushing thro' darkness home.

The bright sun set in his pomp and pride,
As on that eve when the fair boy died,
She gazed from her couch, and a softness fell
O'er her weary heart with the day's farewell;
She spoke, and her voice in its dying tone
Had an echo of feelings that long seem'd flown.
She murmur'd a low sweet cradle song,
Strange midst the din of a warrior throng,
A song of the time when her boy's young cheek
Had glow'd on her breast in its slumber meek;
But something which breathed from that mournful strain
Sent a fitful gust o'er her soul again;
And starting as if from a dream, she cried—
"Give him proud burial at my side!
There, by yon lake, where the palm-boughs wave,
When the temples are fallen, make there our grave."

And the temples fell, tho' the spirit pass'd,
That stay'd not for victory's voice at last;
When the day was won for the martyr-dead,
For the broken heart, and the bright blood shed.

Thro' the gates of the vanquish'd the Tartar steed
Bore in the avenger with foaming speed;
Free swept the flame thro' the idol-fanes,
And the streams flow'd red, as from warrior-veins,
And the sword of the Moslem, let loose to slay,
Like the panther leapt on its flying prey,
Till a city of ruin begirt the shade,
Where the boy and his mother at rest were laid.

Palace and tower on that plain were left,
Like fallen trees by the lightning cleft;
The wild vine mantled the stately square,
The Rajah's throne was the serpent's lair,
And the jungle grass o'er the altar sprung—
This was the work of one deep heart wrung!

Indian Woman's Death-Song
(1828)

An Indian woman, driven to despair by her husband's desertion of her for another wife, entered a canoe with her children, and rowed it down the Mississippi towards a cataract. Her voice was heard from the shore singing a mournful death-song, until overpowered by the sound of the waters in which she perished. The tale is related in [William Hypolitus Keating's *Narrative of* (Major Stephen)] *Long's Expedition to the Source of St. Peter's River* [1825] [F. H.].

Non, je ne puis vivre avec un coeur brisé. Il faut que je retrouve la joie, et que je m'unisse aux esprits libres de l'air.

Bride of Messina,
Translated by MADAME DE STAËL

Let not my child be a girl, for very sad is the life of a woman.

The Prairie[1]

[1] *Trans.* "I cannot live with a broken heart; I must find joy, must unite with the free spirits of the air." *The Bride of Messina* (1803) is by Friedrich von Schiller. **Madame de Staël**: pen-name of Anne-Louise-Germaine Necker de Staël (1766–1817), famous

Down a broad river of the western wilds,
Piercing thick forest glooms, a light canoe
Swept with the current: fearful was the speed
Of the frail bark, as by a tempest's wing
Borne leaf-like on to where the mist of spray
Rose with the cataract's thunder.—Yet within,
Proudly, and dauntlessly, and all alone,
Save that a babe lay sleeping at her breast,
A woman stood. Upon her Indian brow
Sat a strange gladness, and her dark hair wav'd
As if triumphantly. She press'd her child,
In its bright slumber, to her beating heart,
And lifted her sweet voice, that rose awhile
Above the sound of waters, high and clear,
Wafting a wild proud strain, her Song of Death.

....

Roll swiftly to the Spirit's land, thou mighty stream and free!
Father of ancient waters,[2] roll! and bear our lives with thee!
The weary bird that storms have toss'd, would seek the sunshine's calm,
And the deer that hath the arrow's hurt, flies to the woods of balm.

Roll on!—my warrior's eye hath look'd upon another's face,
And mine hath faded from his soul, as fades a moonbeam's trace;
My shadow comes not o'er his path, my whisper to his dream,
He flings away the broken reed—roll swifter yet, thou stream!

The voice that spoke of other days is hush'd within *his* breast,
But *mine* its lonely music haunts, and will not let me rest;
It sings a low and mournful song of gladness that is gone,—
I cannot live without that light—Father of waves! roll on!

Will he not miss the bounding step that met him from the chase?
The heart of love that made his home an ever sunny place?
The hand that spread the hunter's board, and deck'd his couch of yore?—
He will not!—roll, dark foaming stream, on to the better shore!

Some blessed fount amidst the woods of that bright land must flow,
Whose waters from my soul may lave the memory of this wo;
Some gentle wind must whisper there, whose breath may waft away
The burden of the heavy night, the sadness of the day.

And thou, my babe! tho' born, like me, for woman's weary lot,
Smile!—to that wasting of the heart, my own! I leave thee not;
Too bright a thing art *thou* to pine in aching love away,
Thy mother bears thee far, young Fawn! from sorrow and decay.

She bears thee to the glorious bowers where none are heard to weep,
And where th' unkind one hath no power again to trouble sleep;
And where the soul shall find its youth, as wakening from a dream,—
One moment, and that realm is ours.—On, on, dark rolling stream!

Swiss-French woman of letters, political writer, and literary hostess. *The Prairie* (1827) is by James Fenimore Cooper (1789–1851).

[2] **Father of ancient waters:** the Indian name for the Mississippi [River] [F. H.].

Joan of Arc, in Rheims

(1828)

"Jeanne d'Arc avait eu la joie de voir à Chalons quelques amis de son enfance. Une joie plus ineffable encore l'attendait à Rheims, au sein de son triomphe: Jacques d'Arc, son père, y se trouva, aussitôt que de troupes de Charles VII. y furent entrées; et comme les deux frères de notre héroïne l'avaient accompagnée, elle se vit pour un instant au milieu de sa famille, dans les bras d'un père vertueux.
[Jean Masson,] *Vie de Jeanne d' Arc* [1712].[1]

....

[1] *Trans.* "Joan of Arc had the pleasure of seeing some childhood friends in Chalons. A far greater pleasure awaited her in

Thou hast a charmed cup, O Fame!
 A draught that mantles high,
And seems to lift this earth-born frame
 Above mortality:
Away! to me—a woman—bring
Sweet waters from affection's spring.[2]

....

That was a joyous day in Rheims of old,
When peal on peal of mighty music roll'd
Forth from her throng'd cathedral; while around,
A multitude, whose billows made no sound,
Chain'd to a hush of wonder, tho' elate
With victory, listen'd at their temple's gate.

And what was done within?—within, the light
 Thro' the rich gloom of pictur'd windows flowing,
Tinged with soft awfulness a stately sight,
 The chivalry of France, their proud heads bowing
In martial vassalage!—while midst that ring,
And shadow'd by ancestral tombs, a king
Receiv'd his birthright's crown. For this, the hymn
 Swell'd out like rushing waters, and the day
With the sweet censer's misty breath grew dim,
 As thro' long aisles it floated o'er th' array
Of arms and sweeping stoles. But who, alone
And unapproach'd, beside the altar-stone,
With the white banner, forth like sunshine streaming,
And the gold helm, thro' clouds of fragrance
 gleaming,
Silent and radiant stood?—The helm was rais'd,
And the fair face reveal'd, that upward gaz'd,
 Intensely worshipping;—a still, clear face,
Youthful, but brightly solemn!—Woman's cheek
And brow were there, in deep devotion meek,
 Yet glorified with inspiration's trace
On its pure paleness; while, enthron'd above,
The pictur'd Virgin, with her smile of love,
Seem'd bending o'er her votaress.—That slight form!
Was that the leader thro' the battle storm?
Had the soft light in that adoring eye,
Guided the warrior where the swords flash'd high?
'Twas so, even so!—and thou, the shepherd's child,
Joanne, the lowly dreamer of the wild!
Never before, and never since that hour,
Hath woman, mantled with victorious power,
Stood forth as *thou* beside the shrine didst stand,
Holy amidst the knighthood of the land;
And beautiful with joy and with renown,
Lift thy white banner o'er the olden crown,
Ransom'd for France by thee!

 The rites are done.
Now let the dome with trumpet-notes be shaken,
And bid the echoes of the tombs awaken,
 And come thou forth, that Heaven's rejoicing sun
May give thee welcome from thine own blue skies,
 Daughter of Victory!—A triumphant strain,
A proud rich stream of warlike melodies,
 Gush'd thro' the portals of the antique fane,[3]
And forth she came.—Then rose a nation's sound—
Oh! what a power to bid the quick heart bound
The wind bears onward with the stormy cheer
Man gives to Glory on her high career!
Is there indeed such power?—far deeper dwells
In one kind household voice, to reach the cells
Whence happiness flows forth!—The shouts that fill'd
The hollow heaven tempestuously, were still'd
One moment; and in that brief pause, the tone,
As of a breeze that o'er her home had blown,
Sank on the bright maid's heart.—"Joanne!"—
 Who spoke
 Like those whose childhood with *her* childhood
 grew
Under one roof?—"Joanne!"—*that* murmur broke
 With sounds of weeping forth!—She turn'd—she
 knew
Beside her, mark'd from all the thousands there,
In the calm beauty of his silver hair,
The stately shepherd; and the youth, whose joy
From his dark eye flash'd proudly; and the boy,
The youngest-born, that ever lov'd her best:

Rheims, the scene of her triumph: her father James of Arc arrived just as Charles VII's army entered the city; and as our heroine's two brothers had accompanied their father, she found herself for an instant in the midst of her family, in the arms of her good father." **Joan of Arc**: French national heroine (1412–1431), born in Domremy-la-Pucelle, heard holy voices which led her, at the age of 13, to offer her services to the dauphin; in May 1429, she successfully led the French army to raise the English siege of Orleans; in July, she conducted the dauphin to Rheims where he was crowned Charles VII. She was later condemned by the French ecclesiastical court for heresy and burned at the stake on 30 May 1431.

[2] This stanza (and motto) later became lines 1 to 6 of Felicia Hemans's poem "Woman and Fame."

[3] **fane**: temple.

"Father! and ye, my brothers!"—On the breast
Of that grey sire she sank—and swiftly back,
Ev'n in an instant, to their native track
Her free thoughts flowed.—She saw the pomp no
 more—
The plumes, the banners:—to her cabin-door,
And to the Fairy's Fountain in the glade,[4]
Where her young sisters by her side had play'd,
And to her hamlet's chapel, where it rose
Hallowing the forest unto deep repose,
Her spirit turn'd.—The very wood-note, sung
 In early spring-time by the bird, which dwelt
Where o'er her father's roof the beech-leaves hung,
 Was in her heart; a music heard and felt,
Winning her back to nature.—She unbound
 The helm of many battles from her head,
And, with her bright locks bow'd to sweep the
 ground,
 Lifting her voice up, wept for joy, and said,—
"Bless me, my father, bless me! and with thee,
To the still cabin and the beechen-tree,
Let me return!"
 Oh! never did thine eye
Thro' the green haunts of happy infancy
Wander again, Joanne!—too much of fame
Had shed its radiance on thy peasant-name;
And bought alone by gifts beyond all price,
The trusting heart's repose, the paradise
Of home with all its loves, doth fate allow
The crown of glory unto woman's brow.

Madeline: A Domestic Tale[1]

(1828)

Who should it be?—Where shouldst thou look for
 kindness?
When we are sick where can we turn for succour,
When we are wretched where can we complain;
And when the world looks cold and surly on us,
Where can we go to meet a warmer eye
With such sure confidence as to a mother?

JOANNA BAILLIE

"My child, my child, thou leav'st me!—I shall hear
The gentle voice no more that blest mine ear
With its first utterance; I shall miss the sound
Of thy light step amidst the flowers around,
And thy soft-breathing hymn at twilight's close,
And thy "Good-night" at parting for repose.
Under the vine-leaves I shall sit alone,
And the low breeze will have a mournful tone
Amidst their tendrils, while I think of thee,
My child! and thou, along the moonlight sea,
With a soft sadness haply in thy glance,
Shalt watch thine own, thy pleasant land of France,
Fading to air.—Yet blessings with thee go!
Love guard thee, gentlest! and the exile's wo
From thy young heart be far!—And sorrow not
For me, sweet daughter! in my lonely lot,
God shall be with me.—Now, farewell! farewell!
Thou that hast been what words may never tell
Unto thy mother's bosom, since the days
When thou wert pillow'd there, and wont to raise
In sudden laughter thence thy loving eye
That still sought mine:—those moments are gone by,
Thou too must go, my flower!—Yet with thee dwell
The peace of God!—One, one more gaze—
 farewell!"
This was a mother's parting with her child,
A young meek bride on whom fair fortune smil'd,
And wooed her with a voice of love away
From childhood's home; yet there, with fond delay,
She linger'd on the threshold, heard the note
Of her cag'd bird thro' trellis'd rose-leaves float,
And fell upon her mother's neck, and wept,
Whilst old remembrances, that long had slept,
Gush'd o'er her soul, and many a vanish'd day,
As in one picture traced, before her lay.

But the farewell was said; and on the deep,
When its breast heav'd in sunset's golden sleep,
With a calm'd heart, young Madeline ere long
Pour'd forth her own sweet solemn vesper-song,
Breathing of home: thro' stillness heard afar,
And duly rising with the first pale star,
That voice was on the waters; till at last
The sounding ocean-solitudes were pass'd,
And the bright land was reach'd, the youthful world
That glows along the West: the sails were furl'd

[4] **And to the Fairy's Fountain in the glade:** "A beautiful fountain near Domremi, believed to be haunted by fairies, and a favourite resort of Jeanne d'Arc in her childhood" [F. H.].

[1] Originally published in the *Literary Souvenir* for 1828 [F. H.].

In its clear sunshine, and the gentle bride
Look'd on the home that promis'd hearts untried
A bower of bliss to come.—Alas! we trace
The map of our own paths, and long ere years
With their dull steps the brilliant lines efface,
On sweeps the storm, and blots them out with tears.
That home was darken'd soon: the summer breeze
Welcom'd with death the wanderers from the seas,
Death unto one, and anguish—how forlorn!
To her, that widow'd in her marriage-morn,
Sat in her voiceless dwelling, whence with him
  Her bosom's first belov'd, her friend and guide,
Joy had gone forth, and left the green earth dim,
  As from the sun shut out on every side,
By the close veil of misery!—Oh! but ill,
  When with rich hopes o'erfraught, the young high
    heart
  Bears its first blow!—it knows not yet the part
Which life will teach—to suffer and be still,
And with submissive love to count the flowers
Which yet are spared, and thro' the future hour,
To send no busy dream!—*She* had not learn'd
Of sorrow till that hour, and therefore turn'd
In weariness from life: then came th' unrest,
The heart-sick yearning of the exile's breast,
The haunting sounds of voices far away,
And household steps; until at last she lay
On her lone couch of sickness, lost in dreams
Of the gay vineyards and blue-rushing streams
In her own sunny land, and murmuring oft
Familiar names, in accents wild, yet soft,
To strangers round that bed, who knew not aught
Of the deep spells wherewith each word was fraught.
To strangers?—Oh! could strangers raise the head
Gently as *hers* was rais'd?—did strangers shed
The kindly tears which bath'd that feverish brow
And wasted cheek with half-unconscious flow?
Something was there, that thro' the lingering night
Outwatches patiently the taper's light,
Something that faints not thro' the day's distress,
That fears not toil, that knows not weariness;
Love, true and perfect love!—Whence came that
    power,
Uprearing thro' the storm the drooping flower?
Whence?—who can ask?—the wild delirium pass'd,
And from her eyes the spirit look'd at last
Into her *mother's* face, and wakening knew
The brow's calm grace, the hair's dear silvery hue,
The kind sweet smile of old!—and had *she* come,
Thus in life's evening, from her distant home,
To save her child?—Ev'n so—nor yet in vain:
In that young heart a light sprung up again,
And lovely still, with so much love to give,
Seem'd this fair world, tho' faded; still to live
Was not to pine forsaken. On the breast
That rock'd her childhood, sinking in soft rest,
"Sweet mother! gentlest mother! can it be?"
The lorn one cried, "and do I look on thee?
Take back thy wanderer from this fatal shore,
Peace shall be ours beneath our vines once more."

The Memorial Pillar
(1828)

On the road-side between Penrith and Appleby, stands a small pillar, with this inscription:—"This pillar was erected in the year 1656, by Ann, Countess Dowager of Pembroke, for a memorial of her last parting, in this place, with her good and pious mother, Margaret, Countess Dowager of Cumberland, on the 2d April, 1616."—See [Samuel Rogers's] Notes to the *"Pleasures of Memory"* [F. H.].

Hast thou, thro' Eden's wild-wood vales, pursued
Each mountain-scene, magnificently rude,
Nor with attention's lifted eye, revered
That modest stone, by pious Pembroke rear'd,
Which still records, beyond the pencil's power,
The silent sorrows of a parting hour?

ROGERS[1]

Mother and child! whose blending tears
  Have sanctified the place,
Where, to the love of many years,
  Was given one last embrace;
Oh! ye have shrin'd a spell of power,
Deep in your record of that hour!

A spell to waken solemn thought,
  A still, small under-tone,
That calls back days of childhood, fraught
  With many a treasure gone;

[1] The headnote and motto come from *The Pleasures of Memory* (1792) by Samuel Rogers (1763–1855), poet, best known for his *Italy* (1822–1828).

And smites, perchance, the hidden source,
Tho' long untroubled—of remorse.

For who, that gazes on the stone
Which marks your parting spot,
Who but a mother's love hath known,
The *one* love changing not?
Alas! and haply learn'd its worth
First with the sound of "Earth to earth"?

But thou, high-hearted daughter! thou,
O'er whose bright, honour'd head,
Blessings and tears of holiest flow,
Ev'n here were fondly shed,—
Thou from the passion of thy grief,
In its full burst, couldst draw relief.

For oh! tho' painful be th' excess,
The might wherewith it swells,
In nature's fount no bitterness
Of nature's mingling, dwells;
And thou hadst not, by wrong or pride,
Poison'd the free and healthful tide.

But didst thou meet the face no more,
Which thy young heart first knew?
And all—was all in this world o'er,
With ties thus close and true?
It was!—On earth no other eye
Could give thee back thine infancy.

No other voice could pierce the maze
Where deep within thy breast,
The sounds and dreams of other days,
With memory lay at rest;
No other smile to thee could bring
A gladd'ning, like the breath of spring.

Yet, while thy place of weeping still
Its lone memorial keeps,
While on thy name, midst wood and hill,
The quiet sunshine sleeps,
And touches, in each graven line,
Of reverential thought a sign;

Can I, while yet these tokens wear
The impress of the dead,
Think of the love embodied there,
As of a vision fled?
A perish'd thing, the joy and flower
And glory of one earthly hour?

Not so!—I will not bow me so,
To thoughts that breathe despair!
A loftier faith we need below,
Life's farewell words to bear.
Mother and child!—Your tears are past—
Surely your hearts have met at last!

The Homes of England

(1828)

Where's the coward that would not dare
To fight for such a land?

Marmion[1]

The stately Homes of England,
How beautiful they stand!
Amidst their tall ancestral trees,
O'er all the pleasant land.
The deer across their greensward bound
Thro' shade and sunny gleam,
And the swan glides past them with the sound
Of some rejoicing stream.

The merry Homes of England!
Around their hearths by night,
What gladsome looks of household love
Meet in the ruddy light!
There woman's voice flows forth in song,
Or childhood's tale is told,
Or lips move tunefully along
Some glorious page of old.

The blessed Homes of England!
How softly on their bowers
Is laid the holy quietness
That breathes from Sabbath-hours!
Solemn, yet sweet, the church-bell's chime
Floats thro' their woods at morn;
All other sounds, in that still time,
Of breeze and leaf are born.

The Cottage Homes of England!
By thousands on her plains,
They are smiling o'er the silvery brooks,
And round the hamlet-fanes.

[1] Motto comes from *Marmion* (1808), by Sir Walter Scott* (1771–1832).

Thro' glowing orchards forth they peep,
Each from its nook of leaves,
And fearless there the lowly sleep,
As the bird beneath their eaves.

The free, fair Homes of England!
Long, long, in hut and hall,
May hearts of native proof be rear'd
To guard each hallow'd wall!
And green for ever be the groves,
And bright the flowery sod,
Where first the child's glad spirit loves
Its country and its God!

The Image in Lava[1]
(1828)

Thou thing of years departed!
What ages have gone by,
Since here the mournful seal was set
By love and agony!

Temple and tower have moulder'd,
Empires from earth have pass'd,—
And woman's heart hath left a trace
Those glories to outlast!

And childhood's fragile image
Thus fearfully enshrin'd,
Survives the proud memorials rear'd
By conquerors of mankind.

Babe! wert thou brightly slumbering
Upon thy mother's breast,
When suddenly the fiery tomb
Shut round each gentle guest?

A strange, dark fate o'ertook you,
Fair babe and loving heart!
One moment of a thousand pangs—
Yet better than to part!

Haply of that fond bosom
On ashes here impress'd,
Thou wert the only treasure, child!
Whereon a hope might rest.

Perchance all vainly lavish'd
Its other love had been,
And where it trusted, nought remain'd
But thorns on which to lean.

Far better then to perish,
Thy form within its clasp,
Than live and lose thee, precious one!
From that impassion'd grasp.

Oh! I could pass all relics
Left by the pomps of old,
To gaze on this rude monument,
Cast in affection's mould.

Love, human love! what art thou?
Thy print upon the dust
Outlives the cities of renown
Wherein the mighty trust!

Immortal, oh! immortal
Thou art, whose earthly glow
Hath given these ashes holiness—
It must, it *must* be so!

[1] "**The Image in Lava:**" The impression of a woman's form, with an infant clasped to the bosom, found at the uncovering of Herculaneum [F. H.]. The classical cities of Herculaneum and Pompeii, in southern Italy, were buried after Mount Vesuvius erupted in 79 AD. The whole city and its people were preserved, petrified by the lava.

from the *Journal* of Felicia Hemans[1]
(comp. 1828)

"Our home!—what images are brought before us by that one word! The meeting of cordial smiles, and the gathering round the evening hearth, and the interchange of thoughts in kindly words, and the glance of eyes to which our hearts lie open as the day;—there is the true 'City of Refuge;'—where are we to turn when it is shut from us or changed? Who ever thought his home could change? And yet those calm and deep, and still delights, over which the world seems to have no breath of power, they too are like the beautiful summer clouds, tranquil as if fixed to sleep for ever in the pure azure of the skies, yet all the while melting from us, though imperceptibly, 'passing away!'"

[1] Reprinted from *The Works of Mrs. Hemans; with A Memoir of Her Life, by Her Sister,* Edinburgh: Blackwood, 1839, 7 Volumes; Volume I:112.

from SONGS OF THE AFFECTIONS
(1830)

A Spirit's Return
(1830)

"This is to be a mortal,
And seek the things beyond mortality!"[1]
MANFRED

Thy voice prevails—dear Friend, my gentle Friend!
This long-shut heart for thee shall be unseal'd;
And though thy soft eye mournfully will bend
Over the troubled stream, yet once reveal'd
Shall its freed waters flow; then rocks must close
For evermore, above their dark repose.

Come while the gorgeous mysteries of the sky
Fused in the crimson sea of sunset lie;
Come to the woods, where all strange wandering
 sound
Is mingled into harmony profound;
Where the leaves thrill with spirit, while the wind
Fills with a viewless being, unconfined,
The trembling reeds and fountains. Our own dell,
With its green dimness and Aeolian[2] breath,
Shall suit th' unveiling of dark records well—
Hear me in tenderness and silent faith!

Thou knew'st me not in life's fresh vernal noon—
I would thou hadst!—for then my heart on thine
Had pour'd a worthier love; now, all o'erworn
By its deep thirst for something too divine,
It hath but fitful music to bestow,
Echoes of harp-strings broken long ago.

Yet even in youth companionless I stood,
As a lone forest-bird midst ocean's foam;
For me the silver cords of brotherhood
Were early loosed;—the voices from my home
Pass'd one by one, and Melody and Mirth
Left me a dreamer by a silent hearth.

But, with the fulness of a heart that burn'd
For the deep sympathies of mind, I turn'd
From that unanswering spot, and fondly sought
In all wild scenes with thrilling murmurs fraught,
In every still small voice and sound of power,
And flute-note of the wind through cave and bower,
A perilous delight!—for then first woke
My life's lone passion, the mysterious quest
Of secret knowledge; and each tone that broke
From the wood-arches or the fountain's breast,
Making my quick soul vibrate as a lyre,
But minister'd to that strange inborn fire.
Midst the bright silence of the mountain-dells,
In noontide-hours or golden summer-eves,
My thoughts have burst forth as a gale that swells
Into a rushing blast, and from the leaves
Shakes out response;—O thou rich world unseen!
Thou curtain'd realm of spirits!—thus my cry
Hath troubled air and silence—dost thou lie
Spread all around, yet by some filmy screen
Shut from us ever?—The resounding woods,
Do their depths teem with marvels?—and the floods,
And the pure fountains, leading secret veins
Of quenchless melody through rock and hill,
Have they bright dwellers?—are their lone domains
Peopled with beauty, which may never still
Our weary thirst of soul?—Cold, weak and cold,
Is earth's vain language, piercing not one fold
Of our deep being!—Oh, for gifts more high!
For a seer's glance to rend mortality!
For a charm'd rod, to call from each dark shrine,
The oracles divine!
I woke from those high fantasies, to know
My kindred with the earth—I woke to love:—
O gentle friend! to love in doubt and woe,
Shutting the heart the worshipp'd name above,
Is to love deeply—and *my* spirit's dower
Was a sad gift, a melancholy power
Of so adoring;—with a buried care,
And with the o'erflowing of a voiceless prayer,
And with a deepening dream, that day by day,
In the still shadow of its lonely sway,
Folded me closer,—till the world held naught
Save the *one* being to my centred thought.
There was no music but his voice to hear,
No joy but such as with *his* step drew near;
Light was but where he look'd—life where he
 moved.—
Silently, fervently, thus, thus I loved.
Oh! but such love is fearful!—and I knew

[1] Motto is from Byron's *Manfred,** II.iv.527–28. This poem is a response both to *Manfred* and to Percy Shelley's *Alastor.**

[2] **Aeolian:** in Greek myth, Aeolus was the god of the winds; hence, produced by or borne on the wind; aerial.

Its gathering doom:—the soul's prophetic sight
Even then unfolded in my breast, and threw
O'er all things round a full, strong, vivid light,
Too sorrowfully clear!—an under-tone
Was given to Nature's harp, for me alone
Whispering of grief.—Of grief?—be strong, awake!
Hath not thy love been victory, O, my soul?
Hath not its conflict won a voice to shake
Death's fastnesses?—a magic to control
Worlds far removed?—from o'er the grave to thee
Love hath made answer; and *thy* tale should be
Sung like a lay of triumph!—Now return,
And take thy treasure from its bosom'd urn,
And lift it once to light!

In fear, in pain,
I said I loved—but yet a heavenly strain
Of sweetness floated down the tearful stream,
A joy flash'd through the trouble of my dream!
I knew myself beloved!—we breathed no vow,
No mingling visions might our fate allow,
As unto happy hearts; but still and deep,
Like a rich jewel gleaming in a grave,
Like golden sand in some dark river's wave,
So did my soul that costly knowledge keep.
So jealously!—a thing o'er which to shed,
When stars alone beheld the drooping head,
Lone tears! yet ofttimes burden'd with the excess
Of our strange nature's quivering happiness.

But, oh! sweet friend! we dream not of love's might
Till Death has robed with soft and solemn light
The image we enshrine!—Before *that* hour,
We have but glimpses of the o'ermastering power
Within us laid!—*then* doth the spirit-flame
With sword-like lightning rend its mortal frame;
The wings of that which pants to follow fast
Shake their clay-bars, as with a prison'd blast,—
The sea is in our souls!

He died, *he* died,
On whom my lone devotedness was cast!
I might not keep one vigil by his side,
I, whose wrung heart watch'd with him to the last!
I might not once his fainting head sustain,
Nor bathe his parch'd lips in the hour of pain,
Nor say to him, "Farewell!"—He pass'd away—
Oh! had *my* love been there, its conquering sway
Had won him back from death!—but thus removed,
Borne o'er th' abyss no sounding line hath proved,
Join'd with the unknown, the viewless—he became
Unto my thoughts another, yet the same—
Changed—hallow'd—glorified!—and his low grave
Seem'd a bright mournful altar—mine, all mine:—
Brother and friend soon left me *that* sole shrine,
The birthright of the faithful!—*their* world's wave
Soon swept them from its brink.—Oh! deem thou not
That on the sad and consecrated spot
My soul grew weak!—I tell thee that a power
There kindled heart and lip;—a fiery shower
My words were made;—a might was given to prayer,
And a strong grasp to passionate despair,
And a dread triumph!—Know'st thou what I sought?
For what high boon my struggling spirit wrought?
—Communion with the dead!—I sent a cry,
Through the veil'd empires of eternity—,
A voice to cleave them! By the mournful truth,
By the lost promise of my blighted youth,
By the strong chain a mighty love can bind
On the beloved, the spell of mind o'er mind;
By words, which in themselves are magic high,
Armed, and inspired, and wing'd with agony;
By tears, which comfort not, but burn, and seem
To bear the heart's blood in their passion-stream;
I summon'd, I adjured!—with quicken'd sense,
With the keen vigil of a life intense,
I watch'd, an answer from the winds to wring,
I listen'd, if perchance the stream might bring
Token from worlds afar; I taught *one* sound
Unto a thousand echoes; one profound
Imploring accent to the tomb, the sky;
One prayer to night,—"Awake! appear! reply!"

Hast thou been told that from the viewless bourne,
The dark way never hath allow'd return?
That all, which tears can move, with life is fled,
That earthly love is powerless on the dead?
Believe it not!—There is a large lone star,
Now burning o'er yon western hill afar,
And under its clear light there lies a spot,
Which well might utter forth—Believe it not!

I sat beneath that planet,—I had wept
My woe to stillness; every night-wind slept;
A hush was on the hills; the very streams
Went by like clouds, or noiseless founts in dreams,
And the dark tree o'ershadowing me that hour,
Stood motionless, even as the gray church-tower
Whereon I gazed unconsciously:—there came
A low sound, like the tremor of a flame,
Or like the light quick shiver of a wing,
Flitting through twilight woods, across the air;

And I look'd up!—Oh! for strong words to bring
Conviction o'er thy thought!—Before me there,
He, the Departed, stood!—Ay, face to face.—
So near, and yet how far!—his form, his mien,
Gave to remembrance back each burning trace
Within:—Yet something awfully serene,
Pure, sculpture-like, on the pale brow, that wore
Of the once beating heart no token more;
And stillness on the lip—and o'er the hair
A gleam, that trembled through the breathless air;
And an unfathom'd calm, that seem'd to lie
In the grave sweetness of th' illumined eye,
Told of the gulfs between our being set,
And, as that unsheath'd spirit-glance I met,
Made my soul faint:—with *fear?*—Oh! *not* with fear!
With the sick feeling that in *his* far sphere
My love could be as nothing!—But he spoke—
How shall I tell thee of the startling thrill
In that low voice, whose breezy tones could fill
My bosom's infinite?—O friend! I woke
Then first to heavenly life!—Soft, solemn, clear,
Breathed the mysterious accents on mine ear,
Yet strangely seem'd as if the while they rose
From depths of distance, o'er the wide repose
Of slumbering waters wafted, or the dells
Of mountains, hollow with sweet echo-cells;
But, as they murmur'd on, the mortal chill
Pass'd from me, like a mist before the morn,
And, to that glorious intercourse upborne,
By slow degrees, a calm, divinely still,
Possess'd my frame:—I sought that lighted eye,—
From its intense and searching purity
I drank in *soul!*—I question'd of the dead—
Of the hush'd, starry shores their footsteps tread.—
And I was answer'd:—if remembrance there,
With dreamy whispers fill the immortal air;
If Thought, here piled from many a jewel-heap,
Be treasure in that pensive land to keep;
If love, o'ersweeping change, and blight, and blast,
Find there the music of his home at last;
I ask'd, and I was answer'd:—Full and high
Was that communion with eternity,
Too rich for aught so fleeting!—Like a knell
Swept o'er my sense its closing words,—"Farewell,
On earth we meet no more!"—and all was gone
The pale, bright settled brow—the thrilling tone.—
The still and shining eye!—and never more
May twilight gloom or midnight hush restore
That radiant guest!—One full-fraught hour of Heaven,
To earthly passion's wild implorings given,
Was made my own—the ethereal fire hath shiver'd
The fragile censer[3] in whose mould it quiver'd,
Brightly, consumingly!—What now is left?—
A faded world, of glory's hues bereft,
A void, a chain!—I dwell, 'midst throngs, apart,
In the cold silence of the stranger's heart;
A fix'd immortal shadow stands between
My spirit and life's fast-receding scene;
A gift hath sever'd me from human ties,
A power is gone from all earth's melodies,
Which never may return:—their chords are broken.—
The music of another land hath spoken,—
No after-sound is sweet!—this weary thirst!—
And I have heard celestial fountains burst!—
What here shall quench it?
Dost thou not rejoice,
When the spring sends forth an awakening voice
Through the young woods?—Thou dost!—And in that birth
Of early leaves, and flowers, and songs of mirth,
Thousands, like thee, find gladness!—Couldst thou know
How every breeze then summons *me* to go!
How all the light of love and beauty shed
By those rich hours, but woos me to the Dead!
The *only* beautiful that change no more,
The only loved!—the dwellers on the shore
Of spring fulfill'd!—The Dead!—*whom* call we so?
They that breathe purer air, that feel, that know
Things wrapt from us!—Away!—within me pent,
That which is barr'd from its own element
Still droops or struggles!—But the day *will* come—
Over the deep the free bird finds its home,
And the stream lingers midst the rocks, yet greets
The sea at last; and the wing'd flower-seed meets
A soil to rest in:—shall not *I*, too, be,
My spirit-love! upborne to dwell with thee?
Yes! by the power whose conquering anguish stirr'd
The tomb, whose cry beyond the stars was heard,
Whose agony of triumph won thee back
Through the dim pass no mortal step may track,
Yet shall we meet!—that glimpse of joy divine,
Proved thee for ever and for ever mine!

[3] **censer:** vessel in which incense is burnt.

The Two Homes

(1830)

"Oh, if the soul immortal be,
Is not its love immortal too?"

See'st thou my home?—'tis where yon woods are waving,
In their dark richness, to the summer air;
Where yon blue stream, a thousand flower-banks laving,
Leads down the hills a vein of light,—'tis there!

Midst those green wilds how many a fount lies gleaming,
Fringed with the violet, colour'd with the skies!
My boyhood's haunt, through days of summer dreaming,
Under young leaves that shook with melodies.

My home! The spirit of its love is breathing
In every wind that blows across my track;
From its white walls the very tendrils wreathing,
Seem with soft links to draw the wanderer back.

There am I loved—there pray'd for—there my mother
Sits by the hearth with meekly thoughtful eye;
There my young sisters watch to greet their brother—
Soon their glad footsteps down the path will fly.

There, in sweet strains of kindred music blending,
All the home-voices meet at day's decline;
One are those tones, as from one heart ascending,—
There laughs *my* home—sad stranger! where is thine?

Ask'st thou of mine?—In solemn peace 'tis lying,
Far o'er the deserts and the tombs away;
'Tis where *I*, too, am loved with love undying,
And fond hearts wait my step—But where are they?

Ask where the earth's departed have their dwelling;
Ask of the clouds, the stars, the trackless air!
I know it not, yet trust the whisper, telling
My lonely heart that love unchanged is there.

And what is home, and where, but with the loving?
Happy *thou* art, that so canst gaze on thine!
My spirit feels but, in its weary roving,
That with the dead, where'er they be, is mine.

Go to thy home, rejoicing son and brother!
Bear in fresh gladness to the household scene!
For me, too, watch the sister and the mother,
I well believe—but dark seas roll between.

Corinne at the Capitol

(1830)

Les femmes doivent penser qu'il est dans cette carrière bien peu de sorte qui puissent valoir la plus obscure vie d'une femme aimée et d'une mère heureuse.[1]

MADAME DE STAËL

Daughter of th' Italian heaven!
Thou, to whom its fires are given,
Joyously thy car hath roll'd
Where the conqueror's pass'd of old;
And the festal sun that shone,
O'er three[2] hundred triumphs gone,
Makes thy day of glory bright,
With a shower of golden light.

Now thou tread'st th' ascending road,
Freedom's foot so proudly trode;
While, from tombs of heroes borne,
From the dust of empire shorn,
Flowers upon thy graceful head,
Chaplets of all hues, are shed,
In a soft and rosy rain,
Touch'd with many a gemlike stain.

Thou hast gain'd the summit now!
Music hails thee from below;—
Music, whose rich notes might stir
Ashes of the sepulchre;
Shaking with victorious notes

[1] *Trans.* "Women must think that there is very little in this career [of writing/political action] that can be worth [the giving up of] the obscure life of a beloved wife and a happy mother." For Madame de Staël, see "Indian Woman's Death-Song," above. *Corinne* (1807) was de Staël's most famous novel; it tells the story of an inspired and passionate Italian poet, Corinne, who falls in love with an Englishman who finally deserts her to return to his more modest and reserved English fiancée.

[2] **three:** The trebly hundred triumphs.—Byron [F. H.], *Childe Harold,** IV.731.

All the bright air as it floats.
Well may woman's heart beat high
Unto that proud harmony!

Now afar it rolls—it dies—
And thy voice is heard to rise
With a low and lovely tone
In its thrilling power alone;
And thy lyre's deep silvery string,
Touch'd as by a breeze's wing,
Murmurs tremblingly at first,
Ere the tide of rapture burst.

All the spirit of thy sky
Now hath lit thy large dark eye,
And thy cheek a flush hath caught
From the joy of kindled thought;
And the burning words of song
From thy lip flow fast and strong,
With a rushing stream's delight
In the freedom of its might.

Radiant daughter of the sun!
Now thy living wreath is won.
Crown'd of Rome!—Oh! art thou not
Happy in that glorious lot?—
Happier, happier far than thou,
With the laurel on thy brow,
She that makes the humblest hearth
Lovely but to one on earth!

POSTHUMOUS PUBLICATIONS

from THE POETICAL WORKS OF MRS. HEMANS

(Philadelphia, 1836)

Woman and Fame

(1836; comp. 1833)

Happy—happier far than thou,
With the laurel on thy brow;
She that makes the humblest hearth
Lovely but to one on earth.

....

Thou hast a charmèd cup, O Fame,
A draught that mantles high,
And seems to lift this earthly frame
Above mortality.

Away! to me—a woman—bring
Sweet waters from affection's spring.

Thou hast green laurel leaves that twine
Into so proud a wreath;
For that resplendent gift of thine,
Heroes have smiled in death.

Give me from some kind hand a flower,
The record of one happy hour!

Thou hast a voice, whose thrilling tone
Can bid each life-pulse beat,
As when a trumpet's note hath blown,
Calling the brave to meet:
But mine, let mine—a woman's breast,
By words of home-born love be bless'd.

A hollow sound is in thy song,
A mockery in thine eye,
To the sick heart that doth but long
For aid, for sympathy,
For kindly looks to cheer it on,
For tender accents that are gone.

Fame, Fame! thou canst not be the stay
Unto the drooping reed,
The cool, fresh fountain in the day
Of the soul's feverish need:
Where must the lone one turn or flee?
Not unto thee, oh! not to thee!

JOHN CLARE

(1793–1864)

Thresher's son, herdsman, field laborer, "Northamptonshire peasant poet," John Clare benefitted from the vogue of natural genius during this period of literary history. His first volume, *Poems Descriptive of Rural Life and Scenery* (1820), went through three editions within a year, and *The Village Minstrel* (1821) immediately followed to meet demand. Also in 1820 Clare married Martha Turner, who was pregnant with his child, and was introduced by his publisher, John Taylor, to the literary circle of London—Coleridge,* Lamb,* Hazlitt,* De Quincey,* and the poet closest to him in age, John Keats,* whose descriptions of nature Clare found marred by fancy and classical allusion rather than "as [Keats] would have described her had he witnessed the things he describes."

Clare's fortunes declined, however, as tastes changed. His third volume, *The Shepherd's Calendar* (1827) sold only 400 copies in two years. The final volume published during his lifetime, *The Rural Muse* (1835), fared better, but Clare's physical and mental condition was now declining. In 1837 Clare became a voluntary patient at a mental asylum at High Beach, Epping Forest, from which he ventured in 1841 in a delusionary state. He was admitted to the Northampton General Asylum, where he spent the remaining twenty-three years of his life, writing the bulk of his poetry, sometimes from the assumed identity of successful contemporaries.

Much of Clare's poetry remained unpublished until the twentieth century, during the course of which his reputation has grown. Clare's lovingly detailed rendering of natural phenomena, which "combines a designing intellect with a watchful heart," as a recent critic states it, has earned Clare an honorable place among the nature poets of England and America. His poems of social marginality and the growing destitution of village life give an authentic and historically significant accounting of the experience of the rural poor. His asylum poems wage to the end of his life the war of memory, spirit, and imagination against confinement and alienation:

I lost earth's joys, but felt the glow
  Of heaven's flame abound in me,
Till loveliness and I did grow
  The bard of immortality.
. . . .
In every language upon earth,
  On every shore, o'er every sea,
I gave my name immortal birth
  And kept my spirit with the free.
("A Vision")

from THE RURAL MUSE
(1835)

Nutting
(1835; comp. 1821–1824)

The sun had stooped his westward clouds to win
Like weary traveller seeking for an Inn
When from the hazelly wood we glad descried[1]
The ivied gateway by the pasture side
Long had we sought for nutts amid the shade
Where silence fled the rustle that we made
When torn by briars and brushed by sedges rank
We left the wood and on the velvet bank
Of short sward[2] pasture ground we sat us down
To shell our nutts before we reached the town
The near hand stubble field with mellow glower[3]
Showed the dimmed blaze of poppys still in flower
And sweet the molehills smelt we sat upon
And now the thymes in bloom but where is pleasure gone

The Morning Wind
(1835; comp. 1824–1832)

Theres more then music in this early wind
Awaking like a bird refreshed from sleep
And joy what Adam might in eden find
When he with angels did communion keep
It breaths all balm and insence from the sky
Blessing the husbandman with freshening powers
Joys manna from its wings doth fall and lie
Harvests for early wakers with the flowers
The very grass in joys devotion moves
Cowslaps[1] in adoration and delight
This way and that bow to the breath they love
Of the young winds that with the dew pearls play
Till smoaking chimneys sicken the young light
And feelings fairey visions fade away[2]

[1] **descried:** came to see after careful observation.

[2] **sward:** grassy soil; sod.

[3] **glower:** a sullen look; here suggests *luster.*

[1] **Cowslap:** var. of cowslip, a primrose with either yellow or purplish flowers.

[2] **Adam . . . fade away:** Cf. *Paradise Lost,* IX.192–199: "Now whenas sacred light began to dawn / In Eden on the humid flow'rs, that breathed / Their morning incense, when all things that breathe, / From th' earth's great altar send up silent praise / To the Creator, and his nostrils fill / With grateful smell, forth came the human pair / And joined their vocal worship to the choir / Of creatures wanting voice."

The Nightingales Nest
(1835; comp. 1824–1832)

Up this green woodland ride lets softly rove
And list the nightingale—she dwelleth here
Hush let the wood gate softly clap—for fear
The noise may drive her from her home of love
For here Ive heard her many a merry year
At morn and eve nay all the live long day
As though she lived on song—this very spot
Just where that old mans beard all wildly trails
Rude arbours oer the road and stops the way
And where that child its blue bell flowers hath got
Laughing and creeping through the mossy rails[1]
There have I hunted like a very boy
Creeping on hands and knees through matted thorns
To find her nest and see her feed her young
And vainly did I many hours employ
All seemed as hidden as a thought unborn
And where these crimping fern leaves ramp[2] among
The hazels under boughs—Ive nestled down
And watched her while she sung—and her renown
Hath made me marvel that so famed a bird[3]
Should have no better dress than russet brown
Her wings would tremble in her extacy
And feathers stand on end as twere with joy
And mouth wide open to release her heart

[1] **rails:** fence.

[2] **ramp:** grow luxuriously.

[3] **so famed a bird:** Cf. the Greek myth of Philomel; Milton's *Il Penseroso,* ll. 60–64: "Sweet Bird that shunn'st the voice of folly, / Most musical, most melancholy!"; Coleridge's "The Nightingale";* Keats's "Ode to a Nightingale."*

Of its out sobbing songs[4] — the happiest part
Of summers fame she shared — for so to me
Did happy fancys shapen her employ
But if I touched a bush or scarcely stirred
All in a moment stopt — I watched in vain
The timid bird had left the hazel bush
And at a distance hid to sing again
Lost in a wilderness of listening leaves[5]
Rich extacy would pour its luscious strain
Till envy spurred the emulating thrush
To start less wild and scarce inferior songs
For cares with him for half the year remain
To damp the ardour of his speckled breast
While nightingales to summers life belongs
And naked trees and winters nipping wrongs
Are strangers to her music and her rest
Her joys are evergreen her world is wide
— Hark there she is as usual lets be hush
For in this black thorn clump if rightly guest[6]
Her curious house is hidden — part aside
These hazle branches in a gentle way
And stoop right cautious neath the rustling boughs
For we will have another search to day
And hunt this fern strown thorn clump round and round
And where this seeded wood grass idly bows
Well wade right through — it is a likely nook
In such like spots and often on the ground
Theyll build where rude boys never think to look
Aye as I live her secret nest is here
Upon this white thorn stulp[7] — Ive searched about
For hours in vain — there put that bramble bye
Nay trample on its branshes and get near
How subtle is the bird she started out
And raised a plaintive note of danger nigh
Ere we were past the brambles and now near
Her nest she sudden stops — as choaking fear
That might betray her home so even now
Well leave it as we found it — safetys guard
Of pathless solitude shall keep it still
See there shes sitting on the old oak bough
Mute in her fears our presence doth retard
Her joys and doubt turns all her rapture chill
Sing on sweet bird may no worse hap befall
Thy visions then the fear that now decieves
We will not plunder music of its dower
Nor turn this spot of happiness to thrall
For melody seems hid in every flower
That blossoms near thy home — these harebells all
Seems bowing with the beautiful in song
And gaping cuckoo with its spotted leaves
Seems blushing of the singing it has heard
How curious is the nest no other bird
Uses such loose materials or weaves
Their dwellings in such spots — dead oaken leaves
Are placed without and velvet moss within
And little scraps of grass — and scant and spare
Of what seems scarce materials down and hair
For from mans haunts she seemeth nought to win
Yet nature is the builder and contrives
Homes for her childerns comfort even here
Where solitudes deciples[8] spend their lives
Unseen save when a wanderer passes near
That loves such pleasant places — deep adown
The nest is made an hermits mossy cell
Snug lie her curious eggs in number five[9]
Of deadend green or rather olive brown
And the old prickly thorn bush guards them well
And here well leave them still unknown to wrong
As the old woodlands legacy of song

[4] **extacy . . . sobbing songs:** Cf. "Ode to a Nightingale," ll. 57–58.

[5] **distance hid . . . leaves:** Cf. "Ode to a Nightingale," ll. 75–78.

[6] **guest:** guessed.

[7] **stulp:** tree stump.

[8] **deciples:** disciples.

[9] **lie . . . five:** Cf. W. Wordsworth, "The Sparrow's Nest,"* line 1.

POSTHUMOUS PUBLICATIONS

from THE LIFE OF JOHN CLARE

(1865)

I am

(1865; comp. 1842–1864)

I AM — yet what I am, none cares or knows;
My friends forsake me like a memory lost:
I am the self-consumer of my woes —
They rise and vanish in oblivions host,

Like shadows in love frenzied stifled throes
And yet I am, and live—like vapours tost
Into the nothingness of scorn and noise,
Into the living sea of waking dreams,
Where there is neither sense of life or joys,
But the vast shipwreck of my lifes esteems;
Even the dearest that I love the best
Are strange—nay, rather, stranger than the rest.

I long for scenes where man hath never trod
A place where woman never smiled or wept
There to abide with my Creator God,
And sleep as I in childhood sweetly slept,
Untroubling and untroubled where I lie
The grass below, above, the vaulted sky.

from POEMS OF JOHN CLARE
(1920)

The Peasant Poet
(1920; comp. 1842–1864)

He loved the brook's soft sound,
The swallow swimming by,
He loved the daisy-covered ground,
The cloud-bedappled sky.
To him the dismal storm appeared
The very voice of God;
And when the evening rock was reared
Stood Moses with his rod.
And everything his eyes surveyed,
The insects i' the brake,
Were creatures God Almighty made,
He loved them for his sake—
A silent man in life's affairs,
A thinker from a boy,
A peasant in his daily cares,
A poet in his joy.

An Invite to Eternity
(1920; comp. 1842–1864)

Wilt thou go with me, sweet maid
Say, maiden, wilt thou go with me
Through the valley depths of shade,
Of night and dark obscurity,
Where the path hath lost its way,
Where the sun forgets the day,
Where there's nor life nor light to see,
Sweet maiden, wilt thou go with me?

Where stones will turn to flooding streams,
Where plains will rise like ocean waves,
Where life will fade like visioned dreams
And mountains darken into caves,
Say, maiden, wilt thou go with me
Through this sad non-identity,
Where parents live and are forgot,
And sisters live and know us not?

Say, maiden, wilt thou go with me
In this strange death of life to be,
To live in death and be the same
Without this life, or home, or name,
At once to be and not to be—
That was and is not—yet to see
Things pass like shadows and the sky
Above, below, around us lie?

The land of shadows wilt thou trace,
And look, nor know each other's face;
The present mixed with reasons gone,
And past and present all as one?
Say, maiden, can thy life be led
To join the living with the dead?
Then trace thy footsteps on with me;
We're wed to one eternity.

from POEMS OF JOHN CLARE
(1935)

The Mores
(1935; comp. 1821–1824)

Far spread the moorey ground a level scene
Bespread with rush and one eternal green
That never felt the rage of blundering plough
Though centurys wreathed springs blossoms on its brow
Still meeting plains that stretched them far away
In uncheckt shadows of green brown and grey
Unbounded freedom ruled the wandering scene
Nor fence of ownership crept in between

To hide the prospect of the following eye
Its only bondage was the circling sky
One mighty flat undwarfed by bush and tree
Spread its faint shadow of immensity
And lost itself which seemed to eke its bounds
In the blue mist the orisons[1] edge surrounds
Now this sweet vision of my boyish hours
Free as spring clouds and wild as summer flowers
Is faded all—a hope that blossomed free
And hath been once no more shall ever be
Inclosure came and trampled on the grave
Of labours rights and left the poor a slave[2]
And memorys pride ere want to wealth did bow
Is both the shadow and the substance now
The sheep and cows were free to range as then
Where change might prompt nor felt the bonds of
    men
Cows went and came with evening morn and night
To the wild pasture as their common right
And sheep unfolded with the rising sun
Heard the swains shout and felt their freedom won
Tracked the red fallow field and heath and plain
Then met the brook and drank and roamed again
The brook that dribbled on as clear as glass
Beneath the roots they hid among the grass
While the glad shepherd traced their tracks along
Free as the lark and happy as her song
But now alls fled and flats of many a dye
That seemed to lengthen with the following eye
Moors loosing from the sight far smooth and blea[3]
Where swopt the plover in its pleasure free
Are vanished now with commons wild and gay
As poets visions of lifes early day
Mulberry bushes where the boy would run
To fill his hands with fruit are grubbed and done
And hedgrow briars—flower lovers overjoyed
Came and got flower pots—these are all destroyed
And sky bound mores in mangled garbs are left
Like mighty giants of their limbs bereft
Fence now meets fence in owners little bounds
Of field and meadow large as garden grounds
In little parcels little minds to please
With men and flocks imprisoned ill at ease
Each little path that led its pleasant way
As sweet as morning leading night astray
Where little flowers bloomed round a varied host
That travel felt delighted to be lost
Nor grudged the steps that he had taen[4] as vain
When right roads traced his journeys end again
Nay on a broken tree hed sit awhile
To see the mores and fields and meadows smile
Sometimes with cowslaps smothered—then all white
With daiseys—then the summers splendid sight
Of corn fields crimson oer the 'headach' bloomd
Like splendid armys for the battle plumed
He gazed upon them with wild fancys eye
As fallen landscapes from an evening sky
These paths are stopt—the rude philistines thrall[5]
Is laid upon them and destroyed them all
Each little tyrant with his little sign
Shows where man claims earth glows no more divine
On paths to freedom and to childhood dear
A board sticks up to notice 'no road here'
And on the tree with ivy overhung
The hated sign by vulgar taste is hung
As tho the very birds should learn to know
When they go there they must no further go
This was the poor scared freedom bade good bye
And much the[y] feel it in the smothered sigh
And birds and trees and flowers without a name
All sighed when lawless laws enclosure came
And dreams of plunder in such rebel schemes
Have found too truly that they were but dreams

[1] **orison:** var. of horizon.

[2] **Inclosure came . . . slave:** See SOCIETY AND POLITICAL ECONOMY.

[3] **blea:** bleak.

[4] **taen:** taken.

[5] **thrall:** control.

Pastoral Poesy
(1935; comp. 1824–1832)

True poesy is not in words,
    But images that thoughts express,
By which the simplest hearts are stirred
    To elevated happiness.

Mere books would be but useless things
    Where none had taste or mind to read,
Like unknown lands where beauty springs
    And none are there to heed.

But poesy is a language meet,
    And fields are every one's employ;

The wild flower 'neath the shepherd's feet
Look up and gives him joy;

A language that is ever green,
That feelings unto all impart,
As hawthorn blossoms, soon as seen,
Give May to every heart.

An image to the mind is brought,
Where happiness enjoys
An easy thoughtlessness of thought
And meets excess of joys.

And such is poesy; its power
May varied lights employ,
Yet to all minds it gives the dower
Of self-creating joy.

And whether it be hill or moor,
I feel where'er I go
A silence that discourses more
That any tongue can do.

Unruffled quietness hath made
A peace in every place,
And woods are resting in their shade
Of social loneliness.

The storm, from which the shepherd turns
To pull his beaver[1] down,
While he upon the heath sojourns,
Which autumn pleaches[2] brown.

Is music, ay, and more indeed
To those of musing mind
Who through the yellow woods proceed
And listen to the wind.

The poet in his fitful glee
And fancy's many moods
Meets it as some strange melody,
A poem of the woods,

And now a harp that flings around
The music of the wind;
The poet often hears the sound
When beauty fills the mind.

So would I my own mind employ,
And my own heart impress,
That poesy's self's a dwelling joy
Of humble quietness.

[1] **beaver:** hat made of beaver fur.

[2] **pleaches:** bleaches.

Winter Fields

(1935; comp. 1832–1835)

O for a pleasant book to cheat the sway
Of winter—where rich mirth with hearty laugh
Listens and rubs his legs on corner seat
For fields are mire and sludge—and badly off
Are those who on their pudgy[1] paths delay
There striding shepherd seeking driest way
Fearing nights wetshod feet and hacking cough
That keeps him waken till the peep of day
Goes shouldering onward and with ready hook
Progs[2] oft to ford the sloughs[3] that nearly meet
Accross the lands—croodling[4] and thin to view
His loath dog follows—stops and quakes and looks
For better roads—till whistled to pursue
Then on with frequent jump he hirkles[5] through

Cottage Fears

(1935; comp. 1832–1835)

The evening gathers from the gloomy woods
And darkling creeps oer silent vale and hill
While the snug village in nights happy moods
Is resting calm and beautifully still
The windows gleam with light the yelping curs
That guards the henroost from the thieving fox
Barks now and then as somthing passing stirs
And distant dogs the noises often mocks
While foxes from the woods send dismal cries
Like somthing in distress the cottager
Hears the dread noise and thinks of danger nigh
And locks up door in haste—nor cares to stir
From the snug safety of his humble shed
Then tells strange tales till time to go to bed

[1] **pudgy:** filled with puddles.

[2] **Progs:** pokes.

[3] **sloughs:** mud holes.

[4] **croodling:** shrinking from the cold.

[5] **hirkles:** moves carefully through.

JOHN KEATS

(1795–1821)

John Keats was among the most devoted poetic craftsmen of his time. Others had significant extra-literary intentions. Blake, Coleridge, and Wordsworth hoped that their work might enjoy political and religious influence. Shelley admitted to a primary passion for reforming the world. Byron died on behalf of Greek independence. Keats devoted his short span of life to acquiring literary immortality—"I would sooner fail than not to be among the greatest"—yet he could also say that his "mere yearning and fondness for the Beautiful" would keep him writing "even if [his] night's labours should be burnt every morning and no eye ever shine upon them." It seems he meant it. Charles Armitage Brown reported that Keats would often compose on random scraps of paper, which he then discarded or used as bookmarks. Brown rescued from casual oblivion "Ode to a Nightingale."

Keats did not begin life as an artist with much more than a legacy of ambition, passion, and a touch of creative madness. His father, Thomas Keats, worked as a London stable boy, got promoted to head ostler, and married Frances Jennings, the manager's daughter. John was born to the young couple seven months later. The Keats-Jennings business prospered until Thomas suffered a fatal accident in 1804. He left his wife with four children—John, then eight; George, seven; Thomas, four; and Frances Mary (Fanny), ten months. Within two months of her husband's death, Frances Keats remarried, thereby passing on legal ownership of the family business to her second husband. She soon left him for incompatibility, and he revealed his marital motivation by selling the business and disappearing. Placing her children in the care of her mother, Frances moved in with another man. She returned to her children eventually, but died of tuberculosis when John was thirteen. He had nursed her devotedly but unsuccessfully.

In 1811, Keats's appointed guardian, the tea merchant Richard Abbey, removed him from the grammar school at Enfield, where Keats's passion for reading and writing had been fostered under the tutelage of the headmaster's son, Charles Cowden Clarke. Keats was apprenticed to a surgeon and apothecary for several years and then completed his medical training at Guy's Hospital, London, in 1815. During the course of his medical studies, he wrote poetry, attempted Latin translation, and published his first poem, the sonnet "To Solitude." A coterie of radical London writers befriended Keats, and because of the special interest of Leigh Hunt (1784–1859)—poet, essayist, political activist, enthusiast of the arts, and editor of *The Examiner*—Keats began to think seriously of a poetic vocation. Hunt featured the poetry of Keats and Percy Shelley* in an essay entitled "Young Poets." In spring 1817, Keats's first volume, *Poems,* appeared, and he gave up any inclination toward medicine he may have had.

Poems and Keats's second volume, *Endymion* (1818), were viciously reviewed in Tory literary periodicals, but the liberal press also winced at Keats's stylistic affectations—"leafy luxury," "jaunty streams," "lawny slope," "the moon-beamy air," "a sun-beamy tale"—and apparently pretentious ambitions. Reviewing anonymously for the conservative *Blackwood's Magazine* (1817–1980), John Gibson Lockhart (1794–1854) mocked the poems as the "drivelling idiocy" of the "Cockney School of Politics, as well as the Cockney School of Poetry." John Wilson Croker's anonymous review in *The Quarterly Review* (1809–1967) was comparably motivated: "This author is a copyist of Mr. Hunt; but he is more unintelligible, almost as rugged, twice as diffuse, and ten times more tiresome and absurd than his prototype." (See Literary Criticism under AESTHETIC THEORY AND LITERARY CRITICISM.) Percy Shelley believed these reviews brought on Keats's early death; however, Keats's self-criticism was more severe on the point of literary merit, though he took the high road in ignoring the reviewers' political motivations in scorning his social class and lack of university education:

> Praise or blame has but a momentary effect on the man whose love of beauty in the abstract makes him a severe critic of his own Works. My own domestic criticism has given me pain without comparison beyond what Blackwood or the Quarterly could possibly inflict, and also when I feel I am right, no external praise can give me such a glow as my own solitary reperception & ratification of what is fine.

The more difficult issue came to be the moral value of his verse. In his fragmentary epic, *The Fall of Hyperion,* the poem's muse challenges the poet-narrator to prove that he has been more than "a dreaming thing, / A fever of thyself." The challenge was contagious, for it echoed through the century in the work of writers emulative of Keats's aesthetics of intensity, who wished to dwell in a Palace of Art or to create "art for art's sake," but whose public demanded a socially and politically committed art.

Fever was more than a figure of speech for Keats. Besides watching his mother die, he cared for his brother Tom during a painful tubercular decline in 1818 and became aware of his own fatal condition in February 1820, when he coughed blood: "I cannot be deceived in that colour; that drop of blood is my death warrant. I must die." He was twenty-four. Though personal conditions became nearly intolerable after the death of Tom, Keats's creativity flourished in 1819. He was plagued by a severe cough contracted during a wet, cold, and intense walking tour of northern England, Scotland, and Ireland; he was in desperate need of money; and he was deeply in love with a vivacious eighteen-year-old who bore the first name of his mother and sister. Poverty and his developing consumption precluded an intended marriage to Fanny Brawne.

In the first nine months of 1819, however, Keats composed the title poems, *Hyperion,* and the famous odes that make up perhaps the single greatest volume of poetry in the nineteenth century, *Lamia, Isabella, The Eve of St. Agnes, and Other Poems* (1820). It is a commonplace of literary history that the early works of Chaucer, Shakespeare, Spenser, Milton, and Wordsworth fail to compare with Keats's *Lamia* volume. Keats's stylistic development is the special wonder. It represents his expectation that poetry should "surprise by a fine excess." Purged of mannerism in striving for "the true voice of feeling," Keats's poetic line is rich with sound pattern and wordplay, as in the elaborate consonance of "with brede / Of marble men and maidens overwrought," which includes the puns on *brede* ("breed") and *overwrought* (as "delicately formed on" and as "overly excited"). His imagery mingles sense perception in the synaesthesia of touch and smell in such phrases as "soft incense" and of touch and hearing in "smoothest silence." It elicits an empathy that accords with the poet's desire to leave the self behind in experiencing *einfuhling,* or sympathetic identification with the condition of objects, as in "warmed jewels," and with others in "all their limbs / Locked up like veins of metal, crampt and screwed." Using past participles as epithets concentrates energy ("purple-stained mouth," "pale-mouthed prophet," "full-throated song," oaktrees "branch-charmed by the earnest stars"). The exquisite rendering of fleeting, meaningful detail fixes attention on the moment ("through a lowly arched way, / Brushing the cobwebs with his lofty plume"). Adjectives arouse deeper reflection ("starved lips," "unravish'd bride of quietness"). And, of course, as with every great writer, Keats displays the genius of writing lines that one cannot help remembering: "A thing of beauty is a joy for ever"; "Beauty is truth, truth beauty"; "tender is the night"; "Season of mists and mellow fruitfulness"; "first in beauty should be first in might."

However, Keats intended to do more and in a different vein. His apprenticeship had been spent in imitation; early manhood, in reflecting deeply in his remarkable letters upon aesthetics and the direction of contemporary poetry, in staking out his own territory for poetic achievement, and in turning from contemporary "large self worshipers," i.e., Wordsworth, and "careless hectorers in proud bad verse," i.e., Byron, to the tragedies of Shakespeare as an antidote to romantic egotism. Keats's late ambition was to write a "few fine Plays" so that he could realize the inclination of his genius toward the Shakespearean qualities of disinterestedness and impersonality in art, or the *negative capability* to explore ideas and to create characters without self-interest or self-projection. Keats was fond of saying things like, all ideas "end in speculation," and thus, it is best for the poet to be "the most unpoetical of any thing in existence," or lacking an intrusive ego. He claimed that his powerful inclination to empathize threatened extinction of personality in the company of others: "the identity of every one . . . begins to press upon me . . . I am in a very little time anhilated [sic]."

Keats's medical prognosis had been correct. The salubrious air of Italy perhaps provided a few more months of what he called his "posthumous existence," but from September 1820 to his death in February he was wracked with anxiety, bitterness, and remorse over love and immortality. Keats wrote to Fanny Brawne of waking nights:

> "If I should die," said I to myself, "I have left no immortal work behind me—nothing to make my friends proud of my memory—but I have lov'd the principle of beauty in all things, and if I had had time I would have made myself remember'd." Thoughts like these came very feebly whilst I was in health and every pulse beat for you—now you divide with this (may *I* say it?) "last infirmity of noble minds" all my reflection.

Keats died a year to the month after he saw death in his blood. He was buried in the Protestant Cemetery in Rome, his tombstone inscribed as he wished: "Here lies one whose name was writ in water." His lodge at 26 Piazza di Spagna is now the Keats-Shelley Memorial House, in honor of both *poetes maudits* who died in Italy. Shelley was to drown off the coast of Leghorn in a sailing accident with Keats's *Lamia* volume opened in his pocket.

from POEMS
(1817)

How many bards gild the lapses of time
(1817; comp. 1816)

How many bards gild the lapses of time!
  A few of them have ever[1] been the food
  Of my delighted fancy,—I could brood
Over their beauties, earthly, or sublime:
And often, when I sit me down to rhyme,
  These will in throngs before my mind intrude:
  But no confusion, no disturbance rude
Do they occasion; 'tis a pleasing chime.
So the unnumber'd sounds that evening store;
  The songs of birds—the whisp'ring of the leaves—
  The voice of waters—the great bell that heaves
With solemn sound,—and thousand others more,
  That distance of recognizance bereaves,
Make pleasing music, and not wild uproar.

On First Looking into Chapman's Homer
(1816/1817; comp. 1816)

Much have I travell'd in the realms of gold,[1†]
  And many goodly states and kingdoms seen;
  Round many western islands have I been
Which bards in fealty to Apollo hold.
Oft of one wide expanse had I been told
  That deep-brow'd Homer ruled as his demesne;
  Yet did I never breathe its pure serene
Till I heard Chapman[2†] speak out loud and bold:
Then felt I like some watcher of the skies
  When a new planet swims into his ken;
Or like stout Cortez[3†] when with eagle eyes
  He star'd at the Pacific—and all his men
Look'd at each other with a wild surmise—
  Silent, upon a peak in Darien.[4†]

Addressed to the Same
(1817; comp. 1816)

Great spirits now on earth are sojourning;
  He of the cloud, the cataract, the lake,
  Who on Helvellyn's[1] summit, wide awake,
Catches his freshness from archangel's wing:
He of the rose, the violet, the spring,
  The social smile, the chain for freedom's sake:[2]
  And lo!—whose[3] stedfastness would never take
A meaner sound than Raphael's[4] whispering.
And other spirits there are standing apart
  Upon the forehead of the age to come;
These, these will give the world another heart,
  And other pulses. Hear ye not the hum
Of mighty workings?——
  Listen awhile ye nations, and be dumb.

from Sleep and Poetry
(1817; comp. 1816)

"As I lay in my bed slepe full unmete
Was unto me, but why that I ne might

[1] **ever**: always.

[1†] **realms of gold**: Possible associations are Apollo's "Western halls of gold" (Bush) and the treasure of the mythical "El Dorado," sought after by the Spanish conquistadores.

[2†] **Chapman**: A folio English edition of the *Iliad* and *Odyssey*, translated by poet and playwright George Chapman (1559?–1634), was published in 1616.

[3†] **Cortez**; Balboa, not Cortez, discovered the Pacific Ocean in 1513.

[4†] **Darien**: mountain range in what is now eastern Panama.

[1] **He**: Wordsworth. **Helvellyn**: a mountain in England's Lake District, where Wordsworth lived.

[2] **He**: Keats's friend and early mentor, the poet and editor Leigh Hunt (1784–1859), was sentenced to two years' imprisonment in 1813 for libelling the Prince Regent.

[3] **whose**: Keats's friend the painter Benjamin Robert Haydon (1786–1846), whose painting *Christ's Entry into Jerusalem* contains a likeness of Keats.

[4] **Raphael**: Italian Renaissance painter Raffaello Sanzio (1483–1520).

Rest I ne wist, for there n'as erthly wight
[As I suppose] had more of hertis ese
Than I, for I n'ad sicknesse nor disese."[1]
CHAUCER

. . . .

O Poesy! for thee I hold my pen
That am not yet a glorious denizen
Of thy wide heaven—Should I rather kneel
Upon some mountain-top until I feel
A glowing splendour round about me hung,
And echo back the voice of thine own tongue?
O Poesy! for thee I grasp my pen
That am not yet a glorious denizen
Of thy wide heaven; yet, to my ardent prayer,
Yield from thy sanctuary some clear air,
Smoothed for intoxication by the breath
Of flowering bays, that I may die a death
Of luxury, and my young spirit follow
The morning sun-beams to the great Apollo
Like a fresh sacrifice; or, if I can bear
The o'erwhelming sweets, 'twill bring to me the fair
Visions of all places: a bowery nook
Will be elysium—an eternal book
Whence I may copy many a lovely saying
About the leaves, and flowers—about the playing
Of nymphs in woods, and fountains; and the shade
Keeping a silence round a sleeping maid;
And many a verse from so strange influence
That we must ever wonder how, and whence
It came. Also imaginings will hover
Round my fire-side, and haply there discover
Vistas of solemn beauty, where I'd wander
In happy silence, like the clear Meander[2]
Through its lone vales; and where I found a spot
Of awfuller[3] shade, or an enchanted grot,
Or a green hill o'erspread with chequered dress
Of flowers, and fearful from its loveliness,
Write on my tablets all that was permitted,
All that was for our human senses fitted.
Then the events of this wide world I'd seize
Like a strong giant, and my spirit teaze
Till at its shoulders it should proudly see
Wings to find out an immortality.

Stop and consider! life is but a day;
A fragile dew-drop on its perilous way
From a tree's summit; a poor Indian's sleep
While his boat hastens to the monstrous steep
Of Montmorenci.[4] Why so sad a moan?
Life is the rose's hope while yet unblown;
The reading of an ever-changing tale;
The light uplifting of a maiden's veil;
A pigeon tumbling in clear summer air;
A laughing school-boy, without grief or care,
Riding the springy branches of an elm.

O for ten years, that I may overwhelm
Myself in poesy; so I may do the deed
That my own soul has to itself decreed.
Then will I pass the countries that I see
In long perspective, and continually
Taste their pure fountains. First the realm I'll pass
Of Flora, and old Pan:[5] sleep in the grass,
Feed upon apples red, and strawberries,
And choose each pleasure that my fancy sees;
Catch the white-handed nymphs in shady places,
To woo sweet kisses from averted faces,—
Play with their fingers, touch their shoulders white
Into a pretty shrinking with a bite
As hard as lips can make it: till agreed,
A lovely tale of human life we'll read.
And one will teach a tame dove how it best
May fan the cool air gently o'er my rest;
Another, bending o'er her nimble tread,
Will set a green robe floating round her head,
And still will dance with ever varied ease,
Smiling upon the flowers and the trees:
Another will entice me on, and on
Through almond blossoms and rich cinnamon;
Till in the bosom of a leafy world
We rest in silence, like two gems upcurl'd
In the recesses of a pearly shell.

And can I ever bid these joys farewell?
Yes, I must pass them for a nobler life,
Where I may find the agonies, the strife

[1] The author of "The Floure and the Leafe," from which the epigraph is taken, is unknown. It is not Chaucer.

[2] **Meander:** in classical antiquity, a river of Asia Minor flowing into the Aegean, known for its winding course.

[3] **awfuller:** lit., more full of awe.

[4] **Montmorenci:** the falls of Montmorenci in Quebec, Canada.

[5] **Flora, and old Pan:** In classical mythology, Flora was the goddess of flowers and gardens, Pan the god of universal nature.

Of human hearts: for lo! I see afar,
O'er sailing the blue cragginess, a car
And steeds with streamy manes—the charioteer
Looks out upon the winds with glorious fear:
And now the numerous tramplings quiver lightly
Along a huge cloud's ridge; and now with sprightly
Wheel downward come they into fresher skies,
Tipt round with silver from the sun's bright eyes.
Still downward with capacious whirl they glide;
And now I see them on a green-hill's side
In breezy rest among the nodding stalks.
The charioteer with wond'rous gesture talks
To the trees and mountains; and there soon appear
Shapes of delight, of mystery, and fear,
Passing along before a dusky space
Made by some mighty oaks: as they would chase
Some ever-fleeting music on they sweep.
Lo! how they murmur, laugh, and smile, and weep:
Some with upholden[6] hand and mouth severe;
Some with their faces muffled to the ear
Between their arms; some, clear in youthful bloom,
Go glad and smilingly athwart[7] the gloom;
Some looking back, and some with upward gaze;
Yes, thousands in a thousand different ways
Flit onward—now a lovely wreath of girls
Dancing their sleek hair into tangled curls;
And now broad wings. Most awfully intent,
The driver of those steeds is forward bent,
And seems to listen: O that I might know
All that he writes with such a hurrying glow.

The visions all are fled—the car is fled
Into the light of heaven, and in their stead
A sense of real things comes doubly strong,
And, like a muddy stream, would bear along
My soul to nothingness: but I will strive
Against all doubtings, and will keep alive
The thought of that same chariot, and the strange
Journey it went.

. . . .

Will not some say that I presumptuously
Have spoken? that from hastening disgrace
'Twere better far to hide my foolish face?
That whining boyhood should with reverence bow
Ere the dread thunderbolt could reach? How!
If I do hide myself, it sure shall be
In the very fane,[8] the light of Poesy:
If I do fall, at least I will be laid
Beneath the silence of a poplar shade;
And over me the grass shall be smooth shaven;
And there shall be a kind memorial graven.
But off, Despondence! miserable bane!
They should not know thee, who, athirst to gain
A noble end, are thirsty every hour.
What though I am not wealthy in the dower
Of spanning wisdom; though I do not know
The shiftings of the mighty winds that blow
Hither and thither all the changing thoughts
Of man: though no great minist'ring reason sorts
Out the dark mysteries of human souls
To clear conceiving: yet there ever rolls
A vast idea before me, and I glean
Therefrom my liberty; thence too I've seen
The end and aim of Poesy. 'Tis clear
As any thing most true; as that the year
Is made of the four seasons—manifest
As a large cross, some old cathedral's crest,
Lifted to the white clouds. Therefore should I
Be but the essence of deformity,
A coward, did my very eye-lids wink
At speaking out what I have dared to think.
Ah! rather let me like a madman run
Over some precipice; let the hot sun
Melt my Dedalian[9] wings, and drive me down
Convuls'd and headlong! Stay! an inward frown
Of conscience bids me be more calm awhile.
An ocean dim, sprinkled with many an isle,
Spreads awfully before me. How much toil!
How many days! what desperate turmoil!
Ere I can have explored its widenesses.
Ah, what a task! upon my bended knees,
I could unsay those—no, impossible!
Impossible!

For sweet relief I'll dwell
On humbler thoughts, and let this strange assay
Begun in gentleness die so away.
E'en now all tumult from my bosom fades:

[6] **upholden:** upheld.

[7] **athwart:** against.

[8] **fane:** temple.

[9] **Dedalian:** In Greek mythology, the craftsman Dedalus built wings of wax and feathers so he and his son Icarus could escape from King Minos's prison; but Icarus, disobeying his father, flew too near the sun, which melted his wings, and he fell into the sea and drowned.

I turn full hearted to the friendly aids
That smooth the path of honour; brotherhood,
And friendliness, the nurse of mutual good;
The hearty grasp that sends a pleasant sonnet
Into the brain ere one can think upon it;
The silence when some rhymes are coming out;
And when they're come, the very pleasant rout:
The message certain to be done to-morrow—
'Tis perhaps as well that it should be to borrow
Some precious book from out its snug retreat,
To cluster round it when we next shall meet.
Scarce can I scribble on; for lovely airs
Are fluttering round the room like doves in pairs;
Many delights of that glad day recalling,
When first my senses caught their tender falling.
And with these airs come forms of elegance
Stooping their shoulders o'er a horse's prance,
Careless, and grand—fingers soft and round
Parting luxuriant curls;—and the swift bound
Of Bacchus[10] from his chariot, when his eye
Made Ariadne's cheek look blushingly.
Thus I remember all the pleasant flow
Of words at opening a portfolio.[11]

Things such as these are ever harbingers
To trains of peaceful images: the stirs
Of a swan's neck unseen among the rushes:
A linnet starting all about the bushes:
A butterfly, with golden wings broad parted,
Nestling a rose, convuls'd as though it smarted
With over pleasure—many, many more,
Might I indulge at large in all my store
Of luxuries: yet I must not forget
Sleep, quiet with his poppy coronet:
For what there may be worthy in these rhymes
I partly owe to him: and thus, the chimes
Of friendly voices had just given place
To as sweet a silence, when I 'gan[12] retrace
The pleasant day, upon a couch at ease.
It was a poet's house who keeps the keys
Of pleasure's temple. Round about were hung
The glorious features of the bards who sung
In other ages—cold and sacred busts
Smiled at each other. Happy he who trusts
To clear futurity his darling fame!
Then there were fauns and satyrs taking aim
At swelling apples with a frisky leap
And reaching fingers, 'mid a luscious heap
Of vine leaves. Then there rose to view a fane
Of liny marble, and thereto a train
Of nymphs approaching fairly o'er the sward:[13]
One, loveliest, holding her white hand toward
The dazzling sun-rise: two sisters sweet
Bending their graceful figures till they meet
Over the trippings of a little child:
And some are hearing, eagerly, the wild
Thrilling liquidity of dewy piping.
See, in another picture, nymphs are wiping
Cherishingly Diana's[14] timorous limbs;—
A fold of lawny mantle[15] dabbling swims
At the bath's edge, and keeps a gentle motion
With the subsiding crystal:[16] as when ocean
Heaves calmly its broad swelling smoothness o'er
Its rocky marge,[17] and balances once more
The patient weeds, that now unshent[18] by foam
Feel all about their undulating home.

Sappho's[19] meek head was there half smiling down
At nothing; just as though the earnest frown
Of over thinking had that moment gone
From off her brow, and left her all alone.

Great Alfred's[20] too, with anxious, pitying eyes,
As if he always listened to the sighs

[10] **Bacchus:** Lemprière's *Bibliotheca Classica* [1788, 1st ed.], Keats's source for much of his knowledge of Classical mythology, says that "Bacchus loved [Ariadne] after Theseus had deserted her. . . ." One of Keats's favorite paintings was Titian's *Bacchus and Ariadne* (exhibited at the British Institution in 1816), in which Bacchus' chariot is drawn by leopards.

[11] **portfolio:** a folio or large-sized edition of a book.

[12] **'gan:** began to.

[13] **sward:** lawn, turf.

[14] **Diana:** Goddess of the moon and of maidenhood, Diana and her twenty nymphs were sworn to virginity.

[15] **lawny mantle:** garment made of light or sheer fabric ("lawn").

[16] **crystal:** clear water.

[17] **marge:** margin, border.

[18] **unshent:** uninjured, unharmed (OED).

[19] **Sappho:** a bust of the Greek poet Sappho (c. 610–c. 580 BC), from the isle of Lesbos. Her work celebrated love between women.

[20] **Alfred:** Alfred the Great (849–899) united all of England not under Danish rule and translated St. Augustine and Boethius into Old English.

Of the goaded world; and Kosciusko's[21] worn
By horrid suffrance—mightily forlorn.

Petrarch,[22] outstepping from the shady green,
Starts at the sight of Laura; nor can wean
His eyes from her sweet face. Most happy they!
For over them was seen a free display
Of out-spread wings, and from between them shone
The face of Poesy: from off her throne
She overlook'd things that I scarce could tell.
The very sense of where I was might well
Keep Sleep aloof: but more than that there came
Thought after thought to nourish up the flame
Within my breast; so that the morning light
Surprised me even from a sleepless night;
And up I rose refresh'd, and glad, and gay,
Resolving to begin that very day
These lines; and howsoever they be done,
I leave them as a father does his son.

from THE EXAMINER

On Seeing the Elgin Marbles[1]

(1817; comp. 1817)

My spirit is too weak—mortality
Weighs heavily on me like unwilling sleep,
And each imagined pinnacle and steep
Of godlike hardship tells me I must die
Like a sick eagle looking at the sky.
Yet 'tis a gentle luxury to weep
That I have not the cloudy winds to keep
Fresh for the opening of the morning's eye.
Such dim-conceived glories of the brain
Bring round the heart an undescribable feud;
So do these wonders a most dizzy pain,
That mingles Grecian grandeur with the rude
Wasting of old time—with a billowy main—
A sun—a shadow of a magnitude.

[21] **Kosciusko:** Polish patriot and general Thaddeus Kosciusko (1746–1817) led the rebellion against the Russian forces occupying Poland (1791–1794). Keats wrote a poem to him in December 1816.

[22] **Petrarch:** Italian poet Francesco Petrarca (1304–1374) wrote odes and sonnets about his love for Laura de Noves (1308?–1348).

[1] On March 1 or 3 Keats had gone to see the exhibition of Greek sculpture from the Parthenon brought to England by Thomas Bruce, seventh earl of Elgin (1766–1841). The sonnet was published on 9 March 1817, in both *The Examiner* and *The Champion*.

from Letter to Benjamin Bailey

(*22 November 1817*)

My dear Bailey,[1]

. . . I am certain of nothing but of the holiness of the Heart's affections and the truth of Imagination—What the imagination seizes as Beauty must be truth—whether it existed before or not—for I have the same Idea of all our Passions as of Love they are all in their sublime, creative of essential Beauty—In a Word, you may know my favorite Speculation by my first Book and the little song I sent[2] in my last—which is a representation from the fancy of the probable mode of operating in these Matters—The Imagination may be compared to Adam's dream[3]—he awoke and found it truth. I am the more zealous in this affair, because I have never yet been able to perceive how any thing can be known for truth by consequitive reasoning—and yet it must be—Can it be that even the greatest Philosopher ever ~~when~~ arrived at his goal without putting aside numerous objections—However it may be, O for a Life of Sensations rather than of Thoughts! It is 'a Vision in the form of Youth' a Shadow of reality to come—and this consideration has further conv[i]nced me for it has come as auxiliary to another favorite Speculation of mine, that we shall enjoy ourselves here after by having what we called happiness on Earth repeated in a finer tone and so repeated—And yet such a fate can only befall those who delight in sensation rather than hunger as you do after Truth—Adam's dream will do here and seems to be a conviction that

[1] Keats's friend Benjamin Bailey (1791–1853) was at this time a divinity student at Oxford. In September 1817 Keats had lived in Bailey's rooms at Oxford, where he wrote Book 3 of *Endymion*.

[2] **my first Book:** Book 1 of *Endymion* was begun in April 1817. **the little song I sent:** "Ode to Sorrow" was included in a letter to Bailey on 3 November 1817, and later became lines 146 to 181 of Book 4 of *Endymion*.

[3] **Adam's dream:** cf. *Paradise Lost*, VIII.452–490.

Imagination and its empyreal reflection is the same as human Life and its spiritual repetition. But as I was saying—the simple imaginative Mind may have its rewards in the repeti[ti]on of its own silent Working coming continually on the spirit with a fine suddenness—to compare great things with small[4]—have you never by being surprised with an old Melody—in a delicious place—by a delicious voice, fe[l]t over again your very speculations and surmises at the time it first operated on your soul—do you not remember forming to youself the singer's face more beautiful that it was possible and yet with the elevation of the Moment you did not think so—even then you were mounted on the Wings of Imagination so high—that the Prototype must be here after—that delicious face you will see—What a time! I am continually running away from the subject—sure this cannot be exactly the case with a complex Mind—one that is imaginative and at the same time careful of its fruits—who would exist partly on sensation partly on thought—to whom it is necessary that years should bring the philosophic Mind[5]—such an one I consider your's and therefore it is necessary to your eternal Happiness that you not only ~~have~~ drink this old Wine of Heaven which I shall call the redigestion of our most ethereal Musings on Earth; but also increase in knowledge and know all things. I am glad to hear you are in a fair Way for Easter—you will soon get through your unpleasant reading and then!—but the world is full of troubles and I have not much reason to think myself pestered with many—I think Jane or Marianne[6] has a better opinion of me than I deserve—for really and truly I do not think my Brothers illness connected with mine—you know more of the real Cause than they do—nor have I any chance of being rack'd as you have been—you perhaps at one time thought there was such a thing as Worldly Happiness to be arrived at, at certain periods of time marked out—you have of necessity from your disposition been thus led away—I scarcely remember counting upon any Happiness—I look not for it if it be not in the present hour—nothing startles me beyond the Moment. The setting sun will always set me to rights—or if a Sparrow come before my Window I take part in its existince and pick about the Gravel. The first thing that strikes me on hea[r]ing a Misfortune having befalled another is this. 'Well it cannot be helped.—he will have the pleasure of trying the resourses of his spirit, and I beg now my dear Bailey that hereafter should you observe any thing cold in me not to but it to the account of heartlessness but abstraction—for I assure you I sometimes feel not the influence of a Passion or Affection during a whole week—and so long this sometimes continues I begin to suspect myself and the genuiness of my feelings at other times—thinking them a few barren Tragedy-tears—My Brother Tom is much improved. . .

Your affectionate friend
JOHN KEATS—

[4] **to compare . . . small:** cf. *Paradise Lost,* II.921–2: "Nor was his ear less peal'd / With noises loud and ruinous (to compare / Great things with small)"

[5] **years should bring . . . Mind:** cf. Wordsworth's "Ode,"* lines 188–89: "In the faith that looks through death, / In years that bring the philosophic mind."

[6] **Jane or Marianne:** sister of Keats's friend John Hamilton Reynolds. Here Keats refers to their fears that he may have contracted consumption, or tuberculosis. Keats might have become infected with TB while nursing his brother Tom, who died of the disease in November 1818. Keats's mention of Bailey's being "racked" refers to an unsuccessful love affair.

from Letter to George and Tom Keats[1]
21, 27 (?) December 1817

Hampstead Sunday
22 December 1818

MY DEAR BROTHERS

. . . —I have had two very pleasant evenings with Dilke[2] yesterday & today; & am at this moment just come from him & feel in the humour to go on with this, began in the morning, & from which he came to fetch me. I spent Friday evening with Wells & went the next morning to see *Death on the Pale horse.* It is a wonderful picture, when West's[3] age is considered; But there is nothing to be

[1] George (1797–1841) and Tom (1799–1818) were Keats's younger brothers.

[2] **Dilke:** Besides having literary interests, Charles Wentworth Dilke (1784–1864) introduced Keats to his future love, Fanny Brawne.

[3] **West:** American-born painter Benjamin West (1738–1820) was president of the Royal Academy.

intense upon; no women one feels mad to kiss; no face swelling into reality. The excellence of every Art is its intensity, capable of making all disagreeables evaporate, from their being in close relationship with Beauty & Truth—Examine King Lear & you will find this exemplified throughout; but in this picture we have unpleasantness without any momentous depth of speculation excited, in which to bury its repulsiveness—The picture is larger than Christ rejected—I dined with Haydon the sunday after you left, & had a very pleasant day, I dined too (for I have been out too much lately) with Horace Smith & met his two Brothers with Hill & Kingston & one Du Bois, they only served to convince me, how superior humour is to wit in respect to enjoyment—These men say things which make one start, without making one feel, they are all alike; their manners are alike; they all know fashionables; they have a mannerism in their very eating & drinking, in their mere handling a Decanter—They talked of Kean[4] & his low company—Would I were with that company instead of yours said I to myself! I know such like acquaintance will never do for me & yet I am going to Reynolds, on wednesday—Brown[5] & Dilke walked with me & back from the Christmas pantomime. I had not a dispute but a disquisition with Dilke, on various subjects; several things dovetailed in my mind, & at once it struck me, what quality went to form a Man of Achievement especially in Literature & which Shakespeare posessed so enormously—I mean *Negative Capability*, that is when man is capable of being in uncertainties, Mysteries, doubts, without any irritable reaching after fact & reason—Coleridge, for instance, would let go by a fine isolated verisimilitude caught from the Penetralium[6] of mystery, from being incapable of remaining content with half knowledge. This pursued through Volumes would perhaps take us no further than this, that with a great poet the sense of Beauty overcomes every other consideration, or rather obliterates all consideration. Shelley's poem[7] is out & there are words about its being objected too, as much as Queen Mab was. Poor Shelley I think he has his Quota of good qualities, in sooth la!![8] Write soon to your most sincere friend & affectionate Brother

(Signed) John

[4] **Horace Smith . . . Kean:** Poet, novelist, and wit Horace Smith (1779–1849) was an intimate friend of Shelley and Leigh Hunt. His brothers were James and Leonard. Thomas Hill (1760–1840) was a book collector and bon vivant. Edward Dubois (1774–1850) was a wit and man of letters. John Kingston, whom Keats "heartily disliked," was comptroller and then commissioner of stamps. Shakespearean actor Edmund Kean (1789–1833) was the leading tragedian of his day. **Haydon:** See note 3 to "Addressed to the Same."

[5] **Reynolds:** Keats's best friend John Hamilton Reynolds (1794–1852) was a lawyer by profession and a poet by avocation, and introduced Keats to his future publishers James Hessey and John Taylor. **Brown:** Keats's friend (and later host) Charles Armitage Brown (1786–1842). Keats was staying at Brown's house in the north of London when he wrote the great odes of May 1819. From this sentence on, the letter should be dated 27 December or later because the pantomime Keats refers to was held after Christmas (Rollins).

[6] **Penetralium:** Usually used in the plural, *penetralia* means the inner part or inner room.

[7] **Shelley's poem:** Some copies of *Laon and Cythna* had come out early in December 1817.

[8] **in sooth la!!:** Cf. *Antony and Cleopatra,* IV.iv.8: "Sooth, la, I'll help."

from Letter to J. H. Reynolds[1]

3 February 1818
Hampstead Tuesday.

MY DEAR REYNOLDS,

. . . It may be said that we ought to read our Contemporaries. that Wordsworth &c should have their due from us. but for the sake of a few fine imaginative or domestic passages, are we to be bullied into a certain Philosophy engendered in the whims of an Egotist—Every man has his speculations, but every man does not brood and peacock over them till he makes a false coinage and deceives himself—Many a man can travel to the very bourne of Heaven,[2] and yet want confidence to put down his half-seeing. Sancho[3] will invent a Journey heavenward as well

[1] See note 5 to letter to George and Tom Keats.

[2] **the very bourne of Heaven:** Cf. *Hamlet,* III.i.79–80: "The undiscover'd country from whose bourn / No traveller returns."

[3] **Sancho:** The reference is either to Sancho Panzo from *Don Quixote* or to the part of Sancho in the opera *Griselda,* playing at *King's Theatre* in January 1818 (Rollins).

as any body. We hate poetry that has a palpable design upon us—and if we do not agree, seems to put its hand in its breeches pocket. Poetry should be great & unobtrusive, a thing which enters into one's soul, and does not startle it or amaze it with itself but with its subject.—How beautiful are the retired flowers! how would they lose their beauty were they to throng into the highway crying out, "admire me I am a violet! dote upon me I am a primrose! . . . —I will have no more of Wordsworth or Hunt in particular—Why should we be of the tribe of Manasseh, when we can wander with Esau? why should we kick against the Pricks, when we can walk on Roses? Why should we be owls, when we can be Eagles? Why be teased with "nice Eyed wagtails," when we have in sight "the Cherub Contemplation"?—Why with Wordsworths "Matthew with a bough of wilding in his hand" when we can have Jacques[4] "under an oak &c"—The secret of the Bough of Wilding will run through your head faster than I can write it—Old Matthew spoke to him some years ago on some nothing, & because he happens in an Evening Walk to imagine the figure of the old man—he must stamp it down in black & white, and it is henceforth sacred—I don't mean to deny Wordsworth's grandeur & Hunt's merit, but I mean to say we need not be teazed with grandeur & merit—when we can have them uncontaminated & unobtrusive. Let us have the old Poets, & robin Hood Your letter and its sonnets gave me more pleasure than Will the 4th Book of Childe Harold[5] & the whole of any body's life & opinions. In return for your dish of filberts, I have gathered a few Catkins,[6] I hope they'll look pretty.

Y[r] sincere friend and Coscribbler
JOHN KEATS.

[4] **tribe of Manasseh . . . Esau:** cf. Genesis, and Judges 6:15 and 7:23. **Pricks:** Cf. Acts 9:5 and 26:14. **wagtails:** Cf. Leigh Hunt, *Foliage* (1818), xxxiii. **"the Cherub Contemplation":** Cf. Milton, *Il Penseroso,* 54. **Wordsworths "Matthew . . . hand":** Cf. "The Two April Mornings," 59 ff. **Jacques:** *As You Like It,* II.i.31.

[5] **4th Book of Childe Harold:** Byron's fourth canto was published in April 1818.

[6] **filberts:** hazelnuts. **Catkins:** a plant with scaly, drooping leaves, somewhat resembling a cat's tail.

from Letter to John Taylor 27 February 1818

Hampstead 27 Feby-
[London T]

MY DEAR TAYLOR,[1]

. . . It is a sorry thing for me that any one should have to overcome Prejudices in reading my Verses—that affects me more than any hypercriticism on any particular Passage. In *Endymion* I have most likely but moved into the Go-cart from the leading strings.[2] In Poetry I have a few Axioms, and you will see how far I am from their Centre. 1st I think Poetry should surprise by a fine excess and not by Singularity—it should strike the Reader as a wording of his own highest thoughts, and appear almost a Remembrance—2nd Its touches of Beauty should never be half way therby making the reader breathless instead of content: the rise, the progress, the setting of imagery should like the Sun come natural too him—shine over him and set soberly although in magnificence leaving him in the Luxury of twilight—but it is easier to think what Poetry should be than to write it—and this leads me on to another axiom. That if Poetry comes not as naturally as the Leaves to a tree it had better not come at all. . . .

Your sincere and oblig[d] friend
JOHN KEATS—

[1] John Taylor (1781–1864), along with his partner James Augustus Hessey, published *Endymion* (April 1818) and *Lamia, Isabella, the Eve of St. Agnes, and Other Poems* (July 1820).

[2] **Go-cart:** stroller. **leading strings:** strings to support toddlers when beginning to walk.

from Letter to J. H. Reynolds 3 May 1818

Teignmouth May 3[d]

MY DEAR REYNOLDS,

. . . Until we are sick, we understand not;—in fine, as Byron says, "Knowledge is Sorrow";[1] and I go on to say that "Sorrow is Wisdom"—and further for aught we can know for certainty! "Wisdom is folly"

[1] **Byron says . . . Sorrow:** *Manfred,* I.i.10.

. . . I will return to Wordsworth—whether or no he has an extended vision or a circumscribed grandeur—whether he is an eagle in his nest, or on the wing—And to be more explicit and to show you how tall I stand by the giant, I will put down a simile of human life as far as I now perceive it; that is, to the point to which I say we both have arrived at—' Well—I compare human life to a large Mansion of Many Apartments,[2] two of which I can only describe, the doors of the rest being as yet shut upon me—The first we step into we call the infant or thoughtless Chamber, in which we remain as long as we do not think—We remain there a long while, and notwithstanding the doors of the second Chamber remain wide open, showing a bright appearance, we care not to hasten to it; but are at length imperceptibly impelled by the awakening of the thinking principle—within us—we no sooner get into the second Chamber, which I shall call the Chamber of Maiden-Thought, than we become intoxicated with the light and the atmosphere, we see nothing but pleasant wonders, and think of delaying there for ever in delight: However among the effects this breathing is father of is that tremendous one of sharpening one's vision into the ~~head~~ heart and nature of Man—of convincing ones nerves that the World is full of Misery and Heartbreak, Pain, Sickness and oppression—whereby This Chamber of Maiden Thought becomes gradually darken'd and at the same time on all sides of it many doors are set open—but all dark—all leading to dark passages—We see not the ballance of good and evil. We are in a Mist—*We* are now in that state—We feel the "burden of the Mystery,"[3] To this point was Wordsworth come, as far as I can conceive when he wrote 'Tintern Abbey' and it seems to me that his Genius is explorative of those dark Passages. Now if we live, and go on thinking, we too shall explore them. he is a genius and superior [to] us, in so far as he can, more than we, make discoveries, and shed a light in them—Here I must think Wordsworth is deeper than Milton—though I think it has depended more upon the general and gregarious advance of intellect, than individual greatness of Mind . . .

Your affectionate friend
JOHN KEATS

[2] **a large Mansion . . . Apartments**: cf. John 14:2: "In my Father's house are many mansions." Also, Wordsworth's "Tintern Abbey," ll.139–41.*

[3] **"burden of the Mystery"**: cf. Wordsworth, "Tintern Abbey," 38.*

from Letter to Benjamin Bailey 18 July 1818

Inverary July 18th

MY DEAR BAILEY,

. . . I am certain I have not a right feeling towards Women—at this moment I am striving to be just to them but I cannot—Is it because they fall so far beneath my Boyish imagination? When I was a Schoolboy I though[t] a fair Woman a pure Goddess, my mind was a soft nest in which some one of them slept though she knew it not—I have no right to expect more than their reality. I thought them etherial above Men—I find the[m] perhaps equal—great by comparison is very small—Insult may be inflicted in more ways than by Word or action—one who is tender of being insulted does not like to think an insult against another—I do not like to think insults in a Lady's Company—I commit a Crime with her which absence would have not known—Is it not extraordinary? When among Men I have no evil thoughts, no malice, no spleen—I feel free to speak or to be silent—I can listen and from every one I can learn—my hands are in my pockets I am free from all suspicion and comfortable. When I am among Women I have evil thoughts, malice spleen—I cannot speak or be silent—I am full of Suspicions and therefore listen to no thing—I am in a hurry to be gone—You must be charitable and put all this perversity to my being disappointed since Boyhood—Yet with such feelings I am happier alone among Crowds of men, by myself or with a friend or two—With all this trust me Bailey I have not the least idea that Men of different feelings and inclinations are more short sighted than myself—I never rejoiced more than at my Brother's Marriage[1] and shall do so at that of any of my friends—. I must absolutely get over this—but how? The only way is to find the root of evil, and so cure it "with backward mutters of dissevering Power"[2] That is a difficult thing; for an obstinate Prejudice can seldom be produced but from a gordian[3] complication of feelings, which must take time

[1] **my Brother's Marriage**: George married Georgiana Wylie in late May 1818.

[2] **"with backward mutters . . . Power"**: Cf. Milton, *Comus*, 817: "And backward mutters of dissevering power."

[3] **gordian**: The Gordian knot of classical legend was named after the Phrygian peasant Gordius, who tied a yoke to a beam

to unravelled and care to keep unravelled—I could say a good deal about this but I will leave it in hopes of better and more worthy dispositions—and also content that I am wronging no one, for after all I do think better of Womankind than to suppose they care whether Mister John Keats five feet hight likes them or not. You appeard to wish to avoid any words on this subject—don't think it a bore my dear fellow—it shall be my Amen . . .

Your affectionate friend
JOHN KEATS—

from Letter to C. W. Dilke 21 September 1818

MY DEAR DILKE,

. . . —I wish I could say Tom was any better.[1] His identity presses upon me so all day that I am obliged to go out—and although I intended to have given some time to study alone I am obliged to write, and plunge into abstract images to ease myself of his countenance his voice and feebleness—so that I live now in a continual fever—it must be poisonous to life although I feel well. Imagine "the hateful siege of contraries"[2]—if I think of fame of poetry it seems a crime to me, and yet I must do so or suffer—I am sorry to give you pain—I am almost resolv'd to burn this—but I really have not self possession and magninimity enough to manage the thing othe[r]wise—after all it may be a nervousness proceeding from the Mercury[3] . . .

Your sincere friend
JOHN KEATS—

so ingeniously that it was said that whoever could succeed in untying the knot would become the ruler of Asia. Alexander the Great could not untie it, so he cut it with his sword.

[1] Throughout the fall Keats devotedly nursed his brother Tom, who died of tuberculosis in November.

[2] **hateful siege of contraries:** Cf. *Paradise Lost*, IX.119–122: "the more I see / Pleasures about me, so much more I feel / Torment within me, as from the hateful siege / Of contraries."

[3] **Mercury:** At this time Mercury was used as a treatment for syphilis, which Keats believed himself (wrongly, it seems) to be suffering from.

from Letter to Richard Woodhouse 27 October 1818

MY DEAR WOODHOUSE[1]

Your Letter gave me a great satisfaction; more on account of its friendliness, than any relish of that matter in it which is accounted so acceptable in the 'genus irritabile'[2] The best answer I can give you is in a clerklike manner to make some observations on two principle points, which seem to point like indices into the midst of the whole pro and con, about genius, and views and atchievements and ambition and coetera. 1st As to the poetical Character itself, (I mean that sort of which, if I am any thing, I am a Member; that sort distinguished from the wordsworthian or egotistical sublime; which is a thing per se and stands alone[3]) it is not itself—it has no self—it is every thing and nothing—It has no character—it enjoys light and shade; it lives in gusto,[4] be it foul or fair, high or low, rich or poor, mean or elevated—It has as much delight in conceiving an Iago as an Imogen. What shocks the virtuous philosop[h]er, delights the camelion Poet. It does no harm from its relish of the dark side of things any more than from its taste for the bright one; because they both end in speculation. A Poet is the most unpoetical of any thing in existence; because he has no Identity—he is continu-

[1] **Woodhouse:** Lawyer and scholar Richard Woodhouse (1788–1834) was a great admirer of Keats's poetry, and predicted that one day all "Keatsiana" would be invaluable. At the end of Keats's letter, Woodhouse added: "N.B. The above letter was in answer to one which I addressed to Keats on 21 Oct.—on occasion of the malicious & unjust article in the Quarterly Review" (Rollins). The article was a savage review of *Endymion* by John Wilson Croker, who stated he'd been unable to read past Book I, and called Keats a "disciple of the new school of what has been called somewhere Cockney poetry; which may be defined to consist of the most incongruous ideas in the most uncouth language . . ."

[2] **'genus irritabile':** the "irritable race" of poets; Cf. Horace, *Epistles*, II.ii.102.

[3] **a thing per se . . . alone:** Cf. *Troilus and Cressida*, I.ii.15: "They say he is a very man *per se*, / And stands alone."

[4] **gusto:** Cf. Hazlitt, "On Gusto" (1816): "Gusto in art is power or passion defining any object."

ally in for—and filling some other Body—The Sun, the Moon, the Sea and Men and Women who are creatures of impulse are poetical and have about them an unchangeable attribute—the poet has none; no identity—he is certainly the most unpoetical of all God's Creatures. If then he has no self, and if I am a Poet, where is the Wonder that I should say I would ~~right~~ write no more? Might I not at that very instant [have] been cogitating on the Characters of saturn and Ops?[5] It is a wretched thing to confess; but is a very fact that not one word I ever utter can be taken for granted as an opinion growing out of my identical nature—how can it, when I have no nature? When I am in a room with People if I ever am free from speculating on creations of my own brain, then not myself goes home to myself: but the identity of every one in the room begins to to press upon me that, I am in a very little time anhilated—not only among Men; it would be the same in a Nursery of children: I know not whether I make myself wholly understood: I hope enough so to let you see that no dependence is to be placed on what I said that day.

In the second place I will speak of my views, and of the life I purpose to myself—I am ambitious of doing the world some good: if I should be spared that may be the work of maturer years—in the interval I will assay to reach to as high a summit in Poetry as the nerve bestowed upon me will suffer. The faint conceptions I have of Poems to come brings the blood frequently into my forehead—All I hope is that I may not lose all interest in human affairs—that the solitary indifference I feel for applause even from the finest Spirits, will not blunt any acuteness of vision I may have. I do not think it will—I feel assured I should write from the mere yearning and fondness I have for the Beautiful even if my night's labours should be burnt every morning and no eye ever shine upon them. But even now I am perhaps not speaking from myself; but from some character in whose soul I now live. I am sure however that this next sentence is from myself. I feel your anxiety, good opinion and friendliness in the highest degree, and am

Your's most sincerely
JOHN KEATS

[5] **saturn and Ops:** characters in *Hyperion,* which Keats had begun writing in September.

from Letter to George and Georgiana Keats 14 . . . 24 . . . October 1818[1]

MY DEAR GEORGE: . . .

. . . The Miss Reynoldses are very kind to me—but they have lately displeased me much and in this way—Now I am [be]coming the Richardson.[2] On my return, the first day I called they were in a sort of taking or bustle about a Cousin of theirs[3] who having fallen out with her Grandpapa in a serious manner, was invited by Mrs R—— to take Asylum in her house—She is an east indian and ought to be her Grandfather's Heir. At the time I called Mrs R. was in conference with her up stairs and the young Ladies were warm in her praises down stairs calling her genteel, interresting and a thousand other pretty things to which I gave no heed, not being partial to 9 days wonders—Now all is completely changed—they hate her; and from what I hear she is not without faults—of a real kind: but she has othe[r]s which are more apt to make women of inferior charms hate her. She is not a Cleopatra; but she is at least a Charmian.[4] She has a rich eastern look; she has fine eyes and fine manners. When she comes into a room she makes an impression the same as the Beauty of a Leopardess. She is too fine and too concious of her Self to repulse any Man who may address her—from habit she thinks that nothing *particular.*[5] I always find myself more at ease with such a woman; the picture before me always gives me a life and animation which I cannot possibly feel with any thing inferiour—I am at such times too much occupied in admiring to be awkward or on a tremble. I forget myself entirely because I live in her. You will by this time think I am in love with her; so before I go any further I will tell you I am not—she kept me awake one Night as a tune of Mozart's might do—I speak of the

[1] George married Georgiana Wylie in June 1818, after which they left for the United States and settled in Kentucky.

[2] **Miss Reynoldses . . . Richardson:** Jane and Marianne. See the letter to Bailey (22 Nov. 1817, n. 6). *Richardson* suggests the novelist Samuel Richardson, who deals with small matters and intrigues in his fiction.

[3] **a Cousin of theirs:** Jane Cox, born in India.

[4] **Charmian:** Cleopatra's attendant in *Antony and Cleopatra.*

[5] **particular:** flirtatious.

thing as a passtime and an amuzement than which I can feel none deeper than a conversation with an imperial women the very 'yes' and 'no' of whose Lips is to me a Banquet.[6] I dont cry to take the moon home with me in my Pocket no[r] do I fret to leave her behind me. I like her and her like because one has no *sensations*—what we both are is taken for granted—You will suppose I have by this had much talk with her—no such thing—there are the Miss Reynoldses on the look out—They think I dont admire her because I did not stare at her—They call her a flirt to me—What a want of knowledge? she walks across a room in such a manner that a Man is drawn towards her with a magnetic Power. This they call flirting! they do not know things. They do not know what a Woman is. I believe tho' she has faults—the same as Charmian and Cleopatra might have had—Yet she is a fine thing speaking in a worldly way: for there are two distinct tempers of mind in which we judge of things—the worldly, theatrical and pantomimical; and the unearthly, spiritual and etherial—in the former Buonaparte, Lord Byron and this Charmian hold the first place in our Minds; in the latter John Howard, Bishop Hooker[7] rocking his child's cradle and you my dear Sister are the conquering feelings. As a Man in the world I love the rich talk of a Charmian; as an eternal Being I love the thought of you. I should like her to ruin me, and I should like you to save me. Do not think my dear Brother from this that my Passions are head long or likely to be ever of any pain to you—no

"I am free from Men of Pleasure's cares
By dint of feelings far more deep than theirs"

This is Lord Byron,[8] and is one of the finest things he has said—I have no town talk for you, as I have not been much among people—as for Politics they are in my opinion only sleepy because they will soon be too wide awake—Perhaps not—for the long and continued Peace of England itself has given us notions of personal safety which are likely to prevent the reestablishment of our national Honesty—There is of a truth nothing manly or sterling in any part of the Government. There are many Madmen In the Country, I have no doubt, who would like to be beheaded on tower Hill merely for the sake of eclat, there are many Men like Hunt who from a principle of taste would like to see things go on better, there are many like Sir F. Burdett who like to sit at the head of political dinners—but there are none prepared to suffer in obscurity for their Country—the motives of our wo[r]st Men are interest and of our best Vanity—We have no Milton, no Algernon Sidney[9]—Governers in these days loose the title of Man in exchange for that of Diplomat and Minister—We breathe in a sort of Officinal Atmosphere—All the departments of Government have strayed far from Spimpicity[10] which is the greatest of Strength—there is as much difference in this respect between the present Government and oliver Cromwell's, as there is between the 12 Tables of Rome[11] and the volumes of Civil Law which were digested by Justinian. A Man now entitlerd Chancellor has the same honour paid to him whether he be a Hog or a Lord Bacon. No sensation is created by Greatness but by the number of orders a Man has at his Button holes Notwithstand[12] the part which the Liberals take in the Cause of Napoleon I cannot but think he had done more harm to the life of Liberty than any one else could have done: not that the divine right Gentlemen have done or intend to do any good—no they have taken a Lesson of him and will do all the further harm he would have done without any of the good—The worst thing he has done is, that he has taught them how to organize their monstrous armies—The Emperor Alexander it is said intends to divide his Empire as did Diocletian[13]—creating

[6] **Banquet**: cf. *Much Ado about Nothing*, II.iii.21: "his words are a very fantastical banquet."

[7] **John Howard, Bishop Hooker**: prison reformer John Howard (1726–1790) and theologian and author Richard Hooker (1554?–1600), who was not a bishop.

[8] **This is Lord Byron**: not from Byron, but from Leigh Hunt's *The Story of Rimini* (1816) (Rollins).

[9] **Sir F. Burdett**: reformist politician Sir Francis Burdett (1770–1844), later a conservative. **Algernon Sidney**: great-nephew of the poet Sir Phillip Sidney; was a republican leader and martyr (1622–1683). Milton wrote numerous political tracts for the republicans.

[10] **loose**: lose. **Spimpicity**: simplicity.

[11] **Oliver Cromwell**: Oliver Cromwell (1599–1658), republican statesman and commander in chief of the republican forces during the Civil War, installed himself as Lord Protector after dissolving Parliament in 1653, but refused the title of king. **12 Tables of Rome**: the earliest Roman code of laws, drawn up in 451 to 450 BC, whose object was, in part, to reduce patrician privilege. The Roman emperor Justinian (c. 482–565) issued the 50-book *Digesta* in 533.

[12] **Notwithstand**: obsolete variant of "notwithstanding."

[13] **Alexander**: Alexander I of Russia (1777–1825). "Russia is to be divided into three parts, the North, West, and South; over which Alexander will place his three brothers, with the title of

two Czars besides himself, and continuing the supreme Monarch of the whole—Should he do this and they for a series of Years keep peacable among themselves Russia may spread her conquest even to China—I think a very likely thing that China itself may fall Turkey certainly will—Meanwhile european north Russia will hold its horns against the rest of Europe, intrieguing constantly with France. Dilke, whom you know to be a Godwin[14] perfectibil[it]y Man, pleases himself with the idea that America will be the country to take up the human intellect where england leaves off—I differ there with him greatly—A country like the united states whose greatest Men are Franklins and Washingtons will never do that—They are great Men doubtless but how are they to be compared to those our countrey men Milton and the two Sidneys—The one is a philosophical Quaker full of mean and thrifty maxims the other sold the very Charger who had taken him through all his Battles[15]—Those American's are great but they are not sublime Man—the humanity of the United States can never reach the sublime—Brikbeck's[16] mind is too much in the American Stryle [style]—you must endeavour to infuse a little Spirit of another sort into the Settlement, always with great caution, for thereby you may do your descendents more good than you may imagine. If I had a prayer to make for any great good, next to Tom's recovery, it should be that one of your Children should be the first American Poet. I have a great mind to make a prophecy and they say prophecies work out their own fullfillment. . . .

. . . I think Tom has been rather better these few last days—he has been less nervous. I expect Reynolds tomorrow Since I wrote thus far I have met with that same Lady again,[17] whom I saw at Hastings and whom I met when we were going to the English Opera. It was in a street which goes from Bedford Row to Lamb's Conduit Street—I passed her and turrned back—she seemed glad of it; glad to see me and not offended at my passing her before We walked on towards Islington where we called on a friend of her's who keeps a Boarding School. She has always been an enigma to me—she has ~~new~~ been in a Room with you and with Reynolds and wishes we should be acquainted without any of our common acquaintance knowing it. As we went along, some times through shabby, sometimes through decent Street[s] I had my guessing at work, not knowing what it would be and prepared to meet any surprise—First it ended at this Hou{s}e at Islington: on parting from which I pressed to attend her home. She consented and then again my thoughts were at work what it might lead to, tho' now they had received a sort of genteel hint from the Boarding School. Our Walk ended in 34 Gloucester Street Queen Square—not exactly so for we went up stairs into her sitting room—a very tasty sort of place with Books, Pictures a bronze statue of Buonaparte, Music, aeolian Harp; a Parrot a Linnet—A Case of choice Liquers &c &c &. she behaved in the kindest manner—made me take home a Grouse for Tom's dinner—Asked for my address for the purpose of sending more game—As I had warmed with her before and kissed her—I though[t] it would be living backwards not to do so again—she had a better taste: she perceived how much a thing of course it was and shrunk from it—not in a prudish way but in as I say a good taste—She cont[r]ived to disappoint me in a way which made me feel more pleasure than a simple kiss could do—she said I should please her much more if I would only press her hand and go away. Whether she was in a different disposition when I saw her before—or whether I have in fancy wrong'd her I cannot tell—I expect to pass some pleasant hours with her now and then: in which I feel I shall be of service to her in matters of knowledge and taste: if I can I will—I have no libidinous thought about her—she and your George are the only women à près de mon age whom I would be content to know for their mind and friendship alone—I shall in a short time write you as far as I know how I intend to pass my Life—I cannot think of those things now Tom is so unwell and weak. Notwithstand your Happiness and your recommendation I hope I shall

Kings; while he remains supreme head of the whole" (*The Gentleman's Magazine,* September 1818; cited in Rollins). **Diocletian:** In 293 the Roman emperor Diocletian established a "tetrarchy" whereby he and his subordinate, Galerius, ruled in the East, and Maximinian and his subordinate, Constantius Chlorus, ruled in the West.

[14] **Godwin:** Political philosopher and novelist William Godwin* (1756–1836), husband of Mary Wollstonecraft* and father of the future Mary Shelley,* believed that reason taught benevolence, and that man acted according to reason and was perfectible.

[15] **the other sold . . . Battles:** mistaken reference to George Washington's selling of his warhorse Nelson.

[16] **Brikbeck:** English author Morris Birkbeck (1764–1825) founded the town of Albion, IL.

[17] **same Lady again:** probably Mrs. Isabella Jones. The date of the letter here becomes 24 October.

never marry. Though the most beautiful Creature were waiting for me at the end of a Journey or a Walk; though the carpet were of Silk, the Curtains of the morning Clouds; the chairs and Sofa stuffed with Cygnet's down; the food Manna, the Wine beyond Claret, the Window opening on Winander mere, I should not feel—or rather my Happiness would not be so fine, ands my Solitude is sublime. Then instead of what I have described, there is a Sublimity to welcome me home—The roaring of the wind is my wife and the Stars through the window pane are my Children. The mighty abstract Idea I have of Beauty in all things stifles the more divided and minute domestic happiness—an amiable wife and sweet Children I contemplate as a part of that Bea{u}ty. but I must have a thousand of those beautiful particles to fill up my heart. I feel more and more every day, as my imagination strengthens, that I do not live in this world alone but in a thousand worlds—No sooner am I alone than shapes of epic greatness are stationed around me, and serve my Spirit the office of which is equivalent to a king's body guard—then "Tragedy, with scepter'd pall, comes sweeping by"[18] According to my state of mind I am with Achilles shouting in the Trenches or with Theocritus in the Vales of Sicily. Or I throughw my whole being into Triolus[19] and repeating those lines, 'I wander, like a lost soul upon the stygian Banks staying for waftage," I melt into the air with a voluptuousness so delicate that I am content to be alone—These things combined with the opinion I have of the generallity of women—who appear to me as children to whom I would rather give a Sugar Plum than my time, form a barrier against Matrimony which I rejoice in. I have written this that you might see I have my share of the highest pleasures and that though I may choose to pass my days alone I shall be no Solitary. You see therre is nothing spleenical in all this. The only thing that can ever affect me personally for more than one short passing day, is any doubt about my powers for poetry—I seldom have any, and I look with hope to the nighing time when I shall have none. I am as happy as a Man can be—that is in myself I should be happy if Tom was well, and I knew you were passing pleasant days—Then I should be most enviable—with the yearning Passion I have for the beautiful, connected and made one with the ambition of my intellect. Th[i]nk of my Pleasure in Solitude, in comparison of my commerce with the world—there I am a child—there they do not know me not even my most intimate acquaintance—I give into their feelings as though I were refraining from irritating [a] little child—Some think me middling, others silly, others foolish—every one thinks he sees my weak side against my will; when in truth it is with my will—I am content to be thought all this because I have in my own breast so great a resource. This is one great reason why they like me so; because they can all show to advantage in a room, and eclipese from a certain tact one who is reckoned to be a good Poet—I hope I am not here playing tricks 'to make the angels weep':[20] I think not: for I have not the least contempt for my species; and though it may sound paradoxical: my greatest elevations of soul leaves me every time more humbled—Enough of this—though in your Love for me you will not think it enough. . . .

Your anxious and affectionate Brother
JOHN—

[18] **Tragedy . . . sweeping by**: cf. Milton, *Il Penseroso*, 97–98: "Sometime let Gorgeous Tragedy / In Scepter'd Pall come sweeping by."

[19] **Achilles . . . Trenches**: cf. *Iliad*, XVIII.228–29: "Three times across the ditch brilliant Achilleus gave his great cry, / and three times the Trojans and their renowned companions were routed." According to Bailey, this passage was a favorite of Keats's. **Troilus**: cf. *Troilus and Cressida*, III.ii.9–11: "I stalk about her door / Like a strange soul upon the stygian Banks / staying for waftage."

from Letter to George and Georgiana Keats 19 February, 19 March, 15, 21 April 1819

MY DEAR BROTHER & SISTER . . .

. . . I never drink now above three glasses of wine—and never any spirits and water. Though by the bye the other day—Woodhouse took me to his coffee house—and ordered a Bottle of Claret—now I like Claret whenever I can have Claret I must drink it.—'t is the only palate affair that I am at all sensual in—Would it not be a good

[20] **'to make the angels weep'**: cf. *Measure for Measure*, II.ii.121–22: "His glassy essence, . . . / Plays such fantastic tricks before high heaven / As makes the angels weep."

Speck to send you some vine roots—could i[t] be done? I'll enquire—If you could make some wine like Claret to d[r]ink on summer evenings in an arbour! For really 't is so fine—it fills the mouth one's mouth with a gushing freshness—then goes down cool and feverless—then you do not feel it quarelling with your liver—no it is rather a Peace maker and lies as quiet as it did in the grape—then it is as fragrant as the Queen Bee; and the more ethereal Part of it mounts into the brain, not assaulting the cerebral apartments like a bully in a bad house looking for his trul[1] and hurrying from door to door bouncing against the waistcoat; but rather walks like Aladin about his own enchanted palace so gently that you do not feel his step—Other wines of a heavy and spirituous nature transform a Man to a Silenus; this makes him a Hermes—and gives a Woman the soul and imortality of Ariadne for whom Bacchus always kept a good cellar of claret[2]—and even of that he could never persuade her to take above two cups—I said this same Claret is the only palate-passion I have I forgot game I must plead guilty to the breast of a Partridge, the back of a hare, the backbone of a grouse, the wing and side of a Pheasant and a Woodcock *passim* . . . I have not said in any Letter yet a word about my affairs—in a word I am in no despair about them—my poem[3] has not at all succeeded—in the course of a year or so I think I shall try the public again—in a selfish point of view I should suffer my pride and my contempt of public opinion to hold me silent—but for your's and fanny's sake. I will pluck up a spirit, and try again—I have no doubt of success in a course of years if I persevere—but it must be patience—for the Reviews have enervated and made indolent mens minds—few think for themselves—These Reviews too are getting more and more powerful and especially the Quarterly—They are like a superstition which the more it prostrates the Crowd and the longer it continues the more powerful it becomes just in proportion to their increasing weakness—I was in hopes that when people saw, as they must do now, all the trickery and iniquity of these Plagues they would scout them, but no they are like the spectators at the Westminster cock-pit—they like the battle and do not care who wins or who looses . . .

Friday [March] 19th Yesterday I got a black eye—the first time I took a Cr{icket} bat—Brown who is always one's friend in a disaster {app}lied a lee{ch to} the eyelid, and there is no infla{mm}ation this morning though the ball hit me dir{ectl}y on the sight—'t was a white ball—I am glad it was not a clout—This is the second black eye I have had since leaving school—during all my {scho}ol days I never had one at all—we must e{a}t a peck before we die—This morning I am in a sort of temper indolent and supremely careless: I long after a stanza or two of Thompson's[4] Castle of indolence—My passions are all alseep from my having slumbered till nearly eleven and weakened the animal fibre all over me to a delightful sensation about three degrees on this side of faintness—if I had teeth of pearl and the breath of lillies I should call it langour—but as I am I must call it Laziness—In this state of effeminacy the fibres of the brain are relaxed in common with the rest of the body, and to such a happy degree that pleasure has no show of enticement and pain no unbearable frown. Neither Poetry, nor Ambition, nor Love have any alertness of countenance as they pass by me: they seem rather like three figures on a greek vase—a Man and two women—whom no one but myself could distinguish in their disguisement. This is the only happiness; and is a rare instance of advantage in the body overpowering the Mind. I have this moment received a note from Haslam[5] in which he expects the death of his Father who has been for some time in a state of insensibility—his mother bears up he says very well—I shall go to twon tommorrow to see him. This is the world—thus we cannot expect to give way many hours to pleasure—Circumstances are like Clouds continually gathering and bursting—While we are laughing the seed of some trouble is put into ~~he~~ the wide arable land of events—while we are laughing it sprouts is grows and suddenly bears a poison fruit which we must pluck—Even so we have leisure to reason on the misfortunes of our friends; our own touch us too nearly for words. Very few men have ever arrived at

[1] **trul**: for *trull* (prostitute).

[2] **Silenus . . . claret**: Silenus is the jolly, old drunkard of Greek myth, who also served as foster father to Bacchus, the more charming god of epicurean delights and orgies and lover of Ariadne after she had been abandoned, when pregnant, by Theseus. Bacchus gave her a crown of diamonds, which became a constellation after her death. Hermes is Mercury, the crafty and eloquent messenger of the gods and patron of merchants, pickpockets, and thieves.

[3] **my poem**: Reference to *Endymion*.

[4] **Thompson**: James Thomson's *Castle of Indolence* was published in 1748, a few weeks before his death.

[5] **Haslam**: Keats's friend from school days, William Haslam (1795?–1851).

a complete disinterestedness of Mind: very few have been influenced by a pure desire of the benefit of others—in the greater part of the Benefactors ~~of~~ & to Humanity some meretricious motive has sullied their greatness—some melodramatic scenery has facinated them—From the manner in which I feel Haslam's misfortune I perceive how far I am from any humble standard of disinterestedness—Yet this feeling ought to be carried to its highest pitch, as there is no fear of its ever injuring society—which it would do I fear pushed to an extremity—For in wild nature the Hawk would loose his Breakfast of Robins and the Robin his of Worms The Lion must starve as well as the swallow—The greater part of Men make their way with the same instinctiveness, the same unwandering eye from their purposes, the same animal eagerness as the Hawk—The Hawk wants a Mate, so does the Man—look at them both they set about it and procure on[e] in the same manner—They want both a nest and they both set about one in the same manner—they get their food in the same manner—The noble animal Man for his amusement smokes his pipe—the Hawk balances about the Clouds—that is the only difference of their leisures. This it is that makes the Amusement of Life—to a speculative Mind. I go among the Feilds and catch a glimpse of a stoat or a fieldmouse peeping out of the withered grass—the creature hath a purpose and its eyes are bright with it—I go amongst the buildings of a city and I see a Man hurrying along—to what? The Creature has a purpose and his eyes are bright with it. But then as Wordsworth says, "we have all one human heart"[6]—there is an ellectric fire in human nature tending to purify—so that among these human creature[s] there is continully some birth of new heroism—The pity is that we must wonder at it: as we should at finding a pearl in rubbish—I have no doubt that thousands of people never heard of have had hearts comp[l]etely disinterested: I can remember but two—Socrates and Jesus—their Histories evince it—What I heard a little time ago, Taylor[7] observe with respect to Socrates, may be said of Jesus—That he was so great a~~s~~ man that though he transmitted no writing of his own to posterity, we have his Mind and his sayings and his greatness handed to us by others. It is to be lamented that the history of the latter was written and revised by Men interested in the pious frauds of Religion. Yet through all this I see his splendour. Even here though I myself am pursueing the same instinctive course as the veriest human animal you can think of—I am however young writing at random—straining at particles of light in the midst of a great darkness—without knowing the bearing of any one assertion of any one opinion. Yet may I not in this be free from sin? May there not be superior beings amused with any graceful, though instinctive attitude my mind m[a]y fall into, as I am entertained with the alertness of a Stoat or the anxiety of a Deer? Though a quarrel in the streets is a thing to be hated, the energies displayed in it are fine; the commonest Man shows a grace in his quarrel—By a superior being our reasoning[s] may take the same tone—though erroneous they may be fine—This is the very thing in which consists poetry; and if so it is not so fine a thing as philosophy—For the same reason that an eagle is not so fine a thing as a truth—Give me this credit—Do you not think I strive—to know myself? Give me this credit—and you will not think that on my own accou[n]t I repeat Milton's lines

> "How charming is divine Philosophy
> Not harsh and crabbed as dull fools suppose
> But musical as is Apollo's lute"—[8]

No—no for myself—feeling grateful as I do to have got into a state of mind to relish them properly—Nothing ever becomes real till it is experienced—Even a Proverb is no proverb to you till Your Life has illustrated it . . .

[15 April]

Last Sunday I took a Walk towards highgate[9] and in the lane that winds by the side of Lord Mansfield's park I met Mr Green[10] our Demonstrator at Guy's in conversation with Coleridge—I joined them, after enquiring by a look whether it would be agreeable—I walked with him a[t] his alderman-after dinner pace for near two miles I suppose In those two Miles he broached a thousand things—let me see if I can give you a list—Nightingales, Poetry—on Poetical sensation—Metaphysics—Different

[6] **"we have all one human heart"**: cf. Wordsworth, "The Old Cumberland Beggar," line 153: "we have all of us one human heart."

[7] **Taylor**: Keats's publisher and friend John Taylor.

[8] From Milton, *Comus*, 475–77.

[9] **highgate**: a district in the north of London, near Hampstead, where Keats was staying at the time (in Brown's house).

[10] **Mr Green**: From 1815 to 1816 Keats studied at Guy's Hospital in London to become an apothecary and surgeon. **Demonstrator**: Joseph Henry Green (1791–1863) was Keats's "demonstrator" or teaching assistant. Green later became Coleridge's literary executor.

genera and species of Dreams—Nightmare—a dream accompanied ~~with~~ by a sense of touch—single and double touch—A dream related—First and second consciousness—the difference explained between will and Volition—so m[an]y metaphysicians from a want of smoking the second consciousness—Monsters—the Kraken[11]—Mermaids—southey believes in them—southeys belief too much diluted—A Ghost story—Good morning—I heard his voice as he came towards me—I heard it as he moved away—I had heard it all the interval—if it may be called so. He was civil enough to ask me to call on him at Highgate Good Night! . . .

[21 April]

I have been reading lately two very different books Robertson's America and Voltaire's Siecle De Louis xiv It is like walking arm and arm between Pizarro and the great-little Monarch.[12] In How lementabl[e] a case do we see the great body of the people in both instances: in the first, where Men might seem to inherit quiet of Mind from unsophisticated senses; from uncontamination of civilisation; and especially from their being as it were estranged from the mutual helps of Society and its mutual injuries—and thereby more immediately under the Protection of Providence—even there they had mortal pains to bear as bad; or even worse than Baliffs, Debts and Poverties of civilised Life—The whole appears to resolve into this—that Man is originally 'a poor forked creature'[13] subject to the same mischances as the beasts of the forest, destined to hardships and disquietude of some kind or other. If he improves by degrees his bodily accomodations and comforts—at each stage, at each accent there are waiting for him a fresh set of annoyances—he is mortal and there is still a heaven with its Stars abov[e] his head. The most interesting question that can come before us is, How far by the persevering endeavours of a seldom appearing Socrates Mankind may be made happy—I can imagine such happiness carried to an extreme—but what must it end in?—Death—and who could in such a case bear with death—the whole troubles of life which are now frittered away in a series of years, would the[n] be accumulated for the last days of a being who instead of hailing its approach, would leave this world as Eve left Paradise—But in truth I do not at all believe in this sort of perfectibility—the nature of the world will not admit of it—the inhabitants of the world will correspond to itself—Let the fish philosophise the ice away from the Rivers in winter time and they shall be at continual play in the tepid delight of summer. Look at the Poles and at the sands of Africa, Whirlpools and volcanoes—Let men exterminate them and I will say that they may arrive at earthly Happiness—The point at which Man may arrive is as far as the paralel state in inanimate nature and no further—For instance suppose a rose to have sensation, it blooms on a beautiful morning it enjoys itself—but there comes a cold wind, a hot sun—it can not escape it, it cannot destroy its annoyances—they are as native to the world as itself: no more can man be happy in spite, the world[l]y elements will prey upon his nature—The common cognomen of this world among the misguided and superstitious is 'a vale of tears'[14] from which we are to be redeemed by a certain arbitary interposition of God and taken to Heaven—What a little circumscribe[d] straightened notion! Call the world if you Please "'The vale of Soul-making" Then you will find out the use of the world (I am speaking now in the highest terms for human nature admitting it to be immortal which I will here take for granted for the purpose of showing a thought which has struck me concerning it) I say *'Soul making'* Soul as distinguished from an Intelligence—There may be intelligences or sparks of the divinity in millions—but they are not Souls ~~the~~ till they acquire identities, till each one is personally itself. I[n]telligences are atoms of perception—they know and they see and they are pure, in short they are God—how then are Souls to be made? How then are these sparks which are God to have identity given them—so as ever to possess a bliss peculiar to each ones individual existence? How, but by the medium of a world like this? This point I sincerely wish to consider because I think it a grander system of salvation than the chrysteain religion—or rather it is a system of Spirit-creation—This is effected by three grand materials

---

[11] **Kraken**: a mythical Norwegian sea beast.

[12] **Robertson's America**: *The History of America* (1777) by William Robertson (1721–1793) was one of the sources of "On First Looking into Chapman's Homer." **Siècle De Louis xiv**: the greatest historical work of the French author Voltaire (1694–1778). **Pizarro**: Francisco Pizarro (c. 1475–1541) conquered Peru for the Spanish. **great-little Monarch**: reference to Louis, who was called "Louis the Great."

[13] **'a poor forked creature'**: cf. *King Lear*, III.ii.106–108: "unaccomodated man is no more but such a poor, bare, fork'd animal as thou art."

[14] **'a vale of tears'**: possibly from Shelley, "Hymn to Intellectual Beauty,"* l. 17: "This dim vast vale of Tears."

acting the one upon the other for a series of years—These three Materials are the *Intelligence*—the *human heart* (as distinguished from intelligence or Mind) and the *World* or *Elemental space* suited for the proper action of *Mind and Heart* on each other for the purpose of forming the *Soul* or *Intelligence destined to possess the sense of Identity.* I can scarcely express what I but dimly perceive—and yet I think I perceive it—that you may judge the more clearly I will put it in the most homely form possible—I will call the *world* a School instituted for the purpose of teaching little children to read—I will call the *human heart* the *horn Book* used in that School—and I will call the *Child able to read, the Soul* made from that *school* and its *hornbook.* Do you not see how necessary a World of Pains and troubles is to school an Intelligence and make it a soul? A Place where the heart must feel and suffer in a thousand diverse ways! Not merely is the Heart a Hornbook, It is the Minds Bible, it is the Minds experience, it is the teat from which the Mind or intelligence sucks its identity—As various as the Lives of Men are—so various become their souls, and thus does God make individual beings, Souls, Identical Souls of the sparks of his own essence—This appears to me a faint sketch of a system of Salvation which does not affront our reason and humanity—I am convinced that many difficulties which christians labour under would vanish before it—There is one wh[i]ch even now Strikes me—the Salvation of Children—In them the Spark or intelligence returns to God without any identity—it having had no time to learn of, and be altered by, the heart—or seat of the human Passions—It is pretty generally suspected that the chr[i]stian scheme has been coppied from the ancient persian and greek Philosophers. Why may they not have made this simple thing even more simple for common apprehension by introducing Mediators and Personages in the same manner as in the hethen mythology abstractions are personified—Seriously I think it probable that this System of Soul-making—may have been the Parent of all the more palpable and personal Schemes of Redemption, among the Zoroastrians the Christians and the Hindoos. For as one part of the human species must have their carved Jupiter; so another part must have the palpable and named Mediator and saviour, their Christ their Oromanes and their Vishnu[15]—If what I have said should not be plain enough, as I fear it may not be, I will [p]ut you in the place where I began in this series of thoughts—I mean, I began by seeing how man was formed by circumstances—and what are circumstances?—but touchstones of his heart—? and what are touch stones?—but proovings of his hearrt?—and what are proovings of his heart but fortifiers or alterers of his nature? and what is his altered nature but his soul?—and what was his soul before it came into the world and had These provings and alterations and perfectionings?—An intelligences—without Identity—and how is this Identity to be made? Through the medium of the Heart? And how is the heart to become this Medium but in a world of Circumstances?—There now I think what with Poetry and Theology you may thank your Stars that my pen is not very long winded . . .

Your ever Affectionate Brother
(SIGNED) JOHN KEATS—

[15] **Zoroastrians:** Zoroastrianism, an early monotheistic religion based on the dualistic opposition of good and evil spirits, arose in Persia in the sixth century BC from the teachings of the prophet Zoroaster (c. 628–c. 551 BC). **Oromanes:** Keats had read "The History of the Merchant Abudah; Or, The Talisman of Oromanes," in James Ridley's 1764 collection *The Tales of the Genii;* a theatrical production of the story was presented at Drury Lane in April and May of 1819 (Rollins). **Vishnu:** in Hinduism, one of the three aspects of the supreme Godhead (the others being Siva and Brahma).

from Letter to Fanny Brawne[1] 25 July 1819

Sunday Night

MY SWEET GIRL,

. . . Forgive me if I wander a little this evening, for I have been all day employ'd in a very abstr[a]ct Poem[2] and I am in deep love with you—two things which must excuse

[1] Keats first met Frances Brawne (1800–1865) in August or September 1818, after returning from his walking tour with Brown (who had let his half of the house to Fanny's mother and her children while he and Keats were away). Keats quickly fell in love, and they were informally engaged on Christmas Day. In the spring of 1819 the Brawnes moved next door, into the other half of Wentworth Place (also occupied by the Dilkes). After Keats left for Italy in Sept. 1820, he never wrote to Fanny again, and could not bear to look at her letters to him, which were placed (unopened) in his coffin.

[2] **abstr[a]ct Poem:** presumably, the revised version of *Hyperion,* entitled *The Fall of Hyperion. A Dream.**

me. I have, believe me, not been an age in letting you take possession of me; the very first week I knew you I wrote myself your vassal; but burnt the Letter as the very next time I saw you I thought you manifested some dislike to me. If you should ever feel for Man at the first sight what I did for you, I am lost. Yet I should not quarrel with you, but hate myself if such a thing were to happen—only I should burst if the thing were not as fine as a Man as you are as a Woman. Perhaps I am too vehement, then fancy me on my knees, especially when I mention a part of you Letter which hurt me; you say speaking of Mr. Severn[3] "but you must be satisfied in knowing that I admired you much more than your friend." My dear love, I cannot believe there ever was or ever could be any thing to admire in me especially as far as sight goes—I cannot be admired, I am not a thing to be admired. You are, I love you; all I can bring you is a swooning admiration of your Beauty. I hold that place among Men which snubnos'd brunettes with meeting eyebrows do among women—they are trash to me—unless I should find one among them with a fire in her heart like the one that burns in mine. You absorb me in spite of myself—you alone: for I look not forward with any pleasure to what is call'd being settled in the world; I tremble at domestic cares—yet for you I would meet them, though if it would leave you the happier I would rather die than do so. I have two luxuries to brood over in my walks, your Loveliness and the hour of my death. O that I could have possession of them both in the same minute. I hate the world: it batters too much the wings of my self-will, and would I could take a sweet poison from your lips to send me out of it. From no others would I take it. I am indeed astonish'd to find myself so careless of all cha[r]ms but yours—remembring as I do the time when even a bit of ribband was a matter of interest with me. What softer words can I find for you after this—what it is I will not read. Nor will I say more here, but in a Postscript answer any thing else you may have mentioned in your Letter in so many words—for I am distracted with a thousand thoughts. I will imagine you Venus tonight and pray, pray, pray to your star like a Hethen.

Your's ever, fair Star,
JOHN KEATS.

[3] **Mr. Severn**: Keats's friend, the artist Joseph Severn (1793–1879), who later accompanied him to Italy.

from Letter to J. H. Reynolds 21 September 1819

Winchester, Tuesday

MY DEAR REYNOLDS,

. . . How beautiful the season is now—How fine the air. A temperate sharpness about it. Really, without joking, chaste weather—Dian skies—I never lik'd stubble fields so much as now—Aye better than the chilly green of the spring. Somehow a stubble plain looks warm—in the same way that some pictures look warm—this struck me so much in my sunday's walk that I composed upon it. I hope you are better employed than in gaping after weather. I have been at different times so happy as not to know what weather it was—No I will not copy a parcel of verses. I always somehow associate Chatterton[1] with autumn. He is the purest writer in the English Language. He has no French idiom, or particles like Chaucers—'tis genuine English Idiom in English words. I have given up Hyperion—there were too many Miltonic inversions in it—Miltonic verse cannot be written but in an artful or rather artist's humour. I wish to give myself up to other sensations. English ought to be kept up. It may be interesting to you to pick out some lines from Hyperion and put a mark × to the false beauty proceeding from art, and one || to the true voice of feeling. Upon my soul 'twas imagination I cannot make the distinction—Every now & then there is a Miltonic intonation—But I cannot make the division properly. . . .

Ever your affectionate friend
JOHN KEATS—

[1] **Chatterton**: The precocious poetic fabricator Thomas Chatterton (1752–1770) is best known as the author of the "Rowley poems," purporting to be the work of an imaginary fifteenth-century monk, Thomas Rowley, for which Chatterton also fabricated various background documents. In severe poverty, Chatterton committed suicide with arsenic at the age of 18 in a London garrett.

from Letter to George and Georgiana Keats
17, 18 . . . 24 . . . September 1819

Winchester Septr Friday

MY DEAR GEORGE,

. . . My name with the literary fashionables is vulgar—I am a weaver boy to them—a Tragedy would lift me out of this mess. And mess it is as far as it regards our Pockets—But be not cast down any more than I am. I feel I can bear real ills better than imaginary ones. Whenever I find myself growing vapourish, I rouse myself, wash and put on a clean shirt brush my hair and clothes, tie my shoestrings neatly and in fact adonize[1] as I were going out—then all clean and comfortable I sit down to write. This I find the greatest relief—Besides I am becoming accustom'd to the privations of the pleasures of sense. In the midst of the world I live like a Hermit. I have forgot how to lay plans for enjoyment of any Pleasure. I feel I can bear any thing, any misery, even imp[r]isonment—so long as I have neither wife nor child. . . . Nothing strikes me so forcibly with a sense of the rediculous as love—A Man in love I do think cuts the sorryest figure in the world—Even when I know a poor fool to be really in pain about it, I could burst out laughing in his face—His pathetic visage becomes irrisistable. Not that I take Haslam[2] as a pattern for Lovers—he is a very worthy man and a good friend. His love is very amusing. Somewhere in the Spectator[3] is related an account of a Man inviting a party of stutter[e]rs and squinters to his table. 't would please me more to scrape together a party of Lovers, not to dinner—no to tea. The[re] would be no fighting as among Knights of old . . .

[18 September 1819] Saturday

With my inconstant disposition it is no wonder that this morning, amid all our bad times and misfortunes, I should feel so alert and well spirited. At this moment you are perhaps in a very different state of Mind. It is because my hopes are very paramount to my despair. I have been reading over a part of a short poem I have composed lately call'd 'Lamia'[4]—and I am certain there is that sort of fire in it which must take hold of people in some way—give them either pleasant or unpleasant sensation. What they want is a sensation of some sort. . . . On the next Street [sheet, of paper] I will give you a little politics. In every age there has been in England for some two or th[r]ee centuries subjects of great popular interest on the carpet: so that however great the uproar one can scarcely prophesy any material change in the government; for as loud disturbances have agitated this country many times. All civil[iz]ed countries become gradually more enlighten'd and there should be a continual change for the better. Look at this Country at present and remember it when it was even though[t] impious to doubt the justice of a trial by Combat—From that time there has been a gradual change—Three great changes have been in progress—First for the better, next for the worse, and a third time for the better once more. The first was the gradual annihilation of the tyranny of the nobles. when kings found it their interest to conciliate the common people, elevate them and be just to them. Just when baronial Power ceased and before standing armies were so dangerous, Taxes were few. kings were lifted by the people over the heads of their nobles, and those people held a rod over kings. The change for the worse in Europe was again this. The obligation of kings to the Multitude began to be forgotten—Custom had made noblemen the humble servant of kings—Then kings turned to the Nobles as the adorners of the[i]r power, the slaves of it, and from the people as creatures continually endeavouring to check them. Then in every kingdom therre was a long struggle of kings to destroy all popular privileges. The english were the only people in europe who made a grand kick at this. They were slaves to Henry 8th but were freemen under william 3rd at the time the french were abject slaves under Lewis 14th. The example of England, and the liberal writers of france and england sowed the seed of opposition to this Tyranny—and it was swelling in the ground till it burst out in the french revolution—That has had an unlucky termination. It put a stop to the rapid progress of free sentiments in England; and gave our Court hopes of turning back to the despotism of the 16

[1] **adonize:** act like Adonis (Venus's lover).

[2] **Haslam:** see the letter to George and Georgiana Keats (19 Feb.–21 April 1819), n. 5.

[3] **the Spectator:** a popular daily literary periodical edited, and largely written, by Sir Richard Steele (1672–1729) and Joseph Addison (1672–1719) from March 1711 to December 1712, and revived by Addison in 1714. The issue Keats refers to is No. 371, 6 May 1712 (Rollins).

[4] **'Lamia':** Keats began *Lamia* at the end of June, and finished it in early September.

century. They have made a handle of this event in every way to undermine our freedom. They spread a horrid superstition against all inovation and improvement—The present struggle in England of the people is to destroy this superstition. What has rous'd them to do it is their distresses—Perpaps on this account the pres'ent distresses of this nation are a fortunate thing—tho so horrid in the[i]r experience. You will see I mean that the french Revolution put a temporry stop to this third change, the change for the better—Now it is in progress again and I thing in an effectual one. This is no contest beetween whig and tory—but between right and wrong. There is scarcely a grain of party spirit now in England—Right and Wrong considered by each man abstractedly is the fashion. I know very little of these things. I am convinced however that apparently small causes make great alterations. There are little signs wherby we may know how matters are going on—This makes the business about Carlisle the Bookseller of great moment in my mind. He has been selling deistical pamphlets, republished Tom Payne[5] and many other works held in superstitious horror. He even has been selling for some time immense numbers of a work call 'The Deist' which comes out in weekly numbers—For this Conduct he I think has had above a dozen ~~Prosecutions~~ inditements issued against him; for which he has found Bail to the amount of many thousand Pounds—After all they are affraid to prosecute: they are affraid of his defence: it ~~will~~ would be published in all the papers all over the Empire: they shudder at this: the Trials would light a flame they could not extinguish. Do you not think this of great import? You will hear by the papers of the proceedings at Manchester and Hunt's triumphal entry[6] into London—I would take me a whole day and a quire of paper to give you any thing like detail—I will merely mention that it is calculated that 30.000 people were in the streets waiting for him—The whole distance from the Angel Islington to the Crown and anchor[7] was lined with Multitudes. . . .

[24 September 1819]

In the course of a few months I shall be as good an Italian Scholar as I am a french one—I am reading Ariosto[8] at present: not manageing more than six or eight stanzas at a time. When I have done this language so as to be able to read it tolerably well—I shall set myself to get complete in latin and there my learning must stop. I do not think of venturing upon Greek. I would not go even so far if I were not persuaded of the power the knowledge of any language gives one. the fact is I like to be acquainted with foreign languages. It is besides a nice way of filling up intervals &c Also the reading of Dante in [is] well worth the while. And in latin there is a fund of curious literature of the middle ages—The Works of many great Men Aretine and Sanazarius and Machievel[9]—I shall never become attach'd to a foreign idiom so as to put it into my writings. The Paradise lost though so fine in itself is a curruption of our Language—it should be kept as it is unique—a curiosity. a beautiful and grand Curiosity. The most remarkable Production of the world—A northern dialect accommodating itself to greek and latin inversions and intonations. The purest english I think—or what ought to be the purest—is Chatterton's[10]—The Language had existed long enough to be entirely uncorrupted of Chaucer's gallicisms and still the old words are used—Chatterton's language is entirely northern—I prefer the native music of it to Milton's cut by feet I have but lately stood on my guard against Milton. Life to him would be death to me. Miltonic verse cannot be written but it the vein of art—I wish to devote myself to another sensation . . .

[5] **Carlisle the Bookseller**: Richard Carlile (1790–1843) was arrested for republishing Paine's *Age of Reason* and Palmer's *Principles of Deism*. He received a fine of £1500 and three years' imprisonment. **deistical**: from deism, a religion based on human reason which rejected the notion of supernatural intervention. **Tom Payne**: Thomas Paine.*

[6] . . . **Hunt's triumphal entry**: On 16 August 1819, reformist and radical workers, many of them veterans of the Battle of Waterloo, gathered at St. Peter's Field in Manchester. The meeting was brutally dispersed by the military; 11 were killed, and 400 wounded. The incident was dubbed the "Peterloo Massacre." The politician Henry Hunt (1773–1835) presided at the gathering, and was arrested and released on bail.

[7] **Angel Islington**: Islington is a district in the north of London. **Crown and anchor**: formerly a tavern in the Strand; the distance between Islington and the tavern was about three miles.

[8] **Ariosto**: Italian poet Ludovico Ariosto (1474–1533), author of *Orlando Furioso* (1516).

[9] **Aretine**: Pietro Aretino (1492–1556), satirical libertine poet. **Sanazarius**: Italian writer Jacopo Sannazaro (1458–1530), author of *Arcadia* (1504), a prototype of the modern prose pastoral. **Machievel**: Niccolo Machiavelli (1469–1527), Italian political philosopher, best known as the author of *The Prince* (1513).

[10] **Chatterton's**: See the letter to Reynolds (21 September 1819), n. 1.

from THE INDICATOR
(1820)

La Belle Dame sans Mercy[1]
(1820; comp. 1819)

1

Ah, what can ail thee, wretched wight,
Alone and palely loitering;
The sedge[2] is wither'd from the lake,
And no birds sing.

2

Ah, what can ail thee, wretched wight,
So haggard and so woe-begone?
The squirrel's granary is full,
And the harvest's done.

3

I see a lilly on thy brow,
With anguish moist and fever dew;
And on thy cheek a fading rose
Fast withereth too.

4

I met a lady in the meads[3]
Full beautiful, a faery's child;
Her hair was long, her foot was light,
And her eyes were wild.

5

I set her on my pacing steed,
And nothing else saw all day long;
For sideways would she lean, and sing
A faery's song.

6

I made a garland for her head,
And bracelets too, and fragrant zone;[4]
She look'd at me as she did love,
And made sweet moan.

7

She found me roots of relish sweet,
And honey wild, and manna dew;
And sure in language strange she said,
I love thee true.

8

She took me to her elfin grot,
And there she gaz'd and sighed deep,
And there I shut her wild sad eyes—
So kiss'd to sleep.

9

And there we slumber'd on the moss,
And there I dream'd, ah woe betide,
The latest[5] dream I ever dream'd
On the cold hill side.

10

I saw pale kings, and princes too,
Pale warriors, death-pale were they all;
Who cry'd—"La belle Dame sans mercy
Hath thee in thrall!"

11

I saw their starv'd lips in the gloom
With horrid warning gaped wide,
And I awoke, and found me here
On the cold hill side.

12

And this is why I sojourn here
Alone and palely loitering,
Though the sedge is wither'd from the lake,
And no birds sing.

---

[1] The title is probably taken from the poem of the same title by French writer and diplomat Alain Chartier (c. 1385–after 1433). The text reproduced here is that of Leigh Hunt's *Indicator* for 10 May 1820, a short-lived but widely read periodical of 1819–1821. See *Life, Letters, and Literary Remains* (1848)* for the later version.

[2] **sedge:** a marsh grass.

[3] **meads:** meadows.

[4] **fragrant zone:** a girdle or belt made of flowers.

[5] **latest:** last.

from LAMIA, ISABELLA, THE EVE OF ST. AGNES, AND OTHER POEMS

(1820)

The Eve of St. Agnes[1]

(1820; comp. 1819)

1

St. Agnes' Eve—Ah, bitter chill it was!
The owl, for all his feathers, was a-cold;
The hare limp'd trembling through the frozen grass,
And silent was the flock in woolly fold:
Numb were the Beadsman's fingers, while he told[2]
His rosary, and while his frosted breath,
Like pious incense from a censer old,
Seem'd taking flight for heaven, without a death,
Past the sweet Virgin's picture, while his prayer he saith.

2

His prayer he saith, this patient, holy man;
Then takes his lamp, and riseth from his knees,
And back returneth, meagre, barefoot, wan,
Along the chapel aisle by slow degrees:
The sculptur'd dead, on each side, seem to freeze,
Emprison'd in black, purgatorial rails:
Knights, ladies, praying in dumb orat'ries,
He passeth by; and his weak spirit fails
To think how they may ache in icy hoods and mails.

3

Northward he turneth through a little door,
And scarce three steps, ere Music's golden tongue
Flatter'd to tears this aged man and poor;
But no—already had his deathbell rung;
The joys of all his life were said and sung:
His was harsh penance on St. Agnes' Eve:
Another way he went, and soon among
Rough ashes sat he for his soul's reprieve,
And all night kept awake, for sinners' sake to grieve.

4

That ancient Beadsman heard the prelude soft;
And so it chanc'd, for many a door was wide,
From hurry to and fro. Soon, up aloft,
The silver, snarling trumpets 'gan to chide:
The level chambers, ready with their pride,
Were glowing to receive a thousand guests:
The carved angels, ever eager-eyed,
Star'd, where upon their heads the cornice rests,
With hair blown back, and wings put cross-wise on their breasts.

5

At length burst in the argent revelry,[3]
With plume, tiara, and all rich array,
Numerous as shadows haunting fairily
The brain, new stuff'd, in youth, with triumphs gay
Of old romance. These let us wish away,
And turn, sole-thoughted, to one Lady there,
Whose heart had brooded, all that wintry day,
On love, and wing'd St. Agnes' saintly care,
As she had heard old dames full many times declare.

6

They told her how, upon St. Agnes' Eve,
Young virgins might have visions of delight,
And soft adorings from their loves receive
Upon the honey'd middle of the night,
If ceremonies due they did aright;
As, supperless to bed they must retire,
And couch supine their beauties, lily white;
Nor look behind, nor sideways, but require[4]
Of heaven with upward eyes for all that they desire.

---

[1] Keats's narrative is based on the popular superstition that if a maiden performed certain rites on January 20, St. Agnes' Eve, she would have a dream revealing the identity of her future husband. Stanza 6 lists some of the rites. The setting, familial conflicts, and characters of Keats's poem are reminiscent of *Romeo and Juliet.*

[2] **Beadsman:** one hired to pray for his benefactor's family and friends. **told:** counted, or prayed the "Hail Mary" on each bead of the rosary.

[3] **argent revelry:** reference to the brightly dressed revelers in silvery apparel.

[4] **require:** ask.

7

Full of this whim was thoughtful Madeline:
The music, yearning like a god in pain,
She scarcely heard: her maiden eyes divine,
Fix'd on the floor, saw many a sweeping train
Pass by—she heeded not at all: in vain
Came many a tiptoe, amorous cavalier,
And back retir'd, not cool'd by high disdain;
But she saw not: her heart was otherwhere:
She sigh'd for Agnes' dreams, the sweetest of the year.

8

She danc'd along with vague, regardless eyes,
Anxious her lips, her breathing quick and short:
The hallow'd hour was near at hand: she sighs
Amid the timbrels[5] and the throng'd resort
Of whisperers in anger, or in sport;
'Mid looks of love, defiance, hate, and scorn,
Hoodwink'd with faery fancy; all amort,[6]
Save to St. Agnes and her lambs unshorn,
And all the bliss to be before to-morrow morn.

9

So, purposing each moment to retire,
She linger'd still. Meantime, across the moors,
Had come young Porphyro, with heart on fire
For Madeline. Beside the portal doors,
Buttress'd from moonlight, stands he, and implores
All saints to give him sight of Madeline,
But for one moment in the tedious hours,
That he might gaze and worship all unseen;
Perchance speak, kneel, touch, kiss—in sooth such things have been.

10

He ventures in: let no buzz'd whisper tell:
All eyes be muffled, or a hundred swords
Will storm his heart, Love's fev'rous citadel:
For him, those chambers held barbarian hordes,
Hyena foemen, and hot-blooded lords,
Whose very dogs would execrations howl
Against his lineage: not one breast affords
Him any mercy, in that mansion foul,
Save one old beldame,[7] weak in body and in soul.

[5] **timbrels:** tambourines.

[6] **amort:** oblivious.

[7] **beldame:** nurse.

11

Ah, happy chance! the aged creature came,
Shuffling along with ivory-headed wand,
To where he stood, hid from the torch's flame,
Behind a broad hall-pillar, far beyond
The sound of merriment, and chorus bland:
He startled her; but soon she knew his face,
And grasp'd his fingers in her palsied hand,
Saying, "Mercy, Porphyro! hie thee from this place;
They are all here to-night, the whole blood-thirsty race!

12

"Get hence! get hence! there's dwarfish Hildebrand;
He had a fever late, and in the fit
He cursed thee and thine, both house and land:
Then there's that old Lord Maurice, not a whit
More tame for his gray hairs—Alas me! flit!
Flit like a ghost away."—"Ah, gossip dear,
We're safe enough; here in this arm-chair sit,
And tell me how"—"Good Saints! not here, not here;
Follow me, child, or else these stones will be thy bier."

13

He follow'd through a lowly arched way,
Brushing the cobwebs with his lofty plume,
And as she mutter'd "Well-a—well-a-day!"[8]
He found him in a little moonlight room,
Pale, lattic'd, chill, and silent as a tomb.
"Now tell me where is Madeline," said he,
"O tell me, Angela, by the holy loom
Which none but secret sisterhood may see,
When they St. Agnes' wool are weaving piously."

14

"St. Agnes! Ah! it is St. Agnes' Eve—
Yet men will murder upon holy days:
Thou must hold water in a witch's sieve,
And be liege-lord of all the Elves and Fays,
To venture so: it fills me with amaze
To see thee, Porphyro!—St. Agnes' Eve!

[8] **well-a-day:** an expression of sorrow or lamentation. cf. Coleridge's *Christabel,** 264.

God's help! my lady fair the conjuror plays
This very night: good angels her deceive!
But let me laugh awhile, I've mickle[9] time to grieve."

15

Feebly she laugheth in the languid moon,
While Porphyro upon her face doth look,
Like puzzled urchin on an aged crone
Who keepeth clos'd a wond'rous riddle-book,
As spectacled she sits in chimney nook.
But soon his eyes grew brilliant, when she told
His lady's purpose; and he scarce could brook
Tears, at the thought of those enchantments cold,
And Madeline asleep in lap of legends old.

16

Sudden a thought came like a full-blown rose,
Flushing his brow, and in his pained heart
Made purple riot: then doth he propose
A stratagem, that makes the beldame start:
"A cruel man and impious thou art:
Sweet lady, let her pray, and sleep, and dream
Alone with her good angels, far apart
From wicked men like thee. Go, go!—I deem
Thou canst not surely be the same that thou didst seem."

17

"I will not harm her, by all saints I swear,"
Quoth Porphyro: "O may I ne'er find grace
When my weak voice shall whisper its last prayer,
If one of her soft ringlets I displace,
Or look with ruffian passion in her face:
Good Angela, believe me by these tears;
Or I will, even in a moment's space,
Awake, with horrid shout, my foemen's ears,
And beard[10] them, though they be more fang'd than wolves and bears."

18

"Ah! why wilt thou affright a feeble soul?
A poor, weak, palsy-stricken, churchyard thing,
Whose passing-bell may ere the midnight toll;
Whose prayers for thee, each morn and evening,
Were never miss'd."—Thus plaining,[11] doth she bring
A gentler speech from burning Porphyro;
So woful, and of such deep sorrowing,
That Angela gives promise she will do
Whatever he shall wish, betide her weal or woe.

19

Which was, to lead him, in close secrecy,
Even to Madeline's chamber, and there hide
Him in a closet, of such privacy
That he might see her beauty unespied,
And win perhaps that night a peerless bride,
While legion'd fairies pac'd the coverlet,
And pale enchantment held her sleepy-eyed.
Never on such a night have lovers met,
Since Merlin paid his Demon all the monstrous debt.[12]

20

"It shall be as thou wishest," said the Dame:
"All cates and dainties[13] shall be stored there
Quickly on this feast-night: by the tambour frame[14]
Her own lute thou wilt see: no time to spare,
For I am slow and feeble, and scarce dare
On such a catering trust my dizzy head.
Wait here, my child, with patience; kneel in prayer
The while: Ah! thou must needs the lady wed,
Or may I never leave my grave among the dead."

21

So saying, she hobbled off with busy fear.
The lover's endless minutes slowly pass'd;
The dame return'd, and whisper'd in his ear
To follow her; with aged eyes aghast
From fright of dim espial.[15] Safe at last,
Through many a dusky gallery, they gain

[9] **mickle:** much (Scots).

[10] **beard:** to confront or oppose boldly.

[11] **plaining:** complaining.

[12] **Since Merlin . . . debt:** probably refers to the magician Merlin's imprisonment and death brought about by one of his own spells wielded by his beloved Vivien.

[13] **cates and dainties:** Elizabethan terms for delicacies.

[14] **tambour frame:** frame for embroidery.

[15] **From fright of dim espial:** i.e., for fear they would be seen, even in the dim light.

The maiden's chamber, silken, hush'd, and chaste;
Where Porphyro took covert, pleas'd amain.
His poor guide hurried back with agues[16] in her brain.

22

Her falt'ring hand upon the balustrade,
Old Angela was feeling for the stair,
When Madeline, St. Agnes' charmed maid,
Rose, like a mission'd[17] spirit, unaware:
With silver taper's light, and pious care,
She turn'd, and down the aged gossip led
To a safe level matting. Now prepare,
Young Porphyro, for gazing on that bed;
She comes, she comes again, like ring-dove fray'd and
fled.[18]

23

Out went the taper as she hurried in;
Its little smoke, in pallid moonshine, died:
She clos'd the door, she panted, all akin
To spirits of the air, and visions wide:
No uttered syllable, or, woe betide!
But to her heart, her heart was voluble,
Paining with eloquence her balmy side;
As though a tongueless nightingale should swell
Her throat in vain, and die, heart-stifled, in her dell.[19]

24

A casement high and triple-arch'd there was,
All garlanded with carven imag'ries
Of fruits, and flowers, and bunches of knot-grass,
And diamonded with panes of quaint device,
Innumerable of stains and splendid dyes,
As are the tiger-moth's deep-damask'd wings;
And in the midst, 'mong thousand heraldries,
And twilight saints, and dim emblazonings,
A shielded scutcheon blush'd with blood of queens
and kings.

25

Full on this casement shone the wintry moon,
And threw warm gules[20] on Madeline's fair breast,
As down she knelt for heaven's grace and boon;
Rose-bloom fell on her hands, together prest,
And on her silver cross soft amethyst,
And on her hair a glory, like a saint:
She seem'd a splendid angel, newly drest,
Save wings, for heaven:—Porphyro grew faint:
She knelt, so pure a thing, so free from mortal taint.

26

Anon his heart revives: her vespers done,
Of all its wreathed pearls her hair she frees;
Unclasps her warmed jewels one by one;
Loosens her fragrant boddice; by degrees
Her rich attire creeps rustling to her knees:
Half-hidden, like a mermaid in sea-weed,
Pensive awhile she dreams awake, and sees,
In fancy, fair St. Agnes in her bed,
But dares not look behind, or all the charm is fled.

27

Soon, trembling in her soft and chilly nest,
In sort of wakeful swoon, perplex'd she lay,
Until the poppied warmth of sleep oppress'd
Her soothed limbs, and soul fatigued away;
Flown, like a thought, until the morrow-day;
Blissfully haven'd both from joy and pain;
Clasp'd like a missal where swart Paynims pray;
Blinded[21] alike from sunshine and from rain,
As though a rose should shut, and be a bud again.

28

Stol'n to this paradise, and so entranced,
Porphyro gazed upon her empty dress,
And listen'd to her breathing, if it chanced
To wake into a slumberous tenderness;
Which when he heard, that minute did he bless,
And breath'd himself: then from the closet crept,
Noiseless as fear in a wide wilderness,
And over the hush'd carpet, silent, stept,
And 'tween the curtains peep'd, where, lo!—how fast
she slept.

---

[16] **amain**: greatly. **agues**: trembling.

[17] **mission'd**: commissioned. **balustrade**: railing.

[18] **ring-dove**: pigeon or small dove. **fray'd**: frightened.

[19] **tongueless nightingale . . . dell**: Tereus cut out Philomela's tongue after raping her so she could not tell her sister, Procne, of her husband's crime. After she learned of Tereus's crime from a narrative of the event Philomela wove into a robe, Procne served Tereus their son for dinner. All three were transformed into birds—Tereus, a hawk; Procne, a swallow; and Philomela, a nightingale—when Tereus sought to avenge his wife's murder of their child.

[20] **gules**: heraldic term for red.

[21] **swart**: swarthy. **Paynims**: archaic for "pagans" (esp. Muslim). **Blinded**: shielded.

29

Then by the bed-side, where the faded moon
Made a dim, silver twilight, soft he set
A table, and, half anguish'd, threw thereon
A cloth of woven crimson, gold, and jet:—
O for some drowsy Morphean[22] amulet!
The boisterous, midnight, festive clarion,
The kettle-drum, and far-heard clarionet,
Affray his ears, though but in dying tone:—
The hall door shuts again, and all the noise is gone.

30

And still she slept an azure-lidded sleep,
In blanched linen, smooth, and lavender'd,
While he from forth the closet brought a heap
Of candied apple, quince, and plum, and gourd;
With jellies soother than the creamy curd,
And lucent syrops, tinct with cinnamon;
Manna and dates, in argosy transferr'd
From Fez; and spiced dainties, every one,
From silken Samarcand to cedar'd Lebanon.[23]

31

These delicates he heap'd with glowing hand
On golden dishes and in baskets bright
Of wreathed silver: sumptuous they stand
In the retired quiet of the night,
Filling the chilly room with perfume light.—
"And now, my love, my seraph fair, awake!
Thou art my heaven, and I thine eremite:[24]
Open thine eyes, for meek St. Agnes' sake,
Or I shall drowse beside thee, so my soul doth ache."

[22] **Morphean:** Morpheus was a minister of Somnus, god of sleep.

[23] **soother:** smoother. **lucent:** bright, clear. **argosy:** a large merchant ship. **Fez:** Fes, a city in north central Morocco. **Samarcand to cedar'd Lebanon:** Samarkand was a Persian market city famous for its wealth, destroyed in c. 1220 by Genghis Khan and rebuilt as the opulent capital of Tamerlane's empire (c. 1370). The cedars of Lebanon, cf. Psalms 104:16: "The trees of the Lord are full of sap; the cedars of Lebanon, which he hath planted. . . ."

[24] **eremite:** a Christian hermit.

32

Thus whispering, his warm, unnerved arm
Sank in her pillow. Shaded was her dream
By the dusk curtains:—'twas a midnight charm
Impossible to melt as iced stream:
The lustrous salvers in the moonlight gleam;
Broad golden fringe upon the carpet lies:
It seem'd he never, never could redeem
From such a stedfast spell his lady's eyes;
So mus'd awhile, entoil'd in woofed[25] phantasies.

33

Awakening up, he took her hollow lute,—
Tumultuous,—and, in chords that tenderest be,
He play'd an ancient ditty, long since mute,
In Provence call'd, "La belle dame sans mercy":[26]
Close to her ear touching the melody;—
Wherewith disturb'd, she utter'd a soft moan:
He ceased—she panted quick—and suddenly
Her blue affrayed eyes wide open shone:
Upon his knees he sank, pale as smooth-sculptured stone.

34

Her eyes were open, but she still beheld,
Now wide awake, the vision of her sleep:
There was a painful change, that nigh expell'd
The blisses of her dream so pure and deep:
At which fair Madeline began to weep,
And moan forth witless words with many a sigh;
While still her gaze on Porphyro would keep;
Who knelt, with joined hands and piteous eye,
Fearing to move or speak, she look'd so dreamingly.

35

"Ah, Porphyro!" said she, "but even now
Thy voice was at sweet tremble in mine ear,
Made tuneable with every sweetest vow;
And those sad eyes were spiritual and clear:
How chang'd thou art! how pallid, chill, and drear!
Give me that voice again, my Porphyro,
Those looks immortal, those complainings dear!
Oh leave me not in this eternal woe,
For if thou diest, my love, I know not where to go."

[25] **woofed:** woven.

[26] **"La belle dame sans mercy:"** See note 1 to "La Belle Dame sans Merci."

36

Beyond a mortal man impassion'd far
At these voluptuous accents, he arose,
Ethereal, flush'd, and like a throbbing star
Seen mid the sapphire heaven's deep repose;
Into her dream he melted, as the rose
Blendeth its odour with the violet,—
Solution sweet: meantime the frost-wind blows
Like Love's alarum pattering the sharp sleet
Against the window-panes; St. Agnes' moon hath set.

37

'Tis dark: quick pattereth the flaw-blown sleet:
"This is no dream, my bride, my Madeline!"
'Tis dark: the iced gusts still rave and beat:
"No dream, alas! alas! and woe is mine!
Porphyro will leave me here to fade and pine.—
Cruel! what traitor could thee hither bring?
I curse not, for my heart is lost in thine,
Though thou forsakest a deceived thing;—
A dove forlorn and lost with sick unpruned wing."[27]

38

"My Madeline! sweet dreamer! lovely bride!
Say, may I be for aye thy vassal blest?
Thy beauty's shield, heart-shap'd and vermeil[28] dyed?
Ah, silver shrine, here will I take my rest
After so many hours of toil and quest,
A famish'd pilgrim,—saved by miracle.
Though I have found, I will not rob thy nest
Saving of thy sweet self; if thou think'st well
To trust, fair Madeline, to no rude infidel.

39

"Hark! 'tis an elfin-storm from faery land,
Of haggard seeming,[29] but a boon indeed:
Arise—arise! the morning is at hand;—
The bloated wassaillers will never heed:—
Let us away, my love, with happy speed;
There are no ears to hear, or eyes to see,—
Drown'd all in Rhenish and the sleepy mead:[30]
Awake! arise! my love, and fearless be,
For o'er the southern moors I have a home for thee."

40

She hurried at his words, beset with fears,
For there were sleeping dragons all around,
At glaring watch, perhaps, with ready spears—
Down the wide stairs a darkling way they found.—
In all the house was heard no human sound.
A chain-droop'd lamp was flickering by each door;
The arras,[31] rich with horseman, hawk, and hound,
Flutter'd in the besieging wind's uproar;
And the long carpets rose along the gusty floor.

41

They glide, like phantoms, into the wide hall;
Like phantoms, to the iron porch, they glide;
Where lay the Porter, in uneasy sprawl,
With a huge empty flaggon by his side:
The wakeful bloodhound rose, and shook his hide,
But his sagacious eye an inmate owns:[32]
By one, and one, the bolts full easy slide:—
The chains lie silent on the footworn stones;—
The key turns, and the door upon its hinges groans.

42

And they are gone: ay, ages long ago
These lovers fled away into the storm.
That night the Baron dreamt of many a woe,
And all his warrior-guests, with shade and form
Of witch, and demon, and large coffin-worm,
Were long be-nightmar'd. Angela the old
Died palsy-twitch'd, with meagre face deform;
The Beadsman, after thousand aves told,
For aye[33] unsought for slept among his ashes cold.

[27] **unpruned wing**: "not smoothed with the beak" (OED).

[28] **vermeil**: vermillion, a vivid red.

[29] **haggard seeming**: wild or fierce appearance.

[30] **Rhenish . . . sleepy mead**: Rhine wine, and an alcoholic liquid of fermented honey and water.

[31] **arras**: a thick hanging tapestry.

[32] **an inmate owns**: recognizes a resident (of the castle).

[33] **For aye**: forever.

Hyperion: A Fragment[1]

(1820, comp. 1819)

— BOOK I —

Deep in the shady sadness of a vale
Far sunken from the healthy breath of morn,
Far from the fiery noon, and eve's one star,
Sat gray-hair'd Saturn,[2] quiet as a stone,
Still as the silence round about his lair;
Forest on forest hung above his head
Like cloud on cloud. No stir of air was there,
Not so much life as on a summer's day
Robs not one light seed from the feather'd grass,
But where the dead leaf fell, there did it rest.
A stream went voiceless by, still deadened more
By reason of his fallen divinity
Spreading a shade: the Naiad[3] mid her reeds
Press'd her cold finger closer to her lips.

Along the margin-sand large foot-marks went,
No further than to where his feet had stray'd,
And slept there since. Upon the sodden ground
His old right hand lay nerveless, listless, dead,
Unsceptred; and his realmless eyes were closed;
While his bow'd head seem'd list'ning to the Earth,
His ancient mother, for some comfort yet.

It seem'd no force could wake him from his place;
But there came one,[4] who with a kindred hand
Touch'd his wide shoulders, after bending low
With reverence, though to one who knew it not.
She was a Goddess of the infant world;
By her in stature the tall Amazont
Had stood a pigmy's height; she would have ta'en
Achilles by the hair and bent his neck;
Or with a finger stay'd Ixion's wheel.
Her face was large as that of Memphian sphinx,[5]
Pedestal'd haply in a palace court,
When sages look'd to Egypt for their lore.
But oh! how unlike marble was that face:[6]
How beautiful, if sorrow had not made
Sorrow more beautiful than Beauty's self.
There was a listening fear in her regard,
As if calamity had but begun;
As if the vanward clouds of evil days
Had spent their malice, and the sullen rear
Was with its stored thunder labouring up.
One hand she press'd upon that aching spot
Where beats the human heart, as if just there,
Though an immortal, she felt cruel pain:
The other upon Saturn's bended neck
She laid, and to the level of his ear
Leaning with parted lips, some words she spake
In solemn tenour and deep organ tone:
Some mourning words, which in our feeble tongue
Would come in these like accents; O how frail
To that large utterance of the early Gods!
"Saturn, look up! — though wherefore, poor old King?
I have no comfort for thee, no not one:
I cannot say, 'O wherefore sleepest thou?'
For heaven is parted from thee, and the earth
Knows thee not, thus afflicted, for a God;
And ocean too, with all its solemn noise,
Has from thy sceptre pass'd; and all the air
Is emptied of thine hoary majesty.
Thy thunder, conscious of the new command,
Rumbles reluctant o'er our fallen house;
And thy sharp lightning in unpractised hands
Scorches and burns our once serene domain.
O aching time! O moments big as years!
All as ye pass swell out the monstrous truth,
And press it so upon our weary griefs

[1] Hyperion, one of the Titans, was the sun god before Apollo. The mythological background of the poem concerns the defeat of the Titans by the new race of Olympian gods. The characters, scenes, speeches, and implied action bear close resemblance to the opening books of Milton's *Paradise Lost*.

[2] **Saturn:** the son of Uranus (Heaven) and Terra (Earth), and the leader of the Titans.

[3] **Naiad:** a freshwater nymph.

[4] **one:** Saturn's sister Thea, also Hyperion's wife.

[5] **Achilles:** the legendary Greek soldier and hero of the *Iliad*, of proverbial strength. **Ixion's wheel:** "Jupiter, displeased with the insolence of Ixion, banished him from heaven . . . struck him with thunder, and ordered Mercury to tie him to a wheel in hell, which continually whirls round. The wheel was perpetually in motion, therefore the punishment of Ixion was eternal" (Lemprière). **Memphian sphinx:** Memphis was the traditional center of lower Egypt, and the location of the statue of the Sphinx.

[6] **haply:** perhaps. **But oh! how unlike:** "O how unlike the place from whence they fell." *Paradise Lost,* I. 75.

That unbelief has not a space to breathe.
Saturn, sleep on: — O thoughtless, why did I
Thus violate thy slumbrous solitude?
Why should I ope thy melancholy eyes?
Saturn, sleep on! while at thy feet I weep."

As when, upon a tranced summer-night,
Those green-rob'd senators of mighty woods,
Tall oaks, branch-charmed by the earnest stars,
Dream, and so dream all night without a stir,
Save from one gradual solitary gust
Which comes upon the silence, and dies off,
As if the ebbing air had but one wave;
So came these words and went; the while in tears
She touch'd her fair large forehead to the ground,
Just where her falling hair might be outspread,
A soft and silken mat for Saturn's feet.
One moon, with alteration slow, had shed
Her silver seasons four upon the night,
And still these two were postured motionless,
Like natural sculpture in cathedral cavern;
The frozen God still couchant[7] on the earth,
And the sad Goddess weeping at his feet:
Until at length old Saturn lifted up
His faded eyes, and saw his kingdom gone,
And all the gloom and sorrow of the place,
And that fair kneeling Goddess; and then spake,
As with a palsied tongue, and while his beard
Shook horrid with such aspen-malady:
"O tender spouse of gold Hyperion,
Thea, I feel thee ere I see thy face;
Look up, and let me see our doom in it;
Look up, and tell me if this feeble shape
Is Saturn's; tell me, if thou hear'st the voice
Of Saturn; tell me, if this wrinkling brow,
Naked and bare of its great diadem,
Peers like the front of Saturn. Who had power
To make me desolate? whence came the strength?
How was it nurtur'd to such bursting forth,
While Fate seem'd strangled in my nervous grasp?
But it is so; and I am smother'd up,
And buried from all godlike exercise
Of influence benign on planets pale,
Of admonitions to the winds and seas,
Of peaceful sway above man's harvesting,
And all those acts which Deity supreme
Doth ease its heart of love in. — I am gone
Away from my own bosom: I have left
My strong identity, my real self,
Somewhere between the throne, and where I sit
Here on this spot of earth. Search, Thea, search!
Open thine eyes eterne, and sphere them round
Upon all space: space starr'd, and lorn of light;
Space region'd with life-air; and barren void;
Spaces of fire, and all the yawn of hell. —
Search, Thea, search! and tell me, if thou seest
A certain shape or shadow, making way
With wings or chariot fierce to repossess
A heaven he lost erewhile: it must — it must
Be of ripe progress — Saturn must be King.
Yes, there must be a golden victory;
There must be Gods thrown down, and trumpets blown
Of triumph calm, and hymns of festival
Upon the gold clouds metropolitan,
Voices of soft proclaim, and silver stir
Of strings in hollow shells; and there shall be
Beautiful things made new, for the surprise
Of the sky-children; I will give command:
Thea! Thea! Thea! where is Saturn?"

This passion lifted him upon his feet,
And made his hands to struggle in the air,
His Druid locks to shake and ooze with sweat,
His eyes to fever out, his voice to cease.
He stood, and heard not Thea's sobbing deep;
A little time, and then again he snatch'd
Utterance thus. — "But cannot I create?
Cannot I form? Cannot I fashion forth
Another world, another universe,
To overbear and crumble this to nought?
Where is another Chaos?[8] Where?" — That word
Found way unto Olympus, and made quake
The rebel three. — Thea was startled up,
And in her bearing was a sort of hope,
As thus she quick-voic'd spake, yet full of awe.

"This cheers our fallen house: come to our friends,
O Saturn! come away, and give them heart;
I know the covert, for thence came I hither."
Thus brief; then with beseeching eyes she went
With backward footing through the shade a space:
He follow'd, and she turn'd to lead the way

[7] **couchant:** heraldic term for "lying."

[8] **Chaos:** In Greek mythology, Heaven and Earth arose out of primeval Chaos, and Saturn was their son.

Through aged boughs, that yielded like the mist
Which eagles cleave upmounting from their nest.

Meanwhile in other realms big tears were shed,
More sorrow like to this, and such like woe,
Too huge for mortal tongue or pen of scribe:
The Titans fierce, self-hid, or prison-bound,
Groan'd for the old allegiance once more,
And listen'd in sharp pain for Saturn's voice.
But one of the whole mammoth-brood still kept
His sov'reignty, and rule, and majesty;—
Blazing Hyperion on his orbed fire
Still sat, still snuff'd the incense, teeming up
From man to the sun's God; yet unsecure:
For as among us mortals omens drear
Fright and perplex, so also shuddered he—
Not at dog's howl, or gloom-bird's[9] hated screech,
Or the familiar visiting of one
Upon the first toll of his passing-bell,
Or prophesyings of the midnight lamp;
But horrors, portion'd to a giant nerve,
Oft made Hyperion ache. His palace bright,
Bastion'd with pyramids of glowing gold,
And touch'd with shade of bronzed obelisks,
Glar'd a blood-red through all its thousand courts,
Arches, and domes, and fiery galleries;
And all its curtains of Aurorian clouds
Flush'd angerly: while sometimes eagle's wings,
Unseen before by Gods or wondering men,
Darken'd the place; and neighing steeds were heard,
Not heard before by Gods or wondering men.
Also, when he would taste the spicy wreaths
Of incense, breath'd aloft from sacred hills,
Instead of sweets, his ample palate took
Savour of poisonous brass and metal sick:
And so, when harbour'd in the sleepy west,
After the full completion of fair day,—
For rest divine upon exalted couch
And slumber in the arms of melody,
He pac'd away the pleasant hours of ease
With stride colossal, on from hall to hall;
While far within each aisle and deep recess,
His winged minions in close clusters stood,
Amaz'd and full of fear; like anxious men
Who on wide plains gather in panting troops,
When earthquakes jar their battlements and towers.
Even now, while Saturn, rous'd from icy trance,
Went step for step with Thea through the woods,
Hyperion, leaving twilight in the rear,
Came slope upon the threshold of the west;
Then, as was wont, his palace-door flew ope
In smoothest silence, save what solemn tubes,
Blown by the serious Zephyrs,[10] gave of sweet
And wandering sounds, slow-breathed melodies;
And like a rose in vermeil[11] tint and shape,
In fragrance soft, and coolness to the eye,
That inlet to severe magnificence
Stood full blown, for the God to enter in.

He enter'd, but he enter'd full of wrath;
His flaming robes stream'd out beyond his heels,
And gave a roar, as if of earthly fire,
That scar'd away the meek ethereal Hours
And made their dove-wings tremble. On he flared,
From stately nave to nave, from vault to vault,
Through bowers of fragrant and enwreathed light,
And diamond-paved lustrous long arcades,
Until he reach'd the great main cupola;
There standing fierce beneath, he stampt his foot,
And from the basements deep to the high towers
Jarr'd his own golden region; and before
The quavering thunder thereupon had ceas'd,
His voice leapt out, despite of godlike curb,
To this result: "O dreams of day and night!
O monstrous forms! O effigies of pain!
O spectres busy in a cold, cold gloom!
O lank-eared Phantoms of black-weeded pools!
Why do I knew ye? why have I seen ye? why
Is my eternal essence thus distraught
To see and to behold these horrors new?
Saturn is fallen, am I too to fall?
Am I to leave this haven of my rest,
This cradle of my glory, this soft clime,
This calm luxuriance of blissful light,
These crystalline pavilions, and pure fanes,
Of all my lucent empire? It is left
Deserted, void, nor any haunt of mine.
The blaze, the splendor, and the symmetry,
I cannot see—but darkness, death and darkness.
Even here, into my centre of repose,
The shady visions come to domineer,
Insult, and blind, and stifle up my pomp.—

[9] **gloom-bird:** the owl.

[10] **Zephyrs:** soft, warm winds out of the west.

[11] **vermeil:** vermillion, bright red.

Fall!—No, by Tellus and her briny robes![12]
Over the fiery frontier of my realms
I will advance a terrible right arm
Shall scare that infant thunderer, rebel Jove,
And bid old Saturn take his throne again."—
He spake, and ceas'd, the while a heavier threat
Held struggle with his throat but came not forth;
For as in theatres of crowded men
Hubbub increases more they call out "Hush!"
So at Hyperion's words the Phantoms pale
Bestirr'd themselves, thrice horrible and cold;
And from the mirror'd level where he stood
A mist arose, as from a scummy marsh.
At this, through all his bulk an agony
Crept gradual, from the feet unto the crown,
Like a lithe serpent vast and muscular
Making slow way, with head and neck convuls'd
From over-strained might. Releas'd, he fled
To the eastern gates, and full six dewy hours
Before the dawn in season due should blush,
He breath'd fierce breath against the sleepy portals,
Clear'd them of heavy vapours, burst them wide
Suddenly on the ocean's chilly streams.
The planet orb of fire, whereon he rode
Each day from east to west the heavens through,
Spun round in sable curtaining of clouds;
Not therefore veiled quite, blindfold, and hid,
But ever and anon the glancing spheres,
Circles, and arcs, and broad-belting colure,[13]
Glow'd through, and wrought upon the muffling dark
Sweet-shaped lightnings from the nadir deep
Up to the zenith,—hieroglyphics old,
Which sages and keen-eyed astrologers
Then living on the earth, with labouring thought
Won from the gaze of many centuries:
Now lost, save what we find on remnants huge
Of stone, or marble swart;[14] their import gone,
Their wisdom long since fled.—Two wings this orb
Possess'd for glory, two fair argent[15] wings,
Ever exalted at the God's approach:
And now, from forth the gloom their plumes immense
Rose, one by one, till all outspreaded were;
While still the dazzling globe maintain'd eclipse,
Awaiting for Hyperion's command.
Fain[16] would he have commanded, fain took throne
And bid the day begin, if but for change.
He might not:—No, though a primeval God:
The sacred seasons might not be disturb'd.
Therefore the operations of the dawn
Stay'd in their birth, even as here 'tis told.
Those silver wings expanded sisterly,
Eager to sail their orb; the porches wide
Open'd upon the dusk demesnes of night;
And the bright Titan, phrenzied with new woes,
Unus'd to bend, by hard compulsion bent
His spirit to the sorrow of the time;
And all along a dismal rack of clouds,
Upon the boundaries of day and night,
He stretch'd himself in grief and radiance faint.
There as he lay, the heaven with its stars
Look'd down on him with pity, and the voice
Of Coelus,[17] from the universal space,
Thus whisper'd low and solemn in his ear.
"O brightest of my children dear, earth-born
And sky-engendered, Son of Mysteries
All unrevealed even to the powers
Which met at thy creating; at whose joys
And palpitations sweet, and pleasures soft,
I, Coelus, wonder, how they came and whence;
And at the fruits thereof what shapes they be,
Distinct, and visible; symbols divine,
Manifestations of that beauteous life
Diffus'd unseen throughout eternal space:
Of these new-form'd art thou, oh brightest child!
Of these, thy brethren and the Goddesses!
There is sad feud among ye, and rebellion
Of son against his sire. I saw him fall,
I saw my first-born tumbled from his throne!
To me his arms were spread, to me his voice
Found way from forth the thunders round his head!
Pale wox[18] I, and in vapours hid my face.
Art thou, too, near such doom? vague fear there is:
For I have seen my sons most unlike Gods.

[12] **Tellus and her briny robes:** Earth, wife of Heaven; her briny robes are the oceans.

[13] **colure:** "The colures are the two circles, intersecting each other at the poles, which divide the equinoctial and the ecliptic into four equal parts" (*OED*).

[14] **swart:** dark.

[15] **argent:** heraldic term for silver.

[16] **Fain:** eagerly.

[17] **Coelus:** Heaven (or Uranus), father of Saturn and the other Titans.

[18] **wox:** waxed, grew.

Divine ye were created, and divine
In sad demeanour, solemn, undisturb'd,
Unruffled, like high Gods, ye liv'd and ruled:
Now I behold in you fear, hope, and wrath;
Actions of rage and passion; even as
I see them, on the mortal world beneath,
In men who die.—This is the grief, O Son!
Sad sign of ruin, sudden dismay, and fall!
Yet do thou strive; as thou art capable,
As thou canst move about, an evident God;
And canst oppose to each malignant hour
Ethereal presence:—I am but a voice;
My life is but the life of winds and tides,
No more than winds and tides can I avail:—
But thou canst.—Be thou therefore in the van
Of circumstance; yea, seize the arrow's barb
Before the tense string murmur.—To the earth!
For there thou wilt find Saturn, and his woes.
Meantime I will keep watch on thy bright sun,
And of thy seasons be a careful nurse."—
Ere half this region-whisper had come down,
Hyperion arose, and on the stars
Lifted his curved lids, and kept them wide
Until it ceas'd; and still he kept them wide:
And still they were the same bright, patient stars.
Then with a slow incline of his broad breast,
Like to a diver in the pearly seas,
Forward he stoop'd over the airy shore,
And plung'd all noiseless into the deep night.

—BOOK II—

Just at the self-same beat of Time's wide wings
Hyperion slid into the rustled air,
And Saturn gain'd with Thea that sad place
Where Cybele[19] and the bruised Titans mourn'd.
It was a den where no insulting light
Could glimmer on their tears; where their own groans
They felt, but heard not, for the solid roar
Of thunderous waterfalls and torrents hoarse,
Pouring a constant bulk, uncertain where.
Crag jutting forth to crag, and rocks that seem'd
Ever as if just rising from a sleep,
Forehead to forehead held their monstrous horns;
And thus in thousand hugest phantasies
Made a fit roofing to this nest of woe.
Instead of thrones, hard flint they sat upon,
Couches of rugged stone, and slaty ridge
Stubborn'd with iron. All were not assembled:
Some chain'd in torture, and some wandering.
Coelus, and Gyges, and Briareüs,
Typhon, and Dolor, and Porphyrion,[20]
With many more, the brawniest in assault,
Were pent in regions of laborious breath;
Dungeon'd in opaque element, to keep
Their clenched teeth still clench'd, and all their limbs
Lock'd up like veins of metal, crampt and screw'd;
Without a motion, save of their big hearts
Heaving in pain, and horribly convuls'd
With sanguine feverous boiling gurge of pulse.
Mnemosyne was straying in the world;
Far from her moon had Phoebe[21] wandered;
And many else were free to roam abroad,
But for the main, here found they covert drear.
Scarce images of life, one here, one there,
Lay vast and edgeways; like a dismal cirque
Of Druid[22] stones, upon a forlorn moor,
When the chill rain begins at shut of eve,
In dull November, and their chancel vault,[23]
The heaven itself, is blinded throughout night.
Each one kept shroud, nor to his neighbour gave
Or word, or look, or action of despair.
Creüs[24] was one; his ponderous iron mace
Lay by him, and a shatter'd rib of rock
Told of his rage, ere he thus sank and pined.
Iäpetus another; in his grasp,
A serpent's plashy neck; its barbed tongue
Squeez'd from the gorge, and all its uncurl'd length
Dead; and because the creature could not spit
Its poison in the eyes of conquering Jove.
Next Cottus: prone he lay, chin uppermost,
As though in pain; for still upon the flint
He ground severe his skull, with open mouth
And eyes at horrid working. Nearest him

[19] **Cybele:** here, the wife of Saturn (also known as Ops, but sometimes also identified with his mother Tellus).

[20] **Coelus . . . Porphyrion:** all names of Titans.

[21] **Mnemosyne:** goddess of memory; mother of the Muses by Jupiter. **Phoebe:** the mother of Diana, goddess of the moon, but the name could also refer to Diana herself.

[22] **Druid:** the ancient priests of Gaul, Britain, and Ireland, who appear in Irish and Welsh sagas and Christian legends as magicians and wizards.

[23] **chancel:** the area of a church where the altar is located.

[24] **Creüs . . . Caf:** all names of Titans.

Asia, born of most enormous Caf,
Who cost her mother Tellus keener pangs,
Though feminine, than any of her sons:
More thought than woe was in her dusky face,
For she was prophesying of her glory;
And in her wide imagination stood
Palm-shaded temples, and high rival fanes,
By Oxus[25] or in Ganges'[26] sacred isles.
Even as Hope upon her anchor leans,[27]
So leant she, not so fair, upon a tusk
Shed from the broadest of her elephants.
Above her, on a crag's uneasy shelve,
Upon his elbow rais'd, all prostrate else,
Shadow'd Enceladus; once tame and mild
As grazing ox unworried in the meads;
Now tiger-passion'd, lion-thoughted, wroth,
He meditated, plotted, and even now
Was hurling mountains in that second war,
Not long delay'd, that scar'd the younger Gods
To hide themselves in forms of beast and bird.
Not far hence Atlas; and beside him prone
Phorcus, the sire of Gorgons. Neighbour'd close
Oceanus, and Tethys, in whose lap
Sobb'd Clymene among her tangled hair.
In midst of all lay Themis, at the feet
Of Ops the queen all clouded round from sight;
No shape distinguishable, more than when
Thick night confounds the pine-tops with the clouds:
And many else whose names may not be told.
For when the Muse's wings are air-ward spread,
Who shall delay her flight? and she must chaunt
Of Saturn, and his guide, who now had climb'd
With damp and slippery footing from a depth
More horrid still. Above a sombre cliff
Their heads appear'd, and up their stature grew
Till on the level height their steps found ease:
Then Thea spread abroad her trembling arms
Upon the precincts of this nest of pain,
And sidelong fix'd her eye on Saturn's face:
There saw she direst strife; the supreme God
At war with all the frailty of grief,
Of rage, of fear, anxiety, revenge,
Remorse, spleen, hope, but most of all despair.
Against these plagues he strove in vain; for Fate
Had pour'd a mortal oil upon his head,
A disanointing poison: so that Thea,
Affrighted, kept her still, and let him pass
First onwards in, among the fallen tribe.

As with us mortal men, the laden heart
Is persecuted more, and fever'd more,
When it is nighing to the mournful house
Where other hearts are sick of the same bruise;
So Saturn, as he walk'd into the midst,
Felt faint, and would have sunk among the rest,
But that he met Enceladus's eye,
Whose mightiness, and awe of him, at once
Came like an inspiration; and he shouted,
"Titans, behold your God!" at which some groan'd;
Some started on their feet; some also shouted;
Some wept, some wail'd, all bow'd with reverence;
And Ops, uplifting her black folded veil,
Show'd her pale cheeks, and all her forehead wan,
Her eye-brows thin and jet, and hollow eyes.
There is a roaring in the bleak-grown pines
When Winter lifts his voice; there is a noise
Among immortals when a God gives sign,
With hushing finger, how he means to load
His tongue with the full weight of utterless thought,
With thunder, and with music, and with pomp:
Such noise is like the roar of bleak-grown pines;
Which, when it ceases in this mountain'd world,
No other sound succeeds; but ceasing here,
Among these fallen, Saturn's voice therefrom
Grew up like organ, that begins anew
Its strain, when other harmonies, stopt short,
Leave the dinn'd air vibrating silverly.
Thus grew it up—"Not in my own sad breast,
Which is its own great judge and searcher out,
Can I find reason why ye should be thus:
Not in the legends of the first of days,
Studied from that old spirit-leaved book
Which starry Uranus with finger bright
Sav'd from the shores of darkness, when the waves
Low-ebb'd still hid it up in shallow gloom;—
And the which book ye know I ever kept
For my firm-based footstool:—Ah, infirm!
Not there, nor in sign, symbol, or portent
Of element, earth, water, air, and fire,—
At war, at peace, or inter-quarreling
One against one, or two, or three, or all

---

[25] **Oxus:** the classical name for the Amu Darya, which flows through what is now Afghanistan, Uzbekistan, and Turkmenistan, and into the Caspian Sea.

[26] **Ganges:** a sacred river in northeastern India.

[27] **Hope upon her anchor leans:** a traditional emblem of hope. Heb. VI.19: "Hope we have as an anchor of the soul."

Each several one against the other three,
As fire with air loud warring when rain-floods
Drown both, and press them both against earth's face,
Where, finding sulphur, a quadruple wrath
Unhinges the poor world;—not in that strife,
Wherefrom I take strange lore, and read it deep,
Can I find reason why ye should be thus:
No, no-where can unriddle, though I search,
And pore on Nature's universal scroll
Even to swooning, why ye, Divinities,
The first-born of all shap'd and palpable Gods,
Should cower beneath what, in comparison,
Is untremendous might. Yet ye are here,
O'erwhelm'd, and spurn'd, and batter'd, ye are here!
O Titans, shall I say 'Arise!'—Ye groan:
Shall I say 'Crouch!'—Ye groan. What can I then?
O Heaven wide! O unseen parent dear!
What can I? Tell me, all ye brethren Gods,
How we can war, how engine our great wrath!
O speak your counsel now, for Saturn's ear
Is all a-hunger'd. Thou, Oceanus,[28]
Ponderest high and deep; and in thy face
I see, astonied, that severe content
Which comes of thought and musing: give us help!"

So ended Saturn; and the God of the Sea,
Sophist and sage, from no Athenian grove,
But cogitation in his watery shades,
Arose, with locks not oozy, and began,
In murmurs, which his first-endeavouring tongue
Caught infant-like from the far-foamed sands.
"O ye, whom wrath consumes! who, passion-stung,
Writhe at defeat, and nurse your agonies!
Shut up your senses, stifle up your ears,
My voice is not a bellows unto ire.
Yet listen, ye who will, whilst I bring proof
How ye, perforce, must be content to stoop:
And in the proof much comfort will I give,
If ye will take that comfort in its truth.
We fall by course of Nature's law, not force
Of thunder, or of Jove. Great Saturn, thou
Hast sifted well the atom-universe;
But for this reason, that thou art the King,
And only blind from sheer supremacy,
One avenue was shaded from thine eyes,
Through which I wandered to eternal truth.
And first, as thou wast not the first of powers,
So art thou not the last; it cannot be:
Thou art not the beginning nor the end.
From Chaos and parental Darkness came
Light, the first fruits of that intestine broil,
That sullen ferment, which for wondrous ends
Was ripening in itself. The ripe hour came,
And with it Light, and Light, engendering
Upon its own producer, forthwith touch'd
The whole enormous matter into life.
Upon that very hour, our parentage,
The Heavens and the Earth, were manifest:
Then thou first-born, and we the giant-race,
Found ourselves ruling new and beauteous realms.
Now comes the pain of truth, to whom 'tis pain;
O folly! for to bear all naked truths,
And to envisage circumstance, all calm,
That is the top of sovereignty. Mark well!
As Heaven and Earth are fairer, fairer far
Than Chaos and blank Darkness, though once chiefs;
And as we show beyond that Heaven and Earth
In form and shape compact and beautiful,
In will, in action free, companionship,
And thousand other signs of purer life;
So on our heels a fresh perfection treads,
A power more strong in beauty, born of us
And fated to excel us, as we pass
In glory that old Darkness: nor are we
Thereby more conquer'd, than by us the rule
Of shapeless Chaos. Say, doth the dull soil
Quarrel with the proud forests it hath fed,
And feedeth still, more comely than itself?
Can it deny the chiefdom of green groves?
Or shall the tree be envious of the dove
Because it cooeth, and hath snowy wings
To wander wherewithal and find its joys?
We are such forest-trees, and our fair boughs
Have bred forth, not pale solitary doves,
But eagles golden-feather'd, who do tower
Above us in their beauty, and must reign
In right thereof; for 'tis the eternal law
That first in beauty should be first in might:
Yea, by that law, another race may drive
Our conquerors to mourn as we do now.
Have ye beheld the young God of the Seas,
My dispossessor? Have ye seen his face?
Have ye beheld his chariot, foam'd along
By noble winged creatures he hath made?
I saw him on the calmed waters scud,
With such a glow of beauty in his eyes,

[28] **Oceanus**: the god of the oceans.

That it enforc'd me to bid sad farewell
To all my empire: farewell sad I took,
And hither came, to see how dolorous fate
Had wrought upon ye; and how I might best
Give consolation in this woe extreme.
Receive the truth, and let it be your balm."

Whether through poz'd conviction, or disdain,
They guarded silence, when Oceanus
Left murmuring, what deepest thought can tell?
But so it was, none answer'd for a space,
Save one whom none regarded, Clymene;[29]
And yet she answer'd not, only complain'd,
With hectic lips, and eyes up-looking mild,
Thus wording timidly among the fierce:
"O Father, I am here the simplest voice,
And all my knowledge is that joy is gone,
And this thing woe crept in among our hearts,
There to remain for ever, as I fear:
I would not bode of evil, if I thought
So weak a creature could turn off the help
Which by just right should come of mighty Gods;
Yet let me tell my sorrow, let me tell
Of what I heard, and how it made we weep,
And know that we had parted from all hope.
I stood upon a shore, a pleasant shore,
Where a sweet clime was breathed from a land
Of fragrance, quietness, and trees, and flowers.
Full of calm joy it was, as I of grief;
Too full of joy and soft delicious warmth;
So that I felt a movement in my heart
To chide, and to reproach that solitude
With songs of misery, music of our woes;
And sat me down, and took a mouthed shell
And murmur'd into it, and made melody—
O melody no more! for while I sang,
And with poor skill let pass into the breeze
The dull shell's echo, from a bowery strand
Just opposite, an island of the sea,
There came enchantment with the shifting wind,
That did both drown and keep alive my ears.
I threw my shell away upon the sand,
And a wave fill'd it, as my sense was fill'd
With that new blissful golden melody.
A living death was in each gush of sounds,
Each family of rapturous hurried notes,
That fell, one after one, yet all at once,
Like pearl beads dropping sudden from their string:
And then another, then another strain,
Each like a dove leaving its olive perch,
With music wing'd instead of silent plumes,
To hover round my head, and make me sick
Of joy and grief at once. Grief overcame,
And I was stopping up my frantic ears,
When, past all hindrance of my trembling hands,
A voice came sweeter, sweeter than all tune,
And still it cried, 'Apollo! young Apollo!
The morning-bright Apollo! young Apollo!'
I fled, it follow'd me, and cried 'Apollo!'
O Father, and O Brethren, had ye felt
Those pains of mine; O Saturn, hadst thou felt,
Ye would not call this too indulged tongue
Presumptuous, in thus venturing to be heard."

So far her voice flow'd on, like timorous brook
That, lingering along a pebbled coast,
Doth fear to meet the sea: but sea it met,
And shudder'd; for the overwhelming voice
Of huge Enceladus swallow'd it in wrath:
The ponderous syllables, like sullen waves
In the half-glutted hollows of reef-rocks,
Came booming thus, while still upon his arm
He lean'd; not rising, from supreme contempt.
"Or shall we listen to the over-wise,
Or to the over-foolish, Giant-Gods?
Not thunderbolt on thunderbolt, till all
That rebel Jove's whole armoury were spent,
Not world on world upon these shoulders piled,
Could agonize me more than baby-words
In midst of this dethronement horrible.
Speak! roar! shout! yell! ye sleepy Titans all.
Do ye forget the blows, the buffets vile?
Are ye not smitten by a youngling arm?
Dost thou forget, sham Monarch of the Waves,
Thy scalding in the seas? What, have I rous'd
Your spleens with so few simple words as these?
O joy! for now I see ye are not lost:
O joy! for now I see a thousand eyes
Wide glaring for revenge!"—As this he said,
He lifted up his stature vast, and stood,
Still without intermission speaking thus:
"Now ye are flames, I'll tell you how to burn,
And purge the ether of our enemies;
How to feed fierce the crooked stings of fire,
And singe away the swollen clouds of Jove,
Stifling that puny essence in its tent.

[29] **Clymene:** the daughter of Oceanus and Tethys, and mother of Atlas and Prometheus.

O let him feel the evil he hath done;
For though I scorn Oceanus's lore,
Much pain have I for more than loss of realms:
The days of peace and slumberous calm are fled;
Those days, all innocent of scathing war,
When all the fair Existences of heaven
Came open-eyed to guess what we would speak:—
That was before our brows were taught to frown,
Before our lips knew else but solemn sounds;
That was before we knew the winged thing,
Victory, might be lost, or might be won.
And be ye mindful that Hyperion,
Our brightest brother, still is undisgraced—
Hyperion, lo! his radiance is here!"

All eyes were on Enceladus's face,
And they beheld, while still Hyperion's name
Flew from his lips up to the vaulted rocks,
A pallid gleam across his features stern:
Not savage, for he saw full many a God
Wroth as himself. He look'd upon them all,
And in each face he saw a gleam of light,
But splendider in Saturn's, whose hoar locks
Shone like the bubbling foam about a keel
When the prow sweeps into a midnight cove.
In pale and silver silence they remain'd,
Till suddenly a splendour, like the morn,
Pervaded all the beetling gloomy steeps,
All the sad spaces of oblivion,
And every gulf, and every chasm old,
And every height, and every sullen depth,
Voiceless, or hoarse with loud tormented streams:
And all the everlasting cataracts,
And all the headlong torrents far and near,
Mantled before in darkness and huge shade,
Now saw the light and made it terrible.
It was Hyperion:—a granite peak
His bright feet touch'd, and there he stay'd to view
The misery his brilliance had betray'd
To the most hateful seeing of itself.
Golden his hair of short Numidian[30] curl,
Regal his shape majestic, a vast shade
In midst of his own brightness, like the bulk
Of Memnon's[31] image at the set of sun
To one who travels from the dusking east:
Sighs, too, as mournful as that Memnon's harp
He utter'd, while his hands contemplative
He press'd together, and in silence stood.
Despondence seiz'd again the fallen Gods
At sight of the dejected King of Day,
And many hid their faces from the light:
But fierce Enceladus sent forth his eyes
Among the brotherhood; and, at their glare,
Uprose Iäpetus, and Creüs too,
And Phorcus, sea-born, and together strode
To where he towered on his eminence.
There those four shouted forth old Saturn's name;
Hyperion from the peak loud answered, "Saturn!"
Saturn sat near the Mother of the Gods,
In whose face was no joy, though all the Gods
Gave from their hollow throats the name of "Saturn!"

— BOOK III —

Thus in alternate uproar and sad peace,
Amazed were those Titans utterly.
O leave them, Muse! O leave them to their woes;
For thou art weak to sing such tumults dire:
A solitary sorrow best befits
Thy lips, and antheming a lonely grief.
Leave them, O Muse! for thou anon wilt find
Many a fallen old Divinity
Wandering in vain about bewildered shores.
Meantime touch piously the Delphic harp,
And not a wind of heaven but will breathe
In aid soft warble from the Dorian flute;
For lo! 'tis for the Father of all verse.
Flush every thing that hath a vermeil hue,
Let the rose glow intense and warm the air,
And let the clouds of even and of morn
Float in voluptuous fleeces o'er the hills;
Let the red wine within the goblet boil,
Cold as a bubbling well; let faint-lipp'd shells,
On sands, or in great deeps, vermilion turn
Through all their labyrinths; and let the maid
Blush keenly, as with some warm kiss surpris'd.
Chief isle of the embowered Cyclades,
Rejoice, O Delos,[32] with thine olives green,
And poplars, and lawn-shading palms, and beech,
In which the Zephyr breathes the loudest song,

[30] **Numidian:** Numidia was a province of Saharan Africa, southwest of the Carthaginian territories.

[31] **Memnon:** mythical king of Ethiopia. While his colossi were in a state of ruin, their stones were said to sing at dawn.

[32] **Cyclades:** a cluster of islands in the Aegean Sea. **Delos:** one of these islands; Apollo's birthplace, and sacred to him.

And hazels thick, dark-stemm'd beneath the shade:
Apollo is once more the golden theme!
Where was he, when the Giant of the Sun
Stood bright, amid the sorrow of his peers?
Together had he left his mother fair
And his twin-sister[33] sleeping in their bower,
And in the morning twilight wandered forth
Beside the osiers[34] of a rivulet,
Full ankle-deep in lilies of the vale.
The nightingale had ceas'd, and a few stars
Were lingering in the heavens, while the thrush
Began calm-throated. Throughout all the isle
There was no covert, no retired cave
Unhaunted by the murmurous noise of waves,
Though scarcely heard in many a green recess.
He listen'd, and he wept, and his bright tears
Went trickling down the golden bow he held.
Thus with half-shut suffused eyes he stood,
While from beneath some cumbrous boughs hard by
With solemn step an awful Goddess[35] came,
And there was purport in her looks for him,
Which he with eager guess began to read
Perplex'd, the while melodiously he said:
"How cam'st thou over the unfooted sea?
Or hath that antique mien and robed form
Mov'd in these vales invisible till now?
Sure I have heard those vestments sweeping o'er
The fallen leaves, when I have sat alone
In cool mid-forest. Surely I have traced
The rustle of those ample skirts about
These grassy solitudes, and seen the flowers
Lift up their heads, as still the whisper pass'd.
Goddess! I have beheld those eyes before,
And their eternal calm, and all that face,
Or I have dream'd."—"Yes," said the supreme shape,
"Thou hast dream'd of me; and awaking up
Didst find a lyre all golden by thy side,
Whose strings touch'd by thy fingers, all the vast
Unwearied ear of the whole universe
Listen'd in pain and pleasure at the birth
Of such new tuneful wonder. Is't not strange
That thou shouldst weep, so gifted? Tell me, youth,
What sorrow thou canst feel; for I am sad
When thou dost shed a tear: explain thy griefs
To one who in this lonely isle hath been
The watcher of thy sleep and hours of life,
From the young day when first thy infant hand
Pluck'd witless the weak flowers, till thine arm
Could bend that bow heroic to all times.
Show thy heart's secret to an ancient Power
Who hath forsaken old and sacred thrones
For prophecies of thee, and for the sake
Of loveliness new born."—Apollo then,
With sudden scrutiny and gloomless eyes,
Thus answer'd, while his white melodious throat
Throbb'd with the syllables.—"Mnemosyne!
Thy name is on my tongue, I know not how;
Why should I tell thee what thou so well seest?
Why should I strive to show what from thy lips
Would come no mystery? For me, dark, dark,
And painful vile oblivion seals my eyes:
I strive to search wherefore I am so sad,
Until a melancholy numbs my limbs;
And then upon the grass I sit, and moan,
Like one who once had wings.—O why should I
Feel curs'd and thwarted, when the liegeless air
Yields to my step aspirant? why should I
Spurn the green turf as hateful to my feet?
Goddess benign, point forth some unknown thing:
Are there not other regions than this isle?
What are the stars? There is the sun, the sun!
And the most patient brilliance of the moon!
And stars by thousands! Point me out the way
To any one particular beauteous star,
And I will flit into it with my lyre,
And make its silvery splendour pant with bliss.
I have heard the cloudy thunder: Where is power?
Whose hand, whose essence, what divinity
Makes this alarum in the elements,
While I here idle listen on the shores
In fearless yet in aching ignorance?
O tell me, lonely Goddess, by thy harp,
That waileth every morn and eventide,
Tell me why thus I rave, about these groves!
Mute thou remainest—mute! yet I can read
A wondrous lesson in thy silent face:
Knowledge enormous makes a God of me.
Names, deeds, gray legends, dire events, rebellions,
Majesties, sovran voices, agonies,
Creations and destroyings, all at once
Pour into the wide hollows of my brain,
And deify me, as if some blithe wine

[33] **mother . . . twin-sister:** Latona and Diana respectively.

[34] **osiers:** willows.

[35] **awful:** awe-inspiring. **Goddess:** Mnemosyne, mother of the Muses.

Or bright elixir peerless I had drunk,
And so become immortal."—Thus the God,
While his enkindled eyes, with level glance
Beneath his white soft temples, stedfast kept
Trembling with light upon Mnemosyne.
Soon wild commotions shook him, and made flush
All the immortal fairness of his limbs;
Most like the struggle at the gate of death;
Or liker still to one who should take leave
Of pale immortal death, and with a pang
As hot as death's is chill, with fierce convulse
Die into life: so young Apollo anguish'd:
His very hair, his golden tresses famed,
Kept undulation round his eager neck.
During the pain Mnemosyne upheld
Her arms as one who prophesied.—At length
Apollo shriek'd;—and lo! from all his limbs
Celestial
. . . .

Ode to Psyche[1]

(1820; comp. 1819)

O Goddess! hear these tuneless numbers, wrung
  By sweet enforcement and remembrance dear,
And pardon that thy secrets should be sung
  Even into thine own soft-conched ear:
Surely I dreamt to-day, or did I see
  The winged Psyche with awaken'd eyes?
I wander'd in a forest thoughtlessly,
  And, on the sudden, fainting with surprise,
Saw two fair creatures, couched side by side
  In deepest grass, beneath the whisp'ring roof
  Of leaves and trembled blossoms, where there ran
    A brooklet, scarce espied:

'Mid hush'd, cool-rooted flowers, fragrant-eyed,
  Blue, silver-white, and budded Tyrian,[2]
They lay calm-breathing on the bedded grass;
  Their arms embraced, and their pinions too;
  Their lips touch'd not, but had not bade adieu,
As if disjoined by soft-handed slumber,
And ready still past kisses to outnumber
  At tender eye-dawn of aurorean love:
    The winged boy[3] I knew;
  But who wast thou, O happy, happy dove?
    His Psyche true!

O latest born and loveliest vision far
  Of all Olympus' faded hierarchy!
Fairer than Phoebe's sapphire-region'd star,
  Or Vesper,[4] amorous glow-worm of the sky;
Fairer than these, though temple thou hast none,
    Nor altar heap'd with flowers;
Nor virgin-choir to make delicious moan
    Upon the midnight hours;
No voice, no lute, no pipe, no incense sweet
  From chain-swung censer teeming;
No shrine, no grove, no oracle, no heat
  Of pale-mouth'd prophet dreaming.

O brightest! though too late for antique vows,
  Too, too late for the fond believing lyre,
When holy were the haunted forest boughs,
  Holy the air, the water, and the fire;
Yet even in these days so far retir'd
  From happy pieties, thy lucent fans,
  Fluttering among the faint Olympians,
I see, and sing, by my own eyes inspired.
So let me be thy choir, and make a moan
    Upon the midnight hours;
Thy voice, thy lute, thy pipe, thy incense sweet
  From swinged censer teeming;
Thy shrine, thy grove, thy oracle, thy heat
  Of pale-mouth'd prophet dreaming.

Yes, I will be thy priest, and build a fane[5]
  In some untrodden region of my mind,

---

[1] **Psyche**: "nymph whom Cupid married and carried into a place of bliss, where he long enjoyed her company. Venus put her to death because she had robbed the world of her son; but Jupiter, at the request of Cupid, granted immortality to Psyche. The word signifies the soul . . . Psyche is generally represented with the wings of a butterfly [which the word also denotes in Greek], to intimate the lightness of the soul, of which the butterfly is the symbol, and on that account, among the ancients, when a man had just expired, a butterfly appeared fluttering above, as if rising from the mouth of the deceased" (Lemprière).

[2] **Tyrian**: purple, after a purple dye once made at Tyre, in Phoenicia (now Lebanon).

[3] **winged boy**: Cupid.

[4] **Phoebe's sapphire-region'd star**: the moon; see note 21 to *Hyperion*. **Vesper**: the evening star (and another name for the planet Venus).

[5] **fane**: temple.

Where branched thoughts, new grown with pleasant
pain,
Instead of pines shall murmur in the wind:
Far, far around shall those dark-cluster'd trees
Fledge the wild-ridged mountains steep by steep;
And there by zephyrs, streams, and birds, and bees,
The moss-lain Dryads[6] shall be lull'd to sleep;
And in the midst of this wide quietness
A rosy sanctuary will I dress
With the wreath'd trellis of a working brain,
With buds, and bells, and stars without a name,
With all the gardener Fancy e'er could feign,
Who breeding flowers, will never breed the same:
And there shall be for thee all soft delight
That shadowy thought can win,
A bright torch, and a casement ope at night,
To let the warm Love in!

Ode to a Nightingale

(1820; comp. 1819)

1

My heart aches, and a drowsy numbness pains
My sense, as though of hemlock[1] I had drunk,
Or emptied some dull opiate to the drains
One minute past, and Lethe-wards[2] had sunk:
'Tis not through envy of thy happy lot,
But being too happy in thine happiness,—
That thou, light-winged Dryad[3] of the trees,
In some melodious plot
Of beechen green, and shadows numberless,
Singest of summer in full-throated ease.

2

O, for a draught of vintage! that hath been
Cool'd a long age in the deep-delved earth,
Tasting of Flora and the country green,
Dance, and Provençal[4] song, and sunburnt mirth!
O for a beaker full of the warm South,
Full of the true, the blushful Hippocrene,[5]
With beaded bubbles winking at the brim,
And purple-stained mouth;
That I might drink, and leave the world unseen,
And with thee fade away into the forest dim:

3

Fade far away, dissolve, and quite forget
What thou among the leaves hast never known,
The weariness, the fever, and the fret
Here, where men sit and hear each other groan;
Where palsy shakes a few, sad, last gray hairs,
Where youth grows pale, and spectre-thin, and
dies;
Where but to think is to be full of sorrow
And leaden-eyed despairs,
Where Beauty cannot keep her lustrous eyes,
Or new Love pine at them beyond to-morrow.

4

Away! away! for I will fly to thee,
Not charioted by Bacchus and his pards,[6]
But on the viewless wings of Poesy,
Though the dull brain perplexes and retards:
Already with thee! tender is the night,
And haply[7] the Queen-Moon is on her throne,
Cluster'd around by all her starry Fays;
But here there is no light,
Save what from heaven is with the breezes blown
Through verdurous glooms and winding mossy
ways.

5

I cannot see what flowers are at my feet,
Nor what soft incense hangs upon the boughs,
But, in embalmed darkness, guess each sweet
Wherewith the seasonable month endows

[6] **zephyrs**: see note 10 to *Hyperion*. **Dryads**: tree nymphs.

[1] **hemlock**: a sedative, if taken in small doses.

[2] **Lethe-wards**: The river Lethe was the river of forgetfulness in the classical underworld whose waters, when drunk, produced oblivion.

[3] **Dryad**: a tree nymph.

[4] **Provence**: region of southeastern France.

[5] **Hippocrene**: sacred spring associated with poetic inspiration on Mt. Helicon, home of the Muses.

[6] **pards**: leopards. See note 10 to "Sleep and Poetry." "[Bacchus's] expedition into the east is celebrated. He marched, at the head of an army composed of men, as well as of women, all inspired with divine fury, and armed with thyrsuses, cymbals, and other musical instruments. The leader was drawn in a chariot by a lion and a tyger and was accompanied by Pan and Silenus and all the Satyrs" (Lemprière).

[7] **haply**: perhaps.

The grass, the thicket, and the fruit-tree wild;
White hawthorn, and the pastoral eglantine;
Fast fading violets cover'd up in leaves;
And mid-May's eldest child,
The coming musk-rose, full of dewy wine,
The murmurous haunt of flies on summer eves.

6

Darkling[8] I listen; and, for many a time
I have been half in love with easeful Death,
Call'd him soft names in many a mused rhyme,
To take into the air my quiet breath;
Now more than ever seems it rich to die,
To cease upon the midnight with no pain,
While thou art pouring forth thy soul abroad
In such an ecstasy!
Still wouldst thou sing, and I have ears in vain—
To thy high requiem become a sod.

7

Thou wast not born for death, immortal Bird!
No hungry generations tread thee down;
The voice I hear this passing night was heard
In ancient days by emperor and clown:[9]
Perhaps the self-same song that found a path
Through the sad heart of Ruth,[10] when, sick for home,
She stood in tears amid the alien corn;
The same that oft-times hath
Charm'd magic casements, opening on the foam
Of perilous seas, in faery lands forlorn.

8

Forlorn! the very word is like a bell
To toll me back from thee to my sole self!
Adieu! the fancy cannot cheat so well
As she is fam'd to do, deceiving elf.
Adieu! adieu! thy plaintive anthem fades
Past the near meadows, over the still stream,
Up the hill-side; and now 'tis buried deep
In the next valley-glades:
Was it a vision, or a waking dream?
Fled is that music:—Do I wake or sleep?[11]

[8] **Darkling:** in the dark.

[9] **clown:** peasant, rustic.

[10] **Ruth:** cf. the Book of Ruth 2.

[11] **Was it a vision . . . wake or sleep?:** *Midsummer Night's Dream,* IV.1.192–194: "Are you sure / That we are awake? It seems to me / That we sleep, we dream."

Ode on a Grecian Urn

(1820; comp. 1819)

1

Thou still unravish'd bride of quietness,
Thou foster-child of silence and slow time,
Sylvan historian, who canst thus express
A flowery tale more sweetly than our rhyme:
What leaf-fring'd legend haunts about thy shape
Of deities or mortals, or of both,
In Tempe or the dales of Arcady?[1]
What men or gods are these? What maidens loth?
What mad pursuit? What struggle to escape?
What pipes and timbrels?[2] What wild ecstasy?

2

Heard melodies are sweet, but those unheard
Are sweeter; therefore, ye soft pipes, play on;
Not to the sensual ear, but, more endear'd,
Pipe to the spirit ditties of no tone:
Fair youth, beneath the trees, thou canst not leave
Thy song, nor ever can those trees be bare;
Bold lover, never, never canst thou kiss,
Though winning near the goal—yet, do not grieve;
She cannot fade, though thou hast not thy bliss,
For ever wilt thou love, and she be fair!

3

Ah, happy, happy boughs! that cannot shed
Your leaves, nor ever bid the spring adieu;
And, happy melodist, unwearied,
For ever piping songs for ever new;
More happy love! more happy, happy love!
For ever warm and still to be enjoy'd,
For ever panting, and for ever young;
All breathing human passion far above,
That leaves a heart high-sorrowful and cloy'd,
A burning forehead, and a parching tongue.

[1] **Tempe . . . Arcady:** locations of proverbial beauty and happiness in Greece.

[2] **timbrels:** tambourines.

4

Who are these coming to the sacrifice?
To what green altar, O mysterious priest,
Lead'st thou that heifer lowing at the skies,
And all her silken flanks with garlands drest?
What little town by river or sea shore,
Or mountain-built with peaceful citadel,
Is emptied of this folk, this pious morn?
And, little town, thy streets for evermore
Will silent be; and not a soul to tell
Why thou art desolate, can e'er return.

5

O Attic shape! Fair attitude! with brede[3]
Of marble men and maidens overwrought,
With forest branches and the trodden weed;
Thou, silent form, dost tease us out of thought
As doth eternity: Cold Pastoral!
When old age shall this generation waste,
Thou shalt remain, in midst of other woe
Than ours, a friend to man, to whom thou say'st,
"Beauty is truth, truth beauty,"—that is all
Ye know on earth, and all ye need to know.[4]

Ode on Melancholy

(1820; comp. 1819)

1

No, no, go not to Lethe, neither twist
Wolf's bane, tightrooted, for its poisonous wine;
Nor suffer thy pale forehead to be kiss'd
By nightshade, ruby grape of Proserpine;
Make not your rosary of yew-berries,
Nor let the beetle, nor the death-moth be
Your mournful Psyche, nor the downy owl
A partner in your sorrow's mysteries;[1]
For shade to shade will come too drowsily,
And drown the wakeful anguish of the soul.

2

But when the melancholy fit shall fall
Sudden from heaven like a weeping cloud,
That fosters the droop-headed flowers all,
And hides the green hill in an April shroud;
Then glut thy sorrow on a morning rose,
Or on the rainbow of the salt sand-wave,
Or on the wealth of globed peonies;
Or if thy mistress some rich anger shows,
Emprison her soft hand, and let her rave,
And feed deep, deep upon her peerless eyes.

3

She dwells with Beauty—Beauty that must die;
And Joy, whose hand is ever at his lips
Bidding adieu; and aching Pleasure nigh,
Turning to poison while the bee-mouth sips:
Ay, in the very temple of Delight
Veil'd Melancholy has her sovran shrine,
Though seen of none save him whose strenuous tongue
Can burst Joy's grape against his palate fine;
His soul shall taste the sadness of her might,
And be among her cloudy trophies hung.

Lamia

(1820; comp. 1819)

—PART I—

Upon a time, before the faery broods
Drove Nymph and Satyr from the prosperous woods,
Before King Oberon's bright diadem,
Sceptre, and mantle, clasp'd with dewy gem,

[3] **brede**: embroidery.

[4] **"Beauty is truth, . . . all ye need to know**: a textual crux. The first publication of the poem, in the *Annals of the Fine Arts* (Jan. 1820), omits quotation marks, as do transcripts made of the poem by George Keats, Brown, and Dilke. The version of the poem in *Lamia, Isabella, The Eve of St. Agnes, and Other Poems* (1820), which Keats saw through the press, includes quotations, i.e., "Beauty is truth, truth beauty."

[1] **Lethe**: See note 2 to "Ode to a Nightingale." **Wolf's bane**: "a dried, tuberous root . . . formerly much used as a cardiac and respiratory sedative" (Webster's). **nightshade**: a plant with poisonous purple berries; belladonna. **Proserpine**: Hades's wife, and queen of the underworld. **yew-berries**: the poisonous fruit of the yew tree. **beetle**: the death-watch beetle, so named because of the ticking sound it makes. **death-moth**: the death's-head moth, with markings on the thorax resembling a human skull. **Psyche**: See note 1 to "Ode to Psyche."

Frighted away the Dryads and the Fauns[1]
From rushes green, and brakes, and cowslip'd lawns,
The ever-smitten Hermes[2] empty left
His golden throne, bent warm on amorous theft:
From high Olympus had he stolen light,
On this side of Jove's clouds, to escape the sight
Of his great summoner, and made retreat
Into a forest on the shores of Crete.
For somewhere in that sacred island dwelt
A nymph, to whom all hoofed Satyrs knelt;
At whose white feet the languid Tritons[3] poured
Pearls, while on land they wither'd and adored.
Fast by the springs where she to bathe was wont,
And in those meads where sometime she might haunt,
Were strewn rich gifts, unknown to any Muse,
Though Fancy's casket were unlock'd to choose.
Ah, what a world of love was at her feet!
So Hermes thought, and a celestial heat
Burnt from his winged heels to either ear,
That from a whiteness, as the lily clear,
Blush'd into roses 'mid his golden hair,
Fallen in jealous curls about his shoulders bare.

From vale to vale, from wood to wood, he flew,
Breathing upon the flowers his passion new,
And wound with many a river to its head,
To find where this sweet nymph prepar'd her secret
bed:
In vain; the sweet nymph might nowhere be found,
And so he rested, on the lonely ground,
Pensive, and full of painful jealousies
Of the Wood-Gods, and even the very trees.
There as he stood, he heard a mournful voice,
Such as once heard, in gentle heart, destroys
All pain but pity: thus the lone voice spake:
"When from this wreathed tomb shall I awake!
When move in a sweet body fit for life,
And love, and pleasure, and the ruddy strife
Of hearts and lips! Ah, miserable me!"
The God, dove-footed, glided silently
Round bush and tree, soft-brushing, in his speed,
The taller grasses and full-flowering weed,
Until he found a palpitating snake,
Bright, and cirque-couchant[4] in a dusky brake.

She was a gordian[5] shape of dazzling hue,
Vermillion-spotted, golden, green, and blue;
Striped like a zebra, freckled like a pard,[6]
Eyed like a peacock, and all crimson barr'd;
And full of silver moons, that, as she breathed,
Dissolv'd, or brighter shone, or interwreathed
Their lustres with the gloomier tapestries—
So rainbow-sided, touch'd with miseries,
She seem'd, at once, some penanced lady elf,
Some demon's mistress, or the demon's self.
Upon her crest she wore a wannish fire
Sprinkled with stars, like Ariadne's tiar:[7]
Her head was serpent, but ah, bitter-sweet!
She had a woman's mouth with all its pearls complete:
And for her eyes: what could such eyes do there
But weep, and weep, that they were born so fair?
As Proserpine still weeps for her Sicilian air.[8]
Her throat was serpent, but the words she spake
Came, as through bubbling honey, for Love's sake,
And thus; while Hermes on his pinions lay,
Like a stoop'd falcon ere he takes his prey.

"Fair Hermes, crown'd with feathers, fluttering
light,
I had a splendid dream of thee last night:
I saw thee sitting, on a throne of gold,
Among the Gods, upon Olympus old,
The only sad one; for thou didst not hear
The soft, lute-finger'd Muses chaunting clear,

[1] **Nymph:** in classical mythology, one of the minor deities of nature represented as beautiful maidens. **Satyr:** sylvan deity, a deity of the woods, having the lower trunk and legs of a horse or goat and the chest, arms, and head of a man. **King Oberon:** King of the fairies in *A Midsummer Night's Dream.* **Dryads:** tree-nymphs. **Fauns:** satyrs.

[2] **Hermes:** messenger of the gods celebrated for his love affairs.

[3] **Tritons:** many of the sea-deities are called Tritons, but the name is generally applied to those only who are half men and half fishes (Lemprière).

[4] **cirque-couchant:** Keats's pseudo-heraldic coinage for "lying coiled."

[5] **gordian:** see note 3, letter to Bailey, 18 July 1818.

[6] **pard:** leopard.

[7] **tiar:** crown. ". . . Bacchus loved [Ariadne] after Theseus had forsaken her, and he gave her a crown of seven stars, which, after her death, were made a constellation [the Pleiades]" (Lemprière).

[8] **Proserpine:** Demeter's daughter, who was kidnapped from her home in Sicily by Hades, who made her his queen. Lamia, the snake, is of African descent. "Lamiæ [are] certain monsters of Africa, who had the face and breast of a woman, and the rest of their body like that of a serpent" (Lemprière).

Nor even Apollo when he sang alone,
Deaf to his throbbing throat's long, long melodious
moan.
I dreamt I saw thee, robed in purple flakes,
Break amorous through the clouds, as morning breaks,
And, swiftly as a bright Phoebean dart,[9]
Strike for the Cretan isle, and here thou art!
Too gentle Hermes, hast thou found the maid?"
Whereat the star of Lethe[10] not delay'd
His rosy eloquence, and thus inquired:
"Thou smooth-lipp'd serpent, surely high inspired!
Thou beauteous wreath, with melancholy eyes,
Possess whatever bliss thou canst devise,
Telling me only where my nymph is fled,—
Where she doth breathe!" "Bright planet, thou hast
said,"
Return'd the snake, "but seal with oaths,[11] fair God!"
"I swear," said Hermes, "by my serpent rod,
And by thine eyes, and by thy starry crown!"
Light flew his earnest words, among the blossoms
blown.
Then thus again the brilliance feminine:
"Too frail of heart! for this lost nymph of thine,
Free as the air, invisibly, she strays
About these thornless wilds; her pleasant days
She tastes unseen; unseen her nimble feet
Leave traces in the grass and flowers sweet;
From weary tendrils, and bow'd branches green,
She plucks the fruit unseen, she bathes unseen:
And by my power is her beauty veil'd
To keep it unaffronted, unassail'd
By the love-glances of unlovely eyes,
Of Satyrs, Fauns, and blear'd Silenus'[12] sighs.
Pale grew her immortality, for woe
Of all these lovers, and she grieved so
I took compassion on her, bade her steep
Her hair in weïrd syrops, that would keep
Her loveliness invisible, yet free
To wander as she loves, in liberty.
Thou shalt behold her, Hermes, thou alone,
If thou wilt, as thou swearest, grant my boon!"
Then, once again, the charmed God began
An oath, and through the serpent's ears it ran
Warm, tremulous, devout, psalterian.[13]
Ravish'd, she lifted her Circean[14] head,
Blush'd a live damask, and swift-lisping said,
"I was a woman, let me have once more
A woman's shape, and charming as before.
I love a youth of Corinth[15]—O the bliss!
Give me my woman's form, and place me where he is.
Stoop, Hermes, let me breathe upon thy brow,
And thou shalt see thy sweet nymph even now."
The God on half-shut feathers sank serene,
She breath'd upon his eyes, and swift was seen
Of[16] both the guarded nymph near-smiling on the
green.
It was no dream; or say a dream it was,
Real are the dreams of Gods, and smoothly pass
Their pleasures in a long immortal dream.
One warm, flush'd moment, hovering, it might seem
Dash'd by the wood-nymph's beauty, so he burn'd;
Then, lighting on the printless verdure, turn'd
To the swoon'd serpent, and with languid arm,
Delicate, put to proof the lythe Caducean[17] charm.
So done, upon the nymph his eyes he bent
Full of adoring tears and blandishment,
And towards her stept: she, like a moon in wane,
Faded before him, cower'd, nor could restrain
Her fearful sobs, self-folding like a flower
That faints into itself at evening hour:
But the God fostering her chilled hand,
She felt the warmth, her eyelids open'd bland,
And, like new flowers at morning song of bees,
Bloom'd, and gave up her honey to the lees.
Into the green-recessed woods they flew;

[9] **Phoebean dart:** a ray of sunshine. Phoebus was another name for Apollo.

[10] **star of Lethe:** One of Hermes's functions was to conduct the spirits of the dead to Hades, where the river Lethe is located. See also note 2 to "Ode to a Nightingale."

[11] **seal with oaths:** Hermes was untrustworthy. "He . . . not only presided over orators, merchants, and declaimers, but was also the god of thieves, pick-pockets and all dishonest persons . . ." (Lemprière).

[12] **Silenus:** A demi-god, who became the nurse, the preceptor, and attendant of the god Bacchus . . . Silenus is generally represented as a fat and jolly old man, riding on an ass, crowned with flowers, and always intoxicated (Lemprière).

[13] **psalterian:** the psaltery was a medieval stringed instrument.

[14] **Circean:** reference to Circe, the fabled enchantress who turned Odysseus's men into swine in *The Odyssey*.

[15] **youth of Corinth:** Lycius.

[16] **of:** by.

[17] **Caducean:** Hermes bore a wand, called *caduceus*.

Nor grew they pale, as mortal lovers do.

Left to herself, the serpent now began
To change; her elfin blood in madness ran,
Her mouth foam'd, and the grass, therewith besprent,[18]
Wither'd at dew so sweet and virulent;
Her eyes in torture fix'd, and anguish drear,
Hot, glaz'd, and wide, with lid-lashes all sear,[19]
Flash'd phosphor and sharp sparks, without one
cooling tear.
The colours all inflam'd throughout her train,
She writh'd about, convuls'd with scarlet pain:
A deep volcanian yellow took the place
Of all her milder-mooned body's grace;
And, as the lava ravishes the mead,
Spoilt all her silver mail, and golden brede;[20]
Made gloom of all her frecklings, streaks and bars,
Eclips'd her crescents, and lick'd up her stars:
So that, in moments few, she was undrest
Of all her sapphires, greens, and amethyst,
And rubious-argent:[21] of all these bereft,
Nothing but pain and ugliness were left.
Still shone her crown; that varnish'd, also she
Melted and disappear'd as suddenly;
And in the air, her new voice luting soft,
Cried, "Lycius! gentle Lycius!"—Borne aloft
With the bright mists about the mountains hoar
These words dissolv'd: Crete's forests heard no more.

Wither fled Lamia, now a lady bright,
A full-born beauty new and exquisite?
She fled into that valley they pass o'er
Who go to Corinth from Cenchreas' shore;
And rested at the foot of those wild hills,
The rugged founts of the Peraean rills,
And of that other ridge whose barren back
Stretches, with all its mist and cloudy rack,
South-westward to Cleone.[22] There she stood
About a young bird's flutter from a wood,
Fair, on a sloping green of mossy tread,
By a clear pool, wherein she passioned[23]
To see herself escap'd from so sore ills,
While her robes flaunted with the daffodils.

Ah, happy Lycius!—for she was a maid
More beautiful than ever twisted braid,
Or sigh'd, or blush'd, or on spring-flowered lea
Spread a green kirtle[24] to the minstrelsy:
A virgin purest lipp'd, yet in the lore
Of love deep learned to the red heart's core:
Not one hour old, yet of sciential[25] brain
To unperplex bliss from its neighbour pain;
Define their pettish[26] limits, and estrange
Their points of contact, and swift counterchange;[27]
Intrigue with the specious chaos, and dispart[28]
Its most ambiguous atoms with sure art;
As though in Cupid's college she had spent
Sweet days a lovely graduate, still unshent,[29]
And kept his rosy terms in idle languishment.

Why this fair creature chose so fairily
By the wayside to linger, we shall see;
But first 'tis fit to tell how she could muse
And dream, when in the serpent prison-house,
Of all she list,[30] strange or magnificent:
How, ever,[31] where she will'd, her spirit went;
Whether to faint Elysium,[32] or where
Down through tress-lifting waves the Nereids fair
Wind into Thetis'[33] bower by many a pearly stair;
Or where God Bacchus drains his cups divine,
Stretch'd out, at ease, beneath a glutinous[34] pine;
Or where in Pluto's gardens palatine

[18] **besprent:** besprinkled.

[19] **sear:** seared, scorched.

[20] **mead:** meadow. **brede:** embroidery.

[21] **rubious-argent:** ruby-tinted silver.

[22] **Cenchreas:** port of Corinth at the head of the Saronic gulf. **Peraea:** not identified, but perhaps Keats had in mind Piraeum, a town on the west coast of the Isthmus of Corinth. **Cleone:** village south of Corinth on the road to Argos.

[23] **passioned:** had a passion.

[24] **lea:** grassland, pasture. **kirtle:** "a long gown or dress worn during the middle ages by women" (Webster's).

[25] **sciential:** endowed with knowledge.

[26] **pettish:** irksome.

[27] **counterchange:** exchange, alternation.

[28] **dispart:** separate.

[29] **unshent:** unspoiled.

[30] **list:** wanted.

[31] **ever:** always.

[32] **Elysium:** place of bliss inhabited by the souls of the virtuous after death.

[33] **Nereids:** sea-nymphs. **Thetis:** one of the Nereids and mother of Achilles.

[34] **glutinous:** resinous.

Mulciber's columns gleam in far piazzian[35] line.
And sometimes into cities she would send
Her dream, with feast and rioting to blend;
And once, while among mortals dreaming thus,
She saw the young Corinthian Lycius
Charioting foremost in the envious race,
Like a young Jove with calm uneager face,
And fell into a swooning love of him.
Now on the moth-time of that evening dim
He would return that way, as well she knew,
To Corinth from the shore; for freshly blew
The eastern soft wind, and his galley now
Grated the quaystones with her brazen prow
In port Cenchreas, from Egina[36] isle
Fresh anchor'd; whither he had been awhile
To sacrifice to Jove, whose temple there
Waits with high marble doors for blood and incense
rare.
Jove heard his vows, and better'd his desire;
For by some freakful chance he made retire
From his companions, and set forth to walk,
Perhaps grown wearied of their Corinth talk:
Over the solitary hills he fared,
Thoughtless at first, but ere eve's star appeared
His phantasy was lost, where reason fades,
In the calm'd twilight of Platonic shades.[37]
Lamia beheld him coming, near, more near—
Close to her passing, in indifference drear,
His silent sandals swept the mossy green;
So neighbour'd to him, and yet so unseen
She stood: he pass'd, shut up in mysteries,
His mind wrapp'd like his mantle, while her eyes
Follow'd his steps, and her neck regal white
Turn'd—syllabling thus, "Ah, Lycius bright,
And will you leave me on the hills alone?
Lycius, look back! and be some pity shown."
He did; not with cold wonder fearingly,
But Orpheus-like at an Eurydice;[38]
For so delicious were the words she sung,
It seem'd he had lov'd them a whole summer long:
And soon his eyes had drunk her beauty up,
Leaving no drop in the bewildering cup,
And still the cup was full,—while he, afraid
Lest she should vanish ere his lip had paid
Due adoration, thus began to adore;
Her soft look growing coy, she saw his chain so sure:
"Leave thee alone! Look back! Ah, Goddess, see
Whether my eyes can ever turn from thee!
For pity do not this sad heart belie—
Even as thou vanishest so I shall die.
Stay! though a Naiad of the rivers, stay!
To thy far wishes will thy streams obey:
Stay! though the greenest woods be thy domain,
Alone they can drink up the morning rain:
Though a descended Pleiad,[39] will not one
Of thine harmonious sisters keep in tune
Thy spheres,[40] and as thy silver proxy shine?
So sweetly to these ravish'd ears of mine
Came thy sweet greeting, that if thou shouldst fade
Thy memory will waste me to a shade:—
For pity do not melt!"—"If I should stay,"
Said Lamia, "here, upon this floor of clay,
And pain my steps upon these flowers too rough,
What canst thou say or do of charm enough
To dull the nice remembrance of my home?
Thou canst not ask me with thee here to roam
Over these hills and vales, where no joy is,—
Empty of immortality and bliss!
Thou art a scholar, Lycius, and must know
That finer spirits cannot breathe below
In human climes, and live: Alas! poor youth,
What taste of purer air hast thou to soothe

[35] **Pluto**: Roman name for Hades, god of the underworld. **palatine**: palatial. **Mulciber's columns**: Mulciber, the architect of Hell in *Paradise Lost*, built Pandemonium in the Doric style (like the Parthenon) with rows of fluted columns supporting an entablature of three layers of stone.

[36] **Egina**: island southwest of Athens.

[37] **shades**: shadows, as in Plato's "Allegory of the Cave," which are mistaken for reality by the ignorant: "To them, I said, the truth would be literally nothing but the shadows of the images."

[38] **Orpheus-like at an Eurydice**: "The power of Orpheus' music was such that it could move even inanimate things. When his wife Eurydice died, he went down to the infernal regions, and so charmed Pluto that she was released, on condition that Orpheus would not look back until they reached the earth. He was just about to put his foot on the earth when he looked back. Eurydice vanished" (Lemprière).

[39] **Pleiad**: "a name given to seven of the daughters of Atlas. . . . They were placed in the heavens after death, where they formed a constellation . . ." (Lemprière).

[40] **spheres**: in classical times it was believed that the planets travelled inside crystalline globes or spheres whose concentric movements produced harmonious music.

My essence? What serener palaces,
Where I may all my many senses please,
And by mysterious sleights a hundred thirsts appease?
It cannot be—Adieu!' So said, she rose
Tip-toe with white arms spread. He, sick to lose
The amorous promise of her lone complain,[41]
Swooned, murmuring of love, and pale with pain.
The cruel lady, without any show
Of sorrow for her tender favourite's woe,
But rather, if her eyes could brighter be,
With brighter eyes and slow amenity,[42]
Put her new lips to his, and gave afresh
The life she had so tangled in her mesh;
And as he from one trance was wakening
Into another, she began to sing,
Happy in beauty, life, and love, and every thing,
A song of love, too sweet for earthly lyres,
While, like held breath, the stars drew in their
panting fires.
And then she whispered in such trembling tone,
As those who, safe together met alone
For the first time through many anguished days,
Use other speech than looks; bidding him raise
His drooping head, and clear his soul of doubt,
For that she was a woman, and without
Any more subtle fluid in her veins
Than throbbing blood, and that the self-same pains
Inhabited her frail-strung heart as his.
And next she wondered how his eyes could miss
Her face so long in Corinth, where, she said,
She dwelt but half retired, and there had led
Days happy as the gold coin could invent
Without the aid of love; yet in content
Till she saw him, as once she passed him by,
Where 'gainst a column he leant thoughtfully
At Venus' temple porch, 'mid baskets heaped
Of amorous herbs and flowers, newly reaped
Late on that eve, as 'twas the night before
The Adonian[43] feast; whereof she saw no more,
But wept alone those days, for why should she adore?
Lycius from death awoke into amaze,
To see her still, and singing so sweet lays;
Then from amaze into delight he fell
To hear her whisper woman's lore so well;
And every word she spake enticed him on
To unperplexed delight and pleasure known.
Let the mad poets say whate'er they please
Of the sweets of Faeries, Peris,[44] Goddesses,
There is not such a treat among them all,
Haunters of cavern, lake, and waterfall,
As a real woman, lineal indeed
From Pyrrha's pebbles[45] or old Adam's seed.
Thus gentle Lamia judged, and judged aright,
That Lycius could not love in half a fright,
So threw the goddess off, and won his heart
More pleasantly by playing woman's part,
With no more awe than what her beauty gave,
That, while it smote, still guaranteed to save.
Lycius to all made eloquent reply,
Marrying to every word a twinborn sigh;
And last, pointing to Corinth, asked her sweet,
If 'twas too far that night for her soft feet.
The way was short, for Lamia's eagerness
Made, by a spell, the triple league decrease
To a few paces; not at all surmised
By blinded Lycius, so in her comprised.
They passed the city gates, he knew not how,
So noiseless, and he never thought to know.

As men talk in a dream, so Corinth all,
Throughout her palaces imperial,
And all her populous streets and temples lewd,
Muttered, like tempest in the distance brewed,
To the wide-spreaded night above her towers.
Men, women, rich and poor, in the cool hours,
Shuffled their sandals o'er the pavement white,
Companioned or alone; while many a light
Or found them cluster'd in the corniced shade
Of some arch'd temple door, or dusky colonnade.

Muffling his face, of greeting friends in fear,
Her fingers he press'd hard, as one came near
With curl'd gray beard, sharp eyes, and smooth bald
crown,
Slow-stepp'd, and robed in philosophic gown:

[41] **complain:** complaint.

[42] **amenity:** attractiveness, pleasure.

[43] **Adonian:** an annual feast of eight days celebrating the resurrection of Adonis, beloved of Venus.

[44] **Peris:** Persian for good fairies or genii.

[45] **lineal:** descended. **Pyrrha's pebbles:** Pyrrha and Deucalion, the sole survivors of a cataclysmic flood sent by Jupiter in his anger at mankind, repopulated the earth by scattering stones that turned into men and women.

Lycius shrank closer, as they met and past,
Into his mantle, adding wings to haste,
While hurried Lamia trembled: "Ah," said he,
"Why do you shudder, love, so ruefully?
Why does your tender palm dissolve in dew?"—
"I'm wearied," said fair Lamia: "tell me who
Is that old man? I cannot bring to mind
His features:—Lycius! wherefore did you blind
Yourself from his quick eyes?" Lycius replied,
"'Tis Apollonius sage, my trusty guide
And good instructor; but to-night he seems
The ghost of folly haunting my sweet dreams."

While yet he spake they had arrived before
A pillar'd porch, with lofty portal door,
Where hung a silver lamp, whose phosphor glow
Reflected in the slabbed steps below,
Mild as a star in water; for so new,
And so unsullied was the marble hue,
So through the crystal polish, liquid fine,
Ran the dark veins, that none but feet divine
Could e'er have touch'd there. Sounds Aeolian[46]
Breath'd from the hinges, as the ample span
Of the wide doors disclos'd a place unknown
Some time to any, but those two alone,
And a few Persian mutes, who that same year
Were seen about the markets: none knew where
They could inhabit; the most curious
Were foil'd, who watch'd to trace them to their house:
And but the flitter-winged verse must tell,
For truth's sake, what woe afterwards befel,
'Twould humour many a heart to leave them thus,
Shut from the busy world of more incredulous.

— PART II —

Love in a hut, with water and a crust,
Is—Love, forgive us!—cinders, ashes, dust;
Love in a palace is perhaps at last
More grievous torment than a hermit's fast:—
That is a doubtful tale from faery land,
Hard for the non-elect to understand.
Had Lycius liv'd to hand his story down,
He might have given the moral a fresh frown,
Or clench'd it quite: but too short was their bliss
To breed distrust and hate, that make the soft voice
    hiss.

[46] **Sounds Aeolian:** The Aeolian harp or lyre produced musical sounds as the wind passed over its strings.

Besides, there, nightly, with terrific glare,
Love, jealous grown of so complete a pair,
Hover'd and buzz'd his wings, with fearful roar,
Above the lintel[47] of their chamber door,
And down the passage cast a glow upon the floor.

For all this came a ruin: side by side
They were enthroned, in the even tide,
Upon a couch, near to a curtaining
Whose airy texture, from a golden string,
Floated into the room, and let appear
Unveil'd the summer heaven, blue and clear,
Betwixt two marble shafts:—there they reposed,
Where use had made it sweet, with eyelids closed,
Saving a tythe which love still open kept,
That they might see each other while they almost
    slept;
When from the slope side of a suburb hill,
Deafening the swallow's twitter, came a thrill
Of trumpets—Lycius started—the sounds fled,
But left a thought, a buzzing in his head.
For the first time, since first he harbour'd in
That purple-lined palace of sweet sin,
His spirit pass'd beyond its golden bourn
Into the noisy world almost forsworn.
The lady, ever watchful, penetrant,
Saw this with pain, so arguing a want
Of something more, more than her empery
Of joys; and she began to moan and sigh
Because he mused beyond her, knowing well
That but a moment's thought is passion's passing bell.
"Why do you sigh, fair creature?" whisper'd he:
"Why do you think?" return'd she tenderly:
"You have deserted me;—where am I now?
Not in your heart while care weighs on your brow:
No, no, you have dismiss'd me; and I go
From your breast houseless: ay, it must be so."
He answer'd, bending to her open eyes,
Where he was mirror'd small in paradise,
"My silver planet, both of eve and morn!
Why will you plead yourself so sad forlorn,
While I am striving how to fill my heart
With deeper crimson, and a double smart?
How to entangle, trammel up and snare
Your soul in mine, and labyrinth you there
Like the hid scent in an unbudded rose?
Ay, a sweet kiss—you see your mighty woes.

[47] **lintel:** the weight bearing beam above a doorway.

My thoughts! shall I unveil them? Listen then!
What mortal hath a prize, that other men
May be confounded and abash'd withal,
But lets it sometimes pace abroad majestical,
And triumph, as in thee I should rejoice
Amid the hoarse alarm of Corinth's voice.
Let my foes choke, and my friends shout afar,
While through the thronged streets your bridal car
Wheels round its dazzling spokes."—The lady's cheek
Trembled; she nothing said, but, pale and meek,
Arose and knelt before him, wept a rain
Of sorrows at his words; at last with pain
Beseeching him, the while his hand she wrung,
To change his purpose. He thereat was stung,
Perverse, with stronger fancy to reclaim
Her wild and timid nature to his aim:
Besides, for all his love, in self despite,
Against his better self, he took delight
Luxurious in her sorrows, soft and new.
His passion, cruel grown, took on a hue
Fierce and sanguineous as 'twas possible
In one whose brow had no dark veins to swell.
Fine was the mitigated fury, like
Apollo's presence when in act to strike
The serpent—Ha, the serpent! certes,[48] she
Was none. She burnt, she lov'd the tyranny,
And, all subdued, consented to the hour
When to the bridal he should lead his paramour.
Whispering in midnight silence, said the youth,
"Sure some sweet name thou hast, though, by my truth,
I have not ask'd it, ever thinking thee
Not mortal, but of heavenly progeny,
As still I do. Hast any mortal name,
Fit appellation for this dazzling frame?
Or friends or kinsfolk on the citied earth,
To share our marriage feast and nuptial mirth?"
"I have no friends," said Lamia, "no, not one;
My presence in wide Corinth hardly known:
My parents' bones are in their dusty urns
Sepulchred, where no kindled incense burns,
Seeing all their luckless race are dead, save me,
And I neglect the holy rite for thee.
Even as you list[49] invite your many guests;
But if, as now it seems, your vision rests
With any pleasure on me, do not bid
Old Apollonius—from him keep me hid."
Lycius, perplex'd at words so blind and blank,
Made close inquiry; from whose touch she shrank,
Feigning a sleep; and he to the dull shade
Of deep sleep in a moment was betray'd.

It was the custom then to bring away
The bride from home at blushing shut of day,
Veil'd, in a chariot, heralded along
By strewn flowers, torches, and a marriage song,
With other pageants: but this fair unknown
Had not a friend. So being left alone,
(Lycius was gone to summon all his kin)
And knowing surely she could never win
His foolish heart from its mad pompousness,
She set herself, high-thoughted, how to dress
The misery in fit magnificence.
She did so, but 'tis doubtful how and whence
Came, and who were her subtle servitors.
About the halls, and to and from the doors,
There was a noise of wings, till in short space
The glowing banquet-room shone with wide-arched grace.
A haunting music, sole perhaps and lone
Supportress of the faery-roof, made moan
Throughout, as fearful the whole charm might fade.
Fresh carved cedar, mimicking a glade
Of palm and plantain,[50] met from either side,
High in the midst, in honour of the bride:
Two palms and then two plantains, and so on,
From either side their stems branch'd one to one
All down the aisled place; and beneath all
There ran a stream of lamps straight on from wall to wall.
So canopied, lay an untasted feast
Teeming with odours. Lamia, regal drest,
Silently paced about, and as she went,
In pale contented sort of discontent,
Mission'd her viewless servants to enrich
The fretted splendour of each nook and niche.
Between the tree-stems, marbled plain at first,
Came jasper pannels; then, anon, there burst
Forth creeping imagery of slighter trees,
And with the larger wove in small intricacies.
Approving all, she faded at self-will,

[48] **the serpent:** reference to Python, who was slain by Apollo at Delphi. **certes:** certainly (Spenserian).
[49] **list:** wish.

[50] **plantain:** banana tree.

And shut the chamber up, close, hush'd and still,
Complete and ready for the revels rude,
When dreadful guests would come to spoil her
solitude.

The day appear'd, and all the gossip rout.
O senseless Lycius! Madman! wherefore flout
The silent-blessing fate, warm cloister'd hours,
And show to common eyes these secret bowers?
The herd approach'd; each guest, with busy brain,
Arriving at the portal, gaz'd amain,[51]
And enter'd marveling: for they knew the street,
Remember'd it from childhood all complete
Without a gap, yet ne'er before had seen
That royal porch, that high-built fair demesne;
So in they hurried all, maz'd, curious and keen:
Save one, who look'd thereon with eye severe,
And with calm-planted steps walk'd in austere;
'Twas Apollonius: something too he laugh'd,
As though some knotty problem, that had daft[52]
His patient thought, had now begun to thaw,
And solve and melt:—'twas just as he foresaw.

He met within the murmurous vestibule
His young disciple. "'Tis no common rule,
Lycius," said he, "for uninvited guest
To force himself upon you, and infest
With an unbidden presence the bright throng
Of younger friends; yet must I do this wrong,
And you forgive me." Lycius blush'd, and led
The old man through the inner doors broad-spread;
With reconciling words and courteous mien
Turning into sweet milk the sophist's spleen.

Of wealthy lustre was the banquet-room,
Fill'd with pervading brilliance and perfume:
Before each lucid pannel fuming stood
A censer fed with myrrh and spiced wood,
Each by a sacred tripod held aloft,
Whose slender feet wide-swerv'd upon the soft
Wool-woofed carpets: fifty wreaths of smoke
From fifty censers their light voyage took
To the high roof, still mimick'd as they rose
Along the mirror'd walls by twin-clouds odorous.
Twelve sphered tables, by silk seats insphered,[53]
High as the level of a man's breast rear'd
On libbard's[54] paws, upheld the heavy gold
Of cups and goblets, and the store thrice told
Of Ceres' horn,[55] and, in huge vessels, wine
Come from the gloomy tun with merry shine.
Thus loaded with a feast the tables stood,
Each shrining in the midst the image of a God.

When in an antichamber every guest
Had felt the cold full sponge to pleasure press'd,
By minist'ring slaves, upon his hands and feet,
And fragrant oils with ceremony meet
Pour'd on his hair, they all mov'd to the feast
In white robes, and themselves in order placed
Around the silken couches, wondering
Whence all this mighty cost and blaze of wealth
could spring.

Soft went the music the soft air along,
While fluent Greek a vowel'd undersong
Kept up among the guests, discoursing low
At first, for scarcely was the wine at flow;
But when the happy vintage touch'd their brains,
Louder they talk, and louder come the strains
Of powerful instruments:—the gorgeous dyes,
The space, the splendour of the draperies,
The roof of awful richness, nectarous cheer,
Beautiful slaves, and Lamia's self, appear,
Now, when the wine has done its rosy deed,
And every soul from human trammels freed,
No more so strange; for merry wine, sweet wine,
Will make Elysian shades not too fair, too divine.

Soon was God Bacchus at meridian height;
Flush'd were their cheeks, and bright eyes double
bright:
Garlands of every green, and every scent
From vales deflower'd, or forest-trees branch-rent,
In baskets of bright osier'd[56] gold were brought
High as the handles heap'd, to suit the thought
Of every guest; that each, as he did please,
Might fancy-fit his brows, silk-pillow'd at his ease.

What wreath for Lamia? What for Lycius?
What for the sage, old Apollonius?

[51] **amain**: greatly.

[52] **daft**: made sport of.

[53] **sphered tables**: the Greeks made their tables round in imitation of the world. **insphered**: surrounded.

[54] **libbard**: archaic for leopard.

[55] **Ceres' horn**: cornucopia (horn of plenty).

[56] **osier'd**: woven (because baskets were woven from the supple branches of the willow, or osier).

Upon her aching forehead be there hung
The leaves of willow and of adder's tongue;[57]
And for the youth, quick, let us strip for him
The thyrsus,[58] that his watching eyes may swim
Into forgetfulness; and, for the sage,
Let spear-grass and the spiteful thistle wage
War on his temples. Do not all charms fly
At the mere touch of cold philosophy?
There was an awful rainbow once in heaven:
We know her woof, her texture; she is given
In the dull catalogue of common things.
Philosophy will clip an Angel's wings,
Conquer all mysteries by rule and line,
Empty the haunted air, and gnomed mine[59]—
Unweave a rainbow, as it erewhile[60] made
The tender-person'd Lamia melt into a shade.

By her glad Lycius sitting, in chief place,
Scarce saw in all the room another face,
Till, checking his love trance, a cup he took
Full brimm'd, and opposite sent forth a look
'Cross the broad table, to beseech a glance
From his old teacher's wrinkled countenance,
And pledge him. The bald-head philosopher
Had fix'd his eye, without a twinkle or stir
Full on the alarmed beauty of the bride,
Brow-beating her fair form, and troubling her sweet pride.
Lycius then press'd her hand, with devout touch,
As pale it lay upon the rosy couch:
'Twas icy, and the cold ran through his veins;
Then sudden it grew hot, and all the pains
Of an unnatural heat shot to his heart.
"Lamia, what means this? Wherefore dost thou start?
Know'st thou that man?" Poor Lamia answer'd not.
He gaz'd into her eyes, and not a jot
Own'd they the lovelorn piteous appeal:
More, more he gaz'd: his human senses reel:
Some hungry spell that loveliness absorbs;
There was no recognition in those orbs.
"Lamia!" he cried—and no soft-toned reply.
The many heard, and the loud revelry
Grew hush; the stately music no more breathes;
The myrtle sicken'd in a thousand wreaths.
By faint degrees, voice, lute, and pleasure ceased;
A deadly silence step by step increased,
Until it seem'd a horrid presence there,
And not a man but felt the terror in his hair.
"Lamia!" he shriek'd; and nothing but the shriek
With its sad echo did the silence break.
"Begone, foul dream!" he cried, gazing again
In the bride's face, where now no azure vein
Wander'd on fair-spaced temples; no soft bloom
Misted the cheek; no passion to illume
The deep-recessed vision:—all was blight;
Lamia, no longer fair, there sat a deadly white.
"Shut, shut those juggling[61] eyes, thou ruthless man!
Turn them aside, wretch! or the righteous ban
Of all the Gods, whose dreadful images
Here represent their shadowy presences,
May pierce them on the sudden with the thorn
Of painful blindness; leaving thee forlorn,
In trembling dotage to the feeblest fright
Of conscience, for their long offended might,
For all thine impious proud-heart sophistries,
Unlawful magic, and enticing lies.
Corinthians! look upon that gray-beard wretch!
Mark how, possess'd, his lashless eyelids stretch
Around his demon eyes! Corinthians, see!
My sweet bride withers at their potency."
"Fool!" said the sophist, in an under-tone
Gruff with contempt; which a death-nighing moan
From Lycius answer'd, as heart-struck and lost,
He sank supine beside the aching ghost.
"Fool! Fool!" repeated he, while his eyes still
Relented not, nor mov'd; "from every ill
Of life have I preserv'd thee to this day,
And shall I see thee made a serpent's prey?"
Then Lamia breath'd death breath; the sophist's eye,
Like a sharp spear, went through her utterly,
Keen, cruel, perceant,[62] stinging: she, as well
As her weak hand could any meaning tell,
Motion'd him to be silent; vainly so,
He look'd and look'd again a level—No!
"A Serpent!" echoed he; no sooner said,
Than with a frightful scream she vanished:

[57] **The leaves of willow . . . adder's tongue:** emblems of grief and sorrow.

[58] **thyrsus:** a staff topped by a pine cone or a bunch of vine or berries carried by Bacchus and satyrs.

[59] **gnomed mine:** Traditionally, gnomes lived in the earth and guarded precious ores.

[60] **erewhile:** some time ago.

[61] **juggling:** deceitful.

[62] **perceant:** piercing (Spenserian).

And Lycius' arms were empty of delight,
As were his limbs of life, from that same night.
On the high couch he lay!—his friends came round—
Supported him—no pulse, or breath they found,
And, in its marriage robe, the heavy body wound.[63]

To Autumn

(1820; comp. 1819)

1

Season of mists and mellow fruitfulness,
Close bosom-friend of the maturing sun;
Conspiring with him how to load and bless
With fruit the vines that round the thatch-eves run;
To bend with apples the moss'd cottage-trees,
And fill all fruit with ripeness to the core;
To swell the gourd, and plump the hazel shells
With a sweet kernel; to set budding more,
And still more, later flowers for the bees,
Until they think warm days will never cease,
For summer has o'er-brimm'd their clammy cells.

2

Who hath not seen thee oft amid thy store?
Sometimes whoever seeks abroad may find
Thee sitting careless on a granary floor,
Thy hair soft-lifted by the winnowing wind;
Or on a half-reap'd furrow sound asleep,
Drows'd with the fume of poppies, while thy hook
Spares the next swath and all its twined flowers:
And sometimes like a gleaner thou dost keep
Steady thy laden head across a brook;
Or by a cyder-press, with patient look,
Thou watchest the last oozings hours by hours.

3

Where are the songs of spring? Ay, where are they?
Think not of them, thou hast thy music too,—
While barred clouds bloom the soft-dying day,
And touch the stubble-plains with rosy hue;
Then in a wailful choir the small gnats mourn
Among the river sallows, borne aloft
Or sinking as the light wind lives or dies;
And full-grown lambs loud bleat from hilly bourn;
Hedge-crickets sing; and now with treble soft
The red-breast whistles from a garden-croft;[1]
And gathering swallows twitter in the skies.

from Letter to James Rice 14 February 1820

Wentworth Place
Monday Morn.

MY DEAR RICE,[1]

I have not been well enough to make any tolerable rejoinder to your kind Letter. I will as you advise be very chary of my health and spirits. I am sorry to hear of your

[63] Hellenistic philosopher Flavius Philostratus (c. 170–c. 244) wrote *The Life of Apollonius of Tyana*, about a philosophizing mystic of the first century AD. Keats's note to Lamia reads: "Philostratus, in his fourth book *de Vita Apollonii*, hath a memorable instance in this kind, which I may not omit, of one Menippus Lycius, a young man twenty-five years of age, that going betwixt Cenchreas and Corinth, met such a phantasm in the habit of a fair gentlewoman, which taking him by the hand, carried him home to her house, in the suburbs of Corinth, and told him she was a Phoenician by birth, and if he would tarry with her, he should hear her sing and play, and drink such wine as never any drank, and no man should molest him; but she, being fair and lovely, would live and die with him, that was fair and lovely to behold. The young man, a philosopher, otherwise staid and discreet, able to moderate his passions, though not this of love, tarried with her a while to his great content, and at last married her, to whose wedding, amongst other guests, came Apollonius; who, by some probable conjectures, found her out to be a serpent, a lamia; and that all her furniture was, like Tantalus' gold, described by Homer, no substance but mere illusions. When she saw herself descried, she wept, and desired Apollonius to be silent, but he would not be moved, and thereupon she, plate, house, and all that was in it, vanished in an instant: many thousands took notice of this fact, for it was done in the midst of Greece." (Burton's "Anatomy of Melancholy." Part 3. Sect. 2. Memb. 1. Subs. 1.)

[1] **bourn**: stream, or boundary. **treble**: high-pitched song. **red-breast**: robin. **garden-croft**: small field adjoining a house.

[1] **Rice**: James Rice Jr. (b. ?-d. before 12 Feb. 1833).

relapse[2] and hypochondriac symptoms attending it. Let us hope for the best as you say. I shall follow your example in looking to the future good rather than brooding upon present ill.[3] I have not been so worn with lengthen'd illnesses as you have therefore cannot answer you on your own ground with respect to those haunting and deformed thoughts and feelings you speak of. When I have been or supposed myself in health I have had my share of them, especially within this last year. I may say that for 6 Months before I was taken ill I had not passed a tranquil day—Either that gloom overspred me or I was suffering under some passionate feeling, or if I turn'd to versify that acerbated[4] the poison of either sensation. The Beauties of Nature had lost their power over me. How astonishingly (here I must premise that illness as far as I can judge in so short a time has relieved my Mind of a load of deceptive thoughts and images and makes me perceive things in a truer light)—How astonishingly does the chance of leaving the world impress a sense of its natural beauties on us. Like poor Falstaff,[5] though I do not babble, I think of green fields. I muse with the greatest affection on every flower I have known from my infancy—their shapes and coulours as are new to me as if I had just created them with a superhuman fancy—It is because they are connected with the most thoughtless and happiest moments of our Lives—I have seen foreign flowers in hothouses of the most beautiful nature, but I do not care a straw for them. The simple flowers of our sp[r]ing are what I want to see again. . . .

[2] **relapse:** For years Rice had been suffering from an incurable ailment.

[3] **present ill:** On 3 Feb. 1820, Keats suffered a severe hemorrhage in his lungs.

[4] **acerbated:** exacerbated.

[5] **Falstaff:** *Henry V,* II.iii.16: Falstaff "[babbl'd] of green fields" while dying.

Letter to Percy Bysshe Shelley
16 August 1820

Hampstead August 16th

MY DEAR SHELLEY,

I am very much gratified that you, in a foreign country,[1] and with a mind almost over occupied, should write to me in the strain of the Letter beside me. If I do not take advantage of your invitation it will be prevented by a circumstance I have very much at heart to prophesy—There is no doubt that an english winter would put an end to me, and do so in a lingering hateful manner, therefore I must either voyage or journey to Italy as a soldier marches up to a battery. My nerves at present are the worst part of me, yet they feel soothed when I think that come what extreme may, I shall not be destined to remain in one spot long enough to take a hatred of any four particular bed-posts. I am glad you take any pleasure in my poor Poem;[2]—which I would willingly take the trouble to unwrite, if possible, did I care so much as I have done about Reputation. I received a copy of the Cenci,[3] as from yourself from Hunt. There is only one part of it I am judge of; the Poetry, and dramatic effect, which by many spirits now a days is considered the mammon.[4] A modern work it is said must have a purpose, which may be the God—*an artist* must serve Mammon—he must have "self concentration" selfishness perhaps. You I am sure will forgive me for sincerely remarking that you might curb your magnanimity and be more of an artist, and 'load every

[1] **foreign country:** Italy. At this time, the Shelleys were staying in Pisa. Keats had first met Shelley at Hunt's cottage in Dec. 1816. Shelley had written to Keats earlier in the summer of 1820 urging him to come to Italy for his health, offering to put him up at his house.

[2] **my poor Poem:** *Endymion.* Shelley had written: "I have lately read your Endymion again & ever with a new sense of the treasures of poetry it contains, though treasures poured forth with indistinct profusion. This, people in general will not endure, & that is the cause of the comparatively few copies which have been sold. I feel persuaded that you are capable of the greatest things, so you but will" (Shelley's *Letters,* II.221).

[3] **the Cenci:** *The Cenci** is Shelley's drama about incest and parricide (published in the spring of 1820).

[4] **mammon:** god of material wealth.

rift' of your subject with ore.[5] The thought of such discipline must fall like cold chains upon you, who perhaps never sat with your wings furl'd for six Months together. And is not this extraordina[r]y talk for the writer of Endymion? whose mind was like a pack of scattered cards—I am pick'd up and sorted to a pip.[6] My Imagination is a Monastry and I am its Monk—you must explain my metapcs to yourself. I am in expectation of Prometheus[7] every day. Could I have my own wish for its interest effected you would have it still in manuscript—or be but now putting an end to the second act. I remember you advising me not to publish my first-blights, on Hampstead heath—I am returning advice upon your hands. Most of the Poems in the volume I send you[8] have been written above two years, and would never have been publish'd but from a hope of gain; so you see I am inclined enough to take your advice now. I must exp[r]ess once more my deep sense of your kindness, adding my sincere thanks and respects for Mrs Shelley. In the hope of soon seeing you {I} remain

most sincerely {yours,}
JOHN KEATS—

Letter from Joseph Severn to John Taylor[1] 6 March 1821

Rome March 6th 182[1]

MY DEAR SIR

I have tried many times to write you—but no—I could not it has been too much for me to think on it—I have been ill from the fatigue and pain I have suffered—the recollection of poor Keats hangs dreadfully upon me—I see him at every glance—I cannot be alone now—my nerves are so shattered.—These brutal Italians have nearly finished their monstrous business—they have burned all the furniture—and are now scraping the walls—making new windows—new door's—and even a new floor—You will see all the miseries [?] attendant on these laws—I verily think I have suffered more from their cursed cruelties—than from all I did for Keats—These wretches have taken the moments when I was suffering in mind and body—they have inraged me day after day—until I trembled at the sound of every voice—I will try now once more to write you on our poor Keats—you will have but little for I can hardly dare to think on it—but I will write at intervals—and pray you to take it as my utmost endeavour—when I am stronger I will send you every word—the remembrance of this scene of horror will be fresh upon my mind to the end of my days—

Four days previous to his death—the change in him was so great that I passed each moment in dread—not knowing what the next would have—he was calm and firm at its approaches—to a most astonishing degree—he told [me] not to tremble for he did not think that he should be convulsed—he said—"did you ever see any one die" no—"well then I pity you poor Severn—what trouble and danger you have got into for me—now you must be firm for it will not last long—I shall soon be laid in the quiet grave—thank God for the quiet grave—O! I can feel the cold earth upon me—the daisies growing over me—O for this quiet—it will be my first"—when the morning light came and still found him alive—O how bitterly he grieved—I cannot bear his cries—

Each day he would look up in the doctors face to discover how long he should live—he would say—"how long will this posthumous life of mine last"—that look was more than we could ever bear—the extreme brightness of his eyes—with his poor pallid face—were not earthly—~~These fo~~

These four nights I watch him—each night expecting his death—on the fifth day the doctor prepared me

[5] **'load every rift'**: Cf. *The Fairie Queen*, Book II, Canto VII, stanza 28, line 5: "And with rich metall loaded every rifte."

[6] **sorted to a pip**: "Arranged in orderly fashion with all the cards matched" (Rollins).

[7] **Prometheus**: reference to Shelley's *Prometheus Unbound,** published that month.

[8] **the volume I send you**: *Lamia, Isabella, The Eve of St. Agnes, and Other Poems*, published in July 1820. When Shelley's drowned body was recovered, his pocket contained an open copy of this book.

[1] John Taylor, along with his partner James Hessey, had published Keats's last two volumes. The artist Joseph Severn (1793–1879) accompanied the severely ill Keats to Italy in the fall of 1820, and devotedly nursed him on his deathbed in Rome, until the poet died on 23 Feb. 1821. For 20 years after Keats's death Severn stayed on in Rome, and his body lies next to Keats's in the Protestant cemetery there.

for it—23rd at 4 o'clock afternoon—The poor fellow bade me lift him up in bed—he breathed with great difficulty—and seemd to lose the power of coughing up the phlegm—and immense sweat came over him so that my breath felt cold to him—"dont breath on me—it comes like Ice"—he clasped my hand very fast as I held him in my arms—the mucus was boiling within him—it gurgled in his throat—this increased—but yet he seem'd without pain—his eyes look'd upon me with extrem[e] sensibility but without pain—at 11 he died in my arms—The English Nurse had been with me all this {day—} this was something to me—but I was very bad—n{o} sleep that night—The next day the doctor had me over to his house—I was still the same.—these kind people did every thing to comfort me—I must have sunk under it all—but for them—On the following day a cast was taken—and his death made known to the brutes here—yet we kept a strong hand over them—we put them off untill the poor fellow was laid in his grave—On Sunday the second day Dr Clark and Dr Luby with an Italian Surgeon—opened the body—they thought it the worst possible Consumption—the lungs were intirely destroyed—the cells were quite gone—but Doctor Clark will write you on this head—This was another night without sleep to me—I felt worse and worse—On the third day Monday 26th the funeral beasts came—many English requested to follow him—those who did so were Dr Clark & Dr Luby Messrs Ewing—Westmacott—Henderson—Pointer—and the Revd Mr Wolf who read the funeral service—he was buried very near to the monument of Caius Cest[i]us—a few yards from Dr Bell and an infant of Mr Shelly's.[2]—The good hearted Doctor made the man put turfs of daisies upon the grave—he said—"this would be poor Keats's wish—could he know it"—I will write again by next post but I am still but in a poor state—

farewell
Josh Severn

[2] **Caius Cestius**: a first-century BC Roman praetor and tribune of the people. William Shelley was buried on 8 June 1819.

POSTHUMOUS PUBLICATIONS

from THE PLYMOUTH AND DEVENPORT WEEKLY JOURNAL
(1838)

On Sitting Down to Read *King Lear* Once Again
(1838; comp. 1818)

O golden-tongued Romance, with serene lute!
Fair plumed syren, queen of far-away!
Leave melodizing on this wintry day,
Shut up thine olden pages, and be mute.
Adieu! for, once again, the fierce dispute
Betwixt damnation and impassion'd clay
Must I burn through; once more humbly assay
The bitter-sweet of this Shaksperean fruit.
Chief Poet! and ye clouds of Albion,[1]
Begetters of our deep eternal theme!
When through the old oak forest I am gone,
Let me not wander in a barren dream:
But, when I am consumed in the fire,
Give me new phoenix[2] wings to fly at my desire.

Bright star, would I were stedfast as thou art
(1838; comp. 1819)

Bright star, would I were stedfast as thou art—
Not in lone splendor hung aloft the night,

[1] **Albion**: a traditional name for England.

[2] **phoenix**: Egyptian bird of legend that sits in a burning fire of aromatic wood every 500 years to be reborn as a new phoenix.

And watching, with eternal lids apart,
Like nature's patient, sleepless eremite,[1]
The moving waters at their priestlike task
Of pure ablution round earth's human shores,
Or gazing on the new soft-fallen mask
Of snow upon the mountains and the moors;
No—yet still stedfast, still unchangeable,
Pillow'd upon my fair love's ripening breast,
To feel for ever its soft swell and fall,
Awake for ever in a sweet unrest,
Still, still to hear her tender-taken breath,
And so live ever—or else swoon to death.

[1] **eremite:** a Christian hermit.

from LIFE, LETTERS, AND LITERARY REMAINS, OF JOHN KEATS
(1848)

When I have fears that I may cease to be
(1848; comp. 1818)

When I have fears that I may cease to be
Before my pen has glean'd my teeming brain,
Before high piled books, in charactry,
Hold like rich garners the full ripen'd grain;
When I behold, upon the night's starr'd face,
Huge cloudy symbols of a high romance,
And think that I may never live to trace
Their shadows, with the magic hand of chance;
And when I feel, fair creature of an hour,
That I shall never look upon thee more,
Never have relish in the fairy power
Of unreflecting love;—then on the shore
Of the wide world I stand alone, and think
Till love and fame to nothingness do sink.

Ode on Indolence
(1848; comp. 1819)

"They toil not, neither do they spin."[1]

1

One morn before me were three figures seen,
With bowed necks, and joined hands, side-faced;
And one behind the other stepp'd serene,
In placid sandals, and in white robes graced:
They pass'd, like figures on a marble urn,
When shifted round to see the other side;
They came again; as when the urn once more
Is shifted round, the first seen shades return;
And they were strange to me, as may betide
With vases, to one deep in Phidian[2] lore.

2

How is it, shadows, that I knew ye not?
How came ye muffled in so hush a masque?
Was it a silent deep-disguised plot
To steal away, and leave without a task
My idle days? Ripe was the drowsy hour;
The blissful cloud of summer-indolence
Benumb'd my eyes; my pulse grew less and less;
Pain had no sting, and pleasure's wreath no flower.
O, why did ye not melt, and leave my sense
Unhaunted quite of all but—nothingness?

3

A third time pass'd they by, and, passing, turn'd
Each one the face a moment whiles to me;
Then faded, and to follow them I burn'd
And ached for wings, because I knew the three:
The first was a fair maid, and Love her name;
The second was Ambition, pale of cheek,
And ever watchful with fatigued eye;

[1] The epigram is from Matthew 6:28: "And why take ye thought for raiment? Consider the lilies of the field, how they grow; they toil not, neither do they spin."

[2] **Phidian:** Phidias (c. 490–c. 448 BC) is regarded as the greatest of the ancient Greek sculptors, and many of the Elgin Marbles were attributed to him.

The last, whom I love more, the more of blame
Is heap'd upon her, maiden most unmeek,—
I knew to be my demon Poesy.

4

They faded, and, forsooth! I wanted wings:
O folly! What is Love? and where is it?
And for that poor Ambition—it springs
From a man's little heart's short fever-fit;
For Poesy!—no,—she has not a joy,—
At least for me,—so sweet as drowsy noons,
And evenings steep'd in honied indolence;
O, for an age so shelter'd from annoy,[3]
That I may never know how change the moons,
Or hear the voice of busy common-sense!

5

A third time came they by;—alas! wherefore?
My sleep had been embroider'd with dim dreams;
My soul had been a lawn besprinkled o'er
With flowers, and stirring shades, and baffled beams:
The morn was clouded, but no shower fell,
Though in her lids hung the sweet tears of May;
The open casement press'd a new-leaved vine,
Let in the budding warmth and throstle's lay;[4]
O shadows! 'twas a time to bid farewell!
Upon your skirts had fallen no tears of mine.

6

So, ye three ghosts, adieu! Ye cannot raise
My head cool-bedded in the flowery grass;
For I would not be dieted with praise,
A pet-lamb in a sentimental farce!
Fade softly from my eyes, and be once more
In masque-like figures on the dreamy urn;
Farewell! I yet have visions for the night,
And for the day faint visions there is store;
Vanish, ye phantoms, from my idle spright,[5]
Into the clouds, and never more return!

---

[3] **annoy:** annoyance.

[4] **throstle's lay:** the thrush's song.

[5] **spright:** soul.

La Belle Dame sans Merci: A Ballad

(1848; 1820; comp. 1819)

1

O what can ail thee, knight at arms,
Alone and palely loitering?
The sedge has wither'd from the lake,
And no birds sing.

2

O what can ail thee, knight at arms,
So haggard and so woe-begone?
The squirrel's granary is full,
And the harvest's done.

3

I see a lily on thy brow
With anguish moist and fever dew,
And on thy cheeks a fading rose
Fast withereth too.

4

I met a lady in the meads,
Full beautiful, a fairy's child;
Her hair was long, her foot was light,
And her eyes were wild.

5

I made a garland for her head,
And bracelets too, and fragrant zone;
She look'd at me as she did love,
And made sweet moan.

6

I set her on my pacing steed,
And nothing else saw all day long,
For sidelong would she bend, and sing
A fairy's song.

7

She found me roots of relish sweet,
And honey wild, and manna dew,
And sure in language strange she said—
I love thee true.

8

She took me to her elfin grot,
And there she wept, and sigh'd full sore,
And there I shut her wild wild eyes
With kisses four.

9

And there she lulled me asleep,
And there I dream'd—Ah! woe betide!
The latest dream I ever dream'd
On the cold hill's side.

10

I saw pale kings, and princes too,
Pale warriors, death pale were they all;
They cried—"La belle dame sans merci
Hath thee in thrall!"

11

I saw their starv'd lips in the gloam
With horrid warning gaped wide,
And I awoke and found me here
On the cold hill's side.

12

And this is why I sojourn here,
Alone and palely loitering,
Though the sedge is wither'd from the lake,
And no birds sing.

from MISCELLANIES OF THE PHILOBIBLON SOCIETY
(1856–1857)

The Fall of Hyperion: A Dream[1]
(1856; comp. 1819)

—CANTO—

Fanatics have their dreams, wherewith they weave
A paradise for a sect; the savage too
From forth the loftiest fashion of his sleep
Guesses at heaven: pity these have not
Trac'd upon vellum[2] or wild Indian leaf
The shadows of melodious utterance.
But bare of laurel they live, dream, and die;
For Poesy alone can tell her dreams,
With the fine spell of words alone can save
Imagination from the sable charm
And dumb enchantment. Who alive can say
"Thou art no poet; may'st not tell thy dreams"?
Since every man whose soul is not a clod
Hath visions, and would speak, if he had lov'd
And been well nurtured in his mother tongue.
Whether the dream now purposed to rehearse
Be poet's or fanatic's will be known
When this warm scribe my hand is in the grave.

Methought I stood where trees of every clime,
Palm, myrtle, oak, and sycamore, and beech,
With plantane, and spice blossoms, made a screen;
In neighbourhood of fountains, by the noise
Soft showering in mine ears, and, by the touch
Of scent, not far from roses. Turning round,
I saw an arbour with a drooping roof
Of trellis vines, and bells, and larger blooms,
Like floral-censers swinging light in air;
Before its wreathed doorway, on a mound
Of moss, was spread a feast of summer fruits,
Which, nearer seen, seem'd refuse of a meal
By angel tasted, or our mother Eve;
For empty shells were scattered on the grass,
And grape stalks but half bare, and remnants more,
Sweet smelling, whose pure kinds I could not know.
Still was more plenty than the fabled horn[3]
Thrice emptied could pour forth, at banqueting
For Proserpine[4] return'd to her own fields,
Where the white heifers low. And appetite
More yearning than on earth I ever felt
Growing within, I ate deliciously;
And, after not long, thirsted, for thereby
Stood a cool vessel of transparent juice,
Sipp'd by the wander'd bee, the which I took,

---

[1] For the mythological background of Hyperion, see note 1 to *Hyperion: A Fragment*.

[2] **vellum**: a parchment made of thin animal skin, used for writing or printing.

[3] **fabled horn**: cornucopia.

[4] **Proserpine**: After Proserpine was kidnapped by Pluto and made Queen of the underworld, her mother Ceres appealed to Jupiter, who allowed Proserpine to rejoin her mother on earth for half the year. Ceres, in her joy, caused the earth to bloom (accounting for spring and summer).

And, pledging all the mortals of the world,
And all the dead whose names are in our lips,
Drank. That full draught is parent of my theme.
No Asian poppy, nor elixir fine
Of the soon fading jealous caliphat;[5]
No poison gender'd in close monkish cell
To thin the scarlet conclave[6] of old men,
Could so have rapt unwilling life away.
Among the fragrant husks and berries crush'd,
Upon the grass I struggled hard against
The domineering potion; but in vain:
The cloudy swoon came on, and down I sunk
Like a Silenus[7] on an antique vase.
How long I slumber'd 'tis a chance to guess.
When sense of life return'd, I started up
As if with wings; but the fair trees were gone,
The mossy mound and arbour were no more;
I look'd around upon the carved sides
Of an old sanctuary with roof august,
Builded so high, it seem'd that filmed clouds
Might spread beneath, as o'er the stars of heaven;
So old the place was, I remembered none
The like upon the earth; what I had seen
Of grey cathedrals, buttress'd walls, rent towers,
The superannuations of sunk realms,
Or nature's rocks toil'd hard in waves and winds,
Seem'd but the faulture[8] of decrepit things
To that eternal domed monument.
Upon the marble at my feet there lay
Store of strange vessels, and large draperies,
Which needs had been of dyed asbestus wove,
Or in that place the moth could not corrupt,
So white the linen; so, in some, distinct
Ran imageries from a sombre loom.
All in a mingled heap confus'd there lay
Robes, golden tongs, censer, and chafing dish,
Girdles, and chains, and holy jewelries.

Turning from these with awe, once more I rais'd
My eyes to fathom the space every way;
The embossed roof, the silent massy range
Of columns north and south, ending in mist
Of nothing, then to eastward, where black gates
Were shut against the sunrise evermore.
Then to the west I look'd, and saw far off
An image, huge of feature as a cloud,
At level of whose feet an altar slept,
To be approach'd on either side by steps,
And marble balustrade, and patient travail
To count with toil the innumerable degrees.
Towards the altar sober-pac'd I went,
Repressing haste, as too unholy there;
And, coming nearer, saw beside the shrine
One minist'ring; and there arose a flame.
When in mid-May the sickening east wind
Shifts sudden to the south, the small warm rain
Melts out the frozen incense from all flowers,
And fills the air with so much pleasant health
That even the dying man forgets his shroud;
Even so that lofty sacrificial fire,
Sending forth Maian incense,[9] spread around
Forgetfulness of every thing but bliss,
And clouded all the altar with soft smoke,
From whose white fragrant curtains thus I heard
Language pronounc'd. "If thou canst not ascend
These steps, die on that marble where thou art.
Thy flesh, near cousin to the common dust,
Will parch for lack of nutriment — thy bones
Will wither in few years, and vanish so
That not the quickest eye could find a grain
Of what thou now art on that pavement cold.
The sands of thy short life are spent this hour,
And no hand in the universe can turn
Thy hour glass, if these gummed leaves[10] be burnt
Ere thou canst mount up these immortal steps."
I heard, I look'd: two senses both at once
So fine, so subtle, felt the tyranny
Of that fierce threat, and the hard task proposed.
Prodigious seem'd the toil; the leaves were yet
Burning, — when suddenly a palsied chill
Struck from the paved level up my limbs,
And was ascending quick to put cold grasp
Upon those streams that pulse beside the throat:
I shriek'd; and the sharp anguish of my shriek

[5] **caliphat**: allusion to Zobeide, the jealous wife in "The History of Ganem" in *The Arabian Nights,* who drugged the mistress of Caliph.

[6] **the scarlet conclave**: the college of cardinals responsible for electing a new pope from their number when the pope dies.

[7] **Silenus**: See note 12 to *Lamia.*

[8] **faulture**: Keats's coinage for weakness.

[9] **Maian incense**: an epithet suggesting spring-like fragrance; from the goddess Maia.

[10] **gummed leaves**: aromatic leaves.

Stung my own ears—I strove hard to escape
The numbness; strove to gain the lowest step.
Slow, heavy, deadly was my pace: the cold
Grew stifling, suffocating, at the heart;
And when I clasp'd my hands I felt them not.
One minute before death, my iced foot touch'd
The lowest stair; and as it touch'd, life seem'd
To pour in at the toes: I mounted up,
As once fair angels on a ladder flew
From the green turf to heaven.[11]—"Holy Power,"
Cried I, approaching near the horned shrine,
"What am I that should so be sav'd from death?
What am I that another death come not
To choak my utterance sacrilegious here?"
Then said the veiled shadow—"Thou hast felt
What 'tis to die and live again before
Thy fated hour. That thou hadst power to do so
Is thy own safety; thou hast dated on[12]
Thy doom."—"High Prophetess," said I, "purge off
Benign, if so it please thee, my mind's film."
"None can usurp this height," return'd that shade,
"But those to whom the miseries of the world
Are misery, and will not let them rest.
All else who find a haven in the world,
Where they may thoughtless sleep away their days,
If by a chance into this fane[13] they come,
Rot on the pavement where thou rotted'st half."—
"Are there not thousands in the world," said I,
Encourag'd by the sooth[14] voice of the shade,
"Who love their fellows even to the death;
Who feel the giant agony of the world;
And more, like slaves to poor humanity,
Labour for mortal good? I sure should see
Other men here: but I am here alone."
"They whom thou spak'st of are no vision'ries,"
Rejoin'd that voice—"They are no dreamers weak,
They seek no wonder but the human face;
No music but a happy-noted voice—
They come not here, they have no thought to come—
And thou art here, for thou art less than they.
What benefit canst thou do, or all thy tribe,
To the great world? Thou art a dreaming thing;
A fever of thyself—think of the earth;
What bliss even in hope is there for thee?
What haven? Every creature hath its home;
Every sole man hath days of joy and pain,
Whether his labours be sublime or low—
The pain alone; the joy alone; distinct:
Only the dreamer venoms all his days,
Bearing more woe than all his sins deserve.
Therefore, that happiness be somewhat shar'd,
Such things as thou art are admitted oft
Into like gardens thou didst pass erewhile,
And suffer'd in these temples; for that cause
Thou standest safe beneath this statue's knees."
"That I am favored for unworthiness,
By such propitious parley medicin'd
In sickness not ignoble, I rejoice,
Aye, and could weep for love of such award."
So answer'd I, continuing, "If it please,
Majestic shadow, tell me: sure not all
Those melodies sung into the world's ear
Are useless: sure a poet is a sage;
A humanist, physician to all men.
That I am none I feel, as vultures feel
They are no birds when eagles are abroad.
What am I then? Thou spakest of my tribe:
What tribe?"—The tall shade veil'd in drooping white
Then spake, so much more earnest, that the breath
Mov'd the thin linen folds that drooping hung
About a golden censer from the hand
Pendent.—"Art thou not of the dreamer tribe?
The poet and the dreamer are distinct,
Diverse, sheer opposite, antipodes.
The one pours out a balm upon the world,
The other vexes it." Then shouted I
Spite of myself, and with a Pythia's[15] spleen,
"Apollo! faded, far flown Apollo!
Where is thy misty pestilence to creep
Into the dwellings, through the door crannies,
Of all mock lyrists, large self worshipers,
And careless hectorers in proud bad verse.

[11] **As once fair angels:** an allusion to Jacob's ladder. See Genesis 28:12. "Then he dreamed, and behold, a ladder was set up on the earth, and its top reached to heaven; and there the angels of God were ascending and descending on it."

[12] **dated on:** postponed.

[13] **fane:** temple.

[14] **sooth:** smooth.

[15] **Pythia:** "The person that delivered the oracles of the god [Apollo] was a woman, whom they called Pythia . . . [she] was no sooner inspired but she began immediately to swell and foam at the mouth. . . ." (from Potter's *Antiquities of Ancient Greece* [1697], cited in Allott).

Though I breathe death with them it will be life
To see them sprawl before me into graves.
Majestic shadow, tell me where I am:
Whose altar this; for whom this incense curls:
What image this, whose face I cannot see,
For the broad marble knees; and who thou art,
Of accent feminine, so courteous."
Then the tall shade in drooping linens veil'd
Spake out, so much more earnest, that her breath
Stirr'd the thin folds of gauze that drooping hung
About a golden censer from her hand
Pendent; and by her voice I knew she shed
Long treasured tears. "This temple sad and lone
Is all spar'd from the thunder of a war
Foughten long since by giant hierarchy
Against rebellion: this old image here,
Whose carved features wrinkled as he fell,
Is Saturn's; I, Moneta,[16] left supreme
Sole priestess of his desolation."—
I had no words to answer; for my tongue,
Useless, could find about its roofed home
No syllable of a fit majesty
To make rejoinder to Moneta's mourn.
There was a silence while the altar's blaze
Was fainting for sweet food: I look'd thereon
And on the paved floor, where nigh were pil'd
Faggots of cinnamon, and many heaps
Of other crisped spice-wood—then again
I look'd upon the altar and its horns
Whiten'd with ashes, and its lang'rous flame,
And then upon the offerings again;
And so by turns—till sad Moneta cried,
"The sacrifice is done, but not the less
Will I be kind to thee for thy good will.
My power, which to me is still a curse,
Shall be to thee a wonder; for the scenes
Still swooning vivid through my globed brain
With an electral[17] changing misery
Thou shalt with those dull mortal eyes behold,
Free from all pain, if wonder pain thee not."
As near as an immortal's sphered words
Could to a mother's soften, were these last:
But yet I had a terror of her robes,
And chiefly of the veils, that from her brow
Hung pale, and curtain'd her in mysteries
That made my heart too small to hold its blood.
This saw that Goddess, and with sacred hand
Parted the veils. Then saw I a wan face,
Not pin'd by human sorrows, but bright blanch'd
By an immortal sickness which kills not;
It works a constant change, which happy death
Can put no end to; deathwards progressing
To no death was that visage; it had pass'd
The lily and the snow; and beyond these
I must not think now, though I saw that face—
But for her eyes I should have fled away.
They held me back, with a benignant light,
Soft mitigated by divinest lids
Half closed, and visionless entire they seem'd
Of all external things—they saw me not,
But in blank splendor beam'd like the mild moon,
Who comforts those she sees not, who knows not
What eyes are upward cast. As I had found
A grain of gold upon a mountain's side,
And twing'd with avarice strain'd out my eyes
To search its sullen entrails rich with ore,
So at the view of sad Moneta's brow,
I ached to see what things the hollow brain
Behind enwombed: what high tragedy
In the dark secret chambers of her skull
Was acting, that could give so dread a stress
To her cold lips, and fill with such a light
Her planetary eyes; and touch her voice
With such a sorrow. "Shade of Memory!"
Cried I, with act adorant at her feet,
"By all the gloom hung round thy fallen house,
By this last temple, by the golden age,
By great Apollo, thy dear foster child,
And by thy self, forlorn divinity,
The pale Omega[18] of a wither'd race,
Let me behold, according as thou said'st,
What in thy brain so ferments to and fro."—
No sooner had this conjuration pass'd
My devout lips, than side by side we stood,
(Like a stunt bramble by a solemn pine)
Deep in the shady sadness of a vale,
Far sunken from the healthy breath of morn,
Far from the fiery noon, and eve's one star.

[16] **Saturn:** the fallen leader of the Titans. **Moneta:** Jupiter's child by Mnemosyne, goddess of memory; in some accounts, Moneta is also another name for Mnemosyne.

[17] **electral:** electrical.

[18] **Omega:** last letter of the Greek alphabet; proverbially, the end.

Onward I look'd beneath the gloomy boughs,
And saw, what first I thought an image huge,
Like to the image pedestal'd so high
In Saturn's temple. Then Moneta's voice
Came brief upon mine ear, — "So Saturn sat
When he had lost his realms." — Whereon there grew
A power within me of enormous ken,
To see as a God sees, and take the depth
Of things as nimbly as the outward eye
Can size and shape pervade. The lofty theme
At those few words hung vast before my mind,
With half unravel'd web. I set myself
Upon an eagle's watch, that I might see,
And seeing ne'er forget. No stir of life
Was in this shrouded vale, not so much air
As in the zoning[19] of a summer's day
Robs not one light seed from the feather'd grass,
But where the dead leaf fell there did it rest:
A stream went voiceless by, still deaden'd more
By reason of the fallen divinity
Spreading more shade: the Naiad[20] mid her reeds
Press'd her cold finger closer to her lips.
Along the margin sand large footmarks went
No farther than to where old Saturn's feet
Had rested, and there slept, how long a sleep!
Degraded, cold, upon the sodden ground
His old right hand lay nerveless, listless, dead,
Unsceptred; and his realmless eyes were clos'd,
While his bow'd head seem'd listening to the Earth,
His antient mother, for some comfort yet.

It seem'd no force could wake him from his place;
But there came one who with a kindred hand
Touch'd his wide shoulders, after bending low
With reverence, though to one who knew it not.
Then came the griev'd voice of Mnemosyne,
And griev'd I hearken'd. "That divinity
Whom thou saw'st step from yon forlornest wood,
And with slow pace approach our fallen King,
Is Thea,[21] softest-natur'd of our brood."
I mark'd the goddess in fair statuary
Surpassing wan Moneta by the head,
And in her sorrow nearer woman's tears.
There was a listening fear in her regard,
As if calamity had but begun;
As if the vanward clouds of evil days
Had spent their malice, and the sullen rear
Was with its stored thunder labouring up.
One hand she press'd upon that aching spot
Where beats the human heart; as if just there,
Though an immortal, she felt cruel pain;
The other upon Saturn's bended neck
She laid, and to the level of his hollow ear
Leaning, with parted lips, some words she spake
In solemn tenor and deep organ tune;
Some mourning words, which in our feeble tongue
Would come in this-like accenting; how frail
To that large utterance of the early Gods! —
"Saturn! look up — and for what, poor lost King?
I have no comfort for thee, no — not one:
I cannot cry, *Wherefore thus sleepest thou?*[22]
For heaven is parted from thee, and the earth
Knows thee not, so afflicted, for a God;
And ocean too, with all its solemn noise,
Has from thy sceptre pass'd, and all the air
Is emptied of thine hoary majesty.
Thy thunder, captious at the new command,
Rumbles reluctant o'er our fallen house;
And thy sharp lightning in unpracticed hands
Scorches and burns our once serene domain.
With such remorseless speed still come new woes
That unbelief has not a space to breathe.
Saturn, sleep on: — Me thoughtless, why should I
Thus violate thy slumbrous solitude?
Why should I ope thy melancholy eyes?
Saturn, sleep on, while at thy feet I weep."

As when, upon a tranced summer night,
Forests, branch-charmed by the earnest stars,
Dream, and so dream all night, without a noise,
Save from one gradual solitary gust,
Swelling upon the silence; dying off;
As if the ebbing air had but one wave;
So came these words, and went; the while in tears
She press'd her fair large forehead to the earth,
Just where her fallen hair might spread in curls,
A soft and silken mat for Saturn's feet.
Long, long, those two were postured motionless,
Like sculpture builded up upon the grave

[19] **zoning:** bounds, course.

[20] **Naiad:** freshwater deity.

[21] **Thea:** Hyperion's wife and Saturn's sister.

[22] **Wherefore thus sleepest thou:** Milton, *Paradise Lost,* V. 38, "Wherefore sleepest thou, Eve?"

Of their own power. A long awful time
I look'd upon them; still they were the same;
The frozen God still bending to the earth,
And the sad Goddess weeping at his feet;
Moneta silent. Without stay or prop
But my own weak mortality, I bore
The load of this eternal quietude,
The unchanging gloom, and the three fixed shapes
Ponderous upon my senses a whole moon.
For by my burning brain I measured sure
Her silver seasons shedded on the night,
And every day by day methought I grew
More gaunt and ghostly. Oftentimes I pray'd
Intense, that death would take me from the vale
And all its burthens. Gasping with despair
Of change, hour after hour I curs'd myself:
Until old Saturn rais'd his faded eyes,
And look'd around, and saw his kingdom gone,
And all the gloom and sorrow of the place,
And that fair kneeling Goddess at his feet.
As the moist scent of flowers, and grass, and leaves
Fills forest dells with a pervading air
Known to the woodland nostril, so the words
Of Saturn fill'd the mossy glooms around,
Even to the hollows of time-eaten oaks,
And to the windings in the foxes' hole,
With sad low tones, while thus he spake, and sent
Strange musings to the solitary Pan.

"Moan, brethren, moan; for we are swallow'd up
And buried from all godlike exercise
Of influence benign on planets pale,
And peaceful sway above man's harvesting,
And all those acts which deity supreme
Doth ease its heart of love in. Moan and wail.
Moan, brethren, moan; for lo! the rebel spheres
Spin round, the stars their antient courses keep,
Clouds still with shadowy moisture haunt the earth,
Still suck their fill of light from sun and moon,
Still buds the tree, and still the sea-shores murmur.
There is no death in all the universe,
No smell of death—there shall be death—Moan, moan,
Moan, Cybele,[23] moan, for thy pernicious babes
Have chang'd a God into a shaking palsy.
Moan, brethren, moan; for I have no strength left,
Weak as the reed—weak—feeble as my voice—
O, O, the pain, the pain of feebleness.
Moan, moan; for still I thaw—or give me help:
Throw down those imps and give me victory.
Let me hear other groans, and trumpets blown
Of triumph calm, and hymns of festival
From the gold peaks of heaven's high piled clouds;
Voices of soft proclaim, and silver stir
Of strings in hollow shells; and let there be
Beautiful things made new for the surprize
Of the sky children."—So he feebly ceas'd,
With such a poor and sickly sounding pause,
Methought I heard some old man of the earth
Bewailing earthly loss; nor could my eyes
And ears act with that pleasant unison of sense.
Which marries sweet sound with the grace of form,
And dolorous accent from a tragic harp
With large limb'd visions. More I scrutinized:
Still fix'd he sat beneath the sable trees,
Whose arms spread straggling in wild serpent forms,
With leaves all hush'd: his awful presence there
(Now all was silent) gave a deadly lie
To what I erewhile heard: only his lips
Trembled amid the white curls of his beard.
They told the truth, though, round, the snowy locks
Hung nobly, as upon the face of heaven
A midday fleece of clouds. Thea arose
And stretch'd her white arm through the hollow dark,
Pointing some whither: whereat he too rose
Like a vast giant seen by men at sea
To grow pale from the waves at dull midnight.
They melted from my sight into the woods:
Ere I could turn, Moneta cried—"These twain
Are speeding to the families of grief,
Where roof'd in by black rocks they waste in pain
And darkness for no hope."—And she spake on,
As ye may read who can unwearied pass
Onward from the antichamber of this dream,
Where even at the open doors awhile
I must delay, and glean my memory
Of her high phrase: perhaps no further dare.

—CANTO II—

"Mortal, that thou may'st understand aright,
I humanize my sayings to thine ear,
Making comparisons of earthly things;
Or thou might'st better listen to the wind,
Whose language is to thee a barren noise,
Though it blows legend-laden through the trees.
In melancholy realms big tears are shed,

[23] **Cybele:** Saturn's wife and mother of the gods.

More sorrow like to this, and such-like woe,
Too huge for mortal tongue, or pen of scribe.
The Titans fierce, self-hid, or prison-bound,
Groan for the old allegiance once more,
Listening in their doom for Saturn's voice.
But one of our whole eagle-brood still keeps
His sov'reignty, and rule, and majesty;
Blazing Hyperion on his orbed fire
Still sits, still snuffs the incense teeming up
From man to the Sun's God: yet unsecure;
For as upon the earth dire prodigies
Fright and perplex, so also shudders he:
Nor at dog's howl, or gloom-bird's even screech,
Or the familiar visitings of one
Upon the first toll of his passing bell:
But horrors portion'd to a giant nerve
Make great Hyperion ache. His palace bright,
Bastion'd with pyramids of glowing gold,
And touch'd with shade of bronzed obelisks,
Glares a blood red through all the thousand courts,
Arches, and domes, and fiery galeries:
And all its curtains of Aurorian[24] clouds
Flush angerly: when he would taste the wreaths
Of incense breath'd aloft from sacred hills,
Instead of sweets, his ample palate takes
Savour of poisonous brass and metals sick.
Wherefore when harbour'd in the sleepy west,
After the full completion of fair day,
For rest divine upon exalted couch
And slumber in the arms of melody,
He paces through the pleasant hours of ease,
With strides colossal, on from hall to hall;
While, far within each aisle and deep recess,
His winged minions in close cluster stand
Amaz'd, and full of fear; like anxious men
Who on a wide plain gather in sad troops,
When earthquakes jar their battlements and towers.
Even now, while Saturn, rous'd from icy trance,
Goes, step for step, with Thea from yon woods,
Hyperion, leaving twilight in the rear,
Is sloping to the threshold of the west.
Thither we tend."—Now in clear light I stood,
Reliev'd from the dusk vale. Mnemosyne
Was sitting on a square edg'd polish'd stone,
That in its lucid depth reflected pure
Her priestess-garments. My quick eyes ran on
From stately nave to nave, from vault to vault,
Through bowers of fragrant and enwreathed light,
And diamond paved lustrous long arcades.
Anon rush'd by the bright Hyperion;
His flaming robes stream'd out beyond his heels,
And gave a roar, as if of earthly fire,
That scar'd away the meek ethereal hours
And made their dove-wings tremble: on he flared

. . . .

[24] **Aurorian:** Aurora was goddess of the dawn.

from POETICAL WORKS OF JOHN KEATS
(1898)

This living hand, now warm and capable
(comp. 1819)

This living hand, now warm and capable
Of earnest grasping, would, if it were cold
And in the icy silence of the tomb,
So haunt thy days and chill thy dreaming nights
That thou would wish thine own heart dry of blood,
So in my veins red life might stream again,
And thou be conscience-calm'd. See, here it is—
I hold it towards you.

MARY WOLLSTONECRAFT GODWIN SHELLEY

(1797–1851)

The daughter of the best-known feminist and of the most radical philosopher of the day, and the author of the most famous and disturbing literary work of this period, Mary Wollstonecraft Godwin was born on 30 August 1797, eleven days before her mother died of puerperal fever. Until her father's remarriage in 1801, Mary and her half-sister Fanny Imlay were raised by William Godwin* with the help of a governess, Louisa Jones (whom Godwin dismissed in 1800). After his marriage to Mary Jane Clairmont, an unmarried mother of two children, Godwin left the child-rearing to his new wife, who was jealous of Mary's parentage and openly favored her own children, especially William, her son by Godwin. Mary grew up in a household where she felt abandoned and unloved; this conviction intensified when Godwin sent her at the age of 14 to live for two years with strangers, the William Baxter family of Dundee, Scotland.

Returning to visit her family in 1812, Mary met Godwin's latest disciple, an enthusiastic republican/anarchist and poet, Percy Bysshe Shelley.* Two years later, they met again at Godwin's house and soon became lovers, despite Percy's marriage to Harriet Westbrook Shelley. On 28 July 1814, they eloped to France, taking Mary's stepsister Claire Clairmont with them. Seven months later, Mary gave birth prematurely to a baby girl, christened Clara, who lived only 2 weeks. Immediately pregnant again, anxiously living under the threat of bailiffs (Percy's father refused to pay him his inheritance), of Percy's passionate involvement with Claire, and of her father's refusal to see her again, Mary gave birth to her son William on 24 January 1816. Four months later, Mary, Percy, and Claire left England to follow Claire's lover, Lord Byron,* to Geneva. Kept indoors by the coldest summer in a century, telling ghost stories for their amusement, on 16 June 1816 Mary had the "waking dream" which gave birth to the most mythic literary work of this period, the novel *Frankenstein, or the Modern Prometheus* (published in 1818). As many critics have recognized, this novel simultaneously explores the monstrousness of a man's attempt to have a baby without a woman, of Mary's own pregnancy anxieties, of the predictable consequences of contemporary scientific and technological research, and of the aftermath of violent political revolution.

Able to marry Percy Shelley after his first wife Harriet committed suicide on 10 December 1816, Mary Shelley bore a third child, Clara Everina, on 1 September 1817, and published an account of their earlier travels in France, Germany, Switzerland, and Holland, *History of a Six Weeks' Tour* (1817). This account, based on their Journal and letters, tempers Percy's visions of the sublimity of nature, especially of the Alps, with Mary's ability to find signs of domesticity even among the most barren landscapes. After the publication of *Frankenstein* in March 1818, the Shelley entourage (now including the Shelleys; their two children; Claire and her daughter by Byron, Allegra) moved to Italy, never to return to England. Settling in Bagni di Lucca, near Pisa, Mary Shelley began work on her next novel, *Castruccio, Prince of Lucca* (retitled and published as *Valperga* in 1823), a study of masculine egoism and female self-sacrifice in twelfth-century Italy. After Clara Everina's death in September, to which Percy's carelessness contributed, and William's death of malaria on

7 June 1819, Mary descended into a severe depression, partly fuelled by her repressed anger at her husband's parental irresponsibility and womanizing. In addition to his relationship with Claire and his "platonic" love for Emilia Viviani, Percy Shelley may have carried on a sexual liaison with their nursemaid Elise; an infant he described as his "Neapolitan charge" was baptised Elena Adelaide Shelley in Naples on 28 December 1819. The literary product of Mary's depression, the novella *Mathilda,* a story of father-daughter incest, of the separation from a poet-friend who resembles Percy Shelley, and of female suicidal despair, was completed in 1819 (but not published in Mary's lifetime, since Godwin refused to send it on to a publisher).

Cheered by the birth of her fourth child, Percy Florence, on 12 November 1819, Mary completed *Valperga* in 1821 and moved to the Casa Magni in La Spezia, on the coast of western Italy. On 16 June she had a miscarriage which almost killed her. Three weeks later, on 8 July 1822, Percy and his friend Edward Williams were drowned at sea in a storm while sailing their new boat home from Genoa. Mary never recovered from this loss, in part because she blamed herself for Percy's unhappiness in the last months of their marriage. Returning to London to live for the next five years with Jane Williams, her "saving Angel" to whom "for better or worse I am wedded," she dedicated herself to giving Percy Shelley a posthumous literary life, collecting and editing his poetry, writing his biography (in the form of lengthy introductions to his poems), and addressing him regularly in the Journal she kept till the end of her life. Her next novel, *The Last Man,* begun in February 1824, is a powerful exploration of the myriad varieties of human loss and grief, as a typhoid plague relentlessly destroys all human life, save that of Lionel Verney, the last man, with whom Shelley identified herself in her Journal.

Rejecting all offers of marriage (from John Howard Payne and Edward Trelawney and Prosper Merrimee) Mary focused her energies on providing a superior upper-class education for her only surviving child, Percy Florence. She sent him first to Harrow and then to Cambridge University, financially supported only by a £200 annual allowance from Sir Timothy Shelley and by her own extensive literary endeavors. Living alone in Harrow and London, she wrote numerous stories for the annual gift books, contributed entries on the lives of famous literary men to Lardner's *Cabinet Cyclopedia,* wrote essays and reviews for the periodicals, and completed three more novels: *The Adventures of Perkin Warbeck* in 1830 (a historical romance which focuses on political corruption), *Lodore* in 1835 (a study of the social construction of gender), and *Falkner* in 1837 (an analysis of father-daughter relationships and the endurance of guilt). In 1839 she published four volumes of *The Poetical Works of Percy Bysshe Shelley* as well as his *Essays* and *Letters.* In 1840 and again in 1842 and 1843, she travelled with Percy Florence in Italy and Germany, revisiting her old haunts and reflecting on the changing political climate; her moving account of this voyage into the past was published as *Rambles in Germany and Italy in 1840, 1842, and 1843* in 1843. After Percy Florence graduated from Cambridge and inherited his grandfather's estate, Field Place, in Bournemouth, Sussex, Mary found him a congenial wife, the attractive widow Jane St. John, and spent her final years with the couple at Field Place, where one room was kept as a shrine to Percy Shelley. Affectionately nursed by Percy Florence and Jane, she died after a protracted bout of nervous attacks and partial paralysis in 1851.

from The Journals of Mary Shelley
(6–20 March 1815)

March 1815, Monday 6th

find my baby dead
Send for Hogg—talk—a miserable day—in the evening read fall of the Jesuits.[1] H. sleeps here—

Teusday 7

Shelley & Clary go after breakfast to town[2]—Write to Fanny—Hogg stays all day with us talk with him & read the fall of the Jesuits & Rinaldo Renaldini[3] not in good spirits—H. goes at 11.—a fuss.—to bed at 3

Wednesday 8th

Finish Renaldini—talk with Shelley—in very bad spirits but get better—sleep a little in the day—in the evening net—Hogg comes—he goes at ½ 11.—Clary has written for Fanny but she does not come

Thursday 9th

Read & talk—still think about my little baby—'tis hard indeed for a mother to loose a child—Hogg & C.[harles] C.[lairmont] come in the evening—CC goes at 11. Hogg stays all night Read Fontinelle Plurality of Worlds[4]

Friday 10th

Hogg holidays begin—S.[helley] H.[ogg] & C.[lary] go to town—Hogg comes back soon—talk & net—Hogg now remains with us. Put the rooms to rights

Saterday 11th

Very unwell—Hogg goes to town—talk about Clary's going away—nothing settled—I fear it is hopeless—she will not go to Skinner St.—then our house is the only remaining place—I see plainly—what is to be done—Hogg returns—talk & Hogg reads the life of Goldoni[5] aloud.

Sunday 12th

Talk a great deal—not well but better—very quiet all the morning & happy for Clary does not get up till 4—in the evening read Gibbon (333)[6] go to bed at 12—
4 vol

Monday 13th

S.[helley] H.[ogg] & C.[lary] go to town—stay at home net & think of my little dead baby—this is foolish I suppose yet whenever I am left alone to my own thoughts & do not read to divert them they always come back to the same point that I was a mother & am so no longer—Fanny comes wet through she dines & stays the evening—talk about many things—she goes at ½ 9—cut out my new gown— . . .

Sunday 19th

Dream that my little baby came to life again—that it had only been cold & that we rubbed it by the fire & it lived—I awake & find no baby—I think about the little thing all day—not in good spirits . . .

Monday 20th

Dream again about my baby . . .

---

[1] **my baby**: Clara, born on 22 February 1815, prematurely at seven months, died two weeks later, on 6 March. **Hogg**: Thomas Jefferson Hogg (1792–1862), lawyer and author, expelled from Oxford with his best friend, Percy Shelley, in 1812. **fall of the Jesuits**: reference to *Despotism: or, The Fall of the Jesuits* (1811) by Isaac D'Israeli.

[2] **Shelley**: Percy Bysshe Shelley,* with whom Mary had eloped nine months earlier. **Clary**: Claire (born Jane) Clairmont, Mary's stepsister, who had joined them on their elopement and continued to live with them, despite Mary's desire for privacy. **go . . . to town**: to arrange for the burial of the baby.

[3] **Fanny**: Fanny Imlay, daughter of Mary Wollstonecraft and Gilbert Imlay, Mary's half-sister. **Rinaldo Renaldini**: *Rinaldo Rinaldini, der Rauberhauptmann* by Christian August Volpius, trans. as *The History of Rinaldo Rinaldini* by J. Hinckley (1798, trans. 1800).

[4] **C.[harles] C.[lairmont]**: Mary's stepbrother. **Fontinelle . . . Worlds**: reference to Bernard Le Bouvier de Fontenelle, *Conversations on the Plurality of Worlds*, trans. W. Gardiner (1687, trans. 1715).

[5] **Skinner St.**: the home of William and Mary Jane Clairmont Godwin; Claire's mother had insisted she return to live with them and had forbidden her to see Mary and Percy again; Claire had refused. **Goldoni**: reference to *Memoirs of Goldoni (the celebrated Italian dramatist) written by himself* by M. Goldoni, trans. John Black (1787, trans. 1814).

[6] **Gibbon**: reference to Edward Gibbon, *The History of the Decline and Fall of the Roman Empire* (1776–1788), Vol. 4, up to p. 333.

from History of a Six Weeks' Tour[1]

through A Part of France, Switzerland, Germany, and Holland with Letters Descriptive of a Sail Round the Lake of Geneva, and of the Glaciers of Chamouni

(1817)

— *from* CHAPTER 1 —

FRANCE

We now approached scenes that reminded us of what we had nearly forgotten, that France had lately been the country in which great and extraordinary events had taken place. Nogent,[2] a town we entered about noon the following day, had been entirely desolated by the Cossacs. Nothing could be more entire than the ruin which these barbarians had spread as they advanced; perhaps they remembered Moscow and the destruction of the Russian villages; but we were now in France, and the distress of the inhabitants, whose houses had been burned, their cattle killed, and all their wealth destroyed, has given a sting to my detestation of war, which none can feel who have not travelled through a country pillaged and wasted by this plague, which, in his pride, man inflicts upon his fellow.

We quitted the great route soon after we had left Nogent, to strike across the country to Troyes. About six in the evening we arrived at St. Aubin, a lovely village embosomed in trees; but on a nearer view we found the cottages roofless, the rafters black, and the walls dilapidated; —a few inhabitants remained. We asked for milk—they had none to give; all their cows had been taken by the Cossacs. We had still some leagues to travel that night, but we found that they were not post leagues,[3] but the measurement of the inhabitants, and nearly double the distance. The road lay over a desart plain, and as night advanced we were often in danger of losing the track of wheels, which was our only guide. Night closed in, and we suddenly lost all trace of the road; but a few trees, indistinctly seen, seemed to indicate the position of a village. About ten we arrived at Trois Maisons, where, after a supper on milk and sour bread, we retired to rest on wretched beds: but sleep is seldom denied, except to the indolent, and after the day's fatigue, although my bed was nothing more than a sheet spread upon straw, I slept soundly until the morning was considerably advanced.

S***[4] had hurt his ancle so considerably the preceding evening, that he was obliged, during the whole of the following day's journey, to ride on our mule. Nothing could be more barren and wretched than the track through which we now passed; the ground was chalky and uncovered even by grass, and where there had been any attempts made towards cultivation, the straggling ears of corn discovered more plainly the barren nature of the soil. Thousands of insects, which were of the same white colour as the road, infested our path; the sky was cloudless, and the sun darted its rays upon us, reflected back by the earth, until I nearly fainted under the heat. A village appeared at a distance, cheering us with a prospect of rest. It gave us new strength to proceed; but it was a wretched place, and afforded us but little relief. It had been once large and populous, but now the houses were roofless, and the ruins that lay scattered about, the gardens covered with the white dust of the torn cottages, the black burnt beams, and squalid looks of the inhabitants, presented in every direction the melancholy aspect of devastation. One house, a *cabarêt*,[5] alone remained; we were here offered plenty of milk, stinking bacon, sour bread, and a few vegetables, which we were to dress for ourselves.

As we prepared our dinner in a place, so filthy that the sight of it alone was sufficient to destroy our appetite, the people of the village collected around us, squalid with dirt, their countenances expressing every thing that is disgusting and brutal. They seemed indeed entirely detached from the rest of the world, and ignorant of all that was passing in it. There is much less communication between the various towns of France than in England. The use of

[1] Drawing on the journals and letters that she, Percy Shelley, and Claire Clairmont had written during their elopement journey from London to Switzerland and back from July 28–13 September 1814, Mary Godwin published this account of their travels in 1817; the volume included Percy Shelley's poem "Mont Blanc."*

[2] **Nogent**: Nogent-sur-Seine, town in central France, 50 kilometers southwest of Paris, where five months earlier an invading army of Austrians and Russian Cossacks led by Prince Schwarzenburg had been driven back after heavy fighting by Napoleon's army.

[3] **post league**: about three English miles.

[4] **S*****: Percy Bysshe Shelley had sprained his leg the day before, on Thursday, 11 August 1814.

[5] **cabarêt**: nightclub; the village is Echemines, in the Champagne.

passports may easily account for this: these people did not know that Napoleon was deposed, and when we asked why they did not rebuild their cottages, they replied, that they were afraid that the Cossacs would destroy them again upon their return. Echemine (the name of this village) is in every respect the most disgusting place I ever met with.

Two leagues beyond, on the same road, we came to the village of Pavillon, so unlike Echemine, that we might have fancied ourselves in another quarter of the globe; here every thing denoted cleanliness and hospitality; many of the cottages were destroyed, but the inhabitants were employed in repairing them. What could occasion so great a difference? . . .

— *from* CHAPTER 3 —
GERMANY

. . . .

We took our place in the *diligence par-eau*[6] for Cologne, and the next morning (September 4th) departed. This conveyance appeared much more like a mercantile English affair than any we had before seen; it was shaped like a steam-boat, with a cabin and a high deck. Most of our companions chose to remain in the cabin; this was fortunate for us, since nothing could be more horribly disgusting than the lower order of smoking, drinking Germans who travelled with us; they swaggered and talked, and what was hideous to English eyes, kissed one another: there were, however, two or three merchants of a better class, who appeared well-informed and polite.

The part of the Rhine down which we now glided, is that so beautifully described by Lord Byron in his third canto of *Childe Harold*. We read these verses with delight, as they conjured before us these lovely scenes with the truth and vividness of painting, and with the exquisite addition of glowing language and a warm imagination. We were carried down by a dangerously rapid current, and saw on either side of us hills covered with vines and trees, craggy cliffs crowned by desolate towers, and wooded islands, where picturesque ruins peeped from behind the foliage, and cast the shadows of their forms on the troubled waters, which distorted without deforming them. We heard the songs of the vintagers, and if surrounded by disgusting Germans, the sight was not so replete with enjoyment as I now fancy it to have been; yet memory, taking all the dark shades from the picture, presents this part of the Rhine to my remembrance as the loveliest paradise on earth.

We had sufficient leisure for the enjoyment of these scenes, for the boatmen, neither rowing nor steering, suffered us to be carried down by the stream, and the boat turned round and round as it descended.

While I speak with disgust of the Germans who travelled with us, I should in justice to these borderers record, that at one of the inns here we saw the only pretty woman we met with in the course of our travels. She is what I should conceive to be a truly German beauty; grey eyes, slightly tinged with brown, and expressive of uncommon sweetness and frankness. She had lately recovered from a fever, and this added to the interest of her countenance, by adorning it with an appearance of extreme delicacy. . . .

[6] **diligence par-eau**: river-bus. **Cologne**: seaport, commercial and industrial center in West Germany, on the Rhine River.

from Letter to Marianne Hunt
(1819)

Leghorn — June 29th 1819

MY DEAR MARIANNE

Although we have not heard from you or of you for some time I hope you are going on well — that you enjoy our [*your*] health and see your children lively about you —

You see by our hap how blind we mortals are when we go seeking after what we think our good — We came to Italy thinking to do Shelley's health good — but the Climate is not any means warm enough to be of benefit to him & yet it is that that has destroyed my two children[1] — We went from England comparatively prosperous & happy — I should return broken hearted & miserable — I never know one moments ease from the wretchedness & despair that possesses me — May you my dear Marianne never know what it is to loose two only & lovely children in one year — to watch their dying moments — & then at last to be left childless & for ever miserable . . .

[1] Mary Shelley's second daughter, Clara Everina, died on 24 September 1818, at the age of one year, of fever and convulsions, in part exacerbated by Percy Shelley's insistence that Mary bring her from the west coast of Italy to Venice at top speed in the August heat. William Shelley died in Rome on 7 June 1819, of malaria.

from Letter to Maria Gisborne

(1822)

Pisa August 15th 1822

I said . . . that I would send you some account of the last miserable months of my disastrous life. From day to day I have put this off, but I will now endeavour to fulfill my design. The scene of my existence is closed & though there be no pleasure in retracing the scenes that have preceded the event which has crushed my hopes yet there seems to be a necessity in doing so, and I obey the impulse that urges me. I wrote to you either at the end of May or the beginning of June. I described to you the place we were living in:[1]—Our desolate house, the beauty yet strangeness of the scenery and the delight Shelley took in all this—he never was in better health or spirits than during this time. I was not well in body or mind. My nerves were wound up to the utmost irritation, and the sense of misfortune hung over my spirits. No words can tell you how I hated our house & the country about it. Shelley reproached me for this—his health was good & the place was quite after his own heart—What could I answer—that the people were wild & hateful, that though the country was beautiful yet I liked a more *countryfied* place, that there was great difficulty in living—that all our Tuscans would leave us, & that the very jargon of these *Genovese* was disgusting—This was all I had to say but no words could describe my feelings—the beauty of the woods made me weep & shudder—so vehement was my feeling of dislike that I used to rejoice when the winds & waves permitted me to go out in the boat so that I was not obliged to take my usual walk among tree shaded paths, allies of vine festooned trees—all that before I doated on—& that now weighed on me. My only moments of peace were on board that unhappy boat, when lying down with my head on his knee I shut my eyes & felt the wind & our swift motion alone. My ill health might account for much of this—bathing in the sea somewhat relieved me—but on the 8th of June (I think it was) I was threatened with a miscarriage, & after a week of great ill health on sunday the 16th this took place at eight in the morning. I was so ill that for seven hours I lay nearly lifeless—kept from fainting by brandy, vinegar eau de Cologne &c—at length ice was brought to our solitude—it came before the doctor so Claire & Jane were afraid of using it but Shelley overuled them & by an unsparing application of it I was restored. They all thought & so did I at one time that I was about to die—I hardly wish that I had, my own Shelley could never have lived without me, the sense of eternal misfortune would have pressed too heavily upon him, & what would have become of my poor babe? My convalescence was slow and during it a strange occurence happened to retard it. . . . As I said Shelley was at first in perfect health but having over fatigued himself one day, & then the fright my illness gave him caused a return of nervous sensations & visions as bad as in his worst times. I think it was the saturday after my illness while yet unable to walk I was confined to my bed—in the middle of the night I was awoke by hearing him scream & come rushing into my room; I was sure that he was asleep & tried to waken him by calling on him, but he continued to scream which inspired me with such a panic that I jumped out of bed & ran across the hall to Mrs W's room where I fell through weakness, though I was so frightened that I got up again immediately—she let me in & Williams went to S. who had been wakened by my getting out of bed—he said that he had not been asleep & that it was a vision that he saw that had frightened him—But as he declared that he had not screamed it was certainly a dream & no waking vision—What had frightened him was this—He dreamt that lying as he did in bed Edward & Jane came into him, they were in the most horrible condition, their bodies lacerated—their bones starting through their skin, the faces pale yet stained with blood, they could hardly walk, but Edward was the weakest & Jane was supporting him—Edward said—["]Get up, Shelley, the sea is flooding the house & it is all coming down." S. got up, he thought, & went to the his window that looked on the terrace & the sea & thought he saw the sea rushing in. Suddenly his vision changed & he saw the figure of himself strangling me, that had made him rush into my room, yet fearful of frightening me he dared not approach the bed, when my jumping out awoke him, or as he phrased it caused his vision to vanish. All this was frightful enough, & talking it over the next morning he told me that he had had many visions lately—he had seen the figure of himself which met him as he walked on the terrace & said to

[1] **place we were living in:** The Shelleys had been living since May 1822, with their only surviving child, Percy Florence; Claire Clairmont and her daughter by Byron, Allegra Alba; and their friends Edward and Jane Williams at the Casa Magni in Lerici, Italy, on the coast of the Gulf of Spezia, directly west of Pisa. Edward Trelawney (1792–1881), sailor, adventurer, and friend of Byron, was a frequent visitor.

him—"How long do you mean to be content"—No very terrific words & certainly not prophetic of what has occurred. But Shelley had often seen these figures when ill; but the strangest thing is that M[rs] W. saw him. Now Jane though a woman of sensibility, has not much imagination & is not in the slightest degree nervous—neither in dreams or otherwise. She was standing one day, the day before I was taken ill, at a window that looked on the Terrace with Trelawny—it was day—she saw as she thought Shelley pass by the window, as he often was then, without a coat or jacket—he passed again—now as he passed both times the same way—and as from the side towards which he went each time there was no way to get back except past the window again (except over a wall twenty feet from the ground) she was struck at seeing him pass twice thus & looked out & seeing him no more she cried—"Good God can Shelley have leapt from the wall? Where can he be gone?" Shelley, said Trelawny—"No Shelley has past—What do you mean?" Trelawny says that she trembled exceedingly when she heard this & it proved indeed that Shelley had never been on the terrace & was far off at the time she saw him. Well we thought {no} more of these things & I slowly got better. Having heard from Hunt[2] that he had sailed from Genoa, on Monday July 1st S., Edward & Captain Roberts (the Gent. who built our boat) departed in our boat for Leghorn to receive him—I was then just better, had begun to crawl from my bedroom to the terrace; but bad spirits succeded to ill health, and this departure of Shelley's seemed to add insuferably to my misery. I could not endure that he should go—I called him back two or three times, & told him that if I did not see him soon I would go to Pisa with the child—I cried bitterly when he went away. They went & Jane, Claire & I remained alone with the children—I could not walk out, & though I gradually gathered strength it was slowly & my ill spirits encreased; in my letters to him I entreated him to return—"the feeling that some misfortune would happen," I said, "haunted me": I feared for the child, for the idea of danger connected with him never struck me—When Jane & Claire took their evening walk I used to patrole the terrace, oppressed with wretchedness, yet gazing on the most beautiful scene in the world. This Gulph of Spezia is subdivided into many small bays of which ours was far the most beautiful—the two horns of the bay (so to express myself) were wood covered promontories crowned with castles—at the foot of these on the furthest was Lerici on the nearest San[t] Arenzo—Lerici being above a mile by land from us & San Arenzo about a hundred or two yards—trees covered the hills that enclosed this bay & then beautiful groups were picturesquely contrasted with the rocks the castle on [*and*] the town—the sea lay far extended in front while to the west we saw the promontory & islands which formed one of the extreme boundarys of the Gulph—to see the sun set upon this scene, the stars shine & the moon rise was a sight of wondrous beauty, but to me it added only to my wretchedness—I repeated to myself all that another would have said to console me, & told myself the tale of love peace & competence which I enjoyed—but I answered myself by tears—did not my William die? & did I hold my Percy by a firmer tenure?—Yet I thought when he, when my Shelley returns I shall be happy—he will comfort me, if my boy be ill he will restore him & encourage me. I had a letter or two from Shelley mentioning the difficulties he had in establishing the Hunts, & that he was unable to fix the time of his return. Thus a week past. On Monday 8th Jane had a letter from Edward, dated saturday, he said that he waited at Leghorn for S. who was at Pisa That S's return was certain, "but" he continued, "if he should not come by monday I will come in a felucca,[3] & you may expect me tuesday evening at furthest." This was monday, the fatal monday, but with us it was stormy all day & we did not at all suppose that they could put to sea. At twelve at night we had a thunderstorm; T[ue]sday it rained all day & was calm—the sky wept on their graves—on Wednesday—the wind was fair from Leghorn & in the evening several felucca's arrived thence—one brought word that they had sailed monday, but we did not believe them—thursday was another day of fair wind & when twelve at night came & we did not see the tall sails of the little boat double the promontory before us we began to fear not the truth, but some illness—some disagreable news for their detention. Jane got so uneasy that she determined to proceed the next day to Leghorn in a boat to see what was the matter—friday came & with it a heavy sea & bad wind—Jane however resolved to be rowed to Leghorn (since no boat could sail) and busied herself in preparations—I wished her to wait for letters, since friday was letter day—she would not—but the sea

[2] **Hunt:** James Henry Leigh Hunt (1784–1859), poet and editor of the liberal journal *The Examiner,* had come with his wife Marianne and their eight children to Pisa to begin a new journal, *The Liberal,* under Byron's patronage.

[3] **felucca:** small boat propelled by oars or a single sail.

detained her, the swell rose so that no boat would venture out—At 12 at noon our letters came—there was one from Hunt to Shelley, it said—"pray write to tell us how you got home, for they say that you had bad weather after you sailed monday & we are anxious"—the paper fell from me—I trembled all over—Jane read it—"Then it is all over!" she said. "No, my dear Jane," I cried, "it is not all over, but this suspense is dreadful—come with me, we will go to Leghorn, we will post to be swift & learn our fate." We crossed to Lerici, despair in our hearts; they raised our spirits there by telling us that no accident had been heard of & that it must have been known &c—but still our fear was great—& without resting we posted to Pisa It must have been fearful to see us—two poor, wild, aghast creatures—driving (like Matilda)[4] towards the *sea* to learn if we were to be for ever doomed to misery. I knew that Hunt was at Pisa at Lord Byrons' house but I thought that L. B. was at Leghorn. I settled that we should drive to Casa Lanfranchi that I should get out & ask the fearful question of Hunt, "do you know any thing of Shelley?" On entering Pisa the idea of seeing Hunt for the first time for four years under such circumstances, & asking him such a question was so terrific to me that it was with difficulty that I prevented myself from going into convulsions—my struggles were dreadful—they knocked at the door & some one called out "Chi è?" it was the Guiccioli's maid[5] L.B. was in Pisa—Hunt was in bed, so I was to see LB. instead of him—This was a great relief to me; I staggered up stairs—the Guiccioli came to meet me smiling while I could hardly say—"Where is he—Sapete alcuna cosa di Shelley"[6]—They knew nothing—he had left Pisa on sunday—on Monday he had sailed—there had been bad weather monday afternoon—more they knew not. Both LB & the lady have told me since—that on that terrific evening I looked more like a ghost than a woman—light seemed to emanate from my features, my face was very white I looked like marble—Alas. I had risen almost from a bed of sickness for this journey—I had travelled all day—it was now 12 at night—& we, refusing to rest, proceeded to Leghorn—not in despair—no, for then we must have died; but with sufficient hope to keep up the agitation of the spirits which was all my life. It was past two in the morning when we arrived—They took us to the wrong inn—neither Trelawny or Cap[n] Roberts were there nor did we exactly know where they were so we were obliged to wait until daylight. We threw ourselves drest on our beds & slept a little but at 6 o'clock we went to one or two inns to ask for one or the other of these gentlemen. We found Roberts at the Globe. He came down to us with a face which seemed to tell us that the worst was true, and here we learned all that had occurred during the week they had been absent from us, & under what circumstances they had departed on their return. ———Shelley had past most of the time a[t] Pisa—arranging the affairs of the Hunts—& skrewing LB's mind to the sticking place[7] about the journal. He had found this a difficult task at first but at length he had succeeded to his heart's content with both points. M[rs] Mason said that she saw him in better health and spirits than she had ever known him, when he took leave of her sunday July 7th His face burnt by the sun, & his heart light that he had succeeded in rendering the Hunts' tolerably comfortable. Edward had remained at Leghorn. On Monday July 8th during the morning they were employed in buying many things—eatables &c for our solitude. There had been a thunderstorm early but about noon the weather was fine & the wind right fair for Lerici—They were impatient to be gone. Roberts said, "Stay until tomorrow to see if the weather is settled; & S. might have staid but Edward was in so great an anxiety to reach home—saying they would get there in seven hours with that wind—that they sailed! S. being in one of those extravagant fits of good spirits in which you have sometimes seen him. Roberts went out to the end of the mole[8] & watched them out of sight—they sailed at one & went off at the rate of about 7 knots—About three—Roberts, who was still on the mole—saw wind coming from the Gulph—or rather what the Italians call a temporale anxious to know how the boat w[d] weather the storm, he got leave to go up the tower & with the glass discovered them about ten miles out at sea, off Via Reggio, they were taking in their topsails—"The haze of the storm," he said, "hid them from me & I saw them no more when the storm cleared I looked again fancying that I should see them on their return to us—but there was no boat on the sea."—This then was all we knew, yet we did not despair—they might have been

[4] See Mary Shelley, *Mathilda,* ch. 6;* below.

[5] Byron was visiting his mistress, Theresa Guiccioli, at her home, the Casa Lanfranchi, in Pisa, where Hunt was also staying. **Chi è?**: Italian, "Who is it?"

[6] **"Sapete alcuna cosa di Shelley"**: Italian, "Do you know anything about Shelley?"

[7] **sticking place**: Shakespeare, *Macbeth,* I.i.60.

[8] **mole**: massive stone structure, serving as pier or breakwater.

driven over to Corsica & not knowing the coast & Gone god knows where. Reports favoured this belief.—it was even said that they had been seen in the Gulph

We resolved to return with all possible speed—We sent a courier to go from tower to tower along the coast to know if any thing had been seen or found, & at 9 AM. we quitted Leghorn—stopped but one moment at Pisa & proceeded towards Lerici. When at 2 miles from Via Reggio we rode down to that town to know if they knew any thing—here our calamity first began to break on us—a little boat & a water cask had been found five miles off—they had manufactured a piccolissima lancia[9] of thin planks stitched by a shoemaker just to let them run on shore without wetting themselves as our boat drew 4 feet water.—the description of that found tallied with this—but then this boat was very cumbersome & in bad weather they might have been easily led to throw it overboard—the cask frightened me most—but the same reason might in some sort be given for that. I must tell you that Jane & I were not now alone—Trelawny accompanied us back to our home. We journied on & reached the Magra about ½ past ten P.M. I cannot describe to you what I felt in the first moment when, fording this river, I felt the water splash about our wheels—I was suffocated—I gasped for breath—I thought I should have gone into convulsions, & I struggled violently that Jane might not perceive it—looking down the river I saw the two great lights burning at the foce[10]—A voice from within me seemed to cry aloud that is his grave. After passing the river I gradually recovered. Arriving at Lerici we {were} obliged to cross our little bay in a boat—San Arenzo was illuminated for a festa[11]—what a scene—the roaring sea—the scirocco wind—the lights of the town towards which we rowed—& our own desolate hearts—that coloured all with a shroud—we landed; nothing had been heard of them. This was saturday July 13. & thus we waited until Thursday July 25th thrown about by hope & fear. We sent messengers along the coast towards Genoa & to Via Reggio—nothing had been found more than the lancetta,[12] reports were brought us—we hoped—& yet to tell you all the agony we endured during those 12 days would be to make you conceive a universe of pain—each moment intolerable & giving place to one still worse. The people of the country too added to one's discomfort—they are like wild savages—on festa's the men & women & children in different bands—the sexes always separate—pass the whole night in dancing on the sands close to our door running into the sea then back again & screaming all the time one perpetuel air—the most detestable in the world—then the scirocco perpetually blew & the sea for ever moaned their dirge. On thursday 25th Trelawny left us to go to Leghorn to see what was doing or what could be done. On friday I was very ill but as evening came on I said to Jane—"If any thing had been found on the coast Trelawny would have returned to let us know. He has not returned so I hope." About 7 o'clock P.M. he did return—all was over—all was quiet now, they had been found washed on shore—Well all this was to be endured.

Well what more have I to say? The next day we returned to Pisa. And here we are still—days pass away—one after another—& we live thus. We are all together—we shall quit Italy together. Jane must proceed to London if letters do not alter my views I shall remain in Paris.—Thus we live—Seeing the Hunts now & then. Poor Hunt has suffered terribly as you may guess. Lord Byron is very kind to me & comes with the Guiccioli to see me often.

Today—this day—the sun shining in the sky—they are gone to the desolate sea coast to perform the last offices to their earthly remains.[13] Hunt, LB. & Trelawny. The quarantine laws would not permit us to remove them sooner—& now only on condition that we burn them to ashes. That I do not dislike—His rest shall be at Rome beside my child[14]—where one day I also shall join them—Adonais is not Keats's it is his own elegy[15]—he bids you there go to Rome.—I have seen the spot where he now lies—the sticks that mark the spot where the sands cover him—he shall not be there it is too nea[r] Via Reggio—They are now about this fearful office—& I live!

One more circumstance I will mention. As I said he took leave of Mrs Mason in high spirits on sunday—"Never," said she, "did I see him look happier than the last glance I had of his countenance." On Monday he was lost

[9] **piccolissima lancia**: smallest ship's boat.

[10] **foce**: river outlet into the sea.

[11] **festa**: festival.

[12] **lancetta**: ship's boat, dinghy.

[13] **earthly remains**: On 15 August 1822, Byron, Hunt, and Trelawney gathered on the beach near Viareggio where the bodies of Percy Shelley and Edward Williams had been washed ashore and temporarily buried in limestone as a precaution against putrefaction. They dug up and cremated Williams's remains on 15 August and Shelley's on the following day. Shelley's heart, which would not burn, was seized from the fire by Leigh Hunt.

[14] **His rest . . . beside my child**: William Shelley was buried at the Protestant Cemetery in Rome in June 1819.

[15] Cf. P. B. Shelley, "Adonais"* (1821).

—on monday night she dreamt—that she was somewhere—she knew not where & he came looking very pale & fearfully melancholy—she said to him—"You look ill, you are tired, sit down & eat." "No," he replied, "I shall never eat more; I have not a *soldo* left in the world."—"Nonsense," said she, "this is no inn—you need not pay"—"Perhaps," he answered, "it is the worse for that." Then she awoke & going to sleep again she dreamt that my Percy was dead & she awoke crying bitterly & felt so miserable—that she said to herself—"why if the little boy should die I should not feel it in this manner." She [was] so struck with these dreams that she mentioned them to her servant the next day—saying she hoped all was well with us.

Well here is my story—the last story I shall have to tell—all that might have been bright in my life is now despoiled—I shall live to improve myself, to take care of my child, & render myself worthy to join him. soon my weary pilgrimage will begin—I rest now—but soon I must leave Italy—& then—there is an end of all despair. Adieu. . .

Your's ever truly Mary WS.—Pisa

from The Journals of Mary Shelley
(14–15 May 1824)

May 14, 1824

The last man![1] Yes I may well describe that solitary being's feelings, feeling myself as the last relic of a beloved race, my companions, extinct before me . . .

May 15, 1824

This then was the "coming event" that cast its shadow on my last night's miserable thoughts. Byron has become one of the people of the grave[2]—that innumerable conclave to which the beings I best loved belong. I knew him in the bright days of youth, when neither care or fear had visited me: before death had made me feel my mortality and the earth was the scene of my hopes—Can I forget our evening visits to Diodati—our excursions of the lake when he sang the Tyrolese hymn[3]—and his voice was harmonized with winds and waves?—Can I forget his attentions & consolations to me during my deepest misery?

Never.

Beauty sat on his countenance and power beamed from his eye—his faults for the most part weaknesses induced one readily to pardon them. Albe[4]—the dear capricious fascinating Albe has left this desart world

What do I do here? Why am I doomed to live on seeing all expire before me? God grant I may die young—A new race is springing about me—At the age of twenty six I am in the condition of an aged person—all my old friends are gone—I have no wish to form new—I cling to the few remaining—but they slide away & my heart fails when I think by how few ties I hold to the world—Albe, dearest Albe, was knit by long associations—Each day I repeat with bitterer feelings "Life is the desart and the solitude—how populous the grave."[5] and that region to the dearer and best beloved beings which it has torn from me, now adds that resplendent Spirit, whose departure leaves the dull earth dark as midnight

[1] **the last man!:** Mary Shelley had begun writing her novel *The Last Man* (1826) in which a plague destroys all human beings except one, Lionel Verney, who is left to tell the tale.

[2] **Byron . . . grave:** Byron died on 19 April 1824, at Missolonghi, Greece, but the news did not reach England until 14 May.

[3] **visits to Diodati . . . Tyrolese hymn:** The Shelleys visited Byron at his home, the Villa Diodati, on the shore of Lake Geneva in Switzerland, during the summer of 1816 in which Mary Shelley began writing *Frankenstein.* Byron frequently sang the Tyrolese Song of Liberty aloud while boating on the lake.

[4] **Albe:** the Shelleys' nickname for Byron, a pun on "L.B."

[5] **"Life . . . grave":** See Edward Young, *The Complaint, or Night Thoughts* (1742–1744), Night the First, ll. 114–16.

Author's Introduction to The Last Man[1]
(1826)

I visited Naples in the year 1818. On the 8th of December of that year, my companion and I crossed the Bay, to visit

[1] Mary Shelley composed *The Last Man* between February and September 1824; it was published by George Colburn on 23 January 1826. The novel, a *roman à clef* in which many of the characters are thinly disguised portraits of Percy Shelley, Byron, Mary Shelley, and members of their circle, portrays the impact of a universal, inescapable plague upon the citizens of England and Europe. The narrative is written by the only person to recover from the plague, Lionel Verney, and as the introduction indicates, is cast as a prophecy, set in the year 2010 AD.

the antiquities which are scattered on the shores of Baiæ. The translucent and shining waters of the calm sea covered fragments of old Roman villas, which were interlaced by sea-weed, and received diamond tints from the chequering of the sun-beams; the blue and pellucid element was such as Galatea might have skimmed in her car of mother of pearl; or Cleopatra, more fitly than the Nile, have chosen as the path of her magic ship.[2] Though it was winter, the atmosphere seemed more appropriate to early spring; and its genial warmth contributed to inspire those sensations of placid delight, which are the portion of every traveller, as he lingers, loath to quit the tranquil bays and radiant promontories of Baiæ.

We visited the so called Elysian Fields and Avernus:[3] and wandered through various ruined temples, baths, and classic spots; at length we entered the gloomy cavern of the Cumaean Sibyl.[4] Our Lazzeroni[5] bore flaring torches, which shone red, and almost dusky, in the murky subterranean passages, whose darkness thirstily surrounding them, seemed eager to imbibe more and more of the element of light. We passed by a natural archway, leading to a second gallery, and enquired, if we could not enter there also. The guides pointed to the reflection of their torches on the water that paved it, leaving us to form our own conclusion; but adding it was a pity, for it led to the Sibyl's Cave. Our curiosity and enthusiasm were excited by this circumstance, and we insisted upon attempting the passage. As is usually the case in the prosecution of such enterprizes, the difficulties decreased on examination. We found, on each side of the humid pathway, "dry land for the sole of the foot." At length we arrived at a large, desert, dark cavern, which the Lazzeroni assured us was the Sibyl's Cave. We were sufficiently disappointed—Yet we examined it with care, as if its blank, rocky walls could still bear trace of celestial visitant. On one side was a small opening. Whither does this lead? we asked: can we enter here?—"*Questo poi, no,*"[6]—said the wild looking savage, who held the torch; "you can advance but a short distance, and nobody visits it."

"Nevertheless, I will try it," said my companion; "it may lead to the real cavern. Shall I go alone, or will you accompany me?"

I signified my readiness to proceed, but our guides protested against such a measure. With great volubility, in their native Neapolitan dialect, with which we were not very familiar, they told us that there were spectres, that the roof would fall in, that it was too narrow to admit us, that there was a deep hole within, filled with water, and we might be drowned. My friend shortened the harangue, by taking the man's torch from him; and we proceeded alone.

The passage, which at first scarcely admitted us, quickly grew narrower and lower; we were almost bent double; yet still we persisted in making our way through it. At length we entered a wider space, and the low roof heightened; but, as we congratulated ourselves on this change, our torch was extinguished by a current of air, and we were left in utter darkness. The guides bring with them materials for renewing the light, but we had none—our only resource was to return as we came. We groped round the widened space to find the entrance, and after a time fancied that we had succeeded. This proved however to be a second passage, which evidently ascended. It terminated like the former; though something approaching to a ray, we could not tell whence, shed a very doubtful twilight in the space. By degrees, our eyes grew somewhat accustomed to this dimness, and we perceived that there was no direct passage leading us further; but that it was possible to climb one side of the cavern to a low arch at top, which promised a more easy path, from whence we now discovered that this light proceeded. With considerable

[2] **Baiae**: village in the Compania, southern Italy, on the Bay of Naples; in Roman times, a celebrated spa and imperial residence, known for its sumptuous villas. **Galatea**: in Greek mythology, a beautiful sea-nymph; the daughter of Nereus and Doris, sculptured in stone by Pygmalion, who then invoked Venus to bring the statue to life. **Cleopatra**: Queen of Egypt (69–30 BC), beloved by both Julius Caesar and Antony; for a description of her ship, see Shakespeare, *Antony and Cleopatra,* II.ii.195–215.

[3] **Elysian Fields**: in Greek mythology, the region assigned to the blessed dead. **Avernus**: small crater lake in the Compania, southern Italy, which emits sulphuric fumes so strong they kill birds flying over the lake; hence, in antiquity, thought to be the entrance to hell.

[4] **Cumaean Sibyl**: in classical mythology, the most famous of ten sibyls or prophetesses, consulted by Tarquin in Virgil's *Aenead;* she wrote her oracles on tree leaves. Although she burned most of her prophecies or sibylline books, three which according to legend Tarquin purchased from her were kept in the Capitoline at Rome and were consulted at times of emergency; these books were destroyed by fire in the sack of Rome in 83 BC.

[5] **Lazzeroni**: guide.

[6] **"Questo poi, no"**: *trans.* "That won't do!"

difficulty we scrambled up, and came to another passage with still more of illumination, and this led to another ascent like the former.

After a succession of these, which our resolution alone permitted us to surmount, we arrived at a wide cavern with an arched dome-like roof. An aperture in the midst let in the light of heaven; but this was overgrown with brambles and underwood, which acted as a veil, obscuring the day, and giving a solemn religious hue to the apartment. It was spacious, and nearly circular, with a raised seat of stone, about the size of a Grecian couch, at one end. The only sign that life had been here, was the perfect snow-white skeleton of a goat, which had probably not perceived the opening as it grazed on the hill above, and had fallen headlong. Ages perhaps had elapsed since this catastrophe; and the ruin it had made above, had been repaired by the growth of vegetation during many hundred summers.

The rest of the furniture of the cavern consisted of piles of leaves, fragments of bark, and a white filmy substance, resembling the inner part of the green hood which shelters the grain of the unripe Indian corn. We were fatigued by our struggles to attain this point, and seated ourselves on the rocky couch, while the sounds of tinkling sheep-bells, and shout of shepherd-boy, reached us from above.

At length my friend, who had taken up some of the leaves strewed about, exclaimed, "This *is* the Sibyl's cave; these are Sibylline leaves." On examination, we found that all the leaves, bark, and other substances, were traced with written characters. What appeared to us more astonishing, was that these writings were expressed in various languages: some unknown to my companion, ancient Chaldee, and Egyptian hieroglyphics, old as the Pyramids. Stranger still, some were in modern dialects, English and Italian. We could make out little by the dim light, but they seemed to contain prophecies, detailed relations of events but lately passed; names, now well known, but of modern date; and often exclamations of exultation or woe, of victory or defeat, were traced on their thin scant pages. This was certainly the Sibyl's Cave; not indeed exactly as Virgil describes it; but the whole of this land had been so convulsed by earthquake and volcano, that the change was not wonderful, though the traces of ruin were effaced by time; and we probably owed the preservation of these leaves, to the accident which had closed the mouth of the cavern, and the swift-growing vegetation which had rendered its sole opening impervious to the storm. We made a hasty selection of such of the leaves, whose writing one at least of us could understand; and then, laden with our treasure, we bade adieu to the dim hypaethric[7] cavern, and after much difficulty succeeded in rejoining our guides.

During our stay at Naples, we often returned to this cave, sometimes alone, skimming the sun-lit sea, and each time added to our store. Since that period, whenever the world's circumstance has not imperiously called me away, or the temper of my mind impeded such study, I have been employed in deciphering these sacred remains. Their meaning, wondrous and eloquent, has often repaid my toil, soothing me in sorrow, and exciting my imagination to daring flights, through the immensity of nature and the mind of man. For awhile my labours were not solitary; but that time is gone; and, with the selected and matchless companion of my toils, their dearest reward is also lost to me—

> Di mie tenere frondi altro lavoro
> Credea mostrarte; e qual fero pianeta
> Ne' nvidiò insieme, o mio nobil tesoro?[8]

I present the public with my latest discoveries in the slight Sibylline pages. Scattered and unconnected as they were, I have been obliged to add links, and model the work into a consistent form. But the main substance rests on the truths contained in these poetic rhapsodies, and the divine intuition which the Cumaean damsel obtained from heaven.

I have often wondered at the subject of her verses, and at the English dress of the Latin poet. Sometimes I have thought, that, obscure and chaotic as they are, they owe their present form to me, their decipherer. As if we should give to another artist, the painted fragments which form the mosaic copy of Raphael's Transfiguration in St. Peter's;[9] he would put them together in a form, whose mode would be fashioned by his own peculiar

---

[7] **hypaethric:** open to the air, having no roof.

[8] Cf. Francesco Petrarch (1304–1374), sonnet to his dead patron Giacomo Colonna, "Mai non vedranno le mie luci asciutte . . .": "From my tender leaves I expected to present another work to you; and what fierce planet begrudged our being together, O my noble treasure?"

[9] **mosaic copy:** reproduction of painting in small colored pieces of stone or glass that are cemented together. **Raphael:** Raffaello Sanzio of Urbino (1483–1520), Italian Renaissance painter; succeeded Bramante as the architect of St. Peter's, the Papal cathedral in Rome; painted many images of Christ and the Madonna, including a *Transfiguration of Christ.*

mind and talent. Doubtless the leaves of the Cumaean Sibyl have suffered distortion and diminution of interest and excellence in my hands. My only excuse for thus transforming them, is that they were unintelligible in their pristine condition.

My labours have cheered long hours of solitude, and taken me out of a world, which has averted its once benignant face from me, to one glowing with imagination and power. Will my readers ask how I could find solace from the narration of misery and woeful change? This is one of the mysteries of our nature, which holds full sway over me, and from whose influence I cannot escape. I confess, that I have not been unmoved by the development of the tale; and that I have been depressed, nay, agonized, at some parts of the recital, which I have faithfully transcribed from my materials. Yet such is human nature, that the excitement of mind was dear to me, and that the imagination, painter of tempest and earthquake, or, worse, the stormy and ruin-fraught passions of man, softened my real sorrows and endless regrets, by clothing these fictitious ones in that ideality, which takes the mortal sting from pain.

I hardly know whether this apology is necessary. For the merits of my adaptation and translation must decide how far I have well bestowed my time and imperfect powers, in giving form and substance to the frail and attenuated Leaves of the Sibyl.

from Letter to John Murray
(1830)

33 Somerset St.
*Portman Sq 19 Jan^y^*

MY DEAR SIR

Except the occupation of one or two annoyances, I have done nothing but read since I got Lord Byron's life[1] —

I have no pretensions to being a critic — yet I know infinitely well what pleases me — Not to mention the judicious arrangement and happy *tact* displayed by Mr Moore, which distinguish this book — I must say a word concerning the style, which is elegant and forcible. I was particularly struck by the observations on Lord Byron's character before his departure to Greece — and on his return — there is strength and richness as well as sweetness —

The great charm of the work to me, and it will have the same for you, is that the Lord Byron I find there is our Lord Byron — the fascinating — faulty — childish — philosophical being — daring the world — docile to a private circle — impetuous and indolent — gloomy and yet more gay than any other — I live with him again in these pages — getting reconciled (as I used in his lifetime) to those waywardnesses which annoyed me when he was away, through the delightful & buoyant tone of his conversation and manners —

His own letters and journals mirror himself as he was, and are invaluable — There is something cruelly kind in this single volume When will the next come? — impatient before how tenfold now am I so.

Among its many other virtues this book is *accurate* to a miracle I have not stumbled on one mistake with regard either to time place or feeling

I am dear Sir
Your Ob^t^ & Obliged Servant
MARY SHELLEY

from Letter to Maria Gisborne
(1834)

Harrow October 30 Nov. 17

MY DEAREST MARIA

Thank you many times for your kind dear letter — God grant that your constitution may yet bear you up a long time & that you may continue impressed with the idea of your *happiness*. Your expression is not ill applied — the object of tender solicitude — necessary & dear to one whom you love & esteem, you enjoy a greater portion of happiness than many whose lots are less beset by pain — To be loved is indeed necessary — sympathy & companionship are the only sweets "to make the nauseous draught of life go down" — And I, who feel this, live in a solitude, such as since the days of Hermits in the desert, no one was ever before condemned to! I see no one — I speak to none — except perhaps for a chance half hour in the course of a fortnight. I never walk out beyond my garden — because I *cannot* walk alone: — you will say I ought to force myself — so I thought once, & tried — but it would not do — The sense of desolation was too oppressive — I only find relief from the sadness of my position by living a dreamy

[1] The first volume of Thomas Moore's edition of *Byron, Journal and Letters* was published by John Murray on 18 January 1830. The second volume appeared in late December 1830.

existence from which realities are excluded — but going out disturbed this — I wept — my heart beat with a sense of injury & wrong — I was better shut up. Poverty prevents my visiting town — I am too far for visitors to reach me — I must bear to the end — when & what will that be? You say truly that my father-in-law's prolonged life will ruin me — it has done so — twelve years have I spent, the currents of life benumbed by poverty — and meanwhile he does all he can to injure the future prospects of Percy & myself.[1] Of him I think, — life & hope are over for me. You may guess that absorbed in him, I adhere to your advice of cultivating his affection — Fate shews her determination to drive me to him alone — she cuts me off from love, friendship, society, ambition; she gives me him alone — but there is no sympathy in a child — & though I look forward to reaping a subsequent harvest from my sacrifices (how likely to be blighted — he will marry — & there ends a Mother's happiness) yet for the present something more is needed — something not so *unnatural* as my present life. Not that I often feel ennui — I am too much employed — too much a being of dreams — but it hurts me — it destroys the spring of my mind; it makes me at once over sensitive with my fellow creatures, & yet their victim & dupe — it takes all strength from my character — making me, who by nature am too much so — timid. I need to have one resource, a belief in *my good fortune*; this is exchanged after twelve years of *One* Adversity, blotted & sprinkled by *many* adversities, — a dark ground with sad figures painted on it — to a perfect belief in my ill fortune — Percy is spared to me because I am to live — I should be free & die if —— but no — He is a blessing; my heart acknowledges that he is perhaps as great a one as any human being possesses. & indeed, my dear friend, while I suffer I do not repine while he remains, — He is not all you say — he has no ambition — & his talents are not so transcendant as you appear to imagine but he is a fine, spirited, clever Boy — & I think promises good things — If hereafter I have reason to be proud of him — these melancholy days & weeks at Harrow will brighten in my imagination — And they are not Melancholy — I am seldom so — but they are not right — & it will be a good thing if they terminate happily soon At the same time I cannot in the least regret having come here. It was the only way I had of educating Percy in a public school — of which institution, at least here at Harrow, the more I see, the more I like — besides that it was Shelley's wish that his son be brought up at one. It is indeed peculiarly suited to Percy — and whatever he will be — he will be twice as much as if he had been brought up in the narrow confinement of a private school — The boys here have liberty to the verge of licence — yet of the latter, save the breaking of a few windows now & then, there is none. His life is not quite what it would be if he did not live with me — but the greater scope given to the cultivation of the affections is surely an advantage — Then it cultivates his hospitality, since his friends would rather dine badly with him than well at their tutors — He has two who frequent the house — he will not extend the number, for fear of their annoying me — but sometimes he gives breakfasts to 6 or 8 — & so gets a portion of popularity, despite my poverty — this last has caused him to be quizzed[2] now & then — the character I hear from others that he bears among his companions, is that he is very clever, & gives more help than any boy in the school, but is very haughty — it is odd that with me he is yielding either to persuasion or rebuke — but with his Boys — their utmost violence can never make him give in a jot — he can say *No,* which I cannot do — & has lively spirits — & is indeed a strange mixture of Shelley & I — he wants sensibility — but I fancy mine, at his age was almost as covert — except that M[rs] Godwin had discovered long before my excessive & romantic attachment to my Father — he is not cruel to animals, & he likes them but has no tender solicitude about them. But when he has suffered himself he will feel for others — May that day be far off! . . .

[1] Sir Timothy Shelley refused to allow Mary Shelley to publish her biography of his son, on pain of withdrawing the modest annual allowance of £200 that he gave her toward the schooling of his grandson. Percy Florence was now a day-student at Harrow (an elite private school), and would inherit Sir Timothy's estate on his death. Mary Shelley augmented her meagre income by writing stories and essays for the annual journals and the encyclopedias as well as novels. Sir Timothy did not die until 1844, at the age of 91.

[2] **quizzed:** mocked, teased.

from The Journals of Mary Shelley

(21 October 1838)

I have been so often abused by pretended friends for my lukewarmness in the "Good Cause,"[1] that though I disdain

[1] **"Good Cause":** in 1837, the manifesto or "People's Charter" of the Chartist Movement demanded the following "Six

to answer them, I shall put down here a few thoughts on this subject. I am much of a self examiner. Vanity is not my fault, I think—if it is, it is uncomfortable vanity—for I have none that teaches me to be satisfied with myself—far otherwise—And if I use the word disdain—it is that I think my qualities—such as they are—[are] not appreciated from unworthy causes.

In the first place with regard to the "good Cause"—the cause of the advancement of freedom & knowledge—of the Rights of Women &c—I am not a person of Opinions. I have said elsewhere that human beings differ greatly in this—some have a passion for reforming the world: others do not cling to particular opinions. That my Parents & Shelley[2] were of the former class, makes me respect it—I respect such when joined to real disinterestedness, toleration & a clear understanding;—My accusers—after such as these—appear to me mere drivellers. For myself, I earnestly desire the good & enlightenment of my fellow creatures—& see all in the present course tending to the same, & rejoice—but I am not for violent extremes which only tend to bring on an injurious reaction. I have never written a word that is in disfavour of liberalism; that I have not supported it openly in writing arises from the following causes—as far as I know:

That I have not argumentative powers. I see things pretty clearly; but cannot demonstrate them. Besides I feel the counter arguments too strongly. I do not feel that I could say aught to support the cause efficiently—besides that on some topics (especially with regard to my own sex) I am far from making up my mind. I beleive that we are sent here to educate ourselves & that self denial & disappointment & self controul are a part of our education—that it is not by taking away all restraining law that our improvement is to be achieved—& though many things need great amendment—I can by no means go so far as my friends would have me. When I feel that I can say what will benefit my fellow creatures, I will speak,—not before. . . . Then, I recoil from the vulgar abuse of the inimical press; I do more than recoil: . . . I am silent therefore from prudence. I will not put myself so far forward—for then I cannot pause, but shall be dragged further. Proud & sensitive, I act on the defensive—an inglorious position. . . . To hang back, as I do, brings a penalty. I was nursed and fed with a love of glory. To be something great and good was the precept given me by my father: Shelley reiterated it. Alone & poor, I could only be something by joining a party—& there was much in me—the woman's love of looking up & being guided, & being willing to do any thing if any one supported & brought me forward, which would have made me a good partizan—but Shelley died & I was alone—my father from age & domestic circumstances & other things could not *me faire valoir*[3]—none else noticed me—had I been french I had been courted & flattered—& sympathized with. The solitude in which I lived with Shelley—my total friendlessness & want of connection—my first step in life (which except for that it was wrong I never repent on my own account—what ever may have been its effects) my being poor—my horror of pushing—& inability to put myself forward unless led, cherished & supported, all this has sunk me in a state of loneliness no other human being ever before I beleive endured—Except Robinson Crusoe.[4] How many tears & spasms of anguish this solitude has cost me lies buried in my memory—formed to feel pleasure in society—in intercourse with persons of wit & genius & the busy scene of life—how against the hair has fortune ever stroked me!—Well—it is well nigh over.

If I had raved & ranted about what I did not understand—had I adopted a set of opinions & a propagated them with enthusiasm—had I been careless of attack—& eager for notoriety—then the party to which I belonged had gathered round me & I had not been alone.

But since I lost Shelley I have no wish to ally myself to the Radicals—they are full of repulsion to me. Violent without any sense of justice—selfish in the extreme—talking without knowledge—rude, envious & insolent—I wish to have nothing to do with them.

It has been the fashion with these same friends to accuse me of worldliness. There indeed in my own heart & conscience I take a high ground. I may blame or despise myself for not being more of a reformer—I may distrust

---

Points": Universal Suffrage, Vote by Ballot, Annual Parliaments, Payment of Members of Parliament, Abolition of the Property Qualification for the Vote, and Equal Electoral Districts. In 1838, the parliamentary debate concerning the Infants' Custody Bill, which would grant custody of children in a divorce or legal separation to the mother as well as the father, became a referendum on women's rights, championed by Caroline Norton.

[2] **passion for reforming the world**: Percy Shelley admits to such a passion in the same words in his Preface to *Prometheus Unbound*.*

[3] **me faire valoir**: French, "put me forward"; "support me."

[4] **Robinson Crusoe**: protagonist of Daniel Defoe's novel *Robinson Crusoe* (1719–1720) who was shipwrecked alone on a desert island for twenty years.

my own judgement too much—be too indolent—& too timid—but in conduct I am above merited blame.

I like society—I beleive all persons of any talent (who are in good health) do—The soil that gives forth nothing may lie ever fallow—but that which produces—however humble its product—needs cultivation—change of harvest—refreshing dews & refining sun—books do much—but the living intercourse is the vital heat, debarred from that how have I pined & died. I do not abuse my Country—England has many merits—but the usage I have suffered at her hands of neglect & loneliness would have been my dower no where else.

My early friends chose the position of enemies. I had faults—instead of exposing these to a candid mind & tender conscience—I was villified behind my back. I discovered this—I discovered the sad influence exercised there when the grave permitted no appeal—& the sense of my own faults redoubled (erroneously perhaps) the bitter sense of unjust treatment. When I first discovered that a trusted friend[5] had acted thus by me, I was nearly destroyed—my health was shaken. I rememember thinking of Guatamotzin's[6] bed of torture & with a burst of agonizing tears exclaiming I would prefer that to the unutterable anguish a friend's falsehood engendered!—I cannot forget that—it is wrong. She has many virtues—I have no right still to feel sore—but in vain I try to cicatrize[7] the wound—there is no resentment—but the world can never be to me what it was before—trust & confidence & the heart's sincere devotion are gone.—I sought at that time to make acquaintances to divert my mind from the anguish inflicted by a friend. I got entangled in various ways through my ready sympathy & too eager heart. But I never crouched to society—never sought it unworthily—if I have never written to vindicate the Rights of women, I have ever befriended women when oppressed—at every risk I have defended & supported victims to the social system—But I do not make a boast—I do not say aloud—behold my generosity & greatness of mind—for in truth it is simple justice I perform—and so I am still reviled for being worldly.

For the rest—God grant a happier & better day is near. Percy—my all in all—will—I trust—by his excellent understanding—his clear bright sincere spirit & affectionate heart repay me for sad long years of desolation—His career may lead me into the thick of life—or only gild a quiet home—I am content with either. And as I grow older I grow more fearless for myself—I become firmer in my opinions—the experienced—the suffering—the thoughtful may at last speak unrebuked—or careless of rebuke. If it be the will of God that I live I may ally my name yet to the "good Cause"—though I do not expect to please my Accusers.

Thus have I put down my thoughts—I may have deceived myself—I may be vain—I may be in the wrong. I try to examine myself—& such as I have written appears to me the exact truth. . . .

Enough of this! The great work of life goes on—Death draws near—To be better after death than in life is one's hope & endeavour—to be that through self schooling. If I write the above it is that those who love me may hereafter know that I am not all to blame—nor merit the heavy accusations cast on me for not putting myself forward—I *cannot* do that—it is against my nature—as well cast me from a precipice & rail at me for not flying.

[5] Jane Williams and Thomas Jefferson Hogg, whom she later married, had both blamed Mary Shelley for making the last months of Percy Shelley's life unhappy ones; Jane had even told their friends that Percy Shelley was planning to leave Mary.

[6] **Guatamotzin**: Guauhtemoc (1497–1522), Montezuma's nephew and son-in-law, emperor of Mexico (1520–1521), was vanquished and cruelly tortured by Cortés in 1521 (see William Robertson, *History of America,* 1815, Shelley's source).

[7] **cicatrize**: heal by skinning over a wound; create a scar.

from Rambles in Germany and Italy, in 1840, 1842, and 1843
(1843)

—VOLUME ONE—
(1840)

from LETTER 1

. . . Can it, indeed, be true, that I am about to revisit Italy? How many years are gone since I quitted that country![1] There I left the mortal remains of those beloved—my

[1] Mary Shelley left Italy in August 1823, after the drowning of Percy Shelley; she returned with Percy Florence and two of his school friends in June 1840. They spent eight weeks on the shores of Lake Como in northern Italy. Her letters to Claire Clairmont were later edited for this text. In 1842, after Percy's graduation from Cambridge University, they spent the summer in Germany and the winter and spring of 1843 in Italy.

husband and my children, whose loss changed my whole existence, substituting, for happy peace and the interchange of deep-rooted affections, years of desolate solitude, and a hard struggle with the world; which only now, as my son is growing up, is brightening into a better day. The name of Italy has magic in its very syllables. The hope of seeing it again recalls vividly to my memory that time, when misfortune seemed an empty word, and my habitation on earth a secure abode, which no evil could shake. Graves have opened in my path since then; and, instead of the cheerful voices of the living, I have dwelt among the early tombs of those I loved. Now a new generation has sprung up; and, at the name of Italy, I grow young again in their enjoyments, and gladly prepare to share them. You know, also, how grievously my health has been shaken; a nervous illness interrupts my usual occupations, and disturbs the ordinary tenor of my life. Travelling will cure all: my busy, brooding thoughts will be scattered abroad; and, to use a figure of speech, my mind will, amidst novel and various scenes, renew the outworn and tattered garments in which it has long been clothed, and array itself in a vesture all gay in fresh and glossy hues, when we are beyond the Alps. . . .

from LETTER 4

. . . All Italian travellers know what it is, after toiling up the bleak, bare, northern, Swiss side of an Alp, to descend towards ever-vernal Italy. The rhododendron, in thick bushes, in full bloom, first adorned the mountain sides; then, pine forests; then, chesnut groves; the mountain was cleft into woody ravines; the waterfalls scattered their spray and their gracious melody; flowery and green, and clothed in radiance, and gifted with plenty, Italy opened upon us. Thus,—and be not shocked at the illustration, for it is all God's creation,—after dreary old age and the sickening pass of death, does the saint open his eyes on Paradise. Chiavenna is situated in a fertile valley at the foot of the Splugen[2]—it is glowing in rich and sunny vegetation. The inn is good; but the rooms were large and somewhat dreary. So near our bourne, low spirits crept over some of us, I know not why. To me, indeed, there was something even thrilling and affecting in the aspect of the commonest objects around. Every traveller can tell you how each country bears a distinctive mark in the mere setting out of the room of an inn, which would enable a man who had visited it before, if, transported by magic, he opened his eyes in the morning in a strange bed, to know to what country he had been removed. Window-curtains, the very wash-hand stands, they were all such as had been familiar to me in Italy long, long ago. I had not seen them since those young and happy days. Strange and indescribable emotions invaded me; recollections, long forgotten, arose fresh and strong by mere force of association, produced by those objects being presented to my eye, inspiring a mixture of pleasure and pain, almost amounting to agony. . . .

from LETTER 5

. . . This evening P——'s little boat has come; small, indeed, it is. In shape it is something of a sea boat, and it has a keel, and a tiny sail; but it is too small to convey a feeling of safety. I look at it and shudder. I can bring no help, except constant watchfulness; and many an anxious hour it will cause me to pass. Do not call me a grumbler. A tragedy has darkened my life: I endeavour, in vain, to cast aside the fears which are its offspring; they haunt me perpetually, and make too large and too sad a portion of my daily life.

The arrival of the boat, you see, has dashed my spirits, so I break off.—Adieu.

from LETTER 8

. . . I love the Italians. It is impossible to live among them and not love them. Their faults are many—the faults of the oppressed—love of pleasure, disregard of truth, indolence, and violence of temper. But their falsehood is on the surface—it is not deceit. Under free institutions, and where the acquirement of knowledge is not as now a mark inviting oppression and wrong, their love of pleasure were readily ennobled into intellectual activity. They are affectionate, simple, and earnestly desirous to please. There is life, energy, and talent in every look and word; grace and refinement in every act and gesture. They are a noble race of men—a beautiful race of women; the time must come when again they will take a high place among nations. Their habits, fostered by their governments, alone are degraded and degrading; alter these, and the country of Dante and Michael Angelo and Raphael still exists. . . .

from LETTER 9

. . . I always feel renewed and extreme delight as I watch the shadows of evening climb the huge mountains, till the granite peaks alone shine forth glad and bright, and a

---

[2] **Chiavenna . . . Splugen:** Shelley crossed the Rhaetian Alps by the Splugen Pass, which extends from Splugen in southeast Switzerland to Chiavenna in northern Italy.

holy stillness gathers over the landscape. With what serious yet quick joy do such sights fill me; and dearer still is the aspiring thought that seeks the Creator in his works, as the soul yearns to throw off the chains of flesh that hold it in, and to dissolve and become a part of that which surrounds it.

This evening my friends are gone to Como, and I sat long on my favourite seat, listening to the ripplet of the calm lake splashing at my feet; to the murmur of running streams, and to the hollow roar of the mysterious torrent —the *Fiume Latte*[3]—which is borne, softened by distance, from the opposite shore; viewing the magnificent mountain scene, varied by the lights and shadows caused by the setting sun. My heart was elevated, purified, subdued. I prayed for peace to all; and still the supreme Beauty brooded over me, and promised peace; at least there where change is not, and love and enjoyment unite and are one. From such rapt moods the soul returns to earth, bearing with it the calm of Paradise:

> Quale è colui, che sognando vede,
> E dopo 'l sogno la passione impressa
> Rimane, e l'altro alla mente non riede;
> Cotal son io, che quasi tutta cessa
> Mia visione, ed ancor mi distilla
> Nel cor il dolce, che nacque da essa.
> Cosi la neve al sol si dissigilla;
> Cosi al vento nelle feglie lievi
> Si perdea la sentenzia di Sibilla.[4]

It has seemed to me—and on such an evening, I have felt it,—that this world, endowed as it is outwardly with endless shapes and influences of beauty and enjoyment, is peopled also in its spiritual life by myriads of loving spirits; from whom, unawares, we catch impressions, which mould our thoughts to good, and thus they guide beneficially the course of events, and minister to the destiny of man. Whether the beloved dead make a portion of this holy company, I dare not guess; but that such exists, I feel. They keep far off while we are worldly, evil, selfish; but draw near, imparting the reward of heaven-born joy, when we are animated by noble thoughts, and capable of disinterested actions. Surely such gather round me this night, and make a part of that atmosphere of peace and love which it is paradise to breathe.

I had thought such ecstacy as that in which I now was lapped dead to me for ever; but the sun of Italy has thawed the frozen stream—the cup of life again sparkles to the brim. Will it be removed as I turn northward? I fear it will. I grieve to think that we shall very soon leave Cadenabbia—the first sad step towards quitting Italy. . . .

—*from* VOLUME TWO—
(1843)

from LETTER 23

. . . To suffer is a different thing under this sky.[5] They have bad food, they work hard; but Nature is their friend; they are not pinched with cold nor racked by rheumatic pains. Thus my poor woman, in whom I grew interested, had nothing morose—scarcely anything plaintive—about her. *"Sono sempre allegra,"* she said. "I am gay—we ought to be gay." *"Siamo come Dio vuole."* "We live as God pleases, and must not complain. My heart aches when I remember my poor children now in Paradise; I cry when I think of them; and that little fellow," and she cast an anxious, maternal glance on him—"he is not well" (heaven knows, he was not). *"Ma, allegra, Signora"*—"the Virgin will help us;" and she began, in a sweet voice, to sing a plaintive hymn to the Virgin. Poor people! their religion is hung round with falsehood; but it is a great, a real comfort, to them. Sickness and all evil comes from God, and must be borne, therefore, with patience; and the great duty is to be gay under all, and to serve God with a cheerful, as well as a pure, heart. I should have liked to have tried, at least, to have done some real good to this woman, whose countenance, and voice, and conversation, gave her distinction. Nothing could be more simple and unpretending than her talk; but it had a stamp of heart, joined to that touch of the imaginative, peculiar to the Italian peasantry. . . .

I spend the evenings on our terrace. The nights here are wonderful; and I am never weary of observing the loveliness of the skies. Twenty-four o'clock, a moveable hour which is fixed for half an hour after sunset, never, in

---

[3] **Fiume Latte**: literally, "a stream of milk"; a waterfall on the eastern side of Lake Como near Varenna.

[4] Cf. Dante, *Paradiso,* Canto 33 (M. W.), ll. 58–66: "As from a dream one may awake to find / Its passion yet imprinted on the heart, / Although all else is cancelled from the mind, / So of my vision now but little part / Remains, yet in my inmost soul I know / The sweet instilling which it did impart. / So the sun melts the imprint on the snow, / Even so the Sibyl's wisdom that was penned / On light leaves vanished on the winds that blow."

[5] **this sky**: Mary Shelley was in Sorrento, Italy, on the Bay of Naples, from 16 May to 19 July 1843.

this climate, falls later than half-past eight. By that time it is night; but the extreme purity of the atmosphere gives to darkness a sort of brilliancy, such as a black shining object has. The sea is dark and bright at the same time; the high coast around does not assume that gigantic, misty appearance, hills do in the North during dusk, but they stand out as well defined as by day. If there be a moon, we see it floating in mid-air. We perceive at once that it is not a shining shape, plastered, as it were, against the sky; but a ball which, all bright, or partly dusky, hangs pendant. Its light is painfully bright; the extreme glittering whiteness fatigues the eye more than daylight. In the North, we often repine that we have not two moons, so always to enjoy the use of our eyes in the absence of the sun; in the South, the interlunar nights are an agreeable change, at times almost a relief. By the moonlight we can perceive the smoke ascend from the crater of Vesuvius;[6] if she desert the night, a lambent flame shoots up at intervals. I may have wearied you by my various accounts of the evening hours which, to a lover of nature, are so enchanting. In other places a sense of tenderness, a softening influence, has fallen on my heart at that time; but here, the glory of absolute immeasurable beauty mantles all things at all times.

June 20

——Yet not so. Lo! a scirocco[7] comes to blot the scene. Nothing can be stranger than this scirocco: at its first breath, the sea grows dull, leaden, slate-coloured—all its transparency is gone. The view of the opposite shore is hidden in mist. The near mountains wear a deeper green, but have lost all brightness and cast weird shadows on the dull waters. This wind coming from the south-east is with us a land wind. It rolls huge waves on the beach of Naples; but beneath our cliffs the sea is calm—such a calm!—it looks so treacherous, that even if you did not hear of the true state of things, you would hesitate to trust yourself to it. At a short distance from the shore the wind plays wild pranks; here and there it seizes the water as a whirlwind, and you see circles emerge from a centre, spread round and fade away. P—— went out in his boat about a hundred yards from our cavern; even there, though in apparent calm, the skiff was whirled round, and nothing but letting go the sheet on the instant prevented her from being capsized.

The heat is excessive. Every one appears to be seized with feverish illness: nobody wishes to eat or move. The early setting and late rising of the sun in this high latitude, making the nights long, gives the earth and atmosphere time to cool; and it is thus that the heat of summer is often not so oppressive as in the North; otherwise it would be intolerable. Imagine our Dresden length of day with a Neapolitan temperature: no one could bear it and live. But our nights are cool; our early mornings even chill, and thus nature is refreshed: only, this does not occur during the periods of scirocco; then, night and day, the heat lies like a heavy garment round our limbs. Fortunately, three days is its utmost, one or two its usual, extent; it vanishes as it came, no one knows how. Nature and our human spirits come forth as after an eclipse; the world revived looks up and resumes its natural healthy appearance. . . .

[6] **Vesuvius:** active volcano on the eastern shore of the Bay of Naples.

[7] **scirocco:** hot, dry wind, from Africa.

POSTHUMOUS PUBLICATIONS

Mathilda[1]

(1959; comp. 1819)

— CHAPTER I —

It is only four o'clock; but it is winter and the sun has already set: there are no clouds in the clear, frosty sky to reflect its slant beams, but the air itself is tinged with a slight roseate colour which is again reflected on the snow that covers the ground. I live in a lone cottage on a solitary, wide heath: no voice of life reaches me. I see the desolate plain covered with white, save a few black patches that the noonday sun has made at the top of those sharp pointed hillocks from which the snow, sliding as it fell, lay thinner than on the plain ground: a few birds are pecking at the hard ice that covers the pools—for the frost has been of long continuance.

[1] Mary Shelley began the novella *Mathilda,* initially titled *The Fields of Fancy,* in Leghorn, Italy, on Shelley's birthday, 4 August 1819, and completed it in Florence on 9 November 1819. In May 1819, her friend Maria Reveley Gisborne carried the manuscript to London to William Godwin for submission to a publisher, but Godwin refused either to send the novella to a publisher or to return it to Mary. The manuscript was first edited and published by Elizabeth Nitchie in 1959.

I am in a strange state of mind. I am alone—quite alone—in the world—the blight of misfortune has passed over me and withered me; I know that I am about to die and I feel happy—joyous.—I feel my pulse; it beats fast: I place my thin hand on my cheek; it burns: there is a slight, quick spirit within me which is now emitting its last sparks. I shall never see the snows of another winter—I do believe that I shall never again feel the vivifying warmth of another summer sun; and it is in this persuasion that I begin to write my tragic history. Perhaps a history such as mine had better die with me, but a feeling that I cannot define leads me on and I am too weak both in body and mind to resist the slightest impulse. While life was strong within me I thought indeed that there was a sacred horror in my tale that rendered it unfit for utterance, and now about to die I pollute its mystic terrors. It is as the wood of the Eumenides none but the dying may enter; and Oedipus is about to die.[2]

What am I writing?—I must collect my thoughts. I do not know that any will peruse these pages except you, my friend, who will receive them at my death. I do not address them to you alone because it will give me pleasure to dwell upon our friendship in a way that would be needless if you alone read what I shall write. I shall relate my tale therefore as if I wrote for strangers. You have often asked me the cause of my solitary life; my tears; and above all of my impenetrable and unkind silence. In life I dared not; in death I unveil the mystery. Others will toss these pages lightly over: to you, Woodville, kind, affectionate friend, they will be dear—the precious memorials of a heart-broken girl who, dying, is still warmed by gratitude towards you: your tears will fall on the words that record my misfortunes; I know they will—and while I have life I thank you for your sympathy.

But enough of this. I will begin my tale: it is my last task, and I hope I have strength sufficient to fulfill it. I record no crimes; my faults may easily be pardoned; for they proceeded not from evil motive but from want of judgement; and I believe few would say that they could, by a different conduct and superior wisdom, have avoided the misfortunes to which I am the victim. My fate has been governed by necessity, a hideous necessity. It required hands stronger than mine; stronger I do believe than any human force to break the thick, adamantine chain that has bound me, once breathing nothing but joy, ever possessed by a warm love and delight in goodness,—to misery only to be ended, and now about to be ended, in death. But I forget myself, my tale is yet untold. I will pause a few moments, wipe my dim eyes, and endeavour to lose the present obscure but heavy feeling of unhappiness in the more acute emotions of the past.

I was born in England. My father was a man of rank: he had lost his father early, and was educated by a weak mother with all the indulgence she thought due to a nobleman of wealth. He was sent to Eton[3] and afterwards to college; and allowed from childhood the free use of large sums of money; thus enjoying from his earliest youth the independance which a boy with these advantages, always acquires at a public school.

Under the influence of these circumstances his passions found a deep soil where they might strike their roots and flourish either as flowers or weeds as was their nature. By being always allowed to act for himself his character became strongly and early marked and exhibited a various surface on which a quick sighted observer might see the seeds of virtues and of misfortunes. His careless extravagance, which made him squander immense sums of money to satisfy passing whims, which from their apparent energy he dignified with the name of passions, often displayed itself in unbounded generosity. Yet while he earnestly occupied himself about the wants of others his own desires were gratified to their fullest extent. He gave his money, but none of his own wishes were sacrifised to his gifts; he gave his time, which he did not value, and his affections which he was happy in any manner to have called into action.

I do not say that if his own desires had been put in competition with those of others that he would have displayed undue selfishness, but this trial was never made. He was nurtured in prosperity and attended by all its advantages; every one loved him and wished to gratify him. He was ever employed in promoting the pleasures of his companions—but their pleasures were his; and if he bestowed more attention upon the feelings of others than is usual with schoolboys it was because his social temper could never enjoy itself if every brow was not as free from care as his own.

While at school, emulation and his own natural abilities made him hold a conspicuous rank in the forms

[2] See Sophocles, *Oedipus at Colonus*. The Eumenides (literally "the kindly ones") are the Furies who tormented Oedipus for his incestuous affair with his mother, Jocasta.

[3] Eton: the most elite of England's private (called "public") secondary schools.

among his equals; at college he discarded books; he believed that he had other lessons to learn than those which they could teach him. He was now to enter into life and he was still young enough to consider study as a schoolboy shackle, employed merely to keep the unruly out of mischief but as having no real connexion with life—whose wisdom of riding—gaming &c. he considered with far deeper interest—So he quickly entered into all college follies although his heart was too well moulded to be contaminated by them—it might be light but it was never cold. He was a sincere and sympathizing friend—but he had met with none who superior or equal to himself could aid him in unfolding his mind, or make him seek for fresh stores of thought by exhausting the old ones. He felt himself superior in quickness of judgement to those around him: his talents, his rank and wealth made him the chief of his party, and in that station he rested not only contented but glorying, conceiving it to be the only ambition worthy for him to aim at in the world.

By a strange narrowness of ideas he viewed all the world in connexion only as it was or was not related to his little society. He considered queer and out of fashion all opinions that were exploded by his circle of intimates, and he became at the same time dogmatic and yet fearful of not coinciding with the only sentiments he could consider orthodox. To the generality of spectators he appeared careless of censure, and with high disdain to throw aside all dependance on public prejudices; but at the same time that he strode with a triumphant stride over the rest of the world, he cowered, with self-disguised lowliness, to his own party, and although its chief never dared express an opinion or a feeling until he was assured that it would meet with the approbation of his companions.

Yet he had one secret hidden from these dear friends; a secret he had nurtured from his earliest years, and although he loved his fellow collegiates he would not trust it to the delicacy or sympathy of any one among them. He loved. He feared that the intensity of his passion might become the subject of their ridicule; and he could not bear that they should blaspheme it by considering that trivial and transitory which he felt was the life of his life.

There was a gentleman of small fortune who lived near his family mansion who had three lovely daughters. The eldest was far the most beautiful, but her beauty was only an addition to her other qualities—her understanding was clear and strong and her disposition angelically gentle. She and my father had been playmates from infancy: Diana, even in her childhood had been a favourite with his mother; this partiality encreased with the years of this beautiful and lively girl and thus during his school and college vacations they were perpetually together. Novels and all the various methods by which youth in civilized life are led to a knowledge of the existence of passions before they really feel them, had produced a strong effect on him who was so peculiarly susceptible of every impression. At eleven years of age Diana was his favourite playmate but he already talked the language of love. Although she was elder than he by nearly two years the nature of her education made her more childish at least in the knowledge and expression of feeling; she received his warm protestations with innocence, and returned them unknowing of what they meant. She had read no novels and associated only with her younger sisters, what could she know of the difference between love and friendship? And when the development of her understanding disclosed the true nature of this intercourse to her, her affections were already engaged to her friend, and all she feared was lest other attractions and fickleness might make him break his infant vows.

But they became every day more ardent and tender. It was a passion that had grown with his growth; it had become entwined with every faculty and every sentiment and only to be lost with life. None knew of their love except their own two hearts; yet although in all things else and even in this he dreaded the censure of his companions, for thus truly loving one inferior to him in fortune, nothing was ever able for a moment to shake his purpose of uniting himself to her as soon as he could muster courage sufficient to meet those difficulties he was determined to surmount.

Diana was fully worthy of his deepest affection. There were few who could boast of so pure a heart, and so much real humbleness of soul joined to a firm reliance on her own integrity and a belief in that of others. She had from her birth lived a retired life. She had lost her mother when very young, but her father had devoted himself to the care of her education—He had many peculiar ideas which influenced the system he had adopted with regard to her—She was well acquainted with the heroes of Greece and Rome or with those of England who had lived some hundred years ago, while she was nearly ignorant of the passing events of the day: she had read few authors who had written during at least the last fifty years but her reading with this exception was very extensive. Thus although she appeared to be less initiated in the mysteries of life and society than he, her knowledge was of a deeper kind and laid on firmer foundations; and if even her beauty and sweetness had not fascinated him, her understanding would ever have held his in thrall. He looked up to her as his guide, and such was his adoration that he delighted to augment to his own mind the sense of inferiority with which she sometimes impressed him.

When he was nineteen his mother died. He left college on this event and shaking off for a while his old friends he retired to the neighbourhood of his Diana and received all his consolation from her sweet voice and dearer caresses. This short separation from his companions gave him courage to assert his independance. He had a feeling that however they might express ridicule of his intended marriage they would not dare display it when it had taken place; therefore seeking the consent of his guardian which with some difficulty he obtained, and of the father of his mistress which was more easily given, without acquainting any one else of his intention, by the time he had attained his twentieth birthday he had become the husband of Diana.

He loved her with passion and her tenderness had a charm for him that would not permit him to think of aught but her. He invited some of his college friends to see him but their frivolity disgusted him. Diana had torn the veil which had before kept him in his boyhood: he was become a man and he was surprised how he could ever have joined in the cant[4] words and ideas of his fellow collegiates or how for a moment he had feared the censure of such as these. He discarded his old friendships not from fickleness but because they were indeed unworthy of him. Diana filled up all his heart: he felt as if by his union with her he had received a new and better soul. She was his monitress as he learned what were the true ends of life. It was through her beloved lessons that he cast off his old pursuits and gradually formed himself to become one among his fellow men; a distinguished member of society, a Patriot; and an enlightened lover of truth and virtue.—He loved her for her beauty and for her amiable disposition but he seemed to love her more for what he considered her superior wisdom. They studied, they rode together; they were never seperate and seldom admitted a third to their society.

Thus my father, born in affluence, and always prosperous, clombe without the difficulty and various disappointments that all human beings seem destined to encounter, to the very topmost pinnacle of happiness. Around him was sunshine, and clouds whose shapes of beauty made the prospect divine concealed from him the barren reality which lay hidden below them. From this dizzy point he was dashed at once as he unawares congratulated himself on his felicity. Fifteen months after their marriage I was born, and my mother died a few days after my birth.

A sister of my father was with him at this period. She was nearly fifteen years older than he, and was the offspring of a former marriage of his father. When the latter died this sister was taken by her maternal relations: they had seldom seen one another, and were quite unlike in disposition. This aunt, to whose care I was afterwards consigned, has often related to me the effect that this catastrophe had on my father's strong and susceptible character. From the moment of my mother's death until his departure she never heard him utter a single word: buried in the deepest melancholy he took no notice of any one; often for hours his eyes streamed tears or a more fearful gloom overpowered him. All outward things seemed to have lost their existence relatively to him and only one circumstance could in any degree recall him from his motionless and mute despair: he would never see me. He seemed insensible to the presence of any one else, but if, as a trial to awaken his sensibility, my aunt brought me into the room he would instantly rush out with every symptom of fury and distraction. At the end of a month he suddenly quitted his house and, unattended by any servant, departed from that part of the country without by word or writing informing any one of his intentions. My aunt was only relieved of her anxiety concerning his fate by a letter from him dated Hamburgh.[5]

How often have I wept over that letter which until I was sixteen was the only relick I had to remind me of my parents. "Pardon me," it said, "for the uneasiness I have unavoidably given you: but while in that unhappy island, where every thing breathes *her* spirit whom I have lost for ever, a spell held me. It is broken: I have quitted England for many years, perhaps for ever. But to convince you that selfish feeling does not entirely engross me I shall remain in this town until you have made by letter every arrangement that you judge necessary. When I leave this place do not expect to hear from me: I must break all ties that at present exist. I shall become a wanderer, a miserable outcast—alone! alone!"—In another part of the letter he mentioned me—"As for that unhappy little being whom I

[4] **cant:** set form of words repeated mechanically; stock phrases.

[5] **Hamburgh:** city in northern Germany.

could not see, and hardly dare mention, I leave her under your protection. Take care of her and cherish her: one day I may claim her at your hands; but futurity is dark, make the present happy to her."

My father remained three months at Hamburgh; when he quitted it he changed his name, my aunt could never discover that which he adopted and only by faint hints, could conjecture that he had taken the road of Germany and Hungary to Turkey.

Thus this towering spirit who had excited interest and high expectation in all who knew and could value him became at once, as it were, extinct. He existed from this moment for himself only. His friends remembered him as a brilliant vision which would never again return to them. The memory of what he had been faded away as years passed; and he who before had been as a part of themselves and of their hopes was now no longer counted among the living.

— CHAPTER II —

I now come to my own story. During the early part of my life there is little to relate, and I will be brief; but I must be allowed to dwell a little on the years of my childhood that it may be apparent how when one hope failed all life was to be a blank; and how when the only affection I was permitted to cherish was blasted my existence was extinguished with it.

I have said that my aunt was very unlike my father. I believe that without the slightest tinge of a bad heart she had the coldest that ever filled a human breast: it was totally incapable of any affection. She took me under her protection because she considered it her duty; but she had too long lived alone and undisturbed by the noise and prattle of children to allow that I should disturb her quiet. She had never been married; and for the last five years had lived perfectly alone on an estate, that had descended to her through her mother, on the shores of Loch Lomond in Scotland. My father had expressed a wish in his letters that she should reside with me at his family mansion which was situated in a beautiful country near Richmond in Yorkshire. She would not consent to this proposition, but as soon as she had arranged the affairs which her brother's departure had caused to fall to her care, she quitted England and took me with her to her Scotch estate.

The care of me while a baby, and afterwards until I had reached my eighth year devolved on a servant of my mother's, who had accompanied us in our retirement for that purpose. I was placed in a remote part of the house, and only saw my aunt at stated hours. These occurred twice a day; once about noon she came to my nursery, and once after her dinner I was taken to her. She never caressed me, and seemed all the time I stayed in the room to fear that I should annoy her by some childish freak.[6] My good nurse always schooled me with the greatest care before she ventured into the parlour—and the awe my aunt's cold looks and few constrained words inspired was so great that I seldom disgraced her lessons or was betrayed from the exemplary stillness which I was taught to observe during these short visits.

Under my good nurse's care I ran wild about our park and the neighbouring fields. The offspring of the deepest love, I displayed from my earliest years the greatest sensibility of disposition. I cannot say with what passion I loved every thing, even the inanimate objects that surrounded me. I believe that I bore an individual attachment to every tree in our park; every animal that inhabited it knew me and I loved them. Their occasional deaths filled my infant heart with anguish. I cannot number the birds that I have saved during the long and severe winters of that climate; or the hares and rabbits that I have defended from the attacks of our dogs, or have nursed when accidentally wounded.

When I was seven years of age my nurse left me. I now forget the cause of her departure if indeed I ever knew it. She returned to England, and the bitter tears she shed at parting were the last I saw flow for love of me for many years. My grief was terrible: I had no friend but her in the whole world. By degrees I became reconciled to solitude but no one supplied her place in my affections. I lived in a desolate country where

——— there were none to praise
And very few to love.[7]

It is true that I now saw a little more of my aunt, but she was in every way an unsocial being; and to a timid child she was as a plant beneath a thick covering of ice; I should cut my hands in endeavouring to get at it. So I was entirely thrown upon my own resources. The neighbouring minister was engaged to give me lessons in reading, writing, and French, but he was without family and his manners even to me were always perfectly characteristic of

[6] **freak:** whim, caprice.

[7] **there were . . . love:** William Wordsworth, *Lyrical Ballads*, 2nd ed. (1800), "She dwelt among th' untrodden ways . . . ,"* lines 3 to 4.

the profession in the exercise of whose functions he chiefly shone, that of a schoolmaster. I sometimes strove to form friendships with the most attractive of the girls who inhabited the neighbouring village; but I believe I should never have succeeded [even] had not my aunt interposed her authority to prevent all intercourse between me and the peasantry; for she was fearful lest I should acquire the Scotch accent and dialect; a little of it I had, although great pains was taken that my tongue should not disgrace my English origin.

As I grew older my liberty encreased with my desires, and my wanderings extended from our park to the neighbouring country. Our house was situated on the shores of the lake and the lawn came down to the water's edge. I rambled amidst the wild scenery of this lovely country and became a complete mountaineer: I passed hours on the steep brow of a mountain that overhung a waterfall or rowed myself in a little skiff to some one of the islands. I wandered for ever about these lovely solitudes, gathering flower after flower

Ond' era pinta tutta la mia via[8]

singing as I might the wild melodies of the country, or occupied by pleasant day dreams. My greatest pleasure was the enjoyment of a serene sky amidst these verdant woods: yet I loved all the changes of Nature; and rain, and storm, and the beautiful clouds of heaven brought their delights with them. When rocked by the waves of the lake my spirits rose in triumph as a horseman feels with pride the motions of his high fed steed.

But my pleasures arose from the contemplation of nature alone, I had no companion: my warm affections finding no return from any other human heart were forced to run waste on inanimate objects. Sometimes indeed I wept when my aunt received my caresses with repulsive coldness, and when I looked round and found none to love; but I quickly dried my tears. As I grew older books in some degree supplied the place of human intercourse: the library of my aunt was very small; Shakespear, Milton, Pope and Cowper were the strangely assorted poets of her collection; and among the prose authors a translation of Livy and Rollin's[9] ancient history were my chief favourites although as I emerged from childhood I found others highly interesting which I had before neglected as dull.

When I was twelve years old it occurred to my aunt that I ought to learn music; she herself played upon the harp. It was with great hesitation that she persuaded herself to undertake my instruction; yet believing this accomplishment a necessary part of my education, and balancing the evils of this measure or of having some one in the house to instruct me she submitted to the inconvenience. A harp was sent for that my playing might not interfere with hers, and I began: she found me a docile and, when I had conquered the first rudiments, a very apt scholar. I had acquired in my harp a companion in rainy days; a sweet soother of my feelings when any untoward accident ruffled them: I often addressed it as my only friend; I could pour forth to it my hopes and loves, and I fancied that its sweet accents answered me. I have now mentioned all my studies.

I was a solitary being, and from my infant years, ever since my dear nurse left me, I had been a dreamer. I brought Rosalind and Miranda and the lady of Comus[10] to life to be my companions, or on my isle acted over their parts imagining myself to be in their situations. Then I wandered from the fancies of others and formed affections and intimacies with the aerial creations of my own brain—but still clinging to reality I gave a name to these conceptions and nursed them in the hope of realization.[11] I clung to the memory of my parents; my mother I should never see, she was dead: but the idea of [my] unhappy, wandering father was the idol of my imagination. I bestowed on him all my affections; there was a miniature of him that I gazed on continually; I copied his last letter and read it again and again. Sometimes it made me weep; and at others I repeated with transport those words,—"One day I may claim her at your hands." I was to be his consoler, his companion in after years. My favourite vision was that when I grew up I would leave my aunt, whose coldness lulled my conscience, and disguised like a boy I would seek my father through the world. My imagi-

[8] **Ond' era . . . via**: "with which all my path was painted." Cf. Dante Alighieri, *Purgatorio,* XXVIII.42, trans. Charles Singleton; this is where Dante's Matelda first appears.

[9] **Pope**: Alexander Pope (1688–1744), poet and satirist. **Cowper**: William Cowper (1731–1800), poet. **Livy**: Roman historian (59 BC–17 AD). **Rollin**: Charles Rollin (1661–1741), Jansenist French educator, author of *Ancient History* (1725).

[10] **Rosalind . . . lady of Comus**: heroines of Shakespeare's dramas *As You Like It* and *The Tempest* and of Milton's masque *Comus.*

[11] **aerial creations . . . hope of realization**: *Midsummer Night's Dream,* V.i.15–17: "The poet's pen / Turns them to shapes, and gives to aery nothing / A local habitation and a name."

nation hung upon the scene of recognition; his miniature, which I should continually wear exposed on my breast, would be the means and I imaged the moment to my mind a thousand and a thousand times, perpetually varying the circumstances. Sometimes it would be in a desart; in a populous city; at a ball; we should perhaps meet in a vessel; and his first words constantly were, "My daughter, I love thee!" What extatic moments have I passed in these dreams! How many tears I have shed; how often have I laughed aloud.

This was my life for sixteen years. At fourteen and fifteen I often thought that the time was come when I should commence my pilgrimage, which I had cheated my own mind into believing was my imperious duty: but a reluctance to quit my aunt; a remorse for the grief which, I could not conceal from myself, I should occasion her for ever withheld me. Sometimes when I had planned the next morning for my escape a word of more than usual affection from her lips made me postpone my resolution. I reproached myself bitterly for what I called a culpable weakness; but this weakness returned upon me whenever the critical moment approached, and I never found courage to depart.

— CHAPTER III —

It was on my sixteenth birthday that my aunt received a letter from my father. I cannot describe the tumult of emotions that arose within me as I read it. It was dated from London; he had returned! I could only relieve my transports by tears, tears of unmingled joy. He had returned, and he wrote to know whether my aunt would come to London or whether he should visit her in Scotland. How delicious to me were the words of his letter that concerned me: "I cannot tell you," it said, "how ardently I desire to see my Mathilda. I look on her as the creature who will form the happiness of my future life: she is all that exists on earth that interests me. I can hardly prevent myself from hastening immediately to you but I am necessarily detained a week and I write because if you come here I may see you somewhat sooner." I read these words with devouring eyes; I kissed them, wept over them and exclaimed, "He will love me!"—

My aunt would not undertake so long a journey, and in a fortnight we had another letter from my father, it was dated Edinburgh: he wrote that he should be with us in three days. As he approached, his desire of seeing me, he said, became more and more ardent, and he felt that the moment when he should first clasp me in his arms would be the happiest of his life.

How irksome were these three days to me! All sleep and appetite fled from me; I could only read and re-read his letter, and in the solitude of the woods imagine the moment of our meeting. On the eve of the third day I retired early to my room; I could not sleep but paced all night about my chamber and, as you may in Scotland at midsummer, watched the crimson track of the sun as it almost skirted the northern horizon. At day break I hastened to the woods; the hours past on while I indulged in wild dreams that gave wings to the slothful steps of time, and beguiled my eager impatience. My father was expected at noon but when I wished to return to meet him I found that I had lost my way: it seemed that in every attempt to find it I only became more involved in the intricacies of the woods, and the trees hid all trace by which I might be guided. I grew impatient, I wept, and wrung my hands but still I could not discover my path.

It was past two o'clock when by a sudden turn I found myself close to the lake near a cove where a little skiff was moored—It was not far from our house and I saw my father and aunt walking on the lawn. I jumped into the boat, and well accustomed to such feats, I pushed it from shore, and exerted all my strength to row swiftly across. As I came, dressed in white, covered only by my tartan *rachan*,[12] my hair streaming on my shoulders, and shooting across with greater speed than it could be supposed I could give to my boat, my father has often told me that I looked more like a spirit than a human maid. I approached the shore, my father held the boat, I leapt lightly out, and in a moment was in his arms.

And now I began to live. All around me was changed from a dull uniformity to the brightest scene of joy and delight. The happiness I enjoyed in the company of my father far exceeded my sanguine expectations. We were for ever together; and the subjects of our conversations were inexhaustible. He had passed the sixteen years of absence among nations nearly unknown to Europe; he had wandered through Persia, Arabia and the north of India and had penetrated among the habitations of the natives with a freedom permitted to few Europeans. His relations of their manners, his anecdotes and descriptions of scenery whiled away delicious hours, when we were tired of talking of our own plans of future life.

The voice of affection was so new to me that I hung with delight upon his words when he told me what he had

[12] **rachan**: rauchan, a plaid cloak, the traditional dress of Scottish shepherds.

felt concerning me during these long years of apparent forgetfulness. "At first"—said he, "I could not bear to think of my poor little girl; but afterwards as grief wore off and hope again revisited me I could only turn to her, and amidst cities and desarts her little fairy form, such as I imagined it, for ever flitted before me. The northern breeze as it refreshed me was sweeter and more balmy for it seemed to carry some of your spirit along with it. I often thought that I would instantly return and take you along with me to some fertile island where we should live at peace for ever. As I returned my fervent hopes were dashed by so many fears; my impatience became in the highest degree painful. I dared not think that the sun should shine and the moon rise not on your living form but on your grave. But, no, it is not so; I have my Mathilda, my consolation, and my hope."—

My father was very little changed from what he described himself to be before his misfortunes. It is intercourse with civilized society; it is the disappointment of cherished hopes, the falsehood of friends, or the perpetual clash of mean passions that changes the heart and damps the ardour of youthful feelings; lonely wanderings in a wild country among people of simple or savage manners may inure the body but will not tame the soul, or extinguish the ardour and freshness of feeling incident to youth. The burning sun of India, and the freedom from all restraint had rather encreased the energy of his character: before he bowed under, now he was impatient of any censure except that of his own mind. He had seen so many customs and witnessed so great a variety of moral creeds that he had been obliged to form an independant one for himself which had no relation to the peculiar notions of any one country: his early prejudices of course influenced his judgement in the formation of his principles, and some raw college ideas were strangely mingled with the deepest deductions of his penetrating mind.

The vacuity his heart endured of any deep interest in life during his long absence from his native country had had a singular effect upon his ideas. There was a curious feeling of unreality attached by him to his foreign life in comparison with the years of his youth. All the time he had passed out of England was as a dream, and all the interest of his soul, all his affections belonged to events which had happened and persons who had existed sixteen years before. It was strange when you heard him talk to see how he passed over this lapse of time as a night of visions; while the remembrances of his youth standing seperate as they did from his after life had lost none of their vigour. He talked of my mother as if she had lived but a few weeks before; not that he expressed poignant grief, but his description of her person, and his relation of all anecdotes connected with her was thus fervent and vivid.

In all this there was a strangeness that attracted and enchanted me. He was, as it were, now awakened from his long, visionary sleep, and he felt somewhat like one of the seven sleepers, or like Nourjahad,[13] in that sweet imitation of an eastern tale: Diana was gone; his friends were changed or dead, and now on his awakening I was all that he had to love on earth.

How dear to me were the waters, and mountains, and woods of Loch Lomond now that I had so beloved a companion for my rambles. I visited with my father every delightful spot, either on the islands, or by the side of the tree-sheltered waterfalls; every shady path, or dingle[14] entangled with underwood and fern. My ideas were enlarged by his conversation. I felt as if I were recreated and had about me all the freshness and life of a new being: I was, as it were, transported since his arrival from a narrow spot of earth into a universe boundless to the imagination and the understanding. My life had been before as a pleasing country rill, never destined to leave its native fields, but when its task was fulfilled quietly to be absorbed, and leave no trace. Now it seemed to me to be as a various river flowing through a fertile and lovely landscape, ever changing and ever beautiful. Alas! I knew not the desart it was about to reach; the rocks that would tear its waters, and the hideous scene that would be reflected in a more distorted manner in its waves. Life was then brilliant; I began to learn to hope and what brings a more bitter despair to the heart than hope destroyed?

Is it not strange that grief should quickly follow so divine a happiness? I drank of an enchanted cup but gall was at the bottom of its long drawn sweetness. My heart was full of deep affection, but it was calm from its very depth and fulness. I had no idea that misery could arise from love, and this lesson that all at last must learn was taught me in a manner few are obliged to receive it. I lament now, I must ever lament, those few short months of Paradisaical bliss; I disobeyed no command, I ate no

---

[13] **seven sleepers:** legendary third-century Christians of Ephesus who slept for two centuries to escape the persecutions of the Roman Emperor Decius. **Nourjahad:** Persian who claimed he awoke only once every fifty years; his story is told in Frances Sheridan's romance, *History of Nourjahad* (1767).

[14] **dingle:** deep dell or hollow.

apple, and yet I was ruthlessly drive from it. Alas! my companion did, and I was precipitated[15] in his fall. But I wander from my relation—let woe come at its appointed time; I may at this stage of my story still talk of happiness.

Three months passed away in this delightful intercourse, when my aunt fell ill. I passed a whole month in her chamber nursing her, but her disease was mortal and she died, leaving me for some time inconsolable. Death is so dreadful to the living; the chains of habit are so strong even when affection does not link them that the heart must be agonized when they break. But my father was beside me to console me and to drive away bitter memories by bright hopes: methought that it was sweet to grieve that he might dry my tears.

Then again he distracted my thoughts from my sorrow by comparing it with his despair when he lost my mother. Even at that time I shuddered at the picture he drew of his passions: he had the imagination of a poet, and when he described the whirlwind that then tore his feelings he gave his words the impress of life so vividly that I believed while I trembled. I wondered how he could ever again have entered into the offices of life after his wild thoughts seemed to have given him affinity with the unearthly; while he spoke, so tremendous were the ideas which he conveyed that it appeared as if the human heart were far too bounded for their conception. His feelings seemed better fitted for a spirit whose habitation is the earthquake and the volcano than for one confined to a mortal body and human lineaments. But these were merely memories; he was changed since then. He was now all love, all softness: and when I raised my eyes in wonder at him as he spoke the smile on his lips told me that his heart was possessed by the gentlest passions.

Two months after my aunt's death we removed to London where I was led by my father to attend to deeper studies than had before occupied me. My improvement was his delight; he was with me during all my studies and assisted or joined with me in every lesson. We saw a great deal of society, and no day passed that my father did not endeavour to embellish by some new enjoyment. The tender attachment that he bore me, and the love and veneration with which I returned it cast a charm over every moment. The hours were slow for each minute was employed; we lived more in one week than many do in the course of several months, and the variety and novelty of our pleasures gave zest to each.

We perpetually made excursions together. And whether it were to visit beautiful scenery, or to see fine pictures, or sometimes for no object but to seek amusement as it might chance to arise, I was always happy when near my father. It was a subject of regret to me whenever we were joined by a third person, yet if I turned with a disturbed look towards my father, his eyes fixed on me and beaming with tenderness instantly restored joy to my heart. O, hours of intense delight! Short as ye were ye are made as long to me as a whole life when looked back upon through the mist of grief that rose immediately after as if to shut ye from my view. Alas! ye were the last of happiness that I ever enjoyed; a few, a very few weeks and all was destroyed. Like Psyche[16] I lived for awhile in an enchanted palace, amidst odours, and music, and every luxurious delight; when suddenly I was left on a barren rock; a wide ocean of despair rolled around me; above all was black, and my eyes closed while I still inhabited a universal death. Still I would not hurry on; I would pause for ever on the recollections of these happy weeks; I would repeat every word, and how many do I remember, record every enchantment of the faery habitation. But, no, my tale must not pause; it must be as rapid as was my fate,—I can only describe in short although strong expressions my precipitate and irremediable change from happiness to despair.

— CHAPTER IV —

Among our most assiduous visitors was a young man of rank, well informed, and agreeable in his person. After we had spent a few weeks in London his attentions towards me became marked and his visits more frequent. I was too much taken up by my own occupations and feelings to attend much to this, and then indeed I hardly noticed more than the bare surface of events as they passed around me; but I now remember that my father was restless and uneasy whenever this person visited us, and when we talked together watched us with the greatest apparent anxiety although he himself maintained a profound silence. At

[15] **precipitated:** suddenly thrown headlong down, plunged into destruction or ruin.

[16] **Psyche:** Greek maiden beloved by Cupid, who built her a heavenly palace but refused to let her see him, coming to her only in secret at night. Psyche finally lit a lamp while Cupid was sleeping; awaked, Cupid was forced by his mother Venus to abandon Psyche who then wandered the earth, heartbroken, seeking him.

length these obnoxious visits suddenly ceased altogether, but from that moment I must date the change of my father: a change that to remember makes me shudder and then filled me with the deepest grief. There were no degrees which could break my fall from happiness to misery; it was as the stroke of lightning—sudden and entire. Alas! I now met frowns where before I had been welcomed only with smiles: he, my beloved father, shunned me, and either treated me with harshness or a more heart-breaking coldness. We took no more sweet counsel together; and when I tried to win him again to me, his anger, and the terrible emotions that he exhibited drove me to silence and tears.

And this was sudden. The day before we had passed alone together in the country; I remember we had talked of future travels that we should undertake together—there was an eager delight in our tones and gestures that could only spring from deep and mutual love joined to the most unrestrained confidence; and now the next day, the next hour, I saw his brows contracted, his eyes fixed in sullen fierceness on the ground, and his voice so gentle and so dear made me shiver when he addressed me. Often, when my wandering fancy brought by its various images now consolation and now aggravation of grief to my heart, I have compared myself to Proserpine[17] who was gaily and heedlessly gathering flowers on the sweet plain of Enna, when the King of Hell snatched her away to the abodes of death and misery. Alas! I who so lately knew of nought but the joy of life; who had slept only to dream sweet dreams and awoke to incomparable happiness, I now passed my days and nights in tears. I who sought and had found joy in the love-breathing countenance of my father now when I dared fix on him a supplicating look it was ever answered by an angry frown. I dared not speak to him; and when sometimes I had worked up courage to meet him and to ask an explanation, one glance at his face where a chaos of mighty passion seemed for ever struggling made me tremble and shrink to silence. I was dashed down from heaven to earth as a silly sparrow when pounced on by a hawk; my eyes swam and my head was bewildered by the sudden apparition of grief. Day after day passed marked only by my complaints and my tears; often I lifted my soul in vain prayer for a softer descent from joy to woe, or if that were denied me that I might be allowed to die, and fade for ever under the cruel blast that swept over me,

—— for what should I do here,
Like a decaying flower, still withering
Under his bitter words, whose kindly heat
Should give my poor heart life?[18]

Sometimes I said to myself, this is an enchantment, and I must strive against it. My father is blinded by some malignant vision which I must remove. And then, like David,[19] I would try music to win the evil spirit from him; and once while singing I lifted my eyes towards him and saw his fixed on me and filled with tears; all his muscles seemed relaxed to softness. I sprung towards him with a cry of joy and would have thrown myself into his arms, but he pushed me roughly from him and left me. And even from this slight incident he contracted fresh gloom and an additional severity of manner.

There are many incidents that I might relate which shewed the diseased yet incomprehensible state of his mind; but I will mention one that occurred while we were in company with several other persons. On this occasion I chanced to say that I thought Myrrha the best of Alfieri's tragedies;[20] as I said this I chanced to cast my eyes on my father and met his: for the first time the expression of those beloved eyes displeased me, and I saw with affright that his whole frame shook with some concealed emotion that in spite of his efforts half conquered him: as this tempest faded from his soul he became melancholy and silent. Every day some new scene occurred and displayed in him a mind working as [it] were with an unknown horror that now he could master but which at times threatened to overturn his reason, and to throw the bright seat of his intelligence into a perpetual chaos.

[17] **Proserpine:** Persephone, daughter of the Greek deities Zeus and Demeter, seized by Pluto, the god of the underworld. Demeter finally prevailed on Zeus to return her daughter, but since Persephone had eaten a seed of the pomegranate, the food of the dead, she could return to earth for only half of the year; hence, the goddess of fertility and the annual vegetation cycle.

[18] Cf. Fletcher's comedy of the Captain [M. S.]: John Fletcher (1579–1625), *The Captain* (c. 1612), I.iii.237–40.

[19] **David:** second king of Israel; an accomplished harpist and singer, who with song won the love first of Jonathan (I Samuel 18:1) and then of Bathsheba.

[20] In *Myrrha*, or *Mirra*, by Vittorio Alfieri (1749–1803), Mirra's father Ciniro unwittingly forces his daughter to reveal her secret, incestuous love for him (V.ii.160–86). At Percy Shelley's insistence, Mary Shelley had begun a translation of *Mirra* in September 1818.

I will not dwell longer than I need on these disastrous circumstances. I might waste days in describing how anxiously I watched every change of fleeting circumstance that promised better days, and with what despair I found that each effort of mine aggravated his seeming madness. To tell all my grief I might as well attempt to count the tears that have fallen from these eyes, or every sign that has torn my heart. I will be brief for there is in all this a horror that will not bear many words, and I sink almost a second time to death while I recall these sad scenes to my memory. Oh, my beloved father! Indeed you made me miserable beyond all words, but how truly did I even then forgive you, and how entirely did you possess my whole heart while I endeavoured, as a rainbow gleams upon a cataract,[21] to soften thy tremendous sorrows.

Thus did this change come about. I seem perhaps to have dashed too suddenly into the description, but thus suddenly did it happen. In one sentence I have passed from the idea of unspeakable happiness to that of unspeakable grief but they were thus closely linked together. We had remained five months in London, three of joy and two of sorrow. My father and I were now seldom alone or if we were he generally kept silence with his eyes fixed on the ground—the dark full orbs in which before I delighted to read all sweet and gentle feeling shadowed from my sight by their lids and the long lashes that fringed them. When we were in company he affected gaiety but I wept to hear his hollow laugh—begun by an empty smile and often ending in a bitter sneer such as never before this fatal period had wrinkled his lips. When others were there he often spoke to me and his eyes perpetually followed my slightest motion. His accents whenever he addressed me were cold and constrained although his voice would tremble when he perceived that my full heart choked the answer to words proffered with a mien yet new to me.

But days of peaceful melancholy were of rare occurrence: they were often broken in upon by gusts of passion that drove me as a weak boat on a stormy sea to seek a cove for shelter; but the winds blew from my native harbour and I was cast far, far out until shattered I perished when the tempest had passed and the sea was apparently calm. I do not know that I can describe his emotions: sometimes he only betrayed them by a word or gesture, and then retired to his chamber and I crept as near it as I dared and listened with fear to every sound, yet still more dreading a sudden silence—dreading I knew not what, but ever full of fear.

It was after one tremendous day when his eyes had glared on me like lightning—and his voice sharp and broken seemed unable to express the extent of his emotion—that in the evening when I was alone he joined me with a calm countenance, and not noticing my tears which I quickly dried when he approached, told me that in three days he intended to remove with me to his estate in Yorkshire, and bidding me prepare left me hastily as if afraid of being questioned.

This determination on his part indeed surprised me. This estate was that which he had inhabited in childhood and near which my mother resided while a girl; this was the scene of their youthful loves and where they had lived after their marriage; in happier days my father had often told me that however he might appear weaned from his widow sorrow, and free from bitter recollections elsewhere, yet he would never dare visit the spot where he had enjoyed her society or trust himself to see the rooms that so many years ago they had inhabited together; her favourite walks and the gardens the flowers of which she had delighted to cultivate. And now while he suffered intense misery he determined to plunge into still more intense, and strove for greater emotion than that which already tore him. I was perplexed, and most anxious to know what this portended; ah, what could it portend but ruin!

I saw little of my father during this interval, but he appeared calmer although not less unhappy than before. On the morning of the third day he informed me that he had determined to go to Yorkshire first alone, and that I should follow him in a fortnight unless I heard any thing from him in the mean time that should contradict this command. He departed the same day, and four days afterwards I received a letter from his steward telling me in his name to join him with as little delay as possible. After travelling day and night I arrived with an anxious, yet a hoping heart, for why should he send for me if it were only to avoid me and to treat me with the apparent aversion that he had in London. I met him at the distance of thirty miles from our mansion. His demeanour was sad; for a moment he appeared glad to see me and then he checked himself as if unwilling to betray his feelings. He was silent during our ride, yet his manner was kinder than before and I thought I beheld a softness in his eyes that gave me hope.

---

[21] **as a rainbow . . . cataract:** Lord Byron [M. S.]: Cf. the images of the rainbow and cataract in Byron's *Childe Harold's Pilgrimage,** Canto IV (1818), st. 71–72.

When we arrived, after a little rest, he led me over the house and pointed out to me the rooms which my mother had inhabited. Although more than sixteen years had passed since her death nothing had been changed; her work box, her writing desk were still there and in her room a book lay open on the table as she had left it. My father pointed out these circumstances with a serious and unaltered mien, only now and then fixing his deep and liquid eyes upon me; there was something strange and awful in his look that overcame me, and in spite of myself I wept, nor did he attempt to console me, but I saw his lips quiver and the muscles of his countenance seemed convulsed.

We walked together in the gardens and in the evening when I would have retired he asked me to stay and read to him; and first said, "When I was last here your mother read Dante to me; you shall go on where she left off." And then in a moment he said, "No, that must not be; you must not read Dante. Do you choose a book." I took up Spenser and read the descent of Sir Guyon to the halls of Avarice;[22] while he listened his eyes fixed on me in sad profound silence.

I heard the next morning from the steward that upon his arrival he had been in a most terrible state of mind: he had passed the first night in the garden lying on the damp grass; he did not sleep but groaned perpetually. "Alas!" said the old man who gave me this account with tears in his eyes, "it wrings my heart to see my lord in this state: when I heard that he was coming down here with you, my young lady, I thought we should have the happy days over again that we enjoyed during the short life of my lady your mother—But that would be too much happiness for us poor creatures born to tears—and that was why she was taken from us so soon. She was too beautiful and good for us. It was a happy day as we all thought it when my lord married her: I knew her when she was a child and many a good turn has she done for me in my old lady's time—You are like her although there is more of my lord in you—But has he been thus ever since his return? All my joy turned to sorrow when I first beheld him with that melancholy countenance enter these doors as it were the day after my lady's funeral—He seemed to recover himself a little after he had bidden me write to you—but still it is a woful thing to see him so unhappy." These were the feelings of an old, faithful servant: what must be those of an affectionate daughter. Alas! Even then my heart was almost broken.

We spent two months together in this house. My father spent the greater part of his time with me; he accompanied me in my walks, listened to my music, and leant over me as I read or painted. When he conversed with me his manner was cold and constrained; his eyes only seemed to speak, and as he turned their black, full lustre towards me they expressed a living sadness. There was something in those dark deep orbs so liquid, and intense that even in happiness I could never meet their full gaze that mine did not overflow. Yet it was with sweet tears; now there was a depth of affliction in their gentle appeal that rent my heart with sympathy; they seemed to desire peace for me; for himself, a heart patient to suffer; a craving for sympathy, yet a perpetual self denial. It was only when he was absent from me that his passion subdued him,—that he clinched his hands—knit his brows—and with haggard looks called for death to his despair, raving wildly, until exhausted he sank down nor was revived until I joined him.

While we were in London there was a harshness and sullenness in his sorrow which had now entirely disappeared. There I shrunk and fled from him, now I only wished to be with him that I might soothe him to peace. When he was silent I tried to divert him, and when sometimes I stole to him during the energy of his passion I wept but did not desire to leave him. Yet he suffered fearful agony; during the day he was more calm, but at night when I could not be with him he seemed to give the reins to his grief: he often passed his nights either on the floor in my mother's room, or in the garden; and when in the morning he saw me view with poignant grief his exhausted frame, and his person languid almost to death with watching, he wept; but during all this time he spoke no word by which I might guess the cause of his unhappiness. If I ventured to enquire he would either leave me or press his finger on his lips, and with a deprecating[23] look that I could not resist, turn away. If I wept he would gaze on me in silence but he was no longer harsh and although he repulsed every caress yet it was with gentleness.

He seemed to cherish a mild grief and softer emotions although sad as a relief from despair—He contrived in many ways to nurse his melancholy as an antidote to

[22] See Edmund Spenser, *The Faerie Queene* (1589–1591), Book II, canto 7.

[23] **deprecating**: earnestly desiring that something may be removed; pleading against.

wilder passion. He perpetually frequented the walks that had been favourites with him when he and my mother wandered together talking of love and happiness; he collected every relick that remained of her and always sat opposite her picture which hung in the room fixing on it a look of sad despair — and all this was done in a mystic and awful silence. If his passion subdued him he locked himself in his room; and at night when he wandered restlessly about the house, it was when every other creature slept.

It may easily be imagined that I wearied myself with conjecture to guess the cause of his sorrow. The solution that seemed to me the most probable was that during his residence in London he had fallen in love with some unworthy person, and that his passion mastered him although he would not gratify it: he loved me too well to sacrifise me to this inclination, and that he had now visited this house that by reviving the memory of my mother whom he so passionately adored he might weaken the present impression. This was possible; but it was a mere conjecture unfounded on any fact. Could there be guilt in it? He was too upright and noble to *do* aught that his conscience would not approve; I did not yet know of the crime there may be in involuntary feeling and therefore ascribed his tumultuous starts and gloomy looks wholly to the struggles of his mind and not any as they were partly due to the worst fiend of all — Remorse.

But still do I flatter myself that this would have passed away. His paroxisms of passion were terrific but his soul bore him through them triumphant, though almost destroyed by victory; but the day would finally have been won had not I, foolish and presumptuous wretch! hurried him on until there was no recall, no hope. My rashness gave the victory in this dreadful fight to the enemy who triumphed over him as he lay fallen and vanquished. I! I alone was the cause of his defeat and justly did I pay the fearful penalty. I said to myself, let him receive sympathy and these struggles will cease. Let him confide his misery to another heart and half the weight of it will be lightened. I will win him to me; he shall not deny his grief to me and when I know his secret then will I pour a balm into his soul and again I shall enjoy the ravishing delight of beholding his smile, and of again seeing his eyes beam if not with pleasure at least with gentle love and thankfulness. This will I do, I said. Half I accomplished; I gained his secret and we were both lost for ever.

— CHAPTER V —

Nearly a year had passed since my father's return, and the seasons had almost finished their round — It was now the end of May; the woods were clothed in their freshest verdure, and the sweet smell of the new mown grass was in the fields. I thought that the balmy air and the lovely face of Nature might aid me in inspiring him with mild sensations, and give him gentle feelings of peace and love preparatory to the confidence I determined to win from him.

I chose therefore the evening of one of these days for my attempt. I invited him to walk with me, and led him to a neighbouring wood of beech trees whose light shade shielded us from the slant and dazzling beams of the descending sun — after walking for some time in silence I seated myself with him on a mossy hillock — It is strange but even now I seem to see the spot — the slim and smooth trunks were many of them wound round by ivy whose shining leaves of the darkest green contrasted with the white bark and the light leaves of the young sprouts of beech that grew from their parent trunks — the short grass was mingled with moss and was partly covered by the dead leaves of the last autumn that driven by the winds had here and there collected in little hillocks — there were a few moss grown stumps about — The leaves were gently moved by the breeze and through their green canopy you could see the bright blue sky — As evening came on the distant trunks were reddened by the sun and the wind died entirely away while a few birds flew past us to their evening rest.

Well it was here we sat together, and when you hear all that passed — all that of terrible tore our souls even in this placid spot, which but for strange passions might have been a paradise to us, you will not wonder that I remember it as I looked on it that its calm might give me calm, and inspire me not only with courage but with persuasive words. I saw all these things and in a vacant manner noted them in my mind while I endeavoured to arrange my thoughts in fitting order for my attempt. My heart beat fast as I worked myself up to speak to him, for I was determined not to be repulsed but I trembled to imagine what effect my words might have on him; at length, with much hesitation I began:

"Your kindness to me, my dearest father, and the affection — the excessive affection — that you had for me when you first returned will I hope excuse me in your eyes that I dare speak to you, although with the tender affection of a daughter, yet also with the freedom of a friend and equal. But pardon me, I entreat you and listen to me: do not turn away from me; do not be impatient; you may easily intimidate me into silence, but my heart is bursting, nor can I willingly consent to endure for one moment longer the agony of uncertitude which for the last four months has been my portion.

"Listen to me, dearest friend, and permit me to gain your confidence. Are the happy days of mutual love which have passed to be to me as a dream never to return? Alas! You have a secret grief that destroys us both: but you must permit me to win this secret from you. Tell me, can I do nothing? You well know that on the whole earth there is no sacrifise that I would not make, no labour that I would not undergo with the mere hope that I might bring you ease. But if no endeavour on my part can contribute to your happiness, let me at least know your sorrow, and surely my earnest love and deep sympathy must soothe your despair.

"I fear that I speak in a constrained manner: my heart is overflowing with the ardent desire I have of bringing calm once more to your thoughts and looks; but I fear to aggravate your grief, or to raise that in you which is death to me, anger and distaste. Do not then continue to fix your eyes on the earth; raise them on me for I can read your soul in them: speak to me, and pardon my presumption. Alas! I am a most unhappy creature!"

I was breathless with emotion, and I paused fixing my earnest eyes on my father, after I had dashed away the intrusive tears that dimmed them. He did not raise his, but after a short silence he replied to me in a low voice: "You are indeed presumptuous, Mathilda, presumptuous and very rash. In the heart of one like me there are secret thoughts working, and secret tortures which you ought not to seek to discover. I cannot tell you how it adds to my grief to know that I am the cause of uneasiness to you; but this will pass away, and I hope that soon we shall be as we were a few months ago. Restrain your impatience or you may mar what you attempt to alleviate. Do not again speak to me in this strain; but wait in submissive patience the event of what is passing around you."

"Oh, yes!" I passionately replied, "I will be very patient; I will not be rash or presumptuous: I will see the agonies, and tears, and despair of my father, my only friend, my hope, my shelter, I will see it all with folded arms and downcast eyes. You do not treat me with candour; it is not true what you say; this will not soon pass away, it will last for ever if you deign not to speak to me; to admit my consolations.

"Dearest, dearest father, pity me and pardon me: I entreat you do not drive me to despair; indeed I must not be repulsed; there is one thing that although it may torture me to know, yet that you must tell me. I demand, and most solemnly I demand if in any way I am the cause of your unhappiness. Do you not see my tears which I in vain strive against—You hear unmoved my voice broken by sobs—Feel how my hand trembles: my whole heart is in the words I speak and you must not endeavour to silence me by mere words barren of meaning: the agony of my doubt hurries me on, and you must reply. I beseech you; by your former love for me now lost, I adjure you to answer that one question. Am I the cause of your grief?"

He raised his eyes from the ground, but still turning them away from me, said: "Besought by that plea I will answer your rash question. Yes, you are the sole, the agonizing cause of all I suffer, of all I must suffer until I die. Now, beware! Be silent! Do not urge me to your destruction. I am struck by the storm, rooted up, laid waste: but you can stand against it; you are young and your passions are at peace. One word I might speak and then you would be implicated in my destruction; yet that word is hovering on my lips. Oh! There is a fearful chasm; but I adjure you to beware!"

"Ah, dearest friend!" I cried, "do not fear! Speak that word; it will bring peace, not death. If there is a chasm our mutual love will give us wings to pass it, and we shall find flowers, and verdure, and delight on the other side." I threw myself at his feet, and took his hand, "Yes, speak, and we shall be happy; there will no longer be doubt, no dreadful uncertainty; trust me, my affection will soothe your sorrow; speak that word and all danger will be past, and we shall love each other as before, and for ever."

He snatched his hand from me, and rose in violent disorder: "What do you mean? You know not what you mean. Why do you bring me out, and torture me, and tempt me, and kill me—Much happier would [it] be for you and for me if in your frantic curiosity you tore my heart from my breast and tried to read its secrets in it as its life's blood was dropping from it. Thus you may console me by reducing me to nothing—but your words I cannot bear; soon they will make me mad, quite mad, and then I shall utter strange words, and you will believe them, and we shall be both lost for ever. I tell you I am on the very verge of insanity; why, cruel girl, do you drive me on: you will repent and I shall die."

When I repeat his words I wonder at my pertinacious folly. I hardly know what feelings resistlessly impelled me. I believe it was that coming out with a determination not to be repulsed I went right forward to my object without well weighing his replies: I was led by passion and drew him with frantic heedlessness into the abyss that he so fearfully avoided—I replied to his terrific words: "You fill me with affright it is true, dearest father, but you only confirm my resolution to put an end to this state of doubt. I will not be put off thus: do you think that I can live thus fearfully from day to day—the sword in my bosom yet kept from its mortal wound by a hair—a word!—I demand that dreadful word; though it be as a flash of lightning to destroy me, speak it.

"Alas! Alas! What am I become? But a few months have elapsed since I believed that I was all the world to you; and that there was no happiness or grief for you on earth unshared by your Mathilda—your child: that happy time is no longer, and what I most dreaded in this world is come upon me. In the despair of my heart I see what you cannot conceal: you no longer love me. I adjure you, my father, has not an unnatural passion seized upon your heart? Am I not the most miserable worm that crawls? Do I not embrace your knees, and you most cruelly repulse me? I know it—I see it—you hate me!"

I was transported by violent emotion, and rising from his feet, at which I had thrown myself, I leant against a tree, wildly raising my eyes to heaven. He began to answer with violence: "Yes, yes, I hate you! You are my bane, my poison, my disgust! Oh! No!" And then his manner changed, and fixing his eyes on me with an expression that convulsed every nerve and member of my frame—"you are none of all these; you are my light, my only one, my life.—My daughter, I love you!" The last words died away in a hoarse whisper, but I heard them and sunk on the ground, covering my face and almost dead with excess of sickness and fear: a cold perspiration covered my forehead and I shivered in every limb—But he continued, clasping his hands with a frantic gesture:

"Now I have dashed from the top of the rock to the bottom! Now I have precipitated myself down the fearful chasm! The danger is over; she is alive! Oh, Mathilda, lift up those dear eyes in the light of which I live. Let me hear the sweet tones of your beloved voice in peace and calm. Monster as I am, you are still, as you ever were, lovely, beautiful beyond expression. What I have become since this last moment I know not; perhaps I am changed in mien as the fallen archangel. I do believe I am for I have surely a new soul within me, and my blood riots through my veins: I am burnt up with fever. But these are precious moments; devil as I am become, yet that is my Mathilda before me whom I love as one was never before loved: and she knows it now; she listens to these words which I thought, fool as I was, would blast her to death. Come, come, the worst is past: no more grief, tears or despair; were not those the words you uttered?—We have leapt the chasm I told you of, and now, mark me, Mathilda, we are to find flowers, and verdure and delight, or is it hell, and fire, and tortures? Oh! Beloved One, I am borne away; I can no longer sustain myself; surely this is death that is coming. Let me lay my head near your heart; let me die in your arms!"—He sunk to the earth fainting, while I, nearly as lifeless, gazed on him in despair.

Yes it was despair I felt; for the first time that phantom seized me; the first and only time for it has never since left me—After the first moments of speechless agony I felt her fangs on my heart: I tore my hair; I raved aloud; at one moment in pity for his sufferings I would have clasped my father in my arms; and then starting back with horror I spurned him with my foot; I felt as if stung by a serpent, as if scourged by a whip of scorpions which drove me—Ah! Whither—Whither?

Well, this could not last. One idea rushed on my mind; never, never may I speak to him again. As this terrible conviction came upon *him* [*me?*] it melted my soul to tenderness and love—I gazed on him as to take my last farewell—he lay insensible—his eyes closed as [and?] his cheeks deathly pale—Above, the leaves of the beech wood cast a flickering shadow on his face, and waved in mournful melody over him—I saw all these things and said, "Aye, this is his grave!" And then I wept aloud, and raised my eyes to heaven to entreat for a respite to my despair and an alleviation for his unnatural suffering—the tears that gushed in a warm and healing stream from my eyes relieved the burthen that oppressed my heart almost to madness. I wept for a long time until I saw him about to revive, when horror and misery again recurred, and the tide of my sensations rolled back to their former channel: with a terror I could not restrain—I sprung up and fled, with winged speed, along the paths of the wood and across the fields until nearly dead I reached our house and just ordering the servants to seek my father at the spot I indicated, I shut myself up in my own room.

—CHAPTER VI—

My chamber was in a retired part of the house, and looked upon the garden so that no sound of the other inhabitants could reach it; and here in perfect solitude I wept for several hours. When a servant came to ask me if I would take food I learnt from him that my father had returned, and was apparently well and this relieved me from a load of anxiety, yet I did not cease to weep bitterly. At first, as the memory of former happiness contrasted to my present despair came across me, I gave relief to the oppression of heart that I felt by words, and groans, and heart rending sighs: but nature became wearied, and this more violent grief gave place to a passionate but mute flood of tears: my whole soul seemed to dissolve them. I did not wring my hands, or tear my hair, or utter wild exclamations, but as Boccaccio describes the intense and quiet grief [of] Ghismunda over the heart of Guiscardo,[24] I sat with my hands folded, silently letting fall a perpetual stream from my eyes. Such was the depth of my emotion that I had no feeling of what caused my distress, my thoughts even wandered to many indifferent objects; but still neither moving limb or feature my tears fell until, as if the fountains were exhausted, they gradually subsided, and I awoke to life as from a dream.

When I had ceased to weep, reason and memory returned upon me, and I began to reflect with greater calmness on what had happened, and how it became me to act—A few hours only had passed but a mighty revolution had taken place with regard to me—the natural work of years had been transacted since the morning: my father was as dead to me, and I felt for a moment as if he with white hairs were laid in his coffin and I—youth vanished in approaching age, were weeping at his timely dissolution. But it was not so, I was yet young, Oh! far too young, nor was he dead to others; but I, most miserable, must never see or speak to him again. I must fly from him with more earnestness than from my greatest enemy: in solitude or in cities I must never more behold him. That consideration made me breathless with anguish, and impressing itself on my imagination I was unable for a time to follow up any train of ideas. Ever after this, I thought, I would live in the most dreary seclusion. I would retire to the Continent and become a nun; not for religion's sake, for I was not a Catholic, but that I might be for ever shut out from the world. I should there find solitude where I might weep, and the voices of life might never reach me.

But my father; my beloved and most wretched father? Would he die? Would he never overcome the fierce passion that now held pityless dominion over him? Might he not many, many years hence, when age had quenched the burning sensations that he now experienced, might he not then be again a father to me? This reflection unwrinkled my brow, and I could feel (and I wept to feel it) a half melancholy smile draw from my lips their expression of suffering: I dared indulge better hopes for my future life; years must pass but they would speed lightly away winged by hope, or if they passed heavily, still they would pass and I had not lost my father for ever. Let him spend another sixteen years of desolate wandering: let him once more utter his wild comp[l]aints to the vast woods and the tremendous cataracts of another clime: let him again undergo fearful danger and soul-quelling hardships: let the hot sun of the south again burn his passion worn cheeks and the cold night rains fall on him and chill his blood.

To this life, miserable father, I devote thee!—Go!—Be thy days passed with savages, and thy nights under the cope[25] of heaven! Be thy limbs worn and thy heart chilled, and all youth be dead within thee! Let thy hairs be as snow; thy walk trembling and thy voice have lost its mellow tones! Let the liquid lustre of thine eyes be quenched; and then return to me, return to thy Mathilda, thy child, who may then be clasped in thy loved arms, while thy heart beats with sinless emotion. Go, Devoted One, and return thus!—This is my curse, a daughter's curse: go, and return pure to thy child, who will never love aught but thee.

These were my thoughts; and with trembling hands I prepared to begin a letter to my unhappy parent. I had now spent many hours in tears and mournful meditation; it was past twelve o'clock; all was at peace in the house, and the gentle air that stole in at my window did not rustle the leaves of the twining plants that shadowed it. I felt the entire tranquillity of the hour when my own breath and involuntary sobs were all the sounds that struck upon the air. On a sudden I heard a gentle step ascending the stairs; I paused breathless, and as it approached glided into an obscure corner of the room; the steps paused at my door, but after a few moments they again receded, descended the stairs and I heard no more.

This slight incident gave rise in me to the most painful reflections; nor do I now dare express the emotions I felt. That he should be restless I understood; that he should wander as an unlaid ghost and find no quiet from the burning hell that consumed his heart. But why approach my chamber? Was not that sacred? I felt almost ready to faint while he had stood there, but I had not betrayed my wakefulness by the slightest motion, although I had heard my own heart beat with violent fear. He had withdrawn. Oh, never, never, may I see him again! Tomorrow night the same roof may not cover us; he or I must depart. The mutual link of our destinies is broken; we

[24] See Giovanni Boccaccio (1313?–1375), *The Decameron* (1348–1358), Day Four.

[25] **cope**: cloak, canopy, vault.

must be divided by seas—by land. The stars and the sun must not rise at the same period to us: he must not say, looking at the setting crescent of the moon, "Mathilda now watches its fall."—No, all must be changed. Be it light with him when it is darkness with me! Let him feel the sun of summer while I am chilled by the snows of winter! Let there be the distance of the antipodes between us!

At length the east began to brighten, and the comfortable light of morning streamed into my room. I was weary with watching and for some time I had combated with the heavy sleep that weighed down my eyelids: but now, no longer fearful, I threw myself on my bed. I sought for repose although I did not hope for forgetfulness; I knew I should be pursued by dreams, but did not dread the frightful one that I really had. I thought that I had risen and went to seek my father to inform him of my determination to separate myself from him. I sought him in the house, in the park, and then in the fields and the woods, but I could not find him. At length I saw him at some distance, seated under a tree, and when he perceived me he waved his hand several times, beckoning me to approach; there was something unearthly in his mien that awed and chilled me, but I drew near. When at short distance from him I saw that he was dead-lily pale, and clothed in flowing garments of white. Suddenly he started up and fled from me; I pursued him: we sped over the fields, and by the skirts of woods, and on the banks of rivers; he flew fast and I followed. We came at last, methought, to the brow of a huge cliff that over hung the sea which, troubled by the winds, dashed against its base, at a distance. I heard the roar of the waters: he held his course right on towards the brink and I became breathless with fear lest he should plunge down the dreadful precipice; I tried to augment my speed, but my knees failed beneath me, yet I had just reached him; just caught a part of his flowing robe, when he leapt down and I awoke with a violent scream. I was trembling and my pillow was wet with my tears; for a few moments my heart beat hard, but the bright beams of the sun and the chirping of the birds quickly restored me to myself, and I rose with a languid spirit, yet wondering what events the day would bring forth. Some time passed before I summoned courage to ring the bell for my servant, and when she came I still dared not utter my father's name. I ordered her to bring my breakfast to my room, and was again left alone—yet still I could make no resolve, but only thought that I might write a note to my father to beg his permission to pay a visit to a relation who lived about thirty miles off, and who had before invited me to her house, but I had refused for then I could not quit my suffering father. When the servant came back she gave me a letter.

"From whom is this letter," I asked trembling.

"Your father left it, madam, with his servant, to be given to you when you should rise."

"My father left it! Where is he? Is he not here?"

"No; he quitted the house before four this morning."

"Good God! He is gone! But tell how this was; speak quick!"

Her relation was short. He had gone in the carriage to the nearest town where he took a post chaise and horses with orders for the London road. He dismissed his servants there, only telling them that he had a sudden call of business and that they were to obey me as their mistress until his return.

— CHAPTER VII —

With a beating heart and fearful, I knew not why, I dismissed the servant and locking my door, sat down to read my father's letter. These are the words that it contained.

"My dear Child

"I have betrayed your confidence; I have endeavoured to pollute your mind, and have made your innocent heart acquainted with the looks and language of unlawful and monstrous passion. I must expiate these crimes, and must endeavour in some degree to proportionate my punishment to my guilt. You are I doubt not prepared for what I am about to announce; we must seperate and be divided for ever.

"I deprive you of your parent and only friend. You are cast out shelterless on the world: your hopes are blasted; the peace and security of your pure mind destroyed; memory will bring to you frightful images of guilt, and the anguish of innocent love betrayed. Yet I who draw down all this misery upon you; I who cast you forth and remorselessly have set the seal of distrust and agony on the heart and brow of my own child, who with devilish levity have endeavoured to steal away her loveliness to place in its stead the foul deformity of sin; I, in the overflowing anguish of my heart, supplicate you to forgive me.

"I do not ask your pity; you must and do abhor me: but pardon me, Mathilda, and let not your thoughts follow me in my banishment with unrelenting anger. I must never more behold you; never more hear your voice; but the soft whisperings of your forgiveness will reach me and cool the burning of my disordered brain and heart; I am sure I should feel it even in my grave. And I dare enforce this request by relating how miserably I was betrayed into this net of fiery anguish and all my struggles to release myself: indeed if your soul were less pure and bright I would not attempt to exculpate myself to you; I should fear that if I led you to regard me with less abhorrence you might hate vice less: but in addressing you I feel as if I appealed to an angelic judge. I cannot depart without your forgiveness and I must endeavour to gain it, or I must despair. I conjure you therefore to listen to my words, and if with the good guilt may be in any degree extenuated by sharp agony and remorse that rends the brain as madness, perhaps you may think, though I dare not, that I have some claim to your compassion.

"I entreat you to call to your remembrance our first happy life on the shores of Loch Lomond. I had arrived from a weary wandering of sixteen years, during which, although I had gone through many dangers and misfortunes, my affections had been an entire blank. If I grieved it was for your mother, if I loved it was your image; these sole emotions filled my heart in quietness. The human creatures around me excited in me no sympathy and I thought that the mighty change that the death of your mother had wrought within me had rendered me callous to any future impression. I saw the lovely and I did not love, I imagined therefore that all warmth was extinguished in my heart except that which led me ever to dwell on your then infantine image.

"It is a strange link in my fate that without having seen you I should passionately love you. During my wanderings I never slept without first calling down gentle dreams on your head. If I saw a lovely woman, I thought, does my Mathilda resemble her? All delightful things, sublime scenery, soft breezes, exquisite music seemed to me associated with you and only through you to be pleasant to me. At length I saw you. You appeared as the deity of a lovely region, the ministering Angel of a Paradise to which of all human kind you admitted only me. I dared hardly consider you as my daughter; your beauty, artlessness, and untaught wisdom seemed to belong to a higher order of beings; your voice breathed forth only words of love: if there was aught of earthly in you it was only what you derived from the beauty of the world; you seemed to have gained a grace from the mountain breezes—the waterfalls and the lake;[26] and this was all of earthly except your affections that you had; there was no dross, no bad feeling in the composition. You yet even have not seen enough of the world to know the stupendous difference that exists between the women we meet in daily life and a nymph of the woods such as you were, in whose eyes alone mankind may study for centuries and grow wiser and purer. Those divine lights which shone on me as did those of Beatrice upon Dante, and well might I say with him yet with what different feelings

E quasi mi perdei con gli occhi chini.[27]

Can you wonder, Mathilda, that I dwelt upon your looks, your words, your motions, and drank in unmixed delight?

"But I am afraid that I wander from my purpose. I must be more brief for night draws on apace and all my hours in this house are counted. Well, we removed to London, and still I felt only the peace of sinless passion. You were ever with me, and I desired no more than to gaze on your countenance, and to know that I was all the world to you; I was lapped[28] in a fool's paradise of enjoyment and security. Was my love blamable? If it was I was ignorant of it; I desired only that which I possessed, and if I enjoyed from your looks, and words, and most innocent caresses a rapture usually excluded from the feelings of a parent towards his child, yet no uneasiness, no wish, no casual idea awoke me to a sense of guilt. I loved you as a human father might be supposed to love a daughter borne to him by a heavenly mother; as Anchises[29] might have regarded the child of Venus if the sex had been changed; love mingled with respect and adoration. Perhaps also my passion was lulled to content by the deep and exclusive affection you felt for me.

"But when I saw you become the object of another's love; when I imagined that you might be loved otherwise than as a sacred type and image of loveliness and excellence; or that you might love another with a more ardent affection than that which you bore to me, then the fiend awoke within me; I dismissed your lover; and from that moment I have known no peace. I have sought in vain for sleep and rest; my lids refused to close, and my blood was for ever in a tumult. I awoke to a new life as one who dies

[26] **grace from the mountain breezes . . . lake**: cf. Wordsworth, "Three Years She Grew in Sun and Shower": "Nor shall she fail to see / Even in the motions of the storm / Grace that shall mould the maiden's form / By silent sympathy" (ll. 21–25).

[27] Canto IV Vers Ult (M. S.): "And I almost lost myself with eyes downcast" (Dante, *Paradiso,* IV.142).

[28] **lapped**: folded, wrapped.

[29] The child of the mortal Anchises and the goddess of love, Venus, was Aeneas, the founder of Rome and the hero of Virgil's *Aenead.*

in hope might wake in Hell. I will not sully your imagination by recounting my combats, my self-anger, and my despair. Let a veil be drawn over the unimaginable sensations of a guilty father; the secrets of so agonized a heart may not be made vulgar. All was uproar, crime, remorse, and hate, yet still the tenderest love; and what first awoke me to the firm resolve of conquering my passion and of restoring her father to my child was the sight of your bitter and sympathizing sorrows. It was this that led me here: I thought that if I could again awaken in my heart the grief I had felt at the loss of your mother, and the many associations with her memory which had been laid to sleep for seventeen years, that all love for her child would become extinct. In a fit of heroism I determined to go alone; to quit you, the life of my life, and not to see you again until I might guiltlessly. But it would not do: I rated my fortitude too high, or my love too low. I should certainly have died if you had not hastened to me. Would that I had been indeed extinguished!

"And now, Mathilda I must make you my last confession. I have been miserably mistaken in imagining that I could conquer my love for you; I never can. The sight of this house, these fields and woods which my first love inhabited seems to have encreased it: in my madness I dared say to myself—Diana died to give her birth; her mother's spirit was transferred into her frame, and she ought to be as Diana to me. With every effort to cast it off, this love clings closer, this guilty love more unnatural than hate, that withers your hopes and destroys me for ever.

Better have loved despair, and safer kissed her.

No time or space can tear from my soul that which makes a part of it. Since my arrival here I have not for a moment ceased to feel the hell of passion which has been implanted in me to burn until all be cold, and stiff, and dead. Yet I will not die; alas! how dare I go where I may meet Diana, when I have disobeyed her last request; her last words said in a faint voice when all feeling but love, which survives all things else, was already dead, she then bade me make her child happy: that thought alone gives a double sting to death. I will wander away from you, away from all life—in the solitude I shall seek I alone shall breathe of human kind. I must endure life; and as it is my duty so I shall until the grave, dreaded yet desired, receive me free from pain: for while I feel it will be pain that must make up the whole sum of my sensations. Is not this a fearful curse that I labour under? Do I not look forward to a miserable future? My child, if after this life I am permitted to see you again, if pain can purify the heart, mine will be pure: if remorse may expiate guilt, I shall be guiltless.

"I have been at the door of your chamber: every thing is silent. You sleep. Do you indeed sleep, Mathilda? Spirits of Good, behold the tears of my earnest prayer! Bless my child! Protect her from the selfish among her fellow creatures: protect her from the agonies of passion, and the despair of disappointment! Peace, Hope, and Love be thy guardians, oh, thou soul of my soul: thou in whom I breathe![30]

"I dare not read my letter over for I have no time to write another, and yet I fear that some expressions in it might displease me. Since I last saw you I have been constantly employed in writing letters, and have several more to write; for I do not intend that any one shall hear of me after I depart. I need not conjure you to look upon me as one of whom all links that once existed between us are broken. Your own delicacy will not allow you, I am convinced, to attempt to trace me. It is far better for your peace that you should be ignorant of my destination. You will not follow me, for when I banish myself would you nourish guilt by obtruding yourself upon me? You will not do this, I know you will not. You must forget me and all the evil that I have taught you. Cast off the only gift that I have bestowed upon you, your grief, and rise from under my blighting influence as no flower so sweet ever did rise from beneath so much evil.

"You will never hear from me again: receive these then as the last words of mine that will ever reach you; and although I have forfeited your filial love, yet regard them I conjure you as a father's command. Resolutely shake off the wretchedness that this first misfortune in early life must occasion you. Bear boldly up against the storm: continue wise and mild, but believe it, and indeed it is, your duty to be happy. You are very young; let not this check for more than a moment retard your glorious course; hold on, beloved one. The sun of youth is not set for you; it will restore vigour and life to you; do not resist with obstinate grief its beneficent influence, oh, my child! bless me with the hope that I have not utterly destroyed you.

"Farewell, Mathilda. I go with the belief that I have your pardon. Your gentle nature would not permit you to hate your greatest enemy and though I be he, although I have rent happiness from your grasp; though I have passed over your young love and hopes as the angel of destruction, finding beauty and joy, and leaving blight and

[30] **soul of my soul**: see Percy Shelley, "Essay on Love,"* for a discussion of "soul within a soul."

despair, yet you will forgive me, and with eyes overflowing with tears I thank you; my beloved one, I accept your pardon with a gratitude that will never die, and that will, indeed it will, outlive guilt and remorse.

"Farewell for ever!"

The moment I finished this letter I ordered the carriage and prepared to follow my father. The words of his letter by which he had dissuaded me from this step were those that determined me. Why did he write them? He must know that if I believed that his intention was merely to absent himself from me that instead of opposing him it would be that which I should myself require—or if he thought that any lurking feeling, yet he could not think that, should lead me to him would he endeavour to overthrow the only hope he could have of ever seeing me again; a lover, there was madness in the thought, yet he was my lover, would not act thus. No, he had determined to die, and he wished to spare me the misery of knowing it. The few ineffectual words he had said concerning his duty were to me a further proof—and the more I studied the letter the more did I perceive a thousand slight expressions that could only indicate a knowledge that life was now over for him. He was about to die! My blood froze at the thought: a sickening feeling of horror came over me that allowed not of tears. As I waited for the carriage I walked up and down with a quick pace; then kneeling and passionately clasping my hands I tried to pray but my voice was choked by convulsive sobs—Oh the sun shone, the air was balmy—he must yet live for if he were dead all would surely be black as night to me!

The motion of the carriage knowing that it carried me towards him and that I might perhaps find him alive somewhat revived my courage: yet I had a dreadful ride. Hope only supported me, the hope that I should not be too late. I did not weep, but I wiped the perspiration from my brow, and tried to still my brain and heart beating almost to madness. Oh! I must not be mad when I see him; or perhaps it were as well that I should be, my distraction might calm his, and recall him to the endurance of life. Yet until I find him I must force reason to keep her seat, and I pressed my forehead hard with my hands—Oh do not leave me; or I shall forget what I am about—instead of driving on as we ought with the speed of lightning they will attend to me, and we shall be too late. Oh! God help me! Let him be alive! It is all dark; in my abject misery I demand no more: no hope, no good: only passion, and guilt, and horror; but alive! Alive! My sensations choked me—No tears fell yet I sobbed, and breathed short and hard; one only thought possessed me, and I could only utter one word, that half screaming was perpetually on my lips: Alive! Alive!—

I had taken the steward with me for he, much better than I, could make the requisite enquiries—the poor old man could not restrain his tears as he saw my deep distress and knew the cause—he sometimes uttered a few broken words of consolation: in moments like these the mistress and servant become in a manner equals and when I saw his old dim eyes wet with sympathizing tears; his gray hair thinly scattered on an age-wrinkled brow I thought oh if my father were as he is—decrepid and hoary—then I should be spared this pain—

When I had arrived at the nearest town I took post horses and followed the road my father had taken. At every inn where we changed horses we heard of him, and I was possessed by alternate hope and fear. At length I found that he had altered his route; at first he had followed the London road; but now he changed it, and upon enquiry I found that the one which he now pursued led *towards the sea.* My dream recurred to my thoughts; I was not usually superstitious but in wretchedness every one is so. The sea was fifty miles off, yet it was towards it that he fled. The idea was terrible to my half-crazed imagination, and almost overturned the little self possession that still remained to me. I journeyed all day; every moment my misery encreased and the fever of my blood became intolerable. The summer sun shone in an unclouded sky; the air was close but all was cool to me except my own scorching skin. Towards evening dark thunder clouds arose above the horizon and I heard its distant roll—after sunset they darkened the whole sky and it began to rain, the lightning lighted up the whole country, and the thunder drowned the noise of our carriage. At the next inn my father had not taken horses; he had left a box there saying he would return, and had walked over the fields to the town of ——— a seacoast town eight miles off.

For a moment I was almost paralized by fear; but my energy returned and I demanded a guide to accompany me in following his steps. The night was tempestuous but my bribe was high and I easily procured a countryman. We passed through many lanes and over fields and wild downs; the rain poured down in torrents, and the loud thunder broke in terrible crashes over our heads. Oh! What a night it was! And I passed on with quick steps among the high, dank grass amid the rain and tempest. My dream was for ever in my thoughts, and with a kind of half insanity that often possesses the mind in despair, I said aloud: "Courage! We are not near the sea; we are yet several miles from the ocean"—Yet it was towards the sea that our direction lay and that heightened the confusion of my ideas. Once, overcome by fatigue, I sunk on the wet earth; about two hundred yards distant, alone in a large meadow stood a magnificent oak; the lightnings shewed its myriad boughs torn by the storm. A strange idea seized me; a person must have felt all the agonies of doubt concerning the life and death of one who is the whole world to them before they can enter into my feelings—for in that state, the mind working unrestrained by the will makes strange and fanciful combinations with outward circumstances and weaves the chances and changes of nature into an immediate connexion with the event they dread. It was with this feeling that I turned to the old steward who stood pale and trembling beside me; "Mark, Gaspar, if the next flash of lightning rend not that oak my father will be alive."

I had scarcely uttered these words than a flash instantly followed by a tremendous peal of thunder descended on it; and when my eyes recovered their sight after the dazzling light, the oak no longer stood in the meadow—The old man uttered a wild exclamation of horror when he saw so sudden an interpretation given to my prophecy. I started up, my strength returned with my terror; I cried, "Oh, God! Is this thy decree? Yet perhaps I shall not be too late."

Although still several miles distant we continued to approach the sea. We came at last to the road that led to the town of ——— and at an inn there we heard that my father had passed by somewhat before sunset; he had observed the approaching storm and had hired a horse for the next town which was situated a mile from the sea that he might arrive there before it should commence: this town was five miles off. We hired a chaise here, and with four horses drove with speed through the storm. My garments were wet and clung around me, and my hair hung in straight locks on my neck when not blown aside by the wind. I shivered, yet my pulse was high with fever. Great God! What agony I endured. I shed no tears but my eyes wild and inflamed were starting from my head; I could hardly support the weight that pressed upon my brain. We arrived at the town of ——— in a little more than half an hour. When my father had arrived the storm had already begun, but he had refused to stop and leaving his horse there he walked on—*towards the sea.* Alas! it was double cruelty in him to have chosen the sea for his fatal resolve; it was adding madness to my despair.

The poor old servant who was with me endeavoured to persuade me to remain here and to let him go alone—I shook my head silently and sadly; sick almost to death I leant upon his arm, and as there was no road for a chaise dragged my weary steps across the desolate downs to meet my fate, now too certain for the agony of doubt. Almost fainting I slowly approached the fatal waters; when we had quitted the town we heard their roaring. I whispered to myself in a muttering voice—"The sound is the same as that which I heard in my dream. It is the knell of my father which I hear."

The rain had ceased; there was no more thunder and lightning; the wind had paused. My heart no longer beat wildly; I did not feel any fever: but I was chilled; my knees sunk under me—I almost slept as I walked with excess of weariness; every limb trembled. I was silent: all was silent except the roaring of the sea which became louder and more dreadful. Yet we advanced slowly: sometimes I thought that we should never arrive; that the sound of waves would still allure us, and that we should walk on for ever and ever: field succeeding field, never would our weary journey cease, nor night nor day; but still we should hear the dashing of the sea, and to all this there would be no end. Wild beyond the imagination of the happy are the thoughts bred by misery and despair.

At length we reached the overhanging beach; a cottage stood beside the path; we knocked at the door and it was opened: the bed within instantly caught my eye; something stiff and straight lay on it, covered by a sheet; the cottagers looked aghast. The first words that they uttered confirmed what I before knew. I did not feel shocked or overcome: I believe that I asked one or two questions and listened to the answers. I hardly know, but in a few moments I sank lifeless to the ground; and so would that then all had been at an end!

—CHAPTER VIII—

I was carried to the next town: fever succeeded to convulsions and faintings, and for some weeks my unhappy spirit hovered on the very verge of death. But life was yet strong within me; I recovered: nor did it a little aid my returning health that my recollections were at first vague, and that I was too weak to feel any violent emotion. I often said to myself, my father is dead. He loved me with a guilty passion, and stung by remorse and despair he killed himself. Why is it that I feel no horror? Are these circumstances not dreadful? Is it not enough that I shall never more meet the eyes of my beloved father; never more hear his voice; no caress, no look? All cold, and stiff, and dead! Alas! I am quite callous: the night I was out in was fearful and the cold rain that fell about my heart has acted like the waters of the cavern of Antiparos[31] and has changed it to stone. I do not weep or sigh; but I must reason with myself, and force myself to feel sorrow and despair. This is not resignation that I feel, for I am dead to all regret.

I communed in this manner with myself, but I was silent to all around me. I hardly replied to the slightest question, and was uneasy when I saw a human creature near me. I was surrounded by my female relations, but they were all of them nearly strangers to me: I did not listen to their consolations; and so little did they work their designed effect that they seemed to me to be spoken in an unknown tongue. I found if sorrow was dead within me, so was love and desire of sympathy. Yet sorrow only slept to revive more fierce, but love never woke again—its ghost, ever hovering over my father's grave, alone survived—since his death all the world was to me a blank except where woe had stampt its burning words telling me to smile no more—the living were not fit companions for me, and I was ever meditating by what means I might shake them all off, and never be heard of again.

My convalescence rapidly advanced, yet this was the thought that haunted me, and I was for ever forming plans how I might hereafter contrive to escape the tortures that were prepared for me when I should mix in society, and to find the solitude which alone could suit one whom an untold grief seperated from her fellow creatures. Who can be more solitary even in a crowd than one whose history and the never ending feelings and remembrances arising from it is known to no living soul. There was too deep a horror in my tale for confidence; I was on earth the sole depository of my own secret. I might tell it to the winds and to the desart heaths but I must never among my fellow creatures, either by word or look give allowance to the smallest conjecture of the dread reality: I must shrink before the eye of man lest he should read my father's guilt in my glazed eyes: I must be silent lest my faltering voice should betray unimagined horrors. Over the deep grave of my secret I must heap an impenetrable heap of false smiles and words: cunning frauds, treacherous laughter, and a mixture of all light deceits would form a mist to blind others and be as the poisonous simoon[32] to me. I, the offspring of love, the child of the woods, the nursling of Nature's bright self was to submit to this? I dared not.

How must I escape? I was rich and young, and had a guardian appointed for me; and all about me would act as if I were one of their great society, while I must keep the secret that I really was cut off from them for ever. If I fled I should be pursued; in life there was no escape for me: why then I must die. I shuddered; I dared not die even though the cold grave held all I loved; although I might say with Job

> Where is now my hope? For my hope who shall see it? They shall go down together to the bars of the pit, when our rest together is in the dust[33]—

Yes my hope was corruption and dust and all to which death brings us.—Or after life—No, no, I will not persuade myself to die, I may not, dare not. And then I wept; yes, warm tears once more struggled into my eyes soothing yet bitter; and after I had wept much and called with unavailing anguish, with outstretched arms, for my cruel father; after my weak frame was exhausted by all variety of plaint[34] I sank once more into reverie, and once more reflected on how I might find that which I most desired; dear to me if aught were dear, a death-like solitude.

I dared not die, but I might feign death, and thus escape from my comforters: they will believe me united to my father, and so indeed I shall be. For alone, when no voice can disturb my dream, and no cold eye meet mine to check its fire, then I may commune with his spirit; on a lone heath, at noon or at midnight, still I should be near him. His last injunction to me was that I should be happy; perhaps he did not mean the shadowy happiness that I promised myself, yet it was that alone which I could taste. He did not conceive that never again I could make one of the smiling hunters that go coursing after bubbles that break to nothing when caught, and then after a new one with brighter colours; my hope also had proved a bubble, but it had been so lovely, so adorned that I saw none that could attract me after it; besides I was wearied with the pursuit, nearly dead with weariness.

I would feign to die; my contented heirs would seize upon my wealth, and I should purchase freedom. But then

[31] **cavern of Antiparos**: modern Adiparos is one of the Cyclades in the south Aegean, west of Paros, famous for a grotto of great depth.

[32] **simoon**: hot, dry, suffocating sand wind which sweeps across the African and Asiatic deserts in the summer.

[33] Cf. Job 17:15–16.

[34] **plaint**: grieving, lamentation.

my plan must be laid with art; I would not be left destitute, I must secure some money. Alas! to what loathsome shifts must I be driven? Yet a whole life of falsehood was otherwise my portion: and when remorse at being the contriver of any cheat made me shrink from my design I was irresistibly led back and confirmed in it by the visit of some aunt or cousin, who would tell me that death was the end of all men. And then say that my father had surely lost his wits ever since my mother's death; that he was mad and that I was fortunate, for in one of his fits he might have killed me instead of destroying his own crazed being. And all this, to be sure, was delicately put; not in broad words for my feelings might be hurt but

Whispered so and so
In dark hint soft and low[35]

with downcast eyes, and sympathizing smiles or whimpers; and I listened with quiet countenance while every nerve trembled; I that dared not utter aye or no to all this blasphemy. Oh, this was a delicious life quite void of guile! I with my dove's look and fox's heart: for indeed I felt only the degradation of falsehood, and not any sacred sentiment of conscious innocence that might redeem it. I who had before clothed myself in the bright garb of sincerity must now borrow one of divers colours: it might sit awkwardly at first, but use would enable me to place it in elegant folds, to lie with grace. Aye, I might die my soul with falsehood until I had quite hid its native colour. Oh, beloved father! Accept the pure heart of your unhappy daughter; permit me to join you unspotted as I was or you will not recognize my altered semblance. As grief might change Constance[36] so would deceit change me until in heaven you would say, "This is not my child"—My father, to be happy both now and when again we meet I must fly from all this life which is mockery to one like me. In solitude only shall I be myself; in solitude I shall be thine.

Alas! I even now look back with disgust at my artifices and contrivances by which, after many painful struggles, I effected my retreat. I might enter into a long detail of the means I used, first to secure myself a slight maintenance for the remainder of my life, and afterwards to ensure the conviction of my death: I might, but I will not. I even now blush at the falsehoods I uttered; my heart sickens: I will leave this complication of what I hope I may in a manner call innocent deceit to be imagined by the reader. The remembrance haunts me like a crime—I know that if I were to endeavour to relate it my tale would at length remain unfinished. I was led to London, and had to endure for some weeks cold looks, cold words and colder consolations: but I escaped; they tried to bind me with fetters that they thought silken, yet which weighed on me like iron, although I broke them more easily than a girth formed of a single straw and fled to freedom.

The few weeks that I spent in London were the most miserable of my life: a great city is a frightful habitation to one sorrowing. The sunset and the gentle moon, the blessed motion of the leaves and the murmuring of waters are all sweet physicians to a distempered mind. The soul is expanded and drinks in quiet, a lulling medecine—to me it was as the sight of the lovely water snakes to the bewitched mariner—in loving and blessing Nature I unawares, called down a blessing on my own soul. But in a city all is closed shut like a prison, a wiry prison from which you can peep at the sky only.[37] I cannot describe to you what were the frantic nature of my sensations while I resided there; I was often on the verge of madness. Nay, when I look back on many of my wild thoughts, thoughts with which actions sometimes endeavoured to keep pace; when I tossed my hands high calling down the cope of heaven to fall on me and bury me; when I tore my hair and throwing it to the winds cried, "Ye are free, go seek my father!" And then, like the unfortunate Constance, catching at them again and tying them up, that nought might find him if I might not. How, on my knees I have fancied myself close to my father's grave and struck the ground in anger that it should cover him from me. Oft when I have listened with gasping attention for the sound of the ocean mingled with my father's groans; and then wept until my strength was gone and I was calm and faint, when I have recollected all this I have asked myself if this were not madness. While in London these and many other dreadful thoughts too harrowing for words were my portion: I lost all this suffering when I was free; when I saw the wild

[35] Shelley has adapted lines 17 to 18 of S. T. Coleridge's "Fire, Famine, and Slaughter: A War Eclogue" (1798), in which Famine says to Slaughter, "Whisper it, sister! so and so! / In a dark hint, soft and slow."

[36] **Constance:** See Shakespeare, *King John*, III.i.67–74 and III.iv.93–105.

[37] **water snakes . . . mariner:** Cf. S. T. Coleridge, "The Rime of the Ancient Mariner,"* ll. 272–87. **prison . . . sky:** Coleridge, "Frost at Midnight,"* ll. 50–53.

heath around me, and the evening star in the west, then I could weep, gently weep, and be at peace.

Do not mistake me; I never was really mad. I was always conscious of my state when my wild thoughts seemed to drive me to insanity, and never betrayed them to aught but silence and solitude. The people around me saw nothing of all this. They only saw a poor girl broken in spirit, who spoke in a low and gentle voice, and from underneath whose downcast lids tears would sometimes steal which she strove to hide. One who loved to be alone, and shrunk from observation; who never smiled; oh, no! I never smiled—and that was all.

Well, I escaped. I left my guardian's house and I was never heard of again; it was believed from the letters that I left and other circumstances that I planned that I had destroyed myself. I was sought after therefore with less care than would otherwise have been the case; and soon all trace and memory of me was lost. I left London in a small vessel bound for a port in the north of England. And now having succeeded in my attempt, and being quite alone peace returned to me. The sea was calm and the vessel moved gently onwards, I sat upon deck under the open canopy of heaven and methought I was an altered creature. Not the wild, raving and most miserable Mathilda but a youthful Hermitess dedicated to seclusion and whose bosom she must strive to keep free from all tumult and unholy despair[38]—The fanciful nun-like dress that I had adopted; the knowledge that my very existence was a secret known only to myself; the solitude to which I was for ever hereafter destined nursed gentle thoughts in my wounded heart. The breeze that played in my hair revived me, and I watched with quiet eyes the sunbeams that glittered on the waves, and the birds that coursed each other over the waters just brushing them with their plumes. I slept too undisturbed by dreams; and awoke refreshed to again enjoy my tranquil freedom.

In four days we arrived at the harbour to which we were bound. I would not remain on the sea coast, but proceeded immediately inland. I had already planned the situation where I would live. It should be a solitary house on a wide plain near no other habitation: where I could behold the whole horizon, and wander far without molestation from the sight of my fellow creatures. I was not misanthropic, but I felt that the gentle current of my feelings depended upon my being alone. I fixed myself on a wide solitude. On a dreary heath bestrewn with stones, among which short grass grew; and here and there a few rushes beside a little pool. Not far from my cottage was a small cluster of pines the only trees to be seen for many miles: I had a path cut through the furze from my door to this little wood, from whose topmost branches the birds saluted the rising sun and awoke me to my daily meditation. My view was bounded only by the horizon except on one side where a distant wood made a black spot on the heath, that every where else stretched out its faint hues as far as the eye could reach, wide and very desolate. Here I could mark the net work of the clouds as they wove themselves into thick masses: I could watch the slow rise of the heavy thunder clouds and could see the rack as it was driven across the heavens, or under the pine trees I could enjoy the stillness of the azure sky.

My life was very peaceful. I had one female servant who spent the greater part of the day at a village two miles off. My amusements were simple and very innocent; I fed the birds who built on the pines or among the ivy that covered the wall of my little garden, and they soon knew me: the bolder ones pecked the crumbs from my hands and perched on my fingers to sing their thankfulness. When I had lived here some time other animals visited me and a fox came every day for a portion of food appropriated for him and would suffer me to pat his head. I had besides many books and a harp with which when despairing I could soothe my spirits, and raise myself to sympathy and love.

Love! What had I to love? Oh many things: there was the moonshine, and the bright stars; the breezes and the refreshing rains; there was the whole earth and the sky that covers it: all lovely forms that visited my imagination, all memories of heroism and virtue. Yet this was very unlike my early life although as then I was confined to Nature and books. Then I bounded across the fields; my spirit often seemed to ride upon the winds, and to mingle in joyful sympathy with the ambient[39] air. Then if I wandered slowly I cheered myself with a sweet song or sweeter day dreams. I felt a holy rapture spring from all I saw. I drank in joy with life; my steps were light; my eyes, clear from the love that animated them, sought the heavens, and with my long hair loosened to the winds I gave my body and my mind to sympathy and delight. But now my walk was slow—My eyes were seldom raised and

---

[38] **an altered creature . . . unholy despair**: cf. Wordsworth, "The Female Vagrant": "every tear / Dried up, despairing, desolate, on board / A British ship I waked, as from a trance restored."

[39] **ambient**: revolving, surrounding.

often filled with tears; no song; no smiles; no careless motion that might bespeak a mind intent on what surrounded it — I was gathered up into myself—a selfish solitary creature ever pondering on my regrets and faded hopes.

Mine was an idle, useless life; it was so; but say not to the lily laid prostrate by the storm, "Arise, and bloom as before." My heart was bleeding from its death's wound; I could live no otherwise — Often amid apparent calm I was visited by despair and melancholy; gloom that nought could dissipate or overcome; a hatred of life; a carelessness of beauty; all these would by fits hold me nearly annihilated by their powers. Never for one moment when most placid did I cease to pray for death. I could be found in no state of mind which I would not willingly have exchanged for nothingness. And morning and evening my tearful eyes raised to heaven, my hands clasped tight in the energy of prayer, I have repeated with the poet —

> Before I see another day
> Oh, let this body die away![40]

Let me not be reproached then with inutility; I believed that by suicide I should violate a divine law of nature, and I thought that I sufficiently fulfilled my part in submitting to the hard task of enduring the crawling hours and minutes — in bearing the load of time that weighed miserably upon me and that in abstaining from what I in my calm moments considered a crime, I deserved the reward of virtue. There were periods, dreadful ones, during which I despaired — and doubted the existence of all duty and the reality of crime — but I shudder, and turn from the remembrance.

— CHAPTER IX —

Thus I passed two years. Day after day so many hundreds wore on; they brought no outward changes with them, but some few slowly operated on my mind as I glided on towards death. I began to study more; to sympathize more in the thoughts of others as expressed in books; to read history, and to lose my individuality among the crowd that had existed before me. Thus perhaps as the sensation of immediate suffering wore off, I became more human. Solitude also lost to me some of its charms: I began again to wish for sympathy; not that I was ever tempted to seek the crowd, but I wished for one friend to love me. You will say perhaps that I gradually became fitted to return to society. I do not think so. For the sympathy that I desired must be so pure, so divested of influence from outward circumstances that in the world I could not fail of being balked by the gross materials that perpetually mingle even with its best feelings. Believe me, I was then less fitted for any communion with my fellow creatures than before. When I left them they had tormented me but it was in the same way as pain and sickness may torment; something extraneous to the mind that galled it, and that I wished to cast aside. But now I should have desired sympathy; I should wish to knit my soul to some one of theirs, and should have prepared for myself plentiful draughts of disappointment and suffering; for I was tender as the sensitive plant,[41] all nerve. I did not desire sympathy and aid in ambition or wisdom, but sweet and mutual affection; smiles to cheer me and gentle words of comfort. I wished for one heart in which I could pour unrestrained my plaints, and by the heavenly nature of the soil blessed fruit might spring from such bad seed. Yet how could I find this? The love that is the soul of friendship is a soft spirit seldom found except when two amiable creatures are knit from early youth, or when bound by mutual suffering and pursuits; it comes to some of the elect unsought and unaware; it descends as gentle dew on chosen spots which however barren they were before become under its benign influence fertile in all sweet plants; but when desired it flies; it scoffs at the prayers of its votaries; it will bestow, but not be sought.

I knew all this and did not go to seek sympathy; but there on my solitary heath, under my lowly roof where all around was desart, it came to me as a sunbeam in winter to adorn while it helps to dissolve the drifted snow. — Alas the sun shone on blighted fruit; I did not revive under its radiance for I was too utterly undone to feel its kindly power. My father had been and his memory was the life of my life. I might feel gratitude to another but I never more could love or hope as I had done; it was all suffering; even my pleasures were endured, not enjoyed. I was as a solitary spot among mountains shut in on all sides by steep black precipices; where no ray of heat could penetrate; and from which there was no outlet to sunnier fields. And

---

[40] Cf. William Wordsworth, "The Complaint of a Forsaken Indian Woman" (1798), ll. 1–2.

[41] **the sensitive plant:** *Mimosa pudica*, a small variety of mimosa native to Brazil, that closes up and recoils when touched; it is hermaphroditic, i.e., needing only a single plant to reproduce. This plant was frequently invoked at this time as the archetype of female sensibility. Cf. Percy Bysshe Shelley, "The Sensitive-Plant" (1820).

thus it was that although the spirit of friendship soothed me for a while it could not restore me. It came as some gentle visitation; it went and I hardly felt the loss. The spirit of existence was dead within me; be not surprised therefore that when it came I welcomed not more gladly, or when it departed I lamented not more bitterly the best gift of heaven — a friend.

The name of my friend was Woodville. I will briefly relate his history that you may judge how cold my heart must have been not to be warmed by his eloquent words and tender sympathy; and how he also being most unhappy we were well fitted to be a mutual consolation — to each other, if I had not been hardened to stone by the Medusa head[42] of Misery. The misfortunes of Woodville were not of the heart's core like mine; his was a natural grief, not to destroy but to purify the heart and from which he might, when its shadow had passed from over him, shine forth brighter and happier than before.

Woodville was the son of a poor clergyman and had received a classical education. He was one of those very few whom fortune favours from their birth; on whom she bestows all gifts of intellect and person with a profusion that knew no bounds, and whom under her peculiar protection, no imperfection however slight, or disappointment however transitory has leave to touch. She seemed to have formed his mind of that excellence which no dross can tarnish, and his understanding was such that no error could pervert. His genius was transcendant, and when it rose as a bright star in the east all eyes were turned towards it in admiration. He was a Poet. That name has so often been degraded that it will not convey the idea of all that he was. He was like a poet of old whom the muses had crowned in his cradle, and on whose lips bees had fed. As he walked among other men he seemed encompassed with a heavenly halo that divided him from and lifted him above them. It was his surpassing beauty, the dazzling fire of his eyes, and his words whose rich accents wrapt the listener in mute and extatic wonder, that made him transcend all others so that before him they appeared only formed to minister to his superior excellence.

He was glorious from his youth. Every one loved him; no shadow of envy or hate cast even from the meanest mind ever fell upon him. He was, as one the peculiar delight of the gods, railed and fenced in by his own divinity, so that nought but love and admiration could approach him. His heart was simple like a child, unstained by arrogance or vanity. He mingled in society unknowing of his superiority over his companions, not because he undervalued himself but because he did not perceive the inferiority of others. He seemed incapable of conceiving of the full extent of the power that selfishness and vice possesses in the world: when I knew him, although he had suffered disappointment in his dearest hopes, he had not experienced any that arose from the meanness and self-love of men: his station was too high to allow of his suffering through their hardheartedness; and too low for him to have experienced ingratitude and encroaching selfishness: it is one of the blessings of a moderate fortune, that by preventing the possessor from conferring pecuniary favours it prevents him also from diving into the arcana[43] of human weakness or malice — To bestow on your fellow men is a godlike attribute — So indeed it is and as such not one fit for mortality; — the giver like Adam and Prometheus,[44] must pay the penalty of rising above his nature by being the martyr to his own excellence. Woodville was free from all these evils; and if slight examples did come across him he did not notice them but passed on in his course as an angel with winged feet might glide along the earth unimpeded by all those little obstacles over which we of earthly origin stumble. He was a believer in the divinity of genius and always opposed a stern disbelief to the objections of those petty cavillers[45] and minor critics who wish to reduce all men to their own miserable level — "I will make a scientific simile" he would say, "in the manner, if you will, of Dr. Darwin[46] — I consider the alledged errors of a man of genius as the aberrations of

---

[42] **Medusa head:** in Greek mythology, Medusa was one of the three snaky-haired Gorgons who turned all who looked upon them to stone.

[43] **arcana:** hidden things; profound secrets.

[44] **Adam:** the firstborn man in Genesis who was expelled from Paradise for eating the apple of the Tree of Knowledge. **Prometheus:** Greek god who stole fire from the Olympian deities to benefit humanity and was punished for all eternity by Zeus who nailed him to a rock in the Caucasus where a vulture daily tore out his liver. Cf. Byron, "Prometheus";* P. B. Shelley, *Prometheus Unbound;** and M. Shelley, *Frankenstein, or the Modern Prometheus.*

[45] **cavillers:** objectors, those who find fault unfairly or without good reason. **cavil:** a frivolous objection.

[46] **Dr. Darwin:** Erasmus Darwin* (1731–1802), physiologist and poet, early supporter of the theory of evolution and author of a botanical treatise in verse, *Botanic Garden: The Temple of Nature* (1789–1792).

the fixed stars. It is our distance from them and our imperfect means of communication that makes them appear to move; in truth they always remain stationary, a glorious centre, giving us a fine lesson of modesty if we would thus receive it."—

I have said that he was a poet: when he was three and twenty years of age he first published a poem, and it was hailed by the whole nation with enthusiasm and delight. His good star perpetually shone upon him; a reputation had never before been made so rapidly: it was universal. The multitude extolled the same poems that formed the wonder of the sage in his closet: there was not one dissentient voice.

It was at this time, in the height of his glory, that he became acquainted with Elinor. She was a young heiress of exquisite beauty who lived under the care of her guardian: from the moment they were seen together they appeared formed for each other. Elinor had not the genius of Woodville but she was generous and noble, and exalted by her youth and the love that she every where excited above the knowledge of aught but virtue and excellence. She was lovely; her manners were frank and simple; her deep blue eyes swam in a lustre which could only be given by sensibility joined to wisdom.

They were formed for one another and they soon loved. Woodville for the first time felt the delight of love; and Elinor was enraptured in possessing the heart of one so beautiful and glorious among his fellow men. Could any thing but unmixed joy flow from such a union?

Woodville was a Poet—he was sought for by every society and all eyes were turned on him alone when he appeared; but he was the son of a poor clergyman and Elinor was a rich heiress. Her guardian was not displeased with their mutual affection: the merit of Woodville was too eminent to admit of cavil on account of his inferior wealth; but the dying will of her father did not allow her to marry before she was of age and her fortune depended upon her obeying this injunction. She had just entered her twentieth year, and she and her lover were obliged to submit to this delay. But they were ever together and their happiness seemed that of Paradise: they studied together: formed plans of future occupations, and drinking in love and joy from each other's eyes and words they hardly repined at the delay to their entire union. Woodville for ever rose in glory; and Elinor become more lovely and wise under the lessons of her accomplished lover.

In two months Elinor would be twenty one: every thing was prepared for their union. How shall I relate the catastrophe to so much joy; but the earth would not be the earth it is, covered with blight and sorrow, if one such pair as these angelic creatures had been suffered to exist for one another: search through the world and you will not find the perfect happiness which their marriage would have caused them to enjoy; there must have been a revolution in the order of things as established among us miserable earth-dwellers to have admitted of such consummate joy. The chain of necessity ever bringing misery must have been broken and the malignant fate that presides over it would not permit this breach of her eternal laws. But why should I repine at this? Misery was my element, and nothing but what was miserable could approach me; if Woodville had been happy I should never have known him. And can I who for many years was fed by tears, and nourished under the dew of grief, can I pause to relate a tale of woe and death?

Woodville was obliged to make a journey into the country and was detained from day to day in irksome absence from his lovely bride. He received a letter from her to say that she was slightly ill, but telling him to hasten to her, that from his eyes she would receive health and that his company would be her surest medecine. He was detained three days longer and then he hastened to her. His heart, he knew not why, prognosticated misfortune; he had not heard from her again; he feared she might be worse and this fear made him impatient and restless for the moment of beholding her once more stand before him arrayed in health and beauty; for a sinister voice seemed always to whisper to him, "You will never more behold her as she was."

When he arrived at her habitation all was silent in it: he made his way through several rooms; in one he saw a servant weeping bitterly: he was faint with fear and could hardly ask, "Is she dead?" and just listened to the dreadful answer, "Not yet." These astounding words came on him as of less fearful import than those which he had expected; and to learn that she was still in being, and that he might still hope was an alleviation to him. He remembered the words of her letter and he indulged the wild idea that his kisses breathing warm love and life would infuse new spirit into her, and that with him near her she could not die; that his presence was the talisman of her life.

He hastened to her sick room; she lay, her cheeks burning with fever, yet her eyes were closed and she was seemingly senseless. He wrapt her in his arms; he imprinted breathless kisses on her burning lips; he called to her in a voice of subdued anguish by the tenderest names; "Return Elinor; I am with you; your life, your love. Return;

dearest one, you promised me this boon, that I should bring you health. Let your sweet spirit revive; you cannot die near me: What is death? To see you no more? To part with what is a part of myself; without whom I have no memory and no futurity? Elinor die! This is frenzy and the most miserable despair: you cannot die while I am near."

And again he kissed her eyes and lips, and hung over her inanimate form in agony, gazing on her countenance still lovely although changed, watching every slight convulsion, and varying colour which denoted life still lingering although about to depart. Once for a moment she revived and recognized his voice; a smile, a last lovely smile, played upon her lips. He watched beside her for twelve hours and then she died.

— CHAPTER X —

It was six months after this miserable conclusion to his long nursed hopes that I first saw him. He had retired to a part of the country where he was not known that he might peacefully indulge his grief. All the world, by the death of his beloved Elinor, was changed to him, and he could no longer remain in any spot where he had seen her or where her image mingled with the most rapturous hopes had brightened all around with a light of joy which would now be transformed to a darkness blacker than midnight since she, the sun of his life, was set for ever.

He lived for some time never looking on the light of heaven but shrouding his eyes in a perpetual darkness far from all that could remind him of what he had been; but as time softened his grief, like a true child of Nature he sought in the enjoyment of her beauties for a consolation in his unhappiness. He came to a part of the country where he was entirely unknown and where in the deepest solitude he could converse only with his own heart. He found a relief to his impatient grief in the breezes of heaven and in the sound of waters and woods. He became fond of riding; this exercise distracted his mind and elevated his spirits; on a swift horse he could for a moment gain respite from the image that else for ever followed him; Elinor on her death bed, her sweet features changed, and the soft spirit that animated her gradually waning into extinction. For many months Woodville had in vain endeavoured to cast off this terrible remembrance; it still hung on him until memory was too great a burthen for his loaded soul, but when on horseback the spell that seemingly held him to this idea was snapt; then if he thought of his lost bride he pictured her radiant in beauty; he could hear her voice, and fancy her "a sylvan Huntress by his side,"[47] while his eyes brightened as he thought he gazed on her cherished form. I had several times seen him ride across the heath and felt angry that my solitude should be disturbed. It was so long [since] I had spoken to any but peasants that I felt a disagreeable sensation at being gazed on by one of superior rank. I feared also that it might be some one who had seen me before: I might be recognized, my impostures discovered and I dragged back to a life of worse torture than that I had before endured. These were dreadful fears and they even haunted my dreams.

I was one day seated on the verge of the clump of pines when Woodville rode past. As soon as I perceived him I suddenly rose to escape from his observation by entering among the trees. My rising startled his horse; he reared and plunged and the rider was at length thrown. The horse then galloped swiftly across the heath and the stranger remained on the ground stunned by his fall. He was not materially hurt, a little fresh water soon recovered him. I was struck by his exceeding beauty, and as he spoke to thank me the sweet but melancholy cadence of his voice brought tears into my eyes.

A short conversation passed between us, but the next day he again stopped at my cottage and by degrees an intimacy grew between us. It was strange to him to see a female in extreme youth. I was not yet twenty, evidently belonging to the first classes of society and possessing every accomplishment an excellent education could bestow, living alone on a desolate heath—One on whose forehead the impress of grief was strongly marked, and whose words and motions betrayed that her thoughts did not follow them but were intent on far other ideas; bitter and overwhelming miseries. I was dressed also in a whimsical nun-like habit which denoted that I did not retire to solitude from necessity, but that I might indulge in a luxury of grief, and fanciful seclusion.

He soon took great interest in me, and sometimes forgot his own grief to sit beside me and endeavour to cheer me. He could not fail to interest even one who had shut herself from the whole world, whose hope was death, and who lived only with the departed. His personal beauty; his conversation which glowed with imagination and sensibility; the poetry that seemed to hang upon his lips and to make the very air mute to listen to him were

[47] **"a sylvan Huntress by his side"**: Cf. William Wordsworth, "Ruth" (1799), l. 95.

charms that no one could resist. He was younger, less worn, more passionless than my father and in no degree reminded me of him: he suffered under immediate grief yet its gentle influence instead of calling feelings otherwise dormant into action, seemed only to veil that which otherwise would have been too dazzling for me. When we were together I spoke little, yet my selfish mind was sometimes borne away by the rapid course of his ideas; I would lift my eyes with momentary brilliancy until memories that never died and seldom slept would recur, and a tear would dim them.

Woodville for ever tried to lead me to the contemplation of what is beautiful and happy in the world. His own mind was constitutionally bent to a firmer belief in good than in evil and this feeling which must even exhilarate the hopeless ever shone forth in his words. He would talk of the wonderful powers of man, of their present state and of their hopes: of what they had been and what they were, and when reason could no longer guide him, his imagination as if inspired shed light on the obscurity that veils the past and the future. He loved to dwell on what might have been the state of the earth before man lived on it, and how he first arose and gradually became the strange, complicated, but as he said, the glorious creature he now is. Covering the earth with their creations and forming by the power of their minds another world more lovely than the visible frame of things,[48] even all the world that we find in their writings. A beautiful creation, he would say, which may claim this superiority to its model, that good and evil is more easily seperated: the good rewarded in the way they themselves desire; the evil punished as all things evil ought to be punished, not by pain which is revolting to all philanthropy to consider but by quiet obscurity, which simply deprives them of their harmful qualities; why kill the serpent when you have extracted his fangs?

The poetry of his language and ideas which my words ill convey held me enchained to his discourses. It was a melancholy pleasure to me to listen to his inspired words; to catch for a moment the light of his eyes; to feel a transient sympathy and then to awaken from the delusion, again to know that all this was nothing,—a dream —a shadow for which there was no reality for me; my father had for ever deserted me, leaving me only memories which set an eternal barrier between me and my fellow creatures. I was indeed fellow to none. He—Woodville, mourned the loss of his bride: others wept the various forms of misery as they visited them: but infamy and guilt was mingled with my portion; unlawful and detestable passion had poured its poison into my ears and changed all my blood, so that it was no longer the kindly stream that supports life but a cold fountain of bitterness corrupted in its very source. It must be the excess of madness that could make me imagine that I could ever be aught but one alone; struck off from humanity; bearing no affinity to man or woman; a wretch on whom Nature had set her ban.

Sometimes Woodville talked to me of himself. He related his history brief in happiness and woe and dwelt with passion on his and Elinor's mutual love. "She was," he said, "the brightest vision that ever came upon the earth: there was something in her frank countenance, in her voice, and in every motion of her graceful form that overpowered me, as if it were a celestial creature that deigned to mingle with me in intercourse more sweet than man had ever before enjoyed. Sorrow fled before her; and her smile seemed to possess an influence like light to irradiate all mental darkness. It was not like a human loveliness that these gentle smiles went and came; but as a sunbeam on a lake, now light and now obscure, flitting before as you strove to catch them, and fold them for ever to your heart. I saw this smile fade for ever. Alas! I could never have believed that it was indeed Elinor that died if once when I spoke she had not lifted her almost benighted eyes, and for one moment like nought beside on earth, more lovely than a sunbeam, slighter, quicker than the waving plumage of a bird, dazzling as lightning and like it giving day to night, yet mild and faint, that smile came; it went, and then there was an end of all joy to me."

Thus his own sorrows, or the shapes copied from nature that dwelt in his mind with beauty greater than their own, occupied our talk while I railed in my own griefs with cautious secresy. If for a moment he shewed curiosity, my eyes fell, my voice died away and my evident suffering made him quickly endeavour to banish the ideas he had awakened; yet he for ever mingled consolation in his talk, and tried to soften my despair by demonstrations of deep sympathy and compassion. "We are both unhappy—" he would say to me; "I have told you my melancholy tale and we have wept together the loss of that lovely spirit that has so cruelly deserted me; but you hide your griefs: I do not ask you to disclose them, but tell me

[48] **visible frame of things**: cf. Percy Shelley, *Alastor**: "Nature's vast frame, the web of human things" (l. 719).

if I may not console you. It seems to me a wild adventure to find in this desart one like you quite solitary: you are young and lovely; your manners are refined and attractive; yet there is in your settled melancholy, and something, I know not what, in your expressive eyes that seems to seperate you from your kind: you shudder; pardon me, I entreat you but I cannot help expressing this once at least the lively interest I feel in your destiny.

"You never smile: your voice is low, and you utter your words as if you were afraid of the slight sound they would produce: the expression of awful and intense sorrow never for a moment fades from your countenance. I have lost for ever the loveliest companion that any man could ever have possessed, one who rather appears to have been a superior spirit who by some strange accident wandered among us earthly creatures, than as belonging to our kind. Yet I smile, and sometimes I speak almost forgetful of the change I have endured. But your sad mien never alters; your pulses beat and you breathe, yet you seem already to belong to another world; and sometimes, pray pardon my wild thoughts, when you touch my hand I am surprised to find your hand warm when all the fire of life seems extinct within you.

"When I look upon you, the tears you shed, the soft deprecating look with which you withstand enquiry; the deep sympathy your voice expresses when I speak of my lesser sorrows add to my interest for you. You stand here shelterless. You have cast yourself from among us and you wither on this wild plain forlorn[49] and helpless: some dreadful calamity must have befallen you. Do not turn from me; I do not ask you to reveal it: I only entreat you to listen to me and to become familiar with the voice of consolation and kindness. If pity, and admiration, and gentle affection can wean you from despair let me attempt the task. I cannot see your look of deep grief without endeavouring to restore you to happier feelings. Unbend your brow; relax the stern melancholy of your regard; permit a friend, a sincere, affectionate friend, I will be one, to convey some relief, some momentary pause to your sufferings.

"Do not think that I would intrude upon your confidence: I only ask your patience. Do not for ever look sorrow and never speak it; utter one word of bitter complaint and I will reprove it with gentle exhortation and pour on you the balm of compassion. You must not shut me from all communion with you: do not tell me why you grieve but only say the words, 'I am unhappy,' and you will feel relieved as if for some time excluded from all intercourse by some magic spell you should suddenly enter again the pale of human sympathy. I entreat you to believe in my most sincere professions and to treat me as an old and tried friend: promise me never to forget me, never causelessly to banish me; but try to love me as one who would devote all his energies to make you happy. Give me the name of friend; I will fulfill its duties; and if for a moment complaint and sorrow would shape themselves into words, let me be near to speak peace to your vext soul."

I repeat his persuasions in faint terms and cannot give you at the same time the tone and gesture that animated them. Like a refreshing shower on an arid soil they revived me, and although I still kept their cause secret he led me to pour forth my bitter complaints and to clothe my woe in words of gall and fire. With all the energy of desperate grief I told him how I had fallen at once from bliss to misery; how that for me there was no joy, no hope; that death however bitter would be the welcome seal to all my pangs; death the skeleton[50] was to be beautiful as love. I know not why but I found it sweet to utter these words to human ears; and though I derided all consolation yet I was pleased to see it offered me with gentleness and kindness. I listened quietly, and when he paused would again pour out my misery in expressions that shewed how far too deep my wounds were for any cure.

But now also I began to reap the fruits of my perfect solitude. I had become unfit for any intercourse, even with Woodville the most gentle and sympathizing creature that existed. I had become captious and unreasonable: my temper was utterly spoilt. I called him my friend but I viewed all he did with jealous eyes. If he did not visit me at the appointed hour I was angry, very angry, and told him that if indeed he did feel interest in me it was cold, and could not be fitted for me, a poor worn creature, whose deep unhappiness demanded much more than his worldy heart could give. When for a moment I imagined that his manner was cold I would fretfully say to him—"I was at peace before you came; why have you disturbed me? You have given me new wants and now you trifle with me as if my heart were as whole as yours, as if I were not in truth a shorn lamb thrust out on the bleak hill side, tortured by every blast. I wished for no friend, no sympathy.

---

[49] **wild plain forlorn**: Milton, *Paradise Lost,* IX.908–910: "How can I . . . live again in these wild woods forlorn."

[50] **death the skeleton**: Wordsworth, "Yew-Trees," ll. 27–28: "Death the Skeleton / And Time the Shadow."

I avoided you, you know I did, but you forced yourself upon me and gave me those wants which you see with triumph give you power over me. Oh the brave power of the bitter north wind which freezes the tears it has caused to shed! But I will not bear this; go: the sun will rise and set as before you came, and I shall sit among the pines or wander on the heath weeping and complaining without wishing for you to listen. You are cruel, very cruel, to treat me who bleed at every pore in this rough manner."

And then, when in answer to my peevish words, I saw his countenance bent with living pity on me. When I saw him

> Gli occhi drizzo ver me con quel sembiante
> Che madre fa sopra figlioul deliro[51]

I wept and said, "Oh, pardon me! You are good and kind but I am not fit for life. Why am I obliged to live? To drag hour after hour, to see the trees wave their branches restlessly, to feel the air, and to suffer in all I feel keenest agony. My frame is strong, but my soul sinks beneath this endurance of living anguish. Death is the goal that I would attain, but, alas! I do not even see the end of the course. Do you, my compassionate friend, tell me how to die peacefully and innocently and I will bless you: all that I, poor wretch, can desire is a painless death."

But Woodville's words had magic in them, when beginning with the sweetest pity, he would raise me by degrees out of myself and my sorrows until I wondered at my own selfishness: but he left me and despair returned; the work of consolation was ever to begin anew. I often desired his entire absence; for I found that I was grown out of the ways of life and that by long seclusion, although I could support my accustomed grief, and drink the bitter daily draught with some degree of patience, yet I had become unfit for the slightest novelty of feeling. Expectation, and hopes, and affection were all too much for me. I knew this, but at other times I was unreasonable and laid the blame upon him, who was most blameless, and peevishly thought that if his gentle soul were more gentle, if his intense sympathy were more intense, he could drive the fiend from my soul and make me more human. I am, I thought, a tragedy; a character that he comes to see act: now and then he gives me my cue that I may make a speech more to his purpose: perhaps he is already planning a poem in which I am to figure. I am a farce and play to him, but to me this is all dreary reality: he takes all the profit and I bear all the burthen.

— CHAPTER XI —

It is a strange circumstance but it often occurs that blessings by their use turn to curses; and that I who in solitude had desired sympathy as the only relief I could enjoy now find it an additional torture to me. During my father's life time I had always been of an affectionate and forbearing disposition, but since those days of joy alas! I was much changed. I had become arrogant, peevish, and above all suspicious. Although the real interest of my narration is now ended and I ought quickly to wind up its melancholy catastrophe, yet I will relate one instance of my sad suspicion and despair and how Woodville with the goodness and almost the power of an angel, softened my rugged feelings and led me back to gentleness.

He had promised to spend some hours with me one afternoon but a violent and continual rain prevented him. I was alone the whole evening. I had passed two whole years alone unrepining, but now I was miserable. He could not really care for me, I thought, for if he did the storm would rather have made him come even if I had not expected him, than, as it did, prevent a promised visit. He would well know that this drear sky and gloomy rain would load my spirit almost to madness: if the weather had been fine I should not have regretted his absence as heavily as I necessarily must, shut up in this miserable cottage with no companions but my own wretched thoughts. If he were truly my friend he would have calculated all this; and let me now calculate this boasted friendship, and discover its real worth. He got over his grief for Elinor, and the country became dull to him, so he was glad to find even me for amusement; and when he does not know what else to do he passes his lazy hours here, and calls this friendship—It is true that his presence is a consolation to me, and that his words are sweet, and, when he will, he can pour forth thoughts that win me from despair. His words are sweet,—and so, truly, is the honey of the bee, but the bee has a sting, and unkindness is a worse smart than that received from an insect's venom. I will put him to the proof. He says all hope is dead to him, and I know that it is dead to me, so we are both equally fitted for death. Let me try if he will die with me; and as I fear to die alone, if he will accompany to cheer me, and thus he can shew himself my friend in the only manner my misery will permit.

It was madness I believe, but I so worked myself up to this idea that I could think of nothing else. If he dies with

[51] Cf. Dante, *Paradiso*, I.101–102: "she turned her eyes on me with the look that a mother casts on her delirious child."

me it is well, and there will be an end of two miserable beings; and if he will not, then will I scoff at his friendship and drink the poison before him to shame his cowardice. I planned the whole scene with an earnest heart and franticly set my soul on this project. I procured Laudanum[52] and placing it in two glasses on the table, filled my room with flowers and decorated the last scene of my tragedy with the nicest care. As the hour for his coming approached, my heart softened and I wept; not that I gave up my plan, but even when resolved the mind must undergo several revolutions of feeling before it can drink its death.

Now all was ready and Woodville came. I received him at the door of my cottage and leading him solemnly into the room, I said: "My friend, I wish to die. I am quite weary of enduring the misery which hourly I do endure, and I will throw it off. What slave will not, if he may, escape from his chains? Look, I weep; for more than two years I have never enjoyed one moment free from anguish. I have often desired to die; but I am a very coward. It is hard for one so young who was once so happy as I was voluntarily to divest themselves of all sensation and to go alone to the dreary grave; I dare not. I must die, yet my fear chills me; I pause and shudder and then for months I endure my excess of wretchedness. But now the time is come when I may quit life. I have a friend who will not refuse to accompany me in this dark journey; such is my request: earnestly do I entreat and implore you to die with me. Then we shall find Elinor and what I have lost. Look, I am prepared; there is the death draught, let us drink it together and willingly and joyfully quit this hated round of daily life.

"You turn from me; yet before you deny me reflect, Woodville, how sweet it were to cast off the load of tears and misery under which we now labour: and surely we shall find light after we have passed the dark valley. That drink will plunge us in a sweet slumber, and when we awaken what joy will be ours to find all our sorrows and fears past. *A little patience,* and all will be over;[53] aye, a very little patience; for, look, there is the key of our prison; we hold it in our own hands, and are we more debased than slaves to cast it away and give ourselves up to voluntary bondage? Even now if we had courage we might be free. Behold, my cheek is flushed with pleasure at the imagination of death; all that we love are dead. Come, give me your hand, one look of joyous sympathy and we will go together and seek them; a lulling journey; where our arrival will bring bliss and our waking be that of angels. Do you delay? Are you a coward, Woodville? Oh fie! Cast off this blank look of human melancholy. Oh! that I had words to express the luxury of death that I might win you. I tell you we are no longer miserable mortals; we are about to become gods; spirits free and happy as gods.[54] What fool on a bleak shore, seeing a flowery isle on the other side with his lost love beckoning to him from it would pause because the wave is dark and turbid?

What if some little payne the passage have
That makes frayle flesh to fear the bitter wave?
Is not short payne well borne that brings long ease,
And lays the soul to sleep in quiet grave?[55]

"Do you mark my words; I have learned the language of despair: I have it all by heart, for I am Despair; and a strange being am I, joyous, triumphant Despair. But those words are false, for the wave may be dark but it is not bitter. We lie down, and close our eyes with a gentle good night, and when we wake, we are free. Come then, no more delay, thou tardy one! Behold the pleasant potion! Look, I am a spirit of good, and not a human maid that invites thee, and with winning accents (oh, that they would win thee!) says, Come and drink."

As I spoke I fixed my eyes upon his countenance, and his exquisite beauty, the heavenly compassion that beamed from his eyes, his gentle yet earnest look of deprecation and wonder even before he spoke wrought a change in my high-strained feelings taking from me all the sternness of despair and filing me only with the softest grief. I saw his eyes humid[56] also as he took both my hands in his; and sitting down near me, he said:

---

[52] **Laudanum**: opium dissolved in alcohol, prescribed in the nineteenth century as a sedative and for muscular pain and nervous diseases. Addictive, and when taken to excess, fatal. (See SOCIETY AND POLITICAL ECONOMY.)

[53] **"A little patience, and all will be over"**: Shelley here quotes the dying words of her mother, Mary Wollstonecraft.*

[54] **we are about to become gods**: cf. *Milton, Paradise Lost.* Satan to Eve: "ye shall be as gods" (IX.708); Eve to Adam, "I feel / . . . not death, but life / Augmented . . . / . . . / . . . / On my experience, Adam, freely taste, / And fear of death deliver to the winds" (IX.983–989).

[55] Cf. Edmund Spenser, *The Faerie Queene,* Book I, canto 9, xl; these are the words of Despair, who is tempting Red Crosse Knight to die; he is saved by Una.

[56] **humid**: moist, wet.

"This is a sad deed to which you would lead me, dearest friend, and your woe must indeed be deep that could fill you with these unhappy thoughts. You long for death and yet you fear it and wish me to be your companion. But I have less courage than you and even thus accompanied I dare not die. Listen to me, and then reflect if you ought to win me to your project, even if with the overbearing eloquence of despair you could make black death so inviting that the fair heaven should appear darkness. Listen I entreat you to the words of one who has himself nurtured desperate thoughts, and longed with impatient desire for death, but who has at length trampled the phantom under foot, and crushed his sting. Come, as you have played Despair with me I will play the part of Una with you and bring you hurtless from his dark cavern. Listen to me, and let yourself be softened by words in which no selfish passion lingers.

"We know not what all this wide world means; its strange mixture of good and evil. But we have been placed here and bid live and hope. I know not what we are to hope; but there is some good beyond us that we must seek; and that is our earthly task. If misfortune come against us we must fight with her; we must cast her aside, and still go on to find out that which it is our nature to desire. Whether this prospect of future good be the preparation for another existence I know not; or whether that it is merely that we, as workmen in God's vineyard, must lend a hand to smooth the way for our posterity. If it indeed be that; if the efforts of the virtuous now, are to make the future inhabitants of this fair world more happy; if the labours of those who cast aside selfishness, and try to know the truth of things, are to free the men of ages, now far distant but which will one day come, from the burthen under which those who now live groan, and like you weep bitterly; if they free them but from one of what are now the necessary evils of life, truly I will not fail but will with my whole soul aid the work. From my youth I have said, I will be virtuous; I will dedicate my life for the good of others; I will do my best to extirpate evil and if the spirit who protects ill should so influence circumstances that I should suffer through my endeavour, yet while there is hope, and hope there ever must be, of success, cheerfully do I gird myself to my task.

"I have powers; my countrymen think well of them. Do you think I sow my seed in the barren air, and have no end in what I do? Believe me, I will never desert life until this last hope is torn from my bosom, that in some way my labours may form a link in the chain of gold with which we ought all to strive to drag Happiness from where she sits enthroned above the clouds, now far beyond our reach, to inhabit the earth with us. Let us suppose that Socrates, or Shakespear, or Rousseau[57] had been seized with despair and died in youth when they were as young as I am; do you think that we and all the world should not have lost incalculable improvement in our good feelings and our happiness through their destruction? I am not like one of these; they influenced millions: but if I can influence but a hundred, but ten, but one solitary individual, so as in any way to lead him from ill to good, that will be a joy to repay me for all my sufferings, though they were a million times multiplied; and that hope will support me to bear them.

"And those who do not work for posterity; or working, as may be my case, will not be known by it; yet they, believe me, have also their duties. You grieve because you are unhappy; it is happiness you seek but you despair of obtaining it. But if you can bestow happiness on another; if you can give one other person only one hour of joy ought you not to live to do it? And every one has it in their power to do that. The inhabitants of this world suffer so much pain. In crowded cities, among cultivated plains, or on the desart mountains, pain is thickly sown, and if we can tear up but one of these noxious weeds, or more, if in its stead we can sow one seed of corn, or plant one fair flower, let that be motive sufficient against suicide. Let us not desert our task while there is the slightest hope that we may in a future day do this.

"Indeed I dare not die. I have a mother whose support and hope I am. I have a friend who loves me as his life, and in whose breast I should infix a mortal sting if I ungratefully left him. So I will not die. Nor shall you, my friend; cheer up; cease to weep, I entreat you. Are you not young, and fair, and good? Why should you despair? Or if you must for yourself, why for others? If you can never be happy, can you never bestow happiness? Oh! believe me, if you beheld on lips pale with grief one smile of joy and gratitude, and knew that you were parent of that smile, and that without you it had never been, you would feel so pure and warm a happiness that you would wish to live for ever again and again to enjoy the same pleasure.

"Come, I see that you have already cast aside the sad thoughts you before franticly indulged. Look in that

[57] **Socrates:** Greek philosopher (470?–399 BC). **Shakespear:** William Shakespeare, English dramatist (1564–1616). **Rousseau:** Jean-Jacques Rousseau, French political theorist and novelist (1712–1778).

mirror; when I came your brow was contracted, your eyes deep sunk in your head, your lips quivering; your hands trembled violently when I took them; but now all is tranquil and soft. You are grieved and there is grief in the expression of your countenance but it is gentle and sweet. You allow me to throw away this cursed drink; you smile. Oh! Congratulate me, hope is triumphant, and I have done some good."

These words are shadowy as I repeat them but they were indeed words of fire and produced a warm hope in me (I, miserable wretch, to hope!) that tingled like pleasure in my veins. He did not leave me for many hours; not until he had improved the spark that he had kindled, and with an angelic hand fostered the return of something that seemed like joy. He left me but I still was calm, and after I had saluted the starry sky and dewy earth with eyes of love and a contented good night, I slept sweetly, visited by dreams, the first of pleasure I had had for many long months.

But this was only a momentary relief and my old habits of feeling returned; for I was doomed while in life to grieve, and to the natural sorrow of my father's death and its most terrific cause, imagination added a ten-fold weight of woe. I believed myself to be polluted by the unnatural love I had inspired, and that I was a creature cursed and set apart by nature. I thought that like another Cain,[58] I had a mark set on my forehead to shew mankind that there was a barrier between me and them. Woodville had told me that there was in my countenance an expression as if I belonged to another world; so he had seen that sign: and there it lay a gloomy mark to tell the world that there was that within my soul that no silence could render sufficiently obscure. Why when fate drove me to become this outcast from human feeling; this monster with whom none might mingle in converse and love; why had she not from that fatal and most accursed moment, shrouded me in thick mists and placed real darkness between me and my fellows so that I might never more be seen; and as I passed, like a murky cloud loaded with blight, they might only perceive me by the cold chill I should cast upon them; telling them, how truly, that something unholy was near? Then I should have lived upon this dreary heath unvisited, and blasting none by my unhallowed gaze. Alas! I verily believe that if the near prospect of death did not dull and soften my bitter feelings, if for a few months longer I had continued to live as I then lived, strong in body, but my soul corrupted to its core by a deadly cancer, if day after day I had dwelt on these dreadful sentiments I should have become mad, and should have fancied myself a living pestilence: so horrible to my own solitary thoughts did this form, this voice, and all this wretched self appear; for had it not been the source of guilt that wants a name?

This was superstition. I did not feel thus franticly when first I knew that the holy name of father was become a curse to me: but my lonely life inspired me with wild thoughts; and then when I saw Woodville and day after day he tried to win my confidence and I never dared give words to my dark tale, I was impressed more strongly with the withering fear that I was in truth a marked creature, a pariah, only fit for death.

— CHAPTER XII —

As I was perpetually haunted by these ideas, you may imagine that the influence of Woodville's words was very temporary; and that although I did not again accuse him of unkindness, yet I soon became as unhappy as before. Soon after this incident we parted. He heard that his mother was ill, and he hastened to her. He came to take leave of me, and we walked together on the heath for the last time. He promised that he would come and see me again; and bade me take cheer, and to encourage what happy thoughts I could, until time and fortitude should overcome my misery, and I could again mingle in society.

"Above all other admonition on my part," he said, "cherish and follow this one: do not despair. That is the most dangerous gulph on which you perpetually totter; but you must reassure your steps, and take hope to guide you. Hope, and your wounds will be already half healed: but if you obstinately despair, there never more will be comfort for you. Believe me, my dearest friend, that there is a joy that the sun and earth and all its beauties can bestow that you will one day feel. The refreshing bliss of Love will again visit your heart, and undo the spell that binds you to woe, until you wonder how your eyes could be closed in the long night that burthens you. I dare not hope that I have inspired you with sufficient interest that the thought of me, and the affection that I shall ever bear you, will soften your melancholy and decrease the bitterness of your tears. But if my friendship can make you look on life with less disgust, beware how you injure it with suspicion. Love is a delicate sprite and easily hurt by rough jealousy. Guard, I entreat you, a firm persuasion of

---

[58] **Cain**: eldest son of Adam and Eve, branded on his forehead and cast out by God after he murdered his brother Abel; see Genesis 4.

my sincerity in the inmost recesses of your heart out of the reach of the casual winds that may disturb its surface. Your temper is made unequal by suffering, and the tenor of your mind is, I fear, sometimes shaken by unworthy causes; but let your confidence in my sympathy and love be deeper far, and incapable of being reached by these agitations that come and go, and if they touch not your affections leave you uninjured."

These were some of Woodville's last lessons. I wept as I listened to him; and after we had taken an affectionate farewell, I followed him far with my eyes until they saw the last of my earthly comforter. I had insisted on accompanying him across the heath towards the town where he dwelt: the sun was yet high when he left me, and I turned my steps towards my cottage. It was at the latter end of the month of September when the nights have become chill. But the weather was serene, and as I walked on I fell into no unpleasing reveries. I thought of Woodville with gratitude and kindness and did not, I know not why, regret his departure with any bitterness. It seemed that after one great shock all other change was trivial to me; and I walked on wondering when the time would come when we should all four, my dearest father restored to me, meet in some sweet Paradise. I pictured to myself a lovely river such as that on whose banks Dante describes Mathilda gathering flowers, which ever flows

——— bruna, bruna,
Sotto l'ombra perpetua, che mai
Raggiar non lascia sole ivi, nè Luna.[59]

And then I repeated to myself all that lovely passage that relates the entrance of Dante into the terrestrial Paradise; and thought it would be sweet when I wandered on those lovely banks to see the car of light descend with my long lost parent to be restored to me. As I waited there in expectation of that moment, I thought how, of the lovely flowers that grew there, I would wind myself a chaplet and crown myself for joy: I would sing *sul margine d'un rio*,[60] my father's favourite song, and my voice gliding through the windless air would announce to him, in whatever bower he sat expecting the moment of our union, that his daughter was come. Then the mark of misery would have faded from my brow, and I should raise my eyes fearlessly to meet his, which ever beamed with the soft lustre of innocent love. When I reflected on the magic look of those deep eyes I wept, but gently, lest my sobs should disturb the fairy scene.

I was so entirely wrapt in this reverie that I wandered on, taking no heed of my steps until I actually stooped down to gather a flower for my wreath on that bleak plain where no flower grew, when I awoke from my day dream and found myself I knew not where.

The sun had set and the roseate hue which the clouds had caught from him in his descent had nearly died away. A wind swept across the plain, I looked around me and saw no object that told me where I was; I had lost myself, and in vain attempted to find my path. I wandered on, and the coming darkness made every trace indistinct by which I might be guided. At length all was veiled in the deep obscurity of blackest night; I became weary and knowing that my servant was to sleep that night at the neighbouring village, so that my absence would alarm no one; and that I was safe in this wild spot from every intruder, I resolved to spend the night where I was. Indeed I was too weary to walk further: the air was chill but I was careless of bodily inconvenience, and I thought that I was well inured to the weather during my two years of solitude, when no change of seasons prevented my perpetual wanderings.

I lay upon the grass surrounded by a darkness which not the slightest beam of light penetrated—There was no sound for the deep night had laid to sleep the insects, the only creatures that lived on the lone spot where no tree or shrub could afford shelter to aught else—There was a wondrous silence in the air that calmed my senses yet which enlivened my soul; my mind hurried from image to image and seemed to grasp an eternity. All in my heart was shadowy yet calm, until my ideas became confused and at length died away in sleep.

When I awoke it rained:[61] I was already quite wet, and my limbs were stiff and my head giddy with the chill of night. It was a drizzling, penetrating shower; as my dank hair clung to my neck and partly covered my face, I had hardly strength to part with my fingers, the long straight locks that fell before my eyes. The darkness was much dissipated and in the east where the clouds were

---

[59] Cf. Dante, *Purgatorio*, XXVIII.31–33: "quite dark under the perpetual shade, which never lets sun or moon beam enter there."

[60] **sul margine d'un rio**: *trans.* "On the edge of a brook." A song with this title by Robert Birchall was published in London in 1800.

[61] **When I awoke it rained**: Coleridge, *Rime of the Ancient Marinere,** l. 300: "And when I awoke, it rained."

least dense the moon was visible behind the thin grey cloud—

> The moon is behind, and at the full
> And yet she looks both small and dull.[62]

Its presence gave me a hope that by its means I might find my home. But I was languid and many hours passed before I could reach the cottage, dragging as I did my slow steps, and often resting on the wet earth unable to proceed.

I particularly mark this night, for it was that which has hurried on the last scene of my tragedy, which else might have dwindled on through long years of listless sorrow. I was very ill when I arrived and quite incapable of taking off my wet clothes that clung about me. In the morning, on her return, my servant found me almost lifeless, while possessed by a high fever I was lying on the floor of my room.

I was very ill for a long time, and when I recovered from the immediate danger of fever, every symptom of a rapid consumption declared itself. I was for some time ignorant of this and thought that my excessive weakness was the consequence of the fever. But my strength became less and less; as winter came on I had a cough; and my sunken cheek, before pale, burned with a hectic fever. One by one these symptoms struck me; and I became convinced that the moment I had so much desired was about to arrive and that I was dying. I was sitting by my fire, the physician who had attended me ever since my fever had just left me, and I looked over his prescription in which digitalis[63] was the prominent medecine. "Yes," I said, "I see how this is, and it is strange that I should have deceived myself so long; I am about to die an innocent death, and it will be sweeter even than that which the opium promised."

I rose and walked slowly to the window; the wide heath was covered by snow which sparkled under the beams of the sun that shone brightly through the pure, frosty air: a few birds were pecking some crumbs under my window. I smiled with quiet joy; and in my thoughts, which through long habit would for ever connect themselves into one train, as if I shaped them into words, I thus addressed the scene before me:

"I salute thee, beautiful Sun, and thou, white Earth, fair and cold! Perhaps I shall never see thee again covered with green, and the sweet flowers of the coming spring will blossom on my grave. I am about to leave thee; soon this living spirit which is ever busy among strange shapes and ideas, which belong not to thee, soon it will have flown to other regions and this emaciated body will rest insensate on thy bosom

> Rolled round in earth's diurnal course
> With rocks, and stones, and trees.[64]

"For it will be the same with thee, who art called our Universal Mother, when I am gone. I have loved thee; and in my days both of happiness and sorrow I have peopled your solitudes with wild fancies of my own creation. The woods, and lakes, and mountains which I have loved, have for me a thousand associations; and thou, oh, Sun! has smiled upon, and borne your part in many imaginations that sprung to life in my soul alone, and which will die with me. Your solitudes, sweet land, your trees and waters will still exist, moved by your winds, or still beneath the eye of noon, though what I have felt about ye, and all my dreams which have often strangely deformed thee, will die with me. You will exist to reflect other images in other minds, and ever will remain the same, although your reflected semblance vary in a thousand ways, changeable as the hearts of those who view thee. One of these fragile mirrors, that ever doted on thine image, is about to be broken, crumbled to dust. But ever teeming Nature will create another and another, and thou wilt lose nought by my destruction.

"Thou wilt ever be the same. Receive then the grateful farewell of a fleeting shadow who is about to disappear, who joyfully leaves thee, yet with a last look of affectionate thankfulness. Farewell! Sky, and fields and woods; the lovely flowers that grow on thee; thy mountains and thy rivers; to the balmy air and the strong wind of the north, to all, a last farewell. I shall shed no more tears for my task is almost fulfilled, and I am about to be rewarded for long and most burthensome suffering. Bless thy child even in death, as I bless thee; and let me sleep at peace in my quiet grave."

I feel death to be near at hand and I am calm. I no longer despair, but look on all around me with placid affection. I find it sweet to watch the progressive decay of my strength, and to repeat to myself, another day and yet another, but again I shall not see the red leaves of autumn;

[62] Cf. S. T. Coleridge, *Christabel** (1816), ll. 18–19.

[63] **digitalis**: medicine prepared from foxglove, used for a weak heart.

[64] Cf. William Wordsworth, "A Slumber Did My Spirit Seal"* (1800), ll. 7–8.

before that time I shall be with my father. I am glad Woodville is not with me for perhaps he would grieve, and I desire to see smiles alone during the last scene of my life; when I last wrote to him I told him of my ill health but not of its mortal tendency, lest he should conceive it to be his duty to come to me for I fear lest the tears of friendship should destroy the blessed calm of my mind. I take pleasure in arranging all the little details which will occur when I shall no longer be. In truth I am in love with death; no maiden ever took more pleasure in the contemplation of her bridal attire than I in fancying my limbs already enwrapt in their shroud: is it not my marriage dress?[65] Alone it will unite me to my father when in an eternal mental union we shall never part.

I will not dwell on the last changes that I feel in the final decay of nature. It is rapid but without pain: I feel a strange pleasure in it. For long years these are the first days of peace that have visited me. I no longer exhaust my miserable heart by bitter tears and frantic complaints; I no longer reproach the sun, the earth, the air, for pain and wretchedness. I wait in quiet expectation for the closing hours of a life which has been to me most sweet and bitter. I do not die not having enjoyed life; for sixteen years I was happy: during the first months of my father's return I had enjoyed ages of pleasure: now indeed I am grown old in grief; my steps are feeble like those of age; I have become peevish and unfit for life; so having passed little more than twenty years upon the earth I am more fit for my narrow grave than many are when they reach the natural term of their lives.

Again and again I have passed over in my remembrance the different scenes of my short life: if the world is as a stage[66] and I merely an actor on it my part has been strange, and, alas! tragical. Almost from infancy I was deprived of all the testimonies of affection which children generally receive; I was thrown entirely upon my own resources, and I enjoyed what I may almost call unnatural pleasures, for they were dreams and not realities. The earth was to me a magic lantern and I [a] gazer, and a listener but no actor; but then came the transporting and soul-reviving era of my existence: my father returned and I could pour my warm affections on a human heart; there was a new sun and a new earth created to me; the waters of existence sparkled: joy! joy! but, alas! what grief! My bliss was more rapid than the progress of a sunbeam on a mountain, which discloses its glades and woods, and then leaves it dark and blank; to my happiness followed madness and agony, closed by despair.

This was the drama of my life which I have now depicted upon paper. During three months I have been employed in this task. The memory of sorrow has brought tears; the memory of happiness a warm glow the lively shadow of that joy. Now my tears are dried; the glow has faded from my cheeks, and with a few words of farewell to you, Woodville, I close my work; the last that I shall perform.

Farewell, my only living friend; you are the sole tie that binds me to existence, and now I break it. It gives me no pain to leave you; nor can our seperation give you much. You never regarded me as one of this world, but rather as a being, who for some penance was sent from the Kingdom of Shadows; and she passed a few days weeping on the earth and longing to return to her native soil. You will weep but they will be tears of gentleness. I would, if I thought that it would lessen your regret, tell you to smile and congratulate me on my departure from the misery you beheld me endure. I would say: Woodville, rejoice with your friend, I triumph now and am most happy. But I check these expressions; these may not be the consolations of the living; they weep for their own misery, and not for that of the being they have lost. No; shed a few natural tears[67] due to my memory: and if you ever visit my grave, pluck from thence a flower, and lay it to your heart: for your heart is the only tomb in which my memory will be interred.

My death is rapidly approaching and you are not near to watch the flitting and vanishing of my spirit. Do not regret this; for death is too terrible an object for the living. It is one of those adversities which hurt instead of purifying the heart; for it is so intense a misery that it hardens and dulls the feelings. Dreadful as the time was when I pursued my father towards the ocean, and found there only his lifeless corpse; yet for my own sake I should prefer that to the watching one by one his senses fade; his pulse weaken — and sleeplessly as it were devour his life in gazing. To see life in his limbs and to know that

[65] **in love with death . . . marriage dress**: *Romeo and Juliet,* III.ii.136–137: "I'll to my wedding-bed, / And death, not Romeo, take my maidenhead."

[66] **the world is as a stage**: cf. Shakespeare, *As You Like It,* II.vii.139ff: "All the world's a stage / And all the men and women merely players . . ."

[67] **natural tears**: *Paradise Lost,* XII.645: "Some natural tears they dropped, but wiped them soon."

soon life would no longer be there; to see the warm breath issue from his lips and to know they would soon be chill—I will not continue to trace this frightful picture; you suffered this torture once; I never did. And the remembrance fills your heart sometimes with bitter despair when otherwise your feelings would have melted into soft sorrow.

So day by day I become weaker, and life flickers in my wasting form, as a lamp about to lose its vivifying oil. I now behold the glad sun of May. It was May, four years ago, that I first saw my beloved father; it was in May, three years ago that my folly destroyed the only being I was doomed to love. May is returned, and I die. Three days ago, the anniversary of our meeting; and, alas! of our eternal seperation, after a day of killing emotion, I caused myself to be led once more to behold the face of nature. I caused myself to be carried to some meadows some miles distant from my cottage; the grass was being mowed, and there was the scent of hay in the fields; all the earth looked fresh and its inhabitants happy. Evening approached and I beheld the sun set. Three years ago and on that day and hour it shone through the branches and leaves of the beech wood and its beams flickered upon the countenance of him whom I then beheld for the last time. I now saw that divine orb, gilding all the clouds with unwonted splendour, sink behind the horizon; it disappeared from a world where he whom I would seek exists not; it approached a world where he exists not. Why do I weep so bitterly? Why does my heart heave with vain endeavour to cast aside the bitter anguish that covers it "as the waters cover the sea."[68] I go from this world where he is no longer and soon I shall meet him in another.

Farewell, Woodville, the turf will soon be green on my grave; and the violets will bloom on it. There is my hope and my expectation; your's are in this world; may they be fulfilled.

---

[68] Cf. Isaiah 11:9.

LETITIA ELIZABETH LANDON
(*known as* L. E. L.)

(1802–1838)

A childhood prodigy in her ability to memorize long poems, Letitia Landon achieved early fame when she began publishing poetry at the age of 15 in her neighbor William Jerdan's *Literary Gazette.* Her poetry, written with what one critic called a "fatal felicity," consciously assumed the persona of the innocent but rejected female lover. Embracing Edmund Burke's equation of "the beautiful" with a woman who is soft, delicate, tender, submissive, devoted to others, and yet tinged with melancholy, Landon's poetry repetitively constructs the narrative of female love. (See AESTHETIC THEORY.) It is the story of love rejected, love thwarted by fate and circumstances, love known only to be lost. Deriving her plots intertextually from Greek poetry (especially Sappho), medieval courtly love lyrics, and Madame de Staël's *Corinne,* rather than from her personal experiences, Landon consciously created a poetry of "beauty," of "baffled hopes and blighted affections," as her admiring biographer Laman Blanchard put it.

Landon correctly gauged the taste of her time. Her frequent publications between 1820 and 1838—six volumes of poems and four novels, in addition to numerous short stories and over a thousand miscellaneous verses for literary journals and annual giftbooks (one of which, *Heath's Book of Beauty,* she wrote and edited entirely by herself)—earned Landon enough to support separate London establishments for herself and her mother after her father's death in 1825, to send her beloved brother Whittington to Oxford University, and to purchase him a clerical living. Her editor William Jerdan estimated her income at the height of her success at a minimum of £250 sterling per annum, and £2,585 in her lifetime, a fortune by nineteenth-century standards.

But Landon paid a heavy price for her popularity. The first in a long line of female media "stars," she was expected to embody the lovelorn persona her poetry and prose constructed. By temperament affectionate and outgoing, living by herself in rooms above her former boarding school at 22 Hans Place, London, surrounded by female friends and admirers, Landon too easily entered into innocent friendships and correspondences with the painter Daniel Maclise and the Irish journalist William Maginn. These friendships were maliciously read as sexual affairs, especially after her effusive letters to Maginn, addressed to "My dearest William," were released to the press by his jealous wife. The resultant scandal forced Landon to break off her engagement to the ten-year-younger John Foster in 1835.

Once Landon, the commodified icon of female beauty, had been constructed in the public discourse as the fallen woman, she no longer had a viable literary life. Desperate to regain her reputation and literary marketability at the age of 35, she eagerly accepted the only marriage proposal she received, from George Maclean, Governor of the British slave trade outpost at Cape Coast, West Africa. Within seven months of her marriage and emigration to Africa, she was dead.

The reason for her death on 15 October 1838 from an overdose of prussic acid remains a mystery: was it suicide? an accident? murder? or even, possibly, from natural causes, as her mother and brother insisted? Rumors were rife in Britain for years to come, as her readers interpreted her death: killed out of jealousy by Maclean's banished African mistress; overcome by suicidal despair at her life in an uncivilised slave trade post; killed by Maclean in a rage at her poor housekeeping; or dead from a particularly virulent attack of the "spasmodic affections" or hysterical nervous attacks to which she had long been prone. The most likely explanation is that Landon, in an attack of nerves, accidentally took more than the two prescribed drops of her medication, prussic acid. As with Mary Wollstonecraft, the scandal of her death soon erased the value of her work in the public eye.

Landon's writings, published under the diminutive signature of L. E. L., can best be understood as an attempt to commodify the concept of ideal feminine beauty constructed by the patriarchal culture of this period. Landon accepts an essentialist definition of "woman" as "the one who loves," endorsing Byron's dictum in *Don Juan** that love is "woman's whole existence." Her poetry obsessively and repetitively details every nuance of female love, of female sympathy, of female imagination in the service of the affections, always arriving at the same narrative conclusion: such love is futile.

In the poems included here, the woman who loves is inevitably rejected, abandoned, or merely forgotten by her lover. *The Lost Pleiade* rewrites the Greek myth of *Endymion* from the perspective of the abandoned woman, just as the ballad of "The Proud Ladye" refocuses Keat's ballad of "La Belle Dame sans Merci"* on the feelings of the rejected lady. Adeline, in despair at the rejection of her proffered love, grows "wan and pale" and finally takes refuge from the homosocial desire of men in an all-female but still imprisoning community, "Saint Marie's cell." For Landon, the cause of female sorrow and despair is always the reckless, unfeeling, even deliberate, cruelty of men. In "Love's Last Lesson," set in contemporary England, the modest young woman's love is aroused only to be contemptuously dismissed.

"Love's Last Lesson" further suggests that a woman who cannot speak her love cannot speak *at all*. Since her whole existence is love, she has no language but that of love, of the private or domestic affections. She cannot inhabit the public realm of masculine discourse. When a woman does try to carry her commitment to love into the public sphere, as do the female poets in *Erinna* and *A History of the Lyre,* they win fame but experience only a loss of self, even of the air they breathe: Erinna survives "only in others' breath." Landon accepts the doctrine of the separate spheres, the belief that men inhabit the realm of intellect and ambition, women the realm of feeling and the body. Thus when Eulalia in *A History of the Lyre* moves from her secluded home into the public eye, she becomes diseased; when she returns to the domestic realm, having been infected by ambition, she finds only "utter weariness" and death.

Landon's poetry is grounded on the ideological construction of the female as essentially beautiful, essentially loving. By equating the essence of woman with her body, Landon restricted the kind of knowledge that women could possess to physical sensations and the emotions they produce. Landon implicitly endorsed David Hume's sceptical argument that the mind can know only the empirical sensations transmitted through the body, but she confined this argument to the female sex. Landon's heroines are conscious only of what they can experience through the body, on earth; they have no conception of an afterlife. When love dies, they die.

Working from *within* this definition of the female as the beautiful and the loving, Landon's poetry uncovers the emptiness, the self-defeating consequences, of such a social construction of the feminine gender. The beauty of her heroines inevitably fades, leaving them "wan and pale"; even the air they breathe is taken from them: "I lived / Only in others' breath." Her heroines are faithful to the love that constitutes their whole existence, but that love is never reciprocated. Their natural fertility is thus rendered barren. If they attempt to cross the barrier between the private and the public, taking love and beauty into the public sphere, their lifeblood is infected by the fatal plague of ambition and vanity. Landon thus uncovers the nihilism at the core of her culture's hegemonic construction of woman as the Beautiful.

from THE IMPROVISATRICE
(1824)

Sappho's Song[1]
(1824)

Farewell, my lute!—and would that I
Had never waked thy burning chords!
Poison has been upon thy sigh,
And fever has breathed in thy words.

Yet wherefore, wherefore should I blame
Thy power, thy spell, my gentlest lute?
I should have been the wretch I am,
Had every chord of thine been mute.

It was my evil star above,
Not my sweet lute, that wrought me wrong;
It was not song that taught me love,
But it was love that taught me song.

If song be passed, and hope undone,
And pulse, and head, and heart, are flame;
It is thy work, thou faithless one!
But, no!—I will not name thy name;

Sun-god, lute, wreath are vowed to thee!
Long be their light upon my grave—
My glorious grave—yon deep blue sea:
I shall sleep calm beneath its wave!

[1] **Sappho**: early Greek lyric poet who wrote in the sixth century BC. An aristocrat who lived on the island of Lesbos, Sappho is most famous for her love poems addressed to other women. According to later legend, probably unfounded, she killed herself for love (of Phaon, a male youth) by jumping off mount Leucas into the sea.

from THE TROUBADOUR
(1825)

The Proud Ladye.[1]
(1825)

Oh, what could the ladye's beauty match,
An it were not the ladye's pride?
An hundred knights from far and near
Woo'd at that ladye's side.

The rose of the summer slept on her cheek,
Its lily upon her breast,
And her eye shone forth like the glorious star
That rises the first in the west.

There were some that woo'd for her land and gold,
And some for her noble name,
And more that woo'd for her loveliness;—
But her answer was still the same.

"There is a steep and lofty wall,
Where my warders trembling stand,
He who at speed shall ride round its height,
For him shall be my hand."

Many turn'd away from the deed,
The hope of their wooing o'er;
But many a young knight mounted the steed
He never mounted more.

[1] "This ballad is also taken, with some slight change, from a legend in Russell's Germany." [L. E. L.] **Russell's Germany**: reference to *A Tour of Germany* (1824), by John Russell.

At last there came a youthful knight,
From a strange and far countrie,
The steed that he rode was white as the foam
Upon a stormy sea.

And she who had scorn'd the name of love,
Now bow'd before its might,
And the ladye grew meek, as if disdain
Were not made for that stranger knight.

She sought at first to steal his soul
By dance, song, and festival;
At length on bended knee she pray'd
He would not ride the wall.

But gaily the young knight laugh'd at her fears,
And flung him on his steed,—
There was not a saint in the calendar
That she pray'd not to in her need.

She dared not raise her eyes to see
If Heaven had granted her prayer,
Till she heard a light step bound to her side,—
The gallant knight stood there!

And took the ladye ADELINE
From her hair a jewell'd band,
But the knight repell'd the offer'd gift,
And turn'd from the offer'd hand.

And deemest thou that I dared this deed,
Ladye, for love of thee?
The honour that guides the soldier's lance
Is mistress enough for me.

Enough for me to ride the ring,
The victor's crown to wear;
But not in honour of the eyes
Of any ladye there.

I had a brother whom I lost.
Through thy proud crueltie,
And far more was to me his love,
Than woman's love can be.

I came to triumph o'er the pride
Through which that brother fell,
I laugh to scorn thy love and thee,
And now, proud dame, farewell!

And from that hour the ladye pined,
For love was in her heart,
And on her slumber there came dreams
She could not bid depart.

Her eye lost all its starry light,
Her cheek grew wan and pale,
Till she hid her faded loveliness
Beneath the sacred veil.

And she cut off her long dark hair,
And bade the world farewell,
And she now dwells a veiled nun
In Saint Marie's cell.

from THE GOLDEN VIOLET, WITH ITS TALES OF ROMANCE AND CHIVALRY

(1827)

from Sir Walter Manny at His Father's Tomb: The Poet's Epilogue

(1827)

. . . .

My task is ended; it may seem
But vain regret for morning dream,
To say how sad a look is cast
Over the line we know the last.
The weary hind[1] at setting sun
Rejoices over labour done,
The hunter at the ended chase,
The ship above its anchoring-place,
The pilgrim o'er his pilgrimage,
The reader o'er the closing page;
All, for end is to them repose.
The poet's lot is not with those:
His hour in paradise is o'er;
He stands on earth, and takes his share
Of shadows closing round him more,
The feverish hope, the freezing care;
And he must read in other eyes,
Or if his spirit's sacrifice
Shall brighten, touch'd with heaven's own fire,
Or in its ashes dark expire.

[1] **hind**: an agricultural laborer or farm servant.

Then even worse,—what art thou, fame?
A various and doubtful claim
One grants and one denies; what none
Can wholly quite agree upon.
A dubious and uncertain path
At least the modern minstrel hath;
How may he tell, where none agree,
What may fame's actual passport be?

For me, in sooth, not mine the lute
    On its own powers to rely;
But its chords with all wills to suit,
    It were an easier task to try
To blend in one each varying tone
The midnight wind hath ever known.
One saith that tale of battle brand
Is all too rude for my weak hand;
Another, too much sorrow flings
Its pining cadence o'er my strings.
So much to win, so much to lose,
No marvel if I fear to choose.
How can I tell of battle-field,
I never listed brand to wield,[2]
Or dark ambition's pathway try,
In truth I never look'd so high,
Or stern revenge, or hatred fell,
Of what I know not, can I tell?
I soar not on such lofty wings,
My lute has not so many strings;
Its dower is but a humble dower,
    And I who call upon its aid,
My power is but a woman's power,
    Of softness and of sadness made.
In all its changes my own heart
Must give the colour, have its part.
If that I know myself what keys
Yield to my hand their sympathies,
I should say it is those whose tone
Is woman's love and sorrow's own;
Such notes as float upon the gale,
When twilight, tender nurse and pale,
Brings soothing airs and silver dew
The panting roses to renew;
Feelings whose truth is all their worth,
Thoughts which have had their pensive birth
When lilies[3] hang their heads and die,
Eve's lesson of mortality.
Such lute, and with such humble wreath
As suits frail string and trembling breath,
Such, gentle reader, woos thee now.
Oh! o'er it bend with yielding brow:
Read thou it when some soften'd mood
Is on thy hour of solitude;
And tender memory, sadden'd thought,
On the world's harsher cares have wrought.
Bethink thee, kindly look and word
Will fall like sunshine o'er each chord;
That, light as is such boon to thee,
'Tis more than summer's noon to me;
That, if such meed my suit hath won,
I shall not mourn my task is done.

[2] **never listed brand to wield:** L.E.L. uses somewhat archaic language here, signifying that the poet was never inclined to bear or use a sword in battle.

[3] **lilies:** characteristically white, showy flower, symbolically associated with purity, mortality, and innocence; in Christian imagery, an emblem of the Virgin Mary and Christ's resurrection.

Erinna
(1827)

—INTRODUCTORY NOTICE—

Among the obligations I owe to "The Brides of Florence,"[1] and to the information contained in its interesting notes, I must refer particularly for the origin of the present poem. In one of those notes is the first, indeed the only account I ever met with of Erinna. The following short quotation is sufficient for my present purpose:—"Erinna was a poetess from her cradle, and she only lived to the completion of her eighteenth year.—Of Erinna very little is known; there is in the Grecian Anthology a sepulchral epigram by Antipater[2] on this young poetess. A

[1] **"The Brides of Florence":** Randolph Fitz-Eustace, pseud. [W. Fraser], *The Brides of Florence: a play, in five acts: illustrative of the Manners of the Middle Ages; with Historical notes, and minor poems* (London, 1824). The discussion of Erinna, a contemporary of Sappho, appears on pp. 230–33.

[2] **Grecian Anthology:** the Greek or Palatine Anthology, a collection from the tenth century AD of around 4,000 poems, mostly epigrams, written from the seventh century BC to the

poem of the present kind had long floated on my imagination; and this gave it a local habitation and a name.[3] There seemed to me just enough known of Erinna to interest; and I have not attempted to write a classical fiction; feelings are what I wish to narrate, not incidents: my aim has been to draw the portrait and trace the changes of a highly poetical mind, too sensitive perhaps of the chill and bitterness belonging even to success. The feelings which constitute poetry are the same in all ages, they are acted upon by similar causes. Erinna is an ideal not a historical picture,[4] and as such I submit it less to the judgment than to the kindness of my friends.

....

Was she of spirit race, or was she one
Of earth's least earthly daughters, one to whom
A gift of loveliness and soul is given,
Only to make them wretched?

There is an antique gem,[5] on which her brow
Retains its graven beauty even now.
Her hair is braided, but one curl behind
Floats as enamour'd of the summer wind;
The rest is simple. Is she not too fair
Even to think of maiden's sweetest care?
The mouth and brow are contrasts. One so
fraught
With pride, the melancholy pride of thought
Conscious of power, and yet forced to know
How little way such power as that can go;
Regretting, while too proud of the fine mind,
Which raises but to part it from its kind:
But the sweet mouth had nothing of all this;
It was a mouth the rose had lean'd to kiss
For her young sister, telling, now though mute,
How soft an echo it was to the lute.
The one spoke genius, in its high revealing;
The other smiled a woman's gentle feeling.
It was a lovely face: the Greek outline
Flowing, yet delicate and feminine;
The glorious lightning of the kindled eye,
Raised, as it communed with its native sky
A lovely face, the spirit's fitting shrine;
The one almost, the other quite divine.

My hand is on the lyre,[6] which never more
With its sweet commerce, like a bosom friend,
Will share the deeper thoughts which I could trust
Only to music and to solitude.
It is the very grove, the olive grove,
Where first I laid my laurel crown[7] aside,
And bathed my fever'd brow in the cold stream;
As if that I could wash away the fire
Which from that moment kindled in my heart.
I well remember how I flung myself,
Like a young goddess, on a purple cloud
Of light and odour—the rich violets
Were so ethereal in bloom and breath:
And I—I felt immortal, for my brain
Was drunk and mad with its first draught of fame.
'Tis strange there was one only cypress[8] tree,
And then, as now, I lay beneath its shade.
The night had seen me pace my lonely room,
Clasping the lyre I had no heart to wake,
Impatient for the day: yet its first dawn
Came cold as death; for every pulse sank down,
Until the very presence of my hope
Became to me a fear. The sun rose up;
I stood alone 'mid thousands: but I felt
Mine inspiration; and, as the last sweep
Of my song died away amid the hills,
My heart reverb'rated the shout which bore
To the blue mountains and the distant heaven

---

time of the collection itself. The epigram—originally, as with the **sepulchral epigram**, an inscription carved on a burial or other monument—became one of the principal poetic forms of classical Greece, distinguished by its condensation and wit. **Antipater**: Antipater of Sidon (present-day Lebanon), a Greek poet of the first century BC. His epigram on Erinna, who died at the age of nineteen, is in volume II of the Loeb *Greek Anthology* (ed. W. R. Paton).

[3] **a local habitation and a name**: Cf. Shakespeare, *A Midsummer Night's Dream*, V.i.15–17: "the poet's pen . . . gives to airy nothing / A local habitation and a name."

[4] **an ideal not a historical picture**: Landon refers here to Aristotle's opposition in the *Poetics* (section IX) between poetry, which gives "general truth" (what might happen, the typical or universal), and history, which gives "particular facts" (the actual and singular case).

[5] **gem**: a precious stone carved with a design which is either raised in relief (cameo) or cut into the surface (intaglio).

[6] **lyre**: See note 12 to *The Lost Pleiad* below.

[7] **laurel crown**: a crown woven of the leaves and twigs of the bay laurel, a tree native to the Mediterranean and sacred to the Greek god Apollo; the crown was awarded to the victor in athletic, military, or as in this case, poetic contests.

[8] **cypress**: here, the Italian cypress, an evergreen which since ancient times has symbolized mourning.

ERINNA's name, and on my bended knee,
Olympus,[9] I received thy laurel crown.

And twice new birth of violets have sprung,
Since they were first my pillow, since I sought
In the deep silence of the olive grove
The dreamy happiness which solitude
Brings to the soul o'erfilled with its delight:
For I was like some young and sudden heir
Of a rich palace heap'd with gems and gold,
Whose pleasure doubles as he sums his wealth
And forms a thousand plans of festival;
Such were my myriad visions of delight.
The lute, which hitherto in Delphian[10] shades
Had been my twilight's solitary joy,
Would henceforth be a sweet and breathing bond
Between me and my kind. Orphan unloved,
I had been lonely from my childhood's hour,
Childhood whose very happiness is love:
But that was over now; my lyre would be
My own heart's true interpreter, and those
To whom my song was dear, would they not bless
The hand that waken'd it? I should be loved
For the so gentle sake of those soft chords
Which mingled others' feelings with mine own.

Vow'd I that song to meek and gentle thoughts,
To tales that told of sorrow and of love,
To all our nature's finest touches, all
That wakens sympathy: and I should be
Alone no longer; every wind that bore,
And every lip that breathed one strain of mine,
Henceforth partake in all my joy and grief.
Oh! glorious is the gifted poet's lot,
And touching more than glorious: 'tis to be
Companion of the heart's least earthly hour;
The voice of love and sadness, calling forth
Tears from their silent fountain: 'tis to have
Share in all nature's loveliness; giving flowers
A life as sweet, more lasting than their own;
And catching from green wool and lofty pine
Language mysterious as musical;
Making the thoughts, which else had only been
Like colours on the morning's earliest hour,
Immortal, and worth immortality;
Yielding the hero that eternal name
For which he fought; making the patriot's deed
A stirring record for long after-time;
Cherishing tender thoughts, which else had pass'd
Away like tears; and saving the loved dead
From death's worst part—its deep forgetfulness.

From the first moment when a falling leaf,
Or opening bud, or streak of rose-touch'd sky,
Waken'd in me the flush and flow of song,
I gave my soul entire unto the gift
I deem'd mine own, direct from heaven; it was
The hope, the bliss, the energy of life;
I had no hope that dwelt not with my lyre,
No bliss whose being grew not from my lyre,
No energy undevoted to my lyre.
It was my other self, that had a power;
Mine, but o'er which I had not a control.
At times it was not with me, and I felt
A wonder how it ever had been mine:
And then a word, a look of loveliness,
A tone of music, call'd it into life;
A song came gushing, like the natural tears,
To check whose current does not rest with us.

Had I lived ever in the savage woods,
Or in some distant island, which the sea
With wind and wave guards in deep loneliness;
Had my eye never on the beauty dwelt
Of human face, and my ear never drank
The music of a human voice; I feel
My spirit would have pour'd itself in song,
Have learn'd a language from the rustling leaves,
The singing of the birds, and of the tide.
Perchance, then, happy had I never known
Another thought could be attach'd to song
Than of its own delight. Oh! let me pause
Over this earlier period, when my heart
Mingled its being with its pleasures, fill'd
With rich enthusiasm, which once flung
Its purple colouring o'er all things of earth,
And without which our utmost power of thought
But sharpens arrows that will drink our blood.
Like woman's soothing influence o'er man
Enthusiasm is upon the mind;
Softening and beautifying that which is

---

[9] **Olympus:** the highest mountain in Greece (9,750 feet), whose summit in the ancient period was held to be the home of the gods.

[10] **Delphian shades:** referring to Delphi, ancient town in central Greece near the foot of Mount Parnassus; site of a temple to Apollo which housed the Delphic oracle, a priestess through whom the god spoke in response to human questions.

Too harsh and sullen in itself. How much
I loved the painter's glorious art, which forms
A world like, but more beautiful than this;
Just catching nature in her happiest mood!
How drank I in fine poetry, which makes
The hearing passionate, fill'd with memories
Which steal from out the past like rays from clouds!
And then the sweet songs of my native vale,
Whose sweetness and whose softness call'd to mind
The perfume of the flowers, the purity
Of the blue sky; oh, how they stirr'd my soul!—
Amid the many golden gifts which heaven
Has left, like portions of its light, on earth
None hath such influence as music hath.
The painter's hues stand visible before us
In power and beauty; we can trace the thoughts
Which are the workings of the poet's mind:
But music is a mystery, and viewless
Even when present, and is less man's act,
And less within his order; for the hand
That can call forth the tones, yet cannot tell
Whither they go, or if they live or die,
When floated once beyond his feeble ear;
And then, as if it were an unreal thing,
The wind will sweep from the neglected strings
As rich a swell as ever minstrel drew.

A poet's word, a painter's touch, will reach
The innermost recesses of the heart,
Making the pulses throb in unison
With joy or grief, which we can analyse;
There is the cause for pleasure and for pain:
But music moves us, and we know not why;
We feel the tears, but cannot trace their source.
Is it the language of some other state,
Born of its memory? For what can wake
The soul's strong instinct of another world,
Like music? Well with sadness doth it suit
To hear the melancholy sounds decay,
And think (for thoughts are life's great human links,
And mingle with our feelings) even so
Will the heart's wildest pulses sink to rest.

How have I loved, when the red evening fill'd
Our temple with its glory, first, to gaze
On the strange contrast of the crimson air,
Lighted as if with passion, and flung back,
From silver vase and tripod rich with gems,
To the pale statues round, where human life
Was not, but beauty was, which seem'd to have
Apart existence from humanity:
Then, to go forth where the tall waving pines
Seem'd as behind them roll'd a golden sea
Immortal and eternal; and the boughs,
That darkly swept between me and its light,
Were fitting emblems of the worldly cares
That are the boundary between us and heaven;
Meanwhile, the wind, a wilful messenger
Lingering amid the flowers on his way,
At intervals swept past in melody,
The lutes and voices of the choral hymn
Contending with the rose-breath on his wing!
Perhaps it is these pleasures' chiefest charm,
They are so indefinable, so vague.
From earliest childhood all too well aware
Of the uncertain nature of our joys,
It is delicious to enjoy, yet know
No after-consequence will be to weep.
Pride misers with enjoyment, when we have
Delight in things that are but of the mind:
But half humility when we partake
Pleasures that are half wants, the spirit pines
And struggles in its fetters, and disdains
The low base clay to which it is allied.
But here our rapture raises us: we feel
What glorious power is given to man, and find
Our nature's nobleness and attributes,
Whose heaven is intellect; and we are proud
To think how we can love those things of earth
Which are least earthly; and the soul grows pure
In this high communing, and more divine.

This time of dreaming happiness pass'd by,
Another spirit was within my heart;
I drank the maddening cup of praise, which grew
Henceforth the fountain of my life; I lived
Only in others' breath; a word, a look,
Were of all influence on my destiny:
If praise they spoke, 'twas sunlight to my soul;
Or censure, it was like the scorpion's sting.

And yet a darker lesson was to learn—
The hollowness of each: that praise, which is
But base exchange of flattery; that blame,
Given by cautious coldness, which still deems
'Tis safest to depress; that mockery,
Flinging shafts but to show its own keen aim;
That carelessness, whose very censure's chance;
And, worst of all, the earthly judgment pass'd

By minds whose native clay is unredeem'd
By aught of heaven, whose every thought falls foul
Plague-spot on beauty which they cannot feel,
Tainting all that it touches with itself.
O dream of fame, what hast thou been to me
But the destroyer of life's calm content!
I feel so more than ever, that thy sway
Is weaken'd over me. Once I could find
A deep and dangerous delight in thee;
But that is gone. I am too much awake.
Light has burst o'er me, but not morning's light;
'Tis such light as will burst upon the tomb,
When all but judgment's over. Can it be,
That these fine impulses, these lofty thoughts,
Burning with their own beauty, are but given
To make me the low slave of vanity,
Heartless and humbled? O my own sweet power,
Surely thy songs were made for more than this!
What a worst waste of feeling and of life
Have been the imprints of my roll of time,
Too much, too long! To what use have I turn'd
The golden gifts in which I pride myself?
They are profaned; with their pure ore I made
A temple resting only on the breath
Of heedless worshippers. Alas! that ever
Praise should have been what it has been to me—
The opiate of my heart. Yet I have dream'd
Of things which cannot be; the bright, the pure,
That all of which the heart may only dream;
And I have mused upon my gift of song,
And deeply felt its beauty, and disdain'd
The pettiness of praise to which at times
My soul has bow'd; and I have scorn'd myself
For that my cheek could burn, my pulses beat
At idle words. And yet, it is in vain
For the full heart to press back every throb
Wholly upon itself. Ay, fair as are
The visions of a poet's solitude,
There must be something more for happiness;
They seek communion. It had seem'd to me
A miser's selfishness, had I not sought
To share with others those impassion'd thoughts,
Like light, or hope, or love, in their effects.
When I have watch'd the stars write on the sky
In characters of light, have seen the moon
Come like a veiled priestess from the east,
While, like a hymn, the wind swell'd on mine ear,
Telling soft tidings of eve's thousand flowers,
Has it not been the transport of my lute
To find its best delight in sympathy?
Alas! the idols which our hopes set up,
They are Chaldean[11] ones, half gold, half clay;
We trust, we are deceived, we hope, we fear,
Alike without foundation; day by day
Some new illusion is destroyed, and life
Gets cold and colder on towards its close.
Just like the years which make it, some are check'd
By sudden blights in spring; some are dried up
By fiery summers; others waste away
In calm monotony of quiet skies,
And peradventure[12] these may be the best:
They know no hurricanes, no floods that sweep
As a God's vengence were upon each wave;
But then they have no ruby fruits, no flowers
Shining in purple, and no lighted mines
Of gold and diamond. Which is the best,—
Beauty and glory, in a southern clime,
Mingled with thunder, tempest; or the calm
Of skies that scarcely change, which, at the least,
If much of shine they have not, have no storms?
I know not: but I know fair earth or sky
Are self-consuming in their loveliness,
And the too radiant sun and fertile soil
In their luxuriance run themselves to waste,
And the green valley and the silver stream
Become a sandy desert. O! the mind,
Too vivid in its lighted energies,
May read its fate in sunny Araby.[13]
How lives its beauty in each Eastern tale,
Its growth of spices, and its groves of balm!
They are exhausted; and what is it now?
A wild and burning wilderness. Alas!
For such similitude. Too much this is
The fate of this world's loveliest and best.

Is there not a far people, who possess
Mysterious oracles of olden time,
Who say that this earth labours with a curse,
That it is fallen from its first estate,

[11] **Chaldean**: referring to an ancient region in southern Mesopotamia (present-day Iraq), successor to the Babylonian empire in the seventh century BC.

[12] **peradventure**: perhaps, by chance (archaic).

[13] **Araby**: Arabia, which Landon reads through the "Eastern tales" of the *Thousand and One Nights*, a collection of stories from India, Persia, and the Arab world.

And is now but the shade of what it was?
I do believe the tale. I feel its truth
In my vain aspirations, in the dreams
That are revealings of another world,
More pure, more perfect than our weary one,
Where day is darkness to the starry soul.

O heart of mine! my once sweet paradise
Of love and hope! how changed thou art to me!
I cannot count thy changes: thou hast lost
Interest in the once idols of thy being;
They have departed, even as if wings
Had borne away their morning; they have left
Weariness, turning pleasure into pain,
And too sure knowledge of their hollowness.

And that too is gone from me; that which was
My solitude's delight! I can no more
Make real existence of a shadowy world.
Time was, the poet's song, the ancient tale,
Were to me fountains of deep happiness,
For they grew visible in my lonely hours,
As things in which I had a deed and part;
Their actual presence had not been more true:
But these are bubbling sparkles, that are found
But at the spring's first source. Ah! years may bring
The mind to its perfection, but no more
Will those young visions live in their own light;
Life's troubles stir life's waters all too much,
Passions chase fancies, and, though still we dream,
The colouring is from reality.

Farewell, my lyre! thou hast not been to me
All I once hoped. What is the gift of mind,
But as a barrier to so much that makes
Our life endurable,—companionship,
Mingling affection, calm and gentle peace,
Till the vex'd spirit seals with discontent
A league of sorrow and of vanity,
Built on a future which will never be!

And yet I would resign the praise that now
Makes my cheek crimson, and my pulses beat,
Could I but deem that when my hand is cold,
And my lip passionless, my songs would be
Number'd 'mid the young poet's first delights;
Read by the dark-eyed maiden in an hour
Of moonlight, till her cheek shone with its tears;
And murmur'd by the lover when his suit
Calls upon poetry to breathe of love.
I do not hope a sunshine burst of fame,
My lyre asks but a wreath of fragile flowers.
I have told passionate tales of breaking hearts,
Of young cheeks fading even before the rose;
My songs have been the mournful history
Of woman's tenderness and woman's tears;
I have touch'd but the spirit's gentlest chords,—
Surely the fittest for my maiden hand;—
And in their truth my immortality.

Thou lovely and lone star, whose silver light,
Like music o'er the waters,[14] steals along
The soften'd atmosphere; pale star, to thee
I dedicate the lyre, whose influence
I would have sink upon the heart like thine.

In such an hour as this, the bosom turns
Back to its early feelings; man forgets
His stern ambition and his worldly cares,
And woman loathes the petty vanities
That mar her nature's beauty; like the dew,
Shedding its sweetness o'er the sleeping flowers
Till all their morning freshness is revived,
Kindly affections, sad but yet sweet thoughts,
Melt the cold eyes, long, long unused to weep.
O lute of mine, that I shall wake no more!
Such tearful music, linger on thy strings,
Consecrate unto sorrow and to love;
Thy truth, thy tenderness, be all thy fame!

Love's Last Lesson
(1827)

Teach it me, if you can,—forgetfulness![1]
I surely shall forget, if you can bid me;
I who have worshipp'd thee, my god on earth,
I who have bow'd me at thy lightest word.
Your last command, "Forget me," will it not
Sink deeply down within my inmost soul?
Forget thee!—ay, forgetfulness will be
A mercy to me. By the many nights,
When I have wept for that I dared not sleep,—
A dream had made me live my woes again,

[14] **music o'er the waters**: cf. Shakespeare, *The Tempest*, I.ii.392: "This music crept by me upon the waters."

[1] **Teach . . . forgetfulness!**: cf. Byron, *Manfred*,* I.i.135–136: "What wouldst thou with us, son of mortals—say?" Manfred: "Forgetfulness—."

Acting my wretchedness, without the hope
My foolish heart still clings to, though that hope
Is like the opiate which may lull a while,
Then wake to double torture; by the days
Pass'd in lone watching, and in anxious fears,
When a breath sent the crimson to my cheek,
Like the red gushing of a sudden wound;
By all the careless looks and careless words
Which have to me been like the scorpion's stinging;
By happiness blighted, and by thee, for ever;
By thy eternal work of wretchedness;
By all my wither'd feelings, ruin'd health,
Crush'd hopes, and rifled heart, I will forget thee!
Alas! my words are vanity. Forget thee!
Thy work of wasting is too surely done.
The April shower may pass and be forgotten,
The rose fall and one fresh spring in its place,
And thus it may be with light summer love.
It was not thus with mine: it did not spring,
Like the bright colour on an evening cloud,
Into a moment's life, brief, beautiful;
Not amid lighted halls, when flatteries
Steal on the ear like dew upon the rose,
As soft, as soon dispersed, as quickly pass'd;
But you first call'd my woman's feelings forth,
And taught me love ere I had dream'd love's name.
I loved unconsciously: your name was all
That seem'd in language, and to me the world
Was only made for you; in solitude,
When passions hold their interchange together,
Your image was the shadow of my thought;
Never did slave, before his Eastern lord,
Tremble as I did when I met your eye,
And yet each look was counted as a prize;
I laid your words up in my heart like pearls
Hid in the ocean's treasure-cave. At last
I learn'd my heart's deep secret: for I hoped,
I dream'd, you loved me; wonder, fear, delight,
Swept my heart like a storm; my soul, my life,
Seem'd all too little for your happiness;
Had I been mistress of the starry worlds
That light the midnight, they had all been yours,
And I had deem'd such boon but poverty.
As it was, I gave all I could — my love,
My deep, my true, my fervent, faithful love;
And now you bid me learn forgetfulness:
It is a lesson that I soon shall learn.
There is a home of quiet for the wretched,
A somewhat dark, and cold, and silent rest,
But still it is rest, — for it is the grave.

She flung aside the scroll, as it had part
In her great misery. Why should she write?
What could she write? Her woman's pride forbade
To let him look upon her heart, and see
It was an utter ruin; — and cold words,
And scorn and slight, that may repay his own,
Were as a foreign language, to whose sound
She might not frame her utterance. Down she bent
Her head upon an arm so white that tears
Seem'd but the natural melting of its snow,
Touch'd by the flush'd cheek's crimson; yet life-blood
Less wrings in shedding than such tears as those.

And this then is love's ending! It is like
The history of some fair southern clime.
Hot fires are in the bosom of the earth,
And the warm'd soil puts forth its thousand flowers,
Its fruits of gold, summer's regality,
And sleep and odours float upon the air:
At length the subterranean element
Breaks from its secret dwelling-place, and lays
All waste before it; the red lava stream
Sweeps like the pestilence; and that which was
A garden in its colours and its breath,
Fit for the princess of a fairy tale,
Is as a desert, in whose burning sands,
And ashy waters, who is there can trace
A sign, a memory, of its former beauty?
It is thus with the heart; love lights it up
With hopes like young companions, and with joys
Dreaming deliciously of their sweet selves.

This is at first; but what is the result?
Hopes that lie mute in their own sullenness,
For they have quarrel'd even with themselves;
And joys indeed like birds of Paradise:[2]
And in their stead despair coils scorpion-like
Stinging itself; and the heart, burnt and crush'd
With passion's earthquake, scorch'd and wither'd up,
Lies in its desolation, — this is love.

What is the tale that I would tell? Not one
Of strange adventure, but a common tale
Of woman's wretchedness; one to be read
Daily in many a young and blighted heart.

---

[2] **birds of Paradise:** "In Eastern tales, the bird of Paradise never rests on the earth" [L.E.L.]. The bird of paradise is the general name for numerous species of birds native to New Guinea, known for brightly colored plumage and elongated tail feathers.

The lady whom I spake of rose again
From the red fever's couch, to careless eyes
Perchance the same as she had ever been.
But oh, how alter'd to herself! She felt
That bird-like pining for some gentle home
To which affection might attach itself,
That weariness which hath but outward part
In what the world calls pleasure, and that chill
Which makes life taste the bitterness of death.

And he she loved so well,—what opiate
Lull'd consciousness into its selfish sleep?—
He said he loved her not; that never vow
Or passionate pleading won her soul for him;
And that he guess'd not her deep tenderness.

Are words, then, only false? are there no looks,
Mute but most eloquent; no gentle cares
That win so much upon the fair weak things
They seem to guard? And had he not long read
Her heart's hush'd secret in the soft dark eye
Lighted at his approach, and on the cheek
Colouring all crimson at his lightest look?
This is the truth; his spirit wholly turn'd
To stern ambition's dream, to that fierce strife
Which leads to life's high places, and reck'd not
What lovely flowers might perish in his path.

And here at length is somewhat of revenge:
For man's most golden dreams of pride and power
Are vain as any woman-dreams of love;
Both end in weary brow and wither'd heart,
And the grave closes over those whose hopes
Have lain there long before.

from THE VENETIAN BRACELET
(1829)

The Lost Pleiad[1]
(1829)

A story from the stars; or rather one
Of starry fable from the olden time,
When young Imagination was as fresh
As the fair world it peopled with itself.
The Poet's spirit does so love to link
Its feelings, thoughts, with nature's loveliness:
And hence the twilight grove, the lonely spring,
The ocean-caves, the distant planets, all
Were fill'd with radiant creatures; and the heart
Became interpreter, and language made
From its own warm sad sympathies, for those
Of whom the dream was beauty.

He was weary of flinging the feather'd reed,[2]
He was weary of curbing his raven steed;
He heard the gay din from the palace hall,
But he was not in mood for the festival.
There was that crimson, the last on the sky,
Blushes that fade in the moon's cold eye;
The sigh of the flowers arose sweet on the air,
For the breath of the twilight was wandering there.
He look'd to the west, and the tranquil main
Was branch'd with many a life-like vein;
Hues of the rosebud the clouds had cast,
Like a cheek on its mirror in gliding past.
It tempted him forth,—to the lulling gale
Prince CYRIS has open'd his silken sail,
And the little boat went over the sea
Like foam, for it was of ivorie,
And carved and shaped like a wreathed shell,
And it was lined with the rose as well;
For the couch was made of those plumes that fling
The one warm tint 'neath the wood-dove's wing.
O'er the purple sail the golden flowers run,
For it was wrought for a monarch's son;
And as it pass'd on, the air was fill'd
With odours, for only waters distill'd
From clove, and sandal,[3] and cinnamon,
E'er wash'd that boat when its task was done:
'Twas left in the care of maidens three;

[1] **Pleiad**: one of the Pleiades, the seven daughters of Atlas in Greek mythology, who were transformed into stars; also a star cluster in the constellation Taurus. Only six stars of the Pleiades cluster are visible to the naked eye; the missing seventh, corresponding to a daughter who, according to legend, was lost or in hiding, is called the lost Pleiad. The Pleiad was also the name of a group of seven ancient Alexandrian poets and, in emulation of these, a group of seven classical French poets of the sixteenth century.

[2] **the feather'd reed**: arrows.

[3] **sandal**: sandalwood; the name of several aromatic tropical trees, some of them used to make incense or perfume.

Lovely they were as maidens should be;
And in the soft airs that around it flew,
Perhaps their own breath left a perfume too.
—There lay Prince CYRIS, and his mood
Made harmony with the solitude.
—Oh, pleasant is it for the heart
To gather up itself apart;
To think its own thoughts, and to be
Free, as none ever yet were free,
When, prisoners to their gilded thrall,
Vain crowd meets crowd in lighted hall;
With frozen feelings, tutor'd eye,
And smile which is itself a lie.
—Oh, but for lonely hours like these,
Would every finer current freeze;
Those kindlier impulses that glow,
Those clear and diamond streams that flow
Only in crystal, while their birth
Is all unsoil'd with stain of earth.
Ever the Lover hath gainsay'd
The creed his once religion made,—
That pure, that high, that holy creed.
Without which love is vain indeed;
While that which was a veiled shrine,
Whose faith was only not divine,
Becomes a vague, forgotten dream,—
A thing of scorn—an idle theme.
Denied, degraded, and represt,
Love dies beneath the heartless jest.
Oh vain! for not with such can be
One trace of his divinity.
Ever from poet's lute hath flown
The sweetness of its early tone,
When from its wild flight it hath bow'd,
To seek for homage mid the crowd;
Be the one wonder of the night,
As if the soul could be a sight;
As all his burning numbers speak
Were written upon brow and cheek;
And he forsooth must learn its part,
Must choose his words, and school his heart
To one set mould, and pay again
Flattery with flattery as vain;
Till, mixing with the throng too much,
The cold, the vain, he feels as such
Then marvels that his silent lute
Beneath that worldly hand is mute.
—Away! these scenes are not for thee;
Go dream beneath some lonely tree;
Away to some far woodland spring,
Dash down thy tinsel crown, and wring
The scented unguents from thine hair:
If thou dost hope that crown to share
The laurell'd bards immortal wear;
Muse thou o'er leaf and drooping flower,
Wander at evening's haunted hour;
Listen the stockdove's[4] plaining song
Until it bear thy soul along;
Then call upon thy freed lute's strain,
And it will answer thee again.
Oh mine own song, did I not hold
Such faith as held the bards of old,—
That one eternal hope of fame
Which sanctifies the poet's name,
I'd break my lyre in high disdain,
And hold my gift of song as vain
As those forced flowers which only bloom
One hot night for a banquet room.
—But I have wander'd from my tale,—
The ivory bark, the purple sail,
That bore Prince CYRIS o'er the sea,—
Content with that slow ebb to be
Danced on the wave. By nightfall shaded
The red lights from the clouds are faded;
Leaving one palest amber line
To mark the last of day's decline;
And all o'er heaven is that clear blue
The stars so love to wander through.
They're rising from the silent deep,
Like bright eyes opening after sleep.
Young CYRIS watch'd them till their ray
Grew sad—so far they were away.
He felt so earthly, thus to see
What he might never hope to be.
He thought upon earth's loveliest eyes;
  What were they to those shining there?
He thought upon earth's sweetest sighs:
  What were they to the lulling air?
"Oh no, my heart," he mournful sigh'd,
"To thee is that dear boon denied;
That wildering[5] dream whose fair deceit
Makes languid earth a temple meet
For light, such light as dwells above,—

[4] **stockdove:** a wild dove or pigeon which often lives in the hollow trunk, or stock, of a tree.

[5] **wildering:** misleading, bewildering.

I have no faith in thee, false love!
I've knelt at many a beauteous shrine,
And call'd, but thought them not, divine.
I've dived in many a beating heart,
But search'd them only to depart;
For selfish care, or heartless pride,
Were all they ever had to hide.
I'm weary, weary: — one by one,
The life-charms of my youth are gone.
I had a dream of stirring fame, —
It was a promise, and a name,
Thrice glorious, shining from afar,
But nearer earth had touch'd the star;
With toil and trouble won from many,
Yet trembling on the breath of any.
The bard, the warrior, and the sage,
What win they but one lying page,
Where deeds and words, at hazard thrown,
May be or may not be their own?
And pleasure, lighted halls, red wine,
Bright smiles, gay words, have all been mine:
They only left what haunts me now, —
A wasted heart, a weary brow.
Ye distant stars, so calm, so bright,
Would I had portion in your light,
Could read the secrets of your birth, —
Aught, any thing but this dull earth!"
— It was not long, ere, still and deep,
Those restless eyes were closed in sleep.
There lay he like a statue pale,
His canopy that silken sail.
There lay he as Endymion[6] slept
When Dian came to him, and wept
Beside the sleep she might not break.
Love, thus we sorrow for thy sake.
There lay he: — well might CYRIS seem
The being of a poet's dream.
  Ay, beautiful as a star in the sky,
When the clouds are gloom, and the storm is high,
But still in defiance keeps shining on,
Till the shades are past, and the wind is done.
His hair was gold, like the pheasant's wing,
And curl'd like the hyacinth flower in spring;
And his eye was that blue so clear, so dark,
Like the falcon's when flying his highest mark;
And, telling a tale of gallant war,
On his brow was a slight but glorious scar.
His voice had that low and lute-like sound,
Whose echo within the heart is found.
His very faults were those that win
Too dazzling and ready an entrance in.[7]
Daring, and fiery, wild to range,
Reckless of what might ensue from the change;
Too eager for pleasures to fill up the void,
Till the very impatience their nature destroy'd;
Restless, inconstant, he sought to possess, —
The danger was dar'd, and the charm grew less.
But, oh! these were only youth's meteor fires,
The ignis blaze[8] that with youth expires.
  No, never! — the heart should child-like be train'd,
And its wilful waywardness somewhat enchain'd.
— Was it the spell of morning dew
That o'er his lids its influence threw,
Clearing those earthly mists away,
That erst like veils before them lay?
Whether fair dream, or actual sight,
It was a vision of delight;
For free to his charm'd eyes were given
The spirits of the starry heaven.[9]
It was that hour, when each faint dye
  Of rose upon the morning's cheek
Warns the bright watchers of the sky
  Their other ocean home to seek.
He saw the Archer with his bow
Guide now his radiant car below;
He saw the shining Serpent[10] fold

[6] **Endymion**: in Greek mythology, a young shepherd loved by Selene, the goddess of the moon, whose Roman name was Diana. Zeus granted Endymion immortality and eternal youth, but on condition that he remain asleep forever.

[7] **His very faults . . . entrance in**: *Paradise Lost*, IX.734–735: "He ended, and his words replete with guile / Into her heart too easy entrance won."

[8] **ignis blaze**: ignis fatuus, a flickering or phosphorescent light seen over marshy ground at night; possibly caused by the spontaneous combustion of gases released by the decay of plant and animal matter.

[9] **delight . . . heaven**: cf. Wordsworth, "She Was a Phantom of Delight":* "She was a phantom of delight . . . / A lovely Apparition."

[10] **the Archer**: Sagittarius, one of the twelve constellations of the zodiac, traditionally represented as a centaur drawing a bow. **Serpent**: either the Serpens (northern sky) or Hydra (southern sky) constellations. Landon seems also to be drawing

Beneath the wave his scales of gold.
—But, of all the pageants nigh,
Only one fix'd CYRIS' eye:
Borne by music on their way,
Every chord a living ray,
Sinking on a song-like breeze,
The lyre of the Pleiades,
With its seven fair sisters bent
O'er their starry instrument;
Each a star upon her brow,
Somewhat dim in daylight's glow,
That clasp'd the flashing coronet
On their midnight tresses set.
—All were young, all very fair;—
But one,—oh! CYRIS gazed but there,
Each other lip wore sterner mould,—
Fair, but so proud,—bright, but so cold,
And clear pale cheek, and radiant eye,
Wore neither blush, nor smile, nor sigh,
Those sweet signs of humanity.
But o'er CYRENE's[11] cheek the rose,
Like moon-touch'd water, ebbs and flows;
And eyes that droop like Summer flowers
Told they could change with shine and showers.
—The starry lyre[12] has reach'd the sea,
Started young CYRIS to his knee:
Surely her dark eyes met his own;
But, ah! the lovely dream is flown.[13]
—I need not tell how long the day
Pass'd in its weariness away;
I need not say how CYRIS' sight
Pined for the darkness of the night.
But darkness came, and with it brought
The vision which the watcher sought.
He saw the starry lyre arise—
  The seven fair sisters' glittering car—
Till, lost amid the distant skies,
  Each only look'd a burning star.
Again, at morning's dewy hour,
He saw them seek their ocean bow'r;
Again those dark eyes met his own,—
Again the lovely dream is flown.
—Night after night thus pass'd; but now
The young moon wears less vestal brow.
Her silver veil is lined with gold;
Like a crown'd queen, she comes to hold
Her empire in the sky alone,—
No rival near her midnight throne.
Sometimes he fancied o'er the tide
He saw pale phantoms dimly glide:
The moonbeams fell o'er sea and sky,
No other light met CYRIS' eye.
The night,—the morn,—he watch'd in vain,
No starry lyre rose from the main.
—And who were they, the lovely seven,
With shape of earth, and home in heaven?
Daughters of King Atlas[14] they—
He of the enchanted sway;
He who read the mystic lines
Of the planets' wondrous signs;
He the sovereign of the air—
They were his, these daughters fair.
Six were brides, in sky and sea,
To some crown'd divinity;
But his youngest, loveliest one,
Was as yet unwoo'd, unwon.
She's kneeling at her father's side:
What the boon could be denied
To that fair but tear-wash'd cheek,
That look'd so earnest, yet so meek;
To that mouth whose gentle words
Murmur like the wind-lute's chords;
To that soft and pleading eye
Who is there could suit deny?
Bent the king, with look of care,
O'er the dear one kneeling there;
Bent and kiss'd his pleading one,—
Ah, that smile! her suit is won.
—It was a little fountain made
A perfect sanctuary of shade;

---

on the story of Apollo (who drove the chariot of the sun) killing the serpent Python with an arrow.

[11] **Cyrene:** Landon's name for the youngest Pleiad does not correspond to any of the seven traditional names; it was presumably chosen to match Cyris.

[12] **starry lyre:** harp-like stringed instrument associated in ancient Greece with lyric poetry; Landon imagines it as part of the Pleiades constellation, linking the different senses of Pleiad as in note 1 above.

[13] **the lovely dream is flown:** Percy Shelley, *Alastor,** ll. 192ff.

[14] **King Atlas:** father of the seven Pleiades; Titan, condemned by the gods to hold the sky on his shoulders for eternity.

The pine boughs like a roof, beneath
The tapestry of the acacia wreath.
The air was haunted: sounds, and sighs,
The falling waters' melodies;
The breath of flowers, the faint perfume
Of the green pineleaf's early bloom;
And murmurs from the music hung
Ever the woodland boughs among:
His couch of moss, his pillow flowers,
Dreaming away the listless hours—
Those dreams so vague, those dreams so vain,
Yet iron links in lover's chain.—
Prince CYRIS leant: the solitude
Suited such visionary mood;
For love hath delicate delights,—
The silence of the summer nights;
The leaves and buds, whose languid sighs
Seem like the echo of his own;
The wind which like a lute-note dies;
The shadow by the branches thrown,
Although a sweet uncertain smile
Wanders through those boughs the while,
As if the young Moon liked to know
Her fountain mirror bright below;
Linking his thoughts with all of these,
For love is full of fantasies.
—Why starts young CYRIS from his dream?
There is a shadow on the stream,
There is an odour on the air;—
What shape of beauty fronts him there!
He knows her by her clear dark eye,
Touch'd with the light that rules the sky;
The star upon her forehead set,
Her wild hair's sparkling coronet;
Her white arms, and her silvery vest,—
The lovely Pleiad stands confest.
—I cannot sing as I have sung;
My heart is changed, my lute unstrung.
Once said I that my early chords
Were vow'd to love or sorrow's words:
But love has like an odour past,
Or echo, all too sweet to last;
And sorrow now holds lonely sway
O'er my young heart, and lute, and lay.
Be it for those whose unwaked youth
Believes that hope and love are sooth—
The loved, the happy—let them dream
This meeting by the forest stream.
—No more they parted till the night
Call'd on her starry host for light,
And that bright lyre arose on high
With its fair watchers to their sky.
Then came the wanderings long and lonely,
As if the world held them, them only;
The gather'd flower, which is to bear
Some gentle secret whisper'd there;
The seat beneath the forest tree;
The breathless silence, which to love
Is all that eloquence can be;
The looks ten thousand words above;
The fond deep gaze, till the fix'd eye
Casts each on each a mingled dye;
The interest round each little word,
Though scarcely said, and scarcely heard.
Little love asks of language aid,
For never yet hath vow been made
In that young hour when love is new;
He feels at first so deep, so true,
A promise is a useless token,
When neither dreams it can be broken.
Alas! vows are his after-sign!—
We prop the tree in its decline—
The ghosts that haunt a parting hour,
With all of grief, and nought of power;
A chain half sunder'd in the making,—
The plighted vow's already breaking.
From such dreams all too soon we wake;
For, like the moonlight on the lake,
One passing cloud, one waving bough—
The silver light, what is it now?
Said I not that young prince was one
Who wearied when the goal was won;
To whom the charm of change was all
That bound his heart in woman's thrall?
And she now lingering at his side,
His bright, his half-immortal bride,
Though she had come with him to die,
Share earthly tear, and earthly sigh;
Left for his sake her glorious sphere,—
What matter'd that?—she now was here.
At first 'twas like a frightful dream:
Why should such terror even seem?
Again,—again,—it cannot be!
Woe for such wasting misery!—
This watching love's o'erclouding sky,
Though still believing it must clear;

This closing of the trusting eye;
The hope that darkens into fear;
The lingering change of doubt and dread;
All in the one dear presence fled.
Till days of anguish pass'd alone,
Till careless look, and alter'd tone,
Relieve us from the rack, to know
Our last of fate, our worst of woe.
—And she, the guileless, pure, and bright,
Whose nature was her morning's light;
Who deem'd of love as it is given
The sunniest element to heaven;
Whose sweet belief in it was caught
Only from what her own heart taught—
Her woman's heart, that dreamy shrine,
Of what itself made half divine—
CYRENE, when thy shadow came
With thy first step that touch'd the earth,
It was an omen how the same
Doth sorrow haunt all mortal birth.
Thou hast but left those starry spheres
For woman's destiny of tears.
—They parted as all lovers part,—
She with her wrong'd and breaking heart;
But he, rejoicing he is free,
Bounds like the captive from his chain,
And wilfully believing she
Hath found her liberty again:
Or if dark thoughts will cross his mind,
They are but clouds before the wind.
—Thou false one, go!—but deep and dread
Be minstrel curse upon thy head!
—Go, be the first in battle line,
Where banners sweep, and falchions[15] shine;
Go thou to lighted festival,
Be there the peerless one of all;
Let bright cheeks wear yet brighter rays
If they can catch Prince CYRIS' gaze;
Be thine in all that honour'd name
Men hold to emulate is fame:
Yet not the less my curse shall rest,
A serpent coiling in thy breast.
Weariness, like a weed, shall spring
Wherever is thy wandering.

[15] **falchions:** short, broad swords with a curved blade used in the medieval period.

Thy heart a lonely shrine shall be,
Guarded by no divinity.
Thou shalt be lonely, and shalt know
It is thyself hast made thee so.
Thou hast been faithless, and shalt dread
Deceit in aught of fondness said.
Go, with the doom thou'st made thine own!
Go, false one! to thy grave—alone.—
'Twas the red hue of twilight's hour
That lighted up the forest bower,
Where that sad Pleiad look'd her last.
The white wave of his plume is past;
She raised her listening head in vain,
To catch his echoing step again;
Then bow'd her face upon her hand,
And once or twice a burning tear
Wander'd beyond their white command,
And mingled with the waters clear.
'Tis said that ever from that day
Those waters caught their diamond ray.
—The evening shades closed o'er the sky,
The night winds sang their melody:
They seem'd to rouse her from the dream
That chain'd her by that lonely stream.
She came when first the starry lyre
Ting'd the green wave with kindling fire;
"Come, sister," sang they, "to thy place:"
The Pleiad gazed, then hid her face.
Slowly that lyre rose while they sung,—
Alas! there is one chord unstrung.
It rose, until CYRENE's ear
No longer could its music hear.
She sought the fountain, and flung there
The crown that bound her raven hair;
The starry crown, the sparkles died,
Darkening within its fated tide.
She sinks by that lone wave:—'tis past;
There the lost Pleiad breath'd her last.
No mortal hand e'er made her grave;
But one pale rose was seen to wave,
Guarding a sudden growth of flowers,
Not like those sprung in summer hours,
But pale and drooping; each appears
As if their only dew were tears.
On that sky lyre a chord is mute:
Haply[16] one echo yet remains,

[16] **Haply:** by chance, perhaps (archaic).

To linger on the poet's lute,
And tell in his most mournful strains,
—A star hath left its native sky,
To touch our cold earth, and to die;
To warn the young heart how it trust
To mortal vows, whose faith is dust;
To bid the young cheek guard its bloom
From wasting by such early doom;
Warn by the histories link'd with all
That ever bow'd to passion's thrall;
Warn by all—above—below,
By that lost Pleiad's depth of woe,—
Warn them, Love is of heavenly birth,
But turns to death on touching earth.

Revenge
(1829)

Ay, gaze upon her rose-wreath'd hair,
And gaze upon her smile;
Seem as you drank the very air
Her breath perfumed the while;

And wake for her the gifted line,
That wild and witching lay,
And swear your heart is as a shrine,
That only owns her sway.

'Tis well: I am revenged at last;—
Mark you that scornful cheek,—
The eye averted as you pass'd,
Spoke more than words could speak.

Ay, now by all the bitter tears
That I have shed for thee,—
The racking doubts, the burning fears,—
Avenged they well may be—

By the nights pass'd in sleepless care,
The days of endless woe;
All that you taught my heart to bear,
All that yourself will know.

I would not wish to see you laid
Within an early tomb;
I should forget how you betray'd,
And only weep your doom:

But this is fitting punishment,
To live and love in vain,—
O my wrung heart, be thou content,
And feed upon his pain.

Go thou and watch her lightest sigh,—
Thine own it will not be;
And bask beneath her sunny eye,—
It will not turn on thee.

'Tis well: the rack, the chain, the wheel,
Far better hadst thou proved;
Ev'n I could almost pity feel,
For thou art not beloved.

from TRAITS AND TRIALS OF EARLY LIFE
(1836)

"The History of a Child," a story included in Landon's book for children, *Traits and Trials of Early Life*, was assumed by her readers to be an autobiographical account of the fate of female genius. Many of her friends insisted, however, that the story was entirely fictional and that Landon's own childhood had been an exceptionally happy one of constant companionship with her brother Whittington and numerous school-friends.

....

The History of a Child
(1836)

How well I remember it, that single and lonely laurel tree, it was my friend, my confidant. How often have I sat rocking on the one long, pendant branch which dropped even to the grass below. I can remember the strange pleasure I took in seeing my tears fall on the bright shining leaves; often while observing them have I forgotten the grief that led to their falling. I was not a pretty child, and both shy and sensitive; I was silent, and therefore not amusing. No one loved me but an old nurse—why she should have been fond of me I know not, for I gave her much trouble; night after night has she wakened with my crying—but she only wakened to soothe me. She was far advanced in years, but was still strikingly handsome. Her face, with its bold Roman profile, its large black eyes, is still before me as I used to see it bending over my crib, and singing, or rather crooning me to sleep with the old ballad "Barbara Allen."[1] Never will the most finished music, that ever brought the air and perfume of an Italian summer upon its melody—never will it be sweet in my ears as that untaught and monotonous tone. My first real sorrow was her departure; life has been to me unhappy enough, but never has it known a deeper desolation than that first parting. It is as present as yesterday; she had married, and was now about to go to a home of her own. How I hated her husband; with the rest of the nursery he was a popular person, for he had been a sailor, and his memory was stored with wild histories of the Buccaneers; nor was he without his own perils: he had been shipwrecked on the coast of Cornwall,[2] and was once prisoner of war, though rescued before the French vessel made harbour. From any one else with what rapt attention should I have listened to these narratives, but to him I always turned a reluctant ear. Whenever he came, which he often did, into the large old nursery, where the hearth would have sufficed for ten fireplaces of these degenerate days; I used to draw my stool close to my nurse, and, leaning my head on her knee, keep fast hold of her hand—she encouraged this, and used to tell me she would never go away.

The time of her departure was kept a secret, but I knew it; the coach passed the road at the end of the horsechestnut avenue, and one night, they thought that I was asleep, I heard that two days after she was there to meet the coach, and go to London, to go there forever. I buried my face in my pillow, that my crying might not be heard. I slept, and my dreams brought the old avenue, the coach stopping, as vividly as when I really saw them.

I awoke the next morning, pale and heavy-eyed, but I was subject to violent headachs, and all passed off as their effects. Not a word passed my lips of the previous night's discourse. For the first time I felt the bitterness of being deceived; I could have better brooked the approaching separation, had I been trusted with it. But the secrecy made me feel so unworthy and so helpless; young as I was, I should have been proud of my nurse's confidence; at length, after three miserable silent days, the last night came. My nurse gave us all some little keepsake, though without telling her immediate departure. To me she gave a book, for I was, to use her own expression, "a great scholar." That is, I had not the bodily strength for more active amusement, and was therefore very fond of reading; but to-night I had not the heart to look into the pages which at another time would have been greedily devoured. She was hurt at my seeming indifference, and took my brother on her knee, who was all rapture with his windmill; I was very wrong, I could not bear to see him caressed, and pushing him violently aside, entreated her with a passionate burst of tears, to love me, and only me.

We slept in a sort of gallery off the nursery, and the next morning I was up with the earliest daybreak. Taking the greatest care not to awaken my companions, I put on my clothes as well as I could, and stole downstairs. It was scarcely light through the closed windows, and the shadows took all fantastic semblances, and one or two of the chance rays fell upon the pictures in the hall, giving them strange and distorted likenesses. There was one stately lady in black, with a huge white ruff that encircled a face yet paler. The eyes seemed to follow me wherever I moved; cold, glassy, immovable eyes, which looked upon, as if they hated the little trembling thing that was creeping along below. Suddenly a noise like thunder, at least such it seemed in my ears, rang through the hall. I clung to the oaken banisters of the staircase, my very heart died within me, and I could scarcely raise my head from the place in which it had almost unconsciously buried itself, to ascertain the cause of an unusual light: the fact was a shutter had been carelessly fastened, and a gust of wind had caused the iron bar to fall. It was, however, fortunate for me, as in my well arranged plan, I had forgotten one very important point, namely, how I was to leave the home. To unfasten the hall door was utterly beyond my strength; now an obvious method of escape presented itself. I opened the window and sprang out, running thence at full speed till I gained the avenue; there I was secure. Breathless with running, agitated and afraid, it is singular how soon I grew composed, and even cheerful, in the clear bright morning; its gladness entered into my heart. For a moment I almost forgot the purpose that had brought me there at such an hour: the mists were rising from the park, rolling away like waves of some silvery sea, such as I ever after fancied the seas in fairy tales to be. The clouds were warming into deeper crimson every moment, til the smallest leaf on the chestnut trees seemed

[1] **the old ballad of "Barbara Allen":** one of the most famous of the traditional Scottish folk ballads; a tragic and violent love story.

[2] **Cornwall:** county in the southwest of England, on a peninsula known for its rugged coast and a history of piracy and smuggling.

distinct on that bright red sky. How beautifully it was reflected on the lake, and yet it was almost terrible; it seemed to me filled with flame. How huge and dark too rose our two cedars; what a distance did their shadows spread before them; but I then turned to what was brightest. I was delighted to see the dewdrops on the painted speargrass, and the down-balls shining with moisture; it is a common superstition in our part of the country, that wish and blow away the gossamer round, if it goes at one breath your wish will be granted. I caught one eagerly—I blew with all my strength—alas, only a little of the shining down was displaced; I could scarcely see the remainder for tears; at that moment I heard the horn of the coach. I wonder now that I could distinguish at such a distance; I stopped my ears not to hear it again; and the moment after held my breath to listen. At last I caught sight of the coach in a winding of the road; how glad I felt to think that there was still the hill between us. I had never before seen it coming, though I had often watched it drive past on a summer evening: I saw it pass rapidly through the windings of the green hedges, till it began slowly to ascend the hill. Here my attention was drawn from it, by the sight of my nurse and one of her fellow-servants hurrying up the avenue; years—years have passed since then, but even now the pang of that moment is cold at my heart. I was standing with my arm round the slender stem of one of the young trees. I leant my face upon it; but I saw my nurse coming along as distinctly as if I had watched her. The coach stopped at the gate, and the coachman gave a loud and hasty ring, my nurse hurried by without seeing me, another moment and I felt that she was lost to me forever: I sprang forward, I flung my arms around her, I clung to her with the momentary strength of despair; I implored her to take me with her. I said I would work, beg for her, any thing, if she would let me go and be her own child. At first she kissed and coaxed me to loose her, but at last the coachman became impatient of waiting; in the fear of the stage going without her, harassed too by all the perplexities which I have since learnt belong to all departures; she exclaimed in the momentary peevishness of not being able to unclasp my arms,—

"What a tiresome child it is, I shall have the coach go without me."

My arms relaxed their tender and passionate clasp. I stood at her side pale, for I felt the colour go from my cheek back upon my heart; my eyes drank back their tears; I felt then what I never felt before; the perfect self-control of strong excitement, and I bade her civilly good morning. I walked slowly away from the gate without looking back to see her get into the coach, but hearing the horn echo on the air, I ran to a point of rising ground, I caught the last sight of the horses, and flung myself down on the grass; the words "how tiresome the child is," ringing in my ears, as if another person at my side delighted to repeat them in every possible way.

To know yourself less beloved than you love, is a dreadful feeling—alas, how often has the remembrance of that bitter hour come back again by some following hour too sadly like the one that went before. How often have I since exclaimed, "I am not beloved as I love."

The consequence of my being so long on the dewy grass, aided by the agitation that I had endured, brought on one of those violent colds to which I have always been subject. It was poor consolation, the undeniable fact that it had been brought on by my own fault. I never coughed without a sensation of shame. Of all shapes that illness can take, a cough is the worst. Pain can be endured in silence, but a cough is so noisy, it inevitably attracts attention; the echo of mine from the vaulted roof was a perpetual torment to myself, because I knew that others must hear it as well. My cough brought also what was the severest of punishments, it kept me within doors, it prevented my daily visit to the old laurel, where I used to share my luncheon with a favourite old pointer of my father's.

One day, while I was sitting by the window, forced, alas, to be shut, I heard a whining at the door. I opened it, and in bounded the dog, overwhelming me with its caresses. Its large bright brown eyes were fixed upon me with all the depth of human affection. It was a delicious sensation to think that any thing in the world had missed me. Clio[3] was a beautiful creature, with a coat of glossy blackness only broken by a few spots of tan. I have since heard a lovely head of hair compared to the "down of darkness," and to the raven's wing, but the highest compliment that ever passes through my mind is to liken it to the dark silkiness of my darling Clio. The weather being very dry, no dirt could be brought into the house, and the visits of the intruder were a permitted pleasure. Another source of enjoyment too opened upon me. I began to read the book that my nurse had given me; at first the very sight of it was insupportably painful, but one long weary morning when the severity of illness had softened into that langour which needs some quiet amusement, I

[3] **Clio:** The child's beloved dog is named for the muse of history.

opened its pages. It was an epoch in my life, it is an epoch in every child's life, the first reading of Robinson Crusoe.[4] What entire possession it took of my imagination. Henceforth one-half of my time was past on that lovely and lonely island. The only thing that I could not understand were Robinson Crusoe's lamentations over his solitude, to me the most unreasonable things in the world. How little did I share his joy when the English vessel came and bore him once more over the sea to his native England. It was a long time before I had any wish to read the rest. For weeks after reading that book, I lived as if in a dream, indeed I rarely dreamt of any thing else at night. I went to sleep with the cave, its parrots and goats, floating before my closed eyes; I wakened in some rapid flight from the savages landing in their canoes. The elms in our own hedges were not more familiar than the prickly shrubs which formed his palisade; and the grapes whose drooping branches made fertile the wild savannahs. When at length allowed to go into the open air, my enjoyment was tenfold.

We lived in a large, old, and somewhat dilapidated place, only part of the grounds were kept up in their original high order. I used to wander in the almost deserted shrubberies, where the flowers grew in all the luxuriance of neglect over the walks, and the shrubs become trees drooped to the very ground, the boughs heavy with bloom and leaves. In the very heart of one of these was a large deep pond, almost black with the depths of shadow. One bank only was sunny, it had been turf, but one flower after another had taken possession of a situation so favourable. The rododhendron spread its fragile blossom of the softest lilac, beside the golden glories of the Constantinople rose; a variety too of our English roses, had taken root and flourished there. There was the damask, with all its York and Lancaster associations, the white, cold as snow, the little red Ayshire darling, and last, but not least, for it grew with a spendthrift's prodigality, the Chinese rose,[5] a delicate frail stranger, yet the last to shed beauty on even our dark November. Below, the pond was covered with water lilies with the large green leaves that support the loveliest of ivory boats, fit for the fairy queen and her summer court. But these were not the attractions of that solitary pond in my eyes. Its charm was a little island which seemed to float upon the dark water; one side of the pond was covered with ancient willow trees, whose long pendant branches dropped forever over the same mournful mirror. One of these trees, by some natural caprice, shot out direct from the bank, a huge, straight bough that formed a complete bridge to the little island—at least so near that a rapid spring enabled me to gain it.—There was only one tree on this miniature island—a curiously shaped but huge yew tree; it quite rivalled the laurel that used to be my favorite haunt. I would remain hidden in the deep shadows of that gloomy tree, for the whole of my playtime, I was there,

"Monarch of all I survey'd
My right there was none to dispute."[6]

How well I recollect the eagerness with which, one morning, I sprang into its shade. The day before I had been to a juvenile ball given in the neighborhood. I was dressed with unusual care—and I am convinced that dress is the universal passion—and turned to leave the nursery with an unusual glow of complacency, one of the servants smoothing down a rebellious curl. As I past I heard the other say "leave well alone"—and unfortunately I heard the rejoinder also—"Leave ill alone, you mean; did you ever see such a little plain thing." This was but the beginning of my mortifications, that evening was but the first of many coming events that cast their shadows before. Still it was my earliest experience of the bitterness of neglect, and of the solitude of a crowd. I had for several hours the melancholy satisfaction of sitting unnoticed in a corner; at length the lady of the house, in the most cruel kindness, insisted on my dancing. How the first figure of

[4]**Robinson Crusoe**: title of Daniel Defoe's 1719 novel of a man shipwrecked alone on a tropical island; when, after years of solitude, he saves the life of a native of a nearby island, he makes him his servant and gives him the name Friday.

[5]**Constantinople rose**: uncertain; presumably a rose cultivated in Turkey. **damask**: a rose native to the Caucasus region of Russia, cultivated for its fragrant oil, attar of roses. **York and Lancaster**: rival English dynasties whose struggle over the throne of England, lasting from around 1455 to 1485, is known as the Wars of the Roses (the House of York's symbol was the white rose, Lancaster's the red). **Ayshire darling**: a hybrid native to North America but first developed commercially in the eighteenth century in Ayrshire, Scotland. **Chinese rose**: any of numerous forms of Rosa chinensis, a large group of roses cultivated in China, including the various fragrant tea roses.

[6]**"Monarch of all I survey'd . . ."**: adapted from "Verses supposed to be written by Alexander Selkirk," by William Cowper (1731–1800). Selkirk was the historical model for Defoe's fictional Robinson Crusoe.

the quadrille was accomplished I know not. I fancied every one was laughing at me; I had to advance by myself, the room swam round, my head became giddy, I left my unfortunate partner, sprang away, and took refuge in a balcony and a burst of tears. The next morning I had to endure reproof, for I had inflicted the mortification I felt, and the unanswerable question of "What use was my being taught any thing?" In sad truth, at that time, it might have seemed very little use indeed. I was a clever, very clever child, but my mind was far beyond my years, and it lacked the knowledge which alone can teach how to use its powers. Moreover I was wholly deficient in all showy talents; for music I had no ear, for drawing no eye, and dancing was positively terrible to my timid temper. My sensitiveness made any attempt at display a hopeless endeavour. An hundred times has my book been returned because I was too anxious that I might say my lesson well, the words died on my lips, I became confused, speechless, while the tears that rose too readily into my eyes appeared like sullenness. And yet at that moment my heart almost stopped beating with its eagerness to repeat, what in reality I had thoroughly mastered, and whose spirit had become a part of my mind.

Still the imagination conquers the real. My head ached with crying when I reached my darling island, and yet in half an hour I was sitting in the shadow of the yew tree, my arm round Clio's dark and glossy neck, and fancying the pointer an excellent representation of "my man Friday." There was one time in the day, however, when I could never prevail on Clio to be my companion—about six she regularly disappeared, and all my coaxing to keep her at my side was in vain. One afternoon I watched and followed her. She took her way across the long shadows that were now beginning to sweep over the sunny park. She made her way to a small gate that opened on the road, and there lay down patiently awaiting the arrival of her master. I thought I would wait too, for I knew that my father was in the habit of coming in at that gate, as it saved a long round by the road. I soon heard the sound of his horse's hoofs, and felt half inclined to run away. I was so glad that I did not, for my father took me up in his arms and kissed me with the utmost pleasure, saying,—"So you have been waiting for me;" and taking the horse's bridle in one hand, and me in the other, we walked across the park together. I now went to meet him every day; happy, happy hours that I past on that gate, with the pointer at my feet, looking up with its large human eyes, as if to read in mine when I first caught sight of my father. How I hated the winter with its cold cutting air, its thick fog, that put an end to this waiting; winter, that left out the happiest hour of the day. But spring came again, spring that covered one bank with the sweet languor of the pale primrose, and another with the purple arabia[7] of the breathing violet. No flower takes upon me the effect of these. Years, long years past away since I have seen these flowers, other than in the sorted bouquet, and the cultivated garden, but those fair fresh banks rise distinct on my mind's eye. They colour the atmosphere with themselves, their breath rises on the yet perfumed air, and I think with painful pleasure over all that once surrounded them. I think of affections gone down to the grave, and of hopes and beliefs which I can trust no more.

It was in the first week of an unusually forward May, that one afternoon, for I had again begun my watchings by the park gate, that my father produced four volumes and for me. How delicious was the odour of the Russian leather in which they were bound, how charming the glance at the numerous pictures which glanced through the half-opened leaves. The first reading of the Arabian Nights[8] was like the first reading of Robinson Crusoe. For a time, their world made mine—my little, lonely island, dark with the mingled shadow of the yew and the willow, was now deserted, I sought a gayer site, that harmonized better with the bright creations now around me, I found it in a small, oldfashioned flower garden, where the beds, filled with the richest colours, were confined by small edgings of box[9] into every variety of squares, ovals, and rounds. At one end was the beehouse, whence the murmur of myriad insect wings came like the falling of water. Near was a large accacia, now in the prodigality of bloom which comes but every third year; I found a summer palace amid its luxuriant boughs. The delight of reading those enchanted pages, I must even to this day rank as the most delicious excitement of my life. I shall never have courage to read them again, it would mark too decidedly, too bitterly, the change in myself,—I need not. How perfectly I recollect those charming fictions whose fascination was so irresistible! How well I remember the thrill of awe which came over me at the brazen giant sitting alone amid the pathless seas, mighty and desolate till the

---

[7] **purple arabia**: "Arabia" is used figuratively for the fragrance of "the breathing violet," because of Arabia's importance in the trade of spices and perfumes with Europe.

[8] **Arabian Nights**: reference to *Thousand and One Nights*, a collection of Persian studies.

[9] **box**: evergreen shrub used for hedges.

appointed time came for the fated arrow, at whose touch he was to sink down, an unsolved mystery, hidden by the eternal ocean!

How touching the history of Prince Agib[10]—when he arrives at the lovely island, only inhabited by the beautiful boy who dwelt there in solitude and fear till he came! How in the thoughtlessness of youth, they laughed, when sweet confidence had grown up between them, at the prediction which threatened that beloved and gentle child with death at Prince Agib's hand! Fate laughs at human evasion—the fated morning comes—one false step, and even in the very act of tender service, the knife enters the heart of the predestined victim. Prince Agib sees from the thick leaves of the tree where he had taken shelter, the anxious father—anxious, but hopeful—arrive. He comes with music and rejoicing. What does he take back with him? The dead body of his son.

Again, with what all but actual belief did I devour the history of the wondrous lamp,[11] whose possessor had only to wish. For weeks I lived in a world of wishes, and yet it was this dreaming world first led me into contact with the actual. As usual, such knowledge began in sorrow.

One morning, before the period of leaving the schoolroom, I heard the report of a gun. In spite of the intricate path of rivers and boundaries I was then tracing, it still occurred to me to wonder what could lead to a gun's being fired at that time of year. Alas, I learnt only too soon. On going to the accacia I was surprised not to find my usual companion waiting. As to reading in any comfort till I had Clio's soft brown eyes watching me, was impossible. I sent off in search of the truant. Perhaps she had been fastened up. I found my way to the stable, and to the dead body of my favourite. She had been bitten by an adder, and they had been obliged to shoot her. It was one of those shocking spectacles which remain with you for your life. Even now my dreams are haunted with the sight. I believe at first that horror predominated over regret. I could not cry, I stood trembling beside the mangled remains of what I had loved so dearly. I prevailed on one of the servants to bury it near my accacia tree. For days afterwards I did nothing but sob on that grave. How desolate the mornings seemed—how the presence of one real sorrow shook to its very foundations my fairy land. I started from even a moment's forgetfulness as a wrong to the memory of my beloved companion.

At length I began to take an interest in decorating the grave, and planted first one flower and then another. I was not very successful in my gardening attempts, till at length Lucy came to my assistance. Lucy was the grandaughter of an old blind woman who lived near; an aged retainer of some great family, whose small pension had long outlasted the original donors. I have seen many beautiful faces since, but nothing that rises to my memory to be compared with Lucy's childish but exceeding loveliness. She was delicately fair, though constant exposure to the sun had touched the little hands, and the sweet face with soft brown, through which came the most transparent colour that ever caught its red from the rose, or its changefulness from the rainbow. Her hair was of that pale yet rich gold so rarely seen: with the sunshine upon it, it was positively radiant; it shone as the wind lifted some of the long, soft curls. It was a species of beauty too frail, too delicate, and the large blue eyes had that clear, skylike azure, that violet shadow round the orbs, which mark an hereditary tendency to decline. She was in the habit of coming into our gardens to gather roses for distillation.[12] Accustomed from her cradle to strangers and exertion, making friends by a manner whose sweetness was as natural as the smile to her face, Lucy was not the least shy: if she had been, we should never have become acquainted. But when she frankly offered her services to assist in ornamenting the little plot of ground on which my shrubs were drooping, and round which my flowers always made a point of dying; they were accepted on my part with equal surprise and gratitude. Under her more judicious management, the ground was soon covered with leaf and bloom, and every blossom that put forth was a new link in our intimacy.

"I wish I could do any thing to oblige you," was my exclamation at the sight of my first carnation.

"O," exclaimed she, the soft colour warming into her cheek with eagerness, "you are a great reader, would you sometimes come and read to my grandmother?" This I easily obtained permission to do, and that very evening I went with Lucy to Mrs. Selby's. The cottage where she lived stood alone in a little nook between our park and the churchyard; yew trees were on the one side, and our

[10] **Prince Agib:** hero of another story from the *Thousand and One Nights* who unwittingly fulfills a prophecy that he will murder his beloved friend.

[11] **the wondrous lamp:** Cf. the story of Aladdin: the lamp contained a genie who could grant wishes to its possessor.

[12] **roses for distillation:** reference to the process of extracting the essential oils from the rose to make perfume.

cedars on the other, but the garden itself seemed a very fairyland of sunshine; a jessamine covered the front with its long, trailing, green branches, and its white delicate blossoms. The porch was enlivened by that rare and odoriferous shrub, the yellow musk rose; it is the only one I have ever seen, but of a summer evening, it covered that little portal with gold, and filled the whole air with its peculiar and aromatic fragrance. We read of the gales that bear from the shores of Ceylon the breathings of the cinnamon groves. I have always fancied that the musk rose resembles them. Inside, how cool, clean and neat was the room, with its brick floor and large old fireplace, and yet there was only Lucy to do every thing; I have often thought since of the difference between the children of the rich and the children of the poor—the first, kept apart, petted, indulged, and useless;—the second, with every energy in full exercise from the cradle, actively employed, and earning their daily bread, almost from the hour that they begin to eat it. If there is too much of this in the lower classes, if labour be carried into cruelty, there is infinitely too little of it in the higher. The poor child, as Charles Lamb[13] so touchingly expresses it, is not brought, but "dragged out," and if the wits are sharpened, so, too, is the soft, round cheek. The crippled limb and broken constitution attest the effects of the over-early struggle with penury; but the child of rich parents suffers, though in another way; there it is the heart that is crippled, by the selfishness of indulgence and the habit of relying upon others. It takes years of harsh contact with the realities of life to undo the enervating work of a spoilt and overaided childhood. We cannot too soon learn the strong and useful lessons of exertion and self-dependence. Lucy was removed from the heaviest pressure of poverty, but how much did she do that was wonderful in a child of her age! The cottage was kept in the most perfect neatness, and her grandmother's every want watched as only love watches; she was up with the lark, the house was put in order, their own garden weeded, her nosegays collected from all parts, for Lucy was the flower market, the Madeline of our village. Then their dinner was made ready; afterwards, her light song and even lighter step were again heard in the open air, and when evening came on, you saw her in the porch as busily plaiting straw, as if the pliant fingers had only just found employment.

That was my time for visiting at the cottage, when the last red shadows turned the old Gothic lattices of the church into rubies; then, on the low bench beside Lucy, I used to sit and read aloud to her grandmother. She was a very remarkable woman, her tall, stately figure was unbent by age, and her high and strongly marked features were wonderful in expression for a face where the eyes were closed forever. She was a north country woman,[14] and her memory was stored with all those traditions which make so large a portion of our English poetry. Lucy was her only link with the present, but for her affection to that beautiful child, she lived entirely with the past. The old castle where she had chiefly lived, whose noble family had perished from the earth, as if smitten by some strange and sudden doom, the legends connected with their house,—these were her sole topics of discourse. All these legends were of a gloomy tendency, and I used to gaze on her pale, sightless face, and listen to the hollow tones of her voice, till my heart sank within me for fear. But if, by any chance, Lucy left us for a moment, no matter how interesting the narrative, the old woman would suspend her discourse and question me about Lucy's appearance. I did not then understand the meaning of her questions. Alas! how I look back to the hour passed every summer evening in that little shady porch, reading to that blind old woman, Lucy thanking me all the time, with her sweet blue eyes. I have rarely I fear me, been so useful since, certainly never so beloved. It was not to last long: August was now beginning, and it came in with violent thunder storms. One of Lucy's occupations was to gather wild strawberries in a wood at some distance, and nothing could exceed the natural taste with which she used to arrange the bright scarlet fruit amid the vine leaves she fetched from our garden. Returning over the common, she was caught in a tremendous shower, and wet through. The sudden chill struck to a constitution naturally delicate, and in four-and-twenty hours Lucy was no more—I went to see her, unconscious of what had happened. The house was shut up. I felt for the first time in my life, that vague presentiment of evil which is its certain forerunner; I thought only of the aged woman, and entered hastily and yet stealthily in. No one was to be seen in the front room, and I found my way to the one at the back. There were no

[13] **Charles Lamb***: English essayist (1775–1834), author of *Essays of Elia* (1820–1825) and, with his sister Mary, of the classic children's *Tales from Shakespeare* (1807).

[14] **a north country woman**: woman from the northern part of England, which includes the Borders region, source of much of the body of traditional poetry in Britain; cf. Scott's *Minstrelsy of the Scottish Border** (1802–1803).

shutters to the window, and the light streamed through the thin white curtain; it fell on the face of the dead. Beside sat the grandmother, looking the corpse which she became in the course of that night. She never spoke after she felt her child's hand grow cold and stiff in her own. There she lay, that beloved and beautiful girl, her bright hair shining around her, and her face so pale, but with such strange sweetness. I bent down to kiss her, but the touch was death. But why should I go on; I had lost my gentle companion forever.

I have told the history of my childhood, childhood which images forth our after life. Even such has been mine—it has but repeated what it learnt from the first, Sorrow, Beauty, Love and Death.

POSTHUMOUS PUBLICATION

from THE ZENANA
(1839)

Felicia Hemans[1]
(1839; comp. 1836)

No more, no more—oh, never more returning,
Will thy beloved presence gladden earth;
No more wilt thou with sad, yet anxious yearning
Cling to those hopes which have no mortal birth.
Thou art gone from us, and with thee departed,
How many lovely things have vanished too:
Deep thoughts that at thy will to being started,
And feelings, teaching us our own were true.
Thou hast been round us, like a viewless spirit,
Known only by the music on the air;
The leaf or flowers which thou hast named inherit
A beauty known but from thy breathing there:
For thou didst on them fling thy strong emotion,
The likeness from itself the fond heart gave;
As planets from afar look down on ocean,
And give their own sweet image to the wave.

And thou didst bring from foreign lands their
treasures,
As floats thy various melody along;
We know the softness of Italian measures,
And the grave cadence of Castilian song.[2]
A general bond of union is the poet,
By its immortal verse is language known,
And for the sake of song do others know it—
One glorious poet makes the world his own.
And thou—how far thy gentle sway extended!
The heart's sweet empire over land and sea;
Many a stranger and far flower was blended
In the soft wreath that glory bound for thee.
The echoes of the Susquehanna's waters
Paused in the pine-woods words of thine to hear;
And to the wide Atlantic's younger daughters[3]
Thy name was lovely, and thy song was dear.

Was not this purchased all too dearly?—never
Can fame atone for all that fame hath cost.
We see the goal, but know not the endeavour,
Nor what fond hopes have on the way been lost.
What do we know of the unquiet pillow,
By the worn cheek and tearful eyelid prest,
When thoughts chase thoughts, like the tumultuous
billow,
Whose very light and foam reveals unrest?
We say, the song is sorrowful, but know not
What may have left that sorrow on the song;
However mournful words may be, they show not
The whole extent of wretchedness and wrong
They cannot paint the long sad hours, passed only
In vain regrets o'er what we feel we are.
Alas! the kingdom of the lute is lonely—
Cold is the worship coming from afar.

Yet what is mind in woman, but revealing
In sweet clear light the hidden world below,

[1] See Felicia Hemans* (1793–1835). Landon's stanzas, comprised of four quatrains each, recall Wordsworth's quatrains for Felicia Hemans in "Extempore Effusion upon the Death of James Hogg."*

[2] **Italian measures**: Italian lyric poetry, particularly the sonnets and songs of Petrarch and the pastoral romances of Sannazzaro and Tasso, had a key influence on the development of English poetry; Spanish poetry—**Castilian song** in Landon's phrase—had less direct impact, but the work of Lope de Vega and Francisco de Quevedo from the seventeenth century was well known throughout Europe.

[3] **Susquehanna's waters**: river running through New York and Pennsylvania to Chesapeake Bay. **Atlantic's younger daughters**: the lakes and rivers of America.

By quicker fancies and a keener feeling
Than those around, the cold and careless, know?
What is to feed such feeling, but to culture
A soil whence pain will never more depart?
The fable of Prometheus and the vulture[4]
Reveals the poet's and the woman's heart.
Unkindly are they judged—unkindly treated—
By careless tongues and by ungenerous words,
While cruel sneer, and hard reproach, repeated,
Jar the fine music of the spirit's chords.

[4] **The fable of Prometheus and the vulture**: For stealing fire from the gods and giving it to mankind (whom, in some versions of the myth, he had created), the titan Prometheus was chained to a mountain peak in the Caucasus, while an eagle or vulture devoured his constantly regenerating liver.

Wert thou not weary—thou whose soothing numbers
Gave other lips the joy thine own had not?
Didst thou not welcome thankfully the slumbers
Which closed around thy mourning human lot?

What on this earth could answer thy requiring,
For earnest faith—for love, the deep and true,
The beautiful, which was thy soul's desiring,
But only from thyself its being drew.
How is the warm and loving heart requited
In this harsh world, where it awhile must dwell.
Its best affections wronged, betrayed, and slighted—
Such is the doom of those who love too well.
Better the weary dove should close its pinion,
Fold up its golden wings and be at peace:
Enter, O ladye, that serene dominion
Where earthly cares and earthly sorrows cease.
Fame's troubled hour has cleared, and now replying,
A thousand hearts their music ask of thine.
Sleep with a light, the lovely and undying
Around thy grave—a grave which is a shrine.

COMPREHENSIVE CHRONOLOGY AND BIBLIOGRAPHIES

Comprehensive Chronology
(1780–1830)

YEAR	LITERATURE, THE ARTS, AND LITERARY STUDIES	POLITICS AND WAR
1780	Klopstock's *Messiah*; the bolero introduced in Spain, the waltz in Germany and Austria; American Academy of Arts and Sciences established	Gordon Riots in London against Catholic Rights; Holland enters the war against Gr. Br. on behalf of the American Colonies
1781	Schiller, *Die Räuber*; Rousseau, *Confessions*; Fuseli, *The Nightmare* (painting); Johnson, *Lives of the Poets* (1779–1781); Warton, *History of English Poetry* (1774–1781)	Cornwallis surrenders at Yorktown
1782	Frances Burney, *Cecilia*; Kemble debuts as Hamlet; Pierre de Laclos's *Les Liaisons dangereuses*; Cowper, *Poems*	Treaty of Paris between U.S., Gr. Br., France, Spain, and Holland ends the American Revolution
1783	Sophia Lee, *The Recess*; George Crabbe, *The Village*; Blair, *Lectures on Rhetoric and Belles Lettres*; Ritson, ed. *Select Collection of English Songs*	William Pitt becomes Prime Minister
1784	Samuel Johnson dies; Phillis Wheatly dies; David, *The Oath of the Horatii* (painting)	Pitt's India Act makes East India Company answerable to the Crown
1785	Boswell, *Life of Johnson*; Sarah Siddons plays Lady Macbeth for the first time; Cowper, *The Task*	Warren Hastings resigns as Governor-General of India
1786	William Beckford, *Vathek*; Mozart, *The Marriage of Figaro*; Pinkerton, ed. *Ancient Scottish Poems*	Lord Cornwallis becomes Governor-General of India
1787	Mozart, *Don Giovanni*; Warton, ed. *Sidney's Defence of Poetry*	Britain acquires Sierra Leone (Africa) for freed slaves; Committee for the Abolition of the Slave Trade founded in England; U.S. Constitution signed
1788	Gibbon completes *Decline and Fall of the Roman Empire*; J-H. B. Saint-Pierre, *Paul and Virginia*; artist Thomas Gainsborough dies; Giovanni Casanova, *Histoire de me fuite* (memoirs); the *Daily Union Register* becomes the *Times* of London	Temporary insanity of George III; first British shipload of convicts debark at Botany Bay and Sydney; Parliamentary motion to abolish slave trade; Washington elected president of U.S.; trial of Hastings for corruption in governing India; Estates-General summoned in France
1789	Erasmus Darwin, *The Loves of the Plants*	Fall of the Bastille; *Declaration of the Rights of Man*; First Congress convenes at New York; Washington inaugurated as president of U.S.; mutiny on the H.M.S. *Bounty*

YEAR	PHILOSOPHY, EDUCATION, RELIGION, ECONOMICS	SCIENCE, EXPLORATION, MEDICINE, TECHNOLOGY
1780	Catholic pop. of England 70,000; Kennicut's Hebrew Bible	Berthollet and Lavoisier isolate carbon, oxygen, and hydrogen, introducing era of organic analysis and physiological chemistry; Cavendish discovers the formula for water
1781	Kant, *Critique of Pure Reason*	Pennant, *History of Quadrupeds*; Herschel discovers Uranus
1782	Joseph Priestley, *A History of the Corruptions of Christianity*	Harris, *Exposition of English Insects*
1783	Kant, *Prolegomena to Any Future Metaphysics*	First balloon ascent in France by Montgolfier brothers; Bergman, *Outline of Mineralogy*
1784	John Wesley's charter of Wesleyan Methodism	Meikle invents thresher; Adams, *An Essay on Electricity*; Pennant, *Arctic Zoology*
1785	Paley, *Principles of Moral and Political Philosophy*	Salsano invents the seismograph; Bergman, *A dissertation on elective attractions*
1786		M. H. Klaproth discovers uranium
1787		Horace de Saussure takes weather observations from summit of Mont Blanc; *Botanical Magazine* begins pub.; Cavallo, *A Treatise on Magnetism*; Linnaeus, *The Families of Plants* (trans)
1788	Kant, *Critique of Practical Reason*; Lempriere, *Classical Dictionary*	Hutton, *New Theory of the Earth*; Laplace, *Laws of the Planetary System*; Banks founds the *African Association* to enhance trade and exploration; Bolton, *A History of the Fungusses growing about Halifax*
1789	Bentham, *Introduction to the Principles of Morals and Legislation*; Lavater, *Essays on Physiognomy, designed to promote the knowledge and the love of mankind* (trans)	Lavoisier, *Elements of Chemistry*; Galvani's experiments on muscular contractions; first steam-driven cotton factory in Manchester; William Patterson, *Narrative of Four Voyages in the Land of the Hottentots and the Kaffirs*; Darwin, *The Botanic Garden* (–1791)

YEAR	LITERATURE, THE ARTS, AND LITERARY STUDIES	POLITICS AND WAR
1790	Ann Radcliffe, *The Sicilian*; Edmund Malone's *Plays and Poems of Shakespeare* (10 vols.); Ritson, ed., *Ancient Songs*; Ellis, ed., *Specimens of the Early English Poets*	Jacobins under Robespierre become greatest power in France; Louis XVI accepts the Constitution; royal family captured in attempt to flee; mutineers from H.M.S. *Bounty* settle Pitcairn Island
1791	Elizabeth Inchbald, *A Simple Story*; Boswell, *Life of Johnson*; Mozart dies	Sierra Leone devoted to settlement by freed slaves; Legislative Assembly convenes in Paris (Oct. 1791–Sept. 1792); slaves revolt in Santo Domingo; French royal family imprisoned; American *Bill of Rights* ratified; anti-Jacobin riots in Birmingham
1792	Artist Joshua Reynolds dies; architect Robert Adam dies	Denmark is first country to prohibit the slave trade; storming of the Tuileries; French royal family arrested; September Massacres in Paris; Revolutionary Forces defeat Prussians at Battle of Valmy; National Convention convenes (Sept. 1792–Oct. 1795); abolition of the Monarchy; trial of Louis XVI, condemned to death by one vote (361 to 288, with 72 votes for a delay)
1793	Charlotte Smith, *The Old Manor House*; Marquis de Sade, *La philosophie dans le boudoir*; John Flaxman, Illustrations for the *Iliad*; David paints *The Murder of Marat*; Louvre becomes national art gallery; Paganini, age 11, makes debut as violinist	Louis XVI executed (23 Jan.); France declares war on Gr. Br., Holland, Spain; Marat executed; Reign of Terror (1793–1794); French abolish worship of God; Marie Antoinette executed (16 Oct.); first free settlers arrive in Australia
1794	Elizabeth Inchbald, *Nature and Art*; Radcliffe, *The Mysteries of Udolpho*; Godwin, *Caleb Williams*; Percy, *Reliques of Ancient English Poetry* (4th ed.)	Trials of Hardy, Horne Tooke, and Thelwall for High Treason; fall of Robespierre (27 July); end of the Terror; *Habeus Corpus Act* suspended in England
1795	Potter Josiah Wedgwood dies; James Boswell dies; Goethe, *Wilhelm Meisters Lehrjahre*; Beethoven, *Opus 1*	Bread riots in Paris; the Directory convenes as the new government in Paris (1795–1799); John Macarthur introduces sheep breeding to Australian economy; Speenhamland Act provides poor relief in England; Hastings acquitted
1796	Francis Burney, *Camilla*; Mary Hays, *Memoirs of Emma Courtney*; Elizabeth Hamilton, *Letters of a Hindu Raj*; Lewis, *The Monk*	Napoleon Bonaparte's Italian Campaign (1796–1797); French declare war on the Republic of Venice; coup in Paris by republican directors; Napoleon marries Josephine; Catherine of Russia dies

YEAR	PHILOSOPHY, EDUCATION, RELIGION, ECONOMICS	SCIENCE, EXPLORATION, MEDICINE, TECHNOLOGY
1790	Jews in France granted civil liberties; Adam Smith dies; founding of the Clapham Sect; *Monthly Review*, 2nd series (–1825)	First steam-powered rolling mill built in England; Lavoisier's *Elements of Chemistry* (trans); Priestley, *Experiments . . . on Different Kinds of Air*; Bruce, *Travels to discover the source of the Nile*
1791	Wesley dies; Walker, *Critical Pronouncing Dictionary and Exposition of the English Language*; Enfield, *History of Philosophy*	Galvani posits "animal electricity"; Bartram, *Travels through North and South Carolina*
1792	Stock Exchange opens in New York; D. Stewart, *Elements of the Philosophy of the Human Mind* (–1827); Wells, *An Essay Upon Single Vision with Two Eyes*	First gas lights used in England; Buffon, *Natural History of Birds* (9 vols)
1793	Godwin's *Enquiry Concerning Political Justice*	Eli Whitney invents the cotton gin; Donovan, *The Natural History of British Insects* (–1813; 16 vols)
1794	Gibbon dies; Paine, *The Age of Reason*; Paley, *Evidences of Christianity*	First telegraph, Paris to Lille; Darwin, *Zoonomia*; Moises, *A Treatise on the Blood*
1795	Murray, *English Grammar*; Rawlinson Professorship of Anglo-Saxon, Oxford University, est.	Hutton, *Theory of the Earth*; Mungo Park explores Gambia and reaches Niger; first horse-drawn railroad in England; Joseph Bramah invents hydraulic press; France adopts the metric system; François Appert creates the preserving jar; Nicholson, *A Dictionary of Chemistry*
1796	Richard Watson, *An Apology for the Bible*; Hutton, *Mathematical and Philosophical Dictionary*	Stedman, *Narrative of a Five Years Expedition Against the Revolted Negroes of Surinam*, illus. by Blake; physician Edward Jenner introduces smallpox vaccine

YEAR	LITERATURE, THE ARTS, AND LITERARY STUDIES	POLITICS AND WAR
1797	Ann Radcliffe, *The Italian*; Hölderlin, *Hyperion*; Haydn, *Emperor Quartet*; *Anti-Jacobin or Weekly Examiner* published; Taylor translates *Lenore*, famous German ballad	John Adams becomes 2nd president of U.S.; first British mission at Tahiti; Edmund Burke dies; Napoleon defeats Austrians at Rivoli, arrives in Paris to lead invasion of England
1798	Haydn, *The Creation*; Godwin, *Memoirs of Mary Wollstonecraft*; Beethoven, *Pathetique sonata*; Landor, *Gebir*; Philpot, *Introduction to the Literary History of the Fourteenth and Fifteenth Centuries*	French invade Rome, Switzerland; Bonaparte's Egyptian Campaign to dismantle England's Indian empire; Horatio Nelson defeats the French fleet in Battle of the Nile; Irish Rebellion
1799	Mary Hays, *The Victim of Prejudice*; Harriet and Sophia Lee, *Canterbury Tales*; Schiller, *Wallensteins Tod*; Schlegel, *Lucinde*; Beethoven, *Symphony No. 1*; David, *Rape of the Sabine Women* (painting); Turner, *History of the Anglo-Saxons* (–1805)	Napoleon's Syrian Campaign; Napoleon returns to France to lead coup d'état of Brumaire; Napoleon becomes first consul; Sierra Leone made a British Colony; Tallyrand made French Foreign Minister; Washington dies; Pope Pius VI dies while imprisoned in France; Edict of Peking bans import of opium into China
1800	Maria Edgeworth, *Castle Rackrent*; Baillie, *De Montfort* at Drury Lane, with J. P. Kemble and Sarah Siddons; Mme. de Staël, *De la littérature*; Library of Congress established in America; William Cowper dies	Renewal of the French Austrian Campaign; Napoleon crosses Alps with 40,000 men to attack the Austrian flank; British capture Malta
1801	Beethoven, *Moonlight Sonata*; Haydn, *The Seasons*; Todd, *Poetical Works of Milton* (variorium ed); English Catalogue of Books	Treaty of Lunéville dissolves Holy Roman Empire; Concordat between France and the Papacy; Jefferson becomes 3rd president of U.S.; Act of Union between Ireland and Gr. Br.; Toussaint L'Ouverture liberates slaves in Santo Domingo
1802	*Edinburgh Review* and *Cobbett's Weekly Political Register* founded; Cruikshank begins career as illustrator; Scott, *Minstrelsy of the Scottish Border*	Treaty of Amiens between Gr. Br., France, and Spain brings peace to Europe; Napoleon becomes Consul for life; *Health and Morals of Apprentices Act* restricts child labor and introduces 12-hour day
1803	Benjamin West, *Christ Healing the Sick* (painting); sculptures from the Parthenon sent by Lord Elgin to England; Godwin, *Life of Chaucer*; Reed, *First Variorium Shakespeare* (21 vols)	Louisiana Purchase ends risk of powerful French presence in U.S.; France and England return to war

YEAR	PHILOSOPHY, EDUCATION, RELIGION, ECONOMICS	SCIENCE, EXPLORATION, MEDICINE, TECHNOLOGY
1797	Schelling, *Ideen zu einer Philosophie der Natur*; Chateaubriand, *Essai historique, politique, et moral sur les révolutions*; Bank of England refuses to make cash payments; Robison, *Proofs of a Conspiracy against all of the Religions and Governments of Europe*	England begins export of iron; Thomas Bewick, *History of British Birds* (land birds); Euler, *Elements of Algebra*; Vince, *A Complete System of Astronomy* (–1808); Nicholson's *Journal of Natural Philosophy, Chemistry and the Arts* begins pub.
1798	Malthus, *First Essay on the Principle of Population*; Bentham, *Political Economy*; Bell introduces Madras educational system to England; Willich's translation of *Elements of the Critical Philosophy* introduces Kantian philosophy to England	Guinand discovers process for making optical glass; Senefelder invents lithography
1799	Schleiermacher, *Reden über die Religion*; Schelling, *Systems der Naturphilosophie*; Pius VI dies in French custody	Cuvier founds comparative anatomy; Mungo Park, *Travels in the Interior Districts of Africa*; Rosetta Stone found in Egypt; preserved mammoth found in Siberia; T. Beddoes, *Contributions to Physical and Medical Knowledge*
1800	Schelling, *System des transzendentalen Idealismus*; Schlegel's romantic irony introduced in *The Athenaeum*; Herder, *Outlines of a Philosophy of the History of Man* (trans)	Alessandro Volta produces electricity from a cell, resulting in first electric battery; Royal Institution of Great Britain founded to disseminate scientific and technical knowledge; Davy, *Researches . . . Concerning Nitrous Oxide*; Herschel discovers infrared solar rays
1801	Gauss, *Disquisitiones arithmeticae*; *Christian Observor* begins monthly publication by evangelicals; Henry, *An Epitome of Chemistry*	Barrow, *Travels into the Interior of Southern Africa*; Fulton's submarine *The Nautilus*; Lalande catalogues 47,390 stars; First British census; Linnaeus, *Elements of Natural History* (–1802)
1802	Bentham, *Civil and Penal Legislation*; Grotefend deciphers Babylonian cuneiform; Paley, *Natural Theology*	Trevithick builds high-pressure steam engine; Young describes periodic wave motion of light; Dalton's atomic theory; Erasmus Darwin dies; Anna Maria Falconbridge, *Narrative of Two Voyages to the River Sierra Leone*; Cuvier, *Lectures on Comparative Anatomy* (trans); Thomson, *A System of Chemistry*
1803	Cobbett, *Parliamentary Debates* (to become Hansard)	Henry Shrapnel invents the artillery shell; Fulton uses steam to propel a boat on the Seine

YEAR	LITERATURE, THE ARTS, AND LITERARY STUDIES	POLITICS AND WAR
1804	Schiller, *Wilhelm Tell*; Beethoven, *Symphony No. 3*; Turner, *Passage of the St. Gothard* (painting)	Conspiracy against the life of Napoleon discovered; First Empire under Napoleon I revives absolute monarchy (1804–1814); *Code Napoleon*; Jefferson reelected president of U.S.
1805	Chateaubriand, *René*; Paganini's concert tour through Europe; Turner, *The Shipwreck* (painting); Boston Athenaeum founded; Gifford, ed., *The Plays of Massinger*	Coalition of Austria, Russia, Sweden, and Britain against France and Spain; Franco-Spanish fleet defeated at Trafalgar by Nelson, who dies of wounds; Napoleon defeats combined Austrian and Russian forces at Austerlitz; Treaty of Pressburg between France and Austria; Christian literature proscribed in China
1806	Jane and Ann Taylor, *Rhymes for the Nursery*; Rossini's first opera in Rome; Arnim and Bretano collect German folk songs (*Des Knaben Wunderhorn*); Turner paints *Mer de Glace*; Constable draws *Langdale Pikes* and *Helvelyn*	Brothers of Napoleon become kings of Naples and Holland; Holy Roman Empire comes to an end; French wars against Prussia and Russia; Prussian forces routed at battles of Jena and Auerstadt; Napoleon declares the Continent closed to British trade, in effect creating the Continental System; Bligh made governor of Australia to control unruly and anarchic population, but fails; Charles James Fox dies
1807	David, *Coronation of Napoleon* (painting); Thomas Moore, *Irish Melodies*; Mme. de Staël, *Corinne*; Ingram, *On the Utility of Anglo-Saxon Literature*	Slave trade banned throughout British empire; Russians fall back at the battle of Friedland; Treaties of Tilsit with Russia and Prussia; British invade Alexandria; French invade Portugal
1808	Elizabeth Hamilton, *The Cottagers of Glenburnie*; Goethe, *Faust*, part I; Friedrich, *The Cross in the Mountains* (painting); Beethoven, *Symphonies No. 5* and *No. 6*; Hunt founds the *Examiner*; Covent Garden burns down; Lamb, ed., *Specimens of English Dramatic Poets*; Scott, ed., *Works of Dryden* (18 vols)	France invades Spain; Joseph, brother of Napoleon, becomes king of Spain; Peninsular war between England and France begins; under Wellesley, British defeat French at Vimeiro, French agree to evacuate Portugal at Convention of Cintra; Napoleon advances on Spain with army of 150,000; British in retreat; African slave trade prohibited in U.S.
1809	*Quarterly Review* founded; Hannah More, *Coelebs in Search of a Wife*; Ingres, *Dream of Ossian* (painting); Schlegel, *Uber dramatische Kunst und Litteratur*; Irving, *Rip Van Winkle*; Constable, *Malvern Hill* (painting); Haydn dies; Drury Lane theater burns down	James Madison becomes 4th U.S. president; Metternich made Foreign Minister of Austria; Napoleon annexes Papal States, divorces Josephine

YEAR	PHILOSOPHY, EDUCATION, RELIGION, ECONOMICS	SCIENCE, EXPLORATION, MEDICINE, TECHNOLOGY
1804	Immanuel Kant dies; Taylor translates *The Works of Plato* (5 vols)	Trevithick builds locomotive to run on rails; chemist Joseph Priestley dies; Donovan, *The Natural History of British Fishes* (–1808); Parkinson, *Organic Remains of a Former World* (–1811)
1805	Schiller dies	Mungo Park explores Niger River up to Bussa Rapids and drowns; Sarturner isolates morphine
1806	Adelung, *Mithridates, a History of Languages and Dialects*; Boylston Professorship of Rhetoric and Oratory, Harvard College, est.; Taylor trans. *The Works of Aristotle* (10 vols); Jane Marcet, *Conversations on Chemistry*	First gas lighting of cotton mills; Huber, *New observations on the natural history of bees*; Priestley, *Memoirs of Dr. Joseph Priestley* (2 vols)
1807	Hegel, *Phänomenologie de Geistes*	Davy isolates potassium and sodium; Geological Society of London founded; Fulton's steamboat *Clermont* navigates on Hudson River; gas lighting used in London; J. Wilson, *A History of Mountains* (–1810)
1808	Napoleon abolishes the Inquisition in Spain and Italy; Eichhorn, *Geschichte des deutschen Rechts*; *Edinburgh Encyclopedia* (18 vols; –1830)	Dalton, *New System of Chemical Philosophy*, establishes quantitative atomic theory; source of Ganges discovered; excavations at Pompeii
1809	Thomas Paine dies; Ricardo, *The High Price of Bullion, Proof of the Depreciation of Bank Notes*; *Quarterly Review* begins pub	Lamarck, *Philosophie zoologique* advances theory of evolution; McDowell performs successful ovariotomy; Laplace, *System of the World* (trans); Deluc, *An Elementary Treatise on Geology*

YEAR	LITERATURE, THE ARTS, AND LITERARY STUDIES	POLITICS AND WAR
1810	Mme. de Staël, *De l'Allemagne*; Goya, *Los Desastres de la Guerra* (engravings); Crabbe, *The Borough*; Isaiah Thomas, *History of Printing in America*; Chalmers, ed., *Works of the English Poets* (21 vols)	Wellesley (Wellington) defeats French at Salamanca; Joseph Bonaparte abandons Madrid; debate over press coverage in House of Commons; reform bill introduced
1811	Austen, *Sense and Sensibility*; Mary Brunton, *Self-Control*; Goethe, *Aus meinem Leben: Dichtung und Wahrheit*; John Nash designs Regent Street, London	Prince of Wales becomes Regent with declaration of George III's insanity; Austria bankrupt; Russia captures Belgrade; Luddite riots and bread riots in Nottingham
1812	The Brothers Grimm, *Fairy Tales*; Nichols, *Literary Anecdotes of the 18th Century*; Drury Lane theatre, London, rebuilt; Goya, *Portrait of the Duke of Wellington*; Beethoven *Symphonies No. 7* and *No. 8*; Maria Edgeworth, *The Absentee*; Turner, *Hannibal Crossing the Alps* (painting)	Napoleon's Grand Army begins invasion of Russia; French occupy Moscow; the burning of Moscow by Russians (15–19 Sept.); Napoleon's army in retreat and then routed at the Crossing of the Beresina (26–28 Nov.); 100,000 of 600,000 make it back to France; War of 1812 between U.S. and Britain (1812–1814); Madison reelected president
1813	Austen, *Pride and Prejudice*; Robert Southey becomes poet laureate, publishes *Life of Nelson*; London Philharmonic Society founded; Hunt imprisoned until 1815 for libel	Wars of liberation throughout Europe; Napoleon's forces defeated at Battle of Leipzig; Parliament reviews East India Company charter, but prohibits monopoly of trade and extends sovereignty of Crown over EIC's possessions; Simón Bolívar becomes dictator of Venezuela; mass Luddite trial in York
1814	Austen, *Mansfield Park*; Kean's debut as Shylock at Drury Lane; Scott, *Waverley*; Frances Burney, *The Wanderer*; Francis Scott Key, "Defense of Fort McHenry," to become the "Star-Spangled Banner"; Constable paints *The Vale of Dedham*; Dunlop, *History of Fiction*	Allies enter Paris in March; Napoleon banished to Elba; Louis XVIII, brother of Louis XVI, becomes king of France; Congress of Vienna (Sept. 1814–June 1815); British capture and burn Washington, D.C.; Treaty of Ghent ends War of 1812; British receive Cape Colony, South Africa, in Treaty of Paris
1815	Biedermeier style for home furnishings begins; Turner, *Crossing the Brook* (painting); Canova, *The Three Graces* (sculpture); Park, ed., *Heliconia*; Schlegel's *Lectures on Dramatic Art and Literature* translated; Cary translates Dante's *Divine Comedy*; Thurkelin, ed., *De Danorum Rebus Gestis Seculis III et IV* [i.e., *Beowulf*, discovered in Cottonian mss]	France bans the slave trade as part of Treaty of Paris; Napoleon lands at Cannes, Louis flees, Napoleon enters Paris to begin Hundred Days of rule; Allied forces of Austria, Britain, Prussia, and Russia under command of Wellesley, now Duke of Wellington, defeat French forces at Waterloo (18 June); Napoleon surrenders and is exiled to St. Helen's island in South Atlantic; postwar economic depression begins in England (1815–1820) with demobilization of 400,000 men; demands for Reform; Corn Law passes in England

YEAR	PHILOSOPHY, EDUCATION, RELIGION, ECONOMICS	SCIENCE, EXPLORATION, MEDICINE, TECHNOLOGY
1810	Joseph de Maistre, *Essay on the Generation of Political Constitutions*; *Encyclopedia Brittanica*, 4th ed (20 vols); D. Stewart, *Philosophical Essays*	Koenig's power-driven printing press; Gall develops system of phrenology; Appert develops techniques for canning food; Hahnemann founds homeopathy; Buffon, *A History of the Earth and Animated Nature*
1811	Böttiger, *Kunstmythologie*	Sir Charles Bell, *New Idea of the Anatomy of the Brain*; Hooker, *Journal of a Tour of Iceland*
1812	Hegel, *Die objektive Logik*; Genesius, *Hebrew and Chaldaik Dictionary*; Leake, *Greece*	Humphry Davy, *Elements of Chemical Philosophy*; Georges Cuvier, *Recherches sur les ossements fossiles de quadrupèdes*; Hutton, *Tracts on Mathematical and Philosophical Subjects*
1813	Robert Owen, *A New View of Society*; *Annals of Philosophy* begins pub; Townsend, *The character of Moses established for veracity as an historian*	Horrocks's power loom; Davy, *Elements of Agricultural Chemistry*; Cuvier, *Essay on the Theory of the Earth* (trans)
1814	Inquisition restored in Spain; first Anglican bishop appointed in India; Chateaubriand, *De Buonaparte et les Bourbons*; evangelical preacher Joanna Southcott dies, leaving 100,000 followers	*London Times* uses steam-operated press; Higgins, *Experiments and Observations on the Atomic Theory*; Lewis and Clark, *History of the expedition . . . to the sources of the Missouri, thence, . . . to the Pacific Ocean*
1815	Malthus, *An Inquiry into the Nature and Progress of Rent*; Ricardo, *The Influence of a Low Price of Corn on the Profits of Stock*; Dugald Stewart, *Progress of Metaphysical, Ethical, and Political Philosophy*	William Smith's geological map of England and Wales; Apothecaries Act restricts medical practice to qualified doctors; U.S.S. *Fulton*, steam warship; Lamarck, *Histoire naturelle des animaux*; Spurzheim introduces phrenology to England; Bichat, *Physiological Researches on Life and Death* (trans)

YEAR	LITERATURE, THE ARTS, AND LITERARY STUDIES	POLITICS AND WAR
1816	Austen, *Emma*; Elgin Marbles exhibited in British Museum; Rossini, *Barbiere di Siviglia*; Peacock, *Headlong Hall*; Constable, *Weymouth Bay* (painting); Pickering, *Vocabulary . . . of Words . . . Peculiar to the United States*	British force Algiers to end Christian slavery; British ambassador refused reception in Peking; Spa Fields riots
1817	*Blackwood's Magazine* founded; Jane Austen dies; Thomas Moore, *Lalla Rookh*; Hazlitt, *Characters in Shakespeare's Plays*; Mme. de Staël dies; Scott, *Rob Roy*; John Martin paints *The Bard*; Nash designs the orientalist Royal Pavilion, Brighton; Southey, ed., *Malory's Kyng Arthur*	Coercion Acts enacted in reaction to violence by a political mob at Spa Fields, London; James Monroe elected 5th U.S. president; riots in Derbyshire against low wages
1818	Austen, *Northanger Abbey* and *Persuasion*; Peacock, *Nightmare Abbey*; Scott, *Heart of Midlothian*; Mary Shelley publishes *Frankenstein*; Huber and Mohr, "Stille Nacht, heilige Nacht"; Rask, *Investigation on the Origin of the Old Norse or Icelandic Speech*	Habeas Corpus restored; Allied forces leave France
1819	Géricault, *The Raft of the Medusa* (painting); Grimm, *Deutsche Grammatik*; Wilson's *Sanskrit-English Dictionary*	Peterloo Massacre (16 Aug.), in Manchester, England; East India Company establishes first settlement in Singapore
1820	*London Magazine* founded; Scott, *Ivanhoe*; Kean plays Richard III in New York; discovery of the *Venus de Milo*; Chas. Maturin, *Melmoth the Wanderer*	Cato Street conspiracy; George III dies; Prince Regent becomes George IV; 4,000 British colonists settle in South Africa; fomentation of Muslim *jihad* against Punjab Sikhs for acquiescing to British modernization of India (1820–1831); Final Act of Congress of Vienna; Monroe re-elected president
1821	*Manchester Guardian* founded; Constable, *Hay Wain* and *Cloud Studies* (paintings); Severn, portrait of dying John Keats; Goethe, *Wilhelm Meisters Wanderjahre*; Heine, *Poems*; Malone and Boswell, eds., *Third Variorium Shakespeare* (21 vols)	Illicit opium trade in China transferred from Canton to Lintin Island (5,000 chests per annum); Greek War of Independence begins (1821–1831); Sierra Leone, the Gold Coast, and Gambia joined as British West African Settlements; Napoleon dies
1822	Pushkin, *Eugene Onegin*; Stendhal, *De l'amour*; Alfred de Vigny, *Poèmes*; Liszt makes his debut in Vienna; Royal Academy of Music founded; Schubert, *Unfinished Symphony*; Delacroix, *Dante and Virgil Crossing the Styx* (painting); *Sunday Times* founded	Suicide of Castlereagh brings liberals Canning to Foreign Ministry, Peel to Home Affairs, and Huskisson to Board of Trade; Turks invade Greece with an army of 30,000; Liberia founded as a colony for freed American slaves; Massacres of Chios

YEAR	PHILOSOPHY, EDUCATION, RELIGION, ECONOMICS	SCIENCE, EXPLORATION, MEDICINE, TECHNOLOGY
1816	Parliamentary Committee on Education for the Poor; secular education introduced into India; British missionaries invade South Africa	Sir David Brewster invents kaleidoscope; R. T. Laënnec invents stethoscope; Lacroix, *Elementary Treatise on the Differential and Integral Calculus* (trans)
1817	Ricardo, *Principles of Political Economy and Taxation*; Cobbett, *Paper against Gold, the History and Mystery of the Bank of England*; Hegel, *Encyclopedia of the Philosophical Sciences*; Chalmers, *A Series of Discourses on the Christian Revelation, viewed in connection with Modern Astronomy*	John Oxley explores Australian interior; Berzelius discovers selenium and lithium
1818	Dobrovsky, *History of the Czech Language*	Institute of Civil Engineers founded in London; Berzelius's molecular weights of 2,000 compounds; steamship *Savannah* crosses Atlantic in 26 days; Davy, *On the Safety Lamp for Coal Mines*
1819	Schopenhauer, *Die Welt als Wille und Vorstellung*; Jane Marcet, *Conversations on Natural Philosophy*	Oersted discovers electromagnetism; Grisenthwaite, *New Theory of Agriculture*; Combe, *Essays on Phrenology*
1820	Malthus, *Principles of Political Economy*	Scoresby, *Account of the Arctic Regions*; Ampere, *Laws of Electrodynamic Action*; platinum discovered in Russian Urals; P. Huber, *The Natural History of Ants*
1821	Schleiermacher, *Der christliche Glaube*; Saint-Simon, *Du Système industriel*; Rosetta Stone leads to deciphering of hieroglyphics by Champollion	Faraday demonstrates electromagnetic rotation; European population data (in millions): France—30.4; Great Britain—20.8; Italy—18; Austria—12; Germany—26; U.S.—9.6; Barton, *A Flora of North America* (–1823); Jameson, *Manual of Mineralogy*
1822	Colebrooke founds Royal Asiatic Society for the study of Eastern languages	Magendie shows that sensory and motor functions derive from different spinal roots; Daguerre and Bouton invent the diorama; Gr. Br. imports 22,000 pounds of opium

YEAR	LITERATURE, THE ARTS, AND LITERARY STUDIES	POLITICS AND WAR
1823	Cooper, *The Pioneers*; Smirke designs the main facade of the British Museum; Beethoven, *Missa Solemnis*	Turks fall back at Missolonghi, but Greeks unable to take advantage; enactment of Monroe Doctrine
1824	Delacroix, *The Massacres of Chios*; Mary Mitford, *Our Village*; National Gallery, London, founded; Overbeck, *Christ's Entry into Jerusalem* (painting); *Le Globe*, Paris, begins publication; James Hogg, *Private Memoirs and Confessions of a Justified Sinner*; Maria Jane Jewsbury, *Phantasmagoria*; Watt, *Bibliotheca Brittanica*	British war vs. the Ashanti on the Gold Coast of Africa (1824–1827); First Burmese War to protect interests of East India Company (1824–1826); British workers permitted to unionize
1825	Ackermann's gift-book annual, *Forget-me-not* creates publishing craze; Hazlitt, *The Spirit of the Age*; Nash remodels Buckingham Palace	Missolonghi falls to Turks by April; Philhellenism spreads throughout Europe; Greeks under British Protection; John Quincy Adams elected 6th president of the U.S.; French aristocrats compensated for losses suffered in Revolution
1826	Cooper, *The Last of the Mohicans*; Benjamin Disraeli, *Vivian Gray*; Weber, *Oberon* (opera); Mendelssohn, *Overture to A Midsummer Night's Dream*; John Martin, *The Deluge* (painting); Anna Jameson, *The Diary of an Ennuyee*	
1827	Constable, *The Glebe Farm* and *The Corn Field* (paintings); Beethoven dies; Baedeker's first travel guides; Balzac begins *La Comédie humaine* (–1847)	At Battle of Navarino, British, French, and Russian forces destroy Egyptian fleet at harbor; Grecian independence ensured
1828	Edward Bulwer-Lytton, *Pelham*; Dumas, *Les Trois Mousquetaires*; Webster, *American Dictionary of the English Language* (2 vols)	Cabinet of Wellington (1828–1830); Br. Test Act repealed; Russia declares war on Turkey
1829	Turner, *Ulysses Deriding Polyphemous* (painting); Constable paints *Hadleigh Castle*; Poe, *Al Araaf Tamerlane, and Other Poems*; Schlegel dies; Chopin debuts in Vienna; Knapp, *Lectures on American Literature*	July Revolution in France; Turks concede to Grecian Independence in Treaty of Adrianople; Andrew Jackson becomes 7th U.S. president; white manhood suffrage established in most U.S. states; Daniel O'Connell, M.P., agitates to repeal Act of Union between Ireland and Great Britain

YEAR	PHILOSOPHY, EDUCATION, RELIGION, ECONOMICS	SCIENCE, EXPLORATION, MEDICINE, TECHNOLOGY
1823		*The Mechanics' Magazine* (–1897); Cauchy establishes fundamental theorem of calculus; medical journal, *The Lancet,* published; Mackintosh invents water-repellent fabric
1824	Leopold von Ranke, *History of the Latin and Teutonic People, 1494–1535; Westminster Review* begins pub.	J. L. Prévost and J. B. Dumas prove that sperm is required to fertilize the egg; Society for the Prevention of Cruelty to Animals founded; Bichat, *General Anatomy* (trans); Curtis, *British Entomology*
1825	James Mill, *Analysis of the Phenomena of the Human Mind;* Robert Dale Owen and Frances Wright found utopian community in New Harmony, Indiana; Whately, *Essays on Some of the Peculiarities of the Christian Religion*	Stockton-Darlington Railway becomes first successful railway system; Alexander Laing crosses desert from Tripoli, goes on to become first explorer to visit Timbuktu
1826	Jane Marcet, *Conversations on the Evidences of Christianity*	Lobachevsky develops non-Euclidean geometry; first railway tunnel in England; Royal Zoological Society founded
1827	Hallam, *The Constitutional History of England;* John Keble, *The Christian Year*	Fourneyron's water turbine; Ohm's Law defines electrical current potential and resistance; Audubon begins publication of *Birds of North America;* Edward Parry tries reaching North Pole, but does not get beyond 82°45′ N.L., the record for 50 years; Niepce reproduces photographs; John Walker produces friction matches; Ressel obtains patent for screw propellor for steamships; Bellefonds explores Nile to lat. 13°69′ N.L.; Faraday, *Chemical Manipulation*
1828	Dale appointed first professor of English Language and Literature, University of London	Von Baer founds comparative embryology; Wohler's synthesis of urea undermines vitalism and begins organic chemistry; construction of Baltimore and Ohio railway begun
1829	Catholic Emancipation Act in Great Britain; *London Encyclopedia* (29 vols)	British chemist James Smithson wills £100,000 to found Smithsonian in Washington, D.C.; U.S. patent on typewriter granted to William Burt; Stephens, *Systematic Catalogue of British Insects*

YEAR	LITERATURE, THE ARTS, AND LITERARY STUDIES	POLITICS AND WAR
1830	Cobbett, *Rural Rides*; Delacroix, *Liberty Leading the People* (painting); Stendhal, *Le Rouge et le Noir*; Tennyson, *Poems, Chiefly Lyrical*; Maria Jane Jewsbury, *Three Histories*; Catherine Moody Gore, *Women as They Are*; Moore, *Life of Byron*; Channing, *Remarks on American Literature*	George IV dies; Wellington resigns, effectively ending 50 years of Tory rule; Whigs in the Cabinet of Earl Grey adopt Reform as their program; Louis Phillipe begins reign in France (1830–1848)

YEAR	PHILOSOPHY, EDUCATION, RELIGION, ECONOMICS	SCIENCE, EXPLORATION, MEDICINE, TECHNOLOGY
1830	Comte, *Cours de philosophie positive* (?–1842); Phillips, *Protest against the prevailing principles of Natural Philosophy, with the development of a common-sense system*	Lyle begins publication of *Principles of Geology*; Royal Geographic Society founded; steam cars used in London; Liverpool-Manchester Railway opened; Babbage, *Reflections on the Decline of Science in England*

Bibliographies

I. Historical and Cultural Contexts

The French Revolution and Rights of Man

Crossley, Ceri and Ian Small, eds. *The French Revolution and British Culture.* New York: Oxford UP, 1989.

Harrison, John F. C. *The Birth and Growth of Industrial England, 1714–1867.* New York: Harcourt, 1973.

Lefebvre, Georges. *The Coming of the French Revolution,* trans R. R. Palmer. 1947. Princeton, NJ: Princeton UP, 1967.

Mitchell, L. G. Introduction. *The French Revolution, 1790–1794,* vol. 8. *The Writings and Speeches of Edmund Burke,* by gen. ed. Paul Landford. Oxford: Clarendon, 1989.

Philp, Mark, ed. *The French Revolution and British Popular Politics.* Cambridge: Cambridge UP, 1991.

Scrivener, Michael. *Poetry and Reform: Periodical Verse from the English Democratic Press, 1792–1824.* Detroit: Wayne State UP, 1992.

Thrale, Mary, ed. *Selections from the Papers of the London Corresponding Society, 1792–1799.* Cambridge: Cambridge UP, 1983.

Rights of Woman

Davidoff, Leonore and Catherine Hall. *Family Fortunes: Men and Women of the English Middle-Class, 1780–1850.* Chicago: U of Chicago P, 1987.

Kelly, Gary. *Women, Writing, and Revolution 1790–1827.* Oxford: Clarendon, 1993.

Taylor, Barbara. *Eve and the New Jerusalem — Socialism and Feminism in the Nineteenth Century.* New York: Pantheon Books, 1983.

Ty, Eleanor. *Unsex'd Revolutionaries — Five Women Novelists of the 1790s.* Toronto: U of Toronto P, 1993.

Slavery, the Slave Trade, and Abolition

Davis, David Brion. *The Problem of Slavery in Western Culture.* Ithaca: Cornell University Press, 1966.

Dykes, Eva B. *The Negro in English Romantic Thought.* Washington, DC: American UP, 1942.

Hofkosh, Sonia and Alan Richardson, eds. *Romanticism, Race and Imperial Culture.* Bloomington: Indiana UP, 1996.

Midgeley, Clare. *Women against Slavery — The British Campaigns, 1780–1870.* London and New York: Routledge, 1992.

Patterson, Orlando. *Slavery and Social Death — A Comparative Study.* Cambridge: Harvard UP, 1982.

Williams, Eric. *Capitalism and Slavery.* Chapel Hill: U of North Carolina P, 1945.

———. "Golden Age of the Slave System in Britain," *Journal of Negro History,* XXV: 1940.

Society and Political Economy

Cole, G. D. H. and A. W. Filson, eds. *British Working Class Movements: Selected Documents 1789–1875.* 1951. New York: St. Martin's, 1965.

Harrison, John F. C. *The Birth and Growth of Industrial England: 1714–1967.* New York: Harcourt, 1973.

Hayter, Alethea. *Opium and the Romantic Imagination.* London: Faber and Faber, 1968.

Leask, Nigel. *British Romantic Writers and the East: Anxieties of Empire.* Cambridge: Cambridge UP, 1992.

Morse, Hosea Ballou. *The Chronicles of the East India Company Trading to China: 1635–1834.* 4 vols. Taipei: Ch'eng-Wen, 1966.

Parkinson, C. Northcote. *Trade in the Eastern Seas: 1793–1813.* London: Cambridge UP, 1937.

Thompson, E. P. *The Making of the English Working Class.* 1963. London: Victor Gollancz, 1980.

Science and Nature

Averill, James H. "Wordsworth and 'Natural Science': The Poetry of 1798." *The Journal of English and Germanic Philology.* 77 (1978): 232–46.

Bewell, Alan. *Wordsworth and the Enlightenment: Nature, Man, and Society in the Experimental Poetry.* New Haven: Yale UP, 1989.

Eichner, Hans. "The Rise of Modern Science and the Genesis of Romanticism." *Publications of the Modern Language Association.* 97 (1982): 8–30.

Grabo, Carl. *A Newton Among Poets: Shelley's Use of Science in* Prometheus Unbound. 1930. New York: Gordian P, 1968.

Jordanova, Ludmilla, ed. *Languages of Nature: Critical Essays on Science and Literature.* London: Free Association, 1986.

Knight, David M. *Natural Science Books in English: 1600–1900.* New York: Praeger, 1972.

Mellor, Anne K. *Mary Shelley: Her Life, Her Fiction, Her Monsters.* New York: Methuen, 1988. Chap. 5.

Piper, H. W. *The Active Universe: Pantheism and the Concept of the Imagination in the English Romantic Poets.* London: Athlone, 1962.

Wylie, Ian. "Coleridge and the Lunatics," in *The Coleridge Connection: Essays for Thomas McFarland,* eds. Richard Gravil and Molly Lefebure. Houndmills: Macmillan, 1990.

Aesthetic Theory and Literary Criticism

Abrams, M. H. *The Mirror and the Lamp: Romantic Theory and the Critical Tradition.* New York: Norton, 1953.

Barker-Benfield, J. G. *The Culture of Sensibility — Sex and Society in Eighteenth-Century Britain.* Chicago: U of Chicago P, 1992.

Bate, Walter Jackson. *From Classic to Romantic — Premises of Taste in Eighteenth-Century England.* New York: Harper, 1946.

Beer, John, ed. *Questioning Romanticism.* Baltimore: Johns Hopkins UP, 1995.

Hipple, Walter John, Jr. *The Beautiful, the Sublime and the Picturesque in Eighteenth-Century British Aesthetic Theory.* Carbondale: Southern Illinois UP, 1957.

Klancher, Jon P. *The Making of English Reading Audiences 1790–1832.* Madison: U of Wisconsin P, 1987.

McGann, Jerome. *The Romantic Ideology.* Chicago: U of Chicago P, 1983.

Mellor, Anne K. *English Romantic Irony.* Cambridge: Harvard UP, 1980.

Wellek, Rene. *A History of Modern Criticism: The Romantic Age.* New Haven: Yale UP, 1955.

II. GENERAL BIBLIOGRAPHY FOR THE LITERARY PERIOD, 1780–1830

Romanticism and Gender

Feldman, Paula R. and Theresa M. Kelley, eds. *Romantic Women Writers — Voices and Countervoices.* Hanover and London: UP of New England, 1995.

Mellor, Anne K. *Romanticism and Gender.* New York and London: Routledge, Chapman and Hall, 1993.

———, ed. *Romanticism and Feminism.* Bloomington: Indiana UP, 1988.

Ross, Marlon B. *The Contours of Masculine Desire: Romanticism and the Rise of Women's Poetry.* New York and Oxford: Oxford UP, 1989.

Wilson, Carol Shiner and Joel Haefner, eds. *Re-Visioning Romanticism — British Women Writers, 1776–1837.* Philadelphia: U of Pennsylvania P, 1994.

Romanticism and History

Butler, Marilyn. *Romantics, Rebels and Reactionaries — English Literature and Its Background, 1760–1830.* Oxford: Oxford UP, 1981.

Leask, Nigel. *British Romantic Writers and the East — Anxieties of Empire.* Cambridge: Cambridge UP, 1992. rept. 1994.

Manning, Peter. *Reading Romantics — Text and Context.* New York and Oxford: Oxford UP, 1990.

Siskin, Clifford. *The Historicity of Romantic Discourse.* New York and Oxford: Oxford UP, 1988.

III. INDIVIDUAL AUTHORS

Lucy Aikin

Lorimer: A Tale. London, 1814.

Mellor, Anne K. "Distinguishing the Poetess from the Female Poet," in *Approaches to Teaching British Women Poets of the Romantic Period,* ed. Stephen Behrendt and Harriet Linkin. New York: MLA, 1996.

Memoirs of the Court of Elizabeth Queen of England. London, 1818.

Memoirs of the Court of King James the First. London, 1822.

Memoirs of the Court of King Charles the First. London, 1833.

Schnorrenberg, Barbara Brandon. "Lucy Aikin," *New Dictionary of National Biography,* forthcoming.

Jane Austen

Chapman, R. W., ed. *The Works of Jane Austen.* 6 vols. London: Oxford UP, 1954. rev. 1965.

———, ed. *Jane Austen's Letters to her Sister Cassandra and Others.* 2nd ed. London: Oxford UP, 1952. rept. 1969.

Halperin, John. *The Life of Jane Austen.* Baltimore: Johns Hopkins UP, 1984.

Auerbach, Nina. *Communities of Women: An Idea in Fiction.* Cambridge: Harvard UP, 1978.

Brown, Julia Prewitt. *Jane Austen's Novels: Social Change and Literary Form.* Cambridge: Harvard UP, 1979.

Butler, Marilyn. *Jane Austen and the War of Ideas.* Oxford: Clarendon, 1975.

Duckworth, Alistair. *The Improvement of the Estate: A Study of Jane Austen's Novels.* Baltimore: Johns Hopkins UP, 1971.

Harding, D. W. "Regulated Hatred: An Aspect of the Work of Jane Austen," *Scrutiny* 9 (1940): 346–62.

Kaplan, Deborah. *Jane Austen among Women.* Baltimore: Johns Hopkins UP, 1992.

Kirkham, Margaret. *Jane Austen, Feminism and Fiction.* Brighton, England: Harvester, 1983.

Johnson, Claudia. *Jane Austen: Women, Politics, and the Novel.* Chicago: U of Chicago P, 1988.

Mudrick, Marvin. *Jane Austen: Irony as Defense and Discovery.* Berkeley: U of California P, 1968.

Newton, Judith Lowder. *Women, Power and Subversion: Social Strategies in British Fiction, 1778–1860.* Athens: U of Georgia P, 1981.

Roberts, Warren. *Jane Austen and the French Revolution.* New York: St. Martin's, 1979.

Sulloway, Alison G. *Jane Austen and the Province of Womanhood.* Philadelphia: U of Pennsylvania P, 1989.

Tanner, Tony. *Jane Austen.* Cambridge: Harvard UP, 1986.

Joanna Baillie

The Dramatic and Poetical Works of Joanna Baillie. London: Longman, Brown, Green and Longmans, 1851. rept. Hildesheim and New York: Georg Olms Verlag, 1976.

Carhart, Margaret S. *The Life and Work of Joanna Baillie.* New Haven: Yale UP, 1923.

Burroughs, Catherine B. "English Romantic Women Writers and Theatre Theory: Joanna Baillie's Prefaces to the *Plays on the Passions,*" in *Re-Visioning Romanticism.* Ed. Carol Shiner Wilson and Joel Haefner. Philadelphia: U of Pennsylvania P, 1994.

Mellor, Anne. "Joanna Baillie and the Counter-Public Sphere," *Studies in Romanticism* 33 (Winter 1994) 559–67.

Anna Letitia Barbauld

McCarthy, William and Elizabeth Kraft, ed. *The Poems of Anna Letitia Barbauld.* Athens and London: U of Georgia P, 1994.

Aikin, Lucy, ed. *Works of Anna Letitia Barbauld.* 2 vols. London: Longman, 1825, with "Memoir."

Ellis, Grace A., ed. *Memoir, Letters, and a Selection from the Poems and Prose Writings of Anna Letitia Barbauld,* 2 vols. Boston: Osgood, 1874.

Rodgers, Betsy. *Georgian Chronicle: Mrs. Barbauld & Her Family.* London: Methuen, 1958.

William Blake

Erdman, David, ed. *The Poetry and Prose of William Blake.* Garden City, N.J.: Doubleday, 1965.

Bentley, G. E., Jr. *Blake Books.* Oxford: Clarendon, 1977.

King, James. *William Blake—His Life.* New York: St. Martin's, 1991.

Damrosch, Leo. *Symbol and Truth in Blake's Myth.* Princeton: Princeton UP, 1980.

Eaves, Morris. *William Blake's Theory of Art.* Princeton: Princeton UP, 1982.

Erdman, David V. *Blake: Prophet against Empire.* New York: Doubleday, 1954. rev. 1969.

Essick, Robert. *William Blake and the Language of Adam.* Oxford: Clarendon, 1989.

Frye, Northrop. *Fearful Symmetry: A Study of William Blake.* Princeton: Princeton UP, 1947.

Mellor, Anne K. *Blake's Human Form Divine.* Berkeley: U of California P, 1974.

Mitchell, W. J. T. *Blake's Composite Art.* Princeton: Princeton UP, 1978.

Paley, Morton. *The Continuing City: William Blake's Jerusalem.* Oxford: Clarendon, 1983.

Thompson, E. P. *Witness against the Beast: William Blake and Moral Law.* Cambridge: Cambridge UP, 1993.

Robert Burns

Kinsley, James, ed. *The Poems and Songs of Robert Burns.* 3 vols. Oxford: Clarendon, 1968.

Low, Donald A., ed. *The Songs of Robert Burns.* London: Routledge, 1993.

Ferguson, John De Lancey, and G. Ross Roy, eds. *The Letters of Robert Burns.* 2 vols. Oxford: Clarendon, 1985.

Bentman, Raymond. *Robert Burns.* Boston: Twayne, 1987.

Low, Donald A., ed. *Robert Burns: The Critical Heritage.* London: Routledge, 1974.

———, ed. *Critical Essays on Robert Burns.* London: Routledge, 1975.

Mackay, James A. *Burns: A Biography of Robert Burns.* Edinburgh: Mainstream, 1992.

George Gordon Lord Byron

McGann, Jerome J., ed. *Lord Byron: The Complete Poetical Works.* 7 vols. Oxford: Clarendon, 1980–93.

Marchand, Leslie A., ed. *Byron's Letters and Journals.* 12 vols. Cambridge: Harvard UP, 1973–82.

———. *Byron: A Biography.* 3 vols. New York: Knopf, 1957.

———. *Byron: A Portrait.* 1970. Chicago: U of Chicago P, 1979.

Manning, Peter J. *Byron and His Fictions.* Detroit: Wayne State UP, 1978.

McGann, Jerome J. *Fiery Dust: Byron's Poetic Development.* Chicago: U of Chicago P, 1968.

Mellor, Anne K. *English Romantic Irony.* Cambridge: Harvard UP, 1980.

Richardson, Alan. *A Mental Theater: Poetic Drama and Consciousness in the Romantic Age.* University Park: Penn State UP, 1988.

Rutherford, Andrew, ed. *Byron, Augustan and Romantic.* Houndmills: Macmillan, 1990.

Thorslev, Peter L., Jr. *The Byronic Hero: Types and Prototypes.* Minneapolis, U of Minnesota P, 1962.

Trueblood, Paul G. *Lord Byron.* 2nd ed. Boston: Twayne, 1977.

John Clare

Robinson, Eric, and David Powell, eds. *The Later Poems of John Clare, 1837–1864.* 2 vols. Oxford: Clarendon, 1984.

———, eds. *John Clare.* Oxford Standard Authors. New York: Oxford UP, 1984.

Tibble, J. W. and Anne Tibble. *John Clare: A Life.* 1932. rev. Anne Tibble, London: Joseph, 1972.

Barrell, John. *The Idea of Landscape and the Sense of Place, 1730–1840: An Approach to the Poetry of John Clare.* Cambridge: Cambridge UP, 1972.

Haughton, Hugh, Adam Phillips, and Goeffrey Summerfield, eds. *John Clare in Context.* Cambridge: Cambridge UP, 1994.

Storey, Mark. *The Poetry of John Clare: A Critical Introduction.* London: Macmillan, 1974.

Samuel Taylor Coleridge

Coleridge, Ernest Hartley, ed. *The Complete Poetical Works of Samuel Taylor Coleridge.* 2 vols. Oxford: Clarendon-Oxford UP, 1912.

Coburn, Kathleen, gen. ed. *The Collected Works of Samuel Taylor Coleridge.* Bollingen Series 75. Princeton: Princeton UP, 1969–.

Griggs, Earl Leslie, ed. *The Collected Letters of Samuel Taylor Coleridge.* 6 vols. Oxford: Clarendon-Oxford UP, 1956–71.

Coburn, Kathleen, ed. *The Notebooks of Samuel Taylor Coleridge.* 4 vols. to date. New York: Pantheon, 1957–.

Bate, Walter Jackson. *Coleridge.* New York: Macmillan, 1968.

Holmes, Richard. *Coleridge: Early Visions.* New York: Viking, 1989.

Abrams, M. H. *The Mirror and the Lamp: Romantic Theory and the Critical Tradition.* New York: Oxford UP, 1953.

Beer, John. *Coleridge the Visionary.* London: Chatto & Windus, 1959.

Bostetter, Edward E. *The Romantic Ventriloquists: Wordsworth, Coleridge, Keats, Shelley, Byron.* Seattle: U of Washington P, 1963.

Fruman, Norman. *Coleridge, The Damaged Archangel.* New York: Braziller, 1971.

Lowes, John Livingston. *The Road to Xanadu: A Study in the Ways of the Imagination.* 1927. rev. 1930. Princeton: Princeton UP, 1986.

Magnuson, Paul. *Coleridge and Wordsworth: A Lyrical Dialogue.* Princeton: Princeton UP, 1988.

McFarland, Thomas. *Romanticism and the Forms of Ruin: Wordsworth, Coleridge, and the Modalities of Fragmentation.* Princeton: Princeton UP, 1981.

McGann, Jerome J. "*The Ancient Mariner:* The Meaning of the Meanings." In *The Beauty of Inflections: Literary Investigations in Historical Method and Theory.* Oxford: Clarendon-Oxford UP, 1985. 135–72.

Roe, Nicholas. *Wordsworth and Coleridge: The Radical Years.* Oxford: Clarendon-Oxford UP, 1988.

Schneider, Elisabeth. *Coleridge, Opium, and "Kubla Khan."* Chicago: U of Chicago P, 1953.

Thomas De Quincey

Mason, David, ed. *The Collected Writings of Thomas De Quincey.* 14 vols. Edinburgh: Adam and Charles Black, 1890.

De Quincey, Thomas. *Confessions of an English Opium-Eater.* 1822. Oxford: Woodstock Books, 1989.

Lindop, Grevel. *The Opium-Eater: A Life of Thomas De Quincey.* London: Dent, 1981.

Hayter, Alethea. *Opium and the Romantic Imagination.* Berkeley: U of California P, 1970.

Leask, Nigel. *British Romantic Writers and the East: Anxieties of Empire.* Cambridge: Cambridge UP, 1992. chap 3.

McFarland, Thomas. *Romantic Cruxes: The English Essayists and The Spirit of the Age.* Oxford: Clarendon, 1987.

Maria Edgeworth

Butler, Marilyn, and W. J. McCormack, eds. *The Works of Maria Edgeworth.* 12 vols. London: Pickering & Chatto, 1996.

Butler, Marilyn. *Maria Edgeworth: A Literary Biography.* Oxford: Oxford UP, 1972.

Ferguson, Moira. *Subject to Others: British Women Writers and Colonial Slavery, 1670–1834.* New York: Routledge, 1992.

Kowaleski-Wallace, Elizabeth. *Their Fathers' Daughters: Hannah More, Maria Edgeworth & Patriarchal Complicity.* New York and Oxford: Oxford UP, 1991.

MacFadyen, Heather. "Lady Delacour's Library: Maria Edgeworth's *Belinda* and Fashionable Reading," *Nineteenth-Century Literature* 48:4 (March 1994): 423–39.

Olaudah Equiano

The Life of Olaudah Equiano: or, Gustavas Vassa the African, 1789, rept. with a new Introduction by Paul Edwards. 2 vols. London: Dawsons, 1969.

Costanzo, Angelo. *Surprising Narrative: Olaudah Equiano and the Beginnings of Black Autobiography.* New York: Greenwood, 1987.

Edwards, Paul. "Three West African Writers of the 1780's," in *The Slave's Narrative.* Ed. Charles T. Davis and Henry Louis Gates, Jr. Oxford: Oxford UP, 1985. 175–98.

Fichtelberg, Joseph. "Word between Worlds: The Economy of Equiano's Narrative," *American Literary History* 5 (1993): 459–80.

Marren, Susan M. "Between Slavery and Freedom: The Transgressive Self in Olaudah Equiano's Autobiography." *PMLA* 108 (1993): 94–105.

Samuels, Wilfred D. "Disguised Voice in the Interesting Narrative of Olaudah Equiano, or Gustavas Vassa, the African," *Black American Literature Forum* 19 (1985): 64–69.

Felicia Dorothea Browne Hemans

The Works of Mrs. [Felicia] Hemans. 7 vols. London: Thomas Cadell. 1839. Edinburgh: William Blackwood & Sons, 1839.

Chorley, Henry F. *Memorials of Mrs. Hemans, with Illustrations of Her Literary Character from Her Private Correspondence,* 2 vols. London: Saunders and Otley, 1836.

Hughes (later Owen), Harriett Mary [Browne]. *Memoir of the Life and Writings of Felicia Hemans: By Her Sister.* vol. 1 of the 1839 Cadell/Blackwood edition of Hemans' *Works* cited above.

Armstrong, Isobel. *Victorian Poetry: Poetry, poetics and politics.* London and New York: Routledge, 1993. ch. 12.

Clarke, Norma. *Ambitious Heights: Writing, Friendship, Love — The Jewsbury Sisters, Felicia Hemans, and Jane Welsh Carlyle.* London: Routledge, 1990.

Feldman, Paula R. and Theresa M. Kelley, eds. *Romantic Women Writers — Voices and Countervoices.* Hanover and London: UP of New England, 1995. essays by Susan Wolfson (33–68) and Anthony Harding (138–49).

Leighton, Angela. *Victorian Women Poets: Writing against the Heart.* Charlottesville: U of Virginia P, 1993. ch. 1.

Lootens, Tricia. "Hemans and Home: Victorianism, Feminine 'Internal Enemies,' and the Domestication of National Identity," *PMLA* 109 (1994): 238–53.

Mellor, Anne K. *Romanticism and Gender.* New York and London: Routledge, 1993. ch. 6.

Trinder, Peter W. *Mrs. Hemans.* Cardiff: U of Wales, 1984.

Wilson, Carol Shiner and Joel Haefner, eds. *Re-Visioning Romanticism — British Women Writers, 1776–1837.* Philadelphia:

U of Pennsylvania P, 1994. essays by Susan Wolfson (128–66) and Jerome McGann (210–27).

John Keats

Stillinger, Jack, ed. *The Poems of John Keats.* Cambridge: Harvard UP, 1978.

Rollins, Edward Hyder, ed. *The Letters of John Keats.* 2 vols. Cambridge: Harvard UP, 1958.

Bate, Walter Jackson. *John Keats.* 1963. New York: Oxford UP, 1966.

Brooks, Cleanth. *The Well-Wrought Urn: Studies in the Structure of Poetry.* 1947. New York: Harcourt, 1975.

Perkins, David. *The Quest for Permanence: The Symbolism of Wordsworth, Shelley, and Keats.* Cambridge: Harvard UP, 1959.

Sperry, Stuart. *Keats the Poet.* 1973. Princeton: Princeton UP, 1994.

Stillinger, Jack. *The Hoodwinking of Madeline and Other Essays on Keats's Poems.* Urbana: U of Illinois P, 1971.

Vendler, Helen. *The Odes of John Keats.* Cambridge, MA: Harvard UP, 1983.

Waldoff, Leon. *Keats and the Silent Work of the Imagination.* Urbana: U of Illinois P, 1985.

Wolfson, Susan J. *The Questioning Presence: Wordsworth, Keats, and the Interrogative Mode in Romantic Poetry.* Ithaca: Cornell UP, 1986.

Charles Lamb

Lucas, E. V., ed. *The Works of Charles and Mary Lamb.* 7 vols. London: Methuen, 1903–05.

———, ed. *The Letters of Charles Lamb: To Which Are Added Those of His Sister, Mary Lamb.* London: Dent, 1935.

Marrs, Edwin W., ed. *The Letters of Charles and Mary Lamb.* 3 vols. to date. Ithaca: Cornell UP, 1975–.

Courtney, Winifred F. *Young Charles Lamb, 1775–1802.* New York: New York UP, 1982.

Aaron, Jane. *A Double Singleness: Gender and the Writing of Charles and Mary Lamb.* Oxford: Clarendon, 1991.

Barnett, George L. *Charles Lamb.* Boston: Twayne, 1976.

McFarland, Thomas. *Romantic Cruxes: The English Essayists and The Spirit of the Age.* Oxford: Clarendon, 1987.

Letitia Elizabeth Landon

Sypher, E. J., ed. *Poetical Works of Letitia Elizabeth Landon—"L. E. L.".* London, 1873. rept. Delmar, New York: Scholars' Facsimiles & Reprints, 1990.

Complete Works of Letitia Elizabeth Landon. London, 1856.

Blanchard, Laman. *Life and Literary Remains of L. E. L.,* 2 vols. London: Henry Colburn, 1841.

Armstrong, Isobel. *Victorian Poetry—Poetry, poetics and politics.* London and New York: Routledge, 1993. ch. 12.

Leighton, Angela. *Victorian Women Poets: Writing against the Heart.* London: Harvester, 1992, and Charlottesville, Va.: U of Virginia P, 1993. ch. 2.

Mellor, Anne K. *Romanticism and Gender.* New York: Routledge, 1993. ch. 6.

Stephenson, Glennis. *Letitia Landon: The Woman Behind L. E. L.* Manchester: Manchester UP, 1995.

Hannah More

Collected Works of Hannah More, 8 vols. 1799. rept. London: T. Cadell, 1801.

Roberts, William, ed. *Memoirs of the Life and Correspondence of Mrs. Hannah More,* 2 vols. 1834. rept., New York: Harper Brothers, 1836.

Jones, M. G. *Hannah More.* Cambridge: Cambridge UP, 1952.

Kowaleski-Wallace, Elizabeth. *Their Father's Daughters—Hannah More, Maria Edgeworth and Patriarchal Complicity.* New York and Oxford: Oxford UP, 1991.

Myers, Mitzi. "Reform or Ruin: 'A Revolution in Female Manners'," *Studies in Eighteenth-Century Culture,* vol. 11, ed. Harry C. Payne. Madison: U of Wisconsin P, 1982: 199–216.

Pederson, Susan. "Hannah More Meets Simple Simon: Tracts, Chapbooks, and Popular Culture in Late Eighteenth-Century England," *Journal of British Studies* 25. 1 (1986): 84–113.

Amelia Alderson Opie

The Father and Daughter. London, 1801.

Poems. London, 1802.

Adeline Mowbray. London, 1804. rept. London: Pandora, 1986.

Brightwell, Cecilia Lucy, ed. *Memorials of the Life of Amelia Opie.* London: Longman and Brown, 1854.

Eberle, Roxanne. "Amelia Opie's *Adeline Mowbray:* Diverting the Libertine Gaze; or, The Vindication of a Fallen Woman." *Studies in the Novel* 26 (1994): 121–52.

Sydney Owenson, Lady Morgan

The Wild Irish Girl. Dublin, 1806. rept. London: Pandora, 1986.

France. London, 1817.

The O'Briens and the O'Flahertys—A National Tale. Dublin, 1827. rept. London: Pandora, 1988.

France in 1829–30. London, 1830.

Campbell, Mary. *Lady Morgan—The Life and Times of Sydney Owenson.* London: Pandora, 1988.

Stevenson, Lionel. *The Wild Irish Girl—The Life of Sydney Owenson, Lady Morgan.* London: Chapman and Hall, 1936.

Newcomer, James. *Lady Morgan the Novelist.* Lewisburg: Bucknell University Press, 1990.

Mary Prince

Ferguson, Moira, ed. *The History of Mary Prince.* London: Pandora, 1987.

———. *Subject to Others—British Women Writers and Colonial Slavery, 1670–1834.* New York and London: Routledge, 1992. ch. 13.

Paquet, Sandra Pouchet. "The Heartbeat of a West Indian Slave: *The History of Mary Prince.*" *African American Review* 26 (1992): 131–46.

Mary Darby Robinson

Robinson, Maria, ed. *Poetical Works of the Late Mrs. Mary Robinson.* London: 1806. rept. 1828.

———, ed. *Memoirs of the Late Mrs. Robinson, Written by Herself.* London: 1801.

Bass, Robert D. *The Green Dragoon: The Lives of Banastre Tarleton and Mary Robinson.* New York: Henry Holt, 1957.

Fergus, Jan, and Janice Farrar Thaddeus. "Women, Publishers, and Money, 1790–1820," in *Studies in Eighteenth-Century Culture* 17:191–207.

Peterson, Linda H. "Becoming an Author: Mary Robinson's *Memoirs* and the Origins of the Woman Artist's Autobiography," in *Re-Visioning Romanticism.* Eds. Carol Shiner Wilson and Joel Haefner. Philadelphia: U of Pennsylvania P, 1994.

Walter Scott

Lang, Andrew, ed. *Poems and Ballads.* 6 vols. Boston: D. Estes, 1900.

———, ed. *The Waverley Novels.* New York: E. B. Hall, 1892–94.

Grierson, H. J. C., et al., eds. *The Letters of Sir Walter Scott.* 12 vols. London: Constable, 1932–37.

Johnson, Edgar. *Sir Walter Scott: The Great Unknown.* 2 vols. New York: MacMillan, 1970.

Lockhart, J. G. *Memoirs of the Life of Sir Walter Scott.* Philadelphia: Carey Lea & Blanchard, 1837.

Daiches, David. *Sir Walter Scott and His World.* London: Thames and Hudson, 1971.

Duncan, Ian. *Modern Romance and Transformations of the Novel: the Gothic, Scott, and Dickens.* Cambridge: Cambridge UP, 1992.

Ferris, Ina. *The Achievement of Literary Authority: Gender, History, and the Waverley Novels.* Ithaca: Cornell UP, 1991.

Millgate, Jane. *Walter Scott: The Making of the Novelist.* Toronto: U of Toronto P, 1984.

Mary Wollstonecraft Godwin Shelley

Crook, Nora, ed., with Pamela Clemit. *The Novels and Selected Works of Mary Shelley.* 8 vols. London: Pickering & Chatto, 1996.

Robinson, Charles E., ed. *Mary Shelley: Collected Tales and Stories.* Baltimore: Johns Hopkins UP, 1976.

Bennett, Betty T., ed. *The Letters of Mary Wollstonecraft Shelley.* 3 vols. Baltimore: Johns Hopkins UP, 1980–88.

Feldman, Paula R., and Diana Scott-Kilvert, eds. *The Journals of Mary Shelley, 1814–1844.* 2 vols. Oxford: Clarendon, 1987.

Sunstein, Emily W. *Mary Shelley: Romance and Reality.* Boston: Little, 1989.

Baldick, Chris. *In Frankenstein's Shadow—Myth, Monstrosity, and Nineteenth-Century Writing.* Oxford: Clarendon, 1987.

Cantor, Paul. *Creature and Creator—Myth-Making and English Romanticism.* Cambridge: Cambridge UP, 1984.

Fisch, Audrey, Anne Mellor, and Esther Schor, eds. *The Other Mary Shelley—Beyond Frankenstein.* New York: Oxford UP, 1993.

Levine, George, and U. C. Knoepflmacher, eds. *The Endurance of Frankenstein: Essays on Mary Shelley's Novel.* Berkeley: U of California P, 1979.

Mellor, Anne K. *Mary Shelley: Her Life, Her Fiction, Her Monsters.* New York and London: Methuen/Routledge, 1989.

Poovey, Mary. *The Proper Lady and the Woman Writer.* Chicago: U of Chicago P, 1984. chs. 4–5.

Veeder, William. *Mary Shelley & Frankenstein—The Fate of Androgyny.* Chicago: U of Chicago P, 1986.

Percy Bysshe Shelley

Ingpen, Roger, and Walter E. Peck, eds. *The Complete Works of Percy Bysshe Shelley.* 10 vols. London: Ernest Benn, 1926–30.

Reiman, Donald H., and Sharon B. Powers, eds. *Shelley's Poetry and Prose.* New York: Norton, 1977.

Jones, Frederick, ed. *The Letters of Percy Bysshe Shelley.* 2 vols. Oxford: Clarendon, 1964.

White, Newman Ivey. *Shelley.* 2 vols. New York: Knopf, 1940.

———. *The Young Shelley: The Genesis of a Radical.* New York: Macmillan, 1950.

Cameron, Kenneth Neill. *Shelley: The Golden Years.* Cambridge: Harvard UP, 1974.

Gelpi, Barbara. *Shelley's Goddess: Maternity, Language, Subjectivity.* New York: Oxford UP, 1992.

Hogle, Jerrold. *Shelley's Process: Radical Transference and the Process of his Major Works.* New York: Oxford UP, 1988.

Keach, William. *Shelley's Style.* New York: Methuen, 1984.

Pulos, C. E. *The Deep Truth: A Study of Shelley's Scepticism.* Lincoln: U of Nebraska P, 1954.

Reiman, Donald H. *Percy Bysshe Shelley.* 1969. Boston: Twayne, 1990.

Wasserman, Earl R. *Shelley: A Critical Reading.* Baltimore: Johns Hopkins UP, 1971.

Charlotte Turner Smith

Curran, Stuart, ed. *The Poems of Charlotte Smith.* London: Oxford UP, 1993.

Hilbish, Florence. *Charlotte Smith: Poet and Novelist, 1749–1806.* Philadelphia: The Mitre Press, 1941.

Jane Taylor

Barry, F. V., ed. *Jane Taylor, Prose and Poetry.* London: Humphrey Milford, 1924.

Curran, Stuart. "Romantic Poetry: The I Altered," in *Romanticism and Feminism*, ed. Anne K. Mellor. Bloomington: Indiana UP, 1988. 185–207.

Davidoff, Leonore, and Catherine Hall. *Family Fortunes—Men and Women of the English Middle Class, 1780–1850*. Chicago: U of Chicago P, 1987.

McGann, Jerome. "Poetry, 1785–1832," in *The Columbia History of British Poetry*, ed. Carl Woodring and James Shapiro. New York: Columbia UP, 1994. 353–80.

John Thelwall

Poems Chiefly Written in Retirement. 1801. Oxford: Woodstock Books, 1989.

Roe, Nicholas. "Coleridge and John Thelwall. The Road to Nether Stowey." In *The Coleridge Connection: Essays for Thomas McFarland*, eds. Richard Gravil and Molly Lefebure. Basingstoke: 1990.

———. *Wordsworth and Coleridge: The Radical Years*. Oxford: Clarendon, 1988.

Helen Maria Williams

Letters from France, London: 1795, 1796. 8 vols. Ed. with Introduction by Janet Todd. Delmar, New York: Scholars' Facsimiles and Reprints, 1975.

Poems, 2 vols. London, 1786.

Woodward, Lionel-D. *Une Amie Anglaise de la Révolution Française*. Paris: Ancienne Honore Champion, 1930.

Favret, Mary A. *Romantic Correspondence: Women, Politics & The Fiction of Letters*. Cambridge: Cambridge UP, 1993, ch. 3.

Jones, Chris. "Helen Maria Williams and Radical Sensibility," *Prose Studies* 12 (1989): 3–24.

Mellor, Anne K. "English Women Writers and the French Revolution," in *Rebel Daughters: Women and the French Revolution*, ed. Sara E. Melzer and Leslie W. Rabine. New York: Oxford UP, 1992. 255–72.

Watson, Nicola J. *Revolution and the Form of the British Novel, 1790–1825—Intercepted Letters, Interrupted Seductions*. Oxford: Clarendon, 1994.

Mary Wollstonecraft

Todd, Janet, and Marilyn Butler, eds. *The Works of Mary Wollstonecraft*. 8 vols. London: Pickering & Chatto, 1989. New York: New York UP, 1989.

Poston, Carol, ed. *A Vindication of the Rights of Woman*. New York: Norton Critical Edition. rev. ed. 1988. Includes excellent selection of critical essays and bibliography.

Sunstein, Emily W. *The Life of Mary Wollstonecraft*. Boston and Toronto: Little, 1975.

Tomalin, Claire. *The Life and Death of Mary Wollstonecraft*. New York and London: Harcourt, 1974.

Kelly, Gary. *Revolutionary Feminism—The Mind and Career of Mary Wollstonecraft*. New York: St. Martin's, 1992.

Mellor, Anne K. *Romanticism and Gender*. New York and London: Routledge, 1993. ch. 2.

Poovey, Mary. *The Proper Lady and the Woman Writer*. Chicago: U of Chicago P, 1984. chs. 2–3.

Sapiro, Virginia. *A Vindication of Political Virtue—The Political Theory of Mary Wollstonecraft*. Chicago: U of Chicago P, 1992.

Dorothy Wordsworth

Moorman, Mary, ed. *The Journals of Dorothy Wordsworth*. Oxford: Oxford UP, 1971.

Woof, Pamela, ed. *Dorothy Wordsworth: The Grasmere Journals*. Oxford: Oxford UP, 1993.

Levin, Susan M., ed. "The Collected Poems of Dorothy Wordsworth." Appendix One, *Dorothy Wordsworth and Romanticism* by Levin. New Brunswick: Rutgers UP, 1987.

Hill, Alan, ed. *Letters of Dorothy Wordsworth*. Oxford: Oxford UP, 1987.

Gittings, Robert and Jo Manton. *Dorothy Wordsworth*. Oxford: Clarendon, 1985.

Alexander, Meena. *Women in Romanticism: Mary Wollstonecraft, Dorothy Wordsworth, and Mary Shelley*. Totowa, N.J.: Barnes, 1989.

Homans, Margaret. *Women Writers and Poetic Identity*. Princeton: Princeton UP, 1980.

Mellor, Anne K. "Writing the Self / Self Writing: William Wordsworth's *Prelude* / Dorothy Wordsworth's *Journals*." In *Romanticism and Gender*. New York: Routledge, 1993. 144–69.

The Wordsworth Circle. 9 (1978). Special issue on Dorothy Wordsworth.

William Wordsworth

de Selincourt, Ernest, ed. *The Poetical Works of William Wordsworth*. 5 vols. Oxford: Clarendon, 1940–49.

Parrish, Stephen, gen. ed. *The Cornell Wordsworth*. Ithaca: Cornell UP, 1975–.

Gill, Stephen, ed. *William Wordsworth*. Oxford Author Series. New York: Oxford UP, 1984.

Brett, R. L., and A. R. Jones, eds. *Lyrical Ballads: Wordsworth and Coleridge*. New York: Barnes, 1968.

Wordsworth, Jonathan, M. H. Abrams, and Stephen Gill, eds. *The Prelude, 1799, 1805, 1850: Authoritative Texts, Context and Reception, Recent Critical Essays*. New York: Norton, 1979.

Owen, J. W. B., and J. M. Smyser, eds. *Prose Works*. 3 vols. Oxford: Oxford UP, 1974.

de Selincourt, Ernest, et al., eds. *The Letters of William and Dorothy Wordsworth*. 6 vols. Oxford: Clarendon, 1967–.

Darlington, Beth, ed. *The Love Letters of William and Mary Wordsworth*. Oxford: Clarendon, 1981.

Gill, Stephen. *William Wordsworth: A Life*. Oxford: Clarendon, 1989.

Bialostosky, Don H. *Making Tales: The Poetics of Wordsworth's Narrative Experiments*. Chicago: U of Chicago P, 1984.

Chandler, James K. *Wordsworth's Second Nature: A Study of the Poetry and Politics*. Chicago: U of Chicago P, 1984.

Gilpin, George H. *Critical Essays on William Wordsworth.* Boston: G. K. Hall, 1990.
Hartman, Geoffrey. *Wordsworth's Poetry: 1787–1814.* 1964. New Haven: Yale UP, 1971.
Johnston, Kenneth R. *Wordsworth and* "The Recluse." New Haven: Yale UP, 1984.
Kelley, Theresa M. *Wordsworth's Revisionary Aesthetics.* Cambridge: Cambridge UP, 1988.
Levinson, Marjorie. *Wordsworth's Great Period Poems: Four Essays.* Cambridge: Cambridge UP, 1986.
Liu, Alan. *Wordsworth: The Sense of History.* Stanford: Stanford UP, 1989.
Manning, Peter J. *Reading Romantics: Texts and Contexts.* New York: Oxford UP, 1990.
McFarland, Thomas. *Romanticism and the Forms of Ruin: Wordsworth, Coleridge, and the Modalities of Fragmentation.* Princeton: Princeton UP, 1981.
Onorato, Richard J. *The Character of the Poet: Wordsworth in* The Prelude. Princeton, N.J.: Princeton UP, 1971.
Page, Judith W. *Wordsworth and the Cultivation of Women.* Berkeley: U of California P, 1994.
Roe, Nicholas. *Wordsworth and Coleridge: The Radical Years.* Oxford: Clarendon-Oxford UP, 1988.
Sheats, Paul D. *The Making of Wordsworth's Poetry, 1785–1798.* Cambridge: Harvard UP, 1973.
Simpson, David. *Wordsworth's Historical Imagination: The Poetry of Displacement.* New York: Methuen, 1987.
Woodring, Carl. *Wordsworth.* Cambridge: Harvard UP, 1975.
Wordsworth, Jonathan. *William Wordsworth and the Borders of Vision.* Oxford: Clarendon, 1982.

Ann Cromarty Yearsley

Poems on Several Occasions. London, 1784.
Poems on Various Subjects. London, 1787.
The Rural Lyre. London, 1796.

Doody, Margaret Anne. *The Daring Muse—Augustan Poetry Reconsidered.* Cambridge: Cambridge University Press, 1985.
Ferguson, Moira. "Resistance and Power in the Life and Writings of Ann Yearsley," in *The Eighteenth Century: Theory and Interpretation* 27:3. Fall 1986: 247–68.
Landry, Donna. *The Muses of Resistance—Laboring-Class Women's Poetry in Britain, 1739–1796.* Cambridge: Cambridge UP, 1990. ch. 4.
Waldron, Mary. "Ann Yearsley and the Clifton Records," *The Age of Johnson: A Scholarly Annual* 3. Ed. Paul J. Korshin. New York: AMS, 1990.

IV. CHRONOLOGY

Chronological Table. *British Writers,* vol. 3. Gen ed. Ian Scott-Kilvert. New York: Charles Scribner's, 1979.
Chronology 1770–1850. *William Wordsworth and the Age of English Romanticism.* eds. Jonathan Wordsworth, Michael C. Jaye, and Robert Woof. Rutgers: Rutgers UP, 1987.
Drabble, Margaret, ed. *The Oxford Companion to English Literature.* 5th ed. New York: Oxford UP, 1985.
Grun, Bernard. *The Timetables of History: A Horizontal Linkage of People and Events.* 3rd ed. New York: Touchstone, 1991.
Knight, David M. *Natural Science Books in English: 1600–1900.* Praeger: New York, 1972.
Langer, William L. *An Encyclopedia of World History: Ancient, Medieval, and Modern.* 4th ed. Boston: Houghton, 1968.
Parker, William Riley. "The History of English Studies: 1557–1967." Unpublished chronology of books, periodicals, and events. September 1967.

Index of Authors, Titles, and First Lines

Credits

Austen, Jane. Selections from *The Oxford Illustrated Jane Austen.* Ed. R.W. Chapman, 1923. Selections from *Jane Austen's Letters.* Ed. R.W. Chapman, 1952. Reprinted by permission of Oxford University Press.

Anna Letitia Barbauld. Selections from *The Poems of Anna Letitia Barbauld.* Ed. William McCarthy and Elizabeth Kraft, 1994. Reprinted by permission of University of Georgia Press.

William Blake. Selections from *The Poetry and Prose of William Blake.* Ed. David V. Erdman, 1965. Reprinted by permission of Doubleday, Inc.

Edmund Burke. Selections from *The Writings and Speeches of Edmund Burke.* Volume VIII. Selections from *The French Revolution, 1790–1794.* Ed. L.G. Mitchell, 1989. Reprinted by permission of Oxford University Press.

William Burns. Selections from *The Poems and Songs of Robert Burns.* Ed. James Kinsley, 1968. Reprinted by permission of Oxford University Press.

George Gordon, Lord Byron. Selections from *Lord Byron: The Complete Poetical Works.* Ed. Jerome J. McGann, 1980–1993. Reprinted by permission of Oxford University Press. Selections from *Byron's Letters and Journals.* Ed. Leslie A. Marchand. Cambridge, Massachusetts. Reprinted by permission of the Belknap Press of Harvard University. © editorial, Leslie A. Marchand, 1973. © Byron Copyright material, John Murray, 1973.

John Clare. Selections from *John Clare.* Eds. Eric Robinson and David Powell. Oxford University Press, 1984. Selections from *The Later Poems of John Clare, 1837–1864.* Eds. Eric Robinson and David Powell. Associate Ed. Margaret Grainger. © Eric Robinson, 1984. Reprinted by permission of Curtis Brown Limited, London. Selections from *The Poems of John Clare.* Edited with an introduction by J.W. Tibble. © 1935 by J.M.Dent & Sons Limited.

Samuel Taylor Coleridge. Selections from *The Collected Works of Samuel Taylor Coleridge.* Ed. Kathleen Coburn, 1969. Reprinted by permission of Princeton University Press. Selections from *The Letters of Samuel Taylor Coleridge.* Ed. Earl Leslie Griggs, 1956–1971. Reprinted by permission of Oxford University Press. Selections from *Coleridge's Dejection.* Ed. Stephen Maxfield Parrish. © 1988 by Cornell University. Used by permission of the publisher, Cornell University Press.

John Keats. Selections from John Keats reprinted by permission of the publishers of *The Poems of John Keats.* Ed. Jack Stillinger. Cambridge, Massachusetts: The Belknap Press of Harvard University Press. © 1978 by the President and Fellows of Harvard College. Letters from *The Keats Circle: Letters and Papers, 1816–1878.* Ed. Hyder Edward Rollins. Cambridge, Massachusetts: Harvard University Press. © 1948, 1955, 1965 by the President and Fellows of Harvard College. Selected excerpts from Keats's letters reprinted by permission of the publishers from *The Letters of John Keats, 1814–1821.* Ed. Hyder Edward Rollins. Cambridge, Massachusetts: Harvard University Press. © 1958 by the President and Fellows of Harvard College.

Percy Bysshe Shelley. Selections from *Shelley's Poetry and Prose: A Norton Critical Edition.* Selected and edited by Donald H. Reiman and Sharon B. Powers. Reprinted with the permission of W.W. Norton & Company, Inc. © 1977 by Donald H. Reiman and Sharon B. Powers.

Mary Wollstonecraft Shelley. Selections from *The Works of Mary Wollstonecraft.* Ed. Janet Todd and Marilyn Butler, 1989. Reprinted by permission of Pickering and Chatto (Publishers) Limited. Selections from *The Collected Letters of Mary Wollstonecraft.* Ed. Ralph Wardle, 1979. Reprinted by permission of Cornell University Press. Selections from *The Letters of Mary Wollstonecraft Shelley.* Ed. Betty Bennett. Reprinted by permission of Johns Hopkins University Press. Selections from *The Journals of Mary Shelley.* Ed. Paula R. Feldman and Diana Scott-Kilvert, 1987. Reprinted by permission of Oxford University Press.

Charlotte Smith. Selections from *The Poems of Charlotte Smith.* Ed. Stuart Curran, 1993. Reprinted by permission of Oxford University Press.

Dorothy Wordsworth. Selections from *The Journals of Dorothy Wordsworth.* Ed. Mary Moorman, 1971. Selections from *Dorothy Wordsworth: The Grasmere Journals.* Ed. Pamela Woof, 1991. © Pamela Woof, 1991. Reprinted by permission of Oxford University Press. Selections from Appendix One, "The Collected Poems of Dorothy Wordsworth," in *Dorothy Wordsworth and Romanticism.* Susan M. Levin, 1987. © The Trustees of Dove Cottage.

William Wordsworth. Selections from *William Wordsworth: The Prelude, 1798–1799.* Ed. Stephen Maxfield Parrish. © 1977 by Cornell University. Selections from *Lyrical Ballads and Other Poems, 1797–1800.* Eds. James Butler and Karen Green. © 1993 Cornell University. Selections from *Poems, in Two Volumes.* Ed. Jared Curtis. © 1983 Cornell University. Selections from *Home at Grasmere.* Ed. Beth Darlington. © 1977. All used by permission of the publisher, Cornell University Press. Letters from *The Letters of William and Dorothy Wordsworth.* Ed. Ernest de Selincourt. Vol. I rev. by Chester L. Shaver, 1967. Reprinted by permission of Oxford University Press. Selections from *The Love Letters of William and Dorothy Wordsworth.* Ed. Beth Darlington, 1981. © Trustees of Dove Cottage. Reprinted by permission of Oxford University Press.